OPEN A WINDOW

PRENTICE HALL

LITERATURE

Where Great Ideas Happen

OPEN A WINDOW...

TO EXCEPTIONAL LITERATURE

Lead your students to appreciate literature across time and cultures with an unparalleled collection of classic and contemporary selections.

OPEN A WINDOW…

TO LANGUAGE ARTS INTEGRATION

Use literature
as a bridge
to teaching
skills mastery:
critical reading,
writing, grammar,
speaking
and listening…
solid instruction
at the teachable
moment.

OPEN A WINDOW...

TO GROUND-BREAKING TECHNOLOGY

Discover a remarkable multimedia Writing Studio that integrates literature and writing:

writing software, hand–held Electronic Grammar Handbook, Literature Videodiscs, Transparencies for Writing, Audio Prose Library.

OPEN A WINDOW...

TO PRENTICE HALL LITERATURE

WHERE GREAT IDEAS HAPPEN

Student Text

Annotated Teacher's Edition

Teaching Portfolio
(with Computer Test Bank)

Multicultural Library

Great Works Library

Study Guides

Library of Video Classics

Listening to Literature
Audiocassettes

**The Prentice Hall Literature
Writing Studio:**

Bank Street Writer Software

Writer's Helper Software

Franklin Language Master 6000

Literature Videodiscs

Audio Prose Library Audiocassettes

Transparencies for Writing

Front cover art: Interior with a Table, 1921, Vanessa Bell,
Tate Gallery, London, Art Resource, New York

Annotated Teacher's Edition

PRENTICE HALL

LITERATURE
WORLD MASTERPIECES

FOURTH EDITION

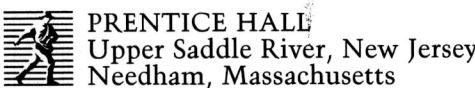

SHIPS RETURNING TO HARBOR AT TEMPOZAN
Yashima Gakutei (1786–1868)

PRENTICE HALL
Upper Saddle River, New Jersey
Needham, Massachusetts

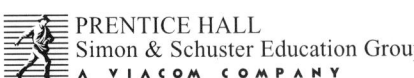

PRENTICE HALL
Simon & Schuster Education Group
A VIACOM COMPANY

ACKNOWLEDGMENTS

Grateful acknowledgment is made to the following for permission to reprint copyrighted material:

Basic Books, Inc.
"Parabolic Ballad" from *Antiworlds and the Fifth Ace* by Andrei Voznesensky. © 1966, 1967 by Basic Books, Inc. Reprinted by permission of Basic Books, Inc., Publishers, New York.

Robert Bly
Excerpts from *Neruda and Vallejo: Selected Poems,* translated by Robert Bly and James Wright, Boston, Beacon Press 1976 ©1972 by Robert Bly. Reprinted with the translator's permission.

Bostonia
Excerpt from "For the Dead and the Living, We Must Bear Witness," dedication speech at the U.S. Holocaust Museum, as printed in the *Bostonia,* Summer 1993.

Judith H. Ciardi
Excerpts from *The Inferno* by Dante Alighieri, translated by John Ciardi. Copyright 1954 and renewed 1982 by John Ciardi. Reprinted by permission of Judith H. Ciardi.

Encyclopaedia Britannica, Inc.
Excerpts from the *Encyclopaedia Britannica,* 15th edition (1979). Reprinted by permission.

Farrar, Straus & Giroux, Inc.
Excerpt from "For the Union Dead" from *For the Union Dead* by Robert Lowell. Copyright © 1956, 1960, 1961, 1962, 1963, 1964 by Robert Lowell. Excerpt from the Preface by Donald Finkel to *A Splintered Mirror: Poetry from the Democracy Movement,* translated by Donald Finkel, additional translations by Carolyn Kizer. Copyright 1991 by Donald Finkel. Reprinted by permission of Farrar, Straus & Giroux, Inc.

John J. Figueroa
Excerpt from an essay titled "Omeros" by John J. Figueroa, © John J. Figueroa, 1991.

HarperCollins Publishers
Excerpt from *The Harper Atlas of the Bible,* edited by James B. Pritchard. Copyright © 1987 by Times Books, Ltd. Lines from "A Letter of Recommendation" from *The Selected Poetry of Yehuda Amichai,* edited and translated by Chana Bloch and Stephen Mitchell. Copyright © 1986 by Chana Bloch and Stephen Mitchell. Reprinted by permission of HarperCollins Publishers.

Henry Holt and Company, Inc.
Excerpts from "Stopping by Woods on a Snowy Evening" from *The Poetry of Robert Frost* edited by Edward Connery Lathem. Copyright 1923, © 1969 by Holt, Rinehart and Winston. Copyright 1951 by Robert Frost. Reprinted by permission of Henry Holt and Company, Inc.

Houghton Mifflin Company
Excerpts from "Loving the Killer" from *Love Poems* by Anne Sexton. Copyright © 1967, 1968, 1969 by Anne Sexton. Reprinted by permission of Houghton Mifflin Company.

Indiana University Press
Excerpt from *An Introduction to Chinese Literature* by Liu Wu-chi, copyright © 1966 by Liu Wu-chi. Excerpt from Ovid, *Metamorphoses,* translated by Rolfe Humphries. Copyright © 1955, by Indiana University Press. Reprinted by permission of Indiana University Press.

Alfred A. Knopf
Excerpt from *A Distant Mirror: The Calamitous 14th Century* by Barbara W. Tuchman. Copyright © 1978 by Barbara W. Tuchman. Excerpt from "The Artist and His Time"

from *The Myth of Sisyphus* by Albert Camus, translated from the French by Justin O'Brien. © copyright 1955, by Alfred A. Knopf, Inc. Reprinted by permission.

Macmillan Publishing Company
From *The Poems of W. B. Yeats: A New Edition,* edited by Richard J. Finneran: "The Scholars," copyright 1919 by Macmillan Publishing Company, renewed 1947 by Bertha Georgie Yeats, and excerpt from "The Second Coming," copyright 1924 by Macmillan Publishing Company, renewed 1952 by Bertha Georgie Yeats. Excerpt from W. B. Yeats Introduction to *Gitanjali* by Rabindranath Tagore (New York: Macmillan 1913). Reprinted by permission of Macmillan Publishing Company.

Martin Secker & Warburg Limited, a division of The Octopus Group Limited and Little, Brown & Company
Excerpt from *The Ironic German: A Study of Thomas Mann* by Erich Heller. Copyright © Erich Heller 1958. Reprinted by permission.

McGraw-Hill, Inc.
Excerpt from *Franz Kafka: A Collection of Criticism,* Leo Hamalian, editor. Reprinted by permission of McGraw-Hill, Inc.

The New York Review of Books
Excerpt from an essay, "East Germany," by Timothy Garton Ash. Copyright © 1990 Nyrev, Inc. Excerpt from "India: The Seed of Destruction" by Anita Desai. Copyright © 1991 Nyrev, Inc. Reprinted with permission of *The New York Review of Books.*

W.W. Norton & Company, Inc.
Excerpt from the Introduction to *Aristotle's Poetics,* translated, with an Introduction and Notes by James Hutton. Copyright © 1982 by W.W. Norton & Company, Inc.

Oxford University Press
"Violins" from Zbigniew Herbert: *Selected Poems,* translated by John and Bogdana Carpenter (1977). Lines from sonnet from Michelangelo: *Life, Letters, and Poetry,* translated by George Bull and Peter Porter (1987). Reprinted by permission of Oxford University Press.

Penguin Books Ltd.
Four verses from *The Rig Veda: An Anthology,* translated by Wendy Doniger O'Flaherty (Penguin Classics, 1981), copyright © Wendy Doniger O'Flaherty, 1981. Reprinted by permission of Penguin Books Ltd.

Princeton University Press
Excerpt from E. A. Speiser's scholarly translation of *Gilgamesh,* from *The Ancient Near East, Volume 1.* James B. Pritchard, editor. Copyright © 1958 Princeton University Press. Reprinted by permission of Princeton University Press.

Random House, Inc.
Excerpt from "The Labyrinth" by W. H Auden. Copyright 1945 and renewed 1973 by W. H. Auden. Reprinted from *W. H Auden: Collected Poems,* edited by Edward Mendelson. Excerpts from *The Aeneid* by Virgil, translated by Robert Fitzgerald. Translation copyright © 1980, 1982, 1983 by Robert Fitzgerald. Reprinted by permission of Random House, Inc.

Charles Scribner's Sons, an imprint of Macmillan Publishing Company
Excerpt from *Love Songs of the New Kingdom,* translated by John L. Foster. Copyright © 1974 by John L. Foster. Reprinted by permission of Charles Scribner's Sons, an imprint of Macmillan Publishing Company.

Twayne Publishers, a division of G. K. Hall & Co., Boston
Excerpt from *Colette* by Joan Hinde Stewart. Copyright 1983 and reprinted with the permission of Twayne Publishers, a division of G. K. Hall & Co., Boston.

University of Chicago Press
Excerpt from Sophocles, *Antigone,* in *The Complete Greek Tragedies* (edited by Grene and Lattimor, 1954). Excerpt from Lattimore (translator), *The Iliad of Homer.* Reprinted by permission of the University of Chicago Press.

University of Texas Press
"Parable of Cervantes and Don Quixote" from *Dreamtigers* by Jorge Luis Borges. Copyright © 1964. All rights reserved. Reprinted by permission of the publisher, University of Texas Press.

Viking Penguin, a division of Penguin Books USA, Inc.
Excerpt from "The Creation" from *God's Trombones* by James Weldon Johnson. Copyright 1927 by The Viking Press, Inc., renewed copyright © 1955 by Grace Nail Johnson. Reprinted by permission of the publisher, Viking Penguin, a division of Penguin Books USA, Inc.

Ehsan Yarshater, Columbia University
"Lament for His Son" from *The Epic of the Kings,* translated by Reuben Levy. Reprinted by permission of Ehsan Yarshater, Columbia University.

Note: Every effort has been made to locate the copyright owner of material reprinted in this book. Omissions brought to our attention will be corrected in subsequent editions.

CONTENTS

WHAT IS INTEGRATED LANGUAGE ARTS?

Sharon Sorenson

formerly with Evansville-Vanderburgh School Corporation
Evansville, Indiana

Those of us who have been in the classroom for more than a few years can recall when there were separate literature, composition, and grammar classes. We were reasonably satisfied teaching literature. We lectured, occasionally asking questions and seeking discussion. The students listened and, for the most part, were successful on the tests we gave on literature. Beyond that, however, we could say little about our students' understanding and even less about their enthusiasm. We were frustrated, for instance, by students who, even though they were superior literature students, wrote miserably poor compositions chock full of grammatical errors. Why, we stormed, couldn't students see the connection between all those grammar rules and their own writing? Why couldn't they write successful, thoughtful, coherent essays about literature? Some of us even cast blame on one another. "If the teacher across the hall really did a good job of teaching grammar last semester, students would know where to put commas this semester," we fumed behind closed doors.

Later, we took a bold step: We decided to do away with some of those separate classes and teach grammar and composition together. We believed integrated grammar and composition classes would be the answer to our prayers. Now, at last, we could have the same students for grammar and composition and know full well that students had been taught the rules and could apply those rules to their writing. Unfortunately, in spite of our hopes, combined grammar and composition classes weren't the answer, either. For the most part, student writing was little improved.

The Writing Process

Next, the writing process took the language arts teaching profession by storm. We began working more carefully with students, talking them through prewriting activities, giving them supervised time to write, modeling the revising process, and talking about proofreading in terms of grammar, usage, and mechanics rules. We increased classroom emphasis on peer editing, cooperative learning, and editorial boards, moving away from transmission of information to transaction, from a teacher-centered classroom to a student-centered one. Suddenly, those old grammar handbooks came off the shelves as students struggled to find rules to support whatever error a proofreader found. Grammar, usage, and mechanics became a relevant part of the writing process as students began to see the purpose behind the rules.

The research had been there all along. "Don't teach grammar in isolation," studies said. "It has no meaning to students if not couched in the context of something useful—like writing."

Let's face it. Would anybody except an English teacher expect Ernest Hemingway to describe the use of gerund phrases in his writing? Would Mark Twain have passed a test that asked him to identify the tense and form of verb phrases such as *could have been revising?* What, then, is the relationship between understanding grammar and writing well? That was the question research posed. Or course, we know now that a student's thorough understanding of grammar is no guarantee that he or she will write well. Accurately, maybe, but not well. Writing, the researchers said, is far more than nouns, commas, and participles that don't dangle.

What Makes Good Writing?

Ah, that was the rub! If writing well takes more than applying grammar rules, what makes good writing? We know the answer: We expect our students to say something when they write! But, we argued, given the tools of grammar, usage, and mechanics, shouldn't they be able to just say it? Apparently not. The problem is that grammar rules don't teach students to think like writers. Or to create sentences, paragraphs, and pages like writers. In fact, to think like writers, students need to study writers. Regularly. Daily. All kinds of writers. Then students can identify with the process of writing as a form of thinking. To write is to think. Bingo! This was the first step toward recognizing the importance of integrated language arts.

Integrated Language Arts and Whole Language

About the same time that this first step started marching in the minds of middle-school and high-school language arts teachers, our colleagues in elementary schools began talking about whole language. Depending on whose definition you accept, whole language can be a thematically structured curriculum or a literature-driven curriculum. In either case, all content areas—language arts, science, social studies, math, art, music—spring from a central theme or a central piece of literature. A story about an ugly duckling, for instance, will lead to a science lesson about why duck feathers repel moisture, a math lesson about the incubation of their eggs, a social studies lesson about their semiannual migratory routes, a language arts lesson about using quotation marks when writing narrative, and similar music and art lessons.

However, we middle- and high-school teachers teach mainly language arts, so the term *whole language* didn't seem entirely appropriate. As a result, most of us began talking about integrated language arts. We followed the same philosophy as our elementary-school colleagues—that the parts should come from the whole—but we framed it in the context of our own teaching world. Thus, the term *integrated language arts* has come to refer to a literature-driven language arts curriculum. We start with a piece of literature—a short story, poem, play, essay, or novel—and incorporate instruction in all of the other language arts skills within its framework; reading, writing, grammar, usage, mechanics, spelling, vocabulary, critical thinking, and speaking and listening. We rely heavily on the teachable moment, teaching, for instance, a vocabulary word the moment it pops up in literature, teaching critical skills as part of the response to literature, teaching grammar as it springs from the discussion of the writer's style, teaching writing as students prepare written responses to the literature, and teaching usage and mechanics during the proofreading process of that written response.

A Changed Classroom

The result is a changed classroom. Some of the changes are hard for us; all of them are proving successful for students. For instance, lesson plans are harder to write because content pops up at unexpected and unanticipated moments, changing the direction of the best-laid plans. Curriculum guides must necessarily become more flexible because we address skills within the context of the literature and at the teachable moment. Classroom strategies and management techniques change because we focus on student-centered activities that meet varying ability levels and respond to individual needs. While the changes are sometimes hard for veteran teachers, the results are changed classrooms that excite students, promote learning, and improve test scores.

What does an integrated language arts classroom look like and sound like? Here's a mythical classroom. As the students settle in their seats, they find a learning log prompt on the overhead projector. Its purpose is to serve as a prereading activity. The prompt asks students to think about an experience they have had in nature. Maybe they have watched a sunset, hiked in the desert, crossed a glacier, or witnessed a severe storm. What did they see? Students begin writing in response to the prompt. The teacher roams the room reading over shoulders, checking for prior knowledge and individual interests, while also preparing students for the experience they will have reading N. Scott Momaday's poem "New World." A few minutes later, the teacher asks students to name the five senses, to give examples of each, and then to return to their learning logs to add the other senses to their descriptions. The teacher gives them three minutes. Afterward, students are asked to reason logically about what the term *sensory language* must mean and, without discussion, to write a one-sentence definition in their logs. The teacher is setting students up for the literary focus of Momaday's poem, using another kind of prereading activity but also employing critical thinking skills. Simultaneously, the teacher is engaging students as active learners. To write is to think. And everyone is participating.

Next it is time for an initial choral reading of the poem. Students simply listen for an overall impression. On a second

reading, however, the teacher stops—at the teachable moment—to ask students to define an unusual word. It is the vocabulary lesson for the day.

Then, to begin getting at the poem's meaning, students do what they were prepared to do before the reading: look for sensory words, an activity completed individually, cooperatively, or in a whole-class setting. After the choral reading of the poem (to say is to think), students read about the author and indicate how understanding his background helps them understand the poem. After further discussion, moving through as complicated an analysis of the literature as makes sense with the given class, the teacher surprises students by asking them to name the verbs in the poem and to identify their tense. After students identify the verbs as present tense, the teacher asks them to substitute the past tense as he or she rereads the poem. Many students recognize that the change in verb tense affects the meaning of the poem—dramatically. So there's the grammar lesson for the day: Use consistent verb tense and use it to convey your message.

Now, back to those learning logs. The prereading activity also functions as a prewriting activity because the teacher now asks students to use their learning log ideas (with the sensory language already in place) to create one or two products: a poem modeled after "New World" or a narrative description of their experience. In the course of students developing their written products, the teacher may refer to the poem to model structure, sensory language, punctuation, even grammar. Not only does that teaching technique reiterate the elements of the author's style, but it stimulates students' thinking. In the course of revising, students cope with unity, coherence, supporting details, transitions, and other techniques of clear writing. In the course of proofreading, peer editors tackle grammar, usage, and mechanics problems and find their solutions. Students who are writing at computers may even use a style checker to analyze their sentence lengths, sentence structure, and readability indices. The lesson is finished in about two days.

What Happens in the Integrated Classroom?

What happened during the integrated language arts lesson? Students addressed all of the language arts skills within the context of the literature. All of the parts came out of the whole. They studied literature—a poem—and literary concepts, including sensory language. They practiced active reading skills—predicting, analyzing, clarifying, visualizing, summarizing. They wrote—in their learning logs to promote active learning and in response to the literature to produce a formal written product. They studied grammar—the use of consistent verb tense and its effect on meaning. They referred to usage and mechanics rules, employed critical thinking skills, and engaged in speaking and listening activities.

Integrated language arts classrooms are as varied as the teachers and students who inhabit them, and the activities are equally varied. They are exciting places where skills, not drills, are taught when the students need them. Some teachers, however, feel frustration because they believe that the teachable moment lacks structure. There is no guarantee, they say, that we will actually cover everything we're supposed to cover; it's just too hit or miss.

Those of us who are highly structured will continue to feel this tugging at our professional consciences. However, look at it this way: If the student isn't using dangling participles, why teach him not to? If he is using them, then teach him, not his classmates, at the teachable moment, referring to his own writing. Or if most of the students face the same problem, do a five-minute minilesson, and then let the practice come in their own writing. Remind yourself what the research tells us: Students don't learn skills in isolation. We can best approach skills from the context or their use—in the literature and in the student's own writing at the moment the student needs them.

The Test

Two teachers told me recently that they put these integrated language arts ideas to the test. They had evenly matched classes, so one teacher taught the traditional grammar units and interspersed them with writing, and the other teacher taught the integrated language arts approach, letting all of the language arts skills spring from the literature. At the end of the year, both classes took the same test (it happened to be a state-mandated one). The class whose teacher had used the integrated approach attained much higher scores than those whose teacher had pounded rules and skills all year.

"Why do you think that happened?" I asked.

"Simple," was one teacher's response. "The kids learn best at the moment they have a need for the knowledge. That's when it makes sense to them, and that's why they remember it. You know," she went on, "it's like someone telling you how to change a flat tire. Only when you really need to know do those instructions matter. I just applied that little analogy to my language arts classroom."

Lots of teachers who faced flat tires in their classrooms have turned to an integrated language arts approach. They like what they find. "It's refreshing," one teacher said, "to find students who really have something to say. The literature discussions provoke thought, the literature itself provides for structure and style, and the writing process makes sense after students see how other writers put it into effect. It's the complete cycle. We read writing to write reading."

Right!

The Prentice Hall Literature Program

OVERVIEW

THE STUDENT BOOK

The Prentice Hall Literature Program is a complete literature program, offering high-quality, appealing, traditional and contemporary literary selections, with study aids that will guide students into, through, and beyond the literature.

Organization

The selections are organized chronologically to present the literature of the world in a historical context. The following list shows the parts, units, and sections into which the selections are organized:

Part 1: Beginnings in the East
  Sumerian, Egyptian, and Hebrew Literature: Egyptian
    Poetry, Hebrew Literature
  Persian and Arabic Literature
Part 2: The Rise of Asia
  Indian Literature
  Chinese Literature: Philosophy, Poetry
  Japanese Literature: Poetry, Prose
Part 3: The Rise of Classical Civilizations
  Ancient Greece: Poetry, Prose, Drama
  Roman Literature: Poetry, Prose
Part 4: Europe in Transition
  The Middle Ages
  The Renaissance
  The Age of Rationalism
  Romanticism and Realism: Poetry, Prose, The New
    Age of Drama
Part 5: The Twentieth Century
  The Modern World: Europe, The Americas, Asia
  The Contemporary World: The Americas, Western
    Europe, Eastern Europe, The Middle East, Africa, Asia

The number and variety of selections offer choice and flexibility in meeting curriculum requirements as well as student needs and interests.

Unique Features

Because the Prentice Hall Literature Program puts emphasis on the reading and appreciation of literature, it offers several unique features to help students become active readers.

Reading Critically Each unit begins with a feature called Reading Critically, which includes a summary of the historical context, the literary movements, and the writers' techniques of the period. This feature is followed by a Model for Reading Critically, which is annotated to demonstrate and explain to students how a good reader might apply this information to the analysis of a selection. This technique actively involves the reader in the text before reading and while reading. Such involvement and reaction are neces-

sary if students are to learn. Students are encouraged to use this technique as they read other selections in the unit. This feature provides a method of scaffolding—giving students help and support while they acquire the skills to become successful readers of literature. To give students further practice with this process, there is an additional selection in the Teaching Portfolio, which students can annotate themselves.

Guide for Interpreting All other selections begin with a Guide for Interpreting. These pages contain useful prereading information. The Guide for Interpreting prepares students for successful reading in the following ways:
• A biography of the author provides insight into how the author came to write the selection.
• Commentaries introduce a noteworthy aspect of the work—literary, thematic, stylistic, or meaning-oriented—and offer an insight into it.
• A motivational writing activity puts students in an appropriate frame of mind.
• A primary source presents a quotation from the writer or a critic that gives an insight into the writer's work or times.
This Guide for Interpreting provides the necessary background to enhance comprehension, motivates students to read, and gives them technical support to read successfully. Each selection is self-contained and complete so that you can use selections in any order that you like.

After Reading

Features at the end of the selection are designed to foster comprehension and encourage constructive response, either personal or literary. These features encourage the growth of skills needed by students to become independent readers. These features comprise the following areas:

Reader's Response This question is designed to prompt the students' personal response to the selection.

Thinking About the Selection These study questions are built upon three levels of comprehension: the literal, the interpretive, and the applied. The questions are grouped by the levels of increasing complexity: recalling (literal), interpreting (inference, analysis), and applying (generalization, extension, judgment). The different levels may be used as appropriate for different ability levels, or may be used to take all students through different levels of thinking.

Analyzing Literature This section develops and reinforces the literary concept or skill introduced on the Guide for Reading page and applies it to the selection. It helps students to understand literary concepts and appreciate writers' techniques, thereby enabling them to respond appropriately to literature.

Critical Thinking and Reading This section introduces students to those critical thinking and critical reading skills that are necessary for understanding literature. It gives them an opportunity to apply these skills to the literary selections.

Understanding Language Knowledge and appreciation of language are developed in this section, which contains activities on language prompted by the selection. The activities may be geared toward helping students appreciate writers' use of language, master skills needed to increase their vocabulary, or prepare for SATs.

Thinking and Writing This is a composition assignment arising from the selection. This assignment, which may be creative or analytical, is process-oriented, suggesting steps for prewriting, drafting, and revising.

Special Features

A number of special features occur throughout this volume: **Cross Currents** present some contemporary or humanities connection to the period or the content of the unit. **Great Works** introduce students to great works of literature, novels and plays that cannot be included in this anthology. This feature places the work in its historical period, indicates the significance of the work, presents a synopsis, and motivates students to read. **Ideas and Insights** provide background or insightful comment on a variety of topics related to the literature. **Themes in World Literature** discuss the universal themes in literature.

Writing About Literature

At the end of each unit is a lesson on writing about literature. Each lesson is structured through the steps of the writing process.

End of Book

A **Handbook of Literary Terms and Techniques** provides an alphabetical guide to the literary terms taught in the Analyzing Literature activities at the end of selections. Each entry provides a full definition of the term or technique with one or more examples. The handbook can be used for preteaching, for review, or as a support for students as they work on individual Analyzing Literature activities.

A **Handbook of Grammar and Revising Strategies** presents strategies for revising common writing problems, with examples of good usage from the literature selections. It also contains a brief overview of the grammar of a sentence, punctuation rules, and correct usage.

TEACHING SUPPORT

THE ANNOTATED TEACHER'S EDITION

The Annotated Teacher's Edition of *Prentice Hall Literature* is designed to be used both for planning and for actual in-class teaching. It offers planning aids and specific teaching suggestions for all selections. This planning and teaching material appears in the side columns next to the reduced student pages of each selection. These annotations, which correspond to the student material on that page, help you give your students positive and relevant experiences with literature by asking the right questions at the right time and by pointing out what is significant.

Preparing the Lesson: Focus

The annotations on the opening pages of the selection help you plan your presentation of the material. Each selection begins with notes that suggest ways to introduce or enhance the prereading instruction or activities presented in the students' Guide for Interpreting. **Pronunciation** notes give help with the pronunciation of writers' names. A **critical evaluation** note indicates one critic's point of view on the writer or the work. A **vocabulary** list presents, in glossary format, words from the selection that might present difficulty in reading; you may wish to preteach these words. An occasional **spelling tip** gives a hint for remembering the spelling of a troublesome word. Objectives for each selection are keyed to the end-of-selection material. This page also includes a complete list of support material for this selection in the Teaching Portfolio and other components of the program. In the column next to the first page of the selection,

you will find a **motivation/prior knowledge** suggestion and a **purpose-setting question** to prepare the students to read. Frequently, **universal themes** notes are given. These suggest other selections in this book that treat themes similar to those under discussion. You may want to use these selections together to integrate and reinforce universal concepts and themes. **ESL strategies** suggest ways to make a selection accessible to ESL students. **Teaching tenth-grade students** suggests an insight or a strategy for making a selection more accessible to students in tenth grade. All of these annotations help you effectively prepare your lesson.

Teaching the Lesson: Presentation

You may use the notes throughout the pages of the selection to direct your discussion in class. As you and your students read the selection, you will find additional notes that enable you to customize the lesson for your class. They let you increase your students' involvement in the work and enrich their reading of it, while enabling them to deal with the particular genres. The following kinds of notes may direct your class discussions:

Master Teacher Notes These tips from master teachers give an approach, a strategy, or a special bit of information that enlivens the selection or increases appreciation.

Humanities Notes For each piece of fine art in the student book, there is a humanities note giving information on the work of art and the artist. These notes generally point out features of the piece of art that relate it to the work of literature with which it is presented. Additionally, the humanities note concludes with questions that you may use if you wish to discuss the art as part of your discussion of the selection.

Enrichment Enrichment notes provide additional information on points of interest that arise in selections. You may use this information to enrich your students' knowledge of the background of a selection and their appreciation of it.

Reading Strategies Strategies to promote student comprehension of the literary text reinforce the emphasis on teaching students to read literature actively.

Clarification Words, phrases, or ideas that might be obstacles to student understanding are clarified to ensure comprehension.

Discussion Throughout the selection, you will find additional questions and points for discussion. These help you proceed through the selection with students, eliciting their understanding and appreciation of significant passages.

Literary Focus To promote understanding of the writer's techniques, literary focus annotations direct attention to those aspects of the selection that reflect the literary concept presented with it.

Critical Thinking and Reading These notes reinforce the critical thinking and reading skills developed throughout the program.

There are probably more notes that you need for presenting any given selection. We emphasize the importance of selecting those annotations that are best suited to your classes and to your course of instruction.

Grammar in Action Grammar in Action notes integrate language arts skills. These notes demonstrate the writer's use of particular grammatical or style points. They present a direct link between grammar and writing.

Additional **commentary** and **primary source** notes add further background or insight to the selection.

Closure and Extension

Answers are provided for all questions in each feature following the selection. Where questions are open-ended, we present a suggested response or we suggest points that students should note in their answers.

The annotations after the selection also include the following:

Challenge These questions take students beyond those given with the instruction.

Publishing Student Writing For many selections, additional notes suggest ways to publish the writing students have done in the Thinking and Writing feature.

Writing Across the Curriculum Where appropriate, you will see suggestions for additional assignments or suggestions for relating the Thinking and Writing assignment to students' work in another discipline.

In addition, you will find teaching suggestions for the special features in the student book—Reading Critically, Cross Currents, Great Works, Background, and Ideas and Insights. You will also find annotations on the unit introductions, relating the information there to specific selections.

THE TEACHING PORTFOLIO

The Teaching Portfolio provides support for teaching and testing all of the selections and skills in *Prentice Hall Literature.*

Fine Art Transparencies

Twenty fine art transparencies with blackline masters are provided in the Teaching Portfolio. These can be used to introduce selections and motivate students to read, or they can be used as additional writing assignments in response to art. Each fine art transparency has a writing assignment for students and a lesson plan for teaching that assignment. Furthermore, the fine art is keyed into the selections through Master Teacher Notes in the Annotated Teacher's Edition.

Beginning of Unit

Each unit begins with a list of objectives and a skills chart listing literary elements and skills covered in the unit. The skills chart also identifies all the blackline masters in the Teaching Portfolio that correlate to each selection.

The Selections Full teaching support is provided for each selection. This support material is organized by selection for your convenience. The support for each selection consists of the following: Teacher Backup, Grammar in Action Worksheet, Usage and Mechanics Worksheet, Vocabulary Check, Analyzing Literature Worksheet,* Critical Thinking and Reading Worksheet,* Language Worksheet* (there are always two of the starred three), and a Selection Test.

Teacher Backup Teacher Backup material is provided for each selection. This material consists of more information about the author, a critical quotation about the author, a summary of the selection, and list of other works by the author. In addition, there is a Check Test that you can use to check if students have read the selection. Help in teaching and evaluating the writing assignment in the student text is provided as well as three alternative composition assignments for the students. One of these is less challenging than the assignment in the student text, one is more challenging, and one requires the student to write in response to literary criticism. Finally, answers to all worksheet activities and tests are provided.

Grammar in Action The Grammar in Action worksheet provides further instruction and practice corresponding to Grammar in Action notes in the Annotated Teacher's Edition.

Usage and Mechanics The Usage and Mechanics Worksheet provides sentences dealing with the selection that contain errors in usage and mechanics. These provide practice in correcting such common problems as run-on sentences, sentence fragments, and subject-verb agreement as well as errors in spelling and punctuation. Additionally, the Grammar in Action skills are incorporated into these sentences. We suggest you have your students correct these sentences orally so that they can discuss each problem.

Vocabulary Check The Vocabulary Check tests mastery of the vocabulary words presented in the Annotated Teacher's Edition on the Guide for Interpreting page before each selection. This blackline master can be used as a test or as an in-class or at-home assignment.

Worksheets The Analyzing Literature Worksheet, Critical Thinking and Reading Worksheet, and Language Worksheet support and expand upon the skills taught at the end of the selection in the student book. If no Understanding Language assignment appears in the student book, one is provided in the Teaching Portfolio.

Selection Test A Selection Test is provided for each selection. This test provides a check for comprehension as well as of mastery of the skills taught at the end of the selection.

Annotated Models For each selection that is annotated as a model in the student book, a selection is provided in the Teaching Portfolio for students to annotate themselves.

End of Unit

Each unit ends with two unit tests: a short-answer test and an essay test. Guidelines are provided for evaluating student responses to the essay test questions. In addition, a list of suggested projects, a bibliography, and list of audio-visual aids follow.

End of Portfolio

At the end of the Teaching Portfolio are models of strong and weak student writing, a guide to evaluating student writing, and writing process activities.

Computer Test Bank

Information about the Computer Test Bank and instructions for receiving the appropriate version are included in the Teaching Portfolio. The Computer Test Bank provides the selection test and unit tests from the Teaching Portfolio on computer disks. The program allows you to modify the selection tests by deleting items from the short-answer selection tests supplied, choosing a different essay question, and

writing your own test questions. You can save your test for future use.

Library of Video Classics

The Library of Video Classics provides videotapes of films made of major works in this level. Each tape is accompanied by a Viewing Guide, which gives background on the film or director, a planning overview for the film, and previewing and after-viewing questions and activities.

Study Guides

Study Guides for major novels and plays are available with *Prentice Hall Literature*. These guides will help you teach many of the works of your choice as part of your total literature program. Each guide contains an overview of the novel or play, chapter-by-chapter lessons, assignments leading to essays and imaginative writing, guidelines for dealing with provocative themes, a bibliography, and blackline masters of skills and a test for the work.

Multicultural Library

This library contains twenty young adult novels by acclaimed writers from diverse backgrounds. The books will have particular appeal in Grades 6–10. Each title is accompanied by a Study Guide.

Great Works Library

This library contains unabridged editions of time-honored classics by major writers. The books will have particular appeal to high-school students. Each title is accompanied by a Study Guide.

Listening to Literature Audiocassettes

A series of audiocassettes is available for each level of *Prentice Hall Literature*. The audiocassettes provide professional readings of selections to enliven classroom learning. Each level is accompanied by a teacher's guide.

Prentice Hall Literature Writing Studio

The Writing Studio provides tools that help the teacher integrate writing instruction with the literature program and facilitate the writing process. We suggest teachers customize their program from the following components:

Bank Street Writer software
Writer's Helper software
Franklin Language Master 6000
Literature Videodiscs
Audio Prose Library audiocassettes
Transparencies for Writing

Skills Chart for Selections in Each Unit

The following chart shows the literary elements and integrated language arts skills covered with each selection. An asterisk (*) indicates that a worksheet appears in the Teaching Portfolio.

SUMERIAN, EGYPTIAN, AND HEBREW LITERATURE

Selection	Analyzing Literature	Critical Thinking and Reading	Understanding Language/ Speaking and Listening	Thinking and Writing	Grammar in Action
Reading Critically					
from *The Epic of Gilgamesh* "Prologue," p. 15 "The Battle with Humbaba," p. 16 "Enkidu's Dream of the Underworld," p. 19	Understanding conflict Understanding an archetypal battle*	Contrasting Gilgamesh and Enkidu Contrasting characters*		Creating an imaginary underworld	Commas that set off added elements*
from *The Epic of Gilgamesh* "The Story of the Flood," p. 23 "The Return," p. 26	Understanding the hero and his quest*	Inferring the purpose of the flood story Inferring the purpose of stories*	Appreciating an Akkadian pun	Comparing and contrasting heroes	The semicolon*
Egyptian Poetry					
"Your Love, Dear Man, Is As Lovely to Me," p. 32 "I Think I'll Go Home and Lie Very Still," p. 33 "The Voice of the Swallow," p. 34	Understanding pastoral poetry*	Inferring the dramatic context*	Appreciating concrete language Appreciating diction*	Writing love poems for fictional characters	
Hebrew Literature					
Genesis 1–3, The Creation and the Fall, p. 40	Understanding archetypes*	Tracing two stories of creation*	Appreciating repetition*	Writing from different perspectives	
Genesis 6–9, The Story of the Flood, p. 47	Understanding the theme of the covenant*	Comparing and contrasting flood stories*	Understanding the King James Version of the Bible*	Adapting the flood story	Pronoun and antecedent agreement*
The Book of Ruth, p. 55	Understanding the Hebrew short story*	Inferring character traits*		Writing about a role model	
1 Samuel 17, David and Goliath, p. 61	Understanding a biblical hero	Appreciating the use of dialogue*	Finding the meaning that fits the context*	Writing a modern "David" story	Evolution of the language*
Psalm 8, p. 67 Psalm 19, p. 68 Psalm 23, p. 69 Psalm 137, p. 70	Understanding parallelism in the Bible* Understanding parallelism in the psalms	Appreciating historical context	Synonyms and antonyms* Reading psalms aloud	Writing a modern psalm	

PERSIAN AND ARABIC LITERATURE

Selection	Analyzing Literature	Critical Thinking and Reading	Understanding Language/ Speaking and Listening	Thinking and Writing	Grammar in Action
Reading Critically					
from the *Shah-nama,* Firdawsi, p. 89	Understanding irony*	Predicting later events*		Writing a letter	Adverb phrases* Using similes*
from *The Rubáiyát,* Omar Khayyám, p. 100	Understanding metaphors*	Recognizing the author's beliefs*		Writing poems in the rubái form	
from the Koran, p. 108	Understanding the Koran*		Translating into modern English*	Writing about Islam	
from the *Gulistan,* Sa'di, p. 112 from the *Divan,* Hafiz, p. 118	Understanding Sufi fables*		Using context clues*	Writing a fable	The colon*
from the *Masnavi,* Rumi, p. 122	Understanding didactic literature*		Understanding symbolism*	Comparing and contrasting writers	
from *The Thousand and One Nights,* p. 128	Understanding folk tales*		Recognizing word origins*	Adapting a folk tale	Transitions*

INDIAN LITERATURE

Selection	Analyzing Literature	Critical Thinking and Reading	Understanding Language/ Speaking and Listening	Thinking and Writing	Grammar in Action
Reading Critically					
from the *Rig Veda,* "Creation Hymn," p. 155	Exploring language's limitations Expressing the inexpressible*	Comparing a poem and a picture Using concrete language*	Identifying concrete and abstract language Using vivid action verbs*	Reflecting on the limits of language	
from the *Rig Veda,* "Night," p. 159	Understanding personification and simile Using simile and personification*	Making inferences*	Using adjectives*		
from the *Taittiriya Upanishad,* "The Mystery of Brahman," p. 162	Understanding the mystery of Brahman*	Appreciating the role of the guru*	Appreciating cross-cultural influences*		

INDIAN LITERATURE (continued)

Selection	Analyzing Literature	Critical Thinking and Reading	Understanding Language/ Speaking and Listening	Thinking and Writing	Grammar in Action
from the *Mahabharata*, "Sibi," p. 168	Understanding the Hindu concept of dharma*		Exploring the connotations of synonyms*	Writing about sacrifice	Understanding the correct use of verb tenses*
from the *Bhagavad-Gita*, "The Yoga of Knowledge," p. 176	Understanding nonattached work*	Appreciating an idea's influence		Applying an Indian concept	Understanding unity and coherence*
from the *Panchatantra*, "Numskull and the Rabbit," p. 184	Understanding an animal fable*	Analyzing the role of the trickster*		Writing an animal fable	

CHINESE LITERATURE

Selection	Analyzing Literature	Critical Thinking and Reading	Understanding Language/ Speaking and Listening	Thinking and Writing	Grammar in Action
Reading Critically					
"Substance, Shadow, and Spirit," T'ao Ch'ien, p. 203	Understanding theme*	Identifying opinions*	Completing sentences	Writing about theme	Using punctuation in poetry*
Philosophy					
from the *Tao Te Ching,* Lao Tzu, p. 210	Understanding Taoism*	Making inferences*		Writing about Taoism	
from *The Analects,* Confucius, p. 214	Understanding Confucianism Understanding literature*	Understanding comparison and contrast*		Comparing and contrasting philosophies	
Poetry					
from *The Book of Songs,* p. 220	Understanding the use of refrain*	Appreciating the effect of incremental variation		Writing a folk song	
T'ao Ch'ien "Poem on Returning to Dwell in the Country," p. 225 "I Built My House Near Where Others Dwell," p. 226	Understanding Shih poetry*		Finding meanings of words naming occupations*	Writing a poem	

CHINESE LITERATURE (continued)

Selection	Analyzing Literature	Critical Thinking and Reading	Understanding Language/ Speaking and Listening	Thinking and Writing	Grammar in Action
Wang Wei "To the Assistant Prefect Chang," p. 230 "The Hill," p. 230 "On an Autumn Evening in the Mountains," p. 231	Understanding Buddhism*	Analyzing the effect of imagery*			
Li Po "The River-Merchant's Wife: A Letter," p. 234 "In the Mountains on a Summer Day," p. 236 "Addressed Humorously to Tu Fu," p. 236 "The Moon at the Fortified Pass," p. 237	Recognizing a persona*	Inferring tone*	Tracing the origins of words*	Writing a response	
Tu Fu "Jade Flower Palace," p. 240 "Sent to Li Po as a Gift," p. 241 "The Return of the Wanderers," p. 242 "Loneliness," p. 242	Appreciating style*	Drawing conclusions about a writer's life	Appreciating the use of color in poetry*	Responding to criticism	
Po Chü-i "Sick Leave," p. 246 "At the End of Spring," p. 246 "To Li Chi'en," p. 247 "Last Poem," p. 248	Appreciating the T'ang poet-official	Finding the implied main idea*	Recognizing analogies*	Writing about the role of poetry	

JAPANESE LITERATURE

Selection	Analyzing Literature	Critical Thinking and Reading	Understanding Language/ Speaking and Listening	Thinking and Writing	Grammar in Action
Reading Critically					
from *Essays in Idleness,* Yoshida Kenko, p. 267	Understanding the Zuihitsu form*	Recognizing cultural characteristics*		Writing from models	Parallelism* Topic sentences and supporting information*

JAPANESE LITERATURE (continued)

Selection	Analyzing Literature	Critical Thinking and Reading	Understanding Language/ Speaking and Listening	Thinking and Writing	Grammar in Action
Poetry					
Kakinomoto Hitomaro "In the Sea of Iwami," p. 276 "I Loved Her Like the Leaves," p. 278	Understanding a choka*		Reading with expression Understanding word analogies*	Writing a choka	
Tanka Ki no Tsurayuki, p. 284 Ono Komachi, p. 284 Priest Jakuren, p. 284 Minamoto no Toshiyori, p. 284	Understanding tanka	Recognizing cultural characteristics*	Appreciating connotations*	Writing a tanka	
Haiku Bashō, p. 288 Yosa Buson, p. 290 Kobayashi Issa, p. 292	Understanding the haiku form* Understanding the haiku form	Comparing forms Considering characteristics of language*	Considering language Appreciating concise language*	Comparing and contrasting poems Writing haiku Writing about Japanese poetry	
Prose					
from *The Pillow Book,* Sei Shōnagon, p. 296	Understanding historical context*	Making inferences about the author*		Writing a dramatization	Varied sentence structures*
The Deserted Crone, Zeami, p. 306	Understanding a Nō play*	Recognizing the Japanese aesthetic Relating the Nō to the Japanese aesthetic*		Writing about a Nō play	Imagery*

ANCIENT GREECE

Selection		Analyzing Literature	Critical Thinking and Reading	Understanding Language/ Speaking and Listening	Thinking and Writing
Reading Critically					
from the *Iliad,* Homer, from Book I, p. 335		Recognizing epic convention*	Defining the epic hero		Explaining the role of Achilleus' anger

ANCIENT GREECE (continued)

Selection	Analyzing Literature	Critical Thinking and Reading	Understanding Language/ Speaking and Listening	Thinking and Writing	Grammar in Action
from the *Iliad,* Homer from Book VI, p. 347 from Book XVIII, p. 355	Analyzing the imagery of Achilleus' shield	Comparing and contrasting characters*	Analyzing oral literature*	Writing about divine causality	Recognizing transitions* Recognizing prepositional phrases and their uses* Recognizing inverted sentence patterns* Recognizing compound verbs*
from the *Iliad,* Homer from Book XXII, p. 366 from Book XXIV, p. 379	Interpreting epic similes*	Understanding ancient codes of ethics*	Identifying English words of Greek origin	Writing about shared humanity	Recognizing uses of the hyphen* Recognizing types of imagery* Using commas to separate basic elements* Using past, present, and future tenses of verbs* Using parallel structure*
Poetry					
Archilochus "Some Barbarian Is Waving My Shield," p. 394 "To the Gods All Things are Easy," p. 394 "A Call to Arms," Callinus, p. 395	Analyzing lyric poetry*	Making inferences*	Recognizing the origins of words*		
Sappho "Awed By Her Splendor," p. 398 "Although They Are," p. 398 "And Their Feet Move," p. 398 "You Know the Place: Then," p. 399 "You May Forget But," p. 400	Analyzing lyric fragments Analyzing personal lyric*	Concrete versus abstract terms*	Comparing translations*	Writing about thematic threads	

ANCIENT GREECE (continued)

Selection	Analyzing Literature	Critical Thinking and Reading	Understanding Language/ Speaking and Listening	Thinking and Writing	Grammar in Action
Sappho "He Is More Than a Hero," p. 401 "Invocation to Aphrodite," p. 402					
"Olympia 11," Pindar, p. 404	Analyzing a victory ode	Imitating an ode			
Prose					
from *History of the Peloponnesian War,* "Pericles' Funeral Oration," Thucydides, p. 408	Analyzing elements of oration	Evaluating persuasive arguments*	Writing for an audience Recognizing Greek word roots*	Writing about leadership	Recognizing unity and coherence*
from the *Apology,* Plato, p. 416	Analyzing dramatic monologue*	Understanding analogy*	Using context clues	Writing a defense	Improving diction*
Drama					
Oedipus the King, Part 1, Sophocles, p. 433	Analyzing tragedy*	Tracing a motif*		Writing about character	Using participles and participial phrases* Setting tone* Using dashes* Maintaining tone*
Oedipus the King, Part 2, Sophocles, p. 457	Analyzing dramatic irony*	Understanding causality		Writing about justice	Understanding narrative*

ROMAN LITERATURE

Selection	Analyzing Literature	Critical Thinking and Reading	Understanding Language/ Speaking and Listening	Thinking and Writing	Grammar in Action
Reading Critically					
from the *Aeneid,* Book II, Virgil, p. 493	Understanding narrative in epic*	Inferring an author's opinion*		Expanding on myth	Recognizing adjectives: Participles* Using prepositional phrases*

ROMAN LITERATURE (continued)

Selection	Analyzing Literature	Critical Thinking and Reading	Understanding Language/ Speaking and Listening	Thinking and Writing	Grammar in Action
from the *Aeneid,* Book IV, Virgil, p. 507	Understanding heroic conflict*	Evaluating divine influence*		Composing a farewell letter	Understanding pronoun-antecedent agreement* Using commas: Parenthetical phrases* Recognizing participles and participial phrases* Using words that create mood*
Poetry					
Catullus "My Woman Says There's Nobody She'd Rather Marry," p. 528 "I Hate Her and I Love Her," p. 528 "I Crossed Many Lands and a Lot of Ocean," p. 528 "My Mind's Sunk So Low, Lesbia, Because of You," p. 529	Evaluating love lyrics*	Understanding subjective reactions*	Interpreting allusions*	Comparing love lyrics	
from the *Metamorphoses,* Ovid, p. 532	Understanding verse narrative	Interpreting symbols*	Understanding similes	Writing about tone	
Prose					
from the *Annals,* Tacitus, p. 538 from *Letters,* Pliny, p. 546	Understanding annals Understanding the epistle	Recognizing cause and effect* Noting an author's attitude*	Finding prefixes* Recognizing the impact of language*	Writing about the news Writing persuasively	Understanding the paragraph*

THE MIDDLE AGES

Selection	Analyzing Literature	Critical Thinking and Reading	Understanding Language/ Speaking and Listening	Thinking and Writing	Grammar in Action
Reading Critically					
from the *Song of Roland,* Cantos 1–68, p. 569	Understanding theme*	Understanding tone*			Using colon and semicolon*

THE MIDDLE AGES (continued)

Selection	Analyzing Literature	Critical Thinking and Reading	Understanding Language/ Speaking and Listening	Thinking and Writing	Grammar in Action
from the *Song of Roland,* Cantos 80–289, p. 581	Understanding the hero*		Understanding words of French origin*	Writing about values	Uses of language: Understanding similes* Uses of language: Understanding personification*
from the *Nibelungenlied,* p. 592	Understanding the tragic flaw*	Understanding hunting rituals*		Composing dialogue	Understanding superlatives*
from *Perceval,* Chrétien de Troyes, p. 602	Understanding the quest*	Interpreting symbols*		Examining goals	Understanding hyperbole*
"The Lay of the Werewolf," Marie de France, p. 612	Understanding Breton lais*	Recognizing symbolism*		Writing from a different perspective	Avoiding comma splices*
from the *Inferno,* Canto I, Dante, p. 622	Interpreting allegory*	Comparing epics*		Composing an allegory	
from the *Inferno,* Canto III, Dante, p. 629	Interpreting imagery*	Understanding cause and effect*	Appreciating dialogue	Describing scenes of horror	Recognizing uses of language imagery*
from the *Inferno,* Canto V, Dante, p. 635	Evaluating first-person point of view*	Comparing and contrasting judgments*	Examining Latin roots*	Writing from another point of view	Making effective use of adjectives*
from the *Inferno,* Canto XXXIV, Dante, p. 641	Understanding personification*	Avoiding "translationese"*	Understanding connotations of words*	Preparing translations	
"Ballade," François Villon, p. 650	Understanding the narrator*	Recognizing tone*	Understanding verb tenses*	Writing an advertisement	

THE RENAISSANCE

Selection	Analyzing Literature	Critical Thinking and Reading	Understanding Language/ Speaking and Listening	Thinking and Writing	Grammar in Action
Reading Critically					
from *The Prince,* Niccolò Machiavelli, p. 669	Understanding Machiavelli's purpose*	Appreciating Machiavelli's art*		Writing a letter as Machiavelli	Developing and supporting a topic*

THE RENAISSANCE (continued)

Selection	Analyzing Literature	Critical Thinking and Reading	Understanding Language/ Speaking and Listening	Thinking and Writing	Grammar in Action
from *Canzoniere,* Petrarch "Laura," p. 676 "The White Doe," p. 678 "Spring," p. 678	Understanding Petrarch's love poems*	Appreciating the Petrarchan sonnet Appreciating the sonnet*		Comparing translations	
from the *Decameron,* "Federigo's Falcon," Giovanni Boccaccio, p. 684	Understanding themes in the *Decameron**	Tracing Boccaccio's influence*	Participating in a storytelling circle	Writing down a story you have told	Using adverb clauses*
Pierre de Ronsard "Roses," p. 692 "When You Are Old," p. 693	Understanding the drama in lyrics*	Appreciating the *carpe diem* theme*		Writing the woman's response	
from *The Tragical History of the Life and Death of Dr. Faustus,* Christopher Marlowe, p. 700	Understanding dramatic irony*	Appreciating historical context*	Completing word analogies	Writing about atomic energy	
The Tempest, Act I, William Shakespeare, p. 709	Understanding exposition Understanding exposition and conflict*	Appreciating Shakespeare's songs	Understanding archaic words*	Contrasting characters	Understanding pronoun reference* Using *that* and *which**
The Tempest, Act II, p. 731	Understanding themes*	Tracing sources	Recognizing diction as a character trait*	Writing as a Caribbean islander	Understanding characterization through diction* Writing humor*
The Tempest, Act III, p. 749	Understanding plot, subplot, and character*		Performing a scene Finding the meaning that fits the context*	Contrasting characters as a clue to theme	Appreciating the evolution of language*
The Tempest, Act IV, p. 763	Understanding Renaissance masques*	Appreciating dramatic speeches*	Appreciating Shakespeare's repetitions	Writing a blank verse soliloquy	Appreciating the uses of language: Poetry and prose*
The Tempest, Act V, p. 773	Understanding the resolution*	Staging a scene	Distinguishing between words*	Writing review guidelines	Establishing tone*

THE AGE OF RATIONALISM

Selection	Analyzing Literature	Critical Thinking and Reading	Understanding Language/ Speaking and Listening	Thinking and Writing	Grammar in Action
Reading Critically					
from "A Modest Proposal," Jonathan Swift, p. 801	Understanding satire*		Using words ironically*		Recognizing compound-complex sentences* Using *who* and *whom**
from *Paradise Lost,* Book IX, John Milton, p. 814	Understanding anastrophe*	Understanding biblical context*	Meaning from context	Collectively describing paradise	Understanding economy of language* Purposes of writing: Understanding persuasive writing*
from *Thoughts,* Blaise Pascal, p. 830	Understanding paradox*	Inferring tone*	Debating		
Jean de La Fontaine "The Boy and the Schoolmaster," p. 836 "The Wolf and the Lamb," p. 838 "The Council Held by the Rats," p. 840	Understanding the fable*	Reasoning	Understanding expressions about animals*	Evaluating a moral	

ROMANTICISM AND REALISM

Selection	Analyzing Literature	Critical Thinking and Reading	Understanding Language/ Speaking and Listening	Thinking and Writing	Grammar in Action
Reading Critically					
from *Faust,* "Prologue in Heaven," Johann Wolfgang von Goethe, p. 863	Recognizing literary models*	Comparing and contrasting depictions*		Writing a dialogue	Using effective reasoning*
from *Faust,* from "The First Part of the Tragedy," Johann Wolfgang von Goethe, p. 869	Understanding legends*		Using context clues*	Planning an adaptation	Supporting an opinion*

ROMANTICISM AND REALISM (continued)

Selection	Analyzing Literature	Critical Thinking and Reading	Understanding Language/ Speaking and Listening	Thinking and Writing	Grammar in Action
"The Bridegroom," Alexander Pushkin, p. 880	Understanding ballads*		Appreciating the effects of verbs and participles*	Comparing and contrasting ballads	
Heinrich Heine "The Lorelei," p. 886 "The Lotus Flower," p. 887	Understanding lyric poetry*	Appreciating concrete words and images*		Writing a lyric poem	
from *The Expiation,* Victor Hugo, p. 890	Understanding the retreat from Russia* Understanding figurative language*		Using words to intensify an effect*	Writing a war poem	
"Ode: Intimations of Immortality from Recollections of Early Childhood," William Wordsworth, p. 896	Understanding romanticism*	Comparing and contrasting ideas*		Responding to a writer's statement	Using common language*
Charles Baudelaire "Invitation to the Voyage," p. 904 "The Albatross," p. 905	Exploring a recurring theme			Writing about theme	
Arthur Rimbaud "Ophelia," p. 908 "Eternity," p. 910	Appreciating borrowed characters	Identifying words that signal cause-and-effect relationships*	Recognizing abstract words*	Extending a characterization	
Prose					
"Two Friends," Guy de Maupassant, p. 914	Understanding realism and naturalism*	Recognizing the author's attitude*		Writing a naturalist story	Using sensory impressions*
"The Overcoat," Nikolai Gogol, p. 992	Understanding a symbol*	Relating symbolism to theme*		Responding to criticism	Recognizing adjective clauses* Recognizing parallelism* Using varied sentence length and structure* Using commas*

ROMANTICISM AND REALISM (continued)

Selection	Analyzing Literature	Critical Thinking and Reading	Understanding Language/ Speaking and Listening	Thinking and Writing	Grammar in Action
"How Much Land Does a Man Need?" Leo Tolstoy, p. 944	Understanding allegory*	Exploring connections among works*	Understanding specific language*	Writing a parable	Recognizing infinitives and infinitive phrases* Punctuating dialogue*
"The Bet," Anton Chekhov, p. 960	Understanding characterization*	Noting the effect of point of view*		Comparing and contrasting stories	Understanding methods of organization*
The New Age of Drama					
A Doll's House, Act I, Henrik Ibsen, p. 969	Understanding a realistic drama*	Writing a dramatic scene*	Recognizing appropriate diction*		Writing realistic dialogue* Using deductive reasoning*
A Doll's House, Act II, p. 989	Understanding characterization*	Making predictions*	Recognizing appropriate diction	Writing a letter	Understanding the four functions of sentences* Recognizing sentence fragments*
A Doll's House, Act III, p. 1105	Recognizing themes*	Appreciating the importance of casting	Recognizing connections of metaphors*	Writing about theme	Understanding purposes of writing: Directions* Recognizing rhetorical and direct questions*

THE MODERN WORLD

Selection	Analyzing Literature	Critical Thinking and Reading	Understanding Language/ Speaking and Listening	Thinking and Writing	Grammar in Action
Reading Critically					
"The Infant Prodigy," Thomas Mann, p. 1039	Recognizing point of view*	Recognizing dramatic irony*		Writing about point of view	Using active and passive voice*

THE MODERN WORLD (continued)

Selection	Analyzing Literature	Critical Thinking and Reading	Understanding Language/ Speaking and Listening	Thinking and Writing	Grammar in Action
Europe					
Rainer Maria Rilke "The Grownup," p. 1055 "Interior of the Rose," p. 1056 "Archaic Torso of Apollo," p. 1057	Interpreting poetry*	Recognizing simile and metaphor*		Writing a poem	
"The Pearls," Isak Dinesen, p. 1066	Understanding setting	Recognizing sensory details*	Understanding phonetic spelling*	Writing a description	Using coordination and subordination* Recognizing infinitives and infinitive phrases*
"The Princess and All the Kingdom," Pär Lagerkvist, p. 1078	Recognizing elements of a fairy tale Interpreting gestures*	Analyzing conflict*		Writing an imitation of a fairy tale	
"The Metamorphosis," Franz Kafka, p. 1084	Understanding modernism*	Relating a work to a writer's life	Choosing the right word*	Responding to a writer's statement	Recognizing adjective clauses* Varying sentence lengths* Using descriptive writing*
Anna Akhmatova "Everything Is Plundered," p. 1114 "I Am Not One of Those Who Left the Land," p. 1115	Understanding acmeism	Understanding imagery*	Comparing translations*		
Boris Pasternak "The Drowsy Garden," p. 1118 "The Weeping Garden," p. 1118	Understanding imagery and figures of speech*	Understanding analogies*			

THE MODERN WORLD (continued)

Selection	Analyzing Literature	Critical Thinking and Reading	Understanding Language/ Speaking and Listening	Thinking and Writing	Grammar in Action
"The Bracelet," Colette, p. 1122	Understanding epiphany*	Sequencing events Identifying cause and effect*	Appreciating word origins	Writing a letter	
Paul Valéry "Caesar," p. 1128 "The Friendly Wood," p. 1129 "Palm," p. 1130	Understanding symbolism*		Understanding denotation and connotation*	Writing using symbolism	
"A Breath of Air," Luigi Pirandello, p. 1134	Understanding plot devices*		Finding antonyms*	Writing a short story	Recognizing tone*
Federico García Lorca "The Guitar," p. 1143 "My Child Went to Sea," p. 1144 "Rider's Song," p. 1145	Recognizing a poet's vision	Interpreting a poet's attitude*		Writing about vision	
Constantine Cavafy "Waiting for the Barbarians," p. 1148 "Artificial Flowers," p. 1150	Understanding irony*	Recognizing situational irony*		Writing about history	
The Americas					
"The Glass of Milk," Manuel Rojas, p. 1154	Understanding point of view*	Recognizing period characteristics*		Exploring a different point of view	Using indirect and direct quotations*
"Sonatina," Rubén Darío, p. 1162	Recognizing distinctive features* Recognizing distinctive themes*	Appreciating tone and atmosphere*		Comparing and contrasting writers	
Gabriela Mistral "Bread," p. 1166 "The Prayer," p. 1168 "Fear," p. 1170	Understanding tone*	Comparing and contrasting tone in poetry*		Responding to fine art	

THE MODERN WORLD (continued)

Selection	Analyzing Literature	Critical Thinking and Reading	Understanding Language/ Speaking and Listening	Thinking and Writing	Grammar in Action
Asia					
"Under Reconstruction," Mori Ōgai, p. 1174	Appreciating changes in Japanese life Appreciating literary symbolism*	Connecting literary works*		Describing a society in transition	Using concrete details*
"My Old Home," Lu Hsun, p. 1182	Appreciating historical context*	Recognizing the author's attitudes*	Finding antonyms	Comparing and contrasting stories	Recognizing prepositional phrases*
"The Artist," Rabindranath Tagore, p. 1192	Understanding conflict*	Relating conflict to theme Contrasting characters*		Writing a continuation of the story	Recognizing appositives*

THE CONTEMPORARY WORLD

Selection	Analyzing Literature	Critical Thinking and Reading	Understanding Language/ Speaking and Listening	Thinking and Writing	Grammar in Action
Reading Critically					
"The Handsomest Drowned Man in the World," Gabriel García Márquez, p. 1213	Appreciating an unusual characterization*		Completing analogies Identifying participial modifiers*	Writing about an extraterrestrial	Recognizing shifting point of view* Appreciating fantastic and concrete details*
The Americas					
"The Garden of Forking Paths," Jorge Luis Borges, p. 1226	Understanding symbols*	Understanding balanced and periodic sentences*		Writing an interactive story	Appreciating understatement*
"House Taken Over," Julio Cortázar, p. 1238	Understanding the fantastic	Making inferences about a story*	Finding the meaning that fits the context*	Writing a fantastic tale	Understanding precise language*
Octavio Paz "Poet's Epitaph," p. 1246 "Fable," p. 1246 "Concord," p. 1246	Appreciating poetic language*	Reading and responding to poetry*	Recognizing prepositions and adverbs*	Writing about paradox	

THE CONTEMPORARY WORLD (continued)

Selection	Analyzing Literature	Critical Thinking and Reading	Understanding Language/ Speaking and Listening	Thinking and Writing	Grammar in Action
"Ode to My Socks," Pablo Neruda, p. 1250	Understanding surrealism*	Learning to interpret*		Writing a surrealistic ode	
Derek Walcott "Sea Grapes," p. 1254 from *Omeros*, p. 1257	Understanding theme through allusion*	Making inferences about allusions	Using etymology*	Writing about an inspirational encounter	
from *Annie John*, Jamaica Kincaid, p. 1264	Understanding reminiscences*	Analyzing the effect of setting*		Writing reminiscences	
Western Europe					
"The Myth of Sisyphus," Albert Camus, p. 1274	Understanding existentialism*		Appreciating the connotations of a word*	Reinterpreting a myth	
Günter Grass "Folding Chairs," p. 1280 "Food for Prophets," p. 1281	Understanding symbolism*	Interpreting symbols and expressions*	Recognizing symbols*		
"The Garden of Stubborn Cats," Italo Calvino, p. 1284	Analyzing theme*	Appreciating tone*		Writing about urbanization	Writing dialogue*
from *Survival in Auschwitz*, Primo Levi, p. 1294	Understanding historical context*	Appreciating details*	Interpreting the language of irony	Writing a personal essay	Using active and passive voice*
Eastern Europe					
"A Song on the End of the World," Czeslaw Milosz, p. 1304	Understanding historical context*	Detecting irony*	Appreciating repetition*	Writing about a quiet hero	
"The First Sally (A) OR Trurl's Electronic Bard," Stanislaw Lem, p. 1308	Understanding satire in science fiction	Making inferences*	Understanding jargon*	Writing a parody	Writing science fiction*
"The One Great Heart," Alexander Solzhenitsyn, p. 1318	Understanding theme*	Appreciating a writer's background*	Understanding phrasing*	Responding to theme	

THE CONTEMPORARY WORLD (continued)

Selection	Analyzing Literature	Critical Thinking and Reading	Understanding Language/ Speaking and Listening	Thinking and Writing	Grammar in Action
"I Am Goya," Andrei Voznesensky, p. 1325	Understanding persona*	Understanding allusions*	Understanding paradox*		
Yevgeny Yevtushenko "Visit," p. 1328 "Weddings," p. 1329	Understanding atmosphere*	Appreciating the speaker's characteristics* Appreciating a poem's ending	Appreciating sensuous language*	Evoking atmosphere	
The Middle East					
"The Happy Man," Najib Mahfouz, p. 1334	Understanding irony and theme* Recognizing a theme*	Anticipating a surprise ending	Using concrete and abstract nouns*	Writing about happiness	Understanding parallelism*
Yehuda Amichai "The Diameter of the Bomb," p. 1342 "From the Book of Esther I Filtered the Sediment," p. 1343	Appreciating figures of speech*	Understanding tone*	Appreciating how language changes*		
Africa					
Léopold Sédar Senghor "Prayer to Masks," p. 1348 "Night of Sine," p. 1350	Understanding negritude*	Relating to features of another culture*		Explaining an original design	
from *Song of Lawino,* Okot p'Bitek, p. 1356	Understanding cultural conflict*	Appreciating figurative language*		Examining cultural conflict	
Wole Soyinka "Season," p. 1362 "Civilian and Soldier," p. 1363	Understanding irony and paradox Understanding irony*	Understanding the poem as a dramatic situation*	Understanding denotation and connotation*		
"The Ultimate Safari," Nadine Gordimer, p. 1366	Understanding social context*	Recognizing point of view*	Using similes*	Writing from a personal perspective	
"Snapshots of a Wedding," Bessie Head, p. 1376	Understanding theme*	Making inferences about tone*	Appreciating abstract and concrete words*	Writing from a different perspective	
"The Winner," Barbara Kimenye, p. 1382	Understanding theme*	Inferring cultural values*		Exploring personal values	
"Tribal Scars or The Voltaique," Ousmane Sembène, p. 1392	Understanding historical context*	Examining conflict*		Writing about a difficult decision	Using adverbs*

THE CONTEMPORARY WORLD (continued)

Selection	Analyzing Literature	Critical Thinking and Reading	Understanding Language/ Speaking and Listening	Thinking and Writing	Grammar in Action
Asia					
"An Astrologer's Day," R. K. Narayan, p. 1410	Understanding situational irony*	Appreciating humor*		Writing a story with a surprise ending	
"Studies in the Park," Anita Desai, p. 1416	Understanding cultural context*	Interpreting epiphanies*		Writing a personal essay	
Pak Tu-jin "August River," p. 1426 "High Mountain Plant," p. 1426	Understanding symbols of nature*	Interpreting poetry*			
"The Jay," Kawabata Yasunari, p. 1430	Analyzing thematic imagery*	Understanding structure*	Appreciating words from Japanese Understanding linking verbs*	Writing from past experience	
"Thought of Hanoi," Nguyen Thi Vinh, p. 1436	Understanding theme*	Appreciating imagery*		Writing a poem with vivid imagery	
Bei Dao "Answer," p. 1440 "Testament," p. 1441 "All," p. 1441 "When Hope Comes Back," Gu Cheng, p. 1442 Shu Ting "Assembly Line," p. 1444 "Also All," p. 1445 "Fairy Tales," p. 1446	Understanding the Misty Poets*	Interpreting imagery*	Appreciating repetition	Comparing and contrasting poems	

ASSESSMENT AND EVALUATION IN PRENTICE HALL LITERATURE

Ruth Townsend
former English Teacher and Teacher Coordinator
Yorktown High School
Yorktown Heights, New York

Marcia Lubell
English Teacher
Yorktown High School
Yorktown Heights, New York

Education . . . Helping the child realize
his [her] potentialities.
—Erich Fromm

There are many valid ways to educate students, to help them achieve success as readers and writers, speakers and listeners. However, the way students' learning is assessed and evaluated often determines the quality of that learning. *Prentice Hall Literature* offers a variety of assessment and evaluation strategies to promote students' progress toward mastery of language arts outcomes.

LEARNING OUTCOMES

The goal of language arts instruction is to make students successful readers, writers, speakers, and thinkers who can demonstrate the following learning outcomes:

1. As readers, students
   - respond personally, aesthetically, and critically to diverse texts
   - collect facts and ideas, discover relationships, and make inferences
   - make critical judgments, analyze, evaluate, and draw conclusions.
2. As writers, students
   - express personal feelings and ideas in a variety of modes
   - communicate information, ideas, and beliefs to a variety of audiences
   - express their ideas critically and evaluatively
   - express their ideas persuasively and provide support for those ideas.
3. As speakers and listeners, students
   - express themselves orally to entertain and to inform
   - interpret information and apply it
   - evaluate ideas according to personal and/or objective criteria.

ASSESSMENT AND EVALUATION OPTIONS

Measuring student growth begins with assessment, an on-going process of gathering information to meet many different evaluation purposes. *Prentice Hall Literature* provides a wide range of assessment strategies and procedures, including testing.

Testing Options
Selection Tests

1. Part A of the Selection Tests contains multiple-choice questions. These types of test items play a role in the initial stages of the assessment and evaluation of your students' growth toward mastery of the learning outcomes. You may use tests on content knowledge as reading checks and as the basis of discussions; you may also use them for collaborative reviews of reading and to prompt personal and critical responses. You may choose to have students work independently or collaboratively to frame their answers to each question and to justify them with textual evidence. You may want students to extend their discussion of the story beyond the printed questions to develop their own questions and to evaluate the universal relevance of the story.

2. Part B of the Selection Test is an essay question. Essay questions offer your students the opportunity to go beyond the limited responses of the multiple-choice items to explore an idea in some depth.

3. Part C of the Selection Test is a Reader's Response question. This type of question elicits a personal reaction to literature.

Other Testing Options

Prentice Hall Literature offers a number of writing assignments and expressive activities that may be used as tests to assess and evaluate your students' mastery of the learning outcomes.

ALTERNATIVE ASSESSMENT OPTIONS

Testing is only one way to measure comprehension of ideas, reasoning process, or problem-solving skills. Assessment is a continuing process linked with curriculum and instruction.

In a student-centered classroom, you assess and evaluate growth in many ways, each of which motivates your students to use language for effective communication. The student-centered classroom enables students to perceive themselves as partners with you in the learning process. That process includes their ability to assess their own competence, determine goals for their own achievement, and judge their own performance. As your students learn to assess and evaluate their own work, they become empowered to take increasing responsibility for their own learning.

You can assist your students in developing self-assessment skills by involving them in the following activities:

Reader's Response Journals
Alternative and Expressive Assignments
Protocols
Peer Review
Collaborative Assessment
Student Portfolios

Reader's Response Journals

Reader's Response Journals help students become conscious of their own thinking process by asking them to make observations of what they read and to respond personally based on those observations. Making observations about a text requires readers to be as objective as possible. Of course, some personal judgment is involved in deciding which details of the text are relevant and appropriate to "observe." However, when making observations students concentrate on factual information and cite concrete details of language or description to back up their observations.

Responding personally to a text is also an important part of active reading. After students have recorded each observation, they react personally, making inferences and predictions, evaluating details, and raising questions. They may question the significance of details they have observed, the meaning of events they have recorded, or the reasons for human behavior they have noted. They may also explore the implications of the connections between what they have read and their own experiences, other pieces of literature, and the world in which they live. Because students' questions are generated by their personal responses to what is otherwise objective and concrete, they can see the relationship between logical inferences and concrete details.

Alternative and Expressive Assignments

Alternative assignments challenge students to present their critical reading responses imaginatively. They make judgments about character development, the significance of plot details and stylistic techniques, including characteristics of diction, imagery, and syntax. Judgments about literary elements may lend support to students' ideas of theme and the universal significance of a text, or they may cause students to rethink or re-envision their initial responses to the reading. These are sample alternative assignments:

Writing letters to real and imagined audiences
Writing in the persona of a character in the text
Comparing literary figures to real people
Writing investigative reports
Writing editorials
Writing human interest stories
Creating speeches in various personae
Creating commercials or advertisements

You will find examples of alternative assignments throughout the student text under Thinking and Writing, in the Annotated Teacher's Edition, and in the Teaching Portfolio.

Expressive assignments stimulate creativity by encouraging students to re-envision the text and to re-create portions of it. Here are some examples of expressive assignments:

Writing a new ending for a selection
Adding scenes
Changing the point of view
Writing a modern version or a parody
Conducting a trial of a character
Holding elections for literary characters
Inventing a newspaper or magazine based on a selection
Writing a poem based on the selection
Making a video

You will find examples of expressive response assignments throughout the student text, in the Teaching Portfolio, and in the Annotated Teacher's Edition.

Protocols

Protocols are descriptions of the thinking and writing process. They enable your students to assess their own learning by providing them with the opportunity to describe the processes they follow in writing, reading, and speaking. Thus, students begin to monitor their progress toward mastery. To prompt the writing of protocols, students answer questions such as these:

What were your content and stylistic goals in this piece?
How successful do you feel you were in meeting those goals?
What gave you difficulty in this assignment?
What new learning came out of writing this piece?

You may adapt this basic protocol to fit your specific assignments.

Peer Review

Peer review offers your students another opportunity to develop other metacognition skills as they learn from each other. Working in pairs or in small groups, students review each other's work and make suggestions for revision of content, form, and mechanics. However, the emphasis of the review changes, depending on what stage in the writing process the peer critique occurs. For example, in the drafting stage students focus on content and development, answering questions like these:

What do you see as the writer's purpose?
For what audience is this piece intended?
What specific details did the writer include to accomplish that purpose?
What additional information would enhance the piece?
What, if anything, would you suggest the writer delete?

In the editing stage the review questions may focus more on form and mechanics. Your students may consider these questions:

What is the topic of each paragraph?
Are the supporting details presented logically?
Are the verb tenses appropriate and consistent?
What corrections do you suggest for improving the language and mechanics of the piece?

You may tailor the peer review to fit specific assignments.

To validate the peer review, you may have your students revise their work, incorporating those suggestions they believe will enhance their final product. Thoughtful peer reviews have a value not only for the students whose pieces are reviewed but for the reviewers who in the process of assessing other students' work are practicing their active reading skills.

Collaborative Assessment

Collaborative assessment offers yet another opportunity for your students to develop an awareness of their thinking and writing processes, enabling you and your students to work together to determine the criteria for evaluating student performance. These criteria, usually identified in the initial stages of an assignment, may change as your students develop their competence as language users. Because they have helped define the criteria for evaluation, your students have a clearer understanding of how to complete the assignment successfully. These criteria form the basis for the writing of their protocols and for peer reviews. Criteria vary but may include these factors:

Accuracy of content
Relevance of detail
Appropriateness of form
Consistency of voice
Variety of sentence structure
Correctness of language mechanics

Collaborative assessment helps your students gain confidence in their ability to participate in evaluating their individual mastery of the learning outcomes.

Student Portfolios

One of the most powerful assessment options available to you and your students is the portfolio. Portfolios are collections of students' work. You may choose to have portfolios contain various drafts of students' work so that you can assess growth during the process of writing a paper, examples of students' best work so that you can assess growth during the year, or a combination of both. For portfolios to be effective learning tools, students must be trained to take responsibility for their own learning. That means they must develop skills for self-assessment.

Once students have taken responsibility for their own learning by working through reader response and critical re-

sponse activities, they have developed the skills necessary to create portfolios. What makes portfolios effective is that they involve students even further in the assessment and evaluation process. To prepare their portfolios, students review a body of their work and select those performance pieces they believe best represent their growth toward mastery of the learning outcomes. They may create several different kinds of portfolios:

Individual Performance Portfolios Your students may create individual portfolios reflecting their performance on a particular unit of study. Students collaborate with you in determining the number and type of pieces to include in the portfolio. Your students also help establish the criteria for evaluation of the portfolio. Individual portfolios may be a collection of videotaped dramatic presentations or speeches, stories, memoirs, poems and/or responses to poems, and personal and analytical essays on a particular theme or literary work.

A sample portfolio for a selection might include student responses to the following assignments:

The Reader's Response Journal
The Selection Test in the Teaching Portfolio
An Alternate Composition from the Teaching Portfolio
The Thinking and Writing assignment in the Student Text

From these assignments, you and your students may decide to include three pieces. By selecting those pieces they believe best reflect their growth toward mastery of the learning outcomes, students reveal their ability to assess their own work. You may also give your students the opportunity to revise any of their selections and to enhance their portfolio with additional pieces that reflect their appreciation and understanding of the text.

Project Portfolios Working collaboratively, your students may create project portfolios that reflect their performance on a particular project. Here too students help define the direction and scope of the project or activity. They work together with you to establish the criteria for evaluation of the project. Project portfolios may be written products such as newspapers, news magazines, or handbooks based on a particular literary work, or they may be performance oriented such as trials, elections, game shows, interview shows, or videos.

Mastery Portfolios At the end of a course your students may compile a mastery portfolio that reflects their best work in the course. You and your students may decide how many pieces to include, what models to have represented, and whether to include early pieces as well as later pieces to demonstrate growth. Creating the portfolio also offers your students an opportunity to revise any work in order to demonstrate mastery.

Portfolio Protocols The most valuable step in the creation of a portfolio is the writing of the protocol in which students describe the rationale behind their portfolio selections, the learning demonstrated in each piece, and their awareness of their strengths and weaknesses as language users. To prompt the writing of the protocols, your students may consider questions like these:

What pieces did you include in your portfolio?
Why did you select these particular pieces?
What learning does each piece reflect?
What insights did you gain about yourself, as a reader, writer, speaker, and listener from creating this portfolio?

Evaluating Portfolios

Even though students have been active participants in the creation and assessment of their portfolios, ultimately it is your responsibility to evaluate the work and assign a grade. Just as your students are guided by clearly defined criteria as they develop their portfolios, you are guided by these same criteria as you evaluate their performance. In general, these criteria reflect concern for content, form, and presentation.

Evaluation of content focuses on the students' abilities to reflect their understanding of or insight into the literature studied, the concepts explored, the issues considered as well as their facility with modes of writing. Mastery is characterized by each student's demonstration of skill in analytical thinking, that is, the ability to summarize, compare, and synthesize.

Evaluation of form focuses on students' mastery of the modes of response, including logical and appropriate organization and sequence, coherence, unity, sophistication of style, and control of language use.

Evaluation of presentation deals with the appearance of the final product—its neatness, its attractiveness, and its appropriateness for the focus of the content.

MASTERY OF LEARNING OUTCOMES

Evaluation of student mastery requires consideration of the desired outcomes for reading, writing, speaking, and listening. The extent to which your students meet the desired outcomes determines their level of mastery of English/language arts skills.

Competent The students who demonstrate competence in reading, writing, speaking, and listening can deal with a wide range of subject matter in a variety of forms. They reveal an ability to see relationships; they can emulate models; they can apply knowledge in a limited number of contexts.

Excellent The students who demonstrate excellence in reading, writing, speaking, and listening can deal with complex and sophisticated subject matter. They discriminate among language forms for specific purposes and make appropriate stylistic judgments. They synthesize their insights in a variety of contexts.

Superior The superior students are characterized by their originality and creativity. They reveal depth of perception, imaginative insights, and authority in all aspects of language use.

CONCLUSION

As an English/language arts teacher you have a wide variety of assessment and evaluation options available to you in *Prentice Hall Literature.* These assessment and evaluation strategies afford you the opportunity to respond to the individual needs of your students.

Bibliography

Benson, Barbara. "Effective Tests: Let Them Write!" *The English Journal,* February 1991.

DeFabio, Roseanne. "Outcomes Projects." State Education Department. Albany, N.Y., 1991.

English Language Arts Syllabus K–12. State Education Department. Bureau of Curriculum Development. Albany, N.Y., 1988.

Johnson, D.W., and Johnson, R. *Circles of Learning: Cooperation in the Classroom.* Alexandria, Va.: ASCD, 1984. New York State English Language Arts Syllabus.

Neubert, Gloria, and McNelis, Sally. "Peer Response: Teaching Specific Revision Suggestions." *The English Journal,* September 1990.

Perrone, Vito. *Expanding Student Assessment.* Alexandria, Va.: ASCD, 1991.

Rosenblatt, L. *The Reader, the Text, and the Poem.* Cambridge, Mass.: Harvard University Press, 1978.

Schwartz, Jeffrey. "Let Them Assess Their Own Learning." *The English Journal,* February 1991.

Shaughnessy, Mina. *Errors and Expectations.* New York: Oxford University Press, 1977.

Tchudi, Stephen. *Planning and Assessing the Curriculum in English Language Arts.* Alexandria, Va.: ASCD, 1991.

Tierney, Robert J., Carter, Mark, and Desai, Laura. *Portfolio Assessment in the Reading-Writing Classroom.* Norwood, Mass.: Christopoher Gordon Publishers, 1991.

Wiggins, Grant. "A True Test: Toward More Authentic and Equitable Assessment." *Phi Delta Kappan,* May 1989.

Wolf, Denny P. "Portfolio Assessment: Sampling Student Work." *Educational Leadership,* April 1989.

ALTERNATE COURSES OF STUDY

Tenth-Grade Course

The following selections are especially appropriate for average tenth-grade students:

One-Semester Course

The following selections are particularly recommended for a one-semester course:

ROMAN LITERATURE
(C. 300 B.C.–A.D. 500)

■ P A R T 4 ■

THE MIDDLE AGES
(A.D. 450–1300)

THE RENAISSANCE
(1300–1650)

THE AGE OF RATIONALISM
(1650–1800)

ROMANTICISM AND REALISM
(1800–1890)

■ P A R T 5 ■

THE MODERN WORLD
(1890–1945)

THE CONTEMPORARY WORLD
(1946–PRESENT)

PRENTICE HALL

LITERATURE

COPPER

BRONZE

SILVER

GOLD

PLATINUM

THE AMERICAN EXPERIENCE

THE BRITISH TRADITION

WORLD MASTERPIECES

PRENTICE HALL

LITERATURE
WORLD MASTERPIECES

FOURTH EDITION

SHIPS RETURNING TO HARBOR AT TEMPOZAN
Yashima Gakutei (1786–1868)

PRENTICE HALL
Upper Saddle River, New Jersey
Needham, Massachusetts

Humanities Note

Fine art, *Ships Returning to Harbor at Tempozan* by Yashima Gakutei (1786–1868). Beginning in the seventeenth century, Japanese traditional painters joined with engravers and printers to produce colored wood block prints of traditional and current subjects. Compared to paintings, these prints were relatively inexpensive, and they immediately became very popular.

The Japanese called these prints Ukiyo-E (pronounced ookee yoh eh), which means "pictures of the floating world" and refers to a moment frozen in time. In the mid-nineteenth century, these prints were exported to the West in book or album form. The unfamiliar aspects of the Ukiyo-E style surprised Westerners: the seeming disregard for the rules of perspective, the flat use of color with no suggestion of three dimensionality, and the expressive, decorative use of pattern. However, the Japanese artists' different point of view greatly influenced the work of James Whistler, Toulouse Lautrec, Edgar Degas and other avant garde artists in France.

An offshoot of Ukiyo-E was the art of Surimono. These highly-refined woodblock prints were produced in limited editions for private buyers to mark special occasions like a holiday or marriage, announce an event, or illustrate a favorite poem. The immaculate Surimono required great technical skill to produce and were printed on the finest paper with the best ink.

The Japanese painter and printmaker Yashima Gakutei specialized in Surimono. He mastered his artistic and printing techniques as a student of the premier woodblock print artist Hiroshige. *Ships Returning to Harbor at Tempozan* is a Surimono print in which the artist reduces the ships and elements of nature, trees, sky and waves to flat decorative patterns. The first boat in the foreground is repeated many times in diminishing sizes, which creates an illusion of distance. The sameness of the ships gives a decorative effect to the print. This effect is enhanced by the stylized rays of the sun, the golden moon on the right, and the soaring cranes above the sails.

Although Japanese artists continued to produce wood block prints, the popularity of Ukiyo-E and Surimono lasted only through the end of the nineteenth century. The advent of photography, magazine illustration, greeting cards, and Japanese interest in Western painting styles brought the art to a virtual halt. Collectors of art have always been interested in beautiful prints like this, and the demand for antique prints is ever increasing. Recently, Ukiyo-E has had a revival among the young artists of Japan who look to masters like Gakutei for their inspiration.

ISBN 0-13-722638-1

3 4 5 6 7 8 9 10   98 97 96

Art credits begin on page 1514.

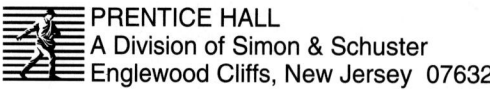

PRENTICE HALL
A Division of Simon & Schuster
Englewood Cliffs, New Jersey 07632

STAFF CREDITS FOR PRENTICE HALL LITERATURE

Publisher: Eileen Thompson

Editorial: Ellen Bowler, Philip Fried, Douglas McCollum, Kelly Ackley,
Barbara Coe, Eric Hausmann, Richard Tortoriello, Amy Fleming,
Megan Mahoney, Jacqueline Regan, Glenn E. Bell

Marketing: Mollie Ledwith, Belinda Loh

National Language Arts Consultants: Ellen Lees Backstrom, Ed.D., Craig A.
McGhee, Karen Massey Riley, Vennisa Travers, Gail Witt

Permissions: Doris Robinson

Design: Susan Walrath, Leslie Osher, Carmela Pereira, AnnMarie Roselli

Visual Research: Libby Forsyth, Emily Rose, Martha Conway

Production: Suse Bell, Joan McCulley, Elizabeth Torjussen, Garret Schenck,
Gertrude Szyferblatt

Publishing Technology: Andrew G. Black, Deborah J. Jones, Kathryn A. Foot,
Monduane Harris, Cleasta Wilburn, Greg Myers

Pre-Press Production: Laura Sanderson, Paula Massenaro, Denise Herckenrath

Print and Bind: Rhett Conklin,

ACKNOWLEDGMENTS

Grateful acknowledgment is made to the following for
permission to reprint copyrighted material:

**The American University in Cairo Press and Saad El-
Gabalawy** "The Happy Man" by Naguib Mahfouz from
Modern Egyptian Short Stories, translated by Saad El-
Gabalawy. Copyright © 1969 as al-Ragul al-Saᶜid.
Translation copyright © 1977, York Press. Reprinted by
arrangement with The American University in Cairo Press
and the translator.

The Asia Society and Nguyen Ngoc Bich "Thoughts of
Hanoi" by Nguyen Thi Vinh from *A Thousand Years of
Vietnamese Poetry,* edited by Nguyen Ngoc Bich.
Copyright 1962, 1967, 1968, 1969, 1970, 1971, 1974 by
The Asia Society and Nguyen Ngoc Bich. Reprinted by
permission.

Basic Books Inc. "I Am Goya" translated by Stanley
Kunitz from *Antiworlds and the Fifth Ace* by Andrei
Voznesensky, edited by Patricia Blake and Max Hayward.
Copyright © 1963 by Encounter Ltd.; copyright © 1966,
1967 by Basic Books, Inc. Reprinted by permission.

Basil Blackwell Publishers, Ltd. "A Modest Proposal"
by Jonathan Swift from *The Norton Anthology of World
Masterpieces,* Volume II, edited by Maynard Mack.
Copyright © 1985, 1979, 1973, 1965, 1956 by W. W.
Norton & Company, Inc. All rights reserved. Reprinted by
permission.

Robert Bly "Ode to My Socks" by Pablo Neruda.
Reprinted from *Neruda and Vallejo: Selected Poems,*

(Continued on page 1511.)

CONTENTS

PART 2
The Rise of Asia
(c. 1400 B.C.–A.D. 1890)

INDIAN LITERATURE
(c. 1400 B.C.–c. A.D. 500)

CHINESE LITERATURE
(1000 B.C.–A.D. 1890)

JAPANESE LITERATURE
(500 B.C.–A.D. 1890)

P A R T 4
Europe in Transition
(450–1890)

THE MIDDLE AGES
(A.D. 450–1300)

THE RENAISSANCE
(1300–1650)

THE AGE OF RATIONALISM
(1650–1800)

ROMANTICISM AND REALISM
(1800–1890)

PART 5
The Twentieth Century
(1890–Present)

THE MODERN WORLD
(1890–1945)

THE CONTEMPORARY WORLD
(1946–Present)

Beginnings in the East
3000 B.C.–A.D. 1400

NEAR EASTERN KINGDOMS
In the Seventh Century B.C.

Oxus R.

Sogdiana

○ Bactra

Bactria

hia

Aria

TIANS

Drangiana

PACTYANS

○ Arachosia

SVLAIMAN MTS.

Indus R.

INDIA

MARE ARABICUM
(Arabian Sea)

Using the Map

Have students study the map and ask them the following questions.

1. What means do you think the ancient Egyptians used to trade with the Assyrians? Why?
2. Why were the Babylonians, whose capital city was Babylon, particularly well situated to engage in commerce?
3. Which geographical features favored the early development of civilization in Egypt and in Mesopotamia (the region labeled the Assyrian Empire on this map)?
4. How do you explain the absence of cities and towns in the region labeled Arabia?
5. What does the location of Phoenicia suggest about the way its inhabitants earned their living?

WALKING LION IN RELIEF (detail)
Babylonian mosaic on walls of processional road
The Metropolitan Museum of Art, New York

Objectives

1 To understand ancient Mesopotamian civilization
2 To understand ancient Egyptian civilization
3 To understand ancient Hebrew civilization

SUMERIAN, EGYPTIAN, AND HEBREW LITERATURE

3000 B.C.–c. 100 B.C.

When the journey was accomplished they arrived at Uruk, the strong-walled city. Gilgamesh spoke to him, to Urshanabi the ferryman, "Urshanabi, climb up onto the wall of Uruk, inspect its foundation terrace, and examine well the brickwork; see if it is not of burnt bricks; and did not the seven wise men lay these foundations? One third of the whole is city, one third is garden, and one third is field, with the precinct of the goddess Ishtar. These parts and the precinct are all Uruk."

—**from *The Epic of Gilgamesh***

Motivation/Prior Knowledge Tell students that they will be learning about the earliest civilizations known to us. Many of our religious, scientific, and philosophical ideas date back to these civilizations. Even the way we build and organize our houses was influenced by these early peoples: The ancient Sumerians developed the first cities in history.

1 Enrichment Tell students that the Tigris-Euphrates Valley, home of ancient Mesopotamian civilization, forms the eastern part of the Fertile Crescent. Shaped like a semicircle, this fertile strip of land stretches from the Persian Gulf around to the Mediterranean Sea. Not only is the Fertile Crescent agriculturally productive, but it is ideally situated for trade. It is located at the point where three continents meet: Asia, Africa, and Europe.

Using the Map
Have students study the map and ask them the following questions:
1. Name five cities included in the area of the earliest Sumerian settlement.
2. Name two cities included in the Empire of Agade that had never before been part of a Mesopotamian kingdom.
3. How did the size and extent of ancient Mesopotamian empires change over time?
4. What, if anything, can you deduce from these changes?
5. Which empire might have found it easiest to convey goods from the Persian Gulf to the Mediterranean Sea? Explain.

MESOPOTAMIA

The Origins of Mesopotamian Civilization

The quotation on the preceding page comes from an epic about an ancient Sumerian king. That it boasts about a city is no accident. When we speak of civilization, we usually mean cities, or at least the high degree of social organization that cities suggest: temples, palaces, arts and crafts, technology, and systems of writing.

About 4,000 years ago, several major civilizations developed in the river valleys of southwest Asia. The region between the Tigris and Euphrates rivers, in modern Iraq, was one of these sites: Mesopotamia, the Greek name for this region, means "the land between the two rivers."

The southeastern part of this region, Sumer, was flat, dry, and arid; moreover, it lacked timber and minerals. Yet overflows from the two rivers made the land fertile and the resulting mud could be baked into brick. To capitalize on these floods, however, farmers had to build irrigation ditches. The need to coordinate the digging and repair of these ditches may have prompted the growth of Sumerian civilization.

The Sumerians

Scholars disagree about the identity of the people or peoples who spoke and wrote Sumerian. In the succession of civilizations that arose in this region, however, theirs was the first, and it influenced the Babylonian and Assyrian civilizations that followed.

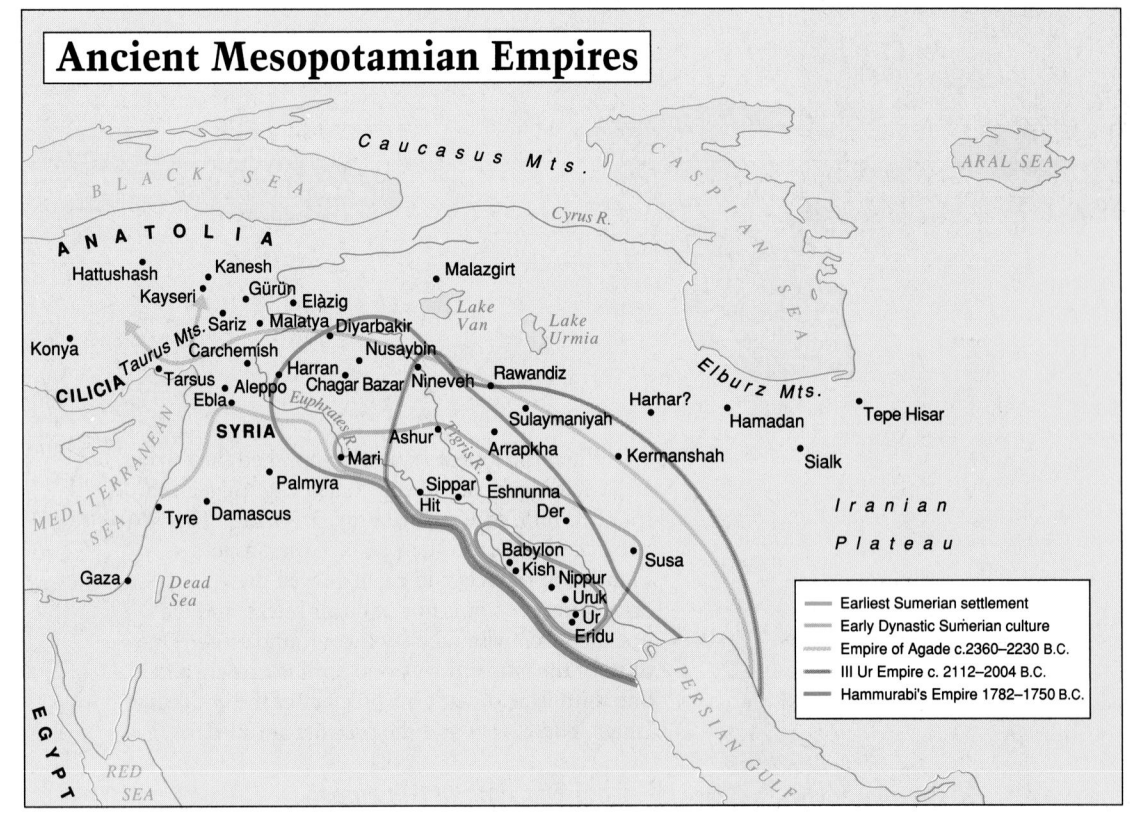

Ancient Mesopotamian Empires

Legend:
- Earliest Sumerian settlement
- Early Dynastic Sumerian culture
- Empire of Agade c.2360–2230 B.C.
- III Ur Empire c. 2112–2004 B.C.
- Hammurabi's Empire 1782–1750 B.C.

As the founders of Mesopotamian civilization, the Sumerians have many "firsts" to their credit. They probably invented the region's earliest system of writing, which developed from simple pictures to the cuneiform, or wedge-shaped, signs familiar to archeologists.

Furthermore, the professional writers called scribes learned this system in Mesopotamia's first schools, called *edubbas*. These scribes were the guardians of Sumeria's rich literary tradition. While much literature circulated in oral form, scribes also recorded and transmitted many of the culture's epics, hymns, historical accounts, myths, and proverbs.

Besides cuneiform writing, the Sumerians developed a system of numeration based on sixty. The Sumerian system led to our 60-second minute, 60-minute hour, and 360-degree circle.

Perhaps the most famous Sumerian "first" was the creation of cities. Many of these urban centers, which were like mini-nations, were actually within sight of one another. At first the main institution in each city was a temple. This temple contained the image of the city's chief god—the Sumerians worshiped many gods—and housed the temple staff: priests who ruled the city, scribes who recorded the crops the temple received from its lands, and artisans. The largest building in the temple complex, and in the city itself, was the ziggurat, a six- or seven-story tower that Sumerians believed the gods could use as a ladder in descending from heaven.

As city-states grew and came into conflict, military leaders replaced priests as rulers. These military leaders eventually became kings, and the king's palace, with its own staff, rivaled the temple in importance.

The Babylonians

One of the greatest Mesopotamian kings was Sargon (c. 2340 B.C.). His new capital city of Agade, located near the site of Babylon, was north of Sumer—the northward shift of power in Mesopotamia would become a continuing trend. Agade contributed its name to the region where Sargon lived (Akkad) and the language he spoke (Akkadian). A Semitic language, related to modern Hebrew and Arabic, Akkadian in its various forms became the tongue of the new northern centers of power, Babylon and Assur.

GROUP OF SUMERIAN FIGURES FROM IRAQ: TELL ASMAR
c. 2700–2500 B.C.
The Oriental Institute of the University of Chicago

Those who spoke Semitic languages, the Semites, were nomadic peoples who migrated to Mesopotamia from the Arabian peninsula. One such group, the Amorites, founded the village of Babylon on the Euphrates River (c. 2000 B.C.). Not until the reign of Hammurabi (c. 1750 B.C.), however, did Babylon come into its own as the capital of a great empire. Hammurabi's kingdom encompassed Sumer, Akkad, and the northern cities of Assur and Nineveh. His famous legal code, engraved on a stone slab, contains 282 laws covering all aspects of daily life. It was based on a principle described as "an eye for an eye": A person who blinded another was punished by being blinded.

Babylonians had a reverent attitude toward Sumerian culture. Babylonian scribes, for instance, learned the Sumerian language and preserved its literature. However, they were far more than slavish imitators. Reshaping a group of Sumerian tales about a legendary king, these scribes fashioned a brilliant Akkadian work that we know today as *The Epic of Gilgamesh* (see page 15).

Humanities Note

Fine art, *Group of Sumerian figures from the Abu Temple, Tell Asmar*, c. 2700–2500 B.C. A tell is a mound or hill covering ancient communities, and Tell Asmar is located at the site of the ancient city of Eshunna (see the map on page 4). Tell Asmar and several other nearby tells were excavated between 1930 and 1936 by the well-known archeologist Henri Frankfort. In addition to these Sumerian sculptures, he found temples, palaces, tablets, and cylinder seals.

These figures are meant to please a god or gods by representing worshipers in the act of offering prayers. The tallest one is about a foot high. Carving these statues from marble, the sculptor followed conic and cylindrical patterns and did not attempt to create a good likeness. One purpose of this simplification was to focus attention on the eyes, which were thought to reveal the soul. The flounced skirts were worn by Sumerian men of this era.

You might want to use the following questions to discuss the art:

1. What do you think these figures are doing? How do you know?
2. What mood do they inspire in you? Why?
3. What geometric shapes did the sculptor use to create these figures? Explain.

2 **Enrichment** Explain to students that the Sumerian school, or *edubba*, had the following personnel: the "school-father," who was in charge of the establishment; the "big brother," or assistant professor, who wrote tablets for students to copy and monitored students' work; "the man in charge of drawing"; "the man in charge of Sumerian"; and officers responsible for attendance and discipline.

Sumerian, Egyptian, and Hebrew
(3000 B.C.–100 B.C.)

Mesopotamian carving of Gudea, a Sumerian city-god, c. 2130 B.C.

Ziggurat at Ur

Humanities Notes

Pictured from left to right:

Gudea was the city-god of Lagash, an independent Sumerian city-state. Gudea had numerous statues of himself placed in the shrines of Lagash, all of which exhibit the same immobile and expressionless face. These statues were carved from diorite, an extremely hard stone favored by many Egyptian sculptors.

A ziggurat is a form of temple common to the Sumerians, Babylonians, and Assyrians. The temples were built because there was a widespread belief that mountaintops were the dwelling places of the gods. These ancient peoples believed they could provide a fit place for their deity by creating artificial mountains of their own. The ziggurat at Ur, pictured here, was built by King Urnammu in c. 2500 B.C. Ziggurats were planned in such a way that when worshipers started at the bottom, they were forced to go around as many corners as possible before reaching the cella—the main room where sacrifices were offered before the statue of the patron god. This sort of angular spiral or "bent-axis approach" is a fundamental characteristic of Mesopotamian religious architecture.

The pyramids of Giza—dating c. 2600 to 1500 B.C.—are situated on the west bank of the Nile River near Cairo, Egypt. There are ten pyramids at Giza, including the three largest and best-preserved Egyptian pyramids pictured here. The Great Pyramid was built for King Khufu; the second was built for King Khafre; and the third for King Menkaure. It is possible that it took 100,000 men, working four-month shifts, to build the Great Pyramid. Since the ancient Egyptians had no machinery, they cut the limestone with copper chisels and saws. Gangs of men dragged the blocks to the site. The upper layers of blocks were dragged up long ramps. Workers then covered the pyramid with an outer coating of white casing stones. The outer stones were so exactly laid that from a distance the pyramid ap-

	−3000	−2500	−2000

HISTORY

- Sumerian city-state develops
- Old Kingdom in Egypt begins
- Promulgation of laws by Sumerian states is common
- Sargon, an Akkadian soldier, establishes the first empire in recorded history
- First Intermediate period in Egypt begins
- Dynasty of Pharaohs in Egypt begins
- Middle Kingdom in Egypt begins
- Second Intermediate period in Egypt begins
- Hammurabi, King of Babylon, establishes empire in Mesopotamia

HUMAN PROGRESS

- Sumerians develop written language in cuneiform
- Egyptians develop hieroglyphics
- Systematic astrological observations in Egypt, India, and China begin
- Egypt introduces calendar of 365 days
- Wrestling becomes the first sport
- The horse is domesticated
- First libraries in Egypt are opened
- The earliest Egyptian mummies are made
- Percussion instruments are added to Egyptian orchestral music
- The Hebrew patriarch Abraham migrates from Ur
- Irrigation system in Egypt begins

LITERATURE

- Gilgamesh, legendary King of Uruk, rules
- Scribal schools in Sumeria are established
- Written composition of *The Epic of Gilgamesh* begins
- Hammurabi's code is established

The Giza Pyramids, Cairo, Egypt

Gold sarcophagus cover, tomb of Tutankhamun

Noah's Ark, illustration for Gutenberg's Bible, c. 1456

Old City of Jerusalem, Israel

-1500   -1000   -500   -100

- New Kingdom in Egypt begins
  - Ikhnaton rules as pharaoh; enforces sun worship in Egypt
    - Tutankhamun inherits throne
    - King Tutankhamun dies
      - Jewish exodus from Egypt begins
        - King David rules

- Solomon succeeds King David
  - Solomon dies; Kingdom of Israel divides into Israel and Judah
    - Assyrians conquer Israel
  - Nebuchadnezzar II, King of Babylonia, rules
    - Nebuchadnezzar seizes Judah, destroys temple in Jerusalem
      - Temple of Jerusalem is restored
      - Persians conquer Egypt

- Egypt revolts against Persia
  - Egypt joins Persia against Greece
    - Persian empire falls to Alexander the Great

- Iron is used instead of bronze
- The Ten Commandments become the basis of Jewish law
- Tapestries are made in Egypt
- Obelisks in Egypt serve as sundials

- First coins are minted
- Ivory carving is practiced in Egypt, Phoenicia, and Sumeria
- Earliest recorded music, a hymn, is written on a tablet in Sumeria
  - Alexander the Great founds the Port of Alexandria

- Oldest parts of Old Testament are composed

- The Book of Ruth is composed
  - Old Testament is assembled

(continued from page 6)

pears to have been cut out of a single white stone.

King Tutankhamun ruled from c. 1347 B.C. until his death in 1339 B.C. He began his reign at the age of nine. Tutankhamun was the son-in-law of King Ikhnaton, the Egyptian ruler who named Aton the sole god of Egypt. Tutankhamun's name means *the living image of Aton*. Although his reign was relatively unimportant, interest in Tutankhamun grew in 1922 after a British archeologist discovered his tomb. The contents of Tutankhamun's tomb included a mummy and the gold sarcophagus—a monumental coffin or tomb—pictured here.

Chapters 6–9 of the Book of Genesis tell the story of Noah and his ark. According to the Bible, Noah was chosen by God to keep people and animals alive during the Great Flood. For 120 years, Noah warned people of the Flood, and in preparation for it, Noah built an ark, or ship. He took into his ark his family and enough animals and birds to repopulate the earth. This illustration from Gutenberg's Bible—the first printed book—depicts Noah's ark during the forty days and forty nights that it rained.

Jerusalem is the disputed capital of Israel. It is the holy city for Jews, Christians, and Muslims. Also called Zion, Jerusalem figures prominently in Jewish and Christian literature as a symbol of the capital of the Messiah. The Old City, pictured here, is the eastern part of Jerusalem. To the east of the Old City lie the Garden of Gethsemane and the Mount of Olives.

Fine art, *Babylonian map of the world*. Some tablets contain surveyors' plans, but this is the only Babylonian map of the world known to have survived. It is about 6 inches long and illustrates a treatise on mythology. It shows the circle of the "Salt Sea" and, beyond it, an area "where the sun is not seen." The parallel lines through the middle of the map are meant to represent the Euphrates River, and the rectangle across these lines stands for the city of Babylon. At the mouth of the Euphrates, in the south, the map shows marsh country.

You might want to use the following questions to discuss the art:

1. What geographical features does this map seem to represent?
2. Does this map seem to be accurate? Explain.
3. What factors might have limited the ancient Babylonians' knowledge of the world?

3 Enrichment Explain to students that Egyptian literature and art began to flourish during the Middle Kingdom period, when Egyptians began to have greater contact with other peoples. A famous story written at this time is the *Tale of Sinuhe*, which tells about the adventures of an Egyptian traveling in foreign lands. This tale later inspired stories about Sinbad the Sailor, one of which found its way into the Persian book of tales entitled *The Thousand and One Nights*. (For an excerpt from this classic—not the story of Sinbad, however—see page 128.)

4 Enrichment Tell students that the Egyptian system of writing, hieroglyphics, appeared in the earliest stages of Egyptian history. Scholars are surprised by the fact that from its first appearance, this system makes use of a rebus-principle. In other words, to take an example from English, the pictures of a bee and of a leaf might be put together to sound out the word *belief*. Usually, this rebus-principle takes some time to develop, so it is unusual to see it be-

BABYLONIAN MAP
OF THE WORLD
British Museum, London

The Assyrians

The Assyrians were a Semitic group that built the city-state of Assur in northern Mesopotamia. For about half a millennium (1100 –600 B.C.), they used their iron weapons and formidable cavalry to battle for control of the land between the two rivers. While Assyrians competed with Babylonians, however, they recognized the superiority of Babylonian and Sumerian culture. The seventh-century Assyrian king Assurbanipal paid homage to that culture by assembling the first great library of the ancient world—more than 20,000 clay tablets in Sumerian and Babylonian cuneiform.

EGYPT

Origins: "The gift of the Nile"

At the time that Sumerian civilization was developing along the Tigris and Euphrates rivers, Egyptian civilization arose along the banks of the Nile in northeastern Africa. The Greek historian Herodotus called Egypt "the gift of the Nile," and he was right. Every July the river would flood, replenishing farmland along its banks with moisture and rich silt. In addition to fertile land, the river provided a watery highway for travel and trade. It was also a source of fish. Without the river's life-giving bounty, Egypt would be as barren as the deserts that surround it.

History: Old, Middle, and New Kingdoms

At first the villages along the Nile were divided into two countries: Upper Egypt in the south and Lower Egypt in the north. Around 3100 B.C., the ruler of Upper Egypt, Menes, conquered Lower Egypt and created a single realm. The history of the pharaohs, or rulers, who led Egypt for the next two thousand years can be divided into the following periods: the Old Kingdom (2700–2200 B.C.), the Middle Kingdom (2050–1800 B.C.), and the New Kingdom (1570–1090 B.C.). In the periods between these eras, Egypt was prey to invasions and civil wars. By and large, however, the geographical barriers of desert and sea protected Egypt from its neighbors and made for a long-lived, stable, and conservative civilization.

Unlike the Mesopotamian kings, who were powerful but human figures, the pharaohs were looked upon as gods. At no time was their godlike power more apparent than in the Old Kingdom. During this period, many pharaohs had peasants and slaves labor to build them giant pyramids. These large structures, some of them made of millions of stones, housed the pharaoh's body, household furniture, and fortune after his death. During the Middle Kingdom, commoners gained more rights, including the privilege of having their own bodies embalmed after death. The New Kingdom, also known as the Empire Age, saw increased contacts with other civilizations and an expansion of Egyptian rule to Palestine and Syria.

Egyptian Society: A Pyramid

Not only was the pyramid a symbol of the afterlife, it was also an image of Egyptian society. At the top, of course, was the pharaoh. Beneath him were the priests, who were important as intermediaries between society and the many Egyptian gods. It was the priests who devised the system of writing called hieroglyphics. Like the Sumerian language, invented at about the same time (c. 3100 B.C.), hi-

ing used from the beginning. By way of explanation, scholars theorize that the Egyptians may have borrowed this principle from the Mesopotamians.

Humanities Note

Fine art, *Sporting boat from Thebes, tomb of Chancellor Meketre*. This model boat from the tomb of a high Egyptian official dates from about 2050 B.C., the time of the Middle Kingdom. The Middle Kingdom was a period when nobles and high officials like Meketre gained more sta-

tus; the pharaohs were no longer the all-powerful rulers they had been during the Old Kingdom.

Notice that the chancellor sits comfortably in the shade of the cabin, while members of his household staff spear fish and bring birds for supper. This activity indicates that he was on an overnight expedition. The matting roof of the cabin could

IPUY AND HIS WIFE RECEIVING OFFERINGS FROM THEIR CHILDREN
Copy of wall paintings from the tomb of Ipuy, c. 1275 B.C.
The Metropolitan Museum of Art, New York

eroglyphics developed from a system based on pictures to one in which symbols could also represent sounds. These symbols were written on papyrus, a paperlike writing material made from reeds that grew by the Nile.

The nobles were on the same level as the priests in society's pyramid. Usually they held important administrative positions in the palace or in the various regions controlled by Egypt. They lived on luxurious estates, and their children could study at schools attached to the various temples. Noble women enjoyed many privileges, such as the right to testify in court and to buy and sell property.

Farther down in the social pyramid, and more numerous, were people of the middle class. These were the artisans, merchants, and physicians who served the ruling class. Lowest and most numerous were the peasants and slaves. Living in low, mudbrick shelters, peasants farmed their small holdings and turned over much of their crops to the pharaoh. In addition, they often had to serve on the pharaoh's construction gangs.

Egyptian Culture

Religion was a key aspect of ancient Egyptian culture. Many of the gods that Egyptians worshiped were associated with forces of nature. Amon-Re, the sun god, was the chief deity. Also important was Osiris, the god of the Nile, whose death and rebirth were linked with the rise and fall of that river. Osiris was the god of the underworld as well and had the power of judging the dead. Egyptians of every social class were extremely concerned about life after death. (See the feature on the Book of the Dead, page 36.)

During the New Kingdom, the pharaoh Amenhotep IV revolutionized Egyptian religion by instituting the worship of a single god: Aton, symbolized by the sun's disk. He changed his name to Akenaton, meaning "It goes well with Aton," and established a new royal city in honor of this god. After his death, however, Egyptians reverted to the worship of many gods.

Like Egypt itself, Egyptian science was also a "gift of the Nile." Since the yearly flooding of the river washed away boundary markers, farmers had to learn methods of surveying. This, in turn, led to the development of geometry. The need to predict the Nile's floods resulted in the creation of a 12-month, 365-day calendar.

SPORTING BOAT
From Thebes, tomb of Chancellor Meketre
The Metropolitan Museum of Art, New York

be rolled up or down depending on the weather. The rawhide shield on this roof could provide defense in case of an attack from the shore.

You might want to use the following questions to discuss the art:
1. Can you pick out Chancellor Meketre? Explain your choice.
2. What do you think the members of his household staff are doing?
3. What clues suggest that this boat was a pleasure craft?
4. How does this boat compare with the yachts of today?

Egyptian literature varied with the mood of the times. In the Old Kingdom, when the power of the pharaoh was unquestioned, literature was characterized by sacred hymns as cold and formal as the great pyramids themselves. As society became less rigidly structured in the Middle Kingdom, literature began to reflect personal feelings. The love poetry of the New Kingdom (see page 32) continued this trend. Its grace and freedom speak to us over thousands of years.

THE HEBREWS

People of the Covenant

At the time the Amorites were founding the village of Babylon (c. 2000 B.C.), another Semitic group migrated westward from Mesopotamia to Canaan, or Palestine. This group, the Hebrews, recorded their history in a sacred text that we now call the Bible. Unlike the Mesopotamians or Egyptians, the Hebrews believed in one god, and a key theme of the Bible was the covenant, or solemn agreement, between God and the Hebrew people. This covenant provided that God would protect the Hebrews from their enemies as long as the Hebrews obeyed him.

Around 1800 B.C., famine forced some of the Hebrews to migrate from Canaan to Egypt. There they were enslaved by the pharaohs. The Bible tells, however, that God inspired a leader called Moses to lead the Hebrews out of their captivity and back to Canaan (c. thirteenth century B.C.). Through Moses, God gave the Hebrews a set of laws called The Ten Commandments. In return for their obedience to these laws and their worship of him, God granted the land of Canaan to the Hebrews as his "chosen people."

The Kingdom of Israel

For several hundred years, the Hebrews battled the Philistines and other peoples for control of this promised land. They finally conquered the region in 1025 B.C. under the leadership of a general named David. He became the ruler of the new Hebrew kingdom of Israel, and Solomon, his son, made Jerusalem into an impressive national capital. There he erected a temple that became the center of worship for the whole nation. After his death in 930 B.C., however, quarrels led to the division of the country into the northern kingdom of Israel and the southern kingdom of Judah.

This division made the two kingdoms more vulnerable, and in 722 B.C. Israel fell to the Assyrians. Not long after, in 586 B.C., Judah was conquered by the Babylonian king Nebuchadnezzar. He destroyed the temple in Jerusalem and carried away many Hebrews to Babylon. At the end of the sixth century B.C., however, another turn of events led to the conquest of the Babylonians by the Persians. Cyrus, the Persian king, allowed the Hebrews to return to their homeland and rebuild the temple.

While ancient Israel never again achieved the power and independence it had enjoyed under David, the Hebrew contribution to Western culture has been of tremendous value.

The Hebrew Legacy

Hebrew monotheism, or belief in a single God, served as a basis for two other world religions, Christianity and Islam. In addition, Hebrew law demonstrated a greater respect for human life than had previously existed in the ancient Near East. Also new was the Hebrews' deep concern with moral behavior.

Uniquely among ancient Near Eastern peoples, the Hebrews saw themselves as actors in a historical drama: As God's chosen people, they would eventually bring his word and his law to the nations of the world. Their sense of a historical mission has influenced our modern idea that history moves forward like an arrow rather than circling and recircling in endless cycles.

AARON IN THE TABERNACLE
Painted wall panel. Synagogue of Dura Europos, third century B.C.

ANCIENT VOICES

Hear me, great ones of Uruk,
I weep for Enkidu, my friend,
Bitterly moaning like a woman mourning
I weep for my brother.
O Enkidu, my brother,
You were the ax at my side,
My hand's strength, the sword in my belt,
The shield before me,
A glorious robe, my fairest ornament;
An evil Fate has robbed me.

from *The Epic of Gilgamesh*

I have not slain men and women . . . I have not stolen grain . . . I have not uttered lies . . . I have not uttered curses . . . I have not stolen cultivated land . . . I have not been an eavesdropper . . . I have not worked witchcraft against the king . . . I have never stopped [the flow of] water . . .

from the Negative Confession, Egyptian Book of the Dead

Praise to thee, O Nile, that issuest forth from the earth and comest to nourish the dwellers in Egypt. Secret of movement, a darkness in the daytime.

from the "Hymn to the Nile"

And God spake all these words, saying,
2 I am the Lord thy God, which have brought thee out of the land of Egypt, out of the house of bondage.
3 Thou shalt have no other gods before me.

the Bible, Exodus 20:1–3

A merry heart maketh a cheerful countenance: but by sorrow of the heart the spirit is broken.

the Bible, Proverbs 15:13

Cast thy bread upon the waters: for thou shalt find it after many days.

the Bible, Ecclesiastes 11:1

To every thing there is a season, and a time to every purpose under the heaven:
2 A time to be born, and a time to die; a time to plant, and a time to pluck up that which is planted.

the Bible, Ecclesiastes 3:1–2

Additional Voices

In the beginning there was no heaven and no earth. There was nothing but water, which was ruled over by the gods Apsu and Tia-mat. No other gods existed.

—from "The Mighty Works of Marduk"

I love a girl, but she lies over there
 on the too far side of the River.
A whole Nile at floodstage rages between,
 and a crocodile hunched on the sand
Keeps motionless guard at the crossing.

—from an Egyptian love poem of the New Kingdom

11 For, lo, the winter is past, the rain is over and gone;
12 The flowers appear on the earth; the time of the singing of birds is come, and the voice of the turtle is heard in our land.

—the Bible, the Song of Solomon 2:11–12

25 The wolf and the lamb shall feed together, and the lion shall eat straw like the bullock; and dust shall be the serpent's meat. They shall not hurt or destroy in all my holy mountain, saith the Lord.

—the Bible, Isaiah 65:25

oped in the _____ of southwest Asia.
2. The most famous Sumerian "first" was the creation of _____.
3. Ancient Egyptian society can be pictured as a giant _____ with the pharaoh on the top and the commoners on the bottom.
4. Unlike Mesopotamian kings, the pharaohs were viewed as _____.

5. The laws that God gave the Hebrews were called _____.

Answers
1. river valleys
2. cities
3. pyramid
4. gods
5. The Ten Commandments

BACKGROUND

THE GILGAMESH EPIC

What Is the Gilgamesh Epic?

The Gilgamesh epic is a long narrative poem about a Sumerian king named Gilgamesh who lived between 2700 and 2500 B.C.—an era about twenty-three times more distant from us than our own Revolutionary War. Although this poem is probably the oldest work you have ever read, its concerns are timeless and universal: how to become known and respected, how to cope with the loss of a dear friend, and how to accept one's own inevitable death.

Unlike modern books, this epic does not have a single author. Stories about King Gilgamesh were told and handed down by Sumerians for hundreds of years after his death. By the twenty-first century B.C., however, these tales existed in written form. When the Babylonians conquered the Sumerians soon afterward, they inherited the Sumerian cultural tradition. A Babylonian author, borrowing from some of these tales, created a unified epic about the legendary Sumerian king. Other Babylonian writers modified the epic and, in the seventh century B.C., it was included in the library of the Assyrian king Ashurbanipal.

The Gilgamesh epic was an international favorite of its time, translated into many ancient Near Eastern languages. After the fall of Babylonia, however, the story survived only in folklore. The written epic was lost until archeologists excavated Ashurbanipal's library in the last century. They discovered the poem written on clay tablets in cuneiform, the wedge-shaped writing used by the Babylonians. Archeologists were especially excited by the portion of the epic describing a great flood, an account remarkably similar to the story of Noah's ark in the Bible.

A Summary of the Story

The men of Uruk, an ancient Sumerian city, complain about the arrogance of Gilgamesh, their king, who is part god and part man. Their lament is heard in heaven, and the goddess Aruru creates Enkidu to contend with Gilgamesh and offer him an outlet for his energy. At first, Enkidu lives like a wild man, on friendly terms with gazelles and other beasts. Then Gilgamesh hears about Enkidu and sends a woman to entice him. She draws him into a relationship, alienates him from the wild beasts, and urges him to search out Gilgamesh in the city-state of Uruk. Meanwhile, Gilgamesh has dreams that foretell the coming of a companion for him. Before Enkidu goes to Uruk, however, he lives with a group of shepherds and protects their herd from wolves and lions.

Entering Uruk, Enkidu confronts Gilgamesh just as the king is about to claim his right to sleep with a subject's bride. Enkidu blocks his way, and the two mighty men wrestle, "holding each other like bulls." Gilgamesh wins after a hard-fought battle, but the king and the wild man become fast friends.

A Name for Himself

Eager to make a name for himself, Gilgamesh takes Enkidu on a mission to slay the giant who guards a distant cedar forest. With the help of the sun-god Shamash, the heroes succeed in killing this giant.

Ishtar, the goddess of love, sees Gilgamesh in his splendor after the victory. She tries to seduce him, offering him gifts like "a chariot of . . . gold." He not only rejects her overtures but recites for her all the ways in which she has wronged her former lovers. Furious, she sends the Bull of Heaven to destroy him. Gilgamesh and Enkidu kill the bull; however, Enkidu dreams that the gods have ordered him to die for helping to kill the giant and the Bull of Heaven. Soon afterward, he does perish.

The Search for Everlasting Life

Gilgamesh bitterly laments his friend's death: *"O Enkidu, my brother / You were the ax at my side, / My hand's strength . . ."* Worried now about his own mortality, Gilgamesh goes in search of everlasting life. He seeks out Utnapishtim, a man who survived the great flood and who will live forever. On his quest Gilgamesh has many adventures. He kills lions in the mountains; passes through the mysterious Mount Mashu, guarded by Man-Scorpions; encounters the winemaker Siduri, who advises him to "be merry, feast, and rejoice"; and crosses the waters of death with the ferryman Urshanabi.

"There Is No Permanence"

When Gilgamesh finally reaches Utnapishtim, he receives the disappointing news that "'There is no permanence.'" Then Utnapishtim tells him the story of the great flood that wiped out all human life but his own. After hearing this story, Gilgamesh tries to resist sleeping for six days and seven nights to prove that he can attain immortality. He is unsuccessful: As with all humans, death is the dark reality; immortality is out of his grasp. Nevertheless, before the hero returns to Uruk with the ferryman Urshanabi, Utnapishtim tells him about a plant, growing underwater, that magically restores youth. Gilgamesh dives for this plant and finds some to take back to Uruk as an offering to his people. On the journey home, however, a serpent steals this sweet flower. The king is bitterly disappointed, but there is nothing he can do. When the travelers reach Uruk, Gilgamesh shows Urshanabi the famous walls of the city.

Sometime later, Gilgamesh dies and is lamented by his "people . . . , great and small." Death, then, completes the cycle of life.

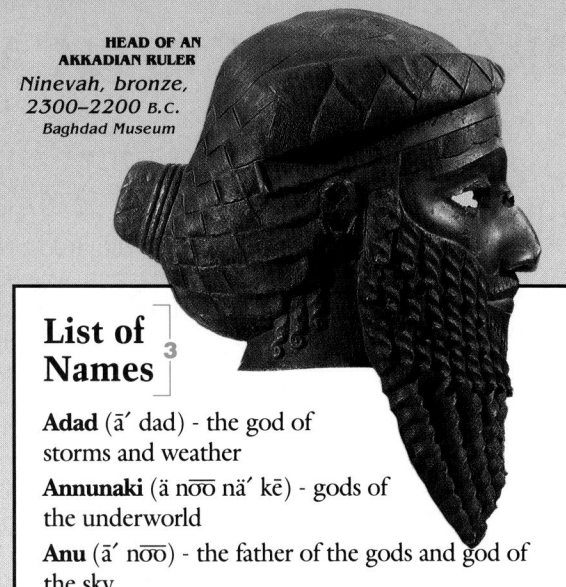

List of Names ⟧ 3

Adad (ā′ dad) - the god of storms and weather

Annunaki (ä nōō nä′ kē) - gods of the underworld

Anu (ā′ nōō) - the father of the gods and god of the sky

Belit-Sheri (bel′ ēt sher′ ē) - the scribe for the underworld gods

Ea (ā′ ä) - the god of the waters and of wisdom; also called **Enki** (eɳ′ kē)

Enkidu (eɳ′ kē dōō) - Gilgamesh's friend and adviser

Enlil (en lil′) - the god of earth, wind, and air

Gilgamesh (gil′ gə mesh′) - the hero of the epic, king of Uruk

Humbaba (hum bä′ bə) - the giant who guards the cedar forest

Irkalla (ir kä′ lə) - the queen of the underworld; also known as **Ereshkigal** (er esh kē′ gäl)

Ishtar (ish′ tär) - the goddess of love

Namtar (näm′ tär) - the god of evil fate

Samuqan (säm′ ōō kän) - the god of cattle

Shamash (shä′ mäsh) - the sun god

Shurrupak (shə rōō′ pək) - an ancient Sumerian city, eighteen miles northwest of Uruk

Urshanabi (ʉr′ shə nä bē) - Utnapishtim's ferryman

Uruk (ōō′ rook) - an ancient Sumerian city on the Euphrates river

Utnapishtim (ʊot nə pēsh′ təm) - the Mesopotamian Noah, survivor of the great flood

Humanities Note

Fine art, *Head of an Akkadian ruler*, 2300–2200 B.C. This bronze head shows why Akkadian art has been praised for its realism. About 1½ feet high, it may be a likeness of the Akkadian King Sargon, who seized control of the city of Kish c. 2334 B.C. Sargon then went on to create a great empire that stretched as far as Ebla in northern Persia.

You might want to use the following questions to discuss the art:

1. Is this sculpture realistic? Why or why not?
2. What does this life-size head reveal about the appearance and personality of the subject?

2 **Enrichment** Explain to students that *The Epic of Gilgamesh* was inscribed on twelve clay tablets in the library of the Assyrian king Assurbanipal. This translation and others, however, include material only from the first eleven tablets. The narrative on the twelfth tablet is often excluded because its chronological relationship to the rest of the story is unclear. In the account on the twelfth tablet, Enkidu is alive. He descends to the underworld to retrieve a drum and beater that have fallen into the realm of the dead. By failing to obey Gilgamesh's instructions, however, he is trapped in the underworld. Gilgamesh requires the assistance of Ea to free his companion. Enkidu, once freed, tells Gilgamesh about the world of the dead.

3 **Enrichment** With regard to pronunciations, tell students that even the experts do not know for certain how the names in this epic were really pronounced. Scholars have, however, made reasonable guesses based for the most part on known Semitic languages.

Give students the following additional pronunciations:

Nergal (nʉr′ gäl) - an underworld god

Ninsun (nin′ sun) - Gilgamesh's mother

Siduri (sə dōō′ rē) - a winemaker

Sumerian, Egyptian, and Hebrew Literature

Historical Context

Situated on the Tigris and Euphrates rivers, ancient Mesopotamia was simultaneously a region of plenty and poverty, opportunity and danger. Frequent floods created rich soil. Yet floods could also be violent and unpredictable, and the summer droughts could turn the soil to dust and wither crops. With its two major rivers, the region was ideally situated for trade. However, the flat alluvial plain, without forests or other natural obstacles, left the region open to invaders.

Between 2500 and 500 B.C., Mesopotamia was invaded repeatedly. Those who built the first great civilization on the two rivers, the Sumerians, gave way to the Babylonians and Assyrians. As often happens, however, the conquerors adopted the culture of the conquered. *The Epic of Gilgamesh* itself is eloquent testimony to this fact. This tale of a Sumerian ruler was shaped by Babylonians and preserved in the library of a great Assyrian king.

Cultural Context

Ancient Near-Eastern religion reflected the insecurities of life in a region threatened by flood and invaders. Mesopotamians believed, for example, that humans were created only to serve the gods. These unpredictable, quarreling, working, eating, drinking, and all-too-human gods had absolute control over human destiny. Also, Mesopotamians envisioned the underworld as a dreary and inhospitable place.

Literary Context

Both the Sumerians and the Babylonians had schools of scribes who created a varied and impressive literature. Among the works they produced were essays, proverbs, dialogues, myths, hymns, and epics. As the Gilgamesh tale passed through the hands of these authors, it was continually reshaped. The Babylonians, who fashioned the epic as we know it today, added the prologue and flood story and emphasized the friendship between Gilgamesh and Enkidu. Most important, they gave the narrative its central theme: the search for immortality.

On the following pages is part of *The Epic of Gilgamesh*. The annotations in the margin point out the historical context, cultural context, and literary context.

The Epic of Gilgamesh

from

translated by N. K. Sandars

Prologue

I will proclaim to the world the deeds of Gilgamesh. This was the man to whom all things were known; this was the king who knew the countries of the world. He was wise, he saw mysteries and knew secret things, he brought us a tale of the days before the flood. He went on a long journey, was weary, wornout with labor, returning he rested, he engraved on a stone the whole story.

Front of lyre from tomb of Queen Pu-abi at Ur. Recitations of epics and tales may have been accompanied by music from lyres like this one.
Early Dynastic period, c. 2685–2290 B.C.
British Museum, London

Cultural Context: Some scholars consider this poem an epic rather than a myth since its protagonist, or main character, is a hero, not a god. The recitation of epics was probably accompanied by music. Sumerians and Babylonians were familiar with such instruments as harps and lyres, drums, and pipes of reed and metal.

Literary Context: The first words of the epic in Akkadian are *Sha nagba imuru,* meaning "He who saw everything" or "he who saw the abyss." They refer to Gilgamesh, who looks into the abyss and finds wisdom.

Historical Context: Ancient Mesopotamians divided history into two parts—before the Flood and after the Flood. Before the Flood great sages ruled the land. These sages received instruction in developing civilization from Ea, the god of the waters and of wisdom. After the Flood kings like Gilgamesh ruled the land.

out differences between Gilgamesh and his companion Enkidu?

ESL Strategy Review each annotation with ESL students to make sure they understand it. Also, pair up each ESL student with a partner who can assist him or her with the questions at the end of the selection.

Teaching Tenth-Grade Students You might want to have tenth-grade students look at and discuss the art on page 15 before they begin reading. This strategy may help ease them into the selection.

Vocabulary

Preteach the following vocabulary words:
endowed (en doud´) *v.*: Gave
rampart (ram´ pärt´) *n.*: A wall or embankment protecting a city or fort
cornice (kôr´ nis) *n.*: A horizontal molding projecting along the top of a wall or building
countenance (koun´ tə nəns) *n.*: Face
immolation (im´ ə lā´ shən) *n.*: Sacrifice
succor (suk´ ər) *n.*: Aid
ecstasy (ek´ stə sē) *n.*: Great joy

Humanities Note

Fine art, *Front of lyre from tomb of Queen Pu-abi at Ur*, c. 2685–2290 B.C. Fashioned from wood, this instrument was meant to give the appearance of a bull making music. The bull was a Sumerian nature deity. Its head, the only part of its body represented on this lyre, is covered with gold leaf and overlaid with lapis-lazuli, a semi-precious blue stone.

You might want to use the following question to discuss the art:

Imagine a recitation of *The Epic of Gilgamesh* accompanied by music from a lyre like this one. How do you think the music would have contributed to the reading?

derstanding an Archetypal Battle, p. 13
Critical Thinking and Reading Worksheet, *Contrasting Characters*, p. 14
Selection Test, pp. 15–16

Presentation

Motivation/Prior Knowledge Tell students that they will be reading about the adventures of a hero who lived almost 5,000 years ago. In many ways, however, this hero resembles the great warriors who are more familiar to them, such as Achilleus and Beowulf or even Conan and Indiana Jones. Have students list the common characteristics of these better known heroes and speculate about the reasons for their appeal.

Universal Themes Other selections that deal with heroic deeds are 1 Samuel 17 (David and Goliath), page 61; the *Iliad*, Books XVIII and XXII, pages 355 and 366; and the *Song of Roland*, page 569.

Purpose-Setting Question How does the Battle with Humbaba bring

Enrichment Excavations at Uruk, the city ruled by Gilgamesh, have proved important in establishing dates for Sumerian civilization. Archeologists dug a pit of about 60 feet and then identified changes that occurred from level to level. Artifacts found in the deepest layers were associated with the earliest settlers in the region. At a somewhat higher level, archeologists uncovered the remains of ancient Sumer's first great buildings (c. 3000 B.C.). Still higher up, they discovered the marble head of a woman (c. 2800 B.C.), which revealed that the early Sumerians had mastered the art of sculpture.

One of the most important finds was a large collection of writing tablets. These enabled archeologists to trace the evolution of cuneiform writing back to its origins as a pictographic system: The picture of a fish, for example, stood for the word *fish*, and the word *mountain* was represented by three half circles that resembled mountains.

Historical Context: The city-state of Uruk was located in what is now southern Iraq. Uruk was a powerful and wealthy city-state. In ancient times, it was a king's chief function to protect his people. **1** Building walls around the city was therefore a notable achievement.

Literary Context: Babylonian writers stressed the friendship between Enkidu and Gilgamesh, which is not such a consistent theme in the Sumerian sources. Gilgamesh sets off to slay Humbaba in order to make a name for himself. The way making a name for yourself grants a type of immortality is another important theme in literature

Literary Context: Humbaba is presented as a personification of what is evil. Since Shamash the sun god—the god of goodness and light—supports Gilgamesh's endeavor, the battle takes on mythic proportions.

When the gods created Gilgamesh they gave him a perfect body. Shamash the glorious sun endowed him with beauty, Adad the god of the storm endowed him with courage, the great gods made his beauty perfect, surpassing all others, terrifying like a great wild bull. Two thirds they made him god and one third man.

In Uruk he built walls, a great rampart, and the temple of blessed Eanna[1] for the god of the firmament Anu, and for Ishtar the goddess of love. Look at it still today: the outer wall where the cornice runs, it shines with the brilliance of copper; and the inner wall, it has no equal. Touch the threshold, it is ancient. Approach Eanna the dwelling of Ishtar, our lady of love and war, the like of which no latter-day king, no man alive can equal. Climb upon the wall of Uruk; walk along it, I say; regard the foundation terrace and examine the masonry: is it not burnt brick and good? The seven sages[2] laid the foundations.

The Battle with Humbaba

When the people of Uruk complain about Gilgamesh's arrogance, the goddess Aruru creates Enkidu to contend with the king and absorb his energies. At first, Enkidu lives like a wild animal and has no contact with other humans. Later, he enters Uruk, loses a wrestling match to Gilgamesh, and becomes his faithful friend. Then the two set off to destroy Humbaba, the giant who guards the cedar forest. As Gilgamesh prepares for battle, Enkidu expresses his fears.

Then Enkidu, the faithful companion, pleaded, answering him, "O my lord, you do not know this monster and that is the reason you are not afraid. I who know him, I am terrified. His teeth are dragon's fangs, his countenance is like a lion, his charge is the rushing of the flood, with his look he crushes alike the trees of the forest and reeds in the swamp. O my lord, you may go on if you choose into this land, but I will go back to the city. I will tell the lady your mother all your glori-

---

1. **In Uruk . . . Eanna:** Uruk was an important city in southern Babylonia, with temples to the gods Anu and Ishtar. Eanna was the temple site where these gods were worshiped.
2. **seven sages:** Legendary wise men who civilized Mesopotamia's seven oldest cities.

Grammar in Action

Commas When writers use introductory material, parenthetical expressions, and nonessential material, they set them off with commas. The following examples illustrate the role of the comma in setting off such added elements:

INTRODUCTORY ADVERB: *Slowly,* they picked up their scattered belongings.

NOUN OF DIRECT ADDRESS: *Bob,* will you come with us?

NONESSENTIAL APPOSITIVE: George, *the great liar,* told us that story.

N. K. Sandars, the translator of *The Epic of Gilgamesh*, often uses commas to set off added elements. As in many epics, descriptive epithets precede or follow the names of gods or heroes. When they follow these names, they are usually set off by commas as nonessential appositives:

Approach Eanna the dwelling of Ishtar, *our lady of love and war,* the like of which no latter-day king, no man alive can equal.

Then Enkidu, *the faithful companion,* pleaded, answering him, . . .

These descriptive phrases, although grammatically "nonessential," add color to the epic and stress key themes—one such theme is the friendship ous deeds till she shouts for joy: and then I will tell the death that followed till she weeps for bitterness." But Gilgamesh said, "Immolation and sacrifice are not yet for me, the boat of the dead[3] shall not go down, nor the three-ply cloth be cut for my shrouding. Not yet will my people be desolate, nor the pyre be lit in my house and my dwelling burnt on the fire. Today, give me your aid and you shall have mine: what then can go amiss with us two? All living creatures born of the flesh shall sit at last in the boat of the West, and when it sinks, when the boat of Magilum sinks, they are gone; but we shall go forward and fix our eyes on this monster. If your heart is fearful throw away fear; if there is terror in it throw away terror. Take your ax in your hand and attack. He who leaves the fight unfinished is not at peace."

Humbaba came out from his strong house of cedar. Then Enkidu called out, "O Gilgamesh, remember now your boasts in Uruk. Forward, attack, son of Uruk, there is nothing to fear." When he heard these words his courage rallied; he answered, "Make haste, close in, if the watchman is there do not let him escape to the woods where he will vanish. He has put on the first of his seven splendors but not yet the other six, let us trap him before he is armed." Like a raging wild bull he snuffed the ground; the watchman of the woods turned full of threatenings, he cried out. Humbaba came from his strong house of cedar. He nodded his head and shook it, menacing Gilgamesh; and on him he fastened his eye, the eye of death. Then Gilgamesh called to Shamash and his tears were flowing, "O glorious Shamash, I have followed the road you commanded but now if you send no succor how shall I escape?" Glorious Shamash heard his prayer and he summoned the great wind, the north wind, the whirlwind, the storm and the icy wind, the tempest and the scorching wind; they came like dragons, like a scorching fire, like a serpent that freezes the heart, a destroying flood and the lightning's fork. The eight winds rose up against Humbaba, they beat against his eyes; he was gripped, unable to go forward or back. Gilgamesh shouted, "By the life of Ninsun my mother and divine Lugulbanda my father, in the Country of the Living, in this Land I have discovered your dwelling; my weak arms and my small weapons I have brought to this Land against you, and now I will enter your house."

So he felled the first cedar and they cut the branches and laid them at the foot of the mountain. At the first stroke Humbaba blazed out, but still they advanced. They felled seven cedars and cut and bound the branches and laid them at the foot of the mountain, and seven times Humbaba loosed his glory on them. As the seventh blaze died out they reached his lair. He slapped his thigh in scorn. He approached like a

---

3. boat of the dead: A ceremonial boat on which the dead were placed.

Cultural Context: Gilgamesh's last statement expresses part of the code of the warrior-king. A battle must be fought to its conclusion. **2**

Literary Context: In calling for Shamash's help, Gilgamesh reveals that he is human and vulnerable, not a god.

Cultural Context: In many Eastern cultures, seven is the number of completion or perfection. Belief in the power of the number seven is apparent even today when we speak of "lucky seven."

2 Enrichment Students may be curious about the geographical location of the cedar forest where the battle with Humbaba takes place. In the Sumerian tales about Gilgamesh, this forest was probably located in the Zagros Mountains northeast of Uruk. However, the Akkadians who created the epic as we know it today probably had a different location in mind. They imagined that the cedar forest was in Lebanon, to the northwest of Gilgamesh's city. This change reflects the greater interest of Babylonian kings in western territories. A change in political realities, therefore, had an important effect on a literary work.

between Gilgamesh and Enkidu.
   Student Activity 1. Find two instances where Sandars uses a comma to set off nouns of direct address. Explain how in each case this use of the comma adds drama to the epic.
   Student Activity 2. Invent your own heroic epithets for Gilgamesh, Shamash, and Humbaba. Then use these phrases as nonessential appositives in a description of Gilgamesh's battle with Humbaba.

Bronze head from Nineveh. Gilgamesh probably looked something like this warrior.
Imperial Akkadian II–III Phase, c. 2415–2290 B.C.
Iraq Museum, Baghdad

noble wild bull roped on the mountain, a warrior whose elbows are bound together. The tears started to his eyes and he was pale, "Gilgamesh, let me speak. I have never known a mother, no, nor a father who reared me. I was born of the mountain, he reared me, and Enlil made me the keeper of this forest. Let me go free, Gilgamesh, and I will be your servant, you shall be my lord; all the trees of the forest that I tended on the mountain shall be yours. I will cut them down and build you a palace." He took him by the hand and led him to his house, so that the heart of Gilgamesh was moved with compassion. He swore by the heavenly life, by the earthly life, by the underworld itself: "O Enkidu, should not the snared bird return to its nest and the captive man return to his mother's arms?" Enkidu answered, "The strongest of men will fall to fate if he has no judgment. Namtar, the evil fate that knows no distinction between men, will devour him. If the snared bird returns to its nest, if the captive man returns to his mother's arms, then you my friend will never return to the city where the mother is waiting who gave you birth. He will bar the mountain road against you, and make the pathways impassable."

Literary Context: Enkidu argues that if Humbaba is spared, he will prove a dangerous foe. Here, Enkidu demonstrates that he is shrewder and less trusting than Gilgamesh.

Humbaba said, "Enkidu, what you have spoken is evil: you, a hireling, dependent for your bread! In envy and for fear of a rival you have spoken evil words." Enkidu said, "Do not listen, Gilgamesh: this Humbaba must die. Kill Humbaba first and his servants after." But Gilgamesh said, "If we touch him the blaze and the glory of light will be put out in confusion, the glory and glamour will vanish, its rays will be quenched." Enkidu said to Gilgamesh, "Not so, my friend. First entrap the bird, and where shall the chicks run then? Afterwards we can search out the glory and the glamour, when the chicks run distracted through the grass."

Literary Context: Gilgamesh seems to be afraid that, when the light goes out, the forest will be in utter darkness.

Gilgamesh listened to the word of his companion, he took the ax in his hand, he drew the sword from his belt, and he struck Humbaba

---

with a thrust of the sword to the neck, and Enkidu his comrade struck the second blow. At the third blow Humbaba fell. Then there followed confusion for this was the guardian of the forest whom they had felled to the ground. For as far as two leagues the cedars shivered when Enkidu felled the watcher of the forest, he at whose voice Hermon and Lebanon used to tremble. Now the mountains were moved and all the hills, for the guardian of the forest was killed. They attacked the cedars, the seven splendors of Humbaba were extinguished. So they pressed on into the forest bearing the sword of eight talents.[4] They uncovered the sacred dwellings of the Anunnaki[5] and while Gilgamesh felled the first of the trees of the forest Enkidu cleared their roots as far as the banks of Euphrates.[6] They set Humbaba before the gods, before Enlil; they kissed the ground and dropped the shroud and set the head before him. When he saw the head of Humbaba, Enlil raged at them. "Why did you do this thing? From henceforth may the fire be on your faces, may it eat the bread that you eat, may it drink where you drink." Then Enlil took again the blaze and the seven splendors that had been Humbaba's: he gave the first to the river, and he gave to the lion, to the stone of execration,[7] to the mountain and to the dreaded daughter of the Queen of Hell.

O Gilgamesh, king and conqueror of the dreadful blaze; wild bull who plunders the mountain, who crosses the sea, glory to him, and from the brave the greater glory is Enki's![8]

Enkidu's Dream
of the Underworld

Gilgamesh rejects the advances of Ishtar, goddess of love. In revenge, she brings the mighty Bull of Heaven down to threaten Uruk. Gilgamesh and Enkidu kill the bull, but Enkidu dreams that the gods have decreed his death for helping to slaughter the bull and Humbaba. Enkidu is furious at his fate until Shamash, the sun god, allays some of his anger. Then Enkidu describes another dream about death.

---

4. talents: Large units of weight and money used in the ancient world.
5. Anunnaki: Gods of the underworld.
6. Euphrates (yōō frāt′ ēz): A river flowing from Turkey generally southward through Syria and Iraq, joining the Tigris River.
7. execration (ek′ si krā′ shən) *n.*: Cursing, denunciation.
8. Enki's: Belonging to Enki, god of wisdom and one of the creators of human beings.

Cultural Context: Enlil was the father of the gods, the most important of the Sumerian deities. There is a conflict of interest between Enlil, who is angry at the death of Humbaba, and Shamash, who helped bring it about. The episode of the flood, which appears later in the epic, reveals further differences among the gods.

Cultural Context: The ancient Sumerians viewed the underworld as a bleak abode where little distinction was made between those who did evil on earth and those who did good. Only leaving loved ones on earth to keep their names alive offered any respite for the dead.

3

3 Enrichment In this portion of the epic, Enkidu visits the underworld in a dream. There is also a Sumerian myth describing the descent of Inanna (the Sumerian goddess of love, called Ishtar by the Akkadians) to the underworld. According to this myth, Inanna wants to wrest control of the underworld from her sister and bitter rival, Ereshkigal, the goddess of death. Inanna's plans misfire, however. Not only does she lose her garments and jewelry in the underworld, but the threatening stare of Ereshkigal turns her into a corpse. Enlil, the father of the gods, refuses to help Inanna, but the god of wisdom, Enki, devises a trick to rescue her.

This myth illustrates what one scholar calls "the ambitious, aggressive, and demanding" nature of Ishtar. Unsatisfied with her own realm, she wants to dominate the world of death as well. However, the myth also illustrates the fearful power that Sumerians attributed to Ereshkigal and the other gods of the underworld.

As a class project, you might divide the class into groups and have each group investigate a myth concerning a journey to the underworld. Then have the group dramatize their myth and present it to their classmates.

mension it had not had before: Gilgamesh as the instrument of the sun god in his battle against the forces of evil.

4 Enrichment Sometime after his death, Gilgamesh himself was deified and given an important role in the Sumerian underworld. According to legend, it was his job to supervise the behavior of the dead and to ensure that they observed a complex set of rules.

Other deities who supervised the dead were the *gallas*, who constituted a kind of underworld police force. Unlike Ereshkigal, Nergal, and other members of the underworld pantheon, however, the *gallas* did not require clothing, weapons, jewelry, or food.

Cultural Context: The underworld, ruled by Ereshkigal (also known as Irkalla) and Nergal, included the deities mentioned here and special officers called *gallas*. The realm of the dead was a large region below the earth,
4 comparable to the sky above. The Sumerians believed that this lower region could be reached through special openings and gates in Uruk and other major cities. Sumerian myth, however, is uncertain as to the exact location of Ereshkigal's seven-gated palace.

As Enkidu slept alone in his sickness, in bitterness of spirit he poured out his heart to his friend. "It was I who cut down the cedar, I who leveled the forest, I who slew Humbaba and now see what has become of me. Listen, my friend, this is the dream I dreamed last night. The heavens roared, and earth rumbled back an answer; between them stood I before an awful being, the somber-faced man-bird; he had directed on me his purpose. His was a vampire face, his foot was a lion's foot, his hand was an eagle's talon. He fell on me and his claws were in my hair, he held me fast and I smothered; then he transformed me so that my arms became wings covered with feathers. He turned his stare towards me, and he led me away to the palace of Irkalla, the Queen of Darkness, to the house from which none who enters ever returns, down the road from which there is no coming back.

"There is the house whose people sit in darkness; dust is their food and clay their meat. They are clothed like birds with wings for covering, they see no light, they sit in darkness. I entered the house of dust and I saw the kings of the earth, their crowns put away forever; rulers and princes, all those who once wore kingly crowns and ruled the world in the days of old. They who had stood in the place of the gods like Anu and Enlil, stood now like servants to fetch baked meats in the house of dust, to carry cooked meat and cold water from the waterskin. In the house of dust which I entered were high priests and acolytes,[9] priests of the incantation[10] and of ecstasy; there were servers of the temple, and there was Etana, that king of Kish whom the eagle carried to heaven in the days of old. I saw also Samuqan, god of cattle, and there was Ereshkigal the Queen of the Underworld; and Belit-Sheri squatted in front of her, she who is recorder of the gods and keeps the book of death. She held a tablet from which she read. She raised her head, she saw me and spoke: 'Who has brought this one here?' Then I awoke like a man drained of blood who wanders alone in a waste of rushes; like one whom the bailiff[11] has seized and his heart pounds with terror."

---

9. **acolytes** (ak′ ə līts′) *n.*: Attendants, faithful followers.
10. **incantation** (in′ kan tā′ shən) *n.*: Chanting of magical words.
11. **bailiff** (bāl′ if) *n.*: Court officer or law officer

Reader's Response *Would you like to have been Gilgamesh's companion? Why or why not?*

THINKING ABOUT THE SELECTION

Clarifying

1. For which qualities and achievements is Gilgamesh praised in the prologue?
2. Briefly summarize the battle with Humbaba.
3. What role do the dead play in the palace of Irkalla?

Interpreting

4. What does the prologue suggest about the values of ancient Mesopotamians?
5. Gilgamesh is described as being "two thirds" a god "and one third man." What conflicts might arise from such a combination?
6. When Gilgamesh and Enkidu debate whether to fight Humbaba, what is Gilgamesh's attitude toward death?
7. How important is Enkidu's role in the battle with Humbaba? Support your opinion with specific passages from the epic.
8. (a) Identify the figure of speech that occurs at the end of the selection. (b) How does it contribute to the mood?

Applying

9. Some scholars have characterized the ancient Mesopotamian outlook on life as pessimistic. Find passages in the epic that support or disprove this assertion and explain your choices.

ANALYZING LITERATURE

Understanding Conflict

An **archetype** is a pattern or theme that recurs in many different cultures. One such archetype, which appears in *The Epic of Gilgamesh*, is the battle between the forces of good (or light) and those of evil (or darkness). It is around this **conflict,** or struggle between two forces, that this episode of the epic is built.

In the battle with the giant Humbaba, Gilgamesh and Enkidu are on the side of goodness and light. They are representatives of Shamash, who is the god of light himself.

1. How does Enkidu's description of Humbaba reveal that the giant is evil?
2. Humbaba is the guardian of a forest. Why might a forest be associated with an evil or demonic being?
3. Does Shamash's role in the battle diminish the heroes' achievement? Why or why not?
4. What other tales have you read or seen dramatized in which the forces of good combat the forces of evil?

CRITICAL THINKING AND READING

Contrasting Gilgamesh and Enkidu

Although friends, Gilgamesh and Enkidu differ in important ways. The king, for example, is a civilized man of the city, while his companion lived in the wilderness among wild beasts. The battle with Humbaba and Enkidu's dream bring out other contrasts between the two heroes.

1. (a) How do Gilgamesh and Enkidu differ in their willingness to fight and willingness to spare their opponent? (b) What do these disagreements suggest about their different natures?
2. Why do you think that Enkidu, rather than Gilgamesh, is marked for death by the gods and dreams about the underworld?

THINKING AND WRITING

Creating an Imaginary Underworld

Enkidu's dream contains a memorable description of the Babylonian Underworld. In "the palace of Irkalla," the mysterious, birdlike dead "sit in darkness" consuming "dust" and "clay." Imagine that you are Enkidu. Continue relating your dream. Take into account such factors as the food, if any, of the dead, their appearance, and the location of this underworld. If you like, you can even include dialogue. When you revise your dream, make sure you have used language that appeals to more than one sense. Will your readers be able to visualize the inhabitants you have created and to see the strange world in which they dwell? Finally, proofread your paper and share it with your classmates.

(continued from bottom of page)

6. He accepts death but does not let its inevitability deter him from winning honor in battle.
7. Enkidu plays a key role by advising Gilgamesh to kill Humbaba and then helping him do it. If Enkidu did not warn Gilgamesh against showing compassion, Humbaba might have survived.
8. (a) Enkidu, awakening from his nightmare, uses a simile to compare himself to someone whom a court officer has seized. (b) The simile helps create a mood of apprehension and fear.
9. Answers will differ. Many students will probably indicate that the picture of the underworld in Enkidu's dream is pessimistic.

ANSWERS TO ANALYZING LITERATURE

1. Enkidu endows Humbaba with an awesome destructiveness, like that of a wild animal or a natural force.
2. Answers will differ. Students may respond that the forest was a place of mystery, where thieves or wild animals might lurk.
3. Answers will differ. Some students may respond that Shamash's role in immobilizing the giant diminishes the heroes' achievement.
4. Answers will differ. Some students may mention the Star Wars movies, in which there is a clear differentiation between the forces of good and the forces of evil.

ANSWERS TO CRITICAL THINKING AND READING

1. (a) Gilgamesh is more willing to fight, but he is also more willing to spare Humbaba. (b) These differences suggest that Enkidu, if less noble and chivalrous, is shrewder.
2. Answers will differ. Students may speculate that the gods decide to vent their anger on Enkidu because he is less important than Gilgamesh.

THINKING AND WRITING

Publishing Student Writing Have students read their descriptions aloud to the class.

Closure and Extension
ANSWERS TO THINKING ABOUT THE SELECTION

1. Gilgamesh is praised for his wisdom, beauty, and courage. He is also praised for bringing his people "a tale of the days before the flood," as well as the story of his own journey, and building the walls and temple of Uruk.
2. When Humbaba emerges from his house of cedar, Gilgamesh prays to Shamash for help. Shamash sends his winds to attack Humbaba. Gilgamesh cuts down seven cedar trees and advances to Humbaba's lair. Humbaba pleads for mercy and Gilgamesh is willing to let him live, but Enkidu advises Gilgamesh to kill the giant. Gilgamesh listens to his companion and together they slay Humbaba.
3. The dead act as servants, carrying food and water.
4. The prologue suggests that they valued courage, wisdom, and beauty. The praise bestowed on the walls of Uruk indicates the importance of the king's role as the protector of his people.
5. He might have longings for immortality that are not appropriate for a mortal man.

GUIDE FOR INTERPRETING

Focus

Literary Focus Have students identify modern heroes who are engaged upon quests. In the film *Raiders of the Lost Ark*, for example, Indiana Jones is searching for the ancient chest containing the stone tablets inscribed with the Ten Commandments. After students cite a number of modern quests, encourage them to analyze how these quests involve ordeals and trials.

Writing/Prior Knowledge Explain to students that "vital knowledge" can refer to anything from background information on one's family to the skills necessary to participate in a sport.

ESL Teaching Strategy Have ESL students tell an ancient legend or tale from their own culture. Then ask them to describe the circumstances in which they first heard this tale. You might also want to make sure that ESL students are seated toward the front of the room, so they can hear what you are saying and have a good view of the chalkboard.

Teaching Tenth-Grade Students You might want to give tenth-grade students a brief synopsis of the flood story before they begin reading it.

Vocabulary

You may want to preteach the following vocabulary words:

ballast (bal´ əst) *n.*: Anything heavy carried in a ship to give stability

heralds (her´ əlds) *n.*: A person who comes before to announce what follows

livid (liv´ id) *adj.*: Black-and-blue; pale, white, or red

travail (trə vāl´) *n.*: Toil; intense pain

consigned (kən sīnd´) *v.*: Handed over; gave up

sluices (slōos´ əz) *n.*: Channels or passages for water, regulated by a gate

from The Epic of Gilgamesh

Commentary

The Hero and His Quest. The turning point of *The Epic of Gilgamesh* is the death of Enkidu. Gilgamesh is deeply troubled by this event: "Hear me, great ones of Uruk, / I weep for Enkidu, my friend, / Bitterly moaning like a woman mourning / I weep for my brother." The king cannot accept the inevitability of death, and with all the energy of his proud and restless nature, he begins a quest, or search, for everlasting life. He determines to find Utnapishtim, survivor of an ancient flood and the only man to whom the gods have granted immortality. Up until this time, Gilgamesh was ambitious for glory. He undertook the battle with the giant Humbaba in order to rid the land of evil and create a name for himself. Now he is not concerned with fame. He does not want survival in story and song but immortal life in his own body.

The hero's **quest**—a search for immortal life or some kind of secret knowledge—is a theme found in the folklore and literature of many peoples. Usually, the hero must suffer a number of ordeals in the course of this search. This suffering can be compared to an initiation. In fact, the initiation into a club or fraternity resembles in a minor way the difficulties faced on a quest. In both situations, suffering leads to special knowledge or privileges.

Like any serious quest, Gilgamesh's journey is dangerous because it takes him past the boundaries of the familiar world. He travels to distant places known only in legend, such as "the great mountains . . . which guard the rising and the setting sun." His appearance, too, becomes less and less civilized as he journeys farther from Uruk. He wears animal skins, and his cheeks look "drawn." Ironically, he is now more of a wild man, just as Enkidu was when he roamed with gazelles and other beasts.

Not only does the king's quest take him over the edge of the map, but it also takes him backward in time to an unimaginably ancient past. In speaking with Utnapishtim, Gilgamesh will be encountering a man whose memories predate any known historical records. He will be journeying back to the legendary beginnings of his people.

Writing

Gilgamesh searches out Utnapishtim to gain a vital piece of knowledge. Describe a conversation in which an adult or a friend gave you vital knowledge about yourself and your place in the world.

Objectives

Thematic
To understand the quest for immortality

Skills
1 To understand the hero and his quest

2 To infer the purpose of the flood story

3 To appreciate an Akkadian pun

4 To compare and contrast heroes

Support Material

Teaching Portfolio
Teacher Backup, p. 17
Grammar in Action, *Using the Semicolon*, p. 21
Usage and Mechanics Worksheet, p. 23
Vocabulary Check, p. 24
Analyzing Literature Worksheet,

from The Epic of Gilgamesh

The Story of the Flood

Enkidu dies, and greatly saddened by his death, Gilgamesh goes on a quest for immortality. He journeys through the mysterious mountain of Manshu, encounters the sun-god Shamash and the goddess Siduri, and travels across the Ocean to Utnapishtim, whose name means "He Who Saw Life." Utnapishtim and his family are the only humans who have been granted immortality. When Gilgamesh asks him how he has defeated death, Utnapishtim tells the following story.

"You know the city Shurrupak, it stands on the banks of Euphrates? That city grew old and the gods that were in it were old. There was Anu, lord of the firmament, their father, and warrior Enlil their counselor, Ninurta the helper, and Ennugi watcher over canals; and with them also was Ea. In those days the world teemed, the people multiplied, the world bellowed like a wild bull, and the great god was aroused by the clamor. Enlil heard the clamor and he said to the gods in council, 'The uproar of mankind is intolerable and sleep is no longer possible by reason of the babel.' So the gods agreed to exterminate mankind. Enlil did this, but Ea because of his oath warned me in a dream. He whispered their words to my house of reeds, 'Reed-house, reed-house! Wall, O wall, harken reed-house, wall reflect: O man of Shurrupak, son of Ubara-Tutu; tear down your house and build a boat, abandon possessions and look for life, despise worldly goods and save your soul alive. Tear down

Detail of alabaster relief from the Palace of King Sargon II (721–705 B.C.) at Khorsabad. This ship, which is transporting timber, conveys some idea of Mesopotamian vessels.
The Louvre, Paris

ues forever, as fame that endures after death, or as an intimation of eternity within our mortal lives. The following selections deal with this theme: the Koran, page 108; Book 24 of Homer's *Iliad,* page 379; Dante's *Inferno,* page 622; and Rimbaud's "Eternity," page 910.

Cultural Note The late American novelist John Gardner was influenced by *The Epic of Gilgamesh* when he wrote *The Sunlight Dialogues* (1972). He went on to translate the epic, in collaboration with John Maier.

Humanities Note
Fine art, *Detail of alabaster relief from the Palace of King Sargon II at Khorsabad,* c. 721–705 B.C. The whole relief shows a number of ships transporting timber, the waves of the sea, and the fish swimming beneath the water's surface. This artist's attempt to indicate depth and perspective is advanced for its time.

You might want to use the following questions to discuss the art:
1. (a) What does this relief suggest about the size and quality of Mesopotamian ships? (b) What does it indicate about methods of transporting goods?
2. Consult the map (page 4) to determine on what waterways ancient Mesopotamians might have voyaged.

1 Enrichment Anu is the Sumerian god of the heavens. At one time the Sumerians believed him to be the greatest god; however, his supreme position was eventually taken over by Enlil, god of the air. Anu was primarily worshiped at Uruk, Gilgamesh's city.

Ea, also known as Enki, was the god who taught humans the arts and crafts of civilization.

2 Clarification Since Ea has taken an oath to exterminate humankind, he cannot warn Utnapishtim directly. Ea, who was the god of wisdom, cleverly bypasses the oath by giving his warning in a dream and by speaking to the wall rather than to Utnapishtim.

Understanding the Hero and His Quest, p. 25
Critical Thinking and Reading Worksheet, *Inferring the Purpose of the Flood Story*, p. 26
Selection Test, pp. 27–28

Spelling Tip Point out to students that the o͞o sound of *sluices* is spelled *ui*. This sound is spelled the

same way in the word *juice*.

Presentation
Motivation/Prior Knowledge Tell students that they will be reading an ancient story about a disastrous flood. Have them describe floods they have experienced, read about, or seen on television news programs. Ask them why floods would

have been even more devastating in ancient times.

Purpose-Setting Question Why do you think Utnapishtim tells Gilgamesh the story of the flood?

Universal Themes The quest for immortality is an important theme in world literature. Immortality can be regarded as life that literally contin-

3 Enrichment Ea once again displays his cleverness. When Utnapishtim expresses his concern about the reaction of the city elders to his ark-building activities, Ea suggests that he tell a half-truth. The words that Utnapishtim uses can refer to a rich harvest or to misfortune. (For more information, see the Understanding Language exercise on page 29.)

4 Discussion You might want to have students compare and contrast this flood story with the one in Genesis 6–9, pages 47–51. For instance, students can compare the size, design, and provisioning of Utnapishtim's boat with those of Noah's ark.

5 Enrichment Adad, the storm god, was worshiped throughout Mesopotamia but, unlike other gods, had no religious center especially devoted to his rites. Storms brought needed water to this arid region. At the same time, they could be quite threatening, as this description suggests.

6 Discussion Have students identify the two similes in this passage and explain how they contribute to the mood evoked by the narrative.

7 Discussion Ask students what is surprising about the description of the gods in this passage. Have them find similes that add to the sense of surprise.

8 Reading Strategy Have students predict how this episode will affect the gods' attitude toward Enlil.

your house, I say, and build a boat. These are the measurements of the barque as you shall build her: let her beam equal her length, let her deck be roofed like the vault that covers the abyss;[1] then take up into the boat the seed of all living creatures.'

"When I had understood I said to my lord, 'Behold, what you have commanded I will honor and perform, but how shall I answer the people, the city, the elders?' Then Ea opened his mouth and said to me, his servant, 'Tell them this: I have learnt that Enlil is wrathful against me, I dare no longer walk in his land nor live in his city; I will go down to the Gulf[2] to dwell with Ea my lord. But on you he will rain down abundance, rare fish and shy wildfowl, a rich harvest-tide. In the evening the rider of the storm will bring you wheat in torrents.'

"In the first light of dawn all my household gathered round me, the children brought pitch and the men whatever was necessary. On the fifth day I laid the keel and the ribs, then I made fast the planking. The ground-space was one acre, each side of the deck measured one hundred and twenty cubits,[3] making a square. I built six decks below, seven in all, I divided them into nine sections with bulkheads between. I drove in wedges where needed, I saw to the punt-poles,[4] and laid in supplies. The carriers brought oil in baskets, I poured pitch into the furnace and asphalt and oil; more oil was consumed in caulking,[5] and more again the master of the boat took into his stores. I slaughtered bullocks for the people and every day I killed sheep. I gave the shipwrights wine to drink as though it were river water, raw wine and red wine and oil and white wine. There was feasting then as there is at the time of the New Year's festival; I myself anointed my head. On the seventh day the boat was complete.

---

1. like . . . abyss: Like the firmament or heaven that covers the depths.
2. Gulf: The abyss, the great depths of the waters, where Ea, also called Enki, was supposed to dwell.
3. cubits: Ancient units of linear measure, about 18–22 inches each (originally, the distance from the elbow to the tip of the middle finger).
4. punt-poles: Poles that are pushed against the bottom of a shallow river or lake in order to propel a boat.
5. caulking (kôk′ iŋ) *v.:* Stopping up cracks or seams with a sealant.

"Then was the launching full of difficulty; there was shifting of ballast above and below till two thirds was submerged. I loaded into her all that I had of gold and of living things, my family, my kin, the beasts of the field both wild and tame, and all the craftsmen. I sent them on board, for the time that Shamash had ordained was already fulfilled when he said, 'In the evening, when the rider of the storm sends down the destroying rain, enter the boat and batten her down.' The time was fulfilled, the evening came, the rider of the storm sent down the rain. I looked out at the weather and it was terrible, so I too boarded the boat and battened her down. All was now complete, the battening and the caulking; so I handed the tiller to Puzur-Amurri the steersman, with the navigation and the care of the whole boat.

"With the first light of dawn a black cloud came from the horizon; it thundered within where Adad, lord of the storm, was riding. In front over hill and plain Shullat and Hanish, heralds of the storm, led on. Then the gods of the abyss rose up; Nergal pulled out the dams of the nether[6] waters, Ninurta the war-lord threw down the dykes, and the seven judges of hell, the Anunnaki, raised their torches, lighting the land with their livid flame. A stupor of despair went up to heaven when the god of the storm turned daylight to darkness, when he smashed the land like a cup. One whole day the tempest raged, gathering fury as it went, it poured over the people like the tides of battle; a man could not see his brother nor the people be seen from heaven. Even the gods were terrified at the flood, they fled to the highest heaven, the firmament of Anu; they crouched against the walls, cowering like curs. Then Ishtar the sweet-voiced Queen of Heaven cried out like a woman in travail: 'Alas the days of old are turned to dust because I commanded evil; why did I command this evil in the council of all the gods? I commanded wars to destroy the people, but are they not my people, for I brought them forth? Now like the spawn of fish they float in the ocean.' The great gods of heaven and of hell wept, they covered their mouths.

---

6. nether (neth′ ər) *adj.:* Below the earth's surface; lower.

Grammar in Action

The Semicolon Skillful writers use semicolons to link two closely related ideas, as follows:

RELATED IDEAS SEPARATED BY A PERIOD: We explored the abandoned house. We were surprised to find a packet of old love letters

RELATED IDEAS LINKED BY A SEMICOLON: We explored the abandoned house; we were surprised to find a packet of old love letters.

In this translation of *The Epic of Gilgamesh*, N. K. Sandars frequently uses a semicolon to connect closely related ideas. The following semicolon links two instructions for building an ark:

. . . let her beam equal her length, let her deck be roofed like the vault that covers the abyss; then take up into the boat the seed of all living creatures.

In the following sentence, the independent clause that comes after the semicolon explains the clause that precedes it:

Then was the launching full of difficulty; there was shifting of ballast above and below till two thirds was submerged.

Flood stories were popular in many different cultures. This picture illustrates an Indian tale called "The Legend of the Fish."

New York Public Library

"For six days and six nights the winds blew, torrent and tempest and flood overwhelmed the world, tempest and flood raged together like warring hosts. When the seventh day dawned the storm from the south subsided, the sea grew calm, the flood was stilled; I looked at the face of the world and there was silence, all mankind was turned to clay. The surface of the sea stretched as flat as a rooftop; I opened a hatch and the light fell on my face. Then I bowed low, I sat down and I wept, the tears streamed down my face, for on every side was the waste of water. I looked for land in vain, but fourteen leagues[7] distant there appeared a mountain, and there the boat grounded; on the mountain of Nisir the boat held fast, she held fast and did not budge. One day she held, and a second day on the mountain of Nisir she held fast and did not budge. A third day, and a fourth day she held fast on the mountain and did not budge; a fifth day and a sixth day she held fast on the mountain. When the seventh day dawned I loosed a dove and let her go. She flew away, but finding no resting-place she returned. Then I loosed a swallow, and she flew away but finding no resting-place she returned. I loosed a raven, she saw that the waters had retreated, she ate, she flew around, she cawed, and she did not come back. Then I threw everything open to the four winds, I made a sacrifice and poured out a libation[8]

---

7. **leagues:** Units of linear measure, varying in different times and countries; usually a league is about three miles.

8. **libation** (lī bā′ shən) *n*.: A liquid poured out as a sacrifice to a god.

12 Discussion Have students identify the first simile in this passage and discuss what it suggests about the Babylonian gods. Also have students explain Ishtar's change of attitude toward the flood. If you think it is appropriate, you can ask students to compare and contrast this passage with Genesis 9:11–15. While Ishtar regrets the flood, she does not make a covenant vow comparable to God's in Genesis.

13 Clarification Point out to students that Ea is asking Enlil to be more merciful toward humankind. Ea does not deny the need to punish sin; however, he emphasizes the need to temper justice with mercy: *"Punish him a little when he breaks loose, / Do not drive him too hard or he perishes."*

14 Discussion Have students speculate about why Enlil grants immortality to Utnapishtim and his wife.

15 Discussion Ask students to analyze this remark. What does it indicate about Gilgamesh's quest for immortality? How is it related to the flood story? Also, have students establish the connection between this remark and the test that Utnapishtim proposes for Gilgamesh.

16 Discussion Have students compare and contrast the attitudes toward Gilgamesh displayed by Utnapishtim and Utnapishtim's wife.

17 Reading Strategy Ask students to look for further evidence of the different attitudes of Utnapishtim and his wife.

on the mountain top. Seven and again seven cauldrons I set up on their stands, I heaped up wood and cane and cedar and myrtle. When the gods smelled the sweet savor, they gathered like flies over the sacrifice. Then, at last, Ishtar also came, she lifted her necklace with the jewels of heaven that once Anu had made to please her. 'O you gods here present, by the lapis lazuli⁹ round my neck I shall remember these days as I remember the jewels of my throat: these last days I shall not forget. Let all the gods gather round the sacrifice, except Enlil. He shall not approach this offering, for without reflection he brought the flood; he consigned my people to destruction.'

"When Enlil had come, when he saw the boat, he was wroth and swelled with anger at the gods, the host of heaven, 'Has any of these mortals escaped? Not one was to have survived the destruction.' Then the god of the wells and canals Ninurta opened his mouth and said to the warrior Enlil, 'Who is there of the gods that can devise without Ea? It is Ea alone who knows all things.' Then Ea opened his mouth and spoke to warrior Enlil, 'Wisest of gods, hero Enlil, how could you so senselessly bring down the flood?

Lay upon the sinner his sin,
Lay upon the transgressor his transgression,
Punish him a little when he breaks loose,
Do not drive him too hard or he perishes;
Would that a lion had ravaged mankind
Rather than the flood,
Would that a wolf had ravaged mankind
Rather than the flood,
Would that famine had wasted the world
Rather than the flood,
Would that pestilence had wasted mankind
Rather than the flood.

It was not I that revealed the secret of the gods; the wise man learned it in a dream. Now take your counsel what shall be done with him.'

"Then Enlil went up into the boat, he took me by the hand and my wife and made us enter the boat and kneel down on either side, he standing between us. He touched our foreheads to bless us saying. 'In time past Utnapishtim was a mortal man; henceforth he and his wife shall live in the distance at the mouth of the rivers.' Thus it was that the gods took me and placed me here to live in the distance, at the mouth of the rivers."

The Return

Utnapishtim said, "As for you, Gilgamesh, who will assemble the gods for your sake, so that you may find that life for which you are searching? But if you wish, come and put it to the test: only prevail against sleep for six days and seven nights." But while Gilgamesh sat there resting on his haunches, a mist of sleep like soft wool teased from the fleece drifted over him, and Utnapishtim said to his wife, "Look at him now, the strong man who would have everlasting life, even now the mists of sleep are drifting over him." His wife replied, "Touch the man to wake him, so that he may return to his own land in peace, going back through the gate by which he came." Utnapishtim said to his wife, "All men are deceivers, even you he will attempt to deceive; therefore bake loaves of bread, each day one loaf, and put it beside his head; and make a mark on the wall to number the days he has slept."

So she baked loaves of bread, each day one loaf, and put it beside his head, and she marked on the wall the days that he slept; and there came a day when the first loaf was hard, the second loaf was like leather, the third was soggy, the crust of the fourth had mold, the fifth was mildewed, the sixth was fresh, and the seventh was still on the em-

---

9. **lapis lazuli** (lap′ is laz′ yōō lī): A sky–blue gemstone.

Primary Source Note

The prose translation of *The Epic of Gilgamesh* by N. K. Sandars is widely respected for its accuracy and readability. Other English versions of the epic do exist, however, including a scholarly verse translation by E. A. Speiser. In his translation of "The Return," Speiser uses brackets, parentheses, and ellipses to indicate missing or mutilated sections of the clay tablet:

Gilgamesh says to him, to Urshanabi, the boatman:
"Urshanabi, this plant is a plant *apart,*
Whereby a man may regain his *life's breath.*
I will take it to ramparted Uruk,
  Will cause [. . .] to eat the plant . . . !
Its name shall be 'Man Becomes Young in Old Age.'
I myself shall eat (it)
  And thus return to the state of my youth."
After twenty leagues they broke off a morsel,
After thirty (further) leagues they prepared
  for the night.
Gilgamesh saw a well whose water was cool.
He went down into it to bathe in the water.

bers. Then Utnapishtim touched him and he woke. Gilgamesh said to Utnapishtim the Faraway, "I hardly slept when you touched and roused me." But Utnapishtim said, "Count these loaves and learn how many days you slept, for your first is hard, your second like leather, your third is soggy, the crust of your fourth has mold, your fifth is mildewed, your sixth is fresh and your seventh was still over the glowing embers when I touched and woke you." Gilgamesh said, "What shall I do, O Utnapishtim, where shall I go? Already the thief in the night has hold of my limbs, death inhabits my room; wherever my foot rests, there I find death."

Then Utnapishtim spoke to Urshanabi the ferryman: "Woe to you Urshanabi, now and forevermore you have become hateful to this harborage; it is not for you, nor for you are the crossings of this sea. Go now, banished from the shore. But this man before whom you walked, bringing him here, whose body is covered with foulness and the grace of whose limbs has been spoiled by wild skins, take him to the washing-place. There he shall wash his long hair clean as snow in the water, he shall throw off his skins and let the sea carry them away, and the beauty of his body shall be shown, the fillet[10] on his forehead shall be renewed, and he shall be given clothes to cover his nakedness. Till he reaches his own city and his journey is accomplished, these clothes will show no sign of age, they will wear like a new garment." So Urshanabi took Gilgamesh and led him to the washing-place, he washed his long hair as clean as snow in the water, he threw off his skins, which the sea carried away, and showed the beauty of his body. He renewed the fillet on his forehead, and to cover his nakedness gave him clothes which would show no sign of age, but would wear like a new garment till he reached his own city, and his journey was accomplished.

Then Gilgamesh and Urshanabi launched the boat onto the water and boarded it, and they made ready to sail away; but the wife of Utnapishtim the Faraway said to him, "Gilgamesh came here wearied out, he is worn out; what will you give him to carry him back to his own country?" So Utnapishtim spoke, and Gilgamesh took a pole and brought the boat in to the bank. "Gilgamesh, you came here a man wearied out, you have worn yourself out; what shall I give you to carry you back to your own country? Gilgamesh, I shall reveal a secret thing, it is a mystery of the gods that I am telling you. There is a plant that grows under the water, it has a prickle like a thorn, like a rose; it will wound your hands, but if you succeed in taking it, then your hands will hold that which restores his lost youth to a man."

When Gilgamesh heard this he opened the sluices so that a sweet-water current might carry him out to the deepest channel; he tied heavy stones to his feet and they dragged him down to the water-bed. There he saw the plant growing; although it pricked him he took it in his hands; then he cut the heavy stones from his feet, and the sea carried him and threw him onto the shore. Gilgamesh said to Urshanabi the ferryman, "Come here, and see this marvelous plant. By its virtue a man may win back all his former strength. I will take it to Uruk of the strong walls; there I will give it to the old men to eat. Its name shall be 'The Old Men Are Young Again'; and at last I shall eat it myself and have back all my lost youth." So Gilgamesh returned by the gate through which he had come, Gilgamesh and Urshanabi went together. They traveled their twenty leagues and then they broke their fast; after thirty leagues they stopped for the night.

Gilgamesh saw a well of cool water and he went down and bathed; but deep in the pool there was lying a serpent, and the serpent sensed the sweetness of the flower. It rose out of the water and snatched it away, and immediately it sloughed its skin and returned to the well. Then Gilgamesh sat down and wept, the tears ran down his face, and he took the hand of Urshanabi; "O Urshanabi, was it for this that I toiled with my hands, is it for this I have wrung out my heart's blood? For myself I have gained nothing; not I, but the beast of the earth has joy of it now. Already the stream has carried it twenty leagues back to the channels where I found it. I found a sign and now I have lost it. Let us leave the boat on the bank and go."

10. **fillet** (fil' it) *n.:* A narrow band worn around the head to hold the hair in place.

A serpent snuffed the fragrance of the plant;
It came up [from the water] and carried off the plant.
Going back it shed [its] slough.

Thereupon Gilgamesh sits down and weeps,
His tears running down over his face.
[He took the hand] of Urshanabi, the boatman:
"[For] whom, Urshanabi, have my hands toiled?
For whom is being spent the blood of my heart?
I have not obtained a boon for myself.

For the earth-lion have I effected a boon!"

Read the translated verses aloud to your students. Ask them to discuss why one translator might choose to work in prose while another chooses poetry.

18 **Discussion** Ask students why Gilgamesh is so despairing when he learns that he has slept for six days.

19 **Discussion** Have students interpret Utnapishtim's motive for banning Urshanabi.

20 **Discussion** Ask students if there is anything ironic in the gift of clothes that "'will wear like a new garment'" only until Gilgamesh reaches his city. To prompt them ask how this present compares with the gift Gilgamesh has been seeking. You can also have students discuss the way in which Gilgamesh's ritual washing marks a turning point in the plot. How, for instance, does it indicate that the quest is at an end?

21 **Discussion** Ask students whether or not there is anything unusual about the timing of this gift of valuable information.

22 **Discussion** Ask students whether they were surprised by Gilgamesh's plan to share the plant with the old men of Uruk. Then have them explain their answers.

23 **Discussion** Have students discuss their reactions to this sudden loss of the magical plant. Also ask them why the snake sloughs its skin "immediately."

Unfinished *Kudurru* (boundary-stone). These boundary-stones, indicating a royal grant of land to a citizen, were set up in the field received from the king. This one depicts a snake like the one that stole Gilgamesh's magical plant.

The Louvre, Paris

24
25

24 **Discussion** Have students compare this passage with the description of the walls of Uruk on page 16. Ask them why this description is repeated. For instance, what do the walls of Uruk symbolize? How is the king's achievement in building them related to his quest for immortality? Will the construction of these walls ensure Gilgamesh a kind of life after death? Why or why not?

25 **Enrichment** Each Sumerian city had a chief, or sponsoring, deity. Ishtar, or Inanna as she was known to the Sumerians, was the chief deity of Uruk.

Master Teacher Note Students might enjoy mapping Gilgamesh's quest. Have them draw Gilgamesh's journey, briefly noting the various adventures that occur along the way. Make sure students use evidence from the text to create their maps; however, where the text does not specify a direction or distance, give students considerable latitude in imagining Gilgamesh's quest. You might ask them to use the map on page 4 as the basis for their own map.

Cooperative Learning Have students work in small groups to create maps of Gilgamesh's quest. Some group members can actually draw the maps, while others can check them against the text or write captions for the various adventures.

Humanities Note

Fine art, *Unfinished Kudurru* (boundary-stone). Archeologists have discovered more than eighty of these boundary-stones, dating from the fourteenth to the seventh century B.C. They proclaimed that the king granted a parcel of land to a citizen. These declarations were accompanied by relief carvings like the ones shown here.

You might want to use the following questions to discuss the art.
1. Why do you think such care and workmanship were devoted to these boundary-stones?
2. Do we have a modern equivalent to the ancient Mesopotamian kudurru? Explain.

After twenty leagues they broke their fast, after thirty leagues they stopped for the night; in three days they had walked as much as a journey of a month and fifteen days. When the journey was accomplished they arrived at Uruk, the strong-walled city. Gilgamesh spoke to him, to Urshanabi the ferryman, "Urshanabi, climb up onto the wall of Uruk, inspect its foundation terrace, and examine well the brickwork; see if it is not of burnt bricks; and did not the seven wise men lay these foundations? One third of the whole is city, one third is garden, and one third is field, with the precinct of the goddess Ishtar. These parts and the precinct are all Uruk."

This too was the work of Gilgamesh, the king, who knew the countries of the world. He was wise, he saw mysteries and knew secret things, he brought us a tale of the days before the flood. He went a long journey, was weary, worn out with labor, and returning engraved on a stone the whole story.

Reader's Response *What kinds of quests, if any, do people go on today?*

THINKING ABOUT THE SELECTION

Clarifying

1. (a) Why do the gods agree to destroy humankind? (b) What causes them to change their minds?
2. List in order the key events that occur after Utnapishtim tells his story.

Interpreting

3. What purpose does the flood story serve in the epic?
4. (a) What evidence is there that Utnapishtim is not entirely sympathetic to Gilgamesh's quest? (b) What might cause Utnapishtim to have mixed feelings about Gilgamesh?
5. When the snake steals the plants, why doesn't Gilgamesh return for more?
6. Which of the following phrases best summarizes Gilgamesh's mood at the end? (a) bitter resignation, (b) pride in the walls of Uruk. Give your reasons for your choice.
7. (a) What insights into life do you think the ancient people who heard this epic gained? (b) What insights did you gain from reading it?

Closure and Extension

ANSWERS TO THINKING ABOUT THE SELECTION

1. (a) There are so many people that their noise disturbs the gods. (b) Even the gods are terrified by the destructiveness of the flood.
2. Gilgamesh sleeps for six days and into a seventh while Utnapishtim's wife bakes a loaf of bread to mark the passing of each day. Before Gilgamesh returns to Uruk with the ferryman, Utnapishtim tells him where he can find a plant to restore youth. Gilgamesh dives under the water to find the plant. On the way back, however, a snake steals it while Gilgamesh is bathing in a pool. When Gilgamesh and the ferryman reach Uruk, Gilgamesh shows his companion the walls of the city.
3. Answers will differ. The flood story may indicate that only one man was destined to be immortal; therefore, Gilgamesh's quest is futile. Another response is that the story is meant to distract Gilgamesh from his quest.
4. (a) Utnapishtim asks, possibly in a sarcastic tone, "As for you, Gilgamesh, who will assemble the gods for your sake, so that you may find

Applying

8. (a) What makes this epic difficult to read? (b) Which passages or ideas did you find the most thought-provoking? Why?
9. What do you think Gilgamesh would find most surprising about our civilization? Least surprising? Explain.

ANALYZING LITERATURE

Understanding the Hero and His Quest

A **hero** is a character whose actions are inspiring or noble. Deeply troubled by the death of his friend Enkidu, Gilgamesh embarks on a quest not for glory but for everlasting life in the flesh. Strangely, both his success and his failure have an accidental quality. Utnapishtim gives him the secret of a magical, restorative plant not in answer to his request but as a parting gift, an afterthought. Similarly, his loss of the plant to a snake, described very briefly, is presented as a chance occurrence.

1. What is the connection between the role of chance or accident and the theme that humans cannot attain everlasting life?
2. Which passages in the epic foreshadow the failure of the quest? Explain.
3. Why is it appropriate that a snake, rather than some other beast, steals the magical plant?
4. Was Gilgamesh's quest a selfish one? Why or why not?
5. When speaking to Urshanabi, Gilgamesh says he has "gained nothing" for his trouble. Do you agree? Give reasons for your answer.

CRITICAL THINKING AND READING

Inferring the Purpose of the Flood Story

The flood narrative was added to a late version of *The Epic of Gilgamesh*, and scholars have disagreed about the role it was meant to play. Jeffrey Tigay, for instance, argues that it was introduced to distract an audience from Gilgamesh's quest. As a result, the suspense would diminish and the audience would be readier to accept the hero's failure to gain immortality. Other critics have asserted that the flood story was meant to show Gilgamesh the futility of his search for everlasting life. According to this viewpoint, the story demonstrates that the bestowal of immortality on Utnapishtim was a unique, unrepeatable event.

Evaluate each of these arguments, citing passages from the text to back up your opinion.

UNDERSTANDING LANGUAGE

Appreciating an Akkadian Pun

Ea, the Mesopotamian god of the waters, was known for his slyness. When Utnapishtim wonders what he will tell his fellow citizens about the ark he is building, Ea gives him a clever speech to recite. This speech contains the Akkadian words *kukku* and *kibati*, which can mean either "bran and wheat" or "misfortune and sorrow." When Utnapishtim uses these words, his listeners think of the first meaning and believe that Enlil "will rain down abundance . . . a rich harvest-tide." The real message, however, is that the god will shower the people with misfortune.

Like Akkadian, most languages have words and phrases with several different, sometimes opposite, meanings. What are the advantages and disadvantages of this characteristic of language?

THINKING AND WRITING

Comparing and Contrasting Heroes

Gilgamesh is a hero on a quest for eternal life. Think of a modern-day hero—from the movies, television, or fiction—who also journeys in search of a goal. Write an essay comparing and contrasting Gilgamesh to this modern hero. Consider such factors as the nature of the goal, the difficulties that must be overcome, the help, if any, that the hero receives, and the hero's ultimate success or failure. When you revise your essay, make sure that you have organized it logically so that readers can follow your comparisons and contrasts.

Egyptian Poetry

Detail of back of throne of Tutankhamun; Queen anointing Tut with perfume
From the tomb of Tutankhamun

Objectives

Thematic

To understand how the theme of love spans the ages

Skills

1 To appreciate concrete language
2 To infer the dramatic context
3 To understand pastoral poetry
4 To appreciate diction
5 To write love poems for fictional characters

GUIDE FOR INTERPRETING

Egyptian Poetry

Commentary

Pastoral Poetry. The term *pastoral* comes from the Latin word for shepherd—*pastor*—but pastoral poetry is not merely about shepherds and shepherdesses. A pastoral poem is one that deals with the pleasures of a simple rural life or that treats the longings and desires of simple people. It is one that, according to Barris Mills, "invites us to forget for a while man's destiny . . . and to indulge ourselves in a daydream of rustic simplicity and romantic love."

Pastoral poetry is written by sophisticated artists who assume the persona of a simple character. In fact, pastoral poetry can be thought of as a type of escapist literature that allows highly civilized readers to experience vicariously what they imagine to be the free and untroubled life of ordinary folk.

The New Kingdom (1570–1085 B.C.) in Egypt was a highly sophisticated period marked by the last great flowering of ancient Egyptian culture. It was a time of expansion abroad—the Egyptian empire reached to the Euphrates River—and increased opportunity at home. Women enjoyed a greater prestige in New Kingdom society than they did in perhaps any other ancient culture. With a legal status equal to that of men, they could will property, initiate a lawsuit, and probably divorce a husband. It is not surprising that such an advanced culture might want to enjoy a vicarious simplicity.

The three poems you are about to read were all written by skillful poets—no doubt highly cultured men. In each the poet assumes a much simpler persona. In the first poem a female character expresses in simple, direct language her longing and devotion. In the second a young boy tells of his lovesickness. In the third a bird-catcher tells of her girlish love.

As you read these poems, no doubt you will find yourself identifying with the direct emotions of the three speakers. Think about how the lives of the sophisticated poets who wrote these poems differed from the lives they presented. How were they able to make you identify so closely with the three characters?

Writing

Even today, the desire to escape from a complicated time is common. Indeed, one critic once said that cowboy-and-Indian movies can be considered pastorals for our time. Explain why you agree or disagree. Do such movies show the untroubled life of ordinary people? Does the violence in these films rule them out as pastorals? Freewrite, exploring your thoughts on this matter.

Language Worksheet, *Appreciating Diction*, p. 36
Selection Test, pp. 37–38

Focus

Literary Focus Ask students if they have read or seen films about people whose lives were simpler than those of contemporary Americans. Encourage students to describe these simpler ways of life and analyze their appeal.

Writing/Prior Knowledge Have students get together in small groups and share their perspectives on western movies before they begin to freewrite. Ask them to discuss the specific questions raised in the assignment.

ESL Teaching Strategy Assign each ESL student a partner who can act as a resource person and answer questions about the text.

Teaching Tenth-Grade Students In order to illustrate the concept of pastoral poetry, you might want to read aloud Christopher Marlowe's poem "The Passionate Shepherd to His Love." Then have students explain why this poem belongs in the pastoral tradition.

Master Teacher Note Have students bring in recordings of contemporary love ballads. Play these recordings in class and write the lyrics of some of these ballads on the chalkboard. Then ask students to compare and contrast these words with the lyrics of the ancient Egyptian poems.

Motivation/Prior Knowledge Tell students that although these poems are thousands of years old, they express feelings that are familiar to us today. In many ways the voices in these poems are even more poignant because we hear them across the expanse of thousands of years.

Purpose-Setting Question For each of these poems, identify the speaker and the situation suggested by his or her words.

Universal Themes You might want to have students compare these love poems with the love poems of Sappho, pages 398–402; Catullus, pages 528–529; Petrarch, pages 676–678; and Baudelaire, pages 904–905.

Cultural Note The translator of these poems, John L. Foster, wrote that he was influenced by "the language used by . . . American poets (Ezra Pound, William Carlos Williams, e. e. cummings, and others) prominent in the earlier decades of the twentieth century and writing in the 'modernist' style."

1 **Discussion** The poet uses concrete images—oil, ritual robes, and incense—familiar to his audience. Ask students what concrete images they would use to express the same feeling in a contemporary love poem.

Humanities Note

Fine art, *Sculpture of a girl carrying cuts of meat in a box, from the tomb of Mekutre,* c. 2009–1998 B.C. This wooden sculpture of a colorfully dressed serving girl was found in the tomb of Mekutre, the chief steward and chancellor of Pharaoh Mentuhotep II. To add color to the figure, the wood was coated with plaster and painted.

You might want to use the following questions to discuss the art.
1. Do you think this sculpture is true to life? Why or why not?
2. Compare and contrast the style of the girl's hair and clothing with contemporary styles.

*From the tomb of Mekutra,
c. 2009–1998 B.C.*
The Metropolitan Museum of Art, New York

Your Love, Dear Man, Is as Lovely to Me

translated by John L. Foster

Your love, dear man, is as lovely to me
As sweet soothing oil to the limbs of the restless,
        as clean ritual robes to the flesh of gods,
As fragrance of incense to one coming home
5   hot from the smells of the street.

It is like nipple-berries ripe in the hand,
        like the tang of grainmeal mingled with beer,
Like wine to the palate when taken with white bread.

        While unhurried days come and go,
10 Let us turn to each other in quiet affection,
        walk in peace to the edge of old age.
And I shall be with you each unhurried day,
        a woman given her one wish: to see
For a lifetime the face of her lord.

THINKING ABOUT THE SELECTION

Interpreting

1. (a) What is the mood of this poem? (b) Identify specific words that contribute to this mood.
2. This poem is filled with similes—figurative comparisons between unlike things. What inferences do you make about the speaker based on the things to which she compares her love?
3. (a) In what ways is this poem timeless? (b) In what ways is it rooted in a specific time and place?

Applying

4. What does this poem reveal about life in Egypt at the time of the New Kingdom?

5. Identify a modern poem or song that is similar to this one and explain your choice.

UNDERSTANDING LANGUAGE

Appreciating Concrete Language

Concrete language is language that appeals to the senses. Among the specific sensations the poet evokes in this poem is the taste of wine and bread.
1. (a) Name all the senses to which the poet appeals. (b) Identify the concrete language that appeals to each sense you have named.
2. How does the concrete language contribute to the speaker's definition of her love?

Closure and Extension

ANSWERS TO THINKING ABOUT THE SELECTION

1. (a) The mood is one of peace and deep devotion. (b) Words and phrases that contribute to this mood are "lovely," "sweet soothing," "unhurried," "quiet affection," and "peace."
2. We can infer that she is alert to the experience of her senses. We might also infer that she is a simple, direct person because her comparisons are down to earth.
3. (a) It is timeless as an expression of devotion and sincere love. (b) The concrete experience referred to in the similes—e.g. "clean ritual robes"—root it in a specific time and place.
4. Answers will differ. Students may refer to the use of oil and incense and the mention of berries, grain, bread, and beer as foods. Especially bright students may speculate about the differences between the "ideal" world of the poem and the actual world of New Kingdom Egypt.
5. Answers will differ, but students should explain their choices.

Musicians with harp, lute, double-pipe, and lyre
c. 1411–1397 B.C.
The Metropolitan Museum of Art, New York

I Think I'll Go Home and Lie Very Still

translated by John L. Foster

I think I'll go home and lie very still,
      feigning[1] terminal illness.
Then the neighbors will all troop over to stare,
      my love, perhaps, among them.
How she'll smile while the specialists
          snarl in their teeth!—

      she perfectly well knows what ails me.

---

1. feigning (fān´ iŋ) *v.*: Pretending.

Reader's Response *Have you ever known anyone who felt lovesick? Describe the symptoms of this "disease."*

THINKING ABOUT THE SELECTION

Interpreting

1. Why will the speaker's love smile when she sees him lying "very still"?
2. Why will the specialists "snarl in their teeth"?
3. What role does irony—the difference between appearance and reality—play in this poem?

Applying

4. Imagine that the young woman the speaker refers to is looking at him as he lies ill in bed. Give a brief account of her thoughts.

CRITICAL THINKING AND READING

Inferring the Dramatic Context

Sometimes a lyric poem, even a small one, contains the seeds of a whole drama. When we read "I think I'll go home and lie very still," for example, we can imagine a character in a play speaking these words. Obviously, he has been disappointed in love.

1. Briefly outline an imaginary play in which this poem is one speech.
2. What do the events leading up to this speech suggest about its tone? Is it sarcastic, amused, angry, ironic, sad, or some combination of these? Give reasons for your choice.

The Voice of the Swallow, Flittering, Calls to Me

translated by John L. Foster

1   The voice of the swallow, flittering, calls to me:
        "Land's alight! Whither away?"
  No, little bird, you cannot entice me,
        I follow you to the fields no more.
  Like you in the dawn mist I rose,
        at sunrise discovered my lover abed
            (his voice is sweeter).
2   "Wake," I said, "or I fly with the swallow."
  5 And my heart smiled back
        when he, smiling, said:
  "You shall not fly,
        nor shall I, bright bird.
            But hand in hand
3   We shall walk the Nileside pathways,
  under cool of branches, hidden
        (only the swallows watching)—
  Wide-eyed girl,
        I shall be with you in all glad places."
10 Can you match the notes of that song, little swallow?
        I am first in his field of girls!
  My heart, dear sister, sings in his hand—
        love never harmed a winged creature.

THINKING ABOUT THE SELECTION

Interpreting

1. The speaker in the poem is a bird-catcher; she captures and tames wild birds. (a) How does the poet weave this occupation into almost every line of the poem? (b) How does the poet play with the themes of wildness and tameness?
2. What does the speaker mean when she says, "My heart, dear sister, sings in his hand—"?
3. Explain the meaning of the last line in the poem.

Applying

4. Egyptian poetry was often sung to the accompaniment of harps, lutes, and other string instruments. (a) What is songlike about this poem? (b) If you were setting this song to music, what instrument would you use?

BIRDS IN A PAPYRUS SWAMP
Akhenaton at Tell el Amarna, c. 1360 B.C.
The Metropolitan Museum of Art, New York

(continued from page 34)

ANALYZING LITERATURE

Understanding Pastoral Poetry

Pastoral poetry is work that depicts the pleasures of a simple rural life or that treats the longings and desires of uncomplicated characters.
1. Imagine a New Kingdom Egyptian with a complex and demanding job—a general, the head of a school of scribes, or a palace adviser in charge of trade with Mesopotamians. Why might such a person have been pleased to read this poem?
2. A critic once declared that "to achieve simplicity in poetry requires a great deal of skill." Using this poem, argue in favor of this observation.

UNDERSTANDING LANGUAGE

Appreciating Diction

Diction refers to a writer's choice of words. In some ways, this choice is like the appropriate selection of clothing. For example, normally you would not turn up at a wedding dressed in dungarees, at least not an ordinary wedding.

John L. Foster, the translator of these Egyptian love poems, made the following statement about his choice of words: "The diction should be unpretentiously colloquial, simple, except when elevated by the power of strong feeling or slipping over into the sometimes slangy verbal patterns of irony or humor. The language should be conversational, quiet, the usages of personal and private speech; for those are the kinds of words for lovers."
1. Do you agree with Foster's statement about the correct diction for these poems? Why or why not?
2. Has he followed his own guidelines in "The Voice of the Swallow, Flittering, Calls to Me"? Support your answer with references to passages in the poem.

THINKING AND WRITING

Writing Love Poems for Fictional Characters

Experiment with diction by writing love poems for different types of characters. Get together with a small group of classmates and think of an unusual couple; for example, a female United States senator and a male ice skater. Discuss the type of love poem that each would write to the other, focusing on the kinds of words and images that he or she would naturally use. The senator, for instance, might make her poem sound like an appeal for votes. Then write a humorous love poem for each of the characters. As you revise these poems, read them to your classmates and ask them how you can make the diction even funnier.

Humanities Note

Fine art, *Birds in a papyrus swamp*, c. 1360 B.C. This mural decorated a wall of Pharaoh Akenaton's palace at Tel el Amarna. The new, more naturalistic style of art that Akenaton introduced is evident in this painting. As opposed to the formalized rendering of men and gods in earlier eras, it presents a simple landscape. Also, while earlier art was chiefly used to decorate tombs, this mural was created for the enjoyment of the living.

You might want to use the following questions to discuss the art:
1. What are some of the differences in style between this mural and the illustration from the Book of the Dead on page 37?
2. Which style do you find more appealing? Why?
3. If you were in charge of decorating buildings for your town or city, where would you place this mural? Explain your choice.

EGYPTIAN BOOK OF THE DEAD

Presentation

Motivation/Prior Knowledge Elicit from students what they know about ancient Egypt and its religion based upon films they have seen and books they have read. Have them speculate as to why movies about ancient Egypt are often mysterious and frightening. Ask them specifically about the process of mummification and its purpose.

1 Enrichment The Egyptians believed that the dead had greater powers than the living. For example, the Book of the Dead contained special magical spells that enabled the deceased to transform themselves into any living thing they desired to be: a falcon, a lotus flower, a crocodile, and so forth.

2 Enrichment Egyptian burial beliefs were influenced by changes in society itself. During the Old Kingdom when the pharaoh ruled supreme, only he was entitled to immortality. In the period between the Old and Middle Kingdoms, however, as the nobles gained more power in society, they too earned the right to a blissful life after death. There is even evidence that the lower classes enjoyed access to the afterworld.

Hollywood and Egypt

How do you picture ancient Egypt? Do you see mysterious pyramids, linen-wrapped mummies, and secret religious ceremonies? Many of our images of ancient Egypt probably derive from Hollywood movies like *The Mummy's Curse*. Surprisingly, however, many observers throughout history have shared this picture of Egypt as an uncanny culture, wise in secret lore.

Why is this so? Although these popular ideas about ancient Egypt are exaggerated and distorted, they do contain a grain of truth. The ancient Egyptians were preoccupied with death and the progress of the soul through the underworld. Their concern, however, reflected an optimistic—not a dark—outlook. They believed in a type of life after death. To prepare for this existence, they collected the numerous spells, confessions, and words of power known as the Egyptian Book of the Dead.

What Is the Egyptian Book of the Dead?

The title Egyptian Book of the Dead incorrectly suggests a single volume. Actually, this title refers to many different texts written in different eras. These texts, inscribed on long papyrus scrolls entombed with the deceased, were a guide for the dead person on the perilous journey through the underworld. They contained, for example, magical spells that would fend off demons and monsters, as well as confessions and assertions of innocence that would help the soul when it came to judgment before Osiris, the Egyptian god of the dead.

It was only through a misunderstanding that nineteenth-century archeologists gave these different scrolls a single name. Tomb-robbers who sold these papyrus texts to archeologists referred to them as *Kitab al-Mayyitun*, which meant nothing more than "dead men's books." The scholars, misinterpreting this term, thought that it referred to a single text: the Egyptian Book of the Dead.

Social Class and the Book of the Dead

Even in death, the rich were better provided for than were the poor. Pharaohs and rich bureaucrats could afford to be buried with a deluxe scroll, rendered by the most skillful scribe. The Papyrus of Ani is an example of such a scroll. Ani was an important official who lived around 1450 B.C. This papyrus "book" unrolls to a length of 78 feet and is about 1 foot wide. It contains a version of the Book of the Dead that is associated with the ancient city of Thebes in southern Egypt. The various chapters are illustrated with pictures in brilliant reds, yellows, blues, and greens. (The illustration on the next page comes from a later era but resembles the pictures in the Papyrus of Ani.)

Egyptians who were not as important had to settle for a cut-rate edition. These were prepared in quantity, with a space left for the name of the purchaser. As might be expected, hastily copied editions had errors in spelling and omissions of words.

Errors appeared even in fine editions. Sometimes these mistakes resulted from the attention given to pictures at the expense of text. At first the pictures, which were not as important as the text,

Primary Source Note

John A. Wilson explains how, as the Old Kingdom ended, much more importance was given to good deeds as a means of gaining eternal life:

Ma'at, "truth, justice, righteousness, right dealing, order," had thus become critically important for the supreme prize of eternal happiness. Meri-ka-Re was advised by his father [the king] "to do *ma'at* whilst thou endurest upon earth." Why? The text goes on to relate royal justice upon earth to the judgment at death: "The council which judges the deficient, thou knowest that they are not lenient on that day of judging the miserable, the hour of doing (their) duty. . . . Do not trust in length of years, for they regard a lifetime as (but) an hour. A man remains over after death, and his deeds are placed beside him in heaps. However, existence yonder is for eternity . . . He who reaches it without wrongdoing shall exist yonder like a god, stepping out freely like the lords of eternity." Whereas those of earlier times had tried to purchase their immortality by huge tombs and elaborate endowment for perpetual offerings, the new emphasis on character shifted the focus from goods to good.

NSIGHTS

PAGE FROM THE "BOOK OF THE DEAD"
c. 1100 B.C.
The British Museum, London

were rendered by the scribe himself in black outline. Gradually, however, they were assigned to skillful artists, who drew them in brilliant color. As people valued these pictures more and more, less attention was given to the text itself. In one case a careless and ignorant scribe copied an entire chapter backwards, ending with the title!

A Travel Guide to the Underworld

In some ways the Egyptian Book of the Dead resembled a travel guide to the underworld. (Travel guides, of course, lack the religious dimension of the Egyptian text.) Just as a contemporary travel guide might inform you about accommodations, traffic, and currency in a foreign country, so the Book of the Dead told the ancient Egyptian what to say and do in the strange country of the hereafter.

For example, on the way to see Osiris, the ruler of the dead, the deceased had to pass through seven great halls. Each of these was supervised by three gods, and unless the deceased could tell each god his or her name, the journey would end. Not knowing the magical names was comparable to arriving at a modern frontier without a passport! Naturally, the names of all the gods were carefully listed in the Book of the Dead.

The ruler of the Egyptian underworld was the god Osiris. His story involved suffering, death, and resurrection. That emphasis on resurrection is why Osiris's story had such an appeal, for the average Egyptian hoped to survive death and live forever. The identity that Egyptians felt with Osiris was so strong that the dead were referred to by name as Osiris. In the Papyrus of Ani, for instance, there are many references to "Osiris Ani." It is as if modern-day Christians referred to themselves in burial ceremonies as Jesus Jones or Jesus Thompson.

The most dramatic moment of the underworld journey was the judgment of the dead by Osiris. As the illustration above indicates, the heart of the deceased—for Egyptians the word "heart" also meant "conscience"—was weighed against a figure of Ma'at, the goddess of law, truth, and justice. Those who were found to be true would live an afterlife of eternal happiness. Souls that failed this test, however, were tortured and destroyed. Such destruction, called "repeated death," was perhaps the greatest fear of the Egyptians. It meant complete extermination.

This conception of judgment, reward, and punishment is common to many cultures, including our own. Compare the Egyptian underworld with that depicted in *The Epic of Gilgamesh* (page 15) or in Dante's *Inferno* (page 622).

Egyptian Burial Practices

Associated with the Book of the Dead were the Egyptian burial practices that have fascinated so many other cultures, including ours. Egyptians believed, for instance, that the preservation of the body was necessary to ensure a satisfactory life after death. They therefore embalmed the dead using a process known today as mummification. (The word *mummy* derives from the Arabic term *mumiyah*, which means "bitumen." It came into use because many people believed the Egyptians employed the mineral bitumen to keep dead bodies from decaying.) Although Egyptian techniques of embalming changed over time, they usually involved the removal of internal organs, treatment of the body with resin—an organic substance from plants—and wrapping the corpse in linen bandages. No Hollywood movie about ancient Egypt omitted these crucial bandages!

HEBREW LITERATURE

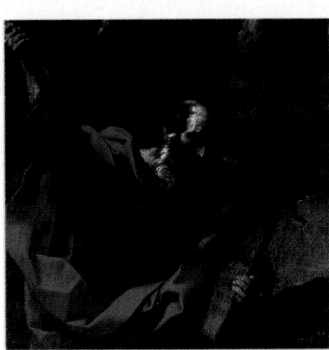

MOSES WITH THE TEN COMMANDMENTS
Guido Reni
Galleria Borghese, Rome

The most important example of Hebrew literature is the Jewish Bible (called by Christians the Old Testament in contrast to the New Testament). If extraterrestrials visited our planet and wanted to understand Western Civilization, we would be well advised to hand them a copy of the Bible.

What Is the Bible?

The word *Bible* came from the Greek word *biblia,* meaning a collection of writings. It is accurate to call the Bible a collection, even a library, rather than a single book. Like an extensive library, it contains many types of books.

Traditionally, the books of the Hebrew Bible have been divided into three main sections. The Torah—from the Hebrew word *tora,* meaning "law"—consists of the first five books of the Bible (Genesis, Exodus, Leviticus, Numbers, and Deuteronomy). While the Torah is largely concerned with the law, it contains important narratives and an account of the world's creation. Another section contains historical accounts like the Book of Samuel. It also contains the writings of the prophets, those who in God's name summoned the Jews to the path of justice and faith. Still another section of the Bible consists of a variety of works: poetry like the Psalms, short stories like the Book of Ruth, and religious dialogues like the Book of Job.

When and How Was the Bible Written?

Who wrote the Bible is a question that has intrigued people over the centuries. Many believe that the Bible is the word of God. Through the workings of divine inspiration, human beings wrote down God's message. It was once believed that Moses himself wrote the first five books of the Bible and that King David composed the Psalms. In the nineteenth century, however, some scholars began to theorize that differences in style and content suggest multiple sources for the Bible. Today some experts infer that the oldest sources for the Torah, for instance, date back to the tenth century B.C. and the most recent to about the fifth century B.C.

What Themes Run Through the Bible?

Despite the diversity of the Bible, it is unified by a few constant themes. Among these are the power, goodness, and mercy of the one God (most other peoples of that era worshiped many gods); the covenant, or solemn agreement, into which he enters with the Hebrew people; the tendency of humans to stray from the right path; and the forgiveness they win from God.

The Bible's Influence

For Jews the Bible was a "Written Temple," sustaining Jewish culture and beliefs when the Temple in Jerusalem and the Jewish nation itself were destroyed.

The Bible has also been of major importance for Muslims and Christians. Translated into Greek, Latin, and every important Western language, it is regarded by Christians as the precursor to the New Testament. Martin Luther, inaugurating Protestantism, translated the Bible into German and stressed its importance for the individual believer. Still another famous translation of the Bible was the English version done by a committee of scholars for King James (1611). The phrasing and cadences of the King James Version —from which the following selections are taken —have influenced the prose and poetry of our language for nearly four hundred years.

GUIDE FOR INTERPRETING

The Creation and the Fall

Commentary

Archetypes. Archetypes are symbols, images, or patterns that appear in the myths, literature, and visual art of many different peoples. Their occurrence at various times and places suggests that they have universal meanings and are not the products of any one culture. Archetypes tend to show that no matter how different human beings may appear on the outside, they are really quite similar.

Often archetypes derive from nature. Trees, for instance, have played an important role in the myths and legends of different peoples. Many cultures conceived of a great tree whose branches reach the heavens and whose roots extend into the depths of the earth. In Norse mythology there was the ash tree Yggdrasil (ig′drə sil′), which bound together the three main realms of the world: heaven, earth, and hell. Many of the peoples who envisioned such a world-tree thought of it as a source of divine knowledge, because it led like a stairway from earth to heaven.

Humans have always been fascinated by snakes, and these creatures—along with their more fantastic cousins, dragons—wind in and out of many of the world's legends. Not every culture, however, has given this archetypal beast the same meaning. In the Near East, snakes were often poisonous, so it is not surprising that they became symbols of evil. Yet in China and Japan, the dragon was a positive symbol.

The following passage from the Bible deals with the most important subject one could imagine: how everything came to be (the word *genesis* comes from the Greek word *gignesthai*, "to be born," and is related to *genus* and *genetic*). Since archetypes embody our most universal and powerful experiences, we can expect to find them in such an account. The emergence of the world from an original ocean of chaos is an archetypal image. Other archetypes in Genesis are the Tree of Knowledge, a world-tree like Yggdrasil, and the "subtil" serpent, a creature of evil.

Writing

Archetypes are not things of the past. These timeless and universal symbols can be found in today's stories and films. List some archetypal images you have encountered in books or viewed on the screen. In addition to the ones mentioned earlier, you might consider the following: a circle or ring as a symbol of completion or loyalty and a crossroad as a symbol of choice or conflict. Then freewrite about one of them.

Literary Focus Explain to students that archetypes often come from experiences with nature that are common to different peoples. Tell them, for example, that in many of the world's legends mountain peaks are associated with deities. Then ask them to consider why such a natural environment was thought of as a suitable dwelling place for gods.

Writing/Prior Knowledge Have students get together in pairs to brainstorm for archetypal images before they freewrite. You might even want to provide each pair with a magazine: Students can look through the advertisements to find archetypes.

ESL Teaching Strategy ESL students may have special problems with biblical language. You may therefore want to review early Modern English verb conjugations with them. The Teaching Portfolio contains a worksheet on the Evolution of Language, page 75, that might be helpful for this purpose.

Teaching Tenth-Grade Students You might want to give tenth-grade students practice in sequencing events by having them list the order in which God creates things as related in the first chapter of Genesis.

Master Teacher Note Read portions of the selection aloud to students so that they can better appreciate the rhythms and repetitions of this magnificent prose. You might also want to ask students to read passages aloud. If possible have them work in small groups and give each group a tape recorder so that students can hear themselves reading.

Language Worksheet, *Appreciating Repetition*, p. 46
Selection Test, pp. 47–48

Genesis 1–3

The Creation and the Fall

King James Version

Presentation

Motivation/Prior Knowledge Tell students that they will be reading the biblical account of the beginning of the world. Ask them to mention some of the things they would expect such an account to explain; for example, the origin of day and night or the way in which plants and animals came to be.

Purpose-Setting Question How does the relationship between humans and God develop and change?

Universal Theme An important theme of this selection is the role of humans in the universe. Other selections that deal with this theme are the poems of Wang Wei, pages 230–231; "Man and the Universe," page 830, by Pascal; "Russia 1812," page 890, by Victor Hugo; and "The Myth of Sisyphus," page 1274, by Albert Camus.

Another selection that deals with the creation of the universe is the "Creation Hymn" from the *Rig Veda*, page 155.

1 Enrichment The word *firmament* derives from the Latin word *firmare,* which means "to strengthen." This Latin word, in turn, comes from the Indo-European root *dher,* which means "to hold, support." In contrast to the chaotic soup of the oceans, the firmament is a solid support.

CHAPTER 1

1 In the beginning God created the heaven and the earth.

2 And the earth was without form, and void; and darkness was upon the face of the deep. And the Spirit of God moved upon the face of the waters.

3 And God said, "Let there be light": and there was light.

4 And God saw the light, that it was good: and God divided the light from the darkness.

5 And God called the light Day, and the darkness he called Night. And the evening and the morning were the first day.

6 And God said, "Let there be a firmament[1] in the midst of the waters, and let it divide the waters from the waters."

7 And God made the firmament, and divided the waters which were under the firmament from the waters which were above the firmament: and it was so.

8 And God called the firmament Heaven. And the evening and the morning were the second day.

9 And God said, "Let the waters under the heaven be gathered together unto one place, and let the dry land appear": and it was so.

10 And God called the dry land Earth; and the gathering together of the waters called he Seas: and God saw that it was good.

11 And God said, "Let the earth bring forth grass, the herb yielding seed, and the fruit tree yielding fruit after his kind, whose seed is in itself, upon the earth": and it was so.

12 And the earth brought forth grass, and herb yielding seed after his kind, and the tree yielding fruit, whose seed was in itself, after his kind: and God saw that it was good.

13 And the evening and the morning were the third day.

14 And God said, "Let there be lights in the firmament of the heaven to divide the day from the night; and let them be for signs, and for seasons, and for days, and years:

15 "And let them be for lights in the firmament of the heaven to give light upon the earth": and it was so.

16 And God made two great lights; the greater light to rule the day, and the lesser light to rule the night: he made the stars also.

17 And God set them in the firmament of the heaven to give light upon the earth,

18 And to rule over the day and over the night, and to divide the light from the darkness: and God saw that it was good.

19 And the evening and the morning were the fourth day.

20 And God said, "Let the waters bring forth abundantly the moving creature that hath life, and fowl that may fly above the earth in the open firmament of heaven."

21 And God created great whales, and every living creature that moveth, which the waters brought forth abundantly, after their kind, and every winged fowl after his kind: and God saw that it was good.

22 And God blessed them, saying, "Be fruitful, and multiply, and fill the waters in the seas, and let fowl multiply in the earth."

---

1. firmament (furm′ ə mənt) *n.*: The sky, viewed poetically as a solid arch or vault.

Primary Source Note

James Weldon Johnson, the black American poet, gave a folk interpretation of the first chapters of Genesis in his poem "The Creation." The poem begins as follows:

And God stepped out on space,
And he looked around and said:
I'm lonely—
I'll make me a world.

And far as the eye of God could see
Darkness covered everything.
Blacker than a hundred midnights
Down in a cypress swamp.

Then God smiled,
And the light broke,
And the darkness rolled up on one side,
And the light stood shining on the other,
And God said: That's good!

23 And the evening and the morning were the fifth day.

24 And God said, "Let the earth bring forth the living creature after his kind, cattle, and creeping thing, and beast of the earth after his kind": and it was so.

25 And God made the beast of the earth after his kind, and cattle after their kind, and every thing that creepeth upon the earth after his kind: and God saw that it was good.

26 And God said, "Let us make man in our image, after our likeness: and let them have dominion[2] over the fish of the sea, and over the fowl of the air, and over the cattle, and over all the earth, and over every creeping thing that creepeth upon the earth."

27 So God created man in his own image, in the image of God created he him; male and female created he them.

28 And God blessed them, and God said unto them, "Be fruitful, and multiply, and replenish the earth, and subdue it: and have dominion over the fish of the sea, and over the fowl of the air, and over every living thing that moveth upon the earth."

29 And God said, "Behold, I have given you every herb bearing seed, which is upon the face of all the earth, and every tree, in the which is the fruit of a tree yielding seed; to you it shall be for meat.

30 "And to every beast of the earth, and to every fowl of the air, and to every thing that creepeth upon the earth, wherein there is life, I have given every green herb for meat": and it was so.

31 And God saw every thing that he had made, and, behold, it was very good. And the evening and the morning were the sixth day.

CHAPTER 2

1 Thus the heavens and the earth were finished, and all the host of them.

2 And on the seventh day God ended his work which he had made; and he rested on the seventh day from all his work which he had made.

3 And God blessed the seventh day, and sanctified it: because that in it he had rested from all his work which God created and made.

---

2. **dominion** (də min′ yən) *n*.: Rule or power to rule.

4 These are the generations of the heavens and of the earth when they were created, in the day that the Lord God made the earth and the heavens,

5 And every plant of the field before it was in the earth, and every herb of the field before it grew: for the Lord God had not caused it to rain upon the earth, and there was not a man to till the ground.

6 But there went up a mist from the earth, and watered the whole face of the ground.

7 And the Lord God formed man of the dust of the ground,[3] and breathed into his nostrils the breath of life; and man became a living soul.

8 And the Lord God planted a garden eastward in Eden; and there he put the man whom he had formed.

9 And out of the ground made the Lord God to grow every tree that is pleasant to the sight, and good for food; the tree of life also in the midst of the garden, and the tree of knowledge of good and evil.

10 And a river went out of Eden to water the garden; and from thence it was parted, and became into four heads.

11 The name of the first is Pison: that is it which compasseth the whole land of Havilah, where there is gold;

12 And the gold of that land is good: there is bdellium[4] and onyx stone.

13 And the name of the second river is Gihon: the same is it that compasseth the whole land of Ethiopia.

14 And the name of the third river is Hiddekel: that is it which goeth toward the east of Assyria. And the fourth river is Euphrates.[5]

15 And the Lord God took the man, and put him into the garden of Eden to dress it and to keep it.

16 And the Lord God commanded the man, saying, "Of every tree of the garden thou mayest freely eat:

---

3. **And the Lord God . . . ground:** The name Adam is said to come from the Hebrew word *'adhāmāh*, meaning "earth."
4. **bdellium** (del′ ē əm): A deep-red gem.
5. **Assyria . . . Euphrates** (yoo frāt′ ēz): Assyria was an ancient empire in southwestern Asia; the Euphrates River flows from East Central Turkey generally southward through Syria and Iraq.

2 Discussion Call students' attention to the repeated phrase "and God saw that it was good." Ask them to note when this phrase usually appears. Then have them explain the effects of this repetition.

3 Discussion Ask students to speculate about the meaning of the words "God created man in his own image." Does image, for example, refer to physical resemblance, like a mirror image?

Then have students compare and contrast the blessing God bestows on man and woman with the one he gives to other creatures (1:22).

4 Discussion Have students contrast this description of creation with the one in 1:27. Which creation scene, for instance, is more vivid? Why?

5 Enrichment Explain that the name *Eden* comes from a Hebrew word meaning "delight." The word *paradise,* a synonym for Eden, comes from Latin and Greek words meaning "park or garden" and from a Persian word, *pardez,* meaning "enclosure or walled place." Ask students why so many peoples thought the best place in the world would be an enclosed garden or park.

Then God reached out and took the light in his hands,
And God rolled the light around in his hands
Until he made the sun;
And he set that sun a-blazing in the heavens.
And the light that was left from making the sun
God gathered it up in a shining ball
And flung it against the darkness,
Spangling the night with the moon and stars.
Then down between
The darkness and the light

He hurled the world;
And God said: That's good! . . ."

17 "But of the tree of knowledge of good and evil, thou shalt not eat of it: for in the day that thou eatest thereof thou shalt surely die."

18 And the Lord God said, "It is not good that the man should be alone; I will make him an help meet for him."

19 And out of the ground the Lord God formed every beast of the field, and every fowl of the air; and brought them unto Adam to see what he would call them: and whatsoever Adam called every living creature, that was the name thereof.

20 And Adam gave names to all cattle, and to the fowl of the air, and to every beast of the field; but for Adam there was not found an help meet for him.

21 And the Lord God caused a deep sleep to fall upon Adam, and he slept: and he took one of his ribs, and closed up the flesh instead thereof;

22 And the rib, which the Lord God had taken from man, made he a woman, and brought her unto the man.

23 And Adam said, "This is now bone of my bones, and flesh of my flesh: she shall be called Woman, because she was taken out of Man."

24 Therefore shall a man leave his father and his mother, and shall cleave unto his wife: and they shall be one flesh.

25 And they were both naked, the man and his wife, and were not ashamed.

CHAPTER 3

1 Now the serpent was more subtil than any beast of the field which the Lord God had made. And he said unto the woman, "Yea, hath God said,'Ye shall not eat of every tree of the garden'?"

2 And the woman said unto the serpent, "We may eat of the fruit of the trees of the garden:

3 "But of the fruit of the tree which is in the midst of the garden, God hath said, 'Ye shall not eat of it, neither shall ye touch it, lest ye die.'"

4 And the serpent said unto the woman, "Ye shall not surely die:

5 "For God doth know that in the day ye eat thereof, then your eyes shall be opened and ye shall be as gods, knowing good and evil."

6 And when the woman saw that the tree was good for food, and that it was pleasant to the eyes, and a tree to be desired to make one wise, she took of the fruit thereof, and did eat, and gave also unto her husband with her; and he did eat.

7 And the eyes of them both were opened, and they knew that they were naked; and they sewed fig leaves together, and made themselves aprons.

8 And they heard the voice of the Lord God walking in the garden in the cool of the day: and Adam and his wife hid themselves from the presence of the Lord God amongst the trees of the garden.

9 And the Lord God called unto Adam, and said unto him, "Where art thou?"

10 And he said, "I heard thy voice in the garden, and I was afraid, because I was naked; and I hid myself."

11 And he said, "Who told thee that thou wast naked? Hast thou eaten of the tree, whereof I commanded thee that thou shouldest not eat?

12 And the man said, "The woman whom thou gavest to be with me, she gave me of the tree, and I did eat."

13 And the Lord God said unto the woman, "What is this that thou hast done?" And the woman said, "The serpent beguiled[6] me, and I did eat."

14 And the Lord God said unto the serpent, "Because thou has done this, thou art cursed above all cattle and above every beast of the field; upon thy belly shalt thou go, and dust shalt thou eat all the days of thy life:

15 "And I will put enmity between thee and the woman, and between thy seed[7] and her seed; it shall bruise thy head, and thou shalt bruise his heel."

16 Unto the woman he said, "I will greatly multiply thy sorrow and thy conception; in sorrow thou shalt bring forth children; and thy desire shall be to thy husband, and he shall rule over thee."

17 And unto Adam he said, "Because thou hast hearkened unto the voice of thy wife, and hast

---

6. **beguiled** (bē gīld') *v.:* Tricked, deceived.
7. **seed:** Descendants.

(continued from bottom of page)

upon its back, I've breasts and
  splat!
On my face the paint's congealing.

The Creation of Adam is perhaps the most famous panel of the
Sistine Chapel ceiling. It shows a
dynamic creator, cloaked in a bil-
lowing cape and surrounded by
angels. Both God and Adam have
the muscular definition of sculpted
forms. While God floats in the air,
Adam is rooted in the earth. Symbolizing creation is the spark of life
that passes from God's forefinger
to Adam's. All the divine energy
seems to be focused on that tenuous, narrow bridge between
Adam and God.

You might want to use the following questions to discuss the
art:

1. Why is God's finger touching
   Adam's?
2. How would you describe the
   look on Adam's face?
3. (a) What mood does the painting convey? (b) Is this mood appropriate to the subject?
4. Compare and contrast this
   painting with the creation scene
   described in the Bible.
5. How would you describe this
   painting to a friend who has
   never seen it?

THE CREATION OF ADAM
Michelangelo
Sistine Chapel ceiling, Rome

Humanities Note

Fine art, *The Creation of Adam* by
Michelangelo. Like his older contemporary Leonardo da Vinci,
Michelangelo Buonarotti (1475–
1564) was truly a Renaissance man.
In addition to being a painter,
Michelangelo was a sculptor, architect, engineer, and poet. His *David*,
a larger-than-life sculpture of the
young biblical hero, embodies the
ideals of the Italian Renaissance:
strength, courage, intelligence, and
nobility. Michelangelo also used biblical themes in his most famous
painting, the ceiling and wall of the
Sistine Chapel in Rome. In addition
to *The Creation of Adam*, the Sistine
ceiling shows *The Flood* (see page
48) and many other scenes and figures from the Bible. As a poet,
Michelangelo wrote humorously and
eloquently about the exhausting labor involved in painting the Sistine
Chapel. For much of the time, he
was awkwardly positioned on a
scaffold:

My beard points skyward, I seem a
  bat

12 **Discussion** Ask students to mention some bitter facts about life that this account explains. Also have them consider why an explanation of a difficulty can help reconcile people to it.

13 **Discussion** Ask students to whom God is referring when he says, "one of us." Also have them explain the difference between the tree of the knowledge of good and evil and the tree of life.

14 **Discussion** Have students explain the emotional power of the final image: the way to paradise barred by a "flaming sword."

15 **Enrichment** The stories that Isaac Bashevis Singer read in Genesis inspired him to become a writer: "I wanted to write stories like the ones I read in the Book of Genesis, every one of them more interesting than any of the secular novels which my brother smuggled into the house. I would say that although I became disappointed in many beliefs, whether religious or scientific, I was never disenchanted in the wondrous art of these stories."

Cultural Note In *Paradise Lost* Milton deals with the theme of the fall of humankind. You might want to ask students to compare and contrast portions of that epic with Genesis 1–3.

Cooperative Learning Have small groups of students research appropriate music to accompany the first chapter of Genesis. Then allow each group to bring in the record it has chosen, play it for the class, and explain the choice.

Closure and Extension

ANSWERS TO THINKING ABOUT THE SELECTION

eaten of the tree, of which I commanded thee, saying 'Thou shalt not eat of it': cursed is the ground for thy sake; in sorrow shalt thou eat of it all the days of thy life;

18 "Thorns also and thistles shall it bring forth to thee; and thou shalt eat the herb of the field;

19 "In the sweat of thy face shalt thou eat bread, till thou return unto the ground; for out of it wast thou taken: for dust thou art, and unto dust shalt thou return."

20 And Adam called his wife's name Eve; because she was the mother of all living.[8]

_____
8. **Mother . . . living:** *Hawwāh,* the Hebrew word translated as Eve, is derived from another Hebrew word meaning "alive" or "a living thing."

21 Unto Adam also and to his wife did the Lord God make coats of skins, and clothed them.

22 And the Lord God said, "Behold, the man is become as one of us, to know good and evil: and now, lest he put forth his hand, and take also of the tree of life, and eat, and live for ever":

23 Therefore the Lord God sent him forth from the garden of Eden, to till the ground from whence he was taken.

24 So he drove out the man; and he placed at the east of the garden of Eden Cherubims,[9] and a flaming sword which turned every way, to keep the way of the tree of life.

_____
9. **Cherubims** (cher' ə bimz): Winged heavenly beings that support the throne of God or act as guardian spirits.

Reader's Response *The purpose of much religious writing is to be awe inspiring. In what ways did you find this account of the creation and the fall awe inspiring?*

PRIMARY SOURCE

The Nobel Prize-winning novelist Isaac Bashevis Singer described his first encounters with Genesis as follows:

"For me, a son and grandson of rabbis, learning the first book of the Pentateuch [the first five books of the Bible] was the greatest event of my life. I often heard my father recite passages of this book in his sermons to his congregation. I knew already that God had created the world in six days and on the seventh day He rested. It may sound strange, but I began to ponder Creation when I was still a little boy—the problems which in my later years I found in philosophical works such as the *Guide for the Perplexed* by Maimonides, in the *Kuzari* of Rabbi Yehuda Halevi, and still later in the works of Plato, Aristotle, and Kant: What is time? What is space? What is eternity? infinity? How can something be created from nothing? God has created the world, but who created God?"

THINKING ABOUT THE SELECTION

Interpreting

1. What meanings are associated with light and darkness in the first chapter of Genesis?
2. (a) What attitude toward nature does Genesis convey? (b) Explain how specific passages contribute to this attitude.
3. Naming is an important theme in Genesis. (a) Find five separate passages in which God names things. (b) How does the act of naming seem to be related to the act of creation itself? (c) What does Adam's ability to name the animals reveal about him?
4. What are the implications of the relationship established between humans and the rest of creation?
5. Why do you think God links "the knowledge of good and evil" with death?

1. Darkness is associated with formlessness and confusion, light with form and all that is "good."
2. (a) Nature is abundant, full of variety, and good. (b) A passage that conveys this attitude is 1:21.
3. (a) "God called the light Day" (1:5); "the darkness he called Night" (1:5); "God called the firmament Heaven" (1:8); "God called the dry land Earth" (1:10); "the gathering together of the waters called he Seas" (1:10). (b) The act of naming seems to be part of the act of creation. (c) His ability to name things reveals a godlike capacity.
4. Humans are given "dominion" over the rest of creation. This fact suggests that humans are somehow above nature.
5. Answers will differ. Perceptive students may point out that animals, who have no knowledge of good and evil, are not aware of their own death as humans are.
6. Answers will differ. Many students will realize that by tempting Eve with divinity, the snake reveals a knowledge of the human desire to be more than human.
7. (a) They made clothing for themselves and they hid from God. (b) These changes reveal that they feel shame and guilt; they are no longer innocent.
8. Answers will differ, but students may realize that the ancient Hebrews valued speech and words highly.
9. Answers will differ, but students should show how their questions arise from the text.

6. Psychology is the study of the mind, of mental and emotional processes, and of human behavior. The serpent in Genesis has been called "the first psychologist." Comment on this observation.

7. (a) Name two ways in which the behavior of Adam and Eve changes after they have eaten the forbidden fruit. (b) What do these changes reveal about their state of mind?

Applying

8. In Genesis God creates the world through speech: "Let there be light," "Let there be a firmament," and so forth. What does God's preference for speech reveal about the ancient Hebrews?

9. This story of creation answers many questions— Why do men work? Why do women experience pain in childbirth?—but it also raises questions. What questions does it inspire you to ask?

ANALYZING LITERATURE

Understanding Archetypes

An **archetype** is an image, symbol, or pattern that appears in the art, literature, or legends of many different peoples. Some archetypes in this portion of Genesis are the ocean from which the world emerges, the trees of knowledge and life, and the evil snake.

1. In Genesis 1:2 an ocean or a large body of water is associated with the world in its unformed state. Why do you think this is so?

2. Many cultures regarded the archetypal world-tree as a link between the human and divine realms. What evidence is there that the trees in Genesis are world-trees?

3. Snakes are archetypal creatures because they inspire such fear and fascination: They can be deadly and hypnotic, and they seem to have a secret knowledge of the earth. How does the reptile in Genesis manifest some or all of these qualities?

4. Compare and contrast the serpent in Gilgamesh (page 27) with that in Genesis.

CRITICAL THINKING AND READING

Tracing Two Stories of Creation

In Genesis there are actually two versions of the creation of the world. The first chapter presents one version, and then the second chapter tells the story again in a somewhat different way.

1. (a) List the order in which living things are created in each version. (b) What are the main differences between these two sequences?

2. In which of these versions do God and man seem to have a closer relationship? Explain.

3. (a) How does the second version fill out the story of the creation of woman? (b) What do the additional details suggest concerning the relationship between man and woman?

UNDERSTANDING LANGUAGE

Appreciating Repetition

The prose of Genesis falls into elaborate patterns, with a great deal of repetition. In Chapter 1, for instance, many verses begin with phrases like "And God said," "And God called," or "And God made." The repeated phrases are like repeated notes or themes in a piece of music. One function of these repetitions is to emphasize the stately progress of creation and the key role that God plays in this process.

1. (a) Small children often like to hear things repeated, even if they know them already. How is repetition related to feelings of comfort and order? (b) Why might repetition be especially important in a description of a world emerging from chaos?

2. Repetition is effective in stressing ideas. (a) What idea, for instance, is stressed in Chapter 1, verses 26 and 27? (b) Why do you think it is stressed?

THINKING AND WRITING

Writing from Different Perspectives

Many writers such as Mark Twain, Arthur Miller, and Thornton Wilder have taken the story of Adam and Eve and told it from a less reverential perspective. The expulsion of Adam and Eve from the Garden of Eden marked the beginning of history and the introduction of evil into the world. It was a momentous event. Think about the several participants in this episode —God, Adam, Eve, and the snake—and how their outlooks could differ. The snake, for instance, could be pretty glib and probably had an excuse for his actions. Write a letter from the point of view of each participant. These letters should contain reflections on the events themselves and explanations of the writer's motives. In revising these letters, make sure that each one reflects its writer's unique perspective.

indicate that man and woman are created together in the first sequence and that they are created after the other creatures. In the second version, man is created before the animals and woman is created after everything else.

2. The relationship is closer in the second sequence.

3. (a) The second story shows God perceiving Adam's loneliness and creating a woman as "an help meet for him." It also indicates that woman was formed from man's rib. (b) The story suggests the closeness between man and woman—they literally come from the same flesh.

ANSWERS TO UNDERSTANDING LANGUAGE

1. (a) Answers will differ. Students may point out that repetition is reassuring; it conveys the feeling that the world is stable and predictable. (b) Answers will differ. Students may indicate that repetition, because it is linked with order, shows that the world is not in danger of falling back into chaos.

2. (a) The idea that God made man and woman in his own image is stressed. (b) Answers will differ. Students may respond that the repetition emphasizes the unique place of humankind in creation.

THINKING AND WRITING

Writing Across the Curriculum

You may want to inform the art department that students are reading this selection. An art teacher can help students find works of art inspired by Genesis 1–3. One example is *The Creation of Adam* by Michelangelo, on page 43. Students can then write about the relationship between the art and the biblical account of creation.

ANSWERS TO ANALYZING LITERATURE

1. An ocean is formless.

2. Answers will differ. Students may point out that eating from the tree of life would give humans godlike powers. The tree is therefore a means of ascending to the heavens.

3. Answers will differ. Students may point out that the snake has an almost hypnotic power over Eve.

4. Answers will differ. Students may indicate, however, that both serpents are crafty and both deprive humans of immortality. The serpent in Genesis is a more developed character in the story.

ANSWERS TO CRITICAL THINKING AND READING

1. (a) In Chapter 1, the order is as follows—light, day, night, heaven, earth, seas, plants, seasons, moon, sun, and stars, fish and fowl, earthly creatures, man and woman; in Chapter 2—earth, heavens, plants, man, Eden, beasts, fish and birds, woman. (b) Answers will differ. Students may

Commentary

Writing

The Story of the Flood

Theme. The **theme** of a work of literature is its central idea, concern, or insight into life. Appearing throughout the Hebrew Bible is the theme of the covenant, or solemn agreement, between God and humankind. The Biblical God is not a remote deity, uninterested in human fate. On the contrary, he displays a great concern about earthly doings. He wants human beings to be just in their behavior toward each other and faithful to him as the unique lord of creation. In return—and this mutual loyalty is the essence of the covenant—he agrees to protect those who keep the faith.

In Exodus, the second book of the Bible, God makes a covenant with the Hebrew people. After rescuing them from Egypt, where they had been enslaved for many generations, he gives them the Ten Commandments on Mount Sinai. This code of laws, with its injunctions against murder, robbery, and adultery, is one of the bases of our modern-day legal system. It is also the foundation of the covenant between God and the people of Israel. If they observe these commandments—and one of them forbids the worship of other gods—he will watch over their destiny and ensure their success.

Typically, God interacts with the Hebrew people through a mediator. It is Moses who climbs to the top of Mount Sinai and, in a dramatic and awesome confrontation with God, receives the Ten Commandments for his people. Much later, when the Hebrews have violated the covenant, God chooses other mediators, the prophets, to express his displeasure.

Covenant sounds like a cold and remote word; however, in the Bible it refers to a divine-human relationship that is warm and intense. It is almost like a marriage bond, and when it is threatened, the anger and resentment are powerful.

In Genesis 6–9 the theme of covenant is first sounded. This time the person chosen by God is Noah; however, the issue is not the fate of the Hebrew people in particular but the viability of creation itself.

What problems threaten life on our planet today? Have we today broken our covenant with the planet? Freewrite about environmental issues—damage to the ozone layer of the atmosphere, pollution, destruction of rain forests—that affect every inhabitant of the earth.

Genesis 6–9

The Story of the Flood

King James Version

CHAPTER 6

1 And it came to pass, when men began to multiply on the face of the earth, and daughters were born unto them,

2 That the sons of God saw the daughters of men that they were fair; and they took them wives of all which they chose.

3 And the Lord said, "My spirit shall not always strive with man, for that he also is flesh: yet his days shall be an hundred and twenty years."

4 There were giants in the earth in those days; and also after that, when the sons of God came in unto the daughters of men, and they bare children to them, the same became mighty men which were of old, men of renown.

5 And God saw that the wickedness of man was great in the earth, and that every imagination of the thoughts of his heart was only evil continually.

6 And it repented the Lord that he had made man on the earth, and it grieved him at his heart.

7 And the Lord said, "I will destroy man whom I have created from the face of the earth; both man, and beast, and the creeping thing, and the fowls of the air; for it repenteth me that I have made them."

1 8 But Noah found grace in the eyes of the Lord.

9 These are the generations of Noah: Noah was a just man and perfect in his generations, and Noah walked with God.

2 10 And Noah begat three sons, Shem, Ham, and Japheth.

11 The earth also was corrupt before God, and the earth was filled with violence.

12 And God looked upon the earth, and, behold, it was corrupt; for all flesh had corrupted his way upon the earth.

13 And God said unto Noah, "The end of all flesh is come before me; for the earth is filled with violence through them; and, behold, I will destroy them with the earth.

14 "Make thee an ark of gopher wood; rooms shalt thou make in the ark, and shalt pitch it within and without with pitch.

15 "And this is the fashion which thou shalt make it of: The length of the ark shall be three hundred cubits,[1] the breadth of it fifty cubits, and the height of it thirty cubits.

16 "A window shalt thou make to the ark, and in a cubit shalt thou finish it above; and the door of the ark shalt thou set in the side thereof; with lower, second, and third stories shalt thou make it.

17 "And behold, I, even I, do bring a flood of waters upon the earth, to destroy all flesh, wherein is the breath of life, from under heaven; and every thing that is in the earth shall die.

18 "But with thee will I establish my covenant;[2] and thou shalt come into the ark, thou, and thy sons, and thy wife, and thy sons' wives with thee. **3**

19 "And of every living thing of all flesh, two of every sort shalt thou bring into the ark, to keep them alive with thee; they shall be male and female.

20 "Of fowls after their kind, and of cattle after their kind, of every creeping thing of the earth

---

1. **cubits:** Ancient units of linear measure, about 18–22 inches each.

2. **covenant** (kuv′ ə nənt) *n.:* A binding and solemn agreement.

derstanding the Theme of the Covenant, p. 56
Critical Thinking and Reading Worksheet, Comparing and Contrasting Flood Stories, p. 57
Language Worksheet, Understanding the King James Version of the Bible, p. 58
Selection Test, pp. 59–60

Art Transparency 1
Passage Through the Red Sea, by Raphael and assistants

Master Teacher Note Place Art Transparency 1, *Passage Through the Red Sea* by Raphael, on the overhead projector. Tell students the story of the Jews' exodus from Egypt. Explain that this painting depicts Moses and the Jews passing safely through the Red Sea as the waters engulf Pharaoh's army. Have them identify Moses, the Hebrews, and Pharaoh's soldiers. Also have them find the pillar of fire and cloud of smoke that show the divine presence. Ask them whether or not this painting is suitable to illustrate the flood that occurred in Noah's time.

Presentation

Motivation/Prior Knowledge
Many students will know the biblical flood story. Elicit some details of the story, such as the length of the flood, the animal and human passengers of the ark, the way in which Noah discovered that the waters had subsided, and the reassuring sign that God gave Noah after the disaster. Have students speculate about why these details are so memorable.

Purpose-Setting Question How does this story show an evolution in the relationship between God and humankind?

Thematic Idea There is a flood story remarkably similar to this one in *The Epic of Gilgamesh,* page 23.

Teaching Tenth-Grade Students Tenth-grade students may be especially intrigued by the size and dimensions of the ark. Have them figure this out and compare these measurements to those of modern ships.

Master Teacher Note Use the overhead projector to show students Art Transparency 1.

1 Enrichment The name *Noah* means "rest or comfort." Ask students to determine why this meaning is appropriate to the biblical hero Noah.

2 Discussion The sons of Noah were regarded as founders of the various peoples inhabiting the earth. Ham was the legendary father of the Canaanites and the Egyptians, Shem of the Israelites, and Japheth of the Sumerians, the Hittites, the Scythians, and many other groups.

3 Literary Focus Point out to students that this is the first mention of the theme of the covenant. Ask them what they can deduce about this agreement from the context.

4 **Clarification** The Hebrews divided beasts into those that were unclean, meaning unfit to eat, and those that were clean. These dietary laws are spelled out in detail in Leviticus, the third book of the Old Testament.

Humanities Note

Fine art, *The Flood*, by Michelangelo. The Italian Renaissance artist Michelangelo Buonarotti (1475–1565) considered himself to be primarily a sculptor. He was therefore somewhat daunted at first by the task of painting the entire ceiling of the Sistine Chapel in Rome. This fresco (a fresco is a painting done on wet plaster) on the ceiling presented particular problems. At first the plaster dried improperly, and the entire painting had to be scraped off and redone.

Despite his problems with *The Flood*, Michelangelo went on to make it a masterpiece. The composition of the picture is such that the eye cannot rest in any particular place but roves from victim to victim. Each of these sufferers is portrayed with great sensitivity.

You might want to use the following questions to discuss the art:

1. (a) On whom does Michelangelo choose to focus, Noah or the victims of the flood? (b) Do you think his choice is justified? Why or why not?
2. Pick out three flood victims and explain how Michelangelo has dramatized their plight.
3. Tell how you would illustrate the story of Noah.

after his kind, two of every sort shall come unto thee, to keep them alive.

21 "And take thou unto thee of all food that is eaten, and thou shalt gather it to thee; and it shall be for food for thee, and for them."

22 Thus did Noah; according to all that God commanded him, so did he.

CHAPTER 7

1 And the Lord said unto Noah, "Come thou and all thy house into the ark; for thee have I seen righteous before me in this generation.

2 "Of every clean beast thou shalt take to thee by sevens, the male and his female: and of beasts that are not clean by two, the male and his female.

3 "Of fowls also of the air by sevens, the male and the female; to keep seed alive upon the face of all the earth.

4 "For yet seven days, and I will cause it to rain upon the earth forty days and forty nights; and every living substance that I have made will I destroy from off the face of the earth."

5 And Noah did according unto all that the Lord commanded him.

6 And Noah was six hundred years old when the flood of waters was upon the earth.

7 And Noah went in, and his sons, and his wife, and his sons' wives with him, into the ark, because of the waters of the flood.

8 Of clean beasts, and of beasts that are not clean, and of fowls, and of every thing that creepeth upon the earth,

9 There went in two and two unto Noah into the ark, the male and the female, as God had commanded Noah.

10 And it came to pass after seven days, that the waters of the flood were upon the earth.

11 In the six hundredth year of Noah's life, in the second month, the seventeenth day of the month, the same day were all the fountains of the great deep broken up, and the windows of heaven were opened.

12 And the rain was upon the earth forty days and forty nights.

13 In the selfsame day entered Noah, and Shem, and Ham, and Japheth, the sons of Noah, and Noah's wife, and the three wives of his sons with them, into the ark;

14 They, and every beast after his kind, and all the cattle after their kind, and every creeping thing that creepeth upon the earth after his kind, and every fowl after his kind, every bird of every sort.

15 And they went in unto Noah into the ark, two and two of all flesh, wherein is the breath of life.

THE FLOOD
Michelangelo
Sistine Chapel ceiling, Rome

Grammar in Action

Agreement of Pronouns and Antecedents Pronouns must agree with their antecedents in person, number, and gender. When such agreement is lacking, readers may be confused as to the writer's meaning.

LACK OF AGREEMENT: The Noah story has been popular, and *they are* found in many medieval manuscripts.

AGREEMENT: The Noah story has been popular, and *it is* found in many medieval manuscripts.

The translators who worked on the King James Version of the Bible were careful to maintain correct pronoun agreement:

And of every living thing of all flesh, *two* [antecedent] of every sort shalt thou bring into the ark, to keep *them* [pronoun] alive with thee; *they* [pronoun] shall be male and female.

In the selfsame day entered *Noah,* and *Shem,* and *Ham,* and *Japheth,* the sons of Noah, and *Noah's wife* [antecedents], and the three wives of his sons with *them* [pronoun], into the ark.

16 And they that went in, went in male and female of all flesh, as God had commanded him: and the Lord shut him in.

17 And the flood was forty days upon the earth; and the waters increased, and bare up the ark, and it was lift up above the earth.

18 And the waters prevailed, and were increased greatly upon the earth; and the ark went upon the face of the waters.

19 And the waters prevailed exceedingly upon the earth; and all the high hills, that were under the whole heaven, were covered.

20 Fifteen cubits upward did the waters prevail; and the mountains were covered.

21 And all flesh died that moved upon the earth, both of fowl, and of cattle, and of beast, and of every creeping thing that creepeth upon the earth, and every man:

22 All in whose nostrils was the breath of life, of all that was in the dry land, died.

23 And every living substance was destroyed which was upon the face of the ground, both man, and cattle, and the creeping things, and the fowl of the heaven; and they were destroyed from the earth: and Noah only remained alive, and they that were with him in the ark.

24 And the waters prevailed upon the earth an hundred and fifty days.

CHAPTER 8

1 And God remembered Noah, and every living thing, and all the cattle that was with him in the ark: and God made a wind to pass over the earth, and the waters asswaged;[3]

2 The fountains also of the deep and the windows of heaven were stopped, and the rain from heaven was restrained;

3 And the waters returned from off the earth continually: and after the end of the hundred and fifty days the waters were abated.

4 And the ark rested in the seventh month, on the seventeenth day of the month, upon the mountains of Ararat.

5 And the waters decreased continually until the tenth month: in the tenth month, on the first

day of the month, were the tops of the mountains seen.

6 And it came to pass at the end of forty days, that Noah opened the window of the ark which he had made:

7 And he sent forth a raven, which went forth to and fro, until the waters were dried up from off the earth.

8 Also he sent forth a dove from him, to see if the waters were abated from off the face of the ground;

9 But the dove found no rest for the sole of her foot, and she returned unto him into the ark, for the waters were on the face of the whole earth: then he put forth his hand, and took her, and pulled her in unto him into the ark.

10 And he stayed yet other seven days; and again he sent forth the dove out of the ark;

11 And the dove came in to him in the evening; and, lo, in her mouth was an olive leaf pluckt off: So Noah knew that the waters were abated from off the earth.

12 And he stayed yet other seven days; and sent forth the dove; which returned not again unto him any more.

13 And It came to pass in the six hundredth and first year, in the first month, the first day of the month, the waters were dried up from off the earth: and Noah removed the covering of the ark, and looked, and, behold, the face of the ground was dry.

14 And in the second month, on the seven and twentieth day of the month, was the earth dried.

15 And God spake unto Noah, saying,

16 "Go forth of the ark, thou, and thy wife, and thy sons, and thy sons' wives with thee.

17 "Bring forth with thee every living thing that is with thee, of all flesh, both of fowl, and of cattle, and of every creeping thing that creepeth upon the earth; that they may breed abundantly in the earth, and be fruitful, and multiply upon the earth."

18 And Noah went forth, and his sons, and his wife, and his sons' wives with him:

19 Every beast, every creeping thing, and every fowl, and whatsoever creepeth upon the earth, after their kinds, went forth out of the ark.

---

3. **asswaged:** Calmed; this is an archaic use of the word *assuaged* as an intransitive verb.

---

5 **Discussion** Have students identify the repetitions in this passage. Then have them explain how the repetitions contribute to the narrative.

6 **Enrichment** Mount Ararat is a mountain in eastern Turkey, near the Armenian and Iranian borders. It is about 17,000 feet high.

7 **Enrichment** The dove appears in many of the world's legends and folk tales and is often closely associated with the divine realm. A dove with an olive branch is a well-known symbol of peace.

8 **Discussion** Have students point out the similarities between this language and the language used in Genesis 1:22. Ask them to explain why God repeats these words.

God's instructions to Noah and the enumeration of the ark's passengers would be especially confusing if the translators did not have pronouns agree with their antecedents.

Student Activity 1. Find three additional examples of correct pronoun agreement in Genesis 6–9.

Student Activity 2. Write a comic account of the flood story. As one of your humorous devices, make sure pronouns and antecedents fail to agree at critical points of the narrative so that a reader will be thoroughly confused. Before revising your account, exchange papers with a classmate and get pointers on how to make your description even funnier.

9 Discussion Ask students how this passage reflects themes that were sounded earlier in Genesis. Also have them identify new elements that did not appear earlier.

10 Discussion Ask students why the rainbow is an especially appropriate symbol of the covenant that God makes with Noah and his sons.

11 Clarification Point out to students that this episode provides a justification for the Hebrew conquest of Canaan and the domination of the Canaanites.

Cooperative Learning Divide the class into small groups and have each group research the Noah story in a folklore reference book (for example, Funk & Wagnalls *Standard Dictionary of Folklore, Mythology, and Legend*, edited by Maria Leach and Jerome Fried). Ask each group to bring in one vivid story or detail that was added to the biblical tale of Noah.

Enrichment The biblical account of Noah is very spare, but it has inspired many folk tales and legends that contain specific, and often entertaining, details. According to one tale, the ass was slow in boarding the ark and Noah shouted in exasperation, "Hurry, even though Satan be with thee." Hearing this curse, the devil interpreted it as an invitation to enter the ark with the ass. This detail, of course, explains why there was still evil in the world after the flood subsided.

20 And Noah builded an altar unto the Lord; and took of every clean beast, and of every clean fowl, and offered burnt offerings on the altar.

21 And the Lord smelled a sweet savor; and the Lord said in his heart, "I will not again curse the ground any more for man's sake; for the imagination of man's heart is evil from his youth; neither will I again smite any more every thing living, as I have done.

22 "While the earth remaineth, seedtime and harvest, and cold and heat, and summer and winter, and day and night shall not cease."

CHAPTER 9

1 And God blessed Noah and his sons, and said unto them, "Be fruitful, and multiply, and replenish the earth.

2 "And the fear of you and the dread of you shall be upon every beast of the earth, and upon every fowl of the air, upon all that moveth upon the earth, and upon all the fishes of the sea; into your hand are they delivered.

3 "Every moving thing that liveth shall be meat for you; even as the green herb have I given you all things.

4 "But flesh with the life thereof, which is the blood thereof, shall ye not eat.

5 "And surely your blood of your lives will I require; at the hand of every beast will I require it, and at the hand of man; at the hand of every man's brother will I require the life of man.

6 "Whoso sheddeth man's blood, by man shall his blood be shed: for in the image of God made he man.

7 "And you, be ye fruitful, and multiply; bring forth abundantly in the earth, and multiply therein."

8 And God spake unto Noah, and to his sons with him, saying,

9 "And I, behold, I establish my covenant with you, and with your seed after you;

10 "And with every living creature that is with you, of the fowl, of the cattle, and of every beast of the earth with you; for all that go out of the ark, to every beast of the earth.

11 "And I will establish my covenant with you; neither shall all flesh be cut off any more by the waters of a flood; neither shall there any more be a flood to destroy the earth."

12 And God said, "This is the token of the covenant which I make between me and you and every living creature that is with you, for perpetual generations:

13 "I do set my bow in the cloud, and it shall be for a token of a covenant between me and the earth.

14 "And it shall come to pass, when I bring a cloud over the earth, that the bow shall be seen in the cloud:

15 "And I will remember my covenant, which is between me and you and every living creature of all flesh; and the waters shall no more become a flood to destroy all flesh.

16 "And the bow shall be in the cloud; and I will look upon it, that I may remember the everlasting covenant between God and every living creature of all flesh that is upon the earth."

17 And God said unto Noah, "This is the token of the covenant, which I have established between me and all flesh that is upon the earth."

18 And the sons of Noah, that went forth of the ark, were Shem, and Ham, and Japheth: and Ham is the father of Canaan.

19 These are the three sons of Noah: and of them was the whole earth overspread.

20 And Noah began to be an husbandman,[4] and he planted a vineyard.

21 And he drank of the wine, and was drunken; and he was uncovered within his tent.

22 And Ham, the father of Canaan, saw the nakedness of his father, and told his two brethren without.

23 And Shem and Japheth took a garment, and laid it upon both their shoulders, and went backward, and covered the nakedness of their father; and their faces were backward, and they saw not their father's nakedness.

24 And Noah awoke from his wine, and knew what his younger son had done unto him.

25 And he said, "Cursed be Canaan; a servant of servants shall he be unto his brethren.

---

4. **husbandman:** An archaic word for farmer.

Closure and Extension

ANSWERS TO THINKING ABOUT THE SELECTION

1. (a) Noah was a righteous and just man. (b) It suggests that he tempers justice with mercy.
2. Answers will differ, but some students may respond as follows. In both accounts evil involves disobedience of God. In Genesis 1–3, however, evil results in the loss of the Garden of Eden, while in Genesis 6–9 it almost results in the loss of the earth itself.
3. Answers will differ. Some students may indicate the image of the dove returning with an olive leaf. This image is particularly vivid because the small detail of the leaf has an immense meaning. Another vivid detail is the rainbow that symbolizes the covenant between God and humankind.
4. Answers will differ. The emotions that students describe should be in keeping with the details of the story.

Challenge The story of Noah and his ark has inspired many folk tales and legends (see Enrichment, at left). Have students use

26 And he said, "Blessed be the Lord God of Shem; and Canaan shall be his servant.

27 "God shall enlarge Japheth, and he shall dwell in the tents of Shem; and Canaan shall be his servant."

28 And Noah lived after the flood three hundred and fifty years.

29 And all the days of Noah were nine hundred and fifty years: and he died.

Reader's Response *Why do you think the story of Noah has such a universal and timeless appeal?*

THINKING ABOUT THE SELECTION

Interpreting

1. (a) What is the meaning of the statement, "Noah walked with God"? (b) What does God's willingness to spare the earth because of Noah suggest?
2. Both Genesis 1–3 and Genesis 6–9 deal with the theme of evil. What is similar and different about their treatment of this theme?
3. Find two details and explain why you think they are especially vivid.

Applying

4. In Biblical narrative the emotions of the characters are often not spelled out. Choose a human character from this story—Noah, his wife, or one of his sons—and indicate the emotions that he or she might have felt at critical points in the story.

ANALYZING LITERATURE

Understanding the Theme of the Covenant

The flood story marks the first Biblical reference to the **theme** of the covenant, a solemn agreement that God makes with humankind. After the waters withdraw, God promises that he will never again send a flood to "destroy all flesh." The sign of this agreement is the rainbow.

1. (a) How does the flood reduce the earth to its appearance in the early stages of creation? (b) How might this fact make humans especially eager to have a covenant?
2. (a) What does God require of Noah and his sons before he makes the covenant? (b) What is the reason for these demands?
3. (a) How does God's giving of all creatures into human hands look back to Genesis 1:26? (b) How do God's commands to Noah look forward to the Ten Commandments?

CRITICAL THINKING AND READING

Comparing and Contrasting Flood Stories

When *The Epic of Gilgamesh* was discovered in the nineteenth century, scholars were amazed that it contained a flood story much like the story of Noah in Genesis.(See *The Epic of Gilgamesh*, pages 23–26.) In each version a chosen man, his family, and various animals survive the flood in an ark, after receiving a divine warning. However, the stories also contrast in significant ways.

1. How do the reasons for initiating the flood differ in each story?
2. (a) Why is each hero chosen to survive? (b) How is each warned in a different way? (c) How are their fates different?
3. What do these stories suggest about the differences between Babylonian and Hebrew cultures?

THINKING AND WRITING

Adapting the Flood Story

Many stories from the Bible have a universal and timeless appeal. Imagine that you are a screenwriter and want to use the key elements of the Noah story in a science-fiction movie. Begin by listing these elements. Then figure out how you can adapt each to an outer-space setting. Write a summary of your story that will convince a producer to finance this film. Include at least a few ideas for specific shots, music, and sound effects that will impress an audience. As you revise your summary, insert a few striking details.

(continued from bottom of page)
ANSWERS TO CRITICAL THINKING AND READING

1. In *The Epic of Gilgamesh*, Enlil initiates the flood because the "clamor" of humankind disturbs him. In Genesis God initiates the flood because he is disturbed by the wickedness of humankind.
2. (a) Ea warns Utnapishtim because of an "oath." God chooses Noah to survive because Noah is a righteous and a just man. (b) Utnapishtim is warned indirectly, in a dream. God, however, speaks to Noah directly. (c) Utnapishtim is granted immortality and lives separated from the rest of humankind. Noah becomes a farmer and dies 350 years after the flood.
3. Answers will differ. Some students may notice that in *The Epic of Gilgamesh*, there is no covenant between the gods and humankind. Students may also realize that the Babylonian gods are frightened by the flood, while God is not frightened by the deluge he causes. In general the Babylonian gods seem more capricious and less powerful than the Hebrew God.

THINKING AND WRITING

Writing Across the Curriculum Have a social studies teacher assist students in researching the ship-building capabilities of the ancient Mesopotamians, Phoenicians, and Hebrews. Students can then write a report comparing ancient ships to the ark described in Genesis 6–9.

---

their answer to the Applying question to create their own folk tale. Remind them that such a tale can contain exaggerations and other humorous elements.

ANSWERS TO ANALYZING LITERATURE

1. (a) In the early stages of creation and during the flood, the earth is covered by swirling, chaotic waters. (b) Answers will differ, but most students will realize that humans would want a covenant to ensure that the earth will not revert to chaos.
2. (a) God requires that they not eat flesh with blood and that they not kill other humans. (b) Answers may differ. Some students will respond that God wants to avoid the evil that existed on the earth before the flood.

Especially perceptive students will recognize that the prohibition against murder echoes God's oath not to destroy the earth.
3. (a) In Genesis 1:26 God gives humans "dominion" over all the animals, just as he does again in Genesis 9:2. (b) God's prohibition against murder anticipates one of the most important of these commandments.

Archeology—the science of digging a hole and spinning a yarn about it.

—Ralph Alexander

Biblical Archeology

Biblical archeology is the search for artifacts and records related to the Bible. This field includes projects as diverse as the quest for Noah's ark and the interpretation of the Dead Sea Scrolls, ancient documents discovered in 1947 near the Israel-Jordan border.

The Search for Noah's Ark

The search for Noah's Ark is more interesting as an adventure story than for any information it is likely to uncover. According to Biblical tradition, the ark landed on Mount Ararat, located near the border of modern Armenia, Iran, and Turkey. For hundreds of years, people who believed the Bible's account were tantalized by the image of the abandoned ark sitting on a mountaintop and waiting to be discovered.

Relics of the ark were reported by historians in the first and third centuries A.D. However, no one bothered to actually climb the mountain until Dr. Friedrich Parrot of Estonia made the attempt in 1829. In a village high on Ararat, he was shown a religious image supposedly made of wood from the ark. The monastery where it was kept, however, was destroyed in 1840 by the mountain's last volcanic eruption. A number of later attempts to reach the mountain's summit ran into trouble when native guides refused to approach what they regarded as holy and forbidden ground.

Elusive Evidence

Although several people have claimed to have actually been in the ark, they have produced no evidence. One searcher did find a fossilized timber fragment on Mount Ararat in 1955. He claimed that it was a piece of the ancient ark, and it was first estimated to be about 5,000 years old. More accurate carbon dating, however, indicated that it was little more than 1,000 years old.

Photographs exist of a so-called "buried ship" on a smaller mountain twenty miles away. Some claim that this is the true ark. People living near this ship, however, say that it belonged to Malik Shah, an ancient ruler of this region.

What Are the Dead Sea Scrolls?

In 1947 several shepherd boys found a trove of ancient scrolls hidden in caves near the Dead Sea. These scrolls were made of papyrus, a paperlike material made from a water plant, and leather. The boys had inadvertently uncovered the hidden library of a religious sect that lived in this arid region about two thousand years ago. Soon archeologists discovered similar materials in other nearby caves, and they also found the remains of the buildings occupied by this mysterious community.

Primary Source Note

The Harper Atlas of the Bible contains the following information about the Essenes, the sect that owned the Dead Sea Scrolls:

The Essenes were a sect the origins of which are unclear but which some scholars believe may have originated in Babylon as a reaction against the religious laxity that had provoked the divine punishment of the exile in c. 587–538 B.C. The members of this New Covenant devoted themselves to the perfect observance of the exact interpretation of the Law. . . .

In about 150 B.C. a faction of the Essenes split off from the main group and made their home at Qumran [the site near the Dead Sea where the Dead Sea Scrolls were found]. Under the leadership of a deposed high-priest, who had taken the name of Teacher of Righteousness, they moved to the solitude of the desert to prepare for the advent of the Messiah. . . .

*　　*　　*

The Essenes' dedication to strict observance of the Law meant that they had an obvious need for copies of the sacred books. Indeed their library

NSIGHTS

DEAD SEA SCROLL, THE MANUAL OF DISCIPLINE
From Col. 2–4, Qumram Cave #1

What Documents Were Found?

Among the documents in these caves were scrolls representing the entire Old Testament, except for the Book of Esther. Also included were documents relating to the religious community itself: a book of rules and teachings and a book describing events that would supposedly occur at the end of the world. Some of the materials found were surprisingly similar to New Testament writings. Scholars concluded that most of these scrolls were written between 100 B.C. and A.D. 100, during the time that this community flourished.

Why Were These Finds Important?

These finds were of dramatic importance for several reasons. First, they provided documentary evidence that the Hebrew Bible existed in its present form since no later than A.D. 70. No such evidence had been previously known. Second, they offered valuable insights into the history of Palestine during the time leading up to the birth of Christ.

Of particular interest was the relationship they suggested between Judaism and Christianity. The

religious sect that maintained this library were Jews who had turned their backs on what they regarded as the worldly life of their fellow Jews. Withdrawing into the desert, they set up their own, strictly governed community. The rules and concerns of this group suggest a connection with early Christian beliefs. Some scholars have even speculated that John the Baptist might have been a member of this community. However, others have discounted this notion.

Continuing Controversies

Not only have the scrolls generated controversies about religious matters, but their publication itself has caused disputes. Surprisingly, not all of them have yet been published, even though the original discoveries were made in the late 1940's. Some feel that the researchers in control of these documents are working too slowly. Others defend the researchers, arguing that they need time to piece together the remaining fragments. This controversy will probably continue until all the scrolls are published.

contained copies of all the books of the Hebrew canon with the exception of Esther. . . .

When the news of the Roman advance preceded the tramp of the Tenth Legion [of the Roman army] down the Jordan valley in A.D. 68, the first concern of the Essenes was to hide their precious manuscripts. At the beginning they wrapped the rolls in linen and sealed them in jars, which were placed in remote caves. However, as time grew short they were forced to dump unprotected manuscripts in hiding places near the settlement, which degenerated into thousands of fragments.

Humanities Note

Dead Sea Scrolls, the Manual of Discipline. The Dead Sea Scrolls belonged to a Jewish religious sect called the Essenes. Seriously concerned with the law and its interpretation, they developed strict codes of behavior to govern their community. The Manual of Discipline contained these rules of behavior. One rule, for instance, required the community to "watch in common for a third of all the nights of the year to read the Book [the Bible] and study the Law and to pray together." (For more about the Essenes, see the Primary Source Note on page 52.)

You might want to use the following questions to discuss the art:
1. What does this photograph reveal about the condition of this document?
2. Basing your answer on what you have learned about the Dead Sea Scrolls, explain why this document looks as it does.

Learning Across the Curriculum
Have a social studies teacher assist students in researching some of the controversies that this archeological find has stirred up. Students can present the results of their researches to the class in an oral report. They should make sure, however, they deal with controversial issues in a fair and objective manner.

Questions
1. Why do you think people find biblical archeology so fascinating?
2. Why do you think it took so long for someone to actually climb the mountain where the ark was reputed to rest?

Activities
1. Have students locate Mt. Ararat and the Dead Sea on the map that appears on page 1.
2. Ask students to bring in information about ancient books and ancient writing materials, like papyrus. Then have them make a model of a codex or a scroll.

Focus

Literary Focus Elicit from students what they know about the short story. Have them discuss such elements as plot, conflict, character, and dialogue. Then tell them they will be reading a story that is nearly 3,000 years old. Ask them to keep in mind the ways that it resembles and differs from modern short stories they have read.

Writing/Prior Knowledge Before students begin to write, have a class discussion about the problems and pleasures of being new in a neighborhood or a school.

ESL Teaching Strategy ESL students may be especially attuned to this story because they themselves are strangers in a new place. Make sure they have the opportunity to contribute to the class discussion. If they have trouble reading the story, pair them with a native-speaking student who can provide assistance.

Teaching Tenth-Grade Students To help tenth-grade students appreciate this story, you might want to preteach some of the information in the teacher's notes about the location of Moab (pages 56–57), customs relating to the harvest (page 56), and the duties of families toward widows (page 58).

Vocabulary

Preteach the following vocabulary words:

glean (glēn) v.: To collect grain left by harvesters

reapers (rē´ perz) n.: Harvesters

nativity (nə tiv´ ə tē) n.: Birth

morsel (môr´ səl) n.: Small piece or portion of food

redeem (ri dēm´) n.: To recover, by paying a fee

raiment (rā´ mənt) n.: Clothing

Commentary

Writing

Primary Source

The Book of Ruth

The Hebrew Short Story. The Book of Ruth is an excellent example of the Hebrew short story, a literary form created relatively early in the history of Israel. Scholars guess that this particular story, for instance, was written sometime between 950 and 700 B.C.

These stories were something new in the literature of the ancient Near East. For the most part, they dispensed with the obvious magical and fairy-tale elements that characterized other Near Eastern tales. Coming relatively early in the birth of a new nation, they had a dual purpose: to entertain their audience and at the same time strengthen their faith. The Book of Ruth, with its skillfully contrasted characters and poetic prose, is ideally suited to both these aims.

Before being written down, the Book of Ruth was probably told orally. Just who told it and where is a matter for guesswork. The story may have been recited at festivals in capital cities and well-known centers of worship; however, it may also have been told in the many small towns that dotted the countryside. Townsfolk could have gathered in the evening at the town spring or gate to hear the story of Ruth and Naomi. The storytellers may have been Levites, members of a Hebrew tribe whose role was to assist with religious ceremonies.

An even more interesting possibility is that "wise women" told this tale. Such female storytellers are mentioned in more than one Biblical narrative; one is selected, for instance, to tell a story to King David (II Samuel 14:1–20).

Ruth chooses to live in the southern part of the Hebrew kingdom, a land that is unfamiliar to her. Some of the problems she faces and the feelings she experiences are probably familiar to you. Freewrite about a time when you were a stranger.

The contemporary novelist Cynthia Ozick feels a special affinity for the Book of Ruth: "Only eighty-five verses tell Ruth's and Naomi's story. To talk of it takes much longer. Not that the greatest stories are the shortest—not at all. But a short story has a stalk-shoot—through which its life rushes, and out of which the flowery head erupts. The Book of Ruth—wherein goodness grows out of goodness, and the extraordinary is found here, and here, and here—is sown in desertion, bereavement, barrenness, death, loss, displacement, destitution. What can sprout from such ash? Then Ruth sees into the nature of Covenant, and the life of the story streams in. Out of this stalk mercy and redemption unfold. . . ."

Objectives

Thematic

To understand Hebrew ideals

Skills

1 To understand the Hebrew short story

2 To write about a role model

Support Material

Teaching Portfolio

Teacher Backup, p. 61

Usage and Mechanics Worksheet, p. 65

Vocabulary Check, p. 66

Analyzing Literature Worksheet, *Understanding the Hebrew Short Story*, p. 67

Critical Thinking and Reading Worksheet, *Inferring Character Traits*, p. 68

Selection Test, pp. 69–70

Spelling Tip Point out to students that although the word *nativity* contains the word *native*, the *e* is dropped when the suffix *ity* is added.

The Book of Ruth

King James Version

CHAPTER 1

1 Now it came to pass in the days when the judges ruled, that there was a famine in the land. And a certain man of Bethlehem-judah went to sojourn in the country of Moab,[1] he, and his wife, and his two sons.

2 And the name of the man was Elimelech, and the name of his wife Naomi, and the name of his two sons Mahlon and Chilion, Ephrathites of Bethlehem-judah. And they came into the country of Moab, and continued there.

3 And Elimelech Naomi's husband died; and she was left, and her two sons.

4 And they took them wives of the women of Moab; the name of the one was Orpah, and the name of the other Ruth: and they dwelled there about ten years.

5 And Mahlon and Chilion died also both of them; and the woman was left of her two sons and her husband.

6 And she arose with her daughters-in-law, that she might return from the country of Moab: for she had heard in the country of Moab how that the Lord had visited his people in giving them bread.

7 Wherefore she went forth out of the place where she was, and her two daughters-in-law with her; and they went on the way to return unto the land of Judah.[2]

8 And Naomi said unto her two daughters-in-law, "Go, return each to her mother's house: the Lord deal kindly with you, as ye have dealt with the dead, and with me.

9 "The lord grant you that ye may find rest, each of you in the house of her husband." Then she kissed them; and they lifted up their voice, and wept.

10 And they said unto her, "Surely, we will return with thee unto thy people."

11 And Naomi said, "Turn again, my daughters: why will ye go with me? are there yet any more sons in my womb, that they may be your husbands?

12 "Turn again, my daughters, go your way; for I am too old to have an husband. If I should say, I have hope, if I should have an husband also tonight, and should also bear sons;

13 "Would ye tarry for them till they were grown? would ye stay for them from having husbands? nay, my daughters; for it grieveth me much for your sakes that the hand of the Lord is gone out against me."

14 And they lifted up their voice, and wept again: and Orpah kissed her mother-in-law; but Ruth clave unto her.

15 And she said, "Behold, thy sister-in-law is gone back unto her people, and unto her gods: return thou after thy sister-in-law."

16 And Ruth said, "Intreat me not to leave thee, or to return from following after thee: for whither thou goest, I will go; and where thou lodgest, I will lodge: thy people shall be my people, and thy God my God:

17 "Where thou diest, will I die, and there will I be buried: the Lord do so to me,[3] and more also, if ought but death part thee and me."

18 When she saw that she was stedfastly minded to go with her, then she left speaking unto her.

---

1. Moab (Mō′ ab′): An ancient kingdom east and south of the Dead Sea, and east of the Jordan River.

2. Judah: The Jewish kingdom in the southern part of Palestine.

---

3. do so to me: Punish me.

Presentation
Motivation/Prior Knowledge Ask students to recall stories or films that showed what it was like to be a stranger in a place. Have them describe vivid details from these stories or films. Then tell them that The Book of Ruth deals with a similar subject.

Purpose-Setting Question How do Ruth's words and actions define her character?

Universal Themes Ruth is a stranger and exile in the land of Judah. The theme of exile also appears in Book II of Virgil's *Aeneid*, page 493. In "My Old Home" by Lu Hsun, page 1182, the author finds that he is a stranger in his former home.

1 Clarification Before the advent of King Saul, Israel's military and tribal leaders in Canaan were called judges. The era during which they ruled dates from about the thirteenth to the eleventh century B.C.

2 Discussion Ask students why this speech is so eloquent. How do the repetitions contribute to its poetic quality? Also, what does it reveal about Ruth?

19 So they two went until they came to Bethlehem. And it came to pass, when they were come to Bethlehem, that all the city was moved about them, and they said, "Is this Naomi?"

20 And she said unto them, "Call me not Noami, call me Mara:[4] for the Almighty hath dealt very bitterly with me.

21 "I went out full, and the Lord hath brought me home again empty: why then call ye me Naomi, seeing the Lord hath testified against me, and the Almighty hath afflicted me?"

22 So Naomi returned, and Ruth the Moabitess, her daughter-in-law, with her, which returned out of the country of Moab: and they came to Bethlehem in the beginning of barley harvest.

CHAPTER 2

1 And Naomi had a kinsman of her husband's, a mighty man of wealth, of the family of Elimelech; and his name was Boaz.

2 And Ruth the Moabitess said unto Naomi, "Let me now go to the field, and glean ears of corn after him in whose sight I shall find grace." And she said unto her, "Go, my daughter."

3 And she went, and came, and gleaned in the field after the reapers: and her hap was to light on a part of the field belonging unto Boaz, who was of the kindred of Elimelech.

4 And, behold, Boaz came from Bethlehem, and said unto the reapers, "The Lord be with you." And they answered him, "The Lord bless thee."

5 Then said Boaz unto his servant that was set over the reapers, "Whose damsel is this?"

6 And the servant that was set over the reapers said, "It is the Moabitish damsel that came back with Naomi out of the country of Moab:

7 "And she said, 'I pray you, let me glean and gather after the reapers among the sheaves': so she came, and hath continued even from the morning until now, that she tarried a little in the house."

8 Then said Boaz unto Ruth, "Hearest thou not, my daughter? Go not to glean in another field, neither go from hence, but abide here fast by my maidens:

9 "Let thine eyes be on the field that they do reap, and go thou after them: have I not charged the young men that they shall not touch thee? and when thou art athirst, go unto the vessels, and drink of that which the young men have drawn."

10 Then she fell on her face, and bowed herself to the ground, and said unto him, "Why have I found grace in thine eyes, that thou shouldest take knowledge of me, seeing I am a stranger?"

11 And Boaz answered and said unto her, "It hath fully been showed me, all that thou hast done unto thy mother-in-law since the death of thine husband: and how thou hast left thy father and thy mother, and the land of thy nativity, and art come unto a people which thou knewest not heretofore.

12 "The Lord recompense thy work, and a full reward be given thee of the Lord God of Israel, under whose wings thou art come to trust."

13 Then she said, "Let me find favor in thy sight, my lord; for that thou hast comforted me, and for that thou hast spoken friendly unto thine handmaid, though I be not like unto one of thine handmaidens."

14 And Boaz said unto her, "At mealtime come thou hither, and eat of the bread, and dip thy morsel in the vinegar." And she sat beside the reapers: and he reached her parched corn, and she did eat, and was sufficed, and left.

15 And when she was risen up to glean, Boaz commanded his young men, saying, "Let her glean even among the sheaves, and reproach her not:

16 "And let fall also some of the handfuls of purpose for her, and leave them, that she may glean them, and rebuke her not."

17 So she gleaned in the field until even, and beat out that she had gleaned: and it was about an ephah[5] of barley.

18 And she took it up, and went into the city: and her mother-in-law saw what she had gleaned: and she brought forth, and gave to her that she had reserved after she was sufficed.

19 And her mother-in-law said unto her, "Where hast thou gleaned today? and where wroughtest thou? blessed be he that did take

---

4. Naomi . . . Mara: In Hebrew, Naomi means "my delight" and Mara "bitter."

5. ephah (ē′ fə): An ancient Hebrew unit of dry measure, estimated at from one third of a bushel to a little over one bushel.

Primary Source Note

Ruth is a stranger in Judah; she comes from the land of Moab. *The Harper Atlas of the Bible* explains the political and geographical relationship between Moab and Israel:

> The Israelites and Moabites were close neighbors who shared a common culture and whose respective histories were intertwined. Periods of peaceful relations (as depicted in the Book of Ruth) were interrupted occasionally by periods of hostilities. . .
>
> Moab, as a geographical designation, refers to the strip of agricultural

land sandwiched between the Dead Sea and the Arabian Desert. The Mujib canyon (the river Arnon of Old Testament times) separates northern Moab from Moab proper. The region of northern Moab was a constantly disputed territory between the Israelites, Ammonites, and Moabites.

> * * *
>
> Moab was good farm and grazing land in ancient times, as it is today. In time of famine, people from Judah might go to Moab in search of food (which is the setting of the Book of Ruth). Mesha [a king of Moab]

Detail from a French illuminated manuscript showing scenes from the story of Ruth
C. A.D. 1250
The Pierpont Morgan Library, New York

knowledge of thee." And she showed her mother-in-law with whom she had wrought, and said, "The man's name with whom I wrought today is Boaz."

20 And Naomi said unto her daughter-in-law, "Blessed be he of the Lord, who hath not left off his kindness to the living and to the dead." And Naomi said unto her, "The man is near of kin unto us, one of our next kinsmen."

21 And Ruth the Moabitess said, "He said unto me also, 'Thou shalt keep fast by my young men, until they have ended all my harvest.'"

22 And Naomi said unto Ruth her daughter-in-law, "It is good, my daughter, that thou go out with his maidens, that they meet thee not in any other field."

23 So she kept fast by the maidens of Boaz to glean unto the end of barley harvest and of wheat harvest; and dwelt with her mother-in-law.

CHAPTER 3

1 Then Naomi her mother-in-law said unto her, "My daughter, shall I not seek rest for thee, that it may be well with thee?

2 "And now is not Boaz of our kindred,[6] with whose maidens thou wast? Behold, he winnoweth barley tonight in the threshing-floor.

3 "Wash thyself therefore, and anoint[7] thee, and put thy raiment upon thee, and get thee down to the floor: but make not thyself known unto the man, until he shall have done eating and drinking.

4 "And it shall be, when he lieth down, that thou shalt mark the place where he shall lie, and thou shalt go in, and uncover his feet, and lay thee down; and he will tell thee what thou shalt do."

5 And she said unto her, "All that thou sayest unto me I will do."

6 And she went down unto the floor, and did according to all that her mother-in-law bade her.

7 And when Boaz had eaten and drunk, and his heart was merry, he went to lie down at the end of the heap of corn: and she came softly, and uncovered his feet, and laid her down.

8 And it came to pass at midnight, that the man was afraid, and turned himself: and, behold a woman lay at his feet.

9 And he said, "Who art thou?" And she answered, "I am Ruth thine handmaid: spread therefore thy skirt over thine handmaid: for thou art a near kinsman."

10 And he said, "Blessed be thou of the Lord, my daughter: for thou hast showed more kindness in the latter end than at the beginning, inasmuch as

---

6. kindred: According to Jewish law, the closest unmarried male relative of Ruth's deceased husband was obligated to marry her.

7. anoint (ə noint´) *v.*: Rub oil or ointment on.

paid annual tribute to Omri and Ahab [kings of Israel] in kind—lambs and wool.

10 **Clarification** Tell students that the "nearer kinsman," or closer relative, of Ruth and Naomi has the prior right to marry Ruth and to buy a parcel of Elimelech's land. Boaz will therefore meet with this man to see whether or not he will exercise this prior right; if not, then Boaz will marry Ruth.

11 **Enrichment** Point out to students that the Book of Ruth often delineates character by means of contrast. Earlier, Orpah and Ruth were contrasted in terms of their devotion to Naomi. Ruth proved the more loving. Now Boaz and the kinsman are contrasted in terms of their willingness to marry Ruth. Ask students what this contrast reveals.

Also ask them why the kinsman is not named. Names are very important in this narrative—Naomi, for instance, renames herself Mara to indicate her bitterness. What does the lack of a name indicate about the kinsman?

12 **Enrichment** Tell students that the business of a city was often transacted at its gate. Here the elders of the city act as witnesses to this transaction. Today such dealings take place in a courtroom or a lawyer's office.

13 **Clarification** Family ties were very important to the ancient Hebrews. Male relatives of a widow therefore had not only a right but an obligation to marry her in order to maintain the family line. Tamar invoked this obligation by insisting that her father-in-law, Judah, marry her after her husband died (Genesis 38).

thou followedst not young men, whether poor or rich.

11 "And now, my daughter, fear not; I will do to thee all that thou requirest: for all the city of my people doth know that thou art a virtuous woman.

10 12 "And now it is true that I am thy near kinsman: howbeit there is a kinsman nearer than I.

13 "Tarry this night, and it shall be in the morning, that if he will perform unto thee the part of a kinsman, well; let him do the kinsman's part: but if he will not do the part of a kinsman to thee, then will I do the part of a kinsman to thee, as the Lord liveth: lie down until the morning."

14 And she lay at his feet until the morning: and she rose up before one could know another. And he said, "Let it not be known that a woman came into the floor."

15 Also he said, "Bring the vail[8] that thou hast upon thee, and hold it." And when she held it, he measured six measures of barley, and laid it on her: and she went into the city.

16 And when she came to her mother-in-law, she said, "Who art thou, my daughter?" And she told her all that the man had done to her.

17 And she said, "These six measures of barley gave he me; for he said to me, 'Go not empty unto thy mother-in-law.'"

18 Then said she, "Sit still, my daughter, until thou know how the matter will fall: for the man will not be in rest, until he have finished the thing this day."

CHAPTER 4

1 Then went Boaz up to the gate, and sat him down there: and behold, the kinsman of whom Boaz spake came by; unto whom he said, "Ho, such a one! turn aside, sit down here." And he turned aside, and sat down.

11
12 2 And he took men of the elders of the city, and said, "Sit ye down here." And they sat down.

3 And he said unto the kinsman, "Naomi, that is come again out of the country of Moab, selleth a parcel of land, which was our brother Elimelech's:

---

8. **vail:** Veil.

---

4 "And I thought to advertise thee, saying, 'Buy it before the inhabitants, and before the elders of my people. If thou wilt redeem it, redeem it: but if thou wilt not redeem it, then tell me, that I may know: for there is none to redeem it beside thee; and I am after thee.'" And he said, "I will redeem it."

5 Then said Boaz, "What day thou buyest the field of the hand of Naomi, thou must buy it also of Ruth the Moabitess, the wife of the dead, to raise up the name of the dead upon his inheritance."

6 And the kinsman said, "I cannot redeem it for myself, lest I mar mine own inheritance: redeem thou my right to thyself; for I cannot redeem it.

7 Now this was the manner in former time in Israel concerning redeeming and concerning changing, for to confirm all things; a man plucked off his shoe, and gave it to his neighbor: and this was a testimony in Israel.

8 Therefore the kinsman said unto Boaz, "Buy it for thee." So he drew off his shoe.

9 And Boaz said unto the elders, and unto all the people, "Ye are witnesses this day, that I have bought all that was Elimelech's, and all that was Chilion's and Mahlon's, of the hand of Naomi.

10 "Moreover Ruth the Moabitess, the wife of Mahlon, have I purchased to be my wife, to raise up the name of the dead upon his inheritance, that the name of the dead be not cut off from among his brethren, and from the gate of his place: ye are witnesses this day."

11 And all the people that were in the gate, and the elders, said, "We are witnesses. The Lord make the woman that is come into thine house like Rachel and like Leah,[9] which two did build the house of Israel: and do thou worthily in Ephratah, and be famous in Bethlehem:

12 "And let thy house be like the house of Pharez, whom Tamar bare unto Judah,[10] of the seed which the Lord shall give thee of this young woman."

---

9. **Rachel . . . Leah:** Wives of Jacob, whose sons, along with those of their handmaids Bilhah and Zilpha, became the founders of the twelve tribes of Israel.

10. **Pharez . . . Judah:** Ruth, like Tamar, was a childless widow who conceived a son with her husband's kinsman.

Master Teacher Note Explain to students that biblical narratives are often characterized by the economy of their means. A modern storyteller might take many pages to tell this same tale. Have students demonstrate the ways in which the narrative is spare and economical. What, for instance, is omitted that might appear in a modern story? Then ask them to decide whether or not this spareness is a virtue.

Cooperative Learning Have students divide into small groups and write additional dialogue for this story. Then have them perform the scenes they have expanded.

Closure and Extension

ANSWERS TO THINKING ABOUT THE SELECTION

1. (a) Answers will differ. Some students may choose Ruth's famous speech to Naomi in 1:16–17. That speech reveals Ruth's exceptional loyalty to Naomi and to God. It foreshadows the restoration of Naomi's good fortune.

13 So Boaz took Ruth, and she was his wife: and when he went in unto her, the Lord gave her conception, and she bare a son.

14 And the women said unto Naomi, "Blessed be the Lord, which hath not left thee this day without a kinsman, that his name may be famous in Israel.

15 "And he shall be unto thee a restorer of thy life, and a nourisher of thine old age: for thy daughter-in-law, which loveth thee, which is better to thee than seven sons, hath born him."

16 And Naomi took the child, and laid it in her bosom, and become nurse unto it.

17 And the women her neighbors gave it a name, saying, "There is a son born to Naomi"; and they called his name Obed: he is the father of Jesse, the father of David.

18 Now these are the generations of Pharez: Pharez begat Hezron,

19 And Hezron begat Ram, and Ram begat Amminadab,

20 And Amminadab begat Nahshon, and Nahshon begat Salmon,

21 And Salmon begat Boaz, and Boaz begat Obed,

22 And Obed begat Jesse, and Jesse begat David.

Reader's Response *What character did you identify with most closely? Why?*

THINKING ABOUT THE SELECTION

Interpreting

1. The Book of Ruth has been praised for its poetic and moving prose. (a) Find a passage that you think is especially poetic. Explain how this passage contributes to the story. (b) Did you feel moved by it? Why or why not?
2. This tale is realistic, yet novelist Cynthia Ozick has said that it is filled with "extraordinary" events. Explain how the Book of Ruth is a mixture of the ordinary and the extraordinary.
3. (a) How does Naomi move from complaint to celebration in this tale? (b) How does this emotional journey reflect the movement of the story from misfortune to restoration of loss?
4. How does the naming of Naomi's descendants—down to David, the greatest king of ancient Israel—reflect the theme of restoration?
5. God does not take a direct part in this story as he does in Genesis 1–3 and 6–9. Yet in some ways he is the most important character in the story. Explain.
6. In what way is this story an attack on racism?

Applying

7. What aspects of the Book of Ruth are timeless and universal? Support your answer.

ANALYZING LITERATURE

Understanding the Hebrew Short Story

The Hebrew short story developed at about the same time the people of Israel were finding their identity as a nation. Early examples of this form, like the Book of Ruth, were realistic; their purpose was to teach and to entertain.

1. (a) How is Ruth a role model in her attitude toward God and her relationships with her fellow humans? (b) In what way does her foreign birth add to her stature?
2. How do the final sentences of the first three chapters foreshadow coming events?
3. Show how the pace of the story varies and explain how this varying pace helps convey the story's message.

THINKING AND WRITING

Writing About a Role Model

Ancient Hebrew storytellers presented Ruth as a person to be imitated. Choose someone you know who could also serve as a role model. Brainstorm to gather some of the admirable deeds that he or she has performed. Then write a narrative of these deeds. Do not praise your subject directly; instead, let his or her actions speak for themselves. As you revise your account, consider inserting memorable dialogue at crucial points.

(continued from bottom of page)

Focus

Literary Focus Have students recall a variety of heroes they have read about or seen in films. Elicit from them the qualities that these heroes displayed, and have students speculate about whether heroes can be classified into various types. For instance, do some heroes rely more on brains or on intuition than on brawn? Also, how are heroes influenced by their nationality or background?

Writing/Prior Knowledge Group students in pairs and have them tell their story to a partner before they begin the writing assignment.

ESL Teaching Strategy Consider assigning each ESL student to an advanced student who can answer questions about the text. The advanced students can also preteach the vocabulary words.

Teaching Tenth-Grade Students Tenth-grade students might enjoy calculating the exact size of Goliath, the weight of his armor, and so forth. The second and third footnotes provide the necessary information for such calculations.

Vocabulary

Preteach the following vocabulary words:

array (ə rā´) n.: Orderly grouping of troops

prevail (prē vāl´) v.: To gain the advantage over someone

dismayed (dis mād´) adj.: Greatly discouraged and afraid

parched (pärcht) adj.: Dried

reproach (ri prōch´) n.: Shame and disgrace

kindled (kin´ dəld) v.: Aroused

disdained (dis dānd´) v.: Regarded or treated someone as unworthy

Commentary

Writing

Primary Source

David and Goliath

A Biblical Hero. Heroes, whether ancient or modern, tend to be bold and resourceful beyond the means of ordinary mortals. These qualities that heroes share, however, should not disguise the differences among them. Every culture exhibits its own customs, beliefs, and outlook in tales of heroism that it passes down from generation to generation.

The adventures of Gilgamesh (see *The Epic of Gilgamesh*, pages 15–28), for example, reflect the pessimism of Mesopotamian civilization. Unaided by the gods, this hero fails in his quest for immortality. His story ends on a note of resignation: Even the greatest kings are subject to death.

In the Bible, however, heroism has meaning only in relation to the covenant, the solemn agreement between God and his people. Heroes and heroines act on God's behalf. This link between the hero and God explains aspects of the David and Goliath story that would otherwise be puzzling. David (c. 1012–972 B.C.), who would become a great king of Israel, is at this point an extremely unlikely hero. He is a mere shepherd boy, without any military training. A family errand brings him to the battlefield where the Jews, under King Saul, are fighting their traditional enemies the Philistines—a people who came to Palestine from Crete in the twelfth century B.C. David's unpromising appearance, however, turns out to be the whole point of the story.

Sometimes people surprise us by what they are able to achieve against all odds. Recall a situation in which you were sure that someone was going to fail. First, list all the factors that seemed to make success impossible; then briefly tell how this person achieved a goal despite everything.

Some contemporary writers have declared that we live in an era of the anti-hero, a person with *un*heroic qualities. In this spirit the novelist Jerome Charyn preferred Saul, the moody and failed king, to the successful David: "I never much cared for David. The little giant-slayer is as competent as any Boy Scout. He has no demons to upset him. . . . Our own lives seem as arbitrary as Saul's. The blessing of his kingship was only another form of curse. . . . If David is history's darling, then we, all the modern fools—liars, jugglers, wizards without song—still have Saul."

Objectives

Thematic

To appreciate a timeless and universal tale about an underdog

Skills

1 To understand a biblical hero

2 To appreciate the use of dialogue

3 To write a modern "David" story

Support Material

Teaching Portfolio

Teacher Backup, p. 71

Grammar in Action Worksheet, *Evolution of the Language*, p. 75

Usage and Mechanics Worksheet, p. 77

Vocabulary Check, p. 78

Critical Thinking and Reading Worksheet, *Appreciating the Use of Di-*

1 Samuel 17

David and Goliath

King James Version

1 Now the Philistines gathered together their armies to battle, and were gathered together at Shochoh, which belongeth to Judah, and pitched between Shochoh and Azekah, in Ephes-dammim.[1]

2 And Saul and the men of Israel were gathered together, and pitched by the valley of Elah, and set the battle in array against the Philistines.

3 And the Philistines stood on a mountain on the one side, and Israel stood on a mountain on the other side: and there was a valley between them.

4 And there went out a champion out of the camp of the Philistines, named Goliath, of Gath, whose height was six cubits and a span.[2]

5 And he had an helmet of brass upon his head, and he was armed with a coat of mail; and the weight of the coat was five thousand shekels[3] of brass.

6 And he had greaves of brass upon his legs, and a target of brass between his shoulders.

7 And the staff of his spear was like a weaver's beam,[4] and his spear's head weighed six hundred shekels of iron: and one bearing a shield went before him.

8 And he stood and cried unto the armies of Israel, and said unto them, "Why are ye come out to set your battle in array? am not I a Philistine, and ye servants to Saul? choose you a man for you, and let him come down to me.

9 "If he be able to fight with me, and to kill me, then will we be your servants: but if I prevail against him, and kill him, then shall ye be our servants, and serve us."

10 And the Philistine said, "I defy the armies of Israel this day; give me a man, that we may fight together."

11 When Saul and all Israel heard those words of the Philistine, they were dismayed, and greatly afraid.

12 Now David was the son of the Ephrathite of Bethlehem-judah, whose name was Jesse; and he had eight sons: and the man went among men for an old man in the days of Saul.

13 And the three eldest sons of Jesse went and followed Saul to the battle: and the names of his three sons that went to the battle were Eliab the firstborn, and next unto him Abinadab, and the third Shammah.

14 And David was the youngest: and the three eldest followed Saul.

15 But David went and returned from Saul to feed his father's sheep at Bethlehem.

16 And the Philistine drew near morning and evening, and presented himself forty days.

17 And Jesse said unto David his son, "Take now for thy brethren an ephah[5] of this parched corn, and these ten loaves, and run to the camp to thy brethren;

---

1. **Philistines . . . in Ephes-dammim** (ē′ fiz dam′ im): The Philistines were a non-Semitic people who came to Palestine from the Aegean in about the twelfth century B.C. Shochoh (shō′ kō) was a town southwest of Bethlehem and Azekah a town west of Jerusalem.

2. **six . . . span:** A cubit is 18 to 22 inches and a span is about 9 inches.

3. **shekels** (shek′ əls): Ancient units of weight equal to about half an ounce.

4. **weaver's beam:** One of the two large rollers of a loom.

5. **ephah** (ē′ fə): An ancient Hebrew unit of dry measure, estimated at from one third of a bushel to a little over one bushel.

alogue, p. 79
Language Worksheet, _Finding the Meaning That Fits the Context_, p. 80
Selection Test, pp. 81–82

Spelling Tip Write the word _kindled_ on the chalkboard. Remind students that even though the second syllable is pronounced _dəld_, it is spelled _dled_.

Presentation
Motivation/Prior Knowledge Many students will be familiar with the story of David and Goliath. Have them tell it and then have them check the details they mentioned against the narrative in the Bible.

Purpose-Setting Question How is David different from the Israelite soldiers fighting under Saul's leadership?

Universal Themes The following selections in the book also deal with the theme of heroism: _The Epic of Gilgamesh_, page 15; the excerpt from _Rustam and Suhrab_, page 89; Book XXII of Homer's _Iliad_, page 366; Book II of Virgil's _Aeneid_, page 493; and the excerpt from the _Song of Roland_, page 569.

1 **Discussion** Ask students how the description of the setting contributes to the drama of the tale.

2 **Discussion** Ask students why Goliath's appearance and armor are described in such great detail.

3 **Discussion** Have students compare David's reaction to Goliath with that of "the men of Israel."

4 **Clarification** Circumcision was the practice of cutting off all or part of the foreskin. Since the Hebrews practiced this rite and the Philistines did not, "uncircumcised" is a term of abuse in this context. It is a synonym for ungodly.

5 **Discussion** Ask students what this exchange reveals about the relationship between David and Eliab. Have them describe similar exchanges they might have had with their own brothers or sisters.

6 **Clarification** Explain to students that a shepherd was expected to defend the flock against wild beasts. David's description of his encounter with a lion and a bear is therefore not implausible.

7 **Literary Focus** Ask students how this passage underscores the relationship between heroism and the covenant.

18 "And carry these ten cheeses unto the captain of their thousand, and look how thy brethren fare, and take their pledge."

19 Now Saul, and they, and all the men of Israel, were in the valley of Elah, fighting with the Philistines.

20 And David rose up early in the morning, and left the sheep with a keeper, and took, and went, as Jesse had commanded him; and he came to the trench, as the host was going forth to the fight, and shouted for the battle.

21 For Israel and the Philistines had put the battle in array, army against army.

22 And David left his carriage in the hand of the keeper of the carriage, and ran into the army, and came and saluted his brethren.

23 And as he talked with them, behold, there came up the champion, the Philistine of Gath, Goliath by name, out of the armies of the Philistines, and spake according to the same words: and David heard them.

24 And all the men of Israel, when they saw the man, fled from him, and were sore afraid.

25 And the men of Israel said, "Have ye seen this man that is come up? surely to defy Israel is he come up: and it shall be, that the man who killeth him, the king will enrich him with great riches, and will give him his daughter, and make his father's house free in Israel."

26 And David spake to the men that stood by him, saying, "What shall be done to the man that killeth this Philistine, and taketh away the reproach from Israel? for who is this uncircumcised Philistine, that he should defy the armies of the living God?"

27 And the people answered him after this manner, saying, "So shall it be done to the man that killeth him."

28 And Eliab his eldest brother heard when he spake unto the men; and Eliab's anger was kindled against David, and he said, "Why camest thou down hither? and with whom hast thou left those few sheep in the wilderness? I know thy pride, and the naughtiness of thine heart; for thou art come down that thou mightest see the battle."

29 And David said, "What have I now done? Is there not a cause?"

30 And he turned from him toward another, and spake after the same manner: and the people answered him again after the former manner.

31 And when the words were heard which David spake, they rehearsed them before Saul: and he sent for him.

32 And David said to Saul, "Let no man's heart fail because of him; thy servant will go and fight with this Philistine."

33 And Saul said to David, "Thou are not able to go against this Philistine to fight with him: for thou art but a youth, and he a man of war from his youth."

34 And David said unto Saul, "Thy servant kept his father's sheep, and there came a lion and a bear, and took a lamb out of the flock:

35 "And I went out after him, and smote him, and delivered it out of his mouth: and when he arose against me, I caught him by his beard, and smote him, and slew him.

36 "Thy servant slew both the lion and the bear: and this uncircumcised Philistine shall be as one of them, seeing he hath defied the armies of the living God."

37 David said moreover, "The Lord that delivered me out of the paw of the lion, and out of the paw of the bear, he will deliver me out of the hand of this Philistine." And Saul said unto David, "Go, and the Lord be with thee."

38 And Saul armed David with his armor, and he put an helmet of brass upon his head; also he armed him with a coat of mail.

39 And David girded his sword upon his armor, and he assayed to go; for he had not proved it. And David said unto Saul, "I cannot go with these; for I have not proved them." And David put them off him.

40 And he took his staff in his hand, and chose him five smooth stones out of the brook, and put them in a shepherd's bag which he had, even in a scrip;[6] and his sling was in his hand: and he drew near to the Philistine.

41 And the Philistine came on and drew near unto David; and the man that bare the shield went before him.

---

6. **scrip** (skrip): Small bag, wallet, or satchel.

Grammar in Action

Evolution of the Language Over the course of 1,500 years, the English language has evolved from Old English (A.D. 450–1150) through Middle English (A.D. 1150–1500) to Modern English (1500–present). The King James Version of the Bible was written during the Modern English period, but it contains words and grammatical forms that are not in use today. Here are some examples:

ARCHAIC WORD: sore (adverb)

MEANING: greatly

EXAMPLE: ". . . all the men of Israel . . . were *sore* afraid."

ARCHAIC VERB CONJUGATION:

Singular
First person: I go
Second person: thou goest   (modern: you go)
Third person: she goeth   (modern: she goes)

Plural
First person: we go
Second person: you go
Third person: they go

THE YOUTHFUL DAVID
Andrea del Castagno
National Gallery of Art, Washington, D.C.

Humanities Note

Fine art, *The Youthful David*, c. 1450–1457, by Andrea del Castagno. Andrea del Castagno (1423–1457) was a masterful painter of the early Italian Renaissance. He won fame at the age of seventeen for a shocking painting of effigies of hanged men. In the course of his brief but illustrious career, he painted frescoes on the ceiling of a Venetian chapel and decorated the hall of a villa with pictures of Dante, Petrarch, and Boccaccio, among others.

Castagno painted *The Youthful David* on a leather shield that was used as decoration at jousts and tournaments. The swirl of David's garments and his wind-tossed hair are set off in stark relief against the dark, stormy background. David's uplifted arm and expression of shocked determination contribute to the drama of this painting.

You might want to use the following questions to discuss the art:

1. (a) What is lying at David's feet? (b) Why is his arm upraised?
2. What stage of the combat between David and Goliath did the artist capture? Explain.
3. (a) How would you describe the mood of this painting? (b) What elements contribute to this mood?
4. Choose a modern hero and describe how you would depict him or her in a painting.

These archaic words and forms give the King James Version an unmistakable flavor. Some scholars have argued that while recent translations of the Bible are more in keeping with modern usage, they are also less poetic. This point is controversial.

Student Activity 1. Find another example of an archaic verb conjugation in this selection. Then identify two archaic words and look them up in a dictionary.

Student Activity 2. Rewrite a passage of this selection using up-to-date English. Then compare your rewritten version with the original. Which sounds better? Why?

42 And when the Philistine looked about, and saw David, he disdained him: for he was but a youth, and ruddy, and of a fair countenance.

43 And the Philistine said unto David, "Am I a dog, that thou comest to me with staves?"[7] And the Philistine cursed David by his gods.

44 And the Philistine said to David, "Come to me, and I will give thy flesh unto the fowls of the air, and to the beasts of the field."

45 Then said David to the Philistine, "Thou comest to me with a sword, and with a spear, and with a shield: but I come to thee in the name of the Lord of hosts, the God of the armies of Israel, whom thou has defied.

46 "This day will the Lord deliver thee into mine hand; and I will smite thee, and take thine head from thee; and I will give the carcasses of the host of the Philistines this day unto the fowls of the air, and to the wild beasts of the earth; that all the earth may know that there is a God in Israel.

47 "And all this assembly shall know that the Lord saveth not with sword and spear: for the battle is the Lord's, and he will give you into our hands."

48 And it came to pass, when the Philistine arose, and came and drew nigh to meet David, that David hasted, and ran toward the army to meet the Philistine.

49 And David put his hand in his bag, and took thence a stone, and slang it, and smote the Philistine in his forehead, that the stone sunk into his forehead; and he fell upon his face to the earth.

50 So David prevailed over the Philistine with a sling and with a stone, and smote the Philistine,

and slew him; but there was no sword in the hand of David.

51 Therefore David ran, and stood upon the Philistine, and took his sword, and drew it out of the sheath thereof, and slew him, and cut off his head therewith. And when the Philistines saw their champion was dead, they fled.

52 And the men of Israel and of Judah arose, and shouted, and pursued the Philistines, until thou come to the valley, and to the gates of Ekron. And the wounded of the Philistines fell down by the way to Shaaraim, even unto Gath, and unto Ekron.

53 And the children of Israel returned from chasing after the Philistines, and they spoiled[8] their tents.

54 And David took the head of the Philistine, and brought it to Jerusalem; but he put his armor in his tent.

55 And when Saul saw David go forth against the Philistine, he said unto Abner, the captain of the host, "Abner, whose son is this youth?" And Abner said, "As thy soul liveth, O king, I cannot tell."

56 And the king said, "Inquire thou whose son the stripling is."

57 And as David returned from the slaughter of the Philistine, Abner took him, and brought him before Saul with the head of the Philistine in his hand.

58 And Saul said to him, "Whose son art thou, thou young man?" And David answered, "I am the son of thy servant Jesse the Bethlehemite."

---

7. **staves** (stāvs) *n.*: Sticks or staffs.

8. **spoiled:** Plundered and pillaged.

Reader's Response *Would you choose David or Saul as a role model for our times? Why?*

Primary Source Note

The Harper Atlas of the Bible summarizes the career of Saul, king of Israel at the time of David's battle with Goliath:

Saul lived approximately 1000 B.C. and belonged to the small Israelite tribe of Benjamin, which was overshadowed by (if not a sub-branch of) the neighboring tribe of Ephraim. Both tribes were settled in the hill country north of Jerusalem, along with various other population elements such as Hivites and Archites. Jerusalem was not yet a city of prominence, of course, and the villagers of the hill country were vulnerable to oppression from all sides. Thus Saul emerged on the scene as a local military hero who led the Benjamin-Ephraimite resistance against surrounding enemies, especially the Philistines. Proclaimed king by his countrymen in response to his early victories, Saul spent the remainder of his career, a reign of unknown duration, defending what thus became the fledgling kingdom of Israel. His public career ended the same way it had begun, in battle. Both Saul and his son Jonathan were killed while fighting the Philistines on the slopes of Mt. Gilboa.

THINKING ABOUT THE SELECTION

Interpreting

1. How does the description of the setting heighten the drama of this one-on-one combat?
2. What devices does the author use to create suspense in building toward the battle of David and Goliath?
3. (a) In what ways do these two opponents represent opposite views of life? (b) How do the descriptions of their weapons emphasize these contrasting outlooks?
4. Is it fair to call the combat between David and Goliath a contest between good and evil? Explain.
5. Is the battle itself an anticlimax or a disappointment in terms of what you expected? Why or why not?

Applying

6. David is in many ways a classic underdog. (a) What advantage does an underdog have in a contest? (b) Why are people naturally sympathetic toward an underdog?

ANALYZING LITERATURE

Understanding a Biblical Hero

We cannot understand Biblical heroes or heroines unless we take into account the covenant, or agreement, between God and the Hebrew people. That covenant calls on God to help his people, if they have faith in him. David is a living example of that faith. His bravery, in fact, is inseparable from his faith in God. David's youth and lack of military experience turn out to be an advantage, because they graphically demonstrate that God is taking a hand in this battle: How else could the boy have won? Also, unlike most heroes, David is not concerned with personal glory. From the time he first sets eyes on Goliath, he is interested solely in defending the honor of God.

1. Identify two speeches in which David shows more concern for God's honor than for his own. Explain your choices.
2. (a) David describes to Saul his role as a shepherd. What does this description suggest about God's role in relation to the Hebrew people? (b) How does the story of David and Goliath illustrate this role?
3. David refuses to use conventional weapons. How is

this refusal a statement about the relationship between the Hebrew people and God?

CRITICAL THINKING AND READING

Appreciating the Use of Dialogue

The author of the tale of David and Goliath skillfully uses dialogue to reveal and contrast character traits. The first speech we hear is that of the giant Goliath. As befits his great stature—the description of his size comes right before the speech—his words themselves are spoken at full volume. This mighty shout of defiance reveals the man's simple mentality: I am a warrior; beat me if you can! The speech that introduces us to David is quite different.

1. (a) If Goliath's words define him as a mighty warrior, what do Jesse's words (17:17–18) suggest about David's role? (b) What is ironic about placing these two speeches so close together?
2. How do Eliab's words reflect a man's response to his kid brother?
3. How does David's speech to Saul reveal a new dimension of the boy's character?
4. (a) Contrast the speeches that David and Goliath make to each other. (b) How do these speeches disclose their different personalities?

THINKING AND WRITING

Writing a Modern "David" Story

Return to your brief account of a person succeeding against all odds and use it to write a modern David-and-Goliath story. First, evaluate your account. If it does not clearly illustrate a person battling against a giant opponent, choose another situation. Remember that in our times, "Goliath" can be a huge institution—a corporation, school, or government—as well as an imposing person. Rather than simply listing the difficulties of the situation, use your descriptions to suggest them to a reader. Also, don't merely tell the reader about your hero or heroine—show this person in action! In revising your story, make sure a reader will understand the qualities that led your "David" to succeed in the end.

(continued from bottom of page)

en for granted. (b) People admire the courage of those who go against the odds.

Challenge Have students read 1 Samuel, chapters 16 and 18–30 to learn more about David.

ANSWERS TO ANALYZING LITERATURE

1. In 17:26 David is more concerned about the insult to God than he is about his own reputation or the danger of Goliath. He demonstrates the same spirit in 17:45–47.
2. (a) It suggests that God is the shepherd of the people of Israel. (b) The story illustrates how God protects his "flock" from danger.
3. His refusal shows that he relies on God's power rather than on his own. He places his faith in the covenant that exists between God and the people of Israel: If Israel has faith, God will deliver it from its enemies.

ANSWERS TO CRITICAL THINKING AND READING

1. (a) Answers will differ, but many students will realize that Jesse's words suggest that David is merely an adolescent running an errand. (b) The irony is that this mere adolescent will kill the mighty boasting warrior.
2. Like an older brother, Eliab thinks of David as a meddling, curious, irresponsible boy.
3. It reveals that he has encountered and overcome serious dangers.
4. Answers will differ, but some students may respond as follows. (a) Goliath is boasting, abusive, and disdainful. David boasts on God's behalf, not on his own. (b) The speeches reveal that Goliath is angry, scornful, and vain, while David is courageous and believes in a power beyond his own.

THINKING AND WRITING

Writing Across the Curriculum You might want to inform the social studies department that students are reading this selection. A social studies teacher can help students research the origins of the Philistine people. Students can then write a report on their findings.

Closure and Extension

ANSWERS TO THINKING ABOUT THE SELECTION

1. Answers will differ, but students may indicate that the valley between the armies is almost like a stage for this combat.
2. Answers will differ. One device that heightens suspense is the verbal

duel that precedes the actual combat.
3. (a) Answers will differ, but many students will recognize that Goliath places his faith in his own strength while David relies on God. (b) Goliath is heavily armored, but David has only a slingshot and a bag of stones.
4. Answers will differ, but students may indicate that the abusive Goliath

does seem to embody evil while the young and appealing David seems a champion of goodness.
5. Answers will differ. Some students may feel that the battle is anticlimactic because it takes place so quickly.
6. Answers will differ, but some students may respond as follows. (a) Underdogs have an advantage because they are underrated and tak-

GUIDE FOR INTERPRETING

Literary Focus Recite Psalm 23 and ask how many students are familiar with it. Ask those who know it to describe the circumstances in which they first read or heard of it. Then tell students that this famous psalm is part of a group of 150 psalms contained in the Bible.

Writing/Prior Knowledge Ask students to bring in song lyrics . Copy these lyrics onto the chalkboard so that students can refer to them when doing the assignment.

ESL Teaching Assignment ESL students may not be familiar with American popular songs. Allow them to use songs from their own language in doing the Writing assignment. If they are willing, have them translate these lyrics for the class.

Teaching Tenth-Grade Students Have tenth-grade students write their own parallel verses, using the techniques of repetition, completion, and negation.

Master Teacher Note Bring in recordings of psalms being sung or chanted and play them for students. This experience will help students appreciate that the psalms were meant to be heard.

Vocabulary

Preteach the following vocabulary words:

avenger (ə venj′ ər) *n.*: Someone who gets revenge for an injury or wrong

tabernacle (tab′ ər nak′ əl) *n.*: Temporary shelter; dwelling place

testimony (tes′ tə mō′ nē) *n.*: Statement made under oath; any affirmation or declaration

statutes (stach′ o̅o̅ts) *n.*: Rules, regulations

redeemer (ri dēm′ ər) *n.*: Rescuer

cunning (kun′ iŋ) *n.*: Skill

raze (rāz) *n.*: Demolish

Commentary

Psalms 8, 19, 23, 137

Parallelism. The Psalms—a word that comes from the Greek *psalmas,* meaning "song"—have been the most popular poems in the Western world. Composed by many psalmists over a long period of time, these 150 poems and hymns were known in Hebrew as "songs of praise." Together they express not only praise but all the feelings that humans experience in relation to God, including fear, gratitude, joy, and despair. Set to music, they earned an important place in the religious service of Jews and Christians alike.

The Jews inherited the form of the psalm from Babylonian and Egyptian sources. As for the verse itself, they used a pattern common in ancient Near Eastern poetry. Guided by this pattern, called **parallelism,** Hebrew poets stated an idea in the first half of a line and then repeated, negated, completed, or otherwise elaborated it in the second half. In Psalm 5, for example, the author uses repetition.

> Give ear to my words, O Lord,
> consider my meditation.

The second half of this line repeats, in a slightly different way, the idea expressed in the first half. Verse 53 of Psalm 78 exhibits another type of parallelism, negation:

> And he led them on safely, so that they feared not,
> but the sea overwhelmed their enemies.

In this case, the second half of the line expresses the opposite, or negation, of the initial idea: They are safe, but their enemies are overwhelmed. Still another type of parallelism involves the completion of an idea (Psalm 59:14):

> And at evening let them return,
> and let them make a noise like a dog, and go round about the
>   city.

Here the second half of the line introduces an image that vividly brings home the meaning of the first statement.

As these examples suggest, parallelism was not a rigid, mechanical system for constructing poems. In the hands of ancient Hebrew poets, it was a means of introducing balance and variation into their work.

Writing

Repetition and variation is a method used in ancient psalms and popular songs. Think of a song whose lyrics are repeated, with slight variations. Then explain why this pattern is effective in evoking a mood or a feeling.

Objectives

Thematic
To understand the variety and art of the Psalms

Skills
1 To understand parallelism in the Psalms

2 To appreciate historical context

3 To read Psalms aloud

4 To write a modern psalm

Support Material

Teaching Portfolio
Teacher Backup, p. 83
Usage and Mechanics Worksheet, p. 87
Vocabulary Check, p. 88
Analyzing Literature Worksheet, *Understanding Parallelism in the Bible*, p. 89

Psalm 8

1 O Lord our Lord, how excellent is thy name in all the earth! who hast set thy glory above the heavens.

2 Out of the mouth of babes and sucklings hast thou ordained[1] strength because of thine enemies, that thou mightest still the enemy and the avenger.

3 When I consider thy heavens, the work of thy fingers, the moon and the stars, which thou hast ordained;

4 What is man, that thou art mindful of him? and the son of man, that thou visitest him?

5 For thou hast made him a little lower than the angels, and hast crowned him with glory and honor.

6 Thou madest him to have dominion over the works of thy hands; thou has put all things under his feet;

7 All sheep and oxen, yea, and the beasts of the field;

8 The fowl of the air, and the fish of the sea, and whatsoever passeth through the paths of the seas.

9 O Lord our Lord, how excellent is thy name in all the earth!

---

1. **ordained** (ôr dānd´) *v.*: Decreed; ordered; established.

DAVID COMPOSING THE PSALMS
Illustration in the Paris Psalter
Bibliothèque Nationale, Paris

THINKING ABOUT THE SELECTION

Interpreting

1. The central theme of Psalm 8 is the role of humankind in the creation. (a) In what verse is this theme first sounded? (b) According to the psalmist, what place do humans occupy in relation to heaven and the rest of creation? (c) What does this unique place suggest about the relationship between humans and God?

2. (a) How does the first verse set the tone of the psalm? (b) What is the effect of repeating part of the first verse in the ninth? (c) How is this repeated praise linked to the central theme of the psalm?

Applying

3. In what ways does this psalm draw upon the first chapter of Genesis?

4. This and many other psalms praise God for his mercy and goodness. Why is poetry an especially effective means of expressing praise?

Language Worksheet, *Synonyms and Antonyms*, p. 90
Selection Test, pp. 91–92
Short Answer Unit Test, pp. 93–95
Essay Questions and Evaluation Guidelines, pp. 97–98

Spelling Tip Students may be tempted to spell *raze* as they do *raise* and *statutes* without the third *t*. Write the words on the chalkboard and warn them about these common errors.

---

1 **Discussion** Ask students what the psalmist means by saying that humans are "a little lower than the angels."

ANSWERS TO THINKING ABOUT THE SELECTION

1. (a) This theme is first sounded in verse 4 (accept verse 5, too). (b) Humans are above the rest of the creation and only "a little lower than the angels." (c) This place suggests that humans enjoy a close and unique relationship with God.

2. (a) The first verse sets a tone of fervent praise. (b) Answers will differ. Some students may respond that the repetition rounds out the poem and emphasizes the praise. (c) Answers will differ. Students may respond that since humans have been given so much by God, it is our duty to praise him.

3. In Genesis 1:28 God gives humans "dominion" over creation; this point is reiterated in verse 6 of the psalm.

4. Answers will differ. Students may indicate that poetry "sings" more than prose and so is better suited to solemn and lofty expressions of emotion.

Humanities Note

Fine art, *David Composing the Psalms*. This picture comes from an illustrated French psalm book dating from the tenth century A.D.

You might want to use the following questions to discuss the art:

1. Identify David and explain your choice.

2. (a) What is the mood of this picture? (b) Does it reflect the mood of Psalm 8? Why or why not?

Psalm 19

1 **Literary Focus** Ask students to explain how the first verse is an example of parallelism.

2 **Discussion** Have students evaluate the effectiveness of this figure of speech. Possible criteria for such an evaluation are (1) vividness and (2) ability to surprise without being outlandish.

3 **Discussion** Ask students how this verse marks a transition from what has gone before.

4 **Discussion** Have students identify the adjectives in this verse and ask them how the connotations of these words contribute to the poem.

ANSWERS TO THINKING ABOUT THE SELECTION

1. The first seems to praise God as the creator of the material universe. The second praises his law and judgments.
2. (a) The sun is personified "as a bridegroom" and "as a strong man" running a race. Students may also indicate that the heavens, the firmament, day, and night are personified because the psalmist says they speak. (b) Answers will differ. Some students may respond that the personification of the sun creates a vivid image and dramatizes the praise.
3. The first section deals with the "wordless speech" mentioned; the second deals with the speech or language of the law.
4. (a) The prayer with which the psalm concludes is in verse 13 (also the second part of verse 12). Verse 14 contains the prayer about the prayer. (b) In the first case, the psalmist wants protection from sin. In the second case, the psalmist wants this prayer and the entire psalm to be accepted by God.
5. Answers will differ, but students should support their responses.
6. Answers will differ; however, students should justify their choices.

1 The heavens declare the glory of God; and the firmament showeth his handywork.

2 Day unto day uttereth speech, and night unto night showeth knowledge.

3 There is no speech nor language, where their voice is not heard.

4 Their line[1] is gone out through all the earth, and their words to the end of the world. In them hath he set a tabernacle for the sun,

5 Which is as a bridegroom coming out of his chamber, and rejoiceth as a strong man to run a race.

6 His going forth is from the end of the heaven, and his circuit unto the ends of it: and there is nothing hid from the heat thereof.

7 The law of the Lord is perfect, converting the soul: the testimony of the Lord is sure, making wise the simple.

8 The statutes of the Lord are right, rejoicing the heart: the commandment of the Lord is pure, enlightening the eyes.

9 The fear of the Lord is clean, enduring for ever: the judgments of the Lord are true and righteous altogether.

10 More to be desired are they than gold, yea, than much fine gold: sweeter also than honey and the honeycomb.

11 Moreover by them is thy servant warned: and in keeping of them there is great reward.

12 Who can understand his errors? cleanse thou me from secret faults.

13 Keep back thy servant also from presumptuous sins; let them not have dominion over me: then shall I be upright, and I shall be innocent from the great transgression.[2]

14 Let the words of my mouth, and the meditation of my heart, be acceptable in thy sight, O Lord, my strength, and my redeemer.

---

1. Their line: Their call.

2. transgression (trans gresh´ ən): Sin.

THINKING ABOUT THE SELECTION

Interpreting

1. Scholars have suggested that this psalm combines two originally distinct poems (1–6 and 7–14). How do these poems differ in what they praise?
2. A personification is a figure of speech in which something nonhuman is described in human terms. (a) Identify the personification in the first part (1–6) of the psalm. (b) How does this personification contribute to the praise that the psalmist expresses?
3. The psalm begins by describing a kind of wordless "speech" spoken by different parts of the creation. This image shows that the world, as God created it, holds together in a coherent, vital way. How does each section of this psalm (1–6 and 7–14) deal with a different type of "speech" or "language"?
4. A prayer is a request or plea directed to God. This psalm is unusual because it ends with a prayer *and* a prayer about this prayer. (a) Identify each of these prayers. (b) What is the author requesting of God in each case?
5. Was the author of this psalm successful in unifying the two poems that make it up? Explain.

Applying

6. In ancient times the psalms were set to music. If you wanted to do a modern setting of Psalm 19, which instrument or instruments would you choose? Explain.

Psalm 23

1 The Lord is my shepherd; I shall not want.

2 He maketh me to lie down in green pastures: he leadeth me beside the still waters.

3 He restoreth my soul: he leadeth me in the paths of righteousness for his name's sake.

4 Yea, though I walk through the valley of the shadow of death, I will fear no evil: for thou art with me; thy rod and thy staff they comfort me.

5 Thou preparest a table before me in the presence of mine enemies: thou anointest my head with oil;[1] my cup runneth over.

6 Surely goodness and mercy shall follow me all the days of my life: and I will dwell in the house of the Lord forever.

---

1. **anointest . . . oil:** To put oil on in a ceremony of blessing.

THE GOOD SHEPHERD
Early Christian marble statue, fourth century
Vatican Museum, Rome

---

1 **Discussion** Ask students why the psalmist chose to describe God as a shepherd.

ANSWERS TO THINKING ABOUT THE SELECTION

1. (a) The Lord is compared to a shepherd and the speaker to one of his flock. (b) The metaphor suggests that God cares for and comforts humans as a shepherd does his flock.
2. (a) Answers will differ. Students may indicate that the tone is, for the most part, tranquil and trusting. (b) Answers will differ. Some words that students may cite are "restoreth," "comfort," and "mercy."
3. Answers will differ. Students who agree may assert that the reality of death becomes most vivid in the fourth verse and that the sixth verse resolves the crisis with a final statement of faith and confidence: "I will dwell in the house of the Lord forever." Students who disagree may argue that even though death is mentioned in the fourth verse, the speaker does not feel threatened because of his faith: "I will fear no evil."
4. Answers will differ. Students may choose the first verse because it states the metaphor that is extended in subsequent verses.
5. The story in 1 Samuel 17 suggests that God, working through David, was acting as a good shepherd to defend his people.
6. Answers will differ. Students may respond that the tone of trust and confidence in God's mercy may be responsible for this use of the psalm.

THINKING ABOUT THE SELECTION

Interpreting

1. An **extended metaphor** is one that is developed at length and includes several points of comparison. (a) Identify the extended metaphor in this psalm. (b) What does this metaphor suggest about the relationship between God and humans?
2. In addition to extending the initial metaphor, the psalmist extends and maintains the tone that characterizes the first verse. (a) Describe the tone, or attitude, reflected in every verse of this psalm. (b) Identify the specific words that contribute to this tone.
3. A critic has argued that, although the dominant tone remains constant, the psalm builds to a crisis in the fourth verse, when the psalmist is threatened by death. This crisis is then resolved in the final verses. Do you agree with this observation? Why or why not?
4. Which verse best summarizes the theme of the psalm? Give reasons for your choice.

Applying

5. How does the image of the Lord as a "shepherd" link this poem with the David and Goliath story?
6. Psalm 23 has earned a reputation as the psalm that people recite when they are in life-threatening situations. What may have caused this psalm to be adopted as a prayer of last resort?

Humanities Note

Fine art, *The Good Shepherd*, fourth century A.D. The origin of this Roman statuette is unknown. It may have been part of a column.

The figure wears a shepherd's garment called an *exomis*. His gentle way of holding the lamb on his shoulders contrasts with the strength of his limbs. The waves of his hair are almost ornamental.

You might want to use the following questions to discuss the art:
1. Why do you think the shepherd is holding the lamb?
2. Explain the title of this sculpture.
3. Does this shepherd correspond to your image of David in 1 Samuel 17? Why or why not?
4. Is the mood of this sculpture in keeping with that of Psalm 23? Explain.

Psalm 137

1 Enrichment Tell students that Babylon was located on the Euphrates River. Refer them to the map on page 4.

2 Enrichment Point out to students that this passage mentions at least one musical instrument that was probably used to accompany the psalms. Other accompanying instruments may have been the lyre (*kinnor*) and the pipe (*ugab*). Both of these are mentioned in Genesis 4:21.

3 Discussion Tell students that this is a famous passage. Ask them why it is so memorable. How might this passage, and the Psalm itself, appeal to anyone suffering in exile?

4 Clarification Edom was a kingdom extending from the Dead Sea to Elath on the Gulf of Aqaba. The Edomites were constant enemies of the Israelites, as this passage suggests.

1 By the rivers of Babylon, there we sat down, yea, we wept, when we remembered Zion.

2 We hanged our harps upon the willows in the midst thereof.

3 For there they that carried us away captive required of us a song; and they that wasted us required of us mirth, saying, "Sing us one of the songs of Zion."

4 How shall we sing the Lord's song in a strange land?

5 If I forget thee, O Jerusalem, let my right hand forget her cunning.

6 If I do not remember thee, let my tongue cleave to the roof of my mouth; if I prefer not Jerusalem above my chief joy.

7 Remember, O Lord, the children of Edom[1] in the day of Jerusalem; who said, "Raze it, raze it, even to the foundation thereof."

8 O daughter of Babylon, who art to be destroyed; happy shall he be, that rewardeth thee as thou hast served us.

9 Happy shall be he, that taketh and dasheth thy little ones against the stones.

---

1. Edom (ē′ dəm): An ancient kingdom in southwest Asia, south of the Dead Sea and east of the Jordan River.

Reader's Response *How do the emotions expressed in Psalm 137 differ from those expressed in the other psalms? Were you surprised by the end of Psalm 137?*

PRIMARY SOURCE

The American poet John Hollander has explained how seventeenth- and eighteenth-century English poets who adapted Psalm 137 toned down its violence:

"The famous opening . . . speaks of a condition of exile: . . . The power of the refusal to perform for the captors grows during the subsequent verses. Hanging the harps, . . . on the trees, abandoning familiar and consoling music, is hardly anything but a violent gesture—it is a slamming down of the piano lid, say, or a closing of the instrument case. With the memory of the lost home that follows, the almost violent power continues: . . . The violent conclusion of the psalm with its curse against *batbavel*, the 'daughter of Babylon' (meaning the city itself, not one of its . . . inhabitants), has been generating throughout the poem. But in English Protestant tradition, the opening image became more and more languorous, and the memory of Jerusalem engendered by the scene more and more nostalgic. . . . Sir John Denham wrote, sometime before 1668, 'Our harps to which we lately sang, / Mute as ourselves, on willows hang.' The unfolding theme of abandonment and neglect, rather than positive, outraged refusal to perform, is far from the point of the Hebrew poem, . . ."

Primary Source Note

The critic Robert Alter explains why medieval and Renaissance poets felt more in tune with the Bible than modern poets have.

In certain respects, the Bible was more directly available as a model of poetic emulation in the Middle Ages and the Renaissance because there was a greater congruence then between biblical poetic practice and the prevalent conceptions of the purpose of poetry than has existed since. The Bible, that is, knows nothing of the personal lyric; the anonymity of all but prophetic poetry in the Bible is an authentic reflection of its fundamentally collective nature. . . .

Now, this collective and traditionalist impulse of biblical poetry accorded nicely with a predisposition of Western poets until the Romantic revolution to conceive of their activity as a transmissible craft, the poet aspiring to be a master artisan rather than a daring explorer of the unique experience of the self.

THINKING ABOUT THE SELECTION

Interpreting

1. (a) How does the situation of this psalmist differ from that of the authors of the other psalms? (b) What special problem does this new situation present?
2. (a) In what way are verses 5–9 an answer to the command in verse 3? (b) What is ironic about this "answer"? (c) How are verses 5–9 also an answer to the question in verse 4?
3. Other psalms appeal to God's mercy and goodness? To which qualities of God does this psalm appeal? Why?

Applying

4. (a) How might poetry, like this psalm, be an especially valuable asset to a people in exile? (b) Explain how other songs, for example, Negro spirituals, have served a similar function.

ANALYZING LITERATURE

Understanding Parallelism in the Psalms

Parallelism is a system by which the psalmists state an idea in the first half of a verse and then repeat, negate, complete, or elaborate on it in the second half. In verse 4 of Psalm 8, for instance, the second half repeats and slightly varies the initial idea:

What is man that thou art mindful of him?
and the son of man, that thou visitest him?

1. Explain the type or types of parallelism exhibited in verses 1, 2, 7, 8, and 10 of Psalm 19.
2. (a) Find two examples of parallelism in Psalm 23. (b) Explain how the parallelism in this psalm contributes to its tone.

CRITICAL THINKING AND READING

Appreciating Historical Context

In addition to serving as an eloquent and bitter lament, this psalm gives an insight into the power politics of the ancient Near East. The southern kingdom of Judah—a remnant of the Jewish state founded by King David around 1000 B.C.—was conquered by the Babylonians in 587 B.C. The Babylonians destroyed the great Temple in Jerusalem built by David's son Solomon. They also forced many Jews, like the author of Psalm 137, to leave their native land and take up residence in Babylon and elsewhere. The Babylonian

ruler Nebuchadnezzar II had been angered by the rebelliousness of Judah's kings, and the enforced exile was an attack on Jewish sovereignty. However, the Babylonians did allow the Jews to practice their religion. In fact, many of the historical books of the Old Testament were composed during this period of exile. The Jews were able to return to Jerusalem and rebuild the temple after the Persian ruler Cyrus II defeated the Babylonians in 539 B.C.

1. (a) How are verses 5 and 6 of the psalm a response to the Babylonian attack on Jewish sovereignty? (b) How did subsequent events make the psalm a prophecy as well as a lament?
2. Why do you think a period of exile might inspire a people to write its history?

SPEAKING AND LISTENING

Reading Psalms Aloud

The psalms have played an important role in the service of worship of Jews and Christians. They are therefore meant to be heard. Get together with a small group of classmates and read these psalms to each other. Before you read a psalm aloud, however, review archaic words like "passeth" and "visitest" so that you will be able to pronounce them without stumbling. Also, be aware of the range of tones in the psalm and reflect these in your reading. In Psalm 137, for example, the speaker expresses sadness, ardent devotion, and anger. Finally, decide on the best places to pause. Each verse is a natural unit, but you can vary the pauses between verses to indicate a close relationship between them or to heighten the drama.

THINKING AND WRITING

Writing a Modern Psalm

Write a modern psalm celebrating something or someone worthy of praise. If you are religious, you can imitate the ancient psalmists and write about God. Or if you prefer, celebrate an inspiring person or a landscape that has touched you deeply. Freewrite about your subject; then use phrases and images from this freewriting in your psalm. Like the ancient Hebrew psalmists, divide your poem into separate verses. You might even want to experiment with parallel construction in a few verses. Express your thoughts and feelings in modern language, however. As you revise your psalm, read it aloud to yourself or a classmate to see whether it "sings."

(continued from bottom of page)
the theme of exile. Ask them to compare and contrast this poem with Psalm 137.

ANSWERS TO ANALYZING LITERATURE

1. Verse 1—repetition; verse 2—repetition (possibly completion); verse 7—repetition (possibly completion); verse 8—repetition; verse 10—repetition.
2. (a) Answers will differ. Verse 2 shows repetition with variation. Verse 4 shows completion. (b) Answers will differ. Students may respond that the balance of the parallel line contributes to the calmness and confidence of the tone.

ANSWERS TO CRITICAL THINKING AND READING

1. (a) They reflect a determination to keep that sovereignty alive, at least in memory. (b) Subsequently Babylon was destroyed, as the psalmist had predicted.
2. Answers will differ. Students might respond that exile would encourage a people to reflect on their past and their identity.

THINKING AND WRITING

Writing Across the Curriculum Inform the music department that students are reading these selections. A music teacher can help students select instruments and/or a piece of music to accompany the psalms they have written.

Closure and Extension

ANSWERS TO THINKING ABOUT THE SELECTION

1. (a) This psalmist lived in exile. (b) He must "sing the Lord's song in a strange land."
2. (a) Verses 5–9 can be interpreted as the "song" that is sung in answer to the captors' demand. (b) The an-

swer is ironic in that it calls for the destruction of the captors' empire. (c) Verses 5–9 show that one can sing "the Lord's song in a strange land"—it is a song of bitterness, a prayer for revenge.

3. This psalm appeals to God's judgment and anger. The speaker wants God to avenge the destruction of the Jewish state.

4. (a) Answers will differ. Students may respond that poetry can help a people retain its identity and purpose. (b) Answers will differ. Students may indicate that spirituals helped blacks to endure slavery and preserve their dignity and faith.

Challenge Have students find a contemporary poem dealing with

Presentation

Motivation/Prior Knowledge Tell students that throughout history, people have wondered whether it is possible to live forever or to contact a realm that is unchanging and eternal. These speculations appear in epics, legends, poems, and stories from every era.

1 **Enrichment** Explain to students that Joseph Campbell, from whom the first quotation is taken, was a college professor who became a national celebrity when he was interviewed by Bill Moyers on public television. Ask them whether they have seen or heard about these interviews. (The collected interviews are also a best-selling book.) Then tell them that Campbell studied myths and legends and identified themes and patterns in the myths of many different peoples.

2 **Enrichment** Read the following lines from Wordsworth's "Ode: Intimations of Immortality . . ." and have students speculate about their meaning:

Our birth is but a sleep and a
   forgetting:
The Soul that rises with us, our
   life's Star,
 Hath had elsewhere its setting,
   And cometh from afar:
   Not in entire forgetfulness,
   And not in utter nakedness,
 But trailing clouds of glory do
   we come
 From God, who is our home.

The Quest for Immortality

"I've lost a lot of friends, as well as my parents. A realization has come to me very, very keenly, however, that I haven't lost them. That moment when I was with them has an everlasting quality about it that is now still with me. What it gave me then is still with me, and there's a kind of intimation of immortality in that."

—Joseph Campbell

The ancient Mesopotamians, Egyptians, and Hebrews were all concerned with the theme of immortality: going beyond the limitations of our brief, mortal existence.

In *The Epic of Gilgamesh*, the Mesopotamians depicted a Sumerian king's personal quest for eternal life. By the conclusion of the epic, it is clear that humans must accept the brevity of their lives. As for the afterlife, it may last forever but it is harsh and unpleasant. The Egyptians were more optimistic, however. Their Book of the Dead provides the deceased with instructions for achieving a happy immortality after death. Hebrew culture had still another perspective on immortality. Paradoxically, eternal life was something in the past. As the Bible indicates, Adam and Eve had the opportunity for such an existence in Eden but forfeited this chance when they disobeyed God. The following passages reflect these different views of immortality:

"'What shall I do, O Utnaphishtim, where shall I go? Already the thief in the night has hold of my limbs, death inhabits my room; wherever my foot rests, there I find death.'"

—from *The Epic of Gilgamesh*

"I am Horus, Prince of Eternity, a fire before your faces, . . ."

—from the Egyptian Book of the Dead

"22 And the Lord God said, 'Behold, the man is become as one of us, to know good and evil: and now, lest he put forth his hand, and take also of the tree of life, and eat, and live for ever:

"23 Therefore the Lord God sent him forth from the garden of Eden. . . ."

—from the Bible, Genesis 3:22–23

The quest for immortality is an important theme in other eras as well. Wordsworth, in his famous poem "Ode: Intimations of Immortality," suggested that every individual is born with an intuitive sense of eternal existence but loses this intuition as he or she matures. Joseph Campbell is building on Wordsworth's notion in the first quotation. Campbell hints that immortality is not a life that literally goes on forever but an intuitive sense of something that is "everlasting." Like Gilgamesh we gain immortality through our deeds. As the American poet Henry Wadsworth Longfellow wrote, "Lives of great men all remind us / We can make our lives sublime, / And, departing, leave behind us / Footprints on the sands of time."

Various selections in the book illustrate many different attitudes toward the issue of immortality. Some reflect a literal belief in a life that continues forever, while others view immortality as a sense of timelessness that penetrates our lives at special moments. The following selections all concern immortality in one form or another:

SUGGESTED READINGS

George Lucas

In his *Star Wars* trilogy, director George Lucas acts as a contemporary mythmaker. In his films he combines the latest in Hollywood special effects with traditional devices, themes, and characters from folklore and literature.

GOOD VERSUS EVIL

Lucas drew on an age-old theme in depicting the battle of good and evil. The conflict between Luke Skywalker, the young hero, and the evil Darth Vader recalls the struggle between Gilgamesh and the giant Humbaba in *The Epic of Gilgamesh*. Just as Luke relies on the Force, Gilgamesh puts his faith in the sun god Shamash, symbol of light and justice.

Another ancient conflict that Lucas's films suggest is the struggle between David and Goliath, described in the Bible. Both David and Luke are young and enthusiastic heroes who are fighting against great odds. Their opponents, Goliath and Darth Vader, are older, more experienced warriors, threatening and evil. While Vader may not be quite as large as Goliath, he is tall and menacing. That his face cannot be seen makes him even more sinister. Also, his voice is deep and resonant—Lucas chose the actor James Earl Jones, known for his deep voice, to speak for Vader.

THE HERO'S COMPANIONS

Often in myths, legends, and fairy tales, heroes are accompanied by companions who help them in their quest. In fairy tales these helpers can be animals. For instance, a frog may dive down into a well and find the lost ring for which a hero is searching, or ants may help a heroine gather together grains of rice in an impossibly short time. Lucas humorously updates these traditions by giving Luke the android helpers C3PO and R2D2.

In *The Epic of Galgamesh*, the hero's companion, Enkidu, is not an animal. He is, however, a wild man, someone who has lived very close to nature. Enkidu's knowledge and advice prove valuable to Gilgamesh in the battle with Humbaba. Luke's hairy sidekick, Chewbacca, is a wild man in the tradition of Enkidu. Han Solo, not as beastly as Chewbacca but wild nevertheless, is also an Enkidu-like companion for Luke.

SPIRITUAL ORDEAL AND TRAINING

Traditional heroes and heroines often undergo a spiritual ordeal that prepares them for victory. This ordeal can involve a journey to the underworld to gain special knowledge. In *The Epic of Gilgamesh*, the Sumerian king must cross the waters of death to find Utnapishtim, the man who can teach him about immortality.

Like Gilgamesh, Luke Skywalker journeys to a strange place in search of spiritual knowledge. In order to complete himself, he must discover his true identity. He visits a distant and murky planet to learn about the Force from the Jedi Master Yoda. When his training is complete, he is ready to confront challenges that would defeat an ordinary person.

ANCIENT TRADITIONS, ALIVE AND WELL

Lucas's use of these and other themes from myth and folklore proves that ancient traditions are alive and well, even in the most up-to-date media. Since these themes reflect our deepest concerns, the chances are that they will endure long past the computer age.

Presentation

Motivation/Prior Knowledge Ask students whether they have seen the *Star Wars* trilogy. Have them describe their favorite characters and episodes from these films. Then tell them that many of the themes and character types in this trilogy are drawn from folklore and world literature.

1 Enrichment Remind students of the way in which each of the *Star Wars* films begins: A statement on the screen declares that the events the viewer will see occur in a time and place far removed from our own. Tell them that this type of beginning is similar to the traditional opening of fairy tales: "Once upon a time . . ." By safely distancing the fairy tale from our immediate concerns, this formulaic beginning allows us to hear the tale in a relaxed and receptive frame of mind. Have students speculate about why it might be important to hear or view a story in a relaxed mood.

2 Enrichment Tell students that the medieval romance *Sir Gawain and the Green Knight* describes a trial and ordeal that the hero must undergo. A mysterious knight gives Sir Gawain the opportunity to cut off his head; however, Sir Gawain must repay this favor in a year. Before the tale is over, Gawain's virtue and courage are put to a severe test.

Autobiographical Incident

Writing an Autobiographical Incident

For most of us, our favorite subject is ourselves. We love telling stories about our lives—our successes, our defeats, our joy, our fear. Sometimes we tell the whole truth; sometimes we embroider our stories a little. When we write about something that actually happened to us, we are writing an autobiographical incident. The word *autobiography* is formed from *auto*, meaning self, *bio*, meaning life, and *graph*, meaning writing. An autobiographical incident is a story about something specific that occurred in your life. The incident has a definite beginning, middle, and end. It may have taken two minutes or two days to complete but not longer. In other words, a summer trip to Canada is too long to be an incident.

For example, epics like *Gilgamesh* are based on actual events. Imagine that the real-life king were to tell about his first meeting with Humbaba. He might tell the event in chronological order and also relate his thoughts and feelings. He would be relating an autobiographical incident.

Writing Assignment

Write an autobiographical incident in which you recall a specific time when an event happened that changed you in a way you didn't expect or when you did something that had results other than the ones you expected. Describe the situation that led to the unexpected consequences. It could center on a surprise or an accident. It might involve an unexpected meeting with a stranger who eventually became a close friend. Remember to use sensory details as you describe the incident. Finish your essay with a paragraph describing how you feel about the incident now, and how your perspective on it has changed from the time when the event took place.

Keep in mind the characteristics of this type of writing. Autobiographical incidents should

- Narrate a story with a central incident
- Provide context that orients readers
- Reveal significance by giving insights and reflecting on incidents
- Have voice and style that reveal the writer's personality

Prewrite

Use clustering to help you select an incident to write about. The diagram illustrates several steps for you. First decide on a general time of your life from which the incident will come, making sure it is at a distance from the present so that you can observe it with some perspective. You might choose between seven and ten years old as your time frame. Put "unexpected events" in the center of a sheet of paper and circle the words. Now close your eyes and think back to several surprises or accidents that happened when you weren't expecting such events. Allow your mind to roam freely, letting one memory trigger another one. You may find general categories like "coincidences" to be useful. Consider those as prompts to find specific occurrences. Open your eyes and write down everything that comes to mind around the circled words. When you have filled the paper, read what you wrote and star those memories that made you feel something as you noted them. You may notice that the starred items have something in common. If they do, write that down too. Looking only at the starred memories, pick the one you remember best to write about.

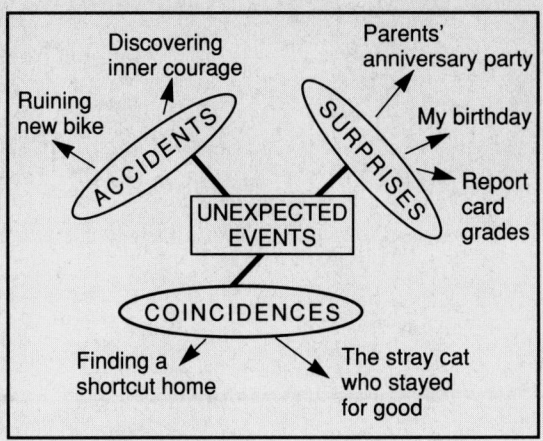

Now think about the specific incident and answer the following questions about it on paper:

- What made the event so memorable?
- What led up to it?
- What made the incident unlikely from the start?
- What sensory details do you recall at that precise time?
- Who were the people with you when the events took place?
- What did you think would change immediately after the event?
- Did your feelings about the event alter with time?
- From your present perspective looking back, how do you feel about it?
- Looking back, what do you think the experience taught you?

Write

Now write your first draft. In your first paragraph, be sure you describe both the unexpected event and what led up to it . While relating the incident, make it vivid by using sights, sounds, tastes, and odors. Name people and places. Give visual de-tails of scenes. Use dialogue. Then explain how you were changed because of this event. Deal with how you were changed immediately following the event. Then explain how a long-range influence has taken time to appreciate.

Collaborate

Ask someone who knows the assignment to read your draft and answer these questions about it.
1. Was the event you described really unexpected?
2. Is your description of it rich in detail?
3. Is it clear how you didn't imagine something like this would happen?
4. Can you distinguish between what you felt about it then and what you feel about it now?
5. Did you clearly state what the incident has meant to your life?

Revise

Rewrite your paper, clarifying all the places your responder found weak. Add vivid words to capture the feelings you had while the coincidence occurred and to depict the feelings you had just afterward. Make your sentences strong and clear.

Before you hand in your work, proofread the final copy.

Publish

You may now wish to share your story with classmates. Choose a partner and exchange the stories you have written. Ask your reader for an honest opinion after the pages are read.

Evaluate

Now consider the paper you finished and the incident it described. As you continue to grow older, do you think the incident will remain important in your life? Will your feelings about it change as you do? You might consider saving the paper to show your children someday.

Clarification Call students' attention to the chart at the top of the page. Tell them that writers sometimes find it helpful to work out their ideas in a visual way. Encourage them to experiment with charts and maps.

Cooperative Learning Pair up students so that they can work together on this phase of the assignment. Have students show their final copy to their partners. You might even want to have students give credit to their partners on the title page; for example, their account might read, "Written by _____; Edited by _____."

Teaching Tenth-Grade Students Tenth-grade students may be interested in reading such autobiographies as Maya Angelou's *I Know Why the Caged Bird Sings* and Richard Rodriguez's *Hunger of Memory.*

Guidelines for Evaluating Writing About Literature Keep in mind the following questions when evaluating students' narratives.
1. Does the student narrate a memorable autobiographical incident?
2. Is the account rich in detail?
3. Does the student show how the event led to unexpected consequences?
4. Does the student include vivid words to describe the feelings aroused by the event and its consequences?
5. Does the account contain any errors in spelling, grammar, or punctuation?

Fine art, *The Court of Gayumarth*. This Persian miniature painting is an illustration from a manuscript made in the city of Shiraz in southern Iran. Like many Persian miniatures, this painting depicts a local ruler surrounded by loyal followers and servants. These figures are skillfully integrated into the surrounding landscape, which extends slightly beyond the borders of the painting. Miniatures such as this one typically portray the Persian landscape as a beautiful, romantic place, filled with exquisite flowers and trees.

Flourishing from the twelfth through the seventeenth centuries, Islamic art is known for its intricate designs. In addition to miniature paintings, Islamic art consists mainly of elaborate rugs and decorative tiles. Despite their deep religious devotion, Islamic artists most frequently focused on secular subjects. When they did choose to depict scenes involving Muhammad, they generally did not show his face. Instead he appeared wearing either a mask or a disguise.

You might want to use the following questions to discuss the art:

1. Which of the figures in this painting is the ruler of Gayumarth?
2. What does this painting suggest about the relationship between the ruler and his court?
3. Islamic paintings such as this one often glorified the reign of a specific ruler. Why might this be the case?
4. How does the scene depicted in this painting compare with your image of Iranian life?

THE COURT OF GAYUMARTH
Arthur M. Sackler Gallery, Smithsonian Institution, Washington, D.C.

Objectives

1. To learn about the history of pre-Islamic Persia
2. To learn about religion in ancient Persia
3. To learn about the rise and the spread of Islam
4. To gain an understanding of the fundamental Islamic beliefs
5. To learn about Persian and Arabic literature

PERSIAN AND ARABIC LITERATURE

c. A.D. 600–A.D. 1400

When the help of God arrives and victory,
And you see human beings entering God's religion
   in hordes,
Then recite the praises for your Lord and seek
   forgiveness of Him.
Indeed, He is relenting.

—Koran, Chapter 110

Focus

Historical Background The Persian and the Arabic people have a long and glorious history. The most significant event in this history is undoubtedly the rise and the spread of the Islamic religion. Prior to the rise of Islam, the Persians practiced an ancient religion known as Zoroastrianism. This religion has almost completely disappeared, however, and today the vast majority of people from this region practice Islam.

Just as Islam has played a major role in the daily lives of most Arabs and Persians, it has had a dramatic impact on Persian and Arabic literature. As students will soon discover, the fundamental beliefs of Islam are evident in most Persian and Arabic literature.

Explain to students that the information about Persian and Arabic history, culture, and religion in this introduction will help them to understand and to appreciate the selections in this unit.

Writing to Learn Have students write a journal entry about their perceptions of life in the Middle East and of the Persian (Iranian) and the Arabic peoples. They should also discuss the sources of their perceptions. As they move through this unit, encourage them to look back at their journal entries and explore the ways in which their perceptions may have changed.

ESL Teaching Strategy If you have any Persian or Arabic students in your class, encourage them to share their knowledge of Persian and Arabic culture, history, and religion with their classmates. This may help to remove any misconceptions that native-speaking students may have about Persian and Arabic people.

Teaching Tenth-Grade Students Many of your tenth-grade students may be taking world history at the same time they are studying world literature. Encourage them to consult their history teachers and their history textbooks to learn more about Persian and Arabic history, culture, and religion.

Motivation/Prior Knowledge Ask students if they have any prior knowledge of Persian and Arabic history, culture, and religion. If they do, encourage them to share what they know with their classmates. If they do not, tell them that they are about to be led on a journey back in time to a distant land—ancient Persia. Explain that they will explore the foundations of Persian society, learn about the rise and fall of the Persian Empire, and delve into the fundamental Islamic beliefs.

Finally have students discuss why it is important to learn about other cultures, such as those of the Persians and the Arabs.

Purpose-Setting Question What are the fundamental beliefs of Islam? What is the role of Islam in Persian and Arabic life? How are Islamic beliefs reflected in Persian and Arabic literature?

1 Enrichment Tell students that the Persians conquered Babylon in 539 B.C. Unlike the Assyrians, who had conquered the city less than two centuries earlier, the Persians left Babylon intact, and it remained a center of commerce and education.

2 Enrichment Tell students that the provinces were known as *satrapies*. To keep the satrapies in check, the Persian rulers appointed people to inspect the provinces at regular intervals.

Over 800 million people in the world today follow the religion of Islam. Spreading from Morocco on the Atlantic Ocean to the island of Mindanao in the Pacific and from the tropical forests of West Africa to the arid steppes of Central Asia, Muslims (followers of Islam) comprise a mosaic of cultures and a myriad of linguistic groups. Yet, for most of their 1,500 years as a religious community, Muslims have relied almost entirely on two languages to express their ideas and record their history. These languages are Persian and Arabic.

PRE-ISLAMIC PERSIA

Origins of the Persian Culture

Sometime after 2000 B.C., a group of Aryan tribes, who had migrated from southern Russia, reached the mountainous region that is now known as Iran and used to be known as Persia. According to archeological evidence, this region had already been inhabited for several thousand years. Yet, because the Aryan tribes were far more advanced than the people who lived in the region at the time of their arrival, they were able to overwhelm the native population and seize control of the land.

The tribal group that settled in Persis, or Pars, a region of central Iran bordering on the Persian Gulf, eventually emerged as one of the most powerful forces in the ancient Middle East. It is from this region that the name *Persian* is derived, and it was among this group of people that the Persian language first evolved.

THE PERSIAN EMPIRE

During the latter half of the sixth century B.C., the Persian king Cyrus the Great began a series of conquests that led to the establishment of a vast and powerful empire. By the time of Cyrus's death in 529 B.C., the Persian Empire stretched from the border of India to Asia Minor and from the edge of Egypt to the coasts of the Black Sea and the Caspian Sea. Cyrus's son-in-law, Darius I, extended the boundaries even farther by conquering Egypt, Afghanistan, and northern India.

DARIUS DYING COMFORTED BY ALEXANDER WHILE ASSASSINS ARE HANGED
From the "Book of Omens"
Musée d'art et d'histoire, Geneve

The Persians proved to be remarkably adept at retaining order throughout their huge empire. They divided the empire into twenty provinces, each with its own governor, who collected taxes and administered the Persian code of laws. To connect these provinces, they built a sophisticated road system and established relay stations with fresh horses along the main roads. By doing so, the Persians made it possible for royal messengers to cover up to 1,500 miles in just ten days.

Another reason for the success of the Persian Empire was the tolerance with which the Persians treated conquered peoples. Not only did they allow conquered peoples to retain some degree of political freedom, but they also showed respect for native customs and religions. By showing this type of tolerance, the Persians were able to minimize dissent and reduce the chance of rebellion.

Despite the effectiveness and tolerance of its rulers, the Persian Empire lasted for only about two centuries. Weakened by its unsuccessful attempts to conquer Greece, the Persian Empire fell to the forces of Alexander the Great in 331 B.C.

RELIGION IN ANCIENT PERSIA

Although the Persian Empire was short-lived, its official state religion, Zoroastrianism, continued to thrive long after its downfall. This religion was founded during the seventh century B.C. by a great teacher named Zarathustra (660? B.C.–583? B.C.), called Zoroaster by the Greeks. After first taking hold in Zoroaster's native land of Balkh (in modern Afghanistan), Zoroastrianism spread throughout the Persian Empire and was made the state religion in about 500 B.C. It remained the dominant Persian religion for over a thousand years, until it was replaced by Islam in the seventh century A.D. Today, Zoroastrianism is practiced by only a handful of people living in India and Pakistan and in remote mountainous regions of Iran and Afghanistan.

Unlike Judaism, Christianity, and Islam, which are monotheistic religions, the underlying philosophy of Zoroastrianism is one of dualism. Zoroaster taught that the world is governed by two opposing gods—Ahura Mazda, or Ormazd, the god of goodness, wisdom, and truth, and Ahriman, the spirit of evil—who are engaged in an enduring battle in which Ahura Mazda will ultimately prevail. According to Zoroaster, people who follow Ahura Mazda and live a life of purity will be rewarded at death with an eternal life in paradise. In contrast, those who follow Ahriman will be condemned to eternal suffering.

THE RISE OF ISLAM

Islam originated during the sixth century A.D. in an area of the Arabian Peninsula that is now part of Saudi Arabia. At the time, most of the Middle East was controlled by either Persia or the Byzantine Empire, two powerful forces that had been at

3 Enrichment Inform students that the sacred book of Zoroastrianism was a collection of hymns and religious poems known as the *Zend Avesta*.

Using the Map
Have students study the map and ask them the following questions:
1. How many miles wide and how many miles long was the Persian Empire at its height?
2. Given the difficulties of long-distance travel at the time, why might it have been difficult for the Persians to maintain control of such a large empire?
3. Why do you think the Persians chose to run the Royal Road from the Persian Gulf to the Mediterranean Sea?
4. What are some of the countries in today's world that are located in the area of the Persian Empire?

The Persian Empire at Its Height

respected historical figures?
4. What emotions does this painting evoke in you? Why?

Persian and Arabic
(c. 600–1400)

Relief, Darius I,
king of ancient Persia

Leaf of Koran, the sacred
book of Islamic religion
*The Metropolitan Museum
of Art, New York*

Pictured from left to right:

Darius I (c. 550–486 B.C.), also known as Darius the Great, was king of ancient Persia from 522 B.C. until his death. Darius took part in the murder of King Bardiya of Persia and seized the throne in 522 B.C. He is pictured here with a Mede official paying homage to him. Darius ruled his vast empire by dividing it into twenty *satrapies,* or provinces. Each province was ruled by satraps, who were responsible only to the Great King. They were checked by generals, ministers of home affairs, and secret police, all of whom were solely accountable to Darius. Darius attempted and failed to conquer Greece in 492 B.C.; he tried and failed again in 490 B.C. He died before he could organize another invasion. Darius was succeeded by his son Xerxes I.

The Koran, which means "something to be recited," is the sacred book of the Islamic religion. According to tradition, the angel Gabriel revealed the Koran (page 108) to Muhammad a little at a time. The revelations began in A.D. 610 and continued until Muhammad's death in 632. This picture shows a leaf from the Koran written in kufic calligraphy. Kufic is an early Arabic alphabet, characterized by its angular letters.

Persia (now Iran), which is bounded by mountains and deserts, provided a plethora of subjects from nature for artists. This bronze lion probably came from the mountainous Luristan (the area that is now western Iran), dating from sometime between 1200 and 700 B.C. During this period artists produced small bronze objects most often depicting animals. By whom and for whom these animal-style bronzes were produced remain a mystery.

---

600   **800**

HISTORY

- Persians take Damascus and Jerusalem; take Holy Cross as booty
- Persians overrun Egypt
  - Damascus becomes capital of the caliphs
  - Arabs destroy Persian Empire; caliphs rule country until 1258
    - The Omayyads become caliphs
      - Arabs conquer Spain
      - Abbasids wipe out Omayyads, obtaining caliphate
      - Arab capital is moved from Damascus to Baghdad

- Arabs sack Rome, damage Vatican
  - Arabs conquer Sicily, make Palermo the captial
    - Asmanid rule in Persia begins
    - Arabs are expelled from central Italy
      - Arabs found Algiers

HUMAN PROGRESS

- Muhammad experiences vision on Mt. Hira
  - Muhammad flees to Medina
  - Muhammad begins dictating the Koran
    - Caliphs organize first news service
      - Arab coinage begins
      - The Great Mosque at Damascus is built

- Golden period of Arabic learning takes place
  - Persian writes book on mathematical equations; term *algebra* is coined
  - School of Astronomy is established at Baghdad
    - Arabs perfect astrolabe

- Persian period of great watercolor painters begins
  - Prime of Arab art, science, and philosophy
    - Arabs bring mathematical notation to Europe

LITERATURE

- Arabs find the famous library with 300,000 papyrus scrolls in Alexandria
- Book-copying industry at Alexandria is destroyed by Arabs
  - Koran is put into 114 chapters

- Earliest records of Persian poetry and literature
  - Augustan Age of Arabian Literature begins
    - Academy of Translations in Baghdad is founded
      - *Hamasa,* collection of Arabian legends, proverbs, and heroic tales, is written
        - Tales of *The Thousand and One Nights* begin
          - Firdawsi is born

Persian bronze
perfume burner

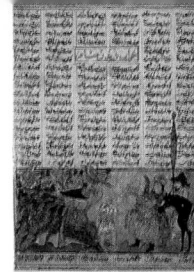

Leaf of the
Persian
epic the
Shah-nama
The Metropolitan
Museum of Art,
New York

Silk medallion rug
*National Gallery of
Art, Washington D.C.*

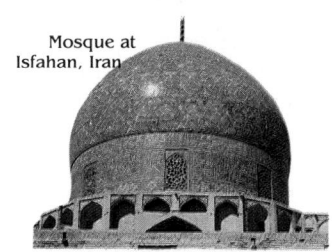

Mosque at
Isfahan, Iran

000   **1200**   **1400**

- Arabs sack Pisa
  - Arabs conquer Sardinia
    - Pisa takes Sardinia from Arabs

- Genghis Khan conquers Persia

- Timur begins successful campaign to Persia

- Arabs become court physicians in Germany
  - Arabs in Spain manufacture paper

- Arab geographical encyclopedia is written
  - Arab geographer explores Sahara Desert

- Firdawsi: *Shah-nama*
  - Firdawsi dies
    - Omar Khayyám is born
- Omar Khayyám dies
  - Sa'Di is born
    - Djelaleddin Rumi is born
- Sa'Di: *The Fruit Garden*
  - Djelaleddin Rumi dies
    - Sa'Di dies
      - Odes Hafiz is born
        - Odes Hafiz dies

The Persian epic the *Shah-nama* (the Book of Kings) was written by Firdawsi (c.940–1020). It is a fictitious account of Persia's rulers throughout the existence of the Persian empire. This page, taken from the original epic, depicts Zal's meeting with his father, Sam. The epic continues with this family line in the excerpt from the *Shah-nama*, page 89. Rustam and his son Suhrab, who are the principal characters in the excerpt, are the descendents of Sam and Zal: Sam is Rustam's grandfather and Zal is his father. Firdawsi completed his epic in 1010.

The Arabs and Persians share a love of portable, richly decorated objects. When the nomads' art of rug making merged with the forms and materials accumulated by craftsmen, the decorative arts reached a peak of lavishness that has lasted throughout history. This Persian silk medallion rug, dated the second half of the sixth century, is one example of the rich art that has been produced in the Near East.

The imperial mosque at Isfahan (1585–1612), pictured here, represents the climax of Persian mosque design. Mosques are large buildings used for worship by members of the Muslim faith. They contain a *mihrab,* or decorated niche, which indicates the direction of the holy city Mecca and the direction one must face to worship. Many mosques also contain a *mimbar,* or pulpit, which is entered by a flight of stairs. Mosques are decorated with abstract and geometric shapes in keeping with the prohibition against imitating God's works.

4 Enrichment Explain to students that the Arabian Peninsula is now divided into a number of countries, including Jordan, Saudi Arabia, Yemen, and Oman.

5 Learning Across the Curriculum Have students conduct research to learn more about the Arabian climate and the traditional way of life of the Arab people. Then hold a class discussion about the ways in which the Arabian climate may have shaped the traditional Arabian way of life.

6 Enrichment Students can learn more about Islam by consulting the Guide for Interpreting on page 107.

7 Enrichment Tell students that the first caliph, named Abu Bakr, was a close friend of Muhammad's.

war for over a century. The Arabian Peninsula, however, remained independent from these two powers. The peninsula was divided into two parts, South Arabia (modern-day Yemen) and North Arabia (the rest of the peninsula), which were culturally and linguistically distinct from each other. For several centuries South Arabia had enjoyed a more advanced civilization. Yet by the sixth century, it was in decline, largely as a result of the decreased importance of sea trade and the slow decay of its agricultural system.

North Arabia, on the other hand, had become a vital part of the overland trade routes between Western Europe and Asia. Camel caravans led by foreign traders carried goods across North Arabia. Some of the Arabs engaged in trade with the foreigners, and through the foreigners they learned about other lands and other cultures. The majority of Arabs, however, had little contact with the foreigners and retained their traditional way of life. For centuries most Arabs had led a nomadic existence, traveling about the arid landscape with flocks of sheep or camels. They were loosely organized into tribes and practiced a variety of ancient tribal religions.

Muhammad, the founder of Islam, was born in A.D. 572 in Mecca, a large town on the trade route between Europe and Asia. At the time Mecca was a city of extremes, where the rich lived in opulent luxury and the poor lived in hopelessness and despair. Profoundly disturbed by these conditions, Muhammad frequently retreated to a mountain cave to meditate. At the age of forty, he had an experience during one of his retreats that dramatically changed his life. He believed that the angel Gabriel came to him and told him that he had been chosen to serve as God's prophet. Muhammad continued to receive such revelations throughout the rest of his life, and he recited them to his followers. After his death, the revelations he had received were arranged into a book called the Koran, which became the sacred scripture of all Muslims.

The central message of the Koran is that there is a single, unique God who is the creator and sustainer of all things. This God is called Allah, which literally means "the God" in Arabic. According to the Koran, it is the duty of all Muslims to submit their wills to Allah, because he is not only their creator and sustainer but is also the one who will judge them at death. This duty is evident in the fact that the word *Islam* actually means "submission."

There are several other duties that are essential to the Islamic faith. Together with the duty of recognizing and submitting to Allah, these duties are known as the Five Pillars of Islam. The second duty requires all Muslims to turn toward the holy city of Mecca and pray five times a day. Muslims are also expected to perform acts of charity. The fourth duty involves fasting during the holy month of Ramadan. Finally, all Muslims are supposed to make at least one pilgrimage to Mecca during their lifetimes.

Although Muhammad taught people to recognize Allah as the only God, he did not discount the principles of Judaism and Christianity. Instead, he believed that these other religions were part of a series of religions sent by God to guide human beings toward good. As a result, Muslims consider both the Torah and the New Testament to be divine scriptures. Yet at the same time, they believe that Islam is the final religion in the series and view it as the perfect religion. Related to this notion is the Muslim belief that Muhammad was the last in a long series of prophets, starting with Adam and including Moses and all of the other prophets mentioned in the Bible.

The Spread of Islam

Because Muhammad also preached the importance of establishing a just and pious society on earth, his message had great appeal among the poor and downtrodden people in Arabian towns such as Mecca and Medina. These people converted to Islam in large numbers, enabling Muhammad to assemble an army of loyal followers. With the support of his followers, Muhammad was able to overpower his enemies and spread his message throughout the Arabian Penninsula.

By the time of Muhammad's death in 632, all of Arabia had been united into an Islamic nation. The leaders of this nation were Muhammad's closest advisers, who were known as caliphs. The caliphs shared Muhammad's belief that Islam was a religion meant not just for Arabs but for the entire human race. Prompted by this belief, they sent out Arab armies to conquer surrounding lands and spread the ideas of Islam throughout the world. Due to the remarkable success of these armies, the Islamic world expanded at a speed unrivaled in world history. Over a period of only several decades, the Arab armies established a massive Islamic empire that extended from Spain and North Africa to Central Asia.

The Islamic religion quickly took hold among the various groups that the Arabs conquered. While some people were forced to convert by the Arab armies, many others did so voluntarily because they were attracted to the teachings of this new religion. Still others became Muslims because they viewed conversion as a means of social and economic advancement in the new empire.

THE BLENDING OF CULTURES

Although they were deeply committed to the idea of converting people to Islam, the Arab leaders did not try to force people to abandon their cultural traditions and beliefs. Instead, the Arabs themselves embraced much of the heritage of their conquered peoples, at the same time as these people were embracing elements of Arab culture. This blending of heritages resulted in the establishment of a vibrant and diverse Islamic civilization, remarkably rich in cultural traditions.

Because Arabic was the official language of Islam, however, it became the dominant language throughout the empire. Although common people continued to use their native languages in their daily lives, Arabic became firmly established as the language of government, scholarship, and literature. By the ninth century, however, some writers had started experimenting with the public use of Persian,

and soon the use of Persian became widespread throughout the eastern Islamic world. Eventually it supplanted Arabic in all areas of life except religious affairs. Although other languages also reemerged in the following centuries, Persian continued to enjoy a position of prominence because of its beauty. This quality is reflected in the Turkish saying, "Arabic is for praying, Turkish is for cursing, and Persian is for courtship."

PERSIAN AND ARABIC LITERATURE

Because of the prominent status of both Persian and Arabic, it is not surprising that a large body of literature exists in each of the two languages. As a result of the blending of cultural traditions that occurred in the Islamic Empire, Persian and Arabic literature share many of the same characteristics. Yet there are also important differences between the two bodies of literature.

Arabic Literature

By the time of Muhammad's birth, the Arabs already possessed a large body of poetry. For centuries, poets from all over Arabia had gathered at first to recite odes (called *qasidas*) praising their own tribe or making fun of others. Although these poems were seldom written down, they were committed to memory by generations of people who appreciated them for the depth of their emotion and the beauty of their imagery. The following is a brief passage from a typical early Arabic poem:

> Your eyes do not shed a tear, except to
>   shatter
> With their lances, the pieces of a broken
>   heart.
>   —from the *Mu'allaqa* of Imru'l-Qays

8 **Enrichment** Explain to students that most of the people in the areas conquered by the Muslim armies were not forced to convert to Islam. Yet non-Muslims living in conquered territories were required to pay a special tax.

9 **Enrichment** Tell students that during the eleventh century the Seljuk Turks invaded the Islamic Empire. Although they had recently converted to Islam, the Seljuk Turks were a warlike people known for their cruelty and mercilessness. When they conquered Palestine in 1071, they showed little tolerance for the Christians and Jews who lived there. In addition it is believed that they tortured many Christian pilgrims who had traveled to Palestine to visit sacred shrines. The intolerance of the Seljuk Turks was the main cause of the First Crusade (1096–1099), in which a massive army of Christian knights traveled to the Middle East, seized control of Jerusalem, and set up four small feudal states in Palestine and Syria.

10 **Enrichment** Tell students that the Islamic Empire was invaded again in the thirteenth century. This time the invaders were the Mongols, who established a massive empire that stretched all the way across China. Later the Ottoman Turks conquered Egypt, Syria, Iraq, and Arabia and established a new Islamic state known as the Ottoman Empire—an empire that lasted until 1918.

Humanities Note

Interior of the Mosque at Córdoba, Spain. The mosque at Córdoba is considered the most magnificent of all the mosques in Spain. The construction of the building began in 785 after the Islamic armies invaded Spain. Because of the continuing growth of the Islamic population, the building was continually being expanded until the end of the tenth century. Although its design is based primarily on the fundamentals of Islamic architecture, its system of two-story arcades forming long aisles may have been inspired by ancient Roman aqueducts that had been built in Spain hundreds of years earlier.

You might want to use the following questions to discuss the art:
1. What can you infer from this picture about the relationship between art and religion in Islamic society?
2. How do you envision the exterior of the mosque at Córdoba? Why?

Even after the rise of Islam, Arabs continued to appreciate such poetry. The works of pre-Islamic poets were committed to paper, and new poets continued to write poetry very similar to the magnificent odes of their predecessors. Arabic prose also began to develop, although the earliest works were religious in nature and dealt, either directly or indirectly, with the text of the Koran. However, as Islamic civilization became increasingly advanced, prose writers expanded into the fields of history, philosophy, and science. Fiction also began to be written, and some of the fictional works produced during the eleventh century are still considered to be among the finest examples of Arabic prose.

In addition to reading works of scholarly and ornate prose, the Islamic Arabs also enjoyed listening to fables and folk tales. Many anonymous collections of such stories exist, but the one entitled *The Thousand and One Nights* (pages 128–134) is by far the most famous. In fact, this collection has become so popular in the Western world that it is probably the most famous of all Arabic works of literature.

PERSIAN LITERATURE

The vibrant literary heritage of the Persian people extends all the way back to the days of the Persian Empire. Yet in the centuries immediately following the Islamic conquest, virtually no literature was written in the Persian language. During the ninth century, however, Persia experienced a literary renaissance that lasted for several hundred years.

Although they also produced historical and geographical works, the Persian prose writers of this period concentrated mainly on books that dealt with ethics and morals. Some of these works—including the *Gulistan*, or "Rose Garden," and the *Bustan*, or "Fruit Garden," by the famous poet and thinker Sa'di (pages 112– 116)—offered moral advice to the general public. Other books offered advice to kings and princes on the nature of virtuous government.

Although there are a number of successful works of Persian prose, the form of literature for which Persia is best known is poetry. Like Arabia, Persia had a longstanding tradition of poetry, which had been used in pre-Islamic times as a means of preserving Persian history. While this type of poetry disappeared in the aftermath of the Islamic conquest, many Persians continued to feel a strong sense of patriotism and longed to retain their national heritage. As a result, during the ninth and tenth centuries, several poets attempted to write epic poems describing Persian history. The most famous of these poems, the *Shah-nama*, or "Epic of Kings," by Firdawsi (pages 89–97), is still considered a national treasure in Iran.

Aside from Firdawsi's epic, the finest poems of the Persian literary renaissance were lyrics. These lyrics reflected the influence of the lighthearted love poetry of the nomadic Arabs. Yet, unlike their Arab predecessors, the Persian lyric poets used complex rhyme schemes and rhythmical patterns.

Another Persian poetic form, the rubái, has been immortalized in the Western world through the translation of *The Rubáiyát*, a collection of verse by the Persian scientist and poet Omar Khayyám. Ironically, this short four-line poetic form was not highly regarded in classical Persian literary circles, and Khayyám was not a widely respected poet.

THE NIGHTINGALE'S LAMENT

Many of the most gifted Persian poets were members of an Islamic sect known as Sufism. The followers of Sufism, known as Sufis, were people who had withdrawn from society to live solitary lives of worship and piety in the hope of achieving a sense of oneness with Allah. The Sufis' attachment to Allah was similar to being in love and caused them to experience such feelings as intoxication, bliss, and pain. Such emotions naturally lend themselves to poetry, and many Sufis, including Sa'di and Hafiz (page 110), and Rumi (page 120), wrote exquisite verses expressing their spiritual feelings in the language of love. These poets often compared themselves to a nightingale that cries out its feelings of love for an inaccessible rose, couched in its bed of thorns.

PERSIAN AND ARABIC VOICES

Praise belongs to God, the Lord of all Being,
the All-merciful, the All-compassionate,
the Master of the Day of Doom.
Thee only we serve. . . .
> **the Koran**

God changes not what is in a people,
until they change what is in themselves.
> **the Koran**

The present life is naught but a diversion and a sport;
surely the Last Abode is Life, did they but know.
> **the Koran**

Come, fill the Cup, and in the fire of Spring
The Winter garment of Repentance fling:
The Bird of Time has but a little way
To fly—and Lo! the Bird is on the Wing.
> **Omar Khayyám,** *The Rubáiyát*

Then Rustam choked, his heart was full of fire,
His eyes of tears. He mounted quick as dust
And came with lamentations to the host
In grievous consternation of his deed.
> **Firdawsi,** the *Shah-nama*

Thee I choose, of all the world, alone;
Wilt thou suffer me to sit in grief?
My heart is as a pen in thy hand,
Thou art the cause if I am glad or melancholy.
> **Rumi**

Return! that to a heart wounded full sore
Valiance and strength may enter in; return!
And Life shall pause at the deserted door. . . .
> **Hafiz**

When eating little has become the nature of a man
He takes it easy when a calamity befalls him.
But when the body becomes strong in affluence
He will die when a hardship overtakes him.
> **Sa'di,** the *Gulistan*

Additional Voices

Wealth and children are the adornment of this present life: but good works, which are lasting, are better in the sight of thy Lord as to recompense.

—The Koran

He makes night seep into the day,
and makes the day seep into the night;
He has subordinated the sun and the moon,
making each of them journey toward a preordained time.

—The Koran

Ah Love! could you and I with Him conspire
To grasp this Sorry Scheme of Things entire,
Would not we shatter it to bits–and then
Remold it nearer to the Heart's Desire!

—**Omar Khayyám**, *The Rubáiyát*

I am a painter, a maker of pictures; every moment I shape a beauteous form,
And then in thy presence I melt them all away.

—**Rumi**

As the tulip shrinks from the cold night air,
So shrank my heart and quailed in the shade . . .

—**Hafiz**

"Drama, comedy, tragedy—all are here," says one scholar of the *Shah-nama*, or *Book of Kings*, the national epic of the Persian people. Since its composition, it has held a special place in Persian society. So important is it that people name their children after characters in this epic, and every Persian who has attended school has read at least a portion of the book. Just as Western students are expected to know Shakespeare and the Bible, Persian students were well versed in the tales of the *Shah-nama*.

Firdawsi (940–1020)

Abu'l-Qasim Firdawsi (ab yōol kā sēm fir dou´ sē) was born in the Persian city of Tus. Because his family belonged to the landed gentry, he had enough money to receive an education and pursue his own interests for most of his life, though he was never extremely rich.

Like other members of his class, Firdawsi was deeply patriotic and was familiar with Persian history. After conducting a great deal of research, he began to write his own history in the form of an epic poem called the *Shah-nama*. He did not fabricate the story in this book, nor did he invent the name. The story was the mythic history of Persia commonly known at this time, and several versions of it had already been called the *Shah-nama*. Yet Firdawsi told this story in a way that surpassed any earlier rendition, and it became the standard version of this national epic.

A National Identity

Iran had been conquered by the Arabs less than two centuries before Firdawsi's birth. Al-though most Persians had converted to Islam by this time, many of them resented the degree to which Arabic words and customs were pervading Persian society. Many people, particularly members of the landed gentry, collected histories of pre-Islamic Persia in order to preserve their sense of national identity.

In writing his *Shah-nama*, Firdawsi made a conscious attempt to avoid using the Arabic words that had entered the Persian vocabulary and were threatening to permanently corrupt the Persian language. For this reason Firdawsi has been credited with rescuing Persian from decay and the *Shah-nama* has come to be seen as the model for a pure Persian style of writing.

The Problem of Money

Firdawsi used all his financial resources in the research and writing of the *Shah-nama*. He then sought out financial support from many of the wealthy people of Tus, but even this did not prove to be enough. As a result, he began looking for financial patronage outside of Tus, and his search led him to Sultan Mahmud (mah´ mood), who ruled much of Persia as well as parts of central Asia and India from his capital of Ghazna (gaz´ na) in Afghanistan. Sultan Mahmud was a patron of the arts. Since he had gathered a large number of scholars and artists at his court, it was not surprising that Firdawsi would hope to be well received in Ghazna. The Sultan apparently agreed to pay Firdawsi handsomely for completing the *Shah-nama* but apparently changed his mind when a minister who had befriended Firdawsi fell out of favor.

FIRDAWSI (far left)
*Manuscript illumination
by Mirza Ali*

More About the Author It is believed that Firdawsi worked on the *Shah-nama* for thirty-five years. Given the fact that the epic consists of more than 60,000 couplets, it certainly seems possible that this could be true. Have students discuss what might motivate a writer to work on a single work for such a long period of time. What qualities must a writer possess to devote so much time to one work?

Cultural Note You might want to encourage your students to locate a copy of Matthew Arnold's poem and to compare and contrast it with Firdawsi's tale. You can then either have student volunteers present their findings to the class, or you can hold a class discussion about the similarities and differences between the two works.

Legend has it that when Firdawsi traveled to Ghazna to receive payment for the *Shah-nama*, Sultan Mahmud gave him only half of the agreed sum. Firdawsi was so disappointed that he distributed the money among three attendants at a bathhouse and immediately left Ghazna for the court of a Persian prince named Shahriyar (shä′ rē yär). This prince was a vassal of Mahmud who, wishing to avoid any trouble with his lord, paid Firdawsi handsomely for his epic on the condition that he still dedicate it to Mahmud. Firdawsi agreed to this condition and took the money, then returned to his home town, where he remained for the last ten years of his life.

The *Shah-nama*

The *Shah-nama* is presented as a history of Persia from the beginning of the world until the conquest of Iran by the Arabs. Since many of the early events occurred before the development of written history, much of the work is drawn from Persian myths and legends. This does not mean that Firdawsi believed he was writing a fictional work, however, since from his perspective and that of his readers the mythic events had actually occurred.

A Struggle Between Good and Evil

The *Shah-nama* is a description of the creation of the world, followed by a portrayal of how the earliest kings of Persia fought the demons of darkness and provided human beings with the basis of civilization. The war between these good kings and the forces of evil continues for over a thousand years. Then King Faridum (fa′ ri d'm) appears and divides the world among his three sons, Iraj (i räj′), Tur (t$\overline{oo}$r), and Salm (sälm). Iraj, the ruler of Persia, is murdered by his brothers. This starts a long and bloody cycle of wars between the Persians and the people of Turan, a land generally identified with the territory of the Turks. The centuries-long struggle forms the background of the *Shah-nama*.

After the description of many legendary dynasties, the epic ends with a description of the reign of Yazdigird (yaz′ di g'rd), the last pre-Islamic ruler of Iran, whose armies were defeated by the Arabs in the middle of the eighth century.

Rustam and Suhrab

The historical narrative serves as a canvas on which Firdawsi has painted some incomparably beautiful and moving stories of romance, intrigue, bravery, cowardice, triumph, and defeat. The most important hero of the entire work is the warrior Rustam (rus′ tam), a mythic figure who appears intermittently over a period of three centuries. The tragic episode of Rustam's confrontation with his son, Suhrab (sə′ räb), is perhaps the most widely read part of the *Shah-nama*. This episode was popularized in the English-speaking world by the English poet Matthew Arnold (1822–1888), who, in 1853, adapted it into an English poem entitled "Suhrab and Rustam."

Focus

Reading Critically The information on this page will help students to read critically Persian and Arabic literature. Discuss the information on this page with your students. Explain that the selection on the following pages is a model for reading critically. The notes in the side column are designed to help students place the selection in its historical, cultural, and literary contexts. Have students read the selection through, commenting on the selection as they read it actively.

Before students begin reading, however, you may want to emphasize that unlike the other selections in this unit, this selection depicts Persia before the rise of Islam. Consequently the selection contains no Islamic elements. In contrast, most of the other selections in the unit are flooded with the teachings of Islam. Urge students to keep this difference in mind as they work their way through the unit.

To give students further practice in the process of reading critically, use the selection in the Teaching Portfolio, "When As My Wailing Is Heard" by Hafiz, page 109, following the Teacher Backup, which students can annotate themselves. Encourage students to use these strategies as they read the rest of the literature in this unit.

Cultural Context If students want to know more about the ancient Persian religion Zoroastrianism, direct their attention to page 79 of the unit introduction.

Persian-Arabic Literature

Historical Context

Persian legend tells us that before the Arab conquest of Iran, the Persians were engaged in a longstanding war with the people of Turan, or the Turkmans. This episode from the *Shah-nama* takes place during the reign of a legendary Persian king named Kaus, at a time when the struggle between the Persians and the Turkmans was raging. In early wars armies commonly sent their best warriors to fight one another in single combat as a means of settling disputes quickly and possibly avoiding a full-scale war. For these reasons the events depicted in the following episode are by no means unrealistic.

Cultural Context

The *Shah-nama* depicts Persia before the Islamic religion of the Arabs became the guiding force in the lives of most Persian people. A central concept of the ancient Persian religion was the battle between good and evil. Evil was seen as a force almost equal to good. Even though the correct moral course for all people was to fight evil at all times, the triumph of good over evil was not guaranteed. In the following episode, Firdawsi depicts this struggle and demonstrates its potentially tragic outcome.

Literary Context

The *Shah-nama* of Firdawsi is an outstanding example of an epic poem. The stories recorded in this work were not invented by Firdawsi, but rather had been known to the Persians for a long time. Firdawsi organized these earlier stories into one long work, using the purest form of the Persian language he knew and all the patriotic zeal he could muster. These two factors have combined to establish the *Shah-nama* as the foremost symbol of Persian national identity and one of the finest examples of Persian literature. Some of the characters who march across the pages of the *Shah-nama* are historic, some legendary, and some semi-legendary.

The annotations that accompany the following selection from the *Shah-nama* point out the work's historical context, cultural context, and literary context.

Objectives

Thematic

To understand how a lack of communication can produce tragic results

Skills

1 To understand irony
2 To write a letter to Suhrab's mother informing her of his death

Support Material

Teaching Portfolio
Teacher Backup, p. 105
Reading Critically, "When As My Wailing Is Heard" by Hafiz, p.109
Grammar in Action Worksheets, *Recognizing Adverb Phrases*, p. 111; *Using Similes*, p. 113

from the Shah-nama
Firdawsi

from Rustam and Suhrab
translated by Arthur and Edmund Warner

Historical Context: *Shah* comes from the Persian word *sāh,* which means rule. *Shah* is the title of any of the former rulers of Iran.

The following excerpt from the Shah-nama *tells the story of the tragic meeting between Rustam, a famous Persian warrior with incredible strength, and his son, Suhrab. Prior to the meeting, Rustam had been unaware of his son's existence. However, Suhrab's mother had revealed to him the identity of his father. Knowing of his father's reputation as the finest warrior in the Persian army, Suhrab devised a plan that he hoped would enable him to meet Rustam. Joining the Turkmans, a people from an area east of the Caspian Sea, in a war against the Persians, Suhrab desired to meet his father in battle and to reveal his identity to him. Suhrab challenged the Persians to send a warrior to meet him in single combat, expecting them to send his father. As it turns out, Rustam is the warrior who comes to meet Suhrab. Yet, because Rustam wears unmarked armor and refuses to reveal his identity, Suhrab is uncertain whether the Persian warrior is, indeed, his father.*

The bright sun shone, the raven night flew low,
Great Rustam donned his tiger-skin cuirass[1]
And mounted on his fiery dragon-steed.
Two leagues divided host from host, and all
5   Stood ready-armed. The hero with a casque[2]
Of iron on his head came on the field.
Suhrab on his side reveling with comrades
Had thus addressed Human:[3] "That lion-man,
Who striveth with me, is as tall as I am
10   And hath a dauntless heart. He favoreth me
In shoulder, breast, and arm, and thou wouldst say
That some skilled workman laid us out by line.

Literary Context: The battle that is about to take place is just one of the vast number of episodes in Firdawsi's monumental epic poem. This episodic organization is a common feature of epic poetry.

---

1. cuirass (kwi ras´) *n.*: A piece of closefitting armor for protecting the breast and back.
2. casque (kask) *n.*: A helmet.
3. Human (hoo´ män): Suhrab's friend and fellow warrior.

Usage and Mechanics Worksheet, p. 115
Vocabulary Check, p. 116
Analyzing Literature Worksheet, *Understanding Irony,* p. 117
Critical Thinking and Reading Worksheet, *Predicting Later Events,* p. 118
Selection Test, pp. 119–120

Spelling Tip Point out to students that both *consternation* and *lamentation* end with the letters *tion.*

Presentation

Motivation for Reading Tell students that the selection they are about to read is a classic example of a tragedy. Have them discuss tragic incidents or situations from books they have read or movies they have seen. For example, they might bring up the tragic deaths of Romeo and Juliet in Shakespeare's play. Ask students what makes tragedy appealing to readers and viewers. Then ask how they are affected by tragic books and movies. Do tragic books and movies ever have a lasting impact on them? Why or why not?

Purpose-Setting Question Could the outcome of the tale have been avoided? Why or why not?

Universal Themes This selection highlights the potentially tragic results of a lack of communication. Many other works of world literature also explore this theme. One such work is Henrik Ibsen's play *A Doll's House* (page 969).

1 **Discussion** Have students discuss the impression of Rustam that is conveyed in the opening passage.

Vocabulary
Preteach the following vocabulary words:
dauntless (dônt´ lis) *adj.*: Fearless
mirthful (murth´ fəl) *adj.*: Merry
magnanimity (mag´ nə nim´ ə tē) *n.*: The ability to rise above pettiness or meanness
malignantly (mə lig´ nənt lē) *adv.*: Very harmfully
wanton (wän´ t'n) *adj.*: Senseless; unprovoked; unjustifiable; deliberately malicious
consternation (kän stər nā´ shən) *n.*: Great fear or shock that makes one feel helpless or bewildered
lamentations (lam´ ən tā´ shənz) *n.*: Outward expressions of grief

Humanities Note

Fine art, *The Birth of Rustam*. This is an example of a type of painting known as the Persian miniature. During the twelfth through the seventeenth centuries, small and elegant paintings such as this one were included in handwritten versions of great Persian literary works. This painting was created during the sixteenth century as an illustration for a version of Firdawsi's *Shah-nama*. Although the artist is not known, it is known that it was produced in the Persian city of Shiraz, which was a thriving artistic center at the time.

This painting is typical of Persian miniatures in several respects. First it is a highly decorative work, consisting of vivid colors, large rectangular areas, and calligraphy that has been integrated into the overall design. In addition it combines several different scenes into a single work, though the viewer's attention is drawn mainly to the action occurring in the center of the painting. Finally, as is typical of Persian miniatures, flowers and designs are strewn throughout the painting.

You might want to use the following questions to discuss the art:

1. Persian miniature paintings often included symbolic details. Which of the elements of this painting might be symbolic, and what do you imagine they symbolize?

2. Do you think this is an ideal illustration for the story of Rustam and Suhrab? Why or why not?

3. If you were an art collector, would you include this painting in your collection? Why or why not?

BIRTH OF RUSTAM
*The Metropolitan Museum
of Art, New York*

His very feet and stirrups move my love
And make me blush, for I perceive in him
15 The marks whereof my mother spake. Moreover
My heart presageth[4] that he must be Rustam,
For few resemble him. I may not challenge

---

4. presageth (pri sāj′ ith) *v.:* Foretells; predicts.

Grammar in Action

Adverb phrases are prepositional phrases that modify verbs, adjectives, or adverbs by pointing out where, when, in what manner, or to what extent. Look at the following examples:

They lighted, tied their chargers to a rock, / And cautiously advanced in mail and casque /*With troubled hearts.*

From sunrise till the shadows grew they strove / Until Suhrab, that maddened elephant, / Reached out, up—leaping with a lion's spring, Caught Rustam's girdle, . . .

Student Activity 1. Identify the adverb phrases in the following passages from "Rustam and Suhrab." (Notice that some of the sentences may contain more than one adverb phrase.)

1. At sunrise, when they woke, Suhrab arrayed / Himself in mail and, mirthful though resolved, / Set forward shouting, ox-head mace in hand.

2. Such puissance as that / Proved an abiding trouble, and he prayed / To God in bitterness of soul to minish / His strength that he might walk like other men.

3. They approached Iran / Through trust in me, and I encouraged them.

4. When day declined and Rustam came not back / There went forth twenty

My sire or lightly meet him in the combat."

Human said: "Rustam oft hath countered me:
This charger is like his, except in action."

At sunrise, when they woke, Suhrab arrayed
Himself in mail and, <u>mirthful</u> though resolved,
Set forward shouting, ox-head mace[5] in hand.
He greeted Rustam smiling, thou hadst said
That they had passed the night in company:
"How went the night? How is't with thee today?
Why so intent on strife? Fling down thine arrows
And scimitar,[6] and drop the hand of wrong.
Let us dismount and, sitting, clear our faces
With wine, and, leaguing in God's sight, repent
Our former strife. Until some other cometh
To battle, feast with me because I love thee,
And weep for shamefastness. In sooth thou comest
From heroes and wilt tell me of thy stock,
For as my foe thou shouldst not hide thy name.
Art thou the famous Rustam of Zabul,
The son of valiant Zal the son of Sam?"

Then Rustam: "Young aspirant! heretofore
We talked not thus but spake last night of wrestling.
I am not to be gulled, attempt it not.
Though thou art young I am no child myself,
But girt to wrestle, and the end shall be
According to the will of Providence.
I have known ups and downs and am not one
To practice guile upon."

Suhrab replied:
"Old man! if thou rejectest my proposals . . . !
I wished that thou shouldst die upon thy bed,
And that thy kin should tomb thy soulless corpse,
But I will end thee if it be God's will."

They lighted, tied their chargers to a rock,
And cautiously advanced in mail and casque
With troubled hearts. They wrestled like two lions
Until their bodies ran with sweat and blood.
From sunrise till the shadows grew they strove
Until Suhrab, that maddened elephant,
Reached out, up-leaping with a lion's spring,
Caught Rustam's girdle, tugged amain as though,
Thou wouldst have said, to rend the earth, and shouting

---

5. mace (mās) *n.*: A heavy, armor-breaking club with a metal head.
6. scimitar (sim´ ə tər) *n.*: A short, curved sword.

Historical Context: The type of one-on-one fighting in which the two warriors are about to engage occurred frequently in early wars, such as the one involving the Persians and the Turkmans.

Cultural Context: In this episode Firdawsi depicts the ongoing struggle between good and evil that is an important part of ancient Persian belief. If the forces of good win out, Rustam and Suhrab will be united. In contrast, if the forces of evil win out, the two will engage in a battle with a tragic result.

2

3

Literary Context: Note the use of metaphors and similes—two important elements of epic poetry.

4

Master Teacher Note If you have any artistically inclined students in your class, you might want to have them prepare an illustration depicting the battle scene between Rustam and Suhrab. Before preparing their illustrations, they should carefully read Firdawsi's descriptions of the two warriors. Once they have finished their drawings, you may want to display them on the bulletin board.

2 Discussion Have students offer reasons why Rustam does not identify himself.

3 Discussion Have students discuss what Suhrab's reply reveals about his character. Why does he not demand his foe to reveal his identity?

4 Discussion Draw students' attention to Firdawsi's comparisons of both Rustam and Suhrab to wild animals. Have them discuss the impression conveyed by these comparisons. What might these comparisons reveal about Persian values?

trusty warriors / To learn the issue.
5. In part through confidence, in part through fate, / In part no doubt through magnanimity, / Suhrab let Rustam go, . . .

Student Activity 2. Write five original sentences that each contain at least one adverb phrase.

5 **Discussion** Have students discuss whether there are any situations in which they feel that it is acceptable to use deception. Is this such a situation? Why or why not?

6 **Enrichment** Draw students' attention to the translator's use of such archaic words as *thou, hadst,* and *spake.* What might have been the translator's reason for having included such words? Would the selection have been more or less effective if he had not used such words? Explain.

7 **Discussion** Have students discuss the meaning of the proverb that Human relates to Suhrab. How does it apply to Suhrab's situation?

8 **Reading Strategy** Have students predict the outcome of the selection. Will Suhrab's prediction turn out to be correct? Why or why not?

5 **Cultural Context:** This was not really a Persian custom. Rustam is actually trying to deceive Suhrab.

Cultural Context: Rustam's deception of Suhrab and Suhrab's reasons for letting him go are indicative of the ongoing struggle between good and evil.

6

7

8

With rage and vengeance hurled him to the ground,
60 Raised him aloft and, having dashed him down,
Sat on his breast with visage, hand, and mouth
Besmirched with dust, as when a lion felleth
An onager,[7] then drew a bright steel dagger
To cut off Rustam's head, who seeing this
65 Exclaimed: "Explain I must! O warrior
That takest lions captive and art skilled
With lasso, mace, and scimitar! the customs
And laws of arms with us are not as yours.
In wrestling none may take a foeman's head
70 The first time that his back is on the ground,
But having thrown him twice and won the name
Of lion then he may behead the foe:
such is our custom."
⠀⠀⠀⠀⠀⠀⠀⠀⠀⠀Thus he sought to 'scape
The dragon's clutches and get off with life.
75 The brave youth hearkened to the old man's words.
In part through confidence, in part through fate,
In part no doubt through magnanimity,
Suhrab let Rustam go, turned toward the plain,
Pursued an antelope that crossed his path,
80 And utterly forgot his recent foe.
When he was far away, Human came up
As swift as dust and asked about the fight.
He told Human what had been said and done,
Who cried: "Alas! young man! art thou indeed
85 So weary of thy life? Woe for thy breast,
Mien, stature, stirrups, and heroic feet!
The mighty lion whom thou hadst ensnared
Thou hast let go and all is still to do.
Mark how he will entreat thee on the day
90 Of battle owing to thy senseless act.
A king once spake a proverb to the point:
'Despise not any foe however weak.'"
⠀⠀He took the very life out of Suhrab,
Who standing sorrowing and amazed replied:
95 "Let us dismiss such fancies from our hearts,
For he will come to fight with me tomorrow,
And thou shalt see a yoke[8] upon his neck."
⠀⠀He went to camp in dudgeon[9] at his deed.

---

7. onager (än′ ə jər) *n.:* A wild ass.
8. yoke (yōk) *n.:* A mark or symbol of subjection or servitude.
9. dudgeon (duj′ ən) *n.:* Anger or resentment.

When Rustam had escaped his foeman's clutch
10 He was again as 'twere a mount of steel.
He went toward a rivulet as one
Who having fainted is himself again.
He drank and bathed, then prayed to God for strength
And victory, not knowing what the sun
15 And moon decreed, or how the turning sky
Would rob him of the crown upon his head.
 The tale is told that Rustam had at first
Such strength bestowed by Him who giveth all
That if he walked upon a rock his feet
20 Would sink therein. Such puissance[10] as that
Proved an abiding trouble, and he prayed
To God in bitterness of soul to minish[11]

---

10. **puissance** (pyoo′ əs səns) *n*.: Strength; power.
11. **minish** (min′ ish) *v*.: Diminish; make small.

9

10

Literary Context: This passage reflects the mythic origin of this episode. As in a myth or legend, Rustam is depicted as being larger than life.

SCENE FROM SHAH-NAMA (BOOK OF KINGS).
The Iranian hero Zal slays Khazarvan, the leader of the invading Turanian army, with his father's ox-head mace.
Attributed to 'Abd ul-Vahhab
The Metropolitan Museum of Art, New York

9 **Discussion** Have students discuss the effect of the similes in this passage. How does a person who has fainted behave after returning to consciousness?

10 **Enrichment** Tell students that the god to whom Rustam is praying is probably Ahura Mazda, or Ormazd, the Zoroastrian god of goodness, wisdom, and truth.

Humanities Note

Fine art, *Scene from the* Shah-nama, attributed to 'Abd ul-Vahhab. This sixteenth-century Persian miniature is from an illustrated version of the *Shah-nama*. As is the case of most illustrations from sixteenth-century editions of the *Shah-nama*, it depicts a heroic moment in the life of a legendary warrior. At the time this painting was produced, the Persians were engaged in fierce combat with both the Ottoman Turks and the Uzbecs. As a result of these ongoing struggles, a sense of national pride was sweeping through Persia—a feeling clearly reflected in the painting.

Like many Persian miniatures, this work was painted from an unusual perspective. At the center of the painting is a hill, surrounded by groups of soldiers on both sides. At the bottom of the hill, the central figures are portrayed from a bird's-eye view. On the top of the hill is a tree, which contributes to the painting's symmetry. This arrangement of elements is designed to dramatize the action in the foreground and to give the illusion that vast numbers of soldiers are about to emerge from behind the hill.

You might want to use the following questions to discuss the art:

1. Do you think this picture glorifies war? Why or why not?
2. What details in this illustration are distinctly Persian?
3. Although this painting depicts neither Rustam nor Suhrab, why is it an appropriate illustration for their battle scene?
4. What do you imagine that it would be like to be one of the soldiers witnessing the battle between Zal and Khazarvan?

11 Discussion Have students name other stories about heroes who lose their strength. Then have them discuss what they know about each of these stories. Ask them what situations in the contemporary world are comparable to that of a hero who has lost his or her strength. One example might be an athlete whose ability has deteriorated with age.

12 Clarification Point out to students that the word *wane* means "to grow less in extent" and that the word *wax* means "to increase in strength, intensity, or volume."

13 Discussion Once again call students' attention to the use of animal metaphors in this passage and have them discuss the effect created by these metaphors.

14 Clarification Remind students of what Rustam told Suhrab when Suhrab was about to kill him. Ask students why Suhrab does not use the same tactic in an effort to save his life. How do students imagine that Rustam would have responded to this use of his own tactic?

15 Discussion Have students explain the meaning of this passage. How does it apply to life in general?

Literary Context: Again, note Firdawsi's use of similes.

Cultural Context: The outcome reflects the ancient Persian belief that evil often triumphs over good.

His strength that he might walk like other men.
According to his prayer his mountain-strength
115 Had shrunk, but face to face with such a task,
And pierced by apprehension of Suhrab,
He cried to God and said: "Almighty Lord!
Protect Thy slave in his extremity.
O holy Fosterer! I ask again
My former strength."
120   God granted him his prayer,
The strength which once had waned now waxed in him.
He went back to the field perturbed and pale
While, like a maddened elephant, Suhrab,
With lasso on his arm and bow in hand,
125 Came in his pride and roaring like a lion,
His plunging charger flinging up the soil.
When Rustam saw the bearing of his foe
He was astounded and gazing earnestly
Weighed in his mind the chances of the fight.
130 Suhrab, puffed up with youthful arrogance,
On seeing Rustam in his strength and grace,
Cried: "Thou that didst escape the lion's claws!
Why com'st thou boldly to confront me? Speak!
Hast thou no interests of thine own to seek?"
135 They tied their steeds while fate malignantly
Revolved o'erhead, and when dark fate is wroth
Flint rocks become like wax. The two began
To wrestle, holding by their leathern belts.
As for Suhrab thou wouldst have said: "High heaven
140 Hath hampered him," while Rustam, reaching, clutched
That warrior-leopard by the head and neck,
Bent down the body of the gallant youth,
Whose time was come and all whose strength was gone,
And like a lion dashed him to the ground;
145 Then, knowing that Suhrab would not stay under,
Drew lightly from his waist his trenchant[12] sword
And gashed the bosom of his gallant son.
   Whenever thou dost thirst for blood and stain
Therewith thy glittering dagger, destiny
150   Will be athirst for thy blood and ordain
Each hair of thine to be a sword for thee.
   Suhrab cried: "Ah!" and writhed. Naught recked he then
Of good or ill. "I am alone to blame,"
He said to Rustam. "Fate gave thee my key.

---

12. **trenchant** (tren′ chənt) *adj.*: Sharp.

Grammar in Action

Similes are explicit comparisons between two dissimilar things, indicated by the words *like* or *as*. Writers use similes to enliven their descriptions and to enable readers to visualize connections that their senses may not be able to perceive. Notice the similes in the following passages from the *Shah-nama*:

. . . *They* wrestled *like two lions* / Until their bodies ran with sweat and blood. (page 91)

. . . *like a maddened elephant, Suhrab,* / With a lasso on his arm and bow in hand, / Came in his pride . . .

Student Activity 1. Identify the similes in each of the following passages from the *Shah-nama*. Then explain the impression conveyed by each simile.
1. When he was far away, Human came up / As swift as dust and asked about the fight.
2. When Rustam had escaped his foeman's clutch / He was again as 'twere a mount of steel.
3. They tied their steeds while fighting malignantly / Revolved o'erhead, and

5 This hump-backed sky reared me to slay me soon.
Men of my years will mock me since my neck
Hath thus come down to dust. My mother told me
How I should recognize my father. I
Sought him in love and die of my desire.
0 Alas! my toils are vain, I have not seen him.
Now wert thou fish, or wrapped like night in gloom,
Or quit of earth wast soaring like a star,
My father would avenge me when he seeth
My pillow bricks.[13] Some chief will say to Rustam:
5 'Suhrab was slain and flung aside in scorn
While seeking thee.'"
              Then Rustam grew distraught,
The world turned black, his body failed; o'ercome
He sank upon the ground and swooned away;
Till coming to himself he cried in anguish:
0 "Where is the proof that thou art Rustam's son?
May his name perish from among the great,
For I am Rustam! Be my name forgotten,
And may the son of Sam sit mourning me!"
  He raved, his blood seethed, and with groans he plucked
5 His hair up by the roots, while at the sight
Suhrab sank swooning till at length he cried:
"If thou indeed art Rustam, thou hast slain me
In wanton malice, for I made advances,
But naught that I could do would stir my love.
0 Undo my breastplate, view my body bare,
Behold thy jewel, see how sires treat sons!
The drums beat at my gate, my mother came
With bloodstained cheeks and stricken to the soul
Because I went. She bound this on mine arm
5 And said: 'Preserve this keepsake of thy father's
And mark its virtue.' It is mighty now,
Now when the strife is over and the son
Is nothing to his sire."
              When Rustam loosed
The mail and saw the gem he rent his clothes,
0 And cried: "Oh! my brave son, approved by all
And slain by me!"
              With dust upon his head
And streaming face he rent his locks until

Literary Context: Note that this passage reveals a different side of Rustam. Despite his actions in this episode, he is by no means an embodiment of evil. In fact, he is the most important hero in the entire *Shah-nama*.

16

17

16 **Literary Context** Explain to students that irony is a contrast between what is stated and what is meant, or between what is expected to happen and what actually happens. Tell them that there are three types of irony: verbal irony, situational irony, and dramatic irony. Verbal irony occurs when the literal meaning of a word or statement is different from the intended meaning. Situational irony occurs when the actual result of an action or situation is different from the expected result. Dramatic irony occurs when the audience perceives something that a character in a literary work does not know. Have them discuss what makes the outcome of "Rustam and Suhrab" ironic. Then have them identify the type of irony being used.

17 **Discussion** Ask students if they can think of any situation more tragic than a father slaying his own son. What other literary works can they think of in which this situation occurs?

---

13. pillow bricks: Blocks of wood or stone, contoured to fit a person's head, used as pillows. When a warrior died, his pillow blocks would be returned to his family.

when dark fate is wroth / Flint rocks became like wax.
4. That warrior-leopard by the head and neck, / Bent down the body of the gallant youth, / Whose time was come and all whose strength was gone, / And like a lion dashed him to the ground; . . .
5. Now wert thou fish, or wrapped like night in gloom, / Or quit of earth wast soaring like a star, / My father would avenge me when he seeth / My pillow bricks.

    Student Activity 2. Write a descriptive paragraph that contains at least five similes or write five separate sentences that each contain one simile.

18 Clarification Explain to students that in this context the word *issue* means "result, consequence, or upshot."

19 Discussion Ask students what is revealed by the Shah's unwillingness to concede defeat to the Turkmans if Rustam has been slain. Do they feel that any type of code of ethical conduct can be applied to war? Why or why not?

20 Reading Strategy Have students predict whether Rustam will be able to convince the Shah to allow the Turkmans to "depart unscathed"?

21 Discussion Ask students if they imagine that Rustam will ever fight again. Why or why not?

18

Historical Context: The Shah reveals that even if Rustam has lost in one-on-one combat, the Persians will not concede defeat to the Turkmans.

19

20

21

His blood ran down.
　　　　　　　　"Nay, this is worse and worse,"
Suhrab said. "Wherefore weep? What will it profit
195 To slay thyself? What was to be hath been."
　　When day declined and Rustam came not back
There went forth twenty trusty warriors
To learn the issue. Both the steeds were standing
Bemoiled with dust, but Rustam was not there.
200 The nobles, thinking that he had been slain,
Went to Kaus[14] in consternation saying:
"The throne of majesty is void of Rustam!"
　　A cry went up throughout the host and all
Was in confusion. Then Kaus bade sound
205 The drums and trumpets, Tus[15] came, and the Shah
Said to the troops: "Dispatch a messenger
That he may find out what Suhrab hath done,
And if there must be mourning through Iran.
None will confront him with brave Rustam dead.
210 We must attack in force and speedily."
　　While clamor raged, Suhrab said thus to Rustam:
"The Turkmans' case is altered since my day
Is done. Use all thine influence that the Shah
May not attack them. They approached Iran
215 Through trust in me, and I encouraged them.
How could I tell, O famous paladin![16]
That I should perish by my father's hand?
Let them depart unscathed, and treat them kindly.
I had a warrior in yonder hold
220 Caught by my lasso. Him I often asked
To point thee out. Mine eyes looked ever for thee.
He told me all but this. His place is void.
His words o'ercast my day, and I despaired.
See who he is and let him not be harmed.
225 I marked in thee the tokens that my mother
Described, but trusted not mine eyes. The stars
Decreed that I should perish by thy hand.
I came like lightning and like wind I go.
In heaven I may look on thee with joy."
230 　　Then Rustam choked, his heart was full of fire,
His eyes of tears. He mounted quick as dust
And came with lamentations to the host

---

14. **Kaus** (kā′ o͞os): The ruler of Persia.
15. **Tus** (to͞os): Troops from the region called Tus.
16. **paladin** (pal′ ə din) *n*.: A knight or a heroic champion.

Primary Source

In the following excerpt from Rueben Levy's prose translation of the *Shah-nama*, Firdawsi laments the death of his own son:

My years have passed sixty and five and no purpose now would be served for me by striving after wealth. Perhaps I should take my own counsel and give a thought to the death of my son. It was my turn to have gone, but it was the younger man who departed and in my agony for him I am a body without a soul. I hasten about dreaming that perchance I may find him; and if I find him I will hasten to him with reproaches, telling him that it was my turn to go and demanding why he has gone, robbing me of hope and tranquility. He had ever been one to take me by the hand when distresses came and now he has taken a path far from his old fellow-wayfarer. Have you perchance found younger companions on the way, since you have so swiftly gone ahead of me? When this young man reached the age of thirty-seven, the world no longer went according to his liking. He has gone and what remains is my grief and sorrow for him; he has steeped my heart and eyes in blood.

In grievous consternation at his deed.
The Iranians catching sight of him fell prostrate
5 And gave God praise that Rustam had returned;
But when they saw the dust upon his head,
His clothes and bosom rent, they questioned him:
"What meaneth this? For whom art thou thus troubled?"
  He told the fearful deed, and all began
0 To mourn aloud with him. His anguish grew.
He told the nobles: "I have lost today
All strength and courage. Fight not with Turan:[17]
I have done harm enough."

---

17. **Turan** (tŏŏ' rän): The Turkmans.

Reader's Response *What thoughts and feelings does this
selection from the* Shah-nama *evoke in you? Can you
imagine the depths of Rustam's grief?*

Literary Context: This
episode is considered by
many readers and critics to
be among the most tragic
works ever written.

THINKING ABOUT THE SELECTION

Interpreting

1. Why does Suhrab begin fighting even though he
   realizes that he may be battling his own father?
2. The heroes of epics such as the *Shah-nama* generally embody many of the dominant attitudes and
   values of their culture. (a) If we assume this to be
   the case with Rustam, what is revealed about
   ancient Persian attitudes through Rustam's use of
   deception to avoid losing his battle? (b) What else
   can you infer, or conclude, about ancient Persian
   values from Rustam's character?
3. (a) What is the significance of the frequent references to fate in this episode? (b) What do these references suggest about Persian beliefs concerning
   the role of fate in people's lives?
4. What lesson could be learned from the tragedy of
   Rustam and Suhrab? Explain.

Applying

5. (a) What literary works can you think of that involve
   tragic struggles between members of the same
   family? (b) In what ways are these works similar to
   and different from "Rustam and Suhrab"?

ANALYZING LITERATURE

Understanding Irony

  Irony is a contrast between what is stated and
what is meant, or between what is expected to happen
and what actually happens. Irony is often painful like
the twisting of a knife in a wound. In what way is this
true of the ironic outcome in "Rustam and Suhrab"?

THINKING AND WRITING

Writing a Letter

  Putting yourself in Rustam's place, write a letter to
Suhrab's mother explaining what has happened. Try to
make your writing style consistent with the manner in
which Rustam speaks in the selection. After you have
finished writing, revise the letter, making sure it clearly
expresses Rustam's feelings. Have you used the proper tone—one that will help Suhrab's mother come to
grips with the tragic event? Once you have revised and
proofread your letter, share it with your classmates.

Now that he is departed, going toward the light, he would surely
choose out a place for his father? Long is the time that has passed
over me and none of my fellow-wayfarers have returned. Surely he
awaits me and is angry at my tarrying? May the All-possessor keep
your spirit ever in brightness! May wisdom ever be the shield that
guards your soul!

  Have students compare Firdawsi's response to his son's death with
Rustam's response to the death of Suhrab. How do they think Firdawsi's
experience might have affected his writing of "Rustam and Suhrab"?

OMAR KHAYYÁM

1050?–1132?

Focus

More About the Author Khayyám's poetry was not well-known in his native land. Yet his achievements in math and science were widely recognized. In addition to reforming the Persian calendar, Khayyám built an observatory in the city of Isfahan in collaboration with other astronomers. He also taught science, philosophy, and mathematics, and at times he even worked as a fortuneteller.

Have students try to think of other writers who earned fame for accomplishments made outside the literary world. For example, they might name the American writers Benjamin Franklin—who made important contributions in the fields of science and diplomacy—and Oliver Wendell Holmes—who taught at Harvard medical school for thirty-five years.

Critical Evaluation Because of the great liberties taken by FitzGerald in his translation, these poems might be viewed as a collaboration between a Persian poet and a Victorian English poet, rather than simply as a translation of Persian poetry. The renowned Argentine writer Jorge Luis Borges once commented that from the merging of the poetic talents of Khayyám and FitzGerald "emerges an extraordinary poet who does not resemble either of them." Have students discuss the idea of a collaboration between a Persian poet and a nineteenth- century English poet. Why might this be viewed as an unusual combination? What might be some of the major differences between the two poets? Why might the merging of Khayyám's and FitzGerald's poetic talents have been so successful?

A Persian poet, scientist, and mathematician, Omar Khayyám (ō′ mar kī yäm′) is probably the best known Islamic poet in the West, where his rubáiyát have been read and appreciated for over a century.

Khayyám was born in a small village outside the Persian city of Nishapur (nē′ shä pōor), a major center of art and learning in the Middle Ages. The name *Khayyám* means "tent-maker" and probably refers to the profession of his ancestors. Although the exact date of his birth is unknown, by 1075 he was already famous as a mathematician and was invited by the local king to participate in the reform of the Persian calendar. In addition to his work in mathematics, Khayyám was also famous for his scholarship in philosophy, history, law, and astrology. Despite his accomplishments in all these fields, he wrote very little: The majority of his scholarly writings are on mathematics, and only a few short works on other subjects are known to exist.

In recent times Omar Khayyám's reputation as a poet has eclipsed his scientific fame. A collection of poetry called *The Rubáiyát* is attributed to him, although we now know that Khayyám did not write the majority of the poems in the collection. One of the oldest known copies of *The Rubáiyát* was handwritten in 1457 and contains only 131 poems, whereas an edition published in 1894 contains 770 poems. This suggests that over the years many poems written by other people have been added to *The Rubáiyát* and ascribed to Khayyám. In fact, scholars who have studied the authenticity of *The Rubáiyát* believe that fewer than twenty of the poems attributed to Khayyám were certainly written by him. The question of authorship, however, is of little concern to Omar Khayyám's admirers, who read and enjoy *The Rubáiyát* to this day.

Why then is Omar Khayyám so well known in the West? Why is *The Rubáiyát* read and enjoyed by so many people outside Khayyám's own country? The success of *The Rubáiyát* is largely the result of an English translation published in 1859 by the noted English scholar Edward Fitz-Gerald (1809–1883). In his translation FitzGerald was less concerned with textual accuracy than with capturing the spirit of the original poems as he interpreted it. He adapted the rubái form to English, trying to re-create the rhyme, rhythm, and mood of the original Persian poems. In doing so FitzGerald created a series of lyrical and energetic poems that are often quite different in content from the original poems. Despite their inaccuracy FitzGerald's rubáiyát are widely recognized for their beauty and have enjoyed enormous popularity throughout the English-speaking world. In fact, a group of ardent admirers of FitzGerald's rubáiyát even formed an Omar Khayyám Club in London in 1892.

The main topics addressed in *The Rubáiyát* are philosophical and religious in nature. Omar Khayyám appears to have been concerned with the fleeting nature of life. This awareness made him pessimistic and, at the same time, prompted him to try to enjoy every instant as much as possible. In *The Rubáiyát* he conveys both his pessimism and his awareness of the preciousness of every moment of a person's life.

Objectives

Thematic
To grasp Khayyám's ideas about the fleeting nature of life.

Skills
1 To understand the use of metaphors

2 To recognize the author's beliefs

3 To write poems in the rubái form

Support Material

Teaching Portfolio
Teacher Backup, p. 121
Usage and Mechanics Worksheet, p. 125
Vocabulary Check, p. 126
Analyzing Literature Worksheet, *Understanding Metaphors*, p. 127
Critical Thinking and Reading Work-

GUIDE FOR INTERPRETING

from The Rubáiyát

Commentary

Metaphor. Omar Khayyám's poems are written in a literary form known as the rubái. This form takes its name from the Arabic word for "four," because each poem consists of four lines, the first, second, and fourth of which rhyme with one another. Because each poem is so short, the poet must use concise and vivid imagery to convey his or her message to the reader. In Persian literature this task is accomplished through the elaborate use of metaphors.

A **metaphor** is a type of comparison that prompts us not only to see the similarities between two seemingly different things but to pretend that one thing actually *is* something totally different. For example, Firdawsi uses two metaphors in the following lines from the *Shah-nama* (page 91): "From sunrise till the shadows grew they strove / Until Suhrab, that maddened elephant, / Reached out, up-leaping with a lion's spring . . ." In the first metaphor we are led to envision Suhrab as a maddened elephant, while the second metaphor prompts us to identify his powerful leap with the spring of a lion.

Persian poets relied on metaphors as a means of exploring the same idea in many different ways. For instance, read the following lines from Omar Khayyám's *The Rubáiyát*: "The wine of life keeps oozing drop by drop, / The leaves of life keep falling one by one." In both lines Khayyám is trying to convey the idea that life is passing by and death is drawing closer. Through his use of metaphors, however, he conveys the idea in two strikingly different ways. In the first line he uses the image of wine spilling slowly out of a bottle or glass as a metaphor for life; in the second he uses leaves falling off a tree for the same purpose. By using these two metaphors in consecutive lines, he captures the reader's interest and adds emphasis to the idea he is trying to convey.

Writing

In the Persian culture, there is a constant awareness of how uncontrollable and fleeting life is, accompanied by a belief that the uncontrollable nature of life adds to its value and makes it more enjoyable. Write a journal entry in which you discuss your own thoughts and feelings about the uncontrollable nature of life.

Literary Focus Point out to students that metaphors are often used in everyday speech. For example, people often refer to lucrative investment opportunities as "goldmines," and football announcers frequently describe strong-armed quarterbacks as "having a rifle." Have students try to think of other examples of metaphors used in everyday speech. Then have them discuss the reasons why people use metaphors. What purposes do metaphors serve in everyday speech?

Writing Before students write their journal entries, you might want to arrange them into groups and have them share their ideas about the uncontrollable nature of life.

ESL Teaching Strategy To accomplish the writing assignment, pair each ESL student with another member of the class. The native-speaking students should read over the assignment with the ESL students to make sure they understand it.

Teaching Tenth-Grade Students Have tenth-grade students take turns reading the poems aloud. After each poem has been read, take some time to discuss its meaning and to answer any questions students may have. In these discussions you should also encourage students to look for connections between the individual poems and have them think about what the poems suggest about Khayyám's attitudes and beliefs.

Vocabulary
Preteach the following vocabulary words:
repentance (ri pent´ ′ns) *n.*: Feeling of sorrow for wrongdoing; remorse
pomp (pämp) *n.*: Splendor; magnificence
myriads (mir´ ē ədz) *n.*: Great number of persons or things
piety (pī´ ə tē) n.: Devotion to religious duties and practices

---

sheet, *Recognizing the Author's Beliefs*, p. 128
Selection Test, pp. 129–130

Spelling Tip Point out to students that the word *repentance* ends with the letters *ance*, not *ence*. Explain that it is easy to confuse these two endings. Tell students that another word that ends with *ance* is *domi-* nance. The word *prominence*, on the other hand, ends in *ence*.

from The Rubáiyát

Omar Khayyám

translated by Edward FitzGerald

I

Wake! For the Sun, who scatter'd into flight
The Stars before him from the Field of Night,
　Drives Night along with them from Heav'n, and strikes
The Sultán's Turret[1] with a Shaft of Light.

VII

Come, fill the Cup, and in the fire of Spring
Your Winter-garment of Repentance fling:
　The Bird of Time has but a little way
To flutter—and the Bird is on the Wing.

VIII

Whether at Naishápúr or Babylon,[2]
Whether the Cup with sweet or bitter run,
　The Wine of Life keeps oozing drop by drop,
The Leaves of Life keep falling one by one.

XII

A Book of Verses underneath the Bough,
A Jug of Wine, a Loaf of Bread—and Thou
　Beside me singing in the Wilderness—
Oh, Wilderness were Paradise enow![3]

---

1. Turret (tŭr´ it) *n*.: A small tower projecting from a large building.
2. Naishápúr (nā shä pōor´) **. . . Babylon** (bab´ ə lən): Naishápúr, also known as Neyshabur and Nī´shä´pur, is a city in northeastern Iran. It was one of the foremost cities of the Persian Empire and was the birthplace of Omar Khayyám. Babylon, an ancient city that was famous for its wealth, luxury, and wickedness, was the capital of the Babylonian Empire, which flourished from 2100 to 689 B.C.
3. enow (i nou´) *adj*.: Enough.

XIII

Some for the Glories of This World; and some
Sigh for the Prophet's Paradise to come;
　Ah, take the Cash, and let the Credit go,
Nor heed the rumble of a distant Drum!

XVI

The Worldly Hope men set their Hearts upon
Turns Ashes—or it prospers; and anon,[4]
　Like Snow upon the Desert's dusty Face,
Lighting a little hour or two—is gone.

XVII

Think in this batter'd Caravanserai[5]
Whose Portals are alternate Night and Day,
　How Sultán after Sultán with his Pomp
Abode[6] his destined Hour, and went his way.

XXVII

Myself when young did eagerly frequent
Doctor and Saint, and heard great argument
　About it and about: but evermore
Came out by the same door where in I went.

XXVIII

With them the seed of Wisdom did I sow,
And with mine own hand wrought to make it
　grow;

---

4. anon (ə nän´) *adv*.: Immediately; at once.
5. Caravanserai (kar´ ə van´ sə rī) *n*.: An inn with a large central court.
6. Abode (ə bōd´) *v*.: Awaited.

RUBÁIYÁT OF OMAR KHAYYÁM

Discussion Which details in this verse give it a distinctive Persian flavor? If these details were changed, would it still be possible to identify the verse as a Persian poem? Why or why not?

5 **Discussion** Ask students what this poem expresses about the place of an individual human in the overall scheme of existence.

6 **Literary Focus** Have students explain the metaphorical meaning of the "Moving Finger." Why is an awareness of the meaning of this metaphor vital to a reader's overall understanding of the poem?

7 **Critical Thinking and Reading** Have students discuss what this verse suggests about Khayyám's attitude toward the world in which he lived.

Cooperative Learning Arrange students into groups of three or four and have them discuss Khayyám's views concerning life and death. In what ways are their own views similar to and different from Khayyám's?

Humanities Note

Fine art, *illustration of* The Rubáiyát *of Omar Khayyám* by Edmund Dulac. Illustrating verse XII, this picture depicts a romantic poet sitting in an idyllic wilderness, poetry book in hand, bread and wine resting on the grass beside him, while his lady leans on a tree branch. The contemplative tone of the picture results mainly from the couple's dreamy gaze into the distance (rather than at each other) and the pinkish early evening light with the first hint of moonlight. The flowing lines of the couple's clothing are echoed in the lines of the tree branches, and the small rocks and plants imitate the patterns of her shawl and jewelry.

You might want to use the following questions to discuss the art:

1. How does the couple depicted in this illustration differ from the one depicted in the illustration on page 101?
2. How does the artist's choice of colors contribute to the mood?

RUBÁIYÁT OF OMAR KHAYYÁM
Edmund Dulac

And this was all the Harvest that I reap'd—
"I came like Water, and like Wind I go."

XLVII

When You and I behind the Veil are past,
Oh, but the long, long while the World shall last,
　　Which of our Coming and Departure heeds
As the Sea's self should heed a pebble-cast.

XLVIII

A Moment's Halt—a momentary taste
Of BEING from the Well amid the Waste—
　　And Lo!—the phantom Caravan has reach'd
The NOTHING it set out from—Oh, make haste!

LXIV

Strange, is it not? that of the myriads who
Before us pass'd the door of Darkness through,
　　Not one returns to tell us of the Road,
Which to discover we must travel too.

LXXI

The Moving Finger writes; and, having writ,
Moves on: nor all your Piety nor Wit
　　Shall lure it back to cancel half a Line,
Nor all your Tears wash out a Word of it.

XCIX

Ah, Love! could you and I with Him conspire
To grasp this sorry Scheme of Things entire,
　　Would not we shatter it to bits—and then
Remold it nearer to the Heart's Desire!

Reader's Response *Which images in these poems do you find especially vivid or striking? Why?*

Closure and Extension

ANSWERS TO THINKING ABOUT THE SELECTION

1. (a) Suggested response: He conveys the impression that the sun is powerful and awe-inspiring. (b) The image of the sun scattering the stars into flight and driving night away conveys the sun's power.

2. Suggested response: Khayyám is suggesting that we focus on our present lives rather than on what will happen after death.

3. Suggested response: Verse XIII focuses on whether people should be more concerned with life on earth or with what happens after death. Verse XVI emphasizes the fleeting nature of life on earth. The fleeting nature of life can be used to support either side of

the argument addressed in verse XIII.

4. (a) He suggests that the world is indifferent to human life and death. (b) He conveys the world's indifference by comparing its reaction to "our Coming and Departure" to the sea's reaction to having a pebble thrown into it.

5. He points out that it is impossible to turn back the clock. Time keeps moving forward.

THINKING ABOUT THE SELECTION

Interpreting

1. (a) What impression of the sun does Khayyám convey in the first verse? (b) How does he convey this impression?
2. In verse XIII, what is the meaning of the line "take the Cash, and let the Credit go"?
3. How do the ideas conveyed in verse XVI relate to those conveyed in verse XIII?
4. (a) In verse XLVII, what does Khayyám suggest about the world's attitude toward human life and death? (b) How does he convey this idea?
5. In verse LXXI, what insight about the passage of time does Khayyám offer?
6. Throughout his *Rubáiyát* Omar Khayyám emphasizes the inevitability of death. (a) Which of these poems best expresses this sentiment to you? Why? (b) Which of the poems best emphasizes the resulting need to enjoy life while it lasts? Why?
7. What themes recur throughout these verses? Explain your answers.
8. What contradictory ideas do you find in these verses? Explain your answer.

Applying

9. According to one Persian poet, "In the rubái the last line thrusts the fingernail into the heart." (a) Now that you have read these rubái, explain the meaning of this quotation. (b) Which last line had this effect on you? Explain.

ANALYZING LITERATURE

Understanding Metaphors

Omar Khayyám uses many different metaphors to describe death and the passage of life. However, he does not intend for all of these metaphors to be interpreted in exactly the same way. Instead, each specific metaphor is used to convey a particular aspect or nuance of the subject. For example, the Drum in verse XIII and the Veil in verse XLVII are both metaphors for death. Yet the Drum is used to convey the inevitable approach of death, while the Veil is used to capture how death separates people from the material world.

1. The Bird in verse VII and the Leaves in verse VIII are both metaphors for life, yet they convey a strikingly different impression of its nature. Explain.
2. In verse XVI, Khayyám uses "Snow upon the Desert's dusty Face" as a metaphor for life. What aspect of life does this metaphor reveal?

3. (a) What metaphor for death does Khayyám present in verse LXIV? (b) What impression does this metaphor convey?
4. The English writer Joseph Addison has written, "When it is placed to an advantage, [a metaphor] casts a kind of glory round it, and darkens a luster through a whole sentence." Explain how this definition fits Omar Khayyám's use of metaphors.

CRITICAL THINKING AND READING

Recognizing the Author's Beliefs

Omar Khayyám was a Muslim, or a follower of the religion of Islam. One of the central doctrines of Islam is the belief in the oneness and absolute authority of God, who is the giver and taker of life. In addition, Muslims believe that life in this world is an extremely brief preparation for the eternal life after death. Although Khayyám wrote extensively about themes central to the Islamic religion, he was not a devout believer. In much of his poetry, it is not God, but fate, that dictates the passage of life.

1. Does Khayyám's message in verse XIII seem to be consistent with Islamic belief? Why or why not?
2. Explain whether or not you think that his message in verse LXIV is consistent with Islamic belief.
3. Khayyám chose to write using the rubái form and metaphors employed by other poets, particularly those writing religious poetry. This decision to conform to an existing pattern is called following a literary norm or poetic convention. Why might a poet choose to follow a norm rather than create his or her own style?

THINKING AND WRITING

Writing Poems in the Rubái Form

Write a poem or a series of poems in the rubái form. Remember that a rubái is a poem of four lines in which the first, second, and fourth lines rhyme. In addition, a good rubái conveys a message to the reader. It is self-contained, so that the reader does not need any further explanation to understand the message. Before you begin writing, decide on the message or idea you wish to convey. Then think of a metaphor for your idea. Try to avoid using very abstract metaphors that will not be easily understood in a four-line poem. When you have written and revised your poem or series of poems, share your work with your classmates.

(continued from bottom of page)

ANSWERS TO ANALYZING LITERATURE

1. Suggested response: Because the bird is beautiful, energetic, and able to fly, it conveys the impression that life is a brief yet wonderful process filled with activities and possibilities. The leaves, on the other hand, convey the impression that life is a process of steady decay, because they just sit passively on tree branches until they wither and fall to the ground.
2. Suggested response: It captures the fleeting, fragile nature of life.
3. (a) He uses "the door of Darkness" as a metaphor for death. (b) Suggested response: This metaphor conveys the impression that death is a mysterious and possibly ominous realm.
4. Answers will differ.

Challenge Have students find an American or British poet who uses metaphors extensively. For example, they might think of William Shakespeare or Emily Dickinson. Have them read at least ten poems by the poet they have chosen. Then have them compare and contrast Khayyám's use of metaphors with the British or American poet's use of metaphors.

ANSWERS TO CRITICAL THINKING AND READING

1. Suggested response: On the surface it does not seem to be consistent with Islamic belief because it suggests we focus on the present life, not on what will happen after death.
2. Suggested response: It does not seem to be consistent with Islamic belief because it suggests Khayyám is uncertain about what will happen after death.
3. Answers will differ. Students may respond that following a norm may increase a poet's chances of becoming successful.

THINKING AND WRITING

Publishing Student Writing You may want to have student volunteers make photocopies of the poems and arrange them into an anthology that can be distributed to the class.

6. (a) Answers will differ. Verses VIII, XVI, XVII, XXVIII, XLVII, XLVIII, LXIV, and LXXI all express the inevitability of death. (b) Answers will differ. Verses VII, XII, XIII, XLVIII all emphasize the need to enjoy life while it lasts.
7. Suggested response: The main recurring themes are the inevitable passage of time, the fleeting nature of life on earth, the inescapability of death, and the need to enjoy life to its fullest.

8. Suggested response: In a number of the verses, he expresses the idea that one should live for the present and try to enjoy life to its fullest. Yet he also points out the fleeting nature of life. The fleeting nature of life on earth can be seen as an important reason why people should be more concerned with what happens after death than with life on earth.
9. (a) Suggested response: The quota-

tion points out that the final lines of these poems tend to be jolting. (b) Answers will differ.

Presentation

Motivation/Prior Knowledge
Have students imagine that they have been asked to translate an American poem, such as Robert Frost's "The Road Not Taken," into a foreign language. Assuming that they are fluent in the chosen language, how would they go about translating the poem? Would they focus on capturing the meaning of the poem? Would they try to re-create the poem's rhythmical pattern and rhyme scheme? Why or why not? Would they try to re-create the poet's use of sound devices? Why or why not?

From this discussion students should become aware of some difficulties involved in translation. Point out that the process is especially difficult when the two languages are as dramatically different as English and Persian. Have students discuss other languages that might be difficult to translate into English.

Enrichment Tell students that the effectiveness of a translation can have a major impact on a reader's response to a work of foreign literature. For example, readers are more likely to respond favorably to a translation that consists of lively and vivid language than to one that consists of dull, monotonous language.

When you think of great world literature, certain writers probably spring to mind. For instance, you might think of Homer, Colette, Leo Tolstoy, and Anton Chekhov. These and other writers deserve the recognition they have received. Yet there are people other than writers who also deserve credit for the international appeal of world literature. These people are translators, the unsung heroes of world literature.

What Does Translation Involve?

At first glance, it may seem that translation requires nothing more than the knowledge of a foreign language. Yet in reality translation requires a wide array of talents. In addition to having a thorough appreciation of the nuances of the original language, translators must have an understanding of all the literary forms and techniques used in the original work. Translators must also be able to adapt these forms and techniques to a second language. At the same time, they must be careful to avoid altering the meaning of the work, and they must try to recapture the original writer's subtle uses of language.

Obviously, translation is not an easy task. Rather, it is an art form that requires both linguistic and literary talents. Because of the literary abilities required, many translators are themselves successful writers.

Edward FitzGerald's *Rubáiyát*

Edward FitzGerald, who translated Omar Khayyám's *The Rubáiyát*, was a nineteenth-century English poet. Yet his translations of *The Rubáiyát* are far more famous than his own poems.

Despite their success, however, FitzGerald's *The Rubáiyát* has also aroused controversy and raised questions about the relative importance of literal accuracy in the art of translation. In translating *The Rubáiyát*, FitzGerald clearly paid much more attention to capturing the form and spirit of the original poems than he did to literal accuracy. As a result, while the beauty of his translations is widely recognized, some scholars have criticized the translations and suggested that they should be regarded as *The Rubáiyát* of FitzGerald rather than *The Rubáiyát* of Khayyám. Even FitzGerald himself admitted that his translations were not altogether accurate, commenting, "I suppose few people have ever taken such pains in translation as I have, though certainly not to be literal."

Comparing Two Translations

Compare Friedrich Rosen's translation of one of the poems from Khayyám's *The Rubáiyát* with FitzGerald's translation of the same poem.

> This old caravanserai which they call a world
> Is the stable of the piebald steed of
>   morning and evening.
> It is a feast which is the remnant of a
>   hundred Jamshids,
> It is a castle which is the resting-place of a
>   hundred Bahrams.
> —Friedrich Rosen

> Think, in this batter'd Caravanserai,
> Whose Portals are alternate Night and Day,

NSIGHTS

How Sultan after Sultan with his Pomp
Abode his destin'd Hour, and went his way.
—Edward FitzGerald

Although Rosen has translated the Persian vocabulary and grammar very accurately, he has not managed to retain the rhyme, meter, and mood of the original poem. As a result, his version lacks the energy and vitality that made the original poem a work of art. In addition, because Rosen chose to include the references to the legendary Persian kings Jamshid and Bahram, anyone unfamiliar with Persian history and culture is likely to have trouble understanding the poem.

FitzGerald, on the other hand, has taken great care to reproduce the rhyme and rhythm of the original poem. At the same time, however, it is clear that he has altered the content of the original poem. For example, he has eliminated the references to Jamshid and Bahram and replaced them with anonymous sultans. Rather than focusing on literal accuracy, FitzGerald has tried to capture the form and intent of the original poem. Although he has succeeded in doing so, some critics might argue that his version is not a true translation of Khayyám's poem but rather an entirely new composition on the same theme as the original Persian poem.

Thinking About Translation

1. Which of the two versions of Khayyám's poem do you think is a better work of literature? Explain.
2. Considering how FitzGerald has altered the content of the original poem, do you think that his version should be regarded as a translation or as a new poem on the same theme as the original poem? Explain.
3. What do the differences between the two versions of Khayyám's poems reveal about the difficulties involved in translating literature?
4. If you were translating Omar Khayyám's *The*

Rubáiyát, how much importance would you place on literal accuracy?

Looking at Different Translations

The following are three different translations of another poem from Khayyám's *The Rubáiyát*. The first is a literal—or word-for-word one. The other two are more poetic. Carefully look over the three translations. Then answer the questions that follow.

We are puppets and the sky is a puppeteer,
From the perspective of reality, not from
    the perspective of metaphor.
What game should we play on the leather
    checkerboard of existence?
We go to the box of nonexistence one by
    one again.
        —Literal Translation

Impotent Pieces of the Game he plays
Upon this Checkerboard of Nights and
    Days;
Hither and thither moves, and checks, and
    slays;
And one by one back in the Closet lays.
        —Edward FitzGerald

We are the playthings and heaven the
    player,
In a manner that is true in word and deed.
Why should we play games on the chess-
    board of life
When we return to death's box, one piece
    at a time?
        —Jamal Elias

1. Which of the two latter translations is closer in meaning to the original poem? Explain.
2. What are the strengths and weaknesses of each of the two latter translations?
3. Which of these translations do you find most effective? Why?

ANSWERS TO THINKING ABOUT TRANSLATION

1. Answers will differ. Students should offer reasons for their choice.
2. Answers will differ. Students may comment that FitzGerald's version should be regarded as an adaptation of Khayyám's poem.
3. Answers will differ. Students may respond that the differences between the translations reveal that it is difficult to recapture both the form and the content of a foreign poem.
4. Answers will differ. Students may respond that they feel literal accuracy should be a translator's primary concern.

ANSWERS TO LOOKING AT DIFFERENT TRANSLATIONS

1. Suggested response: The translation by Jamal Elias is closer in meaning to the original poem.
2. Answers will differ. Students may respond that FitzGerald's translation is lively and entertaining and that Elias's translation is fairly accurate.
3. Answers will differ. Students may prefer FitzGerald's translation because of its lively language.

Additional Questions and Activities

1. How do FitzGerald's and Elias's translations differ in meaning?
2. Do you think that both FitzGerald's and Elias's translations are better works of literature than the literal translation? Why or why not?
3. Have students find two different translations of a poem by a foreign writer other than Khayyám. Then have them compare and contrast the two translations and explain which one they feel is most effective. You may want to have students work in groups of three or four to complete this activity.

THE KORAN

Focus

More About the Koran The Koran begins with the Surah entitled "The Opening." The rest of the Surahs are organized according to length, with the longer Surahs preceding the shorter ones. No one is certain of the order in which the revelations came to Muhammad. Yet it is known that the shorter revelations are generally the earliest ones and that most of the longer revelations came late in Muhammad's life. Have students discuss the reasons why Muhammad's later revelations might have been longer than his earlier revelations. What can be gained from the knowledge of the order in which Muhammad received his revelations?

The Koran is the scripture of the religion of Islam. It is believed to be the Word of Allah, the one true God according to the Muslim faith, and for this reason holds a higher place for Muslims than any other book in the world.

Muslims believe that the Koran is a divine book revealed to their prophet, Muhammad (moo ham´ əd), over the latter third of his life. These revelations first started coming to Muhammad when he was sitting and meditating in a cave outside his home town of Mecca (now one of the two capitals of Saudi Arabia). Suddenly, the angel Gabriel came to him and commanded him to recite something. When Muhammad asked the angel what it was that he wanted him to recite, Gabriel said in Arabic, "Recite in the name of the Lord Who creates." This was followed by the first of the revelations, and as a result is the first line of the Koran revealed to Muhammad. In fact, the name of the book may indeed be taken from this line, because the word *Koran* means "recitation" in Arabic.

It is held that Muhammad continued receiving such revelations from the age of forty until his death approximately twenty years later. He would repeat these revelations in front of his followers who would either memorize them or write them down on bits of parchment, pieces of leather, or clay tablets. Because these words were believed to have been given to Muhammad from God, they were highly valued. In the years after Muhammad's death, the people who had originally memorized or recorded segments of the Koran dispersed over a large area. In addition, some of these people died. Fearing that many parts of revelation would be lost, the leaders of the emerging Islamic community began collecting all the fragments of the revelation that they could locate. Approximately fifteen years after Muhammad's death, they organized these fragments into a book and named it the Koran. Copies of the Koran were then sent to all major cities in the Islamic world with orders that all other unofficial versions of the revelations should be destroyed. The book that they had distributed was then made the official scripture of the Islamic religion.

The revelations of Muhammad are arranged in chapters called Surahs. There are 114 such Surahs in the Koran, varying in length from three or four verses to well over 200 verses. Each one has a title, which is generally an unusual word or phrase appearing early in the Surah.

The earliest copies of the Koran were written in an imperfect Arabic script that included no vowels and used the same symbols for many different consonants. For this reason, unless people were already familiar with the words in the book, it was very difficult for them to follow what they were reading. However, the Arabic script was reformed in the eighth century to include vowels as well as signs to distinguish all consonants from one another. The Koran was then recopied in this script, and it has remained virtually unchanged to this day.

Objectives

Thematic

To understand Islamic beliefs

Skills

1 To grasp the messages of the Surahs from the Koran

2 To write a paper about Islamic beliefs

Support Materials

Teaching Portfolio

Teacher Backup, p. 131

Usage and Mechanics Worksheet, p. 135

Analyzing Literature Worksheet, p. 136

Critical Thinking and Reading, *Making Comparisons and Contrasts*, p.137

GUIDE FOR INTERPRETING

from the Koran

Commentary

The Role of the Koran in the Islamic Religion. In the eyes of Muslims, the Koran is viewed as the most important scripture in the world, but not the only one. They believe that Allah sent a series of heavenly books, or scriptures, to the world. These include the Torah (see page 40), the Psalms of David (see pages 67–70), and the New Testament. The last of these heavenly books is the Koran, which Muslims believe to be the final revelation of Allah. Although Muhammad uttered the words of the Koran, he is not considered its author, but rather is viewed as the transmitter of God's message to humanity. Muslims believe that the Koran, word for word and syllable for syllable, is the exact message of Allah. Because this means that the words used in the Koran are Allah's words, and any translation loses some of its religious value, most Muslims feel that the Koran should be read in Arabic, and that translations are only approximations of the real text. Of course, the vast majority of today's Muslims do not know Arabic and can only read the translations. However, all scholars of Islam use the original Arabic text for their studies.

The belief that the words used in the Koran are divine has had a tremendous impact on the development of the Arabic language. Since it is Allah's speech, and Allah does not make mistakes, Muslims feel that the Koran is grammatically and stylistically perfect. For this reason the Koran is regarded as the best model of the Arabic language and is the basis for all Arabic grammar to this day.

The fundamental message of the Koran is that there is but one God who has created the world and everything that is in it. This God is all-powerful and all-knowing; is just, loving, and merciful; is the Protector and Sustainer of all life; and is our Judge at the end of time. As a result, it is the duty of all people to praise, glorify, and submit to him. The Surahs in the Koran convey this message in many different ways, but none do this more clearly than the the one called "The Opening."

Writing

"The Opening" begins with the line "In the Name of God, the Merciful, the Compassionate." Freewrite, exploring the meaning of the word *compassionate.*

Literary Focus Just as Muslims consider the Koran to be the last in a series of heavenly books, they believe Muhammad was the last in a long series of prophets, starting with Adam and including Moses and all the other prophets mentioned in the Bible. In addition Muslims regard Islam as the last in a series of religions sent by God to guide human beings toward good. Have students compare and contrast these and other Islamic views with the beliefs of other religions with which they are familiar.

Writing/Prior Knowledge Before students begin their freewriting, hold a class discussion in which students talk about people whom they consider to be especially compassionate.

ESL Teaching Strategy Explain to your ESL students that the words *thee* and *thou* are often found in religious works and in poetry but are no longer used in everyday speech. Point out that both of these words replace the pronoun *you.*

Teaching Tenth-Grade Students You may want to read these selections aloud to tenth-grade students so that they hear the beauty of the language. Encourage them to ask questions after you have finished reading each selection.

Language Worksheet, *Translating into Modern English,* p. 138
Selection Test, pp. 139–140

from the # Koran
The Opening
translated by Arthur J. Arberry

In the Name of God, the Merciful, the Compassionate

Praise belongs to God, the Lord of all Being,
the All-merciful, the All-compassionate,
  the Master of the Day of Doom.

Thee only we serve; to Thee alone we pray for succor.[1]
5 Guide us in the straight path,
the path of those whom Thou hast blessed,
not of those against whom Thou art wrathful,
  nor of those who are astray.

---

1. succor (suk´ ər) *n.*: Aid; help; relief.

KORAN, IN NASHTI CALLIGRAPHY
Ibrahim Sultan, grandson of Tame
The Metropolitan Museum of Art, New York

Power
translated by Arthur J. Arberry

In the Name of God, the Merciful, the Compassionate

Behold, We sent it down on the Night of Power;
And what shall teach thee what is the Night of Power?
The Night of Power is better than a thousand months;
  in it the angels and the Spirit descend,
5   by the leave of their Lord, upon every command.
Peace it is, till the rising of dawn.

Humanities Note

Fine art, *Koran, in Nashti Calligraphy,* by Ibrahim Sultan. Calligraphy is the art of fine handwriting—an art form that the Persians brought to a level of elegance matched by few other cultures. The two types of calligraphy used by the Persians and the Arabs are Nashti, the cursive style with rounded letters seen in this example, and the angular style known as Kufic. With its curving arabesques derived from flower shapes and its rhythmic linear design, Nashti script originated as an outgrowth of ancient Middle Eastern patterns in heraldry and decorative art. Often the decorative style of Nashti is combined with Islamic ornament, such as the design surrounding the pages of the Koran.

You might want to use the following questions to discuss the art:.
1. What can you infer about the Persian culture from the use of calligraphy and elaborate ornaments in printing the Koran?
2. Does the design of a book ever affect your appreciation for it?

Daybreak

translated by Arthur J. Arberry

In the Name of God, the Merciful, the Compassionate

Say: "I take refuge with the Lord of the Daybreak
    from the evil of what He has created,
    from the evil of darkness when it gathers,
    from the evil of the women who blow on knots,
    from the evil of an envier when he envies."

3

THINKING ABOUT THE SELECTIONS

Interpreting

1. Why do you think the line "In the Name of God, the Merciful, the Compassionate" is repeated in all three selections?
2. (a) In "The Opening" what is meant by "the strait path"? (b) What is the meaning of the line that reads, "the Master of the Day of Doom"?
3. In the selection entitled "Daybreak," with whom is a person supposed to take refuge, and from what?

Applying

4. "Daybreak" describes several different types of evil. What are some of the types of evil that exist in today's world?

ANALYZING LITERATURE

Understanding the Koran

The selections you have just read are perfect examples of what many of the Surahs, or chapters, of the Koran are like. You may have found some of these verses difficult to understand. Many Islamic scholars also find some Koranic verses difficult to interpret, and over the centuries they have written books in which they have offered their explanations of the Koran. In the eyes of religious Muslims, these books are considered to be vitally important in helping them to understand exactly what God wants them to know and do.

1. "The Night of Power" is believed to be the night on which the last piece of the Koran was revealed to Muhammad. In light of this fact, what do you think is the overall meaning of the selection?
2. Restate the central message of "The Opening" in your own words.
3. "The Opening" is probably the most frequently recited Islamic prayer. Why might this be the case?
4. What is the central message of "Daybreak"?

THINKING AND WRITING

Writing About Islam

Write a paper in which you explain what the three selections from the Koran reveal about Islamic belief. Begin by reviewing the three selections, noting the main ideas they convey. Organize your ideas. Then begin writing your essay. Limit your discussion to what is revealed in the three selections. When you revise make sure your paper is clear and accurate.

(continued from bottom of page)
4. Suggested response: "Daybreak" is simply a pledge to take refuge in Allah from all forms of evil.

THINKING AND WRITING

Writing Across the Curriculum You may want to inform the social studies department about this assignment.

3 Discussion Have students discuss the connotations of the word *daybreak*. What associations do they have with this time of day? What associations do they have with darkness?

Cultural Note The British soldier and writer T. E. Lawrence (1888–1935), better known as Lawrence of Arabia, had an excellent knowledge of the Koran and the Islamic religion. Passionately devoted to the Arabic people, Lawrence led the Arabs in their struggle to win independence from the Turkish Ottoman Empire. Lawrence recounted his involvement with the Arabs in his book *The Seven Pillars of Wisdom* (1927), and his exploits were later captured on screen in the popular film *Lawrence of Arabia*. You might want to rent a videotape of the movie and show it to your class. Then have your students discuss reasons why Lawrence might have become so devoted to the Arab cause.

Cooperative Learning Divide your students into groups of three or four and have them research Lawrence of Arabia or another Westerner who was interested in or adopted the Islamic religion. For example, students might choose a famous athlete, such as Mohammed Ali or Kareem Abdul Jabbar. When conducting their research, students should focus on the role of Islam in the life of the figure they have chosen. Once students have finished their research, they should present their findings to the class.

Closure and Extension

ANSWERS TO THINKING ABOUT THE SELECTIONS

1. Suggested response: It is repeated to emphasize the Muslim belief in and devotion to Allah.
2. (a) Suggested response: It is the path of righteousness and devotion that ultimately leads to Paradise after death.
(b) Suggested response: It emphasizes Allah's power and points out that it is Allah who judges people at death.
3. Suggested response: People are supposed to take refuge with Allah from all forms of evil.
4. Answers will differ. Students might suggest greed, prejudice, and self-centeredness.

ANSWERS TO ANALYZING LITERATURE

1. Suggested response: The selection recounts how Muhammad received his final revelations, stressing the wondrous nature of this event.
2. Suggested response: "The Opening" is a pledge of devotion to Allah and a request for guidance.
3. Answers will differ.

Focus

More About the Authors During his thirty years of traveling, Sa'di visited Asia Minor, Syria, India, and Egypt, and made a pilgrimage to Mecca. For a brief period, he was held captive by the Crusaders. A year after completing his travels, he presented his *Bustan* to Sa'd bin Zangi.

Have students discuss the ways in which traveling can benefit writers. Also have them think of other writers who have traveled extensively. How did the travels of these writers shape their works?

In the years before his poetry earned him the patronage of the rulers of Shiraz, he supported himself by teaching and copying manuscripts. Have your students discuss why writers often support themselves by teaching. Why might writers make good teachers?

Hafiz's poems have been translated into many different languages, including Latin, French, English, German, and Greek. Probably the most famous translator of his poems is the renowned German Romantic Johann Wolfgang von Goethe. Have students discuss why famous writers such as Goethe would choose to translate the works of other writers. Do they imagine that a gifted writer might be a better translator than someone who does not have a talent for writing? Why or why not?

SA'DI (1184–1282)

Sa'di (sä′ dē) is revered for his wit, learning, and elegant style of writing. Persian-speaking people of all ages still read his works for enjoyment and for ethical guidance in their lives.

Sa'di was born in the city of Shiraz, which was a major center of art and literature at the time. His real name was Muslihuddin (mōōs lə hōō dēn′), but he adopted the pseudonym Sa'di to show his appreciation for his royal patron, a local ruler named Sa'd bin Zangi (sä′d bēn zän jē′).

Sa'di was educated in Baghdad, which was the capital of the Islamic world until it was sacked by the Mongols in 1258. In addition to studying at a major university, he was a disciple of several famous religious and mystical teachers. After devoting the first three decades of his life to his education, Sa'di spent approximately thirty years traveling and composing poetry. He then spent another three decades in religious seclusion, devoting much of his time and energy to revising his poems. During the last ten years of his life, he focused on teaching the ways of the mystic and taking care of the needy.

As a writer, Sa'di is known mainly for three major works: the *Bustan*, or "Garden," which is a collection of religious and ethical poems; the *Gulistan*, or "Rose Garden," which is a book of fables; and the *Divan*, or "Collection of Poems," which contains a large number of odes, along with a variety of light, humorous poems.

The *Gulistan* has crossed easily from one culture to another. Its speculations on life and proper behavior are so accessible to Westerners that it has been repeatedly translated since 1787.

HAFIZ (1324–1390)

Hafiz (hä′ fəz) ranks second only to Sa'di among all of the Persian lyric poets. In fact, Hafiz's skill at writing odes even surpasses that of Sa'di, and he is is considered the undisputed master of this form of poetry.

Like Sa'di, Hafiz was born in Shiraz, a city famous for its flowers as well as its poets. Orphaned when very young, he was forced to work as a baker's apprentice in order to support himself. In his free time he attended a local religious school, where he immediately distinguished himself as a student with unusual ability and determination. When he was still a young boy, he memorized the entire Koran—a feat that earned him the title of *Hafiz,* which is the term generally applied to someone who has memorized the Koran.

As a young man, Hafiz gained immediate recognition as an outstanding poet and attached himself to the court at Shiraz. Even though many other rulers tried to entice him to come to their courts, Hafiz spent almost his entire life in his native city, leaving only for short periods of time. Hafiz's love for Shiraz and its beautiful gardens is evident in many of his poems.

Although he also wrote a few prose works, Hafiz's fame rests entirely upon his collected poems, called the *Divan*. Most of the poems in this collection are odes that display his profound understanding of religion as well as his love for his native city. Believing that his *Divan* contains a hidden mystical meaning, many people use the collection as a sort of poetic horoscope: They open the book at random, then study the poem on the page they have turned to, hoping to find guidance.

Objectives

Thematic

To grasp the writers' messages about human conduct

3 To use context clues to determine the meanings of words

Skills

1 To understand Sufi fables
2 To write a fable

Support Material

Teaching Portfolio
Teacher Backup, p. 141
Grammar in Action Worksheet, *Using the Colon,* p. 145
Usage and Mechanics Worksheet, p. 147
Vocabulary Check, p. 148
Analyzing Literature Worksheet,

GUIDE FOR INTERPRETING

Selections by Sa'di and Hafiz

Commentary

Sufism. Picture an ascetic in a threadbare woolen garment abandoning earthly desires and retreating from the world to contemplate God. You are picturing a **Sufi,** a member of a mystical sect within the Islamic religion known as Sufism. The humble attire just described is so essential to these mystics that they draw their name from the Arabic word *suf,* meaning "wool."

Sufis have a particular interest in mystical topics, or matters that are beyond our normal understanding. In order to understand the true nature of God and his relationship to human beings, they feel they must free themselves from material desires and live disciplined lives in which they frequently isolate themselves to engage in prayer and meditation.

Many Sufis use literature as a means of explaining their mystical revelations and their moral and ethical beliefs to others. As a result, some of the most esteemed Persian writers, including Sa'di and Hafiz, were Sufis. When writing prose, Sufis try to make their theme, or central message, as accessible as possible. For example, Sa'di directly states the moral or ethical message at the end of each of the fables in the *Gulistan.* In their poetry the message is frequently less obvious. Because the Sufi writers rely to a great extent on metaphors and symbols, their poetry can often be interpreted on two different levels, a literal level and a symbolic level. Generally, it is necessary to interpret the poems on a symbolic level to decipher their religious message. In addition, many of the symbols and metaphors used by the Sufi writers are tied to nonreligious, sensual pursuits. For example, wine is used as a symbol for religious doctrine and a tavern is used to symbolize a place of religious instruction.

A central theme in Sufi writing is the belief that our life on earth is transitory and constitutes a blink of the eye when compared to the eternal life after death. This idea is accompanied by the belief that people should be more concerned with piety and religious behavior than with worldly pursuits, because when people die their fates rest solely in God's hands. As you read the following selections by Sa'di and Hafiz, look for the messages they convey and note what they reveal about the Sufi beliefs concerning proper moral conduct.

Writing

In one of the sections from "On the Excellence of Contentment," Sa'di explores whether it is better to pursue knowledge or wealth. Write a journal entry in which you examine your own answer to this age-old question.

(continued from bottom of page)
amples of other people or groups of people who have chosen to withdraw from society. Then have them compare and contrast the Sufis with the people and groups of people they have named.

Writing/Prior Knowledge Before having students write their journal entry, you might want to divide your class into two groups and hold a debate about whether it is better to pursue knowledge or wealth.

ESL Teaching Strategy To avoid confusion explain to ESL students that a number of Persian or Arabic terms are used in these selections. These words include *padshah, vizier, amirs,* and *ullemma.* Tell students that it is very important for them to read the footnote that accompanies each of these words.

Adapting to Tenth-Grade Students Explain to tenth-grade students that the messages of the following selections are directly stated in passages of verse.

Vocabulary

Preteach the following vocabulary words:
beneficent (bə nef´ ə s'nt) *adj.*: Charitable
tyrannical (ti ran´ i k'l) *adj.*: Harsh; cruel; unjust;
extortions (ik stôr´ shənz) *n.*: Acts of obtaining money through threats, violence, or misuse of authority
succor (suk´ ər) *n.*: Aid; help; relief
censorious (sen sôr´ ē əs) *adj.*: Inclined to find fault
benevolent (bə nev´ ə lənt) *adj.*: Kindly; charitable
bereave (bi rēv´) *v.*: To deprive or rob

Understanding Sufi Fables, p. 149
Language Worksheet, *Using Context Clues,* p. 150
Selection Test, pp. 151–152
Art Transparency 2
Illustration from *The Book of Omens*

Literary Focus Explain to students that one of the reasons Sufis withdrew from society was that they were deeply disturbed by the evil and suffering they saw in the world around them. Also point out that although the Sufis withdrew from society, they still maintained contact with the outside world through their writing. Have students think of ex-

Spelling Tip Make sure students note the double *n* in the word *tyrannical.* Point out that a double *n* is used in many other words, including *beginning, uncanny,* and *dinner.*

from the # Gulistan

Sa'di

from ## The Manners of Kings

translated by Edward Rehatsek

1

I heard a padshah[1] giving orders to kill a prisoner. The helpless fellow began to insult the king on that occasion of despair, with the tongue he had, and to use foul expressions according to the saying:

> *Who washes his hands of life*
> *Says whatever he has in his heart.*

> *When a man is in despair, his tongue becomes long and he is like a vanquished cat assailing a dog.*

> *In time of need, when flight is no more*
> *   possible,*
> *The hand grasps the point of the sharp*
> *   sword.*

When the king asked what he was saying, a good-natured vizier[2] replied: "My lord, he says: '*Those who bridle their anger and forgive men; for Allah loveth the beneficent.*'"[3]

The king, moved with pity, forbore taking his life, but another vizier, the antagonist of the former, said: "Men of our rank ought to speak noth-ing but the truth in the presence of padshahs. This fellow has insulted the king and spoken unbecomingly." The king, being displeased with these words, said: "That lie was more acceptable to me than this truth thou hast uttered because the former proceeded from a conciliatory disposition and the latter from malignity;[4] and wise men have said: 'A falsehood resulting in conciliation is better than a truth producing trouble.'"

> *He who the shah follows in what he says,*
> *It is a pity if he speaks anything but what is*
> *   good.*

The following inscription was upon the portico of the hall of Feridun:[5]

> *O brother, the world remains with no one,*
> *Bind the heart to the Creator, it is enough.*
> *Rely not upon possessions and this world*
> *Because it has cherished many like thee and*
> *   slain them.*
> *When the pure soul is about to depart,*
> *What boots it if one dies on a throne or on*
> *   the ground?*

---

1. padshah (päd′ shä): King.
2. vizier (vi zir′): A high officer in the government; a minister.
3. *Those who bridle . . . beneficent*: A passage from the Koran. The beneficent are those who are kind and charitable.

4. malignity (mə lig′ nə tē) *n*.: Persistent or intense ill will or desire to do harm to others.
5. Feridun (fer ə dön′): A legendary Persian king whose life is recorded in Firdawsi's *Shah-nama*. Feridun's three sons all died as a result of their dispute concerning who should succeed their father.

6

It is narrated that one of the kings of Persia had stretched forth his tyrannical hand to the possessions of his subjects and had begun to oppress them so violently that in consequence of his fraudulent extortions they dispersed in the world and chose exile on account of the affliction entailed by his violence. When the population had diminished, the prosperity of the country suffered, the treasury remained empty and on every side enemies committed violence.

> Who desires succor in the day of calamity,
> Say to him: "Be generous in times of
>   prosperity."
> The slave with a ring in his ear, if not
>   cherished will depart.
> Be kind because then a stranger will become
>   thy slave.

One day the *Shah-nama* was read in his assembly, the subject being the ruin of the dominion of Zohak[6] and the reign of Feridun. The vizier asked the king how it came to pass that Feridun, who possessed neither treasure nor land nor a retinue, established himself upon the throne. He replied: "As thou hast heard, the population enthusiastically gathered around him and supported him so that he attained royalty." The vizier said: "As the gathering around of the population is the cause of royalty, then why dispersest thou the population? Perhaps thou hast no desire for royalty?"

> It is best to cherish the army as thy life
> Because a sultan reigns by means of his
>   troops.

The king asked: "What is the reason for the gathering around of the troops and the population?" He replied: "A padshah must practice justice that they may gather around him and clemency that they may dwell in safety under the shadow of his government; but thou possessest neither of these qualities."

> A tyrannic man cannot be a sultan
> As a wolf cannot be a shepherd.

> A padshah who establishes oppression
> Destroys the basis of the wall of his own
>   reign.

The king, displeased with the advice of his censorious vizier, sent him to prison. Shortly afterward the sons of the king's uncle rose in rebellion, desirous of recovering the kingdom of their father. The population, which had been reduced to the last extremity by the king's oppression and scattered, now assembled around them and supported them, till he lost control of the government and they took possession of it.

> A padshah who allows his subjects to be
>   oppressed
> Will in his day of calamity become a violent
>   foe.
> Be at peace with subjects and sit safe from
>   attacks of foes
> Because his subjects are the army of a just
>   shahanshah.[7]

7

A padshah was in the same boat with a Persian slave who had never before been at sea and experienced the inconvenience of a vessel. He began to cry and to tremble to such a degree that he could not be pacified by kindness, so that at last the king became displeased as the matter could not be remedied. In that boat there happened to be a philosopher, who said: "With thy permission I shall quiet him." The padshah replied: "It will be a great favor." The philosopher ordered the slave to be thrown into the water so that he swallowed some of it, whereon he was caught and pulled by his hair to the boat, to the stern of which he clung with both his hands. Then he sat down in a corner and became quiet. This appeared strange to the king who knew not what wisdom there was in the preceeding and asked for it. The philosopher replied:

"Before he had tasted the calamity of being drowned, he knew not the safety of the boat; thus also a man does not appreciate the value of immunity from a misfortune until it has befallen him."

---

6. **Zohak** (zä′ hāk): A legendary and tyrannical Persian king who was dethroned by Feridun.

7. **shahanshah** (shä′ hän shä): Emperor or King of kings, usually referred to as a shah.

Commentary

The Role of Love in Sufi Belief Many Sufis believe that the best way to reach God is through love. This is not the physical love of one person for another, but divine love, which is the love of a human being for God. When a person truly loves God, Sufis feel that this love fills the person completely and produces a sense of joy and contentment. In addition Sufis believe that their love for God causes God to love them in return. As a consequence of this mutual love, the Sufi is drawn to God and eventually becomes united with Him. Having become united with God, the person then loses a sense of his or her individuality.

In shedding their sense of individuality, Sufis develop a strong desire to describe their feeling of love to the general public in order to induce people to join them in their union with God. Generally the Sufis consider poetry the best means for conveying their divine love. In their poetry they often use descriptions of intimate relationships between lovers or between friends as metaphors for divine love. Thus a poem that on the surface appears to be an expression of a poet's love for a person is in reality an expression of his or her love for God.

Humanities Note

Fine art, *Salih, Ayyubid King of Syria, conversing with two paupers.* This Persian miniature painting comes from Bukhara, a Persian city that became a center of cultural activity during the sixteenth century when a group of exiled artists settled there. The vivid, enamellike colors seen here are typical of the miniature paintings produced in Bukhara. Another important characteristic of these paintings is the reliance on geometric forms. In this picture note the star-shaped design in front of the throne and the dark cross and other angular divisions of space.

Depicting a Syrian king conversing with two paupers, this painting was intended to serve as an admonition to rulers not to ignore the common people.

You might want to use the following questions to discuss the art:

1. Why do you think the artist placed the king where he did in this picture? How can you tell he is the king?
2. Why do you think artists of Persian miniatures frequently chose to paint scenes that emphasized the splendor of the royal court and the wisdom of the king?
3. In what ways is the purpose of this painting similar to the purpose of story 6 from the *Gulistan*?
4. Do you consider the setting of this painting to be intriguing or exotic? Why or why not?

12 Discussion Have students discuss what they could learn from this passage. How could they apply this lesson to their own lives?

SALIH, AYYUBID KING OF SYRIA, CONVERSING WITH TWO PAUPERS
The Metropolitan Museum of Art, New York

12

O thou full man, barley-bread pleases thee
   not.
She is my sweetheart who appears ugly to
   thee.
To the huris[8] of paradise purgatory seems
   hell.

8. **huris** (hoo´ rēs): The dark-eyed women who in Islamic legend live with the blessed in paradise.

Ask the denizens[9] of hell. To them purgatory
   is paradise.

There is a difference between him whose friend is in his arms
And him whose eyes of expectation are upon the door.

9. **denizens** (den´ i zənz) *n.*: Inhabitants or occupants.

Grammar in Action

A **colon** is used to introduce a quotation that is formal or lengthy or a quotation that does not contain a "he said/she said" expression.

For example, note how the colon is used to introduce the vizier's statement in the following passage from the *Gulistan*:

The vizier said: "As the gathering around of the population is the cause of royalty, then why dispersest thou the population? Perhaps thou hast no desire for royalty?"

In the *Gulistan*, colons are also sometimes used to introduce

quotations that are brief and informal. Normally a comma would be used to introduce such quotations.

Student Activity 1. Find ten instances in the *Gulistan* in which colons are used to introduce quotations. Then for each example explain whether the colon was the appropriate punctuation mark or whether a comma would have been more appropriate.

Student Activity 2. Record a conversation between two or more people. Use both colons and commas to introduce the comments of the people involved. Make sure you use both punctuation marks correctly.

35

I was sitting in a vessel with a company of great men when a boat which contained two brothers happened to sink near us. One of the great men promised a hundred dinars[10] to a sailor if he could save them both. Whilst however the sailor was pulling out one, the other perished. I said: "He had no longer to live and therefore delay took place in rescuing him." The sailor smiled and replied: "What thou hast said is certain. Moreover, I preferred to save this one because, when I once happened to lag behind in the desert, he seated me on his camel, whereas I had received a whipping by the hands of the other. When I was a boy I recited: *He, who doth right, doth it to his own soul and he, who doth evil, doth it against the same.*"[11]

> As long as thou canst, scratch the interior[12]
>   of no one
> Because there are thorns on this road.
> Be helpful in the affairs of a dervish[13]
> Because thou also hast affairs.

---

10. dinars (di närz´) *n.*: Gold coins used in a number of Islamic countries.

11. He, who doth right . . . the same: A passage from the Koran.
12. scratch the interior: Injure the feelings.
13. dervish (dʉr´ vish): A Muslim dedicated to a life of poverty and chastity.

from On the Excellence of Contentment
translated by Edward Rehatsek

2

Two sons of amirs[14] were in Egypt, the one acquiring science, the other accumulating wealth, till the former became the ullemma[15] of the period and the other the prince of Egypt; whereon the rich man looked with contempt upon the faquih[16] and said: "I have reached the sultanate whilst thou hast remained in poverty as before." He replied: "O brother, I am bound to be grateful to the most high Creator for having obtained the inheritance of prophets whilst thou hast attained the inheritance of Pharaoh and of Haman,[17] namely the kingdom of Egypt."

---

14. amirs (ə mirz´): Princes.
15. ullemma (ool´ ləm mä´): A Muslim scholar or person of authority in religion and law.
16. faqih (fə kï´): A scholar of law.
17. pharaoh (fer´ ō) **. . . Haman** (hä´ mən): The pharaohs were the rulers of ancient Egypt. Haman was a Persian courtier who lived during the fifth century B.C. Both Haman and the pharaohs are remembered for their extreme wickedness.

> I am that ant which is trodden under foot
> Not that wasp, the pain of whose sting
>   causes lament.
> How shall I give due thanks for the blessing
> That I do not possess the strength of
>   injuring mankind?

3

I heard that a dervish, burning in the fire of poverty and sewing patch upon patch, said to comfort his mind:

> "We are contented with dry bread and a
>   patched robe
> For it is easier to bear the load of one's own
>   trouble than that of thanks to others."

Someone said to him: "Why sittest thou? A certain man in this town possesses a benevolent nature, is liberal to all, has girded his loins to serve the pious and is ready to comfort every heart. If he becomes aware of thy case, he will consider it an

13 Discussion Have students discuss what they can infer about the narrator's attitude toward life from this comment. Does the comment suggest that people's fates are beyond their control? Why or why not?

14 Discussion Have students discuss how they would have reacted if they had been in the sailor's place. Would they have done everything possible to save both brothers?

15 Literary Focus Have students explain how this passage sums up the message of the story that precedes it. Why do they think Sa'di included this passage?

16 Reading Strategy Have students make inferences about these selections based on the title. How might these selections differ from the selections from "The Manners of Kings"?

17 Discussion Which of the two brothers do students find more deserving of respect? Why?

18 Reading Strategy Have students pause to think about the connection between this passage and the story that precedes it.

19 Clarification Point out that it is likely that the dervish described here is a Sufi.

Master Teacher Note Have students list the various messages of Sa'di's fables and record them on the chalkboard. Then have your students discuss what the messages suggest about Sa'di's attitudes and beliefs. In what ways are Sa'di's attitudes and beliefs similar to and different from their own attitudes and beliefs? Do they feel they can learn anything about the similarities and differences between the Persian and American cultures by reading Sa'di's fables? Why or why not?

20 Discussion Have students react to this comment. Do they agree with this point of view? Why or why not? Why might some of the homeless people in our society share these sentiments?

21 Literary Focus Have students make inferences about Sufi beliefs based on this passage and the story that precedes it.

22 Literary Focus Have students explain how this passage relates to the paragraph that precedes it. Is this connection clear? Why or why not?

23 Enrichment The belief in a drink that bestows immortality is a common element of many folk traditions. Such a belief even prompted the Spanish explorer Ponce de León (1460?–1521) and other explorers to engage in quests to discover the legendary Fountain of Youth in America. Have students discuss why people from a variety of cultures might have shared the belief in an elixir of immortality.

24 Discussion Have students discuss what they could learn from this fable.

Cultural Note Point out to students that writers from a wide array of cultures have written fables. Two examples are the French writer Jean de la Fontaine (page 834) and the American writer James Thurber. Have students discuss possible reasons for the lasting popularity of the fable form.

Cooperative Learning Divide your class into groups of four or five. Then have each group choose a writer who has written fables. Next the groups should read the fables of the writer they have chosen. After reading the fables, the groups should spend some time discussing them. Finally they should report on the fables to their classmates.

obligation to comfort the mind of a worthy person." He replied: "Hush! It is better to die of inanition[18] than to plead for one's necessities before any man."

> It is better to patch clothes and sit in the
>   corner of patience
> Than to write petitions for robes to
>   gentlemen.
> Verily it is equal to the punishment of hell
> To go to paradise as a flunky to one's
>   neighbor.

11

A brave warrior who had received a dreadful wound in the Tatar war was informed that a certain merchant possessed a medicine which he would probably not refuse to give if asked for; but it is related that the said merchant was also well known for his avarice.[19]

> If instead of bread he had the sun in his
>   table-cloth
> No one could see daylight till the day of
>   resurrection.

The warrior replied: "If I ask for the medicine he will either give it or refuse it and if he gives it maybe it will profit me, and maybe not. At any rate the inconvenience of asking it from him is a lethal poison.

---

18. **inanition** (in´ ə nish´ ən) *n.*: Exhaustion from lack of food.
19. **avarice** (av´ ər is) *n.*: Greed for riches.

> Whatever thou obtainest by entreaties from
>   base men
> Will profit thy body but injure thy soul.

And philosophers have said: "If for instance the water of life[20] were to be exchanged for a good reputation, no wise man would purchase it because it is preferable to die with honor than to live in disgrace."

> To eat coloquinth[21] from the hand of a
>   sweet-tempered man
> Is better than confectionary from the hand
>   of an ill-humored fellow.

17

I noticed an Arab of the desert sitting in a company of jewelers at Bosrah and narrating stories to them. He said: "I had once lost my road in the desert and consumed all my provisions. I considered that I must perish when I suddenly caught sight of a bag full of pearls and I shall never forget the joy and ecstasy I felt on thinking they might be parched grain nor the bitterness and despair when I discovered them to be pearls."

> In a dry desert and among moving sand
> It is the same to a thirsty man whether he
>   has pearls or shells in his mouth.
> When a man has no provisions and his
>   strength is exhausted
> It matters not whether his girdle is adorned
>   with pearls or potsherds.[22]

---

20. **the water of life:** According to Middle Eastern legend, a drink that bestows immortality.
21. **coloquinth** (käl´ ə kwinth´) *n.*: The spongy, bitter fruit of a widely cultivated plant of the gourd family.
22. **potsherds** (pät´ shʉrdz´) *n.*: Pieces of broken pottery.

Reader's Response *Literature speaks to us across centuries and across cultures. Which lesson in living from the* Gulistan *would you share with a friend? Why?*

Sufism began in the late seventh and the eighth centuries as a reaction to the worldliness and extravagance of the ruling class. The following is a description by al-Khatib of a visit to Baghdad in 917.

". . . Finally, they came again to the presence of the Caliph Muktadir, whom they found in the Palace of the Crown upon the bank of the Tigris. He was arrayed in clothes of Dabik-stuff embroidered in gold, being seated on an ebony throne overlaid with Dabik-stuff embroidered in gold likewise, and on his head was the tall bonnet called galansuwah. Suspended on the right of the throne were nine necklaces, like prayer beads, and to the left were seven others, all of famous jewels, the largest of which was of such a size that its sheen eclipsed the daylight. Before the Caliph stood five of his sons, three to the right and two to the left. Then the ambassadors, with their interpreter, halted before Muktadir, and stood in the posture of humility, with their arms crossed."

THINKING ABOUT THE SELECTION

Interpreting

1. (a) In the first story from "The Manners of Kings," why does the vizier lie to the king about the prisoner's remarks? (b) What does the the king's reaction to the truth reveal about his character?
2. In story 6 from "The Manners of Kings," Sa'di writes that "a sultan reigns by means of his troops," then goes on to state that a ruler who "establishes oppression destroys the basis of the wall of his own reign." Are these two statements contradictory? Explain.
3. How does the verse at the end of story 2 from "On the Excellence of Contentment" relate to the fable that precedes it?
4. What is ironic, or surprising, about the Arab's reaction to his discovery of the pearls in story 17 from "On the Excellence of Contentment"?
5. In what way are stories 2, 11, and 17 from "On the Excellence of Contentment" similar to one another?

Applying

6. To what other types of situations might the philosopher's lesson in story 7 from "The Manners of Kings" be applied?

ANALYZING LITERATURE

Understanding Sufi Fables

Almost all Sufi writing conveys a religious message. Often, this is done through fables that capture the reader's interest, while at the same time offering them religious instruction. For example, in the *Gulistan* Sa'di uses fables involving kings and other characters from Persian mythology to illustrate his religious teachings.

1. The Sufis believe that it is necessary to treat others with kindness, because we will eventually be either rewarded or punished for our actions. Which of Sa'di's stories convey this idea? Support your answer.
2. The Sufis also believe that people should not be concerned with worldly pursuits, such as the quest for wealth and material objects. Which of Sa'di's stories convey this belief and how do they convey it?
3. The Sufis have an intense awareness of the fleeting nature of life on earth. Which of Sa'di's stories express this awareness? Explain.
4. Name two other lessons that Sa'di teaches in his stories. Then explain how he conveys each of these lessons.
5. According to an Arabian proverb, a fable is "a bridge which leads to truth." Do you think fables are an effective way of revealing truths about life? Explain your answer.

THINKING AND WRITING

Writing a Fable

Write a fable modeled after the ones by Sa'di that you have read. Begin by thinking of a moral message you would like to convey. Then design a story that illustrates this message. The fable does not have to be about kings; it can be about ordinary people or even about animals that think, speak, and act like human beings. Regardless of the characters you use, try to make your fable as interesting and entertaining as possible and end it with a two- or four-line poem that directly states its message. When you revise your fable, make sure your message is apparent both in the main story and in the concluding poem. After you have finished revising, share your fable with your classmates.

(continued from bottom of page)

ANSWERS TO ANALYZING LITERATURE

1. Suggested response: Stories 1, 6, and 35 from "The Manners of Kings" convey this idea. Story 1 emphasizes the importance of compassion and conciliation. Story 6 teaches that rulers must treat their subjects justly. Story 35 demonstrates a potential consequence of mistreating others.
2. Suggested response: All the stories from "On the Excellence of Contentment" convey this belief. Stories 2 and 3 convey the belief by showing the contentment of people who are not wealthy. Story 11 teaches that death is preferable to being beholden to a greedy person. Story 17 demonstrates that material objects do not serve an essential purpose.
3. Suggested response: Story 7 and story 33 from "The Manners of Kings" and stories 3, 11, and 17 from "On the Excellence of Contentment" express this awareness by showing different ways in which life can be quickly stripped away from a person.
4. Answers will differ. Students may point out that story 6 from "The Manners of Kings" teaches that rulers should treat their subjects fairly. They may also note that story 3 from "On the Excellence of Contentment" teaches that people should not rely on others.
5. Answers will differ. Students may respond that fables are effective because they teach lessons in an entertaining manner.

Challenge Have students compare and contrast Sa'di's fables with other fables they have read.

THINKING AND WRITING

Publishing Student Writing You might want to encourage students to submit their fables to the school literary magazine.

Closure and Extension

ANSWERS TO THINKING ABOUT THE SELECTION

1. (a) Suggested response: He lies because he believes in forgiveness. (b) Suggested response: It reveals that he places a high value on conciliation.
2. Suggested response: The two statements are not contradictory. A sultan must have control of the military to retain power, yet having control of the military does not necessarily make the sultan oppressive.
3. Suggested response: The wasp and the ant referred to in the verse represent the two brothers in the story.
4. It is ironic because you would expect the discovery of pearls to make a person happy.
5. Suggested response: All three fables teach that people should not be greedy and should not place too much importance on material possessions.
6. Answers will differ. Students might suggest that the lesson could be applied to wealthy people who do not feel grateful for what they have.

from the Divan
Hafiz

Alive from the Dead
translated by Walter Leaf

LOVE SCENE
Persian miniature from the Bokhara School (late sixteenth–early seventeenth centuries)
The Metropolitan Museum of Art, New York

Returns again to the pleasance the rose, alive from the dead;
Before her feet in obeisance[1] is bowed the violet's head.

The earth is gemmed as the skies are, the buds a zodiac band,
For signs in happy ascendant and sweet conjunction spread.

5 Now kiss the cheek of the Saki[2] to sound of tabor and pipe,
To voice of viol and harpstring the wine of dawntide wed.

The rose's season bereave not of wine and music and love,
For as the days of a man's life her little week is fled.

The faith of old Zoroaster[3] renews the garden again,
10 For lo, the tulip is kindled with fire of Nimrod[4] red.

The earth is even as Eden, this hour of lily and rose;
This hour, alas! Not an Eden's eternal dwellingstead!

The rose with Solomon[5] rides, borne aloft on wings of the wind;
The bulbul's[6] anthem at dawn like the voice of David[7] is shed.

---

1. obeisance (ō bā′ s'ns) *n.*: A gesture of respect.
2. Saki (sā′ kī) *n.*: The wine-pourer.
3. Zoroaster (zō′ rō as′ tər): Zarathustra, a great Persian prophet who lived during the sixth or seventh century B.C. His teachings formed the foundation of Zoroastrianism, the dominant Persian religion before the emergence of Islam.
4. Nimrod (nim′ räd): A figure from the Old Testament, known for his skill as a hunter.
5. Solomon (säl′ ə mən): In Islamic belief, Solomon is a great king and prophet known for his wisdom.
6. bulbul's (bo͞ol′ bo͞olz): The bulbul is the nightingale, a songbird often referred to in Persian poetry as a metaphor for the poet himself.
7. David: In the Old Testament, David is the second king of Israel and the father and predecessor of Solomon. He is considered a prophet in Islam.

Humanities Note

Fine art, *Love Scene*. This Persian miniature was painted during the late sixteenth or early seventeenth century in the Persian city of Bokhara. Controlled by a patron of the arts named Shah Abbas, Bokhara was a major Persian artistic center of the time. Many artists who lived there had fled from other Persian cities that had been overrun by foreign invaders.

The artists of Bokhara formed a school of miniature painting known for its conservative yet tender and romantic style. Rather than focusing on full historical scenes, these artists generally depicted only one or two figures in each painting. As in this painting, the figures were usually surrounded by delicate flowering trees and plants. In depicting both the people and the landscape, the artists used warm, subtle colors.

As a whole, this period of Persian art was characterized by curves rather than straight lines, by delicacy rather than drama, and by a soft and lyrical outlook. Eventually

5 Fill high the bowl to our lord's name 'Imad-ud-Din Mahmud;[8]
Behold King Solomon's Asaph[9] in him incarnated.

Beyond eternity's bounds stretch the gracious shade of his might;
Beneath that shadow, O Hafiz, be thine eternity sped.

6

---

8. Imad-ud-Din Mahmud (ē' mäd ood dīn mä mood'): Hafiz's royal patron.
9. Asaph (ā' säf): In the Bible, Asaph is the chief musician in the ancient temple at Jerusalem in the time of David.

Reader's Response *What did you think this poem would be about when you read the title "Alive from the Dead"?*

THINKING ABOUT THE SELECTION

Interpreting

1. What does Hafiz mean when he writes that the rose has returned "alive from the dead"?
2. How does Hafiz relate the life cycle of the rose to the human experience?
3. Like most other works by Sufi writers, "Alive from the Dead" conveys a message. What is this message?

Applying

4. It is common for writers from a wide variety of cultures and eras to relate the cycles of nature to the human experience. (a) Why do you think this is so? (b) What other literary works can you think of that relate the cycles of nature to the human experience?
5. The next to last stanza of Hafiz's poem is dedicated to one of his patrons. (a) Do you think that a contemporary writer would be likely to include this type of dedication? Why or why not? (b) If not, what difference does this reveal between contemporary writers and writers of Hafiz's time?

UNDERSTANDING LANGUAGE

Using Context Clues

You can often determine the meaning of a word by examining the **context** in which it is used. As a result, when you come across a word with which you are unfamiliar, you should look at the words surrounding it to see if they hint at its meaning. For example, look at the line, "Before her feet in obeisance bowed the violet's head." The word *obeisance* may be unfamiliar to you. However, if you note that the violet's head is bowed and remember that a bow is usually a sign of respect, you should be able to figure out that obeisance means "showing respect."

Try to determine the meaning of the following words from the context in which they are used. Read the line aloud to hear the way the word sounds. Then check your definitions in a dictionary. After you are sure of the definition, write an original sentence using each word.

1. pleasance (line 1)
2. ascendant (line 4)
3. conjunction (line 4)
4. kindled (line 10)
5. incarnated (line 16)

Persian art deteriorated as a result of the combined effects of war, Western influences, indifferent patronage, and a lack of new or original styles. Miniature painting ceased to be a major art form in Persia in the late seventeenth and early eighteenth centuries. Today paintings such as this one suggest a golden, romantic era far removed from the real world.

You might want to use the following questions to discuss the art:
1. Does the scene depicted in this painting seem distant in both time and space? Why or why not?
2. How would you describe the mood of the painting?
3. Considering the mood of the painting and the remoteness of the scene it depicts, do you think it is an appropriate illustration for "Alive from the Dead"? Why or why not?
4. Can you see yourself in the place of one of the people depicted in the painting? Why or why not?

1207–1273

Rumi (rü´ mē) is regarded not only as one of the finest Persian mystical poets but as one of the finest poets the world has ever seen. Muslims from all over the world follow the teachings contained in his poetry and even reenact the whirling dance that Rumi did as part of his mystical exercises. Rumi himself was the founder of the Sufi order known as "Whirling Dervishes." You may have seen films of dervishes performing the hypnotic dance through which they hope to gain enlightenment.

Rumi was born in the central Asian city of Balkh, where his father was a religious instructor. When he was ten years old, his family moved to Anatolia (now known as Turkey), eventually settling in the city of Konya, which was the capital of Anatolia at the time. When Rumi's father died in 1231, Rumi assumed his position as a teacher of religion and quickly developed into a famous Sufi master with a large circle of disciples.

A murder figured importantly in Rumi's life. One day a wandering Sufi named Shams came to Konya. Rumi was so impressed with this man's knowledge that he invited Shams to live in his own house and began spending all his time with his new friend. Rumi's disciples were extremely jealous of this newcomer, but Rumi ignored their complaints. Enraged by their master's unwillingness to listen to them, Rumi's disciples secretly murdered Shams and hid his body in a well. Thinking that his friend had deserted him, Rumi became distraught, and he left Konya in search of Shams. When he returned from his vain search, instead of resuming his teaching duties as his disciples had hoped, he started writing poetry and dedicating it to his lost friend.

Several years after the death of Shams, Rumi met a goldsmith named Zarkub in the market at Konya. Rumi felt that this man was, in fact, Shams appearing in a different form, and he became close friends with Zarkub. Rumi stayed with his new friend until his death but continued writing poems about Shams.

Rumi is remembered primarily for three books: one collection of prose and two works of poetry. The prose work, entitled *Fihi ma Fihi*, or "In It What Is in It," is a collection of religious and mystical sayings. His largest work is a collection of poems dedicated to Shams, entitled *The Divan of Shams*. In addition to Persian poetry, this collection contains some verses in Greek and Turkish, which were the other languages spoken in Konya at the time. Rumi's most famous work is the *Masnavi*, a long poem written at the suggestion of one of his students and intended to provide guidance for his disciples and for future generations.

Rumi had an unusual method of composing. Although some of the verses in the *Masnavi* were written while Rumi was sitting, many others were composed while he was walking around, dancing, or even taking a bath. After having written these verses, he seldom bothered to revise them. For this reason, they are fresh and vibrant when read in Persian, and they convey Rumi's overflowing love for God. The *Masnavi* has stood through time as one of the most important Sufi works ever written, and it has been translated into many languages and analyzed by countless religious and literary scholars.

GUIDE FOR INTERPRETING

from the Masnavi

Commentary

Didactic Literature. Didactic literature is central to many religions. It imparts moral lessons through simple stories that may take the form of short tales or fables. The word *didactic* comes from a Greek word meaning "to teach."

The purpose of didactic literature is not to reveal psychological truths but to define the values of a society. It is not to entertain or to raise questions, but to establish codes of behavior. Therefore, didactic literature often contains aphorisms, or short pointed statements expressing human truths. The stories themselves often end with morals, or principles regarding right and wrong conduct.

Writing

Both of the following selections deal with wisdom. According to Islamic belief, a person must possess wisdom in order to recognize the difference between right and wrong and to know how to behave in a moral way. What do you see as the role of wisdom in our society? How highly do you think wisdom is valued? Freewrite, exploring your answers to these questions.

Primary Source

The Bible often uses concise stories to teach moral truths. One of the most famous of these is the parable of the mustard seed, Mark 5:30–32:

> [30] And he said, "With what can we compare the kingdom of God, or what parable shall we use for it? [31] It is like a grain of mustard seed, which, when sown upon the ground, is the smallest of all the seeds on earth; [32] yet when it is sown it grows up and becomes the greatest of all shrubs, and puts forth large branches, so that the birds of the air can make nests in its shade."

What moral truth do you find in this parable? What other parables do you know that teach moral truths?

Language Worksheet, *Understanding Symbolism*, p. 160
Selection Test, pp. 161–162

Spelling Tip Students may find it easier to spell *degradation* if they remember that it is the noun form of the verb *degrade.*

Literary Focus Have students discuss whether they think that literature can be an effective means of instruction. During the discussion they should explore the following questions: Does a moral principle have more of an impact when it is illustrated by a story? Why or why not? Are there any possible negative implications of using literature as a means of instruction? If so, what are they?

Writing/Prior Knowledge Before students begin freewriting, write the word *wisdom* on the chalkboard. Have students discuss the connotations of the word. In their freewriting they can then draw on the ideas expressed during the discussion.

ESL Teaching Strategy Pair each ESL student with another member of the class. Then have each pair read the following selections together, taking turns reading aloud to each other. The native-speaking student should make sure the ESL student pronounces all the words correctly and should clarify the meanings of any difficult words.

Teaching Tenth-Grade Students To help tenth-grade students grasp the first selection, divide your chalkboard into three columns with the headings: "Wise Man," "Half Wise," and "Fool." Then read the selection aloud with your students, listing the characteristics that Rumi attributes to each of these types of people.

Vocabulary

Preteach the following vocabulary words:
degradation (deg´ rə dā´ shən) *n.*: A lowering in rank, status, or condition
wiles (wīlz) *n.*: Sly tricks
assertions (ə sur´ shənz) *n.*: Positive statements
lamentations (lam´ ən tā´ shənz) *n.*: Outward expressions of grief
ignoramus (ig´ nə rā´ məs) *n.*: A stupid person who lacks knowledge and experience

from the # Masnavi

Rumi

The Marks of the Wise Man, of the Half Wise, and of the Fool

translated by E. H. Whinfield

1 The wise man is he who possesses a torch of his own;
He is the guide and leader of the caravan.
That leader is his own director and light;
That illuminated one follows his own lead.
5 He is his own protector; do ye also seek protection
From that light whereon his soul is nurtured.
2 The second, he, namely, who is half wise,
Knows the wise man to be the light of his eyes.
He clings to the wise man like a blind man to his guide,
10 So as to become possessed of the wise man's sight.
But the fool, who has no particle of wisdom,
Has no wisdom of his own, and quits the wise man.
He knows nothing of the way, great or small,
And is ashamed to follow the footsteps of the guide.
3 15 He wanders into the boundless desert,
Sometimes halting and despairing, sometimes running.
He has no lamp wherewith to light himself on his way,
Nor half a lamp which might recognize and seek light.
He lacks wisdom, so as to boast of being alive,
20 And also half wisdom, so as to assume to be dead.
That half wise one became as one utterly dead
In order to rise up out of his degradation.
If you lack perfect wisdom, make yourself as dead
Under the shadow of the wise, whose words give life.
4 25 The fool is neither alive so as to companion with 'Isa,[1]
Nor yet dead so as to feel the power of 'Isa's breath.
His blind soul wanders in every direction,
And at last makes a spring, but springs not upward.

---

1. 'Isa (ĭ′zä): Jesus, considered by Muslims to be a very important prophet.

society that Rumi would regard as "fools."

wise man. His followers, on the other hand, would have been regarded as "half wise."

One important way in which he provided religious guidance for his followers was by writing instructive verses such as "The Marks of the Wise Man, of the Half Wise, and of the Fool." In these verses he often used metaphors to

**ISKANDAR AND
THE SEVEN WISE MEN**
*Shiraz style, 1475–1485,
from the* Book of
Alexander *by Nizami*
Musée d'Art et d'Histoire, Geneva

Reader's Response *Given Rumi's
definition, which of the people you know
would you consider wise?*

THINKING ABOUT THE SELECTION

Interpreting

1. Explain the statement that "the wise man is he who possesses a torch of his own."
2. How does Rumi's statement that the wise man "is the guide and leader of the caravan" relate to his observations about those who are "half wise"?
3. Why does Rumi comment that people who lack perfect wisdom should make themselves "as dead"?
4. What does Rumi mean when he writes that the fool "is neither alive" nor "yet dead"?

5. Explain Rumi's statement that the fool "at last makes a spring, but springs not upward"?

Applying

6. The American writer and philosopher Ralph Waldo Emerson wrote, "Whoso would be a man must be a nonconformist. . . . Nothing is at last sacred but the integrity of our own mind." (a) What is your reaction to Emerson's comment? (b) How does Emerson's statement relate to the ideas Rumi expresses in this excerpt from the *Masnavi?*

Rumi's message easier to grasp? Why or why not?

Closure and Extension

ANSWERS TO THINKING ABOUT THE SELECTION

1. Suggested response: The statement implies that the wise man is a leader who possesses his own ideas.

2. The "half wise" are the people in the wise man's "caravan."
3. Suggested response: By making themselves "as dead," the people free themselves of their preconceptions and open themselves to the teachings of the wise.
4. Suggested response: He is not "alive" because he does not possess wisdom, and he is not "dead" because he has not freed his mind of precon-

ceptions and opened it to the teachings of the wise.
5. Suggested response: Because he lacks wisdom and has not followed the teachings of the wise, his soul does not spring upward toward salvation and paradise.
6. (a) Answers will differ. Students may respond that they agree with Emerson's comment because they believe that individuality is very important.

(continued from bottom of page)
(b) Suggested response: The "non-conformist" Emerson refers to can be compared with Rumi's "wise man."

Challenge Ask students if they have read any other literary works that express ideas similar to those expressed by Rumi. Then have them compare and contrast the works they have named with Rumi's poem.

Humanities Note

Fine art, *Iskandar and the Seven Wise Men.* In this painting Iskandar (the Persian name for Alexander the Great) is shown consulting seven wise men. Created in Shiraz, Persia, between 1475 and 1485 as an illustration for a manuscript called *The Book of Alexander,* the painting depicts the Macedonian conqueror as a Persian shah. Written by the famous Persian poet Nizami, *The Book of Alexander* describes the period in which Alexander ruled Persia.

This painting is only one of a vast number of Persian artistic works depicting a king receiving counsel from wise men. As in this instance, the works usually depict them as being aged men with turbans and beards.

Notice that in this painting the advisers and the king are all equal in size, though they are positioned at varying distances from the viewer. Rather than attempting to depict space and distances realistically, Persian artists generally used complex overall designs to create decorative, balanced compositions. In this instance the artist has established a pattern by distributing the black and red accents, white turbans, and bunches of flowers throughout the picture.

You might want to use the following questions to discuss the art:
1. What does the fact that Alexander is shown with no throne or attendants suggest about the Persian attitude concerning his rule?
2. What impression of Alexander's advisers does the painting convey?

from the *Masnavi* 123

The Counsels of the Bird

translated by E. H. Whinfield

CONCOURSE OF THE BIRDS
Habib Allah
The Metropolitan Museum of Art, New York

A man captured a bird by wiles and snares;
The bird said to him, "O noble sir,
In your time you have eaten many oxen and sheep,
And likewise sacrificed many camels;
5 You have never become satisfied with their meat,
So you will not be satisfied with my flesh.
Let me go, that I may give you three counsels,
Whence you will see whether I am wise or foolish.
The first of my counsels shall be given on your wrist,
10 The second on your well-plastered roof,
And the third I will give you from the top of a tree.
On hearing all three you will deem yourself happy.
As regards the counsel on your wrist, 'tis this,
'Believe not foolish assertions of anyone!'"
15 When he had spoken this counsel on his wrist, he flew
Up to the top of the roof, entirely free.
Then he said, "Do not grieve for what is past;
When a thing is done, vex not yourself about it."
He continued, "Hidden inside this body of mine
20 Is a precious pearl, ten drachms[1] in weight.
That jewel of right belonged to you,
Wealth for yourself and prosperity for your children.
You have lost it, as it was not fated you should get it,
That pearl whose like can nowhere be found."
25 Thereupon the man, like a woman in her travail,[2]
Gave vent to lamentations and weeping.
The bird said to him, "Did I not counsel you, saying,
'Beware of grieving over what is past and gone'?
When 'tis past and gone, why sorrow for it?
30 Either you understood not my counsel or are deaf.
The first counsel I gave you was this, namely,
'Be not misguided enough to believe foolish assertions.'
O fool, altogether I do not weigh three drachms,
How can a pearl of ten drachms be within me?"

---

1. drachms (dramz) *n.*: An ancient Greek unit of weight approximately equal to the weight of a silver coin of the same name.
2. travail (trav'āl) *n.*: Pains of childbirth.

5 The man recovered himself and said, "Well then,
Tell me now your third good counsel!"
The bird replied, "You have made a fine use of the others,
That I should waste my third counsel upon you!
To give counsel to a sleepy ignoramus
0 Is to sow seeds upon salt land.
Torn garments of folly and ignorance cannot be patched.
O counselors, waste not the seed of counsel on them!"

Reader's Response *How important do you consider the messages that this poem conveys?*

THINKING ABOUT THE SELECTION

Interpreting

1. Why does the bird give his second counsel from the top of the man's roof?
2. (a) What is the meaning of the bird's comment that "to give counsel to a sleepy ignoramus / is to sow seeds upon salt land"? (b) What is the meaning of his statement that "torn garments of folly and ignorance cannot be patched"?
3. Rumi believed that people who were not wise were not capable of grasping his religious and ethical teachings. How does "The Counsels of the Bird" convey this belief?
4. Based on "The Counsels of the Bird," summarize Rumi's ideas about people who are not wise.

Applying

5. Why do you think Rumi chose to write this verse, rather than merely stating his message in one or two sentences?
6. (a) As in Rumi's verse, animals are often used as a means of teaching moral or religious lessons. Why do you think this is so? (b) What other literary works can you think of in which animals are used as a means of teaching moral or religious messages? (c) In what ways are these works similar to and different from "The Counsels of the Bird"?

ANALYZING LITERATURE

Understanding Didactic Literature

In addition to being consumed by his love for God, Rumi was a religious teacher who wanted his students to learn the proper ethical and moral way of life.
1. In your own words, restate Rumi's message.
2. How does this message apply to your life?
3. In what way, if any, is Rumi's all-consuming love for God evident in this selection? Support your answer.

THINKING AND WRITING

Comparing and Contrasting Writers

Write a paper in which you compare and contrast the selections from Rumi's *Masnavi* with the selections from Sa'di's *Gulistan*. Along with two or three of your classmates, review the selections. Then discuss the following questions with the other members of your group: What are the similarities and differences between the literary styles of the two writers? What are the similarities and differences between their messages? How does each writer go about conveying his message? Take notes during your discussion. Then work individually to write your paper. As you write, use passages from the selections for support. When you have finished writing, gather again with the members of your group and read your papers to one another. Discuss ways in which they could be improved.

THE THOUSAND AND ONE NIGHTS

Focus

More About the Work The first standard printed text of *The Thousand and One Nights* appeared in the fifteenth century. Two centuries later, it was introduced to the Western world by the French scholar Antoine Gallard (1646–1715). Since then, many English translations of the work have been produced, and many of the tales have become so well known in the West that they have almost become integrated into Western folklore. Ask your students if they are familiar with any of the tales from *The Thousand and One Nights*. How did they learn about these stories? Do they find the stories entertaining? Why or why not?

The Thousand and One Nights is undoubtedly the most famous work of Arabic prose known to the Western world. Even people who have never heard its name are familiar with many of its tales, which have become part of the large collection of stories that are an important part of most people's childhood. Who has not heard of the voyages of Sindbad the Sailor, or of Aladdin and his magic lamp? These are just two of the many stories contained in this massive book.

The Thousand and One Nights is actually not just one story. Rather, it is a collection of different tales loosely pieced together into one long narrative. The framework that connects all the various tales is the story of the woman-hating King Shahriyar, who marries a different woman each night and puts her to death each morning. To delay her execution, Princess Shaharazad (sometimes spelled Scheherazade) tells him a story each night but withholds its ending until the next day. The tales go on for a thousand and one nights (hence the name of the book). By the time Princess Shaharazad has finished telling her tale, almost three years have passed and King Shahriyar has fallen in love with her and as a result decides not to execute her.

There probably never was a real King Shahriyar or Princess Shaharazad. Nor is there a single author who wrote all of *The Thousand and One Nights*. The Arabic book known by this name today is based on an ancient Persian storybook called the *Hazar Afsaneh (The Thousand Tales)*. This book was translated into Arabic around the year A.D. 850. It was then that the book came to be known as *The Thousand and One Nights*. Following its translation, the book quickly became popular in many Arabic lands. Often, people would gather around professional storytellers in marketplaces and coffeehouses to hear these fantastic tales. Over the years the storytellers embellished the original collection of tales, adding to them many new stories they had invented or heard from other sources. They also changed the names of the people and places, as well as some other details. Consequently, under the influence of these storytellers, *The Thousand and One Nights* was transformed into a genuinely Arabic collection of stories.

Because of the great changes that occurred over time, three different strands of *The Thousand and One Nights* can be identified. The first is the original Persian book and its accompanying framework. This strand is now difficult to distinguish, however, though it is still obvious that certain stories originated from Persian folklore. The story of Princess Shaharazad, which forms the fragile string that loosely connects all the tales in the book, belongs to this strand.

The second strand is set in the Arabic city of Baghdad (now the capital of Iraq) and focuses on the reign of King Harun ar-Rashid. Among the stories included in this strand are the tales of Sindbad and Aladdin. The final strand consists of many short humorous tales that originated in the city of Cairo (now the capital of Egypt). All these strands and the stories they involve are now woven together like a tapestry, so that readers find themselves reading stories within stories, with characters in one tale becoming the narrators of the next one.

Objectives

Thematic

To see how each of these interconnected tales conveys the importance of compassion

Skills

1 To understand folk tales
2 To recognize word origins
3 To write an adaptation of a folk tale

Support Material

Teaching Portfolio

Teacher Backup, p. 163
Grammar in Action Worksheet, *Recognizing Transitions*, p. 167
Usage and Mechanics Worksheet, p. 169
Vocabulary Check, p. 170
Analyzing Literature Worksheet, *Understanding Folk Tales*, p. 171

GUIDE FOR INTERPRETING

from The Thousand and One Nights

Commentary

Folk Tales. Folk tales are stories that were originally handed down orally among the common people of a particular culture. Because they are intended for a general audience, they are told in simple language that can be understood by virtually anyone, regardless of the level of education. Often, these stories relate events that are unrealistic or unlikely to happen in the real world in order to teach a lesson or express a general truth about life. In addition, the characters in folk tales tend to be stereotypes or stock characters embodying a single human trait, quality, or emotion. For example, a character in a folk tale may embody envy or greed.

During the course of history, folk tales have often been transmitted from one culture to another and eventually assimilated into the traditions of the new culture. Yet on the basis of plot and other details, it is usually possible to identify when a folk tale has been adopted from another culture. *The Thousand and One Nights* is a perfect example of the merging of a number of folk traditions. It includes many stories that were originally Persian but have been transformed into Arabic tales, along with many other tales that are of Arabic origin. It is also likely that some of the Persian stories are themselves variations of earlier Indian folk tales. "The Fisherman and the Jinnee," for example, is one of the simplest and oldest tales in *The Thousand and One Nights* and may indeed have originally been an Indian folk tale.

Writing

We have all heard stories about jinnees or seen them on television or in the movies. How do you envision a typical jinnee? What would the jinnee look like? What would cause it to appear? How would it act? Write a journal entry in which you respond to these questions.

Primary Source

The Thousand and One Nights (also known as *The Arabian Nights*) has had a tremendous impact on Westerners. Patricia Barrett Perkins comments on its power to bridge the cultural gap between East and West in her foreword to the tales: "Only a generation or two ago, reading *The Arabian Nights* provided a magic carpet ride to a land and a people most of us would never see or know. Today, when one reads the stories, we not only enter this fascinating and exotic world, but also are better able to understand a land and people who are as close as our television sets. What better way to breach the cultural gap than through their literature?"

Language Worksheet, *Recognizing Word Origins*, p. 172
Selection Test, pp. 173–174

Spelling Tip Point out to students that the *f* sound in the word *blasphemous* is spelled with the letters *ph*.

Literary Focus Tell students that since folk tales were at first transmitted orally from one generation to the next, their authors are seldom known. In addition explain that through the process of retelling, the details of the stories are likely to have changed over the years although their basic plots are likely to have remained the same. Have students compare this process to a situation in which someone recounts an experience to a friend who in turn relates the story to others. Ask students whether it is their impression that stories grow more entertaining or amusing as they are passed on from person to person.

Writing/Prior Knowledge If your students are unfamiliar with jinnees, you might offer them the alternative of writing a journal entry in which they discuss another character from *The Thousand and One Nights*.

ESL Teaching Strategy Because this selection contains some difficult vocabulary, you may want to read it aloud with students. Encourage ESL students to speak up whenever they come across a word they do not understand.

Teaching Tenth-Grade Students Before tenth-grade students begin reading this story, you might want to explain to them that it contains three interwoven tales.

Vocabulary
Preteach the following vocabulary words:
blasphemous (blas´ fə məs) *adj.*: Showing a lack of respect toward God
adjured (ə jŏord´) *v.*: Commanded solemnly
indignantly (in dig´ nənt lē) *adv.*: Angrily or scornfully
resolutely (rez´ ə lŏot´ lē) *adj.*: In a determined, unwavering manner
enraptured (in rap´ chərd) *adj.*: Filled with great pleasure or delight
munificence (myŏo nif´ ə səns) *n.*: Generosity
ominous (äm´ ə nəs) *adj.*: Sinister; threatening

from The Thousand and One Nights

The Fisherman and the Jinnee

translated by N. J. Dawood

Once upon a time there was a poor fisherman who had a wife and three children to support.

He used to cast his net four times a day. It chanced that one day he went down to the sea at noon and, reaching the shore, set down his basket, rolled up his shirt sleeves, and cast his net far out into the water. After he had waited for it to sink, he pulled on the cords with all his might; but the net was so heavy that he could not draw it in. So he tied the rope ends to a wooden stake on the beach and, putting off his clothes, dived into the water and set to work to bring it up. When he had carried it ashore, however, he found in it a dead donkey.

"By Allah,[1] this is a strange catch!" cried the fisherman, disgusted at the sight. After he had freed the net and wrung it out, he waded into the water and cast it again, invoking Allah's help. But when he tried to draw it in he found it even heavier than before. Thinking that he had caught some enormous fish, he fastened the ropes to the stake and, diving in again, brought up the net. This time he found a large earthen vessel filled with mud and sand.

Angrily the fisherman threw away the vessel, cleaned his net, and cast it for the third time. He waited patiently, and when he felt the net grow heavy he hauled it in, only to find it filled with bones and broken glass. In despair, he lifted his eyes to heaven and cried: "Allah knows that I cast my net only four times a day. I have already cast it for the third time and caught no fish at all. Surely He will not fail me again!"

With this the fisherman hurled his net far out into the sea and waited for it to sink to the bottom. When at length he brought it to land he found in it a bottle made of yellow copper. The mouth was stopped with lead and bore the seal of our master Solomon, son of David.[2] The fisherman rejoiced and said: "I will sell this in the market of the coppersmiths. It must be worth ten pieces of gold." He shook the bottle and, finding it heavy, thought to himself: "I will first break the seal and find out what is inside."

The fisherman removed the lead with his knife and again shook the bottle; but scarcely had he done so when there burst from it a great column of smoke which spread along the shore and rose so high that it almost touched the heavens. Taking shape, the smoke resolved itself into a jinnee of such prodigious[3] stature that his head reached the clouds, while his feet were planted on the sand. His head was a huge dome and his mouth as wide as a cavern, with teeth ragged like broken rocks. His

---

1. Allah (al´ lə): The Arabic word for God.

2. Solomon . . . David: In the Old Testament, David and his son Solomon are both great Kings of Israel and are considered prophets by Muslims.

3. prodigious (prə dij´ əs) *n.*: Wonderful; amazing.

legs towered like the masts of a ship, his nostrils were two inverted bowls, and his eyes, blazing like torches, made his aspect fierce and menacing.

The sight of this jinnee struck terror to the fisherman's heart; his limbs quivered, his teeth chattered together, and he stood rooted to the ground with parched tongue and staring eyes.

"There is no god but Allah and Solomon is His Prophet!" cried the jinnee. Then, addressing himself to the fisherman, he said: "I pray you, mighty Prophet, do not kill me! I swear never again to defy your will or violate your laws!"

"Blasphemous giant," cried the fisherman, "do you presume to call Solomon the Prophet of Allah? Solomon has been dead these eighteen hundred years, and we are now approaching the end of time. But what is your history, pray, and how came you to be imprisoned in this bottle?"

On hearing these words the jinnee replied sarcastically: "Well, then; there is no god but Allah! Fisherman, I bring you good news."

"What news?" asked the old man.

"News of your death, horrible and prompt!" replied the jinnee.

"Then may heaven's wrath be upon you, ungrateful wretch!" cried the fisherman. "Why do you wish my death, and what have I done to deserve it? Have I not brought you up from the depths of the sea and released you from your imprisonment?"

But the jinnee answered: "Choose the manner of your death and the way that I shall kill you. Come, waste no time!"

"But what crime have I committed?" cried the fisherman.

"Listen to my story, and you shall know," replied the jinnee.

"Be brief, then, I pray you," said the fisherman, "for you have wrung my soul with terror."

"Know," began the giant, "that I am one of the rebel jinn who, together with Sakhr the Jinnee, mutinied against Solomon, son of David. Solomon sent against me his vizier,[4] Asaf ben Berakhya, who vanquished me despite my supernatural power and led me captive before his master. Invoking the

---

4. **vizier** (vi zir'): A high officer in the government; a minister.

ILLUSTRATION FOR *ARABIAN NIGHTS* FOR "THE FISHERMAN AND THE GENIE (JINNEE)"
Edmund Dulac
New York Public Library

name of Allah, Solomon adjured me to embrace his faith and pledge him absolute obedience. I refused, and he imprisoned me in this bottle, upon which he set a seal of lead bearing the Name of the Most High. Then he sent for several of his faithful jinn, who carried me away and cast me into the middle of the sea. In the ocean depths I vowed; 'I will bestow eternal riches on him who sets me free!' But a hundred years passed away and no one freed me. In the second hundred years of my imprisonment I said: 'For him who frees me I will open up the buried treasures of the earth!' And yet no one freed me. Whereupon I flew into a rage and swore: 'I

from *The Thousand and One Nights*   129

8 **Discussion** Ask students if they think that the jinnee has any justification for killing the fisherman.

9 **Reading Strategy** Have students predict whether the fisherman will be able to find a way to outsmart the jinnee.

10 **Enrichment** Muslims share the Christian belief in a final judgment day, when people will be rewarded or punished, depending on how they conducted their lives.

11 **Discussion** Have students discuss whether the fisherman should believe the jinnee's promise.

12 **Reading Strategy** Have students pause at this point in the story. Make sure they recognize that they have made a transition from one tale into another and that the fisherman is the narrator of the new tale.

13 **Literary Focus** Remind students that this type of interweaving of tales occurs throughout *The Thousand and One Nights*. Considering that the princess had to sustain King Shahriyar's interest in order to avoid being executed, why do students think she chose to weave together a web of interconnected tales rather than just tell one long story?

---

will kill the man who sets me free, allowing him only to choose the manner of his death!' Now it was you who set me free; therefore prepare to die and choose the way that I shall kill you."

"O wretched luck, that it should have fallen on my lot to free you!" exclaimed the fisherman. "Spare me, mighty jinnee, and Allah will spare you; kill me, and so shall Allah destroy you!"

"You have freed me," repeated the jinnee. "Therefore you must die."

"Chief of the jinn," cried the fisherman, "will you thus requite[5] good with evil?"

"Enough of this talk!" roared the jinnee. "Kill you I must."

At this point the fisherman thought to himself: "Though I am but a man and he is a jinnee, my cunning may yet overreach his malice." Then, turning to his adversary, he said: "Before you kill me, I beg you in the Name of the Most High engraved on Solomon's seal to answer me one question truthfully."

The jinnee trembled at the mention of the Name, and, when he had promised to answer truthfully, the fisherman asked: "How could this bottle, which is scarcely large enough to hold your hand or foot, ever contain your entire body?"

"Do you dare doubt that?" roared the jinnee indignantly.

"I will never believe it," replied the fisherman, "until I see you enter this bottle with my own eyes!"

Upon this the jinnee trembled from head to foot and dissolved into a column of smoke, which gradually wound itself into the bottle and disappeared inside. At once the fisherman snatched up the leaden stopper and thrust it into the mouth of the bottle. Then he called out to the jinnee: "Choose the manner of your death and the way that I shall kill you! By Allah, I will throw you back into the sea, and keep watch on this shore to warn all men of your treachery!"

When he heard the fisherman's words, the jinnee struggled desperately to escape from the bottle, but was prevented by the magic seal. He now altered his tone and, assuming a submissive air, as-

---

5. **requite** (ri kwīt´) *v.*: To make return or repayment for.

---

sured the fisherman that he had been jesting with him and implored him to let him out. But the fisherman paid no heed to the jinnee's entreaties[6] and resolutely carried the bottle down to the sea. "What are you doing with me?" whimpered the jinnee helplessly.

"I am going to throw you back into the sea!" replied the fisherman. "You have lain in the depths eighteen hundred years, and there you shall remain till the Last Judgment![7] Did I not beg you to spare me so that Allah might spare you? But you took no pity on me, and He has now delivered you into my hands."

"Let me out," cried the jinnee in despair, "and I will give you fabulous riches!"

"Perfidious[8] jinnee," retorted the fisherman, "you justly deserve the fate of the king in the tale of Yunan and the doctor.

"What tale is that?" asked the jinnee.

THE TALE OF KING YUNAN
AND DUBAN THE DOCTOR

It is related (began the fisherman) that once upon a time there reigned in the land of Persia a rich and mighty king called Yunan. He commanded great armies and had a numerous retinue of followers and courtiers. But he was afflicted with a leprosy[9] which baffled his physicians and defied all cures.

One day a venerable[10] old doctor named Duban came to the king's capital. He had studied books written in Greek, Persian, Latin, Arabic, and Syriac, and was deeply versed in the wisdom of the ancients. He was master of many sciences, knew the properties of plants and herbs, and was above all skilled in astrology and medicine. When this physician heard of the leprosy with which Allah had plagued the king and of his doctors' vain endeavors

---

6. **entreaties** (en trēt´ ēz) *n.*: Earnest requests.
7. **Last Judgment:** The final judgment of humankind at the end of the world.
8. **perfidious** (pər fid´ ē əs) *adj.*: Treacherous.
9. **leprosy** (lep´ rə sē) *n.*: A chronic infectious disease that attacks the skin, flesh, and nerves.
10. **venerable** (ven´ ər ə b'l) *adj.*: Worthy of respect by reason of age and dignity or character.

Grammar in Action

Transitions are words or phrases that clarify the relationship among ideas. In "The Fisherman and the Jinnee," as in most works of fiction, transitions are often used to indicate the order in which events occur. Here are a few examples from pages 110–131:

At this point the fisherman thought to himself . . .
When he heard the fisherman's words . . .
Next morning, *as soon as* the king sat down upon his throne . . .

Student Activity 1. Identify the transitions in the following passages

from "The Fisherman and the Jinnee."
1. So, on the following day, when the king entered the council chamber and was about to call the physician, the vizier kissed the ground before him . . .
2. Then the executioner came forward, blindfolded the doctor and, drawing his sword, held it in readiness for the king's signal.
3. After much difficulty, he turned over the second and the third, moistening his finger with his spittle at every page, and tried to read.
4. But when he tried to draw it in he found it even heavier than before.
5. At this point the fisherman thought to himself: "though I am but a man and he is a jinnee, my cunning may yet overreach his malice."

to cure him, he put on his finest robes and betook himself to the royal palace. After he had kissed the ground before the king and called down blessings upon him, he told him who he was and said: "Great king, I have heard about the illness with which you are afflicted and have come to heal you. Yet will I give you no potion to drink, nor any ointment to rub upon your body."

The king was astonished at the doctor's words and asked: "How will you do that? By Allah, if you cure me I will heap riches upon you, and your children's children after you. Anything you wish for shall be yours and you shall be my companion and my friend."

Then the king gave him a robe of honor and other presents and asked: "Is it really true that you can heal me without draught or ointment? When is it to be? What day, what hour?"

"Tomorrow, if the king wishes," he replied.

The doctor took leave of the king, and hastening to the center of the town rented for himself a house, to which he carried his books, his drugs, and his other medicaments. Then he distilled balsams and elixirs,[11] and these he poured into a hollow polo stick.

Next morning he went to the royal palace and, kissing the ground before the king, requested him to ride to the field and play a game of polo with his friends. The king rode out with his viziers and his chamberlains,[12] and when he had entered the playing field the doctor handed him the hollow club and said: "Take this and grasp it firmly. Strike the ball with all your might until the palm of your hand and the rest of your body begin to perspire. The cure will penetrate your palm and course through the veins and arteries of your body. When it has done its work, return to the palace, wash yourself, and go to sleep. Thus shall you be cured; and peace be with you."

The king took hold of the club and, gripping it firmly, struck the ball and galloped after it with the other players. Harder and harder he struck the ball

---

11. **balsams** (bôl′ səmz) **and elixirs** (i lik′ sərz): Two potions with supposed healing powers.
12. **chamberlains** (chām′ bər linz) *n.*: High officials in the king's court.

as he dashed up and down the field, until his palm and all his body perspired. When the doctor saw that the cure had begun its work, he ordered the king to return to the palace. The slaves hastened to make ready the royal bath and hurried to prepare the linens and the towels. The king bathed, put on his nightclothes, and went to sleep.

Next morning the physician went to the palace. When he was admitted to the king's presence he kissed the ground before him and wished him peace. The king hastily rose to receive him; he threw his arms around his neck and seated him by his side.

For when the king left the bath the previous evening, he looked upon his body and rejoiced to find no trace of the leprosy. His skin had become as pure as virgin silver.

The king regaled the physician sumptuously all day. He bestowed on him robes of honor and other gifts, and when evening came gave him two thousand pieces of gold and mounted him on his own favorite horse. And so enraptured was the king by the consummate skill of his doctor that he kept repeating to himself: "This wise physician has cured me without draught or ointment. By Allah, I will load him with honors and he shall henceforth be my companion and trusted friend." And that night the king lay down to sleep in perfect bliss, knowing that he was clean in body and rid at last of his disease.

Next morning, as soon as the king sat down upon his throne, with the officers of his court standing before him and his lieutenants and viziers seated on his right and left, he called for the physician, who went up to him and kissed the ground before him. The king rose and seated the doctor by his side. He feasted him all day, gave him a thousand pieces of gold and more robes of honor, and conversed with him till nightfall.

Now among the king's viziers there was a man of repellent aspect, an envious, black-souled villain, full of spite and cunning. When this vizier saw that the king had made the physician his friend and lavished on him high dignities and favors, he became jealous and began to plot the doctor's downfall. Does not the proverb say: "All men envy the strong openly, the weak in secret?"

14 Reading Strategy Have students predict how the doctor will attempt to heal the king and whether or not he will be successful.

15 Enrichment If students are unfamiliar with polo, explain that it is a game played on horseback by two teams of four players each, who attempt to drive a small wooden ball through the opponents' goal with a mallet having a long, flexible handle.

16 Enrichment Explain to students that leprosy occurs chiefly among people who live in warm climates. Although it can now be easily treated, it was once a highly feared disease, and throughout most of history, people who had the disease were isolated in special hospitals called leprosariums.

17 Literary Focus Remind students that the characters in folk tales tended to be stereotypes of stock characters embodying a single human trait, quality, or emotion. Ask them what trait, quality, or emotion the vizier embodies.

18 Discussion Have students discuss whether or not they agree with this proverb.

Student Activity 2. Find five more sentences from "The Fisherman and the Jinnee" that contain transitions. Then explain why the story would be more difficult to follow if these transitions were removed.

Student Activity 3. Write a brief account of an interesting or amusing experience you had in the past several weeks. Your account should contain at least five transitions indicating the order of events.

So, on the following day, when the king entered the council chamber and was about to call for the physician, the vizier kissed the ground before him and said: "My bounteous master, whose munificence extends to all men, my duty prompts me to forewarn you against an evil which threatens your life; nor would I be anything but a base-born wretch were I to conceal it from you."

Perturbed at these ominous words, the king ordered him to explain his meaning.

"Your majesty," resumed the vizier, "there is an old proverb which says: 'He who does not weigh the consequences of his acts shall never prosper.' Now I have seen the king bestow favors and shower honors upon his enemy, on an assassin who cunningly seeks to destroy him. I fear for the king's safety."

"Who is this man whom you suppose to be my enemy?" asked the king, turning pale.

"If you are asleep, your majesty," replied the vizier, "I beg you to awake. I speak of Duban, the doctor."

"He is my friend," replied the king angrily, "dearer to me than all my courtiers; for he has cured me of my leprosy, an evil which my physicians had failed to remove. Surely there is no other physician like him in the whole world, from East to West. How can you say these monstrous things of him? From this day I will appoint him my personal physician and give him every month a thousand pieces of gold. Were I to bestow on him the half of my kingdom, it would be but a small reward for his service. Your counsel, my vizier, is the prompting of jealousy and envy. Would you have me kill my benefactor and repent of my rashness, as King Sindbad repented after he had killed his falcon?"

THE TALE OF KING SINDBAD AND THE FALCON

Once upon a time (went on King Yunan) there was a Persian king who was a great lover of riding and hunting. He had a falcon which he himself had trained with loving care and which never left his side for a moment; for even at nighttime he carried it perched upon his fist, and when he went hunting took it with him. Hanging from the bird's neck was a little bowl of gold from which it drank. One day the king ordered his men to make ready for a hunting expedition and, taking with him his falcon, rode out with his courtiers. At length they came to a valley where they laid the hunting nets. Presently a gazelle fell into the snare, and the king said: "I will kill the man who lets her escape!"

They drew the nets closer and closer round the beast. On seeing the king the gazelle stood on her haunches and raised her forelegs to her head as if she wished to salute him. But as he bent forward to lay hold of her, she leaped over his head and fled across the field. Looking round, the king saw his courtiers winking at one another.

"Why are they winking?" he asked his vizier.

"Perhaps because you let the beast escape," ventured the other, smiling.

"On my life," cried the king, "I will chase the gazelle and bring her back!"

At once he galloped off in pursuit of the fleeing animal, and when he had caught up with her, his falcon swooped upon the gazelle, blinding her with his beak, and the king struck her down with a blow of his sword. Then dismounting he flayed the animal and hung the carcass on his saddle-bow.

It was a hot day and the king, who by this time had become faint with thirst, went to search for water. Presently, however, he saw a huge tree, down the trunk of which water was trickling in great drops. He took the little bowl from the falcon's neck and, filling it with this water, placed it before the bird. But the falcon knocked the bowl with its beak and toppled it over. The king once again filled the bowl and placed it before the falcon, but the bird knocked it over a second time. Upon this the king became very angry and, filling the bowl a third time, set it down before his horse. But the falcon sprang forward and knocked it over with its wings.

"Allah curse you for a bird of ill omen!" cried the king. "You have prevented yourself from drinking and the horse also."

So saying, he struck the falcon with his sword and cut off both its wings. But the bird lifted its head as if to say: "Look into the tree!" The king raised his eyes and saw in the tree an enormous serpent spitting its venom down the trunk.

The king was deeply grieved at what he had done and, mounting his horse, hurried back to the palace. He threw his kill to the cook, and no sooner had he sat down, with the falcon still perched on his fist, than the bird gave a convulsive gasp and dropped down dead.

The king was stricken with sorrow and remorse for having so rashly killed the bird which had saved his life.

When the vizier heard the tale of King Yunan, he said: "I assure your majesty that my counsel is prompted by no other motive than my devotion to you and my concern for your safety. I beg leave to warn you that, if you put your trust in this physician, it is certain that he will destroy you. Has he not cured you by a device held in the hand? And might he not cause your death by another such device?"

"You have spoken wisely, my faithful vizier," replied the king. "Indeed, it is quite probable that this physician has come to my court as a spy to destroy me. And since he cured my illness by a thing held in the hand, he might as cunningly poison me with the scent of a perfume. What should I do, my vizier?"

"Send for him at once," replied the other, "and when he comes, strike off his head. Only thus shall you be secure from his perfidy."

Thereupon the king sent for the doctor, who hastened to the palace with a joyful heart, not knowing what lay in store for him.

"Do you know why I have sent for you?" asked the king.

"Allah alone knows the unspoken thoughts of men," replied the physician.

"I have brought you here to kill you," said the king.

The physician was thunderstruck at these words and cried: "But why should you wish to kill me? What crime have I committed?"

"It has come to my knowledge," replied the king, "that you are a spy sent here to cause my death. But you shall be the first to die."

Then he called out to the executioner, saying: "Strike off the head of this traitor!"

"Spare me, and Allah will spare you!" cried the unfortunate doctor. "Kill me, and so shall Allah kill you!"

A royal hunting expedition. Charge of the Faramourz cavaliers, mid-fourteenth century
Musée Reza Abbasi, Teheran, Iran

But the king gave no heed to his entreaties. "Never will I have peace again," he cried, "until I see you dead. For if you cured me by a thing held in the hand, you will doubtless kill me by the scent of a perfume or by some other foul device."

"Is it thus that you repay me?" asked the doctor. "Will you thus requite good with evil?"

But the king said: "You must die; nothing can now save you."

When he saw that the king was determined to put him to death, the physician wept and bitterly repented the service he had done him. Then the executioner came forward, blindfolded the doctor and, drawing his sword, held it in readiness for the king's signal. But the doctor continued to wail, crying: "Spare me, and Allah will spare you! Kill me, and so shall Allah kill you!"

27

Humanities Note

Fine art, *A royal hunting expedition. Charge of the Faramourz cavaliers.* Produced during the mid-fourteenth century, this work is in many ways a typical Persian miniature. The landscape is strikingly beautiful and full of life. In addition the people and the horses are integrated into the landscape in such a masterful manner that they seem almost a natural part of it. Because of the artist's use of brilliant colors and balanced, harmonious blending of details, the picture seems more glorious than reality itself—a characteristic shared by many Persian miniatures. The horses, for example—a favorite subject of Persian artists—are drawn with accuracy and precision, yet they somehow seem more perfect than real horses.

You might want to use the following questions to discuss the art:
1. What impression does the artist convey of the horsemen's relationship with nature?
2. How would you characterize the landscape depicted in this painting?
3. Which details in this painting do or do not correspond to those in "King Sindbad and the Falcon"?
4. Which of the two illustrations for this selection do you prefer? Explain.

25 Discussion Have students explain the point that King Yunan is trying to make by relating this tale to the vizier.

26 Discussion Have students discuss whether or not they consider this turn of events believable. Has the vizier given the king any real cause to change his opinion of the doctor?

27 Discussion Call students' attention to the fact that the fisherman asked the jinnee the same question when the jinnee was about to kill him. Then have them explain the significance of this parallel.

28 Clarification Make sure students recognize that this paragraph is the conclusion of the fisherman's story and that the following paragraph will be the conclusion of the main story.

29 Discussion Have students discuss the relationship between the three stories and the message that the work as a whole conveys.

Cultural Notes One of the many Western writers who took an interest in *The Thousand and One Nights* was the British Romantic poet William Wordsworth. If your students have studied British literature, ask them if they see any similarities between *The Thousand and One Nights* and works by British Romantic poets.

Cooperative Learning Students might be interested in exploring how certain characters from *The Thousand and One Nights* have become integrated into Western culture. Divide students into groups of three or four and have each group choose one of the following characters: the jinnee, Sindbad the Sailor, Ali Baba, Aladdin, or Shaharazad. Have the groups acquaint themselves with the character they have chosen by skimming through *The Thousand and One Nights*. Then have them research the ways in which the character has been integrated into Western culture. For example, they might note cartoons or television programs in which the character has appeared. Once they have finished their research, they should select a spokesperson to present their findings to the class.

Moved by the old man's lamentations, one of the courtiers interceded for him with the king, saying: "Spare the life of this man, I pray you. He has committed no crime against you, but rather has he cured you of an illness which your physicians have failed to remedy."

"If I spare this doctor," replied the king, "he will use his devilish art to kill me. Therefore he must die."

Again the doctor cried: "Spare me, and Allah will spare you! Kill me, and so shall Allah kill you!" But when at last he saw that the king was fixed in his resolve, he said: "Your majesty, if you needs must kill me, I beg you to grant me a day's delay, so that I may go to my house and wind up my affairs. I wish to say farewell to my family and my neighbors and instruct them to arrange for my burial. I must also give away my books of medicine, of which there is one, a work of unparalleled virtue, which I would offer to you as a parting gift, that you may preserve it among the treasures of your kingdom."

"What may this book be?" asked the king.

"It holds secrets and devices without number, the least of them being this: that if, after you have struck off my head, you turn over three leaves of this book and read the first three lines upon the left-hand page, my severed head will speak and answer any questions you may ask it."

The king was astonished to hear this and at once ordered his guards to escort the physician to his house. That day the doctor put his affairs in order and next morning returned to the king's palace. There had already assembled the viziers, the chamberlains, the nabobs,[13] and all the chief offi-

---

13. **nabobs** (nā′ bäbz) *n.*: Very rich or important people; aristocrats.

---

cers of the realm, so that with their colored robes the court seemed like a garden full of flowers.

The doctor bowed low before the king; in one hand he had an ancient book and in the other a little bowl filled with a strange powder. Then he sat down and said: "Bring me a platter!" A platter was instantly brought in, and the doctor sprinkled the powder on it, smoothing it over with his fingers. After that he handed the book to the king and said: "Take this book and set it down before you. When my head has been cut off, place it upon the powder to stanch the bleeding. Then open the book."

The king ordered the executioner to behead the physician. He did so. Then the king opened the book, and, finding the pages stuck together, put his finger to his mouth and turned over the first leaf. After much difficulty he turned over the second and the third, moistening his finger with his spittle at every page, and tried to read. But he could find no writing there.

"There is nothing written in this book," cried the king.

"Go on turning," replied the severed head.

The king had not turned six pages when the venom (for the leaves of the book were poisoned) began to work in his body. He fell backward in an agony of pain, crying: "Poisoned! Poisoned!" and in a few moments breathed his last.

"Now, treacherous jinnee," continued the fisherman, "had the king spared the physician, he in turn would have been spared by Allah. But he refused, and Allah brought about the king's destruction. And as for you, if you had been willing to spare me, Allah would have been merciful to you, and I would have spared your life. But you sought to kill me; therefore I will throw you back into the sea and leave you to perish in this bottle!"

Reader's Response *What is your reaction to the use of the technique of telling tales within tales? Do you find this technique confusing? Why or why not?*

THINKING ABOUT THE SELECTION

Interpreting

1. When the fisherman discovers the bottle in his net, he rejoices because he thinks it is worth a lot of money. Based on the outcome of the tale, explain whether you think he would have been happier if he had found fish in his net rather than the bottle.

2. What trait does the fisherman recognize in the jinnee that allows him to outsmart him?

3. Considering the action that King Yunan eventually takes against the doctor, what is ironic, or surprising, about the vizier's warning to him that "He who does not weigh the consequences of his acts shall never prosper"?

4. (a) What does the fact that King Yunan is so easily deceived by the vizier reveal about his character? (b) Why should he have trusted Duban more than he trusted the vizier?

5. (a) What common thread connects the "Tale of King Sindbad and the Falcon" to "The Fisherman and the Jinnee"? (b) How is the "Tale of King Sindbad and the Falcon" similar in theme to the "Tale of King Yunan and Duban the Doctor"? (c) What effect is created by these interlocking tales?

6. In *The Thousand and One Nights,* "The Fisherman and the Jinnee" is just one of the many tales that Princess Shaharazad tells to King Shahriyar in an effort to delay her execution. How do the situations depicted in "The Fisherman and the Jinnee" relate to the princess's situation?

7. (a) What traits do many of the characters in these tales share? (b) What other characters in selections you have read in this unit share similar traits?

Applying

8. Shaharazad uses storytelling as a means of beguilement. (a) What is it about fiction that allows it to beguile and ensnare the listener? (b) Why is storytelling most effective when the listener and the teller form a close bond or relationship?

ANALYZING LITERATURE

Understanding Folk Tales

Although *The Thousand and One Nights* is now a distinctly Arabic book, many of the folk tales it includes originally came from either Persia or India. As is gener-

ally the case with folk tales, there are no known authors of any of the stories in the book. In addition, the tales that now appear in the book are probably all quite different from their original forms. This is because the details and characters of folk tales generally change a great deal through the process of telling and retelling.

1. What relevance might each story have to the lives of common people?
2. What lessons do the three stories teach?

UNDERSTANDING LANGUAGE

Recognizing Word Origins

Many of the words in the English language were borrowed from other languages. Although the majority of these loan words come from Latin, Greek, and French, there are also many words that originated from other languages, including Persian and Arabic. For example, the word *algebra* comes from the Arabic word *al-jabr,* meaning "the reunion of broken parts."

Find the Arabic word from which each of the following words originated.

1. vizier 4. alchemy
2. nabob 5. admiral
3. sherbet

THINKING AND WRITING

Adapting a Folk Tale

Write an adaptation of the tale of the fisherman's encounter with the jinnee set in contemporary America. Start by gathering with a group of your classmates and brainstorming about the ways in which the tale would be different if it were set in contemporary America. Then, using the ideas from the brainstorming session, work on your own to develop a plot outline. Do not hesitate to make changes in the original plot that you feel would make it more interesting or exciting. When you write the tale, focus on dramatizing the events through dialogue and action, rather than on merely describing them. After you have finished writing, gather again with the members of your group and read your tales to one another. Suggest ways in which they could be improved. When evaluating your classmates' tales, try to make your comments as constructive as possible. Try to avoid being overly critical or overly positive. Also avoid making any criticisms you cannot support, and for each criticism that you do offer, try to suggest a possible remedy.

(continued from bottom of page)

of the story.
6. Suggested response: All the stories deal with characters who are condemned despite the fact that they have done nothing wrong. The same is also true of the princess.
7. (a) Answers will differ. Students may point out that a number of the characters are cruel, rash, and unappreciative. (b) Answers will differ. Students may note that several of the characters from Sa'di's the *Gulistan* share these traits.
8. (a) Answers will differ. Students may respond that fiction can accomplish this because it draws readers out of the real world into a world of fantasy. (b) Answers will differ. Students may respond that a close relationship between the listener and the storyteller increases the likelihood that the listener will take in all the details of the story.

ANSWERS TO ANALYZING LITERATURE

1. Answers will differ. Students may observe that the stories do not deal with situations likely to occur in everyday life, yet the stories teach values that can be applied to anyone's life.
2. Suggested response: The stories teach that people should not behave cruelly or rashly. Instead, people should be compassionate and should reward those who help them.

ANSWERS TO UNDERSTANDING LANGUAGE

1. wazir, "a bearer of burdens"
2. nuwwab, "deputy; viceroy"
3. sharbah, "a drink"
4. al-kimiya, " to pour"
5. amir a' alie, "high leader"

THINKING AND WRITING

Writing Across the Curriculum
You might want to inform the members of your social studies department about this assignment. Social studies teachers may be able to assist students in exploring the differences between contemporary American society and the Arabic society depicted in "The Fisherman and the Jinnee."

Challenge Have students embed one or two inner stories within their adaptation of the story about the fisherman and the jinnee.

Closure and Extension

ANSWERS TO THINKING ABOUT THE SELECTION

1. He would have been happier if he had caught a fish because his life would not have been threatened and he would have had something to show for his day's work.
2. Suggested response: He realizes that

the jinnee is arrogant.
3. The warning is ironic because the king clearly does not weigh the possible consequences of his decision to execute the doctor.
4. (a) Suggested response: It reveals that King Yunan is not a good judge of character and that he is suspicious and rash. (b) Duban had earned his trust by saving his life, while the vizier had done nothing to earn his trust.

5. (a) Suggested response: Both stories deal with characters who requite good with evil. The same is also true of "The Tale of King Yunan and Duban the Doctor." (b) Suggested response: Both stories warn of the consequences of acting rash and teach people to reward those who help them. (c) Answers will differ. Students may respond that the interlocking adds emphasis to the overall theme

The Individual and Society

> "We're in two worlds. We're in our own world, and we're in the world that has been given us outside, and the problem is to achieve a harmonious relationship between the two. . . . One has to build up one's own system that may violate the expectations of the society, and sometimes society doesn't accept that. But the task of life is to live within the field provided by the society that is really supporting you."
> —Joseph Campbell

For people living in the Islamic Empire, the task of living "within the field provided" by society mainly involved adhering to the principles of Islam. This applied to kings and scholars as well as to common men and women. It even applied to people such as the Sufis who isolated themselves from others.

The Islamic beliefs concerning proper conduct, wisdom, and justice recur throughout Persian and Arabic literature. Only those individuals who were guided by these beliefs could achieve a harmonious relationship with society.

> A tyrannic man cannot be a sultan
> As a wolf cannot be a shepherd.
> A padshah who establishes oppression
> Destroys the basis of the wall of his own
>   reign.
> —from the *Gulistan*

"Now treacherous jinnee," continued the fisherman, "had the king spared the physician, he in turn would have been spared by Allah. But he refused, and Allah brought about the king's destruction. And as for you, if you had been willing to spare me, Allah would have been merciful to you, and I would have spared your life. . . ."
—from *The Thousand and One Nights*

Literature provides us with a window not only into Persian and Arabic society but also into a vast array of other societies. It enables us to learn about the expectations of these societies and often offers insights about the impact of these expectations on the lives of individuals.

Sometimes, literary works focus on specific issues concerning the relationship between the individual and society. Henrik Ibsen's play *A Doll's House* (pages 969–1018), for instance, delves into the constraints that nineteenth-century European society placed on women. Another example is Par Lagerkvist's story "The Princess and All the Kingdom," which deals with a ruler's responsibility to his or her society.

The following are some other selections dealing with the theme of the individual and society:

SUGGESTED READINGS

Confucius, from *The Analects*, page 214
Jonathan Swift, "A Modest Proposal," page 801
Alexander Pushkin, "The Bridegroom," page 880
Charles Baudelaire, "The Albatross," page 905

Anton Chekhov, "The Bet," page 960
Franz Kafka, "The Metamorphosis," page 1084
Rabindranath Tagore, "The Artist," page 1192

CROSS CURRENTS

Scheherazade

When we think of *The Thousand and One Nights*, a number of characters immediately spring to mind. We think of Ali Baba, Sinbad the Sailor, and Aladdin and his magic lamp—characters so well known that they almost seem part of our own folk tradition. Yet none of these characters has captured the interest of Western writers, composers, and choreographers more than has Scheherazade (also spelled Shaharazad), the clever princess who staves off her own execution by weaving together a captivating web of tales.

JOHN BARTH

One writer who is especially intrigued by Scheherazade is the contemporary American John Barth (1930–), who views her as the prototypical storyteller. His novella *The Dunyazadiad*, one of three interrelated novellas in his book *Chimera*, is based on Scheherazade and her situation. Like *The Thousand and One Nights*, this novella consists of a web of neatly interconnected stories.

Barth has suggested that Scheherazade's situation parallels the anguish of the contemporary writer. Because her own life was at stake, Scheherazade had to fight desperately to create new narrative possibilities and to sustain King Shahriyar's interest. According to Barth the contemporary writer also faces a desperate struggle to sustain interest and create fresh narrative possibilities because so many ideas and approaches have already been used by earlier writers.

COMPOSERS AND CHOREOGRAPHERS

Scheherazade has also served as an inspiration for a number of musical composers and dance choreographers. Among these is the celebrated Russian composer Nikolai Rimsky-Korsakov (1844–1908), whose free-flowing symphonic suite *Scheherazade* parallels the *The Thousand and One Nights* in structure. The French composer Maurice Ravel (1875–1937) also wrote a piece entitled *Scheherazade* that was inspired by the princess and her situation.

Both Rimsky-Korsakov's and Ravel's compositions have been used as the music for ballets about Scheherezade. Rimsky-Korsakov's piece was used for a ballet choreographed by Michel Fokine that was first performed in 1910. Ravel's piece was used for a ballet choreographed by George Ballanchine that was perfomed in 1975 by the New York City Ballet Company.

Why do you think the story of the tale-weaving princess has captured the imagination of artists across cultures and across the ages?

SCHEHERAZADE AND KING SHAHRIYAR
Anton Pieck
Uitgeversmaatschappij, Amsterdam

Analytical Essay

Writing an Analytical Essay

Analyzing means looking at the parts in order to form conclusions about the whole. Writing an analytical essay about technique requires keen observation and clear thought. Writers must observe the factors to be analyzed and their functions in the literature.

A Good Literary Analysis:

- Begins with a thesis that is briefly stated
- tells how the use of technique works in the literature
- Shows how the technique makes the literature more powerful

For example, one student started to write an analytical essay about the use of connotation in the Koran.

> Connotative language in the Koran creates a powerful, almost frightening tone. The words of God, as Mohammed recited them, strike awe and perhaps fear in the reader.

The writer then proceeded to prove the thesis statement by showing how.·

Writing Assignment

Write an analytical essay in which you show how language choice in the Koran or another work from this unit affects the reader. To do this, you will need to describe the connotative (or emotional) meanings of the words and show how they support their denotative (or literal) meanings.

Prewrite

Form a group of three or four students and brainstorm about the connotations and denotations of key words from the selections. Use a sheet of paper folded in half lengthwise. Label the left side "connotations" and the right side "denotations." Remember that connotations are the associated feelings a word brings to mind. Denotations are the literal meanings of words. Working together on one word at a time, list words or phrases that are rich in connotation and write down all the associated feelings, impressions, and ideas each word brings to mind. You may use a thesaurus and a dictionary to help you.

CONNOTATIONS	DENOTATIONS
wrathful	wrathful
frightening	angry
out of control	furious
avenging angels	raging
demons	
Dad's red face	
complete rage	
ready for violence	

Write

Working individually, examine the brainstormed lists, looking for themes or ideas shared among several of the words. Those similarities create the emotional tone of the work and suggest your thesis statement.

To produce a strong paper, you must

- Have a clear thesis statement. This is the sentence that presents your main idea.
- Support your thesis with evidence from your connotation list. That evidence will form the body of your essay.
- Directly state what your examples prove. Listing examples in isolation is not enough. Make the connections.
- Use your final paragraph to tell how parts fit together in the whole. For instance, tell how the connotation supports the denotation, or how the emotional appeal affects the literal meaning.

Keep in mind that when you write an essay of this nature, you are like a lawyer going to court. Your thesis statement is what you plan to prove, and your examples are the evidence you offer to do it. Be sure you present your evidence in compelling order so you can convince the "jury" (your reader) and win your case.

Collaborate

When your rough draft is finished, return to your group and take turns reading your essays aloud. As each member reads, the group should pretend to be a jury, listening to a lawyer present his or her case in court. It should respond to each essay by examining the following things:

- Is the thesis statement clear? (Do you know what he or she is trying to prove?)
- Does the evidence prove it? (Are you convinced beyond a reasonable doubt?)

- Is there a break in the chain of evidence? (Are you left with unanswered questions?)

The group should render a verdict to the reader/writer based on its answers to the three questions. Then it should offer concrete suggestions about any flaws in the case.

Revise

Rewrite your paper bearing your group's comments in mind. Don't be afraid to rearrange sections of your essay to make your evidence more compelling. For additional power, use a thesaurus to help you select words that have strong connotations beyond their literal meanings. Proofread your paper and prepare a final draft.

Publish

The final jury for your paper is your teacher, who will look for holes in your argument. Before you hand in your paper, be certain your thesis is clear, your examples convincing, and your organization logical. Also, be sure you showed the connection between language choice and meaning.

Evaluate

Having completed this assignment, ask yourself how you feel about the power of language to affect meaning. Have your ideas about words changed since writing this paper? You might consider what happens to people when you address them in words loaded with connotations. If the connotations are good, do they smile? If they are bad, do they shrink from you? Words are powerful instruments. They can create and they can destroy.

Master Teacher Note Explain to students that they should not hesitate to make revisions in their work as they are writing. Point out to students that they can vary the stages of the writing process to find the approach that works best for them. For example, they may find that it works best for them to prepare a formal outline before they begin writing, or they may find that they like to organize their ideas as they are writing.

Publishing Student Writing Once students have finished revising their papers, you may want to have volunteers read their papers to the class. As an alternative, you might want to arrange your students' papers into a bulletin-board display.

Guidelines for Evaluating Writing About Literature Keep the following questions in mind when evaluating students' compositions.
1. Does the paper have a clear thesis statement?
2. Is the thesis statement thoroughly supported with evidence?
3. Is the paper well organized?
4. Does the writer use transitions to connect his or her ideas?

Presentation

The map on pages 140–141 shows Eastern and Southern Asia, c. A.D. 1775. Point out to students that the era of British rule in India is usually dated from 1757. That date marks the British governor Clive's recovery of Calcutta from an Indian ruler. By 1818 the British controlled almost the entire subcontinent.

In 1775 China was under the rule of the Manchu dynasty (1644–1912). The late eighteenth century was the time during which China expanded to its greatest size. By the first part of the nineteenth century, however, the European powers had begun to dominate China.

During the late eighteenth century, Japan was ruled by members of the Ieyasu family. They had established a strong, centralized government that ensured stability at the cost of social progress. A single Dutch trading post at Nagasaki represented the only trading contact maintained with foreigners.

Spain controlled the Philippines in 1775 and would continue to do so until 1898, when it lost the Spanish-American War. In this region of the world, the Spanish frequently fought the Moro pirates but were unable to suppress them until the mid-nineteenth century.

The Rise of Asia

c. 1400 B.C.–A.D. 1890

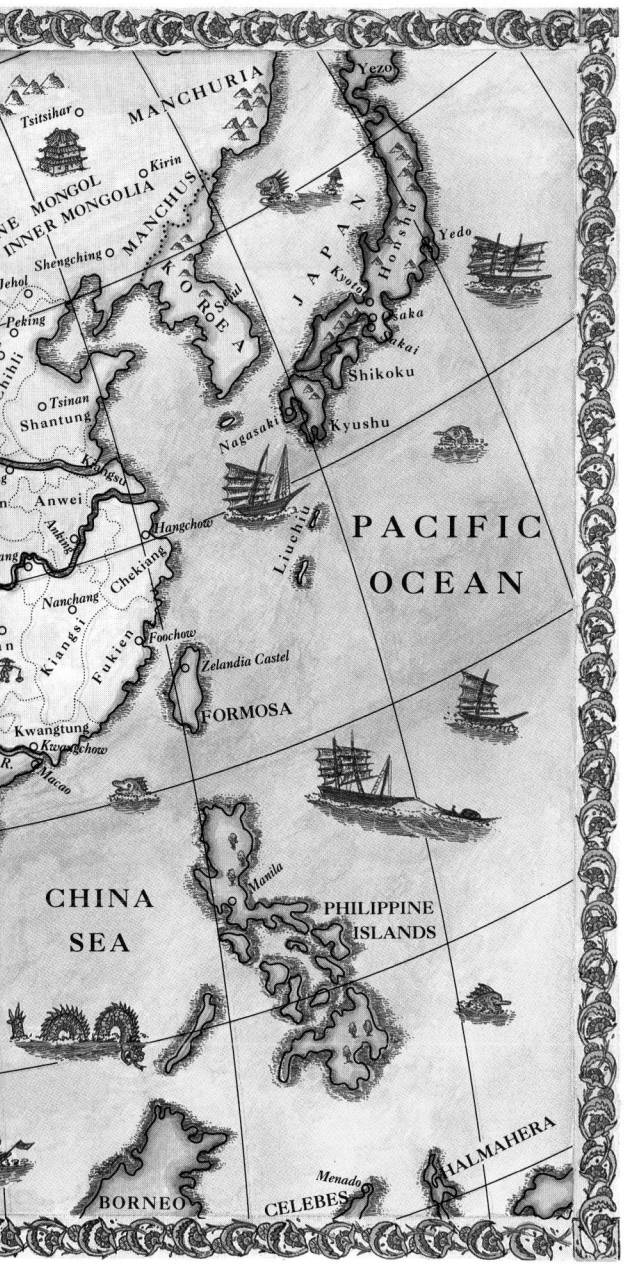

Using the Map

Have students study the map and ask them the following questions.

1. (a) Find Japan on the map. (b) Why do you think it was able to maintain its isolation at this relatively late date?
2. (a) Find the Indus and Ganges rivers in northern India. (b) Name the larger bodies of water into which they flow.
3. In the fourth century B.C., Alexander the Great took his army from Macedonia, an ancient kingdom in southeast Europe, all the way to the Indus River. Using this map, show the direction from which he came.
4. In 1775 Siam was a country in Southeast Asia. Its name is preserved in terms like Siamese twins and Siamese cat. Compare this map with a more up-to-date one and identify the modern name of Siam.
5. Name three countries that bordered on China in 1775.

Fine art, *Krishna's Magic Flute*. Krishna was the most important incarnation of the Hindu god Vishnu, the creator and preserver of the world. The many legends associated with Krishna fall into three main categories: They depict him as a godlike child, as an amorous cowherd, or as a manly hero.

This painting, in which Krishna charms the animals with his flute, depicts him as a cowherd. Not only did the adolescent Krishna charm animals with his flute, but he also used it to lure women from their houses at night. This erotic side of the god's nature was given a religious interpretation, however. His seductive flute music was compared to a divine voice that calls upon humans to abandon earthly pursuits and experience the joys of religion.

Westerners who view this painting may be reminded of the legendary Greek musician Orpheus. The music from his lyre had the power to soothe wild beasts, stop the flow of rivers, and cause the trees to dance.

You might want to use the following questions to discuss the art:

1. How do the lightning bolts in the sky emphasize the power of Krishna's music?
2. Describe the feeling that exists between Krishna and the animals.
3. Do you know of any other god or legendary figure who was a musician? Explain.
4. Why have so many peoples believed that music has the power to charm animals?
5. If Krishna were reborn into our world, what kind of music would he play? Explain.

KRISHNA'S MAGIC FLUTE
Unknown artist; Kangra Valley

Objectives

1 To understand India's geographical setting
2 To understand the history of India
3 To appreciate Indian culture
4 To learn about Indian language and literature

INDIAN LITERATURE

c. 1400 B.C.–c. A.D. 500

In the English-speaking world the strongest Indian influence was felt in America, where Emerson, Thoreau and other New England writers avidly studied much Indian religious literature in translation, and exerted immense influence on their contemporaries and successors, notably Walt Whitman.

—A. L. Basham, *The Wonder That Was India*

What a positive statement Basham makes about Indian literature! However, the influence and importance of Indian literature were not always recognized by Westerners. Contrast the positive statement on the preceding page with the following one by Thomas Babington Macaulay, one of nineteenth-century England's most celebrated writers:

> I have never found one [scholar] who could deny that a single shelf of a good European library was worth the whole native literature of India and Arabia. . . .

Macaulay made this arrogant and inaccurate declaration in a report to the British colonial government on the future of Indian education.

**View of the south gate of
Buddhist monument at Sanchi**

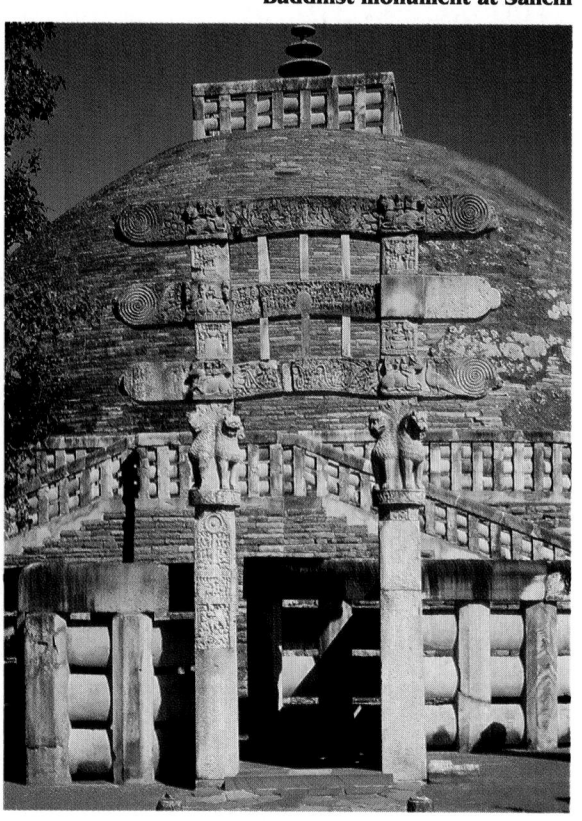

Today such an attitude of superiority is rare. Unfortunately, however, the ignorance that underlies this statement is still prevalent. Even though the Indian literary tradition stretches back over a 3,500-year history, and even though the number of works India has produced far exceeds those of the Greek and Latin traditions, we in the West know relatively little about Indian literature.

Part of the reason for our ignorance is the vastness of the Indian tradition. Not only does it span three and a half millennia, but it includes works written in Sanskrit, Persian, Tamil, and dozens of modern languages derived from these. Only a linguistic genius could read all these works in the original.

In spite of these difficulties, however, scholars have recognized certain texts that are crucial to an understanding of India's dominant Hindu culture. This unit is made up of selections from several of these texts.

THE GEOGRAPHICAL SETTING

India is more a subcontinent than a country. Surrounded by oceans and by the forbidding Himalayan mountains, it has remained isolated for long periods of its history. This isolation was broken periodically by invasions. Often, however, invading peoples became cut off from their original homelands and then were gradually absorbed into the Indian population.

India's geographical isolation probably contributed to the assumption of many Indian thinkers that their subcontinent was the center of the universe.

HISTORY

Early Settlements

Throughout India's long history, there have been hundreds of kingdoms and some very large empires (see the map on page 145). The map of India's political history is a checkerboard of continually changing boundaries between kingdoms that do battle, absorb one another, and then split into new divisions.

First Empires of India, 297 B.C. – A.D. 150

Maurya's Empire 297 B.C.
Bindusara's Empire 272 B.C.
Empire of Asoka 232 B.C.
Western Satraps A.D. 150
Kushan Empire A.D. 150
Satavahana Kingdom A.D. 150

Using the Map
Have students study the map and ask them the following questions.
1. Which of the empires shown on this map encompassed the largest area?
2. Which part of India was not controlled by any of these empires?
3. Name an empire that controlled territory only in the northwest of India.
4. Imagine that you are traveling through India from its southernmost tip to Kasmira in A.D. 150. Name the empires you would pass through on your way.
5. Find the region on the east coast that Asoka conquered but that Bindusara did not.

2 Enrichment Tell students that the Indus Valley Civilization, also known as the Harappa Culture, extended for about 1,000 miles north and south along the Indus River. This civilization was so well organized that even the bricks used in widely separated towns were the same size. Each city had a fortified citadel, and the streets were laid out in a regular plan. In fact the same street plans were followed for almost 1,000 years!

One of the most impressive achievements of this civilization was its drainage system. Each house had a bathroom, and the water from the bathroom drained to sewers beneath the main streets and then to pits. Scholars guess that such an elaborate system must have required a centralized authority to maintain it. Of all ancient peoples, only the Minoans and Romans had comparable drainage systems.

The cultural map of India is much more stable. However, the earliest settlements on the subcontinent are still shrouded in mystery. Nevertheless, we know that some of these early settlers developed an impressive civilization in the northwest, where modern Pakistan and western India are located. This culture—the Indus Valley Civilization, named for the river that runs through the region—was urban and highly sophisticated. It had a system of writing, which survives but has not yet been deciphered. It also had an elaborate religious cult, farms that produced surplus crops, and excellent engineers. We can infer this last fact from the quality of the drainage systems in the ancient cities.

The Aryans and the Dravidians

The Indus Valley Civilization mysteriously ended around 1500 B.C.—the reasons for its demise are still the subject of scholarly debate. Around this same time, people who called themselves Aryans (arʹ ē ənz) migrated into India from the north and west. These people brought with them the hymns of the *Rig Veda*, which expressed their religious

managed to learn Sanskrit. With the aid of Wilkins and friendly Bengali pandits Jones began to learn the language. On the first day of 1784 the Asiatic Society of Bengal was founded, on Jones's initiative, and with himself as president. In the journal of this society, *Asiatic Researches*, the first real steps in revealing India's past were taken. In November 1784 the first direct translation of a Sanskrit work into English, Wilkins's *Bhagavad-Gita*, was completed.

Yoga refers to both a school of thought in Indian philosophy and a spiritual discipline in Hinduism and Buddhism, two of the predominant religions in India. Practicing the discipline of yoga is one way of attaining enlightenment and liberation from ignorance, suffering, and rebirth. Pictured here is an Indian practicing one of the many yogic positions. Much literature has been written about yoga, including the excerpt in this unit—"The Yoga of Knowledge" from the *Bhagavad-Gita*, page 176.

Pictured here is the figure of a musician sculpted from unglazed earthenware, or terra cotta. Music plays an important role in India. Indian music is entirely monodic, or sung by a single voice. Unlike Western music, the Indian tonal system divides the octave into twenty-two segments called *srutis*. A srutis is aproximately one quarter of a whole note in Western music. In addition Indian music consists of numerous *ragas,* or melody types, used as the basis for improvisation. Each raga is ascribed certain ethical and emotional properties and linked with certain seasons or times of day. Legend celebrates the powers of ragas. For example, a raga associated with darkness could, if sung during the day, bring about darkness. Indians consider accompanied song the highest form of music. Among the instruments used for accompaniment are the drum, the vina or harp, and the sitar. The bagpipe, lute, fiddle, oboe, trumpet, flute, cymbal, and gong have also been widely used.

The Ajanta caves, situated in the Ajanta Hills in west-central India, were discovered in 1819. These caves, carved out of the side of a steep ravine, contain stunning examples of Buddhist art, depicting scenes from the life of Buddha. The caves consist of chapels and monasteries dating from c. 200 B.C. to A.D. 650.

This painting of the face of a celestial nymph is an example of the

Indian
(1400 B.C.–A.D. 500)

Indian practicing yoga
The Chester Beatty Library and Gallery of Oriental Art, Dublin

Terracotta figure of a musician

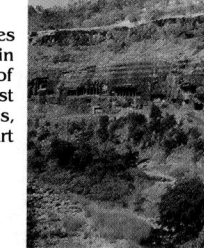

Ajanta caves contain examples of Buddhist monasteries, chapels, and art

	–1400	–1000	–600
HISTORY	• Leprosy is widespread in India	• Formation of the Vedas begins • Upanishad tradition begins	• Mahavira founds Jainism; first known rebel against caste system • Reign of Bimbisara begins
HUMAN PROGRESS		• Indians establish lunar year with 360 days • Medicine breaks from priesthood; anatomical models used • Aryans develop written language, Sanskrit • Mahavira Jina, founder of Jainism, is born • Buddha is born	
LITERATURE	• *Rig Veda*	• Composing of *Taittiriya Upanishad* is believed to have begun	

frescoes that are painted on the walls of the Ajanta caves.

Shiva, one of the three most important divinities in Hinduism, is called the Destroyer. As the counterpart of Vishnu, Shiva the Destroyer periodically destroys the world in order to re-create it. Despite his fearsome characteristics, Shiva's followers believe he is a merciful god. Hindus depict Shiva in many forms, one of which is Nataraja, or Lord of the Cosmic Dance. In this form, shown here, the four-armed Shiva dances on a prostrate demon.

Vishnu, Shiva's counterpart and another of the most important divinities in Hinduism, is called the Preserver.

Hindus believe Vishnu ensures the welfare of humanity. According to tradition Vishnu periodically descends from heaven to earth in one of his *avatars,* or physical forms. He has already apeared in nine avatars, including one as the prince Rama, the hero of the *Ramayana*, and another as the god Krishna, one of the principle characters in the *Bha-*

Face of celestial nymph, Ajanta cave 17

The Hindu god Shiva Nataraja, 11th century

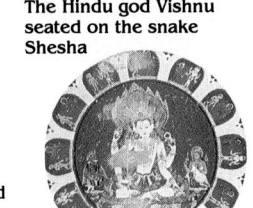
The Hindu god Vishnu seated on the snake Shesha

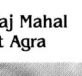
Portrait of Buddha, or Siddhartha Gautama (detail)
The Metropolitan Museum of Art, New

Taj Mahal at Agra

-200   200   500

- Indian Empire: Magadha, "cradle of Buddhism," begins
  - Greeks invade India
  - Alexander the Great leaves India
  - Maurya dynasty begins
    - Asoka conquers India; establishes edicts
- Maurya dynasty ends
- Gupta dynasty begins

- India vina, considered origin of hollow string instruments, is invented
- Indian surgeon performs cataract operations
- Dams are constructed in India
  - Buddha dies
- Building of the Great Stupa in Sanchi, India, begins

- *Ramayana*
- Composing of *Mahabharata* is believed to have begun
- Writing for the *Panchatantra* is believed to have begun
- Kalidasa: *Sakuntala*, Sanskrit drama
  - Scrolls begin to be replaced by books

(continued from bottom of page)

to tradition, when he was a wealthy prince, Buddha wore heavy gold jewelry that stretched his ear lobes. Finally his webbed fingers are believed to be a net by which Buddha gathers his followers.

Emperor Shah Jahan ordered the building of the Taj Mahal at Agra in memorial to his favorite wife, Mumtaz Mahal, in 1629. The building of the Taj Mahal actually began in 1630 and was completed in 1648. One of the most resplendent mausoleums in India, the Taj Mahal was designed by a Turkish architect. The exterior of the tomb is white marble inlaid with semi-precious stones.

gavad-Gita, page 176. Hindus believe Vishnu will return again to earth to destroy all evil and to begin a new Golden Age of humanity. Pictured here is Vishnu seated on the snake Shesha and surrounded by numerous deities.

Buddha, or Siddhartha Gautama, is the founder of Buddhism. Buddha means "enlightened one." Buddhists believe they are in a continuous cycle of death and rebirth. People who have attained enlightenment, however, will reach nirvana, or the final death, thereby breaking the cycle of rebirth. Buddha is one such person. To distinguish Buddha from mortals, artists use established symbols to depict him and his achievements. At the top of Buddha's head is a bump that signifies his special knowledge. His short, curly hair represents a time when Buddha gave up his princely life to devote himself to a new disciplined life. The dot between his eyes symbolizes his special wisdom. His elongated ear lobes refer to the time before his enlightenment. According

3 Enrichment Explain to students that it was once thought that the Arabs devised the use of decimals. We now know, however, that the Arabs gained their knowledge of decimal notation and other mathematical inventions from India. The Arabs even called mathematics "the Indian (art)."

One scholar asserts that without the decimal system, which was invented in India, Europeans would not have been able to make such rapid progress in science and technology. The only alternative to decimal notation was the clumsy system of Roman numerals.

Medieval Indian mathematicians were far more sophisticated than their European counterparts. Indians, for example, achieved a much greater understanding of the concepts of zero and infinity. The mathematician Bhaskara proved that x/0 = infinity. He also proved that infinity remains infinite no matter how many times it is divided. Furthermore Indians calculated the value of pi (the ratio of the circumference of a circle to its diameter) much more accurately than the Greeks had. The Indian value for pi of 3.1416 is very close to the modern figure of 3.14159265+.

4 Enrichment Tell students that a piece of iron the size and weight of the Iron Pillar of Delhi could not have been produced by Europeans until the nineteenth century. The metal of this pillar is so pure that it has withstood the rains of thousands of monsoons without any signs of rust.

ideas (for more information on the Aryans and the *Rig Veda*, see pages 152–154).

Another cultural group, the Dravidians (drə vid´ ē ənz), inhabited southern India in ancient times. We do not know much about the earliest history of these dark-skinned, small-framed people, but we do know that they developed a thriving culture sometime during the first millennium B.C.

Hinduism

The mixture of all these cultures—Indus Valley, Aryan, and Dravidian—contributed to India's Hindu civilization. Hinduism (hin´ do͞o iz´ əm)—the word comes from the Sanskrit word *sindhu*, meaning "river," or more specifically, the Indus River—refers to both a religion and a social system. The Hindu religion recognizes many gods and teaches that the soul can be reborn into countless bodies before it achieves union with a universal soul. Hindu society was rigidly divided into groups, or castes, each of which had its own special duties. (For more information on the Hindu religion and caste system, see pages 164–165.)

The Great Empires

There were many great empires in India's history (see map on page 145). The Emperor Ashoka (ə shō´ kə), who lived in the third century B.C., was one of the first rulers to consolidate much of the subcontinent under his control. Centuries later, the great Hindu king Chandragupta Maurya (chän drə go͞op´ tə mou´ əryə), created an empire even larger than Ashoka's had been. Still later, around A.D. 1200, the Moguls (mo´ gulz) established a great empire in north India—these Islamic rulers were descendants of Genghis Khan (for more about the Moguls, see page 165).

The entire subcontinent, however, was never united under any single political administration until the British succeeded in making India into a colony. While the British did leave a significant mark on the region, we must also remember that they ruled it for a relatively short period, from 1800 to 1947. For most of its history, India has been a collection of kingdoms with ever-changing boundaries.

Unchanging Village Life

History tends to be concerned with political developments—kingdoms lost and kingdoms won—and Indian history as written by Westerners is full of such detail. The real center of interest and enduring value in India, however, is the village. R. K. Narayan described a typical village as follows: "[it] consists of less than a hundred houses, scattered in six crisscross streets. The rice fields stretch away westward and . . . water is obtainable from a well open to the skies in the center of the village. All day the men and women are in the fields, digging, ploughing, transplanting, or harvesting. . . ."

CULTURAL BACKGROUND
Mathematics, Technology, and Medicine

Some of India's cultural achievements are so much a part of our everyday lives that they have lost their identity as Indian discoveries. Among these is our number system. The numerals that we use come from India; they are called Arabic numerals because Arab traders brought them from India to Europe. In addition, ancient Indian mathematicians are responsible for the invention of zero and the decimal notation that this discovery made possible.

Indians also excelled in metalworking. A monument that testifies to their skill is the Iron Pillar of Delhi, a solid metal column 23 feet tall. It was erected sometime during the period A.D. 300–500.

Medicine was another field where Indians distinguished themselves. Ancient Indian physicians were able to set broken bones, knew the importance of keeping wounds clean, and developed plastic surgery long before it was practiced in Europe.

Painting, Sculpture, and Architecture

Indian painters and sculptors were patronized by kings and wealthy merchants. As artists traveled from kingdom to kingdom to show their work, they spread the inventions and secrets of their craft. For the most part, they depicted religious themes. However, their work also reveals the daily life, dress, and pastimes of ancient India, so it is a valuable record for us today.

Primary Source Note

Ashoka, who reigned from about 269 to 232 B.C., was not only a powerful emperor but a humane one as well. In the following edict, he describes a change of heart that he experienced:

When the King, of Gracious Mien and Beloved of the Gods, had been consecrated eight years Kalinga [see the map on page 145] was conquered. One hundred fifty thousand people were thence taken captive, 100,000 were killed, and many more died. Just after the taking of Kalinga

the Beloved of the Gods [Ashoka himself] began to follow Righteousness, to love Righteousness, to give instruction in Righteousness. When an unconquered country is conquered, people are killed, they die, or are made captive. That the Beloved of the Gods finds very pitiful and grievous. . . . Today, if a hundredth or a thousandth part of those who suffered in Kalinga were to be killed, to die, or to be taken captive, it would be very grievous to the Beloved of the Gods. If anyone does him wrong it will be forgiven as far as it can be forgiven.

Among the most notable achievements of Indian art are the frescoes, or wall paintings, in caves near the village of Ajanta in western India. These caves were created by Buddhist monks during the period from the first century B.C. to the seventh century A.D. The vibrant and colorful paintings on their walls depict Buddhist themes.

The artificial caves at Ajanta and elsewhere in western India are also great architectural achievements. Their interiors were designed to imitate the brightly colored halls in which Buddhist monks gathered during the rainy season to recite texts and debate religious questions. One of these cave-temples was carved from the entire side of a mountain. It is 75 feet high, 280 feet long, and 75 feet wide.

Religious Thought

Indian creativity is especially evident in the field of religion. The subcontinent was the birthplace of many important faiths: Hinduism, the dominant religion of India; Buddhism (bood′ iz′m), which is now virtually extinct in India but has spread throughout Asia; Jainism (jīn′ iz′m); and Sikhism (sēk′ iz′m). (See the feature on Indian religion, pages 164–165.)

A revealing fact about Indian religious life is that no Indian language has an exact counterpart for the English word *religion*. The explanation for this state of affairs is that Indians do not divide life into "religious" and "secular" spheres. Instead, religious concerns pervade all aspects of thought in Hindu India. The term that best reflects this universal concern with religious values is **dharma** (dur′ mə). This Sanskrit word refers to the unique

obligations that each person must fulfill in order to maintain harmony in the universe.

The earliest surviving record of Indian religious thought, and the basis of Hinduism, is the collection of hymns known as the *Rig Veda*. These hymns do not set forth religious ideas in a systematic manner. Their homage to the gods of nature, however, sets a tone of devotion and piety that carries down to the present day.

These ancient hymns accompanied elaborate sacrifices to the gods: Some of these rituals lasted as long as a year! The writings that were developed to describe the details of these sacrifices had a profound effect on the way that Hindus thought. This influence shows up, for example, in the structure of India's great epic poem, the *Mahabharata* (mə hä′ bä′ rə tə). Just as a sacrificial ritual was divided into many small parts, the *Mahabharata* was divided into many small episodes told by different narrators.

LANGUAGE AND LITERATURE
The Sacredness of Language

The universal concern with religious values in Hindu life explains the lack of a clear separation between religion and literature. In fact, language itself —the sound of words—was regarded as sacred. An example of this attitude is the practice of repeating the word *om* (ōm) during Hindu prayers. The repetition of this word is a religious act, a means of saying "yes" to the universe.

If language was considered sacred, Sanskrit (san′ skrit′) was viewed as the most perfect of

BUDDHA TEACHING HIS DISCIPLES
Eighteenth century
Victoria and Albert Museum, London

(continued from bottom of page)
they spoke. Individual letters of the alphabet were thought of as gods! Given this orientation, it is not surprising that a special holiness was later attributed to certain syllables, like OM.

Humanities Note
Fine art, *Buddha teaching his disciples*, eighteenth century. Legend has it that the prince Gautama achieved enlightenment after sitting for forty-nine days under a large pipal tree. Thereafter he was called Buddha, which means "the enlightened one." His basic insight was that humans must renounce desire of all kinds in order to achieve nirvana, a blessed state in which individual existence is extinguished. (For more about Buddhism, see page 164.)

After achieving enlightenment Buddha was not sure whether he should teach others what he had discovered. According to legend the god Brahma convinced him to transmit his wisdom to the world. Buddha preached his first sermon to five ascetics near modern Sarnath (see the map on page 145). These ascetics immediately became his disciples, and shortly afterward sixty young men also joined him. He and his followers then preached his message in the region around the Ganges River. In this painting Buddha, with his legs in the lotus position, is seated on a white mat.

You might want to use the following questions to discuss the art:
1. Which of these seated figures is Buddha? Explain your choice.
2. What does the painting suggest about the relationship between Buddha and his disciples?

5 Enrichment Explain to students that unlike most wall paintings, which are done while the plaster is still wet, the paintings in the Ajanta caves were executed after the plaster had dried. In order to see what they were doing, the painters set up metal mirrors to reflect outside light onto the cave walls.

Although these paintings have a religious message, they are valuable records of ancient Indian life. They show, for instance, a whole range of social types, from beggars to beautiful harem women. They also show ancient India's birds, animals, and flowers.

6 Enrichment Explain to students that the most important deity of the Aryans was Indra, who was both a war god and a weather god. He was somewhat similar to Zeus, the chief Greek god. Like Zeus, he had the power to hurl thunderbolts at his enemies.

7 Enrichment Tell students that ancient Indians came to associate the brahmans' power with the words

8 Enrichment Explain to students that the Sanskrit word for *father* is *pitr* and the word for *mother* is *matr*. Have students compare these Sanskrit terms not only with these English words but with their French and Spanish counterparts as well.
French: *père* (father); *mère* (mother)
Spanish: *padre* (father); *madre* (mother)

9 Enrichment Tell students that ancient Indian thinkers began to study phonetics and grammar in order to preserve the original pronunciations and meanings of words in the *Rig Veda*. They believed that these words had to be pronounced properly or else they would not be effective in bringing divine blessings. Also they were aware that Sanskrit was changing: Its grammar was being simplified, certain word endings were disappearing, and older words were falling out of use.

10 Enrichment Point out to students that the Indian dramatist Kalidasa has been compared to Shakespeare. Like Shakespeare, Kalidasa was a lyric poet as well as a great playwright. Kalidasa was also similar to Shakespeare in that he used poetry and prose in his plays, based his plots on coincidences, and presented vivid characters.

In general, however, the conventions of Indian drama were much different from those of European drama. The Indians did not favor tragedies. Individual scenes within plays might be tragic or pathetic, but almost every play had a happy ending.

Cooperative Learning Divide the class into small groups. Have each group do further research on a topic discussed in the introduction. Examples: Indian drama, the Sanskrit language, the Aryans and the Dravidians, and Indian achievements in mathematics and technology. Then have the groups report their findings to the class.

all languages. It is not currently a spoken language, but all of the selections in this unit were written in Sanskrit. (Today we recognize that Sanskrit is related to other ancient Indo-European languages like Latin and Greek.)

Because they believed that language was holy, Indians speculated a great deal about its power to convey ideas and emotions. This speculation led to a greater understanding about how language works. The Sanskrit grammars written by the Indian thinker Panini in the sixth century B.C. are still admired by modern linguists.

The Importance of Memory

Indians placed a great importance on memory, more so perhaps than other ancient cultures did. The traditional way of studying a subject in India was to memorize—completely and perfectly—the *entire* text, and then to hear the teacher explain it. In the case of a sacred text like the *Rig Veda*, every syllable, every accent, every pause in the recitation had to be correct; otherwise, when these hymns were recited during a sacrifice, their power would be lost.

Students of the *Rig Veda* were first taught to memorize all 1,028 hymns in the normal way. One hymn, for example, begins, "I pray to the God of Fire, the household priest. . . ." After memorizing this hymn, each student would be assigned another way to memorize it, for example: "I pray I to pray the to God the of God Fire of the Fire household the priest household. . . ." This second version of the hymn was purposely nonsensical so that the student's act of memory would not be dependent on meaning. These incredible feats of memory took years, of course, and they seem utterly impossible to us. Yet it was just such dedication that preserved the hymns unchanged from 1500 B.C. to the present.

Texts were also written down in ancient India, but Hindus believed that trusting to the written medium involved too great a risk. A written copy could be lost or damaged. Strange as it may seem to us, a person's memory was regarded as a far safer means of preserving a text.

The Evolution of Sanskrit Literature

Ancient Indians had no literary genres like the novel or the short story. Except for poetry and drama, most Sanskrit texts imitated the *Rig Veda* in attempting to convey general and timeless truths. Even the myths that tell the story of the god Krishna —he was the incarnation of Vishnu, one of the three most important Indian deities—deal with abstract principles. The same is true of the animal fables of the *Panchatantra* (pun´ chə tun´ trə). They use vivid language and are disarmingly naive, but their purpose is to enable people to fulfill their dharma.

Indian poetry and drama did not come into their own until centuries after the *Rig Veda* was compiled. The greatest Indian poet was Kalidasa (kä´ lē dä´ sä), who lived sometime between the fourth and sixth centuries A.D. His plays and epic poems set the standards for those two genres.

About the Following Selections

The selections in this unit come from the earliest products of India's literary tradition. Despite the fact that some of these works are 3,500 years old, however, their influence has still been felt in recent times. They inspired the American authors Emerson and Thoreau, the Indian writer Rabindranath Tagore (see page 1190), and the Indian leader who pioneered the methods of nonviolent protest, Mahatma Gandhi.

KRISHNA AND RADHA IN THE RAIN WITH TWO MUSICIANS
Raj-putana School
New Delhi National Museum

Humanities Note
Fine art, *Krishna and Radha in the Rain with Two Musicians*. As previously discussed (see Humanities Note, page 142), the youthful Krishna is portrayed as a lover of *gopies*, or milkmaids. Krishna's amorous adventures are given a religious interpretation in Hinduism: They are understood to represent the soul's relationship with God. In this picture Krishna is shown dancing with Radha, traditionally regarded as his favorite partner.

You might want to use the following questions to discuss the art:
1. What mood does this picture convey?

2. Hindus traditionally interpreted such scenes in a religious way. How could this scene be given a religious interpretation?

INDIAN VOICES

You gods who are all here and who belong to all men, give far-reaching shelter to us and to our cows and horses.

Rig Veda, from "To All the Gods"

When the wise ones fashioned speech with their thought, sifting it as grain is sifted through a sieve, then friends recognized their friendships.

Rig Veda, from "The Origins of Sacred Speech"

Behold the universe in the glory of God: and all that lives and moves on earth. Leaving the transient, find joy in the Eternal: set not your heart on another's possession.

Isa Upanishad

Brahma was before the gods were, the Creator of all, the Guardian of the Universe.

Mundaka Upanishad

OM. This eternal Word is all: what was, what is and what shall be, and what beyond is in eternity. All is OM.

Mandukya Upanishad

The mind of man is of two kinds, pure and impure: impure when in the bondage of desire, pure when free from desire.

Maitri Upanishad

All living creatures are led astray as soon as they are born, by the delusion that this relative world is real.

Bhagavad-Gita, VII. Knowledge and Experience

The faith of each individual corresponds to his temperament. A man consists of the faith that is in him. Whatever his faith is, he is.

Bhagavad-Gita, XVII. Three Kinds of Faith

Who was the artificer at her creation?
Was it the moon, bestowing its own charm?
Was it the graceful month of spring, itself
Compact with love, a garden full of flowers?

Kalidasa

Check Test

1. Two natural barriers that have isolated India geographically are oceans and _____.
2. The main religion of India is _____.
3. The nomads who invaded India in the second millennium and compiled the *Rig Veda* were the _____.
4. The entire Indian subcontinent had never been united under one rule until the coming of the _____.
5. An important Indian contribution to mathematics was the invention of _____.

Answers
1. mountains, or the Himalayan Mountains
2. Hinduism
3. Aryans
4. British
5. zero

Presentation

Motivation/Prior Knowledge
Tell students that these two pages will help them understand the culture and religion of the Aryans, warlike stock breeders who invaded India in the second millennium B.C. Organized into tribes, the Aryans were very much like the warriors described in the Anglo-Saxon epic *Beowulf*.

Critical Evaluation The scholar R. C. Zaehner declared that "the *Rig-Veda*, the oldest of the Samhitas or 'collections,' represents an extraverted and life-accepting type of religion. . . ."

1 Enrichment Tell students that the Aryans invaded India from the northwest, coming through passes in the Hindu Kush mountains and then crossing the Indus River. (Have students trace this route on the map on page 145.) Explain to students that this onslaught was not a single occurrence but a series of invasions.

Point out that the Indus Valley Civilization lay directly along this invasion route. The enemies to whom the Aryans refer in the Vedic hymns—and the references are naturally uncomplimentary—are therefore the survivors of this civilization. In contrast to these city dwellers, the Aryans were a fierce, nomadic people organized in tribes led by rajahs.

Humanities Note

Fine art, *Nandin the Bull*. Nandin was associated with the god Shiva, who was believed to reconcile such opposites as creation and destruction, goodness and evil, rest and ceaseless activity. As the animal on which Shiva rode, Nandin usually had statues or separate shrines at the entrance to Shiva's temples. This statue indicates the resting position in which Nandin was usually portrayed. Also he was often depicted with a decorative collar and various ornaments on his head and back. The worship of Nandin made the killing of any cattle a punishable offense. Even today many Indians refuse to eat

BACKGROUND

THE RIG VEDA

Hinduism, an Indian religion, claims the Vedas as the source of all truth and the basis of its religious beliefs. The earliest and most influential of these sacred texts is the *Rig Veda*.

Compiled around 1400 B.C., the *Rig Veda* is a collection of 1,028 hymns composed by different authors at different times. These hymns are mostly in praise of gods, like the poem "Night" on page 159. The *Rig Veda*, however, also contains poems like "Creation Hymn" (pages 155–156), which speculates about the origin and nature of the universe.

Who Wrote These Ancient Hymns?

The identity of the authors is a mystery. We know only that they were part of the Indo-European race that gradually migrated into the Indian subcontinent from central Europe via what are now Iran and Afghanistan. These Indo-Europeans, who also migrated throughout Europe, referred to themselves as "Aryans," a name that in Sanskrit means "noble" and distinguished the migrants from the native peoples. You can still find traces of this word in the names of countries like *Ire*land and *Iran*.

Wherever they traveled, Indo-Europeans naturally took their language with them. Over a long period of time, modern languages as diverse as English, Greek, French, Polish, Bengali, and Albanian evolved from Indo-European. (Most dictionaries and encyclopedias have a chart of Indo-European languages.) Sanskrit, the language of the *Rig Veda*, is one of the oldest Indo-European tongues.

The Religion of the *Rig Veda*

The poets of the *Rig Veda* clearly were moved by the forces of nature. In many hymns they portray natural phenomena—the sun, the moon, rain, night, wind, storms—as godlike beings. The authors praise these gods for their power and beauty and for the benefits they bring to humankind.

Because the hymns were composed at different times, they indicate different stages of religious thought. There is, however, a general concern with prosperity and comfort. The gods are invoked for protection and sustenance. Unlike later Hindu writings, the hymns place little emphasis on doing good for its own sake. They reflect the preoccupations of an agricultural people who needed rain for their crops, protection from storms, and a sense of security in the terror-filled night.

Later hymns in the *Rig Veda* diverge from this pattern by speculating about the purpose and creation of the universe.

NANDIN THE BULL
Ashmolean Museum, Oxford

beef or to sanction the killing of cows or bulls.

You might want to use the following questions to discuss the art:
1. What mood does this sculpture convey? Explain.
2. Nandin is an animal sacred to the Hindus. Name other examples of animals that have taken on symbolic meaning for various peoples or nations.
3. Why do you think people have given such importance to certain animals?

STATUE OF MOTHER AND CHILD
Indian Museum, Calcutta

The Sacrificial Cult

The *Rig Veda* describes a world in which the forces of nature are both benevolent and threatening. Rain, which is necessary for crops, can also bring catastrophe if it comes at the wrong time. The hymns were therefore recited at sacrificial offerings intended to cultivate the favor of the gods and ward off natural disturbance and chaos.

The earliest Vedic poets sought to placate the gods through offerings of food and drink. They thought that such gifts would incline the forces of nature to perform beneficially for humans. The idea gradually evolved, however, that sacrifice is not only helpful to the gods, because it provides them with sustenance and praise, but is actually necessary for them. Eventually, the notion emerged that sacrifice *controls* the gods and the order of the universe. This belief gave the priests, who supervised the sacrifice, enormous power and influence.

The ancient Vedic cult is still alive in modern India, although it is slowly dying out and being replaced by other religious practices that claim to be based on the *Rig Veda*.

Clues to a Vanished Civilization

The Vedic hymns often allude to stories and myths that were well known at the time. Unfortunately, as readers who are 4,000 years removed from the *Rig Veda*, scholars are often unable to puzzle out every allusion. The poems on the following pages are quite well understood, but in other cases, the myth or story that is referred to has been lost. In these instances scholars have been forced to compare ancient mythologies of other Indo-European traditions to reconstruct what the Vedic poets may have meant.

The *Rig Veda* is the earliest record we have of the Aryan presence in India. As a result the view it gives us of their society and religion is very important, but a bit sketchy. Imagine, for example, the difficulty historians would have 4,000 years from now trying to reconstruct American life based on a modern-day hymn book.

Why Do We Read the *Rig Veda*?

The *Rig Veda* is fascinating not only for its clues to an ancient civilization but also for the ways in which it reflects timeless concerns. Despite all of our advanced technology, we too have our nighttime fears. Also, like the poet of "Creation Hymn," we speculate and wonder about the origin of the universe. If we sometimes express that wonder in terms of quarks and quantum mechanics, we are still challenged by the questions of the millennia-old hymn: "What stirred? Where? In whose protection?"

(continued from bottom of page)

You might want to use the following questions to discuss the art:
1. (a) Describe the feeling that seems to exist between this mother and her child. (b) Which details suggest this feeling?
2. Why do you think the Hindus included such a sculpture in a temple?
3. Compare and contrast this sculpture with Western representations of the Madonna and Child.

2 **Enrichment** To illustrate the importance of rain to the Aryans, read the following excerpt from a hymn dedicated to Parjanya, the Bull, personification of the rain cloud:

Bellow and thunder; lay your seed. Fly in circles around the world in your chariot full of water. Drag the leather water-bag upside down, untied. Let the hills and the valleys become level.

Draw up the enormous bucket and pour it down. Let the streams flow forth, set free. Drench heaven and earth with butter. Let there be a good drinking-place for the cows.

You might want to ask students why the rain would make the hills and the valleys level.

Humanities Note

Fine art, *Statue of mother and child.* This stone carving comes from the city of Khajuraho in northeastern India (see the map on page 145), where more than eighty temples were built. Khajuraho means "city of the gods," and it was a center for Hindu architecture and sculpture during the period A.D. 950–1050. Each temple was designed to represent a mountain range with numerous small peaks surrounding a central peak. Within these temples elaborate sculptures like this one decorated the walls.

Medieval Indian sculpture was warm, joyous, and fanciful. Statues were not meant to be realistic likenesses of particular individuals; they represented idealized images. This idealized mother and child symbolized the life-giving qualities of nature. Decorative details, like the looping necklaces and flower petals seen here, helped convey a sense of joy and contentment.

Focus

Teaching Reading Critically The information on this page will help students understand the *Rig Veda* by placing it in its historical, cultural, and literary contexts. The strategies that students learn to use as they read "Creation Hymn" will also help them in their reading of other selections.

Discuss the information on this page with your students, and explain that the selection that accompanies this page, "Creation Hymn," is a model for reading critically the literature of this period. In the side column there are notes that draw attention to the historical, cultural, and literary contexts of the work. Ask students to read these notes and suggest that they make their own critical comments as they read the selection.

To give students further practice with the process of reading critically, allow them to annotate "Savitri," a selection from the *Mahabharata* adapted by R. K. Narayan, on page 189 of the Teaching Portfolio. Also encourage them to use this approach as they read the other selections in this unit.

Historical Context Scholars speculate that the military techniques of the Aryans, which enabled them to conquer local tribes, were superior to those of the Babylonians or Assyrians.

Cultural Context Cattle were so important to the Aryans that they were a kind of currency. Material value was often computed in terms of number of cattle.

Indian Literature

Historical Context

The *Rig Veda* provides us with a record of the earliest religious and philosophical speculations of the Aryans in India. The date of its compilation, 1400 B.C., is slightly earlier than the Exodus of the Jews from Egypt and several hundred years before the dawn of Greek civilization. At the time the *Rig Veda* was collected, the Aryans were slowly migrating across northwestern India and using their superior weapons to conquer local tribes. The *Rig Veda* provides us with a collection of their hymns and prayers to their gods.

Cultural Context

Darkness is a common image in these poems. Terrifying Night must be praised and placated, but Dawn is the goddess who is hoped for and welcomed. Imagine migrating tribes crossing India's vast lands. Certainly they would fear the dark. Certainly they would long for the dawn. It is worth remembering that today we seldom experience the kind of utter darkness that made the Aryans feel so vulnerable when they were away from the fires of their village.

The many images of breeding and shepherding that appear in the hymns suggest that the Aryans were a pastoral people. Their intimacy with nature is revealed by their worship of natural phenomena and the role of their gods in providing sustenance and protection.

Literary Context

Vedic poets are in awe of nature, but they also desire to control and understand it. By endowing natural forces with the qualities of humans and animals, they make it easier to approach, flatter, and manage these forces. Such attempts at control lead to thoughts about the workings and origin of the world, speculations that will become even more important in later Hindu texts. Of all the Vedic poems, the "Creation Hymn" represents the most self-conscious effort to fathom the world's mysteries.

You will find the "Creation Hymn" on the following page. The annotations in the margin point out the historical context, cultural context, and literary context.

Objectives

Thematic
To understand the religious beliefs and concerns of ancient Indians
Skills
1 To explore language's limitations

2 To compare a poem and a picture
3 To identify abstract and concrete terms
4 To reflect on the limits of language

Support Material

Teaching Portfolio
Teacher Backup, p. 185
Usage and Mechanics Worksheet, p. 193
Analyzing Literature Worksheet, *Expressing the Inexpressible*, p. 194
Critical Thinking and Reading Work-

from the # Rig Veda
Creation Hymn

translated by Wendy Doniger O'Flaherty

Cultural Context: The word *veda* comes from the Sanskrit word meaning knowledge. *Rig* comes from the Sanskrit word meaning praise or hymn. The *Rig Veda*, then, is a collection of hymns expressing the knowledge and wisdom of the Hindu.

1 There was neither non-existence nor existence then; there was neither the realm of space nor the sky which is beyond. What stirred? Where? In whose protection? Was there water, bottomlessly deep?
2 There was neither death nor immortality then. There was no distinguishing sign of night nor of day. That one breathed, windless, by its own impulse. Other than that there was nothing beyond.

Cultural Context: The "Creation Hymn" speculates on the origin of the universe and comments on the gods of nature that are worshiped in the cults. It marks a transition between attempts to control the universe and attempts to understand its workings. Showing an unusual ability to tolerate uncertainty, the poet chooses not to fill the gaps in his knowledge with mythical explanations. The following important ideas in the "Creation Hymn" are characteristic of Hindu thought as a whole: (1) Nonexistence is linked with chaos and evil while existence is associated with order and truth—the purpose of Vedic sacrifice, in fact, is to ward off chaos; (2) Existence is conceived as a bond that is rooted in nonexistence; and (3) Creation begins with desire.

JAMBU-DVIPA
This eighteenth-century A.D. Indian painting is as complex and abstract as the much older "Creation Hymn" from the *Rig Veda*.
Rajastan

sheet, *Using Concrete Language*, p. 195
Language Worksheet, *Using Vivid Action Verbs*, p. 196
Selection Test, pp. 197–198

3 Darkness was hidden by darkness in the beginning; with no distinguishing sign, all this was water. The life force that was covered with emptiness, that one arose through the power of heat.

4 Desire came upon that one in the beginning; that was the first seed of mind. Poets seeking in their heart with wisdom found the bond of existence in nonexistence.

5 Their cord was extended across. Was there below? Was there above? There were seed-placers; there were powers. There was impulse beneath; there was giving-forth above.

6 Who really knows? Who will here proclaim it? Whence was it produced? Whence is this creation? The gods came afterwards, with the creation of this universe. Who then knows whence it has arisen?

7 Whence this creation has arisen—perhaps it formed itself, or perhaps it did not—the one who looks down on it, in the highest heaven, only he knows—or perhaps he does not know.

Reader's Response *Do you think that the questions raised in this hymn can be answered? Why or why not?*

THINKING ABOUT THE SELECTION

Interpreting

1. Identify the images in the poem that suggest the Aryans were an agricultural people. Give reasons for your choices.
2. The poet begins and ends this hymn with questions. Which of the questions are answered and which are not? Explain.
3. A paradox is a statement that seems contradictory but that may in fact be true. Explain what the poet means when he speaks of finding "the bond of existence in nonexistence."

Applying

4. According to Ecclesiasticus 1:3, "The height of heaven, the breadth of the earth, the abyss, and wisdom—who can search them out?" Is the answer to some questions unknowable? Discuss your answer with your classmates.

ANALYZING LITERATURE

Exploring Language's Limitations

In the "Creation Hymn," the poet uses language in unusual ways, because he is trying to hint at ideas that may be beyond the power of words to capture. Ordinarily, we employ language to say what things *are*. The Vedic poet, however, is talking about things that are removed from our common experience, so he uses negative statements to say what something is *not*: "There was *neither* nonexistence nor existence then . . ." This negative formulation teases us out of our usual thought patterns and allows us to experience the mystery of creation.

1. (a) How are the poet's questions another device for expressing the inexpressible? (b) In the end the poet admits his uncertainty. Does this admission make his questions less effective as techniques for communicating the inexpressible? Why or why not?
2. If the ultimate origin of things is beyond the ability of language to describe, why would a writer attempt a description?

CRITICAL THINKING AND READING

Comparing a Poem and a Picture

The picture accompanying the "Creation Hymn" (see page 155) is a much later work of Indian art that uses symbols, lines, and shapes to depict the whole universe. Like the hymn, it attempts to convey something that is ultimately inexpressible.

1. Of course, the poet and the painter use different media. How are they similar, nevertheless, in the ways they express what the mind cannot fully grasp?
2. Why do you think the poet and the painter deliberately made their works complicated and hard to fathom?
3. When we say that poets or painters are trying to convey something that is inexpressible, we are saying that they will inevitably fail in their goal. Under these circumstances what criteria can we use to judge whether such works are effective or ineffective?

UNDERSTANDING LANGUAGE

Identifying Concrete and Abstract Language

Concrete language describes something you can see, touch, taste, hear, or smell. Abstract language refers to something you cannot readily perceive through any of your five senses. Much of the language in "Creation Hymn" is abstract; for example, terms like "nonexistence" and "immortality." Even concrete terms like *water* can seem abstract when they appear in a question and are not related to a specific time or place: "Was there water, bottomlessly deep?"

1. Find another concrete term that is given an abstract feeling in this poem and explain your choice.
2. Why is it appropriate that this poem is more abstract than concrete?

THINKING AND WRITING

Reflecting on the Limits of Language

The Greek philosophers Aristotle and Plato implied that there are no limits to what language can express. On the other hand, the Jewish philosopher Philo Judaeus asserted that some things cannot be expressed in words. Write a paper in which you comment on these two views. Before you write, briefly list the arguments in favor of both positions and draw on the "Creation Hymn" for evidence. Then decide which view you accept. Is language limited in its capacities or not? Can you think of a compromise position that might admit the correctness of both views? In revising your work, make sure you have supported your opinions with convincing evidence from literature and experience.

(continued from bottom of page)
er to move an audience and heighten its awareness of the inexpressible.

Challenge Imagine that you are writing a poem or creating a painting. How would you attempt to convey the inexpressible?

ANSWERS TO UNDERSTANDING LANGUAGE

1. Answers will differ. Some students may respond that "seed-placers" is a concrete term that has an abstract feeling in this poem. It has such a feeling because we do not know where and how the seeds are placed.
2. Most students will realize that the subject of this poem, the creation of the world, is abstract and speculative. It is appropriate therefore that the language is abstract as well.

THINKING AND WRITING

Writing Across the Curriculum
Have students investigate various myths about the origin of the world. One reference work they can use is Funk & Wagnalls *Standard Dictionary of Folklore, Mythology, and Legend* (New York: Harper & Row, 1972). After students have gathered a number of myths, have them work out a classification system: which myths postulate a primeval ocean, which stress the importance of a particular animal, and so forth.

ANSWERS TO ANALYZING LITERATURE

1. (a) Answers will differ. Some students may respond that the poet's questions suggest all that we do *not* know. (b) Answers will differ. Perceptive students may realize that paradoxically this admission expresses well that the origin of things *cannot* be expressed.
2. Answers will differ. Some students may respond that the failed attempt can at least heighten readers' awareness of what *cannot* be expressed.

ANSWERS TO CRITICAL THINKING AND READING

1. Answers will differ. Students may respond that both the poem and the painting contain tangible and recognizable images, but in a context that is not readily grasped.
2. Answers will differ. Students may realize that the complexity of both works indicates that the subjects (creation in the case of the poem and the entire universe in the case of the painting) are also hard to fathom.
3. Answers will differ. Especially perceptive students will realize that such works can be measured by their pow-

Focus

Literary Focus The natural elements were sacred in the Vedic religion. Vedic poets represented the elements as actual persons to whom people talked. Have students find examples of elemental gods and goddesses from Greek mythology, Egyptian religion, or other sources. Ask students if they think our culture views "the elements," or nature, as having a spirit of their own.

Writing/Prior Knowledge Have students recall natural objects they might have talked to as children. Possible examples are the "the man in the moon" and the wishing star in "Star light, star bright." Ask students to compose a description of one verse that clearly refers to human characteristics.

ESL Teaching Strategy ESL students might need clarification of the term *personification.* Explain that the intent of personification is not one of mystery or fantasy but of description. Ordinary examples might clarify the term. Here are some examples students may recognize: the wind howled, the house creaked, the sun beat down on the earth.

Teaching Tenth-Grade Students Suggest that tenth-grade students are baby-sitting for a child who is afraid of the dark. Have them think of ways by which they might explain what night is and how the child will be safe during the night. Then ask students to describe how the poet feels about night and to cite lines from the poem to support their opinions.

Commentary

Writing

Primary Source

from the Rig Veda

Personification and Simile. Like many modern poets, the authors of the *Rig Veda* use figurative language to capture their audience's imagination. Many of the hymns are rich in **personification,** the giving of human characteristics to a nonhuman subject. The poet of "Night," for example, describes the night as a goddess who looks "about . . . with her eyes." Many of the hymns also contain **similes,** comparisons of two apparently dissimilar things by means of a word such as *like* or *as.* For example, in another hymn, "Parjanya, the Bull," the rain god is compared to a charioteer:

> *Like* a charioteer lashing his horses with a whip, he makes his messengers of rain appear.

The Vedic poets use figurative language not only to create memorable images but to make a sometimes violent world seem familiar and understandable. The conquering Aryans rode their horses into northern India. Think how formidable the night must have seemed to them as it descended on this strange land of rich forest and vast open areas cleared for cultivation. How welcome the dawn must have been. How reassuring it must have been to see night and dawn as two goddesses who could be coaxed and placated.

Figurative language is not found only in poems. People often use such language in conversation to describe common occurrences in an uncommon way. Imagine, for example, that you are attending a sports event. Think about the way the crowd bursts into cheers, buzzes with tense excitement, or sighs with disappointment. How might you use personification, simile, or both to describe the crowd's reactions?

The scholar P. Chandra has commented on the oral transmission of the Vedic hymns: "The Vedic literature was oral and not written down until very much later, the first reference to a written Vedic text being in the 10th century A.D. In order to ensure the purity of the Vedas, the slightest change was forbidden, and the priests devised systems of checks and counterchecks, so that there has been virtually no change in these texts for about 3,000 years. Underlying this was the belief that the correct recitation of the Vedas was 'the pivot of the universe' and that the slightest mistake would have disastrous cosmic consequences unless expiated by sacrifice and prayer. The Vedas are still chanted by the Brahmin priests at weddings, initiations, funerals, and the like, in the daily devotions of the priests, and at the now rarely held so-called public sacrifices."

Objectives

Thematic

To understand the ways in which the Vedic poets speculated on the mysteries of the world.

Skills

1 To understand personification
2 To understand simile

Support Material

Teaching Portfolio
Teacher Backup, p. 199
Usage and Mechanics Worksheet, p. 203
Analyzing Literature Worksheet, *Using Simile and Personification,* p. 204
Critical Thinking and Reading Work-

from the Rig Veda
Night

translated by
Wendy Doniger O'Flaherty

1 The goddess Night has drawn near, looking about on many sides with her eyes. She has put on all her glories.

2 The immortal goddess has filled the wide space, the depths and the heights. She stems the tide of darkness with her light.

3 The goddess has drawn near, pushing aside her sister the twilight. Darkness, too, will give way.

4 As you came near to us today, we turned homeward to rest, as birds go to their home in a tree.

5 People who live in villages have gone home to rest, and animals with feet, and animals with wings, even the ever-searching hawks.

6 Ward off the she-wolf and the wolf; ward off the thief. O night full of waves, be easy for us to cross over.

7 Darkness—palpable,[1] black, and painted—has come upon me. O Dawn, banish it like a debt.

8 I have driven this hymn to you as the herdsman drives cows. Choose and accept it, O Night, daughter of the sky, like a song of praise to a conqueror.

---

1. **palpable** (pal'pə bəl) *adj.*: That which can be touched, felt, or handled.

Reader's Response *Are our experiences of the night different from those of the ancient Indian poet? Explain.*

THINKING ABOUT THE SELECTION

Interpreting

1. In the first two verses, the poet tells us that the goddess Night "has put on all her glories" and "stems the tide of darkness with her light." To what do you think the poet is referring?
2. Notice the verbs and verbal phrases that the poet uses in this hymn: *stems, pushing aside, ward off, banish.* What do these words and phrases reveal about the poet's attitude toward the night?
3. Dawn is also a character in this hymn. What does the poet suggest about the relationship between Night and Dawn?

Applying

4. Think about a time in your life when you were completely away from artificial sources of light, for example, when a power failure occurred or you were on an overnight camping trip. Use figures of speech to describe the night as it seemed to you then.

ANALYZING LITERATURE

Understanding Personification and Simile

The hymns of the *Rig Veda* make frequent use of two important figures of speech: **personification,** the giving of human characteristics to a nonhuman subject, and **simile,** the comparison of dissimilar things through the use of words such as *like* or *as.* Both of these devices appear in "Night." The poet personifies the night as a conquering goddess and uses a simile to describe his creation of this poem: "I have driven this hymn to you *as* the herdsman drives cows."

1. For the Aryan, cows would have been a valuable commodity. What does the simile mentioned above suggest about the purpose of the hymn?
2. It has been said that a good simile should first surprise readers and then make them nod their heads in agreement. Does the simile in the seventh verse meet this criterion? Why or why not?
3. Name two ways in which the personification of night would have helped the poet and his audience feel more comfortable in the darkness.

TAITTIRIYA UPANISHAD

Focus

More About the Author The Upanishads themselves are attributed to certain sages who were divorced from society and living in the forest. These authors defied the ritualistic practices of the Vedic cult, yet they incorporated much of the ritual imagery into their literary style, which indicated a move toward inward contemplation and self-realization. The specific writer of this text is unknown.

Pronunciation Note This Upanishad (ōō pän' i shad') is called Taittiriya (tē' tə rē' ə), with the accent on the third syllable, after a Vedic ritualistic work entitled Taittiriya-Brahmana (brä' mə nə).

Humanities Note

Fine art. *Hindu drawing showing tortoise supporting elephants.* This unusual work is called a cosmogram because it is a visual explanation of the creation of the world and the cosmos. Recognizable symbols in this cosmogram include the tortoise, elephants, and a serpent. In the East, the tortoise is frequently featured as the symbol of existence and evolution. Its shell is rounded on top to represent Heaven and square underneath to represent Earth. In view of the tortoise's legendary slowness, it is said to represent natural evolution, rather than rapid, spiritual evolution.

On the tortoise's back are three elephants who signify the supports or caryatids of the universe; on their backs they hold the higher realms of existence.

The serpent that circles the entire design represents energy and, according to some Indian beliefs, the waters of the sea, the spring of life and immortality, and the riches of the spirit.

You might want to use the following questions to discuss the art:
1. What would you imagine a cosmogram of the biblical view of Genesis to look like?
2. Why would a visual representation of philosophy be important to a people?

HINDU DRAWING SHOWING TORTOISE
SUPPORTING ELEPHANTS

The Indian philosophical tradition, one of the richest in the world, has its roots in the Sanskrit texts called the Upanishads (ōō pan' i shadz'). These texts, written by many different authors, date from 1000 to 600 B.C. *Upanishad* in Sanskrit means "to sit nearby," in the sense of sitting near a teacher and learning from him. In accord with this meaning, the Upanishads often treat complicated subjects—such as the nature of reality—in dialogues between teachers and students. The Upanishads also use stories to convey difficult ideas.

The Upanishads and the Vedas

The Upanishads are the final stage in the development of the sacred books called the Vedas. (For a discussion of the longest and oldest of these books, the *Rig Veda*, see pages 152–154.) The teaching in the Upanishads is therefore called *vedanta* (vi dän' tə), which means the conclusion of the Vedas and the final statement of the hidden truth of the Vedas.

Unlike the Vedas, however, the Upanishads tend to diminish the importance of individual gods. Instead of focusing on Night, Dawn, or the gods of the storm so important to farmers, the Upanishads emphasize that there is a *single* principle underlying all existence. This underlying reality, Brahman (brä' mən), is not a god as many people understand the term. It is more of an abstract concept than a personal divinity.

An important theme of the Upanishads is the identification of the atman, or soul, of a person with Brahman. Appearances disguise this identity. However, by means of meditation—a kind of deep and focused thought—we can discover our connection with ultimate reality.

Secret and Dangerous Books

Because they do not stress the gods or rituals of the Vedas, the Upanishads were viewed as a subversive, even dangerous, body of literature. They appear to have been secret books, read only by those who could appreciate their subtle teaching.

The Influence of the Upanishads

Despite their status as secret books, the Upanishads have had a strong influence on Indian philosophy. In the eighth century A.D., for example, one of India's greatest thinkers, Shankara, developed a system of thought based on the Upanishads. He too believed that everything we see, hear, and feel derives from a single ultimate reality. Shankara's philosophy was so popular in India that it became the standard against which all other philosophies were measured.

Beyond the Borders of India

The Upanishads have also had a great influence beyond the borders of India. When they were translated into European languages in the 1800's, their teachings contributed to the Western philosophical tradition.

Objectives

Thematic

To understand the Indian way of exploring the mystery of Brahman

Skills

1 To analyze the mystery of Brahman
2 To appreciate cross-cultural influences in language

Support Material

Teaching Portfolio
Teacher Backup, p. 209
Usage and Mechanics Worksheet, p. 213
Analyzing Literature Worksheet, *Understanding the Mystery of Brahman*, p. 214
Critical Thinking and Reading Work-

GUIDE FOR INTERPRETING

Commentary

from the Taittiriya Upanishad

The Concept of Brahman. The authors of the vedic hymns express the wishes and fears of an agricultural people. They are preoccupied with material well-being—safety in the threatening night, protection from storms, an abundant harvest, and plentiful cattle. The authors of the Upanishads, however, go beyond such concerns. They pursue questions that are highly abstract and philosophical: What is the most important thing in life? What is the most fundamental thing one can know?

Both these questions lead to the central concept of the Upanishads, the idea of **Brahman.** This term, which is difficult to translate, has been rendered in English as "the one, self-existent Impersonal Spirit," "the one, universal Soul," "the Self-existent," and "the Absolute."

You may wonder why translators did not simply express this notion as "God." The answer is that Brahman is neither a god (although it is referred to as "he" and "him" in the following translation) nor an object of worship. As the reality that underlies all appearances, Brahman is something that one "knows." It is the subject of meditation (called *tapas* in the Upanishads), a kind of prayerlike thought that focuses the mind on what is most real.

Since Brahman is such a difficult concept to grasp, it can best be defined by stating what it is *not.* This process is similar to peeling away the layers of an onion. When everything that is mere appearance has been stripped away, the remaining core will be Brahman.

In the Upanishads this type of negative description of Brahman is called "not this, not that." Following is an example of how it works (remember, however, that an Indian thinker would not necessarily share the beliefs of Christians, Muslims, or Jews): We know that the universe existed for millions of years without any form of life, so life is not essential. We know that the universe existed without the Earth, so our planet is not essential. What predates the universe? What underlies the very origin of the universe? According to the Upanishads, the answer—and the core of the onion—is Brahman.

In the following excerpt, a father teaches his son about Brahman through a similar process of peeling away what is not essential.

Writing

The authors of the Upanishads must describe the ultimate abstraction, Brahman, but even an abstract notion like joy or freedom would be hard to put into words. Write a description of such an idea that a younger relative or friend of yours would understand.

Literary Focus In the Upanishads, the primary emphasis is on the attainment of the highest truth. Suggest that students think of Brahman as the highest truth, an object of knowledge received by personal revelation rather than earned by work.

Writing/Prior Knowledge In composition classes students have probably encountered the terms *inductive* and *deductive reasoning.* Ask them to discuss these types of reasoning as ways to perceive reality. You might suggest that students think about the relationship between material and spiritual experience, which Westerners typically think of as separate.

ESL Teaching Strategy ESL Students may need the term *vision* clarified. Explain to students the different meanings of the word. Start by defining vision as the act of seeing with the eye, but point out that vision can also refer to something seen by means other than normal sight. Stress that as it is used in this selection, vision has religious meaning, as the boy is able to "see" something that is not actually visible.

Teaching Tenth-Grade Students Tenth-grade students might appreciate the idea that the levels of discovery Bhrigu undergoes are somewhat like the progression of grades from grammar school through junior and senior high school and on into college. The simpler ideas must be mastered as a foundation for learning and understanding complexities.

sheet, *Appreciating the Role of the Guru,* p. 215
Language Worksheet, *Identifying Words from Different Cultures,* p. 216
Selection Test, pp. 217–218

from the Taittiriya Upanishad
The Mystery of Brahman
translated by Juan Mascaró

From a Bahr al Hayat manuscript Mughal school, c. 1600–1605. Hindus often assume positions like this one when engaging in prayer or meditation.
The Chester Beatty Library and Gallery of Oriental Art, Dublin

Once Bhrigu Varuni went to his father Varuna and said: "Father, explain to me the mystery of Brahman."

Then his father spoke to him of the food of the earth, of the breath of life, of the one who sees, of the one who hears, of the mind that knows, and of the one who speaks. And he further said to him: "Seek to know him from whom all beings have come, by whom they all live, and unto whom they all return. He is Brahman."

So Bhrigu went and practiced *tapas*, spiritual prayer. Then he thought that Brahman was the food of the earth: for from the earth all beings have come, by food of the earth they all live, and unto the earth they all return.

After this he went again to his father Varuna and said: "Father, explain further to me the mystery of Brahman." To him his father answered: "Seek to know Brahman by *tapas*, by prayer, because Brahman is prayer."

So Bhrigu went and practiced *tapas*, spiritual prayer. Then he thought that Brahman was life: for from life all beings have come, by life they all live, and unto life they all return.

After this he went again to his father Varuna and said: "Father, explain further to me the mystery of Brahman." To him his father answered: "Seek to know Brahman by *tapas*, by prayer, because Brahman is prayer."

So Bhrigu went and practiced *tapas*, spiritual prayer. Then he thought that Brahman was mind: for from mind all beings have come, by mind they all live, and unto mind they all return.

After this he went again to his father Varuna and said: "Father, explain further to me the mystery of Brahman." To him his father answered: "Seek to know Brahman by *tapas*, by prayer, because Brahman is prayer."

So Bhrigu went and practiced *tapas*, spiritual prayer. Then he thought that Brahman was reason: for from reason all beings have come, by reason they all live, and unto reason they all return.

He went again to his father, asked the same question, and received the same answer.

So Bhrigu went and practiced *tapas*, spiritual prayer. And then he *saw* that Brahman is joy: for FROM JOY ALL BEINGS HAVE COME, BY JOY THEY ALL LIVE, AND UNTO JOY THEY ALL RETURN.

This was the vision of Bhrigu Varuni which came from the Highest: and he who sees this vision **4** lives in the Highest.

Reader's Response *What is your reaction to Bhrigu's vision?*

THINKING ABOUT THE SELECTION

Interpreting

1. Consider the progression of things that Bhrigu is told to meditate on by his father. Why are the different items—food, life, mind, reason, joy—mentioned in this particular order?
2. (a) Why do you think Bhrigu's father does not recommend scientific investigation as a means of knowing Brahman? (b) Does the text give you any insight into the nature of *tapas?* Explain.

Applying

3. The Upanishads focus on abstract, spiritual matters, while the *Rig Veda* is concerned with material well-being. What do you think this difference reveals about the two societies in which these texts were written?
4. What might Bhrigu's father say about the modern scientific theory that all matter is composed of a few subatomic particles?

ANALYZING LITERATURE

Understanding the Mystery of Brahman

Brahman refers to the reality that underlies everything we see, hear, taste, smell, and feel. Since it is not a god, it is not meant to be worshiped. It can be "known," however, by a process of meditation or focused thought in which we first discover what Brahman is *not*. After everything inessential has been eliminated, the last remaining thing is Brahman. In this excerpt from the Upanishads, we see Bhrigu Varuni going through this process until he discovers the quality—joy—that underlies reason, mind, life, and food.

1. It is clear that by "joy," Varuni means more than a person's brief experience of happiness. What deeper meaning of "joy" does he suggest when he says, "FROM JOY ALL BEINGS HAVE COME, BY JOY THEY ALL LIVE, AND UNTO JOY THEY ALL RETURN"?
2. Use the technique of negative description—"not this, not that"—to define the essence or underlying reality of an individual person. What single quality —memory? intelligence? consciousness?—gives a person his or her identity?

UNDERSTANDING LANGUAGE

Appreciating Cross-Cultural Influences

The original word *Brahman,* referring to the underlying reality of the universe, gave rise to two related words: (1) *Brahmana* (English spelling: Brahman or Brahmin), the term for the priestly class in the Hindu tradition, and (2) *Brahman,* which is spelled the same as the original word but refers to a personified creator-god.

1. Cultured and snobbish members of long-established New England families are called Brahmins. Why do you think they might have been given this name?
2. Use your dictionary to determine why a certain breed of American cattle is referred to as Brahmans.

Closure and Extension

ANSWERS TO THINKING ABOUT THE SELECTION

1. The progression indicates a pattern of eliminating what Brahman is not, moving from the specific to the general, the material to the spiritual.
2. (a) Scientific investigation leads to one definitive, indisputable answer. Brahman must be investigated individually, explored in terms of what the individual can understand and discover for himself or herself. (b) Answers will vary. Although the actual process of *tapas* is not described, perceptive students may recognize it as a form of meditation that increases depth of thought.
3. Vedic society was preoccupied with basic needs of survival, whereas the society of the Upanishads was free from such concerns and able to concentrate on more philosophic issues.
4. Bhrigu's father would probably not accept modern scientific theory because he has an abstract, spiritual perception of the world.

ANSWERS TO ANALYZING LITERATURE

1. He suggests that joy is at the very core of life, giving root to life, sustaining life, and containing life.
2. Answers will vary. One possible answer is memory, because if you don't remember who you are, you have no sense of identity.

ANSWERS TO UNDERSTANDING LANGUAGE

1. Suggested response: The original European settlers of the United States founded colonies in New England. Their descendants therefore regard themselves as members of an elite, comparable to the Brahmins. The Brahmins are the highest ranking Hindu caste.
2. Brahman cattle are a breed of domestic cattle developed from Indian cattle.

Master Teacher Note Explain that the writers of the Upanishads were conducting a spiritual pursuit that necessarily went beyond logical reasoning. By contemplating the nature of the microcosm (the small), the searcher could discover the reality of the macrocosm (the large). Have students think of minor events or situations that are mirrors of larger ones.

Cultural Note In exploring the gap between Indians and Englishmen in *A Passage to India*, E. M. Forster touches on the seemingly impersonal mystery that underlies much of India's religious thought. His character Mrs. Moore sees the echoing "boum" of the Marabar caves as an infinite comment on the smallness of mankind.

Discussion Having read the selection, go back to the title. Ask students: What was the mystery of Brahman? Do students feel that the mystery has been solved?

A Kaleidoscope of Images

The following images are part of the kaleidoscope of Indian religious practices: gigantic bonfires consuming effigies of ten-headed demons; sacred texts that are chanted without interruption for a month at a time; naked ascetics smeared with ashes from sacred fires; and monks absorbed in silent meditation.

As the richness of these images suggests, few places on earth have devoted more creative energy to religious expression than India. It has given the world the religion called Hinduism, which you have been studying when reading the selections from the *Rig Veda* and the Upanishads. In addition, it gave the world Jainism (jīn´ iz'm), Buddhism (bōōd´ iz'm), and Sikhism (sēk´ iz'm). Also, it has added its own flavor to religions like Christianity and Islam.

Jainism and Buddhism arose in the sixth century B.C. in protest against the beliefs of the Vedas and the complex Hindu rituals of sacrifice. Jains—the name of their religion derives from the Sanskrit for "saint," *jina*—renounced earthly pleasures and devoted themselves to protecting all forms of life.

Nirvana: An Extinguished Flame

Buddhism was founded by Siddhartha Gautama (sid där´ tə gou´ tə mə), an Indian prince (563–483 B.C.) and a remarkable personality. Born to a royal family in what is now southern Nepal, he led a protected life. When he left the palace grounds and learned about suffering and death for the first time, he was so affected by this experience that he renounced luxury forever. The former prince became a wandering religious man. After years of fasting and intense study, he achieved nirvana (nir vä´ nə). This Sanskrit word refers to a flame that has gone out for lack of fuel. As its original meaning suggests, nirvana describes a state of being in which the desire for earthly things has been quenched. Gautama was given the name Buddha, Sanskrit for "enlightened one," in recognition of his achievement. Buddha's followers—and the religion he inspired spread as far as China and Japan—seek to reach this same state of blessed emptiness. In emulation of their master, Buddhists also cultivate the virtues of compassion and mercy.

The Sikh religion developed in northern India about two thousand years after the origin of Buddhism and Jainism. Like these two religions, Sikhism rejected the caste system and rituals of Hinduism; however, the Sikhs' belief in a single god set them apart. Gradually the Sikhs developed a strong military tradition and conquered much of the northern Indian region called the Punjab. They adopted the customs of carrying a dagger, wearing a turban, and allowing their hair to grow long. In the nineteenth century, they fought against the British and, when defeated, served in Britain's colonial army.

Islam in India

Seagoing Arab traders brought the Muslim religion to western India in the eighth century. Later, Muslim armies invaded India from the north. The emperor Babur led such an invasion

NSIGHTS

from Afghanistan, and in 1526 he established the Mogul empire with its capital in Delhi. Despite the successes of Muslim rulers, however, Islam never replaced Hinduism as India's main religion.

Under the Mogul emperors (1526–1857), Islamic and Indian traditions mingled to produce a distinctive style of art and architecture. The most famous example of this style is the Taj Mahal, built by a Muslim emperor after the death of his favorite wife. This domed structure is made from white marble decorated with semiprecious stones arranged in intricate designs and Arabic inscriptions.

BHUBANESHVAR TEMPLE

Rebirth: The Body Is an Old Shirt

The best-known religious belief to come out of India—a belief shared by Hindus, Jains, and Buddhists—is the notion that the soul is repeatedly reborn into this world. As the body is cast off like an old shirt, the soul can go to heaven for a period of time or it can be reborn in a human body, an animal, or even an insect.

Whether a soul is reborn in better circumstances depends on a person's deeds—the totality of these deeds is known as karma (kär′ mə). A good and virtuous person, with good karma, will be reborn as a higher-ranking person; for example, an honorable merchant may become a warrior. However, the texts record unpleasant punishments for those with bad karma. A person who steals grain, for instance, will be reborn as a rat, and a priest who steals gold is doomed to be reborn a thousand times as a spider or lizard.

Indian religions tend to view this life as a place of impermanence and inevitable disappointment. Even the good and wonderful things of our lives—friends, family, our daily round of pleasures—will come to an end. Continual rebirth, therefore, can only result in continual suffering. The way to avoid such suffering is to escape from the process of death and rebirth.

Dharma: The Path of Duty

For Hindus the only means to escape rebirth is to perform one's duty—dharma (dur′ mə) is the name given to the duties and responsibilities unique to every individual. Each member of society, even each animal, has a set of prescribed duties. The worst thing a person can do is to try to perform someone else's duty. A famous verse in the *Bhagavad-Gita* says:

> It is better to do one's own duty badly than to do another's well. Death in one's own duty is preferable to another's duty which is fraught with danger.

As you will see in the following selections, Indian myths and stories praise those who perform their duty even in the face of great adversity.

important than the rival sect of the Ajivikas. . . . We owe much to the Jaina monks' love of literature. To copy a manuscript, even a secular one, was considered a work of great religious merit, and thus the old Jaina monasteries of Western India have preserved many rare and otherwise unknown texts, some of which have still to be published, and many of which are of non-Jaina origin.

MAHABHARATA

Focus

More About the _Mahabharata_
The _Mahabharata_ has sometimes been compared to the epics of Homer. Yet the _Mahabharata_ plays a much more active role in contemporary Indian society than Homer's epics do in contemporary Western society. Explain to students that many of the episodes in the _Mahabharata_ are recited by Indian parents to their children. Have them discuss what this reveals about the place of the _Mahabharata_ in Indian culture.

Critical Evaluation The _Mahabharata_ is such a vital part of Indian life that there is a common saying that "if something is not found in the _Mahabharata_ then it is not part of Indian culture." Have students discuss what this saying reveals about the _Mahabharata_. Could this saying be applied to any Western literary works? If so, which ones?

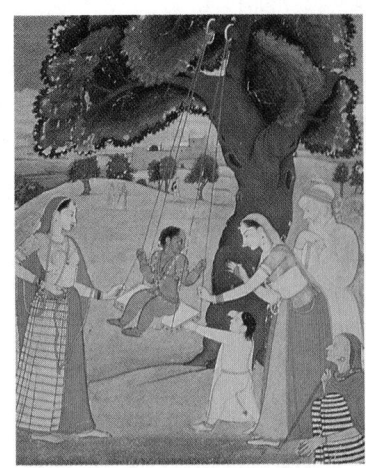

KRISHNA ON THE SWING
British Museum, London

The _Mahabharata_ (mə hä′bä′rə tə) is the world's longest epic. Although it was compiled sometime between 200 B.C. and A.D. 200, Indian storytellers who know it by heart still entertain and instruct their village audiences with recitations from this epic poem.

The Rights to a Kingdom

The myths and tales of the _Mahabharata_ are woven into the fabric of its main story: the account of a fight over the rights to a kingdom. Two branches of a family, the Pandavas and the Kauravas, are involved in this dispute.

The Pandavas and the Kauravas

On one side are the Pandavas, five brothers who were brought up by King Pandu. However, the Pandava boys were really fathered by various Hindu gods and are therefore semi-divine themselves.

These five brothers are all married to the same woman, Draupadi—a situation that came about in an unusual way. In ancient India young princes often competed in a contest to win the hand of an eligible princess. Such a contest was held for the princess Draupadi. One of the Pandavas won the right to marry her by defeating his brothers and the other contestants in sports like wrestling and archery. When the brothers returned home, they proudly announced to their mother that one of them had been victorious. Their mother was distracted at the time and, without looking up to see what the prize was, she told them to share it equally among themselves. Since no virtuous Indian son can refuse to obey his mother, they did what she said and Draupadi became the wife of all five brothers.

The opponents of the Pandavas are the Kauravas, who are the ninety-nine sons of King Pandu's blind brother. (Pandu's brother should have been king, but he was blind and therefore disqualified for kingship, according to ancient Indian traditions.) They are led by the eldest brother, Duryodhana, whose name means "Mr. Dirty Fighter." He challenges the eldest of the Pandavas to a gambling match and uses rigged dice to defeat him. The Pandavas lose everything in this dice game, even their own freedom. Duryodhana gives them back their freedom, but he keeps the kingdom and banishes the five Pandavas to the forest.

Banishment

The banishment or exile of honest rulers by villains is a common theme in world literature. Often the place of banishment, where the hero or heroes must dwell for a time, is uncivilized and primitive but also magical. In Shakespeare's _The Tempest_ (see page 709), this place is an enchanted island. The forest in the _Mahabharata_ has a similar magic and mystery. While the Pandavas live there, they meet various characters who tell them instructive and entertaining stories. Sometimes these stories mirror and comment on the plight of the Pandavas. They learn from these tales how to conduct their lives in exile. The theme of such stories, like "Sibi" on the following pages, is that unrighteous behavior leads one astray while righteous behavior will eventually be rewarded.

Objectives

Thematic
To understand the Indian perspective on sacrifice

Skills
1 To understand the Hindu concept of dharma

2 To explore the connotations of synonyms
3 To write about sacrifice

Support Material

Teaching Portfolio
Teacher Backup, p. 219
Grammar in Action Worksheet, _Understanding the Correct Use of Verb Tenses_, p. 223
Usage and Mechanics Worksheet, p. 225
Vocabulary Check, p. 226

GUIDE FOR INTERPRETING

Mahabharata

Commentary

The Hindu Concept of Dharma. In the Hindu tradition, the duties of each individual were determined by the caste, or group, into which he or she was born. As members of the priestly caste, for example, Brahmans were expected to conduct the ritual sacrifices and set a standard of correct behavior. The code of duty also determined one's behavior as a son or daughter, husband or wife. **Dharma,** a Sanskrit term, referred both to the sum of a person's obligations and to the moral law that governed the world. To perform one's duty, no matter how humble, was to contribute to the well-being of the whole universe.

A major obligation for all Hindus was keeping one's word. Once you promised to do something, for instance, you had to stand by that promise even if circumstances changed. If someone failed to keep a pledge, the person who was wronged might sit in the street outside the offender's house and demand justice. This type of nonviolent protest was especially effective when humble people were lied to by the rich and powerful.

Remember these Indian notions of duty as you evaluate the actions of Sibi in the following story. He is above all a man of his word. Although keeping his promise has dire consequences, he knows that breaking his word will lead to an even more terrible punishment when his soul is reborn.

Writing

Is it ever acceptable to break one's word? Don't answer this question immediately, but take a moment to think of its implications. In responding to this question, cite examples to support your arguments.

Primary Source

R. K. Narayan describes the typical village storyteller, who knows "by heart all the . . . 100,000 stanzas of the *Mahabharata*," beginning an evening session: ". . . the storyteller will dress himself for the part by smearing sacred ash on his forehead and wrapping himself in a green shawl, while his helpers set up a framed picture of some god on a pedestal in the veranda, decorate it with jasmine garlands, and light incense to it. After these preparations, when the storyteller enters to seat himself in front of the lamps, he looks imperious and in complete control of the situation. He begins the session with a prayer, prolonging it until the others join and the valleys echo with the chants, drowning the cry of jackals."

Literary Focus Tell students that the dharma of the Hindu god Brahma is to sustain the world. People are expected to imitate Brahma by fulfilling their specific duties and thereby contributing to the sustenance of the world. Even if people consider their dharma to be inappropriate or unjust, they are required to accept it. If they refuse, it is believed that the Hindu gods will force them to do so.

Have students discuss the role of duty in contemporary American society. Then have them compare and contrast it with the Hindu concept of dharma. Do they think the Hindu concept of dharma could ever be applied to American life? Why or why not?

Writing/Prior Knowledge Before students begin writing, you might want to have a class discussion about the importance of keeping one's word. Ask students whether they lose respect for people who do not keep their word. Why or why not?

ESL Teaching Strategy If you have any Indian students, you might encourage them to share their knowledge of Hinduism and of the *Mahabharata* with the class.

Vocabulary
Preteach the following vocabulary words:
mitigated (mit′ ə gāt′ id) v.: Moderated
caricature (kar′ ə kə chər) n.: A likeness that is so distorted or inferior as to seem ludicrous
concession (kən sesh′ ən) n.: An act or instance of conceding or yielding
grotesque (grō tesk′) adj.: Characterized by distortions or striking incongruities in appearance, shape, or manner
asylum (ə sī′ ləm) n.: Refuge
carrion (kar′ ē ən) n.: The decaying flesh of a dead body
profusely (prə fyo͞os′ lē) adj.: Pouring forth freely

Analyzing Literature Worksheet, *Understanding the Concept of Dharma*, p. 227
Language Worksheet, *Exploring the Connotations of Synonyms*, p. 228
Selection Test, pp. 229–230

Spelling Tip Point out that in the word *asylum* the long i sound is spelled with a *y.*

Teaching Tenth-Grade Students "Sibi" is an accessible and entertaining story that should not pose much of a problem for tenth grade students. To ensure that they do not have any difficulties, however, you may want to read this selection as a class, with student volunteers taking turns reading aloud. Encourage students to raise any questions that arise as the text is being read.

from the Mahabharata

Sibi

adapted by R. K. Narayan

There is a half-moon in the sky today which will disappear shortly after midnight, said the storyteller. I'll select a tale which will end before the moon sets, so that you may all go home when there is still a little light.

The tale concerns a king and two birds. The king was Sibi, who had just performed a holy sacrifice on the banks of the Jumna.[1] The guests were resting in the tree shade after partaking of a feast. The air was charged with the scent of flowers and incense. Sibi went round to make sure that everyone was comfortable. A cool breeze blew from the south, patches of clouds mitigated the severity of the sun in the blue sky, the embers of the holy fire subsided into a soft glow under the ash.

The king, satisfied that all his guests were happy, dismissed his attendants and proceeded to his own corner of the camp to rest under a canopy. He had closed his eyes, half in sleep and half in prayer, when he felt a gust of air hitting him in the face and some object suddenly dropping on his lap. He awoke and noticed a dove, white and soft, nestling in his lap. Its feathers were ruffled in terror and its eyes were shut. It looked so limp that he thought it was dead, but then he noticed a slight flutter of breath. He sat still in order not to frighten away the bird, and looked about for a servant.

Just then a hawk whirled down in pursuit, and perched itself on a low branch of the tree beside the canopy. The hawk exclaimed, "Ah, at last! What a game of hide and seek!"

"What do you want?" asked the king.

"I am addressing myself to that creature on your lap! Never been so much tricked in my life! If every mouthful of food has to be got after such a trial, a nice outlook indeed for the so-called king of birds! As one king to another, let me tell you, the dove nestling in your lap is mine. Throw it back to me."

The king thought over the statement of the hawk and said, "I am indeed honored by a visit from the king of birds, although I had thought till now that the eagle was the king!"

"I am a hawk, not a kite.[2] Know you that the hawk belongs to the kingly race while the kite is a mere caricature of our family, pursuing a career of deception by seeming no bigger than its victim and then attacking it. How often one mistakes a kite for a dove!"

Sibi wanted to divert the attention of the hawk from the subject of the dove and so said, "The kite also goes out of sight when it flies, so don't be offended if we land-bound creatures imagine that the kite floats in the same heaven as the hawk."

The hawk sharpened his beak on the tree-trunk and lifted one leg to display his talons and

---

1. **Jumna** (jum′ nə): A river in northern India, flowing from the Himalayas southwest into the Ganges.

---

2. **kite:** Any of various birds, including the hawk, that prey on insects, reptiles, and small mammals. The hawk is haughtily distinguishing himself from his smaller, less significant cousins.

said, "I'm sorry to see the mistakes you human beings make. The kite no doubt flies—but not beyond the back of the lowest cloud. And you think that it sports in the heavens itself! The only common element between us is that we both have pointed, curved beaks, that's all; but the kite has a taste for helpless little creatures such as mice and sparrows —creatures which we would not care to notice."

The king realized that the subject was once more drifting towards food and diverted the hawk's attention again by saying, "The general notion is that the eagle is the king of birds."

The hawk chuckled cynically. "Ignorant mankind! How the eagle came to be so much respected, I shall never understand; what is there to commend the eagle? Its wingspread? You people are too easily carried away by appearances! Do you know that the hawk can fly just as high as the eagle? And yet you have no regard for us!"

Sibi said, "You can't blame us, we take things as they seem from here! I now know better."

The hawk looked pleased at this concession and said, "Have you ever seen a mountain eagle walk on the ground? Is there anything more grotesque? Don't you agree that the first requirement for kingliness would be grace of movement? Only we hawks have it."

"True, true," said the king. "When I move from my bed to the bathroom, even if alone at night, I catch myself strutting along as in a parade, I suppose!" The king laughed, to entertain the hawk; he thought it might please the bird to be treated as a fellow king. The hawk looked pleased, and the king hoped that it would take itself off after these pleasantries.

The dove slightly stirred on his lap, and he hastened to draw over it his silk scarf. The hawk noticed this and bluntly said, "King, what is the use of your covering the dove? I will not forget that my food, which I have earned by honest chase, is there, unfairly held by you."

The king said, "This bird has come to me for asylum; it is my duty to protect it."

"I may brave your sword and swoop on my prey, and if I die in the attempt the spirits of my ancestors will bless me. We have known no fear for one thousand generations, what should we fear

when the back of our prime ancestor serves as the vehicle of the great god Vishnu?"[3]

Again the king was on the point of correcting him, that it was a golden eagle that Vishnu rode, not a hawk, but he checked himself.

The bird emphasized his own status again. "You who are reputed to be wise, O king, don't confuse me with the carrion birds wheeling over your head. I know where I stand," said the bird, preening its feathers.

The king felt it was time to say something agreeable himself, secretly worrying that he was

---

3. **Vishnu** (vish′ no͞o): The Hindu god known as the Preserver, because he became a human being on nine separate occasions to save humanity from destruction.

A HAWK, FROM AN EIGHTEENTH-CENTURY A.D. INDIAN PAINTING
Victoria and Albert Museum, London

pains to protect it in order to avoid the possibility of even greater suffering in a future lifetime.

6 **Discussion** Have students explain why the king keeps changing the subject.

7 **Discussion** Have students discuss whether they feel that physical grace has anything to do with kingliness. Do they feel, for instance, that it is important for a politician to move in a graceful manner? Why or why not?

8 **Literary Focus** Make sure students notice that the king openly declares that he considers protecting the dove to be part of his dharma.

Humanities Note

Fine art, *A hawk*, from an eighteenth-century Indian painting. This miniature painting reflects the influence of a seventeenth-century Indian emperor named Jahangir, who was both a nature lover and a patron of the arts. An avid bird watcher, he set his artists to work picturing the species of birds known to the court. Dozens of paintings of birds were created for him. Like the painting seen here, these works were painted in a detailed, lifelike style.

You might want to use the following questions to discuss the art:

1. What impression of the hawk does this painting convey?
2. What is the significance of the hawk's being tethered to its perch?
3. Explain whether this is an appropriate illustration for the story.
4. How would you react if you were to encounter a bird similar to the one depicted here? Explain.

9 Literary Focus Because it is the king's duty to protect *all* his subjects, including all types of birds and animals, do your students think he is obligated to ensure the well-being of the hawk? Why or why not?

10 Clarification Tell students that in ancient India, oil was the primary fuel for lamps. Keeping this in mind, have students explain the hawk's analogy.

11 Discussion Do students imagine that a hawk would really pass up prepared food if it were hungry enough? Why or why not?

12 Discussion Have students discuss the common symbolic meaning of hawks and doves. How do these symbolic meanings apply to this story?

13 Discussion If hawks and doves are interpreted symbolically, do students feel there is any truth to the saying, "Hawks eat doves"? Why or why not?

reaching the limits of his wit. The dove nestled within the silk scarf. There was an uneasy pause while the king dreaded what might be coming next.

The hawk suddenly said, "All the world speaks of you as one who has the finest discrimination between right and wrong. And so you have a serious responsibility at this moment. You must not do anything that goes contrary to your reputation. Remember, I am in the agonies of hunger, and you refuse me my legitimate diet. By your act you cause me suffering, you injure me every second that you keep your hold on that parcel of meat. You have attained immeasurable spiritual merit by your deeds of perfection; now this single selfish act of yours will drain away all your merit and you will probably go to hell."

"O infinitely wise bird, does it seem to you that I am holding this dove out of selfishness so that I may eat it myself?"

"I am not so simple-minded," said the bird haughtily. "By selfish I meant that you were thinking of your own feelings, totally ignoring my viewpoint."

"When I recollect the terror in its eye as it fell on my lap, I feel nothing ever matters except affording it protection."

"O prince among princes, food is life, out of food all things exist and stir. Between life and death stands what? Food! I am faint with hunger. If you deny me my food any longer I may die. In a cranny of yonder rock my wife has hatched four eggs, the little ones are guarded by their mother, and all of them await my return home. If I die here of hunger, they will keep peeping out for my return home until they perish of the same hunger. And the sin of ending six lives will be on you. O maharaja,[4] consider well whether you want to save one doubtful life, which is probably half gone already, or six lives. Let not the performance of what seems to you a rightful act conflict with bigger issues. You know all this, king, but choose to ignore the issues. And all this talking only fatigues me and takes me nearer to death. So please spare me further argument."

Sibi said, "I notice that you are an extraordinary bird. You talk wisely, knowledgeably; there is

---

4. **maharaja** (mä´ hə rä´ jə): King.

nothing that you do not know. Your mind journeys with ease at subtle heights of thought. But, bird, tell me, how is it that you fail to notice the sheer duty I owe a creature that cries for protection? As a king is it not my duty?"

"I am only asking for food; food is to life what oil is to a lamp."

"Very well. You see all these people lying around, they have all rested after a feast in which nothing was lacking to satisfy the sixfold demands of the palate. Tell me what you want, and I will spread a feast before you in no time."

"King, the nature of food differs with different creatures. What you call a feast seems to me just so much trash. We observe from our heights all the activity that goes on in your royal kitchen and ever wonder why you take all that trouble with spice, salt, and fire to ruin the taste of God-given stuff. King, I do not want to speak at length. I am famished and I feel my eyes dimming. Have consideration for me too."

"If it is flesh you want, I will ask them to get it for you."

The hawk gave an ironical laugh at this. "See where all this leads you! How are you going to get flesh without killing something else? When you interfere with what God has ordained, you complicate everything."

"What is God's plan, actually? Please enlighten me."

"The dove is intended for me; God has no other purpose in creating it and letting it multiply so profusely. Are you not aware of the ancient saying that hawks eat doves?"

The king thought it over and said, "If you spare this dove, I'll guarantee you food every day in my palace all your life."

"I have already told you, my lord, that your food is inedible. Your assurance of daily feeding does not appeal to me. I hunt for food when I want it. I do not see why I should bother about tomorrow. Hoarding for generations ahead is a human failing, a practice unknown to us. I repeat the ancient saying that hawks eat doves."

The king brooded over the words of the hawk for a moment. "Ask for anything, except this little bird on my lap. I won't give it up, whichever way you may argue."

Grammar in Action

A **tense** is a form of a verb that shows the time of an action or a state of being. There are six different tenses: present, past, future, present perfect, past perfect, and future perfect. To enable readers to grasp time sequences, writers must use these six tenses correctly.

Notice the different tenses used in the following passages from "Sibi":

You *see* (present) all these people *lying* (present) around, they *have* all *rested* (present perfect) after a feast in which nothing *was lacking* (past) to satisfy the sixfold demands of the palate.

I *will ask* (future) for the next best thing. I *want* (present) warm flesh . . .

Student Activity 1. Find the verbs and verb phrases in each of the following sentences. Then identify the tense of each verb or verb phrase.
1. How are you going to get flesh without killing something else?
2. I have already told you, my lord, that your food is inedible.
3. By now the whole camp was astir, watching this incredible duel between the king and the hawk.
4. I will not forget that my food, which I have earned by honest chase, is there, unfairly held by you.

KING SIBI'S SACRIFICE TO THE GOD INDRA
c. Second century
British Museum, London

The hawk tilted its head, rolled its eyes, and said, "So be it. I will ask for the next best thing. I want warm flesh, with warm blood dripping, equal in weight to the dove. We are used to eating only fresh meat, we are not carrion[5] birds, let me remind you. You will have to cut it out of your own body, as I know you will not choose to kill another creature for it."

The king brooded over this. "Yes, but I must consider which part of my body will yield the flesh you want without destroying my life. Give me a little time. Bear your hunger for a moment." And he added, "A ruler has no liberty to die. Many depend on him."

"In the same way as my family," said the hawk.

The king beckoned to an attendant. "Bring a pair of weighing scales."

The attendant was nonplussed. "Your Majesty, how can we find one here, in this remote place?"

The king repeated, "I want a pair of scales for accurate weighing."

"May I send a messenger to fetch one from the city?"

---

5. **carrion** (kar′ ē ən) *adj.*: Feeding on the dead.

"How long will he take?" asked the king.

The courtier made a swift reckoning and declared, "If he rides a galloping horse, he should be back tomorrow at dawn."

The king looked at the hawk, who already seemed to droop. He did not want to hear again about his family on the mountain. It was also time to clear up all this situation and feed the refugee on his lap. He said to the courtier, "Construct a balance immediately with whatever is available here. I'll give you ten minutes!"

"Whoever fails will have his head cut off, I suppose?" sneered the hawk. "That would be truly kinglike, but let me tell you straight away that I am not interested in a cut-off head."

"You shall have my flesh and nothing less," said the king.

They bustled about. By now the whole camp was astir, watching this incredible duel between the king and the hawk. They managed to dangle a beam from the branch of a tree. Suspended from either end was a plate from the kitchen; a pointer, also improvised, marked the dead centre of the beam.

The king looked at the hawk and said, "This is the best we can manage."

14 **Reading Strategy** Have students predict how Sibi will respond to the hawk's request.

15 **Discussion** Have students offer their reactions to the idea of a king sacrificing his own flesh to protect one of his subjects. Have students discuss recent leaders, such as Martin Luther King, who have made major sacrifices for their people.

16 **Enrichment** Tell students that Mahatma Gandhi (1869–1948), the celebrated Indian nationalist and reformer, possessed many of the traits that Sibi exhibits. Like Sibi, Gandhi had great respect for all forms of life and was protective of his people and willing to make sacrifices for them.

Humanities Note

Fine art, *King Sibi's sacrifice to the God Indra*. This stone carving is an example of Ghandaran art, a term used to describe the sculptures produced by a school of artists from the northwestern Indus valley during the first centuries A.D. These sculptures are noted for their finely proportioned bodies and classically styled portrait heads. Although the Ghandaran artists were heavily influenced by Greek sculptures, they typically focused on distinctively Indian subjects. This sculpture, for example, depicts the story of King Sibi from the *Mahabharata*.

You might want to use the following questions to discuss the art:

1. Describe what is happening in the sculpture.
2. In what ways does this sculpture reflect the influence of Greek art?
3. How might an Indian painting of this scene differ from this sculpture?
4. What do you find most interesting about this sculpture?

5. We challenged your integrity; and happily accept defeat.

Student Activity 2. Write a paragraph describing a real or imaginary experience. Use at least three different verb tenses in your paragraph, making sure you use them correctly.

Margin notes (left column)

17 Discussion Ask students if they are surprised that the dove weighs so much. What might be the significance of the dove's heaviness?

18 Discussion Have students discuss what the subjects' reactions reveal about their feelings for King Sibi.

19 Literary Focus Call students' attention to the fact that even in his weakened state the king does not forget his duty to his kingdom.

20 Discussion Have your students offer their reactions to the ending of the story. Were they surprised by this turn of events? Why or why not? Do they imagine that Indian audiences would have been surprised? Why or why not?

Cooperative Learning Your students might be interested in finding other Indian literary works that concern the concept of dharma. Divide your class into groups of three or four. Then have each group find another Indian literary selection that explores the concept of dharma. After reading this selection, the students should prepare an informal oral presentation in which they summarize the selection and explain how it conveys the concept of dharma. Finally each group should select a spokesperson to deliver their presentation to the class.

"I understand. A little fluctuation should not matter in the least. Only I do not want you to lose more flesh than is necessary to balance the dove."

The king did not let the bird finish his sentence, but rose, bearing the dove in his hand. He walked up to the crude scales in order to test them. He addressed the hawk, "Will you step nearer?"

"I can watch quite well from here. Also I can trust you."

The king placed the dove on the right-hand side of the scale pan, which immediately went down, making the king wonder how a little bird which had lain so lightly on his lap could weigh down the balance in this manner.

He wasted no further time in speculation. He sat on the ground, stretched out his leg, and after a brief prayer, incised his thigh with a sharp knife. The courtiers and guests assembled groaned at the sight of the blood. The king gritted his teeth and tore out a handful of flesh and dropped it on the scale.

The pan became bloodstained but the pointer did not move. Someone cursed the dove, "It has the weight of an abandoned corpse. It looks dead, see if it is dead."

Another added, "Just pick it up and fling it to that hawk and be done with it, the miserable creature."

The king was too faint to talk; he gestured to them to stop commenting. He had now only the skin on his right thigh. Still the scales were unbalanced. The king went on to scoop the flesh from his other leg; the pointer was still down.

People averted their eyes from the gory spectacle. The hawk watched him critically.

"O hawk, take all that meat and begone!" they said.

"I have been promised the exact equal weight of the dove," insisted the hawk, at which all those assembled cursed the hawk and drew their swords. The king was faint with pain now, but mustered the last ounce of his strength to command his followers to keep away.

He beckoned to his chief minister to come nearer. "One has no right to end one's life, but this is unforeseen. Even if this means hell to me, I have to face it," he said. Everyone looked at the dove with distaste. "My brother shall be the regent[6] till the prince comes of age."

With this he struggled onto his feet and stepped on the flesh-filled pan. At once the other pan went up and equalized.

The hawk now flitted nearer and said, "This is more than a mouthful for me and my family. How am I to carry you to the mountain?"

The king mumbled feebly, "I did not think of that problem," and added, "You wouldn't have been able to lift the dove either! So bring your family here."

The hawk flapped its wings and rose in the air and swooped down as if to peck at the king's flesh. People shut their eyes, unable to bear the spectacle. But presently they heard divine instruments filling the skies with music. The hawk was gone, but in its place they found Indra,[7] the god with the dazzling crown, armed with the diamond spear, seizing Sibi's hand and helping him down off the weighing scales. A flame rose where the dove had lain, and from the heart of it emerged the God of Fire.

They said, "O king, we put you to a severe test. We challenged your integrity; and we happily accept defeat. You are indeed blessed, and as long as human beings recollect your tale, they will partake of the spiritual merit that you have yourself acquired"—and vanished. The king recovered his energy in a moment, while the pieces of flesh in the scale pan turned to fragrant flowers.

---

6. **regent** (rē′ jənt) *n*.: A person appointed to rule when the king is too young to rule himself.
7. **Indra** (in′ drə): The chief god of the early Hindu religion, often depicted wielding a thunderbolt.

Reader's Response *Was Sibi foolish to keep his promise to the dove regardless of the consequences? Why or why not?*

Commentary

The Story of Yudhishthira "Sibi" parallels another story from the Mahabharata about a king named Yudhishthira. After reaching the end of his life on earth, Yudhishthira reaches the gates of heaven and is greeted by the great god Indra. Yudhishthira requests that his loyal dog be allowed to accompany him through the gates. Indra responds, "In paradise there is no place for men with dogs," and demands that Yudhishthira renounce the dog. Yet Yudhishthira refuses to do so, declaring that he would rather sacrifice his own pleasure than renounce the dog. As it turns out, however, the dog is not an ordinary dog, but rather is the God Dharma himself. In the end Dharma reveals himself to Yudhishthira and leads him into paradise. Like Sibi, Yudhishthira has been put to a test and he has passed.

Interpreting

1. In this story it is clear that Sibi is the hero. Is there a villain? Explain.
2. Each of the two main characters in the story has a duty. How do these duties conflict?
3. (a) What is the first strategy that Sibi adopts to resolve the situation? (b) What does this strategy reveal about Sibi's attitude toward the painful sacrifice he later undertakes?
4. What does the final paragraph suggest about the purpose of this story?

Applying

5. (a) What are the attitudes of our society toward keeping one's word? (b) Compare and contrast these with Indian attitudes.
6. The British writer Christopher Marlowe wrote, "Honor is purchased by the deeds we do." Explain how this statement relates to Sibi.

ANALYZING LITERATURE

Understanding the Hindu Concept of Dharma

Dharma is a Sanskrit term referring to the duties and obligations unique to each person. In the traditional Indian setting, the king was the ultimate protector. Since the king swore to defend all his subjects, an injury to any one of them was a challenge to his integrity. Sibi must therefore fulfill his duty as a king by protecting the dove.

1. Suppose Sibi argued that he could best fulfill his obligations as an Indian king by thinking of the interests of his other subjects and refusing to sacrifice himself for the dove. In your opinion would he be justified? Explain.
2. (a) Describe a recent situation in which a local or national leader has, like Sibi, faced conflicting demands. (b) How did the official resolve the dilemma? (c) Do you agree with his or her solution? Why or why not?
3. In the United States, we do not have kings. How does the United States as an entity take on the role of protecting its citizens?

UNDERSTANDING LANGUAGE

Exploring the Connotations of Synonyms

The **connotations** of a word are the feelings and associations it suggests in addition to its primary meaning. *Chicanery* and *deception* are synonyms, for example, but chicanery connotes some sort of skillful deceit or trick while deception is a more general term for dishonesty.

Duty is a word that explains a great deal in "Sibi." *Integrity, honesty,* and *faithfulness* are all synonyms relating to the proper performance of one's duty. Explore the different connotations of these three synonyms —look them up in a dictionary but use your own words to express the different feelings and associations they evoke. You can also conduct your own experiments in language to distinguish these synonyms from one another. Using each word, try writing three sentences that clearly show the differences in these words.

THINKING AND WRITING

Writing About Sacrifice

Sacrifice involves giving up something important for a goal that is even more important. In this story Sibi is willing to sacrifice his well-being and even his life for his integrity. Describe a sacrifice that someone you have read about, someone you know, or you yourself have undertaken. This sacrifice does not have to involve a life-threatening situation. Remember that physical and mental work can also be forms of sacrifice—in both cases the person is giving up time and energy in order to reach a goal. Begin by recalling the objective for which the person was willing to sacrifice. Freewrite about some of the hardships and difficulties the person encountered. Draw on these notes when you write your description. Imagine that your audience is a group of adults whom you respect. In revising your work, make sure your readers will understand what the person gave up, whether the person reached the goal, and whether the person still believes the sacrifice was justified. Proofread your work and prepare a final draft to share with your classmates.

(continued from bottom of page)

people place more emphasis on keeping one's word than do most of the people in our society.
6. Suggested response: King Sibi "purchases" the honor of the gods through his deeds.

ANSWERS TO ANALYZING LITERATURE

1. Answers will differ. Students may respond that he would be justified in doing so because he must preserve himself to rule his other subjects.
2. (a) Answers will differ. Students should offer an explanation of how the situation they describe is similar to the conflict that Sibi faces. (b) Answers will differ according to the situation that students describe. (c) Answers will differ. Make sure students offer a clear explanation of their opinion.
3. Answers will differ. Students may respond that American citizens are protected by the armed forces.

Challenge Ask students if they think that most political leaders are willing to sacrifice their own well-being to protect their people. Why or why not?

ANSWERS TO UNDERSTANDING LANGUAGE

Answers will differ. Students may respond that the word *integrity* calls to mind the image of a trustworthy politician. The word *honesty* may call to mind situations from their own lives in which they have been tested. The word *faithfulness* may evoke feelings related to a romantic relationship.

The following are examples of the types of sentences that students might come up with:

Having never misled his constituents, the politician was known as a person of *integrity.*

Because Frank's mother had always stressed the importance of *honesty*, he could not lie to her about breaking the vase.

THINKING AND WRITING

Publishing Student Writing You might want to make photocopies of your students' papers and arrange them into a class anthology entitled *Making Sacrifices.*

Closure and Extension

ANSWERS TO THINKING ABOUT THE SELECTION

1. Suggested response: There is no villain in the story. The hawk at first appears to be a villain, but he is actually the god Indra, who is putting Sibi to a test.
2. Suggested response: The hawk has

a duty to feed its family, and Sibi has a duty to protect the dove, who is one of his subjects. By protecting the dove, however, Sibi prevents the hawk from feeding its family.
3. (a) Suggested response: He tries to divert the hawk's attention from the dove. (b) Suggested response: It reveals that he is not eager to make the painful sacrifice that he later undertakes.

4. Suggested response: The last paragraph suggests that there is a lesson to be learned; people should follow the king's example.
5. (a) Answers will differ. Students may respond that our society is fairly lenient toward those who do not keep their word. (b) Answers will differ. Students may respond that the Indian people place more emphasis on keeping one's word than do most of

BHAGAVAD-GITA

EPISODE FROM THE GITA
Prince of Wales Museum, Bombay

For centuries, the *Bhagavad-Gita* (bug´ ə vəd gē´ tä), which means "Song of the Lord," has been one of the most important texts in the Hindu tradition. It has been translated more often and into more languages than any other Sanskrit text, and many Hindu religious teachers have written commentaries on it. This ancient Sanskrit book has also played a role in modern politics. During the struggle for his country's independence, the Indian leader Mahatma Gandhi turned to the *Gita* for inspiration almost daily.

Part of the *Mahabharata*

Although it can be read as a self-contained book, the *Bhagavad-Gita* is actually a small part of India's greatest epic, the *Mahabharata*. This epic is monumentally long, approximately four times the combined length of the *Iliad* and the *Odyssey*! It is a collection of tales that were passed on for many generations by village storytellers. Sometime between 200 B.C. and A.D. 200 —scholars cannot provide a more precise date— these tales were woven together into India's most important epic.

The main story of the *Mahabharata* concerns the conflict between two branches of a family, the Pandavas and the Kauravas, over the rights to a kingdom in northern India. After many episodes, these two groups prepare to fight a battle just north of modern-day New Delhi. The entire *Bhagavad-Gita*, which falls in the middle of the epic, takes place on the battlefield prior to the fighting. The story of the battle, like all the eighteen chapters of the *Gita*, is narrated by a character named Sanjay.

Krishna and Arjuna

Arjuna (är´ jo͞on ə), a Pandava, has chosen his brother-in-law Krishna (krish´ nə) as his charioteer for the battle. (The role of the charioteer in ancient India was more than that of a driver. He was a trusted adviser to the warrior who owned the chariot.) At this early point in the story, Arjuna knows only that Krishna is a special person. He does not yet realize that Krishna is god. That will be dramatically revealed to him in a later chapter of the *Bhagavad-Gita*.

As the poem begins, Arjuna faces a dilemma: He knows it is wrong to kill his cousins and uncles who are on the opposing side, but he also knows that it is his duty to fight. In the first chapter of the *Gita*, he refuses to take part in the battle; dropping his bow, he asks Krishna for advice. We meet this great warrior here in Chapter 2 weeping with frustration and confusion. Krishna, however, bluntly tells him that he must fight.

GUIDE FOR INTERPRETING

Bhagavad-Gita

Commentary

Nonattached Work. Krishna advises Arjuna to fight, but to fight without concern for the results of his actions. This kind of unworried participation, which Krishna calls **nonattached work,** is one of the main themes of the *Bhagavad-Gita*. In order to appreciate this idea, however, it is necessary to understand the caste system that regulated Indian society and the Indian conception of the Atman, or soul.

Indian society was divided into four main castes. The Brahmans, or priests, were the caste with the greatest prestige. Next, in descending order, came the rulers and warriors, the merchants and farmers, and the peasants and laborers. Lowest of all were the untouchables, who performed the most menial and degrading tasks. (Not only were the untouchables considered the lowest of the low, but they weren't even considered a caste.) Caste identity was determined by birth, but Hindus were expected to marry within their caste. They were also required to perform the duties prescribed by their social position: Brahmans presided over sacrifices, warriors fought, merchants traded, and farmers farmed. In advising Arjuna, Krishna reminds him that he is a member of the warrior caste and therefore obligated to fight.

Krishna also knows that Arjuna is worried about hurting his relatives. He tries to allay this fear by pointing out to Arjuna the difference between the body and the Atman. The body may perish in battle, but the Atman is an eternal and unchangeable soul (the same term is also used to describe the source of all souls). When an individual dies, his or her Atman is reborn into another body. Knowing this to be true, Arjuna should not be concerned about the killing that occurs in battle.

As this account of the caste system and the concept of Atman suggests, Krishna is not asking Arjuna to act carelessly or cruelly. He is not urging him to do what he pleases. On the contrary, he wants him to fulfill his social obligations, but to do so with a knowledge of the Atman and without anxiety about the results of his action. Krishna and the *Gita* teach that every action will ultimately be rewarded or punished. It is impossible, however, for anyone to understand this system of rewards and punishments. Arjuna should therefore do the right thing, set his mind at rest, and not expect an immediate reward.

Writing

Is it possible to act out your role in society without concern for the results of your action? Think about the implications of such an attitude. Then list some of the benefits and disadvantages for society if everyone were to act in this manner.

Analyzing Literature Worksheet, *Understanding Nonattached Work,* p. 239

Critical Thinking and Reading Worksheet, *Appreciating an Idea's Influence,* p. 240

Selection Test, pp. 241–242

Literary Focus Have students discuss books or movies that deal with difficult choices, especially those concerning life-and-death situations in wartime. Some students may be able to compare and contrast an older relative's experience during the Vietnam War with the movies that have recently explored the Vietnam experience.

Writing/Prior Knowledge Based on the class discussion of the subjects in the Literary Focus, have students freewrite about what they would do in one or more of the situations discussed.

ESL Teaching Strategy It might be profitable to review capitalization with ESL students. Then discuss the use of capitalization in this selection—It, That, Reality, Changeless, and so forth. Remind them that the authors of this *Gita* used capitalization freely, unlike the way capitalization is used in English and other languages.

Teaching Tenth-Grade Students Ask tenth-grade students to offer their own definitions of the word *soul.* Work at the chalkboard, on the overhead, or at a large-screen computer monitor to develop a class definition. Then help students understand the abstraction of Atman by means of the poem on page 177 of this selection.

Vocabulary

Preteach the following vocabulary words:

scruples (skrōō′ pəlz) *n.*: Feelings of doubt over what is ethical

pervades (pər vādz′) *v.*: Spreads throughout

manifested (man′ ə fest′ id) *v.*: Proved or revealed

discrimination (di skrim′ i nā′ shən) *n.*: Ability to distinguish differences

contemplation (kän′ təm plā′ shən) *n.*: Deep, thoughtful inspection, or mystical meditation

from the Bhagavad-Gita

The Yoga of Knowledge

translated by Swami Prabhavananda and Christopher Isherwood

SANJAYA: Then his eyes filled with tears, and his heart grieved and was bewildered with pity. And Sri Krishna spoke to him, saying:

SRI KRISHNA: Arjuna, is this hour of battle the time for scruples and fancies? Are they worthy of you, who seek enlightenment? Any brave man who merely hopes for fame or heaven would despise them.

What is this weakness? It is beneath you. Is it for nothing men call you the foe-consumer? Shake off this cowardice, Arjuna. Stand up.

ARJUNA: Bhisma and Drona are noble and ancient, worthy of the deepest reverence. How can I greet them with arrows, in battle? If I kill them, how can I ever enjoy my wealth, or any other pleasure? It will be cursed with blood-guilt. I would much rather spare them, and eat the bread of a beggar.

Which will be worse, to win this war, or to lose it? I scarcely know. Even the sons of Dhritarashtra stand in the enemy ranks. If we kill them, none of us will wish to live.

Is this real compassion that I feel, or only a delusion? My mind gropes about in darkness. I cannot see where my duty lies. Krishna, I beg you, tell me frankly and clearly what I ought to do. I am your disciple. I put myself into your hands. Show me the way.

Not this world's kingdom,
Supreme, unchallenged,
No, nor the throne

Of the gods in heaven,
Could ease this sorrow
That numbs my senses!

SANJAYA: When Arjuna, the foe-consuming, the never-slothful, had spoken thus to Govinda, ruler of the senses, he added: "I will not fight," and was silent.

Then to him who thus sorrowed between the two armies, the ruler of the senses spoke, smiling:

SRI KRISHNA: Your words are wise, Arjuna, but your sorrow is for nothing. The truly wise mourn neither for the living nor for the dead.

There was never a time when I did not exist, nor you, nor any of these kings. Nor is there any future in which we shall cease to be.

Just as the dweller in this body passes through childhood, youth and old age, so at death he merely passes into another kind of body. The wise are not deceived by that.

Feelings of heat and cold, pleasure and pain, are caused by the contact of the senses with their objects. They come and they go, never lasting long. You must accept them.

A serene spirit accepts pleasure and pain with an even mind, and is unmoved by either. He alone is worthy of immortality.

That which is non-existent can never come into being, and that which is can never cease to be. Those who have known the inmost Reality know also the nature of *is* and *is not*.

Commentary

Indian Thought and the *Bhagavad-Gita* "The Yoga of Knowledge" propounds the basic philosophy of reincarnation that pervades nearly all Indian thought. Krishna presents the standard definitions of the soul and its relationship to the body as accepted by Hindu belief. He proceeds to reveal himself as the ultimate source of everything and as the object of personal faith and devotion who awards ultimate liberation from the cycle of birth and death described here. As God is detached from the universe, yet involved in its creation, maintenance, and destruction, similarly, human beings must also be detached from their own work. Thus the essence of Krishna's teaching here is, "Believe me and imitate me."

Indian thought has had a profound influence on American writers, specifically Emerson and Thoreau, who, in turn, exerted their influence on Walt Whitman (see A. L. Basham's quote from

That Reality which pervades the universe is indestructible. No one has power to change the Changeless.

Bodies are said to die, but That which possesses the body is eternal. It cannot be limited, or destroyed. Therefore you must fight.

Some say this Atman¹
Is slain, and others
Call It the slayer:
They know nothing.
How can It slay
Or who shall slay It?

Know this Atman
Unborn, undying,
Never ceasing,
Never beginning,
Deathless, birthless,
Unchanging forever.
How can It die
The death of the body?

Knowing It birthless,
Knowing It deathless,
Knowing It endless,

Forever unchanging,
Dream not you do
The deed of the killer,
Dream not the power
Is yours to command it.

Worn-out garments
Are shed by the body:
Worn-out bodies
Are shed by the dweller
Within the body.
New bodies are donned
By the dweller, like garments.

Not wounded by weapons,
Not burned by fire,
Not dried by the wind,
Not wetted by water:
Such is the Atman,
Not dried, not wetted,
Not burned, not wounded,
Innermost element,
Everywhere, always,
Being of beings,
Changeless, eternal,
Forever and ever.

This Atman cannot be manifested to the senses, or thought about by the mind. It is not subject to modification. Since you know this, you should not grieve.

---

1. **Atman** (ät´ mɔn): This term, whose literal meaning is "Self," refers to the eternal, unchanging soul in every conscious being.

ARJUNA AND KRISHNA IN THE CHARIOT, BETWEEN THE TWO ARMIES
Illustration from the Bhagavad-Gita

The Wonder That Was India, page 143). Whitman's "Song of Myself" especially reflects the Indian reincarnation philosophy:

What do you think has become of the young and old men? / And what do you think has become of the women and children? / They are alive and well somewhere, / The smallest sprout shows there is really no death, / And if ever there was it led forward life, and does not wait at the end to arrest it. / And ceas'd the moment life appear'd. / All goes onward and outward, nothing collapses, / And to die is different from what anyone supposed, and luckier.

Ask students to discuss how this passage from "Song of Myself," like the Bhagavad-Gita, suggests that the human soul is involved in a cycle of birth and death.

4 Clarification This passage is somewhat similar to the biblical "ashes to ashes, dust to dust," but it also develops the idea of reincarnation. While the body may change, the essence of the soul does not. How does the idea of reincarnation support the belief in following one's dharma (duty)?

Master Teacher Note The authors of the *Bhagavad-Gita* recognized that paying attention to form does not guarantee substance—an idea of universal appeal. Start a class discussion about why actions are not always indicative of the true nature of a person. Students should be able to recall public figures whose actions exemplify the discrepancy between appearance and reality.

However, the twentieth-century American writer Kurt Vonnegut wrote, "You are what you appear to be." Have students discuss the truth of this statement. Point out that Vonnegut's notion conflicts with the idea of the discrepancy between appearance and reality. Can both ideas be true? Discuss.

Humanities Note
Fine art, *Arjuna and Krishna in the Chariot, Between the Two Armies.* An artist who wanted to continue the Indian tradition of picturing well-known Hindu legends painted this modern version of a scene from the *Bhagavad-Gita*. Like many historic and contemporaneous works, this modern picture's theme is warfare. But Indian art did not typically reflect the violence and war common in India. On the contrary, most Indian miniatures depict pleasurable events and fanciful scenes—art was not meant to imitate reality.

You might want to use the following questions to discuss the art:
1. Do you think it is possible to fully capture or re-create a theme or an event from an earlier period using a modern artistic style?
2. Is the painting on this page successful in capturing the legend about which you're reading?

But if you should suppose this Atman to be subject to constant birth and death, even then you ought not to be sorry.

Death is certain for the born. Rebirth is certain for the dead. You should not grieve for what is unavoidable.

Before birth, beings are not manifest to our human senses. In the interim between birth and death, they are manifest. At death they return to the unmanifest again. What is there in all this to grieve over?

There are some who have actually looked upon the Atman, and understood It, in all Its wonder. Others can only speak of It as wonderful beyond their understanding. Others know of Its wonder by hearsay. And there are others who are told about It and do not understand a word.

He Who dwells within all living bodies remains forever indestructible. Therefore, you should never mourn for anyone.

Even if you consider this from the standpoint of your own caste-duty, you ought not to hesitate; for, to a warrior, there is nothing nobler than a righteous war. Happy are the warriors to whom a battle such as this comes: it opens a door to heaven.

But if you refuse to fight this righteous war, you will be turning aside from your duty. You will be a sinner, and disgraced. People will speak ill of you throughout the ages. To a man who values his honor, that is surely worse than death. The warrior-chiefs will believe it was fear that drove you from the battle; you will be despised by those who have admired you so long. Your enemies, also, will slander your courage. They will use the words which should never be spoken. What could be harder to bear than that?

Die, and you win heaven. Conquer, and you enjoy the earth. Stand up now, son of Kunti, and resolve to fight. Realize that pleasure and pain, gain and loss, victory and defeat, are all one and the same: then go into battle. Do this and you cannot commit any sin.

I have explained to you the true nature of the Atman. Now listen to the method of Karma Yoga.[2] If you can understand and follow it, you will be able to break the chains of desire which bind you to your actions.

In this yoga, even the abortive attempt is not wasted. Nor can it produce a contrary result. Even a little practice of this yoga will save you from the terrible wheel of rebirth and death.

In this yoga, the will is directed singly toward one ideal. When a man lacks this discrimination, his will wanders in all directions, after innumerable aims. Those who lack discrimination may quote the letter of the scripture, but they are really denying its inner truth. They are full of worldly desires, and hungry for the rewards of heaven. They use beautiful figures of speech. They teach elaborate rituals which are supposed to obtain pleasure and power for those who perform them. But, actually, they understand nothing except the law of Karma,[3] that chains men to rebirth.

Those whose discrimination is stolen away by such talk grow deeply attached to pleasure and power. And so they are unable to develop that concentration of the will which leads a man to absorption in God.

The Vedas[4] teach us about the three gunas[5] and their functions. You, Arjuna, must overcome the three gunas. You must be free from the pairs of opposites.[6] Poise your mind in tranquillity. Take care neither to acquire nor to hoard. Be established in the consciousness of the Atman, always.

When the whole country is flooded, the reservoir becomes superfluous. So, to the illumined seer, the Vedas are all superfluous.

You have the right to work, but for the work's sake only. You have no right to the fruits of work. Desire for the fruits of work must never be your motive in working. Never give way to laziness, either.

---

2. **Karma Yoga:** The path of selfless, God-dedicated action.
3. **the law of Karma:** Hindus believe that everyone is reborn many times and that one's actions in each life determine one's fate in future lives.
4. **Vedas:** Sacred books of the Hindus.
5. **gunas:** Three substances that make up the material universe.
6. **opposites:** The world that seems real is composed of illusory opposites like heat and cold.

Grammar in Action

Unity and Coherence To communicate effectively, all parts of a written work must be clearly related. **Unity** occurs when the topic is evident and adequately supported. **Coherence** shows the relationship between the topic and the supporting details as well as between the supporting details themselves.

Bad writers will get carried away with an idea that is only vaguely related to the topic. Failure to show the connection interferes with coherence and unity. In some cases ideas or points that are only vaguely relevant to the topic should be developed somewhere else or omitted altogether.

Coherence involves a relationship of grammatical structure and word choice as well as content. Notice the parallel structure in the paragraph beginning "Die, and you win heaven" on page 178. Each sentence after that also begins with a verb. This paragraph is also structured in pairs of opposites. The transitional word "now" maintains the active sense of the paragraph and, with the word "then" in the next sentence, indicates when the action should be performed. The pronoun "this" shows how the actions will be the cause of avoiding sin. Without all these linking techniques, the reader would have to guess how one idea was intended to follow another.

Perform every action with your heart fixed on the Supreme Lord. Renounce attachment to the fruits. Be even-tempered in success and failure; for it is this evenness of temper which is meant by yoga.

Work done with anxiety about results is far inferior to work done without such anxiety, in the calm of self-surrender. Seek refuge in the knowledge of Brahman.[7] They who work selfishly for results are miserable.

In the calm of self-surrender you can free yourself from the bondage of virtue and vice during this very life. Devote yourself, therefore, to reaching union with Brahman. To unite the heart with Brahman and then to act: that is the secret of non-attached work. In the calm of self-surrender, the seers renounce the fruits of their actions, and so reach enlightenment. Then they are free from the bondage of rebirth, and pass to that state which is beyond all evil.

When your intellect has cleared itself of its delusions, you will become indifferent to the results of all action, present or future. At present, your intellect is bewildered by conflicting interpretations of the scriptures. When it can rest, steady and undistracted, in contemplation of the Atman, then you will reach union with the Atman.

ARJUNA: Krishna, how can one identify a man who is firmly established and absorbed in Brahman? In what manner does an illumined soul speak? How does he sit? How does he walk?

SRI KRISHNA:

> He knows bliss in the Atman
> And wants nothing else.
> Cravings torment the heart:
> He renounces cravings.
> I call him illumined.
> Not shaken by adversity,
> Not hankering after happiness:
> Free from fear, free from anger,

> Free from the things of desire.
> I call him a seer, and illumined.
> The bonds of his flesh are broken.
> He is lucky, and does not rejoice:
> He is unlucky, and does not weep.
> I call him illumined.

> The tortoise can draw in his legs:
> The seer can draw in his senses.
> I call him illumined.

> The abstinent[8] run away from what they
>   desire
> But carry their desires with them:
> When a man enters Reality,
> He leaves his desires behind him.

> Even a mind that knows the path
> Can be dragged from the path:
> The senses are so unruly.
> But he controls the senses
> And recollects the mind
> And fixes it on me.
> I call him illumined.

> Thinking about sense-objects
> Will attach you to sense-objects;
> Grow attached, and you become addicted;
> Thwart your addiction, it turns to anger;
> Be angry, and you confuse your mind;
> Confuse your mind, you forget the lesson of
>   experience;
> Forget experience, you lose discrimination;
> Lose discrimination, and you miss life's only
>   purpose.

> When he has no lust, no hatred,
> A man walks safely among the things of
>   lust and hatred.
> To obey the Atman
> Is his peaceful joy:
> Sorrow melts
> Into that clear peace:
> His quiet mind
> Is soon established in peace.

---

7. **Brahman:** The oversoul of which each individual's Atman is a part.

8. **The abstinent** (ab´ stə nənt): Those who voluntarily do without food, drink, or other pleasures.

---

8 Discussion Krishna claims that those who work only for results are miserable. Ask students to elaborate on his claim. Why might people who work only to meet a goal, only to achieve self-satisfaction, or to please others, be miserable? Suggest that perhaps such an approach to work precludes satisfaction in the work itself. Some students might identify with the idea that studying hard for the sake of earning good grades should not interfere with studying hard to learn, understand, and remember.

9 Enrichment The ways in which human beings can be slaves to vice are obvious, but how can people be slaves to virtue? Asking students to comment on the idea of "the bondage of virtue" might enrich their understanding of this paragraph and the "secret of nonattached work." Ask students to make a connection with the more familiar idea of "too much of a good thing."

10 Literary Focus Ask students to recall their knowledge of the Vedic writings, which suggested that the mind and the emotions were bound together. How does Krishna's philosophy here differ from that conveyed in earlier Vedic hymns?

11 Discussion Here Krishna rephrases one of his earlier teachings, found on page 178: "Those whose discrimination is stolen away by such talk grow deeply attached to pleasure and power. And so they are unable to develop that concentration of the will which leads a man to absorption in God." Ask students to define what Krishna calls "life's only purpose." Once they have offered their answers, ask them to reread page 178 and locate the paragraph that Krishna echoes here on page 179. Ask students: By "life's only purpose" (page 179) does Krishna mean "absorption in God" (page 178)?

Student Activity 1: Write a paragraph about a specific idea in the selection. Make the topic sentence clear and develop it coherently with at least three supporting sentences.

Student Activity 2: Think of three ideas that could be used to explain the idea of dharma (duty). Using transitional words and phrases, organize your ideas in a coherent, unified paragraph. Remember that transitions can be an economical way of contrasting, comparing, and showing results, time order, and location.

PRIMARY SOURCE

What is life like in India today? The contemporary writer Santha Rama Rau gives us a view of an Indian bazaar. "To me an Indian bazaar is a source of endless delight and excitement. It is usually a series of plain wooden stalls on which are piled, with unconscious artistry, brightly colored, fruits, vegetables, spices, gleaming silver jewelry, brilliant silks and cottons, or charming, grotesque painted wooden toys. The vendors who can't afford a stall sit on the sidewalk outside the market, their baskets stacked behind them, their wives in vivid cotton saris crouching in the shade, and in front of them are spread carpets of scarlet chilies drying in the sun, small hills of saffron, tumeric, coriander, ginger, cinnamon—all the magical names from the old days of the spice trade with the Indies. With a worn stone mortar and pestle the vendor or his wife will grind your spices for you, blending them according to your particular taste, and weigh them in tiny brass scales strung on twine and balanced delicately in one hand. In all transactions you receive a pleasantly individual attention—nothing standardized."

Commentary

In Indian philosophy and religion, the human soul is considered to be eternal and indestructible, quite unlike the Jewish or Christian notion of the soul's creation "out of nothing" leading to a final judgment. Though the universe is created and destroyed many times in Hinduism, the souls repeatedly enter different bodies, which experience birth, growth, decay, and death. One's very thoughts at the time of death determine the course of the next incarnation. Unless one is able to be uplifted through right action, karma, or devotion to a sovereign God (i.e., Krishna), he or she is perpetually bound to the cycle of birth and death. Therefore there is a note of urgency in the *Bhagavad-Gita* when Krishna admonishes Arjuna to renounce the fruit of his activities and "think of me."

THINKING ABOUT THE SELECTION

Interpreting

1. Yoga is a Hindu practice by which one seeks union with the universal soul, or Atman, through practices like deep concentration and controlled breathing. Why do you think this selection is entitled "The Yoga of Knowledge"?
2. Krishna says, "When a man enters Reality, / He leaves his desires behind him." Explain what he means by "Reality."
3. Krishna classifies virtue and vice together, although we usually think of them as opposites. Why does he consider them both forms of "bondage"?
4. Why is Krishna's comparison of the "illumined seer" to the tortoise especially apt?
5. A paradox is a statement that seems contradictory. What is paradoxical about Krishna's instilling in Arjuna the urge to "break the chains of desire"?

Applying

6. What would an "illumined seer" find most strange about contemporary American society?

ANALYZING LITERATURE

Understanding Nonattached Work

Nonattached work is the performance of one's caste-duty in a spirit of "calm" and "self-surrender." This calmness comes from the insight that the body and the world are unimportant but the Atman, or soul, is eternal. It is therefore unnecessary, and even harmful, to strive for worldly success and rewards.

Krishna teaches these ideas to Arjuna in two ways. Speaking directly, he provides a poetic and philosophical explanation of terms like the Atman: "Not dried by the wind, / Not wetted by water: / Such is the Atman." However, he also explains these ideas indirectly by telling Arjuna how the person who understands them will behave: "Free from fear, free from anger / Free from the things of desire."

1. Which of these two methods of teaching do you think is the more effective? Explain.
2. The title of this chapter is "The Yoga of Knowledge," yet Krishna's purpose is to motivate Arjuna to act. (a) What do Krishna's words suggest about the relationship between knowledge and action? (b) Is one more important than the other? Explain.

CRITICAL THINKING AND READING

Appreciating an Idea's Influence

Mahatma Gandhi led the Indian struggle to win independence from the British. Influenced by the teachings of the *Bhagavad-Gita*, Gandhi devised a technique which he called the "truth act"—in Sanskrit, the term is *satyagraha* (sut´ yə gru´ hə). He would perform such an act by publicly and dramatically pointing to some injustice and calling on the authorities to remedy it. By performing such acts, he and his followers risked beating and imprisonment. As Krishna recommends in the *Gita*, however, Gandhi continued to fulfill his duty and disregarded the dangers.

In the late 1950's, Martin Luther King adopted Gandhi's nonviolent method of protest and used the "truth act" in the struggle to win equality for African Americans.

1. Through the Civil Rights movement, an ancient Hindu text has profoundly influenced American society. What lessons does this fact suggest?
2. The *Bhagavad-Gita* teaches that the material world is transitory and unreal. (a) Would belief in the world's unreality make it easier to act without regard for the consequences? Explain. (b) Is this belief essential to the technique of *satyagraha*? Why or why not?

THINKING AND WRITING

Applying an Indian Concept

Krishna advises Arjuna to "Be even-tempered in success and failure." Consider this advice and then write a paper describing the ways in which American society either supports this attitude or conveys an opposite message. Begin by listing people in your own life who would welcome this view or would find it odd. What, for instance, would classmates, coaches, teachers, or parents think of Krishna's advice? As you write, support your generalizations with examples based on your experience. In revising your paper, make sure you have ended with a conclusion that summarizes your opinion.

(continued from bottom of page)

satisfaction as well as for monetary rewards.

ANSWERS TO ANALYZING LITERATURE

1. Answers will differ; however, students should explain their choice.
2. (a) Suggested response: His words suggest that knowledge of the Atman will enable a person to act correctly. (b) Answers will differ. Students may respond that both are equally important. Knowledge is crucial, but it also must lead to right action: Arjuna must fight.

ANSWERS TO CRITICAL THINKING AND READING

1. Suggested response: The *Bhagavad-Gita*'s profound influence on American society suggests the timelessness and universality of some of its teachings.
2. (a) Answers will differ. Suggested response: Yes; if the world is unreal then consequences of action are also unreal and unimportant. (b) Yes; the belief that the world is transitory and unreal would empower people to disregard the dangers of being beaten and imprisoned, risks they might not take if they thought the material world was real.

THINKING AND WRITING

Writing Across the Curriculum
You might interest students in doing further historical research on the *Bhagavad-Gita*'s influence on Gandhi or Martin Luther King. As a writing assignment, have students write a short paper on how the *Bhagavad-Gita* influenced Gandhi, King, or both.

Closure and Extension

ANSWERS TO THINKING ABOUT THE SELECTION

1. This selection is appropriately titled "The Yoga of Knowledge" because Krishna urges Arjuna to develop concentration of the will and to clear his intellect from sensory delusions that interfere with complete union and knowledge of Brahman.
2. Reality is the state of absorption in God, the knowledge of Brahman, where one has nothing further to desire.
3. Virtue and vice are both forms of bondage because they both involve attachment to action.
4. Answers will differ. Suggested response: The reference to a tortoise provides a concrete comparison—a vivid image of detaching yourself from the world and retreating from worldly concerns.
5. Breaking the chains of desire necessarily involves the desire to break those chains.
6. Answers will differ but should include examples of how contemporary Americans are generally success-oriented, attached to their work for personal and intellectual

KANGRA VALLEY PAINTING
New York Public Library

Our bookstores are filled with books that claim to teach us how to dress, how to amass a fortune, and how to fix the plumbing. Did ancient India have any "how-to" books? We don't have ancient Indian texts about plumbing, but we do know of a book that taught young princes how to govern a kingdom and conduct their lives. This book is called the *Panchatantra* (pun´ chə tun´ trə), which simply means "a treatise in five chapters."

The Education of Indian Royalty

The education of Indian royalty involved military training, instruction in art and literature, and guidance in the social graces: how to dress, how to behave with women, and how to spend one's leisure time. In addition, from a very early age, these heirs to kingdoms were tutored in the intrigues of politics. This political instruction came from sources ranging from sophisticated handbooks on royal administration to the fables of the *Panchatantra*.

The general world view expressed in these fables is that of an orthodox, righteous Brahman. For instance, the author advocates proper behavior and high moral standards. However, he does not want his readers to be ineffectual or weak. A bit of chicanery to outwit an untrustworthy or too powerful opponent is perfectly acceptable. Also, while the end does not justify the means, according to the *Panchatantra* rulers can take extraordinary measures if a foe threatens to destroy them or their family.

Animal Stories: A Long Tradition

The use of animal stories to teach moral lessons is most familiar to us from Aesop's fables. However, such instructive stories are also an old tradition in India: They are found in both the *Rig Veda* and the Upanishads. Buddhists, too, used these kinds of animal fables to depict previous lives of the Buddha and to teach the principles of compassion and mercy, which are so important to the Buddhist tradition.

An Ancient and Influential Book

The *Panchatantra* is ancient. Yet we cannot say for certain exactly when it was written—sometime between 200 B.C. and A.D. 500 is the best guess. We do know, however, that it has had a wide-ranging influence. In the sixth century A.D., for example, it was translated into Pahlavi, a language of ancient Iran, and there are old Syrian and Arabic versions of these fables as well.

An Unknown Author

We know little about the author of these instructive tales. The collection itself tells us that he was a man named Vishnusharman who was charged with the responsibility of instructing the sons of a king named Amarashakti. The author's name indicates that he was a Brahman and a devotee of the god Vishnu. However, no other details about him have come down to us.

From the fables themselves, we can infer that he was an artist of considerable accomplishments. The tales are woven together in an ingenious way. Also, their mixture of prose and poetry is pleasing and natural. The little verses included in the fables were designed to help students recall the key points—poetry is easier to remember than prose.

GUIDE FOR INTERPRETING

Panchatantra

Commentary

An Indian Animal Fable. A fable is a brief narrative usually containing animal characters with human attributes. Ending with a memorable moral, a fable provides a lesson in life. The purpose of the animal fables in the *Panchatantra* was to teach Indian princes how to govern a kingdom. These entertaining stories gave advice related to political matters and to interpersonal relationships in general.

From a fable called "The Jackal Who Killed No Elephants," for instance, princes learned the importance of knowing themselves and others. This fable tells about a baby jackal who is brought up in a family of lions. Everything goes well until one day the jackal's two lion-cub "brothers" want to attack an elephant. The jackal dissuades them. Later, in the lions' family circle, the lion cubs tease the jackal about his cowardice and he becomes furious. The mother lion calms him down, but when he insists on his courage, she gives him this humorous warning:

> Handsome you are, and valorous;
> You have a scholar's brain:
> But in your family, my boy,
> No elephants are slain.

Taking the hint in good grace, the jackal departs before his brothers grow up, realize he is not a lion, and turn on him.

The moral of the fable is that one must appreciate human limitations and capacities—in oneself and others. Just as jackals and lions have different strengths and weaknesses, so do human beings.

Typical of these fables is the verse that conveys the moral in a graceful, entertaining manner. Memorization is a technique of learning that generally has fallen out of fashion in the United States. In India, however, it was—and still is—an important part of the educational tradition. By memorizing the verse quoted above, a young prince would have ready access to this fable's important lesson.

As you will see in the following story, "Numskull and the Rabbit," the animal kingdom in these fables reflects the society that young princes will one day inhabit. Note, for instance, how the relationship between the lion and the other animals mirrors the interactions between a king and his subjects.

Writing

Does our society have ways of giving young people important advice in an entertaining manner? Do movies, television programs, or popular songs serve this purpose? Freewrite, expressing your views on this subject.

Literary Focus Have students discuss any type of instruction books they know. These can range from simple directions manuals to more complicated books. Use the chalkboard to list examples of this kind of writing. Then have students speculate on what all such titles need to contain in order to be of use.

Have students check the best-seller list. How many books on this list are self-help books—books that show you how to adapt your behavior in order to succeed? Why is this type of book so popular?

Writing/Prior Knowledge Ask students to try to remember the first story they heard that had a moral in it. Have them freewrite about how they felt about the story then and how they feel now about it.

ESL Teaching Strategy Note Explain the characteristics of a fable to ESL students. Ask them to share fables from their own cultures.

Master Teacher Note Use the overhead projector to show students Art Transparency 3, *Hanuman the King goes to Ceylon*. Point out the excitement that surrounds the journey and the turmoil created among the birds by what seems like an invasion. Ask for a response to the choice of colors.

Vocabulary

Preteach the following vocabulary words:

rank (raŋk) *adj*.: Rancid; smelly

sustenance (sus´ ti nəns) *n*.: Support; maintenance

elixir (i lik´ sər) *n*.: Panacea; magical substance

accrue (ə krōō´) *v*.: Come to as an advantage

weal (wēl) *n*.: Welfare

reprobate (rep´ rə bāt´) *n*.: Scoundrel

skulks (skulks) *v*. : Lurks, in a cowardly way

Critical Thinking and Reading Worksheet, *Analyzing the Role of the Trickster,* p. 250
Selection Test, pp. 251–252
Unit Test: Short Answer Questions, pp. 253–255
Essay Questions and Evaluation Guidelines, pp.256–257

Art Transparency 3
Hanuman the King goes to Ceylon,
Indian—Malwa

from the Panchatantra
Numskull and the Rabbit
translated by Arthur W. Ryder

In a part of a forest was a lion drunk with pride, and his name was Numskull. He slaughtered the animals without ceasing. If he saw an animal, he could not spare him.

So all the natives of the forest—deer, boars, buffaloes, wild oxen, rabbits, and others—came together, and with woe-begone countenances,[1] bowed heads, and knees clinging to the ground, they undertook to beseech obsequiously[2] the king of beasts: "Have done, O King, with this merciless, meaningless slaughter of all creatures. It is hostile to happiness in the other world. For the Scripture says:

> A thousand future lives
> > Will pass in wretchedness
> For sins a fool commits
> > His present life to bless.

Again:

> What wisdom in a deed
> > That brings dishonor fell,
> That causes loss of trust,
> > That paves the way to hell?

And yet again:

> The ungrateful body, frail
> > And rank with filth within,
> Is such that only fools
> > For its sake sink in sin.

"Consider these facts, and cease, we pray, to slaughter our generations. For if the master will re-main at home, we will of our own motion send him each day for his daily food one animal of the forest. In this way neither the royal sustenance nor our families will be cut short. In this way let the king's duty be performed. For the proverb says:

> The king who tastes his kingdom like
> > Elixir, bit by bit,
> Who does not overtax its life,
> > Will fully relish it.

> The king who madly butchers men,
> > Their lives as little reckoned
> As lives of goats, has one square meal,
> > But never has a second.

> A king desiring profit, guards
> > His world from evil chance;
> With gifts and honors waters it
> > As florists water plants.

> Guard subjects like a cow, nor ask
> > For milk each passing hour:
> A vine must first be sprinkled, then
> > It ripens fruit and flower.

> The monarch-lamp from subjects draws
> > Tax-oil to keep it bright:
> Has any ever noticed kings
> > That shone by inner light?

> A seedling is a tender thing,
> > And yet, if not neglected,
> It comes in time to bearing fruit:
> > So subjects well protected.

> Their subjects form the only source
> > From which accrue to kings

---

1. **countenances** (koun′ tə nəns əz) *n.*: Faces.
2. **obsequiously** (əb sē′ kwē əs lē) *adv.*: In a manner that shows too great a willingness to serve.

> *Their gold, grain, gems, and varied drinks,*
> *And many other things.*
>
> *The kings who serve the common weal,*
> *Luxuriantly sprout;*
> *The common loss is kingly loss,*
> *Without a shade of doubt."*

After listening to this address, Numskull said: "Well, gentlemen, you are quite convincing. But if an animal does not come to me every day as I sit here, I promise you I will eat you all." To this they assented with much relief, and fearlessly roamed the wood. Each day at noon one of them appeared as his dinner, each species taking its turn and providing an individual grown old, or religious, or grief-smitten, or fearful of the loss of son or wife.

One day a rabbit's turn came, it being rabbit-day. And when all the thronging animals had given him directions, he reflected: "How is it possible to kill this lion—curse him! Yet after all,

> *In what can wisdom not prevail?*
> *In what can resolution fail?*
> *What cannot flattery subdue?*
> *What cannot enterprise put through?*

I can kill even a lion."

So he went very slowly, planning to arrive tardily, and meditating with troubled spirit on a means of killing him. Late in the day he came into the presence of the lion, whose throat was pinched by hunger in consequence of the delay, and who angrily thought as he licked his chops: "Aha! I must kill all the animals the first thing in the morning."

While he was thinking, the rabbit slowly drew near, bowed low, and stood before him. But when the lion saw that he was tardy and too small at that for a meal, his soul flamed with wrath, and he taunted the rabbit, saying: "You reprobate! First, you are too small for a meal. Second, you are tardy. Because of this wickedness I am going to kill you, and tomorrow morning I shall extirpate[3] every species of animal."

Then the rabbit bowed low and said with deference: "Master, the wickedness is not mine, nor the other animals'. Pray hear the cause of it." And the lion answered: "Well, tell it quick, before you are between my fangs."

---

3. extirpate (ek′ stər pāt′) *v.*: Root out, destroy.

FRAGMENT OF AN INDIAN ANIMAL CARPET
Late sixteenth century A.D.
The Textile Museum, Washington, D.C.

"Master," said the rabbit, "all the animals recognized today that the rabbits' turn had come, and because I was quite small, they dispatched me with five other rabbits. But in mid-journey there issued from a great hole in the ground a lion who said: 'Where are *you* bound? Pray to your favorite god.' Then I said: 'We are traveling as the dinner of lion Numskull, our master, according to agreement.' 'Is that so?' said he. 'This forest belongs to me. So all the animals, without exception, must deal with me—according to agreement. This Numskull is a sneak thief. Call him out and bring him here at once. Then whichever of us proves stronger, shall be king and shall eat all these animals.' At his command, master, I have come to you. This is the cause of my tardiness. For the rest, my master is the sole judge."

After listening to this, Numskull said: "Well, well, my good fellow, show me that sneak thief of a lion, and be quick about it. I cannot find peace of mind until I have vented on him my anger against the animals. He should have remembered the saying:

5 **Discussion** Discuss the criterion for the sacrifice. In what way can all these types be spared from society? What are their weaknesses? Why is "grown religious" on the list? Ask your students who would be "volunteered" for sacrifice if it were Americans who made this agreement.

6 **Enrichment** It may seem unusual that it is the tiny rabbit, rather than the bear or the oxen, who decides to challenge the lion. But this serves to emphasize the importance of cleverness over brute strength. The supposedly timid rabbit is often used in animal tales to play a surprising role. Even in American cartoons, Bugs Bunny has been outwitting Elmer Fudd for years.

7 **Discussion** Ask the students why the lion-king doesn't simply eat the rabbit after this tale. Why would the lion never dream that the rabbit might be trying to deceive him?

8 **Discussion** Have the students examine the ways in which the lion has ignored what he says was forgotten by the forest lion. Do the students believe he was ignoring his own advice? What does this say about the lion's state of enlightenment?

Humanities Note

Fine art, *Fragment of an Indian animal carpet*. This brilliant section of a Mughal carpet was made in the sixteenth century. Characteristic of the style are the patterned flora and fauna designs of the Muslim arts and Indian symbols and masklike faces. It shows a series of birds, serpents, rabbits, oxen, and other animals.

You might want to use the following questions to discuss the art:

1. What do these violent images suggest about life in India during the sixteenth century?

2. What different animals can you spot?

3. What details from the pattern seem to contribute most to its beauty?

9 **Reading Strategy** The idea of an enemy in a fortress should sound intimidating. The rabbit as a trickster is trying to flatter the lion in an attempt to fool him. Draw readers' attention to the image and ask students to discuss why that image is used to challenge the lion.

10 **Literary Focus** English-speaking persons have a similar saying that warns, "Look before you leap." In what ways is the Indian proverb more specific or descriptive of the consequences of carelessness?

11 **Discussion** The end of the story is simple, without a stated moral. If your students had to write a moral for the story, how would they phrase it?

12 **Reading Strategy** Of course there is a lesson here. But can it be put simply? Have the students think about the echo in the well and the lion's attacking his own image. Discuss the nature of the illusion and try to have students see the significance of the lion fighting what was *not* there.

Cultural Note The *Panchatantra* has been translated into many languages and distributed widely around the world. Though it is similar in nature to Aesop's *Fables*, scholars have not been able to demonstrate any direct connection between the two. Some experts, however, have argued convincingly that both Chaucer and Shakespeare were influenced to some extent by the *Panchatantra* in one of its many forms.

Collaborative Learning The fable has been used for centuries as a teaching device. Divide students into groups and assign each to find examples from a literary period or area.

Master Teacher Note Discuss and share examples of common adages, aphorisms, sayings, maxims, and proverbs. How are they used today? How does their use characterize the users? What does the reader understand about the lion and the rabbit based on the sayings each uses?

> *Land and friends and gold at most*
> *Have been won when battles cease;*
> *If but one of these should fail,*
> *Do not think of breaking peace.*
>
> *Where no great reward is won,*
> *Where defeat is nearly sure,*
> *Never stir a quarrel, but*
> *Find it wiser to endure."*

"Quite so, master," said the rabbit. "Warriors fight for their country when they are insulted. But this fellow skulks in a fortress. You know he came out of a fortress when he held us up. And an enemy in a fortress is hard to handle. As the saying goes:

> *A single royal fortress adds*
> *More military force*
> *Than do a thousand elephants,*
> *A hundred thousand horse.*
>
> *A single archer from a wall*
> *A hundred foes forfends;*
> *And so the military art*
> *A fortress recommends.*
>
> *God Indra used the wit and skill*
> *Of gods in days of old,*
> *When Devil Gold-mat plagued the world,*
> *To build a fortress-hold.*
>
> *And he decreed that any king*
> *Who built a fortress sound,*
> *Should conquer foemen. This is why*
> *Such fortresses abound."*

When he heard this, Numskull said: "My good fellow, show me that thief. Even if he is hiding in a fortress, I will kill him. For the proverb says:

> *The strongest man who fails to crush*
> *At birth, disease or foe,*
> *Will later be destroyed by that*
> *Which he permits to grow.*

And again:

> *The man who reckons well his power,*
> *Nor pride nor vigor lacks,*
> *May single-handed smite his foes*
> *Like Rama-with-the-ax."*[4]

"Very true," said the rabbit. "But after all it was a mighty lion that I saw. So the master should not set out without realizing the enemy's capacity. As the saying runs:

> *A warrior failing to compare*
> *Two hosts, in mad desire*
> *For battle, plunges like a moth*
> *Headforemost into fire.*

And again:

> *The weak who challenge mighty foes*
> *A battle to abide,*
> *Like elephants with broken tusks,*
> *Return with drooping pride."*

But Numskull said: "What business is it of yours? Show him to me, even in his fortress." "Very well," said the rabbit. "Follow me, master." And he led the way to a well, where he said to the lion: "Master, who can endure your majesty? The moment he saw you, that thief crawled clear into his hole. Come, I will show him to you." "Be quick about it, my good fellow," said Numskull.

So the rabbit showed him the well. And the lion, being a dreadful fool, saw his own reflection in the water, and gave voice to a great roar. Then from the well issued a roar twice as loud, because of the echo. This the lion heard, decided that his rival was very powerful, hurled himself down, and met his death. Thereupon the rabbit cheerfully carried the glad news to all the animals, received their compliments, and lived there contentedly in the forest.

---

4. Rama-with-the-ax: The sixth incarnation of Vishnu. He became angry with the warrior caste and killed them all with his ax. (Rama of the *Ramayana* was the seventh incarnation of Vishnu.)

Reader's Response *Do you know anyone like the lion in this fable? Like the rabbit? Explain.*

THINKING ABOUT THE SELECTION

Interpreting

1. The other animals give the lion both moral and political reasons for stopping his slaughter. (a) Explain two justifications, one moral and one political, that they give. (b) How does the lion's response reveal his character?
2. In what way does the rabbit show himself to be a master psychologist (a person who studies behavior) in his encounter with the lion?
3. How do the poems that the lion and rabbit quote for each other reveal their different natures?
4. What does the rabbit's trick suggest about the identity of the lion's greatest enemy?
5. When good is rewarded or evil punished in an especially fitting way, the result is often called "poetic justice." Why is the conclusion of this fable an example of "poetic justice"?

Applying

6. What moral or morals do you think this fable teaches?

ANALYZING LITERATURE

Understanding an Animal Fable

The *Panchatantra*'s animal fables were like a seminar in government and personal relations for young Indian princes. Although the tone of "Numskull and the Rabbit" is lighthearted, it contains lessons that could save a ruler's life. On one level the forest in this fable is a never-never land, but on another level it reflects a kingdom in which something is seriously wrong.

1. Explain how the initial situation in this fable represents a kingdom that is not working.
2. Imagine a young prince reading this tale. What lessons could he draw from it about the correct behavior of a king?
3. What does the fable suggest about the proper limitations on a king's power?
4. Do political cartoons and comic strips perform the same function in our society as the *Panchatantra* did in ancient India? Explain.

CRITICAL THINKING AND READING

Analyzing the Role of the Trickster

The rabbit in this fable is an example of a type of character well known in folklore, the **trickster.** Whether as a rabbit, spider, coyote, or crafty human, the lovable trickster uses mother wit to overcome the greater strength of others. In African folklore, for instance, the spider Anansi deceives larger animals like the leopard.

The rabbit in this fable expresses the credo of all tricksters—brains over brawn—in a small poem:

> In what can wisdom not prevail?
> In what can resolution fail?
> What cannot flattery subdue?
> What cannot enterprise put through?

His success highlights the weaknesses of the lion, who represents the king.

1. (a) What weaknesses does the lion display? (b) How does the rabbit exploit these weaknesses?
2. Would you say that the rabbit is a virtuous character? Explain.

THINKING AND WRITING

Writing an Animal Fable

Write an animal fable with a trickster character in it. First, choose a human weakness that you would like to satirize, for example, pride, greed, or vanity. Then select an appropriate animal to represent this weakness. Also, choose an animal to be the trickster—in addition to a rabbit, you might want to consider such animals as a fox, raccoon, or weasel. Finally, devise a simple plot in which the more powerful creature is outsmarted by the trickster. Imagine that you are writing this fable for your classmates *and* for younger friends. Include dialogue and details that will amuse both types of readers. Try weaving poetry into your narrative, as the author of the *Panchatantra* does; you can even give the poetry a modern twist by writing it in the form of rap lyrics. As you revise your fable, read it to several classmates and see whether they think it is funny. If possible, perform the same experiment with younger readers.

(continued from bottom of page)

4. Answers will differ. Comic strips are not used to instruct princes in modern America.

Conduct in Life

For Hindus, acting morally meant acting in accordance with dharma. This Sanskrit term refers both to one's own duty and the rules by which the universe is regulated.

While these cosmic rules could not be understood by mortals, one's own duty—dictated by caste and social role—was usually straightforward. It was necessary, however, to fulfill one's duty in a spirit of unworried detachment. Acting in such a way was an admission that mere humans could not comprehend the laws that governed the universe: The best one could do, without a knowledge of cosmic laws, was to fulfill one's obligations as calmly as possible.

In "Sibi," therefore, the king consents to sacrifice himself in order to fulfill his role as a protector of all who live in his realm.

> The king brooded over the words of the hawk for a moment. "Ask for anything, except this little bird on my lap. I won't give it up, whichever way you may argue."
> — from "Sibi"

Likewise, in the *Bhagavad-Gita*, Krishna advises Arjuna to fulfill his duty as a warrior, even though it means killing his relatives. To us these choices may seem unpalatable. For Hindus, however, they represented a praiseworthy respect for dharma.

> But if you refuse to fight this righteous war, you will be turning aside from your duty. You will be a sinner, and disgraced. People will speak ill of you throughout the ages. To a man who values his honor, that is surely worse than death. The warrior-chiefs will believe it was fear that drove you from the battle; you will be despised by those who have admired you so long.
> —Krishna to Arjuna, from the *Bhagavad-Gita*

In other eras and cultures, the problem of right conduct was defined in different terms. For the ancient Hebrews, it meant following the law that was revealed by God to the prophet Moses on Mount Sinai. For the heroes depicted by the Greek poet Homer, however, right conduct was defined by the virtue that is proper to warriors. The following selections illustrate a variety of approaches to the theme of correct behavior:

SUGGESTED READINGS

CROSS CURRENTS

The Beatles

Indian music, with its ancient traditions, influenced one of the newest forms of music in the West: rock-and-roll. This influence was especially apparent in the songs of The Beatles.

GEORGE HARRISON: EASTWARD-LOOKING WESTERNER

George Harrison, the lead guitarist and a vocalist with the group, met some Indian musicians in the winter of 1965 while making the Beatles' feature film *Help*. As a result of this encounter, he began to learn how to play the sitar (si tär´), a lutelike Indian instrument with a long neck, three to seven playing strings, and other strings that vibrate with them.

THE SITAR

Developed during the thirteenth century A.D., the sitar is traditionally used to play Indian compositions called ragas (rä´ gəz). These pieces are based on seventy-two different scales, and a sitar player must constantly adjust metal clasps, or frets, on the instrument's neck to allow for these scales. The resulting sound is somewhat harsh and tinny to a Westerner's ear.

INDIAN MUSIC AND BEATLES' SONGS

In the fall of 1965, George Harrison played the sitar for John Lennon's song "Norwegian Wood." He also used the sitar for "Love You To," a cut on the Beatles' album *Revolver* (1966). That album reflected a great deal of Indian influence. In fact the Beatles called it their "drone" album, referring to the continuous, fixed tone that characterizes some Indian music. To convey such a dronelike quality, the Beatles used only one or two chords for many of the songs.

While no album after *Revolver* was as influenced by Indian traditions, the song "Within You, Without You" from *Sergeant Pepper's Lonely Hearts Club Band* was written for Indian instruments. George, on the sitar, was accompanied by musicians playing the tabla (täb´ la´), two small drums, and the tamboura (täm boor´ ə), a lutelike instrument with a droning sound.

INDIAN PHILOSOPHY

In the mid to late 1960's, vibrations from Indian philosophy were as much in the air as those from Indian music. The Beatles, too, claimed to study Indian thought and were frequently photographed with a self-advertised guru named Maharishi Mahesh Yogi. This flirtation with Indian doctrines may be less important, however, than the influence of Indian music on some of the best rock-and-roll music of our time.

What influences can you find on rock-and-roll today?

Logical Argument

Writing a Logical Argument

Logic—The armory of reason, furnished with all offensive and defensive weapons.

—Thomas Fuller

Logical arguments are meant to persuade. Writing a good logical argument requires you to think like a lawyer in court. You must present a clear case in a reasonable tone; then you must supply evidence in the form of examples that prove your case is valid. If you fail to be reasonable or you fail to supply sufficient supporting evidence, you will not prove your case.

Writing an essay to prove a thesis statement is a step-by-step process. The essay should

- state its thesis clearly
- itemize supporting details
- present convincing arguments
- conclude with links between arguments and proof of the thesis

For example, in the *Bhagavad-Gita* excerpt, page 176, Arjuna does not want to kill people in battle and asks Krishna to guide him. To induce Arjuna to fight, Krishna offers him a logical argument. Krishna uses several approaches, or areas of evidence, to convince Arjuna (ending with "Do this and you cannot commit any sin," page 178).

Writing Assignment

Write an essay in which you write a logical argument to prepare a friend to do something of importance to you.

Prewrite

Choose a subject that interests you. It might be a popular cause—banning nuclear weapons, protecting the environment—or a very private concern—convincing a friend to lend you money to buy tickets to a game. Then take notes about your subject. Next review your notes to discover common threads. Write these ideas down. Then examine the ideas. Their common ground is what they can prove. What these ideas prove is your thesis statement. The process looks like this.

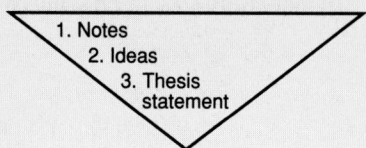

1. Notes
2. Ideas
3. Thesis statement

Write

When you have a clearly stated thesis, follow these steps to write a logical, supported essay.

1. Choose the strongest two or three ideas. The supporting ideas will give you more than enough evidence to prove your thesis.
2. Remember your audience—your friend. Use reasons that will convince him or her.
3. Write a paragraph that states your thesis and how you will prove it (the two or three supporting ideas stated briefly).
4. Go back to your notes and place each note under the idea it relates to. Using the noted page numbers, select the quotes you'll use and list them under the ideas they support. These quotations will give your paper authority.
5. Organize an outline from your supporting ideas and evidence. Look for logical transitions between the ideas to help you decide on a sequence. Here's a sample outline.

Thesis to Prove

- Supporting Idea One
  Example evidence
  Example with transition
- Supporting Idea Two
  Example evidence
  Example with transition
- Supporting Idea Three
  Example evidence
  Example with transition to conclusion

Using your outline as guide, write the body of your essay with one paragraph for each supporting idea. Make sure the topic sentence of each paragraph joins the supporting idea to your thesis. Most of the paragraph should consist of your evidence and statements about what it shows.

Conclude with a brief summation of the most compelling points or a provocative evaluation of your own. Try for a unique ending—perhaps a significant quotation or an intriguing question.

Collaborate

Ask a partner to read your rough draft and respond to it using this guide. Read the draft once quickly, and then follow the steps below.

Guide for Evaluating

(In the thesis paragraph)
- Underline the thesis statement. (If you can't find it, put –10 in the margin.)
- Write small numbers 1, 2, and possibly 3 before the words or phrases that introduce the main supporting ideas. (If you can't find them, write –10 in the margin.)
  (In each body paragraph)
- Put a wavy line under the paragraph's topic sentence if it corresponds to the 1, 2, or 3

you marked in the thesis paragraph. (If you can't find the topic sentence or the topic sentence does not correspond to the number, write –5 in the margin.)
- Read each body paragraph for specific supporting examples. (If there are none, write –10 in the margin. If the examples do not prove the topic sentence adequately, write –5. If the examples are excellent proof of the topic sentence, write +10 in the margin.)
- Look for effective transition words, phrases, or sentences at the end of each paragraph. (For each one you find, write +5 in the margin.)
  (In the concluding paragraph)
- If there is no conclusion, write –10.
- If the paragraph includes something "special" or stylistically effective, write +5 in the margin.

Revise

A minus score indicates work to do. A plus score indicates a solid paper, but it will still profit by fine-tuning the language.

As you revise, remember that a good logical proof uses a reasonable tone, but that does not rule out use of persuasive language. Look for the most compelling words with which to frame your points, but avoid emotionally loaded words.

Publish

Present your argument to your classmates. Let them judge whether they are convinced by your reasons. Would they do what you want them to do?

Evaluate

Put yourself in the place of the friend to whom you wrote the letter. Would you be convinced by your arguments? Has writing this paper altered your own views?

Humanities Note

Fine art, *Two Ladies in a Landscape*. This painting is one of eleven leaves of an album of pictures painted during the Ming dynasty (1368–1644). The Ming dynasty was an era of economic prosperity during which the Chinese people developed an increased interest in the arts. The arts flourished during this period, and Chinese artists produced some of the world's finest paintings, porcelains, and fabrics.

Although the Chinese populace demonstrated a willingness to accept new artistic forms, this willingness was not shared by the Ming court. Court artists found the emperor congenial neither to their ideas nor to their talents. As a result court artists often worked according to past artistic traditions, and little new or original art appeared during this time. The emphasis, therefore, turned to attaining a high level of skill in one's work. Typical of this conservative outlook is this album picture. Paintings such as this one often illustrated traditional Chinese morals and were highly valued for their elegance and beauty.

You might want to use the following questions to discuss the art:

1. How would you characterize the two women depicted in the painting?
2. What does this painting suggest about the relationship between humanity and nature?
3. What is the mood, or atmosphere, of the painting? Support your answer with details from the painting.
4. What emotions does this painting evoke in you? Why?

TWO LADIES IN A LANDSCAPE
Ming Dynasty
The Metropolitan Museum of Art, New York

Objectives

1 To understand the history of the Chinese Empire
2 To understand traditional Chinese government
3 To understand Chinese literature

CHINESE LITERATURE

1000 B.C.–A.D. 1890

Know contentment
And you will suffer no disgrace;
Know when to stop
And you will meet with no danger.
You can then endure.

—the *Tao Te Ching*

Motivation/Prior Knowledge Tell students that they are about to learn about a society with cultural and literary traditions unlike those of any Western nation. Also explain to them that they are going to discover new outlooks on life and views of the world quite unlike their own. What students learn in this introduction and in the literature that follows will help them to understand what it means to be Chinese and to appreciate the unique characteristics of the Chinese people.

Purpose-Setting Question What were the pivotal events in Chinese history? What are the dominant Chinese attitudes and beliefs? What is the role of literature in Chinese society? What are the distinctive qualities of Chinese literature?

1 **Enrichment** Tell students that the river valleys, such as the Yellow River basin, and the coastal plains of central and north-central China continue to support most of the Chinese population because of the good farmland in these regions.

2 **Enrichment** Tell students that the principal Shang god was named Shang Ti. The Shang people believed that Shang Ti and the other gods had the power to produce floods, droughts, and locust plagues.

3 **Enrichment** Explain to students that during the Chou dynasty a social system emerged that remained in place throughout the dynasties that followed. This system was headed by the government officials. Just below them were the landowners. The lower positions of the social hierarchy were occupied by peasants, artisans, merchants, and soldiers.

4 **Enrichment** Tell students that the first Chinese emperor was the Ch'in leader, who assumed the title Shih Huang Ti, meaning "First Emperor." Unfortunately Shih Huang was a ruthless leader who prevented the teaching of different points of view and ordered the burning of all books. Have students discuss

These lines are from the *Tao Te Ching*, one of the great works of Chinese philosophy. Despite what this work teaches, like most people the Chinese have not always known contentment and they have often met with danger. Yet they have endured for over 3,500 years, making China the world's oldest surviving civilization.

HISTORICAL BACKGROUND

Beginnings of Chinese Civilization

The birthplace of Chinese civilization lies in the Yellow River basin in northern China. Several thousand years ago, the people who lived there began establishing permanent farming villages, and by 1600 B.C. they had developed a complex social and economic system. At about this time, an elite group of kings established authority over northern China and founded the Shang dynasty, the first in a long chain of Chinese dynasties.

During the Shang dynasty, China was divided into many small regions, each of which was governed by a different king. Throughout these regions, the people practiced a religion based on the belief that nature was inhabited by many powerful gods and spirits. Hoping to bring themselves good fortune, the people made regular sacrifices to the various gods and to the spirits of their ancestors.

The people of the Shang dynasty made many significant advances. These included the development of new technologies in bronzeworking; the establishment of a decimal system and a twelve-month calendar; and the creation of fine pottery, silk textiles, and jade ornaments. Yet what may be the most important achievement of the Shang people was the development of a system of writing, consisting of over 3,000 characters.

The Chou Dynasty

Around the eleventh century B.C., the Shang dynasty was overthrown by a Central Asian people known as the Chou. The longest of all the Chinese dynasties, the Chou dynasty lasted until 256 B.C. Throughout most of this period, however, China

suffered from severe political disunity and upheaval. Divided into hundreds of small feudal states, each with its own ruler, China was plagued by almost constant warfare for several centuries.

Despite the ongoing bloodshed and political turmoil, the final centuries of the Chou dynasty saw major breakthroughs in Chinese philosophy. This era came to be known as the Hundred Schools period because of the many competing philosophers and teachers who emerged at the time. By far the most influential of these philosophers were Lao Tzu and Confucius, who established two schools of thought—Taoism and Confucianism—that have had an immeasurable impact on Chinese culture. Lao Tzu stressed freedom, simplicity, and the mystical contemplation of nature. Confucius, on the other hand, set forth a code of social conduct and stressed the importance of discipline, morality, and knowledge.

The Ch'in Dynasty

During the third century B.C., the feudal state of Ch'in began conquering the other states one after another. By 221 B.C. it had defeated all of the other states and had succeeded in unifying China. Because of its intolerance of opposing views and its extreme cruelty, the Ch'in dynasty was overthrown within fifteen years. Yet in this short period, the Ch'in rulers made a number of lasting contributions to Chinese civilization. In addition to strengthening the central government and dividing China into provinces, the Ch'in rulers built roads connecting all parts of their empire and patched together the existing walls on the northern borders to form the Great Wall of China. The Ch'in rulers also standardized the Chinese writing system.

The Han Dynasty

The next dynasty, the Han, which lasted for over four hundred years, was one of the most glorious eras of Chinese history. During this period China strengthened its central government, expanded its borders, improved its educational system, made important advances in the arts and sci-

other leaders who have tried to prevent the teaching of different points of view.

5 **Enrichment** Tell students that the most famous Han ruler was Wu Ti, or the "Warrior Emperor." After ascending to the throne in 140 B.C., he succeeded in driving back the Huns, who at the time were threatening China in the north and west.

The Unification of China

0 100 200 Miles
0 100 200 Kilometers

HSIUNGNU

to Chao 300

JUNG

Yellow R.

213

conquered 330

CHAO
conquered
228

YEN
conquered
222

WEI

WEI HAN
conquered 225
CHOU
HAN conquered 230
WEI
occupied 312

CH'IN

CH'I
conquered 221

LU
TENG
SUNG

CH'U
conquered 223

YUEH
(to Ch'u 333)
conquered 223

YELLOW
SEA

SHU
incorporated 316

PA

Yangtze R.

EAST
CHINA
SEA

TIEN

213-11

MINYUEH

211-09

SOUTH
CHINA
SEA

Original Ch'in territory

Ch'in expansion before 300 B.C.

Other major states with
dates of conquest by Ch'in

New areas conquered by Ch'in
after unification

Using the Map

Have students study the map. Then ask them the following questions:

1. Was the state of Ch'in located in the best possible position to control its empire? Why or why not?
2. What obstacles might have prevented the state of Ch'in from establishing an even larger empire?
3. How does the size of the Chinese Empire during the Ch'in dynasty compare with the current size of the United States?
4. How does the size of the Chinese Empire during the Ch'in dynasty compare with the size of China today?

6 **Enrichment** Tell students that in addition to inventing block printing, the Chinese developed movable type, pieces of metal containing Chinese characters that could be combined to form sentences. This development occurred in about 1050. Although Chinese printing techniques spread to Korea and Japan soon after their invention, they did not reach Western Europe for centuries.

ences, and established trade with Europe and western Asia. One of the most significant effects of these trade interactions was the introduction of the Buddhist religion from India. Buddhism, which advocates freedom from worldly desires, would take hold in China during the following centuries and become one of the dominant Chinese schools of thought.

The T'ang Dynasty

When the Han dynasty declined at the end of the second century A.D., China entered a long period of disunity. During this time, China not only suffered through violent internal struggles, but was also frequently attacked by outside invaders from the north and west. Despite these troubles, however, fine arts and literature flourished in China during this era.

The arts flourished even more, however, during the T'ang dynasty, which followed the period of disunity. Lasting for close to 300 years, the T'ang is viewed by many as the Golden Age of Chinese civilization. The T'ang rulers created a Chinese empire that extended from the Pacific Ocean to the borders of Persia and India, and they established the world's most effective system of government. The stability created by this government enabled the Chinese economy to expand dramatically. At the same time, the Chinese peo- 6

Chinese
(1000 B.C.–A.D. 1890)

The Forbidden City, Beijing

Marco Polo entering Beijing

Imaginary portrait of T'ao Ch'ien smelling flowers (detail)
Honolulu Academy of Arts

Emperors ruled China until 1912. The Chinese believed that the emperor was more than human; he was the mediator between heaven and earth. They called the emperor the "son of Heaven" who ruled the "central country." The emperor lived in the Forbidden City in Beijing with his family and servants. Because the emperor was more than human, almost every detail of his life emphasized his uniqueness and superiority over other humans. Yellow, for example, was the imperial color, and the emperor was the only one allowed to write in red. Each emperor also had an official seal that only he used, and the written character representing the emperor's name was banned from use except by the emperor himself.

Marco Polo (c. 1254–c. 1324) was an Italian trader and traveler. In 1271, when Polo was seventeen, he began his journey to China. Three years later he reached Kublai Khan's palace. The khan employed Polo on business in central and northern China and in southeast Asia, including India. In addition Polo served as a government official in the Chinese city of Yanghouz for three years. In 1292, Polo began his return to Italy, acting as escort for the wife of the khan of Persia. After his return in 1295, Polo joined the Venetian forces fighting Genoa and was soon taken prisoner. During his two-year captivity, Polo recorded his travels to China and other lands in *Descriptions of the World*. Scholars copied Polo's book, and it soon became the most widely read book in Europe. Historians believe Polo's recorded travels may have influenced many explorers, including Christopher Columbus.

T'ao Ch'ien (365–427), also known as T'ao Yuan-ming, was born into a family of government officials. He began a career in government service. At thirty-five, however, he resigned from his post and settled on a farm on the ouskirts of a village. There T'ao Ch'ien spent the

−1000	−500	0

HISTORY

- Feudal Age begins
- Feudal state under Chou dynasty begins to decline
- Han dynasty begins
- Feudal age ends
- Han dynasty ends; four centuries of division follow
- Ch'in dynasty begins
- Ch'in dynasty ends

HUMAN PROGRESS

- Brush and ink painting is developed in China
- Chinese book of mathematics
- Confucius is born
- Siddhartha, founder of Buddhism, is born
- First Chinese ships reach India
- Buddha leaves home to devote himself to philosophy and asceticism
- Buddhism is introduced by Emperor Ming-Ti
- Confucius' wander years begin
- Siddhartha dies
- Confucius dies
- Iron used as working metal
- Great Wall of China is built

LITERATURE

- First Chinese dictionary with 40,000 characters
- Chinese script is fully developed
- Oldest Chinese poems in *The Book of Songs*
- Beginning of second period of Chinese literature
- Beginning of third period of Chinese literature
- Beginning of fourth period of Chinese literature
- T'ao Ch'ien is born

rest of his life in semi-reclusiveness. During his later years, T'ao Ch'ien wrote poetry that expressed his philosophy of living tranquilly. His poetry also exhibits his fondness for a few of his favorite activities, including farming and playing the zither—a stringed instrument similar to a dulcimer.

Poet Li Po admiring a waterfall
Honolulu Academy of Arts

Cloisonne vase, Ming Dynasty
The British Museum

Portrait of Kublai Khan, ruler of China during 13th and 14th centuries

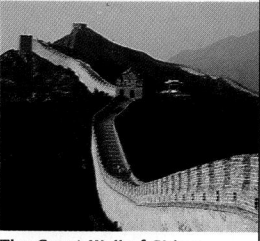

The Great Wall of China

500	1000	1500	1890

- Ch'i dynasty begins
- Ch'i dynasty ends; Wu-Ti becomes emperor
- Sui dynasty ends; T'ang dynasty rules
- China is united under T'ang dynasty
- Tibetan army invades China
- T'ang dynasty ends
- Sung dynasty begins
- Genghis Khan invades China
- Kublai Khan becomes governor
- Kublai Khan founds Yuan dynasty
- Marco Polo visits China
- Kublai Khan dies
- Ming dynasty is founded
- Manchus found Ch'ing dynasty
- Cholera breaks out
- All Chinese ports are open to foreign trade
- China invades Tibet
- First "Opium War" begins
- Second "Opium War" begins

- Great Age of Buddhist Sculpture begins
- Tea is brought to China from India
- Book printing in China begins
- Porcelain is produced
- *Ch'a Ching,* first Chinese tea handbook
- Paper money leads to inflation and state bankruptcy
- Chinese perfect invention of gunpowder
- Great Wall is restored
- China voyages in Indian Ocean begin
- Tea from China is shipped to Europe
- Chinese scientist and naturalist publishes book on new inventions

- T'ao Ch'ien dies
- Lyric poetry of T'ang dynasty promotes everyday Chinese language
- Wang Wei is born
- Li Po is born
- Chinese encyclopedia of 1000 volumes
- Tu-Fu is born
- Po Chü-i dies
- Period of Tchhouen-khi heroic Chinese drama begins
- Po Chü-i is born
- First Chinese plays with music are produced
- *Ching P'ing Mei,* first classic Chinese novel

Li Po (701–762) grew up in Szechwan province. At an early age, Li Po trained himself as a "knight-errant," or selfless avenger of injustices. At twenty-five, he left his home province and wandered widely, spreading his reputation as a poet. In 742, upon recommendation, Li Po was retained as a sort of court poet. Living wildly, he soon fell out of the court's favor and returned to his wanderings. Li Po's fondness for wine is legendary. According to tradition, after drinking heavily Li Po tried to embrace the reflection of the moon in the water and was drowned.

Cloisonné is an art form that was invented in the Middle East but perfected in China, Japan, and France. Cloisonné is enamel work in which the surface decoration is set in hollows formed by thin strips of wire that are welded to a metal plate. The Ming vase pictured here depicts a dragon. In many Eastern cultures, the dragon is a symbol of kingly power. It is a sacred ancestor that lives in the heavens and should be

(continued from bottom of page)
respected by mortals. Dragons are compassionate and generous creatures that can, with their wisdom, guide and protect humans.

Kublai Khan (1216–1294) was the grandson of Genghis Khan. The khan founded the Mongol dynasty that ruled China from 1279 to 1368. He established his capital in Beijing in 1264. By 1279 Kublai Khan had completed his conquest of China. Under his rule art and science flourished, and cultural relations among countries throughout the world were established, in part because of Marco Polo.

The Great Wall of China was erected to protect China from northern invaders. The wall extends approximately 4,000 miles across northern China, from Kansu to Hopeh province on the Yellow Sea. The wall is a conglomeration of many walls built in ancient times. The first wall was built by the Ch'in dynasty in the third century B.C. Laborers were brought in from all over China, many of whom died during the project. The wall's present form dates from the Ming dynasty (1368–1644). Successive invasions from the north have demonstrated that the wall had little military use.

ple made a number of technological advances, including the invention of gunpowder and block printing.

During the T'ang dynasty, the Chinese capital city of Ch'ang-an was the largest and probably the most cosmopolitan city in the world. It attracted visitors not only from Japan, Korea, and Southeast Asia, but also from Persia, India, and Arabia. These visitors absorbed many aspects of T'ang culture and carried them back to their native countries. Eventually, Chinese influence also spread to Europe.

The Sung Dynasty

The Sung dynasty arose in the middle of the tenth century, after peasant revolts ended T'ang rule. Like the T'ang, the Sung dynasty was a time of prosperity for Chinese civilization. Yet life during the Sung dynasty was quite different from what it had been during the T'ang: The Sung was a time characterized by delicacy and refinement, while the T'ang was an era of exuberance. This contrast is ev-

THE LIVES OF THE CHINESE EMPERORS
Tchou Dynasty

ident in the dominant art forms of the two ages—the colorful and vigorous T'ang sculptures and the serene black-and-white Sung landscape paintings.

Neo-Confucianism

Reacting against the Buddhist ideas that had crept into Chinese culture, the Sung philosophers created a new school of thought called Neo-Confucianism—a school that would dominate Chinese intellectual life for the next thousand years. Although the original aim of the Neo-Confucianists was to return to the true teachings of Confucius, they unconsciously incorporated some Buddhist ideas into their philosophy. This blending of Confucian and Buddhist ideas is reflected in the Neo-Confucianist practice of seeking enlightenment through a combination of meditation and moral action.

The Mongol Invasion

During the late twelfth and early thirteenth centuries, northern China was overrun by Mongol invaders led by the ruthless warrior Genghis Khan. In 1279 Genghis Khan's grandson Kublai Khan completed the Mongol conquest of China and established the Yuan dynasty, the first foreign dynasty in China's history.

Because China was only a part of a vast Mongol empire that included much of Central Asia, Russia, India, and Eastern Europe, the Chinese had a great deal of contact with the outside world during the Yuan dynasty. One of the many traders to visit China in this period was Marco Polo, who spent close to two decades in China before returning to his native Venice with glowing reports of the land he had visited.

The Ming Dynasty

During the mid-1300's, the Mongols were driven out of China. In 1368 Chinese rule was reestablished with the foundation of the Ming dynasty. The Ming emperors revived many of the traditions that had preceded the Mongol invasion, and once again the Chinese culture began to flourish. At the same time, however, because of lingering resentment from the Mongol conquest, the emperors tried to avoid foreign influence by limiting Chinese contact with the outside world.

The Ch'ing Dynasty

Ironically, the Ming dynasty was ultimately overthrown by foreign invaders, when armies from Manchuria swept through China during the seventeenth century. In 1644, when the armies completed their conquest, a second foreign dynasty, the Ch'ing, was established. Unlike the Mongols, however, the Manchus adopted many elements of Chinese culture and formed a government modeled after that of the Ming dynasty.

China prospered during the early years of the Ch'ing dynasty. Yet the rapid growth of the Chinese population eventually began to cause major problems for China and its government. These problems contributed to the growing unrest in Chinese society that ultimately toppled the Manchu regime and put an end to imperial rule during the early 1900's.

Traditional Chinese Government

By the time the Ch'ing dynasty was overthrown, imperial rule had lasted in China for over 2,000 years. Throughout most of this period, the Chinese government was organized into a pyramid-shaped hierarchy. At the top of this hierarchy was an all-powerful emperor, and beneath him were numerous national, regional, and local officials of varying ranks. The emperor, known as the Son of Heaven, was a hereditary ruler, who was usually the eldest son of the imperial family. His legitimacy and authority were thought to be bestowed by Heaven. To maintain his position, it was believed that he had to serve Heaven properly. The bureaucratic officials, on the other hand, were often common people, who were selected for official service by means of a nationwide examination.

The Chinese generally believed that service in government was the highest career to which they could aspire. Since an official career carried so much prestige, traditional education was geared toward preparing people for government examinations. Because the examinations tested people's knowledge of the major Chinese works of philosophy and poetry and often required the composition of verse, virtually all government officials were well-versed in literature and philosophy and most famous Chinese poets also served as government officials.

CHINESE LITERATURE

Poetry

As is suggested by the content of civil-service examinations, poetry has always held an especially important place in Chinese culture. Even after the current Communist regime came into power in the mid-twentieth century, poetry continued to be highly valued. In fact, Mao Zedong (1893–1976), the leader of the Communist Revolution, was himself a gifted poet.

The oldest collection of Chinese poetry is *The Book of Songs*, or the *Shih Ching*. Compiled around the sixth century B.C., this collection consists of 305 poems, many of which were originally folk songs, focusing on such themes as farming, love, and war. Throughout Chinese history, *The Book of Songs* has retained an honored status in Chinese society and students have been expected to memorize it.

Despite the importance of *The Book of Songs*, most great Chinese poetry was written after the fall of the Han dynasty. At about the same time that the Han collapsed, poets began writing beautiful, emotive verses using a fairly rigid poetic form known as the *shih* (see page 223). One of the first masters of the *shih* form, T'ao Ch'ien (365–427), is still ranked as one of the finest Chinese poets.

The *shih* form was raised to its greatest heights, however, by the poets of the T'ang dynasty. Among the many talented poets of this period, Wang Wei (706?–761?), Li Po (701–762), Tu Fu (712–770), and Po Chü-i (772–846) are the most highly regarded. A devout Buddhist, Wang Wei is known for his beautiful, contemplative depictions of nature. In contrast, many of Li Po's verses are best described as romantic, imaginative, or playful. Tu Fu, on the other hand, is known for his superb craftsmanship

10 Enrichment Tell students that during the early stages of the Ch'in dynasty China was so prosperous that the Western merchants who reached China in the 1600's and 1700's were extremely impressed by what they saw and began buying large quantities of tea, silk, and porcelain.

11 Discussion Tell students that today the population of China far exceeds one billion people. Then have them discuss some of the problems that such a large population might pose.

12 Discussion Have students compare and contrast the Chinese system of government with other forms of government with which they are familiar.

13 Discussion Have students compare and contrast the role of poetry in traditional Chinese society with the role of poetry in contemporary America.

14 Enrichment Tell students that at one time the Chinese believed that the great philosopher Confucius compiled and edited *The Book of Songs*. Today, however, scholars do not believe this to be the case.

Humanities Note

Fine art, *Confucius*. The Western world developed a fascination with Eastern art soon after Marco Polo established contact with Asia. By the seventeenth and eighteenth centuries, Asian artifacts, paintings, porcelain, silks, and sculpture had become extremely popular in Western Europe. At the same time, a number of Western artists began creating paintings modeled after traditional Chinese works of art. For example, this picture depicts the great Chinese philosopher Confucius in the delicate, refined style characteristic of Chinese paintings.

You might want to use the following questions to discuss the art:

1. What impression does the painting convey of Confucius?
2. Are you intrigued by the people depicted in the painting? Why or why not?

15 Enrichment Tell students that the word *tz'u* means "words" or "lyrics." As this name suggests, *tz'u* poems are written to be set to music. The form first came into being in the eighth century A.D., when poets began composing new lyrics for popular songs. Since the length of the lines in the original songs varied greatly to fit the twists and rhythms of the melodies, the lines of the new lyrics also varied in length. As a result the *tz'u* form is often referred to as "long and short lines," in contrast to the *shih*, in which every line of a given poem has the same number of words.

CONFUCIUS
Chinese style
Bibliothèque Nationale, Paris

and his command of language. Finally, the last of the great T'ang poets, Po Chü-i, wrote many poems attacking the social ills of his time.

Chinese poetry continued to flourish in later ages and new poetic forms emerged, such as the lyrical *tz'u* form. Yet no later group of poets has been able to match the accomplishments of those of the T'ang dynasty, and the T'ang era has come

Chinese Philosophy

Along with poetry, the most highly valued Chinese literary works are philosophical texts. Of these books, the most notable are *The Analects* of Confucius and the *Tao Te Ching* of Lao Tzu—the principal works of Confucianism and Taoism respectively. Another major philosophical work is the *Chuang Tzu* by Lao Tzu's most important disciple, Chuang Tzu. Written in a witty, imaginative style, this book consists of fables and anecdotes that teach the Taoist philosophy and question the principles of Confucianism.

Chinese Fiction and Drama

For the most part, the Chinese have always regarded fiction and drama as inferior to poetry. Despite this fact, however, the Chinese have produced a number of notable dramas and works of fiction.

The golden age of Chinese drama occurred during the Yuan dynasty. By this time, the Chinese already had a longstanding tradition of dramatic entertainments involving singing and dancing. Like these earlier spectacles, the plays produced during the Yuan dynasty combined singing and dancing with dialogue, but they differed from their predecessors in that they had a consistent plot. Among the most famous plays written during this period are *The Western Chamber* by Wang Shifu and *Injustice to Tou O* by Guan Hanqing.

Although the Chinese had a rich oral tradition that included countless legends and folk tales, Chinese fiction did not come into its own until the Ming and Ch'ing dynasties. The major fictional works written during the Ming dynasty include *Romance of the Three Kingdoms*, a long historical tale by Luo Guanzhong, and *The Journey to the West*, an entertaining comic novel by Wu Cheng'en. Yet the most famous Chinese novel, *The Dream of the Red Chamber* by Cao Xuequi, was not written until the eighteenth century. A long, complicated work filled with penetrating psychological insights, this novel chronicles the decline of a prominent aristocratic family.

Check Test

1. The unification of China occurred during the _____ dynasty.
2. Although the T'ang dynasty was an era of disunity, the _____ flourished during this period.
3. During the late twelfth and early thirteenth centuries, northern China was overrun by the _____.
4. The second group of foreign invaders to conquer China were the _____.
5. Chinese civil-service examinations often required the composition of _____.

Answers to Check Test

1. Ch'in
2. arts
3. Mongols
4. Manchus
5. poetry or verse

CHINESE VOICES

In pursuit of learning one knows more every day; in pursuit of the way one does less every day. One does less and less until one does nothing at all, and when one does nothing at all there is nothing that is undone.
   Lao Tzu, the *Tao Te Ching*

The Master said, He who rules by moral force is like the pole-star, which remains in its place while all the lesser stars do homage to it.
   Confucius, *The Analects*

The Master said, Learn as if you were following someone whom you could not catch up, as though you were frightened of losing.
   Confucius, *The Analects*

The life of man is like a shadow-play
Which must in the end return to nothingness.
   T'ao Ch'ien, "Poem on Returning to Dwell in the Country"

You ask what laws rule "failure" or "success"—
Songs of fishermen float to the still shore.
   Wang Wei, "To the Assistant Prefect Chang"

The flowers of the field have dabbled their powdered cheeks;
The mountain grasses are bent level at the waist,
By the bamboo stream the last fragment of cloud
Blown by the wind slowly scatters away.
   Li Po, "Clearing at Dawn"

You must have been suffering from poetry again.
   Li Po, "Addressed Humorously to Tu Fu"

. . . The future
Slips imperceptibly away.
Who can say what the years will bring?
   Tu Fu, "Jade Flower Palace"

The Four Seasons go on for ever and ever:
In all Nature nothing stops to rest
Even for a moment . . .
   Po Chü-i, "Illness"

Chinese Literature

Historical Context

Chinese history is generally divided into dynasties, or periods during which a particular family or group of people reigned. During the earliest dynasties, the Shang (shaŋ) (1766 B.C.–1122 B.C.) and the Chou (chou) (1122 B.C.–221 B.C.), China was divided into many small states. With the rise of the Ch'in (chin) dynasty (221 B.C.–206 B.C.), however, the Chinese states were unified into a large empire with a central government. The Chinese empire lasted for over two thousand years, surviving periods of internal turmoil, attacks from outside invaders, and the rise and fall of numerous dynasties.

The poet T'ao Ch'ien (dou' chē' en) lived during the period known as the Six dynasties (220 A.D.–581 A.D.), one of the most tumultuous eras in Chinese history. Throughout this period, China was in a state of disunity.

Cultural Context

The dominant Chinese attitudes and beliefs have been shaped by three major religious and philosophical schools: Taoism (dou' iz m), Confucianism (kən fyoo' shən iz m), and Buddhism (bood' iz m). Taoism—which stresses freedom, simplicity, and the mystical contemplation of nature—and Confucianism—which stresses discipline and respect for authority—were established prior to the unification of the Chinese states. The third Chinese school of thought, Buddhism, which emphasizes the need to eliminate desires through self-discipline and meditation, was not introduced into Chinese society until the first century A.D. Buddhism flourished during the Six dynasties period, as many Chinese scholars turned away from political and social issues and focused on personal and spiritual concerns.

Literary Context

Throughout most eras of Chinese history, poetry has been a vital part of Chinese life and poets have been among the most highly regarded members of Chinese society. From the second through the twelfth centuries A.D., the dominant Chinese poetic form was the *shih* (shə). *Shih* poems consist of an even number of lines, each of which has the same number of words. During T'ao Ch'ien's time, poets often wrote *shih* poems in which they expressed their personal emotions. Many of these poems have a brooding or troubled tone, though others express calm contentment or even elation.

On the following pages is a poem by T'ao Ch'ien. The annotations that accompany it point out the poem's historical context, cultural context, and literary context.

Substance, Shadow, and Spirit

T'ao Ch'ien

translated by Arthur Waley

Cultural Context: The poet sees the human being as consisting of three elements: Substance (the body), Shadow (fame or reputation), and Spirit. The poem will compare the merits of stressing each of the three aspects of the self.

High and low, wise and simple, all busily hoard up the moments of
    life. How greatly they err!
Therefore I have to the uttermost exposed the bitterness both of
    Substance and Shadow and have made Spirit show how, by following
    Nature, we may dissolve this bitterness.

Literary Context: The poet begins with a prose introduction in which he explains his purpose.

Substance speaks to Shadow:

Heaven and Earth exist forever:
Mountains and rivers never change.
5 But herbs and trees in perpetual rotation
Are renovated and withered by the dews and frosts:
And Man the wise, Man the divine—
Shall he alone escape this Law?
Fortuitously[1] appearing for a moment in the World
10 He suddenly departs, never to return.
How can he know that the friends he has left
Are missing him and thinking of him?
Only the things that he used remain;
They look upon them and their tears flow.
15 Me no magical arts can save,
Though you may hope for a wizard's aid.
I beg you listen to this advice—
When you can get wine, be sure to drink it.

Cultural Context: The question of whether people are like trees, which come back to life every year, relates to the Buddhist belief in reincarnation.

Historical Context: Alchemy and other magical arts aimed at prolonging life flourished during the Six dynasties period.

Cultural Context: These lines refer to one of the prevalent attitudes of the Six dynasties period: "Eat, drink, and be merry, for tomorrow you will die."

Shadow replies:

There is no way to preserve life.
20 Drugs of Immortality are instruments of folly.

Historical Context: This is another reference to alchemy.

---

1. Fortuitously (fôr too′ ə təs lē) *adj.*: Accidentally.

(continued from bottom of page)

1 **Enrichment** Tell students that this selection was influenced by Lao Tzu's *The Tao Te Ching*, page 210. The information they learn from this selection can be applied and reinforced in the following selection.

2 **Discussion** Which aspect of the self does T'ao Ch'ien believe is the most important? Explain.

3 **Discussion** Explain to students that these lines state beautifully the classical Chinese view of humanity's relationship to nature and the Taoist view of a natural pattern, or Tao, of the universe.

4 **Discussion** How are the concepts presented here similar to or different from your own views on nature and life?

5 **Discussion** Restate in your own words what Substance is saying in these lines. Do you agree that when someone dies you will not remember that person unless he or she leaves "things" behind that will remind you of that person? Explain.

6 **Enrichment** Explain to students that "magical arts" and "wizards" refer to the practices of the religious Taoists, who believed in and sought physical immortality. T'ao Ch'ien rejected these pursuits toward immortality.

7 **Discussion** Why does Shadow believe "there is no way to preserve life"? What inherent characteristic does Shadow possess that would make him believe this idea?

Master Teacher Note Make sure students understand the literal meaning of the poem. Then ask three students to role play Substance, Shadow, and Spirit by creating a dialogue consistent with the poet's message. Offer one of the following springboards:
1. You have received an anonymous gift of $500,000.
2. A catastrophe has left you without a family.
3. You learn that you have a fatal illness.

Presentation
Motivation/Prior Knowledge Tell students to imagine that the human self can be divided into various parts that when put together make up the whole person. Ask them to name the aspects they think the human self comprises. Students may suggest the mind, body, soul, breath, and so on. Make a list of their suggestions on the chalkboard. Then ask them to personify each of these aspects by giving them human characteristics. What would their personalities be like? How would they act? You might then have groups of students role play one aspect of the self as they debate which is the most important.

Then tell students that this selection is a conversation among what T'ao Ch'ien believes are the three aspects of the self—substance, shadow, and spirit.

Purpose-Setting Question What does each aspect—substance, shadow, and spirit—contribute to the whole self? What is the theme of this piece?

Fine art, *A Myriad of Trees on Strange Peaks*, attributed to Yen Wen-kuei. Yen Wen-kuei is a well-known Sung dynasty painter who primarily worked in ink on silk.

This picture, which is part of a fan-shaped album page, is typical of Sung landscape art; it possesses the characteristic fusion of mystery and poetry. Like so many Sung paintings, distance and space are indefinite, leaving viewers lost in the expanse of the painting.

In this painting, for example, the jutting mountains, the mysterious fog, the forest, the rocky cliffs, and the distant peaks suggest a mysterious, unknown place. The detail shown in the nearest part of the picture implies that beyond the mists lie other beautiful scenes. The viewer is asked to use his or her imagination to see beyond the artist's vista.

You might want to use the following questions to discuss the art:

1. What scenes do you imagine lie beyond the mists?
2. How does this picture relate to the lines in the poem that read: "You had better go where Fate leads—/Drift on the Stream of Infinite Flux,/Without joy, without fear"?

8 **Enrichment** Tell students that the idea that there is no road to paradise reflects the view that ultimate reality cannot be perceived with common human senses. This idea will be reinforced in Lao Tzu's work.

9 **Enrichment** Tell students that the impermanence of human life is a common theme in the literature in this unit.

A MYRIAD OF TREES ON STRANGE PEAKS
Yen Wen-kuei (Northern Sung Dynasty)

I would gladly wander in Paradise,
But it is far away and there is no road.
Since the day that I was joined to you
We have shared all our joys and pains.
25 While you rested in the shade, I left you awhile:
But till the end we shall be together.
Our joint existence is impermanent:
Sadly together we shall slip away.

Grammar in Action

Unlike prose, poetry does not have any set grammatical rules—poetic license applies equally to content and to written format. For example, poetry has no standard rules of grammar, capitalization, and punctuation. Traditionally the first word in each line of poetry is capitalized, but this too can be altered to fit the needs of the poet. Poets are also not bound by the same grammatical rules governing the use of punctuation marks as prose writers are. They are at liberty to use punctuation in the way that will best suit their purposes or that will create the best effect.

When you read poetry, follow the punctuation marks carefully. The poet is guiding you through the poem by using or not using punctuation. A comma, for example, indicates a slight pause, a semicolon or a colon indicates a longer pause, and a period indicates a complete stop. Remember that when you read poetry, in most cases, you should follow the punctuation, not the breaks in the lines of the poetry. If you read the poem correctly, its rhythm and meaning will be clearer.

Student Activity 1. In groups of three read "Substance, Shadow, and Spirit," incorrectly pausing at the end of every line. Then reread it, carefully

That when the body decays Fame should also go
30 Is a thought unendurable, burning the heart.
    Let us strive and labor while yet we may
    To do some deed that men will praise.
    Wine may in truth dispel our sorrow,
    But how compare it with lasting Fame?

        Spirit expounds:

35 God can only set in motion:
    He cannot control the things he has made.
    Man, the second of the Three Orders,[2]
    Owes his precedence to Me.
    Though I am different from you,
40 We were born involved in one another:
    Nor by any means can we escape
    The intimate sharing of good and ill.
    The Three Emperors[3] were saintly men,
    Yet today—where are they?
45 P'eng[4] lived to a great age,
    Yet he went at last, when he longed to stay.
    And late or soon all go:
    Wise and simple have no reprieve.
    Wine may bring forgetfulness,
50 But does it not hasten old age?
    If you set your hearts on noble deeds,
    How do you know that any will praise you?
    By all this thinking you do Me injury:
    You had better go where Fate leads—
55 Drift on the Stream of Infinite Flux,
    Without joy, without fear:
    When you must go—then go,
    And make as little fuss as you can.

    ———————

    2. **the Three Orders:** Heaven, Man, and Earth.
    3. **the Three Emperors:** Three mythical rulers of ancient times.
    4. **P'eng** (pəŋ): The archetypal Chinese aged man.

Reader's Response *What is your response to the ideas T'ao Ch'ien expresses in this poem? What questions does the poem bring to mind?*

Cultural Context: These lines reflect the Confucian belief that people can achieve a kind of immortality by becoming famous. The Confucians do not believe in reincarnation.

Cultural Context: Here "God" refers not to a supreme deity as in Western religions, but to the force that gives things their form.

Cultural Context: This passage conveys the belief that the spirit separates people from animals, thereby allowing humanity to join Heaven and Earth as one of the Three Orders.

Cultural Context: The final passage reflects the Taoist belief that people should not strive for a long life, pleasure, or fame, but instead should merge with the flow of the universe, of which death is a natural part.

10 **Discussion** Do you agree with Substance's view on fame? Why or why not?

11 **Discussion** What is the tone of Spirit's dialogue? Why does Spirit seem so harsh?

12 **Discussion** Restate in your own words what Spirit is saying in these lines.

ESL Teaching Strategy Explain to ESL students the concept of personification. Help students understand how the conversations among Substance, Shadow, and Spirt can take place. You might explain the abstractions of a human being in terms of cookie dough: When the flour, milk, and eggs are blended, we cannot identify separate ingredients, yet each one has its own importance.

Teaching Tenth-Grade Students Ask tenth-grade students to think about a famous athlete, or music or film star. Discuss the relationship of body, spirit, and reputation. Ask how the body affects reputation. If reputation is damaged, what happens to the body? to the spirit? What happens if the spirit is destroyed? How can the body be damaged? the reputation? What does T'ao Ch'ien's poem say to the famous athlete or music or film star?

following the punctuation marks. Which reading sounds better? Which reading makes more sense? Explain.

   Student Activity 2. Look through the poems in this unit. Find one that does not follow the traditional form of punctuation. Has the poet formed his or her own rules for capitalization and punctuation? Why do you think the poet chose to ignore these rules? What effect do these changes have on the reading of the poem? on the meaning of the poem?

ANSWERS TO THINKING ABOUT THE SELECTION

1. Answers may differ. Suggested responses: (a) He would concern himself with and try to derive satisfaction from the material aspects of life. (b) He would concern himself with and try to gain satisfaction from projecting images he believes would be viewed favorably by others. (c) He would try to do nothing that is contrary to the natural order of the universe and would let the spiritual aspect lead the other two.
2. Answers may differ. Suggested responses: (a) The opening stanza reveals that Substance and Shadow are deluded and must be enlightened by Spirit. (b) One would expect Spirit to be a teacher of sorts.
3. Answers may differ. Suggested responses: (a) Shadow fears impermanence and mortality. (b) Having rejected the quest for physical immortality, Substance wishes to escape from his sorrows.
4. Answers may differ. Suggested responses: (a) Substance replies that life is impermanent. (b) Shadow agrees with this fear of mortality but suggests that achieving fame will supply a certain kind of immortality.
5. Answers may differ. Suggested responses: (a) Spirit takes the role of the leader and refutes both positions. (b) Spirit suggests that life is fate and one should neither go against it nor fear it.
6. Answers may differ. Some students will support one aspect over another, while many may suggest that one must achieve a balance in all aspects of the self.

THINKING ABOUT THE SELECTION

Interpreting

1. In this poem, Ta'o Ch'ien considers the merits of stressing each of the three aspects of the self: Substance (the body), Shadow (fame or reputation), and Spirit. (a) How would a person who chose to stress Substance live his or her life? (b) How would someone who chose to stress Shadow live? (c) How would someone who chose to stress Spirit live?
2. (a) What does the opening stanza reveal about the poet's attitude concerning Substance, Shadow, and Spirit? (b) How does this stanza shape your expectations of the rest of the poem?
3. (a) What fear does Substance express in the second stanza? (b) How does Substance respond to this fear?
4. (a) How does Shadow respond to Substance's approach to life? (b) What alternate approach does Shadow suggest?
5. (a) How does Spirit respond to Substance and Shadow? (b) What alternative does Spirit offer?

Applying

6. Which aspect or aspects of the self do you think that a person should stress in living his or her life? Explain your answer.

ANALYZING LITERATURE

Understanding Theme

The **theme** is the central idea or insight about life that a writer hopes to convey in a work of literature. In some literary works, the theme is directly stated. More often, however, the theme is implied, or revealed indirectly.

1. What is the theme of "Substance, Shadow, and Spirit"?
2. How is the theme revealed? Cite specific passages from the poem in your answer.
3. Many literary works have more than one theme or can be interpreted in more than one manner. Explain why you do or do not think that it is possible to interpret "Shadow, Substance, and Spirit" in more than one way.

UNDERSTANDING LANGUAGE

Completing Sentences

Each of the following sentences is incomplete. Read each sentence carefully. Then choose the lettered word that best completes the sentence.

1. T'ao Ch'ien lived during the _____ Six dynasties era, a period characterized by internal turmoil and disunity.
   a. turbulent   c. primitive
   b. tranquil   d. hateful
2. Because poetry has almost always been an integral part of Chinese life, poets have usually been among the most _____ members of society.
   a. encouraged   c. repected
   b. recognizable   d. repressed
3. Many Chinese poets have been _____ by the ideas of Lao Tzu.
   a. shaped   c. exhibited
   b. influenced   d. aggrandized
4. Thanks to the efforts of a number of gifted poets, Chinese poetry _____ during the T'ang dynasty.
   a. progressed   c. flourished
   b. furbished   d. expanded
5. The Chinese Empire _____ for over two thousand years, surviving periods of internal turmoil and attacks from outside invaders.
   a. endured   c. dominated
   b. struggled   d. flourished

THINKING AND WRITING

Writing About Theme

The theme of "Substance, Shadow, and Spirit" relates to the question of how people should live their lives. Write a paper in which you explain why you do or do not agree with the ideas that T'ao Ch'ien sets forth. Begin by reviewing the poem, paying close attention to the ideas it expresses. Then spend some time clarifying your own thoughts concerning how people should approach their lives. Organize your ideas. Then begin writing your paper, focusing on expressing your thoughts as clearly and concisely as possible. After you have finished writing, make sure that you have varied the length and structure of your sentences and have used transitions to connect your ideas.

ANSWERS TO ANALYZING LITERATURE

1. Answers may differ. As expressed by Spirit, the theme is that you should view life as fate and neither go against it nor fear it, but accept what life gives you.
2. The theme is stated explicitly, particularly in lines 54–58.
3. Answers may differ. Most students will reply that this poem can be interpreted in only one way because its theme is so clearly stated.

ANSWERS TO UNDERSTANDING LANGUAGE

1. (a) turbulent
2. (c) respected
3. (b) influenced
4. (c) flourished
5. (a) endured

THINKING AND WRITING

Writing Across the Curriculum

Inform the social studies or sociology departments that students are reading this selection. These teachers may be able to give students more information about Taoism and the ways in which Taoist philosophy was integrated into the Chinese social system.

Philosophy

VISITING GROUP
Handscroll, Chinese

Humanities Note

Fine art, *Visiting Group*, hand-scroll Chinese print on silk. This painting demonstrates several characteristics of traditional Chinese art: It shows the beauty of nature, the asymmetrical balance found in many Chinese works, and the delicate and rhythmic line favored by traditional Chinese artists.

The composition, in which the major elements of the painting are compacted into the left diagonal area, is also typical of many Chinese works. One famous painter was nicknamed "Old Corner" because his compositions left most of the picture empty. "I show one corner," he remarked, "and if a man cannot find the other three, I need not repeat myself."

The starkly caricatured figures are also characteristic of many Chinese paintings. Each person in this painting has a distinctive look, including the fanciful figure of Kuan-yin, the goddess of Mercy, perched at the end of the boat. The expressive use of lines, which is clearly shown in both the drawing of the figures and in the rocky mountain, contributes to its distinctive look. In addition the sea, which appears in a rippled pattern, sets off the figures and the rest of the landscape.

You might want to use the following questions to discuss the art:

1. How does the artist assure that the two figures in red stand out? Why might he want to focus on them?
2. What mood do the colors in this painting elicit?
3. What kind of people are on this trip? What do you think they will do when they disembark?

LAO TZU

Focus

More About the Author Lao Tzu lived and wrote during the time of enormous political turmoil and intellectual ferment known as the period of the Warring States. China was not yet the unified country of today. Several independent kingdoms, constantly vying for supremacy, launched long and costly wars against one another in which nobles and commoners alike suffered and died.

This period is also known as the golden age of classical Chinese philosophy. The great thinkers of the time diagnosed the ills of Chinese society and proposed ways of resolving China's crisis. Lao Tzu's philosophy, later called Taoism, was one of the earliest and most influential schools of philosophy that emerged during this period.

Ask students how the political climate at the time may have influenced Lao Tzu's writing.

Pronunciation Note In Pin Yin, the system of romanization used in Mainland China, Lao Tzu is also spelled Lao Zi and Lao Tze.

Critical Evaluation According to D. C. Lau, the translator of these selections, "Lao Tzu has had an influence on Chinese thought through the ages all out of proportion to its length." The work, which has been translated more times than any other work of Oriental literature, is composed of only about 5,000 Chinese characters and is written in a style that is "more often than not succinct to the point of obscurity."

Lao Tzu (lou′dzu′), which means "Old Master" or "Ancient One," is the name given to the author of a book called the *Tao Te Ching*, or *The Way and Its Power*, one of the two basic texts of Taoist philosophy.

No one knows exactly who the "Old Master" was or when he lived, though it seems most likely that he lived during the fourth or fifth centuries B.C. Legend has it that he remained in his mother's womb for sixty-two years before birth and emerged as a white-haired old man. According to tradition, he served as Keeper of the Archives in the ancient Chinese kingdom of Chou. Unhappy with the political situation of his day, the legend goes, he mounted a black ox and headed for a western pass, hoping to leave the chaos in China. As he approached the pass, the gatekeeper recognized him as a sage and refused to let him through until he would write down some words of wisdom. Lao Tzu proceeded to write the 5,000-word *Tao Te Ching* and was allowed to depart through the pass. Some say he was 160 years old when he departed, while others put his age at 200.

Perhaps one reason why so many legends have emerged about the author of the *Tao Te Ching* is the mysterious and cryptic nature of the text itself—such an unusual text must have an unusual author. The book is written partly in verse and partly in compact prose. The author speaks of mysteries and secrets, of knowledge that cannot be spoken, and of words that have no meaning but behind which lie profound significance. The ideas expressed in the *Tao Te Ching* frequently contradict both logic and intuition, yet on reflection they seem to contain a truth that is beyond words.

Lao Tzu has two primary concerns: understanding the way of the universe and using that understanding for self-preservation. He is not interested in how to win fame, glory, honor, or wealth, but rather in how to survive. Some of the passages seem to be addressed to a ruler, advising how to ensure the survival of a kingdom in a time of political upheaval. Others are addressed to anyone who wishes to understand the fundamental principles of existence and to use them to preserve himself or herself in a chaotic world.

Objectives

Thematic
To compare the Indian and Taoist concepts of the universe

Skills
To understand Taoism

Support Material

Teaching Portfolio
Teacher Backup, p. 277
Usage and Mechanics Worksheet, p. 281
Vocabulary Check, p. 282
Analyzing Literature Worksheet, *Understanding Taoism*, p. 283

Critical Thinking and Reading Worksheet, *Making Inferences*, p. 284
Selection Test, pp. 285–286

GUIDE FOR INTERPRETING

from the Tao Te Ching

Commentary

Taoism. Along with Buddhism and Confucianism, **Taoism** is one of the three dominant Chinese philosophical schools. The Taoists get their name from the term Tao, which means "Path" or "Way." For the early Chinese, including both Taoists and Confucianists, the Tao was the force that controlled the universe. Confucianists thought of the Tao as a moral force, calling for righteous behavior and respect for one's superiors. In contrast, Taoists did not ascribe human moral qualities to the Tao. They thought of it as being beyond the scope of human concerns, but believed we could see its workings by observing nature.

The *Tao Te Ching* is the primary work expressing the Taoist understanding of the Way. Lao Tzu begins his book by commenting that we are not able to talk about the Way, because whatever we say will be incomplete. He goes on to suggest that we can begin to understand the Way by observing how nature works, though we must be careful not to impose human desires on our observations. In addition, he points out that to appreciate the Way we must find a balance between opposites, because the Way is characterized by regular alterations of contradictory phenomena, such as day and night.

The difference between the Taoist and Confucian understanding of the Tao is hinted at in section III of the *Tao Te Ching*. While Confucius stresses duty and education, and teaches that people should strive to serve society and should honor people of worth, Lao Tzu recommends *not* honoring men of worth, *not* educating people, and *not* encouraging clever people to act. He suggests that placing value on certain people, things, or actions, and labeling them "better" results in undesirable sentiments and situations, such as jealousy and strife. Instead, he argues, people should seek to simplify their lives and should free themselves of desires. Once people have achieved freedom and simplicity, they can focus on the mystical contemplation of nature that will enable them to discover the Way.

In the *Tao Te Ching*, Lao Tzu also applies his understanding of the Way to politics. He suggests that the best type of ruler is one who protects his or her people from material wants, while imposing a minimum of governmental regulations. In addition, he argues that the government, as well as the individual, that seems the weakest is most likely to escape destruction, just as grass that bends with the wind is more likely to survive a storm than a mighty tree.

Writing

Write a journal entry in which you explore your thoughts about Lao Tzu's suggestion that the weakest governments and individuals are the most likely to escape destruction. Do you agree with Lao Tzu?

Literary Focus Students may be familiar with the American political debates during the 1980's about the role of government in society. Many may have heard President Ronald Reagan quote Thomas Jefferson's statement that the government that governs least governs best. Have students compare Lao Tzu's philosophy of government with ours and with other forms of government with which they might be familiar.

Writing/Prior Knowledge From their journal entries, have students develop their own philosophy of government. Ask volunteers to share their philosophy with the class. Then discuss how each might be implemented in our government system.

ESL Teaching Strategy Lao Tzu and Taoism have had a profound effect on Asian culture. Have your Asian students share with the class their insights and understanding of Taoism, Chinese philosophy, and Chinese culture.

Vocabulary

Preteach the following vocabulary words:

myriad (mir´ ē əd) *n.*: Countless; of a highly varied nature

manifestations (man´ ə fes tā´ shənz) *n.*: The world of human reality

manifold (man´ ə fōld´) *adj.*: Many and varied

contention (kən ten´ shən) *n.*: Strife; struggle

calamity (kə lam´ ə tē) *n.*: Deep trouble or misery

submissive (sub mis´ iv) *adj.*: Docile; submitting without resistance

crevices (krev´ is iz) *n.*: Cracks

Master Teacher Note Ask students to imagine that Lao Tzu has spent the past five days with them. Based on what he says in his work, ask them to discuss how he would react to their daily routine, environment, classes, and their ethical, moral, and monetary values.

Teaching Tenth-Grade Students
Some tenth-grade students might have difficulty understanding the concepts inherent in Lao Tzu's work. Ask an advanced student to paraphrase Lao Tzu's work. Then share it with the class.

from the Tao Te Ching

Lao Tzu

translated by D. C. Lau

WHITE CLOUDS OVER XIAO AND XIANG
Wang Chien
*Freer Gallery of Art, Smithsonian Institution,
Washington, D.C.*

I

The way that can be spoken of
Is not the constant way;
The name that can be named
Is not the constant name,
5 The nameless was the beginning of heaven and
    earth;
The named was the mother of the myriad
    creatures.
Hence always rid yourself of desires in order to
    observe its secrets;
But always allow yourself to have desires in order
    to observe its manifestations.
These two are the same
10 But diverge in name as they issue forth.
Being the same they are called mysteries,
Mystery upon mystery—
The gateway of the manifold secrets.

III

Not to honor men of worth will keep the people
from contention; not to value goods which are
hard to come by will keep them from theft; not to
display what is desirable will keep them from being
unsettled of mind.
15   Therefore in governing the people, the sage
empties their minds but fills their bellies, weakens
their wills but strengthens their bones. He always
keeps them innocent of knowledge and free from
desire, and ensures that the clever never dare to act.
    Do that which consists in taking no action, and
order will prevail.

Humanities Note

Fine art, *White Clouds over Xiao and Xiang* by Wang Chien (1598–1677). As an influential and well-known painter during the Ch'ing dynasty, Wang Chien epitomized the Ch'ing style of landscape painting in his work.

Tradition established the rules under which artists painted. These rules included a strict adherence to particular painting styles, to certain subjects, to the relationship of art and philosophy, and to the artist's role in society.

Influential in Chien's work was the Taoist philosophy that nature was mysterious and difficult to understand.

You might want to use the following questions to discuss the art:
1. How does Chien's painting uphold this Taoist belief?
2. According to Chien's painting, what place does man hold in nature? How do you know?
3. How does this painting support the beliefs Lao Tzu expresses in the *Tao Te Ching*?

Rather than fill it to the brim by keeping it upright
Better to have stopped in time;[1]
Hammer it to a point
10 And the sharpness cannot be preserved forever;
There may be gold and jade to fill a hall
But there is none who can keep them.
To be overbearing when one has wealth and position
Is to bring calamity upon oneself.
15 To retire when the task is accomplished
Is the way of heaven.

---

1. **Rather than . . . in time:** These lines refer to a container that stands in position when empty but overturns when full.

XLIII

The most submissive thing in the world can ride roughshod over the hardest in the world—that which is without substance entering that which has no crevices.

That is why I know the benefit of resorting to no action. The teaching that uses no words, the benefit of resorting to no action, these are beyond the understanding of all but a very few in the world.

Reader's Response *What is your immediate reaction to the ideas expressed in these selections from the* Tao Te Ching? *Do the ideas seem unusual or different? Why or why not?*

THINKING ABOUT THE SELECTION

Interpreting

1. To what do the "nameless" and the "named" refer in section I, lines 5 and 6?
2. (a) What values does Lao Tzu expound in section III? (b) How does he apply his belief in freedom from desire to government in this section?
3. In section IX, how do the images in the first six lines relate to the examples of human behavior in the final four lines?
4. What type of behavior does Lao Tzu advocate in section XLIII?

Applying

5. How do the values set forth in section III contrast with the dominant values of American society?
6. How do you think Lao Tzu would view the current Chinese government? Why?
7. Martin Luther King, Jr., and Mahatma Gandhi advocated nonviolence and passive resistance in dealing with one's opponents. How does this approach relate to the ideas of Lao Tzu?

ANALYZING LITERATURE

Understanding Taoism

The Taoist philosophy focuses on the quest to understand the Tao, or Way. Although the Tao is elusive and difficult to define, it has been described as "the source of all being and governor of all life, human and natural, and the basic, undivided unity in which all the contradictions and distinctions of existence are ultimately resolved.

1. How does Lao Tzu capture the elusive, mysterious nature of the Tao in section I?
2. What are the main beliefs expressed in the four selections from the *Tao Te Ching*?
3. How does the style in which the *Tao Te Ching* is written echo the elusive, mysterious nature of the Tao?

THINKING AND WRITING

Writing About Taoism

Write an essay in which you discuss the aspects of the Taoist philosophy that can and cannot be applied to life in our society. Begin by reviewing the Guide for Interpreting page on Taoism and rereading the selections from the *Tao Te Ching*. Note as many Taoist beliefs as you can. Then think about whether each of these beliefs could or could not be applied to life in our society. After arranging your ideas into an outline, begin writing your essay. Make sure that you include an introduction with a clear thesis statement. When you revise your essay, make sure that you have supported each of your opinions with facts, reasons, or details.

(continued from bottom of page)
greed and thus will not harm others.
3. These images are meant to illustrate the principle of moderation in all aspects of human behavior.
4. Answers may differ. Suggested response: He essentially advocates passive behavior that conforms to the principles of natural order.
5. These values are diametrically opposed to the value system implicit in capitalism, which holds the "desirable" as incentive to work and produce.
6. Answers may differ. Suggested response: Lao Tzu might admire communism's rejection of capitalism. But he would consider the current authoritarianism antithetical to the principles of natural order and a laissez faire government.
7. Answers may differ. Suggested response: Lao Tzu argued that passivity overcomes aggression, a concept that was at the heart of the civil disobedience tactics used by both Gandhi and King.

ANSWERS TO ANALYZING LITERATURE

1. He used terse, ambiguous language to suggest in words that which words cannot describe.
2. The main beliefs may be summed up as follows: Everything in the universe has a Tao, or natural way; spiritual knowledge and social tranquillity can be gained by doing nothing contrary to the Tao; and the Tao has two aspects, that which is tangible and that which remains unknown to the senses.
3. The book is written in a deliberately cryptic, terse style that is difficult to understand and thus remains open to many varying interpretations. It emphasizes poetry over logic.

THINKING AND WRITING

Publishing Student Writing Have students share their essays with the class and compare ideas on how Taoist philosophy can and cannot be applied to their lives.

Challenge Tell students that in *The Empire Strikes Back*, the movie sequel to *Star Wars*, Yoda exhibits many of the characteristics of a Taoist sage. Have students watch this movie and list the aspects of Taoist philosophy to which Yoda ascribes.

---

6 **Enrichment** Tell students that one central tenet of Taoist thought is moderation. This passage suggests that nothing should be pushed beyond its natural limit. To do so would be to violate the principles of nature.

7 **Discussion** Name examples of people who have brought calamity upon themselves by going too far.

8 **Discussion** Why does Lao Tzu suggest that the passive can overcome the aggressive?

Closure and Extension

ANSWERS TO THINKING ABOUT THE SELECTION

1. The "nameless" refers to the essence and origin of all things. It is nameless because it cannot be described in words. The "named" refers to the visible, tangible aspects of reality.
2. Answers may differ. Suggested responses: (a) He stresses the values of austerity, virtue, and a laissez faire government, all of which should conform to the natural order of society. (b) He suggests that people free of desire will not develop

551?–479? B.C.

There is a story about Confucius (kən fyoo′ shəs) —more legend than fact. Once when he was out shooting, he would not shoot at a sitting bird. The bird had the disadvantage. Shooting it would not be fair play.

This is only one of the many Confucian ideas that have shaped the pattern of Chinese life for over two thousand years. Yet few details are known about Confucius's life. No writings from Confucius's own hand even exist. *The Analects*, or collected sayings of Confucius, were compiled long after his death by disciples of his disciples. For centuries Confucius was credited with editing several great works of ancient Chinese literature, including the *Book of Songs*, but it is likely that this is only an invention of later Confucians, intended to enhance the reputation of their patron.

The name Confucius is probably a Latinized version of K'ung-Fu-tsu (kʊoŋ′ foo′ dzu′), or Master K'ung. He was a scholar from the state of Lu, now part of Shandong province. Confucius wished to be an adviser to kings but never achieved that goal. Making his living by wandering from place to place instructing any young men who appeared to have talent for learning, he considered himself to be a transmitter of ancient truths. Confucius believed that the values of the ancient golden age were generally ignored by his generation, who seemed to care for outer appearances more than for inner emotions and who appeared to have no sense of decorum. He tried to teach his pupils to become true gentlemen, by which he meant morally and spiritually superior men, as opposed to the gentlemen who received that title by being born into wealthy families.

In all of his teachings, Confucius emphasized the importance of moral conduct. He believed that people in positions of authority, such as political officials, should set extremely high standards for themselves and be lenient with others. When out of office, these people should maintain their high standards, modeling their behavior after that of their superiors.

Confucius probably never imagined the extent to which his ideas would spread and the impact that they would have on Chinese society. Thanks to the efforts of some of his later disciples, primarily Mencius (men′ shē əs), or Meng-tzu, and Hsun Tzu (shun′ dzu′), Confucius's teachings were developed into a philosophy that has had an unparalleled impact on Chinese life, in addition to influencing the lives of people in a number of other countries in East Asia.

GUIDE FOR INTERPRETING

from The Analects

Commentary

Confucianism. The philosophical ideas generated by Confucius led to the development of a system of beliefs called **Confucianism.** Confucianism is the dominant ethical, social, and political philosophy in China. It was the official state doctrine of most of the Chinese emperors from the second century B.C. until the overthrow of the imperial system in 1911. Prior to the beginning of this century, Chinese students memorized four short works of Confucian doctrine, including *The Analects*, as a major part of their elementary and intermediate schooling. These texts were also the basis for the civil service examinations that led to prestigious official posts in the government.

Confucianism is concerned with how people act—with moral behavior. It deals with all types of social units, from the most basic, the family, to the largest, the state, which is seen as an all-encompassing family. In the Confucian system, social relations are based on a system of subordination, with younger family members subordinate to older members, subjects subordinate to government officials, and women subordinate to men. As a result, the family is ruled by an authoritarian father, whom all family members are expected to obey without question; and the state is ruled by an authoritarian king or emperor, whom all people are expected to serve and honor. However, all must be governed by the concept of *ren,* or human-heartedness—a type of loving benevolence toward others.

In addition to respecting and obeying those of superior status, people are expected to conduct themselves in a virtuous manner. The Confucianists believe that Heaven is the supreme moral authority, which dictates an ethical code by which all people must live. People in positions of authority, including the ruler, are expected to conduct themselves in an irreproachable manner and thus serve as models of virtue for their subordinates. Those who fail to follow the moral way of Heaven are considered unworthy to be in a position of authority.

As you read the following selections from *The Analects*, look for what they reveal about the Confucian social system and code of conduct.

Writing

The words of wisdom in *The Analects* are concentrated into short, pithy verses. They are in fact the model for the messages inside many fortune cookies, though fortune cookies were invented in the United States. Try writing five or six of your own sayings, each embodying a truth about social relations between family members or friends.

Literary Focus Confucius saw the relationships between the individual and the state and between the state and heaven to be extensions of familial relationships, such as those between father and son and between husband and wife. Have students compare and contrast the ideal Confucian family with the modern American family. Ask them whether Confucian ideals could be applied in some ways in today's world and to what effect.

Writing/Prior Knowledge Pair up the students in your class. Have them brainstorm ideas for truths and possible sayings.

ESL Teaching Strategy Ask your Asian students to compare what they know of Confucianism to what they have observed in this country. What specific differences in moral conduct do they notice between Chinese and Americans?

Teaching Tenth-Grade Students Ask students to imagine Confucius as a parent. Have students discuss how the Confucian family structure differs from that of the modern American family. Then discuss what Confucius would tell students to do to change their ways of life. Of what part of their lives would he approve?

Vocabulary

Preteach the following vocabulary words:

homage (häm´ ij) *n.*: An act that shows respect

chastisements (chas tīz´ mənts) *n.*: Punishments

ritual (rich´ o͞o əl) n.: The observance of prescribed rules

biased (bī´ əst) *adj.*: Prejudiced; slanted

reverence (rev´ ər əns) *n.*: Respect

ensue (en so͞o´) *v.*: Immediately follow; result

covets (kuv´ its) *v.*: Longs for with envy

from The Analects
Confucius
translated by Arthur Waley

The Master[1] said, To learn and at due times to repeat what one has learnt, is that not after all[2] a pleasure? That friends should come to one from afar, is this not after all delightful? To remain unsoured even though one's merits are unrecognized by others, is that not after all what is expected of a gentleman?

The Master said, A young man's duty is to behave well to his parents at home and to his elders abroad, to be cautious in giving promises and punctual in keeping them, to have kindly feelings towards everyone, but seek the intimacy of the Good. If, when all that is done, he has any energy to spare, then let him study the polite arts.[3]

The Master said, (the good man) does not grieve that other people do not recognize his merits. His only anxiety is lest he should fail to recognize theirs.

The Master said, He who rules by moral force is like the pole-star,[4] which remains in its place while all the lesser stars do homage to it.

The Master said, If out of three hundred *Songs*[5] I had to take one phrase to cover all my teaching, I would say, "Let there be no evil in your thoughts."

The Master said, Govern the people by regulations, keep order among them by chastisements, and they will flee from you, and lose all self-respect. Govern them by moral force, keep order among them by ritual, and they will keep their self-respect and come to you of their own accord.

Mêng Wu Po[6] asked about the treatment of parents. The Master said, Behave in such a way that your father and mother have no anxiety about you, except concerning your health.

The Master said, A gentleman can see a question from all sides without bias. The small man is biased and can see a question only from one side.

The Master said, Yu[7] shall I teach you what knowledge is? When you know a thing, to recognize that you know it, and when you do not know a thing, to recognize that you do not know it. That is knowledge.

The Master said, High office filled by men of narrow views, ritual performed without reverence, the forms of mourning observed without grief— these are things I cannot bear to see!

The Master said, In the presence of a good man, think all the time how you may learn to equal him. In the presence of a bad man, turn your gaze within![8]

---

1. **The Master:** Confucius.
2. **after all:** Even though one does not hold office.
3. **the polite arts:** Such activities as reciting from *The Book of Songs*, practicing archery, and learning proper deportment.
4. **pole-star:** Polaris, the North Star.
5. **three hundred *Songs*:** Poems in *The Book of Songs*.

6. **Mêng Wu Po** (muŋ wōō bó): The son of one of Confucius's disciples.
7. **Yu** (yōō): Tzu-lu, one of Confucius's Disciples.
8. **within:** Within yourself; scrutinize yourself.

OLD TREES BY COLD WATERFALL
Wen Zhengming

6 **Discussion** (Bracketed text on page 216.) Confucian social philosophy looks back to a "golden age" when gentlemen ruled and social relations were conducted in proper fashion. Do you think American society looks to the future or clings to the past? Explain.

ANSWERS TO THINKING ABOUT THE SELECTION

1. Answers may differ. Suggested response: People should be cautious in giving promises because Confucius believed strongly that a firm moral order is founded primarily on the integrity of the individual, particularly the gentleman.
2. Answers may differ. Suggested response: Confucius may have meant that the king should set an example of perfect Confucian morality, thereby drawing others to follow him.
3. Answers may differ. Suggested response: Confucius may have meant that one should examine his own behavior before criticizing that of another.
4. Answers may differ. Suggested response: He may have meant that a gentleman should be moderate in speech and should make sure his actions match his promises.
5. Confucius's belief in humility is upheld by his statements that one should attain moderation in personal conduct and that one should strive to perfect oneself before criticizing others.
6. Answers will differ. Many students may respond that his ideas regarding the family, knowledge, and good men or gentlemen apply most directly to their own lives.
7. (a) Answers will differ. Some students may be reminded of their parents, grandparents, or other elders who cherish the days of old. (b) Answers will differ. Some students may suggest that many people are reluctant to change and, therefore, cling to the way things were in the past.

ANSWERS TO ANALYZING LITERATURE

1. Answers may differ. Suggested response: These passages reveal that the ruler should set a virtuous example for his subjects to follow by treating them with humaneness and righteousness. He should govern by moral force.
2. Answers may differ. Suggested response: The passages reveal that in the hierarchical family, the young should respect and obey their parents and elders.
3. Answers may differ. Suggested response: The passages reveal that education in the classics and in the proper rituals will lead one to become a gentleman. Education is also a key to self-improvement.

The Master said, In old days a man kept a hold on his words, fearing the disgrace that would ensue should he himself fail to keep pace with them.

The Master said, A gentleman covets the reputation of being slow in word but prompt in deed.

6 The Master said, In old days men studied for the sake of self-improvement; nowadays men study in order to impress other people.

The Master said, A gentleman is ashamed to let his words outrun his deeds.

The Master said, He who will not worry about what is far off will soon find something worse than worry close at hand.

The Master said, To demand much from oneself and little from others is the way (for a ruler) to banish discontent.

Reader's Response *If you had lived in China during the time of Confucius, do you think you would have been drawn to Confucius and his ideas? Why or why not?*

THINKING ABOUT THE SELECTION

Interpreting

1. Why does Confucius believe that people "should be cautious in giving promises"?
2. What do you think Confucius means when he says that a ruler should govern people "by moral force"?
3. What do you think Confucius means when he suggests that "in the presence of a bad man" you should "turn your gaze within"?
4. What does Confucius mean when he says, "A gentleman is ashamed to let his words outrun his deeds"?
5. What evidence is there in these passages that Confucius had a strong belief in humility?

Applying

6. Which of Confucius's ideas do you think you could apply to your own life?
7. In two of the passages (page 220), Confucius expresses his belief that life was better during "old days." (a) What people do you know who share this belief with Confucius? (b) Why do you think people often long for "old days"?

ANALYZING LITERATURE

Understanding Confucianism

Confucianism is a philosophy that advocates authoritarian social and political systems and teaches that people should conduct themselves in a humble, respectful, and virtuous manner.

1. What do these passages from *The Analects* reveal about the Confucian beliefs concerning a ruler's treatment of his subjects?
2. What do the passages reveal about the Confucian beliefs concerning how young people should treat their parents?
3. What do the passages reveal about the Confucian attitude concerning education?
4. Imagine that the United States were to adopt Confucianism as a state code of behavior. (a) Name at least three aspects of life that would change. (b) Name three that would stay the same. Explain the reason for each of your choices.

THINKING AND WRITING

Comparing and Contrasting Philosophies

Write an essay in which you compare and contrast the ideas of Lao Tzu and Confucius. Begin by reviewing the Guides for Interpreting on Taoism and Confucianism and by rereading the selections from *The Analects* and the *Tao Te Ching*. Note as many similarities and differences between the two philosophies as you can. Arrange your notes according to corresponding points of contrast. Then write your essay, using passages from *The Analects* and the *Tao Te Ching* for support. When you revise, make sure that you have varied the length and structure of your sentences and have used transitions to link your ideas.

4. Answers may differ. Suggested response: (a) Our government would be an empirical system, not a democratic system; the family structure would change—it would be controlled only by the father; and we would have a more clearly defined social hierarchy. These aspects would change because Confucianism is basically antithetical to our society. (b) We would still have taxes; we would still have a bureaucratic government; and we would still have the same social institutions. These aspects would stay the same because certain institutions are common to most societies—only their structure is different.

THINKING AND WRITING

Writing Across the Curriculum
You may want to inform the history department that students are reading Lao Tzu. History teachers might then help students research and understand the Taoist and Confucian philosophies.

IDEAS AND INSIGHTS

THE THREE SCHOOLS OF THOUGHT

The more you learn about Chinese culture, history, and literature, the more you will realize that the traditional Chinese views of the world contrast sharply with traditional Western outlooks. One of the main reasons for this contrast is that the Chinese culture has been dominated by three schools of thought—Confucianism, Taoism, and Buddhism—that until fairly recently have been almost completely unknown to the Western world.

Confucianism

The official Chinese state doctrine for over two thousand years, Confucianism is more of a social philosophy than a religion. It is primarily concerned with the moral nature of social relationships. It emphasizes the need to respect and obey people in positions of authority, such as heads of households and government officials. At the same time, however, it stresses the need for people in positions of authority to behave in a humane and righteous way.

Taoism

Taoism, in contrast, is more concerned with the relation of humanity to the larger world of nature. In the classical Taoist view, human beings are perceived as being merely one of the many manifestations of nature, on an equal level with all other creatures. Taoism teaches that rather than seeking status, wealth, or power, people should withdraw from society and strive to live a simple life in harmony with nature.

Buddhism

The third school of thought, Buddhism, began to take hold in China in the second century A.D. during the period of disunity that followed the decline of the Han dynasty. Because Buddhism taught that life on earth is filled with suffering and is characterized by emptiness and illusion, it was especially appealing to the people who lived during this period in Chinese history. With its doctrine of reincarnation and its message that people could overcome their suffering through self-discipline, meditation, and moral conduct, Buddhism offered new hope to the people of this time.

Shaping Chinese Views

Through the centuries, elements of all three schools of thought have influenced the way in which Chinese people live. At the same time, however, the original teachings of all three schools have at times become distorted when put into practice. Confucianism, for example, often assumed a rigid form that emphasized the power of those in authority but neglected to stress their obligations to treat their subjects with compassion. Taoism, on the other hand, evolved into a folk religion concerned with finding elixers of immortality and magical charms to cure illnesses. Finally, the aspect of Buddhism that took hold among the common people was the notion that one's behavior in previous lives determines one's fate in the present life. This belief fostered a generally passive and fatalistic attitude toward life among the common people.

Poetry

Humanities Note

Fine art, *Frog on a Lotus Leaf* by Hsiang Sheng-mo. This painting is one of eight leaves of an album of Chinese paintings. It has the design and meticulous attention to detail that many such Chinese paintings of plants and animals have.

Nature was, and still is, a popular subject in Chinese art. The importance of every blade of grass and every creature great and small was a central belief in Chinese philosophy.

Like many Chinese paintings, aspects of the art are symbolic and represent certain tenets of Chinese philosophy. For example, the lotus, which is at "the head of cultivated flowers," is the most beloved and the most sacred of Chinese flora. Buddha sits on a throne of lotus flowers, and it was he who brought the lotus to blossom. The lotus is a symbol of purity and perfection because it grows out of the mud, yet it is clean and pure. In Taoism the lotus represents the summer, fruitfulness, and fertility. The lotus blossom and its leaves are perhaps the most commonly found floral symbols in Chinese art.

The frog is also a familiar and symbolic creature in Chinese art. Referred to as "the heavenly chicken," the frog is considered a delicacy to eat. It was also the subject of many superstitions. Thus this gentle and poetic painting has significance far beyond its apparent simplicity, both as fine art and as a philosophical symbol.

You might want to use the following questions to discuss the art:

1. In what ways is this painting poetic?
2. Why might nature be a popular subject in art and poetry?
3. Why do you think artists pictured one leaf or one tiny creature rather than more dramatic views? What does this choice tell you about their beliefs?

FROG ON LOTUS LEAF
Hsiang Sheng-mo

GUIDE FOR INTERPRETING

Songs 24 and 34

Background

The Book of Songs, also known as the *Book of Odes,* is an anthology of 305 ancient Chinese poems compiled around the sixth century B.C. According to tradition, Confucius chose the poems to be included. Though in reality it is doubtful that Confucius actually selected the poems, he did know them well and recommended their study. Because of his association with the book, it is considered to be one of the classic works of Confucian thought.

The poems in *The Book of Songs* are quite varied and come from many different regions of China. Most of them were originally folk songs describing the daily activities of the people, such as farming, fishing, or gathering herbs. Others focus on love or courtship. In addition, the book contains a group of poems written by courtiers in praise of kings, describing banquets or other court ceremonies.

All of the songs were originally set to music. Some, especially the songs of the court, may have been accompanied by musical instruments, such as bells and drums, as well as by dancing. Though the tunes are long lost, the songs' powerful rhythms are preserved in their four-beat lines.

Because of the book's honored status and its association with Confucius, traditional Chinese interpreters of the poems have stressed their political and social importance, sometimes going to great lengths to find hidden meanings in what appear to be simple love songs. In recent years, however, scholars have tried to strip away the layers of traditional interpretations that have become attached to the poems. They have begun to interpret the ancient songs more literally, appreciating them for their simplicity and directness and using them as a window into the lives of the early Chinese people.

Commentary

Refrain. A **refrain** is a word, phrase, line, or group of lines repeated at regular intervals in a poem or song. Refrains are common in folk songs throughout the world, from ancient China to contemporary America. They are especially important in songs that originated as part of an oral tradition, because they made the songs easier to remember. Since many of the verses in *The Book of Songs* were at first transmitted orally, it is not surprising that most of the verses contain a refrain. In addition to making the songs easier to remember, the refrains emphasize the most important ideas and help to establish a rhythm.

Writing

List some memorable refrains from recent popular songs. Then jot down the reasons why these refrains stick out in your mind.

Focus

Literary Focus Have students discuss the love poetry they have read. Remind students that song lyrics are a form of poetry and can be included in the discussion. What feelings are expressed in love poetry? Why is love poetry so powerful? Why has it lasted through the ages and spanned the globe? Then tell students that these selections from *The Book of Songs,* which is one of the *Five Classics* of Confucian philosophy, are love poems. (The other classics are *The Spring and Autumn Annals,* the *Book of Changes,* the *Book of Rites,* and the *Book of History.*)

Writing/Prior Knowledge Pair up the students in your class. Have them discuss the songs with which they are familiar and share ideas with one another before they begin writing.

ESL Teaching Strategy Ask ESL students to share with the class love poems from their first language. Have students read them in their native language and then either translate them or read a translation of the poems.

Master Teacher Note Remind students that according to tradition, Confucius selected these poems. Discuss how these poems do or do not support Confucius' philosophy.

Teaching Tenth-Grade Students To help tenth-grade students make a connection between poetry and music, ask students to set the poems from *The Book of Songs* to music. They may simply establish rhythm with percussion or create a melody appropriate to the meaning. Have students perform the songs for the class.

Objectives

To understand love poetry

Skills

1 To understand the use of refrain
2 To write a folk song

Support Material

Teaching Portfolio
Teacher Backup, p. 297
Usage and Mechanics Worksheet, p. 301
Analyzing Literature Worksheet, *Understanding Refrain,* p. 302
Critical Thinking and Reading, *Appreciating the Effect of Incremental Variation,* p. 303
Language Worksheet, *Appreciating Adjectives,* p. 304
Selection Test, pp. 305–306

from The Book of Songs

I Beg of You, Chung Tzu

translated by Arthur Waley

24

I beg of you, Chung Tzu
Do not climb into our homestead,
Do not break the willows we have planted.
Not that I mind about the willows,
5 But I am afraid of my father and mother.
Chung Tzu I dearly love;
But of what my father and mother say
Indeed I am afraid.

I beg of you, Chung Tzu,
10 Do not climb over our wall,
Do not break the mulberry trees we have planted.

Not that I mind about the mulberry trees,
But I am afraid of my brothers.
Chung Tzu I dearly love;
But of what my brothers say
15 Indeed I am afraid.

I beg of you, Chung Tzu,
Do not climb into our garden,
Do not break the hard wood we have planted.
Not that I mind about the hard wood,
20 But I am afraid of what people will say.
Chung Tzu I dearly love;
But of all that people will say
Indeed I am afraid.

Reader's Response *The speaker of Song 24 is obviously concerned about what others will think of her actions. How concerned do you think people should be about what others think of their actions?*

STREAMS AND HILLS UNDER FRESH SNOW (detail #1)
Southern Sung Dynasty
The Metropolitan Museum of Art, New York

1. Why is the horizontal scroll particularly appropriate for landscape painting?
2. What is poetic about this painting?
3. How do you feel when you look at this painting? What in this painting evokes these feelings? Explain.

Thick Grow the Rush Leaves

translated by Arthur Waley

34

Thick grow the rush leaves;
Their white dew turns to frost.
He whom I love
Must be somewhere along this stream.
5 I went up the river to look for him,
But the way was difficult and long.
I went down the stream to look for him,
And there in midwater
Sure enough, it's he!

10 Close grow the rush leaves,
Their white dew not yet dry.
He whom I love
Is at the water's side.

Upstream I sought him;
15 But the way was difficult and steep.
Downstream I sought him,
And away in midwater
There on a ledge, that's he!

Very fresh are the rush leaves;
20 The white dew still falls.
He whom I love
Is at the water's edge.
Upstream I followed him;
But the way was hard and long.
25 Downstream I followed him,
And away in midwater
There on the shoals is he!

THINKING ABOUT THE SELECTIONS

Interpreting

1. (a) In Song 24 what is the speaker's relationship with Chung Tzu? Support your answer. (b) What internal struggle is the speaker experiencing?
2. What are the primary emotions expressed by the speaker of Song 34?
3. (a) In which season is Song 34 set? (b) How do the season and the natural images relate to the speaker's emotions?

Applying

4. These songs were written over 2,500 years ago. Are the feelings expressed by the speakers of the two poems as relevant today as they were when the poems were written? Why or why not?

ANALYZING LITERATURE

Understanding the Use of Refrain

A **refrain** is a word, phrase, line, or group of lines repeated at regular intervals in a poem or song. Often, one or two words within a refrain are varied in successive stanzas. This is known as *incremental variation.*

1. Explain why Song 24 would serve as an excellent model of both refrain and incremental variation.
2. Explain how the use of refrain in Song 24 makes the song easy to remember.
3. How does the use of refrain in Song 24 contribute to the poem's rhythm?

THINKING AND WRITING

Writing a Folk Song

Just like the writers of *The Book of Songs*, contemporary folk singers take as their subjects everyday activities and love, courtship, and marriage. Write a folk song of your own in which you use both refrains and incremental variations. Start by thinking of a subject. Then think of some images related to your subject. Write one stanza, then vary the lines slightly in two or more subsequent stanzas.

(continued from bottom of page)
ANSWERS TO ANALYZING LITERATURE

1. Answers may differ. Suggested response: Song 24 is an example of refrain because certain words, such as "the rush leaves," "Their white dew," and "He whom I love" are repeated throughout. It is an example of incremental variation because certain lines are repeated with minor variations, such as "Thick grow the rush leaves," "Close grow the rush leaves," and "Very fresh are the rush leaves."
2. Answers may differ. Suggested response: Song 24 is easy to remember because each stanza is basically the same with the exception of a few minor variations.
3. Answers may differ. Suggested response: A rhythm is established because the lines are either the same or very similar in terms of structure and the number of syllables.

THINKING AND WRITING

Publishing Student Writing Have students set their original poems to music and let them perform their songs for the class. Afterward compile students' work in a class song book, which students can decorate and name. Include the notes to the music. Leave the book out for others to read and enjoy.

Challenge Have students read selections from or portions of one or several of the other *Five Classics.* Then have students read a sampling of the book to the class, report on its contents, and state the reasons that the book is considered a classic of Confucianism.

Closure and Extension

ANSWERS TO THINKING ABOUT THE SELECTION

1. Answers may differ. Suggested responses: (a) They appear to be unmarried lovers. Since Chung Tzu must surmount various obstacles in order to see her, it can be assumed they can meet only in secret. (b) The speaker seems to be struggling with her love for Chung Tzu and her respect for and obedience to her family.
2. Answers may differ. Suggested response : The primary emotions are love and devotion to the one she loves as well as love and respect for her family.
3. Answers may differ. Suggested responses: (a) The season in which this poem is set is spring. (b) The speaker's feelings and longing for her loved one remain strong and constant throughout the beginning and end of spring. In addition spring is often associated with love.
4. Answers may differ. Suggested response : The feelings of love and longing for loved ones that are expressed in these poems are timeless and universal.

T'AO CH'IEN

Focus

More About the Author T'ao Ch'ien is generally known as the father of eremetic poetry, or the poetry of reclusion. What gives T'ao Ch'ien's poetry its sense of freshness and honesty is the manner in which he retired from public life. China scholar Burton Watson has written that since his motives were free of the faddism and hypocrisy that prompted many to retire only for personal gain, T'ao Ch'ien's reclusion "belonged to the highest type—that of the mind and spirit."

Pronunciation Note In the Pin Yin system used in Mainland China, T'ao Ch'ien is spelled Tao Chien.

Critical Evaluation Liu Wu Chi, a scholar of Chinese literature, said of T'ao Ch'ien: "Of all the major Chinese poets, T'ao Ch'ien is perhaps the easiest one for Western readers to appreciate. His poems are relatively free of literary allusions, and do not demand a knowledge of Chinese history and culture to be appreciated. Anyone who enjoys the warm humanity of Robert Frost's poetry will enjoy T'ao Ch'ien's."

Master Teacher Note Choose a favorite poem from the Romantic period to read to the class. You might consider reading one of Heinrich Heine's poems on page 886. Discuss the similarities and differences between the ideas expressed by the Romantic poets and those expressed by T'ao Ch'ien.

A.D. 365–427

An ancient Chinese curse is "May you live in an interesting time." T'ao Ch'ien certainly did. One of the finest ancient Chinese poets, T'ao Ch'ien knew the uncertainty and tumult of a China divided and partially under foreign rule. Yet his poetry transcends the unrest of his day, expressing his vision of how to live tranquilly in a chaotic world.

T'ao Ch'ien, also known as T'ao Yuan-ming (dɔu′ yüän′ miŋ′), was born into a family of government officials who, though of high standing, were impoverished and often did not have enough to eat. After reaching adulthood, T'ao Ch'ien himself began a career in government service in order to support his wife and children. He found it difficult, however, to behave in the subservient manner required of lower-ranking officials. When he was about thirty-five, he refused to obey a request to call on a visiting inspector, remarking, "I will not bow before a scoundrel for five pecks of rice." Later that day he resigned from office and retired to a farm on the outskirts of a village, where he lived for the rest of his life as something of a recluse, though he did have family and friends around him.

During his later years, T'ao Ch'ien devoted most of his energy to writing poetry. Inspired by the serenity of his life in the countryside, T'ao Ch'ien established himself as the foremost member of the "Field and Garden" school of poetry—a school of nature poets who delighted in the simple beauty of the landscapes surrounding farms and villages, rather than in the grandeur of remote mountain peaks and crashing waterfalls. In addition to exhibiting his appreciation for nature, T'ao Ch'ien's poetry reveals his passion for his favorite activities—farming, spending time with his family, drinking wine, writing poetry, playing the zither, and having conversations with his friends.

T'ao Ch'ien's poems reflect the influence of both Confucianism and Taoism. The impact of Confucian thought is evident in T'ao Ch'ien's emphasis on duty and devotion to family, while the influence of Taoism is apparent in his advocacy of seclusion and quiet reflection and in his deep appreciation for nature.

In contrast to the ornate style of many of his contemporaries, T'ao Ch'ien's language is simple, direct, and unpretentious. Because of his directness and his avoidance of literary and historical allusions, his works tend to be extremely accessible, both in Chinese and in translation. Yet, at the same time, his poems are filled with beautiful images and timeless insights. Due to their beauty, accessibility, and insightfulness, T'ao Ch'ien's poems have been enjoyed and appreciated by countless generations of readers and remain among the finest Chinese poems ever written.

Objectives

Thematic

To understand time, impermanence, and nostalgia

Skills

1 To understand *shih* poetry
2 To write a poem

Support Material

Teaching Portfolio

Teacher Backup, p. 307
Usage and Mechanics Worksheet, p. 311
Analyzing Literature Worksheet, *Understanding* Shih *Poetry*, p. 312
Critical Thinking and Reading Worksheet, *Inferring the Author's Attitude from Details*, p. 313
Language Worksheet, *Finding the Meanings of Words Naming Occupations*, p. 314
Selection Test, pp. 315–316

GUIDE FOR INTERPRETING

Poem on Returning to Dwell in the Country; I Built My House Near Where Others Dwell

Literary Forms

Shih Poetry. The *shih* was the dominant Chinese poetic form from the second through the twelfth centuries A.D. The main formal characteristics of *shih* poetry are the following: (1) There are an even number of lines; (2) each line has the same number of words, in most cases five or seven; and (3) rhymes occur at the ends of the even-numbered lines. In addition, *shih* poems often involve the use of parallelism, or couplets that are similar in structure or meaning. The use of this technique contributes to a poem's rhythm and adds emphasis to its main ideas.

Because *shih* poetry evolved over the centuries, it is often divided into two separate classifications: "old style" *shih* poetry and "new style" *shih* poetry. The "old style" *shih* form was extremely flexible, since the poems could be any length, as long as they consisted of an even number of lines of the same length. In contrast, the "new style" *shih* form was fairly rigid, with strict rules governing both length and form. One of those rules was that the two middle couplets in an eight-line *shih* poem had to be parallel in both structure and meaning.

To fully appreciate the *shih* form, you need a basic understanding of the classical Chinese language. Unlike any of the European languages, classical Chinese is not written with a phonetic alphabet, but with characters, or ideograms. For example, the character 木 means "tree" or "wood," and the character for "cart" is 車, representing a bird's-eye view of a two-wheeled cart. Although most of the characters are somewhat more complex than these, the vast majority of classical Chinese words were expressed with one written character, and each character was pronounced with one syllable. As a result, the lines within a *shih* poem would not only consist of the same number of words, but they would also consist of the same number of characters and syllables.

The poems you are about to read are examples of old-style *shih* poetry. However, they are translations of the original Chinese. While most of the features of *shih* poetry are lost in translation, the parallel couplets are often preserved. As you read the following "old style" *shih* poems by T'ao Ch'ien, look for T'ao Ch'ien 's use of parallelism.

Writing

The following poem was inspired by T'ao Ch'ien's decision to leave his government post and move to the countryside. Write a journal entry in which you discuss the advantages and disadvantages of country life.

Literary Focus *Shih* is one of many Chinese poetic forms developed over China's two thousand year literary tradition. Have students discuss the similarities and differences between this form and the forms of Western poetry with which they may be familiar.

Writing/Prior Knowledge Before writing, have students break into small groups and discuss the advantages and disadvantages of country and city life.

ESL Teaching Strategy Ask students to point out cultural references in the poems that distinguish them as Chinese. Then have them suggest substitute words that would be appropriate parallels in their own culture.

Teaching Tenth-Grade Students Have tenth-grade students find lines in T'ao Ch'ien's poetry that illustrate his preference for life's simple pleasures. Discuss whether such simple pleasures are available today. Students should explain why they do or do not think so.

Presentation

Motivation/Prior Knowledge Tell students that they will be reading some of the earliest poems of what became an important mainstream tradition in Chinese poetry—the poetry of the recluse. T'ao chose to reject the society in which most of his peers lived and worked. While few of T'ao's intellectual and literary heirs actually became recluses as T'ao did, many dreamed of and found solace in thinking and writing about the life of the rustic. Have students imagine what their lives would be like if they were to abandon their current life styles and live the life of a recluse.

Purpose-Setting Question What meaning of life does T'ao Ch'ien convey to his readers?

Universal Themes The sense of time, impermanence, and nostalgia that permeates much of T'ao's poetry is a common theme in Western literature as well. You might consider having students also read Pierre de Ronsard's "When You Are Old," page 693; Jorge Luis Borges's "The Garden of Forking Paths," page 1226; Czeslaw Milosz's "A Song on the End of the World," page 1308; and Yevgeny Yevtushenko's "Visit," page 1334.

Humanities Note

Fine art, *Mountain Hermitage* by Wang Meng. During the Yuan dynasty (1260–1368) when Mongol warriors ruled, China was dominated by four "Great Masters" of landscape painting. Among them was Wang Meng, a founder of a new school of "literary" art that directly related poetry and painting.

Wang Meng led a tormented life; he died a political prisoner in a dungeon. His style and influence as a painter, however, were long lasting and of great importance. As a scholar-painter, Wang became an ideal that later generations of artists tried to match.

Wang Meng and the other Great Masters painted using a dry brush and ink technique. Their works were on paper, rather than on the traditional silk.

MOUNTAIN
HERMITAGE
Wang Mer

You might want to use the following questions to discuss the art:
1. For what might the small, hidden hermitage be a symbol?
2. How does this symbol relate to T'ao Ch'ien's beliefs?
3. How does this painting bring together painting with poetry?

Poem on Returning to Dwell in the Country

T'ao Ch'ien

translated by William Acker

Long I have loved to stroll among the hills and
  marshes,
And take my pleasure roaming the woods and
  fields.
Now I hold hands with a train of nieces and
  nephews,
Parting the hazel growth we tread the untilled
  wastes—
Wandering to and fro amidst the hills and mounds
Everywhere around us we see dwellings of ancient
  men.
Here are vestiges[1] of their wells and hearthstones,
There the rotted stumps of bamboo and mulberry
  groves.
I stop and ask a fagot-gatherer:[2]
"These men—what has become of them?"
The fagot-gatherer turns to me and says:
"Once they were dead that was the end of them."
In the same world men lead different lives;
Some at the court, some in the marketplace.
Indeed I know these are no empty words:
The life of man is like a shadow-play
Which must in the end return to nothingness.

---

1. **vestiges** (ves′ tij əz) *n.*: Traces of something that once existed but has passed away or disappeared.
2. **fagot-gatherer:** A person who gathers bundles of sticks, twigs, or branches to be used as fuel.

THINKING ABOUT THE SELECTION

Interpreting

1. What does this poem suggest about T'ao Ch'ien's attitude toward nature?
2. What does the poem suggest about T'ao Ch'ien's attitude toward his family?
3. How does T'ao's observation that "in the same world men lead different lives" relate to the rest of the poem?
4. (a) What is the meaning of T'ao's observation that "the life of man is like a shadow-play"? (b) What details in the poem support this observation?
5. What does this poem suggest about T'ao's attitude toward death?

Applying

6. Explain why you do or do not agree with the views that T'ao Ch'ien expresses in this poem.

ANALYZING LITERATURE

Understanding Shih Poetry

T'ao Ch'ien was one of the last masters of "old style" poetry. Unlike the "new style" poems, which had to be either four or eight lines long, the "old style" poems could be any length, as long as they consisted of an even number of lines of the same length.

1. "Poem on Returning to Dwell in the Country" is an example of "old style" *shih* poetry. However, its form has been dramatically altered in translation. Which, if any, features of the "old style" *shih* are apparent in this translation of the poem?
2. What does the fact that the poem's form was altered reveal about the translator's priorities?
3. Translating poetry is a very difficult task. Imagine that you were going to translate your favorite English poem into another language. What would be your priorities; in other words, what would you hope to maintain from the original poem—its rhythm, its rhyme, the suggested meanings of words, the images, the figures of speech, the look of the poem on the page? Think about this question for a while. Then list your priorities in order of preference. Compare your priorities with those of your classmates. On which items do you agree? On which do you disagree?

(continued from bottom of page)

their religious views and philosophies of life, some students will agree with T'ao's views on time, nature, life, and death; others will disagree.

ANSWERS TO ANALYZING LITERATURE

1. There are no apparent features of the "old style" *shih* in this translation.
2. The translator considered meaning more important than form and structure.
3. Answers may differ. If the poem's meaning is lost without the structure, then structure will be first; if meaning is the most important, then that will come first.

1 Enrichment Tell students that returning to the country is a common theme in Chinese poetry. It meant that the poet had either retired from official life, had resigned an official post in protest to current policy, or had rejected the world and decided to live the life of a recluse.

2 Enrichment Explain to students that T'ao Ch'ien's life differed from those of other recluses in that he brought his family into the country with him. He left society behind but did not live alone.

3 Enrichment Tell students that these lines describe the scene of ancient ruins that the wanderers have stumbled across on their journey. T'ao suggests that they have found the remains of a once great civilization, laid to waste by the passage of time.

4 Enrichment Tell students that the image of the fagot gatherer, or wood gatherer, suggests a lone, forest-dwelling recluse who has rejected the world and is, therefore, wise enough to tell the wanderers what became of the men of old.

5 Discussion Point out to students that these lines echo Lao Tzu's belief in humans' subordination to the eternity of nature and his denial of an afterlife. Ask students to discuss this vision of life and how it compares to that of other philosophical systems.

Closure and Extension

ANSWERS TO THINKING ABOUT THE SELECTION

1. Answers may differ. Suggested response: This poem suggests that, in contrast to humans' impermanence, nature is eternal.
2. Answers may differ. Suggested response: This poem suggests that T'ao Ch'ien believes the family is an important part of the natural life, even of the life of a recluse.
3. Answers may differ. Suggested response: This line invites a comparison between the courtly life led by those of the ancient civilization they had stumbled across and the life led by rustics, such as T'ao and the wood gatherer.
4. Answers may differ. Suggested responses: (a) This line suggests that against the eternity of the universe, humankind is insignificant. (b) At the site of the ancient, dead civilization, the earth still stands, virtually unchanged.
5. The poem suggests that T'ao believes that there is no afterlife and that death, like life, must be accepted as natural.
6. Answers may differ. Depending on

I Built My House Near Where Others Dwell

T'ao Ch'ien

translated by William Acker

I built my house near where others dwell,
And yet there is no clamor of carriages and horses.
You ask of me "How can this be so?"
"When the heart is far the place of itself is distant."
5 I pluck chrysanthemums under the eastern hedge,
And gaze afar towards the southern mountains.
The mountain air is fine at evening of the day
And flying birds return together homewards.
Within these things there is a hint of Truth,
10 But when I start to tell it, I cannot find the words.

Reader's Response *Like the poet, have you too been able to isolate yourself from the clamor of the world? Explain.*

THINKING ABOUT THE SELECTION

Interpreting

1. (a) Why is it paradoxical, or apparently self-contradictory, that though the speaker lives near other people he does not hear the "clamor of carriages and horses"? (b) How does he explain this paradox?
2. If the speaker wanted to be away from the "clamor of carriages and horses" why do you think he built his house near where others dwell?
3. What inference can you make about T'ao's attitude toward nature from lines 5–8?
4. What evidence is there in the poem that T'ao Ch'ien valued solitude?
5. What is the meaning of the final two lines?

Applying

6. Considering the ideas he expresses in this poem, how do you think T'ao Ch'ien would have responded to living in one of today's large, industrial cities? Why?

THINKING AND WRITING

Writing a Poem

What brings you peace and tranquility? Where would you choose to build your house? Write a ten-line poem providing your answer to these questions. Start, as T'ao Ch'ien does, with the words "I built my house." After you have finished, read your poem aloud to see how it sounds. Then prepare a final draft and read it to your classmates.

ers may read and enjoy it.

LANDSCAPE
Lan Yin

Humanities Note

Fine art, *Landscape* by Lan Yin. Lan Yin (1585–c. 1664) lived during the Ming dynasty, when Chinese landscape painting was required to be traditional in style by a conservative and restrictive government. In so doing, Lan Yin revived earlier styles of painting and founded his own school in Hangchou. As seen in this painting, his technique was very skillful, and he used strong, vibrant colors. Many of his works were done with a brush and India ink on gold-speckled paper.

This painting contains a number of characteristic elements of Lan Yin's style. Among them are the diagonally divided picture and his choice of subjects. His subjects are typically figures, landscapes, birds, flowers, rocks, mountains, and bamboo trees.

In addition many of his paintings include calligraphy, or beautiful writing. Including calligraphy in the corner of his painting was intentional. In fact his pieces included calligraphy as much for its meaning as for its design and decorative appeal. In this picture, for example, the calligraphy balances the landscape by filling in the opposite corner of the painting.

Chinese art and calligraphy contain some of the most finely drawn, rhythmic, and delicate lines in all art. Both brushwork and pen drawing are extraordinarily clear and fine. The well-trained Chinese artist is able to control the smallest line detail.

You might want to use the following questions to discuss the art:

1. What does the small size of the man in the picture suggest about the relative importance of people to the world around them?
2. Why do you think most poetry and painting were concerned with country landscapes, rather than with urban or court life?
3. Why do you suppose it was in the interest of the government to ban new styles of art?

WANG WEI

Focus

More About the Author Wang Wei is a classic example of the scholar-official of China's middle ages. In one person he combined the best aspects of Taoist, Confucian, and Buddhist philosophies. As a Confucian scholar, Wang held various government posts over the course of his official career. As a practicing Buddhist, he spent his leisure time composing Taoist- and Buddhist-inspired poems and paintings at his mountain estate near the capital.

Critical Evaluation Wang Wei's poetry is distinguished by its Buddhist sense of life and quiet meditation. According to Burton Watson, a noted scholar of Chinese literature, Wang "gives the impression of viewing the landscape with perfect Buddhist passivity, not seeking to see anything at all, but merely allowing whatever may lie within the scope of vision to register upon his mind."

Master Teacher Note Wang Wei, like some other Chinese poets, lived mostly in seclusion. Discuss why some poets may have lived as recluses and how that seems to have affected their poetry. Ask students to identify images in Wang Wei's poems that suggest his life style.

706?–761?

An accomplished painter as well as a poet, Wang Wei (wän wā) is known for his beautiful and vivid landscape poems and paintings. In fact, both his poetry and his paintings are so striking that it has been said that in Wang Wei's "poetry there are paintings, and in his paintings there is poetry."

Wang Wei established himself early as a talented scholar. By his early teens, he was already writing mature poetry, and he passed the highest Chinese scholarly examination, the *chih-shih*, at the age of twenty-one. As a young adult, he served in various governmental positions and, like many Chinese officials from the earliest times to the present, spent some time in exile when opposing factions were in power. A reclusive man by nature, he eventually chose to withdraw from government service to live in seclusion in the mountains and devote his energy to writing poetry.

While living in the mountains, he studied the Buddhist scriptures with his friend P'ei Ti and became a devout Buddhist. Wang Wei's conversion to Buddhism had a tremendous impact on his later poetry. These poems exhibit the calmness and restraint that are characteristic of Buddhism. They are filled with Buddhist images, such as moonlight, gently flowing water, quiet pine forests, and serene bamboo groves.

A master of four-line "new style" *shih* poetry, Wang Wei had a profound influence on a number of other poets of his day. In fact, Wang was considered the leader of a poetic school, which included Meng Hao-jan (muŋ' hō' jan')(689–740) and Chu Kuang-hsi (choo' koōŋ' shē') (706–760). The members of Wang Wei's school were inspired by Wang's deceptively simple language, his evocative descriptions, and his meditative tone—the same qualities that have established Wang Wei as one of the greatest poets in the history of Chinese literature.

Objectives

Thematic
To understand humanity's relationship with nature

Skills
To understand Buddhism

Support Material

Teaching Portfolio
Teacher Backup, p. 317
Usage and Mechanics Worksheet, p. 321
Analyzing Literature Worksheet, *Understanding Buddhism*, p. 322
Critical Thinking and Reading Worksheet, *Analyzing the Effect of*

Imagery, p. 323
Language Worksheet, *Using Concrete Words*, p. 324
Selection Test, pp. 325–326

GUIDE FOR INTERPRETING

To the Assistant Prefect Chang; On an Autumn Evening in the Mountains; The Hill

Commentary

Buddhism. Buddhism teaches that all life is sorrow and that sorrow is caused by desires. The way to rid one's life of sorrow is to eliminate desire. This can be accomplished through self-discipline, restraint, moral conduct, and meditation.

The Buddhist religion came to China from India during the first century A.D. It is based on the teachings of Siddhartha Gautama (sid där′ tə gout′ ə mə), called the Buddha, a religious title meaning "The Enlightened One" or "The Awakened One"). Siddhartha lived during the fifth century B.C. at approximately the same time as Confucius.

The basic message of Buddhism was elaborated in different ways to form many diverse schools. These range from a devotional salvationist religion that worshiped Buddha and other figures as deities, to an elaborate scholastic form of Buddhism devoted to abstract speculation about reality. The forms of Buddhism that took hold in China were greatly influenced by the existing Chinese beliefs and often ended up being dramatically different from the original Indian forms.

One of the main schools to emerge in China was Ch'an Buddhism (comparable to Zen Buddhism in Japan), which taught that one could attain enlightenment through meditation. Many Chinese of the T'ang dynasty, including Wang Wei, were devotees of this school. The Ch'an Buddhism that prevailed in China during the eighth century combined many ancient Taoist ideas, such as the emphasis on simplicity and solitude, with the Buddhist emphasis on stilling one's desires and striving to find true enlightenment (which might be defined as peace of mind and a calm acceptance of reality).

The impact of Ch'an Buddhism on Chinese poetry is apparent in the frequent use of Buddhist imagery, symbols, and language. Common Ch'an Buddhist images include the full moon, which symbolizes a clean mirror that reflects without passing judgment, and ripples or reflections in water, which symbolize that material substances are constantly changing and that physical appearances are unreal. Examples of Buddhist language include the word *kong,* or "emptiness," which signifies among other things the unreality and vanity of physical perceptions and worldly concerns, and *jing,* or "quietude."

Writing

Quietude, or calmness, is a central notion in Buddhist thought. How important do you think it is to find quietude in life? Freewrite, exploring your answer.

Literary Focus Scholars actively debate the use of nature imagery in the works of the Chinese landscape poets like Wang Wei. Some say the images are used to convey human emotion; others say they reflect a world untouched by human emotion. Have students discuss the two sides of this debate, with reference both to Wang Wei and to other Western poets with whom they are familiar. How does the nature imagery fit in with the tenets of Buddhism?

Writing/Prior Knowledge If space and time allow, have students go to remote, quiet areas of the school or school grounds. Have them reflect on the times they have enjoyed quiet solitude. What did they ponder? What benefits came from spending time calmly and quietly?

ESL Teaching Strategy If you have Chinese students in class, ask them to read aloud in Chinese several of Wang Wei's poems. Let them share with the class the problems in translating poetry from one language to another.

Teaching Tenth-Grade Students Wang Wei writes one poem to Chang, the assistant prefect. Discuss with tenth-grade students why Wang addresses these comments to Chang, the official who asks "what laws rule 'failure' or 'success.'"

AUTUMN HILL AFTER WANG MENG
Ch'ing Dynasty

To the Assistant Prefect[1] Chang

Wang Wei

translated by Cyril Birch

In the evening years given to quietude,
The world's worries no concern of mine,
For my own needs making no other plan
Than to unlearn, return to long-loved woods:
5 I loosen my robe before the breeze from pines,
My lute[2] celebrates moonlight on mountain pass.
You ask what laws rule "failure" or "success"—
Songs of fishermen float to the still shore.

---

1. **Assistant Prefect:** A high-ranking government official.
2. **lute:** Actually, Wang Wei is referring to a ch'in (chin), a Chinese stringed instrument that is placed on the lap or a low table and plucked with both hands.

The Hill

Wang Wei

translated by Arthur Christy

No one can be seen on this silent hill,
But one may hear distant voices.
The rays of the sun filter through the deep foliage
And fall refreshingly on the mosses.

Reader's Response *What is your response to the natural scenes that Wang Wei describes in his poetry? Do you share Wang Wei's love of nature? Why or why not?*

On an Autumn Evening in the Mountains

Wang Wei

translated by Arthur Christy

How clear are the mountains after the new rain!
The dusk of the Autumn evening is pouring in,
As moonbeams filter through the pine trees.
Cool spring-water flows over white stones.
A lone washing-girl returns homeward by the bamboo grove.
The boatman sails his barge through the lotus[1] patch.
Although Spring is long gone
Why cannot I linger over this pleasant view?

_____

1. **lotus** (lōt′ əs) *n.*: A tropical water lily native to Asia and Africa.

RIVER AND MOUNTAINS IN AUTUMN COLOR
Zhao Boju
Palace Museum, Beijing

THINKING ABOUT THE SELECTIONS

Interpreting

1. (a) What does the speaker of "To the Assistant Prefect Chang" mean when he says that he plans to "unlearn"? (b) What is the significance of his loosening his robe?
2. In "To the Assistant Prefect Chang," what do you think is the speaker's definition of failure and success? Support your answer with details from the poem.
3. (a) How would you describe the mood of "The Hill"? (b) What emotions does the poem evoke?
4. In "The Hill," how does Wang Wei capture both the immensity of the natural world and the minute details that make up the natural world?
5. How do the final two lines of "On an Autumn Evening in the Mountains" tie the rest of the poem together?
6. After reading these poems, explain whether you agree with the statement that "there is painting in [Wang Wei's] poetry."

Applying

7. (a) How do you respond to the comment of the speaker of "To the Assistant Prefect Chang" that he is not concerned with the "world's worries"? (b) Explain whether you think that this attitude would be considered acceptable if the speaker were living in our society. (c) Do you consider the attitude to be acceptable? Why or why not?

ANALYZING LITERATURE

Understanding Buddhism

Wang Wei's conversion to Ch'an Buddhism had a tremendous impact on his poetry.
1. In what ways does each of these poems reflect the Ch'an Buddhist emphasis on calmness and restraint?
2. Find at least two Buddhist images and two examples of Buddhist language in these poems.

(continued from bottom of page)

beauty of the spring landscape. The joy of spring and the sadness of age suggested in the rest of the poem are brought together for emotional effect.
6. Answers may differ. Suggested response: The imagery of Wang's poetry is so fresh and vivid that one can almost see the scene he was writing about.
7. Answers may differ. (a) Some students may suggest that it is difficult to abandon worries. Others may respond that it is good advice to follow. (b) Some students might respond that in today's society, there are too many worries, and it is next to impossible to abandon them. (c) Many students may suggest that although the attitude is acceptable, it is an unattainable goal.

ANSWERS TO ANALYZING LITERATURE

1. Answers may differ. Suggested response: The first poem suggests that a life devoted to quietude will enable one to unlearn the ways of the world; the second poem emphasizes the silence of the landscape; the third one suggests a quiet, rustic life style.
2. Answers may differ. Suggested response: The moon is a symbol of enlightenment; the lotus flower is a symbol of the Buddha. Two Buddhist terms and concepts are "unlearn" and "emptiness."

Humanities Note

Fine art, *River and Mountains in Autumn Color* by Zhao Boju. When the Sung Dynasty established its court at Hangchou in 1138, it became a center for artists who relished its civilized environment and natural beauty. Among the artists working at the court was Zhao Boju (1120–1182), who was a descendant of the first Sung emperor. Zhao Boju typically used the blue-green colors of the Tang dynasty, rather than the monochrome browns of the Sung dynasty. In addition to his landscapes, Zhao Boju painted palace pictures showing life in the Chinese court.

Ask students what this painting suggests is beyond the mountains.

Closure and Extension

ANSWERS TO THINKING ABOUT THE SELECTION

1. Answers may differ. Suggested responses: (a) The speaker may mean that he wants to free himself of all the desires and concepts he has accumulated over the years. (b) The act might symbolize an attitude of openness to the landscape around him.
2. Answers may differ. Suggested response: "Failure or success" refers to the worries of the world—the world of humanity's desires—referred to in the second line of the poem.
3. Answers may differ. Suggested responses: (a) The mood is one of solitude and purity in the natural landscape. (b) The poem evokes a sense of sadness offset by the joy the poet finds in viewing the sunlight shining on the moss.
4. Answers may differ. Suggested response: He captures them by juxtaposing opposites. The first two lines suggest vastness; the second two lines describe the scene immediately next to the poet.
5. Answers may differ. Suggested response: The lines contrast the poet's sense of impermanance with the

LI PO

Focus

More About the Author Li Po is considered the incurable romantic of Chinese poetry and a rebel against all artificial conventions. In response to an imperial summons, Li once wrote:

A hundred poems Li Bo wrote after
  a cask of wine
He was asleep in a tavern in
  Ch'ang An
When the Emperor called; he
  would not board the imperial
  barge
But said, "Your humble servant is
  a god of wine."

Pronunciation Note Li Po is spelled Li Bo in the Pin Yin romanization system. His name is also pronounced lē bō or lē bī.

Critical Evaluation According to China scholar Burton Watson, Li Po introduced few innovations either of style or of theme into Chinese poetry. However, "in treating the traditional themes, Li Po often introduces a freshness of outlook and imagery, a narrative skill, and beauty of diction that make his poem the most memorable and satisfying statement on the subject, replacing in popularity the earlier models upon which he drew."

701–762

Li Po (lē' pō') and Tu Fu (tōō' fōō'), two men with very different temperaments, are usually mentioned in one breath as the two supreme masters of Chinese poetry. Both lived in the middle of the T'ang dynasty (618–907), during the Golden Age of Chinese poetry. Though they came from different parts of the country and led very different lives, they became close friends. However, they had contrasting poetic styles. While Tu Fu is recognized for his finely crafted, realistic, socially conscious poems, Li Po is known for his free-spirited, graceful, and lyrical style.

Though the details of Li Po's early life are not clear, he probably grew up in southwestern China, in the region that is now Szechuan province. During his mid-twenties, he moved to eastern China, and throughout the remainder of his life he continued moving from place to place, at first trying to find an outlet for his talents, and later in an imposed exile. For a short time, he held an official literary position in the capital city of Changan, where he came to know Tu Fu. After political conditions made it impossible for him to stay in Changan, he lived in various places in the south, the southwest, and along the Yangtze River.

Li Po was heavily influenced by Taoist thought, especially the magical variant of Taoism known as Neo-Taoism. Neo-Taoists believed in the existence of *hsien,* or "immortals" or "transients"—men of great age, with long white hair and flowing robes, who lived in the mountains nourished only by the wind and dew, and who possessed supernatural powers. Li Po admired the Neo-Taoist thinkers who aspired to become *hsien* by freeing themselves of the desire for possessions and power and by sleeping under the stars and drinking from clear mountain streams. In many of his poems, he speaks of mountains, rivers, and stars, and of the reflection of the moon in the water. In addition, his poetry frequently conveys his love for freedom and his sense of harmony with nature.

His life, however, was by no means austere. Far from living a hermit's existence in the mountains, he is known for his love of wine, women, and song. Many legends have been handed down about his drinking bouts and his intrigues with palace ladies. A popular story, almost certainly untrue, says that he died by drowning when, after he had been drinking, he reached out to grasp the reflection of the moon in a lake.

Li Po's unruly life style is evident in the playful quality of much of his poetry. This quality, along with his vivid imagery and the timeless insights that many of his poems express, has earned his poems a secure place among the finest literary works that China has produced.

Objectives

Thematic
1 To understand the fragility of humankind's life on Earth
2 To understand the loneliness of being separated from a loved one

Skills
1 To recognize a persona
2 To infer tone
3 To write a response

Support Material

Teaching Portfolio
Teacher Backup, p. 327
Usage and Mechanics Worksheet, p. 331
Analyzing Literature Worksheet, *Recognizing a Persona,* p. 332
Critical Thinking and Reading Worksheet, *Recognizing Tone,* p. 333

GUIDE FOR INTERPRETING

Li Po's Poetry

Commentary

Persona. The **persona** is the character assumed by the speaker of a poem or the narrator of a novel or short story. The word *persona* comes from the Latin word for a mask worn in a play. Just as we make the distinction between an actor and the role that he or she plays, we must distinguish between a writer and the character, or persona, whom the writer has created to narrate a work of literature.

In most Chinese poetry, we assume (rightly or wrongly) that the words spoken in the poem accurately represent the personal thoughts of the poet. In other words we assume that the persona and the poet are identical. For example, in T'ao Ch'ien's poems, when the speaker talks of building his house near where others dwell, plucking chrysanthemums beneath the eastern hedge, or strolling with his nieces and nephews, we assume that T'ao Ch'ien is in fact describing his own actions. In this case and in the case of most other *shih* poetry, our assumptions would be correct, because *shih* poems are usually expressions of the poet's feelings, observations, or recollections.

Sometimes, however, the persona is clearly different from the poet. This is especially common in Chinese ballads, songlike poems that tell a story. In Li Po's ballad "The River-Merchant's Wife: A Letter," for example, the speaker is a young woman awaiting the return of her husband, who has gone on a long and dangerous journey up the Yangtze River. Li Po has put on the "mask" of a river-merchant's wife to narrate this tender letter.

When you read literature, ask yourself three questions about persona: Who is the speaker? What is the speaker like? What role is the speaker playing?

Writing

Imagine being separated from someone you love for an extended period of time without being able to contact him or her. Write a journal entry in which you discuss how you feel you would respond to this situation. Then write another entry in which you discuss the ways in which modern methods of communication have made it easier for people to cope with being separated from their loved ones.

Literary Focus Many students may be familiar with the television show *The Wonder Years*. Discuss with students the effect of using the persona of an adult looking back on his childhood years.

You might also have students select a book, a movie, or a television show and discuss its persona. How would the work change if you altered the persona? Would the work be better or worse? Why or why not?

Writing/Prior Knowledge Encourage students to write their journal entry in any form they choose. Some students may wish to compose poetry, while others may choose to write a brief story or the lyrics to a song.

ESL Teaching Strategy Help ESL students understand the fine-tuned word meanings in Li Po's poetry. For example, how does one "stir" a fan? How does wind "trickle"? How does one "grow thin"? How can the moon "lift"? You might pair your ESL students with a native-speaking student. The partner should guide the ESL student through the selection and help him or her better understand Li Po's diction and imagery.

Master Teacher Note Discuss with students how Li Po's theme in "The River Merchant's Wife: A Letter" is echoed in "The Moon at the Fortified Pass." Ask students to explain how altering the persona affects the meaning of each poem.

Teaching Tenth-Grade Students Ask tenth-grade students to bring a favorite ballad to share with the class. The ballads may be in the form of either poetry or the lyrics to a song. Have students compare and contrast these ballads with Li Po's ballad "The River Merchant's Wife: A Letter."

Language Worksheet, *Tracing the Origins of Words*, p. 334
Selection Test, pp. 335–336
Art Transparency 4
Chinese Riders with Swords and Spears, anonymous

The River-Merchant's Wife: A Letter

Li Po

translated by Ezra Pound

While my hair was still cut straight across my
   forehead
I played about the front gate, pulling flowers.
You came by on bamboo stilts, playing horse,
You walked about my seat, playing with blue
   plums.
5 And we went on living in the village of Chōkan:[1]
Two small people, without dislike or suspicion.

At fourteen I married My Lord you.
I never laughed, being bashful.
Lowering my head, I looked at the wall.
10 Called to, a thousand times, I never looked back.

At fifteen I stopped scowling,
I desired my dust to be mingled with yours
Forever and forever and forever.
Why should I climb the lookout?

15 At sixteen you departed,
You went into far Ku-tō-en,[2] by the river of
   swirling eddies.
And you have been gone five months.
The monkeys make sorrowful noise overhead.
You dragged your feet when you went out.
20 By the gate now, the moss is grown, the different
   mosses,
Too deep to clear them away!
The leaves fall early this autumn, in wind.
The paired butterflies are already yellow with
   August
Over the grass in the West garden;
25 They hurt me. I grow older.
If you are coming down through the narrows of
   the river Kiang,[3]
Please let me know beforehand,
And I will come out to meet you
                    As far as Chō-fu-Sa.[4]

___

1. Chōkan (chō′ kän′): The Japanese name for Chángkan (chän gän), a village in eastern China.

___

2. Ku-tō-en (kōō′ tō′ yen′): The Japanese name for Ch'ü-tàng-yen (chü taŋ yen), the shoals at the mouth of the dangerous Yangtze (yäŋ tsə) Gorges, in the upper reaches of the Yangtze River.
3. the river Kiang (kyaŋ): The Yangtze River.
4. Chō-fu-Sa (chō′ fōō′ sä′): The Japanese name for Chang-Feng-Sha (chaŋ fəŋ shä), a village on the Yangtze River, about 200 miles upstream from Chōkan.

___

Reader's Response *If you were the river-merchant's wife, what emotions would you be feeling now?*

THINKING ABOUT THE SELECTION

Interpreting

1. At the time when this poem was written, Chinese marriages were arranged according to custom. What evidence is there in this poem that the marriage between the speaker and the river merchant had been arranged?
2. (a) What is the speaker's attitude toward the river merchant when she first marries him? (b) How is her attitude revealed? (c) How do her feelings about him change as she grows old? (d) How is her change in attitude revealed?
3. How do the natural images in the fourth stanza echo the speaker's feelings?
4. Why do the paired butterflies "hurt" the speaker?
5. "The River-Merchant's Wife: A Letter" was not the original title of Li Po's poem, but was created by the poem's translator, Ezra Pound. Explain whether you think Pound's title for the poem is appropriate.

Applying

6. In what ways does the society depicted in this poem differ from our society? Support your answer.

ANALYZING LITERATURE

Recognizing a Persona

The **persona** is the character assumed by the speaker of a poem or the narrator of a novel or short story. In many Chinese poems, the persona and the poet are identical. In Chinese ballads, however, the speaker is often an imaginary character. For example, the speaker of "The River-Merchant's Wife: A Letter" is the river-merchant's wife herself.

1. How do you think the poem might be different if the speaker had been someone closely acquainted with the river-merchant's wife, rather than the river-merchant's wife herself?
2. How do the speaker's feelings shape your impressions of the situation she describes?
3. Why do you think the river-merchant's wife is not given a name?

THINKING AND WRITING

Writing a Response

Imagine that you are the river merchant addressed by the speaker of this poem. Explore your feelings about your wife, how they have changed in the years

RIVER VILLAGE IN A RAINSTORM
Lu Wen-ying
The Cleveland Museum of Art

since you were first married, and how you feel about being separated from her. Then write a poem addressed to your wife, expressing your feelings. Model the poem after "The River-Merchant's Wife: A Letter." Try to connect the feelings you express to natural images, as Li Po does in his poem. When you have finished writing, revise your poem, making sure that you have conveyed your feelings clearly. Then prepare a final copy of your poem and share it with your classmates.

(continued from bottom of page)
ANSWERS TO ANALYZING LITERATURE

1. Answers may differ. Suggested response: The poem would have been written in the third person rather than the first person. In addition the end of the poem might have described the woman waiting for her husband to return. We would not know her thoughts as intimately as we do.
2. Suggested response: The poem evokes empathy by allowing the reader to have direct contact with the speaker's feelings.
3. Suggested response: The speaker is not given a name so that the poem's impact is timeless and universal rather than linked to a specific person, place, or time.

THINKING AND WRITING

Writing Across the Curriculum
You might inform the history department that students are reading "The River-Merchant's Wife: A Letter." The history teachers might be able to give students more information.

Humanities Note
Fine art, *River Village in a Rainstorm* by Lu Wen-ying. Lu Wen-ying lived during the late fifteenth-century Ming dynasty. This silk-scroll painting depicts a popular subject of landscape artists—the changing seasons and the weather.

In order to show the delicate differences in atmosphere and light that are seen in this painting, the landscape artist held the brush in a variety of ways. (These same ink and brush techniques are also used in calligraphy.) Unlike the flat brushes of Western artists, the Chinese brush is long and thin, coming to a sharp point at the end. When held vertically and by varying the pressure placed on it, the brush will make a variety of thick and thin strokes. Over time many different strokes evolved by also varying the angle at which the brush was held.

Ask the students if they think this painting elicits the same mood as the poem does. Have them explain their answers.

now has but did not have in the beginning.
3. It is revealed through the images of the monkey and autumn, which symbolize the passage of time and the sadness and loneliness she feels.
4. Answers may differ. Suggested response: The butterflies hurt the speaker because, although they are old, they are together, unlike her and her loved one.

5. Answers may differ. Some students may disagree with Pound's choice, thinking it should have reflected either the speaker's love for her husband or her loneliness in his absence. Others may agree that Pound's choice for a title is appropriate because the poem reads as though it were a letter the speaker was writing to her beloved and far away husband.
6. Answers may differ. Suggested re-

sponse: The most apparent difference is that in our society marriages are not arranged. In addition most people wait until they are much older before they get married. Finally, in today's society, technology and the ease of transportation reduce the distance between people.

LANDSCAPE AFTER KAO K'O-KUNG
Lan Ying
The Metropolitan Museum of Art, New York

In the Mountains on a Summer Day

Li Po

translated by Arthur Waley

Gently I stir a white feather fan,
With open shirt sitting in a green wood.
I take off my cap and hang it on a jutting stone;
A wind from the pine trees trickles on my bare head

Addressed Humorously to Tu Fu

Li Po

translated by Shigeyoshi Obata

Here! is this you on top of Fan-ko Mountain,
Wearing a huge hat in the noonday sun?
How thin, how wretchedly thin, you have grown!
You must have been suffering from poetry again.

The Moon at the Fortified Pass

Li Po

translated by Lin Yutang

The bright moon lifts from the Mountain of
    Heaven
In an infinite haze of cloud and sea,
And the wind, that has come a thousand miles,
Beats at the Jade Pass[1] battlements. . . .
China marches its men down Po-têng Road
While Tartar[2] troops peer across blue waters of the
    bay. . . .
And since not one battle famous in history
Sent all its fighters back again,
The soldiers turn round, looking toward the
    border,
And think of home, with wistful eyes,
And of those tonight in the upper chambers
Who toss and sigh and cannot rest.

---

1. **Jade Pass:** A gap in the Great Wall in northeastern China.
2. **Tartar** (tär′ tər): The Tartars were nomadic tribes who originally lived in Mongolia, Manchuria, and Siberia. From A.D. 200 through 400, the Tartars were almost constantly at war with the Chinese. A thousand years later, under the leadership of Genghis Khan, the Tartars conquered China as well as a number of other European and Asian countries.

Reader's Response *How do you think you would feel if you were one of the soldiers in "The Moon at the Fortified Pass"?*

THINKING ABOUT THE SELECTIONS

Interpreting

1. (a) How would you describe the mood, or atmosphere, of "In the Mountains on a Summer Day"? (b) Which details in the poem contribute to this mood?
2. (a) What does "In the Mountains on a Summer Day" suggest about Li Po's attitude toward nature? (b) What does the poem suggest about Li Po's disposition?
3. In "Addressed Humorously to Tu Fu," what does Li Po mean when he says that Tu Fu is "suffering from poetry"?
4. What does the manner in which Li Po addresses Tu Fu suggest about their relationship?
5. "The Moon at the Fortified Pass" is set in northwestern China, a remote and barren region of the country. What details in the poem emphasize the remoteness of the setting?
6. In what ways does the setting of "The Moon at the Fortified Pass" seem appropriate for a battle?
7. (a) In "The Moon at the Fortified Pass," what is the attitude of the soldiers concerning the coming battle? (b) What sort of emotions are they experiencing?

Applying

8. (a) Why do you think that writers often develop close friendships with other writers? (b) What do you think this tendency reveals about the nature of friendship?

CRITICAL THINKING AND READING

Inferring Tone

    The **tone** of a literary work is the author's attitude toward his or her subject and characters. Generally, the tone is revealed through the author's choice of words and details and through his or her portrayal of characters. When you read, it is important to infer the tone.
1. How would you describe the tone of "Addressed Humorously to Tu Fu" and how is it revealed?
2. What is the tone of "The Moon at the Fortified Pass" and how is it revealed?

(continued from bottom of page)

sponses: (a) The poem suggests that the soldiers feel determined and duty-bound to fight. (b) The soldiers were fearful of the imminent battle "since not one battle famous in history/Sent all its fighters back again . . ." They feared death and were wistfully thinking of home and their loved ones, whom they might never see again.
8. Answers may differ. Suggested responses: (a) Writers often develop close friendships with one another because they are of kindred spirit. They often share the same views and philosophies of life and share the same passion for their art. (b) Friendships are often made between people with similar interests and philosophies.

ANSWERS TO CRITICAL THINKING AND READING

1. Li Po develops a lighthearted, humorous poem, as he pokes fun at his friend and fellow poet. This tone is revealed in his use of the exclamation point, the silly rhetorical question he asks, and the conclusion he draws for the reason his friend is thin.
2. Answers may differ. Suggested response: The tone of this poem is both foreboding and sad. The soldiers know that they are to meet in battle as they each march down the road or peer out over the water. They are sadly reminded of the loved ones from whom they are separated as they look wistfully toward home.

Master Teacher Note To help set the mood for the poem "The Moon at the Fortified Pass," place Art Transparency 4, *Chinese Riders with Swords and Spears*, on the overhead projector. What is the tone of this piece? What might the artist's attitude about war be? Then have students read Li Po's poem and look for details that reflect his attitude toward war.

8 Discussion What is Li Po comparing in these lines?

9 Enrichment Throughout its history China faced invasions from the tribes the Chinese called barbarians who lived along their borders. These lines refer to one of these wars.

---

mate with his surroundings contribute to this mood.
2. Answers may differ. Suggested responses: (a) It suggests an attitude of close friendship. To Li Po, the natural world is a place where he can sit back and be totally comfortable, just as if he were in his own living room. (b) This poem suggests that he is happy and relaxed and enjoying his leisure time.
3. Answers may differ. Suggested response: He might mean that either Tu Fu takes poetry too seriously, almost to the point of obsession, or that Li Po occasionally "suffers" from poetry. Either way, it is meant as a playful comment.
4. Answers may differ. Suggested response: The manner in which Li Po addresses Tu Fu suggests that they had a close relationship and that they

shared many common interests.
5. The images of infinite space and great distances in lines 2–3 suggest a remote setting.
6. Answers may differ. Suggested response: The setting is appropriate for battle because the battle takes place on the border and at a point of weakness—at a hole in the Great Wall, which was built to keep invaders out.
7. Answers may differ. Suggested re-

TU FU

More About the Author Tu Fu lived and wrote during the dangerous and difficult days of the An Lushan rebellion, which shook the ruling T'ang dynasty to its very foundation. Although the rebellion was put down at great social and economic cost, the dynasty never fully recovered its former splendor. Legend has it that the rebellion began because the emperor had turned his attentions toward a woman instead of toward ruling the country.

Tu Fu, who was profoundly influenced by the events of his day, wrote stark, striking poems in which he tried to inform his readers about the bleak reality of the times.

Pronunciation Note Tu Fu is also pronounced dōō fōō and is spelled Du Fu in the Pin Yin romanization system.

Critical Evaluation One of Tu Fu's hallmarks was his spirit of innovation. Unlike many of his contemporaries, who preferred the older, established poetic forms, Tu Fu wrote mostly in the new styles and developed many technical innovations. According to the China scholar Burton Watson, "The forward-looking nature of Tu Fu's poetry is attested by the fact that it anticipates so many of the trends of later poetry, and that his reputation grew steadily in the centuries following his death."

712–770

A younger contemporary of Li Po (lē′ pō′), Tu Fu (tōō′ fōō′) was little known and for the most part unappreciated during his own lifetime. Yet he is now regarded as the supreme craftsman of Chinese *shih* poetry.

As a boy Tu Fu was frail and sickly, but he loved to study. Excelling as both a poet and a calligrapher at an extremely early age, he left home when he was about twenty to try to find a place to use his talents. Like most ambitious scholars in China, he decided to pursue a career as a government official. He never held a high position, instead moving from place to place throughout the country filling minor posts. Because of his inability to forge a successful career, Tu Fu spent much of his life in bitter poverty. In addition, his constant travels often forced him to be away from his wife and children, to whom he was deeply devoted.

At the beginning of his career, China was relatively peaceful and prosperous, but during the latter part of his life he witnessed a major rebellion, the destruction of the capital city, and an invasion by Turkic tribes from the northwest. His poems give some of the most vivid accounts of war and destruction in all of Chinese literature, as well as searing indictments of the opulence and extravagance of the court in the face of the extreme poverty of the common people.

Tu Fu's poetry also reveals a great deal about his character and his personal experiences—his love for his family and friends, his frustration at living in poverty, his joy in the simple pleasures of nature, and his disappointment over not being more successful in his political career. In all of his poetry—both the poems that focus on his personal experiences and the poems dealing with social issues—he exhibits his command of the Chinese language and his mastery of the *shih* form. As a result, Tu Fu's poems are admired as much for their form as they are for their content.

Objectives

Thematic
To understand impermanence and humans' relationship to nature

Skills
1 To appreciate style
2 To draw conclusions about a writer's life
3 To respond to criticism

Support Material

Teaching Portfolio
Teacher Backup, p. 337
Usage and Mechanics Worksheet, p. 341
Vocabulary Check, p. 342
Analyzing Literature Worksheet, *Appreciating Style*, p. 343
Language Worksheet, *Appreciating*

GUIDE FOR INTERPRETING

Tu Fu's Poetry

Commentary

Style. The term **style** refers to the manner in which a writer puts his or her ideas into words. It involves the characteristics of a literary work that concern form of expression rather than the thoughts conveyed. In poetry, for example, style is determined by such factors as choice and arrangement of words, length and arrangement of lines, stanza length and format, use of punctuation and capitalization, and use of literary devices. Often, style is contrasted with content, or subject matter, for the purpose of analyzing literature, though in most cases the two are inseparably linked.

Like most of the other poets of his day, Tu Fu mainly used the new-style *shih* form. Because the new-style *shih* form is fairly rigid, dictating the number of lines, the number of words per line, and the rhyme scheme, many stylistic elements were predetermined by a poet's decision to use this form. As a result, most of the distinctive features of a *shih* poet's style related to his or her choice and arrangement of words. Tu Fu, for example, is known for his innovative uses of language, such as his use of nouns and adjectives as verbs and his use of words with double meanings. Because of his innovativeness and his mastery of the language, Tu Fu is known as the supreme stylist in Chinese poetry.

Since all languages have different sound systems and different sets of connotations for each word or image, style is very difficult to reproduce in translation. The blocklike structure of *shih* poetry, for instance, is impossible to capture in a language such as English that has words of differing lengths. For example, consider the original text of Tu Fu's poem "Sent to Li Po as a Gift" in comparison with the translation on page 241. The original poem has only four lines, with seven syllables in each line, while the translation has eleven lines with varying numbers of syllables. End rhymes and internal rhymes are important in the original, but do not appear in the translation. In addition, the words *you* and *your* appear several times in the translation, but their Chinese equivalent cannot be found in the original. These are but a few of the many differences between the original and the translation

When you read poetry in translation, you can seldom be sure which elements of the style reflect the style of the original poet and which are in fact the translator's style. As a result, you should generally avoid trying to analyze an author's style based on a translation.

Writing

Tu Fu frequently uses images from nature to evoke human feelings. Freewrite about the types of natural images that evoke such feelings as loneliness, fear, and despair.

Literary Focus Literary style concerns the use of imagery as well as the types of grammatical constructs a writer chooses for his poetry. The use of imagery often distinguishes the literary style of one poet from another. Have students contrast the particular styles and imagery of other poets they may have read.

Writing/Prior Knowledge Before students begin writing, you might have them look at scenes either around the school or in pictures and in posters that you provide. Have students discuss the feelings that each scene evokes and why they evoke such feelings. Is it the colors? the subject? the memories it conjures up? Then have students complete the writing assignment.

ESL Teaching Strategy In order to help ESL students understand the details of the descriptive poem, suggest that they work in pairs to write a prose description of Tu Fu's poetry.

Vocabulary

Preteach the following vocabulary words:

scurry (skɥr´ ē) *v*.: Run hastily; scamper

courtiers (kôrt´ ē ərz) *n*.: Attendants at a royal court

imperceptibly (im pər sep´ tə blē) *adv*.: Subtly; gradually without notice

immortality (im´ môr tal´ i tē) *n*.: Life everlasting

strenuous (stren´ yoo əs) *adj*.: Vigorous; arduous

hued (hyood) *adj*.: Having some shade or intensity of color

hovers (huv´ ərz) *v*.: Flutters in the air near one place

---

the Use of Color in Poetry, p. 344
Selection Test, pp. 345–346

Master Teacher Note Tu Fu's joy in the simple pleasures of nature seems deeply shadowed by such lines as "The pathos . . . overcomes me" and "I stand alone with ten thousand sorrows." Discuss the possible intention or meaning behind the apparent paradox.

Teaching Tenth-Grade Students
Ask tenth-grade students to find the verbs and verbals in Tu Fu's poems. Then ask them to make general statements about the images created through these verbs and verbals.

Jade Flower Palace

Tu Fu

translated by Kenneth Rexroth

The stream swirls. The wind moans in
The pines. Gray rats scurry over
Broken tiles. What prince, long ago,
Built this palace, standing in
5 Ruins beside the cliffs? There are
Green ghost fires in the black rooms.
The shattered pavements are all
Washed away. Ten thousand organ
Pipes whistle and roar. The storm
10 Scatters the red autumn leaves.
His dancing girls are yellow dust.
Their painted cheeks have crumbled
Away. His gold chariots
And courtiers are gone. Only
15 A stone horse is left of his
Glory. I sit on the grass and
Start a poem, but the pathos[1] of
It overcomes me. The future
Slips imperceptibly away.
20 Who can say what the years will bring?

---

1. pathos (pā´ thäs) *n.:* The quality in something experienced or observed that arouses feelings of pity, sorrow, sympathy, or compassion.

Reader's Response *What feelings does the sight of a decaying building evoke in you?*

CONVERSATION IN AUTUMN
Hua Yen
The Cleveland Museum of Art

In this painting two scholars are having a conversation in a remote little hut in the country. The subject of this piece came from a famous eleventh-century piece of rhymed prose by poet Ou-yang Hsiu. In his work Ou-yang Hsiu described the sounds of autumn. Hua Yen captured the rhythm of Ou-yang Hsiu's words with his delicate brush work, lyrical lines, and varied tones of color. His mountain is exaggeratedly high and mysterious. The quiet around the little hut is emphasized by its isolation and the misty atmosphere. The few landscape details are so varied in technique and so beautifully arranged that the picture has been compared to music.

Ask students what they imagine the two scholars are discussing.

Sent to Li Po as a Gift

Tu Fu

translated by Florence Aysough and Amy Lowell

Autumn comes,
We meet each other.
You still whirl about as a thistledown in the wind.
Your Elixir[1] of Immortality is not yet perfected

5 And, remembering Ko Hung,[2] you are ashamed.
You drink a great deal,
You sing wild songs,
Your days pass in emptiness.
Your nature is a spreading fire,
10 It is swift and strenuous.
But what does all this bravery amount to?

---

1. Elixir (i lik′ sər) *n.*: A supposed remedy for all ailments.

2. Ko Hung (gə hoŏŋ): A Chinese philosopher and alchemist who tried to create an Elixir of Immortality.

THINKING ABOUT THE SELECTION

Interpreting

1. (a) How would you describe the mood, or atmosphere, of "Jade Flower Palace"? (b) Which details contribute to the mood?
2. In "Jade Flower Palace," how does the image of the storm scattering the red autumn leaves relate to the description of the decaying palace?
3. How do the last six lines of "Jade Flower Palace" relate to the rest of the poem?
4. (a) What is the theme, or main point, of "Jade Flower Palace"? (b) How is the theme conveyed?
5. What does "Sent to Li Po as a Gift" suggest about Li Po's character?
6. What does Tu Fu mean when he comments that Li Po's "nature is a spreading fire"?
7. (a) What seems to be Tu Fu's attitude toward Li Po? (b) Is he criticizing Li Po, or teasing him? Explain your answer.
8. Why do you think Tu Fu refers to this poem as a "gift" for Li Po?

Applying

9. If you were Li Po, how would you respond to "Sent to Li Po as a Gift"?

ANALYZING LITERATURE

Appreciating Style

Style refers to the manner in which a writer puts his or her ideas into words. It involves the characteristics of a literary work that concern form of expression rather than the thoughts conveyed. Because forms of expression vary extensively from language to language, style is extremely difficult to reproduce in translation.

The following is a word-for-word transcription of the first four lines of Tu Fu's "Jade Flower Palace":

Stream	swirls	pine	wind	long
Gray	rats	scurry	old	tiles.
Don't	know	what	prince	palace
Left	building	steep	cliff	beneath.

1. What does this transcription reveal about the style of the original poem?
2. What are some of the differences between the style of Rexroth's translation and the style of the original poem?
3. Based on the four-line transcription, do you think that there was any way that Rexroth could have preserved the style of the original poem without altering its meaning? Support your answer.

ANSWERS TO THINKING ABOUT THE SELECTIONS

1. Answers may differ. Suggested responses: (a) The mood is one of quiet melancholy. (b) The time of day, the location, and the birds seeking rest contribute to this mood.
2. Answers may differ. Suggested responses: (a) The images appeal to our sense of sight. (b) Students may disagree on the answer, but most will reply that there are enough images, since his purpose most likely was to evoke certain emotions rather than to paint a scenic picture.
3. Answers may differ. Suggested response: They are both predators.
4. Answers may differ. Suggested responses: (a) He is using the process of nature as a metaphor to represent the behavior of certain people. (b) They illustrate predatory creatures feeding on the unsuspecting. (c) It implies that Tu Fu is like the prey, standing alone with his many worries.
5. Answers may differ. Some students will disagree with Tu Fu's statement, stating that man's actions are antithetical to nature; some, however, may agree.
6. Answers may differ. Suggested response: Sunsets are one of the few common sights of nature throughout the world.

ANSWERS TO CRITICAL THINKING AND READING

Answers may differ. Suggested response: Tu Fu lived during a time of much political intrigue, turmoil, and uncertainty. This poem may have been written under the stress and loneliness of trying to survive in this kind of world.

The Return of the Wanderers

Tu Fu

translated by Arthur Christy

5 The red clouds beneath the setting sun
Cover the massive foothills of the west.
A rose-hued light floods the valleys.
Beautiful birds are seeking their nests for rest.

Reader's Response *What emotions does a sunset evoke in you? How does your reaction compare with Tu Fu's?*

Loneliness

Tu Fu

translated by Kenneth Rexroth

A hawk hovers in air.
Two white gulls float on the stream.
Soaring with the wind, it is easy
To drop and seize
5 Birds who foolishly drift with the current.
Where the dew sparkles in the grass,
The spider's web waits for its prey.
The processes of nature resemble the business of men.
I stand alone with ten thousand sorrows.

THINKING ABOUT THE SELECTIONS

Interpreting

1. (a) How would you describe the mood, or atmosphere, of "The Return of the Wanderers"? (b) Which details contribute to the mood?
2. (a) To which sense do the images in "The Return of the Wanderers" appeal? (b) Explain whether you think that Tu Fu included enough images to create a vivid picture of the scene he describes.
3. In "Loneliness" what is the connection between the images of the birds and the image of the spider?
4. (a) What does the speaker of "Loneliness" mean when he says that "the processes of nature resemble the business of men"? (b) How do the images in the first seven lines relate to this statement? (c) How does the final line fit in with the rest of the poem?

Applying

5. Explain whether you do or do not agree with Tu Fu's statement in "Loneliness" that the "processes of nature" resemble the "business of men."

6. Why do you think that sunsets have captured the interest of people from all cultures and generations?

CRITICAL THINKING AND READING

Drawing Conclusions About a Writer's Life

Tu Fu's poems are usually considered to be truthful expressions of his experiences and feelings. Assuming that this is the case with "Loneliness," explain how the poem relates to what you know about his life.

THINKING AND WRITING

Responding to Criticism

A critic has said that "Li Po's poetry appears to possess a life or vitality of its own, and so well is its art concealed that it gives the impression of being quite artless and unpremeditated. Tu Fu's poetry, on the other hand, is above all serious in purpose and full of deep meaning." Write an essay in which you agree or disagree with this assessment of Li Po and Tu Fu.

THINKING AND WRITING

Publishing Student Writing In small groups have students read their essays aloud. After each student reads, group members should comment on the paper and offer advice for ways of improving it. After all papers have been read, have students write a final draft of their papers.

AUTUMN MOUNTAINS
T'ang Yin (Ming Dynasty)

Humanities Note

Fine art, *Autumn Mountains* by T'ang Yin. During the early Ming dynasty, T'ang Yin (1470–1523) stood out as a leading painter. Despite having to work within the acceptable style of the period, like many of his contemporaries, T'ang Yin made his own contribution to art. For example, he combined a more traditional lyrical style of drawing with a more realistic style, as seen in the rocks in this painting.

In contrast to T'ang Yin, many Chinese artists made little attempt to picture nature realistically. This was in part because to them art was the personal concern of the individual artist. Landscapes such as this one were not made with social aims or in response to any demands by the public. Chinese artists set their own tasks, chose their own poetry or philosophical idea to capture, and worked for themselves and their own self-development; art was generally not a commodity to be bought and sold to the public. Chinese artists therefore avoided painting what was dictated by public demands and tastes. They painted nature as they saw it in their imaginations or through their emotions.

You might want to use the following questions to discuss the art:

1. How did Chinese philosophy contribute to the idea of the reclusive scholar-artist who sought separation from the public and society?

2. Can artists today work as hermits, cut off from social and financial concerns? Explain.

3. How does the choice of subjects of Chinese artists show a separation from worldly influences or concerns?

PO CHÜ-I

Focus

More About the Author Po Chü-i, like Wang Wei, Li Po, and Tu Fu, lived during the T'ang dynasty (618–907). The T'ang is known as China's greatest age—the time during which Chinese culture reached its peak of creativity in the arts, literature, religion, and philosophy. The cultural figures of the T'ang drew on the previous achievements handed down from Chinese history and combined them with new foreign ideas that flowed into China. T'ang China in turn exerted a deep and lasting influence on all the countries of East Asia.

Pronunciation Note Po Chü-i is also pronounced bō jōō yē and is spelled Bo Juyi in the Pin Yin romanization system.

Critical Evaluation Po Chü-i became one of China's most popular poets even during his lifetime. His legacy also spread throughout the whole of East Asia. In Japan, for instance, he was made the subject of a Nō play. His poetry even today is still taught to Japanese school children. Perhaps it is Po's choice of subject matter—the common people and romantic and reflective themes—and the accessibility of his language that have carried his name through the ages. According to Burton Watson, the noted China scholar, "The present-day American reader accustomed to such works as *Blowin' in the Wind* will have no difficulty understanding the concept" of protest underlying much of Po's poetry.

772–846

Po Chü-i (pō′ chü′ ē) was born two years after Tu Fu died, at a time when China was still in turmoil as a result of foreign invasion and internal strife. Deeply troubled by the events of his time, Po Chü-i wrote many poems in which he spoke out bitterly against the social and economic problems that were plaguing the country.

Like many of the great poets of the T'ang dynasty, Po Chü-i was born into a family of minor officials and began exhibiting his literary talents as a young child. At the age of twenty-eight, he passed the highest examination for government service and started a long career as a government official. In 833, when he was sixty-one years old, he was forced to retire because of illness. Although he suffered from ill health for the remainder of his life, he continued writing poetry until he was physically unable to do so.

A dedicated and compassionate man, Po Chü-i devoted his life as a public official to serving people with honesty and integrity. In addition, he firmly believed that the function of literature was to reform society, and much of his earlier poetry describes the sufferings of the common people, resulting from war and the government's indifference to their needs. The subjects of these poems include laborers toiling in the fields, a man who breaks his own arm to avoid serving in the military, weavers whose hands become numb from weaving fine silk for the wealthy, and a charcoal seller whose cartload of charcoal is seized by imperial horsemen for official use. Though Po Chü-i considered these his most important works, he also wrote many quiet, reflective poems describing picturesque scenes or exploring such simple pleasures as taking a nap or eating bamboo shoots.

Po Chü-i took pains to write poetry in a clear and simple style that would be accessible to as many people as possible. It is said that he would read his poems to illiterate women and would revise the poems until the women were able to understand them. Because of the accessibility of his poetry and the relevance of his themes, Po Chü-i was by far the most popular poet of his day and has remained popular throughout the centuries since his death.

Objectives

Thematic
To understand personal lyrics

Skills
1 To appreciate T'ang poet-officials
2 To recognize word analogies
3 To write about the role of poetry

Support Material

Teaching Portfolio
Teacher Backup, p. 347
Usage and Mechanics Worksheet, p. 351
Vocabulary Check, p. 352
Critical Thinking and Reading Worksheet, *Finding the Implied Main Idea*, p. 353

GUIDE FOR INTERPRETING

Po Chü-i's Poetry

Commentary

Chinese Poet-Officials. It is no coincidence that T'ao Ch'ien, Wang Wei, Tu Fu, and Po Chü-i were all both poets and government officials. For most of China's history, from the time of Confucius to the beginning of this century, the roles of scholar and official were closely intertwined. From the Confucian point of view, the highest duty of a scholar was to serve in the government. Conversely, it was the ruler's duty to employ the country's most capable scholars to aid in maintaining order and carrying out imperial policy.

Throughout Chinese history, officials were chosen through a series of examinations offered at the local, regional, and national levels. Although the content of these exams varied from dynasty to dynasty, during the T'ang era they included tests of the ability to write poetry and creative prose, as well as tests on the interpretation of major Chinese literary works. In preparation for a career as an official, children were taught to write poetry as part of their elementary schooling. Because of this early instruction, several famous poet-officials, including Po Chü-i and Tu Fu, were able to achieve success as poets by the age of nine or ten.

The inclusion of poetic composition as part of official examinations reflected the overall Chinese belief that every educated person could and should master the art of writing poetry. In fact, the writing of poetry was considered an important social skill. Social gatherings often included the writing of poems as a form of amusement, and it was common for scholars to write collaborative poetry and to play games involving poetic composition. Poetry was also used as a means of recording daily experiences and observations, serving a role similar to that of a journal or diary.

Writing

In addition to writing poems about official ceremonies and matters of national concern, the poet-officials of the T'ang era wrote many poems about their personal lives. Make a list of events in your own life that you feel would make appropriate topics for a poem. Then briefly describe the thoughts and feelings that you would like to express about each of the events. Finally, you might want to try writing a brief, informal poem about one of the events you have listed, attempting to convey the thoughts and feelings you have described.

Literary Focus Chinese literary theory traditionally has concerned itself with the function or purpose of literature. One of the most famous exponents of this idea was Confucius himself. Po, too, believed poetry should primarily be a vehicle for moral instruction. Have students discuss their views on the role literature plays in our society.

Writing/Prior Knowledge You might have students divide a sheet of paper into three columns, labeling one *school life*, one *family life*, and one *personal life*. Then have students write topics for each of these areas of their lives.

ESL Teaching Strategy Be sure ESL students understand the following figures of speech:
1. ". . . a face . . . buried in the World's dust."
2. ". . . the Fleeting World is but a long dream. . . ."
3. ". . . thoughts grow narrow. . . ."
4. "Since we parted hands. . . ."
5. "Thrice and again the full moon has shown."

You might pair ESL students with native-speaking students as they read Po's work.

Vocabulary

Preteach the following vocabulary words:

hover (huv´ ər) *v.*: To stay suspended in the air

confront (kən frunt´) *v.*: Face; stand before

covetous (kuv´ ə təs) *adj.*: Desirous

awry (ə rī´) *adj.*: Askew

unsubdued (un sub dood´) *v.*: Undiminished; unconquered

superintendence (soo´ pər in ten´ dəns) *n.*: Management; supervision

trifling (trī´ fliŋ) *adj.*: Trivial; shallow

Language Worksheet, *Recognizing Analogies*, p. 354
Selection Test, pp. 355–356

Master Teacher Note Po Chü-i speaks of sickness, sorrow, loneliness, and death; yet the poems reflect a sense of greater calm. Ask students to point out evidence in the poem of this calm and to infer its possible source.

Teaching Tenth-Grade Students Have tenth-grade students individually or in groups summarize each of Po Chü-i's poems. Then ask individuals or groups to compare their summaries.

Sick Leave

Po Chü-i

translated by Arthur Waley

Propped on pillows, not attending to business;
For two days I've lain behind locked doors.
I begin to think that those who hold office
Get no rest, except by falling ill!
5 For restful thoughts one does not need space;
The room where I lie is ten foot square.
By the western eaves, above the bamboo twigs,
From my couch I see the White Mountain rise.
But the clouds that <u>hover</u> on its far-distant peak
10 Bring shame to a face that is buried in the World's dust.

At the End of Spring

Po Chü-i

translated by Arthur Waley

The flower of the pear tree gathers and turns to fruit;
The swallows' eggs have hatched into young birds.
When the Seasons' changes thus <u>confront</u> the mind
What comfort can the Doctrine of Tao give?
5 It will teach me to watch the days and months fly
Without grieving that Youth slips away;
If the Fleeting World is but a long dream,
It does not matter whether one is young or old.
But ever since the day that my friend[1] left my side
10 And has lived an exile in the City of Chiang-ling,
There is one wish I cannot quite destroy:
That from time to time we may chance to meet again.

---

1. **my friend:** Yüan Chēn (yōō än), one of Po Chü-i's closest friends.

To Li Ch'ien[1]

Po Chü-i

translated by Arthur Waley

Worldly matters again draw my steps;
Worldly things again seduce my heart.
Whenever for long I part from Li Ch'ien
Gradually my thoughts grow narrow and covetous.
I remember how once I used to visit you;
I stopped my horse and tapped at the garden gate.
Often when I came you were still lying in bed;
Your little children were sent to let me in.
And you, laughing, ran to the front door
With coat tails flying and cap all awry.
On the swept terrace, green patterns of moss;
On the dusted bench, clean shadows of leaves.
To gaze at the hills we sat in the eastern lodge;

15 To wait for the moon we walked to the
          southern moor,
At your quiet gate only birds spoke;
In your distant street few drums were heard.
Opposite each other all day we talked,
20 And never once spoke of profit or fame.
Since we parted hands, how long has passed?
Thrice and again the full moon has shone.
For when we parted the last flowers were falling,
And today I hear new cicadas[2] sing.
The scented year suddenly draws to its close,
Yet the sorrow of parting is still unsubdued.

1. **Li Ch'ien** (lē chē′en): A friend of Po Chü-i's.

2. **cicadas** (si kā′ dɔz) *n*.: Large, flylike insects with transparent wings. The male cicada makes a loud, shrill sound by vibrating a special organ in its undersurface.

Reader's Response *What picture do you form of the poet after reading these poems?*

SCENES FROM THE LIFE OF T'AO CH'IEN
Ch′ên Hung′ shou
Honolulu Academy of Arts

(continued from bottom of page)
curling clarity to them. Each figure's cloak is bordered several times in parallel curving lines. The heads are large, with distinctive ears and facial features. The figures are curiously unreal and somewhat grotesque.

The scroll, which was much admired by intellectual figures when the artist painted it, was thought to be a model of the "true Chinese spirit" of the classical virtues of selflessness, simplicity, and poetic honesty.

You might want to use the following questions to discuss the art:
1. Why do you think both Ch'ên Hung' shou and Po Chü-i chose as their subjects a poet? What does this suggest about the influence of poets and their work in Chinese society?
2. What were Po Chü-i and T'ao Yüan-ming, the poet pictured here, seeking?
3. What is the tone of this painting? Is it similar to or different from the tone of "To Li Ch'ien"? Explain.

5 **Discussion** Have students recall the Taoist beliefs of Lao Tzu. Why is Po Chü-i worried about being drawn into the concerns of "Worldly matters"?

6 **Discussion** Why is it significant that neither spoke of "profit or fame"?

7 **Discussion** Approximately how much time has passed since Li Ch'ien died?

Humanities Note

Fine art, *Scenes from the Life of T'ao Yüan-ming* by Ch'ên Hung' shou. Ch'ên Hung' shou (1599–1652) worked as a court painter during the Ming dynasty, but, unlike the paintings of the conservative era of his time, his album of figure paintings about the poet T'ao Yüan-ming (365–427) are original in style. This picture is one of a series of paintings illustrating the life of a great Chinese poet—T'ao Yüan-ming, who had been a government official but gave up his career to retire to a country house where he led a simple and exemplary life. Ch'ên Hung' shou's paintings of T'ao Yüan-ming illustrate T'ao Yüan-ming's unpretentious life style.

Dated 1650, the silk handscroll is in a distinctive style, quite unlike that of other artists of his time. Ch'ên Hung's style of figure painting combined a style that was popular hundreds of years earlier with his own exaggerated and slightly satirical style. The figures in this painting, for example, are outlined and lightly shaded. The lines have a sharp,

Last Poem

Po Chü-i

translated by Arthur Waley

They have put my bed beside the unpainted screen;
They have shifted my stove in front of the blue curtain.
I listen to my grandchildren, reading me a book;
I watch the servants, heating up my soup.
5 With rapid pencil I answer the poems of friends;
I feel in my pockets and pull out medicine money.
When this <u>superintendence</u> of <u>trifling</u> affairs is done,
I lie back on my pillows and sleep with my face to the South.

FAN MOUNTED AS ALBUM LEAF: HERMITAGE BY A PINE-COVERED BLUFF
Mid-twelfth century
The Metropolitan Museum of Art, New York

THINKING ABOUT THE SELECTIONS

Interpreting

1. (a) In "Sick Leave," what is the speaker's attitude toward his illness? (b) How is his attitude conveyed?
2. How do the natural images in lines 7–10 of "Sick Leave" contrast with the description of the room in which the speaker is lying?
3. How do you interpret the final two lines of "Sick Leave"?
4. How do the speaker's observations of nature in lines 1–2 of "At the End of Spring" relate to his own life?
5. How does the speaker's admission in the final four lines of "At the End of Spring" conflict with the Taoist emphasis on simplifying one's life and freeing oneself from desires?
6. What do the first four lines of "To Li Ch'ien" reveal about Li Ch'ien's influence on Po Chü-i?
7. How would you describe the dispositions of Po Chü-i and Li Ch'ien when they are together?
8. (a) In what season was "To Li Ch'ien" written? (b) How is the season identified? (c) How does the season add to the impact of the poem?
9. (a) What can you infer, or conclude, from the title "Last Poem"? (b) How do the images in the poem support this inference? (c) Explain whether you think that it was Po Chü-i himself who gave this poem its title.
10. (a) In "Last Poem," what seems to be Po Chü-i's attitude toward his condition? (b) How is his attitude conveyed?

Applying

11. How important are friendships such as the one Po Chü-i describes in "To Li Ch'ien"?
12. What qualities make "Last Poem" as relevant today as it was when it was written?

ANALYZING LITERATURE

Appreciating the T'ang Poet-Officials

From the time of Confucius until the beginning of this century, poetry was such an integral part of Chinese life that every educated person was expected to be able to write poetry. In addition, throughout much of Chinese history a person could not be appointed to government office without possessing poetic talent. As a result, many noted Chinese poets, including Wang Wei, Tu Fu, and Po Chü-i, were also government officials.

1. What does Po Chü-i's poem "Sick Leave" suggest about the demands of public office?
2. How might the ability to write poetry contribute to a person's effectiveness as a government official?
3. In what ways is the role of poetry in traditional Chinese society different from its role in our society?
4. In what ways might our government and our society be different if public officials were given examinations that tested their ability to write poetry?

UNDERSTANDING LANGUAGE

Recognizing Analogies

A verbal analogy is an expression of a relationship between two words. Analogy questions on standardized tests ask you to choose two words that are related in the same way as a given pair. For example,

tall : short : : big : small

The words in capital letters in the following analogies appear in Po Chü-i's poetry. Complete each analogy by choosing the pair of words whose relationship is most similar to that expressed by the capitalized pair.

1. SORROW : GRIEF
   (a) yield : compromise
   (b) surrender : conform
   (c) maturity : youth
   (d) clairvoyant : obtuse
2. MOUNTAIN : PEAK
   (a) automobile : transmission
   (b) church : steeple
   (c) chronometer : timepiece
   (d) museum : exhibit
3. HOVERING : BURIED
   (a) circuitous : direct
   (b) stagnant : immobile
   (c) optimistic : fatalistic
   (d) chaos : unity

THINKING AND WRITING

Writing About the Role of Poetry

Gather with a group of your classmates and discuss the differences between the role of poetry in traditional Chinese society and in our society. (Remember that the lyrics of songs are a form of poetry.) Then use the ideas from the discussion as the basis for a paper in which you compare and contrast the role of poetry in the two societies. After you have finished writing, revise your paper, making sure that you have supported your ideas with facts and details.

(continued from bottom of page)

now listen to his grandchildren read, watch the servants, and answer friends' poems.

11. Answers may differ. Suggested response: Relationships such as theirs are very important to have in one's lifetime.
12. Answers may differ. Suggested response: Its theme is timeless and universal, since everyone eventually must die.

ANSWERS TO ANALYZING LITERATURE

1. This poem suggests that the demands were severe and taxing, leaving little time for relaxation. Illness provided workers with the only opportunity to rest.
2. Answers may differ. Suggested response: Government officials would perhaps be more imaginative, sensitive, and creative.
3. Poetry played an integral role in Chinese society; for example, it was expected that politicians be able to write poetry; writing poetry was even part of their examination for holding public office. Poetry in the United States does not play a big role overall. It is generally either a hobby or something attainable by only a comparatively few scholars and writers.
4. Answers may differ. Suggested response: We would perhaps get a different type of person in office if such examinations and requirements were imposed. Our politicians might be more sensitive to the needs of the people and might be more creative in solving problems.

ANSWERS TO UNDERSTANDING LANGUAGE

1. (a) yield : compromise
2. (b) church : steeple
3. (a) circuitous : direct

THINKING AND WRITING

Publishing Student Writing Have students share their work with classmates. You might also consider sending students' work to a local poet who can read and respond to students' work.

above the "narrow and covetous" matters of everyday life.
7. Answers may differ. Suggested response: Po Chü-i and Li Ch'ien are happy and are enjoying each other's company. They obviously enjoy talking with each another. When Po Chü-i is with Li Ch'ien, he is able to cast away the worldly matters that were creeping into his thoughts.
8. Answers may differ. Suggested re-

sponses: (a) The poem was written in autumn. (b) The flowers are falling and cicadas are singing; the "scented year" is drawing to a close. (c) Autumn is associated with feelings of death and melancholy.
9. Answers may differ. Suggested responses: (a) You can infer that this is the last poem Po Chü-i wrote and that he is close to his death. (b) In the poem, Po Chü-i is ill and is answering

poems from friends as if in a hurry. (c) Some students may suggest Po Chü-i gave this poem its title because he knew he was close to his death; others may suggest that the title was given after Po Chü-i died.
10. Answers may differ. Suggested response: (a) Po Chü-i seems to be thankful that his illness has provided him with the time to appreciate the simple aspects of life. (b) He can

I CHING (THE BOOK OF CHANGE)

The Changes is a book
From which one may not hold aloof.
Its tao is forever changing—
Alteration, movement without rest,
Flowing through the six empty places;
Rising and sinking without fixed law,
Firm and yielding transform each other.
They cannot be confined within a rule;
It is only change that is at work here. . . .

They also show care and sorrow and their
  causes.
Though you have no teacher,
Approach them as you would your parents.

Scholars believe the principle of the hexagrams found in the *I Ching* (ē′ chēŋ), or *The Book of Change*, were discovered on the back of a tortoise shell by the legendary emperor Fu Hsi in the twenty-fourth century B.C. Since then, the *I Ching* has survived as one of the *Five Classics* of Confucian philosophy and has piqued the curiosity of many Westerners.

In China the *I Ching* has primarily been used for divination. It is a

The Eight Kua, trigrams from the ancient classic *I Ching* (*Book of Change*), surrounding the elemental forces yin and yang

guidebook of sorts for interpreting hexagrams, the figures of six lines that indicate the future. The *I Ching* is believed to be one of the oldest extant books in China, with parts of it dating as far back as 3,000 years. Although its authorship and origin are unknown, scholars attribute the basic text to King Wen (115 B.C.) and his son Duke Chou.

The *I Ching* is based on the concept of change—the one constant of the universe. Nothing within the universe is impervious to change. Everything is either being born, developing, decaying, or dying. Although change is never ending, it too proceeds according to certain universal and observable patterns. Understanding these patterns and humankind's place in the universe are at the heart of the *I Ching* and its divining powers.

Also at the heart of the *I Ching* is the Chinese concept of *yin* and *yang*. On a simplified level, yin and yang are opposite poles. For example, yang represents Heaven—active, positive, firm, strong, light, male, and so on; yin represents earth—passive, negative, yielding, weak, dark, female, and so on. Everything exists somewhere between these two poles. Their interblending in varying proportions accounts for the differences that exist in everything in the universe. The *I Ching* pictorially represents this in-

NSIGHTS

Chinese title page to *I Ching*

terblending of yin and yang in its hexagrams.

The *I Ching* is used for divination. A person (the inquirer) would have a question in mind that he or she wants foretold; for example: Is it advisable, under our present circumstances, to go forward with the attack? The hexagrams are then formed using yarrow sticks, the stalks of which grow in sacred places and are the vehicle by which the future is told. With the question in mind and after performing the required rituals and procedures, the inquirer takes forty-nine of the fifty required sticks and systematically eliminates all but three of them. Since hexagrams are read from bottom to top, the first three sticks form the base of the hexagram. The same process is repeated for the top trigram, thereby completing the hexagram. The interpreter then gives his judgment of the figure, consulting the *I Ching*'s commentary and text.

The *I Ching* contains illustrations of sixty-four hexagrams, the total number of possible combinations that can be formed. Based on the interpreter's judgment or reading of the hexagram, he or she suggests ways the inquirer should act, given the circumstances at the time of the inquiry. Sometimes the judgment is to proceed with an action; other times the judgment is a warning that difficulties are insurmountable, and it would be wise to stop or re-

treat. The final decision, however, is left up to the inquirer.

The *I Ching* is arranged in three books: Book I consists of illustrations of the sixty-four hexagrams and the judgment; Images, beautiful sayings that express the human, social, or cosmic application of the hexagram; and King Wen's text. Scholars believe King Wen, following his arrest by Emperor Shing Chu, composed the book during his seven-year captivity. Book II contains the Ten Wings purportedly written by Confucius and his students and disciples. According to tradition, in Book III, both Confucius and Duke Chou added the Decision, commentaries they wrote that clarify the judgment of the hexagram and discuss the philosophy out of which the prediction developed.

Although the *I Ching* is primarily used for divination and philosophy, it also gives practical advice on government, numerology, astrology, cosmology, meditation, and military strategy.

Critical Thinking: Why do you think that throughout the ages people have used devices such as the *I Ching* to foretell their futures? What does the need to know the future indicate about people in general?

Humanities Note

Fine art, *I Ching*. This is the title page of the *I Ching*. The two large Chinese characters read *Chou I*, or *Changes of Chou*, an alternative name of the *Book of Changes*.

ANSWERS TO CRITICAL THINKING

Answers may differ. Suggested responses: Perhaps by knowing the future, we can better understand the present. The need to know about the future implies that people have a natural curiosity to understand themselves better and to understand the unknown.

Closure and Extension

Cooperative Learning In small groups have students research the *I Ching* further, presenting their findings to the class. Groups might research the contents of the three books of the *I Ching*, the sixty-four hexagrams and their meanings, the rituals, and the ways in which the *I Ching* influenced both Confucianism and Taoism.

The Journey Inward

. "When I read [mythology], no matter the culture or origin, I feel a sense of wonder at the spectacle of the human imagination groping to try to understand this existence, to invest in their small journey these transcendent possibilities."
—Joseph Campbell

Like the myths to which Campbell refers, many Chinese literary works lead readers on a journey inward—a journey aimed at attaining an understanding of existence. Many of these works not only attempt to help us better understand our own possibilities and limitations, but also move us toward an awareness of a universal spirit or a higher reality. At the same time, the works often point out the elusiveness of this higher reality.

The way that can be spoken of
Is not the constant way;
The name that cannot be named
Is not the constant name . . .
—Lao Tzu, the *Tao Te Ching*

The Master said, Who shall teach you what knowledge is? When you know a thing, to recognize that you know it, and when you do not know a thing, to recognize that you do not know it.
—Confucius, *The Analects*

Within these things there is a hint of Truth,
But when I start to tell it, I cannot find the words.
—T'ao Ch'ien, "I Built My House Near Where Others Dwell"

When the Seasons' changes thus confront the mind
What comfort can the Doctrine of Tao give?
It will teach me to watch the days and months fly
Without grieving that Youth slips away;
If the Fleeting World is but a long dream,
What does it matter whether one is young or old?
—Po Chü-i, "At the End of Spring"

Chinese literary works are not alone in leading readers on a journey inward. Throughout history, people from all corners of the globe have shared the desire to better understand themselves and their world. Because of this ongoing quest, we can find literary works from almost all cultures and eras that lead us on a journey inward. For instance, "The Bracelet" (page 1122) by the modern French writer Colette leads us on a journey inward that brings us to the discovery that once we lose the freshness of youth we can never regain it. A similar theme is conveyed by British Romantic poet William Wordsworth in his poem "Ode: Intimations of Immortality from Recollections of Early Childhood" (page 896).

The following are some other selections in Prentice Hall *World Masterpieces* that will lead you on a journey inward.

SUGGESTED READINGS

CROSS CURRENTS

Bertolt Brecht (1898–1956)

The German playwright Bertolt Brecht was one of the most innovative dramatists of the modern age. Rejecting the traditional Western approach to theater, he established a new type of drama known as "epic theater." In doing so, he was heavily influenced by traditional Chinese theater.

BRECHT'S EPIC THEATER

A fervent political activist, Brecht used his plays as a means of conveying political and social messages. He felt that audiences would be unlikely to grasp his messages, however, if they became emotionally involved in the stage action. As a result, he created the "epic theater," a dramatic form that employed a variety of techniques to distance the audience from the characters and action and to remind spectators that they were not witnessing real events. If people were prevented from accepting and identifying with the characters and actions, Brecht felt that they would be forced to critically examine what was taking place and would be less likely to miss the play's message.

THE INFLUENCE OF CHINESE DRAMA

Many of the techniques used in Brecht's "epic theater" reflect the influence of traditional Chinese theater. As in Chinese dramas, the actors in Brecht's plays express the awareness that they are being watched and at times directly address the audience. In addition, rather than submerging themselves in the emotions of their characters, the actors merely demonstrate or artificially reproduce these emotions. For example, an actor might demonstrate fear by simply rubbing white makeup on his or her face. Another similarity between Brecht's plays and the Chinese theater is the exaggerated, highly stylized manner in which the actors move. Finally, both types of dramas generally blend dialogue with singing and dancing, performed to the accompaniment of a group of musicians who sit in full view of the audience.

BRECHT'S MOST FAMOUS PLAYS

Brecht's most famous play is probably *The Threepenny Opera* (1928), the play from which the hit song "Mack the Knife" was taken. Among his other well-known dramas are *Measures Taken* (1930), *The Life of Galileo* (1938–1939), and *Mother Courage and Her Children* (1939). The two plays that most clearly exhibit the influence of Chinese theater, however, are *The Good Woman of Setzuan* (1938–1940) and *The Caucasian Chalk Circle* (1944–1945). *The Good Woman of Setzuan* is even set in China, and *The Caucasian Chalk Circle* was inspired by a play written by an anonymous thirteenth-century Chinese playwright.

A scene from Brecht's
Caucasian Chalk Circle

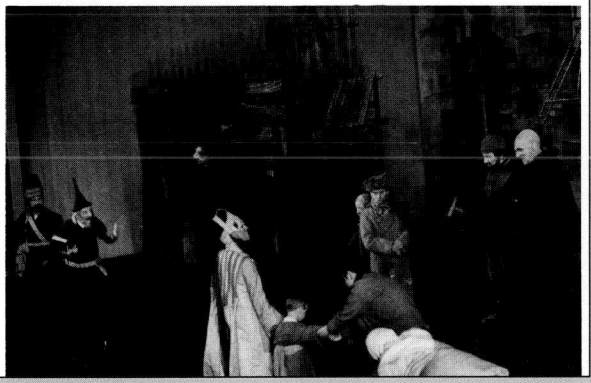

Presentation
Motivation/Prior Knowledge With what they have learned about Chinese poetry and art in this unit, have students discuss the ways in which a Western playwright, such as Bertolt Brecht, might be influenced by and incorporate into his work Chinese philosophy. How might his work differ from that of other Western playwrights? What characteristics might one expect to see in a Brecht performance? Then have students read this feature.

Enrichment Bertolt Brecht initially sought a career in medicine and studied it in school. In 1918 he served as an army medical orderly. In 1926 he privately published his first poems. Although Brecht was primarily a poet, he became famous as a playwright. His most significant contribution to theater was the creation of the epic theater.

Throughout much of his work, Brecht openly struggled between opposing tensions. He struggled between the public and private, the political and lyrical, and the rational and emotional sides of his being.

The following two lines from Brecht's poetry, which are frequently quoted, exhibit a contradiction and the tension he felt most of his life: "The truth is concrete" and "The only truth is in the imagination." Have students discuss the contradiction in these two lines. Which line do they think is more accurate? Why?

Closure and Extension

Student Activity In his literature Brecht struggled between opposing tensions. Have students characterize each of these parts of their beings. What is their private self like? their public self? What is their political self like? How does this differ from their creative, or lyrical, self? What is the rational side like? the emotional side? Then call out situations in which students might find themselves, and ask them which side of their beings dominates the others and why. For example, when they are at a debate, how do they act? Which side is dominant or in control? Other situations you might present are sporting events, recitals, school, home, outings with friends, and so on.

You might continue the discussion by asking if students understand why these opposing sides might be a constant source of tension for someone like Brecht. Were they also a source of tension for the Chinese poets in this unit? Explain. What did many of the poets do to solve or to avoid this tension? What do the students themselves do?

Presentation

Motivation/Prior Knowledge Discuss with students the definition of personal narrative. Then ask them either to name the writers in this unit who wrote personal narratives or to activate their prior knowledge by having them discuss other writers they have read in this anthology or elsewhere who have written personal narratives. If necessary read several examples of narratives to students. Ask them what they liked about the personal narratives. What made each one effective? Then ask students, if they were to write a personal narrative, what would they want to include to make it as expressive and effective as possible? Make a list of students' suggestions on the chalkboard. What are some possible topics they could write about? Finally tell students that in this assignment they will have the opportunity to write their own personal narratives in an essay.

Teaching Tenth-Grade Students Have tenth-grade students write a model so that everyone understands the process of this assignment. To enhance student participation, have students suggest events that have occurred in this class or perhaps those that the entire school attended, such as an assembly. Narrow the possibilities to the two best ones and vote on which of those will be the topic of the class essay. With the help of your students, write a class narrative as outlined in this feature. Then have students write individual narratives.

Personal Narrative Essay

Writing a Personal Narrative

Personal narratives take many forms. Some explore a person's feelings or beliefs. Some relate single events of significance. Others recount a series of events, or incidents, to develop a central theme. All use a personal voice and express the significance of the subject to the writer's life.

Personal essays that relate a series of events can be developed in various ways.

- Find possible cause/effect relationships
- Combine disparate details into new wholes
- Make judgments
- Disclose insights
- Reveal feelings

For example, "The River-Merchant's Wife: A Letter" tells the story of two people's lives together. It uses a chronological sequence of events as its organizing element. Through the words of the wife, we see their childhood history, the developing relationship, its present status, and the wife's intentions for the future. In other words, though simply drawn, the letter contains a personal narrative that develops over time.

Writing Assignment

In a personal narrative essay, write the story of a good relationship you have had that has developed over time. Convey your story through carefully selected incidents that show the changing relationship. Arrange the incidents in chronological order and make them build to a climax that tells something about the importance of the relationship. As with all personal narratives, write in the first person.

Prewrite

Select two possible relationships to write about. For each, write one sentence that depicts a specific, emotional turning point in that relationship. An example follows.

GRANDMOTHER: I hated myself when she ran crying from the room because I'd answered her question honestly.

FORMER BOYFRIEND: Two years later, he still grew quiet and looked down at his feet when I mentioned that last football game.

In a group with three other students, read your two sentences and have the group select the most interesting one for you to write about. Then take turns describing the circumstances surrounding each member's selected sentence. Help one another decide why that scene was significant to the relationship. Write the comments down.

If your theme is not obvious to you, discover it by asking yourself why this relationship is particularly important to you. Write down your thoughts.

Now plot your relationship, as the river merchant's wife did, with one or two events that took place before the one your sentence depicts, then the "sentence" event (which will serve as your emotional center), then an event after that.

Set up a diagram, as on page 255, to separate that special moment from the others. Place them chronologically left to right, but offset the most important one by placing it higher than the others. Choose the other incidents as carefully as you picked the special one. The earlier events will help prepare the reader for the shock or beauty or tenderness of the climax. The concluding event will provide a special perspective from which the central moment can be appreciated.

Remember, as you recount incidents you are developing a theme in your narrative, so the incidents must have both relationship to one another and meaning.

Write

Use your diagram and notes to help you write your narrative. Keep the theme in mind as you write. Be sure to build toward the emotional high point of your essay.

Pay particular attention to your first-person voice. It should portray an individual, not a neutral narrator.

Go back to your notes and diagram as you compose your first draft. Don't worry about perfecting the story at this point. Just be sure it aims at the central episode. Try to give that central event the proportionate emphasis it deserves in the story.

Collaborate

Ask your group to check your plot development. Read the essay to your group, then ask them to physically portray the three or four incidents as if each one were a snapshot or freeze frame. Tell them to strike the poses in the order they occur in your essay. The group should decide how to show the events without your help. Close your eyes while they change poses so all you see is the series of freeze frames. These portrayals should help you

to see if the story of your relationship progresses logically or if you need something more to link the pieces. You should also be able to see if the incidents you've chosen build your theme.

As you observe the sequence of freeze frames, note how each relates to the one before and after it. When the group has finished, ask if it had difficulty portraying any of the events. Difficult places may be unclearly written or insufficiently linked to events before or after.

Now ask someone to read your essay and critique the narrative voice. Does it have character? Is it effective?

Revise

Rewrite your story with the group's comments and your observations in mind. Hear the narrative voice as you write. When you cannot hear it, make language changes.

Keep in mind that smooth transitions between incidents aid readers much as road signs guide motorists.

Publish

Give a copy of your story to someone who can appreciate its personal value. Attach a note, offering to consider any response that would be appropriate. The person you pick may or may not be mentioned in the story, but you should be sure to choose someone who will enjoy understanding you better after reading what you have written.

Evaluate

Consider what you'll do with this essay when it's returned. Would you like to show it to the person in the essay? What conversation might it provoke if you did? Perhaps your having written this narrative essay is the newest chapter in your relationship.

Humanities Note

Fine art, *The Great Wave* by Katsushika Hokusai. This is one of the best-known prints by the world-renowned Japanese printmaker Katsushika Hokusai (1760–1849). One of the foremost designers of a type of print known as ukiyo-e ("the floating world"), Hokusai was a gifted and prolific artist, whose work not only influenced other Japanese artists but also had an impact on the French Impressionists. Despite his success, however, Hokusai lived in poverty throughout his life.

Part of a series of prints entitled *Thirty-six Views of Mount Fuji*, this print depicts a massive wave that seemingly rises far above the distant snow-capped peak of Mount Fuji and almost completely obscures the slim boat on the left side of the print. In this print Hokusai used a new pigment, known as Prussian Blue, that had only recently been imported into Japan through a Dutch trading post.

You might want to use the following questions to discuss the art:

1. How does the artist's inclusion of the distant Mount Fuji help to emphasize the tremendous size and strength of the wave?
2. By including the small boat in the left side of the print, what impression does he convey of the relationship between humanity and nature?
3. Among the most famous prints ever produced, this print is admired by people from all over the world. What might be some reasons for the popularity of this print?
4. What is your response to this painting?

THE GREAT WAVE
Katsushika Hokusai
Museum of Fine Arts, Boston

Objectives

1 To learn about Japanese history
2 To learn about Japanese religious traditions
3 To learn about Japanese literature

JAPANESE LITERATURE
500 B.C.–A.D. 1890

There was a heavy fall of snow. In the evening there were new flurries. The contrast between the snow on the bamboo and the snow on the pines was very beautiful. . . . People make a great deal of the flowers of spring and the leaves of autumn, but for me a night like this, with a clear moon shining on snow, is the best—there is not a trace of color in it. I cannot describe the effect it has on me, weird and unearthly somehow.

**—Lady Murasaki Shikibu
from *The Tale of Genji***

Focus

Historical Context Explain to students that throughout the early stages of its history, Japan was heavily influenced by the Chinese culture. Despite the influence of the Chinese, however, Japan developed its own distinctive cultural traditions, including a vibrant literary heritage. Hoping to prevent its cultural traditions from being affected by outside influences, Japan closed its doors to the outside world in the early 1600's. This marked the beginning of a period of self-imposed isolation that lasted for more than 250 years. Have students speculate about how this period of isolation might have affected Japanese literature.

Explain to students that learning about the era of isolation and about other aspects of Japanese history, culture, and religion will help them to understand and to appreciate the selections in this unit. For this reason it is important for them to read the introduction carefully.

Writing to Learn Have students write a journal entry about their current perceptions of Japanese society. As they move through the unit, they should feel free to look back at their journal entries and think about the ways in which their perceptions may have changed.

ESL Teaching Strategy If you have any Japanese students in your class, it might be interesting to have them share their knowledge of Japanese history, culture, religion, and literature with their classmates.

Teaching Tenth-Grade Students Many tenth-grade students may be taking world history at the same time they are studying world literature. Encourage them to consult their history teachers and their history textbooks to learn more about Japanese history, culture, and religion.

Presentation

Motivation/Prior Knowledge Explain to students that today's Japanese society is remarkably different from what Japan was like just over a hundred years ago. Although students may find it surprising, prior to the mid-nineteenth century, Japan was an undeveloped country with a longstanding social order and firmly entrenched cultural traditions. Tell students that this introduction will lead them on a journey through Japanese history, from the foundation of Japanese society to the establishment of feudalism to the beginning of Japan's modern age.

Purpose-Setting Question What aspects of Japanese history and culture make Japan a unique society? What are the distinctive elements of Japanese history?

Enrichment Tell students that the Japanese name for their country is *Nippon* or *Nihon,* which means "source of the sun."

Using the Map

Have students study the map and ask them the following questions:

1. Throughout much of Japanese history, the central government was unable to control the entire country. How might the physical composition of Japan have contributed to the central government's lack of control?
2. Why would it have been easier for Japan to isolate itself from the rest of the world than it would have been for most other countries?
3. Which of the Japanese islands do you think has the largest population? Why?
4. Today, more than 120 million people live in Japan. What problems do you imagine the size of the population might pose? Why?

The Tale of Genji was the world's first novel. Prince Genji, the central character, was the son of an emperor who presided over a court populated by Japanese lords and ladies about 1,000 years ago. In relating the story of Genji's loves and adventures, Lady Murasaki, who was herself a member of the court, provides readers with a vivid sense of the glittering, colorful lives of the Japanese aristocracy.

Modern readers continue to be drawn to *The Tale of Genji* because of its beauty and its evocative powers. Lady Murasaki's brilliant descriptions of court dress and manners, her command of the subtle inner workings of the mind, and her deep concern for universal questions about life and time have enabled the work to transcend the barriers of both time and culture.

JAPANESE HISTORY
The Roots of Japanese Civilization

The society depicted in Lady Murasaki's novel was one that had taken shape over the course of thousands of years. Although little is known about early Japanese history, it is known that the first inhabitants of the islands arrived there several thousand years ago. Like the earliest members of other cultures, these people survived by hunting, fishing, and gathering plants. By 200 B.C., however, the Japanese people had begun to practice farming and cultivate irrigated rice. At about the same time, a steady flow of immigrants began to arrive from Korea and other areas of continental Asia. This influx of people lasted for seven centuries and resulted in the significant growth in the Japanese population.

As its population grew, Japan began to emerge as a distinct and homogeneous culture. Yet the nation was not politically unified. Instead, Japanese society was divided into tribal organizations called *uji*, or clans, each of which had a well-defined social grouping that was dominated by aristocrats and also included warriors and spiritual leaders. Because the islands' mountainous terrain forced settlements in scattered coastal plains or in narrow valleys divided by sharply rising slopes, the clans were able to remain relatively independent and no central government could be established.

Despite their independence, however, the clans were constantly fighting with one another. During the fourth century, the Yamato emerged as the nation's most powerful clan. The Yamato leaders established a relationship with the Chinese. As a result, many Chinese ideas and beliefs, including those associated with Buddhism and Confucianism, were introduced into Japanese society. Hoping that the Japanese could also learn from the Chinese political system, one of the Yamato leaders, Prince Shotoku Taishi, sent a group of Japanese students to China in 607 to study its government and history.

Following the return of these students, the Yamato leaders set out to reform the Japanese political structure by adopting the Chinese system of centralized imperial rule. They created strong national and local governments with hierarchies of officials who were all subject to the authority of the emperor, who, of course, was a member of the Yamato clan. At the same time, the Japanese began copying many other features of Chinese society. Not only did they copy Chinese architectural and artistic forms and clothing styles, but they also adapted the Chinese system of writing to the Japanese language.

SU TUNG-P'O'S VISIT TO LI CHIEH-CH'IAO
AT THE WIND AND WATER CAVE (detail)
Japanese, Kano School
The Metropolitan Museum of Art, New York

The Heian Age

The central government was able to retain its authority for only a brief period. In 794, a new imperial capital was built at Heian (now Kyoto). During the following years, the Japanese began to lose interest in China. At the same time, the power of the emperor began to diminish. Soon the emperors and their courts were no longer the administrative chiefs of a centralized government. Although the emperor continued to be a respected figure, surrounded by elegant lords and ladies, the real political authority had slipped into the hands of the powerful aristocratic Fujiwara family.

Meanwhile, ambitious and militaristic aristocrats who were not part of the Fujiwara family settled in the Japanese countryside, beyond the reach of the central government. There, they established huge private estates and assembled bands of warriors, hoping to eventually challenge the authority of the Fujiwaras.

Feudal Japan

By 1100 the power of the Fujiwara family had begun to slip away, while the rural lords became increasingly powerful. As a result, Japan was eventually transformed into a feudal society in some ways similar to that of Western Europe at the time. Feudal Japan was dominated by the *samurai* class, which included the militaristic lords, known as *daimyo,* and their bands of warriors, known as *samurai* soldiers. As a symbol of their status, the *samurai* carried a pair of swords. In addition they

Japanese
(500–1890)

"Events of Heian Period," Japanese civil war (detail) *Museum of Fine Arts, Boston*

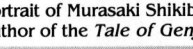

Portrait of Murasaki Shikibu, author of the *Tale of Genji*

Scene from the *Tale of Genji*, 12th century

500	1000

HISTORY

- Great Reform begins
- Imperial Japan begins
- Japanese political law is codified
- Heian (Kyoto) is founded
- Heian Epoch begins
- The period of Engi begins
- Revolt occurs against imperial rule; civil war begins
- Fujiwara domination begins

HUMAN PROGRESS

- Petroleum is used in Japan
- Capital at Nara is built
- Pictorial book printing is first known in Japan
- Earliest extant prints in Japan are produced
- Japan imports Buddhist paintings of T'ang era from China

LITERATURE

- Kakinomoto Hitomaro: *Collection for a Myriad Ages*
- Hitomaro dies
- *Manyoshu: Book of Ten Thousand Leaves*
- Sei Shōnagon begins writing *The Pillow Book*
- *Taketori Monogatari (The Story of the Bamboo Gatherer)*, earliest Japanese narrative
- Ono Komachi: *Kokinshu,* the official imperial anthology of Japanese poetry of preceding 150 years
- Lady Murasaki is born
- Murasaki: *Tale of Genji*
- Lady Murasaki dies

Humanities Notes

Pictured from left to right:

The power and influence of the Heian court declined in the early 1100's. Noble court families lost power to strong rural lords. One of the many conflicts that ensued is depicted here. As a result of these warring families, feudalism emerged as the new system of government. The feudal period in Japan lasted until the latter part of the nineteenth century.

Japanese novelist and diarist Lady Murasaki Shikibu (c. 978–c. 1031) is the celebrated author of *The Tale of Genji*. This tale of adventure and courtly love is one of the first great works of Japanese fiction. Although the exact date of writing is uncertain, some scholars believe it was completed by 1022. After the death of her first husband in 1001, Lady Murasaki's father found her a position in the service of Empress Akiko; she remained there until her death. In *Diaries of Court Ladies of Old Japan*, Lady Murasaki discloses the life and people at her mistress's court.

Some scholars and historians consider *The Tale of Genji* the first novel ever written. It is undisputedly the greatest work of Japanese prose literature. The book details the life of Genji, or "the Shining One," as he was called. Genji was a prince known for his physical attractiveness. One of the main attractions for this novel is its beautiful descriptions of nature and of life in a Japanese court.

In 1185 Japanese warrior and dictator Yoritomo Minamoto (1148–1199) led his clan to victory over the Taira. Soon afterward Minamoto established a new system of military government and became the first *shōgun*. He established his capital at Kamakura. Minamoto's reign marks the end of a long period of civil war and the beginning of feudalism in Japan, which lasted for nearly 750 years. The overthrow of the shōgunate in 1867 marks the beginning of modern Japan.

Nō plays are the oldest of three traditional forms (doll, or puppet,

Portrait of Yoritomo, Japan's first shōgun

Japanese Ko-mote, 15th century Nō mask
Kongo Family Collection, Tokyo

Admiral Perry lands at Kurihama, July 14, 1853
United States Naval Academy Museum

Temple of the Golden Pavilion, Kyoto

1500

1890

- Civil war ends
- Feudal Japan begins
- Kamakura era begins
- Yoritomo becomes first Shogun
  - Kublai Khan invades Japan

- Battle of Sekigahara is fought
  - Great fire of Tokyo occurs
    - Mount Fujiyama erupts
- Tokyo becomes imperial city
  - Feudalism is abolished
  - Famine in Japan occurs
  - Opium War begins
  - Japan is forced to open trade with U.S.
    - Imperial power is restored

- Tea arrives from China
  - Porcelain manufacturing begins

- Japanese magnolia is introduced in England
  - First Japanese railway is founded

- Yoshida Kenko is born
  - Yoshida Kenko: "Essays in Idleness"
    - Development of Japanese Nō Plays
  - Yoshida Kenko dies
  - Zeami is born
    - Zeami dies

- Matsuo Bashō is born
  - Bashō begins journey diaries
  - Matsuo Bashō dies
  - Yosa Buson is born
    - Kobayashi Issa is born
    - Yosa Buson dies
      - Kobayashi Issa dies

and Kabuki being the other two). Nō plays are generally very short and have a highly tragic mood. They were developed in the 1300's from dances performed at religious shrines. They combine history, legend, and Buddhist and Shinto beliefs. The Nō play reached its present form in the 1600's and has remained virtually unchanged ever since. Zeami Motokiyo (1363–1443), author of "The Deserted Crone," page 306, brought the Nō play to its height. Like Greek drama, the Nō play is performed by actors wearing wooden masks who are accompanied by music and choral speaking. Every aspect of the Nō play is highly controlled and follows a specific rule. Thousands of Nō plays were written, but only about 250 are performed today.

Commodore Matthew Perry (1794–1858) is best known for having opened Japanese ports to world trade. In July 1853 Perry sailed the first U.S. Navy ships into Tokyo Bay. His meeting with the highest Japanese officials is pictured here. Shortly after his first meeting, Perry arranged a treaty with Japan, protecting American sailors and property in Japanese waters. Japan had had a previous history of hostility toward foreigners and had sealed itself off from all outside influence. Perry's diplomatic achievements made significant changes in American and European policy toward Japan and brought about changes within Japan.

The Temple of the Golden Pavilion is an example of the symmetrical simplicity of Chinese architecture. Shinto temples, such as this one, were greatly influenced by Chinese architecture, which came to Japan with the introduction of Buddhism. Of greatest importance to the Shinto temple was the landscape setting, the most favored of which was nestled in a forested hillside.

Humanities Note

Fine art, *The Actor Ichimura Mitsuzo as a Samurai* by Torii Kiyomasu II. Torii Kiyomasu II (1694–1716) was the son of a theatrical signboard painter and playbill designer. Although Torii Kiyomasu II began his artistic career by following in his father's footsteps, he soon surpassed his father's accomplishments and established himself as one of the master printmakers of the Edo period. In his prints he used stop-action poses to capture the stylized movements of the actors in the Kabuki theater. Here he portrays a famous actor named Ichimura Mitsuzo, dressed as a samurai. Notice how he has frozen the actor in a graceful pose, with the drapery of his ropes echoing the curved shape of the plant behind him.

You might want to use the following questions to discuss the art:
1. During the period in which this print was produced, artists often used actors as subjects. Why might an actor make a good subject for a work of art?
2. How does attire worn by samurai contrast with the attire worn by warriors from Western countries during the Middle Ages?
3. What might be the reason that the clothing of the Japanese warriors was so different from that worn by Western warriors?
4. What do you find most interesting about this print?

adhered to a strict code of conduct that emphasized bravery, loyalty, and honor.

In 1160 the *daimyo* of the Taira family seized control of Japan from the Fujiwaras. Throughout the next twenty-five years, however, the authority of the Tairas was challenged by the Minamoto family. Finally, in 1185 the Minamotos defeated the Tairas, and Minamoto Yoritomo became the most powerful figure in Japan, establishing his headquarters at Kamakura, near present-day Tokyo. Although Yoritomo claimed to be in the service of the emperor, there was no doubt that he himself was the true ruler of Japan. In 1192 Yoritomo accepted from the emperor the title of *shōgun*, or chief general. As it turned out, he was one of a series of *shōguns*, who ruled Japan for over 500 years.

Despite their military strength, Yoritomo and most of the *shōguns* who followed him were unable to completely control the other *daimyo*. Each *daimyo* continued to rule his own estate, and most thirsted to broaden their power. As a result, Japan existed in a state of constant feudal warfare for hundreds of years.

The Tokugawa Shōgunate

During the late 1500s, a great warrior named Hideyoshi subdued the feuding *daimyo* and gained control of all of Japan. Following his death, one of his deputies, Tokugawa Iyeyasu, seized control of the nation. He became *shōgun* in 1603, and the Tokugawa Shōgunate was established.

Following Tokugawa's assumption of power, a new capital was built at Edo (now Tokyo). Although he allowed the *daimyo* to retain their estates, he ordered them to spend every other year at Edo, and he ordered the families of the *daimyo* to settle permanently in Edo. The *shōgun* also took many other measures to control the *daimyo*, such as spying on them and preventing them from accumulating too much wealth.

To guard against the appearance of any new groups that might challenge established authority, the *shōgun* attempted to freeze Japanese society in its early seventeenth-century form. Social classes were defined by the *shōgun* himself, and people were forbidden to cross class lines. European merchants and Christian missionaries, who had recently arrived and were viewed as potential threats to the *shōgun's* authority, were driven from the country. Following the expulsion of these people, Japanese ports were closed to foreign ships, with the exception of a single Dutch ship that was permitted to call once a year. In addition, the Japanese people were forbidden to leave their home islands, while foreigners having the misfortune of landing in Japan were imprisoned and treated badly. As a result of these measures, Japan was effectively closed to the outside world until the middle of the nineteenth century.

THE ACTOR ICHIMURA MITSUZO AS A SAMURAI
Torii Kiyomasu II
The Metropolitan Museum of Art, New York

The Downfall of Feudalism in Japan

By borrowing the best that China had to offer, Japan had developed into an advanced civilization. The isolation imposed by the Tokugawas, however, came just as sweeping scientific, technological, economic, and political advances were beginning to occur in the West. The Tokugawa leaders kept their eyes on the

West through the annual voyages of the Dutch ships but chose not to share their knowledge. As a result, when an American fleet commanded by Commodore Matthew Perry steamed into Tokyo Bay in 1853, the Japanese people on the shores panicked. They knew only of ships that were propelled by oars and sails.

Perry had come to Japan seeking to open trade. Realizing that the United States was just one of many Western powers seeking to break Japan's isolation, the Tokugawa government eventually signed a treaty with the United States and later signed agreements with several other countries. These treaties not only opened Japan to the outside world, but they also helped to create unrest at home that eventually toppled the Tokugawa regime.

In 1868, after the Shōgunate had toppled, a new government was established in which the new emperor, Meiji, had real authority. Not only did the new government do away with the feudal system, but it also plunged into an effort to reshape Japan into a modern nation equal to the great Western powers. The government's efforts were extremely successful, and by the turn of the century, Japan was well on its way to becoming a major industrial and military power.

RELIGIOUS TRADITIONS

Buddhism and Shintoism

Modern Japanese society is overwhelmingly secular. While religious structures, such as temples and shrines, can be seen everywhere and while many religious traditions are observed, most contemporary Japanese do not think of religion as being central to their lives. This type of attitude, however, was not common in Japan's early history. Two major faiths, Shintoism and Buddhism, were essential elements in the cultural foundations of Japanese society.

The early Japanese practiced simple nature worship. By the sixth century A.D., this practice had assumed the name *Shintoism*, or "the way of the gods," to distinguish it from Buddhism, which had been introduced from China and was gaining popularity in Japan. Central to Shintoism was the popular belief that mountains, streams, lakes, and other elements of nature were inhabited by spirits, known as *kami*. For this reason natural scenes, such as a waterfall, a gnarled tree, or a full moon, inspired reverence in the Japanese people.

Despite its popularity, Buddhism did not compete with Shintoism. Instead, the Japanese found that they could embrace both religions. The Japanese looked to Buddhism to teach them how to overcome the pain, misfortunes, and sorrows of life. Buddhism emphasized the impermanence of life on Earth and taught people to rid themselves of worldly conceits, pleasures, and ambitions. According to Buddhist doctrine, by turning away from worldly things, people could free themselves of the troubles of this life and move toward a blissful eternity.

Japanese Buddhism assumed a number of different forms. The military aristocrats, for example, favored a form of Buddhism known as Zen. In contrast to other Buddhist sects, Zen rejects the notion that salvation is attained outside of this life and this world. Instead, Zen disciples believe that one can attain personal tranquillity and insights into the true meaning of life through rigorous physical and mental discipline.

JAPANESE LITERATURE

Poetry

Poetry is one of the oldest and most popular means of expression and communication in the Japanese culture. Although poetry had already existed for centuries as part of an oral tradition, the first anthology of Japanese poetry, the *Manyoshu*, or "Book of Ten Thousand Leaves," did not appear until the eighth century. Containing over four thousand poems, the anthology includes works by poets from a wide range of social classes, including the peasantry, the clergy, and the ruling class. When viewed as a whole, the anthology makes it clear that poetry was an integral part of daily life in ancient Japanese society, serving as a means through which anyone could chronicle experiences and express emotions.

In the centuries following the publication of the *Manyoshu*, Japanese emperors and their courts became increasingly interested in and supportive of the

7 Enrichment Tell students that the treaties that the Japanese signed with the United States and the major European powers generally benefited the foreign countries more than they benefited the Japanese. Ask students how the unfairness of the treaties might have contributed to the unrest that eventually toppled the Tokugawa regime.

8 Learning Across the Curriculum Students might be interested in learning more about how Japan's isolation came to an end. Encourage them to research this subject in the library and to report their findings to the class.

9 Enrichment Students can learn more about the collapse of the feudal system and the rise of the Meiji regime by reading the Commentary on page 1173.

10 Enrichment Students can learn more about Buddhism by reading the Commentary on page 229.

11 Enrichment If you have already covered the unit on Chinese literature, remind students that poetry was also an integral part of daily life in ancient Chinese society. Do students have the impression that poetry played a more important role in ancient Chinese and Japanese societies than in ancient Western societies? Why or why not?

efforts of poets. The court held regular poetry contests and published a series of poetry anthologies that included the best poems of the time.

Nearly all the poems in these anthologies were written in tanka form, consisting of five lines of five, seven, five, seven, and seven syllables. In previous centuries the choka, consisting of an unlimited number of alternating lines of five and seven syllables, had rivaled the tanka in popularity. However, as the court began playing an active role in establishing poetic standards, an increasing emphasis was placed on brevity, and the choka form was almost completely abandoned.

12 During the age of Japanese feudalism, it became fashionable for groups of poets to work together to write chains of interlocking tanka, known as renga. Each tanka within a renga was divided into verses of seventeen and fourteen syllables, composed by different poets. Eventually, the opening verse of a renga, known as the hokku, developed into a distinct literary form, consisting of three lines of five, seven, and five syllables. The haiku, the name by which this verse form came to be known, soon replaced the tanka as the most popular Japanese verse form and remained so until the end of the nineteenth century.

Prose

Appearing in the early part of the eighth century, the first works of Japanese prose, the *Kojiki*, or "Record of Ancient Matters," and *Nihon Shoki*, or "Chronicles of Japan," focused on Japanese history. The content of Japanese prose changed, however, as the nation evolved.

13 During the Heian Age, the ladies and gentlemen of the court, having few administrative or political duties, kept lengthy diaries and experimented with writing fiction. Among the court ladies who vividly captured the lives of the Heian aristocracy in prose were Murasaki Shikibu and Sei Shōnagon.

Aside from Lady Murasaki's *Tale of Genji*, the most famous early Japanese novel may be *The Tale of Heike*. Written by an unknown author during the thirteenth century, this work presents a striking portrait of war-torn Japan during the early stages of the age of feudalism. Another important work of prose produced during the age of feudalism is *Essays in Idleness*, a loosely organized collection of insights,

YOUNG WOMEN ARRANGING A BOUQUET OF PEONIES
Musée Guimet, Paris

reflections, and observations, written during the fourteenth century by a Buddhist priest named Kenko. Finally, throughout the age of feudalism as well as the Tokugawa period, a vast number of Japanese writers and aristocrats kept diaries and journals that offer vivid accounts of Japanese life at the time.

Drama

The earliest surviving form of Japanese drama, Nō plays, emerged during the fourteenth century. In some respects, the Nō theater is like the drama of ancient Greece: The plays are performed on an almost bare stage by a small but elaborately costumed cast of actors wearing masks; the actors are accompanied by a chorus; and the plays are written either in verse or in highly poetic prose. Yet the dramas themselves are decidedly Japanese, reflecting many Shinto and Buddhist beliefs, along with a number of the dominant Japanese artistic preferences.

Two other theatrical forms developed during the Tokugawa period: Joruri and Kabuki. Joruri (now called Bunraku) is staged using puppets. Kabuki involves lively, melodramatic acting and is staged using elaborate and colorful costumes and sets. Both types of dramas are performed to the accompaniment of an orchestra, and they both generally focus on the lives of common people rather than of aristocrats.

JAPANESE VOICES

How delightful it would be to converse intimately with someone of the same mind, sharing with him the pleasures of uninhibited conversation on the amusing and foolish things of this world, but such friends are hard to find.

Kenko, *Essays in Idleness*

A certain hermit once said, "There is one thing that even I, who have no worldly entanglements, would be sorry to give up, the beauty of the sky."

Kenko, *Essays in Idleness*

In spring it is the dawn that is most beautiful. As the light creeps over the hills, their outlines are dyed a faint red and wisps of purplish cloud trail over them.

Sei Shōnagon, *The Pillow Book*

And so, young though he was, fleeting beauty took its hold upon his thoughts . . .

Lady Murasaki, *The Tale of Genji*

The autumn moon
We saw last year
Shines again: but she
Who was with me then
The years separate forever.

Kakinomoto Hitomaro, "I Loved Her Like the Leaves"

The hanging raindrops
Have not dried from the needles
Of the fir forest
Before the evening mist
Of autumn rises.

Priest Jakuren

On a journey, ill,
And over fields all withered, dreams
Go wandering still.

Bashō

Morning haze:
as in a painting of a dream,
men go their ways.

Yosa Buson

Far-off mountain peaks
Reflected in its eyes:
The dragonfly.

Kobayashi Issa

Additional Voices

Though it seemed a shame to put so lovely a child into man's dress, he was now twelve years old and the time for his Initiation was come. The Emperor directed the preparations with tireless zeal and insisted upon magnificence beyond what was prescribed. . . .

—Lady Murasaki, *The Tale of Genji*

The breezes of spring
Are blowing the ripples astray
Along the water—
Today they will surely melt
The sheet of ice on the pond

—Ki no Tomonori

Nothing but pain and shame in this
  world of men,
But I cannot fly away,
Wanting the wings of a bird.

—Yamanoue Okura

When people meet they are never silent for a moment. There is always talk about something. If you listen to their conversations, most of what they say is meaningless chatter. Their gossip about society and their criticisms of other people cause much harm and little profit, either for themselves or others. When people are gabbling over these things, they never seem to realize that it does neither party any good.

—Yoshida Kenko, *Essays in Idleness*

Japanese Literature

Historical Context

Throughout the early stages of its history, Japan was heavily influenced by the Chinese culture. The Japanese borrowed the Chinese system of writing, adopted the dominant Chinese religions of Confucianism and Buddhism, and even attempted to mimic the Chinese system of centralized imperial rule. The attempt to create a centralized government controlled by an emperor was unsuccessful, however, and most Japanese emperors turned out to be little more than figureheads manipulated by the most powerful family of the time. The leader of the dominant family, who was known as the shogun, was the true ruler of the country, using bands of hired warriors known as samurai to keep order throughout the nation.

Cultural Context

Despite the influence of the Chinese, Japan has developed its own distinctive cultural identity. Certain elements of the Japanese culture, such as the emphasis on family relations and respect for authority, do reflect the impact of Chinese ideas. Other elements, however, are of purely Japanese origin. A number of these elements, including deep appreciation for nature and preference for simplicity, originated from the oldest Japanese religion, Shintoism, which teaches that the Japanese mountains, rivers, and trees are inhabited by numerous gods known as *kami*. Closely tied to the Japanese people's appreciation for nature is their emphasis on perishability, which is reflected in their love for cherry blossoms, which bloom for only a short time, and their undying awareness of the changing of seasons. Two other important aspects of the dominant Japanese tastes are the culture's preference for suggestion, rather than direct statement, and irregularity, rather than perfect symmetry.

Literary Context

The emphasis on simplicity, suggestion, irregularity, and perishability is exhibited in all types of Japanese literature. The vast majority of traditional Japanese poems are extremely brief, reflecting the Japanese preference for simplicity and suggestion; and they generally consist of an uneven number of lines and syllables per line, reflecting the Japanese emphasis on irregularity. In contrast to Japanese poetry, works of Japanese prose are often quite long. However, the dominant Japanese tastes are generally exhibited in the content of these works.

The annotations that accompany the following selection point out the work's historical context, cultural context, and literary context.

Objectives

Thematic
To understand Japanese tastes and attitudes

Skills
1 To understand the *zuihitsu* form

2 To recognize cultural characteristics
3 To write a collection of personal sketches modeled after *Essays in Idleness*

Support Material
Teaching Portfolio
Teacher Backup, p. 369
Reading Critically, "Love's Complaint" by Lady Otomo, p. 373
Grammar in Action Worksheets, *Parallelism*, p.375; *Topic Sentences*, p. 377
Usage and Mechanics Worksheet, p. 379

from Essays in Idleness

Yoshida Kenko

translated by Donald Keene

> **Cultural Context:** Kenko was a Buddhist priest, and the title of his work captures the quiet, contemplative existence that is characteristic of this position.

2

The man who forgets the wise principles of the reigns of the ancient emperors; who gives no thought to the grievances of the people or the harm done the country; who strives for the utmost luxury in everything, imagining this is the sign of magnificence; who acts as if the world were too small for him seems deplorably wanting in intelligence. You will find in Lord Kujō's Testament[1] the instruction, "Make do with whatever you have, from your court costume down to your horses and carriages. Do not strive for elegance." Again, you will find among the writings of the Retired Emperor Juntoku[2] on court ceremonial, "The clothes worn by the emperor should be simple and unassuming."

> **Cultural Context:** Kenko's condemnation of a life of luxury reflects the Japanese emphasis on simplicity.

> **Historical Context:** Although Japanese writers frequently refer to the reigns of various emperors, it is important to keep in mind that most Japanese emperors were little more than ceremonial figureheads.

20

A certain hermit once said, "There is one thing that even I, who have no worldly entanglements, would be sorry to give up, the beauty of the sky." I can understand why he should have felt that way.

> **Cultural Context:** The hermit's remarks reflect the influence of Buddhism, which emphasizes the need to free oneself of material possessions and earthly desires.

21

Looking at the moon is always diverting, no matter what the circumstances. A certain man once said, "Surely nothing is so delightful as the moon," but another man rejoined, "The dew moves me even more." How amusing that they should have argued the point! What could fail to be affecting in its proper season? This is obviously true of the moon and cherry blossoms. The wind seems to have a special power to move men's hearts.

Regardless of the season, however, a clear-flowing stream breaking against rocks makes a splendid sight. I remember how touched I was

> **Cultural Context:** The Japanese associate certain elements of nature with specific seasons. For example, cherry blossoms are associated with spring. The interest in the changing seasons and the accompanying changes in nature reflects the Japanese appreciation of perishability.

---

1. **Lord Kujō's** (kōō′ jōz′) **Testament:** Lord Kujō was the title of Fujiwara no Morosuke (908–960). His testament is a statement of his beliefs.
2. **Emperor Juntoku** (jōōn to kōō): The emperor of Japan from 1197 through 1242.

Vocabulary Check, p. 380
Analyzing Literature Worksheet, *Understanding the Zuihitsu Form*, p. 381
Critical Thinking and Reading Worksheet, *Recognizing Cultural Characteristics*, p. 382
Selection Test, pp.383–384

Spelling Tip Call students' attention to the double *l* in *unsullied* and to the double *s* in *unassuming*.

Presentation

Motivation/Prior Knowledge
Have students discuss the types of behavior that they find agreeable and the types of behavior that bother them. Explain that in *Essays in Idleness* Kenko expresses many of his opinions concerning people's behavior. As students read the following excerpts they should compare and contrast Kenko's views with their own.

Purpose-Setting Question What do these excerpts reveal about Kenko's likes and dislikes?

1 **Reading Strategy** Have students make inferences about the selection based on its title.

2 **Discussion** Have students discuss whether these concerns are applicable to the contemporary world.

3 **Discussion** Have students express their reactions to the hermit's comment. Do they share his attachment to the beauty of the sky? Why or why not?

4 **Discussion** Have students discuss natural images that they associate with each of the four seasons.

Vocabulary

Preteach the following vocabulary words:
deplorably (di plôr′ ə blē) *adv.*: Wretchedly
unassuming (un ə sōō′ miŋ) *adj.*: Modest
unsullied (un sul′ ēd) *adj.*: Unstained
interminable (in tur′ mi nə b'l) *adj.*: Endless
hinterland (hin′ tər land′) *n.*: Back country
expatiating (ik spā′ shē āt iŋ) *v.*: Speaking or writing in great detail
impunity (im pyōō′ nə tē) *n.*: Exemption from punishment, penalty, or harm

5 **Discussion** Have students discuss whether they share Kenko's deep love of nature.

6 **Discussion** Have students discuss whether the observations in this passage are as relevant today as when they were written. Why or why not?

7 **Discussion** Have students describe a situation in which a friend, acquaintance, or family member behaved in the manner that Kenko describes. Do students agree with Kenko's opinion concerning this type of behavior? Why or why not?

8 **Discussion** Do students agree that people should address themselves to one person even if there are many people present? Why or why not? What difference between Japanese and Western culture might Kenko's opinion reflect?

Literary Context: Most Japanese writers were influenced by or were familiar with the works of Chinese poets. In fact, many Japanese writers composed at least some of their poetry in Chinese.

Cultural Context: As a Buddhist priest, Kenko tried to free himself of earthly desires through meditation. At the same time, his Buddhist beliefs caused him to have an inescapable awareness of the instability of human life.

Cultural Context: The Japanese generally believe that people should conduct themselves in a restrained, dignified, and disciplined manner.

when I read the Chinese poem, "The Yüan and Hsiang flow ever east, night and day alike; they never stop an instant to soothe the grieving man."[3] Chi K'ang[4] also has the lines, "The heart rejoices to visit mountains and lakes and see the birds and fish." Nothing gives so much pleasure as to wander to some spot far from the world, where the water and vegetation are <u>unsullied</u>.

29

When I sit down in quiet meditation, the one emotion hardest to fight against is a longing in all things for the past. After the others have gone to bed, I pass the time on a long autumn's night by putting in order whatever belongings are at hand. As I tear up scraps of old correspondence I should prefer not to leave behind, I sometimes find among them samples of the calligraphy[5] of a friend who has died, or pictures he drew for his own amusement, and I feel exactly as I did at the time. Even with letters written by friends who are still alive I try, when it has been long since we met, to remember the circumstances, the year. What a moving experience that is! It is sad to think that a man's familiar possessions, indifferent to his death, should remain unaltered long after he is gone.

56

How boring it is when you meet a man after a long separation and he insists on relating at <u>interminable</u> length everything that has happened to him in the meantime. Even if the man is an intimate, somebody you know extremely well, how can you but feel a certain reserve on meeting him again after a time? The vulgar sort of person, even if he goes on a brief excursion somewhere, is breathless with excitement as he relates as matters of great interest everything that has happened to him. When the well-bred man tells a story he addresses himself to one person, even if many people are present, though the others too listen, naturally. But the ill-bred man flings out his words into the crowd, addressing himself to no one in particular, and describes what happened so graphically that everyone bursts into boisterous laughter. You can judge a person's breeding by whether he is quite impassive even when he tells an amusing story, or laughs a great deal even when relating a matter of no interest.

---

3. **"The Yüan** (yo͞o än) **and Hsiang** (shē äng) **. . . grieving man":** From a poem by the Chinese poet Tai Shu-lun (dī sho͞o lo͞on). The Yüan and the Hsiang are both rivers in China.
4. **Chi K'ang** (jē käng): An ancient Chinese poet.
5. **calligraphy** (kə lig′ rə fē) *n.*: Beautiful handwriting.

Grammar in Action

Parallelism is the arrangement of equal ideas in equivalent grammatical structures. Writers use parallelism to create balance and rhythm and to emphasize important ideas. Notice the following example of parallelism from Donald Keene's translation of *Essays in Idleness*:

. . . *who gives* no thought to the grievances of the people or the harm done the country; *who strives* for the utmost luxury in everything, imagining this is the sign of magnificence; *who acts* as if the world were too small for him . . . (page 267)

Student Activity 1. Find two more examples of parallelism in Keene's translation of *Essays in Idleness*.

Student Activity 2. Correct the faulty parallelism in each of the following sentences by rewriting them so that equal ideas are cast in equivalent grammatical structures.

1. *Essays in Idleness* reflects the Japanese people's emphasis on restraint in behavior, preference for simplicity, and their love of nature.
2. *Essays in Idleness* is a loosely organized collection of insights, reflections, and contains Kenko's observations.
3. According to Kenko, people should remember the lessons of the past,

SUMMER NIGHT
Maruyama Okyo
The Cleveland Museum of Art

It is most distressing, when the good and bad of somebody's appearance or the quality of a certain person's scholarship is being evaluated, for the speaker to refer to himself by way of comparison.

79

A man should avoid displaying deep familiarity with any subject. Can one imagine a well-bred man talking with the air of a know-it-all, even about a matter with which he is in fact familiar? The boor who pops up on the scene from somewhere in the hinterland answers questions with an air of utter authority in every field. As a result, though the man may also possess qualities that compel our admiration, the manner in which he displays his high opinion of himself is contemptible. It is impressive when a man is always slow to speak, even on subjects he knows thoroughly, and does not speak at all unless questioned.

92

A certain man who was learning to shoot a bow aimed at the target with two arrows in his hand. His teacher said, "A beginner should not hold two arrows. It will make him rely on the second arrow and be careless with the first. Each time you shoot you should think not of hitting or missing the target but of making *this* one the decisive arrow." I wonder if

Literary Context: This echoes a passage from *The Pillow Book* by the eleventh-century Japanese writer Sei Shonagon. Shonagon writes that it is hateful "when a man who has nothing in particular to recommend him discusses all sorts of subjects at random as though he knew everything." Japanese writers often indirectly allude to or elaborate on details or ideas from earlier literary works.

9 Discussion Do students agree that it is bad taste for people to refer to themselves by way of comparison? Why or why not?

10 Master Teacher Note Have students describe characters in movies or in a television series who present themselves as know-it-alls. For instance, they might think of Alex from the television series *Family Ties*. Then have students discuss what is appealing and unappealing about the characters they have named.

11 Discussion Have students discuss occasions on which they have performed an activity with the knowledge that they would have a second chance. For example, did they ever take a test, knowing that they would have the opportunity to take it again if they did poorly? How did the knowledge that they could have a second chance affect their performance?

avoid displaying familiarity with any subject, and people should not be careless.

Humanities Note

Fine art, *Summer Night* by Maruyama Okyo. Maruyama Okyo (1733–1795) brought the art of Japanese landscape painting to new heights. While retaining a traditional Japanese style, Okyo devoted himself to picturing animals, plants, and other elements of nature in a more detailed and realistic manner than most earlier Japanese artists. At the same time, he managed to create a mystical, dreamlike atmosphere in many of his paintings, including the one seen here.

You might want to use the following questions to discuss the art:
1. How would you describe the mood, or atmosphere, of this painting?
2. Which details contribute to this atmosphere?
3. Do you think this painting is an appropriate illustration for *Essays in Idleness*? Why or why not?
4. How does the scene depicted in this painting compare with the way in which you envision a typical summer night?

anyone with only two arrows would be careless with one of them in the presence of his teacher. But though the pupil is himself unaware of any carelessness, the teacher will notice it. This caution applies to all things.

A man studying some branch of learning thinks at night that he has the next day before him, and in the morning that he will have time that night; he plans in this way always to study more diligently at some future time. How much harder it is to perceive the laziness of mind that arises in an instant! Why should it be so difficult to do something now, in the present moment?

105

The unmelted snow lying in the shade north of the house was frozen hard, and even the shafts of a carriage drawn up there glittered with frost. The dawn moon shone clear, but its light was not penetrating. In the corridor of a deserted temple a man of obvious distinction sat beside a woman on a doorsill, chatting. Whatever it was they were discussing, there seemed no danger they would run out of things to say. The woman had a charming manner of tilting her head toward the man, and I caught an occasional, enchanting whiff of some exquisite perfume. The scraps of their conversation reaching me made me long to hear the rest.

168

When an old man has acquired surpassing ability in some art and people ask about him, "Once he has gone, who will answer our questions?" it means that he is not living in vain, for he serves as a justification for all old people. However, the very fact that his art has not deteriorated in the least makes him seem rather contemptible, for it means he has spent his whole life doing only one thing. I prefer it when an old man says, "I've forgotten it now." As a rule, even if a man knows his art, people will suspect that he is not really so talented if he keeps chattering on about it. Besides, mistakes will naturally occur. A man is more likely to seem a true master of his art if he says, "I cannot tell for certain."

It is worse still to listen to a man of eminence expatiating on some subject he knows nothing about with a look of self-satisfaction on his face; one cannot very well criticize him, but one is thinking all the while, "What nonsense!"

235

A man with no business will never intrude into an occupied house simply because he so pleases. If the house is vacant, on the other hand, travelers journeying along the road will enter with impunity, and even creatures like foxes and owls, undisturbed by any human presence, will take up their abodes, acting as if the place belonged to them. Tree spirits and other apparitions will also manifest themselves.

---

12 Discussion Have students discuss the reasons people procrastinate. Ask them if they have ever had a problem with procrastination. If so, why?

13 Critical Thinking and Reading Have students discuss other ways in which this passage reflects the Japanese preference for suggestion.

14 Discussion Have students discuss their reactions to the views that Kenko expresses in this passage.

15 Discussion Have students discuss why this passage does not apply to contemporary American life. Do they imagine that it applies to contemporary life in any other societies? If so, which ones?

Cultural Context: This section reflects the Japanese emphasis on suggestion. By referring to the snow as "unmelted," Kenko hints at the fact that it will melt with the coming of spring. Then he offers a fragmentary description of a conversation, leaving it up to the reader to imagine what the conversation was about.

Cultural Context: This passage exhibits the influence of the Chinese philosophy of Confucianism, which teaches that people should strive to acquire knowledge of a variety of subjects and that elderly people should be knowledgeable to be worthy of respect. Confucianism also teaches that a person's studies should not be motivated by the desire to impress other people.

Cultural Context: The reference to "tree spirits and other apparitions" reflects the Shinto belief that the Japanese landscape is inhabited by numerous gods known as *kami* (kə′ mē′).

Grammar in Action

A **topic sentence** expresses the main idea of a paragraph and defines the scope of the paragraph. The rest of the sentences in a paragraph should support the topic sentence by offering examples, details, facts, reasons, or incidents. The first sentence of the following paragraph is an example of a topic sentence, and the sentences that follow support the topic sentence.

A man should avoid displaying deep familiarity with any subject. Can one imagine a well-bred man talking with the air of a know-it-all, even about a matter with which he is in fact familiar? The boor who pops up on the scene from somewhere in the hinterland answers questions with an air of utter authority in every field. As a result, though the man may also possess qualities that compel our admiration, the manner in which he displays his high opinion of himself is contemptible. It is impressive when a man is always slow to speak, even on subjects he knows thoroughly, and does not speak at all unless questioned.

Student Activity 1. Identify the topic sentences and supporting information in two other paragraphs from *Essays in Idleness*.

Student Activity 2. Write an original paragraph in which you express

It is the same with mirrors: being without color or shape of their own, they reflect all manner of forms. If mirrors had color and shape of their own, they would probably not reflect other things.

Emptiness accommodates everything. I wonder if thoughts of all kinds intrude themselves at will on our minds because what we call our minds are vacant? If our minds were occupied, surely so many things would not enter them.

16

Reader's Response *Which section of* Essays in Idleness *spoke most directly to you? Why?*

Kenko (1283?–1352?) Kenko's reputation as a writer rests almost entirely on the tremendous success of his masterpiece, *Essays in Idleness*. A loosely organized collection of insights, reflections, and observations, *Essays in Idleness* has been read and loved by generations and promises to remain popular far into the future.

Although he was born into a high-ranking Shinto family, Kenko became a Buddhist priest as a young adult. At the same time, he developed a reputation as a talented poet. Yet today it is generally felt that his reputation as a poet was undeserved.

In contrast, his reputation as a prose writer has only grown over the centuries. Reflecting his Buddhist beliefs as well as many of the dominant attitudes of his day, *Essays in Idleness* has not only informed and entertained millions of readers, but it has also played a major role in defining the Japanese aesthetic.

your opinion about an issue that you feel is important. Make sure your paragraph has a clear topic sentence and you thoroughly support your topic sentence with facts, reasons, and details.

16 Discussion Have students discuss the tone of this passage. Is Kenko being serious?

Cooperative Learning Point out to students that unlike the Japanese culture, our society tends to emphasize durability and longevity rather than perishability. Divide the class into groups of three or four. Next have each group try to think of elements of American culture that reflect an emphasis on durability and longevity. Then have each group share its examples with the rest of the class.

More About the Author Kenko's appreciation of the perishability of life is reflected throughout *Essays in Idleness*. While human frailty has been a recurring theme throughout the history of literature, Kenko's association of frailty with beauty reflects an essential quality of the Japanese culture. Unlike the traditional Western discomfort with the delicacy of life, the Japanese view frailty as an integral part of beauty and as an element to be celebrated and cherished. Kenko wrote, "If man were never to fade away like the dews of Adashino, never to vanish like the smoke over Toribeyama, but lingered on forever in this world, how things would lose their power to move us! The most precious thing in life is its uncertainty." Have students express their reactions to this view and discuss the ways in which it contrasts with a typical Western outlook.

Critical Evaluation A distinguished Japanese literature scholar writes that Kenko "did not in the least resemble the typical Buddhist monks of the medieval period, who either lived in monasteries or else were hermits. Kenko lived in the city and was as familiar with worldly gossip as with Buddhist doctrine. . . . He did not reject the world. Ultimately this world was not enough, but Kenko seems always to be saying that while we are here we should try to enrich our lives with beauty."

ANSWERS TO THINKING ABOUT THE SELECTION

1. (a) Answers will differ. Appropriate responses include modesty, thoughtfulness, and sensitivity to the beauty of nature. (b) Answers will differ according to the qualities that students name.
2. (a) Answers will differ. Appropriate responses include self-importance, procrastination, and ostentation. (b) Answers will differ according to the qualities that students name.
3. Answers will differ. Students may respond that they feel it is appropriate for people to display deep familiarity with subjects in which they are very knowledgeable.
4. Answers will differ. Students may respond that the lesson can be applied to both schoolwork and athletics.
5. Answers will differ. Students may respond that they can apply Kenko's ideas concerning procrastination to their lives.

Challenge Joseph Addison called idleness "A kind of monster in the creation. All nature is busy about him; every animal he sees reproaches him." Horace called it "masterly inactivity." Compare both views with Kenko's view.

ANSWERS TO ANALYZING LITERATURE

1. Answers will differ. Students may observe that the sections are similar to an artist's sketchbook in that they each portray a different scene or situation.
2. Answers will differ. Students should observe that both forms consist of a seemingly random arrangement of ideas.

Challenge Have students read a literary work in which the stream-of-consciousness technique is used. For example, you might suggest T. S. Eliot's "The Love Song of J. Alfred Prufrock" or Eudora Welty's "The Jilting of Granny Weatherall." Then have students compare and contrast the use of the stream-of-consciousness technique in the work they have chosen with the presentation of ideas and observations in *Essays in Idleness.*

THINKING ABOUT THE SELECTION

Interpreting

1. *Essays in Idleness* represents Kenko's musings on various subjects. (a) Based on these selections, identify at least three qualities you think Kenko values. (b) Which sections support your answers?
2. Like every human being, Kenko has dislikes as well as likes. (a) Identify at least three qualities Kenko dislikes. (b) Which sections support your answers?

Applying

3. Explain whether you agree with Kenko's opinion in section 79 that people "should avoid displaying deep familiarity with any subject."
4. In section 92 Kenko applies the archery instructor's advice that "a beginner should not hold to two arrows" to a student's management of his or her time. To what other types of situations might the archery instructor's advice be applied?
5. Which of Kenko's ideas could you apply to your own life? Explain your answer.

ANALYZING LITERATURE

Understanding the *Zuihitsu* Form

Essays in Idleness is an example of a type of Japanese nonfiction known as *zuihitsu* (zo͞o′ i′ hit′ se′), characterized by its apparent formlessness. The name *zuihitsu* means "follow the brush." The purpose of this type of work is to allow the writer's brush to skip from one topic to the next led only by his or her natural associations.

1. In what way are the the the sections of *Essays in Idleness* similar to illustrations in an artist's sketchbook?
2. Many twentieth-century writers have used a literary device known as the stream-of-consciousness technique, which attempts to capture the random movement of a character's thoughts. What similarities do you see between the stream-of-consciousness technique and the *zuihitsu?*

CRITICAL THINKING AND READING

Recognizing Cultural Characteristics

Essays in Idleness reveals a great deal about the dominant Japanese tastes and attitudes. For example, in section 56 Kenko conveys the Japanese emphasis on restraint in behavior, when he writes that only vulgar people relate their experiences with great excitement.

1. Find another passage in which Kenko conveys the Japanese emphasis on restraint in behavior. Explain your answer.
2. Closely connected to the Japanese emphasis on restraint is the Japanese preference for simplicity. This preference is most clearly reflected in section 2, but it is also subtly exhibited in a number of other sections. Find another section in which this preference is apparent and explain how it is conveyed.
3. In his famous poem "Against Idleness and Mischief," the English poet Isaac Watts wrote, "For Satan finds some mischief still / For idle hands to do." In Western culture idleness is generally frowned upon. Yet Kenko's work is called *Essays in Idleness.* (a) Do you think the Japanese view of idleness might differ from the Western view? (b) How might idleness be beneficial rather than harmful?

THINKING AND WRITING

Writing from Models

Write a short *zuihitsu* modeled after the selections from *Essays in Idleness.* Begin by exploring your thoughts about a variety of different topics, such as nature, music, and personal conduct. Let your mind doodle just as your hand might. Jot down the various ideas you come up with. When you write your *zuihitsu*, do not include transitions or try to make obvious connections between the various sections. Instead, skip from one topic to another in whatever direction your natural associations take you. After you have finished writing, revise your work, making sure you have expressed your ideas clearly.

ANSWERS TO CRITICAL THINKING AND READING

1. Answers will differ. Appropriate responses include sections 2, 79, and 168.
2. Answers will differ. Appropriate responses include sections 20, 21, and 105.
3. (a) Answers will differ. Many students may respond that despite the title of Kenko's work, it is their impression that idleness is frowned upon in contemporary Japanese society. (b) Answers will differ. Students may point out that it allows time for contemplation.

THINKING AND WRITING

Publishing Student Writing Encourage students to submit their papers to the school literary magazine.

Poetry

TRIPTYCH OF SNOW, MOON, AND FLOWER, 1780'S (detail)
Museum of Art, Atami, Japan

Humanities Note

Fine art, *Triptych of Snow, Moon, and Flower.* This is a single panel from a triptych, or three-part work of art. The panels that make up this piece of art are thin, vertical hanging scrolls that are designed to hang side by side on a wall. The panel seen here offers a stylized depiction of snow, while the other two panels focus on the moon and a flower respectively.

Notice how in this panel the artist has directed the viewer's attention to the graceful woman at the center, while hinting at the accumulating snow outside the window. In addition to including a snow-covered tree in the background, the artist indicates a cloud of snow in the traditional Japanese manner by sweeping a stripe of white against a dark sky.

You might want to use the following questions to discuss the art:
1. What is the mood, or atmosphere, of this painting?
2. How does this picture suggest that snowfall is a poetic event?
3. How does the color scheme fit the subject?
4. If you were an artist who had been asked to paint a picture entitled *Snow*, what would you depict? Why?

KAKINOMOTO HITOMARO

Focus

More About the Author Although Hitomaro's reputation as a poet was firmly established by the time the *Manyoshu* was compiled, he did not have a high rank in the courts in which he served. While his position as court poet may be considered prestigious today, it is important to note that during this period, all members of the court, regardless of their rank, were expected to write poetry. Ask students to consider what this suggests about the role of poetry in traditional Japanese society. How does this compare to the role of poetry in contemporary American society?

Pronunciation Note Notice that in the Japanese language all syllables are pronounced with equal emphasis.

Critical Evaluation The authors of *The Princeton Companion to Classical Japanese Literature* write, "[Hitomaro's] personal poems . . . contain elements resembling those in his official poems, in that the individual, personal occasion is set in a context that enables others to share the experience. On these grounds, his poetry is all more or less public in nature, emphasizing the unified, shared nature of the events of human life."

Seventh to Eighth Centuries A.D.

Little is known about the life of Kakinomoto Hitomaro (kä′ kē′ nä′ mō′ tō′ hē′ tō′ mä′ rō′). Yet from his poetry we can infer that he was extremely dignified, genuine, and perceptive. Characterized by these qualities, as well as by an understanding of human nature and an appreciation for the universal quality of certain experiences, Hitomaro's poetry has earned him a reputation as one of the finest writers in the Japanese poetic tradition.

One of the main contributors to the *Manyoshu* (män′ yōō′ shü′), or *Book of Ten Thousand Leaves,* Hitomaro served as the court poet for three Japanese rulers: Temmu (te′mōō′) (reigned 673–686), Jito (jē′ tō′) (reigned 690–697), and Mommu (mō′ mōō′) (reigned 697–707). In his role as court poet, Hitomaro wrote a number of poems extolling the causes of the various emperors and empresses, especially those of Empress Jito, one of the most pious sovereigns in Japanese history. One of these poems, which mourns the death of Jito's son, Prince Takechi (tä′ kä′ chē′), may be the longest traditional Japanese poem, consisting of 159 lines. In other poems Hitomaro relates his personal experiences, both triumphs and tragedies, in a style that enables readers to share his experiences.

In both his public and his personal poems, Hitomaro conveys a sense of optimism; an awareness of human concerns, motivations, and limitations; and a belief in the unity of humanity and nature. Because of the universal quality of the sentiments they express, Hitomaro's poems are in many ways as moving today as they were in his time.

Objectives

Thematic
To grasp the speaker's feelings for his wife and to understand how he is affected by her death

Skills
1 To understand the choka form
2 To recite a poem expressively

Support Material

Teaching Portfolio
Teacher Backup, p. 385
Usage and Mechanics Worksheet, p. 389
Vocabulary Check, p. 390
Analyzing Literature Worksheet, *Understanding a Choka,* p. 391
Language Worksheet, *Completing*

GUIDE FOR INTERPRETING

In the Sea of Iwami;
I Loved Her Like the Leaves

Commentary

Choka. Have you ever read a limerick? Do you know the sonnet form? Just as Western poetry has certain set forms or structures, so too does Japanese poetry. One form is the **choka** (chō′ kä′).

Choka are poems that consist of alternate lines of five and seven syllables with an additional seven-syllable line at the end. Unlike most other traditional Japanese verse forms, there is no limit to the number of lines in a choka, though the longest existing one is fewer than 160 lines long.

Choka frequently end with one or more *envoys,* or pithy summations. These envoys also have a strict structure, consisting of five lines of five, seven, five, seven, and seven syllables. Generally, the envoys elaborate on or summarize the theme, or central idea, of the main poem. For example, the poem "In Praise of Empress Jito" by Kakinomoto Hitomaro, which celebrates both humanity's and nature's devotion to Empress Jito, ends with the following envoy:

> Mountain and river too
> Come near and serve.
> She, in her divinity,
> On foaming torrents
> Rides her royal craft.

Writing

Have you ever been filled with a sense of longing for what isn't? Is there something sweet or even bittersweet about this feeling? Freewrite, exploring your thoughts on this subject.

Primary Source

The Japanese appreciation of nature differs from the dominant Western view. In the following passage, the Japanese novelist Natsume Sōseki relates an anecdote that illuminates the differences. "When I was in England, I was once laughed at because I invited someone for snow-viewing. At another time I described how deeply the feelings of Japanese are affected by the moon, and my listeners were only puzzled. . . . I was invited to Scotland to stay at a palatial house. One day, when the master and I took a walk in the garden, I noted that the paths between the rows of trees were all thickly covered with moss. I offered a compliment, saying that these paths had magnificently acquired a look of age. Whereupon my host replied that he intended soon to get a gardener to scrape all this moss away."

Word Analogies, p. 392
Selection Test, pp. 393–394

Spelling Tip Students should be familiar with the type of tree known as the *pine.* Point out that the verb *pine* has the same spelling.

Literary Focus Emphasize that choka tend to be substantially longer that most other Japanese poems. Of course this is not surprising considering that the two dominant poetic forms, the tanka and the haiku, consist of five and three lines respectively. Ask students to discuss the possible advantages and disadvantages of using a poetic form with no length limitations rather than one with very strict length limitations.

Writing/Prior Knowledge Before students begin freewriting, divide them into groups of three or four and have them share their memories of favorite childhood holidays. Encourage them to relate as many details as possible.

ESL Teaching Strategy If you have any Japanese students in your class, it might be interesting to have them offer their perceptions of the role of poetry in traditional Japanese society.

Teaching Tenth-Grade Students The following poems should not pose much of a problem for tenth-grade students. Consequently you can either have students read the poems independently or have the poems read aloud. To make sure students have fully understood the poems, you might want to have individual students summarize the poems for the class.

Vocabulary

Preteach the following vocabulary words:

strand (strand) *n.*: A rope-like length of anything

coursing (kôrs′ iŋ) *v.*: Moving swiftly

lush (lush) *adj.*: Of luxuriant growth

flout (flout) *v.*: Show contempt for; jeer; scoff

remedy (rem′ ə dē) *n.*: Something that corrects, counteracts, or removes an evil or wrong

pine (pīn) *v.*: To have an intense longing or desire; yearn

trudge (truj) *v.*: To walk wearily or laboriously

In the Sea of Iwami

Kakinomoto Hitomaro

translated by Haxon Ishii, Shigeyoshi Obata, Ralph Hodgson, and Sanki Ichikawa

In the sea of Iwami
By the cape of Kara,
There amid the stones under sea
Grows the deep-sea *miru* weed;
5 There along the rocky strand
Grows the sleek sea tangle.

Like the swaying sea tangle,
Unresisting would she lie beside me—
My wife whom I love with a love
10 Deep as the *miru*-growing ocean.
But few are the nights
We two have lain together.

Away I have come, parting from her
Even as the creeping vines do part.
15 My heart aches within me;
I turn back to gaze—
But because of the yellow leaves
Of Watari Hill,
Flying and fluttering in the air,
20 I cannot see plainly
My wife waving her sleeve to me.

Now as the moon, sailing through the cloud-rift
25 Above the mountain of Yakami,
Disappears, leaving me full of regret,
So vanishes my love out of sight;
Now sinks at last the sun,
Coursing down the western sky.
I thought myself a strong man,
30 But the sleeves of my garment
Are wetted through with tears.

Envoys

My black steed
Galloping fast,
Away have I come,
35 Leaving under distant skies
The dwelling place of my love.

Oh, yellow leaves
Falling on the autumn hill,
Cease a while
40 To fly and flutter in the air,
That I may see my love's dwelling place!

Reader's Response *The theme of love and longing is universal. Of what other poems or songs does "In the Sea of Iwami" remind you? Why?*

Commentary

The Decline of the Choka Although it was one of the main forms used in the *Manyoshu*, the choka virtually disappeared after the eighth century. This decline seems to have resulted from a variety of factors. First the characteristics of the Japanese language—especially the lack of a stress accent and the limited number of word endings—made it difficult to maintain a high level of intensity throughout a long poem. In addition the Japanese emphasis on suggestion, as opposed to statement, resulted in the preference for short, evocative poems rather than poems that fully express the poet's feelings.

Finally the tremendous popularity of Chinese poetry during the eighth and ninth centuries made it fashionable for Japanese poets to write longer poems in Chinese rather than in Japanese. Despite the form's disappearance, however, a number of the choka included in the *Manyoshu* are still ranked among the greatest Japanese poems ever written.

THINKING ABOUT THE SELECTION

Interpreting

1. (a) How would you describe the mood, or atmosphere, of the poem? (b) What elements of the poem help to create the mood?
2. How do the descriptions of the landscape in lines 17 through 27 echo the speaker's feelings?
3. (a) How do the feelings of separation expressed by the speaker support his statement that his love for his wife is as "deep as the *miru*-growing ocean"? (b) Do you find this image effective? Explain why.

Applying

4. Explain whether you think that the feelings expressed in this poem are as relevant today as they were during Hitomaro's time.

ANALYZING LITERATURE

Understanding a Choka

The **choka** is one of the few Japanese verse forms without length limitations. However, many choka end with one or more envoys, or pithy summations, that have a set length of five lines.

1. How do the two envoys in Hitomaro's poem capture the theme, or central idea, of the main poem?
2. Explain whether you think the two envoys could stand by themselves as separate poems.
3. If you count the number of syllables in each line of this translation of Hitomaro's poem, you will notice that it does not correspond to the syllabic structure of the choka form. Why do you think the translators might have chosen to focus on capturing the meaning of the poem rather than on retaining its syllabic structure?

SPEAKING AND LISTENING

Reading with Expression

Recite Hitomaro's poem to your classmates as expressively as possible, trying to capture the speaker's feelings in the tone of your voice. Hesitate only where a pause is indicated by punctuation, by the meanings of words, or by the natural rhythms of the language. Also vary the loudness of your voice, and be sure to speak slowly and clearly so that your classmates can understand you.

FUJI FROM FUTAMI
From the series "Thirty-six Views of Fuji"
Ichiryusai Hiroshige
Minneapolis Institute of Arts

(continued from bottom of page)

ANSWERS TO ANALYZING LITERATURE

1. Suggested response: The images of the falling leaves and the autumn hill and the expression of the speaker's desire to see his loved one's dwelling place convey his sense of longing for her. His sense of longing is also the central message of the main poem.
2. Answers will differ. Students may respond that the envoys could stand as separate poems but would not have as much of an impact as they do as part of the longer work.
3. Suggested response: The translator probably felt that the syllabic structure was less important than the meaning.

Humanities Note

Fine art, *Fuji from Futami* by Ichiryusai Hiroshige. Ichiryusai Hiroshige (who should not be confused with the famous Japanese artist Ando Hiroshige) was a nineteenth-century Japanese artist who specialized in color woodblock prints. This print is part of his series of thirty-six views of Mount Fuji. In each of these prints, the mountain is seen from a different perspective. Here the mountain appears as a small detail on the horizon.

The traditional Japanese art of woodblock printing grew out of a popular school of painting called *Ukiyo-e*, or "pictures of the floating world." The object of *Ukiyo-e* prints was to depict everyday life, emphasizing its impermanence and its pleasures.

When advances in the printmaking process made it possible to produce many color prints in short periods of time, prints began appearing in nearly every urban Japanese home. Prints also began being used to illustrate poetry, fiction, calendars, and travel books.

You might want to use the following questions to discuss the art:

1. This is only one of thousands of works of Japanese art depicting Mount Fuji. Why do you think Mount Fuji has captured the interest of so many artists?
2. In what ways does this print relate to "In the Sea of Iwami"?

Closure and Extension

ANSWERS TO THINKING ABOUT THE SELECTION

1. (a) Suggested response: The mood is sorrowful and lonely. (b) Suggested response: The mood is created by the speaker's references to his aching heart and tear-soaked sleeves.

2. Suggested response: The speaker feels lifeless and helpless like the fluttering leaves. The description of the disappearance of the moon echoes the speaker's separation from his loved one.

3. (a) Suggested response: If the speaker did not care deeply about his wife, he would not be so upset about being separated from her. (b) Answers will differ. Some students may respond that it is an effective image because the ocean is so deep that it is rarely possible to see its floor.

4. Suggested response: The feelings are still relevant because most people in today's world are deeply saddened when they are separated from a loved one.

I Loved Her Like the Leaves

Kakinomoto Hitomaro
translated by Geoffrey Bownas

I loved her like the leaves,
The lush leaves of spring
That weighed the branches of the willows
Standing on the jutting bank
5 Where we two walked together
While she was of this world.
My life was built on her;
But man cannot flout
The laws of this world.
10 To the wide fields where the heat haze shimmers,
Hidden in a white cloud,
White as white mulberry scarf,
She soared like the morning bird
Hidden from our world like the setting sun.
15 The child she left as token
Whimpers, begs for food; but always
Finding nothing that I might give,
Like birds that gather rice-heads in their beaks,
I pick him up and clasp him in my arms.
20 By the pillows where we lay,
My wife and I, as one,
The daylight I pass lonely till the dusk,
The black night I lie sighing till the dawn.
I grieve, yet know no remedy:
25 I pine, yet have no way to meet her.
The one I love, men say,
Is in the hills of Hagai,
So I labor my way there,
Smashing rock-roots in my path,
30 Yet get no joy from it.
For, as I knew her in this world,
I find not the dimmest trace.

Envoys

The autumn moon
We saw last year
35 Shines again: but she
Who was with me then
The years separate forever.

On the road to Fusuma
In the Hikite Hills,
40 I dug my love's grave.
I trudge the mountain path
And think: "Am I living still?"

Reader's Response *Do you sympathize with the poem's speaker? Why or why not? What words come to your mind to describe the speaker's love?*

THINKING ABOUT THE SELECTION

Interpreting

1. The poet begins the poem with a vivid simile, or comparison between unlike things: "I loved her like the leaves." What qualities of leaves make them a particularly appropriate image in this poem?
2. (a) How do the two envoys capture the events and feelings described in the first 32 lines? (b) Explain whether you think that the two envoys could stand by themselves as separate poems.
3. Explain the significance of the speaker's last question.

PLUM BLOSSOMS BY
THE RIVERSIDE IN FEBRUARY
Suzuki Harunobu
Keio Gijuku Library, Japan

Humanities Note

Fine art, *Plum Blossoms by the Riverside in February* by Suzuki Harunobu. Harunobu (1725–1770) is believed to be the inventor of the polychrome woodblock print. Unlike the prints of earlier Japanese artists, his prints contain up to seven or eight colors. Because he was able to include a wide range of colors, he was able to color the backgrounds of his works in accordance with seasonal changes. In this picture, for example, he creates a contrast between the dark background and the light, delicate plum blossoms—a contrast that suggests the transition from winter to spring.

This picture depicts a young man breaking off a branch of the plum tree for the girl standing beside him. Both figures are graceful, fluid forms, with impersonal, mask-like faces. Their faces are so impersonal that some viewers may have difficulty distinguishing the boy from the girl.

You might want to use the following questions to discuss the art:
1. How would you describe the mood of this illustration?
2. Which details contribute to the mood?
3. Explain whether this print makes an appropriate illustration for "I Loved Her Like the Leaves."
4. If you wanted to create a piece of art depicting the transition from winter to spring, what type of scene would you depict? Explain.

Applying

4. Longing for a lost loved one is a universal feeling. What other poems have you read that deal with this theme particularly effectively?

THINKING AND WRITING

Writing a Choka

Write a choka in which you express your feelings about being separated from a person or a group of people about whom you care deeply. Begin by reviewing your freewriting about this subject and underlining any ideas or details that you could use in your choka. Using the ideas and details you have underlined, begin writing your choka. Make sure you use the correct syllabic structure and end your choka with one or two envoys that either elaborate on or summarize the theme of the main poem. When you revise, try to replace any abstract words with concrete words and any vague words with more specific words. After you have finished revising, prepare a final copy of your choka and share it with your classmates.

3. Suggested response: The question suggests that his wife's death has stripped him of his enthusiasm for life.
4. Answers will differ. Two selections that students might name are James Wright's "Complaint" and Robert Hayden's "Those Winter Sundays."

Challenge Have students speculate about whether writing this poem may have helped Hitomaro to cope with the loss of his wife.

THINKING AND WRITING

Publishing Student Writing You might want to have student volunteers arrange the poems into a class anthology. The students should make copies of the poems, choose the order in which they will appear, prepare a cover and a table of contents, and even create some illustrations to accompany the poems.

WOMEN WRITERS IN JAPAN

You come no more, who came so often,
Nor yet arrives a messenger with your letter.
There is—alas!—nothing I can do.
Though I sorrow the black night through
And all day till the red sun sinks,
It avails me nothing. Though I pine,
I know not how to soothe my heart's pain.
— from "Love's Complaint" by Lady
Otomo

One of the main poets represented in the *Manyoshu*, Lady Otomo stands at the beginning of a long line of talented Japanese women writers. Through the ages, many women made vital contributions to the Japanese literary heritage. Not only did they produce some of the finest poetry written in the Japanese language, but they also contributed numerous diaries, essays, and novels. In fact, *The Tale of Genji*, the novel regarded by many as the masterpiece of Japanese literature, was written by a woman, Lady Murasaki Shikibu.

The Tale of Genji

A work of tremendous length and complexity, Shikibu's novel is filled with timeless insights and incredibly beautiful and moving prose. For example, note the following description of the emperor's reaction to the death of his loved one:

But when he thought of the lost lady's voice and form, he could find neither in the beauty of flowers nor in the song of birds any fit comparison. Continually he pined that fate should not have allowed

them to fulfill the vow which morning and evening was ever talked of between them —the vow that their lives should be as the twin birds that share a wing, the twin trees that share a bough. The rustling of the wind, the chirping of an insect would cast him into the deepest melancholy . . .

Murasaki Shikibu's Diary

Like most noted Japanese women writers, Shikibu was a member of the imperial court. In addition to writing *The Tale of Genji*, Shikibu produced a diary that offers vivid insights into the realities of court life during the Heian Age. Her diary is also filled with breathtaking descriptions of nature, such as the following:

As autumn deepens, the beauty of the . . . mansion defies description. The trees by the lake and the grasses by the stream become a blaze of color that intensifies in the evening flow and makes the voices in ceaseless recitation sound all the more impressive. A cool breeze gently stirs, and throughout the night the endless murmur of the stream blends with the sonorous chanting.

Other Heian Diaries

Throughout the Heian Age, diaries served as the vehicle through which the women of the court expressed their most intimate thoughts and emotions. Yet, despite their highly personal nature, many

NSIGHTS

THE CELEBRATED BEAUTY OF THE TEAHOUSE, KAGIYA, AT KASAMORI SHRINE
Suzuki Harunobi,
eighteenth century
The Metropolitan Museum of Art, New York

of these diaries exhibit a level of literary sophistication that has earned them a place among the great works of Japanese literature. For instance, the court lady who wrote the famous *Sarashina Diary* offers many captivating descriptions of her daydreams:

> I lived forever in a dream world. . . . The height of my aspiration was that a man of noble birth, perfect in both looks and manners . . . would visit me just once a year in the mountain village where he would have me hidden . . . There I should live my lonely existence, gazing at the blossoms and the autumn leaves and the moon and the snow, and wait for an occasional splendid letter from him. This is all that I wanted; and in time I came to believe that it would actually happen.

Sei Shōnagon

Another woman of the Heian court, Sei Shōnagon, wrote a treasured book of prose that is neither a diary nor a work of fiction. This work, entitled *The Pillow Book*, is a loosely organized collection of character sketches, descriptions, anecdotes, lists, and witty insights. Some selections from Shōnagon's *Pillow Book* appear on pages 296 through 301.

Women Poets

In addition to prose, the court ladies of the Heian Age and the feudal period also produced many fine collections of poetry. For instance, Lady Dabu, a member of the imperial court of the late 1100's, wrote *The Poetic Memoirs of Lady Dabu*, which includes the following poems:

> Caught in the last rays
> Of the setting sun, the treetops
> Darken in the chilling rain:
> So too my heart is dimmed
> And clouded over in its misery.
>
> In this mountain village
> Snow lies thickly piled,
> And the path is covered:
> How lovingly I shall look
> On the person who will come today.

Thinking About Women Writers

1. Which of the preceding passages or poems did you like most? Why?
2. Why do you imagine that most noted Japanese women writers were members of the imperial court?
3. How does the role of women in the Japanese literary tradition compare with the role of women in other literary traditions with which you are familiar?

ONO KOMACHI

KI NO TSURAYUKI

MINAMOTO NO TOSHIYORI

THE PRIEST JAKUREN HOUSHI

ONO KOMACHI
833–857

A great beauty with a strong personality, Ono Komachi (ō′ nō′ kō′ mä′ chē′) was an early tanka poet whose poems are characterized by their passion and energy. Few details of her life are known. However, a vast number of Japanese legends have been created about her life, and these legends serve as the basis for a well-known series of Nō plays.

KI NO TSURAYUKI
c. 868–964

The chief aide of Emperor Daigo (dī′ gō′), Ki no Tsurayuki (kē′ nō′ tsōōr′ ī′ ōō′ kē′) was one of the leading poets, critics, and diarists of his time. Tsurayuki deserves much of the credit for assembling the *Kokinshu* (kō′ kēn′ shōō′), a collection of over eleven hundred years of the Heian (hā′ än′) Age.

In the preface to the anthology, Tsurayuki vividly captured the character and purpose of traditonal Japanese poetry: "The poetry of Japan, as a seed, springs from the heart of man, creating countless leaves of language . . . In a world full of things man strives to find words to express the impression left on his heart by sight and sound . . . And so the heart of man came to find expression in words for his joy in the beauty of the blossoms, his wonder at the song of birds, and his tender welcome of the mists that bathe the landscapes, as well as his mournful sympathy with the evanescent morning dew."

MINAMOTO NO TOSHIYORI
1055?–1129?

An innovative poet and critic, Minamoto no Toshiyori (mi′ nä′ mō′ tō′ nō′ tō′ shē′ yō′ rē′) rebelled against traditional poetic approaches and helped bring about the acceptance of new descriptive styles. Toshiyori spent his childhood and early adulthood in Kyushu, where his father was governor. Following his father's death, Toshiyori became the leader of a group of inventive poets. Devoting his energy to writing poetry, judging poetry contests, and promoting his literary ideals, he earned a reputation as one of the most respected literary figures of his time. In fact, he received the honor of being chosen by the emperor to compile the *Kinyoshu*, a court anthology consisting of the finest poems of the time.

PRIEST JAKUREN
1139?–1202

Jakuren (jä′ kōō′ rən′) was a Buddhist priest and a prominent tanka poet whose poems are filled with beautiful yet melancholy imagery. After entering the priesthood at the age of twenty-three, Jakuren spent much of his time traveling throughout the Japanese countryside, writing poetry and seeking spiritual fulfillment. He also appeared at numerous poetic gatherings and participated in many poetry contests. In addition to contributing poems to the *Senzishu* (sən′ zē′ shōō′), a court anthology, he produced *Jakuren Hoshi Shu* (hō′ shē′ shōō′), a personal collection of poetry.

GUIDE FOR INTERPRETING

Tanka

Commentary

Tanka. The **tanka** (tän′kə′) is the most prevalent verse form in traditional Japanese literature. In fact, for many centuries the tanka was virtually the only form used by poets who wrote in the Japanese language. Each short poem consists of five lines of five, seven, five, seven, and seven syllables. The enduring popularity of the tanka form resulted partly from the limiting characteristics of the Japanese language, which made it difficult to maintain a high level of intensity throughout a long poem, and from the Japanese preferences for simplicity, suggestion, and irregularity, which are reflected in the brevity of the tanka form, the evocativeness of the poems, and the uneven number of lines and syllables per line. Most tanka include at least one caesura, or pause, often indicated by punctuation in English translations.

Used as a means of communication in ancient Japanese society, tanka often tell a brief story or express a single thought or insight. The most common subjects on which they focus are love and nature. In expressing their feelings of love or their appreciation for nature, tanka poets generally exhibit restraint, relying on clear, powerful imagery to evoke an emotional response rather than using abstract words to directly express their feelings. At the same time, tanka poets often hint at or suggest the existence of a higher reality. For example, the following tanka by Oshikochi Mitsune (osh′ ē′ kō′ chē′ mēt′ sōō′ nā′) conveys the poet's intuitive belief in the spiritual unity between humanity and nature:

> At the great sky
> I gaze all my life:
> For the rushing wind,
> Though it howls as it goes,
> Can never be seen.

The Japanese place more emphasis on the imagery used and the emotions evoked by a tanka than they do on the structure of the poems. In addition, when Japanese tanka are translated into English, the syllabic structure of the poems is often altered, and in some cases the number of lines is also changed. As a result, when you read the following tanka, you should focus more on their content than on their structure, paying special attention to the use of imagery and the emotions and insights expressed.

Writing

Many tanka include striking images from nature. Brainstorm about the images from nature that you find especially powerful or interesting. Note the emotions each image arouses.

Literary Focus Tell students that because suggestion plays such an important role in Japanese poetry, a single poem can often be interpreted in many different ways. Each person brings his or her own experiences and associations to the poem and interprets it accordingly. For this reason students should feel free to interpret the following tanka in their own way, and they should not hesitate to share any of their interpretations.

Writing/Prior Knowledge Before students begin brainstorming, have them sit quietly for several minutes, picturing themselves in a beautiful natural setting, such as the mountains, the oceanside, or a city park. Encourage them to envision as many details of the setting as possible.

ESL Teaching Strategy Make sure ESL students understand the difference between denotation and connotation. Emphasize the importance of connotations, or word associations, in tanka. Urge them to look beyond the denotations, or literal meanings, of the words in these poems.

Teaching Tenth-Grade Students Explain to tenth-grade students that although tanka are very brief, they should not be read quickly. In fact, to fully appreciate a tanka, it is usually necessary to read it several times.

To help students get the most out of these tanka, you might want to take the following approach. First have students read over each tanka on their own. Then have each poem read aloud several times, having students take turns reading. Next go through each poem line by line, having students discuss the associations evoked by each image. Finally have students discuss their overall impressions of each poem.

Tanka

Ki no Tsurayuki

translated by Geoffrey Bownas

When I went to visit
The girl I love so much,
That winter night
The river blew so cold
That the plovers[1] were crying.

———————
1. plovers (pluv′ ərz) *n*.: Wading shore birds with short tails, long, pointed wings, and short, stout beaks.

Ono Komachi

translated by Geoffrey Bownas

Was it that I went to sleep
Thinking of him,
That he came in my dreams?
Had I known it a dream
I should not have wakened.

Priest Jakuren

translated by Geoffrey Bownas

One cannot ask loneliness
How or where it starts.
On the cypress-mountain,[1]
Autumn evening.

———————
1. cypress-mountain: cypress trees are cone-bearing evergreen trees, native to North America, Europe, and Asia.

Minamoto no Toshiyori

translated by Donald Keene

The clustering clouds—
Can it be they wipe away
The lunar shadows?
Every time they clear a bit
The moonlight shines the brighter.

JAPANESE GIRL GARDENING IN A FROZEN GARDEN
Winteri

Reader's Response *In the second tanka, the speaker expresses disappointment that she has awakened from a dream. Have you ever had a similar experience? Explain your answer.*

THINKING ABOUT THE SELECTIONS

Interpreting

1. In the first tanka, what does the speaker's willingness to endure the bitter cold indicate about the depth of his love for the woman he goes to visit?
2. In the second tanka, what do the speaker's comments reveal about her feelings toward the man she dreams about?
3. In the fourth tanka, what seems to be the speaker's attitude toward the clustering clouds? Explain your answer.
4. In the third tanka, how does the image, or word picture, of the cypress-mountain relate to the speaker's observations about loneliness?

Applying

5. Do you think it is more effective to suggest a feeling or to describe it in detail? Explain your answer.

ANALYZING LITERATURE

Understanding Tanka

Often focusing on the subjects of love or nature, tanka use clear, powerful imagery to evoke an emotional response.
1. What emotions are evoked by each of the tanka you have read?
2. How do the images included in each tanka contribute to the emotions that it evokes?
3. Despite the enduring popularity of the tanka form, it is impossible to deny the fact that the form has certain limitations. (a) Name at least two possible limitations of the tanka form. (b) How do you think Japanese poets might have been able to overcome these limitations?

CRITICAL THINKING AND READING

Recognizing Cultural Characteristics

The most prevalent type of poetry in traditional Japanese literature, the tanka reflects a number of the dominant characteristics of the Japanese culture. For example, the brevity of tanka and the uneven number of lines reflect the Japanese preferences for simplicity and irregularity.
1. Filled with striking images from nature, many tanka convey the traditional Japanese emphasis on a harmonious relationship with nature. In which of the tanka you have read do the speakers convey a sense of a spiritual harmony with nature? Explain.
2. Reflecting the Japanese emphasis on suggestion, tanka often hint at a love relationship without actually describing interactions between the people involved. For example, a tanka might describe the feelings of emptiness resulting from a parting with a loved one or convey the sense of anticipation that occurs during a trip to visit a loved one. Which of the tanka you have read fit into this category? Explain.

UNDERSTANDING LANGUAGE

Appreciating Connotations

Because of the brevity of the tanka form, suggestion and association usually play an important role in conveying the meaning of a tanka. Natural associations are known as *connotations*. For example, the word *spring* has a variety of connotations, including warmth, beauty, and rebirth.

List at least two of the connotations of each of the following words from the tanka.
1. winter   4. clouds
2. dreams   5. moonlight
3. evening

THINKING AND WRITING

Writing Tanka

Try your own hand at writing a tanka. Choose as your subject one of the five words in the Understanding Language activity. Then put yourself in a Japanese frame of mind and rely on suggestion and brevity. After finishing your first attempt, check that you have used highly connotative words and images. Then check your form. Does your tanka consist of five lines of five, seven, five, seven, and seven syllables? Prepare a final draft. If you choose, you might even illustrate your tanka.

(continued from bottom of page)

ANSWERS TO ANALYZING LITERATURE

1. Answers will differ. The tanka may evoke many different emotions, including love, longing, hope, loneliness, and a sense of wonder.
2. Answers will differ. Students may note that the images of the winter night and the cold wind in the first tanka both help to create a sense of longing. They may also note that the image of the bright moonlight in the final tanka evokes a sense of wonder.
3. (a) Answers will differ. Students may note that the brevity of the tanka form prevents poets from incorporating specific details into their poems and makes it impossible for them to depict an extended experience. (b) Answers will differ. Students may observe that poets used the power of suggestion to enable readers to detail pictures in their minds.

ANSWERS TO CRITICAL THINKING AND READING

1. Answers will differ. Students may respond that the third and fourth tanka convey a sense of spiritual harmony with nature.
2. Suggested response: The first two tanka fit into this category. The first focuses on a trip to see a loved one. The second focuses on a dream about a loved one.

ANSWERS TO UNDERSTANDING LANGUAGE

Answers may differ. The following are examples of appropriate responses.
1. cold, bitter, long, darkness
2. fantasy, hope, unreality
3. ending, regret, darkness
4. dreariness, hopelessness
5. hope, love, happiness

THINKING AND WRITING

Publishing Student Writing You may want to have students recite their tanka to their classmates.

Challenge Divide your students into groups of three or four and have each group write a series of related tanka.

you consider acquiring this painting? Why or why not?

Closure and Extension

ANSWERS TO THINKING ABOUT THE SELECTION

1. His willingness to endure the bitter cold suggests that he loves her very much. If he did not love her deeply, he probably would have chosen not to make the trip.
2. Suggested response: The fact that she regrets waking from her dream about him suggests that she is deeply attracted to him.
3. Suggested response: The fact that the cypress trees do not change from season to season parallels the constancy of loneliness. In addition, the image of a deserted mountain on an autumn evening conveys a sense of loneliness.
4. Suggested response: The speaker appreciates the clouds because they help make the moonlight seem more brilliant.
5. Answers will differ. Students may respond that it is more effective to suggest a feeling because it encourages readers to draw on their own experiences and associations.

YOSA BUSON

MATSUO BASHŌ

KOBAYASHI ISSA

MATSUO BASHŌ
1644–1694

Generally regarded as the greatest Japanese haiku (hī′kōō′) poet, Matsuo Bashō (ma′tzōō′ō′ ba′shō′) was born in Iga-Ueno into a samurai family. He began studying the writing of poetry at an early age. Following the death of his master in 1666, he moved to Edo (now Tokyo), where he continued to write. After becoming a Zen Buddhist, he moved into an isolated hut on the outskirts of Edo. There, he lived the life of a hermit, supporting himself by teaching and judging poetry contests. He also spent a good deal of time traveling through areas of central and northern Japan, visiting famous places and observing nature. Following the tradition of earlier Japanese recluse-poets, Bashō traveled with only the barest essentials and relied on the hospitality of temples and fellow poets. During his travels he recorded his observations and insights in both poems and meditative travel diaries.

Bashō wrote his best poetry during the final ten years of his life. Reflecting the influence of his Buddhist faith, these poems are written in a direct, simple style. In most of the poems, Bashō conveys his observations of nature through spare yet vivid images. By re-creating his own observations, Bashō hopes to evoke in the reader the same insight or emotional response that he himself experienced.

YOSA BUSON
1716–1783

Although Yosa Buson (yō′sä′bōō′sän′) is widely regarded as the second-greatest Japanese haiku poet, little is known about his life. We do know that Buson lived in Kyoto throughout most of his life and that in addition to being a celebrated poet he was one of the finest painters of his time. In both his paintings and his flawlessly crafted poetry, Buson presents a romantic view of the Japanese landscape, vividly capturing the wonder and mystery of nature. Buson frequently wrote more than one haiku on the same subject. In fact, he wrote a series of at least thirty haiku about spring rain.

KOBAYASHI ISSA
1763–1827

Although his talent was not widely recognized until after his death, Kobayashi Issa (kō′bä′yä′shē′ ē′sä′) is now generally ranked with Bashō and Buson. Born into poverty, Issa struggled throughout his life to support himself and to overcome the loneliness and pain resulting from the deaths of loved ones. His appreciation for the hardships faced by the common people is reflected in his haiku. Filled with simple, humble images, Issa's poems capture the essence of daily life in Japan and convey his compassion for the less fortunate.

GUIDE FOR INTERPRETING

Haiku

Haiku. The **haiku,** which consists of three lines of five, seven, and five syllables, evolved from a form of collaborative poetry known as *renga*. Consisting of chains of interlocking verses of seventeen and fourteen syllables composed by groups of poets, the renga form thrived during the medieval age. Eventually, the *hokku*, the opening verse of a renga, developed into a distinct literary form known as haiku.

Reflecting the dominant tastes of the Japanese culture, haiku are characterized by precision, simplicity, and suggestiveness. Haiku present spare yet clear images that stimulate thought and evoke emotion. Because of the brevity of the haiku form, the images cannot be presented in detail. As a result, haiku employ the power of suggestion to produce detailed pictures in the reader's mind. For example, almost all haiku include a *kigo*, or seasonal word, such as "snow" or "cherry blossoms," that indicates the time of year being described. By establishing the season, the haiku calls to mind all the details and ideas that readers associate with that time of year.

Although some haiku seem to contain only one image, most present an explicit or implicit comparison between two images, actions, or states of being. For example, in the following haiku by Bashō there is an explicit comparison between two actions:

> Poverty's child—
> He starts to grind the rice
> And gazes at the moon.

By contrasting the task of grinding rice with the boy's observation of the moon, Bashō evokes a sense of longing and captures the soothing effect of nature on the human spirit. Sometimes haiku create a contrast by rapidly shifting their focus from the general to the specific or vice versa. For example, in this haiku by Bashō, the reader's eye jumps from an "old pond" to a specific action occurring on the pond:

> An old pond:
> a frog jumps in—
> the sound of water.

Because of their brevity and suggestiveness, haiku demand extra effort on the reader's part. To understand the following haiku, read each one several times and spend some time thinking about each one and exploring the details, thoughts, and emotions that you associate with the images it presents.

Writing

To the Japanese mind, the quality of perishability or impermanence adds to an item's beauty. Write a journal entry exploring your own thoughts about this quality.

Literary Focus Another type of contrast frequently used in haiku is that between the eternal and the momentary. In the haiku that describes the frog leaping into the water, for example, the old pond represents the eternal and the frog's action represents the momentary. Have students discuss the effect created by contrasting the eternal with the momentary. What literary works have they read or movies have they seen in which this type of contrast is presented?

Writing Before your students complete the writing activity, you might want to have a class discussion about the quality of perishability. During the discussion have students try to come up with examples of items that exhibit this quality. For instance, students might mention snow, fresh fruit, and cut flowers.

ESL Teaching Strategy If you have any Japanese students in your class, you may want to have them discuss the distinctive characteristics of the Japanese language and explain how these characteristics affect the composition of poetry. For example, they might discuss the impact of the limited number of word endings in the Japanese language.

Teaching Tenth-Grade Students Tenth-grade students may have already encountered haiku in an earlier grade. Because it is likely that the structure of haiku was emphasized in the earlier course, it is important for you to point out to students that they should be more concerned with the content of the haiku than with their structure.

Vocabulary

Because the language used in haiku generally reflects the Japanese emphasis on simplicity, it rarely poses problems for readers. While the words in a haiku are usually simple, however, they tend to be filled with associations. For this reason students should take the time to appreciate the richness of each word in the following haiku.

Support Material

Teaching Portfolio
Teacher Backup, p. 405
Usage and Mechanics Worksheet, p. 409
Analyzing Literature Worksheet, *Understanding the Haiku Form*, p. 410
Critical Thinking and Reading Work-

sheet, *Considering the Characteristics of Language*, p. 411
Language Worksheet, *Appreciating Concise Language,* p. 412
Selection Test, pp. 413–414

Art Transparency 5
Juman-tsubo Plain at Suzaki, Utagawa Hiroshige

Haiku

Bashō

**translated by Harold G. Henderson (first 3)
and Geoffrey Bownas (last 3)**

The sun's way:
Hollyhocks turn toward it
Through all the rain of May.

Poverty's child—
He starts to grind the rice,
And gazes at the moon.

Clouds come from time to time—
And bring to men a chance to rest
From looking at the moon.

The cuckoo—
Its call stretching
Over the water.

Seven sights were veiled
In mist—then I heard
Mii Temple's bell.[1]

Summer grasses—
All that remains
Of soldiers' visions.

---

1. Mii (mē´ ē´) **Temple's bell:** The bell at Mii Temple is known for its extremely beautiful sound. The temple is located near Otsu, a city in southern Japan.

Reader's Response *Which of these haiku did you find the most evocative? Why?*

THE MONKEY BRIDGE IN KOSHU PROVINCE
Hiroshige hitsu

THINKING ABOUT THE SELECTION

Interpreting

1. How does the first haiku capture the transition between the end of spring and the beginning of summer?
2. How does the third haiku convey a sense of harmony between humanity and nature?
3. Tone refers to a writer's attitude toward his or her subject. (a) How would you characterize the tone of the fifth haiku? (b) How would you characterize the tone of the sixth haiku?

Applying

4. (a) In what ways are Bashō's poems different from the traditional Western poems you have read? (b) What do you think a Western poet might learn from Bashō's poetry?

ANALYZING LITERATURE

Understanding the Haiku Form

Although some haiku seem to contain only one image, most haiku present an explicit or implicit comparison between two images, actions, or states of being. For example, a haiku poet might contrast a distant view of a landscape with a specific detail from the landscape.

1. (a) In which of these haiku does Bashō create a contrast by rapidly shifting his focus from the general to the specific or vice versa? (b) What is the effect of his use of this technique?
2. (a) In which of these haiku does Bashō contrast the momentary with the eternal? (b) What is the effect of this type of contrast?
3. (a) In which of the haiku does Bashō contrast visual images with auditory images? (b) What is the effect of this type of contrast?

CRITICAL THINKING AND READING

Comparing Forms

In reading about traditional Japanese poetic forms, you have probably noticed that various forms share certain structural characteristics, such as the use of five- and seven-syllable lines. These common characteristics result from the fact that new Japanese verse forms generally evolved from established forms.

1. Renga—collaborative poems consisting of chains of interlocking verses of seventeen and fourteen syllables—evolved from the tanka form. How do you think the limitations of the tanka form might have contributed to the development of the renga?
2. Haiku, which have the same structure as the first three lines of a tanka, replaced the tanka as the dominant Japanese verse form during the seventeenth century. (a) How does the emergence of the haiku form reflect the Japanese emphasis on simplicity and suggestiveness? (b) Do you think that less is more in poetry?

UNDERSTANDING LANGUAGE

Considering Language

Unlike English, the Japanese language does not have a stress accent. In fact, all syllables in a Japanese word have equal weight. This characteristic has affected the way the Japanese write poetry.

Another important characteristic of the Japanese language is the limited number of word endings. In Japanese all words end in one of five different vowel sounds. As a result, it is easy to achieve rhyme when writing in Japanese.

1. The most prevalent foot, or rhythmical unit, in American and English poetry is the iamb, which consists of two syllables, the first unaccented and the second accented. Why would the iamb not be a standard feature of Japanese poetry?
2. Considering the easiness of achieving rhyme in Japanese, for what reasons might Japanese poets have chosen not to employ it?

THINKING AND WRITING

Comparing and Contrasting Poems

Haiku and tanka have a number of common characteristics. At the same time, however, there are also a variety of significant differences between the two forms. Write an essay in which you compare and contrast the tanka on page 284 with Bashō's haiku. Begin by reviewing the poems and listing their similarities and differences. Make sure you pay close attention to the content of the poems, as well as to their form. When you write your essay, organize your ideas according to corresponding points of comparison and contrast. When you revise, make sure you have supported each of your main points with passages from the poems.

(continued from bottom of page)

ANSWERS TO ANALYZING LITERATURE

1. (a) Suggested response: This type of shift occurs in the first, second, and fourth haiku. (b) Answers will differ. Students may respond that this type of shift emphasizes the vastness of the world and captures the fact that the world is made up of a myriad of specific details.
2. (a) Suggested response: This type of contrast is used in each of the first four haiku. (b) Suggested response: Students may respond that this type of contrast emphasizes the immortality of nature and the impermanence of human life.
3. (a) He creates this type of contrast in the fourth and the fifth haiku. (b) Answers will differ. Students may respond that the use of this type of contrast helps to create a more complete picture in the reader's mind.

ANSWERS TO CRITICAL THINKING AND READING

1. Answers will differ. Students may respond that the renga enabled poets to explore topics in a more developed manner.
2. (a) Suggested response: The haiku form is even simpler and more concise than the tanka form. As a result, haiku rely to a great extent on the power of suggestion. (b) Answers will differ. Students may comment that they generally find short poems to be more moving than long poems.

ANSWERS TO UNDERSTANDING LANGUAGE

1. It could not be a feature of Japanese poetry because all syllables are pronounced with equal emphasis in the Japanese language.
2. Suggested response: Rhyme is not used because it does not present a challenge to the poet.

THINKING AND WRITING

Publishing Student Writing You may want to have student volunteers read their essays to the class.

Closure and Extension

ANSWERS TO THINKING ABOUT THE SELECTION

1. Suggested response: The sun represents the summer and the rain represents the spring. Therefore the movement of the hollyhock toward the sun suggests the passage from spring to summer.
2. Suggested response: The people are gazing at the moon, which suggests a sense of harmony between humanity and nature. They welcome the coming of the clouds, which also conveys this sense of harmony.
3. (a) Answers may differ. Students may suggest that the tone is characterized by a sense of wonder. (b) Answers may differ. Students may respond that the tone is mournful.
4. (a) Answers will differ. Students will probably note that the haiku are much shorter than most Western poetry. They may also observe that the haiku rely more on the power of suggestion than does most Western poetry. (b) Answers will differ. Students may observe that Western poets could learn to make their poems more concise and to rely more on the power of suggestion.

Motivation/Prior Knowledge
Tell students that it was common for Japanese artists to produce series of prints or paintings depicting the same subject from different perspectives. Point out that Buson sometimes applied this approach to his writing. Have students discuss the effect a series of haiku about the same subject might create.

Purpose-Setting Question What is the cumulative effect of Buson's series of haiku about spring rain?

1 Discussion Have students discuss the emotions evoked by the image of the rat. Do these emotions relate to the final line of the haiku? If so, how?

2 Enrichment Explain to students that the term "spring rain" is associated with a light, gentle rain.

3 Discussion Have students discuss how they envision the man's home and why they see it this way.

4 Discussion Have students discuss any feelings or memories that this haiku brings to mind.

5 Discussion Explain to students that Fuji is one of the most common subjects of Japanese poetry and artwork. Have students discuss what Fuji might symbolize for the Japanese people.

Cooperative Learning Divide your class into groups of three or four. Through research, each group should gather additional information about Bashō, Buson, or Issa, about the haiku form, or about twentieth-century Western writers who were influenced by the haiku. Once all students have completed their research, each group should present their findings to the class.

Closure and Extension

ANSWERS TO THINKING ABOUT THE SELECTION

1. (a) Answers will differ. Students may observe that because rats move very quickly it is difficult to catch sight of them. (b) Answers will differ. Students may respond that the

Haiku

Yosa Buson

translated by Geoffrey Bownas

1 Scampering over saucers—
The sound of a rat.
Cold, cold.

2 Spring rain:
Telling a tale as they go,
Straw cape, umbrella.

Spring rain:
In our sedan
Your soft whispers.

3 Spring rain:
A man lives here—
Smoke through the wall.

4 Spring rain:
Soaking on the roof
A child's rag ball.

5 Fuji[1] alone
Left unburied
By young green leaves.

---

1. Fuji (foo´ jē): Mount Fuji, the highest peak in Japan (12,388 ft.).

THINKING ABOUT THE SELECTION

Interpreting

1. (a) In the first haiku, why do you think Buson focuses on the sound made by the rat rather than describing its appearance? (b) How does the final line of the haiku relate to the image in the first two lines?
2. Buson establishes the setting in the first line of each of his haiku. How does the setting shape your impression of the image in the final two lines of each of these poems?
3. What impression of Mount Fuji does Buson convey in the sixth haiku?

Applying

4. (a) What do you think might have been Buson's purpose in writing a series of haiku, such as the series about spring rain? (b) How might writing a series of haiku help him to overcome some of the limitations of the haiku form?

UNDERSTANDING LANGUAGE

Appreciating Concise Language

Due to their brevity, haiku must be written using concise language. Poets must use precise verbs and nouns, while eliminating any unnecessary words. For example, in the third haiku Buson writes, "In our sedan/Your soft whispers," omitting the words *I hear* or *I listen to*.

1. What words has Buson omitted from the first haiku?
2. What words has he omitted from the fourth haiku?
3. Rewrite the final two lines of the second haiku in the form of a sentence. Which is more effective—the sentence or the haiku? Why?

THINKING AND WRITING

Writing Haiku

Write a series of haiku in which you use vivid imagery to relate your own observations of nature. Imagine that you are writing your haiku for someone who has never seen the scenes you are describing. Start by listing details from nature that you find especially vivid or striking. Then review your list and underline the most effective details. Using your list, begin writing your haiku, focusing on creating clear, precise, and suggestive images. Try to avoid using any unnecessary or abstract words. When you finish writing, revise your haiku, deleting or replacing any vague or unnecessary words.

final line concerns the effect that the sound of a rat produces on people.
2. Suggested response: Each setting arouses certain associations. These associations carry over to the images that follow.
3. Answers may differ.
4. (a) Answers will differ. (b) Suggested response: The use of a series enables him to explore many different aspects of the same subject.

ANSWERS TO UNDERSTANDING LANGUAGE

1. Answers may differ. Appropriate responses include the phrases *I hear* and *I feel*.
2. Answers may differ. Appropriate responses include the phrases *in this hut* and *I see*.
3. Answers will differ. An appropriate response would be, "Wearing straw capes and carrying umbrellas, they tell a tale as they go."

THINKING AND WRITING

Publishing Student Writing Arrange your students' haiku into a class bulletin board display.

SUDDEN SHOWER ON OHASHI BRIDGE
Hiroshige hitsu

Reader's Response *Did the poet capture the way spring rain makes you feel? Explain.*

Commentary

Translating Haiku Due to the dramatic differences between Japanese and English and the unique characteristics of traditional Japanese verse, translating Japanese poetry is a difficult task. Translators must not only attempt to retain the syllabic structure of a poem, but they must also choose English words that have connotations similar to those of the original Japanese words. Because haiku rely so much on suggestiveness, it is extremely vital that the translator accomplish the latter task. Considering that the purpose of haiku is to stimulate insights and evoke emotions, translators generally place far more emphasis on selecting appropriate words than they do on retaining the poem's exact syllabic structure. As a result, English translations of Japanese haiku often do not contain the prescribed number of syllables per line.

Haiku

Kobayashi Issa

translated by Geoffrey Bownas

Melting snow:
And on the village
Fall the children.

Beautiful, seen through holes
Made in a paper screen:
The Milky Way.

1 Far-off mountain peaks
Reflected in its eyes:
The dragonfly.

A world of dew:
Yet within the dewdrops—
Quarrels.

2 Viewing the cherry-blossom:
Even as they walk,
Grumbling.

3 With bland serenity
Gazing at the far hills:
A tiny frog.

Reader's Response *What image in these haiku did you find especially effective? Explain your choice.*

THINKING ABOUT THE SELECTION

Interpreting

1. In the first haiku, Issa suggests that the cycles of human life parallel the falling and melting of snow. If the melting snow (line 1) symbolizes, or represents, death, what is the meaning of the image in line 3?
2. What does the fourth haiku suggest about the possible contrast between people's perceptions of a situation and the reality of that situation?
3. (a) In what ways are the third and sixth haiku similar to each other? (b) How do these poems convey a sense of harmony among the elements of nature?

Applying

4. If you were not aware of the identity of the poet who wrote these haiku, would you be able to guess that the poet was Japanese? Why or why not?

ANALYZING LITERATURE

Understanding the Haiku Form

Because of their brevity, haiku must rely to a great extent on the power of suggestion. For example, most haiku include a *kigo,* or seasonal word, that indicates the time of year being described and calls to mind all the associations that readers have with that time of year.

1. (a) Identify two kigo in Issa's haiku. (b) What season does each of these words call to mind? (c) What are some of the associations that you have with each of these seasons?
2. (a) What emotions does Issa evoke in the first haiku? (b) What emotions does the fourth evoke?
3. What contrast is presented in the fifth haiku?
4. The translator did not follow the pattern of five, seven, and five syllables. What do you think may have been the translator's priorities?

THINKING AND WRITING

Writing About Japanese Poetry

Japanese poetry is unlike that of any other culture. Write an essay in which you examine the unique characteristics of Japanese poetry. Start by reviewing the Guide for Interpreting pages that focus on Japanese poetic forms. Note each unique characteristic of Japanese poetry. Then reread the poems in this unit, looking for examples of each characteristic. When you write your essay, use passages from the poems for support.

Prose

NICHIREN CALMING THE STORM
Kuniyoshi

(continued from bottom of page)

ples' observation of the cherry blossoms and their quibbling.
4. Suggested response: The translator probably focused on choosing English words with the same connotations as the original Japanese words.

Challenge What insight does Issa offer in the fourth haiku? How does this insight apply to human behavior?

Humanities Note

Fine art, *Nichiren Calming the Storm* by Kuniyoshi. Kuniyoshi (1798–1861) was one of the most talented and innovative Japanese printmakers of the nineteenth century. Influenced by Western artistic concepts and techniques, he is known for his realistic portrayal of subjects and his use of brilliant colors. As was the fashion of his day, he produced a number of series of landscape views. He also created a series of prints known as the *Nichiren* series, which includes the print seen here. Made between 1842 and 1848, this series depicts ten different scenes from the life of a famous Buddhist saint and reformer named Nichiren. In ths print he shows Nichiren guiding a boat through massive waves.

You might want to use the following questions to discuss the art:
1. How does the artist emphasize the peril of the people in the small boat?
2. How does the artist's use of color help to dramatize the people's plight?
3. If you were a collector of Japanese art would you want to include this print in your collection? Why or why not?

ements of the landscape. (b) Suggested response: In the third haiku, the mountains are reflected in the dragonfly's eyes, which suggests a sense of harmony. In the sixth haiku, the serenity of the frog suggests a sense of harmony.
4. Answers will differ. Most students will observe that Issa's haiku are much shorter than most traditional Western poetry. Unlike many Western poems,

Issa's haiku do not have a regular rhythm nor do they employ rhyme.

ANSWERS TO ANALYZING LITERATURE

1. (a) Answers will differ. Two *kigo* are "melting snow" and "cherry-blossom." (b) Answers will differ according to the *kigo* that students identify. (c) Answers will differ. Students should be able to explain their various associ-

ations with the seasons they have identified.
2. (a) Answers will differ. Students may respond that the first haiku evokes a sense of hope because it brings to mind the coming of spring. (b) Answers will differ. Students may respond that it evokes a sense of despair because the quarreling of the dewdrops parallels human behavior.
3. He presents a contrast between peo-

SEI SHŌNAGON

Tenth and Eleventh Centuries

A lady-in-waiting for the Empress Sadako (sä′ dä′ kō′) during the last decade of the tenth century, Sei Shōnagon (sä′ ē′ shō′ nä′ gōn′) is responsible for providing us with a detailed portrait of upper-class life in Japan during the Heian Age. Her *Pillow Book*, a collection of personal notes written during her ten years of court service, is filled with character sketches, descriptions, anecdotes, lists, and witty insights. A precursor of the Japanese literary form *zuihitsu*, or *occasional writings*, *The Pillow Book* is widely recognized as one of the finest works of Japanese prose.

Shōnagon was the daughter of a provincial official who was also a noted scholar and poet, and she may have been briefly married to a government official. Aside from what *The Pillow Book* reveals about her years of court service, however, little else is known about her life. In fact, her life following her court service is a complete mystery.

Although few details are known about Shōnagon's life, *The Pillow Book* offers a wealth of insights into her personality. The 185 sections of the book reveal her to be a complex, intelligent, knowledgeable, observant, flirtatious, and quick-witted woman. While she had a tremendous amount of admiration for the imperial family, she seems to have had little respect for the lower social orders. Shōnagon's scorn for the less fortunate, along with her lack of restraint, her judgmen-tal nature, and her competitive attitude toward men, has angered some scholars and critics. Shōnagon even earned criticism from one of her contemporaries—the great Japanese novelist Murasaki Shikibu (mōō′ rä′ sä′ kē′ shē′ kē′ bōō′)—who wrote, "Sei Shōnagon has the most extraordinary air of self-satisfaction . . . Someone who makes such an effort to be different from others is bound to fall in people's esteem, and I can only think that her future will be a hard one. She is a gifted woman, to be sure. Yet, if one gives free rein to one's emotions even under the most inappropriate circumstances, if one has to sample each interesting thing that comes along, people are bound to regard one as frivolous. And how can things turn out well for such a woman?" However, it should be remembered that these two women were not only contemporaries—but rivals!

How is it possible that two of the most important writers of the Heian court were women? At this time boys at court were trained to write in Chinese, much as monks in medieval European courts were trained to write in Latin. Chinese, though, was considered beyond the power of girls, who wrote in low Japanese. This discrimination backfired, however, since more people were able to read low Japanese than Chinese, ensuring the popularity of women writers.

Despite the criticism Shōnagon has received, it is impossible to deny the literary and historical value of her book. Filled with vivid and evocative language, *The Pillow Book* is clearly the work of an extremely gifted writer. When evaluating Japanese works of prose, many critics even rank *The Pillow Book* above Murasaki Shikabu's *The Tale of Genji*, which is widely regarded as the greatest Japanese novel. Among these critics is Arthur Waley, who wrote, "As a writer [Shōnagon] is incomparably the best poet of her time, a fact which is apparent only in her prose . . . Passages such as that about the stormy lake or the few lines about crossing a moonlit river show a beauty of phrasing that Murasaki, a much more deliberate writer, certainly never surpassed."

GUIDE FOR INTERPRETING

from The Pillow Book

Commentary

The Government in Ancient Japan. During the seventh and eighth centuries, a series of reforms occurred in Japan that were aimed at creating a centralized government and diminishing the influence of a number of powerful families that had previously controlled the country. Using the Chinese system as a model, the Japanese leaders created a new governmental hierarchy at both the provincial and national levels. According to the new system, all local officials were to serve as subordinates to a provincial governor who was to be appointed every six years by the national government. At the national level, the government was to be controlled by the emperor, who theoretically had unlimited authority throughout the country. Beneath the emperor there were two branches of government, a religious division and a secular division.

As it turned out, the reforms had little impact on how the country was run. As would be the case in later eras of Japanese history, the emperor ended up being little more than a figurehead, controlled by the most powerful family of the time. During Sei Shōnagon's time, Japan was dominated by the Fujiwara family. Serving as the nation's chancellor, a position not originally included in the new system of government, the leader of the Fujiwara family was the true ruler of the country. In addition, other members of the Fujiwara family had usurped the power of the officials in the various national and provincial divisions and offices that had been established as part of the governmental reforms. As a result, many of the people referred to by title in *The Pillow Book* actually had few official responsibilities.

Despite the essentially ceremonial nature of the positions, members of the Japanese aristocracy placed a great deal of importance on obtaining a government post. The offices were tied closely to social rank, and holders of rank were often given land or servants and were entitled to a variety of privileges, including exemption from military service. Generally, national officials had higher ranks than provincial officials had. Even pets and inanimate objects could receive a rank; in fact, an emperor's cat could have a rank equal to or higher than that of a provincial governor.

As you read the following excerpts from *The Pillow Book*, look for details that indicate the importance that the Japanese aristocracy placed on official titles and social ranks.

Writing

The Pillow Book includes a number of lists, such as a list of things that Sei Shōnagon finds hateful and a list of things that arouse her memories of the past. Prepare a list of things that you find hateful and a list of your favorite activities.

Understanding Historical Context, p. 423
Critical Thinking and Reading Worksheet, *Making Inferences About the Author,* p. 424
Selection Test, pp. 425–426

Literary Focus Have students discuss how first-person accounts, such as diaries and letters, can contribute to our understanding of different cultures and historical periods. What do first-person accounts offer us that most history books do not?

Writing/Prior Knowledge After students have completed their lists, arrange them into groups of three or four. Then have the members of each group discuss what their lists reveal about their personalities. Following these discussions you may want to encourage students to write journal entries in which they reveal the items on their lists and explore how these items relate to their personalities.

ESL Teaching Strategy Pair each of your ESL students with a native-speaking student. Then have the members of each pair take turns reading aloud to each other. The non-ESL student can then clarify the meaning of any words with which the ESL student is unfamiliar.

Teaching Tenth-Grade Students Tenth-grade students may find the form of *The Pillow Book* confusing. Emphasize that *The Pillow Book* is a seemingly disorganized collection of personal notes. Most often these notes seem to have little relation to one another. As a result, students should not look for connections between the following excerpts from Shōnagon's work. Instead they should focus on the meaning of each individual excerpt.

Vocabulary
Preteach the following vocabulary words:
earnest (ʉr′ nist) *adj.*: Serious; not joking
chastised (chas tīzd′) *v.*: Punished
loathsome (lōth′ səm) *adj.*: Detestable
piebald (pī′ bôld′) *adj.*: Covered with patches or spots of two colors
incantations (in′ kan tā′ shanz) *n.*: Chantings of magical words and formulas that are supposed to cast a spell or perform other magic
gesticulate (jes tik′ yə lāt′) *v.*: To make or use gestures to add force to one's speech or as a substitute for speech
inquisitive (in kwiz′ ə tiv) *adj.*: Eager to learn

from The Pillow Book

Sei Shōnagon

translated by Ivan Morris

IN SPRING IT IS THE DAWN

In spring it is the dawn that is most beautiful. As the light creeps over the hills, their outlines are dyed a faint red and wisps of purplish cloud trail over them.

In summer the nights. Not only when the moon shines, but on dark nights too, as the fireflies flit to and fro, and even when it rains, how beautiful it is!

In autumn the evenings, when the glittering sun sinks close to the edge of the hills and the crows fly back to their nests in threes and fours and twos; more charming still is a file of wild geese, like specks in the distant sky. When the sun has set, one's heart is moved by the sound of the wind and the hum of the insects.

In winter the early mornings. It is beautiful indeed when snow has fallen during the night, but splendid too when the ground is white with frost; or even when there is no snow or frost, but it is simply very cold and the attendants hurry from room to room stirring up the fires and bringing charcoal, how well this fits the season's mood! But as noon approaches and the cold wears off, no one bothers to keep the braziers[1] alight, and soon nothing remains but piles of white ashes.

THE CAT WHO LIVED IN THE PALACE

The cat who lived in the Palace had been awarded the headdress of nobility and was called Lady Myōbu. She was a very pretty cat, and His Majesty saw to it that she was treated with the greatest care.

One day she wandered onto the veranda, and Lady Uma, the nurse in charge of her, called out, "Oh, you naughty thing! Please come inside at once." But the cat paid no attention and went on basking sleepily in the sun. Intending to give her a scare, the nurse called for the dog, Okinamaro.

"Okinamaro, where are you?" she cried. "Come here and bite Lady Myōbu!" The foolish Okinamaro, believing that the nurse was in earnest, rushed at the cat, who, startled and terrified, ran behind the blind in the Imperial Dining Room, where the Emperor happened to be sitting. Greatly surprised, His Majesty picked up the cat and held her in his arms. He summoned his gentlemen-in-waiting. When Tadataka, the Chamberlain,[2] appeared, His Majesty ordered that Okinamaro be chastised and banished to Dog Island. The attendants all started to chase the dog amid great confusion. His Majesty also reproached Lady Uma. "We shall have to find a new nurse for our cat," he told her. "I no longer feel I can count on you to look after her." Lady Uma bowed; thereafter she no longer appeared in the Emperor's presence.

The Imperial Guards quickly succeeded in catching Okinamaro and drove him out of the Palace grounds. Poor dog! He used to swagger about so happily. Recently, on the third day of the

---

1. braziers (brā′ zhərz) *n*.: Metal pans or bowls used to hold burning coals or charcoal.

2. Chamberlain (chām′ bər lin) *n*.: A high official in the emperor's court.

Third Month,[3] when the Controller First Secretary paraded him through the Palace grounds, Okinamaro was adorned with garlands of willow leaves, peach blossoms on his head, and cherry blossoms round his body. How could the dog have imagined that this would be his fate? We all felt sorry for him. "When Her Majesty was having her meals," recalled one of the ladies-in-waiting, "Okinamaro always used to be in attendance and sit opposite us. How I miss him!"

It was about noon, a few days after Okinamaro's banishment, that we heard a dog howling fearfully. How could any dog possibly cry so long? All the other dogs rushed out in excitement to see what was happening. Meanwhile a woman who served as a cleaner in the Palace latrines[4] ran up to us. "It's terrible," she said. "Two of the Chamberlains are flogging a dog. They'll surely kill him. He's being punished for having come back after he was banished. It's Tadataka and Sanefusa who are beating him." Obviously the victim was Okinamaro. I was absolutely wretched and sent a servant to ask the men to stop; but just then the howling finally ceased. "He's dead," one of the servants informed me. "They've thrown his body outside the gate."

That evening, while we were sitting in the Palace bemoaning Okinamaro's fate, a wretched-looking dog walked in; he was trembling all over, and his body was fearfully swollen.

"Oh dear," said one of the ladies-in-waiting. "Can this be Okinamaro? We haven't seen any other dog like him recently, have we?"

We called to him by name, but the dog did not respond. Some of us insisted that it was Okinamaro, others that it was not. "Please send for Lady Ukon,"[5] said the Empress, hearing our discussion. "She will certainly be able to tell." We immediately went to Ukon's room and told her she was wanted on an urgent matter.

"Is this Okinamaro?" the Empress asked her, pointing to the dog.

---

3. the third day of the Third Month: The day of the Jōmi Festival, an event during which the dogs in the palace were often decorated with flowers.

4. latrines (lə trēnz´) *n.*: Lavatories.

5. Lady Ukon (o͞o´ kôn´): One of the ladies in the Palace Attendants' Office, a bureau of female officials who waited on the emperor.

TRIPTYCH OF SNOW, MOON, AND FLOWER
(detail depicting Lady Murasaki at her desk)
Shunsho
Museum of Art, Atami, Japan

4 Discussion Have students discuss what the brutality of the chamberlains suggests about the political and social atmosphere in Japan at the time.

5 Discussion Have students explain how Shōnagon evokes sympathy for Okinamaro.

Humanities Note

Fine art, *Triptych of Snow, Moon, and Flower*, Shunsho. This picture is from a three-panel painted screen. The artist, Shunsho (1726–1792), was a painter and a woodblock artist noted for his unusual compositions, his fine brushwork, and his portrayals of beautiful women and famous actors.

The woman depicted in this picture is the famous novelist Murasaki Shikibu. She is shown deep in thought, contemplating her next line. Her chamber is illuminated by the moonlight streaming through the window. Because of the artist's use of angular, overlapping shapes, it is difficult to tell where the walls of the chamber begin or end. This gives the picture a mysterious quality that is heightened by the lack of shadows in the painting.

You might want to use the following questions to discuss the art:

1. What impression of Lady Murasaki does the artist convey?
2. Which details in the painting contribute to this impression?
3. Explain the ways in which this painting is and is not an appropriate illustration for *The Pillow Book*.
4. How productive do you think you would be in an environment such as the one in which Lady Murasaki is depicted?

"Well," said Ukon, "it certainly looks like him, but I cannot believe that this loathsome creature is really our Okinamaro. When I called Okinamaro, he always used to come to me, wagging his tail. But this dog does not react at all. No, it cannot be the same one. And besides, wasn't Okinamaro beaten to death and his body thrown away? How could any dog be alive after being flogged by two strong men?" Hearing this, Her Majesty was very unhappy.

When it got dark, we gave the dog something to eat; but he refused it, and we finally decided that this could not be Okinamaro.

On the following morning I went to attend the Empress while her hair was being dressed and she was performing her ablutions.[6] I was holding up the mirror for her when the dog we had seen on the previous evening slunk into the room and crouched next to one of the pillars. "Poor Okinamaro!" I said. "He had such a dreadful beating yesterday. How sad to think he is dead! I wonder what body he has been born into this time. Oh, how he must have suffered!"

At that moment the dog lying by the pillar started to shake and tremble, and shed a flood of tears. It was astounding. So this really was Okinamaro! On the previous night it was to avoid betraying himself that he had refused to answer to his name. We were immensely moved and pleased. "Well, well, Okinamaro!" I said, putting down the mirror. The dog stretched himself flat on the floor and yelped loudly, so that the Empress beamed with delight. All the ladies gathered round, and Her Majesty summoned Lady Ukon. When the Empress explained what had happened, everyone talked and laughed with great excitement.

The news reached His Majesty, and he too came to the Empress's room. "It's amazing," he said with a smile. "To think that even a dog has such deep feelings!" When the Emperor's ladies-in-waiting heard the story, they too came along in a great crowd. "Okinamaro!" we called, and this time the dog rose and limped about the room with his swollen face. "He must have a meal prepared for

---

6. **ablutions** (ab lōō′ shənz) *n.*: Washings of the body.

him," I said. "Yes," said the Empress, laughing happily, "now that Okinamaro has finally told us who he is."

The Chamberlain, Tadataka, was informed, and he hurried along from the Table Room. "Is it really true?" he asked. "Please let me see for myself." I sent a maid to him with the following reply: "Alas, I am afraid that this is not the same dog after all." "Well," answered Tadataka, "whatever you say, I shall sooner or later have occasion to see the animal. You won't be able to hide him from me indefinitely."

Before long, Okinamaro was granted an Imperial pardon and returned to his former happy state. Yet even now, when I remember how he whimpered and trembled in response to our sympathy, it strikes me as a strange and moving scene; when people talk to me about it, I start crying myself.

OXEN SHOULD HAVE VERY SMALL FOREHEADS

Oxen should have very small foreheads with white hair; their underbellies, the ends of their legs, and the tips of their tails should also be white.

I like horses to be chestnut, piebald, dapple-gray, or black roan, with white patches near their shoulders and feet; I also like horses with light chestnut coats and extremely white manes and tails—so white, indeed, that their hair looks like mulberry threads.

I like a cat whose back is black and all the rest white.

NOTHING CAN BE WORSE

Nothing can be worse than allowing the driver of one's ox-carriage to be poorly dressed. It does not matter too much if the other attendants are shabby, since they can remain at the rear of the carriage; but the drivers are bound to be noticed and, if they are badly turned out, it makes a painful impression.

The servants who follow one's carriage must have at least a few good points. Some people choose slender young men who look as if they were really made to be after-runners, but then let them wear threadbare hunting costumes and trouser-skirts

Grammar in Action

Good writers **vary the length and structure of their sentences** to make their writing smoother and more interesting to read. Notice the sentence variety in the following passage from *The Pillow Book*:

At that moment the dog lying by the pillar started to shake and tremble, and shed a flood of tears. It was astounding. So this really was Okinamaro! On the previous night it was to avoid betraying himself that he had refused to answer to his name. We were immensely moved and pleased. "Well, well, Okinamaro!" I said, putting down the mirror. The that are dark at the hems and actually seem to be of shaded material. This is a great mistake; for, as they amble along beside the carriage, these badly dressed young men do not seem to be part of their master's equipage at all.

The fact is that the people in one's employ should always be decently dressed. To be sure, servants often tear their clothes; but, so long as they have been wearing them for some time, this is no great loss and one can let the matter pass.

Gentlemen who have had official servants allotted to their households must certainly not allow them to go about looking slovenly.[7]

When a messenger or a visitor arrives, it is very pleasant, both for the master and for the members of his household, to have a collection of good-looking pages in attendance.

HATEFUL THINGS

One is in a hurry to leave, but one's visitor keeps chattering away. If it is someone of no importance, one can get rid of him by saying, "You must tell me all about it next time"; but, should it be the sort of visitor whose presence commands one's best behavior, the situation is hateful indeed.

One finds that a hair has got caught in the stone on which one is rubbing one's inkstick, or again that gravel is lodged in the inkstick, making a nasty, grating sound.

Someone has suddenly fallen ill and one summons the exorcist.[8] Since he is not at home, one has to send messengers to look for him. After one has had a long fretful wait, the exorcist finally arrives, and with a sigh of relief one asks him to start his incantations. But perhaps he has been exorcizing too many evil spirits recently; for hardly has he installed himself and begun praying when his voice becomes drowsy. Oh, how hateful!

A man who has nothing in particular to recommend him discusses all sorts of subjects at random as though he knew everything.

_____

7. slovenly (sluv′ ən lē) *adj.*: Careless in appearance, habits, or work; untidy.

8. exorcist (ek′ sôr sist) *n.*: A person who drives evil spirits out or away by ritual prayers or incantations.

An elderly person warms the palms of his hands over a brazier and stretches out the wrinkles. No young man would dream of behaving in such a fashion; old people can really be quite shameless. I have seen some dreary old creatures actually resting their feet on the brazier and rubbing them against the edge while they speak. These are the kind of people who in visiting someone's house first use their fans to wipe away the dust from the mat and, when they finally sit on it, cannot stay still but are forever spreading out the front of their hunting costume or even tucking it up under their knees.

THE OIRAN YOSO-OI SEATED AT HER VANITY
Kitagawa Utamaro
The Metropolitan Museum of Art, New York

12 Discussion Have students discuss the role of clothing in shaping people's impressions of one another. What judgments do we sometimes make about people based on the clothes they wear?

13 Enrichment Explain to students that during the Heian age each Japanese aristocrat had a certain number of servants appointed to him or her depending on his or her rank.

14 Clarification Point out that Shō-nagon's description of the elderly person reflects the Japanese emphasis on proper decorum.

Humanities Note

Fine art, *The Oiran Yoso-oi Seated at Her Vanity* by Kitagawa Utamaro. Utamaro, whose brilliant designs and asymmetrical compositions raised the art of woodcut printing to new heights, was one of the greatest Japanese artists of his time. Not only were his prints widely admired in Japan, but they were also well known in Europe. His prints influenced a number of the French Impressionists.

Utamaro specialized in depicting women, and he had the ability to capture both physical appearance and personality with a few deft strokes of his brush. His favorite subjects were "oirans," the high-ranking courtesans of Edo society. Their elegant hair styles, makeup, and clothing afforded him opportunities for luxuriant color and dynamic design.

You might want to use the following questions to discuss the art:
1. What impression of the two women does the artist convey?
2. How does he convey this impression?

dog stretched itself flat on the floor and yelped loudly, so that the Empress beamed with delight. All the ladies gathered round, and Her Majesty summoned Lady Ukon. When the Empress explained what happened, everyone talked and laughed with great excitement.

Student Activity 1. Find two other paragraphs in which a variety of sentence lengths and structures are used. Then rewrite each of these paragraphs so that the sentences are all similar in length and structure. Finally explain why the original versions of the paragraphs are more effective than the rewritten versions.

Student Activity 2. Find two more paragraphs in which the sentences are varied in length and structure. Then explain how Shōnagon uses sentence variation to sustain the reader's interest and to emphasize certain ideas.

Student Activity 3. Write a paragraph or two describing one of your favorite activities. In writing this paragraph, focus on varying the length and structure of your sentences.

One might suppose that such behavior was restricted to people of humble station; but I have observed it in quite well-bred people, including a Senior Secretary of the Fifth Rank in the Ministry of Ceremonial and a former Governor of Suruga.

I hate the sight of men in their cups who shout, poke their fingers in their mouths, stroke their beards, and pass on the wine to their neighbors with great cries of "Have some more! Drink up!" They tremble, shake their heads, twist their faces, and gesticulate like children who are singing, "We're off to see the Governor." I have seen really well-bred people behave like this and I find it most distasteful.

To envy others and to complain about one's own lot; to speak badly about people; to be inquisitive about the most trivial matters and to resent and abuse people for not telling one, or, if one does manage to worm out some facts, to inform everyone in the most detailed fashion as if one had known all from the beginning—oh, how hateful!

One is just about to be told some interesting piece of news when a baby starts crying.

A flight of crows circle about with loud caws.

THINGS THAT MAKE ONE'S
HEART BEAT FASTER

Sparrows feeding their young. To pass a place where babies are playing. To sleep in a room where some fine incense has been burnt. To notice that one's elegant Chinese mirror has become a little cloudy. To see a gentleman stop his carriage before one's gate and instruct his attendants to announce his arrival. To wash one's hair, make one's toilet, and put on scented robes; even if not a soul sees one, these preparations still produce an inner pleasure.

It is night and one is expecting a visitor. Suddenly one is startled by the sound of raindrops, which the wind blows against the shutters.

THINGS THAT AROUSE
A FOND MEMORY OF THE PAST

Dried hollyhock. The objects used during the Display of Dolls. To find a piece of deep violet or grape-colored material that has been pressed between the pages of a notebook.

It is a rainy day and one is feeling bored. To pass the time, one starts looking through some old papers. And then one comes across the letters of a man one used to love.

Last year's paper fan. A night with a clear moon.

I REMEMBER A CLEAR MORNING

I remember a clear morning in the Ninth Month when it had been raining all night. Despite the bright sun, dew was still dripping from the chrysanthemums in the garden. On the bamboo fences and criss-cross hedges I saw tatters of spider webs; and where the threads were broken the raindrops hung on them like strings of white pearls. I was greatly moved and delighted.

As it became sunnier, the dew gradually vanished from the clover and the other plants where it had lain so heavily; the branches began to stir, then suddenly sprang up of their own accord. Later I described to people how beautiful it all was. What most impressed me was that they were not at all impressed.

Reader's Response *In the first segment, Shōnagon describes the time of day she finds most beautiful in each of the four seasons. What time of day do you find most beautiful in each of the four seasons?*

THINKING ABOUT THE SELECTION

Interpreting

1. How does the first segment reveal Shōnagon's eye for detail?
2. What does the segment entitled "The Cat Who Lived in the Palace" reveal about life in the imperial palace?
3. What does the segment entitled "Nothing Can Be Worse" reveal about the lives of the aristocracy in ancient Japan?
4. Why might Shōnagon have been impressed by the fact that others "were not at all impressed" with the scene she describes in "I Remember a Clear Morning"?

Applying

5. Explain whether you think it would be possible to mistake these excerpts from *The Pillow Book* for the work of a contemporary American writer. If so, what author?
6. Based on these excerpts from *The Pillow Book*, what do you imagine it was like to be a member of the emperor's court in traditional Japanese society?

ANALYZING LITERATURE

Understanding Historical Context

Because the true power in ancient Japan rested in the hands of the dominant family of the time, the government officials, including the emperor, actually had little to do with running the country. Japanese aristocrats, however, still placed a great deal of importance on being appointed to a government post. Appointment to an official post was tied directly to social rank, and by attaining a high rank and the accompanying government position, a person could receive a wide variety of privileges.

1. Find three details or events in the excerpts from *The Pillow Book* that reveal the importance of social rank during Shōnagon's time.
2. As is indicated in the segment about the emperor's cat and the court dog, even a cat could attain a high social rank. How is the punishment that the court dog, Okinamaro, receives for startling the cat indicative of the cat's high social ranking?
3. What is your response to the idea of an animal receiving a high social ranking? Why?

CRITICAL THINKING AND READING

Making Inferences About the Author

Although few details are known about Sei Shōnagon's life, it is possible to make inferences, or draw conclusions, about her personality from her comments and descriptions in *The Pillow Book*. For example, the segment entitled "Nothing Can be Worse" enables you to infer that Shōnagon placed a great deal of importance on physical appearance.

1. What inferences about Shōnagon's personality might you make from the segment entitled "The Cat Who Lived in the Palace"?
2. What inferences about her personality might you make from her list of hateful things?
3. What inferences might you make about the lives of women in Japan during the Heian Age? Support each inference with evidence from the selection.

THINKING AND WRITING

Writing a Dramatization

Some of the incidents described in *The Pillow Book* are so lively and entertaining that they could easily be developed into scenes from a movie or a play. Write a dramatic adaptation of the incident described in "The Cat Who Lived in the Palace." Begin by brainstorming about how the events in this segment could be captured through dialogue and stage directions alone. Develop an outline. Then begin writing your dramatization, making sure your stage directions are clear and specific and your dialogue seems natural and realistic. Also make sure you include a vivid description of the setting. When you finish writing, make sure the way your characters act and talk matches the way Shōnagon portrays them.

(continued from bottom of page)

2. Answers will differ. Students may respond that the list reveals that she dislikes pompous people and that she is bothered by people who talk about subjects about which they know nothing.
3. Answers will differ. Students may conclude that the women of the court were respected and well educated but did not enjoy the same status as men did.

Challenge What inferences can you make about court life in the Heian age from these excerpts from *The Pillow Book*?

THINKING AND WRITING

Publishing Student Writing Have students act out their dramatizations. Make sure every student in the class is given the opportunity to take part in at least one of the dramatizations.

was probably enjoyable because all the members of the court were pampered by servants and had few responsibilities.

ANSWERS TO ANALYZING LITERATURE

1. Answers will differ. Students may cite the treatment that the dog is given because he has a lower rank than the cat. They may also note that people of high rank ride in carriages and wear nice clothes, while servants run beside the carriages in threadbare outfits.
2. Suggested response: The punishment that Okinamaro receives is severe even though the incident was minor and occurred because of a misunderstanding.
3. Answers will differ. Many students will probably respond that they think it is ridiculous that a cat could have a higher social ranking than many people.

ANSWERS TO CRITICAL THINKING AND READING

1. Answers will differ. Students may note that the section reveals that Shōnagon is compassionate and dislikes extreme violence.

Focus

More About the Author Zeami has received enormous acclaim for his critical and theoretical writing about Nō drama. In these writings Zeami repeatedly uses two important terms: *hana,* which refers to outer beauty and the expression of beauty in the arts; and *yugen,* which refers to the unspoken, inner beauty and mystery that exists beneath the *hana.* In describing true dramatic accomplishment, Zeami once wrote, "One must perform in such a way as to bring out this mysterious beauty. When one has mastered *yugen,* he may be said to have reached the highest level, that of perfect artistic enlightenment." Tell students that many critics consider *The Deserted Crone* to be a play that reaches the apex of *yugen.* As they read the play, have them think about the ways in which it exhibits the type of mysterious, inner beauty to which Zeami refers.

Critical Evaluation In his book *The Pleasures of Japanese Literature,* the noted Japanese literary scholar Donald Keene writes: "Zeami, as he matured as both actor and dramatist, rejoiced in the appreciation of his art . . . Unlike the many writers who have predicted that their works would not be fully appreciated until many years had passed, Zeami feared that audiences in the future might not be able to understand [his] plays . . ." What other writers can students think of who feared that future readers or audiences might not be able to appreciate their works?

1363?–1443

No person is more responsible for the enduring success of the Japanese Nō theater than Zeami (zā′ ä′ mē′), who is universally acknowledged as the most gifted and prolific Nō playwright.

The son of Kannami (kä′ nä′ mē′), another significant Nō playwright, Zeami seems to have been born in 1363, although some historians question the accuracy of that date. Like his father, Zeami was an actor and composer, as well as a playwright. An extremely precocious child, Zeami established himself as a successful actor at an early age. In fact, he was only eleven when he first performed before Ashikaga Yoshimitsu (äsh′ ē′ kä′ gä′ yō′ shē′ mē′ tsōō′), the reigning shogun, who was so captivated by the young actor's beauty and grace that he became a patron of both Zeami and the Nō theater.

When Zeami was nineteen or twenty, his father died, and Zeami became the leader of his father's troupe of performers. For the next twenty years or so, Zeami enjoyed the reputation as the leading figure in the Japanese Nō theater. Unfortunately, however, in 1408 Yoshimitsu died, and Zeami lost his governmental patronage.

Throughout the rest of his career as an actor, Zeami was involved in disputes with government officials and other Nō actors, and at the age of seventy he was sent into exile for an unknown reason. According to tradition he died alone in a Buddhist temple shortly after returning from exile.

While it is now impossible to measure Zeami's talent as an actor, it is fairly easy to measure his ability as a playwright. Although scholars are still debating the exact number of plays that should be credited to Zeami (as many as fifty plays have been attributed to him), he is clearly the most prolific Nō playwright. In addition, there is no question that his plays have greater literary value than those of any other Nō playwright. Filled with rich, beautiful, and harmonious imagery, his plays offer universal and timeless insights about human existence.

Zeami is also known for his excellent critical writings in which he described and defined the Nō theater. Although a number of other talented playwrights have excelled as actors and others have excelled as critics, no other figure in any of the world's literary traditions can equal Zeami's accomplishments in acting, playwriting, and criticism.

Objectives

Thematic

To understand the need to come to terms with change and loss

Skills

1 To understand a Nō play
2 To recognize the Japanese aesthetic
3 To write about a Nō play

Support Material

Teaching Portfolio

Teacher Backup, p. 427
Grammar in Action Worksheet, *Using Imagery,* p. 431
Usage and Mechanics Worksheet, p. 433
Vocabulary Check, p. 434
Analyzing Literature Worksheet,

BACKGROUND

THE NŌ THEATER.

The **Nō Theater** is a traditional Japanese dramatic form with a set of firmly established conventions. Because it is strikingly different from any type of Western drama, it is not possible to offer a simple definition of the Nō. It is possible, however, to characterize the theater as a unique and captivating blend of lyrical language, hypnotic singing, music, and dance, involving elaborate costumes and striking masks. The plays are staged in specially designed theaters, using little scenery and few props; and the actors move and deliver their lines in a subtle, highly stylized manner. Due to the simplicity of the set and the subtlety of the actors' performances, the audience at a Nō play must be both attentive and imaginative.

Officially established in the 1300's, Nō plays are deeply grounded in both the Shinto and Buddhist religions. By the time of the theater's inception, elements of these two religions, along with a variety of folk superstitions, had essentially become intertwined into a single dominant Japanese faith. This merging of beliefs is exhibited in Nō plays, which involve the portrayal of Shinto gods and the use of Shinto shrines, while at the same time involving the use of Buddhist language and displaying the Buddhist preoccupation with death. In addition, Nō plays reflect the Japanese folk belief that the mountains and waters of Japan are inhabited by demons and ghosts. In fact, Nō plays may have originally developed as a means of pacifying troubled ghosts who had returned to haunt the living. The plays, which are almost always tragic, often focus on a deceased character who has suffered an injustice and is seeking to gain deliverance from his or her tortures. This character, known as the *shite* (shtā), or "protagonist," is usually the incarnation of a strong emotion, such as loneliness. Because these emotions are universal, the audience is likely to be profoundly moved by the *shite's* situation.

Unlike Western plays, Nō plays almost never involve an external conflict. In fact, the *shite* is the only well-developed character in a Nō play. The other characters, who possess neither names nor personalities, serve mainly to elicit the *shite's* story and to observe the action. These characters include the *waki* (wä´ kē´), or "person at the side," who is usually a wandering monk who has come to visit a sacred shrine and whose role is to ask questions that prompt the *shite* to tell his or her story. A Nō play may also include several other minor characters, including the *tsure* (tsōō´ rä´), or "companion," who accompanies the *shite* but usually appears as no more than a shadow; the *kokata* (kō´ gä´ tə´), or "child parts"; and the *kyogen* (kyō´ gən´), or "rustics" or "menials," who are generally peasants or villagers from the area in which the play is set.

All the roles in a Nō play are played by male actors. Because the actors often wear masks, it is possible for them to play any role—even an elderly man can play the role of a beautiful woman. Because the expressions on the masks do not change, an actor must use other means, such as body movements, to convey a character's emotions. At the same time, the masks create an additional demand for the audience because they muffle the actors' delivery of their lines. The audience is also required to use its imagination when watching actors play certain roles because the actors use the same tone of voice and style of movement regardless of the age and sex of their character.

Understanding a Nō Play, p. 435
Critical Thinking and Reading Worksheet, *Relating the Nō to the Japanese Aesthetic*, p. 436
Selection Test, pp. 437–438

Presentation

Motivation/Prior Knowledge Explain to students that Nō plays are probably dramatically different from any type of drama they have previously seen or read. Consequently it is very important for them to learn about the characteristics of Nō dramas before they begin reading *The Deserted Crone*. Make sure they carefully read through the Background on the Nō theater, and encourage them to refer back to the Background if they encounter any difficulties while reading the play.

Enrichment Tell students that most Nō plays can be divided into three parts. The first part is an introductory section called the *jo*, which is slow and deliberate in pace. This is followed by the *ha*, a longer and faster-moving section in which the story is developed. The third and final section is the *kyu*, which is very fast in pace and is about the same length as the introduction.

Enrichment Tell students that in 1374, after the reigning shōgun witnessed a Nō play for the first time, the Nō became the official entertainment of the shōgun's court. In the following years, the Nō went through its most important period of development—the period in which most of the surviving Nō plays were written.

Using a Diagram Have students study the diagram and ask them the following questions:
1. In what ways is the Nō stage different from the stages with which you are familiar?
2. Why do you think the chorus and the musicians are located on adjoining sides of the stage rather than on the same side or opposite each other?
3. What do you imagine is the purpose of the bridgeway?

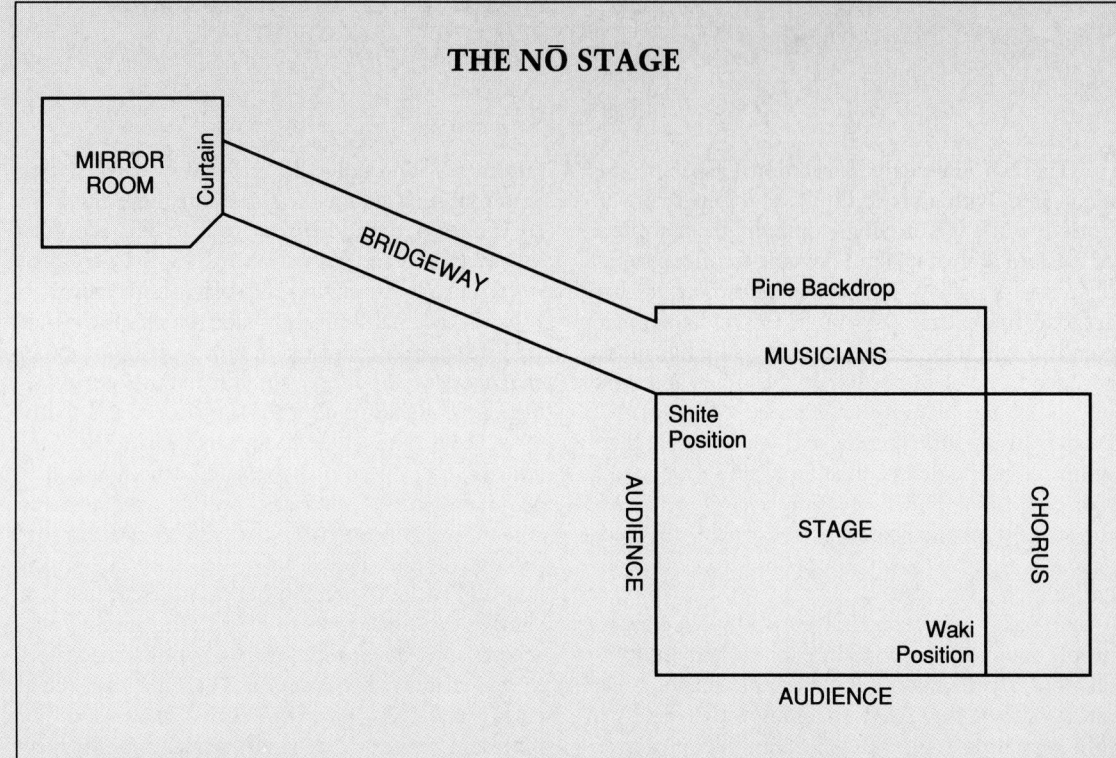

THE NŌ STAGE

MIRROR ROOM
Curtain
BRIDGEWAY
Pine Backdrop
MUSICIANS
Shite Position
AUDIENCE
STAGE
CHORUS
Waki Position
AUDIENCE

In addition to the actors, all Nō plays involve a chorus and an orchestra. The chorus consists of eight to ten men who sit at the side of the stage throughout the play, at times expressing the thoughts of the actors, particularly when the actors are dancing. The orchestra, which includes a flutist and several drummers, accompanies both the chorus and the actors when they sing or declaim their lines.

Although dancing is often a vital part of a Nō play, some plays include little dancing and little movement. In fact, the plays with the least amount of movement generally earn the highest ratings from critics, and the moments within a play that are devoid of action tend to be most appreciated by the audience. Commenting about this fact, Zeami wrote, "When we examine why such moments without action are enjoyable, we find that it is due to the underlying spiritual strength of the actor which unremittingly holds the attention. He does not relax the tension when the dancing or singing comes to an end, but maintains an unwavering inner strength. This feeling of inner strength will faintly reveal itself and bring enjoyment."

Primary Source
Because they had no understanding of or appreciation for the conventions of the Nō, the first Westerners to witness Nō plays responded very negatively. This is reflected in the late nineteenth-century critic W. G. Aston's observation that "The Nō are not classical poems. They are too deficient in lucidity, method, coherence, and good taste to deserve this description. . . . As dramas the Nō have little value. There is no action to speak of, and dramatic propriety and effects are hardly thought of." Ask students why people might be likely to respond negatively to literary forms that are unlike anything they have previously encountered.

GUIDE FOR INTERPRETING

The Deserted Crone

Commentary

The Nō Theater. The Nō performers' subtle expressions of inner strength, along with the beauty of the costumes, the eloquence of the dancing, the mesmerizing quality of the singing, and the mystical, almost supernatural, atmosphere of the performances, has enabled the **Nō theater** to retain its popularity throughout the centuries. In fact, the Nō theater may be more popular today than it ever has been, despite the fact that the format of the plays has changed little over time. As you read "The Deserted Crone," look for the qualities that make the play as beautiful and moving today as it was when it was written. Try to envision a performance of the play, keeping in mind that the actors would be wearing masks and that the play would be staged with little scenery and few props.

Writing

The word *crone* carries strong association. Freewrite about the thoughts and feelings that come to mind when you consider the word crone.

Primary Source

The Nō theater has captured the interest of many twentieth-century Western writers. Commenting on this fact, the Asian literary scholar John D. Yohannan writes: "The fascination which the Japanese Nō drama has had for such outstanding twentieth-century poets as William Butler Yeats and Ezra Pound is no doubt attributable to its highly stylized and self-conscious form. If to the untutored reader or observer the Nō seems primitive, he must remember that primitivism is often the hallmark of sophistication. . . .

"The Nō is characterized by a very slight text which is eked out by elaborate conventions of acting, chanting, and dancing. As in Greek tragedy, which it somewhat resembles, masks and a chorus are used. The role of the latter is to lend emphasis to passages of text and on occasion to speak the lines of a leading character if he is engaged in dancing. Often a character speaks to himself in the third person, with an effect of startling detachment. The text is highly lyrical and stresses, not the action, but the after-effects of the action upon the leading characters—or their ghosts."

Writing/Prior Knowledge Before students begin their freewriting, make sure they are all aware that the word *crone* refers to "an ugly, withered old woman."

ESL Teaching Strategy If you have any Japanese students in your class, you might want to have them share their knowledge of the Nō drama with their classmates.

Teaching Tenth-Grade Students *The Deserted Crone* is a difficult selection that may present a problem for tenth-grade students. Consequently it may be necessary for them to read the play more than once to thoroughly comprehend it. Have them begin by reading the play on their own, focusing on its literal meaning. Then have student volunteers read the play aloud to the rest of the class. Encourage students to raise their hands and ask any questions that come to mind.

Vocabulary

Preteach the following vocabulary words:
solace (säl´ is) *n.*: An easing of grief, loneliness, or discomfort
vista (vis´ tə) *n.*: A view or outlook
serene (sə rēn´) *adj.*: Not disturbed or troubled
reveling (rev´ 'l iŋ) *v.*: Taking much pleasure
pervading (pər vād´ iŋ) *v.*: Passing through; spreading or being diffused throughout
radiance (rā´ dē əns) *n.*: Brightness
perpetual (pər pech´ ōō wəl) *adj.*: Unceasing; constant
delusions (di lōō´ zhəns) *n.*: False beliefs or opinions

Literary Focus Ask students to think about the differences between a realistic, action-packed movie and a slow, subdued play in which the characters and the scenery do not resemble real life. Have students discuss what is demanded of an audience watching a film filled with conflict and dramatic dialogue and involving believable characters.

Then ask them to imagine what it would be like to witness a slow-moving play about unrealistic situations, events, and characters—a drama in which elements are intended to be interpreted symbolically. Why does this type of drama demand more of the audience?

Spelling Tip Point out to students that in the word *solace* the final *s* sound is spelled with the letters *ce*.

The Deserted Crone

Zeami

translated by Stanleigh H. Jones, Jr.

PERSONS

A Traveler from the Capital (*waki*)
Two Companions to the Traveler (*wakizure*)
An Old Woman (*mae-jite*)
The Ghost of the Old Woman (*nochi-jite*)
A Villager (*kyōgen*)

PLACE

Mount Obasute in Shinano Province

TIME

The fifteenth night of the eighth month

[*A* TRAVELER *and* TWO COMPANIONS *from the Capital enter and face each other at stage center. They wear short swords and conical* kasa *hats made of reeds.*]

TOGETHER. *Autumn's height,*
   The full moon's night is near,
   Soon the full moon's glory.
   Let us go and visit Mount Obasute.

[*The* TRAVELER *removes his hat and faces front.*]

TRAVELER. I am a man of the Capital. I have yet to see the moon of Sarashina and this autumn I have bestirred myself at last. I hurry now to Obasute Mountain.

[*He puts his hat back on and faces his* COMPANIONS.]

TOGETHER. *On our journey—*
   Fleeting are the dreams at inns along the way,
   Fleeting are the dreams at inns along the way,
   And once again we take our leave;
   Nights and days in lonely hostels
   Bring us here to famed Sarashina,

[*The* TRAVELER *faces front and takes a few steps forward, then returns to his place.*]

TOGETHER. *We have reached Obasute Mountain,*
   Reached Obasute Mountain.

[*His return indicates that he has arrived. He takes off his hat and faces front.*]

TRAVELER. We have traveled so swiftly that we are here already at Mount Obasute.

COMPANION. Indeed, that is so.

For instance, a few steps may represent several miles or even a week's journey.

Primary Source

The Japanese literary scholar Donald Keene writes:

The solemnity of Nō is what most distinguishes it from other forms of drama. The Japanese enjoy laughing at comedies. Indeed, farces called *Kyogen* have traditionally been performed between the Nō tragedies. . . . Even a Nō that ends happily is performed today with the deliberation and gravity reserved in most parts of the world for funeral rites. The plays are filled with tragic incidents, and on the rare occasions when a character says "How happy I am!" he sounds to the uninitiated spectator like a tortured soul.

The special atmosphere can be detected as soon as one sets foot inside a Nō theater. Before a play there is none of the usual chatter of

[*The* COMPANIONS *move to the* waki-*position. The* TRAVELER *goes to stage center.*]

TRAVELER. Now that I am here at Mount Obasute I see that all is just as I imagined it—the level crest, the infinite sky, the unimpeded thousands of leagues of night flooded by the moon so clear. Yes, here I will rest and tonight gaze upon the moon.

[*The* OLD WOMAN, *wearing the* fukai *mask,[1] slowly starts down the bridgeway. The* TRAVELER *moves to the* waki-*position.*]

OLD WOMAN. You there, traveler, what is it you were saying?

[TRAVELER, *standing, goes downstage left.*]

TRAVELER. I have come from the Capital, and this is my first visit here. But tell me, where do you live?

OLD WOMAN. In this villge, Sarashina. Tonight is that mid-autumn night for which all have waited.

> The moon has hurried the dusk of day,
> And now the high plain of heaven
> Glows in mounting brilliance—
> In all directions, the crystalline night.
> How wonderful the moon this evening!

TRAVELER. Oh, are you from Sarashina? Can you tell me then the spot where in ancient days the old woman was left to die?

[*The* OLD WOMAN *has reached the* shite-*position.*]

OLD WOMAN. You ask of the fate of the old woman of Obasute?—a thoughtless question. But if you mean the remains of the woman who sang:

> "No solace for my heart at Sarashina
> When I see the moon
> Shining down on Mount Obasute,"

They are here in the shadow of the little laurel tree—the remains of an old woman long ago abandoned.

TRAVELER. Then here beneath this tree lie the woman's remains, the woman who was deserted?

---

1. fukai (fōō′ kī′) **mask:** The mask of a woman in her thirties. Generally used for the role of mothers.

OLD WOMAN. Yes, deep in the loam,
Buried in obscure grasses
Cut by the reaper.
Short-lived, they say, as is this world,
And already now . . .

TRAVELER. *It is an ancient tale,*
Yet perhaps attachments still remain.

OLD WOMAN. Yes, even after death . . . somehow . . .

TRAVELER. The dismal loneliness of this moor,

OLD WOMAN. The penetrating wind,

TRAVELER. The lonely heart of autumn.

CHORUS [*for the* OLD WOMAN]. *Even now,*
"No solace for my heart at Sarashina,
No solace for my heart at Sarashina."
At dusk of day on Mount Obasute
The green lingers in the trees,
The intermingled pines and laurels,
The autumn leaves so quickly tinged.
Thin mists drift over One-Fold Mountain—
Folds of faintly dyed cloth;
In a cloudless sky a doleful wind.
Lonely mountain vista,
Remote and friendless landscape.

OLD WOMAN. Traveler, from where have you come?

TRAVELER. I am from the Capital, as I told you, but I have long heard of the beauties of the moon at Sarashina, and I come here now for the first time.

OLD WOMAN. Are you indeed from the Capital? If that is so, then I will show myself with the moon tonight and entertain you here.

TRAVELER. Who are you that you should entertain me tonight?

OLD WOMAN. In truth, I am from Sarashina . . .

TRAVELER. But where do you live now?

OLD WOMAN. Where do I live? On this mountain . . .

TRAVELER. This famous mountain that bears the name . . .

OLD WOMAN. Obasute Mountain of the Deserted Crone.

the audience, even though no one admonishes talkers. The great gleaming expanse of the stage imposes silence, almost like an altar. This is not true of performances of Nō in the countryside, where audiences, rather like those in Southeast Asia, talk, eat, or doze throughout the plays, or even throw money to actors they admire. Initially, however, the Nō plays may have been performed by the priests of a Shinto shrine, not for a human audience but to please the gods by acting out their miracles or the history of their shrines.

At the front of the Nō stage are three steps leading down to ground level. These steps have no function at present-day performances, but no stage is without them. Originally they may have been used by the priests to pass from the shrine to the stage, where they performed for the gods alone.

5 Literary Focus Tell students that the *waki*, or "person at the side," never wears a mask. Ask them how they envision the physical appearance of the *waki* in *The Deserted Crone*.

6 Literary Focus Remind students that all female roles are played by men or boys. The masks and costumes indicate the type of character the actor is playing.

7 Discussion Have students discuss the similarities between the Old Woman's description of the night and the Traveler's description.

8 Clarification Draw students' attention to the *shite* position in the diagram on page 304. Make sure students realize that the Old Woman's assumption of the *shite* position indicates that she is the play's central character. Tell students that the *shite* usually appears in two different forms during the course of a play.

9 Enrichment Tell students that these lines are taken from a poem that is believed to be the inspiration for Zeami's play.

10 Clarification Make sure students realize that the Traveler is suggesting that the woman's spirit may still be attached to the world of the living. Remind students that Nō plays often focus on ghosts who have suffered an injustice and are seeking to gain deliverance from their tortures.

11 Discussion Draw students' attention to the references to autumn. Then have them discuss the types of associations they have with autumn.

12 Literary Focus Remind students that the role of the chorus in a Nō play is to express the thoughts of other characters. What does this passage reveal about the character of the Old Woman?

13 Discussion Have students discuss how this passage exemplifies the Japanese reliance on suggestion. What associations does the passage call to mind?

Humanities Note

Fine art, *The Riverhead at Shijo: Theater and Entertainment District at Shijo Kawara.* In this section of a magnificent painted screen, we see a panorama of life in the center of seventeenth-century Kyoto. Painted on a gold background, the screen is an excellent example of the style and subject matter favored during the Edo period.

This section of the screen depicts several events that are occurring simultaneously. In the center of the painting is a street, lined with ticket windows, running through the theater district of Kyoto. In the foreground in two enclosures suggesting buildings, people are shown watching an entertainer, talking with one another, and looking up to see a tightrope artist, whose rope is overhead. On the other side of the street, a theatrical event is taking place. Sitting in two rows, the audience watches with varying degrees of attention. Altogether these details provide a vivid portrait of life in the Kyoto theater district during the seventeenth century.

You might want to use the following questions to discuss the art:

1. What impression of the Kyoto theater district does this painting convey?
2. How does it convey this impression?
3. Explain the ways in which this painting is and is not an appropriate illustration for *The Deserted Crone.*
4. Would you be interested in visiting the place depicted in this painting? Why or why not?

THE RIVERHEAD AT SHIJO: THEATER AND ENTERTAINMENT DISTRICT AT SHIJO KAWARA (detail)
Museum of Fine Arts, Boston

CHORUS [*for the* OLD WOMAN]. *Even to pro-*
    nounce the name—
  How shameful!
  Long ago I was abandoned here.
  Alone on this mountainside
  I dwell, and every year
  In the bright and full mid-autumn moon
  I try to clear away
  The dark confusion of my heart's attachment.
  That is why tonight I have come before you.

CHORUS [*narrating*]. *Beneath the tree,*
  In the evening shadows,
  She vanished like a phantom,
  Like an apparition[2] . . . *disappeared* . . .

[*She exits.*]

[*The* VILLAGER *enters and stands at the naming-place. He wears a short sword.*]

VILLAGER. I live at the foot of this mountain. Tonight the moon is full, and I think I will climb the mountain and gaze at the moon.

[*He sees the* TRAVELER.]

Ah! There's a gentleman I have never seen before. You sir, standing there in the moonlight, where are you from and where are you bound?

TRAVELER. I am from the Capital. I suppose you live in this neighborhood?

VILLAGER. Yes indeed, I do.

TRAVELER. Then come a bit closer. I have something to ask you.

VILLAGER. Certainly.

[*He kneels at stage center.*]

VILLAGER. You said you had something to ask. What might it be?

TRAVELER. You may be somewhat surprised at what I have to ask, but would you tell me anything you may know about the pleasures of moonviewing at Sarashina and the story of Obasute Mountain?

VILLAGER. That is indeed a surprising request. I do live in this vicinity, it is true, but I have no detailed knowledge of such matters. Yet, would it not appear inhospitable if, the very first time we meet, I should say I know nothing of these things you ask? I will tell you, then, what in general I have heard.

TRAVELER. That is most kind of you.

VILLAGER. Well then, here is the story of Mount Obasute: Long ago there lived at this place a man named Wada no Hikonaga. When he was still a child his parents died and he grew up under the care of an aunt. From the day of his marriage his wife hated his aunt and made many accusations against her. But Hikonaga would not listen to her. At length, however, his wife spoke out so strongly that he forgot his aunt's many years of kindness and bowing to his wife's demands, he said one day to the old woman: "Not far from this mountain is a holy image of the Buddha.[3] Let us go there and make our offerings and prayers." So he brought her to this mountain and in a certain place he abandoned her. Later he looked back at the mountain where now the moon was bright and clear. He wanted to go back and fetch his aunt, but his wife was a crafty woman and she detained him until it was too late. The old woman died and her heart's attachment to this world turned her to stone. Hikonaga later went in search of her, and when he saw the stone he realized the dreadful thing he had done. He became a priest they say. Ever since then the mountain has been called Mount Obasute—Mountain of the Deserted Old Woman. Long ago it seems that the mountain was known as Sarashina Mountain. Well, that is what I know of the story. But why do you ask? It seems such an unusual request.

TRAVELER. How kind of you to tell me this story! I asked you for this reason: As I said a little while ago, I am from the Capital, but I had heard about Sarashina and so I made a special journey here to view the moon. A short while ago, as I was waiting for the moon to rise, an old woman appeared to me

14 **Clarification** Point out that the chorus is now describing the Old Woman rather than speaking for her.

15 **Literary Focus** Remind students that Zeami is not interested in developing the characters of the Traveler and the Villager.

16 **Discussion** Have students respond to the story of the Old Woman. What makes the story especially tragic?

17 **Discussion** Have students discuss why the Old Woman's heart remained attached to the world of the living.

18 **Enrichment** Remind students that it is not unusual for the names of places to change over time. Generally places are renamed to honor a person or a special event. Have students discuss the reasons the people of Sarashina may have renamed their mountain.

19 **Clarification** Make sure students note the frequency of the references to the moon. What effect is created by these frequent references?

---

2. apparition (ap′ ə rish′ ən) *n.*: A strange figure appearing suddenly and thought to be a ghost.

3. Buddha (bōōd′ ə): The religious philosopher and teacher who lived in India (563?–483? B.C.) and founded the Buddhist religion.

20 Clarification Make sure students realize that the Old Woman with whom the Traveler had been speaking is the spirit of the woman who was abandoned on the mountain.

21 Clarification Make sure students realize that the Ghost is the *shite* appearing in a different form.

22 Discussion Tell students that some Nō masks are not all that different from masks they may have worn on Halloween when they were younger. Have students discuss their favorite Halloween costumes and explain what these costumes represented.

23 Discussion Call attention to Zeami's use of allusion. Have students discuss what the use of allusions adds to a play. How do allusions create additional layers of meaning?

24 Discussion Have students discuss the meaning of the Ghost's observation that "this is not the moon of long ago."

25 Discussion Have students discuss the ways in which this passage of dialogue differs from the dialogue in other plays they have read.

26 Clarification Make sure students realize that the chorus is once again speaking for the *shite*.

---

from nowhere and recited to me the poem about Obasute Mountain. She promised to entertain me this night of the full moon, and I asked her who she was. Long ago, she told me, her home was in Sarashina, but now she dwelled on Mount Obasute. She had come here this night in order to dispel the dark confusion of her heart's attachment. No sooner had she spoken than here, in the shadows of this tree, she vanished.

VILLAGER. Oh! Amazing! It must be the old woman's spirit, still clinging to this world, who appeared and spoke with you. If so, then stay awhile; recite the holy scriptures and kindly pray for her soul's repose. I believe you will see this strange apparition again.

TRAVELER. I think so too. I will gaze at the moon and cleanse my heart. For somehow I feel certain I shall see this mysterious figure again.

VILLAGER. If you have any further need of me, please call.

TRAVELER. I will.

VILLAGER. I am at your service.

[*He exits.*]

TRAVELER AND COMPANIONS. *Evening twilight deepens,*
And quickens on the moon which sheds
Its first light-shadows of the night.
How lovely:
Ten thousand miles of sky, every corner clear—
Autumn is everywhere the same.
Serene my heart, this night I shall spend in poetry.
"The color of the moon new-risen—
Remembrances of old friends
Two thousand leagues away."

[*The* GHOST *of the old woman enters, wearing the* uba *mask.*⁴ *She stands at the* shite-position.]

GHOST. *How strange and wonderful this moment,*

---

4. Uba ($\overline{oo}'$ bah′) **mask:** The mask of an old woman who had once been beautiful.

Superb yet strange this moment out of time—
Is my sadness only for the moon tonight?
With the dawn
*Half of autumn will have passed,*⁵
And waiting for it seemed so long.
The brilliant autumn moon of Mount Obasute,
So matchless, flawless I cannot think
I have ever looked upon the moon before;
Unbearably beautiful—
Surely this is not the moon of long ago.

TRAVELER. *Strange,*
In this moonlit night already grown so late
A woman robed in white appears—
Do I dream?—Is it reality?

GHOST. *Why do you speak of dreams?*
That aged figure who came to you by twilight
In shame has come again.

TRAVELER. *What need have you for apologies?*
this place, as everybody knows, is called . . .
Obasute—

GHOST. *Mountain where an old hag dwells.*

TRAVELER. *The past returns,*
An autumn night . . .

GHOST. *Friends had gathered*
To share the moon together . . .
Grass on the ground was our cushion . . .

TRAVELER. *Waking, sleeping, among flowers,*
The dew clinging to our sleeves.

TOGETHER. *So many varied friends*
Reveling in the moonlight . . .
When did we first come together?
Unreal—like a dream.

CHORUS [*for the* GHOST]. *Like the lady-flower nipped by time,*
The lady-flower past its season,
I wither in robes of grass;
Trying to forget that long ago

---

5. Is my sadness . . . will have passed: An allusion to the following lines from a poem by the ancient Japanese poet Fujiwara no Teika (foo′ jě′ wä′ rä′ nō′ tě′ kä′): "Is my sadness only for the sinking moon? / With the dawn half of autumn will have passed."

Grammar in Action

Imagery refers to words or phrases that create mental pictures, or images, that appeal to one or more of the five senses—sight, hearing, touch, smell, and taste. Notice the following images from *The Deserted Crone* and the senses to which they appeal:

Evening twilight deepens, . . .   (sight)

. . . The dew clinging to our sleeves.   (touch)

. . . Tones of string and flute, . . .   (sound)

Student Activity 1. Find the images in each of the following passages from *The Deserted Crone*. Then identify the sense or senses to which each image appeals.

1. At dusk of day on Mount Obasute / The green lingers in the trees, / Intermingled pines and laurels, / The autumn leaves so quickly tinged.
2. Thin mists drift over One-Fold Mountain— / Folds of faintly dyed cloth; / In a cloudless sky a doleful wind.
3. Beneath the tree, / In the evening shadows, / She vanishes like a phantom, . . .
4. Peacocks and parrots call their notes / In harmonies of imitation.

I was cast aside, abandoned,
I have come again to Mount Obasute.
How it shames me now to show my face
In Sarashina's moonlight, where all can see!
Ah, well, this world is all a dream—
Best I speak not, think not,
But in these grasses of remembrance
Delight in flowers, steep my heart in the moon.

[*She gazes upward, then advances a few steps during
the following passage.*]

CHORUS [*for the* GHOST]. *"When pleasure moved me,
    came;*
The pleasure ended, I returned."[6]
Then, as now tonight, what beauty in the sky!

GHOST. *Though many are the famous places*
Where one may gaze upon the moon,
Transcending[7] *all—Sarashina.*

CHORUS [*for the* GHOST]. *A pure full disk of light,*
Round, round, leaves the coastal range,
Cloudless over Mount Obasute.

GHOST. *Even though the vows of the many*
    Buddhas

CHORUS. *Cannot be ranked in terms of high or low,*
None can match the light of Amida's Vow,[8]
Supreme and all-pervading in its mercy.

|7| [*She dances.*]

And so it is, they say,
The westward movement of the sun, the moon, and
    stars
Serves but to guide all living things
Unto the Paradise of the West.
The moon, that guardian who stands on Amida's
    right,

---

6. **"When pleasure . . . I returned"**: An allusion to a
comment by Wang Tzu-yu (wäng′ dzu yōō), a third–century
Chinese nobleman. After traveling by boat to a friend's house
and reaching the gate of the house, Wang left without seeing
his friend. When asked why he did this, Wang responded,
"Moved by pleasure, I came; the pleasure ended, I returned."

7. **transcending** (tran send′ iŋ) *v.*: Going beyond the limits
of.

8. **Amida's Vow:** The vow that all living beings would receive
salvation. Amida is a divine figure in the Buddhist religion.

Nō mask: Demon Ja
Courtesy Mitsui Bunko

Leads those with special bonds to Buddha:
Great Seishi,[9] *"Power Supreme," he is called,*
For he holds the highest power to lighten heavy
    crimes.
Within his heavenly crown a flower shines,
And its jeweled calyx reveals with countless leaves
The pure lands of all the other worlds.[10]
The sounds of the wind in the jeweled tower,
Tones of string and flute,
Variously bewitch the heart.

|28|

---

9. **Seishi** (sē′ shē′): Seishi is another divine figure in the
Buddhist religion.

10. **The pure lands . . . other worlds:** The infinite number
of Buddhist paradises in the universe.

29 Discussion Have students discuss the ways in which Zeami conveys "the inconstancy of the world" in this play. How does the world's inconstancy relate to the Japanese appreciation for perishability?

30 Discussion Have students recall the memories by which her "heart is bound." What are her "unshakable delusions"?

31 Discussion Have students respond to the ending of the play. How is the ending different from the endings of other plays they have seen or read? Why has the Traveler "abandoned" the spirit of the Old Woman? What impact does being abandoned again have on the Old Woman? Why?

Cultural Note The renowned Irish poet William Butler Yeats was so drawn to Nō plays that he borrowed many of the conventions of the Nō when writing his own plays about Irish legends. He wrote, "It is natural that I go to Asia for a stage-convention that has no part in the action. . . . A mask will enable me to substitute for the fact of some commonplace player . . . the fine invention of a sculptor. A mask . . . no matter how close you go is still a work of art . . . and we shall not lose by staying the movement of the features, for deep feeling is expressed by the movement of the whole body."

Cooperative Learning Divide your class into groups of three or four, and assign each group a different feeling, such as longing, doubt, anger, relief, love, and excitement. Ask each group to act out their emotion in the subtle and suggestive style that is characteristic of Nō plays.

Trees by the Pond of Treasures,[11]
Where the lotus blooms red and white,
Scatter flowers along their avenues;
On the water's little waves—
A riot of sweet fragrances.

GHOST. *The incomparable voices of the birds of paradise—*

CHORUS [*for the* GHOST]. *Peacocks and parrots call their notes*
In harmonies of imitation.
Throughout that realm—unimpeded, all-pervading—
The radiance that gives his name—"Light without limit,"[12]
But here the moon through its rift of clouds,
Now full and bright, now dimly seen,
Reveals the inconstancy of this world
Where all is perpetual change.

GHOST. *My sleeves move again in dances*
Of sweet remembered nights of long ago.

[*She continues to dance, her song alternating back and forth between herself and the* CHORUS.]

CHORUS. *"No solace for my heart at Sarashina*
When I see the moon
Shining down on Mount Obasute"
When I see the shimmering moon.

GHOST. *No stranger to the moon,*
I dally among the flowers
For these moments, brief as dew on autumn grasses . . .

---

11. the Pond of Treasures: A pond in the western paradise of Amida.
12. "Light without limit": Another name for Seishi.

CHORUS. *Fleeting as the dew indeed . . .*
Why should I have come here?
A butterfly at play . . .

GHOST. *Fluttering . . .*
Dancing sleeves . . .

CHORUS. *Over and return, over and . . .*

GHOST. *. . . Return, return*
Autumn of long ago.

CHORUS. *My heart is bound by memories,*
Unshakable delusions.
In this piercing autumn wind tonight
I ache with longing for the past,
Hunger after the world I knew—
Bitter world,
*   Autumn,*
*   Friends.*
But even as I speak,
See how the night already pales,
And daylight whitens into morning.
I shall vanish,
The traveler will return.

[*The* TRAVELER *exits.*]

GHOST. *Now, alone,*
Deserted,
A moss-grown wintry hag.

[*She watches the* TRAVELER *depart, and weeps.*]

CHORUS. *Abandoned again as long ago.*
And once again all that remains—
Desolate, forsaken crag,
Mountain of the Deserted Crone.

[*She spreads her arms and remains immobile at the* shite-*position.*]

Reader's Response *In what ways is this play different from other plays you have read or seen? Would you like to see a performance of this play? Why or why not?*

Closure and Extension

ANSWERS TO THINKING ABOUT THE SELECTION

1. (a) Suggested response: The mood is somber, sad, and eerie. (b) Answers will differ. Students may feel that the mood is established through the references to the Old Woman's loneliness and sadness and through the descriptions of the setting.

2. Suggested response: She sings part of the deserted crone's song, she knows the spot where the deserted crone died, and she says that she lives on Obasute Mountain.

3. (a) Suggested response: Autumn is a season that is often associated with sadness and death. (b) The Old Woman was abandoned on a night when the moon was full.

4. (a) She is clinging to this world because she is unable to come to terms with the circumstances of her death. (b) She is unable to do so because she has been abandoned for a second time.

5. (a) Suggested response: This Buddhist preoccupation is clearly reflected in the fact that the play's central character is a spirit who is unable to break her ties to the world of the liv-

THINKING ABOUT THE SELECTION

Interpreting

1. (a) How would you describe the play's mood, or atmosphere? (b) How is the mood established?
2. When the Old Woman first encounters the travelers, what hints about her true identity does she offer?
3. (a) Why is it significant that the play takes place during autumn? (b) Why is it significant that the play takes place on a night when the moon is full?
4. (a) Why is the ghost of the Old Woman "still clinging to this world"? (b) At the end of the play, why is the ghost still unable to break her ties to the world of living?
5. (a) How does the play reflect the Buddhist preoccupation with death and the afterworld? (b) What is the significance of the reference to "Amida's Vow"?
6. How does the play capture the transient nature of life on earth?
7. Why would it be appropriate to characterize this play as a tragedy?

Applying

8. Explain whether you think that this play would have as powerful an impact on today's audiences as it did on the audiences of Zeami's time.

ANALYZING LITERATURE

Understanding a Nō Play

It is extremely difficult to envision the performance of a Nō play by merely reading one. It is possible, however, to appreciate some of the characteristics that contribute to the play's value as a work of literature. For example, a reader can appreciate the depth and beauty of the language and the timeless relevance of the play's theme, or central insight.

1. What is the theme of *The Deserted Crone*?
2. Nō plays often contain recurring images, or word pictures, that relate to the play's theme. What images recur throughout *The Deserted Crone* and how do they relate to the play's theme?

3. Because Nō plays are staged using little scenery and few props, the audience has to use its imagination to visualize the setting. How might Zeami's use of imagery help the audience to do so?

CRITICAL THINKING AND READING

Recognizing the Japanese Aesthetic

Like other Japanese literary forms, the Nō theater reflects several of the aspects of the **Japanese aesthetic.** For example, the Japanese preference for suggestion is reflected in the use of visual imagery to help the audience envision the setting.

1. How is the Japanese preference for suggestion exhibited in the use of masks and in the casting of Nō plays?
2. How does the fact that Nō plays are staged with few props and little scenery reflect the Japanese emphasis on simplicity?
3. How does *The Deserted Crone* reflect the Japanese emphasis on perishability?

THINKING AND WRITING

Writing About a Nō Play

What qualities set *The Deserted Crone* apart from other plays you have read? What are your reactions to the play? What could you learn from it? What do you think it would be like to see a performance of the play? Write a personal essay in which you explore your responses to each of these questions. Before you begin writing, spend some time thinking about the play, keeping each of these questions in mind. Begin your essay with an introduction that pulls together all your ideas. As you write the body of the essay, make sure you support each of your opinions with reasons and details. After you have finished writing, revise your essay, making sure it is well-organized and coherent.

PRIMARY SOURCE

The Japanese aesthetic influences its music too. Raphael Mostel explains the difference between Japanese and Western music. "The traditional Eastern view that time is a fluid gives the music a distinctively elastic flow and ebb, as opposed to the usual Western idea of mechanical ticking. Repeated notes are more likely to imitate the acceleration of a bouncing ball or insect rhythms, rather than a regular, four-square repetition. The phrasings and gestures of traditional Japanese music are drawn from the observation of nature. . . "

Another concern is the synesthetic effect of sounds, that is, sounds chosen because they evoke associations with the other senses (sight, taste, touch, smell). . . ."

(continued from bottom of page)

3. Suggested response: The vividness of the imagery enables audiences and readers to create a picture of the setting in their minds.

ANSWERS TO CRITICAL THINKING AND READING

1. Suggested response: Rather than casting actors whose age and physical appearance match those of the character, masks are worn to suggest what the character might look like.
2. Suggested response: The sets are extremely simple.
3. Suggested response: In a beautiful and moving manner, the play tells the story of how the Old Woman perished.

Challenge What other dominant Japanese tastes does *The Deserted Crone* reflect?

THINKING AND WRITING

Publishing Student Writing Have students read their essays to the class, and use the essays as a springboard for a class discussion about the play.

---

ing. (b) Suggested response: The Old Woman has not received the salvation promised by Amida.

6. Suggested response: The story of the Old Woman's death conveys the transient nature of life. The awareness of the transience of life is heightened by the descriptions of eternal elements of nature, such as the moon and the mountain.

7. Suggested response: The circumstances surrounding the Old Woman's death are tragic. The woman's inability to come to terms with her death and her abandonment at the end of the play are also tragic.

8. Answers will differ. Students may comment that it would have as powerful an impact because the emotions it deals with are still relevant.

ANSWERS TO ANALYZING LITERATURE

1. Suggested response: The play points out the need to come to terms with great loss and change.
2. Answers will differ. Students should note that images of the moon recur throughout the play. These images remind the Old Woman of the night on which she was abandoned.

The Natural World

"Every part of this earth is sacred to my people. Every shining pine needle, every sandy shore, every mist in the dark woods, every meadow, every humming insect. All are holy in the memory and experience of my people."
—Chief Seattle

Chief Seattle was expressing the sentiments of the Native American people. Yet he could also have been speaking for the Japanese. Like the Native Americans, the Japanese are known for their deep appreciation of and respect for nature. In addition, many people in traditional Japanese society also shared the Native Americans' belief in a spiritual unity between humanity and nature.

The Japanese people's attitude toward nature is evident throughout Japanese literature. Japanese poets and prose writers of all ages have expressed a sense of closeness to nature, reveled in its beauty, and conveyed a feeling of reverence toward it.

Looking at the moon is always diverting, no matter what the circumstances. A certain man once said, "Surely nothing is so delightful as the moon," but another man rejoined, "The dew moves me even more." How amusing that they should have argued the point! What could fail to be affecting in its proper season? This is obviously true of the moon and cherry blossoms. The wind seems to have a special power to move men's hearts.
—Yoshida Kenko, *Essays in Idleness*

Clouds come from time to time—
And bring to men a chance to rest
From looking at the moon.
—Bashō, Haiku

I loved her like the leaves,
The lush leaves of spring
That weighed the branches of the willows
Standing on the jutting bank . . .
—Kakinomoto Hitomaro,
"I Loved Her Like the Leaves"

In spring it is the dawn that is most beautiful. As the light creeps over the hills, their outlines are dyed a faint red and wisps of purplish cloud trail over them.
—Sei Shōnagon, *The Pillow Book*

Traveler: Now that I am here at Mount Obasute I see that all is just as I imagined it —the level crest, the infinite sky, the unimpeded thousands of leagues of night flooded by the moon so clear. Yes, here I will rest and tonight gaze upon the moon.
—Zeami, *The Deserted Crone*

Although nature plays an especially important role in Japanese literature, writers from almost all cultures and eras have celebrated nature's beauty and explored humanity's relationship to it. For example, "The Story of the Flood" from *The Epic of Gilgamesh* (page 23) conveys the tremendous power of nature and humanity's inability to predict or control it.

The following are some other selections in Prentice Hall *World Masterpieces* that are concerned with the natural world or its relationship to humanity.

SUGGESTED READINGS

Motivation/Prior Knowledge
Have one student read aloud the quotation by Chief Seattle. Then use Chief Seattle's comment as a springboard for a class discussion about the natural world and humanity's relationship to it. How do students perceive humanity's relationship to nature? Do students feel that people have an obligation to protect nature? Why or why not? What literary works have students read that explore humanity's relationship with nature? What themes do these works convey?

Cultural Note Many American writers have explored humanity's relationship with nature. If your students have studied American literature, have them discuss American literary works that focus on the natural world and its relationship to humanity. For example, they might discuss some of the works of Walt Whitman and Ralph Waldo Emerson.

CROSS CURRENTS

Frank Lloyd Wright (1869–1959)

Considered the greatest American architect to date, Frank Lloyd Wright was heavily influenced by Japanese aesthetics and architectural forms. Wright was introduced to Japanese architecture in 1893 when he had the opportunity to view a small Japanese temple that was exhibited at the Chicago World's Fair. Fascinated by the striking delicacy of the temple, he soon began applying many of the principles of Japanese architecture to his own work.

EARLY WORK

Japanese influence is most evident in Wright's early work. Inspired by the Japanese love for nature, Wright designed his early houses, often referred to as "prairie houses," to harmonize with the midwestern environment. With their low, long roofs, the houses were intended to draw attention to the beauty of the low-lying prairie landscape. Reflecting the Japanese desire for simplicity, Wright avoided applying ornaments or decorations to these houses. Instead, the beauty of the houses results from natural lines, curves, and open spaces. Some of Wright's early houses, most notably the famous Robie house in Chicago, also reflect the Japanese preference for irregularity in their lack of symmetry. Finally, many of Wright's early houses directly reflect Japanese architectural principles in their use of geometric panels, latticework, and openings.

LATER WORK

Wright's later works are recognized mainly for their innovations and originality. It is also clear, however, that these buildings indirectly reflect the influence of Japanese aesthetics. Wright's famous Falling Water House (pictured here) in Bear Run, Pennsylvania, draws attention to the tremendous beauty of its setting, exhibiting the influence of the Japanese emphasis on nature. In addition, the building's lack of symmetry again reflects the Japanese preference for irregularity. Probably the most famous of Wright's later works, the Solomon R. Guggenheim Museum in New York City, also echoes Japanese ideals. Just as Wright had designed other buildings to harmonize with the environment, he constructed the Guggenheim so that the architectural design would harmonize with the artwork. This harmony results mainly from the simplicity of the interior design. Once again reflecting Wright's distaste for ornaments and decorations, the building's beauty results from its natural curves and open spaces. At the same time, the lack of ornamentation draws people's attention to the works of art, in the same way the design of Wright's early houses had drawn people's attention to the landscape.

Motivation/Prior Knowledge
Have students discuss interesting or unusual buildings they have seen. Then explain that they are about to learn about one of the most innovative American architects of the twentieth century, Frank Lloyd Wright. Explain that Wright drew upon Japanese tastes to create unique and beautiful buildings, such as the one seen here. Tell them that many of these buildings were constructed to harmonize with their natural surroundings. Then have them discuss how the building pictured here harmonizes with its natural surroundings.

The Interpretive Essay

Writing an Interpretive Essay

Interpretive essays make and support claims about the meaning of something. The effectiveness of the essay depends not so much on what the writer claims as on the strength of the support the writer includes. Two writers may interpret the meaning of the same work differently, yet both might write strong essays with solid evidence to support their very different interpretations.

Elements of Interpretive Essays

- Point of departure
  gives introduction to subject
  provides context
- Interpretive claims
  present position
- Support (bulk of essay)
  gives evidence, quotes, backup, etc.
- Stance
  defines strong, consistent position that is a step beyond mere claim

Writing Assignment

Write an interpretive essay in which you interpret the meaning of one of the poems in this unit. State the meaning as your thesis and show how the poet's details illuminate it. In your essay you should follow these steps.

- State your interpretive claim ("The poet's haiku shows that _____.")
- Support the claim with evidence ("_____, in the poem, implies that _____.")
- Take a stand on the universal truth, the poem's depiction of it, or both ("I agree with the poet that _____. However, _____.")

Prewrite

Gather information for your essay in several ways. The following diagram shows four channels to explore. Use them in the order that suits you best.

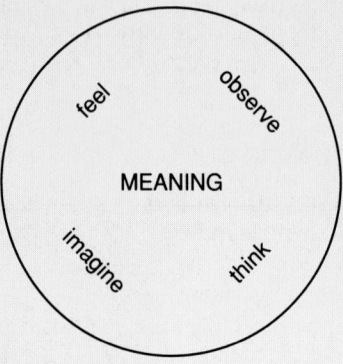

Reread the poem and write down your observations as simple statements. For example:

The sun has a method.
Hollyhocks face the sun.
It rains in May.

Hollyhocks turn toward the sun even in rain when the sun isn't visible.

Reflect on the emotions this poem evokes in you. Don't limit your feeling responses by guessing the emotions the poet expects you to feel. Write down your own feelings. For example:

I feel happy.
I feel hopeful.
I feel strong.
I feel invigorated.

Imagine

Close your eyes and allow your imagination to wander over the image in the poem. Imagine the situation and what lies beyond it. Let your mind's eye roam freely. Then open your eyes and write down the information your imagination produced.

Analyze

Look over the observations, feelings, and imaginings you've written down, and speculate about them. Express the common threads you see in a meaningful statement or two. Then use the best one as your claim, or thesis statement. For example:

Strength and hope always exist, but sometimes you lose sight of them.

Write

Choose the evidence and the arrangement you'll use to support your claim, then write your paper. Offer a point of departure and a claim in your first paragraph. It must include all necessary information such as reference to the poem, its author, and your thesis statement. Support the thesis in your next paragraphs by showing how the haiku reveals the universal truth. Use the information you gathered from observing, feeling, imagining, and analyzing. Proclaim your stance in your final paragraph. Strike a clear position about the universal truth, the poem, or better still, both.

Collaborate

Ask a partner to read your draft and answer the following questions. Remind him or her that you need information and help beyond "Yes" or "No."

- Is the claim clear? What wording could make it sharper?

- Does the claim seem forceful? Uncertain?
- Is the claim supported by the evidence? If it is not, can you point out specific places the evidence seems unrelated or unconvincing?
- Do the thesis and evidence support the stand the writer takes in the last paragraph? What help can you offer?

Revise

Before revising, ask someone to read your essay aloud to you. Listen as if someone else wrote it. This practice gives you an objective distance that may help you catch some problems you might otherwise overlook.

Now, recalling the suggestions your response partner made and the problems you heard when it was read to you, rewrite your paper. Don't be afraid to go back to notes for help, too.

For additional improvement, vary the structure of your sentences to keep the reader's interest.

Publish

Choose a partner with whom you'll appear in an interview show staged for your class. Read each other's essays and then prepare four or five questions to be addressed during the brief exchange that will allow others to watch you discuss the ideas expressed in your papers.

Evaluate

You've discovered a great deal from very little in this paper, taking a poem of few syllables and expanding its meaning to hundreds of words. How do you feel about doing so? Is the poem more meaningful to you now that you've done that process? Is it less meaningful? Consider sharing this paper with someone you care about.

Master Teacher Note Explain to students that they should not hesitate to make revisions in their work as they are writing. Point out to students that they can vary the stages of the writing process to find the approach that works best for them. For example, they may find that it works best for them to prepare a formal outline before they begin writing, or they may find that they like to organize their ideas as they are writing.

Guidelines for Evaluating Writing About Literature Keep the following questions in mind when evaluating students' compositions.
1. Does the student clearly state his or her interpretation of the poem?
2. Is the interpretation valid?
3. Does the student support his or her interpretation with details from the poem?
4. Is the essay well organized?

Presentation

This map of the classical world features the Roman Empire during the time of Caesar. Explain to students that the term *Classical Civilizations* refers to the ancient Greeks and the ancient Romans. Because the Romans borrowed from as well as imitated Greek culture, the classical component of European civilization is primarily Greek.

Greek civilization began to flourish in the third millennium B.C., when the sites of the Athenian Acropolis, Corinth, and Troy were occupied by neolithic craftspeople and artists who left behind evidence of their skill. Later Greeks told legends of King Minos of Crete, said to be the first lawgiver and to sit in judgment over the dead in the underworld. The Minoan palace culture on Crete reached its peak from about 2200 B.C. to 1450 B.C., when the Myceneans took control of Knossos. But by 1100 B.C., the Mycenean palace culture had disappeared, and Greek civilization experienced what historians call the Dark Ages.

During the Dark Ages, despotic monarchs ruled ancient Greece, but by 700 B.C., kings disappeared and tyrants rose to power. Tyrants were strong leaders who imposed order on a politically unstable society. The tyrants of Athens led it to a leadership position in ancient Greece. Eventually, Athens became the center of power for an empire. This increase in power led to the Peloponnesian War with Sparta. Athens lost the war, and in 338 B.C., Philip of Macedon conquered Greece. After his assassination, Alexander conquered the Mediterranean and Asian worlds. But his empire disintegrated with his death. The next world empire was that of Rome.

The Rise of Classical Civilizations

800 B.C.–A.D. 500

Using the Map
Have students study the map and ask them the following questions:
1. Why would Italy's location have facilitated Rome's rise to power?
2. Why would Caesar have regarded Belgae one of the most savage (uncivilized) parts of Gaul?
3. By the time of the Roman Empire, Troy had fallen. The closest settlement to where Troy was located on Asia Minor is Pergamum. Locate Pergamum.
4. If you were traveling from Rome to Athens by boat, in which direction would you sail?
5. Why would the Nile have been a major commercial route?

Humanities Note

Fine art, *The School of Athens* by Raphael. The work of the Italian artist Raffaello Sanzio, or Raphael, (1483–1520) typifies the ideal of the high Renaissance. Though strongly influenced by the enormous talents of Michelangelo and Leonardo da Vinci, Raphael maintained a powerful individualistic style. His seemingly effortless work in the classical vein can be compared to Greek art at its peak of perfection.

The School of Athens is one of the four frescoes Raphael painted in the Signature Room of the Vatican. It epitomizes the humanist ideal of rational truth. The full, stagelike composition is contained within architectural elements thought to be Raphael's visualization of St. Peter's Basilica, then under construction. The two central figures are portraits of the ancient philosophers Plato and Aristotle. Grouped at Plato's side are ancient philosophers and sages concerned with the spiritual world. Grouped with Aristotle are those philosophers and scientists concerned with mankind and nature.

An interesting feature of this fresco is Raphael's playful portraits within portraits. The figure of the philosopher Heraclitus, leaning on a stone block at the base of the stairs, is actually a portrait of the painter Michelangelo. Leonardo da Vinci is the philosopher Plato. Euclid, the mathematician, bent over a geometry problem in the right foreground, is a portrait of Bramante, the creator of St. Peter's Basilica. Raphael, in a final gleeful gesture, painted himself, in a black beret, peeking out from behind the philosopher Sodoma on the far right.

You might want to use the following questions to discuss the art:

1. What do you think prompted Raphael to paint his fellow artists in the exalted company of these philosophers?
2. Which figures in the painting most interest you, and why?

THE SCHOOL OF ATHENS
Raphael
Vatican Museum, Rome

Objectives

1 To understand the historical background of ancient Greek civilization
2 To understand the Golden Age of Athens
3 To understand ancient Greek religion
4 To appreciate ancient Greek literature

ANCIENT GREECE

(c. 800 B.C.–323 B.C.)

. . . never at any other period has so much
energy, beauty, and virtue been developed; never
was blind strength and stubborn force so
disciplined and rendered subject to the will of
man, or that will less repugnant to the dictates of
the beautiful and the true, as during the century
which preceded the death of Socrates. Of no other
epoch in the history of our species have we
records and fragments stamped so visibly with the
image of the divinity in man.

**—Percy Bysshe Shelley
from *A Defense of Poetry***

Motivation/Prior Knowledge Tell students that they will be reading about one of the most influential ancient civilizations. More than any other nation, the Greeks have influenced Western society in many spheres, from literature, philosophy, science, and aesthetics to art, architecture, and language. The legacy of Greek culture has outlived the history of ancient Greece itself.

Enrichment Students might be interested in specific information about the archeological finds of Minoan culture. Wall paintings, statuettes, and other art works offer tantalizing glimpses of palace life: processions, graceful young athletes somersaulting over the horns of charging bulls, tame monkeys, and spectators at a contest. Women are depicted as handling snakes, as having elaborate hairstyles, mascaraed eyes, and form-fitting and revealing gowns. These graceful and sophisticated palace dwellers prized comfort and beauty. Evidence exists of indoor plumbing, wall paintings full of color and motion depicting scenes from nature (blue dolphins cavorting in the waves) and daily life.

HISTORICAL BACKGROUND

The Early Aegeans

The beginnings of civilization are as early in Greek lands as in Egypt and Mesopotamia. In the second millennium B.C., the brilliant Minoan culture (named after the mythical king Minos) flourished on Crete. Archeological finds indicate that the Minoans were sophisticated palace dwellers accustomed to comfort, luxury, and beauty. In its heyday (about 1600 B.C.) Minoan civilization exerted its influence throughout the Greek world through trade and colonization.

Mycenean Civilization (1600–1200 B.C.)

Minoan influence gave rise to the Mycenean palace culture on the Greek mainland. In about 1450 B.C., the Myceneans, Indo-European invaders from the north, seem to have taken control of Knossos, and the thousands of written tablets found there and on the Peloponnese bear witness to impressive record keeping. These tablets are in a syllabic script called Linear B, distinct from the older and still undeciphered Minoan Linear A. In 1952 another amateur, architect Michael Ventris, deciphered Linear B and proved it to be an archaic form of Greek. The Myceneans brought with them their own Indo-European language, but they adopted the commercial and bureaucratic practices of Minoan culture such as recording major transactions and minor details on tablets. Mycenean record keeping anticipated modern, computerized government, prying relentlessly and recording the most trivial details.

The Myceneans probably arrived in Greece about 2100 B.C. From about 1600 to 1200 B.C., their empire flourished. Around 1200 B.C., however, there was widespread destruction in the eastern Mediterranean. The sack of Troy in 1220 B.C. was the last major effort of the Mycenean empire. By 1100 B.C. the sophisticated network of imperial palaces, with complex trade, diplomatic relations, and elaborate written records, had disappeared.

The Dark Age

For about 300 years, we have no written records and few material remains of Greek civilization. One theory holds fire responsible for the destruction of the great Mycenean palaces, arts, skills, wealth, and writing systems. Since no written evidence survives, we call the period after the collapse of Mycenean civilization the Dark Age of Greece.

After the massive upheaval in the eastern Mediterranean between 1250 and 1150 B.C., the vacuum was filled by relatively primitive invaders, the Dorians. During the Dark Age, both on the mainland and in Asia Minor, trade with the East was crucial in the establishment of permanent Greek trading posts. In the eighth century B.C., major colonies were founded throughout Sicily and southern Italy. Greek traders voyaged and settled throughout the Mediterranean from Spain, France, and Italy to what is now Turkey and Syria. Trading posts brought together Phoenicians and Greeks.

To facilitate commercial dealings, the Greeks adapted the Phoenician unvocalized syllabary (set of written signs or characters of a language representing syllables) to their own needs. Their adaptation of the Phoenician syllabary resulted in the first true alphabet. The introduction of the alphabet through trade explains why there is evidence of literacy everywhere in Greece by 750 B.C. Literacy was not restricted to a select class (such as priests or scribes) but seems to have been universal. So efficient was the alphabet that it was adopted first by the Etruscans who traded with the Greeks during the Dark Age and later by the Romans and thus the rest of the Western world.

The Orientalizing Period

Greece emerged from the Dark Age not only with widespread literacy but with epic poems that represent the culmination of a long and rich oral tradition. In the seventh and sixth centuries, art and literature flourished, fostered by an economic boom throughout the Mediterranean. Greek merchants dominated trade from Syria to the Phoeni-

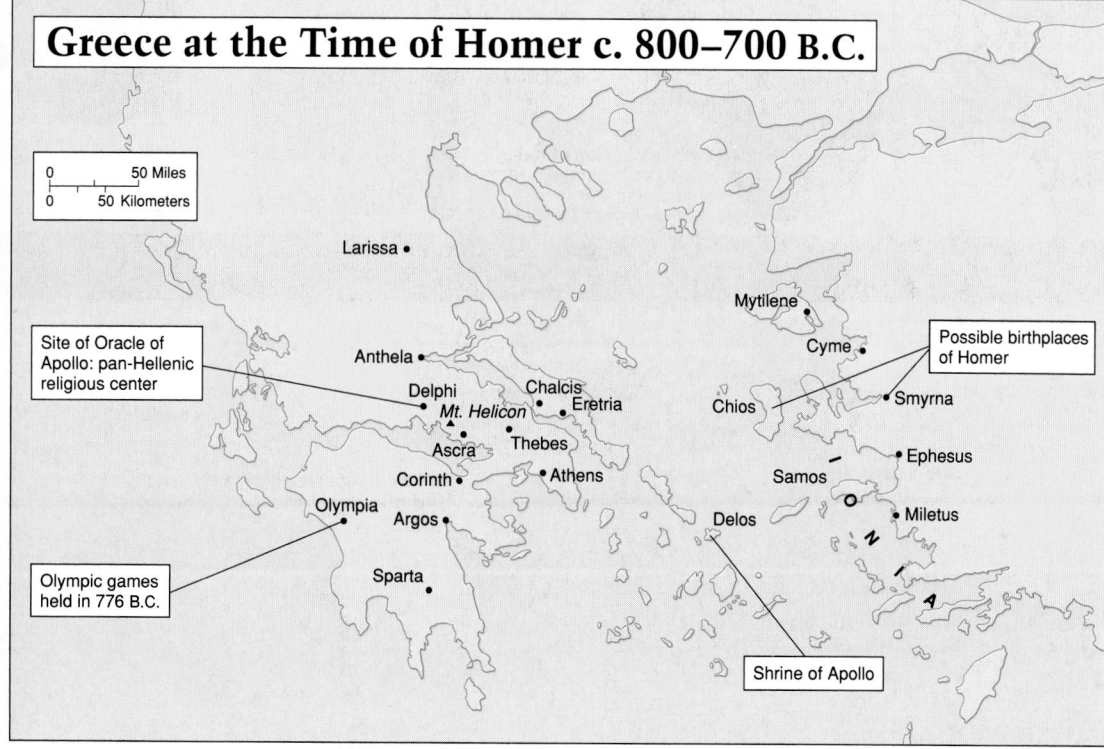

Greece at the Time of Homer c. 800–700 B.C.

0   50 Miles
0   50 Kilometers

Larissa

Site of Oracle of Apollo: pan-Hellenic religious center

Anthela

Delphi
Mt. Helicon
Ascra
Thebes
Corinth
Olympia
Argos
Sparta

Chalcis
Eretria
Athens

Olympic games held in 776 B.C.

Mytilene
Cyme

Chios

Possible birthplaces of Homer

Smyrna

Ephesus
Samos
Delos
Miletus

I O N I A

Shrine of Apollo

Using the Map
Have students study the map and ask them the following questions:
1. Identify the two most powerful city-states and give their approximate locations.
2. Locate Athens. Why would Athens be a strong naval force?
3. Locate Sparta. Why would the Spartans be a formidable land force?
4. What two locations have to do with the worship of Apollo?
5. Based on the geography depicted on the map, what gave rise to Greece's fragmented society?

Clarification Democracy was not the only form of government in Greece, nor was it necessarily the most efficient. Why then did Athenian democracy gain so much prestige? Perhaps one part of the answer lies in the role of Athens as "the savior of Greece" against the invading Persians. In 548 B.C., Cyrus of Persia defeated the pro-Greek Lydian king Croesus. He then moved westward to subdue the rich Ionian Greek cities of Anatolia and the coast of Asia Minor. The next step for the Persians was to turn their formidable troops against mainland Greece. The first invasion was unsuccessful: the Persian fleet was damaged off Mt. Athos in 492 B.C., and in 490 B.C. the Athenians mounted a desperate defense at Marathon, repulsing the Persian army. Their superior numbers and wealth as well as the internal discord in Greece made the Persians' success seem sure. But in 480 B.C., the Athenian fleet, aided by some allies, defeated the vast Persian navy off the island of Salamis near Athens. The war was essentially over after Salamis. Athens had spearheaded Greek resistance and driven off the barbarian invader. Sparta sent no men to Marathon and saw no reason to fight at Salamis, claiming there was no sense in fighting unless the Persians were in the Peloponnese. Athens had saved Greece, and much emphasis was placed on the bravery of the free citizens of a democracy, able to defeat the powerful Persian army.

cian coast, taking advantage of the roads built by the Persian empire; to the west trading posts and colonies were built in Italy, France, and Spain. The importance of long-distance trade in this period cannot be overestimated. Literacy, new currents in art and intellectual history, colonization, and the creation of the polis, or city-state, are ultimately due to trade.

City-states were small, independent cities. The geography of the Greek peninsula and its scattered islands made a fragmented society inevitable. City-states had a common Hellenic heritage, but their differences in custom, political constitution, and dialect fostered rivalry; they were constantly at war with each other.

The Persian War

By the beginning of the fifth century B.C., Athens and Sparta had emerged as the two most powerful city-states. Together, they resisted the Persian invasion of Europe from 490 to 479 B.C. Success in defeating the Persians was largely due to the Athenians at Marathon and, finally, at Salamis.

THE GOLDEN AGE OF ATHENS

Athens' decisive role in spearheading Greek resistance against Persia led to the rise of the Athenian Empire. At the time, Athenian democracy provided citizens with an unprecedented cultural and political environment known as the Golden Age of Athens. During the Golden Age, Athenians were encouraged to develop individually while maintaining steadfast devotion to the community. By contrast, Sparta was a totalitarian state in which individual citizens were subordinate to the state. As a result, the Spartan army was superior to any other Greek force, and the Spartans controlled most of the city-states in the Peloponnese.

Minoan art from Crete is the richest of the Aegean world. After 2000 B.C. Cretan farmers were prosperous and civilized enough to build wealthy private villas or palaces such as Phaestos, the site where this jug was found. As the power and wealth increased at Phaestos and other such villas, a palace bureaucracy grew up and flourished. With the introduction of the potter's wheel, artists were able to produce exquisite ceramics—called Kamares ware—which were decorated with abstract patterns, such as those on this beaked jug. The abstract patterns later gave way to designs drawn from plant and animal life.

In Greek mythology, the Trojan War (c. 1200 B.C.), was a battle between the Greeks and the people of Troy that lasted ten years. The war began after the Trojan prince Paris abducted Helen, the wife of Menelaus of Sparta—the scene painted on this vase. Homer's *Iliad*, page 356, focuses on the events during the final year of the war.

The Parthenon, which means virgin's place, is the sacred temple of the goddess Athena. Athena is the patron deity of Athens, so named in her honor. The Parthenon was built under Pericles, the Athenian statesman and general, between 447 B.C. and 432 B.C. The Parthenon lies on the Acropolis, the sacred hill above Athens. The Parthenon, which was built from white marble, is the pinnacle of Classical Doric architecture. The Doric style is distinguished by its simplicity of form and especially by its fluted columns.

Appearing on the face of this tetradrachm is the head of Apollo, the Greek god of music, poetry, and medicine. The tetradrachm, a silver coin used in ancient Greece, had the approximate value of four drachms, roughly equivalent to nine U.S. dollars. However, with no standard at that time, these coins varied in weight and value in different places.

Ancient Greece (c. 800 B.C.–323 B.C.)

Cretan jug
*Archaeological
Museum,
Heraklion,
Crete*

Paris' abduction of Helen
marks the beginning
of the Trojan War
Museum of Fine Arts, Boston

The Parthenon,
Athens

Tetradrachm with fac
of Greek god Apollo
*Smithsonian Institution,
Washington D.C.*

−800	−700	−600

HISTORY

- Al Mina, Greek trading post on Orotes River, is founded
  - Greek trading post on Ischia is founded
- City-states develop
  - Tyrant governments spread in Greece
  - Solon, Athenian law-giver, is born
- Solon's reforms established

HUMAN PROGRESS

- Orientalizing period in Greek art begins
- Artists migrate throughout the Mediterranean
  - First recorded Olympic Games are held in Greece
  - Greeks invent alphabet based on Phoenician set of syllables
  - Choral and dramatic music develops
    - Etruscans adopt Greek alphabet in Italy
- First Doric columns in Peloponnese are built
  - First Ionic columns on Samos are built
  - Building of Acropolis begins
- Highest development of astronomy in the ancient world begins
  - Pythagoras, philosopher and mathematician, is born
  - Ionian Enlightenment begins
  - First water supply system in Athens is begun

LITERATURE

- Homer composes *Iliad* and *Odyssey*
- Hesiod composes *Theogony* and *Works and Days*
- Archilochus writes poetry using iambic form
- Callinus and Tyrraeus compose choral lyric in Sparta
  - Sappho of Lesbos writes poetry

Theatre of
Epidauros

Statue of
Sophocles,
one of the three
great Greek
tragedians

Great Altar of
Zeus at Pergamon

- Further democratic reforms
  are introduced in Athens
- Pericles is born
- Persian empire annexes
  Greek cities of Ionia
  - Persian Wars begin
    - Themistocles builds navy, defeats Persians off Salamis
      - Periclean Age begins
        - Truce between
          Athens and Sparta established

- Peloponnesian War begins
  - Plague in Athens takes place
    - Periclean Age ends
      - Peloponnesian War ends

- Philip II becomes
  King of Macedonia
  - Philip defeats
    combined forces
    of Greeks
    - Alexander
      begins
      conquering
      empire
      - Alexander
        dies in
        Babylon

- Public libraries in Athens
  are founded
  - Height of Greek choral music
    attained
    - Democritus, father of
      atomic theory, is born
      - Hippocrates, Greek physician,
        is born

- Plato founds The Academy
  - Corinthian columns
    are built
  - Zeno, founder of
    Stoicism, is born
    - Aristotle lays
      foundations of
      musical theory

- Aesop, a former Phrygian slave,
  writes Fables
  - Aeschylus, Greek
    dramatist, is born

- Herodotus: *Histories*
  - Aeschylus: *Seven Against Thebes*
    - Pindar: fourth *Pythian*
      - Sophocles' *Oedipus Rex* is produced
        - Euripides' *Medea* is produced
          - Thucydides begins writing the
            History of the Peloponnesian Wars
            - Pericles' *Funeral Oration*

- Socrates on trial
  - Plato writes *The Republic*, first Utopian writing
    - Plato's *Apology* is delivered
      - Aristotle's *Poetics*

The Theatre at Epidauros in Greece illustrates the simplicity of Hellenic art. This theater, built about 350 B.C., accommodates about 25,000 spectators and is still the site for performances today. The *orchestra* (literally, dancing place), the large circular area in the center, is the place where the chorus dances and sings odes. In the center of the orchestra is a stone on which the statue of the deity honored in the drama is placed. Behind the orchestra is the *proskenion,* the acting area. Behind this area is the *skene,* a structure that serves both as a backdrop and as a dressing room.

Sophocles (c. 496 B.C.–406 B.C.), who was born in Colonus, near Athens, was a renowned tragic dramatist. After his death, Sophocles was immortalized and worshiped as a hero. Statues such as this one were erected in his honor. One of his most famous plays was *Oedipus the King* (c. 429), in which Greek dramatic irony reaches an apex.

Before the time of Alexander the Great, the largest volume of building was found in the Greek cities of Asia Minor. The structures there exhibit an Asian influence, such as the Altar of Zeus at Pergamon. This picture shows the northern projection of the great frieze—the horizontal band decorated with sculptures.

In 478 B.C. the Delian League, a defensive alliance not unlike NATO (North Atlantic Treaty Organization), was formed under the leadership of Athens. The allies took an oath to defend Greece against enemy invasion and, if necessary, to engage in preemptive attack. The responsibility of maintaining a battle-ready fleet fell on Athens, with the allies contributing money rather than men and ships. When some allies showed disgruntlement, Athens crushed the dissidents, making it clear that the Delian League was no voluntary alliance of equals. In 454 B.C. the League's treasury was moved from Delos to Athens, and what was nominally an alliance clearly became the Athenian Empire.

Democracy Under Pericles

The single statesman most closely associated with the Golden Age of Athenian democracy is Pericles. He guided the democratic state at home, fostering the highest ideals of citizen participation, while his hawkish and openly imperialistic foreign policy aroused the resentment of formerly friendly states. His mission seems to have been to establish the glory and supremacy of Athens at all costs, and it is his vision that channeled the city's prosperity into impressive new public architecture and art. Under Pericles, civic festivals grew more splendid, attracting crowds from all over Greece, and even foreigners; artists, poets, scientists, philosophers congregated in Athens. The brief period between the Persian war and the civil war between Athens and Sparta was a "golden age" that left its mark on the intellectual history of the Western world.

The Peloponnesian War

To its allies, however, Athens was no longer "the savior of Greece" but a tyrant city, whose armed forces mercilessly crushed any allies who were unwilling subjects. Greece became polarized between Athens and Sparta, and in 432 B.C. Sparta officially declared war on Athens.

In 430 B.C. Athens was decimated by a severe plague; one of the victims was Pericles. Still, Athens might have won the war had it not decided to fight on too many fronts. In 415 B.C. the Athenian fleet sailed against the rich Greek cities of Sicily, confident of gaining wealth and natural resources to continue the war. The fleet suffered a disastrous defeat, and although the war dragged on, Athens was finally defeated in 404 B.C.

Alexander the Great

After the defeat of Athens, however, not Sparta but Macedon emerged as a world power. Macedon was ruled by King Philip, whose son Alexander soon became known as "the Great" because of his military conquests. Alexander's armies marched south and east, spreading Greek language and culture. In Egypt the city he founded and named after himself, Alexandria, became the cultural and political center of the Mediterranean for centuries. What are now Turkey, Iraq, Iran (Persia), and part of India formed part of Alexander's empire. By his death in 323 B.C., Alexander had transformed the eastern Mediterranean into a Greek empire. The culture of the Alexandrian empire was fundamentally cosmopolitan, and the blend of different cultures that emerged was so strong that it survived the rise and fall of the Roman Empire.

RELIGION

The Gods

The way the Greeks conceived of their gods reveals how they saw the world around them and their role as human beings in the world. As personifications of war, plague, or earthquake, the gods were formidable; but in their anthropomorphic (having human qualities) form they were approachable and even comic. The Greeks perceived their relationship to the gods as one of mutually advantageous exchange. They often held religious festivals in honor of the gods. The most famous example is the Olympic Games, first held in 776 B.C. in honor of Zeus.

The Greek gods were organized in a patriarchal hierarchy with Zeus, "father of the gods and men," at the top. Zeus maintained the precarious balance of forces that makes the world, as the Greeks saw it, possible. Without that balance, chaos (which in Greek means "gaping void") would have taken over—the Greeks had above all a horror of chaos. They perceived the universe as an orderly arrangement (cosmos) in which potentially warring forces were kept in harmony.

All the aspects of nature and human life were represented in the divine hierarchy. Zeus had the sky as his domain; his brother Poseidon ruled the sea, and another brother, Hades, the realm under the earth. Zeus' sister Hera, who was also his wife, was a patroness of marriage. Zeus' daughter Athene embodied intelligence, skill, and military victory. His other children Artemis and Apollo were archer gods. Aphrodite, the goddess of beauty and love, was the wife of Hephaestus (the blacksmith god) and a lover of Ares, the god of war, who was also a child of Zeus. Dionysus, the son of Zeus and a mortal woman, was the god of wine and ecstasy. In one way or another, the Greeks envisioned all the gods as being related to Zeus, and all the legendary heroes claimed to be Zeus' descendants.

The gods intervened in the lives of mortals; in legendary times, they mated with mortals and generally spent time among human beings. They never functioned as mere puppeteers, and they never imposed on a mortal a fate not in keeping with his or her own character. For the Greeks, destiny was simply a recognition of the way things are. The gods did not make reality; they embodied it and were not to blame for human suffering. They gave true signs, but it was the nature of mortals to misinterpret those signs.

LITERATURE

Epic

Out of the Dark Ages came a body of oral epic poetry that was the raw material for the sophisticated epics of Homer, the *Iliad* and the *Odyssey*. Revered as statements of cultural identity, the Homeric epics center on heroes who embody the values of ancient Greek culture. Homer's primary focus is on humanity. The Greek concept of humanity as celebrated by Homer is his greatest contribution to Western literature and Western thought.

Lyric

Of all the genres of Greek literature, lyric poetry loses the most of its flavor over the passage of centuries and in translation. Specifically, the musical quality of lyric, which originally meant "sung to the lyre," weakens in translation. Nevertheless, the Greek lyric voice, intensely individual and personal, influenced the Roman poets and still exerts its influence today.

Philosophy

In the beginning of the sixth century B.C., the Ionian Enlightenment began, out of which came the first scientist-philosophers. The influence of these early thinkers was pervasive. A pupil of the great scientist Anaxagoras taught Socrates (469–399 B.C.), and Socrates' most famous disciple, Plato, owes much to the Ionians too. Plato's vision of a realm of immutable, perfect forms of which this world is a flawed reflection attracted some of the finest minds of later generations, including many Christian theologians.

In his *Republic*, Plato sets forth a theory on the human soul, but his analogy of the soul to a city-state or republic also provides a detailed treatise on government; he served as an adviser to more than one ruler. For the Greeks, the nature and nurture of the soul must be examined in connection with civilized life in a community. So it comes as no surprise that Plato's most famous disciple, Aristotle (384–322 B.C.), became the teacher of Alexander the Great. Aristotle also advocates seeing the universe as a whole and placing humanity in that universe. The philosophers of classical Greece influenced the Romans and all of Western thought.

Tragedy

Greek drama reached its peak in fifth-century Athens. During that time, tragedies and comedies were performed in conjunction with the worship of Dionysus and fertility rituals connected with the seasons and the staple crops of the community. Tragedies dealt with universal issues and indirectly with contemporary politics, but the plots were taken from the same cycle of legends found in the Homeric epics. Themes such as war, incest, and murder were treated seriously.

For Athenians, the tragic competition formed only one part of the communal religious and civic festival. The festival was a time for exploring the fundamental ideas and values that made Athens a unified community. Because the tragic competition was a community event, dramatists were able to bombard their audiences with deeply troubling emotional issues, to examine in public the worst and most hidden fears of the individual. As a group of citizens joined in the celebration of their community's health and prosperity, they could confront such terrors as those in *Oedipus the King* and leave the theater "purged" and intact, to feast with family and friends.

In order of birth, the three great tragedians are Aeschylus, who wrote the Oresteia, the sequence of tragedies composed of *Agamemnon*, *The Libation Bearers*, and the *Eumenides*; Sophocles, who lived until the age of ninety, when he wrote his most powerfully religious play, *Oedipus at Colonus*; and Euripides, perhaps best-known for *The Medea* and *The Bacchae*. Many tragedians wrote plays and won prizes, but we have the works of only these three, who were recognized as the three greatest. Even of their output, we have a very small percentage: The seven surviving tragedies of Aeschylus, for instance, represent not even a tenth of the tragedies he composed. All of the tragedians influenced each

other, and each of them in his own way was daring and innovative.

History

The great tragedians of the fifth century B.C. were essentially engaged in the same pursuit as the epic poets and philosophers, examining the human condition and reflecting on the human's place in the universe. The two great historians of the fifth century B.C. belonged to the same intellectual tradition: Herodotus (484–430 B.C.), who wrote on the Persian Wars, and Thucydides (460–400 B.C.), who wrote about the Peloponnesian War between Athens and Sparta. Thucydides chronicled the rise and decline of the Athenian empire and sought to understand the universal patterns revealed by major historical events. Herodotus, "the father of history," saw in the rise and fall of empires the tragic pattern of prosperity leading to arrogant confidence followed by divine punishment. Like Aeschylus, Herodotus warned that people should never forget that they are subject to human limitations.

Thucydides consciously distinguished himself from Herodotus, whom he considered a storyteller. Instead, Thucydides stressed the scientific method—the role of the historian as researcher and analyst. He saw the Peloponnesian War as one manifestation of the same universal patterns. His self-appointed purpose was to present events so that later generations would avoid making the same mistakes. The Greek historians, like the poets and philosophers, saw themselves as teachers of their fellow-men.

GREEK VOICES

The single best augury is to fight for one's country.
Homer, the *Iliad*

Destiny waits alike for the free man as well as for him enslaved by another's might.
Aeschylus, *The Libation Bearers*

What greater grief than the loss of one's native land.
Euripides, *Medea*

I shall suffer nothing as great as dying with a lack of grace.
Sophocles, *Antigone*

Wonders are many, and none is more wonderful than man.
Sophocles, *Antigone*

The ideal condition would be, I admit, that men should be right by instinct; but since we are all likely to go astray, the reasonable thing is to learn from those who can teach.
Sophocles, *Antigone*

The direction in which education starts a man will determine his future life.
Plato, *The Republic*

There is only one good, knowledge, and one evil, ignorance.
Socrates, *Diogenes Laertius, Lives of Eminent Philosophers*

One's sense of honor is the only thing that does not grow old, and the last pleasure, when one is worn out with age, is not, as the poet said, making money, but having the respect of one's fellow-men.
Thucydides, *History of the Peloponnesian War*

As in the Olympic Games it is not the most beautiful and strongest who receive the crown but those who actually enter the combat, for from those come the victors, so it is those who act that win rightly what is noble and good in life.
Aristotle, *Nicomachean Ethics*

With regard to excellence, it is not enough to know, but we must try to have it and use it.
Aristotle, *Metaphysics*

Additional Voices

I have found power in the mysteries of thought, exaltation in the chanting of the Muses; I have been versed in the reasonings of men; but Fate is stronger than anything I have known.
—**Euripides,** *Alcestis*

Whoso neglects his learning in his youth, loses the past and is dead for the future.
—**Euripides,** *Phrixius*

The hastening of any undertaking begets errors, from which great losses are wont to come; but in holding back there are advantages, perhaps not apparent at the moment, but one may perceive them in time.
—**Herodotus,** *The Histories*

A man is the origin of his actions.
—**Aristotle,** *Metaphysics*

The glorious gifts of the gods are not to be cast aside.
—**Homer,** the *Iliad*

It was built against the will of the immortal gods, and so it did not last for long.
—**Homer,** the *Iliad*

My word, how mortals take the gods to task! / All their afflictions come from us we hear? / And what of their own failings? Greed and folly / double the suffering in the lot of man.
—**Homer,** the *Odyssey*

Friends have all things in common.
—**Plato,** *Dialogues, Phaedrus*

The soul of man is immortal and imperishable.
—**Plato,** *The Republic*

To be conscious that we are perceiving or thinking is to be conscious of our own existence.
—**Aristotle,** *Nicomachean Ethics.*

False words are not only evil in themselves, but they infect the soul with evil.
—**Plato,** the *Phaedo*

APOTHEOSIS OF HOMER
J. A. Dominique Ingres
The Louvre, Paris

The ancient Greeks ascribed the *Iliad* and the *Odyssey*, their two oldest, monumental epic poems to Homer, whom they called simply "The Poet." Nothing certain is known about Homer's life. His name, which means "hostage," gives no clue to his origins, since small wars and raids between neighboring towns were frequent in ancient Greece, and prisoners were routinely held for ransom or sold into slavery. Homer is commonly referred to as the "Ionian bard" or poet; more than likely, he came from Ionia in the Eastern Mediterranean, where eastern and western cultures met and new intellectual currents were born. In support of that theory, the *Iliad* contains several accurate descriptions of the Ionian landscape and its natural features, whereas Homer's grasp of the geography of mainland Greece seems less authoritative.

The legend that Homer was a blind bard may have some basis in fact; if he lived to be an old man, he may simply have become blind. However, the idea of Homer's blindness may have arisen because of its symbolic implications. The Greeks contrasted inner vision with physical vision, as for instance in the case of the blind seer Teiresias and of Oedipus himself, who becomes blind in *Oedipus the King*.

Although Homer's dates are uncertain, the *Iliad* was almost certainly composed late in the eighth century B.C. Historically, however, both epics take place in a long-past heroic age known as the Late Bronze Age. What equipped Homer to depict an era five hundred years before his time? Homer did not create the plot or characters of the epics ascribed to him; rather, he inherited the stories of those epics. Generations of Greeks had preserved orally the subject matter of Homer's epics—the story of the Trojan War and the heroic mythology that pervades both poems. As a result, Homer is the ultimate spokesman of a long and rich tradition of oral poetry, developed over centuries.

From generation to generation, poets transmitted tales of "the glorious feats of men." Many of the stories were about those who fought in the war against Troy (1200 B.C.). A bard might choose to sing of the exploits of a particular war hero, at Troy or elsewhere, about his homecoming, and about his ancestors or his descendants. In the world of Homer's audience, the landed warrior aristocracy claimed descent from the heroes of legend and ultimately from the gods. For such a society, the legends about heroes formed a kind of tribal, and later national, family history.

In fact, the *Iliad* was considered history; children in the fifth century B.C. memorized large sections of the poem and practiced the ethical codes that Homer presents. Even fifth-century Athenians claimed the Homeric gods and heroes as founders or champions of Athens and its people. The fact that Homer's epics were the first poems to be written down partially explains their tremendous influence on later generations of Greeks. Greek lyric poets, dramatists, and philosophers considered themselves Homer's heirs, drawing on his work either to imitate it or to argue with it. As Greek culture spread through the Eastern Mediterranean and west to Italy, Homer's epics formed a common text for a large part of the Western world.

BACKGROUND

THE ILIAD

Form and Structure

Just as the oral tradition supplied Homer with a vast body of legend, it also provided him with the form and structure in which to express the legend. Although Homer was free to choose and shape the story according to his vision of reality, his language, meter, and style were formulaic. Over time, bards developed a fund of useful formulas—expressions, phrases, and extended descriptions that fit into the rhythms of the epic verse line. The building blocks of the epic genre, the invocation *in medias res,* stock epithets, and fixed metrical formulas, were commonly used by the ancient bards.

The Invocation *In Medias Res*

Homer begins the epic powerfully by stating theme and invoking the muse. Muses were omniscient goddesses of poetry, art, music, and dance. From their all-knowing perspective, muses were thought to inspire the poet with the material he needed to recite his story.

Another epic element occurs as the poem begins *"in medias res,"* which is Latin for "in the middle of things." Reading a Greek epic from the beginning is comparable to tuning in to a story already in progress. Homer could begin his poems *in medias res* because the general outline of the story and the main characters were already familiar to his audience. The *Iliad,* like other epics, is a small fragment of a large body of legendary material that formed the cultural and historical heritage of its society.

Stock Epithets

The particular demands of composing and listening to oral poetry gave rise to the use of stock descriptive words or phrases, such as "Thetis of the silver feet" or "resourceful Odysseus." These **stock epithets,** as they are known, are noun-adjective combinations that allowed the reciter to describe an object ("wine-dark sea") or a character ("swift-footed Achilleus") quickly and economically, in terms his audience would recognize. Using formulaic language may have helped the poet shape his story and compose while reciting; but the repetition of familiar expressions also helped the audience to follow the narrative.

Meter

Meter is another essential ingredient to the Homeric epic formula. The Greek epic line is made up of six units, or feet, which have the shape of dactyls (a long syllable followed by two short) or spondees (two long syllables). In English translation, a dactyl is an accented syllable followed by two unaccented syllables, "an´ ger ŏf." A spondee is two accented syllables, "strong´-greaved´." These units can be combined in a variety of ways, but each line ends in a dactyl followed by a spondee. Greek meter is based on the interplay of long and short syllables in words combined so that certain predictable rhythmic patterns emerge and form a structure. Homeric meter probably corresponds to normal speech patterns at the time Homer wrote.

Enrichment The long, formal speech is another epic element, one that is commonly associated with Homeric epic. Homer's characters express their thoughts and feelings by delivering long speeches to other characters. They do not speculate about their emotions or analyze their thought processes; nor does the poet directly reveal the characters' inner workings to his audience. Later Greek and Roman authors, as well as modern writers, give us access to a character's thoughts and feelings through interior monologues and soliloquies. Both of these forms are modeled on the long Homeric speech directed toward an external audience.

Clarification The structure of the verse and the existence of certain word combinations adapted to it did not limit the poet's creativity. Poets mastered the poetic language the way people learn any language; they manipulate it freely. Having mastered the legend and the techniques of epic verse, Homer was able to manipulate his material to his own artistic and imaginative ends.

The building blocks of the epic genre—the invocation *in medias res,* stock epithets, long speeches, and fixed formulas were commonly used by the ancient bards. But because Homer was so influential in Western literature, these same features were imitated in later epics even though they no longer served the same purposes.

Critical Thinking and Reading Worksheet, *Defining the Epic Hero,* p. 460
Selection Test, pp. 461–462

Synopsis

Is This the Face That Launched a Thousand Ships?

The *Iliad* recounts only part of a long series of events in the Trojan War, which was fought, according to legend, because of a quarrel among gods and the resulting incidents of betrayal among mortals. How did the war start? King Peleus and the sea-goddess Thetis were parents of Achilleus, hero of the *Iliad*. When Peleus and Thetis were married, all the gods were invited except Eris, the goddess of discord. Angry at being excluded, Eris tossed a golden apple among the guests; on it was inscribed "for the fairest one." Hera, Athene, and Aphrodite each claimed the prize. They chose the Trojan prince Paris, a handsome and unworldly young man, to decide which goddess was the fairest. Each goddess offered him a bribe, and Paris chose Aphrodite's: She promised to give him the most beautiful woman alive, Helen, who was already married to Menelaos, king of Sparta.

Paris violated the sacred bond of hospitality when he went to Menelaos' court as a guest and abducted his host's wife. Menelaos sought the help of his brother Agamemnon, king of Mycenae and the most powerful ruler of his time. Together with other kings, they mounted an expedition against Troy, to reclaim Helen and to sack a city famed for its opulence. The war lasted for ten years until Troy was finally taken.

Out of a vast body of material, which his audience knew, Homer chose to focus on a period of less than two months in the tenth year of the war. Homer did not concentrate on the war as such, but on the rage of Achilleus and its consequences.

As the Poem Opens

The Greek army beseiging Troy has been stricken by a plague, sent by the god Apollo in punishment for Agamemnon's refusal to ransom a captive girl, Chryseis, daughter of Apollo's priest. Aga-

THE ABDUCTION OF HELEN OF TROY
Guido Reni
The Louvre, Paris

memnon returns the girl to her father, but he replaces her with another female captive, Briseis, who is Achilleus' prize. The two warriors quarrel, and Achilleus withdraws from the battle, depriving the Greeks of their strongest warrior. All the action in the *Iliad* is, more or less directly, the consequence of Achilleus' anger at being dishonored.

Achilleus' Anger

Homer's audience thus sees the war between Greeks and Trojans from the perspective of Achilleus' crisis of identity. Withdrawing from battle is devastating to Achilleus' private and public sense of worth; without exploits, he can only sing of glory and eternal fame instead of achieving it by killing or being killed in battle. Achilleus is "the best of the Achaians," or Greeks, the strongest and swiftest, but he is not the most powerful ruler. The gap between his merit and its rewards leads this young man to question the values of his society, and the worth and meaning of life itself.

CHARACTERS

MORTALS

THE GREEKS (Also called Achaians, Danaans, and Argives)

ACHILLEUS (ə kil´ ē əs): Son of Peleus, a mortal king, and the sea-goddess Thetis. The best warrior among the Achaians; leader of the Myrmidons. Other names: Peleides or Peleion; Aiakides (page 335).

AGAMEMNON (äg ə mem´ nän): King of Mycenae; husband of Klytaimestra; brother of Menelaos. Leader of the Greek expeditionary force. Other name: Atreides (page 336).

AIAS (ī´ əs): The strongest warrior on the Greek side after Achilleus (the Romans called him Ajax) (page 339).

HELEN (hel´ ən): Wife of Menelaos, king of Sparta (page 347).

KLYTAIMESTRA (klī tə mes´ trə): Wife of Agamemnon, sister of Helen (page 339).

MENELAOS (men ə lā´ ōs): King of Sparta and the surrounding area (Lakedaimon). Son of Atreus, brother of Agamemnon, husband of Helen (page 340).

NESTOR (nes´ tər): King of Pylos, belonging to an older generation than the other Greek warriors. He serves as a wise old counselor (page 343).

ODYSSEUS (ō dis´ ē əs): King of Ithaka. The smoothest talker and wiliest thinker among the Greeks; a favorite of the goddess Athene (page 339).

PATROKLOS (pə träk´ lōs): Son of Menoitios, a companion and henchman to Achilleus (page 355).

PELEUS (pel´ ē əs): Father of Achilleus; husband of the goddess Thetis (page 335).

THE TROJANS (Also called Dardanians, and Phrygians)

ANDROMACHE (an dräm´ ə kē): Wife of Hektor (page 349).

ASTYANAX (ə stī´ ə naks): Infant son of Hektor and Andromache. Other name: Skamandrios (page 350).

BRISEIS (bri´ sē is): A Trojan captive girl, named after her father Briseus, given as a prize to Achilleus (page 341).

CHRYSEIS (kri´ sē is): The daughter of Chryses, priest of Apollo. A captive girl given to Agamemnon as his prize (page 339).

HEKTOR (hek´ tər): Son of Priam; leader of the Trojans and their greatest fighter (page 343).

PARIS (par´ is): Son of king Priam and queen Hekabe. Other name: Alexandros (page 347).

PRIAM (prī´ əm): King of Troy; husband of Hekabe, father of Hektor and Alexandros/Paris (page 336).

IMMORTALS

APHRODITE (af rō dī´ tē): Goddess of love, beauty; protects Helen and Alexandros/Paris and favors the Trojans. Other name: Lady of Kypros (page 377).

APOLLO (ə pôl´ ō): The archer god; a god of light (whose epithets are Lykios or Phoebus) and of healing. Apollo not only heals, he visits pestilence on men. He favors and protects the Trojans. Other names: Lykios, Phoebus, Smintheus (page 335).

ARES (a´ rēz): God of war; favors the Trojans (page 360).

ATHENE (a thē´ nə): Daughter of Zeus only (she has no mother). She emerged out of her father's head fully armed and is associated with victory in war and clever thinking and speaking. She protects the Greeks. Other names: Pallas and Tritogeneia (page 341).

HADES (hā´ dēz): Ruler of the underworld. Other name: Aidoneus (page 335).

HERA (her´ ə): Sister and wife of Zeus; favors the Greeks (page 337).

HERMES (hər´ mēz): Messenger god. Other name: Argeiphontes (page 381).

THETIS (thē´ tis): Sea goddess; wife of the mortal Peleus and mother of Achilleus (page 347).

ZEUS (zo͞os): The most powerful of the gods, known as "father of men and gods" (page 335).

Clarification *Achaians* refers to the inhabitants of either of the two Greek regions known as Achaia. But Homer applies the term Achaians to all the Greek forces in the Trojan War; he never calls them Greeks, as we do.

Enrichment Trojans are the inhabitants of the walled Phrygian city Troy, also called Ilium. Although we are reasonably certain that Troy existed, its mythical history is confused. One theory suggests that the Trojans were a group of tribes that formed a federation to share the great walled city of Troy by the time of the Trojan war.

Enrichment One of Achilleus' epithets is "godlike Achilleus"; indeed, he is of semi-divine origin. But unlike the gods, Achilleus is not invulnerable. Share with students the legend of Achilleus' heel, explaining that at his birth, Thetis held him by his heel and dipped his body in the river Styx to make him invulnerable like herself. However, when it came time for Achilleus' fated death, he was lethally wounded in his heel.

Achilleus is vulnerable in more areas than his heel. He is human, and like all humans, he experiences human emotions—grief, fear, and above all, anger. Ask students to think about how Achilleus and the other characters embody aspects of human nature.

ESL Teaching Strategy While reading the *Iliad* for the first time, it is easy to get characters confused. To help students of limited English proficiency learn the characters in the *Iliad*, have them identify the pronoun references. There are several pronoun references that might be confusing to ESL students.

Teaching Tenth-Grade Students Tenth-grade students might be interested in discussing the mythology in the *Iliad*. Have students volunteer what they know about the myths associated with the immortals in the character list on this page.

Clarification Students will notice that both Athene and Hera favor the Greeks. Remind students that both goddesses despised the Trojans because of Paris, who chose Aphrodite over Hera and Athene as "the fairest one" at the wedding of Peleus and Thetis.

from the Iliad, *from* Book I

Historical Context

According to tradition, the *Iliad* was composed in 750 B.C., but its story takes place five hundred years earlier, in the tenth year of the Trojan War. Troy was a major city and trading hub. Greece was not, either in the thirteenth or the eighth century B.C., a single nation; the Achaian expeditionary force was a loose group of independent tribal lords or kings who commanded their own fighting men. Kings did not owe other kings unconditional allegiance. If they did not support another king's policies, they were free to do what Achilleus does in the *Iliad*—take their ships and their men and leave.

Cultural Context

As a product of a long and rich oral tradition, the *Iliad* was a source of culture for the ancient Greeks. They revered the poem as an expression of central truths about human beings and their place in the scheme of the universe. The story in the *Iliad*, which grew from the story of Paris' abduction of Helen and the resulting war of Troy, was firmly planted in Greek culture. Similarly, the values of warfare depicted in the poem—the nobility and glory of the slayers and the humanity and pathos of the slain—were also grounded in the Greek consciousness.

A fundamental element of the Greek code of ethics was honor. It was understood that warriors fought for honor and to ensure a reputation that would outlive them. Honor was expressed tangibly by the prizes distributed to a warrior according to his rank and valor. A warrior's share of booty was thus a visible symbol of his merit, which is why Achilleus and Agamemnon feel so shamed when they must forfeit their prizes in the *Iliad*. Ultimately, a hero's honor depended on how the world saw him, not on how he saw himself.

It is important to read the *Iliad* with sensitivity to Homeric values and to avoid imposing the values of another time and culture on the epic. To fully understand and appreciate the Homeric attitude toward war and death, the modern reader must read through objective lenses.

Literary Context

The *Iliad* as we know it is the end product of an oral poetic tradition of heroic narrative. Since poetry composed in the oral tradition was intended to be heard, not read, the singer of the poem had to fulfill the traditional expectations of his audience. As Homer sang the *Iliad*, his language, style, themes, and portrayal of gods and humans is both formulaic according to convention and original according to his vision of human existence.

from the # Iliad

Homer

from Book I: The Quarrel of Achilleus and Agamemnon

translated by Richmond Lattimore

Sing, goddess,[1] the anger of Peleus' son Achilleus
and its devastation, which put pains thousandfold upon the
  Achaians,[2]
hurled in their multitudes to the house of Hades[3] strong souls
of heroes, but gave their bodies to be the delicate feasting
5 of dogs, of all birds, and the will of Zeus was accomplished
since that time when first there stood in division of conflict
Atreus' son[4] the lord of men and brilliant Achilleus.

What god was it then set them together in bitter collision?
Zeus' son and Leto's, Apollo, who in anger at the king drove
10 the foul pestilence along the host, and the people perished,
since Atreus' son had dishonored Chryses, priest of Apollo,
when he came beside the fast ships of the Achaians to ransom
back his daughter, carrying gifts beyond count and holding
in his hands wound on a staff of gold the ribbons of Apollo
15 who strikes from afar, and supplicated[5] all the Achaians,
but above all Atreus' two sons,[6] the marshals of the people:
"Sons of Atreus and you other strong-greaved[7] Achaians,
to you may the gods grant who have their homes on Olympos[8]

---

1. Sing, goddess: Conventional epic opening whereby the narrator invites a goddess called a muse to inspire in him the epic's story.
2. Achaians (ə kē´ ənz) *n.:* Tribal name for Greeks. Homer also refers to them as Danaans and Argives.
3. Hades (hā´ dēz) *n.:* Lord of the dead.
4. Atreus' son *n.:* Agamemnon (ag´ ə mem´ nän´), king, or chief leader of the Achaians.
5. supplicated (sup´ lə kāt´ əd) *n.:* Requested humbly and earnestly through prayer.
6. Atreus' two sons: Agamemnon and Menelaos (men ə lā´ əs).
7. strong-greaved (stroŋ grēvd´) *adj.:* Well-protected by armor on the legs.
8. Olympos (ō lim´ pəs) *n.:* Mountain in Greece between Thessaly and Macedonia; mythological home of the gods.

Literary Context: Homeric epics have formulaic openings in which the narrator invokes the muse, begins in medias res (in the middle of things), and states the subject and theme of the poem. The *Iliad* is about a fight between Agamemnon, king of the Argives, and Achilleus, their best warrior.

Cultural Context: It is important to understand Apollo's role in the plague in terms of Greek culture. In the eyes of the ancient Greeks, gods and goddesses controlled and directed the events in the *Iliad*. Although the modern reader may interpret the gods symbolically, ancient Greeks perceived them as an actual, formidable presence.

Presentation

Motivation/Prior Knowledge
Tell students that they will be reading about warriors from a distant time and a different culture. Nevertheless, although many of the details of their world will seem alien, many of the basic dilemmas and emotions may seem familiar. Ask students to think about other works they have read or films they have seen which are about unfamiliar times or cultures but which still made them empathize with the characters and feel involved.

Purpose-Setting Question How do the opening lines prepare the audience for the story? How completely are the main issues and characters introduced?

Universal Themes The most fundamental challenge facing all mortals is the need to come to terms with death. Different societies, and different individuals in those societies, face the problem in a variety of ways. Remind students of Gilgamesh and his quest (page 15). Prepare them to think about Aeneas' view of death and life in Virgil's *Aeneid* (page 493), and to compare Aeneas with Achilleus. Later in the Greek unit, students will read about Socrates' view of death in the *Apology* (page 416). Later still in the Middle Ages unit, students will encounter the Christian poet Dante and his very different views of life on earth and death in the Divine Comedy (page 622).

Master Teacher Note In the original Greek, the first word of the *Iliad* is *menis,* "anger," in the direct object case. (You might write the word on the board.) Homer thus indicates immediately what the poem is about. Furthermore, this particular term for anger is used elsewhere only of the gods. It is too powerful for ordinary mortals; thus Homer reminds us of Achilleus' superhuman dimensions and indicates that his anger will be cataclysmic in some way, like the wrath of divinities.

for a condemnation of war as such. People make war, they put up with it, they curse it, they even praise it in songs and verses, but it is not to be judged any more than destiny is . . . The irreparable has the curious property of inducing forgetfulness by paralyzing the imagination and the mem-ory, which retain no trace of its horrors. Yet while the imagination is overpowered by war, it is at the same time stimulated by a brutal shift of lighting that casts the elemental substance of life into relief. War, in the epic, appears first of all as a kind of prolonged spasm re-lated to the rhythms of anger that are always ravaging nature, the great cosmic upheavals. The imagery of the *Iliad* keeps evoking the savage brotherhood between man and the elements.

ACHILLEUS AND AGAMEMNON
Archaeological Museum, Agrigento, Italy

Priam's city⁹ to be plundered and a fair homecoming thereafter,
20 but may you give me back my own daughter and take the ransom,
giving honor to Zeus' son who strikes from afar, Apollo."
Then all the rest of the Achaians cried out in favor
that the priest be respected and the shining ransom be taken;
yet this pleased not the heart of Atreus' son Agamemnon,
25 but harshly he drove him away with a strong order upon him:
"Never let me find you again, old sir, near our hollow
ships, neither lingering now nor coming again hereafter,
for fear your staff and the god's ribbons help you no longer.
The girl I will not give back; sooner will old age come upon her
30 in my own house, in Argos,¹⁰ far from her own land, going
up and down by the loom and being in my bed as my companion.
So go now, do not make me angry; so you will be safer."
So he spoke, and the old man in terror obeyed him,
and went silently away beside the murmuring sea beach.

---

9. **Priam's city:** Troy.
10. **Argos** (är′ gōs′) *n.*: City in the northwest Peloponnese.

Over and over the old man prayed as he walked in solitude
to King Apollo, whom Leto of the lovely hair bore: "Hear me,
lord of the silver bow who set your power about Chryse
and Killa the sacrosanct,[11] who are lord in strength over Tenedos,[12]
Smintheus,[13] if ever it pleased your heart that I built your temple,
if ever it pleased you that I burned all the rich thigh pieces
of bulls, of goats, then bring to pass this wish I pray for:
let your arrows make the Danaans pay for my tears shed."

So he spoke in prayer, and Phoibos Apollo heard him,
and strode down along the pinnacles[14] of Olympos, angered
in his heart, carrying across his shoulders the bow and the hooded
quiver; and the shafts clashed on the shoulders of the god walking
angrily. He came as night comes down and knelt then
apart and opposite the ships and let go an arrow.
Terrible was the clash that rose from the bow of silver.
First he went after the mules and the circling hounds, then let go
a tearing arrow against the men themselves and struck them.
The corpse fires burned everywhere and did not stop burning.

Nine days up and down the host ranged the god's arrows,
but on the tenth Achilleus called the people to assembly;
a thing put into his mind by the goddess of the white arms, Hera,
who had pity upon the Danaans when she saw them dying.
Now when they were all assembled in one place together,
Achilleus of the swift feet stood up among them and spoke forth:
"Son of Atreus, I believe now that straggling backwards
we must make our way home if we can even escape death,
if fighting now must crush the Achaians and the plague likewise.
No, come, let us ask some holy man, some prophet,
even an interpreter of dreams, since a dream also
comes from Zeus, who can tell why Phoibos Apollo is so angry,
if for the sake of some vow, some hecatomb[15] he blames us,
if given the fragrant smoke of lambs, of he goats, somehow
he can be made willing to beat the bane[16] aside from us."

He spoke thus and sat down again, and among them stood up

Literary Context: Homer does not describe the characters in the *Iliad* in great detail. Instead, he repeatedly uses short, formulaic phrases called *stock epithets* to characterize people and make them easily recognizable to his audience. "Goddess of the white arms, Hera," and "Achilleus of the swift feet" are among the stock epithets that appear throughout the poem.

---

11. **sacrosanct** (sak′ rō sāŋkt′) *n*.: Here, a very sacred, holy individual.
12. **Tenedos** (ten′ ə däs) *n*.: Island off the coast of the Troad, the name given to the country of the Trojans.
13. **Smintheus** (smin′ thā əs) *n*.: Another name for Apollo; Smintheus means "rat/mouse god," an appropriate name for him as the god of plague.
14. **pinnacles** (pin′ ə kəlz) *n*.: The highest points of the mountain.
15. **hecatomb** (hek′ ə tōm′) *n*.: A sacrifice to the gods.
16. **bane** (bān) *n*.: Cause of distress or death.

3 Enrichment This is a typical prayer formula: the invocation of the divinity in his or her various guises, especially the aspect of the god most relevant to the suppliant's purpose; the mention of the places the god frequents and protects, especially those closest to the suppliant; and a reminder that a reciprocal relationship has existed in the past between god and suppliant along with a promise to continue that relationship. It is as important to remind the god of favors the god has given as well as grateful offerings he or she has received. Sappho uses this same basic formula in her playful invocation to Aphrodite (page 402).

4 Discussion Draw students' attention to the very concrete, physical image of the angry god. If Apollo is in some ways a personification of plague, for instance, he is also envisioned as an actual, physical, anthropomorphic figure. Point out that anthropomorphic comes from two Greek words, *anthropos*, human, and *morphe*, form.

5 Enrichment Point out that for the Greeks, nine was a magical, formulaic number. What other such numbers are familiar to students? They might respond with seven, or three.

6 Clarification Make sure students understand that although any warrior could call an assembly, it would be normal here for Agamemnon to do so. His failure to take the initiative creates a vacuum filled by Achilleus, who is the best warrior, but who is also younger and not the commander in chief.

weep;
their immortal natures were outraged
by this work of death they had to look at.
They reared their heads, tossed their manes,
beat the ground with their hooves,
and mourned Patroklos, seeing him lifeless, destroyed,

now mere flesh only, his spirit gone,
defenseless, without breath,
turned back from life to the great Nothingness.

Zeus saw the tears of those immortal horses and felt sorry.
"I shouldn't have acted so thoughtlessly
at the wedding of Peleus," he said.

"Better if we hadn't given you as a gift,
my unhappy horses. What business did you have down there,
among pathetic human beings, the toys of fate.
You're free of death, you won't get old,
yet ephemeral disasters torment you.

Men have caught you up in their misery."
But it was for the eternal disaster of death
that those two gallant horses shed their tears.

Kalchas, Thestor's son, far the best of the bird interpreters,[17]
who knew all things that were, the things to come and the things
70   past,
who guided into the land of Ilion[18] the ships of the Achaians
through that seercraft[19] of his own that Phoibos Apollo gave him.
He in kind intention toward all stood forth and addressed them:
"You have bidden me, Achilleus beloved of Zeus, to explain to
75 you this anger of Apollo the lord who strikes from afar. Then
I will speak; yet make me a promise and swear before me
readily by word and work of your hands to defend me,
since I believe I shall make a man angry who holds great kingship
over the men of Argos, and all the Achaians obey him.
80 For a king when he is angry with a man beneath him is too strong,
and suppose even for the day itself he swallow down his anger,
he still keeps bitterness that remains until its fulfillment
deep in his chest. Speak forth then, tell me if you will protect me."
    Then in answer again spoke Achilleus of the swift feet:
85 "Speak, interpreting whatever you know, and fear nothing.
In the name of Apollo beloved of Zeus to whom you, Kalchas,
make your prayers when you interpret the gods' will to the Danaans,
no man so long as I am alive above earth and see daylight
shall lay the weight of his hands on you beside the hollow ships,
90 not one of all the Danaans, even if you mean Agamemnon,
who now claims to be far the greatest of all the Achaians."
    At this the blameless seer[20] took courage again and spoke forth:
"No, it is not for the sake of some vow or hecatomb he blames us,
but for the sake of his priest whom Agamemnon dishonored
95 and would not give him back his daughter nor accept the ransom.
Therefore the archer sent griefs against us and will send them
still, nor sooner thrust back the shameful plague from the Danaans
until we give the glancing-eyed girl back to her father
without price, without ransom, and lead also a blessed hecatomb to
100 Chryse; thus we might propitiate[21] and persuade him."
    He spoke thus and sat down again, and among them stood up
Atreus' son the hero wide-ruling Agamemnon
raging, the heart within filled black to the brim with anger
from beneath, but his two eyes showed like fire in their blazing.

---

17. bird interpreters: People who read the omens believed to be carried by certain ominous birds.
18. Ilion (il′ ē ən) *n.*: Troy, the city of Ilos.
19. seercraft (sē′ ər kraft′) *n.*: Skill used by prophets to foretell events of the future.
20. seer (sē′ ər) *n.*: A person with prophetic powers.
21. propitiate (prō pish′ ē āt) *v.*: Appease; pacify.

Commentary

Throughout the *Iliad*, reciprocity and exchange are the glue that holds a society together, mending the cracks that would split it apart. Exchanging gifts and services is the way *xenia* works, the guest-host relationship that binds together people not related by blood or clan, as if they were brothers. Early in the sixth book, the heroes Glaukos and Diomedes come together to fight in single combat. Before engaging in battle, they ascertain each other's identity. For the Homeric hero, as for Pindar's athletes in a later century, identity means family, clan, as far back as you can trace your lineage. The two men

First of all he eyed Kalchas bitterly and spoke to him:
"Seer of evil: never yet have you told me a good thing.
Always the evil things are dear to your heart to prophesy,
but nothing excellent have you said nor ever accomplished.
5 Now once more you make divination to[22] the Danaans, argue
forth your reason why he who strikes from afar afflicts them,
because I for the sake of the girl Chryseis would not take
the shining ransom; and indeed I wish greatly to have her
in my own house; since I like her better than Klytaimestra
10 my own wife, for in truth she is no way inferior,
neither in build nor stature nor wit, nor in accomplishment.
Still I am willing to give her back, if such is the best way.
I myself desire that my people be safe, not perish.
Find me then some prize that shall be my own, lest I only
15 among the Argives go without, since that were unfitting;
you are all witnesses to this thing, that my prize goes elsewhere."

Then in answer again spoke brilliant swift-footed Achilleus:
"Son of Atreus, most lordly, greediest for gain of all men,
how shall the great-hearted Achaians give you a prize now?
20 There is no great store of things lying about I know of.
But what we took from the cities by storm has been distributed;
it is unbecoming for the people to call back things once given.
No, for the present give the girl back to the god; we Achaians
thrice and four times over will repay you if ever Zeus gives
25 into our hands the strong-walled citadel[23] of Troy to be plundered."

Then in answer again spoke powerful Agamemnon:
"Not that way, good fighter though you be, godlike Achilleus,
strive to cheat, for you will not deceive, you will not persuade me.
What do you want? To keep your own prize and have me sit here
30 lacking one? Are you ordering me to give this girl back?
Either the great-hearted Achaians shall give me a new prize
chosen according to my desire to atone[24] for the girl lost,
or else if they will not give me one I myself shall take her,
your own prize, or that of Aias, or that of Odysseus,
35 going myself in person; and he whom I visit will be bitter.
Still, these are things we shall deliberate again hereafter.
Come, now, we must haul a black ship down to the bright sea,
and assemble rowers enough for it, and put on board it
the hecatomb, and the girl herself, Chryseis of the fair cheeks,

---

22. **make divination** (div´ ə nā´ shən) **to:** To guess or explore the unknown by supernatural means.
23. **citadel** (sit´ ə del´) *n.*: A safe, fortified place of defense in a city.
24. **atone** (ə tōn´) *v.*: Make up for; make amends.

Cultural Context: As commander in chief, Agamemnon is not **11** obliged to give up his rightful prize, but by refusing to surrender her, he jeopardizes his people. He is obligated to protect them, even if that means making a personal **12** sacrifice. Agamemnon, however, does not see surrendering Chryseis as fulfilling his kingly responsibilities. In **13** Agamemnon's eyes, being asked to surrender Chryseis is an insult.

Cultural Context: Once distributed, prizes belong to a warrior and mark his rank. Taking back a prize is like demoting an officer in the same way that Agamemnon feels demoted by having to return his prize.

Cultural Context: The Greeks are almost all young men, warrior princes away from their homes. Their only means to female companionship is capturing Trojan women. Once captured, Trojan women serve as slaves and concubines. These women are possessions, symbols of honor to be traded like other valuable possessions.

---

11 Enrichment Agamemnon is blaming Kalchas for interpreting reality as if he had caused events. Here, Agamemnon is referring to an earlier incident at Aulis, where the fleet was kept from sailing to Troy because Artemis was angered and had stopped the winds. Kalchas explained that to propitiate the goddess, Agamemnon must sacrifice his daughter Iphigeneia. How does Homer indicate that there is a longstanding personal quarrel between the two men?

12 Clarification Although Agamemnon speaks in terms of personal desire and preference, make students aware that the Greek word for prize, *geras*, is a neuter noun, and this is the way both heroes refer to their female captives.

13 Discussion In what ways does stressing how valuable Chryseis is to him put Agamemnon in a stronger bargaining position? Students should be aware of the bargaining strategy here and not be led into speculations about romantic love from alien contexts.

---

discover that their ancestors had established a bond of *xenia,* a relationship that turns strangers (*xenos* means stranger) into allies. Realizing that they are bound not to violate their ancestral guest-friend relationship, the two men (who are on opposite sides of the war) vow not to fight one another and exchange armor as a token of friendship, one that will also be recognizable to others. This symbolic act of reciprocity is based on a fiction of equal exchange. Refusing to take part in the system, as Agamemnon does when he rejects Chryses, and as Achilleus does later in the poem, is to threaten the foundations of civilized community.

14 Discussion "Most terrifying of all men" comes as a surprise. It has the shape of a superlative formulaic compliment but functions both as an insult and as a suggestion that Achilleus is like the war-god Ares, who is described in these terms. Ask students to think about how the quarrel is escalating.

Master Teacher Note Help students focus on the underlying conflict between Agamemnon and Achilleus and on the cause of Achilleus' existential crisis, by having them paraphrase Achilleus' grievance. Once he is dishonored, Achilleus comes face to face with the inevitable imbalance between his being "best of the Achaians," the best warrior and almost a god, but not the "most powerful," or "most lordly," and not the commander in chief. Once students see these basic issues, ask them to think about similar situations they have come across in literature, in films, or in life.

15 Discussion Achilleus has the right to leave. Ask students, however, whether in a culture that prizes courage and prowess in battle above all, it is appropriate for Achilleus, "best of the Achaians," to leave Troy and return home.

16 Discussion Agamemnon taunts Achilleus with accusations of cowardice, boasts that men and Zeus are on his side, and goes on to characterize Achilleus as a quarrelsome bully. How is he manipulating Achilleus? Does he want him to go? (Opinions may differ.) How is Achilleus being forced to go beyond the human system in order not to lose face? That Achilleus has a quick temper is not a lie: Even his beloved companion Patroklos mentions Achilleus' violence and his alacrity to blame his friends.

14 Literary Context: In major epics, the hero is often, in some sense, an exile. Achilleus is not exactly an exile, but he is an outsider from a remote region of the Greek-speaking world. He has been recruited because he is the greatest fighter and because the Greeks cannot hope to capture Troy without him. Achilleus claims to have joined the Greeks out of loyalty to Agamemnon. As you read, look for details that support or refute his claim.

Cultural Context: Customarily, the foremost fighter, by virtue of how hard and how well he fights, is formally recognized by the booty distributed to him. Stripping Achilleus of his prize is like stripping him of a medal of honor and, in turn, threatens his identity as the greatest warrior.

15 Achilleus' complaint that his rewards should equal, if not surpass, Agamemnon's prizes reveals his desire for power. The fact that Agamemnon has the authority to revoke his prize frustrates and angers Achilleus. Rather than accept his status as inferior in power to Agamemnon, Achilleus withdraws from the war.

140 and let there be one responsible man in charge of her,
   either Aias or Idomeneus or brilliant Odysseus,
   or you yourself, son of Peleus, most terrifying of all men,
   to reconcile[25] by accomplishing sacrifice the archer."
      Then looking darkly at him Achilleus of the swift feet spoke:
145 "O wrapped in shamelessness, with your mind forever on profit,
   how shall any one of the Achaians readily obey you
   either to go on a journey or to fight men strongly in battle?
   I for my part did not come here for the sake of the Trojan
   spearmen[26] to fight against them, since to me they have done
150   nothing.
   Never yet have they driven away my cattle or my horses,
   never in Phthia[27] where the soil is rich and men grow great did they
   spoil my harvest, since indeed there is much that lies between us,
   the shadowy mountains and the echoing sea; but for your sake,
   o great shamelessness, we followed, to do you favor,
155 you with the dog's eyes, to win your honor and Menelaos'[28]
   from the Trojans. You forget all this or else you care nothing.
   And now my prize you threaten in person to strip from me,
   for whom I labored much, the gift of the sons of the Achaians.
   Never, when the Achaians sack some well-founded citadel
160 of the Trojans, do I have a prize that is equal to your prize.
   Always the greater part of the painful fighting is the work of
   my hands; but when the time comes to distribute the booty[29]
   yours is far the greater reward, and I with some small thing
   yet dear to me go back to my ships when I am weary with fighting.
165 Now I am returning to Phthia, since it is much better
   to go home again with my curved ships, and I am minded no longer
   to stay here dishonored and pile up your wealth and your luxury."
      Then answered him in turn the lord of men Agamemnon:
   "Run away by all means if your heart drives you. I will not
170 entreat you to stay here for my sake. There are others with me
   who will do me honor, and above all Zeus of the counsels.[30]
   To me you are the most hateful of all the kings whom the gods love.
   Forever quarreling is dear to your heart, and wars and battles;
   and if you are very strong indeed, that is a god's gift.

---

25. reconcile (rek´ ən sīl´) *v*.: Here, bring the mortals into harmony with the gods; make the gods content.
26. Trojan spearmen: Spearmen from Troy.
27. Phthia (thē´ ə) *n*.: Achilleus' home in northern Greece.
28. Menelaos': Refers to Menelaos' honor; Menlaos' wife Helen had been kidnapped by Priam's son Paris.
29. booty (bo̅o̅t´ ē) *n*.: Loot or prizes taken from the enemy during war.
30. counsels (koun´ səlz) *n*.: People whose advice is sought.

Primary Source Note

In Homeric society, a warrior's status is measured by the special privileges granted him in his home community and by the booty allotted to him when a town is plundered or a city is sacked. The clearest expression of how and why the system works is expressed in Book XII of the *Iliad* (lines 310–328). Sarpedon, a son of Zeus, is talking to his friend Glaukos. (Sarpedon will be killed by Patroklos, and although Zeus sheds tears of blood he does not save him because to do so would destroy the precarious balance of the universe.) He says:

Go home then with your own ships and your own companions,
be king over the Myrmidons.[31] I care nothing about you.
I take no account of your anger. But here is my threat to you.
Even as Phoibos Apollo is taking away my Chryseis,
I shall convey her back in my own ship, with my own
followers; but I shall take the fair-cheeked Briseis,
your prize, I myself going to your shelter, that you may learn well
how much greater I am than you, and another man may shrink back
from likening himself to me and contending against me."

   So he spoke. And the anger came on Peleus' son, and within
his shaggy breast the heart was divided two ways, pondering
whether to draw from beside his thigh the sharp sword, driving
away all those who stood between and kill the son of Atreus,
or else to check the spleen within[32] and keep down his anger.
Now as he weighed in mind and spirit these two courses
and was drawing from its scabbard the great sword, Athene
   descended
from the sky. For Hera the goddess of the white arms sent her,
who loved both men equally in her heart and cared for them.
The goddess standing behind Peleus' son caught him by the fair hair,
appearing to him only, for no man of the others saw her.
Achilleus in amazement turned about, and straightway
knew Pallas Athene and the terrible eyes shining.
He uttered winged words and addressed her: "Why have you come
   now,
o child of Zeus of the aegis,[33] once more? Is it that you may see
the outrageousness of the son of Atreus Agamemnon?
Yet will I tell you this thing, and I think it shall be accomplished.
By such acts of arrogance he may even lose his own life."

   Then in answer the goddess gray-eyed Athene spoke to him:
"I have come down to stay[34] your anger—but will you obey me?—
from the sky; and the goddess of the white arms Hera sent me,
who loves both of you equally in her heart and cares for you.
Come then, do not take your sword in your hand, keep clear of
   fighting,
though indeed with words you may abuse him, and it will be that
   way.
And this also will I tell you and it will be a thing accomplished.

---

31. Myrmidons (mur′ mə dänz′) *n.*: Achilleus' warriors from his home in
northern Greece.
32. check the spleen within: Control his bad temper.
33. aegis (ē′ jis) *n.*: The breastplate or shield of Zeus made of goat hide; Zeus
used his aegis to cause storms and panic humans.
34. stay (stā) *v.*: Stop; halt.

Cultural Context: A king
with the best interests of
his kingdom in mind would
not want to humiliate the
most valuable warrior. By
humiliating Achilleus,
Agamemnon preserves his
status as the most
powerful king, who
commands absolute
obedience from even his
most essential warrior.   **17**

Literary Context: The
intervention of
supernatural forces is
characteristic of epic
poetry. In the *Iliad* the gods
descend frequently to
Earth and mingle freely
with mortals.
                         18

Cultural Context: The
gods are a ubiquitous
presence—they are
everywhere, even when
they are visible to only one
person, as Athene is here
visible only to Achilleus.
The Greeks do not
necessarily perceive them
as the ultimate cause of
events. Rather, they are a
deeper and truer way of
perceiving human action
and human thought. The
gods' involvement with
mortals, including the   **19**
intermarriage of gods and
mortals, shows how the
Greeks saw themselves as
inextricably connected with
their universe.

17 Reading Strategy As they read
this passage, have students pay
particular attention to Agamemnon's remarks, "I care nothing
about you. I take no account of
your anger." Would a good commander in chief "care nothing"
about his best fighter? Moreover,
by "taking no account" of
Achilleus' anger, Agamemnon
degrades Achilleus in a way that
undermines the strict heroic
code. Ask students to evaluate
Agamemnon's behavior in these
lines. What are his choices?

18 Discussion Have students think
about how the gods intervene. To
what extent is their action tailored to the character and state
of mind of the human beings involved? Although the Greeks
thought of Athene as real, not a
symbol or allegory, modern readers might think of other explanations for the behavior Homer attributes to Achilleus. What does
the way a culture conceptualizes
human motivation reveal about
that culture's view of the universe
and people's place in it?

19 Discussion To what extent is
Athene's advice in these lines
something Achilleus might have
thought of by himself? In other
words, how is this episode indicative of the connection between human motivation and divine causality, the belief that the
gods control what happens and
what doesn't happen?

Glaukos, why is it you and I are honored before others / with pride of
place, the choice meats and the filled wine-cups / in Lykia, and all men
look on us as if we were immortals, / and we are appointed a great piece
of land by the banks of Xanthos, / good land, orchard and vineyard,
and ploughland for the planting of wheat? / Therefore, it is our duty in
the forefront of the Lykians / to take our stand, and bear our part of the
blazing of battle, / so that a man of the close armored Lykians might
say of us: / "Indeed, these are no ignoble men who are lords of Lykia,
/ these kings of ours, who feed upon the fat sheep appointed / and drink
the exquisite sweet wine, since indeed there is strength / of valor in them,
since they fight in the forefront of the Lykians." / Man, supposing you
and I, escaping this battle, / would be able to live on forever, ageless,
immortal, / so neither would I myself go on fighting in the foremost / nor
would I urge you into the fighting where men win glory. / But now, seeing
that the spirits of death stand close about us / in their thousands, no
man can turn aside nor escape them, / let us go on and win glory for
ourselves, or yield it to others.

Humanities Note

Fine art, *Athene Restraining the Anger of Achilleus* by Giovanni Battista Tiepolo (1696–1770). The fresco *Athene Restraining the Anger of Achilleus* is one of many executed for Count Valmarona in his Vincenzia palazzo in 1757. The subject matter, new to Tiepolo, was taken from Homer's *Iliad*.

Tiepolo's device of using a light washed background with indistinct details provides a dramatic setting for the action in the foreground. Here he has abandoned his palette of bright and cheerful colors for more somber earth tones that infuse a subtle melancholy to the scene.

Tiepolo worked closely on this project with the famed rococo architect, Mingozzi Colonna. The relaxed and expansive nature of Tiepolo's compositions were perfectly suited to architecture of this style. You might want to use the following questions to discuss the art:

1. What do the stance and expression of Agamemnon convey?
2. Is Achilleus' anger accurately portrayed in this painting?

20 Reading Strategy Ask students to discuss how Achilleus sees the relationship between humans and gods as essentially reciprocal. What is Achilleus implying when he says, "If any man obeys the gods, they listen to him also"? Encourage students to think not only about what the characters explicitly say, but also about what they imply.

21 Reading Strategy What do Achilleus' insults, expressed in individualized language, mean? Have students paraphrase them. How do Achilleus' charges reveal the warrior ethic and what is expected of a king and a fighter?

ATHENE RESTRAINING THE ANGER OF ACHILLEUS
Giovanni Battista Tiepolo

210 Some day three times over such shining gifts shall be given you
by reason of this outrage. Hold your hand then, and obey us."
    Then in answer again spoke Achilleus of the swift feet:
"Goddess, it is necessary that I obey the word of you two,
angry though I am in my heart. So it will be better.
If any man obeys the gods, they listen to him also."
215 He spoke, and laid his heavy hand on the silver sword hilt
and thrust the great blade back into the scabbard nor disobeyed
the word of Athene. And she went back again to Olympos
to the house of Zeus of the aegis with the other divinities.
    But Peleus' son once again in words of derision
220 spoke to Atreides,[35] and did not yet let go of his anger:
"You wine sack, with a dog's eyes, with a deer's heart. Never
once have you taken courage in your heart to arm[36] with your people

---

35. Atreides (ə trē′ ə dēz′) *n.*: Literally, son of Atreus; another name for Agamemnon.
36. arm (ärm) *v.*: To prepare clothing and weapons for battle.

Primary Source Note

Achilleus is both greater than a mere mortal because of his divine mother and at the same time bereft of much of the comfort associated with being human. He is mortal, but he has no mortal mother to comfort him and mourn for him. Thetis' very immortality and invulnerability divide her from her mortal son no matter how much she loves him and how deeply his death distresses her. In *On the Iliad*, Rachel Bespaloff focuses on the special poignancy of the bond between Thetis and Achilleus.

This man of passion, driven from restless boredom to frenzied action, is son to a goddess . . . whose grace enfolds him in calm. From the

for battle, or go into ambuscade[37] with the best of the Achaians.
No, for in such things you see death. Far better to your mind
5 is it, all along the widespread host of the Achaians
to take away the gifts of any man who speaks up against you.
King who feeds on your people, since you rule nonentities,[38]
otherwise, son of Atreus, this were your last outrage.
But I will tell you this and swear a great oath upon it:
0 in the name of this scepter, which never again will bear leaf nor
branch, now that it has left behind the cut stump in the mountains,
nor shall it ever blossom again, since the bronze blade stripped
bark and leafage, and now at last the sons of the Achaians
carry it in their hands in state when they administer
5 the justice of Zeus. And this shall be a great oath before you:
some day longing for Achilleus will come to the sons of the
    Achaians,
all of them. Then stricken at heart though you be, you will be able
to do nothing, when in their numbers before man-slaughtering
    Hektor
0 they drop and die. And then you will eat out the heart within you
in sorrow, that you did no honor to the best of the Achaians."

*Nestor, one of the wisest Greek commanders and counselors, advises
Agamemnon and Achilleus to concede to each other; both men refuse. To
appease the gods and spare the Achaians further annihilation,
Agamemnon orders Odysseus to return Chryseis. As compensation for his
lost war prize, Agamemnon abducts Achilleus' Briseis. Dishonored,
Achilleus swears that never again would he join the Achaians in fight-
ing against the Trojans. He convinces Thetis to persuade Zeus to help the
Trojans defeat the Achaians.*

But that other still sat in anger beside his swift ships,
Peleus' son divinely born, Achilleus of the swift feet.
Never now would he go to assemblies where men win glory,
never more into battle, but continued to waste his heart out
5 sitting there, though he longed always for the clamor and fighting.
But when the twelfth dawn after this day appeared, the gods who
live forever came back to Olympos all in a body
and Zeus led them; nor did Thetis forget the entreaties
of her son, but she emerged from the sea's waves early
0 in the morning and went up to the tall sky and Olympos.
She found Kronos' broad-browed son apart from the others
sitting upon the highest peak of rugged Olympos.

---

37. **ambuscade** (am´ bəs kād´) *n.*: A group of people hiding, waiting for a
surprise attack.
38. **nonentities** (nän´ en´ tə tēz) *n.*: People of little or no significance.

depths of that submarine retreat where she dwells with her old father,
Thetis keeps watch over her son, and her vigilance never sleeps . . .
The anxious love that has taught her the lesson of human distress has
also taught her to despise her immortal status. Beside the earth-bound
Achilleus, whom force has made half-god, and violence half-beast,
Thetis herself becomes earthly . . . Outside of Patroklos, the only being
that Achilleus is capable of affection for is Thetis of the fair tresses, the
mother, immortal, and young . . . In the last analysis, it is not through
action that Homer reveals humans' profoundest nature but rather through
humans' way of loving and choosing love. For Hektor, love is the forgetfulness of self. For Achilleus, self is at the center of love.

Cultural Context: Oaths
are sworn to solemnize
promises or threats and to
formalize official
relationships between
individuals, clans, or
states. The gods are
called on to witness the
intention of the speaker,
and it is understood that if
the speaker violates his
oath, the gods will punish
him. Achilleus swears by
the scepter, unchanging
because it is no longer a
living tree, and the symbol
of justice.

Achilleus may appear
to be boasting when he
calls himself the best of
the Achaians, but in his
society, false modesty is
not a virtue; a man who is
the best fighter has earned
the right to say so. No man
should forget, however,
that he is mortal, not a
god.

Cultural Context: In
Achilleus' world, what
society thinks of the hero
is far more important than
what the hero thinks of
himself. Achilleus knows
that he can achieve fame
and glory only through
action. As he sits by his
ships, Achilleus is acutely
aware that as long as he
allows his anger to keep
him from battle, he will be
unable to establish his
reputation.

22

23

24

22 **Discussion** Discuss the fact
that Achilleus keeps stressing
Agamemnon's desire for profit
and unearned goods. Why is
Achilleus so concerned with material things? What do objects
represent for Achilleus?

Master Teacher Note Students
may be prone to think that boasting is unheroic and that true
heroes should be strong, silent,
and at least pretend to self-effac-
ing modesty. Help them see that
the etiquette of Homeric society
is different. Depending on their
individual experiences, students
may be able to compare Homeric heroes with samurai heroes,
with heroes in medieval epic and
romance, as well as with the
more widely familiar "Aw shucks,
'twarnt nothin'" school of the
American Western hero. The only
danger a hero like Achilleus
might run into is forgetting the
limits separating all mortals from
the gods. Achilleus' oath in fact
will be realized in the course of
the poem.

23 **Discussion** Achilleus' great oath
foresees grief for the Achaians.
What do these lines reveal about
Achilleus' suffering? Why is withdrawal from the assembly and
the battle so destructive for him?
In what dilemma is he caught?

24 **Enrichment** The representation
of Thetis in the poem contains
traces of another, much more
powerful goddess figure. The
prophecy that she would bear a
son stronger than his father associates her with a kind of earth-
mother goddess; it was because
of this power that Zeus and Poseidon gave her up and handed
her over to the mortal Peleus.
Her indispensable help enabled
Zeus to be victorious over the
monsters and giants who threatened his throne. She has special
rights to favors from Zeus, and
she is collecting some of what he
owes her now.

Fine art, *The Surrender of Briseis*. The mural *The Surrender of Briseis* is from the House of the Tragic Poet in Pompeii. It was executed shortly before the eruption of Mt. Vesuvius in A.D. 79.

The foreboding atmosphere in this mural is achieved through the use of golden earth tones contrasted with cool grays. The face-less line of soldiers in the rear heighten this effect. Achilleus on his throne in the foreground looks at Briseis being led away; his expression is a mixture of grief and anger. The beach setting is sketchily indicated by the misty outline of the prows of ships in the background.

This mural and others on the same theme attest to the regard ancient Romans had for the ancient Greek poets. You might want to ask students: What do wall paintings of specific scenes from the *Iliad* tell you about the poem's importance in ancient Greek culture?

25 Clarification Thetis' position here is the standard posture of a suppliant.

Cultural Note American authors have turned much less to the *Iliad* than to the *Odyssey* for inspiration, but occasionally epic techniques can be used for comic or ironic effect. For instance, in *Maggie, a Girl of the Streets*, Stephen Crane opens his story with a mock-epic account of a battle of slum urchins in Rum Alley, and throughout the work he uses "Homeric" stock epithets ironically.

Cooperative Learning In group discussions, have students address the Reader's Response question by analyzing how both Agamemnon and Achilleus are at fault and how they both have valid arguments. Each member of the group should contribute to the discussion by referring to specific lines in the text.

THE SURRENDER OF BRISEIS
Pompeii wall painting, A.D. *63–79*
National Museum, Naples

She came and sat beside him with her left hand embracing
his knees, but took him underneath the chin with her right hand
255 and spoke in supplication to lord Zeus son of Kronos:
"Father Zeus, if ever before in word or action
I did you favor among the immortals, now grant what I ask for.
Now give honor to my son short-lived beyond all other
mortals. Since even now the lord of men Agamemnon
260 dishonors him, who has taken away his prize and keeps it.
Zeus of the counsels, lord of Olympos, now do him honor.
So long put strength into the Trojans, until the Achaians
give my son his rights, and his honor is increased among them."

Reader's Response *In Book I, Homer presents both sides of the argument between Achilleus and Agamemnon. Both characters have valid arguments, but both are also at fault. With whom do you side and why?*

Closure and Extension

ANSWERS TO THINKING ABOUT THE SELECTION

1. The army is plague-stricken, and unless the causes are discovered and the plague stopped, the Greeks will perish.
2. Opinions may differ, but students should be prepared to support their viewpoint with specific textual evidence. Suggested response: No, Agamemnon is more interested in his personal pride than what is best for his people. In support of this answer, students might suggest that Agamemnon agrees to return Chryseis, but he demands that she be replaced with Achilleus' prize, and he makes this demand to save face.
3. As a prize of valor, Briseis is a symbol of his status as a warrior.
4. Recognition of a warrior's worth by his peers was seen as payment for his risking his life in battle. Without recognition, he has no reason to fight.
5. On the most immediate level, he is stopped by Athene. He also realizes that to kill Agamemnon would be to violate all the codes of his society and opt for chaos.
6. Achilleus is saying that he is the only

THINKING ABOUT THE SELECTION

Interpreting

1. Identify the problem confronting the characters as the *Iliad* begins and explain why it is of national importance.
2. Assess Agamemnon's sincerity in line 117 when he says he has his people's best interest at heart.
3. Why is Achilleus dishonored when Agamemnon takes Briseis?
4. Explain why Achilleus withdraws from battle.
5. Why does Achilleus decide not to strike Agamemnon?
6. Why does Achilleus predict that the Achaians will drop and die at Hektor's hands? Why does he want them to fail?
7. Explain why honor is so important to Achilleus.

Applying

8. Achilleus' primary objective is to prove himself to be the best, most honorable Greek fighter. Are modern heroes similarly concerned with proving themselves honorable? Explain.

ANALYZING LITERATURE

Recognizing Epic Conventions

An **epic** is a long, narrative poem in which characters of high birth or national status are engaged in a quest, a series of adventures important to the history of a nation or race. The hero is a central, imposing figure of national or international importance and of great historical or legendary significance. Usually, the epic has a vast setting covering great nations. The action consists of valorous deeds requiring superhuman courage and which involve the intervention of supernatural forces. Conventions employed by most epic poets include: beginning in medias res; stating theme in the invocation of the muse; presenting catalogs of warriors, ships, and armies; having the main characters utter long, formal speeches; and using epic similes, elaborate comparisons between two unlike things.

1. Identify the three epic conventions employed in the first lines of the *Iliad*: "Sing goddess, the anger of Peleus' son Achilleus and its devastation, which put pains thousandfold upon the Achaians . . ."
2. Find three examples of the intervention of supernatural forces in Book I.

CRITICAL THINKING AND READING

Defining the Epic Hero

The **epic hero** possesses certain qualities—bravery, superhuman strength, success in battle, and a driving desire to immortalize himself through valorous deeds. All heroes desire eternal glory and fame. Although they achieve that fame by performing heroic deeds for society, they are concerned exclusively with how their individual behavior will immortalize them for future generations. He who shows courage in the face of death is sure to be immortalized as a hero.

With few exceptions, the epic hero is of high birth or of semi-divine origin, as Achilleus is the son of a mortal and the goddess Thetis. Achilleus' mortality is an overwhelming fact of life for him because he knows he is fated to die. Therefore, he strives to achieve a reputation that will survive his death.

One of the most important and recurring epic conflicts is the conflict between hero and king. As stated early in Book I, Agamemnon and Achilleus "stood in division of conflict" in a dispute over honor. Their conflict generates the material for the remainder of the poem.

1. Quote three examples from the text that illustrate Achilleus' heroism.
2. What other characters have you read about who fit the definition of epic hero? Support each of your choices.

THINKING AND WRITING

Explaining the Role of Achilleus' Anger

Achilleus' particular situation may seem distant in time and culture, but his anger and its underlying causes are not limited to his time or his gender. Some ways of seeing him are as a young man rebelling against an older man, as an individual setting himself up against authority, or as a human being confronting the unfairness of the human condition. First choose the way in which you view Achilleus. Next outline a scenario in which a modern Achilleus and a modern Agamemnon confront each other. (Neither character has to be male.) Then develop your sketch into a story based on one critical scene. Revise your story, making sure you have illustrated the role of the hero's anger. Finally, proofread for spelling, grammar, and punctuation errors.

(continued from bottom of page)

ANSWERS TO CRITICAL THINKING AND READING

1. Suggested responses: Agamemnon articulated one of Achilleus' heroic qualities—his godlike status—when he says, "Not that way, good fighter though you be, godlike Achilleus . . ." in line 127. Achilleus himself articulates another of his heroic qualities—being rewarded for his fighting with a prize—when he says: "And now my prize you threaten in person to strip from me, / for whom I labored much, the gift of the sons of the Achaians" in lines 157–158. A third indication of Achilleus' heroic status occurs when he refers to himself as "the best of the Achaians" in line 241.
2. Answers will differ. Students may have read about the semi-divine Sumerian epic hero Gilgamesh, who is engaged in a quest for immortality.

THINKING AND WRITING

Publishing Student Writing Students have a great deal of latitude with this assignment. However, papers should focus on a character of heroic status whose anger dictates his or her character in the same way that Achilleus' does. Have students share their papers in class.

Challenge Ask students what they learned about ancient Greek social and cultural values from Book I of the *Iliad*.

Greek warrior good enough to ward off Hektor. He feels dishonored; by failing without his participation in the fight, the Greeks will realize his worth and their dependence on him.

7. Honor is the only recognized currency in the warrior elite to which Achilleus belongs. Without honor, he has no identity.
8. Students should think about the need to "be the best" as one part of the issue and then about the ways "honor" is accorded excellence. Students may respond that modern heroes do not pursue honor for themselves, or that some seek honor for large groups of people.

ANSWERS TO ANALYZING LITERATURE

1. The three epic conventions are the invocation of the muse (Sing, goddess), the statement of subject and theme (the anger of Achilleus and its devastation), and the opening *in medias res*, since this first line tunes us in to the story in the middle.
2. Suggested response: Apollo's plague with which the epic opens, Athene restraining Achilleus' anger, and Athene asking Zeus to restore Achilleus' honor by helping the Trojans are three examples.

Literary Focus The imagery of Achilleus' shield is important not only as a microcosm of the *Iliad* but as an interval of calm in the passion and fury of the poem. Homer's emphasis on Hephaistos' beautiful artwork is a strong contrast to the savage fighting of the books prior to and immediately following Book XVIII. Homer temporarily sets aside the action of the poem to depict the world beyond Troy. As he focuses on the shield from scene to scene, image after image, he captures the full range of human life.

Writing/Prior Knowledge To help students with the writing assignment, have a class discussion about films they have seen that use an object or a scene to convey meaning. Popular westerns, detective films, and romance fiction can provide examples of ekphrasis. You might also have them think about whether music videos could be considered a form of ekphrasis or not.

ESL Teaching Strategy Students of limited English proficiency might benefit from making inferences from the text. Select passages from the poem and ask ESL students what inferences they draw from the passages.

Teaching Tenth-Grade Students Tenth-grade students might be interested in capturing the full range of their lives on a "shield." Ask students what images and scenes they would include in an ekphrasis of their world.

Vocabulary
Preteach the following vocabulary words:
rebuked (ri byo͞okt´) *v.*:
    Reprimanded
onslaught (än´ slôt) *n.*:
    Violent attack
decreed (dē krēd´) *v.*:
    Officially ordered or
    ordained
incessant (in ses´ 'nt) *adj.*:
    Continual

Commentary

from the Iliad, *from* Books VI and XVIII

Imagery of Achilleus' Shield. Homer's description of Achilleus' shield is as fabulous a piece of art as the shield itself. Using a pattern of images—concrete representations of sensory experiences and abstractions—Homer brings the scenes on the shield to life. He endows the people in the scenes with motion, sound, thought, speech, and action. Contrasting scenes of peace and war, country and city, sowing and harvesting, and dancing and working reflect the intense joy and utter pathos of life as Homer's audience knew it. Ultimately, the images on the shield form a coherent description of human reality.

Homer's extensive description of the shield is often referred to as an *ekphrasis,* an extended description of a work of art, real or imaginary. In a work of literature, an ekphrasis often adds to the main story indirectly, focusing our attention on a symbolic meaning or making us reflect on the main story. Homer's ekphrasis of Achilleus' shield leads us through the world of the *Iliad*, cinematically. In cinematography, the use of a camera takes the place of words; by causing the viewer's eye to follow a slowly moving camera, by focusing on certain details, or by freezing a shot, a film-maker "describes," or "comments on," a scene. Since the images on the shield are thematically connected to events elsewhere in the *Iliad*, Homer's detail of the shield is an indirect comment on the main story.

Remarkably, the shield contains the entire cosmos, or ordered universe. The outer circle is the River Ocean, the boundary of the world. Within the boundary are planets and constellations that form an essential part of the daily life of people who till the soil and live by the seasons. Agriculture, harvest festivals, and marriage rites find their place on the shield. Two cities, one at war and one enjoying peace, represent all the major aspects of life in the *Iliad*—the heroic and tragic reality of war, and the relieving calm of peacetime. In fact, Achilleus' shield is a microcosm of the *Iliad*, and of Homer's world.

Writing

When we read a book or watch a film, certain scenes are more memorable because of the amount and intensity of detail in them. Think of an ekphrasis in a book you have read or a film you have seen. Freewrite about why the description was significant and how it caused you to reflect on the main story.

Objectives

Thematic
To understand the range of human life in the *Iliad*

Skills
1 To analyze the imagery of Achilleus' shield

2 To compare and contrast characters
3 To analyze oral literature
4 To write about divine causality

from the Iliad

from Book VI: The Meeting of Hektor and Andromache

Upon Thetis' request, Zeus intervenes to help the Trojans defeat the Achaians. Bitter fighting resumes, causing the massive death of Trojans and Achaians. Disadvantaged though the Achaians are by Achilleus' absence, they manage to subdue the Trojans. Under Diomedes' leadership, the Achaians drive the Trojan forces back to the Trojan gates and into temporary retreat. Realizing the severity of the Trojan cause, Hektor and his men go to Priam's palace in Troy to urge the gods to take pity on Troy and its people. Next, Hektor tries to persuade Paris to help fight the Achaians.

But Hektor saw him [Paris], and in words of shame he <u>rebuked</u> him:
"Strange man! It is not fair to keep in your heart this coldness.
The people are dying around the city and around the steep wall
as they fight hard; and it is for you that this war with its clamor
has flared up about our city. You yourself would fight with another
whom you saw anywhere hanging back from the hateful encounter.
Up then, to keep our town from burning at once in the hot fire."

Then in answer the godlike Alexandros spoke to him:
"Hektor, seeing you have scolded me rightly, not beyond measure,
therefore I will tell, and you in turn understand and listen.
It was not so much in coldness and bitter will toward the Trojans
That I sat in my room, but I wished to give myself over to sorrow.
But just now with soft words my wife was winning me over
and urging me into the fight, and that way seems to me also
the better one. Victory passes back and forth between men.
Come then, wait for me now while I put on my armor of battle,
or go, and I will follow, and I think I can overtake you."

He spoke, but Hektor of the shining helm gave him no answer,
but Helen spoke to him in words of endearment: "Brother
by marriage to me, who am a nasty witch evil-intriguing,
how I wish that on that day when my mother first bore me
the foul whirlwind of the storm ahead caught me away and
    swept me
to the mountain, or into the wash of the sea deep-thundering

Support Material

Teaching Portfolio
Teacher Backup, p. 463
Grammar in Action Worksheets, *Recognizing Transitions*, p. 469; *Recognizing Prepositional Phrases*, p. 471; *Recognizing Inverted Sentence Patterns*, p. 473; *Recognizing Compound Verbs*, p. 475

Usage and Mechanics Worksheet, p. 477
Vocabulary Check, p. 478
Critical Thinking and Reading Worksheet, *Comparing and Contrasting Characters*, p. 479
Language Worksheet, *Analyzing Oral Literature*, p. 480
Selection Test, pp. 481–482

Presentation

Motivation/Prior Knowledge Tell students that they will be reading a scene not unfamiliar to them from other contexts—a warrior's farewell before leaving for battle, and death. Have them think about such scenes and look for both similarities and differences between this particular scene in the *Iliad* and what they know.

Purpose-Setting Question The opening exchange between Hektor and Paris focuses on two contrasting responses to the heroic code. What can students surmise about the code, and why does Homer develop Paris as a foil to Hektor?

Universal Themes Being torn between love and duty is a recurring topic in many literatures. Aeneas faces the same kind of choice in the *Aeneid* (page 493) as does Lancelot in *Perceval* (page 602).

1 Discussion How do Hektor's words reveal his inability to understand Paris' behavior? Students might note Hektor's assumption that only ill will toward the Trojans could cause a warrior to refuse battle.

2 Clarification Paris' response reveals that he is speaking a "language" different from Hektor's. Paris rejects the notion that his actions are determined by his relationship with the Trojans. What do the students think of his wanting to sit in his room and indulge in his sorrow?

Master Teacher Note Helen holds herself blameworthy and responsible at the same time as she sees that the gods have "brought it about that these vile things must be." Recognizing a divine plan and destiny does not exonerate mortals, who are responsible for what they do. One's destiny is not separate from one's character. Have students discuss this view of predetermination and free will/moral responsibility; it will surface again when they read *Oedipus the King*.

THE ABDUCTION
OF HELEN BY PARIS
Fra Angelico (follower)
National Gallery, London

> where the waves would have swept me away before all these things
>   had happened.
> Yet since the gods had brought it about that these vile things
> 25   must be,
> I wish I had been the wife of a better man than this is,
> one who knew modesty and all things of shame that men say.
> But this man's heart is no steadfast[1] thing, nor yet will it be so
> ever hereafter; for that I think he shall take the consequence.
> 30 But come now, come in and rest on this chair, my brother,
> since it is on your heart beyond all that the hard work has fallen
> for the sake of dishonored me and the blind act of Alexandros,
> us two, on whom Zeus set a vile destiny, so that hereafter
> we shall be made into things of song for the men of the future."

1. steadfast (sted´ fast´) *adj.*: Constant; not fickle or frequently changing.

Then tall Hektor of the shining helm answered her: "Do not,
    Helen,
make me sit with you, though you love me. You will not
    persuade me.
Already my heart within is hastening[2] me to defend
the Trojans, who when I am away long greatly to have me.
Rather rouse this man, and let himself also be swift to action
so he may overtake me while I am still in the city.
For I am going first to my own house, so I can visit
my own people, my beloved wife and my son, who is little,
since I do not know if ever again I shall come back this way,
or whether the gods will strike me down at the hands of the
    Achaians."
    So speaking Hektor of the shining helm departed
and in speed made his way to his own well-established dwelling,
but failed to find in the house Andromache of the white arms;
for she, with the child, and followed by one fair-robed attendant,
had taken her place on the tower in lamentation,[3] and tearful.
When he saw no sign of his perfect wife within the house, Hektor
stopped in his way on the threshold and spoke among the
    handmaidens:
"Come then, tell me truthfully as you may, handmaidens:
where has Andromache of the white arms gone? Is she
with any of the sisters of her lord or the wives of his brothers?
Or has she gone to the house of Athene, where all the other
lovely-haired women of Troy propitiate the grim goddess?"
    Then in turn the hard-working housekeeper gave him an answer:
"Hektor, since you have urged me to tell you the truth, she is not
with any of the sisters of her lord or the wives of his brothers,
nor has she gone to the house of Athene, where all the other
lovely-haired women of Troy propitiate the grim goddess,
but she has gone to the great bastion[4] of Ilion, because she heard
    that
the Trojans were losing, and great grew the strength of the
    Achaians.
Therefore she has gone in speed to the wall, like a woman
gone mad, and a nurse attending her carries the baby."
    So the housekeeper spoke, and Hektor hastened from his home
backward by the way he had come through the well-laid streets. So
as he had come to the gates on his way through the great city,
the Skaian gates,[5] whereby he would issue into the plain, there
at last his own generous wife came running to meet him,
Andromache, the daughter of high-hearted Eëtion;[6]
Eëtion, who had dwelt underneath wooded Plakos,[7]
in Thebe below Plakos, lord over the Kilikian people.[8]
It was his daughter who was given to Hektor of the bronze helm.
She came to him there, and beside her went an attendant carrying

2. hastening (hās′ ə niŋ) *v.*:
Causing to hurry; accelerating.

3. lamentation (lam′ ən tā′
shən) *n.*: Act of expressing
extreme grief.

4. bastion (bas′ chən) *n.*:
Fortified place.

5. Skaian gates (skē′ ən) *n.*:
The northwest gates of Troy.
6. Eëtion (ē ē′ tē on) *n.*: King
of Thebe, a city near Troy.
7. Plakos (plā′ kōs) *n.*:
Mountain dominating Thebe.
8. Kilikian (kil′ i kē′ ən)
people: People in Asian Thebe.

4 Discussion Ask students to
think about the importance of
Hektor's words. How does he
see himself in relationship to his
people?

5 Enrichment Whenever a major
event is at hand, Homer heightens the listener's involvement
and pleasure by preparing for
and delaying the description of
the event itself, thus creating
suspense.

6 Literary Focus Call students' attention to the repetition of the
phrase ". . . has she gone to the
house of Athene, where all the
other / lovely-haired women of
Troy propitiate the grim goddess" in lines 55–56 and 60–61.
Remind students that the repetition of lines and, in some cases,
entire passages, is a feature of
oral literature. In the *Iliad*, Homer
often uses repetition to preserve
the rhythm of the poem; at the
same time, repetition also serves
to reinforce important information
for the listener.

7 Discussion Ask students to describe Andromache's frame of
mind. Can students visualize the
scene or speculate on her emotions?

8 Clarification Students should realize that Hektor, having missed
his wife, is retracing his steps to
the gate and the battlefield. The
last meeting of husband and wife
almost never took place.

9 Enrichment Important characters are introduced with a complete "family history." Ask students why this information is
important in placing a character
in the context of the poem.

Yet since the gods had brought it about that these vile things must be,
/ I wish I had been the wife of a better man than this is, / one who knew
modesty and all things of shame that men say. / But this man's heart
is no steadfast thing, nor yet will it be so / hereafter . . .

    Helen's repetition of the transitions *yet* and *but* suggest her conflicting
feelings about her relationship with Paris and her role in the Trojan War.
    The transitions used in lines 64–68 reveal the urgency in Andromache's
and Hektor's purposes:

"Therefore, she has gone in speed to the wall, like a woman gone mad,

and a nurse attending her carries the baby."

So the housekeeper spoke, and Hektor hastened from his home backward by the way he had come through the well-laid streets. So as he
had come to the gates on his way through the great city.

    Student Activity 1. Find additional transitions in Helen's speech and
explain what relationships the transitions show.
    Student Activity 2. Examine an article from a newspaper or magazine.
Identify the transitions and explain how they are used.

the boy in the fold of her bosom, a little child, only a baby,
Hektor's son, the admired, beautiful as a star shining,
whom Hektor called Skamandrios, but all of the others
Astyanax—lord of the city; since Hektor alone saved Ilion.

80 Hektor smiled in silence as he looked on his son, but she,
Andromache, stood close beside him, letting her tears fall,
and clung to his hand and called him by name and spoke to him:
"Dearest,
your own great strength will be your death, and you have no pity
on your little son, nor on me, ill-starred,[9] who soon must be your
widow;

85 for presently the Achaians, gathering together,
will set upon you and kill you; and for me it would be far better
to sink into the earth when I have lost you, for there is no other
consolation for me after you have gone to your destiny—
only grief; since I have no father, no honored mother.

90 It was brilliant Achilleus who slew my father, Eëtion,
when he stormed the strong-founded citadel of the Kilikians,
Thebe of the towering gates. He killed Eëtion
but did not strip his armor, for his heart respected the dead man,
but burned the body in all its elaborate war-gear
and piled a grave mound over it, and the nymphs[10] of the
95   mountains,
daughters of Zeus of the aegis, planted elm trees about it.
And they who were my seven brothers in the great house all went
upon a single day down into the house of the death god,
for swift-footed brilliant Achilleus slaughtered all of them

100 as they were tending their white sheep and their lumbering oxen;
and when he had led my mother, who was queen under wooded
Plakos,
here, along with all his other possessions, Achilleus
released her again, accepting ransom beyond count, but Artemis
of the showering arrows struck her down in the halls of her father.

105 Hektor, thus you are father to me, and my honored mother,
you are my brother, and you it is who are my young husband.
Please take pity upon me then, stay here on the rampart,[11]
that you may not leave your child an orphan, your wife a widow,
but draw your people up by the fig tree, there where the city

110 is openest to attack, and where the wall may be mounted.
Three times their bravest came that way, and fought there to
storm it
about the two Aiantes[12] and renowned Idomeneus,[13]
about the two Atreidai[14] and the fighting son of Tydeus.[15]
Either some man well skilled in prophetic arts had spoken,
or the very spirit within themselves had stirred them to the
115   onslaught."

Then tall Hektor of the shining helm answered her: "All these
things are in my mind also, lady; yet I would feel deep shame

---

9. ill-starred (il'stärd') *adj.*: Unfavorably influenced by the stars, which were believed to control destiny.

10. nymphs (nimfs) *n.*: Nature goddesses.

11. rampart (ram' pärt') *n.*: A protected embankment of earth where people were safe from attack.

12. Aiantes (ī' an' tēz): There were two people called Aias: one was Aias of Salamis, son of Telamon; and the second was Aias of Lokris, son of Oileus. Aiantes is the name for the two men when spoken of together.

13. Idomeneus (ī' dō men' ā əs): Son of Deukalion, one of the great princes and fighters of the Achaians.

14. Atreidai (ə trē' ə dī'): Refers to the two sons of Atreus, Agamemnon and Menelaos.

15. Tydeus (tə dā' əs): Father of Diomedes, a great Achaian fighter.

---

10 Enrichment Students should note that the name given to the baby by the Trojans connects father and son: Astyanax, "lord of the city," is a living token of Hektor's reputation.

11 Discussion Ask students to recall Helen's speech to Hektor earlier in Book VI, lines 19–34. How is Andromache's plea to Hektor different from Helen's words to him?

12 Reading Strategy Embedded in Andromache's recital of Achilleus' brutality is proof of his capacity for human compassion. In observance of the ancient code of ethics, for example, Achilleus killed Andromache's father, but out of respect for the dead man, he burned him in his armor and gave him his rite of burning. Ask students for another example of Achilleus' respect for ethical codes in this passage. As they read the rest of the *Iliad*, students should pay particular attention to Achilleus' behavior in human and inhuman terms.

13 Discussion Ask students to discuss how Homer suggests the richness of Andromache's love for Hektor. Students undoubtedly have their own ideas about love; ask them to describe love in terms of Andromache's plea to Hektor. You may even want them to paraphrase her plea, or ask them to rewrite her plea in their own words.

14 Discussion Although she does not explicitly say that Achilleus will slay Hektor as he slew her father and brothers, Andromache implies that Hektor will most likely die at Achilleus' hands. Students should keep this scene in mind, as it foreshadows Hektor's death in Book XXII.

Primary Source Note

Helen sees herself and Paris as the subject of bardic song. Early bards composed and recited poems about the stories of people and the stories of gods. In the words of James M. Redfield, in his study *Nature and Culture in the Iliad*,

. . . stories of the gods among themselves are generally lighthearted in tone and are often stories of playful tricks played by one god upon another. The gods live an easy life apart from us, and they live forever; they are in continual conflict but experience no real sorrow or permanent disasters, and out of their conflicts they create the human world. The stories of the gods often tell the origins of things . . .

The stories of heroes, by contrast, are stories of disasters and suffering, sometimes surmounted, more often simply endured. They tell of quarrels, stratagems, labors, and especially battles. These stories are historical, in the sense that they are set in the past, but they are not stories of historical origins. They tell, not of the founding of cities, but of their destruction. Man's life is set in contrast to the gods' life.

**HEKTOR TAKING LEAVE
OF ANDROMACHE**
Angelica Kaufmann
Tate Gallery, London

before the Trojans, and the Trojan women with trailing garments,
if like a coward I were to shrink aside from the fighting;
and the spirit will not let me, since I have learned to be valiant
and to fight always among the foremost ranks of the Trojans,
winning for my own self great glory, and for my father.

15

"Fames of men" (klea andron) is the epic phrase for the heroic story.
This kind of "fame" outlives the "glory" won by men in their lifetime, and
is thus (in Redfield's words) "a specific type of social identity. A man
has a history, and for better or worse he must live with it. His story is
in a certain sense himself—or one version of himself—and, since his
story can survive his personal existence and survive his enactment of
a social role, his story is from one point of view the most real version
of himself. To think of life as a story is different from thinking of it in terms
of praise and blame. A story is more than that; it has a shape—a beginning, middle, and end . . ."

Humanities Note
Fine art, *Hektor Taking Leave of
Andromache* by Angelica Kauffmann. The Swiss-born painter
Maria Anna Angelica Catherine
Kauffmann (1741–1807) was the
daughter of the artist Joseph Johann Kauffmann (1707–1782). As
a recognized child prodigy, she
worked on commissioned portraits
as early as age thirteen. Her father
soon felt he had reached his limit
as her tutor in the arts. He moved
his entire family to Italy to enable
her to receive the finest artistic education. Rather than settle into the
refined position of society portrait
painter, as would have been suitable for a woman artist of her generation, Angelica Kauffmann
chose to become a "history
painter" and did so with remarkable success.

*Hektor Taking Leave of
Andromache* is one of the many
historical paintings on classical
subjects produced by Kauffmann.
Her expertise at composition is
recognizable in the interesting
grouping of the characters in this
dramatic scene. Her figures are
rendered with consummate skill
that bespeaks her years of study
in Italy. Although Kauffmann takes
a somewhat decorative approach,
the pathos of this scene is not lost.

You might want to use the following questions to discuss the
art:
1. What mood do the colors of this
painting create?
2. Do you think this artist makes
Andromache's despair clear?
Explain.

15 Discussion Ask students to analyze Hektor's response to Andromache. What is the importance of
shame for Hektor? Do Hektor's
words suggest that his entire training has left him no choice but to
fight?

For I know this thing well in my heart, and my mind knows it:
there will come a day when sacred Ilion shall perish,
125 and Priam, and the people of Priam of the strong ash spear.
But it is not so much the pain to come of the Trojans
that troubles me, not even of Priam the king nor Hekabe,[16]
not the thought of my brothers who in their numbers and valor
shall drop in the dust under the hands of men who hate them,
130 as troubles me the thought of you, when some bronze-armored
Achaian leads you off, taking away your day of liberty,
in tears; and in Argos you must work at the loom of another,
and carry water from the spring Messeis[17] or Hypereia,[18]
all unwilling, but strong will be the necessity upon you;
135 and some day seeing you shedding tears a man will say of you:
'This is the wife of Hektor, who was ever the bravest fighter
of the Trojans, breakers of horses, in the days when they fought
   about Ilion.'"
So will one speak of you; and for you it will be yet a fresh grief,
to be widowed of such a man who could fight off the day of your
   slavery.
140 But may I be dead and the piled earth hide me under before I
hear you crying and know by this that they drag you captive."

   So speaking glorious Hektor held out his arms to his baby,
who shrank back to his fair-girdled nurse's bosom
screaming, and frightened at the aspect of his own father,
145 terrified as he saw the bronze and the crest with its horse-hair,
nodding dreadfully, as he thought, from the peak of the helmet.
Then his beloved father laughed out, and his honored mother,
and at once glorious Hektor lifted from his head the helmet
and laid it in all its shining upon the ground. Then taking
150 up his dear son he tossed him about in his arms, and kissed him,
and lifted his voice in prayer to Zeus and the other immortals:
"Zeus, and you other immortals, grant that this boy, who is
   my son,
may be as I am, pre-eminent among the Trojans,
great in strength, as am I, and rule strongly over Ilion;
and some day let them say of him: 'He is better by far than his
155   father,'
as he comes in from the fighting; and let him kill his enemy
and bring home the blooded spoils, and delight the heart of his
   mother."

   So speaking he set his child again in the arms of his beloved
wife, who took him back again to her fragrant bosom
160 smiling in her tears; and her husband saw, and took pity upon her,
and stroked her with his hand, and called her by name and spoke
   to her:
"Poor Andromache! Why does your heart sorrow so much for me?
No man is going to hurl me to Hades, unless it is fated,

16. Hekabe (hek′ əb) *n.*: Queen of Troy; wife of Priam.

17. Messeis (mes′ ē is) *n.*: Wellspring in Greece.
18. Hypereia (hī pēr′ ē ə) *n.*: A spring in Thessaly.

but as for fate, I think that no man yet has escaped it
once it has taken its first form, neither brave man nor coward.
Go therefore back to our house, and take up your own work,
the loom and the distaff,[19] and see to it that your handmaidens
ply[20] their work also; but the men must see to the fighting,
all men who are the people of Ilion, but I beyond others."

*Andromache goes home, where she and her handmaidens mourn
Hektor in anticipation of his death. Paris takes arms and joins Hektor
in driving the Achaians out of Troy. Hektor and the Trojans campaign vigorously until they completely drive the Achaians off the battlefield back to their ships. To prevent the Achaians from sailing away,
the Trojans light watchfires and camp on the plain overnight, ready to
attack in the morning. The demoralized Achaian army feels handicapped by Achilleus' absence. To persuade their most valuable fighter to
reconsider and join the battle, Agamemnon sends Aias and Odysseus
on an embassy to Achilleus.*

19. distaff (dis′ taf′) *n.*: A staff on which fibers are wound before being spun into thread.
20. ply (plī) *n.*: Twist into strands.

22 Discussion Hektor's closing words reiterate his view of the values and roles in his society. Have students discuss those values. What are the assumptions he is making about the way men and women should live their lives?

Humanities Note
Fine art, *Odysseus' Mission to Achilleus*, "The Cleophrades Painter." This three-handled water jar, known to ancient Greeks as a hydria, was painted by one of the greatest artists of the late archaic period, the Cleophrades painter (active from 500 B.C. to 475 B.C.). His work was in the "red-figure technique." The red-figure method of painting allows the natural red of the clay to become the color of the figures by blacking out the background.

In his depiction of Odysseus' mission to Achilleus, (c. 485–475 B.C.) the dejected attitude of Achilleus and the pleading posture of Odysseus are simply and clearly captured through the use of a firm flowing line. Odysseus is seated facing Achilleus. Scenes from the Trojan war were a favorite subject for this highly individualistic vase painter.

Ask students what they can tell from the posture of Achilleus.

ODYSSEUS' MISSION TO ACHILLEUS
Cleophrades Painter
Staatlichen Antikensammlungen und Glyptothek, Munich

will come a day when sacred Ilion shall perish, / and Priam, and the people of Priam of the strong ash spear. / But it is not so much the pain to come of the Trojans that troubles me, not even of Priam the king nor Hekabe . . .

Student Activity 2. Locate the other prepositional phrases on page 352. Identify the objects of the prepositions.

23 **Enrichment** Odysseus' mission to Achilleus occurs in Book IX, which marks the turning point of the *Iliad* and focuses on how the foundation of heroic society is threatened by the continued quarrel of Achilleus and Agamemnon. Agamemnon has admitted to a council of elders that he was driven mad or blinded by "Ate," the embodiment of irrational and self-destructive behavior. He makes atonement by offering Achilleus countless gifts and privileges; but of course his power to offer gifts marks his status as superior to that of Achilleus, which Achilleus resents. Achilleus has also lost faith in the system of unequal exchange that lies at the heart of his society. During the embassy scene, Achilleus' surrogate father Phoinix tells a parable, revealing the way an insult should be atoned for and forgiven: He tells about Ate and Prayers. Ate is young, strong, swift, and sound of limb, like Achilleus. She races ahead, doing harm. Prayers, personified as old women, follow after Ate, hobbling, slow-footed, bleary-eyed and wrinkled. It is their task to try to mend what Ate has destroyed. Propitiation and compromise cannot undo what has been done, but they can allow people to settle their accounts without deadly strife and to go on living in a civilized community.

Cultural Note Weaving is traditionally the role of women in ancient Greek society. They make the clothing for the household, and this includes the important task of weaving shrouds for dead family members. They weave stories; complicated representations of legend and myth are described in literature and can be seen on the clothing depicted on vase painting.

In his speech to Achilleus, Odysseus reminds him of his father's advice. Peleus had told Achilleus that the Argives would hold him in higher honor if he did not let the anger of his proud heart get the best of him. Odysseus adds that if Achilleus gives up his anger and joins the Achaians in battle, Agamemnon has promised to give Achilleus numerous war prizes, including the prize he stole: Briseis. Finally, Odysseus pleads with Achilleus to fight, if not in acceptance of Agamemnon's offer, at least for the afflicted Achaians who will honor Achilleus as a god. Agamemnon's offer serves only to drive Achilleus deeper into his pride. Hurt, dishonored, and above all, angry, he refuses to help the Greeks defeat Hektor and the Trojans. Odysseus and Aias return to Agamemnon with the news of their unsuccessful embassy.

23

Reader's Response *Andromache's plea to Hektor to remain with her and their child is one of the most poignant in all literature. What would you have done in Hektor's place? Would you have stayed with her or would you have gone to battle? Explain.*

PRIMARY SOURCE

"The Meeting of Hektor and Andromache" shows how Hektor's loyalty to his family conflicts with his loyalty to Troy. As a husband and father, he is responsible for caring for his wife and child, but as a man and hero, he belongs on the battlefield, fighting for Troy with fellow Trojans. In his response to Andromache's plea that he remain within the safe walls of Troy, Hektor articulates how acutely he feels the conflict. In *The Mortal Hero: An Introduction to Homer's Iliad*, Seth Schein interprets the exchange between Hektor and Andromache as follows:

". . . After expressing both his sorrow at the slavery that awaits her after the inevitable fall of Troy and his wish that he might be dead before he witnesses it, Hektor prays to Zeus and the other gods to make his son outstanding, like himself, as a warrior and ruler among the Trojans. Hektor realizes that the war will lead to the destruction of his city and the enslavement of his wife, but the only wish that he can make for Astyanax is that he be a preeminent warrior and hence a joy to his mother. Even Hektor's final words, meant as encouragement to Andromache, have to do with his 'portion,' with what can't be changed. Just as Achilleus is trapped within the contradictions of a heroism he transcends but to which he has no alternative, so Hektor, as the defender of his city, cannot escape the consequences of a heroic way of life that necessarily involves both his own destruction and the abandonment and destruction of the family he loves more than his city and more than all the world."

Primary Source Note

Achilleus' dilemma is clear in Book IX. He is obsessed with the insult he has suffered, and he has lost faith in the system of honor and exchange that makes a warrior's life possible. Yet he has no other values to substitute for the system he rejects: He wants recompense but reveals the gaping void created by the quarrel:

Not if he gave me ten times as much, and twenty times over / as he possesses now, not if more should come to him from elsewhere, / or gave all that is brought in to Orchomenos, all that is brought in / to Thebes of Egypt, where the greatest possessions lie up in the houses, / Thebes of the hundred gates, where through each of the gates two hundred / fighting men come forth to war with horses and chariots; / not if he gave me gifts as many as the sand or the dust is, / not even so

from Book XVIII:
The Arming of Achilleus

After Achilleus refuses Agamemnon's offer, the Achaian plight rapidly deteriorates; Agamemnon, Diomedes, and Odysseus are wounded. Unyielding, Achilleus still refuses to aid the Achaians, but he agrees to allow Patroklos to fight wearing Achilleus' armor. Disguised as Achilleus, Patroklos manages to drive the Trojans back to the walls of Troy until Apollo intervenes and helps Hektor kill Patroklos. Achilleus' armor then becomes Hektor's. A bitter fight ensues over Patroklos' body, which the Achaians rescue in order to perform the proper funeral rites. Nestor delivers the sorrowful news of Patroklos' death to Achilleus.

Then sighing heavily Achilleus of the swift feet answered her
    [Thetis]:
"My mother, all these things the Olympian brought to
    accomplishment.
But what pleasure is this to me, since my dear companion has
    perished,
Patroklos, whom I loved beyond all other companions,
as well as my own life. I have lost him, and Hektor, who killed
    him,
has stripped away that gigantic armor, a wonder to look on
and splendid, which the gods gave Peleus, a glorious present,
on that day they drove you to the marriage bed of a mortal.
I wish you had gone on living then with the other goddesses
of the sea, and that Peleus had married some mortal woman.
As it is, there must be on your heart a numberless sorrow
for your son's death, since you can never again receive him
won home again to his country; since the spirit within does not
    drive me
to go on living and be among men, except on condition
that Hektor first be beaten down under my spear, lose his life
and pay the price for stripping Patroklos, the son of Menoitios."
    Then in turn Thetis spoke to him, letting the tears fall:
"Then I must lose you soon, my child, by what you are saying,
since it is decreed your death must come soon after Hektor's."
    Then deeply disturbed Achilleus of the swift feet answered her:
"I must die soon, then; since I was not to stand by my companion
when he was killed. And now, far away from the land of his fathers,
he has perished, and lacked my fighting strength to defend him.
Now, since I am not going back to the beloved land of my fathers,

would Agamemnon have his way with my spirit / until he had made good to me all this heartrendering insolence (lines 379–387).

Aias, second only to Achilleus as a fighter, expresses what he finds is wrong and incomprehensible about Achilleus' refusal:

Let us go . . . seeing that Achilleus / has made savage the proud-hearted spirit within his body. / He is hard, and does not remember that friends, affection / wherein we honored him by the ships, far beyond all others. / Pitiless. And yet a man takes from his brother's slayer / the blood price, or the price for a child who was killed, and the guilty / one, when he has largely repaid, stays still in the country, / and the injured man's heart is curbed, and his pride, and his anger / when he has taken the price; but the gods put in your breast a spirit / not to be placated, bad, for the sake of one single / girl . . . (lines 624–638).

Motivation/Prior Knowledge Tell students that they will be reading about a young hero preparing to meet his certain death. Have them remember Hektor's farewell to Andromache as they read about Achilleus' preparing to die in avenging his beloved companion Patroklos, whom he loved more than his own life, as he says.

Purpose-Setting Question What do we learn about Achilleus' frame of mind? What is his attitude toward living and dying?

Universal Themes For Achilleus, risking his life is now inextricably tied to revenge. The toll vengeance takes on the avenger is a recurrent theme in literature. Have students think about this issue when they come to read *The Tempest*, page 709: Prospero has the power to get revenge, and he must use it wisely. Caliban is also attracted by the thought of revenge.

1 **Discussion** Ask students how they respond to this show of deep emotion on Achilleus' part. How has the loss of his friend changed his view of what "honor from Zeus" means?

2 **Enrichment** When Patroklos' corpse is stripped, the armor of Achilleus' father, Peleus, a wedding present from the gods, is lost. Armor mattered to serious warriors: Only Paris seems not to have armor he cares about, but at one point he borrows a corselet from one of his brothers, since it happens to fit him. What does it say about Achilleus' state of mind, however, that he does not dwell on the loss of honor associated with the loss of his father's armor, but on the futility of human bonds and expectations?

3 **Discussion** What is the dramatic effect of Achilleus' certainty that killing Hektor means choosing his own death?

THE FIGHT OVER THE BODY OF PATROKLOS
Giulio Romano
Ducal Palace, Hall of Troy, Mantua, Italy

25 since I was no light of safety to Patroklos, nor to my other
companions, who in their numbers went down before glorious
    Hektor,
but sit here beside my ships, a useless weight on the good land,
I, who am such as no other of the bronze-armored Achaians
in battle, though there are others also better in council—
why, I wish that strife would vanish away from among gods and
30   mortals,
and gall,[1] which makes a man grow angry for all his great mind,
that gall of anger that swarms like smoke inside of a man's heart
and becomes a thing sweeter to him by far than the dripping of
    honey.
So it was here that the lord of men Agamemnon angered me.
35 Still, we will let all this be a thing of the past, and for all our
sorrow beat down by force the anger deeply within us.
Now I shall go, to overtake that killer of a dear life,
Hektor; then I will accept my own death, at whatever
time Zeus wishes to bring it about, and the other immortals.
40 For not even the strength of Herakles[2] fled away from destruction,

1. **gall** (gôl) *n.*: Bitter feeling

2. **strength of Herakles** (her′ ə klēz′): Herakles was worshipped for his physical strength and courage. Born of Zeus and a mortal woman, Herakles was hated by Zeus' jealous wife Hera, who forced him to undertake twelve great labors. On his final adventure, he died from wearing a poisoned tunic.

Grammar in Action

Sentence Structure Experimenting with the length and structure of sentences adds variety to your writing. Paragraphs consisting of sentences that are all structured using normal word order are dull and flat. Normal word order involves the verb following the subject. When the subject follows the verb, order is **inverted**. Normal word order is also inverted when the direct object comes before the subject. In addition to adding variety to your writing, inversion allows you to emphasize ideas economically. For example, Homer emphasizes the number of people Hektor killed by using inverted word order:

"since I was no light of safety to Patroklos, nor to my other / companions, who in their numbers went down before Glorious Hektor" (lines 25–27).

Inverted sentence patterns can also enhance the sense of drama in writing. Note the dramatic effect created when the direct object appears before the subject in line 71:

Ah me. It was an empty word I cast forth on that day.

Placing "word" early in the sentence emphasizes the speaker's sense of defeat and despair. Inversion is a typical sentence pattern in the *Iliad*.

although he was dearest of all to lord Zeus, son of Kronos,[3]
but his fate beat him under, and the wearisome anger of Hera.
So I likewise, if such is the fate which has been wrought for me,
shall lie still, when I am dead. Now I must win excellent glory,
and drive some one of the women of Troy, or some deep-girdled
Dardanian woman,[4] lifting up to her soft cheeks both hands
to wipe away the close bursts of tears in her lamentation,
and learn that I stayed too long out of the fighting. Do not
hold me back from the fight, though you love me. You will not
    persuade me."
In turn the goddess Thetis of the silver feet answered him:
"Yes, it is true, my child, this is no cowardly action,
to beat aside sudden death from your afflicted companions.
Yet, see now, your splendid armor, glaring and brazen,[5]
is held among the Trojans, and Hektor of the shining helmet
wears it on his own shoulders, and glories in it. Yet I think
he will not glory for long, since his death stands very close to him.
Therefore do not yet go into the grind of the war god,
not before with your own eyes you see me come back to you.
For I am coming to you at dawn and as the sun rises
bringing splendid armor to you from the lord Hephaistos."

*Hera sends Iris to persuade Achilleus to rise up and help protect
Patroklos' corpse from the Trojans. Without his armor but with
Athene's protection, Achilleus shows himself at the ditch, terrifying the
Trojans. Hektor, thirsty for glory, orders his men not to retreat.*

                Meanwhile the Achaians
mourned all night in lamentation over Patroklos.
Peleus' son led the thronging[6] chant of their lamentation,
and laid his manslaughtering hands over the chest of his dear friend
with outbursts of incessant grief. As some great bearded lion
when some man, a deer hunter, has stolen his cubs away from him
out of the close wood; the lion comes back too late, and is
    anguished,
and turns into many valleys quartering[7] after the man's trail
on the chance of finding him, and taken with bitter anger;
so he, groaning heavily, spoke out to the Myrmidons:
"Ah me. It was an empty word I cast forth on that day
when in his halls I tried to comfort the hero Menoitios.
I told him I would bring back his son in glory to Opous[8]
with Ilion sacked, and bringing his share of war spoils allotted.
But Zeus does not bring to accomplishment all thoughts in men's
    minds.
Thus it is destiny for us both to stain the same soil[9]
here in Troy; since I shall never come home, and my father,
Peleus the aged rider, will not welcome me in his great house,
nor Thetis my mother, but in this place the earth will receive me.
But seeing that it is I, Patroklos, who follow you underground,

3. **Kronos** (krō′ nŏs):
Supreme deity until he was
superseded by his son Zeus.

4. **Dardanian** (där da′ nē·ən)
women *n.*: Women associated
with Trojan allies.

5. **brazen** (brā′zən) *adj.*: Of
brass or like brass in color.

6. **thronging** (thrôŋ′ iŋ) *adj.*:
Collective.

7. **quartering** (kwôrt′ ər iŋ)
v.: Passing back and forth over
an area.

8. **Opous** (ō′ pəs) *n.*: City in
Lokris, a district in east-central
Greece where Aias ruled.

9. **stain the same soil:** That
is, with blood; die in the same
place.

6 **Discussion** Achilleus accepts the idea of his death and focuses on "excellent glory" for the moment. Have students speculate on the meaning of winning glory if one has rejected the standards and values of the heroic code.

7 **Enrichment** Mourning for the dead is traditionally the task of women, primarily, and it is they who lead the keening and ritual laments in the *Iliad*. Throughout the poem, Achilleus has a maternal side, usually revealed in similes: He likens himself to a mother bird feeding her young in the nest, to a mother whose little girl (Patroklos, in this case) clutches tearfully at her skirt. What does this more feminine and sensitive aspect of Achilleus add to his greatness as a warrior?

8 **Discussion** Have students look carefully at this simile. Achilleus is likened to a father lion, bereft of his cubs. How does he seem in comparison to Hektor, as a father? Does it make sense that his feeling toward Patroklos leads him to think about Patroklos' father, and about his own, both of whom will have lost their sons?

Student Activity 1. Locate other examples of inversions on pages 356–357.

Student Activity 2. Summarize Book VI of the *Iliad*, using inverted sentences wherever you think appropriate. For example, you might use inversion when you want to emphasize an action or an idea, or when you want to enhance the sense of drama.

THE TROJANS
WITHDRAW TO THE
TOWN: HEKTOR ALONE
STOPS TO WAIT FOR
ACHILLEUS
Ilias Ambrosiana

I will not bury you till I bring to this place the armor
and the head of Hektor, since he was your great-hearted murderer.
Before your burning pyre[10] I shall behead twelve glorious
children of the Trojans, for my anger over your slaying.
85 Until then, you shall lie where you are in front of my curved ships
and beside you women of Troy and deep-girdled Dardanian
    women
shall sorrow for you night and day and shed tears for you, those whom
you and I worked hard to capture by force and the long spear
in days when we were storming the rich cities of mortals."

The Achaians wash and anoint Patroklos' body, shroud him, and lament him all night. Meanwhile, Thetis visits Hephaistos to ask him to make Achilleus' new armor.

Hearing her the renowned smith[11] of the strong arms answered her
90   [Thetis]:
"Do not fear. Let not these things be a thought in your mind.
And I wish that I could hide him away from death and its sorrow
at that time when his hard fate comes upon him, as surely
as there shall be fine armor for him, such as another
95 man out of many men shall wonder at, when he looks on it."
    So he spoke, and left her there, and went to his bellows.[12]
He turned these toward the fire and gave them their orders for
    working.
And the bellows, all twenty of them, blew on the crucibles,[13]
from all directions blasting forth wind to blow the flames high

10. pyre (pīr) *n.*: A pile of wood on which a dead body is burned during a funeral.

11. smith (smith) *n.*: The metalworker Hephaistos (hef ī´ stōs).

12. bellows (bel´ ōz) *n.*: Tools used to produce air for blowing fires.
13. crucibles (krōō´ sə bəlz) *n.*: Containers that can resist great heat, for melting or fusing metals.

now as he hurried to be at this place and now at another,
wherever Hephaistos might wish them to blow, and the work went
    forward.
He cast on the fire bronze which is weariless, and tin with it
and valuable gold, and silver, and thereafter set forth
upon its standard the great anvil,[14] gripped in one hand
the ponderous[15] hammer, while in the other he grasped the
    pincers.[16]

First of all he forged[17] a shield that was huge and heavy,
elaborating[18] it about, and threw around it a shining
triple rim that glittered, and the shield strap was cast of silver.
There were five folds composing the shield itself, and upon it
he elaborated many things in his skill and craftsmanship.

He made the earth upon it, and the sky, and the sea's water,
and the tireless sun, and the moon waxing[19] into her fullness,
and on it all the constellations that festoon[20] the heavens,
the Pleiades and the Hyades and the strength of Orion
and the Bear, whom men give also the name of the Wagon,
who turns about in a fixed place and looks at Orion
and she alone is never plunged in the wash of the Ocean.

On it he wrought in all their beauty two cities of mortal
men. And there were marriages in one, and festivals.
They were leading the brides along the city from their maiden
    chambers
under the flaring of torches, and the loud bride song was arising.
The young men followed the circles of the dance, and among them
the flutes and lyres kept up their clamor as in the meantime
the women standing each at the door of her court admired them.
The people were assembled in the market place, where a quarrel
had arisen, and two men were disputing over the blood price
for a man who had been killed. One man promised full restitution[21]
in a public statement, but the other refused and would accept
    nothing.
Both then made for an arbitrator,[22] to have a decision;
and people were speaking up on either side, to help both men.
But the heralds kept the people in hand, as meanwhile the elders
were in session on benches of polished stone in the sacred circle
and held in their hands the staves[23] of the heralds who lift their
    voices.
The two men rushed before these, and took turns speaking their
    cases,
and between them lay on the ground two talents of gold, to be
    given
to that judge who in this case spoke the straightest opinion.[24]

But around the other city were lying two forces of armed men
shining in their war gear. For one side counsel was divided
whether to storm and sack, or share between both sides the
    property

14. anvil (an'vəl) *n.*: An iron block on which metal objects are hammered into shape.
15. ponderous (pän' dər əs) *adj.*: Very heavy.
16. pincers (pin' sərz) *n.*: Tool used to grip objects.
17. forged (forjd) *v.*: Made by heating and hammering metal into shape.
18. elaborating (ē lab' ə rāt' iŋ) *n.*: Decorating carefully and in great detail.
19. waxing (waks' iŋ) *v.*: Growing gradually larger in phases.
20. festoon (fes tōōn') *v.*: Adorn.

11

21. restitution (res' tə tōō' shən) *n.*: Reimbursement; an act of making up for loss or damage.
22. arbitrator (är' bə trāt' ər) *n.*: A person chosen to judge and settle a dispute.

12

23. staves (stāvz) *n.*: Plural of staff. Heralds carried a staff as a mark of office; they could command attention or silence by pounding it on the ground. It served the same function as a judge's gavel.

24. straightest opinion: Wisest and fairest opinion.

13

Master Teacher Note Students should try to visualize the shield. Constructing a diagram on the board might help students "place" the scene and visualize the shield. The shield is encompassed by the Ocean River (lines 234–235), which bounds the earth that human beings inhabit. But the shield also includes the heavens and constellations and the natural universe with its cyclical seasons.

11 Discussion The two cities, one at peace and one at war, suggest all the activities of mankind and all the aspects of the *Iliad*, which includes the peacetime world largely through its similes. What activity is first described in the city at peace? What does marriage stand for?

12 Discussion What is significant about the dispute taking place in the city at peace? What is the quarrel about? Call students' attention to the fact that the quarrel scene includes a vivid description of a tribal council. Students may have read, heard about, or seen portrayals of similar mechanisms for solving disputes within a community and averting blood feuds in other close-knit groups.

13 Discussion How does the city at war make us think about Troy? In what ways does the shield, contained within the poem, also contain in microcosm the poem itself?

She looked over his shoulder
    For vines and olive trees,
Marble well-governed cities
    And ships upon untamed seas,
But there on the shining metal
    His hands had put instead
An artificial wilderness
    And a sky like lead.

A plain without a feature, bare and brown,
    No blade of grass, no sign of neighborhood,
Nothing to eat and nowhere to sit down,
    Yet, congregated on its blankness, stood
    An unintelligible multitude.
A million eyes, a million boots in line,
Without expression, waiting for a sign.

and all the possessions the lovely citadel held hard within it.
But the city's people were not giving way, and armed for an
    ambush.
Their beloved wives and their little children stood on the rampart
to hold it, and with them the men with age upon them, but
    meanwhile
the others went out. And Ares led them, and Pallas Athene.
These were gold, both, and golden raiment[25] upon them, and they
    were
beautiful and huge in their armor, being divinities,
and conspicuous from afar, but the people around them were
    smaller.
These, when they were come to the place that was set for their
    ambush,
in a river, where there was a watering place for all animals,
there they sat down in place shrouding[26] themselves in the bright
    bronze.
But apart from these were sitting two men to watch for the rest of
    them
and waiting until they could see the sheep and the shambling
    cattle,
who appeared presently, and two herdsmen went along with them
playing happily on pipes, and took no thought of the treachery.[27]
Those others saw them, and made a rush, and quickly thereafter
cut off on both sides the herds of cattle and the beautiful
flocks of shining sheep, and killed the shepherds upon them.
But the other army, as soon as they heard the uproar arising
from the cattle, as they sat in their councils, suddenly mounted
behind their light-foot horses, and went after, and soon overtook
    them.
These stood their ground and fought a battle by the banks of the
    river,
and they were making casts at each other with their spears bronze-
    headed;
and Hate was there with Confusion among them, and Death the
    destructive;
she was holding a live man with a new wound, and another
one unhurt, and dragged a dead man by the feet through the
    carnage.[28]
The clothing upon her shoulders showed strong red with the
    men's blood.
All closed together like living men and fought with each other
and dragged away from each other the corpses of those who had
    fallen.
  He made upon it a soft field, the pride of the tilled land,
wide and triple-plowed, and many plowmen upon it
who wheeled their teams at the turn and drove them in either
    direction.

Line markers: 145, 14, 15, 150, 155, 160, 165, 16, 170

25. raiment (rā′ mənt) *n.*: Apparel; clothing.

26. shrouding (shroud′ iŋ) *v.*: Wrapping to shelter and protect.

27. treachery (trech′ ər ē) *n.*: Disloyalty or treason.

28. carnage (kär′ nij) *n.*: Dead bodies on a battlefield.

14 Enrichment Early Greek poetry contains relatively few words for colors (red/gold, yellow-green, blue/purple/black predominate) but lays great stress on contrasting degrees of brightness, on the quality of light reflected off different surfaces. Have students visualize the shield as an artifact made up of differently colored textured metals, with figures and objects depicted in higher or lower relief, and so casting shadows.

Enrichment A representation of an ancient Greek object depicting a detailed scene in relief might help students visualize the shield. Or students might be reminded of extremely detailed and complex scenes carved in wood that can be found in medieval, Baroque, and Renaissance art.

15 Literary Focus Draw students' attention to the way narrative interpretation forms part of the description of the scene. What elements are purely "descriptive" of the visual object? What elements form the narrative?

16 Discussion Have students consider Homer's technique of using peacetime similes in battle scenes. How does Homer's juxtaposition of human activity in battle with human activity in a nonmartial context invite us to reflect on the many aspects of human life?

Grammar in Action

Compound Verbs A **compound verb** consists of two or more verbs that are joined by a conjunction and have the same subject. Use compound verbs to indicate two closely related actions.

It is important to distinguish between compound verbs and compound sentences. Compound sentences consist of two complete subject-verb predications, separated by a comma. For example,

"These were gold, both, and golden raiment upon them, and they were beautiful and huge in their armor, being divinities . . ." as excerpted is a compound sentence; it has a subject (these) and a verb (were), followed by a comma, a conjunction, and another subject (they) and a verb (were).

Compound verbs have only one subject, and they are not separated by commas. Lines 161–162 contain an example of a compound verb: "These stood their ground and fought a battle by the banks of the river . . ." You will notice that your translation of the *Iliad* contains several compound verbs incorrectly separated by commas: "About he made a field-ditch of dark metal, and drove all around this a fence of tin." In correct grammatical construction, there are no commas between verbs in a compound verb.

Student Activity 1. Locate examples of compound verbs on pages 360–361.

And as these making their turn would reach the end-strip of the field,
a man would come up to them at this point and hand them a flagon
of honey-sweet wine, and they would turn again to the furrows[29]
in their haste to come again to the end-strip of the deep field.
The earth darkened behind them and looked like earth that has been plowed
though it was gold. Such was the wonder of the shield's forging.

   He made on it the precinct[30] of a king, where the laborers
were reaping with the sharp reaping hooks in their hands. Of the cut swathes[31]
some fell along the lines of reaping, one after another,
while the sheaf-binders caught up others and tied them with bind-ropes.
There were three sheaf-binders who stood by, and behind them
were children picking up the cut swathes, and filled their arms with them
and carried and gave them always; and by them the king in silence
and holding his staff stood near the line of the reapers, happily.
And apart and under a tree the heralds made a feast ready
and trimmed a great ox they had slaughtered. Meanwhile the women
scattered, for the workmen to eat, abundant white barley.

   He made on it a great vineyard heavy with clusters,
lovely and in gold, but the grapes upon it were darkened
and the vines themselves stood out through poles of silver. About them
he made a field-ditch of dark metal, and drove all around this
a fence of tin; and there was only one path to the vineyard,
and along it ran the grape-bearers for the vineyard's stripping.
Young girls and young men, in all their light-hearted innocence,
carried the kind, sweet fruit away in their woven baskets,
and in their midst a youth with a singing lyre played charmingly
upon it for them, and sang the beautiful song for Linos
in a light voice, and they followed him, and with singing and whistling
and light dance-steps of their feet kept time to the music.

   He made upon it a herd of horn-straight oxen. The cattle
were wrought of gold and of tin, and thronged in speed and with lowing
out of the dung of the farmyard to a pasturing place by a sounding
river, and beside the moving field of a reed bed.
The herdsmen were of gold who went along with the cattle,
four of them, and nine dogs shifting their feet followed them.
But among the foremost of the cattle two formidable[32] lions
had caught hold of a bellowing[33] bull, and he with loud lowings
was dragged away, as the dogs and the young men went in pursuit of him.

29. **furrows** (fur´ ōz) *n.*: Narrow grooves made in the ground by plows.

30. **precinct** (prē´ siŋkt´) *n.*: A section or division of land under one rule.
31. **swathes** (swäthz) *n.*: Wrapped bundles of wheat.

32. **formidable** (for´ mə də bəl) *adj.*: Arousing fear; difficult to overcome.
33. **bellowing** (bel´ ō iŋ) *v.*: Roaring powerfully.

17 **Discussion** Have students discuss the similarities and contrasts in the rhythm and eagerness of the farmers at work and of the soldiers on the battlefield.

18 **Enrichment** Ask students if they have seen paintings of reapers from other cultures and centuries. For Homer's audience, farming scenes would have been familiar. Ask students how evoking a familiar scene makes the message of the shield seem personal and universal.

19 **Enrichment** That the field being plowed is sacred land allotted to the king of the community makes this harvesting scene a community endeavor, as the feast prepared for the laborers also suggests.

20 **Clarification** Communal harvesting, feasting, singing and dancing, and marrying were for the Greeks at the heart of a well-knit and healthy community. They were also the elements celebrated in Athenian comedy in the fifth century B.C. In the context of a religious and civic festival in honor of Dionysus that spanned the entire agricultural year, the Athenians celebrated their *polis,* or city-state, and its values, especially in comic drama.

21 **Literary Focus** Ask students to discuss what words are purely visual and what words suggest other senses.

Student Activity 2. Were the examples you found correctly punctuated? Correct those that were not.

HEPHAISTOS MAKING ARMOR FOR ACHILLEUS
The Dutuit painter,
c. 480 B.C.
Museum of Fine Arts, Boston

210 But the two lions, breaking open the hide of the great ox,
gulped the black blood and the inward guts, as meanwhile the herdsmen
were in the act of setting and urging the quick dogs on them.
But they, before they could get their teeth in, turned back from the lions,
but would come and take their stand very close, and bayed, and kept clear.
And the renowned smith of the strong arms made on it a meadow
215 large and in a lovely valley for the glimmering sheepflocks,
with dwelling places upon it, and covered shelters, and sheepfolds.
And the renowned smith of the strong arms made elaborate on it
a dancing floor, like that which once in the wide spaces of Knosos³⁴

34. Knosos (näs′ əs): Capital of the Minoan empire, ruled by King Minos.

Daidalos[35] built for Ariadne[36] of the lovely tresses.[37]
And there were young men on it and young girls, sought for their
    beauty
with gifts of oxen, dancing, and holding hands at the wrist. These
wore, the maidens long light robes, but the men wore tunics
of finespun work and shining softly, touched with olive oil.
And the girls wore fair garlands on their heads, while the young
    men
carried golden knives that hung from sword-belts of silver.
At whiles[38] on their understanding feet they would run very lightly,
as when a potter crouching makes trial of his wheel, holding
it close in his hands, to see if it will run smooth. At another
time they would form rows, and run, rows crossing each other.
And around the lovely chorus of dancers stood a great multitude
happily watching, while among the dancers two acrobats
led the measures of song and dance revolving among them.
    He made on it the great strength of the Ocean River
which ran around the uttermost rim of the shield's strong
    structure.
    Then after he had wrought this shield, which was huge and
    heavy,
he wrought for him a corselet brighter than fire in its shining,
and wrought him a helmet, massive and fitting close to his temples,
lovely and intricate work, and laid a gold top-ridge along it,
and out of pliable tin wrought him leg-armor. Thereafter
when the renowned smith of the strong arms had finished the
    armor
he lifted it and laid it before the mother of Achilleus.
And she like a hawk came sweeping down from the snows of
    Olympos
and carried with her the shining armor, the gift of Hephaistos.

Reader's Response *At some point, everyone feels wronged by
another person. Some people insist on "getting even." Others
turn the other cheek. Is revenge ever justifiable? Is it ever
productive? Explain your answers.*

THINKING ABOUT THE SELECTION

Interpreting

1. (a) Why does Helen wish she had been swept away
by the storm on the day of her birth? (b) How do her
words reveal the difference between her and her
husband, Paris?

2. Hektor tells Andromache he would feel deep shame
if he did not fight the Achaians. What do his feelings
indicate about the values of his society?

3. (a) By saying that no one, brave man or coward,
has escaped fate, what is Hektor indicating about
his own mortality? (b) Whom would you consider
the braver man—Hektor or Paris? Why?

35. **Daidalos** (dā´ də lōs): An
artist-engineer famous for
constructing the labyrinth in
which lived the man-eating
Minotaur (half bull, half man),
and for making wings out of
wax. When he and his son
Icarus used the wings to fly,
Icarus came too near the sun,
the wax melted, and he
plunged to his death in the sea.

36. **Ariadne** (a´ rē ad´ nē):
Daughter of Minos and
princess of Knossos, who
helped prince Theseus escape
from the labyrinth after killing
the Minotaur. Theseus later
married her younger sister
Phaidra.

37. **tresses** (tres´əz) *n.*: Locks
of hair.

38. **At whiles:** At times.

(continued on page 364)

(continued from page 363)

corresponding to the warrior code by which Achilleus and Hektor live.

4. In their answers, students should note that the *Iliad*, unlike the quote from *Macbeth*, accepts reality and affirms human life, while looking unflinchingly at ugliness and tragedy. Understanding the shield as a microcosm of the *Iliad*, students should see that the inclusion of the constellations, placing human activities in the context of the seasonal cycle, and looking unjudgmentally at ambush and a murder trial alongside harvest festivals assumes life is meaningful.

ANSWERS TO CRITICAL THINKING AND READING

1. Hektor's parents are both mortal; he is associated with a wife and a baby; he is viewed by others as human rather than as a destructive force.

2. Hektor's reasons for winning glory are associated with his community—what the Trojans will think of him. He is also concerned with protecting his family. Achilleus' reasons for winning glory are purely for himself.

ANSWERS TO UNDERSTANDING LANGUAGE

1. Suggested response: The epithets, such as "gray-eyed goddess Athene," are similar to epithets found in nursery rhymes like "Peter, Peter, Pumpkin Eater."

2. Answers may differ. Students should notice the repetition of lines and phrases and the pattern of referring to characters using their epithets.

THINKING AND WRITING

Publishing Student Writing Invite students to share their analysis of divine causality in class. Encourage class members to respond to the papers being read.

Challenge Encourage students to go to the library and look at a copy of the *Iliad* in its entirety. Students may want to read other books in the *Iliad*. Book IX would be of particular interest to students while they're studying Books VI and XVIII.

4. (a) Why does Achilleus blame himself for Patroklos' death? (b) Is his self-incrimination justified? Why or why not?
5. What causes Achilleus to overcome his intense fury and join the fighting?
6. Hephaistos says that he wishes he could forge a shield that would protect Achilleus from his "hard fate." (a) Based on your reading of the *Iliad* so far, is it ever possible for human beings to escape their fate? Explain. (b) What role do Achilleus' personal characteristics play in bringing about his fate?
7. (a) What insights into life do we receive from the scenes on Achilleus' shield? (b) In what two ways is the shield truly "a gift from Hephaistos"?

Applying

8. Both Hektor and Achilleus make a conscious decision to confront death, which makes them heroic in the eyes of ancient Greeks. Does modern society consider people who consciously confront death heroic? Explain.
9. The Greek playwright Sophocles wrote, "Fate has terrible power. / You cannot escape it by wealth or war. / No fort will keep it out, no ships outrun it." In your opinion, how does the contemporary view of fate differ from the ancient Grecian view?

ANALYZING LITERATURE

Analyzing the Imagery of Achilleus' Shield

In his description of Achilleus' shield, Homer's **imagery** captures the complex world of the *Iliad*. The marriage ceremonies and harvest festivals of one of the cities on the shield represent the joyous side of life, while the city beleaguered by two armies contains images of the pathos of war.

1. How are images of violence on the shield balanced by images of plowing and harvesting?
2. What is the significance of the Ocean River that runs around the outermost rim of the shield?
3. From the text, find images of war and peace and discuss ways in which they correspond with the human nature of characters in the *Iliad*.
4. In *Macbeth*, William Shakespeare wrote, "Life's but a walking shadow, a poor player, / That struts and frets his hour upon the stage / And then is heard no more. It is a tale / Told by an idiot, full of sound and fury, / Signifying nothing." Compare and contrast the view of life presented in this quotation with that presented on Achilleus' shield.

CRITICAL THINKING AND READING

Comparing and Contrasting Characters

According to the heroic code of ethics, male characters in the *Iliad* must fight to win glory, for their families and for themselves. Each hero, however, responds differently to the warrior code he learned since childhood. Consider how differently Achilleus and Hektor behave as heroes.

1. Which hero is characterized as being more human? Find examples to support your answer.
2. Contrast Achilleus' reasons for winning glory with Hektor's reasons.

UNDERSTANDING LANGUAGE

Analyzing Oral Literature

The *Iliad* was composed to be heard. The bard telling the story used dramatic delivery and accompanied himself on a lyre, much as skilled storytellers today use musical accompaniment. Fairy tales, tall tales, folk tales, and ballads grew out of an oral tradition as well. As a result of the oral tradition, noticeable language patterns emerged.

1. What kinds of cues, repetitions, and other features do you notice in the *Iliad* that remind you of other forms of oral literature?
2. What techniques of oral storytelling have you noticed in the *Iliad*? What effects do these techniques have on the listener?

THINKING AND WRITING

Writing About Divine Causality

Mortals in the *Iliad* believe in divine causality, the idea that the gods cause human successes or failures. However, the gods' interference is in keeping with the personality of the character. In other words, the gods do not make anyone do anything that that person is not willing to do deep down in his or her being. The critic Martin Hammond has said of this, "Divine causation will work through human inclination." Choose one incident from the *Iliad* that has to do with divine causality. Jot down notes about the causes of the incident. Then write an essay in which you show how divine interference is consistent with the nature of the character involved. When you revise, make sure you have clearly shown both natural and supernatural causes for the incident. Finally, proofread your paper.

Objectives

Thematic
To understand the tragedy of the *Iliad*

Skills
1 To interpret epic similes

2 To understand ancient codes of ethics
3 To identify English words of Greek origin
4 To write about shared humanity

Support Material

Teaching Portfolio
Teacher Backup, p. 483
Grammar in Action Worksheets, *Recognizing Uses of the Hyphen*, p. 489; *Recognizing Types of Imagery*, p. 491; *Using Commas to Separate Basic Elements*, p. 493; *Using Past, Present, and Future*

GUIDE FOR INTERPRETING

from the Iliad, *from* Books XXII and XXIV

Commentary

Epic Similes. Throughout the *Iliad*, Homer connects the immediate scenes he is describing with the wider world of his audience's experience through the use of **epic similes,** elaborate figures of speech that express likeness between two unlike objects. The two things likened to one another must be similar in some way, but frequently the difference is as striking as the likeness. For instance, a man, when struck, may fall like a tree, or Greeks and Trojans fighting over the dead body of Patroklos may look, superficially, like workers stretching an animal hide. Homeric similes achieve a complex effect with great economy of effort. In Books XXII and XXIV, similes invite the audience to view episodes from a different perspective, often from Hektor's perspective.

Achilleus' pursuit of Hektor, and their confrontation, is the culmination of a process set in motion at the opening of the poem, when Achilleus' withdrawal from battle leaves Hektor without a superior opponent. Since the death of Patroklos, the audience has been waiting with mounting suspense for the predicted death of Hektor, which will in turn be followed by Achilleus' death. When Achilleus and Hektor meet, Homer slows his pace with a series of similes, prolonging the pursuit and delaying the inevitable confrontation.

In the first simile in Book XXII, (ll. 42–45) Homer compares Achilleus to a hawk, sure and swift, chasing a trembling, screaming dove: "As when a hawk . . . makes his effortless swoop for a trembling dove but she slips away . . ." The dove is getting away, although the hawk seems likely to win. Homer's audience was used to hunting and might have felt more admiration for the hawk than sympathy with the dove. A later simile (ll. 92–96) compares Achilleus to a hound cornering a fawn: "as a dog in the mountains who has flushed from his covert a deer's fawn . . ." Whereas the dove in the first simile may have stood a chance, the fawn is unquestionably doomed. An especially poignant simile in ll. 102–104 compares Hektor's feelings of helplessness to the feelings of paralysis in a dream, where we want desperately to run but cannot move: "As in a dream a man is not able to follow one who runs . . ." The simile connects Hektor's feelings with an experience that most people have had, which in turn causes the audience to identify, if not sympathize, with Hektor.

Writing

The first lines of the *Iliad* announce its subject —"the anger of Peleus' son Achilleus and its devastation." Before you read the last part of the poem, freewrite, predicting the consequences of Achilleus' rage.

Tenses of Verbs, p. 495; *Using Parallel Structures,* p. 497
Usage and Mechanics Worksheet, p. 499
Vocabulary Check, p. 500
Analyzing Literature Worksheet, *Interpreting Similes,* p. 501

Critical Thinking and Reading Worksheet, *Understanding Ancient Codes of Ethics,* p. 502
Selection Test, pp. 503–504

Literary Focus Have students think about how similes can help readers understand and conceptualize something they might otherwise see simplistically. Sometimes a simile makes us see, hear, or feel something with precision; but the act of comparison itself adds complexity to our perception.

Writing/Prior Knowledge Before they begin freewriting, have students get together in small groups and brainstorm about how they might use figurative language and comparisons to describe violent rage. How might they envision the consequences of powerful anger or fury?

ESL Teaching Strategy Because the epic similes in the *Iliad* are so elaborate and drawn out, ESL students might need to concentrate on them more heavily than on other parts of the poem. You might ask ESL students to paraphrase verbally the epic similes they encounter.

Teaching Tenth-Grade Students Ask your tenth-grade students to tell you what the *Iliad* has taught them about ancient Greek cultural values. What do they know now that they didn't know before they started reading the *Iliad*? Then ask them what the *Iliad* has taught them about human nature and life.

Vocabulary

Preteach the following vocabulary words:
reproach (ri prōch´) *n.*: An expression of blame
unremittingly (un´ ri mit´ iŋ lē) *adv.*: Persistently
beguilement (bē gīl´ mənt) *n.*: Trickery; deceit
avenger (ə ven´ jər) *n.*: One who takes revenge
implored (im plord´) *v.*: Asked or begged earnestly

Presentation

Motivation/Prior Knowledge
Tell students that in Book XXII, Hektor is represented as very human, in contrast to Achilleus, who has been seen in recent books as a natural force, fighting gods, glutting the river with corpses, destroying all in front of him like uncontrolled fire. Have students think about other stories they have encountered in which a human figure meets a superhuman one. How often does the little guy win, and in what kind of genre?

Purpose-Setting Question How does knowing that Hektor will die influence the way we read the story of his fight with Achilleus?

Universal Themes In folk tales, science fiction, romance epics, and many other genres, the underdog, because of his or her very humanity, may beat the troll, the big bully, or "the system." We usually root for the sympathetic underdog and are saddened if he or she is defeated—as often happens in "real life." Have students think about David and Goliath in the Old Testament (page 61), Caliban in *The Tempest* (page 709), and Gregor Samsa in Kafka's *The Metamorphosis* (page 1084).

1 **Reading Strategy** Homer's depictions of characters are acutely perceptive to human nature. As they read, students should pay attention to their emotional reactions to characters; then they should consider what Homer does to elicit these emotional responses. For example, how does seeing Hektor's desire to retreat and his fear of having his brother say "I told you so" make us empathize with him?

2 **Discussion** Ask students to discuss Hektor's emotions. What makes him feel guilty, and how does he envision his shame?

Armed in his divine armor, Achilleus returns to war to avenge Patroklos' death; he kills every Trojan in his path. During combat with Hektor's half-brother Agenor, Apollo assumes Agenor's shape and diverts Achilleus from Troy, allowing Trojan troops to take refuge in the city. Priam and Hekabe try unsuccessfully to convince Hektor to stay within the walls of Troy, safe from Achilleus. However, furious Hektor is determined to fight Achilleus.

Deeply troubled he [Hektor] spoke to his own great-hearted spirit:
"Ah me! If I go now inside the wall and the gateway,
Poulydamas[1] will be first to put a reproach upon me,
since he tried to make me lead the Trojans inside the city
5 on that accursed night when brilliant Achilleus rose up,
and I would not obey him, but that would have been far better.
Now, since by my own recklessness I have ruined my people,
I feel shame before the Trojans and the Trojan women with trailing
robes, that someone who is less of a man than I will say of me:
10 'Hektor believed in his own strength and ruined his people.'
Thus they will speak; and as for me, it would be much better
at that time, to go against Achilleus, and slay him, and come back,
or else be killed by him in glory in front of the city.
Or if again I set down my shield massive in the middle
15 and my ponderous helm, and lean my spear up against the rampart
and go out as I am to meet Achilleus the blameless
and promise to give back Helen, and with her all her possessions,
all those things that once in the hollow ships Alexandros
brought back to Troy, and these were the beginning of the quarrel;
20 to give these to Atreus' sons to take away, and for the Achaians
also to divide up all that is hidden within the city,
and take an oath thereafter for the Trojans in conclave[2]
not to hide anything away, but distribute all of it,
as much as the lovely citadel keeps guarded within it;
25 yet still, why does the heart within me debate on these things?
I might go up to him, and he take no pity upon me
nor respect my position, but kill me naked so, as if I were
a woman, once I stripped my armor from me. There is no
way any more from a tree or a rock to talk to him gently
30 whispering like a young man and a young girl, in the way
a young man and a young maiden whisper together.

1. Poulydamas (pôl′ ə däm′ əs): Fighter and seer who frequently opposed his brother Hektor's reckless strategy.

2. conclave (kän′ klāv′) *n*.: Private or secret meeting.

Primary Source Note

Hektor's courage is all the more poignant and impressive because he has to conquer fear. He has appealed to people for thousands of years as a kind of Everyman. The modern Greek poet Constantine Cavafy makes this connection eloquently in his poem "Trojans":

Our efforts are those of men prone to disaster;
our efforts are like those of the Trojans.
We just begin to get somewhere,
begin to gather a little strength,
grow almost bold and hopeful,
when something always comes up to stop us:
Achilleus leaps out of the trench in front of us
and terrifies us with his violent shouting.

Our efforts are like those of the Trojans.
We think we'll change our luck
by being resolute and daring,
so we move outside ready to fight.

But when the big crisis comes,

HEKTOR AND ANDROMACHE FROM THE DESTRUCTION OF TROY
Franco-Flemish tapestry
The Metropolitan Museum of Art, New York

Humanities Note

Fine art, *Hektor and Andromache*, Franco-Flemish tapestry. Woven tapestries were often commissioned by the nobility of the fifteenth century for use as decorative coverings for the cold stone walls of their castles and châteaus. First an artist would paint a "cartoon" (specific diagram) for the weaver to follow. Then the master weaver would weave the design on a full-sized loom in vegetable-dyed wools.

Hektor and Andromache is a detail from a Flemish tapestry (c. 1472–1474) produced in Tournai, a center for tapestry making. The scene shows Hektor preparing to fight Achilleus in spite of the pleas of Andromache and Priam. Architectural elements are used to denote setting and enclose the scene. The multilayered composition, consisting of many figures in medieval garb, creates a highly decorative effect. The text woven across the top explains the scene. It has led some historians to believe that the inspiration for this tapestry design came from an illuminated manuscript.

You might encourage students to think about the art they have seen so far in this unit. There are several pieces in different styles, created out of different artistic periods, some of which depict scenes from the *Iliad* in details that are uncharacteristic of the poem's temporal setting. Suggest that the different artistic renditions illustrate universal interest in Homer's *Iliad*. What accounts for such universal interest?

You might want to use the following questions to discuss the art:

1. Why might the artist have depicted these figures from the *Iliad* in fifteenth-century clothing?
2. What other art form does a tapestry reveal?

our boldness and resolution vanish;
our spirit falters, paralyzed,
and we scurry around the walls
trying to save ourselves by running
  away.

Yet we're sure to fail. Up there,
high on the walls, the dirge has already begun.
They're mourning the memory, the
aura of our days.
Priam and Hekuba mourn for us bitterly.

Better to bring on the fight with him as soon as it may be.
We shall see to which one the Olympian grants the glory."
So he pondered, waiting, but Achilleus was closing upon him
35 in the likeness of the lord of battles, the helm-shining warrior,
and shaking from above his shoulder the dangerous Pelian[3]
ash spear, while the bronze that closed about him was shining
like the flare of blazing fire or the sun in its rising.
And the shivers took hold of Hektor when he saw him, and he could no longer
stand his ground there, but left the gates behind, and fled, frightened,
40 and Peleus' son went after him in the confidence of his quick feet.
As when a hawk in the mountains who moves lightest of things flying
makes his effortless swoop for a trembling dove, but she slips away
from beneath and flies and he shrill screaming close after her
45 plunges for her again and again, heart furious to take her;
so Achilleus went straight for him in fury, but Hektor
fled away under the Trojan wall and moved his knees rapidly.
They raced along by the watching point and the windy fig tree
always away from under the wall and along the wagon-way
and came to the two sweet-running well springs. There there are double
50 springs of water that jet up, the springs of whirling Skamandros.
One of these runs hot water and the steam on all sides
of it rises as if from a fire that was burning inside it.
But the other in the summer-time runs water that is like hail
55 or chill snow or ice that forms from water. Beside these
in this place, and close to them, are the washing-hollows
of stone, and magnificent, where the wives of the Trojans and their lovely
daughters washed the clothes to shining, in the old days
when there was peace, before the coming of the sons of the Achaians.
60 They ran beside these, one escaping, the other after him.
It was a great man who fled, but far better he who pursued him
rapidly, since here was no festal[4] beast, no ox-hide
they strove for, for these are prizes that are given men for their running.
No, they ran for the life of Hektor, breaker of horses.
65 As when about the turnposts racing single-foot horses
run at full speed, when a great prize is laid up for their winning,
a tripod or a woman, in games for a man's funeral,
so these two swept whirling about the city of Priam
in the speed of their feet, while all the gods were looking upon them.
70 First to speak among them was the father of gods and mortals;
"Ah me, this a man beloved whom now my eyes watch

3. **Pelian** (Pel′ ē ən) *adj.*: Belonging to Peleus, Achilleus' father.

4. **festal** (fes′ təl) *adj.*: Of a joyous celebration.

Grammar in Action

Hyphens have several uses. One important use of the hyphen is to separate compound adjectives. For example, "sweet-running well springs" contains a hyphenated compound adjective. The dozens of compound adjectives in the *Iliad* provide lush, imagistic details.

The epithets you have encountered in the *Iliad* are composed of hyphenated compound adjectives. "Swift-footed Achilleus" and "gray-eyed Athene" are only two of the many epithets with which you are now familiar. Hyphenating compound adjectives and using them as epithets enabled

Homer to preserve the meter of his poem and provide the audience with ways to recognize characters for their most outstanding qualities.

It is important, however, not to confuse all hyphenated compound adjectives as epithets. The compound adjectives in the following passage are not epithets: "But the other in the summer-time runs water that is like hail / or chill snow or ice that forms from water. Beside these in this place, and close to them, are the washing-hollows of stone . . ." Only hyphenated compound adjectives used to describe or identify characters are epithets.

Student Activity 1. Locate all the compound adjectives on pages 368–369. If the examples you find are epithets, label them as such.

being chased around the wall; my heart is mourning for Hektor
who has burned in my honor many thigh pieces of oxen
on the peaks of Ida[5] with all her folds, or again on the uttermost
part of the citadel, but now the brilliant Achilleus
drives him in speed of his feet around the city of Priam.
Come then, you immortals, take thought and take counsel, whether
to rescue this man or whether to make him, for all his valor,
go down under the hands of Achilleus, the son of Peleus."

Then in answer the goddess gray-eyed Athene spoke to him:
"Father of the shining bolt, dark misted, what is this you said?
Do you wish to bring back a man who is mortal, one long since
doomed by his destiny, from ill-sounding death and release him?
Do it, then; but not all the rest of us gods shall approve you."

Then Zeus the gatherer of the clouds spoke to her in answer:
"Tritogeneia,[6] dear daughter, do not lose heart; for I say this
not in outright anger, and my meaning toward you is kindly.
Act as your purpose would have you do, and hold back no longer."

So he spoke, and stirred on Athene, who was eager before this,
and she went in a flash of speed down the pinnacles of Olympos.

But swift Achilleus kept unremittingly after Hektor,
chasing him, as a dog in the mountains who has flushed from his
    covert[7]
a deer's fawn follows him through the folding ways and the valleys,
and though the fawn crouched down under a bush and be hidden
he keeps running and noses him out until he comes on him;
so Hektor could not lose himself from swift-footed Peleion.
If ever he made a dash right on for the gates of Dardanos
to get quickly under the strong-built bastion, endeavoring
that they from above with missiles thrown might somehow defend
    him,
each time Achilleus would get in front and force him to turn back
into the plain, and himself kept his flying course next the city.
As in a dream a man is not able to follow one who runs
from him, nor can the runner escape, nor the other pursue him,
so he could not run him down in his speed, nor the other get clear.
How then could Hektor have escaped the death spirits, had not
Apollo, for this last and uttermost time, stood by him
close, and driven strength into him, and made his knees light?
But brilliant Achilleus kept shaking his head at his own people
and would not let them throw their bitter projectiles[8] at Hektor
for fear the thrower might win the glory, and himself come second.
But when for the fourth time they had come around to the well
    springs
then the Father balanced his golden scales, and in them
he set two fateful portions of death, which lays men prostrate;[9]
one for Achilleus, and one for Hektor, breaker of horses,
and balanced it by the middle; and Hektor's death-day was heavier

---

5. **Ida** (ī′ də) *n.*: Mountain near the site of Troy.

6. **Tritogeneia** (trī′ tō jen′ ē ə): Another name for Athene, who was born near Lake Tritonis in a part of Africa.

7. **covert** (kuv′ ərt) *n.*: A hiding place.

8. **projectiles** (prō jek′ təlz) *n.*: Objects designed to be thrown forward.

9. **prostrate** (präs′ trāt) *adj.*: Flat; face downward; completely overcome.

---

7 **Clarification** In the preceding books, Achilleus' superhuman (or subhuman) fury has led to the threat of chaos. The gods have been fighting bitterly among themselves on the battlefield; the river Scamander, glutted with corpses, has risen up in fury to fight Achilleus' fire with water; Hades, lord of the underworld, has shrieked in terror. Achilleus has seen war in all its horror, personified. Zeus' thought of sparing Hektor threatens to plunge the universe into disorder. Ask students to think about the power of Zeus: What are its limits?

8 **Literary Focus** Have students look carefully at adjectives and verbs. How do they make the scene vivid? Do they serve to slant our sympathies in any direction?

9 **Discussion** Have students think about how this simile works. The unchanging distance between the two runners is initially seen from above, from the vantage point of a spectator. But the dream forces us to think of our own dreams, to empathize with the feeling of heart-pounding effort, anxiety, and paralysis we can experience in dreams. So we move from being viewers to participating vicariously.

10 **Discussion** Have students discuss how Homer's question in lines 105–107 acknowledges the fact that the listener or reader is involved in the poem, thinking about how the nightmare impasse can be broken.

11 **Enrichment** The weighing of lots is called *psychostasia* in Greek and is a popular subject for vase painting in antiquity. Zeus' action is a graphic way of conceptualizing what a human's portion (the Greek equivalent for what Romans called fate) means, and how the gods too are subservient, finally, to some more impersonal force.

Student Activity 2. Find as many compound adjective epithets as you can from Books I, VI, XVIII, and XXII of the *Iliad*.

and dragged downward toward death, and Phoibos Apollo
   forsook[10] him.
But the goddess gray-eyed Athene came now to Peleion
and stood close beside him and addressed him in winged words:
   "Beloved
of Zeus, shining Achilleus, I am hopeful now that you and I
120 will take back great glory to the ships of the Achaians, after
we have killed Hektor, for all his slakeless[11] fury for battle.
Now there is no way for him to get clear away from us,
not though Apollo who strikes from afar should be willing to
   undergo
much, and wallow[12] before our father Zeus of the aegis.
125 Stand you here then and get your wind again, while I go
to this man and persuade him to stand up to you in combat."
   So spoke Athene, and he was glad at heart, and obeyed her,
and stopped, and stood leaning on his bronze-barbed ash spear.
   Meanwhile
Athene left him there, and caught up with brilliant Hektor,
130 and likened herself in form and weariless voice to Deïphobos.[13]
She came now and stood close to him and addressed him in
   winged words:
"Dear brother, indeed swift-footed Achilleus is using you roughly
and chasing you on swift feet around the city of Priam.
Come on, then; let us stand fast against him and beat him back
   from us."
135 Then tall Hektor of the shining helm answered her: "Deïphobos,
before now you were dearest to me by far of my brothers,
of all those who were sons of Priam and Hekabe, and now
I am minded all the more within my heart to honor you,
you who dared for my sake, when your eyes saw me, to come forth
140 from the fortifications, while the others stand fast inside them."
   Then in turn the goddess gray-eyed Athene answered him:
"My brother, it is true our father and the lady our mother, taking
my knees in turn, and my companions about me, entreated
that I stay within, such was the terror upon all of them.
145 But the heart within me was worn away by hard sorrow for you.
But now let us go straight on the fight hard, let there be no
   sparing
of our spears, so that we can find out whether Achilleus
will kill us both and carry our bloody war spoils back
to the hollow ships, or will himself go down under your spear."
150 So Athene spoke and led him on by beguilement.
Now as the two in their advance were come close together,
first of the two to speak was tall helm-glittering Hektor:
"Son of Peleus, I will no longer run from you, as before this
I fled three times around the great city of Priam, and dared not
155 stand to your onfall. But now my spirit in turn has driven me
to stand and face you. I must take you now, or I must be taken.

---

10. forsook (fôr sŏŏk´) v.: Abandoned.

11. slakeless (slāk´ ləs) adj.: Unable to be satisfied or lessened.

12. wallow (wäl´ ō) v.: Move heavily and clumsily.

13. Deïphobos (dā´ i fō´ bōs): Son of Priam; powerful Trojan fighter.

Primary Source Note

Before the death of Patroklos, Achilleus ransomed captives and was merciful. When he returns to the battlefield in his hopeless and grim endeavor to undo Patroklos' death by destroying everyone and everything, Achilleus is inhumanly cruel. Because of his deep despair, his own life and death hold no meaning to him. In Book XXI (lines 99–113) he encounters Lykaon, whom he had captured earlier, before the action of the *Iliad* began. He had sold the youth rather than kill him. It is the boy's tragic bad luck to run into Achilleus again, just after being ransomed out of slavery by a guest-friend of his father's. He begs for his life, thinking he is talking to the same man who sold him for a hundred oxen, gave him bread to eat, and respected him as a suppliant. But this new Achilleus, who refuses to eat, who sees life and death as equally meaningless, has this to say to Lykaon before killing him:

   Poor fool, no longer speak to

Come then, shall we swear before the gods? For these are the
    highest
who shall be witnesses and watch over our agreements.
Brutal as you are I will not defile you, if Zeus grants
to me that I can wear you out, and take the life from you.
But after I have stripped your glorious armor, Achilleus,
I will give your corpse back to the Achaians. Do you do likewise."
    Then looking darkly at him swift-footed Achilleus answered:
"Hektor, argue me no agreements. I cannot forgive you.
As there are no trustworthy oaths between men and lions,
nor wolves and lambs have spirit that can be brought to agreement
but forever these hold feelings of hate for each other,
so there can be no love between you and me, nor shall there be
oaths between us, but one or the other must fall before then
to glut with his blood Ares the god who fights under the
    shield's guard.
Remember every valor of yours, for now the need comes
hardest upon you to be a spearman and a bold warrior.
There shall be no more escape for you, but Pallas Athene
will kill you soon by my spear. You will pay in a lump for all those
sorrows of my companions you killed in your spear's fury."
    So he spoke, and balanced the spear far shadowed, and threw it;
but glorious Hektor kept his eyes on him, and avoided it,
for he dropped, watchful, to his knee, and the bronze spear flew
    over his shoulder
and stuck in the ground, but Pallas Athene snatched it, and
    gave it
back to Achilleus, unseen by Hektor shepherd of the people.
But now Hektor spoke out to the blameless son of Peleus:
"You missed; and it was not, o Achilleus like the immortals,
from Zeus that you knew my destiny; but you thought so;
    or rather
you are someone clever in speech and spoke to swindle me,
to make me afraid of you and forget my valor and war strength.
You will not stick your spear in my back as I run away from you
but drive it into my chest as I storm straight in against you;
if the god gives you that; and now look out for my brazen
spear. I wish it might be taken full length in your body.
And indeed the war would be a lighter thing for the Trojans
if you were dead, seeing that you are their greatest affliction."
    So he spoke, and balanced the spear far shadowed, and threw it,
and struck the middle of Peleïdes' shield, nor missed it,
but the spear was driven far back from the shield, and Hektor was
    angered
because his swift weapon had been loosed from his hand in a vain[14]
    cast.
He stood discouraged, and had no other ash spear; but lifting
his voice he called aloud on Deïphobos of the pale shield,

14. **vain** (vān) *adj.*: Ineffective; fruitless; unprofitable.

me of ransom, nor argue it. / In the time before Patroklos came to the day of his destiny, / then it was the way of my heart's choice to be sparing / of the Trojans, and many I took alive and disposed of them. / Now there is not one who can escape death, if the gods send / him against my hands in front of Ilion, not one / of all the Trojans and beyond others the children of Priam. / So, friend, you die also. Why all this clamor about it? / Patroklos also is dead, who was better by far than you are. / Do you not see what a man I am, how huge, how splendid / and born of a great father, and the mother who bore me immortal? / Yet even I have also my death and my strong destiny, / and there shall be a dawn or an afternoon or a noontime / when some man in the fighting will take the life from me also, / either with a spearcast or an arrow flown from the bowstring.

17 **Enrichment** Remind students that there are several options in dealing with a dead opponent. The winner might strip the armor but return the body. Hektor did strip Patroklos' armor and did not wish to return the corpse, although the Greeks were able to retrieve it by fighting. Hektor is now asking for Achilleus to follow a more merciful course than Hektor himself followed with Patroklos.

18 **Discussion** Ask students what Achilleus is implying about how much the heroic code can apply to him and Hektor now, when he talks about men and lions, wolves and lambs. Why is he certain he will kill Hektor?

19 **Discussion** Have students discuss what they think about Athene's helping Achilleus the way she does. Does her intervention seem unfair? Could her intervention be another way of visualizing or expressing the way circumstances sometimes go wrong for individuals, as they do for Hektor in his conflict with Achilleus?

20 **Literary Focus** Hektor has not seen Athene, but the reader has. How does Athene's appearance make us evaluate Achilleus' boast? Would his words seem reasonable (given the code that allows warriors to speak this way to each other) if we did not know—as he does not—that he is doomed?

21 **Clarification** With Athene's intervention, Homer implies the limitations of the human understanding of reality. Hektor's aim is good, but he is still unlucky, despite his skill. For Homer and his audience, Athene gave Achilleus back his spear even though he missed Hektor; she made Hektor's good throw harmless. We might say Achilleus was so swift he snatched back his spear, and Hektor was too overwrought and relieved to notice; or that Hektor's aim was good but his throw was not strong enough, and Achilleus' shield—a gift from Hephaistos, after all—was strong enough to deflect the spear.

22 Discussion Have students discuss Hektor's reaction once he realizes Deiphobos is what we might call a figment of his imagination, or what the Greeks saw as a divinity in disguise. Why do students think he resolves to die fighting?

23 Literary Focus Hektor, earlier compared to a dove and a fawn, is now compared to an eagle swooping down on a lamb or hare out of the high clouds. What does this simile convey about Hektor's frame of mind?

24 Discussion Have students discuss the appearance and effect of Achilleus' armor as he puts it to use.

25 Clarification The evening star, Hesperus, is the brightest in the sky. At the same time, Hesperus is associated with the west, where the sun sets, and thus with Hades and death.

26 Enrichment Remind students that Hektor is wearing Achilleus' old armor, which was given to Peleus and then to Achilleus, who lent it to Patroklos. Achilleus eyes the armor for a weak spot in which to slay Hektor. While Achilleus sees nothing in common between himself and Hektor, what might Homer be suggesting about the common mortality among humans as Achilleus eyes the weak spot in his old armor?

27 Discussion Have students discuss Achilleus' words to Hektor. How do they feel about his words? To what extent is he concerned with his own honor?

and asked him for a long spear, but Deïphobos was not near him.
And Hektor knew the truth inside his heart, and spoke aloud:
200 "No use. Here at last the gods have summoned me deathward.
I thought Deïphobos the hero was here close beside me,
but he is behind the wall and it was Athene cheating me,
and now evil death is close to me, and no longer far away,
and there is no way out. So it must long since have been pleasing
205   before this
to Zeus, and Zeus' son who strikes from afar, this way; though
they defended me gladly. But now my death is upon me.
Let me at least not die without a struggle, inglorious,
but do some big thing first, that men to come shall know of it."
   So he spoke, and pulling out the sharp sword that was slung
210 at the hollow of his side, huge and heavy, and gathering
himself together, he made his swoop, like a high-flown eagle
who launches himself out of the murk of the clouds on the flat
   land
to catch away a tender lamb or a shivering hare; so
Hektor made his swoop, swinging his sharp sword, and Achilleus
215 charged, the heart within him loaded with savage fury.
In front of his chest the beautiful elaborate great shield
covered him, and with the glittering helm with four horns
he nodded; the lovely golden fringes were shaken about it
which Hephaistos had driven close along the horn of the helmet.
220 And as a star moves among stars in the night's darkening,
Hesper, who is the fairest star who stands in the sky, such
was the shining from the pointed spear Achilleus was shaking
in his right hand with evil intention toward brilliant Hektor.
He was eyeing Hektor's splendid body, to see where it might best
225 give way, but all the rest of the skin was held in the armor,
brazen and splendid, he stripped when he cut down the strength of
   Patroklos;
yet showed where the collar-bones hold the neck from the
   shoulders,
the throat, where death of the soul comes most swiftly; in this
   place
brilliant Achilleus drove the spear as he came on in fury,
and clean through the soft part of the neck the spearpoint was
230   driven.
Yet the ash spear heavy with bronze did not sever the windpipe,
so that Hektor could still make exchange of words spoken.
But he dropped in the dust, and brilliant Achilleus vaunted above
   him:
"Hektor, surely you thought as you killed Patroklos you would be
235 safe, and since I was far away you thought nothing of me,
o fool, for an avenger was left, far greater than he was,
behind him and away by the hollow ships. And it was I;
and I have broken your strength; on you the dogs and the vultures

---

Grammar in Action

The *Iliad* is rich in imagery—descriptive language that appeals to the senses. Literally, an image is a concrete representation of a sensory experience. Images communicate the richness and the emotional complexity of experience. Through imagery, writers capture the vividness of an object or experience, giving the reader a sense of immediacy, as if he or she were actually part of the experience.

   Many of the images in the *Iliad* are part of epic similes, elaborate comparisons between two unlike objects that surprisingly have something in common. Notice the imagery in the following simile:

So he spoke, and pulling out the sharp sword that was slung / at the hollow of his side, huge and heavy, and gathering / himself together, he made his swoop, like a high-flown eagle / who launches himself out of the murk of the clouds on the flat land / to catch away a tender lamb or a shivering hare (lines 209–213).

   The image of the hunting eagle going in for the kill gives the reader a clear picture of Hektor's action. Moreover, the image provided Homer with an economical way of describing Hektor within the constraints of meter.

   The image of an eagle in line 211 is a specific one, but Homer also uses images in a broader sense. Achilleus' shield, for example, is an image of

HEKTOR KILLED BY ACHILLEUS
Peter Paul Rubens

Humanities Note

Fine art, *Hektor Killed by Achilleus* by Peter Paul Rubens. Throughout his career, Peter Paul Rubens (1577–1640) was fascinated with historical and classical subjects. The painting *Hektor Killed by Achilleus* is an homage to the works of Homer. The massive figures, locked in fatal combat, are painted with vigor and passion. The most striking quality of this work is the amazing light that radiates throughout. The architectural frame of columns and the laurels enhance the classic theme.

This prolific Flemish painter is considered to be the greatest northern European exponent of the Baroque movement. His art acts on the emotions of the viewer with an overwhelming blend of illusion, color, light, and movement.

You might want to use the following questions to discuss the art:

1. What is your emotional response to this painting?
2. Do the colors of this painting affect the emotional tone?

28 Enrichment One of the worst threats in the *Iliad*, and among the worst fears people express, is that a corpse will be left uncremated and unburied, to be eaten by vultures and dogs. In fact, this never actually happens in the poem.

29 Discussion Ask students how these lines highlight Hektor's vulnerability and Achilleus' refusal to compromise.

shall feed and foully rip you; the Achaians will bury Patroklos."

In his weakness Hektor of the shining helm spoke to him:
"I entreat you, by your life, by your knees, by your parents,
do not let the dogs feed on me by the ships of the Achaians,
but take yourself the bronze and gold that are there in abundance,
those gifts that my father and the lady my mother will give you,
and give my body to be taken home again, so that the Trojans
and the wives of the Trojans may give me in death my rite of
    burning."[15]

But looking darkly at him swift-footed Achilleus answered:
"No more entreating of me, you dog, by knees or parents.

28

29

15. rite of burning: Proper funeral ritual of burning the dead body.

the realm of human experience. And throughout the *Iliad* there are image themes, patterns of images that reinforce thematic ideas. An example of an image theme in the *Iliad* is the destructive force of fire, which ravages irrationally and impartially, destroying everything in its path, much like Achilleus.

Student Activity 1. Locate another epic simile from pages 372–373 and identify the image in the simile. Explain the significance of the image in the simile.

Student Activity 2. Choose three or more images from what you have read in the *Iliad* so far. Discuss the images in terms of the larger issues in the *Iliad*, such as morality, humanity, war, peace, rage, or grief.

30 Enrichment Achilleus' grief and rage make him wish he could eat Hektor's flesh raw, as if he were a savage beast. Hekabe later wishes she could eat Achilleus' liver. In some cultures, even today, warriors eat the flesh of their vanquished enemies. For Homer this kind of cannibalism is no longer anything practiced by anyone, but it has become a rhetorical statement, an expression of the inhuman savagery of grief and anger.

31 Literary Focus Ask students what Hektor's phrase "heart of iron" implies about Achilleus' humanity. What does Hektor's dying prophecy suggest about mortality and the way people should act?

32 Discussion Why does Achilleus answer Hektor even when Hektor is dead? What does his answer say about Achilleus?

33 Discussion Ask students to consider how Homer presents Hektor to us. How do students feel about the Greeks' stabbing Hektor's corpse?

34 Discussion What does the treatment of Hektor's corpse, and the taunts uttered over him, suggest about his stature? What feelings are aroused in the reader?

35 Literary Focus In line 288 Achilleus shifts abruptly from deliberating about an end to the war to his concern with Patroklos' corpse. What does this emphasis suggest about his priorities? Is the war important to him? Why has he killed Hektor?

I wish only that my spirit and fury would drive me
to hack your meat away and eat it raw for the things that
you have done to me. So there is no one who can hold the dogs
  off
from your head, not if they bring here and set before me ten times
and twenty times the ransom, and promise more in addition,
not if Priam son of Dardanos should offer to weigh out
your bulk in gold; not even so shall the lady your mother
who herself bore you lay you on the death-bed and mourn you:
no, but the dogs and the birds will have you all for their feasting."
  Then, dying, Hektor of the shining helmet spoke to him:
"I know you well as I look upon you, I know that I could not
persuade you, since indeed in your breast is a heart of iron.
Be careful now; for I might be made into the gods' curse
upon you, on that day when Paris and Phoibos Apollo
destroy you in the Skaian gates, for all your valor."
  He spoke, and as he spoke the end of death closed in upon him,
and the soul fluttering free of the limbs went down into Death's
  house
mourning her destiny, leaving youth and manhood behind her.
Now though he was a dead man brilliant Achilleus spoke to him:
"Die: and I will take my own death at whatever time
Zeus and the rest of the immortals choose to accomplish it."
  He spoke, and pulled the brazen spear from the body, and laid it
on one side, and stripped away from the shoulders the bloody
armor. And the other sons of the Achaians came running about
  him,
and gazed upon the stature and on the imposing beauty
of Hektor; and none stood beside him who did not stab him;
and thus they would speak one to another, each looking at his
  neighbor:
"See now, Hektor is much softer to handle than he was
when he set the ships ablaze with the burning firebrand."
  So as they stood beside him they would speak, and stab him.
But now, when he had despoiled[16] the body, swift-footed brilliant
Achilleus stood among the Achaians and addressed them in winged
  words:
"Friends, who are leaders of the Argives and keep their counsel:
since the gods have granted me the killing of this man
who has done us much damage, such as not all the others together
have done, come, let us go in armor about the city
to see if we can find out what purpose is in the Trojans,
whether they will abandon their high city, now that this man
has fallen, or are minded to stay, though Hektor lives no longer.
Yet still, why does the heart within me debate on these things?
There is a dead man who lies by the ships, unwept, unburied:
Patroklos: and I will not forget him, never so long as

Line numbers: 250, 255, 260, 265, 270, 275, 280, 285, 290

16. **despoiled** (dē spoild') v.: Deprived of value and honor.

Commentary

The *Iliad* looks unflinchingly, and frequently, at death. This is a poem concerned with mortality, with humans' need to find reasons to live although death is inevitable. Because they are mortal, human beings are always potentially tragic. They have something to lose, and so their actions are important. The gods, by contrast, who can never die, remain essentially comic and frivolous.

Men die frequently in the *Iliad*. Each death is different, but all are equally horrible and final. In death scenes Homer's lens zooms compassionately and sympathetically in on what physically happens to the body. Other writers note the vulnerability of the human body with revulsion and despair; Homer looks with tenderness at how fragile humanity is and with wonder that human beings—vulnerable, ephemeral creatures—are capable of so much.

When talking to the immortal horses who weep over Patroklos in Book XVII, Zeus says, "of all living creatures that breathe and move along the earth, nothing is more wretched than man"; but that very wretchedness is what makes humanity great.

I remain among the living and my knees have their spring beneath me.
And though the dead forget the dead in the house of Hades,
even there I shall still remember my beloved companion.
But now, you young men of the Achaians, let us go back, singing
a victory song, to our hollow ships; and take this with us.
We have won ourselves enormous fame; we have killed the great
    Hektor
whom the Trojans glorified as if he were a god in their city."
    He spoke, and now thought of shameful treatment for glorious
    Hektor.
In both of his feet at the back he made holes by the tendons
in the space between ankle and heel, and drew thongs of ox-hide
    through them,
and fastened them to the chariot so as to let the head drag,
and mounted the chariot, and lifted the glorious armor inside it,
then whipped the horses to a run, and they winged their way
    unreluctant.
A cloud of dust rose where Hektor was dragged, his dark hair was
    falling
about him, and all that head that was once so handsome was
    tumbled
in the dust; since by this time Zeus had given him over
to his enemies, to be defiled in the land of his fathers.
    So all his head was dragged in the dust; and now his mother
tore out her hair, and threw the shining veil far from her
and raised a great wail as she looked upon her son; and his father
beloved groaned pitifully, and all his people about him
were taken with wailing and lamentation all through the city.
It was most like what would have happened, if all lowering
Ilion had been burning top to bottom in fire.
His people could scarcely keep the old man in his impatience
from storming out of the Dardanian gates; he implored them
all, and wallowed in the muck before them calling on each man
and naming him by his name: "Give way, dear friends,
and let me alone though you care for me, leave me to go out
from the city and make my way to the ships of the Achaians.
I must be suppliant to this man, who is harsh and violent,
and he might have respect for my age and take pity upon it
since I am old, and his father also is old, as I am,
Peleus, who begot and reared him to be an affliction
on the Trojans. He has given us most sorrow, beyond all others,
such is the number of my flowering sons he has cut down.
But for all of these I mourn not so much, in spite of my sorrow,
as for one, Hektor, and the sharp grief for him will carry me
    downward
into Death's house. I wish he had died in my arms, for that way
we two, I myself and his mother who bore him unhappy,

36 **Discussion** How does Achilleus' evaluation of Hektor both serve to glorify Achilleus and remind us of Hektor's stature, which we may have forgotten in focusing on his vulnerability?

37 **Enrichment** The mutilation and maltreatment of the corpse violates heroic etiquette, as the stabbing of Hektor's corpse by the mob did.

38 **Literary Focus** Point out Homer's use of contrast and specificity in these lines. Ask students how Homer makes the scene more immediate and poignant.

39 **Clarification** Call students' attention to the fact that in mourning Hektor, the people of Ilion are also mourning the fall of Troy (which has not yet happened). Ask students to explain the connection between the mourning of Hektor and the mourning of Troy.

40 **Discussion** How is Priam's grief made particular? What does his lament convey about Hektor and his relationship with his father? Can it be compared with Achilleus' lament for Patroklos?

Humanities Note

Fine art, *Achilleus Dragging the Body of Hektor*, Attic hydria painting. This vase painting on an Athenian hydria (water jar) is executed in the early "black-figure" style of vase painting. Depth is achieved through the intricate layering of the somewhat flat figures. The variation in movement and direction of the figures serves to heighten the drama of the scene. This dense composition creates a rich decorative effect that is contained by the stylized floral border.

Pots such as this were an important part of Greek artistic activity in the late archaic period. Today they are the only evidence we have of this style of Greek painting.

You might want to ask students whether this painting captures the chaos of the scene.

41 Enrichment Priam's lament is individual. As a woman, Hekabe has a much more clearly defined role. It is the role of women to lead a ritual lament, in which the chief mourner weaves together very personal and particular elements with certain ritual commonplaces. Her lament is a solo, supported by a sort of choral lament. Ritual lament can still be found in rural areas of Greece, in a Christian framework.

42 Clarification That Andromache excels at weaving is an indication of her being a good wife. The fact that she is engaged in weaving while Hektor is fighting is another indication.

might so have glutted[17] ourselves with weeping for him and
    mourning."

So he spoke, in tears, and beside him mourned the citizens.
But for the women of Troy Hekabe led out the thronging
chant of sorrow: "Child, I am wretched. What shall my life be
335 in my sorrows, now you are dead, who by day and in the night
were my glory in the town, and to all of the Trojans
and the women of Troy a blessing throughout their city. They
    adored you
as if you were a god, since in truth you were their high honor
while you lived. Now death and fate have closed in upon you."
340 So she spoke in tears but the wife of Hektor had not yet
heard: for no sure messenger had come to her and told her
how her husband had held his ground there outside the gates;
but she was weaving a web in the inner room of the high house,
a red folding robe, and inworking[18] elaborate figures.
345 She called out through the house to her lovely-haired handmaidens

17. glutted (glut´ əd) *v.:* Filled; sated.

18. inworking (in´ wər´ kiŋ) *v.:* Sewing into fabric.

ACHILLEUS DRAGGING THE BODY OF HEKTOR (detail)
Museum of Fine Arts, Boston

Grammar in Action

Use **commas** to separate the basic elements of your sentences. Commas add clarity of expression to writing by indicating the brief pause the writer intends the reader to make when reading or speaking. Some of the basic elements separated by commas are coordinate adjectives ("brilliant, swift-footed Achilleus"); three or more words, phrases, or clauses in a series; and two independent clauses joined by a coordinating conjunction to form a compound sentence.

In the *Iliad* many sentences contain complex series of phrases and clauses that are set off by commas, making them easier to follow. For ex-ample, notice the phrases separated by commas in the following passage:

But for all of these I mourn not so much, in spite of my sorrow, / as for one, Hektor, and the sharp grief for him will carry me downward / into Death's house (lines 327–329).

Commas never separate two independent clauses (clauses that can stand alone as sentences). Two independent clauses separated by a comma make a comma splice, which is grammatically incorrect.

Student Activity 1. Write a well-organized summary of Book XVIII of the *Iliad*, using commas correctly.

to set a great cauldron over the fire, so that there would be
hot water for Hektor's bath as he came back out of the fighting;
poor innocent, nor knew how, far from waters for bathing,
Pallas Athene had cut him down at the hands of Achilleus.
She heard from the great bastion the noise of mourning and
    sorrow.
Her limbs spun, and the shuttle dropped from her hand to the
    ground.
    Then she called aloud to her lovely-haired handmaidens: "Come
    here.
Two of you come with me, so I can see what has happened.
I heard the voice of Hektor's honored mother; within me
my own heart rising beats in my mouth, my limbs under me
are frozen. Surely some evil is near for the children of Priam.
May what I say come never close to my ear; yet dreadfully
I fear that great Achilleus might have cut off bold Hektor
alone, away from the city, and be driving him into the flat land,
might put an end to that bitter pride of courage, that always
was on him, since he would never stay back where the men were in
    numbers
but break far out in front, and give way in his fury to no man."
    So she spoke, and ran out of the house like a raving woman
with pulsing heart, and her two handmaidens went along with her.
But when she came to the bastion and where the men were
    gathered
she stopped, staring, on the wall; and she saw him
being dragged in front of the city, and the running horses
dragged him at random toward the hollow ships of the Achaians.
The darkness of night misted over the eyes of Andromache.
She fell backward, and gasped the life breath from her, and far off
threw from her head the shining gear that ordered her headdress,
the diadem[19] and the cap, and the holding-band woven together,
and the circlet,[20] which Aphrodite the golden once had given her
on that day when Hektor of the shining helmet led her forth
from the house of Eëtion, and gave numberless gifts to win her.
And about her stood thronging her husband's sisters and the wives
    of his brothers
and these, in her despair for death, held her up among them.
But she, when she breathed again and the life was gathered back
    into her,
lifted her voice among the women of Troy in mourning:
"Hektor, I grieve for you. You and I were born to a single
destiny, you in Troy in the house of Priam, and I
in Thebe, underneath the timbered[21] mountain of Plakos
in the house of Eëtion, who cared for me when I was little,
ill-fated he, I ill-starred. I wish he had never begotten me.
Now you go down to the house of Death in the secret places
of the earth, and left me here behind in the sorrow of mourning,

19. diadem (dī′ ə dem′) *n*.: A
decorated cloth headband
worn as a crown.
20. circlet (sur′ klit) *n*.: A
ring or circular band worn on
the head.

21. timbered (tim′ bərd)
adj.: Covered with trees.

43

44

45

46

47

43 Literary Focus Ask students how Homer stresses the irony and poignancy of Andromache's activity and her expectations. You might also ask students to whom line 348 is addressed.

44 Reading Strategy Suggest that students pay careful attention to the precise description of the physical symptoms Andromache experiences. Have students similarly experienced strong emotions? You might also suggest that students keep this passage in mind when they read Sappho.

45 Discussion What is Andromache's view of Hektor's heroism? Does it correspond to Hektor's view of his heroism?

46 Literary Focus Homer combines formulaic elements to achieve subtle and particular effects. For instance, line 370 is a standard formula for death; in this case Andromache is not actually dead, but the shock and grief she experiences (which cause her to faint) are strong enough to be like death. (Similarly, when Achilleus hears of Patroklos' death, he stretches out on the ground, in the dust, and the formulas used to describe his response are those normally used of dead warriors.) As Andromache falls, she loses her bridal headgear (gifts of Aphrodite, and the mark of her status as Hektor's wife) as a warrior might be stripped of the armor that identifies him and marks his status.

47 Discussion How does Andromache's lament reflect her particular relationship with Hektor? Why does she wish she had never been born?

Student Activity 2. Identify three or more passages from the *Iliad* that have a number of basic elements separated by commas. In each passage underline the basic elements.

48

49

50

48 **Discussion** What do Andromache's words reveal about the way her society sees the reciprocal relationship between father and son?

49 **Literary Focus** Point out that the poem itself ends with the funeral of Hektor and with ritual laments for him. Here the lament addressed to Hektor focuses on one repercussion of his dying: what will happen to his son. Ask students how Andromache's description of the life awaiting Astyanax reveals about how one's place in the Trojan community is defined. For the listeners, Andromache's vivid evocation of Astyanax's fate is made even more poignant because the misfortune she envisions still assumes Troy will not fall, but the poet knows, and we know, that Troy will be captured and the Greeks will dash the boy to his death from the top of the wall.

50 **Reading Strategy** How does Andromache's despair that Hektor's corpse will not have the treatment and the burial it deserves influence our view of Achilleus' treatment of the body?

a widow in your house, and the boy is only a baby
who was born to you and me, the unfortunate. You cannot help
    him,
390 Hektor, any more, since you are dead. Nor can he help you.
Though he escape the attack of the Achaians with all its sorrows,
yet all his days for your sake there will be hard work for him
and sorrows, for others will take his lands away from him. The day
of bereavement leaves a child with no agemates to befriend him.
395 He bows his head before every man, his cheeks are bewept,[22] he
goes, needy, a boy among his father's companions,
and tugs at this man by the mantle, that man by the tunic,
and they pity him, and one gives him a tiny drink from a goblet,
enough to moisten his lips, not enough to moisten his palate.
400 But one whose parents are living beats him out of the banquet
hitting him with his fists and in words also abuses him:
'Get out, you! Your father is not dining among us.'
And the boy goes away in tears to his widowed mother,
Astyanax, who in days before on the knees of his father
405 would eat only the marrow or the flesh of sheep that was fattest.
And when sleep would come upon him and he was done with his
    playing,
he would go to sleep in a bed, in the arms of his nurse, in a soft
bed, with his heart given all its fill of luxury.
Now, with his dear father gone, he has much to suffer:
410 he, whom the Trojans have called Astyanax, lord of the city,
since it was you alone who defended the gates and the long walls.
But now, beside the curving ships, far away from your parents,
the writhing worms will feed, when the dogs have had enough of
    you,
on your naked corpse, though in your house there is clothing laid up
415 that is fine-textured and pleasant, wrought by the hands of women.
But all of these I will burn up in the fire's blazing,
no use to you, since you will never be laid away in them;
but in your honor, from the men of Troy and the Trojan women."
    So she spoke, in tears; and the women joined in her mourning.

22. bewept (bē wept') *adj.*: Wet with tears.

Reader's Response *How did you react to Achilleus' treatment of Hektor after his death? Explain your reaction.*

Commentary

The *Iliad* is a life-affirming poem, despite the ubiquitousness of death. And, just as Achilleus' shield encompasses all aspects of human existence, so the poem keeps ordinary, peacetime activities in view even during the most violent scenes of carnage. One way Homer includes the richness of peacetime life in his war poem is by using reference points from peaceful contexts: measuring distance by how long it takes mules to plow a furrow, or pinpointing the time of day by saying it is when a woodcutter thinks of preparing his evening meal after a good day's work in the woods. But the most consistent and economical way of bringing the fullness of life beyond the battlefield is through similes.

Similes create vivid images and force the reader to reflect on war, life, and death. The pain Agamemnon feels when he is wounded is as sharp as a woman's labor pains in Book XI; as Greeks and Trojans fight over the corpse of Patroklos, they are compared to workers employed by some man to stretch a huge ox hide, slippery with grease, and they stand around in a circle and pull the hide evenly, working together toward a common goal in Book XVI; Achilleus' horses trampling corpses are likened to oxen crushing barley in Book XX. The similes are almost numberless. Some are macabre, like the comparison of a corpse-glutted river amid the fire of the twenty-first

from Book XXIV: Achilleus and Priam

Achilleus and the Greeks perform Patroklos' funeral rites. Following the funeral, they hold a feast. The next morning, in honor of Patroklos, the Greeks hold funeral games—chariot races, discus throwing, boxing, and wrestling.

And the games broke up, and the people scattered to go away,
    each man
to his fast-running ship, and the rest of them took thought of their
    dinner
and of sweet sleep and its enjoyment; only Achilleus
wept still as he remembered his beloved companion, nor did sleep
who subdues all come over him, but he tossed from one side to the
    other
in longing for Patroklos, for his manhood and his great strength
and all the actions he had seen to the end with him, and the
    hardships
he had suffered; the wars of men; hard crossing of the big waters.
Remembering all these things he let fall the swelling tears, lying
sometimes along his side, sometimes on his back, and now again
prone on his face; then he would stand upright, and pace turning
in distraction along the beach of the sea, nor did dawn rising
escape him as she brightened across the sea and the beaches.
Then, when he had yoked running horses under the chariot
he would fasten Hektor behind the chariot, so as to drag him,
and draw him three times around the tomb of Menoitios' fallen
son, then rest again in his shelter, and throw down the dead man
and leave him to lie sprawled on his face in the dust. But Apollo
had pity on him, though he was only a dead man, and guarded
the body from all ugliness, and hid all of it under the golden
aegis, so that it might not be torn when Achilleus dragged it.
  So Achilleus in his standing fury outraged great Hektor.
The blessed gods as they looked upon him were filled with
    compassion
and kept urging clear-sighted Argeïphontes[1] to steal the body.
There this was pleasing to all the others, but never to Hera
nor Poseidon, nor the girl of the gray eyes,[2] who kept still
their hatred for sacred Ilion as in the beginning,
and for Priam and his people, because of the delusion of Paris[3]
who insulted the goddesses when they came to him in his
    courtyard

ACHILLEUS
Detail from the fresco
"Thetis Consoling Achilles"
Giovanni Battista Tiepolo
The Room of the Iliad, Villa Valmarana, Venice

1. Argeïphontes (är′ gā ə fon′ tēz): Another name for Hermes, a messenger of Zeus known for his trickery and thieving; he also conducted the souls of the dead to Hades.
2. girl of the gray eyes: A formulaic phrase used to describe Athene.
3. delusion of Paris: As judge of a beauty contest among Aphrodite, Hera, and Athene, he chose Aphrodite after she bribed him with Helen.

Presentation
Motivation/Prior Knowledge Tell students that they will be reading about an encounter between opponents who, for a moment, surpass their differences to find their common humanity. Ask students to think about similar encounters in literature, like those in Dostoevsky's *Crime and Punishment*. Students might also explore the realm of history and current events for analogous instances.

Purpose-Setting Question Does Homer make Achilleus' grief seem obsessive?

Universal Themes Obsessive grief over the death of a loved one is a recurrent theme in world literature. Have students recall *The Epic of Gilgamesh* (page 15), for example. Grief over the irrevocable loss of a loved one who has not died reaches catastrophic proportions in the case of Dido, in the *Aeneid* (page 493).

Humanities Note
Fine art, Detail from fresco *Thetis Consoling Achilleus*, from the Villa Valmarona, Vincenza, by Giovanni Battista Tiepolo. The Italian artist Giovanni Battista Tiepolo (1696–1770) is considered a master of rococo fresco painting. In 1757 he was commissioned to execute fresco paintings in a palazzo near Vincenza by Count Valmarona. With the assistance of his ten-year-old son, he painted a series of frescoes on classical subjects considered to be among his finest work.

    This detail of Achilleus is from one of the frescoes devoted to scenes from the *Iliad*. It clearly demonstrates Tiepolo's skill and sensitivity when rendering human figures on so difficult a surface as wet plaster. This fine portrait captures the melancholic introspection of the grieving Achilleus.

    You might want to ask students their opinions about what Achilleus is thinking in this painting.

book to a large, bubbling caldron full of aromatic, fatty pork. Others evoke natural beauty, comparing a fallen soldier to a felled poplar.

Master Teacher Note Apollo's speech restates concisely some crucial issues. Make certain that students can analyze the speech and understand his message. Outlining the speech on the board with the help of the class might be a good way to prepare for discussion. What are Apollo's accusations? In how many ways does he say that Achilleus is not acting like a human being but a savage lion? What are the attributes of civilized people, according to this contrast? Apollo reiterates what Aias said in the embassy scene about becoming reconciled to the loss of a loved one. What do the Greeks feel about the limits of grief and vengeance? Call attention to the implications of Apollo's last line: In refusing to bury the corpse, and insisting on defiling it above ground, Achilleus not only violates the rituals of human society, he upsets the natural order. (In Sophocles' drama *Antigone*, Kreon's refusal to bury the nephew who fell in civil war is seen as a violation of the natural order and a cause of pestilence.)

30 and favored her who supplied the lust that led to disaster.
But now, as it was the twelfth dawn after the death of Hektor,
Phoibos Apollo spoke his word out among the immortals:
"You are hard, you gods, and destructive. Now did not Hektor
burn thigh pieces of oxen and unblemished goats in your honor?
35 Now you cannot bring yourselves to save him, though he is only
a corpse, for his wife to look upon, his child and his mother
and Priam his father, and his people, who presently thereafter
would burn his body in the fire and give him his rites of burial.
No, you gods; your desire is to help this cursed Achilleus
40 within whose breast there are no feelings of justice, nor can
his mind be bent, but his purposes are fierce, like a lion
who when he has given way to his own great strength and his haughty
spirit, goes among the flocks of men, to devour them.
So Achilleus has destroyed pity, and there is not in him
45 any shame; which does much harm to men but profits them also.
For a man must some day lose one who was even closer
than this; a brother from the same womb, or a son. And yet
he weeps for him, and sorrows for him, and then it is over,
for the Destinies put in mortal men the heart of endurance.
50 But this man, now he has torn the heart of life from great Hektor,
ties him to his horses and drags him around his beloved
     companion's
tomb; and nothing is gained thereby for his good, or his honor.
Great as he is, let him take care not to make us angry;
for see, he does dishonor to the dumb earth in his fury."
55   Then bitterly Hera of the white arms answered him, saying:
"What you have said could be true, lord of the silver bow, only
if you give Hektor such pride of place as you give to Achilleus.
But Hektor was mortal, and suckled at the breast of a woman,[4]
while Achilleus is the child of a goddess, one whom I myself
60 nourished and brought up and gave her as bride to her husband
Peleus, one dear to the hearts of the immortals, for you all
went, you gods, to the wedding; and you too feasted among them
and held your lyre, o friend of the evil, faithless forever."
    In turn Zeus who gathers the clouds spoke to her in answer:
65 "Hera, be not utterly angry with the gods, for there shall not
be the same pride of place given both. Yet Hektor also
was loved by the gods, best of all the mortals in Ilion.
I loved him too. He never failed of gifts to my liking.
Never yet has my altar gone without fair sacrifice,
70 the smoke and the savor of it, since that is our portion of honor.
The stealing of him we will dismiss, for it is not possible
to take bold Hektor secretly from Achilleus, since always
his mother is near him night and day; but it would be better
if one of the gods would summon Thetis here to my presence
75 so that I can say a close word to her, and see that Achilleus
is given gifts by Priam and gives back the body of Hektor."

4. suckled at the breast of a woman: Was breast-fed as an infant by a mortal woman, not a goddess.

Grammar in Action

In the *Iliad*, the use of the three basic **verb tenses**—past, present, and future—is especially helpful because we are reading about events that happened in the past, that are happening in the present, and that are prophesied to happen in the future. Some passages intermingle past, present, and future tenses, combining the three to show the history of the characters, the importance of what they endure in the present, and the knowledge of what they will face in the future.

So Achilleus *has destroyed* pity, and there *is not* in him / any shame;

which *does much* harm to men but *profits* them also, / For a man *must some day lose* one who was even closer / than this; a brother from the same womb, or a son. And yet / he *weeps* for him, and *sorrows* for him, and then it *is over*, / for the Destinies *put* in mortal men the heart of endurance. / But this man, now he *has torn* the heart of life from great Hektor, / *ties* him to his horses and *drags* him around his beloved companion's / tomb; and nothing *is gained* thereby for his good, or his honor (lines 44–52).

In this speech Apollo acknowledges Achilleus' lack of pity and shame

On Olympos, Zeus orders Thetis to tell Achilleus to return Hektor's body to Priam. Then Zeus commands Iris to tell Priam to ransom his son by bringing gifts to Achilleus. Concerned for Priam's safety, Zeus tells Hermes to guide Priam through the hollow Achaian ships. Hermes assures Priam that the gods preserved Hektor's body from defilement even while Achilleus dragged the corpse for nine days.

So Hermes spoke, and went away to the height of Olympos,
but Priam vaulted down to the ground from behind the horses
and left Idaios where he was, for he stayed behind, holding
in hand the horses and mules. The old man made straight for the
  dwelling
where Achilleus the beloved of Zeus was sitting. He found him
inside, and his companions were sitting apart, as two only,
Automedon the hero and Alkimos, scion[5] of Ares,
were busy beside him. He had just now got through with his
  dinner,
with eating and drinking, and the table still stood by. Tall Priam
came in unseen by the other men and stood close beside him
and caught the knees of Achilleus in his arms, and kissed the hands
that were dangerous and manslaughtering and had killed so many
of his sons. As when dense disaster closes on one who has
  murdered
a man in his own land, and he comes to the country of others,
to a man of substance, and wonder seizes on those who behold
  him,
so Achilleus wondered as he looked on Priam, a godlike
man, and the rest of them wondered also, and looked at each
  other.
But now Priam spoke to him in the words of a suppliant:
"Achilleus like the gods, remember your father, one who
is of years like mine, and on the door-sill of sorrowful old age.
And they who dwell nearby encompass him and afflict him,
nor is there any to defend him against the wrath, the destruction.
Yet surely he, when he hears of you and that you are still living,
is gladdened within his heart and all his days he is hopeful
that he will see his beloved son come home from the Troad.
But for me, my destiny was evil. I have had the noblest
of sons in Troy, but I say not one of them is left to me.
Fifty were my sons, when the sons of the Achaians came here.
Nineteen were born to me from the womb of a single mother,
and other women bore the rest in my palace; and of these
violent Ares broke the strength in the knees of most of them,
but one was left me who guarded my city and people, that one
you killed a few days since as he fought in defense of his country,
Hektor; for whose sake I come now to the ships of the Achaians
to win him back from you, and I bring you gifts beyond number.
Honor then the gods, Achilleus, and take pity upon me

5. scion (sī′ ən) *n.*: Descendant; offspring.

3 Clarification Call students' attention to the fact that Achilleus has eaten, so the food he offers Priam is not just an ordinary meal; it is part of the guest-host etiquette, xenia, a relationship that imposes at least the trust of hospitality and at best the duty of kinship between strangers or even enemies.

4 Reading Strategy Ask students to consider how the poet wants us to see Priam's entrance. Why does Homer use "tall" instead of another adjective to describe Priam? Moreover, in line 88, why does Homer dwell on the description of Achilleus' hands?

5 Literary Focus Point out the reversal of expectations in this simile, which is perhaps the most complex and surprising simile in the poem. Lead students to see how it reverses ordinary expectations and mirrors the way war turns everything upside down. It is normal for a man who has committed a crime and been exiled to seek refuge and purification at the court of a powerful king. But Priam is a king, in his own country. He has come to beg Achilleus, who is far from home and who has murdered Priam's son, as if Priam were a murderer fallen on hard times, an exile, come to a foreign land to seek protection and ritual purification from a wealthy man. Have students consider how the simile is connected with the admiration Achilleus and his men feel for Priam, "a godlike man."

6 Discussion Point out to students that Priam opens his speech with a standard rhetorical strategy, connecting himself, the one who asks for a favor, with the listener or potential granter of that favor. Ask students about the effectiveness of Priam's comparing and contrasting himself to Peleus.

both in the past and at present, and he predicts that Achilleus may someday suffer a greater loss and be humbled by the experience. Pay special attention to the different verb tenses in the passage.

   Student Activity 1. Identify the verb tenses of the italicized words in the passage from the *Iliad*.

   Student Activity 2. Locate another passage from the *Iliad* in which verb tenses are similarly combined.

7 Discussion Each man is weeping for his own losses. Have students discuss Achilleus' and Priam's grief. How is their grief, which is individual and separate, also shared? How does Homer make us aware of both their comradeship and of what separates them? Remind students that Hektor killed Patroklos, as Achilleus killed Hektor.

8 Discussion What do Achilleus' expressions in these lines indicate about the Greeks' views of human needs?

9 Literary Focus Remind students that the dying Hektor told Achilleus he had a "heart of iron" (Book XXII, line 260). Reinforce what Hektor meant: that Achilleus was incapable of human emotions, like mercy or empathy. Ask students to consider how Achilleus uses the phrase "heart of iron" in line 130. Ask them if it is in character for Achilleus to admire Priam's inhuman daring and endurance.

10 Discussion Discuss with students how these words mark a radical change in Achilleus, who has obstinately resisted the same kind of moralizing aimed at him by others. Remind students of his vow in Book XVIII, never to forget Patroklos, even after his own death. How does the sentiment he expresses now reflect on his own obsessive grieving and rage at the opening of Book XXIV?

11 Discussion Ask students to discuss the meaning of the parable of the two urns. Can some people expect to have nothing but evil and bad luck in their lives?

12 Discussion Ask students to discuss how Homer represents the human condition. How does Homer suggest that Achilleus is now able to see another's point of view? Do we expect such empathy of Achilleus?

remembering your father, yet I am still more pitiful;
I have gone through what no other mortal on earth has gone
    through;
115 I put my lips to the hands of the man who has killed my children."
    So he spoke, and stirred in the other a passion of grieving
for his own father. He took the old man's hand and pushed him
gently away, and the two remembered, as Priam sat huddled
at the feet of Achilleus and wept close for manslaughtering Hektor
120 and Achilleus wept now for his own father, now again
for Patroklos. The sound of their mourning moved in the house.
    Then
when great Achilleus had taken full satisfaction in sorrow
and the passion for it had gone from his mind and body, thereafter
he rose from his chair, and took the old man by the hand, and set
    him
125 on his feet again, in pity for the gray head and the gray beard,
and spoke to him and addressed him in winged words: "Ah,
    unlucky,
surely you have had much evil to endure in your spirit.
How could you dare to come alone to the ships of the Achaians
and before my eyes, when I am one who have killed in such
    numbers
130 such brave sons of yours? The heart in you is iron. Come, then,
and sit down upon this chair, and you and I will even let
our sorrows lie still in the heart for all our grieving. There is not
any advantage to be won from grim lamentation.
Such is the way the gods spun life for unfortunate mortals,
that we live in unhappiness, but the gods themselves have no
135   sorrows.
There are two urns[6] that stand on the door-sill of Zeus. They are
    unlike
for the gifts they bestow:[7] an urn of evils, an urn of blessings.
If Zeus who delights in thunder mingles these and bestows them
on man, he shifts, and moves now in evil, again in good fortune.
But when Zeus bestows from the urn of sorrows, he makes a
140   failure
of man, and the evil hunger drives him over the shining
earth, and he wanders respected neither of gods nor mortals.
Such were the shining gifts given by the gods to Peleus
from his birth, who outshone all men beside for his riches
145 and pride of possession, and was lord over the Myrmidons. Thereto
the gods bestowed an immortal wife on him, who was mortal.
But even on him the god piled evil also. There was not
any generation of strong sons born to him in his great house
but a single all-untimely child he had, and I give him
150 no care as he grows old, since far from the land of my fathers
I sit here in Troy, and bring nothing but sorrow to you and your
    children.

6. urns (urnz) *n.*: Vases with pedestals.

7. bestow (bē stō′) *v.*: Give.

Primary Source Note

Homer illustrates the need to bury the dead, and the gulf that must separate them from the living, when Patroklos appears to Achilleus in a dream. Achilleus has fallen asleep, exhausted from dragging Hektor's corpse around, obsessed with the memory of Patroklos. But the apparition says:

You sleep, Achilleus; you have forgotten me; but you were not / careless of me when I lived, but only in death. Bury me / as quickly as may be, let me pass through the gates of Hades. / The souls, the images of dead men, hold me at a distance, / and will not let me cross the riv-

PRIAM PLEADING WITH ACHILLEUS FOR THE BODY OF HEKTOR
Gavin Hamilton

Humanities Note
Fine art, *Priam Pleading with Achilleus for the Body of Hektor* by Gavin Hamilton. The Scottish painter Gavin Hamilton (1732–1798) was born to a noble family. His financial independence allowed him the freedom to live and work in Rome for most of his life. Hamilton's neoclassical paintings reflect his genuine desire to re–create the art of ancient Greece and Rome.

Hamilton began painting large-scale illustrations of the story of the *Iliad* in the 1760's. His scholarly knowledge of Homer's work and his interest in accurate historical detail are apparent in the painting *Priam Pleading with Achilleus for the Body of Hektor*. The figures, painted life-sized, have a shallow friezelike quality. The heavy color maintains the austere formal quality of the painting.

You might want to use the following questions to discuss the art:
1. What is the atmosphere of the painting?
2. How does the painting enhance your understanding of the scene depicted?

And you, old sir, we are told you prospered once; for as much
as Lesbos, Makar's hold,[8] confines[9] to the north above it
and Phrygia from the north confines, and enormous Hellespont,
of these, old sir, you were lord once in your wealth and your
    children.
But now the Uranian gods[10] brought us, an affliction upon you,
forever there is fighting about your city, and men killed.
But bear up, nor mourn endlessly in your heart, for there is not
anything to be gained from grief for your son; you will never
bring him back; sooner you must go through yet another sorrow."
  In answer to him again spoke aged Priam the godlike:
"Do not, beloved of Zeus, make me sit on a chair while Hektor
lies yet forlorn among the shelters; rather with all speed
give him back, so my eyes may behold him, and accept the ransom
we bring you, which is great. You may have joy of it, and go back
to the land of your own fathers, since once you have permitted me
to go on living myself and continue to look on the sunlight."
  Then looking darkly at him spoke swift-footed Achilleus:
"No longer stir me up, old sir. I myself am minded
to give Hektor back to you. A messenger came to me from Zeus,
my mother, she who bore me, the daughter of the sea's ancient.
I know you, Priam, in my heart, and it does not escape me

8. **Makar's hold:** The land ruled by Makar, the legendary lord of Lesbos.
9. **confines** (kən fīnz') *v.*: Contains within its boundaries.
10. **Uranian gods:** Descendants of Uranus, god of the sky.

13

13 Discussion Remind students of the parable of the urns, line 136. In the context of the parable, ask students how Achilleus' words can suggest some consolation. Suggest that accepting loss and coming to an end of mourning, realizing that one cannot bring back the dead, is more generally an understanding of the uncertainty of fortune and the unhappiness of human life. How is this view a consolation for Achilleus?

er and mingle with them, / but I wander as I am by Hades' house of the wide gates. / And I call upon you in sorrow, give me your hand; no longer / shall I come back from death, once you give me my rite of burning. / . . . Then in answer to him spoke swift-footed Achilleus: / "How is it, o hallowed head of my brother, you have come back to me / here, and tell me all these several things? Yet surely / I am accomplishing all, and I shall do as you tell me. / But stand closer to me, and let us, if only for a little, embrace, and take full satisfaction from the dirge of sorrow.

Achilleus tries to embrace Patroklos, but the spirit returns underground, "like vapor," and Achilleus realizes that "there is no real heart of life" in the phantom, although it looks and sounds just like a living man.

that some god led you to the running ships of the Achaians.
For no mortal would dare come to our encampment, not even
175 one strong in youth. He could not get by the pickets, he could not
lightly unbar the bolt that secures our gateway. Therefore
you must not further make my spirit move in my sorrows,
for fear, old sir, I might not let you alone in my shelter,
suppliant as you are; and be guilty before the god's orders."
180   He spoke, and the old man was frightened and did as he told him.
The son of Peleus bounded to the door of the house like a lion,
nor went alone, but the two henchmen[11] followed attending,
the hero Automedon and Alkimos, those whom Achilleus
honored beyond all companions after Patroklos dead. These two
185 now set free from under the yoke the mules and the horses,
and led inside the herald, the old king's crier, and gave him
a chair to sit in, then from the smooth-polished mule wagon
lifted out the innumerable spoils for the head of Hektor,
but left inside it two great cloaks and a fine spun tunic
190 to shroud the corpse in when they carried him home. Then
    Achilleus
called out to his serving-maids to wash the body and anoint[12] it
all over; but take it first aside, since otherwise Priam
might see his son and in the heart's sorrow not hold in his anger
at the sight, and the deep heart in Achilleus be shaken to anger
195 that he might not kill Priam and be guilty before the god's orders.
Then when the serving-maids had washed the corpse and anointed it
with olive oil, they threw a fair great cloak and a tunic
about him, and Achilleus himself lifted him and laid him
on a litter, and his friends helped him lift it to the smooth-polished
200   mule wagon. He groaned then, and called by name on his beloved
    companion:
"Be not angry with me, Patroklos, if you discover,
though you be in the house of Hades, that I gave back great
    Hektor
to his loved father, for the ransom he gave me was not unworthy.
I will give you your share of the spoils, as much as is fitting."
205   So spoke great Achilleus and went back into the shelter
and sat down on the elaborate couch from which he had risen,
against the inward wall, and now spoke his word to Priam:
"Your son is given back to you, aged sir, as you asked it.
He lies on a bier.[13] When dawn shows you yourself shall see him
210 as you take him away. Now you and I must remember our supper.
For even Niobe,[14] she of the lovely tresses, remembered
to eat, whose twelve children were destroyed in her palace,
six daughters, and six sons in the pride of their youth, whom
    Apollo
killed with arrows from his silver bow, being angered
215 with Niobe, and shaft-showering Artemis killed the daughters;
because Niobe likened herself to Leto of the fair coloring

11. henchmen (hench´ mən) *n.*: Male attendants, helpers, followers.

12. anoint (ə noint´) *v.*: Rub with oil or ointment to make holy or sacred.

13. bier (bir) *n.*: A coffin and its supporting platform.

14. Niobe (nī ō´ bē): Wife of Amphion, one of the two founders of Thebes.

14 Discussion Ask students to think about how Achilleus' sudden anger affects our view of his self-control and hospitality when we are forced to think about his violent temper and potential for murder.

15 Discussion Remind students of Andromache's weaving and of her despair that Hektor would not be buried in fine shrouds as should be his due. Ask students to discuss why it matters to the living how the dead will be treated.

16 Discussion Achilleus now shows self-awareness and awareness of others. Have students discuss the significance of Achilleus' ability to envision Priam's response to Hektor's maltreated corpse and his own subsequent reaction.

17 Clarification Tell students that in Book XXIII a vision of Patroklos appeared to Achilleus in a dream as he slept in exhaustion after dragging Hektor's corpse, and Patroklos asked to be buried immediately. You might also ask students why Achilleus needs to ask for Patroklos' forgiveness. How is Achilleus now showing his willingness to accept his society's rules for dealing with loss?

18 Discussion Call students' attention to Achilleus' insistence on sharing a meal with Priam, who has refused food since Hektor's death, as Achilleus himself refused to eat after the death of Patroklos. What does Achilleus' gesture say about his frame of mind? What might this scene of *xenia* reveal about the way Priam and Achilleus have momentarily entered a divinely protected sphere?

Grammar in Action

Parallelism involves the construction of sentences in which grammatical elements of equal rank are similarly expressed. Parallel constructions add clarity and coherence to writing. An example of faulty parallel construction is as follows:

My test score revealed exceptional analytical ability but that I make too many careless errors.

The construction is faulty because it pairs a noun, "analytical ability," with a clause, "that I make too many careless errors." To make the sentence parallel, change the noun to a clause:

My test score revealed that I have exceptional analytical ability but that I make too many careless errors.

Note the parallel structure in these lines from the *Iliad*:

He could not get by the pickets, he could not / lightly unbar the bolt that secures our gateway (lines 175–176).

So spoke great Achilleus and went back into the shelter and sat down on the elaborate couch from which he had risen (lines 206–207).

and said Leto had borne only two, she herself had borne many;
but the two, though they were only two, destroyed all those
    others.
Nine days long they lay in their blood, nor was there anyone
to bury them, for the son of Kronos made stones out of
the people; but on the tenth day the Uranian gods buried them.
But she remembered to eat when she was worn out with weeping.
And now somewhere among the rocks, in the lonely mountains,
in Sipylos,[15] where they say is the resting place of the goddesses
who are nymphs, and dance beside the waters of Acheloios,[16]
there, stone still,[17] she broods on the sorrows that the gods
    gave her.
Come then, we also, aged magnificent sir, must remember
to eat, and afterwards you may take your beloved son back
to Ilion, and mourn for him; and he will be much lamented."

So spoke fleet Achilleus and sprang to his feet and slaughtered
a gleaming sheep, and his friends skinned it and butchered it fairly,
and cut up the meat expertly into small pieces, and spitted them,
and roasted all carefully and took off the pieces.
Automedon took the bread and set it out on the table
in fair baskets, while Achilleus served the meats. And thereon
they put their hands to the good things that lay ready before them.
But when they had put aside their desire for eating and drinking,
Priam, son of Dardanos, gazed upon Achilleus, wondering
at his size and beauty, for he seemed like an outright vision
of gods. Achilleus in turn gazed on Dardanian Priam
and wondered, as he saw his brave looks and listened to him
    talking.
But when they had taken their fill of gazing one on the other,
first of the two to speak was the aged man, Priam the godlike:
"Give me, beloved of Zeus, a place to sleep presently, so that
we may even go to bed and take the pleasure of sweet sleep.
For my eyes have not closed underneath my lids since that time
when my son lost his life beneath your hands, but always
I have been grieving and brooding over my numberless sorrows
and wallowed in the muck about my courtyard's enclosure.
Now I have tasted food again and have let the gleaming
wine go down my throat. Before, I had tasted nothing.

Achilleus calls a twelve-day truce while the Trojans perform Hek-
tor's funeral rites. Kassandra watches as her father Priam approaches
Troy in his chariot. She sees her brother Hektor's body drawn by the
mules on a litter.

She [Kassandra] cried out then in sorrow and spoke to the entire
    city:
"Come, men of Troy and Trojan women; look upon Hektor
if ever before you were joyful when you saw him come back living

15. Sipylos (si′ pə lōs′): A mountain in Asia Minor.
16. Acheloios (ə kē′ loi ōs′): A river near Mount Sipylos in Asia Minor.
17. stone still: According to legend, Niobe boasted of having more and better children than Leto. To avenge their insulted mother, Apollo and Artemis killed Niobe's children. Niobe turned to stone while weeping over her loss.

19 Literary Focus Authors and the characters in their works may re-shape a story to fit their own particular needs. Achilleus is retelling the myth for his own purposes: to show that even the most extreme misfortune and the most extreme grief must be finite for human beings. His particular moral, that even Niobe stopped weeping and ate, and that her grief numbed her so much she turned into a dark rock down whose face water flows like tears, is inserted in his version just before the traditional ending of the tale. Does he expect Priam to stop grieving for Hektor, or simply to pause long enough to recognize that he himself is alive and so needs to eat?

20 Literary Focus The preparation of a feast or a meal shared in some formal way is always described in formulaic language. Have students think about why repeating a standard description is appropriate to an act that is performed in a set, ritualized way. What is the significance of a shared meal such as the one between Achilleus and Priam?

21 Discussion After their shared meal, Achilleus and Priam look at each other with admiration. Ask students to think about how Priam sees Achilleus and how Achilleus sees Priam.

22 Discussion Ask students what parallels they can draw between Priam's behavior since Hektor's death and Achilleus' earlier behavior. Suggest that Priam's and Achilleus' obsessive grief can be seen as a denial of the boundaries separating the living from the dead.

    In the first sentence, two past perfect verbs are paired, and in the second sentence, two past tense verbs are paired.
    Student Activity 1. Find three or more examples of parallel structure on pages 384–385.
    Student Activity 2. Write a synopsis of what you have read in the *Iliad* using correct parallel construction.

23 Discussion Ask students to discuss what the Trojans' behavior when his body is brought back suggests about Hektor's relationship to his people. Students should also consider whether lines 256–266 could have been written as a reaction to Achilleus' death. What is fundamentally different between the two men?

24 Discussion How does the formalized, ritual mourning that is led by professional mourners help those whose grief is more personal to express and face their loss?

25 Reading Strategy Have students reread Andromache's speech to Hektor in Book VI and Andromache's words when she first hears of Hektor's death. Ask students how these earlier scenes affect the way we respond to her formal dirge now.

26 Discussion Andromache now also envisions the fate we know awaits Astyanax. Ask students how she places the cruel murder of her baby son in the context of Hektor's greatness as a warrior.

255 from battle; for he was a great joy to his city, and all his people."
    She spoke, and there was no man left there in all the city
nor woman, but all were held in sorrow passing endurance.
They met Priam beside the gates as he brought the dead in.
First among them were Hektor's wife and his honored mother
260 who tore their hair, and ran up beside the smooth-rolling wagon,
and touched his head. And the multitude, wailing, stood there
    about them.
And now and there in front of the gates they would have lamented
all day till the sun went down and let fall their tears for Hektor,
except that the old man spoke from the chariot to his people:
265 "Give me way to get through with my mules; then afterwards
you may sate[18] yourselves with mourning, when I have him inside
    the palace."
    So he spoke, and they stood apart and made way for the wagon.
And when they had brought him inside the renowned house, they
    laid him
then on a carved bed, and seated beside him the singers
270 who were to lead the melody in the dirge,[19] and the singers
chanted the song of sorrow, and the women were mourning beside
    them.
Andromache of the white arms led the lamentation
of the women, and held in her arms the head of manslaughtering
    Hektor:
"My husband, you were lost young from life, and have left me
275 a widow in your house, and the boy is only a baby
who was born to you and me, the unhappy. I think he will never
come of age, for before then head to heel this city
will be sacked, for you, its defender, are gone, you who guarded
the city, and the grave wives, and the innocent children,
280 wives who before long must go away in the hollow ships,
and among them I shall also go, and you, my child, follow
where I go, and there do much hard work that is unworthy
of you, drudgery for a hard master; or else some Achaian
will take you by hand and hurl you from the tower[20] into horrible
285 death, in anger because Hektor once killed his brother,
or his father, or his son; there were so many Achaians
whose teeth bit the vast earth, beaten down by the hands of
    Hektor.
Your father was no merciful man in the horror of battle.
Therefore your people are grieving for you all through their city,
290 Hektor, and you left for your parents mourning and sorrow
beyond words, but for me passing all others is left the bitterness
and the pain, for you did not die in bed, and stretch your arms to
    me,
nor tell me some last intimate word that I could remember
always, all the nights and days of my weeping for you."

18. sate (sāt) *n.*: Satisfy or gratify.

19. dirge (durj) *n.*: A funeral hymn.

20. hurl you from the tower: Hektor's infant son Astyanax was eventually hurled from the walls after the fall of Troy.

So she spoke in tears, and the women were mourning about her.
Now Hekabe led out the thronging chant of their sorrow:
"Hektor, of all my sons the dearest by far to my spirit;
while you still lived for me you were dear to the gods, and even
in the stage of death they cared about you still. There were others
of my sons whom at times swift-footed Achilleus captured,
and he would sell them as slaves far across the unresting salt water
into Samos, and Imbros, and Lemnos[21] in the gloom of the mists.
    You,
when he had taken your life with the thin edge of the bronze sword,
he dragged again and again around his beloved companion's
tomb, Patroklos', whom you killed, but even so did not
bring him back to life. Now you lie in the palace, handsome
and fresh with dew, in the likeness of one whom he of the silver
bow, Apollo, has attacked and killed with his gentle arrows."

So she spoke, in tears, and wakened the endless mourning.
Third and last Helen led the song of sorrow among them:
"Hektor, of all my lord's brothers dearest by far to my spirit:
my husband is Alexandros, like an immortal, who brought me
here to Troy; and I should have died before I came with him;
and here now is the twentieth year upon me since I came
from the place where I was, forsaking the land of my fathers. In
    this time
I have never heard a harsh saying from you, nor an insult.
No, but when another, one of my lord's brothers or sisters, a fair-
    robed
wife of some brother, would say a harsh word to me in the palace,
or my lord's mother—but his father was gentle always, a father
indeed—then you would speak and put them off and restrain them
by your own gentleness of heart and your gentle words. Therefore
I mourn for you in sorrow of heart and mourn myself also
and my ill luck. There was no other in all the wide Troad
who was kind to me, and my friend; all others shrank when they
    saw me."

So she spoke in tears, and the vast populace grieved with her.
Now Priam the aged king spoke forth his word to his people:
"Now, men of Troy, bring timber into the city, and let not
your hearts fear a close ambush of the Argives. Achilleus
promised me, as he sent me on my way from the black ships
that none should do us injury until the twelfth dawn comes."

He spoke, and they harnessed to the wagons their mules and
    their oxen
and presently were gathered in front of the city. Nine days
they spent bringing in an endless supply of timber. But when
the tenth dawn had shone forth with her light upon mortals,
they carried out bold Hektor, weeping, and set the body
aloft a towering pyre for burning. And set fire to it.

21. Samos (sā′ mōs′),
Imbros (im′brōs′), **Lemnos**
(lem′ nōs): Islands in the
Aegean Sea.

27 **Enrichment** In the context of formal mourning, only women sing dirges; so here Hekabe speaks, but Priam does not; his silence suggests that he has accepted his traditional role in coming to terms with Hektor's death. Draw students' attention to lines 302–306, in which Hekabe expresses the wisdom that grief, mourning, and revenge cannot undo death. Her words also suggest that Achilleus' vengeance is finally an ineffectual and meaningless way to exorcise his grief; only accepting death and respecting ritual can help.

28 **Discussion** Ask students if they are surprised that Helen, the cause of all the trouble in the first place, has a role in lamenting Hektor's death. What does she reveal about Hektor's personality and behavior and her relationship to him? What does she reveal about herself when she speaks well of Hektor and Priam but lodges a complaint against Hekabe and others?

29 **Discussion** Ask students to consider whether it heightens our involvement in the funeral to realize that the private truce arranged by Achilleus with Priam is brief and the war will continue.

But when the young dawn showed again with her rosy fingers,
The people gathered around the pyre of illustrious Hektor.
But when all were gathered to one place and assembled together,
340 first with gleaming wine they put out the pyre that was burning,
all where the fury of the fire still was in force, and thereafter
the brothers and companions of Hektor gathered the white bones
up, mourning, as the tears swelled and ran down their cheeks.
  Then
they laid what they had gathered up in a golden casket
345 and wrapped this about with soft robes of purple, and presently
put it away in the hollow of the grave, and over it
piled huge stones laid close together. Lightly and quickly
they piled up the grave-barrow, and on all sides were set watchmen
for fear the strong-greaved Achaians might too soon set upon
  them.
350 They piled up the grave-barrow and went away, and thereafter
assembled in a fair gathering and held a glorious
feast within the house of Priam, king under God's hand.
  Such was their burial of Hektor, breaker of horses.

Reader's Response *Throughout the poem, Homer's focus is on humanity and what it means to be human. What do you think it means to be human?*

THINKING ABOUT THE SELECTION

Interpreting

1. Hektor makes a fatal decision when he decides to stay outside the Skaian gates. Explain how both divine and human causation bring about his decision.
2. On his golden scale, Zeus places two portions of death, one for Achilleus and one for Hektor. (a) Why do you think Hektor's portion is heavier? (b) What does this image reveal about the Greek view of destiny, or, the way life has to be?
3. Hektor pleads with Achilleus not to defile his corpse but to give him his proper rite of burning. (a) What does Achilleus' refusal of Hektor's dying wish suggest about him? (b) In your opinion, what type of man has Achilleus become?
4. What does the act of dragging Hektor's body symbolize?
5. What does Homer's description of Achilleus as he mourns Patroklos reveal about Achilleus?
6. When Priam ransoms Hektor's body from Achilleus, Achilleus describes the two urns that stand on Zeus' doorsill. What do the contents of these two urns indicate about human life?
7. (a) How does the ending show the workings of divine pity? (b) How does it also show the workings of human pity?
8. In your own words, what is the human tragedy presented in the *Iliad*?

Applying

9. The ritual of burial helps the Trojans endure the unendurable. What rituals do we have today that help us bear the human tragedy?

ANALYZING LITERATURE

Interpreting Epic Similes

The elaborate comparisons prevalent in Books XXII and XXIV of the *Iliad* are **epic similes.** Homer compares certain characters and situations in the *Iliad* to objects or occurrences that his audience is familiar with, thus drawing them into the experience of the poem. Homeric similes enable both ancient and modern audiences to identify with the action taking place in the poem.

1. Read the following simile: "And as a star moves among stars in the night's darkening, / Hesper, who is the fairest star who stands in the sky, such / was the shining from the pointed spear Achilleus was shaking / in his right hand with evil intention toward brilliant Hektor." (a) What could the fairest star and Achilleus' spear have in common to lead Homer to make the comparison in this epic simile? (b) How does the comparison portray Achilleus?
2. Find two more epic similes, explain their comparisons, and tell how they invite the audience to identify with the story.

CRITICAL THINKING AND READING

Understanding Ancient Codes of Ethics

In the *Iliad*, funeral rites are elaborate. They provide a way of celebrating the life and acknowledging the worth of the dead person. They also help the living come to terms with grief and loss so that they can separate themselves from the dead and go on living. First the corpse must be prepared for burial. Then those close to the deceased must give voice to their mourning in ritual laments that follow a comfortingly familiar pattern, but that also allow for personal detail. Following the ritual laments, the corpse is burned on a funeral pyre, and the ashes are later buried.

Another sacred code of behavior had to do with hospitality, *xenia*. It was customary to offer a stranger food, drink, and shelter before asking his or her name or business. Neither the host nor the guest was to violate the bond of hospitality; wronging a host or a guest was a crime punishable by Zeus in his role as Zeus Xenios. Ties of xenia could bind persons unrelated by blood, and their descendants, in a strong alliance.

1. What does Achilleus hope to accomplish by defiling Hektor's corpse?
2. How do the gods respond to Achilleus' action?
3. Why does Achilleus arrange a truce so that Hektor can be buried?

4. What role do rituals play in bridging private and public worlds in the *Iliad*?
5. Achilleus insists on sharing food with Priam although he has already eaten. What is the role of shared food in the context of hospitality? In the context of grief and accepting loss?
6. How does the meeting of Priam and Achilleus in Achilleus' tent stretch the limits of the guest-host relationship?

UNDERSTANDING LANGUAGE

Identifying English Words of Greek Origin

Greek language is a substantial part of the rich cultural legacy of ancient Greece; many English words are Greek in origin. For example, the English word *democracy* comes from the Greek root *demos,* meaning "people." The books you have read from the *Iliad* contain several words that have Greek roots. *Generation* (Book XXIV, line 148) comes from the Greek word *genos,* meaning "race" or "kind." Names of Greek gods and heroes also have roots used in English. *Auto* in *Automedon* (Book XXIV, line 83) is the Greek word for self. Among the English words we get from *auto* are *autograph, autobiography,* and *autonomous.* Can you think of other English words from *auto?*

1. Today we associate Achilleus with his heel. Use a dictionary to determine what we mean when we refer to someone's "Achilles' heel."
2. In line 336 of Book XXIV, notice the Greek root *pyre.* What does it mean and what English words come from *pyre?*

THINKING AND WRITING

Writing About Shared Humanity

Priam's tears of loss over Hektor's death move Achilleus to realize that his own father would have been similarly devastated at the thought of Achilleus dead on the battlefield. That realization breaks down the strict heroic code Achilleus lives by, and the two men shed tears of sadness in recognition of their common human condition. Write the first draft of an essay in which you analyze the scene between Achilleus and Priam and discuss the ways in which it illustrates their shared humanity. Revise the first draft, making sure you have supported your discussion with examples from the text. Finally, proofread for spelling and mechanical errors.

(continued from bottom of page)

2. Zeus finds it inappropriate; Apollo explains that Achilleus' refusal to accept death and to honor the dead threatens the order of the world.
3. Achilleus has realized his own humanity and has accepted that there is nothing meaningful to take the place of the customs and rituals of his society.
4. Private grief, unchanneled and uncontrolled, turns human beings into savage beasts, into iron stone or destructive fire. Rituals make continued life in the human community possible.
5. (a) Sharing food is an acknowledgment of common humanity; all living creatures need to eat. Giving and accepting food stresses man's interdependence. (b) Acknowledging the need to eat expresses a willingness to go on living.
6. Ultimate enemies, the two men find a common bond in a kind of no-man's land protected by *Zeus xenios,* the god who joins strangers and enemies in a reciprocal dependence.

ANSWERS TO UNDERSTANDING LANGUAGE

1. Someone's "Achilles' heel" is his or her vulnerable spot.
2. (a) Pyre means fire. (b) Answers will differ. Suggested answers are pyromania and pyrostat.

THINKING AND WRITING

Writing Across the Curriculum
Part of students' discussion of the shared humanity of Priam and Achilleus will involve a discussion of Greek cultural values and customs.

You might want to inform the social studies department that students are reading the *Iliad.* History teachers might help students incorporate the poem's historical context into their papers.

Challenge Ask students to explore those books of the *Iliad* that they did not read for more examples of epic similes and scenes of shared humanity.

mortality and about the tension between man's potential greatness and his vulnerability.
9. Answers will differ. Suggested response: with such "rituals" as wakes, funerals, and religious services.

ANSWERS TO ANALYZING LITERATURE

1. (a) The brightness of the two objects compared triggers the simile. (b) Achilleus seems more than human; the evening star is also associated with death.
2. Answers will differ. Students should be careful to select similes of epic proportions, not simple comparisons

using *like* or *as.* They should also identify the comparison and explain why the comparison is something to which the audience can relate.

ANSWERS TO CRITICAL THINKING AND READING

1. Achilleus really wants to undo Patroklos' death; this is why his attempts to defile Hektor cannot satisfy him.

THE DISCOVERY OF TROY

"I did what no one else has ever done and no one else could ever do . . . Europe and America are dazzled by my discovery of the ancient city of Troy—that Troy which the archaeologists of all countries have searched for in vain for two thousand years." This is how Heinrich Schliemann, self-made millionaire and amateur archeologist, described his achievement in unearthing what he believed to be Troy. Before Schliemann's discovery in 1870, many people believed that Troy was built by Homer's imagination; after Schliemann, no one could deny that an historic Troy had existed.

The world at large has taken Schliemann at his own estimation. The glamour and the glory of finding Homer's Troy and digging up a golden treasure have gone to him. Without his obsession, his ruthlessness, and his wealth, perhaps the dusty, vermin-infested little village covering the site of Troy would have gone on hiding the ruins of the ancient city forever. However, the truth is a bit different from Schliemann's boast.

His success aroused an uproar: he had been digging on privately owned land without the owners' permission and without notifying the government. Archeological scholars were also horrified: Schliemann was just digging, like a dog after a bone, look-ing for his vision of the Homeric city and its treasures, bashing his way through everything he thought more modern and tossing it carelessly aside.

Ironically, though, in his eagerness and ignorance, Schliemann completely missed Homeric Troy. His younger friend and protégé, archeologist Wilhelm Dorpfeld, continued the excavations after Schliemann's death. He found that where Schliemann dug, the only remains of Priam's city were parts of a house and a wall that Schliemann had passed by with contempt, thinking that they were Macedonian, from about a thousand years later than the Trojan war.

The responsible excavation of Troy was not completed until the years 1932–1938, when the American archeologist Carl Blegan from the University of Cincinnati finished the job and repaired as much as he could of the damage Schliemann had done. Posterity is dazzled by Schliemann the visionary raider and by the buried golden treasure he found; but if the earth yields up information about history and ancient cultures, it is because of the painstaking and unglamorous work of scholars like Blegan who pay attention to fragments of pottery, cooking utensils, and farming tools—things that never make the headlines.

SCHLIEMANN'S EXCAVATION OF ANCIENT TROY

Poetry

THETIS BRINGING ARMOR TO ACHILLEUS
Archeological Museum, Gela, Italy

THE DEATH OF HEKTOR
Fifth century B.C.
Vatican Museum, Rome

Archilochus
c. 680 B.C.–c. 640 B.C.

The first and most influential Greek lyric poet is Archilochus (är kil′ ə kəs). Born on the island of Paros, Archilochus was the illegitimate son of a distinguished aristocrat and a slave-woman. Poverty drove him to become a mercenary soldier and join the second colonizing expedition to Thasos, an island off the Thracian coast.

Archilochus' work is priceless evidence of seventh-century frontier life in Thasos during its gold rush. Settlers there lived in constant danger from Thracian tribesmen and other rival prospectors. Living in an era of widespread colonization, constant warfare, and rapid social change provided Archilochus with the material for his lyrics. In them, he reflects the aggressive, bellicose nature of his world.

During his time as a soldier on Thasos, Archilochus fell in love with a local girl named Neobule (nē ob′ yōō lē). To Archilochus' distress, her father, Lycambes (IT kam′ bēz), forbade their marriage. Embittered, Archilochus avenged himself with biting, satirical poems about Neobule's family. According to tradition, Archilochus' savage poems about Neobule and her father shamed them so deeply that they hanged themselves.

Archilochus was an aggressive individualist, famous chiefly for his highly personal, intensely emotional lyrics. Unlike Homer, Archilochus had no use for heroics. He had no illusions about war and scorned heroic ideals. Having been freed from aristocratic concerns, he was liberal with his biting satire. Archilochus attacked all strata of society—the powerful and the powerless, the rich and the poor.

Archilochus was celebrated in antiquity for the sound of his poetry and the bite of his wit. The sound suggests bursts of anger; the bite is so intense that a twelfth-century archbishop called him "scorpion-tongued." Although Archilochus was popular throughout antiquity, only fragments of his poetry have survived.

Callinus
c. 680 B.C.–630 B.C.

Callinus (kə IT′ nəs) of Ephesos (ē fē′ sōs), a contemporary of Archilochus, is also known as one of the first elegists, poets who combined the meter of epic (hexameter) with a more lyrical pentameter line to form elegiac couplets. Little is known about Callinus, and only one fragment of his poetry survives. In his only remaining poem, Callinus encourages his fellow citizens to resist the invading barbaric Cimmerians.

Callinus' poem deviates from the personal, unheroic lyrics of Archilochus. Callinus seems to defend the heroic ideal, especially the patriotic ethic coined later by the Roman Horace, *Dulce et decorum est pro patria mori,* "It is sweet and proper to die for the fatherland."

GUIDE FOR INTERPRETING

Archilochus' and Callinus' Lyrics

Commentary

Lyric Poetry. The early Greeks defined **lyric poetry** as the emotional expression of a singer accompanied by a lyre. Except for the lyre, this definition applies today. Lyric poetry is still defined as the expression of individual experience and personal emotion. The lyric poem is short, presents a single experience, and results in a single effect, usually involving the poet's emotions.

Lyric poetry is melodic; in other words, it creates music with words. Greek lyric is composed in a variety of meters, with different patterns made up of long and short syllables. Greek verse is characterized by syllable length and changes in pitch rather than by stress. English verse, on the other hand, depends on patterns of stressed and unstressed syllables for its rhythm. The meter of Archilochus' poetry, the way it sounds according to the long and short Greek syllables and the accented and unaccented syllables in English translation, conveys his fierce emotional commitment to his ideas.

Ancient lyricists like Archilochus are important both for their contribution to our literary heritage and for the insight they provide into the Greek personality. They reveal a great deal about how the Greeks perceived their world and how they responded to the problems posed by ancient life. The remaining fragments of Archilochus' and Callinus' poetry are examples of how two Greek poets responded to the world very differently.

"A Call to Arms," the only remaining fragment of Callinus' poetry, is more of a public, heroic lyric. It echoes the heroic ethic that pervades the earlier Greek epic poetry.

Writing

Put yourself in the place of a youth growing up in ancient Greece. Freewrite, exploring your thoughts on going to battle.

Primary Source

Ancient lyrics, particularly those of Archilochus and Callinus, were recited publicly well into the fifth century B.C. The fifth-century rhetorician and critic Gorgias saw lyric poetry as having a magical effect on listeners.

"When a person hears it [lyric] there comes over him a tremor of fear and a compassion that moves to tears and a longing that issues in grief: though confronted with vicissitudes in the course of events and the lives of characters that have nothing to do with him, his soul so responds to words that it experiences the emotions of others as if they were its own . . . The divine incantation of words gives rise to pleasure, puts an end to grief: becoming one and the same with the soul's faculty of discernment, the power of incantation bewitches, persuades, and transforms with its magic."

Literary Focus Archilochus and Callinus offer very different views of a soldier's duty. Stress that we are able to determine their views because their poems are lyric in form; that is, they are expressions of individual experience and personal emotion. Have students think about their own encounters with the self-sacrificial heroic code and the cynical survivalist view toward dying in battle.

Writing/Prior Knowledge To help students complete the writing assignment, it might help to ask them to draw from other works they have read about people in wartime. Students may have seen reruns of the series *M.A.S.H.* on television, or the recent movies and documentaries made on the war in Vietnam; some may have read *The Red Badge of Courage* or *Catch 22*. What kinds of factors influence soldiers' points of view?

ESL Teaching Strategy Since these poems are short, ESL students may benefit from reading the poems aloud. You may want to read the poems to them and ask students to infer the authors' attitudes toward war based on what they heard in your reading.

Teaching Tenth-Grade Students To reinforce the characteristics of lyric poetry for tenth-grade students, give them time in class to read the poems. Ask them, as they read, to write down on a separate paper those words or phrases that reflect the speakers' personal thoughts and feelings. Then ask them to discuss the personal qualities they found in the lyrics.

Support Material
Teaching Portfolio
Teacher Backup, p. 505
Usage and Mechanics Worksheet, p. 509
Analyzing Literature Worksheet, *Analyzing Lyric Poetry*, p. 510
Critical Thinking and Reading Worksheet, *Making Inferences*, p. 511

Language Worksheet, *Recognizing the Origins of Words*, p. 512
Selection Test, pp. 513–514

Some Barbarian Is Waving My Shield

Archilochus

translated by Richmond Lattimore

Some barbarian is waving my shield, since I was obliged to
    leave that perfectly good piece of equipment behind
under a bush. But I got away, so what does it matter?
    Let the shield go; I can buy another one equally good.

To the Gods All Things Are Easy

Archilochus

translated by Richmond Lattimore

To the gods all things are easy. Many times from circumstance
of disaster they set upright those who have been sprawled at length
on the ground, but often again when men stand planted on firm feet,
these same gods will knock them on their backs, and then the evils come,
so that a man wanders homeless, destitute, at his wit's end.

THINKING ABOUT THE SELECTION

Interpreting

1. What does the narrator of "Some Barbarian Is Waving My Shield" mean by saying, "But I got away, so
   what does it matter"?
2. In your own words, rephrase the narrator's conclusion of "Some Barbarian Is Waving My Shield."
3. What does "To the Gods All Things Are Easy" suggest about how the narrator perceives fate?
4. The Roman author Horace is famous for saying,
   "Dulce et decorum est pro patria mori," which
   means, "It is sweet and proper to die for your country." Locate three examples from "A Call to Arms"
   that illustrate the ethic Horace describes.

Applying

5. Give examples of how you or people you are familiar with respond to the major issues of the day in
   ways that are similar to Archilochus' and Callinus'
   narrators.
6. The American writer Ralph Waldo Emerson wrote,
   "A hero is no braver than an ordinary man, but he is
   brave five minutes longer." (a) How do you think the

A Call to Arms

Callinus

translated by Richmond Lattimore

How long will you lie idle, and when will you find some courage,
    you young men? Have you no shame of what other cities will say,
you who hang back? You think you can sit quiet in peacetime.
    This is not peace, it is war which has engulfed our land.

4

5   A man, as he dies, should make one last throw with his spear.
It is a high thing, a bright honor, for a man to do battle
    with the enemy for the sake of his children, and for his land
and his true wife; and death is a thing that will come when the spinning
    Destinies make it come. So a man should go straight on
10 forward, spear held high, and under his shield the fighting
    strength coiled ready to strike in the first shock of the charge.
When it is ordained that a man shall die, there is no escaping
    death, not even for one descended from deathless gods.
Often a man who has fled from the fight and the clash of the thrown
      spears
15 goes his way, and death befalls him in his own house,
and such a man is not loved nor missed for long by his people;
    the great and the small alike mourn when a hero dies.
For all the populace is grieved for the high-hearted warrior
    after his death; while he lives, he is treated as almost divine.
20 Their eyes gaze on him as if he stood like a bastion before them.
    His actions are like an army's, though he is only one man.

5

---

4 Discussion What is familiar from Homer? What is different? Would Homer have mentioned "what other cities will say"? What assumptions about national (vs. tribal or individual) honor and shame lie behind this line?

5 Discussion How does Callinus view destiny? Why should a man die in battle rather than at home?

Master Teacher Note Ask students to discuss what a Vietnam veteran might think of this poem compared to what a World War II fighter pilot would think. The film *Apocalypse Now* and the novel/film *Catch 22* would provide students with interesting contemporary frames of reference. Note that both films are intended for mature audiences.

Cultural Note The world of the mercenary, to which Archilochus belongs, has a much more cynical view of friendship (or *xenia*) than the old heroic world. In a fragment he writes, "Glaukos [using the name of the hero who exchanges armor with his ancestral guest-friend Diomedes in the *Iliad*], soldier of fortune, will be your friend, until the fighting begins."

Cooperative Learning Divide students into groups of up to five; have them share ideas about what it might feel like to be living in a small community under attack by tribesmen they consider savage, who speak another language, and whose religious beliefs and cultural practices differ from their own.

ancient Greeks would have responded to this definition? (b) How do you respond to it?

ANALYZING LITERATURE

Analyzing Lyric Poetry

Lyric poetry, whether private or public, creates a unified impression because of its intensity of emotion. Archilochus' lyrics express private concerns, whereas Callinus' lyric, while intensely emotional, is meant to inspire young Greek men against invading barbarians.

Using the heroic code of ethics, Callinus appeals to his fellow citizens' sense of honor and community. Callinus' lyric is a public poem, to be acted out.
1. Using examples from the poem, discuss how "Some Barbarian Is Waving My Shield" is a lyric of private expression.
2. What unified impression does "A Call to Arms" create?
3. Do you consider Callinus' poem inspirational? Explain.
4. What songs can you think of from American history that have a similar purpose to Callinus' lyric?

tor overcoming fear, which makes him a human hero in the way Achilleus is not. (b) Answers will differ. Encourage students to give reasons for their responses.

ANSWERS TO ANALYZING LITERATURE

1. Answers will vary but should focus on the use of the first-person pronoun and the consistently "I-centered"

    point of view.
2. The ethic begins and ends with the subordination of the individual to the needs, values, and reputation of the country.
3. Answers will vary but should be substantiated by explaining why the poem does or does not rouse the listener to action. Students might think of a coach's pregame pep talk as belonging to the same genre.

4. "The Battle Hymn of the Republic" might be one familiar example and, of course, "The Star-Spangled Banner."

Focus

More About the Authors Sappho's biography is difficult to disentangle from the legends that sprang up about her, many of them based on readings and misreadings of her poetry. She belonged to the aristocracy, and her family was involved in local politics. Along with many aristocrats, Sappho was exiled as a result of factional strife. She emigrated to Sicily, where she spent some time before being allowed to return from exile.

Pindar was intensely Theban—a member of a very conservative, tradition-bound aristocracy that still revered the values of the Homeric heroic world. In some ways, his education as a descendant of those old epic heroes, nobles who were constantly aware of how they were connected to the gods and to other nobles in distant communities, gave him the best preparation for becoming a pan-hellenic poet—one who celebrated victors in athletic contests that themselves look back to the world of Patroklos' funeral games.

Critical Evaluation: Sappho Plato called Sappho "the tenth muse," and the geographer Strabo called her "a marvel." He said that "In all the centuries since the beginning of history we know of no woman who can be said to rival her as a poet." Her contemporary, fellow-aristocrat and compatriot Alkaios called her "violet-tressed, holy, sweet-smiling Sappho."

Critical Evaluation: Pindar The Roman poet Horace wrote: "As a river pours down a mountain, swollen / by showers of rain, spilling over its banks, / so Pindar rages and the deep of his voice / pours ever onward . . ."

Sappho
c. 630 B.C.–c. 570 B.C.

Late in the seventh century B.C., the fame of the early lyric poets was eclipsed by Sappho (sa′ fō) of Lesbos, one of the most prolific ancient lyricists. Sappho wrote nearly five hundred poems, only a small fraction of which remain, intact or in fragments. In the bulk of her surviving poems, she addresses various girls of Lesbos, female companions who formed a circle around her. Some critics believe that Sappho was the priestess of a *thiasos* (thī′ ə sōs), an organized group of women who worshiped Aphrodite. Recent scholars, however, maintain that the circle of girls evident in her poetry were students, or apprentices, who studied poetry and the lyre with Sappho.

Her poetry was admired in antiquity; Plato praised her, and the Roman poets Catullus, Horace, and Ovid alluded to her in their work. In fact, at least six Greek comedies parodied her on the late Greek comic stage. Those plays are now lost, but from them sprang a number of legends about Sappho that were the source of disapproval and, later, hatred of her and her work. For example, according to legend, she was short, dark, and ugly, she was a prostitute, and she committed suicide by throwing herself off a cliff after the ferryman Phaon did not return her love. Although these legends are now discredited, they led the Bishop of Constantinople to order all copies of Sappho's work burned early in the Middle Ages. As a result of the bishop's order and a general loss of classical manuscripts during the Middle Ages, no collection of Sappho's poetry survived the medieval period.

Interest in Sappho revived in the Renaissance when scholars used lines quoted by other Greek and Latin writers to reconstruct Sappho's work. Then in 1879 an incredible discovery in an ancient Egyptian trash site uncovered poems by Sappho. Later archaeological digs in the 1890's brought to light shredded papyrus scrolls of Sappho's poetry; the scrolls had been used to wrap mummies and to stuff crocodiles.

Pindar
522 B.C.–c. 440 B.C.

There is little solid information about Pindar's (pin′ där) life. He wrote in a century full of intellectual and political ferment. Although he was born in Thebes, which stood outside the intellectual movements of the time, as a youth he spent a great deal of time away from his provincial birthplace and may have studied music and poetry in Athens, the intellectual hub of classical Greece.

In his twenties he was commissioned by a great aristocratic family to write an ode in honor of their son's victory in the Olympic double foot-race. Eventually, Pindar was commissioned to write for many athletic victors and in so doing became a poet of pan-Hellenic status. He was sought after by powerful monarchs and nobles, and he spent time at the courts of the fabulously wealthy Sicilian tyrants. Like Sappho, the great fame he achieved in his lifetime lasted through antiquity. The Roman poet Horace, for example, considered Pindar to be a poet of unrivaled eloquence and originality.

Objectives

Thematic

To appreciate the personal aim of lyric poetry

Skills

1 To analyze lyric fragments
2 To analyze personal lyric
3 To compare translations
4 To write about thematic threads
5 To analyze a victory ode
6 To imitate an ode

GUIDE FOR INTERPRETING

Sappho's and Pindar's Poetry

Commentary

Personal Lyric. Sappho was truly a lyric poet, singing or chanting poems to her own accompaniment on the lyre. Some of her poems, such as the epithalamia, or wedding songs, have a public orientation, but most of her poems emphasize her private preoccupations, reflecting a fierce attachment to her female companions. Such concern with the private individual is important, in a literary and cultural context. After Sappho, exclusive emphasis on private life and personal affairs did not recur until the Hellenistic Age, after Alexander's death (323 B.C.). We should not assume, however, that Sappho was unconcerned with public affairs, such as the revolution on Lesbos, her birthplace; she simply chose not to write about public concerns. To her, love was of supreme importance.

The musical quality of her poems heightens their emotional quality. Since she intended for the poems to be sung, their musical element is the focal point through which Sappho conveys her emotions. Although some of her most emotionally charged lines may be lost, the remaining fragments reflect the intensity of her poetic voice.

Victory Ode. The most formal, ceremonial, and complex lyric is the ode. Pindar was commissioned to write victory odes to honor the winners of prestigious athletic events, such as boxing or wrestling. These victory odes were designed to be sung and danced by a chorus of citizens. In his day Pindar's odes were more than poems; they were celebratory processionals—a whole people joyfully united to pay homage to a young athletic hero. The modern reader cannot fully appreciate the "Pindaric experience" because when the odes were collected and studied in the third century B.C., they were stripped of their musical and choreographic notations. As a result, the victory odes as we know them are somewhat like an opera libretto (the words or text) without a musical score. Unlike most opera libretti, however, Pindar's poetry can stand on its own. Pindar did not merely commemmorate in song the victor's name and family, the festival where he competed, and the type of contest he won. Weaving together history and myth in an original way, Pindar tailored each ode to the occasion, using daring new imagery. Thus, Pindar made the moment of victory timeless, giving the victor, his ancestors, and his community a kind of permanence and immortality.

Writing

Both Sappho and Pindar celebrated what was most meaningful to them in their poems. Is it easier to write about something for which you have strong feelings or about a subject you can explore objectively? Why?

Literary Focus Have students think about poems or songs that express intensely personal emotions and others that celebrate another person, someone whose achievements shine forth in a larger context. The celebratory lyrics for "John Brown's Body" are an example. Or students might be familiar with a ballad for Goodman, Schwerner, and Chaney, who died in the Civil Rights movement of the 1960's.

Writing/Prior Knowledge Have students share ideas about how to make an intensely personal experience vivid and moving to others. In other words, how can a writer make others feel what he or she feels? The writer has to make the experience matter to the reader or listener so that a heroic accomplishment seems both particular and important beyond the individual.

ESL Teaching Strategy ESL students will find these short, fragmentary poems less daunting than Homer's epic. At the same time, ESL students might be confused by the general lack of punctuation in Sappho's shorter fragments. Explain the lack of punctuation by discussing the poems as ancient fragments, or reconstructions of Sappho's work. It might help ESL students to supply punctuation where they hear it.

Teaching Tenth-Grade Students To enhance tenth-grade students' understanding of lyric poetry, have them suggest possible topics for lyrics. They may name subjects of lyrics they have already read or subjects they think would make good lyric poems.

Support Material

Teaching Portfolio
Teacher Backup, p. 515
Usage and Mechanics Worksheet, p. 519
Analyzing Literature Worksheet, *Analyzing Personal Lyric*, p. 520
Critical Thinking and Reading Worksheet, *Concrete vs. Abstract*

Terms, p. 521
Language Worksheet, *Comparing Translations*, p. 522
Selection Test, pp. 523–524
Art Transparency 6
Munich Olympic Games, 1972, by Jacob Lawrence

Although They Are

Sappho

translated by Mary Barnard

Although they are

Only breath, words
which I command
are immortal

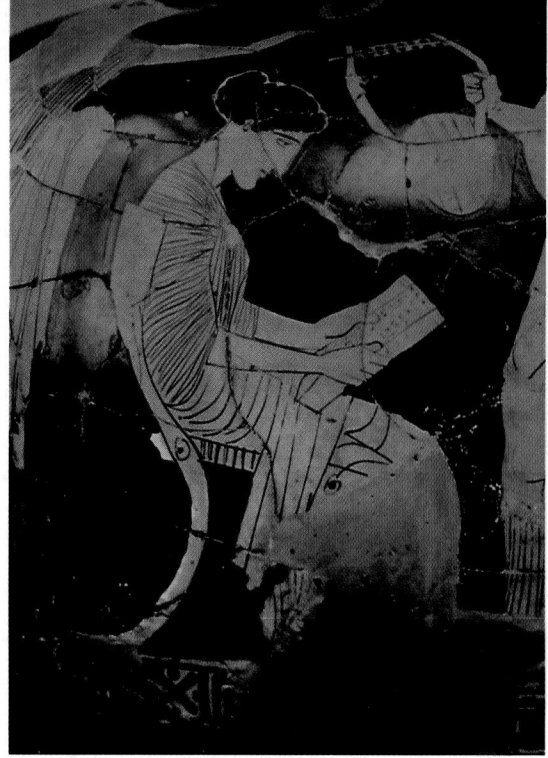

SAPPHO
Detail of a Greek vase painting, c. 440 B.C.

Awed by Her Splendor

Sappho

translated by Mary Barnard

Awed by her splendor

Stars near the lovely
moon cover their own
bright faces
      when she
is roundest and lights
earth with her silver

And Their Feet Move

Sappho

translated by Mary Barnard

And their feet move

Rhythmically as tender
feet of Cretan girls[1]
danced once around an

altar of love, crushing
a circle in the soft
smooth flowering grass

---

1. Cretan (krēt′ ′n) **girls** *n*.: Girls from Crete, an island in the eastern Mediterranean Sea.

You Know the Place: Then

Sappho

translated by Mary Barnard

You know the place: then

Leave Crete and come to us
waiting where the grove is
pleasantest, by precincts

5 sacred to you; incense
smokes on the altar, cold
streams murmur through the

apple branches, a young
rose thicket shades the ground
and quivering leaves pour

down deep sleep; in meadows
where horses have grown sleek
among spring flowers, dill

scents the air. Queen! Cyprian![1]
15 Fill our gold cups with love
stirred into clear nectar

---

1. **Cyprian** (si′ prē ən) *n*.: Name Sappho uses
to address the goddess Aphrodite.

Reader's Response *What contemporary
singer do you think is most like Sappho?
Explain your answer.*

THINKING ABOUT THE SELECTION

Interpreting

1. (a) What two objects does Sappho personify in "Awed by Her Splendor"? (b) What effect does personification have in this poem?
2. In what way might "Awed by Her Splendor" also apply to people?
3. (a) Why does the speaker of "Although They Are" claim that her words are immortal? (b) What does her claim suggest about the effects of poetry?
4. "And Their Feet Move" leaves the reader with a definite picture of what happens in the poem. Describe the picture as you see it and explain how the poem led you to your picture.
5. What two requests does the speaker of "You Know the Place: Then" make of Aphrodite?
6. For what is the speaker of "You Know the Place: Then" waiting?

Applying

7. The speaker of "Although They Are" correctly predicted that her words were immortal. Think of ways in which our culture gives permanence to itself.

ANALYZING LITERATURE

Analyzing Lyric Fragments

Although few of Sappho's lyrics have survived intact, the remaining fragments shed light on her art. Many of Sappho's fragments suggest that she regarded love as being imposed on the individual from the outside world. In her view, love was connected with the laws and movements of the universe. Vivid images of external forces illustrate how Sappho perceived her passions as being connected with the forces of nature, or the gods.

1. Locate the references to love in "And Their Feet Move," and explain how each reference reflects how Sappho saw the relationship between love and nature.
2. The moon has a gravitational pull on the earth. How does the image of the moon in "Awed by Her Splendor" suggest that the moon might have a similar effect on human beings?
3. How does Sappho present love as being imposed by external forces in "You Know the Place: Then"?

4 **Reading Strategy** Ask students who they think "you" is in the first line. How do the opening lines suggest familiarity or assume a prior relationship between the speaker and "you"?

Master Teacher Note In all her poems, Sappho uses precise, sensuous language to involve all the listeners' senses and to evoke strong feelings. She imposes a very personal and human-centered vision of people, places, and things, forcing us to visualize and respond to the world as she does. Have students identify the senses to which Sappho appeals in "You Know the Place: Then."

5 **Discussion** Ask students to consider why Sappho does not open the poem with a formal invocation but saves the goddess's title for the end. How does indirectly invoking a longstanding relationship resemble or differ from the kind of prayer formula students may recall from Chryses' invocation of Apollo in the first book of the *Iliad*?

Challenge Invite students to write a complete version of one of Sappho's fragments. Ask students to choose the fragment that most intrigues them and to imagine how the poem would have appeared in its entirety. Then ask students to write their complete version of the poem. Remind students that they may start at any point, using the fragment as the beginning, as the end, or somewhere in the middle of the complete poem. Remind students that their poem should be consistent with the fragment of Sappho's poem.

ANSWERS TO ANALYZING LITERATURE

1. There is a direct and indirect reference. The direct reference to love is the altar of love, presumably an altar of worship for Aphrodite, goddess of love. The circle "their feet" crush in the grass connects their action with the natural world. The dance itself is an indirect reference to love, the love implicit in the worship of the god for whom the girls are dancing. Both references reflect the notion of the gods as a natural force, imposing passions on mortals.
2. Suggested response: The personification of the moon and the moon's action, lighting the earth with "her silver," suggests that the moon has a strong effect on the earth and its inhabitants.
3. The act of invoking Aphrodite and requesting love from her suggests that love comes not from within an individual but from forces outside the individual.

You May Forget But

Sappho

Two Translations

translated by Mary Barnard

You may forget but

Let me tell you
this: someone in
some future time
will think of us

SAPPHO
L. Alma Tadema
The Walters Art Gallery, Baltimore

translated by Richmond Lattimore

But I claim there will be some who remember us
when we are gone.

Primary Source

The poet/scholar/critic Anne Carson shows a deep understanding of the poem Mary Barnard titles "He Is More Than a Hero" when she writes,

The poem floats toward us on a stage set. But we have no program. The actors go in and out of focus anonymously. The action has no location. We don't know why the girl is laughing nor what she feels about this man. He looms beyond the footlights, somewhat more than mortal in line 1 . . ., and dissolves at line 2 into a pronoun . . . so in-

He Is More Than a Hero

Sappho

Two Translations

translated by Mary Barnard

He is more than a hero

He is a god in my eyes—
the man who is allowed
to sit beside you—he

who listens intimately
to the sweet murmur of
your voice, the enticing

laughter that makes my own
heart beat fast. If I meet
you suddenly, I can't

speak—my tongue is broken;
a thin flame runs under
my skin; seeing nothing,

hearing only my own ears
drumming, I drip with sweat;
trembling shakes my body

and I turn paler than
dry grass. At such times
death isn't far from me

translated by Richmond Lattimore

Like the very gods in my sight is he who
sits where he can look in your eyes, who listens
close to you, to hear the soft voice, its sweetness
    murmur in love and

5 laughter, all for him. But it breaks my spirit;
underneath my breast all the heart is shaken.
Let me only glance where you are, the voice dies,
    I can say nothing,

but my lips are stricken to silence, under-
10 neath my skin the tenuous flame suffuses;
nothing shows in front of my eyes, my ears are
    muted in thunder.

And the sweat breaks running upon me, fever
shakes my body, paler I turn than grass is;
15 I can feel that I have been changed, I feel that
    death has come near me.

definite that scholars cannot agree on what it means. The poet who is staging the mise-èn-scene steps mysteriously from the wings of a relative clause at line 5 . . . and takes over the action.

It is not a poem about the three of them as individuals, but about the geometrical figure formed by their perception of one another, and the gaps in that perception. It is an image of distances between them. Thin lines of force coordinate the three of them . . .

2 Enrichment This is Sappho's most famous poem, and it is widely translated. Here is poet/scholar /critic Anne Carson's translation for you to share with your students.

> He seems to me equal to gods that man
> who opposite you
> sits and listens close
> to your sweet speaking
>
> and lovely laughing—oh it puts the heart in my chest on wings
> for when I look at you, a moment, then no speaking is left in me
>
> no: tongue breaks, and thin fire is racing under skin
> and in eyes no sight and drumming
> fills ears
>
> and cold sweat holds me and shaking
> grips me all, greener than grass
> I am dead—or almost
> I seem to me.

3 Clarification Any translator must decide whether to keep the meter of the original. Lattimore has reproduced Sappho's meter, as has Catullus in his Latin version. Barnard has not, perhaps thinking it sounds artificial in English. Another decision a translator must make is how much to incorporate interpretation into a translation. The original does not say "more than a hero," but Barnard has included this phrase. Ask students to consider what Barnard's purpose might have been by adding the phrase "more than a hero."

4 Discussion Lead students through the two translations, helping them think about the choices each translator has made: for instance, Barnard's "is allowed" and "intimately" correspond to which phrases in Lattimore's version?

Invocation to Aphrodite

Sappho

translated by Richmond Lattimore

SAPPHO AND ALCAEUS
Staatliche Antikensammlungen und Glyptothek, Munich

Reader's Response *Which Sappho poem was the most powerful for you? Explain your answer.*

Throned in splendor, deathless, O Aphrodite,
child of Zeus, charm-fashioner, I entreat you
not with griefs and bitternesses to break my
    spirit, O goddess;

standing by me rather, if once before now
5 far away you heard, when I called upon you,
left your father's dwelling place and descended,
    yoking the golden

chariot to sparrows, who fairly drew you
down in speed aslant the black world, the bright air
trembling at the heart to the pulse of countless
    fluttering wingbeats.

10 Swiftly then they came, and you, blessed lady,
smiling on me out of immortal beauty,
asked me what affliction was on me, why I
    called thus upon you,

what beyond all else I would have befall my
tortured heart: "Whom then would you have Persuasion
force to serve desire in your heart? Who is it,
15   Sappho, that hurt you?

Though she now escape you, she soon will follow;
though she take not gifts from you, she will give
    them:
though she love not, yet she will surely love you
    even unwilling."

In such guise come even again and set me
20 free from doubt and sorrow; accomplish all those
things my heart desires to be done; appear and
    stand at my shoulder.

THINKING ABOUT THE SELECTION

Interpreting

1. In "You May Forget But," the speaker claims that her people will be remembered well beyond their years. What does her claim suggest about the Greek perception of death?
2. Explain why the reference to death at the end of "He Is More Than a Hero" is a figurative reference.
3. What is the source of the narrator's grief in "Invocation to Aphrodite"? What repeated references help identify the source?
4. What causes Sappho such intense pain in "Invocation to Aphrodite"?

Applying

5. The narrator of "He Is More Than a Hero" describes an experience in which her emotions cloud her ability to think clearly. What other situations, such as fear, can cause people's emotions to interfere with reason? What can people do in these situations?

ANALYZING LITERATURE

Analyzing Personal Lyric

In Sappho's **personal lyrics,** her principal subject is love, sometimes expressed very simply and tenderly and sometimes with passionate fire. Sappho's lyrics also have a melodic quality because of their meter, or recurring rhythmic patterns. Since she composed her poems to be sung to the lyre, establishing a recognizable rhythmic pattern was important.

1. Using references from the poem, discuss the ways in which "He Is More Than a Hero" is a personal lyric.
2. What elements of "Invocation to Aphrodite" characterize it as a personal lyric?
3. Although a personal lyric is not meant to inspire others, how are Sappho's lyrics nevertheless powerful and moving?

UNDERSTANDING LANGUAGE

Comparing Translations

Translating words or phrases from one language to another involves a great deal of sensitivity to both languages, particularly in the case of poetry. The translator must be careful to preserve the poem's original meaning and structure within the limits of a different language. Differences in translations of the same poem are partially due to each translator's interpretation.

Many of Sappho's short fragments lend themselves to similar translations. For example, both Mary Barnard and Richmond Lattimore convey the same general meaning in their translations of "You May Forget But": the speaker claims that people in the future will think of her and her people. Yet there are differences in the two translations that are worth considering. Barnard's version emphasizes the future by saying that someone in the future will think of the speaker and her people. She makes no mention of their being gone, though that is implied. Lattimore, on the other hand, states directly that they will be remembered when they are gone. His version emphasizes their death. Notice how Barnard and Lattimore translate Sappho's Greek very differently in "He Is More Than a Hero." One striking difference is the way in which each translator describes the man in the beginning of the poem. Barnard uses a metaphor to describe him, saying that he *is* a god; Lattimore uses a simile, saying that he is *like* a god. Such differences affect how the reader interprets the poem.

1. Contrast the reference to the speaker's heart in the first half of each translation.
2. Which translation of the following lines do you think best captures the intensity of the speaker's experience? Explain.

   Barnard: ". . . I drip with sweat; trembling shakes my body . . ."
   Lattimore: "And the sweat breaks running upon me, fever / shakes my body . . ."

3. How does the difference in the way each translator ends the poem affect your interpretation of both versions?

THINKING AND WRITING

Writing About Thematic Threads

After you read several of Sappho's poems, certain themes emerge as a pattern. One of the strongest themes evident in her poems is love. Another theme stresses the lasting importance of words, indicating that she valued poetry. Tracing thematic patterns in Sappho's poems will enhance your understanding of what she valued. Write an essay in which you trace a common theme through two or more of the Sappho poems you have read. First, select the poems and jot down details that convey the theme. As you revise, make sure you have referred to the poems to support your theme. Finally, proofread for coherence, spelling, and punctuation.

(continued from bottom of page)
ANSWERS TO ANALYZING LITERATURE

1. "He Is More Than a Hero" describes love with passionate fire and has a recognizable rhythmic pattern.
2. "Invocation to Aphrodite" is also an intensely personal expression, involving the speaker's personal desires. Students should also mention the poem's rhythm.
3. Answers will differ. Suggested response: The poems appeal to emotions and desires common to everyone.

ANSWERS TO UNDERSTANDING LANGUAGE

1. In Barnard's translation, the speaker's heart beats fast in response to enticing laughter, while in Lattimore's translation her heart is shaken in response to the laughter she hears.
2. Answers will differ; either answer is acceptable, provided that the student explains his or her choice.
3. Answers will differ but should include the student's interpretation and the reasons for that interpretation.

THINKING AND WRITING

Publishing Student Writing The assignment "Writing About Thematic Threads" calls for sophisticated literary analysis. Suggest that students submit their papers to the school literary magazine or newspaper. Or you might want students to share their papers in small group discussions of four or more people.

Challenge Mary Barnard and Richmond Lattimore have translated several of Sappho's poems. Students might like to compare their translations of more of Sappho's poems. Or they might try exploring different translators, like Anne Carson and Willis Barnstone.

Closure and Extension

ANSWERS TO THINKING ABOUT THE SELECTION

1. The speaker's claim suggests that the Greeks viewed death as final for people but not for their reputations or their accomplishments.
2. The speaker describes an emotional experience that traumatizes her to the

point where she feels that she could die. However, the experience is not literally life threatening.
3. The narrator's "tortured heart" is the source of her grief. The repeated references are to the narrator's heart.
4. Doubt and sorrow afflict the narrator.
5. Answers will differ. Students might suggest being angry with a loved one or being saddened by the absence of a close friend. Students should also

suggest ways in which they deal with such situations.

Olympia 11

Pindar

translated by Richmond Lattimore

There is a time when men need most favoring
gales;[1] there is a time for water from the sky,
the rainy children of cloud.
But if by endeavor[2] a man win fairly, soft-spoken
    songs
5 are given, to be a beginning of men's
speech to come and a trusty pledge for great
    achievements.

Abundant is such praise laid up for Olympian
winners. My lips have good will
to marshal[3] these words; yet only
by God's grace does a man blossom in accordance[4]
10   with his mind's wisdom.
Son of Archestratos,[5] know
that for the sake, Agesidamos,[6] of your boxing

1 I shall enchant in strain of song a glory upon
   your olive wreath of gold
15 and bespeak the race of the West Wind Lokrians.[7]
   There acclaim him; I warrant you,
   Muses, you will visit no gathering cold to strangers
   nor lost to lovely things
   but deep to the heart in wisdom, and spearmen
       also. No thing, neither hot-colored fox
2 nor loud lion, may change the nature born in his
20   blood.

---

1. gales (gālz) *n*.: Breezes.
2. endeavor (en dev′ ər) *n*.: Earnest attempt at achievement.
3. marshal (mär′ shəl) *n*.: To direct ceremoniously.
4. accordance (ə kôrd′ 'ns) *n*.: Agreement; harmony.
5. Archestratos (ärk əs trā′ tōs): Father of Agesidamos.
6. Agesidamos (ə ges′ i dä′ mōs): Victor in the boys' boxing competition in 476 B.C.
7. West Wind Lokrians (lō krē′ ənz) *n*.: Lokris was a city on the Gulf of Corinth in Greece; "West Wind Lokrians" were Greek-speaking people from the colony of Lokris in southern Italy.

THINKING ABOUT THE SELECTION

Interpreting

1. What do favoring gales and water from the sky represent in the first lines of the poem?
2. What are the soft-spoken songs to which the speaker refers in line 4?
3. What does the speaker mean by saying that "only by God's graces does a man blossom in accordance with his mind's wisdom"?

Applying

4. In what ways does the tradition Pindar glorifies survive today?

ANALYZING LITERATURE

Analyzing a Victory Ode

Pindar's **victory odes** are elaborate choral poems written to praise a victorious athlete. The most basic element of the victory ode is the name of the victorious athlete in one of the four great games, Olympian, Pythian, Nemean, or Isthmian. The victor's family, also named, commission the poet to honor their son in an ode to be sung or performed at their home, which also deserves mention in the ode. The whole community unites to celebrate the winner for what is perceived as a civic triumph. Another essential element includes a reference to the muses who inspire the poet; since they preside over victory celebrations, they authorize the poet to praise the winner. The formula is simple, but Pindar makes each ode a unique celebration of magnificent achievement.

1. Locate the elements of the victory ode formula in "Olympia 11."
2. By referring to the poem, explain how Pindar heightens his language to meet the glory of the event.

THINKING AND WRITING

Imitating an Ode

Pindar was not only admired but imitated in antiquity. It was not unusual for a poet to "Pindarize" his work in imitation and in honor of Pindar. Choose an athletic hero and write a "pindaric" ode about the athlete's victory. (Your hero can be male or female, famous or common.) Keep in mind that you are celebrating an achievement you think worthy of the utmost praise. As you revise, check to see whether you have included the elements of the victory ode. Finally, proofread for grammatical errors.

Prose

ATTIC RED-FIGURED CUP, C. 480
Antikenmuseum und Skulpturhalle, Basel

Humanities Note

Fine art, *Attic Red-figured Cup*, Douris Painter. The Attic vase decorator who signed his works "Douris made it" was one of the premier painters of the first third of the fifth century B.C. He was primarily a cup painter who produced over 200 known works. His finely decorated kylix (shallow-stemmed cups) were used for drinking the watered wine favored by ancient Greeks at their festivals and banquets.

Pictured is a detail of a piece by the Douris painter called the *Schoolmaster Cup*. It is a fine example of his more mature style. The rounded figures are painted with a sure, calm hand. A characteristic of this painter is his careful attention to the hands and drapery of each figure. This striking picture was inspired by the painter's observation of an everyday scene.

You might want to use the following questions to discuss the art:

1. What activities do you see depicted on the scene?
2. How does the scene connect with your reading thus far in the unit?

THUCYDIDES

Focus

More About the Author Although he was born in Thrace, Thucydides was connected with the old, conservative nobility of Athens. His family's longstanding involvement in political life probably shaped Thucydides' historical methods.

He examined the war from a political, military, and psychological angle. He was keenly interested in the politics of the war. He also studied the technical aspects of the war, particularly the difficulties in warfare between a powerful land force, Sparta, and a powerful naval force, Athens.

But his principal aim was to study human behavior in wartime. He was famous for being a pessimist; the moral decline he noticed as the war dragged on caused him to predict the "inevitable corrosion of the human spirit."

Critical Evaluation Writing on the philosophy of history, R. G. Collingwood says, ". . . the dominant influence on Thucydides is . . . Hippocratic medicine. Hippocrates was not only the father of medicine, he was also the father of psychology, and his influence is evident not only in such things as the Thucydidean description of the plague, but in such studies in morbid psychology as the description of war-neurosis in general and the special instances of it in the Corcyrean revolution and Melian dialogue. Herodotus may be the father of history, but Thucydides is the father of psychological history."

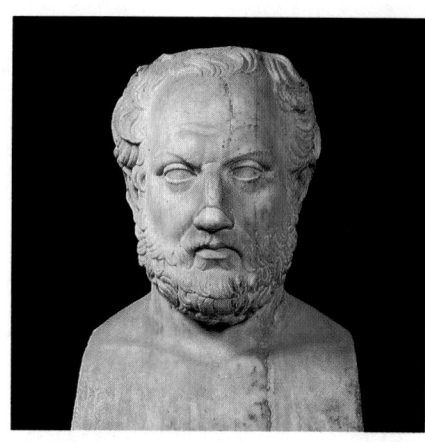

460 B.C.–404 B.C.

The Athenian Thucydides (thu si′ di dēz′) was an important military magistrate in the Peloponnesian War, the long and bloody conflict between Athens and Sparta that ended with the fall of the Athenian empire. During his command of a fleet based at Thasos (thā′ sōs), he failed to protect the crucial Athenian colony of Amphipolis (am fip′ ə lis) from a surprise Spartan attack. He went to trial for his military failure and was exiled for twenty years until the war ended.

Exile provided him with the opportunity to observe the war from a distance. He took notes of events as they occurred, researched extensively, and recorded firsthand accounts of events told to him by Athenians and Spartans. Using the information he gathered, he wrote his historical masterpiece, the *History of the Peloponnesian War*. As a result of his objective, scientific approach to history, Thucydides is known as the greatest historian in antiquity and one of the most influential historians ever.

Beyond what he reveals about himself in the course of his narrative, there is no certain information about his life. He appointed himself historian of the war at its outset and called it the "greatest war of all." Ultimately, he laid the foundations of modern historical methods.

In the first stages of his work, he took notes on events that he participated in or observed from a distance. Then he rewrote and arranged his notes into a consecutive narrative. Finally, he elaborated the narrative so that it would not read merely as a record of events. Unfortunately, he died before he could complete the History; it ends abruptly six years before the war ended, though all the speeches are very polished. Thucydides is believed to have died a sudden and violent death in 404 B.C., shortly after Athens' defeat.

Thucydides believed that history could be understood in terms of human behavior. Consequently, he presented character studies of leading Athenian and Spartan statesmen in which he examined the human mind in wartime. Through the speeches he included in his History, he articulated the motives and ambitions of both armies impartially. He aimed to teach people so that they would avoid making the same mistakes he witnessed in the war.

With a passion for truth, Thucydides refused to "accept all stories of ancient times in an uncritical way," and he adhered to rigorous standards of accuracy. Achieving accuracy was, by his own admission, difficult when he had to reconstruct speeches. Since he used speeches to paint a kind of moral portrait, he may have given himself freedom in shaping the speeches while maintaining their basic truth. In his words:

"I have found it difficult to remember the precise words used in the speeches which I listened to myself and my various informants have experienced the same difficulty; so my method has been, while keeping as closely as possible to the general sense of the words that were actually used, to make the speakers say what, in my opinion, was called for by each situation."

To what extent he relied on his opinion in reconstructing *Pericles' Funeral Oration* is uncertain, but he was a great admirer of Pericles, and he probably heard Pericles deliver the annual speech honoring the Athenian war dead in the winter of 430.

Objectives

Thematic
To understand the glory of being an Athenian and the Athenian concept of democracy

Skills
1 To analyze the elements of oration
2 To understand writing for an audience
3 To write about leadership

GUIDE FOR INTERPRETING

Pericles' Funeral Oration

Commentary

Oration. An **oration** is a formal speech intended to inspire its listeners and incite them to action. Orators use an impassioned delivery to appeal to the audience's religious, moral, or patriotic emotions. Oration was of major cultural interest in Classical times.

Classical oration has seven identifiable parts: (1) the opening, intended to capture the audience's attention; (2) the narration, a recital of facts; (3) the exposition, or definition, of terms to be explained and issues to be proved; (4) the proposition to clarify the points and state exactly what is to be proved; (5) a confirmation to address the arguments for and against the proposition; (6) the confutation, or refutation, to refute the opposing arguments; and (7) the conclusion, or epilogue, to summarize the arguments and stir the audience.

Pericles was one of Athens' ten generals, or *strategoi* (strat′ ə goi̇̄), and the greatest Athenian politician in the early days of the war. Although his speech is in isolation a glowing account of Athens and Athenian democracy, it is not a complete picture of Athens as an imperial power. In fact, later in the war, Pericles was the target of angry criticism for his aggressive, expansionist policies.

Writing

Oration is often called the art of persuasion. Take a stand on an issue of social importance and list ways in which you would appeal to an audience's emotions in supporting your views.

Primary Source

In his introduction Thucydides made the following comments on his historical aims: "And with regard to my factual reporting of the events of the war I have made it a principle not to write down the first story that came my way, and not even to be guided by my own general impressions; either I was present myself at the events which I have described or else I heard of them from eyewitnesses whose reports I have checked with as much thoroughness as possible. Not that even so the truth was easy to discover: different eyewitnesses give different accounts of the same events, speaking out of partiality for one side or the other or else from imperfect memories. And it may well be that my history will seem less easy to read because of the absence in it of a romantic element. It will be enough for me, however, if these words of mine are judged useful by those who want to understand clearly the events which happened in the past and which (human nature being what it is) will, at some time or other and in much the same ways, be repeated in the future. My work is not a piece of writing designed to meet the taste of an immediate public, but was done to last forever."

Literary Focus Have students think about how often rhetoric—persuasive words and arguments that lead the listener to the course of action desired by the speaker—plays a crucial role in everyday life. Students might think of Dr. Martin Luther King's "I Have a Dream" speech; of presidential addresses, from the Gettysburg address to John F. Kennedy's famous Berlin Wall speech in 1962 to more recent examples.

Writing/Prior Knowledge Divide students into small groups of about four and have them brainstorm for examples of orations they have either read or heard recently. Have students, in writing, explain how their examples fit the definition of oration and why the oration is or is not effective.

ESL Teaching Strategy Explain to ESL students that unlike the epic and lyric poetry they have been reading, "Pericles' Funeral Oration" is a nonfictional reconstruction of Pericles' speech. Have all class members read parts of the speech aloud so that ESL as well as native English-speaking students can appreciate its persuasive qualities by hearing them.

Teaching Tenth-Grade Students Encourage tenth-grade students as they read to highlight those parts of Pericles' speech that seem especially persuasive.

Vocabulary
Preteach the following vocabulary words:
exploits (eks′ ploits′) *n.*: Remarkable acts of brilliance or boldness
undeterred (un′ dē turd′) *adv.*: Undiscouraged
liberality (lib′ ər al′ i tē) *n.*: Generosity
manifold (man′ə fold) *adj.*: Many, various
tangible (tan′ jə b'l) *adj.*: Substantial
reproaches (ri prōch′ ez) *n.*: Expressions of blame
culmination (kul′ mə nā′ shən) *n.*: Highest point or climax

Support Material

Teaching Portfolio
Teacher Backup, p. 525
Grammar in Action Worksheet, *Recognizing Unity and Coherence*, p. 529
Usage and Mechanics Worksheet, p. 531
Vocabulary Check, p. 532
Critical Thinking and Reading Work-
sheet, *Evaluating Persuasive Arguments* p. 533
Language Worksheet, *Recognizing Greek Word Roots*, p. 534
Selection Test, pp. 535–536

from History of the Peloponnesian War

Thucydides

Pericles' Funeral Oration

translated by Rex Warner

In the same winter the Athenians, following their annual custom, gave a public funeral for those who had been the first to die in the war. These funerals are held in the following way: two days before the ceremony the bones of the fallen are brought and put in a tent which has been erected, and people make whatever offerings they wish to their own dead. Then there is a funeral procession in which coffins of cypress wood are carried on wagons. There is one coffin for each tribe, which contains the bones of members of that tribe. One empty bier is decorated and carried in the procession: this is for the missing, whose bodies could not be recovered. Everyone who wishes to, both citizens and foreigners, can join in the procession, and the women who are related to the dead are there to make their laments at the tomb. The bones are laid in the public burial-place, which is in the most beautiful quarter outside the city walls. Here the Athenians always bury those who have fallen in war. The only exception is those who died at Marathon,[1] who, because their achievement was considered absolutely outstanding, were buried on the battlefield itself.

When the bones have been laid in the earth, a man chosen by the city for his intellectual gifts and for his general reputation makes an appropriate speech in praise of the dead, and after the speech all depart. This is the procedure at these burials, and all through the war, when the time came to do so, the Athenians followed this ancient custom. Now, at the burial of those who were the first to fall in the war, Pericles, the son of Xanthippus,[2] was chosen to make the speech. When the moment arrived, he came forward from the tomb and, standing on a high platform, so that he might be heard by as many people as possible in the crowd, he spoke as follows:

"Many of those who have spoken here in the past have praised the institution of this speech at the close of our ceremony. It seemed to them a mark of honor to our soldiers who have fallen in war that a speech should be made over them. I do not agree. These men have shown themselves valiant in action, and it would be enough, I think, for their glories to be proclaimed in action, as you have just seen it done at this funeral organized by the state. Our belief in the courage and manliness

---

1. **Marathon** (mar´ ə thän´) *n*.: Ancient Greek village near Athens where the Athenians defeated the Persians in 490 B.C.

2. **Xanthippus** (zan´ thi pəs): Victorious Athenian general in the war against Persia, and a member of one of the most illustrious noble families of Athens.

of so many should not be hazarded on the goodness or badness of one man's speech. Then it is not easy to speak with a proper sense of balance, when a man's listeners find it difficult to believe in the truth of what one is saying. The man who knows the facts and loves the dead may well think that an oration tells less than what he knows and what he would like to hear: others who do not know so much may feel envy for the dead, and think the orator over-praises them, when he speaks of exploits that are beyond their own capacities. Praise of other people is tolerable only up to a certain point, the point where one still believes that one could do oneself some of the things one is hearing about. Once you get beyond this point, you will find people becoming jealous and incredulous.[3] However, the fact is that this institution was set up and approved by our forefathers, and it is my duty to follow the tradition and do my best to meet the wishes and the expectations of every one of you.

"I shall begin by speaking about our ancestors, since it is only right and proper on such an occasion to pay them the honor of recalling what they did. In this land of ours there have always been the same people living from generation to generation up till now, and they, by their courage and their virtues, have handed it on to us, a free country. They certainly deserve our praise. Even more so do our fathers deserve it. For to the inheritance they had received they added all the empire we have now, and it was not without blood and toil that they handed it down to us of the present generation. And then we ourselves, assembled here today, who are mostly in the prime of life, have, in most directions, added to the power of our empire and have organized our state in such a way that it is perfectly well able to look after itself both in peace and in war.

"I have no wish to make a long speech on subjects familiar to you all: so I shall say nothing about the warlike deeds by which we acquired our power or the battles in which we or our fathers gallantly resisted our enemies, Greek or foreign. What I want to do is, in the first place, to discuss the spirit in which we faced our trials and also our constitution and the way of life which has made us great. After that I shall

speak in praise of the dead, believing that this kind of speech is not inappropriate to the present occasion, and that this whole assembly, of citizens and foreigners, may listen to it with advantage.

"Let me say that our system of government does not copy the institutions of our neighbors. It is more the case of our being a model to others, than of our imitating anyone else. Our constitution is called a democracy because power is in the hands not of a minority but of the whole people. When it is a question of settling private disputes, everyone is equal before the law; when it is a question of putting one person before another in positions of public responsibility, what counts is not membership of a particular class, but the actual ability which the man possesses. No one, so long as he has it in him to be of service to the state, is kept in political obscurity[4] because of poverty. And, just as our political life is free and open, so is our day-to-day life in our relations with each other. We do not get into a state with our next-door neighbor if he enjoys himself in his own way, nor do we give him the kind of black looks which, though they do no real harm, still do hurt people's feelings. We are free and tolerant in our private lives; but in public affairs we keep to the law. This is because it commands our deep respect.

"We give our obedience to those whom we put in positions of authority, and we obey the laws themselves, especially those which are for the protection of the oppressed, and those unwritten laws which it is an acknowledged shame to break.

"And here is another point. When our work is over, we are in a position to enjoy all kinds of recreation for our spirits. There are various kinds of contests and sacrifices regularly throughout the year; in our own homes we find a beauty and a good taste which delight us every day and which drive away our cares. Then the greatness of our city brings it about that all the good things from all over the world flow in to us, so that to us it seems just as natural to enjoy foreign goods as our own local products.

"Then there is a great difference between us and our opponents, in our attitude toward military

10

---

3. **incredulous** (in krej′ ōō ləs) *adj.*: Disbelieving; doubtful or skeptical.

4. **obscurity** (əb skyōōr′ ə tē) *n.*: State of being unclear and easily misunderstood.

3 Discussion Ask students: What two problems in appealing to a large audience, gathered for the funeral of kin and strangers alike, does the speaker address here?

4 Clarification Point out the complication in Pericles' maneuvering in this paragraph. He manages to praise the dead for their outstanding heroism, defuse charges that he is exaggerating, recognize incredulity and envy as a reasonable human reaction, and disclaim responsibility at the same time as he stresses he is performing a "duty" at the express request of the listeners themselves.

5 Enrichment The Athenians prided themselves enormously on being *autochthonous people,* that is, people who were sprung from the very soil of their land, not people who had come to Athens from some other place.

6 Clarification Pericles is not only reminding his listeners of how their ancestors have kept Athens a free country by defending it against all attackers, but of how the generation that fought off the Persians also laid the foundations for the Athenian maritime empire.

7 Discussion Ask students to think about how Pericles reminds his listeners that they are also fighting men who have fought to aggrandize the empire. How does his reminder reinforce his comments about earlier generations?

8 Literary Focus Call students' attention to the rhetorical ploy here: claiming that one does not want to say something but saying it in the process.

9 Discussion Ask students to discuss why Pericles concentrates more on national spirit, the laws, and the Athenian way of life than on military heroism. Why does military heroism matter less to Pericles?

10 Discussion Have students consider why it is important that Athens is a model and not an imitator when it comes to its democratic constitution.

security. Here are some examples: Our city is open to the world, and we have no periodical deportations[5] in order to prevent people observing or finding out secrets which might be of military advantage to the enemy. This is because we rely, not on secret weapons, but on our own real courage and loyalty. There is a difference, too, in our educational systems. The Spartans, from their earliest boyhood, are submitted to the most laborious training in courage; we pass our lives without all these restrictions, and yet are just as ready to face the same dangers as they are. Here is proof of this: When the Spartans invade our land, they do not come by themselves, but bring all their allies with them; whereas we, when we launch an attack abroad, do the job by ourselves, and, though fighting on foreign soil, do not often fail to defeat opponents who are fighting for their own hearths and homes. As a matter of fact none of our enemies has ever yet been confronted with our total strength, because we have to divide our attention between our navy and the many missions on which our troops are sent on land. Yet, if our enemies engage a detachment[6] of our forces and defeat it, they give them-

---

5. **deportations** (dē′ pôr tā′ shƏnz) *n.*: Orders that force people to leave the country.
6. **engage a detachment:** Enter into conflict with troops.

WARRIOR CARRYING HIS DEAD COMPANION
Detail of Greek vase
Staatliche Antikensammlungen und Glyptothek, Munich

selves credit for having thrown back our entire army; or, if they lose, they claim that they were beaten by us in full strength. There are certain advantages, I think, in our way of meeting danger voluntarily, with an easy mind, instead of with a laborious training, with natural rather than with state-induced courage. We do not have to spend our time practicing to meet sufferings which are still in the future; and when they are actually upon us we show ourselves just as brave as these others who are always in strict training. This is one point in which, I think, our city deserves to be admired. There are also others:

"Our love of what is beautiful does not lead to extravagance; our love of the things of the mind does not make us soft. We regard wealth as something to be properly used, rather than as something to boast about. As for poverty, no one need be ashamed to admit it: the real shame is in not taking practical measures to escape from it. Here each individual is interested not only in his own affairs but in the affairs of the state as well: even those who are mostly occupied with their own business are extremely well-informed on general politics—this is a peculiarity of ours: we do not say that a man who takes no interest in politics is a man who minds his own business; we say that he has no business here at all. We Athenians, in our own persons, take our decisions on policy or submit them to proper discussions: for we do not think that there is an incompatibility between words and deeds; the worst thing is to rush into action before the consequences have been properly debated. And this is another point where we differ from other people. We are capable at the same time of taking risks and of estimating them beforehand. Others are brave out of ignorance; and, when they stop to think, they begin to fear. But the man who can most truly be accounted brave is he who best knows the meaning of what is sweet in life and of what is terrible, and then goes out undeterred to meet what is to come.

"Again, in questions of general good feeling there is a great contrast between us and most other people. We make friends by doing good to others, not by receiving good from them. This makes our friendship all the more reliable, since we want to keep alive the gratitude of those who are in our debt by showing continued good will to them: whereas the feelings of one who owes us something lack the same enthusiasm, since he knows that, when he repays our kindness, it will be more like paying back a debt than giving something spontaneously. We are unique in this. When we do kindnesses to others, we do not do them out of any calculations of profit or loss: we do them without afterthought, relying on our free liberality. Taking everything together then, I declare that our city is an education to Greece, and I declare that in my opinion each single one of our citizens, in all the manifold aspects of life, is able to show himself the rightful lord and owner of his own person, and do this, moreover, with exceptional grace and exceptional versatility.[7] And to show that this is no empty boasting for the present occasion, but real tangible fact, you have only to consider the power which our city possesses and which has been won by those very qualities which I have mentioned. Athens, alone of the states we know, comes to her testing time in a greatness that surpasses what was imagined of her. In her case, and in her case alone, no invading enemy is ashamed at being defeated, and no subject can complain of being governed by people unfit for their responsibilities. Mighty indeed are the marks and monuments of our empire which we have left. Future ages will wonder at us, as the present age wonders at us now. We do not need the praises of a Homer, or of anyone else whose words may delight us for the moment, but whose estimation of facts will fall short of what is really true. For our adventurous spirit has forced an entry into every sea and into every land; and everywhere we have left behind us everlasting memorials of good done to our friends or suffering inflicted on our enemies.

"This, then, is the kind of city for which these men, who could not bear the thought of losing her, nobly fought and nobly died. It is only natural that every one of us who survives them should be willing to undergo hardships in her service. And it was for this reason that I have spoken at such length about our city, because I wanted to make it clear that for us there is more at stake than there is for others who lack our advantages; also I wanted my words of praise for the dead to be set in the bright light of evidence. And now the most important of these words has been spoken. I have sung the praises of our city; but it was the courage and gallantry of these men, and of people like them, which made her splendid. Nor would you find it true in the case of many of the Greeks, as it is true of them, that no words can do more than justice to their deeds.

"To me it seems that the consummation[8] which has overtaken these men shows us the meaning of manliness in its first revelation and in its final proof. Some of them, no doubt, had their faults; but what we ought to remember first is their gallant conduct against the enemy in defense of their native land. They have blotted out evil with good, and done more service to the commonwealth than they ever did harm in their private lives. No one of these men weakened because he wanted to go on enjoying his wealth: no one put off the awful day in the hope that he might live to escape his poverty and grow rich. More to be desired than such things, they chose to check the enemy's pride. This, to them, was a risk most glorious, and they accepted it, willing to strike down the enemy and relinquish everything else. As for success or failure, they left that in the doubtful hands of Hope, and when the reality of battle was before their faces, they put their trust in their own selves. In the fighting, they thought it more honorable to stand their ground and suffer death than to give in and save their lives. So they fled from the reproaches of men, abiding[9] with life and limb the brunt of battle; and, in a small moment of time, the climax of their lives, a culmination of glory, not of fear, were swept away from us.

"So and such they were, these men—worthy of their city. We who remain behind may hope to be spared their fate, but must resolve to keep the same daring spirit against the foe. It is not simply a question of estimating the advantages in theory. I could tell you a long story (and you know it as well as I do) about what is to be gained by beating the ene-

---

7. **versatility** (vʉr′ sə til′ ə tē) *n*.: Competence in a variety of occupations.

8. **consummation** (kän′ sə mā′ shən) *n*.: State of supreme perfection, skillfulness, and expertise.
9. **abiding** (ə bīd′ iŋ) *v*.: Enduring; putting up with.

12 Enrichment Tell students that the phrase "Athens is the education of Greece" is a famous one. The Greek word for education is *paideia*, and it is rich in connotations. It includes all the moral and ethical values of a community, as well as what we might more narrowly include in the meaning of education. Ask students to discuss Pericles' claim for the citizens Athenian education produces.

13 Discussion Have students discuss why the greatness of the city is important in justifying the sacrifice Athens has exacted. How does Pericles link the public and the personal when he points out why Athenians have a lot to lose?

14 Discussion Ask students to think about why Pericles has waited so long to talk about the specific men who are being buried at the moment. Would these same words have had the same effect if he had uttered them at the beginning of his speech? Why or why not?

---

tice how everything Pericles says relates to one of his two propositions. Moreover, when he makes a claim within a paragraph, he supports his claim with examples. Here are some examples: "Our city is open to the world . . . this is because we rely, not on secret weapons, but on our own real courage and loyalty." A few sentences later, after claiming that Athens is superior to Sparta, he says, "Here is proof of this . . ." and proceeds to cite examples as proof.

Once he has sung the praises of Athens, he moves to his next topic, the courage of the men who died fighting for Athens. He then describes the strength of these men and their accomplishments. By developing his topics through careful and logical organization of supporting details, Pericles achieves unity and coherence.

Student Activity 1. Find three more examples of unity and coherence from "Pericles' Funeral Oration" and explain how Pericles achieves unity and coherence in each example.

Student Activity 2. Examine "Pericles' Funeral Oration" for examples of details that you think detract from the unity and coherence of the speech. Explain your answers.

15 Discussion Discuss Pericles' suggestion that his audience should become "lovers of Athens." What does he mean? Ask students if they are familiar with this concept, and if so, in what context?

16 Discussion Call students' attention to the terms Pericles uses: glory, fame, honor, immortality. How is his message different from or similar to what students have seen in the *Iliad*?

17 Discussion Discuss the ways in which Pericles suggests the parents of the dead soldiers confront their grief and loss. To what extent does he understand and value personal mourning?

18 Enrichment You might mention to students that the Romans, who were essentially always at war, rewarded the production of children by granting all sorts of special privileges and exemptions to those who had sired at least three legitimate children. How does Pericles depict childbearing as both a private and public function here?

19 Enrichment Tell students that children of war heroes were supported at public expense, as were victorious athletes. Suggest that students keep this in mind when they read the *Apology* (page 416).

Cultural Note The ideals expressed in this oration have exerted great influence, both during the heyday of the British Empire under Queen Victoria and more recently in the United States. Consider, for example, the speeches of Franklin Delano Roosevelt and John F. Kennedy.

Cooperative Learning How we honor our dead as a nation says a great deal about our articulated system of values. Have students work in small groups to research funeral orations in honor of those who have died serving their country. For instance, what has been said, by whom, and in what circumstances, about those who died in the space-shuttle disaster in 1986?

my back. What I would prefer is that you should fix your eyes every day on the greatness of Athens as she really is, and should fall in love with her. When you realize her greatness, then reflect that what made her great was men with a spirit of adventure, men who knew their duty, men who were ashamed to fall below a certain standard. If they ever failed in an enterprise, they made up their minds that at any rate the city should not find their courage lacking to her, and they gave to her the best contribution that they could. They gave her their lives, to her and to all of us, and for their own selves they won praises that never grow old, the most splendid of sepulchers[10]—not the sepulcher in which their bodies are laid, but where their glory remains eternal in men's minds, always there on the right occasion to stir others to speech or to action. For famous men have the whole earth as their memorial: it is not only the inscriptions on their graves in their own country that mark them out; no, in foreign lands also, not in any visible form but in people's hearts, their memory abides and grows. It is for you to try to be like them. Make up your minds that happiness depends on being free, and freedom depends on being courageous. Let there be no relaxation in face of the perils of the war. The people who have most excuse for despising death are not the wretched and unfortunate, who have no hope of doing well for themselves, but those who run the risk of a complete reversal in their lives, and who would feel the difference most intensely, if things went wrong for them. Any intelligent man would find a humiliation caused by his own slackness more painful to bear than death, when death comes to him unperceived, in battle, and in the confidence of his patriotism.

"For these reasons I shall not commiserate[11] with those parents of the dead, who are present here. Instead I shall try to comfort them. They are well aware that they have grown up in a world where there are many changes and chances. But this is a good fortune—for men to end their lives with honor, as these have done, and for you honorably to lament them: their life was set to a measure where death and happiness went hand in hand. I

know that it is difficult to convince you of this. When you see other people happy you will often be reminded of what used to make you happy too. One does not feel sad at not having some good thing which is outside one's experience: real grief is felt at the loss of something which one is used to. All the same, those of you who are of the right age must bear up and take comfort in the thought of having more children. In your own homes these new children will prevent you from brooding over those who are no more, and they will be a help to the city, too, both in filling the empty places, and in assuring her security. For it is impossible for a man to put forward fair and honest views about our affairs if he has not, like everyone else, children whose lives may be at stake. As for those of you who are now too old to have children, I would ask you to count as gain the greater part of your life, in which you have been happy, and remember that what remains is not long, and let your hearts be lifted up at the thought of the fair fame of the dead. One's sense of honor is the only thing that does not grow old, and the last pleasure, when one is worn out with age, is not, as the poet said, making money, but having the respect of one's fellow men.

"As for those of you here who are sons or brothers of the dead, I can see a hard struggle in front of you. Everyone always speaks well of the dead, and, even if you rise to the greatest heights of heroism, it will be a hard thing for you to get the reputation of having come near, let alone equaled, their standard. When one is alive, one is always liable to the jealousy of one's competitors, but when one is out of the way, the honor one receives is sincere and unchallenged.

"Perhaps I should say a word or two on the duties of women to those among you who are now widowed. I can say all I have to say in a short word of advice. Your great glory is not to be inferior to what God has made you, and the greatest glory of a woman is to be least talked about by men, whether they are praising you or criticizing you. I have now, as the law demanded, said what I had to say. For the time being our offerings to the dead have been made, and for the future their children will be supported at the public expense by the city, until they come of age. This is the crown and prize which she offers, both to the dead and to their

---

10. **sepulchers** (sep′ əl kərz) *n*.: Graves.
11. **commiserate** (kə miz′ ər āt′) *v*.: Show grief or sorrow.

Commentary

Pericles' words to Athenian women express succinctly the official view on the role of women, whom Aristotle, in the next century, classified, along with slaves, as intrinsically inferior to men. Athenian women were not citizens, even if both their parents were citizens. They could not plead for themselves in court, nor could they hold any public office, nor could they control property. They were forever wards of a male kinsman, never treated as adults or as free agents. Their only public functions were religious, and they were, as so frequently was the case, assigned special roles when it came to birth and death.

Ironically, Pericles' own partner in life was a foreign woman, Aspasia, famous for her education, charm, and wit. Pericles could not marry her, since she was not born of citizen parents, but he cherished her company and valued her good judgment. Their contemporaries said she wrote his speeches.

children, for the ordeals which they have faced. Where the rewards of valor are the greatest, there you will find also the best and bravest spirits among the people. And now, when you have mourned for your dear ones, you must depart."

Reader's Response *Do you agree that the "rewards of valor" motivate people to be brave and sacrifice their lives for their country? Explain.*

THINKING ABOUT THE SELECTION

Interpreting

1. By calling the Athenian system of government a model to others, what emotions was Pericles trying to arouse in his audience?
2. What is Pericles suggesting about the nature of Athenians when he says that the Spartan "laborious training in courage" is unnecessary for the Athenians?
3. Interpret Pericles' remark that a man who has no interest in politics has no business in Athens.
4. In honoring the war dead, what two things does Pericles say their death accomplished? Explain what each accomplishment meant.
5. Interpret Pericles' claim that "happiness depends on being free, and freedom depends on being courageous."
6. How should the honor of the war dead console people who mourn them?
7. How do Pericles' comments about women reflect the status of women in Athenian society?

Applying

8. Discuss how public figures whom you have heard speak use oration. Think about Martin Luther King, Bill Clinton, or even a good coach's pep talk.

ANALYZING LITERATURE

Analyzing Elements of Oration

An **oration** is a persuasive speech intended to inspire people and to incite them to action. Carefully planned, an oration has certain recognizable parts: the opening, the narration of facts, the definition of terms to be explained, the proposition, a confirmation addressing the arguments for or against the proposition, a refutation of the opposing arguments, and the conclusion summarizing the arguments.

1. What is Pericles' proposition? Where does he state his proposition most clearly?
2. List the arguments that Pericles presents in support of his proposition.

3. How does Pericles use the Spartans to address opposing viewpoints?
4. What is inspiring about the concluding paragraph of Pericles' oration?

SPEAKING AND LISTENING

Writing for an Audience

Since Pericles was writing for an audience, he had to use language that would appeal to his listeners. Writing to be heard rather than read placed demands on Pericles' word choice and tone of delivery. He tried, at all times, to communicate a sense of the glory of being an Athenian. To achieve that sense of glory, he appealed to his audience's religious, moral, and above all, patriotic beliefs and assumptions.

1. Locate three passages that seem more powerful heard rather than read.
2. Give an example of how Pericles appeals to his audience's morality.
3. In your opinion what is Pericles' most successful appeal to his audience's patriotism?

THINKING AND WRITING

Writing About Leadership

Pericles was the greatest Athenian statesman. According to Thucydides, he was a "man chosen by the city for his intellectual gifts and for his general reputation." Using details from his speech, write an essay in which you discuss qualities of leadership. For example, Pericles displays his ability to lead by saying: "What I would prefer is that you should fix your eyes every day on the greatness of Athens as she really is, and should fall in love with her." Make a list of similar examples and organize them into an outline of your essay on leadership. Begin with an introduction in which you define leadership and discuss why leadership is important in wartime. Refer to Pericles' speech as you develop your essay, using examples of how Pericles represents leadership. Finally, proofread your paper, making sure you have supported your thesis.

PLATO

Focus

More About the Author On his father's side, legend has it that Plato could trace his descent to the old kings of Athens and the god Poseidon. Plato's mother was descended from old aristocratic stock, related to the great lawgiver Solon. Her cousin Critias was a versatile author, one of the "beautiful people" of Athens in his youth and the leader of the Thirty Tyrants who bathed the city in blood. Her brother Charmides was also disastrously involved in the repressive aristocratic politics of the Thirty. Both these men appear in Plato's dialogues and had been part of Socrates' circle. Plato's stepfather was a wealthy member of Pericles' circle. In other times, Plato would have become a leader of the democratic state; by the time he was a young adult, his uncles, promising in their youth to be brilliant leaders, had distinguished themselves in infamy, as destroyers of the democracy and leaders of a regime akin to the totalitarian dictatorships of the 1930's in Europe or the French Revolutionary government under Robespierre.

Critical Evaluation One distinguished critic of Plato's work writes, "There is in every man . . . a poet who dies young. In Plato the poet did not die, but was translated and transmuted into the philosopher and the prose artist . . . The anecdote that on meeting Socrates Plato burned his youthful experiments in tragedy with an apt quotation from Homer may symbolize both the revolution in his mind caused by Socrates' conversation and the lifelong conflict of poetry and philosophy in his soul . . ."

You might want to ask students if they can see any evidence of Plato's skill as a dramatic poet in the *Apology*.

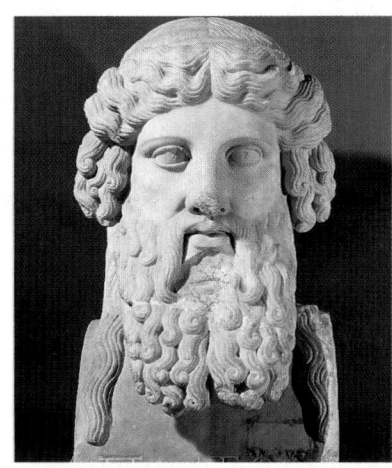

429 B.C.–347 B.C.

Plato is considered the most influential thinker in the history of Western culture. So revered was he in his day and throughout history that Plato's written work has survived practically undamaged and more completely than that of any other ancient Greek writer. Originally named Aristocles (ə ris′ tə klēz′), he took the nickname Plato, meaning "broad-shouldered." He was born during the Golden Age of Athens to a prominent family active in Athenian politics. Belonging to an aristocratic and influential family groomed him to be a political leader like Pericles, but the political corruption he observed in his youth led him to withdraw from political activity. However, Plato's life changed and gained direction once he met the philosopher Socrates (sok′ rə tēz): He turned his attention to philosophy, the love of wisdom.

Although the Athens of Plato's youth was experiencing a period of cultural flowering, it was also engaged in a devastating war with Sparta, which ended with Athens' defeat in 404 B.C. After this, a repressive government called the Thirty Tyrants ruled Athens for a year until democracy was restored. At the same time, self-proclaimed thinkers called Sophists (from *sophia,* wisdom) wandered the streets teaching Athenian youths the art of rhetoric, the ability to use language effectively and persuasively. Sophist teaching came to be considered empty, however, since it had little grounding in morals or values.

In the midst of this intellectual ferment, the philosopher Socrates wandered the streets, shabbily dressed and unbathed, questioning people about their ideas and values. He believed that the unexamined life was not worth living, and so he questioned daily the meaning of virtue, the value of knowledge, and the importance of truth. He compared himself to a gadfly because he knew he was an annoying presence, pressing others to think more clearly about their values and ideals. In Socrates' view, a consistently thorough examination of beliefs was the path to wisdom and goodness. Plato was one of a group of young men who collected about Socrates, drawn to his magnetic personality. In fact, Plato is responsible for nearly all the information we have about Socrates.

The Platonic dialogues constitute a portrait of Socrates, a representation of his interests, his method, and his self-appointed mission to teach by questioning. Socrates was critical of local politicians and their ways of governing, and he advocated a moral code that was independent of religious dictates, one that would not change with the changing governments. Plato portrays him as unwavering in his fidelity to the philosophic life at the ultimate cost of his own. In 399 B.C. certain prominent Athenian democrats who suspected Socrates of anti-democratic activity brought him to trial for atheism (belief that no gods exist) and corrupting Athenian youth. He was convicted and sentenced to drink a brew made from hemlock, a poisonous herb.

After Socrates' death, Plato withdrew from Athens to travel in Italy, Cyrene, Sicily, and Egypt. On his return he founded the Academy, the first European university and institution of pure research. Plato spent the next twenty years of his life directing the Academy, lecturing, and discussing philosophical and mathematical questions with members of the school.

Objectives

Thematic
To understand the Socratic view of wisdom

2 To understand analogy
3 To write a defense

Skills
1 To analyze dramatic monologue

GUIDE FOR INTERPRETING

from the Apology

Commentary

Dramatic Monologue. Plato wrote the *Apology* as a representation or dramatic re-creation of what Socrates said at his trial. Most of Plato's writing took the form of dialogue, or conversation between two people, but Socrates' speech in defense of himself functions as a **dramatic monologue,** an elaborate and revealing speech by one person.

The original speech, as delivered by Socrates in 399 B.C., in court before his accusers and the jurors was a public oration. In order to refute his opponents' accusations and public opinion in general, Socrates' aim was to persuade and teach by appealing to his audience's better sentiments. The stakes were high—his life. His speech, as we have it, is a text by Plato, written much later for a different audience. What Plato has produced is an oration that functions like a dramatic monologue in which Socrates presents a defense and explanation of his life's mission, the pursuit of wisdom. Although it is difficult to distinguish between what Socrates actually said and what Plato put into his mouth, scholars agree that the *Apology* provides a clear picture of the historical Socrates. The Socrates immortalized in Plato's writings is a live and picturesque character who gives voice to the philosophical ideas Plato revered.

Plato regarded the spoken word as superior to the written. The dialogues, refinements upon the actual method Socrates employed in discussion with others, reflect his dedication to the spoken word as an avenue to wisdom. The whole character of thought, according to Plato, is the dialogue of a mind with itself. The mind asks itself a question and offers several replies at random. In the process of thinking, the mind refines and reflects on those replies in an attempt to clarify and organize them. The conversation in Plato's dialogues illustrates his understanding of the thought process.

Similarly, the *Apology* is a dramatic portrait of Socrates as he faces his accusers and his judges. As he articulates his defense, the audience sees the movement of his thought. That movement is comparable to the debate among conflicting voices that occurs within an individual mind. The private drama of an inner argument becomes the public drama of an audible discussion in the *Apology.*

The *Apology* is a defiant speech in which Socrates makes no compromises. He upholds his moral position, refusing to betray his life's work. In no uncertain terms, he promises to keep persuading people to be concerned chiefly with improving their souls.

Writing

The path to wisdom is central to Socrates' and Plato's teachings. How do you define wisdom? How do you think wisdom can be attained? Freewrite, exploring your answers.

Literary Focus Have students discuss their own experience with dramatic monologues, or speeches, in defense of a person's character or way of life. How can justifying something specific lead to arguing for a set of values?

Writing/Prior Knowledge To help students arrive at their own definitions of wisdom, ask them to think about people they would consider wise. They might name legendary or historical figures, people who are especially visible in contemporary society, or people from their personal lives. Ask students what outstanding qualities make these people wise.

ESL Teaching Strategy Explain to ESL students that in first-person narration, the narrator speaks from his or her point of view, using the pronoun "I." As a result, the reader of first-person narration learns most about the narrator.

Teaching Tenth-Grade Students Start a discussion with tenth-grade students about the reliability of the narrator in first-person narration. Ask them if they have ever doubted narrators who used the first-person point of view. Then ask students, as they read, to look for passages in which Socrates seems unreliable.

Vocabulary

Preteach the following vocabulary words:

eloquence (el´ə kwəns) *n.*: Fluent, persuasive speech

affidavit (af´ə dā´vit) *n.*: Legal document

lamented (lə ment´ id) *v.*: Felt deep sorrow for

avenged (ə venjd´) *v.*: Here, vindicated

exhorting (eg zôr´ tiŋ) *v.*: Urging

impudence (im´ pyo͞o dəns) *n.*: Rashness; boldness

piety (pī´ ə tē) *n.*: Respect for the gods

indictment (in dīt´mənt) *n.*: Formal accusation

---

from the Apology

Plato

translated by Benjamin Jowett

How you, O Athenians, have been affected by my accusers, I cannot tell; but I know that they almost make me forget who I was—so persuasively did they speak; and yet they have hardly uttered a word of truth. But of the many falsehoods told by them, there was one which quite amazed me;—I mean when they said that you should be upon your guard and not allow yourselves to be deceived by the force of my eloquence. To say this, when they were certain to be detected as soon as I opened my lips and proved myself to be anything but a great speaker, did indeed appear to me most shameless—unless by the force of eloquence they mean the force of truth; for if such is their meaning, I admit that I am eloquent. But in how different a way from theirs! Well, as I was saying, they have scarcely spoken the truth at all; but from me you shall hear the whole truth: not, however, delivered after their manner in a set oration duly ornamented with words and phrases. No, by heaven! but I shall use the words and arguments which occur to me at the moment; for I am confident in the justice of my cause: at my time of life I ought not to be appearing before you, O men of Athens, in the character of a juvenile orator—let no one expect it of me. And I must beg of you to grant me a favor:—If I defend myself in my accustomed manner, and you hear me using the words which I have been in the habit of using in the agora,[1] at the tables of the money-changers, or anywhere else, I would ask you not to be surprised, and not to interrupt me on this account. For I am more than seventy years of age, and appearing now for the first time in a court of law, I am quite a stranger to the language of the place; and therefore I would have you regard me as if I were really a stranger, whom you would excuse if he spoke in his native tongue, and after the fashion of his country:—Am I making an unfair request of you? Never mind the manner, which may or may not be good; but think only of the truth of my words, and give heed to that: let the speaker speak truly and the judge decide justly.

. . .

Well, then, I must make my defense, and endeavor to clear away in a short time, a slander which has lasted a long time. May I succeed, if to succeed be for my good and yours, or likely to avail me in my cause! The task is not an easy one; I quite understand the nature of it. And so leaving the event with God, in obedience to the law I will now make my defense.

I will begin at the beginning, and ask what is the accusation which has given rise to the slander of me, and in fact has encouraged Meletus to prefer[2] this charge against me. Well, what do the slanderers say? They shall be my prosecutors, and I will sum up their words in an affidavit: "Socrates is an evildoer, and a curious person, who searches into things under the earth and in heaven, and he makes the worse appear the better cause; and he teaches the aforesaid doctrines to others." Such is the nature of the accusation: it is just what you have yourselves seen in the comedy of Aristo-

---

1. agora (ag′ ə rə) *n*.: Term for ancient Greek marketplace.

2. prefer (prē fur′) *v*.: To put before a magistrate or court.

Primary Source Note

In an autobiographical letter written at the end of his life, Plato writes:

When I was young, I had the same experience that comes to so many: I thought that, as soon as I should be my own master, I should enter public life . . . Some of the leaders were relatives and friends of mine, and they at once invited me to cooperate . . . No wonder that, young as I was, I imagined they would bring the state under their management from an iniquitous to a right way of life . . . It was not long before I saw these men make the former constitution seem like a paradise. In particphanes,[3] who has introduced a man whom he calls Socrates, going about and saying that he walks in air, and talking a deal of nonsense concerning matters of which I do not pretend to know either much or little—not that I mean to speak disparagingly[4] of anyone who is a student of natural philosophy. I should be very sorry if Meletus could bring so grave a charge against me. But the simple truth is, O Athenians, that I have nothing to do with physical speculations. Very many of those here present are witnesses to the truth of this, and to them I appeal. Speak then, you who have heard me, and tell your neighbors whether any of you have ever known me hold forth in few words or in many upon such matters. . . . You hear their answer. And from what they say of this part of the charge you will be able to judge of the truth of the rest.

. . .

I dare say, Athenians, that some one among you will reply, "Yes, Socrates, but what is the origin of these accusations which are brought against you; there must have been something strange which you have been doing? All these rumors and this talk about you would never have arisen if you had been like other men: tell us, then, what is the cause of them, for we should be sorry to judge hastily of you." Now, I regard this as a fair challenge, and I will endeavor to explain to you the reason why I am called wise and have such an evil fame.[5] Please to attend then. And although some of you may think that I am joking, I declare that I will tell you the entire truth. Men of Athens, this reputation of mine has come of a certain sort of wisdom which I possess. If you ask me what kind of wisdom, I reply, wisdom such as may perhaps be attained by man, for to that extent I am inclined to believe that I am wise; whereas the persons of whom I was speaking have a superhuman wisdom, which I may fail to describe, because I have it not myself; and he who says that I have, speaks falsely, and is taking away my character. And here, O men of Athens, I

must beg you not to interrupt me, even if I seem to say something extravagant. For the word which I will speak is not mine. I will refer you to a witness who is worthy of credit; that witness shall be the god of Delphi[6]—he will tell you about my wisdom, if I have any, and of what sort it is. You must have known Chaerephon; he was early a friend of mine, and also a friend of yours, for he shared in the recent exile of the people, and returned with you. Well, Chaerephon, as you know, was very impetuous in all his doings, and he went to Delphi and boldly asked the oracle to tell him whether—as I was saying, I must beg you not to interrupt—he asked the oracle to tell him whether any one was wiser than I was, and the Pythian prophetess answered, that there was no man wiser. Chaerephon is dead himself; but his brother, who is in court, will confirm the truth of what I am saying.

Why do I mention this? Because I am going to explain to you why I have such an evil name. When I heard the answer, I said to myself, What can the god mean? and what is the interpretation of this riddle? for I know that I have no wisdom, small or great. What then can he mean when he says that I am the wisest of men? And yet he is a god, and cannot lie; that would be against his nature. After long consideration, I thought of a method of trying the question. I reflected that if I could only find a man wiser than myself, then I might go to the god with a refutation[7] in my hand. I should say to him, "Here is a man who is wiser than I am; but you said that I was the wisest." Accordingly I went to one who had the reputation of wisdom, and observed him—his name I need not mention; he was a politician whom I selected for examination—and the result was as follows: When I began to talk with him, I could not help thinking that he was not really wise, although he was thought wise by many, and still wiser by himself; and thereupon I tried to explain to him that he thought himself wise, but was not really wise; and the consequence was that he hated me, and his enmity[8] was shared by several

---

3. **comedy of Aristophanes** (ar i stäf′ ə nēz): The comic play *Clouds*, a satire on Socrates, written by Aristophanes, an ancient Greek playwright.
4. **disparagingly** (di spar′ ij iŋ lē) *adj.*: Disrespectfully; in a way that discredits or belittles.
5. **fame:** Reputation.

6. **god of Delphi** (del′ fī′) *n.*: Apollo.
7. **refutation** (ref′ yə tā′ shən) *n.*: Something that proves an argument false or wrong.
8. **enmity** (en′ mə tē) *n.*: Bitter attitude; hostility.

1 **Discussion** Have students think about Socrates' strategy. While stating his respect and admiration for scientists, how is he also dissociating himself from them?

2 **Clarification** The Greek word for "wise" also means skilled, expert in some craft or field. Ask students if they think Socrates exploits the broad range of connotations for wisdom. How does he define wisdom and establish a hierarchy?

3 **Discussion** In addition to stressing his piety by calling on Apollo as a witness, Socrates is also claiming ultimate authority (not his own) for his words and actions. Ask students if they can see why some might have found him arrogant.

4 **Enrichment** Chaerephon was both a devoted disciple of Socrates and a well-known, ardent democrat who had been exiled for his beliefs. Socrates had never gone into exile and was viewed with suspicion by a jury of democrats who had suffered repression under the tyrants. Their leader had been Socrates' "pupil" Critias. By reminding the jury of Chaerephon, he is in effect calling a political character reference.

5 **Discussion** Ask students what rhetorical ploy Socrates is using. Since Apollo, god of prophecy, can never be wrong (students should remember this when they come to *Oedipus the King*), what outcome can listeners expect of Socrates' attempts to refute the oracle?

ular they tried to send Socrates, my friend, then advanced in years—a man whom I should not hesitate to call the most righteous man then living—with other persons, to arrest one of the citizens by violence for execution. Their purpose . . . was to implicate Socrates . . . in their proceedings. He refused, preferring to face any danger rather than be a party to their infamous deeds. Seeing all this and other things as bad, I was disgusted and drew back from the evils of the time.

Not long afterwards the Thirty fell and the whole constitution was changed. Once more I was attracted, though less eagerly, towards taking an active part in politics. In these unquiet times much was still going on that might move one to disgust, and it was no wonder that, during the revolutionary changes, some took savage vengeance upon their enemies; but on the whole the returning exiles showed great moderation. Unfortunately, however, some of the men in power brought my friend Socrates to trial on an abominable charge, the very last that could be made against Socrates—the charge of impiety. He was condemned and put to death—he who had refused to share the infamy of arresting one of his accusers' own friends when they themselves were in exile and misfortune.

who were present and heard me. So I left him, saying to myself, as I went away: Well, although I do not suppose that either of us knows anything really beautiful and good, I am better off than he is,—for he knows nothing, and thinks that he knows; I neither know nor think that I know. In this latter particular, then, I seem to have slightly the advantage of him. Then I went to another who had still higher pretensions to wisdom, and my conclusion was exactly the same. Whereupon I made another enemy of him, and of many others besides him.

Then I went to one man after another, being not unconscious of the enmity which I provoked, and I lamented and feared this: but necessity was laid upon me,—the word of God, I thought, ought to be considered first. And I said to myself, Go I must to all who appear to know, and find out the meaning of the oracle. And I swear to you, Athenians, by the dog I swear!—for I must tell you the truth—the result of my mission was just this: I found that the men most in repute[9] were all but the most foolish; and that others less esteemed were really wiser and better. I will tell you the tale of my wanderings and of the "Herculean" labors,[10] as I may call them, which I endured only to find at last the oracle irrefutable. After the politicians, I went to the poets; tragic, dithyrambic,[11] and all sorts. And there, I said to myself, you will be instantly detected; now you will find out that you are more ignorant than they are. Accordingly I took them some of the most elaborate passages in their own writings, and asked what was the meaning of them—thinking that they would teach me something. Will you believe me? I am almost ashamed to confess the truth, but I must say that there is hardly a person present who would not have talked better about their poetry than they did themselves. Then I knew that not by wisdom do poets write poetry, but by a sort of genius and inspiration; they

are like diviners[12] or soothsayers[13] who also say many fine things, but do not understand the meaning of them. The poets appeared to me to be much in the same case; and I further observed that upon the strength of their poetry they believed themselves to be the wisest of men in other things in which they were not wise. So I departed, conceiving myself to be superior to them for the same reason that I was superior to the politicians.

At last I went to the artisans. I was conscious that I knew nothing at all, as I may say, and I was sure that they knew many fine things; and here I was not mistaken, for they did know many things of which I was ignorant, and in this they certainly were wiser than I was. But I observed that even the good artisans fell into the same error as the poets;—because they were good workmen they thought that they also knew all sorts of high matters, and this defect in them overshadowed their wisdom; and therefore I asked myself on behalf of the oracle, whether I would like to be as I was, neither having their knowledge nor their ignorance, or like them in both; and I made answer to myself and to the oracle that I was better off as I was.

This inquisition[14] has led to my having many enemies of the worst and most dangerous kind, and has given occasion also to many calumnies.[15] And I am called wise, for my hearers always imagine that I myself possess the wisdom which I find wanting in others: but the truth is, O men of Athens, that God only is wise; and by his answer he intends to show that the wisdom of men is worth little or nothing; he is not speaking of Socrates, he is only using my name by way of illustration, as if he said, He, O men, is the wisest, who, like Socrates, knows that his wisdom is in truth worth nothing. And so I go about the world obedient to the god, and search and make inquiry into the wisdom of any one, whether citizen or stranger, who appears to be wise; and if he is not wise, then in

---

9. in repute (ri pyoōt′): Here, regarded as being wise.
10. Herculean (hər kyoō lē′ ən) **labors:** In a fit of madness, the hero Hercules killed his children. The Delphic oracle told him to perform twelve labors as punishment. Through these twelve feats, Hercules won immortality.
11. dithyrambic (dith ə ram′ bik) *adj.*: Used to describe impassioned, choric hymns that honor Dionysus, the god of wine.

12. diviners (də vīn′ ərz) *n.*: People who interpret divine omens.
13. soothsayers (soōth′ sā′ ərz) *n.*: People who foretell the future.
14. inquisition (in′ kwə zish′ ən) *n.*: Severe and intensive questioning.
15. calumnies (kal′ əm nēz) *n.*: False, malicious statements meant to slander.

Primary Source Note

In his comic but also fundamentally serious encomium on Socrates, delivered in Plato's *Symposium*, Alcibiades presents Socrates as a hero, as a poet and enchanter, and as more than human.

. . . the really wonderful thing about him is that he is like no other human being, living or dead. If you are looking for a parallel to Achilleus, you can find it in [the most able of the Spartan generals] Brasidas and others; if Pericles is your subject you can compare him to Nestor and Antenor [the Trojan elder statesman in the *Iliad*, as Nestor is to the Greeks]—and they do not exhaust the possibilities; and you can make similar comparisons in other cases. But our friend here is so extraordinary, both in his person and in his conversation, that you will never be able to find anyone even remotely resembling him either in antiquity or in the present generation, unless you go beyond humanity altogether and have recourse to images of Silenus and satyr which I am using myself in this speech . . .

vindication[16] of the oracle I show him that he is not wise; and my occupation quite absorbs me, and I have no time to give either to any public matter of interest or to any concern of my own, but I am in utter poverty by reason of my devotion to the god.

There is another thing:—young men of the richer classes, who have not much to do, come about me of their own accord; they like to hear the pretenders examined, and they often imitate me, and proceed to examine others; there are plenty of persons, as they quickly discover, who think that they know something, but really know little or nothing; and then those who are examined by them instead of being angry with themselves are angry with me: This confounded Socrates, they say; this villainous misleader of youth!—and then if somebody asks them, Why, what evil does he practice or teach? they do not know, and cannot tell; but in order that they may not appear to be at a loss, they repeat the ready-made charges which are used against all philosophers about teaching things up in the clouds and under the earth, and having no gods, and making the worse appear the better cause; for they do not like to confess that their pretense of knowledge has been detected—which is the truth; and as they are numerous and ambitious and energetic, and are drawn up in battle array and have persuasive tongues, they have filled your ears with their loud and inveterate[17] calumnies.

. . .

Some one will say: And are you not ashamed, Socrates, of a course of life which is likely to bring you to an untimely end? To him I may fairly answer: There you are mistaken: a man who is good for anything ought not to calculate the chance of living or dying; he ought only to consider whether in doing anything he is doing right or wrong—acting the part of a good man or of a bad. Whereas, upon your view, the heroes who fell at Troy were

16. **vindication** (vin′ də kā′ shən) *n.*: Defense.

17. **inveterate** (in vet′ ər it) *adj.*: Firmly established over time; deep rooted.

THE SCHOOL OF PLATO
Mosaic
National Museum, Naples

Humanities Note

Fine art, *The School of Plato*, mosaic. *The School of Plato* mosaic was taken from a Roman villa outside Pompeii. This carefully composed scene resembles a painting in its fine shading and modeling of forms and details, all achieved by setting minute squares of colored glass (tesserae) into cement. Ancient Romans used mosaics as decorative elements on floors, in place of carpets, and sometimes on walls.

In the mosaic *The School of Plato*, the group of philosophers are gathered beneath a tree to exchange ideas. In the upper right corner, the Acropolis and Parthenon identify the location as Athens. The skill of the mosaicist is seen in the variety of expressions on the face of each man. Plato is identified as the third figure from the left. The scene is framed with an exquisitely crafted border of twined fruit, flowers, and masks.

You might want to use the following questions to discuss the art:
1. How would you describe this mosaic to a friend who had not seen it? Be specific.
2. What is the mood of this mosaic?

10 **Discussion** Ask students to think back to what Pericles said about people who have no interest in politics. (He said they have no business in Athens.) If political involvement is essential to being a good citizen of Athens, why is it important for Socrates to explain that he is not "minding his own business," instead of the state's, but rather acting as a devoted servant of the god?

11 **Clarification** You might point out to students that Socrates' argument here is not wholly disingenuous. Socrates actually spent a good deal of time in private homes with bright young men of this circle.

not good for much, and the son of Thetis[18] above all, who altogether despised danger in comparison with disgrace; and when he was so eager to slay Hektor, his goddess mother said to him, that if he avenged his companion Patroklus, and slew Hektor, he would die himself—"Fate," she said, in these or the like words, "waits for you next after Hektor"; he, receiving this warning, utterly despised danger and death, and instead of fearing them, feared rather to live in dishonor, and not to avenge his friend. "Let me die forthwith," he replied, "and be avenged of my enemy, rather than abide here by the beaked ships, a laughingstock and a burden of the earth." Had Achilles any thought of death and danger? For wherever a man's place is, whether the place which he has chosen or that in which he has been placed by a commander, there he ought to remain in the hour of danger; he should not think of death or of anything but of disgrace. And this, O men of Athens, is a true saying.

Strange, indeed, would be my conduct, O men of Athens, if I, who, when I was ordered by the generals whom you chose to command me at Potidaea and Amphipolis and Delium,[19] remained where they placed me, like any other man, facing death—if now, when, as I conceive and imagine, God orders me to fulfill the philosopher's mission of searching into myself and other men, I were to desert my post through fear of death, or any other fear; that would indeed be strange, and I might justly be arraigned in court for denying the existence of the gods, if I disobeyed the oracle because I was afraid of death, fancying that I was wise when I was not wise. For the fear of death is indeed the pretense of wisdom, and not real wisdom, being a pretense of knowing the unknown; and no one knows whether death, which men in their fear apprehend to be the greatest evil, may not be the greatest good. Is not this ignorance of a disgraceful sort, the ignorance which is the conceit that a man

knows what he does not know? And in this respect only I believe myself to differ from men in general, and may perhaps claim to be wiser than they are:—that whereas I know but little of the world below, I do not suppose that I know: but I do know that injustice and disobedience to a better, whether God or man, is evil and dishonorable, and I will never fear or avoid a possible good rather than a certain evil. And therefore if you let me go now, and are not convinced by Anytus, who said that since I had been prosecuted I must be put to death; (or if not that I ought never to have been prosecuted at all); and that if I escape now, your sons will all be utterly ruined by listening to my words—if you say to me, Socrates, this time we will not mind Anytus, and you shall be let off, but upon one condition, that you are not to inquire and speculate in this way anymore, and that if you are caught doing so again you shall die;—if this was the condition on which you let me go, I should reply: Men of Athens, I honor and love you; but I shall obey God rather than you, and while I have life and strength I shall never cease from the practice and teaching of philosophy, exhorting[20] any one whom I meet and saying to him after my manner: You, my friend,—a citizen of the great and mighty and wise city of Athens,—are you not ashamed of heaping up the greatest amount of money and honor and reputation, and caring so little about wisdom and truth and the greatest improvement of the soul, which you never regard or heed at all? And if the person with whom I am arguing, says: Yes, but I do care; then I do not leave him or let him go at once; but I proceed to interrogate and examine and cross-examine him, and if I think that he has no virtue in him, but only says that he has, I reproach him with undervaluing the greater, and overvaluing the less. And I shall repeat the same words to every one whom I meet, young and old, citizen and alien, but especially to the citizens, inasmuch as they are my brethren. For know that this is the command of God; and I believe that no greater good has ever happened in the State than my service to the God. For I do nothing but go about persuading you all, old and young alike, not to take thought for your persons or your prop-

---

18. son of Thetis: Achilleus, epic hero of the *Iliad* who, after being dishonored, put his country and his friend Patroklos in danger by refusing to join in battle.

19. Potidaea (pä ti dē′ ə) **and Amphipolis** (am fi′ pə lis) **and Delium** (dē′ lē əm): Three of the battles in which Socrates fought in the Peloponnesian War.

20. exhorting (eg zôrt′ iŋ) *v.:* Urging earnestly by warning.

---

erties, but first and chiefly to care about the greatest improvement of the soul. I tell you that virtue is not given by money, but that from virtue comes money and every other good of man, public as well as private. This is my teaching, and if this is the doctrine which corrupts the youth, I am a mischievous person. But if anyone says that this is not my teaching, he is speaking an untruth. Wherefore, O men of Athens, I say to you, do as Anytus bids or not as Anytus bids, and either acquit me or not; but whichever you do, understand that I shall never alter my ways, not even if I have to die many times.

Men of Athens, do not interrupt, but hear me; there was an understanding between us that you should hear me to the end: I have something more to say, at which you may be inclined to cry out; but I believe that to hear me will be good for you, and therefore I beg that you will not cry out. I would have you know, that if you kill such an one as I am, you will injure yourselves more than you will injure me. Nothing will injure me, not Meletus nor yet Anytus—they cannot, for a bad man is not permitted to injure a better than himself. I do not deny that Anytus may, perhaps, kill him, or drive him into exile, or deprive him of civil rights; and he may imagine, and others may imagine, that he is inflicting a great injury upon him: but there I do not agree. For the evil of doing as he is doing—the evil of unjustly taking away the life of another—is greater far.

And now, Athenians, I am not going to argue for my own sake, as you may think, but for yours, that you may not sin against the God by condemning me, who am his gift to you. For if you kill me you will not easily find a successor to me, who, if I may use such a ludicrous[21] figure of speech, am a sort of gadfly;[22] given to the State by God; and the State is a great and noble steed[23] who is tardy in his motions owing to his very size, and requires to be stirred into life. I am that gadfly which God has attached to the State, and all day long and in all places am always fastening upon you, arousing and persuading and reproaching you. You will not easily find another like me, and therefore I would advise you to spare me. I dare say that you may feel out of temper (like a person who is suddenly awakened from sleep), and you think that you might easily strike me dead as Anytus advises, and then you would sleep on for the remainder of your lives, unless God in his care of you sent you another gadfly. When I say that I am given to you by God, the proof of my mission is this:—if I had been like other men, I should not have neglected all my own concerns or patiently seen the neglect of them during all these years, and have been doing yours, coming to you individually like a father or elder brother, exhorting you to regard virtue; such conduct, I say, would be unlike human nature. If I had gained anything, or if my exhortations had been paid, there would have been some sense in my doing so; but now, as you will perceive, not even the impudence of my accusers dares to say that I have ever exacted or sought pay of anyone; of that they have no witness. And I have a sufficient witness to the truth of what I say—my poverty.

Some one may wonder why I go about in private giving advice and busying myself with the concerns of others, but do not venture to come forward in public and advise the State. I will tell you why. You have heard me speak at sundry[24] times and in diverse places of an oracle or sign which comes to me, and is the divinity which Meletus ridicules in the indictment. This sign, which is a kind of voice, first began to come to me when I was a child; it always forbids but never commands me to do anything which I am going to do. This is what deters me from being a politician. And rightly, as I think. For I am certain, O men of Athens, that if I had engaged in politics, I should have perished long ago, and done no good either to you or to myself. And do not be offended at my telling you the truth: for the truth is, that no man who goes to war with you or any other multitude, honestly striving against the many lawless and unrighteous deeds which are done in a State, will save his life; he who will fight for the right, if he would live

---

21. **ludicrous** (loo′ di krəs) *adj.*: Absurd; ridiculous.
22. **gadfly** (gad′ flī′) *n.*: Horsefly; Socrates uses "gadfly" as a metaphor for himself as he annoys people by trying to rouse them from complacency and apathy.
23. **steed** (stēd) *n.*: A horse.

---

24. **sundry** (sun′ drē) *adj.*: Various.

18 **Literary Focus** Plato has a keen sense of how to create ambiance, how to use "dramatic business" in his writings. Ask students to notice how he suggests what is going on among the jury and spectators, without letting anyone other than Socrates speak, and without intervening as a narrator. From Socrates' repeated injunctions and pleas that the jury not interrupt, cry out, and shout him down, how do students reconstruct the scene? Why might the listeners be responding as they do?

19 **Discussion** Discuss how Socrates turns the tables by arguing that to spare him is in the best interests of the jury rather than his own. Point out that his strategy is a variation on the usual argument that something is beneficial both to the speaker and the person to be persuaded.

20 **Enrichment** Point out that Socrates was famous for his earthy style and his use of concrete examples from everyday life. The analogy to a gadfly is an example of the kind of vivid and earthy analogy Socrates was fond of using in all his teaching. Ask students if Socrates' precise picture of the gadfly and the horse is an apt description of his activity and of the state as constituted by its citizens.

21 **Clarification** The "other men" to whom Socrates refers are sophists, who taught for pay, often for very large fees.

22 **Clarification** Socrates' "little divine voice" has fascinated readers for thousands of years. The most plausible view, in light of everything Plato has written, is that when a man has reached the stage of enlightenment and harmony with the immutable and divine that Socrates had attained, he can "hear" moral dissonance as other men cannot.

retreat from Delium. I was then serving in the cavalry, whereas he was an infantryman, and after the rout had begun I came upon him marching along in company with Laches, and called out to them not to be down-hearted, and assured them that I would not desert them. And here I had an even better chance of observing Socrates than at Potidaea, because being mounted I had less occasion to be frightened myself. In the first place I noticed that he was far cooler than Laches, and next, if I may borrow an expression from you, Aristophanes, that he was using just the same gait as he does in Athens, "strutting along with his head in the air and casting side-long glances," quietly observing the movements of friend and foe, and making it perfectly plain even at a distance that he was prepared to put up a strong resistance to any attack.

even for a brief space, must have a private station and not a public one.

. . .

Now, do you really imagine that I could have survived all these years, if I had led a public life, supposing that like a good man I had always maintained the right and had made justice, as I ought, the first thing? No, indeed, men of Athens, neither I nor any other man. But I have been always the same in all my actions, public as well as private, and never have I yielded any base compliance[25] to those who are slanderously termed my disciples, or to any other. Not that I have any regular disciples. But if any one likes to come and hear me while I am pursuing my mission, whether he be young or old, he is not excluded. Nor do I converse only with those who pay; but any one, whether he be rich or poor, may ask and answer me and listen to my words; and whether he turns out to be a bad man or a good one, neither result can be justly imputed[26] to me; for I never taught or professed to teach him anything. And if any one says that he has ever learned or heard anything from me in private which all the world has not heard, let me tell you that he is lying.

. . .

Well, Athenians, this and the like of this is all the defense which I have to offer. Yet a word more. Perhaps there may be some one who is offended at me, when he calls to mind how he himself on a similar, or even a less serious occasion, prayed and entreated the judges with many tears, and how he produced his children in court, which was a moving spectacle, together with a host of relations and friends; whereas I, who am probably in danger of my life, will do none of these things. The contrast may occur to his mind, and he may be set against me, and vote in anger because he is displeased at me on this account. Now, if there be such a person among you,—mind, I do not say that there is,—to him I may fairly reply: My friend, I am a man, and like other men, a creature of flesh and blood, and not "of wood or stone," as Homer says; and I have

a family, yes, and sons, O Athenians, three in number, one almost a man, and two others who are still young; and yet I will not bring any of them hither in order to petition you for an acquittal. And why not? Not from any self-assertion or want of respect for you. Whether I am or am not afraid of death is another question, of which I will not now speak. But, having regard to public opinion, I feel that such conduct would be discreditable to myself, and to you, and to the whole State. One who has reached my years, and who has a name for wisdom, ought not to demean himself. Whether this opinion of me be deserved or not, at any rate the world has decided that Socrates is in some way superior to other men. And if those among you who are said to be superior in wisdom and courage, and any other virtue, demean themselves in this way, how shameful is their conduct! I have seen men of reputation, when they have been condemned, behaving in the strangest manner: they seemed to fancy that they were going to suffer something dreadful if they died, and that they could be immortal if you only allowed them to live; and I think that such are a dishonor to the State, and that any stranger coming in would have said of them that the most eminent men of Athens, to whom the Athenians themselves give honor and command, are no better than women. And I say that these things ought not to be done by those of us who have a reputation; and if they are done, you ought not to permit them; you ought rather to show that you are far more disposed to condemn the man who gets up a doleful[27] scene and makes the city ridiculous, than him who holds his peace.

But, setting aside the question of public opinion, there seems to be something wrong in asking a favor of a judge, and thus procuring[28] an acquittal, instead of informing and convincing him. For his duty is, not to make a present of justice, but to give judgment; and he has sworn that he will judge according to the laws, and not according to his own good pleasure; and we ought not to encourage you, nor should you allow yourselves to be encouraged, in this habit of perjury[29]—there can be no

---

25. **base compliance:** Giving in to unjustified demands out of self-interest or cowardice.
26. **imputed** (im pyōō′ təd) *v*.: Attributed to; charged to.

27. **doleful** (dōl′ fəl) *adj*.: Mournful; melancholy.
28. **procuring** (prō kyoor′ iŋ) *v*.: Securing; obtaining.
29. **perjury** (pur′ jə rē) *n*.: Act of lying while under lawful oath.

Grammar in Action

Diction, the words a writer chooses and the way he or she uses these words, is one of the most distinctive stylistic marks of a writer. There are four levels of diction: formal, informal, colloquial, and slang. Formal diction refers to the level of word choice common in lofty discourse and "serious" books. Informal diction is conversational—relaxed, but polite and cultivated. Colloquial diction refers to everyday usage, accepted among our immediate neighbors, but not necessarily universally acceptable; some colloquial terms and constructions may be common in a particular group of people while

being unfamiliar to other groups. Slang diction includes newly coined words and phrases that are not a part of formal usage.

Skilled writers manipulate their diction to communicate specific ideas, to set the tone of their writing, and to elicit certain responses from the reader. For example, Pericles' diction in his *Funeral Oration* is patriotic and persuasive. Plato's diction in the *Apology* is sophisticated, logical, and defensive; like Pericles, Socrates is trying to persuade his audience. The study of diction in the *Apology* is an interesting one because we know that we are reading Plato's account of what Socrates said at his trial. Naturally we question how much of the *Apology* is Socrates' diction and how much of it is Plato's.

piety in that. Do not then require me to do what I consider dishonorable and impious and wrong, especially now, when I am being tried for impiety on the indictment of Meletus. For if, O men of Athens, by force of persuasion and entreaty I could overpower your oaths, then I should be teaching you to believe that there are no gods, and in defending should simply convict myself of the charge of not believing in them. But that is not so—far otherwise. For I do believe that there are gods, and in a sense higher than that in which any of my accusers believe in them. And to you and to God I commit my cause, to be determined by you as is best for you and me.

There are many reasons why I am not grieved, O men of Athens, at the vote of condemnation. I expected it, and am only surprised that the votes are so nearly equal; for I had thought that the majority against me would have been far larger; but now, had thirty votes gone over to the other side, I should have been acquitted. And I may say, I think, that I have escaped Meletus. I may say more; for without the assistance of Anytus and Lycon, any one may see that he would not have had a fifth part of the votes, as the law requires, in which case he would have incurred a fine of a thousand drachmae.

And so he proposes death as the penalty. And what shall I propose on my part, O men of Athens? Clearly that which is my due. And what is my due? What returns shall be made to the man who has never had the wit to be idle during his whole life; but has been careless of what the many care for —wealth, and family interests, and military offices, and speaking in the assembly, and magistracies, and plots, and parties. Reflecting that I was really too honest a man to be a politician and live, I did not go where I could do no good to you or to myself; but where I could do the greatest good privately to every one of you, thither I went, and sought to persuade every man among you that he must look to himself, and seek virtue and wisdom before he looks to his private interests, and look to the State before he looks to the interests of the State; and that this should be the order which he observes in all his actions. What shall be done to such an one? Doubtless some good thing, O men of Athens, if he has his reward; and the good should be of a

kind suitable to him. What would be a reward suitable to a poor man who is your benefactor, and who desires leisure that he may instruct you? There can be no reward so fitting as maintenance in the Prytaneum,[30] O men of Athens, a reward which he deserves far more than the citizen who has won the prize at Olympia in the horse or chariot race, whether the chariots were drawn by two horses or by many. For I am in want, and he has enough; and he only gives you the appearance of happiness, and I give you the reality. And if I am to estimate the penalty fairly, I should say that maintenance in the Prytaneum is the just return.

Perhaps you think that I am braving you in what I am saying now, as in what I said before about the tears and prayers. But this is not so. I speak rather because I am convinced that I never intentionally wronged anyone, although I cannot convince you—the time has been too short; if there were a law at Athens as there is in other cities, that a capital cause should not be decided in one day, then I believe that I should have convinced you. But I cannot in a moment refute great slanders; and, as I am convinced that I never wronged another, I will assuredly not wrong myself. I will not say of myself that I deserve any evil, or propose any penalty. Why should I? Because I am afraid of the penalty of death which Meletus proposes? When I do not know whether death is a good or an evil, why should I propose a penalty which would certainly be an evil? Shall I say imprisonment? And why should I live in prison, and be the slave of the magistrate of the year—of the Eleven?[31] Or shall the penalty be a fine, and imprisonment until the fine is paid? There is the same objection. I should have to lie in prison, for money I have none, and cannot pay. And if I say exile (and this may possibly be the penalty which you will affix), I must indeed be blinded by the love of life, if I am so irrational as to expect that when you, who are my own citizens, cannot endure my discourses[32] and words, and have

---

30. Prytaneum (pri tā′ nē əm) *n*.: The place in which the Prytanes, representatives of the city, entertained distinguished visitors and winners of athletic contests at Olympia.

31. the Eleven: Committee in charge of prisons and public executions.

32. discourses (dis′ kôrs′ əz) *n*.: Formal communication of ideas as in speeches.

Student Activity 1. Find a passage from the *Apology* that strikes you with its diction.

Student Activity 2. What response does the diction in the *Apology* elicit from you? Explain, using examples from the text.

---

27 Clarification To discourage frivolous charges and malicious harassment, Athenian law provides that someone whose charges are in essence discredited by a jury must pay a substantial fine.

28 Enrichment There was a system of public recognition for service to the state for Olympic winners or war heroes and their families. Ask students to discuss the logic of Socrates' assertion that he deserves to be rewarded as a state benefactor. What might the jury's reaction be? Inform students that for the first vote, 281 people voted against Socrates and 220 voted for his acquittal; after his proposal of an alternative to the death penalty, the votes were 360 for the death penalty, 141 against. Ask students to account for the difference between the two rounds of voting.

29 Enrichment The point Socrates is making was also made by Xenophanes of Colophon (c. 570–c. 480 B.C.): "Now, supposing a man were to win the prize . . . at Olympia . . . such a man will obtain honor in the citizens' sight, and be given a front seat and be on display at all civic occasions, and he would be given his meals all at the public expense, and be given a gift from the city . . . all this would be granted to him, and yet he would not deserve it as I do. Better than brute strength . . . is the wisdom that is mine. But custom is careless in all these matters, and there is no justice in putting strength on a level above wisdom which is sound." If there is an athletic victor, "the city will not, on account of this man, have better government . . ."

30 Discussion Ask students to think about why Socrates dismisses the most lenient penalty, a fine; why he rejects imprisonment; and especially how he rejects exile.

found them so grievous and odious[33] that you will have no more of them, others are likely to endure me. No, indeed, men of Athens, that is not very likely. And what a life should I lead, at my age, wandering from city to city, ever changing my place of exile, and always being driven out! For I am quite sure that wherever I go, there, as here, the young men will flock to me; and if I drive them away, their elders will drive me out at their request; and if I let them come, their fathers and friends will drive me out for their sakes.

Some one will say: Yes, Socrates, but cannot you hold your tongue, and then you may go into a foreign city, and no one will interfere with you? Now, I have great difficulty in making you understand my answer to this. For if I tell you that to do as you say would be a disobedience to the God, and therefore that I cannot hold my tongue, you will not believe that I am serious; and if I say again that daily to discourse about virtue, and of those other things about which you hear me examining myself and others, is the greatest good of man, and that the unexamined life is not worth living, you are still less likely to believe me. Yet I say what is true, although a thing of which it is hard for me to persuade you. Also, I have never been accustomed to think that I deserve to suffer any harm. Had I money I might have estimated the offense at what I was able to pay, and not have been much the worse. But I have none, and therefore I must ask you to proportion the fine to my means. Well, perhaps I could afford a mina,[34] and therefore I propose that penalty: Plato, Crito, Critobulus, and Apollodorus, my friends here, bid me say thirty minae, and they will be the sureties.[35] Let thirty minae be the penalty; for which sum they will be ample security to you.

. . .

Not much time will be gained, O Athenians, in return for the evil name which you will get from the detractors[36] of the city, who will say that you killed Socrates, a wise man; for they will call me

---

33. odious (ō′ dē əs) *adj.*: Disgusting; offensive.
34. mina (mī′ nə) *n.*: A very small sum of money.
35. sureties (shoor′ ə tēz) *n.*: People who take responsibility for another person's debts.
36. detractors (dē trakt′ ərz) *n.*: Here, people who belittle.

wise, even although I am not wise, when they want to reproach you. If you had waited a little while, your desire would have been fulfilled in the course of nature. For I am far advanced in years, as you may perceive, and not far from death. I am speaking now not to all of you, but only to those who have condemned me to death. And I have another thing to say to them: You think that I was convicted because I had no words of the sort which would have procured my acquittal—I mean, if I had thought fit to leave nothing undone or unsaid. Not so; the deficiency which led to my conviction was not of words—certainly not. But I had not the boldness or impudence or inclination to address you as you would have liked me to do, weeping and wailing and lamenting, and saying and doing many things which you have been accustomed to hear from others, and which, as I maintain, are unworthy of me. I thought at the time that I ought not to do anything common or mean when in danger: nor do I now repent of the style of my defense; I would rather die having spoken after my manner, than speak in your manner and live. For neither in war nor yet at law ought I or any man to use every way of escaping death. Often in battle there can be no doubt that if a man will throw away his arms, and fall on his knees before his pursuers, he may escape death; and in other dangers there are other ways of escaping death, if a man is willing to say and do anything. The difficulty, my friends, is not to avoid death, but to avoid unrighteousness; for that runs faster than death. I am old and move slowly, and the slower runner has overtaken me, and my accusers are keen and quick, and the faster runner, who is unrighteousness, has overtaken them. And now I depart hence condemned by you to suffer the penalty of death,—they too go their ways condemned by the truth to suffer the penalty of villainy and wrong; and I must abide by my award—let them abide by theirs. I suppose that these things may be regarded as fated,—and I think that they are well.

And now, O men who have condemned me, I would fain prophesy to you; for I am about to die, and in the hour of death men are gifted with prophetic power. And I prophesy to you who are my murderers, that immediately after my departure punishment far heavier than you have inflicted on

Primary Source Note

Plato's dialogue *Crito* shows Socrates in prison awaiting execution and discoursing with his young friends, who desperately want to save him. They have the money to bribe the jailers and help him escape, but Socrates refuses and explains his reasons by putting on a dramatic dialogue, a courtroom interrogation of himself as defendant by personified Laws and Constitution of Athens. Even if the laws are applied in an unjust way, even if the state is wrong, an individual who has made a commitment to the legal system of the democratic city-state cannot engage in the criminal act of ignoring the laws and thus overthrowing the state. The laws cover every aspect of a citizen's life, from birth to death. Socrates therefore has the laws speak to him as parents to a wayward son, in their argument against his fleeing to evade the death penalty:

. . . since you have been born

me will surely await you. Me you have killed because you wanted to escape the accuser, and not to give an account of your lives. But that will not be as you suppose: far otherwise. For I say that there will be more accusers of you than there are now; accusers whom hitherto I have restrained: and as they are younger they will be more inconsiderate with you, and you will be more offended at them. If you think that by killing men you can prevent some one from censuring your evil lives, you are mistaken; that is not a way of escape which is either possible or honorable; the easiest and the noblest way is not to be disabling others, but to be improving yourselves. This is the prophecy which I utter before my departure to the judges who have condemned me.

Friends, who would have acquitted me, I would like also to talk with you about the thing which has come to pass, while the magistrates are busy, and before I go to the place at which I must die. Stay then a little, for we may as well talk with one another while there is time. You are my friends, and I should like to show you the meaning of this event which has happened to me. O my judges—for you I may truly call judges—I should like to tell you of a wonderful circumstance. Hitherto the divine faculty of which the internal oracle is the source has constantly been in the habit of opposing me even about trifles, if I was going to make a slip or error in any matter; and now as you see there has come upon me that which may be thought, and is generally believed to be, the last and worst evil. But the oracle made no sign of opposition, either when I was leaving my house in the morning, or when I was on my way to the court, or while I was speaking, at anything which I was going to say; and yet I have often been stopped in the middle of a speech, but now in nothing I either said or did touching the matter in hand has the oracle opposed me. What do I take to be the explanation of this silence? I will tell you. It is an intimation[37] that what has happened to me is good, and that those of us who think that death is an evil are in error. For the customary sign would surely have opposed me had I been going to evil and not to good.

Let us reflect in another way, and we shall see that there is great reason to hope that death is a good; for one of two things—either death is a state of nothingness and utter unconsciousness, or, as men say, there is a change and migration of the soul from this world to another. Now, if you suppose that there is no consciousness, but a sleep like the sleep of him who is undisturbed even by dreams, death will be an unspeakable gain. For if a person were to select the night in which his sleep was undisturbed even by dreams, and were to compare with this the other days and nights of his life, and then were to tell us how many days and nights he had passed in the course of his life better and more pleasantly than this one, I think that any man, I will not say a private man, but even the great king will not find many such days or nights, when compared with the others. Now, if death be of such a nature, I say that to die is gain; for eternity is then only a single night. But if death is the journey to another place, and there, as men say, all the dead abide, what good, O my friends and judges, can be greater than this? If, indeed, when the pilgrim arrives in the world below, he is delivered from the professors of justice in this world, and finds the true judges who are said to give judgment there, Minos and Rhadamanthus and Aeacus and Triptolemus,[38] and other sons of God who were righteous in their life, that pilgrimage will be worth making. What would not a man give if he might converse with Orpheus and Musaeus and Hesiod[39] and Homer? Nay, if this be true, let me die again and again. I myself, too, shall have a wonderful interest in there meeting and conversing with Palamedes,[40] and Ajax[41] the son of Telamon, and any other ancient hero who has suffered death through an unjust judgment; and there will be no small pleasure, as I think, in comparing my own sufferings with theirs. Above all, I shall then be able to continue my search into true and false knowledge; as in this world, so also in the next;

_____

37. **intimation** (in′ tə mā′ shən) *n*.: Indirect suggestion.

38. **Minos** (min′ ōs) **and Rhadamanthus** (rad ə man′ thəs) **and Aeacus** (ē a′ kəs) **and Triptolemus** (trip′ tô′ lə məs): Models of just judges in life and after death.
39. **Orpheus** (ôr′ fē əs) **and Musaeus** (myoo′ sā əs) **and Hesiod** (hes′ ē əd): Poets and religious teachers.
40. **Palamedes** (pal′ ə mē dez): One of the Greek chieftains at Troy who was unjustly executed for treason.
41. **Ajax** (ā′ jaks): Greek warrior who committed suicide after Achilleus' arms were given to Odysseus as the bravest Greek warrior.

35 Clarification Dying men were thought to have special powers to prophesy the truth; students might recall Hektor's dying prophecy to Achilleus on the battlefield. What is Socrates' prophecy?

36 Clarification Here, Socrates is alluding to a belief widely held, although not officially sanctioned, as early as in the fifth century B.C., that the soul was immortal and suffered a variety of fates after death, depending on the individual's conduct in life; for Plato and others, this belief was linked with the belief in reincarnation, or the transmigration of souls.

37 Discussion Explain that Socrates associates himself with two categories of men: the ancient poets—of whom the first two he mentions are legendary figures—viewed as the founders of lyric, dramatic, epic, and didactic poetry; and epic heroes, insufficiently valued or misunderstood by men and so driven to an unjust death. Ask students to think about why Socrates places himself alongside both these groups.

Enrichment In Plato's *Symposium* Alcibiades compares Socrates to the mythical flute player Marsyas, whose divinely inspired melodies could throw listeners into a trance. "But you, Socrates, are so far superior to Marsyas that you produce the same effect by mere words without any instrument . . . a speech by you or even a . . . report of what you have said stirs us to the depths and casts a spell over us, men and women and boys alike."

and brought up and educated, can you deny . . . that you were our child and servant, both you and your ancestors? And if this is so, do you imagine that what is right for us is equally right for you, and that whatever we try to do to you, you are justified in retaliating? You did not have equality of rights with your father or your employer—supposing you had one—to enable you to retaliate. You were not allowed to answer back when you were scolded or to hit back when you were beaten . . . Do you expect to have such license against your country and its laws that if we try to put you to death in the belief that it is right to do so, you on your part will try your hardest to destroy your country and us its laws in return?

. . . Are you so wise as to have forgotten that compared with your mother and father and all the rest of your ancestors your country is something far more precious, more venerable, more sacred, and held in greater honor both among gods and among all reasonable men? . . . Both in war and in the law courts and everywhere else you must do whatever your city and your country command . . .

Humanities Note

Fine art, *The Death of Socrates* by Jacques Louis David. The French artist Jacques Louis David (1748–1825) was an eminent historical painter and the leader of the neoclassical movement in French art. David aspired in his paintings to precisely represent events and personalities of the historic past and to "imitate nature in her most beautiful and perfect form."

You might want to use the following questions to discuss the art:

1. What do the emotional expressions of the figures in David's painting suggest?
2. Does the painting capture the atmosphere of the scene as you would have imagined it?

38 Clarification Reinforce the fact that the heroes of myth and legend were as real to the Greeks as historical figures. Ask students how they interpret Socrates' vision of life in the Underworld. Is he being humorous?

39 Discussion Ask students to identify and discuss Socrates' final message to those whom he has succeeded in persuading "in accordance with universal justice," as he would say. What is Plato indicating about Socrates' piety and the charges against him?

Master Teacher Note Part of what Plato does is to demonstrate that none of the factors that influence and deflect ordinary men—public opinion, the threat of death, money, family—make Socrates change his nature or veer from his course. Have students reflect back on the speech as a whole: How does this steadfastness of purpose make itself felt at each stage of the proceedings? Have students also think about what Pindar says about inborn nature in "Olympia 11" (page 404). How does Plato present Socrates in the heroic tradition as more than human, and as a new kind of hero even greater than the old Homeric heroes?

THE DEATH OF SOCRATES
Jacques Louis David
The Metropolitan Museum of Art, New York

and I shall find out who is wise, and who pretends to be wise, and is not. What would not a man give, O judges, to be able to examine the leader of the great Trojan expedition; or Odysseus or Sisyphus,[42] or numberless others, men and women too! What infinite delight would there be in conversing with them and asking them questions! In another world they do not put a man to death for asking questions: assuredly not. For besides being happier than we are, they will be immortal, if what is said is true.

Wherefore, O judges, be of good cheer about death, and know of a certainty, that no evil can happen to a good man, either in life or after death. He and his are not neglected by the gods; nor has my own approaching end happened by mere chance. But I see clearly that the time had arrived when it was better for me to die and be released from trouble; wherefore the oracle gave no sign.

---

42. Sisyphus (sis′ ə fəs): In Greek mythology, a king of Corinth, famous for his cunning.

For which reason, also, I am not angry with my condemners, or with my accusers; they have done me no harm, although they did not mean to do me any good; and for this I may gently blame them.

Still, I have a favor to ask of them. When my sons are grown up, I would ask you, O my friends, to punish them; and I would have you trouble them, as I have troubled you, if they seem to care about riches, or anything, more than about virtue; or if they pretend to be something when they are really nothing,—then reprove[43] them, as I have reproved you, for not caring about that for which they ought to care, and thinking that they are something when they are really nothing. And if you do this, both I and my sons will have received justice at your hands.

The hour of departure has arrived, and we go our ways—I to die, and you to live. Which is better God only knows.

---

43. reprove (ri pro͞ov′) *v.*: Express disapproval of.

Reader's Response *Imagine yourself as a juror at Socrates' trial. Would his speech have moved you? Would you have condemned him or not? Explain your answer.*

Closure and Extension

ANSWERS TO THINKING ABOUT THE SELECTION

1. The philosopher's mission is to seek virtue and wisdom.
2. He must stop inquiring and speculating about wisdom, which is unacceptable to Socrates because he feels the unexamined life is not worth living, and he regards himself as following God's command.
3. (a) He respects the law, even if he disagrees with it. (b) He has no fear of death because he doesn't know what death will bring.
4. (a) Answers will differ. Suggested response: He makes people uncomfortable by calling attention to their weaknesses and their faults. (b) Answers will differ. Suggested response: Perhaps people are afraid of the truth.
5. (a) He considers the improvement of the soul the greatest improvement of all. (b) Answers will differ.
6. Socrates prophesies that they will have more accusers from whom they can never escape.
7. Answers will differ. Suggested response: Socrates makes no sacrifice because he refuses to compromise.

THINKING ABOUT THE SELECTION

Clarifying

1. According to Socrates, what is the philosopher's mission?
2. Socrates would have been allowed to live on one condition. What is that condition, and why is it unacceptable to him?

Interpreting

3. (a) Why does Socrates insist on obeying the law? (b) What is his attitude toward death?
4. Socrates compares himself to a gadfly. (a) Why do you think the Athenians view him as an annoyance? (b) Why does his pursuit of the truth disturb people?
5. (a) Why does Socrates insist that private concerns are more important than public issues? (b) Do you agree with him? Why or why not?
6. Why does Socrates see his accusers as condemned by the truth?
7. Does Socrates make a sacrifice in the Apology? Explain your answer.

Applying

8. Socrates is willing to die for his beliefs. Under no circumstance will he compromise his principles. What do you think about his refusal to compromise? Evaluate both the fairness of Socrates' condemnation and his reaction to his accusers.
9. How would Socrates have been treated in today's world? Imagine him in different cultures with which you are familiar and describe how he would be treated for his practices.

ANALYZING LITERATURE

Analyzing Dramatic Monologue

In a **dramatic monologue,** a character in a dramatic situation, or crisis, addresses a silent listener. The most famous examples of dramatic monologues are poems, such as Robert Browning's "My Last Duchess" and Alfred, Lord Tennyson's "Ulysses." Plato's Apology, though not a poem, functions as a dramatic monologue for two important reasons. First, the Apology is an intimate portrait of Socrates revealing his mind. Second, it provides telling information about the audience, Socrates' accusers and judges. For example, their intolerance of his behavior implies that they are insecure about their own beliefs. At no time is Socrates insecure about his approach to life.

1. Socrates insists that only the examined life is worth living. How does he support his claim? What does his claim reveal about him?
2. Socrates considers himself wise for unusual reasons. Discuss his reasons, and explain whether you agree that they make him wise.
3. Socrates says, "I would rather die after having spoken after my manner, than speak in your manner and live." What can you infer about the audience's manner? Explain.

CRITICAL THINKING AND READING

Understanding Analogy

An **analogy** is a comparison of two things that are alike in some way. An unfamiliar object or idea may be clarified if it is compared to a more familiar object or idea through analogy. Analogy is especially useful when arguing to convince or persuade an audience, as Socrates does in the Apology.

1. The most famous analogy from the Apology occurs when Socrates compares himself to a gadfly. How does his analogy increase your understanding of his crisis?
2. Socrates also compares himself to Achilleus, hero of the Iliad. What does Socrates' comparison reveal about his perception of the philosopher's role?
3. Locate another analogy from the Apology and explain its significance in terms of Socrates' defense.

THINKING AND WRITING

Writing a Defense

The term apology as Plato uses it means defense. Using what Socrates said at his trial, Plato wrote a defense of Socrates, whom he revered as a teacher and a friend. In the first part of the Apology, Plato portrays Socrates refuting the charges against him. After the refutation, Socrates discusses the reasons why he cannot accept the possible alternatives to a death sentence. Finally, he concludes his defense by accepting his condemnation. Choose someone in current affairs or in history whose beliefs you admire and write a defense similar to Plato's Apology. Define his or her beliefs and argue for them. As in the Apology, write your defense from the character's point of view. Use analogies to increase the impact of your defense. As you revise, make sure you have adequately supported your character's beliefs. Proofread your paper. Then present it to your class as a dramatic monologue.

(continued from bottom of page)

ANSWERS TO CRITICAL THINKING AND READING

1. Answers will differ. The analogy to a gadfly should make students appreciate how people perceived him as an annoyance and how desperately they wanted to be rid of him.
2. The comparison reveals that he perceives the philosopher's role as that of a hero's, who thinks not of death but of honor and righteous deeds even in the face of danger.
3. As he speculates about death, he compares death to a deep, undisturbed sleep. His attitude about death is an important issue in the Apology because he chooses death over less severe punishments.

THINKING AND WRITING

Writing Across the Curriculum Students interested in theater might want to consult a drama instructor for suggestions as to how to make their defense speeches dramatic.

Challenge Encourage students to read more of the Apology or other Platonic dialogues like Crito and Symposium.

8. Answers will differ. Suggested response: Socrates' condemnation was unfair because there is no evidence that he was harming or endangering anyone.
9. In today's world, particularly United States society, people would not take him seriously. In any totalitarian government he would be imprisoned.

ANSWERS TO ANALYZING LITERATURE

1. He examines life for truth, virtue, and the improvement of the soul. Students might infer that without constantly improving the soul, one is stagnating quickly toward death. Socrates' claim reveals his unwavering fidelity to the human soul.
2. Unlike people who pretend to know

but who really know nothing, Socrates neither knows nor pretends to know.
3. Answers will differ. Suggested response: The audience doesn't share Socrates' concern for the human soul because they keep interrupting him, and they have condemned him to die.

Drama

Humanities Note

Fine art, *Theater Masks,* Roman mosaic. The Romans were great lovers of entertainment and also of the decorative arts. In this mosaic the Romans pay tribute both to drama and mosaic art. The minute squares of colored glass, called tessarae, that make up this mosaic imitate the quality of a painting in the delicate shadings and gradations of color they reflect. The tesserae in this mosaic are remarkably small in size. Only a master craftsman could have created such a realistic effect using this exceedingly difficult medium. The subject is one familiar to people who flocked to their open air arenas to see enactments of tragedy and comedy.

You might want to use the following questions to discuss the art:

1. Are these masks familiar to you? If so, how do they resemble or differ from other theater masks you might have seen?

2. How do you interpret the juxtaposition of the comedy and tragedy masks?

ROMAN MOSAIC; THEATER MASKS

SOPHOCLES

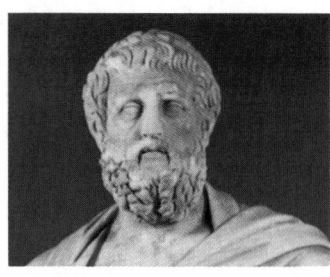

496 B.C.–406 B.C.

Sophocles' (sof′ ə klēz) life corresponded with the splendid rise and tragic fall of fifth-century Athens. At sixteen, he was one of the young men chosen by the city to perform a choral ode, dancing and singing in a public celebration of Athens' naval victory over the Persians at Salamis. In 443 B.C. he was one of the treasurers of the imperial league, organized to resist Persia. With Pericles, Sophocles served as one of the generals in the war against the island of Samos, which later tried to secede from the Athenian league. In 411 B.C., he was also appointed to a special government committee when Athens' expedition to Sicily failed. He died in 406 B.C., two years before Athens surrendered to Sparta in the Peloponnesian War.

Sophocles' life also coincided with the rise and fall of the Golden Age of Greek tragedy. His career as a dramatist began in 468 B.C. when he entered the Dionysia (di′ ə nē′ sē ə), the annual theatrical competition sacred to the god Dionysus (di′ ə nī′ səs). Competing against the established and brilliant playwright Aeschylus (es′ kə ləs), Sophocles won first prize. Over the next 62 years, he wrote over 120 plays, 24 of which won first prize; those that didn't come in first placed second.

Sophocles was an innovative dramatist who made significant contributions to Greek tragedy. Originally, Greek drama was presented in an open-air theater with few sets or props. Sophocles expanded the use of stage machinery and sets, which intensified the dramatic performance. For instance, he was the first to use the *mechane,*

a crane used to lower the gods "miraculously" onto the stage. A god appearing at the end of the play to wrap up loose ends was called by the Romans, *deus ex machina* (dā′ əs eks mäk′ ē nə) to signify a contrived ending, an unexpected last-minute reprieve, the intervention of a supernatural force in the nick of time.

Originally, plays were presented by the Chorus, or group of singers. Eventually, two actors stepped out of the Chorus to take on individual roles. Sophocles increased the number of singers in the chorus and introduced a third speaking part to the Greek stage. The addition of a third actor allowed for more dramatically complex dialogue than that of the earlier Aeschylean plays. And unlike Aeschylus, who wrote three interconnected plays, Sophocles wrote single dramas of concentrated action.

In addition to his technical innovations, Sophocles is known for his profound fidelity to universal human experience. In his plays the world order consists of human beings, nature, and the inscrutable forces of gods and fate. Sophocles suggests that although a person's place in the cosmic order cannot be fully understood, human beings can be held responsible for their actions. Gods can predetermine or influence human action, but they do not necessarily direct a character. In a mysterious and incomprehensible world where suffering is not always justified, people are responsible for finding out where they belong in the universe; then they must take moral responsibility for their lives.

Only seven of Sophocles' plays have survived intact, carefully reconstructed in 303 B.C. by Athenians concerned with preserving such a crucial part of their literary heritage. The extant plays are: *Ajax, The Women of Trachis, Antigone, Oedipus the King, Electra, Philoctetes,* and finally, *Oedipus at Colonus,* which was published posthumously. *Oedipus the King* has often been considered not only the masterpiece among Sophocles' creations but the most important and influential drama ever written.

BACKGROUND

OEDIPUS THE KING

Critical Evaluation The English Romantic poet Percy Bysshe Shelley was trained as a classical scholar and modeled himself on the great poets of ancient Greece. In his preface to his verse drama, *The Cenci*, in 1819, he argues that great poets transmute familiar stories: "The deepest and the sublimest tragic compositions, *King Lear* and the two plays in which the tale of Oedipus is told, were stories which already existed in tradition, as matters of popular belief and interest, before Shakespeare and Sophocles made them familiar to the sympathy of all succeeding generations of mankind." Have students think about how writers transform familiar mythical or plot elements; students may be familiar with Thornton Wilder's *Our Town*.

Enrichment At the outset of the play, Oedipus and his city are presented as one. Identifying the ruler with the land, seeing him as responsible for the prosperity or barrenness of everything in his realm, is an ancient practice. In the *Odyssey*, Homer has Odysseus in disguise praise Penelope in these terms:

> your fame goes up to heaven, / as of some king who, as a blameless man and god-fearing, / and ruling as lord over many powerful people, / upholds the way of good government, and the black earth yields him / barley and wheat, his trees are heavy with fruit, his sheepflocks / continue to bear young, and the sea gives him fish, because of / his good leadership, and his people prosper under him.

The tragic quality of the Oedipus myth made the story prime material for Sophocles' tragic play. For this reason Greek tragedy's most celebrated critic, Aristotle, used *Oedipus the King* as a point of reference in his *Poetics*.

Now since in the finest kind of tragedy the structure should be complex and not simple, and since it should also be a representation of terrible and piteous events (that being the special mark of this type of imitation) in the first place, it is evident that good men ought not to be shown passing from prosperity to misfortune, for this does not inspire either pity or fear, but only revulsion; nor evil men rising from ill fortune to prosperity, for this is the most untragic plot of all—it lacks every requirement, in that it neither elicits human sympathy nor stirs pity or fear, since the first is felt for a person whose misfortune is undeserved and the second for someone like ourselves—pity for the man suffering undeservedly, fear for the man like ourselves—and hence neither pity nor fear would be aroused in this case. We are left with the man whose place is between these extremes. Such is the man who on the one hand is not preeminent in virtue and justice, and yet on the other hand does not fall into misfortune through vice or depravity, but falls because of some mistake; one among the number of the highly renowned and prosperous, such as Oedipus . . .

Sophocles produced *Oedipus the King* in the early years of the Peloponnesian War, when Athenians were re-evaluating accepted standards and traditions. Athens was also being afflicted by a terrible plague that ravaged both the civilian population and the troops and sent Athens into a state of anarchy. *Oedipus the King*, set in ancient Thebes, reflects the Athenian crisis: As the play begins, Thebes is suffering from a plague, and the city's political leadership is being challenged.

The Oedipus Myth

The Oedipus myth was deeply rooted in the consciousness of Sophocles' community. Cadmus, the founder of Thebes, angered Apollo by killing the god's favorite snake. As punishment, the descendants of Cadmus lived under a curse prophesied to each generation by Apollo's oracle. According to prophecy, if Laius, king of Thebes, had a son by Jocasta, his queen, that son would kill his father and marry his mother. In response to the prophecy, Laius had a rivet driven between Oedipus' infant ankles and instructed a household servant to leave him on Mt. Cithaeron to die from exposure to the elements. Instead, the servant pitied the infant Oedipus and, without revealing his identity, gave him to a shepherd. In turn, the shepherd gave Oedipus to Merope, the wife of Polybus, king of Corinth. They named him Oedipus (swollen foot) for the wounds in his feet.

As a young man, Oedipus was taunted for not being the true son of King Polybus. Deeply troubled, Oedipus consulted the oracle of Apollo at

Primary Source Note

The Oedipus myth has captivated many dramatists, from the Roman Seneca to the French playwrights Voltaire, Gide, and Cocteau, to the contemporary American Woody Allen. Each culture and period imposes its own concerns on the myth. In 1934, in Paris, Jean Cocteau first produced his version, *The Infernal Machine*. His view of man in relation to divinity, fate, or universal order is a radical rereading of Sophocles. The action is introduced by the Voice, which addresses the audience:

For the gods really to enjoy themselves, their victim must fall from a great height. Years come and go in prosperity. Two daughters and two sons complicate the monstrous union. The people love their king. But the plague suddenly descends upon them. The gods accuse an anonymous criminal of infecting the country and demand that he shall be driven out. From one discovery to another, and as if intoxicated by misfortune, Oedipus, in the end, finds himself up against the wall. The trap shuts. All becomes clear. With her red scarf, Jocasta hangs herself. With the golden brooch of the hanging woman, Oedipus puts out his eyes.

TWO SPHINXES SURMOUNTED BY TWO LIONS
Egyptian relief from tomb at Xanthes

Humanities Note

Fine art, *Two Sphinxes Surmounted by Two Lions*. The ancient Greeks took the Egyptian image of the half-lion, half-human creature, the sphinx, to be the ultimate symbol of enigma and mystery. This interpretation of the sphinx has continued through the centuries and still applies today.

In this ancient Egyptian relief carving from a tomb at Xanthes, each sphinx has the head of a woman as well as wings. While this carving was certainly used as a decorative motif, the artist's real purpose was to provide the spirit of the dead with two sentries or guardians.

You might want to use the following questions to discuss the art:

1. Did the Egyptian relief meet your expectations of what the sphinx would look like?
2. Does the Egyptian relief capture the spirit of enigma and mystery associated with the sphinx? Explain.

Delphi about the accusation. But before he could ask his question, the priestess, Pythia, drove him away from Apollo's shrine, declaring that Oedipus would kill his father and marry his mother. Horrified at the prophecy, Oedipus fled Corinth, the home of his supposed parents, in an attempt to avoid fulfilling the prophecy.

Not far from Delphi, Oedipus met a man in a chariot whose charioteer demanded that Oedipus move aside. When he refused the charioteer drove his horses forward, so that a wheel of the car grazed Oedipus' foot. As the chariot passed him, someone inside struck Oedipus on the head with a goad. Enraged, Oedipus killed the rider and charioteer and continued on his way.

Eventually, Oedipus found his way to Thebes. Upon arrival he found the city in turmoil. A female monster called the Sphinx was terrorizing the Thebans, eating them one by one. Before eating her victims, the Sphinx would ask them a riddle: "What is it that goes on four legs in the morning, two at midday, and three in the evening?" Unfor-

tunately, the Sphinx would continue tormenting the Thebans until someone answered the riddle. Worse yet, a nearby king, Damasistratus, reported that king Laius had been killed on his way to Delphi. The preoccupied Thebans had no time to seek the murderer. Creon's priority was to find someone who could save Thebes from the Sphinx by solving her riddle. He offered the hand of his sister Jocasta, Laius' widow, and a share in the kingdom to any man who could answer the Sphinx correctly.

Oedipus visited the Sphinx with the correct answer: "Man, who crawls in infancy, walks upright in his prime, and leans on a cane in old age." The Sphinx flung herself to her death, and Oedipus was made king of Thebes with Jocasta as his wife. After he ruled for almost two decades, Thebes was visited with a plague because Laius' murderer was living in Thebes unpunished for his crime. Oedipus opened an investigation immediately to locate the murderer and relieve Thebes of the plague. At this point in the Oedipus story, Sophocles begins the play.

Spectator, this machine you see here wound up to the full in such a way that the spring will slowly unwind the whole length of a human life, is one of the most perfect constructed by the infernal gods for the mathematical destruction of a mortal.

Literary Focus Have students discuss their own experience with literature or films whose plots revolve around good intentions leading to catastrophe, or actions resulting in an unexpected or undesired outcome. They might consider to what extent characters act in avoidable ignorance and to what extent no human being could have made a better decision, given the information available.

Writing/Prior Knowledge In pairs or groups of four, have students talk about situations in which some decision or action of theirs resulted in the opposite of their intention. Do they feel they should have known better, or that they could not have been expected to act differently?

ESL Teaching Strategy Pair ESL students with native-speaking students and have everyone read scenes from the play aloud. The native-speaking student should act as a drama coach for the ESL student.

Teaching Tenth-Grade Students Tenth-grade students might like to discuss the mythology of the Oedipus story. Ask students to share what they know about the myth. Students may also be familiar with Oedipus in the more modern, psychological context. Making the connection between what we now call the Oedipus complex and the ancient Oedipus myth will be a good springboard for reading the play.

Vocabulary

Preteach the following vocabulary words:

blight (blīt) *n.*: Destructive disease

dispatch (di spach´) *v.*: Kill

ordinance (or´ d'n əns) *n.*: Decree of fate

haven (hā vən) *n.*: Safe place

compliance (kəm plī´ əns) *n.*: A giving in to a request

disquiets (dis kwī´ əts) *v.*: Disturbs

malignant (mə lig´ nənt) *adj.*: Very harmful

Commentary

Writing

Oedipus the King, Part I

Tragedy. Drama probably evolved from ritual chants and dances performed by an all-male chorus in honor of Dionysus, the god of wine. In the fifth century B.C., Athens began to hold a cycle of religious festivals throughout the year to honor Dionysus and to celebrate the harvesting of grapes and the production of wine.

Tragedies dealt with universal issues and indirectly with contemporary politics, but the plots were taken from the same cycle of legends in the Homeric epics. Dramatists presented their audience with deeply troubling emotional issues as they publicly examined the worst and most hidden fears of the individual.

The chorus of dancers and singers plays an active part in the play. Often, members of the chorus serve as confidants and advisers to the principal characters. The parodos is presented as the chorus enters. The chorus faces in one direction for the strophe and in the opposite for the antistrophe. Notice how the use of the strophe and the antistrophe create tension in the play. As you read, notice how the chorus reacts to events. In what ways does the chorus serve as the voice of public opinion?

Tragedy recounts an important series of events in the life of a protagonist of high birth or noble status. The causally related events culminate in a catastrophe in which the protagonist, through his or her own actions, is brought low. To the ancients the plot of a drama was like the tying and untying of a knot. Therefore, a well-constructed tragedy includes an introduction of the conflict, the rising action, in which the conflict between the hero and his or her opposing forces occurs, and the climax, or turning point of the play. From the climax, the falling action stresses the forces opposing the hero and leads logically to the disaster with which the play must end. Inevitably, the play ends in a catastrophe that marks the tragic fall of the hero, who is ennobled by facing his or her destiny courageously and accepting his or her responsibility in the downfall. Oedipus is in rebellion against the universe and the frailty of his own flesh and free will.

Most human beings, consciously or unconsciously, strive to achieve happiness and avoid disaster. While that is a healthy approach to life, human imperfections and limitations inevitably interfere with such aspirations. Recall a time when you were committed to a cause of action that in retrospect turned out badly. Freewrite, exploring what you did. Discuss your feelings as you looked ahead to the project and as you looked back on it.

Objectives

Thematic

To understand how human beings cannot escape their fates

Skills

1 To analyze tragedy

2 To trace a motif

3 To use context clues

4 To write about character

Support Material

Teaching Portfolio

Teacher Backup, p. 549

Grammar in Action Worksheets, *Using Participles and Participial Phrases*, p. 555; *Setting Tone*, p. 557; *Using Dashes*, p. 559; *Maintaining Tone*, p. 561

Oedipus the King

Sophocles

translated by David Grene

CHARACTERS

Oedipus, King of Thebes
Jocasta, His Wife
Creon, His Brother-in-Law
Teiresias, an Old Blind Prophet
A Priest

First Messenger
Second Messenger
Herdsman
A Chorus of Old Men of Thebes

Part I

[*Scene: In front of the palace of Oedipus at Thebes. To the right of the stage near the altar stands the Priest with a crowd of children. Oedipus emerges from the central door.*]

OEDIPUS. Children, young sons and daughters of
    old Cadmus,[1]
why do you sit here with your suppliant crowns?[2]
The town is heavy with a mingled burden
of sounds and smells, of groans and hymns and
    incense;
I did not think it fit that I should hear
of this from messengers but came myself,—
I Oedipus whom all men call the Great.
              [*He turns to the* PRIEST.]
You're old and they are young; come, speak for
                      them.

10   What do you fear or want, that you sit here
suppliant? Indeed I'm willing to give all
that you may need; I would be very hard
should I not pity suppliants like these.

PRIEST. O ruler of my country, Oedipus,
you see our company around the altar;
15   you see our ages; some of us, like these,
who cannot yet fly far, and some of us
heavy with age; these children are the chosen
among the young, and I the priest of Zeus.
Within the marketplace sit others crowned
20   with suppliant garlands,[3] at the double shrine
of Pallas[4] and the temple where Ismenus
gives oracles by fire.[5] King, you yourself
have seen our city reeling like a wreck

---

1. **Cadmus** (kad′ məs) *n.*: Mythical founder and first king of Thebes, a city in central Greece where the play takes place.
2. **suppliant** (sup′ lē ənt) **crowns:** Wreaths worn by people who ask favors of the gods.
3. **suppliant garlands** *n.*: Branches wound in wool, which were placed on the altar and left there until the suppliant's request was granted.
4. **double shrine of Pallas:** The two temples of Athena.
5. **temple where Ismenus gives oracles by fire:** Temple of Apollo, located by Ismenus, the Theban river, where the priests studied patterns in the ashes of sacrificial victims to foretell the future.

already; it can scarcely lift its prow
out of the depths, out of the bloody surf.
A blight is on the fruitful plants of the earth,
A blight is on the cattle in the fields,
a blight is on our women that no children
are born to them; a God that carries fire,
a deadly pestilence,[6] is on our town,
strikes us and spares not, and the house of
    Cadmus
is emptied of its people while black Death
grows rich in groaning and in lamentation.[7]
We have not come as suppliants to this altar
because we thought of you as of a God,
but rather judging you the first of men
in all the chances of this life and when
we mortals have to do with more than man.
You came and by your coming saved our city,
freed us from tribute which we paid of old
to the Sphinx,[8] cruel singer. This you did
in virtue of no knowledge we could give you,
in virtue of no teaching; it was God
that aided you, men say, and you are held
with God's assistance to have saved our lives.
Now Oedipus, Greatest in all men's eyes,
here falling at your feet we all entreat you,
find us some strength for rescue.
Perhaps you'll hear a wise word from some God,
perhaps you will learn something from a man
(for I have seen that for the skilled of practice
the outcome of their counsels live the most).
Noblest of men, go, and raise up our city,
go,—and give heed. For now this land of ours
calls you its savior since you saved it once.
So, let us never speak about your reign
as of a time when first our feet were set

secure on high, but later fell to ruin.
Raise up our city, save it and raise it up.
Once you have brought us luck with happy
    omen;
be no less now in fortune.
If you will rule this land, as now you rule it,
better to rule it full of men than empty.
For neither tower nor ship is anything
when empty, and none live in it together.

OEDIPUS. I pity you, children. You have come full
    of longing,
but I have known the story before you told it
only too well. I know you are all sick,
yet there is not one of you, sick though you are,
that is as sick as I myself.
Your several sorrows each have single scope
and touch but one of you. My spirit groans
for city and myself and you at once.
You have not roused me like a man from sleep;
know that I have given many tears to this,
gone many ways wandering in thought,
but as I thought I found only one remedy
and that I took. I sent Menoeceus' son
Creon, Jocasta's brother, to Apollo,
to his Pythian temple,[9]
that he might learn there by what act or word
I could save this city. As I count the days,
it vexes me what ails him; he is gone
far longer than he needed for the journey.
But when he comes, then, may I prove a villain,
if I shall not do all the God commands.

PRIEST. Thanks for your gracious words. Your
    servants here
signal that Creon is this moment coming.

OEDIPUS. His face is bright. O holy Lord Apollo,
grant that his news too may be bright for us
and bring us safety.

PRIEST. It is happy news,
I think, for else his head would not be crowned
with sprigs of fruitful laurel.[10]

---

6. **pestilence** (pes′ tə ləns) *n.*: A fatal, contagious disease of epidemic proportions.

7. **lamentation** (lam′ ən tā′ shən) *n.*: Act of expressing deep sorrow and grief.

8. **Sphinx** (sfinks) *n.*: A winged female monster who ate Theban men who could not answer her riddle: "What is it that walks on four legs at dawn, two legs at midday, and three legs in the evening, and has only one voice; when it walks on most feet, it is weakest?" Creon, appointed ruler of Thebes, offered the kingdom and the hand of his sister Jocasta to anyone who could answer the riddle. Oedipus saved Thebes by answering correctly, "Man, who crawls in infancy, walks upright in his prime, and leans on a cane in old age." Outraged, the Sphinx destroyed herself, and Oedipus became King of Thebes.

9. **Pythian** (pith′ ē ən) **temple**: The shrine of Apollo at Delphi, below Mount Parnassus in central Greece.

10. **sprigs of fruitful laurel:** Laurel symbolized triumph; a crown of laurel signified good news.

Grammar in Action

Tone refers to the author's attitude toward his or her subject. When a writer feels strongly about an issue, he or she may choose to write about it in a serious tone. Or a writer might use an ironic tone to discuss an issue he or she considers ridiculous. Tone can be formal, informal, solemn, somber, playful, condescending, anxious, happy, or any other possible attitudes. The effectiveness of a literary work, whether it communicates the author's intentions, can depend largely on the skill with which the author establishes tone.

In *Oedipus the King*, Thebes is in a crisis. The tone is serious because the Thebans are concerned about their city. They urgently need to discover the causes of the plague, and they are solemn while they wait for Creon to return with the answer from Apollo. The tone in this early scene sets

OEDIPUS. We will know soon,
he's within hail. Lord Creon, my good brother,
what is the word you bring us from the God?

[CREON *enters.*]

CREON. A good word,—for things hard to bear
themselves
if in the final issue all is well
I count complete good fortune.

OEDIPUS. What do you mean?
What you have said so far
leaves me uncertain whether to trust or fear.

CREON. If you will hear my news before these
others
I am ready to speak, or else to go within.

OEDIPUS. Speak it to all;
the grief I bear, I bear it more for these
than for my own heart.

CREON. I will tell you, then,
what I heard from the God.
King Phoebus[11] in plain words commanded us
to drive out a pollution from our land,
pollution grown ingrained within the land;
drive it out, said the God, not cherish it,
till it's past cure.

OEDIPUS. What is the rite
of purification? How shall it be done?

CREON. By banishing a man, or expiation[12]
of blood by blood, since it is murder guilt
which holds our city in this destroying storm.

OEDIPUS. Who is this man whose fate the God pronounces?

CREON. My Lord, before you piloted[13] the state
we had a king called Laius.

OEDIPUS. I know of him by hearsay.[14] I have not
seen him.

---

11. King Phoebus (fē´ bəs): Apollo, god of sun.
12. expiation (eks´ pē ā´ shən) *n.*: The act of making amends for wrongdoing.
13. piloted (pī´ lət əd) *v.*: Led or guided through difficulty.
14. hearsay (hir´ sā´) *n.*: Rumor; gossip.

CREON. The God commanded clearly: let some
one
punish with force this dead man's murderers.

OEDIPUS. Where are they in the world? Where
would a trace
of this old crime be found? It would be hard
to guess where.

CREON. The clue is in this land;
that which is sought is found;
the unheeded thing escapes:
so said the God.

OEDIPUS. Was it at home,
or in the country that death came upon him,
or in another country traveling?

CREON. He went, he said himself, upon an
embassy,[15]
but never returned when he set out from home.

OEDIPUS. Was there no messenger, no fellow
traveler
who knew what happened? Such a one might tell
something of use.

CREON. They were all killed save one. He fled in
terror
and he could tell us nothing in clear terms
of what he knew, nothing, but one thing only.

OEDIPUS. What was it?
If we could even find a slim beginning
in which to hope, we might discover much.

CREON. This man said that the robbers they
encountered
were many and the hands that did the murder
were many; it was no man's single power.

OEDIPUS. How could a robber dare a deed like
this
were he not helped with money from the city,
money and treachery?[16]

CREON. That indeed was thought.
But Laius was dead and in our trouble
there was none to help.

---

15. embassy (em´ bə sē) *n.*: An important mission or errand.
16. treachery (trech´ ər ē) *n.*: Disloyalty or treason.

---

6 Discussion The oracle has spoken clearly, but the information can be interpreted correctly only by those who have all the pieces of the puzzle. Ask students how we relate to the characters in the play, especially the protagonist, since we have more information than the characters.

7 Literary Focus Call students' attention to the ship-of-state metaphor. Do students think it is apt?

8 Literary Focus Sophocles introduces another dominant image: hunting. Oedipus as a tracker, hunting down prey, is also Oedipus the hunter whose arrow will hit the true mark but miss the target he thinks he sees.

9 Clarification Point out to students that only one man killed Laius. Have them discuss why a slave who came home, having survived an attack that killed his master the king, might say that the party was surrounded by robbers rather than saying a single man was involved.

10 Discussion What is Oedipus' assumption? Is it political conspiracy?

---

the tone for the play. Notice the desperation in the following lines:

Once you have brought us luck with happy omen;
be no less now in fortune.
If you will rule this land, as now you rule it,
better to rule it full of men than empty.

For neither tower nor ship is anything
when empty, and none live in it together.

The repetition of the word *empty* in the metaphor that compares the state to a ship conveys the Thebans' desperation.

Now notice the hopeful tone when Oedipus and the priest see that Creon has returned with news from Apollo.

His face is bright. O holy Lord Apollo, grant that his news too may be bright for us and bring us safety.

Again, the repetition of the word *bright* in connection with the image of Creon's facial expression conveys Oedipus' hope.

Student Activity. What other adjectives would you use to describe the tone set on pages 434–435? Cite examples from the text to support your answers.

11 Discussion Ask students to think about the different ways in which Sophocles uses irony to make us feel both sympathetic and superior to Oedipus. How are we engaged and distanced because we know something the character does not?

Master Teacher Note Students often mistake the terms *strophe* and *antistrophe* for the names of characters. Explain that these are titles for corresponding lyric stanzas: Half the chorus sings and dances the strophe and the other half, in response, sings and dances the antistrophe. Poet/composers may have a pair of stanzas correspond internally, or have a strophe correspond to a subsequent strophe and an antistrophe correspond to another antistrophe. Some odes have a third element called an *epode*. Details of meter are unimportant, but students should remember that each choral passage was accompanied by instrumental music, and the members of the chorus both sang the lyrics and danced to the music.

12 Clarification As the chorus reminds the gods that they have helped Thebes before, we are also reminded that Apollo has in effect sent Oedipus both to save the city by killing the sphinx and to bring destruction on the city in working out his own destiny.

13 Literary Focus Point out to students the way in which Sophocles weaves together navigation and hunting metaphors.

14 Discussion Ask students why the chorus focuses on children and women of childbearing age as victims of the plague.

OEDIPUS. What trouble was so great to hinder you
150   inquiring out the murder of your king?

CREON. The riddling Sphinx induced[17] us to neglect
   mysterious crimes and rather seek solution
   of troubles at our feet.

OEDIPUS. I will bring this to light again. King Phoebus
155   fittingly took this care about the dead,
   and you too fittingly.
   And justly you will see in me an ally,
   a champion of my country and the God.
   For when I drive pollution from the land
160   I will not serve a distant friend's advantage,
   but act in my own interest. Whoever
   he was that killed the king may readily
   wish to dispatch me with his murderous hand;
   so helping the dead king I help myself.
   Come, children, take your suppliant boughs and
165   go;
   up from the altars now. Call the assembly
   and let it meet upon the understanding
   that I'll do everything. God will decide
   whether we prosper or remain in sorrow.

170 PRIEST. Rise, children—it was this we came to seek,
   which of himself the king now offers us.
   May Phoebus who gave us the oracle
   come to our rescue and stay the plague.
            [*Exit all but the* CHORUS.]

CHORUS.
   Strophe
   What is the sweet spoken word of God from the
175   shrine of Pytho[18] rich in gold
   that has come to glorious Thebes?
   I am stretched on the rack of doubt, and terror
     and trembling hold
   my heart, O Delian Healer,[19] and I worship full
   of fears

for what doom you will bring to pass, new or
180   renewed in the revolving years.
   Speak to me, immortal voice,
   child of golden Hope.

   Antistrophe
   First I call on you, Athene, deathless daughter of
     Zeus,
   and Artemis, Earth Upholder,
185   who sits in the midst of the marketplace in the
     throne which men call Fame,
   and Phoebus, the Far Shooter, three averters of
     Fate,[20]
   come to us now, if ever before, when ruin
     rushed upon the state,
   you drove destruction's flame away
   out of our land.

   Strophe
190   Our sorrows defy number;
   all the ship's timbers are rotten;
   taking of thought is no spear for the driving
     away of the plague.
   There are no growing children in this famous
     land;
   there are no women bearing the pangs of
     childbirth.
195   You may see them one with another, like birds
     swift on the wing,
   quicker than fire unmastered,
   speeding away to the coast of the Western God.[21]

   Antistrophe
   In the unnumbered deaths
   of its people the city dies;
   those children that are born lie dead on the
     naked earth
200   unpitied, spreading contagion of death; and
     gray-haired mothers and wives
   everywhere stand at the altar's edge, suppliant,
     moaning;

---

17. induced (in doost′) *v*.: Persuaded; caused.
18. Pytho (pī′ thō) *n*.: Another name for Delphi, location of Apollo's oracular shrine. Delphi is the principal religious center for all Greeks.
19. Delian Healer: Born on the island of Delos, Apollo's title was Healer; he caused and averted plagues.

20. three averters of Fate: The chorus is praying to three gods, Athene, Artemis, and Apollo, as a triple shield against death.
21. Western god: Because the sun sets in the west, god of night, Death.

Primary Source Note

Sophocles wrote *Oedipus the King* when war-torn Athens had just been ravaged by a severe plague that devastated the city, killing its people and undermining faith in the laws and religious customs of the commonwealth. In his *History of the Peloponnesian War*, the historian Thucydides, himself a surviving plague victim, describes how the epidemic spread wildly because the population was crowded in unsanitary conditions inside the fortification walls.

The dead lay as they had died, one on top of another; the dying wallowed in the streets, crawling about the fountains, craving water. The sick were lodged in the temples too, which were crammed with the corpses of those who had died there; for the violence of the calamity was so great that men did not know where to turn and showed reckless disregard of all law, human and divine. The funeral customs which had always been observed were now universally violated, and each buried his dead as best he could. Many, reduced to nothing because so many had died in their household, lost all shame and when they found a pyre

15 Clarification The mythological references and the anguished lyric language of the chorus in this strophe may be hard for students to grasp at first reading. Students should be aware that the chorus is saying the plague is as devastating as war. You might also point out that for the Athenian audience, engaged in war, the reference to Ares and to the devastation of war would add poignancy to the lament about the plague. The free association between Ares as the God "who burns us" and the heat of the sun leads the chorus to wish Ares would turn back in his course, seeing him as the Sun God Helios who races through the sky in his golden chariot. They want the War God to "set" in the sea, so night, and symbolically death, will give place to daylight.

the hymn to the healing God[22] rings out but
   with it the wailing voices are blended.
05 From these our sufferings grant us, O golden
   Daughter of Zeus,[23]
glad-faced deliverance.

   Strophe
There is no clash of brazen[24] shields but our
   fight is with the War God,[25]

a War God ringed with the cries of men, a
210   savage God who burns us;
grant that he turn in racing course backwards
   out of our country's bounds
to the great palace of Amphitrite[26] or where the
   waves of the Thracian sea
deny the stranger safe anchorage.
215 Whatsoever escapes the night
   at last the light of day revisits;

15

---

22. **healing God:** Apollo.
23. **Golden Daughter of Zeus:** Athene.
24. **brazen** (brā′ zən) *adj.*: Of brass or like brass in color.
25. **War God:** Ares.

---

26. **Amphitrite** (am′ fi trīt′ ē): Sea goddess who was the wife of Poseidon, god of the sea.

---

prepared by someone else, they would throw their own dead kinsman on first and set fire to the pyre; or they would throw their own dead on top of a stranger's already burning corpse and run away.

There were other and worse forms of lawlessness which the plague introduced . . . Men who had up to now concealed what they took pleasure in now grew bolder. Seeing sudden change and mutability—how the rich died in a moment and those who had nothing suddenly inherited property—they reflected that life and riches were transitory and resolved to enjoy themselves while they could, valuing only pleasure . . . The pleasure of the moment and any sort of thing that led to it replaced both honor and expediency. No fear of gods or law of man deterred a criminal. Those who saw all [good and bad] perishing alike concluded that the worship or neglect of the gods made no difference. Nor was there any reason to fear punishment for offenses against human law: no one would live long enough to be called to account . . .

16 **Enrichment** The chorus (whose members are, of course, Athenian citizens although they are playing the part of Thebans on stage) invokes Dionysus, who is a descendant of the house of Cadmus. Ask students to think about what effect the invocation might have on the audience, sitting in the theater during the city's festival in honor of Dionysus. Remind students that the dramatic performances were part of a larger context of religious and civic rituals, and that the altar of Dionysus was at the center of the stage area, always visible. The priest of Dionysus was also one of the dignitaries sitting in the center of the first row, on special seats.

17 **Reading Strategy** Ask students what Oedipus is claiming in these lines. Why do they think Sophocles has chosen this particular way to have Oedipus say, "I've never heard the story, and I have nothing to do with the murder"? Oedipus thinks of himself as a "stranger" to the city and to the royal house; he is tragically mistaken.

18 **Discussion** The end of Oedipus' impassioned curse, proclaimed by him as ruler against the "unknown murderer(s)" is full of irony. Ask students how they respond to his curse. What does it say about human knowledge that Oedipus, renowned for his intelligence, cannot see what is plain to us, with our hindsight?

so smite the War God, Father Zeus,
beneath your thunderbolt,
for you are the Lord of the lightning, the
220   lightning that carries fire.

    Antistrophe
And your unconquered arrow shafts, winged by
    the golden corded bow,
Lycean King,[27] I beg to be at our side for help;
and the gleaming torches of Artemis with which
    she scours the Lycean hills,
225   and I call on the God with the turban of gold,[28]
    who gave his name to this country of ours,
the Bacchic God with the wind-flushed face,[29]
Evian One,[30] who travel
with the Maenad company,[31]
combat the God that burns us
with your torch of pine;
for the God that is our enemy is a God
230   unhonored among the Gods.

             [OEDIPUS *returns.*]

OEDIPUS. For what you ask me—if you will hear my
    words,
and hearing welcome them and fight the plague,
you will find strength and lightening of your
    load.

235   Hark to me; what I say to you, I say
as one that is a stranger to the story
as stranger to the deed. For I would not
be far upon the track if I alone
were tracing it without a clue. But now,
since after all was finished, I became
240   a citizen among you, citizens—
now I proclaim to all the men of Thebes:
who so among you knows the murderer

---

27. **Lycean** (lī sē´ ən) **King:** Apollo, whose title Lykios means god of light.
28. **God with the turban of gold:** Dionysus, god of wine, who was born of Zeus and a woman of Thebes, the first Greek city to honor him. He wears an oriental turban because he has come from the East.
29. **Bacchic** (bak´ ik) **God with the wind-flushed face:** Refers to Dionysus, who had a youthful, rosy complexion; Bacchus means riotous god.
30. **Evian One:** Dionysus, called Evios because his followers address him with the ritual cry "evoi."
31. **Maenad company:** Female followers of Dionysus.

---

by whose hand Laius, son of Labdacus,
died—I command him to tell everything
to me,—yes, though he fears himself to take the
245   blame
on his own head; for bitter punishment
he shall have none, but leave this land
    unharmed.
Or if he knows the murderer, another,
a foreigner, still let him speak the truth.
250   For I will pay him and be grateful, too.
But if you shall keep silence, if perhaps
some one of you, to shield a guilty friend,
or for his own sake shall reject my words—
hear what I shall do then:
255   I forbid that man, whoever he be, my land,
my land where I hold sovereignty[32] and throne;
and I forbid any to welcome him
or cry him greeting or make him a sharer
in sacrifice or offering to the Gods,
260   or give him water for his hands to wash.
I command all to drive him from their homes,
since he is our pollution, as the oracle
of Pytho's God[33] proclaimed him now to me.
So I stand forth a champion of the God
265   and of the man who died.
Upon the murderer I invoke[34] this curse—
whether he is one man and all unknown,
or one of many—may he wear out his life
in misery to miserable doom!
270   If with my knowledge he lives at my hearth
I pray that I myself may feel my curse.
On you I lay my charge to fulfill all this
for me, for the God, and for this land of ours
destroyed and blighted, by the God forsaken.

275   Even were this no matter of God's ordinance
it would not fit you so to leave it lie,
unpurified, since a good man is dead
and one that was a king. Search it out.
Since I am now the holder of his office,
280   and have his bed and wife that once was his,
and had his line not been unfortunate

---

32. **sovereignty** (säv´ rən tē) *n.*: Supreme authority.
33. **Pytho's God:** Apollo.
34. **invoke** (in vōk´) *v.*: Summon; cause to appear.

Grammar in Action

A **participle** is a verb that is used as an adjective to modify a noun. Form participles by adding *ing* or *ed* to the infinitive verb. A participle that ends in *ing* is a present participle, while one that ends in *ed* is a past participle. Perfect participles are formed with the word *having* and a past participle. It is important not to confuse verbs and participles. Used as a verb, the word *gleaming* indicates the action of Artemis' torches. But in the play, *gleaming* functions as a participle, modifying torches, "the gleaming torches of Artemis."

When participles have modifiers and complements, the entire set of words is called a **participial phrase,** which also acts as an adjective.

On you I lay my charge to fulfill all this
for me, for the God, and for all this land of ours
destroyed and blighted, by the God forsaken (lines 272–274).

In this passage, "destroyed" and "blighted" are participles modifying "land" in the participial phrase "and for this land of ours destroyed and blighted."

Participles and participial phrases should be placed close to the word

we would have common children—(fortune leaped
upon his head)—because of all these things,
I fight in his defense as for my father,
and I shall try all means to take the murderer
of Laius the son of Labdacus
the son of Polydorus and before him
of Cadmus and before him of Agenor.
Those who do not obey me, may the Gods
grant no crops springing from the ground they plow
nor children to their women! May a fate
like this, or one still worse than this consume them!
For you whom these words please, the other Thebans,
may Justice as your ally and all the Gods
live with you, blessing you now and for ever!

CHORUS. As you have held me to my oath, I speak:
I neither killed the king nor can declare
the killer; but since Phoebus set the quest
it is his part to tell who the man is.

OEDIPUS. Right; but to put compulsion[35] on the Gods
against their will—no man can do that.

CHORUS. May I then say what I think second best?

OEDIPUS. If there's a third best, too, spare not to tell it.

CHORUS. I know that what the Lord Teiresias
sees, is most often what the Lord Apollo
sees. If you should inquire of this from him
you might find out most clearly.

OEDIPUS. Even in this my actions have not been sluggard.[36]
On Creon's word I have sent two messengers
and why the prophet is not here already
I have been wondering.

CHORUS.   His skill apart
there is besides only an old faint story.

OEDIPUS. What is it?
I look at every story.

CHORUS.   It was said
that he was killed by certain wayfarers.

OEDIPUS. I heard that, too, but no one saw the
315   killer.

CHORUS. Yet if he has a share of fear at all,
his courage will not stand firm, hearing your curse.

OEDIPUS. The man who in the doing did not shrink
will fear no word.

CHORUS.   Here comes his prosecutor:
320   led by your men the godly prophet comes
in whom alone of mankind truth is native.
[*Enter* TEIRESIAS, *led by a little boy.*]

OEDIPUS. Teiresias, you are versed in everything,
things teachable and things not to be spoken,
things of the heaven and earth-creeping things.
325   You have no eyes but in your mind you know
with what a plague[37] our city is afflicted.
My lord, in you alone we find a champion,
in you alone one that can rescue us.
Perhaps you have not heard the messengers,
330   but Phoebus sent in answer to our sending
an oracle declaring that our freedom
from this disease would only come when we
should learn the names of those who killed King Laius,
and kill them or expel from our country.
335   Do not begrudge us oracles from birds,
or any other way of prophecy
within your skill; save yourself and the city,
save me; redeem the debt of our pollution
that lies on us because of this dead man.
We are in your hands; pains are most nobly
340   taken
to help another when you have means and power.

TEIRESIAS. Alas, how terrible is wisdom when
it brings no profit to the man that's wise!

---

35. compulsion (kəm pul′ shən) *n*.: A driving force; coercion.
36. sluggard (slug′ ərd) *adj*.: Lazy or idle.

---

37. plague (plāg) *n*.: A contagious, deadly, epidemic disease.

This I knew well, but had forgotten it,
345 else I would not have come here.

OEDIPUS.   What is this?
How sad you are now you have come!

TEIRESIAS.   Let me
go home. It will be easiest for us both
to bear our several destinies to the end
if you will follow my advice.

OEDIPUS.   You'd rob us
350 of this your gift of prophecy? You talk
as one who had no care for law nor love
for Thebes who reared you.

TEIRESIAS. Yes, but I see that even your own words
miss the mark; therefore I must fear for mine.

355 **OEDIPUS.** For God's sake if you know of anything,
do not turn from us; all of us kneel to you,
all of us here, your suppliants.

TEIRESIAS. All of you here know nothing. I will not
bring to the light of day my troubles, mine—
rather than call them yours.

360 **OEDIPUS.**   What do you mean?
You know of something but refuse to speak.
Would you betray us and destroy the city?

Commentary

Illusory Certainties In his *Poetics*, Aristotle points out that "the best tragedies are founded on the stories of a few houses," among them the families of Oedipus, Atreus/Thyestes/Orestes, and others "for whom it came about that they either did something terrible or had something terrible done to them." And he calls Euripides "the most tragic" of the poets, because so many of his tragedies center on the right kind of reversal (peripeteia) and recognition (anagnorisis). Reversal occurs when "the action veers around to its opposite," and it goes hand in hand with recognition, "a change from ignorance to knowledge, producing kinship [often translated as "love"] or enmity."

The Greeks believed that it was appropriate to "do good to one's *philoi* (kin, friends, allies, loved ones) and harm to one's *echthroi* (enemies, the opposite category to philoi). Terrible confusion and tragedy must result when the clear lines separating "friend" from "foe" or "insider" from "outsider" dissolve. In the house of Atreus, rivalry between the brothers Atreus and Thyestes leads to murder and cannibalism; in the next generation, Clytemnestra with the help of her lover and her husband's cousin Aegisthus murders her husband, Agamemnon; she in turn is murdered by her son, Orestes, who is bound to kill his mother and draw her curse upon himself because he must avenge his murdered father or submit to a more terrible

TEIRESIAS. I will not bring this pain upon us both,
neither on you nor on myself. Why is it
you question me and waste you labor? I
will tell you nothing.

OEDIPUS. You would provoke a stone! Tell us, you
villain,
tell us, and do not stand there quietly
unmoved and balking[38] at the issue.

TEIRESIAS. You blame my temper but you do not
see
your own that lives within you; it is me
you chide.[39]

OEDIPUS. Who would not feel his temper rise
at words like these with which you shame our
city?

TEIRESIAS. Of themselves things will come,
although I hide them
and breathe no word of them.

OEDIPUS.   Since they will come
tell them to me.

TEIRESIAS.   I will say nothing further.
Against this answer let your temper rage
as wildly as you will.

OEDIPUS.   Indeed I am
so angry I shall not hold back a jot
of what I think. For I would have you know
I think you were complotter[40] of the deed
and doer of the deed save in so far
as for the actual killing. Had you had eyes
I would have said alone you murdered him.

TEIRESIAS. Yes? Then I warn you faithfully to keep
the letter of your proclamation and
from this day forth to speak no word of greeting
to these nor me; you are the land's pollution.

OEDIPUS. How shamelessly you started up this
taunt!
How do you think you will escape?

---

38. balking (bôk′ iŋ) v.: Obstinately refusing to act.
39. chide (chīd) v.: Scold.
40. complotter (käm plät′ ər) n.: Person who plots against
another person.

TEIRESIAS.   I have.
I have escaped; the truth is what I cherish
and that's my strength.

OEDIPUS.   And who has taught you
truth?
Not your profession surely!

TEIRESIAS.   You have taught me,
for you have made me speak against my will.

OEDIPUS. Speak what? Tell me again that I may
learn it better.

TEIRESIAS. Did you not understand before or
would you
provoke me into speaking?

OEDIPUS.   I did not grasp it,
not so to call it known. Say it again.

TEIRESIAS. I say you are the murderer of the king
whose murderer you seek.

OEDIPUS.   Not twice you shall
say calumnies[41] like this and stay unpunished.

TEIRESIAS. Shall I say more to tempt your anger
more?

OEDIPUS. As much as you desire; it will be said
in vain.

TEIRESIAS.   I say that with those you
love best
you live in foulest shame unconsciously
and do not see where you are in calamity.[42]

OEDIPUS. Do you imagine you can always talk
like this, and live to laugh at it hereafter?

TEIRESIAS. Yes, if the truth has anything of strength.

OEDIPUS. It has, but not for you; it has no strength
for you because you are blind in mind and ears
as well as in your eyes.

TEIRESIAS.   You are a poor wretch
to taunt me with the very insults which
every one soon will heap upon yourself.

---

41. calumnies (kal′ əm nēz) n.: False and malicious
statements; slander.
42. calamity (kə lam′ ə tē) n.: Extreme misfortune that leads
to disaster.

23 **Discussion** Many critics have attributed Oedipus' "flaw" to his sharp temper. Ask students if they think Oedipus' outbursts are unprovoked or that his suspiciousness is not based on reasonable (even if ultimately false) conjecture.

24 **Discussion** What is Teiresias implying about the seer's role? Discuss the way in which he hints at the inevitable and inexorable unfolding of a divine plan.

25 **Enrichment** The Athenians were not wholly unfamiliar with collusion between politicians and the clergy. The historian Herodotus reports that the leader of one political faction, in the early days of the democracy, got the Spartan Cleomenes to send a herald to Athens demanding the expulsion from Athens of Cleisthenes, a successful political rival, along with a large number of his associates. The excuse was that Cleisthenes was under a curse and the city must "drive out the pollution." Before the beginning of the Peloponnesian War, the Spartans again used this device, demanding the expulsion of Pericles from Athens on the same grounds.

26 **Discussion** Teiresias' retort confirms Oedipus in his assumptions about a political conspiracy. Have students discuss how this affects the audience, who understands Teiresias in the way that Oedipus does not.

27 **Clarification** The term rendered as "those you love best" has a rich range of connotations in Greek; its primary sense is "those who are your closest in kin," but it is also used by extension to refer to those who are like kin by virtue of being "most trusted allies," "dearest friends," or "most beloved." Ask students how multiple meanings of the term would contribute to the ironic dimension of Teiresias' exchange with Oedipus.

dents if they think Teiresias sounds reasonable. Is Oedipus justified in feeling infuriated?

---

curse. Medea, betrayed by her husband, Jason, murders her own sons. The nearest and dearest of kin become the other, the enemy. In Oedipus' case as well, the distinctions between alien and citizen, stranger and son—so apparently clear—cease to exist.

In comedy, finding out who you really are almost invariably entails discovering that the stranger is really a native son or daughter, the pauper and scullery maid are royalty; the beloved who seemed unattainable because of social class, money, or birth is really an eligible spouse. Tragedy reveals all your certainties to be illusory.

OEDIPUS. Your life is one long night so that you cannot
hurt me or any other who sees the light.

TEIRESIAS. It is not fate that I should be your ruin,
Apollo is enough; it is his care
425 to work this out.

OEDIPUS.   Was this your own design
or Creon's?

TEIRESIAS.   Creon is no hurt to you,
but you are to yourself.

OEDIPUS. Wealth, sovereignty and skill outmatching skill
for the contrivance[43] of an envied life!
430 Great store of jealousy fill your treasury chests,
if my friend Creon, friend from the first and loyal,
thus secretly attacks me, secretly
desires to drive me out and secretly
suborns[44] this juggling, trick devising quack,
435 this wily beggar who has only eyes
for his own gains, but blindness in his skill.
For, tell me, where have you seen clear, Teiresias,
with your prophetic eyes? When the dark singer,
the sphinx, was in your country, did you speak
440 word of deliverance to its citizens?
And yet the riddle's answer was not the province
of a chance comer. It was a prophet's task
and plainly you had no such gift of prophecy
from birds nor otherwise from any God
445 to glean a word of knowledge. But I came,
Oedipus, who knew nothing, and I stopped her.
I solved the riddle by my wit alone.
Mine was no knowledge got from birds.
And now you would expel me,
450 because you think that you will find a place
by Creon's throne. I think you will be sorry,
both you and your accomplice, for your plot
to drive me out. And did I not regard you
as an old man, some suffering would have taught you
455 that what was in your heart was treason.

CHORUS. We look at this man's words and yours, my king,
and we find both have spoken them in anger.
We need no angry words but only thought
how we may best hit the God's meaning for us.

TEIRESIAS. If you are king, at least I have the right
460 no less to speak in my defense against you.
Of that much I am master. I am no slave
of yours, but Loxias', and so I shall not
enroll myself with Creon for my patron.
Since you have taunted me with being blind,
465 here is my word for you.
You have your eyes but see not where you are
in sin, nor where you live, nor whom you live with.
Do you know who your parents are? Unknowing
470 you are an enemy to kith and kin
in death, beneath the earth, and in this life.
A deadly footed, double striking curse,
from father and mother both, shall drive you forth
out of this land, with darkness on your eyes,
475 that now have such straight vision. Shall there be
a place will not be harbor to your cries,[45]
a corner of Cithaeron[46] will not ring
in echo to your cries, soon, soon,—
when you shall learn the secret of your marriage,
480 which steered you to a haven in this house,—
haven no <u>haven</u>, after lucky voyage?
And of the multitude of other evils
establishing a grim equality
between you and your children, you know nothing.
485 So, muddy with contempt my words and Creon's!
Misery shall grind no man as it will you.

OEDIPUS. Is it endurable that I should hear
such words from him? Go and a curse go with you!
Quick, home with you! Out of my house at once!

TEIRESIAS. I would not have come either had you
490 not called me.

---

43. contrivance (kən trī′ vəns) *n.*: The act of devising or scheming.
44. suborns (sə bôrnz′) *v.*: Instigates a person to commit perjury.

45. harbor to your cries: A place that will house or contain your cries; sentence means: Is there any place that won't be full of your cries?
46. Cithaeron (si′ thər än) *n.*: Mountain, near Thebes, on which Oedipus was abandoned as an infant.

OEDIPUS. I did not know then you would talk like
a fool—
or it would have been long before I called you.

TEIRESIAS. I am a fool then, as it seems to you—
but to the parents who have bred you, wise.

OEDIPUS. What parents? Stop! Who are they of all
the world?

TEIRESIAS. This day will show your birth and will
destroy you.

OEDIPUS. How needlessly your riddles darken
everything.

TEIRESIAS. But it's in riddle answering you are
strongest.

OEDIPUS. Yes. Taunt me where you will find me
great.

TEIRESIAS. It is this very luck that has destroyed
you.

OEDIPUS. I do not care, if it has saved this city.

TEIRESIAS. Well, I will go. Come, boy, lead me
away.

OEDIPUS. Yes, lead him off. So long as you are
here,
you'll be a stumbling block and a vexation;[47]
once gone, you will not trouble me again.

TEIRESIAS.   I have said
what I came here to say not fearing your
countenance:[48] there is no way you can hurt me.
I tell you, king, this man, this murderer
(whom you have long declared you are in search
of,
indicting him in threatening proclamation
as murderer of Laius)—he is here.
In name he is a stranger among citizens
but soon he will be shown to be a citizen
true native Theban, and he'll have no joy
of the discovery: blindness for sight
and beggary for riches his exchange,
he shall go journeying to a foreign country

tapping his way before him with a stick.
He shall be proved father and brother both
to his own children in his house; to her   520
that gave him birth, a son and husband both;
a fellow sower in his father's bed
with that same father that he murdered.
Go within, reckon that out, and if you find me   525
mistaken, say I have no skill in prophecy.

[*Exit separately* TEIRESIAS *and* OEDIPUS.]

CHORUS.
Strophe
Who is the man proclaimed
by Delphi's prophetic rock
as the bloody handed murderer,
the doer of deeds that none dare name?
Now is the time for him to run   530
with a stronger foot

---

47. vexation (veks ā′ shən) *n.:* That which causes annoyance
and distress.
48. countenance (koun′ tə nəns) *n.:* Facial expressions that
reveal a person's feelings.

God's meaning for us" (lines 456–459).
But Oedipus' anger stems from his refusal to accept the truth about the uncertainties he faces, while Teiresias' anger is in response to Oedipus' refusal. Unlike Oedipus, Teiresias has authoritative knowledge. He makes no accusations; he simply tells the truth.

Student Activity 1. Analyze the speeches on page 442 and explain how tone is achieved in each speech.

Student Activity 2. Examine the dialogue between Oedipus and Teiresias on page 443. How does Sophocles achieve and maintain tone in this dialogue?

comes from a verb meaning to "hit" or "reach the mark") in human affairs was becoming central. The more uncertain things seemed, the more fluidity people saw in the world around them, the more important blind luck seemed. As they read, students should think about how Teiresias, Oedipus, and the chorus speak from different perspectives on "luck."

33 Literary Focus One of the ironies in the play is that the structure of its plot is essentially comic, that is, suited to a story with a happy ending. Normally the stranger who proves to be a citizen gains rewards; what does Teiresias say will happen to this "stranger"?

34 Literary Focus Remind students of the earlier use of agricultural imagery. What is the effect of using this metaphor here?

Master Teacher Note Even scholars used to the conventions of ancient tragedy have poked fun at the way tragic choruses always seem to miss the point, not to notice even a murder taking place within earshot, or to go off into a lyric outburst that seems irrelevant. But the role of the chorus is very important; in some ways the chorus is like us, both engaged and passive, both a participant and an observer. The members of the chorus were citizens; many members of the audience would have danced and sung in a chorus; for Sophocles' audience, the chorus is in some way Everyman, an Athenian citizen. Ask students to think about the chorus's responses. Why does the chorus seem not to understand Teiresias' prophecy, which to us seems quite explicit? Students might consider how the chorus models for the audience the propensity of human beings not to hear what shocks or frightens them, not to understand when they are "in the thick of things," what with hindsight seems all too obvious.

Discussion Questions

35 Discussion Ask students to identify the dominant metaphor in these lines. Oedipus has represented himself as a tracker; what is the effect of having the chorus speak of itself now as a tracker, or a pack of hunting hounds? Why might the chorus envision the "unknown murderer" as nonhuman, a wild animal living in forests and caverns, in untamed nature outside the polis?

36 Discussion Ask students why the chorus is reluctant to believe Teiresias. On what is the Thebans' allegiance to Oedipus based?

37 Discussion Ask students how they respond to Oedipus' outburst. How has he moved from conjecture to certainty? Is he justified?

---

than Pegasus[49]
for the child of Zeus leaps in arms upon him
with fire and the lightning bolt,
535 and terribly close on his heels
are the Fates that never miss.

Antistrophe
Lately from snowy Parnassus
clearly the voice flashed forth,
bidding each Theban track him down,
540 the unknown murderer.
In the savage forests he lurks and in
the caverns like
the mountain bull.
He is sad and lonely, and lonely his feet
545 that carry him far from the navel of earth;[50]
but its prophecies, ever living,
flutter around his head.

Strophe
The augur[51] has spread confusion,
terrible confusion;
550 I do not approve what was said
nor can I deny it.
I do not know what to say;
I am in a flutter of foreboding;
I never heard in the present
555 nor past of a quarrel between
the sons of Labdacus and Polybus,
that I might bring as proof
in attacking the popular fame
of Oedipus, seeking
560 to take vengeance for undiscovered
death in the line of Labdacus.

Antistrophe
Truly Zeus and Apollo are wise
and in human things all knowing;
but amongst men there is no
565 distinct judgment, between the prophet
and me—which of us is right.
One man may pass another in wisdom
but I would never agree

---

with those that find fault with the king
570 till I should see the word
proved right beyond doubt. For once
in visible form the Sphinx
came on him and all of us
saw his wisdom and in that test
he saved the city. So he will not be condemned
575 by my mind.

[*Enter* CREON.]

CREON. Citizens, I have come because I heard
deadly words spread about me, that the king
accuses me. I cannot take that from him.
If he believes that in these present troubles
580 he has been wronged by me in word or deed
I do not want to live on with the burden
of such a scandal on me. The report
injures me doubly and most vitally—
for I'll be called a traitor to my city
585 and traitor also to my friends and you.

CHORUS. Perhaps it was a sudden gust of anger
that forced that insult from him, and no
judgment.

CREON. But did he say that it was in compliance
with schemes of mine that the seer told him
lies?

590 **CHORUS.** Yes, he said that, but why, I do not know.

CREON. Were his eyes straight in his head? Was his
mind right
when he accused me in this fashion?

CHORUS. I do not know; I have no eyes to see
what princes do. Here comes the king himself.

[*Enter* OEDIPUS.]

OEDIPUS. You, sir, how is it you come here? Have
595 you so much
brazen-faced daring that you venture in
my house although you are proved manifestly[52]
the murderer of that man, and though you tried,
openly, highway robbery of my crown?
600 For God's sake, tell me what you saw in me,
what cowardice or what stupidity,
that made you lay a plot like this against me?

---

49. **Pegasus** (peg′ ə səs): A winged horse.
50. **navel of earth:** A cavity of Mount Parnassus from which mysterious vapors arose to inspire Pythia, priestess of the Oracle of Apollo at Delphi.
51. **augur** (ô′ gər) *n.*: Fortuneteller or prophet; refers here to Teiresias.

52. **manifestly** (man′ ə fest lē) *adv.*: Clearly proven with evidence.

Commentary

Oedipus as Athens the Tyrant City Thucydides represents the Athenian demos, the citizen body, as quick to get angry and violent in retaliation against "enemies," such as rebellious allies or unsuccessful generals. At times the popular assembly would repent on the next day some order of summary execution that had been voted; sometimes it was not too late to reverse the decision. At other times the damage had already been done by the time cooler heads prevailed. While Pericles was alive, he controlled the assembly, even when the Athenians accused him the way Oedipus accuses Creon. In the *History of the Peloponnesian War*, Thucydides quotes Pericles as saying,

I was expecting this outburst of indignation; the causes of it are not unknown to me. And I have summoned an assembly that I may remind you of your resolutions and reprove you for your inconsiderate anger against me, and want of fortitude in misfortune.

In the ensuing patriotic and hawkish speech, he chides Athenians for being weak (in comparison to Pericles himself), unable to face a "great reverse," or peripeteia, steadfastly. "Anything which is sudden and unexpected

Did you imagine I should not observe
the crafty scheme that stole upon me or
seeing it, take no means to counter it?
Was it not stupid of you to make the attempt,
to try to hunt down royal power without
the people at your back or friends? For only
with the people at your back or money can
the hunt end in the capture of a crown.

CREON. Do you know what you're doing? Will you listen
    to words to answer yours, and then pass judgment?

OEDIPUS. You're quick to speak, but I am slow to grasp you,
    for I have found you dangerous,—and my foe.

CREON. First of all hear what I shall say to that.

OEDIPUS. At least don't tell me that you are not guilty.

CREON. If you think obstinacy[53] without wisdom
    a valuable possession, you are wrong.

OEDIPUS. And you are wrong if you believe that one,
    a criminal, will not be punished only
    because he is my kinsman.

CREON.   This is but just—
    but tell me, then, of what offense I'm guilty?

OEDIPUS. Did you or did you not urge me to send
    to this prophetic mumbler?

CREON.   I did indeed,
    and I shall stand by what I told you.

OEDIPUS. How long ago is it since Laius . . .

CREON. What about Laius? I don't understand.

OEDIPUS. Vanished—died—was murdered?

CREON.   It is long,
    a long, long time to reckon.

OEDIPUS.   Was this prophet
    in the profession then?

CREON.   He was, and honored
    as highly as he is today.

OEDIPUS. At that time did he say a word about me?

CREON. Never, at least when I was near him.

OEDIPUS. You never made a search for the dead man?

CREON. We searched, indeed, but never learned of anything.

OEDIPUS. Why did our wise old friend not say this then?

CREON. I don't know; and when I know nothing, I usually hold my tongue.

OEDIPUS.   You know this much,
    and can declare this much if you are loyal.

CREON. What is it? If I know, I'll not deny it.

OEDIPUS. That he would not have said that I killed Laius
    had he not met you first.

CREON.   You know yourself
    whether he said this, but I demand that I
    should hear as much from you as you from me.

OEDIPUS. Then hear,—I'll not be proved a murderer.

CREON. Well, then. You're married to my sister.

OEDIPUS.   Yes,
    that I am not disposed to deny.

CREON.   You rule
    this country giving her an equal share
    in the government?

OEDIPUS.   Yes, everything she wants
    she has from me.

CREON.   And I, as thirdsman[54] to you,
    am rated as the equal of you two?

---

53. obstinacy (äb′ stə nə sē) *n.*: Stubbornness; state of being unyielding to reason. Creon means that Oedipus cannot see or refuses to see the facts.

54. thirdsman (thərdz′ mən) *n.*: Third in line, or one person in a group of three.

38 Literary Focus Ask students to discuss the irony in Oedipus' use of hunting imagery to describe Creon's supposed ambition. Also, what is ironic about Oedipus' reference to the role of the philoi, political "friends" or backers and "kinsmen"?

39 Discussion Ask students to discuss the way Oedipus sentences Creon before allowing him to plead his case. To what extent is the pressure Oedipus is under a plausible explanation, if not a justification, for his rashness?

40 Enrichment Students should note that the exchange between the two men is very much like courtroom interrogation and cross-examination. To an Athenian audience, this way of finding out the facts and of determining guilt, mitigating circumstances, etc., was familiar. Both the Athenians themselves and their detractors talk about Athens as a "city of lawcourts" and of its citizens as devoted to litigation. Although they could poke fun at themselves, the Athenians prized their legal system because it afforded citizens a way to secure justice without violence.

One of the casualties of the Athenian empire was the legal system as it applied to allies and other noncitizens. As a "tyrant city" Athens meted out summary and often brutal retribution or "justice." Students should think about Oedipus not only as an individual but as an embodiment of imperial Athens, the polis tyrannos.

and utterly beyond calculation," like the plague, "coming on top of other misfortunes," throws men into emotional disarray. Stressing the greatness of the Athenian empire, he uses the same terms Oedipus uses to talk about his own rule: wealth and skill/intelligence. Furthermore, Athens is like a tyrant who cannot afford to lose:

. . . you are bound to maintain the imperial dignity of your city in which you all take pride . . . And do not imagine that you are fighting about a simple issue, freedom or slavery; you have an empire to lose, and there is the danger to which the hatred of your imperial rule has exposed you . . . by this time your empire has become a tyranny which in the opinion of mankind may have been unjustly gained, but which cannot be safely surrendered . . .

OEDIPUS. Yes, and it's there you've proved yourself false friend.

CREON. Not if you will reflect on it as I do.
655   Consider, first, if you think any one
  would choose to rule and fear rather than rule
  and sleep untroubled by a fear if power
  were equal in both cases. I, at least,
  I was not born with such a frantic yearning
660   to be a king—but to do what kings do.
  And so it is with every one who has learned
  wisdom and self-control. As it stands now,
  the prizes are all mine—and without fear.
  But if I were the king myself, I must
665   do much that went against the grain.
  How should despotic[55] rule seem sweeter to me
  than painless power and an assured authority?
  I am not so besotted[56] yet that I
  want other honors than those that come with
    profit.
  Now every man's my pleasure; every man greets
670   me;
  now those who are your suitors fawn on me,—
  success for them depends upon my favor.
  Why should I let all this go to win that?
  My mind would not be traitor if it's wise;
675   I am no treason lover, of my nature,
  nor would I ever dare to join a plot.
  Prove what I say. Go to the oracle
  at Pytho and inquire about the answers,
  if they are as I told you. For the rest,
680   if you discover I laid any plot
  together with the seer, kill me, I say,
  not only by your vote but by my own.
  But do not charge me on obscure opinion
  without some proof to back it. It's not just
685   lightly to count your knaves as honest men,
  nor honest men as knaves. To throw away
  an honest friend is, as it were, to throw
  your life away, which a man loves the best.
  In time you will know all with certainty;
690   time is the only test of honest men,
  one day is space enough to know a rogue.

---

55. **despotic** (des pät′ ik) *adj.*: Absolute; unlimited; tyrannical.
56. **besotted** (bē sät′ əd) *v.*: Stupefied; foolish.

CHORUS. His words are wise, king, if one fears to fall.
  Those who are quick of temper are not safe.

OEDIPUS. When he that plots against me secretly
695   moves quickly, I must quickly counterplot.
  If I wait taking no decisive measure
  his business will be done, and mine be spoiled.

CREON. What do you want to do then? Banish me?

OEDIPUS. No, certainly; kill you, not banish you.

CREON. I do not think that you've your wits about
700   you.

OEDIPUS. For my own interests, yes.

CREON.   But for mine, too,
  you should think equally.

OEDIPUS.   You are a rogue.

CREON. Suppose you do not understand?

OEDIPUS.   But yet
705   I must be ruler.

CREON.   Not if you rule badly.

OEDIPUS. O, city, city!

CREON.   I too have some share
  in the city; it is not yours alone.

CHORUS. Stop, my lords! Here—and in the nick of time
710   I see Jocasta coming from the house;
  with her help lay the quarrel that now stirs you.
                [*Enter* JOCASTA.]

JOCASTA. For shame! Why have you raised this foolish squabbling
  brawl? Are you not ashamed to air your private
  griefs when the country's sick? Go in, you, Oedipus,
715   and you, too, Creon, into the house. Don't magnify
  your nothing troubles.

CREON.   Sister, Oedipus,
  your husband, thinks he has the right to do
  terrible wrongs—he has but to choose between
720   two terrors: banishing or killing me.

Commentary

Tragedies were performed in the context of a religious and civic festival, honoring the god Dionysus, provider of the grapes and the wine that constituted one of the city's major exports, and the patron goddess Athene. The inhabitants all came together to reaffirm their cohesion as a community. On the tragic stage, issues deeply affecting both the private individual and the citizen as a member of his or her polis were presented in such a way as to "arouse pity and fear" and to effect a purging of those (toxic) emotions in the viewers.

Audiences could see Oedipus, in Bernard Knox's words, as "an example to all mankind of the existence and authority of divine presence and of the fundamental ignorance of man," and as an embodiment of the Athenian "tyranny" or empire. Oedipus is both the individual spectator as a human being and a way of expressing the single "mind and body" of the demos, the community made up of many individuals functioning as

45 Discussion Have students discuss the chorus's advice to Oedipus. How might Sophocles' audience respond to the many levels of *philos,* meaning both friend and kinsman? What might those in the audience who wanted party strife in Athens to end think about this rift between former political allies?

46 Discussion Ask students to describe the chorus's dilemma. Oedipus wants to force the citizens to express their genuine love for him by taking sides against Creon. How do they see the demands on their loyalty in the light of a more broadly viewed patriotism?

Enrichment An interesting illustration of the sun personified as Apollo is the English poet Shelley's "Song of Apollo." Students might enjoy reading it, particularly the stanzas that follow:

". . . My footsteps pave the clouds with fire; the caves / Are filled with my bright presence, and the air / Leaves the green Earth to my embraces bare.

"The sunbeams are my shafts with which I kill / Deceit, that loves the night and fears the day. / All men who do, or even imagine ill / Fly me; and from the glory of my ray / Good minds, and open actions take new might / Until diminished, by the reign of night.

"I feed the clouds, the rainbows and the flowers / With their aetherial colours; the moon's globe / And the pure stars in their eternal bowers / Are cinctured with my power as with a robe; / Whatever lamps on Earth or Heaven may shine / Are portions of one spirit; which is mine."

OEDIPUS. He's right, Jocasta; for I find him plotting
with knavish[57] tricks against my person.

CREON. That God may never bless me! May I die accursed, if I have been guilty of
one tittle[58] of the charge you bring against me!

JOCASTA. I beg you, Oedipus, trust him in this, spare him for the sake of this his oath to God,
for my sake, and the sake of those who stand here.

CHORUS. Be gracious, be merciful, we beg of you.

OEDIPUS. In what would you have me yield?

CHORUS. He has been no silly child in the past. He is strong in his oath now.
Spare him.

OEDIPUS. Do you know what you ask?

735 **CHORUS.** Yes.

OEDIPUS. Tell me then.

CHORUS. He has been your friend before all men's eyes; do not cast him away dishonored on an obscure conjecture.

OEDIPUS. I would have you know that this request of yours
740 really requests my death or banishment.

CHORUS. May the Sun God,[59] king of Gods, forbid! May I die without God's blessing, without friends' help, if I had any such thought. But my spirit is broken by my unhappiness for my
745 wasting country; and this would but add troubles amongst ourselves to the other troubles.

---

57. **knavish** (nāv′ ish) *adj.*: Deceitful.
58. **tittle** (tit′ ′l) *n.*: A very small particle.

---

59. **Sun God:** Apollo.

parts of a whole. Understanding this helps us to get away from the absurdity of looking for some narrowly individual character flaw in Oedipus that might justify his suffering. It also helps us to see that the chorus, in lines 959–999, is talking about Athens and speaking as a group of Athenians to a group of Athenians, the very people who had heard Pericles describe their city thus:

Know that our city has the greatest name in all the world because she has never yielded to misfortunes, but has sacrificed more lives and endured severer hardships in war than any other; wherefore also she has the greatest power of any state up to this day . . . In talking of how Athens will be remembered, he says "of all the Hellenes, we ruled over the greatest number of Hellenic subjects . . . we withstood our enemies . . . in the most terrible wars . . . we were the inhabitants of a city endowed with every sort of wealth and greatness." He boasts that Athens will be emulated, envied, and he concludes, "to be hateful and offensive has ever been at the time the fate of those who have aspired to empire.

47 Literary Focus Point out the implicit ship-of-state metaphor. Have students think about why it is particularly appropriate for the Athenian maritime empire to think of rule in terms of navigation.

Speaking to the Athenians after the plague and working up their enthusiasm for war, Pericles says: "I too have never mentioned it before, nor would I now, because the claim may seem too arrogant, if I did not see that you are unreasonably depressed. You think your empire is confined to your allies, but I say that of the two divisions of the world accessible to man, the land and the sea, there is one of which you are absolute masters, and have, or may have the dominion to any extent which you please." He goes on to say no power, no nation on earth can hinder the Athenian navy from penetrating anywhere it might wish to sail.

48 Discussion Have students discuss how Jocasta's view of prophets is similar to Oedipus' view.

49 Discussion Ask students to discuss how Jocasta's "proof" that oracles are meaningless and should not be heeded actually proves the opposite of what she intends. What meaning do we see in her concluding statement that Apollo shows what he wants to reveal by himself?

50 Discussion How does Oedipus interpret Jocasta's speech? Ask students what the phrases "a wandering of the soul" and "I could run mad" suggest. Students should also think about how his reaction influences the reader's feelings toward him.

OEDIPUS. Well, let him go then—if I must die ten times for it,
or be sent out dishonored into exile.
It is your lips that prayed for him I pitied,
750 not his; wherever he is, I shall hate him.

CREON. I see you sulk in yielding and you're dangerous
when you are out of temper; natures like yours
are justly heaviest for themselves to bear.

OEDIPUS. Leave me alone! Take yourself off, I tell you.

CREON. I'll go, you have not known me, but they
755 have,
and they have known my innocence.

[*Exit.*]

CHORUS. Won't you take him inside, lady?

JOCASTA. Yes, when I've found out what was the matter.

CHORUS. There was some misconceived suspicion of a story, and on the other side the sting of in-
760 justice.

JOCASTA. So, on both sides?

CHORUS. Yes.

JOCASTA. What was the story?

CHORUS. I think it best, in the interests of the
765 country, to leave it where it ended.

OEDIPUS. You see where you have ended, straight of judgment
although you are, by softening my anger.

CHORUS. Sir, I have said before and I say again—be sure that I would have been proved a madman,
770 bankrupt in sane council, if I should put you away, you who steered the country I love safely when she was crazed with troubles. God grant that now, too, you may prove a fortunate guide for us.

JOCASTA. Tell me, my lord, I beg of you, what was it
775 that roused your anger so?

OEDIPUS.   Yes, I will tell you.
I honor you more than I honor them.
It was Creon and the plots he laid against me.

JOCASTA. Tell me—if you can clearly tell the quarrel—

OEDIPUS.   Creon says
780 that I'm the murderer of Laius.

JOCASTA. Of his own knowledge or on information?

OEDIPUS. He sent this rascal prophet to me, since he keeps his own mouth clean of any guilt.

JOCASTA. Do not concern yourself about this matter;
785 listen to me and learn that human beings have no part in the craft of prophecy.
Of that I'll show you a short proof.
There was an oracle once that came to Laius,—
I will not say that it was Phoebus' own,
790 but it was from his servants—and it told him that it was fate that he should die a victim at the hands of his own son, a son to be born of Laius and me. But, see now, he.
the king, was killed by foreign hignway robbers at a place where three roads meet—so goes the
795 story;
and for the son—before three days were out after his birth King Laius pierced his ankles and by the hands of others cast him forth upon a pathless hillside. So Apollo
800 failed to fulfill his oracle to the son,
that he should kill his father, and to Laius also proved false in that the thing he feared, death at his son's hands, never came to pass.
So clear in this case were the oracles,
805 so clear and false. Give them no heed, I say;
what God discovers need of, easily he shows to us himself.

OEDIPUS.   O dear Jocasta,
as I hear this from you, there comes upon me
810 a wandering of the soul—I could run mad.

JOCASTA. What trouble is it, that you turn again and speak like this?

OEDIPUS.   I thought I heard you say that Laius was killed at a crossroads.

JOCASTA. Yes, that was how the story went and still that word goes round.

OEDIPUS.   Where is this place, Jocasta, where he was murdered?

Grammar in Action

Dashes are punctuation marks that indicate an abrupt break in thought. Like commas, semicolons, and parentheses, dashes signal pause, but dashes signal a more striking, dramatic pause. Dashes are frequently used in punctuating fast-paced dramatic scenes to capture the quick verbal exchange of the speakers.

Use a single dash to indicate an abrupt change of thought.

Well, let him go then—if I must die ten times for it, or be sent out dishonored into exile (lines 747–748).

A single dash can also emphasize additional or explanatory information at the end of a sentence.

Sir, I have said before and I say again—be sure that I would have been proved a madman, bankrupt in sane council, if I should put you away . . . (lines 768–771).

Sometimes dashes are used in pairs to emphasize interrupting information in the middle of the sentence.

He was a tall man and his hair was grizzled—nearly white—and in his form not unlike you (lines 825–826).

JOCASTA. Phocis is the country and the road splits there, one of two roads from Delphi, another comes from Daulia.

OEDIPUS. How long ago is this?

JOCASTA. The news came to the city just before you became king and all men's eyes looked to you. What is it, Oedipus, that's in your mind?

OEDIPUS. What have you designed, O Zeus, to do with me?

JOCASTA. What is the thought that troubles your heart?

OEDIPUS. Don't ask me yet—tell me of Laius— How did he look? How old or young was he?

JOCASTA. He was a tall man and his hair was grizzled already—nearly white—and in his form not unlike you.

OEDIPUS. O God, I think I have called curses on myself in ignorance.

JOCASTA. What do you mean? I am terrified when I look at you.

OEDIPUS. I have a deadly fear that the old seer had eyes. You'll show me more if you can tell me one more thing.

JOCASTA. I will. I'm frightened,—but if I can understand, I'll tell you all you ask.

OEDIPUS. How was his company? Had he few with him when he went this journey, or many servants, as would suit a prince?

JOCASTA. In all there were but five, and among them a herald;[60] and one carriage for the king.

OEDIPUS. It's plain—it's plain—who was it told you this?

JOCASTA. The only servant that escaped safe home.

840 **OEDIPUS.** Is he at home now?

JOCASTA. No, when he came home again and saw you king and Laius was dead, he came to me and touched my hand and begged that I should send him to the fields to be 845 my shepherd and so he might see the city as far off as he might. So I sent him away. He was an honest man, as slaves go, and was worthy of far more than what he asked of me.

OEDIPUS. O, how I wish that he could come back 850 quickly!

JOCASTA. He can. Why is your heart so set on this?

OEDIPUS. O dear Jocasta, I am full of fears that I have spoken far too much; and therefore I wish to see this shepherd.

855 **JOCASTA.** He will come; but, Oedipus, I think I'm worthy too to know what it is that <u>disquiets</u> you.

OEDIPUS. It shall not be kept from you, since my mind has gone so far with its forebodings. Whom 860 should I confide in rather than you, who is there of more importance to me who have passed through such a fortune? Polybus was my father, king of Corinth,[61] and Merope, the Dorian,[62] my mother. 865 I was held greatest of the citizens in Corinth till a curious chance befell me as I shall tell you—curious, indeed, but hardly worth the store I set upon it. There was a dinner and at it a man, 870 a drunken man, accused me in his drink of being bastard. I was furious but held my temper under for that day.

_____
60. herald (her′ əld) n.: Person who makes proclamations and carries messages.

_____
61. Corinth (kôr′ inth): City at the western end of the isthmus (Greece) that joins the Peloponnesus to Boeotia.
62. Dorian (dôr′ ē ən) n.: One of the main branches of the Hellenes; the Dorians invaded the Peloponnesus.

51 Clarification Point out to students that Oedipus doesn't hear everything we hear. How do we respond to "in his form not unlike you"? Have students think about how our own reactions are manipulated as we follow this rapid dialogue. When Jocasta describes Laius, at first Oedipus seems to grasp everything we already know. How does Sophocles encourage us to believe that?

52 Discussion As Oedipus begins his speech, he speaks to Jocasta in a way appropriate to a loving husband confiding in his wife. But his manner of speaking is also suggestive of the ways in which Jocasta is the closest kin he has. Ask students how our awareness of the double relationship between Oedipus and Jocasta positions us to listen to the narrative. Have students think about the different ways in which Oedipus, Jocasta, and the audience can interpret the past events Oedipus relates. How does this illustration of the way hindsight gives a different shape or meaning to "facts" or events make us reflect on the amount of understanding we can bring to bear on our own immediate situation?

Or, double dashes set off complete sentences within a construction.

There was an oracle once that came to Laius,—I will not say that it was Phoebus' own, but it was from his servants—and it told him that it was fate . . . (lines 788–791).

Note the superfluous comma after "Laius"—normally, you do not need a comma and a dash. Use one or the other, but remember that dashes should never replace commas, semicolons, and parentheses. Use dashes only to emphasize important information, but be careful not to overuse them.

Student Activity 1. Identify the ways in which dashes are used in the following lines: 779–780, 795–799, 809–810, 823–824, 831–832, 838, 865–868.

Student Activity 2. Summarize what you have read of the play using dashes to emphasize important information.

53 **Discussion** Ask students to discuss Oedipus' reaction to Apollo's prophecy. What can we surmise from his words about the way the Greeks thought about the acts of pollution (marrying his mother and patricide) Oedipus unwittingly commits.

54 **Discussion** Tell students that some critics have faulted Oedipus for fleeing and trying to escape his destiny. Ask students what they would have done under the circumstances. What do they feel about Oedipus' attempt to take action rather than to submit passively?

55 **Clarification** Remind students that travel in antiquity was dangerous; no police or other kinds of recourse or protection were available to a traveler on a desolate country road. Students might think about a solitary rider or walker in an isolated stretch of country in the old American Wild West running into a party like that of Laius. Oedipus describes how the quarrel between himself and Laius arose, escalated, and ended in violence. Ask students to consider who was at fault, and whether the event is represented in a way that makes us sympathize with one party rather than the other.

56 **Discussion** Why Oedipus suffers this fate has troubled viewers and critics for millennia. His fate is decreed before he does anything, indeed before his birth—Laius is told that if he bears a son, that son will kill him. Ask students to react to the gods' malevolence.

57 **Discussion** Why does Oedipus seem less certain that he is the murderer? Possibly he clings to a last shred of hope that the last witness will exonerate him. Why does Jocasta say the man cannot unsay his earlier testimony?

Next day I went and taxed[63] my parents with it;
they took the insult very ill from him,
875 the drunken fellow who had uttered it.
So I was comforted for their part, but
still this thing rankled[64] always, for the story
crept about widely. And I went at last
to Pytho, though my parents did not know.
880 But Phoebus sent me home again unhonored
in what I came to learn, but he foretold
other and desperate horrors to befall me,
that I was fated to lie with my mother,
and show to daylight an accursed breed
885 which men would not endure, and I was
   doomed
to be murderer of the father that begot me.
When I heard this I fled, and in the days
that followed I would measure from the stars
the whereabouts of Corinth—yes, I fled
890 to somewhere where I should not see fulfilled
the infamies[65] told in that dreadful oracle.
And as I journeyed I came to the place
where, as you say, this king met with his death.
Jocasta, I will tell you the whole truth.
When I was near the branching of the
895   crossroads,
going on foot, I was encountered by
a herald and a carriage with a man in it,
just as you tell me. He that led the way
and the old man himself wanted to thrust me
900 out of the road by force. I became angry
and struck the coachman who was pushing me.
When the old man saw this he watched his
   moment,
and as I passed he struck me from his carriage,
full on the head with his two pointed goad.[66]
905 But he was paid in full and presently
my stick had struck him backwards from the car
and he rolled out of it. And then I killed them
all. If it happened there was any tie
of kinship twixt this man and Laius,

---

63. **taxed** (takst) *v.*: Imposed a burden on; put a strain on.
64. **rankled** (raŋ′ kəld) *v.*: Caused to have long-lasting anger and resentment.
65. **infamies** (in′ fə mēz) *n.*: Items of notorious disgrace and dishonor.
66. **goad** (gōd) *n.*: Sharp, pointed stick used to drive animals.

---

910 who is then now more miserable than I,
what man on earth so hated by the Gods,
since neither citizen nor foreigner
may welcome me at home or even greet me,
but drive me out of doors? And it is I,
915 I and no other have so cursed myself.
And I pollute the bed of him I killed
by the hands that killed him. Was I not born
   evil?
Am I not utterly unclean? I had to fly
and in my banishment not even see
920 my kindred nor set foot in my own country,
or otherwise my fate was to be yoked
in marriage with my mother and kill my father,
Polybus who begot me and had reared me.
Would not one rightly judge and say that on me
925 these things were sent by some malignant God?
O no, no, no—O holy majesty
of God on high, may I not see that day!
May I be gone out of men's sight before
I see the deadly taint of this disaster
come upon me.

930 **CHORUS.** Sir, we too fear these things. But until
you see this man face to face and hear his story,
hope.

OEDIPUS. Yes, I have just this much of hope—to
wait until the herdsman comes.

JOCASTA. And when he comes, what do you want
with him?

935 **OEDIPUS.** I'll tell you; if I find that his story is the
same as yours, I at least will be clear of this guilt.

JOCASTA. Why what so particularly did you learn
from my story?

OEDIPUS. You said that he spoke of highway *robbers*
940 who killed Laius. Now if he uses the same number, it was not I who killed him. One man cannot
be the same as many. But if he speaks of a man
traveling alone, then clearly the burden of the
guilt inclines toward me.

JOCASTA. Be sure, at least, that this was how he
945 told the story. He cannot unsay it now, for everyone in the city heard it—not I alone. But, Oedipus, even if he diverges from what he said then,

---

Commentary

The Elusive Tragic Flaw For hundreds of years, critics have performed prodigious contortionist feats in order to locate Oedipus' "tragic flaw," that character fault that would make him deserve his horrendous fate. Others, like Sigmund Freud, have called this play a "tragedy of fate." Critics who think Oedipus could have avoided his fate had he stayed put forget the unerring truth of Apollo's oracle, which announces things as they are; they argue that, had Oedipus not tried to fight his destiny, he could have avoided fulfilling the prophecy. Consider, however, what that would mean: Oedipus,

58 **Discussion** Have students discuss how each fact meant to disprove the prophecy is nonsense; what effect does it have on the audience to have the very arguments that lead her to this conclusion prove that her skepticism is wrong?

Master Teacher Note Make certain students understand the choral song by helping them express the meaning of each stanza in their own words. Call students' attention to the fact that the chorus turns to divine (vs. human) law in the strophe. Students should also see that the "me" of the chorus is also the "me" of the Athenian audience.

59 **Enrichment** "Insolence breeds the tyrant" is common traditional wisdom, found in Aeschylus and other poets too. Wealth breeds arrogance, which in turn characterizes the tyrant, someone who revels in unchecked power and comes to think of himself as more than human. The result is a fall, since to forget that mortals are not gods is always disastrous.

he shall never prove that the murder of Laius squares rightly with the prophecy—for Loxias declared that the king should be killed by his own son. And that poor creature did not kill him surely,—for he died himself first. So as far as prophecy goes, henceforward I shall not look to the right hand or the left. 965

OEDIPUS. Right. But yet, send some one for the peasant to bring him here; do not neglect it.

JOCASTA. I will send quickly. Now let me go indoors. I will do nothing except what pleases you. 970
[*Exit.*]

CHORUS.
  Strophe
May destiny ever find me
pious in word and deed
prescribed by the laws that live on high:
laws begotten in the clear air of heaven,
whose only father is Olympus;
no mortal nature brought them to birth,
no forgetfulness shall lull them to sleep;
for God is great in them and grows not old.

  Antistrophe
Insolence[67] breeds the tyrant, insolence
if it is glutted with a surfeit,[68] unseasonable,
    unprofitable,
climbs to the rooftop and plunges
sheer down to the ruin that must be,
and there its feet are no service.

59

---

67. **Insolence** (in′ sə ləns) *n.*: Arrogance; bold disrespectfulness.
68. **surfeit** (sur′ fit) *n.*: Excessive supply.

believing his adoptive parents to be his real parents, should have decided to stay at home and risk crime and pollution. It is only reasonable that he try to fight his destiny; but it is inevitable that he fulfill it.

Why is it inevitable? Not because Oedipus has a quick temper, nor because he relies too much on human reason. What was destined to happen would have happened anyway, one way or another; it happened in the way it did because Oedipus was who he was. For the ancient Greeks, fate could be visualized like weaving: The parameters are fixed, as are some elements of the final cloth; some variation is possible, but it will not change the size of the cloth. What this play reveals is that because they are human, all mortals have limited vision; they do not have all they need to see clearly what the target should be, and so they miss the mark, as a hunter's arrow may miss its target. The Greek word for "missing the mark" is *hamartia*, often translated as "tragic flaw." Hamartia can have ethical overtones, but it always maintains its basic meaning as well. For Aristotle, being who you are, and in the culture or situation that constrains you, prevents you from sorting out all the information at hand, so you "miss the mark."

But I pray that the God may never
abolish the eager ambition that profits the state.
For I shall never cease to hold the God as our
   protector.

Strophe

975 If a man walks with haughtiness
of hand or word and gives no heed
to Justice and the shrines of Gods
despises—may an evil doom
980 smite him for his ill-starred pride of heart!—
if he reaps gains without justice
and will not hold from impiety
and his fingers itch for untouchable things.
When such things are done, what man shall
   contrive
to shield his soul from the shafts of the God?

985 When such deeds are held in honor,
why should I honor the Gods in the dance?

Antistrophe
No longer to the holy place,
to the navel of earth I'll go
to worship, nor to Abae
990 nor to Olympia,
unless the oracles are proved to fit,
for all men's hands to point at.
O Zeus, if you are rightly called
the sovereign lord, all-mastering,
let this not escape you nor your ever-living
995   power!
The oracles concerning Laius
are old and dim and men regard them not.
Apollo is nowhere clear in honor; God's service
   perishes.

Reader's Response *Put yourself in Oedipus' place. What mixed emotions must he be feeling at this point in the drama?*

THINKING ABOUT THE SELECTION

Interpreting

1. How would you characterize Oedipus as a ruler?
2. Oedipus has two main interests in locating Laius' murderer. One is to lift the plague from Thebes. (a) What is Oedipus' second reason for wanting to bring justice to the murderer? (b) How is his second reason significant in terms of plot?
3. Although Teiresias is blind, he has authoritative vision. (a) Interpret his claim that "Of themselves things will come, although I hide them and breathe no word of them." (b) What is ironic about a seer being blind?
4. Teiresias says, "You blame my temper but you do not see / your own that lives within you." What else does Oedipus reveal about his character in his exchange with Teiresias?

5. Discuss the references to darkness, blindness, and vision, in Teiresias' speech in lines 460–486.
6. (a) Why does Oedipus distrust Creon? (b) How does Creon try to prove that he has no interest in being king of Thebes?
7. In terms of the plot, what is significant about the exact time when Oedipus comes to the crossroad where he kills the people in the carriage?
8. (a) What reasons does Jocasta give for not having faith in the prophecy? (b) In terms of their approach to destiny, what do Jocasta and Oedipus have in common?
9. (a) What role does the Chorus play in heightening the dramatic tension of this play? (b) If you were producing a modern-dress version of this play, explain whether you would include the chorus and why.
10. Why is it futile for Oedipus to try to escape the circumstances of his life?

Applying

11. When Oedipus claims, "But yet / I must be ruler," Creon replies, "Not if you rule badly." (a) What insights does Sophocles provide about the rights of the ruler and of the ruled? (b) How do these ideas correspond with those in contemporary American life?

ANALYZING LITERATURE

Analyzing Tragedy

Certain conditions must exist in tragedies. First, tragic characters must be of high birth or noble status in society. Second, they must experience a series of events that threaten their positions. These events should have a causal relationship; each event affects the next, so that every action is crucial to the plot. Finally, tragic characters must suffer a tragic fall through their own actions. The gods interfere to some degree; they may even determine the outcome of the plot. However, they never direct the plot or the characters' actions. Characters are responsible for their own actions—that is what renders tragedy tragic. A person who dies after an air conditioner falls on his or her head as he or she passes underneath it is not a tragic character because that person made no conscious choice. The event was simply an accident. Tragic characters, on the other hand, choose their destinies. It is their choices that cause their downfalls.

1. Based on what you have read thus far, what choices does Oedipus make?
2. What choices does Jocasta make?
3. Explain the relationship between the following events: (a) The riddling Sphinx terrorizes Thebes and (b) Thebes suffers a plague.

CRITICAL THINKING AND READING

Tracing a Motif

A **motif** is a design or recurrent image or idea. The motif of the quest for knowledge is apparent from the beginning of *Oedipus the King*. In the priest's speech, he refers to "speaking," "teaching," "hearing," and "learning," all of which are associated with knowledge. Oedipus' initial desire to learn the identity of who murdered Laius is really a consuming desire to know his own identity.

1. Trace the knowledge motif from the beginning of the play to line 998 by noting examples of Oedipus in his quest for knowledge.

2. How does Teiresias figure in the quest for knowledge?
3. Of what does the chorus try to convince Oedipus about knowledge?

UNDERSTANDING LANGUAGE

Using Context Clues

As you read world literature, you may encounter unfamiliar words. Sometimes you need to consult a dictionary to learn the meanings of unfamiliar words. But often you can determine meaning from the context in which the word is used. To use context clues, examine the sentence in which the word appears. You may also need to study the material leading up to the sentence. Information in the material surrounding the reference will help you define the word or words you don't know. Consider the following example from line 28 of *Oedipus the King*: ". . . a *blight* is on our women that no children are born to them." From the information about women being unable to bear children, we know that a *blight* is something that prevents growth.

1. In line 47 you find the word *entreat*. (a) Using the context clues in the sentence, define *entreat*. (b) Now compare your definition with a dictionary definition of *entreat*.
2. Find the word *rogue* in line 691. What context clues helped you determine its meaning?
3. (a) Identify two more words from Part I of the play that you needed to use context clues to understand. (b) What context clues did you use?

THINKING AND WRITING

Writing About Character

Oedipus is probably the most famous tragic character of Greek drama. He is also one of the most complex. Write an essay in which you examine his character. First make notes about him. What are his dominant qualities? Is he moral? Is he fair? Is he guilty? Remember that tragic heroes fall from dignity and grace because of their characters. How do you see Oedipus' character as causing his tragic fall, based on what you have read so far? After you have completed your notes, write the first draft of your essay. When you revise make sure you have organized your information logically. Have you included enough details to support your points? Finally, proofread your essay and prepare a final draft.

(continued from bottom of page)

crossroads; go to Thebes; investigate Laius' murder so that the killer will be found and the plague will be lifted.
2. Jocasta chooses to abandon her and Laius' infant son.
3. Oedipus solves the riddle and saves Thebes, but he also brings a plague on Thebes because he unknowingly killed King Laius.

ANSWERS TO CRITICAL THINKING AND READING

1. Students should include some or all of the following: Oedipus knows the answer to the riddle of the Sphinx, which makes him king of Thebes and responsible for finding out why Thebes is suffering a plague. Once he knows why, he must know who killed Laius. Finally, Oedipus seeks to know whether the man he killed at the crossroads was his father.
2. Teiresias, who knows everything, tries to show Oedipus that he doesn't know where he lives, whom he lives with, and who he is.
3. The chorus explains that human knowledge is limited and divine knowledge is beyond humans' capacity of understanding.

ANSWERS TO UNDERSTANDING LANGUAGE

1. (a) Suggested response: beg: to ask earnestly (*Webster's New World Dictionary*). (b) Answers will differ. Ask students to identify which context clues help indicate the meaning of the word.
2. Answers will differ. Suggested response: The preceding sentence sets up a contrast between honest men and a rogue, indicating that a rogue is opposite to an honest man.
3. Answers will differ.

THINKING AND WRITING

Publishing Student Writing Suggest that students share their papers in class and compare discussions of Oedipus' character.

Challenge Suggest that students go to the library and read literary criticism on *Oedipus the King*.

ing against Oedipus for the kingdom. (b) Creon says that he now enjoys all the prizes of the kingdom without having to be the king and live in fear.
7. It is the same time that King Laius was murdered.
8. (a) She says that Laius was killed by robbers, and she admits to leaving her and Laius' infant son on a hill to die. (b) They both go to great lengths to avoid destiny.

9. (a) The chorus heightens the dramatic tension by providing commentary on the action. (b) Answers will differ.
10. Oedipus, like everyone else, cannot change the circumstances of his life. No matter where he goes and what he does to avoid his fate, destiny finds him.
11. (a) Bad rulers no more deserve to rule than people deserve to be ruled

by them. (b) In contemporary American life, people in powerful political positions lose them if they prove corrupt or incompetent.

ANSWERS TO ANALYZING LITERATURE

1. He chooses to: run away from the prophecy that he will kill his father and marry his mother; kill the men at the

THE DELPHIC ORACLE

Presentation

Motivation/Prior Knowledge Students know from reading the first part of *Oedipus the King* that Oedipus became king of Thebes by solving the riddle of the Sphinx. Students will remember exchanging jokes and riddles as children. They may even continue to do so now. Ask students to explore the significance of riddles—why is it entertaining to tell riddles, and why is trying to solve them fun?

Enrichment Share with students the myth behind Apollo's establishment of the oracle at Delphi. According to one legend, Apollo traveled to Delphi, where he killed a huge serpent, after which he had to leave and be purified. On his way back to Delphi, Apollo looked for other spots to establish his oracle. He had his eye on the spring Telphusa, but the territorial nymph of that spring convinced him to go to Delphi instead. Once he realized why the jealous nymph sent him to Delphi, he returned to Telphusa and dried up the spring. Next he set out in search of men to serve as keepers of the oracle. He met a Cretan ship in the Mediterranean, assumed the shape of a giant blue dolphin, and caused the astounded crew to sail toward the nearest port at Delphi. Then he revealed himself to them and commanded them to establish a shrine of Apollo Delphinius, "He of the Dolphin." Legend also states that he made a woman named Phenomoe the first Pythia, or prophetess of his oracles.

The Oracle of Apollo at Delphi, which the Greeks called the navel or center of the world, was where Greeks and foreigners alike traveled from all over the Mediterranean to seek the advice of the god who knew all things and who always spoke the truth. The Oracle enjoyed such prestige from about 750 B.C. onward that people believed it had always been there, and that at the very beginning of time, before Apollo's temple was built there, Earth herself had prophesied at Delphi.

What kinds of questions did the Oracle answer? States and rulers who wanted to know if they should go to war, or when and where they should found a colony, consulted the oracle. Nobody would consider amending the constitution or establishing a new religious festival without advice from Delphi. The Oracle might have suggested how to handle a difficult criminal case, or how to go about economic ventures.

Wealthy and powerful states and individuals thanked Apollo by offering gifts to the temple such as enormous sums of gold and silver. Soon there wasn't enough room in the temple to hold the treasures Delphi amassed; in any case, powerful states and rulers wanted to show their magnificence by paying for the construction of impressive buildings, treasuries to hold their valuable gifts. These lined the Sacred Way along which pilgrims and visitors passed en route to the temple.

One of the enormous number of visitors to Delphi was the fifth-century historian Herodotus, who has left us descriptions of intricately crafted ivory statues with precious metals and gems. Herodotus also describes solid-gold bowls or jars over eight feet in height. These offerings served to show gratitude and to ensure good relations with the temple. They also provided visible proof of how rich and powerful the donors were.

Apollo spoke through his priestess, the Pythia, who fell into a divine trance and gave voice to his responses. The Pythia was so named because of the Python, a monstrous serpent who guarded the spot. When Apollo came to Delphi, he slew Python and established his oracle there. But the Pythia gave audience only once a month, and crowds of travelers might make the long and difficult journey only to be turned away without an answer. Not only states and kings asked the Oracle's advice; private individuals came from all over looking for answers to their personal problems. Should I marry? Is it a good idea to go on a trip? Should I move to a new city? Anyone could attempt to get an answer from Apollo, provided he or she had the price of a modest fee, a ritual cake, and a goat or sheep to sacrifice.

Donations of money and food helped maintain the temple priests and bureaucrats. Crowds came to Delphi seeking some help in navigating the uncharted waters of life, and the place became a tourist attraction, just as pilgrimage sites are throughout the world. Even if you didn't get an answer from Apollo, you could see the splendid gifts of the fabulously wealthy and feel you were getting a glimpse of the rich and famous. If you were lucky, you might even catch sight of some of the rich and famous themselves. The local people

NSIGHTS

THE APOLLO BELVEDERE
Roman marble copy
probably of Greek origin
Vatican Museum, Rome

Humanities Note

Fine art, *The Apollo Belvedere*. This statue is a larger-than-life-sized Roman sculpture fashioned of Carrara marble. It is thought to be a copy of a Greek bronze statue that stood before Apollo's temple in the Athenian marketplace. This unusual piece was unearthed in the early sixteenth century and brought into the Vatican collection by Pope Julius II. Its placement in the garden of the Belvedere Chapel, where it remains to this day, gives the statue its name.

The elegance of the pose and smooth modeling of the skin suggests the hand of a master sculptor. He interprets the god Apollo as the embodiment of youth and vitality. In 1632 it was decided that the assistant to Michelangelo, Giovanni Angelo Montorsoli, would restore this sculpture. He added the missing arms, which carried a laurel branch and a bow, symbolic of this god's powers. These restorations were removed in 1925.

The neoclassical artists of the eighteenth century revered this sculpture as the epitome of ideal Greek beauty. Its purity of interpretation and stylized classical form has provided a continuing source of inspiration for artists who look to Greco-Roman antiquity for their subjects.

You might want to use the following questions to discuss the art:

1. Do you consider this statue "godlike"? Why or why not?
2. Why do you think restorations were removed from the sculpture in the twentieth century?

catered to the visitors, offering lodging, food, and souvenirs at exorbitant prices. To compare the bustle at Delphi with the Vatican, Lourdes, or Disney World at certain times of the year would not be out of line.

Sometimes Apollo gave straightforward answers, and many went away pleased: A general who had usurped the throne could get the god's approval and be legitimate; a state could say Apollo was solidly behind a new set of laws or a decision to wage war on a neighbor; and many people must have launched themselves into marriage or set out on a trip with a sense that they were doing the right thing. But often the answers were ambiguous riddles that needed to be solved with care and subtlety. Apollo knew all and always spoke the truth, but human limitations could misinterpret his response. For instance, when king Croesus of Lydia, fabled for his wealth, asked if he should invade Persia, the Oracle responded "If you do, you will destroy a great kingdom." He took this as a green light and invaded Persia as he had planned. But against everyone's expectations, he was defeated. Too late, with twenty-twenty hindsight, he realized that the "great kingdom" was his own.

Apollo's riddles always proved the god right and always tested the mental agility of the interpreter. At times, it seemed that no one could be expected to interpret the oracle correctly, especially when an apparently clear answer proved to mean something very different from what you would reasonably have expected. For instance, a man who was told he would be killed "in the sea" met his death in a forest, but it turned out that the locals used to call that neck of the woods "the sea."

With the oracle, there was always room for human ingenuity and courage. Human beings were not always stumped. In the folk tradition, being good at making up and solving riddles is what gives the underdog a chance. Think about how often the clever little guy outwits the slow-witted giant or monster, from Odysseus against the Cyclops to the hobbit Bilbo Baggins against the Gollum. Getting the riddle by the tail and using it cleverly is what helped the small state of Athens defeat the powerful Persian army in 480 B.C. When the Persians were attacking Athens, the old-fashioned conservatives wanted to hole up in the Acropolis, the fortified citadel with its wooden walls. The admiral of the Athenian fleet, an able strategist named Themistocles, wanted to risk a naval engagement, which he saw as the only chance to outmaneuver the Persians. Debate raged, and there was no agreement. So the Athenians asked Apollo at Delphi for advice, and the Pythia answered that Athens would be saved by "a wooden wall." This is a riddle, Themistocles asserted; what the god means is not a literal wooden wall, but a figurative one, made up of wooden ships. He won the argument, Athens won a naval battle off the island of Salamis, and the Persians were driven back.

The Oracle of Apollo at Delphi was a going concern for about a thousand years, but its heyday was during the classical period, from about 580 B.C. to 320 B.C. The Christian emperor Theodosius closed the sanctuary in A.D. 390.

Literary Focus One way to think about the form of the play is that its basic plot occurs commonly in folk tales. Someone has been exposed by the biological parents and either left to die or left to be found and raised by others. In any case the infant is brought up by foster parents, proves his or her innate worth or nobility, and is eventually "recognized" as who she or he really is: A "reversal" of fortune from humble to great takes place. Since the audience knows the Oedipus myth, dramatic irony exploits our expectations of the recognition of who Oedipus really is and the reversal of his fortune.

Writing/Prior Knowledge Have students form groups and brainstorm for examples of situations in which an unpleasant truth was preferable to comfortable ignorance. Examples can come from the public or political sphere, or students may wish to share incidents from their private spheres.

ESL Teaching Strategy Point out to ESL students that in drama, dialogue advances the action. Discuss the role of dialogue in *Oedipus the King*.

Teaching Tenth-Grade Students Ask tenth-grade students to trace the unraveling of the plot. When is the climax? What is the resolution?

Vocabulary

Preteach the following vocabulary words:

checked (chekt) *v.*: Restrained

lineage (lin´ e ij) *n.*: Ancestry

beneficent (bə nef´ ə s'nt) *adj.*: Kind, helpful

consonant (kän´ sə nənt) *adj.*: In harmony or agreement

gratify (grat´ i fī) *v.*: Please

dirge (durj) *n.*: Funeral song

visitant (viz´ it ənt) *n.*: Visitor, guest

reverence (rev´ ər əns) *n.*: Attitude of respect

Oedipus the King, Part II

Commentary

Dramatic Irony. Dramatic irony is the contradiction between what the character thinks and what the audience knows to be true. The words or acts of a character may carry meaning that is understood by the audience but completely unperceived by the character. *Oedipus the King* is famous for its dramatic irony. The most outstanding example occurs when the Messenger tells Jocasta that Oedipus' father, believed to be Polybus, is dead; the audience knows that in reality, Oedipus' father is Laius and that, unknowingly, Oedipus killed Laius on his way to Thebes. Although the audience knows more about Oedipus' history than he does, Sophocles gradually reveals to Oedipus his past. That gradual revelation builds suspense as Oedipus relentlessly pursues the knowledge that will eventually cause his downfall.

Sophocles' use of dramatic irony brings to light the play's knowledge motif. Oedipus is determined "to know" himself and the universe. In Greek, Oedipus is spelled Oidipous; the first part of his name, "Oidi-," resembles a form of the Greek verb "to know." Ironically, only Oedipus knew the answer to the riddle of the Sphinx, which made him savior and king of Thebes. Yet, unknowingly, Oedipus is the cause of Thebes' plague. What is even more ironic, Oedipus doesn't know what is most important in his life: his identity. All his actions generate from his thirst for knowledge, but some of his most important actions, such as killing his father, are based on ignorance. In turn, any knowledge he obtains, he acts on immediately. For example, when he learns of the plague, he sends Creon to Delphi. When he learns of Laius' murder, he sends for Teiresias. Finally, he learns his identity from the Herdsman, and he swiftly takes action. Ultimately, the knowledge Oedipus relentlessly seeks causes his downfall.

Writing

Write briefly about why knowledge, even if it is not pleasing, is important. Think of historical situations in which knowledge of the truth, even if it made the public uncomfortable, was important to people.

Background

In Greek drama, performances took place in a large outdoor theater that held up to 15,000 spectators. Actors—all men—did not rely on facial expression or vocal inflection; they performed in oversized masks and used large physical gestures. As a result, dialogue is the principal form of dramatic expression. From dialogue, the audience gets a sense of character. Actions, particularly violent actions, take place offstage and are described onstage by messengers.

Objectives

Thematic

To understand tragedy

Skills

1 To analyze dramatic irony
2 To understand causality
3 To write about justice

Support Material

Teaching Portfolio

Teacher Backup, p. 569

Grammar in Action Worksheet, *Understanding Narrative*, p. 573

Usage and Mechanics Worksheet, p. 575

Vocabulary Check, p. 576

Analyzing Literature Worksheet, *Analyzing Dramatic Irony*, p. 577

Critical Thinking and Reading Worksheet, *Understanding Causality*, p. 578

Selection Test, pp. 579–580

Oedipus the King

Part II

[*Enter* JOCASTA, *carrying garlands.*]

JOCASTA. Princes of the land, I have had the
    thought to go
to the Gods' temples, bringing in my hand
garlands and gifts of incense, as you see.
For Oedipus excites himself too much
at every sort of trouble, not conjecturing,[1]
like a man of sense, what will be from what was,
but he is always at the speaker's mercy,

---

1. conjecturing (kən jek′ chər iŋ) *v.*: Inferring or predicting
from incomplete evidence.

when he speaks terrors. I can do no good
by my advice, and so I came as suppliant
to you, Lycaean Apollo, who are nearest.
These are the symbols of my prayer and this
1010 my prayer: grant us escape free of the curse.
Now when we look to him we are all afraid;
he's pilot of our ship and he is frightened.

[*Enter* MESSENGER.]

MESSENGER. Might I learn from you, sirs, where is
    the house of Oedipus? Or best of all, if you
1015 know, where is the king himself?

CHORUS. This is his house and he is within doors.
    This lady is his wife and mother of his children.

3 Reading Strategy Students should notice that throughout this scene, the messenger tries almost comically to be the bearer of good tidings, deserving a reward. Have students point out each attempt to please or comfort his listeners that backfires.

Master Teacher Note "Dearest" (line 1039) in the Greek simultaneously means "closest kin." It is the superlative of the adjective philos, from which we derive many English words along the models of philanthropic and philately or bibliophile and hemophilia. You might write *philos* on the board and list derivatives students can generate. Probably the most basic and certainly the most ancient use of philos is to denote something inseparably part of you, like your hand, heart, or eyes. Oedipus' use of "dearest" to Jocasta is both common and appropriate, as well as resonant and ironic for the audience.

4 Discussion Ask students how they respond to Oedipus' violent reaction of relief. Does he seem arrogant? Do they pity him? What shapes their reactions?

5 Reading Strategy Have students think about the repercussion of Jocasta's attitude in these lines. She voices precisely the same attitude Thucydides describes when he writes about the effects of the plague (see Primary Source pages 436–437): seize the day, live for the moment's pleasure, nothing is predictable, and nothing makes sense. Why might such an attitude seem dangerous to Sophocles?

6 Discussion How does the fact that Oedipus should derive comfort from what ought to be bad news highlight the way in which everything is turned upside down in this legend?

MESSENGER. God bless you, lady, and God bless your household! God bless Oedipus' noble wife!

1020 JOCASTA. God bless you, sir, for your kind greeting! What do you want of us that you have come here? What have you to tell us?

3 ⌐ MESSENGER. Good news, lady. Good for your house and for your husband.
  ⌐

1025 JOCASTA. What is your news? Who sent you to us?

MESSENGER. I come from Corinth and the news I bring will give you pleasure. Perhaps a little pain too.

JOCASTA. What is this news of double meaning?

MESSENGER. The people of the Isthmus will choose Oedipus to be their king. That is the rumor 1030 there.

JOCASTA. But isn't their king still old Polybus?

MESSENGER. No. He is in his grave. Death has got him.

JOCASTA. Is that the truth? Is Oedipus' father dead?

MESSENGER. May I die myself if it be otherwise!

1035 JOCASTA. [*to a servant*] Be quick and run to the King with the news! O oracles of the Gods, where are you now? It was from this man Oedipus fled, lest he should be his murderer! And now he is dead, in the course of nature, and not killed by Oedipus.

[*Enter* OEDIPUS.]

OEDIPUS. Dearest Jocasta, why have you sent for 1040 me?

JOCASTA. Listen to this man and when you hear reflect what is the outcome of the holy oracles of the Gods.

OEDIPUS. Who is he? What is his message for me?

JOCASTA. He is from Corinth and he tells us that 1045 your father Polybus is dead and gone.

OEDIPUS. What's this you say, sir? Tell me yourself.

MESSENGER. Since this is the first matter you want clearly told: Polybus has gone down to death. You may be sure of it.

1050 OEDIPUS. By treachery or sickness?

MESSENGER. A small thing will put old bodies asleep.

OEDIPUS. So he died of sickness, it seems,—poor old man!

MESSENGER. Yes, and of age—the long years he had measured.

OEDIPUS. Ha! Ha! O dear Jocasta, why should one look to the Pythian hearth?[2] Why should one look
to the birds screaming overhead? They prophesied 1055
that I should kill my father! But he's dead,
and hidden deep in earth, and I stand here
who never laid a hand on spear against him,— 1060
unless perhaps he died of longing for me,
and thus I am his murderer. But they,
the oracles, as they stand—he's taken them
away with him, they're dead as he himself is,
and worthless.

JOCASTA.   That I told you before now.

1065 OEDIPUS. You did, but I was misled by my fear.

JOCASTA. Then lay no more of them to heart, not one.

OEDIPUS. But surely I must fear my mother's bed?

JOCASTA. Why should man fear since chance is all in all
for him, and he can clearly foreknow nothing?
Best to live lightly, as one can, unthinkingly.
As to your mother's marriage bed,—don't fear it.
Before this, in dreams too, as well as oracles,
many a man has lain with his own mother.
But he to whom such things are nothing bears
his life most easily.

1075 OEDIPUS. All that you say would be said perfectly
if she were dead; but since she lives I must
still fear, although you talk so well, Jocasta.

JOCASTA. Still in your father's death there's light of comfort?

---

2. **Pythian hearth** (pi′ thē ən härth) *n*.: The Delphic oracle that prophesied Oedipus' crime.

Primary Source Note
Sigmund Freud, "the father of psychoanalysis," made the "Oedipus Complex" a household word, familiar to many who have never read what Freud himself wrote. What we must not forget is that Freud, like every other thinker and writer, is the product of a particular time and culture, whatever his claims to universality might be. Here is what he wrote in *The Interpretation of Dreams*, in 1900:

The action of the play [Sophocles' *Oedipus the King*] consists in nothing other than the process of revealing, with cunning delays and ever-mount-

OEDIPUS. Great light of comfort; but I fear the living.

MESSENGER. Who is the woman that makes you afraid?

OEDIPUS. Merope, old man, Polybus' wife.

MESSENGER. What about her frightens the queen and you?

OEDIPUS. A terrible oracle, stranger, from the gods.

MESSENGER. Can it be told? Or does the sacred law forbid another to have knowledge of it?

OEDIPUS. O no! Once on a time Loxias said that I should lie with my own mother and take on my hands the blood of my own father. And so for these long years I've lived away from Corinth; it has been to my great happiness; but yet it's sweet to see the face of parents.

MESSENGER. This was the fear which drove you out of Corinth?

OEDIPUS. Old man, I did not wish to kill my father.

MESSENGER. Why should I not free you from this fear, sir, since I have come to you in all goodwill?

OEDIPUS. You would not find me thankless if you did.

MESSENGER. Why, it was just for this I brought the news,— to earn your thanks when you had come safe home.

OEDIPUS. No, I will never come near my parents.

MESSENGER. Son, it's very plain you don't know what you're doing.

OEDIPUS. What do you mean, old man? For God's sake, tell me.

MESSENGER. If your homecoming is checked by fears like these.

OEDIPUS. Yes, I'm afraid that Phoebus may prove right.

MESSENGER. The murder and the incest?[3]

OEDIPUS.   Yes, old man;
1105 that is my constant terror.

MESSENGER.   Do you know
that all your fears are empty?

OEDIPUS.   How is that,
if they are father and mother and I their son?

1110 **MESSENGER.** Because Polybus was no kin to you in blood.

OEDIPUS. What, was not Polybus my father?

MESSENGER. No more than I but just so much.

OEDIPUS.   How can
my father be my father as much as one
that's nothing to me?

---

3. **incest** (in´ sest) *n*.: Sexual intercourse between persons closely related.

9

7 Clarification Loxias is a title of Apollo meaning "interpreter." It refers to Apollo's prophetic knowledge of the will of Zeus.

8 Reading Strategy Students will already have analyzed Oedipus' choices in the first part of the play. Now have them think about the deeper meanings of his choices. By refusing to go near his parents, and thus, theoretically, eliminating the chance of fulfilling the oracle, what is he really avoiding? Lead students to realize that Oedipus' stubborn (and futile) attempt to avoid fulfilling the oracle is really a blatant denial of who he is. Students should continue to look for the connection between his approach to destiny and his identity throughout the second half of the play.

9 Clarification Make sure students realize that the Greeks viewed incest as an unnatural act. As in most cultures, incest was taboo in Greek culture. Nietzsche interprets the incest motif as a means of understanding the secrets of nature. "How else could one force nature to surrender her secrets except by opposing her and winning a victory, by means of the unnatural? . . . the very man who solves the riddle of nature—that double-constituted Sphinx—must also . . . break the holiest laws of nature."

ing excitement—a process that can be likened to the work of a psychoanalysis—that Oedipus himself is the murderer of Laius, but further that he is the son of the murdered man and of Jocasta . . .

Freud goes on to say that the play is known as a "tragedy of destiny," which moves us because the supreme will of the gods thwarts mankind's vain attempts to escape evil and suffering. Yet other stories that are also "tragedies of destiny" leave us unmoved.

If *Oedipus Rex* moves a modern audience no less than it did the contemporary Greek one, the explanation can only be that its effect does

not lie in the contrast between destiny and human will, but is to be looked for in the particular nature of the material on which that contrast is exemplified. There must be something which makes a voice within us ready to recognize the compelling force of destiny in the *Oedipus* . . . his destiny moves us only because it might have been ours—because the oracle laid the same curse upon us before our birth as upon him.

10 Discussion Ask students to determine the underlying social tension. Why might Oedipus want to discredit the messenger and therefore discount his information? How does the messenger's rebuke point to a common human condition distinct from the artificial differences of wealth and status?

11 Literary Focus Point out to students that Sophocles builds suspense by doling out information bit by bit and postponing the crisis. Remind students that in the *Iliad* Homer builds suspense by postponing the fatal confrontation between Achilleus and Hektor.

MESSENGER.　　　　　Neither he nor I
　begat you.

OEDIPUS.　　　　　Why then did he call me
　son?

MESSENGER.　A gift he took you from these hands
1115　of mine.

OEDIPUS.　Did he love so much what he took from
　another's hand?

MESSENGER.　His childlessness before persuaded him.

OEDIPUS.　Was I a child you bought or found when I
　was given to him?

MESSENGER.　　　　　On Cithaeron's slopes
　in the twisting thickets you were found.

OEDIPUS.　　　　　And why
1120　were you a traveler in those parts?

MESSENGER.　　　　　I was
　in charge of mountain flocks.

OEDIPUS.　　　　　You were a shepherd?
　A hireling vagrant?[4]

MESSENGER.　　　　　Yes, but at least at that
　time
　the man that saved your life, son.

OEDIPUS.　What ailed me when you took me in
1125　your arms?

MESSENGER.　In that your ankles should be witnesses.

OEDIPUS.　Why do you speak of that old pain?

MESSENGER.　　　　　I loosed you;
　the tendons of your feet were pierced and fettered,[5]—

OEDIPUS.　My swaddling clothes[6] brought me a
1130　rare disgrace.

MESSENGER.　So that from this you're called your
　present name.[7]

OEDIPUS.　Was this my father's doing or my
　mother's?
　For God's sake, tell me.

MESSENGER.　　　　　I don't know, but he
1135　who gave you to me has more knowledge than I.

OEDIPUS.　You yourself did not find me then? You
　took me from someone else?

MESSENGER.　　　　　Yes, from another
　shepherd.

---

4. hireling vagrant (hīr′ liŋ vā′ grənt): Person who wanders from place to place and works at odd jobs.
5. fettered (fet′ ərd): *n*.: Shackled or chained.
6. swaddling (swäd′ liŋ) **clothes:** Long, narrow bands of cloth wrapped around infants in ancient times.
7. your present name: "Oedipus" means "swollen foot."

OEDIPUS. Who was he? Do you know him well
enough to tell?

MESSENGER. He was called Laius' man.

OEDIPUS. You mean the king who reigned here in
the old days?

MESSENGER. Yes, he was that man's shepherd.

OEDIPUS. Is he alive
still, so that I could see him?

MESSENGER. You who live here
would know that best.

OEDIPUS. Do any of you here
know of this shepherd whom he speaks about
in town or in the fields? Tell me. It's time
that this was found out once for all.

CHORUS. I think he is none other than the peasant
whom you have sought to see already; but
Jocasta here can tell us best of that.

OEDIPUS. Jocasta, do you know about this man
whom we have sent for? Is he the man he
mentions?

JOCASTA. Why ask of whom he spoke? Don't give
it heed;
nor try to keep in mind what has been said.
It will be wasted labor.

OEDIPUS. With such clues
I could not fail to bring my birth to light.

JOCASTA. I beg you—do not hunt this out—I beg
you,
if you have any care for your own life.
What I am suffering is enough.

OEDIPUS. Keep up
your heart, Jocasta. Though I'm proved a slave,
thrice slave, and though my mother is thrice
slave,
you'll not be shown to be of lowly lineage.

JOCASTA. O be persuaded by me, I entreat you;
do not do this.

OEDIPUS. I will not be persuaded to let be
the chance of finding out the whole thing clearly.

JOCASTA. It is because I wish you well that I
give you this counsel—and it's the best counsel.

OEDIPUS. Then the best counsel vexes me, and has
for some while since.

JOCASTA. O Oedipus, God help you!
God keep you from the knowledge of who you
are!

OEDIPUS. Here, some one, go and fetch the
shepherd for me;
and let her find her joy in her rich family!

JOCASTA. O Oedipus, unhappy Oedipus!
that is all I can call you, and the last thing
that I shall ever call you.

CHORUS. Why has the queen gone, Oedipus, in
wild
grief rushing from us? I am afraid that trouble
will break out of this silence.

OEDIPUS. Break out what will! I at least shall be
willing to see my ancestry, though humble.
Perhaps she is ashamed of my low birth,
for she has all a woman's high-flown pride.
But I account myself a child of Fortune,[8]
beneficent Fortune, and I shall not be
dishonored. She's the mother from whom I
spring;
the months, my brothers, marked me, now as
small,
and now again as mighty. Such is my breeding,
and I shall never prove so false to it,
as not to find the secret of my birth.

CHORUS.
Strophe
If I am a prophet and wise of heart
you shall not fail, Cithaeron,
by the limitless sky, you shall not!—
to know at tomorrow's full moon
that Oedipus honors you,
as native to him and mother and nurse at once;
and that you are honored in dancing by us, as
finding favor in sight of our king.

---

8. child of Fortune: Since Fortune, or good luck, saved him
from death, Oedipus refuses to feel shame at being illegitimate
or of humble origins.

20 Clarification Make certain that students understand what the chorus, in its rather desperate desire to have things work out well for Oedipus, is saying. Oedipus has been revealed to be a foundling, not Polybus' son. He himself thinks he may be the son of a poor man or even a slave. But he feels the pride of a "self-made man" in his success and has said he is not a snob like Jocasta. Now the chorus recalls all the myths in which the foundling, "no man's son," turns out to be the child of a god. They suggest that a nymph bore him on the mountain to the god Pan or to Dionysus; that Apollo fathered him, perhaps with a mortal woman; or that Hermes, another god who wandered in the wilds, fathered him.

21 Discussion Ask students to consider why Sophocles might have the chorus express the most extravagant hopes and optimistic fantasy just before the entrance of the final witness, the herdsman who holds the key to all the past events.

22 Discussion Ask students to discuss how the messenger's well-meaning efforts to jog the old herdsman's memory remind us of the way a cross-examiner might try to get a recalcitrant witness to "remember" in court. Is it effective to have the information revealed in part by the messenger, who does not understand the force of what he is revealing? Why might Sophocles choose this way of getting the information across?

23 Discussion Have students discuss why the old man is reluctant to answer. What does he hope will be gained by silence?

1200 Apollo, to whom we cry, find these things
pleasing!

Antistrophe

Who was it bore you, child? One of
the long-lived nymphs[9] who lay with Pan[10]—
the father who treads the hills?
Or was she a bride of Loxias, your mother? The
grassy slopes

20

1205 are all of them dear to him. Or perhaps Cyllene's
king,[11]
or the Bacchants' God that lives on the tops
of the hills received you a gift from some
one of the Helicon Nymphs, with whom he
mostly plays?

[*Enter an old man, led by* OEDIPUS' *servants.*]

OEDIPUS. If some one like myself who never met
him

21 1210 may make a guess,—I think this is the herdsman,
whom we were seeking. His old age is
consonant
with the other. And besides, the men who bring
him
I recognize as my own servants. You
perhaps may better me in knowledge since
1215 you've seen the man before.

CHORUS.   You can be sure
I recognize him. For if Laius
had ever an honest shepherd, this was he.

OEDIPUS. You, sir, from Corinth, I must ask you
first,
1220 is this the man you spoke of?

MESSENGER.   This is he
before your eyes.

OEDIPUS.   Old man, look here at me
and tell me what I ask you. Were you ever
a servant of King Laius?

1225 HERDSMAN.   I was,—
no slave he bought but reared in his own house.

---

9. **nymphs** (nimfs) *n.*: Minor female divinities with youthful, beautiful, and amorous qualities; "nymph" means young woman.
10. **Pan:** Arcadian shepherd god who lived in the mountains, danced and sang with the nymphs, and played his pipes.
11. **Cyllene's king:** Hermes, the messenger god.

OEDIPUS. What did you do as work? How did you
live?

HERDSMAN. Most of my life was spent among the
flocks.

OEDIPUS. In what part of the country did you live?

1230 HERDSMAN. Cithaeron and the places near to it.

OEDIPUS. And somewhere there perhaps you knew
this man?

HERDSMAN. What was his occupation? Who?

OEDIPUS.   This man here,
have you had any dealings with him?

1235 HERDSMAN.   No—
not such that I can quickly call to mind.

MESSENGER. That is no wonder, master. But I'll
make him remember what he does not know. For
I know, that he well knows the country of
1240 Cithaeron, how he with two flocks, I with one
kept company for three years—each year half a
year—from spring till autumn time and then
when winter came I drove my flocks to our fold
home again and he to Laius' steadings. Well—am
1245 I right or not in what I said we did?

HERDSMAN. You're right—although it's a long time
ago.

MESSENGER. Do you remember giving me a child
to bring up as my foster child?

HERDSMAN.   What's this?
Why do you ask this question?

MESSENGER.   Look old man,
1250 here he is—here's the man who was that child!

HERDSMAN. Death take you! Won't you hold your
tongue?

OEDIPUS.   No, no,
do not find fault with him, old man. Your words
are more at fault than his.

HERDSMAN.   O best of masters,
1255 how do I give offense?

OEDIPUS.   When you refuse
to speak about the child of whom he asks you.

Primary Source Note

In 1871 the German philosopher Friedrich Nietzsche (who began his career as a professor of Greek) wrote about Sophocles' treatment of Oedipus, in *The Birthplace of Tragedy*:

The figure who suffers most on the Greek stage, the unfortunate Oedipus, was understood by Sophocles as the noble human being destined for error and misery despite his wisdom, but who nevertheless through his monstrous suffering exerts a magical healing power on all around him, a force that persists after his death.

Nietzsche here alludes to the last play Sophocles wrote, *Oedipus at Colonus*, in which Oedipus is purified by King Theseus of Athens and becomes in death a deified hero and protector of the city. The spot where he is buried becomes sacred ground, reminding us that in both Greek and Latin, words meaning "holy" or "consecrated" can also mean "polluted" and "untouchable."

The noble human being does not sin; this is the poet's profound message: his action may subvert every law, the natural order, even the moral world itself, but precisely through his same action he will create a higher

HERDSMAN. He speaks out of his ignorance, without meaning.

OEDIPUS. If you'll not talk to <u>gratify</u> me, you will talk with pain to urge you.

HERDSMAN.   O please, sir, don't hurt an old man, sir.

OEDIPUS. [*to the servants*]   Here, one of you, twist his hands behind him.

HERDSMAN.   Why, God help me, why? What do you want to know?

OEDIPUS.   You gave a child to him,—the child he asked you of?

HERDSMAN.   I did. I wish I'd died the day I did.

OEDIPUS.   You will unless you tell me truly.

HERDSMAN.   And I'll die far worse if I should tell you.

OEDIPUS.   This fellow is bent on more delays, as it would seem.

HERDSMAN. O no, no! I have told you that I gave it.

OEDIPUS. Where did you get this child from? Was it your own or did you
1270 get it from another?

HERDSMAN.   Not my own at all; I had it from some one.

OEDIPUS. One of these citizens? or from what house?

HERDSMAN. O master, please—I beg you, master, please don't ask me more.

OEDIPUS.   You're a dead man if I
1275 ask you again.

HERDSMAN.   It was one of the children of Laius.

OEDIPUS.   A slave? Or born in wedlock?

24 Clarification In the Athenian law-courts, the testimony of slaves was admissible only under physical torture. Oedipus' threats to the old slave may sound more brutal to us than they did to Sophocles' audience.

Enrichment As Aristotle notes, Sophocles has kept all the irrational elements in the Oedipus story outside the play. Within the play we see Oedipus play the hand that has been dealt him, and we must decide what kind of man he is. Aristotle finds plot (literally, action) all important because it is through action that essential character is revealed. At different points in his treatise *The Nicomachean Ethics* he says, "We acquire the virtues by first exercising them . . . We become just by doing just acts, temperate by doing temperate acts, brave by doing brave acts;" and "the good state of mind may exist without producing any good result, as in a man who is asleep or in some other way quite inactive, but the good activity cannot . . ." Character, in some inner and abstract sense separate from action, is not of interest to Aristotle, insofar as it is at all detectable.

magical sphere of influences which will build a new world on the ruins of the old world which has been overturned. This is what the poet, who is also a religious thinker, wants to convey.

    After discussing Sophocles' two Oedipus plays and concluding that Sophocles first shows us "the abyss" and then the "light-picture," a healing Nature shows us after the shattering glance into the abyss, Nietzsche goes on to consider further "the substance of the myth."

    Oedipus, murderer of his father, husband of his mother, interpreter of the riddle of the Sphinx! What does the mysterious trinity of these deeds of destiny reveal? In Oedipus' case, "when the boundary dividing present and future, the rigid law of individuation and . . . the intrinsic spell of nature are broken by magic and prophecy, an extraordinarily unnatural act (here incest) must be the cause."

25 Discussion Why does the herdsman shrink from saying what he has been forced to tell? Why does Oedipus—although he realizes what information the herdsman will impart—feel compelled to hear the truth uttered aloud? Some critics have faulted Oedipus for insisting on the truth, as if discovering the truth is what leads to his destruction and not finding it out would make everything all right. (This is in fact Jocasta's position.) Have students think about this point of view: Does it convince them? What are the assumptions that make it possible? What if any are its merits?

26 Clarification In this rapid-fire dialogue which the Greeks called *stichomythia*, perhaps most aptly rendered into English as "shuttle-speech," the questions and answers follow on one another so closely that the two speakers, and indeed an answer-question-answer pattern may share the same line of verse. Ask students how the pace here differs from that of other scenes. Is Sophocles' choice to make things move very rapidly at this point effective?

27 Discussion What fairy tales can the students think of in which a child is sent out to be killed but spared by the executioner, out of pity? What is different about Oedipus' story? For instance, in how many stories is the person who orders the child's killing a stepparent? What kinds of endings do the fairy tales usually have? How is the child's savior rewarded?

HERDSMAN. O God, I am on the brink of frightful speech.

OEDIPUS. And I of frightful hearing. But I must hear.

HERDSMAN. The child was called his child; but she within,
1280 your wife would tell you best how all this was.

OEDIPUS. *She* gave it to you?

HERDSMAN.   Yes, she did, my lord.

OEDIPUS. To do what with it?

1285 **HERDSMAN.**   Make away with it.

OEDIPUS. She was so hard—its mother?

HERDSMAN.   Aye, through fear
of evil oracles.

OEDIPUS.   Which?

HERDSMAN.   They said that he
should kill his parents.

OEDIPUS.   How was it that you
1290 gave it away to this old man?

HERDSMAN.   O master,
I pitied it, and thought that I could send it

off to another country and this man
was from another country. But he saved it
for the most terrible troubles. If you are
the man he says you are, you're bred to misery.   1330

OEDIPUS. O, O, O, they will all come,
all come out clearly! Light of the sun, let me
look upon you no more after today!
I who first saw the light bred of a match
accursed, and accursed in my living
with them I lived with, cursed in my killing.
                                [*Exit all but the* CHORUS.]   1335

CHORUS.
    Strophe
O generations of men, how I
count you as equal with those who live
not at all!
What man, what man on earth wins more
of happiness than a seeming
and after that turning away?
Oedipus, you are my pattern of this,
Oedipus, you and your fate!
Luckless Oedipus, whom of all men
I envy not at all.

    Antistrophe
In as much as he shot his bolt
beyond the others and won the prize
of happiness complete—
O Zeus—and killed and reduced to nought
the hooked taloned maid of the riddling
    speech,[12]
standing a tower against death for my land:
hence he was called my king and hence
was honored the highest of all
honors; and hence he ruled
in the great city of Thebes.

    Strophe
But now whose tale is more miserable?
Who is there lives with a savager fate?
Whose troubles so reverse his life as his?

O Oedipus, the famous prince
for whom a great haven
the same both as father and son

---
12. hooked taloned maid of the riddling speech: The
Sphinx; talons are claws.

---

sufficed for generation,
how, O how, have the furrows plowed
by your father endured to bear you, poor
    wretch,
and hold their peace so long?

    Antistrophe
Time who sees all has found you out
against your will; judges your marriage
    accursed,
begetter and begot at one in it.

O child of Laius,   1335
would I had never seen you.
I weep for you and cry
a dirge of lamentation.

To speak directly, I drew my breath   1340
from you at the first and so now I lull
my mouth to sleep with your name.
                            [*Enter* A SECOND MESSENGER.]

SECOND MESSENGER. O Princes always honored by
    our country,
what deeds you'll hear of and what horrors see,
what grief you'll feel, if you as true born
    Thebans
care for the house of Labdacus's sons.   1345
Phasis nor Ister[13] cannot purge[14] this house,
I think, with all their streams, such things
it hides, such evils shortly will bring forth
into the light, whether they will or not;
and troubles hurt the most   1350
when they prove self-inflicted.

CHORUS. What we had known before did not fall
    short
of bitter groaning's worth; what's more to tell?

SECOND MESSENGER. Shortest to hear and tell—our
    glorious queen Jocasta's dead.   1355

CHORUS.   Unhappy woman! How?

SECOND MESSENGER. By her own hand. The worst
    of what was done
you cannot know. You did not see the sight.

---
13. Phasis (fā´ sis) **nor Ister** (is´ tər) *n*.: Rivers that flow to
the Black Sea.
14. purge (pərj) *v*.: Cleanse of guilt or sin.

---

28 **Discussion** Have students discuss why Oedipus wants never
again to see the light of sun now
that the truth has been clearly revealed.

29 **Enrichment** Point out to students
that the chorus refers to Oedipus
as a "pattern," a paradigm. He exemplifies the fate of mankind, to be
subject to mutability, to be "luckless" when seeming most favored
by "luck." Do the chorus's words
suggest that Oedipus did anything
to deserve his fate?

30 **Literary Focus** As the chorus
points out, Oedipus' story exemplifies *peripeteia*, reversal, at its
most extreme. His greatness is at
the opposite end of the curve,
balanced by his utter wretchedness. Does the chorus imply that
his "savage fate" was caused by
him or was to be avoided by him?
It is important to establish clearly
what Sophocles himself does or
does not imply because this play
more than any other has been interpreted so often and from so
many cultural perspectives alien
to Sophocles.

31 **Literary Focus** Call students' attention to the metaphor of Time.
Why is Time the tracker, flushing
prey from hiding, appropriate in
this play? In what sense does Time
"judge" Oedipus?

32 **Enrichment** Choruses, which in
Sophoclean plays represent the
nonheroic, common citizen, frequently meditate on the ways in
which affection brings suffering,
because it makes us vulnerable to
loss and pity.

33 **Enrichment** Terrible events like
murder and suicide take place offstage, "in the house," rather than
in public. Besides being a stage
convention of the ancient theater,
this convention keeps what is intensely personal out of public view,
enclosed in the "haven," the house
and the family. Why is the desire to
keep the personal hidden particularly in character for Jocasta?

Yet in so far as I remember it
you'll hear the end of our unlucky queen. 1360
When she came raging into the house she went
straight to her marriage bed, tearing her hair
with both her hands, and crying upon Laius
long dead—Do you remember, Laius,
that night long past which bred a child for us 1365
to send you to your death and leave
a mother making children with her son?
And then she groaned and cursed the bed in which
she brought forth husband by her husband, children
by her own child, an infamous double bond. 1370
How after that she died I do not know,—
for Oedipus distracted us from seeing.
He burst upon us shouting and we looked
to him as he paced frantically around,
begging us always: Give me a sword, I say, 1375
to find this wife no wife, this mother's womb,
this field of double sowing whence I sprang
and where I sowed my children! As he raved
some god showed him the way—none of us there.
Bellowing terribly and led by some 1380
invisible guide he rushed on the two doors,—
wrenching the hollow bolts out of their sockets,
he charged inside. There, there, we saw his wife
hanging, the twisted rope around her neck.
When he saw her, he cried out fearfully 1385
and cut the dangling noose. Then, as she lay,
poor woman, on the ground, what happened after,
was terrible to see. He tore the brooches—
the gold chased brooches fastening her robe—
away from her and lifting them up high 1390
dashed them on his own eyeballs, shrieking out
such things as: they will never see the crime
I have committed or had done upon me!
Dark eyes, now in the days to come look on
forbidden faces, do not recognize 1395
those whom you long for—with such imprecations[15]
he struck his eyes again and yet again

---

15. imprecations (im´ prĭ kā´ shənz) *n.:* Acts of cursing and invoking evil.

with the brooches. And the bleeding eyeballs gushed
and stained his beard—no sluggish oozing drops
but a black rain and bloody hail poured down. 1400

So it has broken—and not on one head
but troubles mixed for husband and for wife.
The fortune of the days gone by was true
good fortune—but today groans and destruction
and death and shame—of all ills can be named 1405
not one is missing.

CHORUS. Is he now in any ease from pain?

SECOND MESSENGER.   He shouts
for some one to unbar the doors and show him
to all the men of Thebes, his father's killer,
his mother's—no I cannot say the word, 1410
it is unholy—for he'll cast himself,
out of the land, he says, and not remain
to bring a curse upon his house, the curse
he called upon it in his proclamation. But
he wants for strength, aye, and some one to guide him; 1415
his sickness is too great to bear. You, too,
will be shown that. The bolts are opening.
Soon you will see a sight to waken pity
even in the horror of it.

                    [*Enter the blinded* OEDIPUS.]

CHORUS. This is a terrible sight for men to see! 1420
I never found a worse!
Poor wretch, what madness came upon you!
What evil spirit leaped upon your life
to your ill-luck—a leap beyond man's strength!
Indeed I pity you, but I cannot 1425
look at you, though there's much I want to ask
and much to learn and much to see.
I shudder at the sight of you.

OEDIPUS. O, O,
where am I going? Where is my voice 1430
borne on the wind to and fro?
Spirit, how far have you sprung?

CHORUS. To a terrible place whereof men's ears
may not hear, nor their eyes behold it.

OEDIPUS. Darkness! 1435
Horror of darkness enfolding, resistless,
unspeakable visitant sped by an ill wind in haste!

Grammar in Action

Narrative writing, an important part of ancient Greek drama, tells a story or relates a series of events. Tragedies in particular use narrative, especially when describing significant actions that occur offstage. For example, violence takes place offstage and is narrated for the audience. Surprisingly, narration doesn't detract from the drama of the event. Rather, the narrative brings offstage events to life in vivid and gory detail.

In order for narration to capture the event or series of events, it must meet the pace, or speed at which the action moves. The pace may be

madness and stabbing pain and memory
of evil deeds I have done!

40 **CHORUS.** In such misfortunes it's no wonder
if double weighs the burden of your grief.

OEDIPUS. My friend,
you are the only one steadfast, the only one that
attends on me;
you still stay nursing the blind man.
45 Your care is not unnoticed. I can know
your voice, although this darkness is my world.

CHORUS. Doer of dreadful deeds, how did you
dare
so far to do despite to your own eyes?
What spirit urged you to it?

50 **OEDIPUS.** It was Apollo, friends, Apollo,
that brought this bitter bitterness, my sorrows to
completion.
But the hand that struck me
was none but my own.
Why should I see
55 whose vision showed me nothing sweet to see?

CHORUS. These things are as you say.

OEDIPUS. What can I see to love?
What greeting can touch my ears with joy?
Take me away, and haste—to a place out of the
way!
60 Take me away, my friends, the greatly miserable,
the most accursed, whom God too hates
above all men on earth!

CHORUS. Unhappy in your mind and your
misfortune,
would I had never known you!

65 **OEDIPUS.** Curse on the man who took
the cruel bonds from off my legs, as I lay in the
field.
He stole me from death and saved me,
no kindly service.
Had I died then
I would not be so burdensome to friends.

70 **CHORUS.** I, too, could have wished it had been so.

OEDIPUS. Then I would not have come

to kill my father and marry my mother
infamously.[16]
Now I am godless and child of impurity,
begetter in the same seed that created my
wretched self.
1475 If there is any ill worse than ill,
that is the lot of Oedipus.

CHORUS. I cannot say your remedy was good;
you would be better dead than blind and living. **42**

OEDIPUS. What I have done here was best
1480 done—don't tell me

---

16. **infamously** (in′ fə məs lē) *adv.*: Scandalously;
disgracefully or dishonorably.

39 **Discussion** Have students discuss what Oedipus means when he says that Apollo was the curse, but he himself is the agent of his own blinding. Is he blaming Apollo? Is he suggesting that he is not a mere passive victim because he took it upon himself to put out his own eyes?

40 **Discussion** Does it seem reasonable to students that Oedipus feels he cannot bear to look on anything in the world outside himself any more?

41 **Literary Focus** What ironies are involved in Oedipus' curse on the man who saved him? Why is he disturbed that his friends pity him and feel pain for him?

42 **Discussion** Ask students if they agree with the chorus that Oedipus would be better dead. What might Oedipus' decision to go on living in blindness, exile, and suffering say about his heroic stature?

slow to build suspense, or fast to convey dramatic excitement. In the messenger's narration of Jocasta's death and Oedipus' self-inflicted blinding, the fast pace captures the hastiness and tragedy of Oedipus' irreversible actions.

One device used to heighten the drama of the narrative is the use of dashes. Notice how the messenger uses dashes to emphasize the most horrifying actions in the cursed event. Diction also intensifies the narrative. Oedipus paced "frantically around"; his bleeding eyeballs "gushed and stained his beard"; and "today groans and destruction and death and shame—of all ills can be named not one is missing."

As you reread the messenger's narration, think about how it accomplishes more than just relating the events in vivid and gory detail for the audience. Narrative can also comment on the event, as the messenger encapsulates the severity of Oedipus' actions and interprets the scene for the audience, who did not witness it for themselves.

Student Activity 1. Examine the messenger's narrative and evaluate its effectiveness in bringing the scene to life.

Student Activity 2. If you were seeing the play, would you prefer to see the actual events rather than having them narrated to you? Explain.

43 Clarification Focus students' attention on Oedipus' claim that his deeds deserve "worse punishment than hanging." Ask students to think about how he sees his own pollution in relation to Jocasta's. Point out that in ancient Greek society, the taboos against parricide and son-mother incest are much stronger than those against killing children, for instance.

44 Discussion What does Oedipus mean by saying "It is sweet to keep our thoughts out of the range of hurt"? Why would being deaf and blind, a "locked up carcass," keep one from suffering? Suggest that Oedipus' rejection of reality is the kind of rejection that characterizes some mental disorders.

45 Discussion Now that Oedipus is blind, where is his inner vision turned? What does the sequential, visual detail of "crossroads, and hidden glade, oak and the narrow way at the crossroads, that drank . . . blood" suggest about what he is reliving and "seeing"?

46 Clarification Exile and the death penalty are appropriate punishments for murder; from earliest antiquity, the Greeks had purification rituals in which they cast pollution, or the polluted objects that could localize and so remove pollution, into the sea.

47 Literary Focus Ask students to think about Creon's tone. His desire to hide Oedipus in the house, to enclose the "family scandal," is reminiscent of Jocasta. What does this correspondence imply?

otherwise, do not give me further counsel.
I do not know with what eyes I could look
upon my father when I die and go
under the earth, nor yet my wretched mother—
those two to whom I have done things deserving
worse punishment than hanging. Would the sight
of children, bred as mine are, gladden me?
No, not these eyes, never. And my city,
its towers and sacred places of the Gods,
of these I robbed my miserable self
when I commanded all to drive *him* out,
the criminal since proved by God impure
and of the race of Laius.

To this guilt I bore witness against myself—
with what eyes shall I look upon my people?
No. If there were a means to choke the fountain
of hearing I would not have stayed my hand
from locking up my miserable carcass,[17]
seeing and hearing nothing; it is sweet
to keep our thoughts out of the range of hurt.

Cithaeron, why did you receive me? why
having received me did you not kill me straight?
And so I had not shown to men my birth.

O Polybus and Corinth and the house,
the old house that I used to call my father's—
what fairness you were nurse to, and what foulness
festered beneath! Now I am found to be
a sinner and a son of sinners. Crossroads,
and hidden glade, oak and the narrow way
at the crossroads, that drank my father's blood
offered you by my hands, do you remember
still what I did as you looked on, and what
I did when I came here? O marriage, marriage!
you bred me and again when you had bred
bred children of your child and showed to men
brides, wives and mothers and the foulest deeds
that can be in this world of ours.

Come—it's unfit to say what is unfit
to do.—I beg of you in God's name hide me

somewhere outside your country, yes, or kill me,
or throw me into the sea, to be forever
out of your sight. Approach and deign to touch me
for all my wretchedness, and do not fear.
No man but I can bear my evil doom.

CHORUS. Here Creon comes in fit time to perform
or give advice in what you ask of us.
Creon is left sole ruler in your stead.

OEDIPUS. Creon! Creon! What shall I say to him?
How can I justly hope that he will trust me?
In what is past I have been proved towards him
an utter liar.

[*Enter* CREON.]

CREON.   Oedipus, I've come
not so that I might laugh at you nor taunt you
with evil of the past. But if you still
are without shame before the face of men
reverence at least the flame that gives all life,
our Lord the Sun, and do not show unveiled
to him pollution such that neither land
nor holy rain nor light of day can welcome.

[*To a servant.*]

Be quick and take him in. It is most decent
that only kin should see and hear the troubles
of kin.

OEDIPUS.   I beg you, since you've torn me from
my dreadful expectations and have come
in a most noble spirit to a man
that has used you vilely[18]—do a thing for me.
I shall speak for your own good, not for my own.

CREON. What do you need that you would ask of me?

OEDIPUS. Drive me from here with all the speed you can
to where I may not hear a human voice.

CREON. Be sure, I would have done this had not I
wished first of all to learn from the God the course
of action I should follow.

---

17. **carcass** (kär′ kəs) *n*.: Dead body of an animal; scornful, as used here for the human body.

18. **vilely** (vī′ lē) *adv*.: Wickedly.

Primary Source Note

In 442 B.C., about twenty years before he wrote *Oedipus the King*, Sophocles wrote *Antigone*, naming the play after Oedipus' daughter. Even then he was attracted to the same problem of humanity's great powers and ultimate limits, and he shows the same distrust of Protagoras' view that "man is the measure of all things." In one of the odes he explores human nature:

Many the wonders but nothing walks stranger than man.
This thing crosses the sea in the winter's storm,
making his path through the roaring waves.

And she, the greatest of gods, the earth—
ageless she is, and unwearied—he wears her away
as the ploughs go up and down from year to year
and his mules turn up the soil.

Language, and thought like the wind
and the feelings that make the town,
he has taught himself, and shelter against the cold,
refuge from rain. He can always help himself.
He faces no future helpless. There's only death

OEDIPUS. But his word
has been quite clear to let the parricide,[19]
the sinner, die.

CREON. Yes, that indeed was said.
But in the present need we had best discover
what we should do.

OEDIPUS. And will you ask about
a man so wretched?

CREON. Now even you will trust
the God.

OEDIPUS. So. I command you—and will
beseech you—
to her that lies inside that house give burial
as you would have it; she is yours and rightly
you will perform the rites for her. For me—
never let this my father's city have me
living a dweller in it. Leave me live
in the mountains where Cithaeron is, that's
called
my mountain, which my mother and my father
while they were living would have made my
tomb.
So I may die by their decree who sought
indeed to kill me. Yet I know this much:
no sickness and no other thing will kill me.
I would not have been saved from death if not
for some strange evil fate. Well, let my fate
go where it will.
Creon, you need not care
about my sons; they're men and so wherever
they are, they will not lack a livelihood.
But my two girls—so sad and pitiful—
whose table never stood apart from mine,
and everything I touched they always shared—
O Creon, have a thought for them! And most
I wish that you might suffer me to touch them
and sorrow with them.

[*Enter* ANTIGONE *and* ISMENE, OEDIPUS' *two
daughters.*]

O my lord! O true noble Creon! Can I
really be touching them, as when I saw?
What shall I say?
Yes, I can hear them sobbing—my two darlings!

1585 and Creon has had pity and has sent me
what I loved most?
Am I right?

CREON. You're right: it was I gave you this
because I knew from old days how you loved
them
as I see now.

OEDIPUS. God bless you for it,
1590 Creon,
and may God guard you better on your road
than he did me!
O children,
where are you? Come here, come to my hands,
a brother's hands which turned your father's eyes,
those bright eyes you knew once, to what you
1595 see,
a father seeing nothing, knowing nothing,
begetting you from his own source of life.
I weep for you—I cannot see your faces—
I weep when I think of the bitterness
1600 there will be in your lives, how you must live
before the world. At what assemblages
of citizens will you make one? To what
gay company will you go and not come home
in tears instead of sharing in the holiday?
And when you're ripe for marriage, who will
1605 he be,
the man who'll risk to take such infamy
as shall cling to my children, to bring hurt
on them and those that marry with them? What
curse is not there? "Your father killed his father
and sowed the seed where he had sprung
1610 himself
and begot you out of the womb that held him."
These insults you will hear. Then who will marry
you?
No one, my children; clearly you are doomed
to waste away in barrenness unmarried.
Son of Menoeceus,[20] since you are all the
1615 father
left these two girls, and we, their parents, both
are dead to them—do not allow them wander
like beggars, poor and husbandless.
They are of your own blood.

52

---
19. **parricide** (par′ ə sīd) *n*.: Murderer of one's father.

20. **Son of Menoeceus** (men oi′ kəs): Creon.

48 Discussion Ask students to contrast their feelings toward Oedipus and Creon. Oedipus is very emotional, and the chorus—even the messenger—have shown that they empathize. Does Creon's punctilious coolness and even impatience surprise us?

49 Literary Focus Ask students to consider why Oedipus emends "command" to "beseech." What does his choice of words reveal about his ingrained habits and his new sense of himself?

50 Discussion Ask students how Oedipus' vision at this point recalls the chorus's initial vision of the unknown murderer, living like an animal in a forest or mountain cavern.

51 Clarification Oedipus is reeling from shock, and his words up to this point reveal the way in which his mind darts about in horror from one thought to another, always circling back to the horrible realization of his monstrous pollution. He now begins to sound more calm and rational. Why does Sophocles choose this moment to have him talk about having been saved from death for a strange fate, and thus not being destined to be killed by a human being? What does "let my fate go where it will" suggest about the way he views the gods, his role on earth, and the future?

52 Discussion How are we affected by Oedipus' love for his children? If students have read the *Iliad*, they might compare parts of Oedipus' speech to his daughters with what Andromache and Hektor say when they look ahead to their son's life as an orphan. How is Oedipus' speech like a funeral lament?

that he cannot find an escape from. He has contrived
refuge from illnesses once beyond all cure.

Clever beyond all dreams
the inventive craft that he has
which may drive him one time or another to well or ill.
When he honors the laws of the land and the gods' sworn right
high indeed is his city; but stateless the man
who dares to dwell with dishonor . . .

1620　And do not make them equal with myself
　　　in wretchedness; for you can see them now
　　　so young, so utterly alone, save for you only.
　　　Touch my hand, noble Creon, and say yes.
　　　If you were older, children, and were wiser,
1625　there's much advice I'd give you. But as it is,
　　　let this be what you pray: give me a life
　　　wherever there is opportunity
　　　to live, and better life than was my father's.

CREON.　Your tears have had enough of scope; now
1630　　go within the house.

OEDIPUS.　I must obey, though bitter of heart.

CREON.　In season, all is good.

OEDIPUS.　Do you know on what conditions I
　　　obey?

CREON.　　　　　You tell me them,
1635　and I shall know them when I hear.

OEDIPUS.　　　　That you shall send me
　　　out
　　　to live away from Thebes.

CREON.　　　　That gift you must ask of
　　　the God.

OEDIPUS.　But I'm now hated by the Gods.

CREON.　　　　　So quickly you'll obtain
1640　your prayer.

OEDIPUS.　You consent then?

CREON.　　　　　What I do not mean, I do
　　　not use to say.

OEDIPUS.　Now lead me away from here.

CREON.　　　　　Let go the children, then,
　　　and come.

1645 OEDIPUS.　Do not take them from me.

CREON.　Do not seek to be master in everything,
　　　for the things you mastered did not follow you
　　　throughout your life.

　　　　　　[*As* CREON *and* OEDIPUS *go out.*]

CHORUS.　You that live in my ancestral Thebes,
　　　behold this Oedipus,—
　　　him who knew the famous riddles and was a
　　　　man most masterful;
　　　not a citizen who did not look with envy on his
1650　　lot—
　　　see him now and see the breakers of misfortune
　　　　swallow him!
　　　Look upon that last day always. Count no
　　　　mortal happy till
　　　he has passed the final limit of his life secure
　　　　from pain.

Reader's Response *Do you sympathize with Oedipus? What makes you sympathize with him, or what makes you blame him?*

THINKING ABOUT THE SELECTION

Interpreting

1. What do you think Oedipus means by calling himself "a child of fortune"?
2. Interpret the Chorus' remark: "Time who sees all has found you out against your will."
3. What is significant about Oedipus' blinding himself, especially with Jocasta's brooches?
4. In lines 1450–1453, Oedipus says that Apollo brought his bitterness to completion, but the hand that struck him was his own. What does his statement reveal about him at this point in the play?
5. Why does Oedipus insist that he is better off blind and living than dead?
6. Throughout the play, Oedipus tries desperately to avoid his fate, and at the same time, learn his identity. How are his two goals inextricably connected?
7. How does Oedipus' accepting of his fate ennoble him?
8. Creon says to Oedipus: "Do not seek to be master in everything, for the things you mastered did not follow you throughout your life." Support Creon's claim with evidence from the play.
9. Explain the wisdom of the famous lines that end this play: "Count no / mortal happy till / he has passed the final limit of his life secure / from pain."

Applying

10. Accident or chance figures prominently in the Oedipus story. Can you think of contemporary situations in which chance plays a major role?

ANALYZING LITERATURE

Analyzing Dramatic Irony

Oedipus the King is famous for its **dramatic irony,** the contradiction in what the character thinks and what the audience knows to be true. Throughout the play, Oedipus is continually making statements that carry meaning, and sometimes double meaning, perceptible to the audience but not to him. Sophocles' use of dramatic irony is especially effective in building suspense in his play, since the audience knows the story and its outcome. Dramatic irony also reinforces that aspect of Oedipus' character that refuses to open its eyes and ears to the external world, which has the answers he so desperately seeks.

1. Analyze the scene in which the messenger informs Jocasta and Oedipus that "Oedipus' father" is dead. Discuss the scene in terms of dramatic irony.
2. Locate another example of dramatic irony and analyze it for its significance in the play.

CRITICAL THINKING AND READING

Understanding Causality

Causality is a crucial element of Greek tragedy. The series of events that comprise the tragic plot must have a causal relationship so that the actions build on one another to create feelings of both mounting suspense and inevitability. By solving the riddle of the Sphinx, Oedipus relieves Thebes of the terrible monster, but eventually, as their king, he is the cause of a more destructive plague. Similarly, the character's relationship to the action is the causal, inevitable result of the character's personality. As the play unfolds, we see how each action Oedipus takes, how each choice he makes shapes the next one. Ultimately, every choice he makes is the only one his character, or personality, will allow.

1. Find two causally related events and discuss their significance to the plot.
2. Determine how, by the end of the play, Oedipus has become the answer to the Sphinx's riddle.

THINKING AND WRITING

Writing About Justice

One of the predominant themes in *Oedipus the King* is the justice of the universe. In Greek, justice is *díkê*. Díkê in Homer's world meant getting one's fair portion. To Sophocles, *díkê* signified trial, judgment, and penalty. Write an essay in which you show how Oedipus is on trial in the play. Define the charges against him and describe his defense. In your conclusion determine whether justice has been achieved. When you revise make sure you have quoted lines from the play to support your assertions. Proofread your paper for spelling and punctuation and share it with your classmates.

(continued from bottom of page)

may marry his mother. When Jocasta reminds him that Polybus' death should comfort him, he replies that he fears the living, which he should, since Jocasta is indeed alive and is his mother as well as his wife.

2. Oedipus' referring to himself as coming from the womb of beneficent fortune is an example of dramatic irony because the audience knows that the womb from which he sprang is actually Jocasta's.

ANSWERS TO CRITICAL THINKING AND READING

1. The shepherd gives the abandoned infant Oedipus to a messenger, who gives the baby to Polybus and Merope. Oedipus runs away from Polybus and Merope to avoid fulfilling the prophecy that he would kill his father and marry his mother; in avoiding that very prophecy, he fulfills it. Another example of causally related events is the fact that by solving the riddle of the sphinx, Oedipus becomes king of Thebes and pollutes the city with his presence as murderer of its former king.

2. Oedipus has acted out a human's life span, depicted in the answer to the riddle.

THINKING AND WRITING

Publishing Student Writing Students will benefit from hearing one another's interpretations of justice in the play. Ask for volunteers to share their essays.

Challenge Students who were intrigued by *Oedipus the King* should read *Oedipus at Colonus.*

citizens.

6. His identity as Laius' and Jocasta's son is his fate, as it was decreed that he would kill his father and marry his mother.

7. As a true tragic hero, he accepts his destiny rather than run away from it through death.

8. Answers will vary. Students should explain that Oedipus tried to be in control of his destiny by eluding the or-

acle; he tried to be in control of Thebes by answering the riddle; but despite his efforts to maintain control, he could not avoid his destiny and suffered a tragic fall.

9. Suffering is part of life, and no one can be completely happy, that is, without pain, except in death.

10. Answers will differ. Students may suggest natural disasters or political elections.

ANSWERS TO ANALYZING LITERATURE

1. Since Oedipus and Jocasta think Polybus is Oedipus' father, they are greatly relieved when they hear that he died, and not by Oedipus' hand. The audience, however, knows that Polybus is not Oedipus' father. Furthermore, Oedipus still fears that he

Presentation

Motivation/Prior Knowledge Tell students that they will be reading excerpts from Aristotle's *Poetics*, one of the most important guides to the critical reading of Greek tragedy. All students of *Oedipus the King* should be familiar with Aristotle's *Poetics*, specifically, with his definition of tragedy.

Clarification Expand on Aristotle's definition of tragedy with his discussion of plot and character: "For tragedy is not an imitation of men but of actions and of life. It is in action that happiness and unhappiness are found, and the end we aim at is a kind of activity, not a quality; in accordance with their characters men are of such and such a quality, in accordance with their actions they are fortunate or the reverse. Consequently, it is not for the purpose of presenting their characters that the agents engage in action, but rather it is for the sake of their actions that they take on the characters they have. Thus, what happens—that is, the plot—is the end for which a tragedy exists, and the end or purpose is the most important thing of all."

Aristotle (ar′ is tät′ ′l) was a celebrated scientist-philosopher whose ideas constitute a large part of our intellectual and cultural history. His *Poetics* is considered the first example of literary criticism in Western literature. The *Poetics* gained prestige in the sixteenth century during the Renaissance. Since then, it has been one of the most important guides to the critical reading of drama, especially Greek tragedy.

The *Poetics* is not about poetry, but about the art of poetry, based on a scientific understanding of art. Using a scientific approach, Aristotle methodically defines tragedy as ". . . an imitation of an action that is serious, complete, and possessing magnitude; in embellished language, each kind of which is used separately in the different parts; in the mode of action and not narrated; and effecting through pity and fear the catharsis of such emotions."

The "imitation of an action" is plot, the combination and organization of events. Imitation is the key word in the first part of Aristotle's definition. Actors, however engaging and believable, are at all times imitating life. Watching someone imitate a tragic action, such as Oedipus blinding himself, is horrifying and disturbing, but at the same time, it is tolerable because it is an imitation rather than an actual, irreversible action.

Aristotle considers plot the most important element of tragedy. An effective dramatist constructs the actions of plot completely and in an orderly way, leading to a specific end. Once achieved, that ending reveals the universal truth the playwright wishes to convey.

I have posited that tragedy is an imitation of an action that is a whole and complete in itself and of a certain magnitude—for a thing may be a whole, and yet have no magnitude to speak of. Now a thing is a whole if it has a beginning, a middle, and an end. A beginning is that which does not come necessarily after something else, but after which it is natural for another thing to exist or come to be. An end, on the contrary, is that which naturally comes after something else, either as its necessary sequel or as its usual [and hence probable] sequel, but itself has nothing after it. A middle is that which both comes after something else and has another thing following it. A well-constructed plot, therefore, will neither begin at some chance point nor end at some chance point . . . the events which are the parts of the plot must be so organized that if any one of them is displaced or taken away, the whole will be shaken and put out of joint . . .

Oedipus the King would suffer such disjointedness if one of its parts were to be removed.

Aristotle also comments on the nature of tragedy. What makes a subject tragic? Tragic subjects are not freak accidents that arouse sympathy in the audience. Rather, tragedy involves a causal, inevitable sequence of events connected intimately with the personality of the tragic character. Aristotle explains:

Primary Source Note

In the introduction to his translation of the *Poetics*, James Hutton gives the following biography of Aristotle:

Aristotle had entered Plato's Academy in 367 B.C. when he was seventeen, the age at which, according to a comic poet of the period, young men made their choice between the horses and philosophers. He was born at Stagira in northern Greece; his father, Nicomachus, who died in Aristotle's boyhood, had been the physician and friend of King Amyntas II of Macedonia, the father of Philip and grandfather of Alexan- der. Consciousness of belonging to a medical family may have influenced Aristotle's ways of thought; the Macedonian connection certainly played a role in his personal fortunes. The rise and triumph of Macedonian power was the overshadowing historical fact of his time. He remained a member of the Academy for twenty years, until he was thirty-seven, and no doubt in this time advanced his thinking in its characteristic directions; most of his philosophical dialogues were probably published in this period . . . He formed a school of his own outside [Athens'] city walls in a grove sacred to Apollo Lycaeus and the Muses, whence the school was later known as the Lyceum . . . The next years

NSIGHTS

And it is not only an action complete in itself that tragedy represents; it also represents incidents involving pity and fear, and such incidents are most effective when they come unexpectedly and yet occur in a causal sequence in which one thing leads to another. For occurring in this way, they will have more of the marvelous about them than if they came to pass of themselves and by accident.

Aristotle's ideas on what makes a tragic plot tragic have shed light on the way critics interpret Oedipus as a tragic character. Like his definition of plot, Aristotle's definition of character, particularly a tragic character, is one we maintain today.

First and foremost is that the characters be good. The personages will have character if, as aforesaid, they reveal in speech or in action what their moral choices are, and a good character will be one whose choices are good . . . In the characters and plot construction alike, one must strive for that which is either necessary or probable, so that whatever a character of any kind says or does may be the sort of thing such a character will inevitably or probably say or do and the events of the plot may follow one after another either inevitably or with probability.

Another quality of tragedy closely connected with Aristotle's definition of plot is the arousal of pity and fear in the audience. "For the plot should be so constructed that even without seeing the play, anyone who merely hears the events unfold will shudder and feel pity as a result of what is happening—which is precisely what one would experience in listening to the plot of Oedipus."

In Aristotle's definition, pity and fear in

tragedy effect what he calls the "catharsis of such emotions." Aristotle's terminology in this part of the definition is the subject of debate. What did he mean by catharsis? It is generally accepted that the catharsis of such emotions means the purgation, in the medical sense of exciting emotions to allay them and, thus, rid the spectator of them.

Pity and fear are also evoked through recognition and reversal, as in *Oedipus the King*. Aristotle defines recognition and reversal in terms of Sophocles' play.

Reversal is . . . a change from one state of affairs to its exact opposite, and this . . . should be in conformance with probability or necessity. For example, in *Oedipus* the messenger comes to cheer Oedipus by relieving him of fear with regard to his mother, but by revealing his true identity, does just the opposite of this . . . Recognition, as the word itself indicates, is a change from ignorance to knowledge, leading either to friendship or to hostility on the part of those persons who are marked for good fortune or bad. The best form of recognition is that which is accompanied by a reversal, as in the example from *Oedipus* . . . A recognition joined thus with a reversal will be fraught with pity or with fear (the type of action tragedy is presumed to imitate) because misery and happiness alike will come to be realized in recognitions of this kind.

Recognition and reversal involve the tragic character recognizing his or her role in the reversal of fortune, or "tragic fall." Oedipus' tragic fall has been attributed to what the Greeks call *hamartia*. Hamartia is often mistranslated as tragic flaw, but it actually means an "error in judgment" or "missing the mark," which is precisely what Oedipus does.

Clarification Students have read that the tragic hero suffers a tragic fall through character. The hero makes choices that are consistent with his or her character, and these choices cause the hero to fall tragically. Therefore, tragic heroes always cause their own suffering. Clarify this concept for students with Aristotle's discussion of causality: "In the characters and the plot construction alike, one must strive for that which is either necessary or probable, so that whatever a character of any kind says or does may be the sort of thing such a character will inevitably or probably say or do and the events of the plot may follow one after another either inevitably or with probability. (Obviously, then, the denouement of the plot should arise from the plot itself and not be brought about 'from the machine,' as it is on Medea and in the embarkation scene in the *Iliad*. The machine is to be used for matters lying outside the drama, either antecedents of the action which a human being cannot know, or things subsequent to the action that have to be prophesied and announced; for we accept it that the gods see everything. Within the events of the plot itself, however, there should be nothing unreasonable, or if there is, it should be kept outside the play proper, as is done in the *Oedipus* of Sophocles.)"

were no doubt occupied with teaching and research. His surviving works give us a good idea of the broad range of his lectures. The collection of the constitutions of 158 cities, perhaps begun earlier, was probably now completed. With his relative the historian Callisthenes, he extracted from the archives of Delphi a list of the victors in the Pythian games, and he compiled similar lists of the victors at Olympia, and from the Athenian archives extracted the records of the dramatic contests. He is also said to have collected the first great library of antiquity. In 323, however, the news of Alexander's death in Babylon set off a new wave of anti-Macedonian fervor in Athens. A baseless charge of impiety was

brought against Aristotle, and he withdrew to his property at Calchis in Euboea, a Macedonian stronghold, reportedly saying that the Athenians must not be permitted "to sin twice against philosophy." Here in the next year he died from a chronic ailment at the age of sixty-two.

The Hero

> "Furthermore, we have not even to risk the adventure alone, for the heroes of all time have gone before us. The labyrinth is thoroughly known. We have only to follow the thread of the hero path, and where we had thought to find an abomination, we shall find a god. And where we had thought to slay another, we shall slay ourselves. Where we had thought to travel outward, we will come to the center of our own existence. And where we had thought to be alone, we will be with all the world."
>
> —Joseph Campbell

The heroic code of ancient Greece demands excellence—being the best in any given situation. First, a hero's reputation as the best requires exploits through which he has earned the respect and admiration of his comrades. They bestow him with merit, the mark of a true hero in ancient Greece, where what the world thinks of the individual takes precedence over what the individual thinks of himself. Therefore, he must earn merit by achieving fame and honor through killing or being killed in battle.

Epic heroes have common characteristics. Traditionally, they have bravery, superhuman strength, success in battle, courage in confronting death, and the desire to win glory and fame. Almost all heroes are of high birth or semi-divine ancestry, which makes them highly influential characters. And all are engaged in a long and dangerous quest journey in which they must overcome obstacles and suffer hardships to reach their goals.

Epic heroes become especially interesting when they depart from the heroic code as Achilleus does in the *Iliad*.

> But that other still sat in anger beside his swift ships, / Peleus' son divinely born, Achilleus of the swift feet. Never now would he go to assemblies where men win glory, / never more into battle, but continued to waste his heart out / sitting there, though he longed always for the clamor and fighting.

Achilleus is not the first example of an epic hero. The Prologue of the Sumerian *Epic of Gilgamesh* introduces us to Gilgamesh, who also embodies the qualities of a hero: He possesses superhuman knowledge, he is engaged in a quest journey, and he immortalizes himself not only through his deeds but by giving those deeds permanence by engraving them in stone.

> I will proclaim to the world the deeds of Gilgamesh. This was the man to whom all things were known; this was the king who knew the countries of the world. He was wise, he saw mysteries and knew secret things, he brought us a tale of the days before the flood. He went on a long journey, was weary, wornout with labor, returning he rested, he engraved on a stone the whole story.

The central theme of the *Epic of Gilgamesh* is the search for immortality, which is of utmost importance to epic heroes.

SUGGESTED READINGS

from *The Epic of Gilgamesh*, "The Battle with Humbaba," page 16
I Samuel 17, page 61
Virgil, from the *Aeneid*, Book II, page 493

from *The Nibelungenlied*, "How Siegfried Was Slain," page 592
Pär Lagerkvist, "The Princess and All the Kingdom," page 1078

Presentation

Motivation/Prior Knowledge Ask students to discuss the heroes about which they have read. What made Achilleus a hero? Do they consider Socrates a hero? What are Oedipus' heroic characteristics? Although the heroic code of ancient Greece is not necessarily applicable to all cultures, the heroes of world literature through the ages seem to echo one another's qualities.

Enrichment In the next unit, students will be reading about the Roman epic hero, Aeneas. Aeneas of Virgil's *Aeneid* is engaged in a quest to found Rome. His devotion to fulfilling the commands of the gods that he establish a home for the Trojans in Italy conflicts with his personal desires, particularly with regard to Queen Dido. When Aeneas' passion for Dido seems to be interfering with his mission, Jove sends Mercury to him saying:

. . . No son like this did his enchanting mother / Promise to us . . . He was to be the ruler of Italy, / Potential empire, armorer of war; / To father men from Teucer's noble blood / And bring the whole world under law's dominion. / If glories to be won by deeds like these / Cannot arouse him, if he will not strive / For his own honor, does he begrudge his son, / Ascanius, the high strongholds of Rome? / What has he in mind? What hope, to make him stay / Amid a hostile race, and lose from view / Ausonian progeny, Lavinian lands. / The man should sail: that is the whole point.

Because of his serious devotion to duty, Aeneas is often called the prototype of the ideal Roman ruler. His heroic qualities reflect the Roman ideals that characterized the ordered Roman government for two centuries.

CROSS CURRENTS

Nikos Kazantzakis

Nikos Kazantzakis (kä´ zän dzä´ kēs´) lived by the motto "Reach what is beyond your grasp," a command in keeping with the terrifyingly exacting standards of his father and grandfather, Cretan freedom fighters. Kazantzakis saw himself as a freedom fighter too, using the pen rather than the sword as his weapon, fighting for freedom not from the Turks who occupied Crete when he was a boy but from ignorance, malice, fear, and laziness. His forefathers had taken part in armed struggle against oppressive conquerors; he, in turn, viewed life as a struggle, and the human soul as a battlefield on which opposing forces like good and evil confront each other. He believed that life on earth is necessary and good. His view of the world and people's role in it was certainly fully formed when he began working on his most monumental work in 1925, a modern sequel to Homer's *Odyssey*, which he entitled simply *The Odyssey* (only the English translation subtitles the poem "A Modern Sequel").

Odysseus is the greatest of Kazantzakis' "grandfathers," as he says. The other two spiritual grandfathers he claims are Digenis (di´ jə nis) Akritas (ə krē´ təs), and El Greco. The first is a hero of medieval Greek epic, a courageous border guard whose birth brought together two races. The second is the Cretan painter Kyriakos (kē´ rē ä´ kōs) or Domenico Theotokopoulos (thē ō tō kō´ pə lōs) (c. 1548–1625), nicknamed El Greco (or "the Greek") in Spain, where he became famous. These "ancestors" on whom Kazantzakis models himself all explore new frontiers, living on the cutting edge of history and human progress. Odysseus especially appealed to Kazantzakis because he was a masterful

ANTHONY QUINN AS ZORBA THE GREEK

spinner of tales, a hero who prevailed by his quick intelligence rather than by his brawn. Like Odysseus, who roamed the world in search not only of his island kingdom but of his true identity, Kazantzakis traveled all over the world, never forgetting his own true quest, to liberate the soul and the divinity within himself.

Like the ancient historian Herodotus, Kazantzakis saw a pattern in the rise and fall of civilizations. Cultures grow powerful because people are trying to overcome obstacles. But with security, laziness sets in, and new cultures, still striving to get ahead, seize power. His view is essentially optimistic: Even when it looks as if barbarians are destroying a more sophisticated civilization, Kazantzakis sees the need for change in a positive light. Like Goethe's *Faust*, Kazantzakis' *Odysseus* abhors stagnation; he values striving above all, embracing life in all its manifestations.

Kazantzakis published tirelessly: journals, articles, children's books, translations (including verse translations of both Homeric epics), and plays. The most popular, and in many ways the most appealing, works he wrote were novels. One, *Zorba the Greek*, was made into a movie starring Anthony Quinn that captured the imagination of viewers all over the world.

Like Socrates, Kazantzakis wanted to be a gadfly, to goad the mentally sluggish into activity. Some heroes bring about change with the sword, but Kazantzakis believed that the more lasting victories are won by the pen.

Presentation

Motivation/Prior Knowledge Ask students what they think it means to reflect. Some people are characterized as reflective. Many writers write reflective novels and poems. What makes these people and their works reflective? Lead students to realize that whenever they think seriously about an experience and draw conclusions about it, they are reflecting. Ask students to think about some of the long passages in the *Iliad* in which Achilleus reflected on his dilemma. Long narrative speeches in the *Iliad* are also reflective of past experiences and what these experiences proved. Students should also recall their knowledge of *Pericles' Funeral Oration* and Plato's *Apology*, which also have elements of reflection. Have students discuss what was being reflected in these works. You might want to come back to the discussion once students have studied the characteristics of a reflective essay. Then have students think about outstanding features of their lives that would make good topics for reflective essays.

Teaching Tenth-Grade Students Tenth-grade students might share ideas for their own papers. Ask students to talk about possible topics from their lives. Hearing one another's ideas might be a good anchor for tenth-grade students as they approach the assignment.

The Reflective Essay

Writing a Reflective Essay

In a very real sense, the writer writes in order to teach himself, to understand himself, to satisfy himself . . . ."
—Alfred Kazin

To reflect, to ponder, to muse—what do these words mean? They mean to think about, to play with ideas, to turn over in your mind. A good reflective essay expresses thoughts about life. When you write a reflective essay, you use the experiences of your own life to reach conclusions about life in general. In other words you play with your thoughts on events in your own life to get the big picture. Such exploration leads to understanding of both yourself and your place in the world.

Characteristics of a Reflective Essay

- emotional openness
- intimacy
- natural style
- analytical reasoning
- thoughtfulness

Several of Sappho's lyrics indicate that she reflected on the timeless nature of her work "Although they are / Only breath, words / which I command / are immortal," she wrote. "But I claim there will be some who remember us when we are gone." Having reflected, she knew she would live on through her poetry. People live after their deaths in many ways. They continue to exist in the memories of loved ones, through the fruitful consequences of their deeds, in the children they engender, and in the art they create.

Writing Assignment

In a reflective essay, write about some aspect of your life you hope others will remember you by. Center your essay on one event used as an example of the characteristic or deed you hope will stand out. Finish the essay with an explanation of why you hope this aspect of yourself will be remembered and how it can affect the world.

Prewrite

You will need to gather information from your past to help you choose a topic. If you have a favorite method of recalling your past, feel free to use it, but here is a new idea you might try.

Fold a blank piece of paper in thirds, like a business letter; then fold it in half lengthwise. Open it out and you will have a page divided into six sections.

Now sit quietly and reflect on your life from birth to age ten. Recall the best events during that time, focusing on two or three. Choose the best event of your life from that time and in the top left section of your paper draw something simple to represent it.

Now move forward in time, reflecting on your life between ten years old and the present. Again, select several significant events and choose the most meaningful. Represent it in a simple drawing in the top right section of your page.

Once again reflect on your life, considering only the past year this time. Select your best success or greatest achievement and draw its symbol in the center left section of your page.

In the center right section represent in a simple drawing the happiest moment of an average day. Now move your thoughts forward and answer this hypothetical question: If you had only one year to live and were guaranteed success in whatever you tried to do, what would you attempt? Draw something to symbolize your answer in the lower left section.

Finally, answer another question. What three words would you most like people to say of you? Write those words in the remaining section of the page. You now have a page filled with representations of good times, successes, and hopes. Look them over and see what they have in common. The common thread could be the topic for your paper. Choose one of the incidents represented in the top four sections and center your essay around it.

Now think about the event you have chosen and answer the following questions.

- **What exactly do I want people to remember about me?**
- **What part of the event best shows that?**
- **Why is this legacy important to me?**
- **What can it give the world?**

Write

Using your page of drawings and list of answers for information, write your essay. Be sure you give a general statement about your topic as a point of departure. Describe the incident you have chosen, emphasizing the parts that best illustrate your uniqueness. Conclude by explaining why you want this aspect of your life to be remembered and how it will affect the world.

Remember, your material is personal, and you may have difficulty maintaining a distance from it. Try imagining the event as if it happened to someone else. Notice the difference between your feelings when it happened and what you feel about it now.

Collaborate

Ask someone who knows the assignment to read your draft and answer these questions about it.

- **Is the aspect of the writer's uniqueness clear?**
- **Is it clear why the writer treasures it?**
- **Can you see the link between the event described and how the writer wants to be remembered?**

Revise

Using the information you received from your partner, rewrite your paper. Be specific rather than general. Try to choose words and phrases that will make your reader feel as well as think.

A good paper will also give particular attention to narrative voice. It should be warm and personal, yet mature.

Publish

Before you hand in your work, give it to someone who knows you very well. Ask that person to read the piece and to say whether it is characteristic of you. Answer whatever questions arise from your reader's comments.

Evaluate

Has writing this essay changed your view of life in any way? Consider what you have learned about yourself from this assignment and perhaps keep it to ponder in the future.

Fine art, *Aeneas at Delos* by Claude Lorrain. This work is by Claude Gelée (1600–1682) of Lorraine, now called Claude Lorrain and in England known simply as Claude. He was one of the great French Classical painters. At age thirteen he ran away to Rome and became apprenticed to a decorative painter. In time he became the most exclusive classical landscape painter of his day.

Aeneas at Delos is one of many paintings Lorrain did on themes from the *Aeneid*. It fully expresses his love for ancient things. As in all of his work, the human figure is subordinate to the vast and airy expanse of landscape. The horizon, swathed in misty blue, draws the viewer's eye toward infinity. The cool, shimmering light that permeates the painting creates a dreamlike atmosphere of beauty.

You might want to use the following questions to discuss the art:
1. How does looking at this scene make you feel?
2. How would you evaluate the artist's use of color?
3. What impression is created by having the tree placed so prominently in the center?
4. Do your own fantasies of exotic places like Delos have counterparts in this illustration?

AENEAS AT DELOS
Claude Lorrain
National Gallery, London

Objectives
1 To understand the historic setting
2 To trace the birth and death of the empire
3 To develop an understanding of Roman religion
4 To see the influence of Greek thought on Rome
5 To become acquainted with genres used by Roman authors

ROMAN LITERATURE

c. 300 B.C.–A.D. 500

Aeneas said:
                    "Your ghost,
Your sad ghost, father, often before my mind,
Impelled me to the threshold of this place.
My ships ride anchored in the Tuscan sea.
But let me have your hand, let me embrace you,
Do not draw back."
                    At this his tears brimmed
   over
And down his cheeks. And there he tried three
   times
To throw his arms around his father's neck,
Three times the shade untouched slipped through
   his hands,
Weightless as wind and fugitive as dream.

—Virgil

Focus
The words spoken here attempt to define the important relationship that Romans had with their parents. Virgil has his main character Aeneas, the mythic founder of Rome, encounter the shade of his deceased father in the underworld. His previously unemotional attitude gives special significance to the passage and underscores the high regard in which Romans held their parents.

Writing/Prior Knowledge Before starting the unit, have students briefly discuss what they already know about Rome. Let them freewrite about the way Romans entertained themselves or about the way the Romans left a lasting impression on later Western civilization.

ESL Teaching Strategy Locate Rome on a map for all students. Tell students that Rome gave its language—Latin—to the world. Ask students whether their native language is a Romance language—a language based on Latin. Examples of Romance languages are Spanish, French, and Italian. Show how *mea domina* ("my lady" in Latin) becomes *madame* in French, *doña* in Spanish, and *donna* in Italian. Even English is influenced by Latin. Here the word becomes *madam*. You might also point out how *madonna* translates into "my lady."

Teaching Tenth-Grade Students Many of your tenth-grade students will be studying French, Spanish, or Latin. Ask them to discuss what they have learned about ancient Rome in their foreign language class. Write these details on the chalkboard.

Presentation

Motivation/ Prior Knowledge
Many movies and historical novels are set in ancient Rome. In fact, your students may know more about ancient Rome than they think they do. Have students list the associations that they make with Rome. List the words on the chalkboard. Allow time for a dozen or more ideas to be collected. Briefly evaluate each concept.

Purpose-Setting Question Is it fair to say that no other group from antiquity had a greater influence on Europe than the Romans? Why or why not?

1 Discussion Have students discuss how other countries followed Rome's pattern as they rose to dominance as world powers.

2 Enrichment Tell students that part of Hannibal's success stemmed from his unexpected use of elephants as beasts of burden during his foreign campaign against Rome.

Much of the Roman spirit is captured in its essence by the passage on the preceding page. The speaker, Aeneas, is the legendary founder of the Roman people and he has traveled far and wide in his efforts to satisfy the requirements of his singular destiny. He has finally arrived in the section of the underworld set aside for the honorable and has come here as much to learn of his future as to pay tribute to his deceased father. At this pivotal point in the most widely acclaimed work of Latin literature, he shows an emotional dimension that is as welcome as it is uncharacteristic of what the stereotypical Roman has come to be for readers in the twentieth century.

Rome's history is both long and complex. Its range and diversity are best understood through the history of her people and the stages of change that led Romans from kingdom to republic to empire, as well as through the place of religion in the Roman world view and the influence of Greek thinking on the formation of the Roman way of life. This will focus on a literature that has a richness and a depth that are at least as impressive—even if it is not as original or as ambitious—as that of other cultures.

EARLIEST HISTORY

Until Rome emerged as a significant power in the fourth century B.C., Italy was dominated by two powerful non-Italian peoples. To the north, the Etruscans held sway; to the south, Greek cities dominated. Both these cultures, with their maritime empires, enjoyed a level of civilization Rome would not achieve for many centuries. Nevertheless, a distinct culture was emerging in Latium, one that would eventually be known as "Roman."

Rise of Rome

Because the soil was difficult to farm, the Latins learned to value hard work. Surrounded by Etruscan and Greek powers, early Latin settlements unified into towns that joined in self-defense; the strongest city in this group was Rome. Tradition assigns Rome's founding to 753 B.C. and that of the republic to 508 B.C. In the early period, Rome was ruled by kings, advised by a council of elders. Offices were held by members of the ruling class, the patricians. Rome learned a great deal from the Etruscans. The constitution framed in the late sixth century B.C. owed much to them. Some of the early kings were Etruscan by birth.

Rome's rise to power was fueled by the fear of invasion. Rome first headed a defensive Latin League, then subjugated her allies. By 275 B.C. Rome had defeated all other Italian groups, as well as the Gauls and the Etruscans. African and Asian countries recognized Rome as a world power.

The Punic Wars

Secure at home, Rome began to have problems abroad. Carthage had ruled the seas to the south and saw the need to fight for control of Sicily. The first of three Punic wars lasted for over twenty years (264–241 B.C.). Rome won, and to this period belongs the first flowering of Roman literature and the arts.

Despite its defeat, Carthage did not give up its desire to dominate the area. In 217 B.C. the Carthaginian general Hannibal crossed the Alps from Spain into Italy. The Romans were defeated at first, but adversity led to stubborn resistance. Hannibal, fighting on alien soil, was eventually exhausted, and Carthage was again defeated in 201 B.C.

Rome's second victory over Carthage marks a turning point in Roman foreign policy. Waging aggressive rather than defensive wars, Rome fought successfully against Macedon and against what is now Spain and Portugal. The Roman senate sanc-

ARCH OF CONSTANTINE, ROME

Humanities Note

Triumphal arch, *The Arch of Constantine in Rome*; photo by A. J. Hartman. Triumphal arches are typical Roman monuments built to commemorate the achievements of Roman emperors and generals. They are covered in relief sculpture that chronicled events that led to victories.

The Arch of Constantine is the last of the great triumphal arches built in Rome (c. A.D. 315). While it is a handsome structure with a white marble facade enhanced by yellow marble columns, the relief panels and medallions that decorate it are not entirely original. Many are taken from other public monuments around Rome with features of the other emperors reworked to resemble Constantine. The relief work that is original is in a different, more rigid style that does not compare favorably with the older relief carvings. This monument was dedicated to Constantine by the senate and people for his defeat of the tyrant Maxentius.

You might want to use the following questions to discuss the art:
1. What impression do you get when you first look at this arch?
2. What tributes are created today that are comparable to this arch?
3. What feature of the arch seems to you to contribute most to its beauty?

tioned the use of brutal repression, and native populations were subjected to murder and pillage. The Roman sack of Corinth in Greece shocked the Mediterranean world. Rome's brutality became so notorious that allied kings prudently willed their kingdoms to Rome, in the sometimes vain hope of avoiding merciless wars of annexation.

The third and last war against Carthage (149–146 B.C.) was unprovoked. Rome wanted no competition in the wine and oil export trade. The purpose of the war was to annex Carthage as a province, so that Roman landlords could buy or lease the fertile land cheaply.

Civil Wars

By the late second century B.C., Roman society was dominated by large plantation owners, who owned thousands of slaves, and who had driven out small landholders. The society was divided between the conservative, plantation-owning senatorial aristocracy who wanted the rights of all other groups curtailed and the more "liberal" or "democratic" senatorial aristocrats who saw that the state was harmed by the loss of the small farmers. As poorer citizens sank into an underclass, they became more prone to rioting. Occasionally groups of slaves were able to run away and mount revolts. Reform was necessary.

Two brothers emerged as reformers. Tiberius Gracchus and his younger brother Caius tried to save the state by passing a grain law, giving the vote to more people, and improving the army. Tiberius was assassinated by opponents and Caius was removed from power. In the aftermath, the senate allowed powerful generals to struggle for control of the state. Roman history from the time of the Gracchus brothers to the victory of Augustus a century later looks like a series of heavyweight championship bouts. The contestants invariably both belonged to the senatorial class, frequently starting out as allies and partners before becoming rivals to the death.

Matters began to settle when Gaius Julius Caesar overcame his enemies and was elected to power in 46 B.C. His dictatorship was to last only two years, to March 15, 44 B.C., when he was assassinated by a group of senators headed by Brutus and Cassius. Their victory was short-lived, however. One of Caesar's generals, Mark Antony, defeated the senatorial party. He was forced to rely on the help of Caesar's young grandnephew Octavius, a favorite of Caesar's veterans. Mark Antony and Octavius shared power until 32 B.C., when they too began to fight. After he defeated Antony in 30 B.C., Octavius was elected consul with special emergency powers. His honorific title, *imperator* (from which we derive "emperor"), was a military one, "commander in chief," and he began using the name Augustus.

THE BIRTH OF THE EMPIRE

Augustus' reign is marked by a flowering of literature and architecture. His official program was to restore the old republic, and he was a patron of poets and other artists who could make real his vision of the ideal state. He instituted religious and legal reforms that were meant to promote old-fashioned virtues. His desire to return to the old days fostered a good deal of innovation, including ambitious new building programs.

Augustus ruled for over forty years. Thirty years of inept rulers followed Augustus' leadership. Tiberius, his successor, was a poor and repressive ruler. He was followed by his corrupt grandnephew Caligula (A.D. 37–41), who terrorized Rome and was killed by his bodyguards, who turned the throne over to his weak uncle Claudius (A.D. 41–54). After Claudius was poisoned, Nero, who is known primarily for his excesses, came to power. His death in A.D. 68 sparked a contest for control among generals. Vespasian was the leader who gained power. For twelve years he and his son Titus ruled well, but Vespasian's younger son, Domitian, soon brought Rome back to the cruel excesses of Caligula and Nero. Informers lurked everywhere and anyone could be put to death at whim. After Domitian's "accidental" death in A.D. 96, he was succeeded by a series of sane rulers, chosen by the senate and succeeding each other through adoption.

These extremes of the first century A.D. were repeated again and again during the full length of the Roman Empire. The quality of leadership during the time was as uneven as it was unpredictable.

Ancient Rome (300 B.C.–A.D. 500)

The Colosseum, Rome

Pont du Gard aqueduct

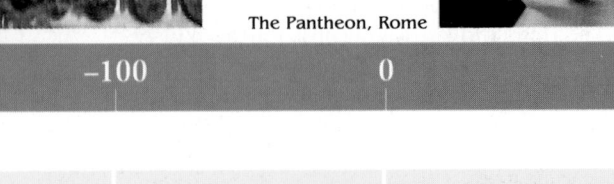

The Pantheon, Rome

Humanities Notes

Pictured from left to right:

The Colosseum, or Flavian, amphitheater is the largest outdoor theater in Rome. Building of the Colosseum began during the reign of Emperor Vespasian in about A.D. 75; it was completed in A.D. 80 under the reign of Vespasian's son. Accommodating approximately 45,000 spectators, the Colosseum was the site of mock naval battles, gladitorial combats, and other public entertainment. According to tradition, persecuted Christians were forced to battle wild animals in the Colosseum. After A.D. 405, the Colosseum was abandoned. During the Middle Ages, stones from the amphitheater were used to construct new buildings.

Pont du Gard is an example of the stone aqueducts built in Rome during the latter part of the first century B.C. Aqueducts are the channels by which water traveled from its source to areas great distances away. Although many Romans considered aqueducts as engineering rather than architectural feats, their design and proportions are illustrative of the height of architectural achievement the ancient Romans attained.

The original Pantheon, which means "place for all gods" in Greek, was built by Agrippa in 27 B.C. It was later destroyed and rebuilt by Hadrian in A.D. 126. Many of the engineering techniques used to rebuild the Pantheon are still used today. Hadrian dedicated the temple to all the Roman gods. From 609 to 1185, however, the Pantheon was converted into a Christian church. It is now a national shrine and the burial place for Italian national heroes.

One of Rome's great military leaders and statesmen was Julius Caesar (c.100–44 B.C.). In 60 B.C. Caesar allied himself with Marcus Crassus and Gnaeus Pompey, forming the First Triumvirate. In 49 B.C., however, Pompey's suspicions of Caesar grew, and he ordered Caesar to give up his army. In reply Caesar led 50,000 soldiers into Pompey's territory in Italy; his

HISTORY

- First Punic War against Carthage begins
- First Punic War ends
- Second Punic War against Hannibal begins
- Second Punic War ends
- Third and last Punic War begins
- Third Punic War ends
- Tiberius' and Caius Gracchus' reforms begin
- Roman Civil War begins
- Pompey becomes consul in Rome
- Caesar starts the civil war
- Caesar and Pompey form alliance with Marcus Lucius Crassus; First Triumverate
- Rome is destroyed by fire
- Brutus and Cassius Longinus lead attack and murder of Caesar
- Senate names Octavian Augustus "Exalted One"; he becomes first Roman Emperor
- Rome enters period of Pax Romana, "Roman Peace"

HUMAN PROGRESS

- Ball games, dice playing, and board games become well known
- Gladiators in Rome begin public combats
- Flaminian Way from Rome to Rimini is constructed
- First stone bridge in Rome is built
- Earliest known paved streets are in Rome
- First water clock invented in Rome
- Building of new Julian forum in Rome begins
- Earliest oboe is made in Rome
- Julian calendar of 365.25 days is adopted; leap year is introduced
- Building of the Pantheon at Rome is begun
- Romans learn to use soap from Gauls

LITERATURE

- Plautus is born
- Plautus dies
- Catullus is born
- Virgil is born
- Catullus dies
- Ovid is born
- Virgil begins *Aeneid*
- *Aeneid* is published
- Virgil dies
- Ovid: *Metamorphosis*
- Ovid is banished to Tomis
- Ovid dies
- Tacitus is born
- Pliny the Younger is born

Statue of
Julius Caesar

Gladiator in combat with leopard

Statue of Augustus,
first Roman emperor,
1st century

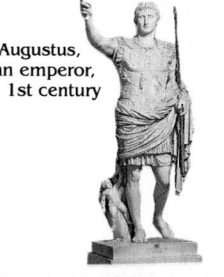

100	200	300	400	500

- Rome begins to decline after Marcus Aurelius dies and Rome suffers civil wars
- Great plague in Roman Empire begins
- Rome celebrates its 1,000th anniversary
- Roman Empire divides into western and eastern empires
- Constantine reunites two empires of Rome, is sole emperor
- Seat of Roman Empire is moved to Constantinople
- Constantine the Great dies
- Rome splits again into western and eastern empires
- Western Roman Empire falls

- Pantheon is completed
- The great plague in Rome occurs
- Baths of Caracalla in Rome are built
- Roman citizenship is given to every freeborn subject in empire
- Edict of Milan establishes toleration of Christianity
- Codex Theodosianus, summary of Roman law
- Boethius is born

- Pliny the Younger dies
- Tacitus: *Historiae*
- Tacitus dies
- Earliest religious plays recorded
- Augustine is born
- Augustine dies

actions provoked a civil war that lasted until 45 B.C. Because of his many victories, the people of Rome regarded Caesar as the undisputed leader of the Roman world and granted him the powers of dictator for ten years. He was later made dictator for life. This statue of Caesar shows him wearing the uniform of a Roman general. On March 15, 44 B.C.—the Ides of March—Mark Antony and Gaius Cassius led Caesar's assassination.

Gladiators were a class of professional fighters who performed for exhibition. Gladiatorial combats usually took place in amphitheaters—such as the Colosseum—before immense audiences. As many as 5,000 and as few as 100 pairs fought on the appointed day. Often the pairs were unequally matched, pairing heavily armed men with ones who were unarmed or armed with crude and ineffective armaments. At times men were paired with wild animals. Defeated gladiators were usually killed by the victor, unless they were spared by the consent of the audience. In the beginning gladiatorial combats were among slaves or prisoners, including Christians. Soon the popularity of the combats grew to such proportions that even the ruling class participated in the competitions. They continued until about A.D. 405.

Augustus (63 B.C.–A.D. 14) was the first Roman emperor. He was born Caius Octavius, then on adoption took the name Caius Julius Caesar Octavian. (He was the grandson of Julius Caesar's sister.) He was granted the honorary title Augustus by the senate in 27 B.C. His reign—later referred to as the Augustan Age—was the beginning of Pax Romana, or Roman Peace. Augustus' reforms were significant and far reaching. He is responsible for changing Rome from a military dictatorship to a constitutional rule, building a new forum, improving and beautifying streets, and setting up fire and police protection. This statue was made by an unknown sculptor during Augustus' reign.

Using the Map

The map depicting the Roman empire at the death of Augustus shows the extent of his influence throughout the area surrounding Rome. Have students study its information carefully. Then you may wish to use these questions:

1. Approximately how many miles is it from Sicily to Rome?
2. In what direction would you travel to go from Rome to Carthage?
3. Name the city at the mouth of the Nile River.
4. What are the names of the provinces bordering Aquitania?
5. If you traveled from Gades to Rome, would it be shorter to sail or to go by land?

Answers
1. 200
2. Southwest
3. Alexandria
4. Lugdunensis, Narbonensis, and Tarraconensis
5. Sail

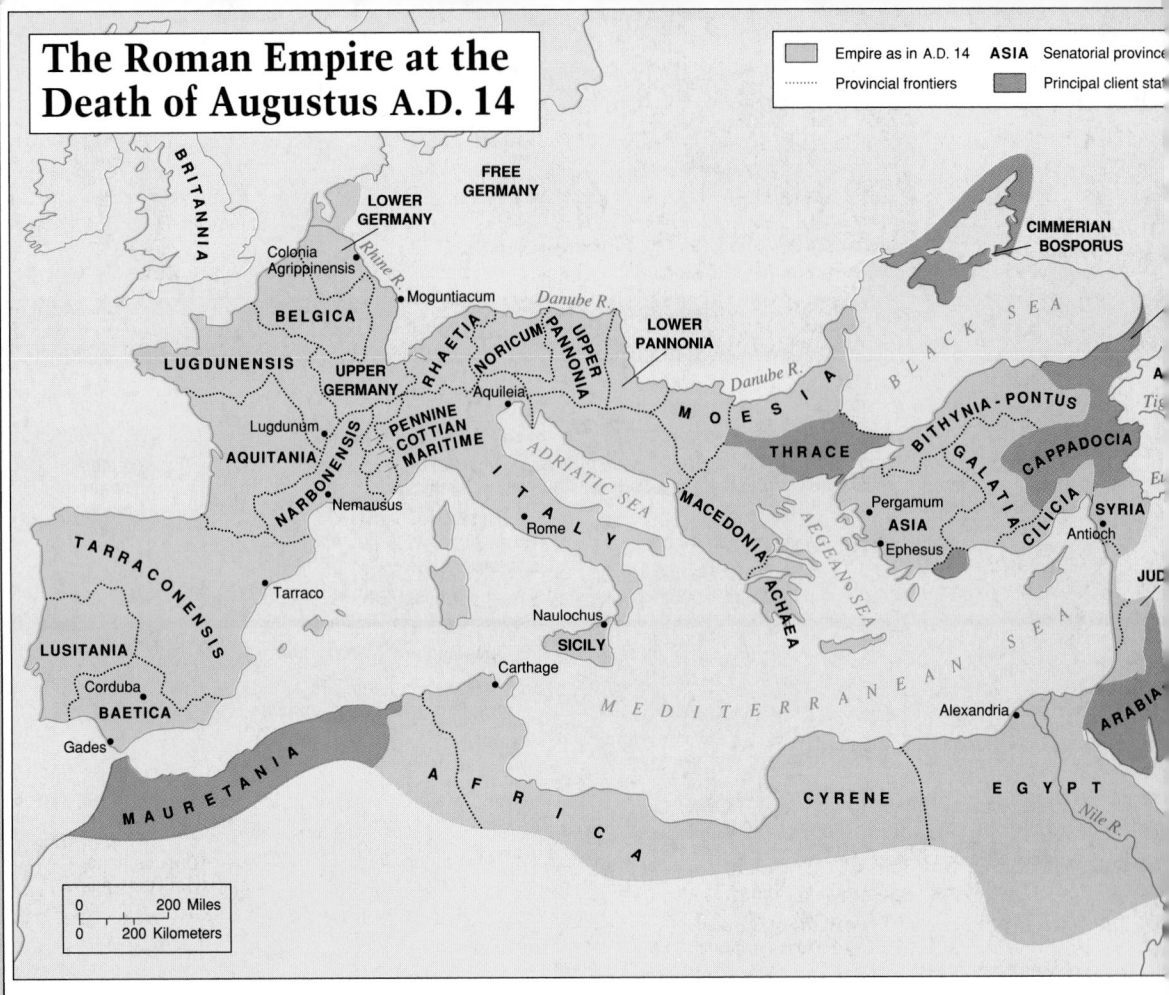

The Roman Empire at the Death of Augustus A.D. 14

The Dismemberment of the Roman Empire

The dinosaurs didn't become extinct overnight, and neither did the Roman Empire. The empire was under stress both at home and abroad, with its very size making it vulnerable on its frontiers. Wandering tribes were attracted by its wealth. Germans had traditionally formed the imperial palace guard; increasingly, Germans, Huns, and their allies provided manpower for the army. The size of the empire also led inevitably to a split between the eastern and western parts, a division that was recognized in the third century A.D. when the empire began to be ruled by two emperors. The center of intellectual life of the empire shifted to the east, with Greek as the official language. The eastern Roman Empire survived intact longer than did the western, where the empire fell both militarily and culturally to invaders from the north who replaced it with a multitude of essentially Germanic kingdoms.

ROMAN RELIGION

From the earliest period, religion played a central role in the organization of Rome. The leader of religious ceremonies, called the King of Sacred Rites, was aided by priestly colleges, all of whose members were patricians (belonging to the senatorial class). These were the *flamines* (burners of offerings), the

Humanities Note

Sculpture, *Enea, Anchise, and Ascanio* by Gianlorenzo Bernini. Gianlorenzo Bernini (1598–1680) was the son of a Tuscan sculptor. This artist of staggering ability and achievement was primarily a sculptor but also produced magnificent paintings, poetry, and architecture. He was instrumental in the design and building of St. Peter's Basilica in Rome. A child prodigy who sculpted a bust at age eight, Bernini was proclaimed at age eleven, by Pope Paul V, to be the "new Michelangelo."

The sculpture *Enea, Anchise, and Ascanio* (Aeneas, Anchises, and Ascanius) was produced in the years 1618–1619 under the patronage of the powerful Cardinal Sciopione Borghese. It represents Bernini's first attempt to sculpt a marble block of this size. The resulting vigor and elasticity of form characterize his work. The precarious grouping of Anchises on the shoulder of Aeneas with the child Ascanius slipping off the oval base creates dramatic tension. The genius of this work astounded the Roman artistic community.

Beginning with this work and continuing for the following fifty years to his death, Bernini dominated the artistic scene in Rome.

You might want to use the following questions to discuss the art:
1. What is the first impression you get from this sculpture?
2. What are the most impressive details of the work?

salii (priests of the war-god Mars, in whose honor they danced in armor), the *luperci* (the wolf-brotherhood, who on certain holidays ran around the sacred boundary of the city to drive away evil spirits and assure the fertility of women and flocks), the *pontifices* (religious and ritual advisers to the king, guardians of religious and civil law, who made pronouncements or "pontificated" on important matters). These last offices, the pontifices, were important, and emperors showed their power by assuming the title of Chief Pontifex.

Rome Versus Greece

Roman religion shows a basic difference between the mentality of the Romans and that of the Greeks. Unlike the Greeks, Romans were obsessed with correct ritual, and they had a practice unknown to the Greeks (*instauratio*), beginning a public religious ceremony all over again if any detail went wrong. On one occasion, a major ceremony was begun again from scratch three times before it could be completed.

The Romans' view of destiny was also essentially non-Greek. The Latin word *fatum* ("fate") means a command or decree to be obeyed. The Greek word *moira*, nearly synonymous with destiny, means a share or an allotment, like a plot of land given to you to cultivate.

Native Gods

The Romans were polytheistic, believing in many gods, and their native deities reveal the Romans' concern with home, cattle, and agriculture. With a strongly developed family religion, centered in respect for the father, the Romans worshiped the *genius,* or master and head of the household. From the worship of the family *genius,* or ancestor of the clan, and the obedience owed a living father, it was not such a big step for the Romans to see themselves as dutiful sons subservient to an emperor who was patriarchal. They worshiped the *manes,* or spirits of dead ancestors, the *penates,* or spirits who guard the wealth of the storehouse, and the *lares,* spirits who watch over fields and paths. Both individual households and the state worshipped Vesta, the goddess of the domestic hearth. Janus is another guardian of enclosures, looking both ways with his two faces, alert to keep outsiders outside the gates. The Romans had many gods of springs, wells, trees. They tended to see the divinity in things rather than to create a fully developed human figure to whom they assigned attributes. Venus, for instance, who came to be equated with the Greek love goddess Aphrodite, was originally an unpersonified force: Her name is a type of word reserved for things, not people, in Latin. This same non-particularizing tendency of the Romans is revealed in their worship of abstractions like Peace and Hope.

Greek Influences

Through contact with Greek religion, literature, and art, the Romans came to see their own gods as corresponding to Greek gods, and they also adopted some of the Greek divinities. Jupiter (also called Jove), the sky god, corresponds to Zeus; his wife, Juno, to Hera; Neptune, the sea god, to Poseidon; Dis to Hades, god of the underworld; Minerva to Athene, weaver and artisan; Diana, the virgin huntress, to Artemis, sister of Apollo; Mercury to Hermes, the messenger; Vulcan, the blacksmith, to Hephaestus, to name some of the most important figures. The Roman god Liber eventually came to be seen as Dionysus, god of wine.

ROMAN LITERATURE

Epic and Drama

Until Rome defeated Carthage in 241 B.C. and emerged as a world power, educated Romans still conducted their foreign policy and read

ENEA, ANCHISE, AND ASCANIO

3 **Clarification** Tell students that Greek and Roman relationships were tense and that Romans frequently critiized Greek culture even while borrowing much from it.

3. Is the person of Aeneas being given a tribute by the artist? Explain.
4. Why would you be interested in Aeneas' story after seeing this work of art?

Humanities Note

Architecture, *Interior of the Pantheon, Rome*. The Pantheon (c. A.D. 118–25) in Rome is a superb monument to Roman engineering skill. A simple cylindrical building topped by a small dome on the outside, the interior was designed to inspire awe with its vast captured space lit beautifully and strangely by an unglazed opening at the top of the dome.

While this photograph does not convey the magnificence of the open dome, it does show the architect's use of polished, colored stone to achieve highly decorative effects. The pavement exhibits alternating squares and circles of yellow marble and purple granite on a white marble field. This pattern follows the overall design theme of circle and square on which the building is based. The walls of the lower half repeat that color scheme in marble of yellow and purple. Above the entablature (architectural element above the columns), the coloration changes to cooler tones of green and white marble.

The coffers (square recesses) of the dome once again repeat the square and circle theme by their placement in the circular dome. In ancient times they were gilded to create a magnificent effect.

You might want to use the following questions to discuss the art:

1. What impressions are created by the repeated use of circles and squares?
2. What buildings in the United States resemble the Pantheon?
3. What is your general impression of this interior?

their literature in Greek. After winning their victory, Romans needed a literature of their own, and a number of native writers translated and adapted Homer and Greek drama into Latin.

To the period immediately following the first war with Carthage belongs the birth of Roman historical epic. This time saw the first Latin epic in a work that influenced subsequent generations, including Virgil, the poet who authored the *Aeneid* (page 488) in the first century B.C.

Drama also flourished in this early period, with elaborate productions of tragedy and comedy presented at public expense. Plautus (254–184 B.C.) emerged as the master of Roman comedy. His younger contemporary Terence wrote polished comedies of morals with sensitive characterization. Both writers have influenced centuries of Western drama.

In the Late Republic (after about 86 B.C.), drama gradually became less popular, but epic continued to flourish. The masterpiece of the Latin tradition is Virgil's *Aeneid*; after him imitations of Homeric epic were left to minor poets with little to say. Under Nero, the brilliant young poet Lucan (A.D. 39–65) wrote a popular and influential hexameter epic on the Roman civil war.

Two other works of epic proportions also stand out, but both are anti-epics in their emphasis because they do not promote the values traditionally connected with heroics. In the *Metamorphoses*, Ovid (page 530) composed a monumental poem based on myths about changing shapes; Augustus saw the work as a subtle attack on established religion and rulers, skillfully penned by a poet talented enough to compose a patriotic work had he wanted. Under Nero, the courtier Petronius wrote a massive volume (*Satyricon*) in prose and verse, often thought to be the first picaresque novel, or novel whose protagonist is a rogue.

History and Biography

Latecomers on the literary scene, the Romans knew that they needed to create a history for themselves. They invented a legendary history that associated them with Troy. In their prose works, they examined recent history and sought to find in great men's lives the causes of major events. The historical works of Tacitus, who lived from A.D. 55 to 117, illustrate how his keen analytical approach incorporates the very Roman elements of the public oration and the biography of public figures.

Lyric Poetry

Lyric poetry for the Romans was an essentially derivative form, although the greatest poets transformed their models. For instance, Catullus and Horace, poets of the first century B.C., imitated Greek forms but created poems essentially Roman in their point of view. So did Virgil in his minor works before composing the *Aeneid*. Horace and Virgil were sponsored by the government and sometimes produced verse that promoted the glory of the state. Other lyric poets in the last years of the Republic and in the Empire frequently saw the choice to write personal lyric as a refusal to write patriotic epic or "serious" works.

Philosophy

In the area of philosophy, the Romans were masterful imitators and adapters rather than original thinkers. The major philosophical work in Latin literature is a poem by Lucretius (Titus Lucretius Carus, c. 99–55 B.C.), on *The Nature of the Universe*. In his work, he combines the atomic theory of Democritus and Epicurus, Greek thinkers who explained the world in exclusively materialistic terms, to present a compelling view of a world in which physical phenomena and events are due to the random combination of particles rather than the caprices of the gods. He urges a way of life that promotes freedom from violent emotion and irrational behavior.

ROMAN VOICES

A friend is, as it were, a second self.
Cicero, *On Friendship*

I came, I saw, I conquered.
Julius Caesar, from **Suetonius,** *Lives of the Caesars*

All life is a struggle in the dark.
Lucretius, *On the Nature of the Universe*

I have written a book that neither the wrath of love, nor fire, nor the sword, nor devouring age shall be able to destroy.
Ovid, *Metamorphoses*

I was in love with loving.
Augustine, *Confessions*

There are tears everywhere and human suffering touches the soul.
Virgil, the *Aeneid*

What is more fun than to put away our cares?
Catullus, *Songs*

I found Rome a city of bricks and I left it a city of marble.
Augustus Caesar, from **Suetonius,** *Lives of the Caesars*

Absence makes the heart grow fonder.
Sextus Propertius, *Elegies*

The greatest reverence is due the young.
Juvenal, *Satires*

Seize the day, put no trust in tomorrow.
Horace, *Epodes*

All art is but an imitation of nature.
Seneca, *Epistles*

Additional Voices

Time bears away all things, even our minds.
—**Virgil,** *Eclogues*

To like and dislike the same things, that is indeed true friendship.
—**Sallust Crispus,** *The War with Catiline*

Oh this age! How tasteless and ill-bred it is!
—**Catullus,** *Poem XLIII*

I love treason but hate the traitor.
—Julius Caesar, from **Plutarch,** *Lives*

More worship the rising than the setting sun.
—Pompey, from **Plutarch,** *Lives*

Better late than never.
—**Livy,** *History*

What fools these mortals be.
—**Seneca,** *Epistles*

Cooperative Learning Allow students to join in teams, and have partners select special topics in history, religion, or literature for reports on Roman thought. Encourage groups not to overlap in their research. Schedule time for each team report.

Check Test
1. The Punic Wars were fought by Rome against _____.
2. Rome became a _____, after being a kingdom and before becoming an empire.
3. The single greatest ruler in the early empire was _____.
4. Much of Roman religion was influenced by the country of _____.
5. The _____ is Virgil's masterpiece about the hero who brought his people to Rome from Troy.

Answers
1. Carthage
2. Republic
3. Augustus
4. Greece
5. *Aeneid*

More About the Author Virgil was Augustus' poet laureate, the literary architect of the new Rome, whose epic was part of a program that included monuments, works of art, and legislation. Although he was part of Augustus' inner circle, Virgil never became embroiled in political intrigue. He preferred to write in seclusion, away from the capital. He wrote slowly and spent much time on revision. We know that it took him seven years to finish his *Georgics*, a philosophic poem on the value of labor, and at that rate it would have averaged out to less than a single line each day!

Everyone who mentions him seems to agree about Virgil's gentleness and shyness. Ask students to think about how his character might add depth to what could have been a piece of imperial propaganda in other hands.

Critical Evaluation Dante Alighieri chooses Virgil as his first guide on the spiritual journey he describes in the *Divine Comedy*. In *Inferno*, Canto I, lines 79–87, he describes Virgil as "that fount which pours forth so broad a stream of speech / . . . O glory and light of other poets, may the long study / and the great love that made me search your volume avail me. / You are my master and my author. / From you alone I took the fair style / that has done me honor."

One author's admiration for another may best be expressed through imitation. Invite students to bear this in mind as they read Virgil, thinking back on Homer, and to remember both Homer and Virgil when they come to Dante. Can they think of English or American authors they have read who imitate one another?

70–19 B.C.

Publius Vergilius Maro (pub´ li əs vʉr jəl´ i əs ma´ ro), unquestionably the greatest Roman poet, was born near Mantua in what was then the province of Gaul. Virgil's childhood experiences on his family's farm marked his outlook in a profound and permanent way. He was to remain, for his entire life, a person sensitive to nature and acutely aware of the beauty and wisdom of the natural world.

When Virgil was eleven years old, Julius Caesar came to govern Gaul. His arrival opened Virgil's eyes to a world different from his father's farm in a backwater town. Virgil traveled to study in various cities, including Rome. It was there that he took courses in rhetoric—the construction and delivery of speeches that was so essential a part of instruction for young Romans being trained for public affairs. But though he was trained as a lawyer, he never pursued a legal career.

He felt the effects of the ongoing civil war directly, for when Mark Antony, a factional leader, needed to reward his soldiers with land grants in 41 B.C., he confiscated many farms, including Virgil's. During this time, Virgil withdrew from the turmoil of the capital. He retreated to Naples and there began the study of Epicureanism, a Greek philosophy of materialism that received widespread attention throughout the Roman world after the publication of a poem by Lucretius (*On The Nature of the Universe*). Soon afterward, Octavius gave Virgil back his land, recognizing his poetic genius. Understandably, Virgil felt deep and enduring gratitude to Octavius (Augustus) all his life. Virgil became the official poet of the empire, but although he was welcome at court, he remained a country boy, spending as much time as he could on an estate Augustus gave him in the south of Italy. His shyness was notorious, and his friends called this tall, dark, retiring man with a delicate constitution Parthenias (par´ the ni əs), or "the virgin."

Virgil's early works were poetry collections called *Eclogues (Bucolics)* and *Georgics*. In these poems, he reworked the tradition of Greek pastoral poetry, highly artificial poems composed by sophisticated city dwellers about the loves of herdsmen singing in an idealized country landscape. The Italian countryside and the hard work of a farmer's life were vividly real to Virgil, and his poems are full of serious, realistic touches. Throughout, he idealizes the return to peace made possible by Augustus after the long civil war. In 40 B.C. he wrote the fourth *Eclogue*, a poem on peace that assured his reputation among later Christians. In it he talks about a return to the golden age, the birth of a divine child, a poisonous serpent trampled underfoot, and the earth bearing fruit by itself. Christians believed Virgil had predicted the birth of Jesus and considered him an honorary Christian and a prophet. In the Middle Ages, people used the *Aeneid* as a kind of fortunetelling device, finding out the future by "Virgilian lots," that is, opening the *Aeneid* at random and pointing at a line of verse.

Virgil's great work was the Aeneid, Rome's national epic and the greatest single work of Latin literature. It assured him an unassailable place in the history of world literature.

BACKGROUND

THE AENEID

A National Epic

Augustus' new empire needed a national epic. The Greeks had Homer's epics, venerated by Greeks and Romans alike; Rome had nothing comparable. Impressive works had been produced in theater and in prose, and outstanding works, like *On the Nature of the Universe* by Lucretius, which could rival certain types of earlier achievements by the Greeks, could be found. However, there was no national epic for Roman citizens whose patriotism might be aroused by an inspirational mythic account of their origins.

Virgil undertook to remedy that lack, spending the last eleven years of his life working on his epic. Virgil belonged to a literate and self-conscious society, far removed from the oral tradition of Homer's times. He wrote many drafts, revising and polishing his verse "like a she-bear licking her cubs into shape," as he put it. When he fell ill after a hard voyage and died, he left instructions to destroy the manuscript he thought imperfect. Naturally, and luckily, Augustus intervened and saved the work.

The challenge facing Virgil was enormous. He had to compose a single national epic that would make Rome seem at least as venerable as Greece, with a place in legendary history. He had to prove that Rome's new epic equaled Homer's as a work of literature. In twelve books of dactylic hexameter (Homer's meter), Virgil set out to combine and transform the forty-eight books of Homer's two epics, presenting a myth explaining Rome's founding and legitimatizing Augustus' empire while ascertaining its right to rule the world in perpetuity. His poem would rival Homer's *Iliad* and *Odyssey* because of its literary sophistication and because it reflected the self-awareness of the new era in which he lived and the superior values of an ideal Roman state.

The *Aeneid* is fundamentally a Roman work, and Virgil consistently modifies Homer's Greek values. For instance, he imitates Homer's book on funeral games in honor of dead heroes but incorporates several changes. For example, while Homer stresses individual excellence when the Achaians compete to honor Patroklos, Virgil's Trojans, like good Romans, excel in group events when they compete in honor of Anchises, and good teamwork is what gains victory.

Virgil makes his purpose clear with his opening words, "Arms and the man I sing." The word "Arms" or warfare recalls the setting of the *Iliad*, but signals a departure from Homer's focus on the "wrath" of an individual hero. These words suggest the tension pervading the poem, between the hero's duty to his people and his personal desires— a thoroughly Roman idea.

The Story itself

Virgil opens the *Aeneid* with an invocation calling on the Muse to remind him of why Aeneas, an exiled hero who survived the destruction of his native Troy, had to suffer so much before he could found Rome. It is Juno, queen of heaven, who persecutes the Trojan hero. She is still angry that his cousin Paris judged her to be less fair than Aeneas' mother, Venus, during a beauty competition. This anger creates an undercurrent of divine tension that will explain many events in the story.

Enrichment Virgil's preparation for his epic began in his late adolescence when he began to write poems that are now lost. His major efforts prior to the composition of the *Aeneid* included *The Eclogues* and *The Georgics*. He spent the last twelve years of his life creating his epic at the rate of approximately one line a day.

Clarification Latin prosody, like its Greek counterpart, enabled Virgil to work comfortably within a highly structured, nearly rigid verse framework. His genius stemmed from his ability to enhance such an apparently inflexible circumstance with a color and vitality that are unparalleled in world literature. It is not surprising that so many later poets (Dante in Italy, Joyce in Ireland, Kazantzakis in Greece, and others) were directly and powerfully influenced by him.

AENEAS AND DIDO
P. N. Guérin
The Louvre, Paris

Virgil begins his story, as Homer does, in the middle of the action (*in medias res*). We first see Aeneas on the high seas, about to land safely in Italy when Juno engineers a storm that wrecks his fleet. He is tossed violently about and lands at last on the African coast not far from Carthage, a city being erected by Queen Dido. Since the town is destined to become Rome's archenemy in later times, it is ironic that now Aeneas is welcomed so generously. Love wins out. The queen is a widow; Venus has tricked her into becoming romantically involved with the hero whose wife was killed during the Greek conquest of Troy.

Book II contains Aeneas' account of the fall of Troy. He tells the story vividly, sadly explaining how Creusa, his wife, was lost and how he managed to save his father, Anchises, and son, Ascanius, while leading a small group to the safety of exile.

Book III recounts how he led the fleet away from the Phrygian coast and across the seas. Aeneas' father, Anchises, dies, and the devoted hero's emptiness is filled with a wordless sorrow.

Aeneas stays with Dido in Carthage, leading her to believe in the future of their romantic union. But Aeneas is visited by Mercury, a messenger god sent by Jupiter, who reminds the hero of his destiny to found the city of Rome, a new Troy to be located on the west coast of Italy. He sails away, dutifully bound to his destiny. Dido kills herself after cursing the future of Carthaginian-Roman affairs that will conclude in the bitter Punic Wars.

An interlude in Sicily precedes the completion of the next part of Aeneas' journey during which he descends to the underworld. After viewing the frightening wonders that await the souls of the dead, Aeneas is able to visit with his father's shade (or ghost) and to receive paternal encouragement for his future tasks.

Next, Aeneas arrives in Latium where he is accepted by Latinus, the king who offers his daughter, Lavinia, to the Trojan in marriage. But the girl's mother, Queen Amata, is prompted by Juno to renounce Aeneas and encourage an earlier suitor, Turnus, to fight for the future of the throne.

War begins. Aeneas joins forces with Evander, a local opponent of Turnus. While Aeneas is away, Turnus attacks the Trojan camp. His assault is not entirely successful. But it does pin down his opponents and cuts off any means of escape. The bloody conflicts inspire a heavenly debate.

When Aeneas does return to camp, he enters battle and shows himself to be a more worthy and honorable fighter than the boastful Turnus. He demonstrates respect for opponents he kills, while Turnus mocks those who are slain.

The allies of Turnus and Aeneas continue the bloody conflict throughout Books XI and XII of the *Aeneid*. Finally, the contestants meet in single combat. Aeneas is victorious. His triumph assures the success of his future in Italy and he is left to wed Lavinia in order to begin the sequence that will result in Rome's founding.

CHARACTERS

MORTALS

AENEAS (i nē´ əs): A Trojan noble, son of the goddess of Love (Venus) and a mortal (Anchises). In the *Iliad* Aeneas appears as a very minor character. Since he played no important role in Greek mythology, it was possible for Virgil to invent a history for him making him the ancestor of the Romans (page 493).

ASCANIUS (as kā´ nē əs): Aeneas' son by his Trojan wife, Creusa. Other name: Ilus (after Ilium, Troy's other name) and Iulus, which would make him an ancestor of the Julians, the family to which Julius Caesar and Augustus belonged. In this way Augustus can claim to be descended from Venus (page 511).

CALCHAS (kal´ kəs): Chief priest and interpreter of omens for the Greek army at Troy (page 499).

DIDO (dī´ dō): Daughter of King Belus of Tyre. When her brother murdered her husband for his money, she led her people to Carthage. When Aeneas abandons her, she kills herself, swearing that the Romans and Carthaginians will be enemies. Other name: Elissa (ə lis´ ə) (page 507).

IARBAS (ē är´ bəs): An African king, son of the ram-headed Libyan god Hammon, equated by Virgil with Jupiter. Offered Dido his protection when she came to Libya and wanted to marry her, but she rejected him for Aeneas (page 507).

LAOCOÖN (lā äk´ ə wän´): A priest of Neptune at Troy who tries to warn the Trojans against the wooden horse but is attacked by monstrous sea-serpents who strangle him and his sons (page 495).

LAOMEDON (lā äm´ ə dän´): King of Troy, son of Troy's founder Ilus (whose name Ascanius shares).

He promised to reward Neptune and Apollo for building Troy's walls, but cheated the gods when their work was done (page 520).

PRIAM (prī´ əm): King of Troy at the time of the Trojan war, father of Hektor and Paris. He was killed by Achilleus' son (page 494).

ULYSSES (yoo lis´ ēz): Roman name for Odysseus, king of Ithaca, who fought at Troy and was known as a resourceful man and a skilled liar (page 493).

IMMORTALS

DIS (dis): God of the underworld. Other name: Pluto (page 523).

JUNO (joo´ nō): Wife of Jupiter, hostile to the Trojans and a patroness of Carthage; goddess of marriage. In this poem, she is the relentless enemy of Aeneas and stands for irrational anger (page 509).

JUPITER (joo´ pə tər): The supreme sky god, equivalent to Zeus. Other name: Jove (page 516).

PALLAS (pal´əs): She sided with the Greeks in the Trojan war. Other names: Athene or Minerva (page 494).

PHOEBUS (fē´ bəs): Sun god, god of archery, healing, and prophecy. The word means "bright one." Other name: Apollo (page 499).

PROSERPINA (prō sɹ´ pi nə): The same as the Greek Persephone. Daughter of Ceres, the goddess of crops, she was abducted by her uncle Dis (Pluto) to be his bride in the underworld. By threatening to make the earth barren, her mother secured her release above ground for half of each year (page 523).

Reading Critically The purpose of this page is to guide students in the critical reading of literature written by Roman authors. The information here will enable students to place a work of literature in its historical context, identify the literary movements of the time, and appreciate the techniques used by writers to convey the ideas of the period.

As you discuss this information with your class, explain that Book II of the *Aeneid* by Virgil, on the facing page, is a model for reading critically. The side columns contain notes that draw students' attention to elements that reflect the historical, cultural, and literary contexts that inform the work of art.

To give students further practice with the process of reading critically, use the selection from Ovid's *Metamorphoses* ("Orpheus and Eurydice") in the Teaching Portfolio, page 597, which students can annotate themselves. Encourage students to use these strategies as they read the literature in this unit.

Teaching to Ability Levels For **less advanced** students, you might discuss the exact location of Troy before reading about its fall. (See map on page 484.) More advanced students might be given a chance to explain what they already know about the excavation of the city.

For Further Study Biographical information on Virgil appears on page 488, and another section from the *Aeneid* begins on page 507.

from the Aeneid, Book II

Historical Context

In 29 B.C. Augustus quashed all opposition and took power, putting an end to over a hundred years of civil warfare in Rome. Many who had experienced the violence and terror of the late Republic welcomed the promise of peace. Augustus marked the beginning of his reign by funding an ambitious building program and supporting poets and artists. The most lasting monument to his reign was not one of the many splendid public buildings he put up but Virgil's monumental epic, which assured Rome a place in world history and literature.

Cultural Context

When they defeated the Carthaginians in 241 B.C., the Romans achieved the status of a world power before they had any national literature or any claim to cultural sophistication. From that time on, they strove to create a legendary history that would make their culture seem as ancient and venerable as their conquered peoples'. Greeks and Egyptians had developed astronomy, philosophy, art, and literature, but the Romans prided themselves on their homespun virtues even if they sometimes paid only lip service to them: loyalty to family and state, obedience, self-denial and endurance, and the ability to manage an operation well. Virgil builds on this ideal of the Roman statesman in shaping the character of Aeneas.

Literary Context

Romans as well as Greeks venerated the Homeric epics, the most ancient texts of Greek literature. To take his place alongside Homer, Virgil uses the same meter as Homer, situates his story at the time of the fall of Troy (1200 B.C., incidentally almost four hundred years before Carthage was actually founded), and adopts conventions such as invoking the muse, involving Olympian gods in the action, and beginning the story *in medias res* or in midstream. He also draws on later Greek romance, epic, tragedy, and lyric as well as on his Latin predecessors in epic, dramatic, and lyric poetry. The *Aeneid* recalls, recombines, and transforms all the major works of the Greek and Roman tradition to make a new, original, and fundamentally Roman work.

On the following pages is a selection from Book II of the *Aeneid*. The annotations in the margin point out the historical, cultural, or literary context.

from the Aeneid

Virgil

Book II: How They Took the City

translated by Robert Fitzgerald

Presentation
Motivation/Prior Knowledge Tell students they will be reading the story of the defeat and the destruction of a city told by a survivor. Ask students to think about other accounts of invasions or defeats they have read or heard. Then remind them that one side's defeat is the other side's victory. What is the importance of point of view? How is perspective distinct from "facts"?

Purpose-Setting Question What mood does Aeneas set at the beginning of his explanation of Troy's ruin? How do you imagine an audience would respond to such an account?

Book I of the Aeneid *begins: "I sing of warfare and a man at war." That man at war is the Trojan prince Aeneas, who embodies the Roman ideal of devotion to duty as he performs his mission to found the Roman people. He and his men set sail from Troy, only to encounter a series of adversities on their way to Italy.*

After a storm stirred up by jealous Juno, Aeneas and his men reach Carthage, where Queen Dido holds a banquet in the Trojans' honor. Disguised as Aeneas' son, Cupid (Amor) attends the banquet and causes Dido to fall in love with Aeneas. To prolong his stay, Dido asks Aeneas to recount the fall of Troy and his subsequent wanderings, which he does as Book II begins.

The room fell silent, and all eyes were on him,
As Father Aeneas from his high couch began:

"Sorrow too deep to tell, your majesty,
You order me to feel and tell once more:
5 How the Danaans[1] leveled in the dust
The splendor of our mourned-forever kingdom—
Heartbreaking things I saw with my own eyes
And was myself a part of. Who could tell them,
Even a Myrmidon[2] or Dolopian[3]
10 Or ruffian of Ulysses,[4] without tears?
Now, too, the night is well along, with dewfall
Out of heaven, and setting stars weigh down
Our heads toward sleep. But if so great desire

Cultural Context: Aeneas is called "Father," since he is the leader of his people. The Roman senators were called "fathers" and the emperor "the father of the nation." At banquets, the ancients reclined on couches placed around a low table. A "high couch" corresponds to the head table, where important guests were placed.

Literary Context: In the first book, the story began *in medias res*. The fall of Troy, the logical beginning of Aeneas' story, is told only now. It is typical for Virgil to have one character give information to another rather than telling the reader himself. Thus the story is recounted in the first person and is shaped by the teller's (Aeneas') perspective.

Vocabulary
Preteach the following vocabulary words:
sheathed (shē*th*d) *v.*: Covered; enclosed
sinister (sin´ is tər) *adj.*: Threatening; dishonest
scion (sī´ ən) *n.*: A bud; descendent
perjured (pʉr´ jərd) *adj.*: Falsely given under oath
demented (di ment´ id) *adj.*: Mentally deranged
embarking (im bark´ iŋ) *v.*: Beginning; putting aboard
reparation (rep ə ra´ shən) *n.*: Restoration; a repairing

---

1. **Danaans** (dā´ nənz): Tribal name for Greeks.
2. **Myrmidon** (mʉr´ mə dän): Myrmidons were soldiers of Achilles.
3. **Dolopian** (də lō´ pē ən): Person from Thessaly, a Greek ally.
4. **Ulysses** (yo͞o lis´ ēz): Roman name for Odysseus, a Greek warrior.

Critical Thinking and Reading Worksheet, *Inferring Author's Opinion*, p. 605
Language Worksheet, *Analyzing Tone*, p. 606
Selection Test, pp. 607–608

1 **Discussion** How does Virgil suggest the emotions of the Trojans and the Greeks (lines 18–29)? Call attention to "so many years," for instance. Whose point of view does this phrase suggest? Do Greeks and Trojans experience the same *fact* differently?

2 **Discussion** Aeneas shifts to "we" (line 34). How does this pronoun modulate the tone of the preceding section? From whose point of view is this section told? How does Virgil make us see through Trojan eyes? Have students discuss the technique in lines 36–45.

Cultural Context: Pallas Athene was notoriously pro-Greek and hostile to the Trojans. Many versions of the sack of Troy were told in epics and tragedies, and the trick of the Trojan horse was part of all of them. Virgil draws on the tradition while emphasizing the Trojan point of view.

Literary Context: By having the Trojans rush out on a kind of ancient sightseeing tour of the abandoned Greek camp, Virgil deftly calls to mind the setting of the *Iliad*. The indirect quotations allow Virgil to evoke, with very few words, the animated and joyous chatter of the milling crowd of Trojans.

Moves you to hear the tale of our disasters,
15 Briefly recalled, the final throes[5] of Troy,[6]
However I may shudder at the memory
And shrink again in grief, let me begin.

Knowing their strength broken in warfare, turned
Back by the fates, and years—so many years—
20 Already slipped away, the Danaan captains
By the divine handicraft of Pallas built
A horse of timber, tall as a hill,
And <u>sheathed</u> its ribs with planking of cut pine.
This they gave out to be an offering
25 For a safe return by sea, and the word went round.
But on the sly they shut inside a company
Chosen from their picked soldiery by lot,
Crowding the vaulted caverns in the dark-—
The horse's belly—with men fully armed.

30 Offshore there's a long island, Tenedos,[7]
Famous and rich while Priam's kingdom[8] lasted,
A treacherous anchorage now, and nothing more.
They crossed to this and hid their ships behind it
On the bare shore beyond. We thought they'd gone,
35 Sailing home to Mycenae[9] before the wind,
So Teucer's town[10] is freed of her long anguish,
Gates thrown wide! And out we go in joy
To see the Dorian[11] campsites, all deserted,
The beach they left behind. Here the Dolopians
40 Pitched their tents, here cruel Achilles lodged,
There lay the ships, and there, formed up in ranks,
They came inland to fight us. Of our men
One group stood marveling, gaping up to see
The dire gift of the cold unbedded goddess,
The sheer mass of the horse.

---

5. **throes** (thrōz) *n*.: Acts of struggling.
6. **Troy** (troi): A city in Asia Minor, home of the Trojans.
7. **Tenedos** (ten′ ə dōs): Island off the coast of Troy.
8. **Priam's kingdom:** Troy.
9. **Mycenae** (mī sē′ nē): Greek city ruled by Agamemnon, a principal character in the *Iliad*.
10. **Teucer's** (tōō′ sərz) **town**: Troy; Teucer, from Crete, was the original king of Troy.
11. **Dorian** (dôr′ ē ən): *adj*.: Greek.

Commentary

Like all educated Romans, Virgil was schooled in the art of public speaking. Citizens were trained to plead cases in a court of law or to speak for or against legislation in the senate. Many Roman authors enjoyed vigorous legal or political careers—for instance Cicero, Pliny, and Tacitus. Others, like Catullus, Virgil, or Ovid, used their education in their writing and more or less avoided law or politics. Everyone, however, knew the rules of the game, and the same techniques used to convince a jury can be found in the speeches of Virgil's characters or in the fictitious letters of Ovid's heroines.

In creating the figure of Sinon, who is wholly his invention, Virgil shows consummate skill in building a character. His portrayal is many-layered: Sinon, as a superb confidence man, creates his own plausible fictional character; simultaneously, Virgil reveals Sinon as a treacherous liar.

In creating the character of Sinon, Virgil not only succeeds in showing off his own rhetorical skills as a speech-making poet, but he also establishes a standard, with this virtuoso performance, against which to measure other such speeches.

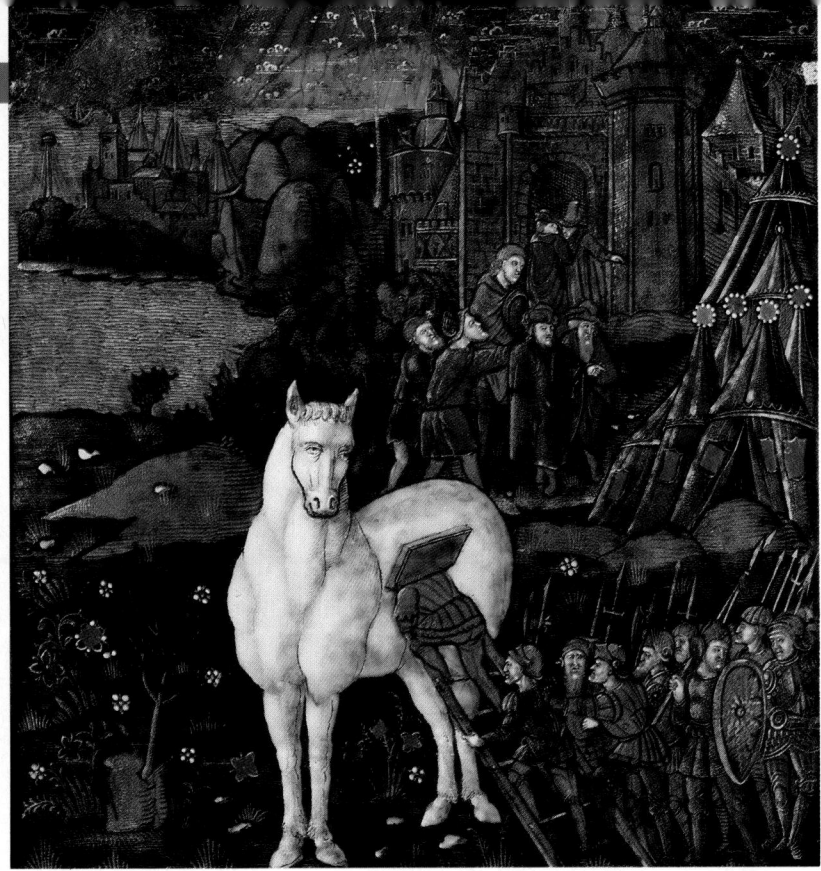

THE WOODEN HORSE OF TROY
*Limoges Master of the
Aeneid, sixteenth century*
The Louvre, Paris

Humanities Note
Fine art, *The Wooden Horse of Troy*, unknown artist. This complex rendering of the Trojan horse (c. 1525–1540) is not, as you might think, a painting on canvas or on paper. Instead it is an extraordinary example of the art of enamel painting. This technique employs colored glass powders fused to a copper or a silver base, using a frame.

This extremely difficult process was brought to the status of high art by the fifteenth– and sixteenth–century French artists of the city of Limoges. By applying the powdered glass with a brush, fine details could be captured.

The name of the artist who created this series of plaques on the themes of the *Aeneid* has been lost. It is thought, however, that they might be the work of Jean I. Penicaud, known as "The Master of the *Aeneid*."

You might want to use the following questions to discuss the art:
1. Did this look like an oil painting when you first saw it?
2. How does this artist's conception of the Trojan horse compare to your own notion of it?
3. Think of a person you know to whom this kind of artwork would be special. Explain why that person might value such work.
4. Choose one element of the illustration that you would extract and another that you would add if you were going to depict this scene differently. Explain your choices.

               Thymoetes[12] shouts
It should be hauled inside the walls and moored
High on the citadel[13]—whether by treason
Or just because Troy's fate went that way now.
Capys[14] opposed him; so did the wiser heads:
"Into the sea with it," they said, "or burn it,
Build up a bonfire under it,
This trick of the Greeks, a gift no one can trust,
Or cut it open, search the hollow belly!"

Contrary notions pulled the crowd apart.
Next thing we knew, in front of everyone,
Laocoön[15] with a great company
Came furiously running from the Height,[16]

3

Literary Context: The figure of the prophet who tells the truth but is not heeded is familiar from Greek literature; one of many examples is Teiresias, whom Oedipus refuses to believe. The type reflects a universal truth: no one wants to listen to bad news.

---

12. **Thymoetes** (thī mœi′ tēz): A Trojan leader.
13. **citadel** (sit′ ə del) *n.*: A safe, fortified place of defense in a city.
14. **Capys** (kā′ pis): A Trojan leader.
15. **Laocoön** (lā äk′ə wän′): Trojan priest of the god Neptune.
16. **the Height:** The Acropolis.

3 Discussion Call students' attention to the way Aeneas offers two different, or perhaps complementary, interpretations of Thymoetes' advice. What are they? What is Aeneas' view, with hindsight?

4 **Discussion** Ask students to look closely at the verbs used here. What images does Sinon evoke?

5 **Discussion** How is the wooden horse made to seem like a living creature? Students should think about words like *flank, belly,* and *groaning.*

6 **Clarification** A device Virgil is fond of is the proleptic (from a Greek word meaning "anticipate") adjective. Ask students to think about "bloody steel." Is the steel bloody to begin with, before it is used to strike? The position of the adjective would indicate that, but logic leads us to see that the steel becomes bloody only after the act of violence. The effect is to compress time, to make the reader see the anticipation of the act, the act itself, and the result in a single frame.

7 **Discussion** Ask students to look for shifts in perspective throughout Aeneas' narrative. For instance, in line 79 the words "but now look" make us feel we are witnessing a scene as it takes place. What shift of perspective is assumed in lines 82–86? What difference does it make that lines 87–89 are framed by Aeneas' editorial comments to his listeners?

8 **Discussion** Ask students to visualize the scene described in lines 87–90. Where does their sympathy lie as they see the prisoner jeered by the mob? When have they witnessed such a scene, either in life or in a book or film? Was their reaction the same in each case?

Literary Context: An archetype is a character who seems to embody certain readily identifiable character traits or to enact familiar experiences. Ulysses is such a character. To his friends he is a resourceful man and a persuasive speaker; to his foes, a rogue and a shameless liar. In contemporary movies Captain Kirk in *Star Trek* and the streetwise police detective in almost any action-suspense movie are similar types.

Literary Context: The "unknown fellow" is Sinon, who is wholly Virgil's creation, and his lying story is free invention. His "sinuous" name and the hissing words he uses in Latin mark him as the proverbial snake in the grass. He is as twisty and talented as Ulysses, his pretended enemy, and better suited for the job because no one knows him.

And still far off cried out: "O my poor people,
Men of Troy, what madness has come over you?
60 Can you believe the enemy truly gone?
A gift from the Danaans, and no ruse?[17]
Is that Ulysses' way, as you have known him?
Achaeans[18] must be hiding in this timber,
Or it was built to butt against our walls,
65 Peer over them into our houses, pelt
The city from the sky. Some crookedness
Is in this thing. Have no faith in the horse!
Whatever it is, even when Greeks bring gifts
I fear them, gifts and all."
He broke off then
70 And rifled his big spear with all his might
Against the horse's flank, the curve of belly.
It stuck there trembling, and the rounded hull
Reverberated[19] groaning at the blow.
If the gods' will had not been sinister,
75 If our own minds had not been crazed,
He would have made us foul that Argive[20] den
With bloody steel, and Troy would stand today—
O citadel of Priam,[21] towering still!

But now look: hillmen, shepherds of Dardania,[22]
80 Raising a shout, dragged in before the king
An unknown fellow with hands tied behind—
This all as he himself had planned,
Volunteering, letting them come across him,
So he could open Troy to the Achaeans.
85 Sure of himself this man was, braced for it
Either way, to work his trick or die.
From every quarter Trojans run to see him,
Ring the prisoner round, and make a game
Of jeering at him. Be instructed now
90 In Greek deceptive arts: one barefaced deed
Can tell you of them all.
As the man stood there, shaken and defenseless,

---

17. **ruse** (rōōz) *n.*: Trick.
18. **Achaeans** (ə kē′ ənz): Greeks.
19. **Reverberated** (ri vʉr′ bə rāt′ əd) *v.*: Echoed repeatedly.
20. **Argive** (är′ gīv) *adj.*: Generalized name for Greek.
21. **Priam** (prī′ əm): King of Troy.
22. **Dardania** (där′ dā′ nē ə): Generalized name for Troy and its surrounding area.

Grammar in Action

Adjectives: Participles Participles that are not part of phrases are most commonly adjectives. Although they are formed from verbs, they have the quality of adjectives in that they modify nouns and pronouns (the *rounded* hull, line 72, and an *unknown* fellow, line 81, are examples), and they most frequently end with *–ing* or *–ed.*

It is sometimes difficult to distinguish a participle used as an adjective from a passive voice. The criterion should be whether the participle modifies the subject, as a predicate adjective with a linking verb, or whether it describes an action.

PASSIVE VOICE: It was *built* to butt against our walls. (line 64)

PREDICATE ADJECTIVE: Our own minds had not been *crazed.* (line 75)

Participles used as adjectives should refer clearly to a specific noun or pronoun; there should be no doubt about what is modified. Otherwise the participle dangles or is misrelated.

Student Activity 1. Pick out all the participles used as adjectives on page 497 (There are eight: *braced, shaken, whimpering, taking, trumped-up,*

Looking around at ranks of Phrygians,[23]
"Oh god," he said, "what land on earth, what seas
Can take me in? What's left me in the end,
Outcast that I am from the Danaans,
Now the Dardanians will have my blood?"

The whimpering speech brought us up short; we felt
A twinge for him. Let him speak up, we said,
Tell us where he was born, what news he brought,
What he could hope for as a prisoner.
Taking his time, slow to discard his fright,
He said:
     "I'll tell you the whole truth, my lord,
No matter what may come of it. Argive
I am by birth, and will not say I'm not.
That first of all: Fortune has made a derelict
Of Sinon,[24] but the witch
Won't make an empty liar of him, too.
Report of Palamedes[25] may have reached you,
Scion of Belus' line,[26] a famous man
Who gave commands against the war. For this,
On a trumped-up charge, on perjured testimony,
The Greeks put him to death—but now they mourn him,
Now he has lost the light. Being kin to him,
In my first years I joined him as companion,
Sent by my poor old father on this campaign,
And while he held high rank and influence
In royal councils, we did well, with honor.
Then by the guile and envy of Ulysses—
Nothing unheard of there!—he left this world,
And I lived on, but under a cloud, in sorrow,
Raging for my blameless friend's downfall.
Demented, too, I could not hold my peace
But said if I had luck, if I won through
Again to Argos,[27] I'd avenge him there.
And I roused hatred with my talk; I fell
Afoul now of that man. From that time on,

---

23. **Phrygians** (fri′ gē ənz): Trojans.
24. **Sinon** (sī′ non): A lying Greek.
25. **Palamedes** (pal′ ə mē′ dēz): A Greek warrior who advised Agamemnon to abandon the war against Troy; he was brought down by Ulysses, who forged proof that Palamedes cooperated with the enemy in the Trojan war.
26. **Scion of Belus'** (bel′ əs) **line:** Descendant of Belus, king of Egypt and father of Dido, queen of Carthage.
27. **Argos** (är′ gōs): Home city of Agamemnon and Menelaus; a generalized name for Greece.

Literary Context: Sinon's pitiful appeal is a rhetorical ploy to win the Trojans' sympathy. Their response shows them and, by extension, their ancestors, the Romans, as generous and forgiving, in contrast to the treacherous Greeks. They are helpless against the skillful web of lies hung on a few facts. Like a secret agent, Sinon establishes a false identity attractive to his listeners.

9 **Discussion** Call students' attention to the way Virgil has structured Aeneas' account so as to reproduce in Aeneas' listeners the same kind of rapidly shifting emotional response as the Trojans experienced. Ask them to consider how Aeneas' editorial remarks also give us the kind of perspective and hindsight the Trojans lacked.

10 **Enrichment** The story of Palamedes was popular. Although no tragedies about him have survived, Virgil and his audience knew many portrayals of Palamedes on stage. The honest hero who advised against the war and was framed by the unscrupulous Ulysses and put to death as a traitor was a familiar and sympathetic hero. Ask students if they have come across similar figures in history or in literature. How might associating oneself with such a figure give one instant credibility?

---

perjured, being, sent; some are included in participial phrases); identify the noun or pronoun that each modifies.

    Student Activity 2. Write a paragraph describing the Trojans' reaction to the wooden horse; include in it two examples of participles used solely as adjectives and two participles used as parts of verbs in the passive voice.

Day in, day out, Ulysses
Found new ways to bait and terrify me,
130 Putting out shady rumors among the troops,
Looking for weapons he could use against me.
He could not rest till Calchas served his turn—
But why go on? The tale's unwelcome, useless,
If Achaeans are all one,
135 And it's enough I'm called Achaean, then
Exact the punishment, long overdue;
The Ithacan[28] desires it; the Atridae[29]
Would pay well for it."

        Burning with curiosity,
We questioned him, called on him to explain—
140 Unable to conceive such a performance,
The art of the Pelasgian.[30] He went on,
Atremble, as though he feared us:

               "Many times
The Danaans wished to organize retreat,
To leave Troy and the long war, tired out.

---

28. **Ithacan** (ith′ ə kən) *n.*: Ulysses, who comes from Ithaca in western Greece.
29. **Atridae** (ā′ tri dē) *n.*: Agamemnon and Menelaus, the two sons of Atreus.
30. **Pelasgian** (pəl az′ gē ən) *n.*: An early inhabitant of Greece.

FALL OF TROY
Limoges Master of Aeneid
The Metropolitan Museum of Art, New York

Humanities Note

Fine art, *The Fall of Troy*, is an enamel plaque attributed to an unknown artist. Enameling, fusing powdered glass to metal with heat, is one of the most ancient of the decorative arts. The artisans of the city of Limoges, France, brought this craft to the status of fine art in the fifteenth century with the invention of a process called *grisaille,* or enamel painting.

    The Fall of Troy is an enamel plaque produced in Limoges during the fifteenth century. It admirably demonstrates the similarity of this difficult medium to painting. The smooth, shiny surface and glowing colors are perfectly suited to the subtle detail of the scene.

This plaque is one in a series of seventy-four similar plaques, all depicting various scenes from the *Aeneid*. The true identity of the artist is unknown. It is thought that he may have been Jean I. Penicaud, a master of enamel painting who is sometimes called the "Master of the *Aeneid*" because of his fondness for the subject.

    You might want to use the following questions to discuss the art:

1. Can you identify various characters from the story in this scene?
2. Are they shown as you would expect to see them?

If only they had done it! Heavy weather
At sea closed down on them, or a fresh gale
From the Southwest would keep them from embarking,
Most of all after this figure here,
This horse they put together with maple beams,
Reached its full height. Then wind and thunderstorms
Rumbled in heaven. So in our quandary[31]
We sent Eurypylus[32] to Phoebus' oracle,[33]
And he brought back this grim reply:
"Blood and a virgin slain
You gave to appease the winds, for your first voyage
Troyward, O Danaans. Blood again
And Argive blood, one life, wins your return."

When this got round among the soldiers, gloom
Came over them, and a cold chill that ran
To the very marrow. Who had death in store?
Whom did Apollo call for? Now the man
Of Ithaca hauled Calchas out among us
In tumult, calling on the seer to tell
The true will of the gods. Ah, there were many
Able to divine the crookedness
And cruelty afoot for me, but they
Looked on in silence. For ten days the seer
Kept still, kept under cover, would not speak
Of anyone, or name a man for death,
Till driven to it at last by Ulysses' cries—
By prearrangement—he broke silence, barely
Enough to designate me for the altar.
Every last man agreed. The torments each
Had feared for himself, now shifted to another,
All could endure. And the infamous day came,
The ritual, the salted meal, the fillets[34] . . .
I broke free, I confess it, broke my chains,
Hid myself all night in a muddy marsh,
Concealed by reeds, waiting for them to sail
If they were going to.
                    Now no hope is left me
Of seeing my home country ever again,
My sweet children, my father, missed for years.

---

31. quandary (kwän′ də rē) *n.*: State of uncertainty.
32. Eurypylus (yoo rip′ ə ləs): A Greek.
33. Phoebus' oracle: The oracle of Apollo at Delphi.
34. fillets (fil′ its) *n.*: Woolen bands worn by sacrificial victims.

Historical Context: The fake oracular utterance refers to Agamemnon's sacrificing his daughter, Iphigeneia, so the winds would blow and his fleet could sail to Troy from Aulis. In Euripides' dramatic version of the myth, Odysseus (Ulysses), with the deceitful cooperation of the seer Calchas, engineers the human sacrifice for his own ambitious ends. Virgil would expect his audience to remember not only the myth in general but the popular Euripidean play.

Cultural Context: Victims were symbolically sprinkled with grain and garlanded with white fillets before being sacrificed to the gods. Virgil frequently, as here, uses a few concrete details to suggest a whole scene.

13 Literary Focus One device that Sinon uses to make the fictitious scene vivid is oblique quotation. Have students look at lines 160–161 and consider how the information might have been conveyed differently. What is the effect of not specifying the speaker? Do the students feel as if they are eavesdropping?

14 Discussion Ask students to think about how Sinon is working to arouse sympathy and increase his credibility. What is the purpose of "confessing" a weakness?

15 Discussion Ask students what devices Sinon uses to make this fictitious scene seem like something he experienced and is recalling.

3. Has anything been added to the illustration that confuses you?
4. Are you surprised that the artist would have done so many pieces based on a single book? Why or why not?

Primary Source

In his pioneering essay "Epic and Novel" (collected in *The Dialogic Imagination*), M. M. Bakhtin writes:

"The world of the epic is the national heroic past: it is a world of 'beginnings' and 'peak times' in the national history, a world of fathers and founders of families, a world of firsts and bests. The important point here is not that the past constitutes the content of the epic. The formally constitutive feature of the epic as a genre is rather the transferral of a represented world into the past . . . The epic has been from the beginning a poem about the past, and the authorial position immanent in the epic and constitutive for it (that is, the position of one who utters the epic word) is the environment of a man speaking about a past that is to him inaccessible, the reverent point of view of a descendent."

16 Literary Focus This section is the standard peroration, the grand finale of a speech. Making the final grand play for the audience's pity and mercy is typical of courtroom oratory. Normally, this commonplace marks the end of a speech and contains what the speaker is asking his audience to do. In Sinon's case this is only the preliminary stage of his performance; what he really wants the Trojans to do is not contained in the speech at all.

17 Discussion Priam's total acceptance of Sinon seems to be what Sinon wanted. It is simply a precondition for Sinon's speech of persuasion. Ask students to notice how Virgil indicates that a new phase of the episode is beginning.

18 Discussion Have students think about "unfettered." How does the adjective not only reiterate Priam's freeing of Sinon but recall Sinon's entrance? Why does Virgil want us to recall that the Trojans have trusted him and set him free although he was in their power?

19 Discussion Aeneas has commented frequently, before this, on what he reports, interrupting his narrative to remind his audience that Sinon is lying. Now he makes such a comment in lines 198–199, but then quotes Sinon's long speech in its entirety, without interruption (lines 199–258). What is Virgil's purpose in exposing not only Dido but us, his readers, to Sinon's speech without mediation? If we are moved by Sinon's words and taken in by his narrative and argument, what will our attitude be toward the Trojans?

16 Cultural Context: From at least the time of the First Punic War (264 B.C.), it was a popular Roman stance to look down on Greeks as frivolous and impractical. One of the ways Romans said "relax and have fun" was "act like a Greek." Here Virgil plays on this national prejudice, presenting the Greeks as stage actors and the Trojans (or Romans) as **17** men too serious to understand play-acting and tricks. The first comedies and tragedies produced in Rome were **18** borrowed from the Greek stage.

Cultural Context: Falsely swearing a solemn oath was a serious offense. During the long years of the civil wars in Rome, however, Virgil's audience would have seen more than one solemn oath of state made only to be broken. Aeneas may be thinking that only Greeks are treacherous, but Virgil wants his audience to think about treachery as a human problem.

Perhaps the army will demand they pay
For my escape, my crime here, and their death,
Poor things, will be my punishment. Ah, sir,
185 I beg you by the gods above, the powers
In whom truth lives, and by what faith remains
Uncontaminated to men, take pity
On pain so great and so unmerited!"

For tears we gave him life, and pity, too.
190 Priam himself ordered the gyves[35] removed
And the tight chain between. In kindness then
He said to him:
                    "Whoever you may be,
The Greeks are gone; forget them from now on;
You shall be ours. And answer me these questions:
195 Who put this huge thing up, this horse?
Who designed it? What do they want with it?
Is it religious or a means of war?"

These were his questions. Then the captive, trained
In trickery, in the stagecraft of Achaea,
200 Lifted his hands unfettered[36] to the stars.
"Eternal fires of heaven," he began,
"Powers inviolable, I swear by thee,
As by the altars and blaspheming swords
I got away from, and the gods' white bands[37]
205 I wore as one chosen for sacrifice,
This is justice, I am justified
In dropping all allegiance to the Greeks—
As I had cause to hate them; I may bring
Into the open what they would keep dark.
210 No laws of my own country bind me now.
Only be sure you keep your promises
And keep faith, Troy, as you are kept from harm
If what I say proves true, if what I give
Is great and valuable.
                        The whole hope
215 Of the Danaans, and their confidence
In the war they started, rested all along
In help from Pallas. Then the night came
When Diomedes and that criminal,

---

35. gyves (gīvz) *n.*: Fetters or shackles used to restrain.
36. unfettered (un´ fet´ ərd) *adj.*: Unchained; unrestrained.
37. god's white bands: Fillets.

Grammar in Action

Prepositional Phrases Phrases made up of prepositions and their objects are modifiers, used as either adjectives or adverbs. As adjectives they usually modify nouns (means *of war,* line 197) while as adverbs they modify verbs (rested . . . *in help,* lines 216–217), adjectives (trained *in trickery,* lines 198–199), or other adverbs (blaspheming swords . . . away *from,* lines 203–204).

Note that a gerund, a verbal noun, can be the object of a preposition (I am justified *in dropping,* lines 206–207), and a participle, a verbal adjective, can be modified by a prepositional phrase (desecrating *with bloody hands,* line 222).

Student Activity 1. Pick out from page 501 three prepositional phrases used as adjectives and ten used as adverbs, listing the word modified as well as the phrase itself. Indicate whether the adverb phrases modify verbs, adjectives, or other adverbs.

Student Activity 2. Write a paragraph in which you tell in your own words Sinon's explanation for the construction of the wooden horse and the penalty involved in transporting it into Troy. Include three prepositional phrases used as adjectives and three used as adverbs.

Ulysses, dared to raid her holy shrine.
They killed the guards on the high citadel
And ripped away the statue, the Palladium,[38]
Desecrating with bloody hands the virginal
Chaplets[39] of the goddess. After that,
Danaan hopes waned and were undermined,
Ebbing away, their strength in battle broken,
The goddess now against them. This she made
Evident to them all with signs and portents.
Just as they set her statue up in camp,
The eyes, cast upward, glowed with crackling flames,
And salty sweat ran down the body. Then—
I say it in awe—three times, up from the ground,
The apparition of the goddess rose
In a lightning flash, with shield and spear atremble.
Calchas divined at once that the sea crossing
Must be attempted in retreat—that Pergamum[40]
Cannot be torn apart by Argive swords
Unless at Argos first they get new omens,
Carrying homeward the divine power
Brought overseas in ships. Now they are gone
Before the wind to the fatherland, Mycenae,
Gone to enlist new troops and gods. They'll cross
The water again and be here, unforeseen.
So Calchas read the portents. Warned by him,
They set this figure up in reparation
For the Palladium stolen, to appease
The offended power and expiate[41] the crime.
Enormous, though, he made them build the thing
With timber braces, towering to the sky,
Too big for the gates, not to be hauled inside
And give the people back their ancient guardian.
If any hand here violates this gift
To great Minerva, then extinction waits,
Not for one only—would god it were so—
But for the realm of Priam and all Phrygians.
If this proud offering, drawn by your hands,
Should mount into your city, then so far

---

38. Palladium (pə lā′ dē əm) *n.*: A statue of Pallas (Athene) at her shrine in Troy. According to the oracle, Troy could not be captured as long as the Palladium remained in place.

39. Chaplets (chap′ lits) *n.*: Fillets; garlands.

40. Pergamum (pʉr′ gə məm) *n.*: The citadel of Troy.

41. expiate (eks′ pē āt′) *v.*: Atone for; make amends for.

Literary Context: Sinon's narrative is so full of believable details that we forget he is lying. One effect of the vivid narrative is to create an indelible impression of Greek brutality and cunning.

Cultural Context: Why does Calchas say that the Greeks must go back to Argos and start the expedition all over again? Beginning a religious ceremony all over again if it is spoiled by some inauspicious sign (like a sacrificial victim stumbling on its way to the altar, or a priest mispronouncing a word) is a Roman custom, unknown to the Greeks. Virgil may be suggesting that the Greeks are well informed about Trojan (Roman) customs or he may be blurring the distinction between Greeks and Trojans.

Literary Context: Finally, Sinon comes to the purpose of his entire performance, to have the Trojans take the wooden horse behind their gates. To achieve his end, he has to establish credibility, a difficult assignment. Virgil has created a chilling picture of an agent slyly left behind in order to be captured. He may have had a model in one of the many intriguing political figures of his time.

20 Discussion Encourage students not only to think about all the senses to which these lines appeal but also to discuss how making listeners recall or vicariously experience physical reactions might serve to make the content of the narrative more convincing.

21 Discussion Lead students to see that Sinon has finally reached the real purpose of this entire charade. How does he explain not only the existence of the wooden horse but also its size?

22 Discussion Sinon does not want the Trojans to discover the hidden men. He intends to have them breach their walls in order to take in the horse. Have students see that he achieves his purpose not by telling them to do so directly, but by making them think that if they do, they will be outwitting the Greeks.

23 **Discussion** Discuss how this conclusion is the purpose of Aeneas' speech.

Humanities Note

Fine art, *The Trojans Defending Their City*, is another plaque in the series of seventy-four scenes illustrating Virgil's *Aeneid* (c. 1525–1540). Executed in the extremely difficult medium of enamel on copper, this scene has all the detail and the life of the German woodcut illustration on which it is based. As in Grüninger's woodcut, perspective is achieved through scale. The figures in the foreground are larger than those in the distance and thus seem closer. The Trojan horse is made a focal point merely by the contrast of its white color against the dark background.

It is thought these tiles were created to line the walls of a small study for a member of the French nobility.

You might want to use the following questions to discuss the art:
1. How would you feel upon entering a room lined with these miniature masterpieces?
2. Did you picture the city of Troy with walls that seemed medieval?
3. Why do you think the artist depicted it in this way?
4. What do you enjoy best about this scene?

Cultural Note Students might think about how much "classical" rhetoric is used in the world around them, in political speeches or in advertisements. Examples abound in literature as well. Students might think of the king and the duke in Mark Twain's *Huckleberry Finn*, of Sinclair Lewis's *Elmer Gantry*, or of Manley Pointer in Flannery O'Connor's "Good Country People."

Literary Context: Virgil must deal with the undeniable historical fact that the Greeks defeated the Trojans. Since the Romans did not have much respect for losers, 23 the poem must show how the Greeks won only through unscrupulous cunning, not superior courage or strength, while the Trojans defeated themselves through their own generosity, honesty, and mercy.

As the walls of Pelops' town[42] the tide of Asia
Surges in war: that doom awaits our children."

260 This fraud of Sinon, his accomplished lying,
Won us over; a tall tale and fake tears
Had captured us, whom neither Diomedes
Nor Larisaean Achilles[43] overpowered,
Nor ten long years, nor all their thousand ships.

Despite warnings that Greeks are hiding in the horse, the Trojans bring the horse inside the walls of Troy. During the night, the horse emits the Greeks, who are ready for combat. Aeneas is also ready. In fierce spirit, he and his men fight against desperate odds. His fury increases when he sees Helen, whom he blames for the war. As he lunges to kill her in an attempt to avenge his people, his mother calms him.

Aeneas returns home, arms himself, and takes his family, Anchises, Iulus, and his wife, Creusa, out of the city. On the way out, Aeneas loses sight of Creusa and hides his father and son while he searches frantically for his wife. She dies in the chaos, but her spirit appears to Aeneas, urging him not to mourn her. She repeats the prophecy that peace and a great kingdom await him. Toward daybreak, Aeneas finds a crowd of refugees gathered for exile, waiting for him to lead them to safety. He does so, with characteristic courage.

---

42. **Pelops'** (pel´ əps) **town:** Argos. Pelops was an early king of Mycenae and an ancestor of Menelaus and Agamemnon.
43. **Larisaean Achilles** (lə ris´ ´ē ən ə kil´ ēz): Achilles, the foremost Greek warrior, was so called after Larissa, a town in his homeland of Thessaly.

THE TROJANS DEFENDING THEIR CITY
Attributed to the Limoges Master of the Aeneid, c. 1530–1540
The Metropolitan Museum of Art, New York

THINKING ABOUT THE SELECTION

Clarifying

1. (a)Why do some of the Trojans fear the wooden horse? (b) How do the Trojans feel about the horse at the end of Sinon's performance?
2. Who does Sinon say he is, and what reasons does he give for running away from the Greeks?

Interpreting

3. Think about how Sinon first appears "on stage," and what nonverbal stage business accompanies his words. As Virgil calls attention to Sinon's acting, how does he help us see Sinon's theatrical flair?
4. Sinon tells a moving story to the Trojans, who spare him and offer him a home. Do you think Virgil draws parallels between him and Aeneas, telling the story of his own misfortunes to Dido, who has offered him protection and a home? Explain your answer.
5. (a) Sinon's speech is filled with convincing but wholly fabricated portents and oracles. What do you think this might suggest to Aeneas and his listeners about the Greeks' reverence for the gods? (b) In contrast, how do the Trojans' reactions to these portents and oracles cast a favorable light on them?

Applying

6. Think of some reasons why someone might want to infiltrate a group in our own day. (a) Would an approach like Sinon's work? Explain your answer. (b) What tactics of Sinon's would be most useful?

ANALYZING LITERATURE

Understanding Narrative in Epic

Virgil presents a large proportion of his story through speeches. He invites us to experience the teller's perspective and to enter into his or her mind. In Book II Virgil introduces Aeneas' narrative, then yields the floor to him. Aeneas is speaking especially to Dido, and we must remember that he is aiming his story at her. At the same time, Virgil is aware of the external audience (us). Aeneas' eyewitness account contains the speeches of others, especially the performance by Sinon. Sinon's speech has such immediacy that it takes us in, so we can experience why the Trojans were duped.

1. What makes Sinon's false stories seem real?
2. Look at his description of the soldiers' response to the false oracle (lines 158–161). What words are most vivid?
3. Look at the shrine's violation (lines 220–233). What is the effect of words like "bloody," or "salty"?

CRITICAL THINKING AND READING

Inferring an Author's Opinion

Like Homer, Virgil seldom interjects his own point of view in the narrative. He may describe a character as "pious" or "wretched," but he avoids telling his readers what to think. By reading between the lines, however, we can make inferences about the author's opinions.

1. What inferences can you draw about Virgil's view of human nature? Find evidence to support your answer. How would Virgil answer this question?
2. How do people deceive themselves and allow others to deceive them? Find evidence for your answer.

THINKING AND WRITING

Expanding on Myth

Imagine that you are a Greek warrior in the horse. Freewrite, exploring your thoughts and feelings. What are you experiencing? You can feel, smell, touch, and hear, but it is too dark to see. Then, building on the descriptions of the Trojan horse and other people's reactions to it, like Laocoön's striking the belly, write the first draft of a first-person narrative. When you revise, make sure you have recounted the events in order. Check to see that you have included details. Proofread and share your paper.

(continued from bottom of page)

might work in infiltrating a group today if a person with his coldheartedness played that role. (b) His poker face and his ability to lie well would be the elements most useful for such deceit.

ANSWERS TO ANALYZING LITERATURE

1. His ability to seem sincere is the quality that makes Sinon's stories seem real.
2. "Cold" and "to the very marrow" suggest specific physical reactions. The reproduced questions "Who . . . ? Whom . . . ?" make the reader hear what is going on in the men's minds and what they are whispering. The sudden, violent intervention of Ulysses "among us" puts the reader in the middle of that terrified assembly.
3. The words used often appeal to the senses. They let us see, hear, or taste the actions.

ANSWERS TO CRITICAL THINKING AND READING

1. It is clear that Virgil's view is mixed. He can as readily create dishonest characters as he can fashion those who are faultless. If asked, Virgil might say that human nature was dual and that it showed a capacity for goodness as well as for evil.
2. People deceive themselves by turning away from factual evidence and by believing what suits them best. It is for the same reasons that they allow others to deceive them as well.

Closure and Extension

ANSWERS TO THINKING ABOUT THE SELECTION

1. (a) They fear the horse because any gift from Greeks would seem uncharacteristic of such an opponent. (b) By the end of Sinon's speech, the Trojans are divided in their opinion about the horse. Some remain suspicious. Others are reassured.

2. Sinon presents himself as an opponent to the war who was framed by Ulysses. He says that he fled to save his life.

3. He helps us see Sinon's flair by having him pause in his speech to mime terror (line 102) and feign fear (line 142). Virgil also has him swear and cry.

4. Answers will differ. It is not likely that Virgil intended such a parallel to be entertained. He would not have compared Sinon's deceit to the early relationship between Aeneas and Dido.

5. (a) The ease with which Sinon makes up divine utterances suggests a cynical disrespect for the gods. (b)The Trojans, by contrast, seem like a godfearing people who are being exploited in part because of their respect for the divine order of things.

6. (a) Yes, an approach like Sinon's

TRACING AENEAS' JOURNEY

Motivation/Prior Knowledge Students should know something about the geography of the Mediterranean Sea in order to appreciate much of what Aeneas experienced during his stormy journey from Troy to Rome. Remind them of the importance of maps and charts for crews, like the one on the starship *Enterprise*, who wish to calculate times and distances before setting out on long trips. Ask them if they think Aeneas himself might have had maps to direct his adventures.

The *Aeneid* is truly a national epic—one that glorifies and exalts Rome and the destiny of the Roman people. Its hero, Aeneas, personifies the traits that Roman people held dear—a heightened sense of duty and of responsibility to the state. During his seven years of wandering, Aeneas underwent many hardships, but he consoled himself with the knowledge of his great destiny to found Rome.

The Wanderings of Aeneas

The *Aeneid* begins "in medias res," which means "in the middle of things." Aeneas is in Carthage, near the end of his journey to Italy. Here he tells Queen Dido the story of the fall of Troy and his subsequent wanderings.

Troy was a wealthy and powerful city-state on the western coast of modern Turkey. After a siege that lasted ten years, Troy finally fell to the Greeks. Learning of the prophesy that he would found a great nation, Aeneas and a small band of refugees set sail.

Aeneas sails from Troy to Aenos, then through a safe passage between two islands to Delos, where he stops to worship Apollo. Apollo sends them to the island of Crete, the "cradle" of their race. From Crete, Aeneas sails for three stormy days until he reaches the Strophades, islands in the Ionian Sea. After he and his Trojans feast there and pray, they set sail for Ithaca.

In Ithaca, Aeneas meets a prophet who maps the remainder of the journey for him. The prophet advises Aeneas to avoid sailing too close to the rocky Sicilian coast where deadly waves crash ships against the rocks. According to the prophet, if Aeneas sets sail west around Sicily, he will come to Cumae, where a priestess will sing the oracles and guide him safely to the end of his journey.

Heeding the prophet's warning, Aeneas and the Trojans sail on to Cumae, but on the way, Aeneas' father, Anchises, dies on the shoreline of Drepanum on the coast of Sicily. Devastated, Aeneas sets sail but is thrown off his route by a violent storm. He reaches Carthage on the coast of Africa, where, under the influence of the gods, he meets and falls in love with queen Dido.

During their romantic interlude, Aeneas is reminded of his ultimate destiny. He leaves Dido brokenhearted and sets sail for Cumae, only to be foiled this time by a violent storm that takes him back to Drepanum.

Next, Aeneas drives his fleet to Cumae, where he meets the priestess Sybil, who will show him his fate by leading him through the underworld. After emerging from the underworld, he sets sail for Latium in central Italy. He turns his course to land and realizes that he and his fleet have reached the Latin shore. Their voyage is complete. His descendant, Romulus, will go on to found the city of Rome in 753 B.C.

Reading a Map

The map on the right represents part of the ancient world. Specifically, it plots the wanderings of Aeneas from Troy to central Italy. The heavy line represents the route that Aeneas took from Troy, where he began his journey, to Latium, or Rome. Bodies of water are labeled, indicating

NSIGHTS

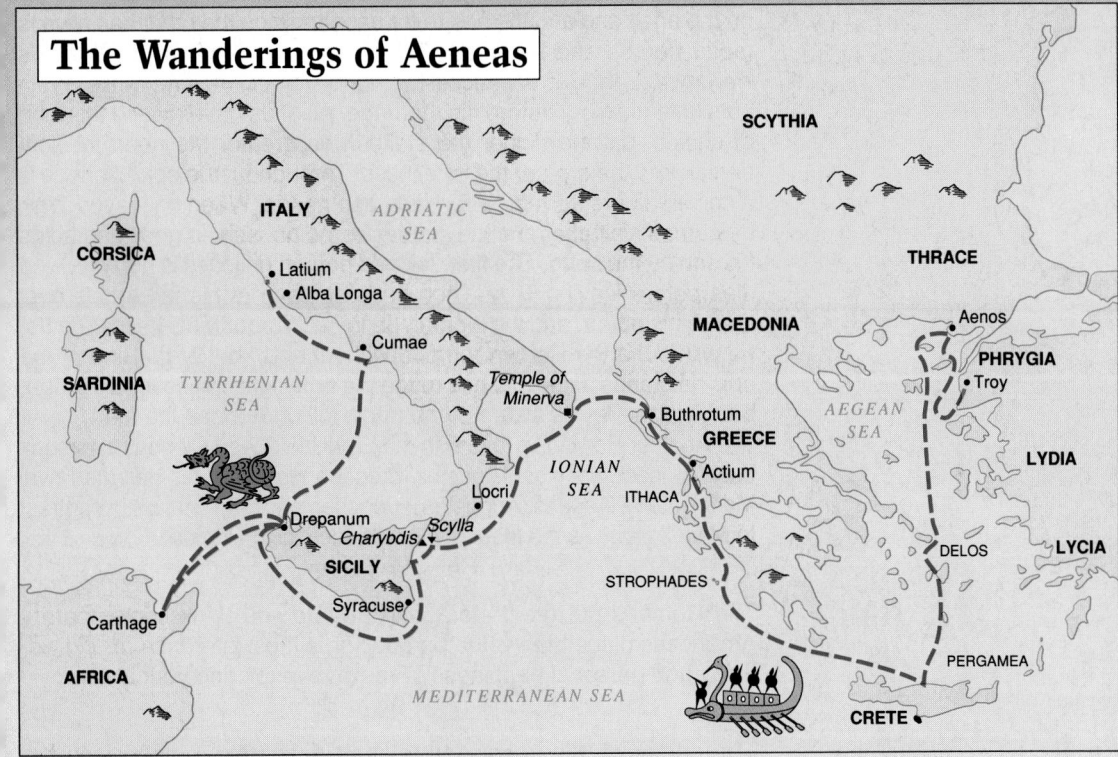

The Wanderings of Aeneas

(Map showing locations including: SCYTHIA, ITALY, CORSICA, ADRIATIC SEA, Latium, Alba Longa, Cumae, SARDINIA, TYRRHENIAN SEA, THRACE, MACEDONIA, Aenos, PHRYGIA, Troy, Temple of Minerva, Buthrotum, GREECE, AEGEAN SEA, LYDIA, Actium, Locri, IONIAN SEA, ITHACA, Drepanum, Charybdis, Scylla, SICILY, DELOS, LYCIA, Syracuse, STROPHADES, Carthage, AFRICA, MEDITERRANEAN SEA, PERGAMEA, CRETE)

ANSWERS TO CRITICAL THINKING QUESTIONS

1. He would have had false starts because there are so many places along the route. They were already settled by others who did not want outsiders.
2. It is a natural rival because its location allows it to dominate the southwestern section of the Mediterranean Sea.
3. The natural outcome of the policies was to justify the expansion of the nations as they reached beyond their original borders.

Enrichment You may wish to use the following questions after students have studied the map:
1. In what direction would you sail from Carthage to Rome?
2. In what direction would you travel from Greece to Italy?
3. What island is north of Sardinia?
4. Name the sea to the west of Greece.
5. Name the country north of Greece.

Answers
1. North
2. West
3. Corsica
4. Ionian
5. Macedonia

which seas Aeneas had to cross. From the map, you should get a sense of the great distance Aeneas had to travel and the natural obstacles he had to overcome.

CRITICAL THINKING

1. One of the most interesting facets of Aeneas' journey is the geography of where he goes. Locate Troy and then trace Aeneas' journey to central Italy. Based on the geography of the area, why would Aeneas have met with so many false landfalls and abortive attempts to resettle?
2. According to myth, Juno tried to prevent Aeneas from reaching Italy because she knew of Rome's eventual destiny to destroy her beloved city of Carthage. Look at the location of Carthage. Why would Rome have considered Carthage a rival for control of the western Mediterranean?
3. **Cooperative Learning** One of Virgil's purposes in writing the *Aeneid* was to justify Rome's "national destiny" toward empire. In the nineteenth century, the United States promulgated the concept of "manifest destiny." Working with a group of students, compare Rome's idea of "national destiny" with the United States' idea of "manifest destiny." What was the outcome of both policies? Report your findings to your classmates.

Focus

Literary Focus Have students discuss stories or films that involve a choice between conflicting obligations. Remind them of recent or classic films that deal with tensions similar to the ones that will force Aeneas and Dido apart. Ask if they believe choices are easier or harder when a society does not have a clear and unified view of where duty lies.

Writing/Prior Knowledge Divide the class into small groups and have each group brainstorm to come up with one or two examples of a difficult choice they can imagine having to make between what they want for themselves and what they feel they should do.

Vocabulary

Preteach the following vocabulary words:
quandaries (kwän´ drēz) *n.*: Uncertainties; dilemmas.
throes (thrōz) *n.*: Spasms; pangs of pain
qualms (kwämz) *n.*: Misgivings
progeny (präj´ ə nē) *n.*: Children
plummeted (plum´ it id) *v.*: Dropped; plunged
reproachful (ri prōch´ fəl) *adj.*: Full of blame
dissolution (dis´ ə loo´ shən) *n.*: Disintegration: ending

from the Aeneid, Book IV

Commentary

Heroic Conflict. The conflict between duty to some higher authority on the one hand and the desire for happiness on the other has always faced heroes and heroines. For instance, in Chrétien de Troyes's *Perceval*, Lancelot sacrifices his honor for Guinevere, while Yvain puts knightly glory before his marriage. All of us have to face this kind of choice, but the higher the stakes, the greater the need for self-denial, and the greater the loneliness. Throughout the epic, Aeneas is a solitary figure, torn between duty and needs. When he leaves Troy, he carries his father and the statues of the household gods and holds his son by the hand. The first beloved person he loses is his wife, who dies before leaving Troy. Then he is stripped of his father, his best friend, his nurse, and the woman he loves. Through his descendants, he will found the Roman "empire without end," but at the end of the epic he stands alone. He has made the only right choice for a Roman, but Virgil makes us aware of the tragic toll on Aeneas the man.

Another Roman, in love with the Egyptian queen Cleopatra, forsook duty. At least this was Augustus' propaganda about his defeated rival Mark Antony. Aeneas, Augustus' supposed ancestor, stands in contrast to Mark Antony as the ideal of the self-sacrificing Roman.

Writing

The Romans put great stock on duty. Do you think contemporary Americans place high value on duty, or is the preference for individuality and personal happiness? Freewrite, exploring your answer.

Primary Source

The author of this translation, Robert Fitzgerald, emphasized the relationship between Troy and Rome in his commentary on Book IV. When reading his statement, it is important to remember the Punic Wars between Rome and Carthage. The Carthaginians crossed the Alps to invade Italy in 218 B.C. This event would have been on the Roman reader's mind when reading the exchange between Aeneas and Dido. Fitzgerald writes: "All of this, and a great deal more, came to the mind of the Roman reader as Virgil in his exordium told of the Tyrian settlement dear to Juno, implacable enemy of the Trojans, just as Carthage in days to come would be, year after year for many, the most dangerous enemy of Rome. The adventure of Aeneas and his people as guests of the Carthaginian queen would seem . . . as narrow an escape as that of Rome when beset by Carthage. Dido indeed in her final curse called for future strife without quarter between her descendants and those of Aeneas and prayed for one Carthaginian in particular, aliquis ultor, 'someone to avenge me.' At this the Roman reader murmured 'Hannibal.'"

Objectives

Thematic

To understand the way passion can upset the course of events

Skills

1 To understand heroic conflict

2 To evaluate divine influence

3 To analyze persuasive language

4 To compose a farewell letter

from the Aeneid

Book IV: The Passion of the Queen

The queen,[1] for her part, all that evening ached
With longing that her heart's blood fed, a wound
Or inward fire eating her away.
The manhood of the man, his pride of birth,
Came home to her time and again; his looks,
His words remained with her to haunt her mind,
And desire for him gave her no rest.
                When Dawn
Swept earth with Pheobus' torch[2] and burned
    away
Night-gloom and damp, this queen, far gone and
    ill,
Confided to the sister of her heart:
"My sister Anna, quandaries and dreams
Have come to frighten me—such dreams!
            Think what a stranger
Yesterday found lodging in our house:
How princely, how courageous, what a soldier.
I can believe him in the line of gods,
And this is no delusion. Tell-tale fear
Betrays inferior souls. What scenes of war
Fought to the bitter end he pictured for us!
What buffetings awaited him at sea!
Had I not set my face against remarriage
After my first love died and failed me, left me
Barren and bereaved—and sick to death
At the mere thought of torch and bridal bed—
I could perhaps give way in this one case
To frailty. I shall say it: since that time
Sychaeus, my poor husband, met his fate,[3]
And blood my brother shed stained our hearth
    gods,

This man alone has wrought upon me so
And moved my soul to yield. I recognize
30 The signs of the old flame, of old desire.
But O chaste life, before I break your laws,
I pray that Earth may open, gape for me
Down to its depth, or the omnipotent[4]
With one stroke blast me to the shades, pale
    shades
35 Of Erebus[5] and the deep world of night!
That man who took me to himself in youth
Has taken all my love; may that man keep it,
Hold it forever with him in the tomb."

At this she wept and wet her breast with tears.
But Anna answered:
40   "Dearer to your sister
Than daylight is, will you wear out your life,
Young as you are, in solitary mourning,
Never to know sweet children, or the crown
Of joy that Venus brings? Do you believe
45 This matters to the dust, to ghosts in tombs?
Granted no suitors up to now have moved you,
Neither in Libya[6] nor before, in Tyre—
Iarbas[7] you rejected, and the others,
Chieftains bred by the land of Africa
50 Their triumphs have enriched—will you contend
Even against a welcome love? Have you
Considered in whose lands you settled here?
On one frontier the Gaetulans,[8] their cities,

---

1. The queen: Dido, queen of Carthage, a rich commercial center in Africa; Carthage was originally a colony of Tyre, a principal city of the Phoenicians.
2. Phoebus' torch: The sun.
3. his fate: Sychaeus was murdered by Pygmalion, Dido's brother and king of Tyre.

4. the omnipotent (ăm nip′ ə tənt) *n.*: The almighty Jupiter, also known as Jove, who has power over everything.
5. Erebus (e′ rə bəs) *n.*: The lower depths of Hades, the underworld.
6. Libya (lib′ ē ə) *n.*: North African country where Carthage was located.
7. Iarbas (ē är′ bəs) *n.*: An African king and one of Dido's suitors.
8. Gaetulans (gē′ too l′nz) *n.*: Savage African people who lived southwest of Carthage.

Support Material

Teaching Portfolio
Teacher Backup, p. 609
Grammar in Action Worksheets: *Pronoun-Antecedent Agreement,* p. 615; *Use of Commas: Parenthetical Phrases,* p. 617; *Participles and Participial Phrases,* p. 619; *Using Words That Create Mood,* p.

621
Usage and Mechanics Worksheet, p. 623
Vocabulary Check, p. 624
Analyzing Literature Worksheet, *Understanding Heroic Conflict,* p. 625
Language Worksheet, *Analyzing Persuasive Language,* p. 626
Selection Test, pp. 627–628

Presentation

Motivation/Prior Knowledge Tell students they are about to read a tragic love story. Ask what kinds of things love is most frequently compared to.

Purpose-Setting Question Why does Virgil not begin with Dido's speech to Anna?

Universal Themes Falling in love with the wrong person, or with the right person under the wrong circumstances, is a recurrent topic in literature. In tragic plots such a story ends unhappily. In comic plots the wrong person turns out to be the right person after all. Catullus' poems about Lesbia (pages 528–529) and Ovid's tale of Pyramus and Thisbe (page 532) tell unhappy stories but not in Virgil's high tragic mode. Happier endings occur in Boccaccio's "Federigo's Falcon" (page 684) and in Shakespeare's *The Tempest* (page 709).

1 Master Teacher Note When students see a word like *passion,* what comes to mind? After a brief discussion of their associations with the word, you might use this opportunity to build vocabulary by explaining that the word comes from the Latin word *passio,* which means "suffering."

2 Discussion Have students look at the choice of words in the opening lines. How does Virgil prepare the reader for the story's tragic outcome?

3 Discussion Point out that Dido experiences a conflict.

4 Enrichment There was a Roman ideal that a matron should be *univira,* a one-man woman.

5 Discussion Does Anna's advice seem reasonable? What feelings toward Dido motivate her?

6 Discussion Anna builds on a fear of hostile tribes. For the Romans, constantly fighting to stave off invasion of their frontiers, her concern would seem very reasonable.

7 Discussion In Book I, Juno appears as the ruthless persecutor of Aeneas. From the point of view of the Carthaginians, whose patron goddess she is, her intervention seems beneficent.

Humanities Note

Fine art, *Meeting of Dido and Aeneas* by Jacopo Amigoni. The Italian painter Jacopo Amigoni (1675–1752) worked in the Venetian rococo style. High regard and demand for his work brought him to England, Germany, and finally Spain, where he became court painter for Ferdinand VI.

Meeting of Dido and Aeneas (c. 1717) is a fresco (painting done on a wet plaster wall) from the Bavarian castle of Schleissheim.

You might want to use the following questions to discuss the art:

1. How does the decorative style of this fresco compare to that of the enameled plaques?
2. Which do you feel more suitably illustrates the *Aeneid*? Please explain your answer.
3. What details from the story you read have not been included?

THE MEETING OF DIDO AND AENEAS
Jacopo Amigoni, 1730

```
     People invincible in war—with wild
 55  Numidian horsemen,⁹ and the offshore banks,
     The Syrtës;¹⁰ on the other, desert sands,
     Bone-dry, where fierce Barcaean nomads¹¹ range.
     Or need I speak of future wars brought on
     From Tyre, and the menace of your brother?
 60  Surely by dispensation of the gods
```

———
9. Numidian (noo mid′ ē ən) **horsemen:** Horsemen of the most powerful local tribe.
10. Syrtës (sər′ tēz) *n*.: Treacherous sandbanks off the North African coast.
11. Barcaean nomads (bär kē′ ən): Wanderers from Barca, a city in north Africa. Barca is also the family name of the Carthaginian Hannibal, Rome's arch enemy. This reference predicts the Punic Wars between Rome and Carthage.

```
     And backed by Juno's will, the ships from Ilium¹²
     Held their course this way on the wind.
                                              Sister,
     What a great city you'll see rising here,
     And what a kingdom, from this royal match!
 65  With Trojan soldiers as companions in arms,
     By what exploits will Punic¹³ glory grow!
     Only ask the indulgence of the gods,
     Win them with offerings, give your guests ease,
     And contrive reasons for delay, while winter
```

———
12. Ilium (il′ ē əm) *n*.: Troy.
13. Punic (pyoo′ nik) *adj*.: Carthaginian.

Commentary

Imagery in the Aeneid: Presenting a Subtext Virgil uses imagery to influence his readers' reactions to characters and events. Without needing to make editorial comments or to interpret, Virgil suggests possible interpretations by his use of figurative language. Recurrent use of the serpent and the flame in metaphors and similes dominate the story of Dido. But serpents (for instance, the monstrous sea snakes that killed Laocoön when he sought to warn the Trojans against the wooden horse, or the serpent Sinon, whose very name hisses and is sinuous like a snake) and flames (also likened to serpents with their flickering tongues) also play a large part in the story of the fall of Troy. As these same images dominate the "siege" of Dido, readers are invited to associate the downfall of Dido and her city with the betrayal of Priam and the destruction of Troy. As usual Virgil aims at no simplistic contrasts or equations: He wants the reader to consider a multiplicity of associations and interpretations, to realize the complexity of human existence.

Another pervasive image in the story of Dido is that of the wounded animal. The extended simile in lines 92–98 both likens Dido to a gentle and graceful animal (a doe) and makes us identify with her suffering, confusion, and frenzied but vain flight. At the same time, by allowing us to associate

Gales rage, drenched Orion[14] storms at sea,
And their ships, damaged still, face iron skies."

This counsel fanned the flame, already kindled,
Giving her hesitant sister hope, and set her
Free of scruple. Visiting the shrines
They begged for grace at every altar first,
Then put choice rams and ewes to ritual death
For Ceres Giver of Laws; Father Lyaeus,[15]
Phoebus,[16] and for Juno[17] most of all
Who has the bonds of marriage in her keeping.
Dido herself, splendidly beautiful,
Holding a shallow cup, tips out the wine
On a white shining heifer,[18] between the horns,
Or gravely in the shadow of the gods
Approaches opulent altars. Through the day
She brings new gifts, and when the breasts are
    opened
Pores over organs, living still, for signs.[19]
Alas, what darkened minds have soothsayers!
What good are shrines and vows to maddened
    lovers?
The inward fire eats the soft marrow away,
And the internal wound bleeds on in silence.

Unlucky Dido, burning, in her madness
Roamed through all the city, like a doe
Hit by an arrow shot from far away
By a shepherd hunting in the Cretan woods—
Hit by surprise, nor could the hunter see
His flying steel had fixed itself in her;
But though she runs for life through copse and
    glade
The fatal shaft clings to her side.

                                            Now Dido
Took Aeneas with her among her buildings,
Showed her Sidonian[20] wealth, her walls prepared,
And tried to speak, but in mid-speech grew still.
When the day waned she wanted to repeat
The banquet as before, to hear once more
In her wild need the throes of Ilium,
And once more hung on the narrator's words.
Afterward, when all the guests were gone,
And the dim moon in turn had quenched her light,
And setting stars weighed weariness to sleep,
Alone she mourned in the great empty hall
And pressed her body on the couch he left:
She heard him still, though absent—heard and saw
    him.
Or she would hold Ascanius in her lap,
Enthralled by him, the image of his father,
As though by this ruse to appease a love
Beyond all telling.

                        Towers, half-built, rose
No farther; men no longer trained in arms
Or toiled to make harbors and battlements
Impregnable.[21] Projects were broken off,
Laid over, and the menacing huge walls
With cranes unmoving stood against the sky.

As soon as Jove's dear consort[22] saw the lady
Prey to such illness, and her reputation
Standing no longer in the way of passion,
Saturn's daughter[23] said to Venus:
                                            "Wondrous!
Covered yourself with glory, have you not,
You and your boy, and won such prizes, too.
Divine power is something to remember
If by collusion[24] of two gods one mortal
Woman is brought low.
                            I am not blind.
Your fear of our new walls has not escaped me,
Fear and mistrust of Carthage at her height.

---

14. Orion (ô rī′ ən) *n.*: A great mythological hunter; after his death he became a constellation whose setting in November signaled the onset of storms at sea.

15. Ceres Giver of Laws; Father Lyaeus: Ceres and Father Lyaeus (Bacchus) control the crops essential to the colonists' survival.

16. Phoebus: Apollo, whose title is also "Founder."

17. Ceres . . . and for Juno: Dido prays to these gods, all of whom are connected with the founding of cities, when she is about to abandon her responsibilities as founder of Carthage.

18. heifer (hef′ ər) *n.*: Young cow.

19. for signs: It was Roman practice to inspect the inner organs of sacrificial victims and interpret irregular or unusual features as signs of what the future held in store.

---

20. Sidonian (sī dō′ nē ən) *adj.*: Of Sidon; Dido fled the Phoenician city Sidon to found Carthage.

21. Impregnable (im preg′ nə b'l) *adj.*: Incapable of being captured or forcefully entered.

22. consort (kän′ sôrt) *n.*: Here, wife; refers to Juno.

23. Saturn's daughter: Refers to Juno; both Jupiter and Juno were offspring of Saturn.

24. collusion (kə lōō′ zhən) *n.*: Secret agreement for fraudulent purpose; conspiracy.

from the *Aeneid*, Book IV   509

---

8 Discussion A common theme for Virgil is how people hear what they want to, and go against their better judgment. Have the students think about how brief "set her free of scruple" is compared to her earlier long recital of the obstacles of the new attachment.

9 Discussion What does Virgil imply about superstition and soothsayers? How does he weigh Dido's consultation of the gods against her consuming malady?

10 Discussion Have students look closely at this extended simile. What scene is evoked in detail? What do students associate with the image of a wounded doe?

11 Discussion Ask students to think about how Virgil describes Dido's troubled soul, her obsession. How does he evoke the mood of Dido's sleepless night? Can they visualize the scenes? (Virgil has frequently been called a very cinematic poet. Can students see why?)

12 Enrichment The very visual description of a city where monumental building projects—not unlike the ones Augustus was undertaking in Rome—are halted suddenly is Virgil's way of showing the far-reaching effects of Dido's passion. She is not just a love-sick girl, she is the ruler of a nation and the founder of a new city. In becoming paralyzed she paralyzes and betrays her city. Her choice (forced on her by factors stronger than she is) has repercussions far beyond herself. Romans might be led to think (with horror) of what it would mean if Augustus were to act like Dido.

Aeneas with the unknowing hunter/shepherd, he suggests that we are not to consider Aeneas consciously guilty of her suffering. (Unlike Sinon, who sets out to betray and destroy the Trojans, Aeneas acts as an unwitting agent of destruction.) Have students look for images of fire, snakes, wounds, illness, and madness. What "subtext" does recurring imagery provide? What kind of richness does it add to the story being told more directly? Another way to think about this is what would be lost if there were no figurative language?

But how far will it go? What do you hope for,
Being so contentious?[25] Why do we not
Arrange eternal peace and formal marriage?
135 You have your heart's desire: Dido in love,
Dido consumed with passion to her core.
Why not, then, rule this people side by side
With equal authority? And let the queen
Wait on her Phrygian lord, let her consign
140 Into your hand her Tyrians as a dowry."

Now Venus knew this talk was all pretense,
All to divert the future power from Italy
To Libya; and she answered:
                              "Who would be
So mad, so foolish as to shun that prospect
145 Or prefer war with you? That is, provided
Fortune is on the side of your proposal.
The fates here are perplexing: would one city
Satisfy Jupiter's will for Tyrians
And Trojan exiles? Does he approve
150 A union and a mingling of these races?
You are his consort: you have every right
To sound him out. Go on, and I'll come, too."

But regal Juno pointedly replied:
"That task will rest with me. Just now, as to
155 The need of the moment and the way to meet it,
Listen, and I'll explain in a few words.
Aeneas and Dido in her misery
Plan hunting in the forest, when the Titan
Sun comes up with rays to light the world.
160 While beaters in excitement ring the glens
My gift will be a black raincloud, and hail,
A downpour, and I'll shake heaven with thunder.
The company will scatter, lost in gloom,
As Dido and the Trojan captain come
165 To one same cavern. I shall be on hand,
And if I can be certain you are willing,
There I shall marry them and call her his.
A wedding, this will be."
                          Then Cytherëa,
13 Not disinclined, nodded to Juno's plea,
170 And smiled at the stratagem[26] now given away.

---

25. **contentious** (kən ten´ shəs) *adj.*: Ready to argue; belligerent.
26. **stratagem** (strat´ ə jəm) *n.*: Trick or scheme to deceive an enemy in war.

Dawn came up meanwhile from the Ocean stream,
And in the early sunshine from the gates
Picked huntsmen issued: wide-meshed nets and snares,
Broad spearheads for big game, Massylian horsemen[27]
175 Trooping with hounds in packs keen on the scent.
But Dido lingered in her hall, as Punic
Nobles waited, and her mettlesome hunter
Stood nearby, cavorting[28] in gold and scarlet,
Champing his foam-flecked bridle. At long last
180 The queen appeared with courtiers in a crowd,
A short Sidonian cloak edged in embroidery
Caught about her, at her back a quiver
Sheathed in gold, her hair tied up in gold,
And a brooch of gold pinning her scarlet dress.
185 Phrygians came in her company as well,
And Iulus, joyous at the scene. Resplendent[29]
Above the rest, Aeneas walked to meet her,
To join his retinue[30] with hers. He seemed—
Think of the lord Apollo in the spring
190 When he leaves wintering in Lycia[31]
By Xanthus torrent,[32] for his mother's isle
Of Delos,[33] to renew the festival;
Around his altars Cretans,[34] Dryopës,[35]
And painted Agathyrsans[36] raise a shout,
195 But the god walks the Cynthian ridge[37] alone
And smooths his hair, binds it in fronded laurel,[38]
Braids it in gold; and shafts ring on his shoulders.
So elated and swift, Aeneas walked
With sunlit grace upon him.

---

27. **Massylian** (mə si´ lē ən) **horsemen:** Horsemen from west of Carthage.
28. **cavorting** (kə vôrt´ iŋ) *v.*: Leaping or prancing about happily.
29. **Resplendent** (ri splen´ dənt) *adj.*: Shining brightly; dazzling.
30. **retinue** (ret´ 'n yōō) *n.*: Train of attendants, followers, or servants.
31. **Lycia** (lish´ē ə) *n.*: Region of Asia Minor allied to Troy.
32. **Xanthus torrent:** The Scamander River, near Troy.
33. **Delos** (dē´läs) *n.*: Island in the Aegean where Apollo (Phoebus) was born.
34. **Cretans** (krē´ tənz): People from Crete, a large island in the Mediterranean, south of Greece.
35. **Dryopës** (drī´ ō pēz): People from northern Greece.
36. **Agathyrsans** (ag´ ə thir´ sənz): Inhabitants of Scythia, regions of Europe and Asia north of the Black Sea.
37. **Cynthian ridge** (kin´ thē ən): Hill on Delos.
38. **fronded laurel:** Leafy wreath.

Grammar in Action

Pronoun-Antecedent Agreement Since a pronoun takes the place of a noun, every pronoun refers to some noun or noun phrase called its *antecedent* that must agree with the pronoun in gender, number, and person, but not necessarily in case. The case of a pronoun depends on its use in the sentence.

AGREEMENT IN GENDER: *Dido* consumed with passion to *her* core (line 136)

AGREEMENT IN NUMBER: As *Dido and the Trojan captain* come . . . there I shall marry *them*. (lines 164–167)

AGREEMENT IN PERSON: *My* gift will be a black rain cloud . . . and *I'll* shake heaven with thunder. (lines 161–163)

AN EXCEPTION: The pronoun *that* in the construction *that is* (line 145) is part of a formal connective and does not have an antecedent.

                    Soon the hunters,
Riding in company to high pathless hills,
Saw mountain goats shoot down from a rocky
      peak
And scamper on the ridges; toward the plain
Deer left the slopes, herding in clouds of dust
In flight across the open lands. Alone,
the boy Ascanius, delightedly riding
His eager horse amid the lowland vales,
Outran both goats and deer. Could he only meet
Amid the harmless game some foaming boar,
Or a tawny lion down from the mountainside!

Meanwhile in heaven began a rolling thunder,
And soon the storm broke, pouring rain and hail.
Then Tyrians and Trojans in alarm—
With Venus' Dardan grandson[39]—ran for cover

Here and there in the wilderness, as freshets[40]
Coursed from the high hills.
215   Now to the self-same cave
Came Dido and the captain of the Trojans.
Primal Earth herself and Nuptial Juno[41]
Opened the ritual, torches of lightning blazed,
High Heaven became witness to the marriage,
And nymphs cried out wild hymns from a
220   mountain top.
       That day was the first cause of death, and first
Of sorrow. Dido had no further qualms
As to impressions given and set abroad;
225 She thought no longer of a secret love
But called it marriage. Thus, under that name,
She hid her fault.
                      Now in no time at all
Through all the African cities Rumor goes—

---

40. freshets (fresh′ its) *n*.: Streams of fresh water that flow into the sea.
41. Nuptial (nup′ shəl) **Juno:** Juno was the goddess of marriage.

39. Venus' Dardan grandson: Ascanius.

DIDO AND AENEAS TAKE
SHELTER IN A CAVE
*Illuminated
manuscript page
of* Aeneid
*Biblioteca Apostolica,
Vatican City*

Student Activity 1. Pick out the twelve pronouns in lines 186–199 and name the antecedent of each. The pronouns are: *her, his, hers, he, he, his, his, his, it, it, his, him.*

Student Activity 2. Write a paragraph in which you tell in your own words Juno's plan for bringing about Dido's and Aeneas' marriage. Include in your paragraph at least five pronouns with clearly expressed antecedents.

15 Discussion Ask students to think about lines 204–209. How does Virgil suggest that Ascanius is experiencing a hunt different from the adults'? What are his fantasies and daydreams? Did any of your students like fantasy adventures like Grail Quest or Dungeons and Dragons when they were Ascanius' age?

16 Clarification Marriage torches and joyful hymns were part of the Roman marriage ceremony. The lightning that replaces the torches is ill-omened, and the nymphs' shrill keening suggests a funeral, not a wedding.

Humanities Note

Fine art, *Dido and Aeneas Take Shelter in a Cave*, is a miniature painting on parchment from a fifth-century A.D. Roman manuscript known today as the *Vatican Virgil*.

The ancient artist made little attempt to employ the use of perspective in this painting. The sheltered couple in the roughly rendered cave are on the same plane as the guard and horses. Their somewhat larger size is the only indication that they are in the foreground. In contrast to the clumsy depth of the painting, the figures are handled with sensitive detail. The folds of their clothing and the facial expressions are delicately rendered. This combination of fine detail and flat perspective gives the pleasing overall effect of a jewel-toned tapestry.

You might want to use the following questions to discuss the art:

1. If the title of this painting were unknown to you, would you know that the couple were in a cave?
2. What do you like most about this painting?
3. What effect does the small size of the illustration have on your perception of it?

17 Master Teacher Note Write a definition of *rumor* on the board, e.g., "unverified information of uncertain origin usually spread by word of mouth." Explain to students that Virgil is using personification and allegory in talking about Rumor. How is Rumor described? What kind of a creature is she?

18 Discussion What creature can the students think of with so many eyes, tongues, mouths, and ears? (Have they come across other descriptions of a crowd or a mob that make it seem like a single monstrous creature?)

19 Literary Focus Ask students if they find "evenhandedly" an incongruous adjective in this context. What irony is involved?

20 Discussion How does Virgil see human gossip? What motivates it? How much truth is there in it?

21 Discussion Remind students of Virgil's similar oblique quotation of unattributed speech in Sinon's lying tale. What is gained by not saying "people said that . . ." but rather reproducing what seem like snatches of overheard conversation?

22 Discussion Why is Rumor "scabrous" and her course "twisting"?

23 Master Teacher Note Notice that the point of view serves to slant any speaker's presentation of "facts." Have students read larbas' prayer carefully.

24 Discussion Have students think about larbas' view of all Trojans as effeminate easterners. Ask them to think about the way people use stereotypes and racial, ethnic, or sexist slurs when they feel threatened or envious.

25 Discussion What does Virgil want us to understand about the state of mind of both lovers? Ask students to recall lines 286–287 later.

26 Discussion What is the tone of Jupiter's speech?

Nimble as quicksilver among evils. Rumor
Thrives on motion, stronger for the running,
230 Lowly at first through fear, then rearing high,
She treads the land and hides her head in cloud.
As people fable it, the Earth, her mother,
Furious against the gods, bore a late sister
To the giants Coeus[42] and Enceladus,[43]
235 Giving her speed on foot and on the wing:
Monstrous, deformed, titanic. Pinioned,[44] with
An eye beneath for every body feather,
And, strange to say, as many tongues and buzzing
Mouths as eyes, as many pricked-up ears,
240 By night she flies between the earth and heaven
Shrieking through darkness, and she never turns
Her eyelids down to sleep. By day she broods,
On the alert, on rooftops or on towers,
Bringing great cities fear, harping on lies
245 And slander evenhandedly with truth.
In those days Rumor took an evil joy
At filling countrysides with whispers, whispers,
Gossip of what was done, and never done:
How this Aeneas landed, Trojan born,
250 How Dido in her beauty graced his company,
Then how they reveled all the winter long
Unmindful of the realm, prisoners of lust.

These tales the scabrous[45] goddess put about
On men's lips everywhere. Her twisting course
255 Took her to King Iarbas, whom she set
Ablaze with anger piled on top of anger.
Son of Jupiter Hammon[46] by a nymph,
A ravished Garamantean,[47] this prince
Had built the god a hundred giant shrines,
260 A hundred altars, each with holy fires
Alight by night and day, sentries[48] on watch,
The ground enriched by victims' blood, the doors

---

42. Coeus (kē′ əs): Titan son of Ge (Earth) and Uranus (Sky).
43. Enceladus (en kel′ ə dəs): Titan who fought against Jupiter.
44. Pinioned (pin′ yənd) *adj.*: Winged; feathered.
45. scabrous (skab′ rəs) *adj.*: Scandalous.
46. Jupiter Hammon: Jupiter is here equated with the Libyan god Hammon, who has a ram's head.
47. Garamantean (gar′ ə man′ tē ən) *n.*: A person from south of Carthage in Africa.
48. sentries (sen′ trēz) *n.*: Military men posted to guard against and warn of danger.

Festooned[49] with flowering wreaths. Before his
    altars
King Iarbas, crazed by the raw story,
265 Stood, they say, amid the Presences,
With supplicating hands,[50] pouring out prayer:
"All powerful Jove, to whom the feasting Moors[51]
At ease on colored couches tip their wine,
Do you see this? Are we then fools to fear you
270 Throwing down your bolts? Those dazzling fires
Of lightning, are they aimless in the clouds
And rumbling thunder meaningless? This woman
Who turned up in our country and laid down
A tiny city at a price, to whom
275 I gave a beach to plow—and on my terms—
After refusing to marry me has taken
Aeneas to be master in her realm.
And now Sir Paris with his men, half-men,
His chin and perfumed hair tied up
280 In a Maeonian[52] bonnet, takes possession.
As for ourselves, here we are bringing gifts
Into these shrines—supposedly your shrines—
Hugging that empty fable."
                                        Pleas like this
From the man clinging to his altars reached
285 The ears of the Almighty. Now he turned
His eyes upon the queen's town and the lovers
Careless of their good name; then spoke to
    Mercury,
Assigning him a mission:
                                        "Son, bestir yourself,
Call up the Zephyrs,[53] take to your wings and
    glide.
290 Approach the Dardan captain where he tarries
Rapt[54] in Tyrian Carthage, losing sight
Of future towns the fates ordain. Correct him,
Carry my speech to him on the running winds:
No son like this did his enchanting mother
295 Promise to us, nor such did she deliver
Twice from peril at the hands of Greeks.
He was to be the ruler of Italy,

---

49. Festooned (fes tōond′) *adj.*: Adorned.
50. supplicating hands: Hands in position of prayer.
51. Moors (moorz) *n.*: Here, Africans.
52. Maeonian (mī ō′ nē ən) *adj.*: Of Maeonia, a region of Lydia in Asia Minor.
53. Zephyrs (zef′ ərz): The west winds.
54. Rapt (rapt) *adj.*: Completely absorbed or engrossed.

Commentary

Virgil's Aeneas as Epic Hero Readers have often found it hard to identify with Aeneas, whose ability to sacrifice himself (and others) for his mission may arouse admiration but may fail to engage our emotions the way Achilles' passionate hot-headedness and existential anguish, or Odysseus' very personal involvement with his country and his family tend to do. One of Virgil's editors, T. E. Page, says ". . . Virgil is unhappy in his hero. Compared with Achilles, his Aeneas is but the shadow of a man. He is an abstraction typifying the ideal Roman, in whom reverence for the gods and manly courage combine . . ." He upbraids Aeneas for "doing exactly what he ought to do

Potential empire, armorer of war;
To father men from Teucer's noble blood
And bring the whole world under law's dominion.
If glories to be won by deeds like these
Cannot arouse him, if he will not strive
For his own honor, does he begrudge his son,
Ascanius, the high strongholds of Rome?
What has he in mind? What hope, to make him
  stay
Amid a hostile race, and lose from view
Ausonian progeny,⁵⁵ Lavinian lands?⁵⁶
The man should sail: that is the whole point.
Let this be what you tell him, as from me."

He finished and fell silent. Mercury
Made ready to obey the great command
Of his great father, and he first tied on
The golden sandals, winged, that high in air
Transport him over seas or over land
Abreast of gale winds; then he took the wand
With which he summons pale souls out of Orcus⁵⁷
And ushers others to the undergloom,
Lulls men to slumber or awakens them,
And opens dead men's eyes. This wand in hand,
He can drive winds before him, swimming down
Along the stormcloud. Now aloft, he saw
The craggy flanks and crown of patient Atlas,⁵⁸
Giant Atlas, balancing the sky
Upon his peak—his pine-forested head
In vapor cowled, beaten by wind and rain.
Snow lay upon his shoulders, rills cascaded
Down his ancient chin and beard a-bristle
Caked with ice. Here Mercury of Cyllenë⁵⁹
Hovered first on even wings, then down
He plummeted to sea-level and flew on
Like a low-flying gull that skims the shallows
And rocky coasts where fish ply close inshore.

So, like a gull between the earth and sky,
The progeny of Cyllenë, on the wing
From his maternal grandsire, split the winds
To the sand bars of Libya.
                    Alighting tiptoe
On the first hutments,⁶⁰ there he found Aeneas
Laying foundations for new towers and homes.
He noted well the swordhilt the man wore,
Adorned with yellow jasper;⁶¹ and the cloak
Aglow with Tyrian dye upon his shoulders—
Gifts of the wealthy queen, who had inwoven
Gold thread in the fabric. Mercury
Took him to task at once:
                    "Is it for you
To lay the stones for Carthage's high walls,
Tame husband that you are, and build their city?
Oblivious of your own world, your own kingdom!
From bright Olympus he that rules the gods
And turns the earth and heaven by his power—
He and no other sent me to you, told me
To bring this message on the running winds:
What have you in mind? What hope, wasting your
  days
In Libya? If future history's glories
Do not affect you, if you will not strive
For your own honor, think of Ascanius,
Think of the expectations of your heir,
Iulus, to whom the Italian realm, the land
Of Rome, are due."
                    And Mercury, as he spoke,
Departed from the visual field of mortals
To a great distance, ebbed⁶² in subtle air.
Amazed, and shocked to the bottom of his soul
By what his eyes had seen, Aeneas felt
His hackles rise, his voice choke in his throat.
As the sharp admonition⁶³ and command
From heaven had shaken him awake, he now
Burned only to be gone, to leave that land
Of the sweet life behind. What can he do? How
  tell

---

55. **Ausonian progeny** (präj′ ə nē) *n.*: Italian lineage.
56. **Lavinian** (lə vin′ ē ən) **lands**: Lavinium was the first Trojan settlement in Italy.
57. **Orcus** (ôr′ kəs) *n.*: The underworld.
58. **patient Atlas** (at′ ləs) *n.*: Atlas was a high mountain range in western North Africa. By "patient Atlas" Virgil is referring to the legend of Titan Atlas, who revolted against Zeus; as punishment, Zeus made him hold up the sky on his shoulders.
59. **Cyllenë** (si lēn′ ē) *n.*: Highest mountain in the Peloponnese and birthplace of Mercury.

60. **hutments** (hut′ mənts) *n.*: Group of huts, as in an army camp.
61. **jasper** (jas′ pər) *n.*: Opaque quartz stone.
62. **ebbed** (ebd) *v.*: Faded away; disappeared.
63. **admonition** (ad′ mə ni′ shən) *n.*: Reprimand.

27 Discussion Why does Virgil dwell on the properties of the wand?

28 Literary Focus Call attention to the way a sort of implied metaphor (Mercury has wings on his sandals, and so flies; but the description of his flight equates him to a bird.) introduces an extended simile.

29 Discussion Along with Mercury we see Aeneas for the first time since his union with Dido. (Up to now we have seen him through the eyes of Rumor and Iarbas.) What is he wearing? (Dressed in Dido's gifts, he has also "gone native" and is becoming a Carthaginian. Romans would have thought of Mark Antony's alliance with Cleopatra of Egypt and of his wearing eastern garb.)

30 Discussion What kind of language is Mercury using? What do students think of a phrase like "tame husband"? Is Mercury just quoting Jupiter? What is different about his speech?

31 Discussion Aeneas' extreme physical reaction is described in detail. Ask students why they think Aeneas reacts so violently. Can they imagine an experience that would evoke the same kind of response?

---

and saying exactly what he ought to say. Once only he exhibits human frailty, and then it is to show that as a human being he can be contemptible. He accepts the love of Dido and then abandons her to despair and death."

Samuel Johnson is quoted as having said the Romans "would never have borne Virgil's description of Aeneas' treatment of Dido, if she had not been a Carthaginian." Many have shared the view expressed by Charles James Fox that Aeneas is "always either insipid or odious." Such attacks on Aeneas seem to ignore his anguish, the way that he suppresses all individualistic or "selfish" emotion, whenever he can, burying his feelings inside an apparently unshakable shell, as if he were willing an oak tree to grow up around him and encase him. At the end of the poem, he experiences extreme rage and grief over the death of the young Italian Pallas, who had been entrusted to him by the boy's father, good king Evander, who is also a kind of surrogate father for Aeneas. These violent emotions—love turned into murderous hatred toward the boy's killer—compel Aeneas to slay a man admitting defeat and begging for mercy, and that is the last view Virgil gives us of Aeneas. He is not "insipid," nor can he be dismissed as simply "odious."

The impassioned queen and hope to win her over?
What opening shall he choose? This way and that
370 He let his mind dart, testing alternatives,
Running through every one. And as he pondered
This seemed the better tactic: he called in
Mnestheus, Sergestus and stalwart Serestus,[64]
Telling them:
    "Get the fleet ready for sea,
375 But quietly, and collect the men on shore.
Lay in ship stores and gear."
      As to the cause
For a change of plan, they were to keep it secret,
Seeing the excellent Dido had no notion,
No warning that such love could be cut short;
380 He would himself look for the right occasion,
The easiest time to speak, the way to do it.
The Trojans to a man gladly obeyed.

The queen, for her part, felt some plot afoot
Quite soon—for who deceives a woman in love?
385 She caught wind of a change, being in fear
Of what had seemed her safety. Evil Rumor,
Shameless as before, brought word to her
In her distracted state of ships being rigged
In trim for sailing. Furious, at her wits' end,
390 She traversed the whole city all aflame
With rage, like a Bacchantë[65] driven wild
By emblems shaken, when the mountain revels
Of the odd year possess her, when the cry
Of Bacchus rises and Cithaeron[66] calls
395 All through the shouting night. Thus it turned out
She was the first to speak and charge Aeneas:

"You even hoped to keep me in the dark
As to this outrage, did you, two-faced man,
And slip away in silence? Can our love
400 Not hold you, can the pledge we gave not hold
 you,
Can Dido not, now sure to die in pain?
Even in winter weather must you toil
With ships, and fret to launch against high winds
For the open sea? Oh, heartless!

        Tell me now,
405 If you were not in search of alien lands
And new strange homes, if ancient Troy remained,
Would ships put out for Troy on these big seas?
Do you go to get away from me? I beg you,
By these tears, by your own right hand,[67] since I
410 Have left my wretched self nothing but that—
Yes, by the marriage that we entered on,
If ever I did well and you were grateful
Or found some sweetness in a gift from me,
Have pity now on a declining house!
415 Put this plan by, I beg you, if a prayer
Is not yet out of place.
Because of you, Libyans and nomad kings
Detest me, my own Tyrians are hostile;
Because of you, I lost my integrity
420 And that admired name by which alone
I made my way once toward the stars.
        To whom
Do you abandon me, a dying woman,
Guest that you are—the only name now left
From that of husband? Why do I live on?
425 Shall I, until my brother Pygmalion comes
To pull my walls down? Or the Gaetulan
Iarbas leads me captive? If at least
There were a child by you for me to care for,
A little one to play in my courtyard
430 And give me back Aeneas, in spite of all,
I should not feel so utterly defeated,
Utterly bereft."
      She ended there.
The man by Jove's command held fast his eyes
And fought down the emotion in his heart.
435 At length he answered:
        "As for myself, be sure
I never shall deny all you can say,
Your majesty, of what you meant to me.
Never will the memory of Elissa[68]
440 Stale for me, while I can still remember
My own life, and the spirit rules my body.
As to the event, a few words. Do not think
I meant to be deceitful and slip away.
I never held the torches of a bridegroom,

---

64. **Mnestheus** (nes′ thē əs), **Sergestus** (sər jes′ təs) **and stalwart Serestus** (sər es′ təs): Trojan leaders.
65. **Bacchantë** (bə kän′ tē) *n*.: A female follower of Bacchus in a trance at the Dionysian (Bacchan) festival.
66. **Cithaeron** (kith ē′ ran) *n*.: Mountain in Greece near Thebes, sacred to Bacchus.

67. **by your own right hand:** The hand with which Aeneas pledged his love and which Dido interprets as a vow of marriage.
68. **Elissa** (ə lis′ ə): Another name for Dido.

Grammar in Action
Use of Commas: Parenthetical Phrases A parenthetical phrase, one that interrupts the direct movement of a sentence, should be set off or enclosed by *two* commas:

The queen, *for her part,* felt some plot afoot. (line 383)

Evil Rumor, *shameless as before,* brought word to her. (lines 386–387)

Nouns used in direct address are treated as parenthetical phrases and punctuated identically:

AENEAS DEPARTING FROM CARTHAGE
Limoges Master of the Aeneid
The Metropolitan Museum of Art, New York

Never entered upon the pact of marriage.
If Fate permitted me to spend my days
By my own lights, and make the best of things
According to my wishes, first of all
I should look after Troy and the loved relics

Left me of my people. Priam's great hall
Should stand again; I should have restored the
450   tower
Of Pergamum for Trojans in defeat.
But now it is the rich Italian land

---

40 **Discussion** Have students paraphrase what Aeneas is saying. Have students think about truthfulness and tact. For instance, lines following 443 may be honest but insensitive. Call attention to lines following 445. Why is Aeneas so cruel? Does he know he is being cruel? (Remind students of the doe—unwitting hunter simile.) What does Aeneas mean? Could one say that Dido and Aeneas are now talking in different "languages?"

Humanities Note

Fine art, *Aeneas Departing from Carthage,* is a scene from Virgil's *Aeneid* created by an unknown French artist in the city of Limoges (c. 1525–1540). Utilizing the unusual medium of colored glass powders fused to copper with heat known as enamel painting, this artist duplicated a German woodcut from a series printed by Johann Grüninger of Strasbourg.

The jewellike colors of the enamel enhance the lively composition. Small details, such as facial expression and the drape of cloth, are sensitively rendered despite the difficult medium. This plaque and the seventy-three others done by the same artist on the theme of Virgil's *Aeneid* are attributed to Jean I. Penicaud, the so-called "Master of the *Aeneid.*"

You might want to use the following questions to discuss the art:

1. How do you feel about the medieval appearance of the figures in this artwork?
2. Do you feel it is appropriate to Virgil's tale?
3. How would you change this illustration if you had the chance?
4. What do you believe is this work's most memorable feature?

All you can say, *your majesty,* of what you meant to me. (lines 436–437)

The test for a parenthetical expression is that its removal allows the sentence to remain structurally intact.

Student Activity 1. Rewrite lines 415–432, removing all parenthetical phrases enclosed by commas. What effect does this deletion have on the content of the message?

Student Activity 2. Recast Dido's speech to Aeneas (lines 397–432) in your own words, including in your version at least five parenthetical phrases correctly punctuated.

Apollo tells me I must make for: Italy,
Named by his oracles. There is my love;
455 There is my country. If, as a Phoenician,
You are so given to the charms of Carthage,
Libyan city that it is, then tell me,
Why begrudge the Teucrians new lands
For homesteads in Ausonia?[69] Are we not
460 Entitled, too, to look for realms abroad?
Night never veils the earth in damp and darkness,
Fiery stars never ascend the east,
But in my dreams my father's troubled ghost[70]
Admonishes and frightens me. Then, too,
465 Each night thoughts come of young Ascanius,
My dear boy wronged, defrauded of his kingdom,
Hesperian lands[71] of destiny. And now
The gods' interpreter, sent by Jove himself—
I swear it by your head and mine—has brought
470 Commands down through the racing winds! I say
With my own eyes in full daylight I saw him
Entering the building! With my very ears
I drank his message in! So please, no more
Of these appeals that set us both afire.
475 I sail for Italy not of my own free will."

During all this she had been watching him
With face averted, looking him up and down
In silence, and she burst out raging now:

"No goddess was your mother. Dardanus
480 Was not the founder of your family.
Liar and cheat! Some rough Caucasian cliff[72]
Begot you on flint. Hyrcanian[73] tigresses
Tendered their teats to you. Why should I palter?
Why still hold back for more indignity?
485 Sigh, did he, while I wept? Or look at me?
Or yield a tear, or pity her who loved him?

---

69. Ausonia (ô sō′ nē ə) *n.*: A generalized term for Italy.
70. father's troubled ghost: Aeneas' father, Anchises, died in Sicily just before strong winds diverted Aeneas to Carthage.
71. Hesperian (hes par′ ē ən) **lands:** Hesperia means "the Western Land"; another name for Italy.
72. Caucasian (kô kā′ zhən) **cliff:** The Caucasus, a mountain range near the Caspian Sea, was a cruel and outlandish place. Dido is accusing Aeneas of being as unfeeling as a rock; she's saying that he's not human, that no human being or goddess was responsible for his birth; he was given birth by Mt. Caucasus and flint, and nursed by savage tigresses.
73. Hyrcanian (hir kā′ nē ən) *adj.*: Of Hyrcania, a savage land near the Caspian Sea.

What shall I say first, with so much to say?
The time is past when either supreme Juno
Or the Saturnian father[74] viewed these things
490 With justice. Faith can never be secure.
I took the man in, thrown up on this coast
In dire need, and in my madness then
Contrived a place for him in my domain,
Rescued his lost fleet, saved his shipmates' lives.
495 Oh, I am swept away burning by furies!
Now the prophet Apollo, now his oracles,
Now the gods' interpreter, if you please,
Sent down by Jove himself, brings through the a
His formidable commands! What fit employmen
500 For heaven's high powers! What anxieties
To plague serene immortals! I shall not
Detain you or dispute your story. Go,
Go after Italy on the sailing winds,
Look for your kingdom, cross the deepsea swell!
505 If divine justice counts for anything,
I hope and pray that on some grinding reef
Midway at sea you'll drink your punishment
And call and call on Dido's name!
From far away I shall come after you
With my black fires, and when cold death has
510   parted
Body from soul I shall be everywhere
A shade to haunt you! You will pay for this,
Unconscionable! I shall hear! The news will
    reach me
Even among the lowest of the dead!"

515 At this abruptly she broke off and ran
In sickness from his sight and the light of day,
Leaving him at a loss, alarmed, and mute
With all he meant to say. The maids in waiting
Caught her as she swooned and carried her
520 To bed in her marble chamber.
                                    Duty-bound,
Aeneas, though he struggled with desire
To calm and comfort her in all her pain,
To speak to her and turn her mind from grief,
And though he sighed his heart out, shaken still
525   With love of her, yet took the course heaven
        gave him
And went back to the fleet. Then with a will
The Teucrians fell to work and launched the shi

---

74. Saturnian father: Jupiter.

Grammar in Action

Participles and Participial Phrases When a participle takes an object or is modified by an adverb or a prepositional phrase, the group of words taken together is called a participial phrase; this phrase is used as an adjective:

The gods' interpreter, *sent by Jove himself.* (line 468)

I saw him / *Entering the building!* (lines 471–472)

Oh, I am swept away *burning by furies!* (line 495)

A participial phrase is generally a compressed or shortened version of an adjective clause; since the nature of poetry requires condensation of ideas, this construction is frequently found in poetry.

Student Activity 1. Pick out five participial phrases from page 516. For each one substitute a subordinate clause. Example: Apollo tells me that I must make for Italy, *which was named for his oracles.*

Student Activity 2. List all the participial phrases from page 517 and the nouns they modify. Point out that *repaid with interest* (line 579) is not a participial phrase but part of an infinitive clause.

Along the whole shore: slick with tar each hull
Took to the water. Eager to get away,
530 The sailors brought oar-boughs out of the woods
With leaves still on, and oaken logs unhewn.
Now you could see them issuing from the town
To the water's edge in streams, as when, aware
Of winter, ants will pillage a mound of spelt[75]
535 To store it in their granary; over fields
The black battalion moves, and through the grass
On a narrow trail they carry off the spoil;
Some put their shoulders to the enormous weight
Of a trundled grain, while some pull stragglers in
540 And castigate[76] delay; their to-and-fro
Of labor makes the whole track come alive.
At that sight, what were your emotions, Dido?
Sighing how deeply, looking out and down
From your high tower on the seething shore
545 Where all the harbor filled before your eyes
With bustle and shouts! Unconscionable Love,
To what extremes will you not drive our hearts!
She now felt driven to weep again, again
To move him, if she could, by supplication,
550 Humbling her pride before her love—to leave
Nothing untried, not to die needlessly.

"Anna, you see the arc of waterfront
All in commotion: they come crowding in
From everywhere. Spread canvas calls for wind,
555 The happy crews have garlanded the sterns.
If I could brace myself for this great sorrow,
Sister, I can endure it, too. One favor,
Even so, you may perform for me.
Since that deserter chose you for his friend
560 And trusted you, even with private thoughts,
Since you alone know when he may be reached,
Go, intercede with our proud enemy.
Remind him that I took no oath at Aulis[77]
With Danaans to destroy the Trojan race;
565 I sent no ship to Pergamum. Never did I
Profane his father Anchisës' dust and shade.
Why will he not allow my prayers to fall
On his unpitying ears? Where is he racing?
Let him bestow one last gift on his mistress:

---

75. spelt (spelt) *n.*: A primitive species of wheat.
76. castigate (kas′ tə gāt′) *v.*: Punish or rebuke.
77. Aulis (ô′ lis) *n.*: Greek seaport from which the Greek fleet left for Troy.

570 This, to await fair winds and easier flight.
Now I no longer plead the bond he broke
Of our old marriage, nor do I ask that he
Should live without his dear love, Latium,
Or yield his kingdom. Time is all I beg,
575 Mere time, a respite[78] and a breathing space
For madness to subside in, while my fortune
Teaches me how to take defeat and grieve.
Pity your sister. This is the end, this favor—
To be repaid with interest when I die."

580 She pleaded in such terms, and such, in tears,
Her sorrowing sister brought him, time and again.
But no tears moved him, no one's voice would he
Attend to tractably.[79] The fates opposed it;
God's will blocked the man's once kindly ears.
585 And just as when the north winds from the Alps
This way and that contend among themselves
To tear away an oaktree hale with age,
The wind and tree cry, and the buffeted trunk
Showers high foliage to earth, but holds
590 On bedrock, for the roots go down as far
Into the underworld as cresting boughs
Go up in heaven's air: just so this captain,
Buffeted by a gale of pleas
This way and that way, dinned all the day long,
595 Felt their moving power in his great heart,
And yet his will stood fast; tears fell in vain.

    On Dido in her desolation now
Terror grew at her fate. She prayed for death,
Being heartsick at the mere sight of heaven.
600 That she more surely would perform the act
And leave the daylight, now she saw before her
A thing one shudders to recall: on altars
Fuming with incense where she placed her gifts,
The holy water blackened, the spilt wine
605 Turned into blood and mire.[80] Of this she spoke
To no one, not to her sister even. Then, too,
Within the palace was a marble shrine
Devoted to her onetime lord, a place
She held in wondrous honor, all festooned
610 With snowy fleeces and green festive boughs.
From this she now thought voices could be heard

---

78. respite (res′ pit) *n.*: An interval of temporary rest.
79. tractably (trak′ tə blē) *adv.*: Compliantly.
80. mire (mīr) *n.*: An area of wet, soggy ground.

51 Discussion How does Virgil indicate the eagerness and haste of Aeneas' men? Why does he choose the simile of the ants? Ask students to visualize the simile. Where are the men situated in relation to the scurrying ants?

52 Discussion Both Homer and Virgil almost never address a character directly as "you." When they do so, it has a special effect. Why does Virgil address Dido this way? (Also make sure students realize that the ant simile corresponds to Dido's position, looking down at the shore from her high tower.) How does Virgil make certain we see things from Dido's point of view?

53 Discussion Virgil as narrator comments or moralizes here. What might he want us to think about Dido's plight? Why does he say "our hearts"?

54 Discussion What kind of glimpse do we have about Aeneas' relationships and life in the palace before Mercury's message?

55 Discussion Dido has earlier called Aeneas "husband," and "guest." Now she calls him "our proud enemy." What does this suggest about the spectrum of her feelings? Does she still love him?

56 Master Teacher Note Make certain the students think about this long simile. How does Virgil make us see Aeneas? What is he feeling? What do students think line 596 means? (Those who think Aeneas a cad think only Anna's tears are meant; it is typical of Virgil to intend ambiguity where he creates it. Aeneas' tears also fail to move him, since he has made himself insensitive to his own suffering.)

57 Discussion What is Dido's state of mind?

58 Enrichment Pantheus and Orestes are among the familiar mad protagonists of the tragic stage, but Virgil means his readers to remember a large number of tragic figures destroyed by madness or passion or some irrational behavior.

59 Discussion Call students' attention to the way Virgil tells us what to think of Dido's state of mind, and then to the way he presents her, as having the apparent lucidity and the slyness characteristic of certain kinds of mental disorders. You might also ask students to think about the way Dido stages a kind of minidrama to fool Anna. She has seen herself as a kind of tragic heroine from the Athenian stage; now she plays the part.

60 Discussion Dido's lying speech to Anna is a fabrication of plausible falsehoods, like Sinon's. What do the students think about her stratagem to persuade Anna?

And words could be made out, her husband's
   words,
Calling her, when midnight hushed the earth;
And lonely on the rooftops the night owl
615 Seemed to lament, in melancholy notes,
Prolonged to a doleful cry. And then, besides,
The riddling words of seers in ancient days,
Foreboding sayings, made her thrill with fear.
In nightmare, fevered, she was hunted down
620 By pitiless Aeneas, and she seemed
Deserted always, uncompanioned always,
On a long journey, looking for her Tyrians
In desolate landscapes—
            as Pentheus[81] gone mad
Sees the oncoming Eumenidës[82] and sees
625 A double sun and double Thebes appear,[83]

---

81. Pentheus (pen´ thē əs) *n.*: King of Thebes, slain by Maenad followers of Bacchus.
82. Eumenidës (yōō men´ i dēz) *n.*: Literally, "the kindly-minded ones"; refers to the Furies, avengers of bloodshed, powers of Hell.
83. A double sun and double Thebes appear: Bacchus inspired Pentheus with an alcoholic spirit, making him see double.

Or as when, hounded on the stage, Orestës[84]
Runs from a mother armed with burning brands
With serpents hellish black,
And in the doorway squat the Avenging Ones,[85]

630 So broken in mind by suffering, Dido caught
Her fatal madness and resolved to die.
She pondered time and means, then visiting
Her mournful sister, covered up her plan
With a calm look, a clear and hopeful brow.

635 "Sister, be glad for me! I've found a way
To bring him back or free me of desire.
Near to the Ocean boundary, near sundown,
The Aethiops[86] farthest territory lies,
Where giant Atlas turns the sphere of heaven
640 Studded with burning stars. From there
A priestess of Massylian stock has come;
She had been pointed out to me: custodian

---

84. Orestës (ô res´ tēz) *n.*: The son of Agamemnon and Clytemnestra; Orestes killed Clytemnestra to avenge her murder of Agamemnon.
85. Avenging Ones: The Furies.
86. The Aethiops (ē´ thē ōps´) *n.*: People from Ethiopia or general term for the deepest or southernmost Africa.

DIDO, QUEEN OF CARTHAGE ABANDONED BY AENEAS
National Museum, Naples

Humanities Note

Fine art, *Dido Abandoned by Aeneas*, is an example of a fresco found in ancient ruins. The city of Pompeii, buried by the eruption of Mount Vesuvius in A.D. 79, provides us with the only undamaged record of the art of Roman mural painting. The inhabitants of this once fashionable resort used mural art to decorate and to expand the visual dimensions of their houses.

The subjects of these murals include architectural elements, such as columns and marble panels, to make the interior seem more richly appointed, window openings with vistas of gardens and lakes to create the illusion of space, and scenes from literature or myth used as decorative, intellectual stimulation.

The fresco *Dido Abandoned by Aeneas* takes its inspiration from Virgil's *Aeneid*. The artist presents the scene very much like a stage tableau. The figures seem frozen in a moment of drama. Executed in light strokes that simply demark light and shade, the style is almost impressionistic. The unknown Augustan artist has successfully combined this decorative wall treatment with homage to the works of Virgil.

You might want to use the following questions to discuss the art:
1. How does Queen Dido seem to feel about the departure of Aeneas in this fresco?

Of that shrine named for daughters of the west,
Hesperidës;[87] and it is she who fed
The dragon, guarding well the holy boughs
With honey dripping slow and drowsy poppy.
Chanting her spells she undertakes to free
What hearts she wills, but to inflict on others
Duress[88] of sad desires; to arrest
The flow of rivers, make the stars move backward,
Call up the spirits of deep Night. You'll see
Earth shift and rumble underfoot and ash trees
Walk down mountainsides. Dearest, I swear
Before the gods and by your own sweet self,
It is against my will that I resort
For weaponry to magic powers. In secret
Build up a pyre in the inner court
Under the open sky, and place upon it
The arms that faithless man left in my chamber,
All his clothing, and the marriage bed
On which I came to grief—solace for me
To annihilate all vestige[89] of the man,
Vile as he is: my priestess shows me this."

While she was speaking, cheek and brow grew
	pale.
But Anna could not think her sister cloaked
A suicide in these unheard-of rites;
She failed to see how great her madness was
And feared no consequence more grave
Than at Sychaeus' death. So, as commanded,
She made the preparations. For her part,
The queen, seeing the pyre in her inmost court
Erected huge with pitch-pine and sawn ilex,[90]
Hung all the place under the sky with wreaths
And crowned it with funereal cypress boughs.
On the pyre's top she put a sword he left
With clothing, and an effigy on a couch,
Her mind fixed now ahead on what would come.
Around the pyre stood altars, and the priestess,
Hair unbound, called in a voice of thunder
Upon three hundred gods, on Erebus,

On Chaos,[91] and on triple Hecatë,[92]
Three-faced Diana. Then she sprinkled drops
Purportedly from the fountain of Avernus.[93]
Rare herbs were brought out, reaped at the new
	moon
685 By scythes of bronze, and juicy with a milk
Of dusky venom; then the rare love-charm
Or caul torn from the brow of a birthing foal
And snatched away before the mother found it.
Dido herself with consecrated grain
690 In her pure hands, as she went near the altars,
Freed one foot from sandal straps, let fall
Her dress ungirdled, and, now sworn to death,
Called on the gods and stars that knew her fate.
She prayed then to whatever power may care
695 In comprehending justice for the grief
Of lovers bound unequally by love.

The night had come, and weary in every land
Men's bodies took the boon of peaceful sleep.
The woods and the wild seas had quieted
700 At that hour when the stars are in mid-course
And every field is still; cattle and birds
With vivid wings that haunt the limpid lakes
Or nest in thickets in the country places
All were asleep under the silent night.
705 Not, though, the agonized Phoenician queen:
She never slackened into sleep and never
Allowed the tranquil night to rest
Upon her eyelids or within her heart.
Her pain redoubled; love came on again,
710 Devouring her, and on her bed she tossed
In a great surge of anger.
							So awake,
She pressed these questions, musing to herself:

"Look now, what can I do? Turn once again
To the old suitors, only to be laughed at—
715 Begging a marriage with Numidians
Whom I disdained so often? Then what? Trail

---

87. Hesperidës (hes par´ i dēz´) *n*.: The daughters of
Hesperus, "the Western maidens," keepers of a garden of
golden apples which was guarded by a dragon.
88. Duress (doo res´) *n*.: The use of force; compulsion.
89. vestige (ves´ tij) *n*.: Trace or sign of existence.
90. ilex (i´ leks): Oak.

91. Chaos (kā´ äs) *n*.: Greek personification of the state of
disorder that preceded the universe.
92. triple Hecatë (hek´ə tē): Title of Diana as goddess of
sorcery, goddess of the moon, and the virgin huntress; thus,
"Three-faced Diana."
93. Avernus (ə vʉr´ nəs´) *n*.: A lake in southern Italy that
supposedly led to the underworld.

2. What emotion do the women around her seem to convey?
3. Could the artist have been trying to flatter Dido in this work?
4. Discuss some detail of this illustration that you do not favor.

65 Discussion Is Dido's view of matters reasonable, or is she raving? Is it at all reasonable for her to be thinking of taking her people and following Aeneas? What does her sarcastic tone suggest about her state of mind? Ask students how they respond to her addressing herself in the second person (line 723). Is she being theatrical? Is she divided in her mind?

66 Discussion Why does Dido think she must die? Ask students to explore the different reasons Virgil suggests.

67 Discussion Is Dido at all justified in thinking Anna responsible for her yielding to love? What loss does she lament, what self-image does she have? Do students believe that she now sees Aeneas as her real "enemy"? What does she hold against him, in addition to his leaving her?

68 Discussion Why is Aeneas feeling at peace and able to sleep? How does Virgil mean us to see the contrast with Dido?

69 Discussion Mercury's appearance is, for Aeneas, a divine sign. How does Virgil also allow us to see this dream as psychologically plausible? Might Aeneas have intuited Dido's mood? Might he have worries that are surfacing out of his subconscious mind?

70 Discussion In what ways are the last two lines in Mercury's speech in character for Mercury?

71 Discussion Virgil again stresses the men's desire for action. Does their eagerness to go, once Aeneas shows he is ready, suggest anything about how they felt while Aeneas seemed to be happy as Dido's consort?

72 Discussion Remind students of the way in which the heroes in the *Iliad* are concerned with not being laughed at and not losing face.

The Ilian ships and follow like a slave
Commands of Trojans? Seeing them so agreeable,
In view of past assistance and relief,
720 So thoughtful their unshaken gratitude?
Suppose I wished it, who permits or takes
Aboard their proud ships one they so dislike?
Poor lost soul, do you not yet grasp or feel
The treachery of the line of Laömedon?[94]
725 What then? Am I to go alone, companion
Of the exultant sailors in their flight?
Or shall I set out in their wake, with Tyrians,
With all my crew close at my side, and send
The men I barely tore away from Tyre
730 To sea again, making them hoist their sails
To more sea-winds? No: die as you deserve,
Give pain quietus with a steel blade.

                 Sister,
You are the one who gave way to my tears
In the beginning, burdened a mad queen
735 With sufferings, and thrust me on my enemy.
It was not given me to lead my life
Without new passion, innocently, the way
Wild creatures live, and not to touch these depths.
The vow I took to the ashes of Sychaeus
740 Was not kept."

           So she broke out afresh
In bitter mourning. On his high stern deck
Aeneas, now quite certain of departure,
Everything ready, took the boon of sleep.
In dream the figure of the god returned
745 With looks reproachful as before: he seemed
Again to warn him, being like Mercury
In every way, in voice, in golden hair,
And in the bloom of youth.

               "Son of the goddess,
Sleep away this crisis, can you still?
750 Do you not see the dangers growing round you,
Madman, from now on? Can you not hear
The offshore westwind blow? The woman hatches
Plots and drastic actions in her heart,
Resolved on death now, whipping herself on
755 To heights of anger. Will you not be gone
In flight, while flight is still within your power?
Soon you will see the offing boil with ships

---

94. **Laomedon** (lā ăm′ ə dän′) *n.*: A king of Troy who cheated Neptune and Apollo out of their promised reward for building the walls of Troy.

And glare with torches; soon again
The waterfront will be alive with fires,
760 If Dawn comes while you linger in this country.
Ha! Come, break the spell! Woman's a thing
Forever fitful and forever changing."

At this he merged into the darkness. Then
As the abrupt phantom filled him with fear,
765 Aeneas broke from sleep and roused his crewmen:
"Up, turn out now! Oarsmen, take your thwarts!
Shake out sail! Look here, for the second time
A god from heaven's high air is goading me
To hasten our break away, to cut the cables.
770 Holy one, whatever god you are,
We go with you, we act on your command
Most happily! Be near, graciously help us,
Make the stars in heaven propitious[95] ones!"

He pulled his sword aflash out of its sheath
775 And struck at the stern hawser. All the men
Were gripped by his excitement to be gone,
And hauled and hustled. Ships cast off their
    moorings,
And an array of hulls hid inshore water
As oarsmen churned up foam and swept to sea.

780 Soon early Dawn, quitting the saffron bed
Of old Tithonus,[96] cast new light on earth,
And as air grew transparent, from her tower
The queen caught sight of ships on the seaward
    reach
With sails full and the wind astern, She knew
785 The waterfront now empty, bare of oarsmen.
Beating her lovely breast three times, four times,
And tearing her golden hair,

               "O Jupiter,"
She said, "will this man go, will he have mocked
My kingdom, stranger that he was and is?
790 Will they not snatch up arms and follow him
From every quarter of the town? and dockhands
Tear our ships from moorings? On! Be quick
With torches! Give out arms! Unship the oars!

---

95. **propitious** (prō pish′ əs) *adj.*: Favorable; boding well.
96. **Tithonus** (tith′ ō nəs) *n.*: Son of Laömedon; beloved of the goddess Aurora. He is "old" because Aurora asked Jupiter to grant him eternal life, but she forgot to ask for his eternal youth.

Grammar in Action

Using Words That Create Mood Writers choose specific words deliberately to create a particular mood. For example, when Virgil wants his readers to sense the haste and immediacy of Aeneas' departure from Carthage, he employs short, strong, direct verbs: *gripped, hauled, hustled, churned* (lines 776–779). In Mercury's warning to the sleeping Aeneas (lines 748–759), Virgil uses words suggesting violence and peril and heat: *dangers, plots, drastic actions, whipping, heights of anger;* the port will *boil* with ships and *glare* with torches and be alive with *fire.*

In describing early Dawn (lines 780–782), however, he uses very dif-

What am I saying? Where am I? What madness
Takes me out of myself? Dido, poor soul,
Your evil doing has come home to you.
Then was the right time, when you offered him
A royal scepter. See the good faith and honor
Of one they say bears with him everywhere
The hearthgods of his country! One who bore
His father, spent with age, upon his shoulders!
Could I not then have torn him limb from limb
And flung the pieces on the sea?[97] His company,
Even Ascanius could I not have minced
And served up to his father at a feast?[98]
The luck of battle might have been in doubt—
So let it have been! Whom had I to fear,
Being sure to die? I could have carried torches
Into his camp, filled passageways with flame,
Annihilated father and son and followers
And given my own life on top of all!
O Sun, scanning with flame all works of earth,
And thou, O Juno, witness and go-between
Of my long miseries; and Hecatë,
Screeched for at night at crossroads in the cities;
And thou, avenging Furies, and all gods
On whom Elissa dying may call: take notice,
Overshadow this hell with your high power,
As I deserve, and hear my prayer!
If by necessity that impious[99] wretch
Must find his haven and come safe to land,
If so Jove's destinies require, and this,
His end in view, must stand, yet all the same
When hard beset in war by a brave people,
Forced to go outside his boundaries
And torn from Iulus, let him beg assistance,
Let him see the unmerited deaths of those
Around and with him, and accepting peace
On unjust terms, let him not, even so,

830 Enjoy his kingdom or the life he longs for,
But fall in battle before his time and lie
Unburied on the sand![100] This I implore,
This is my last cry, as my last blood flows.
Then, O my Tyrians, besiege with hate
835 His progeny and all his race to come:
Make this your offering to my dust. No love,
No pact must be between our peoples;[101] No,
But rise up from my bones, avenging spirit![102]
Harry with fire and sword the Dardan countrymen
840 Now, or hereafter, at whatever time
The strength will be afforded. Coast with coast
In conflict, I implore, and sea with sea,
And arms with arms: may they contend in war,
Themselves and all the children of their children!"

845 Now she took thought of one way or another,
At the first chance, to end her hated life,
And briefly spoke to Barcë, who had been
Sychaeus' nurse; her own an urn of ash
Long held in her ancient fatherland.
                                    "Dear nurse,
850 Tell Sister Anna to come here, and have her
Quickly bedew herself with running water
Before she brings our victims for atonement.[103]
Let her come that way. And you, too, put on
Pure wool around your brows.[104] I have a mind
855 To carry out that rite to Stygian Jove[105]
That I have readied here, and put an end
To my distress, committing to the flames
The pyre of that miserable Dardan."

---

97. And flung the pieces on the sea: What Medea does to
her brother when she flees with Jason after they obtain the
golden fleece. With this allusion, Dido is equating herself with
the tragic heroine most famous for murdering her own
children to punish her husband, Jason, for his infidelity.
98. And served up to his father at a feast: Again, Dido
equates herself with tragic heroines driven to unnatural
violence by a husband's betrayal. Refers to the sisters Procne
and Philomela; specific details vary, but the husband of one
sister rapes his sister-in-law. In response, the sisters chop up the
rapist's son and serve him as stew.
99. impious (im´ pē əs) *adj.*: Irreverent or disrespectful of the
gods.

100. Unburied on the sand: Dido's wish here is actually a
prophecy; Aeneas meets resistance in Italy and has to leave
Ascanius to go beg aid from Evander, an Italian king, who asks
Aeneas to change his people's name to Latins. Since Aeneas
eventually drowns in an Italian river, the reward for all his
struggles comes not during his life, but in the glory of his
succeeding generations.
101. between our peoples: Romans and Carthaginians
would fight three wars, all of which Rome won, and the last of
which destroyed Carthage.
102. avenging spirit: Hannibal; Dido foresees the
Carthaginian general Hannibal's invasion of Italy in the third
century B.C., which did not result in Rome's capture.
103. atonement (ə tōn´ mənt) *n.*: Amends for wrongdoing.
104. Pure wool around your brows: Band worn around
suppliant's head.
105. Stygian (stig´ ē ən) **Jove:** Jupiter, so called because of
the river Styx, which flowed through the underworld, where he
was lord.

76

73 Discussion Dido interrupts her violent raving with lines that suggest
she has a brief moment of lucidity.
What is the ironic effect of having
her go on to say, with apparent
good sense and reasonableness,
"then was the right time . . ." and
regret that she did not act differently?

74 Enrichment Dido again recalls
some of the most horrifying of the
Greek myths, popular in tragic
drama. In what ways has she
moved out of the world of history,
which Aeneas inhabits, and into
the world of literary legend?

75 Discussion Remind students of
the sack of Troy, the account of
which was narrated by Aeneas and
moved Dido. Here she sees
herself as the Greek sacker of
Troy. Discuss how she views herself at this time.

76 Discussion Dido's curse refers to
the long and bloody Punic Wars.
The irony, of course, is that Dido's
descendants were defeated by
the Romans. In her choice of personal passion over the duties of
being a good ruler, Dido is represented as having destroyed her
own people.

---

ferent diction, choosing delicate, radiant words like *saffron* bed, new *light*
on earth, air grew *transparent*.

Student Activity 1. Pick out those words in Dido's speech (lines
794–844) that specifically suggest her anger at Aeneas and her vengefulness. Analyze the quality of these words. Why, for example, are *minced* (line
804) and *annihilated* (line 810) more mood-setting than *cut up* and
destroyed?

Student Activity 2. Write two paragraphs describing a day in school;
in the first, create a negative mood by the use of forceful verbs; in the second,
create a positive mood with favorable adjectives.

77 Discussion What does "with an old woman's eagerness" evoke? Notice how visual this passage is. In Book I, Virgil describes how Cupid, disguised as the boy Ascanius, is walking next to Aeneas and taking extra big steps to keep up with his father. Here he pauses to visualize the old nurse's stiff-jointed bustling.

78 Discussion Draw attention to the way Virgil economically suggests a happier scene: Dido asking her lover Aeneas for his sword as a special gift and his giving it to her. Does her reaction to Aeneas' clothes and to their bed, as well as the opening of her prayer, help us see how Dido feels about Aeneas?

79 Discussion Dido delivers her own epitaph here. Lines 877–879 correspond to an epitaph fitting for a Homeric hero and a good king. What made Dido lose this fame that she had earned for herself? (She did everything any man could do; why was she then undone by being a woman?)

80 Discussion Ask students what her kissing the bed and her last words indicate about her feelings as she dies.

81 Discussion Dido has repeatedly called Aeneas her "enemy." Here Carthage is likened to a city sacked by a hostile army. What in fact is the hostile force that destroyed Carthage?

At this with an old woman's eagerness
860 Barcë hurried away. And Dido's heart
Beat wildly at the enormous thing afoot.
She rolled her bloodshot eyes, her quivering
        cheeks
Were flecked with red as her sick pallor grew
Before her coming death. Into the court
865 She burst her way, then at her passion's height
She climbed the pyre and bared the Dardan
        sword—
A gift desired once, for no such need.
Her eyes now on the Trojan clothing there
And the familiar bed, she paused a little,
870 Weeping a little, mindful, then lay down
And spoke her last words:
                        "Remnants dear to me
While god and fate allowed it, take this breath
And give me respite from these agonies.
I lived my life out to the very end
875 And passed the stages Fortune had appointed.
Now my tall shade goes to the underworld.
I built a famous town, saw my great walls,
Avenged my husband, made my hostile brother
Pay for his crime. Happy, alas, too happy,
880 If only the Dardanian keels[106] had never
Beached on our coast." And here she kissed the
        bed.
"I die unavenged," she said, "but let me die.
This way, this way,[107] a blessed relief to go
Into the undergloom. Let the cold Trojan,
885 Far at sea, drink in this conflagration[108]
And take with him the omen of my death!"

Amid these words her household people saw her
Crumpled over the steel blade, and the blade
Aflush with red blood, drenched her hands. A
        scream
890 Pierced the high chambers. Now through the
        shocked city
Rumor went rioting, as wails and sobs
With women's outcry echoed in the palace

And heaven's high air gave back the beating din,
As though all Carthage or old Tyre fell
895 To storming enemies,[109] and, out of hand,
Flames billowed on the roofs of men and gods.
Her sister heard and trembling, faint with terror,
Lacerating her face, beating her breast,
Ran through the crowd to call the dying queen:

900 "It came to this, then, sister? You deceived me?
The pyre meant this, altars and fires meant this?
What shall I mourn first, being abandoned? Did
        you
Scorn your sister's company in death?
You should have called me out to the same fate!
905 The same blade's edge and hurt, at the same hour,
Should have taken us off. With my own hands
Had I to build this pyre, and had I to call
Upon our country's gods, that in the end
With you placed on it there, O heartless one,
910 I should be absent? You have put to death
Yourself and me, the people and the fathers
Bred in Sidon, and your own new city.
Give me fresh water, let me bathe her wound
And catch upon my lips any last breath
915 Hovering over hers."
                        Now she had climbed
The topmost steps and took her dying sister
Into her arms to cherish, with a sob,
Using her dress to stanch the dark blood flow.
But Dido trying to lift her heavy eyes
920 Fainted again. Her chest-wound whistled air.
Three times she struggled up on one elbow
And each time fell back on the bed. Her gaze
Went wavering as she looked for heaven's light
And groaned at finding it. Almighty Juno,
925 Filled with pity for this long ordeal
And difficult passage, now sent Iris[110] down
Out of Olympus to set free
The wrestling spirit from the body's hold.
For since she died, not at her fated span

---

106. Dardanian keels (kēlz): Aeneas' Trojan ships.
107. This way, this way: In Latin, this repetition indicates two thrusts of the sword.
108. conflagration (kän′ flə grā′ shən) *n.*: Huge, destructive fire.

---

109. To storming enemies: Refers to the destruction of Carthage in the third Punic War.
110. Iris (ī′ ris) *n.*: As in the *Iliad*, a divine messenger. Iris is sometimes identified with the rainbow as in line 935: humid Iris.

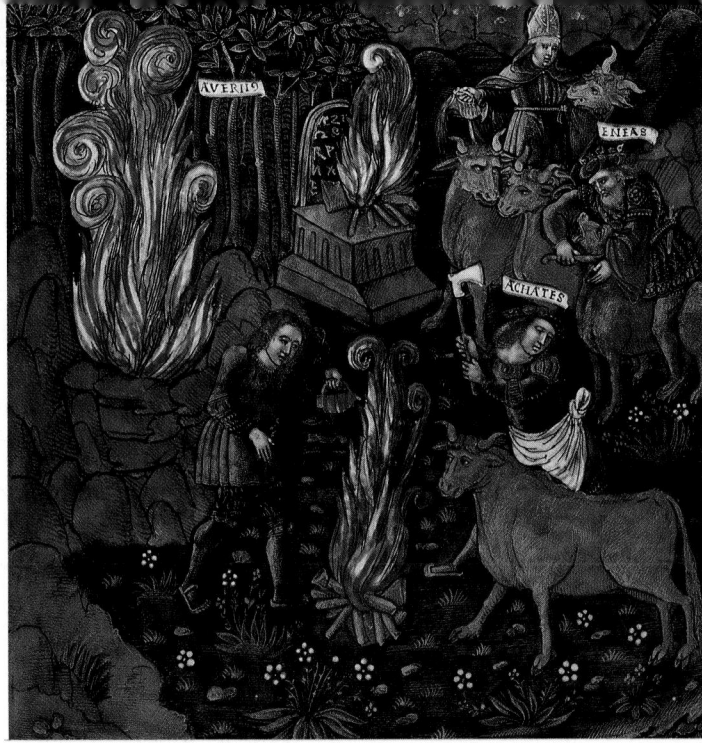

AENEAS OFFERS SACRIFICE
TO GODS OF THE LOWER
WORLD
**Limoges Master
of the Aeneid**
Walters Art Gallery, Baltimore

Humanities Note
Fine art, *Aeneas Offers Sacrifice
to the Gods of the Lower World* is
an enamel painting on copper
(c.1525–1540) from Limoges,
France. The images are outlined in
black on a white ground, which
causes the transparent colored
enamels to glow like jewels. This
intense coloring coupled with the
finely rendered details makes this
work comparable to a fine miniature painting.

You might want to use the following questions to discuss the art:
1. Do you think the strength and
   intensity of the colors of this
   enamel are different from those
   of a painting?
2. Why do you think this artist
   chose Virgil as a subject for his
   works?
3. What do you believe are the
   best sources of inspiration for
   most artists?

Cooperative Learning Have students think carefully about Dido's
death scene. Can they visualize it?
What visual details does Virgil provide? What mood does he create?
Then divide students into small
study groups. Have each group
choose one death scene from a
work they know and compare it
with this one. What elements seem
universal? What elements are culturally determined?

Nor as she merited, but before her time
Enflamed and driven mad, Proserpina[111]
Had not yet plucked from her the golden hair,
Delivering her to Orcus of the Styx.
So humid Iris through bright heaven flew
On saffron-yellow wings, and in her train
A thousand hues shimmered before the sun.
At Dido's head she came to rest.
                              "This token
Sacred to Dis[112] I bear away as bidden
And free you from your body."
                              Saying this,
She cut a lock of hair. Along with it
Her body's warmth fell into dissolution,
And out into the winds her life withdrew.

---

111. Proserpina (prō´ sʉr´ pi nə) *n.*: Queen of the
Underworld who was thought to cut a lock of hair as a sacrifice
before a human died. Since Dido killed herself rather than wait
for her fate, Proserpina could not cut the lock, but Juno sent
Iris to cut it.
112. Dis (dis) *n.*: Roman name for Hades, god of the
underworld.

*After he arrives at Cumae in Italy, Aeneas visits
the Sibyl's cave to hear the Delian prophecy and to
seek advice from his father's spirit in the underworld.
Once Aeneas prays and makes sacrifices to the gods,
Sibyl agrees to lead him through the underworld.
Upon meeting Anchises, Aeneas learns his destiny:
Through a child born to Aeneas late in life, the Trojan race will rule in Alba Longa, and Mars will father Romulus, under whose auspices Rome will prosper. After he relates the future glories of the Roman
Empire, Anchises also tells Aeneas of wars he must
fight. For the remainder of the epic, Virgil emphasizes
the role of the hero to society as Aeneas fights valiant-
ly to achieve his destiny and found Rome.*

Reader's Response *Many readers find fault
with Aeneas for his dismissal of Dido in Book
IV. Do you blame him? Decide for yourself if
he has hurt her on purpose. Explain your
reasons for judging the situation as you have.*

Closure and Extension

ANSWERS TO THINKING ABOUT THE SELECTION

1. (a) Dido refers to her pledge and calls their union a marriage. (b) Aeneas swears his affection but claims there was no binding contract. (c) Answers will differ because Virgil lets us sympathize with Dido.
2. Answers will differ. Some will suggest that Aeneas would have comforted her and given in to his feelings. He shows that capacity earlier.
3. Dido changes into a possessed, lovesick person, because she is overcome by passion.
4. (a) By emphasizing the violence of the emotions imposed on Dido by the superhuman forces, Virgil draws attention to her powerlessness to resist emotion. (b) The images of sickness and madness are associated with irresponsibility.
5. Answers will differ. Many will say that what they have learned directly influences their behavior.

ANSWERS TO ANALYZING LITERATURE

1. Answers will differ. Many will say that Aeneas is feeling bitterness and confusion.

ANSWERS TO CRITICAL THINKING AND READING

1. Mercury awaits no response because there is nothing that Aeneas could say that would mean anything.
2. Aeneas reacts as if he's just been shocked from a dream.
3. He springs to action to prepare the fleet.
4. Answers will differ. Some will say that he does, by claiming he has no choice. Others will say he does not, because he does not tell her immediately about his plan.
5. Answers will differ. Almost all will say that Aeneas was totally controlled by the divine influence in his life.

THINKING AND WRITING

Writing Across the Curriculum

You may wish to inform the art department about the reading of Virgil's account of the love between Dido and Aeneas. Students could be directed toward finding famous paintings of other star-crossed couples that have been depicted by painters through the ages. A writing assignment could be worked into the composition of captions for such illustrations that can be brought to class for display.

Challenge Teams of students might consult maps of the area to calculate the exact distances between Troy, Carthage, and Rome. They could then estimate the sailing time, with assistance from a science teacher, that might have been needed by Aeneas to make the trip from place to place. Have one team member search for appropriate sources to learn about seasonal weather conditions. Another might find information on navigational hazards in the areas.

THINKING ABOUT THE SELECTION

Interpreting

1. (a) How does Dido refer to her marriage with Aeneas? (b) How does Aeneas see it? (c) Which (if either) of them is more accurate? Support your answer with details from the selection.
2. Dido's second embittered speech ends with a curse and a threat. What do you think would have happened if Aeneas had reacted as Virgil says he wished to? Find evidence to support your answer.
3. Virgil first presents Dido as a chaste widow and strong leader, bound by duty to her people and her dead husband. Explain how and why she changes.
4. (a) What do you infer about the value Virgil places on self-control as opposed to passion? Support your answer. (b) Look for images of sickness and madness. With what are they associated?

Applying

5. In our own society, people often think about self-control and passion and define and redefine love. Think about lyrics of popular songs and about phrases such as "I'm crazy about you." How does the way people have learned to think about romantic love influence their behavior?

ANALYZING LITERATURE

Understanding Heroic Conflict

A **conflict** is a struggle between opposing forces. Aeneas is "pious," wholly loyal to the gods, his family, and his country. Like Hector in the *Iliad*, he defines himself in terms of his duties. His formal coldness to Dido hides a conflict she does not understand. Roman men remained *in patria potestate* (under the legal control of their fathers) as long as their fathers were alive; Anchises' influence is so strong that even after his death, his ghost calls Aeneas to task for shirking his duty to his son. For a dutiful Roman to resist the nightly harassment by his father's disapproving ghost is hard enough; to question a command from Jove is unthinkable. Aeneas is given no time to answer Mercury, who flies off before he finishes speaking. Galvanized by the shock, Aeneas springs to obedient action. Look carefully at lines 361–367, 369–371, 433–434, and 521–526 again. Make note of what Aeneas is feeling and discuss what he would do if he felt he had any choices.

CRITICAL READING AND THINKING

Evaluating Divine Influence

People are influenced to act by many different factors, but in Greek and Roman epics the major factor is often the gods. Homer's gods bicker with mortals, express sympathy, cajole. While representing superhuman forces, they relate to human beings more intimately than Virgil's gods. While the Greek goddess Thetis talks to her son Achilleus, strokes him, weeps for him, the Roman goddess Venus looks out for Aeneas' glory, but, as he complains, she never touches him or talks to him like a mother. Dictatorial commands and riddling signs come down from on high and drive Aeneas from one stage of his trials to the next. From the night of Troy's fall, Aeneas is singled out for duty, and to disobey is out of the question.

1. Why does Mercury fly off before the last words?
2. What is Aeneas' physical reaction to the message?
3. What does he do when he pulls himself together?
4. While his attempt to justify his departure to Dido seems cold to her, is he actually making an attempt to help her? Explain your answer.
5. Imagine that you are Aeneas. How would you evaluate the impact of divine influence on you?

THINKING AND WRITING

Composing a Farewell Letter

The farewell scene is especially poignant. Reread it and jot down notes that help you fix in your mind the "memories" of their affair. Then imagine that you are Aeneas. You have a second chance to tell Dido what you are feeling. Write the first draft of a farewell letter appealing to her emotions and reason. Be specific, tactful, and comforting. You want very much for her to understand you. Reread your letter as if you were Dido. Does Aeneas convince you? What would make the letter more persuasive? Finally, proofread your letter and prepare a final draft.

Poetry

AENEID
Biblioteca Riccardiana, Firenze, Italy

Humanities Note

Illumination, *Aeneid*. The art of the illuminated manuscript did not begin with the religious texts of Europe.

Greco-Roman artists pursued this art long before the establishment of Christianity. The early Christian artists, in fact, often copied from earlier pagan texts.

The miniature shown here is from a secular manuscript devoted to the *Aeneid* of Virgil. Though small in size (5"x7"), the detail rivals that of larger scale paintings. The men and tiny ships seem fragile in the face of the fury of the vast sea. The brilliant colors, handmade by this ancient artist through the arduous grinding of natural materials, enhance the startling quality of the scene.

Without these ancient manuscripts, the art of Greco–Roman painting would be lost to us.

You might want to use the following questions to discuss the art:

1. Can you describe what is taking place in this scene?
2. What impression do you receive from the darkness of the colors?
3. What dimensions add most to the confusion of this depiction?
4. Choose a friend to whom you would give this painting as a gift. Then explain your choice.

CATULLUS

c. 87–c. 54 B.C.

Gaius Valerius Catullus (gā′ əs va ler′ ē ′əs′ kə tul′ əs) was born in Verona, in the affluent and cultured province of Cisalpine Gaul, to a prosperous and well-connected family. As a prominent local citizen, his father played host to the provincial governor Julius Caesar, who remained a family friend. Catullus came to Rome in his early twenties armed with introductions to the best families. Witty, wealthy, and well-educated, the gifted young poet was always welcome in the drawing rooms of the literary and elegant rich.

The most glamorous social circle was presided over by Clodia (Pulcher) Metelli, who with her brother set the tone for the wild set of the high aristocracy. Descended from an old noble family and married to a powerful man, she combined position and wealth with chic beauty. She was a notorious flirt and seductress. Her political enemy, the straight-laced Cicero, implied that she would not stop short of murder when he publicly attacked her as the "Medea of the Palatine" (the

area of Rome where the wealthiest lived) and a "two-bit Clytemnestra." (Both women are famous in myth as murderers.) Clodia immediately captivated Catullus, who wrote dazzling, passionate love lyrics to her. With a powerful immediacy that still grips us, his poems convey his mixed feelings—his ecstatic happiness, his depression, his bitterness at still loving a woman who betrayed and manipulated him. As a man, Catullus may not have been a match for Clodia, but as a poet he had the final word.

Catullus did not spend all his time loving and languishing over Clodia. He established himself as accomplished and "learned" (to use his own term), a poet whose polished verses rivaled those of his Greek predecessors, including Sappho. He wrote scathing and hilarious political invective that attacked Julius Caesar (who took it in stride) and other prominent men; occasional poems; a mini-epic on the marriage of Peleus and Thetis; a long piece in exotic eastern rhythms on the savage worship of the goddess Cybele. We know he spent a brief period in the foreign service, although he showed no interest in pursuing a career at law despite his training. With some of his friends, he joined the staff of a senator sent out to govern Bithynia (on the Asian side of modern Turkey). He painted a witty picture of his tour of duty, full of self-irony and satiric wit. Others made fortunes in the provinces and returned with abundant gratuities; not so Catullus. But we should be careful not to take his "starving poet" pose too seriously: he owned estates near fashionable Tivoli outside Rome and at Sirmione on Lake Garda; he had a private library in Rome; and he traveled on his own yacht.

Catullus died sometime in his early thirties. His fame lives on in his poetry. The love lyrics especially have ensured his reputation for thousands of years and inspired many successors and imitators including the English poets Spenser, Jonson, Herrick, Keats, and Tennyson.

Objectives

Thematic

To appreciate the accomplishment of lyric poetry

Skills

1 To practice evaluating love lyrics
2 To learn how to compare love lyrics

GUIDE FOR INTERPRETING

My Woman Says There's Nobody She'd Rather Marry; I Hate Her and I Love Her; I Crossed Many Lands and a Lot of Ocean; My Mind's Sunk So Low, . . .

Commentary

Lyric Poetry. One of the oldest and most subjective of poems, the love **lyric** plumbs the depths of human emotion. The lyric is strongly unified by sensual impressions and takes its name from the lyre, a harplike stringed instrument. It is significant that the word for poem was the same as the word for song. Recitations, therefore, resembled recitals in that the voice rose and fell with the flow of each line of verse, although no written music marked each note. (For an example from Greek lyric poetry, reread Sappho's verses on pages 398–402.)

The love lyric follows rhythmic patterns that take shape in proportion to the intensity of personal expression. Varying widely along with its breadth of subject matter, romantic verse is characterized by honest glimpses of the ups and downs of love. In Catullus' short verses, the focus shifts from ecstatic joy in the poet's beloved to the acute pain of loss that marked Catullus' unpredictable attachment to Clodia, whose public reputation could not be tarnished by her private life. To shroud her identity and honor Sappho, who lived on the island of Lesbos, Catullus addressed the poems to the character Lesbia, a name that mimics the metrical pattern of Clodia's name.

A key element of Catullus' literary expression is his ability to capture the lover's fragile emotional state. He makes us share his exuberant joy when Clodia returns his love and his despair when she does not. His experience seems universal. The poems seem so spontaneous that we forget they are not diary entries but crafted works of art. Though the emotions are real, Catullus sat down and expressed them in complex verse rhythms, sometimes transforming the poems of other writers of love lyrics. Catullus appears the victim of Clodia's fickleness, but his version of the affair has won readers ever since.

Love lyrics can deal with other types of love than the love between a man and a woman. The funeral elegy to his brother shows Catullus' genius. We do not notice his skill; what comes across is pure emotion. Just as funeral rituals control and channel raw anguish, the poem gives a manageable shape to Catullus' grief over his brother's death and his sense that the funeral rites cannot fully express his love or console him for his bitter loss.

Writing

Virgil defined love simply as "the fire," while Plato called it "a grave mental disease." Freewrite, exploring your own definition of love.

Literary Focus Ask students to think about popular songwriters and current singers whose lyrics make a strong statement today about romantic relationships. How much do the lyrics tell us about the singers' lives? Does knowing biographical information from another source change the way we evaluate the lyrics? What contradictions can exist between self-revelation through art and biographical facts? Have students give evaluations of the lyrics of singers like Debbie Gibson, Paul McCartney, or Bruce Springsteen.

Writing/Prior Knowledge Pair up students and have them interview each other about their ideas concerning love's madness. Prompt them to decide how they think most people would respond to Plato's claim before they explore their own feelings as they freewrite.

ESL Teaching Strategy Read any one of the poems aloud to ESL students while they read it silently. Preteach any troublesome vocabulary. Have students close their books and copy down the text from your dictation. Allow them to correct their written passages for errors in capitalization, spelling, and punctuation.

Master Teacher Note Use these epigrammatic poems to introduce the term and concept of **oxymoron**. Explain that it is a rhetorical figure that joins incongruous or contradictory terms to create an epigrammatic effect. Write the term and definition on the board. Then have students think of examples (cheerful pessimist or idiot savant). How does linking the incongruous work?

Support Material

Teaching Portfolio
Teacher Backup, p. 629
Usage and Mechanics Worksheet, p. 633
Analyzing Literature Worksheet, *Evaluating Love Lyrics*, p. 634
Critical Thinking and Reading Worksheet, *Understanding Subjective Reactions*, p. 635

Language Worksheet, *Interpreting Allusions*, p. 636
Selection Test, pp. 637–638

My Woman Says There's Nobody She'd Rather Marry

Catullus

translated by Carl Sesar

My woman says there's nobody she'd rather marry
than me, not even Jupiter himself if he asked her.
She says, but what a woman says to a hungry lover
you might as well scribble in wind and swift water.

I Crossed Many Lands and a Lot of Ocean

Catullus

translated by Carl Sesar

I crossed many lands and a lot of ocean
to get to this painful ceremony, my brother,
so I could finally give you gifts for the dead,
and waste time talking to some silent ashes
being that you're not here yourself with me.
Fate did wrong, my brother, to tear us apart.
But I bring you these offerings now anyway,
after the old custom our parents taught us.
Take them, soaked with your brother's tears,
and forever more, my brother, goodbye.

I Hate Her and I Love Her

Catullus

translated by Carl Sesar

I hate her and I love her. Don't ask me why.
It's the way I feel, that's all, and it hurts.

THINKING ABOUT THE SELECTION

Interpreting

1. (a) Find lines from Catullus' poems that indicate that Lesbia's words are insincere. (b) Discuss the effect of these words on the poet.
2. Explain how "I Hate Her and I Love Her" summarizes Catullus' experiences with Lesbia.
3. Which poem indicates that Catullus has lost respect for himself during his love affair? Explain his feelings.
4. (a) Why does Catullus consider his journey over "many lands and a lot of ocean" futile? (b) Why does he bring offerings anyway?

Applying

5. In "My Mind's Sunk So Low, Lesbia, Because of You," Catullus claims "I couldn't . . . stop loving you,

My Mind's Sunk So Low, Lesbia, Because of You

Catullus

translated by Carl Sesar

My mind's sunk so low, Lesbia, because of you,
wrecked itself on your account so bad already,
I couldn't like you if you were the best of women,
or stop loving you, no matter what you do.

LESBIA AND HER SPARROW
Sir Edward John Poynter

no matter what you do." Do you think there are things people cannot stop themselves from doing, even if they try? Explain.

ANALYZING LITERATURE:

Evaluating Love Lyrics

A significant part of Catullus' success is his ability to convince the reader of his sincerity. Even though his statements are short, they are packed with compelling evidence of the poet's honest evaluation of personal struggles.

Cite phrases that substantiate the following statements about Catullus:
1. He is a dutiful son.

2. He knows his love for Lesbia is doomed.
3. He believes Lesbia is misleading him.

THINKING AND WRITING

Comparing Love Lyrics

Current music contains lyrics as filled with emotion and introspection as those of Sappho or Catullus. Select a set of lines and draw up a list of comparisons between Catullus' work and that of the modern lyricist. Organize your thoughts into a paragraph in which you compare statements about a single emotion, such as passion, grief, or despair. Summarize with a strong conclusion about the universality of that emotion. Read your paper aloud and evaluate your own ability to focus on a single feeling.

OVID

More About the Author During the miserable decade he spent in exile, Ovid wrote autobiographical poetry. He kept a sort of verse journal in the form of letters to friends in Rome. He complained that no one spoke Latin, so he had to talk to himself. His fear of forgetting his Latin is hyperbolic, since his style and sly wit come across undiminished in his descriptions of life on the frontier.

Ovid dealt with exile by writing constantly. Ask students to discuss what they know about other authors, like Aleksandr Solzhenitzyn or Primo Levi, forced by repressive regimes to undergo exile or imprisonment.

Critical Evaluation Seneca the Elder (55 B.C.–A.D. 41) notes that Ovid had a good ear for rhetorical excess and avoided it in speeches. His poetry, however, contained flaws, and Seneca claims that some of these faults were included deliberately. He asserts that some friends once asked Ovid to let them write down three of the verses they wanted him to strike; he agreed, as long as he could write down three he must be allowed to keep. When the two lists were compared, they were identical!

43 B.C.–A.D. 18

Publius Ovidius Naso (pub′li əs ov i′di əs′ nā′sō) known as Ovid (äv id) was born in the mountainous region of Abruzzi east of Rome the year after Julius Caesar's assassination. He was educated by the best tutors and trained in law. He chose, however, to devote his talents not to law but to poetry, to the irritation of his father. Ovid's choice suited his social-butterfly personality, but it was not wholly frivolous. Augustus' Rome left little room for a brilliant political career; the civil wars were over and life was again peaceful and secure. The political strife that could hurl a politician to meteoric success was not in evidence. However, Augustus was a patron of the arts who sponsored poets.

Ovid loved Rome and the life of urban sophisticates. He showed no interest in the official imperial version of an ideal Roman state based on the old puritanical virtues of the early Republic. He delighted in describing the glittering life of the rich and elegant, with malicious wit and an eye for beauty and extravagance. He took Rome by storm by producing a seducer's handbook (*The Art of Love*), advice to the lovelorn (*Cures for Love*), a beauty manual (*Cosmetics, or How to Care for Your Face*), fictitious love letters from the pens of mythical heroines, and an ambitious fifteen-book poem, in the dactylic hexameter of Homer (see page 330) which had recently been polished for use in Latin by Virgil. His mythological epic, the *Metamorphoses* (met′ ə môr′ fə sēz) (transformations) displays to best advantage Ovid's technical skill as a maker of verse and a teller of stories and has been so influential that it is still used as a handbook by novices learning to write.

By A.D. 8, Ovid's popularity was at its peak. He seemed imperturbable. Then, suddenly, giving no reason, Augustus banished him to a desolate stretch of Asia Minor along the Black Sea at Tomis where the local population spoke no Latin. For a lover of Roman high society and the Latin tongue, banishment at Tomis was almost worse than death. Ovid says he was banished because of "a poem and a blunder." The blunder may have been knowing too much about the antics of puritanical Augustus' racy female relatives. The poem was probably not *The Art of Love*, banned from public libraries after Ovid was exiled, but published ten years before. More likely, the *Metamorphoses*, stringing together stories of seduction and violence involving gods, was what annoyed the emperor most, for it was now obvious that Ovid had both the skill to undertake a major epic and the impertinence to use his talents to mock the emperor's program of moral reform. For years Ovid tried to petition and write his way to a reprieve. In exile he wrote a verse calendar of Roman religious holidays and self-pitying autobiographical verse epistles, or letters. Augustus never yielded. Ovid died at 61 years of age without ever again seeing the Rome he loved so much.

Objectives

Thematic
To appreciate an ancient treatment of a universal theme

Skills
1 To understand verse narrative
2 To learn about interpreting symbols
3 To appreciate and understand the use of similes
4 To learn to write about tone

GUIDE FOR INTERPRETING

from the Metamorphoses

Verse Narrative. In the *Metamorphoses* Ovid uses the form of the epic, books of verse in the tradition of Homer and Virgil, who wrote heroic epics. Other authors used the same meter to write long didactic works that were meant to teach lessons. Playing against this venerable tradition, Ovid chooses not to tell the story of a great historical event or a famous hero but rather weaves together a large group of myths about gods, demigods, and mortals. The stories are all connected by a shared theme, that of changing shapes or metamorphoses. For example, Daphne turns into a tree to avoid Apollo's unwanted advances. Arachne boasts about her weaving and is turned into a spider for comparing her talents to those of a goddess. Individual stories make up the smallest narrative units. Ovid dovetails one story into another using a variety of techniques: He may tell more than one story about the same character; use a minor figure from one myth as the protagonist of the next; have characters tell each other stories; or group together stories by place, family, or topic. Clusters of closely connected stories form larger narrative units.

As with most storytelling, the purpose of Ovid's verse narrative is to interest and entertain the reader. He describes two appealing characters, sets out the causes of the conflict in their relationship, and leads the events to an identifiable conclusion much as the writer of short fiction would narrate a tall tale or short story, or a newspaper reporter would relate a newsworthy event or feature. In addition to characters, action, and conflict, the verse narrative contains atmosphere, tone, and theme, which are the other elements essential to storytelling.

What sets verse narrative apart from a short story, tale, or newspaper article? The lines, written in rhythmic, lyrical style, contain an identifiable number of accented beats. Remember, though, that you are reading a translation, not the original Latin. The translator has taken Ovid's classical Latin verse and rephrased it into English but has refrained from forcing the rhythm into an explicit singsong cadence.

Writing

History and literature are filled with great love stories. Brainstorm, listing pairs of famous lovers. For example, you might list Mark Antony and Cleopatra, John Alden and Priscilla Mullen, King Arthur and Guinevere, Porgy and Bess, Pocahontas and Captain John Smith, Queen Elizabeth I and Sir Walter Raleigh, or Eloise and Abelard. Then choose one pair. Freewrite, relating the details of their story.

Literary Focus Have students think about other stories of young lovers kept apart by adults who did not take them seriously. Shakespeare's *Romeo and Juliet* provides a tragic version of this theme, as does the musical based on it, *West Side Story*.

Writing/Prior Knowledge Divide the class into small groups and have students discuss the usual cycle in boy-meets-girl stories. Have students share ideas before they freewrite about the love story they choose to retell.

ESL Teaching Strategy Summarize the selection orally for students before assigning it as a reading exercise. Be sure to stop your summary at the climax in order to motivate the students to read.

Master Teacher Note Display art transparency 7 to show the class another of Poussin's idealizations of antiquity. Identify Orpheus as the lyre player in the foreground to the right.

Vocabulary

Preteach the following vocabulary words:
chink (chiŋk) *n.*: Crack; a narrow opening
futile (fyo͞ot´ 'l) *adj.*: Useless; vain
cunning (kun´ iŋ) *adj.*: Skillful; clever
quenched (kwench't) *v.*: Extinguished; slaked
boxwood (bäks wo͝od´) *n.*: A tree or shrub
scabbard (skab´ ərd) *n.*: Sheath or case for a sword
begrudge (bi gruj´) *v.*: Feel ill will

Support Material

Teaching Portfolio
Teacher Backup, p. 639
Usage and Mechanics Worksheet, p. 643
Vocabulary Check , p. 644
Critical Thinking and Reading Worksheet, *Interpreting Symbols*, p. 645
Language Worksheet, *Understanding Similes*, p. 646

Selection Test, pp. 647–648
Art Transparency 7
Orpheus and Eurydice, Nicolas Poussin

Spelling Tip Put the word *quenched* on the chalkboard. Point out that almost all words in English that begin with the letter *q* use the letter *u* as the next letter. *Qintar* and *qiviut* are exceptions. Ask students to list ten words they know that follow the general rule.

from the Metamorphoses

Ovid

The Story of Pyramus and Thisbe

translated by Rolfe Humphries

"Next door to each other, in the brick-walled city
Built by Semiramis,[1] lived a boy and girl,
Pyramus, a most handsome fellow, Thisbe,
Loveliest of all those Eastern girls.[2] Their nearness
5 Made them acquainted, and love grew, in time,
So that they would have married, but their parents
Forbade it. But their parents could not keep them
From being in love: their nods and gestures
    showed it—
You know how fire suppressed burns all the fiercer.
10 There was a chink in the wall between the houses,
A flaw the careless builder had never noticed,
Nor anyone else, for many years, detected,
But the lovers found it—love is a finder, always—
Used it to talk through, and the loving whispers
15 Went back and forth in safety. They would stand
One on each side, listening for each other,
Happy if each could hear the other's breathing,
And then they would scold the wall: 'You envious
    barrier,
Why get in our way? Would it be too much to ask
    you
20 To open wide for an embrace, or even
Permit us room to kiss in? Still, we are grateful,
We owe you something, we admit; at least
You let us talk together.' But their talking
Was futile, rather; and when evening came
They would say *Good-night!* and give the good-
25   night kisses

That never reached the other.
                    "The next morning
Came, and the fires of night burnt out, and
    sunshine
Dried the night frost, and Pyramus and Thisbe
Met at the usual place, and first, in whispers,
Complained, and came—high time!—to a
30   decision.
That night, when all was quiet, they would fool
Their guardians, or try to, come outdoors,
Run away from home, and even leave the city.
And, not to miss each other, as they wandered
In the wide fields, where should they meet? At
35   Ninus'
Tomb, they supposed, was best; there was a tree
    there,
A mulberry-tree, loaded with snow-white berries,
Near a cool spring. The plan was good, the
    daylight
Was very slow in going, but at last
40 The sun went down into the waves, as always,
And the night rose, as always, from those waters.

And Thisbe opened her door, so sly, so cunning,
There was no creaking of the hinge, and no one
Saw her go through the darkness, and she came,
45 Veiled, to the tomb of Ninus, sat there waiting
Under the shadow of the mulberry-tree.
Love made her bold. But suddenly, here came
    something!—
A lioness, her jaws a crimson froth
With the blood of cows, fresh-slain, came there for
    water,
50 And far off through the moonlight Thisbe saw her

---

1. **the brick-walled city/Built by Semiramis** (si mir′ ə mis): Babylon.
2. **Eastern girls:** Girls from Assyria, an ancient empire in southwest Asia in the upper Tigris River region.

And ran, all scared, to hide herself in a cave,
And dropped her veil as she ran. The lioness,
Having quenched her thirst, came back to the
    woods, and saw
The girl's light veil, and mangled it and mouthed
    it
With bloody jaws. Pyramus, coming there
Too late, saw tracks in the dust, turned pale, and
    paler
Seeing the bloody veil. 'One night,' he cried,
'Will kill two lovers, and one of them, most surely,
Deserved a longer life. It is all my fault,
I am the murderer, poor girl; I told you
To come here in the night, to all this terror,
And was not here before you, to protect you.
Come, tear my flesh, devour my guilty body,
Come, lions, all of you, whose lairs lie hidden
Under this rock! I am acting like a coward,
Praying for death.' He lifts the veil and takes it
Into the shadow of their tree; he kisses
The veil he knows so well, his tears run down
Into its folds: 'Drink my blood too!' he cries,
And draws his sword, and plunges it into his body,
And, dying, draws it out, warm from the wound.
As he lay there on the ground, the spouting blood
Leaped high, just as a pipe sends water spurting
Through a small hissing opening, when broken
With a flaw in the lead, and all the air is sprinkled.
The fruit of the tree, from that red spray, turned
    crimson,
And the roots, soaked with the blood, dyed all the
    berries
The same dark hue.
            "Thisbe came out of hiding,
Still frightened, but a little fearful, also,
To disappoint her lover. She kept looking
Not only with her eyes, but all her heart,
Eager to tell him of those terrible dangers,
About her own escape. She recognized
The place, the shape of the tree, but there was
    something
Strange or peculiar in the berries' color.
Could this be right? And then she saw a quiver
Of limbs on bloody ground, and started backward,
Paler than boxwood, shivering, as water
Stirs when a little breeze ruffles the surface.
It was not long before she knew her lover,

LANDSCAPE WITH PYRAMUS AND THISBE
Nicolas Poussin
Stadelsches Kunstinstitut, Frankfurt-am-Main, Germany

And tore her hair, and beat her innocent bosom
With her little fists, embraced the well-loved body,
Filling the wounds with tears, and kissed the lips
Cold in his dying. 'O my Pyramus,'
95 She wept, 'What evil fortune takes you from me?
Pyramus, answer me! Your dearest Thisbe
Is calling you. Pyramus, listen! Lift your head!'
He heard the name of Thisbe, and he lifted
His eyes, with the weight of death heavy upon
    them,
100 And saw her face, and closed his eyes.
                        "And Thisbe
Saw her own veil, and saw the ivory scabbard
With no sword in it, and understood. 'Poor boy,'
She said, 'So, it was your own hand,
Your love, that took your life away. I too
105 Have a brave hand for this one thing, I too
Have love enough, and this will give me strength
For the last wound. I will follow you in death,
Be called the cause and comrade of your dying.
Death was the only one could keep you from me,
Death shall not keep you from me. Wretched
110 parents
Of Pyramus and Thisbe, listen to us,
Listen to both our prayers, do not begrudge us,
Whom death has joined, lying at last together
In the same tomb. And you, O tree, now shading
115 The body of one, and very soon to shadow
The bodies of two, keep in remembrance always
The sign of our death, the dark and mournful
    color.'
She spoke, and fitting the sword-point at her breast, 6

6 **Enrichment** Tell students that Thisbe stands in a tradition of heroic Roman noblewomen who commit suicide to avoid dishonor and to show eternal loyalty to their husbands.

Humanities Note

Fine art, *Landscape with Pyramus and Thisbe* by Nicolas Poussin. Nicolas Poussin (1596–1665) is considered to be one of the greatest of the French Classical Painters.

Landscape with Pyramus and Thisbe demonstrates Poussin's passion for ancient art and literature. The vast landscape dwarfs the figures in this tragic scene. The storm-tossed trees and darkened sky add to the dramatic tension of the composition.

You might want to use the following questions to discuss the art:
1. Despite the small scale of the characters in this painting, do you feel the artist manages to convey Thisbe's concern and fright?
2. How does he achieve this?
3. What associations do you make with the colors used by the artist?

Cooperative Learning The class as a group could put together an informal skit or play dramatizing the story. Acting out the scenes can highlight the importance of tone.

Commentary

Ovid was so popular and so much imitated by later writers that we may forget that writing a long epic based on stories like "How the Leopard Got His Spots" was a revolutionary step. He himself sees his achievement as monumental and worthy of eternal fame.

In Augustan Rome, however, transformation was not limited to ancient myth. After Julius Caesar was assassinated, Augustus declared him a god. At the public games held in 43 B.C. to celebrate his apotheosis, a comet shone for seven days and was taken to be the soul of Caesar. Ovid writes about the deification of Aeneas and that of Julius. His long and flowery ac-count contains some lines whose tone is ambiguous and risky: "We cannot think him mortal, our Augustus, / Therefore Julius must be made a god / To justify his son."

ANSWERS TO THINKING ABOUT THE SELECTION

1. (a) He blames himself for asking her to meet at a dangerous place. (b) Thisbe shows no evidence of blaming him.
2. (a) Suggest an answer that will refer to the parents' being touched by Thisbe's prayer. (b) They show their change by using a single urn.
3. Answers may differ. Many will note Ovid's high tone.
4. The change seems appropriate because the colors symbolize their lost love.
5. Various answers will be given, but many will focus on the senselessness of love.

ANSWERS TO ANALYZING LITERATURE

1. Answers may differ. Most will suggest that the strength of the plot would be effective in either prose or poetry.
2. Pyramus and Thisbe become tragic victims to an encounter with a lion after they plan to meet secretly.
3. Several could be named including Nikos Kazantzakis' The Odyssey: A Modern Sequel and T. S. Eliot's "The Waste Land."

ANSWERS TO CRITICAL THINKING AND READING

1. The wall stands as a dual factor that separates the lovers at the same time that it allows them to converse.
2. Answers may differ. Some may suggest that white stands for innocence and red for violence.

ANSWERS TO UNDERSTANDING LANGUAGE

1. Suggested answers could include references to discord.
2. A tactile sensation could include the touch of any surface with regular ridges.
3. Answers will differ. Her reaction could be compared to an inconstant wind that disturbs a mild day.

THINKING AND WRITING

Writing Across the Curriculum

Have students involve an art teacher in the selection of colors that will be used for an illustration of this story. Ask students to write

---

Fell forward on the blade, still warm and reeking
With her lover's blood. Her prayers touched the
120   gods,
And touched her parents, for the mulberry fruit
Still reddens at its ripeness, and the ashes
Rest in a common urn."

Reader's Response *The story of Pyramus and Thisbe, like that of Romeo and Juliet to which it is compared, is about the rashness of young love. What advice would you have given to Pyramus and Thisbe?*

THINKING ABOUT THE SELECTION

Interpreting

1. (a) Why does Pyramus blame himself for bringing harm to Thisbe? (b) Does Thisbe share his attitude?
2. (a) Why do you think that the parents relent in their opposition to their children? (b) How do they show their change of heart?
3. How does Ovid show us that this love is tragic?
4. Is the final metamorphosis fitting? Explain.

Applying

5. Philip Barry has defined love as "two minds without a single thought." Discuss your reactions to this definition.

ANALYZING LITERATURE

Understanding Verse Narrative

Verse narrative combines the elements of poetry and storytelling. Like poetry, it has lines written in verse that have a specific rhythm. Like storytelling, it recounts a tale that has a start, a middle, and an end.
1. Would this story have been as effective if it had been written in prose, not verse? Explain your answer.
2. Summarize the events in the story.
3. Give examples of modern verse narratives.

CRITICAL THINKING AND READING

Interpreting Symbols

Verse narrative makes use of symbols. Symbols are often used in myth, allowing authors to use signs to represent other things.

In Ovid's story there are symbols. The brick wall that divides the rooms of the friends is one. The mulberry tree near the tomb is another.
1. What meaning could the wall have for the lovers

that it does not have for anyone else?
2. What meanings are there for the tree's two colors?

UNDERSTANDING LANGUAGE

Understanding Similes

Similes bring freshness and clarity to a story. A **simile** makes a comparison between two dissimilar items by using the words *like* or *as*. For example, a simile invites us to see the blood from Pyramus' wound gushing as water does from a cracked pipe. And when Thisbe shudders in fright upon first seeing her friend's corpse, she is compared to the surface of a lake that shivers when a breeze ruffles its surface.

Ovid intends his readers to perceive his characters more clearly because of his use of such comparisons. Recall his simile in lines 88–90, the one that describes Thisbe's reaction to the corpse of Pyramus.
1. What associations do you make with the surface of water being stirred?
2. Describe the scene's tactile and visual sensations.
3. To what other activity in nature could Thisbe's reaction be compared? Explain.

THINKING AND WRITING

Writing About Tone

Tone is the author's personal attitude toward a composition. There are varied ways in which the author can respond, such as with bitterness or humor. Make a list of adjectives to describe the way Ovid feels. How would you define his regard for the young friends or for their parents? Does he seem to be judging anyone? Next write a description depicting his attitude toward the story. Exchange your first draft with a partner. Try to add tips to each other's work before revising these descriptions. Then expand them into paragraphs that should be proofread for errors.

---

notes for color choices before starting the illustration.

Challenge Have students volunteer to trace the influence of this story in both *Romeo and Juliet* and *West Side Story*. Ask them to prepare lists of ways in which the plots overlap and to also contrast the ways in which the stories differ.

Schedule a discussion of the findings.

Prose

Humanities Note

Fine art, *Orpheus Charming the Animals*, is a Roman mosaic. Composed on tiny squares of colored glass called *tesserae* set in cement, this representation of Orpheus has a naive, forthright quality. The color scheme is based on the contrast between the figure and the white background. The details of dress and landscape are skillfully rendered in this difficult medium.

Roman mosaics are a durable art that has withstood the ravages of time. From them we are able to obtain clues about the more fragile and rare art of Greco-Roman panel painting.

You might want to use the following questions to discuss the art:

1. What is the instrument used by Orpheus to charm the animals?
2. Do you find mosaic art an adequate way to represent an idea?
3. What do you find most impressive about this work?
4. How would you change some dimension of the work in order to improve it?

TACITUS

c. A.D. 55–117

The worldview and the works of Publius Cornelius Tacitus (pub′li əs kôr nel′yəs us tas′i təs) were shaped by the tumultuous era in which he lived. The Roman republic had come to an end in 30 B.C. after death throes lasting for a hundred years of civil war. Augustus Caesar took control and founded the empire. Even his rule was marked by a loss of liberty for his subjects; senators merely rubber-stamped his decisions, and his displeasure could mean (as in Ovid's case) perpetual exile, with no legal right of appeal. Nonetheless, Augustus was an able and sane leader, and under him the empire enjoyed relative peace and prosperity. His immediate successors, however, form a parade of irresponsible, capricious individuals who managed the state poorly. Understandably, many Romans longed for the days when a dutiful citizen could play an important role in governing the state.

Tacitus had not only survived the sometimes brief and always repressive reigns of over half a dozen emperors, he even managed a successful public career as a brilliant trial lawyer and judge. He seems to have been able to do that by keeping his political views to himself and spending some of the most dangerous years away from Rome, in a government office overseas. When the vicious emperor Domitian died in A.D. 96, to be succeeded by reasonable men, Tacitus returned to Rome and enjoyed a distinguished public career (first as consul in Rome and then as proconsul in Asia). He was also finally able to turn his pen against the depraved rule of Augustus' earlier successors.

Through his incisive *Histories* and *Annals*, Tacitus helped shape the world's opinion of the excesses of Augustus' first successors, particularly Nero, the last of the Julio-Claudian line, who is rumored to have sung while Rome burned. Nero's capricious and amoral sadism made itself felt especially among those closest to him. To be Nero's relative or close friend often marked one for an untimely death. But it was his persecution of vulnerable groups like the early Christians that earned him a lasting reputation for savagery.

Tacitus planned to write about good emperors like Nerva and Trajan, and perhaps about Augustus as well, but he died before he had the chance. Perhaps he could not bring himself to turn his keen analytic gaze on good government for fear of having to see its imperfections. He has left us an unforgettable condemnation of the abuses of power. Through his silence and the constantly implied contrast between the evils he describes and the Roman republic, he has left us an idealized but not fundamentally untrue picture of the republic as a state governed by law and informed by a respect for individual freedom.

Focus

More About the Author Tacitus survived the bloody reign of Domitian by keeping his own counsel. Unlike the garrulous Pliny, he says very little about himself, mentioning only that his official honors were "begun by Vespasian, increased by Titus, and further advanced by Domitian" and that he spent four years in some province in an official capacity. Ask students if they think historians should speak about themselves and their involvement with events as they write accounts of their times.

Critical Evaluation Michael Grant, the historian and translator of Tacitus, writes, "Tacitus is always deeply preoccupied with the discrepancy between fact and impression. . . . Another of his particular interests is group psychology, with its crosscurrents and irrationalities." Grant thinks Tacitus was not able to believe that any autocrat can be good.

Ask students if their own study of history has prompted them to believe certain things about those who hold great political power.

Master Teacher Note Since Tacitus was only seven years old when the great fire of Rome took place, his account is not an eyewitness report; however, he may have consulted with survivors. Have students consider, as they read, the ways in which Tacitus might have altered his account had he experienced the disaster as an adult.

Objectives

Thematic
To understand the cause-and-effect relationships that explain the interrelatedness of history

Skill
To define and understand what annals are

GUIDE FOR INTERPRETING

from the Annals

Commentary

Annals. Annals are a literary form similar to journals, diaries, histories, or chronicles. Derived from the Latin word *annus,* or "year," annals are a year-by-year account of a sequence of events, such as Tacitus' retelling of the major events during the first century of the Roman Empire. The cause-and-effect strategy of these narratives establishes the interrelatedness of history. The purpose of writing in this form is to unfold for the reader an ongoing cycle, thereby revealing how reaction to one situation leads to later events.

In order to do justice to all aspects of history, writers of annals must draw on a variety of sources of information. Sometimes the material for annals comes from eyewitness accounts, possibly even the writer's own participation or observation. Other likely sources are written journals, diaries, newspapers, magazines, movies, television and radio programs, letters, and fiction, including novels, plays, and short stories.

Sometimes writers resort to rumor, innuendo, or surmise. Such guesswork often clouds the true nature of an era, leaving later generations with a biased account. Yet, because of the dearth of data, reliance on questionable sources may be unavoidable. This situation often arises during a period of governmental secrecy.

For the benefit of the reader, Tacitus openly rates his source material. He begins his description with lucid details, attesting to his firm grip on fact. He names geographical locations, times, and participants, such as the feeding of fire victims with corn from Ostia at one quarter sesterce per pound. Because he approaches his subject from a factual point of view, he convinces the reader that what he says is true.

When Tacitus ventures into the gray area of drawing conclusions, his intent is clear. For example, he tells us that Nero profited from the burning of Rome during the years of rebuilding. Then he explains how subsequent public works enriched the emperor. Because Tacitus makes no attempt to deceive, the reader is forewarned and can judge accordingly whether the writer makes a convincing case for his opinions.

Writing

Imagine that you witnessed one of the major events in American history. Drawing on your own knowledge, freewrite about the event.

students of the value of some sources and the unreliable nature of others. Ask them to evaluate the reliability of newspapers, press bulletins, interviews, and leaked information.

Writing/Prior Knowledge Pair up students and have them discuss the events about which they will freewrite. Have them state whether they have strong opinions about the event they have chosen, which will influence how they depict the occurence.

ESL Teaching Strategy After the class has finished reading the passage, assign several specific paragraghs to each ESL student to be read silently. Then ask each one to summarize his or her reading orally in a round-robin fashion. This exercise not only serves to stimulate interest but also improves listening and speaking skills.

Support Material

Teaching Portfolio

Teacher Backup, p. 649

Grammar in Action Worksheet, *Understanding the Paragraph*, p. 653

Usage and Mechanics Worksheet, p. 655

Vocabulary Check, p. 656

Critical Thinking and Reading Worksheet, *Recognizing Cause and Ef-*

fect, p. 657

Language Worksheet, *Finding Prefixes*, p. 658

Selection Test, pp. 659–660

Spelling Tip Write the word *demarcation* on the chalkboard. Point out that the *ka* sound of the third syllable uses *ca* as its spelling. Mention other words that do the same. Then

mention that there is an alternate spelling using the *ka* (demarkation) that is also correct.

Literary Focus Ask students how notes might be taken for an assignment that calls for the writing of an annal about a world leader. Remind students of the value of some sources and the unreliable nature of

from the Annals

Tacitus

from The Burning of Rome

translated by Michael Grant

Now started the most terrible and destructive fire which Rome had ever experienced. It began in the Circus,[1] where it adjoins the Palatine and Caelian hills.[2] Breaking out in shops selling inflammable goods, and fanned by the wind, the conflagration instantly grew and swept the whole length of the Circus. There were no walled mansions or temples, or any other obstructions, which could arrest it. First, the fire swept violently over the level spaces. Then it climbed the hills—but returned to ravage the lower ground again. It outstripped every counter-measure. The ancient city's narrow winding streets and irregular blocks encouraged its progress.

Terrified, shrieking women, helpless old and young, people intent on their own safety, people unselfishly supporting invalids or waiting for them, fugitives and lingerers alike—all heightened the confusion. When people looked back, menacing flames sprang up before them or outflanked them. When they escaped to a neighboring quarter, the fire followed—even districts believed remote proved to be involved. Finally, with no idea where or what to flee, they crowded onto the country roads, or lay in the fields. Some who had lost everything— even their food for the day—could have escaped, but preferred to die. So did others, who had failed to rescue their loved ones. Nobody dared fight the flames. Attempts to do so were prevented by menacing gangs. Torches, too, were openly thrown in, by men crying that they acted under orders. Perhaps they had received orders. Or they may just have wanted to plunder unhampered.

Nero was at Antium.[3] He only returned to the city when the fire was approaching the mansion he had built to link the Gardens of Maecenas to the Palatine. The flames could not be prevented from overwhelming the whole of the Palatine, including his palace. Nevertheless, for the relief of the homeless, fugitive masses he threw open the Field of Mars, including Agrippa's public buildings, and even his own Gardens. Nero also constructed emergency accommodation for the destitute multitude. Food was brought from Ostia[4] and neighboring towns, and the price of corn was cut to less than ¼ sesterce[5] a pound. Yet these measures, for all their

---

1. Circus (sur´ kəs) *n.*: In ancient Rome, games and chariot races were held in the Circus, an oval arena surrounded by tiers of seats.
2. Palatine and Caelian (pal´ ə tīn´ and kē´ lē ən) **hills:** Where Nero's imperial palaces were located.

3. Antium (an´ tē əm) *n.*: Town in central Italy where Nero was born.
4. Ostia (äs´ tē ə) *n.*: Roman port at the mouth of the Tiber River.
5. sesterce (ses´ tərs) *n.*: Roman coin, equal in value to two and a half cents.

THE BURNING OF ROME
Hubert Robert

popular character, earned no gratitude. For a rumor had spread that, while the city was burning, Nero had gone on his private stage and, comparing modern calamities with ancient, had sung of the destruction of Troy.

By the sixth day enormous demolitions had confronted the raging flames with bare ground and open sky, and the fire was finally stamped out at the foot of the Esquiline Hill. But before panic had subsided, or hope revived, flames broke out again

Commentary

Objectivity and Bias in Tacitus' *Annals* Tacitus creates the appearance of objectivity because he reports facts accurately, labels rumors as such, and implies that one interpretation of events is more plausible than another without saying so outright. By guiding the reader through his arrangement of material, he creates the impression that truth is being offered.

At the same time Tacitus also builds into his narrative elements of bias against Nero. When he recounts Nero's aggressive rebuilding program, for instance, he ends on a sour note and prompts the reader to question Nero's motives.

in the more open regions of the city. Here there were fewer casualties; but the destruction of temples and pleasure arcades was even worse. This new conflagration caused additional ill-feeling because it started on Tigellinus' estate[6] in the Aemilian district. For people believed that Nero was ambitious to found a new city to be called after himself.

Of Rome's fourteen districts only four remained intact. Three were leveled to the ground. The other seven were reduced to a few scorched and mangled ruins. To count the mansions, blocks, and temples destroyed would be difficult. They included shrines of remote antiquity, such as Servius Tullius' temple of the Moon, the Great Altar and holy place dedicated by Evander to Hercules, the temple vowed by Romulus to Jupiter the Stayer, Numa's sacred residence, and Vesta's shrine containing Rome's household gods. Among the losses, too, were the precious spoils of countless victories, Greek artistic masterpieces, and authentic records of old Roman genius. All the splendor of the rebuilt city did not prevent the older generation from remembering these irreplaceable objects. It was noted that the fire had started on July 19th, the day on which the Senonian Gauls[7] had captured and burnt the city. Others elaborately calculated that the two fires were separated by the same number of years, months, and days.[8]

But Nero profited by his country's ruin to build a new palace. Its wonders were not so much customary and commonplace luxuries like gold and jewels, but lawns and lakes and faked rusticity—woods here, open spaces and views there. With their cunning, impudent[9] artificialities, Nero's architects and engineers, Severus and Celer, did not balk at effects which Nature herself had ruled out as impossible.

They also fooled away an emperor's riches. For they promised to dig a navigable canal from Lake Avernus to the Tiber estuary,[10] over the stony shore and mountain barriers. The only water to feed the canal was in the Pontine marshes. Elsewhere, all was precipitous or waterless. Moreover, even if a passage could have been forced, the labor would have been unendurable and unjustified. But Nero was eager to perform the incredible; so he attempted to excavate the hills adjoining Lake Avernus. Traces of his frustrated hopes are visible today.

In parts of Rome unfilled by Nero's palace, construction was not—as after the burning by the Gauls without plan or demarcation. Street-fronts were of regulated alignment, streets were broad, and houses built round courtyards. Their height was restricted, and their frontages protected by colonnades. Nero undertook to erect these at his own expense, and also to clear debris from building-sites before transferring them to their owners. He announced bonuses, in proportion to rank and resources, for the completion of houses and blocks before a given date. Rubbish was to be dumped in the Ostian marshes by corn-ships returning down the Tiber.

A fixed proportion of every building had to be massive, untimbered stone from Gabii[11] or Alba[12] (these stones being fireproof). Furthermore, guards were to ensure a more abundant and extensive public water supply, hitherto diminished by irregular private enterprise. Householders were obliged to keep fire-fighting apparatus in an accessible place; and semidetached houses were forbidden—they must have their own walls. These measures were welcomed for their practicality, and they beautified the new city. Some, however, believed that the old town's configuration had been healthier, since its narrow streets and high houses had provided protection against the burning sun, whereas now the shadowless open spaces radiated a fiercer heat.

---

6. **Tigellinus' estate** (ti jel ē′ nəs): Land belonging to Tigellinus, second to Nero in power.
7. **Senonian Gauls** (sə nō′ nē ən gôlz): Barbarians from Gaul, an ancient region in western Europe; they burned Rome in 390 B.C.
8. **the same number of years, months, and days:** 418 years, months, and days.
9. **impudent** *adj.*: Shamelessly bold and disrespectful; saucy.

10. **Tiber estuary** (tī′ bər es′ choo wer′ē): The wide mouth of the Tiber, a river in central Italy that flows south through Rome.
11. **Gabii** (gäb′ ē ē) *n.*: Ancient Roman town where Romulus, legendary founder of Rome, was reared. Gabii supposedly resisted a siege and was an important city until it was overshadowed by Rome.
12. **Alba** (äl′ bə) *n.*: Alba Longa, powerful ancient Roman city; legendary birthplace of Romulus and Remus.

Grammar in Action

Paragraph Development The main idea of a paragraph can be developed in a number of ways: by the use of detail, definition, example, comparison and contrast, or a combination of these.

Development by detail is probably the most common of these. Tacitus uses it when he describes the effects of the fire in the paragraph:

Of Rome's fourteen districts only four remained intact. Three were . . . separated by the same number of years, months, and days.

We see a combination of detail and contrast in the final paragraph:

A fixed proportion of every building . . . open spaces radiated a fiercer heat.

Student Activity 1. For each of the six paragraphs on page 541, state the central idea (you may or may not find it in a topic sentence) and the method of paragraph development used in each.

Student Activity 2. Write a paragraph about some contemporary disaster with which you are familiar. Use any one of the listed types of paragraph development, and indicate which one you are using.

So much for human precautions. Next came attempts to appease heaven. After consultation of the Sibylline Books,[13] prayers were addressed to Vulcan, Ceres, and Proserpina. Juno, too, was propitiated.[14] Women who had been married were responsible for the rites—first on the Capitol, then at the nearest sea-board, where water was taken to sprinkle her temple and statue. Women with husbands living also celebrated ritual banquets and vigils.

But neither human resources, nor imperial munificence, nor appeasement of the gods, eliminated sinister suspicions that the fire had been instigated. To suppress this rumor, Nero fabricated scapegoats—and punished with every refinement the notoriously depraved Christians (as they were popularly called). Their originator, Christ, had been executed in Tiberius' reign[15] by the governor of Judaea,[16] Pontius Pilatus. But in spite of this temporary setback the deadly superstition had broken out afresh, not only in Judaea (where the mischief had started) but even in Rome. All degraded and shameful practices collect and flourish in the capital.

First, Nero had self-acknowledged Christians arrested. Then, on their information, large numbers of others were condemned—not so much for incendiarism[17] as for their antisocial tendencies. Their deaths were made farcical. Dressed in wild animals' skins, they were torn to pieces by dogs, or crucified, or made into torches to be ignited after dark as substitutes for daylight. Nero provided his Gardens for the spectacle, and exhibited displays in the Circus, at which he mingled with the crowd—or stood in a chariot, dressed as a charioteer. Despite their guilt as Christians, and the ruthless punishment it deserved, the victims were pitied. For it was felt that they were being sacrificed to one man's brutality rather than to the national interest.

Meanwhile Italy was ransacked for funds, and the provinces were ruined—unprivileged and privileged communities alike. Even the gods were included in the looting. Temples at Rome were robbed, and emptied of the gold dedicated for the triumphs and vows, the ambitions and fears, of generations of Romans. Plunder from Asia and Greece included not only offerings but actual statues of the gods. Two agents were sent to these provinces. One, Acratus, was an ex-slave, capable of any depravity. The other, Secundus Carrinas, professed Greek culture, but no virtue from it percolated to his heart.

Seneca,[18] rumor went, sought to avoid the odium of this sacrilege by asking leave to retire to a distant country retreat, and then—permission being refused—feigning a muscular complaint and keeping to his bedroom. According to some accounts one of his former slaves, Cleonicus by name, acting on Nero's orders intended to poison Seneca but he escaped—either because the man confessed or because Seneca's own fears caused him to live very simply on plain fruit, quenching his thirst with running water.

At this juncture there was an attempted breakout by gladiators at Praeneste.[19] Their army guards overpowered them. But the Roman public, as always terrified (or fascinated) by revolution, were already talking of ancient calamities such as the rising of Spartacus.[20] Soon afterwards a naval disaster occurred. This was not on active service; never had there been such profound peace. But Nero had ordered the fleet to return to Campania by a fixed date regardless of weather. So, despite heavy seas the steersmen started from Formiae. But when they tried to round Cape Misenum a southwesterly gale drove them ashore near Cumae and destroyed numerous warships and smaller craft.

As the year ended omens of impending misfortune were widely rumored—unprecedentedly fre-

---

13. Sibylline (si′ bə lēn′) **Books:** Books of prophecies by Sibyl, Apollo's priestess at Cumae, a city in southwest Italy near Naples.
14. propitiated (prō pish′ ē āt əd) *n.:* Appeased.
15. Tiberius' (tī bir′ ē əs) **reign:** Tiberius was emperor of Rome A.D. 14–37.
16. Judaea (jōō dē′ ə) *n.:* Ancient region of South Palestine.
17. incendiarism (in sen′ dē ə riz′m) *n.:* Willful destruction of property by fire.

18. Seneca (sen′ ə kə) *n.:* Philosopher and minister of Nero.
19. Praeneste (prī nest′): A town in central Italy.
20. Spartacus (spärt′ ə kəs) *n.:* Ancient Thracian slave and gladiator who led a slave revolt.

9 Discussion Have students discuss what Tacitus' personal attitude toward the Christians may be. Ask them whether he uses "deadly superstition" and "mischief" as his own words or simply employs such words to reproduce the propaganda spread by Nero for effect.

10 Literary Focus Have students think about the sequence of events depicted here. Have them list the chronology of this paragraph's description of the persecution of Christians.

11 Clarification Ask students why Tacitus mentions an insignificant and unsuccessful jailbreak. Mentioning the slave uprisings of the sort led by Spartacus during the civil wars suggests certain connotations. Make sure students see that the implied reference to the civil wars leads to the irony of the fleet's destruction in peacetime. The implication is that all by himself Nero is worse than any enemy or than civil uprisings.

quent lightning; a comet (atoned for by Nero, as usual, by aristocratic blood); two-headed offspring of men and beasts, thrown into the streets or discovered among the offerings to those deities to whom pregnant victims are sacrificed. Near Placentia a calf was born beside the road with its head fastened to one of its legs. Soothsayers deduced that a new head was being prepared for the world—but that it would be neither powerful nor secret since it had been deformed in the womb and given birth by the roadside.

Reader's Response *Nero is frequently regarded as the most ruthless and corrupt of all the Caesars, the one most obviously twisted by the apparently limitless power of his office. After reading this selection, do you think that such power always weakens leaders morally? Why? If power does tempt people to be ruthless, what could be done to help them resist such temptations?*

PRIMARY SOURCE

Modern critics have mixed opinions about Tacitus' ability to deal fairly with the events he describes. Will Durant, one of the most popular and widely read historians of our century, condemns his lack of objectivity but also credits Tacitus for possessing many good qualities. He writes:

"If, despite our surprise in finding a sermon and a drama where we looked for history, we must nevertheless rank Tacitus among the greatest of historians, it is because the power of his art redeems the limitations of his view. Above all, he sees intensely, sometimes deeply, always vividly. The portraits he draws stand out more clearly, stride the stage more livingly, than any other in historical literature."

In explaining the specific reason why the author of the Annals disappoints him, Durant continues: "Tacitus was wrong in scorning philosophy—that is, perspective; all his faults are due to a lack of it. If he could have disciplined his pen to the service of the open mind, he would have placed his name first on the list of those who have labored to give form and permanence to the memory and heritage of mankind."

THINKING ABOUT THE SELECTION

Interpreting

1. Tacitus describes in detail Nero's attempts to help the Romans during the fire. (a) What effect is then created by his recounting the rumor of the incident of Nero's singing while Rome burned? (b) Why does he describe the event as rumor, not fact?
2. (a) Describe the spirit in which the newly coined term "Christian" was used in Tacitus' day. (b) What seems to be Tacitus' position on Nero's treatment of the Christians?
3. (a) Did you find this account objective or opinionated? Find evidence to support your answer. (b) How do you think Tacitus has influenced later thought on the nature of Nero's reign?

Applying

4. (a) Why do you think Tacitus holds Nero up to public scorn as an example of tyranny and immorality? (b) What can a historian accomplish by these tactics?

ANALYZING LITERATURE

Understanding Annals

Annals are written accounts of events year by year in chronological order. Because events follow one another in time order, the reader learns how one situation triggers later events. For example, after the fire destroys ten of Rome's fourteen districts, two architects, Severus and Celer, begin reconstruction. Their extravagant plans include a scam by which they propose to dig a navigable canal 172 miles over mountains.

1. Place the following events in probable time order:
   a. The fire ends near the Esquiline Hill.
   b. Nero returns from Antium.
   c. Nero participates in a mock wedding.
   d. Fire breaks out in the Circus.
   e. Vesta's shrine is destroyed.
2. To what extent do historians record history and to what extent do they create it? Discuss your answer with your classmates.
3. How has modern technology changed the nature of annals?

CRITICAL THINKING AND READING

Recognizing Cause and Effect

An **effect** is what happens; a **cause** is what makes something happen. Tacitus is careful to relate events of Nero's reign to identifiable causes. For example, he links a suspicious fire with the emperor's need for a scapegoat. After the fire Nero initiates persecutions of Christians, whom he kills in cruel spectacles.

Relate the following effects to an earlier cause:
1. Italy is ransacked for funds.
2. Seneca feigns illness.
3. Gladiators attempt a breakout.
4. A naval disaster occurs.

UNDERSTANDING LANGUAGE

Finding Prefixes

A **prefix** is a letter or group of letters attached to the beginning of a word to change its meaning. Some prefixes add a negative meaning. For example, *irregular* means "not regular"; *unselfishly* means "not selfishly"; and *incredible* means "not credible." Locate five other examples of words with negative prefixes. On a separate piece of paper, underline the prefix and state its meaning. Then explain how each word affects the tone of the sentence in which it appears.

THINKING AND WRITING

Writing About the News

Today many people receive all their information about current events from television. But how much information do you really get from televized news? Watch a half-hour news show with a stopwatch in hand. (If you do not have a stopwatch, adapt these instructions to a regular clock or watch.) Stop your watch whenever a commercial comes on and do not start again until a news story begins. Stop when special features come on—sports, weather—or when the newscasters simply patter. Based on your findings, write the first draft of an essay telling how well informed a person can be about current events by watching television news. When you revise, make sure your information supports your conclusion.

(continued from bottom of page)

ANSWERS TO CRITICAL THINKING

1. This was done because of Nero's efforts to rebuild Rome.
2. He did this to avoid witnessing Nero's sacrilege of temple robbing.
3. It seemed opportune while the provinces were in turmoil.
4. It happened because Nero ordered the fleet to return regardless of the weather.

ANSWERS TO UNDERSTANDING LANGUAGE

de-formed/not
in-decently/not
un-selfishly/not
im-possible/not
ir-replaceable/not
Answers about how they affect sentence tone will vary.

THINKING AND WRITING

Writing Across the Curriculum
You may wish to inform the science department about the attention being given to Rome's conflagration. Ask students to gather information about the temperatures of fire at different stages of combustion. A chart could be constructed dealing with the colors of flame, and students could write captions for each illustration.

Challenge Tell students that Tacitus was influenced by both Herodotus and Thucydides. Have volunteers go to a library and have them consult the opening pages of the works of those Greek writers and take note of the purposes for their writings. Schedule a report on their findings.

---

evidence of his objectivity. Others may point to the characterization of Nero to show how opinionated it is. (b) Answers will differ. Many students will probably say that Tacitus convinced most historians to regard Nero's reign as the low point of Roman history.

4. (a) Tacitus did this because he distrusted all autocrats, especially those who were as excessive as Nero. (b)

It is by such means that historians can ruin the reputations of their subjects. But they can also use criticism to expose the dishonesty of tyrants.

ANSWERS TO ANALYZING LITERATURE

1. c, d, b, a, e
2. They record history to the extent that they do no more than report events in

a journalistically objective way. They create it whenever they embellish events or characters with imagined background or fabricated dialogue.
3. Modern technology has made it much easier for annalists to give the illusion of completeness or the façade of comprehensiveness.

PLINY

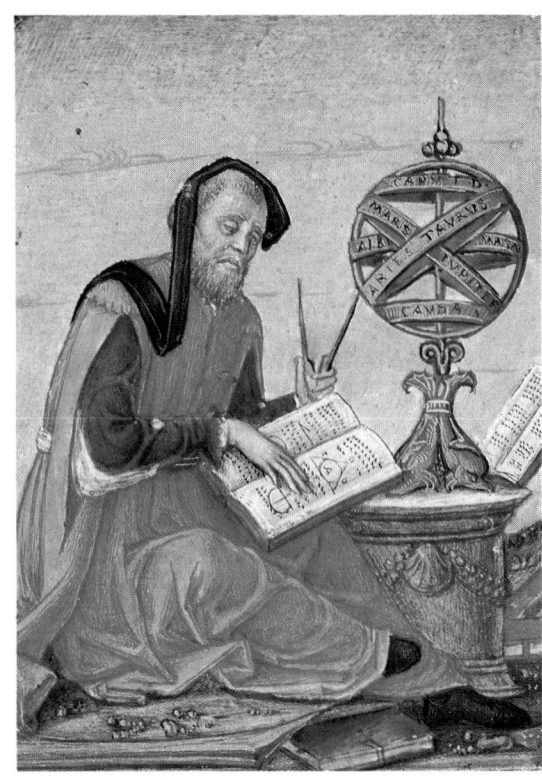

c. A.D. 62–112

Son of a wealthy, distinguished family, Gaius Plinius Caecilius Secundus, (gā′ əs pli′ ne yəs se sil′ yas se kun′ das), or Pliny the Younger, was born near Lake Como in the Po Valley near what is now the Italian-Swiss border. He enjoyed a comfortable life and a successful career as an attorney in Rome. Gaining a fund of knowledge and guidance from his uncle and guardian, Pliny the Elder, who was a cavalry expert and the author of the first Roman encyclopedia, the younger Pliny served his country in various civil-service posts, including judge, financial manager of Syria, and governor of Bithynia. This last appointment, made in A.D. 112, was a natural consequence of his earlier involvement with the defense of two former governors of Bithynia who were accused of extortion. His knowledge of their affairs and his awareness of the financial administration of the area combined to prompt Trajan to select him for the position when the emperor removed the province from senatorial control.

Two great men influenced Pliny. From youth to the end of his life, he emulated his uncle's practice of using every spare moment for reading, note-taking, study, and reflection. From Cicero, an idol of the previous generation, Pliny learned the basics of oratory and writing and gained notoriety for brilliant forensic performances in Rome's law courts. He published a famous encomium (or eulogy) to the Emperor Trajan, but the bulk of Pliny's fame rests on his 370 collected epistles. These letters detail the minutiae of daily life in first-century Rome and provide the author with the chance to comment on all the many aspects of human and natural history that held such fascination for him.

Some of the most famous observations that he detailed are found in numbers 16 and 20 of Book VI. They were written to the historian Tacitus and contain an account of the events of August 24, A.D. 79, when Mount Vesuvius near the Bay of Naples on Italy's western coast erupted. From this readable eyewitness account of the destructive power of the volcano that resulted in his uncle's death, Pliny the Younger delineates the effects of mass hysteria, which swirl around his family estate, and the importance of setting a calm, controlled example in the face of imminent death.

Pliny's style serves as a model to aspiring writers. His letters are succinct, organized, and articulate. He obviously intended them for later publication in a semi-autobiographical collection. The general tone and nature of his epistolary essays reveal an optimistic, bookish Roman gentleman who took stock of the events of his day and recorded them for the education of future generations.

GUIDE FOR INTERPRETING

from Letters of the Younger Pliny

Commentary

Epistle. As a literary form, the **epistle** differs from the private letter or personal note. Intended as a formal observation or essay for the benefit of a distant individual or group of readers, the epistle makes a conscious effort to impart information or critical opinion about manners, life style, religion, or significant political or historical events. The epistle writer deliberately avoids the spontaneity and witty banter of less formal letters in order to maintain an elevated tone. The purpose of the epistle is didactic; the writer attempts to instruct the reader, alter current thinking, or establish a particular outlook.

Pliny employs the epistle as a means of expressing his personal philosophy about the milieu of first-century Rome as well as about life in general. He touches on many topics of universal interest, particularly friendship, marriage, social order, deportment, leisure, worship, sports, travel, food, the arts, and finance. His fluent style, which is brief, to the point, and undecorated, uplifts the reader at the same time that it conveys instruction, reflection, and advice. Without preaching or moralizing, Pliny manages to convince his audience of the worth of his point of view. To Pliny, proper conduct in the face of adversity is not only desirable but vital to a well-ordered life.

In his letter to Tacitus concerning the eruption of Vesuvius, Pliny begins with an explanation of purpose—he is writing in response to Tacitus' questions about the death of Pliny the Elder. Before launching a chronological narrative of events, Pliny comments on the value of living an active, worthwhile life and of recording the events for posterity. Then, without further commentary, he describes the catastrophe that causes his uncle to sail from Misenum harbor on August 24 to rescue a friend and to inspect the cause of the destruction.

Pliny selects details with care and emphasizes sense impressions, such as the shape and color of the cloud over Vesuvius, the smell of the fumes, and the appearance of his uncle's body after death. To express himself clearly, Pliny relies upon cause-and-effect narration, particularly in explaining why his uncle sets out on so dangerous a mission, how he behaves under stress, and what causes contribute to his death.

Writing

Compose a quick, chatty note to a good friend from whom you are separated in which you describe some natural phenomenon, such as a severe snowstorm, tornado, flood, drought, or heat wave.

Language Worksheet, *Recognizing Impact of Language*, p. 668
Selection Test, pp. 669–670
Essay Questions and Evaluation Guidelines, p. 674

Spelling Tip Write the word *phenomenon* on the chalkboard. Ask students to guess how to spell the plural form. Mention words like alumnus/alumni and stadium/stadia that have irregular plural endings in English before explaining that the correct answer is *phenomena*.

Literary Focus Literary epistles are addressed to a real person. They are also meant to be published. Pliny always focuses on a single topic in each of his epistles. Have students speculate on how a single focus distinguishes a literary piece from a "real" letter.

Writing/Prior Knowledge Ask students to describe the visual impressions that they will include in their notes on natural disasters.

ESL Teaching Strategy Ask each ESL student to formulate two short-answer questions based on the reading passage. Then have the students exchange papers so that each can answer another's questions. Returning papers to original writers for direction will enable them to determine how well their work was understood.

Teaching Tenth-Grade Students This passage is made particularly gripping by Pliny's involvement in it; his affection for his uncle is obvious. Direct tenth-grade students' attention to Pliny's technique of revealing many facets of his uncle's character by recounting incidents in which his uncle was involved rather than by making laudatory statements.

Vocabulary

Preteach the following vocabulary words:
posterity (päs ter´ə tē) *n.*: Future generations
phenomenon (fi näm´ ə nän´) *n.*: Unusual event or person
subsided (səb sīd´ id) *v.*: Sank; became less active
blotched (bläch't) *v.*: Covered with blemishes
pumice (pum´ is) *n.*: Spongy rock
debris (də brē´) *n.*: Bits and pieces of rubbish
allay (ə lā´) *v.*: To rest

from Letters
Pliny

The Eruption of Vesuvius
translated by Betty Radice

To Cornelius Tacitus[1]

Thank you for asking me to send you a description of my uncle's death[2] so that you can leave an accurate account of it for posterity; I know that immortal fame awaits him if his death is recorded by you. It is true that he perished in a catastrophe which destroyed the loveliest regions of the earth,[3] a fate shared by whole cities and their people, and one so memorable that it is likely to make his name live forever: and he himself wrote a number of books of lasting value: but you write for all time and can still do much to perpetuate his memory. The fortunate man, in my opinion, is he to whom the gods have granted the power either to do something which is worth recording or to write what is worth reading, and most fortunate of all is the man who can do both. Such a man was my uncle, as his own books and yours will prove. So you set me a task I would choose for myself, and I am more than willing to start on it.

My uncle was stationed at Misenum,[4] in active command of the fleet. On 24 August, in the early afternoon, my mother drew his attention to a cloud of unusual size and appearance. He had been out in the sun, had taken a cold bath, and lunched while lying down, and was then working at his books. He called for his shoes and climbed up to a place which would give him the best view of the phenomenon. It was not clear at that distance from which mountain the cloud was rising (it was afterwards known to be Vesuvius); its general appearance can best be expressed as a being like an umbrella pine, for it rose to a great height on a sort of trunk and then split off into branches, I imagine because it was thrust upwards by the first blast and then left unsupported as the pressure subsided, or else it was borne down by its own weight so that it spread out and gradually dispersed. Sometimes it looked white, sometimes blotched and dirty, according to the amount of soil and ashes it carried with it. My uncle's scholarly acumen[5] saw at once that it was important enough for a closer inspection, and he ordered a boat to be made ready, telling me I could come with him if I wished. I replied that I preferred to go on with my studies, and as it happened he had himself given me some writing to do.

As he was leaving the house he was handed a message from Rectina, wife of Tascius whose house

---

1. **Cornelius Tacitus** (kôr nēl′ yəs tas′ i təs): Roman historian; wrote the *Annals*.
2. **my uncle's death:** Pliny the Elder.
3. **regions of the earth:** Pompeii.
4. **Misenum** (mī sē′ nəm): The northern arm of the bay of Naples.

5. **acumen** (ə kyo͞o′ mən) *n*.: Keenness; shrewdness.

was at the foot of the mountain, so that escape was impossible except by boat. She was terrified by the danger threatening her and implored him to rescue her from her fate. He changed his plans, and what he had begun in a spirit of inquiry he completed as a hero. He gave orders for the warships to be launched and went on board himself with the intention of bringing help to many more people besides Rectina, for this lovely stretch of coast was thickly populated. He hurried to the place which everyone else was hastily leaving, steering his course straight for the danger zone. He was entirely fearless, describing each new movement and phase of the portent[6] to be noted down exactly as he observed them. Ashes were already falling, hotter and thicker as the ships drew near, followed by bits of pumice and blackened stones, charred and cracked by the flames: then suddenly they were in shallow water, and the shore was blocked by the debris from the mountain. For a moment my uncle wondered whether to turn back, but when the helmsman[7] advised this he refused, telling him that Fortune stood by the courageous and they must make for Pomponianus at Stabiae.[8] He was cut off there by the breadth of the bay (for the shore gradually curves round a basin filled by the sea) so that he was not as yet in danger, though it was clear that this would come nearer as it spread. Pomponianus had therefore already put his belongings on board ship, intending to escape if the contrary wind fell. This wind was of course full in my uncle's favor, and he was able to bring his ship in. He embraced his terrified friend, cheered and encouraged him, and thinking he could calm his fears by showing his own composure, gave orders that he was to be carried to the bathroom. After his bath he lay down and dined; he was quite cheerful, or at any rate he pretended he was, which was no less courageous.

Meanwhile on Mount Vesuvius broad sheets of fire and leaping flames blazed at several points, their bright glare emphasized by the darkness of night. My uncle tried to allay the fears of his companions by repeatedly declaring that these were nothing but bonfires left by the peasants in their terror, or else empty houses on fire in the districts they had abandoned. Then he went to rest and certainly slept, for as he was a stout man his breathing was rather loud and heavy and could be heard by people coming and going outside his door. By this time the courtyard giving access to his room was full of ashes mixed with pumice stones, so that its level had risen, and if he had stayed in the room any longer he would never have got out. He was wakened, came out and joined Pomponianus and the rest of the household who had sat up all night. They debated whether to stay indoors or take their chance in the open, for the buildings were now shaking with violent shocks, and seemed to be swaying to and fro as if they were torn from their foundations. Outside on the other hand, there was the danger of falling pumice stones, even though these were light and porous;[9] however, after comparing the risks they chose the latter. In my uncle's case one reason outweighed the other, but for the others it was a choice of fears. As a protection against falling objects they put pillows on their heads tied down with cloths.

Elsewhere there was daylight by this time, but they were still in darkness, blacker and denser than any ordinary night, which they relieved by lighting torches and various kinds of lamp. My uncle decided to go down to the shore and investigate on the spot the possibility of any escape by sea, but he found the waves still wild and dangerous. A sheet was spread on the ground for him to lie down, and he repeatedly asked for cold water to drink. Then the flames and smell of sulfur which gave warning of the approaching fire drove the others to take flight and roused him to stand up. He stood leaning on two slaves and then suddenly collapsed, I imagine because the dense fumes choked his breathing by blocking his windpipe which was constitutionally[10] weak and narrow and often inflamed. When daylight returned on the 26th —two days after the last day he had seen—his body was found intact and uninjured, still fully clothed and looking more like sleep than death.

---

6. **portent** (pôr′ tent) *n.*: Here, an unfortunate, ominous event.

7. **helmsman** (helmz′ mən) *n.*: Person who steers a ship.

8. **Stabiae** (stə bī′ ə): Four miles south of Pompeii.

9. **porous** (pôr əs) *adj.*: Full of openings.

10. **constitutionally** (kän′ sti too′ shən əl ē) *adj.*: In physique; by nature.

4 Literary Focus Make students aware of how Pliny uses antithesis to depict his uncle's Stoic heroism. Here he "hurried" where everyone else is "hastily leaving." Have students find contrasts throughout the letter between Pliny's own bookishness and his uncle's need to act, and between his uncle's courage and the agitation felt by others. Have them comment on how the author's attitude is reflected in such passages.

5 Discussion Why is Pliny at pains to prove that his uncle certainly slept? Have students think about why this detail is important as part of the portrait of Pliny the Elder.

6 Clarification Students should recognize the point that Pliny is making. Make sure they realize that although all reached the same decision, only Pliny's uncle reached it through calm, rational thought, free from panic.

7 Enrichment By filling these molds with plaster, archeologists have made casts that capture the appearance of these citizens of Pompeii at the instant of their death so long ago.

Master Teacher Note Ask students to imagine that their own town or city was unexpectedly frozen in time, like Pompeii, and then rediscovered 2,000 years later. What would excavators see? What would be preserved that would not have been chosen to be put into a time capsule?

Cultural Note In A.D. 79 the prosperous resort of Pompeii was buried virtually instantaneously. For the next 1,700 years it was hidden from view, until some workers digging a canal found some statues. Subsequent excavations revealed the complete city caught in action: villas of the rich, account ledgers of a devious banker, election posters, fast-food shops, and graffiti. We see that daily life in Pompeii was in many ways just like our own.

Cooperative Learning You might have students get together in small groups and agree on a list of up to ten things that would be preserved for posterity if their own town were "frozen" on an average afternoon.

Humanities Note

Fine art, *The Eruption of Vesuvius and the Death of Pliny,* artist unknown.

In the latter part of the eighteenth century, the excavation of Pompeii greatly inspired the imaginations of European artists. The painting *The Eruption of Vesuvius and the Death of Pliny* reflects this interest. The mid-nineteenth-century painter was most likely familiar with the historic letter written by Pliny the Younger. Indeed the swirl of smoke is a prominent feature in this dramatic painting. Narrative scenes of antiquity continued to be a popular inspiration for artists through the end of the nineteenth century.

You might want to use the following questions to discuss the art:

1. Does this artist's interpretation help you visualize the events?
2. How would a photographer today approach the dangerous assignment of capturing a catastrophe?
3. What else could the artist have included to make this more engaging?
4. What dimension of this illustration do you find most impressive?

THE ERUPTION OF VESUVIUS AND THE DEATH OF PLINY
P. H. de Valencieme
Musée des Augustins, Toulouse, France

Meanwhile my mother and I were at Misenum, but this is not of any historic interest, and you only wanted to hear about my uncle's death. I will say no more, except to add that I have described in detail every incident which I either witnessed myself or heard about immediately after the event, when reports were most likely to be accurate. It is for you to select what best suits your purpose, for there is a great difference between a letter to a friend and history written for all to read.

Reader's Response *Acts of bravery inspire us. Think of some action you witnessed or know about that was heroic. What did you think of the person who took risks to help another, as Pliny's uncle did? Is the act of bravery more likely to be instinctive or the result of serious consideration?*

Primary Source Note

In many ways Pliny was his own best audience, and although he can poke fun at himself, he also takes his talent as an orator and author quite seriously. In a letter to a friend, to whom he is sending a speech he delivered in court with great success, he writes, "'Away with all this,' he said, 'and put aside whatever you have begun!' [a quote from *Aeneid* VIII, 439, where Vulcan is about to fashion the armor of Aeneas] You may be reading something or writing—put it down and take up my speech; like Vulcan's arms, it is divine. Could conceit go further? But, seriously, compared with my other speeches it is very fine, and I am quite content to rival myself. . . . It is long, but I feel sure it will be as popular as a short one, for the interest is kept up by the lively arrangement of the abundant material, the frequent use of short anecdotes, and the variety of oratorical style. Much of it is in the grand manner and full of fire . . . but there are long sections in a plainer style . . . I gave full play to my feelings of wrath and indignation, and steered my course through this vastly important case with the wind full in my favor. . . ."

THINKING ABOUT THE SELECTION

Interpreting

1. (a) What picture of Pliny the Elder does his nephew want the reader to form? (b) How does Pliny the Younger convince the reader of the dangers?
2. (a) How does Pliny the Younger keep his uncle's actions from seeming hasty or foolhardy? (b) Why is Rectina important to the narration?
3. (a) Why does Pliny the Younger admire people of action who can also express their actions in writing? (b) Would Pliny the Younger describe himself as such a person? Explain your answer.
4. Give some likely causes of Pliny the Elder's death.
5. Explain Pliny the Younger's final remark to Tacitus about the difference between a friendly letter and history.

Applying

6. Describe some examples from recent history that prove the uncle's remark that "Fortune stands by the courageous."
7. The great Roman orator Cicero called courage "that virtue which champions the cause of right," while Seneca called it "a scorner of things which inspire fear." (a) How do you think Pliny the Younger would define courage? (b) What is your definition of courage?

ANALYZING LITERATURE

Understanding the Epistle

An important feature of the epistle is the inclusion of a second-person reader, addressed as "you." Even though Pliny the Younger is writing a descriptive essay about his uncle death's as a result of a volcanic eruption, he speaks directly to Tacitus, the receiver of the epistle. Yet the personal involvement of a receiver does not diminish the objectivity of Pliny the Younger's reportage.

1. Why has Tacitus asked for Pliny the Younger's help?
2. What does he intend to do with the resulting information?
3. (a) How does Pliny the Younger justify the accuracy of his report to Tacitus? (b) Are his comments convincing? Explain.
4. In your own words, how is the effect of an epistle different from that of an essay?

CRITICAL THINKING AND READING

Noting an Author's Attitude

In his opening paragraph, Pliny the Younger implies that his uncle is a more fortunate man than is Tacitus because Pliny the Elder was both a man of action and a successful writer.

1. Apply the following statements to the lives of Pliny the Elder, Pliny the Younger, and Tacitus. Justify your answers with historical fact.
   a. Saw the eruption of Vesuvius
   b. Wrote about the eruption
   c. Investigated the eruption
   d. Saved people from the eruption
   e. Survived the eruption
2. Is Pliny's attitude toward Tacitus justified? Support your answer.

UNDERSTANDING LANGUAGE

Recognizing the Impact of Language

In the section of the third paragraph that describes the uncle's reply to the helmsman, Pliny the Younger intentionally depicts his uncle as a gallant hero under fire.

1. What words seem like an indirect quotation of Pliny the Elder?
2. How will these words affect later evaluations of the uncle's actions?
3. Choose one sentence that creates a vivid picture of this courageous man. Rewrite this sentence to create the opposite impression.

THINKING AND WRITING

Writing Persuasively

Pliny the Younger makes it clear from the beginning that he hopes to influence history by replying to Tacitus' request for information. Jot down facts concerning the author's description of historical events. From your notes write a summary in which you persuade your audience that Pliny intended to influence others to admire his uncle, Pliny the Elder. When you revise make sure you have adequately supported your claims. Proofread your paper and share it with your classmates.

(continued from bottom of page)

THEMES IN WORLD LITERATURE

Journeys to the Underworld

> "The way down to Avernus is easy going—night and day the door of the Dark God is open wide—but to retrace your steps, to reclimb to the upper air: what a task, what toil!"
>
> —from the *Aeneid*, Book VI

Presentation/Prior Knowledge
Tell students that journeys to the underworld are plentiful and popular. Mention some movies, like *Journey to the Center of the Earth*, that have characters who make great adventures as part of a quest to attempt to understand the world better. Explain that some theorists believe that knowledge cannot be attained without taking some risks. Ask if they can think of any stories they know in which characters have been tempted to search beyond reasonable limits to find information.

Master Teacher Strategy You may wish to suggest that students can illustrate their conception of the underworld by drawing depictions of Hades. Notify the art department to see if supplies can be provided for this undertaking as a special project for which students may be given dual credit.

Journeys to the underworld are a common theme in world literature. Halfway through the *Aeneid*, the guide who prepares Aeneas for his challenging journey through the underworld speaks the words quoted above. She is the Sybil of Cumae, whose duty it is to brace him for a descent beyond Avernus, the gateway to the underworld.

Because he is eager to lead the survivors of Troy to their promised homeland, he wanders over lands and seas. Much of the way, Aeneas has his old father, Anchises, as mentor and friend. But after Anchises' death, Aeneas must travel alone, deciding the fate not only of his small band but also of the images of Troy's gods that he carries with him.

Like Hercules, Orpheus, and Odysseus before him, Aeneas is required to be almost superhuman in order to fulfill his duty. He must journey to Hades to find knowledge. He must take the hard path and persist despite many challenges.

Aeneas searches for a golden bough, the magical pass that will allow him entrance to the hidden world below. Aeneas locates the golden bough and he moves on with the Sybil to escort him toward the smelly entrance to Hades.

Aeneas performs ritual acts. Moans from the earth and the howling of deathly creatures rise up. His guide plunges down the steep slope. Aeneas, obedient to his fate, follows.

The journey through Hades leads Aeneas past silent dreads. He views Hades' fearful sights. Forging a way along dangerous waters, Aeneas confronts souls newly arrived in Hades.

Charon, the ugly ferryman, out of respect for the golden bough, carries Aeneas across the river that circles Hades. Past Cerberus, the three-headed dog, past the stony face of Dido, his recently lost love, the Trojan warrior treads the dark path through throngs of victims who fell during the Trojan conflict. Urged on by his guide, Aeneas ponders the sufferings of those who are punished for their sins.

The scene shifts to groves where Anchises greets his son. The two survey the future greatness for which Aeneas undertook his journey. They see the souls of those who prepare themselves for rebirth. Anchises points them out by name—Romulus, the Scipios, Pompey, the Gracchi, Julius Caesar, and Augustus Caesar, for whom Virgil wrote his epic poem.

Supported by his father's wisdom Aeneas walks the last steps with Anchises's shade. At the Ivory Gate, the old man speeds Aeneas to the upper air, where the warrior sets out to guide the faithful toward a new Troy.

Like Homer's Odysseus, Aeneas accepts the grim challenge of such a hellish journey. He braces himself with superhuman strength and succeeds in learning what is both distasteful and necessary. The quest of his journey is worth the effort. Armed with the belief that his voyage paves the way for future greatness, Aeneas suffers no regrets.

These readings have underworld journeys.

SUGGESTED READINGS

The Epic of Gilgamesh, "Enkidu's Dream of the Underworld," page 19

Dante Alighieri, the *Divine Comedy*, page 622

CROSS CURRENTS

The Planning of Washington, D.C.

Cities evolve slowly and often without any real planning. During the initial stages of a city's existence, transportation may follow waterways. Eventually, streets and residences duplicate the contours of the land as homes and businesses find locations to suit individual needs. In contrast to this free-spirited growth, Washington, D.C., began from the very specific plans of Major Pierre Charles L'Enfant, a French military engineer.

In 1790 a commission began to create a national capital at the direction of President Washington. They situated the city that was intended to honor both Christopher Columbus and the first President on ten square miles along the Potomac River. As the permanent seat of the government, it was to house the individual federal departments as well as centers of learning and culture.

The oldest structure, the White House, was designed by James Hoban and was completed in 1792 to serve as a residence for the Presidents and their families. The original building suffered a major loss in August 1814, when the British set fire to its interior, reducing it to a shell. Redecorated with Ionic porticoes on the north and south ends of the building, it reflects the same scrolled capitals at the heads of its columns that decorate the ruins of Rome's Temple of Saturn and Temple of Fortune Virilis.

The Capitol building takes its name from the Capitoline Hill, one of Rome's seven hills and the site of the imposing Temple of Jupiter. Designed by William Thorton, the Capitol stands on Jenkins' Hill at the end of a 400-foot mall. Extending into a north and a south wing, the Capitol is basically Roman in style.

The key feature, the dome topped by a cupola, suggests the architecture of one of Rome's most enduring architectural feats, the Pantheon, a massive round temple honoring all the gods. The rotunda of the Capitol is a stabilizing force of the architect's plan. This central chamber beneath the soaring dome houses paintings and sculpture that constitute a significant portion of the nation's art treasures.

At the end of the Capitol's facade is an imposing triangular pediment atop Corinthian columns. This stylistic detail, a duplicate of the exterior plan of the Pantheon, gives a sense of order and proportion to the marble structure. The two wings symbolize the balance of powers that comprise the legislature from which emanates law and order.

In a direct line with the Capitol lie the Lincoln Memorial and the Washington Monument. In the classic spirit of the ancient world, these two architectural marvels epitomize the esthetically satisfying geometric shapes found in Imperial Rome. The Lincoln Memorial suggests the spare, but noble architecture typical of the Roman Forum. In stark contrast, the single thrust of marble that constitutes the Washington Monument echoes Egyptian influence, which brought obelisks to Rome during the era when Roman military leaders courted the grain centers surrounding ancient Alexandria.

Without the influence of Rome's lines, Washington, D.C., might have sprung up in a helter-skelter fashion. Fortunately, through the planning of presidential commissions, the nation's capital has captured the lasting beauty of Rome and created a style of building that continues to give a sense of dignity and order to the working center of the American republic.

Firsthand Biography

Writing a Firsthand Biography

A biography is a story of a person's life. If you wanted to write a biography, where would you start? Probably, if you could, you would start with the person himself or herself. A firsthand biography is a biography written from information that comes directly from the subject—the person whose life is being written about. Usually the writer gets information from the subject through personal interviews.

Characteristics of Firsthand Biography

- Sharply drawn characters
  personality
  actions
  physical traits
- Incidents to support characterization
- Details showing how or why the subject is important to the writer
- Tone revealing writer's attitude toward subject

Although it is not firsthand biography, the story that Virgil tells about Dido's love and loss in the *Aeneid* exemplifies many of the characteristics of personal biography. Threaded together with narrative are a series of reports about what the queen says and does concerning the progress of her love for and loss of Aeneas. The narrator focuses the reader, comments on the circumstances without biasing the reader's judgment of the events, and then returns to specific information from Dido that allows the reader to experience what she felt. Virgil provides a context for Dido's story by recounting Anna's and Aeneas' reactions and the actions of the controlling gods as well.

Writing Assignment

Write a firsthand biography about someone you know very well. In it, recount the story of a significant love this person has had or a significant loss he or she has suffered. An older relative or friend with whom you have close contact is a perfect choice. You might choose your grandmother and ask her about falling in love with your grandfather. In your biography, use specific details to make the readers experience for themselves your subject's story.

Prewrite

Tell your subject about your assignment well in advance of the date when the paper is due. Make an appointment for the interview ahead of time. If you have access to a tape recorder, ask permission to tape the interview. Never tape someone without getting permission first. Be on time for your interview.

Prepare your interview questions in advance by anticipating what you want to know about your subject. Be sure your questions cover Who? What? When? Where? and How? You will also need to provide yourself with plenty of specific detail, so plan to ask: What did the place look like then? Do you remember any smell in the air? How did you feel at that moment? What did you hear while this was happening?

Here is a checklist of things to remember about the interview.

- Be punctual and patient.
- Arrive with tape recorder, pen, pad, and list of questions.
- Be prepared to stay for as long as it takes to complete the interview.
- Be flexible and ready to create substitute questions.

When you conclude your interview, thank your subject sincerely and offer to show your rough draft when it is finished.

Now you will need to review the tape or your notes and transcribe key points from your interview. Organize this information toward a good paper by reflecting on the progress of the love or the loss. Go back and review parts of your notes or tape when you get confused.

Use questions in sequence to give order to your plan. Ask yourself the following questions.
1. Where and when did the story begin?
2. What was the next significant event?
3. What happened then?
4. Where is the natural ending for the story?

Be sure to list specific details in each of these answers. Include mention of sights, sounds, smells, or words spoken. Note the places where narrative will have to connect key passages to one another. Make transitions over gaps as smooth as possible. If you notice the need for more information, contact your subject again and use the chance to review accuracy while getting additional details.

Write

As you write, remember that accuracy is paramount, but portraying your subject as real and vital is important also. If the information is too clinically exhibited, you will have something more akin to an FBI report than a firsthand biographical essay.

Use your notes as you write and capture the flavor of the love or the loss with as many specific, telling details as you can. Do remember that as narrator, your voice should be clear, strong, and positive. You may suggest interpretations in the narrative, but you should not render judgments. For example, your narrative voice might say, "She felt desolate when he was away for so long," but it should not add, "He shouldn't have gone at all."

Collaborate

Take your draft to your subject and ask him or her to read it for accuracy. Note this person's comments so you can adjust your final draft accordingly. You will want to please your subject with the portrayal, so take all comments into consideration. It is a good idea to have a fellow student read the draft for style, too, pointing out places you were too general or too dull.

Revise

Rewrite your essay with your responders' comments in mind. Strive for accuracy above all, but keep the narrative lively.

Publish

With your subject's permission, send your paper to the editor of your school newspaper or to the moderator of the literary magazine. If they cannot use the piece, ask if they know of any local competitions that are requesting submissions for such articles.

While awaiting a response, you might consider making a visual gift for your source. Search the story for one line, perhaps a single sentence quotation, that seems to be the emotional center of the story. Use calligraphy to reproduce the line on a parchment that might be suitable for framing.

Evaluate

How do you feel about having been responsible for recounting someone's story? Has your relationship with this person changed? Consider giving a copy of your essay to your subject in thanks for helping you.

Then ask yourself how you would respond if someone approached you with a similar request. Would you share a part of your life so openly? Reevaluate your questions again and see if you would want to have answered such inquiries if they were addressed to you.

Presentation

The European Transition map on this page depicts the political borders that divided the continent in approximately 1560. Point out to students that the Holy Roman Empire still existed and that it included lands that would eventually become part of the nations of France and Germany.

Call students' attention to the fact that there are different terms for the unique governments of various areas. At this time in Europe there are *principalities* in Poland, Lithuania, and Moldavia. Norway, France, and Spain are *kingdoms*. The Moscovite *Dominions* are north of the *Khanate* of the Crimea. The Ottoman *Empire* stretches in a southeasterly direction away from the Holy Roman *Empire*.

In order to have students understand the complexity that would in some places lead slowly to a future uniformity, note that Italy at this time is separated into many rival city states. It includes the kingdom of Naples, the Papal states, and the Venetian republic. These will not become unified until the middle of the nineteenth century.

Europe in Transition

(450–1890)

EUROPE
About 1560

o *Smolensk*

MUSCOVITE

DOMINIONS

CIPALITY

OF

HUANIA

Kiev

KHANATE
OF THE
CRIMEA

Dnieper R.   *Don R.*

Bug R.

Dniester R.

Prut R.

P. OF

MOL-

NIA   DAVIA

ALLACHIA

harest O

be R.

SEA OF
AZOV

B L A C K   S E A

L I A

Constantinople

E M P I R E

EGEAN

SEA

o *Smyrna*

Cyprus

Crete

Using the Map

You might want to ask the following questions about the map:

1. What geographic explanation can you provide for the isolation of Ireland?
2. Why would its location provide the Holy Roman Empire with a crucial role in European politics?
3. In what areas do you find the fewest cities and centers of commercial activity? How would you explain this?
4. Why would the location of Sicily make it a likely target for invasion by rival sea powers?
5. Of what importance would the islands of the Aegean be for commerce with the east?

Humanities Note

Tapestry, *Hunt of the Unicorn*, artist unknown. The *Hunt of the Unicorn* is a set of six magnificent tapestries woven in the workshops of Tornai beginning about 1480 for Anne of Brittany upon the occasion of her marriage to Louis XII. They chronicle the various stages of the hunt for the rare and lovely mythic beast, the unicorn.

This tapestry, second in the series, is often called "The Fountain." It shows hunters witnessing an enchanting scene. An assembly of animals will not drink until the unicorn has dipped his magical horn into the water, thereby insuring its purity.

The designer of these tapestries is unequalled in the skill of expressing the beauties of plants and animals as well as the subtle nuances of human appearance. The extraordinary weavers of Tornai did these designs every justice with this masterful interplay of jewel-toned wools with threads of silver and gold.

You might want to use the following questions to discuss the art:

1. These hangings are sometimes referred to as "thousand-flowers" style tapestries. What do you think prompts that description?
2. What attracts your eye most as you first see this art?
3. Can you identify all the animals that are depicted here?
4. What details could have been added to enhance the beauty of this tapestry?

THE HUNT OF THE UNICORN, II—UNICORN DIPS HORN INTO STREAM
Franco-Flemish tapestry
The Metropolitan Museum of Art, New York

Objectives

1 To acquire an overview of the Middle Ages
2 To learn how Rome's fall forced Europe to use a new political structure
3 To trace the contribution of the German tribes to the new order
4 To investigate the purposes and outcomes of the crusades
5 To appreciate how life was changed by ideas that would lead to a renaissance

THE MIDDLE AGES
A.D. 450–1300

The knight rode up the cliff until
he reached the summit of the hill.
He looked around him from that stand
but saw no more than sky and land.
He cried, "What have I come to see?
Stupidity and trickery!
May God dishonor and disgrace
the man who sent me to this place!
He had the long way round in mind,
when he told me that I would find
a manor when I reached the peak.
Oh, fisherman, why did you speak?
For if you said it out of spite
you tricked me badly." He caught sight
of a tower starting to appear
down in a valley he was near,
and as the tower came into view,
if people were to search, he knew,
as far as Beirut, they would not
find a finer tower or spot.

—**Chrétien de Troyes**

Focus
The words spoken here by the knight in search of the Holy Grail embody the theme of the search that was so important a part of life in the Middle Ages. As people did in antiquity and as we continue to do today, men and women during medieval times constantly sought answers to religious, political, and social questions that perplex humanity. Just as there is a mysterious element in Chrétien De Troyes's passage, so too can students expect to find intrigue and a sense of wonder in this unit on the Middle Ages in Europe.

Writing/Prior Knowledge Before starting the unit, have students dictate ideas they have about what life was like in the Middle Ages. These can be listed on the chalkboard. Let them then choose one of the notions listed and briefly prewrite about that single idea. Then have them file the writing in their writing portfolios so that it can be consulted and evaluated after the unit is studied.

ESL Teaching Strategy Have ESL students consult the map on pages 554–555. Have them locate the most important kingdoms of Europe and become familiar with the relationships of those areas to each other.

Teaching Tenth-Grade Students Have tenth-grade students turn their attention to the illustration on pages 556–557. Ask them to explain why they think the scene is or is not representative of life in the Middle Ages.

BOAR AND BEAR HUNT
Devonshire Hunting Tapestries
Victoria and Albert Museum, London

The passage on the previous page, taken from Chrétien de Troyes's *Perceval,* contains the musings of a knight searching for the Holy Grail (Christ's chalice). He laments the fact that he trusted a stranger, the fisherman, and believes that his journey has ended in confusion and loss. When he spies a distant tower, he finds strength and faith once more, regarding the tower with all the hope he can find in his heart.

Such vacillations between faith and doubt are commonplace for characters in the literature of the Middle Ages. Instead of being regarded any longer as a period of conformity, medieval Europe is looked upon now as a time of variety and rich complexity. The search for the Grail and the hunt for the unicorn are parallels for the quest undertaken by the greatest writer of the time, Dante, in his journey through the hellish realm of the inferno while pursuing salvation he believes awaits him in paradise. That quest, as various in its forms as it is central to the mind-set of the age, appears throughout the literature of the time.

THE MIDDLE AGES

Scholars usually refer to the historical period between A.D. 400 and 1300 as the Middle Ages. There is a peculiar problem surrounding the use of this name. If this age is in fact "middle," what is it nestled between? The Middle Ages may be seen as a historical filling, sandwiched between the Latin civilization of the Roman Empire and the later rediscovery of the classical civilizations of Greece and Rome in the Renaissance.

The dates of the Middle Ages are somewhat arbitrary. The fifth century, a period marked by the rapid decay of those institutions that held the Roman Empire together, is the beginning of this period. The end, however, is more complex an issue. The Renaissance occurred first in the south of Europe. The early fourteenth century brought the rediscovery of classical forms in art and architecture, with excellent editions of Greek and Roman works produced in Italy. In northern Europe, however, these innovations were slower to happen and were not in place until the end of the fifteenth century.

ROME'S FALL AND A NEW EUROPEAN STRUCTURE

In the third century A.D., Rome was master of most of Europe. The empire extended from England in the north to Africa in the south, from Portugal in the west to Syria in the east. Ultimately, this territory was far too large to administer, both politically and militarily. The Roman Empire was then divided into two distinct empires, with the emperor of the west ruling from Rome and the emperor in the east ruling from Constantinople.

The northern frontiers of the empire had been experiencing pressure for some time from several Germanic tribes. For centuries before, the northern border had remained stable. However, a sudden population explosion among these tribes triggered a need for expansion. This need for more territory and a strong warlike disposition provoked what is sometimes called the "barbarian invasions." In reality, the incursion of the Germanic tribes into Roman territory more accurately resembled a mass migration sporadically marked by hostilities. Germanic historians, sensitive about using the word invasion, call this period in history the *Volkerwanderung*—the wandering of the peoples.

The Germanic Contribution

Hardly a portion of the old western Roman Empire was left untouched by the various Germanic tribes: Lombards, Visigoths, and Ostrogoths settled in Italy; Visigoths in southern France and Spain; Franks in northern France; Angles and Saxons in England. The presence of these peoples radically changed the political structure of what was until then a unified empire. As these tribes began to dominate the land in which they settled, they established individual kingdoms, dissolving once and for all the Roman hegemony.

Each tribe brought with it a distinct tribal structure that evolved into the feudal system shaping medieval Europe. The act of vassalage, the backbone of feudalism in which one lord swears allegiance to another in exchange for privileges or "feuds," originated in the political organization of these tribes. The concepts of kingship, knighthood, and chivalry all emerged from these Germanic people.

Wherever they settled in the empire, the Germanic tribes were quickly converted to Christianity, which had become the official religion of the empire by A.D. 353. Because of this religious conversion, their political institutions also became Christianized. With their adoption of Roman religion, they also adopted Latin, the official language of the

Presentation
Motivation/Prior Knowledge
Have students list associations they make about the Middle Ages. Briefly evaluate each concept.

Purpose-Setting Question Is it fair for any age, complex and rich in its own right, to be labeled "middle" by historians because the periods before and after it seem more important?

1 Discussion Ask students if they regard it as unfair for tribes to be called "barbaric," as these people sometimes are.

Using the Map
The map depicting Europe in the thirteenth century shows the area that produced the literature used in this unit. Have students study its information carefully. Then you may wish to ask the following questions:
1. Approximately how many miles is it from Dublin to Paris?
2. In what direction would you travel to get from Toledo to Rome?
3. Name the island south of Corsica.
4. What country is west of Spain?
5. If you were sailing from Coimbra to Rome, would you pass Palermo along the shortest route?

Answers
1. 400
2. East
3. Sardinia
4. Portugal
5. No

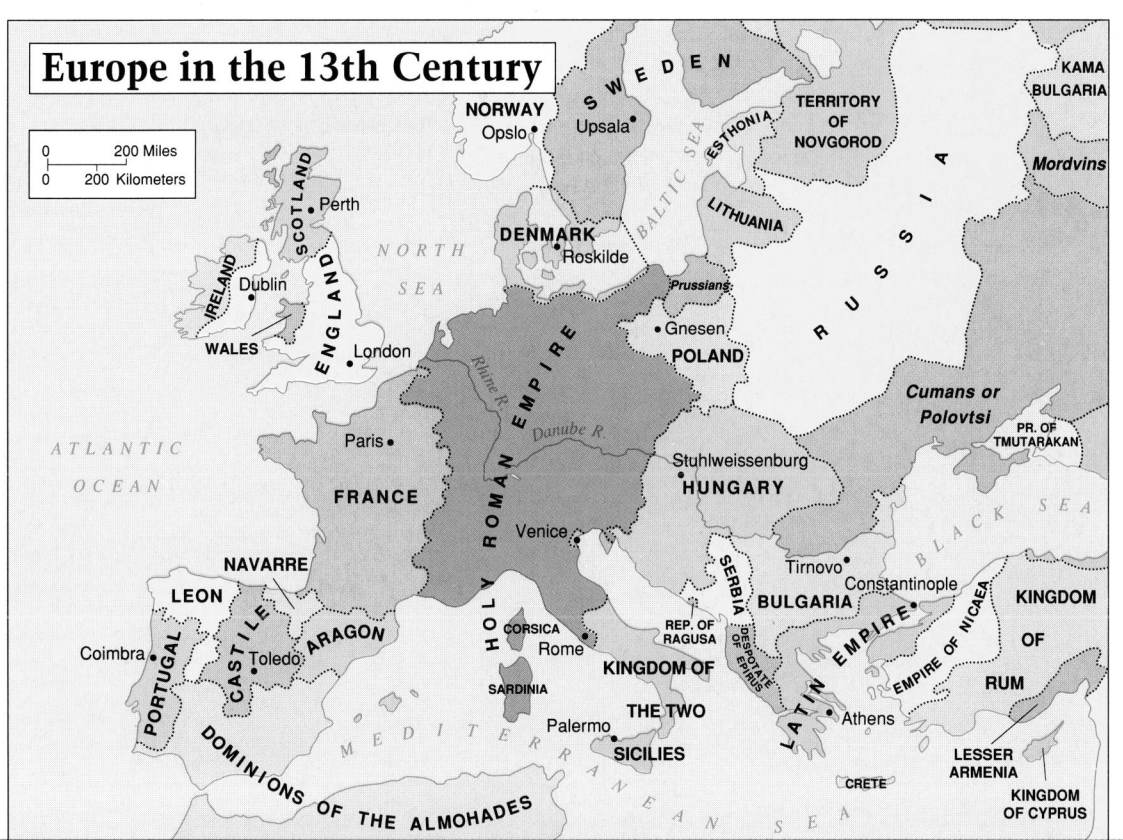

Europe in the 13th Century

The Norman conquest,
Bayeux Tapestry
*With special authorization
of the City of Bayeux*

Richard the Lionheart
in combat with Saladin

Statue of
Charlemagne,
famous ruler
of the Middle Ages

Humanities Notes

Pictured from left to right:

The Bayeux Tapestry is an embroidery that chronicles the Norman conquest of William the Conqueror in 1066. The detail pictured here depicts the arrival of William at Penvesey. This valuable tapestry documents the history and the costumes of the Middle Ages. Tradition attributes the tapestry to William's wife, Queen Matilda, and her handmaidens. However, it is more recently believed to be of later origin and is possibly the work of several English embroiderers.

This painting depicts the conflict between England's King Richard I (or Richard the Lionheart) and Saladin, a Muslim warrior and great opponent of the crusades. In 1189, following Saladin's capture of Jerusalem, Richard set out on the Third Crusade to try to recapture and reclaim the Holy City. In 1192 Richard and Saladin concluded a treaty that allowed Christians access to the holy places of Jerusalem. Both Richard and Saladin were known for their chivalry, and their conflict has been celebrated in chivalric romance literature.

Charlemagne, or Charles the Great (742–814), was one of the most famous rulers of the Middle Ages. Charlemagne and his brother Carloman were the rulers of the Frankish kingdom, an area that is now Belgium, France, Luxembourg, the Netherlands, and part of western Germany. When his brother died in 771, Charlemagne was the sole ruler. After the fall of the West Roman Empire in A.D. 400, Charlemagne revived the political and cultural life of Europe. Among other reforms, he established the feudal system of government, which lasted for the next 400 years. In addition, Charlemagne protected and extended the power of the Christian church. To strengthen his alliance further, on Christmas Day, A.D. 800, Pope Leo III crowned Charlemagne emperor of the Romans. This act led to the Holy Roman Empire, which lasted until 1806. When Charlemagne died in 814, his empire fell.

	450	650	850
HISTORY		• Arthur, king of the Britons, is killed in battle • Plague in Europe ends • London is first mentioned	• Battle of Tours is fought • Charlemagne is crowned emperor • Leo IV, Byzantine emperor, is seated • Charlemagne dies; is succeeded by Louis the Pious
HUMAN PROGRESS		• Chess in India begins • The first church bell in Rome is rung	• Water wheels for mill drive are used in Europe • Three-field system of farming develops
LITERATURE			• Greek, instead of Latin, becomes official language of the Eastern Roman Empire • *Beowulf* • Minuscule handwriting at Charlemagne's scholastic institutions is developed

In 597 Saint Augustine went to England from Rome to convert the English to Christianity. He founded the Canterbury Cathedral and became the first archbishop of Canterbury. This early cathedral was burned and rebuilt several times. Archbishop Lanfranc began building the cathedral in its present state in 1070; it was completed in 1180. It was only after the death of Thomas Becket (1118–1170), English martyr and archbishop of Canterbury, that the cathedral became a famous holy place and the object of holy pilgrimages. Chaucer's *The Canterbury Tales* are stories told by a fictional group of pilgrims on their way to Canterbury.

During the Middle Ages, knights became a social order. Membership in the order became a mark of distinction, and knights were expected to abide by a code of chivalry—a code of behavior and ethics. The word *knight* comes from the Old English word *cnight*, which means "household retainer." Knights vowed their loyalty to a king or lord and de-

Canterbury Cathedral

Knights joining in
combat, c.1250

"The Hunt of
the Unicorn,"
Flemish tapestry
*The Metropolitan
Museum of Art,
New York*

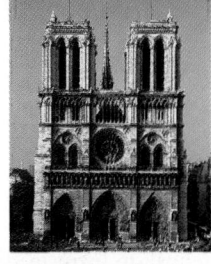

Notre Dame

1050   1250   1300

- Alfred the Great,
  king of England, is crowned
- Charles III becomes king of France;
  unites the empire of Charlemagne
  - Feudalism develops

- Canute becomes king of England
  - Macbeth is murdered by Malcolm
    - Saxons defeated at Hastings
    - Canterbury becomes England's religious center
      - First Crusade to reclaim Holy Land begins
        - Crusaders capture Jerusalem
        - Henry I becomes king of England
          - Thomas Becket,
            archbishop of
            Canterbury, is murdered

- Third Crusade begins
  - King John of England
    seals Magna Carta
    - Crusades
      end
    - Pope Gregory IX
      establishes Inquisition
        - Marco Polo
          visits China

- Crossbow comes into
  use in France
- Calibrated candles to measure the time
  are used in England
  - Vikings develop the art of shipbuilding;
    discover Greenland
    - First Viking colonies are established
      in Greenland by Eric the Red
      - Systematic musical notation is developed

- English monks excel in embroidery
- Astrolabes arrive in Europe
  - Construction of Tower of London begins
    - First paper is
      manufactured in Spain
    - Chess is introduced in England
      - Earliest horse races
        are run in England
        - Engagement rings
          come into fashion

- The first court jesters
  in European courts perform
  - Hats come
    into fashion
    - Eyeglasses
      are invented

- Farces first appear
  - *The Exeter Book,*
    collection of English poetry
    - *Beowulf,* written
      in Old English

- *Song of Roland*
  - Earliest miracle play in
    England
    - *Poem of El Cid*
    - Marie de France is born
      - Chrétien de Troyes: *Lancelot,*
        romance of courtly love
        - Legendary era of
          Robin Hood begins
          - *Nibelungenlied*

- *Elder Edda,* a collection of Norse
  myths and legends, first appears
  - First known sonnet
    appears in Italy
  - Dante
    is born

(continued from bottom of page)
an example of the early achievement of Gothic architecture in France. Among the most significant features of Gothic architecture are the cathedral's flying buttresses—arched exterior supports—and the large stained-glass windows. This picture shows the main entrance of the cathedral, which stands on a small island on the Seine River in the heart of Paris.

fended his land or household from enemies. Pictured here are two orders of knights in combat.

Tapestries—one of the oldest techniques in textile art—flourished in Europe in the Middle Ages. Pieces from this period most often depicted scenes from daily life, the Bible, history, or mythology—like the unicorn pictured here. *The Unicorn in Captivity* is one part of a series of tapestries known as *The Hunt of the Unicorn.* Many Medieval tapestries, like this one, have a background of *millefleurs,* which means "a thousand flowers." Tapestries were made of wool and served as both decoration and insulation against the cold. When many kings and nobles traveled, they took their tapestries with them. Some even hung them in their tents on battlefields.

In 1163 Pope Alexander III laid the cornerstone of the Notre Dame Cathedral; it was completed in 1250. Notre Dame, which means "Our Lady" or "the Virgin Mary," is

2 **Clarification** Tell students that Latin was still used for saying Mass by the Roman Catholic Church until the 1960's, when Vatican Council II suggested that the vernacular be used.

3 **Discussion** Ask students how they would feel about being guided by a person from another age and culture. Discuss what they think it means for a writer to choose such a person for that role.

western Church, as their language. Many linguists believe that the Romance languages, which are descendents of Latin, such as French, Spanish, and Italian, owe their modern differences to the various Germanic tribes that learned Latin in an imperfect manner. Nonetheless, many words of Germanic origin, especially within the spheres of warfare and feudalism, exist in these languages.

A Clash of Cultures

One of the main reasons for the "middleness" of the Middle Ages is that this period is viewed as an interruption in the transmission of Latin culture. Scholars have traditionally viewed these Germanic tribes as ultimately eliminating certain elements of Latin culture. One was a single unifying language. Latin was now being used only by the Church and in various royal chanceries. By the eighth century, the Church recommended that priests no longer preach in Latin since the populace was not able to understand a sermon preached in it.

This new linguistic situation created a division in the transmission of culture. Two cultures existed side by side: a learned culture, the property of learned clerics, written in Latin; and a popular culture, composed in the various vernaculars, that had a more common appeal, though the division was not absolute. As medieval society evolved and education became more available with the growth of the universities, these two cultures at times intersected. A splendid example of the fusion of these traditions is Dante's *Divine Comedy* (1307), in which a great figure from Latin antiquity, the poet Virgil, acts as Dante's guide in this vernacular odyssey.

Perhaps the greatest Germanic contribution to this emerging popular culture was a new poetic form, the epic—a long, narrative, heroic poem. Certainly, epic poetry existed in Classical Latin, but these Latin poems, such as Virgil's *Aeneid*, were extremely refined and literary. The Germanic epics existed in oral form centuries before they were written down. Their verse form is irregular, and they were meant to be performed to stimulate a warrior's courage before battle. The Spanish *Poem of the Cid* and the French *Song of Roland*, although

written in medieval Spanish and medieval French respectively, are descendants of this ancient Germanic tradition.

A NEW THREAT

In A.D. 711 the Muslims, or Moors, inspired by the rapid success of their subjugation of the Middle East and North Africa, swept into Spain and quickly conquered all but a few mountain strongholds. The Muslim advance into Europe's heartland was not stopped until A.D. 732, when Charles Martel, "the Hammer," defeated the Moors at the Battle of Tours, in central France. Shortly thereafter, the struggle between Christianity and Islam began to emerge as one of the most important forces in medieval Europe.

Christendom reacted quickly to this threat. In Spain, the *Reconquista* (reconquest) was initiated. The reconquest was carried out on two fronts. The first was launched from the mountain strongholds of the Visigothic kingdoms in north-central Spain. At first, the gains came slowly, but as time passed, the Christian resistance grew stronger and the Moors began to yield territory until several independent Christian kingdoms emerged. The two principal kingdoms were the Kingdoms of Leon and Castile. The *Poem of the Cid* (1150), composed during this time, tells the story of Spain's national hero, Ruy Díaz de Vivar, who helped spearhead the expansion of these Christian kingdoms against the Moors.

The second front against the Saracens was initiated by Charlemagne, who crossed the Pyrenees into Spain to aid in the reconquest. The *Song of Roland* (1100) (page 569) relates the tragedy that befell Charlemagne's nephew, Roland, during this Spanish campaign.

A NEW STABILITY

The Reemergence of Learning

In A.D. 800 on Christmas Day, Charles, King of the Franks, or Charlemagne, was crowned Holy Roman Emperor by Pope Leo III. This event represents the complete integration of the Germanic peoples into the mainstream of European society. In addition, Charles's taking the title and office so tied to the traditions of the ancient Roman Empire was an attempt at creating a new unified political order and revealed a need and willingness to revive some kind of historical continuity. There is little doubt that at this time Europe needed all the unity it could muster.

As Europe's southern front against the Moors stabilized, people began to turn their attention to matters unrelated to war. Motivated by Charlemagne's patronage, monks began to refine the writing system. A new writing style emerged called the Carolingian minuscule. It was far easier to read than that produced earlier, ensuring more accurate copies of manuscripts. New grammars of Latin were written, which then had a stabilizing effect on documents being written in Latin. Before these events, many documents and texts were produced in a language that was often a mixture of Latin and whatever language the writer spoke.

This new standardization of Latin grammar, which had been in decay since the fragmentation of the Roman Empire, also highlighted the differences between the various spoken languages and Latin. For the first time, a small number of people saw the need to write in the everyday languages they spoke instead of in Latin. At first this movement started slowly. In the second half of the eleventh century, a group of poets began writing verse in Provençal, a Romance language spoken in the south of France. This poetic school started in the courts of certain powerful lords. The poetry of the troubadours, as these poets are called, sang the praises of love. Because they were affiliated with the courts and often the lords themselves were great poets, the theme of their poetry was known as courtly love.

These poets had a large impact on the me-

THE CROWNING OF CHARLEMAGNE
AND OTHER SCENES FROM HIS LIFE
V. de Beauvais
Musée Condé, Chantilly, France

dieval cultural landscape. They traveled to Italy, Spain, northern France, and England, where their poetic traditions quickly took hold. People now began to write poetry in their own languages instead of in Latin. By the twelfth century, the courts of the great feudal lords throughout Europe emerged as famous literary centers. Chrétien de Troyes (page 600), writing at the court of France's Marie de Champagne in the twelfth century, developed a new poetic form, the courtly romance, that combined the elements of courtly love with the longer, narrative form of the romance.

THE CRUSADES

Having contained the Islamic threat in Europe, the Christian kings responded to a call from the papacy to begin an offensive against the Saracens to regain the Holy Land. In 1095 Pope Urban II gave a speech at Clermont in France urging Christian nobles to undertake a crusade to recapture the

HISTORY OF EMPERORS,
SULEYMAN AGAINST THE CHRISTIANS
Bibliothèque de l'arsenal, Paris

Humanities Note
Illumination, *The Crowning of Charlemagne*, artist unknown. The emperor Charlemagne was a favorite subject for illumination and study in the Middle Ages. King Charles V of France revived historic interest in this great leader. That interest led to the establishment of Charlemagne as a cult figure.

In his day Charlemagne was a firm champion of books, libraries, and illumination. He sponsored many projects to promote the literary arts. His appearance in this manuscript is a suitable tribute to this legendary hero.

You might want to use the following questions to discuss the art:
1. What colors are the most engaging in this work?
2. How would you describe the figures in the lower left detail?
3. How does the artist show the esteem that his subjects have for Charlemagne?
4. What would you add to this coronation scene in order to magnify the greatness of Charlemagne?

Humanities Note
Illuminated manuscript, *Suleyman Against the Christians*, artist unknown. This illumination is from a work, *History of Emperors*, produced by a manuscript workshop in France. The brutality of this type of warfare is clearly shown in the somber tones of black and gray. In direct contrast, the painterly delicacy of the landscape and the tiny details of clothing and equipment give a decorative, almost pretty quality to the work.

The wealthy French nobility commissioned many such works, including histories of all kinds, from workshops comprised of scribes and illuminators. Many artists would work on a single volume to speed production. This resulted in variations in the style of illustration.

You might want to use the following questions to discuss the art:
1. Do you think the costumes of the various warriors are authentic to the time of Suleyman?
2. Comment on the artists' ability as nature painters.
3. Does this illustration use color that you regard as appropriate?
4. What is the first impression you receive upon seeing this illustration?

sacred shrines seized by the Moors in the east. Urban's sermon was perhaps one of the most effective orations in history. The pope claimed he was not ready for the intense fervor generated by his discourse. One year later the first crusade was launched. This army, under the leadership of several powerful lords, initially met with great success. They regained Jerusalem in 1099, but the Arabs quickly reorganized and began to exploit the internal discord of the crusaders. By 1187 Jerusalem was once again under Islamic domination.

Several crusades were subsequently undertaken. Their success was minimal because the European lords were more interested in protecting and expanding their own domains than in pursuing any international cooperative venture. With nationalism beginning to take hold in Europe, there arose a natural antagonism between the single most important international office, the Church, and the various kingdoms. This conflict of interest between the papacy and the secular order reshaped the political landscape of Europe. One of the most famous victims of this controversy was Dante Alighieri (page 618). Exiled from his native Florence in 1302 for opposing papal meddling in Florentine politics, he expressed his aversion to the worldly pursuits of the papacy as a recurring theme in the *Inferno*.

Despite their limited military success, the crusades had a tremendous impact on medieval civilization. As they returned from the Middle East, the crusaders brought back with them new spices, textiles, and other products. A demand for these new and exotic items inspired commerce. This trading created a new merchant class centered at first in the Italian city-states of Genoa, Florence, and Venice, but new markets were soon created. Small towns in Europe were quickly transformed into large trading centers. By the end of the crusades in 1291, the bourgeoisie was well on its way to emerging as an important and dominating class in many parts of Europe.

As the medieval city grew, so did the new centers of learning. By 1300 medieval people had at their disposal more than fourteen universities in Europe. The University of Paris was the most eminent center of theology and philosophy in the western world, and the University of Bologna was the most important center for the study of law and rhetoric.

The rapid urbanization of Europe also had a dark side. The rise of the new middle class also highlighted the problems of the underprivileged majority. Poverty and plague, a highly contagious disease carried by ship-borne rats, were an everyday fact of life for the urban underclass. This dark side of medieval life found its highest expression in the pen of the Parisian poet François Villon (page 648). A convicted criminal and consort of thieves, Villon scornfully described the seamy side of life in the medieval city.

Transformation of Medieval Life

Despite problems of plague and poverty, the opening of trade with the East had an irreversible impact on medieval life. New capital generated by commerce stimulated the quest for learning, and the production of classical manuscripts began to flourish. Explorers began to search for quicker trade routes, and new worlds were discovered. This cultural momentum spilled over into a new epoch in which people began to reinterpret and transform medieval traditions and institutions with an unprecedented vitality. This cultural transformation was already underway in Italy by 1300, though in the north, it was slower. By 1500, however, Europe was completely immersed in a new period, the Renaissance.

SPHERE CODEX
Marco d'Avogaro
Biblioteca Estenso, Modena, Italy

VOICES FROM THE MIDDLE AGES

In every adversity of fortune, to have been happy is the most unhappy kind of misfortune.
Boethius, *On the Consolation of Philosophy*

It is better never to begin a good work than, having begun it, to stop.
Venerable Bede, *Ecclesiastical History of the English Church and People*

The voice of the people is the voice of God.
Alcuin, *Letter to Charlemagne*

God is that, the greater than which cannot be conceived.
St. Anselm, *Proslogion*

Riches and power are but gifts of blind fate, whereas goodness is the result of one's own merit.
Heloise, *Letter to Abelard*

Assist the reduced fellowman, either by a considerable gift or by teaching him a trade, so that he may earn an honest livelihood. This is the highest step and the summit of charity's golden ladder.
Maimonides, *Charity's Eighth Degree*

Where there is peace and meditation, there is neither anxiety nor doubt.
Francis of Assisi, *The Counsels of St. Francis*

To sit alone in the lamplight with a book spread out before you, and hold intimate converse with men of unseen generations—such is a pleasure beyond compare.
Yoshida Kenko, *Essays in Idleness*

For you [Virgil] are my true master and first author,
the sole maker from whom I drew the breath
of that sweet style whose measures have brought me honor.
Dante, the *Inferno*

Additional Voices

"Will is to grace as a horse is to a rider."
—**Augustine**, *On Freedom*

"I was in love with loving."
—**Augustine**, *Confessions*

"All things are filled full of signs, and it is a wise man who can learn about one thing from another."
—**Plotinus**, *Enneads*

"When you are in Rome live in the Roman style; when you are elsewhere live as they live elsewhere."
—**St. Ambrose**, *Letters*

In A.D. 1066 a fleet of Norman knights set sail for England under the leadership of their duke, William, in order to settle a dispute with Harold, king of England. William met and defeated Harold in battle on the field at Hastings. In one of the histories of the Norman conquest of England, written only four years after the Battle of Hastings, the historian Wace writes of a *jongleur,* or minstrel, named Taillefer who, while riding at the head of William's army, led the Norman knights into battle singing "of Charlemagne and of Roland and of Olivier and of the vassals who died at Roncesvalles." Taillefer was, of course, referring to Charles the Great of France and referring to events that had occurred almost three hundred years earlier. He was singing a version of the *Song of Roland*; perhaps not the same version of the poem we have today but very likely something similar.

Origin of the Epic

According to some, French literature begins with the *Song of Roland,* or *Chanson de Roland.* This long historical poem about a medieval knight is by far the best known and most studied of all medieval epic poems. Despite its popularity, scholars are hard-pressed to say just when the *Song of Roland* was written or who its author was. The manuscript that today can be viewed at Oxford University, England, dates from the decades after A.D. 1100 and is written in the Norman dialect of Old French. Scholars do agree, however, that the original poem must be dated much earlier.

The *Song of Roland*'s author remains as much a mystery as does its date. The poem concludes with these lines in Old French: *Ci falt la geste que Turol-* *dus declinet* ("Thus concludes the deeds of which Turold _____"). Just what *did* Turold do? The last word is left untranslated because we cannot be entirely certain exactly what *declinet* means in this context. It could mean "translate" or "compose" or "recite." However, these three tasks are very different, and Turold's relationship to the *Song of Roland* clearly depends on how you translate this word.

Theme of the Poem

Central to the medieval epic are the deeds, or *gestes,* of heroic figures. *Geste* is a French word derived from the Latin word *gesta,* meaning "things done, deeds." For this reason an epic poem is also called a *chanson de geste* or "song of deeds." The *Song of Roland* treats one of the great themes of medieval heroic literature: the deeds surrounding Charlemagne and his court.

Charlemagne, or Charles the Great, was king of the Franks from 768 to 814 and also emperor of the Holy Roman Empire from 800 to 814. Because Charlemagne ruled France about 300 years before the *Song of Roland* was composed, there is a considerable distance between the poem and the events it narrates. The *Song of Roland* both transforms and aggrandizes a rather modest historical event. In A.D. 778, Charlemagne intervened in a dispute in Spain between two rival Moorish rulers. The Moors were Muslims from northwest Africa who invaded Spain in the eighth century. Forced to return to France because of a Saxon uprising, Charlemagne's rear guard, captained by his nephew Roland, was attacked and decimated by a band of Basques while crossing the Pyrenees.

THE CORONATION OF CHARLEMAGNE
Bibliothèque l'Arsenal, Paris

Humanities Note

Illumination, *The Coronation of Charlemagne*, artist unknown. The crowning of Charlemagne as king of the Franks occurred in 768. He was made emperor of the Holy Roman Empire in 800. This illustration is one of many that celebrates the greatness of its subject. As a protector of the Church, as a patron of the arts, and as a leader responsible for political and military stability, Charlemagne represented many things during and after his life. Artistic and literary tributes to him are commonplace.

You might want to use the following questions to discuss the art:

1. What is the first impression you receive from this illustration?
2. How does the artist call attention to the elevated and royal bearing of the subject?
3. What symbols of authority are present in the scene?
4. What could be added to this illustration to increase the dignity of its subject?

To a man the rear guard perished in the narrow valley of Roncesvalles (ron´ sə´ valz). In the *Song of Roland*, the poet employs poetic license. Facts are changed—the Basques become Moors—certainly a more contemporary and meaningful foe for both the twelfth-century poet and a public involved in the Crusades to recover the Holy Lands from the Muslims. Charlemagne, thirty-eight at the time of the massacre at Roncesvalles, is transformed into a two-hundred-year-old-or-more miraculous figure. Because Roland is the victim of a treacherous betrayal, his demise is narrated far more dramatically than history could ever have seen it. Feudal betrayal and revenge are in fact the themes on which the *Song of Roland* hinges.

The Structure of the Poem

Both thematically and structurally, the *Song of Roland* is the quintessential epic. Epics flourished at a time when oral transmission was the only way in which a poet could guarantee he or she would be heard. The *jongleur* would stand in a public square and sing or chant the poem, perhaps accompanying himself or herself on a type of fiddle or harp. When you read the poem, you will see how its structure reveals a certain oral quality. The stanzas, *laisses* (les), are of unequal length, allowing for the *jongleur* to pause and improvise. Unlike much medieval poetry, the *chanson de geste* does not rhyme. Instead of rhyme, where both vowels and consonants must sound alike, the poet makes use of a technique called *assonance,* where only the stressed vowels of the lines in a stanza need to match (rain, stay). With every new stanza, the poet would change the assonance, signaling a change in narrative to the public. It would have been a far more difficult task to have the final words of such a long poem rhyme. Assonance made the poet's task of creating and improvising on large passages that much easier.

As you read the *Song of Roland*, pay attention to both the themes and structure of the poem. Always keep in mind that the poem was meant to be performed. Symmetry and contrast are the poet's favorite techniques. Every betrayal is punished and the descriptions are so clear and vivid that the public could never confuse the pattern of good and evil established early in the poem.

Commentary

Paradox in the *Song of Roland* Throughout the *Song of Roland*, and in epic poetry in general, hyperbole and exaggerations are used. Frequently, Charlemagne's age or the power of the count is overdrawn. The reasons for such figures are part of the preservation of the epic form in an almost self-conscious gesture. In the case of Charlemagne's age, it was a popular myth to believe that the king lived for hundreds of years. It is also a comment on the epic form itself. The *Song of Roland*, as many epics, serves two paradoxical functions: the work is both "timely," that is, it describes a specific historical moment, and "timeless," that is, everlasting and not measured. The singers or composers of the tale were aware that they were singing an old song.

Literature of the Middle Ages

Historical Context

In the Middle Ages, the epic poem was the common person's way of perceiving his or her own history. Written histories existed, but only for the educated cleric. Written in Latin, they were not accessible to most people. Epic poems in the Middle Ages had their origins in the great halls of the Germanic tribes. Unlike the more refined versions of history created by Latin-speaking clerics, the epic was concerned with basic themes and concepts that bound societies together. It was more important to express notions of feudal loyalty and personal valor, ideals that prevented the extinction of the tribe, than to insist on factual accuracy. The early Germanic epics dealt with the conflicting values of their traditional mythology and their newly discovered Christianity. The *Song of Roland* was created by the Franks, a Germanic tribe that invaded or settled in France, or *Francia,* the land of the Franks.

Cultural Context

As the epic migrated southward along with the various Germanic tribes, the focus and purpose of this poetic form changed. There was an urgent new mission for which this genre, or type of literature, was perfectly suited. With the Muslims comfortably settled in Spain and southern France, Christendom was directly menaced. New heroes were needed to inspire a crusade against the Islamic threat. These long poems, dramatically performed in town squares and court halls, informed, entertained, and called the populace to war against the Saracen (Muslim) threat. They create a clear picture of the proud hero judged on his bravery in battle and his loyalty to his king or lord.

Literary Context

Because it was intended for recital and was influenced by an oral tradition in its composition, the *Song of Roland* should not be regarded in the same way as epics like Dante's *Divine Comedy* or Virgil's *Aeneid.* It would be far more appropriate to think of the Homeric traditions of the *Iliad* and the *Odyssey* when evaluating the achievement of this work.

On the following pages there are selected passages from the *Song of Roland.* The annotations in the margins point out the historical context, cultural context, and literary context.

from the Song of Roland

translated by Frederick Goldin

1

Charles the King, our Emperor, the Great,
has been in Spain for seven full years,
has conquered the high land down to the sea.
There is no castle that stands against him now,
no wall, no citadel left to break down—
except Saragossa, high on a mountain.
King Marsilion holds it, who does not love God,
who serves Mahumet and prays to Apollin.[1]
He cannot save himself: his ruin will find him there. AOI.[2]

13

"Barons, my lords," said Charles the Emperor,
"King Marsilion has sent me messengers,
wants to give me a great mass of his wealth,
bears and lions and hunting dogs on chains,
seven hundred camels, a thousand molting[3] hawks,
four hundred mules packed with gold of Araby,
and with all that, more than fifty great carts;
but also asks that I go back to France:
he'll follow me to Aix,[4] my residence,
and take our faith, the one redeeming faith,
become a Christian, hold his march lands[5] from me.
But what lies in his heart? I do not know."
And the French say: "We must be on our guard!" AOI.

---

1. Mahumet . . . Apollin: The prophet Mohammed (A.D. 570–632), the founder of Islam, and a god whose name, Apollin, derives from the Greek god Apollo. The point is that, from the perspective of the author, Marsilion does not follow the true Christian faith. He and his men are referred to as pagans or Saracens.
2. AOI: These three mysterious letters appear at certain moments throughout the text, 180 times in all. No one has ever adequately explained them, though every reader feels their effect.
3. molting: Shedding their feathers.
4. Aix (eks): A city in southeastern France.
5. march lands: A frontier province or territory.

Historical Context: The *Song of Roland* begins with Charlemagne supposedly on pilgrimage to the holy places in Spain. He decided to take Spain away from the Moors, who invaded Spain in A.D. 711 and at this time controlled most of the country.

Cultural Context: In this poem the Moors, who are Islamic, are constantly confused with pre-Christian pagans who count Apollo in their pantheon of gods. Mahumet is another name for Mohammed, the founder of Islam. The meaning of *AOI* at the end of a line is in dispute. However, some scholars feel that it was a type of formulaic device that signaled a stop.

1 **Enrichment** Have students figure out where these places may have actually been.

2 **Discussion** Ask students what they think Ganelon means here.

14

The Emperor has told them what was proposed.
Roland the Count will never assent to that,
25 gets to his feet, comes forth to speak against it;
says to the King: "Trust Marsilion—and suffer!
We came to Spain seven long years ago,
I won Noples for you, I won Commibles,
I took Valterne and all the land of Pine,
30 and Balaguer and Tudela and Seville.
And then this king, Marsilion, played the traitor:
he sent you men, fifteen of his pagans—
and sure enough, each held an olive branch;
and they recited just these same words to you.
35 You took counsel with all your men of France;
they counseled you to a bit of madness:
you sent two Counts across to the Pagans,
one was Basan, the other was Basile.
On the hills below Haltille, he took their heads.
40 They were your men. Fight the war you came to fight!
Lead the army you summoned on to Saragossa!
Lay siege to it all the rest of your life!
Avenge the men that this criminal murdered!" AOI.

Historical Context: The poet's knowledge of Spanish geography is not very good. Balaguer and Tudela are in the northeast near the Pyrenees. Seville, however, is in southern Spain, nowhere near these cities and well within Moorish control.

15

The Emperor held his head bowed down with this,
45 and stroked his beard, and smoothed his mustache down,
and speaks no word, good or bad, to his nephew.
The French keep still, all except Ganelon:
he gets to his feet and comes before King Charles,
how fierce he is as he begins his speech;
50 said to the King: "Believe a fool—me or
another—and suffer! Protect your interest!
When Marsilion the King sends you his word,
that he will join his hands and be your man,[6]
and hold all Spain as a gift from your hands
55 and then receive the faith that we uphold—
whoever urges that we refuse this peace,
that man does not care, Lord, what death we die.
That wild man's counsel must not win the day here—
let us leave fools, let us hold with wise men!" AOI.

Cultural Context: Feudalism was the economic, political, and social system of medieval Europe. Land, worked by serfs who were bound to it, was held by vassals. Overlords gave vassals rights to the land in exchange for military service. A baron was a tenant of the king or of any high-ranking lord. Ganelon's counsel, although laced with treachery, is a good example of the interaction of the barons with their king, a necessary component of feudal society.

---

6. he will join his hands . . . man: Part of the gesture by which a vassal swore allegiance to a lord; the lord enclosed the joined hands of his vassal with his own hands.

20

"My noble knights," said the Emperor Charles,
choose me one man: a baron from my march,[7]
to bring my message to King Marsilion."
And Roland said: "Ganelon, my stepfather."
The French respond: "Why, that's the very man!
Pass this man by and you won't send a wiser."
And hearing this Count Ganelon began to choke,
pulls from his neck the great furs of marten
and stands there now, in his silken tunic,
eyes full of lights, the look on him of fury,
he has the body, the great chest of a lord;
stood there so fair, all his peers gazed on him;
said to Roland: "Madman, what makes you rave?
Every man knows I am your stepfather,
yet you named me to go to Marsilion.
Now if God grants that I come back from there,
you will have trouble: I'll start a feud with you,
it will go on till the end of your life."
Roland replies: "What wild words—all that blustering!
Every man knows that threats don't worry me.
But we need a wise man to bring the message:
if the King wills, I'll gladly go in your place."

21

Ganelon answers: "You will not go for me. AOI.
You're not my man, and I am not your lord.
Charles commands me to perform this service:
I'll go to Marsilion in Saragossa.

---

7. **a baron . . . march:** Charlemagne wants them to choose a baron from an outlying region and not one of the Twelve Peers, the circle of his dearest men.

Literary Context:
Roland's exchange with Ganelon shows how the poem can be read as a blood-feud between a stepson and his stepfather. Blood-feud is a common theme in French epic poetry.

Literary Context:
Roland's rejoinder to Ganelon is one of the great ironic moments in the poem. Roland's tone is one of superiority laced with bitterness.

3 **Discussion** What image do rich furs suggest? Have students discuss the connotations of the clothing.

4 **Master Teacher Note** Have students keep in mind Roland's boast: "Every man knows that threats don't worry me." Early on, Roland's arrogance and pride are established. Have students list other examples of Roland's pride as they read through the tale.

5 **Discussion** Ask students how Ganelon establishes his relationship, or lack of it, with Roland. Why does he disclaim him in such terms?

Humanities Note

Fine art, *Gold Sarcophagus of Charlemagne*, artist unknown. The gold sarcophagus of the emperor Charlemagne is a reliquary that holds the leader's bones. Made in the thirteenth century of gilded silver and copper, this box is a masterpiece of the metalworker's art.

The scene in this detail shows the emperor flanked by two saints. The architectural elements of arches and columns richly frame these figures. Other sides of the shrine show scenes from Charlemagne's life in repoussé (raised design).

You might want to use the following questions to discuss the art:

1. What other people mentioned in this textbook used sarcophagi to honor their dead?
2. Do you think this shrine is a suitable monument?
3. How would you describe the expression on Charlemagne's face?
4. What is the most impressive detail of this work of art?

GOLD SARCOPHAGUS OF CHARLEMAGNE

And I tell you, I'll play a few wild tricks
before I cool the anger in me now."
When he heard that, Roland began to laugh. AOI.

27

Count Ganelon goes away to his camp.
90 He chooses, with great care, his battle-gear,
picks the most precious arms that he can find.
The spurs he fastened on were golden spurs;
he girds his sword, Murgleis, upon his side;
he has mounted Tachebrun, his battle horse,
95 his uncle, Guinemer, held the stirrup.
And there you would have seen brave men in tears,
his men, who say: "Baron, what bad luck for you!
All your long years in the court of the King,
always proclaimed a great and noble vassal!
100 Whoever it was doomed you to go down there—
Charlemagne himself will not protect that man.
Roland the Count should not have thought of this—
and you the living issue of a mighty line!"
And then they say: "Lord, take us there with you!"
105 Ganelon answers: "May the Lord God forbid!
It is better that I alone should die
than so many good men and noble knights.
You will be going back, Lords, to sweet France:
go to my wife and greet her in my name,
and Pinabel, my dear friend and peer,
110 and Baldewin, my son, whom you all know:
give him your aid, and hold him as your lord."
And he starts down the road; he is on his way. AOI.

28

Ganelon rides to a tall olive tree,
there he has joined the pagan messengers.
115 And here is Blancandrin,[8] who slows down for him:
with what great art they speak to one another.
Said Blancandrin: "An amazing man, Charles!
conquered Apulia, conquered all of Calabria,[9]
crossed the salt sea on his way into England,

---

8. **Blancandrin:** An envoy from King Marsilion.
9. **Apulia** (ə pyōōl′ yə) . . . **Calabria** (kə lä′ brē ə): Regions in southeastern Italy.

Literary Context: Notice how skillfully the storyteller sets up the conflict. Ganelon must go along with the plan to be able to carry out his treachery. His betrayal, however, is purely personal. Ganelon loves his "sweet France"; it is Roland whom he hates, although the reason for the hatred is never explained.

Historical Context: The events in this poem take place in A.D. 778. However, the poet takes liberties with history and includes events that did not happen until almost three hundred years later—the poet's own time, not Charlemagne's. England is included as a French tributary because the poem was written shortly after the Norman conquest of England in A.D. 1066.

6 **Enrichment** Tell students that the yew is a type of coniferous evergreen tree.

won its tribute, got Peter's pence[10] for Rome:
what does he want from us here in our march?"
Ganelon answers: "That is the heart in him.
There'll never be a man the like of him." AOI.

30

Said Blancandrin: "A wild man, this Roland!
wants to make every nation beg for his mercy
and claims a right to every land on earth!
But what men support him, if that is his aim?"
Ganelon answers: "Why, Lord, the men of France.
They love him so, they will never fail him.
He gives them gifts, masses of gold and silver,
mules, battle horses, brocaded silks, supplies.
And it is all as the Emperor desires:
he'll win the lands from here to the Orient." AOI.

Cultural Context: It is necessary for a feudal lord to share the booty with his men. This would maintain their loyalty and morale.

31

Ganelon and Blancandrin rode on until
each pledged his faith to the other and swore
they'd find a way to have Count Roland killed.
They rode along the paths and ways until,
in Saragossa, they dismount beneath a yew.
There was a throne in the shade of a pine,
covered with silk from Alexandria.
There sat the king who held the land of Spain,
and around him twenty thousand Saracens.
There is no man who speaks or breathes a word,
poised for the news that all would like to hear.
Now here they are: Ganelon and Blancandrin.

Literary Context: Again, we see the poet's talent at generating irony. Ganelon's mentioning of Roland is infused with bitterness.

6

36

Now Ganelon drew closer to the King
and said to him: "You are wrong to get angry,
for Charles, who rules all France, sends you this word:
you are to take the Christian people's faith;
he will give you one half of Spain in fief,[11]
the other half goes to his nephew: Roland—
quite a partner you will be getting there!

Cultural Context: Ganelon and Blancandrin swear an oath to each other. The feudal code must be observed even in plotting treachery.

---

10. Peter's pence: A tribute of one penny per house "for the use of Saint Peter," that is, for the Pope in Rome.
11. in fief (fēf): Held from a lord in return for service.

7 **Discussion** Note the repetition of the figure of the horse in these lines. Ask students why the horse is described here four times and in four different ways. What does each difference signify?

8 **Discussion** Note the figure of speech employed here. Ask your students why Charlemagne uses the phrase "the life of my body."

Literary Context: Ganelon's description of what will happen to Marsilion if he rejects the peace is horrifying given that Marsilion is a king and therefore Charlemagne's peer.

7

If you refuse, if you reject this peace,
he will come and lay siege to Saragossa;
155 you will be taken by force, put into chains,
and brought straight on to Aix, the capital.
No saddle horse, no war horse for you then,
no he-mule, no she-mule for you to ride:
you will be thrown on some miserable dray;
160 you will be tried, and you will lose your head.
Our Emperor sends you this letter."
He put the letter in the pagan's right fist.

37

Marsilion turned white; he was enraged;
he breaks the seal, he's knocked away the wax,
165 runs through the letter, sees what is written there:
"Charles sends me word, this king who rules in France:
I'm to think of his anger and his grief—
he means Basan and his brother Basile,
I took their heads in the hills below Haltille;
170 if I want to redeem the life of my body,
I must send him my uncle: the Algalife.[12]
And otherwise he'll have no love for me."
Then his son came and spoke to Marsilion,
said to the King: "Ganelon has spoken madness.
175 He crossed the line, he has no right to live.
Give him to me, I will do justice on him."
When he heard that, Ganelon brandished his sword;
he runs to the pine, set his back against the trunk.

38

8

Literary Context: We see here why it was important for Ganelon and Blancandrin to swear an oath to each other. It is this "deceit with honor" that saves Ganelon from the Moors.

King Marsilion went forth into the orchard,
180 he takes with him the greatest of his men;
Blancandrin came, that gray-haired counselor,
and Jurfaleu, Marsilion's son and heir,
the Algalife, uncle and faithful friend.
Said Blancandrin: "Lord, call the Frenchman back.
185 He swore to me to keep faith with our cause."
And the King said: "Go, bring him back here, then."
He took Ganelon's right hand by the fingers,
leads him into the orchard before the King.
And there they plotted that criminal treason. AOI.

12. **Algalife:** Caliph, an Islamic leader.

39

Said Marsilion: "My dear Lord Ganelon,
that was foolish, what I just did to you,
I showed my anger, even tried to strike you.
Here's a pledge of good faith, these sable furs,
the gold alone worth over five hundred pounds:
I'll make it all up before tomorrow night."
Ganelon answers: "I will not refuse it.
May it please God to reward you for it." AOI.

42

Said the pagan: "Truly, how I must marvel
at Charlemagne, who is so gray and white—
over two hundred years, from what I hear;
gone through so many lands a conqueror,
and borne so many blows from strong sharp spears,
killed and conquered so many mighty kings:
when will he lose the heart for making war?"
"Never," said Ganelon, "while one man lives: Roland!
no man like him from here to the Orient!
There's his companion, Oliver, a brave man.
And the Twelve Peers, whom Charles holds very dear,
form the vanguard, with twenty thousand Franks.
Charles is secure, he fears no man alive." AOI.

44

"Dear Lord Ganelon," said Marsilion the King,
"What must I do to kill Roland the Count?"
Ganelon answers: "Now I can tell you that.
The King will be at Cize,[13] in the great passes,
he will have placed his rear-guard at his back:
there'll be his nephew, Count Roland, that great man,
and Oliver, in whom he puts such faith,
and twenty thousand Franks in their company.
Now send one hundred thousand of your pagans
against the French—let them give the first battle.
The French army will be hit hard and shaken.
I must tell you: your men will be martyred.
Give them a second battle, then, like the first.
One will get him, Roland will not escape.

---

13. **Cize:** A pass through the Pyrenees mountains.

Cultural Context: Keeping with feudal custom, King Marsilion offers Ganelon reparation for having offended him and doubting his embassy.

Literary Context: The structure of the description of Charlemagne's rear guard is almost identical in this laisse and in laisse 41. Such symmetry is common throughout the poem.

9

10

11

HISTORICAL MIRROR: SCENES
FROM LIFE OF CHARLEMAGNE
V. de Beauvais
Musée Conde, Chantilly, France

12 Discussion Again Marsilion tests Ganelon's loyalty with Ganelon's acceptance of the gift.

13 Enrichment Note the terms "mass" and "matin." Ask students what point about Charlemagne is made by suggesting that he participate in two types of prayers.

Humanities Note

Illumination, *Scenes from the Life of Charlemagne*, artist unknown. There were frequent medieval contacts between the courts of Anjou, France, and Naples, Italy. In both courts the art of illumination flourished. Scribes and illuminators from both countries gathered at these cultural centers.

Scenes from Life of Charlemagne is an illumination from a manuscript of the *Speculum Historiale* by V. de Beauvais. It was produced in the scriptorium of the Cava Abbey in Naples and is preserved there to this day. The richness of detail and the light modeling of the figures show the strong influence of the Anjou school on this unknown Neapolitan painter.

You might want to use the following questions to discuss the art:

1. Explain what you think the value of a work from the Middle Ages might be.
2. How do you suppose this artist developed ideas for this illumination?
3. Comment on the use of color in this work of art.
4. What impression do you receive first from this depiction?

Historical Context:
Marsilion displays remarkable religious tolerance in this passage. The Spanish Moors were far more tolerant of other religions than were the Christians. Under Moorish domination, Christians, Jews, and Muslims usually lived harmoniously.

225 Then you'll have done a deed, a noble deed,
and no more war for the rest of your life!" AOI.

52

Marsilion took Ganelon by the shoulder
and said to him: "You're a brave man, a wise man.
Now by that faith you think will save your soul,
230 take care you do not turn your heart from us.
I will give you a great mass of my wealth,
ten mules weighed down with fine Arabian gold;
and come each year, I'll do the same again.
Now you take these, the keys to this vast city:
235 present King Charles with all of its great treasure;
then get me Roland picked for the rear-guard.
Let me find him in some defile or pass,
I will fight him, a battle to the death."
Ganelon answers: "It's high time that I go."
240 Now he is mounted, and he is on his way. AOI.

54

The Emperor rose early in the morning,
the King of France, and has heard mass and matins.[14]
On the green grass he stood before his tent.
Roland was there, and Oliver, brave man,
245 Naimon the Duke, and many other knights.
Ganelon came, the traitor, the foresworn.

---

14. matins (mat´ins): Morning prayers.

Grammar in Action

Colon and Semicolon The *colon* has a number of uses. These include the following: to introduce a list after an independent clause, to introduce quotes, to introduce summative remarks, and to introduce an appositive following an independent clause. For example:

Ganelon answers: "It's high time that I go."

The *semicolon* is used to join independent clauses that express similar or contrasting ideas. In effect, a semicolon stands midway between a period, which separates sentences, and a comma, which joins sentences more closely than does the semicolon. For example:

The day goes by; now the darkness of night.

The style of much of the *Song of Roland* uses simply constructed phrases and sentences brought together in juxtaposition through the use of colons and semicolons.

Student Activity 1. Find additional passages in the *Song of Roland* where colons and semicolons are used.

With what great cunning he commences his speech;
said to the King: "May the Lord God save you!
Here I bring you the keys to Saragossa.
And I bring you great treasure from that city,
and twenty hostages, have them well guarded.
And good King Marsilion sends you this word:
Do not blame him concerning the Algalife:
I saw it all myself, with my own eyes:
    four hundred thousand men, and all in arms,
their hauberks on, some with their helms[15] laced on,
swords on their belts, the hilts enameled gold.
who went with him to the edge of the sea.
They are in flight: it is the Christian faith—
they do not want it, they will not keep its law.
They had not sailed four full leagues[16] out to sea
when a high wind, a tempest swept them up.
They were all drowned; you will never see them;
if he were still alive, I'd have brought him.
As for the pagan King, Lord, believe this:
before you see one month from this day pass,
he'll follow you to the Kingdom of France
and take the faith—he will take your faith, Lord,
and join his hands and become your vassal.
He will hold Spain as a <u>fief</u> from your hand."
Then the King said: "May God be thanked for this.
You have done well, you will be well rewarded."
Throughout the host they sound a thousand trumpets.
The French break camp, strap their gear on their pack-horses.
They take the road to the sweet land of France. AOI.

56

The day goes by; now the darkness of night.
Charlemagne sleeps, the mighty Emperor.
He dreamt he was at Cize, in the great passes,
and in his fists held his great ashen lance.
Count Ganelon tore it away from him
and brandished it, shook it with such fury
the splinters of the shaft fly up toward heaven.
Charlemagne sleeps, his dream does not wake him.

---

15. hauberks (hô´ bərks) . . . **helms:** Chain mail armor and helmets, respectively.
16. four full leagues: About twelve nautical miles.

Literary Context: Ganelon's speech is truly cunning. It is a wonderful fiction and easily persuades Charlemagne. Like many good liars, Ganelon convinces Charlemagne by telling him what he wants to hear. **14** In this epic poem, Charlemagne is often easily deceived, perhaps the result of his not being able to imagine that anyone would betray him. **15**

Cultural Context: The feudal customs are vividly displayed in Ganelon's speech. The joining of hands was the ceremony by which one lord became another's vassal. A vassal was a person who held land from and pledged fealty, or loyalty, to an overlord in return for his protection. **16**

Historical Context: At the time of the actual events of the *Song of Roland*, Charlemagne had not yet been crowned emperor.

Literary Context: Charlemagne believes these prophetic dreams are sent from God. Charlemagne has another **17** dream right before Roland's death. Belief in the prophetic power of dreams was common during the Middle Ages.

14 Discussion Point out the cliché "with my own eyes." Ask students why they think this cliché is attributed to Ganelon? What effect does it have on our perception of him as a character.

15 Enrichment It might be important to point out how the religious war or crusade must be constantly defended, perhaps as a justification.

16 Clarification Point out how it is important for Ganelon to depict Marsilion as a pagan; discuss the depiction of non-Christians in the poem.

17 Discussion The description of the dream seems to end on a frustrating note. Ask students why Charlemagne's dream does not wake him.

Student Activity 2. Compose a paragraph describing the army that makes the journey in this epic. Be sure to use colons and semicolons at appropriate intervals.

18 **Discussion** What can we infer from the context?

19 **Discussion** Ask students to discuss the importance of the vanguard in military operations.

20 **Discussion** Where have we read this line before? Why does the *Song of Roland* repeat this?

21 **Discussion** What other kind of pack animal, besides a horse, might he be referring to? Discuss the significance of such animals to military campaigns.

22 **Enrichment** Notice how the list of Ganelon's gifts progresses from the familiar to the exotic in each line. What do mules and horses connote? What do camels and lions connote?

Literary Context: Roland's tone here is extremely ironic. Roland senses Ganelon's betrayal. His use of the term "stepfather" resounds with bitterness.

Historical Context: Al-mansur, the "victorious one," was the name of a fierce Arab warrior who sacked Barcelona in A.D. 985. His name was feared by the Spanish Christians. The poet uses the word *almacur* to refer to any fierce Arab knight.

58

The day goes by, and the bright dawn arises.
Throughout that host. . . .[17]
285 The Emperor rides forth with such fierce pride.
"Barons, my lords," said the Emperor Charles,
"look at those passes, at those narrow defiles—
pick me a man to command the rear-guard."
Ganelon answers: "Roland, here, my stepson.
290 You have no baron as great and brave as Roland."
When he hears that, the King stares at him in fury;
and said to him: "You are the living devil,
a mad dog—the murderous rage in you!
And who will precede me, in the vanguard?"
295 Ganelon answers, "Why, Ogier of Denmark,[18]
you have no baron who could lead it so well."

59

Roland the Count, when he heard himself named,
knew what to say, and spoke as a knight must speak:
"Lord Stepfather, I have to cherish you!
300 You have had the rear-guard assigned to me.
Charles will not lose, this great King who rules France,
I swear it now, one palfrey, one war horse—
    while I'm alive and know what's happening—
one he-mule, one she-mule that he might ride,
Charles will not lose one sumpter,[19] not one pack horse
305 that has not first been bought and paid for with swords."
Ganelon answers: "You speak the truth, I know." AOI.

68

King Charles the Great cannot keep from weeping.
A hundred thousand Franks feel pity for him;
and for Roland, an amazing fear.
310 Ganelon the criminal has betrayed him;
got gifts for it from the pagan king,
gold and silver, cloths of silk, gold brocade,
mules and horses and camels and lions.
315 Marsilion sends for the barons of Spain,
counts and viscounts and dukes and almaçurs,

---

17. host . . . : The second part of the line is unintelligible in the manuscript.
18. Ogier (ō′ ji er) **of Denmark:** One of Charlemagne's best-known knights.
19. sumpter (sump′ tər): A pack animal.

and the emirs,[20] and the sons of great lords:
four hundred thousand assembled in three days.
In Saragossa he has them beat the drums,
they raise Mahumet upon the highest tower:
no pagan now who does not worship him
and adore him. Then they ride, racing each other,
search through the land, the valleys, the mountains;
and then they saw the banners of the French.
The rear-guard of the Twelve Companions
will not fail now, they'll give the pagans battle.

---

20. **almaçurs** (ål mə sŭrz´) . . . **emirs** (e mirz´): Titled

THINKING ABOUT THE SELECTION

Interpreting

1. In Canto 13, what motivates Charlemagne to list the tribute that Marsilion is planning to send him?
2. Why do you think Roland nominates Ganelon to bear Charlemagne's message to the Moors?
3. Analyze Roland and Ganelon's exchange in Canto 20. (a) Who wins this verbal joust? (b) Why?
4. When Roland is appointed to the rear guard by Ganelon, his first words are: "Lord Stepfather, I have to cherish you." Why do you think he says this?
5. (a) After Ganelon delivers his message, what does Marsilion's son mean when he says, "Give him to me, I will do justice on him"? (b) Why does Marsilion change his mind about Ganelon?

Applying

6. Imagine telling this story from the Saracen point of view. (a) How would it be different? (b) How would it be the same? (c) What accounts for the similarities and differences?
7. The poet of the *Song of Roland* takes a minor historical incident and in a way blows it out of proportion. He can do this because 300 years separate the event from his public. The distortion of historical facts is a common occurrence, especially in film and fiction. Truth is often passed over for what makes a good story. What historical events can you think of that were not accurately depicted in a movie you have seen or a novel you have read?

ANALYZING LITERATURE

Understanding Theme

The **theme** of a work of literature is the insight it gives into life. The *Song of Roland* may be considered an epic dealing with the theme of betrayal. Within the confines of medieval society, betrayal of one's lord or vassal was considered the greatest violation of the feudal code. What further darkens the *Song of Roland* is the fact that all this betrayal occurs in one family. First Roland betrays his stepfather by recommending his embassy to the pagans. Then Ganelon betrays his stepson by appointing him to the rear guard.

1. What is the poet's attitude to this treachery?
2. Can we blame Ganelon for ultimately plotting Roland's demise? Support your answer.
3. How does the poet guarantee Roland's status as hero and Ganelon's as villain?

CRITICAL THINKING AND READING

Understanding Tone

The structure of the *Song of Roland* may be interpreted as a series of persuasive speeches interspersed by narrative interludes. Critical to these speeches is the tone the author establishes for each character in the work. For example, Charlemagne's tone is almost always solemn and measured.

1. Analyze Charlemagne's diction in laisse 13. (a) What elements make this passage solemn? (b) How is Charlemagne's speech measured?
2. Analyze laisses 20 and 21. How does their tone differ from that in laisse 13?

GUIDE FOR INTERPRETING

Focus

Literary Focus Have students discuss their ideas of what makes a person heroic. Have them mention movies they have seen recently that heralded the heroics of courageous persons. Remind them of characters like Aeneas or Achilles and about readings they may have done in ancient literature. Prompt them to compare and contrast heroes from antiquity and those of the contemporary world.

Writing/Prior Knowledge Pair off students in the class and have them discuss the elements of good stories before listing the elements.

ESL Teaching Strategy Ask ESL students to explain the difference between setting and dialogue. Then have them decide which is more important for a good story.

Teaching Tenth-Grade Students Most likely tenth-grade students will recall reading about the adventures of Odysseus from the previous year. Ask them to discuss the qualities that made Odysseus a hero.

Vocabulary

Preteach the following vocabulary words:
gonfalons (gän´ fə ləns) *n.*: Flags identifying certain princes or states
hefting (heft´ iŋ) *v.*: Weighing
valor (val´ər) *n.*: Bravery
reproach (ri proch´) *v.*: Blame, accuse
prowess (prou´ is) *n.*: Ability
travail (trəv´ āl) *n.*: Labor, work
pommel (pum´ él) *n.*: Knob at the front and tip of a saddle bow

Commentary

from the Song of Roland

The Hero. The *Song of Roland* is an epic poem and, as such, deals with the heroic deeds of great men. You may have read other, more ancient epic poems, such as the *Iliad* or the *Aeneid*, which also sing of the exploits of heroes such as Achilleus, Hektor, and Aeneas. The *Song of Roland* shares much with these poems, but because of a different set of historical circumstances there are also many differences.

Like the heroes in ancient epics, the heroes in the *Song of Roland* are not perfect. Roland is the personification of the flawed hero. He is brave but he is not discreet; he is strong but careless; he is fearless but proud. Roland's flaws become his undoing. The more he resists blowing his horn, the more he ensures both his greatness and the doom of his mission. Roland's strength and pride go hand in hand but are not compatible qualities. Many of the characters in the *Song of Roland* possess similar contradictory qualities. Charlemagne is portrayed as wise and restrained. Many times in the poem, however, he is lacking in forcefulness and is easily persuaded by his advisers. Charlemagne and Roland may be perceived as mirror images.

In the earlier epics, heroism was a personal, individual attribute. Achilleus, Ajax, and Hektor fought for the glory of their own names. This is not the case in the *Song of Roland*. In the medieval epic, the heroic image is shaped by the feudal system and serves something larger than the individual. The *Song of Roland* has a larger political mission. Roland's heroism and valor serve Christianity, his king, and his "sweet France."

Dante Alighieri, the great thirteenth-century Italian poet, wrote that in order for literature to be considered great, it must espouse three themes: God, love, and valor. As you continue reading medieval literature, you will see that God, love, and valor are recurring themes. Within the *Song of Roland*, the three literary values that are so crucial to the medieval mind existed in a nested fashion. Roland's valor underlies his Christian zeal and his love for his country.

Writing

To the medieval person, valor, love, and God were the necessary elements for a good story. List which elements and themes are necessary in order to have a good story today.

Objectives

Thematic
To appreciate the role of the hero

Skills
1 To understand the hero
2 To write about values

Support Material

Teaching Portfolio
Teacher Backup, p. 699
Grammar in Action Worksheets, *Similes*, p. 703; *Understanding Personification*, p. 705
Usage and Mechanics Worksheet, p. 707
Vocabulary Check, p. 708

Analyzing Literature Worksheet, *Understanding the Hero*, p. 709
Language Worksheet, *Understanding Words of French Origin*, p. 710
Selection Test, pp. 711–712

from the Song of Roland

translated by Frederick Goldin

80

Oliver climbs to the top of a hill,
looks to his right, across a grassy vale,
sees the pagan army on its way there;
and called down to Roland, his companion:
5 "That way, toward Spain: the uproar I see
    coming!
All their hauberks, all blazing, helmets like flames!
It will be a bitter thing for our French.
Ganelon knew, that criminal, that traitor,
when he marked us out before the Emperor."
10 "Be still, Oliver," Roland the Count replies.
"He is my stepfather—my stepfather.
    I won't have you speak one word against him."

81

Oliver has gone up upon a hill,
sees clearly now: the kingdom of Spain,
and the Saracens assembled in such numbers:
helmets blazing, bedecked with gems in gold,
those shields of theirs, those hauberks sewn with
    brass,
and all their spears, the gonfalons¹ affixed;
cannot begin to count their battle corps,
there are too many, he cannot take their number.
And he is deeply troubled by what he sees.
He made his way quickly down from the hill,
came to the French, told them all he had seen.

82

Said Oliver: "I saw the Saracens,
no man no earth ever saw more of them—
one hundred thousand, with their shields, up in
    front,
helmets laced on, hauberks blazing on them,
the shafts straight up, the iron heads like flames—
you'll get a battle, nothing like it before.

_____

1. gonfalons (gän´ fə länz´): Battle flags.

My lords, my French, may God give you the
    strength.
30 Hold your ground now! Let them not defeat us!"
And the French say: "God hate the man who runs!
We may die here, but no man will fail you." AOI.

83

Said Oliver: "The pagan force is great;
from what I see, our French here are too few.
Roland, my companion, sound your horn then,
35 Charles will hear it, the army will come back."
Roland replies: "I'd be a fool to do it.
I would lose my good name all through sweet
    France.
40 I will strike now, I'll strike with Durendal,²
the blade will be bloody to the gold from striking!
These pagan traitors came to these passes
    doomed!
I promise you, they are marked men, they'll die."
    AOI.

87

Roland is good, and Oliver is wise,
both these vassals men of amazing courage:
45 once they are armed and mounted on their horses,
they will not run, though they die for it, from
    battle.
Good men, these Counts, and their words full of
    spirit.
Traitor pagans are riding up in fury.
Said Oliver: "Roland, look—the first ones,
50 on top of us—and Charles is far away.
You did not think it right to sound your olifant:³
if the King were here, we'd come out without
    losses.

_____

2. Durendal (dü ren däl´): Roland's sword, whose name
most likely means "enduring."
3. olifant: Roland's horn, whose name derives from
"elephant" because it was carved from a tusk.

Presentation

Motivation/Prior Knowledge Tell students they will continue to read the *Song of Roland*. Call upon their prior knowledge by asking them to review the story so far and to predict what will happen in the coming sections. Remind them of the heroic emphasis in Roland's character. Ask them to remain constantly mindful of the duty and responsibility of a true hero. Suggest that they keep that in mind as they read.

Purpose-Setting Question Why does it seem necessary for heroes to run the risk of death in their various exploits? Can someone be heroic without being willing to do that?

1 **Discussion** What does the figure "helmets like flames" mean here?

2 **Discussion** Note the repetition and expansion. Again and again the *Song of Roland* will repeat similar descriptive lines. Why?

3 **Discussion** Note the use of the term *marked men*. In what sense are they marked?

HISTORY OF EMPERORS: THE BATTLE OF RONCESVALLES, DEATH OF ROLAND
French illuminated manuscript

Now look up there, toward the passes of Aspre—
you can see the rear-guard: it will suffer.
55 No man in that detail will be in another."
Roland replies: "Don't speak such foolishness—
shame on the heart gone coward in the chest.
We'll hold our ground, we'll stand firm— we're
   the ones!
We'll fight with spears, we'll fight them hand to
   hand!" AOI.

89

60 And now there comes the Archbishop Turpin.[4]
He spurs his horse, goes up into a mountain,
summons the French; and he preached them a
   sermon:
"Barons, my lords, Charles left us in this place.
We know our duty: to die like good men for our
   King.
65 Fight to defend the holy Christian faith.
Now you will have a battle, you know it now,
you see the Saracens with your own eyes.
Confess your sins, pray to the Lord for mercy.
I will absolve you all, to save your souls.
70 If you die here, you will stand up holy martyrs,
you will have seats in highest Paradise."
The French dismount, cast themselves on the
   ground;
the Archbishop blesses them in God's name.
He commands them to do one penance: strike.

91

75 Roland went forth into the Spanish passes
on Veillantif,[5] his good swift-running horse.
He bears his arms—how they become this man!—
grips his lance now, hefting it, working it,
now swings the iron point up toward the sky,
80 the gonfalon all white laced on above—
the golden streamers beat down upon his hands:
a noble's body, the face aglow and smiling.
Close behind him his good companion follows;
the men of France hail him: their protector!
85 He looks wildly toward the Saracens,
and humbly and gently to the men of France;
and spoke a word to them, in all courtesy:
"Barons, my lords, easy now, keep at a walk.
These pagans are searching for martyrdom.
90 We'll get good spoils before this day is over,
no king of France ever got such treasure!"
And with these words, the hosts are at each other.
   AOI.

93

Marsilion's nephew is named Aëlroth.
He rides in front, at the head of the army,
95 comes on shouting insults against our French:
"French criminals, today you fight our men.
One man should have saved you: he betrayed you.
A fool, your King, to leave you in these passes.
This is the day sweet France will lose its name,
100 and Charlemagne the right arm of his body."

---

4. Archbishop Turpin: The archbishop of Rheims (*ra*ns), a city in northeastern France.

5. Veillantif (vā yän tēf'): The name of Roland's horse means "wide awake."

When he hears that—God!—Roland is outraged!
He spurs his horse, gives Veillantif its head.
The Count comes on to strike with all his might,
smashes his shield, breaks his hauberk apart,
and drives: rips through his chest, shatters the
     bones,
knocks the whole backbone out of his back,
casts out the soul of Aëlroth with his lance;
which he thrusts deep, makes the whole body
     shake,
throws him down dead, lance straight out,[6] from
     his horse;
he has broken his neck; broken it in two.
There is something, he says, he must tell him:
"Clown! Nobody! Now you know Charles is no
     fool,
he never was the man to love treason.
It took his valor to leave us in these passes!
France will not lose its name, sweet France! today.
Brave men of France, strike hard! The first blow is
     ours!
We're in the right, and these swine in the wrong!"
     AOI.

105

Roland the Count comes riding through the field,
holds Durendal, that sword! it carves its way!
and brings terrible slaughter down on the
     pagans.
To have seen him cast one man dead on another,
the bright red blood pouring out on the ground,
his hauberk, his two arms, running with blood,
his good horse—neck and shoulders running with
     blood!
And Oliver does not linger, he strikes!
and the Twelve Peers, no man could reproach them;
and the brave French, they fight with lance and
     sword.
The pagans die, some simply faint away!
Said the Archbishop: "Bless our band of brave men!"
Munjoie![7] he shouts—the war cry of King Charles.
     AOI.

110

The battle is fearful and full of grief.
Oliver and Roland strike like good men,
the Archbishop, more than a thousand blows,
and the Twelve Peers do not hang back, they
     strike!
135 the French fight side by side, all as one man.
The pagans die by hundreds, by thousands:
whoever does not flee finds no refuge from death,
like it or not, there he ends all his days.
And there the men of France lose their greatest
     arms;
140 they will not see their fathers, their kin again,
or Charlemagne, who looks for them in the passes.
Tremendous torment now comes forth in France,
a mighty whirlwind, tempests of wind and
     thunder,
rains and hailstones, great and immeasurable,
145 bolts of lightning hurtling and hurtling down:
it is, in truth, a trembling of the earth.
From Saint Michael-in-Peril to the Saints,
from Besançon to the port of Wissant,[8]
there is no house whose veil of walls does not
     crumble.
150 A great darkness at noon falls on the land,
there is no light but when the heavens crack.
No man sees this who is not terrified,
and many say: "The Last Day! Judgment Day!
155 The end! The end of the world is upon us!"
They do not know, they do not speak the truth:
it is the worldwide grief for the death of Roland.

130

And Roland says: "We are in a rough battle.
I'll sound the olifant, Charles will hear it."
Said Oliver: "No good vassal would do it.
160 When I urged it, friend, you did not think it right.
If Charles were here, we'd come out with no
     losses.
Those men down there—no blame can fall on
     them."
Oliver said: "Now by this beard of mine,

---

6. lance straight out: The lance is held, not thrown, and
used to knock the enemy from his horse. To throw one's
weapons is savage and ignoble.

7. Munjoie! (mun zhwä´): Mount joy! The origin of this war-
cry is not known for certain.

---

8. Saint Michael-in-Peril . . . Saints . . . Besançon (bə zän
sōn´) **. . . Wissant** (wə sän´): Four points marking out tenth-
century France.

5 **Discussion** Note how the line reflects the poetic structure of the
Song of Roland itself. Each line of
the poem is like a soldier doing
battle. Side by side, each line sits
alone; but collectively they constitute the strength of an army.

6 **Enrichment** Be sure to point out
the allusion here. The darkness
signifies both Christ's crucifixion
and the apocalyptic judgment day.

7 Discussion Point out to students how the threat of death is emphasized by suggesting not merely dead bodies, but "coffins."

8 Discussion Point out to students how the description of Roland's end is exaggerated: Not only does he bleed, but he explodes with blood. Discuss the significance of the description.

9 Clarification In addition to the use of simile, it is important to point out to students the use of antithesis. Charlemagne is not only too old, but so old that he is like an infant.

10 Enrichment The word *travail* here has importance, because not only does it suggest great work or effort, but it carries with it the sense of its etymological twin, the word *travel*.

If I can see my noble sister, Aude,[9]
165 once more, you will never lie in her arms!" AOI.

131

And Roland said: "Why are you angry at me?"
Oliver answers: "Companion, it is your doing.
I will tell you what makes a vassal good:
  it is judgment, it is never madness;
restraint is worth more than the raw nerve of a fool.
170 Frenchmen are dead because of your wildness.
And what service will Charles ever have from us?
If you had trusted me, my lord would be here,
we would have fought this battle through to the end,
Marsilion would be dead, or our prisoner.
175 Roland, your prowess—had we never seen it!
  And now, dear friend, we've seen the last of it.
No more aid from us now for Charlemagne,
a man without equal till Judgment Day,
you will die here, and your death will shame France.
We kept faith, you and I, we were companions;
  and everything we were will end today.
180 We part before evening, and it will be hard." AOI.

132

Turpin the Archbishop hears their bitter words,
digs hard into his horse with golden spurs
and rides to them; begins to set them right:
"You, Lord Roland, and you, Lord Oliver,
185 I beg you in God's name do not quarrel.
To sound the horn could not help us now, true,
but still it is far better that you do it:
let the King come, he can avenge us then—
these men of Spain must not go home exulting!
Our French will come, they'll get down on their feet,
190 and find us here—we'll be dead, cut to pieces.
They will lift us into coffins on the backs of mules,
and weep for us, in rage and pain and grief,
and bury us in the courts of churches;
195 and we will not be eaten by wolves or pigs or dogs."
Roland replies, "Lord, you have spoken well." AOI.

---

9. Aude (ō′ də): Roland's intended bride.

133

Roland has put the olifant to his mouth,
he sets it well, sounds it with all his strength.
The hills are high, and that voice ranges far,
200 they heard it echo thirty great leagues away.
King Charles heard it, and all his faithful men.
And the King says: "Our men are in a battle."
And Ganelon disputed him and said:
"Had someone else said that, I'd call him liar!" AOI.

134

205 And now the mighty effort of Roland the Count:
he sounds his olifant; his pain is great,
and from his mouth the bright blood comes leaping out,
and the temple bursts in his forehead.
That horn, in Roland's hands, has a mighty voice:
210 King Charles hears it drawing through the passes.
Naimon heard it, the Franks listen to it.
And the King said: "I hear Count Roland's horn;
he'd never sound it unless he had a battle."
Says Ganelon: "Now no more talk of battles!
215 You are old now, your hair is white as snow,
the things you say make you sound like a child.
You know Roland and that wild pride of his—
what a wonder God has suffered it so long!
Remember? he took Noples without your command:
220 the Saracens rode out, to break the siege;
they fought with him, the great vassal Roland.
Afterward he used the streams to wash the blood
from the meadows: so that nothing would show.
He blasts his horn all day to catch a rabbit,
225 he's strutting now before his peers and bragging—
who under heaven would dare meet him on the field?
So now: ride on! Why do you keep on stopping?
The Land of Fathers lies far ahead of us." AOI.

135

The blood leaping from Count Roland's mouth,
230 the temple broken with effort in his forehead,
he sounds his horn in great travail and pain.
King Charles heard it, and his French listen hard.
And the King said: "That horn has a long breath!"
Naimon answers: "It is a baron's breath.
235 There is a battle there, I know there is.

Grammar in Action

Writers often use figurative language to make a point or to emphasize something. A *simile* evokes comparison, in much the same way that a metaphor does. However, similes always employ the term *like* or *as*, so that there is no confusion and the comparison as well as the distinction are maintained.

STRAIGHTFORWARD: The sun was red and round.

FIGURATIVE: The sun looked like a lush, ripe orange.

Both sentences describe the sun in similar ways. The first uses straightforward language; the second uses metaphoric language, suggesting a point of comparison. However, because the writer uses the preposition *like* to construct this image, the reader is not confused as to whether an orange or the sun is being described.

Figurative language is important in the *Song of Roland*.

Example: "You are old now, your hair is white as snow, / the things you say make you sound like a child."

Rather than say, simply, that his hair is white, the comparison of

He betrayed him! and now asks you to fail him!
Put on your armor! Lord, shout your battle cry,
and save the noble barons of your house!
You hear Roland's call. He is in trouble."

136

The Emperor commanded the horns to sound,
the French dismount, and they put on their armor:
their hauberks, their helmets, their gold-dressed
  swords,
their handsome shields; and take up their great
  lances,
the ganfalons of white and red and blue.
The barons of that host mount their war horses
and spur them hard the whole length of the pass;
and every man of them says to the other:
"If only we find Roland before he's killed,
we'll stand with him, and then we'll do some
  fighting!"
What does it matter what they say? They are too late.

138

High are the hills, and tenebrous,[10] and vast, AOI.
the valleys deep, the raging waters swift;
to the rear, to the front, the trumpets sound:
they answer the lone voice of the olifant.
The Emperor rides on, rides on in fury,
the men of France in grief and indignation.
There is no man who does not weep and wail,
and they pray God: protect the life of Roland
till they come, one great host, into the field
and fight at Roland's side like true men all.
What does it matter what they pray? It does no
  good.
They are too late, they cannot come in time. AOI.

156

Roland the Count fights well and with great skill,
but he is hot, his body soaked with sweat;
has a great wound in his head, had much pain,
his temple broken because he blew the horn.
But he must know whether King Charles will
  come;

———
10. tenebrous (ten′ ə brəs) *adj.*: Dark, gloomy.

draws out the olifant, sounds it, so feebly.
The Emperor drew to a halt, listened.
270 "Seigneurs," he said, "it all goes badly for us—
My nephew Roland falls from our ranks today.
I hear it in the horn's voice: he hasn't long.
Let every man who wants to be with Roland
ride fast! Sound trumpets! Every trumpet in this
  host!"
275 Sixty thousand, on these words, sound, so high
the mountains sound, and the valleys resound.
The pagans hear: it is no joke to them;
cry to each other: "We're getting Charles on us!"

160

Say the pagans: "We were all born unlucky!
280 The evil day that dawned for us today!
We have lost our lords and peers, and now comes
  Charles—
that Charlemagne!—with his great host. Those
  trumpets!
that shrill sound on us—the trumpets of the
  French!
And the loud roar of that Munjoie! This Roland
285 is a wild man, he is too great a fighter—
What man of flesh and blood can ever hope
to bring him down? Let us cast at him, and leave
  him there."
And so they did: arrows, wigars, darts,
lances and spears, javelots dressed with feathers;
struck Roland's shield, pierced it, broke it to
290 pieces,
ripped his hauberk, shattered its rings of mail,
but never touched his body, never his flesh.
They wounded Veillantif in thirty places,
struck him dead, from afar, under the Count.
The pagans flee, they leave the field to him.
295 Roland the Count stood alone, on his feet.[11]

161

The pagans flee, in bitterness and rage,
strain every nerve running headlong toward Spain,
and Count Roland has no way to chase them,

———
11. The pagans flee . . . feet: This respite granted to Roland
and Turpin after the pagans have fled and before these heroes
die is an act of overwhelming grace and the sign of the two
men's blessedness.

"snow" is suggested, intensifying the quality of his hair. Similarly, "sound like a child" says more than that the spoken words are simple.

Student Activity 1. Find additional passages in the poem where similes are used to exaggerate or provide a vivid description.

Student Activity 2. Write a brief description of a common activity such as sharpening your pencil or brushing your teeth. Use similes to evoke the quality of your experience.

he has lost Veillantif, his battle horse;
300 he has no choice, left alone there on foot.
He went to the aid of Archbishop Turpin,
unlaced the gold-dressed helmet, raised it from his
    head,
lifted away his bright, light coat of mail,
305 cut his under tunic into some lengths,
stilled his great wounds with thrusting on the strips;
then held him in his arms, against his chest,
and laid him down, gently, on the green grass;
and softly now Roland entreated him:
310 "My noble lord, I beg you, give me leave:
our companions, whom we have loved so dearly,
are all dead now, we must not abandon them.
I want to look for them, know them once more,
and set them in ranks, side by side, before you."
315 Said the Archbishop: "Go then, go and come back.
The field is ours, thanks be to God, yours and
    mine."

168

Now Roland feels that death is very near.
His brain comes spilling out through his two ears;
prays to God for his peers: let them be called;
320 and for himself, to the angel Gabriel;
took the olifant: there must be no reproach!
took Durendal his sword in his other hand,
and farther than a crossbow's farthest shot
he walks toward Spain, into a fallow land,[12]
325 and climbs a hill: there beneath two fine trees
stand four great blocks of stone, all are of marble;
and he fell back, to earth, on the green grass,
has fainted there, for death is very near.

169

High are the hills, and high, high are the trees;
there stand four blocks of stone, gleaming of
330   marble.
Count Roland falls fainting on the green grass,
and is watched, all this time, by a Saracen:
who has feigned death and lies now with the
    others,

---

12. **fallow land:** Land plowed but not seeded for one or more growing seasons.

has smeared blood on his face and on his body;
335 and quickly now gets to his feet and runs—
a handsome man, strong, brave, and so crazed
    with pride
that he does something mad and dies for it:
laid hands on Roland, and on the arms of Roland,
and cried: "Conquered! Charles's nephew
    conquered!
340 I'll carry this sword home to Arabia!"
As he draws it, the Count begins to come
    round.

170

Now Roland feels: *someone taking his sword!*
opened his eyes, and had one word for him:
"I don't know you, you aren't one of ours";
345 grasps that olifant that he will never lose,
strikes on the helm beset with gems in gold,
shatters the steel, and the head, and the bones,
sent his two eyes flying out of his head,
dumped him over stretched out at his feet dead;
350 and said: "You nobody! how could you dare
lay hands on me—rightly or wrongly: how?
Who'll hear of this and not call you a fool?
Ah! the bell-mouth of the olifant is smashed,
the crystal and the gold fallen away."

171

355 Now Roland the Count feels: his sight is gone;
gets on his feet, draws on his final strength,
the color on his face lost now for good.
Before him stands a rock; and on that dark rock
in rage and bitterness he strikes ten blows:
360   the steel blade grates, it will not break, it stands
    unmarked.
"Ah!" said the Count, "Blessed Mary, your help!
Ah Durendal, good sword, your unlucky day,
for I am lost and cannot keep you in my care.
The battles I have won, fighting with you,
365 the mighty lands that holding you I conquered,
that Charles rules now, our King, whose beard is
    white!
Now you fall to another: it must not be
a man who'd run before another man!
For a long while a good vassal held you:
there'll never be the like in France's holy land."

Grammar in Action

Personification is the giving of human qualities to inanimate objects. Writers frequently use personification to enliven text or engage the reader more fully.

STRAIGHTFORWARD: The room was cold and poorly lit.
PERSONIFIED: The lonely room trembled from a lack of warmth and light.

The straightforward example gives nothing more than a simple description. It does not paint a scene, nor does it suggest motivation. However, the example employing personification provides a more telling description. Here

the room takes on the qualities of a person or animal; it appears nervous, shy, and perhaps even in poor health. The room seems alive.

In the *Song of Roland*, inanimate objects are frequently given animate qualities.

For example:

Now Roland feels death coming over him,
death descending from his temple to his heart.

Here, death is like a person climbing down a stairway through the home of Roland's body.

SCENE SHOWING
THE DEATH OF ROLAND
*V. de Beauvais, fifteenth-
century manuscript*
Musée Condé, Chantilly, France

173

Roland the Count strikes down on a dark rock,
and the rock breaks, breaks more than I can tell,
and the blade grates, but Durendal will not break,
the sword leaped up, rebounded toward the sky,
The Count, when he sees that sword will not be
  broken,
softly, in his own presence, speaks the lament:
"Ah Durendal, beautiful, and most sacred,
the holy relics in this golden pommel!
Saint Peter's tooth and blood of Saint Basile,
a lock of hair of my lord Saint Denis,
and a fragment of blessed Mary's robe:[13]
your power must not fall to the pagans,
you must be served by Christian warriors.
May no coward ever come to hold you!
It was with you I conquered those great lands
that Charles has in his keeping, whose beard is
  white,
the Emperor's lands, that make him rich and
  strong."

174

Now Roland feels: death coming over him,
death descending from his temples to his heart.

---

13. Saint Peter's tooth . . . Mary's robe: Such relics—remains of holy men and women—were thought to have miraculous power.

He came running underneath a pine tree
and there stretched out, face down, on the green
390   grass,
lays beneath him his sword and the olifant.
He turned his head toward the Saracen hosts,
and this is why: with all his heart he wants
King Charles the Great and all his men to say,
395   he died, that noble Count, a conqueror;
makes confession, beats his breast often, so feebly,
offers his glove, for all his sins, to God. AOI.

176

Count Roland lay stretched out beneath a pine;
he turned his face toward the land of Spain,
400   began to remember many things now:
how many lands, brave man, he had conquered;
and he remembered: sweet France, the men of his
  line,
remembered Charles, his lord, who fostered him:
cannot keep, remembering, from weeping, sighing;
405   but would not be unmindful of himself:
he confesses his sins, prays God for mercy:
"Loyal Father, you who never failed us,
who resurrected Saint Lazarus from the dead,[14]

---

14. Saint Lazarus . . . Daniel from the lions: A reference to two famous miracles described in the Bible (Luke 16:19–31 and Daniel 6:16–23, respectively).

Student Activity 1. Find additional passages in the poem where personification is used.

Student Activity 2. Write a brief description using personification to dramatize or heighten effect. Use a simple, everyday object, such as a bicycle or a pair of shoes, as your subject.

15 Enrichment Note the adjective *tenebrous* (dark, gloomy), used in line 251. It has been transformed into an actual toponym (or place name). Ask students to identify other names of places that describe figuratively their locations, such as Sleepy Hollow or Death Valley. What legends are associated with such places?

and saved your servant Daniel from the lions:
410 now save the soul of me from every peril
for the sins I committed while I still lived."
Then he held out his right glove to his Lord:[15]
Saint Gabriel took the glove from his hand.
He held his head bowed down upon his arm,
415 he is gone, his two hands joined, to his end.
Then God sent him his angel Cherubin
and Saint Michael, angel of the sea's Peril;
and with these two there came Saint Gabriel:
they bear Count Roland's soul to Paradise.

177

420 Roland is dead, God has his soul in heaven.
The Emperor rides into Rencesvals;[16]
there is no passage there, there is no track,
no empty ground, not an elle,[17] not one foot,
that does not bear French dead or pagan dead.
King Charles cries out: "Dear Nephew, where are
425   you?
Where is the Archbishop? Count Oliver?
Where is Gerin, his companion Gerer?
Where is Otun, where is Count Berenger,
Yves and Yvoire, men I have loved so dearly?
430 What has become of Engeler the Gascon,
Sansun the Duke, and Anseïs, that fighter?
Where is Gerard the Old of Roussillon,
and the Twelve Peers, whom I left in these passes?"
And so forth—what's the difference? No one
    answered.
435 "God!" said the King, "how much I must regret
I was not here when the battle began";
pulls his great beard, a man in grief and rage.
His brave knights weep, their eyes are filled with
    tears,
twenty thousand fall fainting to the ground;
440 Duke Naimon feels the great pity of it.

180

God made great miracles for Charlemagne,
for on that day in heaven the sun stood still.
The pagans flee, the Franks keep at their heels,

---

15. he held out . . . to his Lord: A ritual act of resignation to a feudal lord.
16. Rencesvals: The old form of Roncevaux (rôns vō′), the pass in the Pyrenees mountains where Roland was ambushed.
17. elle (el): A unit of measure equal to an arm's length, or about forty-five inches.

---

catch up with them in the Vale Tenebrous,
445 chase them on spurring hard to Saragossa,
and always killing them, striking with fury;
cut off their paths, the widest roads away:
the waters of the Ebro[18] lie before them,
very deep, an amazing sight, and swift;
and there is no boat, no barge, no dromond,[19]
450   no galley.
They call on Tervagant, one of their gods.
Then they jump in, but no god is with them:
those in full armor, the ones who weigh the most,
sank down, and they were many, to the bottom;
455 the others float downstream: the luckiest ones,
who fare best in those waters, have drunk so much,
they all drown there, struggling, it is amazing.
The French cry out: "Curse the day you saw
    Roland!" AOI.

King Marsilion loses his right hand in the battle with Charlemagne but escapes to Saragossa and enlists the aid of Balignant, another pagan. Charlemagne, however, kills Balignant in combat and defeats his army. Then, after capturing Saragossa, the emperor returns home.

270

The Emperor has come home again to Aix.
460 In iron chains, the traitor Ganelon
stands before the palace, within the city.
He has been bound, and by serfs, to a stake;
they tie his hands with deerhide straps and thongs,
and beat him hard, with butcher's hooks, with
    clubs—
465 for what better reward has this man earned?
There he stands, in pain and rage, awaiting his
    trial.

Pinabel, one of Ganelon's kinsmen, threatens to kill anyone who recommends that Ganelon be hanged. The emperor's advisers then suggest freeing Ganelon, a piece of advice that enrages Charlemagne. At this point, however, Tierri volunteers to fight Pinabel. When Tierri wins, against all odds, the French agree that Ganelon must die.

---

18. Saragossa (sar ə gäs′ ə) **. . . Ebro** (ā′ brô): The city of Saragossa in northeastern Spain is on the Ebro River.
19. dromond (drom′ ənd): A fast sailing galley.

Bavarians and Alemans returned,
and Poitevins, and Bretons, and Normans,
and all agreed, the Franks before the others,
Ganelon must die, and in amazing pain.
Four war horses are led out and brought forward;
then they attach his two feet, his two hands.
These battle horses are swift and spirited,
four sergeants come and drive them on ahead
toward a river in the midst of a field.

Ganelon is brought to terrible perdition,
all his mighty sinews are pulled to pieces,
and the limbs of his body burst apart;
on the green grass flows that bright and famous blood.
480 Ganelon died a traitor's and recreant's[20] death.
Now when one man betrays another, it is not right
    that he should live to boast of it.

---

20. recreant's (rek′ rē ənts): Coward's.

Reader's Response *Think of a time when you, like Roland, were reluctant to ask for help as Roland is during the attack. What part did pride play in your hesitancy? Do you now regret not turning to someone for help?*

THINKING ABOUT THE SELECTION

Clarifying

1. (a) At the start of this selection, why does Olivier reproach Roland? (b) How is the dispute settled?
2. Explain the fate of the person who attempts to steal Roland's sword.

Interpreting

3. Explain Archbishop Turpin's role in the battle.
4. Consider the following line: "Roland is good, and Olivier is wise." (a) Explain the distinction the poet makes. (b) Is this distinction of value?
5. (a) Describe Roland's relationship to his sword. (b) Why do you think this relationship is important?

Applying

6. Ganelon has been labeled a traitor. (a) Tell whether Ganelon fits your definition of a traitor. (b) Discuss with your classmates situations in which Ganelon might be labeled very differently.

ANALYZING LITERATURE

Understanding the Hero

Roland is a flawed and imperfect hero whose imperfections have severe consequences for those around him. Roland is brave and is prepared to sacrifice himself for the greater good. His flaw, however, lies in his obsession with his own personal glory rather than with the safety of his companions and his "sweet France." This is nowhere better seen than in laisse 131 where Olivier confronts Roland with his own folly and describes the ideal feudal hero: "I will tell you what makes a vassal good: it is judgment, it is never madness." Like a hero of classical tragedy, Roland's flaw is his pride. But in a medieval epic, this pride must be seen in the added dimension of feudal society. The hero must answer to something larger and more important than himself.

Discuss the evolution of Roland and Olivier's friendship throughout the poem.
1. What is Olivier's literary function?
2. In what ways is Olivier the ideal epic hero?
3. In what ways is he not?

THINKING AND WRITING

Writing About Values

Think about the system of values that is described in the poem. What motivates Roland and his companions to behave as they do? Write an essay in which you describe the values espoused in the *Song of Roland*. Support your ideas with quotes. As you revise your work, make sure your argument proceeds in a logical fashion.

DIETRICH OF BERN OVERTHROWS HAGEN; KRIEMHILD WATCHES FROM THE DOOR
Staatsbibliothek Preussicher Kulturbesitz
West Berlin, Germany

Composed over eight hundred years ago, *The Nibelungenlied* (nē′ bə lŏŏŋ′ ən lēt′) is one of the great works of German literature. Linking the epic form to the very different concerns of courtly romance, this tale of murder and revenge highlights the relationship between Kriemhild and Siegfried, while honoring the traditional significance given to clothing, festivals, and jewelry in medieval literature. However, the theme of forgiveness and salvation so central to romance is replaced by pure vengeance in this epic.

Who wrote *The Nibelungenlied*? As with many medieval epics, authorship is uncertain. Because of the detailed description of Passau in Austria, this epic is often ascribed to Walther von der Vogelweide (fō′ gel vī′ də), an outstanding lyric poet whose patron was the bishop of Passau. But such slim internal evidence should be mistrusted without specific mention of the author by contemporaries. Most critics agree that the author was a cleric, an educated member of religious orders, and that any further attempt to identify him would be futile.

Nor would further attempts necessarily be appropriate. In discussing the problem, the scholar Arthur Thomas Hatto writes: "His anonymity was deliberate, in obedience to the ancient convention that as preservers, renewers, and interpreters of the poetic traditions of famous deeds believed really to have taken place, they should not name themselves as the 'authors' of their poems."

The Nibelungenlied is a tragedy in two parts. The first describes the life and death of Siegfried. He falls in love with Kriemhild, the Burgundian princess, when he hears of her great beauty. In order to marry her, he must help her brother, Gunther, the king, win the hand of Brunhild, a maiden warrior. He does so disguised as a vassal. She is conquered but is then disturbed to see Siegfried marry Kriemhild. Siegfried has also stolen Brunhild's belt and ring. When she derides Kriemhild for acting like a powerful queen, the latter shows her the tokens that suggest her dishonor. Brunhild then calls for revenge. Her loyal servant Hagan plots with Gunther to murder Siegfried. Kriemhild stupidly reveals Siegfried's vulnerable spot, between the shoulders.

The vengeful Kriemhild is the heroine of the work's second part. Hagen takes Siegfried's treasure and sinks it in the Rhine. This leaves Kriemhild helpless. She must marry Attila the Hun in order to regain her lost power. In the guise of reconciliation, she invites her family to visit. Many are murdered. Trapped by her plan, the remaining Burgundian heroes defend themselves bravely and slaughter the forces of their host. But finally, Gunther and Hagen are captured and executed. Attila's queen must be killed in order to put an end to this bloodshed, but the kingdom of Burgundy has been virtually destroyed.

GUIDE FOR INTERPRETING

from The Nibelungenlied

Commentary

Tragic Flaw. A **tragic flaw** is a character trait that brings about the hero's downfall. Understanding the role of the tragic flaw in epic is crucial to reading *The Nibelungenlied.* Siegfried is exuberant, courageous, and loyal. However, he acts without thinking. Everything he does is related to his love of Kriemhild, especially the vanquishing of Brunhild and the gift of the ring and belt. This love in turn seems destined and beyond his control. He loves her before he even sees her. But this excessive love blinds him to the interests of others and harms his loyalty to Gunther. Like Achilles' heel, Siegfried's one vulnerable spot—his excessive love for Kriemhild—leads to his downfall.

Siegfried is not the only tragic figure in this work. Some critics argue that all the characters have tragic flaws. Because they are so consumed with one dominant emotion they do not think about the consequences of their actions. Gunther loves Brunhild so much that he is willing to kill his best friend for her. Hagen's loyalty to Brunhild blinds him to Siegfried's innocence and to the injustice of the murder. Kriemhild's pride is even stronger than her love for Siegfried and becomes a blind vengefulness, which causes her to seek the destruction of her own family. Brunhild, who never seems to feel love for anyone, also evolves from a proud maiden to a vengeful matron. *The Nibelungenlied* stands out among medieval epics because it is constructed around the actions of many heroes, rather than around one or two dominant figures. This work is more concerned with the complexity of the many delicate relationships that make up society than it is with the characterization of one outstanding person.

The epic hero is an incomplete person, usually dominated by one emotion (love, hatred, or loyalty) and incapable of a balanced, reasonable consideration of the problems at hand. The epic hero leaps into action without careful thought.

Although Siegfried is warned of his fate by his wife's dream, he ignores all signs of doom and throws himself eagerly into the hunt with Gunther and Hagen. He is unaware of Brunhild's grievance. His trust in his friends, while admirable, becomes his downfall.

The passage you are about to read is the account of Siegfried's death, the pivotal point of the epic. Hagen, fiercely loyal to Brunhild, wishes to avenge her dishonor. Gunther, forgetting his debt to the Nibelung hero, agrees to the plot. Siegfried's prowess in hunting reflects his heroism in battle, but it also reminds us of his lack of moderation. Look for the fatal flaw that leads to Siegfried's death.

Writing

Superhuman heroes such as Superman are part of our popular culture. Choose one and freewrite about his or her tragic flaw.

Literary Focus Have students discuss their own thoughts about films or stories that include characters who are superhuman. Many students will be familiar with film depictions and comic book renditions of Batman and Superman. Ask them if they think superheroes need to display some mortal qualities.

Writing/Prior Knowledge Have students tell each other about their own ideas concerning tragic flaws before they begin freewriting.

ESL Teaching Strategy Pair off the ESL students with partners. Let them collaborate on lists that use adjectives to describe the heroic and human qualities of the character about whom they will write.

Teaching Tenth-Grade Students Have tenth-grade students talk about how their younger brothers and sisters believe in characters like the Hulk or Mighty Mouse. Ask them to speculate on whether such beliefs in early childhood have any influence on our later ideas about heroes.

> **Vocabulary**
> Preteach the following vocabulary words:
> unrestrained (un ri strānd´) *v.*: Not checked or controlled
> malice (mal´ is) *n.*: Ill will; spite
> thwarted (thwôrt´ əd) *v.*: Hindered; frustrated
> sinister (sin´ is tər) *adj.*: Wicked; threatening harm
> intrepid (in trep´ id) *adj.*: Brave; fearless
> quiver (kwiv´ ər) *n.*: Case load of arrows
> foray (fôr´ ā) *n.*: Sudden attack; raid

derstanding a *Tragic Flaw*, p. 721
Critical Thinking and Reading Worksheet, *Understanding the Significance of Rituals*, p. 722
Selection Test, pp. 723–724

from The Nibelungenlied

How Siegfried Was Slain

translated by A. T. Hatto

The fearless warriors Gunther and Hagen treacherously proclaimed a hunt in the forest where they wished to chase the boar, the bear, and the bison—and what could be more daring? Siegfried rode with their party in magnificent style. They took all manner of food with them; and it was while drinking from a cool stream that the hero was to lose his life at the instigation of Brunhild, King Gunther's queen.

Bold Siegfried went to Kriemhild while his and his companions' hunting-gear was being loaded onto the sumpters in readiness to cross the Rhine,[1] and she could not have been more afflicted. "God grant that I may see you well again, my lady," he said, kissing his dear wife, "and that your eyes may see me too. Pass the time pleasantly with your relations who are so kind to you, since I cannot stay with you at home."

Kriemhild thought of what she had told Hagen, but she dared not mention it and began to lament that she had ever been born. "I dreamt last night—and an ill-omened dream it was—" said lord Siegfried's noble queen, weeping with unrestrained passion, "that two boars chased you over the heath and the flowers were dyed with blood! How can I help weeping so? I stand in great dread of some attempt against your life.—What if we have offended any men who have the power to

vent their malice on us? Stay away, my lord, I urge you."

"I shall return in a few days time, my darling. I know of no people here who bear me any hatred. Your kinsmen without exception wish me well, nor have I deserved otherwise of them."

"It is not so, lord Siegfried. I fear you will come to grief. Last night I had a sinister dream of how two mountains fell upon you and hid you from my sight! I shall suffer cruelly if you go away and leave me." But he clasped the noble woman in his arms and after kissing and caressing her fair person very tenderly, took his leave and went forthwith. Alas, she was never to see him alive again.

They rode away deep into the forest in pursuit of their sport. Gunther and his men were accompanied by numbers of brave knights, but Gernot and Giselher stayed at home. Ahead of the hunt many horses had crossed the Rhine laden with their bread, wine, meat, fish, and various other provisions such as a King of Gunther's wealth is bound to have with him.

The proud and intrepid hunters were told to set up their lodges on a spacious isle in the river on which they were to hunt, at the skirt of the greenwood over toward the spot where the game would have to break cover. Siegfried, too, had arrived there, and this was reported to the King. Thereupon the sportsmen everywhere manned their relays.[2]

---

1. **sumpters . . . Rhine:** Sumpters are pack horses, and the Rhine River flows from eastern Switzerland north through Germany, then west through the Netherlands into the North Sea.

2. **relays:** Fresh horses to relieve tired ones.

"Who is going to guide us through the forest to our quarry, brave warriors?" asked mighty Siegfried.

"Shall we split up before we start hunting here?" asked Hagen. "Then my lords and I could tell who are the best hunters on this foray into the woods. Let us share the huntsmen and hounds between us and each take the direction he likes—and then all honor to him that hunts best!" At this, the hunters quickly dispersed.

"I do not need any hounds." said lord Siegfried, "except for one tracker so well fleshed that he recognizes the tracks which the game leave through the wood: then we shall not fail to find our quarry."

An old huntsman took a good sleuth-hound and quickly led the lord to where there was game in abundance. The party chased everything that was roused from its lair, as good hunting-men still do today. Bold Siegfried of the Netherlands killed every beast that his hound started, for his hunter was so swift that nothing could elude him. Thus, versatile as he was, Siegfried outshone all the others in that hunt.

The very first kill was when he brought down a strong young tusker,[3] after which he soon chanced on an enormous lion. When his hound had roused it he laid a keen arrow to his bow and shot it so that it dropped in its tracks at the third bound. Siegfried's fellow-huntsmen acclaimed him for this shot. Next, in swift succession, he killed a wisent, an elk, four mighty aurochs,[4] and a fierce and monstrous buck—so well mounted was he that nothing, be it hart or hind, could evade him. His hound then came upon a great boar, and, as this turned to flee, the champion hunter at once blocked his path, bringing him to bay; and when in a trice the beast sprang at the hero in a fury, Siegfried slew him with his sword, a feat no other hunter could have performed with such ease. After the felling of this boar, the tracker was returned to his leash and Siegfried's splendid bag was made known to the Burgundians.

---

3. **tusker** (tusk′ ər): Wild boar.
4. **wisent** (vē′ zənt) . . . **aurochs** (ô′ räks′): The European bison and wild oxen.

"If it is not asking too much, lord Siegfried," said his companions of the chase, "do leave some of the game alive for us. You are emptying the hills and woods for us today." At this the brave knight had to smile.

There now arose a great shouting of men and clamor of hounds on all sides, and the tumult grew so great that the hills and the forest re-echoed with it—the huntsmen had unleashed no fewer than four and twenty packs! Thus, many beasts had to lose their lives there, since each of these hunters was hoping to bring it about that *he* should be given the high honors of the chase. But when mighty Siegfried appeared beside the campfire there was no chance of that.

The hunt was over, yet not entirely so. Those who wished to go to the fire brought the hides of innumerable beasts, and game in plenty—what

SIEGFRIED'S DEATH
Cover illustration showing a detail from the Hundeshagen Codex, the only surviving Nibelungen manuscript with illustrations
Handschriftenabteilung, Staatsbibliothek Preussischer Kulturbesitz, West Berlin, Germany

5 **Clarification** Note how the narrative shifts here and addresses the reader directly.

6 **Enrichment** The term *quiver*, from the vocabulary list, has an interesting history. It is from the Old French word *cuivre* and is probably of Teutonic (Germanic) origin. Many French words are of German rather than Latin origin.

7 **Discussion** Ask students what qualities convey the sense that Siegfried is "the very image of a hunting man."

loads of it they carried back to the kitchen to the royal retainers! And now the noble King had it announced to those fine hunters that he wished to take his repast, and there was one great blast of the horn to tell them that he was back in camp.

At this, one of Siegfried's huntsmen said: "Sir, I have heard a horn-blast telling us to return to our lodges.—I shall answer it." There was much blowing to summon the companions.

"Let us quit the forest, too," said lord Siegfreid. His mount carried him at an even pace, and the others hastened away with him but with the noise of their going they started a savage bear, a very fierce beast.

"I shall give our party some good entertainment," he said over his shoulder. "Loose the hound, for I can see a bear which will have to come back to our lodges with us. It will not be able to save itself unless it runs very fast." The hound was unleashed, and the bear made off at speed. Siegfried meant to ride it down but soon found that his way was blocked and his intention thwarted, while the mighty beast fancied it would escape from its pursuer. But the proud knight leapt from his horse and started to chase it on foot, and the animal, quite off its guard, failed to elude him. And so he quickly caught and bound it, without having wounded it at all—nor could the beast use either claws or teeth on the man. Siegfried tied it to his saddle, mounted his horse, and in his high-spirited fashion led it to the campfire in order to amuse the good knights.

And in what magnificent style Siegfried rode! He bore a great spear, stout of shaft and broad of head; his handsome sword reached down to his spurs; and the fine horn which this lord carried was of the reddest gold. Nor have I ever heard tell of a better hunting outfit: he wore a surcoat of costly black silk and a splendid hat of sable,[5] and you should have seen the gorgeous silken tassels on his quiver, which was covered in panther-skin for the sake of its fragrant odor![6] He also bore a bow so

---

5. **surcoat . . . sable** (sā′ bəl): A surcoat is a loose, short cloak worn over armor, and sable is the costly fur of the marten.
6. **panther-skin . . . odor:** The odor of panther-skin was supposed to lure other animals and therefore help with the hunt.

strong that apart from Siegfried any who wished to span it would have had to use a rack. His hunting suit was all of otter-skin, varied throughout its length with furs of other kinds from whose shining hair clasps of gold gleamed out on either side of this daring lord of the hunt. The handsome sword that he wore was Balmung, a weapon so keen and with such excellent edges that it never failed to bite when swung against a helmet. No wonder this splendid hunter was proud and gay. And (since I am bound to tell you all) know that his quiver was full of good arrows with gold mountings and heads a span[7] in width, so that any beast they pierced must inevitably soon die.

Thus the noble knight rode along, the very image of a hunting man. Gunther's attendants saw him coming and ran to meet him to take his horse—tied to whose saddle he led a mighty bear! On dismounting, he loosed the bonds from its muzzle and paws, whereupon all the hounds that saw it instantly gave tongue. The beast made for the forest and the people were seized with panic. Affrighted by the tumult, the bear strayed into the kitchen—and how the cooks scuttled from their fire at its approach! Many caldrons were sent flying and many fires were scattered, while heaps of good food lay among the ashes. Lords and retainers leapt from their seats, the bear became infuriated, and the King ordered all the hounds on their leashes to be loosed—and if all had ended well they would have had a jolly day! Bows and spears were no longer left idle, for the brave ones ran toward the bear, yet there were so many hounds in the way that none dared shoot. With the whole mountain thundering with people's cries the bear took to flight before the hounds and none could keep up with it but Siegfried, who ran it down and then dispatched it with his sword. The bear was later carried to the campfire, and all who had witnessed this feat declared that Siegfried was a very powerful man.

The proud companions were then summoned to table. There were a great many seated in that meadow. Piles of sumptuous dishes were set before the noble huntsmen, but the butlers who were to

---

7. **span:** Nine inches

Grammar in Action

Comparatives and Superlatives

Perhaps the most familiar example of a superlative, a form that compares adjectives or adverbs to three or more other things, is from *Sleeping Beauty*: "Mirror, Mirror on the wall: who is the fairest of them all?"

Most adjectives and adverbs have three forms: the positive, comparative, and superlative. For example:

POSITIVE: The CD player is cool.
COMPARATIVE: Jason's CD is cooler than Judy's.

SUPERLATIVE: My CD is the coolest of all.

The positive form is descriptive without being comparative. The comparative form should be used to compare two things. The superlative is used when comparing three or more things.

Siegfried's horn was described as being made of "the reddest gold." In other words, it was the most red of all gold. Furthermore, Siegfried says: "Unless we hunters are *better* looked after, I'll not be a companion of the hunt." He is using the comparative form.

Student Activity 1. Find additional passages in the story where comparatives and superlatives are used. Explain how this language contributes pour their wine were very slow to appear. Yet knights could not be better cared for than they and if only no treachery had been lurking in their minds those warriors would have been above reproach.

"Seeing that we are being treated to such a variety of dishes from the kitchen," said lord Siegfried, "I fail to understand why the butlers bring us no wine. Unless we hunters are better looked after, I'll not be a companion of the hunt. I thought I had deserved better attention."

"We shall be very glad to make amends to you for our present lack," answered the perfidious[8] King from his table. "This is Hagen's fault—he wants us to die of thirst."

"My very dear lord," replied Hagen of Troneck, "I thought the day's hunting would be away in the Spessart and so I sent the wine there. If we go without drink today I shall take good care that it does not happen again."

"Damn those fellows!" said lord Siegfried. "It was arranged that they were to bring along seven panniers of spiced wine and mead[9] for me. Since that proved impossible, we should have been placed nearer the Rhine."

"You brave and noble knights," said Hagen of Troneck, "I know a cool spring nearby—do not be offended!—let us go there."—A proposal which (as it turned out) was to bring many knights into jeopardy.

Siegfried was tormented by thirst and ordered the board to be removed all the sooner in his eagerness to go to that spring at the foot of the hills. And now the knights put their treacherous plot into execution.

Word was given for the game which Siegfried had killed to be conveyed back to Worms on wagons, and all who saw it gave him great credit for it.

Hagan of Troneck broke his faith with Siegfried most grievously, for as they were leaving to go to the spreading lime-tree he said: "I have often been told that no one can keep up with Lady Kriemhild's lord when he cares to show his speed. I wish he would show it us now."

"You can easily put it to the test by racing me to the brook," replied gallant Siegfried of the Netherlands. "Then those who see it shall declare the winner."

"I accept your challenge," said Hagen.

"Then I will lie down in the grass at your feet, as a handicap," replied brave Siegfried, much to Gunther's satisfaction. "And I will tell you what more I shall do. I will carry all my equipment with me, my spear and my shield and all my hunting clothes." And he quickly strapped on his quiver and sword. The two men took off their outer clothing and stood there in their white vests. Then they ran through the clover like a pair of wild panthers. Siegfried appeared first at the brook.

Gunther's magnificent guest who excelled so many men in all things quickly unstrapped his sword, took off his quiver, and after leaning his great spear against a branch of the lime, stood beside the rushing brook. Then he laid down his shield near the flowing water, and although he was very thirsty he most courteously refrained from drinking until the King had drunk. Gunther thanked him very ill for this.

The stream was cool, sweet, and clear. Gunther stooped to its running waters and after drinking stood up and stepped aside. Siegfried in turn would have liked to do the same, but he paid for his good manners. For now Hagen carried Siegfried's sword and bow beyond his reach, ran back for the spear, and searched for the sign on the brave man's tunic. Then, as Siegfried bent over the brook and drank, Hagen hurled the spear at the cross, so that the hero's heart's blood leapt from the wound and splashed against Hagen's clothes. No warrior will ever do a darker deed. Leaving the spear fixed in Siegfried's heart, he fled in wild desperation, as he had never fled before from any man.

When lord Siegfried felt the great wound, maddened with rage he bounded back from the stream with the long shaft jutting from his heart. He was hoping to find either his bow or his sword, and, had he succeeded in doing so, Hagen would have had his pay. But finding no sword, the gravely

---

8. **perfidious** (pər fid′ ē əs) *adj.*: Treacherous.
9. **panniers** (pan′ yərz) . . . **mead** (mēd): Panniers are baskets and mead is an alcoholic liquor made of fermented honey and water

8 **Enrichment** Worms is a city in Germany.

9 **Enrichment** Here the term *lime–tree* does not refer to the common green citrus fruit, but is an old form for the linden, a tree with large green leaves and yellow flowers. Its flowers are famous for helping bees produce honey.

to the mood and atmosphere of the tale.

Student Activity 2. Write a brief description of your most favorite and least favorite foods. Use comparative and superlative adjectives to create a hierarchy of edibles.

10 Discussion Be sure to point out to students the repetition of d's in the passage. The phrase "damage is done" is a cliché of alliteration.

Cultural Note The composer Richard Wagner was greatly inspired by The *Nibelungelied*. He wrote four dramatic operas based on the epic. The style of his music is considered meliorating and serious. For more about his work, see the Cross Currents section on page 653.

Cooperative Learning Translating a text from one literary form to another may be a challenging exercise. Divide the class into small groups and have each team select a different passage. Have them rewrite the section in verse form. A further challenge would be to have them use the original form, which had a rhyme pattern of *aabb* with each line consisting of six syllables, then seven, then six, and so on.

wounded man had nothing but his shield. Snatching this from the bank he ran at Hagen, and King Gunther's vassal was unable to elude him. Siegfried was wounded to death, yet he struck so powerfully that he sent many precious stones whirling from the shield as it smashed to pieces. Gunther's noble guest would dearly have loved to avenge himself. Hagen fell reeling under the weight of the blow and the riverside echoed loudly. Had Siegfried had his sword in his hand it would have been the end of Hagen, so enraged was the wounded man, as indeed he had good cause to be.

The hero's face had lost its color and he was no longer able to stand. His strength had ebbed away, for in the field of his bright countenance he now displayed Death's token. Soon many fair ladies would be weeping for him.

The lady Kriemhild's lord fell among the flowers, where you could see the blood surging from his wound. Then—and he had cause—he rebuked those who had plotted his foul murder. "You vile cowards," he said as he lay dying. "What good has my service done me now that you have slain me? I was always loyal to you, but now I have paid for it. Alas, you have wronged your kinsmen so that all who are born in days to come will be dishonored by your deed. You have cooled your anger on me beyond all measure. You will be held in contempt and stand apart from all good warriors."

The knights all ran to where he lay wounded to death. It was a sad day for many of them. Those who were at all loyal-hearted mourned for him, and this, as a gay and valiant knight, he had well deserved.

The King of Burgundy too lamented Siegfried's death.

10 "There is no need for the doer of the deed to weep when the damage is done," said the dying man. "He should be held up to scorn. It would have been better left undone."

"I do not know what you are grieving for," said Hagen fiercely. "All our cares and sorrows are over and done with. We shall not find many who will dare oppose us now. I am glad I have put an end to his supremacy."

"You may well exult," said Siegfried. "But had I known your murderous bent I should easily have guarded my life from you. I am sorry for none so much as my wife, the lady Kriemhild. May God have mercy on me for ever having got a son who in years to come will suffer the reproach that his kinsmen were murderers. If I had the strength I would have good reason to complain. But if you feel at all inclined to do a loyal deed for anyone, noble King," continued the mortally wounded man, "let me commend my dear sweetheart to your mercy. Let her profit from being your sister. By the virtue of all princes, stand by her loyally! No lady was ever more greatly wronged through her dear friend. As to my father and his vassals, they will have long to wait for me."

The flowers everywhere were drenched with blood. Siegfried was at grips with Death, yet not for long, since Death's sword ever was too sharp. And now the warrior who had been so brave and gay could speak no more.

When those lords saw that the hero was dead they laid him on a shield that shone red with gold, and they plotted ways and means of concealing the fact that Hagen had done the deed. "A disaster has befallen us," many of them said. "You must all hush it up and declare with one voice that Siegfried rode off hunting alone and was killed by robbers as he was passing through the forest."

"I shall take him home," said Hagen of Troneck. "It is all one to me if the woman who made Brunhild so unhappy should come to know of it. It will trouble me very little, however much she weeps."

Reader's Response *Hagen says, "All our cares and sorrows are over and done with," but others say, "A disaster has befallen us." Which opinion do you think is more accurate? Explain. What do you think will happen next?*

THINKING ABOUT THE SELECTION

Interpreting

1. (a) In the opening dialogue between Kriemhild and Siegfried, how do you think she feels about her relatives? (b) What does Siegfried say about them and what does this indicate to you about his character?
2. (a) Describe Kriemhild's dream. (b) Interpret it.
3. (a) Why do you think so much time and attention are given to Siegfried's pursuit of the bear? (b) What is the tone of this passage?
4. Why does it seem strange that Gunther and Hagen kill Siegfried?

Applying

5. The writer Robert Service writes, "Fate has written a tragedy; its name is 'The Human Heart.'"
   (a) Explain how his words relate to Siegfried.
   (b) Explain how they relate to life in general.

ANALYZING LITERATURE

Understanding the Tragic Flaw

Ties of kinship and loyal friendship held medieval society together. In *The Nibelungenlied* we see that betrayal of even the least of these ties leads to the collapse of social hierarchy and thus to large-scale destruction. This betrayal is inevitably linked to the flawed nature of the epic hero or heroine. Siegfried's betrayal of Brunhild is thoughtless and thus linked to his rashness and consuming love. Gunther's and Hagen's betrayal of Siegfried is caused by blind love and loyalty. It seems that the inborn nature of these people leads inevitably to betrayal. The destruction that follows is fated, and the characters never hesitate or question their own actions. Therefore, Kriemhild sees in advance that Siegfried will die because it is fated.

In spite of Siegfried's mistake, he does not deserve to die, and Gunther betrays his friendship by participating in the murder and breaking his blood ties with Kriemhild. All the actions have consequences. Selfish behavior is ultimately self-destructive because it destroys society, which consists of many bonds and ties with others.

1. (a) What other signs can you find of Siegfried's thoughtlessness? (b) Explain its cause.
2. What signs can you find of Hagen's vengefulness?
3. Explain whether these characters control their fates.

CRITICAL THINKING AND READING

Understanding Hunting Rituals

A ritual is made up of set forms and rites. Although hunting was necessary for survival in the Middle Ages, it was also a type of ritual with almost religious significance. Noblemen proved their courage and strength by hunting large game. The larger the animal, the greater the prestige of the hunter. Siegfried's pursuit of beasts proves him to be the greatest hero in this story, where hunting is a sort of contest, but one in which competing hunters are supposed to cooperate. Thus, hunting reinforces bonds of kinship and friendship.

In medieval literature hunting often symbolizes the quest for truth. In the hunt the hero confronts certain aspects of himself and reevaluates his place in society. The heroic hunter prefers to meet his prey in what almost becomes hand-to-hand combat. As he confronts the boar, he confronts his own natural instincts of survival.

In medieval romance and epic, the hunter often becomes the hunted. This reversal is as old as the Greek myth of Actaeon, who was torn to pieces by his own dogs. Thus, the fragility of life is underscored, and the hero identifies with his prey. The hunt is also a chivalrous pursuit. The hero faces the animal directly. He is supposed to fight only the strongest animals or most worthy opponents. The contests are to be won fairly. When men hunt men, an unnatural pursuit, they can win only by betrayal. Thus, Siegfried's openness in the hunt contrasts with Hagen's and Gunther's cowardice.

1. (a) What is the role of the dogs in the hunt? (b) Do they have human equivalents in this passage? Explain.
2. (a) Explain whether you regard the hunting scene as realistic. (b) What do you think is its purpose?
3. How does Siegfried's death become part of the hunting ritual?

THINKING AND WRITING

Composing Dialogue

Imagine that one of the knights loyal to Siegfried returns to tell Kriemhild what has happened. Which details would he give her of the hunt and the death of the hero? How would Kriemhild react? What words would she use to explain her response? Write your version of the conversation between the knight and Kriemhild. When you revise, make sure the language and sentiments are in keeping with their characters. Mention the main characters involved in the story. Then proofread your work. With a classmate playing the other role, present the dialogue aloud.

THE CODE OF CHIVALRY

Roots in Feudalism

The medieval chivalric code of knightly behavior evolved slowly out of the feudal system, itself the result of a fusion of German and Roman cultures. As Germanic tribes settled throughout western Europe, they adopted the popular and well established legal Roman system of land holding. Those nobles who bore arms and led warriors extended their protection to landowners who were not able to afford to defend themselves with the needed force. In exchange the nobles actually held the title to the land of those they protected. Thus the warrior caste came to hold the power and wealth in medieval Europe.

Under the reign of Charles Martel of the Franks, grandfather of Charlemagne, horsemen became essential to warfare. Having noticed that the Arab superiority in battle was linked to the domination of their armies by cavalry, he decided to form his own mounted elite. He granted land to his followers, or vassals, so that they could afford to maintain their mounted troops. These vassals parceled out their various lands to their own followers in turn. In addition, they required military service from them as part of the mutually satisfactory arrangement. The lord had a group of loyal knights ready to serve him in battle at a moment's notice. This definition of roles proved to be advantageous to all.

The knights (caballari) had to be physically strong to handle the demands of their duties. They also needed to be experienced horsemen, accustomed to the saddle and the road. In addition, it was necessary for them to be well trained in the use of weapons. They were trained in childhood to understand how their various weapons were made, and they also learned how to repair them.

Beginnings of Chivalry

The political and military landscape of the eighth and ninth centuries forced changes on the relationships that existed in earlier times. As the presence of Saracens and other invaders began to diminish by the tenth century, the importance and usefulness of these warlike qualities diminished as well. Now the potential adversary was usually not a foreigner but a more familiar face to be treated with the respect and consideration due a comrade. Moral qualities took on more and more meaning for the knights. Absolute loyalty to the lord was crucial. A courage that went beyond the merely physical had to accompany prowess. The dutiful and conscientious knight took on an obligation to defend his lord's honor and power and also to defend those weaker than himself. Above all, he could not attack those of lower social station.

Defending Christendom

As the knight fought for glory and renown, he began to offer his services to the greater glory of God. Roland defends not only Charlemagne's territory and fame, but in a larger sense Christendom. Perceval's greatest quest is to seek out the Holy Grail in a mission that is more spiritual than military. The Crusades were the crowning glory of Christian knighthood in that each vassal fought for his most powerful lord and suzerain, God himself.

NSIGHTS

THE MEDIEVAL SINGER OF LOVE SONGS COUNT VON TOGGENBURG
Illumination from the early fourteenth century

Life at Court

At court, this gallantry took on special dimensions that changed the nature of relationships between men and women. A true knight swore to defend all women against unfair oppression and to uphold their honor in every circumstance. This cult of honor was not limited to the service of women exclusively but extended itself to all social interactions at the court. The honorable knight, as chivalrous as he was constant, would be loyal to his lord, his family, and his comrades-at-arms in an unstinting way. He had to be willing to risk his life for all these people.

A Good Name

The changed circumstances brought about a novel way of viewing the purpose and duty of knighthood. Rather than seeking out material fortune, the good knight had to love honor for honor's sake. For the glory of his good name, he was to seek out adventures in which he righted wrongs, destroyed evil monsters or men, or defended the helpless without hope of recompense. He had to make good on his word. If he ever promised something would be done, it had to be accomplished no matter what travail needed to be overcome in the process. In addition, the dutiful knight also had to be unfailingly polite and courteous, even in the face of rude behavior. And he could take on only a fair or just fight.

Softening a Brutal System

Obviously, this code of chivalry was impossibly idealistic. But this view of the perfect knight, consistently offered by the *chansons de geste* (medieval epics) and by medieval romance, humanized and softened a brutal feudal system based on warlike qualities. Although chivalry reinforced the existing caste system along behavioral lines—the "lowest" members of society, the villains or peasants, were considered rude and uncultured—it also represented an attempt to check to some small degree the unrelenting oppression of this less powerful class. Mercy is a practice that can be ascribed in some part to the chivalric code.

Evidence, of course, indicates that this idealistic behavior existed mostly in the literature of the time, not in life. It is difficult to estimate how great an influence these notions would have had on the day-to-day protocol of life for the majority of people. But the portrayal of social bonds based on ideals rather than on pure practical need may well have led to greater social coherence in medieval Europe. Relationships based on material goods would have been too easily subject to change; a more permanent relationship based on moral obligation would be lasting. Such strong relationships would be the basis for a more lasting and strong community, in which whole families and villages worked together.

Eventually, chivalry died out because of its dependence on horsemanship. As longbows came increasingly into use, the knight in cumbersome armor on an easily stopped horse became very vulnerable. At various battles in the fourteenth century, the French cavalry were essentially useless in the face of the longbow and were destroyed. The idea of "fighting fair," of one knight facing another on horseback in a deadly sort of joust, died as well. Chivalry, a compelling idea, simply did not function in the real world.

CHRÉTIEN DE TROYES

Focus

More About the Author Very little is known about the author, Chrétien de Troyes. We do know that he was from Brittany, a region in northwestern France. This area is populated by Celts who fled from Britain, and who still speak a Celtic language today. Breton mythology is Celtic. The story of Perceval fits well into the traditions of dragons, enchanted forests, and mysterious elements that abound in Celtic legend.

Pronunciation Note Troyes is pronounced as *trwa*. Remind students that in French the *r* is guttural and that the final *s* is rarely pronounced.

Critical Evaluation "Perceval" is an excellent example of the poetic tradition of the Romance. The term *Romance* means different things to different people. The city of Rome figures in its base. Originally, the word referred to anything that was written in a language that was descended from Latin. We still speak of Romance languages, like Spanish, French, and Italian. Later the term was used to designate a literary narrative.

1135?–1190?

Chrétien de Troyes (cr'ā t'yan' də tr'wä') was one of the first and most gifted authors of Arthurian romance. Little is known about his life. He probably came from the town of Troyes, in the Champagne region of France. The name *Chrétien* (Christian) may simply be an indication of his religion.

Most of what we know about de Troyes is taken from his works. He seems to have been well educated, and his work reflects the inspiration of three cultures: Latin, Provençal (from southern France), and Breton (from Brittany in northwest France). Most of his romances are based on Breton mythology, known to us as Arthurian legends. His *Tristan and Iseut* has been lost, but *Yvain, Lancelot,* and *Perceval,* all tales of the knights of Arthur's Round Table, remain.

Yvain and *Lancelot* explore the conflict between love and the knight's chivalric duty to seek out new adventures and to bring greater glory to himself and to his feudal suzerain, or lord. Lancelot sacrifices his honor for his love of Guinevere, even posing as a common criminal, the ultimate dishonor, in order to save her. Yvain, on the other hand, abandons his marriage in favor of the quest for knightly glory and soon learns the foolishness of his choice.

The quest in *Perceval* is of the most perfect type, in that it is spiritual. De Troyes's version of this story is the earliest we have of the Grail legend—

the search for the Holy Grail, or the cup from which Christ drank at the Last Supper. According to medieval legend, this cup, as well as the lance that pierced Christ's side during the crucifixion, still existed and were hidden away in a magical castle. Sometime in the late Middle Ages, the legend of Arthur and his knights became inextricably linked to that of the Grail. The ultimate quest was for this mystical object, which would allow Arthur to found a new holy kingdom. However, only a pure knight would be able to find the Grail, and no knight in Arthur's kingdom was virtuous enough to find and take it. Thus, Arthur's kingdom eventually crumbled. In the Grail legend, pagan myth and Christian religion are mixed together to form the most enduring legend of the Middle Ages.

Perceval is one of the few knights virtuous enough even to see the Grail. His mother raised him in isolation because she had lost her husband and two other sons to chivalric combat. But Perceval meets some knights, and his first ambition is to be one of them. He goes to Arthur's court, becomes one of the most valiant knights, and sets out on a quest for the Grail.

In the course of his wanderings, Perceval comes upon a mysterious castle, that of the paralyzed "Fisher-King." He witnesses a strange ceremony in which a lance dripping blood and a golden vessel (the Grail) are carried around. Having been told not to speak until spoken to, he does not ask what these objects are or what the ceremony means. The next morning, when he has finally decided to ask the question, the inhabitants of the castle have disappeared. When he leaves the castle, it disappears.

Finally, he learns that had he asked the question, the Fisher-King would have been cured, Perceval himself would have earned salvation and eternal happiness, and peace would have reigned in the world. He is determined to find the Grail again and sets out on his endless quest with his friend Gauvain. Although Perceval has many adventures, de Troyes never finished the romance.

Objectives

Thematic
To appreciate the role of faith in literature

Skills
1 To understand the quest
2 To interpret symbols
3 To examine goals

Support Material

Teaching Portfolio

Teacher Backup, p. 725
Grammar in Action, *Hyperbole,* p. 729
Usage and Mechanics Worksheet, p. 731
Vocabulary Check , p. 732
Analyzing Literature Worksheet,

Understanding the Quest . . . , p. 733
Critical Thinking and Reading Worksheet, *Interpreting Symbols*, p. 734
Selection Test, pp. 735–736

GUIDE FOR INTERPRETING

from Perceval

Commentary

The Quest. Every worthy knight had to undertake a difficult quest. The medieval **quest** was the pursuit, through a series of adventures, or trials, of something or someone of special importance. Whatever was sought had a spiritual or personal significance. The knight had to voyage far, face monsters and evil men, and vanquish them all with his special force. Through the quest the knight matured and so became even more worthy in the eyes of the court.

The quest is Celtic, not Christian, in origin. Often, when a Celtic tribe was threatened by famine or by a neighboring tribe, the bravest of the leaders would travel by land or by sea to find a new home for his people. We know that the Celts migrated a great deal. Wales and Britanny in particular were in constant communication with each other.

By the time of Chrétien de Troyes, the quest had taken on a clearly defined spiritual dimension. Invariably, this quest is undertaken by a young, immature knight who is confident of his power and unaware of his own limitations. At some point he faces an insurmountable problem. He must admit a defeat of sorts and confess his own weakness. Then he may call for help from others. Thus, the brave knight learns that courage and force are not the only elements of a great man. He learns to participate in society, and that his importance rests in his ties to others. Only then is he granted exceptional enlightenment; he is allowed to see or understand beyond what ordinary people know. With this special knowledge, he is equipped to lead his society and to help others. Therefore, the quest is a symbol of the maturation process, with its trials and its triumphs.

Almost every medieval romance is based on this pattern. Unlike the epic hero, who stands almost alone in his glory, the medieval hero must recognize his place as a small part of the larger whole that is society. Relationships, familial or social, are crucial to him. Love, the building-block of any relationship, becomes central. The medieval hero's quest almost always involves a loved one. Perceval may seem to be an exception, but he is not. His love is for God. The love relationship that is at the core of every romance enables the hero to take a fuller part in the world around him. This relationship is what distinguishes the hero of the romance from the epic hero.

Writing

In modern society, a quest could be a long journey, hard work, a series of difficult decisions, perhaps even some personal danger. The most demanding quest could include all these aspects. Make a list of ten things that you would be willing to strive for in this way.

Literary Focus Arthurian legend translates well to film. Ask students if they have seen any of the movies that have been made about variations of the legend. Mention *Excalibur, Camelot,* and *The Sword in the Stone* by Disney. Ask students why they believe these shows are so popular.

Writing/Prior Knowledge Have students discuss their own sense of adventure. Have them think back to the childhood adventures that entailed trips to the supermarket or barbershop when a short journey might take on mythic dimensions for an active youngster's mind. Discuss their sense of what mystery might be involved in such memories.

ESL Teaching Strategy Ask ESL students if they ever consider learning English to be both a quest and an adventure. Have them mention what difficulties they have already overcome and list what hurdles they still face.

Teaching Tenth-Grade Students Tenth-grade students should find the tale of Perceval quite accessible. Tell students to keep in mind that Perceval is just a youth. Have them picture someone their own age as they read about his quest.

> **Vocabulary**
> Preteach the following vocabulary words:
> sovereign (säv´ rən) *adj.*: Chief, superior
> elated (i lāt´ əd) *v.*: Happy, joyful
> serene (sə rēn´) *adj.*: Clear, calm, peaceful
> ebony (eb´ ən ē) *n.*: Hard durable wood, black
> legate (leg´ it) *n.*: Envoy, assistant to governor
> nutmeg (nut´ meg) *n.*: Aromatic seed
> pomegranate (päm´ gran´ it) *n.*: A round fruit

from # Perceval

Chrétien de Troyes

The Grail

translated by Ruth Harwood Cline

The youth began his journey from
the castle, and the daytime whole
he did not meet one living soul:
no creature from the wide earth's span,
5 no Christian woman, Christian man
who could direct him on his way.
The young man did not cease to pray
the sovereign father, God, Our Lord,
if He were willing, to accord
10 that he would find his mother still
alive and well. He reached a hill
and saw a river at its base.
So rapid was the current's pace,
so deep the water, that he dared
15 not enter it, and he declared,
"Oh God Almighty! It would seem,
if I could get across this stream,
I'd find my mother, if she's living."
He rode the bank with some misgiving
20 and reached a cliff, but at that place
the water met the cliff's sheer face
and kept the youth from going through.
A little boat came into view;
it headed down the river, floating
25 and carrying two men out boating.
The young knight halted there and waited.
He watched the way they navigated
and thought that they would pass the place
he waited by the cliff's sheer face.
30 They stayed in midstream, where they stopped
and took the anchor, which they dropped.
The man afore,[1] a fisher, took

a fish to bait his line and hook;
in size the little fish he chose
35 was larger than a minnow grows.
The knight, completely at a loss,
not knowing how to get across,
first greeted them, then asked the pair,
"Please, gentlemen, nearby is there
40 a bridge to reach the other side?"
To which the fisherman replied,
"No, brother, for besides this boat,
the one in which we are afloat,
which can't bear five men's weight as charge,
45 there is no other boat as large
for twenty miles each way and more,
and you can't cross on horseback, for
there is no ferry, bridge, nor ford."
"Tell me," he answered, "by Our Lord,
50 where I may find a place to stay."
The fisherman said, "I should say
you'll need a roof tonight and more,
so I will lodge you at my door.
First find the place this rock is breached
55 and ride uphill, until you've reached
the summit of the cliff," he said.
"Between the wood and riverbed
you'll see, down in the valley wide,
the manor house where I reside."
60 The knight rode up the cliff until
he reached the summit of the hill.
He looked around him from that stand
but saw no more than sky and land.
He cried, "What have I come to see?
65 Stupidity and trickery!
May God dishonor and disgrace

---

1. **afore** (ə fôr'): Before.

the man who sent me to this place!
He had the long way round in mind,
when he told me that I would find
a manor when I reached the peak.
Oh, fisherman, why did you speak?
For if you said it out of spite,
you tricked me badly!" He caught sight
of a tower starting to appear
down in a valley he was near,
and as the tower came into view,
if people were to search, he knew,
as far as Beirut,[2] they would not
find any finer tower or spot.
The tower was dark gray stone, and square,
and flanked by lesser towers, a pair.
Before the tower the hall was laid;
before the hall was the arcade.[3]
On toward the tower the young man rode
in haste and called the man who showed
the way to him a worthy guide.
No longer saying he had lied,
he praised the fisherman, elated
to find his lodgings as he stated.
The youth went toward the gate and found
the drawbridge lowered to the ground.
He rode across the drawbridge span.
Four squires awaited the young man.
Two squires came up to help him doff
his arms and took his armor off.
The third squire led his horse away
to give him fodder, oats, and hay.
The fourth brought a silk cloak, new-made,
and led him to the hall's arcade,
which was so fine, you may be sure
you'd not find, even if you were
to search as far as Limoges,[4] one
as splendid in comparison.
The young man paused in the arcade,
until the castle's master made
two squires escort him to the hall.
The young man entered with them all
and found the hall was square inside:

---

2. Beirut (bā rōōt'): The capital of Lebanon and a seaport on the Mediterranean.

3. arcade (är kād') *n.*: A passage with an arched roof or any covered passageway.

4. Limoges (lē mōzh'): A city in west central France.

THE DAMSEL OF THE HOLY GRAIL
(The tradition that the Grail was carried by a damsel goes back to the original Grail romance, Chrétien de Troyes's *Perceval*. Rossetti has emphasized the religious symbolism by adding the dove as a symbol of the Holy Spirit.)
The Tate Gallery

Humanities Note
Fine art, *The Damsel of the Holy Grail* by Dante Gabriel Rossetti. The British artist Dante Gabriel Rossetti (1828–1882) was a poet as well as a painter. *The Damsel of the Holy Grail* is a watercolor painted in 1857. The single figure that fills the picture is fashioned with a spare and angular grace. Her hair and expression provide an almost mystical appearance. The symbolism of the dove and the covered basket of bread enhance this effect.

The inspiration for this painting came from the fertile imagination of the artist. His model for this and many other paintings was Elizabeth Siddal, a fellow poet and painter, who became his wife.

You might want to use the following questions to discuss the art:
1. What do you think the dove symbolizes in this painting?
2. Why do you think the artist chose to fill the entire picture with a single figure?
3. What adjectives would you use to describe the damsel?
4. What is the impression you receive when viewing this illustration for the first time?

3 **Discussion** The reference to Beirut is important because it shows what an exaggeration he is trying to make. Today we might say something like "all the way to China" to make a similar point. Note that Beirut is in the Middle East.

4 **Discussion** Note the use of figurative language to make a simple description. Discuss with students whether this improves the passage.

5 **Enrichment** *Demoiselle* is a French word for young lady. Some students will be more familiar with the term *mademoiselle*.

6 **Discussion** Discuss why so much space is given to this elaborate description.

4

it was as long as it was wide;
110 and in the center of its span
he saw a handsome nobleman
with grayed hair, sitting on a bed.
The nobleman wore on his head
a mulberry-black sable cap
115 and wore a dark silk robe and wrap.
He leaned back in his weakened state
and let his elbow take his weight.
Between four columns, burning bright,
a fire of dry logs cast its light.
120 In order to enjoy its heat,
four hundred men could find a seat
around the outsized fire, and not
one man would take a chilly spot.
The solid fireplace columns could
125 support the massive chimney hood,
which was of bronze, built high and wide.
The squires, one squire on either side,
appeared before their lord foremost
and brought the youth before his host.
130 He saw the young man, whom he greeted.
"My friend," the nobleman entreated,
"don't think me rude not to arise;
I hope that you will realize
that I cannot do so with ease."
135 "Don't even mention it, sir, please,
I do not mind," replied the boy,
"may Heaven give me health and joy."
The lord rose higher on the bed,
as best he could, with pain, and said,
140 "My friend, come nearer, do not be
embarrassed or disturbed by me,
for I command you to come near.
Come to my side and sit down here."
The nobleman began to say,
145 "From where, sir, did you come today?"
He said, "This morning, sir, I came
from Belrepeire, for that's its name."
"So help me God," the lord replied,
"you must have had a long day's ride:
150 to start before the light of morn
before the watchman blew his horn."
"Sir, I assure you, by that time
the morning bells had rung for prime,"[5]

---

5. prime: The first hour of the daylight, usually 6 A.M.

the young man made the observation.
155 While they were still in conversation,
a squire entered through the door
and carried in a sword he wore
hung from his neck and which thereto
he gave the rich man, who withdrew
160 the sword halfway and checked the blade
to see where it was forged and made,
which had been written on the sword.
The blade was wrought, observed the lord,
of such fine steel, it would not break
165 save with its bearer's life at stake
on one occasion, one alone,
a peril that was only known
to him who forged and tempered it.
The squire said, "Sir, if you permit,
170 your lovely blonde niece sent this gift,
and you will never see or lift
a sword that's lighter for its strength,
considering its breadth and length.
Please give the sword to whom you choose,
175 but if it goes to one who'll use
the sword that he is given well,
you'll greatly please the demoiselle.
The forger of the sword you see
has never made more swords than three,
180 and he is going to die before
he ever forges any more.
No sword will be quite like this sword."
Immediately the noble lord
bestowed it on the newcomer,
185 who realized that its hangings were
a treasure and of worth untold.
The pommel[6] of the sword was gold,
the best Arabian or Grecian;
the sheath's embroidery gold Venetian.
190 Upon the youth the castle's lord
bestowed the richly mounted sword
and said to him, "This sword, dear brother,
was destined for you and none other.
I wish it to be yours henceforth.
195 Gird on the sword and draw it forth."
He thanked the lord, and then the knight
made sure the belt was not too tight,
and girded on the sword, and took

---

6. pommel (pum´ əl) *n*.: The knob on the end of the hilt of a sword or dagger.

Grammar in Action

Hyperbole Often writers use exaggerations in order to make their writing effective and memorable. These exaggerations are called *hyperbole*.

SIMPLE LANGUAGE: The books were *very heavy*.

HYPERBOLIC LANGUAGE: The *towering stack of leaden* books was so heavy that each and every word on the page *weighed like an unchiseled boulder*.

Note how the first description is bland and forgettable. The second is dramatic, extravagant, and overblown.

Perceval is a text full of hyperbole.

In order to enjoy its heat
four hundred men could find a seat
around the outsized fire, and not
one man would take a chilly spot.

A simpler description would be: The fire was large.

the bare blade out for a brief look.
Then in the sheath it was replaced:
it looked well hanging at his waist
and even better in his fist.
It seemed as if it would assist
the youth in any time of need
to do a brave and knightly deed.
Beside the brightly burning fire
the youth turned round and saw a squire,
who had his armor in his care,
among the squires standing there.
He told this squire to hold the sword
and took his seat beside the lord,
who honored him as best he might.
The candles cast as bright a light
as could be found in any manor.
They chatted in a casual manner.
Out of a room a squire came, clasping
a lance of purest white: while grasping
the center of the lance, the squire
walked through the hall between the fire
and two men sitting on the bed.
All saw him bear, with measured tread,
the pure white lance. From its white tip
a drop of crimson blood would drip
and run along the white shaft and
drip down upon the squire's hand,
and then another drop would flow.
The knight who came not long ago
beheld this marvel, but preferred
not to inquire why it occurred,
for he recalled the admonition
the lord made part of his tuition,[7]
since he had taken pains to stress
the dangers of loquaciousness.[8]
The young man thought his questions might
make people think him impolite,
and that's why he did not inquire.
Two more squires entered, and each squire
held candelabra, wrought of fine
pure gold with niello work design.[9]
The squires with candelabra fair
were an extremely handsome pair.

At least ten lighted candles blazed
in every holder that they raised.
The squires were followed by a maiden
245 who bore a grail, with both hands laden.
The bearer was of noble mien,[10]
well dressed, and lovely, and serene,
and when she entered with the grail,
the candles suddenly grew pale,
250 the grail cast such a brilliant light,
as stars grow dimmer in the night
when sun or moonrise makes them fade.
A maiden after her conveyed
a silver platter past the bed.
255 The grail, which had been borne ahead,
was made of purest, finest gold
and set with gems; a manifold
display of jewels of every kind,
the costliest that one could find
260 in any place on land or sea,
the rarest jewels there could be,
let not the slightest doubt be cast.
The jewels in the grail surpassed
all other gems in radiance.
265 They went the same way as the lance:
they passed before the lord's bedside
to another room and went inside.
The young man saw the maids' procession
and did not dare to ask a question
270 about the grail or whom they served;
the wise lord's warning he observed,
for he had taken it to heart.
I fear he was not very smart;
I have heard warnings people give:
275 that one can be too talkative,
but also one can be too still.
But whether it was good or ill,
I do not know, he did not ask.
The squires who were assigned the task
280 of bringing in the water and
the cloths obeyed the lord's command.
The men who usually were assigned
performed these tasks before they dined.
They washed their hands in water, warmed,

---

7. the admonition . . . tuition: The warning that the lord made part of his teaching.

8. loquaciousness (lō kwā′ shəs nis) *n*.: Talkativeness.

9. niello (nē el′ ō) **work design:** Deep black inlaid work used to decorate metal.

---

10. grail (grāl) **. . . mien** (mēn): The grail is the legendary cup or platter used by Jesus at the Last Supper and by Joseph of Arimathea to collect drops of Jesus' blood at the crucifixion. Mien signifies "appearance."

7 **Discussion** Discuss with students what might be meant by describing the sword as "better in his fist."

8 **Discussion** Point out the alliteration in this line. Ask students to find other alliterative passages in the text.

Student Activity 1. Find additional passages in *Perceval* where hyperbole is used. Judge how they stand out.

Student Activity 2. Write a brief description of an everyday household task. Then use hyperbolic language to exaggerate the difficulty of the undertaking.

Illustrated manuscript, *Kundry and Feirefiz Ride to the Grail Castle Where a Feast Is Held*, artist unknown. This is an illumination from the German manuscript of *Perceval* from the middle of the thirteenth century. In an unusual approach, this artist shows three different scenes from the text displayed in horizontal bands on a single page. The first band shows Arthur and King Gramoflanz in their tents; the second concerns their meeting; the bottom band shows Perceval, Kundry, and Feirefiz approaching the Grail Castle. Each scene is crowded with figures and detail resulting in a lively presentation of the story.

You might want to use the following questions to discuss the art:

1. What have you ever seen that is similar to this multiple format?
2. Does this artist attempt to show depth through the use of perspective?
3. How would you respond if someone criticized this artist for being too ambitious in this illustration?
4. What could be changed to improve this work of art?

and then two squires, so I'm informed,
brought in the ivory tabletop,
made of one piece: they had to stop
and hold it for a while before
the lord and youth, until two more
squires entered, each one with a trestle.[11]
The trestles had two very special,
rare properties, which they contained
since they were built, and which remained
in them forever: they were wrought
of ebony, a wood that's thought
to have two virtues: it will not
ignite and burn and will not rot;
these dangers cause no harm nor loss.
They laid the tabletop across
the trestles, and the cloth above.
What shall I say? To tell you of
the cloth is far beyond my scope.
No legate, cardinal, or pope
has eaten from a whiter one.
The first course was of venison,
a peppered haunch, cooked in its fat,
accompanied by a clear wine that
was served in golden cups, a pleasant,
delicious drink. While they were present
a squire carved up the venison.
He set the peppered haunch upon
a silver platter, carved the meat,
and served the slices they would eat
by placing them on hunks of bread.
Again the grail passed by the bed,
and still the youth remained reserved
about the grail and whom they served.
he did not ask, because he had
been told so kindly it was bad
to talk too much, and he had taken
these words to heart. He was mistaken;
though he remembered, he was still
much longer than was suitable.
At every course, and in plain sight,
the grail was carried past the knight,
who did not ask whom they were serving,
although he wished to know, observing

in silence that he ought to learn
about it prior to his return.
330 So he would ask: before he spoke
he'd wait until the morning broke,
and he would ask a squire to tell,
once he had told the lord farewell
and all the others in his train.
335 He put the matter off again
and turned his thoughts toward drink and food.
They brought, and in no stingy mood,
the foods and different types of wine,
which were delicious, rich and fine.
340 The squires were able to provide
the lord and young knight at his side
with every course a count, king, queen,
and emperor eat by routine.
At dinner's end, the two men stayed
345 awake and talked, while squires made
the beds and brought them fruit: they ate
the rarest fruits: the nutmeg, date,
fig, clove, and pomegranate red.
With Alexandrian gingerbread,
350 electuaries[12] at the end,
restoratives, a tonic blend,
and pliris archonticum
for settling his stomachum.
Then various liqueurs were poured
355 for them to sample afterward:
straight piment, which did not contain
sweet honey or a single grain
of pepper, wine of mulberries,
clear syrups, other delicacies.
360 The youth's astonishment persisted;
he did not know such things existed.
"Now, my dear friend," the great lord said,
"the time has come to go to bed.
I'll seek my room—don't think it queer—
365 and you will have your bed out here
and may lie down at any hour.
I do not have the slightest power
over my body anymore
and must be carried to my door."
370 Four nimble servants, strongly set,

---

11. **trestle** (tres´ əl) *n.*: A frame consisting of a horizontal
beam fastened to two pairs of spreading legs.

---

12. **electuaries** (ē lek´ choo er´ ēz): Medicines made by
mixing drugs with honey or syrup to form a paste. Pliris
archonticum, mentioned two lines later, is such a medicine.

9 **Discussion** *Rare* is a word that
has rich meaning. It can mean
thin, uncommon, or excellent.
Discuss with students what they
think its meaning is here.

10 **Discussion** *Ebony* commonly
refers to the color black. Here it
means a tree of very dark wood,
probably the one from which
Christ's cross was made. Discuss
the special elements of the wood.

11 **Discussion** The feast alludes to
The Last Supper. Discuss the significance of that event with students.

12 Discussion Ask if students have ever been in a similar situation. Discuss how it feels to awaken under those circumstances.

came in and seized the coverlet
by its four corners (it was spread
beneath the lord, who lay in bed)
and carried him away to rest.
375 The others helped the youthful guest.
As he required, and when he chose,
they took his clothing off, and hose,
and put him in a bed with white,
smooth linen sheets; he slept all night
380 at peace until the morning broke.
But when the youthful knight awoke,
12 ⌐ he was the last to rise and found
that there was no one else around.
⌐ Exasperated and alone,
385 he had to get up on his own.
He made the best of it, arose,
and awkwardly drew on his hose
without a bit of help or aid.
He saw his armor had been laid
390 at night against the dais' head
a little distance from his bed.
When he had armed himself at last,
he walked around the great hall past
the rooms and knocked at every door
395 which opened wide the night before,
but it was useless: juxtaposed,[13]
the doors were tightly locked and closed.
He shouted, called, and knocked outside,
but no one opened or replied.
400 At last the young man ceased to call,
walked to the doorway of the hall,
which opened up, and passed through there,
and went on down the castle stair.
His horse was saddled in advance.
405 The young man saw his shield and lance
were leaned against the castle wall

---

13. **juxtaposed** (juks' tə pōzd) *adj.*: Put side by side or close together.

upon the side that faced the hall.
He mounted, searched the castle whole,
but did not find one living soul,
410 one servant, or one squire around.
He hurried toward the gate and found
the men had let the drawbridge down,
so that the knight could leave the town
at any hour he wished to go.
415 His hosts had dropped the drawbridge so
the youth could cross it undeterred.
The squires were sent, the youth inferred,
out to the wood, where they were set
to checking every trap and net.
420 The drawbridge lay across the stream.
He would not wait and formed a scheme
of searching through the woods as well
to see if anyone could tell
about the lance, why it was bleeding,
425 about the grail, whom they were feeding,
and where they carried it in state.
The youth rode through the castle gate
and out upon the drawbridge plank.
Before he reached the other bank,
430 the young man started realizing
the forefeet of his horse were rising.
His horse made one great leap indeed.
Had he not jumped well, man and steed
would have been hurt. His rider swerved
435 to see what happened and observed
the drawbridge had been lifted high.
He shouted, hearing no reply,
"Whoever raised the bridge," said he,
"where are you? Come and talk to me!
440 Say something to me; come in view.
There's something I would ask of you,
some things I wanted to inquire,
some information I desire."
His words were wasted, vain and fond;
445 no one was willing to respond.

Reader's Response *Imagine that Perceval had a companion and you are this person. What advice would you have given Perceval?*

THINKING ABOUT THE SELECTION

Interpreting

1. (a) Why do you think Perceval cannot find the castle at first? (b) Why is he eventually able to find it?
2. (a) What is unusual about the Fisher-King? (b) What do you think may be causing this condition? Support your answer.
3. (a) Why does the Fisher-King give Perceval the special sword? (b) Explain the importance of this sword.
4. (a) Describe the ceremony with the Grail and the lance. (b) Why do you think the squire and the maiden carry them around again and again?
5. (a) Why does the Fisher-King have these two objects? (b) Who do you think he is?

Applying

6. Perceval has been told not to speak until spoken to and not to ask unnecessary questions. Obviously, he should have made an exception here. What situations can you think of in modern life where one should make an exception to this rule? In other words, when is it absolutely necessary to speak or to ask questions?

ANALYZING LITERATURE

Understanding the Quest

A quest usually contains some element of mystery, but this scene from Perceval is almost obscure. De Troyes wants his readers to share in the confusion felt by his young hero. Perceval is lost, and even when he is given specific directions, he cannot seem to find the castle. When he finds the castle, he does not seem to know the lord. As he eats dinner, he is witness to an odd ceremony that he does not understand. Yet he obstinately refuses to inquire about it.

The strangest element of all is that the next day there is no one in the castle. Perceval finds himself alone, full of questions, but it is too late. Only through a long and arduous search will he even find out what the castle and its lord were. In this way, Perceval is a sort of universal person. De Troyes wants the reader to see how little anyone knows, compared to divine wisdom: Human ignorance is so great that we must ask questions constantly in order to be able to live.

1. Describe Perceval's chief character traits.
2. Find at least three examples of Perceval's apparent confusion.

3. (a) In each case how might he have cleared up the confusion? (b) What is the result of his not clearing up this confusion?
4. What does Perceval learn at the end of this episode?

CRITICAL THINKING AND READING

Interpreting Symbols

A symbol is an object that stands for something beyond itself. For example, a rose might stand for, or symbolize, love, and a sword, a battle. In romance, almost every image has a symbolic meaning in addition to its literal one. For example, the cliff upon which Perceval finds himself can be said to symbolize the dangers of life, the obstacles he will meet. The river may represent his own incapacity to overcome those obstacles. The boat of the Fisher-King on the river could stand for the fragility of human life in the face of the dangers symbolized by the river and the protection of this life by unseen forces.

1. What do you think the castle symbolizes? Find evidence to support your answer.
2. What might the sword dripping blood symbolize? Find evidence to support your answer.
3. Christ has been referred to as "a fisher of men." Does this information shed light on the meaning of the Fisher-King? Explain.

THINKING AND WRITING

Examining Goals

What would be worth striving for? A car? A college education? The approval of someone you love? How would you go about achieving something that will not be given easily to you? Freewrite, exploring your answers to these questions. Then write the first draft of an essay examining your goals. Write one paragraph about something you would be willing to strive for. Describe your goal and tell why it is worth such effort. Then, in two or more paragraphs, draw up your plans. How would you go about achieving this goal? In several more paragraphs, describe the problems you think might arise during such a modern "quest." Conclude by telling how your quest would end. Do you think you can achieve this goal, or is it impossible? Explain. As you revise your work, make sure the paragraphs all fit together to make one coherent whole. Make sure your language is dramatic and appealing. Finally, proofread your essay and prepare a final draft.

MARIE DE FRANCE

c. 1155–1190

Focus

More About the Author It would be an injustice not to point out how rare it is to find a female writer in early periods of European literature. In fact, up until recent times, European women who wrote often took male pseudonyms. However, there are several female courtly poets who wrote Provençal love poems.

This would be a good opportunity to discuss with the class why students think we have so few examples of early women's writing.

Critical Evaluation We know very little about the life of Marie de France. Using the reading on page 610 as a backdrop for her life and culture, have students speculate on her character. What was she probably like? Do we as readers anticipate a different type of writing from her as a woman? Why? What types of differences could we expect? As students read through the selection, ask them to search for anything they regard as particularly feminine in the author's attitude. Then discuss whether an author's gender is important in literary criticism.

Little is known about the life of Marie de France, one of the finest storytellers of the Middle Ages. Yet her works, read by Boccaccio and Chaucer, were crucial to the development of the short story. We know that she lived and wrote in the French-speaking English court of the late twelfth century, about one hundred years after the Norman Conquest. De France was well educated and devout, undoubtedly noble, and perhaps even the illegitimate sister of Henry II of England. Her name suggests she came from France.

Her works reflect the cultural diversity of her era by combining elements of the classical, Christian, and Celtic cultures. For example, in Saint Patrick's Purgatory, which de France translated from Latin, the hero travels to another land where he learns some of the secrets of the Christian faith. The theme of a voyage to another world, usually the magical world of the dead, is typical of Celtic mythology. But here, the theme also reinforces Christian morality. The animal *Fables,* which de France translated from English, serve a similar moral purpose, which is in harmony with Aesop's classic works.

The theme of de France's most original work, the lais (lā), is passionate love rather than marital duty. The lais are short stories, written in verse, which combine folkloric elements of magic with the newly popular theme of courtly love. In an era when most marriages were not based on love, but on political or economic interest, courtly love sprang up as a radical departure from the ecclesiastically accepted norm. Courtly love was initially depicted as the hopeless adoration of a distant woman by a young man of inferior social standing. De France revised this definition of love to achieve a more realistic view of relations between the sexes. As she makes clear in her lais "Fresne," social standing should not be a concern in a relationship. Two lovers should be allowed to choose each other because of a spiritual or passionate affinity. Ideally, this choice results in marriage, and in the marriage, each partner should be loyal to the other even in the most trying of circumstances. Here, de France along with other courtly authors of the twelfth century, is setting the foundations for our more modern ideas about love.

The unnamed wife of "The Lay of the Werewolf" is tested by very trying circumstances indeed. Her husband disappears for days on end, and she suspects him of being unfaithful. The truth of his double nature drives her to the extreme of locking him into his wolfly form. The author condemns that decision with the moral absolutism of medieval Catholicism. She then has her story aim toward the earthly salvation of a man torn by the dual aspects of his good and evil nature.

Objectives

Thematic
To understand transformations in literature

Skills
1 To understand Breton Lais
2 To recognize symbolism
3 To write from different perspectives

Support Material

Teaching Portfolio
Teacher Backup, p. 737
Grammar in Action Worksheet, *Avoiding Comma Splices*, p. 741
Usage and Mechanics Worksheet, p. 743
Vocabulary Check, p. 744
Analyzing Literature Worksheet,

Understanding Breton Lais, p. 745
Critical Thinking and Reading Worksheet, *Understanding Symbolism*, p. 746
Selection Test, pp. 747–748

GUIDE FOR INTERPRETING

The Lay of the Werewolf

Commentary

Superstition and Symbol. The werewolf in "The Lay of the Werewolf" has to be read in two ways. He is the creation of superstition and is also a symbol that de France uses to reveal the dual aspect of humanity.

The ancient Greeks wrote that people could be transformed into wolves, remain in that form for years, and then return to their human form. Medieval intellectuals were ready to dismiss werewolves as mere hallucinations. Others believed these creatures truly existed and lived among them in human form. For medieval people they were either demons or men being punished for horrible sins.

This belief was fueled by the brutality of life in the Middle Ages. The natural world was still quite threatening, and wolves were the very real embodiment of that threat. They still wandered the forests of Europe and even ventured into villages at night to snatch up small livestock. Wolves were even rumored to prowl in large cities like Rome. The embattled peasants, racked by war and famine, would listen to the eerie howls with chills running down their spines. They could not help but feel that these creatures were diabolical.

As frightening as these animals were, human behavior could hardly be distinguished from the wolves' own predatory habits. Children disappeared often, perhaps carried off by wolves, but more likely abandoned in the woods by parents who could no longer afford to feed them. Only vagabonds and thieves dared to venture into those woods, and they were more terrifying than the wolves. They would murder travelers for even the smallest amount of money, so great was their misery. The brutality of life in the Middle Ages diminished the distance between human and animal behavior.

This human/bestial duality is explored on a more personal level in "The Lay of the Werewolf." The wolf behaves like the perfect courtier, saluting his king with the proper feudal gesture. It is his wife who seems less than human in her actions, which condemn her husband to life as an animal. In this reversal of expected behavior, de France contradicts the popular medieval notion that a person's appearance announces his or her character and affirms the sad reality that appearances deceive and that often good people suffer for no reason other than "bad fortune." Through her use of the werewolf, de France combats the effects of the very superstition that created such a monster.

Writing

Shape-shifting, or changing from one form to another, is a theme in many works of popular entertainment. Choose one of these works and freewrite, describing the shape-shifting.

Literary Focus Many students will be familiar with stories about the process of transformation or metamorphosis. Allow those who have read it to explain Franz Kafka's "The Metamorphosis," page 1084, in which the narrator awakes to discover that he is changed to a dung beetle. Ask students what makes movies about vampires and werewolves either comic or horrifying.

Writing/Prior Knowledge Have students discuss the best and worst transformations that could happen to them. In their dreams would they be likely to be soaring eagles or bored poodles?

ESL Teaching Strategy Pair students off and encourage native-speaking students to coach ESL students so that ESL students can develop drawings that might help describe their tales of transformation.

Teaching Tenth-Grade Students Ask tenth-grade students if they believe in Bigfoot or twentieth-century dinosaurs. Remind them that werewolves were a real threat for the medieval period. Ask them to mention places that today have to deal with the menace of animals that enter populated areas.

Vocabulary

Preteach the following vocabulary words:

esteemed (ə stēmd) v.:
   Valued, respected
vesture (ves chər) n.:
   Clothing, wrapping
raiment (ra´ mənt) n.:
   Clothing, attire
importunity (im´pôr toon´ ə tē) n.: Persistence
fealty (fē´əl tē) n.: Duty, fidelity
abases (ə bās´ əz) v.
   Lowers, brings down
chidden (chid´ ən) v.:
   Scolded, reproved

The Lay of the Werewolf

Marie de France

translated by Eugene Mason

Amongst the tales I tell you once again, I would not forget the Lay of the Werewolf. Such beasts as he are known in every land. Bisclavaret he is named in Brittany; whilst the Norman[1] calls him Garwal.

It is a certain thing, and within the knowledge of all, that many a christened man has suffered this change, and ran wild in woods, as a Werewolf. The Werewolf is a fearsome beast. He lurks within the thick forest, mad and horrible to see. All the evil that he may, he does. He goeth to and fro, about the solitary place, seeking man, in order to devour him. Hearken, now, to the adventure of the Werewolf, that I have to tell.

In Brittany there dwelt a baron who was marvelously esteemed of all his fellows. He was a stout knight, and a comely, and a man of office and repute. Right private was he to the mind of his lord, and dear to the counsel of his neighbors. This baron was wedded to a very worthy dame, right fair to see, and sweet of semblance. All his love was set on her, and all her love was given again to him. One only grief had this lady. For three whole days in every week her lord was absent from her side. She knew not where he went, nor on what errand. Neither did any of his house know the business which called him forth.

On a day when this lord was come again to his house, altogether joyous and content, the lady took him to task, right sweetly, in this fashion,

---

1. Brittany (brit′ 'n ē) ... **Norman:** Brittany is a region of northwestern France, adjacent to Normandy.

"Husband," said she, "and fair, sweet friend, I have a certain thing to pray of you. Right willingly would I receive this gift, but I fear to anger you in the asking. It is better for me to have an empty hand, than to gain hard words."

When the lord heard this matter, he took the lady in his arms, very tenderly, and kissed her.

"Wife," he answered, "ask what you will. What would you have, for it is yours already?"

"By my faith," said the lady, "soon shall I be whole. Husband, right long and wearisome are the days that you spend away from your home. I rise from my bed in the morning, sick at heart, I know not why. So fearful am I, lest you do aught to your loss, that I may not find any comfort. Very quickly shall I die for reason of my dread. Tell me now, where you go, and on what business! How may the knowledge of one who loves so closely, bring you to harm?"

"Wife," made answer the lord, "nothing but evil can come if I tell you this secret. For the mercy of God do not require it of me. If you but knew, you would withdraw yourself from my love, and I should be lost indeed."

When the lady heard this, she was persuaded that her baron sought to put her by with jesting words. Therefore she prayed and required him the more urgently, with tender looks and speech, till he was overborne, and told her all the story, hiding naught.

"Wife, I become Bisclavaret. I enter in the forest, and live on prey and roots, within the thickest of the wood."

After she had learned his secret, she prayed and entreated the more as to whether he ran in his raiment, or went spoiled of vesture.

"Wife," said he, "I go naked as a beast."

"Tell me, for hope of grace, what you do with your clothing?"

"Fair wife, that will I never. If I should lose my raiment, or even be marked as I quit my vesture, then a Werewolf I must go for all the days of my life. Never again should I become man, save in that hour my clothing were given back to me. For this reason never will I show my lair."

"Husband," replied the lady to him, "I love you better than all the world. The less cause have you for doubting my faith, or hiding any tittle from me. What savor is here of friendship? How have I made forfeit of your love; for what sin do you mis-

trust my honor? Open now your heart, and tell what is good to be known."

So at the end, outwearied and overborne by her importunity, he could no longer refrain, but told her all.

"Wife," said he, "within this wood, a little from the path, there is a hidden way, and at the end thereof an ancient chapel, where oftentimes I have bewailed my lot. Near by is a great hollow stone, concealed by a bush, and there is the secret place where I hide my raiment, till I would return to my own home."

On hearing this marvel the lady became sanguine[2] of visage, because of her exceeding fear. She dared no longer to lie at his side, and turned over

---

2. **sanguine** (saŋ' gwin) *adj.*: Reddish; ruddy.

A WEREWOLF ATTACKING A MAN
Fifteenth-century German colored woodcut

4 Enrichment *Tittle*, from the Latin word *titulus* (title or label) means "a tiny part." The word seems to sound like its meaning. Ask students to suggest other words that have this property.

Humanities Note

Woodcut, *A Werewolf Attacking a Man*, artist unknown. The earliest form of printing in Europe was the wood block of the fifteenth century. Not only was the wood block used for printing letters but also for illustrations. Images were deeply cut in reverse into soft wood. The block was then inked and pressed onto paper, leaving an image in black and white.

A Werewolf Attacking a Man is a woodcut illustration from this era.

You might want to use the following questions to discuss the art:

1. Why do you think this artist chooses to show the werewolf only as a wolf?
2. What does the illustration tell you about the nature of life in fifteenth-cen-tury Germany?
3. What details could be added to improve this work?
4. What adjectives would you use to describe this illustration?

5 Discussion Bisclavaret is tricked by his wife in his absence, and the betrayal is committed by a kiss. Discuss what the narrator is suggesting in this passage. Have them define *treachery*.

6 Discussion Although the werewolf cannot speak, he can most certainly bark and growl. Ask students if this line should be read straightforwardly. Discuss what humor might be suggested by the claim "he cannot speak."

7 Discussion The translator's choice of the term *venery* is interesting. Although the word is from the old French term *venerie*, to hunt, it also has an etymological twin, *venery*, from Venus, the goddess of love.

in her mind, this way and that, how best she could get her from him. Now there was a certain knight of those parts, who, for a great while, had sought and required the lady for her love. This knight had spent long years in her service, but little enough had he got thereby, not even fair words, or a promise. To him the dame wrote a letter, and meeting, made her purpose plain.

"Fair friend," said she, "be happy. That which you have coveted so long a time, I will grant without delay. Never again will I deny your suit. My heart, and all I have to give, are yours, so take me now as love and dame."

Right sweetly the knight thanked her for her grace, and pledged her faith and fealty. When she had confirmed him by an oath, then she told him all this business of her lord—why he went, and what he became, and of his ravening[3] within the wood. So she showed him of the chapel, and of the hollow stone, and of how to spoil the Werewolf of his vesture. Thus, by the kiss of his wife, was Bisclavaret betrayed. Often enough had he ravished his prey in desolate places, but from this journey he never returned. His kinsfolk and acquaintance came together to ask of his tidings, when this absence was noised abroad. Many a man, on many a day, searched the woodland, but none might find him, nor learn where Bisclavaret was gone.

The lady was wedded to the knight who had cherished her for so long a space. More than a year had passed since Bisclavaret disappeared. Then it chanced that the King would hunt in that self-same wood where the Werewolf lurked. When the hounds were unleashed they ran this way and that, and swiftly came upon his scent. At the view the huntsman winded on his horn, and the whole pack were at his heels. They followed him from morn to eve, till he was torn and bleeding, and was all adread lest they should pull him down. Now the King was very close to the quarry, and when Bisclavaret looked upon his master, he ran to him for pity and for grace. He took the stirrup within his paws, and fawned upon the prince's foot. The King was very fearful at this sight, but presently he called his courtiers to his aid.

"Lords," cried he, "hasten hither, and see this marvelous thing. Here is a beast who has the sense of man. He abases himself before his foe, and cries for mercy, although he cannot speak. Beat off the hounds, and let no man do him harm. We will hunt no more today, but return to our own place, with the wonderful quarry we have taken."

The King turned him about, and rode to his hall, Bisclavaret following at his side. Very near to his master the Werewolf went, like any dog, and had no care to seek again the wood. When the King had brought him safely to his own castle, he rejoiced greatly, for the beast was fair and strong, no mightier had any man seen. Much pride had the King in his marvelous beast. He held him so dear, that he bade all those who wished for his love, to cross the Wolf in naught, neither to strike him with a rod, but ever to see that he was richly fed and kenneled warm. This commandment the Court observed willingly. So all the day the Wolf sported with the lords, and at night he lay within the chamber of the King. There was not a man who did not make much of the beast, so frank was he and debonair.[4] None had reason to do him wrong, for ever was he about his master, and for his part did evil to none. Every day were these two companions together, and all perceived that the King loved him as his friend.

Hearken now to that which chanced.

The King held a high Court, and bade his great vassals and barons, and all the lords of his venery[5] to the feast. Never was there a goodlier feast, nor one set forth with sweeter show and pomp. Amongst those who were bidden, came that same knight who had the wife of Bisclavaret for dame. He came to the castle, richly gowned, with a fair company, but little he deemed whom he would find so near. Bisclavaret marked his foe the moment he stood within the hall. He ran toward him, and seized him with his fangs, in the King's very presence, and to the view of all. Doubtless he would have done him much mischief, had not the King called and chidden him, and threatened him with a rod. Once, and twice, again, the Wolf set

---

3. ravening (rav′ ən iŋ) *n*.: Greedy searching for prey.

4. debonair (deb′ ə ner′) *adj*.: Pleasant and friendly.

5. venery (ven′ ə rē): The act or practice of hunting game.

Grammar in Action

Comma Splices

Sentences with comma splices, which create the incorrect division of sentences, are problems because they contain sentences with independent clauses that have been too weakly separated.

COMMA SPLICE: It is pouring outside, I forgot my raincoat today.

REVISED: It is pouring outside, and I forgot my raincoat today.

REVISED: It is pouring outside; I forgot my raincoat today.

In order to correct a comma splice, you have these choices: (1) use a coordinating conjunction; (2) use a colon or semicolon; (3) make the clauses into separate sentences; (4) revise the sentences by subordinating one of the clauses.

Consider this sentence from *The Lay of the Werewolf*:

Often enough had he ravished his prey in desolate places, but from his journey he never returned.

The two independent clauses are joined by punctuation (the comma) and by a conjunction (*but*). Imagine how confusing this would be had there

THE WEREWOLF OF ESCHENBACH, GERMANY
Colored engraving, 1685

8 **Discussion** The phrase *mad dog* is probably meant as an irony. Bisclavaret is both figuratively and literally a crazed canine.

Humanities Note

Wood engraving, *The Werewolf of Eschenbach*, artist unknown. *The Werewolf of Eschenbach* is a colored wood engraving produced in Germany in 1685. The artist shows the werewolf walking upright and wearing a man's garment. The man looks back at this fearsome monster as he tries to escape.

The supernatural werewolf continues to inspire the imaginations of today's readers. Movies and television contribute to keeping the legend alive.

You might want to use the following questions to discuss the art:

1. How does this artist's conception of the werewolf compare to others you have seen?
2. Where might you see a werewolf today?
3. How frightening is this illustration?
4. What is the most engaging part of this work?

upon the knight in the very light of day. All men marveled at his malice, for sweet and serviceable was the beast, and to that hour had shown hatred of none. With one consent the household deemed that this deed was done with full reason, and that the Wolf had suffered at the knight's hand some bitter wrong. Right wary of his foe was the knight until the feast had ended, and all the barons had taken farewell of their lord, and departed, each to his own house. With these, amongst the very first, went that lord whom Bisclavaret so fiercely had assailed. Small was the wonder that he was glad to go.

No long while after this adventure it came to pass that the courteous King would hunt in that forest where Bisclavaret was found. With the prince came his wolf, and a fair company. Now at nightfall the King abode within a certain lodge of that country, and this was known of that dame who before was the wife of Bisclavaret. In the morning the lady clothed her in her most dainty apparel, and hastened to the lodge, since she desired to speak with the King, and to offer him a rich present. When the lady entered in the chamber, neither man nor leash might restrain the fury of the Wolf. He became as a mad dog in his hatred and malice. Breaking from his bonds he sprang at the lady's face and bit the nose from her visage. From every side men ran to the succor of the dame. They beat off the wolf from his prey, and for a little would have cut him in pieces with their swords. But a certain wise counselor said to the King,

"Sire, hearken now to me. This beast is always with you, and there is not one of us all who has not known him for long. He goes in and out amongst us, nor has molested any man, neither done wrong or felony to any, save only to this dame, one only time as we have seen. He has done evil to this lady, and to that knight, who is now the husband of the dame. Sire, she was once the wife of that lord who was so close and private to your heart, but who went, and none might find where he had gone. Now, therefore, put the dame in a sure place, and question her straitly, so that she may tell—if perchance she knows thereof—for what reason this Beast holds here in such mortal hate. For many a strange deed has chanced, as well we know, in this marvelous land of Brittany."

been no conjunction.

Student Activity 1. Find additional sentences in the passage where independent clauses are joined by punctuation and conjunctions.

Student Activity 2. Write a brief series of simple sentences describing the members of your family. Revise the sentences by expanding them into more complicated forms. Use appropriate punctuation.

The King listened to these words, and deemed the counsel good. He laid hands upon the knight, and put the dame in surety in another place. He caused them to be questioned straitly, so that their torment was very grievous. At the end, partly because of distress, and partly by reason of her exceeding fear, the lady's lips were loosed, and she told her tale. She showed them of the betrayal of her lord, and how his raiment was stolen from the hollow stone. Since then she knew not where he went, nor what had befallen him, for he had never come again to his own land. Only, in her heart, well she deemed and was persuaded, that Bisclavaret was he.

Straightway the King demanded the vesture of his baron, whether this were to the wish of the lady, or whether it were against her wish. When the raiment was brought him, he caused it to be spread before Bisclavaret, but the Wolf made as though he had not seen. Then that cunning and crafty counselor took the King apart, that he might give him a fresh rede.[6]

"Sire," said he, "you do not wisely, nor well, to set this raiment before Bisclavaret, in the sight of all. In shame and much tribulation must he lay

___

6. **rede** (rēd): Counsel; advice.

aside the beast, and again become man. Carry your wolf within your most secret chamber, and put his vestment therein. Then close the door upon him, and leave him alone for a space. So we shall see presently whether the ravening beast may indeed return to human shape."

The King carried the Wolf to his chamber, and shut the doors upon him fast. He delayed for a brief while, and taking two lords of his fellowship with him, came again to the room. Entering therein, all three softly together, they found the knight sleeping in the King's bed, like a little child. The King ran swiftly to the bed and taking his friend in his arms, embraced and kissed him fondly, above a hundred times. When man's speech returned once more, he told him of his adventure. Then the King restored to his friend the fief that was stolen from him, and gave such rich gifts, moreover, as I cannot tell. As for the wife who had betrayed Bisclavaret, he bade her avoid his country, and chased her from the realm. So she went forth, she and her second lord together, to seek a more abiding city, and were no more seen.

The adventure that you have heard is no vain fable. Verily and indeed it chanced as I have said. The Lay of the Werewolf, truly, was written that it should ever be borne in mind.

___

Reader's Response: *If you were the wife in this story, would you inquire so persistently about your husband's absences? How would you respond to his confession?*

___

PRIMARY SOURCE

Werewolf stories were dismissed in ancient Rome just as quickly as they are today by moviegoers. But during the time of Marie de France, that was not the case. In his *Encyclopedia of Monsters*, Daniel Cohen reports:

"Many individuals were executed for being werewolves. The medieval attitude represents a mixture of pagan lore about shape-shifting and Christian theology. The medieval werewolf was not merely a man changed to a wolf. The werewolf was some sort of demon or servant of the Devil. Werewolf and witchcraft were closely intertwined in the medieval mind. Such unnatural transformation had to be the work of the Devil."

THINKING ABOUT THE SELECTION

Interpreting

1. The only name de France mentions in this story is "Bisclavaret," which means "werewolf." Why doesn't she give real names to the characters in this story?
2. (a) Why does the wife turn to the second knight for help? (b) Why does she agree to marry him?
3. (a) Why does the werewolf tear his wife's nose off? (b) What effect would such a disfigurement have on a person in the Middle Ages?
4. (a) Why does de France insist that this story must be true? (b) Do you think she believes it?
5. Find evidence of the oral tradition in this lay. For example, in the first sentence, the storyteller appears to be speaking directly to her audience.

Applying

6. (a) How would you justify the wife's actions if you were defending her in court? (b) If you were the judge, how would you sentence her? Why?

ANALYZING LITERATURE

Understanding Breton Lais

De France's *lais* are based on similar verse stories told by Breton minstrels who traveled from village to village, accompanying their singing on the harp. Often these *jongleurs* (zhōn′ glërz′), as they were called, performed acrobatics in the village square in order to attract an audience. They lived on whatever this audience gave them, so they entertained well.

These minstrels were the guardians of Celtic culture, which was largely oral in the Middle Ages, so they memorized many stories. They probably originated in central Europe, but by the Middle Ages, they inhabited Brittany (on the west coast of France), Wales, and Ireland.

The Celts believed that the dead lived on the earth, that the springs, rivers, mountains, and forests were guarded by gods or spirits, and that animals had human consciousness and supernatural powers. Even today, stories of magical encounters with ghosts and fairy-people are told in Breton villages.

1. Very few people could read in the Middle Ages, so much information was passed on orally. (a) What do you think would happen to the content of stories that were not written down? (b) How do you think communication in an oral culture, dependent on memory, might differ from modern communication?

2. Many authors criticized the *jongleurs* for their exaggerated stories. (a) Why would written culture be considered superior to oral culture? (b) Why might the minstrels have been so popular?

CRITICAL THINKING AND READING

Recognizing Symbolism

In the *lais,* each story is structured around a symbolic animal or object. These symbols represent abstractions, such as a family bond, the concept of freedom, or a person's character. In "The Lay of the Werewolf," Marie de France uses the symbolism of the werewolf in a new way, by inventing the disconcerting and implausible situation of a woman married to a werewolf. While she does not attempt to deny the frightening nature of the husband's transformation, she is more concerned with the wife's reaction, which seems hasty and which demonstrates a lack of patience and loyalty. Notice, for example, how quickly the wife responds to the situation and how opportunistically she joins with the other knight to plot against a husband who had never directly harmed her. While the husband is a wolf only in form, the wife is wolflike in her behavior.

Cite specific passages to contrast the characterization of the wife with the description of the werewolf.

1. How does de France describe the wife?
2. How does she describe the werewolf?
3. What might his shape-shifting symbolize?
4. Who is the real monster? Explain.

THINKING AND WRITING

Writing from a Different Perspective

Put yourself in a medieval frame of mind. Imagine that a daughter of Bisclavret's ex-wife is born without a nose and wants to know why this has happened. Since the story is common knowledge, the mother must include a version of it in her explanation. But of course she would retell it from her own perspective. Write the wife's reply as a story. First think about which details of de France's story the woman would emphasize and which she would omit. Review especially the beginning of the story with its characterization of werewolves and the initial revelation. As you revise, be sure that this new version consistently supports the wife's point of view. Proofread your story to prepare a final draft. Read it aloud to see if it persuades your classmates. If not, ask for suggestions to make your story more convincing.

1265–1321

Dante Alighieri (dän´ tā al əg yer´ ē), whose visions of Hell have haunted centuries of people since the Middle Ages, was born in Florence, Italy, in May of 1265. Dante's Florence was a place of political turbulence, divided between two rival political factions, the Guelphs and the Ghibellines. The Ghibellines favored the primacy of the Holy Roman emperor in Italian politics, while the Guelphs supported the Roman pontiff. Even after the Ghibellines were expelled from Florence, the Guelphs could not unify the city-state and were themselves divided into two parties, the White (supporting the empire) and the Black (supporting the papacy).

Dante was born into a well-to-do merchant family. Although his father, Alighiero di Bellincione (al əg yer´ ō dē bel lēn çō´ nə), was only moderately involved in Florentine politics and remained relatively unscathed by the political troubles, the same cannot be said of Dante.

Dante was probably educated at the University of Bologna, where he studied law and rhetoric. Not only was Bologna Europe's most prestigious center of legal and rhetorical training, but it was also a city with a great poetical tradition. It was here that Dante came in contact with a new school of poets who sought to free poetry from its old confines of church and court. As a result, he produced a great number of lyric poems and formulated a poetic language that would culminate in the *Divine Comedy*.

Soon, however, Dante became embroiled in the political controversies of his time. He fought against the Ghibellines from Arezzo in the Battle of Campaldino in 1289. In 1295 he became an official in the Florentine commune. Dante belonged to the White faction of the Guelphs at a time when the pope, Boniface VIII, had decided to support the Blacks. The Black Guelphs, aided by the pope and the French, came to power in Florence and in 1302 Dante found himself exiled from his beloved home, never to return. Although he attempted through letters and treatises to regain some influence on papal and Italian politics, these were to no avail. Dante died in Ravenna in northern Italy in 1321.

Finished only shortly before his death, the *Divine Comedy* was the poetic journey of a man struggling to reconcile himself to a bitter political exile through the triumph of love. Guiding him on his pilgrimage for temporal and spiritual salvation was his beloved Beatrice. Dante may have seen the model for his ideal guide, Beatrice Portinari, only twice in his life, when he was nine years old and then again nine years later. Nonetheless, Beatrice, whose name means "she who blesses," became for Dante the force that led him out of his despair and into spiritual renewal. She was first the subject of most of his love poetry, but his quest for happiness in this secular role did not suffice. She became the object of his religious quest and the symbol of spiritual purity that he met at the top of the mountain of Purgatory. Such idealization of Beatrice linked her to the Virgin Mary, herself the object of cultlike adoration in the Middle Ages.

BACKGROUND

THE DIVINE COMEDY

The *Inferno* is the first of three parts of the *Divine Comedy*. Dante's journey begins on Good Friday, the commemoration of Christ's Crucifixion, and ends on the vigil of Easter Sunday, the celebration of Christ's Resurrection. The *Divine Comedy* thus takes the reader on a journey that symbolically begins in a despairing world not yet redeemed by Christ's Crucifixion and ends with the poet's return as a man, renewed in hope, having beheld the beatific vision of divine grace.

Central to Dante's conception and execution of all his work is his preoccupation with the number three, inspired by the Christian concept of Father, Son, and Holy Ghost united in one trinity. Not only is the *Divine Comedy* the last in a poetic trilogy but it is itself composed of three parts. Each part is composed of thirty-three cantos if we exclude the first canto of the *Inferno*, which is the only canto that takes place on Earth. Within each canto, the verse form the poet uses is called *terza rima*, which is composed of three lines. Thus from one of the smallest poetical units, the verse, to the larger project of the *Divine Comedy* and its ultimate place in the Dantean corpus, the number three is crucial.

In fact, the spiritual quest of the *Divine Comedy* takes place over the space of three days. On Good Friday, Dante finds himself lost and directionless in a dark forest. Abandoned by hope and in despair, he undertakes his quest for belonging and ultimate salvation. He is led through Hell by Virgil, who is sent down by Beatrice to guide her admirer through his spiritual journey. Virgil, perhaps the Latin poet most widely read in the Middle Ages, has special significance as a pre-Christian prophet

because of his fourth Eclogue, in which he discusses the birth of a potential savior of the Roman people. Medieval people, obsessed with relating the pagan past to the present Christian experience, were constantly justifying reading ancient literature by means of such interpretations.

The various sinners with whom Dante meets and the punishments they suffer serve as warnings to him to change his life for the better. The images and events depicted in the *Purgatorio* and the *Paradiso*, the last two sections of the *Comedy*, reinforce the lessons of the *Inferno*.

The Circles of Hell

Hell is organized according to the gravity of the sin involved. In this work, however, there is a tension between the theological classification of sin and Dante's personal agenda. The farther Dante descends into the pit, the more serious the crimes committed by the people who surround him. Sometimes these crimes have been committed against God, the Church, and other people; but each of Dante's enemies finds his or her own special place in Hell. In this way Dante avenges himself on those responsible for his exile. It is ultimately his pen that condemns them to their eternal literary damnation.

The virtuous pagans, whom Dante admires but who do not know about Christ, rest peacefully in Limbo, a place without pain or hope where medieval thinking places the souls of unbaptized children and righteous people who lived before Christ's birth. They are closely followed by the lustful, the gluttonous, the avaricious, the prodigal, and the

Critical Evaluation In *Mimesis*, Erich Auerbach writes of Dante:

The themes which the *Comedy* introduces represent a mixture of sublimity and triviality which, measured by the standards of antiquity, is monstrous. Of the characters which appear in it, some belong to the recent past or even to the contemporary present and not all of them are carefully chosen. Quite often they are frankly represented in all the humble realism of their spheres of life. And in general, as every reader is aware, Dante knows no limits in describing with meticulous care and directness things which are humdrum, grotesque, or repulsive.

The concept of the sublime is a useful guide in approaching the *Inferno*. The sublime is often associated with infinity, darkness, terror, and mystery; in contrast the beautiful is perceived as finite, calm, light, and knowable. It is this "monstrous" contrast that fuels much of the power of Dante's writing. Ask students to consider things that combine the good and the terrible in interesting ways.

Humanities Note

Fine art, *Poets Emerge from Hell* by Gustave Doré. Gustave Doré (1832–1883), a self-taught artist, was the most well-known and widely admired illustrator of the late nineteenth century. Drawing in perfect scale and proportion seems to have come naturally to him. In *Poets Emerge from Hell*, Dante and Virgil are depicted looking skyward from a ledge. Rock climbing was a favorite pastime of Doré's, and his familiarity with rock formations and aerial views is evident in this scene.

You might want to use the following questions to discuss the art:

1. What do you think these figures are discovering?
2. What mood does the setting of the drawing convey to you?
3. How could Doré have done this scene in a way that you would find more interesting?

wrathful. These relatively harmless sinners are separated from the heretics by the forbidding Wall of Dis. Even further isolated by the bloody river of Phlegethon are the violent, murderers, suicides, and blasphemers. Dante and Virgil must be carried down a steep precipice by the monster Geryon to the Malebolge, the realm of the fraudulent. Here the most hated of Dante's enemies, such as Boniface VIII, are tormented. But the lowest circle of Hell is reserved for traitors. For Dante, Lucifer, frozen into the lowest depths, is the ultimate traitor. It is easy to see why Dante finds in the demon's mouth Brutus and Cassius, who betrayed Caesar, and Judas Iscariot, who betrayed Jesus Christ.

Purgatory

Virgil carries Dante down through the bottom of Hell and then up toward the mountain of *Purgatorio*. The organization of Purgatory, with its movement toward redemption, is the mirror image of Hell. Not surprisingly, none of Dante's enemies are to be found in this realm of hope. Traitors thus begin their long climb toward Paradise at the bottom of the mountain. They are preceded by the envious, the wrathful, and the other lesser sinners. At the top of the mountain, and at the verge of salvation, Dante finds the lustful, confused by their pursuit of physical rather than spiritual love. His contemplation of love preambles his encounter with Beatrice, the personification of perfect love. At this point, Virgil can go no farther and Beatrice must become Dante's guide.

Paradise

As Dante has confronted the wages of sin in the *Inferno* and *Purgatorio*, so he contemplates the rewards of love in the *Paradiso*. It is love that ultimately saves humankind and enables Dante to gaze upon the mystical rose. Saints, angels, the Virgin Mary, and God all reside in that vision. Having seen all that without being able to describe its inexpressible beauty, Dante returns to his earthly life, renewed in his quest for ultimate redemption.

The Vernacular

Dante broke with tradition by writing in the Italian vernacular. By not writing his masterpiece in Latin, he made it available not only to the learned but to anyone who read Italian.

GUIDE FOR INTERPRETING

from the Inferno, Canto I

Commentary

Allegory. An **allegory** (al′ ə gôr′ ē) is the discussion of one subject by disguising it as another, which resembles the first in some striking way. In an allegory the characters, the setting, and the plot have a hidden or symbolic meaning beyond their literal meaning. For example, rather than speaking directly of school, a disgruntled student might discuss it as a prison in which he does time. The principal becomes a warden, teachers become guards, the classroom a cell, a weekend becomes a furlough, and summer ultimately a three-month parole. All of these images together comprise the allegory of school as a prison.

An allegory teaches a moral lesson. Especially in medieval literature, allegory is the use of visible, physical reality to explain or express the invisible or intangible. Allegories can be read on two levels—the literal and the symbolic. It can be argued that the gods of the Greek Pantheon form an allegory of nature, with each god representing a different natural force or phenomenon. Poseidon represents the sea, Zeus the sky, Hades the earth. Apollo is the sun. Demeter and Dionysius represent the food and drink necessary to human survival. Their capricious behavior toward the human race resembles the arbitrary violence and benevolence of nature.

Writing

Describe someone who has helped you solve a difficult problem or series of problems in your life. How did that person help you? What did he or she do?

Primary Source

George Holmes, a literary historian, points out the source of Dante's masterpiece: "The model that gave Dante the idea of the *Inferno* was Virgil's *Aeneid*, Book VI . . . Virgil's underworld has many resemblances to Dante's Hell. . . . There is a general parallelism, not only in the physical arrangements and in many poetic details, but in the general idea of Hell as a place where punishment can be observed and also where shades of the friendly dead can be interrogated about their fate. The inspiration for the *Inferno*, and very likely the inspiration for the whole *Comedy*, arose out of Dante's enthusiasm for Virgil."

Presentation

Motivation/Prior Knowledge Tell students that they will be reading a piece of writing that chronicles a complicated journey. This journey has several purposes for the narrator. Call upon their prior knowledge by asking them what other journeys they have encountered through their reading. Ask them to recall dimensions of those other stories.

Purpose-Setting Question Have students pay attention to the early clues to Dante's journey. In what ways does the author identify himself as a "pilgrim"? What is the setting for his journey?

Universal Themes The search for salvation is a theme that is common throughout the literature of the world. Variations of its different dimensions can be found in many different cultures.

Remind students of the longing that fills the heart of Aeneas during his journey toward salvation in the *Aeneid*, page 493. Point out that less heroic characters can also be found striving for a less conspicuous sort of salvation, as is done in Tagore's *The Artist*, page 1192.

1 Discussion Note the contradiction between the "our" and the "I." Dante shifts between the poetic and empirical voice, reflecting his own preoccupation with the personal and political nature of his "journey."

2 Discussion Draw students' attention to the narrator's "drugged" state. What sense does Dante's narcotic state give his tale?

from the Inferno

Dante Alighieri

translated by John Ciardi

Canto I

The Dark Wood of Error

Midway in his allotted threescore years and ten, Dante comes to himself with a start and realizes that he has strayed from the True Way into the Dark Wood of Error (Worldliness). As soon as he has realized his loss, Dante lifts his eyes and sees the first light of the sunrise (the Sun is the Symbol of Divine Illumination) lighting the shoulders of a little hill (The Mount of Joy). It is the Easter Season, the time of resurrection, and the sun is in its equinoctial rebirth.[1] This juxtaposition of joyous symbols fills Dante with hope and he sets out at once to climb directly up the Mount of Joy, but almost immediately his way is blocked by the Three Beasts of Worldliness: THE LEOPARD OF MALICE AND FRAUD, THE LION OF VIOLENCE AND AMBITION, and THE SHE-WOLF OF INCONTINENCE.[2] These beasts, and especially the She-Wolf, drive him back despairing into the darkness of error. But just as all seems lost, a figure appears to him. It is the shade of VIRGIL,[3] Dante's symbol of HUMAN REASON.

Virgil explains that he has been sent to lead Dante from error. There can, however, be no direct ascent past the beasts: the man who would escape them must go a longer and harder way. First he must descend through Hell (The Recognition of Sin), then he must ascend through Purgatory (The Renunciation of Sin), and only then may he reach the pinnacle of joy and come to the Light of God. Virgil offers to guide Dante, but only as far as Human Reason can go. Another guide (BEATRICE, symbol of DIVINE LOVE) must take over for the final ascent, for Human Reason is self-limited. Dante submits himself joyously to Virgil's guidance and they move off.

Midway in our life's journey,[4] I went astray
   from the straight road and woke to find myself
   alone in a dark wood. How shall I say

what wood that was! I never saw so drear,
5   so rank, so arduous[5] a wilderness!
   Its very memory gives a shape to fear.

Death could scarce be more bitter than that place!
   But since it came to good, I will recount
   all that I found revealed there by God's grace.

10 How I came to it I cannot rightly say,
   so drugged and loose with sleep had I become
   when I first wandered there from the True Way.

Note: Footnotes adapted from text by John Ciardi.

1. equinoctial rebirth: After the vernal equinox, which occurs about March 21, days become longer than nights.
2. INCONTINENCE: Lack of self-restraint, especially with regard to sexual activity.
3. Virgil (vur′ jəl): A great Roman poet (70–19 B.C.).

---

4. Midway in our life's journey: The Biblical life span is threescore years and ten—seventy years. The action opens in Dante's thirty-fifth year, i.e., A.D. 1300.
5. so rank, so arduous: So overgrown, so difficult to cross.

THE FOREST, INFERNO I
Gustave Doré

Humanities Note

Fine art, *The Forest* by Gustave Doré. The French artist Gustave Doré (1832–1883) published several large-scale illustrated books at the height of his career. Selecting authors whose work he admired, Doré lavishly illustrated these deluxe editions with engravings of his drawings. Dante's *Inferno*, one of the works selected, enjoyed tremendous success.

The Forest is one of the full-page illustrations that appeared in the book. The poet, standing alone in the tangled wood, looks warily around.

You might want to use the following questions to discuss the art:

1. Why do you suppose the figure is looking around?
2. How does the artist achieve the sense of mystery that pervades this drawing?
3. What do you find most intriguing about this illustration?

3 **Discussion** Be sure to point out to students Dante's use of simile. Ask students to suggest other ways to describe the narrator's state.

4 **Discussion** Ask students what Dante might mean by "the holy hour and sweet season." What time of day and year is the setting for his tale? Why is this significant?

5 **Enrichment** Explain Dante's use of "ravening and wasted." Have students look up the terms. How is *ravening* different from *ravenous*.

6 **Discussion** Ask students how Dante's description of a miser is slightly different from the usual sense of the term.

But at the far end of that valley of evil
  whose maze had sapped my very heart with fear!
15 I found myself before a little hill

and lifted up my eyes. Its shoulders glowed
  already with the sweet rays of that planet[6]
  whose virtue leads men straight on every road,

and the shining strengthened me against the fright
20   whose agony had wracked the lake of my heart
  through all the terrors of that piteous night.

Just as a swimmer, who with his last breath
  flounders ashore from perilous seas, might turn
  to memorize the wide water of his death—

25 so did I turn, my soul still fugitive
  from death's surviving image, to stare down
  that pass that none had ever left alive.

And there I lay to rest from my heart's race
  till calm and breath returned to me. Then rose
30   and pushed up that dead slope at such a pace

each footfall rose above the last.[7] And lo!
  almost at the beginning of the rise
  I faced a spotted Leopard,[8] all tremor and flow
and gaudy pelt. And it would not pass, but stood
35   so blocking my every turn that time and again
  I was on the verge of turning back to the wood.

---

6. that planet: The sun. Medieval astronomers considered it a planet. It is also symbolic of God as He who lights man's way.

7. each footfall . . . last: The literal rendering would be: "So that the fixed foot was ever the lower." "Fixed" has often been translated "right" and an ingenious reasoning can support that reading, but a simpler explanation offers itself and seems more competent: Dante is saying that he climbed with such zeal and haste that every footfall carried him above the last despite the steepness of the climb. At a slow pace, on the other hand, the rear foot might be brought up only as far as the forward foot. This device of selecting a minute but exactly centered detail to convey the whole of a larger action is one of the central characteristics of Dante's style.

8. a spotted Leopard: The three beasts that Dante encounters undoubtedly are taken from the Bible, Jeremiah 5:6. Many additional and incidental interpretations have been advanced for them, but the central interpretation must remain as noted. They foreshadow the three divisions of Hell (incontinence, violence, and fraud) which Virgil explains at length in Canto XI, 16–111.

This fell at the first widening of the dawn
  as the sun was climbing Aries with those stars
  that rode with him to light the new creation.[9]

40 Thus the holy hour and the sweet season
  of commemoration did much to arm my fear
  of that bright murderous beast with their good
    omen.

Yet not so much but what I shook with dread
  at sight of a great Lion that broke upon me
45   raging with hunger, its enormous head

held high as if to strike a mortal terror
  into the very air. And down his track,
  a She-Wolf drove upon me, a starved horror

ravening and wasted beyond all belief.
50   She seemed a rack for avarice,[10] gaunt and
    craving.
  Oh many the souls she has brought to endless
    grief!

She brought such heaviness upon my spirit
  at sight of her savagery and desperation,
  I died from every hope of that high summit.

55 And like a miser—eager in acquisition
  but desperate in self-reproach when Fortune's
    wheel
  turns to the hour of his loss—all tears and
    attrition[11]

I wavered back; and still the beast pursued,
  forcing herself against me bit by bit
60   till I slid back into the sunless wood.

---

9. Aries . . . new creation: The medieval tradition had it that the sun was in the zodiacal sign of Aries at the time of the Creation. The significance of the astronomical and religious conjunction is an important part of Dante's intended allegory. It is just before dawn of Good Friday A.D. 1300 when he awakens in the Dark Wood. Thus his new life begins under Aries, the sign of creation, at dawn (rebirth) and in the Easter Season (which commemorates the resurrection of Jesus). Moreover the moon is full and the sun is in the equinox, conditions that did not fall together on any Friday of 1300. Dante is obviously constructing poetically the perfect Easter as a symbol of his new awakening.

10. a rack for avarice: An instrument of torture for greed.

11. attrition: Weakening; wearing away.

And as I fell to my soul's ruin, a presence
   gathered before me on the discolored air,
   the figure of one who seemed hoarse from long
      silence.

At sight of him in that friendless waste I cried:
   "Have pity on me, whatever thing you are,
   whether shade or living man." And it replied:

"Not man, though man I once was, and my
      blood
   was Lombard, both my parents Mantuan.[12]
   I was born, though late, *sub Julio*,[13] and bred

in Rome under Augustus in the noon
   of the false and lying gods.[14] I was a poet
   and sang of old Anchises' noble son

who came to Rome after the burning of Troy.[15]
   But you—why do *you* return to these distresses
   instead of climbing that shining Mount of Joy

which is the seat and first cause of man's bliss?"
   "And are you then that Virgil and that fountain
   of purest speech?" My voice grew tremulous:

"Glory and light of poets! now may that zeal
   and love's apprenticeship that I poured out
   on your heroic verses serve me well!

For you are my true master and first author,
   the sole maker from whom I drew the breath
   of that sweet style whose measures have brought
      me honor.

85 See there, immortal sage, the beast I flee.
   For my soul's salvation, I beg you, guard me
      from her,
   for she has struck a mortal tremor through me."

And he replied, seeing my soul in tears:
   "He must go by another way who would escape
90 this wilderness, for that mad beast that fleers[16]

before you there, suffers no man to pass.
   She tracks down all, kills all, and knows no glut,
   but, feeding, she grows hungrier than she was.

She mates with any beast, and will mate with more
95 before the Greyhound comes to hunt her down.
   He will not feed on lands nor loot, but honor

and love and wisdom will make straight his way.
   He will rise between Feltro and Feltro,[17] and in
      him
   shall be the resurrection and new day

100 of that sad Italy for which Nisus died,
   and Turnus, and Euryalus, and the maid
      Camilla.[18]
   He shall hunt her through every nation of sick
      pride

till she is driven back forever to Hell
   whence Envy first released her on the world.
105 Therefore, for your own good, I think it well

you follow me and I will be your guide
   and lead you forth through an eternal place.
   There you shall see the ancient spirits tried

---

12. Lombard . . . Mantuan: Lombardy is a region of
northern Italy; Mantua, the birthplace of Virgil, is a city in that
region.

13. *sub Julio*: In the reign of Julius Caesar. It would be more
accurate to say that he was born during the lifetime of Caesar
(102?–44 B.C.). Augustus did not begin his rule as dictator
until long after Virgil's birth, which occurred in 70 B.C.

14. under Augustus . . . lying gods: Augustus, the grandnephew of Julius Caesar, was the emperor of Rome from 27
B.C. to A.D. 14. The "lying gods" are the false gods of classical
mythology.

15. and sang . . . Troy: Virgil's epic poem, the *Aeneid*,
describes the destruction of Troy by the Greeks and the
founding of Roman civilization by the Trojan Aeneas, son of
Anchises (an kī' sēz').

---

16. fleers (flirz): Laughs scornfully.

17. the Greyhound . . . Feltro and Feltro: The Greyhound
almost certainly refers to Can Grande della Scala (1290–1329),
a great Italian leader born in Verona, which lies between the
towns of Feltre and Montefeltro.

18. Nisus . . . Camilla: All were killed in the war between the
Trojans and the Latians when, according to legend, Aeneas led
the survivors of Troy into Italy. Nisus and Euryalus (*Aeneid*
IX) were Trojan comrades-in-arms who died together. Camilla
(*Aeneid* XI) was the daughter of the Latian king and one of the
warrior women. She was killed in a horse charge against the
Trojans after displaying great gallantry. Turnus (*Aeneid* XII)
was killed by Aeneas in a duel.

---

7 **Discussion** Note how the author
draws attention to his craft and
profession.

8 **Discussion** Dante claims Virgil as
a mentor. Ask students what he
means by "true master and first
author." Why does he praise Virgil?

9 **Discussion** In what sense does
Dante mean "sweet style"? Explain
to students that Dante was initially
a major exponent of the Italian
poetic school known as the
dolce stil' nuovo (dol' shā stēl nōō
ō' və), "the sweet new style." He
later departed from this school of
lyric poetry to compose his long
narrative masterpiece.

10 **Discussion** Ask students what Dante might mean by "souls in fire and yet content in fire." What does this line suggest about the inhabitants' sense of their surroundings?

Master Teacher Note Dante relies on the aid of others to guide him through his journey. Ask students what other tales of journey, in both literal and figurative senses, rely on a knowledgeable guide to help the narrator along his or her way. What journeys have they themselves taken and who were their guides? Ask students what qualities they think make a guide helpful and a journey fruitful?

in endless pain, and hear their lamentation
110 as each bemoans the second death[19] of souls.
Next you shall see upon a burning mountain[20]

10 souls in fire and yet content in fire,
knowing that whensoever it may be
they yet will mount into the blessed choir.

115 To which, if it is still your wish to climb,
a worthier spirit[21] shall be sent to guide you.
With her shall I leave you, for the King of Time,

who reigns on high, forbids me to come there[22]
since, living, I rebelled against his law.
120 He rules the waters and the land and air

------

19. the second death: Damnation. "This is the second death, even the lake of fire." (the Bible, Revelation 20:14)
20. a burning mountain: The Mountain of Purgatory, described in the second book of Dante's *Divine Comedy*.
21. a worthier spirit: Beatrice.
22. forbids me to come there: Salvation is only through Christ in Dante's theology. Virgil lived and died before the establishment of Christ's teachings in Rome and cannot therefore enter Heaven.

and there holds court, his city and his throne.
Oh blessed are they he chooses!" And I to him:
"Poet, by that God to you unknown,

lead me this way. Beyond this present ill
125 and worse to dread, lead me to Peter's gate[23]
and be my guide through the sad halls of Hell."

And he then: "Follow." And he moved ahead in
silence, and I followed where he led.

------

23. Peter's gate: The gate of Purgatory. (See *Purgatorio* IX, 76ff.) The gate is guarded by an angel with a gleaming sword. The angel is Peter's vicar (Peter, the first pope, symbolized all popes; i.e., Christ's vicar on earth) and is entrusted with the two great keys.

Some commentators argue that this is the gate of Paradise, but Dante mentions no gate beyond this one in his ascent to Heaven. It should be remembered, too, that those who pass the gate of Purgatory have effectively entered Heaven.

The three gates that figure in the entire journey are the gate of Hell (Canto III, 1–11), the gate of Dis (Canto VIII, 79–113, and Canto IX, 86–87), and the gate of Purgatory, as above.

Reader's Response *If you were Dante, what emotions would you be feeling now? Explain.*

THINKING ABOUT THE SELECTION

Clarifying

1. Describe the appearance of the three animals.
2. (a) How is Virgil described? (b) Why does Dante describe him in this way?

Interpreting

3. Why is it appropriate that Virgil is Dante's guide?
4. (a) Explain the significance of the straight road. (b) Of the dark wood.

5. What does his attempt to climb the hill represent, and why is he confronted by the beasts?
6. What does the prediction about the she-wolf and the hound tell you about Dante's purpose in writing the *Inferno*? Is he more concerned with spiritual matters or with temporal problems such as politics? (b) How does he manage to put the two together?
7. (a) In what ways does Dante represent a person living in Florence in the late thirteenth century? (b) In what ways does he represent all people?

Commentary

Translation as an Act of Composition The translation used in this section is that of the American poet John Ciardi. This translation is popular and critically acclaimed. Though it does not maintain accuracy on a lexical level, it does convey the spirit of the original work.

Translation, however, is both an act of composition and betrayal; each translation of a work represents a decomposition and rewriting of that work. The word *translation*, derived from the Latin *translatus* (past participle of *transferre*, to move from one place to another), often means to move or change into "one's own" language. Literature, like language, is a kind of

social property and the act of translating is like buying a new house: The structure remains quite the same but the change of ownership gives the home a different quality.

Applying

8. Assuming that you were undertaking a journey such as Dante's, whom would you choose as your guide and why? Would you choose a literary figure, a political figure, or some other prominent person? Explain your choice and in doing so tell why there would be special advantages that stemmed from your decision.

ANALYZING LITERATURE

Interpreting Allegory

In an allegory the characters, the setting, and the plot all have a symbolic meaning as well as a literal one. Three animals pose obstacles for Dante in this canto: the leopard, the lion, and the she-wolf. These animals are real threats, but they also represent abstract ideas. For example, there is an old story about the leopard changing his coat (adding spots) in order to trick the other animals. Therefore it is easy to see how Dante can construct an allegory of fraud and deceit using the leopard. How might the other animals fit into Dante's allegorical structure? Which beasts would be natural choices?

1. (a) What do people normally say about lions? (b) What do you think the lion in this canto might represent?
2. (a) Why does Dante describe the wolf as the most threatening of the three animals? (b) What or who, then, might the greyhound represent, and why would it be appropriate for him to chase the wolf from Italy?

THINKING AND WRITING

Composing an Allegory

Think about a strong emotion you have felt at some point in your life. This emotion could be love, anger, sadness, or disgust. Could you associate an animal or an object with this emotion? A singing bird could represent happiness, for example. A soft bed might represent comfort. In what way would you describe the animal or object in order to convey all the important aspects of this feeling? Write a brief essay in which you convey your emotion through the description of the object or animal. As you revise your work, think as the reader would. Is your allegory clear without being too obvious? Your reader should still have to guess at the meaning of your description.

COMMENTARY

Tracing Influences

Dante is basing his *Divine Comedy* in part on classical epics, particularly Virgil's *Aeneid*, which tells the story of the founding of Rome. Aeneas, the epic hero, flees Troy and wanders throughout the Mediterranean region in his quest for a new land. In Book VI of the *Aeneid*, Virgil describes Aeneas's descent into Hades, which is divided into the Elysian Fields, where the souls of good men and women wander, and the realm of punishment, where the souls of the wicked suffer. Aeneas is guided by the Cumean Sybil and protected by a golden bough as he makes the arduous journey of self-discovery. The importance of this episode for Dante's work is hinted at by the numerous details the later poet transposes from the classical epic. The boatman of Hades, Charon, is found again in Dante's Hell. Dante finds himself in places, like Cocytus, that originated in the classical Hades. But Dante replaces pagan ceremonies and creeds with his own religious beliefs. Virgil can explain the images of horror to Dante and protect him from danger, but he cannot place the meaning of these visions in the larger context of Christianity. Dante must do this for himself.

(continued from bottom of page)

reflecting contemporary concerns. (b) He transcends the politics of his day and gains a universality by being ecumenical.
8. Answers will differ. Be sure that students explain their choices for guides.

ANSWERS TO ANALYZING LITERATURE

1. (a) People often say lions are cruel. (b) This lion may represent pride or cruelty.
2. He describes the wolf as more threatening because it is ravenous. (b) The greyhound might then symbolize some future prince who might liberate Italy from the poverty that kept people in need.

THINKING AND WRITING

Writing Across the Curriculum You may want to inform the art department that students are reading this selection. An art teacher might wish to comment on the illustrations by Doré. As a writing assignment, students might compose a brief response to the illustration on page 623.

Challenge Tell students that Dante believed Virgil to be prophetic. Ask them to trace and explain the story that the Roman author made predictions concerning the birth of a miraculous child in his *Eclogues*.

Closure and Extension

ANSWERS TO THINKING ABOUT THE SELECTION

1. The leopard has a gaudy pelt; the lion has an enormous head; and the wolf looks wasted and ravenous.
2. (a) Virgil is said to be hoarse from long silence and also the fountain of purest speech. (b) He is described with admiration, like a beloved schoolmaster.
3. It is appropriate because he is regarded as the greatest poet in antiquity.
4. (a) Answers may differ. Some will say it is the direct path that leads in the right direction. (b) Answers will differ. It seems to suggest confusion and a loss of direction.
5. It represents an attempt to search for the truth. He is confronted by beasts, symbolizing his own faults, that may prevent him from attaining the truth.
6. (a) Answers may differ. Some will say that he is equally concerned with spiritual and temporal problems. (b) He joins the concerns by seeing his exile as a religious yearning for home.
7. (a) He represents such a person by

Teaching Portfolio

Focus

Literary Focus Have students discuss their own experiences with films or stories that include images of horror or grotesqueness. Many students have seen *The Wizard of Oz* and will remember the scene with the flying monkeys. The creatures resembled a frightening combination of animal and human qualities.

Writing/Prior Knowledge Pair up the students in class. Have them share their ideas and tell each other about what they think is the most frightening, ghastly image.

ESL Teaching Strategy Pair each ESL student with another member of the class. Let the partners discuss ways in which they can both contribute to the drawings of ghoulish images appropriate for any infernal depiction.

Teaching Tenth-Grade Students Mention to tenth-grade students that Dante's continued success stems in part from each generation's ability "to see" his infernal regions. Let students describe what his words have already let them see. Discuss whether or not Dante could do more in opening the eyes of his readers.

Vocabulary

Preteach the following vocabulary words:

putrid (pyōō′ trid) *adj.*: Rotten, stinking

despicable (des′ pik ə b′l) *adj.*: Deserving to be despised, contemptible

lamentation (lam′ən ta′ shən) *n.*: Weeping, wailing

scorn (skôrn) *v.*: Discredit

rout (rout) *v.*: Chase out, disband

reprimand (rep′ rə mand) *v.*: Chastise, blame

throngs (throŋs) *n.*: Crowds, mobs

Commentary

from the Inferno, Canto III

Imagery. Imagery is the use of words and details to create vivid pictures in the reader's mind. One way the writer creates vivid images is through repetition. From the beginning of this canto, the reader should share in Dante's trepidation, which is underscored by the anaphora, the insistent repetition, found in the inscription on the Gate of Hell: "I AM THE WAY INTO THE CITY OF WOE. / I AM THE WAY TO A FORSAKEN PEOPLE. / I AM THE WAY INTO ETERNAL SORROW." This repetition echoes the never-ending punishments to be found in Hell and reminds us of the endless nature of this suffering. The "Neutral" people, those who chose neither side in religious or political controversies, constantly run around in a large circle. They can never stop running. Dante repeats the notion of circling and entrapment frequently in this canto.

Another way of creating vivid images is by appealing to the senses. Dante assails our sense of hearing in order to convey the horror of this situation. Before he even sees the sinners, he hears "sighs and cries and wails . . . A confusion of tongues and monstrous accents toiled / in pain and anger. Voices hoarse and shrill / and sounds of blows, all intermingled . . ." He also appeals to our sense of sight. When Virgil says "look, and pass on," Dante finally sees this horde, goaded on by wasps and hornets, and even recognizes a few of them. By delaying this recognition, Dante emphasizes the unfamiliar nature of this situation. The sinners are grotesque and deformed by their torment.

After this first frightening encounter with Hell, the two voyagers are confronted by the boatman, Charon. But his anger is mitigated when Virgil reminds him of the higher authority that has instigated Dante's pilgrimage. Thus is established the rhythm of menace and protection that moves the narrative along through Dante's trials.

In describing the passage over the Acheron, Dante uses several images to evoke the staggering numbers of the damned. They are compared to the leaves in autumn, to flocks of birds. It is no wonder that Dante describes all his senses as "shattered," since they must take in sights and sounds that are completely unfamiliar to him. He is clearly overwhelmed by what he sees, and his inability to continue his narration conveys the unspeakably horrible nature of his surroundings. Thus silence becomes crucial to Dante's literary method.

Writing

Have you ever been to a house of horrors in an amusement park, or seen a horror movie? Write down a list of things that shocked or frightened you. What exactly made these details seem horrible?

Objectives

Thematic
To understand how Dante's images contribute to the horror of the *Inferno*

Skills
1 To understand how to interpret imagery
2 To appreciate cause and effect relationships
3 To appreciate dialogue
4 To be able to describe scenes of horror

Support Material

Teaching Portfolio
Teacher Backup, p. 759
Grammar in Action Worksheet, *Imagery* p. 763
Usage and Mechanics Worksheet, p. 765
Vocabulary Check, p. 766
Analyzing Literature Worksheet,

Canto III

The Vestibule of Hell
The Opportunists

The Poets pass the Gate of Hell and are immediately assailed by cries of anguish. Dante sees the first of the souls in torment. They are THE OPPORTUNISTS, those souls who in life were neither for good nor evil but only for themselves. Mixed with them are those outcasts who took no sides in the Rebellion of the Angels.[1] They are neither in Hell nor out of it. Eternally unclassified, they race round and round pursuing a wavering banner that runs forever before them through the dirty air; and as they run they are pursued by swarms of wasps and hornets, who sting them and produce a constant flow of blood and putrid matter which trickles down the bodies of the sinners and is feasted upon by loathsome worms and maggots who coat the ground.

The law of Dante's Hell is the law of symbolic retribution. As they sinned so are they punished. They took no sides, therefore they are given no place. As they pursued the ever-shifting illusion of their own advantage, changing their courses with every changing wind, so they pursue eternally an elusive, ever-shifting banner. As their sin was a darkness, so they move in darkness. As their own guilty conscience pursued them, so they are pursued by swarms of wasps and hornets. And as their actions were a moral filth, so they run eternally through the filth of worms and maggots which they themselves feed.

Dante recognizes several, among them POPE CELESTINE V,[2] but without delaying to speak to any of these souls, the Poets move on to ACHERON,[3] the first of the rivers of Hell. Here the newly arrived souls of the damned gather and wait for monstrous CHARON[4] to ferry them over to punishment. Charon recognizes Dante as a living man and angrily refuses him passage. Virgil forces Charon to serve them, but Dante swoons with terror, and does not reawaken until he is on the other side.

I AM THE WAY INTO THE CITY OF WOE.
I AM THE WAY TO A FORSAKEN PEOPLE.
I AM THE WAY INTO ETERNAL SORROW.

SACRED JUSTICE MOVED MY ARCHITECT.
5 I WAS RAISED HERE BY DIVINE OMNIPOTENCE,
PRIMORDIAL[5] LOVE AND ULTIMATE INTELLECT.

ONLY THOSE ELEMENTS TIME CANNOT WEAR[6]
WERE MADE BEFORE ME, AND BEYOND TIME I
   STAND.[7]
ABANDON ALL HOPE YE WHO ENTER HERE.[8]

10 These mysteries I read cut into stone
   above a gate. And turning I said: "Master,
   what is the meaning of this harsh inscription?"

And he then as initiate to novice:[9]
   "Here must you put by all division of spirit
15   and gather your soul against all cowardice.

---

1. the Rebellion of the Angels: In Christian tradition, Satan and other angels who rebelled against God were cast out of heaven; see the Bible, Revelation 12:7–9.
2. POPE CELESTINE V: He lived from 1215 to 1296.
3. ACHERON (ak´ ər än´)

---

4. CHARON (ker´ən)
5. PRIMORDIAL (prī môr´ dē əl): Existing from the beginning.
6. ONLY . . . WEAR: The Angels, the Empyrean (the highest heaven), and the First Matter are the elements time cannot wear, for they will last to all time. Man, however, in his mortal state, is not eternal. The Gate of Hell, therefore, was created before man.
7. AND BEYOND . . . STAND: So odious is sin to God that there can be no end to its just punishment.
8. ABANDON . . . HERE: The admonition, of course, is to the damned and not to those who come on Heaven-sent errands. The Harrowing of Hell (see Canto IV, note 8) provided the only exemption from this decree, and that only through the direct intercession of Christ.
9. as initiate to novice: as one who knows to one who does not.

Interpreting Imagery, p. 767
Critical Thinking and Reading Worksheet, *Understanding Cause and Effect*, p.768
Selection Test, pp. 769–770

1 Discussion Ask students what other place they can think of that could be described as a scene of "pandemonium." Does the word necessarily have a negative sense?

2 Clarification The reference to Milton may seem a bit confusing to students, especially if you are following a chronological approach to this textbook. It is important here to point out the translation process: Often new words must be employed that carry a different meaning and historical sense than was possible at the time of the original text. Of course, this particular linguistic problem is especially important because most of Dante's work is devoted to creating a new poetic language. Writers in the English Renaissance shared many of the same problems: They too had to justify the use of a vernacular, English, for important religious and political documents, rather than the use of the classical languages.

3 Enrichment Point out to students how the inhabitants here have been rejected by both Heaven and Hell. There is a bit of comedy, even if unintended, in Dante's description. It is like the old joke: "They said you weren't fit to live with pigs, but I defended you: I said you were."

4 Discussion Ask students to imagine situations where death might seem welcome because of some circumstance. Have them discuss alternatives to despair.

5 Discussion Point out the use of personification in this line.

6 Discussion Note the images of circles as endless. Ask students how this might contribute to the larger themes in Dante's work?

This is the place I told you to expect.
Here you shall pass among the fallen people,
souls who have lost the good of intellect."

So saying, he put forth his hand to me,
20 and with a gentle and encouraging smile
he led me through the gate of mystery.

Here sighs and cries and wails coiled and recoiled
on the starless air, spilling my soul to tears.
A confusion of tongues and monstrous accents toiled

25 in pain and anger. Voices hoarse and shrill
and sounds of blows, all intermingled, raised
tumult and pandemonium[10] that still

whirls on the air forever dirty with it
as if a whirlwind sucked at sand. And I,
30 holding my head in horror, cried: "Sweet Spirit,

what souls are these who run through this black haze?"
And he to me: "These are the nearly soulless
whose lives concluded neither blame nor praise.

They are mixed here with that despicable corps
35 of angels who were neither God nor Satan,
but only for themselves. The High Creator

scourged[11] them from Heaven for its perfect beauty,
and Hell will not receive them since the wicked
might feel some glory over them." And I:

40 "Master, what gnaws at them so hideously
their lamentation stuns the very air?"
"They have no hope of death," he answered me,

"and in their blind and unattaining state
their miserable lives have sunk so low
45 that they must envy every other fate.

No word of them survives their living season.
Mercy and Justice deny them even a name.
Let us not speak of them: look, and pass on."

I saw a banner there upon a mist.
50 Circling and circling, it seemed to scorn all pause.
So it ran on, and still behind it pressed

a never-ending rout of souls in pain.
I had not thought death had undone so many
as passed before me in that mournful train.

55 And some I knew among them; last of all
I recognized the shadow of that soul
who, in his cowardice, made the Great Denial.[12]

At once I understood for certain: these
were of that retrograde[13] and faithless crew
60 hateful to God and to His enemies.

These wretches never born and never dead
ran naked in a swarm of wasps and hornets
that goaded them the more the more they fled,

and made their faces stream with bloody gouts
65 of pus and tears that dribbled to their feet
to be swallowed there by loathsome worms and maggots.

Then looking onward I made out a throng
assembled on the beach of a wide river,
whereupon I turned to him: "Master, I long

70 to know what souls these are, and what strange usage

---

10. **pandemonium** (pan′ də mō′ nē əm): A word coined by Milton to describe the demons' capital in hell, it now means any place or scene of noise and wild disorder.
11. **scourged:** Whipped

12. **who, in . . . Denial:** This is almost certainly intended to be Celestine V, who became pope in 1294. He was a man of saintly life, but allowed himself to be convinced by a priest named Benedetto that his soul was in danger since no man could live in the world without being damned. In fear for his soul he withdrew from all worldly affairs and renounced the papacy. Benedetto promptly assumed the mantle himself and became Boniface VIII, a pope who became for Dante a symbol of all the worst corruptions of the church. Dante also blamed Boniface and his intrigues for many of the evils that befell the city of Florence. Celestine's great guilt is that his cowardice (in selfish terror for his own welfare) served as the door through which so much evil entered the church.
13. **retrograde:** Moving backward.

Grammar in Action

Imagery Writers often use imagery to emphasize or clarify a point. Imagery is the use of terms that repeat or echo a particular quality. For example, a writer may employ an image of bells by describing their sound (ringing) or their use (in churches, at the entrances of homes).

Dante employs imagery throughout the *Inferno*. Students will notice that a particular image or group of images seems to guide each canto. In Canto III, "The Vestibule of Hell," the idea of decay and general unpleasantness is echoed throughout the lines of this section. For example, the image is repeated through words such as "despicable corpse," "gnaws," "miserable," "wretches," "bloody gouts," "tears and pus," and "loathsome worms and maggots."

Student Activity 1. Have students list words in the canto that repeat other images. Some themes the students might choose are movement, light, or carnality.

Student Activity 2. Have students write a descriptive paragraph employing a particular image by using different words to evoke the same sense. Their subject should be something or someone familiar to them: the food in the school cafeteria, a pet, or an old sweater.

makes them as eager to cross as they seem to be
  in this infected light." At which the Sage:

"All this shall be made known to you when we
  stand
  on the joyless beach of Acheron." And I
  cast down my eyes, sensing a reprimand

in what he said, and so walked at his side
  in silence and ashamed until we came
  through the dead cavern to that sunless tide.

There, steering toward us in an ancient ferry
  came an old man[14] with white bush of hair,
  bellowing: "Woe to you depraved souls! Bury

here and forever all hope of Paradise:
  I come to lead you to the other shore,
  into eternal dark, into fire and ice.

And you who are living yet, I say begone
  from these who are dead." But when he saw me
  stand
  against his violence he began again:

"By other windings[15] and by other steerage
  shall you cross to that other shore. Not here! Not
  here!
  A lighter craft than mine must give you passage."

And my Guide to him: "Charon, bite back your
  spleen:
  this has been willed where what is willed must be,
  and is not yours to ask what it may mean."[16]

---

14. an old man: Charon. He is the ferryman of dead souls
across the Acheron in all classical mythology.

15. By other windings: Charon recognizes Dante not only
as a living man but as a soul in grace, and knows, therefore,
that the Infernal Ferry was not intended for him. He is
probably referring to the fact that souls destined for Purgatory
and Heaven assemble not at his ferry point, but on the banks
of the Tiber (a river that runs through Rome), from which
they are transported by an Angel.

**16. Charon, bite back your spleen . . . to ask what it may
mean:** Virgil tells Charon to suppress his bad temper, because
God has ordained that Dante shall make this journey. Charon
has no right to question or oppose God's orders.

The steersman of that march of ruined souls,
95 who wore a wheel of flame around each eye,
  stifled the rage that shook his woolly jowls.

But those unmanned and naked spirits there
  turned pale with fear and their teeth began to
  chatter
  at sound of his crude bellow. In despair

100 they blasphemed God,[17] their parents, their time
  on earth,
  the race of Adam, and the day and the hour
  and the place and the seed and the womb that
  gave them birth.

---

17. they blasphemed God: They cursed God. The souls of
the damned are not permitted to repent, for repentance is a
divine grace.

CHARON, THE RIVER ACHERON, INFERNO III
Gustave Doré

Humanities Note
Fine art, *Charon, The River Acheron* by Gustave Doré. This is a full-page illustration for a lavish volume of Dante's *Inferno* published by Doré. His interpretation of the boatman who conveys lost souls to hell is imbued with a nightmarish quality. The architectural splendor of the cliffs seems like an insurmountable barrier against escape while the waves look as if they were tossing the river with help from ill winds. The haggard figure of Charon seems lit from within and casts a glow on the waters around his craft.

You might want to use the following questions to discuss the art:
1. What is your initial reaction to this illustration?
2. Do you feel that the artist has captured the image Dante described in his poem?
3. What is the most engaging aspect of this illustration?

7 **Enrichment** This line crops up again and again in literary history. Students reading American literature will remember it as a common entry in early reading primers: "In Adam's fall we sinned all."

8 **Discussion** Point out to students the repeating images of a downward, spiraling motion. What words does Dante use to create this image? As readers, how do they imagine this to "feel"?

But all together they drew to that grim shore
where all must come who lose the fear of God.
105 Weeping and cursing they come for evermore,

and demon Charon with eyes like burning coals
herds them in, and with a whistling oar
flails on the stragglers to his wake[18] of souls.

As leaves in autumn loosen and stream down
110 until the branch stands bare above its tatters
spread on the rustling ground, so one by one

the evil seed of Adam in its Fall[19]
cast themselves, at his signal, from the shore
and streamed away like birds who hear their call.

115 So they are gone over that shadowy water,
and always before they reach the other shore
a new noise stirs on this, and new throngs
gather.

"My son," the courteous Master said to me,
"all who die in the shadow of God's wrath
converge to this from every clime and
120   country.

And all pass over eagerly, for here
Divine Justice transforms and spurs them so

---

18. wake: A watch over a corpse before burial, with a pun on waking up.
19. Fall: This word has at least three different meanings: the season fall, the fall of all humans with the sin of Adam and Eve, and the fall of individual sinners.

their dread turns wish: they yearn for what they
fear.[20]

No soul in Grace comes ever to this crossing;
125 therefore if Charon rages at your presence
you will understand the reason for his cursing."

When he had spoken, all the twilight country
shook so violently, the terror of it
bathes me with sweat even in memory:

the tear-soaked ground gave out a sigh of wind
130 that spewed itself in flame on a red sky,
and all my shattered senses left me. Blind,

like one whom sleep comes over in a swoon,[21]
I stumbled into darkness and went down.

---

20. they yearn . . . fear: Hell (allegorically Sin) is what the souls of the damned really wish for. Hell is their actual and deliberate choice, for divine grace is denied to none who wish for it in their hearts. The damned must, in fact, deliberately harden their hearts to God in order to become damned. Christ's grace is sufficient to save all who wish for it.
21. swoon: The act of fainting. This device (repeated at the end of Canto V) serves a double purpose. The first is technical: Dante uses it to cover a transition. We are never told how he crossed Acheron; for that would involve certain narrative matters he can better deal with when he crosses Styx (stiks), another river of the underworld, in Canto VII. The second is to provide a point of departure for a theme that is carried through the entire descent: the theme of Dante's emotional reaction to Hell. These two swoons early in the descent show him most susceptible to the grief about him. As he descends, pity leaves him, and he even goes so far as to add to the torments of one sinner. The allegory is clear: we must harden ourselves against every sympathy for sin.

Reader's Response *Imagine that you are Dante reading the inscription cut in stone above the gate. What would be your reaction?*

THINKING ABOUT THE SELECTION

Clarifying

1. What is Virgil's advice to Dante, spoken at the Gate of Hell?
2. Who are the souls tortured in this canto?
3. What is Charon's reaction to Dante's attempt to cross the river Acheron?
4. How does Virgil silence Charon?

Interpreting

5. What message does this canto provide about those who cannot or will not make a commitment to God? Support your answer with details from the canto.
6. Based on what you know of his life, why might Dante harbor special repugnance toward the indecisive?
7. (a) Find three examples of the use of assonance, or repetition of vowel sounds, in this canto. (b) What effect is created by the use of assonance?
8. (a) Does the image of souls as fallen leaves merely convey a sense of great numbers, or does it contribute to the despairing tone of this canto? (b) What are the other possible interpretations of this image?

Applying

9. Charon tells the souls to "Bury / here and forever all hope of Paradise." Is hope necessary for happiness? Explain your answer.

ANALYZING LITERATURE

Interpreting Imagery

In this canto Dante begins his description of Hell, which becomes for the reader an assault on all the senses. As we read his harrowing descriptions of the sounds, sights, and even smells of Hell, we come to share in Dante's repugnance at the horrors the poet encounters.

1. List the sounds that Dante uses to convey the terrors of hell.
2. List the details that appeal to the sense of sight.
3. Which images hint at the sense of touch, smell, or taste? Why would he have chosen these particular images?
4. Why do you think Dante dwells on the physical realities of Hell?

CRITICAL THINKING AND READING

Understanding Cause and Effect

A **cause** is what makes something happen. An **effect** is what actually happens. In Dante's vision a person's sins cause his or her placement in Hell.

1. (a) Why are the nearly soulless in Hell? (b) How does their punishment fit their sin?
2. (a) Why are the despicable corps of angels in Hell? (b) How does their punishment fit their crime?

UNDERSTANDING LANGUAGE

Appreciating Dialogue

Dialogue is conversation between characters. Dante's journey and growth are established by his constant dialogue with his guide and teacher, Virgil. This dialogue gives direction and purpose to the potentially meaningless sufferings that Dante witnesses in Hell. Dante relies on Virgil to guide and protect him. The relationship is one of teacher to pupil, or as Dante states, of "initiate to novice." Dante, in this canto, consistently asks questions that demonstrate his inexperience and awe toward the mysteries of Hell. Virgil allays Dante's fears with detailed explanation. Their dialogue evolves into one moral voice.

1. Find three questions that Dante asks of Virgil and put them in your own words.
2. What are Virgil's responses to Dante's questions?
3. Based on their dialogue, how would you rate Virgil as a teacher? Support your answer.

THINKING AND WRITING

Describing Scenes of Horror, Scenes of Woe

Imagine yourself as Dante. Take your list of details from a horror movie or a house of horrors. Do you think Dante would have reacted to the same things you did? Using as a model Dante's ability to capture and describe the horrifying, write a multiparagraph essay describing your experience in a house of horrors or watching a horror film. As you reread your work, try to create images that are vivid and realistic.

Focus

Literary Focus Stories are often told from the perspective of a person other than the author. This explains why the narrator differs from the author. Have students talk about their experiences of appropriating stories or attributing their own tales to someone else. Ask them to think about point of view as they begin reading this canto,

Writing/Prior Knowledge Have students discuss the two quotations about reason. Let them spend some time trying to evaluate how valid either definition is before starting to freewrite.

ESL Teaching Strategy Pair off the ESL students in class with partners. Have each couple draw up a list of the things that reason allows human beings to do. Then ask each to report on how those things may or may not separate people from animals that do not enjoy the use of reason. Then have students discuss the limits of human reason.

from the Inferno, Canto V

Commentary

Point of View. Every narrative is written from a particular perspective known as the **point of view.** Dante wrote the *Divine Comedy* in the first person in order to underscore the personal nature of his literary pilgrimage and in order to establish a bond with the reader. As he marvels at the sights and situations around him, the reader sees these events and images through his eyes, and to some extent accepts his judgments.

In fact, though, the Dante of the *Divine Comedy* is really a literary character created to express the judgments and opinions of Dante the poet. Dante the poet is writing from the point of view of a man who has already made his spiritual journey and who has reached certain conclusions. He must now persuade his reader to follow him on that journey by means of a sympathetic version of himself and by an intriguing narrative. For example, it is Dante the poet who has consigned Boniface VIII to the lowest depths of Hell, even though Boniface is not even dead. Dante the character/voyager merely inquires of Virgil why there is a place reserved for Boniface in Hell and thus is far more innocent and harmless than the poet himself. Dante the poet condemns Paolo and Francesca, the adulterers, to Hell, while Dante the voyager feels great pity for them when he hears their story. At first Dante the poet depicts the illicit lovers as merely part of a great number of lustful people, compared to flocks of birds. This initial image recalls the description in Canto III of the indecisive and has the effect of depersonalizing and dehumanizing these people. At this point the punishment is emphasized. But when Dante addresses the lovers and they answer eloquently, the pilgrim and, through him, the reader are moved to sympathy. So the reader is drawn into the tension between condemnation of sin and the desire to spare others from suffering. This tension is just the first step in a long lesson about the necessity of suffering in the presence of sin.

Writing

The sinners in Circle Two of Hell are denied the pure light of reason. The Greek philosopher Aristotle called reason "That by which the soul thinks and judges," while the Roman writer Cicero called it "The light and lamp of life." Freewrite, exploring your own definition of reason.

Objectives

Thematic

To witness the punishment of the condemned

Skills

1 To evaluate first-person point of view

2 To compare and contrast judgments

3 To examine Latin roots

4 To write from another point of view

Support Material

Teaching Portfolio

Teacher Backup, p. 771

Grammar in Action Worksheet, *Effective Adjectives*, p. 775

Usage and Mechanics Worksheet, p. 777

Analyzing Literature Worksheet, *Evaluating First-Person Point of View*, p 778

Canto V

Circle Two: *The Carnal*

The Poets leave Limbo and enter the SECOND CIRCLE. Here begin the torments of Hell proper, and here, blocking the way, sits MINOS,[1] the dread and semi-bestial judge of the damned who assigns to each soul its eternal torment. He orders the Poets back; but Virgil silences him as he earlier silenced Charon, and the Poets move on.

They find themselves on a dark ledge swept by a great whirlwind, which spins within it the souls of the CARNAL, those who betrayed reason to their appetites. Their sin was to abandon themselves to the tempest of their passions: so they are swept forever in the tempest of Hell, forever denied the light of reason and of God. Virgil identifies many among them.[2] SEMIRAMIS is there, and DIDO, CLEOPATRA, HELEN, ACHILLES, PARIS, and TRISTAN. Dante sees PAOLO and FRANCESCA swept together, and in the name of love he calls to them to tell their sad story. They pause from their eternal flight to come to him, and Francesca tells their history while Paolo weeps at her side. Dante is so stricken by compassion at their tragic tale that he swoons once again.

So we went down to the second ledge alone;
  a smaller circle[3] of so much greater pain
  the voice of the damned rose in a bestial moan.

5 There Minos sits, grinning, grotesque, and hale.[4]
  He examines each lost soul as it arrives
  and delivers his verdict with his coiling tail.

That is to say, when the ill-fated soul
  appears before him it confesses all,[5]
10   and that grim sorter of the dark and foul

decides which place in Hell shall be its end,
  then wraps his twitching tail about himself
  one coil for each degree it must descend.

The soul descends and others take its place:
15   each crowds in its turn to judgment, each confesses,
  each hears its doom and falls away through space.

"O you who come into this camp of woe,"
  cried Minos when he saw me turn away
  without awaiting his judgment, "watch where you go

20 once you have entered here, and to whom you turn!
  Do not be misled by that wide and easy passage!"
  And my Guide to him: "That is not your concern;

---

1. MINOS (mī′ näs′): Like all the monsters Dante assigns to the various offices of Hell, Minos is drawn from classical mythology. He was the son of Europa and of Zeus who descended to her in the form of a bull. Minos became a mythological king of Crete, so famous for his wisdom and justice that after death his soul was made judge of the dead. In the *Aeneid*, Virgil presents him fulfilling the same office at Aeneas' descent to the underworld. Dante, however, transforms him into an irate and hideous monster with a tail.

2. many among them: The following are famous lovers from legend and history. They are identified more fully in the notes to this canto. Their names are pronounced as follows: Semiramis (si mir′ ə mis); Dido (dī′ dō); Cleopatra (klē′ ō pa′ trə); Achilles (ə kil′ ēz); Tristan (tris′ tən); Paolo (pä′ ō lō); Francesca (frän chä′ skə).

---

3. a smaller circle: The pit of Hell tapers like a funnel. The circles of ledges accordingly grow smaller as they descend.
4. hale (hāl): Healthy.
5. it confesses all: Just as the souls appeared eager to cross Acheron, so they are eager to confess even while they are filled with dread. Dante is once again making the point that sinners elect their Hell by an act of their own will.

Presentation

Motivation/Prior Knowledge Tell students that Dante finds in the second circle of hell Dido, Cleopatra, and Helen. What sin might these three share in common?

Purpose—Setting Question Why would passion be abhorrent to the medieval mind?

Universal Themes The concept of the battle between body and mind is found here and throughout literature. Remind students of the attention paid to the theme in Virgil's *Aeneid*, page 507, and in Milton's *Paradise Lost*, page 814.

Enrichment The word *carnival* shares some meanings of the word *carnal*. The term carnival is borrowed from the medieval Italian phrase *carne vale*, meaning "O flesh farewell!" and was associated with the celebration that comes before the beginning of the Lenten season, which required Christians to abstain from meat for the forty days that preceded Easter. Explain to students that the Mardi Gras celebration in New Orleans is a continuation of this custom. Ask students what other forms of amusement combine both a jubilation and a sense of darkness.

Critical Thinking and Reading Worksheet, *Comparing and Contrasting Judgments*, p. 779
Language Worksheet, *Latin Roots*, p. 780
Selection Test, pp. 781–782
Essay Questions and Evaluation Guidelines, p. 807

THE LUSTFUL, INFERNO V
Gustave Doré

it is his fate to enter every door.
   This has been willed where what is willed must be,
   and is not yours to question. Say no more."

25 Now the choir of anguish, like a wound,
   strikes through the tortured air. Now I have come
   to Hell's full lamentation,[6] sound beyond sound.

I came to a place stripped bare of every light
   and roaring on the naked dark like seas
30 wracked by a war of winds. Their hellish flight

of storm and counterstorm through time foregone,
   sweeps the souls of the damned before its charge.
   Whirling and battering it drives them on,

------

6. Hell's full lamentation: It is with the second circle that the real tortures of Hell begin.

and when they pass the ruined gap of Hell[7]
   through which we had come, their shrieks begin
35 anew.
   There they blaspheme the power of God eternal.

And this, I learned, was the never ending flight
   of those who sinned in the flesh,[8] the carnal and lusty
   who betrayed reason to their appetite.

40 As the wings of wintering starlings bear them on
   in their great wheeling flights, just so the blast
   wherries[9] these evil souls through time foregone.

Here, there, up, down, they whirl and, whirling, strain
   with never a hope of hope to comfort them,
45 not of release, but even of less pain.

As cranes go over sounding their harsh cry,
   leaving the long streak of their flight in air,
   so come these spirits, wailing as they fly.

And watching their shadows lashed by wind, I cried:
50 "Master, what souls are these the very air
   lashes with its black whips from side to side?"

"The first of these whose history you would know,"
   he answered me, "was Empress of many tongues.[10]
55 Mad sensuality corrupted her so

------

7. the ruined gap of hell: At the time of the Harrowing of Hell a great earthquake shook the underworld, shattering rocks and cliffs. Ruins resulting from the same shock are noted in Canto XII, 34, and Canto XXI, 112ff. At the beginning of Canto XXIV, the Poets leave the *bolgia*—an Italian word meaning "ditch"—of the Hypocrites by climbing the ruined slabs of a bridge that was shattered by this earthquake.
8. those who sinned in the flesh: Here begin the punishments for the various sins of Incontinence (the sins of the She-Wolf). In the second circle are punished those who sinned by excess of sexual passion. Since this is the most natural sin and the sin most nearly associated with love, its punishment is the lightest of all to be found in Hell proper. The Carnal are whirled and buffeted endlessly through the murky air (symbolic of the beclouding of their reason by passion) by a great gale (symbolic of their lust).
9. wherries (hwer´ ēz): Transports.
10. Empress of many tongues: Semiramis, a legendary queen of Assyria who assumed full power at the death of her husband, Ninus (nī´ nəs).

------

that to hide the guilt of her debauchery[11]
  she licensed all depravity alike,
  and lust and law were one in her decree.

She is Semiramis of whom the tale is told
  how she married Ninus and succeeded him
  to the throne of that wide land the Sultans hold.

The other is Dido;[12] faithless to the ashes
  of Sichaeus, she killed herself for love.
  The next whom the eternal tempest lashes

is sense-drugged Cleopatra. See Helen[13] there,
  from whom such ill arose. And great Achilles,[14]
  who fought at last with love in the house of
    prayer,

And Paris. And Tristan."[15] As they whirled above
  he pointed out more than a thousand shades
  of those torn from the mortal life by love.

I stood there while my Teacher one by one
  named the great knights and ladies of dim time;
  and I was swept by pity and confusion.

At last I spoke: "Poet, I should be glad
  to speak a word with those two swept together[16]
75 so lightly on the wind and still so sad."

And he to me: "Watch them. When next they
    pass,
  call to them in the name of love that drives
  and damns them here. In that name they will
    pause."

Thus, as soon as the wind in its wild course
  brought them around, I called: "O wearied
80   souls!
  if none forbid it, pause and speak to us."

As mating doves that love calls to their nest
  glide through the air with motionless raised
    wings,
  borne by the sweet desire that fills each breast—

85 Just so those spirits turned on the torn sky
  from the band where Dido whirls across the air;
  such was the power of pity in my cry.

"O living creature, gracious, kind, and good,
  going this pilgrimage through the sick night,
90 visiting us who stained the earth with blood,

were the King of Time our friend, we would pray
    His peace
  on you who have pitied us. As long as the wind
  will let us pause, ask of us what you please.

---

11. debauchery (dē bôch′ ə rē): Indulgence in sensual pleasure.

12. Dido: Queen and founder of Carthage, an ancient kingdom in northern Africa. She had vowed to remain faithful to her husband, Sichaeus (sə kē′ əs), but she fell in love with Aeneas. When Aeneas abandoned her she stabbed herself on a funeral pyre she had had prepared.

  According to Dante's own system of punishments, she should be in the Seventh Circle (Canto XIII) with the suicides. The only clue Dante gives to the tempering of her punishment is his statement that "she killed herself for love." Dante always seems readiest to forgive in that name.

13. Cleopatra . . . Helen: Cleopatra was a queen of Egypt (51–49; 48–30 B.C.), and the mistress of the powerful Romans Julius Caesar and Mark Antony. Helen was the beautiful wife of the King of Sparta. According to legend, the Trojan War was started when she was forcibly taken away to Troy by Paris, a son of the Trojan king, Priam.

14. Achilles: He was the greatest warrior on the Greek side during the Trojan War. Achilles is placed among this company because of his passion for Polyxena (pō lik′ sə nə), the daughter of Priam. For love of her, he agreed to desert the Greeks and to join the Trojans, but when he went to the temple for the wedding (according to the legend Dante has followed) he was killed by Paris.

15. Tristan: A knight sent to Ireland by King Mark of Cornwall to bring back the princess Isolde (i sōl′ də) to be the king's bride. Isolde and Tristan fell in love and tragically died together.

---

16. those two swept together: Paolo and Francesca. Dante's treatment of these two lovers is certainly the tenderest and most sympathetic accorded any of the sinners in Hell, and legends immediately began to grow about this pair.

  The facts are these. In 1275 Giovanni Malatesta, (jō vä′ nē mäl ə te′ stä) of Rimini, called Giovanni the Lame, a somewhat deformed but brave and powerful warrior, made a political marriage with Francesca, daughter of Guido da Polenta (gwē′ dō dä pō len′ tä) of Ravenna. Francesca came to Rimini and there an amour grew between her and Giovanni's younger brother Paolo. Despite the fact that Paolo had married in 1269 and had become the father of two daughters by 1275, his affair with Francesca continued for many years. It was sometime between 1283 and 1286 that Giovanni surprised them in Francesca's bedroom and killed both of them.

4 Cultural Note Dante writes that Dido "killed herself for love." The concepts of love and death seem antithetical, but "dying for love" is a common theme in literature. Ask students how they have seen it treated in any other works with which they are familiar.

    Student Activity 1. Have students list other strings of adjectives employed by Dante in this canto.

    Student Activity 2. Have students write a brief description of their classroom or bedroom, employing adjectives.

5 Discussion Note how each stanza begins with the same word: Love. This type of repetition is called anaphora. Ask students how this is similar to and different from rhyme? What effect does this have on the meaning of the lines? How is it like an incantation? Ask students what chants they know. How do they remember them? Where is the "power" in the chant?

6 Enrichment Students will probably think of *Romeo and Juliet* while reading this passage. Although Shakespeare's drama was written well after the *Divine Comedy*, the comparison will prove useful. Remind students that *Romeo and Juliet* is set in Verona and Mantua, two towns in northern Italy. What comparisons and contrasts can the students bring to the tale of Paolo and Francesca?

The town where I was born lies by the shore
95 where the Po[17] descends into its ocean rest
with its attendant streams in one long murmur.

Love, which in gentlest hearts will soonest bloom
seized my lover with passion for that sweet body
from which I was torn unshriven[18] to my doom.

100 Love, which permits no loved one not to love,
took me so strongly with delight in him
that we are one in Hell, as we were above.[19]

Love led us to one death. In the depths of Hell
Caïna waits for him[20] who took our lives."
105 This was the piteous tale they stopped to tell.

And when I had heard those world-offended
    lovers
I bowed my head. At last the Poet spoke:
"What painful thoughts are these your lowered
    brow covers?"

When at length I answered, I began: "Alas!
110 What sweetest thoughts, what green and young
    desire
led these two lovers to this sorry pass."

Then turning to those spirits once again,
I said: "Francesca, what you suffer here
melts me to tears of pity and of pain.

115 But tell me: in the time of your sweet sighs
by what appearances found love the way
to lure you to his perilous paradise?"

---

17. Po (pō): A river of northern Italy.
18. unshriven: Unconfessed and so with her sin unforgiven.
19. that we . . . above: At many points of the *Inferno* Dante makes clear the principle that the souls of the damned are locked so blindly into their own guilt that none can feel sympathy for another, or find any pleasure in the presence of another. The temptation of many readers is to interpret this line romantically: i.e., that the love of Paolo and Francesca survives Hell itself. The more Dantean interpretation, however, is that they add to one another's anguish (a) as mutual reminders of their sin, and (b) as insubstantial shades of the bodies for which they once felt such great passion.
20. Caïna . . . him: Giovanni Malatesta was still alive at the writing. His fate is already decided, however, and upon his death, his soul will fall to Caïna, the first ring of the last circle (Canto XXXII), where lie those who performed acts of treachery against their kin.

And she: "The double grief of a lost bliss
is to recall its happy hour in pain.
120 Your Guide and Teacher knows the truth of this.

But if there is indeed a soul in Hell
to ask of the beginning of our love
out of his pity, I will weep and tell:

On a day for dalliance we read the rhyme
125 of Lancelot,[21] how love had mastered him.
We were alone with innocence and dim time.[22]

Pause after pause that high old story drew
our eyes together while we blushed and paled;
but it was one soft passage overthrew

130 our caution and our hearts. For when we read
how her fond smile was kissed by such a lover,
he who is one with me alive and dead

breathed on my lips the tremor of his kiss.
That book, and he who wrote it, was a pander.[23]
135 That day we read no further." As she said this,

the other spirit, who stood by her, wept
so piteously, I felt my senses reel
and faint away with anguish. I was swept

by such a swoon as death is, and I fell,
140 as a corpse might fall, to the dead floor of Hell.

---

21. the rhyme . . . Lancelot: The story exists in many forms. The details Dante makes use of are from an Old French version.
22. dim time: The olden time depicted in the Lancelot story. This phrase was added by the translator; the original reads, "We were alone, suspecting nothing."
23. That book . . . pander: *Galeotto,* the Italian word for "pander," is also the Italian rendering of the name of Gallehault, who in the French Romance Dante refers to here, urged Lancelot and Guinevere on to love. A pander is a go-between in a love affair.

Reader's Response *Do you admire people who throw caution to the wind or people who show a tendency to do everything in moderation? Explain your answer.*

Commentary

High and Low Art Much respected art combines both high and low forms of culture. Just as both dandies and groundlings made up the audience of Shakespeare's plays, so do works themselves often combine the varied aspects of culture.

Dante's writing also attempts to combine diverse aspects of culture. Through his choice of language, he bridges these opposite ends of culture and raises the low form to a high level of art. He does this by writing in the vernacular, Italian, and rejecting the classical language of Latin.

Dante's goals were many. In one sense he was trying to directly address his audience. Every day we employ many different registers (modes of speaking) depending on purpose and audience. Remind students that among themselves they often use slang or colloquial language. Have students write a series of brief monologues. In each monologue the student will employ a different language mask: in one, he or she will play a typical teenager (slang); in another, a child (baby talk); and in another, the mask of the teacher (the language of authority).

THINKING ABOUT THE SELECTION

Clarifying

1. (a) Describe the creature that guards this circle of Hell. (b) Explain how he indicates his judgment.
2. List as many of the people named by Virgil as inhabiting this circle as you can remember.
3. (a) Where is the person who killed Paolo and Francesca going to go when he dies? (b) Why?

Interpreting

4. Interpret Virgil's remark, "It is his fate to enter every door." Explain its literal and figurative meanings.
5. Why are the lustful blown about by the wind?
6. What is the truth behind Francesca's statement, "The double grief of a lost bliss / is to recall its happy hour in pain"?
7. Why does Dante feel sympathy for the sinners?

Applying

8. Often, people do things that might seem quite harmless but in fact cause great harm to others. Which is more important, the mistake itself, or the result of that error? For example, is it wrong to cheat on a test or lie on a college application even if no one gets hurt? How would you argue the two different views of this issue?

ANALYZING LITERATURE

Evaluating First-Person Point of View

Canto V contains a tale within a tale, and both are related in the first person. As Francesca tells her story, she draws the pilgrim into the tragedy that has befallen her. She captures his sympathy immediately by addressing him as "gracious, kind, and good" and invokes God to show her gratitude to him. Her repetition of the word *love* and her description of this emotion as a noble sentiment render her argument all the more convincing. The pilgrim is immediately touched and anguished. Francesca continues her story by speaking of herself as a courtly, innocent girl. She never directly speaks of her transgression and leaves the listener and reader to think that she is unjustly punished. Thus the poet shows us the danger of the same language he himself uses. Anyone may mislead others by omitting certain details and emphasizing others. Here the reader learns to distrust the first-person narrative that has previously engaged his or her sympathy.

1. (a) How do you think Paolo might tell this story? (b) Would he choose the same details? Explain.

2. (a) What impression do you form of Francesca? (b) What impression do you form of Paolo?
3. Imagine that you are a prosecuting attorney. How might the impression you create of Paolo and Francesca be different from that in Francesca's story?

CRITICAL THINKING AND READING

Comparing and Contrasting Judgments

A **judgment** is a conclusion you reach after examining the facts. Virgil, the voice of reason in this canto, judges the lustful much more harshly than does his disciple, Dante. He points out clearly how their own behavior brought about their downfall and caused their condemnation to this circle of Hell. His language is harsh, direct, and concise: "The other is Dido; faithless to the ashes / of Sichaeus, she killed herself for love."
1. How does Virgil judge Paolo and Francesca?
2. How does Dante judge Paolo and Francesca?
3. Which judgment do you think Dante the poet wants you to agree with? Explain.

UNDERSTANDING LANGUAGE

Examining Latin Roots

Many words in English share Latin roots. Canto V deals with the punishment of the souls of the carnal, people who have committed sins of the flesh. The English word *carnal* is based on the Latin word *carnalis,* meaning fleshly as opposed to spiritual. The root is *carn,* which gives us many other English words.

Find the meaning of each of the following words. Explain how each relates to *carnalis.*
a. carnal   d. carnival
b. carnivore   e. incarnate
c. carnivorous

THINKING AND WRITING

Writing from Another Point of View

Imagine that Virgil is traveling through Hell alone and encounters Paolo and Francesca. How would his conversation with them be different from Dante's? If you were Virgil, what would you say? Look over what Virgil does say in the fifth Canto; compare his language and his tone to those of Dante. Then in four paragraphs retell the story from Virgil's point of view. As you revise, compare your language to Virgil's and be sure you have maintained a consistent point of view.

(continued from bottom of page)

ANSWERS TO ANALYZING LITERATURE

1. (a) Answers will differ. He might tell it from a more bitter point of view. (b) He would probably choose other details.
2. (a) She seems attractive and sad. (b) He seems detached and is not described in detail.
3. A prosecutor would emphasize their legal status as in-laws.

ANSWERS TO CRITICAL THINKING AND READING

1. He seems to judge them gently.
2. Dante also sympathizes with them.
3. Answers will differ. Most will say he wants us to agree with Virgil.

ANSWERS TO UNDERSTANDING LANGUAGE

a. sensual
b. flesh-eating mammal
c. flesh-eating
d. a sensual celebration
e. made from flesh or into flesh

THINKING AND WRITING

Publishing Student Writing Have students make notes from the readings of Virgil's remarks. Have them read those notes aloud before starting to retell the story. Encourage students to value and benefit from each other's notes.

Closure and Extension

ANSWERS TO THINKING ABOUT THE SELECTION

1. (a) Minos is a grotesque half-man, half-animal. (b) He delivers his judgments by coiling his tail.
2. Semiramis, Dido, Cleopatra, Helen, Achilles, Paolo, Francesca, Paris, and Tristan are mentioned here.
3. (a) He will go to Caina. (b) He will go there because it is set aside for those who killed family members.
4. Answers will differ. Attention will be paid to the fact that Minos is condemned to judge all who enter Hell.
5. They are blown because the wind symbolizes passions that swept away reason in them.
6. Answers will differ. Most will say her sadness is doubled by the fact that she can recall a happy time.
7. He feels sympathy because he himself was a lover.
8. Answers will differ. All will contend with the issues of fairness, practicality, and the consequences of dishonesty.

GUIDE FOR INTERPRETING

Literary Focus Have students discuss their own ideas about films or television shows that use personification. Remind them of images in advertisements that use smiling toilet bowls or telephone books with fingers that do the walking. Ask them what they think of the effectiveness of such techniques.

Writing/Prior Knowledge Pair up the students in your class. Have them share ideas and tell each other about their emotions of fear before they begin freewriting.

ESL Teaching Strategy To accomplish the writing assignment, pair each ESL student with another member of the class. The native-speaking student should act as a coach discussing the ways in which the ESL student might develop drawings to illustrate the freewriting exercise.

Teaching Tenth-Grade Students Before reading Dante's version of Satan, have tenth-grade students speculate on how he will be depicted. Give each student a chance to explain why he or she anticipates some special detail in the portrait of evil.

from the Inferno, Canto XXXIV

Commentary

Personification. Personification is the portrayal of a concept by granting it a human identity. The Greeks and Romans personified phenomena by creating gods that evoked aspects of nature. Poseidon personified the sea and Apollo the sun.

Dante uses both historical and mythological figures to represent the various sins. He goes to great lengths to fashion them an appropriate punishment. In fact, it is the punishment itself that makes the reader aware of the sins that these people have committed. A good example would be Paolo and Francesca. As Dante discovers, they are the personification of lust. They are swept around this circle of hell just as they were swept away by their passions in life. This idea of appropriate punishment is linked to personification. Together, sin, its personification, and punishment create an allegorical system.

Of course, Satan is the ultimate personification of evil. In him, evil is depicted as a hideous three-faced monster. He is frozen into the very bottom of Hell, isolated as far as possible from God and humanity, a suitable punishment for the cold-hearted betrayal of the ultimate good.

Writing

Films often personify evil. They may represent evil as a demonic car or as a plant. Create your own personification of evil.

Commentary

This is the end of an odyssey into Hell. But for Dante, this is merely the first of three stages of his pilgrimage toward salvation. In the cantos you have read, you have seen how Dante creates a transition from one circle of hell to another. Dante succeeds by making constant use of bridges, river crossings, and other images of travel. When he is confronted with an obstacle, Dante conveniently faints, allowing Virgil or his own narrative to carry him from one circle to another.

At the end of the *Inferno*, Dante must prepare for the continuation of his voyage in yet another realm. Satan is used as a bridge over which Virgil and Dante climb into the next world. Virgil must carry the weakened Dante over the obstacle, as he did many times before in the *Inferno*. What is new here is the contrast that Dante uses to lead his reader to a new world of hope and salvation. He contrasts the dark world of Hell with the dazzling light of Purgatory. And so he moves from the "lightless" to the "shining" world. This image summarizes Dante's journey.

Objectives

Thematic

To see how the *Inferno* concludes

Skills

1 To develop an *understanding of personification*

2 To learn how to avoid "translationese"

3 To prepare translations

Support Material

Teaching Portfolio
Teacher Backup, p. 783
Usage and Mechanics Worksheet, p. 787
Analyzing Literature Worksheet, *Understanding Personification*, p. 788
Critical Thinking and Reading Worksheet, *Avoiding "Translationese"*

Canto XXXIV

Circle Nine: *Cocytus*[1]

Round Four: Judecca

The Center

Compound Fraud

The Treacherous to Their Masters

Satan

"On march the banners of the King," Virgil begins as the Poets face the last depth. He is quoting a medieval hymn, and to it he adds the distortion and perversion of all that lies about him. "On march the banners of the King—of Hell."[2] And there before them, in an infernal parody of Godhead, they see Satan in the distance, his great wings beating like a windmill. It is their beating that is the source of the icy wind of Cocytus, the exhalation of all evil.

All about him in the ice are strewn the sinners of the last round, JUDECCA, named for Judas Iscariot.[3] These are TREACHEROUS TO THEIR MASTERS. They lie completely sealed in the ice, twisted and distorted into every conceivable posture. It is impossible to speak to them, and the Poets move on to observe Satan.

He is fixed into the ice at the center to which flow all the rivers of guilt; and as he beats his great wings as if to escape, their icy wind only freezes him more surely into the polluted ice. In a grotesque parody of the Trinity, he has three faces, each a different color, and in each mouth he clamps a sinner whom he rips eternally with his teeth. JUDAS ISCARIOT is in the central mouth: BRUTUS and CASSIUS[4] in the mouths on either side.

Having seen all, the Poets now climb through the center, grappling hand over hand down the hairy flank of Satan himself—a last supremely symbolic action—and at last, when they have passed the center of all gravity, they emerge from Hell. A long climb from the earth's center to the Mount of Purgatory awaits them, and they push on without rest, ascending along the sides of the river Lethe, till they emerge once more to see the stars of Heaven, just before dawn on Easter Sunday.

"On march the banners of the King of Hell,"
　my Master said. "Toward us. Look straight ahead:
　can you make him out at the core of the frozen shell?"

Like a whirling windmill seen afar at twilight,
5　or when a mist has risen from the ground—
　just such an engine rose upon my sight

stirring up such a wild and bitter wind
　I cowered for shelter at my Master's back,
　there being no other windbreak I could find.

10　I stood now where the souls of the last class
　(with fear my verses tell it) were covered wholly;
　they shone below the ice like straws in glass.

Some lie stretched out; others are fixed in place
　upright, some on their heads, some on their soles;
15　another, like a bow, bends foot to face.

---

1. Cocytus (kō sī′ təs): This Greek word means "wailing."

2. On march the banners of the King—of Hell: The hymn was written in the sixth century by Venantius Fortunatus, Bishop of Poitiers. The original celebrates the Holy Cross, and is part of the service for Good Friday to be sung at the moment of uncovering the cross.

3. Judas Iscariot (is ker′ ē ət): The disciple who betrayed Jesus; see the Bible, Matthew 26:14, 48.

4. BRUTUS and CASSIUS: They took part in a plot against Julius Caesar.

p. 789
Language Worksheet, *Understanding Connotations of Words*, p. 790
Selection Test, pp. 791–792
Essay Questions and Evaluation
　Guidelines, p. 807

Presentation

Motivation/Prior Knowledge This canto is the end of the *Inferno*, but it is also the beginning of the *Purgatory*. Ask students if they have ever seen a movie whose ending tells them that a sequel is inevitable. Ask them to mention some, like *Star Wars*, where evil is overcome but not entirely conquered.

Purpose-Setting Question Ask students to keep in mind that this last canto serves as both a beginning and an ending. How do the images present this dual role? What other signs does Dante provide the reader to convey this message?

Master Teacher Note Have students mention their own versions of punishment for crimes they believe call for special penalties. Without naming names, prompt them to evaluate the kinds of punishments that are routinely given to criminals for various acts.

Reading Strategy The subject of this canto is those "who are treacherous to their masters." Ask students why they think Dante fills Hell with such inhabitants.

1 Discussion Ask students why Dante includes the phrase "with fear my verses tell it" in parentheses?

2 Discussion Note Dante's use of juxtaposition. Discuss with students why these images are paired.

3 Discussion Point out how Dante addresses the reader so directly. Discuss with students why he makes this gesture so late in this story.

4 Discussion Note the alliteration in "weirdly wonderful." Discuss with students why this image is somewhat contradictory.

5 Discussion Again note the alliteration here. Discuss its impact on the listener.

6 Clarification Note that Dante gives the reader a seemingly literal explanation of why this Bolgia is encased in ice.

7 Discussion Discuss why the image of cannibalism seems so especially repugnant to Dante.

8 Discussion Discuss with the class why it is significant that Brutus suffers without making any noise or complaint?

When we had gone so far across the ice
    that it pleased my Guide to show me the foul creature[5]
    which once had worn the grace of Paradise,

he made me stop, and, stepping aside, he said:
20   "Now see the face of Dis![6] This is the place
    where you must arm your soul against all dread."

Do not ask, Reader, how my blood ran cold
    and my voice choked up with fear. I cannot write it:
    this is a terror that cannot be told.

25 I did not die, and yet I lost life's breath:
    imagine for yourself what I became,
    deprived at once of both my life and death.

The Emperor of the Universe of Pain
    jutted his upper chest above the ice;
30   and I am closer in size to the great mountan

the Titans[7] make around the central pit,
    than they to his arms. Now, starting from this part,
    imagine the whole that corresponds to it!

If he was once as beautiful as now
35   he is hideous, and still turned on his Maker,
    well may he be the source of every woe!

With what a sense of awe I saw his head
    towering above me! for it had three faces:[8]
    one was in front, and it was fiery red;

40 the other two, as weirdly wonderful,
    merged with it from the middle of each shoulder
    to the point where all converged at the top of the skull;

the right was something between white and bile;
    the left was about the color that one finds
45   on those who live along the banks of the Nile.

Under each head two wings rose terribly,
    their span proportioned to so gross a bird:
    I never saw such sails upon the sea.

They were not feathers—their texture and their form
50   were like a bat's wings—and he beat them so
    that three winds blew from him in one great storm:

it is these winds that freeze all Cocytus.
    He wept from his six eyes, and down three chins
    the tears ran mixed with bloody froth and pus.[9]

55 In every mouth he worked a broken sinner
    between his rake-like teeth. Thus he kept three
    in eternal pain at his eternal dinner.

For the one in front the biting seemed to play
    no part at all compared to the ripping: at times
60   the whole skin of his back was flayed away.

"That soul that suffers most," explained my Guide,
    "is Judas Iscariot, he who kicks his legs
    on the fiery chin and has his head inside.

Of the other two, who have their heads thrust forward,
65   the one who dangles down from the black face
    is Brutus: note how he writhes without a word.

And there, with the huge and sinewy arms,[10] is the soul
    of Cassius,—But the night is coming on[11]
    and we must go, for we have seen the whole."

---

5. the foul creature: Satan.

6. Dis (dis): In greek mythology, the god of the lower world or the lower world itself. Here it stands for Satan.

7. Titans: Giant deities who were overthrown by Zeus and the Olympian gods of Greece.

8. three faces: Numerous interpretations of these three faces exist. What is essential to all explanation is that they be seen as perversions of the qualities of the Trinity.

9. bloody froth and pus: the gore of the sinners he chews, which is mixed with his saliva.

10. huge and sinewy arms: The Cassius who betrayed Caesar was more generally described in terms of Shakespeare's "lean and hungry look." Another Cassius is described by Cicero (*Catiline* III) as huge and sinewy. Dante probably confused the two.

11. the night is coming on: It is now Saturday evening.

JUDECCA—LUCIFER
Gustave Doré

Humanities Note
Fine art, *The Judecca-Lucifer* by Gustave Doré. This is a fine example of the illustrations Doré produced for his deluxe edition of Dante. The artist's use of strong contrasts between light and dark allows the rendering of fine details without sacrificing the overall darkness of the composition. Doré's Lucifer is a nightmarish figure who blends into the dark background and appears to the viewer almost as a surprise. His lurking presence dwarfs the human souls before him. The craggy rock formations add to the barren eeriness of the scene.

You might want to use the following questions to discuss the art:

1. How does Doré's conception of the devil compare with others you have seen?
2. How does this drawing make you feel?
3. How does Doré's depiction compare with that of Dante's?
4. What interests you most in this illustration?

Then, as he bade, I clasped his neck, and he,
   watching for a moment when the wings
   were opened wide, reached over dexterously[12]

and seized the shaggy coat of the king demon;
   then grappling matted hair and frozen crusts
   from one tuft to another, clambered down.

When we had reached the joint where the great thigh
   merges into the swelling of the haunch,
   my Guide and Master, straining terribly,

turned his head to where his feet had been
   and began to grip the hair as if he were climbing,[13]
   so that I thought we moved toward Hell again.

"Hold fast!" my Guide said, and his breath came shrill[14]
   with labor and exhaustion. "There is no way
   but by such stairs to rise above such evil."

85 At last he climbed out through an opening
   in the central rock, and he seated me on the rim;
   then joined me with a nimble backward spring.

I looked up, thinking to see Lucifer
   as I had left him, and I saw instead
90 his legs projecting high into the air.

Now let all those whose dull minds are still vexed
   by failure to understand what point it was
   I had passed through, judge if I was perplexed.

---

12. dexterously: Skilfully.
13. as if he were climbing: They have passed the center of gravity and so must turn around and start climbing.

---

14. his breath came shrill: In Canto XXIII, 85, the fact that Dante breathes indicates to the Hypocrites that he is alive. Virgil's breathing is certainly a contradiction.

"Get up. Up on your feet," my Master said.
95   "The sun already mounts to middle tierce,[15]
  and a long road and hard climbing lie ahead."

It was no hall of state we had found there,
  but a natural animal pit hollowed from rock
  with a broken floor and a close and sunless air.

100 "Before I tear myself from the Abyss,"
  I said when I had risen, "O my Master,
  explain to me my error in all this:

where is the ice? and Lucifer—how has he
  been turned from top to bottom: and how can
    the sun
105 have gone from night to day so suddenly?"

And he to me: "You imagine you are still
  on the other side of the center where I grasped
  the shaggy flank of the Great Worm of Evil

which bores through the world—you *were* while I
    climbed down,
110 but I turned myself about, you passed
  the point to which all gravities are drawn.

You are under the other hemisphere where you
    stand;
  the sky above us is the half opposed
  to that which canopies the great dry land.

115 Under the midpoint of that other sky
  the Man[16] who was born sinless and who lived
  beyond all blemish, came to suffer and die.

You have your feet upon a little sphere
  which forms the other face of the Judecca.
120 There it is evening when it is morning here.

And this gross Fiend and Image of all Evil
  who made a stairway for us with his hide
  is pinched and prisoned in the ice-pack still.

On this side he plunged down from heaven's height,
125 and the land that spread here once hid in the sea
  and fled North to our hemisphere for fright,[17]

And it may be that moved by that same fear,
  the one peak[18] that still rises on this side
  fled upward leaving this great cavern[19] here."

130 Down there, beginning at the further bound
  of Beelzebub's[20] dim tomb, there is a space
  not known by sight, but only by sound

of a little stream[21] descending through the hollow
  it has eroded from the massive stone
135 in its endlessly entwining lazy flow."

My Guide and I crossed over and began
  to mount that little known and lightless road
  to ascend into the shining world again.

He first, I second, without thought of rest
140 we climbed the dark until we reached the point
  where a round opening brought in sight the blest

and beauteous shining of the Heavenly cars.
And we walked out once more beneath the Stars.[22]

---

15. middle tierce: According to the church's division of the day for prayer, tierce is the period from about six to nine A.M. Middle tierce, therefore, is seven-thirty. In going through the center point, they have gone from night to day. They have moved ahead twelve hours.

16. the Man: Jesus, who suffered and died in Jerusalem, which was thought to be the middle of the earth.

17. fled North . . . for fright: Dante believed that the Northern hemisphere was mostly land and the Southern hemisphere water. Here he explains the reason for this state of affairs.

18. the one peak: The Mount of Purgatory.

19. this great cavern: The natural animal pit of line 98. It is also "Beelzebub's dim tomb," line 131.

20. Beelzebub's (bē el′ zə bubz): Beelzebub, which in Hebrew means "god of flies," was another name for Satan.

21. a little stream: Lethe (lē′ thē). In classical mythology, the river of forgetfulness, from which souls drank before being born. In Dante's symbolism it flows down from Purgatory, where it has washed away the memory of sin from the souls who are undergoing purification. That memory it delivers to Hell, which draws all sin to itself.

22. Stars: As part of his total symbolism, Dante ends each of the three divisions of the *Divine Comedy* with this word. Every conclusion of the upward soul is toward the stars, God's shining symbols of hope and virtue. It is just before dawn of Easter Sunday that the Poets emerge—a further symbolism.

THINKING ABOUT THE SELECTION

Interpreting

1. Why are the figures in Satan's mouth considered traitors?
2. Why does Dante choose to represent the most terrible part of Hell as a frozen lake?
3. Why does Virgil have to carry Dante out of Hell by climbing over Satan?
4. Dante himself called punishment "the sword of heaven." (a) First explain the meaning of this statement. (b) Then tell how it applies to Canto XXXIV.
5. What does Dante learn from this experience?

Applying

6. What elements in Dante's depiction of the pit of Hell are designed to strike terror in the hearts of readers?

ANALYZING LITERATURE

Understanding Personification

Satan is the quintessential representation of evil. In the Bible he is represented as a slithering serpent, hissing his treachery to Eve. In Dante's description of Satan, he is the "Emperor of the Universe of Pain." However, he is rendered motionless in the ice. His kingdom and therefore his power is thus limited.

1. Which details make Satan particularly repulsive?
2. In what way does Dante's description of Satan indicate that evil is not necessarily frightening for the Godly human being?

CRITICAL THINKING AND READING

Avoiding "Translationese"

The translator is confronted with many problems when he or she begins to transfer a literary work from one language to another. One of these problems is how to avoid "translationese"; or how to make a translation sound natural and appeal to a particular audience, while at the same time being faithful to the meaning of the original language.

This problem is heightened when the text is in verse, as it is in the *Divine Comedy*. The translator must decide whether to use prose or poetry. If the translator uses verse, then will he or she use a poetic form that is familiar to the intended audience? If there is a gap between what the audience expects and what the translator offers, it is usually because the style of the translation is not appropriate for its public.

1. Imagine that you are John Ciardi preparing your translation of the *Inferno*. Why did you decide to translate it using verse instead of prose?
2. Imagine that you are translating the work. What decisions would you make that are different from Ciardi's?

THINKING AND WRITING

Preparing Translations

Reread these lines from the third canto:

I AM THE WAY INTO THE CITY OF WOE.
I AM THE WAY TO A FORSAKEN PEOPLE.
I AM THE WAY INTO ETERNAL SORROW.

SACRED JUSTICE MOVED MY ARCHITECT.
I WAS RAISED HERE BY DIVINE OMNIPOTENCE,
PRIMORDIAL LOVE AND ULTIMATE INTELLECT.

ONLY THOSE ELEMENTS TIME CANNOT WEAR
WERE MADE BEFORE ME, AND BEYOND TIME I STAND.
ABANDON ALL HOPE YE WHO ENTER HERE.

Paraphrase Ciardi's translation of Dante. The simplest tool at your disposal is a dictionary of synonyms. For example, *woe* could be substituted by *sorrow, pain,* or *tragedy. Forsaken* could be replaced by the words *abandoned, forgotten,* or *forlorn.* Try to find equivalent words for every important noun, verb, or adjective in this passage. Pick out the most striking or appropriate synonyms and then put them together to create your own version of the inscription. As you revise your work, see if a different ordering of the material might be more effective or poetic. Do you think your version conveys Dante's meaning well? Is it easy to read and understand?

THE POET AS OUTLAW

What picture comes to mind when you think of a poet? Someone who is somewhat unworldly? Someone who is naive? Someone unconcerned with the day-to-day routines of life? Or do you see a romantic figure? Someone dashing and perhaps living slightly outside the law?

In the Middle Ages, two outlaw poets were Dante Alighieri and François Villon.

Dante was actually condemned as an outlaw and exiled from Florence. However, in the *Inferno*, he reverses his own situation. Here he condemns those who condemned him and demonstrates how they are themselves outlaws in the eyes of God. In listing their crimes, he shows himself in the end to be the pure adherent of true spiritual goodness. His linking of spiritual good to the outcast status calls upon a long-standing tradition in the medieval Church. According to this tradition, this world is so corrupt that those who seem good may in fact be evil; and those who are condemned as base or bad may in fact be good, since they do not accept the wicked system. In a materialistic and evil society, poverty, isolation, and a lack of social graces may in fact be virtues. Here the Christian condemnation of social hierarchy based on material wealth comes in direct conflict with courtly society, where nobility is directly connected to property. Thus Dante, in his harsh condemnation of the materialistic popes and leaders of Florence, is merely returning to the Christian ideal of poverty.

François Villon (1431–?) was the archetypal poet/outlaw or *voyou* (petty criminal), living in the margins of society, constantly in trouble with the law until his disappearance in 1463. In his "Ballad of the Hanged Men," Villon links himself to this poet-as-outlaw tradition when he asks the sneering observer whether he is really superior to the condemned criminal. From his vantage point as an admitted criminal and outcast, Villon is free to criticize the violent and materialistic society he sees around him. He holds his own flawed character up as a mirror-image of France in the late Middle Ages. Since he has confessed his own guilt and does not need to pretend to be a good man, he can at least seem to be more direct, open, and honest than those who are restrained by a strict code of conduct.

Do not forget, however, that a poet who describes himself as an outlaw is creating another mask, one that is the opposite of the courtly role. Dante is not really being honest; he is merely offering Dante's point of view. Villon offers his criticism in a direct style, but he is still expressing his personal opinion. The literary role of the poet as outlaw thus becomes more important than the actual biography of the poet.

The literary role of the social outcast dates back at least as far as Roman satire, particularly that of the first century A.D. Of course, in Greek literature Thersites of the *Iliad*, constantly playing his own rude nature off against the heroic ideal, is one of the earliest antiheroes. But the Roman poets Juvenal and Martial, and the author Petronius, offer sustained portrayals of the poet as a poverty-stricken con artist trying to eke out his living by his wits. Still, the most celebrated outcast before the Middle Ages was Ovid, exiled at the beginning of the first century A.D. by Tiberius, for some unknown crime. He complained bitterly of his unjust sentence in poetic letters. Juvenal's, Martial's, and Ovid's works were available at least to the scholars of the late Middle Ages, and admiration for their work was joined with some amount of sympathy for their unruly natures.

This sympathy arose in part from the decline of the courtly ideal, already underway in the twelfth century. Anticourtly characters were already prominent in both romance and in epic. Arthur's rude vassal Keu (or Kay) is one outstanding example; the treacherous but compelling Ganelon of the *Song of Roland* is another.

With the rise of materialism and corruption in the Church, medieval monks, who had access to many literary sources, began to produce satires critical of society at large and Church hierarchy in particular. Quickly, the rude, devious, and disloyal character became a respected antihero, trying to get the better of the corrupt and impersonal social system. Short-verse stories known as *fabliaux* vaunted the superior wit of the disenfranchised peasant over the courtly noble, and praised trickery as a crucial skill for survival. Rutebeuf (died 1280) chronicled his own miserable life as a starv-

MEZZETIN
Antoine Watteau
Musée Condé,
Chantilly, France

ing poet, thus raising the social outcast to the status of true hero.

The tradition continues. In the nineteenth century, Arthur Rimbaud was the most striking example of the poet as outlaw. In the twentieth century, the poets of the Beat Generation, in some ways precursors of punk, drew inspiration from both Villon and Rimbaud. Some consider rock bands the troubadors—or singing poets—of our society. What poets as outlaws can you name today?

Humanities Note

Fine art, *Mezzetin*, by Antoine Watteau. Mezzetin or Mezzetino, a sharp-tongued valet with a ready wit, was a stock character in Italian comedy. The role was a standard one for the traveling band of actors who put on improvised comedic performances to the great delight of the French public.

The French painter Antoine Watteau (1684–1721) based many of his paintings on such characters. The spontaneous magic of the theater groups to which they belonged were a great inspiration to him.

This painting shows a character in a typical pose while playing a guitar. The sketchy nature of the painting stems from the fact that Watteau often based his works on sketches done beforehand. This Mezzetin seems sad and introspective. The viewer may wonder what sort of song he is playing.

A subtle melancholy pervades the work of Antoine Watteau. It is thought that his constant battle with tuberculosis might have contributed to this darkness of mood. His artistic work was very important in the development of the French rococo style and his death at the age of thirty-seven was an unfortunate loss to the world of art.

You might want to ask the following questions to discuss the art:

1. What sort of music do you think the Mezzetin is playing?
2. Do you think anyone is listening to him?
3. What poets or singers today could be placed in this tradition?
4. Give instructions on how you would have today's counterpart painted.

FRANÇOIS VILLON

Focus

More About the Author François Villon seemed to lead a most improbable, if not contradictory, life. Although he was born into a troubled family, and he was supposed to be both a thief and murderer, he was also a student. Be sure to tell students that the University of Paris (and its most prestigious school, the Sorbonne) is one of the world's oldest universities.

Pronunciation Note Explain to students that the name of François Villon has a unique pronunciation in French. The author's name is pronounced frän swä vē yä.

In French the letters *oi* are pronounced like the English *w*. The double *l* is pronounced like a *y*.

Critical Evaluation The ballade is an old verse form that was originally set to music. The term *ballade* is derived from the old Provençal word *balar*, "to dance." Originally it was thought to be a verse form of dancing.

The most popular form of the ballade consists of three eight-line stanzas rhyming *ababbcbc*, with a four-line envoi reading *bcbc*. The last line of the first stanza serves as a refrain repeated in the last line of each stanza and of the envoi. This complicated rhyme scheme makes the ballade a difficult poem to write.

1431– c. 1463

François Villon (frän swä′ vē yōn′), born in 1431 into a poor family, is considered the precursor of modern French poetry. With his vivid images and his terse, direct style, he turned poetry away from the delicate allegory of the Late Middle Ages toward the more immediate problems of everyday life. He wrote a great deal of satirical poetry, in which he describes the lively streets and inhabitants of Paris.

Quite understandably, death was also an important theme in Villon's poetry. He lost his family when he was a young child. Life was harsh in fourteenth-century France, but Villon compounded the usual difficulties by running with the roughest crowds in Paris. Although he studied at the Sorbonne, Paris offered more opportunities for crime than for honorable advancement to the young poet. He quickly became involved in brawls among students and even killed a priest. Although he was pardoned because of the circumstances, he merely continued his dissolute

life, mostly stealing and robbing to make a living.

Yet his poetry was admired by members of the royal family. By 1461 he had written his *Testament*, a long satirical poem in the form of a will. In this poem, considered to be one of his finest works, Villon leaves everything he owns, and much that he does not own, to friends and enemies. He also wrote many lyric poems, some of which won contests. But even this admiration for his poetic genius could not spare him the death sentence when he was arrested again.

Villon wrote the ballad you are about to read, thinking that he would soon be hanged. In it he begs those witnessing the execution and laughing at the dead men not to judge the dead. He points out that nobody is perfect and that every person needs to be forgiven.

In this ballad and in many other poems, Villon expresses his strong desire for redemption, to live a good life, even as he shows his incapacity for wise behavior. He is torn between good and evil and sees this as the dilemma of every person. He conveys this personal crisis by using simple language and realistic imagery. The imagery of the *"Ballade des pendus"* ("The Ballad of the Hanged Men") is brutal and even grotesque. Villon is trying to shock his reader into understanding the gravity of his own situation as well as that of the condemned men. It is this direct, personal address to the reader that makes Villon's poetry so engaging or moving. This emphasis on the humanity of each individual, no matter how bad a criminal, gives his poetry force even today.

Mystery surrounds the end of Villon's life. Apparently, he was not executed. The death sentence was annulled, but Villon was exiled from Paris for ten years. From this moment on, no more is heard of the poet. Did he refuse to leave Paris, and was he executed? Was he killed in a street fight? Or did he go to live happily on in England or Italy? The intriguing hypotheses merely contribute to the rather romantic portrait of Villon as the *"poète maudit"* (the accursed poet), isolated from the mainstream of French society.

Objectives

Thematic
To understand the intent of poems that remind readers of mortality

Skills
1 To learn about the role of narrator
2 To understand how to infer tone
3 To write an advertisement

Support Material

Teaching Portfolio
Teacher Backup, p. 793
Usage and Mechanics Worksheet, p. 797
Analyzing Literature Worksheet, *Understanding the Narrator*, p. 798
Critical Thinking and Reading Worksheet, *Recognizing Tone*, p. 799

GUIDE FOR INTERPRETING

Ballade

Commentary

The Narrator. In "Ballade" Villon uses a common device, the first-person narrator, with a startling innovation. The narrators are dead men talking to passers-by to win their pity. This use of the first person is an effective ploy to engage the reader's sympathy.

A speaker returning from the dead is not infrequent in medieval or even classical literature: Achilles returns in the *Odyssey*, and Aeneas speaks to the dead in Virgil's epic. In the Middle Ages, the dead held special importance because of their prophetic powers. After death one was supposed to learn all that had and would happen on Earth and finally understand the difference between good and evil and the importance of one's own actions. The dead often gave valuable advice in order to direct actions toward the best path.

But Villon's use of the first person creates a tension between repulsion and sympathy. First he presents the cry for pity. The reader doesn't even know that the men are already hanged until the fifth line. Then he is confronted with the grotesque nature of the dead bodies. One imagines the witnesses turning away in disgust.

In the second stanza, the dead men continue by admitting their guilt. But they excuse themselves by pleading ignorance. They call for the prayers of others. Thus the reader is drawn back to their human plight. And finally the reader is included by the refrain, repeated from the first stanza, of "But pray God that he absolve us all." It is becoming clear that God must pardon every man or woman.

This sense of togetherness is immediately undercut in the third stanza by the horrifying description of decay. Because Villon has made the reader identify with the dead men in the second stanza, this horror is intensified and personalized. Rather than turning away, the reader begins to feel the suffering of these men. He or she can vividly imagine hanging up there with the others. By alternating horror and pity, Villon has driven home the lesson that no one is immune from this terrible fate. Human beings should show compassion to one another, rather than judging and mocking one another, for they never know when they might suffer. We are all saved from such suffering only by luck or, according to Villon, "the grace of God."

Writing

Imagine that you are an advertising writer working for a charitable organization (one that helps poor children, the elderly, victims of disasters like earthquakes or hurricanes, victims of disease, and the like). You have decided to write an advertisement from the point of view of a person helped by your organization. How would you gain the attention and sympathy of the public? What would the child, the elderly person, the sick or hurt person, say?

Literary Focus One of the most important things about this ballade by Villon is the unique narrative voice that the author chooses to adopt: that of the deceased. Ask students about other works, like Masters's *Spoon River Anthology*, that have unlikely or unbelievable narrators. Some may wish to discuss the similarities that exist between this narrator and the one created by Eliot for *The Love Song of J. Alfred Prufrock*.

Writing/Prior Knowledge Pair up the students in class. Have them share ideas and tell each other about their experiences with disasters, in preparation for the prewriting.

ESL Teaching Strategy Pair off the ESL students with partners in each class. Have both students list and define adjectives and verbs that are likely to be used in writing assignments on disasters.

Teaching Tenth-Grade Students Ask tenth-grade students to list the means by which executions are carried out to end the lives of those condemned for crimes. Have them discuss whether any of those means might be "cruel and unusual." Tell them about the debate between states that have capital punishment (Florida) and states that do not (New York).

Language Worksheet, *Understanding Verb Tenses*, p. 800
Selection Test, pp. 801–802
Essay Questions and Evaluation Guidelines, p. 807

Ballade

François Villon

translated by Galway Kinnell

1 Brother humans who live on after us
Don't let your hearts harden against us
For if you have pity on wretches like us
More likely God will show mercy to you
You see us five, six, hanging here
As for the flesh we loved too well
A while ago it was eaten and has rotted away
And we the bones turn to ashes and dust
Let no one make us the butt of jokes
2 But pray God that he absolve us all.

Don't be insulted that we call you
Brothers, even if it was by Justice
We were put to death, for you understand
Not every person has the same good sense
Speak up for us, since we can't ourselves
Before the son of the virgin Mary[1]
That his mercy toward us shall keep flowing
Which is what keeps us from hellfire
We are dead, may no one taunt us
But pray God that he absolve us all.

The rain has rinsed and washed us
The sun dried us and turned us black
Magpies and ravens have pecked out our eyes
And plucked our beards and eyebrows
Never ever can we stand still
Now here, now there, as the wind shifts
At its whim it keeps swinging us
Pocked by birds worse than a sewing thimble
Therefore don't join in our brotherhood
But pray God that he absolve us all.

---

1. **son . . . Mary:** Jesus Christ.

Prince Jesus, master over all
Don't let us fall into hell's dominion
We've nothing to do or settle down there
Men, there's nothing here to laugh at
But pray God that he absolve us all.

Reader's Response *The speakers address their audience as "Brother humans." Were you able to identify with them, in spite of their predicament? Explain.*

THINKING ABOUT THE SELECTION

Interpreting

1. (a) What is the speakers' purpose in the first stanza? (b) In the last?
2. Explain the effect of the description of these men.
3. Explain how the poem's purpose is achieved.

Applying

4. Medieval criminals were executed in public. As civilization progessed, executions were made private or banned. However, capital punishment is debated today. What stand do you take? Why?

ANALYZING LITERATURE

Understanding the Narrator

The narrator in "Ballade" is unusual—the dead. Although most literary "voices of the dead" are voices of wisdom and experience, in this poem Villon has chosen

**OVIDE MORALISE
(WHEEL OF FORTUNE)**
Chrétien Legouais

Humanities Note

Illumination, *Ovide Moralise—
Wheel of Fortune*, authored and
probably illustrated by Chrétien
Legouais. Representative of the
role of chance in human affairs,
the wheel of fortune was a subject much pondered in the Middle Ages. The artist's interpretation of the wheel of fortune
shown here is based on simply
outlined forms contrasted with
the dark, geometric-patterned
background. The blindfolded
goddess indifferently turns the
wheel that will plunge the ruler at
the top to unknown depths while
elevating another figure to prominence at the same time. The figures on the wheel symbolize the
powers that rule mankind. They
are rendered by this artist with
humor and pathos.

You might want to use the
following questions to discuss
the art:
1. Can you think of where we
   might find a wheel of fortune
   today?
2. What is the most engaging dimension of this illustration?
3. Do you think that today's
   wheel of fortune has any connection to the one conceived
   in the Middle Ages: Explain
   your answer.

to undercut the traditional approach. His dead men are
not voices of authority. They are criminals.
1. What lesson do these criminals teach?
2. Do you think this poem would have been as effective if it had been narrated by someone watching
   the hanged men? Why?

CRITICAL THINKING AND READING

Inferring Tone

Tone is the way in which an author expresses his
or her attitude or emotions toward a particular subject
through his or her style. An author's tone may be serious, comic, or ironic, for example. A serious tone is
usually equated with sincerity, but readers should be
skeptical of any discussion of sincerity in literature.

Villon conveys an impression of sincerity by his
particular use of the first-person narrators. His speakers call out to their "brothers." They point out their
revolting condition, rather than hiding it, and they
openly admit their guilt. Why would the reader not trust

them? At the moment where doubt is assuaged by this
serious tone, Villon shifts tone to the ironic: "Not every
person has the same good sense." In essence, the
dead men are saying: "Don't blame us; we were not as
sensible as you are."
1. (a) Think about the effect of this line. Can it be serious, if these same men are asking that God pardon
   all men? (b) Are others good and only these bad?
2. (a) How is this line a turning point in the poem? (b)
   What does it force the reader to do?

THINKING AND WRITING

Writing an Advertisement

Refer to your notes for the ad for charity. As you
write up your version of the ad, think about how you
would present the need for help. At what point would it
be appropriate to use irony? How would you use it?
Read the ad aloud in class to see what effect it has on
your classmates and revise to improve the tone of your
work.

THINKING AND WRITING

Writing Across the Curriculum
You may wish to inform the social
studies department that the students will be reading this poem. It
might be possible to invite two
teachers with opposing views on
capital punishment to come for a
point/counterpoint discussion in
class. Students could then write
responses to the comments they
hear while deciding how to formulate their own opinions on the matter.

that an onlooker could provoke readers as well as the executed do.

ANSWERS TO CRITICAL
THINKING

1. (a) Answers will differ. It could be serious because of their desperate
   circumstance. (b) The point seems to

be that no one is either all good or all
bad.
2. (a) The line is a turning point because
   it begins a new direction. (b) It forces
   the reader to see morality from the
   point of view of the condemned.

Types of Love

> "The troubadours were very much interested in the psychology of love. They're the first ones in the west who really thought of love as we do now—as a person-to-person relationship."
> —Joseph Campbell, *The Power of Myth*

Writers in every age have written about love. Since romance plays so fundamental a part in life, it is not surprising that literature dealing with the theme is plentiful and popular. Medieval writers, depicting love as having many different dimensions, were as concerned with love as were writers in other ages.

Some of their works dealt with the love between parent and child. Other works dealt with the love of God or the virtues expected of those who would follow God's commandments. Middle Ages authors also gave tribute to the love of friends, of spouses, and of patriots. Variations on the theme of love were as plentiful at that time as they have been since then.

Concern for a loved one is found in *The Nibelungenlied*.

> I fear you will come to grief, lord Seigfried . . . Last night I had a sinister dream of how two mountains fell upon you and hid you from my sight! I shall suffer cruelly if you go away and leave me.
> —*The Nibelungenlied*

Here the wife of the hero frets about his mortality. She transforms her fears to dreams that deal with a plot that will take his life. She exhibits the same concerns as have wives in other ages when beset by the risks faced by warriors.

Medieval writers wrote patriotic verses and professed allegiance to the military champions of their day. Did any medieval leader receive more noteworthy attention than Charlemagne? These opening lines from the *Song of Roland* echo with a sense of pride and a civic love that create a tribute to Charlemagne's fatherliness as well as an homage to him as a military leader.

> Charles the King, our Emperor, the Great
> has been in Spain for seven full years,
> has conquered the high land down to the
>   sea.
> There is no castle that stands against him
>   now,
> no wall, no citadel to break down —
>   —The *Song of Roland*

Medieval authors also expressed their love of God. They did this frequently and eloquently. No writer is credited with being able to voice such sentiments with higher authority than the Italian poet Dante. He believes in the power of an omnipotent God whose love is capable of permeating all existence.

> The glory of Him who makes all things
>   rays forth
> Through all the universe, and is reflected
> from each thing in proportion to its
>   worth.
>   —Dante, *The Divine Comedy*

Such remarks about the types of love are readily found in literature earlier and later than the European Middle Ages.

SUGGESTED READINGS

Presentation
Motivation/Prior Knowledge Tell students that the topic of love has always received tremendous attention from writers and poets. Have them begin a discussion by listing as many different kinds of love as they can. Compile the list on the chalkboard. Combine and eliminate suggestions as it becomes necessary.

The Operas of Richard Wagner

The great German composer Richard Wagner (1813–1883) drew on the traditional literature of his people for inspiration for his operas. Perhaps his finest work, *Der Ring des Nibelungen* (*The Ring of the Nibelungens*) is based on the tales and stories in the medieval classic *The Nibelungenlied*. Made up of four interwoven operas, the *Ring* cycle changes the focus of the original from human beings to the gods. The war saga is overshadowed by a divine conflict—Wotan, king of the gods, battles for control of the world.

THE CYCLE

In the first opera, *Das Rheingold*, Wotan has giants build him a fort. When the giants call for payment, he suggests they be given the hoard of Rhinegold, stolen by the dwarf Alberich, king of the Nibelungs, who has fashioned a ring that can control the world. Threatened, Wotan and Loge steal the hoard, but Alberich curses the ring, predicting death for the gods. Wotan ransoms Freia with the hoard. Upon receiving this payment, one giant kills the other, and the surviving giant guards the hoard. The gods enter their fort, Valhalla, hoping to regain the ring.

THE VALKYRIE AND SIEGFRIED

In the opera, the *Die Walküre* (*The Valkyrie*), Wotan decides to create heroes to recover the ring. He marries a mortal and has twins, Siegmund and Sieglinde. Sieglinde is sold to Hunding, a warrior, but meets Siegmund and flees with him. The Valkyrie Brunnhilde, daughter of Wotan and Erda, is told to defend Hunding against Siegmund. Hunding kills Siegmund, but Brunnhilde carries off Sieglinde to protect her and, having given her the pieces of Siegmund's sword, sends her to the forest where a dragon guards the ring. Wotan puts Brunnhilde in a coma and foretells her death.

In the opera *Siegfried*, another dwarf raises Siegfried and refashions Siegmund's sword out of fragments. Siegfried finds the hoard, slays the dragon, and is told to marry Brunnhilde. Siegfried awakens Brunnhilde, whose love imposes immortality on her.

CONCLUSION

In the final opera, *Die Gotterdämmerung* (*The Twilight of the Gods*), the Fates predict the world's end. The king of the Gibichungs, Gunther, is forming wedding plans for himself and for his sister Gutrune. Hagen proposes that Gunther trick Siegfried into bringing Brunnhilde to be his bride by having the hero fall in love with Gutrune. The plan works. Disguised as Gunther, Siegfried takes a ring from Brunnhilde and claims her as Gunther's bride.

Hagen is told to kill Siegfried. Gunther arrives at court and Siegfried's deception is uncovered. In revenge he is killed for the trick, but his funeral pyre destroys the gods and their fortress.

TRANSFORMATIONS

Wagner transforms the *Nibelungenlied*, an epic about petty characters, into a story of superheroes who can be destroyed only by fate. In the *Niebelungenlied*, Brunnhilde's jealousy destroys Siegfried, and Kriemhild vengefully eliminates the Burgundians. In the *Ring*, Brunnhilde and Siegfried are controlled by evil forces, yet their love is undying and pure. It is the gods themselves who are tainted by greed. The composer of the *Nibelungenlied* showed readers how men and women harm themselves by their refusal to control their own emotions. But Wagner saw human beings as pawns. Yet human beings can rise above their weakness to a new dignity when they accept that fate.

WRITING ABOUT LITERATURE

Guidelines for Evaluating Writing About Literature Keep the following questions in mind when evaluating students' compositions.
1. Does the composition clearly state the criteria for judgment?
2. Has the writer used specific evidence to show how the hero measures up against each criterion?
3. Has the student given a clear final judgment on the topic?
4. Does the composition contain any errors in spelling, grammar, or punctuation?

Evaluation

Writing an Evaluation

Nothing, it appears to me, is of greater value in a man than the power of judgment; and the man who has it may be compared to a chest filled with books, for he is the son of nature and the father of art.

Pietro Aretino, letter to Fausto Longiano, December 17, 1537, tr. Samuel Putnam

Evaluations do more than express personal likes and dislikes. A good evaluation is a judgment based on established criteria. Sometimes criteria for judgment are given and need not be questioned, but most of the time a writer must carefully select criteria against which to measure the subject.

People can be evaluated as easily as films, novels, chocolate cakes, or sports cars. Certain categories of people, such as villains or heroes, seem to have some obvious criteria by which they are normally measured. In the *Nibelungenlied*, for example, Siegfried is, by all criteria, a hero. Even facing a treacherous death, he meets or exceeds any measure by which a hero can be judged. The episode depicts Siegfried as bold, noble, swift, versatile, loyal, strong, courageous, acclaimed, and of surpassing ability—all heroic attributes.

Writing Assignment

How do you judge whether someone is a hero? Select as your criteria three items you consider to be a complete and significant measure of heroism. Then write an essay in which you evaluate the heroism of a character.

Be sure to

- state the criteria for judgment
- use specific evidence to show how your hero measures against each criterion

- state your clear, final judgment of his worth

Evaluate one of the characters you encountered in this unit or suggest one of your own.

Prewrite

Establish criteria: Brainstorm to list the qualities you think make a person a hero. Pick your hero. You can write an excellent evaluation about an imperfect hero, so pick a hero you like, not one you necessarily believe is perfect.

Measure your hero against each criterion, one at a time. Try measuring your hero on a scale of 1 to 10 by putting an X on the line in the place you think your hero falls. (Assume 1 is not at all heroic, and 10 is ideal heroism for each.) Here's an example:

ROLAND AS HERO

	1	2	3	4	5	6	7	8	9	10
brave										x
self-sacrificing								x		
steadfast							x			
unwavering								x		

Select specific evidence to prove each measurement. List the examples and find a persuasive order in which to present them.

Assess your character as a hero. Your hero need not be a "10" on all points for you to conclude he or she is a hero. All things are matters of degree. You can write a strong, valid evaluation of a hero who does not get top marks; your evaluation may be even more interesting if he or she does not. In fact, you can write an excellent evaluation showing that he or she is not a hero at all. But whatever it is, your assessment must be clear.

Write

When you have clearly stated your final judgment, you are ready to present your evaluation in writing. Clearly introduce your subject and the criteria for judgment in the first paragraph. Consider beginning with a shocking statement, a quotation, an anecdote, or some other means of capturing your reader's attention. You may state your assessment in the first paragraph or save it for the last.

Then write a separate paragraph to examine your hero as he or she fits each criterion. You may evaluate by using personal judgments or you may cite some external authority to support your decision. Use your notes to help you prove each measurement with specific evidence. Pay attention to transition words and phrases between the paragraphs.

Include an overall assessment of your subject as a hero in your final paragraph. This paragraph should exhibit a strong, confident tone and leave the reader satisfied and convinced. Remember that a tentative tone and voice kills evaluations. Your reader must feel you write from strong convictions. If you use weak or vague words or sentence structures, you appear to question your own assessments and your reader will too.

Collaborate

Ask someone to read and respond to your draft. Record your partner's responses to the following questions. If one is available, use a tape machine.

- Did I choose any wrong criteria? What would you have chosen?
- Is my set of criteria a complete tool for measuring a hero? If not, what is missing?
- Did I apply the criteria accurately to this hero in each instance?

- Did my specific evidence prove the hero belonged where I put him or her on each criteria scale? If not, where did I go wrong?
- From the criteria and evidence I supplied, do you find my judgment of the hero accurate? If not, where are the weak spots?

Revise

Using the taped responses to guide you, revise your evaluation. If your responder found any criterion weak or inaccurate, go back to the beginning and choose another to replace it. It is better to do that than to labor over a paper you know is weak.

Remember to keep your audience firmly in mind as you write. Think about how much or how little your audience knows about your subject so that you can address their needs. You cannot convince your readers if you lose them.

Publish

After proofreading your evaluation, finish another draft that includes all revisions. Then send a copy of your work to a class committee that has been created to selct the most interesting of the evaluations.

Evaluate

Judgments are interesting things. They change not only with changing criteria but also with passing time. Consider keeping this paper to review in the future. You may find you judge your evaluation differently later.

For now, ask a classmate to read your evaluation and to explain how successful your writing seems to be.

Humanities Note

Fine art, *Parnassus* (1509–1511) by Raphael. Raphael Sanzio (1483–1520), known simply as Raphael, was one of the great Italian Renaissance painters. Among his major works were frescoes (wall paintings) in public buildings. This picture is one of several frescoes he did for a chamber in the papal buildings.

Parnassus is a mountain in Greece. In ancient times it was considered a place sacred to Apollo, Dionysus, and the Muses, goddesses who were patrons of the various arts. The choice of this sacred mountain as a subject indicates the Renaissance admiration for classical Greek culture.

The god Apollo sits in the center of the painting, under the tree. Since he is the god of music and poetry, it is appropriate that he is playing a viol. Apollo is surrounded by twenty-eight figures representing Muses and great poets. As you face the picture, the group to Apollo's left includes the declaiming Homer, a blind man in a dark robe; next to him is Dante's profiled figure. On the other side of Homer is Virgil. To the right of Apollo are the Muses; Thalia, the Muse of comedy and pastoral poetry, holds a comic mask. In the lower left hand portion of the painting, Sappho holds a scroll inscribed with her name. Other famous writers who have been identified in this painting are Ovid, Horace, and Boccaccio.

You might want to use the following questions to discuss the art:

1. How can you tell that Raphael admired ancient Greek culture?
2. How does Raphael express his belief in the importance of balance, proportion, and harmony?
3. Suppose you wanted to create a fresco to honor modern writers. (a) Whom would you include? (b) How would you design the fresco? Why? (c) In what type of building would you have it painted?

PARNASSUS
Raphael

Objectives

1 To understand the historical background of the Renaissance

2 To understand the cultural background of the Renaissance

3 To understand the literary background of the Renaissance

THE RENAISSANCE

(1300–1650)

Of course Sacred Scripture is the basic authority in everything; yet I sometimes run across ancient sayings or pagan writings—even the poets'—so purely and reverently expressed, and so inspired, that I can't help believing their authors' hearts were moved by some divine power.

—from "The Godly Feast," by Erasmus

Focus

Writing to Learn Have students write down what they know about the Renaissance. Tell them that it is not important that their ideas be precise or correct at this point. Also, encourage them to paint word pictures of what everyday life was like in those times. Ask them to keep their notes, and when they have finished reading the introduction, have them look at this assignment to see whether they can revise it.

ESL Teaching Strategy Have ESL students report to the class on what was occurring in their cultures during the Renaissance in Western Europe.

Teaching Tenth-Grade Students Many tenth-grade students will be taking world history. Encourage them to apply what they learn in that course to their study of this unit.

HISTORICAL BACKGROUND

A World of Countryside and Villages

The quotation on the preceding page shows how close in spirit the Renaissance—the period between 1350 and 1550 in Italy and 1500 and 1650 in England—was to the classical period. In many physical respects, too, Western Europe during the Renaissance was closer to ancient times than to our own era. It was a world of countryside and villages, not cities. A large city in the middle of the fourteenth century was a city of 100,000 people, about the size of Boise, Idaho, today. London had about 70,000 people and Paris in 1328 was a giant city with 274,000. Even the largest cities, however, were small enough so that bees often blundered into the streets from neighboring fields.

Status and Rank

It was a time when rank and status mattered a great deal. This concern could be revealed in little ways. For instance, an inferior took his hat off when speaking to a superior, while the superior kept his hat on his head. Violating this rule might lead to a whipping.

The primary source of status was land, not money. When a man became rich through trade, he usually bought property and attempted to marry his daughters to established nobility. He was trying in this way to ennoble his family and move out of the class into which he was born. He might even hire scholars to "discover" noble ancestors in his family background.

A Time of Little Security

For every social class, however, the Renaissance was a time of insecurity and uncertainty. The Black Plague (see page 680) devastated Europe in 1348, at the very beginning of the Italian Renaissance, and periodic outbreaks continued for three hundred years. This disease, however, was only the worst of many. The cities were breeding places for sickness: Open sewers ran down the center of the narrow, unpaved streets and into the nearby rivers, and these unsanitary conditions produced outbreaks of dysentery.

PEASANT DANCE
Pieter Brueghel
Vienna Kunsthistorisches

MAP OF FLORENCE
Museo de Firenze, Firenze, Italy

In addition to sickness, other disasters contributed to the insecurity of the times. With the exception of castles and churches, most buildings were built of wood, and fire in cities was a constant hazard. Since there was no insurance to cover losses from fire, it was possible to be wealthy one moment and destitute the next.

The Increasing Power of Kings

Against this backdrop of general insecurity, the power of kings tended to increase during the Renaissance. This centralization of power helped to create the nations we are familiar with today. Kings helped consolidate their power by creating bureaucracies to rule the realm. The men they chose for these bureaucracies were often not high nobility; they were minor nobility or even men of middle-class origins eager to serve the king and make their fortunes. For example, Cardinal Wolsey, Henry VIII's most important minister, was the son of a butcher. The movement of men like Wolsey from class to class encouraged writers to notice a new kind of individual whose status resulted from his own talents rather than from his family name.

While the power of kings was on the rise, the great nobility were becoming less important. Their mighty castles, for instance, were threatened by the introduction of gunpowder in the later middle ages. Castle walls became vulnerable to cannon shot.

Similarly, the knights who fought for the nobles were no longer such powerful and imposing figures. Despite their heavy armor, they could be toppled by a well-placed bullet.

CULTURAL BACKGROUND

Humanism

Perhaps the most important cultural movement of the Renaissance was humanism, which advocated a return to classical studies and ideals. This movement began in fifteenth-century Italy, and among the first humanists were the famous writers Petrarch and Boccaccio.

Most humanists were wandering scholars who made their living by teaching or by acting as diplomats. They were above all students of the ancient languages, especially Greek, Latin, and Hebrew.

Their motto was *ad fontes,* meaning "back to the sources"—back to the earlier and purer roots of good language and good literature. As the humanist movement developed in Italy, its followers made an effort to master once more the Greek language and to recover Greek texts, from Homer and Sophocles to Plato and Thucydides. For the first time in a thousand years, the intellectual life of Western Europe was directly influenced by the works of Greek writers known before only by inaccurate summaries or inadequate quotation.

(continued from bottom of page)

by Filippo Brunelleschi. It dominates the smaller buildings. On the far right is the Pitti Palace in the center of a walled area; today it houses a great museum. Medieval towers rise from the walls surrounding the city, but the newer, classically styled buildings, like the cathedral, show the changing landscape of the Renaissance.

Fishermen with nets can be seen on the river, while several men are being ferried across in a small boat. On the shore the carcass of a dead horse is being eaten by vultures. This curious addition to the otherwise attractive picture of the city indicates the strong contrasts that characterized Renaissance Florence. It was set in the idyllic Tuscan countryside but was constantly menaced by the neighboring cities of Pisa, Milan, and Siena. Despite the rise of wealthy families, many of the city's natives lived in primitive medieval conditions. While Florence was the cradle of the Renaissance, for many of its citizens it was also a city of turmoil, poverty, and political intrigue.

You might want to use the following questions to discuss the art:

1. Can you identify both medieval and Renaissance styles of architecture in this picture? Explain.
2. What can you deduce about life in Florence from this picture?
3. What evidence is there in this picture that Florence was menaced by neighboring cities?
4. Why do you think city views like this one were so popular after the invention of printing?
5. What would a panoramic view of your city or town reveal?

are peasants rather than nobles or members of the middle class.
2. How does the composition, or placement of the figures, contribute to the painting?
3. What is Brueghel's attitude toward his subject? Explain.
4. What could a historian learn about sixteenth-century life by looking at this painting?

Humanities Note

Fine art, *Map of Florence.* The first version of this panoramic view was made in about 1486. Originally a woodcut, this picture was later published in a series of city views that was widely distributed after the invention of the printing press. Florence, like the other cities in the

book, was depicted as attractive and bustling. The artist included himself (in the lower right corner) seated on a hill overlooking the city.

Major Renaissance landmarks can be identified in this view. The Arno River divides the city. On the left is the great dome of Florence's cathedral, designed

Pictured from left to right:
During the Renaissance, Florence was the intellectual and artistic center of Italy. The Florence Cathedral, depicted here, is only one example of Renaissance Italian architecture. Although construction of the cathedral began in the fourteenth century, it was not completed until the middle of the following century.

The lute is a pear-shaped, 11-stringed instrument that was most popular among the English and Europeans during the late Middle Ages and the Renaissance. During this period, the lute was written about extensively and was featured in much literature.

Martin Luther (1483–1546) was the German leader of the Protestant Reformation. He alone symbolizes the split between Protestants and Roman Catholics. His reforms and influence were far reaching. For example, his German translation of the Bible is considered a masterpiece and was perhaps the single force to create the modern German language. In addition, millions have read his book *Small Catechism of 1529*, which outlines how Christians should live and what they should believe. Among his many reforms within the Church was his belief that the language of the people, not Latin, should be used for worship. Although he was both highly praised and criticized and even excommunicated for his beliefs, Luther stands as one of the most influential and significant leaders of the Renaissance.

The Renaissance (1300–1650)

Artist drawing lute

Florence Cathedral

Portrait of Martin Luther, German leader of the Protestant reformation

| 1300 | 1350 | 1400 | 1450 |

HISTORY

- Aztecs establish Mexico City
- Bubonic plague originates in India
- The Hundred Years' War begins
- Black Death devastates Europe
- Great Schism begins
- Richard II is murdered

HUMAN PROGRESS

- First scientific weather forecasts begin
- Tennis becomes an outdoor sport in England
- Arab geographer explores Sahara Desert
- Building of the Bastille begins in Paris
- Playing cards replace dice in Germany
- Printing is invented
- Gutenberg invents his press; prints complete edition of the Bible

LITERATURE

- Dante is exiled for opposing the pope
- Petrarch begins *Canzoniere*
- Boccaccio begins *The Decameron*
- Chaucer begins *The Canterbury Tales*
- Ecclesiastical drama flourishes in Italy
- Modern English develops from Middle English
- Vatican Library is founded

Portuguese navigator Ferdinand Magellan's ship *Victoria* (detail)

Polish astronomer Nicolaus Copernicus observing skies at night

Leonardo da Vinci's drawing, "Man in Ornothopter"

Elizabeth I, Queen of England

1500   1550   1600   1650

- Spanish Inquisition begins
- Russians explore Siberia
- Columbus lands in the New World
- Spain and Portugal sign Treaty of Tordesillas
- Ponce de León discovers Florida
- Martin Luther's reform movement begins
- Pope Leo X excommunicates Luther

- Magellan sails around the world
- Henry VIII issues Act of Supremacy
- German civil war begins
- Henry VIII dies
- Elizabeth I becomes queen of England
- Black Plague kills 20,000 in London
- Francis Drake returns from circumnavigating the world

- Mary, Queen of Scots, is executed
- English navy defeats Spanish Armada
- Queen Elizabeth I dies; is succeeded by James I
- Jamestown Colony is established
- 30 Years' War begins
- Mayflower lands at New England

- Ballet is introduced
- Canterbury Cathedral is finished
- Balboa sights Pacific Ocean
- Chocolate is introduced in Spain
- Martin Luther: Small Catechism of 1529

- Nicolaus Copernicus: *On the Revolutions of the Heavenly Bodies*

- Galileo is born
- Mercantilism begins
- Galileo investigates law of gravity
- Kepler notes elliptical orbit of planets
- First printing press in U.S.

- Dante's *Divine Comedy* is printed
- Chaucer's *The Canterbury Tales* is printed
- German magician Georg Faust, prototype of Faust legend, is born

- Machiavelli: *The Prince*
- Du Bellay: *Defense and Praise of the French Language*
- William Shakespeare is born
- Ronsard: *La Franciade*

- Ronsard: *Sonnets for Helen*
- Montaigne: *Essays,* his first book
- Marlowe: *Doctor Faustus*
- Globe Theatre is built
- Cervantes: *Don Quixote,* part I
- Globe Theatre is destroyed by fire

- Cervantes: *Don Quixote,* part II
- William Shakespeare dies

On September 20, 1519, Portuguese navigator Ferdinand Magellan set sail on the first expedition around the world. On October 18, 1520, Magellan discovered a passage off the southern tip of South America, which led from the Atlantic Ocean to another ocean. This passage was later named the Strait of Magellan. Magellan named the new

ocean the Pacific, which means "peaceful" because compared to the stormy Atlantic Ocean, the Pacific appeared calm. Magellan's voyage proved that the world is round, not flat as many had previously believed. The voyage also led to future European expeditions to the Pacific.

Polish astronomer Nicolaus Copernicus (1473–1543) was the founder of the first modern European theory of planetary motion and the father of modern astronomy. Copernicus claimed that the sun was at the center of the universe and all the planets revolved around it. His beliefs opposed the earlier theories of Greek astonomer Ptolemy, who be-

---

(continued from bottom of page)

lieved the earth was at the center of the universe. Although Copernicus could not prove his theory of planetary motion, it was mathematically sound. He demonstrated his theories in his book *On the Revolutions of the Heavenly Spheres*, which he dedicated to Pope Paul III. He completed his book around 1530, but it was not published until 1543 when Copernicus was near death. The Copernican system was the basis on which modern astronomy was built.

Although he is best-known as an Italian painter, Leonardo da Vinci was also an accomplished engineer and scientist. Due to his insatiable curiosity about the physical world, da Vinci experimented in geology, botany, hydraulics, and mechanics. His resulting drawings, which were depicted with scientific precision and artistry, ranged from flying machines to anatomical studies of people, animals, and plants. The drawing pictured here shows one of da Vinci's flying machines that he called an ornothopter.

Queen Elizabeth (1533–1603), daughter of Henry VIII and Anne Boleyn (who was executed in 1536), was one of England's most renowned and influential rulers. Under her reign from 1558 until her death in 1603, England's economy, military power, and culture flourished. Her reign, also called the Golden Age or the Elizabethan Age, marks a time of great achievement in England and the time when England was united as a nation. Elizabeth's court became a center for poets, musicians, writers, and scholars. Among the most recognized writers of this time were William Shakespeare, Edmund Spenser, and Walter Raleigh.

The humanists were concerned with more than language or art, however. They saw the classics as a treasury of moral and practical wisdom, works that would illuminate their own world. They believed that while the imitation of antiquity begins with written style, it also embraces the way in which the ancients lived. To learn how to write good Latin was felt to be the first step toward living a good life.

The Humanist Myth

According to the humanists, the Middle Ages were "dark" because the Germanic tribes that had invaded Rome, the Goths, had destroyed classical civilization. Humanists believed that with the rediscovery of classical learning, these "dark" times had given way to an age of "enlightenment." True learning had been reborn.

Today scholars no longer accept this belief, which might be called the Humanist Myth, without qualifications. We realize, for instance, that medieval culture had many great accomplishments and that a number of medieval beliefs continued into the Renaissance. At the same time, we recognize that the Renaissance did bring an important new emphasis on classical studies.

Christian Humanism

Humanism started in Italy, and as it moved northward it changed somewhat in character. The enthusiasm for classical antiquity remained, but it was joined by a Christian fervor. This slightly different movement, called Christian humanism, tended to look back to early Christian as well as classical sources. One of the greatest Christian humanists, Desiderius Erasmus, published the first translation of the New Testament (1516) from Greek into Latin since Saint Jerome had translated it a thousand years before.

Christian humanists stressed the importance of the active, as opposed to the contemplative, life.

PORTRAIT OF ERASMUS
Quentin Metsys
National Gallery, Rome

This emphasis represented a break with medieval thinkers, who believed that a quiet life devoted to God was best. Christian humanists also emphasized the importance of a Christian life as opposed to Christian doctrine: In other words, what a person knows is less important than how he or she acts.

These thinkers ridiculed the performing of mechanical and external acts in the place of inner worship. They attacked pilgrimages to holy places and the purchase of indulgences, or supposed reductions of a sinner's punishment in purgatory after death. In this way Christian humanism prepared for the more radical protests of the Reformation.

The Reformation

During the Renaissance there was an increasing dissatisfaction with the Church. As that institution became a great secular power with immense wealth, extensive territory, and its own armies, some believed that it was losing its spiritual mission.

In 1517 an obscure German professor of theology, Martin Luther, nailed to a cathedral door his "ninety-five theses." This statement, arguing that the Church had no power to cancel any punishments after death, made Luther famous. As the Catholic Church attempted to silence him, he found himself adopting positions that the Church believed were heretical. He asserted, for instance, that salvation and damnation were not affected by one's *works*—by what one did. They were determined by one's *faith*. In addition, he deemphasized the spiritual power of the priesthood and the importance of church ritual. Instead, he stressed the significance of the Bible and the God-given inner light that enables individual Christians to interpret it.

Luther's reform of the Church gave birth to a movement called the Reformation and to the new Protestant (the word comes from the word *to protest*) denominations. As a result, all of Europe divided into religious camps. The Catholic Church was strong in Spain, Italy, and parts of France and Germany. On the other hand, various Protestant groups dominated in Switzerland, Germany, parts of France, and eventually in England and Scotland. The religious debates soon escalated into war, and in France the civil conflict led to more than a half century of bloodshed.

A Changing World and Universe

Not only were religious truths being questioned, but the face of the globe was changing with each new voyage of discovery. (See the map below.) Renaissance explorers greatly enlarged European notions of geography: In 1492, for instance, Columbus sailed to the West Indies, and in 1519 Magellan began a voyage around the world.

The image of the universe itself was gradually changing. According to older views, the earth was the center of the universe, surrounded by the sphere of the moon and beyond it the spheres of the visible planets and the fixed stars. While the heavens were perfect and eternal, the earth was a place of corruption and decay. The astronomer Copernicus (1473–1543), however, argued that the earth was not the center of the universe—it revolved around the sun. Equally disturbing was the discovery of Galileo (1564–1642) that the heavens were not perfect. Looking through the newly invented telescope, he discovered that the moon was rough and cratered and that there were spots on the sun that appeared and vanished.

A Changing View of Human Nature

Tradition held that the created world was organized into a hierarchy with God at the top and stones, mere dead matter, at the bottom. Humans had a fixed place in this "chain of being" between the angels and the beasts. In the fifteenth century, however, an Italian humanist named Pico della Mi-

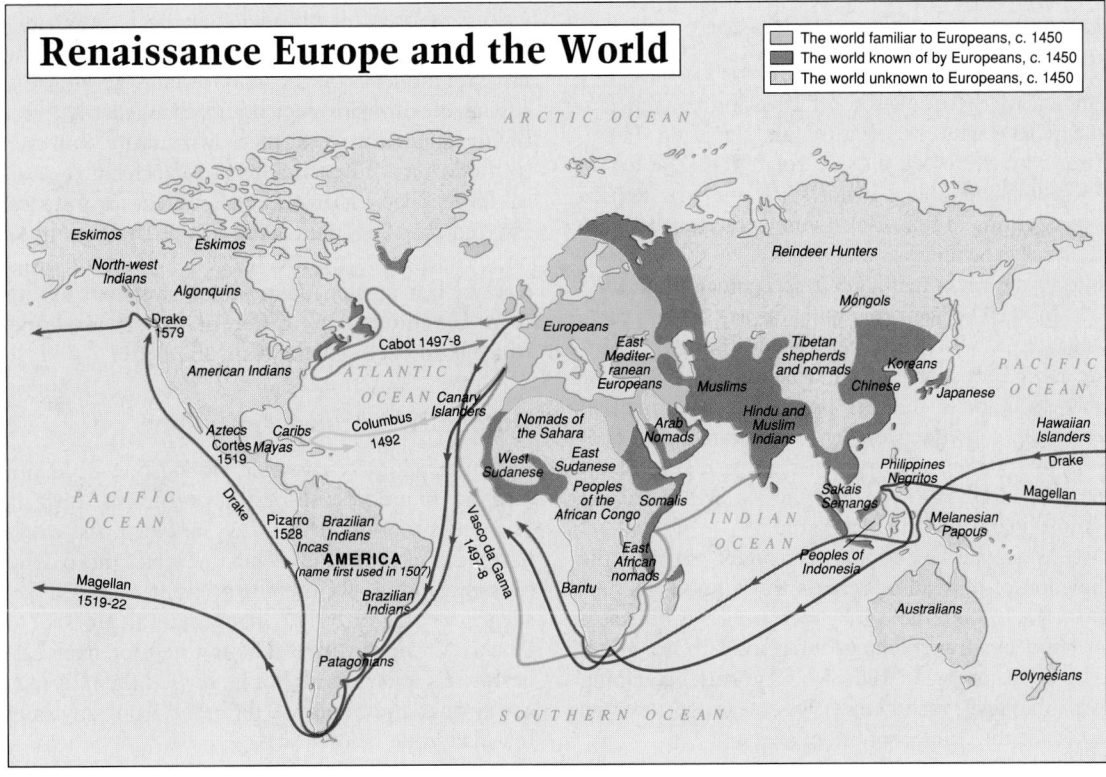

Renaissance Europe and the World

The world familiar to Europeans, c. 1450
The world known of by Europeans, c. 1450
The world unknown to Europeans, c. 1450

6 Enrichment Tell students that the old view of the cosmos was that the earth was divided into four "layers"—a zone of earth at the center, surrounded by zones of water, air, and fire. The traditional explanation of gravity assumed that each substance has a desire to find its natural "place." Stones fall and flames rise because each substance is seeking its "home."

7 Enrichment Tell students that in a letter on sunspots, Galileo wrote that they could be seen without the aid of a telescope: "If in church some day Your Excellency sees the light of the sun falling upon the pavement at a distance from some broken windowpane, you may catch this light upon a flat white sheet of paper, and there you will perceive the spots." Students might want to try this experiment for themselves.

Using the Map
Have students study the map and ask them the following questions:
1. Compare the relative size of the world familiar to Europeans and of the world unknown to Europeans.
2. (a) Which parts of Africa were best known to Europeans in 1450? (b) Why do you think these parts, and not others, were familiar?
3. Which explorer helped to open India to trade, and when did he sail?
4. Which explorer began an expedition that circumnavigated the globe?
5. Name three peoples not known to Europeans in 1450.

Indeed the times were still dark and mankind was perpetually reminded of the miseries and disasters wrought by those Goths who had destroyed all sound scholarship. But, thanks to God, learning has been restored in my age to its former dignity and enlightenment. . . .

Now every method of teaching has been restored and the study of language has been revived: of Greek, without which it is disgraceful for a man to call himself a scholar, and of Hebrew, Chaldean and Latin. The elegant and accurate art of printing, which is now in use, was invented in my time by divine

inspiration, as by contrast, artillery was inspired by diabolical suggestion. The whole world is full of learned men. . . .

Fine art, *Copernican Universe*, 1576. This diagram showing the Copernican model of the universe is from a treatise by the sixteenth-century British mathematician Leonard Digges. The sun is at the center of a series of concentric circles representing the orbits of the six planets then known: Mercury, Venus, Earth, Mars, Jupiter, and Saturn. The earth is the large circle above the center sun and is shown with the moon orbiting around it. Surrounding the solar system is the great star-filled cosmos.

The sun is emanating its traditional rays, the sky is a traditional blue, and night is indicated by the filling in of the lower half of the outer circles.

You might want to use the following questions to discuss the art:

1. Why do you think so many people were threatened by this model of the universe?

2. How would you modify this diagram to bring it up to date?

8 Enrichment Explain to students that one of the most radical thinkers of the Renaissance was Giordano Bruno (1548–1600), an Italian philosopher. Although Bruno supported the Copernican view of the world, he also believed that our perception of reality is based on the position from which we view it. He therefore rejected the notion of absolute truth. Bruno was killed by the Inquisition because his philosophy called into question the authority of the Church.

Check Test

1. The primary source of status during the Renaissance was _____.

2. During this era the power of kings _____.

3. The most important cultural movement of the Renaissance was _____.

4. Renaissance scholars greatly admired the civilizations of ancient _____ and _____.

5. The thinker who initiated the Reformation was _____.

COPERNICAN UNIVERSE
From Thomas Digges's supplement to the 1576 edition of Leonard Digges's Prognostication Everlasting

randola (1463–1494) argued that human nature was not fixed. By emphasizing the beast in oneself one could in effect become a beast; by relying on reason one could rise to the level of the angels. This view of human nature celebrated a person's capacity not to inherit a place in the world, but to make a place for oneself.

LITERARY BACKGROUND

Literature as a Branch of Rhetoric

In the Renaissance literature was classified as a branch of rhetoric—the art of using spoken language to teach, give pleasure, and persuade. Literature was therefore closely related to the art of speechmaking, and it is not surprising that Renaissance writing is full of elaborate speeches. It is also unusually playful in its treatment of language, showing off the tricks that a good speechmaker can use.

In keeping with this spirit of play, writers often engaged in what have been called "thought experiments." They would make a hypothesis—"imagine that such-and-such were possible"—and then explore the consequences. In Shakespeare's *The Tempest*, for example, Prospero's island is a kind of experimental laboratory where the writer can try out various ideas about human nature.

As a branch of rhetoric, literature also had the function of persuading readers to do good. Its purpose was to train the will by increasing our horror of evil and by strengthening our resolve to act good. The vivid image of Marlowe's Faustus bargaining with the devil, for instance, was meant to show an audience the dangers of pride.

Literature and the Vernacular

The Renaissance saw a new emphasis on the vernacular languages: Italian, French, Spanish, German, Dutch, and English. This was a period of linguistic patriotism, and many of the great works of the period were written in the vernacular. This emphasis on vernacular languages, however, does not mean that Latin was unimportant. Erasmus and many of the great humanists wrote primarily in Latin. Nevertheless, during the Renaissance the vernacular became the dominant medium for art.

Humanism and Literature

The Renaissance showed its independence not only in the emphasis placed on the vernacular but even in its relationship to classical authors. Humanism naturally led to a revival of classical forms: Many writers wrote epics modeled in part on Virgil's *Aeneid*, odes modeled on the odes of Horace, and histories modeled on the work of Pliny and Tacitus. Just as the Romans copied and changed the forms of Greek literature to fit their own culture, however, so the writers of Renaissance Europe changed classical forms. The Italian author Petrarch, for instance, asserted that "we must write just as the bees make honey, not keeping the flowers [works of other writers] but turning them into a sweetness all our own, blending many different flavors into one, which shall be unlike them all, and better."

Originality Through Imitation

In reading Renaissance works, one need not look for brand-new stories or new forms. Instead, one needs to look for the ways in which past works have been altered to give them new and more complex meanings. Of the thirty-eight plays Shakespeare wrote, only two had original plots (*The Tempest* is one of them). The rest he took from earlier writers and revised, but he revised them in such a way that they became different from anything that had gone before.

Answers
1. land
2. increased
3. humanism
4. Greece, Rome
5. Martin Luther

RENAISSANCE VOICES

One must therefore be a fox to recognize traps, and a lion to frighten wolves.

Machiavelli, *The Prince*, 17

Here I stand; I can do no other. God help me. Amen.

Martin Luther, Speech at the Diet of Worms

Iron rusts from disuse; stagnant water loses its purity and in cold weather becomes frozen; even so does inaction sap the vigor of the mind.

Leonardo da Vinci, *The Notebooks*, I, chap. 2

Philosophy is written in this grand book—I mean the universe—which stands continually open to our gaze, but it cannot be understood unless one first learns to comprehend the language and interpret the characters in which it is written. It is written in the language of mathematics, and its characters are triangles, circles, and other geometrical figures, . . .

Galileo, from *The Controversy on the Comets of 1618*

To laugh is proper to man.

François Rabelais, *Gargantua and Pantagruel*

Was this the face that launched a thousand ships,
And burnt the topless towers of Ilium?
Sweet Helen make me immortal with a kiss.
Her lips suck forth my soul; see, where it flies.

Christopher Marlowe, from *The Tragical History of Doctor Faustus*

To be, or not to be: that is the question.

William Shakespeare, from *Hamlet*, III, i

I have
Immortal longings in me.

William Shakespeare, from *Antony and Cleopatra*, V, ii

As for me, there are many times when I do not hesitate to hope confidently that the souls of Virgil and Horace are sanctified.

Erasmus, from *The Godly Feast*

What do I know?

Montaigne

Additional Voices

To be able to say how much you love is to love but little.

—**Petrarch**, "To Laura in Death," Canzone 137

Poor naked wretches, wheresoe'er you are,
That bide the pelting of this pitiless storm,
How shall your houseless heads and unfed sides,
Your looped and windowed raggedness, defend you
From seasons such as these?

—**William Shakespeare**, from *King Lear*, III, iv

Now I have described to you as truthfully as I could the structure of this commonwealth, which I think the best, and indeed the only one which can rightfully be called by that name. In other places where they speak of the common good, every man is looking out for his own good. But in Utopia where there is no private property and where they zealously pursue the public business, there the name commonwealth is doubly deserved.

—**Sir Thomas More**, from *Utopia*

The nature of all other beings is limited and constrained within the bounds of laws prescribed by Us [God]. Thou [humankind], constrained by no limits, in accordance with thine own free will, in whose hand We have placed thee, shalt ordain for thyself the limits of thy nature.

—**Pico della Mirandola**, from "Oration on the Dignity of Man"

If, Lord, thy love for me is strong
As this which binds me unto thee,
What holds me from thee, Lord, so long,
What holds thee, Lord, so long from me?

—**Teresa of Avila**, "If, Lord, Thy Love for Me Is Strong"

NICCOLÒ MACHIAVELLI

1469–1527

Niccolò Machiavelli (nē´ kô lô´ mak´ ē ə vel´ ē) embodied one side of Renaissance culture in his fearless devotion to reason and his concern with worldly rather than religious goals. Like Dante he was a citizen of Florence, Italy, and played an important role in advancing that city's interests. Eventually forced out of office by political changes, he produced many of his literary, historical, and political works during his involuntary retirement.

We know little about Machiavelli's early life. Born to a family of poor Florentine nobility, he was educated in the classics and was proficient in Latin. (At that time Latin was the language of diplomacy as well as of scholarship.) In 1498 he was appointed secretary to the governing body of Florence. The duties of the post were many, and they involved him in frequent diplomatic trips to the various Italian and European powers that dealt with Florence: France, Spain, Germany, and the Italian city-states. From these places he sent home descriptions of the strengths and weaknesses of the rulers and governments he observed.

Florence had need of such information. At that time Italy was made up of small states frequently at war with one another. In addition, these states were often at the mercy of France and Spain, which used Italy as a battleground for their rivalries. Florence was especially vulnerable. In 1594 the city had driven out the family of merchant princes, the Medici (med´ ə chē´), who had unofficially ruled the city for three generations. Although Florence became a self-govern-ing republic, the Medici were always attempting to make a comeback. Meanwhile, the city was weakened by internal clashes between the nobles and the smaller merchants, who wanted more political power.

During his years in government, Machiavelli worked faithfully as an ambassador, as a civil servant, and even as a man of war, directing a successful siege of the town of Pisa. Eventually, however, Spanish forces overthrew the Florentine Republic and restored the rule of the Medici. Machiavelli was too closely identified with the former government to keep his position long. Indeed, he may briefly have been tortured on suspicion of having joined in an anti-Medici plot.

The years after 1512 were enormously frustrating for Machiavelli. Poor and out of favor, he tried desperately to work in government again. While he preferred a republic, he was willing to settle for the Medici rule if the new rulers would only allow him to engage in political activity. The works he wrote during his enforced retirement were meant in part to recommend him to the Medici. As he wrote in a letter, he wanted to demonstrate that "for the fifteen years while I have been studying the art of the state, I have not slept or been playing. . . ." His most famous work, *The Prince*, was dedicated to a member of the Medici family.

The dating of many of his works is uncertain, but most of them were probably written during this period of political inactivity. In addition to *The Prince*, he wrote a comedy, *Mandrake, a History of Florence*, a treatise entitled *Art of War*, and a political work entitled the *Discourses on the First Ten Books of Livy*. (Livy was a Roman historian who lived from 59 B.C. to A.D. 17.)

Eventually Machiavelli did succeed in attracting the favor of the Medici. After giving him some minor positions, they assigned him to oversee the reconstruction of the walls around Florence in order to make them invulnerable to attack by artillery. He died the following year while on a diplomatic mission.

BACKGROUND

THE PRINCE
by Niccolò Machiavelli

In *The Prince* Machiavelli stresses the degree to which his views of political morality differ from those of previous writers. Where other theorists discuss how rulers *ought* to act, Machiavelli says that he deals with how rulers do act. Where others say that public deeds should reflect private morality, Machiavelli insists that personal morality has no place in politics. Rulers are not saved by their goodness but by their strength, cunning, and ability.

Politics Is a Jungle

Machiavelli claims that humans are corrupt and that they are likely to be motivated not by loyalty or patriotism but by self-interest. For instance, in arguing that no ruler should keep his word when it is in his interest to break it, he says, "if all men were good, this would be a bad precept but since they are evil and would not keep a pledge to you, then you need not keep yours to them."

Traditional political philosophy distinguished humans from animals largely by their capacity to reason and act morally. By contrast, Machiavelli stresses our kinship with the beasts: "there are two ways of fighting, by means of law and by means of force. The first belongs properly to man, the second to animals; but since the first is often insufficient, it is necessary to resort to the second. Hence a Prince must know how to both use what is proper to man and what is proper to beasts." Politics is a jungle; therefore, on occasion, it is necessary for the successful ruler to act with the strength of a lion or the cunning of a fox.

His image of a successful prince differs sharply from the standard vision of the Good King. For a humanist like Erasmus, the Good King is simply a supremely good man—indeed, an ideal Christian. He should love his subjects and never act like a tyrant. He should avoid wars of aggression and cherish the arts of peace.

Machiavelli's prince, however, is above all concerned to retain or extend his kingdom by any means that will work. His principal business is war and the financing of war: He is aggressive, wily, ruthless, and prudent. In addition, he is aware of how much depends on chance, which Machiavelli calls Fortune, and how much on the willingness to take necessary risks. Conventional morality, according to Machiavelli, is foolishness for such a ruler and will lose him his state. He therefore advises rulers that it is better to be miserly than to be generous and to be feared than to be loved.

Patriotism: The Inspiration for His Beliefs

Machiavelli's abandonment of political morality resulted from more than a simple disbelief in people's goodness. It grew out of his patriotism and the condition in which he saw Italy—prey to its own internal bickering and humiliated by the great European powers. His concern in this book is to offer advice to a ruler who will unite Italy and drive out its foreign invaders. His own preference, as he makes clear in the *Discourses*, is not for a kingship but for a republic. He had come to believe, however, that in the present situation only a prince acting with energy and clear-sighted ruthlessness could unite Italy.

from The Prince

Historical Context

Renaissance Italy was divided into small states, each with its own form of government and its own laws. Machiavelli's Florence was one of the most brilliant of these states. Since the twelfth century, it had prospered from its trade, production of cloth, and banking. It was, however, weakened by internal rivalries and by the tendency of political factions to bring in outsiders to support their bids for power. This tendency made Florence easy prey to the aggression of other Italian states, European powers like France and Spain, and the bands of soldiers who roamed Italy selling themselves to the highest bidder.

Cultural Context

Political philosophy goes back to the Greek philosophers Plato (see page 414) and Aristotle, both of whom Machiavelli had read in translation. Romans like Cicero and the historians Livy and Tacitus carried on this tradition of thought. One of Machiavelli's literary works was a lengthy essay on the writings of Livy, in which he considered the conditions that make for a successful republic. Machiavelli's work thus develops a tradition of political philosophy revived from the ancient world. Yet Machiavelli believed that his work differed from that of his predecessors because he dealt with how things were and not how they ought to be.

Literary Context

The form that Machiavelli gives his work was commonly used in the Renaissance. It is a treatise on the education of a prince, discussing the qualities that a good prince possesses and the education necessary to create those qualities. Erasmus had written such a book in his *Education of a Christian Prince*, as had many other humanists (for a discussion of humanism, see pages 659–662). These books usually stressed the need for the prince to act like a kindly father to his subjects. Machiavelli, on the other hand, concerns himself with one thing only: how the prince is to survive in a dangerous and uncertain world. The religious emphasis that so often appears in humanist writings about kingship is nowhere apparent in *The Prince*.

Objectives

Thematic

To understand the work of a political thinker whose influence is still felt today

Skills

1 To understand Machiavelli's purpose
2 To appreciate Machiavelli's art
3 To write a letter as Machiavelli

from The Prince

Niccolò Machiavelli

translated by Luigi Ricci
revised by E.R.P. Vincent

Cultural Context: The word *prince* derives from the Latin *princeps,* meaning "leader or general." To us it signifies "a young ruler"; however, Machiavelli used it in keeping with its origin to mean "the ruler of a state."

CHAPTER XV

Of the Things for Which Men, and Especially Princes, Are Praised or Blamed

It now remains to be seen what are the methods and rules for a prince as regards his subjects and friends. And as I know that many have written of this, I fear that my writing about it may be deemed presumptuous, differing as I do, especially in this matter, from the opinions of others. But my intention being to write something of use to those who understand, it appears to me more proper to go to the real truth of the matter than to its imagination; and many have imagined republics and principalities which have never been seen or known to exist in reality; for how we live is so far removed from how we ought to live, that he who abandons what is done for what ought to be done, will rather learn to bring about his own ruin than his preservation. A man who wishes to make a profession of goodness in everything must necessarily come to grief among so many who are not good. Therefore it is necessary for a prince, who wishes to maintain himself, to learn how not to be good, and to use this knowledge and not use it, according to the necessity of the case.

Leaving on one side, then, those things which concern only an imaginary prince, and speaking of those that are real, I state that all men, and especially princes, who are placed at a greater height, are reputed for certain qualities which bring them either praise or blame. Thus one is considered liberal, another *misero* or miserly (using a Tuscan term, seeing that *avaro* with us still means one who is rapaciously[1] acquisitive and *misero* one who makes grudging use of his own); one a free giver, another rapacious; one cruel, another merciful; one a breaker of his word, another trustworthy; one effeminate and pusillanimous,[2]

Literary Context: Machiavelli calls attention to the way in which his own writing differs from that of contemporaries like Erasmus, who advises princes to act with Christian virtue. Such writers, he suggests, avoid the truth about human nature, pretending that people are loyal, honest, and patriotic.

---

1. **rapaciously** (rə pā′ shəs lē) *adv.*: Greedily.
2. **pusillanimous** (pyo͞o′ si lan′ ə məs) *adj.*: Cowardly.

LORENZO THE MAGNIFICENT
The famous Italian merchant prince Lorenzo the Magnificent, a contemporary of Machiavelli, was an astute politician and a patron of the arts.
Giorgio Vasari

another fierce and high-spirited; one humane, another haughty; one lascivious,[3] another chaste; one frank, another astute; one hard, another easy; one serious, another frivolous; one religious, another an unbeliever, and so on. I know that everyone will admit that it would be highly praiseworthy in a prince to possess all the above-named qualities that are reputed good, but as they cannot all be possessed or observed, human conditions not permitting of it, it is necessary that he should be prudent enough to avoid the scandal of those vices which would lose him the state, and guard himself if possible against those which will not lose him, but if not able to, he can indulge them with less scruple. And yet he must not mind incurring the scandal of those vices, without which it would be difficult to save the state, for if one considers well, it will be found that some things which seem virtues would, if followed, lead to one's ruin, and some others which appear vices result in one's greater security and wellbeing.

CHAPTER XVI

Of Liberality and Niggardliness[4]

Beginning now with the first qualities above named, I say that it would be well to be considered liberal; nevertheless liberality such as the world understands it will injure you, because if used virtuously and in the proper way, it will not be known, and you will incur the disgrace

---

3. **lascivious** (lə siv′ ē əs) *adj.*: Lustful.
4. **Niggardliness** (nig′ ərd lē nis) *n.*: Stinginess.

---

of the contrary vice. But one who wishes to obtain the reputation of liberality among men, must not omit every kind of sumptuous display, and to such an extent that a prince of this character will consume by such means all his resources, and will be at last compelled, if he wishes to maintain his name for liberality, to impose heavy taxes on his people, become extortionate, and do everything possible to obtain money. This will make his subjects begin to hate him, and he will be little esteemed being poor, so that having by this liberality injured many and benefited but few, he will feel the first little disturbance and be endangered by every peril. If he recognizes this and wishes to change his system, he incurs at once the charge of niggardliness.

A prince, therefore, not being able to exercise this virtue of liberality without risk if it be known, must not, if he be prudent, object to be called miserly. In course of time he will be thought more liberal, when it is seen that by his parsimony[5] his revenue is sufficient, that he can defend himself against those who make war on him, and undertake enterprises without burdening his people, so that he is really liberal to all those from whom he does not take, who are infinite in number, and niggardly to all to whom he does not give, who are few. In our times we have seen nothing great done except by those who have been esteemed niggardly; the others have all been ruined. Pope Julius II,[6] although he had made use of a reputation for liberality in order to attain the papacy, did not seek to retain it afterwards, so that he might be able to wage war. The present King of France[7] has carried on so many wars without imposing an extraordinary tax, because his extra expenses were covered by the parsimony he had so long practiced. The present King of Spain,[8] if he had been thought liberal, would not have engaged in and been successful in so many enterprises.

For these reasons a prince must care little for the reputation of being a miser, if he wishes to avoid robbing his subjects, if he wishes to be able to defend himself, to avoid becoming poor and contemptible, and not to be forced to become rapacious; this niggardliness is one of those vices which enable him to reign. If it is said that Caesar[9] attained the empire through liberality, and that many others have reached the highest positions through being liberal or being thought so, I would reply that you are either a prince already or else on the way to become one. In the first case, this liberality is harmful; in the second, it is certainly

---

5. **parsimony** (pär′ sə mō′ nē) *n*.: A tendency to be over-careful in spending.
6. **Pope Julius II:** He served as pope from 1503 to 1513, restoring the Papal States to the church and sponsoring great artists such as Michelangelo and Raphael.
7. **King of France:** Louis XII (1462–1515).
8. **King of Spain:** Ferdinand II (1452–1516), who drove the Moors from Spain and unified the country.
9. **Caesar:** Julius Caesar (102?– 44 B.C.) made himself dictator of the Roman Empire.

Cultural Context: It was commonly believed that Christians should be secretive about their generosity. For Machiavelli, such generosity is useless because it will not gain the prince the reputation he may need to survive as a ruler. In other words, Machiavelli is concerned with the *reputation* for generosity, and even this reputation may lead a prince to spend money he does not have, ultimately weakening his rule.

Historical Context: Machiavelli draws examples from recent history to prove his point. His use of actual historical figures as examples is in keeping with his argument that he is talking about the way people really act. 1

Cultural Context: Like any Renaissance scholar versed in the classics, Machiavelli uses figures out of ancient history to support his points.

Teaching Tenth-Grade Students Ask tenth-grade students to work in small groups to list the main points of Chapter XVI. Ask each student to select one point from Machiavelli's argument with which they disagree. Each student should create an argument to persuade the class that Machiavelli is wrong on this point. Then group members can share their arguments with one another.

Master Teacher Note Suggest that students incorporate the glosses into their reading as follows: read the glossed passage, read the gloss, and then reread the passage. Tell them that although this method will slow down their reading, it will give them added insights into the text. Emphasize that rereading the passage with the gloss in mind is an especially important stage of this process.

Also, explain to them that experienced readers often pause to think about what an author has said.

Cooperative Learning Have small groups of students do further research on some of the figures Machiavelli mentions; for example, Louis XII, Ferdinand II, and Pope Julius II.

1 **Enrichment** Tell students that in 1508 Pope Julius II asked Michelangelo to paint the ceiling of the Sistine Chapel in Rome. Michelangelo worked for four long years on this painting, and his relationship with Julius II was quite stormy. Students can read more about this encounter between two headstrong men in Irving Stone's biography of Michelangelo, *The Agony and the Ecstasy*.

Machiavelli is masterful at marshaling arguments to support his points. Notice, for example, his approach in the first paragraph of Chapter XVI. He wants to demonstrate that "liberality such as the world understands it will injure you." First he creates an either-or situation: a ruler can either be quietly generous or he can advertise his generosity. Then he shows how each choice is problematic. Virtuous liberality, because secret, will have no effect. However, advertised liberality will get a prince into trouble; typically, Machiavelli demonstrates this point by spelling out the results of an action in detail.

Student Activity 1. Choose another one of Machiavelli's paragraphs and describe how he supports his main point.

Student Activity 2. Write a persuasive paragraph of your own and support your argument by using Machiavelli's technique of spelling out consequences in detail.

2 **Enrichment** Provide students with additional background information on Cyrus, Alexander, and Caesar. Cyrus was a king of Persia in the sixth century B.C. In 550 B.C. he led the Persians in a revolt against the Medes and he went on to conquer Asia Minor and the Fertile Crescent. Not only was Cyrus a great general, but he was a shrewd politician as well. He treated conquered peoples with mercy and allowed them to continue practicing their religion and customs. His son-in-law Darius finished the work of organizing the Persian Empire into governable units, called satrapies.

Alexander the Great lived during the fourth century B.C. He was perhaps the greatest military leader of all time. Leading the seasoned Macedonian army (Macedonia is north of Greece) he conquered Greece, Egypt, the Fertile Crescent, Asia Minor, and portions of India. The Persian Empire was only a portion of the area he controlled. For the first time, East and West were united under a single rule. Alexander, who had been a pupil of Aristotle, was devoted to Greek thought and customs, and he founded Greek cities throughout Asia. Like Cyrus, however, he was tolerant of the beliefs of those he conquered. Alexander's blending of East and West led to a new Hellenistic culture whose center was Alexandria, a city founded by the conqueror in Egypt.

Julius Caesar (first century B.C.) was a Roman general who campaigned successfully in Spain and Gaul (modern France). When the Roman Senate ordered Caesar to disband his army, he refused and took his men into Rome. He seized control of the city, and in 44 B.C. he was appointed dictator for life by the Senate. That same year, however, he was assassinated by a conspiracy of men led by Gaius Cassius and Marcus Brutus.

Cultural Context: Here again Machiavelli opposes the ideas of most humanists. These writers stress that a prince should, if possible, never engage in war, and if he does so should spare the lives and possessions of those he conquers.

Literary Context: Machiavelli returns to one of the key themes of his book: the danger for a prince in being hated or looked down upon. If a prince is hated, his subjects will *want* to overthrow him. If he is looked down upon, they will not be afraid to overthrow him.

necessary to be considered liberal. Caesar was one of those who wished to attain the mastery over Rome, but if after attaining it he had lived and had not <u>moderated</u> his expenses, he would have destroyed that empire. And should anyone reply that there have been many princes, who have done great things with their armies, who have been thought extremely liberal, I would answer by saying that the prince may either spend his own wealth and that of his subjects or the wealth of others. In the first case he must be sparing, but for the rest he must not neglect to be very liberal. The liberality is very necessary to a prince who marches with his armies, and lives by plunder, sack and ransom, and is dealing with the wealth of others, for without it he would not be followed by his soldiers. And you may be very generous indeed with what is not the property of yourself or your subjects, as were Cyrus, Caesar, and Alexander,[10] for spending the wealth of others will not <u>diminish</u> your reputation, but increase it, only spending your own resources will injure you. There is nothing which destroys itself so much as liberality, for by using it you lose the power of using it, and become either poor and <u>despicable</u>, or, to escape poverty, rapacious and hated. And of all things that a prince must guard against, the most important are being despicable or hated, and liberality will lead you to one or other of these conditions. It is, therefore, wiser to have the name of a miser, which produces disgrace without hatred, than to incur of necessity the name of being rapacious, which produces both disgrace and hatred.

---

10. **Cyrus . . . Alexander:** Cyrus the Great (died 529 B.C.) was the founder of the Persian Empire; Alexander the Great (356–323 B.C.) conquered Greece and much of Asia.

Reader's Response *Have you observed anyone, in public or private life, who acts as Machiavelli suggests in this book? Explain.*

Commentary

Machiavelli's Epigrammatic Style Machiavelli's epigrammatic style is nowhere better typified than in his comment that "There is nothing which destroys itself so much as liberality, for by using it you lose the power of using it, and become either poor and despicable, or, to escape poverty, rapacious and hated." The statement seems paradoxical at first, but the thought is typical in insisting on the probable consequences of the prince's action. After the initial, paradoxical opening, Machiavelli suggests that the consequences are *either* one thing *or* another, giving readers the impression that they see all the possibilities and that none of them are good.

Liberality is one of those aristocratic virtues for which Machiavelli has no patience, because it ultimately puts the prince in a situation where he has to rely on others for money. Machiavelli's ideal is that of a prince who is never dependent on anyone else.

THINKING ABOUT THE SELECTION

Interpreting

1. Why is it necessary for a prince to learn how to do evil?
2. (a) According to Machiavelli, what are the pitfalls of generosity for a prince? (b) When is it necessary for a prince to be generous, and why is it necessary at those times?
3. Explain what Machiavelli means when he says, "There is nothing which destroys itself so much as liberality, for by using it you lose the power of using it. . . ."
4. The adjective *tough-minded* means "shrewd and unsentimental." Is it accurate to say that Machiavelli constantly urges rulers to be tough-minded? Explain.

Applying

5. Is Machiavelli's advice appropriate for a modern head of state? Why or why not?

ANALYZING LITERATURE

Understanding Machiavelli's Purpose

Machiavelli's purpose in *The Prince* is to give useful advice to a leader who will unite Italy and drive out the foreigners who have victimized its people. In keeping with this aim, he shrugs off the traditional notion of a good king and rejects the Christian virtues of mercy, charity, and kindness. At the same time, he stresses the qualities that will help a prince survive and conquer. As he sets forth his program, Machiavelli argues that he is concerned with human beings as they really are, not as they are imagined to be.

1. For Machiavelli, what views of human nature represent the "real truth" and what notions are imaginary?
2. How does Machiavelli try to convince the reader that he is discussing things as they really are?
3. How free is Machiavelli's prince to do whatever he wants to do?
4. In what ways does Machiavelli suggest that the prince must not consider conventional Christian morality?

CRITICAL THINKING AND READING

Appreciating Machiavelli's Art

At first it seems as if *The Prince* is written without any art: There are few metaphors or eloquent passages. Yet this plainness is itself an artful device, calculated to make the unpopular arguments seem truthful and self-evident. Related to this deliberate plainness is the way in which Machiavelli spells out the results of actions in detail, to stress that everything the prince does will affect his ability to stay in power. Still another example of Machiavelli's hidden art is his use of **antithesis,** the opposing of one idea to another. Antithesis appears, for instance, in his repeated either/or constructions: ". . . you are *either* a prince already *or* else on the way to become one." These antitheses give Machiavelli's prose a hard-edged clarity and imply quietly that there is no middle road by which one may act. A prince must make hard choices or risk losing power.

1. Look carefully at the first paragraph of Chapter XVI ("Beginning now . . ."). (a) How does Machiavelli stress the results of actions? (b) Why does he emphasize cause and effect?
2. How does he use antithesis to advance his argument in the final paragraph of Chapter XVI ("For these . . .")?

THINKING AND WRITING

Writing a Letter as Machiavelli

Machiavelli's principles go well beyond his own age. People have used them as a way of making sense of our own world too. Imagine that you are Machiavelli and want to give advice to a modern politician, whether the President of the United States, your senator, or the mayor of your town. Suggest how this leader might carry out his or her policies using Machiavellian principles. First freewrite about the ways in which these principles could be applied in our time. Then use your notes in drafting a letter to the politician you choose. You might even want to experiment with some of Machiavelli's stylistic devices, such as antithesis and the detailed spelling out of results. When you revise your letter, make sure you have not only given advice but also have supported it with convincing arguments.

(continued from bottom of page)

Challenge Which American politician, living or dead, would Machiavelli have most admired? Explain.

ANSWERS TO ANALYZING LITERATURE

1. For Machiavelli the "real truth" is that humans are motivated by the basest instincts. A belief in the goodness of human beings is imaginary.
2. Answers will differ. Students may respond that he gives real-life examples; he uses a clear, insistent style; and he organizes his arguments logically.
3. Answers will differ. Many students will notice that the prince is not very free. He always has to think about the effects of his wishes on his primary goal—to maintain his power.
4. Answers will differ. Students may point to the first paragraph of Chapter XV, in which Machiavelli warns that a prince must learn how *not* to be good.

ANSWERS TO CRITICAL THINKING AND READING

1. (a) He shows, event by event, what will occur if a prince tries to acquire a reputation for generosity. (b) Answers will differ. Students may respond that he emphasizes cause and effect to demonstrate that what he is saying is completely realistic.
2. Against the argument that Caesar attained his empire through generosity, Machiavelli puts forward an either-or statement: "you are either a prince already or else on the way to become one." By dealing with each side of this proposition, he gives the impression that he has covered all possibilities. Machiavelli also uses an antithetical statement toward the end of the paragraph: "There is nothing which destroys itself so much as liberality for by using it you lose the power of using it, and become *either* poor and despicable, *or,* to escape poverty, rapacious and hated." This either-or statement makes it seem as if he understands the bitter choices that reality demands of a prince.

THINKING AND WRITING

Publishing Student Writing Have students create a political newsletter called *The Machiavellian*, in which they can publish their letters.

Closure and Extension

ANSWERS TO THINKING ABOUT THE SELECTION

1. A prince must learn to do evil because most men are not good and a man who does only good will not do well among such men.
2. (a) If a prince is quietly liberal, his liberality will not be known and he will gain a reputation as someone who is stingy. If a prince is ostentatiously liberal, he will spend much money and be forced to tax his subjects, who will grow to hate him. (b) Liberality is necessary when a prince is spending the wealth of others; for example, when he is distributing booty. Without such liberality, his soldiers would not follow him.
3. Through his generosity, a prince will spend his money and become poor. As a poor man, he will no longer be capable of generosity.
4. Answers will differ, but most students will realize that Machiavelli does urge rulers to be tough-minded. For instance, rulers must not mind being thought stingy, because a too-easy generosity will endanger their position.
5. Answers will differ.

PETRARCH

Focus

More About the Author As an adolescent Petrarch had already developed what he later described as "an unquenchable thirst for literature." His father, however, wanted him to be a lawyer and was afraid that literature would distract him from more profitable legal studies. According to a famous anecdote, Petrarch's father once hurled the boy's literary books into a fire. Petrarch pleaded with his father and finally convinced him to retrieve copies of Cicero and Virgil from the flames.

Critical Evaluation The critic John Humphreys Whitfield asserted that Petrarch "stands between the dying medieval period and the Renaissance, which he ushered in. Although it cannot be claimed that he had much influence on the economic and political forces of his time, the artistic and moral outlook that characterizes the new age can be traced directly to this one man's mind and work."

1304–1374

Francesco Petrarca, whom the English called Petrarch (pē′ trärk′), was the greatest Italian poet of the fourteenth century. As a writer he was equally at home in Italian and Latin, and his self-centered talent set a pattern for lyric poetry over the next three centuries.

Like many humanists (for a discussion of humanism, see pages 659–662), Petrarch traveled extensively, moving from place to place over his long life. He was born in 1304, in Arezzo; his father, a lawyer, had been exiled from Florence in the same civil conflict that resulted in Dante's banishment. When Petrarch was eight, his family moved to the French city of Avignon, the home of the papal court. In 1320 he went to Bologna to study law but began at this time to read classical works and to write poetry. Returning to Avignon in 1326, he first saw the Laura whom he celebrates in his love poetry.

Who was this Laura who inspired Petrarch to write some of the world's greatest love poetry? She may have been Laura de Noyes, the wife of Hugues de Sade. Petrarch himself creates a picture of her as golden-haired, beautiful, and rich. Whoever she was, her beauty inspired Petrarch to a love that lasted twenty years until her death in the Great Plague of 1348.

In the 1320's Petrarch edited the text of the Roman historian Livy, and in 1337 he made his first trip to Rome. This trip inspired him, and on returning he began two ambitious projects in Latin, an epic entitled *Africa*, about the ancient wars between Rome and Carthage, and *On Famous Men*, biographical accounts of classical figures. His view of himself as representing a new Latin cultural flowering was encouraged in 1341 when the city of Rome crowned him a "laureate" poet—in ancient times a laurel crown was a mark of poetic distinction. Inspired by the revival of interest in classical learning, Petrarch dreamed of the time when a revived Roman state would unite all Italy. Consequently, he approved when in 1344 a new Roman republic was proclaimed. The republic proved short-lived, but Petrarch never regretted his support of it.

During his middle years, he distanced himself increasingly from the Avignon court, traveling in Italy or living in his small house in the French countryside. He wrote a great deal, mostly in Latin. A characteristic dialogue, *On the Solitary Life*, stresses the importance of independence and retirement from the activity of business and politics. His humanist studies fed his writing. When, for instance, he discovered the correspondence of the Roman writer Cicero in the Cathedral of Verona, these Latin letters gave him a model for his own—small personal essays discussing himself and other subjects.

During the final twenty years of his life, Petrarch moved permanently to northern Italy—to Milan for some years, then to Padua, to Venice, and eventually to a house he had built near Padua in the Eugenean hills. His writing at this time took on a more Christian emphasis. In the same years, he revised and completed his two major Italian works: the *Triumphs*, which envision the ultimate triumph of the soul in death, and the *Canzoniere* (kän tsô nyer′ ē). He died in 1374.

Petrarch's work centers on himself. The Latin letters, dialogues, and treatises examine his own thoughts with extraordinary subtlety and depth, while his Italian poetry exhaustively analyzes his uncertainties in love. It is this self-analysis and self-proclamation that made him a model for subsequent Renaissance writers.

Objectives

Thematic
To understand Renaissance concepts of love

Skills
1 To understand Petrarch's love poems
2 To appreciate the Petrarchan sonnet
3 To compare translations

GUIDE FOR INTERPRETING

Laura; The White Doe; Spring

Commentary

Petrarch's Love Poems. Although Petrarch tended to belittle his Italian poetry, his collection of Italian poems, the *Canzoniere*, is the work of a lifetime. The earliest lyrics were written in the 1320's, and Petrarch continued to revise and reorganize the sequence in the five years before his death. Altogether it consists of 366 poems divided into two parts, concerning his relation to Laura "in life" and "in death" (Laura dies before the sequence is complete). The *Canzoniere* also includes many sonnets on political and religious matters not directly related to Laura. She forms the center of its universe but not all of it. The poems in the sequence are mostly fourteen-line **sonnets,** but other forms also appear. Among these are **canzoni** (kän tsô´ nē), lyrics with intricate stanzas.

The sequence gives us little specific information about Laura herself. Indeed, one of Petrarch's contemporaries doubted—against his protests—that she existed at all! Her importance in the sequence lies in her effect on the poet, whose desire for her is never fulfilled. This "Petrarchan" scenario, in which the lovers never reach fulfillment, would become a standard model for generations of poets.

Petrarch understands his desire for Laura in opposite ways. On the one hand, he sees it as a force that will lead him toward the divine. On the other he sees it as a dangerous impulse leaving him prey to the worst aspects of his own nature. His uncertainty about how to evaluate the experience leads to his characteristic use of the **oxymoron,** a phrase that joins two logically contradictory terms like "pleasant pain." In Petrarch the two terms often suggest a mind at war with itself. This internal debate is another of the legacies Petrarch left to later writers.

In dwelling on his situation, Petrarch often uses **allegory,** or extended metaphor; for instance, in one poem he compares his love to a dangerous voyage on a stormy sea, guided by the blind pilot Cupid (the god of love). Or in "The White Doe," page 678, he describes the years of his loving Laura as a day during which he follows a perfect white doe. This poem also typifies Petrarch's response to the beauty of the natural world; many of his sonnets use images from nature to explore his inner experience.

Writing

Petrarch's poetry provided an influential model for the ups and downs of two people in love. What models are there today for how people fall in love and how love-relationships develop? Write a journal entry considering the models suggested by movies, television sitcoms, or soap operas.

Literary Focus Have students discuss how their favorite musical performers sing about love. Love is touched on in all genres of popular music, from country and western to rap and from rhythm and blues to heavy metal. Encourage students to quote the lyrics of their favorite love songs and to compare the way love is treated in various songs and musical genres.

Writing/Prior Knowledge Before students write in their journals, have them work in groups of three or four, with each group creating a list of examples of romantic relationships found on television or in the movies. Each group's list should include at least six model relationships, three from television and three from the movies.

Vocabulary

Preteach the following vocabulary words:
radiant (rā´ dē ənt) *adj.*: Shining brightly
unearthly (un ərth´ lē) *adj.*: Supernatural; ghostly
dreary (drir´ ē) *adj.*: Gloomy; cheerless
sated (sāt´ əd) *v.*: Satisfied; filled
exults (eg zults´) *v.*: Rejoices greatly
sojourn (sō´ jurn) *n.*: Visit
gracious (grā´ shəs) *adj.*: Kind; courteous; charming

Support Material

Teaching Portfolio
Teacher Backup, pp. 839–842
Usage and Mechanics Worksheet, p. 843
Vocabulary Check, p. 844
Analyzing Literature Worksheet, *Understanding Petrarch's Love Poems,* p. 845

Critical Thinking and Reading Worksheet, *Appreciating the Sonnet,* p. 846
Selection Test, pp. 847–848
Spelling Tip Write the word *sojourn* on the chalkboard and point out to students that it contains the root of the word *journey.* Its second syllable is therefore spelled with an *ou* and not simply a *u.*

Presentation

Motivation/Prior Knowledge
Tell students that they are about to read three fourteenth-century love poems. Ask them to use what they know about contemporary love poems and songs to predict the kinds of statements and images they might encounter in Petrarch's work. Encourage discussion of student responses and suggest that students keep their predictions in mind as they read each poem.

Purpose-Setting Question Do you think Petrarch presents a realistic portrait of Laura? Why or why not?

Universal Themes You might want to compare and contrast these poems with the following love poems from various cultures and eras: Egyptian love poems, page 32; "Thick Grow the Rush Leaves," page 221; Ki no Tsurayuki's "When I Went to Visit," page 284; Ronsard's "When You Are Old," page 693; Charles Baudelaire's "Invitation to the Voyage," page 904; and Rubén Darío's "Sonatina," page 1162.

1 Clarification Tell students that the phrase "radiant west" is a reference to the setting sun. Ask them how this image links the description of Laura's eyes in line 3 to that of the speaker's love in lines 7–8.

2 Discussion Ask students to infer the attitude of the unnamed "you" in lines 6 and 13. Have them speculate on his or her relationship to the speaker.

3 Discussion Remind students that the bow referred to in the last line is Cupid's. Then ask them to explain the literal meaning of the line. What does the "unbent" bow symbolize? What is the "wound" that "bleeds" and whose wound is it?

4 Discussion Ask students how the vivid description in lines 1–5 hints at the response in the final line.

BIRTH OF VENUS
Sandro Botticelli

from # Canzoniere

Francesco Petrarch

Laura

translated by Morris Bishop

She used to let her golden hair fly free
   For the wind to toy and tangle and molest;
   Her eyes were brighter than the radiant west.
   (Seldom they shine so now.) I used to see
5 Pity look out of those deep eyes on me.
   ("It was false pity," you would now protest.)
   I had love's tinder[1] heaped within my breast;
   What wonder that the flame burned furiously?

She did not walk in any mortal way,
10   But with angelic progress; when she spoke,
   Unearthly voices sang in unison.
She seemed divine among the dreary folk
   Of earth. You say she is not so today?
   Well, though the bow's unbent,[2] the wound
     bleeds on.

---

1. tinder (tin′ dər) *n.*: Dry, easily flammable material used for starting a fire.

2. though the bow's unbent: Though she is older and does not have her original beauty; the bow referred to is Cupid's.

Humanities Note

Fine art, *Birth of Venus* by Sandro Botticelli. The great early Renaissance artist Botticelli (1444–1510) was born in Florence, Italy. His many important commissions include frescoes for the Sistine Chapel in Rome and a series of illustrations for Dante's *Divine Comedy*.

Botticelli loved Classical works and sought to picture the gods as the potent spirits they were to the ancient Greeks and Romans. In *Birth of Venus*, commissioned for a Medici villa, he portrays the goddess of love, emerging from the sea in a shell.

You might want to use the following questions to discuss the art.

1. (a) Who was Venus? (b) What was the name of her Greek counterpart?
2. How does Botticelli's placement of the various figures contribute to the work?

(continued from bottom of page)

Noli me tangere for Caesar's I am,
And wild for to hold, though I seem tame.

Notes: *list*—wishes: *Noli me tangere*—Touch me not.

You may want to ask students to compare these poems. Points of comparison include the attitude of each speaker toward the lady, the use of the doe-metaphor (Petrarch follows his doe, while Wyatt hunts his), the characterization of the two ladies (Wyatt's lady seems unfaithful), the tone of voice (Petrarch is fondly reminiscent, Wyatt weary and embittered), and the intended audience (Petrarch speaks to himself or to a reader, Wyatt to others who would "hunt" the lady).

Humanities Note

Fine art, *Detail of Three Graces* from *Primavera* [Spring] by Sandro Botticelli. The three Graces were ancient Greek goddesses representing beauty, charm, and grace. They were associated with the Muses, the goddesses of art, and with Venus. Botticelli and other Renaissance Italians may even have regarded the Graces as emanations of Venus.

In *Primavera* the Graces dance beside Venus, who is decorously clothed and wears the cap of a Florentine married woman. The scene is set in an orange grove, and the oranges in the trees could symbolize the coat of arms of the Medicis.

Botticelli is famous for the linear rhythms of his paintings. The vertical lines of the trees in the background make an excellent backdrop for the rhythmic curves of the dancing trio.

You might want to use the following questions to discuss the art:

1. Which details suggest that these women are goddesses representing beauty, charm, and grace?
2. How does Botticelli convey the feeling of a dance?
3. What type of music would you choose to accompany this painting? Explain.

Primary Source Note

The English poet Sir Thomas Wyatt (1503–1542) wrote an imitation of Petrarch's "The White Doe," which shows how brilliantly an imitation can depart from and comment on the original:

Whoso list to hunt, I know where is an hind.

But as for me, alas, I may no more.
The vain travail hath wearied me so sore
I am of them that farthest cometh behind.
Yet may I, by no means, my wearied mind
Draw from the deer, but as she fleeth afore,
Fainting I follow. I leave off therefore,

Since in a net I seek to hold the wind.
Who list her hunt, I put him out of doubt,
As well as I, may spend his time in vain;
And graven with diamonds in letters plain
There is written, her fair neck round about,

from Canzoniere

Francesco Petrarch

The White Doe

translated by Anna Maria Armi

A pure-white doe in an emerald glade
Appeared to me, with two antlers of gold,
Between two streams, under a laurel's shade,
At sunrise, in the season's bitter cold.

5 Her sight was so suavely[1] merciless
That I left work to follow her at leisure,
Like the miser who looking for his treasure
Sweetens with that delight his bitterness.

Around her lovely neck "Do not touch me"
10 Was written with topaz[2] and diamond stone,
"My Caesar's will has been to make me free."

Already toward noon had climbed the sun,
My weary eyes were not <u>sated</u> to see,
When I fell in the stream and she was gone.

---

1. **suavely** (swäv´ lē): In a smoothly gracious manner.
2. **topaz** (tō´ paz´): A yellow gem.

Spring

translated by Morris Bishop

Zephyr[1] returns, and scatters everywhere
New flowers and grass, and company does bring,
Procne and Philomel,[2] in sweet despair,
And all the tender colors of the Spring.
5 Never were fields so glad, nor skies so fair;
And Jove <u>exults</u> in Venus'[3] prospering.
Love is in all the water, earth, and air,
And love possesses every living thing.
But to me only heavy sighs return
10 For her who carried in her little hand
My heart's key to her heavenly <u>sojourn</u>.
The birds sing loud above the flowering land;
Ladies are <u>gracious</u> now.—Where deserts burn
The beasts still prowl on the ungreening
    sand.

---

1. **Zephyr** (zef´ ər): The west wind.
2. **Procne** (präk´ nē) **and Philomel** (fil´ ō mel´): In Greek mythology, Philomel was a princess of Athens raped by Tereus, husband of her sister Procne. The gods changed Philomel into a nightingale, Procne into a swallow, and Tereus into a hawk.
3. **Jove . . . Venus':** Jove was the chief god in Roman mythology, and Venus was the goddess of love.

Reader's Response *What do you imagine Petrarch's Laura was like?*

THINKING ABOUT THE SELECTION

Clarifying

1. Name four details about Laura that the speaker recalls in "Laura."
2. In "The White Doe," what details of time and season does he mention?

Interpreting

3. The speaker in "Laura" contrasts present and past. (a) What are the common qualities of the details he remembers about Laura? (b) How does she seem to have changed? (c) What aspects of the situation remain unchanged?
4. In "Spring," written after Laura's death, the speaker uses contrast differently in dealing with the theme of time. (a) What does he emphasize about the spring? (b) What contrasts with the springtime scene? (c) How do you interpret the surprising ending of the poem?
5. What physical and spiritual qualities characterize the Laura of these poems?

Applying

6. Petrarch was a fourteenth-century writer. (a) In what ways are the feelings or situations he describes recognizable today? (b) In what ways are they out-of-date?

ANALYZING LITERATURE

Understanding Petrarch's Love Poems

Petrarch's poetry often uses **allegory,** an extended metaphor in which the lover's experience is dramatized by being described in terms of something else. An elaborate allegory occurs in "The White Doe," though the final line of "Spring" also compares the poet's inner state to a landscape. Petrarch's most characteristic figure of speech, however, is the **oxymoron**—two words that form a logical contradiction and often express conflicting feelings.

1. (a) What is the meaning and effect of the following oxymorons: "sweet despair" ("Spring"); "suavely merciless" ("The White Doe")? (b) How does the second oxymoron prepare for lines 7–8?
2. In the initial vision of Laura in "The White Doe," which details suggest that the doe is really the lady?
3. (a) What references to time occur in "The White Doe"? (b) What do they mean?

4. (a) What is the meaning of the writing around the doe's neck? (b) What kind of "freedom" does the message suggest?

CRITICAL THINKING AND READING

Appreciating the Petrarchan Sonnet

The Petrarchan sonnet is a fourteen-line poem divided by the rhymes into two parts, an eight-line **octave** followed by a six-line **sestet.** The octave has only two rhyme-sounds and usually rhymes abbaabba; the sestet has either two or three rhyme-sounds combined in one of many different patterns. This division into two parts gives the sonnet's meaning a statement/response form: The octave often takes a position that the sestet contradicts or modifies or develops in a different manner. Petrarch did not invent the sonnet, but his practice established it as the dominant lyric form in the Renaissance.

1. Identify the rhyme scheme of each sonnet (the rhyme-scheme of "The White Doe" is not that of the Italian original, which is too difficult to render in English).
2. How does the sestet of "Spring" modify the octave?
3. What change in emphasis comes with the sestet of "Laura"?
4. All three sonnets end with sudden changes in the final line. In each case, what is the meaning and effect of the change?

THINKING AND WRITING

Comparing Translations

Poetic translations are rarely exact. The demands of the rhyme scheme, among other things, force the translator to depart from the literal meaning of the original. A literal prose translation of the sestet of "Spring" reads as follows: "But to me, alas, come back heavier sighs, which she draws from my deepest heart, she who carried off to Heaven the keys to it; and the singing of little birds, and the flowering of meadows, and virtuous gentle gestures in beautiful ladies are a wilderness and cruel, savage beasts." List some of the changes introduced by the poetic translator, Morris Bishop. What does he add? How does the tone change in the final lines? How is the sentence structure different? Then write a paper saying which version you prefer, and why. Finally, revise the essay, making sure to support your judgment with references to the particular differences you noticed.

(continued from bottom of page)

ANSWERS TO ANALYZING LITERATURE

1. (a) "sweet despair"—sorrow that somehow has an attractive taste to it; "suavely merciless"—unforgiving and cruel yet graceful and appealing. (b) Answers will differ. Students may respond that the oxymoron prepares for the paradox in line 8.
2. Answers will differ. Most students, however, will recognize that the word "appeared" suggests a nonliteral reading of "doe." Also, the speaker's idealized description of the doe ("pure-white," "antlers of gold") suggests that it is an ideal or symbolic creature.
3. (a) Time references include "sunrise" and "toward noon." (b) Answers will differ. Most students will recognize that these time references symbolize stages in the speaker's love for Laura.
4. (a) The writing means that Laura is untouchable and cannot or will not return the speaker's affection. (b) Answers will differ. Some students may respond that a powerful person (a Caesar) has protected Laura from other relationships.

ANSWERS TO CRITICAL THINKING AND READING

1. "Laura"—abbaabba cdedce; "The White Doe"—ababcddc efefef; "Spring"—abbaabba cdcdcd.
2. The sestet introduces the speaker's feelings, which contrast with the springlike mood of the octave.
3. In line 13 the poet reveals that Laura is no longer the radiant young beauty he has been describing.
4. Answers will differ, but students should give the meaning and the effect of the change.

THINKING AND WRITING

Publishing Student Writing Have students read their essays aloud.

Closure and Extension

ANSWERS TO THINKING ABOUT THE SELECTION

1. Laura had golden hair; deep, bright eyes; an angelic walk; and a voice that evoked harmonies of unearthly singers.
2. Time references include "at sunrise" and "toward noon." References to

season include spring "colors," "New flowers and grass," "fair" skies, and birdsong.
3. (a) They portray her as a radiant beauty. (b) She seems to have grown old. (c) The speaker's love for her remains unchanged.
4. (a) He emphasizes its freshness, tenderness, activity, and joyfulness. (b) The speaker's mood contrasts with this scene. (c) Answers will differ.

Some students may respond that the last image represents the poet's desolation.
5. The Laura of these poems seems to be lovely, graceful, and refined, yet also distant.
6. Answers will differ.

THE BLACK PLAGUE

"The Deadly Plague"

The *Decameron* of Giovanni Boccaccio begins by describing the most terrible event of the fourteenth century, one that probably killed a third of the population in Western Europe. In 1348, says Boccaccio, "the deadly plague broke out in the great city of Florence, . . ." Those afflicted with the disease were covered with swellings that grew to "the size of a common apple or egg." Soon these swellings gave way to "black or livid spots appearing on the arms, thighs, and the whole person." Few of the sick lived and most died after the third day.

This sickness was called the Black Plague, but we know it as Bubonic Plague, a disease that originates in parts of Africa and Asia. At intervals of hundreds of years, it erupts into the rest of the world. The Bubonic Plague is carried by a kind of flea that lives on rodents—in fourteenth-century Europe, on the black rats that were everywhere in the overcrowded and dirty cities and in the countryside as well. The rats would die from the disease and the fleas might transfer to a nearby person. It was largely a matter of chance whether or not one was bitten by a plague-bearing flea.

Boccaccio's contemporaries, however, lacked our medical knowledge. It seemed a terrible mystery why some towns or families were spared, others would lose many members, and still others would die to the last person. Like many writers, Boccaccio ascribes the plague to astrological forces or to God's punishment for people's misdeeds. The plague, however, was known to strike good people as well as bad: Priests, many of whom attended the dying, seem to have died more frequently than laypersons.

Doctors had two theories about how the plague spread. It was either seen as the effect of a poisonous air or mist, or it was thought to be spread by human contact. As Boccaccio points out, this second theory caused the healthy to shun the sick: "The calamity had instilled such horror into the hearts of men and women that brother abandoned brother, uncles, sisters, and wives left their dear ones to perish and, what is more serious and almost incredible, parents avoided visiting or nursing their very children, as though these were not their own flesh. . . . Many who might perhaps have lived if they had been tended, perished of this neglect." Current fear of AIDS victims suggests a contemporary parallel.

The plague was the more devastating because fourteenth-century medicine had no cures and, indeed, tended to hasten patients' death. Medieval and Renaissance medical science had, of course, no way of understanding the bacilli that caused the plague. The best medical opinion held that the body was dominated by four different fluid "humors"—blood, phlegm, yellow bile, and black bile—and that each of these humors had a different physical and psychological effect. (Blood, for instance, made one cheerful; black bile made one melancholy and shy.) In the healthy individual, these humors were all in balance, each of them canceling out the bad effects of the others. Sickness consisted of an excess of one humor over another. The primary cure for such an excess was bleeding the patient to get rid of the excessive humor. Tragically, this bleeding weakened patients, making them more likely to die.

The Search for Scapegoats

Faced with this horrible and mysterious disease, people looked for someone to blame. Arabs were accused in Spain and lepers elsewhere. It was

Primary Source Note

Historian Barbara Tuchman pointed out that people were completely ignorant of the causes of the plague:

Of the real carriers, rats and fleas, the 14th century had no suspicion, perhaps because they were so familiar. Fleas, though a common household nuisance, are not once mentioned in contemporary plague writings, and rats only incidentally, although folklore commonly associated them with pestilence. The legend of the Pied Piper arose from an outbreak of 1284. The actual plague bacillus, *Pasturella pestis*, remained undiscovered for another 500 years. Living alternately in the stomach of the flea and the bloodstream of the rat who was the flea's host, the bacillus in its bubonic form was transferred to humans by the bite of either rat or flea. It traveled by virtue of *Rattus rattus*, the small medieval black rat that lived on ships, as well as by the heavier brown or sewer rat. What precipi-

NSIGHTS

(continued from bottom of page)

the Jews, however, who suffered the most. There was already a great deal of prejudice against them in medieval society. Now, however, Jews were accused of poisoning wells and spreading plague, and there was an upsurge of anti-Semitic passion starting in France and spreading to Switzerland and Germany. Thousands of Jews were massacred or burned alive in German cities.

Effects of the Plague

Boccaccio, like many other witnesses, points out that the onslaught of the plague resulted in a breakdown of the civil order. In the country peasants ceased to till the fields: There seemed no point in sowing in the spring when one was likely to die before the harvest. In the city, too, business virtually stopped. Some people locked themselves in their houses; others, by contrast, spent their time drinking in the taverns. Both types of people died.

The constant dying dulled citizens' sense of individual dignity, and ordinary rituals of mourning were shortened or entirely discarded. This was the practice for the more well-to-do. The poor and the middle class, according to Boccaccio, suffered even worse trials: "More wretched still were the circumstances of the common people and, for a great part, of the middle class, for, confined to their homes either by hope of safety or by poverty, and restricted to their own sections, they fell sick daily by thousands. There, devoid of help or care, they died almost without redemption. A great many breathed their last in the public streets, day and night. . . ."

Boccaccio sums up the moral and psychological effects of the plague in a terrible sentence: "Death had become so common that no more attention was given to human lives than would be given to goats brought to slaughter nowadays."

Over the spring and summer of 1348 the plague spread northward and westward over Europe; by the fall it attacked England. By the time the plague ceased in 1350, London may have lost thirty thousand, or four in ten, and the countryside was seriously depopulated. Even then it did not stop. It continued to erupt at irregular intervals—in 1361, 1368–1369, 1371, 1375, 1390, and 1405, and indeed for the next three hundred years.

There is much disagreement about the long-term effects of the plague. It may have hastened an already beginning decline in European population and so, paradoxically, brought about improved conditions for those who remained alive. Before the plague there was a surplus of available labor; afterward there were fewer laborers, who were able to charge more for their services.

Most noticeable was the way in which the plague intensified people's sense of human mortality. Both life and joy were short; nothing earthly was certain. In the sixteenth century, the English writer Thomas Nashe composed a "Litany in Time of Plague," whose refrain sums up this mood:

> Rich men, trust not in wealth,
> Gold cannot buy you health;
> Physic [the doctor] himself must fade,
> All things to end are made.

LORD, HAVE MERCY ON LONDON
English woodcut on the Great Plague of 1665

3 Enrichment Explain to students that one effect of the plague in cities was a breakdown in arrangements for street cleaning and sewage disposal.

Humanities Note

Fine art, *Lord, Have Mercy on London,* 1665. This English woodcut depicts the Great Plague of London which, in the years 1664–1665, killed about one sixth of the city's population.

In making a woodcut, an artist cuts away wood to leave raised lines that accept the printing ink. Paper is placed on the woodcut, rubbed, and pulled away, leaving a reverse image of the design. The first book illustrated with woodcuts and set with movable type was published in 1461. Within ten years woodcutting was an industry, with designers and cutters creating illustrations for books that could now be mass produced.

You might want to use the following questions to discuss the art:

1. What symbols did the artist use to depict the plague?
2. How does this woodcut compare with contemporary posters that warn about AIDS?

Questions

1. Name three ways in which the plague disrupted fourteenth-century society.
2. (a) Why do you think people looked for scapegoats to blame for their suffering? (b) Do modern calamities inspire a similar search for scapegoats? Explain.

Activities

1. Have students read and report on Boccaccio's description of the plague in the *Decameron.*
2. Ask students to draw a diagram illustrating the transmission of the plague bacillus from rats to fleas to humans.

tated the turn of the bacillus from innocuous to virulent form is unknown, but the occurrence is now believed to have taken place not in China but somewhere in central Asia and to have spread along the caravan routes. Chinese origin was a mistaken notion of the 14th century based on real but belated reports of huge death tolls in China from drought, famine, and pestilence which have since been traced to the 1330's, too soon to be responsible for the plague that appeared in India in 1346.

The phantom enemy had no name. Called the Black Death only in later recurrences, it was known during the first epidemic simply as the Pestilence or Great Mortality. Reports from the East, swollen by fearful imaginings, told of strange tempests, and "sheets of fire" mingled with huge hailstones. . . . In another version, "foul blasts of wind" from the fires carried the infection to Europe "and now as some suspect it cometh round the seacoast." Accurate observation in this case could not make the mental jump to ships and rats because no idea of animal- or insect-borne contagion existed.

IOANNES BOCCACCIO

1313–1375

Far from being a musty old classic, Boccaccio's (bô kät´ chôz) book of stories the *Decameron* has delighted readers and inspired writers for half a millennium. Like many best-selling novels of our own time, it has been made into a popular movie: the *Decameron* (1971), directed by Pier Paolo Pasolini.

Boccaccio was the illegitimate son of a Florentine merchant, an associate of a well-known banking family. His father sent him at the age of ten to work in one of his firm's banks in Naples. This southern Italian city was ruled by the Frenchman Robert of Anjou, whose court was known for its splendor and sophistication. As a member of the banking firm that lent this ruler money, Boccaccio was able to attend court functions, and he later remembered this period of his life as a time of gaiety and pleasure.

Boccaccio's father tried to make his son into a businessman and later into a lawyer specializing in church law; however, Boccaccio showed little interest in either field. He did, however, start to write at the Neapolitan court and wrote prolifically for the rest of his life. His early works, written mostly in Italian, include several long narratives. One of them, *Filocolo*, demonstrates Boccaccio's deep insights into human motives and behavior.

In 1340 financial problems caused Boccaccio's family to recall him to Florence, and he had to leave behind the cultivated court that he loved. His letters suggest that the return to what seemed at first a petty, middle-class, money-grubbing environment was difficult. However, this move provided essential experience for the future author of the *Decameron*, a book dealing with all kinds and classes of people. As time passed, Boccaccio became more sympathetic to Florence. Indeed, he actively engaged in Florentine politics, serving as an ambassador to other countries—a role that humanist scholars often played.

In 1350 Boccaccio met Petrarch (see page 674), the only contemporary whose gifts matched his own. This meeting blossomed into a lifelong friendship. Boccaccio admired Petrarch greatly, and Petrarch's example encouraged him in his own humanist studies (for a discussion of humanism, see pages 659–662). He produced a series of scholarly Latin works arising out of his vast reading in classical literature. Among these were biographies entitled "Of Famous Women," prose accounts "Of the Fall of Famous Men," and—dearest to his heart—a treatise on classical mythology, "On the Genealogy of the Gods." (The word *genealogy* means "a study of family descent.") With the help of a Greek collaborator, he produced the first European translation of Homer's works into Latin. He also wrote a biography of Dante (see page 618), and in his last year began an important commentary on the *Divine Comedy*.

Boccaccio would have regarded these scholarly Latin works—rather than the *Decameron*, written in Italian—as his greatest achievement. Indeed, he was famous for them throughout the Renaissance. By contrast, the *Decameron* appears to be a work of amusement, of easy popular writing at a distance from humanist seriousness. Yet these stories are extremely artful and show an extraordinary variety of tone and subject matter.

GUIDE FOR INTERPRETING

from the Decameron

Commentary

The Novella. Boccaccio's *Decameron* is a group of one hundred short prose tales or *novelle* (singular: *novella,* a word that means "a small new thing"). Rather than telling the stories directly, Boccaccio creates a fictional background or frame for the book. He imagines that ten young people of good families—seven women and three men—leave Florence for the country to escape the plague. To pass the time, each of them tells a story a day for ten days (the word *decameron* means "ten days").

Ten was considered a perfect number in medieval and Renaissance times, and the one hundred stories recall the one hundred cantos of Dante's *Divine Comedy.* Boccaccio's book, however, could not be more unlike Dante's poem. Where Dante's work deals with the afterlife, Boccaccio's stories concern people in this world. Also, when religion is a subject, Boccaccio's treatment is usually satirical. The first story, for instance, describes the deathbed confession of a corrupt notary. This man succeeds in convincing a gullible priest that he is all but a saint—the triumphant last trick of a successful con artist!

While the con man is a frequent figure in the *Decameron,* Boccaccio's work is striking for its variety of subject and mood. The frame-tale, in which we see the ten young people speaking, dancing, or playing in the lovely countryside, presents an image of a joyful human community. Within this frame there are stories of many different kinds—accounts of practical jokes, narratives of sexual adventure, and tales of ideal love, among others.

The story of Federigo degli Alberighi is told on the Fifth Day of the *Decameron.* It is a tale of ideal love in which Federigo and his Lady are each models of courteous behavior. The extremity of Federigo's actions shows his absolute devotion to Monna Giovanna and his willingness to sacrifice everything for his love. By one set of standards, his behavior may seem misguided and fanatical: He is so concerned with his love that he ruins himself. Boccaccio, however, does nothing to suggest that such devotion is wrong. On the contrary, he presents it as the natural result of a truly noble and chivalrous character.

Writing

Federigo's action in this story is extremely generous. Describe an incident you heard about or observed in which someone displayed great generosity.

Literary Focus Have students discuss what they know about the Islamic folk tale collection *The Thousand and One Nights* (see page 128). Many of them will mention the stories of Sinbad and Aladdin. Others may know that all of the tales are part of a larger story involving a young woman named Scheherazade, who postpones her execution by entertaining the king with her clever tales. Explain to students that Boccaccio's decision to use a frame story in the *Decameron* may have been influenced by his reading *The Thousand and One Nights.* Have them consider the advantages of having such a frame story.

Writing/Prior Knowledge Have students work in pairs to develop lists of simple acts of generosity. Have them discuss what makes these simple acts special. These lists and discussions can be the springboard for identifying and describing greater acts of generosity.

ESL Teaching Strategy Ask ESL students to tell the class about the meaning of generosity in their culture.

Vocabulary

Preteach the following vocabulary words:
courtly (kôrt´ lē) *adj.*: Dignified; polite; elegant
sumptuous (sump´ chōō əs) *adj.*: Costly; lavish
frugally (frōō´ gə lē) *adv.*: Thriftily; economically
deference (def´ ər əns) *n.*: Courteous regard or respect
affably (af´ fə blē) *adv.*: In a friendly manner
impertinence (im pʉrt´´n əns) *n.*: Insolence; impudence
despondent (di spän´ dənt) *adj.*: Dejected; hopeless

Support Material

Teaching Portfolio
Teacher Backup, p. 849
Grammar in Action Worksheet, *Adverb Clauses*, p. 853
Usage and Mechanics Worksheet, p. 855
Vocabulary Check, p. 856
Analyzing Literature Worksheet,

Understanding the Decameron, p. 857
Critical Thinking and Reading Worksheet, *Tracing Boccaccio's Influence*, p. 858
Selection Test, pp. 859–860
Art Transparency 9
Haymaking (detail), Pieter Brueghel the Elder

Spelling Tip Write *frugally* and *affably* on the chalkboard. Call students' attention to the fact that each word has a double consonant.

from the # Decameron

Giovanni Boccaccio

Federigo's Falcon

translated by G. H. McWilliam

Once Filomena had finished, the queen, finding that there was no one left to speak apart from herself (Dioneo being excluded from the reckoning because of his privilege), smiled cheerfully and said:

It is now my own turn to address you, and I shall gladly do so, dearest ladies, with a story similar in some respects to the one we have just heard. This I have chosen, not only to acquaint you with the power of your beauty over men of noble spirit, but so that you may learn to choose for yourselves, whenever necessary, the persons on whom to bestow your largesse,[1] instead of always leaving these matters to be decided for you by Fortune, who, as it happens, nearly always scatters her gifts with more abundance than discretion.

You are to know, then, that Coppo di Borghese Domenichi, who once used to live in our city and possibly lives there still, one of the most highly respected men of our century, a person worthy of eternal fame, who achieved his position of pre-eminence by dint of his character and abilities rather than by his noble lineage, frequently took pleasure during his declining years in discussing incidents from the past with his neighbors and other folk. In this pastime he excelled all others, for he was more coherent, possessed a superior memory, and spoke with greater eloquence. He

had a fine repertoire, including a tale he frequently told concerning a young Florentine called Federigo, the son of Messer Filippo Alberighi, who for his deeds of chivalry and courtly manners was more highly spoken of than any other squire in Tuscany. In the manner of most young men of gentle breeding, Federigo lost his heart to a noble lady, whose name was Monna[2] Giovanna, and who in her time was considered one of the loveliest and most adorable women to be found in Florence. And with the object of winning her love, he rode at the ring, tilted, gave sumptuous banquets, and distributed a large number of gifts, spending money without any restraint whatsoever. But since she was no less chaste than she was fair, the lady took no notice, either of the things that were done in her honor, or of the person who did them.

In this way, spending far more than he could afford and deriving no profit in return, Federigo lost his entire fortune (as can easily happen) and reduced himself to poverty, being left with nothing other than a tiny little farm, which produced an income just sufficient for him to live very frugally, and one falcon of the finest breed in the whole world. Since he was as deeply in love as ever, and felt unable to go on living the sort of life in Florence to which he aspired, he moved out to Campi,

---

1. **largesse** (lär jes′) *n.*: Generous gifts.

2. **Monna:** Lady.

where his little farm happened to be situated. Having settled in the country, he went hunting as often as possible with his falcon, and, without seeking assistance from anyone, he patiently resigned himself to a life of poverty.

Now one day, while Federigo was living in these straitened circumstances, the husband of Monna Giovanna happened to fall ill, and, realizing that he was about to die, he drew up his will. He was a very rich man, and in his will he left everything to his son, who was just growing up, further stipulating that, if his son should die without legitimate issue, his estate should go to Monna Giovanna, to whom he had always been deeply devoted.

Shortly afterward he died, leaving Monna Giovanna a widow, and every summer, in accordance with Florentine custom, she went away with her son to a country estate of theirs, which was very near Federigo's farm. Consequently this young lad of hers happened to become friendly with Federigo, acquiring a passion for birds and dogs; and, having often seen Federigo's falcon in flight, he became fascinated by it and longed to own it, but since he could see that Federigo was deeply attached to the bird, he never ventured to ask him for it.

And there the matter rested, when, to the consternation of his mother, the boy happened to be taken ill. Being her only child, he was the apple of his mother's eye, and she sat beside his bed the whole day long, never ceasing to comfort him. Every so often she asked him whether there was anything he wanted, imploring him to tell her what it was, because if it was possible to acquire it, she would move heaven and earth to obtain it for him.

After hearing this offer repeated for the umpteenth time, the boy said:

"Mother, if you could arrange for me to have Federigo's falcon, I believe I should soon get better."

On hearing this request, the lady was somewhat taken aback, and began to consider what she could do about it. Knowing that Federigo had been in love with her for a long time, and that she had never deigned to cast so much as a single glance in his direction, she said to herself: "How can I possibly go to him, or even send anyone, to ask him for this falcon, which to judge from all I

have heard is the finest that ever flew, as well as being the only thing that keeps him alive? And how can I be so heartless as to deprive so noble a man of his one remaining pleasure?"

Her mind filled with reflections of this sort, she remained silent, not knowing what answer to make to her son's request, even though she was quite certain that the falcon was hers for the asking.

At length, however, her maternal instincts gained the upper hand, and she resolved, come what may, to satisfy the child by going in person to Federigo to collect the bird, and bring it back to him. And so she replied:

"Bear up, my son, and see whether you can start feeling any better. I give you my word that I shall go and fetch it for you first thing tomorrow morning."

Next morning, taking another lady with her for company,[3] his mother left the house as though intending to go for a walk, made her way to Federigo's little cottage, and asked to see him. For several days, the weather had been unsuitable for hawking, so Federigo was attending to one or two little jobs in his garden, and when he heard, to his utter astonishment, that Monna Giovanna was at the front door and wished to speak to him, he happily rushed there to greet her.

When she saw him coming, she advanced with womanly grace to meet him. Federigo received her with a deep bow, whereupon she said:

"Greetings, Federigo!" Then she continued: "I have come to make amends for the harm you have suffered on my account, by loving me more than you ought to have done. As a token of my esteem, I should like to take breakfast with you this morning, together with my companion here, but you must not put yourself to any trouble."

"My lady," replied Federigo in all humility, "I cannot recall ever having suffered any harm on your account. On the contrary I have gained so much that if ever I attained any kind of excellence, it was entirely because of your own great worth and the love I bore you. Moreover I can assure you

---

3. **taking . . . company:** A young woman of the upper classes would not go out unaccompanied.

(continued from bottom of page)

bird and as such embodies the last outward sign of Federigo's gentility. Yet he is willing to part with it in order to offer one more thing to his beloved.

In the story it is precisely this willingness not to consider consequences that bears fruit. His act is rewarded with both Giovanna's hand and her property. The story ends somewhat slyly, mentioning that after gaining these, Federigo managed his finances "more prudently."

5 **Literary Focus** Ask students to explain how Federigo's response to his impoverishment demonstrates nobility of spirit.

6 **Clarification** Inform students that the custom of leaving the city for the country during the summer was common among the nobility throughout Europe. Poor sanitation combined with summer heat and humidity to make cities like Florence breeding grounds for diseases such as malaria and cholera. Those who could, escaped for the summer, even when the plague was not raging.

7 **Literary Focus** Have the students consider how the illness of Monna Giovanna's son helps to show the nobility of her character.

8 **Clarification** Make sure students understand that Monna Giovanna's fear that without the falcon her son might not get well is literal. So too is her concern for Federigo's health without the falcon.

9 **Discussion** Ask students to discuss why Monna Giovanna's visit would be considered making amends for Federigo's suffering.

10 **Discussion** Have the class consider Federigo's response. Ask them how his comment illustrates Petrarch's vivid oxymoron "sweet despair" (see line 3 of "Spring," page 678).

Commentary

Federigo's Generosity Although many of Boccaccio's stories deal with the middle class, this story is very much concerned with the aristocratic virtue of generosity. Federigo is introduced as a young man known for his deeds of chivalry, and from the beginning he is willing to give up all his wealth for Monna Giovanna. His lavishness has a positive side because it is part of a larger kind of generosity. Federigo is someone who holds back nothing. He "loses his heart" to the lady, and his subsequent actions simply elaborate this openness of spirit.

When his money is spent, he returns to his small farm with no sign of bitterness over his failure to attract Monna Giovanna's attention. Indeed he still sees his love as the high point of his life, and he does not complain about his poverty until he is unable to give Giovanna a breakfast befitting her. His final act, killing the falcon, epitomizes his unhesitating devotion to his love. The falcon is a noble

11 **Clarification** Explain to students that although his poverty reduced Federigo to living on his tiny farm, he was not a working farmer. A peasant family farmed the land for him. They provided the main share of the farm's crops to Federigo as rent.

12 **Discussion** The storyteller emphasizes Federigo's lack of understanding of his own poverty before Monna Giovanna's visit. Why is this significant? What does it tell us about Federigo's concern for wealth and his overall character?

Humanities Note

Fine art, *Robert Cheseman* by Hans Holbein the Younger. Holbein (c. 1498–1543) was born in Augsburg, Germany, and is considered one of the finest portrait painters of all time. His father, uncle, and brother were also painters. The religious wars of the sixteenth century caused European artists to turn from traditional religious subjects. Holbein was able to make his mark in portraiture. At the age of twenty-eight, he left Germany and traveled to England, becoming the court artist of King Henry VIII.

Holbein's art did not reflect the upheaval of his time. In the last ten years of his life, however, he painted about 150 portraits of the royalty and nobility of England that convey the flavor of court life.

Holbein died during a plague in London.

You might want to use the following questions to discuss the art:

1. Which lines from the story would you choose as a caption for this painting? Explain your choice.
2. Does Robert Cheseman, the subject of this portrait, match your image of Federigo? Why or why not?
3. What does this portrait suggest about Cheseman's personality, station in life, and interests?
4. Did the invention of photography make it unnecessary for

ROBERT CHESEMAN
Hans Holbein, The Younger

that this visit which you have been generous enough to pay me is worth more to me than all the money I ever possessed, though I fear that my hospitality will not amount to very much."

So saying, he led her unassumingly into the house, and thence into his garden, where, since there was no one else he could call upon to chaperon her, he said:

"My lady, as there is nobody else available, this good woman, who is the wife of the farmer here, will keep you company whilst I go and see about setting the table."

Though his poverty was acute, the extent to which he had squandered his wealth had not yet been fully borne home to Federigo; but on this particular morning, finding that he had nothing to

painters to continue to do portraits? Explain.

Grammar in Action

An **adverb clause** is a subordinate clause that modifies a verb, adjective, or verbal. It does this by pointing out where, when, in what manner, to what extent, under what condition, or why. It is a clause because it contains a subject and a verb, but these are not the main subject and verb of the sentence. Following are examples of adverb clauses (the clause and the word it modifies are italicized):

Kevin wanted to *write* the postcard *before he left Rome for Milan.*
Sarah was *happy as she welcomed her cousins to her party.*

set before the lady for whose love he had entertained so lavishly in the past, his eyes were well and truly opened to the fact. Distressed beyond all measure, he silently cursed his bad luck and rushed all over the house like one possessed, but could find no trace of either money or valuables. By now the morning was well advanced, he was still determined to entertain the gentlewoman to some sort of meal, and, not wishing to beg assistance from his own farmer (or from anyone else, for that matter), his gaze alighted on his precious falcon, which was sitting on its perch in the little room where it was kept. And having discovered, on picking it up, that it was nice and plump, he decided that since he had nowhere else to turn, it would make a worthy dish for such a lady as this. So without thinking twice about it he wrung the bird's neck and promptly handed it over to his housekeeper to be plucked, dressed, and roasted carefully on a spit. Then he covered the table with spotless linen, of which he still had a certain amount in his possession, and returned in high spirits to the garden, where he announced to his lady that the meal, such as he had been able to prepare, was now ready.

The lady and her companion rose from where they were sitting and made their way to the table. And together with Federigo, who waited on them with the utmost deference, they made a meal of the prize falcon without knowing what they were eating.

On leaving the table they engaged their host in pleasant conversation for a while, and when the lady thought it time to broach the subject she had gone there to discuss, she turned to Federigo and addressed him affably as follows:

"I do not doubt for a moment, Federigo, that you will be astonished at my impertinence when you discover my principal reason for coming here, especially when you recall your former mode of living and my virtue, which you possibly mistook for harshness and cruelty. But if you had ever had any children to make you appreciate the power of parental love, I should think it certain that you would to some extent forgive me.

"However, the fact that you have no children of your own does not exempt me, a mother, from the laws common to all other mothers. And being bound to obey those laws, I am forced, contrary to my own wishes and to all the rules of decorum and propriety, to ask you for something to which I know you are very deeply attached—which is only natural, seeing that it is the only consolation, the only pleasure, the only recreation remaining to you in your present extremity of fortune. The gift I am seeking is your falcon, to which my son has taken so powerful a liking, that if I fail to take it to him I fear he will succumb to the illness from which he is suffering, and consequently I shall lose him. In imploring you to give me this falcon, I appeal, not to your love, for you are under no obligation to me on that account, but rather to your noble heart, whereby you have proved yourself superior to all others in the practice of courtesy. Do me this favor, then, so that I may claim that through your generosity I have saved my son's life, thus placing him forever in your debt."

When he heard what it was that she wanted, and realized that he could not oblige her because he had given her the falcon to eat, Federigo burst into tears in her presence before being able to utter a single word in reply. At first the lady thought his tears stemmed more from his grief at having to part with his fine falcon than from any other motive, and was on the point of telling him that she would prefer not to have it. But on second thoughts she said nothing, and waited for Federigo to stop crying and give her his answer, which eventually he did.

"My lady," he said, "ever since God decreed that you should become the object of my love, I have repeatedly had cause to complain of Fortune's hostility towards me. But all her previous blows were slight by comparison with the one she has dealt me now. Nor shall I ever be able to forgive her, when I reflect that you have come to my poor dwelling, which you never deigned to visit when it was rich, and that you desire from me a trifling favor which she has made it impossible for me to concede. The reason is simple, and I shall explain it in few words.

"When you did me the kindness of telling me that you wished to breakfast with me, I considered it right and proper, having regard to your excellence and merit, to do everything within my power to prepare a more sumptuous dish than those I would offer to my ordinary guests. My thoughts

13 **Discussion** Ask students to consider what the phrase "without thinking twice" tells us about Federigo's character.

14 **Reading Strategy** Have students pause here to predict Monna Giovanna's reaction to news of the falcon's death. You might also ask them to predict Federigo's reaction when he learns the real reason for her visit.

15 **Discussion** Ask students why Monna Giovanna felt an appeal to Federigo's noble heart would be appropriate.

16 **Discussion** Have students consider what Federigo's assertion that God "decreed" his love says about his view of love. Ask them whether or not they subscribe to this view.

17 **Enrichment** Point out that despite the strong religious feelings of the time, belief in the role of Fortune was also strong. Fortune, usually personified as a woman, was a combination of fate (that which happens because it is meant to) and luck (that which happens by chance). Have students compare Federigo's remarks about Fortune with those of the storyteller on page 684.

I enjoy *walking* in the park *after school lets out.*

Notice that an adverb clause begins with a subordinating conjunction.

The translator of the *Decameron* makes frequent use of adverb clauses:

"*When she saw him coming,* she *advanced* with womanly grace to meet him." (page 685)

Student Activity 1. Find two additional examples of adverb clauses on page 687. For each example, identify the subject and verb of the clause and the word or words that the clause modifies.

Student Activity 2. Write five sentences of your own using adverb clauses. Vary your sentences so that you show adverb clauses modifying verbs, adjectives, and verbals.

therefore turned to the falcon you have asked me for and, knowing its quality, I reputed it a worthy dish to set before you. So I had it roasted and served to you on the trencher this morning, and I could not have wished for a better way of disposing of it. But now that I discover that you wanted it in a different form, I am so distressed by my inability to grant your request that I shall never forgive myself for as long as I live."

In confirmation of his words, Federigo caused the feathers, talons and beak to be cast on the table before her. On seeing and hearing all this, the lady reproached him at first for killing so fine a falcon, and serving it up for a woman to eat; but then she became lost in admiration for his magnanimity⁴ of spirit, which no amount of poverty had managed to diminish, nor ever would. But now that her hopes of obtaining the falcon had vanished she began to feel seriously concerned for the health of her son, and after thanking Federigo for his hospitality and good intentions, she took her leave of him, looking all despondent, and returned to the child. And to his mother's indescribable sorrow, within the space of a few days, whether through his disappointment in not being able to have the falcon, or because he was in any case suffering from a mortal illness, the child passed from this life.

---

4. **magnanimity** (mag′ nə nim′ ə tē) *n*.: Noble generosity.

After a period of bitter mourning and continued weeping, the lady was repeatedly urged by her brothers to remarry, since not only had she been left a vast fortune but she was still a young woman. And though she would have preferred to remain a widow, they gave her so little peace that in the end, recalling Federigo's high merits and his latest act of generosity, namely to have killed such a fine falcon in her honor, she said to her brothers:

"If only it were pleasing to you, I should willingly remain as I am; but since you are so eager for me to take a husband, you may be certain that I shall never marry any other man except Federigo degli Alberighi."

Her brothers made fun of her, saying:

"Silly girl, don't talk such nonsense! How can you marry a man who hasn't a penny with which to bless himself?"

"My brothers," she replied, "I am well aware of that. But I would sooner have a gentleman without riches, than riches without a gentleman."

Seeing that her mind was made up, and knowing Federigo to be a gentleman of great merit even though he was poor, her brothers fell in with her wishes and handed her over to him, along with her immense fortune. Thenceforth, finding himself married to this great lady with whom he was so deeply in love, and very rich into the bargain, Federigo managed his affairs more prudently, and lived with her in happiness to the end of his days.

Reader's Response *Do you think Federigo was noble or misguided in serving up his falcon? Explain.*

THINKING ABOUT THE SELECTION

Interpreting

1. (a) How does Monna Giovanna view Federigo's love for her? (b) What is the difference between saying that she "took no notice" of his love and saying that she did not notice it? (c) Why is this distinction important?
2. (a) What social and moral problems arise when Monna Giovanna's son asks her to obtain Federigo's falcon? (b) What does her resolution of these problems reveal about her character?
3. (a) How is Federigo's decision to kill his falcon similar to Monna's decision to ask him for it? (b) How do both these actions relate to the theme of "magnanimity"?
4. (a) In what way are the two main characters models of behavior? (b) Do they have any faults? Explain.
5. How is this a story about loss and restoration, for both Monna and Federigo?

Applying

6. Did you find it disappointing that Monna Giovanna "would have preferred to remain a widow" after her husband died instead of marrying Federigo immediately? Explain.
7. How do the ideals of love expressed in this story differ from current notions of romantic love?

ANALYZING LITERATURE

Understanding Themes in the *Decameron*

Boccaccio uses the stories of the *Decameron* to explore a number of key themes from different perspectives. In "Federigo's Falcon" he focuses on the theme of nobility of spirit. He presents Federigo as the embodiment of this virtue, and in various ways he returns to the idea of nobility throughout the story. The first paragraph of the story itself, beginning "You are to know, then, . . ." sets up the themes and values of this tale.

1. (a) How does the storyteller characterize the principal figures in the tale? (b) What values does she implicitly endorse?
2. Explain how Federigo demonstrates nobility in at least three ways.
3. (a) Contrast Federigo's attitudes toward money at the beginning and end of the story. (b) Does this contrast reveal a conflict about this subject on the part of the storyteller? Explain.

CRITICAL THINKING AND READING

Tracing Boccaccio's Influence

Boccaccio's book was immediately popular, and its tales were repeated by author after author—by his friend Petrarch, by the English poet Geoffrey Chaucer, and others. Also, Boccaccio's use of the frame-tale to unify a series of stories dealing with different themes became a model for many subsequent writers. Finally, his ability to center a story on a particular image or object reappears in the work of later writers like Maupassant (see page 912) and Joyce.

In this story the falcon itself is the focus.

1. (a) When is the falcon first mentioned in the story? (b) What do we know of Federigo's attitude toward it?
2. How does it symbolize the central values of the story, both before and after it is sacrificed?

SPEAKING AND LISTENING

Participating in a Storytelling Circle

Boccaccio pretends that the stories of the *Decameron* were made up and told by a group of seven women and three men. Organize your own storytelling group with several classmates. Decide on a theme that will run through the stories all of you tell. Possible themes include generosity, love, greed, trickery, and so forth. Have each member of your group make up and relate a story that exemplifies the chosen theme. In devising your story, imagine a series of events that will illustrate the theme and then add specific details that will make the story vivid for your audience. Remember that the story need not be true. If you want, exaggerate the details to make your point more strongly.

THINKING AND WRITING

Writing Down a Story You Have Told

Now create a written version of the story you have told. You will find that you need to change the story as you put it down on the page because your voice and gestures can no longer do some of the work for you. First write it out as you told it. Then revise it, adding details that will help the reader understand your tone and purpose without hearing your voice. As you revise the story, ask members of your group to read it and decide whether it has lost anything in the transition to the page. Also, make sure your first paragraph suggests, directly or indirectly, the theme that your story will touch on.

(continued from bottom of page)

his heart to a noble lady, discreetly retires when the love is not reciprocated, maintains his devotion even in poverty, and sacrifices what is most dear to him to please her. All these actions reveal a selfless, generous, and noble nature.

3. (a) At the start of the story, he spends himself into poverty to prove his love. At the end, he is frugal with the wealth he gains by marrying Monna Giovanna. (b) Answers will differ. Students may respond that the narrator doesn't approve of Federigo's reckless spending but forgives him for it because it is done for love. At the end of the story, the narrator clearly endorses Federigo's new-found prudence.

ANSWERS TO CRITICAL THINKING AND READING

1. (a) The falcon is first mentioned after Federigo has wasted his wealth and retired to his tiny farm. (b) We know that he loves to hunt with it and that he values it highly.
2. Answers will differ. Students may respond that the falcon's handsomeness and courage correspond to Federigo's nobility. Also the falcon represents the last remaining symbol of his former station in life. His sacrifice of the falcon verifies his nobility of character.

THINKING AND WRITING

Publishing Student Writing You might want to collect the tales that students have written and publish them in one large book.

---

to the highest ideals of people of their class and character. Federigo suffers with dignity. Monna Giovanna behaves morally in refusing to acknowledge his love and when she is forced to ask a favor of him, does so with the greatest sensitivity. (b) Answers will differ. Some students may feel that Monna Giovanna is cruel in ignoring Federigo's love and that Federigo's devotion is excessive. The storyteller

makes it clear that Federigo is careless with money.
5. Monna Giovanna loses her husband and son; Federigo loses his heart, wealth, and social standing. Their marriage at the story's end returns wealth and love to Federigo and a noble husband to Monna Giovanna.
6. Answers will differ.
7. Answers will differ.

ANSWERS TO ANALYZING LITERATURE

1. (a) Federigo is praised for his courtly manners and deeds of chivalry. Monna Giovanna is described as beautiful and chaste. (b) The narrator endorses good breeding, gentle manners, romantic love, beauty, and self-sacrifice.
2. Answers will differ. Students may point out that he appropriately loses

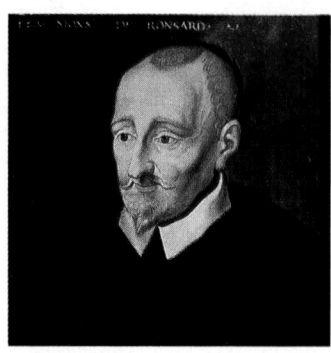

1524–1585

Pierre de Ronsard (pē er´ də rōn sàr´) was called "the Prince of Poets" by his contemporaries, and the title fitted his range and ambition. A key figure in the second half of the sixteenth century, he introduced classical forms and themes into French poetry and wrote verse of many different kinds—epic, satire, political commentary, as well as the odes and sonnets for which he is famous.

The youngest son in a family of minor French nobility, he was born in the family château in 1524. From an early age he was prepared for a diplomatic career and served as an attendant in the royal household. At the age of thirteen, he accompanied Princess Madeleine of France when she married the Scottish king, and Ronsard remained in Scotland for several years. Shortly before his sixteenth birthday, however, he was stricken with an illness that left him partly deaf, ending his chances as a diplomat.

After spending some time at home, Ronsard turned his energy and ambition to study and eventually to poetry. In 1544 he entered the Collège de Coqueret run by Jean Dorat, one of the most learned humanists of the French Renaissance. There he formed part of the group called the *Pléiade,* based on a name the Greeks had given to a constellation of seven stars. The literary stars of this group studied Greek and Latin authors and created a program for a rebirth of French poetry. The *Pléiade* preached—and practiced—the imitation of classical forms and themes in French as a means of enriching the language and building a great modern literature.

Ronsard was slow to publish his work, but in 1550 he released his first four books of odes, modeled on the work of the classical poets Pindar and Horace. The following year he published a book of love poetry addressed largely to a woman named Cassandre. From then on he wrote a great deal: a fifth book of odes, a book of hymns based on mythology, and a book of sensual love poetry called *Folies* (the word *folie* in French means both "madness" and "passion"). Ronsard's ambition and range were extraordinary. He saw poetry as a kind of inspired discipline with the poet acting as a receiver and transmitter of divine energies. At times this vision could lead to self-importance and heavy-handedness, but it often resulted in exciting and vibrant work.

Ronsard received financial support from the Catholic Church, but in an age when some were intolerant in their beliefs, he was open-minded and conciliatory. During the wars between Catholics and Protestants that divided France, he wrote his *Discours des misères de ce temps* ("Discourse on the calamities of this time"). In this work, without abandoning his Catholicism, he pleaded for an end to the bloodshed that was destroying the country.

In 1572 he published the first four books of his *Franciade*, a patriotic epic about France in imitation of Virgil's *Aeneid*; however, he never completed this work. His last major sequence of love poems, the *Sonnets pour Hélène*, appeared in 1578.

Ronsard's seriousness about his calling made him an untiring reviser of his poetry. During his later years, as his friends gradually died before him, he revised his collected works over and over, preparing a seventh and final edition just before his own death in 1585.

Ronsard's verse varies enormously. At its best, however, it is marked by an intensity, an energy, and a deep feeling for the natural world. These qualities are evident in the sonnets on the following pages.

GUIDE FOR INTERPRETING

Commentary

Roses; When You Are Old

Drama in Lyric Poetry. Lyric poetry is usually defined as "the personal expression of thoughts and emotions." However, it is also true that lyric poetry often suggests a dramatic context. If a male poet writes as a rejected lover, for instance, the poem may invite readers to imagine the woman who rejected him, the rival who won her affections, and the events leading up to the rejection. In other words the individual lyric may seem like a single speech in a larger drama.

Renaissance poets were particularly fond of dramatizing themselves, and it was common then to compare the world to a stage on which we play different parts. In their lyrics poets often adopted one of many possible roles—lover, mourner, wise counselor, seducer. We therefore refer to the **speaker** of such a poem rather than identifying the particular voice of the lyric with the poet. Writers are after all more complex than any single part they play.

In the sonnets that follow, Ronsard plays two familiar roles, those of mourner and lover, and in each poem goes through at least one change of mood. In each the poet addresses a lady, though for different purposes. The first is an **elegy**, or lament, for a dead lady. To express his sorrow, the poet develops an elaborate **simile**—a comparison using the word *like* or *as*—between a human being and a flower. Ronsard frequently uses the image of a flower to stress human mortality: Like individual flowers the body dies. Yet this is—and was in Ronsard's time—a cliché. Poets had compared human beings, and especially women, to flowers for at least two thousand years before he wrote this sonnet. Ronsard knew that the comparison was dangerously familiar but decided to take the risk. It is worth considering, therefore, how he makes the simile fresh again and how he uses it to dramatize his feelings at the lady's death.

The scenario of the second sonnet differs. Here the poet plays the role of a rejected lover. He argues that the lady owes him something, because his verse will enable people to remember how beautiful she was long after she is old. This, too, is a familiar situation in sonnet writing, and the final line that asks her to "pluck the roses of the world today" is close to a translation of a famous line by the Roman poet Horace. Again, it is worth considering how Ronsard injects new life and drama into a well-known scenario.

Writing

List five scenarios that occur in boy-meets-girl situations. Then imagine the different types of poems that each scenario might inspire.

Literary Focus Have students describe roles they played as younger children in pretend games: rock singer, firefighter, star athlete, and so forth. Once a number of roles have been identified, discuss the attributes associated with each role. Point out that these roles have a purpose in expressing some part of themselves. As role players, in other words, they were (and are) like poets creating "speakers" for their poems.

Writing/Prior Knowledge Pair up students within each group. Have them role-play a conversation that might come from each type of situation. Then have students do the writing assignment.

ESL Teaching Strategy Ask ESL students to listen to a reading of the poem and to identify the visual images in it. Then ask students to select a flower that is native to their cultures. Working with a native-speaking student, each ESL student can write ten phrases that present visual images of the chosen flower.

Vocabulary

Preteach the following vocabulary words:
oppressive (ə pres´ iv) *adj.*: Causing great discomfort
languishing (laŋ´ gwish iŋ) *v.*: Becoming weak
reposes (ri pōz´ əz) *v.*: Rests
fidelities (fə del´ ə tēz) *n.*: Faithful devotions to a loved one
crone (krōn) *n.*: Ugly, withered old woman
disdain (dis dān´) *n.*: Scorn

Support Material

Teaching Portfolio
Teacher Backup, p. 861
Usage and Mechanics Worksheet, p. 865
Vocabulary Check, p. 866
Analyzing Literature Worksheet, *Understanding the Dramatic Situation*, p. 867

Critical Thinking and Reading Worksheet, *Appreciating the* Carpe Diem *Theme*, p. 868
Selection Test, pp. 869–870
Spelling Tip Write the word *oppressive* on the chalkboard and remind students that it has two doubled consonants.

Roses

Pierre de Ronsard

translated by Vernon Watkins

PORTRAIT OF REMBRANDT'S
MOTHER AS THE
PROPHETESS HANNA
Rembrandt van Rijn

1

As one sees on the branch in the month of May the rose
In her beautiful youth, in the dawn of her flower,
When the break of day softens her life with the shower,
Make jealous the sky of the damask[1] bloom she shows:
5 Grace lingers in her leaf and love sleeping glows
Enchanting with fragrance the trees of her bower,
But, broken by the rain or the sun's oppressive power,

2

Languishing she dies, and all her petals throws.
Thus in thy first youth, in thy awakening fair
10 When thy beauty was honored by lips of Earth and Air,
Atropos[2] has killed thee and dust thy form reposes.
O take, take for obsequies[3] my tears, these poor showers,
This vase filled with milk, this basket strewn with flowers,
That in death as in life thy body may be roses.

---

1. **damask** (dam′ əsk): Deep pink or rose.
2. **Atropos** (a′ trə päs′): In Greek and Roman mythology, the goddess who cuts the thread of life.
3. **obsequies** (äb′ si kwēz′): Funeral rites or ceremonies.

THINKING ABOUT THE SELECTIONS

Interpreting

1. (a) In "Roses" what contrast does Ronsard create between the first six lines and the next two? (b) Which words and images emphasize the contrast?
2. (a) When do you first notice that the speaker is addressing a woman? (b) When do you first realize she is dead? (c) What is the effect of these delayed recognitions?
3. The funeral rites at the end of the poem are pagan, not Christian. Why do you think Ronsard avoids expressing the Christian hope that the lady's soul has gone to heaven?
4. (a) In "When You Are Old," what does "it" (line 5) refer to? (b) What is "love's benefit" (line 7)?
5. In "When You Are Old," what is the poet's attitude toward the changes that time brings?

Applying

6. At the end of "Roses," the poet offers the lady a vase of milk and a basket of flowers. (a) What similar types of offerings do people make today when they are in mourning? (b) Why do you think those in mourning make such gestures?

ANALYZING LITERATURE

Understanding the Drama in Lyrics

Lyrics are "personal expressions of emotion," but they often suggest a dramatic context. In each of Ronsard's sonnets, for instance, the speaker adopts a particular attitude in a particular situation. In "Roses" the dramatic situation is a pagan funeral; in "When You Are Old," it is a situation in which the speaker feels he has not gained the favors he deserves. Each sonnet, how-

When You Are Old

Pierre de Ronsard

translated by Humbert Wolfe

When you are old, at evening candle-lit
beside the fire bending to your wool,
read out my verse and murmur, "Ronsard writ
this praise for me when I was beautiful."
And not a maid but, at the sound of it,
though nodding at the stitch on broidered stool,
will start awake, and bless love's benefit

whose long fidelities bring Time to school.
I shall be thin and ghost beneath the earth
10 by myrtle shade in quiet after pain,
but you, a crone, will crouch beside the hearth
mourning my love and all your proud disdain.
And since what comes tomorrow who can say?
Live, pluck the roses of the world today.

3
4
5

Reader's Response *Did you find these two poems dramatic? Why or why not?*

---

ever, holds back knowledge of the situation until the sestet (the final six lines).

1. (a) What is the effect of holding back this knowledge in "When You Are Old"? (b) Does this strategy serve similar purposes in both poems?
2. In "When You Are Old," Ronsard might have said directly, "I'm preserving your beauty for when you are old." What is the advantage of having the lady express this idea (lines 3–4)?
3. (a) If you were the speaker of this poem, what tone of voice would you use in the first four lines? (b) How and where would you change your tone of voice in the following lines? Explain.

CRITICAL THINKING AND READING
Appreciating the *Carpe Diem* Theme

Carpe diem (kär pe dī′ em) is Latin for "seize the day"—in other words, make use of the present time, for as the Latin poet Catullus puts it, once we are dead we will "sleep one unending sleep." This theme is common in seduction poetry, in which poets usually urge women to enjoy love while they can. The *carpe diem* theme, however, reflects a larger concern with the way that time limits human life and forces one to use the goods that the world offers.

1. (a) Each sonnet is about the effects of time on a particular woman. What is similar about the treatment of time in each poem? (b) What is different?
2. Each poem has a final line in which the word *roses* is important. (a) What do roses stand for in each poem? (b) In each poem how does the final line sum up the meaning?

THINKING AND WRITING
Writing the Woman's Response

The speaker of "When You Are Old" is a scorned and slightly self-pitying lover. Write a response to the poem in the voice of the woman he is addressing. First imagine yourself in her place. Freewrite about the situation that led to your rejection of the speaker. Then list ways in which you feel that his argument in the poem —as to why you should give in and love him—is flawed. Using your freewriting and your list, write a response, possibly imagining a future situation different from the one the speaker imagines for you. Be funny if you want. If you'd like, try writing your response as another sonnet. Finally, revise your response, making sure it answers the points made by the speaker in the poem.

THE ADVENTURES OF DON QUIXOTE
by Miguel de Cervantes Saavedra

To dream the impossible dream
—*Man of La Mancha*

Literature is filled with dreamers—people who hook their wagon to a star or try to lasso the moon. But perhaps the best-known dreamer of all is Don Quixote de La Mancha.

Battling with Windmills

Don Quixote is an old Spanish gentleman who believes he is a knight—even though knights have not ridden in Spain for hundreds of years. Undisturbed by this fact, Don Quixote forever sees perilous adventures where others see only humdrum realities. In the most famous episode from the book, he charges straight into the flailing arms of a monstrous giant. This giant, however, turns out to be a windmill:

"At that moment a slight wind arose, and the great sails began to move. At the sight of which Don Quixote shouted: 'Though you wield more arms than the giant Briareus, you shall pay for it!' Saying this, he commended himself with all his soul to his Lady Dulcinea, beseeching her aid in his great peril. Then, covering himself with his shield and putting his lance in the rest, he urged Rocinante forward at a full gallop and attacked the nearest windmill, thrusting his lance into the sail. But the wind turned it with such violence that it shivered his weapon in pieces, dragging the horse and his rider with it, and sent the knight rolling badly injured across the plain."

Larger-Than-Life Characters

The flamboyant knight Don Quixote is really Alonso Quexana, who lives in the village of La Mancha. At the beginning of the novel, we learn that Quexana "was verging on fifty, of tough constitution, lean-bodied, thin-faced, a great early riser and a lover of hunting." Having a great deal of time on his hands, he devotes

DON QUIXOTE
Honoré Daumier

DON QUIXOTE
Eighteenth-century engraving

Humanities Note

Fine art, *Don Quixote,* eighteenth-century engraving. The art of engraving involves cutting lines in wood, metal, or some other material, inking the surface, and then using it to print. The earliest known engravings printed on paper were done in the mid-1400's. Combined with the development of the printing press, engraving made it possible for a wider audience to enjoy works of art.

This French engraving shows an episode from the book in which Don Quixote and Sancho, blindfolded on a wooden horse, are being mocked.

You might want to use the following questions to discuss the art:

1. Explain what seems to be occurring in this scene.
2. Who is at the center of the picture?
3. How did the artist use the character's gestures, as well as light and shade, to dramatize the scene?
4. Engraving made it possible for a wider audience to enjoy pictures like this one. Do you think that computer graphics may prove to be as revolutionary a development as engraving? Explain.

1 **Enrichment** Tell students that the Spanish philosopher Miguel de Unamuno (1864–1936) wrote a book about Don Quixote that has been translated as *Our Lord Don Quixote*. The Spanish thinker José Ortega y Gasset (1883–1955) wrote a book on Quixote as well. Translated as *Meditations on Quixote*, it was published by Norton.

himself to reading about knights and chivalry. This reading soon becomes an "odd and foolish" passion. His dreams are, as William Shakespeare calls dreams in Romeo and Juliet, "Children of an idle brain / Begot of nothing but vain fantasy." However, intoxicated with these dreams of glory, Quexana decides that he will become a knight himself. He fits out an old horse named Rocinante, salvages a rust-eaten suit of armor, and gloriously renames himself Don Quixote de la Mancha. Since every knight needs a lady to worship from afar, Don Quixote chooses as his inspiration "a very good-looking farm girl" named Aldonza Lorenzo. In keeping with his mad make-believe, however, he gives her the more noble-sounding name Dulcinea del Toboso.

Just as he re-creates himself, Don Quixote proceeds to remake the world as well. Ordinary inns become castles, windmills are transformed into giants, and servant-women are transfigured into aristocratic ladies-in-waiting. No reality can resist Don Quixote's fabulous imagination. Even the adventure of the windmills cannot convert him to a sane view of the world. He attributes this disaster not to his own error but to the arts of an enchanter, who "turned those giants into windmills, to cheat me of the glory of conquering them."

Accompanying Don Quixote on his exploits is a poor laborer named Sancho Panza, for whom windmills are simply windmills. Panza is a reverse image of Don Quixote in almost every respect. If Don Quixote is long and lean and lunatic, Sancho Panza is short and squat and often sensible. For instance, after being battered by the windmill, Don Quixote declares that he will tear down a limb from an oak and do great deeds with it. As usual, however, Sancho Panza has more practical considerations in mind: "'With God's help,' replied Sancho Panza, 'and I believe it all as your worship says. But sit a bit more upright, sir, for you seem to be riding lop-sided. It must be from the bruises you got when you fell.'" Nevertheless, Sancho Panza is also gullible enough to believe Don Quixote's promise that he, Sancho Panza, will become the governor of an island—as soon as Don Quixote can conquer one for him.

This knight and squire ride from one ludicrous adventure to another and keep on riding after the book ends: Like a handful of other literary characters, they are larger than life. Great philosophers have pondered the meaning of their exploits, and famous artists have depicted them on canvas. They

Fine art, *Don Quixote's Dream* from *Le Petit Journal Agricole*, May 21, 1905. This illustration comes from a French journal whose name translates as The Little Agricultural Newspaper.

The illustration shows Quixote in his armchair, presumably reading a book about knights, dragons, and beautiful maidens. This book inspires him with the wildest dreams, which are depicted around the chair, and he raises his sword as if to slay imagined enemies.

You might want to use the following questions to discuss the art:

1. What is occurring in this illustration?
2. What side of Don Quixote does the picture emphasize?

Enrichment The lyrics of the most popular song from *Man of La Mancha* are as follows:

To dream the impossible dream,
To fight the unbeatable foe,
To bear with unbearable sorrow,
To run where the brave dare not go;
To right the unrightable wrong,
To love, pure and chaste, from afar,
To try, when your arms are too weary,
To reach the unreachable star!
This is my Quest
To follow that star,
No matter how hopeless,
No matter how far,
To fight for the right
Without question or pause,
To be willing to march into hell
For a heavenly cause!
And I know, if I'll only be true to this glorious Quest,
That my heart will lie peaceful and calm when I'm laid to my rest.
And the world will be better for this,
That one man, scorned and covered with scars,
Still strove, with his last ounce of courage,
To reach the unreachable stars!

Encourage interested students to find and listen to the album of this musical.

DON QUIXOTE'S DREAM
Illustration from
Le Petit Journal Agricole,
May 21, 1905

have even become the main characters of a contemporary musical entitled *Man of La Mancha*.

A Comedy of Errors

As Don Quixote sallies forth in search of ogres, giants, and evil knights, he and Sancho get into countless scrapes with mule-drivers, innkeepers, thieves, shepherds, students, and peasants.

One particularly hilarious incident occurs at an inn that Don Quixote mistakes for a great castle. He imagines that a serving woman is a highborn lady who has fallen in love with him. At night, when she passes by his bed on her way to her boyfriend, Don Quixote thinks she is coming to see him. Stopping her, he nobly rejects her love out of loyalty to Dulcinea. Her boyfriend, seeing her with Don Quixote, becomes jealous and attacks the poor knight. Hearing this noise, the innkeeper runs to punish his servant. She hides next to the sleeping Sancho Panza, who is scared to death when he finds a mysterious lump in his bed and begins to lash out. The servant, in turn, flails away at Sancho Panza. Then the mule-driver begins to beat Sancho Panza too, and the innkeeper assaults the serving-woman. At this point, the innkeeper's light goes out and a police officer, also a guest at the inn, launches himself into this confused heap of bodies. Discovering the unconscious Don Quixote, the officer yells "Murder!" and runs to search for a light.

This comedy of errors continues and becomes even more confusing. When it ends, however, with bruises all around, Don Quixote immediately charges into another adventure. Seeing two clouds of dust on the horizon, he believes that two armies are attacking each other. Sancho Panza tries to warn him that these "armies" are two flocks of sheep. Disregarding Sancho Panza's pleas, Don Quixote hurls himself at the sheep and instigates still another scene of whirling confusion.

Theme: Reality and Fantasy

While *The Adventures of Don Quixote* is filled with comic scenes like these, it has serious themes as well: The central concern of the novel is the relationship between reality and fantasy. Sancho Panza sees the solid, realistic world of windmills and mule-drivers, while Don Quixote is lost in a fluid,

Primary Source Note

The Argentinian Jorge Luis Borges wrote the following prose poem about Cervantes entitled *Parable of Cervantes and Don Quixote* (for more about Borges, see page 1224):

Weary of his land of Spain, an old soldier of the king sought solace in Ariosto's vast geographies [Ariosto was an Italian poet who lived from 1474 to 1533], in that valley of the moon where misspent dream-time goes, and in the golden idol of Mohammed stolen by Montalban.

In gentle mockery of himself he conceived a credulous man who, unsettled by the marvels he read about, hit upon the idea of seeking noble deeds and enchantments in prosaic places called El Toboso or Montiel.

Defeated by reality, by Spain, Don Quixote died in his native fantastic world of giants and evil knights. Cervantes may be saying that each of these perspectives is necessary for a complete picture of life.

Don Quixote is not simply a mad old man. Despite the battering he receives from people and objects, he never forsakes his devotion to higher ideals. Without the imagination that he brings to life, the world would be a dull place indeed. Cervantes conveys this idea by showing how Sancho Panza gradually comes to recognize Don Quixote's nobility. One of the most touching moments of the novel comes at the end, when the dying Don Quixote renounces his fantasies. Sancho Panza, usually a realist, protests against this renunciation and becomes an eloquent spokesman for Don Quixote's fantasies: "'Oh, don't die, dear master!' answered Sancho in tears. 'Take my advice and live many years. For the maddest thing a man can do in this life is to let himself die just like that, without anybody killing him, but just finished off by his own melancholy. Don't be lazy, look you, but get out of bed, and let's go out into the fields dressed as shepherds, as we decided to. Perhaps we shall find the lady Dulcinea behind some hedge, disenchanted and as pretty as a picture.'"

The Author

Miguel de Cervantes Saavedra led a life that was every bit as exciting as Don Quixote's. Cervantes also displayed, on many occasions, the almost foolhardy bravery that was so characteristic of his elderly knight.

Born into a poor family, Cervantes received little education. At the age of twenty, he joined the Spanish army and shortly afterward fought in the battle of Lepanto against the Turks. This naval battle saw the destruction of the Turkish fleet by the combined forces of Spain and Italy. Cervantes was among the 30,000 soldiers carried by the Spanish and Italian galleys. Although he was ill when the battle began, he plunged into the fighting and was wounded twice in the chest and once in the left arm. For the rest of his life, he regarded his crippled arm as a badge of honor.

Cervantes went on to fight in a number of other battles, but he was captured by pirates while sailing home from the wars. Sold into slavery in Algiers, he repeatedly tried to escape. Although he was always recaptured, his bravery so impressed the Algierians that they did not put him to death. After five years ransom money from Spain set him free.

Back in Spain, Cervantes showed another kind of bravery in facing difficult economic circumstances. He eventually found a bookkeeping job with the government to support his large household. Problems with his account books, however, led to his imprisonment on two occasions. According to legend Cervantes began writing *Don Quixote* during one of these spells in jail. When the first part of the novel appeared in 1604, it was a great success; however, Cervantes received only a small sum from his publisher. At his death in 1616, he was still a poor man.

It is clear that Cervantes invested his true wealth—his keen observation, playfulness, and power of imagination—in the creation of his novel. That is why it remains, as one translator has called it, "One of the best adventure stories in the world."

Read *The Adventures of Don Quixote* for yourself. See if you come to identify with the great dreamer —Don Quixote. Do you come to agree with Alfred, Lord Tennyson: "Dreams are true while they last, and do we not live in dreams?"

MIGUEL DE
CERVANTES SAAVEDRA

village around 1614. He was survived only briefly by Miguel de Cervantes.

For both of them, for the dreamer and the dreamed, the tissue of that whole plot consisted in the contraposition of two worlds: the unreal world of the books of chivalry and the common everyday world of the seventeenth century.

Little did they suspect that the years would end by wearing away the disharmony. Little did they suspect that La Mancha and Montiel and the knight's frail figure would be, for the future, no less poetic than Sinbad's haunts or Ariosto's vast geographies.

For myth is at the beginning of literature, and also at its end.

CHRISTOPHER MARLOWE

1564–1593

Christopher Marlowe was one of the first great English Renaissance dramatists and a master of blank verse, or unrhymed iambic pentameter. He is known for the five powerful plays of his brief maturity and some superb poems and translations.

Marlowe's life was short, obscure, and violent. He was born in 1564, the year of Shakespeare's birth, in Canterbury. The son of a shoemaker, he attended the King's School in Canterbury and then earned a B.A. degree from Corpus Christi College, Cambridge, in 1584. Little is known for certain about his life after this point. Though he earned an M.A. degree from Cambridge in 1587, he probably did not attend school constantly from 1584 to 1587. He may even have worked as a messenger or secret agent for the Elizabethan government, spending time in the French city of Rouen. That city was a haven for English Catholic exiles and a center for plots against the Protestant Elizabethan regime.

Eventually he moved to London and between 1587 and 1593 wrote a series of plays, including the two parts of *Tamburlaine, The Jew of Malta,* *The Massacre at Paris, Edward II,* and *Doctor Faustus.* The hero of each play is a powerful, amoral figure, a man of unbounded ambition who sets himself against conventional limits, whether political, sexual, or religious. Tamburlaine, for instance, is a hero who rises from shepherd to king, conquering an empire in Asia Minor, and is halted in his conquests only (in Part II) by his own death. In his ten-act rise to power, he is often cruel, never repentant, always magnificent. In *Doctor Faustus*, by contrast, the hero's great ambition is ironically undercut: His belief in his own power is ultimately a delusion.

The heroes of Marlowe's plays are all great *speakers* and Marlowe's powerful blank verse is their perfect medium of expression. Elizabethan playwrights had used unrhymed iambic pentameter before, but Marlowe is the first to give it the resounding energy a later poet referred to when he spoke of "Marlowe's mighty line." Marlowe's verse is typically end-stopped, meaning that each line is a more or less complete unit of grammar and rhythm. His example helped make blank verse the standard medium of the Elizabethan theater.

Marlowe was unorthodox in his opinions and his life. His work treated controversial topics —seizure of political power, homosexuality, religion—and sometimes he was in trouble with the law. (Once he was even tried on a charge of murder, though he was acquitted.) He came to have a reputation for heretical opinions and on May 20, 1593, was brought before a government council on charges of speaking against the doctrines of the Church of England. He was not imprisoned, however, and before the case was resolved he was killed in a tavern brawl at the age of twenty-nine.

Marlowe's work is marked by a magnificent fearlessness in tackling dangerous issues and by a powerful sense of irony; it hovers between tragedy and grim, ironic comedy. *Doctor Faustus*, about a man who sells his soul to the devil for magical powers, demonstrates all of these qualities.

Objectives

Thematic

To understand a key archetype of Western culture, the "devil's bargain"

Skills

1 To understand dramatic irony
2 To appreciate historical context
3 To complete word analogies
4 To write about atomic energy

GUIDE FOR INTERPRETING

from The Tragical History of the Life and Death of Doctor Faustus

Commentary

Dramatic Irony. A playwright is using **dramatic irony** when the audience of a play, knowing more than the characters, recognizes meanings in their speeches and actions that they do not intend. When in *Oedipus Rex* the king announces he will find the murderer responsible for the plague in Thebes, he does not dream that the man is himself. Yet the audience, knowing the story, recognizes the irony of Oedipus' statement. Marlowe is a master of dramatic irony, and in *Doctor Faustus* the irony cuts against a hero who misunderstands his own nature.

Marlowe found the outlines of the story in the English translation of a book about an actual German who lived between 1480 and 1540 in the Protestant city of Wittenberg. The title of the book was *The Historie of the damnable life and deserved death of Doctor John Faustus*. It is obvious from this title, with the words "damnable" and "deserved," that the account condemned Faustus. In the centuries after Marlowe, by contrast, Romantic and post-Romantic writers held up Faustus as a positive example. For them, he embodied a heroic willingness to risk everything in order to go beyond human limits.

Marlowe's treatment of the legend is powerfully ironic, suggesting the hero's self-destructiveness. Faustus is, like Marlowe himself, a brilliant man with a gift for powerful and challenging speech. When he invokes the devil, however, he is out of his depth. He believes that giving up his soul will give him a godlike power to satisfy all his wishes. It turns out, nevertheless, that in giving up his soul, Faustus surrenders his chances of human satisfaction. Having gained the power to do anything, he loses an eternity of God's love. No pleasure the world offers is worth that loss.

Furthermore, it appears that the powers the devil allows him are limited; as the play continues, he is forced increasingly to do the devil's will, not his own. Thinking that he will become godlike and all-powerful, Faustus eventually becomes a powerless sufferer distracting himself with magic shows while he awaits his damnation. The play thus comments on the Renaissance theme of a person's power to determine his or her own nature. Faustus believes he can make himself into a demigod but finds that he has merely given himself into the hands of the devil. These ironies are hinted at even when Faustus first calls up the devil Mephistophilis in Act I, Scene 3.

Writing

Faustus is tempted by the idea that he will become all-powerful. Freewrite, exploring the allure of power.

Literary Focus Ask students if they have ever seen the kind of thriller or horror film where a character innocently enters a room in which a murderer lurks behind a curtain or door. Have them describe how the tension in the scene becomes nearly unbearable because the audience knows what the character does not—the killer is about to pounce. The unknowing character, however, may do or say things that seem ironic to the knowing audience. Tell students that the same principle of dramatic irony is at work in this scene from Marlowe's play.

Writing/Prior Knowledge Before students begin writing, divide the class into small groups and have each group discuss the various types of power that people can exercise in today's society. Then have students discuss the kind of temptation that each type of power might present.

Vocabulary

Preteach the following vocabulary words:
incantations (in´ kan tā´ shənz) *n*.: Chanting of magical words
resolute (rez´ ə lo͞ot´) *adj*.: Determined
proficient (prō fish´ ənt) *adj*.: Skilled
pliant (plī´ ənt) *adj*.: Compliant; obedient
aspiring (ə spīr´ iŋ) *adj*.: Ambitious to get something (participle used as adjective)
fortitude (fôrt´ ə to͞od´) *n*.: Strength
incurred (in kʉrd´) *v*.: Brought upon oneself
potentate (pōt´'n tāt) *n*.: Ruler

Support Material

Teaching Portfolio
Teacher Backup, p. 871
Usage and Mechanics Worksheet, p. 875
Vocabulary Check, p. 876
Analyzing Literature Worksheet, *Understanding Dramatic Irony*, p. 877
Critical Thinking and Reading Work-
sheet, *Appreciating Historical Context*, p. 878
Selection Test, pp. 879–880

Spelling Tip Write the word *proficient* on the chalkboard and remind students that its final syllable is spelled *ient*, not *ent*. The spelling is somewhat tricky because the *i* is silent.

from The Tragical History of the Life and Death of Dr. Faustus

Christopher Marlowe

Act I
Scene 3

[*Thunder. Enter* LUCIFER *and* FOUR DEVILS. FAUSTUS *to them with this speech*]

FAUSTUS. Now that the gloomy shadow of the night,
Longing to view Orion's drizzling look,
Leaps from th'Antarctick world unto the sky,
And dims the Welkin[1] with her pitchy breath,
5 Faustus, begin thine <u>incantations</u>
And try if devils will obey thy hest,
Seeing thou hast prayed and sacrificed to them.
Within this circle is Jehova's name
Forward and backward anagrammatized:[2]
10 The abbreviated names of holy saints,
Figures of every adjunct to the heavens,
And characters of signs and evening stars,
By which the spirits are enforced to rise.
Then fear not, Faustus, to be <u>resolute</u>
15 And try the utmost magic can perform.

[*Thunder*]

Sint mihi dei acherontis propitii, valeat numen triplex Jehovae, ignei areii, aquatani spiritus salvete: orientis princeps Belzebub, inferni ardentis monarcha et demigorgon, propitiamus vos, ut appareat, et surgat

---
1. **Welkin:** Sky or vault of heaven.
2. **Jehova's name ... anagrammatized** (an´ ə gram´ ə tīzd): Jehovah, the holy name of God in the Old Testament, has been spelled backwards and forwards in a magical rite.

---

20 *Mephostophilis . . . quod tumeraris: per Jehovam, gehennam, et consecratam aquam quam nunc spargo; signumque crucis quod nunc facio; et per vota nostra ipse nunc surgat nobis dicatus Mephostophilis.*[3]

[*Enter a* DEVIL.]

I charge thee to return and change thy shape.
25 Thou art too ugly to attend on me.
Go, and return an old Franciscan friar:
That holy shape becomes a devil best.

[*Exit* DEVIL.]

I see there's virtue[4] in my heavenly words.
Who would not be <u>proficient</u> in this art?
30 How <u>pliant</u> is this Mephostophilis!
Full of obedience and humility,
Such is the force of magic and my spells.
Now, Faustus, thou are conjuror laureate:[5]
Thou canst command great Mephostophilis.
35 *Quin redis Mephostophilis fratris imagine.*[6]

[*Enter* MEPHOSTOPHILIS.]

---
3. **Sint . . . Mephostophilis:** May the gods of the underworld (Acheron) be kind to me; may the triple deity of Jehovah be gone; to the spirits of fire, air, and water, greetings. Prince of the east, Beelzebub, monarch of the fires below, and Demogorgon, we appeal to you so that Mephostophilis may appear and rise. . . . Why do you delay? By Jehovah, hell and the hallowed water which I now sprinkle, and the sign of the cross, which I now make, and by our vows, let Mephostophilis himself now arise to serve us.
4. **virtue:** Power, as well as goodness.
5. **conjuror laureate:** The greatest magician.
6. **Quin . . . imagine:** Why do you not return, Mephostophilis, in the appearance of a friar?

Commentary

Where Is Hell? Faustus wishes to think of hell as a particular place, but the truth is worse. Hell is a state of mind; it consists in the terrible absence of God's love. All creatures are created, according to Christian doctrine, with the desire for their creator, and angels and human beings have a fundamental need to join with God and rest in him. Without this rest in the divine, humans are bound to an eternally unsatisfied quest for satisfaction.

One of the best Renaissance readers of this play was John Milton, who portrayed his Satan as haunted by the same incompleteness that bedevils Faustus. In the first book of *Paradise Lost* Satan, adopting something like Faustus' position, boasts that the hell that surrounds him is not going to destroy his inner fortitude (lines 249–256):

Farewell happy fields
Where joy for ever dwells; hail horrors, hail
Infernal world, and thou profoundest hell

MEPHOSTOPHILIS. Now, Faustus, what wouldst
thou have me do?

FAUSTUS. I charge thee wait upon me whilst I live,
To do whatever Faustus shall command,
Be it to make the moon drop from her sphere,
Or the ocean to overwhelm the world.

MEPHOSTOPHILIS. I am a servant to great Lucifer,
And may not follow thee without his leave.
No more than he commands must we perform.

FAUSTUS. Did not he charge thee to appear to me?

MEPHOSTOPHILIS. No, I came now hither of mine
own accord.

FAUSTUS. Did not my conjuring speeches raise
thee? Speak.

MEPHOSTOPHILIS. That was the cause, but yet *per
accidens;*[7]
For when we hear one rack the name of God,
Abjure[8] the scriptures and his savior Christ,
We fly in hope to get his glorious soul.
Nor will we come unless he use such means
Whereby he is in danger to be damned.
Therefore the shortest cut for conjuring
Is stoutly to abjure all godliness
And pray devoutly to the prince of hell.

FAUSTUS. So Faustus hath already done, and holds
this principle:
There is no chief but only Belzebub,[9]
To whom Faustus doth dedicate himself.
This word "damnation" terrifies not me,
For I confound hell in elysium.
My ghost be with the old philosophers.[10]
But leaving these vain trifles of men's souls,
Tell me, what is that Lucifer, thy lord?

MEPHOSTOPHILIS. Arch-regent and commander
of all spirits.

---

7. *per accidens:* By the immediate, not the ultimate, cause.
8. **Abjure** (ab joor´) *v.:* Give up, renounce.
9. **Belzebub** (bel´ zə bub): The chief devil, whose name
means "god of flies" in Hebrew.
10. **For I . . . philosophers:** I think that hell is really
elysium. In Greek mythology, elysium was the dwelling place of
the virtuous after death. In Dante's *Inferno,* it is a pleasant
abode for righteous pagans in a special part of hell.

---

65 **FAUSTUS.** Was not that Lucifer an angel once?

MEPHOSTOPHILIS. Yes, Faustus, and most dearly
loved of God.

FAUSTUS. How comes it then that he is prince of
devils?

MEPHOSTOPHILIS. Oh, by aspiring pride and
insolence,
For which God threw him from the face of
heaven.

70 **FAUSTUS.** And what are you that live with Lucifer?

MEPHOSTOPHILIS. Unhappy spirits that fell with
Lucifer,
Conspired against our God with Lucifer,
And are forever damned with Lucifer.

FAUSTUS. Where are you damned?

75 **MEPHOSTOPHILIS.** In hell.

FAUSTUS. How comes it then that thou art out of
hell?

MEPHOSTOPHILIS. Why, this is hell, nor am I out of
it.
Think'st thou that I that saw the face of God
And tasted the eternal joys of heaven,
80 Am not tormented with ten thousand hells
In being deprived of everlasting bliss?
Oh, Faustus, leave these frivolous[11] demands,
Which strike a terror to my fainting soul.

FAUSTUS. What, is great Mephostophilis so
passionate
85 For being deprived of the joys of heaven?
Learn thou of Faustus manly fortitude,
And scorn those joys thou never shalt possess.
Go, bear these tidings to great Lucifer,
Seeing Faustus hath incurred eternal death
90 By desperate thoughts against Jove's deity.
Say he surrenders up to him his soul,
So he will spare him four and twenty years,
Letting him live in all voluptuousness,[12]
Having thee ever to attend on me,
95 To give me whatsoever I shall ask,

---

11. **frivolous** (friv´ ə ləs) *adj.:* Of little value, trifling.
12. **voluptuousness** (və lup´ choo əs nis) *n.:* Indulgence in
sensual delights and pleasures.

---

3 **Literary Focus** Ask students to
consider how an actor might
read Mephostophilis's question
in line 36. What irony is Faustus
missing, and how does his response underscore his lack of
awareness?

4 **Literary Focus** Have students
explain the difference between
these two explanations of
Mephostophilis's presence. What
is ironic about Mephostophilis's
correction of Faustus? How does
this irony undercut Faustus's pre-
tentions to power?

5 **Enrichment** Faustus thinks of
hell as elysium. Even if that were
so, however, Faustus would not
be virtuous enough to earn ad-
mittance.

6 **Discussion** Ask students what
Faustus's dismissal of "men's
souls" as "vain trifles" suggests
about him.

7 **Discussion** Have students note
Mephostophilis's self-description
as one of the "unhappy spirits
that fell with Lucifer." Are they
surprised by his frank use of the
adjective "unhappy"? Why doesn't
he use flattery, lies, and false
promises to seduce Faustus?

8 **Discussion** Tell students that
this is one of the most famous
lines in the play. Ask them how
it points up a crucial difference
between Faustus's and Mephostophilis's conceptions of hell.

9 **Discussion** Ask students whether
these lines reflect genuine surprise on Faustus's part. If so, why
is he so surprised?

10 **Reading Strategy** Ask students
to paraphrase lines 84–87. Ask
them how they are similar to
Faustus's speeches in lines
28–34 and 37–40.

11 **Discussion** Have students compare Faustus's understanding of
"eternal death" with that of
Mephostophilis (lines 78–81).

Receive thy new possessor: one
who brings
A mind not to be changed by place
or time.
The mind is its own place, and in itself
Can make a heav'n of hell, a hell of
heav'n.
What matter where, if still I be the
same. . . .

Later, when he flies to Paradise and realizes that he cannot
enjoy it, he sees that what he said
is true in a way he never meant. If
the mind is its own "place" then
there is no escape from oneself:
"Which way I fly is hell; myself am
hell" (IV.75).

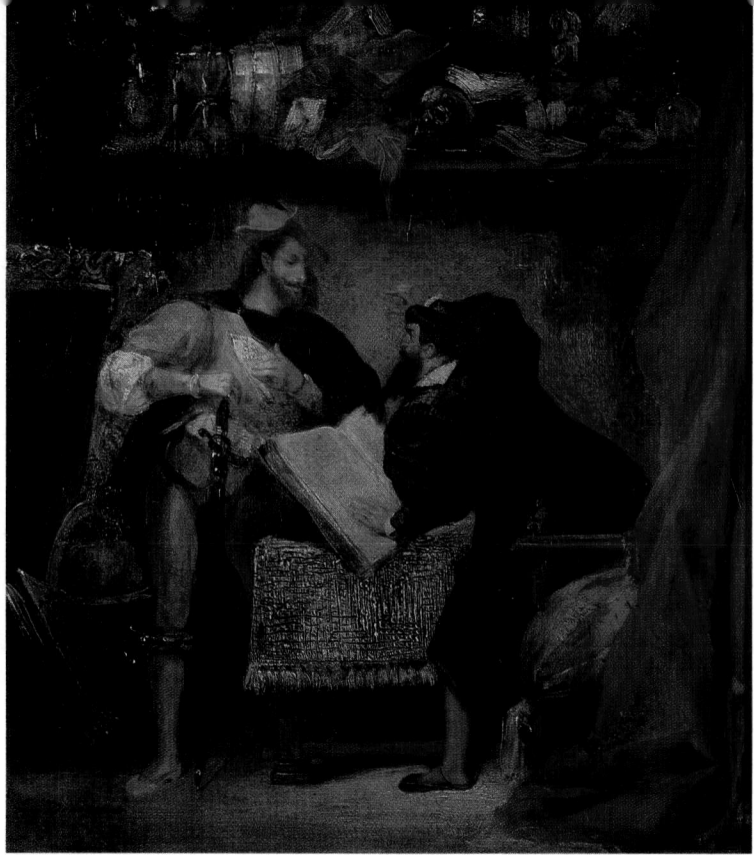

MEPHISTOPHELES
APPEARS BEFORE
FAUST
Eugène Delacroix
Trustees of The
Wallace Collection,
London

To tell me whatsoever I demand,
To slay mine enemies and to aid my friends
And always be obedient to my will.
Go, and return to mighty Lucifer,
100 And meet me in my study at midnight,
And then resolve me of thy master's mind.

12 MEPHOSTOPHILIS. I will, Faustus.

[*Exit*]

FAUSTUS. Had I as many souls as there be stars,
I'd give them all for Mephostophilis.
105 By him I'll be great emperor of the world,
And make a bridge through the air

To pass the ocean. With a band of men
I'll join the hills that bind the Affrick[13] shore,
110 And make that country continent to Spain,
And both contributory to my crown.
The Emperor shall not live but by my leave,
Nor any potentate of Germany.
Now that I have obtained what I desired,
115 I'll live in speculation of this art[14]
Till Mephostophilis return again.

[*Exit*]

---

13. Affrick: African.
14. speculation of this art: Deep study of this art.

Reader's Response *What further requests
do you think Faustus will make of the devil?*

Notice how Delacroix uses Faust's uplifted right hand and Mephistopheles' hand poised on his sword to suggest the drama of this moment.

You might want to use the following questions to discuss the art:
1. Identify Mephistopheles and Faust, and explain how you knew who they were.

2. How did the artist make this scene dramatic?
3. Compare the emotions that Faust and Mephistopheles seem to be feeling.
4. This picture was painted more than 200 years after Marlowe lived, and it was meant to illustrate Goethe's *Faust*. Does it go well with Marlowe's play? Explain.

Interpreting

1. (a) Why do you think Faustus wants to learn about the fall of Lucifer, prince of the damned? (b) How might Lucifer's fate have a relevance for Faustus that he has not guessed?
2. (a) How does Faustus imagine hell? (b) What does Mephistophilis mean by saying, "this is hell nor am I out of it"?
3. When he tells the devil to learn courage from his example, does Faustus look brave, foolish, or both? Explain.
4. What do the benefits that Faustus hopes to gain reveal about him?

Applying

5. Is it possible for people who do not believe in the devil or an afterlife to "sell their souls"? Explain.

ANALYZING LITERATURE

Understanding Dramatic Irony

Dramatic irony results when the audience knows more than the characters and sees more in their words and actions than they do. In this scene the audience realizes more clearly than Faustus just what he will gain and what he will lose. While he dismisses his soul as a "trifle," it is in fact his free center. To give it up is to give up his right to make his own decisions. While Faustus believes he will gain power to do whatever he wants, he is in fact only able to do whatever the devil will allow him to do. Words like "obedient" and "command" signal the irony. Faustus fantasizes that he will *command* Mephistophilis but in fact he agrees to *obey* Lucifer. In giving up his soul, he loses himself, becoming Lucifer's servant.

1. (a) How much does Mephistophilis actually say he will do for Faustus? (b) Contrast this with what Faustus believes Mephistophilis will do for him.
2. Why won't Mephistophilis continue to answer Faustus about Lucifer's fall?
3. How does Mephistophilis contrast with Faustus in his language, his attitudes, and his self-knowledge?

CRITICAL THINKING AND READING

Appreciating Historical Context

Many Renaissance writers believed in the power of magic. They also believed that magic was always performed by spirits invisible to human beings, spirits who would carry out human wishes. This vision of magic means, in effect, that unlike God, who can make things happen simply by willing them, magicians are dependent. Their words alone will do nothing; all they can do is try to make spirits obey their commands.

1. What is the purpose of Faustus' long incantation and what does it seem to achieve?
2. When Mephistophilis appears, Faustus comments, "I see there's virtue in my heavenly words." (a) What does he mean by "heavenly"? (b) How does his use of the word characterize his values?
3. Mephistophilis comments that the quickest way to bring the devil is simply to "pray devoutly to the prince of hell." What ironic light does this remark cast on Faustus' magic?

UNDERSTANDING LANGUAGE

Completing Word Analogies

A word analogy is a type of test in which you are asked to see the relationship between words. Two common relationships are similarities and differences. **Synonyms** are words that have similar meanings; **antonyms** are words that have opposite meanings.

Identify the relationship in the first pair of words in each item below. Then complete the second pair in each item with a word expressing the same relationship.

1. INCANTATION : SPELL : : HOVER:
   a. height   b. plane   c. float   d. hovel
2. FRIVOLOUS : IMPORTANT : : DILIGENT:
   a. indolent   b. indigent   c. skillful   d. deleterious

THINKING AND WRITING

Writing About Atomic Energy

Write a newspaper editorial about the pros and cons of atomic energy, making allusions to Marlowe's *Doctor Faustus*. First freewrite about the ways in which atomic energy resembles the Renaissance concept of magic. What might be a modern equivalent to Faustus' desire for power? When you write your editorial, consider whether the positive uses of this twentieth-century "magic" justify its dangers if misused. Imagine that you are writing for an audience of your classmates. In revising your editorial, make sure you have explained the connection, or lack of connection, between the Faust legend and modern decisions about atomic energy.

(continued from bottom of page)

is terrifying.
3. Answers will differ. Many students will respond that Mephostophilis tends to speak more briefly, with less exaggeration, and he knows much better than Faustus what damnation really involves. He knows what Faustus is losing.

ANSWERS TO CRITICAL THINKING AND READING

1. Its purpose is to compel Mephostophilis's presence. It seems to bring him, although Mephostophilis explains he came because he hoped to get Faustus's soul.
2. (a) Answers will differ. Some students may say that he means powerful or effective. Others may argue that he is being maliciously ironic. (b) His use of the word indicates that he values power and is willing to risk everything for it.
3. Faustus's magic is shown to have no power beyond announcing the weakness of his soul and his submission to Lucifer's power.

ANSWERS TO UNDERSTANDING LANGUAGE

1. c. float
2. a. indolent

THINKING AND WRITING

Publishing Student Writing
Have students create an editorial page on which they can place their editorials. Then display these editorial pages in the classroom.

Challenge The English comedians Peter Cook and Dudley Moore made a humorous film based on the Faust legend. Explain how you would adapt this story to modern times and make it humorous as well.

2. (a) Faust wants to think that hell is elysium, a happy pagan paradise. (b) Answers will differ. Some students may respond that Mephostophilis knows hell is not a place. It is the absence of God's love.
3. Answers will differ. Many students will realize that he looks foolish because he does not really understand what losing his soul means. Some students may feel that his bravado is based on

a certain amount of bravery.
4. Answers will differ. Many students will respond that his requests reveal he is eager for tangible, material power. For all his learning, he does not seem to realize the importance of the intangible soul.
5. Answers will differ. Most students will realize that even those who do not believe in God can betray themselves, giving away control of their lives for illusory satisfactions.

ANSWERS TO ANALYZING LITERATURE

1. (a) Mephostophilis promises only that he will return with Lucifer's response to Faustus's offer. (b) Faustus believes that he will have Mephostophilis in his power for twenty-four years.
2. Answers will differ, but students may realize that Mephostophilis won't go on because the truth about his state

WILLIAM SHAKESPEARE

1564–1616

More About the Author It is difficult for us to believe today, nurtured as we are on Romantic conceptions of authorship, that Shakespeare did not arrange for the publication of his plays. They were first collected for publication in 1623, by Shakespeare's fellow actors John Heminges and Henry Condell. If students express surprise at this fact, tell them that Shakespeare may have thought of himself more as a craftsman than as an author in our sense of the word.

Critical Evaluation The critic Mark Van Doren made the following evaluation of Shakespeare's artistry:

> It is literally true that while we read a play of Shakespeare's we are in it. We may be drawn in swiftly or slowly—in most cases it is swiftly—but once we are there we are enclosed. That is the secret, and it is still a secret, of Shakespeare's power to interest us. He conditions us to a particular world before we are aware that it exists; then he absorbs us in its particulars. We scarcely say to ourselves, this world exists; nor do we pause to note how consistent each thing in it is with every other. Our attention is on the details, which we take in as details should be taken in, one at a time. Meanwhile there is for us no other world.

Ben Jonson declared of Shakespeare, "He was not of an age, but for all time!" Most readers today, seconding this judgment, would agree that William Shakespeare is the only English writer comparable in stature to such figures as Homer, Sophocles, and Dante. This measure of his worth is based not on his lyric poems, excellent though they are, but on the thirty-eight complete plays he wrote over a period of less than twenty-five years: tragedies, comedies, histories, and romances.

Scholars often observe how little we know about such a great writer. That is true in one important sense: His inner life is a mystery to us. Nevertheless, we know many of the outward facts about his life as an upwardly mobile middle-class Elizabethan (someone living during the reign of Queen Elizabeth: 1558–1603).

He was born in 1564 in the small town of Stratford-on-Avon. His father, John Shakespeare, was a well-to-do maker of gloves who was for a time the equivalent of Stratford's mayor. William undoubtedly attended the grammar school at Stratford, but unlike Marlowe did not go on to study at a university.

In November of 1582, he married Anne Hathaway, who gave birth to a daughter, Susanna, in 1583 and to twins, Hamnet and Judith, in 1585. Hamnet was to die at the age of eleven; the girls married and lived to be sixty-six and seventy-nine.

Eventually, like many Englishmen he moved to the rapidly growing capital of London, where he gravitated to the theater. By 1595 he had established himself as a shareholder in the theatrical group organized by the great tragic actor Richard Burbage, the Lord Chamberlain's Company. Shakespeare was one of its actors and its chief playwright. During the 1590's he wrote two "tetralogies," or groups of four plays, about English history; several tragedies; many comedies; an extraordinary sonnet sequence; and two narrative poems.

In 1598 Burbage's company built the Globe Theatre, where most of the plays Shakespeare wrote afterward were performed. His major work in the second half of his career included a series of tragedies from *Julius Caesar* (1599) to *Coriolanus* (1607–1608), as well as several grim comedies. In his final phase (1608–1611), he produced four plays which are now called "romances," works that blend the happy ending of comedy with elements of tragic violence. *The Tempest* is one of these.

Shakespeare prospered as a shareholder in the King's Men (the name given to the Lord Chamberlain's Company after the death of Queen Elizabeth). He bought property in Stratford and helped his father acquire the right to bear a coat of arms. Sometime around 1612 he retired to his home town, where he died in 1616. His collected plays, which did not appear during his lifetime, were published in 1623 by two fellow members of his company.

In an age notorious for verbal abuse, few people seem to have spoken ill of him. Ben Jonson said that "he was indeed honest, and of an open and free nature; had an excellent fancy [imagination], brave notions, and gentle expressions."

The Tempest, which is the last of Shakespeare's romances, is often seen as his farewell to the stage. Like the playwright its hero is an artist—a magician, whose stagey effects move his audience to a new view of themselves. Whatever its relationship to Shakespeare's life, however, this play is surely his final statement about the possibilities of his art.

Commentary

No Illusion of "Real Life" The roots of Elizabethan theater are in nonillusionistic drama, drama where there is no attempt at surface realism—no suggestion that what happens on stage imitates in its details what happens in actual life. The medieval mystery cycles emphasized the divine *significance* of what was happening in the biblical episodes presented and its implications for the salvation of the audience. Characters, including God himself, often commented on events, addressing the audience to spell out the meaning of their actions. But the mystery playwrights were not concerned with the psychological probability of what was dramatized, or with detailed historical truth.

Shakespeare is similarly concerned with presenting his ideas as vividly and as powerfully as possibly, but—particularly in the comedies and romances—he is not concerned to give an illusion of "real life." Improbabilities abound in the plots, and various conventions govern the presentation of action and character. Indeed *The Tempest* often forces on an audience an awareness that they are watching a play. This drama is illusionistic in many other ways as well: People do not actually speak blank verse, nor (usually) do they fall in love at first sight; nor do they speak their thoughts aloud in coherent sentences when they're alone.

BACKGROUND

SHAKESPEAREAN DRAMA

Medieval Plays

Two native dramatic traditions influenced English Renaissance theater, the *Mystery Cycles* and *Morality* plays. The mysteries—their name refers to the religious mysteries that are treated in them—dramatized Christian history from the creation of the world to the Last Judgment. The plays were performed yearly for summer church festivals in the towns of northern and central England.

These plays were produced by the local craft guilds of the city: butchers, glovers, weavers, and so forth. They would be acted on small stages erected on carts, and the carts would move from place to place in the city. A spectator standing in one location would therefore see a series of plays showing him where he stood in the history of the world, from the fall of Adam to the end of time.

The mystery plays were once praised for their vitality and coarse humor. Today, however, we recognize the complexity with which they compare and contrast historical events. From the mystery plays, Shakespearean drama gains its characteristic largeness and sweep, its blending of comedy and seriousness, and its closeness to the audience—an audience the actors often address directly.

Morality plays were often allegorical; in other words, the characters and actions have a symbolic meaning. The most famous of these plays is *Everyman,* in which the central character (a person who stands for Every Person) finds that he must die and looks desperately for aid in this crisis. However, he learns that he must journey to death alone. His earthly friends, characters with symbolic names like Goods, Kindred, and Knowledge, all forsake him; only the Good Deeds he has done will accompany him beyond the grave.

These morality plays trained both playwright and audience to notice allegorical characters who embodied attitudes or ideas. Marlowe's *Doctor Faustus* (see pages 700–702), for instance, is the story of *Everyman* with an unhappy ending. Similarly, in *The Tempest* Shakespeare creates two partly allegorical characters, Ariel and Caliban, the first symbolizing freedom and playful artistry and the second representing bondage to the earth and the body.

In contrast to the mystery plays, the morality plays were acted by professionals. These troupes of actors traveled from place to place, acting in bear-baiting grounds (where bears tied to a stake were attacked by dogs), inn-yards, and the great houses of the nobility.

The First Theaters

In 1576 an actor-carpenter named James Burbage, the father of Richard, built the first theater in London. Called simply The Theater, this building gave a permanent base to his company, the Lord Chamberlain's Men. Other theaters followed, including the Swan, the Rose (the foundations of which have recently been rediscovered), and the Globe (also recently rediscovered), in which most of Shakespeare's plays were acted. These theaters were large round or polygonal structures several stories high and could seat three or four thousand people. Depending on what they paid, patrons could sit on benches in the several galleries, stand on the ground near the stage, or even sit on the stage itself.

The stage was about six feet high and projected out into the center of the theater instead of lying behind a curtain, as the stage usually does today. Around it was a section of the floor called the "pit," where the lowest-paying customers stood and watched the performance. Plays were performed during daylight hours and, since theaters were open at the top, the audience in the pit must have been rained on in bad weather. Performances were probably noisy affairs with vendors selling nuts and oranges in the pit. The recent excavations of the Swan have uncovered mounds of discarded hazelnut shells.

City officials disliked the theaters and did what they could to discourage them. In the summer, for instance, they often closed the theaters during outbreaks of plague on the grounds that they helped spread the disease. On such occasions the players went back to their wandering existence, touring in towns outside London.

The Renaissance Stage

Shakespeare's stage had little scenery, though there were elaborate costumes: We have records detailing the large sums spent on satin and velvet. Despite the lack of scenery, the stage could suggest a great deal to the audience. Horizontally, for instance, the stage symbolized the world, and scenes could change rapidly from one location to another because there was no heavy scenery to move. A special "upper stage" at the back enabled characters to play balcony scenes. The audience learned where the characters were by what they said. The first three lines of *The Tempest*, for instance, let the audience know at once that they were watching a ship in a storm.

Vertically, the stage suggested the universe. Over the stage a canopy studded with stars represented the heavens; below the stage was a space representing hell. A trapdoor led to the spaces beneath the stage, just as it did in the medieval mystery plays.

Out of this door devils could appear. In *Doctor Faustus* a good angel was lowered from the heavens to give Faustus advice he refuses to take, while at the end of the play the devils ascended from below to drag the Doctor off to hell. The stage therefore reminded the audience of humanity's place on earth between hell and heaven.

Tragedies, Histories, Comedies, Romances

Dramatic critics of the eighteenth century commented on Shakespeare's tendency to mix "kings and clowns" in his plays. This mixing of tragic and comic elements is a characteristic of the English Renaissance stage and especially of Shakespeare.

Such blending was easier during the Renaissance because the definition of types of drama was loose and vague. There were often so many traditions to draw from—Classical, Italian, and native English—that an audience would have few expectations of a comedy beyond laughter and a happy ending. Tragedy was usually defined simply as a story with an unhappy ending. More specifically, it was the story of a person who falls from prosperity to misery because of fate or sinful behavior. Shakespearean tragedy goes beyond this simple definition to focus on the complexities of human psychology.

History plays and tragedies shared many elements. In Shakespeare's history plays, however, his emphasis is more political than psychological. These plays focused on the threats to rulers and the attempts of English kings to justify their claims to the throne.

At the end of his career, Shakespeare wrote four comedies that have come to be called his "romances." These were not primarily love stories, though they all include a love plot. Shakespeare's romances have the happy endings of comedy, but they hint at violence in a way not typical of his early comedy. Before the opening of *The Tempest*, for instance, there has been the seizure of a kingdom followed by an indirect attempt at murder and an attempted rape. The action of the play itself contains two more attempted murders, and three men go mad. Yet in the romances, as opposed to the tragedies, the violence and ugliness are contained. Shakespeare makes the audience aware that the play is not "realistic." It is not life but art.

Blank Verse

Shakespearean drama, like most English Renaissance verse drama, is written in unrhymed iambic pentameter, or **blank verse**.

Rhythm in English poetry results mainly from repeated patterns of stressed and unstressed syllables. The pattern of stresses in a poem is called its **meter**, and the meter is made up of several basic units called **feet**. A foot is usually composed of a stressed syllable joined with one or more unstressed syllables. The basic foot for most English verse is the **iamb** (adjective: **iambic**), which consists of an unaccented syllable followed by an accented syllable, as in the word *ăwáy*. Five iambic feet make an iambic pentameter line, as follows:

Ĭmprĭsŏnĕd thóu dĭdst páinfŭllў rĕmáin

or:

Thĕre's nóthĭng ĭll căn dwéll ĭn súch ă témplĕ

As in the second quotation, the blank verse of *The Tempest* often has an extra unaccented syllable at the end of the line. This dangling syllable is called a **feminine ending**.

If iambic pentameter were repeated without variation, it would be as boring as a metronome. Poets writing blank verse therefore vary the iambic pattern. Sometimes this variation occurs simply because the accents in longer words are never equally strong. In the first line quoted above, for instance, the first syllable of "painfully" gets a stronger accent than the third. Shakespeare will also frequently substitute one or more *different* feet for the normal iambic feet in the line. There are five alternate feet in English:

foot	adjective	description
trochee (trō´ kē)	trochaic	strong-weak: *fálliňg*
anapest (an´ ə pest´)	anapestic	weak-weak-strong: *tŏ thĕ wóods*
dactyl (dak´ til)	dactylic	strong-weak-weak: *cráftĭlў*
spondee (spän´ dē)	spondaic	strong-strong: *slów! slów!*
pyrrhic (pir´ ik)	pyrrhic	weak-weak: *wĭn-/dŏw ŏf*

The substitutions can occur for emphasis. In the following line from *The Tempest*, which describes Ferdinand's sorrow at his father's supposed death, the trochee emphasizes the weeping:

Wéepĭng ăgáin thĕ kíng mў fáthĕr's wráck

The use of the trochee in the first foot, as in this line, is a common substitution.

Rhythm can also characterize. The spondees in the second and third feet of the following line suggest Caliban's crudeness and roughness:

Thĕ frésh *spríngs, brínĕ-píts, bárrĕn* pláce ănd fértĭlĕ

A key aspect of rhythm is the pause within the line, called the **caesura** (si zyʊʊr´ ə). There is a *caesura* (marked ‖) in almost all blank verse lines, and it usually falls toward the middle, though it can occur anywhere. In Miranda's lines "Dashed all to pieces. O the cry did knock," the caesura comes halfway through the third foot (after "pieces").

Taken together, this placing of accents and pauses creates a complex rhythm that gives Shakespeare's verse its characteristic movement.

To **scan** a line, or analyze its rhythm, first read the line aloud, accenting the words in a way that makes the meaning clear. Then put the slanted line ´ over the heavy syllables, and a horseshoe symbol ˘ over the light ones. Finally, divide the line into feet, remembering that most feet in the line (though possibly not the last one) will end with a stressed syllable.

3 Enrichment Another topic you may want to cover in connection with blank verse is the texture of Shakespeare's language. Students may not be accustomed to thinking of linguistic texture.

To acquaint them with this concept, call their attention to the way in which certain painters apply paint heavily to a canvas while others apply it sparingly. Tell them that, like paint, words have a texture. In order to familiarize themselves with this texture, they should read a passage aloud, listening for patterns of vowels and consonants. As an example, read aloud the following passage from *The Tempest* (I.ii.395–400): "Full fathom five thy father lies; / Of his bones are coral made; / Those are pearls that were his eyes; / Nothing of him that doth fade / But doth suffer a sea change / Into something rich and strange." Point out to students the pattern of *f* sounds in the first two lines, the pattern of short *o* sounds in "Of," "Nothing," "of," "doth," and "suffer," and the *s* sounds in "suffer," "sea," "something," and "strange."

Explain to students that Shakespeare had a magnificent awareness of such textures and so was able to weave patterns of sound into rich tapestries. Also, just as he uses rhythms to characterize—Caliban often speaks in heavy spondees—he uses sounds in the same way. Point out to students the vibrant long *i* sounds in Ariel's first speech (I.ii.189–191): "All hail, great master! Grave sir, hail! *I* come / To answer th*y* best pleasure; be't to fl*y*, / To swim, to d*i*ve into the f*i*re, to r*i*de. . . ."

This pattern helps to characterize Ariel as a lively, mercurial spirit.

GUIDE FOR INTERPRETING

Focus

Literary Focus Have students re-call their favorite episodes of television programs or their fa-vorite movies. Ask them to de-scribe the central conflict of each drama. Then have them remember how they learned about the back-ground information necessary to understand the conflict. Explain to them that every drama requires exposition.

Writing/Prior Knowledge Before students begin writing, have them specify the location of their imag-inary world. Once they have a def-inite place in mind, it will be easier to do the assignment. Have stu-dents share their completed as-signments with their classmates.

Vocabulary

Preteach the following vocabulary words:
mischance (mis chans´) *n.*:
     Unlucky accident
blasphemous (blas´ fə məs)
     adj.: Irreverent or
     profane
inquisition (in´ kwə zish´ ən)
     n.: Questioning
perfidious (pər fid´ ē əs)
     adj.: Treacherous
inveterate (in vet´ ər it) *adj.*:
     Deep-rooted
manifold (man´ ə fold´) *adj.*:
     Having many and
     various forms or parts
abhorred (ab hôrd´) *adj.*:
     Detested
unmitigable (un mit´ ə gə
     b´l) *adj.*: That which
     cannot be lessened or
     eased

Commentary

The Tempest, Act I

Exposition. An enchanted island, a magician with a beautiful daugh-ter, two not-quite-human servants: These sound like the ingredients of a fairy tale. Shakespeare's problem at the start of *The Tempest* is to make this fairy tale believable. He must intrigue us with his drama and give us the necessary background information, a task usually referred to as **exposition.**

Shakespeare provides the exposition in the two scenes of Act I. He catches our interest immediately with a scene on a ship founder-ing in a storm. The Boatswain tries desperately to keep the craft from shipwreck, but the frightened, angry courtiers of King Alonso of Naples get in his way and curse him in their fear. In this scene there is, significantly, no clear figure of authority. As the Boatswain says, "What cares these roarers [the winds] for the name of king?"

The following scene contrasts dramatically with the first in stressing Prospero's control. He dwells on a nearby island, and it turns out that his magical illusions have made the storm. Prospero proceeds to lecture his daughter Miranda, dominate his servants Ariel and Caliban, and master the shipwrecked Ferdinand, son of King Alonso. We quickly learn, however, that Prospero has not always been in command. He was Duke of Milan, but he was unlaw-fully deprived of his kingdom by his brother Antonio, with Alonso's help. Abandoned with his child on a leaky ship, he came to the island where he now lives. It is no wonder that he feels the need to assert his authority in this place of refuge.

Prospero now has a plan to regain his dukedom. Putting his scheme into action, he has caused Alonso and his courtiers, includ-ing Prospero's brother Antonio, to be shipwrecked on the island. Prospero does not share his plan with the audience, but Act I sug-gests some of his intentions. He will use the magical island as a kind of experimental laboratory to test and teach the other characters. In some cases he will transform them completely. The first example of such transformation occurs when Miranda and Ferdinand fall in love. Prospero makes it clear to the audience, though not to them, that he wants this to happen. The disorienting strangeness of the island will then cause other changes in the way the characters see themselves and the world.

Writing

If you had the magical powers to create a little world just as you wanted it, what would you include? Jot down five things that you would make part of your world. Then explain why each of these things is important to you.

Objectives

Thematic
To understand the mixture of fairy tale and realistic elements in *The Tempest*

Skills
1 To understand exposition
2 To appreciate Shakespeare's songs
3 To contrast characters

Support Material

Teaching Portfolio
Teacher Backup, p. 881
Grammar in Action Worksheets, *Pronoun Reference*, p. 885; *Using That and Which*, p. 887
Usage and Mechanics Worksheet, p. 889
Vocabulary Check, p. 890

The Tempest

William Shakespeare

CHARACTERS

The Scene: An uninhabited island.

Alonso, King of Naples
Sebastian, his brother
Prospero, the right Duke of Milan
Antonio, his brother, the usurping Duke
    of Milan
Ferdinand, son to the King of Naples
Gonzalo, an honest old councilor
Adrian and Francisco, lords
Caliban, a savage and deformed slave
Trinculo, a jester
Stephano, a drunken butler

Master of a ship
Boatswain
Mariners
Miranda, daughter to Prospero
Ariel, an airy spirit
Iris
Ceres
Juno ———— [presented by] spirits
Nymphs
Reapers
[Other Spirits Attending on Prospero]

Act I

Scene i. *On a ship at sea.*

[*A tempestuous noise of thunder and lightning heard. Enter a* SHIPMAS-
TER *and a* BOATSWAIN.]

    MASTER. Boatswain!

    BOATSWAIN. Here, master. What cheer?[1]

    MASTER. Good,[2] speak to th' mariners! Fall to't yarely,[3] or we run
    ourselves aground. Bestir, bestir!   [*Exit.*]

[*Enter* MARINERS.]

5 **BOATSWAIN.** Heigh, my hearts! Cheerly, cheerly, my hearts! Yare,
    yare! Take in the topsail! Tend to th' master's whistle![4] Blow till
    thou burst thy wind, if room enough![5]

1. What cheer? What is your
will? What do you wish?
2. Good: Good fellow.
3. yarely: Vigorously; briskly;
quickly.
4. whistle: A high-pitched
whistle used to give orders.
5. Blow . . . enough: This is
addressed to the wind and
means, "Blow until you split or
burst as long as we are in the
open sea and have room to
maneuver."

Master Teacher Note Students may not fully understand how to use the side glosses as they read. It might be helpful to give them alternate strategies for using such glosses. If they do not want to be interrupted, for instance, they can read through a scene quickly, getting its general sense without referring to the notes. Then they can go back and use the notes to clarify confusing passages. Another strategy would involve referring to each note as they read. Point out that the location of the glosses is designed to facilitate ready reference. Above all, encourage them to be patient. Tell them that the English language has changed since Shakespeare's day, so inevitably his plays will sound somewhat foreign to them. Explain to them, however, that after a little bit of practice, they will get the feel of Elizabethan English.

2 Discussion Point out to students that the play opens with a scene of confusion and distress. Ask them how the title of the play hints at such a scene. Also ask them how the confusion in nature is mirrored by a confusion among the passengers. For instance, ask them how the normal relationships between noblemen and sailors are turned topsy-turvy.

3 Discussion Ask students which portion of this speech most aptly summarizes the general confusion and disruption of relationships among the passengers. Have them give reasons for their choice.

4 Enrichment Students may not realize how small Renaissance boats were in comparison to the ocean liners and carriers of today. Tell them that Renaissance ships were generally about 60 feet long and less than 20 feet wide. In a tempest, a boat of this size would seem quite small indeed.

Videodisc If you have *Shakespeare in Rehearsal: The Tempest* on Videodisc, you can easily show students brief segments that connect directly to scenes from the play or comment on issues related to characters and scenes. The

[*Enter* ALONSO, SEBASTIAN, ANTONIO, FERDINAND, GONZALO, *and others.*]

ALONSO. Good boatswain, have care. Where's the master? Play the men.[6]

10   BOATSWAIN. I pray now, keep below.

ANTONIO. Where is the master, bos'n?

BOATSWAIN. Do you not hear him? You mar our labor. Keep your cabins; you do assist the storm.

GONZALO. Nay, good, be patient.

15   BOATSWAIN. When the sea is. Hence! What cares these roarers[7] for the name of king? To cabin! Silence! Trouble us not!

GONZALO. Good, yet remember whom thou hast aboard.

BOATSWAIN. None that I more love than myself. You are a councilor; if you can command these elements to silence and work the
20   peace of the present,[8] we will not hand[9] a rope more. Use your authority. If you cannot, give thanks you have lived so long, and make yourself ready in your cabin for the mischance of the hour, if it so hap. Cheerly,[10] good hearts! Out of our way, I say.

[*Exit.*]

6. **Play the men:** Make the men work.

7. **roarers:** Loud, noisy characters (here referring either to the waves or to Alonso, Antonio, and Gonzalo).

8. **command . . . present:** Order the raging storm to stop and bring peace to the present (as in the function or job of the king's councilor).
9. **hand:** Handle.
10. **Cheerly:** Quickly.

Videodisc notes throughout the play will suggest key points at which you may want to incorporate a Videodisc segment into your lesson.

GONZALO. I have great comfort from this fellow. Methinks he hath
no drowning mark upon him; his complexion is perfect gallows.[11]
Stand fast, good Fate, to his hanging! Make the rope of his destiny our cable, for our own doth little advantage.[12] If he be not
born to be hanged, our case is miserable.

[Exit with the rest.]

[Enter BOATSWAIN.]

BOATSWAIN. Down with the topmast! Yare! Lower, lower! Bring her
to try with main course.[13] *[A cry within.]* A plague upon this
howling! They are louder than the weather of our office.[14]

[Enter SEBASTIAN, ANTONIO, *and* GONZALO.]

Yet again? What do you here? Shall we give o'er[15] and drown?
Have you a mind to sink?

SEBASTIAN. A pox o' your throat,[16] you bawling, blasphemous,
incharitable dog!

BOATSWAIN. Work you, then.

ANTONIO. Hang, cur! Hang, you insolent noisemaker! We are less
afraid to be drowned than thou art.

GONZALO. I'll warrant him for[17] drowning, though the ship were no
stronger than a nutshell and as leaky as an unstanched[18] wench.

BOATSWAIN. Lay her ahold, ahold! Set her two courses! Off to sea
again! Lay her off![19]

[Enter MARINERS *wet.]*

MARINERS. All lost! To prayers, to prayers! All lost! *[Exit.]*

BOATSWAIN. What, must our mouths be cold?

GONZALO. The King and Prince at prayers! Let's assist them,
For our case is as theirs.

SEBASTIAN.   I am out of patience.

ANTONIO. We are merely[20] cheated of our lives by drunkards.
This wide-chopped[21] rascal—would thou mightst lie drowning
The washing of ten tides![22]

GONZALO.   He'll be hanged yet,
Though every drop of water swear against it
And gape at wid'st to glut him.

[A confused noise within] "Mercy on us!"
"We split, we split!" "Farewell, my wife and children!"
"Farewell, brother!" "We split, we split, we split!"

[Exit BOATSWAIN.]

ANTONIO. Let's all sink wi' th' King.

---

11. no drowning . . . gallows: This alludes to a popular proverb, "He that's born to be hanged need fear no drowning."

12. for . . . advantage: Our own (destiny) will not save us from drowning.

13. Bring . . . course: A nautical term meaning "Bring the ship about to try to hold the course."

14. They . . . office: The passengers are noisier than the storm or our work.

15. give o'er: Give up.

16. pox . . . throat: A plague or curse on your throat.

17. warrant him for: Guarantee him against.

18. unstanched: Not checked or stopped.

19. Lay . . . off: Get control. Bring her back on course. Get the ship out to sea. Get her away from shore.

20. merely: Totally; completely.

21. wide-chopped: Big-mouthed; talkative.

22. ten tides: Pirates were tied down on the shore and left to drown by the washing of tides over them, usually three.

---

5 Discussion Have students explain the ironic humor of Gonzalo's speech. Ask them how "the rope of" the sailor's "destiny" can be a "cable," or lifeline, for the passengers. Also ask them what effect the humor has in this scene of distress and confusion, and what it suggests about the outcome of the scene.

6 Clarification Tell students that a boatswain was a petty officer in charge of the deck crew, the rigging, and so forth. Ask them what sort of a fellow this boatswain seems to be.

7 Discussion Have students contrast the reactions of Sebastian and Antonio with those of Gonzalo. Ask them how, from the beginning of the play, Shakespeare suggests differences between the various characters.

8 Discussion Ask students what the boatswain means by this remark.

9 Enrichment Point out to students the use of offstage noises and voices to add to the confusion of the scene. Ask students how this scene might be staged in a modern proscenium theater, with all its resources for special effects and lighting.

⌨ Videodisc Introduce students to the play by showing the opening segment of the *Shakespeare in Rehearsal: The Tempest* Videodisc. Explain to students that they will be observing an imaginary rehearsal of the play under the direction of William Shakespeare himself.

Frames 2370 to 4310

SEBASTIAN.   Let's take leave of him.

[*Exit with* ANTONIO.]

55 GONZALO. Now would I give a thousand furlongs of sea for an acre
of barren ground—long heath,²³ brown furze,²⁴ anything. The
wills above be done, but I would fain²⁵ die a dry death.   [*Exit.*]

Scene ii. The island. In front of Prospero's cell.

[*Enter* PROSPERO *and* MIRANDA.]

   MIRANDA. If by your art, my dearest father, you have
   Put the wild waters in this roar, allay them.
   The sky, it seems, would pour down stinking pitch
   But that the sea, mounting to th' welkin's cheek,¹
5   Dashes the fire out. O, I have suffered
   With those that I saw suffer! A brave² vessel
   (Who had no doubt some noble creature in her)
   Dashed all to pieces! O, the cry did knock
   Against my very heart! Poor souls, they perished!
10   Had I been any god of power, I would
   Have sunk the sea within the earth or ere³
   It should the good ship so have swallowed and
   The fraughting⁴ souls within her.

   PROSPERO.   Be collected.
   No more amazement.⁵ Tell your piteous⁶ heart
   There's no harm done.

   MIRANDA.   O, woe the day!

15 **PROSPERO.**   No harm.
   I have done nothing but in care of thee,
   Of thee my dear one, thee my daughter, who
   Art ignorant of what thou art, naught knowing
   Of whence I am, nor that I am more better⁷
20   Than Prospero, master of a full poor cell,
   And thy no greater father.⁸

   MIRANDA.   More to know
   Did never meddle⁹ with my thoughts.

   PROSPERO.   'Tis time
   I should inform thee farther. Lend thy hand
   And pluck my magic garment from me. So.

[*Lays down his robe.*]

25   Lie there, my art. Wipe thou thine eyes; have comfort.
   The direful spectacle of the wrack,¹⁰ which touched
   The very virtue¹¹ of compassion in thee,
   I have with such provision¹² in mine art

Side notes (right margin):

23. **heath:** Heather, a shrub that grows on open wasteland.
24. **furze:** Gorse, a shrub that puts forth yellow flowers.
25. **fain:** Rather.

1. **welkin's cheek:** Sky's clouds.

2. **brave:** Splendid.

3. **ere:** Before.

4. **fraughting;** Laden, referring back to the ship, which is loaded with a cargo of souls.

5. **amazement:** Bewilderment; alarm; consternation.

6. **piteous:** Filled with pity; compassionate.

7. **more better:** Of higher rank.

8. **thy . . . father:** Your father, who is no greater than master of a poor cave.

9. **meddle:** Mix.

10. **wrack:** Wreck.
11. **virtue:** Essence.
12. **provision:** Prevision; foresight.

Side notes (left margin):

10 **Enrichment** Tell students that Miranda's name comes from a form of the Latin word *mirari*, which means "to wonder at." This same Latin word appears in the English word *admiration*. Explain that Shakespeare chose this name deliberately, because it suggests an important side of Miranda's character.

11 **Discussion** Ask students how Miranda's first speech reveals her character. Do they have a clue as yet about how her name relates to her nature?

12 **Discussion** Ask students what kind of a father Prospero seems to be.

13 **Discussion** Have students contrast the mood of this scene with that of the first scene.

14 **Enrichment** Tell students that in his last plays, the romances, Shakespeare introduces elements of tragedy and violence, but then distances them and renders them harmless. The transformation of the real tempest to a magician's illusion—"There's no harm done"—is an example of this strategy.

15 **Enrichment** Tell students that the name *Prospero* comes from a Latin word meaning "favorable or fortunate." Ask them to keep this meaning in mind as they listen to Prospero's account of his past. Have them speculate about the ways in which Prospero has been fortunate and unfortunate.

16 **Literary Focus** Point out to students that Shakespeare uses Miranda's ignorance about her past to set up the exposition that Prospero will provide. As Prospero informs Miranda about their past, he will be informing the audience as well.

17 **Enrichment** Explain to students that stage business and the movement of props can have a symbolic meaning. Have them consider why Shakespeare has Prospero remove his "magic garment" before telling how he and Miranda came to the island.

So safely ordered that there is no soul—
30 No, not so much perdition[13] as an hair
Betid[14] to any creature in the vessel
Which thou heard'st cry, which thou saw'st sink.
  Sit down;
For thou must now know farther.

MIRANDA.   You have often
Begun to tell me what I am; but stopped
35 And left me to a bootless[15] inquisition,
Concluding, "Stay; not yet."

PROSPERO.   The hour's now come;
The very minute bids thee ope thine ear.
Obey, and be attentive. Canst thou remember
A time before we came unto this cell?
40 I do not think thou canst, for then thou wast not
Out[16] three years old.

MIRANDA.   Certainly, sir, I can.

PROSPERO. By what? By any other house or person?
Of anything the image tell me that
Hath kept with thy remembrance.

MIRANDA.   'Tis far off,
45 And rather like a dream than an assurance
That my remembrance warrants. Had I not
Four or five women once that tended me?

PROSPERO. Thou hadst, and more, Miranda, but how is it
That this lives in thy mind? What seest thou else
50 In the dark backward and abysm of time?[17]
If thou rememb'rest aught ere thou cam'st here,
How thou cam'st here thou mayst.

MIRANDA.   But that I do not.

PROSPERO. Twelve year since, Miranda, twelve year since,
Thy father was the Duke of Milan and
A prince of power.

55 MIRANDA.   Sir, are not you my father?

PROSPERO. Thy mother was a piece of virtue,[18] and
She said thou wast my daughter; and thy father
Was Duke of Milan; and his only heir
And princess, no worse issued.[19]

MIRANDA.   O the heavens!
60 What foul play had we that we came from thence?
Or blessèd was't we did?

---

13. **perdition:** loss.
14. **Betid:** Befell; happened.

15. **bootless:** Pointless; fruitless; useless.

16. **out:** Beyond; past; more than.

17. **abysm of time:** Depths of the past.

18. **piece of virtue:** Example of perfection and purity.

19. **no worse issued:** No less royal.

---

18 Discussion Have students speculate as to why Prospero hesitated to inform his daughter in the past. Why does he overcome his hesitation now?

19 Enrichment Explain to students that some scholars have identified Miranda with the heart, or emotions, and Prospero with the intellect. Ask students whether the evidence up to this point supports that interpretation.

20 Literary Focus Explain to students that without Miranda's responses and questions, the exposition would be contained in a long, unbroken speech by Prospero. Ask them why such a speech might not be dramatically effective. Then ask them to decide, as they read, whether the by-play between Miranda and Prospero does in fact make the exposition more lively.

21 Enrichment Point out to students that the word *dream* is repeated many times throughout this play. Just as Miranda's past now seems like a dream to her, the events of the play will often appear strange and dreamlike to the characters.

22 Enrichment Tell students that this memorable phrase illustrates the way in which Shakespeare plays with the language. The word *backward*, which is usually an adverb or adjective, becomes a noun here. Shakespeare's unusual use of this word emphasizes the distance and dimness of the events that Prospero is describing.

23 Clarification Milan is a city in northern Italy. During the Renaissance, many Italian cities were states unto themselves. Italy did not become a united country until the nineteenth century.

24 **Clarification** Remind students that Prospero's brother Antonio has already made an appearance, in the first scene.

25 **Clarification** By "liberal arts" Prospero means all those studies that contribute to a general rather than a specifically vocational education.

PROSPERO.   Both, both, my girl!
By foul play, as thou say'st, were we heaved thence,
But blessedly holp²⁰ hither.

MIRANDA.   O, my heart bleeds
To think o' th' teen²¹ that I have turned you to,
65   Which is from²² my remembrance! Please you, farther.

24   **PROSPERO.** My brother and thy uncle, called Antonio—
I pray thee mark me—that a brother should
Be so perfidious!—he whom next thyself
Of all the world I loved, and to him put
70   The manage of my state, as at that time
Through all the signories²³ it was the first,
And Prospero the prime duke, being so reputed
25   In dignity, and for the liberal arts

20. holp: Helped.

21. teen: Misery.

22. from: Gone from.

23. signories: Feudal estates; seigneuries; principalities.

Commentary

The Exchange Between Prospero and Miranda Not only does the exchange between Prospero and Miranda provide the audience with necessary background, but it also develops Prospero's relation to his daughter. Prospero takes off his magical cloak before he speaks with Miranda in order to distinguish between his roles as magician and father. His authority as a father depends on Miranda's loving obedience, not on his power to compel her to do what he wants. Prospero, however, appears uneasy without his power. He repeatedly worries (lines 67, 78, 87) that Miranda is not paying attention, although her answers suggest she is. When the talk ends, he abruptly resumes his magician's role by putting Miranda to sleep.

This powerful magician therefore seems ambivalent about giving up the control which comes with his art. The history that he tells his daughter illuminates his ambivalence. As a duke, Prospero seems to have preferred his study to the throne-room. In other words he was more comfortable with his magic than with the complexities of human interaction.

The island is, indeed, an expanded study in which Prospero can control events with his magical art. Like a small god, he is able to do whatever he wants. In fact, students might wonder why Prospero, who seems not to have

Without a parallel. Those being all my study,
75 The government I cast upon my brother
And to my state grew stranger, being transported
And rapt in secret studies. Thy false uncle—
Dost thou attend me?

MIRANDA.   Sir, most heedfully.

PROSPERO. Being once perfected[24] how to grant suits,
80 How to deny them, who t' advance, and who
To trash for overtopping,[25] new-created
The creatures that were mine, I say—or changed 'em,
Or else new-formed 'em[26]—having both the key
Of officer and office, set all hearts i' th' state
85 To what tune pleased his ear, that now he was
The ivy which had hid my princely trunk
And sucked my verdure[27] out on't. Thou attend'st not?

MIRANDA. O, good sir, I do.

PROSPERO.   I pray thee mark me.
I thus neglecting worldly ends, all dedicated
90 To closeness[28] and the bettering of my mind—
With that which, but by being so retired,
O'erprized all popular rate, in my false brother
Awaked an evil nature,[29] and my trust,
Like a good parent, did beget of him
95 A falsehood in its contrary as great
As my trust was, which had indeed no limit,
A confidence sans bound. He being thus lorded—
Not only with what my revenue yielded
But what my power might else exact, like one
100 Who having into truth—by telling of it,[30]
Made such a sinner of his memory
To credit[31] his own lie, he did believe
He was indeed the Duke, out o' th' substitution
And executing th' outward face of royalty
105 With all prerogative.[32] Hence his ambition growing—
Dost thou hear?

MIRANDA.   Your tale, sir, would cure deafness.

PROSPERO. To have no screen between this part he played
And him he played it for, he needs will be
Absolute Milan.[33] Me (poor man) my library
110 Was dukedom large enough. Of temporal[34] royalties
He thinks me now incapable; confederates
(So dry he was for sway[35]) wi' th' King of Naples
To give him annual tribute, do him homage,
Subject his coronet to his crown, and bend

24. **perfected:** Skilled at.

25. **trash for overtopping:**
Hold back from going too fast
or being too ambitious; "trash"
refers to a cord or leash used in
training dogs.

26. **new-created . . . 'em:**
[He] remade my staff—either
by replacing those I had chosen
with others loyal to him or by
turning my people against me.

27. **verdure:** Green
vegetation—health and vigor.

28. **closeness:** Seclusion.

29. **With . . . nature:** By
devoting myself to higher
things, which is beyond
popular understanding, I
aroused evil in my brother.

30. **like . . . it:** Like one
truly entitled to what my
power commanded by simply
claiming the right.

31. **credit:** Believe.

32. **out . . . prerogative:** By
substituting for me and
pretending he was royalty with
all its rights and privileges.

33. **Absolute Milan:** Duke in
fact, not just in pretense.
34. **temporal:** In time; of this
world.
35. **dry . . . sway:** Thirsty
for power; we would say
"hungry for power."

26 **Discussion** Ask students whether Prospero's neglect of his responsibilities reveals a flaw in his character.

27 **Enrichment** Explain to students that in addition to breaking up Prospero's exposition, this interruption might reveal a kind of nervous testiness on Prospero's part. If so, why does Prospero feel nervous?

28 **Discussion** Ask students if there is an ironic contrast between the current Prospero, a powerful magician, and the Prospero of the past.

29 **Enrichment** Prospero's behavior was in conflict with the Renaissance belief in the importance of the active life. In the Middle Ages, many thinkers believed that a quiet life devoted to God was best. During the Renaissance, however, writers like Erasmus stressed the importance of displaying Christian virtues in a life of action and responsibility.

30 **Discussion** If students have read the selection from Machiavelli's *The Prince*, ask them how Machiavelli might have reacted to Prospero's account of his loss of the dukedom.

enjoyed ruling, should wish to leave his island. Early in the scene, he answers the question, telling Miranda that he has done everying "in care of " her (line 16). He is growing old, and when he dies Miranda will be alone and helpless on the island. She—not he—needs a society in which she can flourish. Furthermore, Prospero's awareness that he is aging is an acknowledgment that he is *not* a god and that, as a mortal, his immortality on earth will come through Miranda's offspring. So even though leaving the island means losing his magical powers, he plans to make this sacrifice.

31 **Clarification** Prospero is complaining here that in order to win the King of Naples to his side, Antonio had to subject Milan to the rule of Naples. During the Italian Renaissance, city-states like Milan and Naples constantly vied for power and influence.

32 **Clarification** Prospero and Miranda might have been abandoned in any of the small seas—the Ligurian, Tyrrhenian, Adriatic, or Ionian—that surround Italy. All these smaller seas, however, flow into the Mediterranean Sea, where Prospero's magic island is presumably located.

33 **Discussion** Ask students to identify the personifications in this passage. Then ask them to explain what these personifications contribute to the meaning. You might also have students compare and contrast this passage with the descriptions of the tempest in the opening scene.

31
115   The dukedom, yet unbowed (alas, poor Milan!),
    To most ignoble stooping.

MIRANDA.   O the heavens!

PROSPERO. Mark his condition,[36] and th' event;[37] then tell me
    If this might be a brother.

MIRANDA.   I should sin
    To think but nobly of my grandmother.
    Good wombs have borne bad sons.

120 PROSPERO.   Now the condition.
    This King of Naples, being an enemy
    To me inveterate, hearkens my brother's suit;
    Which was, that he, in lieu o' th' premises[38]
    Of homage and I know not how much tribute,
125   Should presently extirpate me and mine
    Out of the dukedom and confer fair Milan,
    With all the honors, of my brother. Whereon,
    A treacherous army levied, one midnight
    Fated to th' purpose, did Antonio open
130   The gates of Milan; and, i' th' dead of darkness,
    The ministers[39] for th' purpose hurried thence
    Me and thy crying self.

MIRANDA.   Alack, for pity!
    I, not rememb'ring how I cried out then,
    Will cry it o'er again; it is a hint[40]
    That wrings mine eyes to't.

135 PROSPERO.   Hear a little further,
    And then I'll bring thee to the present business
    Which now's upon's; without the which this story
    Were most impertinent.[41]

MIRANDA.   Wherefore did they not
    That hour destroy us?

PROSPERO.   Well demanded, wench.
140   My tale provokes that question. Dear, they durst not,
    So dear the love my people bore me; nor set
    A mark so bloody on the business; but,
    With colors fairer, painted their foul ends.
    In few,[42] they hurried us aboard a bark;
145   Bore us some leagues to sea, where they prepared
    A rotten carcass of a butt,[43] not rigged,
    Nor tackle, sail, nor mast; the very rats
    Instinctively have quit it. There they hoist us,
    To cry to th' sea that roared to us; to sigh

36. condition: The terms of agreement with Naples.
37. event: The outcome.

38. in lieu o' th' premises: In return for promises.

39. ministers: Agents.

40. hint: Occasion.

41. impertinent: Inappropriate; not pertinent; beside the point.

42. In few: With little explanation; using few words.

43. butt: A contemptuous reference to a ship; a tub.

Grammar in Action

Correct pronoun reference requires that a pronoun refer back to an antecedent that is clearly stated or clearly understood. The following is an example of vague pronoun reference.

    VAGUE: John said that he was a gourmet chef. His wife, however, claimed that he could not even toast bread without burning it. *This* ruined the dinner for all the guests.

    The antecedent of the pronoun *this* is neither clearly stated nor clearly understood. This vague pronoun reference can be corrected as follows:

    CORRECT: John said that he was a gourmet chef. His wife, however, claimed that he could not even toast bread without burning it. *This argument* ruined the dinner for all the guests.

    The pronoun references in *The Tempest* are clear, so that readers always understand to which antecedent a pronoun refers:
    Some food we had, and some fresh water, that
    A noble Neapolitan, Gonzalo,
    Out of *his* charity, who being then appointed
    Master of this design, did give us, with

150 To th' winds, whose pity, sighing back again,
Did us but loving wrong.

MIRANDA.   Alack, what trouble
Was I then to you!

PROSPERO.   O, a cherubin
Thou was that did preserve me! Thou didst smile,
Infused with a fortitude from heaven,
155 When I have decked the sea with drops full salt,⁴⁴
Under my burden groaned; which raised in me
An undergoing stomach,⁴⁵ to bear up
Against what should ensue.

MIRANDA.   How came we ashore?

PROSPERO. By providence divine.
160 Some food we had, and some fresh water, that
A noble Neapolitan, Gonzalo,
Out of his charity, who being then appointed
Master of this design, did give us, with
Rich garments, linens, stuffs, and the necessaries
165 Which since have steaded much.⁴⁶ So, of his gentleness,
Knowing I loved my books, he furnished me
From mine own library with volumes that
I prize above my dukedom.

MIRANDA.   Would I might
But ever see that man!

PROSPERO.   Now I arise.
170 Sit still, and hear the last of our sea sorrow.
Here in this island we arrived; and here
Have I, thy schoolmaster, made thee more profit
Than other princess' can,⁴⁷ that have more time
For vainer hours, and tutors not so careful.

175 MIRANDA. Heavens thank you for't! And now I pray you, sir—
For still 'tis beating in my mind—your reason
For raising this sea storm?

PROSPERO.   Know thus far forth.
By accident most strange, bountiful Fortune
(Now my dear lady⁴⁸) hath mine enemies
180 Brought to this shore; and by my prescience⁴⁹
I find my zenith⁵⁰ doth depend upon
A most auspicious star, whose influence
If now I court not, but omit,⁵¹ my fortunes
Will ever after droop. Here cease more questions.
185 Thou art inclined to sleep. 'Tis a good dullness,

44. decked . . . salt: Decorated the sea with tears.

45. undergoing stomach: Underlying courage.

46. steaded much: Been of much use.

47. princess' can: Princesses have.

48. Now . . . lady: Now my supporter.
49. prescience: Knowledge before an event.
50. zenith: Highest fortune.
51. omit: ignore.

34 **Clarification** Explain to students that the Hebrew word *kerub* means "an angelic being." In Renaissance art and the art of other eras, cherubs are represented as beautiful, winged children. Prospero's description, of course, suggests that Miranda is not entirely an earthly being. Ask students what qualities of her personality suggest an angelic nature.

35 **Discussion** Remind students of the definition of dramatic irony and ask them how this statement is an example of it.

36 **Enrichment** Tell students that the Romans worshiped Fortuna, goddess of fortune, who was depicted with a ship's rudder and a cornucopia. These symbols indicated her control of fate and her ability to bestow bounty on lucky individuals. This personification of Fortune as a woman was also common during the Middle Ages and the Renaissance. It even survives, though faintly, in our own time, most notably in the phrase "fickle fortune."

37 **Literary Focus** Point out to students that with these words, Prospero abruptly finishes with this phase of the exposition. From this point on, he will take no one, except Ariel, into his confidence.

38 **Enrichment** Tell students that this is a minor example of Prospero's powers. As a white magician, Prospero controls nature by means of (in the words of critic Irving Ribner) "the disciplined use of holy knowledge." By contrast, black magicians (like the witch Sycorax, Caliban's mother, mentioned later in this scene) derived their power from the devil. Shakespeare's audience would not have thought of Prospero as a supernatural being. Learned men and women of Shakespeare's time believed that with intelligence and discipline they could gain powers like those Prospero displays. The boundary between science and magic was not as clearly delineated as it is today.

Rich garments, linens, stuffs, and the necessaries
Which since then have steaded much. So, of *his* gentleness,
Knowing I loved my books, *he* furnished me
From mine own library with volumes that
I prize above my dukedom.

It is clear, for instance, that the italicized pronouns all refer back to Gonzalo.

Student Activity Find two other passages in the first act where Shakespeare uses correct pronoun reference while describing a complex, involved action.

And give it way. I know thou canst not choose.

[MIRANDA *sleeps*.]

Come away,[52] servant, come! I am ready now.
Approach, my Ariel! Come!

39 [*Enter* ARIEL.]

40
41
ARIEL. All hail, great master! Grave sir, hail! I come
190   To answer thy best pleasure; be't to fly,
  To swim, to dive into the fire, to ride
  On the curled clouds. To thy strong bidding task
  Ariel and all his quality.[53]

PROSPERO.   Hast thou, spirit,
  Performed to point,[54] the tempest that I bade thee?

42
195 ARIEL. To every article.
  I boarded the King's ship. Now on the beak,
  Now in the waist, the deck,[55] in every cabin,
  I flamed amazement.[56] Sometime I'd divide
  And burn in many places; on the topmast,
200   The yards, and boresprit[57] would I flame distinctly,[58]
  Then meet and join. Jove's lightnings, the precursors
  O' th' dreadful thunderclaps, more momentary
  And sight-outrunning were not. The fire and cracks
  Of sulfurous roaring the most mighty Neptune
205   Seem to besiege, and make his bold waves tremble;
  Yea, his dread trident shake.

PROSPERO.   My brave spirit!
  Who was so firm, so constant, that this coil[59]
  Would not infect his reason?

ARIEL.   Not a soul
  But felt a fever of the mad and played
210   Some tricks of desperation. All but mariners
  Plunged in the foaming brine and quit the vessel,
  Then all afire with me. The King's son Ferdinand,
  With hair up-staring[60] (then like reeds, not hair),
  Was the first man that leapt; cried "Hell is empty,
  And all the devils are here!"

215 PROSPERO.   Why, that's my spirit!
  But was not this nigh shore?

ARIEL.   Close by, my master.

PROSPERO. But are they, Ariel, safe?

43
ARIEL.   Not a hair perished.
  On their sustaining[61] garments not a blemish,

52. **Come away:** Come here.

53. **quality:** Others like Ariel who make up his band of spirits.

54. **to point:** To the smallest detail; with absolute precision.

55. **Now . . . deck:** Now on the prow, now amidships, now on the rear deck or poop.
56. **flamed amazement:** Caused terror by appearing as fire.
57. **boresprit:** Bowsprit.
58. **distinctly:** In distinct or separate places.

59. **coil:** Tumult; uproar.

60. **up-staring:** Standing up on end.

61. **sustaining:** Supporting by keeping them afloat.

But fresher than before; and as thou bad'st me,
In troops I have dispersed them 'bout the isle.
The King's son have I landed by himself,
Whom I left cooling of the air with sighs
In an odd angle of the isle, and sitting,
His arms in this sad knot. [*Illustrates with a gesture.*]

PROSPERO.   Of the King's ship,
The mariners, say how thou hast disposed,
And all the rest o' th' fleet.

ARIEL.   Safely in harbor
Is the King's ship; in the deep nook where once
Thou call'dst me up at midnight to fetch dew
From the still-vexed Bermoothes,[62] there she's hid;
The mariners all under hatches stowed,
Who, with a charm joined to their suff'red labor,[63]
I have left asleep. And for the rest o' th' fleet,
Which I dispersed, they all have met again,
And are upon the Mediterranean flote[64]
Bound sadly home for Naples,
Supposing that they saw the King's ship wracked
And his great person perish.

PROSPERO.   Ariel, thy charge
Exactly is performed; but there's more work.
What is the time o' th' day?

ARIEL.   Past the mid season.[65]

PROSPERO. At least two glasses.[66] The time 'twixt six and now
Must by us both be spent most preciously.

ARIEL. Is there more toil? Since thou dost give me pains,[67]
Let me remember[68] thee what thou hast promised,
Which is not yet performed me.

PROSPERO.   How now? Moody?
What is't thou canst demand?

ARIEL.   My liberty.

PROSPERO. Before the time be out? No more!

ARIEL.   I prithee,
Remember I have done thee worthy service,
Told thee no lies, made thee no mistakings, served
Without or grudge or grumblings. Thou did promise
To bate me a full year.[69]

PROSPERO.   Dost thou forget
From what a torment I did free thee?

---

62. Bermoothes: Bermudas.

63. suff'red labor: The work they had done.

64. flote: Sea.

65. mid season: Noon.

66. two glasses: Two o'clock; the turning of two hourglasses.

67. pains: Hard work.
68. remember: Remind.

69. bate . . . year: Reduce my servitude by a full year.

---

44 Discussion Ask students how Ariel reveals a tendency to mock humans.

45 Enrichment Remind students that Shakespeare would have just read about the shipwreck of the *Sea Adventure* on the island of Bermuda. Point out to them how, in his imagination, Bermuda is linked with Prospero's magic island.

46 Clarification Naples is located on the southwestern coast of Italy.

47 Discussion Ask students whether Prospero's apparent anxiety about the time reflects an anxiety about his ability to carry off his plan.

48 Enrichment Point out to students that the theme of liberty versus slavery runs through the entire play. Have them look for the ways in which various characters express this theme.

☙ Videodisc Have students view the segment on the *Shakespeare in Rehearsal: The Tempest* Videodisc where the actors dramatize this scene between Ariel and Prospero. Point out to students that although Ariel is played by a person, we are to imagine he is a sprite that is capable of flying and casting spells on other characters.

Frames 6875 to 17095

49 Literary Focus Explain to students that in addition to illuminat-
ing the relationship between Prospero and Ariel, this rebuke also
provides an exposition of past
events for the audience.

50 Enrichment Tell students that
Sycorax, Caliban's mother, was a
black witch and therefore in
league with the devil. In that respect, she resembles the protagonist of Marlowe's play *The Tragical History of the Life and Death
of Doctor Faustus*, page 700.

51 Enrichment Explain to students
that in the early sixteenth century,
Algiers was captured by the Turks.
It then became the base for Muslim fleets that preyed upon merchant ships in the Mediterranean.

ARIEL.   No.

PROSPERO. Thou dost; and think'st it much to tread the ooze
Of the salt deep,
To run upon the sharp wind of the North,
255   To do me business in the veins[70] o' th' earth
When it is baked[71] with frost.

ARIEL.   I do not, sir.

PROSPERO. Thou liest, malignant thing! Hast thou forgot
The foul witch Sycorax,[72] who with age and envy[73]
Was grown into a hoop? Hast thou forgot her?

ARIEL. No, sir.

PROSPERO.   Thou hast. Where was she born? Speak!
260   Tell me!

ARIEL. Sir, in Argier.[74]

PROSPERO.   O, was she so? I must
Once in a month recount what thou hast been,
Which thou forget'st. This damned witch Sycorax,
For mischiefs manifold, and sorceries terrible

70. veins: Underground
streams.
71. baked: Hardened.

72. Sycorax: The name of the
witch, possibly made up from
two or more Greek words.
73. envy: Spite.

74. Argier: Algiers in North
Africa.

Commentary

Ariel and Caliban Prospero's two servants, Ariel and Caliban, are alike in
their wish to be free, but different in all other respects. Each corresponds
to a different side of Prospero. Ariel is a natural spirit, one of those invisible
inhabitants of the world that Renaissance writers believed were everywhere.
He is neither human nor moral: His language, his habits, and his impulses
suggest that he responds to Prospero's enjoyment of play and magical creation. This affinity is reflected in the delight Prospero takes in Ariel's bravura
staging of an illusory shipwreck (lines 195–206, 208–214).

Caliban, by contrast, is the son of a witch and a demon, and as such
is half human and half beast. Like Ariel he is amoral, but he is moved not
by love of play but by his bodily appetites. He is responsive to his physical
nature rather than his reason, and remains unrepentant for his attempted
rape of Miranda, seeing her as a potential mother of other Calibans.

Point out to students the differences between the language of Ariel and
Caliban. Ariel tends to emphasize verbs, especially verbs of motion: "All
hail, great master! Grave sir, hail! I *come* / To answer thy best pleasure; be't
to *fly*, / To *swim*, to *dive* into the fire, to *ride* / On the curled clouds." (lines
189–192) Caliban, on the other hand, tends to stress a series of concrete

265   To enter human hearing, from Argier,
        Thou know'st, was banished. For one thing she did
        They would not take her life. Is not this true?

ARIEL. Ay, sir.

PROSPERO. This blue-eyed hag was hither brought with child
270   And here was left by th' sailors. Thou, my slave,
        As thou report'st thyself, wast then her servant.
        And, for thou wast a spirit too delicate
        To act her earthy and abhorred commands,
        Refusing her grand hests,[75] she did confine thee,
275   By help of her more potent ministers,[76]
        And in her most unmitigable rage,
        Into a cloven pine; within which rift
        Imprisoned thou didst painfully remain
        A dozen years; within which space she died
280   And left thee there, where thou didst vent thy groans
        As fast as millwheels strike. Then was this island
        (Save for the son that she did litter here,
        A freckled whelp, hagborn) not honored with
        A human shape.

ARIEL.   Yes, Caliban her son.

285 **PROSPERO.** Dull thing, I say so! He, that Caliban
        Whom now I keep in service. Thou best know'st
        What torment I did find thee in; thy groans
        Did make wolves howl and penetrate the breasts
        Of ever-angry bears. It was a torment
290   To lay upon the damned, which Sycorax
        Could not again undo. It was mine art,
        When I arrived and heard thee, that made gape
        The pine, and let thee out.

ARIEL.   I thank thee, master.

PROSPERO. If thou more murmur'st, I will rend an oak
295   And peg thee in his knotty entrails till
        Thou hast howled away twelve winters.

ARIEL.   Pardon, master.
        I will be correspondent[77] to command
        And do my spriting gently.[78]

PROSPERO.   Do so; and after two days
        I will discharge thee.

ARIEL.   That's my noble master!
300 What shall I do? Say what? What shall I do?

PROSPERO. Go make thyself like a nymph o' th' sea. Be subject
        To no sight but thine and mine, invisible

75. hests: Orders.
76. more potent ministers: More powerful agents.

77. correspondent: Obedient.
78. gently: Graciously.

52 Discussion Ask students how Sycorax is a kind of mirror-image of Prospero.

53 Discussion Have students decide what, if anything, Miranda and Sycorax's child have in common.

54 Enrichment Explain to students that the name *Caliban* is an anagram for cannibal. Then tell them that in creating Caliban, Shakespeare may have been influenced by Europeans' negative reports about encounters with Native Americans. (The French philosopher Montaigne took a different, more positive view of Native Americans in his essay "On Cannibals.")

    Shakespeare may also have been influenced by traditional depictions of a creature known as the European wild man. This mythical creature, governed by lust rather than reason, appeared in paintings and was represented in court entertainments.

55 Discussion Ask students whether Ariel should be more grateful to his master and whether Prospero is justified in threatening him.

nouns: ". . . And then I loved thee / And showed thee all the qualities o' th' isle, / The fresh *springs*, brine *pits*, barren *place* and fertile. / Cursed be I that did so! All the charms / Of Sycorax—*toads*, *beetles*, *bats*, light on you!" (lines 336–340) His early complaint, "I must eat my dinner," says much about him.

56 **Enrichment** Tell students that the word *strange*, in various forms, appears quite often in the play. Have them find additional examples and, if possible, link the repetition of this word to one or more of the play's themes.

57 **Discussion** Ask students why Caliban's labors are necessary to Prospero. Also ask them why Prospero calls Caliban "earth." How does this use of the word "earth" point up the contrast between Caliban and Ariel? Finally, you might ask students how Caliban should speak his lines and what kind of costume he should wear.

58 **Master Teacher Note** Have students research the costumes used for Ariel and Caliban in different productions of *The Tempest*. Students can sketch the most memorable costumes and show these sketches to the rest of the class. A book that illustrates such costumes is *The Annotated Shakespeare*, edited by A. L. Rowse (New York: Greenwich House, 1984).

59 **Enrichment** Point out to students that Caliban has a kind of eloquence, even when he curses. Have them look for additional examples of this eloquence and consider what it reveals about his character.

60 **Discussion** Ask students how Caliban's claim that Prospero has usurped the island relates to Prospero's loss of his dukedom. How seriously does Shakespeare intend us to take Caliban's claim?

To every eyeball else. Go take this shape
And hither come in't. Go! Hence with diligence!　　[*Exit* ARIEL.]

305　Awake, dear heart, awake! Thou hast slept well.
　　　Awake!

MIRANDA. The strangeness of your story put
　　　Heaviness[79] in me.

PROSPERO.　　　　　Shake it off. Come on.
　　　We'll visit Caliban, my slave, who never
　　　Yields us kind answer.

MIRANDA.　　　　　　　'Tis a villain, sir,
　　　I do not love to look on.

310 PROSPERO.　　　　　　　But as 'tis,
　　　We cannot miss[80] him. He does make our fire,
　　　Fetch in our wood, and serves in offices
　　　That profit us. What, ho! Slave! Caliban!
　　　Thou earth, thou! Speak!

CALIBAN. [*Within*]　　　　There's wood enough within.

315 PROSPERO. Come forth, I say! There's other business for thee.
　　　Come, thou tortoise! When?

[*Enter* ARIEL *like a water nymph.*]

　　　Fine apparition! My quaint[81] Ariel,
　　　Hark in thine ear.　　　　　　　　　[*Whispers.*]

ARIEL.　　　　　My lord, it shall be done.　　[*Exit.*]

PROSPERO. Thou poisonous slave, got by the devil himself
320　Upon thy wicked dam, come forth!

[*Enter* CALIBAN.]

CALIBAN. As wicked dew as e'er my mother brushed
　　　With raven's feather from unwholesome fen
　　　Drop on you both! A southwest[82] blow on ye
　　　And blister[83] you all o'er!

325 PROSPERO. For this, be sure, tonight thou shalt have cramps,
　　　Side-stitches that shall pen thy breath up. Urchins[84]
　　　Shall, for that vast of night that they may work,[85]
　　　All exercise on thee; thou shalt be pinched
　　　As thick as honeycomb, each pinch more stinging
　　　Than bees that made 'em.

330 CALIBAN.　　　　　　I must eat my dinner.
　　　This island's mine by Sycorax my mother,
　　　Which thou tak'st from me. When thou cam'st first,

79. **Heaviness:** Sleepiness.

80. **miss:** Manage without.

81. **quaint:** Clever; ingenious.

82. **southwest:** A wind believed to carry the plague.
83. **blister:** Give you blisters, or sores
84. **Urchins:** Goblins.
85. **vast . . . work:** The long period of the night when goblins are permitted to do as they wish.

Grammar in Action

Using That and Which The pronoun *that* refers to people or things, while the pronoun *which* refers only to things.

　EXAMPLES: The play, which is one of my favorites, is being performed tonight.

　The actress *that* (or *who*, not *which*) impressed you at the audition will be here soon.

　In Shakespeare's time, however, the rules of grammar were not as defined as they are now. You might therefore find him using these pronouns as we do, but you may also find him using the pronoun *which* for people:

PROSPERO. For this, be sure, tonight thou shalt have cramps,
　　　Side-stitches *that* shall pen thy breath up . . .
CALIBAN. For I am all the subjects *that* you have,
　　　Which first was mine own king; . . .

　In the first example, Shakespeare uses the pronoun *that* because Prospero is referring to a thing—side-stitches. In the next example, Shakespeare has Caliban correctly use *that* to refer to subjects. However, he also has

Thou strok'st me and made much of me; wouldst give me
Water with berries in't; and teach me how
335 To name the bigger light, and how the less,
That burn by day and night. And then I loved thee
And showed thee all the qualities o' th' isle,
The fresh springs, brine pits, barren place and fertile.
Cursed be I that did so! All the charms
340 Of Sycorax—toads, beetles, bats, light on you!
For I am all the subjects that you have,
Which first was mine own king; and here you sty⁸⁶ me
In this hard rock,⁸⁷ whiles you do keep from me
The rest o' th' island.

PROSPERO.   Thou most lying slave,
345 Whom stripes⁸⁸ may move, not kindness! I have used thee
(Filth as thou art) with humane care, and lodged thee
In mine own cell till thou didst seek to violate
The honor of my child.

CALIBAN. O ho, O ho! Would't had been done!
350 Thou didst prevent me; I had peopled else
This isle with Calibans.

MIRANDA.   Abhorrèd slave,
Which any print of goodness wilt not take,
Being capable of all ill!⁸⁹ I pitied thee,
Took pains to make thee speak, taught thee each hour
355 One thing or other. When thou didst not, savage,
Know thine own meaning, but wouldst gabble like
A thing most brutish, I endowed thy purposes
With words that made them known. But thy vile race,
Though thou didst learn, had that in't which good natures
360 Could not abide to be with. Therefore wast thou
Deservedly confined into this rock, who hadst
Deserved more than a prison.

CALIBAN. You taught me language, and my profit on't
Is, I know how to curse. The red plague rid⁹⁰ you
For learning⁹¹ me your language!

365 **PROSPERO.**   Hagseed, hence!
Fetch us in fuel. And be quick, thou'rt best,⁹²
To answer other business. Shrug'st thou, malice?
If thou neglect'st or dost unwillingly
What I command, I'll rack thee with old cramps,
370 Fill all thy bones with aches, make thee roar
That beasts shall tremble at thy din.

CALIBAN.   No, pray thee.
[*Aside*] I must obey. His art is of such pow'r

---

86. sty: Lodge or pen up, as in a pigsty.
87. rock: Cave.

88. stripes: Whiplashes.

89. print . . . ill: Impression of goodness will not take since you are capable only of making an evil impression.

90. rid: Destroy.
91. learning: Teaching.

92. thou'rt best: You'd better.

---

61 Discussion To what is Caliban referring?

62 Enrichment Point out to students that Shakespeare uses rhythm to help characterize Caliban. In these two lines, for instance, the spondees and trochees suggest his roughness. Have the students scan these lines to confirm this observation.

63 Enrichment Shakespeare portrays Caliban as a creature who is unable to control his lust, like the so-called wild men depicted in European art.

64 Enrichment It appears as if Prospero tried to educate Caliban but that the education did not "take." Renaissance Europeans speculated about the extent to which Native Americans could be civilized.

65 Discussion Ask students whether they think Prospero is upset by his failure to educate and improve Caliban. Have them support their answers with evidence from the play.

✿ Videodisc To prepare students for understanding the relationship between Prospero and Caliban, play the segment on the *Shakespeare in Rehearsal: The Tempest* Videodisc that dramatizes this scene.

Frames 17195 to 22862

66

> It would control my dam's god, Setebos,[93]
> And make a vassal of him.

PROSPERO.   So, slave; hence!   [*Exit* CALIBAN.]

67 [*Enter* FERDINAND; *and* ARIEL *(invisible), playing and singing.*]

Ariel's song.

375 Come unto these yellow sands,
        And then take hands:
     Curtsied when you have and kissed
        The wild waves whist,[94]
     Foot it featly[95] here and there;
380 And, sweet sprites, the burden bear.
        Hark, hark!
        [*Burden, dispersedly*[96]] Bow, wow!
     The watchdogs bark.
        [*Burden, dispersedly*] Bow, wow!
     Hark, hark! I hear
     The strain of strutting chanticleer[97]
385   Cry cock-a-diddle-dow.

FERDINAND. Where should this music be? I' th' air or th' earth?
     It sounds no more; and sure it waits upon
     Some god o' th' island. Sitting on a bank,
     Weeping again the King my father's wrack,
390 This music crept by me upon the waters,
     Allaying both their fury and my passion[98]
     With its sweet air. Thence I have followed it,
     Or it hath drawn me rather; but 'tis gone.
     No, it begins again.

68

Ariel's song.

395 Full fathom five[99] thy father lies;
        Of his bones are coral made;
     Those are pearls that were his eyes;
        Nothing of him that doth fade
     But doth suffer a sea change
400 Into something rich and strange.
     Sea nymphs hourly ring his knell;
                    [*Burden*] Ding-dong.
     Hark! Now I hear them—ding-dong bell.

FERDINAND. The ditty does remember my drowned father.
     This is no mortal business, nor no sound
405 That the earth owes.[100] I hear it now above me.

PROSPERO. The fringed curtains of thine eye advance[101]
     And day what thou seest yond.

93. Setebos: The name of a South American Indian god who was mentioned in a travel book by a sixteenth-century Englishman.

94. kissed . . . whist: Kissed the wild waves into silence.

95. featly: Nimbly.

96. *Burden, dispersedly:* A stage direction calling for a background sound of dogs and later of a crowing rooster.

97. chanticleer: Rooster, originally the name of the rooster character in popular medieval fables.

98. passion: Emotion; sorrow.

99. Full fathom five: Fully or completely at a depth of 30 feet in water.

100. owes: Owns; possesses.

101. advance: Look up.

Commentary

Music in *The Tempest* Ariel's songs introduce the theme of music in the play and its relation to Prospero's magical art. In Renaissance writing music is often a symbol of the orderly nature of the cosmos and humans' ability to imitate that order. The connection between music and magic goes back to early cultures, in which magical incantations were used.

In this scene Ferdinand says (lines 390–392) that Ariel's music has calmed not only himself but the sea. The first song stresses this calming and harmonizing power. Ariel calls on his listeners to enter into a dance, and the waves that seem to have sunk the ship are to be "kissed" into silence. The mysterious second song describes a transformation that the king's drowned body undergoes deep within the sea. While the living bones and eyes become things which are gemlike and beautiful, the adjectives "rich and strange" emphasize that the change is not completely positive. Living flesh is exchanged for what is lovely but lifeless. The eerie beauty of the song perfectly fits Ariel, who lacks the human passions of sympathy and grief.

As for Ferdinand, the music seems to put him in a mood of wonder beyond grief. It has "drawn" him (line 393), and his bewilderment leaves him without defenses when he first sees Miranda.

MIRANDA.　　　　　　　　　　What is't? A spirit?
Lord, how it looks about! Believe me, sir,
It carries a brave form. But 'tis a spirit.

410　**PROSPERO.** No, wench; it eats, and sleeps, and hath such senses
As we have, such. This gallant which thou seest
Was in the wrack; and, but he's something stained
With grief (that's beauty's canker), thou mightst call him
A goodly person. He hath lost his fellows
And strays about to find 'em.

415　**MIRANDA.**　　　　　　　　　　I might call him
A thing divine; for nothing natural
I ever saw so noble.

PROSPERO.　　　　　　　*[Aside]* It goes on, I see,
As my soul prompts it. Spirit, fine spirit, I'll free thee
Within two days for this.

FERDINAND.　　　　　　　　　Most sure, the goddess
420　On whom these airs attend! Vouchsafe my prayer
May know if you remain[102] upon this island,
And that you will some good instruction give
How I may bear me[103] here. My prime request,
Which I do last pronounce, is (O you wonder!)
If you be maid or no?

425　**MIRANDA.**　　　　　　　　　No wonder, sir,
But certainly a maid.

FERDINAND.　　　　　　　My language? Heavens!
I am the best of them that speak this speech,
Were I but where 'tis spoken.

PROSPERO.　　　　　　　　　How? The best?
What wert thou if the King of Naples heard thee?

430　**FERDINAND.** A single[104] thing, as I am now, that wonders
To hear thee speak of Naples. He does hear me;
And that he does I weep. Myself am Naples,
Who with mine eyes, never since at ebb, beheld
The King my father wracked.

MIRANDA.　　　　　　　　　Alack, for mercy!

435　**FERDINAND.** Yes, faith, and all his lords, the Duke of Milan
And his brave son being twain.[105]

PROSPERO.　　　　　　　*[Aside]* The Duke of Milan
And his more braver daughter could control[106] thee,
If now 'twere fit to do 't. At the first sight
They have changed eyes.[107] Delicate Ariel,

---

102. remain: Live; dwell.

103. bear me: Behave; conduct myself.

104. single: Helpless; alone; solitary.

105. twain: Two.

106. control: Disprove; prove wrong.
107. changed eyes: Exchanged glances like lovers.

---

69 Clarification Remind students that the only men Miranda has seen are her father and Caliban. It is not surprising, therefore, that Ferdinand makes such an impression on her.

70 Clarification Explain to students that this aside by Prospero indicates that it was his plan all along for Miranda and Ferdinand to fall in love.

Also, you might want to review for students the differences between an aside, a soliloquy, and a dramatic speech. Ask them why, in this play, asides by Prospero might serve an especially important function.

71 Discussion Ask students how Ferdinand's reaction to Miranda mirrors her own reaction to him.

72 Discussion Have students explain what Ferdinand means by saying, "I am the best of them that speak this speech, . . ." Also have them consider why he makes this statement.

73 **Discussion** Ask students what Prospero means by this statement. Have them decide whether or not they agree with Prospero. Then point out to them that throughout the play, Prospero stands for discipline and chastity.

74 **Discussion** Have students discuss Miranda's linking of outer and inner beauty. Is her statement true? What does it reveal about her experience of the world?

75 **Discussion** Ask students what Ferdinand's reaction to Prospero's unjust accusations reveals about the young man.

76 **Discussion** Ask students why Prospero replies so "ungently" to his daughter. Does this response reflect his true feelings? Why or why not?

440   I'll set thee free for this. [*To* FERDINAND] A word, good sir.
I fear you have done yourself some wrong.[108] A word!

MIRANDA. Why speaks my father so ungently? This
Is the third man that e'er I saw; the first
That e'er I sighed for. Pity move my father
To be inclined my way!

445   FERDINAND.   O, if a virgin,
And your affection not gone forth, I'll make you
The Queen of Naples.

PROSPERO.   Soft, sir! One word more.

73   [*Aside*] They are both in either's pow'rs. But this swift business
I must uneasy make, lest too light winning
Make the prize light. [*To* FERDINAND] One word more! I
450   charge thee
That thou attend me. Thou dost here usurp
The name thou ow'st[109] not, and hast put thyself
Upon this island as a spy, to win it
From me, the lord on't.

FERDINAND.   No, as I am a man!

455   MIRANDA. There's nothing ill can dwell in such a temple.

74   If the ill spirit have so fair a house,
Good things will strive to dwell with't.

PROSPERO.   Follow me.
[*To* MIRANDA] Speak not you for him; he's a traitor. [*To*
FERDINAND] Come!
I'll manacle thy neck and feet together;
460   Sea water shalt thou drink; thy food shall be
The fresh-brook mussels, withered roots, and husks
Wherein the acorn cradled. Follow!

FERDINAND.   No.

75   I will resist such entertainment till
Mine enemy has more pow'r.
            [*He draws, and is charmed from moving.*]

MIRANDA.   O dear father,
465   Make not too rash a trial of him, for
He's gentle and not fearful.[110]

PROSPERO.   What, I say,

76   My foot my tutor?[111] [*To* FERDINAND] Put thy sword up,
traitor—
Who mak'st a show but dar'st not strike, thy conscience
Is so possessed with guilt! Come, from thy ward![112]
470   For I can here disarm thee with this stick[113]
And make thy weapon drop.

108. **done . . . wrong:** Spoken falsely.

109. **ow'st:** Own.

110. **gentle . . . fearful:** Of good birth and courageous.

111. **My . . . tutor?** Am I to be taught by one so far below me?

112. **ward:** Position of defense.

113. **stick:** Prospero's magic wand.

77 Clarification Tell students that sometimes Shakespeare's lines also hint at stage directions. What direction does this line suggest?

MIRANDA.   Beseech you, father!

PROSPERO. Hence! Hang not on my garments.   **77**

MIRANDA.   Sir, have pity.
     I'll be his surety.

PROSPERO.   Silence! One word more
     Shall make me chide thee, if not hate thee. What,
475 An advocate for an impostor? Hush!

79 **Enrichment** Inform students that Shakespeare often contrasts characters to illuminate their different natures. Ferdinand is now, like Caliban, a slave of Prospero. Yet how does Ferdinand differ from Caliban in his response to Miranda and to his loss of liberty?

Explain, too, that the last part of Ferdinand's speech relates to the theme of freedom and slavery. Have them keep this remark in mind as they read about Caliban's bid for liberty.

80 **Enrichment** Ferdinand's comment about liberty also relates to Ariel's desire for freedom. Ask students how Ferdinand and Ariel compare in their attitudes toward liberty and service.

Cooperative Learning Divide the class into small groups and have each group practice performing a scene or portion of a scene from the first act.

Closure and Extension

ANSWERS TO THINKING ABOUT THE SELECTION

1. In the first scene, the ship appears to sink in the tempest. Prospero, however, asserts that "no harm" has been done.
2. Prospero's brother, Antonio, usurped his dukedom and then arranged to put Prospero and Miranda out to sea in a decrepit vessel. Gonzalo, while following these orders, provided them with supplies and books. Their ship took them to this island.
3. Prospero used his magic to free Ariel from "a cloven pine" in which Sycorax had confined him. Prospero learned about the island from Caliban, but when Caliban tried to rape Miranda, Prospero used his magic to enslave him.
4. (a) Sebastian and Antonio are more insolent and less humorous than Gonzalo. (b) The difference suggests that Gonzalo might be a better man.
5. Prospero may have been too involved in his studies, neglecting the responsibilities of power. He may be afraid of the complexities of human interactions.
6. (a) Prospero is angry at Caliban. He is pleased by Ariel's service, and

Thou think'st there is no more such shapes as he,
Having seen but him and Caliban. Foolish wench!
To th' most of men this is a Caliban,
And they to him are angels.

MIRANDA.   My affections
480 Are then most humble. I have no ambition
To see a goodlier man.

PROSPERO. [*To* FERDINAND] Come on, obey!
Thy nerves[114] are in their infancy again
And have no vigor in them.

FERDINAND.   So they are.
My spirits, as in a dream, are all bound up.
485 My father's loss, the weakness which I feel,
The wrack of all my friends, nor this man's threats
To whom I am subdued, are but light to me,
Might I but through my prison once a day
Behold this maid. All corners else o' th' earth
490 Let liberty make use of.[115] Space enough
Have I in such a prison.

PROSPERO. [*Aside*]   It works. [*To* FERDINAND] Come on.
[*To* ARIEL] Thou hast done well, fine Ariel! [*To* FERDINAND]
Follow me.
[*To* ARIEL] Hark what thou else shalt do me.

MIRANDA.   Be of comfort.
My father's of a better nature, sir,
495 Than he appears by speech. This is unwonted
Which now came from him.

PROSPERO.   Thou shalt be as free
As mountain winds; but then[116] exactly do
All points of my command.

ARIEL.   To th' syllable.

PROSPERO. [*To* FERDINAND] Come, follow. [*To* MIRANDA]
Speak not for him.   [*Exit.*]

114. nerves: Sinews; muscles; strength.

115. All . . . of: Let freedom be in all the rest of the world.

116. but then: Until then.

Reader's Response *What is your first impression of Prospero?*

---

when he scolds him, he does so without the rancor he shows toward Caliban. (b) Ariel is a more willing and efficient servant and seems to share Prospero's delight in play and magical creation. (c) He is domineering toward both of them and seems to be afraid that they will escape from him.
7. Answers will differ. Most students will respond that Prospero loves his daughter but realizes she lacks experience and does not take her fully into his confidence. Perceptive students will notice that he is uneasy in the role of a father, without the accouterments of his magic.
8. (a) The opening scene evokes a mood of distress and fear. The second scene is calm. (b) In the second scene Prospero appears to be in complete control and assures his daughter that the tempest was only an illusion.
9. (a) Answers will differ. Students may indicate the transformation of Alonso in Ariel's song. Also, the music transforms Ferdinand's grief into wonder. (b) Answers will differ. Most students will see that Prospero's magic is the cause of the magical transformations in the play.
10. Answers will differ. Some students may feel that Prospero will teach the

THINKING ABOUT THE SELECTION

Clarifying

1. How does the apparent fate of the ship at the end of the first scene differ from its fate according to Prospero?
2. What events caused Prospero and his daughter to settle on the island?
3. How did he gain power over his servants Ariel and Caliban?

Interpreting

4. (a) How does the attitude of Sebastian and Antonio toward the Boatswain differ from that of Gonzalo? (b) What does this difference reveal about the characters?
5. What fault in Prospero may have led to his loss of the dukedom?
6. (a) Are there differences in Prospero's treatment of Ariel and of Caliban? (b) What are the reasons for those differences? (c) Are there also underlying similarities in his treatment of them? Explain.
7. How would you describe the relationship between Miranda and her father?
8. (a) How does the mood of the opening scene contrast with the mood at the start of scene ii? (b) What accounts for the contrast?
9. (a) Transformation is a key theme of the play. In addition to Miranda and Ferdinand falling in love, what other transformation occurs in Act I? (b) What is the relationship between magic and transformation?

Applying

10. What do you think Prospero will do to those who have stolen his dukedom?

ANALYZING LITERATURE

Understanding Exposition

Exposition refers to the way in which a playwright provides essential background information in the opening scenes of a play. In Act I of *The Tempest*, Shakespeare introduces all the main characters, establishes the setting, summarizes the events leading up to the present moment, and touches on the important theme of magical transformation.

1. (a) How does Shakespeare try to make Prospero's explanations to Miranda less tedious for the audi-

ence? (b) Is this device successful? Why or why not?
2. How do the first two scenes complement each other as introductions to Alonso, Antonio, and Gonzalo?
3. The essence of drama is **conflict**, or the struggle between two or more characters or within a character. What conflicts are revealed or hinted at in Act I?

CRITICAL THINKING AND READING

Appreciating Shakespeare's Songs

Shakespeare's songs are not simply pleasant diversions from the action. Frequently they sum up the meaning of a scene or the situation of a character. Ariel's mysterious song "Full fathom five" (I.ii.395–402) calms both the waters and Ferdinand's grief. It makes death by drowning seem like a weird and lovely transformation, and it anticipates the other transformations Prospero's art will bring about in the play.

1. Ariel says Alonso's bones will become "coral" and his eyes "pearls." What is similar about both these transformations?
2. Lines 398–400 sum up the song. (a) Paraphrase them, spelling out in your own words what Ariel says. (b) What in the original does your paraphrase fail to capture?
3. (a) What are the implications of the words "rich and strange"? (b) What does the second adjective add to the first?

THINKING AND WRITING

Contrasting Characters

Caliban and Ariel are both "natives" of the island and Prospero's servants. However, Shakespeare contrasts them in many ways—in their interests, their actions, their language, their personalities, and their relation to Prospero. Reread their first long speeches and freewrite about the differences between the two. Then use your notes to write a paper contrasting these characters. Explain the motivations that give rise to their contrasting natures. In revising your essay, make sure your opening paragraph states what you feel is the central difference between them.

(continued from bottom of page)

and some of the passengers on the ship. It also reveals a serious conflict between Prospero and Caliban and a milder one between Prospero and Ariel. While Prospero and Ferdinand also seem to be at odds, there is a suggestion that this conflict is only apparent. Perceptive students may also realize that the second scene suggests a conflict within Prospero, who may be nervous about leaving his charmed island.

ANSWERS TO CRITICAL THINKING AND READING

1. Answers will differ. Students may respond that in each case a part of the human body becomes something nonhuman, more enduring, and of a gemlike nature. Also, both transformations are unusual or strange. Especially perceptive students may point out the eerie qualities of this change from living tissue to lifeless pearls or coral.
2. (a) The sea changes every part of his body into something valuable and unusual. (b) Answers will differ; however, most students will realize that their summaries fail to capture the haunting beauty of the original.
3. (a) Answers will differ. Students may respond that these words suggest Alonso is being magically transformed and made into something valuable but also something cold and lifeless. (b) Answers will differ. Some students will indicate that it makes the transformation seem more unusual, as if in a fairy tale. It also introduces a cold, eerie note.

THINKING AND WRITING

Writing Across the Curriculum
Inform the social studies department that you are reading this selection. Ask a social studies teacher to assist students in researching the British expedition that was shipwrecked on Bermuda. Then have students write a report on this expedition.

evil-doers a lesson but then forgive them.

Challenge Find a piece of music that could serve as the strange music of Prospero's island.

ANSWERS TO ANALYZING LITERATURE

1. (a) Prospero interrupts his exposition to ask whether Miranda is paying attention. (b) Answers will differ. Some students may feel that this device is not successful because it is too transparent and artificial. Others may point out that it is effective because it reveals Prospero's nervousness about

speaking only as a father and not as a magician.
2. In the first scene these men reveal their characters through their words and actions in a crisis. In the second scene Prospero gives us his perspective on these men.
3. Answers will differ. In the first scene there is a conflict between humans and nature. The second scene reveals a conflict between Prospero

Literary Focus Explain to students that Renaissance speculations about human nature were fueled by the discovery of the New World and the Native Americans who inhabited it. Ask students to imagine how we would react if one of our space probes encountered evidence of extraterrestrial civilizations. How might such a discovery affect our conceptions of living matter, intelligence, and the place of humans in the universe? Tell students that the discovery of the New World was an event of this magnitude for Renaissance Europeans.

Writing/Prior Knowledge Divide the class into small groups and have each group create a list of guidelines by which to judge a civilized person. Then have students do the assignment.

ESL Teaching Strategy Give ESL students the opportunity to report to the class on their culture's ideas about civilized behavior.

Vocabulary

Preteach the following vocabulary words:

spendthrift (spend´ thrift´) *n.*: A person who spends money carelessly

paragon (par´ ə gän´) *n.*: A model of perfection

beseech (bē sēch´) *v.*: Ask earnestly

importuned (im´ pôr tōōnd´) *v.*: Asked for urgently

mettle (met´ 'l) *n.*: Courage, spirit

supplant (sə plant´) *v.*: Take someone's place through force or plotting

credulous (krej´ ōō ləs) *adj.*: Tending to believe too readily

Commentary

Writing

The Tempest, Act II

Themes. Are humans naturally good? Are civilized Europeans better than people from different regions of the world? These are questions that troubled Shakespeare and other Renaissance writers, and they still have meaning for our own time. Shakespeare dealt with these issues as a playwright, by dramatizing them as **themes,** or central concerns, of *The Tempest.*

Shakespeare's thoughts about such matters were no doubt influenced by Montaigne's "On Cannibals," an essay he was reading when he wrote the play. In his skeptical fashion, Montaigne challenges the notion that Renaissance Europeans are superior to the "barbaric" Native Americans. He suggests that such "civilized" customs as torture are less reasonable and more barbaric than the practices of the natives. Also, he describes the customs of a variety of different peoples in order to undercut the complacency of Europeans. Such variety reveals that European culture is one of many and not the embodiment of human reason.

The Tempest offers a dramatic proving ground for Montaigne's ideas. In this play men from a European court come to an uncivilized island. Although the play is set in the Mediterranean, the island conveys the feeling of a new and unexplored world. (Shakespeare may have been influenced in his depiction of Prospero's island by accounts of a shipwreck in Bermuda in 1609.) On the island the Europeans confront two human beings, Miranda and Caliban, who have not been exposed to Europe. Neither is entirely savage, of course, for both have been brought up by Prospero. However, the play repeatedly insists on a comparison between "civilized" and "uncivilized" behavior, especially in the Caliban scenes. As in Montaigne's essay, the Europeans come out looking worse in such comparisons.

What do you think makes a person truly civilized? Is it dress, proper behavior, knowledge of culture, or other attributes? Spend some time freewriting about this topic.

Objectives

Thematic

To understand Renaissance perspectives on civilization and culture

Skills

1 To understand themes
2 To trace sources
3 To recognize diction as a character trait
4 To write as a Caribbean Islander

Act II

Scene i. *Another part of the island.*

[*Enter* ALONSO, SEBASTIAN, ANTONIO, GONZALO, ADRIAN, FRANCISCO, *and others.*]

GONZALO. Beseech you, sir, be merry. You have cause
  (So have we all) of joy; for our escape
  Is much beyond our loss. Our hint of[1] woe
  Is common; every day some sailor's wife,
5 The master of some merchant,[2] and the merchant,
  Have just our theme of woe. But for the miracle,
  I mean our preservation, few in millions
  Can speak like us. Then wisely, good sir, weigh
  Our sorrow with our comfort.

ALONSO.   Prithee, peace.

10 **SEBASTIAN.** [*Aside to* ANTONIO] He receives comfort like cold porridge.[3]

ANTONIO. [*Aside to* SEBASTIAN] The visitor[4] will not give him o'er so.[5]

SEBASTIAN. Look, he's winding up the watch of his wit; by and by it
15 will strike.

GONZALO. Sir—

SEBASTIAN. [*Aside to* ANTONIO] One. Tell.[6]

GONZALO. When every grief is entertained, that's offered
  Comes to the entertainer—

20 **SEBASTIAN.** A dollar.[7]

GONZALO. Dolor[8] comes to him, indeed. You have spoken truer
  than you purposed.

SEBASTIAN. You have taken it wiselier[9] than I meant you should.

GONZALO. Therefore, my lord—

25 **ANTONIO.** Fie, what a spendthrift is he of his tongue!

ALONSO. I prithee, spare.[10]

GONZALO. Well, I have done. But yet—

SEBASTIAN. He will be talking.

ANTONIO. Which, of he or Adrian, for a good wager, first begins to
30 crow?

---

1. **hint of:** Occasion for.

2. **master . . . merchant:** Captain of a ship owned by a merchant.

3. **porridge:** A kind of thick soup made with peas; hence there is an indirect pun on the word "peace."

4. **visitor:** A person who "visits" the sick or elderly and offers comfort.

5. **give . . . so:** Give up so easily; quickly stop offering unwanted comfort.

6. **One. Tell:** That's the first. Keep count.

7. **dollar:** English pronunciation of the German *taler*, silver coin.

8. **Dolor:** A Latin word meaning "pain" or "grief." The word was pronounced very much like "dollar."

9. **wiselier:** More wittily; more cleverly.

10. **prithee, spare:** Please spare me all this cleverness; please shut up.

2 Enrichment Explain to students how the succession of brief remarks affects the pace of the play. To illustrate your point, have several students perform this passage.

3 Discussion Ask students what this mockery reveals about the mockers, Sebastian and Antonio.

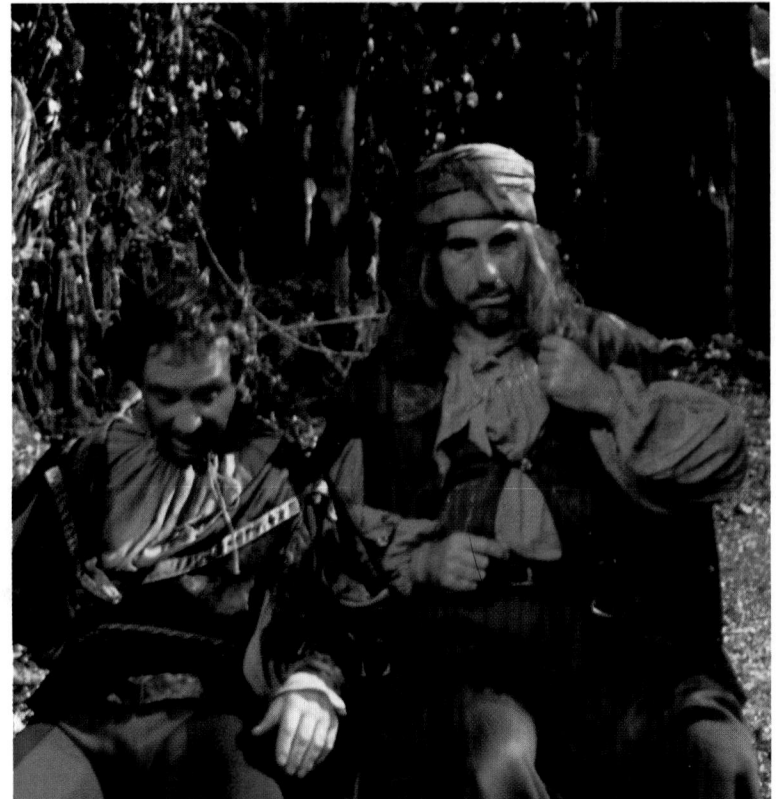

SEBASTIAN. The old cock.[11]

ANTONIO. The cock'rel.

SEBASTIAN. Done! The wager?

ANTONIO. A laughter.

35 **SEBASTIAN.** A match!

ADRIAN. Though this island seem to be desert—

ANTONIO. Ha, ha, ha!

SEBASTIAN. So, you're paid.

ADRIAN. Uninhabitable and almost inaccessible—

40 **SEBASTIAN.** Yet—

ADRIAN. Yet—

ANTONIO. He could not miss't.

11. old cock: Old rooster, Gonzalo.

ADRIAN. It must needs be of subtle, tender, and delicate temperance.[12]

45 **ANTONIO.** Temperance was a delicate wench.

SEBASTIAN. Ay, and a subtle, as he most learnedly delivered.

ADRIAN. The air breathes upon us here most sweetly.

SEBASTIAN. As if it had lungs, and rotten ones.

ANTONIO. Or as 'twere perfumed by a fen.

50 **GONZALO.** Here is everything advantageous to life.

ANTONIO. True; save means to live.

SEBASTIAN. Of that there's none, or little.

GONZALO. How lush and lusty the grass looks! How green!

ANTONIO. The ground indeed is tawny.

55 **SEBASTIAN.** With an eye of green[13] in't.

ANTONIO. He misses not much.

SEBASTIAN. No; he doth but mistake the truth totally.

GONZALO. But the rarity of it is—which is indeed almost beyond
credit—

60 **SEBASTIAN.** As many vouched rarities are.

GONZALO. That our garments, being, as they were, drenched in the
sea, hold, notwithstanding, their freshness and glosses, being
rather new-dyed than stained with salt water.

ANTONIO. If but one of his pockets could speak, would it not say he
65 lies?[14]

SEBASTIAN. Ay, or very falsely pocket up his report.[15]

GONZALO. Methinks our garments are now as fresh as when we put
them on first in Afric, at the marriage of the King's fair daughter
Claribel to the King of Tunis.

70 **SEBASTIAN.** 'Twas a sweet marriage, and we prosper well in our return.

ADRIAN. Tunis was never graced before with such a paragon to[16] their
queen.

GONZALO. Not since widow Dido's time.

75 **ANTONIO.** Widow? A pox o' that! How came that "widow" in?
Widow Dido!

SEBASTIAN. What if he had said "widower Aeneas"[17] too? Good
Lord, how you take it!

---

12. **temperance:** Mild climate. Also, moderation, and among Puritans, the name of a woman, as in the next line.

13. **eye of green:** Patch of green here and there in the parched earth.

14. **If . . . lies?** If one of Gonzalo's pockets could speak, wouldn't it prove him a liar by being water stained?

15. **pocket . . . report:** Cover up Gonzalo's lie by not being stained. Gonzalo can't win either way.

16. **to:** For.

17. **Widow Dido . . . widower Aeneas:** An allusion to a great love story in the national epic of Rome, the *Aeneid* by Virgil.

---

4 Clarification A fen is a low-lying piece of land that is swampy or marshy and therefore has an unpleasant odor.

5 Clarification The famous Shakespeare scholar George Lyman Kittredge explained this line as follows: "To 'pocket up' an insult or injury was to accept it without resentment as one accepts money that is one's due. Sebastian's thin jest implies that the pocket would be a false knave to allow such a lie to be told about it."

6 Clarification Dido entertained Aeneas at ancient Carthage, a city believed to be near present-day Tunis in North Africa.

7 Clarification Antonio mocks Gonzalo because it is peculiar to refer to the legendary lovers Aeneas and Dido as widower and widow, even though both had married previously. Despite Gonzalo's virtues, he is pedantic and long-winded. Antonio and Sebastian are cruel and shallow but not entirely inaccurate in their perception of Gonzalo.

8 Enrichment Inform students that in the *Aeneid*, Virgil tells how Dido fell in love with Aeneas when he was shipwrecked at Carthage. Later, Jupiter ordered Aeneas to abandon her and she killed herself.

This tragic story of love and abandonment is mentioned in a comic context, but the theme of abandonment recurs throughout the play in more serious contexts. Prospero and Miranda were, of course, abandoned at sea and, at the end of the play, Prospero will have to abandon his enchanted island.

ADRIAN. "Widow Dido" said you? You make me study of that. She
80   was of Carthage, not of Tunis.

GONZALO. This Tunis, sir, was Carthage.

ADRIAN. Carthage?

GONZALO. I assure you, Carthage.

ANTONIO. His word is more than the miraculous harp.[18]

85 SEBASTIAN. He hath raised the wall and houses too.

ANTONIO. What impossible matter will he make easy next?

SEBASTIAN. I think he will carry this island home in his pocket and
    give it his son for an apple.

ANTONIO. And, sowing the kernels of it in the sea, bring forth more
90   islands.

GONZALO. Ay!

ANTONIO. Why, in good time.

GONZALO. [*To* ALONSO] Sir, we were talking that our garments seem
    now as fresh as when we were at Tunis at the marriage of your
95   daughter, who is now Queen.

ANTONIO. And the rarest that e'er came there.

SEBASTIAN. Bate,[19] I beseech you, widow Dido.

ANTONIO. O, widow Dido? Ay, widow Dido!
GONZALO. Is not, sir, my doublet as fresh as the first day I wore it?
100   I mean, in a sort.[20]

ANTONIO. That "sort" was well fished for.

GONZALO. When I wore it at your daughter's marriage.

ALONSO. You cram these words into mine ears against
    The stomach of my sense.[21] Would I had never
105   Married my daughter there! For, coming thence,
    My son is lost; and, in my rate,[22] she too,
    Who is so far from Italy removed
    I ne'er again shall see her. O thou mine heir
    Of Naples and of Milan, what strange fish
    Hath made his meal on thee?

110 FRANCISCO.   Sir, he may live.
    I saw him beat the surges under him
    And ride upon their backs. He trod the water,
    Whose enmity he flung aside, and breasted
    The surge most swol'n that met him. His bold head
115   'Bove the contentious waves he kept, and oared

18. miraculous harp: The harp of Amphion, son of the Greek god Zeus, was played so perfectly that the stones for the walls of the city of Thebes slid into place by themselves. Gonzalo's words are more miraculous than the harp because they created a whole city by mistakenly identifying ancient Carthage with modern Tunis.

19. Bate: With the exception of.

20. in a sort: In a manner of speaking.

21. You . . . sense: You force comfort upon me so that it revolts against common sense.
22. rate: View; opinion.

Himself with his good arms in lusty stroke
To th' shore, that o'er his wave-worn basis bowed,
As stooping to relieve him. I no doubt
He came alive to land.

ALONSO. No, no, he's gone.

SEBASTIAN. [*To* ALONSO] Sir, you may thank yourself for this great
120   loss,
That would not bless our Europe with your daughter,
But rather loose her to an African,
Where she, at least, is banished from your eye
Who hath cause to wet the grief on't.

ALONSO. Prithee, peace.

125 **SEBASTIAN.** You were kneeled to and <u>importuned</u> otherwise
By all of us; and the fair soul herself
Weighed, between loathness and obedience, at
Which end o' th' beam should bow.²³ We have lost your son,
I fear, forever. Milan and Naples have
130   Moe²⁴ widows in them of this business' making
Than we bring men to comfort them.
The fault's your own.

ALONSO. So is the dear'st²⁵ o' th' loss.

GONZALO. My Lord Sebastian,
The truth you speak doth lack some gentleness,
135   And time to speak it in. You rub the sore
When you should bring the plaster.

SEBASTIAN. Very well.

ANTONIO. And most chirurgeonly.²⁶

GONZALO. [*To* ALONSO] It is foul weather in us all, good sir,
When you are cloudy.

SEBASTIAN. [*Aside to* ANTONIO] Foul weather?

ANTONIO. [*Aside to* SEBASTIAN] Very foul.

140 **GONZALO.** Had I plantation²⁷ of this isle, my lord—

ANTONIO. He'd sow't with nettle seed.

SEBASTIAN. Or docks, or mallows.

GONZALO. And were the king on't, what would I do?

SEBASTIAN. Scape being drunk for want of wine.

GONZALO. I' th' commonwealth I would by contraries²⁸
145   Execute all things. For no kind of traffic²⁹

---

23. Which . . . bow: To which should she yield.

24. Moe: More.

25. dear'st: Costliest.

26. chirurgeonly: As a surgeon might.

27. plantation: The right of colonization.

28. by contraries: Against prevailing customs.
29. traffic: Trade or business.

---

14 Master Teacher Note Students may not be fully aware how Shakespeare often fills out an iambic line when shifting to another speaker. Point out to them, for instance, how this occurs in line 119, and explain that the end of Francisco's speech, combined with Alonso's brief interjection, are counted as one line. Have them find other examples of this device. Then ask them to consider how the play might be different if every speech had to end with a complete iambic line.

15 Discussion Ask students what this reproach, timed as it is, reveals about Sebastian.

16 Discussion Ask students whether Gonzalo is correct. What does the remark suggest about Gonzalo?

17 Clarification Explain to students that the word *chirurgeon* is an archaic form of the modern word *surgeon*. This older word derives from the Middle English *cirurgian* and the Old French *cirurgien*.

18 Enrichment Tell students that Antonio and Sebastian react as if Gonzalo is beginning another one of his tedious lectures. Antonio purposely misconstrues "plantation" as "planting." Ask students, however, whether Gonzalo might have a motive other than the pleasure of hearing himself speak.

19 Enrichment Point out to students that Gonzalo is hearkening back to the Garden of Eden, mentioned in the first books of Genesis (see page 40). Before Adam and Eve were banished from Eden, they did not have to earn their living by the sweat of their brows. In addition to this implicit biblical allusion, Gonzalo refers explicitly to the classical myth of the Golden Age (see the Primary Source Note below and Enrichment note 20).

20 Enrichment Provide students with background on the Golden Age to which Gonzalo refers. Explain that in classical times, the history of the world was divided into various ages, each characterized by a different metal. The Golden Age was supposedly a time of universal peace. It was to history as spring is to the seasonal cycle. During this period the world was ruled by Cronus (Saturn). Zeus (Jupiter) presided over the following period, called the Silver Age. This period, not as happy as the first, was followed by progressively worse epochs, the Bronze Age and the Iron Age. These latter ages saw an increase in strife and the disappearance of justice and piety from the world.

21 Reading Strategy Have students predict how the sudden appearance of Ariel will transform this scene.

Would I admit; no name of magistrate;
Letters[30] should not be known; riches, poverty,
And use of service,[31] none; contract, succession,[32]
Bourn, bound of land, tilth, vineyard, none;[33]
150 No use of metal, corn, or wine, or oil;
No occupation; all men idle, all;
And women too, but innocent and pure;
No sovereignty.[34]

SEBASTIAN.   Yet he would be king on't.

ANTONIO. The latter end of his commonwealth forgets the
155   beginning.

19 GONZALO. All things in common nature should produce
Without sweat or endeavor. Treason, felony,
Sword, pike, knife, gun, or need of any engine[35]
Would I not have; but nature should bring forth,
160 Of it[36] own kind, all foison,[37] all abundance,
To feed my innocent people

SEBASTIAN. No marrying 'mong his subjects?

ANTONIO. None, man, all idle—knaves.

20 GONZALO. I would with such perfection govern, sir,
T' excel the Golden Age.

165 SEBASTIAN. [*Loudly*]   Save his Majesty!

ANTONIO. [*Loudly*] Long live Gonzalo!

GONZALO.   And—do you mark me, sir?

ALONSO. Prithee, no more. Thou dost talk nothing to me.

GONZALO. I do well believe your Highness; and did it to minister occasion[38] to these gentlemen, who are of such sensible[39] and
170   nimble lungs that they always use to laugh at nothing.

ANTONIO. 'Twas you we laughed at.

GONZALO. Who in this kind of merry fooling am nothing to you; so you may continue, and laugh at nothing still.

ANTONIO. What a blow was there given!

175 SEBASTIAN. And it had not fall'n flatlong.[40]

GONZALO. You are gentlemen of brave <u>mettle</u>; you would lift the moon out of her sphere if she would continue in it five weeks without changing.

21 [*Enter* ARIEL (*invisible*) *playing solemn music.*]

SEBASTIAN. We would so, and then go a-batfowling.[41]

30. **Letters:** Education; learning.
31. **service:** Servants.
32. **succession:** Inheritance.
33. **Bourn . . . none:** No boundaries or enclosures of land, farms, vineyards.
34. **I' th' commonwealth . . . sovereignty:** This entire speech by Gonzalo represents a rejection of the civilization of Shakespeare's day. Many of the ideas and even words are very close to an English translation of an essay by the great French writer Montaigne. The essay presented an idealized picture of American Indian life. It also was an early depiction of life in what has come to be called the "state of nature."
35. **engine:** Weapon.
36. **it:** Its.
37. **foison:** Rich harvest.

38. **minister occasion:** Offer an opportunity.
39. **sensible:** Sensitive.

40. **flatlong:** The flat side of the sword.

41. **We . . . a-batfowling:** We would use the light of the moon to hunt birds at night attracted by light and knock them down with bats or clubs.

Primary Source Note

Gonzalo's account of an imaginary utopia is taken at times verbatim from Montaigne's essay "On Cannibals." In this essay Montaigne describes the natives of the New World as inhabitants of a "golden age" before the fall:

This is a nation . . . in which there is no kind of commerce, no knowledge of letters, no science of numbers, no title of magistrate or of political superior, no habit of service, riches or poverty, no contracts, no inheritance, no divisions of property, only leisurely occupations, no respect for any kinship but the common ties, no clothes, no agriculture, no met-als, no use of corn or wine. The very words denoting lying, treason, deceit, greed, envy, slander, and forgiveness have never been heard.

Yet Shakespeare changes everything while keeping many of Montaigne's actual phrases. For where Montaigne is reporting what he has heard about an actual South American Indian tribe, Gonzalo is imagining an ideal commonwealth. Shakespeare stresses the imaginary nature of this utopia. It is informed by a courtier's nostalgia, a wish for a world that is simpler and less corrupt than his own. (Gonzalo had, however unwillingly, helped to unseat Prospero years before.) The speech is less a serious attempt to create

180 **ANTONIO.** Nay, good my lord, be not angry.

GONZALO. No, I warrant you; I will not adventure my discretion so
weakly.[42] Will you laugh me asleep? For I am very heavy.

ANTONIO. Go sleep, and hear us.
[*All sleep except* ALONSO, SEBASTIAN, *and* ANTONIO.]

185 **ALONSO.** What, all so soon asleep? I wish mine eyes
Would, with themselves, shut up my thoughts. I find
They are inclined to do so.

SEBASTIAN.   Please you, sir
Do not omit the heavy offer of it.
It seldom visits sorrow; when it doth,
It is a comforter.

190 **ANTONIO.**   We too, my lord,
Will guard your person while you take your rest,
And watch your safety.

ALONSO.   Thank you. Wondrous heavy.
                              [ALONSO *sleeps. Exit* ARIEL.]

SEBASTIAN. What a strange drowsiness possesses them!

ANTONIO. It is the quality o' th' climate.

SEBASTIAN.   Why
195 Doth it not then our eyelids sink? I find not
Myself disposed to sleep.

ANTONIO.   Nor I: my spirits are nimble.
They fell together all, as by consent.
They dropped as by a thunderstroke. What might,
Worthy Sebastian—O, what might?—No more!
200 And yet methinks I see it in thy face,
What thou shouldst be. Th' occasion speaks thee,[43] and
My strong imagination sees a crown
Dropping upon thy head.

SEBASTIAN.   What? Art thou waking?

ANTONIO. Do you not hear me speak?

SEBASTIAN.   I do; and surely
205 It is a sleepy language, and thou speak'st
Out of thy sleep. What is it thou didst say?
This is a strange repose, to be asleep
With eyes wide open; standing, speaking, moving,
And yet so fast asleep.

ANTONIO.   Noble Sebastian,
210 Thou let'st thy fortune sleep—die, rather; wink'st[44]
Whiles thou art waking.

---

42. **not adventure . . .
weakly:** I will not risk my
reputation by responding to
such weak wit.

43. **occasion speaks thee:**
Opportunity offers you.

44. **wink'st:** Close your eyes.

---

22 **Enrichment** Remind students that
Prospero used his magic in the
first act to put Miranda to sleep.

23 **Discussion** Ask students whether
they think the kindness displayed
by Antonio and Sebastian is genuine.

24 **Enrichment** Point out to students
the echoing and reechoing word
strange, which has already been
heard in Ariel's song about Alonso's magical transformation
(I.ii.400), Alonso's lament for Ferdinand (II.i.109), and elsewhere.

25 **Discussion** Now that Antonio and
Sebastian are plotting to usurp
Alonso's kingdom, ask students
whether this conspiracy surprises
them. If it does not, have them explain how Shakespeare hinted it
was coming.

26 **Enrichment** Point out to students
the references to sleep and waking. Many of the characters in the
play express uncertainty as to
whether they are waking or sleeping. This theme relates to the feeling of strangeness that pervades
the magical island. This disorienting strangeness, in turn, calls into
question the conventional boundaries between reality and illusion.

Explain to students that in a
well-made play, like *The Tempest*,
there is an intertwining of themes.

---

the ideal state than a somewhat muddled attempt to imagine a world without
the evil behavior he deplores but is unable to evade.

Shakespeare further complicates the speech by having Antonio and
Sebastian comment sardonically but accurately on its inadequacies: Gonzalo
does indeed forget, when he decries "sovereignty," that he began by proclaiming himself king. On a more profound level, Gonzalo's view of human
nature differs from that of Sebastian and Antonio. Gonzalo believes that civilization is corrupting and that without it, human beings would be good.

SEBASTIAN. Thou dost snore distinctly;
There's meaning in thy snores.

ANTONIO. I am more serious than my custom. You
Must be so too, if heed me; which to do
Trebles thee o'er.[45]

215 **SEBASTIAN.** Well, I am standing water.[46]

ANTONIO. I'll teach you how to flow.

SEBASTIAN. Do so. To ebb
Hereditary sloth instructs me.

ANTONIO. O,
If you but knew how you the purpose cherish
Whiles thus you mock it; how, in stripping it,
220 You more invest it![47] Ebbing men, indeed,
Most often do so near the bottom run
By their own fear or sloth.

SEBASTIAN. Prithee, say on,
The setting of thine eye and cheek proclaim
A matter[48] from thee; and a birth, indeed,
Which throes thee much[49] to yield.

225 **ANTONIO.** Thus, sir:
Although this lord of weak remembrance, this
Who shall be of as little memory
When he is earthed,[50] hath here almost persuaded
(For he's a spirit of persuasion, only
230 Professes to persuade[51]) the King his son's alive,
'Tis as impossible that he's undrowned
As he that sleeps here swims.

SEBASTIAN. I have no hope
That he's undrowned.

ANTONIO. O, out of that no hope
What great hope have you! No hope that way is
235 Another way so high a hope that even
Ambition cannot pierce a wink beyond,
But doubt discovery there.[52] Will you grant with me
That Ferdinand is drowned?

SEBASTIAN. He's gone.

ANTONIO. Then tell me,
Who's the next heir of Naples?

SEBASTIAN. Claribel.

240 **ANTONIO.** She that is Queen of Tunis; she that dwells
Ten leagues beyond man's life;[53] she that from Naples

45. **Trebles thee o'er:** Triples your present power.
46. **standing water:** Still water; not moving water, as between the tides.

47. **in stripping . . . invest it:** While seeming to deny ambition, you shape it all the more.

48. **matter:** Something of importance.
49. **throes thee much:** Gives you much pain.

50. **earthed:** Buried.

51. **For . . . persuade:** For he (Gonzalo) is the very spirit of conviction and is nothing more than a professional persuader.

52. **Ambition . . . there:** The eye of ambition cannot see beyond the present, and even doubts what it sees there.

53. **Ten . . . life:** Ten leagues (infinitely) farther than one could travel in a lifetime.

27 **Discussion** Ask students whether this conversation reflects a change in mood on the part of Antonio and Sebastian. If so, have students account for this change.

28 **Master Teacher Note** Students may not be fully aware that Shakespeare weaves together strands of imagery in his plays. First review with them the definition of imagery. Then point out all the water images in these lines. Ask students to recall any other water images from the first part of the play. Some of them are sure to remember Ariel's song about the transformation of Alonso's drowned body. Instruct students to look for additional examples of water imagery as they continue to read. Tell them to look for other types of imagery as well.

You may even want to encourage students to keep records of the various types of imagery, by act, scene, and line number. Remind them, however, that it is not enough to simply record images. They should also try to figure out how an image, or a pattern of images, relates to the themes of the play.

If students want to read more about images in Shakespeare's plays, refer them to *Shakespeare's Imagery*, by Carolyn Spurgeon.

Commentary

The Courtiers' Conspiracy The conspiracy hatched by Antonio and Sebastian recalls Antonio's original usurpation of Prospero's dukedom and displays with full clarity the evil that supposedly civilized men can commit. Students might consider why Prospero encourages this would-be crime by putting the rest of the court to sleep while Sebastian and Antonio remain awake. Their response to this situation shows how the island encourages the characters to be more overtly themselves. Just as Ferdinand and Miranda exhibit their natural sympathy and goodness, Sebastian and Antonio act out their basest instincts.

These two courtiers are moved by greed and the desire to dominate others. In the absence of a police force, they feel ready to do whatever they can manage. Students might consider Antonio's attitude toward conscience (lines 270–284), for it clearly sums up his attitude toward others. He does not fear conscience because he hardly believes it exists. Real things are material things, like a chilblain on the foot, or the "obedient steel" with which he plans to murder Alonso. (This belief is common to many Shakespearean villains, from Richard III to Lady Macbeth.)

The language of sleep and dream which appears so often in the play appears here as well (lines 193–213). Antonio's imagination, however, is lim-

Can have no note—unless the sun were post;[54]
The man i' th' moon's too slow—till newborn chins
Be rough and razorable;[55] she that from whom
245 We all were sea-swallowed, though some cast[56] again,
And by that destiny, to perform an act
Whereof what's past is prologue, what to come,
In yours and my discharge.

SEBASTIAN.   What stuff is this? How say you?
'Tis true my brother's daughter's Queen of Tunis;
250 So is she heir of Naples; 'twixt which regions
There is some space.

ANTONIO.   A space whose ev'ry cubit
Seems to cry out "How shall that Claribel
Measure us back to Naples? Keep in Tunis,
And let Sebastian wake!" Say this were death
255 That now hath seized them, why, they were no worse
Than now they are. There be that can rule Naples
As well as he that sleeps; lords that can prate
As amply and unnecessarily
As this Gonzalo; I myself could make
260 A chough of as deep chat.[57] O, that you bore
The mind that I do! What a sleep were this
For your advancement! Do you understand me?

SEBASTIAN. Methinks I do.

ANTONIO.   And how does your content
Tender[58] your own good fortune?

SEBASTIAN.   I remember
You did supplant your brother Prospero.

265 ANTONIO.   True.
And look how well my garments sit upon me,
Much feater[59] than before. My brother's servants
Were then my fellows; now they are my men.

SEBASTIAN. But, for your conscience—

270 ANTONIO. Ay, sir, where lies that? If 'twere a kibe,[60]
'Twould put me to my slipper; but I feel not
This deity in my bosom. Twenty consciences
That stand 'twixt me and Milan, candied be they
And melt, ere they molest! Here lies your brother,
275 No better than the earth he lies upon—
If he were that which now he's like, that's dead—
Whom I with this obedient steel (three inches of it)
Can lay to bed forever; whiles you, doing thus,

54. **post:** Mail courier.

55. **till . . . razorable:** Until newborn babes grow beards and have to shave.

56. **cast:** Cast up on shore; survive.

57. **I . . . chat:** I myself could make a crow sound as profound as Gonzalo.

58. **Tender:** Think of.

59. **feater:** More attractively; more fittingly.

60. **kibe:** An inflammation of the heel caused by cold.

29 **Teaching Tenth-Grade Students** Have tenth-grade students prepare a chart to keep track of the various conspiracies in the play.

30 **Enrichment** Inform students that many expressions that are now proverbial in the language were coined by Shakespeare. One example is the phrase, "What's past is prologue." Other examples, culled from *Bartlett's Familiar Quotations*, are "Sweet are the uses of adversity" (*As You Like It*, II.i.12); "Frailty, thy name is woman" (*Hamlet*, I.ii.146); and "I am a man / More sinned against than sinning" (*King Lear*, III.ii.59), to name only a few.

Not only was Shakespeare a great phrasemaker, but he also had a tremendous vocabulary. In his plays he uses about 30,000 words, and scholars estimate that the size of the average person's vocabulary today is about 15,000 words.

You might want to refer students to Bartlett's and have them identify other proverbial expressions that first appeared in Shakespeare's plays. You might also want to ask them to analyze what makes some of these phrases so memorable.

31 **Reading Strategy** Remind students that Prospero's magic made this conspiracy possible. Ask them why he might have given Sebastian and Antonio the chance to hatch their plot.

ited to an earthly "crown" (lines 202–203). The spiritual blindness of these men points up a secondary association of the sleep metaphor, the idea that the speakers are spiritually "asleep" and therefore unable to wake and see what is really present in the world. Prospero's attempt in the play will be to awaken this sleeping conscience.

To the perpetual wink for aye might put
280 This ancient morsel, this Sir Prudence, who
Should not upbraid our course. For all the rest,
They'll take suggestion as a cat laps milk;
They'll tell the clock[61] to any business that
We say befits the hour.

SEBASTIAN.   Thy case, dear friend,
285 Shall be my precedent. As thou got'st Milan,
I'll come by Naples. Draw thy sword. One stroke
Shall free thee from the tribute which thou payest,
And I the King shall love thee.

ANTONIO.   Draw together;
And when I rear my hand, do you the like,
To fall it on Gonzalo.   [*They draw.*]

290 SEBASTIAN.   O, but one word!

[*Enter* ARIEL (*invisible*) *with music and song.*]

ARIEL. My master through his art foresees the danger
That you, his friend, are in, and sends me forth
(For else his project dies) to keep them living.
                      [*Sings in* GONZALO's *ear.*]

                      While you here do snoring lie,
295   Open-eyed conspiracy
                           His time doth take.
                      If of life you keep a care,
                      Shake off slumber and beware.
                           Awake, awake!

ANTONIO. Then let us both be sudden.

300 SEBASTIAN. [*Wakes.*]   Now good angels
Preserve the King!   [*The others wake.*]

ALONSO. Why, how now? Ho, awake! Why are you drawn?
Wherefore this ghastly looking?

GONZALO.   What's the matter?

SEBASTIAN. Whiles we stood here securing your repose,
305 Even now, we heard a hollow burst of bellowing
Like bulls, or rather lions. Did't not wake you?
It struck mine ear most terribly.

ALONSO.   I heard nothing.

ANTONIO. O, 'twas a din to fright a monster's ear,
To make an earthquake! Sure it was the roar
Of a whole herd of lions.

61. tell the clock: agree to.

Grammar in Action

Diction refers to a person's choice of words. A sailor, for instance, will probably use many nautical terms in his speech:

BOATSWAIN. Down with the topmast! Yare! Lower, lower! Bring her to try with main course. (*The Tempest*, I.i.33-34)

A courtier, on the other hand, might use many terms relating to government:

GONZALO. I' th' commonwealth I would by contraries

Execute all things. For no king of traffic
Would I admit; no name of magistrate;

Shakespeare is always keenly aware of diction. Not only does he give his characters the words appropriate to their trade or station, but he also gives them language that reveals personality. Caliban, for instance, being an earthy creature, uses words related to the earth and to ways of moving over it:

CALIBAN. All the infections that the sun sucks up
From *bogs*, *fens*, *flats*, on Prosper fall, and make him

310 **ALONSO.**   Heard you this, Gonzalo?

GONZALO. Upon mine honor, sir, I heard a humming,
And that a strange one, too, which did awake me.
I shaked you, sir, and cried. As mine eyes opened,
I saw their weapons drawn. There was a noise,
315   That's verily.⁶² 'Tis best we stand upon our guard,
Or that we quit this place. Let's draw our weapons.

ALONSO. Lead off this ground, and let's make further search
For my poor son.

GONZALO.   Heavens keep him from these beasts!
For he is, sure, i' th' island.

ALONSO.   Lead away.

320 **ARIEL.** Prospero my lord shall know what I have done.
So, King, go safely on to seek thy son.   [*Exit.*]

⌐ 35 ¬

Scene ii. Another part of the island.

[*Enter* CALIBAN *with a burden of wood. A noise of thunder heard.*]

CALIBAN. All the infections that the sun sucks up
From bogs, fens, flats, on Prosper fall, and make him
By inchmeal¹ a disease! His spirits hear me,
And yet I needs must curse. But they'll nor pinch,
5   Fright me with urchin shows,² pitch me i' th' mire,
Nor lead me, like a firebrand,³ in the dark
Out of my way, unless he bid 'em. But
For every trifle are they set upon me;
Sometime like apes that mow⁴ and chatter at me,
10   And after bite me; then like hedgehogs which
Lie tumbling in my barefoot way and mount
Their pricks at my footfall; sometime am I
All wound with adders, who with cloven tongues
Do hiss me into madness.

[*Enter* TRINCULO.]

                        Lo, Now, lo!
15   Here comes a spirit of his, and to torment me
For bringing wood in slowly. I'll fall flat.
Perchance he will not mind me.   [*Lies down.*]

TRINCULO. Here's neither bush nor shrub to bear off⁵ any weather
at all, and another storm brewing; I hear it sing i' th' wind. Yond
20   same black cloud, yond huge one, looks like a foul bombard⁶
that would shed his liquor. If it should thunder as it did before,
I know not where to hide my head. Yond same cloud cannot

---

62. **verily:** The truth.

1. **By inchmeal:** Inch by inch.

2. **urchin shows:** Visions of hobgoblins.

3. **Nor . . . firebrand:** Nor lead me astray with such illusions as the will-o'-the-wisp.

4. **mow:** Make faces.

5. **bear off:** Protect against.

6. **bombard:** A large jug made of leather.

⌐ 36 ¬

⌐ 37 ¬

---

but fall by pailfuls. What have we here? A man or a fish? Dead or alive? A fish! He smells like a fish; a very ancient and fishlike smell; a kind of not of the newest Poor John.[7] A strange fish! Were I in England now, as once I was, and had but this fish painted,[8] not a holiday fool there would but give a piece of silver. There would this monster make a man;[9] any strange beast there makes a man. When they will not give a doit[10] to relieve a lame beggar, they will lay out ten to see a dead Indian. Legged like a man! and his fins like arms! Warm, o' my troth! I do now let loose my opinion, hold it no longer. This is no fish, but an islander, that hath lately suffered by a thunderbolt. [*Thunder.*] Alas, the storm is come again! My best way is to creep under his gaberdine; there is no other shelter hereabout. Misery acquaints a man with strange bedfellows. I will here shroud[11] till the dregs of the storm be past. [*Creeps under* CALIBAN'*s garment.*]

[*Enter* STEPHANO, *singing* (*a bottle in his hand*).]

STEPHANO.   I shall no more to sea, to sea;
                          Here shall I die ashore.

This is a very scurvy[12] tune to sing at a man's funeral. Well, here's my comfort.   [*Drinks.*]

             The master, the swabber, the boatswain, and I,
                 The gunner, and his mate,
             Loved Mall, Meg, and Marian, and Margery,
                 But none of us cared for Kate.
                 For she had a tongue with a tang,
                 Would cry to a sailor "Go hang!"
             She loved not the savor of tar nor of pitch;
             Yet a tailor might scratch her where'er she did itch.
                 Then to sea, boys, and let her go hang!

This is a scurvy tune too; but here's my comfort.   [*Drinks.*]

CALIBAN. Do not torment me! O!

STEPHANO. What's the matter? Have we devils here? Do you put tricks upon 's with savages and men of Inde, ha? I have not scaped drowning to be afeard now of your four legs. For it hath been said, "As proper a man as ever went on four legs cannot make him give ground"; and it shall be said so again, while Stephano breathes at' nostrils.

CALIBAN. The spirit torments me. O!

STEPHANO. This is some monster of the isle, with four legs, who hath got, as I take it, an ague.[13] Where the devil should he learn our language? I will give him some relief, if it be but for that. If I can recover[14] him, and keep him tame, and get to

7. Poor John: A type of fish similar to codfish.

8. painted: The picture of the fish painted on a sign would advertise the show.

9. make a man: Make a person's fortune.

10. doit: A coin of the lowest value.

11. shroud: Cover myself.

12. scurvy: Despicable.

13. ague: A feverish ailment characterized by violent shivering, similar to malaria.

14. recover: Cure.

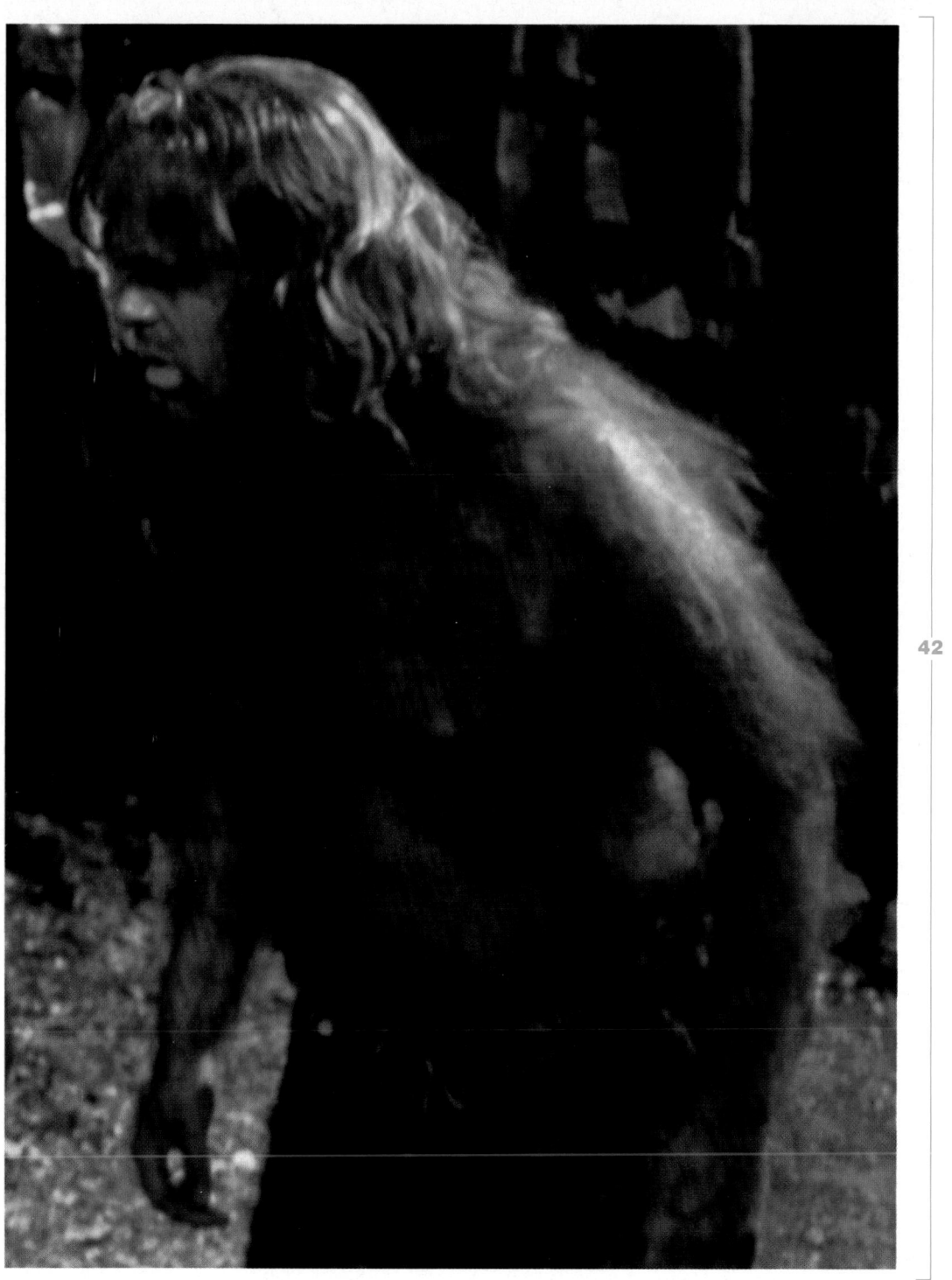

42

42 Discussion Ask students whether the Caliban pictured here is in keeping with their image of Caliban.

65 Naples with him, he's a present for any emperor that ever trod on neat's leather.[15]

CALIBAN. Do not torment me, prithee; I'll bring my wood home faster.

STEPHANO. He's in his fit now and does not talk after the wisest. 70 He shall taste of my bottle; if he have never drunk wine afore, it will go near to remove his fit. If I can recover him and keep him tame, I will not take too much for him.[16] He shall pay for him that hath him, and that soundly.

CALIBAN. Thou dost me yet but little hurt. Thou wilt anon;[17] I know it by thy trembling. Now Prosper works upon thee.

75 **STEPHANO.** Come on your ways, open your mouth; here is that which will give language to you, cat.[18] Open your mouth. This will shake your shaking, I can tell you, and that soundly. [*Gives* CALIBAN *drink.*] You cannot tell who's your friend. Open your chaps[19] again.

80 **TRINCULO.** I should know that voice. It should be—but he is drowned; and these are devils. O, defend me!

STEPHANO. Four legs and two voices—a most delicate monster! His forward voice now is to speak well of his friend; his backward voice is to utter foul speeches and to detract. If all the wine in my 85 my bottle will recover him, I will help his ague. Come! [*Gives drink.*] Amen! I will pour some in thy other mouth.

TRINCULO. Stephano!

STEPHANO. Doth thy other mouth call me? Mercy, mercy! This is a devil, and no monster. I will leave him; I have no long spoon.[20]

90 **TRINCULO.** Stephano! If thou beest Stephano, touch me and speak to me; for I am Trinculo—be not afeard—thy good friend Trinculo.

STEPHANO. If thou beest Trinculo, come forth. I'll pull thee by the lesser legs. If any be Trinculo's legs, these are they. [*Draws him* 95 *out from under* CALIBAN*'s garment.*] Thou art very Trinculo indeed! How cam'st thou to be the siege[21] of this mooncalf?[22] Can he vent Trinculos?

TRINCULO. I took him to be killed with a thunderstroke. But art thou not drowned, Stephano? I hope now thou art not drowned. 100 Is the storm overblown? I hid me under the dead mooncalf's gaberdine for fear of the storm. And art thou living, Stephano? O, Stephano! two Neapolitans scaped!

STEPHANO. Prithee do not turn me about; my stomach is not constant.

15. **trod on neat's leather:** Walked on cowhide; an ancient folk saying.

16. **I . . . him:** However much I get for him will not be enough.

17. **anon:** Soon.

18. **cat:** An allusion to a popular saying of the day: "Ale will make a cat talk."

19. **chaps:** Slang for mouth.

20. **long spoon:** Another allusion to a proverb: "He who eats with the devil must have a long spoon."

21. **siege:** Human waste; excrement.

22. **mooncalf:** Monster.

Grammar in Action

In creating this humorous scene, Shakespeare relied heavily on a device called **dramatic irony**—in other words, the audience is aware of something that the characters do not know. Such irony can be used in tragedy or comedy. In the Greek tragedy *Oedipus Rex*, for instance, we know much earlier than Oedipus that he has killed his own father. This knowledge gives us a sense of terror and foreboding.

In this comic scene from *The Tempest*, we know that Caliban is mistaken to believe that Stephano is a god. In this case, however, our knowledge provokes laughter rather than terror. We feel an amused superiority as he mistakes Stephano and Trinculo for heavenly beings:

CALIBAN. These be fine things, and if they be not sprites,
    That's a brave god and bears celestial liquor.
    I will kneel to him.

The exaggerated actions that accompany such mistakes (Caliban later kneels to his new god) accentuate the humor.

Student Activity 1. Trinculo calls Caliban a "poor credulous monster." Show how, from the audience's point of view, all three of these characters

105 CALIBAN. [*Aside*] These be fine things, and if they be not sprites.
That's a brave god and bears celestial liquor.
I will kneel to him.

STEPHANO. How didst thou scape? How cam'st thou hither? Swear
by this bottle how thou cam'st hither. I escaped upon a butt of
110 sack which the sailors heaved o'erboard—by this bottle which I
made of the bark of a tree with mine own hands since I was cast
ashore.

CALIBAN. I'll swear upon that bottle to be thy true subject, for the
liquor is not earthly.

115 STEPHANO. Here! Swear then how thou escap'dst.

TRINCULO. Swum ashore, man, like a duck. I can swim like a duck,
I'll be sworn.

STEPHANO. Here, kiss the book. [*Gives him drink.*] Though thou
canst swim like a duck, thou art made like a goose.

120 TRINCULO. O Stephano, hast any more of this?

STEPHANO. The whole butt,²³ man. My cellar is in a rock by th' sea-
side, where my wine is hid. How now, mooncalf? How does
thine ague?

CALIBAN. Hast thou not dropped from heaven?

125 STEPHANO. Out o' th' moon, I do assure thee. I was the Man i' th'
Moon when time was.²⁴

CALIBAN. I have seen thee in her, and I do adore thee. My mistress
showed me thee, and thy dog, and thy bush.²⁵

STEPHANO. Come, swear to that; kiss the book. [*Gives him drink.*] I
130 will furnish it anon with new contents. Swear. [CALIBAN *drinks.*]

TRINCULO. By this good light, this is a very shallow monster! I
afeard of him? A very weak monster. The Man i' th' Moon? A
most poor credulous monster! Well drawn,²⁶ monster, in good
sooth!

135 CALIBAN. I'll show thee every fertile inch o' th' island; and I will
kiss thy foot. I prithee, be my god.

TRINCULO. By this light, a most perfidious and drunken monster!
When's god's asleep, he'll rob his bottle.

CALIBAN. I'll kiss thy foot. I'll swear myself thy subject.

140 STEPHANO. Come on then. Down, and swear!

TRINCULO. I shall laugh myself to death at this puppy-headed monster. A most scurvy monster! I could find in my heart to beat
him—

48

49

23. **butt:** A large cask of wine.

50

24. **when time was:** Once
upon a time; in time past.

51

25. **thee . . . bush:**
According to popular legend,
the man in the moon was
exiled there because he
gathered firewood on Sunday, a
day of rest and prayer.
Gathering firewood was
considered work. His dog was
with him at the time.

52

26. **Well drawn:** Good long
drink of wine.

---

48 **Discussion** Ask students how
Caliban's reaction to Stephano
and Trinculo parodies Miranda's
reaction to Ferdinand. What does
Caliban's readiness to worship
Stephano reveal about Caliban?
What does it suggest about the
"civilization" of Stephano and Trinculo?

49 **Literary Focus** Point out to students that there are many images
in this scene in which humans are
compared to animals. Ask them
how this imagery relates to the
theme of civilized versus uncivilized behavior.

50 **Enrichment** Indicate to students
that Caliban is speaking in prose.
In previous scenes and in his
aside (lines 105–107), he speaks
in blank verse. Still later in the
scene, he speaks in blank verse
again. Have students account for
these changes.

51 **Discussion** If Caliban knew the
popular legend about the man in
the moon, why might he have felt
an affinity with this figure?

52 **Enrichment** Point out to students
that Stephano keeps blasphe-
mously referring to the bottle of
liquor as "the book," an allusion to
the Bible. There is also a suggestion that this "book" is somehow
like Prospero's book of magical
spells: Liquor too can work magic,
or so Caliban believes. Soon he
will want to exchange his old master, Prospero, for a new and supposedly greater magician,
Stephano.

---

are "poor credulous" monsters.

Student Activity 2. Tell about a real-life situation that was humorous
because you knew something that others did not.

53 Discussion Ask students how the conspiracy of Caliban, Stephano, and Trinculo resembles and differs from that of Antonio and Sebastian. Also ask them how this conspiracy is a kind of ironic comment on that of the courtiers.

54 Enrichment Point out to students that Caliban, as an earthy creature, seems to have a special knowledge of nature.

55 Discussion Have students compare and contrast Caliban with his fellow plotters.

56 Discussion Have students explain what Caliban's song reveals about his concept of freedom. How do his ideas about freedom differ from those of Ferdinand and Ariel?

Enrichment The Trinculo-Stephano subplot allows Shakespeare to reflect on civilization and its values. Caliban's meeting with Stephano and Trinculo recapitulates his initial meeting with Prospero. He swears allegiance, promises to let them know about the island, and is "civilized" by them in a way that parodies his original encounter with Prospero. But where Prospero taught him language, Stephano teaches him to drink. Even the idea of civilized "elevation" is parodied here in the "elevation" brought on by drunkenness. Caliban typically finds it impossible *not* to be a servant. Although he exits praising his new freedom (line 172), he has in fact only gotten a new master (line 171).

Students should consider, in the context of this and earlier scenes, just how the "civilized" characters appear: What gives them the right to call themselves civilized beings? What distinguishes "civilized" from "uncivilized" natures? It is certainly not Christian charity: Trinculo's comment that people will pay more to see a dead Indian than to relieve a lame beggar (lines 29–30) suggests that many Europeans are considerably less sensitive than Miranda, whose first speech shows her empathy for the sailors of the shipwrecked vessel. Stephano's "civilization" seems to consist of his

STEPHANO. Come, kiss.

145 **TRINCULO.** But that the poor monster's in drink. An abominable monster!

CALIBAN. I'll show thee the best springs; I'll pluck thee berries;
I'll fish for thee, and get thee wood enough.
A plague upon the tyrant that I serve!
150 I'll bear him no more sticks, but follow thee,
Thou wondrous man.

TRINCULO. A most ridiculous monster, to make a wonder of a poor drunkard!

CALIBAN. I prithee let me bring thee where crabs[27] grow;
155 And I with my long nails will dig thee pignuts,[28]
Show thee a jay's nest, and instruct thee how
To snare the nimble marmoset.[29] I'll bring thee
To clust'ring filberts,[30] and sometimes I'll get thee
Young scamels[31] from the rock. Wilt thou go with me?

160 **STEPHANO.** I prithee now, lead the way without any more talking.
Trinculo, the King and all our company else being drowned, we
will inherit here. Here, bear my bottle. Fellow Trinculo, we'll fill
him by and by again. [CALIBAN *sings drunkenly.*]

CALIBAN. Farewell, master; farewell, farewell!

165 **TRINCULO.** A howling monster! A drunken monster!

CALIBAN.   No more dams I'll make for fish,
                Nor fetch in firing
                At requiring,
                Nor scrape trenchering,[32] nor wash dish
170   'Ban, 'Ban, Ca—Caliban
                Has a new master. Get a new man!

Freedom, high day! High day, freedom! high day, freedom!

STEPHANO. O brave monster! Lead the way. [*Exit.*]

27. crabs: Crabapples.
28. pignuts: Roots or other underground tubers; earthnuts.

29. marmoset: A small New World monkey.
30. filberts: Hazel trees.
31. scamels: An unknown word. Perhaps a misspelling of "seamels" or "sea mews," a sea gull, which often builds its nest on the rocks that line the shore.

32. trenchering: Wooden platters used as dishes for food.

Reader's Response *Does Caliban remind you of any other character you have seen on a television show or in a film? Explain.*

possession of a keg of wine.

Closure and Extension

ANSWERS TO THINKING ABOUT THE SELECTION

1. (a) Antonio tells Sebastian that Claribel cannot interfere because she is so far from Naples; that he, Antonio, has successfully usurped a kingdom; and

that conscience is an insignificant, immaterial thing. (b) Ariel causes the sleepers to wake.
2. Caliban mistakes Trinculo for an evil spirit, Stephano mistakes Caliban and Trinculo for monsters, and Caliban mistakes Stephano for a god.
3. Their treatment of Gonzalo reveals their cruelty.
4. Just as Antonio and Sebastian try to execute their plan, Prospero sends

Ariel to wake the sleepers.
5. (a) Stephano and Trinculo are stock characters. (b) Answers will differ. Some students will respond that since audiences have been amused by these "types" before, the chances are that they will be amused again.
6. Where Prospero taught Caliban to speak, Stephano teaches him to drink. Stephano's ironic reference to his bottle as "the book" recalls Pros-

THINKING ABOUT THE SELECTION

Clarifying

1. (a) How does Antonio persuade Sebastian to kill Alonso? (b) What interrupts them?
2. What misunderstandings occur in scene ii?

Interpreting

3. How does Sebastian and Antonio's treatment of Gonzalo foreshadow their plotting against Alonso?
4. In what way does Prospero's magic make the evil that emerges in the first scene less threatening?
5. **Stock characters** are predictable characters used in many different literary works; they are stereotypes who do not grow or change. (a) Which characters in the second scene are stock characters? (b) Why are such characters effective for comic purposes?
6. How does Stephano's treatment of Caliban recall and parody Prospero's attempt to civilize his servant?
7. (a) How does the action in the second scene mirror that in the first? (b) What is different about the mood of the second scene?

Applying

8. How is Stephano's treatment of Caliban similar to the way in which some European explorers and settlers treated Native Americans?

ANALYZING LITERATURE

Understanding Themes

The **themes** of a play are the central ideas that it explores. One of the key themes of *The Tempest*, inspired by Montaigne's essay "On Cannibals," is the true nature of civilization. Caliban is an "uncivilized" native of Prospero's island; his kinship to animals is suggested when Stephano, seeing Caliban and Trinculo under the coat, takes them for "some monster." Yet this scene is ironic about the Englishmen as well. They are as foolish as Caliban although they have the "advantages" of a civilized upbringing.

1. How does the island cause the nobly born Europeans to reveal their true natures as well?
2. How would you describe the "civilization" of Antonio and Sebastian?
3. Is there anything appealing about Caliban's barbaric nature? Explain.

CRITICAL THINKING AND READING

Tracing Sources

Shakespeare all but quotes Montaigne's essay "On Cannibals" when Gonzalo describes the imaginary kingdom he would govern (II.144–165). However, a study of this speech reveals how Shakespeare adapted sources to his own purposes, even when he followed their language closely. Here Montaigne's ideas about the "golden age" are placed in a dramatic context. They become the speculations of a good-hearted, if slightly muddled, courtier, who longs for a simpler life.

1. How does this speech reflect Gonzalo's own view of human nature?
2. (a) What criticisms do Antonio and Sebastian make of Gonzalo's ideas? (b) Are these criticisms accurate, merely cynical, or both? Explain.
3. How do Gonzalo and his detractors differ in their views of primitive man?

UNDERSTANDING LANGUAGE

Recognizing Diction as a Character Trait

The words and phrases a character uses can show a great deal about the character. Ariel's musical rhyming speech, for example, helps convey the airy quality and goodness of this cheery sprite. By contrast, the speech of Caliban, particularly at the beginning of Act II, Scene ii, portrays him as primarily an evil and soulless animallike being, whom Prospero taught to speak but who learned only to "curse." How does Gonzalo's diction help to characterize him as a man of goodness? Use examples from the play to support your answer.

THINKING AND WRITING

Writing as a Caribbean Islander

Perhaps you were born on a Caribbean island. If not, you can certainly imagine that you are a citizen of a Caribbean nation. As a Caribbean islander, you would probably respond to Shakespeare's portrayal of Caliban in a much different way. You might, for instance, view this character as a reflection of Shakespeare's European prejudices. Try the following experiment. Join with a classmate and arrange for one of you to play the part of a native of Trinidad and the other a citizen of modern-day England. Each of you has just read *The Tempest* and you are writing each other about your reactions to Caliban. The first letter should come from the Trinidadian and the second from the citizen of England; however, each should have a chance to reply to the other's views with a second letter. Finally, put the letters together with a jointly written preface in which you outline the differences in attitude.

(continued from bottom of page)

lieves in the essential goodness of human beings, once separated from the corrupting influences of civilization.

2. (a) They accuse him of being inconsistent, creating a monarchy and then inadvertently making it a democracy. They also deliberately misinterpret his reference to innocence as a ban on marriage. (b) Answers will differ. Most students will realize that they are right in pointing out Gonzalo's inconsistency and possibly accurate in suggesting that his plan is muddleheaded. However, most students will also realize that the courtiers' criticisms do reveal their shallow cynicism.
3. Gonzalo believes in the innocence of primitive man, while Antonio and Sebastian are obviously more skeptical, even cynical, about this belief.

ANSWERS TO UNDERSTANDING LANGAGE

Gonzalo uses words like "innocent" and "pure" to describe the citizens of his ideal commonwealth. Such words are never on the lips of Antonio and Sebastian.

THINKING AND WRITING

Publishing Student Writing Have each pair of students bind their letters and make them available for the class to read.

pero's books of magic and his attempts to teach Caliban. Also, Prospero's endeavor to civilize Caliban is parodied by Stephano's "elevation" of Caliban's spirits by means of drink.

7. (a) In both scenes characters plot to take over a kingdom that is not theirs. (b) In the first scene the mood is serious, while in the second it is comic and ridiculous.
8. Answers will differ.

ANSWERS TO ANALYZING LITERATURE

1. Answers will differ. Students may respond that since the Europeans are taken out of civilized surroundings, they are freer to express their essential natures.
2. Most students will realize that their "civilization" is only a thin veneer of

dress and manners.

3. Answers will differ. Some students may be favorably impressed by his sense of poetry and knowledge of nature. Some may even feel that his gullibility is appealing.

ANSWERS TO CRITICAL THINKING AND READING

1. The speech reveals that Gonzalo be-

GUIDE FOR INTERPRETING

Focus

Literary Focus Ask students to describe their favorite movies and novels. Some of these are bound to have subplots. Have students identify these subplots and explain how they mirror and comment on the main plot.

Writing/Prior Knowledge Discuss this question with the class before they begin to write. Suggest situations that might bear on this issue; for example, twins who grow up together or apart.

ESL Teaching Strategy Have ESL students earn extra credit by rewriting scenes in modern English. Small groups of native-speaking students can then act out these adaptations for ESL students.

Teaching Tenth-Grade Students Have tenth-grade students work in groups to diagram the relationships between the main plot and the subplots.

Cooperative Learning Assign a team of students to each of the plots. Have each team study the development of its plot in this act and then predict how it will be resolved at the end of the play.

The Tempest, Act III

Commentary

Plot, Subplot, and Character. Picture the workings of an old-fashioned watch, with big wheels and small wheels intermeshed and precisely turning. This image conveys something of the way a drama works as well. The biggest wheel is the main **plot,** or sequence of events. As it turns it engages with one or more smaller wheels, which are the **subplots,** or less important actions.

In Shakespeare's *The Tempest*, plot and subplot are intermeshed with particular care and precision. The main events of the play relate to Prospero's plan to test and teach Alonso, Sebastian, and Antonio. Several of the subplots reflect and comment on the main story. One of these subplots concerns the relationship between Miranda and Ferdinand. The comical scheming of Caliban and his new masters is still another subplot; it provides a kind of distorted, funhouse reflection of the more dangerous conspiracy of the courtiers.

As the wheels of plot and subplot turn, the play reveals the true nature of each **character** by means of contrast. Caliban and Miranda, for instance, contrast as two "island children" and Caliban and Ferdinand as Miranda's suitors, both made by Prospero to carry wood. Meanwhile Caliban and Antonio are both would-be king killers. These contrasts are also designed to make the audience think about the way in which a person's character is formed. Is the nature one is born with more important than the upbringing, or "nurture" as the Elizabethans called it, that one is given?

Writing

Which do you think is more important in forming a person's character, nature or upbringing? Jot down experiences and observations that support your point of view.

Primary Source

One modern scholar, G. Blakemore Evans, argues that *The Tempest* has little in the way of plot: "Actually, there is not very much plot in *The Tempest*. There is the love of Ferdinand and Miranda, which Prospero has to pretend to oppose (though we know he doesn't), lest it all seem too easy to the lovers. And there are the two conspiracies, but Prospero is so powerful and so well informed that we can feel little suspense about the outcome of either one. Each of the three strands of plot, however, leads up to a spectacle, and in this way, by theatrical means, Shakespeare makes up for the lack of dramatic tension. The disappearing banquet, the masque of the classical goddesses, and the three drunks parading in stolen finery offer variety and display."

Objectives

Thematic
To consider how nature and nurture both contribute to a person's character

Skills
1 To understand plot, subplot, and character
2 To perform a scene
3 To find the meaning that fits the context
4 To contrast characters as a clue to theme

Act III

Scene i. In front of Prospero's cell.

[*Enter* FERDINAND, *bearing a log.*]

FERDINAND. There be some sports are painful, and their labor
    Delight in them sets off;[1] some kinds of baseness
    Are nobly undergone, and most poor matters
    Point to rich ends. This my mean task
5   Would be as heavy to me as odious, but
    The mistress which I serve quickens[2] what's dead
    And makes my labors pleasure. O, she is
    Ten times more gentle than her father's crabbed;
    And he's composed of harshness. I must remove
10   Some thousands of these logs and pile them up.
    Upon a sore injunction.[3] My sweet mistress
    Weeps when she sees me work, and says such baseness
    Had never like executor. I forget;[4]
    But these sweet thoughts do even refresh my labors,
    Most busiest when I do it.[5]

[*Enter* MIRANDA; *and* PROSPERO (*behind, unseen*).]

15 MIRANDA.   Alas, now pray you,
    Work not so hard! I would the lightning had
    Burnt up those logs that you are enjoined to pile!
    Pray set it down and rest you. When this burns,
    'Twill weep[6] for having wearied you. My father
20   Is hard at study; pray now rest yourself;
    He's safe for these three hours.

FERDINAND.   O most dear mistress,
    The sun will set before I shall discharge
    What I must strive to do.

MIRANDA.   If you'll sit down,
    I'll bear your logs the while. Pray give me that;
    I'll carry it to the pile.

25 FERDINAND.   No, precious creature,
    I had rather crack my sinews, break my back,
    Than you should such dishonor undergo
    While I sit lazy by.

MIRANDA.   It would become me
    As well as it does you; and I should do it
30   With much more ease; for my good will is to it,
    And yours it is against.

PROSPERO. [*Aside*]   Poor worm, thou art infected!
    This visitation[7] shows it.

---

1. sets off: Cancels or balances the pain.

2. quickens: Enlivens; animates; brings to life.

3. Upon a sore injunction: Upon a threat of harsh punishment.

4. I forget: I neglect my chores.

5. Most . . . it: A corrupted text, generally interpreted to mean "my thoughts of my mistress are busiest when I am hardest at work."

6. weep: Ooze a resinous sap.

7. visitation: Visit.

Presentation

Motivation/Prior Knowledge
Remind students that Prospero is now menaced by two conspiracies. Ask them how they think he will deal with these threats. Will he deal with each conspiracy in the same way?

Purpose-Setting Question
How do the events of the subplots mirror and comment on the main sequence of events?

Master Teacher Note As students read, they should think about the roles of the natural, supernatural, and unnatural worlds in the play. The action of the play moves from the natural world (the ship being tossed by the storm) into a supernatural one (Prospero's island). In this supernatural realm, Antonio and Sebastian disclose their unnatural designs. Have a group of students work on a mural that depicts these three elements by means of thematic statements, quotations from the play, and pictures.

Vocabulary
Preteach the following vocabulary words:
odious (ō´ dē əs) *adj.*: Disgusting; offensive
jocund (jäk´ ənd) *adj.*: Cheerful
surfeited (sur´ fit əd) *adj.*: Filled
plummet (plum´ it) *n.*: A lead weight hung at the end of a line, used to determine how deep water is

Support Material

Teaching Portfolio
Teacher Backup, p. 909
Grammar in Action Worksheet, *The Evolution of Language*, p. 913
Usage and Mechanics Worksheet, p. 915
Vocabulary Check, p. 916
Analyzing Literature Worksheet, *Understanding Plot, Subplot, and Character*, p. 917
Language Worksheet, *Finding the Meaning That Fits the Context*, p. 918
Selection Test, pp. 919–920

Spelling Tip Write the word *surfeit* on the chalkboard and remind students that the vowel in the second syllable is spelled *ei*, not *i*.

Commentary

Ferdinand and Caliban, Ferdinand and Miranda Shakespeare probably intended to suggest parallels between Ferdinand and Caliban. Both are male, both are Miranda's "suitors," and both act as Prospero's servants. Also, the anger that Prospero feels toward Caliban he pretends to feel toward Ferdinand, so that he will value Miranda as she deserves to be valued.

The differences between these two characters, however, are equally important. Caliban is imprisoned not only by Prospero's threats but by his own violent impulses: He is a "slave" to his passions and hence to anyone who claims to be able to gratify them. Ferdinand, by contrast, feels free. In his opening speech, he declares that his labors are "pleasures" because Miranda is nearby to cheer him on. He will swear to marry her "with a heart as willing / As bondage e'er of freedom" (III.i.88–89). Marrying her is a kind of emancipation.

Ferdinand and Miranda, in good romance fashion, tend to idealize each other (III.i.37–48). Both wish to spare one another hardship, showing a sympathy that suggests the match between them may be a good one. In this scene Miranda gradually shifts her allegiance from her father to her lover, disobeying Prospero to tell Ferdinand her name (III.i.36–37).

MIRANDA. You look wearily.

FERDINAND. No, noble mistress, 'tis fresh morning with me
When you are by at night. I do beseech you,
35 Chiefly that I might set it in my prayers,
What is your name?

MIRANDA. Miranda. O my father,
I have broke your hest to say so!

FERDINAND. Admired Miranda![8]
Indeed the top of admiration, worth
What's dearest to the world! Full many a lady
40 I have eyed with best regard, and many a time
Th' harmony of their tongues hath into bondage
Brought my too diligent ear. For several virtues
Have I liked several women; never any
With so full soul but some defect in her
45 Did quarrel with the noblest grace she owed,
And put it to the foil.[9] But you, O you,
So perfect and so peerless, are created
Of every creature's best.

MIRANDA. I do not know
One of my sex; no woman's face remember,
50 Save, from my glass, mine own. Nor have I seen
More that I may call men than you, good friend,
And my dear father. How features are abroad
I am skilless[10] of; but, by my modesty
(The jewel in my dower), I would not wish
55 Any companion in the world but you;
Nor can imagination form a shape,
Besides yourself, to like of. But I prattle
Something too wildly, and my father's precepts
I therein do forget.

FERDINAND. I am, in my condition,
60 A prince, Miranda; I do think, a king
(I would not so), and would no more endure
This wooden slavery than to suffer
The fleshfly blow[11] my mouth. Hear my soul speak!
The very instant that I saw you, did
65 My heart fly to your service; there resides,
To make me slave to it; and for your sake
Am I this patient log-man.

MIRANDA. Do you love me?

FERDINAND. O heaven, O earth, bear witness to this sound,
And crown what I profess with kind event

8. Admired Miranda: "Admire" comes from the Latin *to wonder* and the name "Miranda" derives from the Latin *mirandus* meaning "wonderful."

9. put it to the foil: Put it to the test, which it failed.

10. skilless: Ignorant.

11. blow: Befoul; contaminate; pollute.

---

1 Literary Focus Remind students of Caliban's attitude toward his physical labors and have them contrast this attitude with Ferdinand's. What accounts for the difference? You might also ask students to compare and contrast Caliban and Ferdinand in other ways.

2 Discussion Ask students what this violation of her father's command reveals. Does it suggest an internal conflict? Does it disclose that she is growing up in some way or entering a period of transition?

3 Discussion Ferdinand presents himself as more experienced than Miranda, but ask students whether he is in some ways as naive as she.

4 Clarification Point out to students that Ferdinand suddenly remembers his father's death and so promotes himself to king. His parenthetical remark, "I would not so," indicates that he would rather see his father alive than be king in his place.

5 Discussion Ask students how likely it is that people would fall in love at first sight. Does Shakespeare succeed in making you believe in this love? If so, how?

As Prospero views the scene, his comments reveal different perspectives on the encounter between the two young lovers. His first aside, "Poor worm, thou art infected," suggests compassion for Miranda as she falls in love and will be subject to all the confusions attendant on that state. However, Prospero's second comment (III.i.74–76) stresses the goodness of their union. His final remark (III.i.92–96) reminds the audience that this is all part of his "plot," and his final line emphasizes his responsibility for what has occurred.

If I speak true! If hollowly, invert
What best is boded me[12] to mischief! I,
Beyond all limit of what else i' th' world,
Do love, prize, honor you.

MIRANDA.   I am a fool
To weep at what I am glad of.

PROSPERO. [*Aside*]   Fair encounter
Of two most rare affections! Heavens rain grace
On that which breeds between 'em!

FERDINAND.   Wherefore weep you?

MIRANDA. At mine unworthiness, that dare not offer
What I desire to give, and much less take
What I shall die to want.[13] But this is trifling;[14]
And all the more it seeks to hide itself,
The bigger bulk it shows. Hence, bashful cunning,
And prompt me, plain and holy innocence!
I am your wife, if you will marry me;
If not, I'll die your maid. To be your fellow[15]
You may deny me; but I'll be your servant,
Whether you will or no.

FERDINAND.   My mistress, dearest,
And I thus humble ever.

MIRANDA.   My husband then?

FERDINAND. Ay, with a heart as willing
As bondage e'er of freedom.[16] Here's my hand.

MIRANDA. And mine, with my heart in't; and now farewell
Till half an hour hence.

FERDINAND.   A thousand thousand!
   [*Exit* (FERDINAND *and* MIRANDA *in different directions*).]

PROSPERO. So glad of this as they I cannot be,
Who are surprised withal;[17] but my rejoicing
At nothing can be more. I'll to my book;
For yet ere suppertime must I perform
Much business appertaining.[18]   [*Exit.*]

Scene ii. Another part of the island.

[*Enter* CALIBAN, STEPHANO, *and* TRINCULO.]

STEPHANO. Tell me not! When the butt is out, we will drink water;
not a drop before. Therefore bear up and board 'em![1] Servant
monster, drink to me.

Sidenotes

12. **What . . . me:** What good fortune will be given me.

13. **want:** Lack; be without.
14. **But . . . trifling:** But words cannot express my feelings.

15. **fellow:** Partner.

16. **as willing . . . freedom:** As eagerly as a prisoner is to gain his freedom.

17. **withal:** By it all.

18. **appertaining;** Relating (to my plans).

1. **bear . . . 'em:** An old seaman's expression meaning "drink up."

Margin Discussion Notes

6 **Discussion** Have students compare this aside with Prospero's first aside (lines 31–32). How does each comment reveal a different perspective on the encounter between Ferdinand and Miranda? What do these comments suggest about Prospero and his relationship with his daughter?

7 **Discussion** Ask students how this declaration is in keeping with Miranda's character. What is similar about the attitudes toward service that Ferdinand and Miranda display? Have you ever encountered, in books or movies, a female character as forthright and direct as Miranda? Explain.

8 **Discussion** Ask students how this speech serves as a transition to the next scene. How does it remind viewers of Prospero's position outside and above the action of the play?

9 **Discussion** Have students describe how the mood changes abruptly with this speech. Does the shift from poetry to prose contribute to this change? If so, how? Why is it important for a playwright to evoke different, and sometimes contrasting, moods?

Grammar in Action

The Evolution of the English Language The words of a language change over time. Some words take on new or different meanings. We use the word *ecstasy* to mean "a state of being overpowered by emotion; great joy." In Shakespeare's time, however, this word could also signify insanity or mental disease. Some words drop out of the language entirely. For example, *whilom* ("at one time") and *whereat* ("at which point") are no longer regularly used in speech or writing, except for special effects. Similarly, certain verb conjugations have changed over the years. Instead of saying he (she, it) *hath*, we say he (she, it) *has*.

Since Shakespeare lived almost 400 years ago, it is inevitable that some of the words he used have changed in meaning or dropped out of use. Following are some examples:

TRINCULO. "Lord" *quoth* he? That a monster should be such a natural!

CALIBAN. *Lo, lo,* again! Bite him to death, I *prithee.*

The verb *quoth* means "says," *lo* is an old-fashioned interjection meaning "look!," and *prithee* is an archaic form of "beg you" or "please."

TRINCULO. Servant monster? The folly of this island! They say
5   there's but five upon this isle; we are three of them. If th' other
    two be brained like us, the state totters.

STEPHANO. Drink, servant monster, when I bid thee; thy eyes are
    almost set in thy head.

TRINCULO. Where should they be set else? He were a brave monster
10   indeed if they were set in his tail.

STEPHANO. My man-monster hath drowned his tongue in sack.² For
    my part, the sea cannot drown me. I swam, ere I could recover
    the shore, five-and-thirty leagues off and on, by this light. Thou
    shalt be my lieutenant, monster, or my standard.³

15 **TRINCULO.** Your lieutenant, if you list;⁴ he's no standard.

STEPHANO. We'll not run, Monsieur Monster.

TRINCULO. Nor go neither; but you'll like dogs, and yet say noth-
    ing neither.

STEPHANO. Mooncalf, speak once in thy life, if thou beest a good
20 mooncalf.

CALIBAN. How does thy honor? Let me lick thy shoe. I'll not serve
    him; he is not valiant.

TRINCULO. Thou liest, most ignorant monster; I am in case to justle
    a constable.⁵ Why, thou deboshed⁶ fish thou, was there ever man
25   a coward that hath drunk so much sack as I today? Wilt thou
    tell a monstrous lie, being but half a fish and half a monster?

CALIBAN. Lo, how he mocks me! Wilt thou let him, my lord?

TRINCULO. "Lord" quoth he? That a monster should be such a nat-
    ural!⁷

30 **CALIBAN.** Lo, lo, again! Bite him to death, I prithee.

STEPHANO. Trinculo, keep a good tongue in your head. If you
    prove a mutineer—the next tree!⁸ The poor monster's my sub-
    ject, and he shall not suffer indignity.

CALIBAN. I thank my noble lord. Wilt thou be pleased to hearken
35   once again to the suit I made to thee?

STEPHANO. Marry,⁹ will I. Kneel and repeat it; I will stand, and so
    shall Trinculo.

[*Enter* ARIEL, *invisible.*]

CALIBAN. As I told thee before, I am subject to a tyrant,
    A sorcerer, that by his cunning hath
40   Cheated me of the island.

---

2. **sack:** A white wine.

3. **standard:** Standard-bearer, but Caliban can barely stand.
4. **if you list:** If you wish. In sailor's jargon, "list" means "lean to one side," as an injured ship or a drunken man.

5. **I am . . . constable:** I am in good enough condition to fight a policeman.
6. **deboshed:** Drunken; debauched.

7. **natural:** Fool; idiot.

8. **the next tree:** An elliptical expression for "You'll hang from the next tree."

9. **Marry:** An exclamation meaning "By the Virgin Mary!"

---

10 **Clarification** This may be a humorous allusion, on Shakespeare's
part, to the theme of the ideal commonwealth set forth by Gonzalo.

11 **Enrichment** Point out to students
the variety of names that Stephano
bestows on Caliban. He calls him
"Servant monster," "man-monster,"
"Monsieur Monster," and "Mooncalf." In Shakespeare's time a
mooncalf was "a monstrosity." This
variety of terms not only indicates
Stephano's drunken state but it
also suggests Caliban's formlessness: He is neither completely human nor completely nonhuman.

12 **Clarification** Forgetting where he
is, Trinculo asserts that in his
drunken bravado, he is ready to
take on a policeman. This statement, of course, is an ironic comment on Trinculo's valor.

13 **Discussion** Ask students how the
interactions among these three
characters parody the relationships between a king and his
courtiers.

14 **Reading Strategy** Have students
predict what Ariel will do as Caliban kneels and pleads his suit before Stephano.

   Student Activity 1. Identify five other archaic words in this act and look
them up in a dictionary.
   Student Activity 2. Write a short speech for Caliban, in poetry or prose,
and use at least three archaic terms. Make sure that the speech is in keeping
with Caliban's character.

15 Clarification Remind students that Ariel is invisible. It is natural, therefore, that Caliban and Stephano believe that Trinculo exclaimed, "Thou liest."

16 Discussion Have students comment on Caliban's evaluation of Stephano. Is Caliban, in his way, as naive as Miranda?

ARIEL. Thou liest.

CALIBAN.   Thou liest, thou jesting monkey thou!
I would my valiant master would destroy thee.
I do not lie.

STEPHANO. Trinculo, if you trouble him any more in's tale, by this
45   hand, I will supplant some of your teeth.

TRINCULO. Why, I said nothing.

STEPHANO. Mum then, and no more. Proceed.

CALIBAN. I say by sorcery he got this isle;
From me he got it. If thy greatness will
50   Revenge it on him—for I know thou dar'st,
But this thing[10] dare not—

STEPHANO. That's most certain.

10. **this thing:** Trinculo.

CALIBAN. Thou shalt be lord of it, and I'll serve thee.

STEPHANO. How now shall this be compassed? Canst thou bring me
to the party?

CALIBAN. Yea, yea, my lord ! I'll yield him thee asleep,
Where thou mayst knock a nail into his head.

ARIEL. Thou liest; thou canst not.

CALIBAN. What a pied[11] ninny's this! Thou scurvy patch![12]
I do beseech thy greatness, give him blows
And take his bottle from him. When that's gone,
He shall drink naught but brine, for I'll not show him
Where the quick freshes[13] are.

STEPHANO. Trinculo, run into no further danger! Interrupt the
monster one word further and, by this hand, I'll turn my mercy
out o' doors and make a stockfish[14] of thee.

TRINCULO. Why, what did I? I did nothing. I'll go farther off.

STEPHANO. Didst thou not say he lied?

ARIEL. Thou liest.

STEPHANO. Did I so? Take thou that! [*Strikes* TRINCULO.] As you
like this, give me the lie another time.

TRINCULO. I did not give the lie. Out o' your wits, and hearing
too? A pox o' your bottle! This can sack and drinking do. A
murrain[15] on your monster, and the devil take your fingers!

CALIBAN. Ha, ha, ha!

STEPHANO. Now forward with your tale. [*To* TRINCULO] Prithee,
stand further off.

CALIBAN. Beat him enough. After a little time
I'll beat him too.

STEPHANO.   Stand farther. Come, proceed.

CALIBAN. Why, as I told thee, 'tis a custom with him
I' th' afternoon to sleep. There thou mayst brain him,
Having first seized his books, or with a log
Batter his skull, or paunch[16] him with a stake,
Or cut his wezand[17] with thy knife. Remember
First to possess his books; for without them
He's but a sot,[18] as I am, nor hath not
One spirit to command. They all do hate him
As rootedly as I. Burn but his books.
He has brave utensils[19] (for so he calls them)
Which, when he has a house, he'll deck withal.
And that most deeply to consider is

---

11. **pied:** Many colored.
12. **patch:** Jester.

13. **freshes:** Freshwater streams.

14. **stockfish:** Dried and salted codfish.

15. **murrain:** Cattle disease.

16. **paunch:** Stab him in the belly.
17. **wezand:** Throat; windpipe.
18. **sot:** Fool.

19. **utensils:** Household furnishings.

---

17 Discussion Ask students whether or not they were shocked by the brutality of this image. Does it introduce a note of seriousness into this scene of bumbling conspiracy?

18 Master Teacher Note Point out to students the stage direction indicated by these lines. In order to help them appreciate the humor of this scene, have them block it out like a director. How do the positions of the characters change as the scene continues? What gestures do they make? How do they show that they are drunk?

19 Enrichment Tell students that in addition to being humorous, this scene reveals a world of misunderstanding, confusion, and brutality. These characters' plans and perceptions are as shapeless and ill-formed as Caliban himself. Like the "man-monster" Caliban, Stephano and Trinculo do not seem fully human.

20 Discussion Ask students what this comment suggests about Caliban. Why wouldn't he be the first to attack Trinculo? Why would he join in, however, "After a little time"?

21 Discussion Point out to students how many times Caliban mentions Prospero's books of magic. Why is Caliban so insistent about possessing and destroying these books? Also, why does Caliban proffer so many alternate ways of killing Prospero? Do you think that he has dreamed about this often? If so, why do you think he has never done it himself? Finally, is it true that all of Prospero's spirits hate him as much as Caliban does?

22 Discussion How does this statement parallel Miranda's speech about Ferdinand (III.i.50–55)?

23 Enrichment Call students' attention to Caliban's obsession with sex and self-replication. Read them his remark in the first act (ii.349–351), when Prospero reminds him of his attempted rape of Miranda: "O ho, O ho! Would't had been done! / Thou didst prevent me; I had peopled else / This isle with Calibans." Now it seems that he has given up his own ambition to people "This isle with Calibans." Instead, he recommends that Stephano create a race of Stephanos.

24 Enrichment Call students' attention to the fact that as Stephano's ambitions expand, he promotes Caliban from lieutenant (line 14) and subject (line 32) to viceroy.

25 Enrichment Stephano apologizes with a kind of royal magnanimity and condescension, feeling himself already the king of the island.

26 Discussion Have students compare what Stephano and Trinculo "teach" Caliban with what Prospero taught him. What is the theme of Stephano and Trinculo's little ditty?

27 Discussion Ask students to describe the tone in which Caliban asks this question. For instance, is he astonished that his master Stephano should be afraid of anything?

The beauty of his daughter. He himself
Calls her a nonpareil.[20] I never saw a woman
95 But only Sycorax my dam and she;
But she as far surpasseth Sycorax
As great'st does least.

STEPHANO.   Is it so brave a lass?

CALIBAN. Ay, lord. She will become thy bed, I warrant,
And bring thee forth brave brood.

STEPHANO. Monster, I will kill this man. His daughter and I will be
100 King and Queen—save our Graces!—And Trinculo and thyself
shall be viceroys. Dost thou like the plot, Trinculo?

TRINCULO. Excellent.

STEPHANO. Give me thy hand. I am sorry I beat thee; but while thou
liv'st, keep a good tongue in thy head.

105 **CALIBAN.** Within this half hour will he be asleep.
Wilt thou destroy him then?

STEPHANO.   Ay, on mine honor.

ARIEL. This will I tell my master.

CALIBAN. Thou mak'st me merry; I am full of pleasure.
Let us be jocund. Will you troll the catch[21]
110 You taught me but whilere?[22]

STEPHANO. At thy request, monster, I will do reason, any reason.
Come on, Trinculo, let us sing. [*Sings.*]

          Flout 'em and scout[23] 'em
          And scout 'em and flout 'em!
115   Thought is free.

CALIBAN. That's not the tune.
            [ARIEL *plays the tune on a tabor*[24] *and pipe.*]

STEPHANO. What is this same?

TRINCULO. This is the tune of our catch, played by the picture of
Nobody.[25]

120 **STEPHANO.** If thou beest a man, show thyself in thy likeness. If thou
beest a devil, take't as thou list.

TRINCULO. O, forgive me my sins!

STEPHANO. He that dies pays all debts. I defy thee. Mercy upon us!

CALIBAN. Art thou afeard?

125 **STEPHANO.** No, monster, not I.

---

20. nonpareil: From the French, meaning "without equal."

21. Will . . . catch: Will you sing the tune?
22. but whilere: Just now.

23. scout: Mock.

24. tabor: Small drum.

25. picture of Nobody: Possibly an allusion to a comedy called *No-body and Some-body.*

Commentary

Caliban and His Co-conspirators This funny, nasty scene partly parodies the earlier plotting of Antonio and Sebastian against Alonso. As Antonio advises Sebastian to kill Alonso, so Caliban advises Stephano to "knock a nail" into Prospero's head. While the courtiers represent the perversion of reason, however, this trio represents its almost total absence.

Note how irritable Caliban and his co-conspirators are with one another. Together they embody a mini-court, a parody of the larger court surrounding Alonso, and court intrigue is reduced to brutal obviousness. Both Caliban and Trinculo seem to want to gain the favor of Stephano, their "king," and

to dominate the other; hence Caliban's "Beat him enought. After a little time / I'll beat him too" (lines 78–79).

Yet for all his nastiness Caliban has a depth that both his "civilized" companions lack. Caliban typically speaks the blank verse normal for "higher" characters, while Stephano and Trinculo speak prose. Also, Caliban appreciates Ariel's music far more than his two companions (lines 126–134). In Caliban's speech music is associated again with imaginative vision; it makes him sleep and dream of a somewhat physical version of divine beauty ("The clouds methought would open and show riches / Ready to drop upon me"). The image of Caliban crying to sleep again is strikingly *human* and the

CALIBAN. Be not afeard; the isle is full of noises,
　Sounds and sweet airs that give delight and hurt not.
　Sometimes a thousand twanling instruments
　Will hum about mine ears; and sometime voices
130　That, if I then had waked after long sleep,
　Will make me sleep again; and then, in dreaming,
　The clouds methought would open and show riches
　Ready to drop upon me, that, when I waked,
　I cried to dream again.

135 STEPHANO. This will prove a brave kingdom to me, where I shall have
　my music for nothing.

CALIBAN. When Prospero is destroyed.

STEPHANO. That shall be by and by; I remember the story.

TRINCULO. The sound is going away; let's follow it, and after do
140　our work.

STEPHANO. Lead, monster; we'll follow. I would I could see this ta-
　borer; he lays it on.

TRINCULO. [*To* CALIBAN] Wilt come? I will follow Stephano.
　　　　　　　　　　　　　　　　　　　　[*Exit.*]

Scene iii. Another part of the island.

[*Enter* ALONSO, SEBASTIAN, ANTONIO, GONZALO, ADRIAN, FRANCISCO,
etc.]

GONZALO. By'r Lakin,[1] I can go no further, sir;
　My old bones aches. Here's a maze trod indeed
　Through forthrights and meanders.[2] By your patience,
　I needs must rest me.

ALONSO.　　　　　　　　Old lord, I cannot blame thee,
5　Who am myself attached[3] with weariness
　To th' dulling of my spirits. Sit down and rest.
　Even here I will put off my hope, and keep it
　No longer for my flatterer. He is drowned
　Whom thus we stray to find; and the sea mocks
10　Our frustrate search on land. Well, let him go.

ANTONIO. [*Aside to* SEBASTIAN] I am right glad that he's so out of
　hope.
　Do not for one repulse forgo the purpose
　That you resolved t' effect.

SEBASTIAN. [*Aside to* ANTONIO] The next advantage
　Will we take throughly.

1. By'r Lakin: Dialect, meaning "By our Lady."

2. forthrights and meanders: Straight and wandering paths.

3. attached: Afflicted; seized.

speech as a whole suggests an unexpected depth to his brute nature. He's responsive to heavenly beauty in a way the two clowns are not. The music of the island mirrors the divine music of the spheres, and the potential goodness in Caliban is nowhere clearer than it is here in his capacity to value it.

28 Discussion Ask students how Caliban's reaction to the mysterious music differs from his companions'? How does his reaction reveal an unexpected side of his personality?

29 Enrichment Explain to students that the strange music of the island suggests the music of the spheres, a divine music associated with the movement of the heavens. Elizabethans believed that the universe consisted of a series of nine concentrically nested shells. The earth was at the center. Around the earth were the celestial spheres, each of which contained a heavenly body. The outermost sphere, called the *primum mobile*, or "first mover," carried all the others around the earth from east to west in a complete circle every twenty-four hours. Meanwhile, over longer and varying periods of time, each heavenly body moved from west to east around the earth.

The spheres were thought to emit a divine music as they circled the earth, a music symbolizing the harmony and perfection of the universe. Classical astronomers believed that this music resulted from friction. Some Renaissance thinkers, however, believed that the music came from the singing of angels. Adam and Eve could hear this music in Eden. After being banished from paradise, however, humans no longer had the capacity to hear these celestial harmonies.

The music that pervades Prospero's island therefore suggests a prelapsarian, Edenic world.

30 Discussion Ask students what is similar about the action in both these scenes. How does this similarity provide an effective transition?

31 **Discussion** Ask students how Prospero's physical position in this scene symbolizes his position and role in the play. Have them turn back to the picture of the second Globe Theatre (page 706) and imagine exactly where Prospero might have stood.

32 **Clarification** According to legend, the phoenix was an Arabian bird that periodically experienced death and rebirth. It lived for 500 years, then burned itself on a pyre. A new phoenix arose from the ashes. The Greek historian Herodotus asserted that the phoenix was red and golden and looked something like an eagle.

33 **Discussion** Ask students how Sebastian and Antonio's reaction to this scene is atypical of them. Can this reaction serve to mobilize their better selves? Explain.

34 **Discussion** Why is it appropriate that Gonzalo, rather than Antonio or Sebastian, make this observation?

35 **Discussion** Have students explain the meaning of Prospero's comment.

ANTONIO. [Aside to SEBASTIAN] Let it be tonight;
15   For, now they are oppressed with travel, they
    Will not nor cannot use such vigilance
    As when they are fresh.

SEBASTION. [*Aside to* ANTONIO] I say tonight. No more.

[*Solemn and strange music; and* PROSPERO *on the top[4] (invisible). Enter several strange* SHAPES, *bringing in a banquet; and dance about it with gentle actions of salutations; and, inviting the King etc. to eat, they depart.*]

ALONSO. What harmony is this? My good friends, hark!

GONZALO. Marvelous sweet music!

20 **ALONSO.** Give us kind keepers,[5] heavens! What were these?

SEBASTIAN. A living drollery.[6] Now I will believe
    That there are unicorns; that in Arabia
    There is one tree, the phoenix' throne; one phoenix
    At this hour reigning there.

ANTONIO.   I'll believe both;
25   And what does else want credit, come to me,
    And I'll be sworn 'tis true. Travelers ne'er did lie,
    Though fools at home condemn 'em.

GONZALO.   If in Naples
    I should report this now, would they believe me
    If I should say I saw such islanders?
30   (For certes[7] these are people of the island)
    Who, though they are of monstrous shape, yet note,
    Their manners are more gentle, kind, than of
    Our human generation you shall find
    Many—nay, almost any.

PROSPERO.   [*Aside*] Honest lord.
35   Thou hast said well; for some of you there present
    Are worse than devils.

ALONSO.   I cannot too much muse[8]
    Such shapes, such gesture, and such sound, expressing
    (Although they want the use of tongue) a kind
    Of excellent dumb discourse.

PROSPERO.   [*Aside*] Praise in departing.[9]

FRANCISCO. They vanished strangely.

40 **SEBASTIAN.**   No matter, since
    They have left their viands[10] behind; for we have stomachs.
    Will't please you taste of what is here?

---

4. on the top: A stage direction indicating that Prospero is to stand at the rear of the stage or possibly on a structure above it so as to seem invisible to the characters onstage.

5. kind keepers: Good protectors or guardian angels.
6. living drollery: A puppet show, such as Punch 'n' Judy, but using live actors; perhaps a masque.

7. certes: Certain; sure.

8. muse: Wonder at; ponder.

9. Praise in departing: Keep your praise until you leave.

10. viands: Food.

Commentary

The Illusory Feast Feasts are often associated with community and a special bond between host and guest. Germanic kings, for instance, would reward their followers with food and gifts, and these followers would reiterate their allegiance to the throne. In Homer's *Iliad*, guests and hosts who had broken bread together were prohibited from doing each other harm.

Prospero plays on these associations in order to remind the courtiers of the ideal of community. Then he abruptly dissolves the feast on the grounds that Alonso, Sebastian, and Antonio are not worthy of it. Indeed they are unworthy to live among other people because they have broken the essential bonds of humanity by attempting to murder Prospero. The broken ceremony of the feast thus symbolizes the sinfulness of the court.

Notice, too, how Prospero's illusions function. The courtiers are at first shocked by the strange spirits into believing that there is more in the world than they would have thought (lines 21–34). Their often acid skepticism is temporarily laid to rest and they are lost in wonder. As the banquet vanishes, however, they are shocked into a new awareness of their guilt. The three are confused even further by being *told* that Ariel has made them mad: Their sure sense of the world is undermined, and as a result they do go mad. Alon-

ALONSO.   Not I.

GONZALO. Faith, sir, you need not fear. When we were boys,
    Who should believe that there were mountaineers
45 Dewlapped[11] like bulls, whose throats had hanging at 'em
    Wallets of flesh? Or that there were such men
    Whose heads stood in their breasts? Which now we find
    Each putter-out of five for one will bring us
    Good warrant of.[12]

    ALONSO.   I will stand to, and feed;
50 Although my last, no matter, since I feel
    The best is past. Brother, my lord the Duke,
    Stand to, and do as we.

[*Thunder and lighting. Enter* ARIEL, *like a harpy;*[13] *claps his wings upon the table; and with a quaint device*[14] *the banquet vanishes.*]

    ARIEL. You are three men of sin, whom destiny—
    That hath to instrument[15] this lower world
55 And what is in't—the never-surfeited sea
    Hath caused to belch up you and on this island,
    Where man doth not inhabit, you 'mongst men
    Being most unfit to live. I have made you mad;
    And even with suchlike valor men hang and drown
    Their proper selves.[16]
               [ALONSO, SEBASTIAN, *etc. draw their swords.*]
60   You fools! I and my fellows
    Are ministers of Fate. The elements,
    Of whom your swords are tempered,[17] may as well
    Wound the loud winds, or with bemocked-at-stabs
    Kill the still-closing waters, as diminish
65 One dowle that's in my plume.[18] My fellow ministers
    Are like invulnerable.[19] If you could hurt,
    Your swords are now too massy for your strengths[20]
    And will not be uplifted. But remember
    (For that's my business to you) that you three
70 From Milan did supplant good Prospero;
    Exposed unto the sea, which hath requit it,[21]
    Him and his innocent child; for which foul deed
    The pow'rs delaying, not forgetting, have
    Incensed the seas and shores, yea, all the creatures,
75 Against your peace. Thee of thy son, Alonso,
    They have bereft; and do pronounce by me
    Ling'ring perdition (worse than any death
    Can be at once) shall step by step attend
    You and your ways; whose wraths to guard you from,
80 Which here, in this most desolate isle, else falls

---

11. **Dewlapped:** Having loose skin hanging from the neck like that of certain animals, such as cows and bulls.

12. **Each . . . warrant of:** Ordinary travelers (who take out insurance at which they are repaid five-to-one) confirm nowadays that such fanciful creatures actually exist.

13. **harpy:** A mythical figure from ancient Greece who pursued those guilty of wrongdoing.

14. **a quaint device:** A stage mechanism, such as a puff of smoke and a trapdoor, that aids the banquet hidden by Ariel's harpy wings to "vanish."

15. **to instrument:** As its instrument.

16. **even with . . . selves:** With courage granted by madness men kill themselves.

17. **tempered:** Made.

18. **dowle . . . plume:** Fluffy little feather in my covering of feathers.

19. **My fellow . . . invulnerable:** My companions are as incapable of being harmed (as I am).

20. **If you . . . strengths:** But even if you could hurt us, your swords are too heavy for your strength.

21. **requit it:** Avenged that wrong.

---

36 Discussion Ask students why it is appropriate for Ariel to come in the shape of a harpy. Why is it fitting that the banquet vanish?

37 Discussion Have students consider the tone with which Ariel should speak these lines. Does this speech show Ariel in a different light than usual? If so, how? Is it fair to call this speech the climax, or at least a climactic point, of the play?

38 Enrichment Point out to students that even the sea rejects these men. It "belches" them up, an image of rejection suitable for a scene in which a banquet has vanished.

39 Discussion Have students describe the action that occurs while Ariel is speaking. Encourage them to find words and phrases in the speech that suggest certain actions.

40 Enrichment Tell students that critics have often praised this play for the artistry of its blank verse. This passage is an excellent example of Shakespeare's skill. As Ariel describes the lingering punishment that Alonso will suffer, the verse itself mimics the slow punishment in its movement. The thought is eked out, constantly interrupted—first by the noun of direct address, then by the line end, the semicolon, the line end again, and the parentheses. Notice that none of the lines is a complete thought; each continues across the enjambment, as if simulating the slow, tortuous pace of "perdition."

---

so is moved by suicidal passion, and Antonio and Sebastian (fittingly) by homicidal violence.

41 Discussion How does the end of the speech point toward the resolution of the play's main conflict? How does the conclusion of the speech relate to the containment and distancing of evil in Shakespeare's romances?

42 Discussion Have students compare this appearance of the spirits with their first appearance. What accounts for the change in their behavior?

43 Enrichment Point out to students that Prospero takes great relish in Ariel's performance. Prospero is an agent of justice, but he is also a showman who wants justice performed with an attention to artistic detail.

44 Discussion Ask students what the phrasing of this line indicates about Prospero's acceptance of Ferdinand?

45 Discussion Have students explain why Gonzalo is the only person not driven mad by Ariel's speech.

46 Enrichment Point out to students how this passage contributes to the music imagery that pervades the play. The whole earth itself seems to resonate with the awe-inspiring music of Alonso's guilt. Also, the images of water, wind, and thunder recall the tempest with which the play began.

47 Discussion Ask students to compare and contrast the ways in which Alonso, Antonio, and Sebastian react to Ariel's speech. How is each man's reaction in keeping with his personality?

Upon your heads, is nothing but heart's sorrow[22]
And a clear life ensuing.

[*He vanishes in thunder; then, to soft music, enter the* SHAPES *again, and dance with mocks and mows,[23] and carrying out the table.*]

PROSPERO. Bravely the figure of this harpy hast thou
    Performed, my Ariel; a grace it had, devouring.[24]
85 Of my instruction hast thou nothing bated
    In what thou hadst to say. So, with good life
    And observation strange, my meaner ministers
    Their several kinds have done.[25] My high charms work,
    And these, mine enemies, are all knit up
90 In their distractions. They now are in my pow'r;
    And in these fits I leave them, while I visit
    Young Ferdinand, whom they suppose is drowned,
    And his and mine loved darling.   [*Exit above.*]

GONZALO. I' th' name of something holy, sir, why stand you
    In this strange stare?

95 ALONSO.   O, it is monstrous, monstrous!
    Methought the billows spoke and told me of it;
    The winds did sing it to me; and the thunder,
    That deep and dreadful organ pipe, pronounced
    The name of Prosper; it did bass my trespass.[26]
100 Therefore my son i' th' ooze is bedded; and
    I'll seek him deeper than e'er plummet sounded
    And with him there lie mudded.   [*Exit.*]

SEBASTIAN.   But one fiend at a time,
    I'll fight their legions o'er![27]

ANTONIO.   I'll be thy second.

             [*Exit* SEBASTIAN *and* ANTONIO.]

GONZALO. All three of them are desperate; their great guilt,
105 Like poison given to work a great time after,
    Now 'gins to bite the spirits. I do beseech you,
    That are of suppler joints, follow them swiftly
    And hinder them from what this ecstasy[28]
    May not provoke them to.

ADRIAN.   Follow, I pray you.   [*Exit all.*]

Reader's Response *If you were Prospero, how would you punish Alonso, Antonio, and Sebastian?*

---

22. nothing . . . sorrow: Nothing but sincere repentance (will protect you from the wrath of the avenging powers).

23. mocks and mows: Derisive gestures and grimaces.

24. a grace . . . devouring: Your performance had an all-consuming grace.

25. with good life . . . done: With true-to-life acting and close attention to my wishes, your lower-ranking companions—my agents—have performed their parts according to their natures.

26. bass my trespass: The bass part of nature's thunderous music made clear to me the wrong I did Prospero.

27. But one fiend . . . o'er: If they but put one devil against me at a time, I'll fight their armies to the last demon.

28. ecstasy: Insanity.

THINKING ABOUT THE SELECTION

Clarifying

1. How do you know that Prospero approves of the growing love between Ferdinand and Miranda?
2. What strategy does Ariel employ to confuse Caliban and his fellow plotters?
3. (a) What does the disguised Ariel say to the banqueters when the banquet vanishes? (b) How does each of them react?

Interpreting

4. (a) How does Prospero haunt this act, although he does not make a formal appearance in any scene? (b) In what way is he different from all the other characters?
5. In his "music" speech, Caliban speaks of sleep and dreaming (III.ii.126–134). (a) What other moments in this act stress dream or illusion? (b) How are dreams or strange visions related to the theme of transformation?
6. A feast usually suggests celebration and welcome. Why is an interrupted feast especially suitable for Prospero's purposes in the final scene of this act?

Applying

7. Gonzalo says that Sebastian, Antonio, and Alonso are affected by the "poison" of their guilt. How is guilt like a "poison"?

ANALYZING LITERATURE

Understanding Plot, Subplot, and Character

Unlike a novelist, a dramatist cannot speak to his audience directly. Shakespeare therefore uses the **plot** and **subplots,** or main and secondary actions, to comment on situations and reveal complexities of **character.** In this act the first two scenes deal with subplots that lend perspective to the primary actions in the final scene. For instance, Caliban's bestial urge to "knock a nail into" Prospero's head underscores the baseness and ingratitude of the two courtiers who want to seize Alonso's kingdom. In addition, contrasts between characters reveal traits that were not at first apparent. Such contrasts also suggest ideas about the way in which humans develop.

1. How do the events of the first scene provide an ironic comment on the actions of the two subsequent scenes?

2. (a) How does Caliban reveal himself to be more eloquent than Stephano or Trinculo? (b) What does this quality suggest about his character?
3. (a) If Caliban and Miranda had the same upbringing, why are they so different? (b) What does this difference suggest about the relative importance of nature versus nurture?

SPEAKING AND LISTENING

Performing a Scene

Get together with a group of classmates to perform a scene from this act. When you have decided who will take each part, study the text and note the important words you want to stress in your reading. Remember that as long as you begin right after the previous speaker stops, you can take your time with a speech. Make the meaning of the words clear to listeners. Also, read with the emotions you imagine the character feels.

UNDERSTANDING LANGUAGE

Finding the Meaning That Fits the Context

The specific meanings of many words are determined by context. The word *foil* (Scene i, line 46) has a number of possible meanings. When Ferdinand says, ". . . And put it to the foil," you know what kind of foil he means.

Use the context to determine the meaning of each of the following italicized words.
1. ". . . 'Twill *weep* for having wearied you." (i, 19)
2. ". . . Did *quarrel* with the noblest grace she owed; . . ." (i, 45)

THINKING AND WRITING

Contrasting Characters as a Clue to Theme

Write an essay in which you demonstrate how Shakespeare explores themes by contrasting characters. For example, you might want to show how contrasts between Miranda and Caliban throw light on the theme of nature versus nurture. Or you can discuss the contrast between Caliban and Stephano and what it suggests about civilized versus uncivilized behavior. Begin by freewriting about the likenesses and differences between two characters. Draw on these notes as you write your paper. In revising your work, make sure your first paragraph clearly states how the contrast between the characters illuminates a theme.

(continued from bottom of page)

mation. For instance, the illusory feast is meant to make the courtiers and the king aware of their guilt and therefore ready to change.
6. Answers will differ. Many students will respond that by interrupting the feast, Prospero shows the nobles that their guilt renders them unfit for celebration or welcome.
7. Answers will differ. Students may respond that as poison destroys one's physical well-being, guilt can destroy one's self-esteem or even sanity.

Challenge What problems in staging would this act have presented to an Elizabethan theater company? How might they have solved these problems?

ANSWERS TO ANALYZING LITERATURE

1. Ferdinand and Miranda are in harmony and want only to help each other. Their love and sympathy contrasts ironically with the brainless greed of the clowns and the cynical evil of the courtiers.
2. (a) His response to the music of the island (III.ii.126–134) is both eloquent and deeply felt. Stephano and Trinculo, who speak in prose rather than poetry are not capable of such a response. (b) Caliban's speech suggests that he is responsive to harmony and reason and therefore can be redeemed.
3. (a) Answers will differ. Students may indicate that their parents were very different. (b) Answers will differ. Some students may feel that the difference between them suggests the decisive influence of nature in determining character.

ANSWERS TO UNDERSTANDING LANGUAGE

1. Ooze a resinous sap, as if it is crying
2. Dispute with and undermine

THINKING AND WRITING

Writing Across the Curriculum You might want to inform the science department that you are reading a selection. Ask a science teacher to speak to the class about the modern scientific perspective on nature vs. nurture. As a writing assignment, students can research and report on an aspect of this issue that interests them.

Closure and Extension

ANSWERS TO THINKING ABOUT THE SELECTION

1. Twice in asides Prospero declares his positive feelings about the match (III.i.74–75, 93–94).
2. He makes Caliban and Stephano think that Trinculo is accusing Caliban of lying. Then he frightens Stephano

and Trinculo with his music.
3. (a) He tells them that they have sinned and that he has made them "mad." (b) Alonso becomes suicidal and Sebastian and Antonio become homicidally violent.
4. (a) He watches the encounter between Ferdinand and Miranda, his agent Ariel confuses the clown-conspirators, and he is present but invisible to the other characters at the in-

terrupted banquet scene.(b) He is in some sense both an actor in this play and its director. He is in control of the action.
5. (a) Answers will differ. Many students will mention the strange and illusory feast that Prospero's spirits prepare for Alonso and his courtiers. (b) Answers will differ. Some students may respond that visions and dreams are a key part of the process of transfor-

Focus

Literary Focus Ask students whether they have ever attended a rock concert, light show, fireworks display, or masquerade party. Have them describe these spectacles as vividly as possible. Then tell them that Act IV of *The Tempest* features a spectacle, called a masque, that was popular during the Renaissance.

Writing/Prior Knowledge Have students discuss these questions in small groups before starting the assignment.

ESL Teaching Strategy Have ESL students tell the class about spectacles that are popular in their cultures. Also, before ESL students read this act, you may want to summarize the actions in the masque and identify the mythological characters who take part in it.

Teaching Tenth-Grade Students Tenth-grade students may enjoy designing costumes and selecting music for the masque. You might also ask them to expand the plot diagrams they started to create for Act III.

Cooperative Learning Have the teams created at the beginning of Act III continue to study their plots. Ask them to review and, if necessary, revise their predictions after reading this act.

Vocabulary
Preteach the following vocabulary words:
austerely (ô stir´ lē) adv.: Sternly
vexations (veks ā´ shənz) n.: Annoyances
ardor (är´ dər) n.: Passion
temperate (tem´ pər it) adj.: Moderate; self-restrained
cankers (kaŋ´ kərz) v.: Becomes infected with corruption

Commentary

The Tempest, Act IV

Renaissance Masques. In Act IV Prospero celebrates the engagement of Ferdinand and Miranda with a spectacle that is like a combination of a light show and a masquerade party. Such spectacles, called **masques**, were an artistic form that flourished in the courts and noble houses of Europe during the later Renaissance. Usually performed indoors, masques used elaborate scenic and lighting effects to commemorate occasions like holidays, marriages, and homecomings. They didn't so much tell stories as present visions: The maskers would assume the characters of classical gods and goddesses and present in their dances a symbolic interpretation of the event being celebrated.

Since Prospero's masque celebrates the marriage of Ferdinand and Miranda, it is about marriage. It gives us an image of the harmonious world Prospero wishes to create, and the love that it celebrates is pure. The divine characters associated with passion, Venus and Cupid, are absent from the show. Instead, the chief mythological characters are Juno, queen of the gods, who saw as her most important role that of being wife to Zeus, and Ceres, the goddess of fertility.

Shakespeare stresses the artificiality of the masque—its distance from ordinary life—by the verse form. It is written in iambic pentameter couplets, whose rhymes make the speech sound less natural than blank verse.

The performance of the masque is interrupted when Prospero suddenly remembers Caliban's plot to kill him. Caliban and Stephano are not serious enemies, but the plot reminds Prospero that he is not all-powerful. It recalls Antonio's more successful plot twelve years earlier. The force of this memory causes the show to end, and Prospero gives a speech which suggests that all human efforts are as transient as the fragile masque.

Writing

Describe a moment when something you had worked hard to create or organize—a painting, a story, a meeting, or a party—failed because of someone's interference. How did you feel? What did you do?

Objectives

Thematic
To appreciate the way in which spectacles can communicate ideas

Skills
1 To understand Renaissance masques
2 To appreciate dramatic speeches
3 To appreciate Shakespeare's repetitions
4 To write a blank verse soliloquy

Support Material

Teaching Portfolio
Teacher Backup, pp. 921–924
Grammar in Action Worksheet, *Poetry and Prose*, pp. 925–926
Usage and Mechanics Worksheet, p. 927
Vocabulary Check, p. 928
Analyzing Literature Worksheet, *Understanding Renaissance*

Act IV

Scene i. *In front of Prospero's cell.*

[*Enter* PROSPERO, FERDINAND, *and* MIRANDA.]

PROSPERO. If I have too austerely punished you,
Your compensation makes amends; for I
Have given you here a third of mine own life,
Or that for which I live; who once again
5   I tender to thy hand. All thy vexations
Were but my trials of thy love, and thou
Hast strangely[1] stood the test. Here, afore heaven,
I ratify this my rich gift. O Ferdinand,
Do not smile at me that I boast her off,[2]
10 For thou shalt find she will outstrip all praise
And make it halt[3] behind her.

FERDINAND.   I do believe it
Against an oracle.[4]

PROSPERO. Then, as my gift, and thine own acquisition
Worthily purchased, take my daughter. But
15 If thou dost break her virgin-knot before
All sanctimonious[5] ceremonies may
With full and holy rite be minist'red,
No sweet aspersion[6] shall the heavens let fall
To make this contract grow;[7] but barren hate,
20 Sour-eyed disdain, and discord shall bestrew
The union of your bed with weeds so loathly
That you shall hate it both. Therefore take heed,
As Hymen's lamps shall light you.[8]

FERDINAND.   As I hope
For quiet days, fair issue, and long life,
25 With such love as 'tis now, the murkiest den,
The most opportune place, the strong'st suggestion
Our worser genius can,[9] shall never melt
Mine honor into lust, to take away
The edge[10] of that day's celebration
30 When I shall think or Phoebus' steeds[11] are foundered[12]
Or Night kept chained below.[13]

PROSPERO.   Fairly spoke.
Sit then and talk with her; she is thine own.
What, Ariel![14] My industrious servant, Ariel!

[*Enter* ARIEL.]

ARIEL. What would my potent master? Here I am.

---

1. **strangely:** Wonderfully.

2. **boast her off:** Praise her to the sky.

3. **halt:** Limp.

4. **I do . . . oracle:** I believe you even if a prophet should say otherwise.

5. **sanctimonious:** Sacred; holy.
6. **aspersion:** Ritual sprinkling of water, as in a religious ceremony.
7. **this contract grow:** This marriage develop into a family.
8. **As . . . you:** As the lamps of the god of marriage burn clearly to light your way at the wedding ceremony.
9. **worser genius can:** Bad demon can make. (In medieval times, everyone had a good demon and a bad demon or set of angels watching over him or her. This was an inheritance from the ancient Greeks, who believed everyone had a personal demon.)
10. **The edge:** Intense pleasure.
11. **Phoebus' steeds:** The horses of Apollo the sun god. They pulled the sun god's chariot across the sky from dawn to dusk.
12. **foundered:** Made lame.
13. **below:** Below the horizon.
14. **What, Ariel!:** Here, Ariel! Come here, Ariel!

Masques, p. 929
Critical Thinking and Reading Worksheet, *Appreciating Dramatic Speeches,* p. 930
Selection Test, pp. 931–932

Spelling Tip Write the word *ardor* on the chalkboard and point out to students that the second syllable is spelled with an *o* even though it may sound like *er.*

Presentation

Motivation/Prior Knowledge Encourage students to think about the problem that a dramatist like Shakespeare faced in writing a fourth act. The third act contains a climax of sorts and the fifth act, a resolution. There is a danger, therefore, that the fourth act will drag. Ask students

how the masque might help sustain audience interest.

Master Teacher Note Give students more background information on masques. These spectacles may have evolved from a custom practiced by middle-class citizens on holidays. They would disguise themselves in elaborate, often grotesque, costumes and serenade their neighbors. Among the upper classes, it was customary for maskers and musicians to appear at a party, perform a skit, and then either unmask themselves and remain or depart still wearing their masks. Italy was the first country in which masques were incorporated into court entertainment. England adopted this custom, and English court masques grew more and more elaborate. Finally, these masques became allegorical pageants in which the characters recited poetry written for the occasion. Under King James I, these poetic speeches were written by Ben Jonson. The magnificent stage settings were designed by a great Renaissance architect, Inigo Jones.

1 Enrichment Point out to students that the resolution of this drama will involve several different kinds of loss for Prospero. His granting permission for Miranda to marry Ferdinand is one kind of loss. Although he will still see her, she will not be *his* again in the same way. As he says to Ferdinand, in giving her away, he is giving "a third" of his "own life." His unselfishness matches the unselfishness that the lovers have shown toward each other.

Ask students if this context makes Prospero's testing of Ferdinand more understandable.

2 Discussion Explain to students that Prospero stands for chastity and self-discipline. As this speech indicates, his feelings about these matters run deep. Have students consider why Prospero feels so strongly about self-control. Is he responding to Caliban's attempted rape of Miranda? Is he remembering the passions of those who attempted to murder him? Do you think Prospero is too nervous about his daughter's honor? Why or why not?

3 Enrichment Remind students that in the previous scene, Miranda began to shift her allegiance from her father to her lover. Here, as if to balance that movement, Ferdinand swears his allegiance to Prospero's principles of discipline and self-control.

4

35 PROSPERO. Thou and thy meaner fellows your last service
Did worthily perform; and I must use you
In such another trick. Go bring the rabble,[15]
O'er whom I give thee pow'r, here to this place.
Incite them to quick motion; for I must
40 Bestow upon the eyes of this young couple
Some vanity[16] of mine art. It is my promise,
And they expect it from me.

ARIEL.   Presently?

PROSPERO. Ay, with a twink.

ARIEL. Before you can say "Come" and "Go,"
45 And breathe twice and cry, "So, so,"
Each one, tripping on his toe,
Will be here with mop[17] and mow.
Do you love me, master? No?

5

PROSPERO. Dearly, my delicate Ariel. Do not approach
50 Till thou dost hear me call.

ARIEL.   Well; I conceive.[18]   [*Exit.*]

6

PROSPERO. Look thou be true.[19] Do not give dalliance[20]
Too much the rein; the strongest oaths are straw
To th' fire i' th' blood. Be more abstemious,[21]
Or else good night your vow!

FERDINAND.   I warrant you, sir.
55 The white cold virgin snow upon my heart
Abates the ardor of my liver.

7

PROSPERO.   Well.
Now come, my Ariel; bring a corollary[22]
Rather than want a spirit. Appear, and pertly!
No tongue! All eyes! Be silent.   [*Soft music*]

[*Enter* IRIS.[23]]

8

60 IRIS. Ceres,[24] most bounteous lady, thy rich leas[25]
Of wheat, rye, barley, fetches,[26] oats, and peas;
Thy turfy mountains, where live nibbling sheep,
And flat meads thatched with stover,[27] them to keep;
Thy banks with pionèd and twillèd-brims,[28]
65 Which spongy April at thy hest betrims
To make cold nymphs chaste crowns; and thy broom groves,
Whose shadow the dismissèd bachelor loves,
Being lasslorn; thy pole-clipt[29] vineyard;
And thy sea-marge,[30] sterile and rocky-hard,
70 Where thou thyself dost air[31]—the queen o' the' sky,[32]
Whose wat'ry arch and messenger am I,
Bids thee leave these, and with her sovereign grace,

15. **rabble:** The lower-ranking spirits; mob or disorderly collection of lower-class individuals.

16. **vanity:** Trifle; small, unimportant thing.

17. **mop:** Grin or gesture.

18. **conceive:** Comprehend; understand.
19. **Look . . . true:** (addressed to Ferdinand and Miranda, who were embracing): Stop that! Be faithful to your promise.
20. **dalliance:** Amorous play; playful lovemaking.
21. **abstemious:** Moderate; sparing.
22. **corollary:** An extra spirit.
23. **Iris:** In classical mythology, a goddess who served as a messenger of the gods. Iris rode the rainbow to deliver her messages.
24. **Ceres:** The Roman goddess of the earth and agriculture.
25. **leas:** Meadows.
26. **fetches:** Vegetables, also clover, alfalfa, and soybeans.
27. **meads . . . stover:** Meadows having grasses used to feed cattle or sheep.
28. **pionèd and twillèd:** Undercut by the stream and retained by interwoven branches.
29. **pole-clipt:** Pruned.
30. **sea-marge:** The margin of the sea; seashore.
31. **Where . . . air:** Where you yourself stroll on holiday.
32. **queen o' th' sky:** Juno, the Roman goddess, queen of the gods.

Commentary

The Masque Masques were elaborate productions created to celebrate important court occasions. They made use of elaborate scenery and much of their action was danced; the dialogue formed a comparatively small part of the whole. Also, masques usually developed a vision of a guiding ideal—the monarch's court was presented as an embodiment of virtue.

The masque that Prospero stages for the couple presents a vision of marriage as a harmonious union of opposite qualities. The stress on harmony appears in the figure of Iris, who is associated with the rainbow. The rainbow

is itself an emblem of divine promise (see Genesis 9:11–17, page 50); it quite literally unites heaven with earth (lines 80–81). Another image of opposites united is that of the nymphs and the reapers. The nymphs are "natural" creatures, denizens of the brooks, while the reapers are human. Nature joins with art in a dance that figures forth a divine harmony.

The masque world differs from the world of the island in several important ways. The masque is written in more formal verse. Its setting (lines 60–70) suggests England, not the Mediterranean. Finally, the masque characters lack the complexity of real human beings. Prospero has created a harmonious vision by excluding many of the human passions that might trou-

[JUNO *descends.*[33]]

Here on this grass plot, in this very place,
To come and sport; her peacocks fly amain.[34]

75 Approach, rich Ceres, her to entertain.

[*Enter* CERES.]

CERES. Hail, many-colored messenger, that ne'er
Dost disobey the wife of Jupiter,[35]
Who, with thy saffron wings, upon my flow'rs
Diffusest honey drops, refreshing show'rs,
80 And with each end of thy blue bow dost crown
My bosky[36] acres and my unshrubbed down,
Rich scarf to my proud earth. Why hath thy queen
Summoned me hither to this short-grassed green?

IRIS. A contract of true love to celebrate
85 And some donation freely to estate[37]
On the blessed lovers.

CERES.   Tell me, heavenly bow,
If Venus[38] or her son,[39] as thou dost know,
Do now attend the Queen? Since they did plot
The means that dusky Dis[40] my daughter got,[41]
90 Her and her blind boy's[42] scandaled[43] company
I have forsworn.

---

33. *Juno descends:* A stage direction indicating that Juno is slowly lowered from the ceiling of the stage.
34. amain: Speedily. (Juno's chariot was drawn by peacocks.)

35. Jupiter: In Roman mythology, the ruler of the gods.
36. bosky: Woodsy.
37. estate: Bestow.
38. Venus: The Roman goddess of love.
39. her son: Cupid, the Roman god of love.
40. Dis: The Roman god of the underworld.
41. my daughter got: An allusion to the classical myth of the abduction of Proserpine. Proserpine, the daughter of Ceres, was carried off by Dis to his underworld kingdom where he made her queen.
42. blind boy's: Cupid's; he was often shown blindfolded.
43. scandaled: Scandalous.

---

ble it: greed, lust, and ambition. Of course, these are the very passions that got Prospero into trouble in Milan. In this respect, the masque is an extreme version of the island itself.

12 **Enrichment** There are two ancient cities named Paphos in southwest Cyprus. Archeologists have found ruins on the site of the older city that date back to 3000 B.C.

13 **Literary Focus** Ask students to whom Iris is referring when she refers to "this man and maid." Also have them explain the allegorical meaning of this little incident. How does it relate to the action of the play?

14 **Literary Focus** Point out to students that the meter of the blessing song is different from that of the dialogue. The song is written in trochaic tetrameter (a trochaic meter with four feet to the line), while the dialogue is written in iambic pentameter. Have students verify this difference for themselves.

15 **Discussion** Ask students to compare and contrast this masque with the banquet that spirits serve in Act III (for more on the masque and the banquet, see the Commentary below).

16 **Enrichment** Point out to students that Ferdinand's enthusiasm for Prospero's art causes him to speak in rhyme, as if he were part of the masque!

IRIS.   Of her society
Be not afraid; I met her Deity
Cutting the clouds towards Paphos,[44] and her son
Dove-drawn with her. Here thought they to have done
95   Some wanton charm upon this man and maid,
Whose vows are, that no bed-right shall be paid
Till Hymen's torch be lighted. But in vain;
Mars's hot minion[45] is returned again;[46]
Her waspish-headed son[47] has broke his arrows,
100 Swears he will shoot no more, but play with sparrows
And be a boy right out.[48]

[JUNO *alights.*]

CERES.   Highest queen of state,
Great Juno, comes; I know her by her gait.

JUNO. How does my bounteous sister? Go with me
To bless this twain, that they may prosperous be
105 And honored in their issue.

[*They sing.*]

JUNO.   Honor, riches, marriage blessing,
             Long continuance, and increasing,
             Hourly joys be still[49] upon you!
             Juno sings her blessings on you.
110 [CERES.] Earth's increase, foison plenty,
             Barns and garners never empty,
             Vines with clust'ring bunches growing,
             Plants with goodly burden bowing;
             Spring come to you at the farthest
115   In the very end of harvest.[50]
             Scarcity and want shall shun you,
             Ceres' blessings so is on you.

FERDINAND. This is a most majestic vision, and
Harmonious charmingly. May I be bold
To think these spirits?

120 PROSPERO.   Spirits, which by mine art
I have from their confines called to enact
My present fancies.

FERDINAND.   Let me live here ever!
So rare a wond'red[51] father and a wise
Makes this place Paradise.

[JUNO *and* CERES *whisper, and send* IRIS *on employment.*]

PROSPERO.   Sweet now, silence!
125 Juno and Ceres whisper seriously.
There's something else to do. Hush and be mute,
Or else your spell is marred.

44. Paphos: A major center for the worship of Venus, on Cyprus.

45. Mars's hot minion: Venus, who was the mistress of Mars, the Roman god of war.
46. returned again: Returned home to Paphos.
47. waspish-headed son: Cupid, who was thought of as having a sharp sting like a wasp because of his arrows.
48. boy right out: An ordinary boy, like all other boys.

49. still: Forever; always.

50. Spring . . . harvest: As summer ends may spring begin—in other words, may there never be a winter in your lives.

51. wond'red: Wonderful.

Commentary

The Dissolution of the Masque Like the banquet in the previous act, the masque dissolves suddenly. The dissolution of the masque, however, is not part of Prospero's plan, as the interruption of the feast was. For the first time in the play, something happens which Prospero has not expected. The masque vanishes when he abruptly remembers Caliban and realizes that he needs to deal with his plot instead of creating petty illusions. Although Caliban is not a real threat, the abruptness of the masque's vanishing and Prospero's anger suggest that with the thought of Caliban comes the memory of all the other, more formidable evils that Prospero will have to face in Milan. The memory of Caliban thus reminds Prospero of his ultimate helplessness when he leaves the island and with it, his magic.

Prospero's speech (lines 146–163), which is meant to reassure Ferdinand, is paradoxically rather disturbing. The old magician draws a parallel between the masque and the world itself, with the implication that ultimately all earthly creations are transient. Indeed, in a curious moment Prospero speaks of "the great globe itself" which will pass away in a last judgment,

IRIS. You nymphs, called Naiades,[52] of the windring[53] brooks,
With your sedged crowns and ever-harmless looks,
130　Leave your crisp[54] channels, and on this green land
Answer your summons; Juno does command.
Come, temperate nymphs, and help to celebrate
A contract of true love; be not too late.

[Enter certain NYMPHS.]

You sunburned sicklemen, of August weary,
135　Come hither from the furrow and be merry.
Make holiday; your rye-straw hats put on,
And these fresh nymphs encounter everyone
In country footing.[55]

[Enter certain REAPERS, properly habited. They join with the NYMPHS in a graceful dance; towards the end whereof PROSPERO starts suddenly and speaks;[56] after which, to a strange, hollow, and confused noise, they heavily[57] vanish.]

PROSPERO. *[Aside]* I had forgot that foul conspiracy
140　Of the beast Caliban and his confederates
Against my life. The minute of their plot
Is almost come. *[To the SPIRITS]* Well done! Avoid![58] No more!

FERDINAND. This is strange. Your father's in some passion
That works him strongly.

MIRANDA.　　　　　　　Never till this day
145　Saw I him touched with anger so distempered.[59]

PROSPERO. You do look, my son, in a movèd sort,[60]
As if you were dismayed; be cheerful, sir.
Our revels now are ended. These our actors,
As I foretold you, were all spirits and
150　Are melted into air, into thin air;
And, like the baseless fabric of this vision,
The cloud-capped towers, the gorgeous palaces,
The solemn temples, the great globe itself,
Yea, all which it inherit,[61] shall dissolve,
155　And, like this insubstantial pageant faded,
Leave not a rack[62] behind. We are such stuff
As dreams are made on, and our little life
Is rounded with a sleep. Sir, I am vexed.
Bear with my weakness; my old brain is troubled.
160　Be not disturbed with my infirmity.
If you be pleased, retire into my cell
And there repose. A turn or two I'll walk
to still my beating mind.

FERDINAND, MIRANDA.　　　We wish your peace.
　　　　　　　[Exit FERDINAND with MIRANDA.]

---

52. **Naiades:** Water nymphs, minor goddesses of classical mythology who were usually represented as lovely young women.
53. **windring:** Wandering.
54. **crisp:** Having little waves.

55. **footing:** Dancing.

56. **speaks:** Prospero breaks the spell, which required silence.
57. **heavily:** Reluctantly.

58. **Avoid:** Depart.

59. **distempered:** Fierce; intense.
60. **movèd sort:** Troubled state of mind.

61. **it inherit:** Inhabit it.

62. **rack:** Windswept cloud.

---

but the Globe Theatre was the structure in which most of Shakespeare's plays were performed. The Elizabethan audience listening to the speech, therefore, is included in this vision of transience.

---

17 Enrichment Point out to students that the dance of the nymphs and reapers symbolizes a union of nature and humanity (see Commentary, pages 764–765).

18 Discussion Ask students if Prospero has ever before shown such surprise? Is Caliban's plot alone enough to cause him such discomfort? What incident might Caliban's conspiracy remind him of? How is the dissolution of the masque different from the dissolution of the feast in the previous act?

19 Enrichment Tell students that this is one of Shakespeare's most famous speeches. Like another famous Shakespearean speech—"All the world's a stage" in *As You Like It*—it depicts human life as a pageant or drama. This speech, however, emphasizes the transitory nature of life, as if the world itself were a stage set that will one day be taken down. Point out to students that in line 153, Shakespeare makes a punning reference to the Globe Theatre where many of his plays had been produced.

20 Discussion Point out to students that Prospero began this speech to reassure Ferdinand. Is the speech in fact reassuring? Why or why not? Ask students to consider what Prospero means by "We are such stuff as dreams are made on. . . ." Are we sleeping? If so, why is our little life "rounded with a sleep"? The effect of this imagery is to reemphasize the transitory nature of the world. Encourage students to remember other moments in which the imagery of sleep and dreaming occurs; for example, Ferdinand's feeling that he is "bound up" as if dreaming (I.ii.484) and Antonio's rhetoric of sleep and vision when proposing murder (II.i.196–212). Ask students to consider why Shakespeare focuses so much attention on sleep and dreams. How does this imagery connect with the play's insistent questioning of the nature of reality?

PROSPERO. Come with a thought! I thank thee, Ariel. Come.

[*Enter* ARIEL.]

ARIEL. Thy thoughts I cleave to. What's thy pleasure?

165　PROSPERO.　　　　　　　　　　　　　　　　　Spirit,
　　　We must prepare to meet with Caliban.

ARIEL. Ay, my commander. When I presented[63] Ceres,
　　　I thought to have told thee of it, but I feared
　　　Lest I might anger thee.

170　PROSPERO. Say again, where didst thou leave these varlets?[64]

ARIEL. I told you, sir, they were red-hot with drinking;
　　　So full of valor that they smote the air
　　　For breathing in their faces, beat the ground
　　　For kissing of their feet; yet always bending[65]
175　Towards their project. Then I beat my tabor;
　　　At which like unbacked[66] colts they pricked their ears,
　　　Advanced[67] their eyelids, lifted up their noses
　　　As they smelt music. So I charmed their ears
　　　That calflike they my lowing followed through
180　Toothed briers, sharp furzes, pricking goss,[68] and thorns,
　　　Which ent'red their frail shins. At last I left them
　　　I' th' filthy mantled[69] pool beyond your cell,
　　　There dancing up to th' chins, that the foul lake
　　　O'erstunk their feet.

PROSPERO.　　　　　　　　This was well done, my bird.
185　Thy shape invisible retain thou still.
　　　The trumpery[70] in my house, go bring it hither
　　　For stale[71] to catch these thieves.

ARIEL.　　　　　　　　　　　I go, I go.　　　[*Exit.*]

PROSPERO. A devil, a born devil, on whose nature
　　　Nurture can never stick; on whom my pains,
190　Humanely taken, all, all lost, quite lost!
　　　And as with age his body uglier grows,
　　　So his mind cankers. I will plague them all,
　　　Even to roaring.

[*Enter* ARIEL, *loaden with glistering apparel, etc.*]

　　　　　　　Come, hang them on this line.[72]

[PROSPERO *and* ARIEL *remain, invisible. Enter* CALIBAN, STEPHANO, *and* TRINCULO, *all wet.*]

CALIBAN. Pray you tread softly, that the blind mole may not
195　Hear a foot fall. We now are near his cell.

---

63. presented: This is ambiguous. It could mean that Ariel acted the part of Ceres or, in the role of Iris, introduced Ceres and the entire pageant.
64. varlets: Low, vile rascals.

65. bending: Heading.

66. unbacked: Untrained and hence unsaddled.
67. Advanced: Raised.

68. goss: Shrubs.

69. mantled: Covered, as with a polluted foam or scum.

70. trumpery: Fancy-looking, gaudy, cheap clothes.
71. stale: Bait.

72. line: A linden tree.

---

21 Enrichment Point out to students that Ariel's reply, "Thy thoughts I cleave to," indicates a particularly close relationship between Prospero and his servant. *To cleave* means "to adhere or cling to." In Genesis 2:24, for example, the text reads, "Therefore shall a man leave his father and his mother, and shall cleave unto his wife: and they shall be one flesh." If Shakespeare had this reference in mind, he might have imagined that Prospero and Ariel were indeed married in some way. Master and servant, however, are soon to separate.

22 Enrichment Point out to students the vividness of this image. In saying "As they smelt music," Shakespeare makes use of a device called *synesthesia,* an image in which the senses are deliberately confused. Several hundred years later, the French poets Baudelaire and Rimbaud, pages 902 and 906, used this same device to simulate a visionary perception of reality. In his famous sonnet "Correspondences," for example, Baudelaire wrote: "All scents and sounds and colors meet as one. / Perfumes there are as sweet as the oboe's sound, / Green as the prairies, fresh as a child's caress, / —And there are others, rich, corrupt, profound . . ."

23 Discussion Ask students why it is especially fitting that Caliban and his companions end up in a stinking pool.

24 Discussion Have students consider why Prospero is so angry at the thought of Caliban's plot against him. Is he primarily angered by the thought of his lost effort in trying to civilize Caliban? Or is he upset at the thought that his failure with Caliban indicates the limitations of his power (which he will soon abandon entirely)?

Grammar in Action

Poetry and Prose It was a convention of Shakespeare's theater that noble characters usually spoke in poetry while commoners, who were often comic characters, talked in prose. Not only did commoners talk in prose, but they also tended to use colloquialisms and slang. In some cases they even spoke in dialect, the speech of a certain region.

　　　Caliban is exceptional in that he speaks in both poetry and prose, perhaps to emphasize his mixed nature. The contrast between Caliban's poetry and the prose of his clownish companions lends the monster a certain no-

STEPHANO. Monster, your fairy, which you say is a harmless fairy, has done little better than played the Jack[73] with us.

TRINCULO. Monster, I do smell all horse piss, at which my nose is in great indignation.

200 **STEPHANO.** So is mine. Do you hear, monster? If I should take a displeasure against you, look you—

TRINCULO. Thou wert but a lost monster.

CALIBAN. Good my lor, give me thy favor still.
Be patient, for the prize I'll bring thee to
205 Shall hoodwink[74] this mischance. Therefore speak softly.
All's hushed as midnight yet.

TRINCULO. Ay, but to lose our bottles in the pool—

STEPHANO. There is not only disgrace and dishonor in that, monster, but an infinite loss.

210 **TRINCULO.** That's more to me than my wetting. Yet this is your harmless fairy, monster.

STEPHANO. I will fetch off my bottle, though I be o'er ears[75] for my labor.

CALIBAN. Prithee, my king, be quiet. Seest thou here?
215 This is the mouth o' th' cell. No noise, and enter.
Do that good mischief which may make this island
Thine own forever, and I, thy Caliban,
For aye thy footlicker.

STEPHANO. Give me thy hand. I do begin to have bloody thoughts.

220 **TRINCULO.** O King Stephano! O peer![76] O worthy Stephano, look what a wardrobe here is for thee!

CALIBAN. Let 't alone, thou fool! It is but trash.

TRINCULO. O, ho, monster! We know what belongs to a frippery.[77] O King Stephano!

225 **STEPHANO.** Put off that gown, Trinculo! By this hand, I'll have that gown!

TRINCULO. Thy Grace shall have it.

CALIBAN. The dropsy[78] drown this fool! What do you mean
To dote thus on such luggage?[79] Let 't alone,
230 And do the murder first. If he awake,
From toe to crown he'll fill our skins with pinches,
Make us strange stuff.

STEPHANO. Be you quiet monster. Mistress line, is not this my jerkin?[80] [*Takes it down.*] Now is the jerkin under the line.[81]

---

73. Jack: Knave; also will-o'-the-wisp.

74. hoodwink: Hide.

75. o'er ears: Underwater (in the polluted pool).

76. O King . . . peer: Alludes to a popular song.

77. a frippery: A shop selling old, secondhand clothes.

78. dropsy: An ailment caused by excessive accumulation of fluid in the body.
79. luggage: Encumbrance; burdens.
80. jerkin: A sleeveless, hip-length jacket.
81. under the line: Under the linden tree. Also a play on the word "line," which can refer to the line on maps marking the equator—see the next sentence.

---

25 **Discussion** Ask students how this exchange reveals differences between Caliban and his fellow plotters. How does Caliban show himself to be more focused and resolute?

26 **Enrichment** Point out to students that the only thing to which Caliban can seem to aspire is eternal servitude: "For aye thy footlicker."

27 **Enrichment** Tell students that Stephano's line is a parody of what an assassin in a tragedy might say. For instance, just before Macbeth kills Duncan he sees an imaginary dagger: "I see thee still; / and on thy blade and dudgeon gouts of blood, / Which was not so before. There's no such thing. / It is the bloody business which informs / Thus to mine eyes." (II.ii.45–49).

28 **Discussion** Ask students whether Caliban's opinion of his companions might be changing now. What is he beginning to understand about them?

---

bility, even when he expresses his slavishness. In the following quotation, he also shows that he is more intelligent and focused than his loutish partners:

TRINCULO. Ay, but to lose our bottles in the pool—

STEPHANO. There is not only disgrace and dishonor in that, monster, but an infinite loss.

TRINCULO. That's more to me than my wetting. Yet this is your harmless fairy, monster.

CALIBAN. Prithee, my king, be quiet. Seest thou here?
This is the mouth o' th' cell. No noise, and enter.
Do that good mischief which may make this island
Thine own forever, and I, thy Caliban,
For aye thy footlicker.

Student Activity. Find another passage where Caliban's poetry contrasts strongly with the prose of his co-conspirators. Explain how the contrast helps to characterize Caliban.

Enrichment Point out to students that the silly punning of this "court" is a parody of the bitter wit of the courtiers Antonio and Sebastian.

30 **Discussion** Ask students why it is appropriate that the three be hunted as if they were prey. How were they themselves the hunters only a moment before? How does their punishment resemble and differ from the punishment meted out to the courtiers?

31 **Discussion** Ask students how this speech serves as a transition to the final act. How does it mark an important turning point in the plot?

235   Now, jerkin, you are like to lose your hair and prove a bald jerkin.[82]

TRINCULO. Do, do![83] We steal by line and level,[84] and't like[85] your Grace.

STEPHANO. I thank thee for that jest. Here's a garment for't. Wit
240   shall not go unrewarded while I am king of this country. "Steal by line and level" is an excellent pass of pate.[86] There's another garment for't.

TRINCULO. Monster, come put some lime[87] upon your fingers, and away with the rest.

245   CALIBAN. I will have none on't. We shall lose our time
And all be turned to barnacles,[88] or to apes
With foreheads villainous low.

STEPHANO. Monster, lay-to your fingers; help to bear this away
where my hogshead of wine is, or I'll turn you out of my
250   kingdom. Go to, carry this.

TRINCULO. And this.

STEPHANO. Ay, and this.

[*A noise of hunters heard. Enter divers* SPIRITS *in shape of dogs and hounds, hunting them about;* PROSPERO *and* ARIEL *setting them on.*]

255   PROSPERO. Hey, Mountain, hey!

ARIEL. Silver! There it goes, Silver!

PROSPERO. Fury, Fury! There, Tyrant, there! Hark, hark!

[CALIBAN, STEPHANO, *and* TRINCULO *are driven out.*]

Go, charge my goblins that they grind their joints
With dry convulsions,[89] shorten up their sinews
With agèd cramps,[90] and more pinch-spotted make them
Than pard or cat o' mountain.[91]

ARIEL.   Hark, they roar!

260   PROSPERO. Let them be hunted soundly. At this hour
Lie at my mercy all mine enemies.
Shortly shall all my labors end, and thou
Shalt have the air at freedom. For a little,
Follow, and do me service.   [*Exit.*]

Reader's Response *Music is an important part of this and other acts. How do you think the "strange music" of the island would sound?*

---

82. Now . . . bald jerkin: Sailors crossing the equator were believed to lose their hair from high fevers contracted in the tropics.
83. Do, do: Fine, fine.
84. line and level: Plumb line and carpenter's level, tools used as rules for making straight lines.
85. and't like: And if it please.
86. pass of pate: Thrust of wit.
87. lime: Birdlime, a sticky substance used to trap birds—thieves are supposed to have sticky fingers.
88. barnacles: North European geese that breed in the frigid Arctic.

89. dry convulsions: Violent spasms that cause bones to grind against one another.
90. agèd cramps: Cramps such as the elderly might get.
91. pard . . . mountain: Leopard or wildcat.

THINKING ABOUT THE SELECTION

Clarifying

1. (a) Which goddesses join in the masque? (b) What kinds of blessings do they bestow on the couple? (c) Who else joins the masque?
2. What causes Caliban and the others to turn aside from their plot?

Interpreting

3. What are Prospero's motives in creating the masque for Ferdinand and Miranda?
4. How does this broken-off "show" resemble and differ from the "show" of the disrupted feast in Act III?
5. (a) How does the final part of the act contrast with the masque? (b) Why do you think Prospero is especially angry at Caliban?

Applying

6. If you were a director, how would you present the masque so that it would keep the attention of a modern audience?

ANALYZING LITERATURE

Understanding Renaissance Masques

The **Renaissance masque** was a spectacle in which courtiers, dressed in elaborate costumes, acted and danced a vision of harmony and order. On occasion masques celebrated engagements, as Prospero does here. If one interprets the masque as Prospero's ideal vision of marriage, many of the details make sense.

1. Why should Juno and Ceres—respectively, the queen of the gods and the goddess of fertility—be involved in the masque?
2. Why should Iris, goddess of the rainbow and traditionally a messenger, play a role?
3. A Renaissance audience saw its own ideals and beliefs reflected in masques. What modern kinds of performances or spectacles symbolize our beliefs?

CRITICAL THINKING AND READING

Appreciating Dramatic Speeches

In Shakespearean drama the long speeches that characters make are not necessarily static and predictable. Sometimes characters will come to new realiza-

tions or experience different feelings *as* they speak. Prospero's famous speech about the masque (IV.i.146–163), for instance, begins as an attempt to reassure Ferdinand, but it becomes a statement that is far from reassuring.

1. (a) Which words and phrases in the speech indicate that Prospero's first intention was to reassure Ferdinand? (b) How and where does this initial emphasis change?
2. In this speech "the great globe" refers to the world but may refer as well to the Globe Theatre, in which the play was acted. How might the comment about the "globe" affect the audience?
3. To whom is Prospero referring when he says, "*We are such stuff / As dreams are made on [of]*"?
4. This speech is sometimes regarded as Shakespeare's own farewell to the stage. Is this a reasonable inference? Explain.

UNDERSTANDING LANGUAGE

Appreciating Shakespeare's Repetitions

Sometimes Shakespeare repeats a single word throughout a play, so that it gains more and more meaning. In *The Tempest*, for example, he repeats the word *strange* (or variations of it like *strangely*). It appears at least three times in Act IV; in i. 7, i. 143, and i. 232. Explain the meaning of the word in each passage and tell how its repeated use relates to the theme of magical transformation. Also, be alert to the appearance of this word as you read the final act.

THINKING AND WRITING

Writing a Blank Verse Soliloquy

A **soliloquy** is a revealing speech spoken by a character when he or she is alone. Write a soliloquy for one of the characters at a moment of crisis. For example, you could write a speech for Alonso when he thinks he is responsible for his son's death or for Miranda when she decides to marry Ferdinand and leave the island. Brainstorm about the thoughts and emotions that would go through the character's mind; then write out the speech in blank verse (see page 707 for a discussion of blank verse). You will find it easier to do this if you spend some time reading aloud the blank verse of this play. Finally, when you revise your speech, read it aloud and change passages that feel or sound clumsy.

Closure and Extension

ANSWERS TO THINKING ABOUT THE SELECTION

1. (a) Iris, Ceres, and Juno. (b) They bless the couple with "Honor, riches," long life, and plenty. (c) nymphs and reapers.
2. First Ariel charms them with his music and drives them into a dirty pool.

Then Stephano and Trinculo are distracted by fancy-looking, cheap clothes that Ariel hangs on a line.
3. Answers will differ. Students may respond that he wants to impress on them the importance of chastity and self-discipline.
4. Answers will differ. Students may respond that both are shows that Prospero puts on, acted by his spirits, and both are meant to have an ed-

ucational function, persuading the courtiers to reformation and the lovers to chastity. Both dissolve suddenly. However, the dissolution of the masque is not part of Prospero's plan.
5. (a) The masque is a highly formal performance of allegorical characters that indicates the importance of chastity. The final part of the act shows the bumbling of clowns who are motivated by lust and ambition.

(continued from bottom of page)

(b) Answers will differ. Students may respond that Caliban's attempt, although ludicrous, reminds him of the successful usurpation of his kingdom years before.
6. Answers will differ. Students may indicate the importance of lighting and costumes.

ANSWERS TO ANALYZING LITERATURE

1. These goddesses symbolize, respectively, lawful matrimony and the abundance that self-control will bring.
2. Answers will differ. Students may point out that Iris, as a rainbow, symbolizes harmony and the link between heaven and earth. In Genesis 9 the rainbow is a symbol of God's covenant with humankind.
3. Answers will differ. Students may mention rock concerts, baseball games, and parades on various holidays.

ANSWERS TO CRITICAL THINKING AND READING

1. (a) In lines 146–147, Prospero tells Ferdinand, "be cheerful, sir." (b) Answers will differ. Some students may cite line 148, while others may indicate line 150, 151, or 156–157.
2. The audience might feel that they, too, would vanish with the theater.
3. Answers will differ. Students may indicate that he is referring simultaneously to the characters in the masque, the characters in the play, and all humans.
4. Answers will differ. Some students may feel that it has enough resonance to suggest this meaning.

ANSWERS TO UNDERSTANDING LANGUAGE

In i.7 "strangely" means "wonderfully." In i.143 it means "unusual or odd." In i.232 it means "peculiar," with a suggestion that the suffering of the clowns will be grotesque. The repetitions of the word contribute to a sense of wonder. In a world so "strange," anything is possible, including Prospero's magic.

THINKING AND WRITING

Publishing Student Writing Have students read their soliloquies aloud to the class.

Focus

Literary Focus Have students describe the resolution of some of their favorite comic novels or movies. Make a list on the chalkboard of the elements common to these resolutions. Then ask the students to look for these elements in the resolution of *The Tempest*.

Writing/Prior Knowledge Pair up students in your class. Have them tell each other about their sacrifice before they begin to write.

ESL Teaching Strategy Have ESL students tell the class about stories of sacrifice that are well known in their culture. Also, give ESL students practice in reading Shakespeare's verse aloud so that it does not seem so strange to them.

Teaching Tenth-Grade Students Point out to tenth-grade students that the theme of power is important in this play. Have them work in groups to identify the kinds of power that are described in the play. Which kinds of power are most effective? Why?

Cooperative Learning Have groups of students research different productions of *The Tempest*. They can use such references as *The Annotated Shakespeare* by A. L. Rowse and the autobiographies of actors like Olivier and Gielgud. Ask each group to report to the class on its findings.

Vocabulary

Preteach the following vocabulary words:
penitent (pen´ i tənt) *adj.*: Truly sorry
abjure (ab jōōr´) *v.*: Give up; renounce
wrangle (raŋ ´gəl) *v.*: Dispute
auspicious (ôs pi´ shəs) *adj.*: Favorable

The Tempest, Act V

Commentary

The Resolution. *The Tempest* is a play in which the **resolution,** or solving, of the conflicts is not absolutely tidy. One of the traditional marks of comedy is a final scene in which all the characters come together in a renewed community. Shakespeare's last play certainly fits this pattern. However, Prospero's mixed feelings at the finale may leave the audience with a bittersweet taste.

Prospero has been the god of this little island world. As a larger-than-life character, he has engineered the happy ending that in most comedies is the work of Fortune or Divine Providence. In a final transformation, however, he must give up the godlike powers he has displayed. Physically removing his magician's cloak, he puts on the costume of the Duke of Milan. This transformation prepares him to leave the "bare island" on which he has been able to work miracles and to reassume his place in the real world. Yet he is not entirely happy about this change. The world has many dukes, but the island has only one Prospero: To leave the island is to give up a world in which he *can* play God for one in which he is only mortal. Accordingly, Prospero seems a bit sad amid the general rejoicing.

Early in the play, Prospero says to Miranda, "I have done nothing but in care of thee" (I.ii.16), and the conclusion of the play bears this out. He could choose to continue on his magical island; however, after his death, Miranda would be helpless. His decision to let her fall in love and leave the island is therefore a sacrifice he undertakes for her. He is glad to do it, but he is also sorrowfully aware of the loss of his magic.

Writing

Tell about a time when you gave up something you loved because you felt there was something more important that made such a sacrifice necessary.

Primary Source

The well-known critic Mark Van Doren made the following comment about a much-argued point, the possible link between Shakespeare and his main character: "Is Shakespeare Prospero, and is his magic the art with which he has fabricated thirty-seven plays? Is he now burying his book—abandoning the theater—and retiring where every third thought will be his grave? . . . Answers are not too easy. Shakespeare has never dramatized himself before, and it may not have occurred to him to do so now. . . . It can be doubted, in other words, that Shakespeare sat down solemnly to decorate his life's work with a secret signature."

Objectives

Thematic
To understand a Shakespearean perspective on imagination and reality

Skills
1 To understand the resolution
2 To stage a scene
3 To write review guidelines

Support Material

Teaching Portfolio
Teacher Backup, p. 933
Grammar in Action Worksheet, *Establishing Tone*, p.937
Usage and Mechanics Worksheet, p. 939
Vocabulary Check, p. 940
Analyzing Literature Worksheet, *Understanding the Resolution*, p. 941

Act V

Scene i. In front of Prospero's cell.

[*Enter* PROSPERO *in his magic robes, and* ARIEL.]

1

PROSPERO. Now does my project gather to a head.
My charms crack not, my spirits obey, and time
Goes upright with his carriage.¹ How's the day?

ARIEL. On the sixth hour, at which time, my lord,
You said our work should cease.

5 **PROSPERO.**   I did say so
When first I raised the tempest. Say, my spirit,
How fares the King and 's followers?

ARIEL.   Confined together
In the same fashion as you gave in charge,
Just as you left them—all prisoners, sir,
10 In the line grove which weather-fends² your cell.
They cannot budge till your release.³ The King,
His brother, and yours abide all three distracted,
And the remainder mourning over them,
Brimful of sorrow and dismay; but chiefly
15 Him that you termed, sir, the good old Lord Gonzalo.
His tears runs down his beard like winter's drops
From eaves of reeds.⁴ Your charm so strongly works 'em.
That if you now beheld them, your affections
Would become tender.

PROSPERO.   Dost thou think so, spirit?

ARIEL. Mine would, sir, were I human.

20 **PROSPERO.**   And mine shall.
Hast thou, which art but air, a touch, a feeling
Of their afflictions, and shall not myself,
One of their kind, that relish all as sharply,
Passion as they, be kindlier moved than thou art?
25 Though with their high wrongs I am struck to th' quick,
Yet with my nobler reason 'gainst my fury
Do I take part. The rarer action is
In virtue than in vengeance. They being penitent,
The sole drift of my purpose doth extend
30 Not a frown further. Go, release them, Ariel.
My charms I'll break, their senses I'll restore,
And they shall be themselves.

ARIEL.   I'll fetch them, sir.   [*Exit.*]

---

1. **carriage:** Burden.

2. **weather-fends:** Protects from inclement weather.
3. **till your release:** Until you free them.

4. **eaves of reeds:** Thatched roofs.

2
3
4

Presentation

Motivation/Prior Knowledge
Have students imagine that they are Prospero as the last act begins. How would they deal with Caliban and his crew? Would they invent new punishments for the courtiers?

Purpose-Setting Question How does Prospero feel about giving up his magical powers?

Master Teacher Note Encourage students to think about the significance of Prospero's divesting himself of his powers. Why is such a rejection of magical powers necessary for the resolution of the play? Have students consider similar or comparable acts of sacrifice they have witnessed or heard about.

1 Discussion Ask students why Prospero is dressed "in his magic robes" for the final scene. Have them recall a previous time when he removed his robes. Why did he take them off that time? Do you think he will remove them again in this act? Why or why not?

2 Discussion Ask students what Gonzalo's extreme sorrow reveals about him. Have them evaluate the simile used to describe his crying. Is it vivid and effective? Explain.

3 Clarification Remind students that Ariel is not human and therefore has no direct knowledge of human passions. However, even he is moved by the plight of Antonio, Sebastian, and Alonso.

4 Literary Focus Ask students how this declaration could serve as Prospero's credo. How does it point toward the resolution of the play's central conflict?

Language Worksheet, *Distinguishing Between Words*, p. 942
Selection Test, pp. 943–944
Short Answer Unit Test, p. 945
Essay Questions and Evaluation Guidelines, p. 949

Spelling Tip Write the word *auspicious* on the chalkboard. Point out to students that, except for the first letter, it is spelled in the same way as the word *suspicious*.

PROSPERO. Ye elves of hills, brooks, standing lakes, and groves,
And ye that on the sands with printless foot
35 Do chase the ebbing Neptune, and do fly him⁵
When he comes back; you demi-puppets that
By moonshine do the green sour ringlets⁶ make,
Whereof the ewe not bites; and you whose pastime
Is to make midnight mushrumps,⁷ that rejoice
40 To hear the solemn curfew; by whose aid
(Weak masters⁸ though ye be) I have bedimmed
The noontide sun, called forth the mutinous winds,
And 'twixt the green sea and the azured vault
Set roaring war; to the dread rattling thunder
45 Have I given fire and rifted Jove's stout oak
With his own bolt; the strong-based promontory
Have I made shake and by the spurs⁹ plucked up
The pine and cedar; graves at my command
Have waked their sleepers, oped, and let 'em forth
50 By my so potent art. But this rough magic
I here abjure; and when I have required
Some heavenly music (which even now I do)
To work mine end upon their senses that¹⁰
This airy charm is for, I'll break my staff,
55 Bury it certain fathoms in the earth,
And deeper than did ever plummet sound
I'll drown my book.   [*Solemn music*]

[*Here enters* ARIEL *before; then* ALONSO, *with a frantic gesture, attended by* GONZALO; SEBASTIAN *and* ANTONIO *in like manner, attended by* ADRIAN *and* FRANCISCO. *They all enter the circle which* PROSPERO *had made, and there stand charmed; which* PROSPERO *observing, speaks.*]

A solemn air, and the best comforter
To an unsettled fancy, cure thy brains,
60 Now useless, boiled within thy skull! There stand,
For you are spell-stopped.
Holy Gonzalo, honorable man,
Mine eyes, ev'n sociable to show of thine,
Fall fellowly drops.¹¹ The charm dissolves apace;
65 And as the morning steals upon the night,
Melting the darkness, so their rising senses
Begin to chase the ignorant fumes that mantle
Their clearer reason. O good Gonzalo,
My true preserver, and a loyal sir
70 To him thou follow'st, I will pay thy graces
Home¹² both in word and deed. Most cruelly
Didst thou, Alonso, use me and my daughter.
Thy brother was a furtherer in the act.
Thou art pinched for't now, Sebastian. Flesh and blood,
75 You, brother mine, that entertained ambition,

5. **fly him:** Race with him.

6. **green sour ringlets:** Small circles of darker grass that accompany circles of mushrooms.
7. **mushrumps:** Mushrooms.
8. **Weak masters:** Not powerful magicians.

9. **spurs:** roots.

10. **their senses that:** The senses of those whom.

11. **sociable . . . drops:** Identifying with the tears in your eyes, mine also drop tears in sympathy.

12. **pay . . . home:** Repay your kindness fully.

Primary Source Note

Prospero's speech (lines 33–50) seems to be based on a passage in Ovid's *Metamorphoses* (VII.193–208) describing the conjuring of Medea, a legendary sorceress. As with the passage from Montaigne in Act II (lines 147–164), Shakespeare imitates it closely while changing its meaning utterly:

O Earth, provider of the herbs of magic,
O winds, O little breezes, O streams, O mountains,
O lakes, O groves, O gods of the groves, O gods
Of night, come, help me, help me, help me!

You have before this, when I wanted, seen me
Make streams return to their sources, while their banks
Wondered; you have seen me still the angry oceans,
Rouse the calm waters, drive the clouds away
Or marshall them together, exile winds,
Recall them; you have seen me break the fangs
Of serpents with my charms and incantations,
Root up the rocks from the soil, root up the oak trees,
Move forests, shake the mountains, make earth rumble,
Call ghosts from graveyards. I can make the moon

Expelled remorse and nature;[13] whom, with Sebastian
(Whose inward pinches therefore are most strong),
Would here have killed your king, I do forgive thee,
Unnatural though thou art. Their understanding
80 Begins to swell, and the approaching tide
Will shortly fill the reasonable shore,
That now lies foul and muddy. Not one of them
That yet looks on me or would know me. Ariel,
Fetch me the hat and rapier in my cell.
85 I will discase[14] me, and myself present
As I was sometime Milan, Quickly, spirit!
Thou shalt ere long be free.

[*Exit* ARIEL *and returns immediately.*]

[ARIEL *sings and helps to attire him.*]

Where the bee sucks, there suck I;
In a cowslip's bell I lie;
90 There I couch when owls do cry.
On the bat's back I do fly
After summer merrily.
Merrily, merrily shall I live now
Under the blossom that hangs on the bough.

95 **PROSPERO.** Why, that's my dainty Ariel! I shall miss thee,
But yet thou shalt have freedom; so, so, so.
To the King's ship, invisible as thou art!
There shalt thou find the mariners asleep
Under the hatches. The master and the boatswain
100 Being awake, enforce them to this place,
And presently,[15] I prithee.

ARIEL. I drink the air before me, and return
Or ere your pulse twice beat.   [*Exit.*]

GONZALO. All torment, trouble, wonder, and amazement
105 Inhabits here. Some heavenly power guide us
Out of this fearful country!

PROSPERO.   Behold, sir King,
The wrongèd Duke of Milan, Prospero.
For more assurance that a living prince
Does now speak to thee, I embrace thy body,
110 And to thee and thy company I bid
A hearty welcome.

ALONSO.   Whe'r[16] thou be'st he or no,
Or some enchanted trifle[17] to abuse me,
As late I have been, I not know. Thy pulse
Beats, as of flesh and blood; and, since I saw thee,
115 Th' affliction of my mind amends, with which,

13. **nature:** Natural feeling (of brotherly affection and loyalty).

14. **discase:** Disrobe.

15. **presently:** Quickly.

16. **Whe'r:** Whether.
17. **trifle:** A ghost.

6 **Discussion** Have students explain this metaphor. Why is the imagery of flowing tides especially appropriate for this play?

7 **Enrichment** Point out to students that dress can have important symbolic meaning in a play. By divesting himself of his magical robes and donning the clothes he used to wear, Prospero is making an important statement. He is ratifying his previous rejection of magic (lines 50–57) and affirming his return to the world as an ordinary man.

8 **Discussion** Have students consider how this little song reflects Ariel's nature. Why is Ariel feeling so happy? What kind of life will he lead? How does Prospero's response to this song reveal his sympathy and humanity? Do you think Ariel will miss Prospero as much as Prospero misses Ariel? Why or why not?

9 **Discussion** Ask students how Shakespeare uses rhythms and sounds to reflect the different states of mind of these two characters.

Darken, the car of the Sun turn pale at my singing,
The Dawn turn pale with my poisons.

Medea summons spirits to help her; however, Prospero names them affectionately as he prepares to give them up. Then, of course, he becomes entranced with his powers and declares he has waked the dead. At that point, however, he turns away from the temptation of magical powers to a humbler and smaller sense of himself (see Enrichment note, above).

10 **Discussion** Ask students why Prospero makes a point of embracing Gonzalo *first*.

11 **Enrichment** Call students' attention to the difference between Antonio's genuine contrition and Sebastian's frightened and bitter aside. Neither Sebastian nor Antonio expresses remorse for what he has done. In fact, these two hardly make any further comments beyond a few remarks about the appearance of Caliban, Trinculo, and Stephano. It is unusual in Shakespeare for villains to be forgiven without any corresponding show of penitence. Ask students how they would handle this problem as a director. What would they have the two courtiers communicate with their body language? Would they instruct them to act humble and penitent or secretly angry?

I fear, a madness held me. This must crave[18]
(And if this be at all[19]) a most strange story.
Thy dukedom I resign and do entreat
Thou pardon me my wrongs. But how should Prospero
Be living and be here?

120   **PROSPERO.**   First, noble friend,
10   Let me embrace thine age, whose honor cannot
Be measured or confined.

  GONZALO.   Whether this be
Or be not, I'll not swear.

  PROSPERO.   You do yet taste
Some subtleties[20] o' th' isle, that will not let you
125   Believe things certain. Welcome, my friends all.
  [*Aside to* SEBASTIAN *and* ANTONIO] But you, my brace of lords, were I so minded,
I here could pluck his Highness' frown upon you,
And justify[21] you traitors. At this time
I will tell no tales.

11   **SEBASTIAN** [*Aside*]   The devil speaks in him.

18. crave: Yearn for; desire intensely.
19. And . . . all: And if this be real.

20. taste some subtleties: Sense some deceptions, an allusion to popular pastries made to look like castles, ships, and the like.

21. justify: Prove.

Commentary

The Resolution Prospero's treatment of the courtiers has been prepared for at the beginning of the scene, where he decides to be merciful. Vengeance is God's, and Prospero in being merciful is acting not as a Divine Judge but as a human being who, sinful himself, needs to grant mercy to others. The limits that he places on himself are dramatized (lines 85–94) when he removes his magician's garb and assumes that of a duke. The gesture recalls his earlier removing of his cloak to talk with Miranda in Act I, but that gesture was half-hearted. Here by contrast the gesture is permanent.

Ariel's song (lines 88–94) embodies everything that Prospero is giving up as he leaves the island: an existence of pure, amoral, delightful play, far from the cares of human existence.

While Prospero's treatment of Gonzalo is full of love and welcome, his treatment of Sebastian and Antonio is threatening. Nothing suggests that the two villains have experienced a change of heart. Prospero feels that he can control their viciousness only by threatening them with exposure (lines 126–129). The return to Milan means a return to dealing with unprincipled characters like these, and so it's no wonder if Prospero seems a bit melancholy in this final, happy scene. Miranda's naive praise of the courtiers (lines

PROSPERO.   No.

130 For you, most wicked sir, whom to call brother
     Would even infect my mouth, I do forgive
     Thy rankest fault—all of them; and require
     My dukedom of thee, which perforce I know
     Thou must restore.

ALONSO.   If thou beest Prospero,

135 Give us particulars of thy preservation;
     How thou hast met us here, whom three hours since
     Were wracked upon this shore; where I have lost
     (How sharp the point of this remembrance is!)
     My dear son Ferdinand.

PROSPERO.   I am woe[22] for't, sir.

140 **ALONSO.** Irreparable is the loss, and patience
     Says it is past her cure.

PROSPERO.   I rather think
     You have not sought her help, of whose soft grace
     For the like loss I have her sovereign aid
     And rest myself content.

ALONSO.   You the like loss?

145 **PROSPERO.** As great to me, as late,[23] and supportable
     To make the dear loss, have I means much weaker
     Than you may call to comfort you; for I
     Have lost my daughter.

ALONSO.   A daughter?
     O heavens, that they were living both in Naples,

150 The King and Queen there! That they were, I wish
     Myself were mudded in that oozy bed
     Where my son lies. When did you lose your daughter?

PROSPERO. In this last tempest. I perceive these lords
     At this encounter do so much admire

155 That they devour their reason, and scarce think
     Their eyes do offices[24] of truth, their words
     Are natural breath. But, howsoev'r you have
     Been justled from your senses, know for certain
     That I am Prospero, and that very duke

160 Which was thrust forth of Milan, who most strangely
     Upon this shore, where you were wracked, was landed
     To be the lord on't. No more yet of this;
     For 'tis a chronicle of day by day,
     Not a relation for a breakfast, nor

165 Befitting this first meeting. Welcome sir;
     This cell's my court. Here have I few attendants,

22. woe: Sorry.

23. As . . . late: As great a loss to me as to you, and as recent a one.

24. do offices: Perform the functions.

12 Enrichment Call students' attention to the anger ill-concealed by this speech of forgiveness. The words are cold and grudging, as if the forgiveness were rational but not emotional. Prospero begins by refusing to call Antonio "brother." Then, when he grants forgiveness, the word "forgive" seems to take much less stress than the words "rankest fault." Not content to let the matter rest there, Prospero emphasizes that there was more than one such fault! In the very next breath, he demands his dukedom back in the most imperative manner. Some forgiveness!

13 Discussion Students will realize that Prospero is deceiving Antonio for the moment. Ask them, however, in what sense Prospero has lost a daughter.

14 Discussion Ask students what a director can learn from Prospero's remarks about the other characters. How should these characters be looking?

181–184) is shadowed by Prospero's wiser, sadder view: "'Tis new to thee."

And subjects none abroad.[25] Pray you look in.
My dukedom since you have given me again,
I will requite you with as good a thing,
170 At least bring forth a wonder to content ye
As much as me my dukedom.

25. **abroad:** Elsewhere on this island.

15 [*Here* PROSPERO *discovers*[26] FERDINAND *and* MIRANDA *playing at chess.*]

26. **discovers:** Reveals.

MIRANDA. Sweet lord, you play me false.

FERDINAND.   No, my dearest love,
I would not for the world.

MIRANDA. Yes, for a score of kingdoms you should wrangle,
And I would call it fair play.[27]

27. **for a score . . . play:** If we were really playing for high stakes and you cheated me, I'd call it fair play.

175 ALONSO.   If this prove
16   A vision of the island, one dear son
Shall I twice lose.

SEBASTIAN   A most high miracle!

FERDINAND. Though the seas threaten, they are merciful.
I have cursed them without cause.   [*Kneels.*]

ALONSO.   Now all the blessings
180 Of a glad father compass thee about!
Arise, and say how thou cam'st here.

MIRANDA.   O, wonder!
How many goodly creatures are there here!
17   How beauteous mankind is! O brave new world
18   That has such people in't!

PROSPERO.   'Tis new to thee.

185 ALONSO. What is this maid with whom thou wast at play?
Your eld'st[28] acquaintance cannot be three hours.
Is she the goddess that hath severed us
And brought us thus together?

28. **eld'st:** Longest.

FERDINAND.   Sir, she is mortal;
But by immortal providence she's mine.
190 I chose her when I could not ask my father
For his advice, nor thought I had one. She
Is daughter to this famous Duke of Milan,
Of whom so often I have heard renown.
But never saw before; of whom I have
195 Received a second life; and second father
This lady makes him to me.

ALONSO.   I am hers.
But, O, how oddly will it sound that I
Must ask my child forgiveness!

PROSPERO.   There, sir, stop.
Let us not burden our remembrance with
A heaviness that's gone.

200 **GONZALO.**   I have inly wept,
Or should have spoke ere this. Look down, you gods,
And on this couple drop a blessèd crown!
For it is you that have chalked forth the way
Which brought us hither.

ALONSO.   I say amen, Gonzalo.

205 **GONZALO.** Was Milan thrust from Milan that his issue
Should become kings of Naples? O, rejoice
Beyond a common joy, and set it down
With gold on lasting pillars. In one voyage
Did Claribel her husband find at Tunis,
210 And Ferdinand her brother found a wife
Where he himself was lost; Prospero his dukedom
In a poor isle; and all of us ourselves
When no man was his own.

ALONSO. [*To* FERDINAND *and* MIRANDA] Give me your hands.
Let grief and sorrow still embrace his heart
That doth not wish you joy.

215 **GONZALO.**   Be it so! Amen!

[*Enter* ARIEL, *with the* MASTER *and* BOATSWAIN *amazedly following.*]

O, look, sir; look, sir! Here is more of us!
I prophesied if a gallows were on land,
This fellow could not drown. Now, blasphemy,
That swear'st grace o'erboard,[29] not an oath on shore?
220 Hast thou no mouth by land? What is the news?

BOATSWAIN. The best news is that we have safely found
Our king and company; the next, our ship,
Which, but three glasses[30] since, we gave out split,
Is tight and yare[31] and bravely rigged as when
We first put out to sea.

225 **ARIEL.**   [*Aside to* PROSPERO] Sir, all this service
Have I done since I went.

PROSPERO.   [*Aside to* ARIEL] My tricksy spirit!

ALONSO. These are not natural events; they strengthen
From strange to stranger. Say, how came you hither?

BOATSWAIN. If I did think, sir, I were well awake,
230 I'd strive to tell you. We were dead of sleep
And (how we know not) all clapped under hatches;
Where, but even now, with strange and several noises

**29. blasphemy . . .
o'erboard:** Irreverent curses
that threw salvation into
the sea.

30. glasses: Hours.
31. yare: Shipshape.

22

Enrichment Point out to students how Shakespeare adds vivid details like these to bring to life characters' descriptions of offstage events.

23 **Enrichment** Call students' attention to the frequent, affectionate exchanges between Ariel and Prospero in this act. They seem to reach an almost feverish pitch. Prospero may take a particular joy in Ariel's tricks because they represent Prospero's own farewell as a magician.

24 **Enrichment** Explain to students that this remark has a humorous, ironic flavor, anticipating the ludicrous show that Caliban and his companions will make.

25 **Discussion** Ask students how both Trinculo and Caliban ironically echo Miranda's speech (line 183).

26 **Clarification** Remind students that Setebos was the god of Caliban's mother, Sycorax.

Of roaring, shrieking, howling, jingling chains,
And more diversity of sounds, all horrible,
235 We were awaked; straightway at liberty;
Where we, in all our trim, freshly beheld
Our royal, good, and gallant ship, our master
Cap'ring to eye her.[32] On a trice, so please you,
Even in a dream, were we divided from them
And were brought moping[33] hither.

240 ARIEL. [*Aside to* PROSPERO]   Was't well done?

PROSPERO. [*Aside to* ARIEL] Bravely, my diligence. Thou shalt be
free.

ALONSO. This is as strange a maze as e'er man trod,
And there is in this business more than nature
Was ever conduct[34] of. Some oracle
Must rectify our knowledge.

245 PROSPERO.   Sir, my liege,
Do not infest your mind with beating on
The strangeness of this business. At picked leisure,
Which shall be shortly, single I'll resolve you
(Which to you shall seem probable) of every
250 These happened accidents;[35] till when, be cheerful
And think of each thing well. [*Aside to* ARIEL] Come hither,
spirit.
Set Caliban and his companions free.
Untie the spell. [*Exit* ARIEL.] How fares my gracious sir?
There are yet missing of your company
255 Some few odd lads that you remember not.

[*Enter* ARIEL, *driving in* CALIBAN, STEPHANO, *and* TRINCULO, *in their
stolen apparel.*]

STEPHANO. Every man shift for all the rest, and let no man take care
of himself; for all is but fortune. *Coraggio,*[36] bully-monster,
coraggio!

TRINCULO. If these be true spies which I wear in my head, here's a
260 goodly sight.

CALIBAN. O Setebos, these brave spirits indeed!
How fine my master is! I am afraid
He will chastise me.

SEBASTIAN.   Ha, ha!
What things are these, my Lord Antonio?
Will money buy 'em?

265 ANTONIO.   Very like. One of them
Is a plain fish and no doubt marketable.

PROSPERO. Mark but the badges[37] of these men, my lords,
Then say if they be true.[38] This misshapen knave,

32. master . . . her: Our captain dancing to see her.

33. moping: Dazed.

34. conduct: Conductor.

35. accidents: Occurrences.

36. *Coraggio:* Italian, meaning courage.

37. badges: Insignia worn by servants to indicate the master they serve.

38. true: Honest.

Grammar in Action

Establishing Tone The term *tone* refers to an author's attitude toward the subject and the audience. The following words are a few of those that can be used to describe tone:

DESCRIPTIONS OF TONE: indifferent, appreciative, admiring, adoring, optimistic, proud, contemptuous, objective, disappointed, respectful, approving, surprised, angry, ironical, indignant, hostile, suspicious, amused

Frequently an author's tone is not straightforward. In that case you may need to use more than one adjective to describe it. For example, you can say that an author takes a tone of respectful amusement.

Authors rely on the connotations, or emotional associations, of words to establish tone. In *The Tempest* Shakespeare repeats the word *strange* to establish a tone of wonder and amazement:

ALONSO. This is as strange a maze as e'er man trod,
And there is in this business more than nature
Was ever conduct of . . .

In this speech Shakespeare even uses a pun (a maze = amaze) to re-

His mother was a witch, and one so strong
270 That could control the moon, make flows and ebbs,
And deal in her command without her power.³⁹
These three have robbed me, and this demi-devil
(For he's a bastard one) had plotted with them
To take my life. Two of these fellows you
275 Must know and own; this thing of darkness I
Acknowledge mine.

CALIBAN.   I shall be pinched to death.

ALONSO. Is not this Stephano, my drunken butler?

SEBASTIAN. He is drunk now. Where had he wine?

ALONSO. And Trinculo is reeling ripe. Where should they
280 Find this grand liquor that hath gilded 'em?
How cam'st thou in this pickle?

TRINCULO. I have been in such a pickle, since I saw you last, that I
fear me will never out of my bones. I shall not fear flyblowing.⁴⁰

SEBASTIAN Why, how, now, Stephano?

285 STEPHANO. O, touch me not! I am not Stephano, but a cramp.

PROSPERO. You'd be king o' the isle, sirrah?

STEPHANO. I should have been a sore⁴¹ one then.

ALONSO. This is a strange thing as e'er I looked on.

PROSPERO. He is as disproportioned in his manners
290 As in his shape. Go, sirrah, to my cell;
Take with you your companions. As you look
To have my pardon, trim it handsomely.

CALIBAN. Ay, that I will; and I'll be wise hereafter,
And seek for grace. What a thrice-double ass
295 Was I to take this drunkard for a god
And worship this dull fool!

PROSPERO.   Go to! Away!

ALONSO. Hence, and bestow your luggage where you found it.

SEBASTIAN. Or stole it rather.
                    [*Exit* CALIBAN, STEPHANO, *and* TRINCULO.]

PROSPERO. Sir, I invite your Highness and your train
300 To my poor cell, where you shall take your rest
For this one night; which, part of it, I'll waste⁴²
With such discourse as, I not doubt, shall make it
Go quick away—the story of my life,
And the particular accidents gone by
305 Since I came to this isle. And in the morn

---

39. without her power:
Without the moon's authority.

27

40. flyblowing: An
infestation of maggots.

41. sore: Pained or angry.

28

42. waste: Spend.

---

27 **Discussion** Point out to students
the strong feelings that lie behind
Prospero's words. What are these
feelings and what accounts for
them? Does this speech indicate
that Prospero has truly forgiven
Caliban? Why or why not?

28 **Discussion** Ask students whether
or not Prospero will pardon his servant. What realization does Caliban have? Do you think that he
will "be wise hereafter"? Explain.

---

inforce the sense of wonder.

Student Activity 1. Find two other words or phrases in this act that contribute to the tone of wonder and explain each of your choices.

Student Activity 2. Imagine that Miranda has returned to Naples as
Ferdinand's wife and as a queen. Write a speech for her, in prose or poetry.
Decide on the tone you want the speech to convey and use words whose
connotations will contribute to that tone.

I'll bring you to your ship, and so to Naples,
Where I have hope to see the nuptial
Of these our dear-beloved solemnizèd;
And thence retire me to my Milan, where
Every third thought shall be my grave.

310 **ALONSO.**   I long
To hear the story of your life, which must
Take[43] the ear strangely.

43. Take: Hold; sound.

PROSPERO.   I'll deliver[44] all;
And promise you calm seas, auspicious gales,
And sail so expeditious that shall catch
315 Your royal fleet far off. [*Aside to* ARIEL] My Ariel, chick,
That is thy charge. Then to the elements
Be free, and fare thou well! [*To the others*] Please you, draw near.
                    [*Exit all.*]

44. deliver: Tell.

EPILOGUE

Spoken by Prospero

Now my charms are all o'erthrown,
And what strength I have's mine own,
Which is most faint. Now 'tis true
I must be here confined by you,
5 Or sent to Naples. Let me not,
Since I have my dukedom got
And pardoned the deceiver, dwell
In this bare island by your spell;
But release me from my bands[1]
10 With the help of your good hands.[2]
Gentle breath[3] of yours my sails
Must fill, or else my project fails,
Which was to please. Now I want
Spirits to enforce, art to enchant;
15 And my ending is despair
Unless I be relieved by prayer,[4]
Which pierces so that it assaults
Mercy itself and frees all faults.
As you from crimes would pardoned be,
20 Let your indulgence[5] set me free.   [*Exit.*]

FINIS

1. bands: Pledges; promises.
2. hands: Applause.
3. Gentle breath: Approving comments.

4. prayer: My plea, request, or petition.

5. indulgence: Generosity; also, remission from sins according to Roman Catholic doctrine.

Reader's Response *Imagine what happens to each of the main characters after the play has ended.*

Commentary

The Epilogue The epilogue plays on the relation between the character and the actor who portrays him: The actor speaks to the audience partly as actor and partly as the character. The "bare island" is the isle but also the stage projecting out into the middle of the audience (see the picture, page 706). The actor asks for applause, but Prospero asks for the prayers of the audience, which the image of clapping hands reduplicates.

Now that Prospero has accomplished his plan, he has no power other than the physical powers of an aging man. This new sense of helplessness brings an associated concern with mercy and forgiveness. Prospero who has shown his mercy for the courtiers now asks the audience to pray that God will be merciful to him. The final couplet extends the chain of forgiveness one link further. If the audience itself wishes to be pardoned by God, it will in turn pardon the Prospero/actor.

THINKING ABOUT THE SELECTION

Clarifying

1. Why does Prospero show mercy to his foes?
2. What will he do to show he has rejected his "rough magic"?
3. (a) What services does Ariel perform for his master in this act? (b) How will Ariel be rewarded?
4. How does Miranda's view of the courtiers differ from her father's?
5. In what way has Caliban changed?

Interpreting

6. Compare and contrast Prospero with Ariel.
7. (a) What quality does Miranda reveal when she exclaims, "O brave new world . . ."? (b) How do you think Shakespeare wants us to view her remark? Explain.
8. What do you think Antonio's silence indicates about his state of mind?
9. (a) What does Prospero mean when he says in the epilogue, "Now my charms are all o'er-thrown, / And what strength I have's mine own, / Which is most faint"? (b) How does his request for "Mercy" relate to his own behavior toward Antonio and Sebastian?

Applying

10. What other works have you read (or films have you seen) in which the protagonist must renounce power to achieve a goal?

ANALYZING LITERATURE

Understanding the Resolution

The **resolution,** or solving, of the conflicts in the final act is not without a touch of sadness. True, on the surface all is well. The subplots and main plot come to satisfactory conclusions: Miranda and Ferdinand will marry, Caliban and his companions are thwarted in their scheme, and Alonso is genuinely sorry for what he did. By means of Prospero, however, Shakespeare hints at an unresolved conflict about the relationship of art (or magic and enchantment) to the real world.

1. (a) In what part of Prospero's "farewell to magic" speech (V.i.33–57) does he seem to dwell on his powers? (b) How do the words "But" and "rough" in line 50 indicate a sudden change of feeling? (c)

How does the speech as a whole reveal his conflict about giving up his powers?
2. (a) What does he mean when he says, at the end of the play, "Every third thought shall be my grave" (V.i.309)? (b) What does this statement suggest about his attitude toward returning to the real world?

CRITICAL THINKING AND WRITING

Staging a Scene

Get together with a few classmates, choose your favorite scene from *The Tempest*, and brainstorm to gather ideas about staging it in a modern theater. Consider such factors as the set, costumes, and lighting. (Even Shakespeare's company may have staged this play in an indoor theater with more elaborate scenery and lighting effects than the Globe had.) If Prospero appears in your scene, how would you stress his power? How would you costume Ariel and Caliban? Would you have two levels for actors to play on, as the Renaissance stage often had (see page 706)? Ask the best artist among you to sketch the group's design for a set and costumes. Then have everyone in the group contribute notes to explain how the set, costumes, and lighting would be used for the scene.

THINKING AND WRITING

Writing Review Guidelines

Imagine that you are a newspaper editor writing guidelines for reporters who will review *The Tempest*. These reporters are unfamiliar with the play, so you will have to instruct them on what to look for. First, list the categories that they should consider, such as set, costumes, lighting, acting, and direction. Under each category jot down some notes about the key issues. For example, what are the major themes that a director should try to convey? What should they expect of the actor who plays Prospero? How should he move and speak? Draw on your notes in writing the guidelines. Remember that such guidelines should be in the form of listed items, brief and to the point. In revising your work, make sure you have neither left out anything essential nor overwhelmed the reporters with too many details.

Presentation

Motivation/Prior Knowledge Ask students what they know about the discovery of the New World by Renaissance Europeans. Have them discuss the various explorers they have read about; for example, Columbus, Amerigo Vespucci, Drake, and Cabot. Then ask them to imagine what it would have been like to sail with these men.

Enrichment Explain to students that the Renaissance was a time of discovery and exploration in many different fields. Scientists like Galileo applied mathematics to problems in physics and began to formulate the laws of motion. Artists also experimented, developing a systematic approach to perspective. They used mathematical principles to simulate the way the eye sees things at a distance.

While artists were learning how to simulate distance, daring explorers were actually sailing beyond the horizon. Their voyages to unknown regions of the globe were made possible by the development of better ships and by the improvement of navigational devices. These expeditions were also made possible by newly powerful kings. Such rulers wanted to fill their coffers with gold, discover trade routes to the East, and claim new land for their empires.

From our present-day perspective, the most important result of these explorations was the discovery of the New World.

The New World

Renaissance Europeans did not discover the New World: They rediscovered it. Centuries before, the greatest sailors of their time, the Vikings, had ventured as far as North America. It is even misleading to assert that the Vikings discovered our continent, however. A prior claim belongs to the peoples who migrated to the Americas over land bridges from Asia thousands of years earlier. These were the ancestors of Native Americans.

From the European point of view, however, the unexpected land mass barring the way to China was a *New World*. This term was first used by Amerigo Vespucci (ä me rē´ gō ves pōōt´ chē), who explored the coastline of Central America in the early sixteenth century. Vespucci was lucky with names, and besides the term *New World,* he also contributed his own first name to the continent.

Like Christopher Columbus, Vespucci was an Italian sailing for Spain. Throughout most of the fifteenth century, Spain had lagged behind Portugal in sponsoring voyages of exploration. Spain's Christian rulers were distracted by the wars they were fighting with Muslims for control of Spanish territory. In 1492, however, Ferdinand and Isabella drove the Muslims out of their last stronghold, Granada. With this victory, Christian Spain could turn its attention to the competition for gold, trade routes, and colonies.

The Conquerors

The religious wars that had torn Spain proved to be an advantage as well as a distraction. They were a breeding ground for tough soldiers. Once the wars had ended, these men required an outlet for their greed, love of battle, and commitment to spreading their religion. The New World was the perfect arena for their vast ambitions: It was dangerous and unexplored, and according to legend, it hid in the depths of its jungles, golden cities of incredible wealth. As they fought their way through this new continent, these Spanish soldiers of fortune earned the name of conquistadores (kän kwis´ tə dôr´ ēz´), or conquerors.

The two most successful conquerors were Hernando Cortes (hər nan´ dō kôr tes´) and Francisco Pizarro (frän thēs´ kô pē thär´ rô). Born of poor families, they used their cunning, bravery, and skill to establish New World empires larger than many European countries. Their conquests, however, can be viewed from different perspectives. By any standards, the courage and audacity of these men was astonishing. Yet they also demonstrated an incredible arrogance, destroying Native American civilizations that were centuries old.

The Conquest of Mexico

When Cortes landed on the coast of Mexico in 1519, his entire force consisted of about 500 soldiers and 16 horses. With a shrewdness that would have pleased his contemporary Machiavelli, Cortes realized that many of the central Mexican tribes controlled by the Aztec Indians were prepared to revolt. He made these tribes his allies in his campaigns against the Aztec empire.

NSIGHTS

PORTUGUESE MAP OF BRAZIL, 1519

Two other factors contributed to his success. First, the Aztec had never seen horses before and were terrified by the sight of cavalrymen. The few horses that Cortes had brought, therefore, were worth whole divisions of soldiers. Second, he was lucky enough to gain the help of a captured Indian princess, Malinche, or Doña Marina, as the Spanish called her. She spoke Nahuatl, the Aztec language, and served as a translator. Perhaps even more important, she was a valued adviser. Her shrewdness in dealing with Montezuma, the Aztec ruler, enabled Cortes to take him prisoner without a struggle.

The conquest of the Aztec, however, involved bloody fighting as well as clever diplomacy. You can read a full account of these events and the story of Pizarro's exploits in two books by the American historian William H. Prescott, *The Conquest of Mexico* and *The Conquest of Peru*.

The Encounter of Different Cultures

No moment is more dramatic than the encounter of two different cultures, and Prescott captures this drama in his description of the Spaniards' approach to the Aztec capital, Tenochtitlán (tä nōch tē tlän'). After a long and difficult march, Cortes and his men saw "the fair city of Mexico, with her white towers and pyramidal temples, . . . the far-famed 'Venice of the Aztecs.'" (Like Venice, the Aztec capital was surrounded by water and crisscrossed by canals.) Soon Montezuma came to meet them "on a royal palanquin blazing with burnished gold. It was borne on the shoulders of nobles. . . ." Atop this enclosed com-

partment was "a canopy of gaudy feather-work, powdered with jewels, and fringed with silver." The Aztec emperor and Cortes met for the first time: "In Montezuma, Cortes beheld the lord of the broad realms he had traversed, whose magnificence and power had been the burden of every tongue. In the Spaniard, on the other hand, the Aztec prince saw the strange being whose history seemed to be so mysteriously connected with his own. . . ."

Later that evening, the Spaniards fired their artillery to celebrate their arrival in the capital and impress the Aztec: "The thunders of the ordnance reverberating among the buildings and shaking them to their foundations, the stench of the sulphureous vapor that rolled in volumes above the walls of the encampment, reminding the inhabitants of the explosions of the great *volcán* [volcano], filled the hearts of the superstitious Aztecs with dismay."

The noise and stink of those cannon seem to foretell the troubled future of Latin America—from the downfall of the Native American empires, to the revolt against Spanish and Portuguese rule in the early 1800's. An echo of that angry artillery can be heard even in current Latin American struggles.

Humanities Note

Fine art, *Portuguese Map of Brazil*, 1519. In 1494 Portugal and Spain signed the Treaty of Tordesillas. This treaty provided for a boundary line that ran north and south about 1,100 miles in the western Atlantic. All newly discovered lands west of the line were given to Spain, while Portugal could colonize any lands east of the line. In 1500 Pedro Cabral, a Portuguese explorer, was blown off course and landed in Brazil. Since it lay east of the boundary line, he claimed it for Portugal.

This map shows Brazil nineteen years after Cabral claimed it for Portugal.

You might want to use the following questions to discuss the map:

1. What does this map reveal about the ships used by the Portuguese in the early sixteenth century?
2. Describe the scenes that the artist has depicted in Brazil.
3. What do these scenes suggest about the Portuguese conception of that country?

Questions

1. Who discovered the New World before the Renaissance Europeans?
2. Why did Spain lag behind Portugal at first in sponsoring voyages of exploration?
3. Who were the conquistadors?
4. Name the two most famous conquistadors.
5. Which empires did these men conquer?

Activities

1. Have students research and report on Aztec contributions to our cuisine; for instance, chocolate.
2. Ask students to trace on a map the route Cortés took in conquering Mexico.
3. Ask students to read all or part of Prescott's *The Conquest of Mexico* or *The Conquest of Peru* and report on their reading to the class.

Knowledge and Power

Presentation

Motivation/Prior Knowledge Tell students that the Renaissance witnessed a new emphasis on the power of humans to understand and alter their environment. Just as Machiavelli described how rulers could stay in power by playing off factions against one another, Leonardo da Vinci studied the interplay of muscles so that he could depict his subjects with greater accuracy and power.

Enrichment Explain to students that Sir Francis Bacon was a statesman who served Queen Elizabeth and King James I. He was also a famous essayist and thinker. Bacon was an important supporter of Renaissance science, although it has been claimed that he did not fully understand the application of mathematical principles to physics. He attacked the medieval practice of assuming that certain general laws were true and then applying them to particular instances. Instead, Bacon emphasized the importance of gathering data before formulating general laws. In his description of a utopia in *The New Atlantis* (1627), he anticipated the founding of scientific associations like The Royal Society (1660).

> "Knowledge is power."
> —Sir Francis Bacon

An important theme in Renaissance thought was the power of people to understand and alter both nature and human nature. Sir Francis Bacon, for instance, proposed collecting a large number of facts, from every field, and then using this data for the betterment of humankind. Bacon probably put too much emphasis on the value of facts in themselves, but his concern with knowledge as a source of power was in tune with the times.

In the field of political science, Machiavelli demonstrated how a ruler, through a knowledge of human nature and the techniques of statecraft, could outwit opponents and stay in power. This philosophy was suited to a period that witnessed a tremendous increase in social mobility. In politics, as in science, power was the fruit of knowledge.

> "... it is necessary for a prince, who wishes to maintain himself, to learn how not to be good, and to use this knowledge and not use it, according to the necessity of the case."
>
> —Machiavelli, *The Prince*

The Renaissance philosopher Pico della Mirandola emphasized human mobility in a slightly different sense. He declared that through knowledge and imagination, people had the power to raise themselves to the heights of the angels or lower themselves to the level of beasts.

While della Mirandola viewed the connection between knowledge and power in a positive light, Christopher Marlowe saw the dangers in human freedom. He demonstrated in *Doctor Faustus* how a wish to go beyond human limits could lead to damnation.

> "Had I as many souls as there be stars,
> I'd give them all for Mephostophilis.
> By him I'll be great emperor of the world."
>
> —Christopher Marlowe, *Dr. Faustus*

Shakespeare, in *The Tempest,* is not as pessimistic as Marlowe, but he too is concerned with the limits of knowledge and power.

> "... graves at my command
> Have waked their sleepers, oped, and let
>   'em forth
> By my so potent art. But this rough magic
> I here abjure; and when I have required
> Some heavenly music (which even now I do)
> To work mine end upon their senses that
> This airy charm is for, I'll break my staff,
> Bury it certain fathoms in the earth,
> And deeper than did ever plummet sound
> I'll drown my book."
>
> —William Shakespeare, *The Tempest*

The theme of knowledge and power has been a concern in many different cultures and eras. In *The Epic of Gilgamesh,* for instance, a Sumerian king goes on a quest for knowledge that will enable him to become immortal. The following selections also deal with this theme:

SUGGESTED READINGS

CROSS CURRENTS

Modern Love Poetry: Laura's Revenge on Petrarch

LAURA HAS HER SAY

Petrarch wrote sonnet after sonnet to his beloved Laura, admiring her from afar and expressing every slightest change in his feelings for her. Not only did he create a famous series of poems, but he set the style for love poetry for centuries to come. He spawned generations of male poets who wrote longingly of distant, unattainable women. The exalted status of these many Lauras only emphasized the fact that they were adored objects rather than real people. As it used to be said about children, they were meant to be seen and not heard.

What would have happened, however, if Laura herself had written sonnets? Would she have expressed gratitude for Petrarch's devotion or scolded him for his selfish concern with his own feelings? Would she have been more down-to-earth about love than her well-known admirer?

We can answer these questions because, in contrast to the Renaissance, our own era has produced many excellent women poets. By focusing on one who is known for her love sonnets, we can allow a modern Laura her say.

EDNA ST. VINCENT MILLAY, A MODERN LAURA

The poet Edna St. Vincent Millay (1892–1950) anticipated the concerns and attitudes of the women's movement that arose in the 1960's. Her sonnets, some Petrarchan in form and some Shakespearean, are a ringing declaration of female independence. At the beginning of one, for instance, she tells a man,

"I shall forget you presently, my dear,
So make the most of this, your little day,
Your little month, your little half a year,
Ere I forget, or die, or move away."

So much for Petrarchan devotion, on Laura's part anyway!

HER REFUSAL TO BE OWNED

Millay's sonnets are not without warmth or affection, but she refuses to acknowledge that a man, even a man she has loved, owns or controls her in some way. To a man who is rejecting her she declares,

"Here might you bless me; what you cannot do
Is bow me down, who have been loved by you."

HONESTY ABOUT PHYSICAL ATTRACTION

At other times, Millay frankly expresses physical attraction for a man. It is refreshing to hear such praise from a woman, as if Laura had turned the tables and written about *Petrarch's* "gold hair" and "fair eyes":

"For there is that about you in this light—
A yellow darkness, sinister of rain—
Which sturdily recalls my stubborn sight
To dwell on you, and dwell on you again.
And I am made aware of many a week
I shall consume, remembering in what way
Your brown hair grows about your brow
and cheek,
And what divine absurdities you say."

The "divine absurdities" in the last line may be an affectionate reference to the man's expressions of love. Is there a hint, however, that Millay is praising this good-looking man even for the general silliness of his remarks? If so, this would be especially ironic, considering the countless times that men have condescendingly praised attractive women for their inane prattling.

Presentation

Motivation/Prior Knowledge Remind students that Laura was the woman Petrarch wrote about and admired from afar. Read aloud to them one or more of his poems on pages 676 and 678 and encourage them to speculate about Laura's personality. Then ask them what kind of poetry they think she would have written.

Enrichment Tell students that during her life, Millay was one of the most popular poets in America. She was famous both for her poetry and for her bohemian lifestyle. Shortly after her graduation from Vassar, she moved to Greenwich Village in New York City (the Village had been discovered by artists in 1910). In 1922 she won the Pulitzer Prize for her book of poems *The Ballad of the Harp Weaver*. Her sonnets have been collected and published under the title *Edna St. Vincent Millay: Collected Sonnets* (New York: Washington Square Press, 1960).

Her friend Edmund Wilson evaluated her work as follows: "Edna St. Vincent Millay seems to me one of the only poets writing in English in our time who have attained to anything like the stature of great literary figures."

Cause and Effect

Writing About Cause and Effect

A cause is what makes something happen. An effect is what happens. For every event or effect, there is a cause. When you discuss causes and effects, you consider the reasons why things happen. Strong writing about cause and effect gives you a chance to weigh the consequences of one thing upon another. This may take many forms, but all of them bear some common characteristics.

Characteristics of Cause-and-Effect Writing

- Traces connections between situations and consequences
- Relies on logic
- Explores cause-and-effect relationships through detail, description, or example

For example, in "The Prince," Machiavelli uses cause and effect to assert his beliefs about the ways in which apparent virtues become vices and apparent vices can be virtues in people with power. Through his rational examination of cause and effect, Machiavelli convinces his reader that he is right, even if the reader does not want to admit the truth of what he is saying. The reader may say, "It should not be this way," but it is almost impossible to say, "It is not this way." Good writing about cause and effect convinces, even in the face of doubt, because it relies on logic.

Writing Assignment

Write, as Machiavelli did, about people who have power. Think of a boss, a political leader, a military leader, or someone you know in a position of power. With that person and position in mind, show how a virtue can become a vice and a vice can become a virtue. Use cause-and-effect reasoning to convince your reader. Apply one of the following "virtue/vice" pairs from the excerpt to the person and position you selected.

- cruel/merciful
- hard/easy
- serious/frivolous
- religious/unbeliever

Prewrite

The Subject

Begin by choosing your subject, say "the mayor," and a pair of qualities, say "serious/lighthearted." Then think how the qualities apply to the person and position you plan to write about. Fold a blank sheet of paper into quarters. In the top left quarter, write all the positives about the person being serious. In the top right quarter, write all the negatives about the person being serious. Do not edit your thoughts. Then do the same regarding all the positives and negatives about the person being lighthearted in the bottom quarters.

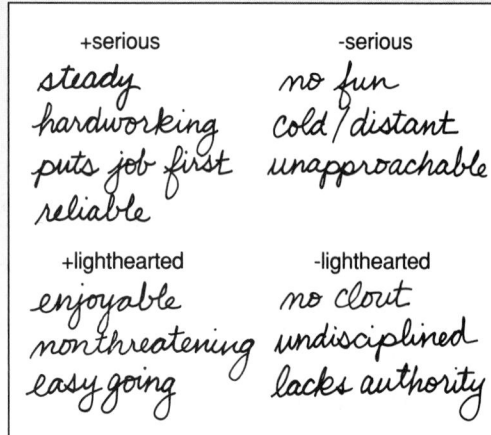

+serious
steady
hardworking
puts job first
reliable

-serious
no fun
cold/distant
unapproachable

+lighthearted
enjoyable
nonthreatening
easy going

-lighthearted
no clout
undisciplined
lacks authority

Remember that personal bias will only get in your way and weaken your argument. You may wish your person were more lighthearted, but you must be willing to embrace the opposite view; if he or she were more lighthearted, he or she might command less authority. If you cannot set aside personal biases, you will not convince your reader.

Collect your thoughts to show how the virtue becomes a vice and the vice a virtue. Make your statements in "if . . . then" form, so the cause and effect are clear. For example, if the mayor were not so hardworking, the job would not get done.

Format

You will be composing an essay from the notes you made. They may not have a clear sequence, but your essay must. Decide where to begin, what to save for the body of your composition, and what to hold for the conclusion.

Write

When you have clearly written your cause-and-effect statements about both the apparent vice and the apparent virtue, you are ready to form your essay. Begin by stating your position clearly. Prove your point by expressing both sides of the virtue with examples and then express both sides of the vice with examples.

If you get stuck while writing, go back to thinking. Brainstorm, talk to a friend about it, or give what you have written to someone for advice. Writing is seldom a neatly linear step-by-step process. Being stuck means you need to go back, and doing so usually clarifies problems.

Collaborate

Ask someone who doesn't know the assignment to respond to your draft. Tell your partner to check your logic by taking the opposite approach to all you say in the paper. Ask your partner to argue with you each step of the way. Use a tape machine to record remarks or take notes about arguments, even if they seem silly. His or her remarks will show you weak spots you can strengthen when you revise. Notice how Machiavelli anticipated counterarguments and supplied ready answers to them.

Revise

As you revise your paper, plug the holes your partner pointed out by adding counterargument statements and supplying reasons these arguments do not prevail. Use statements such as Machiavelli did: "If it is said that . . . I would reply that . . ." or "And should anyone reply that . . . I would answer by saying that . . ."

Publish

Why not test this essay in a different way? Contact the person you wrote about or someone in a similar position. Arrange to have your essay considered and give the person several days to read the story. Then set up a brief meeting during which you can listen to the person's response.

Evaluate

Now what do you really think about your subject? Did writing this paper help you see a side you had not considered before? Consider keeping the paper to ponder later.

Clarification Explain to students that the writing process is not unidirectional and irreversible. Professional writers often move from stage to stage in an odd, unpredictable pattern. Encourage your students to adopt a similar freedom in their use of the writing process.

Further Reading If students need further motivation, explain to them that military histories, accounts of scientific discoveries, and detective stories often rely on clear delineations of cause-and-effect relationships. They might want to sample some of the following books:

Conan Doyle, Sir Arthur. *The Hound of the Baskervilles*: Perhaps the best Sherlock Holmes mystery.

Hart, Basil Liddell. *History of World War II*: A vivid, readable military history.

Roueche, Bertrand. *Eleven Blue Men*: An excellent account of medical detection.

Guidelines for Evaluating Writing About Literature Keep the following questions in mind when evaluating students' compositions:
1. Does the composition clearly explain how a virtue can become a vice and a vice can become a virtue?
2. Does the composition effectively use cause-and-effect reasoning?
3. Is the composition clearly organized so that the thoughts flow smoothly from one paragraph to the next?
4. Does the composition contain any errors in spelling, grammar, or punctuation?

Fine art, *Reading from Molière, about 1728* by Jean-François de Troy. The French painter Jean-François de Troy (1679–1752) received his early artistic training from his father, a fashionable portrait painter in Paris. His later education in Rome led to his acceptance by the French Academy and eventual patronage by King Louis XV. In this painting each person is depicted in a flattering way. This was a habit of de Troy's that added greatly to his popularity. His works were not enjoyed for their deep intellectual meaning. Instead they made light and charming representations of the appearances of his wealthy patrons. Today they can be viewed as a true, if somewhat glorified, record of the life styles of the French nobility of the eighteenth century.

You might want to use the following questions to discuss the art:

1. Do you think people today entertain themselves less frequently by reading in groups?
2. What has replaced this activity today?
3. Do these people seem to be enjoying themselves?
4. What impression does this painting give of reading?

READING FROM MOLIÈRE ABOUT 1728
Jean-François de Troy
Dowager Marchioness of Cholmondeley

Objectives

1 To acquire an overview of the Age of Rationalism
2 To trace the rise of humanism
3 To evaluate the importance of Neoclassicism
4 To understand the relationships of Rationalism with nature, science, the Church, and art
5 To investigate the triumphs of the Age of Rationalism

THE AGE OF RATIONALISM
1650–1800

From time to time Pangloss would say to Candide:

"There is a chain of events in this best of all possible worlds; for if you had not been turned out of a beautiful mansion at the point of a jackboot for the love of the Lady Cunegonde, and if you had not been involved in the Inquisition, and had not wandered over America on foot, and had not struck the Baron with your sword, and lost all those sheep you brought from Eldorado, you would not be here eating candied fruit and pistachio nuts."

"That's true enough," said Candide; "but we must go and work in the garden."

—Voltaire

In the preceding words from the last page of Voltaire's *Candide*, two of the book's leading characters continue the debate that has stretched for the length of the novel. Cause-and-effect relationships, the place of chance in life, and the ability of good people to persevere in the face of unfair hardships are considered again and again by Pangloss, the optimistic teacher, and by Candide, his uncertain student.

LOUIS XIV AND MOLIÈRE
Jean-August-Dominique Ingres

In the same way Pangloss believes that Candide's final position resulted from his earlier experiences, the Age of Rationalism was the product of its parts. If its satirists had not lampooned hypocrisy, if its philosophers had not trusted reason, if its explorers had not mapped the continents, then the world would not have seemed—as it did to many living then—to be the best one possible. But they had, and for a while writers like Molière, Swift, La Fontaine, and Pascal were able to provide a sparkling display of enlightenment that has remained distinct in the history of literature.

OVERVIEW

The late seventeenth and eighteenth centuries were a time of concern for truth as revealed through reason. Philosophers of the Age of Rationalism challenged traditions, folk wisdom, and other unscientific beliefs and attempted to replace them with laws derived from contemplation and analysis of natural phenomena. During this time of enlightenment, reason was accepted as the greatest authority in matters of art and the intellect.

Leaning upon the structure of arithmetic, algebra, geometry, and the newly evolved study of calculus, the application of rationalism required considerable training. As Galileo, a forerunner of the rationalist movement, pointed out, "Truth is written in the great book of Nature, but only he can read it who can decipher the letters in which it is written." Rationalism soon came to be connected with great depth of thought, maturity, and scholarly training.

THE RISE OF HUMANISM

Two famous spokesmen, Sir Thomas More and Desiderius Erasmus, formed the nucleus of a group of Oxford University reformers who fostered the tenets of humanism and rationalism by reviving interest in the writings of ancient Greek and Roman authors. The humanist creed, firmly grounded in classical philosophies, allotted dignity and worth to each individual while it championed the creativity of the human mind.

The humanists elevated the importance of human beings. As More muses in *Utopia*, it seems strange "that gold, which in itself is so useless a thing, should be everywhere so much esteemed, that even men for whom it was made, and by whom it has its value, should yet be thought of less value than it is." To More, lives on Earth were not only valuable, but also perfectible if people would educate themselves and rely on inborn mental powers. The humanists maintained that by virtue and restraint, educated people could purify institutions, end war, and achieve lasting happiness.

Rationalism and the Church

The humanists urged liberalization of the Church. To them life on Earth was most important, with less thought going to fear of death and preparation for the hereafter. Humanists insisted that people, once freed of the paralyzing fear of damnation, could rise to greater heights of virtue and good works, thereby assuring their salvation. These beliefs met opposition from those who maintained that emphasis should be on God, not on human beings.

THE IMPORTANCE OF NEOCLASSICISM

Humanists revived the study of ancient Greek and Roman authors such as Plato and Cicero. They felt that the importance of classical thought was not only in its substance, but also in its form. Because of their natural bent toward symmetry and unity, the ancients provided a worthy model to Rationalists, who sought an appropriate balance of style and subject matter. This uncustomary blend of biblical and pagan images and philosophies formed the basis of major poetic works, notably those of Spenser and Milton.

Milton applied his talents to a re-creation of the ancient epic form based upon a crucial biblical subject—the fall of humanity. Like Spenser before him, Milton crafted graceful, sonorous lines of verse by imitating the classical style of Homer and Virgil. He emphasized Adam and Eve's ability to reason as they faced the alluring temptations and specious arguments of Satan, the wily fallen angel.

Rationalism and Nature

The rise of rationalism, which exalted the use of the intellect above all other human powers, coincided with a renewed interest in nature. Through a contemplation of the natural world, Rationalists evolved an appreciation for and acceptance of certain rules of human behavior, which they called human nature. Both nature and reason were allied with the order that Rationalists sought to impose on their world, thereby replacing enmity with harmony.

John Locke carried his philosophy into the realm of education with his "Essay Concerning the Human Understanding." In this influential work, he stated, "No man's knowledge here can go beyond his experience." As Locke described the human mind, it is merely a *tabula rasa,* a blank slate on which experiences and observations of nature are recorded. By denying the existence of prenatal, and therefore unlearned, ideas, Locke placed a stronger emphasis on reflection and the satisfaction of natural curiosity. Jefferson, Washington, and the other founders of American democracy were heavily influenced by this movement toward individual rights to study and learn firsthand.

Artists and musicians, too, expressed a fervent interest in the natural environment. Among the notable painters of outdoor scenes were Jean Watteau, François Boucher, and Antonio Canaletto. As musical expressions of external nature, Antonio Vivaldi created his "Four Seasons," Wolfgang Amadeus Mozart wrote *Eine Kleine Nachtmusik,* (*A Little Night Music*), and Franz Joseph Haydn composed his "Sun" quartets.

Even the more mundane aspects of life bore the emphasis of external nature. A whole social milieu based on the consumption of coffee, a panacea for many ailments, produced the English coffeehouses. For greater relief of tensions, people made regular pilgrimages to spas and hot springs. At Bath, England, the most famous of the watering places, sufferers from backaches, arthritis, migraine headaches, skin disorders, and a host of debilitating ills submerged in the waters, breathed its sulphur-laden fumes, coated their limbs with curative mud, and drank daily doses from the springs in order to partake of a natural form of healing.

Probably the most graphic representation of

1 **Discussion** Have students consider whether the debate between religion and science still continues in our own day. Discuss some topics that seem to divide the two sides.

2 **Discussion** Ask students why they think people often search for some magic solutions to life's problems. Discuss some of the things besides coffee to which people have turned in their desire to make life less tense.

St. Petersburg, Russia,
built by Peter the Great

Portrait of
English scientist
Sir Isaac Newton

Humanities Notes

Pictured from left to right:

Peter the Great, the czar of Russia from 1682 to 1725, wanted an outlet to the sea and a port for trade through the Baltic Sea; in 1703 he built the city of St. Petersburg. By 1712 Peter moved the capital from Moscow to St. Petersburg and made it the intellectual center of Russia. The city was immortalized in the works of some of Russia's greatest writers, including Pushkin, Dostoevsky, and Tolstoy. Since Peter's rule, St. Petersburg has gone through three name changes: In 1914 it was changed to Petrograd and in 1924 it was named Leningrad, after the founder of the Soviet Communist Party—Lenin. In 1991, the name was changed back to St. Petersburg. In 1918 Moscow replaced St. Petersburg (then Petrograd) as Russia's capital.

Sir Isaac Newton (1642–1727) is considered one of the greatest scientists who ever lived. During the period between 1664 and 1666, this English scientist and mathematician discovered the law of gravity and the properties of white light and developed calculus. (German mathematician Gottfried Leibniz is also credited with developing calculus.) For a short period of time, Newton worked at England's mint. He was warden of the mint in 1696 and master in 1699. In 1705 Queen Anne knighted Newton in recognition of his services in the mint and for his scientific accomplishments. He died in 1727 and was buried in Westminster Abbey, where England's most notable kings, queens, and subjects are buried.

Rembrandt (1606–1669) is celebrated as the greatest Dutch painter. He began studying painting in 1621, when he was a young boy. During his lifetime Rembrandt amassed more than 600 paintings, 300 etchings, 1,400 drawings, and 100 self-portraits; a countless number of other works have been lost. *Syndics of the Drapers' Guild*, pictured here, represents the height of Dutch portrait painting and illustrates Rembrandt's mas-

1650	1675	1700

HISTORY

- Louis XIV begins reign in France
- Great Plague of London begins
- Great fire of London takes place

- Peter the Great becomes czar of Russia
- James II becomes king of England
- Glorious Revolution in Britain begins
- Bill of Rights becomes law in Britain

- Act of Settlement is passed
- War of Spanish Succession begins
- Peter the Great begins building St. Petersburg

HUMAN PROGRESS

- Italian astronomer introduces his map of the moon
- First fountain pens and stockings are manufactured in France
- Ice cream becomes popular dessert in France
- Dutch scientist develops primitive microscope, discovers living single-cell organisms

- French found boarding school for girls
- Isaac Newton publishes book of mathematical proofs
- John Locke: *Two Treatises on Government*
- First address directory is published in France

- First daily newspaper begins publication
- Witch executions end in England
- Syringe is invented
- Daniel Fahrenheit constructs mercury thermometer

LITERATURE

- Molière: *Tartuffe*
- Molière: *The Misanthrope*
- John Milton: *Paradise Lost*
- La Fontaine's first collection of fables is published
- Pascal: *Pensées*, published posthumously

- John Locke: *Essay Concerning Human Understanding*
- Daniel Defoe begins weekly newspaper, *The Review*, while in prison
- *The Evening Post*, the first evening paper, is issued in England
- First literary magazine, *The Tatler*, begins publication
- First Copyright Act is passed
- Alexander Pope: "The Rape of the Lock"

terful handling of light and shadow to create atmosphere. Despite his success as a painter, Rembrandt had financial difficulties. He lived in a style beyond his means and collected art on a scale he could not afford. In 1666 he declared bankruptcy; his house and possessions were sold at auction in 1667 and 1668. He died one year later.

King Louis XIV built the Palace of Versailles, pictured here, in the mid-1600's. The palace served as the royal residence of France for more than 100 years. It took more than 40 years to complete the 1,300-room palace. It is now considered an example of French classical architecture at its height. During the French Revolution, Parisian mobs

stormed the palace and destroyed most of the palace's furniture and art. Although it was never again used as a royal residence, the palace was the place where several important treaties were signed, including the 1919 treaty that ended World War I and established the League of Nations and the 1871 treaty that ended the Franco-Prussian War.

Rembrandt's
"Syndics of
the Drapers' Guild"

Palace of
Versailles, Paris

"The Spirit of
'76," American
Revolution

Portrait of Austrian
composer Wolfgang
Amadeus Mozart

"Night of August 4, 1789,"
French Revolution

1725	1750	1775	1800

- Peter the Great dies; is succeeded by his wife, Catherine
  - Treaty of Seville is established among France, Spain, and England
  - George Washington is born
- Seven Years' War begins
  - Seven Years' War ends
  - Stamp Act is passed
  - Boston Tea Party takes place
  - American Revolution begins
  - Declaration of Independence is signed
  - American Revolution ends
  - Louis XVI begins reign
- Fall of the Bastille takes place; French Revolution begins
  - Bill of Rights in U.S.

- First coffee is planted in Brazil
- Sign language is invented in Portugal
  - Wedgwood develops new methods of pottery making
  - Assembly of 35-volume *Encyclopedia* begins in France
- Eli Whitney invents the cotton gin
  - Vaccination against smallpox is introduced

- Jonathan Swift: *Gulliver's Travels*
  - Jonathan Swift: *A Modest Proposal*
- Charles de Montesquieu dies
  - Voltaire: *Candide*

(continued from bottom of page)

music by the time he was five. At six he played for the Austrian empress at her court in Vienna. During his short life, Mozart wrote over 600 works, many of which were written by the time he was thirteen. In his late twenties, Mozart earned a meager living primarily by teaching and giving public concerts. His financial difficulties persisted until his death at the age of thirty–five.

This picture illustrates the rising of the French middle class in 1789 against the absolute monarchy of King Louis XIV, which some believe marks the beginning of the French Revolution. Although historians disagree on the exact cause of the Revolution, they do agree that the conflict quickly became a movement of reform and a struggle for the middle class to gain power in the government. One of the most famous early events of the Revolution was the capture of the Bastille, a royal fortress and despised symbol of oppression, by a crowd in Paris. Today the French celebrate Bastille Day on July 14, the national holiday of republican France. During the course of the Revolution, a series of elected legislatures ruled France. One of these ruling bodies ordered the execution of King Louis XVI and Marie Antoinette. Thousands of others died at the guillotine during this period, which was later called the Reign of Terror. The Revolution ended in 1799 when General Napoleon Bonaparte took control of the French government.

In February 1775 the British Parliament declared that the Massachusetts colony was in open rebellion against British rule. On April 18 approximately 700 British soldiers marched toward Lexington and Concord, Massachusetts, to end the rebellion. Britain's plan was discovered and Paul Revere was sent to ride to Concord to warn people that the British, or the redcoats, were coming. One day later British soldiers and American patriots clashed at Lexington and Concord, Massachusetts, and the American Revolutionary War began. A year later, on July 4, 1776, the Declaration of Independence was adopted and the United States of America was born. This painting, entitled *The Spirit of '76*, commemorates the birth of that new nation.

Austrian composer Wolfgang Amadeus Mozart (1756–1791) was one of the greatest composers of the classical period. When Mozart was four years old, his father taught him to play the harpsichord, violin, and organ. He began composing

Enrichment The map depicting Europe in 1763 shows the location of the countries that produced the writers whose work is contained in this unit. Have students study its information carefully. Then you may want to ask the following questions:

1. Approximately how many miles is it from Madrid to Lisbon?
2. In what direction would you travel to go from Ireland to Spain?
3. Name the island north of Sardinia.
4. What country is east of Portugal?
5. If you were sailing from Sicily to Algeria, would you pass Corsica along the shortest route?

Answers
1. 300 miles
2. South
3. Corsica
4. Spain
5. No

3 Clarification Mention to students that this scientist is the one who first noticed and then predicted the course of the comet that is named after him. Have students share whatever they can about that phenomenon.

the connection between nature and rationalism is the formal English garden, which is still in vogue throughout the British Isles and in parts of continental Europe as well as in Williamsburg, Virginia, Tryon Palace, North Carolina, and other English settlements in the New World. Laid out with the precision of a draftsman's T-square and compass, the symmetrical rows of flowers and shrubs formed a visible monument to the Rationalists' urge for balance and control and often culminated in a sundial, fountain, or gazebo. Carefully thought out and cultivated so that the owner could make the best use of soil, light, natural contours of the land, waterways, and the passage of the seasons, these landscapes have survived to our own times as though they were artworks in foliage.

Rationalism and Science

At the same time, scientists were unlocking numerous secrets of the universe. Isaac Newton published a book of mathematical proofs in 1687 and shed light on the nature of gravity and the motion of the planets around the sun. Other scientists were breaking new ground. Edmund Halley produced a detailed study of heavenly bodies. Anton van Leeuwenhoek invented the microscope for the observation of one-celled organisms. Robert Boyle defined the chemical elements, and Edward Jenner began inoculations for smallpox, the scourge that had either scarred, maimed, or killed a significant portion of the world's population. Practical knowledge, including the invention of the syringe, air pump, mercury thermometer, pendulum and mainspring clocks, and cotton gin, introduced effective ways to solve old problems. The establishment of the Greenwich Observatory in 1675 helped regulate the perception of time and focused expert attention on changes in the weather and the movements of the moon and stars. Across a wide span of human activities, people were employing rationalism not only as a systematized means of thought, but also as a way to regulate and improve their daily existence.

Europe in 1763

THE GREAT FIRE 1666
Marcus Willemsz Doornik
Guildhall Library, London

Humanities Note

Cartography, *The Great Fire* by Marcus Willemsz Doornik. When it is done with skill, a map can reveal much of the creativity of an artist through the use of color, lettering, design, and decoration. *The Great Fire* by Doornik is an example of the map as a work of art. This aerial view of old London is decorated with an inset view of the city in flames. The interest of the map is further enhanced by the boats in the river and the careful gradations of color. This map is not only interesting to historians, it gives pleasure to any viewer because it is a source of visual pleasure.

You might want to use the following questions to discuss the art:

1. How does this map differ from others you may have seen?
2. Do you think the map's purpose is historical or artistic?
3. Do you feel the decorative quality of this map detracts from its utility?
4. What revisions might be made to improve your estimation of this map?

4 Discussion Mention some of the uses of encyclopedias, such as their use in research and editing. Discuss with students how difficult their own schooling would be if there were no such collections available. Have them speculate on how long it would take a small committee of students to compile a decent encyclopedia on skateboarding, current teen fashion, or a similarly interesting topic.

Rationalism and the Literary Art

Literature too profited from rationalism, which left its mark on poets, essayists, playwrights, and journalists. Writers put new emphasis on practicality by publishing the first daily newspaper in 1702. Seven years later Joseph Addison and Richard Steele produced the first literary magazines, *The Tatler* and *The Spectator*, which proved to be major successes, bringing humorous essays and witty commentary on daily topics to the average reader. In France, Denis Diderot assembled and edited a multivolume encyclopedia of world knowledge. Because his commentary on social and governmental institutions often clashed with accepted principles, his work suffered repeated censorship and repression. Upon its completion after twenty-five years of toil, the *Encyclopédie* became a symbol of tolerance and freedom of expression, key elements of the intellectual enlightenment characteristic of the Age of Rationalism.

Against the backdrop of popularized literature and more objective reference works, figures of great literary significance produced classic works, including Charles de Montesquieu's wise and perceptive essays and letters; Daniel Defoe's stark, intense description of the bubonic plague in *The Journal of the Plague Years* and his classic adventure tale *Robinson Crusoe*; Molière's *The Misanthrope* and *Tartuffe*, comedies of human vice and virtue; Jonathan Swift's powerful satires *A Tale of a Tub* and *Gulliver's Travels*; Voltaire's philosophical *Candide*; as well as John Milton's literary epics *Paradise Lost* and *Paradise Regained* and his drama *Samson Agonistes*.

The Triumphs of the Age of Rationalism

Overall, the Age of Rationalism was a time of progress and betterment in human affairs. In Russia, Czar Peter the Great streamlined the military, introduced modern printing methods, reformed the calendar and tax system, built a new capital at St. Petersburg, and educated peasants in order to improve their lives. Throughout Europe and the New World, persecution of suspected witches ceased. Ex-

You might want to use the following questions to discuss the art:

1. What is the first impression you receive from this work?
2. Explain whether you think the artist is trying to glorify the Revolution.
3. What is the difference between propaganda and art that is used for politics?

Cooperative Learning Let students join in teams to research projects on how the ideas of the Age of Rationalism led to the revolutions in France and America. Encourage students to look for parallels. Schedule time for each team report.

Check Test

1. The Age of Rationalism is regarded as a time of _____ .
2. Desiderius Erasmus was a leading writer who championed the ideas of _____ .
3. Because of its emphasis on the human instead of the divine, rationalism seemed to conflict with _____ .
4. The establishment of the _____ in 1675 helped to regulate Europe's perception of time and space.
5. The Age of Rationalism sparked revolutions in _____ and _____ .

Answers

1. enlightenment
2. humanism
3. religion (or the Church)
4. Greenwich Observatory
5. America and France

plorers of the North American continent pushed westward and southward into the wilderness, reaching the extremes of the Mississippi River and the Great Salt Lake and making contact with heretofore unknown tribes of Indians. England survived both the Great Plague in 1665 and the Great Fire of London the following year. Through the creations of Sir Christopher Wren, who designed and rebuilt fifty-two churches modeled primarily on the order and regularity of Italian Renaissance originals, the city was revitalized. Wren's most notable achievement was St. Paul's Cathedral, which still serves as the site of royal ceremonies of state. The chronicler of this memorable period, Samuel Pepys, unwittingly preserved the tenor of the times in his diary, which covers the major political and historical upheavals of his era alongside a host of mundane affairs, from the cooking of a shank of meat to the foibles of servants, from an evening at the theater to a boat ride on the Thames.

The ideas of rationalism sparked two great revolutions—one in the New World, one in Europe. Throughout the British colonies along the east coast of America, voices of dissatisfaction grew during the 1750's and 1760's. From the ports of Boston and New York, a consistent barrage of complaints streamed forth about taxation, repression, rights, and representation. Dissidents like Benjamin Franklin and Thomas Paine authored material that incorporated ideas borrowed from European theorists opposed to old regimes, with notions of potential created by the vast, unbridled frontiers that stretched across the new continent in what seemed like a limitless way. When the debates heated beyond the point where they could be controlled, violence broke out. By the 1770's a full scale revolution was at hand. George Washington embodied the forceful-

TAKING OF THE BASTILLE

ness and ingenuity that represented so much of his fellow citizens' hopes. His military campaigns were ultimately successful, and the young country found in him a just, imaginative first chief executive. With good fortune a nation was founded on a constitution that not only reflected much of the best thought of previous decades but also contained the resilience to outlast the strains of future years.

In France the situation was different. Unlike the boundless, recently mapped stretches of America, France's own territory seemed weighed down by a tired discrepancy between the nobility and the masses. A few aristocrats held a great percent of the country's wealth. Authors like Voltaire resented the monarchy. The unwillingness of the privileged few to alleviate the misery of many became more and more a point of contention that citizens endlessly debated in the courts and pubs of the land.

But the end result of this seething discontent had results parallel to those in America a decade earlier. Injustices inflamed oratory, and in turn revolt exploded across the land. The 1789 uprising started in the streets of Paris and spread through the provinces, finally resulting in the establishment of a republic. But unlike its American counterpart, the French experiment soon returned much of the power won from the displaced monarchy to a single leader in the form of Napoleon Bonaparte, who set up the Consulate in 1799. Despite the numerous links that bind the French and American revolutions to common sources and inspirations, they are not processes that run on parallel lines to a mutual conclusion. Indeed, in some ways they show that the pangs of the Age of Rationalism were capable of signaling the births of very different children.

VOICES OF RATIONALISM

We have just enough religion to make us hate, but not enough to make us love one another.

Jonathan Swift, *Thoughts on Various Subjects,* from *Miscellanies*

Reading is to the mind what exercise is to the body.

Sir Richard Steele, *Tatler* (1709–1711), No. 49

It is better to risk saving a guilty person than to condemn an innocent one.

Voltaire, *Zadig*

I disapprove of what you say, but I will defend to the death your right to say it.

Voltaire, Attributed

After us the deluge!

Madame Pompadour

In the strict sense of the term, a true democracy has never existed, and never will exist.

Jean Jacques Rousseau, *The Social Contract*

Let them eat cake.

Marie-Antoinette

Do you wish people to think well of you? Don't speak well of yourself.

Blaise Pascal, *Thoughts*

For in fact what is man in nature? A Nothing in comparison with the Infinite, an All in comparison with Nothing, a mean between nothing and everything.

Blaise Pascal, *Pensées*

Birth is nothing without virtue, and we have no claim to share in the glory of our ancestors unless we strive to resemble them.

Molière, *Don Juan*

Great crimes come never singly; they are linked / To sins that went before.

Racine, *Phaedre*

Additional Voices

People use thought only to justify their wrongdoings, and speech only to conceal their thoughts.

—**Voltaire,** *Letters*

Early to bed, early to rise, makes a man healthy, wealthy, and wise.

—**Ben Franklin,** *Poor Richard's Almanac*

I can be expected to look for truth but not to find it.

—**Denis Diderot,** *Philosophic Thoughts*

Man is born free, and everywhere he is in chains.

—**Jean Jacques Rousseau,** *The Social Contract*

The Age of Rationalism

Historical Context

During the Age of Rationalism, poverty was the dominant condition in Ireland. Policies made by the English led to suffering and starvation. Since the twelfth century, the Irish had protested the interference of outsiders, particularly the English, in their politics and the usurpation of lands by absentee landlords who seemed to the Irish to show little concern for exploited people. Yet no political or military action has freed the Irish from outsiders. The ongoing struggle that is referred to by the Irish themselves as "The Troubles" continues to disrupt life in the northern section that remained under the control of England after the southern counties created the Republic of Ireland in 1922. This conflict is the context against which Jonathan Swift's "A Modest Proposal" must be placed in order to be understood.

Cultural Context

For Jonathan Swift, the improvement of living standards for his fellow countrymen became a focus of his life. From the publication of "A Modest Proposal" in 1729, he earned the respect of the Irish, who perceived some of the English landlords as a species of insensitive parasites draining Ireland of its resources and sapping it of vitality. Swift devoted his effort to the betterment of Ireland.

Rural Irish farmers and people who fish, long a source of ridicule for the polished, sophisticated Londoners who visited their shores on vacation, fought the social image that placed them in a poor light. A major source of contention between the two cultures was the difference in their religions. From early times, the English Protestants were most stringently opposed to "popery," or Catholicism, which they assumed to be the root cause of Ireland's poverty and backwardness. The Irish, on the other hand, adhered to a religion that gave them hope and bound them under one uplifting philosophy.

Literary Context

Under the leadership of Jonathan Swift, Ireland discovered its literary powers, and later spokespersons advanced the cause. Once the Irish established an Irish National Theater and produced playwrights, poets, historians, and novelists of the stature of John Millington Synge, William Butler Yeats, Lady Augusta Gregory, and James Joyce, their subservience to English literary domination and superiority ceased. Writers like Swift drew upon the current affairs for inspiration for their writing and used satire to ridicule their subjects.

On the following pages is an article by Swift. The annotations in the margin point out the historical, cultural, and literary context.

A Modest Proposal

Jonathan Swift

For Preventing the Children of poor People in Ireland from being a Burden to their Parents or Country, and for making them beneficial to the Public

It is a melancholy object to those who walk through this great town,[1] or travel in the country when they see the streets, the roads, and cabin doors crowded with beggars of the female sex, followed by three, four, or six children, all in rags and importuning[2] every passenger for an alms. These mothers, instead of being able to work for their honest livelihood, are forced to employ all their time in strolling to beg sustenance for their helpless infants; who, as they grow up, either turn thieves for want of work, or leave their dear native country, to fight for the Pretender[3] in Spain, or sell themselves to the Barbados.[4]

I think it is agreed by all parties that this prodigious[5] number of children in the arms, or on the backs, or at the heels of their mothers, and frequently of their fathers, is, in the present deplorable state of the kingdom, a very great additional grievance; and therefore whoever could find out a fair, cheap, and easy method of making these children sound and useful members of the commonwealth, would deserve so well of the public as to have his statue set up for a preserver of the nation.

But my intention is very far from being confined to provide only for the children of professed beggars: it is of a much greater extent and shall take in the whole number of infants at a certain age who are born of parents in effect as little able to support them as those who demand our charity in the streets.

As to my own part, having turned my thoughts for many years upon this important subject and maturely weighed the several schemes

---

1. **this great town:** Dublin.
2. **importuning** (im´pôr t $\overline{oo}$ n´iŋ) *v.*: Troubling with requests or demands.
3. **the Pretender:** James Edward (1688–1766), son of King James II of England. Although his father had lost the throne in the Revolution of 1688, many people felt that he was the legitimate claimant to the throne.
4. **Barbados:** At the time, Barbados was a British possession with a thriving sugar industry. In hope of escaping from their poverty, many Irish sold their services to the owners of sugar plantations in return for passage to Barbados.
5. **prodigious** (prə dij´ əs) *adj.*: Enormous; huge.

of other projectors,[6] I have always found them grossly mistaken in their computation. It is true, a child just dropped from its dam may be supported by her milk for a solar year with little other nourishment: at most not above the value of two shillings, which the mother may certainly get, or the value in scraps, by her lawful occupation of begging; and it is exactly at one year old that I propose to provide for them in such a manner, as, instead of being a charge upon their parents or the parish, or wanting food and raiment for the rest of their lives, they shall, on the contrary, contribute to the feeding and partly to the clothing of many thousands.

There is likewise another great advantage in my scheme, that it will prevent those voluntary abortions and that horrid practice of women murdering their bastard children, alas! too frequent among us, sacrificing the poor innocent babes, I doubt more to avoid the expense than the shame, which would move tears and pity in the most savage and inhuman breast.

The number of souls in Ireland being usually reckoned one million and a half, of these I calculate there may be about two hundred thousand couples whose wives are breeders; from which number I subtract thirty thousand couples, who are able to maintain their own children—although I apprehend there cannot be so many, under the present distresses of the kingdom—but this being granted, there will remain a hundred and seventy thousand breeders. I again subtract fifty thousand for those women who miscarry, or whose children die by accident or disease within the year. There only remain a hundred and twenty thousand children of poor parents annually born. The question therefore is how this number shall be reared and provided for; which, as I have already said, under the present situation of affairs, is utterly impossible by all the methods hitherto proposed. For we can neither employ them in handicraft or agriculture; we neither build houses (I mean in the country) nor cultivate land. They can very seldom pick up a livelihood by stealing until they arrive at six years old, except where they are of towardly parts;[7] although I confess they learn the rudiments much earlier; during which time they can, however, be properly looked upon only as probationers; as I have been informed by a principal gentleman in the county of Cavan, who protested to me that he never knew above one or two instances under the age of six, even in a part of the kingdom so renowned for the quickest proficiency in that art.

I am assured by our merchants that a boy or a girl before twelve years old is no salable commodity; and even when they come to this age they will not yield above three pounds, or three pounds and half a crown at most, on the Exchange; which cannot turn to account either

---

6. **projectors:** Planners.
7. **of towardly parts:** Unusually talented.

THE WIDOWER
Sir Samuel Luke Fildes
Art Gallery of New South Wales, Sydney

Humanities Note
Fine art, *The Widower* by Sir Samuel Luke Fildes. Sir Luke Fildes (1843–1927) first achieved recognition as an illustrator for a weekly newspaper "The Graphic" and for the last work of Dickens, *Edwin Drood*. His paintings are classified as belonging to the British social realism school. He sought, through his work, to inform people of the misery and injustice suffered by London's poor. He painted scenes such as *The Widower* (1876) with compassion and realism. Here he addresses the plight of a man who has lost his helpmate. He cannot leave his children to go to work, and because he has no money, he cannot pay someone to care for them. Fildes's graphic depiction of this dilemma evokes instant sympathy from the viewer.

Fildes achieved great success with his socially conscious paintings. Unfortunately, this success dimmed his drive to continue to use his painting talent to crusade against injustice. He spent his affluent late years as a fashionable portrait painter.

You might want to use the following questions to discuss the art:

1. What feelings does this painting evoke in you?
2. What elements of the work inspire those feelings?

to the parents or the kingdom, the charge of nutriment and rags having been at least four times that value.

I shall now therefore humbly propose my own thoughts, which I hope will not be liable to the least objection.

I have been assured by a very knowing American of my acquaintance in London that a young, healthy child well nursed is at a year old a most delicious, nourishing, and wholesome food, whether stewed, roasted, baked, or boiled; and I make no doubt that it will equally serve in a fricassee, or ragout.[8]

I do therefore humbly offer it to public consideration that of the hundred and twenty thousand children already computed, twenty thousand may be reserved for breed, whereof only one-fourth part to be males; which is more than we allow to sheep, black cattle, or swine; and my reason is that these children are seldom the fruits of marriage, a circumstance not much regarded by our savages; therefore one male will be sufficient to serve four females. That the remaining hundred thousand may, at a year old, be offered in sale to the persons of quality

Cultural Context: In many parts of Europe at this time, the stereotype of the American was that of a barbarian.

---

8. **ragout** (ra gōō′) *n.*: A highly seasoned stew of meat and vegetables.

time, only to spare my pocket?'. . ." "No, we had rather talk with you, than drink with you. . . ." "But if you had supped with me, as in all reason you ought to have done, you must have drank with me. . . . A bottle of wine; two shillings. . . . Two and two, is four; and one is five: just two and sixpence a piece. There, Pope, there's half-a-crown for you; and there's another for you, sir: for I won't save anything by you I am determined." This was all said and done with his usual seriousness on such occasions; and in spite of every thing we could say to the contrary, he actually obliged us to take the money.

5 Literary Focus Point out to students that Swift exaggerates the stereotypical view of Americans for satiric effect. As late as the nineteenth century, Americans were commonly regarded as barbarians unworthy of notice. In his famous 1820 remarks, for example, Sydney Smith noted the poor opinion in which Americans and their culture were held: "In the four quarters of the globe, who reads an American book? or goes to an American play? or looks at an American picture or statue?"

6

Historical Context: Notice the sly reference to English landlords, whom Swift charges with the terrible poverty of the land.

Cultural Context: The speaker makes reference to a common belief that a diet of fish increases fertility. The English, many of whom were ardent anti-Catholics, were apt to make jokes about the Catholic customs of Ireland, one of which was the consumption of fish during Lent, the forty-day period that precedes Easter.

7

8

and fortune through the kingdom; always advising the mother to let them suck plentifully in the last month, so as to render them plump and fat for a good table. A child will make two dishes at an entertainment for friends; and when the family dines alone, the fore or hind quarter will make a reasonable dish; and seasoned with a little pepper or salt will be very good boiled on the fourth day, especially in winter.

I have reckoned upon a medium[9] that a child just born will weigh twelve pounds, and in a solar year, if tolerably nursed, will increase to twenty-eight pounds.

I grant this food will be somewhat dear,[10] and therefore very proper for landlords, who, as they have already devoured most of the parents, seem to have the best title to the children.

Infants' flesh will be in season throughout the year, but more plentiful in March, and a little before and after: for we are told by a grave author,[11] an eminent French physician, that fish being a prolific diet, there are more children born in Roman Catholic countries about nine months after Lent than at any other season; therefore reckoning a year after Lent, the markets will be more glutted than usual, because the number of popish infants is at least three to one in this kingdom; and therefore it will have one other collateral[12] advantage, by lessening the number of papists among us.

I have already computed the charge of nursing a beggar's child (in which list I reckon all cottagers, laborers, and four-fifths of the farmers) to be about two shillings per annum, rags included; and I believe no gentleman would repine[13] to give ten shillings for the carcass of a good fat child, which, as I have said, will make four dishes of excellent nutritive meat, when he hath only some particular friend or his own family to dine with him. Thus the squire will learn to be a good landlord and grow popular among his tenants; the mother will have eight shillings net profit and be fit for work until she produces another child.

Those who are more thrifty (as I must confess the times require) may flay the carcass; the skin of which artificially[14] dressed will make admirable gloves for ladies and summer boots for fine gentlemen.

As to our city of Dublin, shambles[15] may be appointed for this purpose in the most convenient parts of it, and butchers we may be assured will not be wanting; although I rather recommend buying the children alive and dressing them hot from the knife as we do roasting pigs.

---

9. **medium:** Average.
10. **dear:** Expensive.
11. **a grave author:** François Rabelais (1494?–1553), a French humorist.
12. **collateral** (kə lat′ ər əl) *adj.*: Accompanying or existing in a subordinate, corroborative, or indirect relationship.
13. **repine** (ri pīn′) *v.*: Complain; fret.
14. **artificially:** Artfully.
15. **shambles:** Slaughterhouses.

A very worthy person, a true lover of his country, and whose virtues I highly esteem, was lately pleased, in discoursing on this matter, to offer a refinement upon my scheme. He said that many gentlemen of this kingdom having of late destroyed their deer, he conceived that the want of venison might be well supplied by the bodies of young lads and maidens, not exceeding fourteen years of age nor under twelve; so great a number of both sexes in every county being now ready to starve for want of work and service and these to be disposed of by their parents, if alive, or otherwise by their nearest relations. But with due deference to so excellent a friend and so deserving a patriot, I cannot be altogether in his sentiments; for as to the males, my American acquaintance assured me from frequent experience that their flesh was generally tough and lean, like that of our schoolboys, by continual exercise, and their taste disagreeable; and to fatten them would not answer the charge. Then as to the females it would, I think, with humble submission, be a loss to the public, because they soon would become breeders themselves; and besides it is not improbable that some scrupulous people might be apt to censure such a practice (although indeed very unjustly) as a little bordering upon cruelty, which, I confess, hath always been with me the strongest objection against any project, how wellsoever intended.

But in order to justify my friend, he confessed that this expedient was put into his head by the famous Salmanaazor,[16] a native of the island Formosa, who came from thence to London above twenty years ago and in conversation told my friend that in his country when any young person happened to be put to death, the executioner sold the carcass to persons of quality as a prime dainty; and that in his time the body of a plump girl of fifteen, who was crucified for an attempt to poison the emperor, was sold to his imperial majesty's prime minister of state, and other great mandarins of the court, in joints from the gibbet,[17] at four hundred crowns. Neither indeed can I deny that if the same use were made of several plump young girls in this town, who, without one single groat to their fortunes, cannot stir abroad without a chair,[18] and appear at the playhouse and assemblies in foreign fineries which they never will pay for, the kingdom would not be the worse.

Some persons of a desponding spirit are in great concern about the vast number of poor people who are aged, diseased, or maimed; and I have been desired to employ my thoughts what course may be taken to ease the nation of so grievous an encumbrance. But I am not in the

---

16. **Salmanaazor** (sal´ mən ā´ zər): George Psalmanazar (1679?–1763), a Frenchman who claimed to be a native of Formosa and wrote a false account of life in Formosa, in which he described cannibalism.

17. **gibbet** (jib´ it) *n*.: Gallowslike structure from which the bodies of criminals were hung after execution.

18. **chair:** Sedan chair, an enclosed seat carried on poles by men.

Literary Context: Notice the ironic tone here. Certainly this proposal is more than "a little bordering on cruelty."

9

poraries that Erasmus satirizes in his 1509 *Praise of Folly* and the satire of knighthood in Cervantes's *Don Quixote*, 1605–1615.

Satire took to the stage in seventeenth-century England in the plays of Ben Jonson. In France, Molière's dramas satirized such types as hypocrites, social climbers, and medical frauds.

What scholars have dubbed "The Golden Age of Satire" began in England in the eighteenth century. Gay's *Beggar's Opera* (1728) was followed by the brilliant satires of Pope, Addison, Fielding, Austen, and Smollett. Swift, the most notable satirist of the age, even became the victim of political reprisal because of the ferocity of his work.

least pain upon that matter; because it is very well known that they are every day dying and rotting, by cold and famine, and filth and vermin, as fast as can be reasonably expected. And as to the younger laborers, they are now in almost as hopeful a condition: they cannot get work, and consequently pine away for want of nourishment to a degree that if at any time they are accidentally hired to common labor, they have not strength to perform it; and thus the country and themselves are in a fair way of being soon delivered from the evils to come.

I have too long digressed and therefore shall return to my subject. I think the advantages by the proposal which I have made are obvious and many, as well as of the highest importance.

For first, as I have already observed, it would greatly lessen the number of papists, with whom we are yearly overrun, being the principal breeders of the nation, as well as our most dangerous enemies; and who stay at home on purpose with a design to deliver the kingdom to the Pretender, hoping to take their advantage by the absence of so many good Protestants,[19] who have chosen rather to leave their country than stay at home and pay tithes against their conscience to an idolatrous[20] Episcopal curate.

---

19. **absence of . . . Protestants:** Swift is referring to the absentee landlords.
20. **idolatrous** (ī däl´ ə trəs) *adj.*: Having, or showing excessive admiration or devotion.

AWAITING ADMISSION TO THE CASUAL WARD
Sir Samuel Luke Fildes, R.A.
The Tate Gallery, London

Secondly, the poorer tenants will have something valuable of their own, which by law may be made liable to distress,[21] and help to pay their landlord's rent; their corn and cattle being already seized, and money a thing unknown.

Thirdly, whereas the maintenance of a hundred thousand children, from two years old and upwards, cannot be computed at less than ten shillings apiece per annum, the nation's stock will be thereby increased fifty thousand pounds per annum, besides the profit of a new dish introduced to the tables of all gentlemen of fortune in the kingdom who have any refinement in taste. And the money will circulate among ourselves, the goods being entirely of our own growth and manufacture.

Fourthly, the constant breeders, besides the gain of eight shillings sterling per annum by the sale of their children, will be rid of the charge of maintaining them after the first year.

Fifthly, this food would likewise bring great custom to taverns, where the vintners will certainly be so prudent as to procure the best receipts[22] for dressing it to perfection, and consequently have their houses frequented by all the fine gentlemen who justly value themselves upon their knowledge in good eating, and a skillful cook, who understands how to oblige his guests, will contrive to make it as expensive as they please.

Sixthly, this would be a great inducement to marriage, which all wise nations have either encouraged by rewards or enforced by laws and penalties. It would increase the care and tenderness of mothers toward their children, when they were sure of a settlement for life, to the poor babes, provided in some sort by the public, to their annual profit instead of expense. We should soon see an honest emulation among the married women, which of them could bring the fattest child to the market. Men would become as fond of their wives during the time of their pregnancy as they are now of their mares in foal, their cows in calf, or sows when they are ready to farrow; nor offer to beat or kick them (as it is too frequent a practice) for fear of a miscarriage.

Many other advantages might be enumerated. For instance, the addition of some thousand carcasses in our exportation of barreled beef, the propagation of swine's flesh, and improvement in the art of making good bacon, so much wanted among us by the great destruction of pigs, too frequent at our tables, and are no way comparable in taste or magnificence to a well-grown fat yearling child, which roasted whole will make a considerable figure at a lord mayor's feast, or any other public entertainment. But this and many others I omit, being studious of brevity.

Supposing that one thousand families in this city would be constant customers for infants' flesh, besides others who might have it at

---

21. **distress:** The legal seizure of property or goods to satisfy a debt.
22. **receipts:** Recipes.

11

12

13

14

flay the carcass.
OBJECTIVE CASE: To *whom* did you give the essay? He is the writer of *whom* we spoke.

Student Activity 1. Find additional examples of Swift's use of *who* and *whom* in "A Modest Proposal."

Student Activity 2. Write a brief summary of the essay in which you use *who* and *whom* in at least two sentences.

15 Literary Focus Call students' attention to the sentence "I can think of no one objection that will possibly be raised against this proposal." Ask them how this statement summarizes the entire "Modest Proposal." Discuss the "one objection" that lies at the heart of the speaker's argument.

16 Discussion Ask students to consider the effect of the discussion of expedients, coming as they do after the narrator's "Modest Proposal." Students should understand that these are the measures Swift would like exacted to relieve Ireland's poverty, oppression, and overpopulation.

17 Enrichment Tell students that the expedients the speaker lists here are in fact measures that Swift had previously put forth in such tracts as his "Proposal for the Universal Use of Irish Manufacturers."

Discussion Ask students how the tone on this page differs from the tone on the previous page. Have them find specific examples that show how the tone in this passage is angrier and more bitter than previously, as the speaker now proposes sensible measures that could relieve mass suffering. Make sure that students understand that this is the climax of the essay.

Reading Strategy After students have read the long paragraph on this page beginning "I can think," have them rephrase Ireland's problems as Swift sees them.

Literary Context: Swift darkens his irony by noting that infants' flesh would make a good meal for the celebration of religious rites, such as weddings and christenings.

15

Literary Context: Swift reaches a peak of irony at this point. While the narrator presents his own conclusion, Swift, from line 8 on, presents a series of practical remedies for the problems ailing Ireland. Critics praise this work for its ability to sustain satire without losing control.

16

17

Literary Context: Notice the bitter sarcasm of these lines. Sarcasm is often employed in irony.

merry meetings, particularly weddings and christenings, I compute that Dublin would take off annually about twenty thousand carcasses; and the rest of the kingdom (where probably they will be sold somewhat cheaper) the remaining eighty thousand.

I can think of no one objection that will possibly be raised against this proposal, unless it should be urged that the number of people will be thereby much lessened in the kingdom. This I freely own, and it was indeed one principal design in offering it to the world. I desire the reader will observe that I calculate my remedy for this one individual kingdom of Ireland, and for no other that ever was, is, or, I think, ever can be upon earth. Therefore let no man talk to me of other expedients: of taxing our absentees at five shillings a pound; of using neither clothes nor household furniture, except what is of our own growth and manufacture; of utterly rejecting the materials and instruments that promote foreign luxury; of curing the expensiveness of pride, vanity, idleness, and gaming in our women; of introducing a vein of parsimony,[23] prudence, and temperance; of learning to love our country, wherein we differ even from Laplanders[24] and the inhabitants of Topinamboo;[25] of quitting our animosities and factions, nor act any longer like the Jews, who were murdering one another at the very moment their city was taken;[26] of being a little cautious not to sell our country and consciences for nothing; of teaching landlords to have at least one degree of mercy toward their tenants; lastly, of putting a spirit of honesty, industry, and skill into our shopkeepers, who, if a resolution could now be taken to buy only our native goods, would immediately unite to cheat and exact upon us in the price, the measure, and the goodness, nor could ever yet be brought to make one fair proposal of just dealing, though often and earnestly invited to it.

Therefore, I repeat, let no man talk to me of these and the like expedients, till he hath at least a glimpse of hope that there will ever be some hearty and sincere attempt to put them in practice.

But as to myself, having been wearied out for many years with offering vain, idle, visionary thoughts, and at length utterly despairing of success, I fortunately fell upon this proposal; which, as it is wholly new, so it hath something solid and real, of no expense and little trouble, full in our own power, and whereby we can incur no danger in disobliging England. For this kind of commodity will not bear exportation, the flesh being of too tender a consistency to admit a long continuance in

23. **parsimony** (pär´ sə mō´ nē) *n.*: Stinginess.
24. **Laplanders**: Inhabitants of Lapland, a region in Northern Europe, including the northern parts of Norway, Sweden, and Finland.
25. **Topinamboo** (tō pēn´ əm bōō): An area of Brazil.
26. **city was taken:** While the Romans were besieging Jerusalem in A.D. 70, fighting was taking place among rival factions of the city's inhabitants.

Grammar in Action

Sentences can be classified by their function (statement, question, command, exclamation) or by their structure (simple, compound, complex, and compound-complex). Writers select the specific sentence types that will most clearly convey their ideas. Many authors use a mix of all four types, depending on their audience and purpose. **Compound-complex sentences**, which contain at least two main clauses and at least one subordinate clause, allow writers to express interlocking relationships between sentence elements. The following compound-complex sentence contains a subordinate clause followed by two main clauses. (The subordinate clause is underlined once;

main clauses are underlined twice.)

Although the long promised government reforms were finally instituted, many people had already been compelled to leave the country, and some had been reduced to abject poverty.

Note how Swift conveys his point in this compound-complex sentence:

But as to myself, having been wearied for many years with offering vain, idle, visionary thoughts, and at length utterly despairing of success, I fortunately fell upon this proposal; which, as it is wholly new, so it hath salt, although perhaps I could name a country[27] which would be glad to eat up our whole nation without it.

After all, I am not so violently bent upon my own opinion as to reject any offer proposed by wise men, which shall be found equally innocent, cheap, easy, and effectual. But before something of that kind shall be advanced in contradiction to my scheme, and offering a better, I desire the author or authors will be pleased maturely to consider two points. First, as things now stand, how they will be able to find food and raiment for a hundred thousand useless mouths and backs? And secondly, there being a round million of creatures in human figure throughout this kingdom, whose whole subsistence put into a common stock would leave them in debt two millions of pounds sterling, adding those who are beggars by profession to the bulk of farmers, cottagers, and laborers, with their wives and children, who are beggars in effect; I desire those politicians who dislike my overture and may perhaps be so bold to attempt an answer, that they will first ask the parents of these mortals whether they would not at this day think it a great happiness to have been sold for food at a year old in the manner I prescribe, and thereby have avoided such a perpetual scene of misfortunes as they have since gone through by the oppression of landlords, the impossibility of paying rent without money or trade, the want of common sustenance with neither house nor clothes to cover them from the inclemencies of weather, and the most inevitable prospect of entailing the like or greater miseries upon their breed forever.

I profess, in the sincerity of my heart, that I have not the least personal interest in endeavoring to promote this necessary work, having no other motive than the public good of my country, by advancing our trade, providing for infants, relieving the poor, and giving some pleasure to the rich. I have no children by which I can propose to get a single penny, the youngest being nine years old, and my wife past childbearing.

18

---

27. **a country:** England.

Reader's Response *Imagine that you were one of the Irish living during Swift's time. How would you react? Imagine that you were English. Would your reaction be different? Explain.*

Master Teacher Note Explore with students how governments in other countries today are dealing with the kind of mass social suffering caused by abject poverty, overpopulation, and outside oppression that Swift satirizes in "A Modest Proposal."

Reading Strategy Have students reread the opening page of the essay. Ask them how the first page of the essay and the last page are similar. Discuss how the essay's conclusion summarizes the problems the speaker introduced in the beginning.

18 **Discussion** Ask students why they think Swift ends his essay with a disclaimer. Explore with them how this ending adds to the satire.

Cultural Note Many contemporary satirists have been influenced by Jonathan Swift's writings. American novelist Nathanael West's savage dissection of the Hollywood film society in his 1939 book *The Day of the Locust* is similar to and different from Swift's "A Modest Proposal."

Cooperative Learning How writers gather their ideas, write their drafts, and revise their work is a subject that might intrigue students. Divide the class into small groups of three or four. Have each group select a writer they have already studied in *World Masterpieces* for whom previous drafts exist. Then have them research primary source material to determine how this writer composed and polished his or her work.

something solid and real, of no expense and little trouble, full in our own power, and whereby we can incur no danger in dislodging England.

Student Activity 1. Find additional compound-complex sentences in the essay. Isolate and label each part.

Student Activity 2. Write two compound-complex sentences of your own. Make sure that the elements are correctly joined.

JONATHAN SWIFT

1667–1745

A man of two countries, Jonathan Swift excelled in two realms—religion and literature. Pulled in various philosophical directions, he often resorted to adroit satire as a means of expressing discontent with untenable political situations. His most famous work, *Gulliver's Travels* (1726), ridicules the political clash of Whigs and Tories during a notorious intrigue with the Stuarts.

Swift was born in Dublin, Ireland, of English parents. Though his father died before his birth, Swift received a worthy education in Dublin at Trinity College, where he obtained an M.A. in 1688. Disenchanted with Ireland, he sought a position as secretary and moved to Moor Park, Surrey, in England. Under the mentorship of Sir William Temple, Swift met important figures and immersed himself in a swirling political milieu for ten years.

Disappointed by various factors in England, he return to Ireland in 1694, was ordained an Anglican priest, and took a job as country parson in Kilroot. Eventually, he wearied of the post and returned to Temple's employ. During this period he produced *A Tale of a Tub*, a witty, pungent burlesque of religious squabbling, and *The Battle of the Books*, an equally clever satire of vain and obtuse intellectuals. He associated with Eng-

land's most prominent writers, notably Pope, Congreve, and Gay. They were members of the Scriblerus Club, a literary fraternity formed in 1713 to satirize "all the false tastes in learning." His pamphlets and articles from this era reveal Swift's refinement of his most powerful literary weapon, the incongruities of satire.

In 1709 Swift, pledging allegiance to the Whigs, undertook a mission to England on behalf of the financially strapped Irish church. His plea for a remission of taxation placed him in the thick of controversy. In order to improve his chances of bringing support to those he wished to help, Swift changed loyalties, siding with the Tories and establishing his name as a keen and literate adversary.

Returning once more to Dublin in 1713, Swift served as dean of St. Patrick's, continuing his assault on English oppression. He returned to London in 1726 to publish *Gulliver's Travels* anonymously. Three years later, he wrote *A Modest Proposal*, for which he is acclaimed a master of irony.

The last years of Swift's life were filled with travail. Continually dependent upon patrons and ecclesiastical officials, he was never financially self-sufficient. He formed close attachments to two women, Esther Johnson and Esther Vanhomrigh, but declined to marry. His chief regret was that he never became a bishop. Partially paralyzed by a brain disorder and suffering from vertigo and deafness, he was declared insane in 1742 and died three years later.

Critics continue a longstanding debate about Jonathan Swift and his works. Some label him an outsider and a crusty, uncompromising misanthrope; others, aware of his dedication to the church, applaud his crusade for the betterment of humankind. Whatever his importance to history, he was a master craftsman of irony and satire. In a frequently quoted letter to Alexander Pope, Swift said: "When you think of the world give it one more lash at my request . . . I hate and detest that animal called man; although I heartily love John, Thomas, etc."

THINKING ABOUT THE SELECTION

Interpreting

1. Why does Swift stress facts and details to support his outrageous proposal?
2. How does Swift make subtle stabs at the American and English nations?
3. Why is the speaker so careful to point out that he himself anticipates no profit from the system of selling infants for food?
4. Swift uses the word *modest* to describe his proposal. (a) On what level is it anything but modest? (b) On what level is it actually quite modest indeed?

Applying

5. Suggest other ways in which an overpopulated country can deal with poverty. Cite examples from Third World countries to substantiate your answer.

ANALYZING LITERATURE

Understanding Satire

Satire is a blend of humor and wit that seeks to improve weaknesses in human character and behavior by holding them up to ridicule and sarcasm. The contemporary humorist Jules Feiffer called it "creating a logical argument that, followed to its end, is absurd." As a means of expressing a writer's outrage and dismay, satire surprises readers by producing laughter.

1. What improvement might Swift expect in the absentee landlords in England?
2. How does "A Modest Proposal" remind landlords of their humanitarian responsibilities?
3. Many reader's have problems with satire. Even in our own time, readers have condemned Swift's essay because they have taken it at face value. Why do you think it is so difficult to read satire?

THINKING AND WRITING

Composing Satire

Consider some issue involving human suffering in today's world, such as homeless people, political refugees, crime, or terrorism. As Swift did, propose an outlandish solution to the problem. Before you start writing, list facts and details that support your solution. From your notes compose the first draft of your proposal while concealing your opinions with an air of composed detachment and objectivity. Read your satire aloud to a partner and ask for suggestions on how you can sharpen your attack. Rewrite to refine your satiric technique. Then proofread your satire and prepare a final draft.

COMMENTARY

The literature of Swift's era was rife with satire and accompanying irony. The forerunners of modern magazines, the *Tatler* and the *Spectator*, were rich in wit and humor based on political and social situations of the times. But Swift carried his use of irony beyond the level of tweaking the public's chin. For Swift, the poignant situation that reduced whole families to begging and crime for daily subsistence was adequate reason for a sustained work of biting satire. To emphasize the difference between the surface meaning and the underlying reality, Swift resorts to heavy irony, a device that implies the seriousness of a situation while recognizing only the mask that covers it. For example, the speaker suggests that his proposal is modest, while in truth, it is an abominable suggestion that infants would serve as a crop to be raised and marketed. Cloaked in an emotionless detachment, the satirist pretends to remain above the incongruity, carrying his discourse to great lengths and maintaining his calm throughout. It is this feigned objectivity that so stirs the reader, who perceives Swift's real intentions.

Most critics emphasize the voice of the proposer while explaining how "A Modest Proposal" should be understood. David Nokes, author of a study on Swift, makes the following claim.

"The Proposer is a complex character. Swift does not make him completely obtuse to the hideous implications of what he suggests. There is a nervous cough in his voice . . . which entreats us into a conspiracy of silence. It is a mealy-mouthed nervousness that wishes to be absolved from any unmentioned or unmentionable offensiveness in what is promised. We sense a guilty conscience in his institutional declarations of humanity"

JOHN MILTON

1608–1674

A deliberate, serious, upright man, John Milton lived a life filled with turmoil. His personal life leaves little doubt that brilliance and steadfastness did not assure him lasting happiness. He married for the first of three times in 1642 and separated a short time later. After three years he was reunited with his first wife, who died while their daughters were still young. He suffered the deaths of his beloved second wife as well as an infant daughter in 1658. His own health was poor at this time. He maintained a chilly distance from his three remaining daughters and was regarded by many as difficult and cantankerous. On the other hand, Milton cultivated a host of friends and loved music all his life, generously garnishing his writing with melodic touches in both rhythm and sound. For over three hundred years, biographers have attempted to piece together these conflicting views of so complex a personality, leaving him as great an enigma today as he was to his associates.

Milton studied and taught at Cambridge and in 1632 withdrew for six years to his father's country estate to prepare himself for a challenge that was to remain unclear to him for years. Realizing that his knowledge of language and literature far surpassed the ordinary, Milton honed his talents by giving himself worthy literary assignments. After he had developed his writing skills, he felt equal to the task he chose as the center of his career—writing an English epic.

Because Milton sided with the Puritans in their political battle against the Royalists and their established church, he threw himself into bitter controversies concerning free speech, church reform, divorce, and the divine right of kings. Two of his lesser works, "Areopagitica" and "On the Tenure of Kings and Magistrates," demonstrate his ability to adapt his style from lyrical and epic poetry to logic and argumentation. During this intense period of public dissension, Milton underwent the most trying of his private sufferings, while going slowly blind.

Undeterred from his objective, Milton set out in 1658 to select a subject for his great national epic. Rejecting King Arthur as a possible focus for a work intended to appeal to a nation, he chose a more universal theme and wrote about the fall of Adam in the Garden of Eden. Working through a tedious process of dictation followed by painstaking revision, Milton refined the memorable lines of his greatest work, *Paradise Lost,* elevating his status among readers of English and assuring himself lasting influence and importance. His choices of subject matter for later major works proved as noble as the first, particularly the second epic poem, *Paradise Regained*, and *Samson Agonistes*, a classical tragedy about a ruined Biblical giant.

John Milton was a literary genius, a man of deep religious and ethical conviction, and a shaper of public opinion. The turmoil of his life, so inextricably bound up with one of England's revolutionary eras, led to his being branded a traitor to the throne. Yet Milton maintained his composure and championed his beliefs in difficult times, a testimony to his strength of character.

GUIDE FOR INTERPRETING

Commentary

from Paradise Lost

Anastrophe. One of the most challenging and sometimes puzzling aspects of Milton's majestic, sonorous lines is his frequent use of **anastrophe,** the inversion or rearrangement of normal sentence elements. For example, the line "Thus the orb he roamed . . ." (lines 35–36) makes clearer English sense as "Thus he roamed the orb . . ." By moving the direct object from before the subject to its usual position after the verb, the statement rings truer to the ear and is easier to comprehend.

Other examples are not so casually reworded. Not only is the poet's vocabulary elevated and his imagery difficult, but the placement of subject, verb, and complements frequently confuses the reader, who is more accustomed to standard arrangement of grammatical structure in literary works. For instance,

> Him fast sleeping soon he found
> In labyrinth of many a round self-rolled,
> His head in the midst, well stored with subtle wiles . . .
> (lines 52–54)

A simplified wording requires a few changes, as in "He soon found him fast asleep self-rolled in a labyrinth of many a round, his head in the midst, fully stocked with subtle wiles."

The purpose of anastrophe is more than mere literary whim or casual variation. A skilled poet utilizes every nuance of rhythm, alliteration, and word music to suggest meaningful and innovative connections between words. For example,

> Indeed? Hath God then said that of the fruit
> Of all these garden trees ye shall not eat . . . ?
> (lines 277–278)

In this example Milton deliberately separates subject and verb ("ye shall not eat") from the completer of the thought ("of the fruit"). His purpose is clear—he saves the verb to the end of the line for rhetorical emphasis. In this way, Milton makes the commission of the crime more significant than the forbidden food itself.

Writing

One of the most famous lines in English poetry comes from *Paradise Lost.* Satan tells his angels that it is "better to reign in Hell than serve in Heaven." Freewrite, exploring the emotions that would lead someone to make such a statement.

Literary Focus Ask students to write five sentences in the usual subject-verb-object order. Then, have students rework the sentences to achieve anastrophe. Discuss how anastrophe can be used to achieve emphasis, variation, and logic in writing.

ESL Teaching Strategy ESL students may have difficulty with the inverted sentences. Periodically have ESL students identify the subjects and verbs of Milton's sentences.

Teaching Tenth-Grade Students Memorizing verse often reveals meanings of words, connections between lines, and images in the poem that might otherwise go unnoticed. Ask tenth-grade students to memorize any twenty-five lines of *Paradise Lost.* Once they have memorized, ask them what associations they made as they memorized, and what stands out about the lines they learned.

Writing/Prior Knowledge Before students begin to write, discuss figures from television shows, films, or novels who have fallen prey to various temptations. Guide students to explore how these fictitious stories are similar to and different from the real-life experiences they are going to write about.

Vocabulary

Preteach the following vocabulary words:

arbiter (är´ bət ər) *n.*: One who judges or decides

cherubim (cher´ ə bim) *n.*: Heavenly angels

woodbine (wŏŏd´ bīn´) *n.*: Type of climbing vine

turret (tur´ it) *n.*: A protruding structure

fraudulent (frô´ jə lənt) *adj.*: False; deceitful

importune (im´ pôr tōōn´) *v.*: To urgently demand

credulous (krej´ ōō ləs) *adj.*: Easily convinced

elocution (el´ ə kyōō´ shən) *n.*: The art of speaking

engorged (en gôrjd´) *v.*: Ate greedily

Support Material

Teaching Portfolio
Teacher Backup, p. 973
Grammar in Action Worksheets, *Using Economy of Language,* p. 977; *Recognizing Purposes of Writing: Persuasive,* p. 979
Usage and Mechanics Worksheet, p. 981

Vocabulary Check, p. 982
Analyzing Literature Worksheet, *Understanding Anastrophe,* p. 983
Critical Thinking and Reading Worksheet, *Understanding Biblical Context,* p. 984
Selection Test, pp. 985–986

from Paradise Lost

John Milton

from Book IX

The epic opens just after Satan and several legions of angels, who joined him in a revolt against God, have been driven out of Heaven into Hell. There, Satan rallies his angels, comforting them with the possibility of regaining Heaven and commenting that it is "better to reign in Hell than serve in Heaven." Satan then journeys out of Hell and, after deceiving the archangel Uriel into providing him with directions, ventures onto earth. Climbing to the top of the Tree of Life, Satan looks down on Paradise, observing Adam and Eve in their bliss. After Uriel warns the archangel Gabriel that one of the banished angels may have invaded the earth, Satan is caught whispering in the ear of Eve, while she lies asleep in her bower. After he has been discovered, Satan flees from Paradise. Recognizing Adam and Eve's vulnerability, God sends the archangel Raphael to Paradise to tell Adam and Eve the story of Satan's fall from Heaven and to warn them of the danger that Satan presents. As the following excerpt opens, Satan is circling the earth, plotting re-entry into Paradise.

    The sun was sunk, and after him the star
Of Hesperus,[1] whose office is to bring
Twilight upon the Earth, short arbiter
'Twixt day and night, and now from end to end
5 Night's hemisphere had veiled the horizon round,
When Satan, who late fled before the threats
Of Gabriel out of Eden, now improved
In meditated fraud and malice, bent
On man's destruction, maugre what might hap
10 Of heavier on himself,[2] fearless returned.

---

1. Hesperus (hes′ pər əs): The evening star.
2. maugre . . . himself: Despite the threat of more severe punishments.

By night he fled, and at midnight returned
From compassing the Earth—cautious of day
Since Uriel, regent of the sun, descried
His entrance, and forewarned the cherubim
15 That kept their watch. Thence, full of anguish, driven,
The space of seven continued nights he rode
With darkness; thrice the equinoctial line[3]
He circled, four times crossed the car of Night
From pole to pole, traversing each colure;[4]
20 On the eighth returned, and on the coast averse
From entrance or cherubic watch by stealth
Found unsuspected way. There was a place
(Now not, though sin, not time, first wrought the change)
Where Tigris[5] at the foot of Paradise
25 Into a gulf shot under ground, till part
Rose up a fountain by the Tree of Life.
In with the river sunk and with it rose
Satan, involved in rising mist; then sought
Where to lie hid. Sea he had searched and land
30 From Eden over Pontus, and the pool
Maeotis, up beyond the river Ob;[6]
Downward as far antarctic; and, in length,
West from Orontes to the ocean barred
At Darien, thence to the land where flows

---

3. line: The equator.
4. He circled . . . each colure: The colures are the two imaginary circles of the celestial spheres that intersect at the poles. By continually circling the earth, Satan is able to keep himself hidden in darkness.
5. Tigris (tī′ gris): A river in the Middle East.
6. Pontus . . . Maeotis . . . Ob: Pontus is the Black Sea; the pool Maeotis refers to the swamps of the sea of Azov, the northern arm of the Black Sea; the Ob is a river in western Siberia.

Primary Source Note

Authors often keep "commonplace books" in which they jot down their ideas and record excerpts from their readings that might prove useful. A little more than one hundred years ago, Milton's commonplace book was found. The 250-page notebook contains entries in Latin and English arranged under headings such as liberty, games, war, moral evil, plagues, poetry, food, and highway robbery. Following are three sample entries translated into English from Latin by Glenn McCrea, from *The Works of John Milton* (vol. XVIII, Columbia Edition).

"A man's courage depends not upon his body but upon his reason, which is for a human being the strongest safeguard and defense. That is clear from the fact that a man by this single help of reason masters even the strongest animals and is able if he so desires to do them harm."

"Why does God permit evil? So that reason can support virtue. For virtue is attested by evil, is illuminated and trained. As Lactantius says: that Reason and Judgement may have a field in which they may exercise themselves by choosing the things that are good and shunning the things that are evil; although even these reasons are not satisfactory."

"Why good men who are otherwise outstanding present the ap-

35 Ganges and Indus.[7] Thus the orb he roamed
With narrow search, and with inspection deep
Considered every creature, which of all
Most opportune might serve his wiles, and found
The serpent subtlest beast of all the field.[8]
40 Him, after long debate, irresolute
Of thoughts revolved,[9] his final sentence chose
Fit vessel, fittest imp[10] of fraud, in whom
To enter, and his dark suggestions hide
From sharpest sight; for in the wily snake
45 Whatever sleights none would suspicious mark,
As from his wit and native subtlety
Proceeding, which, in other beasts observed,
Doubt[11] might beget of diabolic power
Active within beyond the sense of brute. . . .
50 Like a black mist low-creeping, he held on
His midnight search, where soonest he might find
The serpent. Him fast sleeping soon he found
In labyrinth of many a round self-rolled,
His head the midst, well stored with subtle wiles:
55 Not yet in horrid shade or dismal den,
Nor nocent[12] yet, but on the grassy herb,
Fearless, unfeared, he slept. In at his mouth
The devil entered, and his brutal sense,
In heart or head possessing, soon inspired
60 With act intelligential; but his sleep
Disturbed not, waiting close[13] th' approach of
     morn.
     Now whenas sacred light began to dawn
In Eden on the humid flowers, that breathed
Their morning incense, when all things that
     breathe
65 From th' Earth's great altar send up silent praise
To the Creator, and his nostrils fill
With grateful smell, forth came the human pair

And joined their vocal worship to the choir
Of creatures wanting voice; that done, partake
70 The season,[14] prime for sweetest scents and airs;
Then còmmune how that day they best may ply
Their growing work; for much their work outgrew
The hands' dispatch of two gardening so wide:
And Eve first to her husband thus began:
75   "Adam, well may we labor still[15] to dress
This garden, still to tend plant, herb, and flower,
Our pleasant task enjoined; but till more hands
Aid us, the work under our labor grows,
Luxurious by restraint: what we by day
80 Lop overgrown, or prune, or prop, or bind,
One night or two with wanton growth derides,
Tending to wild. Thou, therefore, now advise,
Or hear what to my mind first thoughts present.
Let us divide our labors; thou where choice
85 Leads thee, or where most needs, whether to wind
The woodbine round this arbor, or direct
The clasping ivy where to climb; while I
In yonder spring[16] of roses intermixed
With myrtle find what to redress till noon.
90 For while so near each other thus all day
Our task we choose, what wonder if so near
Looks intervene and smiles, or object new
Casual discourse draw on, which intermits
Our day's work, brought to little, though begun
95 Early, and th' hour of supper comes
     unearned!" . . .

*Adam expresses reservations about separating
from Eve because of the danger posed by Satan. However, after warning Eve that Satan may try to use
deception to lead her into disobeying God's will, he
agrees to let her part from him.*

Soft she withdrew, and like a wood nymph light,
Oread or dryad, or of Delia's train,[17]
Betook her to the groves, but Delia's self

---

7. West from Orontes . . . Ganges and Indus: Satan flew
west from the Orontes River in southwestern Asia, across the
Atlantic Ocean to the Isthmus of Panama (Darien), then across
the Pacific Ocean and southeastern Asia to India, the land of
the Ganges and Indus rivers.
8. serpent . . . field: Milton's description of the serpent
echoes the description in the Bible (Genesis 3:1).
9. irresolute . . . revolved: Unable to decide among his
revolving thoughts.
10. imp: Offshoot.
11. Doubt: Suspicion.
12. nocent: Harmful.
13. close: Secretly.

14. The season: The morning.
15. still: Continually.
16. spring: Growth.
17. Oread . . . dryad . . . Delia's train: In Greek and Roman
mythology, oread is a mountain nymph, and dryad is a wood
nymph. Delia is an alternative name for Diana (Roman
mythology) or Artemis (Greek mythology), the goddess of
hunting and the moon. Whenever Delia hunted she was
accompanied by a train of nymphs.

4 **Enrichment** To depict the universe, Milton used the old Ptolemaic cosmography, although he knew of Galileo's work. According to Ptolemy Earth was at the center of the universe, surrounded by ten transparent shells holding the moon, the planets, and the fixed stars. The firmament in which the fixed stars were embedded was considered the outer boundary of everything.

5 **Literary Focus** Have students identify the anastrophe in this line. Then have them discuss how it serves to shift the emphasis from Satan to his planned deeds.

6 **Discussion** Call students' attention to the words *altar* and *praise.* Have them consider what these words suggest about Earth before the Fall.

7 **Enrichment** According to some original outlines, now among the Milton manuscripts at Trinity College, Milton first planned to write a drama. He wanted to use large choruses to recite a great tale of biblical and medieval events. Since he saw the stage chiefly as a way to glorify God and explain his ways to humankind, he wanted the government to take over the theaters and upgrade them. Ask students whether they think *Paradise Lost* would have been more effective as a drama rather than an epic.

8 **Discussion** Discuss with students the implications of Eve's suggestion.

Master Teacher Note Have students reconstruct the conversation between Adam and Eve summarized here. You might want to have students write out formal dialogue, or present improvisations in small groups or as a class.

pearance in a striking degree of minds that are sluggish, small, and
at first glance seem to be worth nothing. Lactantius replied; that they
may have the means of exercising every day the greatest of the
virtues, namely, patience."

In gait surpassed and goddesslike deport,
100 Though not as she with bow and quiver armed,
But with such gardening tools as art yet rude,
Guiltless of fire had formed, or angels brought.
To Pales, or Pomona, thus adorned,
Likest she seemed, Pomona when she fled
105 Vertumnus, or to Ceres in her prime,
Yet virgin of Proserpina from Jove.[18]
Her long with ardent look his eye pursued
Delighted, but desiring more her stay.
Oft he to her his charge of quick return
110 Repeated; she to him as oft engaged
To be returned by noon amid the bower,
And all things in best order to invite
Noontide repast, or afternoon's repose.
O much deceived, much failing, hapless Eve,
115 Of thy presumed return! Event perverse!
Thou never from that hour in Paradise
Found'st either sweet repast, or sound repose;
Such ambush hid among sweet flowers and shades
Waited with hellish rancor imminent[19]
120 To intercept thy way, or send thee back
Despoiled of innocence, of faith, of bliss.
For now, and since first break of dawn, the fiend,
Mere serpent in appearance, forth was come,
And on his quest, where likeliest he might find
125 The only two of mankind, but in them
The whole included race, his purposed prey.
In bower and field he sought, where any tuft
Of grove or garden-plot more pleasant lay,
Their tendance[20] or plantation for delight;
130 By fountain or by shady rivulet
He sought them both, but wished his hap might find
   Eve separate; he wished, but not with hope
Of what so seldom chanced; when to his wish,
Beyond his hope, Eve separate he spies . . .

135 As when a ship by skillful steersman wrought
Nigh[21] river's mouth or foreland, where the wind
Veers oft, as oft so steers and shifts her sail:
So varied he, and of his tortuous train
Curled many a wanton[22] wreath in sight of Eve,
140 To lure her eye: she busied heard the sound
Of rustling leaves, but minded not, as used
To such disport before her through the field,
From every beast, more duteous at her call
Than at Circean call the herd disguised.[23]
145 He bolder now, uncalled before her stood:
But as in gaze admiring; oft he bowed
His turret crest, and sleek enameled neck,
Fawning, and licked the ground whereon she trod.
His gentle dumb expression turned at length
150 The eye of Eve to mark his play: he, glad
Of her attention gained, with serpent tongue
Organic, or impulse of vocal air,[24]
His fraudulent temptation thus began:
   "Wonder not, sovereign mistress, if perhaps
155 Thou canst, who art sole wonder; much less arm
Thy looks, the heaven of mildness, with disdain,
Displeased that I approach thee thus, and gaze
Insatiate, I thus single, nor have feared
Thy awful brow, more awful thus retired.
160 Fairest resemblance of thy Maker fair,
Thee all things living gaze on, all things thine
By gift, and thy celestial beauty adore
With ravishment beheld, there best beheld
Where universally admired: but here
165 In this enclosure wild, these beasts among,
Beholders rude and shallow to discern
Half what in thee is fair, one man except,
Who sees thee?[25] (and what is one?) who shouldst be seen
A goddess among gods, adored and served
170 By angels numberless, thy daily train."

---

18. Pales . . . Pomona . . . Vertumnus . . . Ceres . . . Proserpina . . . Jove: Pales is the Roman goddess of flocks; Pomona is the Roman goddess of fruits and fruit trees. Pomona married Vertumnus, the Roman god of the changing seasons, after he had pursued her for some time. Proserpina is the daughter of Ceres, the Roman goddess of agriculture, and Jove, or Jupiter, the ruler of the Roman gods. Like Eve, Pales, Pomona, and Ceres are patronesses of agriculture.
19. imminent: Threatening.
20. tendance: The object of their tending.

21. Nigh (nī) *adv.*: near.
22. wanton (wän´ t'n) *adj.*: Unrestrained.
23. Circean . . . disguised: In the *Odyssey* by the Greek poet Homer, Circe, an enchantress who turned men into swine, was attended by an obedient herd.
24. with serpent . . . vocal air: When he spoke, Satan either used the actual tongue of the serpent or he used his own powers to create sound waves in the air.
25. these beasts . . . sees thee: The beasts are unable to fully appreciate Eve's beauty; Adam is the only occupant of the Garden who can.

Commentary

Milton's description of the Garden of Eden integrates elements from the entire European tradition of gardens, paradise, and beautiful islands. Much of what he wrote would be familiar to the audience of his day, who knew the various conventions he adapted to suit his needs.

Originally the word *paradise* meant a "walled enclosure, garden, or pleasure park." Seventeenth-century European gardens might seem like a paradise to us today, for they were not the patches of lawn or clumps of scraggly tomatoes that comprise our "gardens." Rather, these gardens were private estates and parks, lushly planted in astonishing geometrical patterns. They were also stocked with wildlife for the enjoyment of their wealthy owners. Such lavish gardens were idealized settings for contemplation and learning.

In fashioning his view of paradise, Milton took some ideas from Sidney's description of the garden in "Arcadia" and others from the setting of Spencer's "Faerie Queene." The Garden he ultimately created for *Paradise Lost* thus has elements from many sources while being uniquely Miltonic.

The elevated, walled garden where Adam and Eve reside occupies the low level of a steep, rugged hill covered by wild shrubs and tangled bushes. Various kinds of trees are arranged in tiers like the seats of an auditorium.

SATAN IN HIS ORIGINAL GLORY
William Blake
The Tate Gallery, London

A hedge encloses the plateau at the garden's edge. The sides of the wooded hill are part of a symbolic head topped by the green band of the wall (a crown) and a circle of blooming fruit trees. The entire scene is illuminated by the glorious light of the sun. The image suggests the power of humanity as well as the beauty and security of paradise.

13 Discussion Discuss with students Eve's initial reaction to the serpent's ability to speak. Focus on how her amazement and uneasiness suggest that the serpent's unnatural ability cannot be for the good of humanity.

Master Teacher Note A great deal has been written about the actual and symbolic nature of the Tree of Knowledge. You might want to organize small groups of students to research some of this material and then share it with the class. Compare what their research discovers about the Tree to Milton's description of it.

14 Literary Focus Have students identify the anastrophe in this line. Then have them rewrite the line to eliminate the inversion. Discuss which version they prefer and why. Concentrate on how each version uses logic, emphasis, and variation. Have students justify their preference with specific reasons.

15 Discussion Ask students how the serpent explains his ability to speak. Then discuss what his explanation implies about the Tree of Knowledge and about Eve.

16 Reading Strategy Have students summarize these lines. Then discuss how the serpent's flattery here builds on his previous explanations. Ask students to predict what other arguments they think the serpent might present, based on what he has said thus far.

So glozed²⁶ the tempter, and his proem²⁷ tuned;
Into the heart of eve his words made way,
Though at the voice much marveling: at length,
Not unamazed, she thus in answer spake:
175 "What may this mean? Language of man pronounced
By tongue of brute, and human sense expressed?
The first at least of these I thought denied
To beasts, whom God on their creation-day
Created mute to all articulate sound;
180 The latter I demur,²⁸ for in their looks
Much reason, and in their actions oft appears.
Thee, serpent, subtlest beast of all the field
I knew, but not with human voice endued:²⁹
Redouble then this miracle, and say,
185 How cam'st thou speakable of mute,³⁰ and how
To me so friendly grown above the rest
Of brutal kind, that daily are in sight?
Say, for such wonder claims attention due."
　　To whom the guileful tempter thus replied:
190 "Empress of this fair world, resplendent Eve!
Easy to me it is to tell thee all
What thou command'st and right thou shouldst be obeyed:
I was at first as other beasts that graze
The trodden herb, of abject thoughts and low,
195 As was my food, nor aught but food discerned
Or sex, and apprehended nothing high:
Till on a day, roving the field, I chanced
A goodly tree far distant to behold
Loaden with fruit of fairest colors mixed,
200 Ruddy and gold; I nearer drew to gaze;
When from the boughs a savory odor blown,
Grateful to appetite, more pleased my sense
Than smell of sweetest fennel, or the teats
Of ewe or goat dropping with milk at even,
205 Unsucked of lamb or kid,³¹ that tend their play.
To satisfy the sharp desire I had

Of tasting those fair apples, I resolved
Not to defer: hunger and thirst at once,
Powerful persuaders, quickened at the scent
210 Of that alluring fruit, urged me so keen.
About the mossy trunk I wound me soon,
For, high from ground, the branches would require
Thy utmost reach, or Adam's: round the tree
All other beasts that saw, with like desire
215 Longing and envying stood, but could not reach.
Amid the tree now got, where plenty hung
Tempting so nigh, to pluck and eat my fill
I spared³² not; for such pleasure till that hour
At feed or fountain never had I found.
220 Sated at length, ere long I might perceive
Strange alteration in me, to degree
Of reason in my inward powers, and speech
Wanted not long, though to this shape retained.³³
Thenceforth to speculations high or deep
225 I turned my thoughts, and with capacious mind
Considered all things visible in Heaven,
Or Earth, or middle,³⁴ all things fair and good:
But all that fair and good in thy divine
Semblance, and in thy beauty's heavenly ray
230 United I beheld: no fair³⁵ to thine
Equivalent or second, which compelled
Me thus, though importune perhaps, to come
And gaze, and worship thee of right declared
Sovereign of creatures, universal dame."
235 　　So talked the spirited³⁶ sly snake: and Eve
Yet more amazed, unwary thus replied:
　　"Serpent, thy overpraising leaves in doubt
The virtue of that fruit, in thee first proved.
But say, where grows the tree, from hence how far?
240 For many are the trees of God that grow
In Paradise, and various, yet unknown
To us; in such abundance lies our choice,
As leaves a greater store of fruit untouched,
Still hanging incorruptible, till men

---

26. glozed: Flattered.
27. proem: Introduction.
28. demur: Am in doubt about.
29. endued: Endowed.
30. How . . . mute: How you acquired the ability to speak after being mute.
31. more pleased . . . lamb or kid: According to popular superstition, serpents sharpened their sight by rubbing their eyes with fennel, a plant of the parsley family, and they drank the milk of sheep and goats.

---

32. spared: Refrained.
33. I might . . . shape retained: Although he retained his exterior shape, his inward powers were altered, and he gained the ability to speak.
34. middle: The air.
35. fair: Beauty.
36. spirited: Possessed by a spirit.

Grammar in Action

Writers try to present their ideas in as concise a manner as possible. **Economical language** eliminates all words, phrases, and clauses that add nothing to the writing. This does not mean that sentences have to be short, but rather that every word must serve a specific purpose. By selecting the most economical language, writers can provide the concrete and specific details that make meaning clear. Economy of language is especially important in poetry. In *Paradise Lost*, for example, Milton often inverts sentence elements and eliminates unnecessary words for economy, as follows:

WORDY: So as she said this, her hand rashly moved in this evil hour / She reached forth to the fruit, she plucked some of it and then she ate some of it.

ECONOMICAL: So saying, her rash hand in evil hour / Forth reaching to the fruit, she plucked, she eat. (402–403)

Notice how in the second passage Milton has eliminated unnecessary words, words already understood, and wordy phrases. In other instances he uses the active over the passive voice and appositives to add detail and

245 Grow up to their provision, and more hands
Help to disburden Nature of her bearth."[37]
    To whom the wily adder,[38] blithe and glad:
"Empress, the way is ready, and not long,
Beyond a row of myrtles, on a flat,
250 Fast by a fountain, one small thicket past
Of blowing[39] myrrh and balm: if thou accept
My conduct, I can bring thee thither soon."
    "Lead then," said Eve. He leading swiftly rolled
In tangles, and made intricate seem straight,
255 To mischief swift. Hope elevates, and joy
Brightens his crest; as when a wandering fire
Compact of unctuous vapor,[40] which the night
Condenses, and the cold environs round,
Kindled through agitation to a flame
260 (Which oft, they say, some evil spirit attends),
Hovering and blazing with delusive light,
Misleads th' amazed night-wanderer from his way
To bogs and mires, and oft through pond or pool,
There swallowed up and lost, from succor far:
265 So glistered the dire snake, and into fraud
Led Eve our credulous mother, to the tree
Of prohibition,[41] root of all our woe:
Which when she saw, thus to her guide she spake:
    "Serpent, we might have spared our coming
      hither,
270 Fruitless to me, though fruit be here to excess,
The credit of whose virtue rest with thee;[42]
Wondrous indeed, if cause of such effects!
But of this tree we may not taste nor touch:
God so commanded, and left that command
275 Sole daughter of his voice;[43] the rest,[44] we live
Law to ourselves; our reason is our law."
    To whom the tempter guilefully replied:
"Indeed? Hath God then said that of the fruit
Of all these garden trees ye shall not eat,
Yet lords declared of all in earth or air?"

---

37. bearth: The word *bearth* is used to associate the bearing of fruit with giving birth.
38. adder (ad′ ər): Snake.
39. blowing: Blooming.
40. Compact . . . vapor: Composed of oily vapor.
41. tree of prohibition: Prohibited tree.
42. The credit . . . with thee: You must remain the only evidence of the fruit's power.
43. Sole daughter . . . voice: His only order.
44. the rest: In everything else.

280   To whom thus Eve, yet sinless: "Of the fruit
Of each tree in the garden we may eat,
But of the fruit of this fair tree amidst
The garden, God hath said, 'Ye shall not eat
285 Thereof, nor shall ye touch it, lest ye die.'"
    She scarce had said, though brief, when now
      more bold
The tempter, but with show of zeal and love
To man, and indignation at his wrong,
New part puts on, and as to passion moved,
290 Fluctuates disturbed, yet comely, and in act
Raised,[45] as of some great matter to begin.
As when of old some orator renowned
In Athens or free Rome, where eloquence
Flourished, since mute, to some great cause
    addressed,
295 Stood in himself collected, while each part,
Motion, each act, won audience ere the tongue,
Sometimes in height began, as no delay
Of preface brooking,[46] through his zeal of right.
So standing, moving, or to height upgrown
300 The tempter all impassioned thus began:
    "O sacred, wise, and wisdom-giving plant,
Mother of science![47] How I feel thy power
Within me clear, not only to discern
Things in their causes, but to trace the ways
305 Of highest agents, deemed however wise.
Queen of this universe! do not believe
Those rigid threats of death. Ye shall not die;
How should ye? by the fruit? it gives you life
To[48] knowledge; by the Threatener? look on me,
310 Me who have touched and tasted, yet both live,
And life more perfect have attained than Fate
Meant me, by venturing higher than my lot.
Shall that be shut to man, which to the beast
Is open? Or will God incense his ire
315 For such a petty trespass, and not praise
Rather your dauntless virtue, whom the pain
Of death denounced, whatever thing death be,
Deterred not from achieving what might lead
To happier life, knowledge of good and evil?

---

45. Raised: Poised.
46. in height . . . preface brooking: Skipping the preface, the orator begins with the middle of his speech.
47. science: Knowledge.
48. To: In addition to.

17 Discussion Have students discuss the significance of Eve's allowing the serpent to lead her to the Tree. Help students see that the serpent has already ensnared Eve by his eloquence.

18 Clarification People in Milton's day (and for centuries to come) feared the damp night air. Evil spirits eager to steal babies, suffocate sleepers, and spoil stores of food and drink were thought to roam on night winds. Only the reckless opened their windows at night or roamed after dark.

19 Reading Strategy Ask students to rephrase Eve's remarks in their own words. Make sure students understand that God forbade Adam and Eve only one thing: eating the fruit of the Tree. Discuss how God's actions suggest the importance of the command. You might also want to talk about how Eve's remarks underscore the severity of her later disobedience.

20 Discussion Ask students to consider the effect of this passage, coming as it does after Eve's explanation that they were not allowed to eat of the Tree. Guide students to see that the repetition reinforces the horror of the transgression.

21 Discussion Have students isolate each of the arguments Satan uses to tempt Eve. Ask them to explain why they think his arguments are successful.

Enrichment In Book IV Satan was able to face the truth about himself and to admit that he had done wrong. The arguments he presents here show that his commitment to evil has destroyed much of his original goodness and intelligence.

maintain economy.
    Student Activity 1. Find additional passages in the excerpt from *Paradise Lost* that employ economical language. Explain what stylistic devices Milton used to achieve economy of language.
    Student Activity 2. Write a brief summary of the entire excerpt. Without sacrificing detail, summarize what you have read as economically as possible.

PARADISE LOST: SATAN

Detail from the painting *Satan Watching the Endearments of Adam and Eve*
William Blake
Huntington Library, San Marino, California

320 Of good, how just![49] Of evil, if what is evil
Be real, why not known, since easier shunned?
God therefore cannot hurt ye, and be just;
Not just, not God: not feared then, nor obeyed:
Your fear itself of death removes the fear.[50]
325 Why then was this forbid? Why but to awe,
Why but to keep ye low and ignorant,
His worshipers? He knows that in the day
Ye eat thereof, your eyes that seem so clear,
Yet are but dim, shall perfectly be then
330 Opened and cleared, and ye shall be as gods,
Knowing both good and evil, as they know.
That ye should be as gods, since I as man,
Internal[51] man, is but proportion meet,
I, of brute, human; ye, of human, gods.
335 So ye shall die perhaps, by putting off
Human, to put on gods:[52] death to be wished,
Though threatened, which no worse than this can
bring.

And what are gods that man may not become
As they, participating[53] godlike food?
340 The gods are first, and that advantage use
On our belief, that all from them proceeds.
I question it; for this fair Earth I see,
Warmed by the sun, producing every kind,
Them nothing: if they all things,[54] who enclosed
345 Knowledge of good and evil in this tree,
That whoso eats thereof forthwith attains
Wisdom without their leave? And wherein lies
Th' offense, that man should thus attain to know?
What can your knowledge hurt him, or this tree
350 Impart against his will, if all be his?
Or is it envy, and can envy dwell
In heavenly breasts?[55] These, these, and many more
Causes import[56] your need of this fair fruit.
Goddess humane, reach then, and freely taste!"
355 He ended, and his words, replete with guile,
Into her heart too easy entrance won:
Fixed on the fruit she gazed, which to behold

---

49. Of good, how just!: How just to have knowledge of good!
50. the fear: Eve's fear of God.
51. Internal: Intellectual.
52. putting off . . . gods: Satan's words are a perversion of a passage from the Bible (Colossians 3:9–10).

---

53. participating: Sharing.
54. if they all things: If they produced all things.
55. Or is it . . . heavenly breasts: An allusion to the Roman poet Virgil's *Aeneid* (1.15).
56. import: Suggest.

Grammar in Action

Persuasion in writing attempts to move an audience to action or to adopt certain beliefs. As one of the major forms of discourse, persuasion is found in such fields as advertising and politics. There are three main ways readers can be persuaded: by an appeal to their reason, their emotions, and their ethics (standards of appropriate behavior). Sometimes the appeal to reason is called "argumentation" and the appeal to emotion and ethics "persuasion."

The serpent's speech to Eve is an example of persuasive writing, as it attempts to convince Eve to disobey God. Notice the different ways that the serpent attempts to persuade Eve in the following examples.

Might tempt alone, and in her ears the sound
Yet rung of his persuasive words, impregned[57]
With reason, to her seeming, and with truth;
Meanwhile the hour of noon drew on, and waked
An eager appetite, raised by the smell
So savory of that fruit, which with desire,
Inclinable now grown to touch or taste,
Solicited her longing eye; yet first
Pausing a while, thus to herself she mused:
  "Great are thy virtues, doubtless, best of fruits,
Though kept from man, and worthy to be
    admired,
Whose taste, too long forborne, at first essay
Gave elocution to the mute, and taught
The tongue not made for speech to speak thy
    praise:
Thy praise he also who forbids thy use
Conceals not from us, naming thee the Tree
Of Knowledge,[58] knowledge both of good and
    evil;
Forbids us then to taste; but his forbidding
Commends thee more, while it infers the good
By thee communicated, and our want:
For good unknown, sure is not had, or had
And yet unknown, is as not had at all.[59]
In plain[60] then, what forbids he but to know?
Forbids us good, forbids us to be wise!
Such prohibitions bind not. But if death
Bind us with after-bands, what profits then
Our inward freedom? In the day we eat
Of this fair fruit, our doom is, we shall die.
How dies the serpent? He hath eaten and lives,
And knows, and speaks, and reasons, and discerns,
Irrational till then. For us alone
Was death invented? Or to us denied
This intellectual food, for beasts reserved?
For beasts it seems: yet that one beast which first
Hath tasted, envies not, but brings with joy
The good befallen him, author unsuspect,[61]
Friendly to man, far from deceit or guile.

395 What fear I then, rather what know to fear
Under this ignorance of good and evil,
Of God or death, of law or penalty?[62]
Here grows the cure of all, this fruit divine,
Fair to the eye, inviting to the taste,
400 Of virtue[63] to make wise: what hinders then
To reach and feed at once both body and mind?"
  So saying, her rash hand in evil hour
Forth reaching to the fruit, she plucked, she eat.[64]
Earth felt the wound, and nature from her seat
405 Sighing through all her works gave signs of woe,
That all was lost. Back to the thicket slunk
The guilty serpent, and well might, for Eve,
Intent now wholly on her taste, naught else
Regarded; such delight till then, as seemed,
410 In fruit she never tasted, whether true
Or fancied so, through expectation high
Of knowledge; nor was godhead from her
    thought.[65]
Greedily she engorged without restraint,
And knew not eating death:[66] satiate at length,
415 And heightened as with wine, jocund and boon,[67]
Thus to herself she pleasingly began:
  "O sovereign, virtuous, precious of all trees
In Paradise! of operation blest
To sapience,[68] hitherto obscured, infamed,[69]
420 And thy fair fruit let hang, as to no end
Created; but henceforth my early care,
Not without song each morning, and due praise
Shall tend thee, and the fertile burden ease
Of thy full branches offered free to all;
425 Till dieted by thee I grow mature
In knowledge, as the gods who all things know;
Though others[70] envy what they cannot give;
For had the gift been theirs, it had not here

---

57. impregned: Impregnated.
58. Conceals . . . Knowledge: The name that God has given
the tree calls attention to the tree's magical powers.
59. For good . . . at all: An unknown good is like no good at
all.
60. In plain: In plain terms.
61. author unsuspect: An unquestionable authority.

62. rather what . . . or penalty: In her ignorance, Eve feels
uncertain about what she should fear.
63. virtue: Power.
64. eat: Ate.
65. godhead from her thought: Eve thought that she
would achieve godhead, or divinity, immediately.
66. knew not eating death: She did not know that she was
eating death.
67. jocund and boon: Joyous and free.
68. sapience: Wisdom.
69. infamed: Made infamous.
70. others: Other gods.

27

28

430

435

440

29

445

450

455

30

Main text (Paradise Lost)

Thus grown. Experience, next to thee I owe,
430 Best guide; not following thee I had remained
In ignorance; thou open'st Wisdom's way,
And giv'st access, though secret she retire.
And I perhaps am secret; Heaven is high,
High and remote to see from thence distinct
435 Each thing on Earth; and other care perhaps
may have diverted from continual watch
Our great Forbidder,[71] safe with all his spies
About him. But to Adam in what sort[72]
440 Shall I appear? Shall I to him make known
As yet my change, and give him to partake
Full happiness with me, or rather not,
But keep the odds[73] of knowledge in my power

Without co-partner? so to add what wants
In female sex, the more to draw his love,
445 And render me more equal, and perhaps,
A thing not undesirable, sometime
Superior: for, inferior, who is free?[74]
This may be well: but what if God have seen
And death ensue? Then I shall be no more,
450 And Adam, wedded to another Eve,
Shall live with her enjoying, I extinct;
A death to think. Confirmed then I resolve,
Adam shall share with me in bliss or woe:
So dear I love him, that with him all deaths
455 I could endure, without him live no life."[75]

---

71. Our great Forbidder: God. Eve's reference to God as a "great Forbidder" is indicative of Eve's corruption.
72. sort: Guise.
73. odds: Balance.

74. Superior: for . . . free: Eve's conception of freedom now echoes that of Satan.
75. without . . . life: Since Eve is now sentenced to death, there is no chance of her "living" without Adam.

Reader's Response *Have you ever wanted something, as Eve wanted the fruit, that you knew was probably harmful? How did you resist the temptation it represented? In what way does such experience strengthen people as they grow? Try to explain the value of that experience as best you can.*

Margin notes (left column)

27 Reading Strategy Have students closely analyze this scene to see what effect the Fall has on Eve. They should see that she eats to excess as never before. Ask students to isolate the words that suggest gluttony, the most immediate consequence. Have them predict how Eve might now act toward Adam.

28 Clarification Point out to students that Eve is now so confused that God becomes the "Great Forbidder" and the angels He has sent to protect her have become "His spies."

29 Discussion Ask students to analyze Eve's attitude toward Adam as revealed in these lines. Point out that she is now selfish and already tempted to deceive him.

30 Reading Strategy Have students speculate what Adam's reaction will be when Eve tells him of her deed. Have them cite the specific lines that support their predictions.

Cultural Note Milton had a strong influence on later poets. Wordsworth, for example, cherished Milton, and thought of himself as his poetic heir. In his poem "Prelude," for example, Wordsworth swears that he is following in Milton's footsteps, that like Milton he wants to create a great English epic. Wordsworth also wrote a sonnet that reveals the high esteem in which he held the great poet.

Cooperative Learning The rest of *Paradise Lost*, especially the conclusion, might intrigue students. Divide the class into small groups. Have each group select another book in the epic, read it, and share their findings with the rest of the class in the form of a brief oral report.

PRIMARY SOURCE

In explaining the delay and the inspiration of his epic, Milton said that it was a work "not to be obtained by the invocation of Dame Memory and her Siren daughters, but by devout prayer to that eternal spirit who can enrich with all utterance and knowledge, and sends out his seraphim, with the hallowed fire of his altar, to touch and purify the lips of whom he pleases."

Closure and Extension

ANSWERS TO THINKING ABOUT THE SELECTION

1. The tempter has been cut off from life, and once Adam and Eve have been tempted, they symbolically begin life.

2. Satan spies the serpent, "subtlest beast of all," asleep in a coil and climbs in the beast's mouth. Because of the serpent's subtlety, he will most likely be successful in tempting Eve.

3. Answers will vary. (a) Students might suggest that Adam is obedient and conservative, while Eve is curious and willing to explore where she has been forbidden. (b) Eve wants knowledge of good and evil; she sees that the serpent ate of the fruit and did not die; she thinks she should not fear what she does not know.

4. (a) At first Eve thinks she will be more attractive to Adam if she has the knowledge he lacks. (b) She cannot bear the thought of Adam wedded to someone else if Eve does in fact die for her transgression.

5. Answers will vary. (a) Satan might be considered heroic for leading Adam and Eve out of ignorance. (b) Humankind has the power to choose between good and evil, but to choose,

THINKING ABOUT THE SELECTION

Interpreting

1. Why is it significant that the tempter achieves entrance into Paradise through the Tree of Life?
2. Why does Satan choose the serpent as an appropriate vessel for himself?
3. (a) Compare and contrast Adam and Eve. (b) Why is the serpent able to convince Eve to eat the fruit?
4. (a) Why is Eve reluctant to share the fruit with Adam? (b) Explain her reasons for changing her mind?
5. (a) In what ways can Satan be described as heroic? (b) In what way do his actions lead to the eventual salvation of humankind?

Applying

6. Why are people easily seduced by evils, even when they know that the consequences may be severe? Apply your answer to common social tempters, such as alcohol, tobacco, or other such drugs.
7. The American humorist Josh Billings once called Satan "the father of lies." Billings then added, "but he neglected to patent the idea, and the business now suffers from competition." (a) First show how Satan proves to be "the father of lies" in this excerpt from *Paradise Lost*. (b) Then explain the second part of Billings's statement and show how it applies to contemporary life.

ANALYZING LITERATURE

Understanding Anastrophe

By means of anastrophe, Milton reshapes the English sentence as he writes of serious matters. The realignment of subject/verb/complement slows the absorption of each line, causing the reader to pay more attention to words that fall in unusual positions, such as a direct object at the beginning of a sentence. Reread lines 429–455. Select three examples of anastrophe to restate in standard English. Make changes in the wording where necessary.

CRITICAL THINKING AND READING

Understanding Biblical Context

Employing his extensive knowledge of literature, Milton composed this segment of *Paradise Lost* from an extension of six Biblical verses found in Genesis 3:

1–6. Read this short segment (page 42) from the Bible and answer these questions concerning Milton's contribution to the original.
1. How does the poet make the serpent seem more alluring?
2. How does the conversation between Eve and the serpent demonstrate the tempter's persuasiveness?
3. Why does the poet conclude with Eve's misgivings about her future relationship with Adam?

UNDERSTANDING LANGUAGE

Meaning from Context

Often literature from an earlier period employs common words in unusual settings. When these words are surrounded by clues to their use, the reader can derive their meaning without resorting to footnotes or a dictionary. For example, in line two, *office* refers to the duty or task that Hesperus performs rather than the more common meaning of a room where business is conducted. Using context clues in the following phrases define each underlined word.
1. Soft as she withdrew (line 96)
2. Such gardening tools as art yet rude (line 101)
3. Of his tortuous train curled many a wanton wreath (line 139)
4. Above the rest of brutal kind (line 186)

THINKING AND WRITING

Collectively Describing Paradise

Join with a small group of students and create a single view of paradise. Work separately on lists of phrases that describe the perfect world in terms of atmosphere, activities, foods, and companions. Then come together for an in-depth discussion of varied opinions. Weed out ideas on which individuals cannot agree. Using your final list, draft a first version of the group's description of paradise. Exchange papers and make concrete suggestions to flesh out one another's picture. Return to your original work and incorporate the ideas your classmates have proposed. Strive for a polished description filled with imaginative detail. Let this finished product reflect the best of your thinking on the topic. Proofread for any errors before you complete it.

(continued from bottom of page)
could live no life without him."

ANSWERS TO CRITICAL THINKING AND READING

1. Milton makes the serpent seem more alluring by depicting him as an intelligent, knowledgeable, reasonable creature, confident in what he says to Eve.
2. He dispels all her doubts.
3. Her misgivings are what lead her to share the fruit with Adam.

ANSWERS TO UNDERSTANDING LANGUAGE

1. Gentle or gently
2. Sophisticated yet rough or crude
3. Trail he left behind
4. Animal

THINKING AND WRITING

Writing Across the Curriculum
Students taking art might want to illustrate the description of Paradise.

Challenge Ambitious students might want to explore the parallels between the story of the Fall in Genesis and *Paradise Lost*. Encourage students to find the allusions to Genesis in Book IX of *Paradise Lost*.

they must have knowledge and understanding of what they choose.
6. Answers will vary. Students may note that people are easily seduced by alcohol, tobacco, and other drugs because of their availability and because other people tempt or persuade them to indulge in the same way that Satan tempts Eve.
7. (a) Satan lies to Eve about having eaten the fruit himself, and he suggests

that once humans eat of the fruit they will be like the gods. (b) Students might suggest that contemporary politicians, television personalities such as TV evangelists, and highly visible businesspeople have been caught in scandalous lies having to do with stealing money, cheating on taxes, and abusing illegal substances.

ANSWERS TO ANALYZING LITERATURE

Answers will vary. Three possible examples are: (1) lines 435–437 "and Our Great Forbidder may have been diverted from continual watch by other care . . ." (2) lines 440–441 "Shall I make my change known to him . . . ." (3) lines 454–455 "I love him so dearly that I could endure all deaths with him but

GREAT WORK

TARTUFFE
by Molière

A Neoclassic Comedy

In Molière's neoclassic comedy *Tartuffe*, a religious fanatic, Orgon, gets duped by a religious hypocrite, Tartuffe. *Tartuffe* is a social comedy, a form that French playwrights of the seventeenth century used to analyze aspects of contemporary society. Molière is considered a master of French social comedy and is credited with establishing it as an enduring type of drama. He is most popular for his comic, critical insight into character types like the hypocrite, the misanthrope, quack doctors, and hypochondriacs.

Poking Fun at the Bourgeoisie

Under King Louis XIV, who reigned from 1643 to 1715, there were basically three classes in France: the aristocracy, the peasantry, and the bourgeoisie, the affluent middle class. Orgon and his family are members of the bourgeoisie, as was Molière, who liked to poke fun at the middle class for its pretensions and affectations. Through his satirical portrayal of Orgon and his family, Molière exposes the absurdities of the bourgeoisie.

As the play opens, Orgon's mother, Madame Pernelle, is condemning her son's family: his second wife Elmire; his daughter Mariane and her maid Dorine; Cleante, Orgon's brother-in-law; and Damis, Orgon's son. Madame Pernelle is an overbearing, egotistical, opinionated woman who finds her son's house appalling and its inhabitants indecent and immoral. Ironically, the only person held high in her esteem is the hypocrite Tartuffe, who poses as a pious, virtuous man, but who is actually the embodiment of everything Madame Pernelle finds abhorrent. Tartuffe has tricked Orgon into thinking that he is a truly devout man who lives in poverty because of his generosity to the poor. He appears to shun earthly pleasures and material objects in favor of spiritual pursuits. Out of pity and admiration, Orgon takes him in as a guest because, in Orgon's words,

> His is a pure and saintly indigence
> Which far transcends all worldly pride and pelf.
> He lost his fortune, as he says himself,
> Because he cared for Heaven alone, and so
> Was careless of his interests here below.
> I mean to get him out of his present straits
> And help him to recover his estates—
> Which, in his part of the world, have no small fame.
> Poor though he is, he's a gentleman just the same.

Orgon's delusion about Tartuffe steadily worsens throughout the play and ultimately jeopardizes Orgon's family's security.

Rhymed Couplets

Tartuffe consists mainly of one rhymed couplet after another, from the first act to the last. Because dialogue comprised of couplets is hard to take seriously, the rhymed couplets in Tartuffe reinforce the absurdities Molière wants to expose. In the following lines from Act I, for example, Molière shows the audience how Madame Pernelle is alone in her reverence for Tartuffe; all the other characters, with the exception of Orgon, see through his pretense.

DORINE. Surely it is a shame and a disgrace
To see this man usurp the master's place—
to see this beggar who, when first he came,
Had not a shoe or shoestring to his name
So far forget himself that he behaves
As if the house were his, and we his slaves.

MADAME PERNELLE. Well, mark my words,
   your souls would fare far better
If you obeyed his precepts to the letter.

DORINE. You see him as a saint. I'm far less
   awed;
In fact, I see right through him. He's a
   fraud.

MADAME PERNELLE. Nonsense!

DORINE. His man Laurent's the same, or worse;
I'd not trust either with a penny purse.

MADAME PERNELLE. I can't say what his
   servant's morals may be;
His own great goodness I can guarantee.
You all regard him with distaste and fear
Because he tells you what you're loath to
   hear,
Condemns your sins, points out your
   moral flaws,

And humbly strives to further Heaven's
   cause.

Madame Pernelle's absurd criticism of the other characters makes the audience doubt her credibility and question whether Tartuffe is really deserving of such lavish praise. According to her, her grandson is a fool, her granddaughter is secretive, her daughter-in-law dresses too elaborately, Dorine is impudent, and Cleante's worldly counsel is sinful. In contrast to Madame Pernelle, the people she admonishes seem normal, rational people. Their logical evaluation of Tartuffe provides the audience with insight into his true character.

Reason and Common Sense

Molière wrote in an age that relied on Christian principles, common sense, and rational behavior. Even in religious matters, people were expected to

Clarification *Tartuffe* is often subtitled "The Impostor" or "The Hypocrite" in various productions of the play. Tartuffe can assume any pose and become master of it. While he convinces Orgon and Madame Pernelle that he is a pious, humble man, the reader and the audience see his hypocrisy almost immediately. Tartuffe's talent lies in his ability to recognize and exploit the weaknesses in his victims.

Reading Strategy As students read either *Tartuffe* in its entirety or the excerpts featured here, have them look for Tartuffe's main weakness. What causes his downfall? Students should notice that Tartuffe's lust for Elmire exposes him for the hypocrite he is.

Enrichment Neoclassic comedy emphasizes rational behavior. In *Candide*, Voltaire ridicules the irrational acceptance of a popular philosophy. Earlier in England Jonathan Swift was similarly concerned with rational behavior. Many of Molière's characters, even when their behavior is absurd, maintain that they are acting on the most rational motives. Molière depicts these characters as exasperated with the social majority for not behaving as rationally as they themselves do.

behave rationally, not with the affected zeal and piety that Tartuffe practices. Faith was to be sincere, not showy or vain. *Tartuffe* is an example of how in neoclassic plays, drama mirrored reality. Playwrights demonstrated the morality of a rational universe. Molière uses Cleante and Dorine to articulate the rational principles of the play. Throughout the play, Cleante exclaims that Orgon has lost his common sense, and Dorine is never shy with her witty, sensible opinions. Cleante's speeches to Orgon at the end of Act I are especially insightful.

> CLEANTE. . . . There's a vast difference, so it
> seems to me,
> Between true piety and hypocrisy:
> How do you fail to see it, may I ask?
> Is not a face quite different from a mask?
> Cannot sincerity and cunning art,
> Reality and semblance, be told apart?
> Are scarecrows just like men, and do you
> hold
> That a false coin is just as good as gold?
> Ah, Brother, man's a strangely fashioned creature
> Who seldom is content to follow Nature,
> But recklessly pursues his inclination
> Beyond the narrow bounds of moderation,
> And often, by transgressing Reason's laws,
> Perverts a lofty aim or a noble cause . . .

Unfortunately Orgon is not convinced. In Act II he takes steps to make Tartuffe his son-in-law, much to his daughter Mariane's horror.

At the time, paternal authority was held in the highest respect. Orgon feels justified, therefore, as he tyrannically orders Mariane to marry Tartuffe, whom she despises; she wants to marry a man named Valere. But the more loudly she objects, the more insistent Orgon is about her marriage to Tartuffe. Fortunately for Mariane, Dorine helps her stall the wedding. Yet the character most influential in preventing the dreaded marriage is Tartuffe himself as he makes a pass at his gracious host's wife in Act III.

Elmire agrees not to tell Orgon about Tartuffe's advances provided he help persuade Orgon to allow Mariane to marry Valere. However, Elmire's stepson Damis, who overheard Tartuffe confess his secret passion for Elmire, is not as forgiving. Damis exposes Tartuffe, telling Orgon how Tartuffe disgracefully proposed to Elmire. In turn, Tartuffe confesses, hypocritically calling himself the most sinful, worthless man in the world. Instead of being furious with Tartuffe, Orgon becomes enraged with Damis and disinherits him, making Tartuffe his sole heir. To Orgon, Tartuffe is worth more than his wife, children, and the rest of the family. Orgon gives him deed and title to everything he owns.

Moderation and Extremes

Molière exposes the absurdities of extremist behavior. Orgon's rash, impulsive behavior in his obsession with Tartuffe, Tartuffe's pretense of being the most sinful person on earth, Mariane's subservience to her father's wish that she marry

Tartuffe, and Damis's violent reaction to Tartuffe all illustrate the danger of extremist behavior. In contrast, Cleante urges the characters to exercise moderation. Specifically, he reprimands Orgon for his extravagant reaction once Orgon accepts that Tartuffe is a hypocrite. Elmire tricks Tartuffe into admitting his desire for her while Orgon is hiding under the table, listening. Convinced that the "pious Tartuffe" is indeed a fraud, Orgon orders him out of his house, only to be reminded that Tartuffe is now the master of the house and that if anyone is to get out, it is Orgon. Orgon swears to hate and persecute all pious men, when Cleante reminds him of the trouble such an extremist attitude has caused him in the past.

Ah, there you go—extravagant as ever!
Why can you not be rational? You never
Manage to take the middle course, it seems,
But jump, instead, between absurd
    extremes.
You've recognized your recent grave
    mistake
In falling victim to a pious fake;
Now, to correct that error, must you
    embrace
An even greater error in its place,
And judge our worthy neighbors as a whole
By what you've learned of one corrupted
    soul?
Come, just because one rascal made you
    swallow
A show of zeal which turned out to be

              hollow,
        Shall you
            conclude that all
        men are deceivers,
And that, today, there are no true believers?
Let atheists make that foolish inference;
Learn to distinguish virtue from pretense,
Be cautious in bestowing admiration,
And cultivate a sober moderation.
Don't humor fraud, but also don't asperse
True piety; the latter fault is worse,
And it is best to err, if err one must,
As you have done, upon the side of trust.

The play doesn't end here. But what do you think happens? Will Orgon be forced to leave his home now that he has signed the deed over to Tartuffe? Should he? Form groups with your classmates and predict the outcome of the play. Based on what you know about the characters and Molière's motivations as a neoclassic dramatist, decide on an appropriate ending for the play. Then read the play to learn Tartuffe's fate.

LITHOGRAPH OF MOLIÈRE IN ECOLE DES FEMMES
François Delpech
Musée de l'Arsenal, Paris

Enrichment In neoclassic comedy, the audience views a series of scenes in which the absurd actions of the main character deviate from socially acceptable behavior. These situations continue until the audience can judge both the character and society. When the characters have been fully exposed, the play should end, and the audience should be able to evaluate their absurdities. Some critics argue that *Tartuffe* could have been ended sufficiently after the fourth act. However, Molière continues the play for another act. According to some critics, Act V of *Tartuffe* contributes nothing to the play and can be interpreted as an attempt to flatter the king. If students are reading *Tartuffe* in its entirety, ask them to consider whether they think Act V adds anything to the total view of the play.

BLAISE PASCAL

Focus

More About the Author After his wife's death in 1626, Pascal's father Etienne gave up his law practice to oversee his children's education. At mealtimes, for example, the family discussed such topics as how gunpowder works, the effects of lightning, and the refraction of light. Although a scholar and mathematician himself, Etienne allowed time for lighter pursuits, including theater and fairs. Etienne's efforts were successful: His daughter Jacqueline was a literary prodigy, while his son Blaise became a brilliant mathematician. In his twenties, for example, Blaise tested Galileo's theories, paving the way for the development of hydro-dynamics. He invented the syringe, the hydraulic press, and formulated "Pascal's law," the principle that fluid transmits pressure equally in all directions. His later studies laid the foundation for the fields of probability and calculus. Ask students to discuss how such a brilliant and rigorous scientific background might complement a writer's talents.

Critical Evaluation Like most great writers, Pascal has met with divided critical opinion. While none challenge his genius, not everyone agrees with his ideas. Cardinal Newman, for example, wrote that "the gifted Pascal, in the work on which his literary fame is mainly founded (*Pensées*), does not approve himself to a Catholic judgement." A recent critic, by contrast, hailed Pascal as "an original thinker in the strongest sense of the word." You might want to ask students what other writers they have read whose work has evoked such sharp difference of opinion.

1623–1662

Blaise Pascal (blǝz pȧs kȧl′), the French mathematician, physicist, and philosopher, was born in Clermont-Ferrand and acclaimed in adolescence as a mathematical prodigy. In 1631 his family moved to Paris, and then to Rouen in 1639. From childhood, Pascal's poor health led him to cultivate in relative solitude a brilliant scientific career. He manifested his mathematical genius at the age of twelve by independently rediscovering Euclid's first thirty-two propositions of geometry. At sixteen, he was already admired for his various mathematical treatises by the greatest mathematicians of the day.

In two years' time, Pascal engineered the world's first calculator, called *la machine arithmétique.* He went on to apply new scientific research methods to studies of the cycloid, air pressure, the vacuum, and the mechanical theory of the natural world. He was one of the first to systematize the science of probability.

In January 1646 Pascal was introduced to a new Christian sect known as *Jansenism.* Jansenism held that holiness is humanity's real goal, but few are chosen to receive God's grace and ultimate salvation.

November 23, 1654, marks a real "conversion" for Pascal, for he claims to have been visited that night by Jesus Christ in a mystical experience, an event he recorded in his *Memorial.* In that same year, his niece was miraculously cured of a fistula shortly after the nuns of the famous Port-Royal convent applied a relic of the Holy Thorn to her wound. These events sealed his religious fervor as well as his increasingly humble attitude toward science.

With even greater enthusiasm he sought a harmony between mathematical certainty and moral truths. When the Catholic Church officially condemned several of the Jansenists' propositions in 1656, Pascal feverishly defended the "heretical" beliefs in a satirical work, *Letters from the Provinces.* In 1657 he began writing what are known as the *Pensées.* In them he hoped to integrate scientific progress with the notion of humankind's fallen state. He also hoped to reconcile his individual conscience with the Church he loved so much.

Although suffering from poor health, Pascal worked steadily until the end of his short life. In 1662, the year of his death, he even oversaw the opening of a carriage transport line.

In recognition of his achievements, the modern computer language Pascal is named after him. Many later philosophers have acknowledged their intellectual debts to him and he continues to be recognized widely as an important physicist and mathematician. Few of his widely quoted sayings are cited more frequently than the one which claims that "things are always at their best in their beginning."

Objectives

Thematic

To understand how thought elevates human beings

Skills

1 To understand paradox

2 To infer tone
3 To stage a debate
4 To write an argument

GUIDE FOR INTERPRETING

from Thoughts

Commentary

Philosophical Writing and Paradox. In Blaise Pascal's philosophical writings, he distinguishes between two kinds of knowledge. The first is derived from the sciences of authority, such as theology. It is there that truth is revealed to readers in sacred writings. The second, called the sciences of reason, requires the active exercise of a person's thought and experience to provide truths of a different order. In an effort to make religious and scientific truths compatible, Pascal planned to write an *Apology of Christianity*. The book was intended to prove to people of all religions that it is only through Jesus Christ and the Christian religion that individuals can truly be saved.

Pascal made a preliminary outline for his *Apology*, but he died before he was able to complete the text. Most of the *Pensées*, or *thoughts*, from which "Man and the Universe" is taken, are really only Pascal's notes for the *Apology*. Some he re-wrote many times; others are only sentence fragments jotted down hastily on scraps of paper. Some of these "thoughts" illustrate Pascal's rigorous, logical mind, for they draw on mathematical and scientific vocabulary and methods of argumentation. In fact, many resemble the structure of a geometric proof. Other "thoughts" are examples of his more poetic side and even appear in the manuscript in "stanzas" as poetry.

The *Pensées* are an important example of philosophic writing. Philosophic texts are meant to persuade the reader of the rightness of the author's position. To be successful, the author must make the arguments clear and the rhetoric interesting. In other words, a didactic text—one that teaches—must appeal not only to our reason, but also to our hearts and our sense of aesthetics. Pascal employs both scientific and literary means to argue his position.

Paradox is an idea or situation that appears to contradict itself but that is nevertheless true. In the *Pensées* two opposite but parallel movements lead to the text's central paradox. First, Pascal reduces the apparently infinitely great and large to its actual humbled position relative to the vastness of creation. Second, he changes perspective in order to view the same object as a world in itself relative to the number and complexity of its divisions. The infinitely small itself paradoxically encompasses an infinity of parts. Paradoxically, greatness is shown to be the illusion of relative perspective.

Writing

Imagine that you are on a space mission to explore the universe. On each planet you visit, you must catalogue every life form. How would you proceed? What tools would you need? What might you expect to find? How would you determine which life forms are intelligent? Freewrite, exploring your answers to these questions.

Literary Focus Remind students that paradox is a statement or situation that seems to contradict itself. Discuss with students how writers who deal with complex philosophical or religious ideas often use paradox to illustrate the complexity of their subjects. One such writer was the seventeenth-century Puritan John Donne. In one of his "Holy Sonnets," Donne appeals to God paradoxically to break his proud spirit so that he may achieve salvation: "That I may rise and stand, o'erthrow me." Discuss with students the paradox in this line and the usefulness of paradox in philosophical writing.

Writing/Prior Knowledge Pair up students in the class. Have them share their plans and ideas before they begin to chart or freewrite. Encourage them to exchange ideas about what they would look for and what equipment they would use.

ESL Teaching Strategy ESL students might struggle with Pascal's comparisons. Stress that Pascal compares "man" and the "Universe" in terms of their relationship to each other. Discuss the analogy of the size of a mite as compared to the size of the mite's body parts.

Teaching Tenth-Grade Students Ask tenth-grade students to discuss what is unique about human beings.

Vocabulary

Preteach the following vocabulary words:

imperceptible (im pər sep´ tə bəl) *adj.*: Not plain to the senses

prodigy (präd´ ə jē) *n.*: Wondrous thing

mite (mīt) *n.*: A tiny creature

globules (gläb´ yo͞olz) *n.*: Tiny drops of liquid

depository (dē päz´ ə tôr´ ē) *n.*: Storehouse

haughty (hôt´ ē) *adj.*: Conceited, arrogant

beatitude (bē at´ ə to͞od) *n.*: Perfect happiness

Support Material

Teaching Portfolio
Teacher Backup, p. 987
Usage and Mechanics Worksheet, p. 991
Vocabulary Check, p. 992
Analyzing Literature Worksheet, *Understanding Paradox*, p. 993
Critical Thinking and Reading Work-

sheet, *Inferring Tone*, p. 994
Selection Test, pp. 995–996

Man and the Universe

Blaise Pascal

translated by O. W. Wight

All this visible world is but an imperceptible point in the ample bosom of nature. No idea approaches it. In vain we extend our conceptions beyond imaginable spaces: we bring forth but atoms, in comparison with the reality of things. It is an infinite sphere, of which the center is everywhere, the circumference nowhere. In fine, it is the greatest discernible character of the omnipotence[1] of God that our imagination loses itself in this thought.

Let man, having returned to himself, consider what he is compared to what is; let him regard himself as a wanderer into this remote province of nature; and let him, from this narrow prison wherein he finds himself dwelling (I mean the universe), learn to estimate the earth, kingdoms, cities, and himself at a proper value.

What is man in the midst of the infinite? But to show him another prodigy equally astonishing, let him seek in what he knows things the most minute; let a mite exhibit to him in the exceeding smallness of its body parts incomparably smaller, limbs with joints, veins in these limbs, blood in these veins, humors[2] in this blood, globules in these humors, gases in these globules; let him, still dividing these last objects, exhaust his powers of conception, and let the ultimate object at which he can arrive now be the subject of our discourse;

he will think, perhaps, that this is the minutest atom of nature. I will show him therein a new abyss.[3] I will picture to him not only the visible universe, but the conceivable immensity of nature, in the compass of this abbreviation of an atom. Let him view therein an infinity of worlds, each of which has its firmament, its planets, its earth, in the same proportion as the visible world; and on this earth animals, and in fine mites, in which he will find again what the first have given; and still finding in the others the same things, without end, and without repose, let him lose himself in these wonders, as astonishing in their littleness as the others in their magnitude; for who will not marvel that our body, which just before was not perceptible in the universe, itself imperceptible in the bosom of the all, is now a colossus, a world, or rather an all, in comparison with the nothingness at which it is impossible to arrive?

For, in fine, what is man in the midst of nature? A nothing in comparison with the infinite, an all in comparison with nothingness: a mean between nothing and all. Infinitely far from comprehending the extremes, the end of things and their principle are for him inevitably concealed in an impenetrable secret; equally incapable of seeing the nothingness whence he is derived, and the infinity in which he is swallowed up.

What can he do, then, but perceive some appearance of the midst of things, in eternal de-

---

1. omnipotence (äm nip′ ə təns) *n*.: The state or quality of having unlimited power or authority.
2. humors (hyo͞o′ mərz) *n*.: Any of the four fluids formerly considered responsible for a person's health and disposition.

3. abyss (ə bis′) *n*.: A deep fissure in the earth; bottomless gulf.

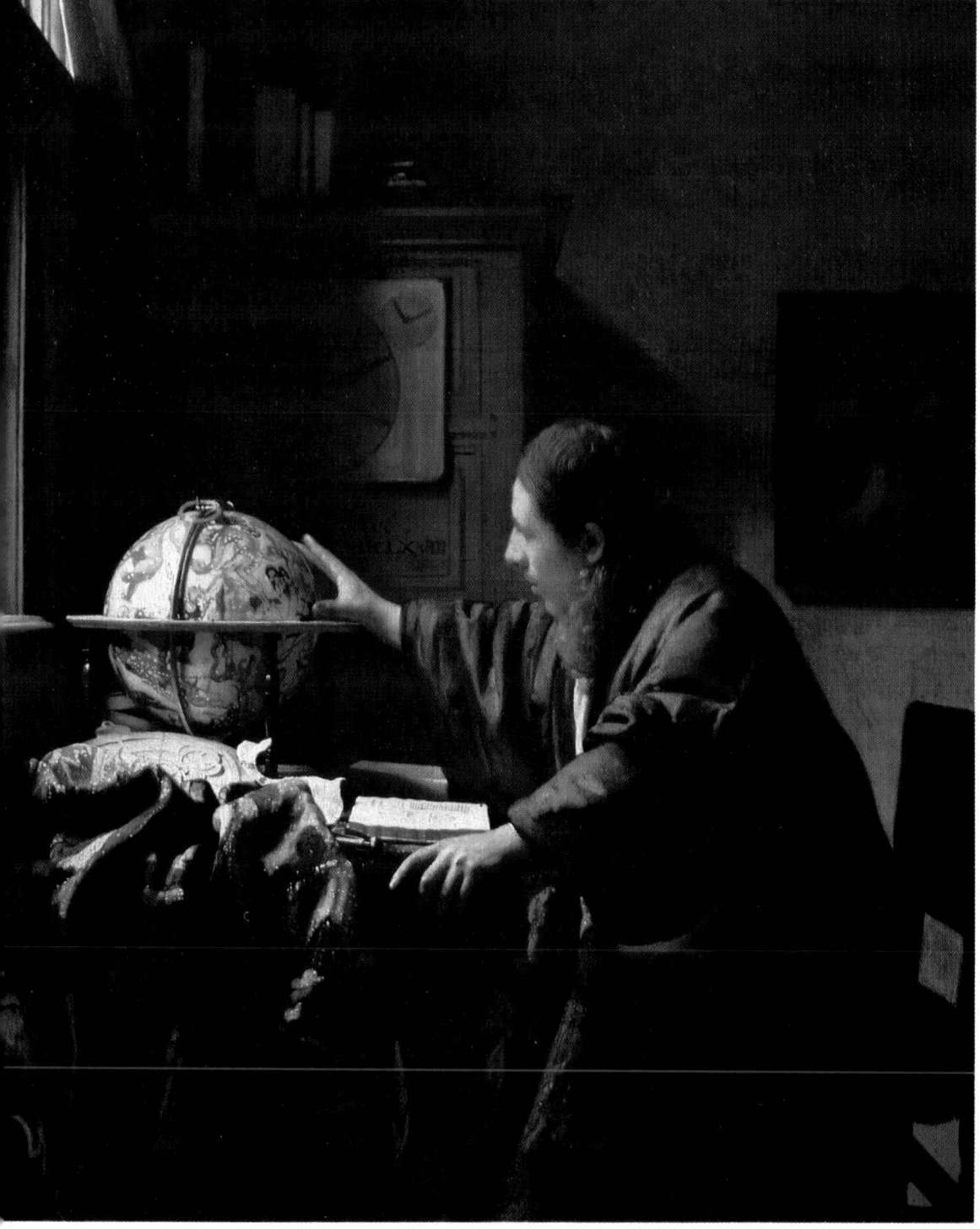

THE ASTRONOMER
Jan Vermeer

concentrate on the language of the piece rather than any overall structure, meaning, or form. As a result, these critics tend to value highly elements of complexity, such as irony and paradox.

New Criticism flourished in the 1940's and 1950's. Its main supporters were Cleanth Brooks, Robert Penn Warren, Allen Tate, R. P. Blackmur, John Crowe Ransom, and occasionally I. A. Richards. Although other critical theories have since taken center stage, the impact of the New Critics is still evident today. Cleanth Brooks, for example, gave the word *paradox* a place in critical terminology by maintaining that it is "the language appropriate and inevitable to poetry" in contrast to the nonparadoxical or explicit language of science. According to this definition, there is little place for paradox in nonpoetical works, such as novels, short stories, and essays. How, then, might we explain Pascal's extensive use of paradox in a philosophical work such as "Man and the Universe"?

Discuss with students the validity of Brooks's definition and the New Critics' approach to literature. Should we consider the author's biography when analyzing his or her work? Are writers' opinions important to an accurate analysis of their writing?

spair of knowing either their principle or their end? All things have sprung from nothingness, and are carried onward to the infinite. Who shall follow this astonishing procession of things? The Author of these wonders comprehends them; no other can . . .

Let us know then our range; we are something and not all. What we have of being deprives us of the knowledge of first principles, which spring from nothingness, and the little that we have of being conceals from us the view of the infinite.

Our intellect holds in the order of things intelligible the same rank as our body in the extent of nature.

Limited in every way, this state which holds the mean between two extremes is found in all our powers . . .

Such is our true state. This is what renders us incapable of certain knowledge and absolute ignorance. We drift on a vast midst always uncertain and floating, driven from one extreme toward the other. This is the state natural to us, and yet the most contrary to our inclination: we burn with desire to find a firm seat and an ultimate constant basis, in order to build upon it a tower that shall reach to the infinite; but our whole foundation cracks, and the earth opens to the abyss.

What a chimera,[4] then, is man! What a novelty, what a monster, what a chaos, what a subject of contradiction, what a prodigy! A judge of all things, feeble worm of the earth, <u>depository</u> of the truth, *cloaca*[5] of uncertainty and error, the glory and the shame of the universe!

---

4. **chimera** (ki mir′ ə) *n.*: A fabulous monster.
5. ***cloaca*** (klō ā′ kə) *n.*: Sewer.

Know then, <u>haughty</u> man, what a paradox[6] you are to yourself. Humble yourself, impotent reason; be silent, imbecile nature; learn that man infinitely surpasses man, and hear from your master your true condition, which you are ignorant of. Listen to God.

For, in fine, if man had never been corrupted, he would enjoy in his innocence both truth and happiness with assurance. And if man had never been anything more than a corrupted being, he would have no idea either of truth or of beatitude. But, unhappy as we are, and more than if there were no grandeur in our condition, we have an idea of happiness, and we cannot reach it; we feel an image of the truth, and possess but falsehood: incapable of absolute ignorance and of certain knowledge, so manifest is it that we have been in a degree of perfection from which we are unfortunately fallen!

Man is but a reed, the weakest in nature, but he is a thinking reed. It is not necessary that the entire universe arm itself to crush him. A breath of air, a drop of water, suffices to kill him. But were the universe to crush him, man would still be more noble than that which kills him, because he knows that he dies; and the universe knows nothing of the advantage it has over him.

Our whole dignity consists, then, in thought. Our elevation must be derived from this, not from space and duration, which we cannot fill. Let us endeavor, then, to think well: this is the principle of ethics.

---

6. **paradox** (par′ ə däks′) *n.*: A person, situation, or act that seems to have contradictory or inconsistent qualities.

Reader's Response *How would you answer the question raised by Pascal about the importance of human beings in the midst of the infinite? Do you believe he is right when he claims that "our whole dignity consists in thought"?*

Master Teacher Note Explain to students that Pascal often used probability in his writings about Christianity. He reasoned that the value of eternal happiness is infinite and that although the probability of gaining such happiness by religion may be small, it is infinitely greater than by any other course of human action.

4 **Critical Thinking and Reading** Ask students why the tone Pascal uses here and throughout is especially effective for his argument.

Enrichment Tell students that the Pascals encountered Jansenism firsthand in 1646 when Etienne's injured leg was treated by two Jansenists, amateur bonesetters practicing their art as part of their faith. During the three months they stayed with the Pascals, the entire family adopted the faith.

5 **Clarification** Make sure students understand that Pascal rejected proofs by reason alone: He insisted that humanity must begin with self-knowledge.

Cooperative Learning Students might be intrigued to explore how writers integrate other fields into their work. Have small groups of students examine other works in *World Masterpieces* for allusions to natural sciences, mathematics, or other related or unrelated fields of study. They might start with Goethe's *Faust* (page 863).

Primary Source Note

In a short work entitled "The Art of Persuasion," Pascal defined the excellence he sought throughout his life:

Excellence of whatever kind is not to be found in things that are extraordinary or peculiar. We raise ourselves to reach them and move away from them: more often we have to stoop down. The best books are those whose readers feel that they have been written about themselves. Nature, which alone is good, is completely familiar and commonplace. I am therefore in no doubt that these rules, being the true ones, should be simple, unsophisticated, natural, as they are . . . We must not allow our minds to be awkward: tense, clumsy manners fill it with a sort of foolish presumption by an elevation which is foreign to it and by a vain and ridiculous inflation instead of a solid and vigorous nourishment. And one of the main reasons that drive those who embark on this kind of knowledge from the true path they ought to follow is the idea we have that good things are out of reach by calling them great, lofty, elevated, sublime. That ruins everything. I should like to call them low, familiar, common; these names are more fitting; I hate those inflated words . . .

THINKING ABOUT THE SELECTION

Clarifying

1. In the beginning of this passage, how does Pascal describe the earth?
2. (a) What does Pascal think of people who believe they can know everything? (b)What does he ultimately conclude about our ability to acquire knowledge?

Interpreting

3. Pascal illustrates the relationship of human beings to the infinite in two ways; one comparison is concrete and visual, the other mathematical. (a) First identify these comparisons. (b) Then explain the meaning of each.
4. (a) What metaphor does Pascal use to describe the extent of Nature itself? (b) What does this metaphor suggest?
5. (a) What passages indicate Pascal's notion of a hierarchy or order of natural things? (b) Where do people fit in to that natural order?
6. (a) In this essay, what kind of certainty does the philosopher reach by the end of the argument? (b) Of what is the author sure?

Applying

7. (a) If you were Pascal writing this passage today, what would you choose to illustrate the infinitely small and the infinitely large? (b) How would you make your choice?

ANALYZING LITERATURE

Understanding Paradox

At the heart of this essay is a **paradox**—or seemingly contradictory truth. Like so many philosophers before him, Pascal searches to understand a human being's nature and place in the universe. Images of movement abound to create a paradoxical state of mind. People constantly aspire "upward"—as in their burning desire to build an ever-growing tower of certainty—only to find themselves ever spiraling "downward" when their reason fails and they fall into the abyss of uncertainty and despair. According to Pascal, only religion can supply comfort and security from vanity and ignorance.

1. Explain Pascal's statement, "Know then, haughty man, what a paradox you are to yourself."
2. What two seemingly contradictory things would happen if human beings had never been corrupted?

CRITICAL THINKING AND READING

Inferring Tone

Tone refers to an author's attitude toward the material being presented. In this essay Pascal plays the role of the confident master who will lead the reader on a journey toward religious knowledge.

1. (a) Describe Pascal's attitude when he writes, "What a paradox, then, is man! What a novelty, what a monster, what a chaos, what a subject of contradiction, what a prodigy!" (b) Which of these terms have negative or positive associations?
2. In his next to last paragraph, Pascal describes man in a paradoxical way by calling him a "thinking reed." How does this metaphor show a positive or negative attitude toward human nature?
3. Some critics accuse Pascal of seeing happiness as impossible—and thus of being pessimistic. (a) Do you think his view is pessimistic? (b) In what ways does he demonstrate this pessimism, and in what ways could he be optimistic?

SPEAKING AND LISTENING

Staging a Debate

Although science has benefited humankind, it has also left behind it a trail of destruction. Choose an advance of modern science: for example, medical technology that prolongs life, or nuclear power. Form two panels. Let one side debate how this breakthrough has aided human beings; the other how it has caused harm. Modeling your method of argumentation on that of Pascal, use as many stylistic devices as possible—for example, vocabulary drawn from mathematics and science, and concrete metaphors.

THINKING AND WRITING

Writing an Argument

Imagine once again that you are a space explorer, this time sent to a galaxy far from the Milky Way. There, on some other planet, you have succeeded in devising a means of communicating with its intelligent life form. Using Pascal's language, how would you describe human beings and their earthly society to the alien? Would you characterize people as purely rational, or are they also intuitive and imaginative? Devise an argument as Pascal might have to convince this other intelligence that your view of man is valid. When you revise, make sure your argument is sound. Proofread your paper and prepare a final draft.

(continued from bottom of page)

7. Answers will differ. Students might choose to compare their own bookshelves to huge university or public libraries, or the smallest plant to a vast jungle.

ANSWERS TO ANALYZING LITERATURE

1. Although humans' ability to reason gives them an advantage over the universe, they are still subordinate to God's infinite wisdom.
2. Pascal claims that human beings would enjoy truth and happiness in their innocence, but at the same time, they would have no idea of truth or of beatitude.

ANSWERS TO CRITICAL THINKING AND READING

1. (a) Pascal sees the human intellect as drifting in uncertainty in an attempt to find a firm seat in the universe, while the human condition is inferior to the supreme wisdom of God. (b) *Novelty* and *prodigy* have positive associations. *Monster, chaos,* and *contradiction* have negative associations.
2. Answers will differ. Students might suggest that although Pascal sees human beings as reeds, our ability to think gives us an advantage over the universe.
3. (a) Answers will differ. Students may argue that his view is not entirely pessimistic, that he considers people noble.(b) He demonstrates pessimism by placing human beings in uncertain, inferior positions, but he can be perceived as optimistic because he emphasizes people's ability to think and to think well.

ANSWERS TO THINKING AND WRITING

Writing Across the Curriculum Science teachers might provide students with specific scientific information that students can use in their papers.

Challenge Encourage students to research Pascal's scientific accomplishments further.

Closure and Extension

ANSWERS TO THINKING ABOUT THE SELECTION

1. He describes the earth as an infinite sphere.
2. (a) He considers them haughty. (b) It dignifies us.
3. (a) The concrete comparison likens human beings to small dungeons in the vast universe. The mathematical comparison calls the human being a middle point between all and nothing. (b) The concrete comparison illustrates the relative insignificance of human beings in the vast scope of the universe, while the mathematical comparison suggests humans' importance relative to nothingness.
4. (a) Pascal compares nature to an infinity of worlds. (b) Man is an atom in this infinity.
5. (a) Possible answers are the passages in which Pascal uses the analogy of the mite, the infinity of worlds, and the state of innocence and corruption. (b) People are reeds, but they are thinking reeds, which dignifies them.
6. (a) Pascal is certain of the limitations of human reason. (b) The principle of ethics is to think well.

JEAN DE LA FONTAINE

1621–1695

An early French example of the somewhat absentminded professor, Jean de La Fontaine (zhän də là fŏn ten′) delighted his seventeenth-century audience as well as later generations with an outpouring of short stories, poems, and fables. While learning to compose verses, La Fontaine dabbled with the possibilities of studying law, entering the priesthood, or following his father's profession of forest ranger before he settled on a literary career. An admirer and imitator of ancient poets and playwrights, he began publishing his own stories in his early thirties and continued to write for nearly forty years.

La Fontaine, like many creative people of the era, depended upon patrons for his room and board. He enjoyed the semi-permanent patronage of various hosts and hostesses, choosing to remain in the stimulating social, artistic surroundings of Paris rather than with his wife and son in his quiet hometown of Château Thierry. During his long residency in the French capital he met and befriended some of the greatest minds of the age, including Racine, Molière, and Boileau. Still, the poet failed to charm the single most influential personality in western Europe, Louis XIV, upon whose assent depended La Fontaine's election to the Royal Society, the inner circle to which French writers aspired.

La Fontaine's work relies heavily on adaptations of early authors and contains idiomatic statements of ethics and philosophy, often in the form of homilies or wise sayings. One of the major sources of his stories is the beast fables of Aesop, the semi-legendary sixth-century B.C.Greek slave and storyteller from the island of Samos. One of the best-loved works by both authors, "The Ant and the Grasshopper," is a moralistic, yet entertaining tale that contrasts the frolicsome grasshopper with the frugal, hard-working ant, who collects stores of food to carry him through the winter.

La Fontaine employs retellings of these succinct, homespun animal stories to depict human idiosyncrasies, such as cowardice, curiosity, greed, and laziness. By putting animals in the place of humans, La Fontaine creates droll restatements of themes that continue to capture the imagination of his readers. Stopping short of heavy-handed preaching, the stories contain common-sense reminders that delight as they instruct, in the characteristic style of a man whose own life was marred by frequent carelessness, improvidence, and lapses of memory.

So popular have his 238 fables become that French schoolchildren memorize them in their entirety and dramatize them as recital pieces. The French language is heavily salted with La Fontaine's witty aphorisms, such as "The sign brings customers," "A hungry stomach cannot hear," "On the wings of Time grief flies away," and "He knows the universe, and himself he does not know."

Focus

More About the Author Relatively little is known about Jean de La Fontaine: He left no memoirs and few letters. The few documents that do survive provide tantalizing hints about his life, however. From a marriage contract, we know that twenty-six year old Jean married fourteen-year old Marie Hericart on November 19, 1647. Their only child, Charles, was born in 1653. An agreement dated 1658 is especially intriguing. In it the couple agreed legally to divide their property, but whether this was done to relieve their financial difficulties or effect a marital separation cannot be determined. Although the couple lived together on-and-off for another fifteen years, the marriage did not endure, and they parted ways permanently in l671.

La Fontaine's exile to Limoges in 1663 is similarly shrouded in mystery. Whether voluntarily or by force, it appears that La Fontaine was sent away to prevent him from becoming embroiled in his patron's disgrace. In 1664 he applied for a license in Paris to publish a book, indicating that his exile was relatively brief.

As with many other great writers whose lives must be pieced together from scraps, La Fontaine's work stands on its own.

Pronunciation Note We have provided for students the French pronunciation for the name La Fontaine, where the last syllable is pronounced "ten." You may prefer to use the English pronunciation (la fon tān′).

Critical Evaluation David Lee Rubin has recently pointed out that "La Fontaine's work runs a grave risk of being taken for granted, underread, misread and finally misjudged" because many of his readers imagine his work is aimed primarily at children. If students have already studied American literature, you might ask them how this description fits Twain's *Adventures of Huckleberry Finn*.

Objectives

Thematic
To understand the importance of fables

Skills
1 To understand the fable
2 To reason
3 To evaluate a moral

Support Material

Teaching Portfolio
Teacher Backup, p. 997
Usage and Mechanics Worksheet, p. 1001
Vocabulary Check, p. 1002
Analyzing Literature Worksheet, *Understanding the Fable*, p. 1003
Understanding Language Worksheet, *Understanding Expressions About Animals*, p. 1004
Selection Test, pp. 1005–1006

Art Transparency 10
Cat and Mouse by James Lloyd

GUIDE FOR INTERPRETING

from Fables

Commentary

The Fable. An appealing combination of elements, the **fable** dramatizes a short lesson or principle of behavior through the antics of animals who speak and interact as though they were human. The structure of the fable varies, but it usually situates a clearly worded moral at either the beginning or the end. Focusing on a single compressed episode, the thrust of the piece turns on an implied frailty or fault of character, which is often the object of satire.

The fable is a popular mainstay of literature. Permeating all levels of writing, it has influenced Western society through the works of Aesop and his Roman collector, Phaedrus, before being retold in the writings of La Fontaine. Other important fabulists include Horace, the Roman poet who relates the story of the city mouse and the country mouse; Chaucer, who incorporates the tale of Chanticleer and the fox in his *Canterbury Tales*; Rudyard Kipling, the author of *The Jungle Books* and *Just So Stories*; and Joel Chandler Harris, whose Uncle Remus stories emphasize the wisdom of weaker animals who must use their wits to survive the attacks of stronger, more ferocious beasts.

La Fontaine's own brand of animal lore was well suited to the neoclassical age. His aphorisms, based on the mind-over-emotions philosophy of seventeenth-century moralists, instruct the reader in prudent living. Making no attempt to mask the severity of the outcome should weaker beings fail to apply forethought in matters of survival, La Fontaine characteristically dwells on the dangers that lurk in seemingly innocent surroundings.

A key feature of the beast fable is its carefully worked-out statement of advice—or moral—based on crucial information, such as personal safety, thought for the future, hard work, perseverance, and sharing. Because they are readily understood by youngsters, these fables remain a staple of children's literature. Parents, themselves brought up on moralistic writing, favor retellings of certain beast stories in order to pass along these useful bits of wisdom. Current children's writers continue the tradition in storybook, comic strip, and cartoon, as is obvious in episodes depicting Babar, Paddington Bear, Winnie the Pooh, Snoopy and Woodstock, Garfield, Roadrunner and Wile E. Coyote, and the animal characters created by Dr. Seuss.

Writing

Most of us remember our favorite childhood stories fondly. Think back to one that has special meaning for you and review the parts of it that you recall most vividly. Freewrite, explaining why you selected that particular story. Try to tell why you think certain sections stand out so memorably.

Literary Focus Have students brainstorm for a list of clichés that have emerged from fables. They might suggest such familiar sayings as "a bird in the hand is worth two in the bush," "haste makes waste," "the early bird catches the worm," and "a stitch in time saves nine." List samples on the chalkboard. Then discuss how moral lessons from different fables have become an important part of our culture.

Writing/Prior Knowledge Divide students in groups of three or four. Have them share childhood stories before they begin writing.

ESL Teaching Strategy Encourage ESL students to share fables from their native cultures with the class.

Teaching Tenth-Grade Students Tenth-grade students have probably encountered fables, such as Aesop's fables, earlier in their education. Ask them to discuss the fables with which they are familiar and why they think these fables have universal appeal.

Vocabulary

Preteach the following vocabulary words:

exemplifies (eg zem′ plə fīz′) *v.*: Shows by example

reproof (ri prōōf′) *n.*: A scolding

precepts (prē′ septs) *n.*: Rules of conduct

rill (ril) *n.*: A little brook

roil (roil) *v.*: To make muddy

vengeance (ven′ jəns) *n.*: Revenge for an injury

impending (im pend′ iŋ) *v.*: About to happen

The Boy and the Schoolmaster

Jean de La Fontaine

translated by Elizur Wright

Wise counsel is not always wise,
  As this my tale exemplifies.
A boy, that frolicked on the banks of Seine,[1]
Fell in, and would have found a watery grave,
5 Had not that hand that planteth ne'er in vain
A willow planted there, his life to save.
While hanging by its branches as he might,
A certain sage preceptor[2] came in sight;
  To whom the urchin cried, "Save, or I'm
    drowned!"
10 The master, turning gravely at the sound,
Thought proper for a while to stand aloof,
And give the boy some seasonable reproof.

  "You little wretch! this comes of foolish
    playing,
  Commands and precepts disobeying.

15 A naughty rogue, no doubt, you are,
Who thus requite your parents' care.
Alas! their lot I pity much,
Whom fate condemns to watch o'er such."
This having coolly said, and more,
20 He pulled the drowning lad ashore.

This story hits more marks than you suppose.
All critics, pedants,[3] men of endless prose,—
  Three sorts, so richly blessed with progeny.[4]
  The house is blessed that doth not lodge
    any,—
25 May in it see themselves from head to toes.
  No matter what the task,
    Their precious tongues must teach;
  Their help in need you ask.
    You first must hear them preach.

---

1. Seine (sān): A river in northern France.
2. preceptor (prē sep′ tər) *n.*: A teacher.

3. pedants (ped′ 'ntz) *n.*: People who lay unnecessary stress on minor or trivial points of learning.
4. progeny (präj′ ə nē) *n.*: Children, descendants, or offspring.

THINKING ABOUT THE SELECTION

Interpreting

1. How does this fable show that those who give wise advice are not always wise?
2. In what way is it true that "this story hits more marks than you suppose"?
3. What is La Fontaine's attitude toward "critics, pedants, men of endless prose"?

Applying

4. Explain how the truth of La Fontaine's tale applies to life today.

THINKING AND WRITING

Evaluating a Moral

    Refer to a book of quotations and list some of the instructive morals that La Fontaine used in his fables. Select one to explain in a single essay. Give examples from modern life that express the value of his advice. Read your essay aloud to a small group and have members discuss whether you selected effective models to typify La Fontaine's message. Then have each member of your group write a notation that gives an evaluation of your essay. These can be collected and read privately by the author of the essay.

The Wolf and the Lamb

Jean de La Fontaine

translated by Elizur Wright

That innocence is not a shield,
    A story teaches, not the longest.
The strongest reasons always yield
    To reasons of the strongest.

5 A lamb her thirst was slaking
    Once at a mountain rill.
A hungry wolf was taking
    His hunt for sheep to kill,
When spying on the streamlet's brink
10 This sheep of tender age,
He howled in tones of rage,
How dare you roil my drink?
Your impudence[1] I shall chastise!
Let not your majesty, the lamb replies,
15   Decide in haste or passion;
For, sure, 'tis difficult to think

In what respect or fashion
My drinking here could roil your drink,
Since on the stream your majesty now faces
I'm lower down, full twenty paces.
20   You roil it, said the wolf; and more, I know
You cursed and slandered me a year ago.
O no! How could I such a thing have done!—
    A lamb that has not seen a year,
    A suckling of its mother dear?
25 Your brother then. But brother I have none.
    Well, well, what's all the same,
    'Twas someone of your name.
Sheep, men, and dogs, of every nation,
30   Are wont to stab my reputation,
    As I have truly heard.
    Without another word,
He made his vengeance good,—
    Bore off the lambkin to the wood,
35   And there without a jury,
Judged, slew, and ate her in his fury.

----

1. **impudence** (im´ pyoo dəns) *n.*: Shamelessness; immodesty.

Reader's Response *What cautions would you have given to the lamb about the dangers of the mountain?*

Primary Source Note

As critic Frank Hamel observed in his book *Jean de la Fontaine*, it is upon the Fables that the poet's reputation rests. Explaining their appeal in the author's day, Hamel remarks: "The Fables were so spontaneous, so full of unexpected surprises and quaint conceits. The idea of inanimate objects and animate objects other than man being shown to possess traits and passions akin to the human—an idea that had existed from the earliest ages—had in spite of its antiquity something novel, stimulating, and provocative in it to people who were surfeited with heroic romance, love-songs, and historical epics."

Although "the composition contains no rapid succession of events, no intricate puzzles of plot, no clashes of interest, no tangle of threads to be unravelled, no bewildering number of characters; there is a central idea, one incident . . . and a moral!" To Hamel, the moral "gives a point to the whole, as salt savours meat. Noth-

Illustration for "The Wolf and the Lamb" for a 1756 publication of *The Fables of La Fontaine*

Oudry

THINKING ABOUT THE SELECTION

Interpreting

1. Why does the author select the lamb and the wolf, rather than any other sort of animals, as adversaries?
2. How does the lamb employ logic to stave off a potential attack?
3. Why does the lamb's strategy fail?
4. Which words denote the wolf's tendency toward violence and how do his actions show him to be violent?
5. Which character has "the strongest reasons" and which "reasons of the strongest" for doing what is done in the story?

Applying

6. Compare this fable to world situations in which strong nations reside alongside weak nations. How do weak nations keep from being overrun?

CRITICAL THINKING AND READING

Reasoning

The wolf determines to attack the lamb and trounces each of the lamb's arguments, concluding with the comment that "sheep, men, and dogs, of every nation / Are wont to stab my reputation." Have a discussion in a small group on the fallacy, or fault, of the wolf's logic. Summarize your conclusions in writing.

(continued from bottom of page)
traditional symbol of viciousness.
2. The lamb argues logically that she is not roiling the wolf's water since she is standing twenty paces below it, that she could not have cursed the wolf a year ago because she had not yet been born, and that neither could her brother have cursed him because she has no brother.
3. The wolf is eager to seek vengeance on any victim, regardless of what is logical.
4. *Hungry, kill, chastise, stab, vengeance, slew,* and *fury* are among possible answers.
5. The lamb has the strongest reasons, but the wolf reasons the strongest.
6. Answers will differ. Suggested response: Weak nations, like Switzerland, Austria, and Cambodia, maintained neutrality in an attempt to remain independent. Eventually, however, weak nations do get overrun.

ANSWERS TO CRITICAL THINKING AND READING

Suggested response: The wolf creates his own reputation by his violent actions, and therefore, no one stabs it by discussing the wolf's ferocity; they simply tell the truth.

Humanities Note

Fine art, *Illustration for "The Wolf and the Lamb"* by Jean Baptiste Oudry. Jean Baptiste Oudry (1686–1755) was a French painter and master engraver. In the early part of his career, Oudry was chiefly a portrait painter. He is remembered for his hunting scenes and animal portraits.

Shortly before his death, Oudry produced many fine illustrations for a literary work he much admired, "La Fontaine." "*The Wolf and the Lamb*" is from this 1755 edition. These illustrations were favorites of the French people for many years.

You might want to use the following questions to discuss the art:
1. What instance in the fable is the artist illustrating?
2. How would you evaluate his success in illustrating that instance?

---

ing is wanting to complete the sense of intellectual satisfaction, provided only the art of the fabulist be of the best. And La Fontaine's art in this class of literature was of the very best and has perhaps never been equalled, in spite of the great names . . . with which his has been linked." Other critics agree.

"What La Fontaine is in the 'Contes' all the world knows," wrote Saint-Beuve; "what he is in fable the world also knows and feels, but it is much less easy to explain it. Authors of intelligence have tried the same style and failed; they have put in action, according to precept, animals, trees, men, hiding a sly meaning, a healthy moral, under their little dramas; and then to their surprise they are judged inferior to their illustrious predecessor."

ANSWERS TO THINKING ABOUT THE SELECTION

1. The lamb, a standard symbol of innocence, pits her logic against the wiliness and ferocity of the wolf, a

The Council Held by the Rats

Jean de La Fontaine

translated by Elizur Wright

Old Rodilard, a certain cat,
    Such havoc of the rats had made,
'Twas difficult to find a rat
    With nature's debt unpaid.
5   The few that did remain,
      To leave their holes afraid,
    From usual food abstain,
      Not eating half their fill.
    And wonder no one will,
10 That one who made on rats his revel,
    With rats passed not for cat, but devil.
    Now, on a day, this dread rat-eater,
    Who had a wife, went out to meet her;
    And while he held his caterwauling,[1]
15 The unkilled rats, their chapter calling,
    Discussed the point, in grave debate,
    How they might shun impending fate.
      Their dean, a prudent rat,
    Thought best, and better soon than late,
20   To bell the fatal cat;
    That, when he took his hunting round,

The rats, well cautioned by the sound,
Might hide in safety underground;
    Indeed he knew no other means.
25   And all the rest
      At once confessed
    Their minds were with the dean's.
No better plan, they all believed,
Could possibly have been conceived.
30 No doubt the thing would work right well,
If anyone would hang the bell.
    But, one by one, said every rat,
    I'm not so big a fool as that.
The plan, knocked up in this respect,
35 The council closed without effect,
And many a council I have seen,
Or reverend chapter with its dean,
    That, thus resolving wisely,
    Fell through like this precisely.

40   To argue or refute
      Wise counselors abound;
    The man to execute
      Is harder to be found.

---

1. caterwauling (kat′ ər wôl′ iŋ) *v.*: Screeching; wailing.

Reader's Response *What advice would you have given to the rats?*

**Illustration for "The Council Held by the Rats"
for a 1756 publication of** *The Fables of La Fontaine*
Oudry

Humanities Note

Fine art, *Illustration for "The Council Held by the Rats"* by Jean Baptiste Oudry. This fanciful engraving was produced by the French artist Jean Baptiste Oudry (1686–1755) as an illustration for the fables of "La Fontaine." The wit and humor of this artist is evident in this amusing scene. Oudry is well known for his skill at rendering animals. He does not take this skill seriously in this case as he shows rats and a cat in human clothing walking upright to great comic effect.

Oudry spent his last years designing tapestries for the weaving centers of Gobelin and Beauvais. His appreciation of the fables of "La Fontaine" prompted him to take time out from these activities to produce illustrations for a deluxe edition of the work. He completed the drawings but did not live to see the edition published.

You might want to use the following questions to discuss the art:

1. What other form of visual art uses animals in human persona for an amusing effect?
2. Do you find this a suitable illustration for this fable?

THINKING ABOUT THE SELECTION

Interpreting

1. Why do the rats choose this particular moment in the story for their debate?
2. How is the death of a rat "nature's debt unpaid"?
3. Explain whether you agree with the author that it is easier to find observers who seek to give advice than doers?

Applying

4. What methods do humans use to protect one animal species against attack by another?

ANALYZING LITERATURE

Understanding the Fable

Through a brief tale with animal characters, the fable teaches a moral lesson. From this story of the rats and the predatory cat has come the phrase "belling the cat." Join in a discussion about the current meaning of the saying. Draw up a list of people who might be "belled" in certain circumstances. Decide whether the aphorism, or saying, is still applicable to modern dilemmas. Add commentary about your own attempts to "bell" a dangerous "cat."

Closure and Extension

ANSWERS TO THINKING ABOUT THE SELECTION

1. Because the cat is involved in a noisy debate with his wife, they can hear the cat's whereabouts.
2. The rat is the natural food of the cat and could fall prey to the cat at any moment that the cat seeks nourishment.
3. It is easier to find counselors than doers because planning difficult jobs involves no risk. However, doing difficult jobs could bring destruction to the doer.
4. Answers will vary. Some people have cats declawed, keep dogs on a leash, and cover birdfeeders to keep out squirrels.

ANSWERS TO ANALYZING LITERATURE

Lists will vary. Students might suggest that people who steal and cheat be belled. However, students might decide that the solution is not applicable in today's world, particularly in the United States where it would be considered unconstitutional.

CANDIDE
by Voltaire

Most of us are entertained when moviemakers or authors thrust us into the misadventures of characters who venture through the mad, mad world of comedy. We are thrilled to be a part of narrow escapes or to watch near misses of catastrophic proportions. We are intrigued by the apparent innocence of wicked villains or by the unexpected goodness of inconsistent evildoers. And what is more fun than encounters with characters who will not stay dead and buried?

That same contagious magic fills the pages of *Candide*, a novel by Voltaire, the father of the French Revolution and a writer who used satire to retaliate against what bothered him most.

The Story of a Good Boy

The story begins in the eighteenth-century castle of Baron Thunder-ten-tronckh in Westphalia. There, in what his teacher insists on repeatedly and annoyingly calling the best of all possible worlds, are the adolescent Candide and his girlfriend Cunegonde. They are taught to believe in the innocence and goodness of all things by the famous Doctor Pangloss. But misfortune soon arrives when Candide and Cunegonde are caught kissing

by her father, the baron: He slaps Cunegonde and boots Candide from the estate. So begins an intercontinental whirlwind that will take Candide from Holland to Portugal to South America to France to England to Venice and finally to Turkey, while surviving disasters, tortures, mayhem, and massacres in an attempt to become reunited with Cunegonde.

Candide, whose name means "the innocent one," is drafted into the Bulgarian army and exposed to the horrors of war before escaping to peaceful Holland. There he meets his former teacher Pangloss, who is destitute but still convinced that all is for the best. Candide is told that invaders ransacked Westphalia and that Cunegonde is dead.

With Jacques, Candide and Pangloss sail to Portugal. They arrive just as an earthquake devastates the port of Lisbon, an event that is paralleled by an event that had upset Voltaire several years before he wrote *Candide*. Thousands of innocent people are killed in the earthquake. To appease God and prevent further damage, the authorities sacrifice strangers: Pangloss is hanged; Candide is flogged. Candide manages to escape and is reunited with "thought-dead" but quite alive Cunegonde. Candide flees Europe with Cunegonde after he kills two men who had assailed her.

Identifying with Candide

Readers identify with the main characters while wondering whether Pangloss could possibly be right about the state of the world. Voltaire expects his readers to ask themselves the same questions that haunt his characters: If all these bad things happen to innocent people, how can life be fair, or how can this be the best of all possible worlds?

Overriding the philosophical overtones, however, is the knowledge that Voltaire is writing satire. Voltaire does not let the reader forget his comic intention. He never treats the foibles of his time with a heavy hand.

Onward to Eldorado

With the proper authorities in pursuit of him for the murder of the men, Candide tries to hide in South America with Cunegonde. However, Cunegonde is held prisoner by a local governor, and Candide must leave her behind as he continues to elude his pursuers. He sets out for more adventures in several countries with Cacambo, his loyal and devoted valet. Eventually they arrive in Eldorado, a legendary paradise where citizens have all they could possibly ever want—except variety. Bored by the lack of challenge and sure that he cannot be happy without Cunegonde, Candide leaves the land of plenty with the hope of finding her again.

Before, during, and after his Eldoradoan venture, Candide crosses paths with an unlikely array of misfits, priests, savages, and soldiers. Many are comic stereotypes. One, Martin, becomes a constant companion for the remainder of the adventure. Martin and his pessimism are counterparts to Pangloss and his unrelieved hopefulness. With Cacambo they start back for Europe with the hope of locating Cunegonde and finding the happiness that has eluded Candide in so ridiculous a way.

Other Stories of Misadventures

Though these adventures may seem too absurd, traditions in earlier European literature exist in which young heroes like Candide are celebrated. Voltaire was certainly aware of a work by the Roman writer Petronius, the *Satyricon*, in which a student spends time on a roller-coaster-type ride through Rome's back alleys.

Humanities Note

Fine art, *Candide and the Marchioness*, artist unknown. This illustration of the young Candide is part of a series done for a French edition of Voltaire's masterpiece during World War I. Along with a dozen other depictions, it shows various stages in the hero's life as he bumps his way from the court of Baron Thunder-ten-tronckh to his final salvation in the Turkish gardens where he labors joyfully at the conclusion of his book. *Candide and the Marchioness* illustrates the first meeting of the lovers in the opening chapter of the novel.

You might want to use the following questions to discuss the art:
1. How can you tell that the figures in this painting are attracted to each other?
2. What does her clothing suggest about the marchioness?
3. How would you describe the expression of the marchioness?
4. What impression do you receive of these characters as a couple?

Themes

The chief inspiration for Voltaire's *Candide*, however, is not literary. Instead, it is deeply personal and involves the heart as well as the mind of the great writer. In 1755 Europe was shocked by news from Lisbon about a terrible earthquake that claimed nearly 25,000 lives. Voltaire channeled his shock into a long poem he wrote shortly after the event, an act that also enabled him to express his grief over the death of his friend Madame Du Chatelet. Writing *Candide* five years later, he targeted the popular philosophic idealism that urged students to accept the premise that their world was the best of all possible worlds.

That idealism was championed by the German author Gottfried Wilhelm Leibnitz, who believed that God is beneficent and that the world is perfect. Leibnitz was not alone in such beliefs, though it was widely believed that he was personally attacked by being portrayed as Doctor Pangloss in the satiric characterization in *Candide*. Voltaire turns his wit against social snobbery, piratical violence, and mercantile opportunism. He directs barbs at prostitutes as well as at priests. Kings and queens are as vulgar as the lowborn who populate his works.

Candide is above all a comic work with a predictably happy ending. Just as its wit contributed to a successful Broadway musical, *Candide* has offered readers through the ages a pleasurable reading experience. It not only provides a memorable introduction to one of Europe's most influential writers, but it also lets the reader watch a master satirist at work. Like Swift in "A Modest Proposal" and Molière in *Tartuffe*, Voltaire uses the extremes of situation and character to explode pretension and deliver blow after blow to the arrogance or stupidity of his intended subjects. Just as film satires or *Mad* magazine concoct circumstances that are as unlikely as they are believable, so too does Voltaire's *Candide* provide readers with scene after scene of spoof, goof, and guffaw. But while in most passages hilarity may be more obvious than the serious message, important questions are left unanswered.

> What place has fortune in life?
> Why do the innocent suffer unfairly?
> Are people never constant enough to be reliable?
> Is it possible to find some escape from a fate that seems haphazard?

For all the seriousness of its author's convictions—and Voltaire was beaten as well as imprisoned for his criticisms of society in his day—readers almost always come away from *Candide* with a sense of vivacity and sympathy for an author who preferred to be giddy rather than sour. Literary historian William Bottiglia reports: "In the judgment of his contemporaries Voltaire was above all a great dramatist, formal poet, and philosopher." The brief acquaintance with his animated characters in Candide makes it possible to appreciate how he was valued and loved by the students of his time who, when giving tribute to him at his funeral in Paris, placed a banner across his casket inscribed with the words: "He gave birth to human reason / He taught us to be free."

2 **Discussion** Ask students to name movies they have seen recently that deal with topics in a satirical manner. Discuss the plots of such shows. Try to determine what makes the absurdities they use so believable.

3 **Enrichment and Challenge** Have students continue the list of inquiries on page 845 that enumerates some of life's unanswerable questions. Ask some students to find brief responses that have been given to comparable questions by poets or philosophers.

Eldorado and the Longing for Paradise

> "Before the Fall man was placed in the garden to dress it and to keep it. After the Fall he was condemned to work as a punishment."
> —William F. Botiglia
> "Voltaire's *Candide*: Analysis of a Classic"

During the Age of Rationalism writers frequently commented on the quest for Eldorado, a mythical place where riches were free. If they didn't directly compare the utopian dream to the Eden described in Genesis, then they used terms similar to biblical ones to depict the desire of their characters to regain a heaven from which they felt exiled. But none contended that paradise could be quickly located, recognizing that a tremendous disparity exists between an imaginary dream world and the all-too-human real world. The Age of Rationalism knew that dreams of utopia were just that, dreams.

Pascal gives an opinion on this topic directly in *Pensées*.

> "If man had never been corrupted, he would enjoy in his innocence both truth and happiness with assurance. And if man had never been anything more than a corrupted being, he would have no idea either of truth or of beatitude. But, unhappy as we are . . . we have an idea of happiness, and we cannot reach it; we feel an image of the truth, and possess but falsehood: incapable of absolute ignorance and of certain knowledge, so manifest is it that we have been in a degree of perfection from which we are unfortunately fallen!"

Elsewhere, as in Milton's *Paradise Lost*, the insight is given by a character. Here is Eve, for example, speaking with Adam before the downfall about the pleasure of their efforts.

> Adam, well may we labor still to dress /
> This garden, still to tend plant, herb, and flower / Our pleasant task enjoined; but till more hands / Aid us, the work under our labor grows, / Luxurious by restraint.

Voltaire, regarded by many as the author who most forcefully reflects the many currents and counter-currents of the Age of Rationalism, brings his inquisitive main character in *Candide* to the country of Eldorado itself halfway through his adventurous search for the perfect world. In his innocence Candide at first believes that he may have stumbled onto *the* answer to his question. "It is probably the country where all goes well," he asserts, "for there must obviously be some such place." But after learning about the customs of the people and about the lack of active competition that Voltaire believed gave life so much of its purpose, Candide sours on the place and decides to move on.

"If we stay here," he confides to his friend, "we shall be no different from anybody else; but if we go back to the old world with a mere 12 sheep laden with Eldorado stones (gold), we shall be richer than all the kings of Europe put together."

Unlike others of his time, Candide will conclude that routine human effort can provide the basis for re-establishing society in the garden for which it was intended. Work, he believes, brings happiness.

In other ages writers as diverse as Dante (page 618) and Baudelaire (page 902) will take up the theme of a lost, idyllic place.

SUGGESTED READINGS

Dante, *The Divine Comedy*, page 618

Charles Baudelaire, "Invitation to a Voyage," page 904

CROSS CURRENTS

Bruce Chatwin

Hailed as an unconventional master writer of travelogue and adventure, Bruce Chatwin produced a series of succinct episodic books that defy classification. Blending the elements of landscape, people, history, myth, anecdote, and etymology, Chatwin won critical and popular acclaim on both sides of the Atlantic Ocean for his meticulously pieced literary mosaics. His most successful works include *The Viceroy of Ouidah* (1980), *On the Black Hill* (1982), *Songlines* (1987), *Uzt* (1988), and his masterpiece, *In Patagonia* (1977).

BACKGROUND

A native of Sheffield in Yorkshire, England, Chatwin pursued a zigzag path to success. Labeled a "dimwit and a dreamer" at Marlborough College because he made a mediocre showing in Greek and Latin, he threw himself into the study of France and all things French. The upshot of his obsession was employment at Sotheby's, the world-famous art auction house, where Chatwin rose from porter to auctioneer and ultimately to director of impressionist art. Then acute problems with his eyesight forced him to change directions, and he began a study of archeology at the University of Edinburgh.

Over the years, Chatwin evolved an interest in nomadic peoples that comprised the subject matter of his first book. Because of his early curiosity about the restless wanderings of certain world tribes, he began traveling to out-of-the-way places, notably Patagonia, which forms the southern tip of South America. The connecting point for around-the-world travelers before the Panama Canal diverted shipping traffic to Central America, Patagonia became a crossroads for every sort—from simple native shepherds to rascals and brigands to visionaries who sought a respite from the acquisitiveness and commerciality of America and Europe.

IN PATAGONIA

Lured by his grandmother's careful stewardship of a treasured piece of sloth skin that her cousin sea captain Charles Milward had entrusted to her, Chatwin pinpointed the exact locale from which the strange item originated. On a meandering walking tour from Buenos Aires, Argentina, southward and on through Chile, Chatwin collected a bizarre montage of items and observations that he ultimately wove into a chronicle of his six-month journey. *In Patagonia* received better than favorable attention for its focused objectivity, humor, and exotica, eventually developing into a best seller.

The book affords readers an intriguing mix of charming and, at times, austere vignettes. Chatwin interposes brief glimpses of Ferdinand Magellan, Sir Francis Drake, Charles Darwin, Butch Cassidy and the Sundance Kid, as well as merchants, missionaries, and settlers from central Europe, Scotland, and Wales.

THE PERIPATETIC CHATWIN

In the style of Voltaire's *Candide*, Chatwin followed the dictates of his spirit, collecting data and experiences, which, like rough chunks of raw ore, he processed into the refined materials of his spare but engaging travel books. Continuing his journeys from Patagonia to Brazil to Dahomey, Africa, to aboriginal Australia and the sheepcotes of Wales, Chatwin maintained the outlook of the utopian, ever looking forward to new vistas. For Chatwin, the shards of knowledge from other cultures formed the core of his life's work. With the grace of a master storyteller, he crafted significant and pleasurable armchair travels.

Problem Solution

Writing a Problem Solution

What is the problem? According to Henry J. Kaiser, "Problems are only opportunities in work clothes." In other words, by doing the work of solving a problem, we often create possibilities for ourselves.

You have probably noticed that authors often write about problems and their solutions. For example, in "A Modest Proposal," Jonathan Swift considered the problem of human misery and poverty among the Irish. By proposing an out-landish solution—that children be bought and sold as food—Swift captured his reader's attention and focused it on the need for more serious considera-tion of the problem he so outrageously addressed.

Whether the problem solving is contained in an editorial, an essay, or a television interview, prob-lem-solution writing shares several characteristics.

Characteristics of Problem Solution Writing

- Engages reader by addressing him or her directly
- Reveals shared concern to reader
- Analyzes problem
- Proposes solution to problem
- Shows
  Practicality of solution
  Ways to put solution into effect
  Benefits of solution
- Convinces reader to accept solution

Writing Assignment

Swift considered a problem that was a major social issue of his time. Think about your own time. What pressing social issue would you like to address? For example, you might choose the prob-lem of homelessness, of toxic waste disposal, or of nuclear weapons. Swift's form for his writing was modeled on the political tracts of his day. Use as your structure the more contemporary forum for addressing problems—the television interview.

Prewrite

The Subject

Start by selecting a problem. To do this you might thumb through a daily newspaper or news magazine, look at a television newscast or docu-mentary, or simply take a look at the world around you. Choose something that moves you. To get your readers involved, you have to make the sub-ject important to them; therefore, make sure it is important to you.

Next, address your problem. Consider it from all angles. Gather examples, anecdotes, facts, and statistics about your problem from newspapers, books, magazines, and reference materials. Trying to solve a pressing social issue without information is like trying to run a car on empty.

Then make a list in which you

- define your problem
- suggest your solution
- cite reasons why your solution is best
- say why other remedies are not effective
- put your reasons in a logical order

Form

Think about the television interviews you have seen in which the host and guest have examined a problem. Usually these shows follow a certain format.

Television Interview

- Host asks questions that define a problem
- Guest offers insightful answers with solutions
- Host asks questions about alternative remedies
- Guest rebuts by reviewing weaknesses of other resolutions
- Host "wraps up" or summarizes at end

Write

Using the list you made about your problem and the format outline, write the script of a television interview. Be sure to state your problem in the beginning and propose your solution soon after. Then give your specific reasons. Refer to the list you made to be sure you have covered everything. Remember to sum up at the end. However, give punch to your summary statement so that you leave your reader feeling that your solution is the only answer to the problem.

Collaborate

Find someone who does not know the assignment—mothers and fathers are good for this—and have this person read your writing. Ask your reader two questions: (1) Is your format recognizable? and (2) Does your argument convince your reader that you are right about the solution to the problem? Have your reader point out both strong points in your writing and spots where either your format or your reasoning broke down.

Revise

Rewrite your paper, bearing in mind your responder's remarks. Don't be afraid to change what you wrote. If you believe something should be added, put it in. If something needs to be cut, then cut it. For an additional improvement, add some words that are currently popular on television interview shows.

Before you finalize your draft, think again about how sound your reasoning has been. Are your statements consistent with known facts? Does your solution coincide with the views of knowledgeable and reliable authorities? Have you avoided logical fallacies? Did you make the mistake of using propaganda devices?

Publish

One way to publish your writing is to present it as an actual television interview. Work with a partner. Decide who will be the host and who the guest. Rehearse until you feel you have your roles down perfectly. Then using the front of your classroom as your television set, present your interview to your classmates.

Evaluate

How do you know if your interview was a success? First, find out if it had an effect on the people who saw it. Ask your classroom audience what they thought of it. Did you make the problem meaningful to them? Did you convince them of the rightness of your solution? Are they likely to take any action as a result of your interview?

Next, find out what it meant to you. Do you feel differently about the problem as a result of your research and writing? Will you now take any steps to solve the problem? Would you at least like to try? Consider keeping the paper you wrote and reviewing it a year or two from now. Perhaps things will have changed.

Guidelines for Evaluating Writing About Literature Keep the following questions in mind when evaluating students' compositions:
1. Does the piece engage the reader by addressing him or her directly?
2. Does the work contain evidence of concern that the reader will recognize?
3. Does the television script analyze the problem and propose a solution?
4. Is the solution believable and practical?
5. Is the reader convinced that the solution is attractive?

Fine art, *Terrace at Sainte-Adresse* by Claude Monet. As a young painter, Monet (1840–1926)—along with a number of other talented French painters, including Manet, Pissarro, and Renoir—became dissatisfied with the dominant artistic approach in Europe at the time. Consequently, Monet and the other painters formed a new artistic school that came to be known as Impressionism. The Impressionists, who derived their name from Monet's 1872 painting *Impression: Sunrise*, focused on capturing the transient colors of nature as they appeared at any given moment and as affected by weather, distance, and surrounding objects. To accomplish this, they often used dabs of broken color and continuous expanses of pure light.

Sainte-Adresse, the setting of this painting, is the place where Monet spent most of his childhood. The figures in the painting are members of Monet's family, gazing at the sea from their terrace. The sort of casual, unstaged scene depicted in this painting is typical not only of Monet but of the Impressionists in general.

You might want to use the following questions to discuss the art:

1. What impression does the painting convey of the scene it depicts?
2. Would you describe the painting as realistic? Why or why not?
3. If you were an art collector, would you want to include this painting in your collection? Why or why not?

TERRACE AT SAINTE-ADRESSE
Claude Oscar Monet
The Metropolitan Museum of Art, New York

Objectives

1 To understand the historical developments that occurred in Europe during the nineteenth century
2 To understand the developments in industry and science that occurred during the nineteenth century and to grasp the implications of these developments
3 To understand the developments in literature that occurred in Europe during the nineteenth century

ROMANTICISM AND REALISM
1800–1890

Would you realize what Revolution is, call it Progress; and would you realize what Progress is, call it Tomorrow.

—Victor Hugo

Throughout Europe, the nineteenth century was an age marked by revolutions, progress, and hope for the future. It was a time during which people often became swept up in democratic idealism and patriotic fervor. Yet it was also an era characterized by unfulfilled expectations and by the emergence of new problems and new approaches to life. All these aspects of nineteenth-century life captured the interest of the writers of the time and shaped the literature they produced.

DEVELOPMENTS IN HISTORY

The Seeds of Revolution

The revolutionary spirit that swept throughout most of Europe during the nineteenth century had its roots in the ideas of the political and social philosophers John Locke (1632–1704) and Jean Jacques Rousseau (1712–1778). After having lived through a bitter civil war in his native land of England, Locke published *Two Treatises on Government*. In this book he argued that governments were established by the people to keep order in society and to protect the peoples' rights to life, liberty, and property. As long as the government protected the rights of the people, the people had an obligation to obey and support the government. If the government did not perform its duty, however, Locke believed that the people had a right to rebel.

THE RETREAT FROM MOSCOW, NOVEMBER 3, 1812
Pelerin

Rousseau's ideas were even more radical than those of his predecessor. He saw society as a force of evil that infringed on personal liberty and happiness. "Man is born free," he wrote, "and everywhere he is in chains." He reasoned that humanity should revert to its natural state, abandoning its stifling social institutions and outworn philosophies, and listening instead to nature, instinct, and intuition.

Revolution in America and Europe

Inspired by the ideas of such thinkers as Locke and Rousseau, the American colonists revolted against British rule and declared their independence in 1776. The Americans went on to defeat the British and establish the world's first democratic government. They also created a constitution that protected the rights of all American citizens.

The success of the American Revolution helped to stir political unrest throughout Europe, especially in France, where people were becoming increasingly unhappy with the policies of King Louis XVI. In 1789 the unrest in France erupted into a revolution, and in the years that followed the monarchy was abolished and France was declared a republic. Early in 1793 the leaders of the newly established republican government executed the king. This event marked the beginning of a period of extreme violence and bloodshed that came to be known as the Reign of Terror—a period during which over 4,000 people were executed.

In 1799 a successful and popular young general, Napoleon Bonaparte, assumed political power in France. Five years later, he made himself emperor. Although in many respects Napoleon ruled as a military dictator, he did accomplish many domestic reforms, such as helping to establish educational opportunities for all French citizens and creating a code of laws. In addition, he aroused a strong sense of nationalism among the French people.

The Empire of Napoleon

Map legend:
- French territories ruled directly from Paris c. 1810
- States ruled by members of Napoleon's family c. 1810
- Other dependent states c. 1810
- British or British occupied territory
- Battles: French victory / French defeat

0   200 Miles
0   200 Kilometers

NORWAY · Stockholm · SWEDEN · DENMARK · Copenhagen · Edinburgh · UNITED KINGDOM OF GREAT BRITAIN AND IRELAND · NORTH SEA · Amsterdam · London · Antwerp · Brussels · WESTPHALIA · PRUSSIA · Berlin · GRAND DUCHY OF WARSAW · RUSSIA · CONFEDERATION OF THE RHINE · Prague · Rhine R. · AUSTRIA · MOLDAVIA · ATLANTIC OCEAN · FRANCE · HELVETIC REPUBLIC · Geneva · Munich · Vienna · Danube R. · WALLACHIA · Alps · ILLYRIAN PROVINCES · Lyons · Venice · OTTOMAN · BLACK SEA · Marseilles · Florence · ADRIATIC SEA · MONTENEGRO · Toulon · PIOMBINO · Cattaro · EMPIRE · PORTUGAL · CATALONIA · Rome · Naples · KINGDOM OF NAPLES · SPAIN · Palermo · SICILY · Gibraltar · MEDITERRANEAN SEA · Pyrenees

Europe at War

Between 1792 and 1815, France was almost constantly at war with other European nations. At first France defended itself against monarchies that were frightened by the Revolution and hoped to destroy it. Later, after Napoleon came to power, France embarked on a series of military conquests in which it seized control of almost all Europe as far east as the Russian border.

In 1812, however, Napoleon overextended himself by invading Russia. There, his army suffered a disastrous defeat that marked the beginning of his downfall. Napoleon's final defeat came in 1815 at the Battle of Waterloo, when his forces were overpowered by an allied army led by Great Britain.

Although Napoleon dominated Europe for only a brief period, his conquests had a lasting impact on the continent. His armies were responsible for spreading many of the achievements of the French Revolution throughout Europe. In the lands Napoleon conquered, for example, he introduced his code of laws, abolished serfdom, and encouraged religious toleration.

While such reforms were welcomed by many, public opinion turned against Napoleon when his occupying forces began assessing high taxes and conscripting local men into his armies. As resentment of the French grew in the occupied lands and in other countries, strong feelings of nationalism emerged throughout Europe.

Revolutions and Reactions

Following the collapse of Napoleon's empire, a large group of national delegates gathered in Vienna to restore order to Europe. Led by the Austrian statesman Klemens von Metternich, the delegates took measures to reestablish the traditions that had

1 Enrichment Tell students that in 1814 the allied armies of Britain, Austria, Russia, and Prussia captured Paris. Forced to abdicate from the throne, Napoleon went into exile on the island of Elba, off the coast of Italy. Napoleon returned to Paris a year later, however, and again proclaimed himself emperor, but Napoleon's second reign was short-lived. One hundred days after his reemergence, he was easily defeated at Waterloo by the allied forces commanded by the Duke of Wellington. Following this crushing defeat, Napoleon was forced back into exile on the island of St. Helena, where he died in 1821.

Using the Map

Have students study the map. Then ask them the following questions:

1. Where did the majority of French defeats occur?
2. How does the size of Napoleon's empire compare with the size of the Roman Empire at its height (see the map on page 484)?
3. How does the size of Napoleon's empire compare with the size of the Persian Empire at its height (see the map on page 79)?
4. Which of the nations depicted in this map either no longer exist or have become part of larger countries?

Portrait of Napoleon Bonaparte, emperor of France

Portrait of German composer Ludwig van Beethoven

Humanities Notes

Pictured from left to right:

Napoleon Bonaparte—Napoleon I—crowned himself emperor of the French in 1804. During his ten-year reign, "the Little Corporal" created an empire that spanned most of central and western Europe. Napoleon's downfall was due in part because of his pride and stubbornness and because of his betrayal of many people. All around him people began to desert him. Finally, his commanders insisted he give up the throne. The French crowned Louis XVIII king and exiled Napoleon to Elba in 1814. The following year Napoleon escaped and returned to France. During the Hundred Days—the period from his escape to his final defeat at Waterloo—Napoleon ruled once again. After Waterloo Napoleon was once again exiled, this time to the barren island of St. Helena, off the coast of west Africa. He died of cancer in 1821.

Ludwig van Beethoven (1770–1827) composed some of the world's greatest music. Beethoven's musical talents emerged at an early age. He learned to play the violin and the piano from his father. He began to compose his own scores in the late 1780's. Throughout his career Beethoven greatly influenced music. Before his time composers wrote music for religious services and social functions and to teach. Beethoven freed music from these earlier constraints; people began to listen to and appreciate his music for its own sake. In the late 1790's, Beethoven began to lose his hearing. He became totally deaf toward the end of his life, but it did not impede his composing. Among his most famous works are the Third, Fifth, Sixth, and Ninth symphonies and the opera *Fidelio*.

The steam locomotive—one of the many developments in the latter part of the Industrial Revolution—was invented by England's Richard Trevithick in 1804. The first American–built steam locomotive was designed and tested by John Stevens in 1826. The *Stourbridge*

Timeline: 1800 — 1810 — 1820 — 1830 — 1840

HISTORY

- Louisiana Purchase takes place
- Napoleon proclaims himself emperor of France
- War of 1812 begins
- Napoleon's unsuccessful invasion of Russia takes place
- Napoleon is defeated at Waterloo; exiled
- German states pass Carlsbad Decrees
- Napoleon dies in exile
- Mexico wins independence from Spain
- Queen Victoria begins reign of Britain

HUMAN PROGRESS

- First electric battery is developed in Italy
- Successful test of the *Clermont,* a paddle-wheeled steamship, takes place
- Erie Canal is completed
- First steam-powered locomotive is run
- Charles Darwin sails to Galapagos Islands
- Samuel Morse invents the telegraph
- Development of photography begins

LITERATURE

- William Wordsworth: "Ode: Intimations of Immortality"
- Goethe: *Faust,* Part I
- George Gordon, Lord Byron begins "Don Juan"
- Heinrich Heine: *Book of Songs*
- Honoré de Balzac: *Les Chouans*
- Alexander Pushkin: *Eugene Onegin*
- Nikolai Gogol: *Dead Souls*

First steam locomotive
Stourbridge Lion

Charles Darwin's
ship H.M.S. *Beagle*

Alexander Graham Bell making
first long-distance phone call

1850	1860	1870	1880	1890

- *The Communist Manifesto*
- • Second Empire is declared in France
- • Crimean War begins
- • U.S. Civil War begins
- • Emancipation Proclamation frees American slaves
- • Franco-Prussian War begins
- • Adolf Hitler is born

- • Steel production improves in Europe
- • Crystal Palace is built in London
- • Neanderthal Man discovered
- • Charles Darwin: *On the Origin of Species* and *The Descent of Man*
- • First railroad spans North America
- • Suez Canal is completed
- • First underwater telegraph cable across the Atlantic Ocean is laid
- • American iron and steel production grows
- • Alexander Graham Bell invents the telephone
- • Internal combustion engine is developed

- • Heinrich Heine: *Romanzero*
- • Walt Whitman: *Leaves of Grass*
- • Gustave Flaubert: *Madame Bovary*
- • Charles Baudelaire: *The Flowers of Evil*
- • Charles Dickens: *Great Expectations*
- • Victor Hugo: *Les Misérables*
- • Emile Zola: *Thérèse Raquin*
- • Charles Dickens: *A Tale of Two Cities*
- • Leo Tolstoy: *Anna Karenina*
- • Fyodor Dostoevsky: *The Brothers Karamazov*
- • Henrik Ibsen: *A Doll's House*
- • Guy de Maupassant: "Ball of Fat," first published short story
- • Chekhov: *Tales of Melpomene,* his first collection of stories

Lion, pictured here, was the first full-sized locomotive to run in North America. Imported from England c. 1829, the *Stourbridge Lion* was too heavy for American tracks and was not a commercial success. Many of the early locomotives weighed 3 to 6 tons but could pull only a few light cars.

From 1831 to 1836, Charles Darwin (1809–1882) served as a naturalist with a British scientific expedition aboard the H.M.S. *Beagle*. The expedition studied plants and animals throughout the world. His studies aboard the *Beagle* convinced him that through millions of years all species of plants and animals have evolved, or developed gradually, from a few common ancestors. He documented his theories and presented them at a meeting with scientists in 1858. Darwin's theories of evolution and natural selection created a wave of controversy and challenged the biblical account of the Creation that is still debated today.

Pictured here is Alexander Graham Bell (1847–1922) making the first long-distance call in 1892 from New York City to Chicago. Bell, an American scientist, educator, and inventor conceived the idea of transmitting speech by electric waves as early as 1865. By 1875 he was experimenting with a multiple harmonic telegraph. On March 10, 1876, he transmitted the first complete sentence, "Watson, come here; I want you." That same year Bell introduced the telephone to the world at the American Academy of Arts and Sciences in Philadelphia. The Bell Telephone Company was organized a year later.

existed before the French Revolution. Yet, although they were able to restore royal authority throughout Europe, they were unable to erase the desire for political and social justice. As a result, the rest of the century was marked by an ongoing conflict between traditional political beliefs and democratic ideals.

Nowhere was this conflict more apparent than in France. In the aftermath of Napoleon's downfall, royal rule had been reestablished. In 1830, however, when the king took measures to restrict the people's freedom, the people revolted and forced him out of power. Although this revolt brought about a number of important reforms, it did not bring an end to the monarchy, and a new king was put into place. When another revolution occurred in 1848, however, a second French republic was established. Yet the Second Republic lasted for only four years, and it was not until 1870 that a third French republic was established.

The French uprisings of 1830 and 1848 inspired revolts in many other European countries, including Belgium, Poland, Italy, Austria, and Hungary. Yet most of the revolts were unsuccessful.

In 1848 a movement also arose among the German people aimed at unifying the many German states into a single nation controlled by a democratic government. Like the revolts in the other European nations, this movement was thwarted. In 1871, however, after Prussia defeated France in the Franco-Prussian War, the Prussian prime minister, Otto von Bismarck, did succeed in unifying the German states. Yet while the newly established German empire was a source of pride for nationalists, it was a major disappointment for reformers. The new government was authoritarian and militaristic and scorned such democratic ideals as freedom and equality.

Similarly, Russian reformers had little success in bringing about political and social changes. In 1825 the forces of the Russian ruler, known as the czar, crushed a revolt by army officers who wanted to establish a constitutional government. Efforts to free the nation's forty million serfs were somewhat more successful. In 1861 these people, who had been bound to the service of wealthy landowners, were granted their freedom. At about the same time, the government also modified its censorship policies and loosened restrictions on its universities. Yet aside from these changes, Russia remained virtually untouched by reform throughout the nineteenth century.

INDUSTRIALISM AND SCIENCE

Political and social movements were not the only forces that brought about changes in European life during the nineteenth century. Industrialization transformed the lives of millions of people and helped to bring about the emergence of a new and powerful social class. In addition, scientific advances occurred that began to change the way in which people viewed themselves and their world.

The Industrial Revolution began in Great Britain during the second half of the eighteenth century. By the middle of the nineteenth century, industrialization had spread throughout Europe, and urban factories were springing up in cities across the continent. Because of the development of steam engines and other mechanical devices, along with advances in the coal and steel industries and great improvements in transportation, these factories were capable of producing mass quantities of an increasing variety of goods. To produce these goods, however, these factories needed a large number of workers to run the machines.

As a result of the need for factory workers, along with the re-

THE GLEANERS
Jean-François Millet

duced need for farm workers brought about by advances in agriculture, increasing numbers of people began moving out of rural areas and into the urban industrial centers. The cities were generally unequipped to handle the growth in their populations, however. As a result, most factory workers were forced to crowd into poorly built housing settlements near their workplaces. In these settlements it was common for a family of eight or ten to live in a single room. Clean water was often unavailable, and there were no systems of public sanitation.

The conditions in the factories themselves were no better than in the slums in which workers lived. Men, women, and even young children were expected to work twelve hours a day six days a week for very low wages. In addition, the workers were forced to work with machines that emitted toxic fumes and made great amounts of noise, and virtually no measures were taken to ensure worker safety. Accidents occurred frequently, and injured workers received no compensation.

In addition to reshaping the lives of the working class, the Industrial Revolution resulted in the emergence of a large middle class composed of factory and mine owners, bankers, and merchants. As the century progressed, the middle class became increasingly wealthy and powerful and began to challenge the longstanding authority of the landed aristocracy.

At the same time industrialization was bringing about changes in the traditional European social structure, developments in science and philosophy were occurring that had a dramatic impact on the way people lived and thought. Some of these developments sparked controversy. The theories of British biologist Charles Darwin, for example, created a tremendous uproar that shook the entire Western world. According to Darwin, all forms of life evolve, or change, over a long period of time. Simpler forms of life evolve into more complex forms, and new forms evolve out of older ones. Darwin believed that this occurred because all beings struggled with each other for the necessities of life. Only the fittest survived this competition and passed their superior characteristics onto subsequent generations.

Because they felt that Darwin's theories contradicted the Bible, many people attacked his ideas.

Others, however, embraced Darwin's ideas and applied them to the social and political issues of the 1800's. The English philosopher Herbert Spencer, for example, used Darwin's theories as an explanation for the inequalities of life.

Another controversial theory was set forth by the German philosophers Friedrich Engels and Karl Marx. Horrified by the dreadful working conditions in nineteenth-century factories and angered by economic and social inequalities, Marx and Engels called for the abolishment of capitalism. They went on to propose the establishment of a system of public land and factory ownership known as communism. Although the ideas of Marx and Engels did not have an impact on European politics until the twentieth century, they did influence a number of nineteenth-century writers, including the Russian novelist Leo Tolstoy.

NINETEENTH-CENTURY LITERATURE

Shaped by the major events and developments of the time, four major literary movements dominated nineteenth-century literature: Romanticism, Realism, Naturalism, and Symbolism.

Romanticism

The first of these movements, Romanticism, emerged in the late 1700's out of the revolutionary spirit fueled by the uprisings in America and France. Although there were many differences in the concerns and approaches of the various writers associated with this movement, they generally shared a desire to discard the dominant forms and approaches of the eighteenth century and to forge a new type of literature. Unlike eighteenth-century writers, who generally used scientific observation and logic as sources of inspiration, the Romantics tended to be inspired by their imaginations and their inner feelings and emotions. The Romantics also had a deep interest in ordinary people and favored the use of simple, common language. In contrast, eighteenth-century writers tended to be most interested in the lives of upper-class people and used ornate, elevated language.

5 **Enrichment** In his novel *Hard Times*, Charles Dickens offers a description of a typical nineteenth-century European factory town. He refers to it as "a town of machinery and tall chimneys, out of which interminable serpents of smoke trailed themselves forever and ever, and never got uncoiled. It had a black canal in it, and a river that ran purple with ill-smelling dye, and vast piles of buildings full of windows where there was a rattling and trembling all day long, and where the piston of the steam engine worked monotonously up and down, like the head of an elephant in a state of melancholy madness."

6 **Enrichment** Dickens goes on to describe the mundane lives of the people who live in the town. He writes that the people were "equally like one another . . . all went in and out at the same hours, with the same sound on the pavement, to do the same work and to whom every day was the same as yesterday and tomorrow, and every year the counterpart of the last and the next."

7 **Enrichment** Tell students that the conditions for workers did improve somewhat as the century progressed. In fact, in France and Britain wages nearly doubled during the last half of the nineteenth century. In addition, a number of nations took steps to improve working conditions in the factories.

Among the other important characteristics of the Romantics were their deep love and appreciation for nature, their interest in the folklore of the Middle Ages, their fascination with the cultures of the Orient and the Middle East and in the supernatural, their sense of optimism, their emphasis on individualism, their refusal to accept human limitations, and their desire for social change. Again, most of these characteristics contrast with the dominant tendencies of eighteenth-century writers.

The many writers associated with Romanticism include Wolfgang von Goethe (page 861), Alexander Pushkin (page 878), Heinrich Heine (page 884), Victor Hugo (page 888), and William Wordsworth (page 894). In his preface to *Lyrical Ballads* (1798), a collection of poetry he co-authored with fellow British poet Samuel Taylor Coleridge, Wordsworth outlined many of the dominant principles of Romanticism. He stressed the need to use "language really used by men," emphasized the role of nature as a source of inspiration, and asserted that poetry should be a "spontaneous overflow of powerful feelings."

Realism and Naturalism

During the middle of the nineteenth century, a new literary movement known as Realism emerged partly as a reaction against Romanticism and partly as a result of the industrial and scientific developments that were transforming society. Led by the French writers Honoré de Balzac and Gustave Flaubert and the Russian writers Leo Tolstoy (page 942) and Fyodor Dostoevsky, the Realists sought to portray life as faithfully and accurately as possible. Aroused by an awareness of social inequalities, along with concerns about the negative effects of industrialization, the Realists confronted many of the harsh realities of nineteenth-century life. Often, they de-

LA TRINITE DES MONTS (THE TRINITY OF THE MOUNTAINS)
Camile Corot

picted the lives of working-class people faced with poverty and other hardships. In doing so, they presented a pessimistic view of the world that contrasted sharply with the optimistic vision of the Romantics.

Another literary movement, known as Naturalism, grew out of the Realistic movement. Like the Realists, the Naturalists attempted to depict life accurately. Yet the Naturalists, who were led by the French writer Émile Zola, differed from the Realists in that they possessed a well-defined view of the world that they imposed on their works. Influenced by the ideas of Darwin and Spencer, the Naturalists believed that a person's fate is determined by heredity, chance, and environment. As a result, the Naturalists frequently depicted characters whose lives were shaped by forces of society and nature they could neither understand nor control.

Symbolism

The last of the major nineteenth-century literary movements, Symbolism, emerged in France toward the end of the century. Believing that the ideas and emotions that people experience are personal and difficult to communicate, the Symbolists avoided directly stating their own ideas and emotions. Instead they tried to suggest meaning through the use of clusters of symbols.

The Symbolist movement was restricted to poetry and did not involve a vast number of writers. Yet the Symbolists influenced many twentieth-century writers, including Paul Valéry (page 1126), and their work offers important clues about the type of poetry that would take hold during the Modern Age.

ROMANTIC AND REALISTIC VOICES

And this is all that I have found—
The impossibility of knowledge!
    Goethe, *Faust,* Part I

Every woman is the gift of a world to me.
    Heinrich Heine, *Ideas*

The supreme happiness of life is the conviction that we are loved.
    Victor Hugo, *Les Misérables*

One impulse from a vernal wood
May teach you more of man,
Of moral evil and of good,
Than all the sages can.
    William Wordsworth, "The Tables Turned"

Nature is a temple whose living colonnades
Breath forth a mystic speech in fitful sighs;
Man wanders among symbols in those glades
Where all things watch him with familiar eyes.
    Charles Baudelaire, "Correspondences"

So long as man remains free he strives for nothing so incessantly and so painfully as to find someone to worship.
    Fyodor Dostoevsky, *The Brothers Karamozov*

Besides considerations as to possible transfers and promotions likely to result from Ivan Ilyich's death, the mere fact of the death of a near acquaintance aroused, as usual, in all who heard of it the complacent feeling that, "it is he who is dead and not I."
    Leo Tolstoy, *The Death of Ivan Ilyich*

Six feet from his head to his heels was all he needed.
    Leo Tolstoy, "How Much Land Does a Man Need?"

All Russia is our orchard.
    Anton Chekhov, *The Cherry Orchard*

I believe that, before all else, I'm a human being, no less than you—or anyway, I ought to try to become one.
    Henrik Ibsen, *A Doll's House*

Additional Voices

And for a long time yet, led by some wondrous power, I am fated to journey hand in hand with my strange heroes and to survey the surging immensity of life, to survey it through the laughter that all can see and through the tears unseen and unknown by anyone.

    —Nikolai Gogol, *Dead Souls*

I am a sick man . . . I am a spiteful man. I am an unattractive man.

    —Fyodor Dostoevsky, *Notes from Underground*

Bliss was it in that dawn to be alive . . .
France standing on top of golden hours
And human nature seemed born again

    —William Wordsworth, *The Prelude*

With every autumn that comes I bloom again;
It is good for my health, it is good, this Russian cold;
I fall afresh in love with the habit of being;
Sleep flies early, and hunger is in its place,
The blood romps joyfully through my heart,
Desire seethes up—I laugh again, I am young, . . .

    —Alexander Pushkin, *Autumn*

BACKGROUND

THE FAUST LEGEND

Origin of the Legend

Few historical figures have fueled the imagination of the Western world as much as the German scholar and magician Johann Faust (or Faustus), who lived from about 1480 to 1540. Because he traveled widely, performing magical feats and demonstrating mystical powers, Faust was well known throughout Germany. Many Germans of the time considered him a fraud, but Martin Luther, the leader of the Protestant Reformation, believed that he had satanic powers. Even during Faust's life, he was the subject of legends. In fact, his story became part of the folk legends of the Middle Ages. According to many of them, Faust had sold his soul to the devil in exchange for youth, knowledge, and magical powers.

In 1587 *Faustenbach*, a crude, loosely organized narrative about the life of Faust, was published in Germany. Written by an anonymous author, the book not only drew upon the existing tales about Faust, but it also attributed to Faust numerous stories about other legendary magicians, such as Merlin. Concluding with Faust's death and descent into Hell, the book had a major impact on readers throughout Europe. The book was first translated into English in 1592 under the title *The History of the Damnable Life and Deserved Death of Doctor John Faustus*.

Literary Works

The English translation was the immediate source for English writer Christopher Marlowe's play *The Tragical History of the Life and Death of Doctor Faustus* (page 700). Completed in 1604, Marlowe's play portrays Faust as a dignified yet tragic character whose quest for unattainable knowledge and power prompts him to contract his soul to the Devil. As in the earlier book, the play ends in Faust's eternal damnation. In contrast, in the German writer Gotthold Lessing's (1729–1781) unfinished Faust play (1784), Faust's pursuit of unlimited knowledge is depicted as a noble quest that will ultimately end in the character's reconciliation with God. Goethe's poetic drama *Faust* also offers a sympathetic portrayal of the legendary magician. Goethe transforms Faust into a Romantic hero, embodying the ideal of limitless spiritual aspirations.

Goethe's *Faust* was by no means the last literary work to draw upon the German legend. Other well-known writers who have treated the legend include the nineteenth-century poets Heinrich Heine (1797–1856) and Paul Valéry (1871–1945) and the modern novelist Thomas Mann (1875–1955). Aside from the plays of Marlowe and Goethe, Mann's *Doktor Faustus* (1947) is probably the most famous literary work connected to the Faust legend. In this novel Mann subtly links the downfall of a demonic composer to the tragic events that occurred in Germany during the first half of the twentieth century.

Art and Music

The Faust legend has inspired musicians and artists as well as writers. Among the many works of art to depict Faust are the paintings of the noted French artist Eugène Delacroix (1798?–1863). The most famous musical composition derived from the German legend is probably the opera *Faust* (1859) by French composer Charles Gounod (1818–1893).

JOHANN WOLFGANG VON GOETHE

1749–1832

Because of the tremendous diversity of his talents and interests, Johann (yö´ hän) Wolfgang von Goethe (gö´ tə) is best described as a true Renaissance man. Not only was he a gifted writer, but he was also a scientist, a painter, a statesman, a philosopher, and an educator.

The son of a wealthy lawyer, Goethe was born in the German town of Frankfurt am Main. After receiving a thorough education from private tutors, he was sent to the University of Leipzig to study law. More interested in the arts than in law, Goethe spent most of his free time in Leipzig writing poetry, studying art, and attending concerts. Forced to leave the University of Leipzig because of illness, Goethe decided to complete his legal studies in Strasbourg. There he came under the influence of Johann Gottfried Herder, the leader of a new literary movement called *Sturm und Drang,* or "Storm and Stress." A precursor of Romanticism, this movement stressed the need to rebel against the existing literary conventions and emphasized the importance of feelings and emotions.

After finishing his legal studies in 1771, Goethe practiced law for a brief period, during which he wrote *The Sorrows of Young Werther* (1774), an autobiographical novel inspired by an unhappy love affair and the suicide of one of his friends. One of the most important novels of the eighteenth century, *The Sorrows of Young Werther* earned Goethe international fame.

A year after the novel's publication, Goethe accepted an invitation to the court of the reigning duke of Weimar, Charles Augustus. Developing a close friendship with the duke, Goethe lived in Weimar for the rest of his life, and for ten years he served as the duke's chief minister. Finding that his official duties along with his involvement in another unsuccessful love affair were hindering his writing, he made a secret journey to Italy in 1786. He remained there for two years, writing, traveling, painting, and studying classical culture.

Shortly after returning to Weimar, Goethe fell in love with Christiane Vulpus, whom he eventually married. He also became the director of the court theater and began devoting much of his energy to scientific studies. Yet he found himself in need of someone who shared his literary talents and interests. This need was filled when he developed a close friendship with the noted German writer Friedrich von Schiller (1759–1805). Schiller provided Goethe with valuable guidance and advice concerning his writing and assisted him in revising a number of his important works.

Probably the most notable of these works was *Faust.* Having read the incomplete version of this work that Goethe had published in 1790, Schiller helped convince Goethe to return to it. With Schiller's advice and direction, Goethe revised what he had already written and added a prologue. Unfortunately, however, Schiller died three years before *Faust, Part I* (1808) was published. Despite the death of his beloved friend and colleague, Goethe continued to work on *Faust* throughout the remainder of his life, and a year after his death *Faust, Part II* (1833) was published.

Faust was by no means the only literary work that Goethe completed during the late eighteenth and early nineteenth centuries. Among his other notable works are his novels *Wilhelm Meister's Apprenticeship* (1795), *Elective Affinities* (1809), and *Wilhelm Meister's Travels* (1821–1829), and his autobiographical work *Poetry and Truth* (1811–1833). By the time of his death, Goethe had become a legendary figure throughout the Western world, and a steady stream of people traveled to Weimar to visit him.

READING CRITICALLY

The Literature of 1800–1890

Historical Context

The events with the greatest impact on European life during the early 1800's were the Industrial Revolution and the French Revolution and its aftermath. After sparking debate throughout Europe among those who believed in democracy and those who favored the existing political and social orders, the French Revolution, which had been born out of democratic idealism, ultimately resulted in the ascension of Napoleon. Driven by a desire to export the ideas of the French Revolution, Napoleon waged war across the continent until he was finally defeated at Waterloo in 1815. At the same time, industrialization was having a profound social and economic impact on most European nations, leading to the rise of capitalism and the growth of a new and powerful social class. Industrial development also resulted in the emergence of new problems, however, such as pollution and the exploitation of factory workers.

Cultural Context

The French Revolution and the Industrial Revolution, along with the ideas of eighteenth-century philosophers Jean Jacques Rousseau and Immanuel Kant, gave rise to a variety of new European cultural attitudes and beliefs. Influenced by the French revolutionary spirit and by the writings of Rousseau, who argued that society infringes on personal liberty, many writers and thinkers of the early nineteenth century stressed the need for freedom and equality. These beliefs were accompanied by an emphasis on individuality and personal feelings, which reflected the teachings of Kant. The early nineteenth-century writers and thinkers were also influenced by industrialization, which prompted them to emphasize the importance of nature and the need to return to a simpler way of life.

Literary Context

The writers and thinkers mentioned in the previous paragraph were part of a major intellectual, artistic, and literary movement known as Romanticism. Along with an emphasis on nature and personal emotions and a belief in freedom, equality, and individuality, the Romantics stressed spontaneity and the use of the imagination and expressed a concern for common people. Other characteristics of Romanticism include an appreciation for folk traditions and an interest in the supernatural. The Romantic movement thrived until about the middle of the century, when it was replaced by another movement known as Realism, which stressed the accurate portrayal of life.

The annotations that accompany the following selection point out its historical context, cultural context, and literary context.

from Faust

Johann Wolfgang von Goethe

Prologue in Heaven

translated by Louis MacNeice

Literary Context: Goethe's poetic drama is based on a German legend about a man whose desire for forbidden knowledge leads him to make a contract with the Devil. Goethe's use of the legend reflects the Romantic interest in medieval folklore.

Literary Context: This scene is modeled after the interchange between God and the Devil in the Book of Job.

[*The* LORD. *The* HEAVENLY HOSTS. MEPHISTOPHELES[1] *following. The* THREE ARCHANGELS[2] *step forward.*]

RAPHAEL. The chanting sun, as ever, rivals
The chanting of his brother spheres
And marches round his destined circuit—
A march that thunders in our ears.
His aspect cheers the Hosts of Heaven
Though what his essence none can say;
These inconceivable creations
Keep the high state of their first day.

GABRIEL. And swift, with inconceivable swiftness,
The earth's full splendor rolls around,
Celestial radiance alternating
With a dread night too deep to sound;
The sea against the rocks' deep bases
Comes foaming up in far-flung force,
And rock and sea go whirling onward
In the swift spheres' eternal course.

MICHAEL. And storms in rivalry are raging
From sea to land, from land to sea,
In frenzy forge the world a girdle
From which no inmost part is free.
The blight of lightning flaming yonder
Marks where the thunderbolt will play;
And yet Thine envoys, Lord, revere
The gentle movement of Thy day.

Literary Context: These descriptions reflect the Romantic love of and appreciation for nature. Notice how words like *whirling, raging,* and *frenzy* create an emotional intensity.

---

1. MEPHISTOPHELES (mef´ ə stäf´ə lēz´): The devil.
2. THREE ARCHANGELS: The three chief angels, Raphael, Gabriel, and Michael.

Presentation

Motivation/Prior Knowledge Tell students that the "Prologue in Heaven" includes a conversation between God and the devil. Have students speculate about what this conversation will be like. What might they discuss? What attitudes toward each other might they convey? What might be the outcome of their conversation?

Purpose-Setting Question What agreement does God reach with the devil? What are God's reasons for making this agreement with the devil?

ESL Teaching Strategy "The Prologue in Heaven" contains some difficult vocabulary that may pose a problem for ESL students. Consequently, you may want to read aloud the selection to these students and clarify the meanings of any words with which they are unfamiliar.

Teaching Tenth-Grade Students Have tenth-grade students read the selection silently in class. Then have students summarize the events Goethe dramatizes in the selection.

Vocabulary
Preteach the following vocabulary words:
inconceivable (in´ kan sē´ və bə´l) *adj.*: That cannot be thought of
envoys (en´ voiz) *n.*: Messengers
fervent (fur´ vənt) *adj.*: Intensely devoted or urgent
ferment (fur´ ment) *n.*: A state of excitement or agitation
primal (prī´ məl) *adj.*: Original; primitive
intuitions (in´ tōō ish´ ənz) *n.*: Things learned without the conscious use of reasoning
eschew (es chōō´) *v.*: Shun

Support Material

Teaching Portfolio
Teacher Backup, p. 1017
Reading Critically, from *Notes from Underground* by Fyodor Dostoevsky, p. 1021
Grammar in Action Worksheet, *Effective Reasoning,* p. 1027
Usage and Mechanics Worksheet,
p. 1029
Vocabulary Check, p. 1030
Analyzing Literature Worksheet, *Recognizing Literary Models,* p. 1031
Critical Thinking and Reading Worksheet, *Comparing and Contrasting Depictions,* p. 1032
Selection Test, pp. 1033–1034

Spelling Tip Write the word *eschew* on the chalkboard. Circle the last four letters and point out to students that they form the word *chew.*

Literary Context: The Devil, here called Mephistopheles (mef′ e stäf′ ə lēz′), is treated more sympathetically in Goethe's *Faust* than he had been in such earlier works as Milton's *Paradise Lost*. This treatment reflects the idealism and optimism of the Romantics.

Literary Context: The Romantics questioned whether the use of reason could lead to any significant form of knowledge.

Historical Context: Although *Faust* is not set during a specific time period, the *Prologue in Heaven* was written between 1797 and 1806, a period during which most of Europe was at war.

25 **CHOIR OF ANGELS.** Thine aspect cheers the Hosts of Heaven
  Though what Thine essence none can say,
    And all Thy loftiest creations
    Keep the high state of their first day.
  [*Enter* MEPHISTOPHELES.]

MEPHISTOPHELES. Since you, O Lord, once more approach and ask
30 If business down with us be light or heavy—
    And in the past you've usually welcomed me—
    That's why you see me also at your levee.[3]
    Excuse me, I can't manage lofty words—
    Not though your whole court jeer and find me low;
35 My pathos[4] certainly would make you laugh
    Had you not left off laughing long ago.
    Your sums and worlds mean nothing much to me;
    How men torment themselves, that's all I see.
    The little god of the world, one can't reshape, reshade him;
40 He is as strange today as that first day you made him.
    His life would be not so bad, not quite,
    Had you not granted him a gleam of Heaven's light;
    He calls it Reason, uses it not the least
    Except to be more beastly than any beast.
45 He seems to me—if your Honor does not mind—
    Like a grasshopper—the long-legged kind—
    That's always in flight and leaps as it flies along
    And then in the grass strikes up its same old song.
    I could only wish he confined himself to the grass!
50 He thrusts his nose into every filth, alas.

  LORD. Mephistopheles, have you no other news?
    Do you always come here to accuse?
    Is nothing ever right in your eyes on earth?

  MEPHISTOPHELES. No, Lord! I find things there as downright bad as
      ever.
55 I am sorry for men's days of dread and dearth;
    Poor things, *my* wish to plague 'em isn't fervent.

  LORD. Do you know Faust?

  MEPHISTOPHELES.   The Doctor?[5]

  LORD.   Aye, my servant.

---

3. **levee** (lev′ ē) *n*.: A morning reception held by a person of high rank.
4. **pathos** (pā′ thäs) *n*.: Suffering.
5. **Doctor:** Doctor of Philosophy.

Grammar in Action

Once you have gathered evidence about a subject, it is important for you to use **effective reasoning** to draw valid conclusions from your evidence. There are two types of formal reasoning, *inductive* and *deductive*. Inductive reasoning moves from specific facts to a conclusion, or generalization, based on those facts. A valid generalization is a statement supported by evidence that holds true in a large number of cases. Deductive reasoning, on the other hand, moves from the general to the specific. When you use this type of reasoning, you start with a general statement that is assumed to be true and apply that statement to specific cases. However, all the supporting facts and evidence must be verified before you can consider the conclusion valid. The following is an example of deductive reasoning from the "Prologue in Heaven":

Mephistopheles recognizes that people who are frustrated by their unquenchable desires are likely to succumb to his temptations. Faust is frustrated by his unquenchable desire for knowledge and experience. Consequently, Mephistopheles reasons that Faust is likely to succumb to his temptation.

MEPHISTOPHELES. Indeed! He serves you oddly enough, I think.
The fool has no earthly habits in meat and drink.
The <u>ferment</u> in him drives him wide and far,
That he is mad he too has almost guessed;
He demands of heaven each fairest star
And of earth each highest joy and best,
And all that is new and all that is far
Can bring no calm to the deep-sea swell of his breast.

LORD. Now he may serve me only gropingly,
Soon I shall lead him into the light.
The gardener knows when the sapling first turns green
That flowers and fruit will make the future bright.

MEPHISTOPHELES. What do you wager? You will lose him yet,
Provided *you* give *me* permission
To steer him gently the course I set.

LORD. So long as he walks the earth alive,
So long you may try what enters your head;
Men make mistakes as long as they strive.

MEPHISTOPHELES. I thank you for that; as regards the dead,
The dead have never taken my fancy.
I favor cheeks that are full and rosy-red;
No corpse is welcome to my house;
I work as the cat does with the mouse.

LORD. Very well; you have my permission.
Divert this soul from its <u>primal</u> source
And carry it, if you can seize it,
Down with you upon your course—
And stand ashamed when you must needs admit:
A good man with his groping <u>intuitions</u>
Still knows the path that is true and fit.

MEPHISTOPHELES. All right—but it won't last for long.
I'm not afraid my bet will turn out wrong.
And, if my aim prove true and strong,
Allow me to triumph wholeheartedly.
Dust shall he eat—and greedily—
Like my cousin the Snake[6] renowned in tale and song.

LORD. That too you are free to give a trial;
I have never hated the likes of you.

---

6. **my cousin the Snake:** In Genesis, the devil assumes the form of a serpent in order to tempt Eve to eat from the Tree of Knowledge.

Literary Context: The Romantics applauded and celebrated the type of unbounded spiritual aspirations exhibited by Faust. **1**

Cultural Context: This type of optimistic attitude was common at the time when the work was written.

Literary Context: God's statement reflects the Romantic belief that people should be led by intuition and emotion rather than by reason. **2**

3
4

If Mephistopheles has evidence that people who are frustrated by their unquenchable desires are indeed likely to succumb to his temptations, then his conclusion can be considered valid. If he does not have evidence of this fact, however, his conclusion must be regarded as invalid.

Student Activity. Identify each of the following items as examples of either inductive reasoning or deductive reasoning. Then explain whether each is valid or invalid.

1. God has faith in all of humankind. Faust is a person. Therefore, God has faith in Faust.

2. All people have been given the ability to use reason. Faust is a person. Therefore, Faust has the ability to use reason.

3. Mephistopheles believes that he is superior to Faust. Therefore, he must believe that he is superior to all of humanity.

MEPHISTOPHELES
Eugène Delacroix

Of all the spirits of denial
The joker is the last that I eschew.
Man finds relaxation too attractive—
Too fond too soon of unconditional rest;
100 Which is why I am pleased to give him a companion
Who lures and thrusts and must, as devil, be active.
But ye, true sons of Heaven, it is your duty
To take your joy in the living wealth of beauty.
The changing Essence which ever works and lives
105 Wall you around with love, serene, secure!
And that which floats in flickering appearance
Fix ye it firm in thoughts that must endure.

CHOIR OF ANGELS. Thine aspect cheers the Hosts of Heaven
Though what Thine essence none can say,
110 And all Thy loftiest creations
Keep the high state of their first day.
[*Heaven closes.*]

MEPHISTOPHELES. [*Alone*] I like to see the Old One now and then
And try to keep relations on the level.
It's really decent of so great a person
To talk so humanely even to the Devil.

Reader's Response *What do you imagine will be the outcome of Mephistopheles's wager with the Lord? Explain your answer.*

Literary Context: This is the end of the first of the many episodes of Goethe's *Faust*. The episodic nature and the rapid pace of the work reflect the restlessness of the Romantic spirit.

THINKING ABOUT THE SELECTION

Interpreting

1. (a) How would you characterize Mephistopheles as he appears in the *Prologue in Heaven*? (b) What is his attitude toward humanity?
2. Given Mephistopheles's description of him (lines 58–67), what type of person do you imagine that Faust is?
3. What is the meaning of the analogy that God makes between himself and a gardener (lines 68–69)?
4. (a) What is God's attitude toward Mephistopheles? (b) How is his attitude conveyed?

Applying

5. (a) Explain whether you agree with the Lord's statement that "Men make mistakes as long as they strive" (line 75). (b) For what types of things should people strive? (c) What types of mistakes, if any, do you think people cannot afford to make?

ANALYZING LITERATURE

Recognizing Literary Models

Goethe's *Prologue* is modeled after God's exchange with Satan in the Book of Job. Yet in the Book of Job, God does not offer a reason for allowing Satan to function, while in the *Prologue* God explains his decision to allow Mephistopheles to tempt Faust and suggests that the devil serves a valuable purpose.

1. What reason does God give for allowing Mephistopheles to attempt to "divert [Faust's] soul from its primal source"?
2. According to God what overall purpose does the devil serve?
3. How do God's reasons for allowing the devil to tempt Faust and his comments about the devil's overall purpose shape your expectations of the outcome of Goethe's play?

CRITICAL THINKING AND READING

Comparing and Contrasting Depictions

Goethe's *Faust* is one of many literary works in which the Devil appears as a character. Yet Goethe treats the Devil more sympathetically than he is treated in such other works as Milton's *Paradise Lost* (page 814) and Marlowe's *Dr. Faustus* (page 700).

1. In *Paradise Lost* Milton explains how Satan was cast out of Heaven for revolting against God. Then he offers the following description of how Satan was affected by his banishment: "But his doom / Reserved him to more wrath; for now the thought / Both of lost happiness and lasting pain / Torments him; round he throws his baleful eyes / That witnessed huge affliction and dismay, / Mixed with obdurate pride and steadfast hate." Explain why Mephistopheles as he appears in the *Prologue in Heaven* is a more sympathetic character than Satan as he is described by Milton.
2. In Marlowe's *Dr. Faustus*, Mephistopheles angrily remarks to Faust, "Think'st thou that I that saw the face of God / And tasted the eternal joys of heaven, / Am not tormented with ten thousand hells / In being deprived of everlasting bliss?" Based on this passage, how does the disposition of Marlowe's Mephistopheles appear to contrast with that of Goethe's Mephistopheles?

THINKING AND WRITING

Writing a Dialogue

Write a dialogue between God and Mephistopheles modeled after the interchange between the two characters in Goethe's *Prologue*. Begin by deciding how you want to portray Mephistopheles. Next determine what the two characters will discuss. Then write your dialogue, focusing on conveying your intended impression of Mephistopheles.

(continued from bottom of page)

Challenge How does the behavior of the devil in the "Prologue in Heaven" compare with his behavior in Genesis (page 40)?

ANSWERS TO ANALYZING LITERATURE

1. He wants to prove to the devil that a "good man with his groping intuitions / Still knows the path that is true and fit."
2. The devil keeps people from becoming complacent.
3. Answers will differ. Many students may respond that they are led to believe that the devil will be unable to win Faust's soul.

ANSWERS TO CRITICAL THINKING AND READING

1. Suggested response: Milton's Satan is a hateful villain thirsting for revenge. Goethe's Satan seems almost playful by comparison.
2. Suggested response: Marlowe's Satan is filled with anguish and despair. Goethe's Satan seems much more contented.

THINKING AND WRITING

Publishing Student Writing Divide students into pairs and have them act out their dialogues for the rest of the class.

Closure and Extension

ANSWERS TO THINKING ABOUT THE SELECTION

1. (a) Suggested response: He is shrewd and cynical and has a surprising sense of humor. (b) Suggested response: He has little respect for or faith in humanity.
2. Suggested response: He is a restless seeker of knowledge and experience.
3. God's relationship to humanity is like a gardener's relationship to his or her plants. Just as a gardener expects his plants to grow and ripen, God expects humanity to mature.
4. (a) He is tolerant of Mephistopheles. (b) Suggested response: He says that he has never hated Mephistopheles and he allows him to compete for Faust's soul.
5. (a) Answers will differ. Many students will probably respond that making mistakes is part of being human. (b) Answers will differ. Some students will probably respond that students should strive to reach reasonable goals. (c) Answers will differ. Students may respond that people cannot afford to make mistakes that hurt other people.

GUIDE FOR INTERPRETING

Literary Focus To clarify the distinctions between myths, folk tales, and legends, you may want to offer students an American example of each. Tell students that some Native American tribes still have living myths. The kachinas of the Pueblo Indians, for example, are mythical figures, whose purposes include bringing rain for the spring crops. Examples of American folk tales include the stories of Paul Bunyan. Explain that although there were undoubtedly some tall, brawny lumberjacks in the upper Midwest, Paul Bunyan is not based on any real historical figure. Johnny Appleseed, on the other hand, is an example of a legendary figure, because the stories about him are derived from the exploits of a real person named John Chapman, who devoted his life to planting apple trees.

Ask students to try to name other figures from American myths, legends, and folk tales.

Writing/Prior Knowledge The class discussion about American myths, legends, and folk tales can serve as a starting point for students' brainstorming. However, you may want to tell students that their lists should not be limited to American folklore.

Teaching Tenth-Grade Students Read this selection aloud to tenth-grade students. Pause periodically to answer any questions that have come to students' minds.

ESL Teaching Strategy You might want to encourage ESL students to share some of their culture's tales about the devil or other evil figures. Encourage native-speaking students to ask questions about the tales that the ESL students share.

Commentary

from The First Part of the Tragedy

Legends. Folklore is one of the many elements that set one culture apart from another. It consists of all the stories, sayings, and beliefs passed from one generation to the next, often by word of mouth, among a specific group of people. Along with **myths** and **folk tales, legends** are one of the main types of stories included in the folk tradition. Unlike myths—which usually involve gods or other supernatural beings—and folk tales—which often involve heroes who perform improbable feats—legends are believed to have a basis in truth. Through the process of being retold, however, the actions and events described in a legend have become increasingly exaggerated or distorted until the fantastic aspects of the story far outweigh the realistic aspects.

Most often associated with common people, folklore usually reveals a great deal about the attitudes, fears, and beliefs of a particular cultural group. By examining the folklore of various groups of people, it is possible not only to learn about cultural differences but also to discover the many concerns shared by people from almost all cultures. For example, the various folk traditions reveal that most cultural groups, at one time or another, have been deeply concerned with the power, unpredictability, and uncontrollability of nature.

Prior to the Romantic Movement, European writers rarely turned to legends and other types of folklore when searching for ideas for their works. Instead, they most often used classical (Greek and Roman) or earlier European literary works as models or sources of inspiration. Unlike their predecessors, the Romantics were deeply interested in the folk traditions of the Middle Ages. This interest stemmed from the Romantics' concern for common people, everyday language, and ordinary life, along with their fascination with the mysterious, the supernatural, and the past. Not only did folklore offer them a window into the everyday concerns and superstitions of common people, but it also gave them a sense of the type of language these people used and provided them with intriguing ideas for their works. In addition to using folklore as a source of inspiration, the Romantics wrote many works that were directly based on stories from the folk tradition. Goethe's *Faust* and Alexander Pushkin's "The Bridegroom" (page 880) are just two examples of such works.

Writing

Brainstorm about the various legends, myths, and folk tales that you have read, listing each one you think of. After completing your list, jot down some notes about how you could develop a short story or poem based on one of these legends, myths, or folk tales.

Objectives

Thematic
To understand the restless nature of the human spirit

Skills
1 To understand legends

2 To use context clues to interpret the meanings of words

3 To plan a film adaptation of Goethe's play

from **Faust**

from **The First Part of the Tragedy**

NIGHT

[*In a high-vaulted narrow Gothic¹ room* FAUST, *restless, in a chair at his desk.*]

FAUST. Here stand I, ach, Philosophy
  Behind me and Law and Medicine too
  And, to my cost, Theology—
  All these I have sweated through and through
  And now you see me a poor fool
  As wise as when I entered school!
  They call me Master, they call me Doctor,
  Ten years now I have dragged my college
  Along by the nose through zig and zag
  Through up and down and round and round
  And this is all that I have found—
  The impossibility of knowledge!
  It is this that burns away my heart;
  Of course I am cleverer than the quacks,
  Than master and doctor, than clerk and priest,
  I suffer no scruple or doubt in the least,
  I have no qualms about devil or burning,
  Which is just why all joy is torn from me,
  I cannot presume to make use of my learning,
  I cannot presume I could open my mind
  To proselytize² and improve mankind.

  Besides, I have neither goods nor gold,
  Neither reputation nor rank in the world;
  No dog would choose to continue so!

---

1. **Gothic** (gäth′ ik) *adj.*: Of a style of architecture characterized by the use of ribbed vaulting, flying buttresses, pointed arches, and steep, high roofs.
2. **proselytize** (präs′ ə li tīz′) *v.*: To try to convert.

25 Which is why I have given myself to Magic
  To see if the Spirit may grant me to know
  Through its force and its voice full many a
    secret,
  May spare the sour sweat that I used to pour out
  In talking of what I know nothing about,
30 May grant me to learn what it is that girds
  The world together in its inmost being,
  That the seeing its whole germination, the
    seeing
  Its workings, may end my traffic in words. . . .

After summoning the Earth Spirit and finding it unwilling to assist him in his quest for knowledge, Faust lapses into a state of despair. He decides to end his life by drinking a cup of poison, but abruptly changes his mind when he hears the tolling of church bells and the singing of choruses, celebrating the arrival of Easter. Setting out on a walk through the countryside with Wagner, his assistant, Faust is inspired by the beauty of spring and soothed by the peasants' expressions of admiration and affection for him. When he returns to his study, however, his sense of contentment quickly dissipates. Alerted by the growling of his dog, Faust becomes aware of another presence in the room. When Faust threatens to use magic to defend himself against the unseen intruder, Mephistopheles comes forward from behind the stove, disguised as a traveling scholar. Faust soon becomes aware of Mephistopheles's true identity, and he is intrigued by the possibility of establishing a contract with the devil. However, Faust falls asleep before the two can reach an agreement. In the following scene, Mephistopheles returns to the study to resume his discussion with Faust.

Presentation

Motivation/Prior Knowledge After reading the "Prologue in Heaven," students should have a good sense of what will happen in "The First Part of the Tragedy." They know that Mephistopheles will be trying to win Faust's soul. They also know that Faust has an unquenchable thirst for knowledge and experience, and they have some sense of Satan's personality. Review this prior knowledge with them, emphasizing the Romantic characteristics of the story.

Purpose-Setting Question Why is Faust willing to consider Mephistopheles's offer?

Master Teacher Note Once again, have students recall other literary works they have read in which characters were tempted by the devil. Instruct them to keep these works in mind as they read the following selection and to think about the ways in which the other works are similar to and different from Goethe's play.

1 Discussion Have students discuss the feelings that Faust conveys in these opening lines. How does he make his frustration immediately clear?

2 Discussion Have students explain why Faust has taken up the study of magic.

Vocabulary

Preteach the following vocabulary words:
germination (jʉr′ mə nā′ shən) *n.*: The process of sprouting
obstinate (äb′ stə nit) *adj.*: Stubborn
asunder (ə sun′ dər) *adv.*: Into parts or pieces
egoist (ē′ gō ist) *n.*: A person who is self-centered
fetters (fet′ ərz) *n.*: Shackles
tenacity (tə nas′ ə tē) *n.*: Persistence; stubbornness
insatiableness (in sā′ shə b′l nəs) *n.*: The quality of being impossible to fill

Support Material

Teaching Portfolio
Teacher Backup, p. 1035
Grammar in Action Worksheet, *Supporting an Opinion*, p. 1039
Usage and Mechanics Worksheet, p. 1041
Vocabulary Check, p. 1042
Analyzing Literature Worksheet,

Understanding Legends, p. 1043
Language Worksheet, *Using Context Clues*, p. 1044
Selection Test, pp. 1045–1046

Spelling Tip Write the word *asunder* on the chalkboard. Point out to students that it can be separated into two other words, *as* and *under*.

3 **Discussion** Ask students to explain why Faust has to say "come in" three times.

4 **Clarification** Remind students that Mephistopheles was dressed as a traveling scholar the first time he visited Faust. This time he is dressed in "a suit of scarlet trimmed with gold." Make sure students note Mephistopheles's explanation for his change of clothes.

5 **Clarification** Have a student summarize the thoughts that Faust expresses in this passage.

6 **Enrichment** Share with students Walter Kaufmann's translation of the final two lines of this passage: "And thus existence is for me a weight, / Death is desirable, and life I hate." Which translation do students think has a more powerful impact? Why? What sound device is used in both translations of these two lines?

7 **Discussion** Ask students to explain Mephistopheles's remark. To whom is he referring? What is the "brown juice" that this person failed to drink?

8 **Speaking and Listening** To help students appreciate the lyricism of this passage, you may want to have a student read it aloud to the rest of the class. Then have students discuss the sound devices that are used in this passage.

[*The same room. Later.*]

FAUST. Who's knocking? Come in! *Now* who wants
  to annoy me?

MEPHISTOPHELES. [*Outside door*] It's I.

35 FAUST.   Come in!

MEPHISTOPHELES. [*Outside door*] You must say
  "Come in" three times.

FAUST. Come in then!

MEPHISTOPHELES. [*Entering*] Thank you; you
  overjoy me.
  We two, I hope, we shall be good friends;
40 To chase those megrims³ of yours away
  I am here like a fine young squire today,
  In a suit of scarlet trimmed with gold
  And a little cape of stiff brocade,
  with a cock's feather in my hat
45 And at my side a long sharp blade,
  and the most succinct advice I can give
  Is that you dress up just like me,
  So that uninhibited and free
  You may find out what it means to live.

50 FAUST. The pain of earth's constricted life, I fancy,
  Will pierce me still, whatever my attire;
  I am too old for mere amusement,
  Too young to be without desire.
  How can the world dispel my doubt?
55 You must do without, you must do without!
  That is the everlasting song
  Which rings in every ear, which rings,
  And which to us our whole life long
  Every hour hoarsely sings.
60 I wake in the morning only to feel appalled,
  My eyes with bitter tears could run
  To see the day which in its course
  Will not fulfill a wish for me, not one;
  The day which whittles away with obstinate
    carping
65 All pleasures—even those of anticipation,
  Which makes a thousand grimaces to obstruct
  My heart when it is stirring in creation.

And again, when night comes down, in anguish
I must stretch out upon my bed
70 And again no rest is granted me,
For wild dreams fill my mind with dread.
The God who dwells within my bosom
Can make my inmost soul react;
The God who sways my every power
75 Is powerless with external fact.
And so existence weighs upon my breast
And I long for death and life—life I detest.

MEPHISTOPHELES. Yet death is never a wholly
  welcome guest.

FAUST. O happy is he whom death in the dazzle of
  victory
80 Crowns with the bloody laurel in the battling
  swirl!
Or he whom after the mad and breakneck dance
He comes upon in the arms of a girl!
O to have sunk away, delighted, deleted,
Before the Spirit of the Earth, before his might!

85 MEPHISTOPHELES. Yet I know someone who failed
  to drink
  A brown juice on a certain night.

FAUST. Your hobby is espionage—is it not?

MEPHISTOPHELES. Oh I'm not omniscient⁴—but I
  know a lot.

FAUST. Whereas that tumult in my soul
90 Was stilled by sweet familiar chimes
Which cozened the child that yet was in me
With echoes of more happy times,
I now curse all things that encompass
The soul with lures and jugglery
95 And bind it in this dungeon of grief
With trickery and flattery.
Cursed in advance be the high opinion
That serves our spirit for a cloak!
Cursed be the dazzle of appearance
100 Which bows our senses to its yoke!
Cursed be the lying dreams of glory,
The illusion that our name survives!
Cursed be the flattering things we own,
Servants and plows, children and wives!

---

3. **megrims** (mē′ grəmz) *n.*: Low spirits.

4. **omniscient** (äm nish′ ənt) *adj.*: Knowing all things.

Grammar in Action

One of the main skills involved in analyzing works of literature is the ability to **support opinions** with details from the selection. For instance, when you offer your interpretation of the theme of a literary work, you must be able to support your interpretation with passages from the work that in some way convey this theme.

Student Activity 1. Support each of the following opinions about Goethe's Faust with details from the selection.
1. Faust is a very intelligent man.

2. Mephistopheles is very clever.
3. The Lord is compassionate and forgiving.
4. Faust is a personification of the unquenchable Romantic spirit.
5. Mephistopheles is portrayed as having a sense of humor.

Student Activity 2. Write a paragraph in which you support either one of the opinions from Activity 1 or one of your own opinions about the play.

Cursed be Mammon[5] when with his treasures
He makes us play the adventurous man   140
Or when for our luxurious pleasures
He duly spreads the soft divan![6]
A curse on the balsam of the grape!
A curse on the love that rides for a fall!
A curse on hope! A curse on faith!
And a curse on patience most of all!

[*Invisible* SPIRITS *sing.*]

SPIRITS.   Woe! Woe!
             You have destroyed it,   145
             The beautiful world
             By your violent hand
             'Tis downward hurled!
             A half-god has dashed it asunder!
             From thunder
             We bear off the rubble to
                  nowhere
             And ponder   150
             Sadly the beauty departed.
             Magnipotent
             One among men,
             Magnificent
             Build it again,
             Build it again in your breast!
             Let a new course of life
             Begin
             With vision abounding
             To welcome it in!

MEPHISTOPHELES. These are the juniors
             Of my faction.
             Hear how precociously[7] they
                  counsel
             Pleasure and action.
             Out and away
             From your lonely day
             Which dries your senses and your
                  juices
             Their melody seduces.

Stop playing with your grief
                  which battens
Like a vulture on your life, your
                  mind!
The worst of company would
                  make you feel
That you are a man among
                  mankind.
Not that it's really my proposition
To shove you among the
                  common men:
Though I'm not one of the
                  Upper Ten,
If you would like a coalition
With me for your career through
                  life,
I am quite ready to fit in,
I'm yours before you can say
                  knife.
I am your comrade;
If you so crave,
I am your servant, I am your
                  slave.

FAUST. And what have I to undertake in return?

MEPHISTOPHELES. Oh it's early days to discuss what   155
     that is.

FAUST. No, no, the devil is an egoist
     And ready to do nothing gratis
     Which is to benefit a stranger.
     Tell me your terms and don't prevaricate![8]   160
     A servant like you in the house is a danger.

MEPHISTOPHELES. I will bind myself to your service
     in this world,
     To be at your beck and never rest nor slack;
     When we meet again on the other side,
     In the same coin you shall pay me back.

FAUST. The other side gives me little trouble;
     First batter this present world to rubble,   165
     Then the other may rise—if that's the plan.
     This earth is where my springs of joy have
          started,
     And this sun shines on me when brokenhearted;

---

5. Mammon (mam′ ən): Generally, mammon refers to riches regarded as an object of worship and greedy pursuit; here, the word is used to refer to the devil, as an embodiment of greed.
6. divan (di van′) *n*.: A large, low couch or sofa, usually without armrests or a back.
7. precociously (pri kō′ shəs lē) *adv*.: Exhibiting maturity to a point beyond that which is normal for the age.

---

8. prevaricate (pri var′ ə kāt′) *v*.: To tell an untruth.

Humanities Note

Fine art, *Mephistopheles Appears to Faust* by Eugène Delacroix. This is another of the seventeen lithographs that Delacroix created for a French edition of *Faust.* The process of lithography was invented in 1796 by the playwright Aloys Senefelder. To create a lithograph, an artist produces a drawing, which is then etched onto a smooth stone. The stone is then inked with a roller and used to make prints. Delacroix was only one of many nineteenth-century artists to use this process. Others include Goya, Manet, Degas, and Whistler.

You might want to use the following questions to discuss the art:

1. Which scene from the play do you think this lithograph illustrates? Explain.
2. How does Faust's study, as it is portrayed here, fit his personality?
3. Which lines from the play would you choose as a caption for this illustration? Why?
4. If you were an artist who had decided to prepare a lithograph depicting this scene, how would your depiction of the scene compare with Delacroix's?

MEPHISTOPHELES APPEARS TO FAUST
Eugène Delacroix

Primary Source

Goethe's Mephistopheles has always intrigued readers and critics. One of Goethe's contemporaries, Madame de Staël, a French advocate of the German Romantic movement, wrote:

Faust . . . cannot be exceeded in boldness of conception, and the recollection of this production [she had seen the play staged] is always attended with a sensation of giddiness. The devil is the hero of the piece; the author has not conceived him like a hideous phantom, such as he is usually represented to children; he has made him, if we may so express ourselves, the Evil Being *par excellence,* before whom all others . . . are only novices, scarcely worthy to be servants of Mephistopheles. . . . Goethe wanted to display in this character, at once real and fanciful, the bitterest pleasantry that contempt can inspire, and at the same time an audacious gaiety that amuses.

If I can first from them be parted,
Then let happen what will and can!
I wish to hear no more about it—
Whether there too men hate and love
Or whether in those spheres too, in the future,
There is a Below or an Above.

MEPHISTOPHELES. With such an outlook you can
    risk it.
Sign on the line! In these next days you will get
Ravishing samples of my arts;
I am giving you what never man saw yet.

FAUST. Poor devil, can *you* give anything ever?
Was a human spirit in its high endeavor
Even once understood by one of your breed?
Have you got food which fails to feed?
Or red gold which, never at rest,
Like mercury runs away through the hand?
A game at which one never wins?
A girl who, even when on my breast,
Pledges herself to my neighbor with her eyes?
The divine and lovely delight of honor
Which falls like a falling star and dies?
Show me the fruits which, before they are
    plucked, decay   225
And the trees which day after day renew their
    green!

MEPHISTOPHELES. Such a commission doesn't alarm
    me,
I have such treasures to purvey.
But, my good friend, the time draws on when we   230
Should be glad to feast at our ease on something
    good.

FAUST. If ever I stretch myself on a bed of ease,
Then I am finished! Is that understood?   235
If ever your flatteries can coax me
To be pleased with myself, if ever you cast
A spell of pleasure that can hoax me—
Then let *that* day be my last!
That's my wager!

MEPHISTOPHELES. Done!

FAUST.   Let's shake!
If ever I say to the passing moment
"Linger a while! Thou art so fair!"
Then you may cast me into <u>fetters</u>,

I will gladly perish then and there!
Then you may set the death bell tolling,
Then from my service you are free,   210
The clock may stop, its hand may fall,
And that be the end of time for me!

MEPHISTOPHELES. Think what you're saying, we
    shall not forget it.

FAUST. And you are fully within your rights;   215
I have made no mad or outrageous claim.
I shall stay as I am, I am a slave—
Whether yours or another's, it's all the same.

MEPHISTOPHELES. I shall this very day at the
    College Banquet[9]
Enter your service with no more ado,
But just one point—As a life-and-death   220
    insurance
I must trouble you for a line or two.

FAUST. So you, you pedant, you too like things in
    writing?
Have you never known a man? Or a man's
    word? Never?
Is it not enough that my word of mouth
Puts all my days in bond forever?   225
Does not the world rage on in all its streams
And shall a promise hamper *me*?
Yet this illusion reigns within our hearts
And from it who would be gladly free?
Happy the man who can inwardly keep his
    word;
Whatever the cost, he will not be loath to pay!
But a parchment, duly inscribed and sealed,
Is a bogy[10] from which all wince away.
The word dies on the tip of the pen
And wax and leather lord it then.
What do you, evil spirit, require?
Bronze, marble, parchment, paper?
Quill or chisel or pencil of slate?
You may choose whichever you desire.

MEPHISTOPHELES. How can you so exaggerate   240
    With such a hectic rhetoric?

---

9. **the College Banquet:** The *Doctorschmaus,* a dinner given
by a successful candidate for a Ph.D. degree.
10. **bogy** (bō′ gē) *n.*: Anything one especially, and often
needlessly, fears.

15 Clarification Have a student summarize Faust's complaint in a single sentence.

16 Discussion Ask students what must happen in order for Faust to lose his bet. What will happen to Faust if and when he does lose his bet? Will Mephistopheles lose his bet with the Lord even if he wins his bet with Faust? Why or why not?

17 Discussion Have students note the use of parallelism in this passage. What is the effect of Goethe's use of this device?

18 Discussion Have students explain why Mephistopheles wants the agreement recorded in writing.

19 Discussion Do students agree with Faust's observations concerning a person's word? Why or why not?

20 Enrichment Some critics have noted that Faust and Mephistopheles share certain personality traits. One of these traits is a penchant for ridicule. Here Faust is mocking the devil's need for a written contract. Have students find a passage in which Mephistopheles ridicules something or someone.

Any little snippet is quite good—
And you sign it with one little drop of blood.

FAUST. If that is enough and is some use,
245   One may as well pander to your fad.

MEPHISTOPHELES. Blood is a very special juice.

FAUST. Only do not fear that I shall break this contract.
What I promise is nothing more
Than what all my powers are striving for.
250   I have puffed myself up too much, it is only
Your sort that really fits my case.
The great Earth Spirit has despised me
And Nature shuts the door in my face.
The thread of thoughts is snapped asunder,
255   I have long loathed knowledge in all its fashions.
In the depths of sensuality
Let us now quench our glowing passions!
And at once make ready every wonder
Of unpenetrated sorcery!
260   Let us cast ourselves into the torrent of time,
Into the whirl of eventfulness,
Where disappointment and success,
Pleasure and pain may chop and change
As chop and change they will and can;
265   It is restless action makes the man.

MEPHISTOPHELES. No limit is fixed for you, no bound;
If you'd like to nibble at everything
Or to seize upon something flying round—
Well, may you have a run for your money!
270   But seize your chance and don't be funny!

FAUST. I've told you, it is no question of happiness.
The most painful joy, enamored hate, enlivening
Disgust—I devote myself to all excess.
My breast, now cured of its appetite for knowledge,
275   From now is open to all and every smart,
And what is allotted to the whole of mankind
That will I sample in my inmost heart,
Grasping the highest and lowest with my spirit,
Piling men's weal and woe upon my neck,
280   To extend myself to embrace all human selves
And to founder in the end, like them, a wreck.

MEPHISTOPHELES. O believe *me,* who have been chewing

285   These iron rations many a thousand year,
No human being can digest
This stuff, from the cradle to the bier.[11]
This universe—believe a devil—
Was made for no one but a god!
He exists in eternal light
290   But *us* he has brought into the darkness
While *your* sole portion is day and night.

FAUST. I will all the same!

MEPHISTOPHELES.   That's very nice.
295   There's only one thing I find wrong;
Time is short, art is long.
You could do with a little artistic advice.
Confederate with one of the poets
And let him flog his imagination
To heap all virtues on your head,
300   A head with such a reputation:
Lion's bravery,
Stag's velocity,
Fire of Italy,
Northern tenacity.
305   Let *him* find out the secret art
Of combining craft with a noble heart
And of being in love like a young man,
Hotly, but working to a plan.
Such a person—*I'd* like to meet him;
"Mr. Microcosm"[12] is how I'd greet him.
310

FAUST. What am I then if fate must bar
My efforts to reach that crown of humanity
After which all my senses strive?

MEPHISTOPHELES. You are in the end . . . what you are.
You can put on full-bottomed wigs with a million locks,
315   You can put on stilts instead of your socks,
You remain forever what you are.

FAUST. I feel my endeavors have not been worth a pin
When I raked together the treasures of the human mind,

---

11. **bier** (bir) *n.:* A coffin and its supporting platform.
12. **Mr. Microcosm:** Man regarded as the epitome of the world.

If at the end I but sit down to find
No new force welling up within.
I have not a hair's breadth more of height,
I am no nearer the Infinite.

MEPHISTOPHELES. My very good sir, you look at
    things   345
Just in the way that people do;
We must be cleverer than that
Or the joys of life will escape from you.
Hell! You have surely hands and feet,
Also a head and you-know-what;
The pleasures I gather on the wing,
Are they less mine? Of course they're not!
Suppose I can afford six stallions,
I can add that horsepower to my score
And dash along and be a proper man
As if my legs were twenty-four.   355
So good-bye to thinking! On your toes!
The world's before us. Quick! Here goes!
I tell you, a chap who's intellectual
Is like a beast on a blasted heath
Driven in circles by a demon
While a fine green meadow lies round beneath.

FAUST. How do we start?

MEPHISTOPHELES.   We just say go—and skip.
But please get ready for this pleasure trip.
    [*Exit* FAUST.]
Only look down on knowledge and reason,
The highest gifts that men can prize,
Only allow the spirit of lies
To confirm you in magic and illusion,
And then I have you body and soul.
Fate has given this man a spirit
Which is always pressing onward, beyond
    control,   350
And whose mad striving overleaps
All joys of the earth between pole and pole.
Him shall I drag through the wilds of life
And through the flats of meaninglessness,
I shall make him flounder and gape and stick
And to tease his insatiableness
Hang meat and drink in the air before his
    watering lips;
In vain he will pray to slake his inner thirst,
And even had he not sold himself to the devil
He would be equally accursed.

Reader's Response *Which, if any, of the sentiments that Faust expresses in the selection do you share? Explain your answer.*

THINKING ABOUT THE SELECTION

Clarifying

1. What are the terms of the agreement between Faust and Mephistopheles?
2. What plans concerning Faust does Mephistopheles convey in his closing monologue?

Interpreting

3. (a) How would you characterize Faust's state of mind in the opening scene? (b) What does he mean when he says that he has discovered "the impossibility of knowledge"? (c) What does he mean when he expresses his desire to "end [his] traffic in words"?
4. Why is Faust so willing to make an arrangement with the Devil?
5. (a) What is Faust's attitude concerning death? (b) What does Mephistopheles mean when, after listening to Faust, he says, "Yet I know someone who failed to drink / A brown juice on a certain night"?
6. Why does Faust question whether a devil can understand a human being?

Enrichment Speaking of *Faust*, Goethe once commented,

> It is not in my line, as a poet, to strive to embody anything *abstract.* I receive in my mind impressions, and those of a sensual, animated, charming, varied, hundredfold kind, just as a lively imagination presented them; and I had, as a poet, nothing more to do than artistically to round off and elaborate such views and impressions, and by means of a lively representation so to bring them forward that others might receive the same impression in hearing or reading my representation of them.

Cooperative Learning Students might enjoy working in groups to create their own stories about a character who bargains with the devil. Divide your class into groups of three of four. Then have the members of each group work together to write their story. When the groups have finished their stories, have them either read them aloud or dramatize them in front of the rest of the class.

Closure and Extension

ANSWERS TO THINKING ABOUT THE SELECTION

1. Mephistopheles will serve Faust until the day on which Faust becomes pleased with himself. On that day Faust will die.
2. Mephistopheles intends to tease Faust's appetite for experience but never let him satisfy it. He is going to drag Faust "through the wilds of life" and do everything he can to torment him.
3. (a) He is in a state of deep despair. (b) Suggested response: Despite all his learning, he feels as if he knows nothing of real value. (c) He wants to abandon his scholarly pursuits.
4. He is so tired of his present life that he is willing to try anything. In addition, the devil offers him earthly joys, which he has never experienced.
5. (a) Suggested response: He is unafraid of death and even claims that he longs for it. (b) He is revealing that he is aware that Faust tried to take his own life but was unable to.

(continued on page 876)

(continued from page 875)

6. Suggested response: Faust believes that the Devil has no appreciation for human emotions.
7. (a) Suggested response: He is a very intelligent man with an unquenchable thirst for knowledge and experience. (b) Suggested response: He is clever and manipulative.
8. (a) Suggested response: Faust is the embodiment of these aspects of Romanticism. (b) Suggested response: The Romantic emphasis on excess and spontaneity is reflected in Faust's behavior.
9. Answers will differ. Students may respond that Faust would be no happier in today's world, because he would still be unable to answer life's ultimate questions.

Challenge If you were a director who was staging a production of *Faust*, whom would you choose to play the role of Faust? Why? Whom would you choose to play the role of Mephistopheles? Why?

ANSWERS TO ANALYZING LITERATURE

1. Suggested response: In the legend, Faust agrees to sell his soul to the devil. In Goethe's play, Faust agrees that he will die only when he is pleased with himself.
2. (a) Suggested response: Unlike Dr. Faustus, who is in search of power, Faust wants only to experience all the joys and sorrows of humanity. (b) Answers may differ. Students should note that Faust's desire reflects the Romantic thirst for experience.
3. Answers will differ. Students may note that people who believe that these types of events can occur would be likely to interpret the work as a warning.

ANSWERS TO UNDERSTANDING LITERATURE

1. *tumult:* agitation; commotion
2. *egoist:* self-centered person; *gratis:* free
3. *insatiableness:* inability to be satisfied

THINKING AND WRITING

Publishing Student Writing You may want to arrange students' papers into a class bulletin-board display.

---

7. (a) How would you characterize Faust based on his comments and actions in this selection? (b) What is revealed about Mephistopheles through his interactions with Faust?
8. The Romantic Movement was characterized by a sense of restlessness accompanied by an unlimited, unquenchable thirst for experience. (a) How are these aspects of Romanticism reflected in this selection? (b) How does the selection reflect the Romantic emphasis on excess and spontaneity?

Applying

9. Explain whether you think that Faust would be more satisfied if he were living in today's world.

ANALYZING LITERATURE

Understanding Legends

The German Faust legend has inspired many literary works, including Goethe's *Faust*. In the original legend, Faust sells his soul to the Devil in exchange for youth, knowledge, and magical powers.
1. How does the agreement that Goethe's Faust makes with Mephistopheles differ from the agreement that Faust makes in the original legend?
2. In Christopher Marlowe's *The Tragical History of the Life and Death of Doctor Faustus*, a literary work based on the Faust legend written during the Renaissance, Faust is driven to sell his soul to the Devil by his desire to attain unlimited power through black magic. (a) How does this desire differ from that of Goethe's Faust? (b) What do the different impulses that led Marlowe's Faustus and Goethe's Faust to make the pact suggest about the times each writer lived in?
3. At the time of its origin, the Faust legend was widely believed to be true. In contrast, when Goethe's *Faust* was published, few people believed that the type of events it depicted could actually happen. How do you think people's beliefs concerning the plausibility of the events might affect the way in which they respond to a work such as Goethe's *Faust*?

UNDERSTANDING LANGUAGE

Using Context Clues

Some of the words that Louis MacNeice uses in his translation of *Faust* may not be familiar to you. In many cases, however, you may be able to determine the meanings of unfamiliar words by examining the context in which they are used.

Try to define each of the italicized words by looking at their context. Then check your definitions in a dictionary.
1. "Whereas that *tumult* in my soul / Was stilled by sweet familiar chimes / Which *cozened* the child that yet was in me / With echoes of more happy times, . . ."
2. "No, no, the devil is an *egoist* / And ready to do nothing *gratis* / Which is to benefit a stranger."
3. "I shall make him flounder and gape and stick / And to tease his *insatiableness* / Hang meat and drink in the air before his watering lips; . . ."

THINKING AND WRITING

Planning an Adaptation

Imagine that you are a film producer who has been hired to create a film adaptation of Goethe's *Faust* set in contemporary America. Then prepare a memorandum to a screenwriter explaining the ways in which the original text should be changed to fit a modern setting. Your memorandum should focus only on the parts of Goethe's poetic drama you have read. Begin by thinking about the ways in which Faust's feelings and desires would be different if he were living today. Then think about how the dialogue and actions should be changed to appeal to a contemporary audience. Should Faust and Mephistopheles be portrayed in a more amusing manner? Should more action be included? Should any special effects be used? Once you have a good idea of the changes that should be made, begin writing your memo. Make sure you explain each change as clearly and concisely as possible. After you have finished writing, have one of your classmates read your memo to see if your instructions are clear. Finally, keeping your classmate's comments in mind, revise your memo and prepare a final copy.

Poetry

SPRING AT BARBIZON
Jean-François Millet

ALEXANDER PUSHKIN

1799–1837

Alexander Pushkin's brief life was abruptly ended when he was mortally wounded in a duel. Despite its apparent pointlessness, Pushkin's violent death seems to be in some respects a fitting end to the life of this brilliant yet extremely rebellious poet. Throughout most of his life, Pushkin aroused controversy because of his political beliefs and his unrestrained behavior in both his public and private lives. His poetic talents, however, were never a matter of dispute, and he is now widely regarded as the finest poet Russia has ever produced.

Pushkin was born in Moscow into an aristocratic family. Because of his parents' busy social schedule, he was often cared for by his grandmother and his nurse, Arina Rodionovna. These women made contributions to his education that would later influence his poetry: His grandmother taught him the history of his ancestors, and his nurse told him stories from Russian folklore.

After graduating from school, Pushkin went into government service, accepting a post in the foreign office at St. Petersburg. There he aroused the suspicion of the government by associating with political rebels and writing poems in which he called for democratic rule and an end to serfdom. In 1820 the government acted upon its suspicion by reappointing Pushkin to a post in a remote province in southern Russia. During the five years Pushkin spent in southern Russia, he enhanced his reputation as a writer by producing a series of Romantic poems known as the "southern cycle," and he began working on his masterpiece, the verse novel *Yevgeny Onegin* (1833). At the same time, he infuriated his superiors by behaving in an unrestrained and sometimes violent manner. Pushkin's behavior resulted in his dismissal from civil service in 1824 and his banishment to his family's estate near the city of Pskov (pskôf).

While living at the estate, Pushkin was extremely lonely and unhappy. Yet his isolation enabled him to channel most of his energy into his writing. He spent much of his time interacting with the peasants who lived on the estate, learning about their life styles and absorbing their legends and folk songs. He also wrote a number of his finest poems, including "The Bridegroom" (1825), which clearly reflect the influence of both peasant life and Russian folklore.

In 1826, following the ascension of Czar Nicholas I, who admired Pushkin's writing, Pushkin was allowed to return to Moscow. Although the new czar promised governmental reforms, he refused to abandon the government's practice of censoring literary works. With the czar himself serving as Pushkin's censor, Pushkin once again became the object of the government's distrust and was eventually put under police surveillance. Despite the limitations placed on his personal and literary freedom, Pushkin's talent as a writer continued to blossom. In the late 1820's and early 1830's, he produced some of his finest works, including his collection of prose tales *Tales of the Late I. P. Belkin* (1830).

After marrying Natalya Goncharova in 1831, Pushkin moved to St. Petersburg and grudgingly returned to government service. His new wife had little interest in his literary pursuits and pushed him into becoming involved in the social life of the Imperial Court. Pushkin came to hate his new life, and his rebellion against it ultimately resulted in the duel that cost him his life.

GUIDE FOR INTERPRETING

The Bridegroom

(continued from bottom of page)

Commentary

The Folk Ballad and the Literary Ballad. Alexander Pushkin was a master of **narrative poetry,** or poetry that tells a story. A number of his poems, including "The Bridegroom," are examples of a specific type of narrative poetry known as the **literary ballad.** The term literary ballad is used to distinguish ballads written by known authors from **folk ballads,** or those that are composed anonymously and are part of an oral tradition. Aside from the issue of authorship and the means by which they are transmitted, however, there is virtually no distinction between the two types of ballads. Literary ballads are generally inspired by and written in imitation of folk ballads. For example, "The Bridegroom" was inspired by the Russian folk ballads that Pushkin learned during his years of exile on his family's estate.

Folk ballads are an important part of the literary heritages of almost every culture. In most cultures the folk ballad was one of the earliest literary forms, thriving in the centuries preceding the development of written literature. Passed from person to person and generation to generation by word of mouth, folk ballads were usually intended to be sung and frequently included refrains, or repeated lines or stanzas, that made them easier to remember. Developing out of the legends, beliefs, and experiences of common people, folk ballads often reveal a great deal about the cultures from which they originated. Generally, folk ballads are composed in simple, straightforward language and focus on situations from the everyday lives of common people. Among the most common themes of folk ballads are physical courage, disappointed love, jealousy, and revenge.

Folk ballads also tend to share a number of other common elements. In most folk ballads, little attention is paid to characterization and description. In addition, the story of a folk ballad is usually developed to a great extent through dialogue, and the transitions between the episodes in a folk ballad tend to be abrupt. Finally, many folk ballads end with a summary stanza that draws the story to a close.

As you read "The Bridegroom," notice the ways in which it resembles a typical folk ballad. Also look for what the poem reveals about traditional Russian culture.

Writing

What are dreams? In the past, people thought that dreams foretold the future or revealed secrets of past events. Freewrite, exploring your thoughts on the nature of dreams.

---

probably old British and American standards, such as "Barbara Allen," "Lord Randall," and "The Golden Valley."

You might also want to bring in recordings of ballads by twentieth-century songwriters such as Bob Dylan and Woodie Guthrie. Explain that these ballads are similar to literary ballads in that they are by known authors.

Writing/Prior Knowledge Before students begin freewriting, have students discuss some of the more interesting or unusual dreams they have had.

Teaching Tenth-Grade Students Have tenth-grade students read the selection aloud in class. Explain that before the advent of television and movies, folk ballads often served as popular entertainment. As students read, have them consider how successful as popular entertainment this ballad might have been to a nineteenth-century audience.

ESL Teaching Strategy Because folk ballads reveal a great deal about the cultures from which they orginate, it might be interesting to have ESL students recite or discuss some of the folk ballads of their native lands.

Vocabulary

Preteach the following vocabulary words:
distraught (dis trôt´) *adj.*: Extremely troubled
brocaded (brō kād´ əd) *adj.*: Made from rich cloth with a raised design
oppresses (ə pres´ əz) *v.*: Worries; troubles
clamor (klam´ ər) *n.*: Uproar
betokens (bi tō k´nz) *v.*: Indicates
throng (thrôn) *n.*: A large crowd
blanches (blanch´ əz) *v.*: Turns pale

Spelling Tip Call students' attention to the double *p* and the double *s* in the word *oppresses.*

Support Material

Teaching Portfolio
Teacher Backup, p. 1047
Usage and Mechanics Worksheet, p. 1051
Vocabulary Check, p. 1052
Analyzing Literature Worksheet, *Understanding Ballads*, p. 1053
Language Worksheet, *Appreciating the Effects of Verbs and Participles*, p. 1054
Selection Test, pp. 1055–1056

Art Transparency 11
Bride and Groom by Amedeo Modigliani.

Literary Focus A way to introduce folk and literary ballads is to play recordings of ballads for your students. Nearly every folk singer includes folk ballads in his or her repertoire. It is possible to find recordings of folk ballads from nations throughout the world and from a variety of regions of the United States. The easiest ones to find are

Motivation/Prior Knowledge
Have students imagine what it would be like to be forced to marry someone they were afraid of. How might they try to get out of this situation? What would they do if they could not get out of it?

Purpose-Setting Question
What happened during the three days Natasha was missing?

Universal Themes Writers from a wide range of cultures and literary eras have expressed the need for people to convey their fears. For example, in his story "A Breath of Air" (page 1134), the Italian writer Luigi Pirandello depicts a grand-father who is unable to express his fear that his family is witholding important information from him.

Master Teacher Note Pushkin wrote "The Bridegroom" while living in isolation on his parents' estate. Although it is possible to overemphasize external influences on the poet's choice of subject, you might want to re-mind students of where Pushkin was living at the time he wrote the poem. As they read the poem, have them speculate about Pushkin's state of mind at the time he wrote the poem.

To set the appropriate mood for the poem, place Art Transparency 11, *Bride and Groom* by Amedeo Modigliani, on an over-head projector. Have students express their reactions to the paint-ing and discuss their impressions of the subjects of the painting

1 Reading Strategy Have students note the poem's title and have them keep it in mind as they are reading. Ask them to consider why Pushkin entitled the poem "The Bridegroom," considering that most of the poem focuses on the bride.

2 Discussion What do students think might have happened to Natasha? Why does she choose not to tell her parents about it?

3 Discussion Have students dis-cuss why Natasha might be so frightened by the handsome man in the *troika*.

The Bridegroom

Alexander Pushkin

translated by D. M. Thomas

For three days Natasha,
The merchant's daughter,
Was missing. The third night,
She ran in, distraught.
5   Her father and mother
Plied her with questions.
She did not hear them,
She could hardly breathe.

Stricken with foreboding[1]
10 They pleaded, got angry,
But still she was silent;
At last they gave up.
Natasha's cheeks regained
Their rosy color.
15 And cheerfully again
She sat with her sisters.

Once at the shingle-gate
She sat with her friends
—And a swift troika[2]
20 Flashed by before them;
A handsome young man
Stood driving the horses;
Snow and mud went flying,
Splashing the girls.

25 He gazed as he flew past,
And Natasha gazed.
He flew on. Natasha froze.
Headlong she ran home.
"It was he! It was he!"

30 She cried. "I know it!
I recognized him! Papa,
Mama, save me from him!"

Full of grief and fear,
They shake their heads, sighing.
35 Her father says: "My child,
Tell me everything.
If someone has harmed you,
Tell us . . . even a hint."
She weeps again and
40 Her lips remain sealed.

The next morning, the old
Matchmaking woman
Unexpectedly calls and
Sings the girl's praises;
45 Says to the father: "You
Have the goods and I
A buyer for them:
A handsome young man.

"He bows low to no one,
50 He lives like a lord
With no debts nor worries;
He's rich and he's generous,
Says he will give his bride,
On their wedding-day,
55 A fox-fur coat, a pearl,
Gold rings, brocaded dresses.

"Yesterday, out driving,
He saw your Natasha;
Shall we shake hands
60 And get her to church?"
The woman starts to eat
A pie, and talks in riddles,

---

1. **foreboding** (fôr bōd′ iŋ) *n.*: A prediction or presentiment.
2. **troika** (troi′ kə) *n.*: A Russian carriage or sleigh drawn by a specially trained team of three horses abreast.

4 Literary Focus Have students discuss what this stanza suggests about Russian customs at the time of the poem. What does it suggest about the status of young women in Russia at the time?

5 Discussion Have students dis-cuss whether these characteris-tics are any indication that the handsome young man will be a good husband.

THE LIGHTS OF MARRIAGE
Marc Chagall
Kunsthaus, Zurich

While the poor girl
Does not know where to look.

"Agreed," says her father;
"Go in happiness
To the altar, Natasha;
It's dull for you here;
A swallow should not spend
All its time singing,
It's time for you to build
A nest for your children."

Natasha leaned against
The wall and tried
To speak—but found herself
Sobbing; she was shuddering
And laughing. The matchmaker
Poured out a cup of water,
Gave her some to drink,
Splashed some in her face.

Her parents are distressed.
Then Natasha recovered,

And calmly she said:
"Your will be done. Call
85 My bridegroom to the feast,
Bake loaves for the whole world,
Brew sweet mead[3] and call
The law to the feast."

"Of course, Natasha, angel!
90 You know we'd give our lives
To make you happy!"
They bake and they brew;
The worthy guests come,
The bride is led to the feast,
95 Her maids sing and weep;
Then horses and a sledge[4]

With the groom—and all sit.
The glasses ring and clatter,
The toasting-cup is passed

8

---

3. mead (mēd) *n*.: A beverage made of fermented honey and water.
4. sledge (slej) *n*.: Sleigh.

Commentary

Pushkin's Poetic Forms The critic Janko Lavrin noted that in discussing Pushkin "one is struck by the difficulty of finding a definition which would cover all his works. A classicist, a romantic, and a realist in turns, he defies any attempts at being reduced to a single literary school or to a specified 'ism.'" Lavrin points out that in matters of prosody Pushkin followed the lead of Mikhail Lomonosov, a scientist, scholar, and poet, who introduced tonic meter as the most suitable medium for the Russian language. "Pushkin," wrote Lavrin, "brought the medium to the height of flexibility and perfection.

Parallel with that there was a less conspicuous trend modeled on the rhythm of the folk-song or even more frequently of the pseudo-folk-song, which created a tradition of its own. . . . But whatever he used, he . . . imparted to his poems a new inflection, a new texture, and above all a conversational ease, combined with a short-hand realism. . . ."

9 **Reading Strategy** Have students answer the bridegroom's question based on the information that has been provided up to this point.

10 **Discussion** Have students discuss the impression of this setting that the bride conveys. Does it seem ominous? Why or why not?

11 **Discussion** Do students think these furnishings seem out of place in a forest hut? If so, how do they explain them?

12 **Reading Strategy** Have students predict the events that will follow the entrance of the girl and the twelve young men.

13 **Literary Focus** As is typically the case with ballads, a great deal of information has been left out of "The Bridegroom." Have students speculate about the identity of the beautiful girl. Why is she there? Why is she sad? Explain to students that there are no right or wrong answers to these questions.

14 **Discussion** Are students surprised by this turn of events? Why or why not? How does it help explain the state of terror that has plagued the bride throughout the poem? What is the identity of the eldest brother?

100 From hand to hand in tumult,[5]
The guests are drunk.

BRIDEGROOM
"Friends, why is my fair bride
Sad, why is she not
Feasting and serving?"

105 The bride answers the groom:
"I will tell you why
As best I can. My soul
Knows no rest, day and night
I weep; an evil dream
110 Oppresses me." Her father
Says: "My dear child, tell us
What your dream is."

"I dreamed," she says, "that I
Went into a forest,
115 It was late and dark;
The moon was faintly
Shining behind a cloud;
I strayed from the path;
Nothing stirred except
120 The tops of the pine-trees.

"And suddenly, as if
I was awake, I saw
A hut. I approach the hut
And knock at the door
125 —Silence. A prayer on my lips
I open the door and enter.
A candle burns. All
Is silver and gold."

BRIDEGROOM
"What is bad about that?
130 It promises wealth."

BRIDE
"Wait, sir, I've not finished.
Silently I gazed
On the silver and gold,
The cloths, the rugs, the silks,

135 From Novgorod,[6] and I
Was lost in wonder.

"Then I heard a shout
And a clatter of hoofs . . .
Someone has driven up
140 To the porch. Quickly
I slammed the door and hid
Behind the stove. Now
I hear many voices . . .
Twelve young men come in,

145 "And with them is a girl,
Pure and beautiful.
They've taken no notice
Of the ikons,[7] they sit
To the table without
150 Praying or taking off
Their hats. At the head,
The eldest brother,

At his right, the youngest;
At his left, the girl.
155 Shouts, laughs, drunken clamor . . ."

BRIDEGROOM
"That betokens merriment."

BRIDE
"Wait, sir, I've not finished.
The drunken din goes on
And grows louder still.
160 Only the girl is sad.

"She sits silent, neither
Eating nor drinking;
But sheds tears in plenty;
The eldest brother
165 Takes his knife and, whistling,
Sharpens it; seizing her by
The hair he kills her
And cuts off her right hand."

---

5. tumult (tōō′ mult) *n*.: Noisy commotion.

---

6. Novgorod (nôv′ gồ rồt′): A city in the northwestern part of the Soviet Union.
7. ikons (ī′ känz): icons, images of Jesus, Mary, a saint, or another sacred Christian religious figure.

Closure and Extension

ANSWERS TO THINKING ABOUT THE SELECTION

1. (a) She was lost in a forest, where she witnessed a murder, leaving her very upset. (b) Suggested response: She was probably afraid that no one would believe her, or that one of the twelve brothers would harm her. (c) It is revealed at the wedding.
2. (a) It is ironic that the murderer wants to marry Natasha, who witnessed the crime. (b) Suggested response: She has a matter-of-fact, callous attitude toward the marriage. She regards Natasha as a piece of property rather than as a person.
3. (a) Suggested response: He feels that it is time for Natasha to have children of her own. (b) Suggested response: He is suggesting that there is a time in people's lives when they have to give up their freedom and settle down.
4. (a) She knows that the man she is going to marry is a murderer. (b) Suggested response: It was not a dream. She actually witnessed these events.
5. Suggested response: He is trying to prevent his actions from being revealed.

"Why," says the groom, "this
Is nonsense! Believe me,
My love, your dream is not evil."
She looks him in the eyes.
"And from whose hand
Does this ring come?"
The bride said. The whole throng
Rose in the silence.

With a clatter the ring
Falls, and rolls along
The floor. The groom blanches,
180 Trembles. Confusion . . .
"Seize him!" the law commands.
He's bound, judged, put to death.
Natasha is famous!
Our song at an end.

15

Reader's Response *Did you find this poem gripping and suspenseful? Why or why not? Were you surprised by the outcome? Explain.*

THINKING ABOUT THE SELECTION

Interpreting

1. (a) Where was Natasha during the three days she was missing, and why was she distraught when she returned? (b) Why does she refuse to reveal this information to her parents? (c) How is the information eventually revealed?
2. (a) What is ironic, or surprising, about the matchmaker's visit? (b) How would you describe the matchmaker's attitude toward the arranged marriage?
3. (a) What seems to be the father's motivation for agreeing to the marriage? (b) What does the father mean by the metaphor, "A swallow should not spend / All its time singing"?
4. (a) Why does Natasha become hysterical when her father and the matchmaker are arranging her wedding? (b) Do you think Natasha actually had the "evil dream" she describes? Explain your answer.
5. Why does the bridegroom repeatedly interrupt Natasha to offer interpretations of her "dream"?
6. What is the significance of the fact that the men in Natasha's story "take no notice / Of the ikons"?
7. (a) How does Natasha's behavior at the end of the poem contrast with her behavior at the beginning? (b) Why does she become famous?

Applying

8. Until fairly recently, arranged marriages were common in a variety of cultures. (a) What do you see as the main advantages and disadvantages of arranged marriages? (b) Explain whether you think the practice of arranging marriages could ever work in our society.

ANALYZING LITERATURE

Understanding Ballads

Like most literary ballads, "The Bridegroom" exhibits a number of the common elements and characteristics of traditional folk ballads. For example, as in most folk ballads, the story of "The Bridegroom" is developed to a large extent through dialogue.

1. How would you describe the language used in "The Bridegroom," and why is it appropriate for a literary ballad?
2. In most folk ballads, little attention is paid to characterization and description. Does this hold true in "The Bridegroom"? Explain your answer.
3. What elements or characteristics of traditional Russian society does the poem reveal? Support your answer.

THINKING AND WRITING

Comparing and Contrasting Ballads

Write a paper in which you compare and contrast "The Bridegroom" with a literary ballad by a writer from a different culture. With a group of classmates, look for other examples of ballads. Examples include *The Rime of the Ancient Mariner* and "La Belle Dame sans Merci" by English Romantic poets Samuel Taylor Coleridge and John Keats. After your group has gathered a number of different examples, choose the one that you like best and work individually to write your paper.

HEINRICH HEINE

More About the Author Throughout his life Heine felt like an outsider. Brought up as a Jew in a nation plagued by anti-Semitism, Heine developed an inescapable sense of alienation at an early age. According to the critic S. S. Prawer, Heine considered himself "a Jew among Germans, a German among Frenchman, a Helene among Jews, a rebel among the bourgeois, and a conservative among revolutionaries." Have students discuss how Heine's sense of isolation and alienation might have shaped his writing. Then have them come up with examples of other writers who have experienced a similar sense of alienation.

Critical Evaluation In the year Heine died, the English novelist George Eliot wrote an essay about him in which she called Heine "a surpassing lyric poet, who has uttered our feelings for us in delicious song; a humorist, who touches leaden folly with the magic wand of his fancy, and transmutes it into the fine gold of art—who sheds his sunny smile on human tears, and makes them a beauteous rainbow on the cloudy background of life; a wit, who holds in his mighty hand the most scorching lightings of satire; an artist... in spite of all the charges against him...who has spoken wise and brave words on behalf of his fellow men...."

1797–1856

The German poet Heinrich Heine (hīn′ riH hī′ nə) filled the shoes of two different writers. On one hand, he was a brilliant love poet whose works have been set to music by such famous composers as Robert Schumann and Franz Schubert. On the other hand, he was a gifted satirist and political writer whose fierce attacks on repression and prejudice made him a highly controversial figure in his native land.

The son of a struggling Jewish merchant, Heine was born in the city of Düsseldorf. Throughout his childhood he was heavily influenced by his generous but strict uncle, Salomon Heine, a wealthy banker. With his uncle's financial support, Heine received a university education and earned a degree in law in 1825. He never practiced law, however, choosing to ignore his uncle's wishes and to pursue a career as a writer. In 1827 he gained prominence as a poet with the publication of *The Book of Songs* (1827), a collection of poetry still regarded by many readers as his finest work. Reflecting the influence of the Romantic poets, the love poems in this collection were inspired by Heine's deep attachment to his uncle's daughter, Amalie, whose fear of her father's reaction made it impossible for her to return Heine's affection.

Attracted by the continuing political upheaval in France, Heine moved to Paris in 1831 and made it his permanent home. While witnessing the establishment of limited democracy in France, he became increasingly critical of the political and social situation in Germany. After he published his criticisms in *The Romantic School* (1833–1835) and "On the History of Religion and Philosophy in Germany" (1834–1835), his popularity was overshadowed by outrage in his native land. In fact, the German government was so angered by these works that it imposed a ban on all his books and made it clear that he was no longer welcome to return to his homeland.

In addition to angering the German government and people, Heine's works had infuriated his uncle, and by the time his uncle died in 1844, he had almost completely cut Heine out of his will. Badly in need of money, Heine began a highly publicized legal battle over his uncle's estate. The case ended in a settlement that allotted Heine more of the estate but granted his uncle's family the right to censor his works.

By the late 1840's, all of Heine's other difficulties were eclipsed by his failing health. Having contracted a progressive spinal disease, Heine had become paralyzed and had gone partially blind. Throughout the final eight years of his life, he was bedridden and in extreme pain. Yet he continued writing until his death.

Even after his death, Heine remained an object of controversy in Germany. Riots broke out in several German cities when attempts were made to erect monuments in his honor; and when the Nazis assumed power in the 1930's, many of his works were suppressed and those that were published were attributed to an unknown author. In the aftermath of World War II, Heine has also become a controversial figure in other European countries and in the United States, because of the similarities of his political beliefs to Marxism. Yet despite all the controversy that has surrounded him, he is still generally regarded as one of the finest writers of the nineteenth century.

Objectives

Thematic
To understand the alluring power of beauty

Skills
1 To write a lyric poem
2 To understand lyric poetry

GUIDE FOR INTERPRETING

The Lorelei; The Lotus Flower

Commentary

Lyric Poetry. Lyric poems, or lyrics, are brief poems that express the writer's personal thoughts and feelings. As the origin of the word *lyric* reveals, these poems were originally written to be sung to the accompaniment of a stringed musical instrument called a lyre. While most lyrics are no longer set to music, the poems still tend to be melodic, like songs, and generally focus on producing a single, unified effect.

The lyric form enjoyed tremendous popularity in Europe during the Middle Ages, when lyric poems were composed and sung by traveling poets known as troubadours. During the Renaissance, European poets continued to use the lyric form, although their lyrics were often not meant to be set to music. After declining in popularity during the Age of Rationalism, the lyric reemerged as a dominant poetic form during the late eighteenth and early nineteenth centuries. By completely abandoning musical accompaniments and focusing on making their poems as powerful, energetic, and evocative as possible, the poets of this period raised the lyric form to new heights. One of the most talented lyric poets of this time was Heinrich Heine. Although Heine did not write his lyrics with the intention of setting them to music, he frequently used the rhythmical patterns of popular folk songs, and a number of famous composers were so inspired by his poems that they wrote musical accompaniments to many of them.

Like countless other lyrics from various cultures and literary eras, many of Heine's lyrics focus on the subject of love. However, there is often a current of irony and cynicism that runs beneath the surface of his love poems. As you read the following lyrics by Heine, look for this underlying current of cynicism.

Writing

What types of situations and experiences from your own life might make suitable topics for lyric poetry? List as many appropriate situations and experiences as you can think of. Then jot down some details and images that you might use in a poem about some of these situations and experiences.

Primary Source

While Heine's lyric poems soothed and entertained readers and inspired musicians, his political writing sparked controversy. In the following passage, he presents a grim, disturbing portrait of the future: "Wild, dark times are rumbling toward us. . . . The future smells of Russian leather, of godlessness and of much whipping. I advise our grandchildren to come into the world with very thick skins on their backs."

Literary Focus If students have difficulty with the definition of a lyric poem, you may want to point out that the term as it is used today is very broad. Any poem that is fairly short and is not a narrative can be classified as a lyric. Given this broad definition, have students name lyric poems that they read in previous literature courses.

Writing/Prior Knowledge Before students prepare their lists, you might want to have a class discussion about the types of situations and experiences that make ideal topics for lyric poetry.

Teaching Tenth-Grade Students In "The Lotus Flower," Heine develops an extended metaphor. Before reading this poem, you may want to take some time to make sure tenth-grade students have a clear sense of what a metaphor is. If they seem uncomfortable with this term, you may want to have them read or review the information about metaphors in the Guide for Interpreting on page 99.

ESL Teaching Strategy If you have any Asian students, have them discuss what they know about the symbolic meaning of the lotus flower in their culture of origin.

> ### Vocabulary
> Preteach the following vocabulary words:
> devoured (di vourd´) *v.*: Consumed or destroyed with devastating force
> wooer (wo͞o´ ər) *n.*: Suitor
> mutely (myo͞ot´ lē) *adv.*: Silently
> exhales (eks hālz´) *v.*: Breathes out

Support Material

Teaching Portfolio
Teacher Backup, p. 1057
Usage and Mechanics Worksheet, p. 1061
Vocabulary Check, p. 1062
Analyzing Literature Worksheet, *Understanding Lyric Poetry*, p. 1063
Critical Thinking and Reading Work-

sheet, *Appreciating Concrete Words and Images*, p. 1064
Selection Test, pp. 1065–1066

Spelling Tip Make sure students note the double *l* in both *enthralling* and *impelled.*

Presentation

Motivation/Prior Knowledge If your students have studied mythology, you can lead into "The Lorelei" by discussing the three sirens from Greek mythology. These sea nymphs lived on an island surrounded by dangerous rocks. They sang so enchantingly that sailors who heard them were lured toward them until the sailors' ships were destroyed by the rocks. In the *Odyssey*, Odysseus thwarted them by having himself lashed to the mast and plugging the ears of his men. After students have read Heine's poem, have them compare the lorelei with the sirens.

Purpose-Setting Question Why is the boatman unable to resist the lorelei's song?

Master Teacher Note "The Lorelei," which was set to music by Friedrich Schiller, has achieved the status of a familiar German folk song, comparable to Robert Burns's "Auld Lang Syne" in English. Your school's music department or foreign language department may have a recording of the song in German. If so, see if you can borrow it and play it for your students.

1 Discussion Have students discuss the images in this stanza that convey the lorelei's physical appeal.

2 Discussion Does it seem to students that the Lorelei recognizes her destructive powers? If she does, why does she continue to use them?

Closure and Extension

ANSWERS TO THINKING ABOUT THE SELECTION

1. (a) Suggested response: The Romantic appreciation for nature is reflected in the idyllic description of the setting in the second stanza. (b) Suggested response: The poem originates from the speaker's sadness and his memory of a legendary tale.
2. (a) Suggested response: The lorelei is beautiful and irresistible. (b) Suggested response: Heine describes the lorelei as "more lovely than a vi-

The Lorelei

Heinrich Heine

translated by Aaron Kramer

I cannot explain the sadness
That's fallen on my breast.
An old, old fable haunts me,
And will not let me rest.

5 The air grows cool in the twilight,
And softly the Rhine[1] flows on;
The peak of a mountain sparkles
Beneath the setting sun.

More lovely than a vision,
10 A girl sits high up there;
Her golden jewelry glistens,
She combs her golden hair.

With a comb of gold she combs it,
And sings an evensong;
15 The wonderful melody reaches
A boat, as it sails along.

The boatman hears, with an anguish
More wild than was ever known;
He's blind to the rocks around him;
20 His eyes are for her alone.

—At last the waves devoured
The boat, and the boatman's cry;
And this she did with her singir.g,
The golden Lorelei.

_____
1. Rhine (rīn): A river in western Europe.

Reader's Response *How do you envision the lorelei? Explain. What is it about this vision that is so alluring and haunting?*

THINKING ABOUT THE SELECTION

Interpreting

1. Like most of Heine's early poems, "The Lorelei" contains many elements of Romanticism. (a) How does this poem reflect the Romantic appreciation for nature? (b) How does this poem reflect the Romantic belief that poetry should originate from the heart and the imagination?
2. According to German legend, the lorelei was a sea nymph whose singing on a rock in the Rhine River lured sailors to shipwrecks. (a) What impression of the lorelei does Heine convey in his poem? (b) Which images, or word pictures, contribute to this impression?
3. (a) Why does the lorelei's singing cause the boatman "anguish / More wild than was ever known"? (b) What do you think might be the words that the lorelei sings? Use your imagination since there is no right or wrong answer to this question.

Applying

4. To what types of situations in real life could you relate the legend of the lorelei? Explain your answer.

THINKING AND WRITING

Writing a Lyric Poem

Write a lyric poem in which you express your thoughts and feelings surrounding a situation or experience from your own life. Begin by reviewing the list of situations and experiences that you prepared before reading "The Lorelei." Choose the one you feel would make the best topic for a poem. Then brainstorm for images and details that you can use in your poem. When you write your poem, do not worry about rhythm and rhyme. Instead, focus on conveying your thoughts and emotions as vividly and concretely as possible. After you have finished writing, set your poem aside for a couple of days. Then look at it with a fresh eye and see if there are any changes that you would like to make.

sion" and describes her beautiful hair and jewelry. Her irresistible nature is conveyed through her ability to lure the boatman onto the rocks.

3. (a) Suggested response: The boatman is so attracted to the lorelei and feels such longing that he abandons caution. (b) Answers will differ. Students might suggest that the lorelei invites sailors to come closer.

4. Suggested response: It applies to any

irresistible attraction that is unattainable or destructive or both.

THINKING AND WRITING

Publishing Student Writing
Encourage students to submit their poems to the school literary magazine.

The Lotus Flower

Heinrich Heine

translated by Edgar Alfred Bowring

The lotus flower is troubled
    At the sun's resplendent[1] light;
With sunken head and sadly
    She dreamily waits for the night.

5 The moon appears as her wooer,
    She wakes at his fond embrace;
For him she kindly uncovers
    Her sweetly flowering face.

She blooms and glows and glistens,
10   And mutely gazes above;
She weeps and exhales and trembles
    With love and the sorrows of love.

---

1. resplendent (ri splen′ dənt) *adj.*: Shining brightly; dazzling.

Reader's Response *What emotions does this poem arouse in you? Why?*

THINKING ABOUT THE SELECTION

Interpreting

1. Heine's description of the lotus flower is an example of an extended metaphor, or a well-developed comparison between two seemingly dissimilar things. (a) To what is he comparing the lotus flower? (b) How does he develop the metaphor of the lotus flower throughout the poem? (c) What impression does Heine convey of the lotus flower?
2. What do you think Heine means when he refers to "the sorrows of love" in the final line?
3. (a) What human traits does the lotus flower embody? (b) What people do you know who exhibit these traits?

Applying

4. What are some elements or processes of nature that you might relate to your own experiences? Explain your answer.

ANALYZING LITERATURE

Understanding Lyric Poetry

Both "The Lorelei" and "The Lotus Flower" are examples of Heine's early lyric poetry. As is the case with many of his early lyrics, "The Lorelei" was clearly inspired by his unreturned love for his uncle's daughter.
1. What similarities do you think Heine might have seen between the legend of the lorelei and his situation with his uncle's daughter?
2. What does this poem suggest about Heine's emotions surrounding his cousin's refusal to return his affection?
3. What does "The Lotus Flower" suggest about Heine's attitude toward love?
4. Do you think that "The Lotus Flower" might have been inspired by his experiences with his cousin? Explain your answer.

Presentation

Motivation/Prior Knowledge Have students discuss the types of associations that flowers bring to mind. Make sure they recognize that flowers often evoke feelings of love.

Purpose-Setting Question To what is Heine comparing the lotus flower? What is the effect of this comparison?

1 Discussion Call students' attention to the use of rhyme in this stanza. Considering the importance of sound in lyric poetry, why might lyric poetry be especially difficult to translate?

2 Discussion Draw students' attention to the use of parallelism in this stanza. Have students discuss the effect that is created by Heine's use of parallelism.

Enrichment The German-born novelist and critic Ludwig Lewisohn viewed Heine as a transitional figure between Romanticism and Realism. He wrote: "How could Heine have had the divine simplicity of the earth-rooted poets? He was, as he himself said, the last of the romantics; he was the first of the realists...." Lewisohn goes on to note "the notorious poem endings in which the romantic mood is riven, loveliness flung into the icy light of common day, and the critical intelligence crashes through the poetic vision—these endings are the symbols of the tragic division between Heine himself and rise, by virtue of the potency and magic of his personality, into symbols of the two major moods that in both literature and life struggle for supremacy in modern civilization."

Closure and Extension

ANSWERS TO THINKING ABOUT THE SELECTION

1. (a) He is comparing the lotus flower to a woman in love. (b) During the course of the poem, the lotus flower "wakes," then "blooms and glows and glistens." (c) Suggested response: The lotus flower is beautiful yet shy and fragile.
2. Suggested response: He suggests that love is inevitably tied to sorrow.
3. (a) Suggested response: It embodies love, timidity, beauty, and sensitivity. (b) Answers will differ. Make sure students explain their responses.
4. Answers will differ. One possible response is a thunderstorm that might reflect a student's anger about a specific situation.

ANSWERS TO ANALYZING LITERATURE

1. Suggested response: Like the lorelei, she was distant and unattainable.
2. Suggested response: It suggests that he was wracked with wild anguish and could think of nothing else.
3. Suggested response: It suggests that he had an idealized view of love but recognized its accompanying sorrows.
4. Answers will differ. Students may suggest that they do not think it was inspired by his cousin because the lotus flower reacts positively to the moon's expression of love.

Challenge Compare and contrast the outlook on love presented in "The Lotus Flower" with the outlook presented in "The Lorelei."

VICTOR HUGO

1802–1885

The French Romantic writer Victor Hugo (hyo͞o′ gō) was so popular in his native country that well over a million mourners flooded onto the streets of Paris to pay tribute to him following his death. Because of his beautiful, energetic lyric poetry and his vocal support for a republican government, Hugo attained the status of a hero among the French people. In fact, the French people's admiration for Hugo was probably exceeded only by Hugo's tremendous admiration for himself—a trait reflected in his suggestion that Paris be renamed *Hugo* in his honor.

Hugo was born in Besançon in 1802, the son of a high-ranking officer in Napoleon's army. Because of his father's constant travels with the imperial army, Hugo was frequently uprooted during his childhood, spending periods of time in the cities of Naples, Madrid, and Paris. Of all the places in which he lived, he most appreciated Paris, which he called the birthplace of his soul.

Hugo's talents as a writer were first recognized during his teens when he won a poetry contest sponsored by the French Academy. Encouraged by his success, he began pouring all his energy into writing and studying poetry. In 1819 he founded a literary magazine in which he published many of his own articles about the prominent French poets of the time. Three years later, in the same year in which he married his childhood sweetheart, Adèle Foucher, he published his first collection of poetry, *Odes et poésies diverses*.

Hugo's career as a writer continued to blossom with the publication of his first novel, *Han d'islande* (1823), and two more collections of verse. Continuing to write at a prolific pace, Hugo produced three plays, *Cromwell* (1827), *Marion de Lorme* (1829), and *Hernani* (1830), which earned him public recognition and established him as the leading French Romantic writer. His fame as a writer continued to grow with the publication of one of his most popular novels, *The Hunchback of Notre-Dame* (1831).

Many of Hugo's following works were devoted to expressing his political and social beliefs. The focus of these works hinted that Hugo would soon become more involved with his political concerns than with his writing. In addition to his political involvement, Hugo was distracted from his writing by his overwhelming grief resulting from the drowning of his daughter Léopoldine and by his love affair with the actress Juliette Drouet.

Following the revolution of 1848 and the reestablishment of a republican form of government, Hugo was elected to the post of deputy to the national assembly. In this position he acted as a champion of workers and fought for educational reforms. However, when Napoleon III seized power and appointed himself emperor, Hugo was forced to flee to Brussels. Hugo spent nineteen years in exile, first in Brussels and later on the islands of Jersey and Guernsey. During this period he continued his involvement in politics and produced his most stirring piece of social commentary, the novel *Les Misérables*. Published in 1870, the year in which Napoleon III fell from power and the Third Republic was established, the novel was a tremendous success, and Hugo returned to his homeland in triumph.

Following his return to France, Hugo once again became active in the French government. He was greatly shaken by the deaths of his two sons in 1871 and 1873, however, and his energy and zest for life began to fade. At the age of seventy-six, he became seriously ill. Yet he managed to continue writing until his death.

GUIDE FOR INTERPRETING

from The Expiation

Commentary

Napoleon's Invasion of Russia. An excerpt from Hugo's long poem *The Expiation*, "Russia 1812" depicts the long, tragic retreat of Napoleon's Grand Army following their unsuccessful invasion of Russia in 1812. After waging war throughout Europe, achieving victory in Italy, Austria, and parts of Germany, and building a large and constantly growing empire, Napoleon had set his sights on Russia in the spring of 1812. Tensions had been mounting for several years between the two countries, following Russian czar Alexander I's refusal to aid Napoleon in his ongoing battles with England, Spain, and Portugal. As a result, it was no surprise when 453,000 French troops crossed into Russia and began marching toward Moscow, and the Russians had already prepared a strategy that would ultimately enable them to thwart Napoleon's invasion.

The strategy of the Russian forces was to withdraw as Napoleon's army advanced. In doing so, the Russians avoided becoming involved in major clashes with the French forces, while at the same time luring Napoleon's army farther and farther away from its sources of supplies. When the French army reached Moscow in September of 1812, hoping to find food and shelter, they found instead that it had been abandoned, completely stripped of supplies, and set on fire. Realizing that it would be pointless to continue his advance, Napoleon ordered his troops to retreat.

During their march across the frigid, barren Russian plains, the French soldiers were constantly subjected to attacks by Russian snipers. In addition they were faced with the premature onset of the harsh Russian winter. Forced to trudge through heavy snow without adequate clothing or enough food to eat, countless French soldiers died from frostbite and starvation. By the time the retreat had ended, two thirds of the Grand Army had died and only 10,000 French soldiers remained fit for combat.

The unsuccessful invasion of Russia signaled the beginning of the end for Napoleon and his empire. With his forces severely depleted, Napoleon quickly began to lose hold of the lands he had conquered. In 1815, after being defeated by the British at Waterloo, Napoleon was overthrown and forced into permanent exile on the island of St. Helena.

Writing

How do you imagine the French people might have reacted to Napoleon's unsuccessful invasion of Russia? How do you imagine other European nations might have reacted to the failure of Napoleon's Russian campaign? Freewrite, exploring your responses to these questions.

(continued from bottom of page)
them share any prior knowledge they have of Napoleon and the Napoleonic Wars.

Teaching Tenth-Grade Students Because a knowledge of this poem's historical background is vital to students' understanding of the poem, you may want to have tenth-grade students read aloud the Commentary in class. Then take some time to discuss Napoleon's invasion of Russia, making sure students grasp the devastating impact that the retreat from Moscow had on the French army.

ESL Teaching Strategy Read the poem aloud to ESL students, stopping to define any difficult words. Then ask them to summarize the poem in their own words. This will enable you to correct any misunderstandings ESL students have about the poem.

Vocabulary
Preteach the following vocabulary words:
dregs (dregz) *n.*: A small amount remaining
submerges (səb mʉrj´ əz) *v.*: Covers over
solitude (säl´ ə tōōd´) *n.*: Seclusion, isolation, or remoteness
avenger (ə venj´ er) *n.*: Someone or something that takes vengeance
shroud (shroud) *n.*: A cloth sometimes used to wrap a corpse for burial
obsessed (əb sest´) *v.*: Preoccupied
leaden (led´ ´n) *adj.*: Depressed; dispirited

Spelling Tip Call students attention to the fact that the letter *s* appears three times in the word *obsessed.*

Language Worksheet, *Using Words to Intensify an Effect*, p. 1074
Selection Test, pp. 1075–1076

Literary Focus The great prose classic of the Napoleonic wars is Leo Tolstoy's novel *War and Peace*. Napoleon appears in person only a few times in the novel, but he is never far from the thoughts of most of the characters. The French retreat from Moscow—the subject of the following excerpt from *The Expiation*—is covered vividly and at length in the novel. A moving description of the French retreat also appears in German author Emil Ludwig's biography *Napoleon*.

Napoleon's retreat from Moscow was one of the monumental events in world history, a disaster of epic proportions for the French. It has been portrayed in art, music, and films as well as in literature. Ask students if they can name any of these other works based on the world-shaking events of 1812.

Writing/Prior Knowledge Before students begin freewriting, have *from* # The Expiation

Victor Hugo

Russia 1812

translated by Robert Lowell

The snow fell, and its power was multiplied.
For the first time the Eagle[1] bowed its head—
dark days! Slowly the Emperor returned—
behind him Moscow! Its onion domes still
    burned.
5 The snow rained down in blizzards—rained and
    froze.
Past each white waste a further white waste rose.
None recognized the captains or the flags.
Yesterday the Grand Army, today its dregs!
No one could tell the vanguard[2] from the flanks.
10 The snow! The hurt men struggled from the
    ranks,
hid in the bellies of dead horses, in stacks
of shattered caissons.[3] By the bivouacs,[4]
one saw the picket[5] dying at his post,
still standing in his saddle, white with frost,
15 the stone lips frozen to the bugle's mouth!
Bullets and grapeshot[6] mingled with the snow,
that hailed . . . The Guard, surprised at shivering,
    march
in a dream now; ice rimes the gray mustache.
The snow falls, always snow! The driving mire
20 submerges; men, trapped in that white empire,

have no more bread and march on
    barefoot—gaps!
They were no longer living men and troops,
but a dream drifting in a fog, a mystery,
mourners parading under the black sky.
25 The solitude, vast, terrible to the eye,
was like a mute avenger everywhere,
as snowfall, floating through the quiet air,
buried the huge army in a huge shroud.
Could anyone leave this kingdom? A crowd—
30 each man, obsessed with dying, was alone.
Men slept—and died! The beaten mob sludged
    on,
ditching the guns to burn their carriages.
Two foes. The North, the Czar.[7] The North was
    worse.
In hollows where the snow was piling up,
35 one saw whole regiments fallen asleep.
Attila's dawn, Cannaes of Hannibal![8]
The army marching to its funeral!
Litters, wounded, the dead, deserters—swarms,
crushing the bridges down to cross a stream.
40 They went to sleep ten thousand, woke up four.
Ney,[9] bringing up the former army's rear,
hacked his horse loose from three disputing
    Cossacks[10] . . .

---

1. **Eagle:** The standard of Napoleon's military forces.
2. **vanguard** (van′ gärd′) *n.*: The part of an army that goes ahead of the main body in an advance.
3. **caissons** (kā′ sänz) *n.*: Two-wheeled wagons used for transporting ammunition.
4. **bivouacs** (biv′ waks) *n.*: Temporary encampments.
5. **picket** (pik′ it) *n.*: A soldier responsible for guarding a body of troops from surprise attack.
6. **grapeshot** (grāp shät′) *n.*: A cluster of small iron balls fired from a canon.

---

7. **the Czar** (zär): The Russian emperor.
8. **Attila's . . . Hannibal:** References to the defeat of Attila, the leader of the Huns, at Gaul in A.D. 451, and to the final victory of Hannibal, the Carthagian general who invaded Rome in 218 B.C.
9. **Ney** (nā): The French officer in charge of the defense of the rear in the retreat from Moscow.
10. **Cossacks** (käs′ aks): People of southern Russia, famous as horsemen and cavalrymen.

CAMPAGNE DE FRANCE, 1814 (NAPOLEON'S ARMY IN RETREAT)
Ernest Meissonier

Humanities Note

Fine art, Campagne de France, 1814 by Ernest Meissonier. Meissonier (1815–1891) was a renowned French painter, sculptor, etcher, and lithographer. Although influenced by the Dutch artists of the seventeenth century, his detailed, precise, and meticulously researched work reflects the scientific spirit of his own age. He often painted military subjects, producing numerous depictions of Napoleon's various campaigns. This painting, which depicts the French army in retreat near the end of Napoleon's reign, is considered one of Meissonier's greatest works.

You might want to use the following questions to discuss the art:

1. How does the painting convey the fact that Napoleon's army is in retreat?
2. How would you describe the mood, or atmosphere, of the painting?
3. How does the mood of this painting mirror that of Hugo's poem?
4. How does this portrayal of Napoleon compare with other depictions of Napoleon you have seen?

Primary Source

Charles Baudelaire, another great French poet who was a younger contemporary of Hugo, greatly admired Hugo. "Never was royalty more legitimate," he wrote in an 1861 essay, "more natural, more acclaimed by gratitude....When one recalls what French poetry was before he appeared, and what a rejuvenation it has undergone since he came...."

Baudelaire marveled at the range of Hugo's subject matter: "As for love, war, family pleasures, the sorrows of the poor, national splendors, all that which is peculiar to man and which constitutes the domain of the genre painter and the history painter, what have we seen that is richer and more concrete than the lyrical poetry of Victor Hugo?"

Elsewhere in the essay, Baudelaire touches on the magnitude and nature of Hugo's vision: "The excessive, the immense are the natural domain of Victor Hugo; he moves in it as if in his native atmosphere. The genius which he has always displayed in painting *all the monstrosity* surrounding man is truly prodigious."

All night, the *qui vive?*[11] The alert! Attacks;
retreats! White ghosts would wrench away our
  guns,

3 45 or we would see dim, terrible squadrons,
circles of steel, whirlpools of savages,
rush sabering through the camp like dervishes.[12]
And in this way, whole armies died at night.

The Emperor was there, standing—he saw.
50 This oak already trembling from the ax,
watched his glories drop from him branch by
  branch:
chiefs, soldiers. Each one had his turn and
  chance—

4 they died! Some lived. These still believed his star,
and kept their watch. They loved the man of war,

---

11. *qui vive?* (kē vēv): "Who lives?" (French).
12. dervishes (dɜr′ vish əz) *n.*: Muslims dedicated to lives of
poverty and chastity.

55 this small man with his hands behind his back,
whose shadow, moving to and fro, was black
behind the lighted tent. Still believing, they
accused their destiny of *lèse-majesté*.[13]
His misfortune had mounted on their back.
60 The man of glory shook. Cold stupefied[14]
him, then suddenly he felt terrified.
Being without belief, he turned to God:
"God of armies, is this the end?" he cried.
And then at last the expiation[15] came,
65 as he heard someone call him by his name,
someone half-lost in shadow, who said, "No,
Napoleon." Napoleon understood,
restless, bareheaded, leaden, as he stood
before his butchered legions in the snow.

---

13. *lèse-majesté* (lez ma zhes tā′): "Injured majesty" or
"treason" (French).
14. stupefied (stoo′ pə fīd′) *v.*: Stunned; made dull or
lethargic.
15. expiation (ek′ spē ā′ shən) *n.*: Reparation; atonement.

Reader's Response *Do you find Hugo's
descriptions of the suffering of the French
forces convincing? Why or why not? What
emotions do these descriptions arouse? Why?*

---

3 Literary Focus Remind students that during the retreat the French troops were constantly subjected to attacks by Russian snipers. How do students think these attacks might have affected the morale of the French soldiers?

4 Discussion Have students discuss how it could be possible that the French soldiers still believe in and love Napoleon, in spite of the disastrous outcome of the Russian campaign.

5 Discussion Have students explain what Hugo means when he writes "at last the expiation came."

Cultural Note Many British and American writers have expressed admiration for Victor Hugo. In fact, the British poet Alfred, Lord Tennyson was so drawn to Hugo's writing that he wrote a poem in Hugo's honor entitled "To Victor Hugo."

Cooperative Learning Students might be interested in learning more about the retreat from Russia or about another major event in the Napoleonic Wars. Divide your class into groups of three or four. Then have each group research a specific event that occurred during the Napoleonic Wars. After the groups have finished their research, have them present their findings to the rest of the class.

Enrichment In his critical study of Victor Hugo, John Porter Huston summarizes the poet's early reflections on his art: "All poetry begins in question of form, language, and style, and the state of the language at the time of a poet's beginnings can be favorable, as during the Baroque period, or unpropitious, as after Racine. Form cannot be separated from idea, expression from content. Hugo steers clearly away from all emotional fallacies about the nature of art and goes beyond the often superficial (if essential) distinction between the Romantic and the Classic."

Interpreting

1. (a) What does Hugo mean when he writes that the snow's "power was multiplied" (line 1)? (b) What is the effect of his frequent repetition of the word *snow* in the first stanza?
2. How does Hugo emphasize the coldness and barrenness of the landscape?
3. What does he mean when he writes, "The solitude, vast, terrible to the eye, / was like a mute avenger everywhere"?
4. (a) At the beginning of the second stanza, what metaphor does Hugo use in describing the downfall of the French army? (b) Why is this metaphor appropriate?
5. Considering that Napoleon is described as being "without belief," why is it ironic, or surprising, that Napoleon questions God about his fate?
6. (a) What other examples of irony can you find in Hugo's poem? (b) How do they add to the poem's impact?
7. (a) What seems to be Hugo's attitude toward Napoleon? (b) How is his attitude revealed?
8. What overall impression is Hugo trying to convey in this poem? Support your answer with details from the poem.
9. (a) How does Hugo's method of depicting the French retreat compare to the manner in which a painter might depict the same event? (b) How does Hugo's depiction compare to the manner in which a filmmaker might depict the event?

Applying

10. (a) What impact, if any, do literary works such as Hugo's have on your attitude toward war? (b) Explain whether you do or do not think that literature is an effective means of protesting war.

ANALYZING LITERATURE

Understanding the Retreat from Russia

"Russia 1812" is a realistic and shocking depiction of one of the most tragic events in French history, the Grand Army's retreat from Moscow in 1812.
1. How does Hugo capture the devastating impact of the retreat from Russia on the French army as a whole?
2. How does he capture the suffering that each individual soldier experienced during the retreat?
3. What does this poem suggest about the surviving soldiers' loyalty to their leader?
4. Considering the success of most of his previous military expeditions, why is it ironic that Napoleon is ultimately defeated by the forces of nature rather than by an opposing army?
5. What does the French retreat from Russia reveal about the role of nature in determining the course of human history?

THINKING AND WRITING

Writing a War Poem

Write a poem describing a battle or another type of scene from a war. Begin by brainstorming about the depiction of war in books you have read or in movies or television news programs you have seen. You might also want to take a look at some accounts of battles written by soldiers who participated in them. Develop a list of words and details you could use in your poem. Then underline the words and details that you feel are most effective. Using these words and details, begin writing your poem. Do not worry about rhythm or rhyme. Instead, focus on creating vivid, precise images that will evoke an emotional response from the reader. After you have finished writing, revise your poem, making sure it conveys the impression that you want it to. Finally, proofread your poem, prepare a final copy, and share it with your classmates.

(continued from bottom of page)

to have an ambivalent attitude toward Napoleon. (b) Suggested response: Hugo has the "God of armies" forgive Napoleon, but Hugo seems unconvinced that the soldiers' continuing faith in their leader is justified.
8. Suggested response: He is trying to convey the idea that war is violent, brutal, and destructive.
9. (a) Answers will differ. Students might note that Hugo creates vivid pictures with words, just as an artist creates vivid pictures with paints. (b) Answers will differ. Students might respond that like Hugo, a filmmaker would be likely to focus on the suffering and destruction caused by the retreat from Russia.
10. (a) Answers will differ. Many students may respond that works such as Hugo's only confirm their attitude toward war. (b) Answers will differ. Many students may feel that literary works are an effective means of protesting war.

Challenge In what ways might this poem be different if it focused on the French Revolution rather than on the retreat from Russia?

ANSWERS TO ANALYZING LITERATURE

1. Suggested response: He includes many details that spell out the magnitude of the defeat.
2. Suggested response: Many of his descriptions focus on individual soldiers.
3. It suggests that they remain loyal to Napoleon despite the suffering they have experienced.
4. Suggested response: Even an "invincible" army cannot defeat the forces of nature.
5. Suggested response: It reveals that nature often plays a major role in shaping human history.

THINKING AND WRITING

Writing Across the Curriculum
You may want to encourage students to consult their history teachers to help them come up with details to use in their war poems.

Closure and Extension

ANSWERS TO THINKING ABOUT THE SELECTION

1. (a) Suggested response: The snow kept falling harder and harder. (b) Suggested response: It emphasizes the misery that the snow causes the French army.
2. Suggested response: The only colors named are white and black. In addition, he uses such words as frost, frozen, ice, solitude, and shroud.
3. Suggested response: He suggests that the cold, barren, isolated Russian landscape is taking revenge on the French army.
4. (a) Napoleon is compared to an oak tree about to fall. (b) Suggested response: Oak trees are known for their strength and toughness, qualities for which Napoleon was famous.
5. If he does not believe in God, it seems pointless to question God.
6. (a) Answers will differ. One example of irony is the fact that the soldiers still love Napoleon even though he is the underlying cause of their suffering. (b) Suggested response: They show the cruel, sometimes contradictory aspects of war.
7. (a) Suggested response: He seems

WILLIAM WORDSWORTH

Focus

More About the Author William Wordsworth spent eight years at Hawkshead Grammar School on the shores of Esthwaite Water, two miles from Lake Windermere, in the Lake District of northern England. It is an area of magnificent natural beauty that Wordsworth called the "dear native regions." At Hawkshead he received a rigorous classical education that prepared him well for Cambridge University, which he attended after his graduation from Hawkshead. During his spare time while he was at Hawkshead, he was free to explore the rivers, lakes, and mountains. He also became a skilled ice skater and mountain climber.

Have students discuss the impact that Wordsworth's experiences at Hawkshead might have had on his writing. Do his experiences at Hawkshead help to explain why his love for nature is readily apparent throughout his poetry? Why or why not?

Critical Evaluation The critic George W. Meyer has written,

The "Intimations Ode" is Wordsworth's greatest short poem and one of the most complex utterances in English verse....As the clouded sun sets at the end of the poet's day, the simplest natural object can provoke thoughts that lead to faith in immortality and are, therefore, "too deep for tears."...Whatever else the "Ode" may affirm, it says... that the origins of man's joy are fundamental, inevitable, and indestructible.

1770–1850

Few writers have ever had more of an impact on the world of literature than William Wordsworth. With the publication of *Lyrical Ballads* (1798), the collection of poetry that he coauthored with Samuel Taylor Coleridge, Wordsworth dramatically altered the direction of English poetry. The collection represented a dramatic departure from English poetic traditions and the establishment of a new type of poetry. This type of poetry would come to be known as Romanticism, and Wordsworth would come to be regarded as the greatest English Romantic poet.

Wordsworth was born in northern England. When he was only eight, his mother died, and he was sent away to boarding school in the English Lake District. There he developed the deep love for nature that would later play a vital role in shaping his poetry. Five years after the death of his mother, his father also died, and William, his three brothers, and his sister, Dorothy, were placed under the guardianship of two uncles.

While in college, Wordsworth became a strong supporter of the French Revolution, passionately advocating the ideas of democracy and equal rights. However, with the onset of the Reign of Terror, in which thousands of people were executed, he became increasingly disillusioned with the French Revolution. This disillusionment, along with his uncertainty concerning his direction as a poet, brought him to the verge of an emotional collapse. Yet he was able to avoid a breakdown by finding solace in his memories of his childhood and his love for the countryside.

In 1795, after a friend died and left him a significant sum of money, Wordsworth and his sister, Dorothy, settled into a cottage in the country. This tranquil environment proved to be the perfect setting for Wordsworth, allowing him to engage in the type of reflection that fueled his writing. Moving to the country also enabled Wordsworth to meet Coleridge, who provided him with strong encouragement, calling him "the best poet of the age." Wordsworth and Coleridge quickly became close friends, meeting almost daily to exchange ideas and compose poetry. Their frequent meetings resulted in the publication of *Lyrical Ballads*, which established both Wordsworth and Coleridge as important and highly innovative poets.

In 1802 Wordsworth married a woman he had known since childhood, and they eventually had five children. During the early 1800's, Wordsworth also wrote many of his best poems, including "Ode: Intimations of Immortality." Unfortunately, however, these years also marked the beginning of a series of personal tragedies that would have a profound impact on his outlook on life. These tragedies included the deaths of two of his children and his brother John, the physical and psychological decline of his sister, and a bitter quarrel with Coleridge that resulted in a long break in their relationship. Despite these events Wordsworth's reputation as a poet grew steadily during this period, and he was able to achieve financial security. At the same time, he became increasingly conservative in his personal beliefs.

In 1843 Wordsworth was appointed British poet laureate. Seven years later, he died. Shortly after his death, *The Prelude*, his long, autobiographical poem, considered by many to be his masterpiece, was published, further enhancing his already lofty reputation.

Objectives

Thematic
To understand how people's experiences and observations lose their freshness as they grow older

Skills
1 To understand Romanticism
2 To compare and contrast ideas
3 To write a response to a writer's statement

GUIDE FOR INTERPRETING

Ode: Intimations of Immortality

Commentary

Romanticism. Romanticism was a major literary and cultural movement that emerged out of the revolutionary spirit of the late 1700's. Although there were many differences in the concerns and approaches of the various Romantic writers, they generally shared a desire to discard the dominant ideas and techniques of the eighteenth century and to forge a new type of literature. Unlike eighteenth-century writers, who located the source of poetry outside the poet, the Romantics viewed poetry as the highly personal expression of the inner thoughts and emotions of the individual poet. Associated with this view was the Romantic belief that poetic composition should be a spontaneous act, arising from the impulses of the heart and the imagination. Eighteenth-century writers, on the other hand, viewed poetic composition as an intellectual activity that required a thorough knowledge of literary traditions and rules.

Shaped by the democratic ideals of the French Revolution, Romanticism was also characterized by an interest in ordinary people. This interest was reflected in the Romantics' use of the language of common people and in their depiction of situations from everyday life. Yet their portrayal of ordinary life was colored by their imaginations to enable readers to view the commonplace in a fresh and wondrous manner. Once again, these tendencies represented a sharp break from the methods of their predecessors, who used ornate language and depicted the lives of upper-class people.

Related to the Romantics' interest in common people was their fascination with the folklore and superstitions that were an integral part of everyday life during the Middle Ages. This was accompanied by an attraction to the mysterious and the supernatural and to the "exotic" cultures of the Orient and the Middle East. These interests also contrasted with those of eighteenth-century writers, whose primary source of inspiration was classical (Greek and Roman) literature.

Another characteristic of the Romantics was their deep love and appreciation for nature. Developing partly as a reaction to the consequences of industrialization, the Romantics' attraction to nature is evident in the titles of many of their poems. Because the Romantics were most concerned with the thoughts and emotions that nature aroused in them, their descriptions of natural scenes are usually colored by their feelings and their imaginations.

Writing

The French Revolution had a major impact on nineteenth-century European life. Write a journal entry in which you discuss some recent events that have had a major impact on life in the United States.

(continued from bottom of page) isolate and even alienate themselves from society, rebelling against the eighteenth-century view of writers as an integral part of society.

Writing/Prior Knowledge You may want to define the word *recent* for students. Events that historians are likely to consider recent—perhaps those since 1945—could easily seem ancient to young people. Yet it is much easier to assess the impact of World War II than it is to assess the impact of more recent events, such as the political changes in Eastern Europe.

Teaching Tenth-Grade Students You may want to read this poem aloud to tenth-grade students. Pause after each stanza and have students discuss the ideas it conveys.

ESL Teaching Strategy Pair each ESL student with a native-speaking student and have them read through the poem together, taking turns reading aloud. Instruct the native speaker to clarify the meaning of any words the ESL student does not understand.

Vocabulary
Preteach the following vocabulary words:
celestial (sə les´ chəl) *adj.*: Of the heavens
adorning (ə dôrn´ iŋ) *v.*: Adding beauty, splendor, or distinction to
semblance (sem´ bləns) *n.*: Outward form or appearance
obstinate (äb´ stə nit) *adj.*: Stubborn
listlessness (list´ lis nəs) *n.*: Spiritlessness
radiance (rā´ dē əns) *n.*: Brightness
habitual (hə bich´ ơo wəl) *adj.*: Done by habit

Support Material

Teaching Portfolio
Teacher Backup, p. 1077
Grammar in Action Worksheet, *Using Common Language*, p. 1081
Usage and Mechanics Worksheet, p. 1083
Vocabulary Check, p. 1084
Analyzing Literature Worksheet, *Understanding Romanticism*, p. 1085
Critical Thinking and Reading Worksheet, *Comparing and Contrasting Ideas*, p. 1086
Selection Test, pp. 1087–1088

Literary Focus Tell students that other dominant Romantic attitudes include a sense of optimism, a desire to transcend human limitations, and an emphasis on individuality. The idea of refusing to accept limitations is reflected in Wolfgang von Goethe's *Faust* (page 863), which focuses on a character whose desire for the unattainable prompts him to bargain with the devil. Also point out that related to the Romantic emphasis on individuality was the effort of a number of Romantic writers to

Spelling Tip Tell students that it might help them to spell *listlessness* if they divide it into the following parts: *list, less,* and *ness.*

Ode: Intimations of Immortality from Recollections of Early Childhood

William Wordsworth

The Child is Father of the Man;
And I could with my days to be
Bound each to each by natural piety.[1]

1

There was a time when meadow, grove, and
    stream,
The earth, and every common sight,
        To me did seem
        Appareled in celestial light,
5 The glory and the freshness of a dream.
It is not now as it hath been of yore;—
        Turn wheresoe'er I may,
          By night or day,
The things which I have seen I now can see no
    more.

2

10   The Rainbow comes and goes,
          And lovely is the Rose,
          The Moon doth with delight
Look round her when the heavens are bare,
          Waters on a starry night
15   Are beautiful and fair;
          The sunshine is a glorious birth;
          But yet I know, where'er I go,
That there hath past away a glory from the earth.

3

Now, while the birds thus sing a joyous song,
20   And while the young lambs bound
          As to the tabor's sound,[2]
To me alone there came a thought of grief:
A timely utterance gave that thought relief,
          And I again am strong:
25 The cataracts[3] blow their trumpets from the steep;
No more shall grief of mine the season wrong;
I hear the Echoes through the mountains throng,
The Winds come to me from the fields of sleep,
          And all the earth is gay;
30   Land and sea
          Give themselves up to jollity,
          And with the heart of May
          Doth every Beast keep holiday;—
          Thou Child of Joy,
35 Shout round me, let me hear thy shouts, thou
    happy Shepherd-boy!

4

Ye blessed Creatures, I have heard the call
          Ye to each other make; I see
The heavens laugh with you in your jubilee;
          My heart is at your festival,
40   My head hath its coronal,[4]
The fullness of your bliss, I feel—I feel it all.

---

1. The Child . . . natural piety: The concluding lines from Wordsworth's poem "My Heart Leaps Up."

---

2. tabor's (tā´ bərz): A tabor is a small drum.
3. cataracts (kat´ ə rakts´) *n.*: Large waterfalls.
4. coronal (kôr´ ə n'l) *n.*: A circlet of wild flowers, worn by shepherd boys in May.

Oh evil day! if I were sullen
While Earth herself is adorning,
   This sweet May-morning,
And the Children are culling
   On every side,
In a thousand valleys far and wide,
Fresh flowers; while the sun shines warm,
And the Babe leaps up on his Mother's arm:—
   I hear, I hear, with joy I hear!
   —But there's a Tree, of many, one,
A single Field which I have looked upon,
Both of them speak of something that is gone:
   The Pansy at my feet
   Doth the same tale repeat:
Whither is fled the visionary gleam?
Where is it now, the glory and the dream?

5

Our birth is but a sleep and a forgetting:
The Soul that rises with us, our life's Star,[5]
   Hath had elsewhere its setting,
   And cometh from afar:
   Not in entire forgetfulness,
   And not in utter nakedness,
But trailing clouds of glory do we come
   From God, who is our home:
Heaven lies about us in our infancy!
Shades of the prison-house begin to close
   Upon the growing Boy,
But He beholds the light, and whence it flows,
   He sees it in his joy;
The Youth, who daily farther from the east
   Must travel, still is Nature's Priest,
   And by the vision splendid
   Is on his way attended;
At length the Man perceives it die away,
And fade into the light of common day.

6

Earth fills her lap with pleasures of her own;
Yearnings she hath in her own natural kind,
And, even with something of a Mother's mind,
   And no unworthy aim,

---

5. **Star:** The sun.

The homely[6] Nurse doth all she can
To make her Foster-child, her Inmate Man,
   Forget the glories he hath known,
And that imperial palace whence he came.

7

Behold the Child among his new-born blisses,
85 A six years' Darling of a pigmy size!
See, where 'mid work of his own hand he lies,
Fretted[7] by sallies of his mother's kisses,
With light upon him from his father's eyes!
See, at his feet, some little plan or chart,
90 Some fragment from his dream of human life,
Shaped by himself with newly-learnèd art;
   A wedding or a festival,
   A mourning or a funeral;
    And this hath now his heart,
95   And unto this he frames his song:
    Then will he fit his tongue
To dialogues of business, love, or strife;
   But it will not be long
   Ere[8] this be thrown aside,
100   And with new joy and pride
The little Actor cons another part;
Filling from time to time his "humorous stage"[9]
With all the Persons, down to palsied[10] Age,
That Life brings with her in her equipage;
105   As if his whole vocation
   Were endless imitation.

8

Thou, whose exterior semblance doth belie
   Thy Soul's immensity;
Thou best Philosopher, who yet dost keep
110 Thy heritage, thou Eye among the blind,
That, deaf and silent, read'st the eternal deep,
Haunted forever by the eternal mind,—
   Mighty Prophet! Seer blest!

---

6. **homely:** Simple and friendly.
7. **Fretted:** Irritated.
8. **Ere:** Before.
9. **"humorous stage":** From a sonnet by the English poet Samuel Daniel (1562–1619).
10. **palsied** (pôl′ zēd) *v.*: Afflicted with palsy, a condition involving the paralysis of voluntary muscles.

---

4 **Enrichment** For many years this poem was interpreted as "Wordsworth's conscious farewell to his art, a dirge sung over his departing powers. In a well-known essay published in 1950, the American critic Lionel Trilling argued that such an interpretation is inaccurate, contending that the intent of the ode is positive. Trilling went on to characterize the poem as "a welcoming of new powers and a dedication to a new poetic subject." Tell students that Trilling's interpretation is widely accepted today.

5 **Discussion** Have students explain why the idea expressed in this line is paradoxical. Then have them discuss the possible meaning of the paradox.

6 **Clarification** You may want to take a couple of minutes to explain to students that Wordsworth's poem is based on the idea that a person's soul exists separately before birth and that people gradually lose their awareness of their soul's immortality as they grow older.

7 **Discussion** Have students discuss what these lines suggest about the nature of the soul's preexistence.

8 **Enrichment** Tell students that the "six-years' Darling" to which Wordsworth refers is Samuel Taylor Coleridge's six-year-old son Hartley.

9 **Enrichment** Tell students that Samuel Taylor Coleridge objected to these lines, commenting that they contained "thoughts and images too great for the subject." Do students agree with Coleridge's objection? Why or why not?

Primary Source

When this poem was first published, Wordsworth prefaced it with a rather long prose explanation. The following is the first part of his explanation:

This was composed during my residence at Town End, Grasmere. Two years at least passed between the writing of the first four stanzas and the remaining part. To the attentive and competent reader the whole sufficiently explains itself, but there may be no harm in adverting here to particular feelings or *experiences* of my own mind on which the structure of the poem partly rests. Nothing was more difficult for me in my childhood than to admit the notion of death as a state applicable to my own being. I have said elsewhere

  A simple child,
That lightly draws its breath,
And feels its life in every limb,
What should it know of death?

But it was not so much from feelings of animal vivacity that my difficulty came as from a sense of the indomitableness of the spirit within me.

Ode: Intimations of Immortality from Recollections of Early Childhood   897

Fine art, *Weymouth Bay from the Downs Above Osmington Mills* by John Constable. Along with J.M.W. Turner, John Constable (1776–1837) dominated English landscape painting during the nineteenth century. He viewed painting as an inquiry into the laws of nature—almost as a branch of natural philosophy. Consequently, the Romantic appreciation for nature is as evident in Constable's paintings as it is in Wordsworth's poetry.

As is the case in many of his paintings, Constable devotes a great deal of attention to the sky in this work. In a letter to a friend, Constable wrote: "That landscape painter who does not make his skies a very material part of his composition, neglects to avail himself of one of his greatest aids . . . It will be difficult to name a class of landscape in which the sky is not . . . the chief organ of sentiment."

You might want to use the following questions to discuss the art:

1. What impression of nature does this painting convey?
2. What thoughts and emotions does the painting evoke? Why?
3. If you were to prepare a caption for this painting using lines from Wordsworth's poem, which lines would you choose? Why?
4. Would you like to visit the place depicted in this painting? Why or why not?

WEYMOUTH BAY FROM THE DOWNS ABOVE OSMINGTON MILLS
John Constable
The Museum of Fine Arts, Boston

115   On whom those truths do rest,
Which we are toiling all our lives to find,
In darkness lost, the darkness of the grave;
Thou, over whom thy Immortality
Broods like the Day, a Master o'er a Slave,
120 A Presence which is not to be put by;
Thou little Child, yet glorious in the might

Of heaven-born freedom on thy being's height,
Why with such earnest pains dost thou provoke
The years to bring the inevitable yoke,
125 Thus blindly with thy blessedness at strife?
Full soon thy Soul shall have her earthly freight,
And custom lie upon thee with a weight,
Heavy as frost, and deep almost as life!

Grammar in Action

As Wordsworth indicated in his preface to the *Lyrical Ballads*, he felt that poets should construct their poems **with the use of common language.** He believed that the simple, unadorned language of the people conveys ideas and emotions more effectively than does the elaborate, ornamental language favored by earlier poets. Note the simple, common language used in the following passage from "Ode: Intimations of Immortality from Recollections of Early Childhood":

Thanks to the human heart by which we live,
Thanks to its tenderness, its joys, and fears,
To me the meanest flower that blows can give
Thoughts that do often lie too deep for tears.

Student Activity 1. Rewrite each of the following passages using elaborate, ornamental language. Then compare each of your passages with the original and explain which one you think is more effective.

1. To me alone there came a thought of grief: / A timely utterance gave that

9

O joy! that in our embers
Is something that doth live,
That nature yet remembers
What was so fugitive!
The thought of our past years in me doth breed
Perpetual benediction:[11] not indeed
For that which is most worthy to be blest;
Delight and liberty, the simple creed
Of Childhood, whether busy or at rest,
With new-fledged hope still fluttering in his
breast:—
    Not for these I raise
    The song of thanks and praise;
    But for those obstinate questionings
    Of sense and outward things,
    Fallings from us, vanishings;
    Blank misgivings of a Creature
Moving about in worlds not realized,[12]
High instincts before which our mortal Nature
Did tremble like a guilty Thing surprised:
    But for those first affections,
    Those shadowy recollections,
    Which, be they what they may,
Are yet the fountain light of all our day,
Are yet a master light of all our seeing;
    Uphold us, cherish, and have power to make
Our noisy years seem moments in the being
Of the eternal Silence: truths that wake,
    To perish never;
Which neither listlessness, nor mad endeavor,
    Nor Man nor Boy
Nor all that is at enmity[13] with joy,
Can utterly abolish or destroy!
    Hence in a season of calm weather
    Though inland far we be,
Our Souls have sight of that immortal sea
    Which brought us hither,
    Can in a moment travel thither,
And see the Children sport upon the shore,
And hear the mighty waters rolling evermore.

10

Then sing, ye Birds, sing, sing a joyous song!
    And let the young Lambs bound
170   As to the tabor's sound!
We in thought will join your throng,
    Ye that pipe and ye that play,
    Ye that through your hearts today
    Feel the gladness of the May!
What though the radiance which was once so
175   bright
Be now forever taken from my sight,
    Though nothing can bring back the hour
Of splendor in the grass, of glory in the flower;
    We will grieve not, rather find
180   Strength in what remains behind;
    In the primal sympathy
Which having been must ever be;
    In the soothing thoughts that spring
    Out of human suffering;
185   In the faith that looks through death,
In years that bring the philosophic mind.

11

And O, ye Fountains, Meadows, Hills, and Groves,
Forebode not any severing of our loves!
Yet in my heart of hearts I feel your might;
190 I only have relinquished one delight
To live beneath your more habitual sway.
I love the Brooks which down their channels fret,
Even more than when I tripped lightly as they;
The innocent brightness of a new-born Day
195   Is lovely yet;
The Clouds that gather round the setting sun
Do take a sober coloring from an eye
That hath kept watch o'er man's mortality;
Another race hath been, and other palms are won.[14]
200 Thanks to the human heart by which we live,
Thanks to its tenderness, its joys, and fears,
To me the meanest flower that blows can give
Thoughts that do often lie too deep for tears.

---

11. **benediction** (ben´ ə dik´ shən) *n.*: A blessing.
12. **not realized:** That seem unreal.
13. **enmity** (en´ mə tē) *n.*: Hostility; antagonism.

---

14. **Another race . . . are won:** In ancient Greece, branches or wreaths of palm were often awarded to the victors of foot races.

thought relief, / And I again am strong: . . .
2. Shades of the prison-house begin to close / Upon the growing Boy, / But He beholds the light, and whence it flows, / He sees it in his joy; . . .
3. Earth fills her lap with pleasures of her own; / Yearnings she had in her own natural kin, . . .
4. At length the man perceives it die away, / And fade into the common light of day.

Student Activity 2. Write a brief poem describing one of your favorite places. Use the same kind of language that you use in everyday speech.

Fine art, *Banks of the Seine at Champrosay* by Pierre Auguste Renoir. Renoir (1841–1919) was a member of a late-nineteenth-century school of painters known as the Impressionists. As the name suggests, these painters focused on capturing a momentary visual impression of a scene rather than trying to capture a scene in an accurate and detailed manner. The Impressionists frequently used nature as the subject for their paintings, and they often explored the changing effects of light.

This painting was produced during the early part of Renoir's career, when he was living in the north of France. The bright colors and fluid brushstrokes are typical of Impressionist works.

You might want to use the following questions to discuss the art:

1. What impression does this painting convey of the scene it depicts? Explain.
2. In what ways is this painting similar to and different from the painting by John Constable on page 898?
3. Explain why you think this painting is or is not an appropriate illustration for Wordsworth's poem.
4. If you were an art collector, would you want to include this painting in your collection? Why or why not?

**BORDS DE LA SEINE AT CHAMPROSAY
(BANKS OF THE SEINE AT CHAMPROSAY)**
Pierre Auguste Renoir

Reader's Response *What are your earliest memories? What thoughts and feelings do you associate with these memories?*

PRIMARY SOURCE

In the preface to *Lyrical Ballads*, Wordsworth outlined many of the main principles of Romanticism, including the Romantic interest in the daily life and language of common people:

"The principal object, then, which I propose to myself in these poems was to choose incidents and situations from common life, and to relate or describe them, throughout, as far as was possible, in a selection of language really used by men; and, at the same time, to throw over them a certain coloring of imagination, whereby ordinary things should be presented to the mind in an unusual way; and, further, and above all, to make these incidents and situations interesting by tracing in them, truly, though not ostentatiously, the primary laws of our nature: chiefly, as far as regards the manner in which we associate ideas in a state of excitement. Low and rustic life was generally chosen, because in that condition, the essential passions of the heart find a better soil in which they can attain maturity, are less under restraint, and speak a plainer and more emphatic language. . . . The language, too, of these men is adopted . . . because such men hourly communicate with the best objects from which the best part of language is originally derived; and because from their rank in society and the sameness and narrow circle of their intercourse, being less under the influence of social vanity they convey their feelings and notions in simple and unelaborated expressions."

Closure and Extension

ANSWERS TO THINKING ABOUT THE SELECTIONS

1. (a) He conveys this idea in the line, "It is not now as it hath been of yore." (b) He writes that he knows "That there hath past away a glory from the earth."
2. (a) He conveys the impression that the elements of nature have a joyous and harmonious relationship. (b) Suggested response: Viewing the joyous relationship among the elements of nature should fill a person's heart with the same type of joy that he or she feels when seeing something for the first time.
3. (a) Suggested response: He writes, "The Soul that rises with us . . . Hath had elsewhere its setting." He then goes on to describe the process of forgetting about our soul's prior existence. (b) Suggested response: The process of forgetting the soul's immortality parallels the loss of freshness.
4. (a) He suggests that a child learns by studious and continuous imitation of older people. (b) Suggested response: He seems to feel that the process of imitation contributes to the loss of freshness.

THINKING ABOUT THE SELECTION

Interpreting

1. (a) In the first stanza, how does Wordsworth suggest that common experiences lose their freshness as people grow older? (b) How does he develop this idea in the second stanza?

2. (a) In the third and fourth stanzas, what impression does Wordsworth convey of the relationship among the elements of nature? (b) How does his portrayal of nature relate to the idea of having a fresh outlook on life?

3. Wordsworth's poem is based on the idea that a person's soul exists separately before birth and after death and that people gradually lose their awareness of their soul's immortality as they grow older. (a) How is this idea conveyed in the fifth and sixth stanzas? (b) How does this idea relate to the notion that common experiences lose their freshness as people grow older?

4. (a) In the final lines of the seventh stanza, what does Wordsworth suggest about the role of imitation in the process of learning? (b) How does Wordsworth feel about the effect of imitation on the growing child?

5. What does Wordsworth mean when he writes that "in our embers / Is something that doth live" (lines 129–130)?

6. For what aspect of childhood does Wordsworth express "thanks and praise" in stanza 9?

7. (a) In stanza 10 how is Wordsworth comforted by his insights concerning the immortality of the soul? (b) How does he further convey his sense of comfort in the final stanza?

8. (a) How do Wordsworth's observations in the final stanza contrast with those in the opening stanza? (b) What is the significance of the difference between these two stanzas?

Applying

9. Have you found that common observations and experiences have lost their freshness as you have grown older? Explain your answer.

ANALYZING LITERATURE

Understanding Romanticism

Like most of Wordsworth's poetry, "Ode: Intimations of Immortality" reflects many of the dominant characteristics of the Romantic movement. For example, like most Romantic works, the poem is written in the simple, direct language of ordinary people.

1. How does Wordsworth's poem reflect the Romantics' love of nature? In your answer cite specific details from the poem.

2. Explain how Wordsworth's descriptions of nature are colored by his emotions and his imagination.

3. In Romantic poetry nature often serves as a stimulus for human thought and emotion. How does Wordsworth use this technique in the third stanza?

4. In his preface to the *Lyrical Ballads*, Wordsworth defined his poetry as "emotion recollected in tranquillity." How does this definition apply to "Ode: Intimations of Immortality"?

5. Romanticism was also characterized by a sense of optimism and a desire to transcend human limitations. How does this poem reflect these characteristics?

6. The Romantics were also known for their emphasis on individuality. Does this poem reflect this emphasis? Explain.

CRITICAL THINKING AND READING

Comparing and Contrasting Ideas

The Greek philosopher Plato argued that the soul exists apart from the body before birth and after death. He also claimed that the knowledge of the soul's immortality is lost at the moment of birth and can be recovered only through philosophical contemplation.

How are Plato's ideas similar to and different from those that Wordsworth expresses in his poem?

THINKING AND WRITING

Responding to a Writer's Statement

In his preface to the *Lyrical Ballads*, Wordsworth wrote that the poet "considers man and nature as essentially adapted to each other, and the mind of man as naturally the mirror of the fairest and most interesting qualities of nature." Write a paper in which you examine how this statement applies to "Ode: Intimations of Immortality." Start by reviewing the poem, noting the passages that relate to Wordsworth's statement. Organize your notes. Then write your paper, using passages from the poem for support. When you have finished writing, revise your paper, making sure you have expressed your ideas clearly and in an organized manner. Finally, proofread your paper and share it with your classmates.

(continued from bottom of page)
ANSWERS TO ANALYZING LITERATURE

1. Suggested response: Nature, along with childhood, is the focus of the poem. Throughout the poem he includes idyllic images of many elements of nature.

2. Suggested response: The natural images are generally presented in an idyllic, almost dreamlike, manner.

3. Suggested response: His observations of nature prompt him to regain his sense of freshness.

4. Suggested response: The poem fits this definition well. It is a reflective poem, based on childhood delight that the poet recalls as an adult.

5. Suggested response: Despite recognizing the loss of the freshness of youth, the poem offers a positive outlook and conveys a sense of harmony between humanity and nature.

6. Suggested response: It does reflect this emphasis, because it focuses on the experiences of a single individual.

ANSWERS TO CRITICAL THINKING AND READING

Both Plato and Wordsworth convey a belief in the preexistence of the soul. Yet Plato suggests that the knowledge of the soul's immortality vanishes at the moment of birth. Wordsworth, on the other hand, suggests that this knowledge disappears gradually.

THINKING AND WRITING

Publishing Student Writing You might want to arrange students' papers into a class bulletin-board display.

---

5. Suggested response: Even though we, like embers, are dying, there is a spark that offers hope of rekindling.

6. He expresses praise from "obstinate questionings."

7. (a) Suggested response: Even though he will never again see the radiance he saw in childhood, he will "find / Strength in what remains" and in a "faith that looks through death." (b) Suggested response: He describes the comfort that nature offers him.

8. (a) Suggested response: In the first stanza, he is sad that he no longer sees nature's "celestial light." In the final stanza, he suggests that he still loves nature as much as ever. (b) Suggested response: He has come to a mature understanding of his relationship to the natural world.

9. Answers will differ. Many students will probably respond that common observations have lost their freshness as they have grown older.

Challenge There is some evidence that Wordsworth did not actually believe in the soul's preexistence. If that is true, why did he incorporate this belief into his poem?

CHARLES BAUDELAIRE

More About the Author When Charles Baudelaire first encountered the work of Edgar Allan Poe, he was amazed—it was as if he had found his artistic twin. "In 1847 or 1846," Baudelaire wrote, "I came across some fragments of Poe; I experienced an extraordinary turmoil . . . I discovered, believe me if you will, poems and stories that I had thought of, only vaguely, confusedly, in a disorganized fashion, and which Poe had managed to put together and perfect." After translating some of Poe's poems and short stories into French, Baudelaire wrote, "Do you know why I translated Poe so patiently? Because he was like me. The first time I opened a book of his I saw, with horror and delight, not just subjects I had dreamt of, but *sentences* I had thought of, and written by him twenty years before."

Ask students if they have ever read works by a writer whose thoughts seemed to mirror their own. If so, have them discuss what this experience was like. How did it make them feel?

Critical Evaluation In his biography of Baudelaire, Alex de Jonge observes, ". . . It was given to this luckless man to write the greatest poetry of his age, poetry born of loss and disaster which he turned into a strange beauty, sometimes savage, sometimes erotic, sometimes soothing—the swaying rocking calm of an adult lullaby. Baudelaire's poetry inaugurated the language and the idioms of modern poetry." Ask students to comment on which parts of this assessment, if any, could be applied to Poe.

CHARLES BAUDELAIRE

1821–1867

Known almost as much for his highly unconventional life style as for his poetry, Charles Baudelaire (shärl bōd ler') was one of the most colorful, startling, and innovative poets of the nineteenth century. Attempting to break away from the Romantic tradition, Baudelaire created poems that are objective rather than sentimental and celebrate the city and the artificial rather than nature. Yet despite Baudelaire's conscious revolt against Romanticism, his work still exhibits the imaginative and mystical qualities that are typical of much Romantic poetry. In fact, Baudelaire's work is in many ways similar to the poetry of the American Romantic writer Edgar Allan Poe.

Baudelaire was born in Paris in 1821. When he was six years old, his father died, and a year later his mother married a prominent military officer. Detesting his new stepfather, he lapsed into a period of rebellion and conflict that lasted through his high school years. Expelled from school in 1839, he nevertheless passed his final exams and threw himself into the Bohemian life style of the Parisian artistic community, determined to become a writer. Disapproving of his life style, his family decided to send him on an ocean voyage to India in 1841. Before his boat reached its destination, however, he returned to France to claim his share of his late father's money. Even

though he did not complete the voyage, the trip had a profound impact on his imagination.

In 1842 he settled into a magnificent apartment in Paris and began living a life of rebellion and extravagance. Constantly questing for sensual pleasures, he became involved in a controversial love affair and he held wild and lavish parties. In less than two years, he squandered half his inheritance; as a result, his mother and stepfather took control of his finances, allotting him only a small monthly allowance. Refusing to adapt his life style to his limited income, Baudelaire was in debt throughout the remainder of his life, and at times he was even forced to move from one residence to another to escape from bill collectors.

Despite his financial troubles, he managed to find plenty of time for writing and socializing. After publishing two short stories, "The Young Enchanter" and "Fanfarlo," he translated a number of Poe's stories and poems into French. At the same time, he was writing and collecting poems for his masterpiece, *Flowers of Evil.* Appearing in 1857, *Flowers of Evil* was immediately banned by the French government for containing six poems that were judged to be obscene and immoral. When the second edition of the book was published in 1861, these six poems were omitted and thirty-five new poems were added.

In 1862 Baudelaire began experiencing the symptoms of the illness that would eventually cause his death. Two years later, he exiled himself in Belgium, where he intended to give a series of lectures. Overcome by paralysis in the spring of 1866, he was brought back to Paris, where he died in his mother's arms in August of 1867. At his funeral his friend Théodore de Banville remarked that "the author of *Flowers of Evil* is not only a poet of talent, he is a poet of genius."

Unfortunately, Baudelaire's talents were not widely recognized during his lifetime. Following his death, however, his reputation rapidly blossomed and he came to be considered one of the finest nineteenth-century poets.

Objectives

Thematic
To understand how our imaginations can enable us to escape to an alternate world

Skills
1 To explore a recurring theme
2 To write about theme

GUIDE FOR INTERPRETING

Invitation to the Voyage; The Albatross

Commentary

Theme. The **theme** is the central idea or insight about life that a writer hopes to convey in a literary work. Often certain themes recur throughout a writer's work. In fact, some themes recur not only throughout the works of a single writer but throughout the literature of an entire culture or era or even throughout the literature of a variety of cultures and eras.

Many of the recurring themes in Baudelaire's poetry had not been explored by earlier poets and were considered startling and innovative when they first appeared. Among these were his erotic themes, or themes related to both the emotional and physical aspects of human love relationships. These themes aroused a great deal of controversy and earned Baudelaire a reputation in some circles as an obscene and immoral poet. Baudelaire was also one of the first poets to express the belief that people are torn by an inner conflict between good and evil and to delve into themes concerning the artificiality, ugliness, and corruption of industrial society. Although he was painfully aware of the negative aspects of industrial cities, Baudelaire had a deep love for cities, especially Paris. While recognizing the ugly and evil aspects of cities and other elements of industrial society, Baudelaire expressed the belief that it was possible to extract beauty from ugliness and evil. This idea provided him with the title for his collection of poetry *The Flowers of Evil.*

Another recurring theme in Baudelaire's poetry is that it is possible for people to use their imaginations to escape to an alternative world. In exploring this theme, he leads readers on imaginary journeys to ideal, dreamlike places. Often, these places are located in childhood or in faraway tropical lands. Baudelaire believed that escaping from reality in this manner enabled people to experience moments of ecstasy. Yet he also felt that these types of escapes were fleeting and that people were likely to be overcome by a sense of disillusionment when they returned to reality.

Writing

You have been invited on an imaginary journey. Where will you go? Freewrite, creating your own imaginary place.

Background

"Invitation to the Voyage" had several sources of inspiration. The most immediate source was probably his love for an actress named Marie Daubrun, whom he once begged to "be [his] guardian angel, [his] Muse, [his] Madonna, and lead [him] on the path to Beauty." In addition, many of the images in the poem are clearly based on his memories of his ocean voyage toward India in 1841. Finally, other images in the poem reflect his love for Dutch landsape pantings.

(continued from bottom of page)
ably similar to those of the Modernists.

As Baudelaire's case suggests, the recurring themes in a writer's work almost always reflect that writer's outlook on life. Have students discuss the outlook of writers with whom they are familiar. Then have them explore ways in which the outlook of these writers is reflected in the themes of their works.

Writing/Prior Knowledge Before students begin freewriting, have them discuss some of the imaginary places they visited as a child. How do they view these places now that they have grown older?

Teaching Tenth-Grade Students You may want to offer tenth-grade students some information about the albatross. Explain that it is a bird found mainly in the South Pacific. With a wingspan that extends up to nine feet, it excels at flying and gliding. During the 1800's, albatrosses were often slaughtered for their feathers and wings.

ESL Teaching Strategy To accomplish the writing assignment, pair each ESL student with a native-speaking student. The native-speaking student can act as a coach, making sure the ESL student understands the assignment and answering any questions the ESL student may have.

Vocabulary

Preteach the following vocabulary words:
treacherous (trech´ ər əs) *adj.*: Untrustworthy
luster (lus´tər) *n.*: Brightness
profferring (präf´ ər iŋ) *v.*: Offering
swells (swelz) *n.*: Large waves that move steadily without breaking
ply (plī) *v.*: To sail regularly back and forth across
diversion (də vʉr´ zhən) *n.*: Distraction of attention
jeering (jir´ iŋ) *v.*: Taunting

Support Material

Teaching Portfolio
Teacher Backup, p. 1089
Usage and Mechanics Worksheet, p. 1093
Vocabulary Check, p. 1094
Analyzing Literature Worksheet, *Exploring a Recurring Theme*, p. 1095

Critical Thinking and Reading Worksheet, *Identifying Realistic and Fantastic Details*, p. 1096
Selection Test, pp. 1097–1098
Art Transparency 12, *Yachting Basin* by Jean Dufy

Spelling Tip Point out to students that the word *reach* is embedded in the word *treacherous.*

Literary Focus Tell students that unlike the Romantics, Baudelaire was not drawn to nature. In fact, he favored the artificial over the natural and the city over the countryside. He did not believe in the fundamental goodness of humanity, but rather in its inherent evil. Out of these beliefs emerged the themes of Baudelaire's poetry—themes often remark-

Invitation to the Voyage

Charles Baudelaire

translated by Richard Wilbur

SEASCAPE AT SAINTES-MARIES DE LA MER (detail)
Vincent van Gogh
National Museum Vincent van Gogh, Amsterdam

My child, my sister, dream
How sweet all things would seem
Were we in that kind land to live together
And there love slow and long,
5 There love and die among
Those scenes that image you, that sumptuous[1]
weather.
Drowned suns that glimmer there
Through cloud-disheveled[2] air
Move me with such a mystery as appears
10 Within those other skies
Of your treacherous eyes
When I behold them shining through their tears.

There, there is nothing else but grace and
measure,
Richness, quietness, and pleasure.

15 Furniture that wears
The luster of the years
Softly would glow within our glowing chamber,
Flowers of rarest bloom
Proffering their perfume
20 Mixed with the vague fragrances of amber;
Gold ceilings would there be,
Mirrors deep as the sea,
The walls all in an Eastern splendor hung—
Nothing but should address
25 The soul's loneliness,
Speaking her sweet and secret native tongue.

There, there is nothing else but grace and
measure,
Richness, quietness, and pleasure.

See, sheltered from the swells
30 There in the still canals
Those drowsy ships that dream of sailing forth;
It is to satisfy
Your least desire, they ply
Hither through all the waters of the earth.
35 The sun at close of day
Clothes the fields of hay,
Then the canals, at last the town entire
In hyacinth and gold:
Slowly the land is rolled
40 Sleepward under a sea of gentle fire.

There, there is nothing else but grace and
measure,
Richness, quietness, and pleasure.

---

1. **sumptuous** (sump′ choo wəs) *adj.*: Magnificent or splendid.
2. **disheveled** (di shev′ ′ld) *adj.*: Disarranged and untidy.

Reader's Response *Would you like to go on the type of voyage that Baudelaire describes? Why or why not?*

The Albatross

Charles Baudelaire

translated by Kate Flores

Ofttimes, for diversion, seafaring men
Capture albatross, those vast birds of the seas
That accompany, at languorous[1] pace,
Boats plying their way through bitter straits.

5 Having scarce been taken aboard
These kings of the blue, awkward and shy,
Piteously their great white wings
Let droop like oars at their sides.

This wingèd voyager, how clumsy he is and weak!
10 He just now so lovely, how comic and ugly!
One with a stubby pipe teases his beak,
Another mimics, limping, the cripple who could fly!

The Poet resembles this prince of the clouds,
Who laughs at hunters and haunts the storms;
15 Exiled to the ground amid the jeering pack,
His giant wings will not let him walk.

---

1. **languorous** (laŋʹ gər əs) *adj.*: Lacking vigor or vitality.

THINKING ABOUT THE SELECTION

Interpreting

1. (a) What impression does Baudelaire convey of the "kind land" he describes? (b) Which details contribute to this impression?
2. (a) Which of the details in the second stanza reveal that this poem was partially inspired by Baudelaire's memories of his 1841 voyage toward India? (b) Which details in the third stanza reveal that the poem was also partially inspired by Dutch landscape paintings? (c) In what ways is this poem similar to a landscape painting?
3. How do the images Baudelaire uses in describing the "kind land" relate to the ideas he expresses in the poem's refrain?
4. (a) How would you characterize the sailors' treatment of the albatross? (b) How do you think Baude-

laire wants readers to respond to the sailors' treatment of the albatross?
5. "The Albatross" may have been inspired by an incident that Baudelaire actually witnessed during his ocean voyage in 1841. Which details in the first three stanzas create the impression that the poem was based on a real-life experience?
6. (a) How does Baudelaire relate the treatment of the albatross to the life of a poet? (b) Which details used in describing the albatross could also be applied to a poet?
7. What does Baudelaire mean when he comments that the poet's "giant wings will not let him walk"?
8. What message is Baudelaire trying to convey about the life of a poet?

Applying

9. (a) Explain whether the world that Baudelaire describes in "Invitation to the Voyage" is the type of place you would be drawn to. (b) How does the place Baudelaire describes compare to your ideal world?

ANALYZING LITERATURE

Exploring a Recurring Theme

One of the recurring themes in Baudelaire's poetry is the expression of the desire to escape to an exotic and ideal alternative world. Often, as is the case with "Invitation to the Voyage," the idea of escaping to an alternative world is closely linked to an expression of love.
1. What impression of love does Baudelaire convey by linking it to the idea of escaping to an ideal, dreamlike world?
2. Why would the world that Baudelaire describes be an ideal place to pursue a love relationship?
3. In this poem Baudelaire evokes a sense of longing for the place he describes. How do you think this sense of longing might relate to Baudelaire's feelings about love?

THINKING AND WRITING

Writing About Theme

Write a paper in which you state the theme of "The Albatross" and discuss the methods that Baudelaire uses to convey this theme. Make sure you support your statement of theme with details and passages from the poem.

(continued from bottom of page)

7. Suggested response: The poet's ability to soar makes it difficult for him or her to cope with the mundane realities of everyday life.
8. Suggested response: He is suggesting that poets experience a sense of isolation and alienation from the rest of society.
9. (a) Answers will differ. Many students will respond that they would be drawn to the world Baudelaire describes. (b) Answers will differ. Some students will respond that Baudelaire's ideal world is similar to their own.

ANSWERS TO ANALYZING LITERATURE

1. Suggested response: He creates the impression that escaping to an alternate world can be a wonderful experience.
2. Suggested response: The place he describes has a very romantic atmosphere.
3. Suggested response: It suggests that he longs for an ideal love but has not been able to find it.

THINKING AND WRITING

Publishing Student Writing Have students read their papers aloud. Then use these readings as a springboard for a class discussion about Baudelaire's poetry.

Motivation/Prior Knowledge Have students discuss their conception of poets. Do they feel that poets are somehow different from other people? If so, why? Explain that a number of nineteenth-century poets, including Baudelaire, felt alienated from the rest of the society. Ask students how a poet might go about expressing this sense of alienation.

Purpose-Setting Question What is Baudelaire suggesting about the life of a poet?

1 **Discussion** Have students discuss the albatross's reaction to its captivity.

2 **Discussion** Ask students to explain why the sailors make fun of the captured albatross. Do people sometimes treat other people in this manner?

3 **Discussion** If the albatross resembles a poet, what do students think the "giant wings" represent?

Closure and Extension

ANSWERS TO THINKING ABOUT THE SELECTION

1. (a) Suggested response: He conveys the impression that it is a wonderful, exotic land of calm beauty. (b) Suggested response: These details include his references to sumptuous weather and drowsy ships in quiet

canals.
2. (a) His references to "fragrances of amber," "gold ceilings," and the "walls all in an Eastern splendor." (b) His references to "the still canals." (c) Suggested response: It is filled with rich visual imagery.
3. Suggested response: The details reinforce the ideas of grace, richness, calmness, and pleasure.
4. (a) They are cruel to it. (b) Suggested

response: He wants readers to be angered by the treatment of the bird and to feel sympathy for it.
5. Suggested response: The details are specific and realistic.
6. (a) Suggested response: He suggests that both have special gifts but suffer from misunderstanding and cruelty. (b) Suggested response: Both are awkward and shy but have the ability to soar.

ARTHUR RIMBAUD

Focus

More About the Author When Arthur Rimbaud was sixteen, he wrote his now-famous "Letter of a Seer" to his friend Paul Demeny. In this letter he spoke of the poet as a visionary, as one who "searches his soul, inspects it, tries it, learns it," and who virtually creates a new language. He wrote, "The poet makes himself a seer by a long, immense, and reasoned *derangement* of *all the senses.* All the forms of love, suffering, folly, he searches in himself, he boils down in himself so as to keep nothing of them but the quintessences." Eventually, "He reaches the *unknown!*" Through poetry, Rimbaud prophesied, he would become "a *seer . . . a SEER!*"

Ask students to comment on Rimbaud's goal. Do they find Rimbaud's sentiments unusual for a sixteen-year-old? Are they surprised that he gave up writing poetry only three years later?

Critical Evaluation Critics have expressed amazement at the precocious brilliance of Rimbaud, whose entire body of poetry was written between the ages of fifteen and nineteen. The British critic Arthur Simmons wrote, "He invents new ways of saying things, not because he is a learned artist, but because he is burning to say them, and he has none of the hesitations of knowledge. He leaps right over or through the conventions that had been standing in everybody's way . . ."

1854–1891

A poet of rare genius, Arthur Rimbaud (år tür´ ra*n* bō´) stopped writing poetry at the age of nineteen and embarked on a life of rebellion and adventure that has inspired scores of writers, musicians, and artists during the last one hundred years.

The son of an army captain, Rimbaud was born in the town of Charlesville in northeastern France. His parents separated when he was six, and he was raised by his mother, with whom he had an extremely stormy relationship. A brilliant student, Rimbaud first earned recognition for his poetry at the age of eight and was first published when he was only fifteen. Despite his early academic and literary achievements, Rimbaud was unsatisfied with life in Charlesville, and in 1870 he ran away to Paris but was arrested for traveling without a train ticket. After his former schoolmaster paid his fine, Rimbaud returned home, only to run away two more times during the coming year.

In August of 1871, Rimbaud sent some of his poems to the renowned French poet Paul Verlaine. Feeling that the poems were the work of an extremely gifted writer, Verlaine invited Rimbaud to visit him in Paris and even paid for Rimbaud's train fare. Rimbaud lived in Paris for close to a year, meeting many of the most prominent poets of the day, writing some of his finest poetry, and arousing controversy because of his rebellious, undisciplined life style. He also developed an extremely close relationship with Verlaine, who eventually abandoned his wife and traveled to London with the younger poet. There, the two poets became involved in frequent quarrels that ulti-

mately resulted in Verlaine's attempt to murder his young follower. While Verlaine was serving a two-year prison sentence, Rimbaud remained in London, where he lived in poverty, while continuing to write poetry and maintaining his wild bohemian life style.

In January of 1875, after Verlaine was released from prison, Rimbaud had his last meeting with Verlaine, during which he gave Verlaine the manuscript for his collection of prose poems, *Illuminations.* By the time Verlaine had the collection published in 1876, Rimbaud had abandoned writing and begun traveling around the world seeking adventure. Rimbaud's travels took him as far as Egypt, Cyprus, Indonesia, and Ethiopia; and he had stints as a soldier in the Dutch colonial army and as a performer in a traveling circus. In addition he worked as a coffee exporter and a gunrunner, and through his involvement in these occupations he managed to amass a fairly sizable amount of money.

While Rimbaud was living in Ethiopia, his reputation as a poet was growing in France. His *Illuminations* earned widespread acclaim among critics and writers and was applauded as the work of a mature, imaginative, innovative, and remarkably talented poet. Yet it seems that Rimbaud was almost completely unaware of the praise his work was receiving. Having developed close ties to the Ethiopian natives, he had immersed himself in native life. He was forced to return to France in April of 1891, however, after having developed a tumor on his knee. Unfortunately, even the best European doctors of the time could not save him, and in November of 1891 he died in the French city of Marseilles.

By the time of his death, Rimbaud's poetry had already begun to influence other writers; and during the twentieth century, his life style has become a model for such vagabond writers, artists, and musicians as Jack Kerouac and Bob Dylan. In addition, Rimbaud has been the subject of several biographies, and a number of literary works have been written about his relationship with Verlaine.

Objectives

Thematic

To grasp the eternal elements of nature

Skills

1 To appreciate borrowed characters

2 To write an extended characterization

3 To recognize abstact words

Support Material

Teaching Portfolio

Teacher Backup, p. 1099
Usage and Mechanics Worksheet, p. 1103
Vocabulary Check, p. 1104
Critical Thinking and Reading Worksheet, *Identifying Words that Signal Cause-and-Effect Relation-*

ships, p. 1105
Language Worksheet, *Recognizing Abstract Words*, p. 1106
Selection Test, pp. 1107–1108

Spelling Tip Tell students that they may find it helpful to break the word *obsession* into its three syllables and sound each syllable out.

GUIDE FOR INTERPRETING

Ophelia; Eternity

(continued from bottom of page)

Commentary

Characters from Previous Literary Works. One of the many ways in which writers draw upon the accomplishments of earlier writers is by borrowing, reusing, or redefining characters from previous literary works. In fact, in many cases a writer will borrow not only the characters but also the plot from an earlier literary work, reshaping and recasting it to create a new and original work of literature. For example, both Christopher Marlowe's *Dr. Faustus* (page 700) and Johann Wolfgang von Goethe's *Faust* (page 863) are based on the Faust legend from German folklore. Yet the numerous differences between the two works reveal that each writer has transformed the legend into his own distinctive literary work.

Borrowing characters enables writers to enhance the meaning of their literary works, because borrowed characters already possess the personality traits that were revealed in the work in which they first appeared. In other words readers who are familiar with borrowed characters are likely to already have an understanding of certain aspects of their personalities. Writers can then either develop the reader's appreciation for a character by building upon the existing personality traits, or they can provide the reader with a new perspective of the character by presenting a portrait of the character that in some way contradicts the earlier writer's portrayal.

Arthur Rimbaud borrows a character from *Hamlet* in his poem "Ophelia." In Shakespeare's play, Ophelia is a beautiful, innocent, modest, impressionable, and frail young maiden who is in love with Hamlet, the play's protagonist. Tortured by his inability to avenge his father's death, Hamlet, who had previously courted Ophelia, casts her away and claims that he never actually loved her. Hamlet then mistakenly kills Ophelia's father, Polonius, while attempting to stab his father's murderer. Unable to cope with her father's death coupled with Hamlet's rejection, Ophelia loses her sanity and becomes completely absorbed with singing and gathering flowers, which she laces in her hair. Eventually, she is found drowned in a river, and her death prompts a strong emotional reaction from Hamlet. In his poem Rimbaud builds upon Shakespeare's characterization of Ophelia, while probing into possible explanations for her death.

Writing

Select one of your favorite characters from a literary work or a movie. Then write a journal entry in which you discuss your impressions of the character's personality. At the end of your entry, explore the ways in which you would further develop the character if you were to create a new literary work or movie involving him or her.

erary works, movies, songs, or musical productions that draw on the Arthurian legend. Ask them why they think that the legend of Arthur has captured people's imaginations for so long.

Writing/Prior Knowledge Before students begin writing their journal entries, have them discuss some of their favorite characters from movies and literary works.

Teaching Tenth-Grade Students Because it is highly unlikely that tenth-grade students have read *Hamlet*, you might want to spend extra time going over the information about Ophelia in the Commentary. Explain to students that they will have a difficult time in understanding Rimbaud's poem if they are unfamiliar with Ophelia's role in *Hamlet*.

ESL Teaching Strategy Use these poems as a vocabulary lesson. Pair each ESL student with a bright native-speaking student. Ask the pairs to read the poems and to look up each word that either one or both of them do not know. Then have them discuss the definitions and possible uses of each word until both of them are sure they understand every word.

Vocabulary

Preteach the following vocabulary words:
flourish (flʉr´ ish) *v.*: Thrive
obsession (əb sesh´ ən) *n.*: Preoccupation with an idea, desire, or emotion
strains (strānz) *n.*: Traces
courtier (kôr´ tē ər) *n.*: An attendant at a royal court
sentinel (sen´ ti nəl) *n.*: A person or animal responsible for guarding a group
sanctions (saŋk´ shənz) *n.*: Rules of conduct
genesis (jen´ ə sis) *n.*: Beginning

Literary Focus You may want to introduce the subject of borrowed characters by tracing the history of the legend of King Arthur. Whether a real King Arthur existed in sixth-century Wales is unknown, although Geoffrey of Monmouth treated Arthur as a historical figure in his *History of the Kings of England*, written in Latin during the twelfth cen- tury. Despite Geoffrey of Monmouth's factual treatment of the subject, Arthur and his knights had already become the stuff of legend. By the fourteenth century, King Arthur's nephew, Sir Gawain, appeared in a metrical romance, *Sir Gawain and the Green Knight*. A century later, Sir Thomas Mallory completed *Morte d'Arthur*, a vivid account of the lives of King Arthur and his knights. In subsequent centuries, many other authors wrote works focusing on characters from the Arthurian legend. These works include Alfred, Lord Tennyson's *Idylls of the King* and Mark Twain's *A Connecticut Yankee in King Arthur's Court*.

Have students think of other lit-

Ophelia[1]

Arthur Rimbaud

translated by Daisy Aldan

I

On the calm black wave where the stars sleep
Floats white Ophelia like a great lily,
Floats very slowly, lying in her long veils . . .
—From the distant woods, the <u>flourish</u> of the kill.

5 For more than a thousand years sad Ophelia
White phantom, passes, on the long black river.
For more than a thousand years her sweet
   <u>obsession</u>
Whispers her love to the evening breeze.

The wind embraces her breasts and unfolds her
   great veils
10 In a corolla[2] gently rocked by the waters;

Trembling willows weep on her shoulder,
Reeds lean on her lofty pensive[3] brow.

Bruised water lilies sigh about her;
Sometimes in a sleeping alder tree she awakens
15 A nest; a tiny wing-flutter escapes;
Mysterious sounds fall from the golden stars.

II

O pale Ophelia! fair as snow!
You died, child, yes, carried off by a river!
Because the winds falling from the great cliffs of
   Norway
20 Spoke low to you of fierce freedom;

Because a wind, tearing your long hair,
Bore strange shouts to your dreaming spirit;

---

1. Ophelia: A character from Shakespeare's *Hamlet* who loses her sanity and eventually drowns in a river, after Hamlet refuses to return her love.

2. corolla (kə räl′ ə) *n.*: The petals, or inner floral leaves, of a flower.

---

3. pensive (pen′ siv) *adj.*: Thinking deeply or seriously, often of sad or melancholy things.

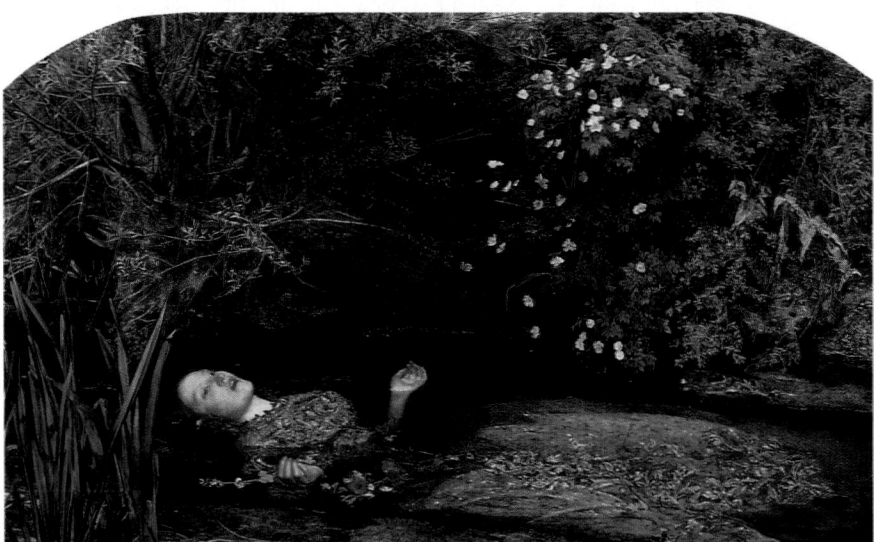

OPHELIA
John Everett Millais
Tate Gallery, London

Humanities Note

Fine art, *Ophelia* by John Everett Millais. Millais (1829–1896) was a highly regarded nineteenth-century English artist. For a brief period, he was a member of the Pre-Raphaelite Brotherhood, a group of painters dedicated to revitalizing craftsmanship, design, and decorative naturalism in an increasingly machine-dominated society. Throughout his career, Millais was known for his detailed, realistic paintings and illustrations. Because of his attention to detail, his works were often used to illustrate the writings of major British writers.

You might want to use the following questions to discuss the art:

1. What impression of Ophelia does this painting convey?
2. How does the artist's depiction of Ophelia compare with Rimbaud's depiction?
3. If you had to choose a piece of music to accompany this poem and this painting, what would you select?

Because your heart listened to the strains of
Nature
In the wails of the tree and the sighs of the nights.

25 Because the voice of mad seas, immense rattle,
Bruised your child's heart, too sweet and too
human;
Because on an April morning, a handsome pale
courtier,
A sorry fool, sat mutely at your feet!

Heaven! Love! Freedom! What a dream, O
Foolish girl!

30 You melted toward him as snow near flame:
Your words were strangled by your great visions
—And the terrible Infinite frightened your blue
eyes!

III

And the Poet says you come at night
To gather flowers in the rays of the stars;
35 And he has seen on the water, lying in her long
veils,
White Ophelia floating, like a great lily.

Reader's Response *What are your
impressions of Ophelia after reading
Rimbaud's poem? What are your feelings
about her?*

THINKING ABOUT THE SELECTION

Interpreting

1. How are light and dark colors used as a means of establishing Ophelia's purity and innocence?
2. (a) How does Rimbaud personify, or attribute human qualities to, nature in this poem? (b) What purpose does his personification of nature serve?
3. What natural current symbolizes, or represents, Ophelia's loss of contact with reality?
4. How does the final stanza reinforce the ideas conveyed in Part I?

Applying

5. Explain whether you think that most people would be able to cope with the type of loss and rejection that Ophelia experienced.

ANALYZING LITERATURE

Appreciating Borrowed Characters

Although Ophelia is one of the major characters in Shakespeare's *Hamlet,* the play focuses mainly on Hamlet and his painful internal struggle to overcome his idealistic, thoughtful, and compassionate nature and avenge his father's death. In his poem, however,

Rimbaud focuses entirely on Ophelia and the suffering that she experienced.

1. In Shakespeare's play Ophelia is portrayed as a simple, gentle, naive, and beautiful maiden. Explain whether Rimbaud's depiction of Ophelia is consistent with Shakespeare's depiction. In your explanation cite specific details from the poem.
2. What does Rimbaud mean when he writes that Ophelia was "too human" (line 26)?
3. What does Rimbaud's poem suggest about the reasons for Ophelia's death?
4. Explain whether it would be possible to understand this poem without some familiarity with the character of Ophelia from Shakespeare's play.

THINKING AND WRITING

Extending a Characterization

Write a poem or a short story in which you use at least one character from one of your favorite movies or literary works. If you want, you can use the character that you discussed in your journal entry. Before you begin you should decide whether you want to build upon or contradict the way in which the character is depicted in the film or literary work. Then you should brainstorm for ideas that you can use in your poem or

(continued from bottom of page)

3. It suggests that she went mad and was seduced to her death by the churning of the wind and the "voice of the mad seas."
4. It would not be possible to understand the poem without some knowledge of the play.

THINKING AND WRITING

Publishing Student Writing You might want to make photocopies of students' poems and short stories and arrange them into a class anthology.

5 **Discussion** Have students discuss what Rimbaud means when he writes that Ophelia's heart "listened to the strains of nature."

6 **Discussion** Have students discuss what Rimbaud means when he writes that Ophelia's heart was "too human."

7 **Literary Focus** Explain that the "handsome pale courtier" is Hamlet. Have students discuss the impression of Hamlet that Rimbaud conveys in these lines.

Cooperative Learning Have a group of students research the life of Paul Verlaine, with whom Rimbaud had a notorious and stormy relationship. Have students explore not only Verlaine's poetry, but also his life style. Once the students have presented their findings, explain that the wild life styles of Rimbaud and Verlaine, never the norm for poets of previous ages, became fixed in many people's minds as the typical life style of a poet.

Closure and Extension

ANSWERS TO THINKING ABOUT THE SELECTION

1. The darkness of the river highlights Ophelia's whiteness, which represents purity and innocence.
2. (a) Suggested response: He describes the elements of nature surrounding Ophelia as if they were

mourning her death. (b) Answers will differ. Students may respond that the emotions that Rimbaud attributes to nature parallel his own emotions.
3. The wind symbolizes her loss of contact with reality.
4. Suggested response: Both Part I and the final stanza convey the impression that Ophelia's spirit has lived on.
5. Answers will differ. Students may respond that many people would be

able to cope with the situation.

ANSWERS TO ANALYZING LITERATURE

1. His depiction is consistent with Shakespeare's. He depicts Ophelia as sad, loving, and childlike.
2. Suggested response: He is suggesting that she was too vulnerable and sensitive.

Eternity

Arthur Rimbaud

translated by Francis Golffing

1   I have recovered it.
What? Eternity.
It is the sea
Matched with the sun.

2   5 My <u>sentinel</u> soul,
Let us murmur the vow
Of the night so void
And of the fiery day.

  Of human <u>sanctions</u>,
10 Of common transports,
You free yourself:
You soar according . . .

From your ardor[1] alone,
Embers of satin,
15 Duty exhales,
Without anyone saying: at last.

Never a hope;
No genesis.
Skill with patience . . .
20 Anguish is certain.

I have recovered it.
What? Eternity.
It is the sea
Matched with the sun.

---

1. ardor (är′ dər) *n.*: Emotional warmth; passion.

THINKING ABOUT THE SELECTION

Interpreting

1. In this poem Rimbaud expresses the desire to escape from "human sanctions" and "common transports." How do the first and last stanzas relate to this desire?
2. (a) What does Rimbaud mean when he refers to the sea "matching" the sun? (b) How is Rimbaud's juxtaposition of the sea and the sun similar to his juxtaposition of night and day (lines 7–8)?
3. How does Rimbaud's statement that "anguish is certain" (line 20) relate to the rest of the poem?

Applying

4. What does eternity represent to you and how do you think it relates to your life?

UNDERSTANDING LANGUAGE

Recognizing Abstract Words

In "Eternity" Rimbaud uses a number of abstract words, or words that express qualities that exist apart from any particular object. However, he links most of these words with concrete images, or word pictures that appeal to one or more of the five senses. For example, Rimbaud links the abstract concept of *eternity* to the sea and the sun.

Define each of the following words from "Eternity." Then think of a concrete image that conveys the qualities expressed by the abstract word.

1. duty
2. hope
3. patience
4. anguish

Prose

LEO NIKOLAEVICH TOLSTOY RESTING IN A FOREST
I. E. Repin
Tretyakov Gallery, Moscow

GUY DE MAUPASSANT

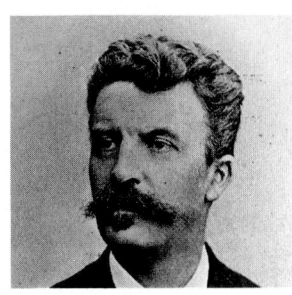

1850–1893

Focus

More About the Author Many authors have earned lasting fame with the publication of their first novel, but few have done so with the publication of their first short story. Guy de Maupassant is one who did. His short story "Ball of Fat" made him an instant celebrity. The story even won praise from the great French realist Gustave Flaubert. In a letter to Maupassant, Flaubert wrote, "I have been longing to tell you that I consider 'Ball of Fat' a *masterpiece.* Yes, young man, nothing more nor less than a masterpiece." Flaubert went on to predict, "That little tale will *live,* I promise you." Have students discuss what an endorsement from an established writer such as Flaubert might mean to a young writer.

Critical Evaluation The English novelist Virginia Woolf praised Maupassant's realism: "In English fiction there are a number of writers who gratify our sense of belief—Defoe, Swift, Trollope . . . , for example; among the French, one instantly thinks of Maupassant. Each of them assures us that things are precisely as they say they are. What they describe happens actually before our eyes. We get from their novels the same sort of refreshment and delight that we get from seeing something actually happen in the street below." Have students keep Woolf's comments in mind as they read the following story.

Few short story writers are as well-known as Guy de Maupassant (gē´ də mō pä sän´). Characterized by their realistic depiction of life, their underlying pessimism, their inescapable irony, and their surprise endings, Maupassant's stories have been enjoyed by generations of readers throughout the Western world and have influenced a number of twentieth-century writers.

Born in 1850 into an aristocratic and educated family, Maupassant spent his youth in Normandy. After graduating from high school, he joined the French armed forces and fought in the Franco-Prussian War. His experiences in the armed service had a profound impact on him and later surfaced in many of his literary works. Following his service in the army, Maupassant settled in Paris, where he worked as a government clerk. Although he detested his job, it provided him with the opportunity to closely observe the lives of French bureaucrats and enabled him to stockpile a wealth of material that he would later use in his short stories.

While living in Paris, Maupassant also began developing his skills as a writer, guided by the famous French writer Gustave Flaubert, who was a personal friend of Maupassant's mother. Maupassant also became a part of a circle of writers led by the French novelist Émile Zola. With Zola's encouragement and support, Maupassant published his first short story, "Ball of Fat," in 1880. The story earned him immediate fame, and from that point on he was able to devote himself exclusively to literary activities.

Maupassant went on to establish himself as a prolific and extremely popular writer, and his success made him a wealthy man. With the royalties he received from his first volume of short stories, *Madame Tellier's Establishment* (1881), he bought a large house in Normandy, and his earnings from his novels *A Woman's Life* (1883) and *Bel-Ami* (1884) enabled him to buy a yacht. As early as 1881, he wrote that he was "drawn by an imperious desire for Africa, by the nostalgia of an unknown desert," and he traveled to Algeria, where he stored away memories that he later used in writing *Au Soleil* (1884). His observations of the Mediterranean coast while traveling aboard his yacht en route to Algeria also provided him with material for his writing, which he later used in *Sur l'eau* (1888) and *La Vie errante* (1890).

Despite his enjoyment of life in the open air, Maupassant was plagued by health problems and frequent bouts of depression. In 1889 his brother Hervé had to be sent to an insane asylum and soon after Guy de Maupassant's psychological state began to deteriorate. After trying to take his own life, Maupassant himself was committed to an asylum, where he died in 1893.

Maupassant's inner turmoil is reflected in his later stories, which deal with the fantastic and the supernatural. These stories contrast with the majority of the three hundred short stories that he wrote, however. Although most of his stories present a somewhat grim and uncomplimentary portrait of the world, they depict life realistically and accurately. In "Two Friends," for example, Maupassant presents a graphic depiction of the violence and destruction of war.

Objectives

Thematic

To recognize the disturbing realities of war

Skills

1 To understand Realism and Naturalism

2 To recognize the author's attitudes

3 To write a naturalist story

GUIDE FOR INTERPRETING

Two Friends

Commentary

Realism and Naturalism. Emerging during the middle of the nineteenth century, **Realism** was a literary movement that in many ways contrasted with Romanticism. Unlike the Romantics, who often portrayed improbable, fantastic situations and events, the Realists sought to depict life as faithfully and accurately as possible. Led by the French writers Honoré de Balzac and Gustave Flaubert, the Realists wrote novels and short stories that delved deeply into the realities of a small group of people or a small portion of the world. For example, Flaubert's novel *Madame Bovary* (1857) presents an unflattering portrait of the lives of the inhabitants of a typical French provincial town. As is the case in *Madame Bovary*, the Realists generally focused on the lives of lower-class and middle-class characters. In depicting the lives of people faced with poverty and other hardships, the Realists confronted many of the harsh realities of the nineteenth-century world, often presenting pessimistic visions of the world dramatically different from the optimistic vision of the Romantics.

Another nineteenth-century literary movement, known as **Naturalism,** grew out of the Realistic movement. Like the Realists, the Naturalists attempted to depict life truthfully and accurately. Yet, while the Realists searched for the truths of existence by delving beneath the surface of everyday life, the Naturalists already possessed a well-defined view of the universe, which they imposed on their works. Led by the French writer Émile Zola, the Naturalists believed that a person's fate is determined by heredity, chance, and the elements of his or her environment. As a result, the Naturalists frequently depicted characters whose lives were shaped by forces of nature or society they could not understand or control. Despite their underlying powerlessness, the characters in Naturalist works generally conduct themselves with strength and dignity in the face of adversity, and in doing so affirm the significance of their existence.

Because he was briefly a member of a circle of writers led by Zola, Maupassant is sometimes classified as a Naturalist. However, Maupassant not only rejected the idea of having any sort of label attached to his writing, but he even denounced the Naturalist movement several years after leaving Zola's literary circle. Yet, despite his rejection of Naturalism, it cannot be denied that elements of Naturalism are visible in many of his stories.

Writing

Write a journal entry in which you discuss what it would be like if the United States were invaded by a powerful foreign army and a war were being fought on our own soil.

(continued from bottom of page)
theory of natural selection. Ask students to explain how the Naturalists' approach to writing reflects Darwin's theories.

Writing/Prior Knowledge Before students begin writing their journal entries, you may want to have a class discussion about the ways in which war affects the lives of civilians.

Teaching Tenth-Grade Students Make sure tenth-grade students understand the historical context of this story. Explain that the story is set in France during the Franco-Prussian War, a conflict in which the French were badly defeated. At the time of the story, the Germans had established a blockade around Paris, cutting off the city's access to supplies. Have students briefly discuss what life might have been like for a civilian in Paris during the siege. Explain to students that they are about to find out how two fictional Frenchmen responded to this situation.

ESL Teaching Strategy If any ESL students are from countries in which wars have been fought during the last several decades, you might want to have them offer their or their parents' impressions of the impact of these wars on daily life.

Vocabulary
Preteach the following vocabulary words:
jovial (jō′ vē əl) *adj.*: Genial and gay
pillaging (pil′ ij iŋ) *v.*: Plundering; looting
superimposed (sōō′ pər im pōzd′) *v.*: Placed on top of something else
jauntiness (jôn′ tē nəs) *n.*: Perkiness
draught (draft) *n.*: The amount of fish caught in one day
tranquil (traŋ′ kwəl) *adj.*: Calm
placidly (plas′ id lē) *v.*: Calmly

Support Material

Teaching Portfolio
Teacher Backup, p. 1109
Grammar in Action Worksheet, *Using Sensory Impressions*, p. 1113
Usage and Mechanics Worksheet, p. 1115
Vocabulary Check, p. 1116
Analyzing Literature Worksheet, *Understanding Realism and Naturalism*, p. 1117
Critical Thinking and Reading Worksheet, *Recognizing the Author's Attitude*, p. 1118
Selection Test, pp. 1119–1120

Spelling Tip Point out to students that the *s* sound in the word *placidly* is spelled with a *c*.

Literary Focus After students have finished reading about the two movements, ask them to explain why it is possible for Realism to show no signs of Naturalism but impossible for Naturalism not to be tied to Realism. Also point out that the leader of the Naturalist movement, Émile Zola, was an ardent supporter of Charles Darwin and his

Two Friends

Guy de Maupassant

translated by Gordon R. Silber

The following story is set during the Franco-Prussian War. Beginning on July 19, 1870, the war had resulted from the Prussian prime minister Otto von Bismarck's belief that a war with France would strengthen the bond between the German states, along with French emperor Napoleon III's feeling that a successful conflict with Prussia would help him to gain support among the French people. As it turned out, the French army was no match for the German forces. After a series of victories, one of which ended in the capture of Napoleon III, the German army established a blockade around Paris on September 19, 1870. Led by a provisional government, Paris managed to hold out until January 28, 1871, though the city's inhabitants were plagued by famine and a sense of hopelessness. As de Maupassant's story begins, the city is on the verge of surrender.

Paris was blockaded, starved, in its death agony. Sparrows were becoming scarcer and scarcer on the rooftops and the sewers were being depopulated. One ate whatever one could get.

As he was strolling sadly along the outer boulevard one bright January morning, his hands in his trousers pockets and his stomach empty, M.[1] Morissot, watchmaker by trade but local militiaman for the time being, stopped short before a fellow militiaman whom he recognized as a friend. It was M. Sauvage, a riverside acquaintance.

Every Sunday, before the war, Morissot left at dawn, a bamboo pole in his hand, a tin box on his back. He would take the Argenteuil[2] railroad, get off at Colombes,[3] and walk to Marante Island. As soon as he arrived at this ideal spot he would start to fish; he fished until nightfall.

Every Sunday he would meet a stout, jovial little man, M. Sauvage, a haberdasher[4] in Rue Notre-Dame-de-Lorette, another ardent fisherman. Often they spent half a day side by side, line in hand and feet dangling above the current. Inevitably they had struck up a friendship.

Some days they did not speak. Sometimes they did; but they understood one another admirably without saying anything because they had similar tastes and responded to their surroundings in exactly the same way.

On a spring morning, toward ten o'clock, when the young sun was drawing up from the tranquil stream wisps of haze which floated off in the direction of the current and was pouring down its vernal warmth on the backs of the two fanatical anglers,[5] Morissot would sometimes say to his neighbor, "Nice, isn't it?" and M. Sauvage would answer, "There's nothing like it." And that was enough for them to understand and appreciate each other.

On an autumn afternoon, when the sky, reddened by the setting sun, cast reflections of its scarlet clouds on the water, made the whole river crimson,

---

1. **M.:** Abbreviation for Monsieur (mə syö´), or "Mister" or "Sir" (French).

2. **Argenteuil** (ȧr zhän tö´ i): A city located across the Seine from Colombes.
3. **Colombes** (kôl ômb´): A city in north-central France, close to Paris.
4. **haberdasher** (hab´ ər dash´ ər) *n.*: A person who is in the business of selling men's clothing.
5. **anglers** (aŋ´ glərz) *n.*: People who fish.

lighted up the horizon, made the two friends look as ruddy as fire, and gilded the trees which were already brown and beginning to tremble with a wintery shiver, M. Sauvage would look at Morissot with a smile and say, "Fine sight!" And Morissot, awed, would answer, "It's better than the city, isn't it?" without taking his eyes from his float.

As soon as they recognized one another they shook hands energetically, touched at meeting under such changed circumstances. M. Sauvage, with a sigh, grumbled, "What goings-on!" Morissot groaned dismally, "And what weather! This is the first fine day of the year."

The sky was, in fact, blue and brilliant.

They started to walk side by side, absent-minded and sad. Morissot went on, "And fishing! Ah! Nothing but a pleasant memory."

"When'll we get back to it?" asked M. Sauvage.

They went into a little café and had an absinthe,[6] then resumed their stroll along the sidewalks.

Morissot stopped suddenly, "How about another, eh?" M. Sauvage agreed, "If you want." And they entered another wine shop.

On leaving they felt giddy, muddled, as one does after drinking on an empty stomach. It was mild. A caressing breeze touched their faces.

The warm air completed what the absinthe had begun. M. Sauvage stopped. "Suppose we went?"

"Went where?"

"Fishing, of course."

"But where?"

"Why, on our island. The French outposts are near Colombes. I know Colonel Dumoulin; they'll let us pass without any trouble."

Morissot trembled with eagerness: "Done! I'm with you." And they went off to get their tackle.

An hour later they were walking side by side on the highway. They reached the villa which the Colonel occupied. He smiled at their request and gave his consent to their whim. They started off again, armed with a pass.

Soon they passed the outposts, went through the abandoned village of Colombes, and reached the edge of the little vineyards which slope toward the Seine.[7] It was about eleven.

Opposite, the village of Argenteuil seemed dead. The heights of Orgemont and Sannois dominated the whole countryside. The broad plain which stretches as far as Nanterre[8] was empty, absolutely empty, with its bare cherry trees and its colorless fields.

Pointing up to the heights, M. Sauvage murmured, "The Prussians are up there!" And a feeling of uneasiness paralyzed the two friends as they faced this deserted region.

"The Prussians!" They had never seen any, but for months they had felt their presence—around Paris, ruining France, pillaging, massacring, starving the country, invisible and all-powerful. And a kind of superstitious terror was superimposed on the hatred which they felt for this unknown and victorious people.

Morissot stammered, "Say, suppose we met some of them?"

His Parisian jauntiness coming to the surface in spite of everything, M. Sauvage answered, "We'll offer them some fish."

But they hesitated to venture into the country, frightened by the silence all about them.

Finally M. Sauvage pulled himself together: "Come on! On our way! But let's go carefully." And they climbed over into a vineyard, bent double, crawling, taking advantage of the vines to conceal themselves, watching, listening.

A stretch of bare ground had to be crossed to reach the edge of the river. They began to run, and when they reached the bank they plunged down among the dry reeds.

Morissot glued his ear to the ground and listened for sounds of anyone walking in the vicinity. He heard nothing. They were indeed alone, all alone.

Reassured, they started to fish.

Opposite them Marante Island, deserted, hid them from the other bank. The little building which had housed a restaurant was shut up and looked as if it had been abandoned for years.

---

6. **absinthe** (ab′ sinth)*n*.: A type of liqueur.

7. **the Seine** (sān): A river in northern France, flowing northwest through Paris into the English Channel.

8. **Nanterre** (nä*n* ter′): Another city located on the Seine.

4 **Discussion** Have students explain why the two characters are no longer able to go fishing.

5 **Discussion** Have students discuss what leads the two men to their decision to go fishing. Do students think this is a wise decision? Why or why not?

6 **Discussion** Ask students why the Colonel smiles at the men's request. What, if anything, does the Colonel's smile suggest about his attitude toward the two men and their request?

7 **Discussion** Have students discuss the possible significance of Maupassant's use of the word *armed* in the final sentence of this paragraph. Is there any irony in his use of the word? Explain.

8 **Reading Strategy** Some readers have a tendency to skip passages of description. Tell students that because Maupassant's stories tend to be very spare, it is important for them to read his descriptions carefully. Point out that this passage highlights the lifelessness of the countryside. Ask students why the lifelessness of the countryside is important.

9 **Reading Strategy** Have students predict what might actually happen if the two friends did encounter some Prussian soldiers.

so distinctly that we believe we see them before our eyes and find them more real than reality itself. He makes them live, but he does not judge them . . . His indifference is equal to that of nature; it astonishes me, it irritates me. I would like to know what is the inner belief and feeling of this pitiless, robust, and good-natured man.

Humanities Note

Fine art, *Les Maisons Cabassud à la Ville d'Avray* by Jean Baptiste Camille Corot. A predecessor of the Impressionists, Corot (1796–1875) was one of the first French painters devoted to capturing the vitality and freshness of nature. Deeply attached to the many facets of the French landscape, Corot enjoyed depicting the forests of Brittany and the coast of Normandy. Another of his favorite painting sites was northern France, especially the town of Avray, which is the subject of this painting.

You might want to use the following questions to discuss the art:

1. How would you describe the mood, or atmosphere, of this painting?
2. How does the painting convey a sense of harmony between humanity and nature?
3. Do you think that this painting is an appropriate illustration for the story? Why or why not?
4. Does the scene depicted in the painting seem inviting? Why or why not?

LES MAISONS CABASSUD À LA VILLE D'AVRAY
(THE CABASSUD HOUSES IN THE TOWN OF AVRAY)
Camille Corot

M. Sauvage caught the first gudgeon.[9] Morissot got the second, and from then on they pulled in their lines every minute or two with a silvery little fish squirming on the end, a truly miraculous draught.

Skillfully they slipped the fish into a sack made of fine net which they had hung in the water at their feet. And happiness pervaded their whole being, the happiness which seizes upon you when you regain a cherished pleasure of which you have long been deprived.

The good sun was pouring down its warmth on their backs. They heard nothing more; they no longer thought about anything at all; they forgot about the rest of the world—they were fishing!

---

9. **gudgeon** (guj′ ən) *n*.: A small, European freshwater fish.

Grammar in Action

The term **sensory impressions** refers to what people see, hear, feel, smell, and taste. To enable readers to identify with the characters, fiction writers often describe the sensory impressions of their characters. For example, note how Guy de Maupassant captures the sensory impressions of M. Sauvage and M. Morissot in the following passages from "Two Friends":

The good sun was pouring down their backs. (sense of touch)
They heard nothing more. (sense of hearing)
Morissot turned and saw, over the bank to the left, the great silhouette of Mount Valérien wearing a white plume on its brow, powdersmoke, which it had just spit out. (sense of sight)

Student Activity 1. Identify the sense or senses to which each of the following sensory impressions appeals.
1. "But suddenly a dull sound which seemed to come from under ground made the earth tremble."
2. "Then more followed, and time after time the mountain belched forth death-dealing breath, breathed out milky-white vapor which rose slowly in the calm sky and formed a cloud above the summit."

But suddenly a dull sound which seemed to come from under ground made the earth tremble. The cannon were beginning.

Morissot turned and saw, over the bank to the left, the great silhouette of Mount Valérien wearing a white plume on its brow, powdersmoke which it had just spit out.

And almost at once a second puff of smoke rolled from the summit, and a few seconds after the roar still another explosion was heard.

Then more followed, and time after time the mountain belched forth death-dealing breath, breathed out milky-white vapor which rose slowly in the calm sky and formed a cloud above the summit.

M. Sauvage shrugged his shoulders. "There they go again," he said.

As he sat anxiously watching his float bob up and down, Morissot was suddenly seized by the wrath which a peace-loving man will feel toward madmen who fight, and grumbled, "Folks sure are stupid to kill one another like that."

M. Sauvage answered, "They're worse than animals."

And Morissot, who had just pulled in a bleak, went on, "And to think that it will always be like this as long as there are governments."

M. Sauvage stopped him: "The Republic[10] wouldn't have declared war—"

Morissot interrupted: "Under kings you have war abroad; under the Republic you have war at home."

And they started a leisurely discussion, unraveling great political problems with the sane reasonableness of easygoing, limited individuals, and found themselves in agreement on the point that men would never be free. And Mount Valérien thundered unceasingly, demolishing French homes with its cannon, crushing out lives, putting an end to the dreams which many had dreamt, the joys which many had been waiting for, the happiness which many had hoped for, planting in wives' hearts, in maidens' hearts, in mothers' hearts, over there, in other lands, sufferings which would never end.

"That's life for you," opined M. Sauvage.

"You'd better say 'That's death for you,'" laughed Morissot.

But they shuddered in terror when they realized that someone had just come up behind them, and looking around they saw four men standing almost at their elbows, four tall men, armed and bearded, dressed like liveried[11] servants, with flat caps on their heads, pointing rifles at them.

The two fish lines dropped from their hands and floated off down stream.

In a few seconds they were seized, trussed up, carried off, thrown into a rowboat and taken over to the island.

And behind the building which they had thought deserted they saw a score of German soldiers.

A kind of hairy giant who was seated astride a chair smoking a porcelain pipe asked them in excellent French: "Well, gentlemen, have you had good fishing?"

Then a soldier put down at the officer's feet the sack full of fish which he had carefully brought along. The Prussian smiled: "Aha! I see that it didn't go badly. But we have to talk about another little matter. Listen to me and don't get excited.

"As far as I am concerned, you are two spies sent to keep an eye on me. I catch you and I shoot you. You were pretending to fish in order to conceal your business. You have fallen into my hands, so much the worse for you. War is like that.

"But—since you came out past the outposts you have, of course, the password to return. Tell me that password and I will pardon you."

The two friends, side by side, pale, kept silent. A slight nervous trembling shook their hands.

The officer went on: "No one will ever know. You will go back placidly. The secret will disappear with you. If you refuse, it is immediate death. Choose."

They stood motionless, mouths shut.

The Prussian quietly went on, stretching out his hand toward the stream: "Remember that with-

---

10. The Republic: The provisional republican government that assumed control when Napoleon III was captured by the Prussians.

---

11. liveried (liv′ ər ēd) *adj.*: Uniformed.

12 Critical Thinking and Reading Point out to students that the apparent beliefs of a third-person narrator do not necessarily reflect those of the author. Thus, it can be tricky to try to extract Maupassant's personal attitudes from the narrator's observations. Still, when the narrator notes that "Morissot was suddenly seized by a wrath which a peace-loving man will feel toward madmen who fight," a reader can probably assume that Maupassant shares Morissot's, Sauvage's, and the narrator's view of war.

13 Discussion Have students discuss how this observation may have been shaped by France's plight at the time. What, if anything, does this comment suggest about M. Morissot's political beliefs?

14 Literary Focus Ask students to discuss how this paragraph reflects the views of the Naturalists.

15 Discussion Ask students why the reader is immediately aware of the identity of these men.

16 Discussion Maupassant often gives the reader very little to go on in trying to understand a character's motives and beliefs. Ask students what, if anything, can be said about the Colonel's character based on this brief speech.

17 Discussion Do students think that the two friends know the password? Why or why not?

18 Literary Focus Do students think that fate has put the two friends in this unfortunate position? Or are the two men themselves responsible for their predicament?

---

3. "Morissot glued his ear to the ground and listened for sounds of anyone walking in the vicinity. He heard nothing."
4. "But they shuddered in terror when they realized that someone had just come up behind them, and looking around they saw four men standing almost at their elbows, four tall men, armed and bearded, dressed like liveried servants, with flat caps on their heads, pointing rifles at them."
5. "On a spring morning, toward ten o'clock, when the young sun was drawing up from the tranquil stream wisps of haze which floated off in the direction of the current and was pouring down its vernal warmth on the backs of the two fanatical anglers, . . ."

Student Activity 2. Write a paragraph describing your own participation in an activity you especially enjoy. Focus on conveying your sensory impressions, making sure to include impressions appealing to at least three different senses.

19 Discussion If the two men did in fact know the password and chose to reveal it, do students think the Prussian officer would have spared them as he had promised? Why or why not?

20 Discussion Ask students how they would characterize the two men's behavior in their final moments.

21 Enrichment Students should recognize the irony of this sequence of events. The two friends, who were going to eat their fish, will presumably have fish eat them. Meanwhile, the German officer, who has had the two friends executed (as they trembled and squirmed like fish), has now given orders to have the fish fried while they are still alive. Have students discuss the parallels between the fate of the two men and the fate of the fish. Then ask them whether they regard this ending as naturalistic. Why or why not?

Cultural Note Maupassant's short stories have influenced many twentieth-century American fiction writers. If students have already studied American literature, have them discuss any similarities between Maupassant's story and some of the twentieth-century American short stories they have read.

Cooperative Learning Students might be interested in learning more about the Franco–Prussian War. Divide them into groups of three or four. Then have each group research a specific topic related to the war, such as the major causes of the war. Once the groups have completed their research, have them share their findings with the rest of the class.

in five minutes you will be at the bottom of that river. Within five minutes! You have relatives, of course?"

Mount Valérien kept thundering.

The two fishermen stood silent. The German gave orders in his own language. Then he moved his chair so as not to be near the prisoners and twelve men took their places, twenty paces distant, rifles grounded.

The officer went on: "I give you one minute, not two seconds more."

19 Then he rose suddenly, approached the two Frenchmen, took Morissot by the arm, dragged him aside, whispered to him, "Quick, the password? Your friend won't know. I'll pretend to relent."

Morissot answered not a word.

The Prussian drew M. Sauvage aside and put the same question.

M. Sauvage did not answer.

They stood side by side again.

And the officer began to give commands. The soldiers raised their rifles.

Then Morissot's glance happened to fall on the sack full of gudgeons which was lying on the grass a few steps away.

20 A ray of sunshine made the little heap of still squirming fish gleam. And he almost weakened. In spite of his efforts his eyes filled with tears.

He stammered, "Farewell, Monsieur Sauvage."

M. Sauvage answered, "Farewell, Monsieur Morissot."

They shook hands, trembling from head to foot with a shudder which they could not control.

The officer shouted, "Fire!"

The twelve shots rang out together.

M. Sauvage fell straight forward, like a log. Morissot, who was taller, tottered, half turned, and fell crosswise on top of his comrade, face up, as the blood spurted from his torn shirt.

The German gave more orders.

His men scattered, then returned with rope and stones which they tied to the dead men's feet. Then they carried them to the bank.

Mount Valérien continued to roar, its summit hidden now in a mountainous cloud of smoke.

Two soldiers took Morissot by the head and the feet, two others seized M. Sauvage. They swung the bodies for a moment then let go. They described an arc and plunged into the river feet first, for the weights made them seem to be standing upright.

There was a splash, the water trembled, then grew calm, while tiny wavelets spread to both shores.

A little blood remained on the surface.

The officer, still calm, said in a low voice: "Now the fish will have their turn."

And he went back to the house.

And all at once he caught sight of the sack of gudgeons in the grass. He picked it up, looked at it, smiled, shouted, "Wilhelm!"

A soldier in a white apron ran out. And the Prussian threw him the catch of the two and said: "Fry these little animals right away while they are still alive. They will be delicious."

Then he lighted his pipe again.

Reader's Response *Did you find this story especially shocking or disturbing? If so, why? Do you think that a story such as this can have a lasting impact on readers? Why or why not?*

Primary Source

In the following passage, the literary critic Branden Matthews discusses Maupassant's growth as a writer:

"The inquirers who should read his stories in the strict sequence of their production could not fail to be struck with the first awakening of his curiousity about human feeling; and they might easily trace the steady growth of his interest in psychological states. Telling us at first bluntly and barely what his characters did, he came in time to find his chief pleasure in suggesting to us not only what they felt, but especially what they vaguely feared. Toward the end of his brief career the thought of death and the dread of mental disease seemed to possess him more and more with a haunting horror that kept recurring with pathetic persistence."

Given Matthews's observation, do students think that Maupassant wrote "Two Friends" early or late in his career?

Closure and Extension

ANSWERS TO THINKING ABOUT THE SELECTION

1. (a) Suggested response: The mood is characterized by bleakness and a sense of desperation. (b) Suggested response: It is established in the first paragraph through the image of Parisians eating sparrows and rats.

THINKING ABOUT THE SELECTION

Interpreting

1. (a) What is the mood, or atmosphere, of the story? (b) How and when is the mood established?
2. (a) How does Maupassant characterize the friendship between M. Morissot and M. Sauvage? (b) What motivates the two men to go fishing?
3. (a) What is the significance of the fact that the villages of Colombes and Argenteuil and the surrounding areas are deserted? (b) How does the emptiness of the landscape foreshadow, or hint at, the events that occur later in the story?
4. (a) Considering the outcome of the story, what is ironic, or surprising, about M. Sauvage's remark that if they met the Prussians they would "offer them some fish"? (b) What is ironic about the happiness that the men feel when they begin to fish? (c) What is ironic about M. Morissot's remark, "That's death for you"?
5. What is the significance of the two men's comments concerning war and its relation to republics and monarchies?
6. How does the description of the physical appearance and actions of the Prussian soldiers support the two men's earlier impressions of the Prussian forces?
7. (a) How would you characterize the Prussian officer's manner and outlook on life? (b) How does his outlook on life compare to that expressed by the two fishermen prior to the arrival of the Prussians?
8. How does the suddenness of the story's climax contribute to its effectiveness?
9. (a) What effect does Maupassant produce by juxtaposing the execution of the fishermen with the frying of the fish? (b) What is the effect of his juxtaposition of the peacefulness of fishing with the violence of war?

Applying

10. (a) If you were in the place of one of the two friends in Maupassant's story, would you have gone fishing? Why or why not? (b) Should the two friends be blamed for their own deaths? Why or why not?

ANALYZING LITERATURE

Understanding Realism and Naturalism

Although Maupassant rejected the idea of being labeled as either a Realist or a Naturalist, certain elements of these two movements are readily apparent in his works. For example, like most Realist stories, "Two Friends" focuses on working-class characters and depicts events in a grimly accurate manner.

1. How does Maupassant's use of actual place names contribute the realistic quality of the story?
2. How does Maupassant's graphic depiction of the deaths of M. Morissot and M. Sauvage contribute to the story's realistic quality?
3. Naturalist works often present a pessimistic vision of the world. Explain whether this is the case with Maupassant's story.
4. The characters in Naturalist works are frequently depicted as having little control over their fates. Explain whether this is the case with M. Morrisot and M. Sauvage in "Two Friends."

CRITICAL THINKING AND READING

Recognizing the Author's Attitude

To fully appreciate the meaning and significance of a literary work, you must be able to recognize the author's attitude toward his or her subject. A writer's attitude is generally revealed through his or her depiction of characters and choice of words and details.

1. What does this story suggest about Maupassant's attitude toward war?
2. What details in the story reveal Maupassant's attitude?
3. (a) What message about war is Maupassant trying to convey? (b) How successful is he at achieving his purpose?

THINKING AND WRITING

Writing a Naturalist Story

Write a short story that focuses on characters who find themselves at the mercy of forces they can neither understand nor control. Begin by gathering with a group of your classmates and brainstorming for ideas. Jot down the ideas that you find most interesting. Then develop one of the ideas into a plot for a short story. As you write your story, remember that you should try to make it as accurate and realistic as possible. When you have finished writing, revise your story, making sure the characters are well developed and that the dialogue seems natural and realistic. After you have finished revising your story, share it with your classmates.

(continued from bottom of page)

8. Suggested response: It reinforces the disturbing, shocking nature of the events.
9. (a) Suggested response: Both are treated as unimportant "little animals." (b) Suggested response: It helps to accentuate the brutality of war.
10. (a) Answers will differ. (b) Answers will differ.

Challenge Is the French colonel partially responsible for the death of the two friends? Why or why not?

ANSWERS TO ANALYZING LITERATURE

1. Suggested response: The use of real place names makes the story seem like a historical account.
2. Suggested response: Maupassant's detailed depiction of their deaths creates a vivid, realistic picture in the reader's mind. It makes readers feel as if they have actually witnessed the event.
3. Suggested response: It is the case with the story. Maupassant seems to think that wars are inevitable, that their cruelty is inherent, and that they cause needless destruction.
4. Answers will differ. Many students will respond that the characters caused their own death by deciding to go fishing.

ANSWERS TO CRITICAL THINKING AND READING

1. Suggested response: Maupassant thinks that war is violent, cruel, and destructive.
2. Suggested response: The two characters' observations about war reflect Maupassant's attitude. His brutal depiction of the two characters' death also reflects his attitude.
3. (a) Suggested response: His message is that war is cruel and impersonal and that the biggest losers in war are the common people. (b) Answers will differ. Many students will say that he succeeds in achieving his purpose through his graphic depiction of events.

THINKING AND WRITING

Publishing Student Writing Encourage students to submit their stories to the school literary magazine.

2. (a) Suggested response: It is a friendship based solely on a mutual love of fishing. (b) Their thoughts are muddled by the absinthe they have been drinking.
3. (a) They are deserted because the Prussians have seized control of the region, and the French residents have fled. (b) Suggested response: The emptiness reflects the fact that the Prussians are in control of the region,

and the Prussians pose great danger to the two friends.
4. (a) Suggested response: It is ironic because the Prussians do in fact end up eating the fish after they have executed the two men. (b) Suggested response: It is ironic because their happiness is about to be replaced by terror and death. (c) Suggested response: Their death follows very soon after the remark.

5. Answers will differ.
6. Suggested response: The Prussians are very large and rugged looking.
7. (a) Suggested response: He is brusque and puts his military duty above humanity. (b) Suggested response: His outlook contrasts sharply with that of the two men. They think war is stupid. He seems to unquestioningly accept it and performs his duties in a cold, businesslike manner.

NIKOLAI GOGOL

1809–1852

During his short life, Nikolai Gogol (nē′ kồ lī′ gō′ gəl) established himself as one of the finest and most influential Russian writers of the nineteenth century, creating works characterized by a unique blend of Romanticism, Realism, and comedy.

The son of a small landowner, Gogol was born in the Ukraine. As a teenager, he suffered from feelings of isolation and discontent and turned to writing as a means of expressing these emotions. After graduating from high school in 1828, he moved to St. Petersburg (Leningrad in the former Soviet Union), hoping to forge an exciting and fulfilling life. He lived there for eight years, working mostly as a minor civil servant and a private tutor, and also briefly serving as a history professor at the University of St. Petersburg. At the same time, he established himself as a successful writer, publishing his first collection of short stories, *Evenings on a Farm Near Dikanka*, in 1832. In these stories Gogol paints a vivid, detailed portrait of Ukrainian life, into which he introduces elements of the supernatural, such as water nymphs, witches, and magicians.

In his second and third collections of stories, *Mirgorod* (1835) and *Arabesques* (1835), Gogol continued to blend realism with fantasy, while adding touches of humor. His sense of humor came to the forefront in his first play, *The Inspector General* (1836), a satirical comedy that pokes fun at the Russian government. Gogol's depiction of Russian bureaucrats as being gullible and dishonest created a controversy that prompted Gogol to leave Russia and settle in Rome.

While living in Rome, Gogol began devoting all his energy to writing *Dead Souls* (1842), his longest and most ambitious work. When this novel was published, it was immediately lauded as Gogol's masterpiece. Unlike earlier Russian novels, *Dead Souls* depicts everyday Russian life without flattery and without exaggeration. As a result, it is generally regarded as the first Russian Realistic novel.

In 1842 Gogol also published his most famous short story, "The Overcoat." In the remaining years of his life, however, he produced very little. Feeling that he had a serious moral lesson to teach, Gogol was deeply disturbed by the fact that many people thought of him as a storyteller and a humorist. While suffering from constant psychological turmoil and frequent bouts of physical illness, he worked on a second volume of *Dead Souls*, in which he hoped to convey a more positive message. But after ten years of unrewarding work on this project, he directed his servant to put the unfinished manuscript into an oven and burn it. Ten days later he died.

It is unfortunate that Gogol was dissatisfied with his work and his reputation when he died. In the years since his death, he has come to be recognized not only for his storytelling ability and his use of humor, but also for his awareness of life's ironies and injustices and his understanding of human nature. In addition, because of his grimly accurate portrayal of nineteenth-century Russian life, he has come to be regarded as the founder of Russian Realism, although many of his works contain elements of the supernatural.

GUIDE FOR INTERPRETING

Commentary

The Overcoat

Symbol. A **symbol** is a person, place, or thing that has a meaning in itself and also represents something larger than itself. For example, a flag symbolizes the character, attitude, and values of the country it represents.

While some symbols are easy to interpret, others are complex, having a number of possible meanings. The overcoat in Gogol's story is an example of an extremely complex symbol. If we pay close attention to the main character Akaky's thoughts and feelings about the overcoat, as well as the ways in which it seems to affect his character, we become aware that the overcoat has a wide array of different meanings.

Noticing that the overcoat makes other people look at him differently than they did before, Akaky starts to see himself differently. He feels like a new person, so he starts to have new thoughts. He begins to look at things as if for the first time—he notices posters in store windows, pays attention to women, starts going to parties. As a result, the overcoat becomes a symbol of Akaky's new identity and his new outlook on the world.

At the same time, the overcoat also comes to represent security, warmth, and companionship. The coat protects Akaky from the biting cold, encircling him with warmth, like a mother's womb. In addition, because the coat is so well constructed, Akaky envisions it as a lifelong companion, a permanent friend.

As the story progresses, the overcoat continues to generate and accumulate new meanings—even after its owner has died. Often the symbolic meanings of the overcoat contrast sharply with one another. For example, though the overcoat represents Akaky's "security blanket," implying the security of childhood, or protectedness of something well known and familiar, it also represents all the risks of novelty—new thoughts, new feelings, new desires.

The various, often contradictory, symbolic meanings of the overcoat are closely tied to the story's theme, or central message. As you read the story, note as many of the overcoat's symbolic meanings as you can, and think about what these symbolic meanings suggest about the story's theme.

Writing

As is the case in "The Overcoat," material possessions can have a dramatic impact on the way people view themselves. Write a journal entry in which you explore the reasons for this phenomenon. Offer some examples of the types of material possessions that can affect people in this way and discuss any instances in which a material possession has had this type of impact on you.

(continued from bottom of page)

phasis on freedom, justice, and equality. What symbols are used to represent other countries? What symbols are used in television commercials? For what other purposes are symbols used in everyday life?

Writing/Prior Knowledge Before students begin their journal entries, have a class discussion in which students provide examples of the types of material possessions that can have an impact on the way people view themselves.

Teaching Tenth-Grade Students You may want to have tenth-grade students read the story aloud in class. Pause occasionally to discuss Akaky's personality, his involvement with other characters, and the ways in which he changes after he acquires the overcoat.

ESL Teaching Strategy Read over the story's footnotes with ESL students, making sure they fully understand each definition.

Vocabulary

Preteach the following vocabulary words:

contrived (kən trīvd´) *adj.*: Not spontaneous or natural

indiscriminately (in´ dis krim´ ə nit lē) *adv.*: Randomly

vestibule (ves´ tə byōōl´) *n.*: A small entrance hall or room

conjecturing (kən jek´ cher iŋ) *v.*: Guessing

embellished (im bel´ isht) *v.*: Ornamented; adorned

exorbitant (ig zôr´ bə tənt) *adj.*: Excessive

irrefutable (i ref´ yoo tə b´l) *adj.*: That cannot be disproved

subordinate (sə bôr´ də nit) *n.*: A person who is inferior in rank, power, or importance

Spelling Tip Call students' attention to the double *l* in the word *embellished* and to the double *r* in the word *irrefutable*.

Literary Focus Have students discuss the role of symbols in everyday life. For example, point out that many people buy certain types of cars or certain types of clothes to symbolize their wealth or their social status. Also make sure students note the many symbols (the bald eagle, for example) used to represent the United States and its em-

The Overcoat

Nikolai Gogol

translated by Andrew R. MacAndrew

Once, in a department . . . but better not mention which department. There is nothing touchier than departments, regiments, bureaus, in fact, any caste of officials. Things have reached the point where every individual takes an insult to himself as a slur on society as a whole. It seems that not long ago a complaint was lodged by the police inspector of I forget which town, in which he stated clearly that government institutions had been imperiled and his own sacred name taken in vain. In evidence he produced a huge volume, practically a novel, in which, every ten pages, a police inspector appears, and what's more, at times completely drunk. So, to stay out of trouble, let us refer to it just as *a department.*

And so, once, in *a department,* there worked a clerk. This clerk was nothing much to speak of: he was small, somewhat pockmarked, his hair was somewhat reddish and he even looked somewhat blind. Moreover, he was getting thin on top, had wrinkled cheeks and a complexion that might be aptly described as hemorrhoidal. But that's the Petersburg[1] climate for you.

As to his civil-service category (for first a man's standing should be established), he was what is called an eternal pen-pusher, a lowly ninth-class clerk, the usual butt of the jeers and jokes of those writers who have the congenial[2] habit of biting those who cannot bite back.

The clerk's name was Shoenik. There is no doubt that this name derives from shoe but we know nothing of how, why, or when. His father, his grandfather, and even his brother-in-law wore boots, having new soles put on them not more than three times a year.

His first name was Akaky, like his father's, which made him Akaky Akakievich. This may sound somewhat strange and contrived but it is not contrived at all, and, in view of the circumstances, any other name was unthinkable. If I am not mistaken, Akaky Akakievich was born on the night between the 22nd and the 23rd of March. His late mother, an excellent woman and the wife of a clerk, had made all the arrangements for the child's christening, and, while she was still confined to her bed, the godparents arrived: the worthy Ivan Yeroshkin, head clerk in the Senate, and Arina Whitetumkin, the wife of a police captain, a woman of rare virtue.

The new mother was given her pick of the following three names for her son: Mochius, Sossius, and that of the martyr, Hotzazat. "That won't do," Akaky's late mother thought. "Those names are . . . how shall I put it . . ." To please her, the godparents opened the calendar at another page and again three names came out: Strifilius, Dulius, and Varachasius.

"We're in a mess," the old woman said. "Who ever heard of such names? If it was something like Varadat or Varuch, I wouldn't object . . . but Strifilius and Varachasius . . ."

So they turned to yet another page and out came Pavsicachius and Vachtisius.

---

1. **Petersburg:** St. Petersburg, a city in northwestern Russia, known as Leningrad in the former Soviet Union.
2. **congenial** (kən jēn′ yəl) *adj.*: Friendly; sympathetic.

**SELF-PORTRAIT BETWEEN
CLOCK AND BED (detail)**
Edvard Munch
Munch-Museet, Olso

4 **Enrichment** Explain that prior to the invention of carbon paper and photocopiers, people had to be hired to copy documents by hand. Have students discuss what they imagine it would be like to be employed as a copy clerk. Does it seem like a job that any of them would like to have? Why or why not?

Humanities Note
Fine art, *Self-Portrait Between Clock and Bed* by Edvard Munch. Born in Oslo, Norway, Munch (1863–1944) was a painter and graphic artist whose life was filled with tragedy and hardships, including the death of many members of his family, frequent bouts of ill health, and a number of unhappy love affairs. Consequently, it is not surprising that his work portrays the psychic anguish and ultimate loneliness of modern life. In describing his aim as a painter, he once wrote, "I shall paint living people who breathe, feel, suffer, and love. The sacredness of this will be understood and people will take off their hats as though they were in church."

You might want to use the following questions to discuss the art:
1. How would you describe the mood, or atmosphere, of this painting?
2. How would you characterize the person depicted in the painting?
3. Does this person remind you of Akaky Akakievich? If so, how?
4. What emotions does this painting evoke in you? Why?

"Well, that's that," the mother said. "That settles it. He'll just have to be Akaky like his father."

So that's how Akaky Akakievich originated.

And when they christened the child it cried and twisted its features into a sour expression as though it had a foreboding that it would become a ninth-class clerk.

Well, that's how it all happened and it has been reported here just to show that the child couldn't have been called anything but Akaky.

No one remembers who helped him get his appointment to the department or when he started working there. Directors and all sorts of chiefs came and went but he was always to be found at the same place, in the same position, and in the same capacity, that of copying clerk. Until, after a while, people began to believe that he must have been born just as he was, shabby frock coat, bald patch, and all.

In the office, not the slightest respect was shown him. The porters didn't get up when he passed. In fact, they didn't even raise their eyes, as if nothing but an ordinary fly had passed through the reception room. His chiefs were cold and despotic[3] with him. Some head clerks would just

_____
3. **despotic** (de spät´ ik) *adj.*: Of or like an absolute ruler; tyrannical.

thrust a paper under his nose without even saying, "Copy this," or "Here's a nice interesting little job for you," or some such pleasant remark as is current in well-bred offices. And Akaky Akakievich would take the paper without glancing up to see who had put it under his nose or whether the person was entitled to do so. And right away he would set about copying it.

The young clerks laughed at him and played tricks on him to the limit of their clerkish wit. They made up stories about him and told them in front of him. They said that his seventy-year-old landlady beat him and asked him when the wedding would be. They scattered scraps of paper which they said was snow over his head. But with all this going on, Akaky Akakievich never said a word and even acted as though no one were there. It didn't even affect his work and in spite of their loud badgering he made no mistakes in his copying. Only when they tormented him unbearably, when they jogged his elbow and prevented him from getting on with his work, would he say:

"Let me be. Why do you do this to me? . . ."

And his words and the way he said them sounded strange. There was something touching about them. Once a young man who was new to the office started to tease him, following the crowd. Suddenly he stopped as if awakened from a trance and, after that, he couldn't stand the others, whom at first he had deemed decent people. And for a long time to come, during his gayest moments, he would suddenly see in his mind's eye the little, balding clerk and he would hear the words, "Let me be. Why do you do this to me?" and within those words rang the phrase, "I am your brother." And the young man would cover his face with his hands. Later in life, he often shuddered, musing about the wickedness of man toward man and all the cruelty and vulgarity which are concealed under refined manners. And this, he decided, was also true of men who were considered upright and honorable.

It would be hard to find a man who so lived for his job. It would not be enough to say that he worked conscientiously—he worked with love. There, in his copying, he found an interesting, pleasant world for himself and his delight was re-flected in his face. He had his favorites among the letters of the alphabet and, when he came to them, he would chuckle, wink and help them along with his lips so that they could almost be read on his face as they were formed by his pen.

Had he been rewarded in proportion with his zeal, he would, perhaps to his own surprise, have been promoted to fifth-class clerk. But all he got out of it was, as his witty colleagues put it, a pin for his buttonhole and hemorrhoids to sit on.

Still, it would be unfair to say that no attention had ever been paid him. One of the successive directors, a kindly man, who thought Akaky Akakievich should be rewarded for his long service, suggested that he be given something more interesting than ordinary copying. So he was asked to prepare an already drawn-up document for referral to another department. Actually, all he had to do was to give it a new heading and change some of the verbs from the first to the third person. But Akaky Akakievich found this work so complicated that he broke into a sweat and finally, mopping his brow, he said:

"Oh no, I would rather have something to copy instead."

After that they left him to his copying forever. And aside from it, it seemed, nothing existed for him.

He never gave a thought to his clothes. His frock coat, which was supposed to be green, had turned a sort of mealy reddish. Its collar was very low and very narrow so that his neck, which was really quite ordinary, looked incredibly long—like the spring necks of the head-shaking plaster kittens which foreign peddlers carry around on their heads on trays. And, somehow, there was always something stuck to Akaky Akakievich's frock coat, a wisp of hay, a little thread. Then too, he had a knack of passing under windows just when refuse happened to be thrown out and as a result was forever carrying around on his hat melon rinds and other such rubbish.

Never did he pay any attention to what was going on around him in the street. In this he was very different from the other members of the pen-pushing brotherhood, who are so keen-eyed and observant that they'll notice an undone strap on the bottom of someone's trousers, an observation that unfailingly molds their features into a sly sneer. But even when Akaky Akakievich's eyes were resting on something, he saw superimposed on it his own well-formed, neat handwriting. Perhaps it was only when, out of nowhere, a horse rested its head on his shoulder and sent a blast of wind down his cheek that he'd realized he was not in the middle of a line but in the middle of a street.

When he got home he would sit straight down to the table and quickly gulp his cabbage soup, followed by beef and onions. He never noticed the taste and ate it with flies and whatever else God happened to send along. When his stomach began to feel bloated, he would get up from the table, take out his inkwell, and copy papers he had brought with him from the office. And if there weren't any papers to copy for the office, he would make a copy for his own pleasure, especially if the document were unusual. Unusual, not for the beauty of its style, but because it was addressed to some new or important personage.

Even during those hours when light has completely disappeared from the gray Petersburg sky and the pen-pushing brotherhood have filled themselves with dinner of one sort or another, each as best he can according to his income and his preference; when everyone has rested from the scraping of pens in the office, from running around on their own and others' errands; when the restless human being has relaxed after the tasks, sometimes unnecessary, he sets himself; and the clerks hasten to give over the remaining hours to pleasure—the more enterprising among them rushes to the theater, another walks in the streets, allotting his time to the inspection of ladies' hats; another spends his evening paying compliments to some prettyish damsel, the queen of a small circle of clerks; another, the most frequent case, goes to visit a brother clerk, who lives somewhere on the third or fourth floor, in two small rooms with a hall of a kitchen and some little pretensions[4] to fashion, a lamp or some other article bought at great sacrifice, such as going without dinner or outside pleasures—in brief, at the time when all clerks have dispersed among the lodgings of their friends to play a little game of whist, sipping tea from glasses and nibbling biscuits, inhaling the smoke from their long pipes, relaying, while the cards are dealt, some bit of gossip that has trickled down from high society, a thing which a Russian cannot do without whatever his circumstances, and even, when there's nothing else to talk about, telling once again the ancient joke about the commandant to whom it was reported that someone had hacked the tail off the horse of the monument to Peter the First[5]—in a word, when everyone else was trying to have a good time, Akaky Akakievich was not even thinking of diverting himself.

No one had ever seen him at a party in the evening. Having written to his heart's content, he would go to bed, smiling in anticipation of the morrow, of what God would send him to copy.

Thus flowed the life of a man who, on a yearly salary of four hundred rubles,[6] was content with his lot. And perhaps it would have flowed on to old age if it hadn't been for the various disasters which are scattered along life's paths, not only for ninth-class clerks, but even for eighth-, seventh-, sixth-class clerks and all the way up to State Councilors, Privy Councilors, and even to those who counsel no one, not even themselves.

In Petersburg, there's a formidable enemy for all those who receive a salary in the neighborhood of four hundred rubles a year. The enemy is none other than our northern cold, although they say it's very healthy.

Between eight and nine in the morning, at just the time when the streets are filled with people walking to their offices, the cold starts to mete out indiscriminately such hard, stinging flicks on noses that the wretched clerks don't know where to put them. And when the cold pinches the brows and brings tears to the eyes of those in high positions, ninth-class clerks are completely defenseless. They can only wrap themselves in their threadbare overcoats and run as fast as they can the five or six

---

4. **pretensions** (pri ten′ shənz) *n.*: Claims.

5. **Peter the First:** The czar, or ruler, of Russia from 1682 through 1725.
6. **rubles** (r o͞o′ b'lz) *n.*: The ruble is the Russian monetary unit.

10 **Enrichment** Akaky's interest in the letters addressed to important personages foreshadows the role that an important personage will play later in his life. Have students speculate about the nature of that role.

11 **Discussion** Have students discuss the impression that Gogol conveys of life in St. Petersburg. Which details contribute to this impression? Does it seem like a place in which students would like to live? Why or why not?

12 **Discussion** Ask students what Akaky's refusal to "even think about diverting himself" reveals about his character.

13 **Enrichment** Tell students that Gogol often creates humor by making a flat statement, then modifying it, taking some of the edge off. Here, for example, after making a strong case for the brutality of winters in St. Petersburg, he adds, "although they say it's very healthy."

14 **Discussion** Have students discuss what is revealed by the fact that the people's overcoats are "threadbare."

15 Discussion Do students feel that it is unfair of the clerks to make fun of Akaky's overcoat? Why or why not?

16 Clarification Make sure students note that Gogol is poking fun at literary conventions.

17 Discussion Here, as in many other places in the story, the narrator interrupts himself to interject an opinion. Have students discuss whether or not the narrator of "The Overcoat" plays a more active role than do the narrators of most other literary works they have read.

18 Discussion Although the story may seem realistic up to this point, some critics maintain that the devil is at work throughout. One critic has claimed that this toenail "may evoke the devil's hooves." Have students discuss the devil theory and have them keep it in mind as they continue reading the story.

19 Discussion Have students discuss what Petrovich's wife's reference to him as a "one-eyed buzzard" suggests about her feelings for him.

blocks to the office. Once arrived, they have to stamp their feet in the vestibule until their abilities and talents, which have been frozen on the way, thaw out once again.

Akaky Akakievich had noticed that for some time the cold had been attacking his back and shoulders quite viciously, try as he might to sprint the prescribed distance. He finally began to wonder whether the fault did not lie with his overcoat. When he gave it a good looking-over in his room, he discovered that in two or three places—the shoulders and back—it had become very much like gauze. The cloth was worn so thin that it let the draft in, and, to make things worse, the lining had disintegrated.

It must be noted that Akaky Akakievich's overcoat had also been a butt of the clerks' jokes. They had even deprived it of its respectable name, referring to it as the old dressing gown. And, as far as that goes, it did have a strange shape. Its collar shrank with every year, since it was used to patch other areas. And the patching, which did not flatter the tailor, made the overcoat baggy and ugly.

Having located the trouble, Akaky Akakievich decided to take the cloak to Petrovich, a tailor who lived somewhere on the fourth floor, up a back stairs, and who, one-eyed and pockmarked as he was, was still quite good at repairing clerks' and other such people's trousers and frock coats, provided he happened to be sober and hadn't other things on his mind.

We shouldn't, of course, waste too many words on the tailor, but since it has become the fashion to give a thorough description of every character figuring in a story, there's nothing to be done but to give you Petrovich.

At first he was called just Grigory and was the serf of some gentleman or other. He began to call himself Petrovich when he received his freedom and took to drinking rather heavily on all holidays, on the big ones at first and then, without distinction, on all church holidays—on any day marked by a little cross on the calendar. In this he was true to the traditions of his forefathers, and, when his wife nagged him about it, he called her impious and a German. Now that we've mentioned his wife, we'd better say a word or two about her, too. But unfor-

tunately very little is known about her, except that Petrovich had a wife who wore a bonnet instead of a kerchief, but was apparently no beauty, since, on meeting her, it occurred to no one but an occasional soldier to peek under that bonnet of hers, twitching his mustache and making gurgling sounds.

Going up the stairs leading to Petrovich's place, which, to be honest about it, were saturated with water and slops and exuded that ammonia smell which burns your eyes and which you'll always find on the back stairs of all Petersburg houses—going up those stairs, Akaky Akakievich was already conjecturing how much Petrovich would ask and making up his mind not to pay more than two rubles.

The door stood open because Petrovich's wife was cooking some fish or other and had made so much smoke in the kitchen that you couldn't even see the cockroaches. Akaky Akakievich went through the kitchen without even seeing Mrs. Petrovich and finally reached the other room, where he saw Petrovich sitting on a wide, unpainted wooden table, with his legs crossed under him like a Turkish pasha.[7]

He was barefoot, as tailors at work usually are, and the first thing Akaky Akakievich saw was Petrovich's big toe, with its twisted nail, thick and hard like a tortoise shell. A skein of silk and cotton thread hung around Petrovich's neck. On his knees there was some old garment. For the past three minutes he had been trying to thread his needle, very irritated at the darkness of the room and even with the thread itself, muttering under his breath: "It won't go through, the pig, it's killing me, the bitch!" Akaky Akakievich was unhappy to find Petrovich so irritated. He preferred to negotiate when the tailor was a little under the weather, or, as his wife put it, "when the one-eyed buzzard had a load on." When caught in such a state, Petrovich usually gave way very readily on the price and would even thank Akaky Akakievich with respectful bows and all that. True, afterwards, his wife would come whining that her husband had charged too

---

7. **pasha** (pə shä′) *n.*: A high civil or military official.

Grammar in Action

An adjective clause is a subordinate clause that modifies a noun or a pronoun by providing additional information. Adjective clauses are usually introduced by relative pronouns—which, that, who, whom, whose—which, in addition to joining the subordinate clause to the independent clause, serve as sentence elements within the adjective clause. Note the adjective clauses in the following passages from "The Overcoat":

And the patching, *which did not flatter the tailor,* made the overcoat look baggy and ugly.

Going up the stairs leading to Petrovich's place, *which,* to be honest about it, *were saturated with water and slops.* . . .

Student Activity. Identify the adjective clauses in each of the following passages from "The Overcoat."

1. Having located the trouble, Akaky Akakievich decided to take the cloak to Petrovich, a tailor who lived somewhere on the fourth floor, up a back stairs, and who, one-eyed and pockmarked as he was, was still quite good at repairing clerks' and other such people's trousers and frock coats, . . .

little because he was drunk; but all you had to do was add ten kopeks[8] and it was a deal.

This time, however, Petrovich seemed to be sober and therefore curt, intractable,[9] and likely to charge an outrageous price. Akaky Akakievich realized this and would have liked to beat a hasty retreat, but the die was cast. Petrovich had fixed his one eye on him and Akaky Akakievich involuntarily came out with:

"Hello, Petrovich."

"Wish you good day, sir," said Petrovich and bent his eye toward Akaky Akakievich's hands to see what kind of spoil he had brought him.

"Well, Petrovich, I've come . . . see . . . the thing is . . . to . . ."

It should be realized that Akaky Akakievich used all sorts of prepositions, adverbs and all those meaningless little parts of speech when he spoke. Moreover, if the matter were very involved, he generally didn't finish his sentences and opened them with the words: "This, really, is absolutely, I mean to say . . ." and then nothing more—he had forgotten that he hadn't said what he wanted to.

"What is it then?" Petrovich asked, looking over Akaky Akakievich's frock coat with his one eye, the collar, the sleeves, the back, the tails, the buttonholes, all of which he was already acquainted with, since, repairs and all, it was his own work. That's just what tailors do as soon as they see you.

"Well, it's like this, Petrovich . . . my cloak, well, the material . . . look, you can see, everywhere else it's very strong, well, it's a bit dusty and it looks rather shabby, but it's not really . . . look, it's just in one place it's a little . . . on the back here, and here too . . . it's a little worn . . . and here on this shoulder too, a little—and that's all. There's not much work . . ."

Petrovich took Akaky Akakievich's old dressing gown, as his colleagues called it, spread it out on the table and looked it over at length. Then he shook his head and, stretching out his hand, took from the windowsill a snuffbox embellished with

---

8. **kopeks** (kō′ peks) *n.*: A kopek is a Russian monetary unit equal to a hundredth of a ruble.
9. **intractable** (in trak′ tə b'l) *adj.*: Hard to manage; unruly or stubborn.

the portrait of a general, though just what general it was impossible to tell since right where his face used to be there was now a dent glued over with a piece of paper. Taking some snuff, Petrovich spread the overcoat out on his hands, held it up against the light and again shook his head. Then he turned the overcoat inside out, with the lining up, and shook his head again. Then, once more, he removed the snuffbox lid with its general under the piece of paper, and, stuffing snuff into his nose, closed the box, put it away, and finally said:

"No. It can't be mended. It's no use."

At these words, Akaky Akakievich's heart turned over.

"But why can't it be, Petrovich?" he said in the imploring voice of a child. "Look, the only trouble is that it's worn around the shoulders. I'm sure you have some scraps of cloth . . ."

"As for scraps, I suppose I could find them," Petrovich said, "but I couldn't sew them on. The whole thing is rotten. It'd go to pieces the moment you touched it with a needle."

"Well, if it starts to go, you'll catch it with a patch . . ."

"But there's nothing for patches to hold to. It's too far gone. It's only cloth in name—a puff of wind and it'll disintegrate."

"Still, I'm sure you can make them hold just the same. Otherwise, really, Petrovich, see what I mean . . ."

"No," Petrovich said with finality, "nothing can be done with it. It's just no good. You'd better make yourself some bands out of it to wrap round your legs when it's cold and socks aren't enough to keep you warm. The Germans thought up those things to make money for themselves."—Petrovich liked to take a dig at the Germans whenever there was a chance.—"As to the overcoat, it looks as if you'll have to have a new one made."

At the word "new" Akaky Akakievich's vision became foggy and the whole room began to sway. The only thing he saw clearly was the general with the paper-covered face on the lid of Petrovich's snuffbox.

"What do you mean a *new* one?" he said, talking as if in a dream. "I haven't even got the money . . ."

20 **Reading Strategy** Based on the information in this paragraph, how do students predict the outcome of Akaky's meeting with Petrovich? How does Gogol create a sense of impending doom?

21 **Discussion** Have students discuss what Akaky's manner of speaking reveals about his character. What might be the reason that he talks in this manner?

22 **Discussion** Given the earlier description of Akaky's coat, do students imagine that Petrovich is a good tailor? Why or why not?

23 **Discussion** Do students think Petrovich is being honest and straightforward with Akaky? Why or why not?

24 **Discussion** Ask students why Akaky's heart turns over when he finds out his overcoat cannot be mended.

25 **Reading Strategy** Have students review the preceding pages to find an earlier detail that reflects Petrovich's inclination to "take a dig at the Germans."

2. Akaky Akakievich went through the kitchen without even seeing Mrs. Petrovich and finally reached the other room, where he saw Petrovich sitting on a wide, unpainted wooden table, . . .
3. When caught in such a state, Petrovich usually gave way very readily on the price . . .
4. But unfortunately very little was known about her, except that Petrovich had a wife who wore a bonnet instead of a kerchief, . . .
5. Once arrived, they have to stamp their feet in the vestibule until their abilities and talents, which have been frozen on the way, thaw out again.

Margin annotations

26 Discussion Ask students what Petrovich is trying to accomplish by setting the price of the overcoat at one hundred and fifty rubles. Why does he like "strong effects"?

27 Discussion Ask students why Petrovich feels that he has to "uphold his own honor as well as that of the entire tailoring profession."

28 Discussion Have students discuss the reason Akaky was unable to foresee that he would need a new overcoat.

29 Reading Strategy Tell students that it is important for them to keep in mind the cultural context of the story. In the society in which Akaky lives, it is not possible to simply go into a clothing store and buy an overcoat off the rack. Instead, a person has to hire a tailor to make a new overcoat. Ask students how the fact that overcoats have to be custom-made might contribute to their high cost.

30 Discussion Have students discuss why Petrovich suggests costly features, such as silver-plated clasps, when he knows that Akaky is hard-pressed for money.

Main text

"A new one," Petrovich repeated with savage calm.

"Well, but if I really had to have a new one, how would it be that . . ."

"That is, what will it cost?"

"Yes."

26 "Well, it will be over one hundred and fifty rubles," Petrovich said, pursing his lips meaningfully. He liked strong effects, he liked to perplex someone suddenly and then observe the grimace that his words produced.

"A hundred and fifty rubles for an overcoat!" shrieked the poor Akaky Akakievich, shrieked perhaps for the first time in his life, since he was always noted for his quietness.

"Yes, sir," said Petrovich, "but what an overcoat! And if it is to have marten on the collar and a silk-lined hood, that'll bring it up to two hundred."

"Please, Petrovich, please," Akaky Akakievich said beseechingly, not taking in Petrovich's words or noticing his dramatic effects, "mend it somehow, just enough to make it last a little longer."

"No sir, it won't work. It would be a waste of labor and money."

27 Akaky Akakievich left completely crushed. And when he left, Petrovich, instead of going back to his work, remained for a long time immobile, his lips pursed meaningfully. He was pleased with himself for having upheld his own honor as well as that of the entire tailoring profession.

28 Akaky Akakievich emerged into the street feeling as if he were in a dream. "So that's it," he repeated to himself. "I never suspected it would turn out this way . . ." and then, after a brief pause, he went on: "So that's it! Here's how it turns out in the end, and I, really, simply couldn't have foreseen it." After another, longer pause, he added: "And so here we are! Here's how things stand. I in no way expected . . . but this is impossible . . . what a business!" Muttering thus, instead of going home, he went in the opposite direction, without having the slightest idea of what was going on.

As he was walking, a chimney sweep brushed his dirty side against him and blackened his whole shoulder; a whole bucketful of lime was showered over him from the top of a house under construction. But he noticed nothing and only when he bumped into a watchman who, resting his halberd[10] near him, was shaking some snuff out of a horn into his calloused palm, did he come to a little and that only because the watchman said:

"Ya hafta knock my head off? Ya got the whole sidewalk, ain'tcha?"

This caused him to look about him and turn back toward home. Only then did he start to collect his thoughts and to see his real position clearly. He began to talk to himself, not in bits of phrases now but sensibly, as to a wise friend in whom he could confide.

"Oh no," he said, "that wasn't the moment to speak to Petrovich. Right now he's sort of . . . his wife obviously has given him a beating . . . that sort of thing. It'd be better if I went and saw him Sunday morning. After Saturday night, his one eye will be wandering and he'll be tired and in need of another drink, and his wife won't give him the money. So I'll slip him a quarter and that will make him more reasonable and so, for the overcoat . . ." Thus Akaky Akakievich tried to reassure himself, and persuaded himself to wait for Sunday.

When that day came, he waited at a distance until he saw Petrovich's wife leave the house and then went up. After his Saturday night libations, Petrovich's eye certainly was wandering. He hung his head and looked terribly sleepy. But, despite all that, as soon as he learned what Akaky Akakievich had come about, it was if the devil had poked him.

"It can't be done," he said. "You must order a new one."

Here Akaky Akakievich pressed the quarter on him.

"Thank you," Petrovich said. "I'll drink a short one to you, sir. And as to the overcoat, you can stop worrying. It's worthless. But I'll make you a first-rate new one. That I'll see to."

Akaky Akakievich tried once more to bring the conversation around to mending, but Petrovich, instead of listening, said:

"I'll make you a new one, sir, and you can count on me to do my best. I may even make the collar fastened with silver-plated clasps for you."

---

10. halberd (hal′ bərd) *n.*: A combination spear and battle-ax.

At this point Akaky Akakievich saw that he'd have to have a new overcoat and he became utterly depressed. Where was he going to get the money? There was of course the next holiday bonus. But the sum involved had long ago been allotted to other needs. He had to order new trousers, to pay the cobbler for replacing the tops of his boots. He owed the seamstress for three shirts and simply had to have two items of underwear which one cannot refer to in print. In fact, all the money, to the last kopek, was owed, and even if the director made an unexpectedly generous gesture and allotted him, instead of forty rubles, a whole forty-five or even fifty, the difference would be a drop in the ocean in the overcoat outlay.

It is true Akaky Akakievich knew that, on occasions, Petrovich slapped on heaven knows what exorbitant price, so that even his wife couldn't refrain from exclaiming:

"Have you gone mad, you fool! One day he accepts work for nothing, and the next, something gets into him and makes him ask for more than he's worth himself."

But he also knew that Petrovich would agree to make him a new overcoat for eighty rubles. Even so, where was he to find the eighty? He could perhaps scrape together half that sum. Even a little more. But where would he get the other half? . . . Let us, however, start with the first half and see where it was to come from.

Akaky Akakievich had a rule: whenever he spent one ruble, he slipped a copper into a little box with a slot in its side. Every six months, he counted the coppers and changed them for silver. He'd been doing this for a long time and, after all these years, had accumulated more than forty rubles. So this came to one half. But what about the remaining forty rubles?

Akaky Akakievich thought and thought and decided that he would have to reduce his regular expenses for an entire year at least. It would mean going without his evening tea; not burning candles at night, and, if he absolutely had to have light, going to his landlady's room and working by her candle. It would mean, when walking in the street, stepping as carefully as possible over the cobbles and paving stones, almost tiptoeing, so as not to wear out the soles of his boots too rapidly, and giving out his laundry as seldom as possible, and, so that it shouldn't get too soiled, undressing as soon as he got home and staying in just his thin cotton dressing gown, which, if time hadn't taken pity on it, would itself have collapsed long ago.

It must be admitted that, at first, he suffered somewhat from these restrictions. But then he became accustomed to them somehow and things went smoothly again. He even got used to going hungry in the evenings, but then he was able to feed himself spiritually, carrying within him the eternal idea of his overcoat-to-be. It was as if his existence had become somehow fuller, as if he had married and another human being were there with him, as if he were no longer alone on life's road but walking by the side of a delightful companion. And that companion was none other than the overcoat itself, with its thick padding and strong lining that would last forever. In some way, he became more alive, even stronger-minded, like a man who has determined his ultimate goal in life.

From his face and actions all the marks of vacillation and indecision vanished.

At times, there was even a fire in his eyes and the boldest, wildest notions flashed through his head—perhaps he should really consider having marten put on the collar? The intensity of these thoughts almost distracted his attention from his work. Once he almost made a mistake, which caused him to exclaim—true, very softly—"Oof!" and to cross himself.

At least once each month he looked in on Petrovich to discuss the overcoat—the best place to buy the material, its color, its price . . . Then, on the way home, a little worried but always pleased, he mused about how, finally, all this buying would be over and the coat would be made.

Things went ahead faster than he had expected. Beyond all expectations, the director granted Akaky Akakievich not forty, nor forty-five, but a whole sixty rubles. Could he have had a premonition that Akaky Akakievich needed a new overcoat, or had it just happened by itself? Whatever it was, Akaky Akakievich wound up with an extra twenty rubles. This circumstance speeded matters up. Another two or three months of moderate hunger

31 **Discussion** Have students discuss what this information suggests about the size of Akaky's salary. Remind students that Akaky does not spend any of his money on social or recreational activities. Considering that Akaky is a devoted worker, does it seem as if he is paid a fair salary? Why or why not?

32 **Discussion** Ask students how Akaky knows that Petrovich will make him an overcoat for eighty rubles.

33 **Discussion** Have students respond to the sacrifices that Akaky plans to make. Are these the type of sacrifices that most contemporary Americans make when they are saving for something?

34 **Literary Focus** Have students discuss what the overcoat is starting to symbolize in Akaky's mind.

35 **Clarification** Tell students that having marten put on the collar would significantly increase the cost of the overcoat. Considering this fact, ask students why Akaky would even consider having this done.

36 **Reading Strategy** Have students predict whether or not the overcoat will live up to Akaky's expectations.

37 Discussion Ask students if it seems that Petrovich takes great pride in his work. Do they think most tailors would put so much time and effort into making a single overcoat? Why or why not?

38 Discussion Considering the time and effort that Petrovich puts into making the overcoat, do students think that twelve rubles seem like a fair fee? Remind them that Akaky's Christmas bonus—sixty rubles—is five times as large as Petrovich's fee. How do they imagine that Petrovich manages to live on such a small income?

39 Discussion Have students discuss why Gogol describes the day on which Petrovich brings Akaky the overcoat as "the most solemn day" in Akaky's life.

40 Literary Focus Ask students why the overcoat has such a powerful effect on Akaky. How do they think this effect relates to the overcoat's symbolic meaning?

41 Discussion Have students discuss how Akaky's acquisition of the overcoat seems to change the other clerks' attitude toward him. Why might the acquisition of a material object, such as an overcoat, make them more accepting of him?

and he had almost all of the eighty rubles he needed. His heartbeat, generally very quiet, grew faster.

As soon as he could, he set out for the store with Petrovich. They bought excellent material, which is not surprising since they had been planning the move for all of six months, and a month had seldom gone by without Akaky Akakievich dropping into the shop to work out prices. Petrovich himself said that there was no better material to be had.

For the lining they chose calico, but so good and thick that, Petrovich said, it even looked better and glossier than silk. They did not buy marten because it was too expensive. Instead they got cat, the best available—cat which at a distance could always be taken for marten. Petrovich spent two full weeks on the overcoat because of all the quilting he had to do. He charged twelve rubles for his work—it was impossible to take less; it had been sewn with silk, with fine double seams, and Petrovich had gone over each seam again afterwards with his own teeth, squeezing out different patterns with them.

It was—well, it's hard to say exactly which day it was, but it was probably the most solemn day in Akaky Akakievich's life, the day Petrovich finally brought him the overcoat. He brought it in the morning, just before it was time to go to the office. There couldn't have been a better moment for the coat to arrive, because cold spells had been creeping in and threatened to become even more severe. Petrovich appeared with the coat, as befits a good tailor. He had an expression of importance on his face that Akaky Akakievich had never seen before. He looked very much aware of having performed an important act, an act that carries tailors over the chasm which separates those who merely put in linings and do repairs from those who create.

He took the overcoat out of the gigantic handkerchief—just fresh from the wash—in which he had wrapped it to deliver it. The handkerchief he folded neatly and put in his pocket, ready for use. Then he took the coat, looked at it with great pride and, holding it in both hands threw it quite deftly around Akaky Akakievich's shoulders. He pulled and smoothed it down at the back, wrapped

it around Akaky Akakievich, leaving it a little open at the front. Akaky Akakievich, a down-to-earth sort of man, wanted to try out the sleeves. Petrovich helped him to pull his arms through and it turned out that with the sleeves too it was good. In a word, it was clear that the coat fitted perfectly.

Petrovich didn't fail to take advantage of the occasion to remark that it was only because he did without a signboard, lived in a small side street, and had known Akaky Akakievich for a long time that he had charged him so little. On Nevsky Avenue, nowadays, he said, they'd have taken seventy-five rubles for the work alone. Akaky Akakievich had no desire to debate the point with Petrovich—he was always rather awed by the big sums which Petrovich liked to mention to impress people. He paid up, thanked Petrovich, and left for the office wearing his new overcoat.

Petrovich followed him and stood for a long time in the street, gazing at the overcoat from a distance. Then he plunged into a curving side street, took a shortcut, and reemerged on the street ahead of Akaky Akakievich, so that he could have another look at the coat from another angle.

Meanwhile, Akaky Akakievich walked on, bubbling with good spirits. Every second of every minute he felt the new overcoat on his shoulders and several times he even let out a little chuckle of inward pleasure. Indeed, the overcoat presented him with a double advantage: it was warm and it was good. He didn't notice his trip at all and suddenly found himself before the office building. In the porter's lodge, he slipped off the overcoat, inspected it, and entrusted it to the porter's special care.

No one knows how, but it suddenly became general knowledge in the office that Akaky Akakievich had a new overcoat and that the old dressing gown no longer existed. Elbowing one another, they all rushed to the cloakroom to see the new coat. Then they proceeded to congratulate him. He smiled at first, but then the congratulations became too exuberant, and he felt embarrassed. And when they surrounded him and started trying to persuade him that the very least he could do was to invite them over one evening to drink to the coat, Akaky Akakievich felt completely at a loss, didn't know what to do with himself, what to say or how to talk himself out of it. And a few minutes later, all red in the face, he was trying rather naively to convince them that it wasn't a new overcoat at all, that it wasn't much, that it was an old one.

In the end, a clerk, no lesser person than an assistant to the head clerk, probably wanting to show that he wasn't too proud to mingle with those beneath him, said:

"All right then, I'll do it instead of Akaky Akakievich. I invite you all over for a party. Come over to my place tonight. Incidentally, it happens to be my birthday today."

Naturally the clerks now congratulated the head clerk's assistant and happily accepted his invitation. Akaky Akakievich started to excuse himself, but he was told that it would be rude on his part, a disgrace, so he had to give way in the end. And lat-

WORKERS RETURNING HOME
Edvard Munch
Munch-Museet, Oslo

er he was even rather pleased that he had accepted, since it would give him an opportunity to wear the new coat in the evening too.

Akaky Akakievich felt as if it were a holiday. He arrived home in the happiest frame of mind, took off the overcoat, hung it up very carefully on the wall, gave the material and the lining one more admiring inspection. Then he took out that ragged item known as the old dressing gown and put it next to the new overcoat, looked at it and began to laugh, so great was the difference between the two. And long after that, while eating dinner, he snorted every time he thought of the dressing gown. He felt very gay during his dinner, and afterwards he did no copying whatsoever. Instead he wallowed in luxury for a while, lying on his bed until dark. Then, without further dallying, he dressed, pulled on his new overcoat and went out.

It is, alas, impossible to say just where the party-giving clerk lived. My memory is beginning to fail me badly and everything in Petersburg, streets and houses, has become so mixed up in my head that it's very difficult to extract anything from it and to present it in an orderly fashion. Be that as it may, it is a fact that the clerk in question lived in a better district of the city, which means not too close to Akaky Akakievich.

To start with, Akaky Akakievich had to pass through a maze of deserted, dimly lit streets, but, toward the clerk's house, the streets became lighter and livelier. More pedestrians began flashing by more often; there were some well-dressed ladies and men with beaver collars. And, instead of the drivers with their wooden, fretworked sledges[11] studded with gilt nails, he came across smart coachmen in crimson velvet caps, in lacquered sledges, with bearskin lap rugs. He even saw some carriages darting past with decorated boxes, their wheels squeaking on the snow.

Akaky Akakievich gazed around him. For several years now he hadn't been out in the evening. He stopped before the small, lighted window of a shop, staring curiously at a picture of a pretty woman kicking off her shoe and thereby showing

---

11. **sledges** (slej′ əz) *n*.: Sleighs.

her whole leg, which was not bad at all; in the background, some man or other with side whiskers and a handsome Spanish goatee was sticking his head through a door leading to another room. Akaky Akakievich shook his head, snorted, smiled and walked on. Why did he snort? Was it because he had come across something that, although completely strange to him, still aroused in him, as it would in anyone, a certain instinct—or did he think, as many clerks do, along the following lines: "Well, really, the French! If they are after something . . . that sort of thing . . . then, really! . . ." Maybe he didn't even think that. After all, one can't just creep into a man's soul and find out everything he's thinking.

At last he reached the house in which the head clerk's assistant lived. And he lived in style, on the second floor, with the staircase lighted by a lantern. In the hall, Akaky Akakievich found several rows of galoshes. Amidst the galoshes, a samovar was hissing and puffing steam. All around the walls hung overcoats and cloaks, some with beaver collars and others with velvet lapels. The noise and talk that could be heard through the partition became suddenly clear and resounding when the door opened and a servant came out with a tray of empty glasses, a cream jug, and a basket of cookies. It was clear that the clerks had arrived long before and had already drunk their first round of tea.

Akaky Akakievich hung his coat up and went in. In a flash, he took in the candles, the clerks, the pipes, the card tables, while his ears were filled with the hubbub of voices rising all around him and the banging of chairs being moved. Awkwardly, he paused in the middle of the room, trying to think what to do. But he had been noticed and his arrival was greeted with a huge yell. Immediately everybody rushed out into the hall to have another look at his new overcoat. Akaky Akakievich felt a bit confused, but, being an uncomplicated man, he was rather pleased when everyone agreed that it was a good overcoat.

Soon, however, they abandoned him and his overcoat and turned their attention, as was to be expected, to the card tables.

The din, the voices, the presence of so many people—all this was unreal to Akaky Akakievich.

Primary Source

Gogol has often been applauded for his innovativeness as a writer. In an article on "The Overcoat," the literary critic John Middleton Murry wrote:

Over and over again in reading "The Overcoat," we come up with sentences and paragraphs in which we feel, as it were, a new life stirring, the birth of new sensitiveness to human experience. The range of man's responsiveness is being definitely extended.

The sense of new possibilities that he gives us is Gogol's great fascination. Old limitations are breaking down; the face-to-face vision of eight-

eenth-century "common sense" is giving way not so much to a new method as to the potentiality of many new methods. Gogol looks more intently at what is before him, now he glances altogether sideways. His scrutiny is sometimes more microscopic, sometimes more fantastic than that of any of his predecessors in his own country or abroad. He looks harder, and looks from a different direction.

He had no idea how to behave, where to put his hands, his feet, or, for that matter, his whole body. He sat down near a card table, stared at the cards and peeked in turn into the faces of the players. In a little while he got bored and began to yawn, feeling rather sleepy—it was long past his usual bedtime. He wanted to take leave of the host, but they wouldn't let him go. He really had to toast his new overcoat with champagne, they insisted. They made Akaky Akakievich drink two glasses of champagne, after which he felt that the party was becoming gayer, but nevertheless he was quite unable to forget that it was now midnight and that he should have gone home long ago.

In spite of everything his host could think up to keep him, he went quietly out into the hall, found his overcoat, which to his annoyance was lying on the floor, shook it, carefully removed every speck he could find on it, put it on and walked down the stairs and out into the street.

The street was still lighted. Some little stores, those meeting places for servants and people of every sort, were open, while others, although closed, still showed a long streak of light under their doors, which indicated that the company had not yet dispersed and that the menservants and maids were finishing up their gossip and their conversations, leaving their masters perplexed as to their whereabouts.

Akaky Akakievich walked along in such a gay mood that, who knows why, he almost darted after a lady who flashed by him like a streak of lightning, every part of her body astir with independent, fascinating motion. Still, he restrained himself immediately, went back to walking slowly and even wondered where that compulsion to gallop had come from.

Soon there stretched out before him those deserted streets which, even in the daytime, are not so gay, and, now that it was night, looked even more desolate. Fewer street lamps were lit—obviously a smaller oil allowance was given out in this district. Then came wooden houses and fences; not a soul around, nothing but glistening snow and the black silhouettes of the low, sleeping hovels with their shuttered windows. He came to the spot where the street cut through a square so immense that the houses opposite were hardly visible beyond its sinister emptiness.

God knows where, far away on the edge of the world, he could see the glow of a brazier[12] by a watchman's hut.

Akaky Akakievich's gay mood definitely waned. He could not suppress a shiver as he stepped out into the square, a foreboding of evil in his heart. He glanced behind him and to either side—it was like being in the middle of the sea. "No, it's better not to look," he thought, and walked on with his eyes shut. And when he opened them again to see if the other side of the square was close, he saw instead, standing there, almost in front of his nose, people with mustaches, although he couldn't make out, exactly who or what. Then his vision became foggy and there was a beating in his chest.

"Why, there's my overcoat," one of the people thundered, grabbing him by the collar.

Akaky Akakievich was just going to shout out "Help!" when another brought a fist about the size of a clerk's head up to his very mouth, and said:

"You just try and yell . . ."

Akaky Akakievich felt them pull off his coat, then he received a knee in the groin. He went down on his back and after that he lay in the snow and felt nothing more.

When he came to a few minutes later and scrambled to his feet, there was no one around. He felt cold and, when he realized that the overcoat was gone, desperate. He let out a yell. But his voice didn't come close to reaching the other side of the square.

Frantic, he hollered all the way across the square as he scrambled straight toward the watchman's hut. The watchman was standing beside it, leaning on his halberd, and gazing out across the square, wondering who it could be running toward him and shouting. At last Akaky Akakievich reached him. Gasping for breath, he began shouting at him—what sort of a watchman did he think he was, hadn't he seen anything, and why the devil had he allowed them to rob a man? The watchman said he had seen no one except the two men who

---

12. **brazier** (brā′ zhər) *n*.: A metal pan or bowl used to hold burning coals or charcoal.

50 Discussion Have students discuss how Gogol makes it clear that despite his acquisition of the overcoat, Akaky still does not fit in with the other clerks. Does it seem as if he wants to fit in?

51 Discussion Ask students why Akaky finds his overcoat lying on the floor.

52 Discussion Have students discuss whether Akaky's attraction to this lady seems out of character.

53 Discussion Call students' attention to the rapid shift in the mood of the story. Have them explain what brings about this shift. Ask them to speculate about what might be foreshadowed by the "sinister emptiness" to which Gogol refers.

54 Discussion Have students respond to this sequence of events. Do they feel sorry for Akaky? Is there any way he could have prevented his overcoat from being stolen? Do they think he has any hope of getting it back? Why or why not?

55 Discussion Keeping in mind what the overcoat has come to represent to Akaky, what do students think will become of him now that it has been stolen?

had stopped Akaky Akakievich in the middle of the square, who he had thought were friends of his, and that instead of hollering at the watchman, he'd better go and see the police inspector tomorrow and the inspector would find out who had taken the overcoat.

Akaky Akakievich hurried home; he was in a terrible state. The little hair he had left, on his temples and on the back of his head, was completely disheveled,[13] there was snow all down one side of him and on his chest and all over his trousers. His old landlady, hearing his impatient banging on the door, jumped out of bed and, with only one shoe on, ran to open up, clutching her nightgown at the neck, probably out of modesty. When she saw the state Akaky Akakievich was in, she stepped back.

56 When he told her what had happened, she threw up her hands and said that he should go straight to the borough Police Commissioner, that the local police inspector could not be trusted, that he'd just make promises and give him the run-around. So it was best, she said, to go straight to the borough Commissioner. In fact, she even knew him because Anna, her former Finnish cook, had now got a job as a nanny at his house. And the landlady herself often saw him driving past their house. Moreover, she knew he went to church every Sunday and prayed and at the same time looked cheerful and was obviously a good man. Having heard her advice, Akaky Akakievich trudged off sadly to his room and somehow got through the night, though exactly how must be imagined by those who know how to put themselves in another man's place.

57 Early the next morning, he went to the borough Commissioner's. But it turned out that he was still asleep. He returned at ten and again was told he was asleep. He went back at eleven and was told that the Commissioner was not home. He tried again during the dinner hour but the secretaries in the reception room would not let him in and wanted to know what business had brought him. For once in his life Akaky Akakievich decided to show some character and told them curtly that he must see the Commissioner personally, that

---

13. disheveled (di shev′ ′ld) *adj.*: Disarranged and untidy.

they'd better let him in since he was on official government business, that he would lodge a complaint against them and that then they would see.

The secretaries didn't dare say anything to that and one of them went to call the Commissioner. The Commissioner reacted very strangely to Akaky Akakievich's story of the robbery. Instead of concentrating on the main point, he asked Akaky Akakievich what he had been doing out so late, whether he had stopped off somewhere on his way, hadn't he been to a house of ill repute. Akaky Akakievich became very confused and when he left he wasn't sure whether something would be done about his overcoat or not.

That day he did not go to his office for the first time in his life. The next day he appeared, looking very pale and wearing his old dressing gown, which now seemed shabbier than ever. His account of the theft of his overcoat touched many of the clerks, although, even now, there were some who poked fun at him. They decided on the spot to take up a collection for him but they collected next to nothing because the department employees had already had to donate money for a portrait of the Director and to subscribe to some book or other, on the suggestion of the section chief, who was a friend of the author's. So the sum turned out to be the merest trifle.

Someone, moved by compassion, decided to help Akaky Akakievich by giving him good advice. He told him that he had better not go to his local inspector because, even supposing the inspector wanted to impress his superiors and managed to recover the coat, Akaky Akakievich would still find it difficult to obtain it at the police station unless he could present irrefutable proof of ownership. The best thing was to go through a certain important personage who, by writing and contacting the right people, would set things moving faster. So Akaky Akakievich decided to seek an audience with the important personage.

Even to this day, it is not known exactly what position the important personage held or what his duties consisted of. All we need to know is that this important personage had become important quite recently and that formerly he had been an unimportant person. And even his present position was

---

Grammar in Action

Parallelism is the arrangement of equal ideas in equivalent grammatical structures. Writers use parallelism to create balance and rhythm and to emphasize important ideas. Note the following example of parallelism from Andrew R. MacAndrew's translation of "The Overcoat":

He returned at ten and again was told he was asleep. *He went* back at eleven and was told that the Commissioner was not home. *He tried* again during dinner hour but the secretaries in the reception room would not let him in and wanted to know what business had brought him.

Student Activity 1. Find five more examples of parallelism from Andrew R. MacAndrew's translation of "The Overcoat." Then explain the effect created by each of these examples.

Student Activity 2. Write a few paragraphs describing an especially enjoyable or exciting experience that you have had recently. In your composition, use parallelism to create a rhythm and to emphasize your main ideas.

---

unimportant compared with other, more important ones. But there is always a category of people for whom somebody who is unimportant to others is an important personage. And the personage in question used various devices to play up his importance: for instance, he made the civil servants of lower categories come out to meet him on the stairs before he'd even reached his office; and a subordinate could not approach him directly but had to go through proper channels. That's the way things are in Holy Russia—everyone tries to ape his superior.

They say that one ninth-class clerk, when he was named section chief in a small office, immediately had a partition put up to make a separate room, which he called the conference room. He stationed an usher at the door who had to open it for all those who came in, although the conference room had hardly enough space for a writing table, even without visitors. The audiences and the manner of our important personage were impressive and stately, but quite uncomplicated. The key to his system was severity. He liked to say: "Severity, severity, severity," and as he uttered the word for the third time, he usually looked very meaningfully into the face of the person he was talking to. True, it was not too clear what need there was for all this severity since the ten-odd employees who made up the whole administrative apparatus of his office were quite frightened enough as it was. Seeing him coming, they would leave their work and stand to attention until he had crossed the room. His usual communication with his inferiors was full of severity and consisted almost entirely of three phrases: "How dare you!" "Who do you think you're talking to?" and "Do you appreciate who I am?" Actually, he was a kindly man, a good friend and obliging, but promotion to a high rank had gone to his head, knocked him completely off balance, and he just didn't know how to act. When he happened to be with equals, he was still a decent fellow, and, in a way, by no means stupid. But whenever he found himself among those who were below him—even a single rank—he became impossible. He fell silent and was quite pitiable, because even he himself realized that he could have been having a much better time. Sometimes he was obviously longing to join some group in a lively conversation, but he would be stopped by the thought that he would be going too far, putting himself on familiar terms and thereby losing face. And so he remained eternally in silent, aloof isolation, only occasionally uttering some monosyllabic sounds, and, as a result, he acquired a reputation as a deadly bore.

It was to this important personage that Akaky Akakievich presented himself, and at a most unpropitious[14] moment to boot. That is, very unpropitious for him, although quite suitable for the important personage. The latter was in his office talking gaily to a childhood friend who had recently come to Petersburg and whom he hadn't seen for many years. This was the moment when they announced that there was a man named Shoenik to see him.

"Who's he?" the personage wanted to know.

"Some clerk," they told him.

"I see. Let him wait. I am not available now."

Here it should be noted that the important personage was greatly exaggerating. He was available. He and his friend had talked over everything imaginable. For some time now the conversation had been interlaced with lengthy silences, and they weren't doing much more than slapping each other on the thigh and saying:

"So that's how it is, Ivan Abramovich."

"Yes, indeed, Stepan Varlamovich!"

Still Akaky Akakievich had to wait, so that his friend, who had left the government service long ago and now lived in the country, could see what a long time employees had to wait in his reception room.

At last, when they had talked and had sat silent facing each other for as long as they could stand it, when they had smoked a cigar reclining in comfortable armchairs with sloping backs, the important personage, as if he had just recalled it, said to his secretary who was standing at the door with papers for a report:

"Wait a minute. Wasn't there a clerk waiting? Tell him to come in."

Seeing Akaky Akakievich's humble appearance and his wretched old frock coat, he turned abruptly to face him and said: "What do you want?"

---

14. **unpropitious** (un prə pish′ əs) *adj.*: Unfavorable.

62 **Discussion** Have students discuss the impression that Gogol conveys of the government bureaucracy. What seems to be his attitude toward the bureaucracy? How is his attitude conveyed?

63 **Reading Strategy** After being given this information about the "important personage," how do students predict he will respond to Akaky's troubles?

64 **Enrichment** Point out to students that the important personage's speechlessness before his subordinates parallels Akaky's speechlessness before his superiors. Encourage students to look for other such parallels as they continue reading the story.

65 **Discussion** Ask students to explain why the important personage forces Akaky to wait.

66 **Discussion** Have students offer their opinions of the important personage at this point in the story. Do they consider him to be a sympathetic character? Why or why not? Does Gogol want him to be viewed as a sympathetic character? Explain.

67 Enrichment Point out to students that the very important personage wants to impress people, to stand out. In contrast, Akaky strives for anonymity.

68 Master Teacher Note Have two student volunteers act out the exchange between Akaky and the important personage. Make sure the students express the appropriate emotions as they deliver their lines.

69 Discussion Have students discuss why the important personage's words have such a powerful impact on Akaky.

70 Discussion Have students discuss what the important personage's reaction to Akaky's distress reveals about his character.

71 Discussion Do students think that the important personage is responsible for Akaky's illness? Why or why not?

72 Discussion Have students discuss the tone of this passage. Why does Gogol use a sarcastic, bantering tone even when discussing Akaky's imminent death?

67 He spoke in the hard, sharp voice which he had deliberately developed by practicing at home before a mirror an entire week before he had taken over his present exalted position.

Akaky Akakievich, who had felt properly subdued even before this, felt decidedly embarrassed. He did his best, as far as he could control his tongue, to explain what had happened. Of course, he added even more than his usual share of phrases like "that is to say" and "so to speak." The overcoat, he explained, was completely new and had been cruelly taken away from him and he had turned to the important personage, that is to say, come to him, in the hope that he would, so to speak, intercede for him somehow, that is to say, write to the Superintendent of Police or, so to speak, to someone, and find the overcoat.

For some unimaginable reason the important personage found his manner too familiar.

"My dear sir," he answered sharply, "don't you know the proper channels? Do you realize whom you're addressing and what the proper procedure should be? You should first have handed in a petition to the office. It would have gone to the head clerk. From him it would have reached the section head, who would have approached my secretary and only then would the secretary have presented it to me. . . ."

"But, Your Excellency," said Akaky Akakievich, trying to gather what little composure he had and feeling at the same time that he was sweating terribly, "I, Your Excellency, ventured to trouble you because secretaries, that is to say . . . are, so to **68** speak, an unreliable lot. . . ."

"What, what, what?" demanded the important personage. "Where did you pick up such an attitude? Where did you get such ideas? What is this insubordination that is spreading among young people against their chiefs and superiors?"

The important personage, apparently, had not noticed that Akaky Akakievich was well over fifty. Thus, surely, if he could be called young at all it would only be relatively, that is, to someone of seventy.

"Do you realize to whom you are talking? Do you appreciate who I am? Do you really realize, do you, I'm asking you?"

Here he stamped his foot and raised his voice to such a pitch that there was no need to be an Akaky Akakievich to be frightened.

And Akaky Akakievich froze completely. He staggered, his whole body shook, and he was quite unable to keep his feet. If a messenger hadn't rushed over and supported him, he would have collapsed onto the floor. They carried him out almost unconscious.

And the important personage, pleased to see that his dramatic effect had exceeded his expectations, and completely delighted with the idea that a word from him could knock a man unconscious, glanced at his friend to see what he thought of it all and was pleased to see that the friend looked somewhat at a loss and that fear had extended to him too.

Akaky Akakievich remembered nothing about getting downstairs and out into the street. He could feel neither hand nor foot. In all his life he had never been so severely reprimanded by a high official, and not a direct chief of his at that. He walked open-mouthed through a blizzard, again and again stumbling off the sidewalk. The wind, according to Petersburg custom, blew at him from all four sides at once, out of every side street. In no time it had blown him a sore throat and he got himself home at last quite unable to say a word. His throat was swollen and he went straight to bed. That's how severe the effects of an adequate reprimand can be.

The next day he was found to have a high fever. Thanks to the generous assistance of the Petersburg climate, the illness progressed beyond all expectations. A doctor came, felt his pulse, found there was nothing he could do and prescribed a poultice.[15] That was done so that the patient would not be deprived of the beneficial aid of medicine. The doctor added, however, that, by the way, the patient had another day and a half to go, after which he would be what is called kaput. Then, turning to the landlady, the doctor said:

"And you, my good woman, I'd not waste my time if I were you. I'd order him the coffin right

---

15. **poultice** (pōl′ tis)*n*.: A hot, soft, moist mass, sometimes spread on cloth and applied to an inflamed part of the body.

Grammar in Action

Good writers **vary the length and structure of their sentences** to make their writing smoother and more interesting to read. Note the sentence variety in the following passage from Andrew R. MacAndrew's translation of "The Overcoat":

Akaky Akakievich remembered nothing about getting downstairs and out into the street. He could feel neither hand nor foot. In all his life he had never been so severely reprimanded by a high official, and not a direct chief of his at that. He walked open-mouthed through a blizzard, again and again stumbling off the sidewalk. The wind, according to Petersburg custom, blew at him from all four sides at once, out of every side street. In no time it had blown him a sore throat and he got himself home at last quite unable to say a word. His throat was swollen and he went straight to bed. That's how severe the effects of an adequate reprimand can be.

Student Activity 1. Find two other paragraphs in which a variety of sentence lengths and structures are used. Then rewrite each of these para-

THE SCREAM
Edvard Munch
Nasjonalgalleriet, Oslo

73 **Clarification** Point out to students that even in the face of death, Akaky is treated with indifference and a lack of respect.

74 **Discussion** Have students discuss the qualities that make Akaky an especially tragic figure.

75 **Discussion** Have students discuss the significance of the apparitions that appear before Akaky's eyes.

Humanities Note
Fine art, *The Scream* by Edvard Munch. Munch was heavily influenced by the strong colors and patterns of the French painter Paul Gauguin. In turn, Munch influenced many of the twentieth-century German Expressionists.

The Scream is probably the most famous of Munch's paintings. Most critics interpret it as a disturbing vision of neurotic panic—a mind cracking under prolonged anxiety. Notice how the swirling patterns of the background mirror the person's distressed state of mind.

You might want to use the following questions to discuss the art:
1. What effect do you imagine that Munch hoped this painting would have on viewers?
2. What details in the painting most contribute to Munch's intended effect? Why?
3. To what details in "The Overcoat" can this painting be related?
4. What emotions does this painting arouse in you? Why?

away. A pine one. The oak ones, I imagine, would be too expensive for him."

Whether Akaky Akakievich heard what for him were fateful words, and, if he heard, whether they had a shattering effect on him and whether he was sorry to lose his wretched life, are matters of conjecture. He was feverish and delirious the whole time. Apparitions,[16] each stranger than the last, kept crowding before him. He saw Petrovich and ordered

an overcoat containing some sort of concealed traps to catch the thieves who were hiding under his bed, so that every minute he kept calling his landlady to come and pull out the one who had even slipped under his blanket. Next, he would ask why his old dressing gown was hanging there in front of him when he had a new overcoat. Then he would find himself standing before the important personage, listening to the reprimand and repeating over and over: "I am sorry, Your Excellency, I am sorry."

Then he began to swear, using the most frightful words, which caused his old landlady to cross

---

16. **Apparitions** (ap′ ə rish′ ənz) *n*.: Things that appear unexpectedly or in extraordinary ways.

---

graphs so that the sentences are all similar in length and structure. Finally, explain why the original versions of the paragraphs are more effective than the rewritten versions.

Student Activity 2. Find two more paragraphs in which the sentences are varied in length and structure. Then explain how Gogol uses sentence variation to sustain the reader's interest and to emphasize certain ideas.

Student Activity 3. Write a paragraph or two describing a place you have visited that had an important impact on you. In writing this paragraph, focus on varying the length and structure of your sentences.

76 Literary Focus Have students discuss what this reference to the overcoat suggests about its symbolic meaning.

77 Discussion Ask students what type of impact Akaky's death seems to have on the people at his office. What is the significance of the fact that he is immediately replaced by a new clerk. How does this detail help to convey the impersonal nature of the government bureaucracy?

78 Enrichment Point out to students that up to this point "The Overcoat" is a realistic story. Now, however, Gogol adds an element of the fantastic. Point out that Gogol wrote this story just as the Romantic movement was about to be supplanted by Realism. Have students discuss how this story reflects elements of both Romanticism and Realism.

79 Literary Focus Have students discuss how the ghost's quest for the overcoat adds to the overcoat's symbolic meaning.

80 Discussion Have students discuss the absurdity of the order given to the police to catch the ghost "dead or alive." Why do they think Gogol included this detail?

herself in horror; never in her life had she heard anything like it from him, and what made it even worse was that they came pouring out on the heels of the phrase, "Your Excellency." After that he talked complete nonsense and it was impossible to make out anything he was saying, except that his disconnected words kept groping for that lost overcoat of his. Then, at last, poor Akaky Akakievich gave up the ghost.

They did not bother to seal his room or his belongings because there were no heirs and, moreover, very little to inherit—namely, a bundle of goose quills, a quire of white government paper, three pairs of socks, a few buttons that had come off his trousers, and the old dressing-gown coat already mentioned. God knows whom they went to; even the reporter of this story did not care enough to find out.

They took Akaky Akakievich away and buried him. And Petersburg went on without him exactly as if he had never existed. A creature had vanished, disappeared. He had had no one to protect him. No one had ever paid him the slightest attention. Not even that which a naturalist pays to a common fly which he mounts on a pin and looks at through his microscope. True, this creature, who had meekly borne the office jokes and gone quietly to his grave, had had, toward the end of his life, a cherished visitor—the overcoat, which for a brief moment had brightened his wretched existence. Then a crushing blow had finished everything, a blow such as befalls the powerful of the earth. . . .

A few days after his death, a messenger from his office was sent to his lodgings with an order summoning him to report immediately; the chief was asking for him. But the messenger had to return alone and to report that Akaky Akakievich could not come.

"Why not?" he was asked.

"Because," the messenger said, "he died. They buried him four days ago."

That is how the department found out about Akaky Akakievich's death, and the next day a new clerk sat in his place: he was much taller and his handwriting was not as straight. In fact, his letters slanted considerably.

But who would have imagined that that was not the end of Akaky Akakievich, that he was fated to live on and make his presence felt for a few days after his death as if in compensation for having spent his life unnoticed by anyone? But that's the way it happened and our little story gains an unexpectedly fantastic ending. Rumors suddenly started to fly around Petersburg that a ghost was haunting the streets at night in the vicinity of the Kalinkin Bridge. The ghost, which looked like a little clerk, was purportedly searching for a stolen overcoat and used this pretext to pull the coats off the shoulders of everyone he met without regard for rank or title. And it made no difference what kind of coat it was—cat, beaver, fox, bearskin, in fact any of the furs and skins people have thought up to cover their own skins with.

One of the department employees saw the ghost with his own eyes and instantly recognized Akaky Akakievich. However, he was so terrified that he dashed off as fast as his legs would carry him and so didn't get a good look; he only saw from a distance that the ghost was shaking his finger at him. Complaints kept pouring in, and not only from petty employees, which would have been understandable. One and all, even Privy Councilors, were catching chills in their backs and shoulders from having their overcoats peeled off. The police were ordered to catch the ghost at any cost, dead or alive, and to punish him with due severity as a warning to others. And what's more, they nearly succeeded.

To be precise, a watchman caught the ghost red-handed, grabbed it by the collar, in Kiryushkin Alley, as it was trying to pull the coat off a retired musician who, in his day, used to tootle on the flute. Grabbing it, he called for help from two colleagues of his and asked them to hold on to it for just a minute. He had, he said, to get his snuffbox out of his boot so that he could bring some feeling back to his nose, which had been frostbitten six times in his life. But it was evidently snuff that even a ghost couldn't stand. The man, closing his right nostril with his finger, had hardly sniffed up half a fistful into the left when the ghost sneezed so violently that the three watchmen were blinded by the resulting shower. They all raised their fists to wipe

Grammar in Action

Commas are used to separate a number of basic elements and to set off many different elements within sentences. They are used to separate two independent clauses; to separate three or more words, phrases, or clauses in a series; to separate adjectives of equal rank; to set off introductory words, phrases, or clauses; to set off parenthetical expressions; and to set off nonessential expressions. Note the use of commas in each of the following passages from "The Overcoat":

. . . a bundle of goose quills, a quire of white government paper, three pairs of socks, a few buttons that had come off his trousers, and the old dressing-gown coat already mentioned. (used to separate items in a series)

A few days after his death, a messenger from his office was sent to his lodgings . . . (used to separate introductory material)

Student Activity. Explain the purpose served by the commas in each of the following passages from "The Overcoat."
1. To be precise, a watchman caught the ghost red-handed, grabbed it by

their eyes and, when they could see again, the ghost had vanished. They even wondered whether they had really held him at all. After that, watchmen were so afraid of the ghost that they felt reluctant to interfere with live robbers and contented themselves with shouting from a distance: "Hey you! On your way!"

And the clerk's ghost began to haunt the streets well beyond the Kalinkin Bridge, spreading terror among the meek.

However, we have completely neglected the important personage, who really, in a sense, was the cause of the fantastic direction that this story—which, by the way, is completely true—has taken. First of all, it is only fair to say that, shortly after poor Akaky Akakievich, reduced to a pulp, had left his office, the important personage felt a twinge of regret. Compassion was not foreign to him—many good impulses stirred his heart, although his position usually prevented them from coming to the surface. As soon as his visiting friend had left the office, his thoughts returned to Akaky Akakievich. And after that, almost every day, he saw in his mind's eye the bloodless face of the little clerk who had been unable to take a proper reprimand. This thought was so disturbing that a week later he went so far as to send a clerk from his office to see how Akaky Akakievich was doing and to find out whether, in fact, there was any way to help him. And when he heard the news that Akaky Akakievich had died suddenly of a fever, it was almost a blow to him, even made him feel guilty and spoiled his mood for the whole day.

Trying to rid himself of these thoughts, to forget the whole unpleasant business, he went to a party at a friend's house. There he found himself in respectable company and, what's more, among people nearly all of whom were of the same standing so that there was absolutely nothing to oppress him. A great change came over him. He let himself go, chatted pleasantly, was amiable, in a word, spent a very pleasant evening. At supper, he drank a couple of glasses of champagne, a well-recommended prescription for inducing good spirits. The champagne gave him an inclination for something special and so he decided not to go home but instead to pay a little visit to a certain well-known lady named Karolina Ivanovna, a lady, it seems, of German extraction, toward whom he felt very friendly. It should be said that the important personage was no longer a young man, that he was a good husband, the respected father of a family. His two sons, one of whom already had a civil-service post, and his sweet-faced sixteen-year-old daughter, who had a slightly hooked but nevertheless pretty little nose, greeted him every day with a "Bonjour,[17] Papa." His wife, a youngish woman and not unattractive at that, gave him her hand to kiss and then kissed his. But although the important personage was quite content with these displays of family affection, he considered it the proper thing to do to have, for friendship's sake, a lady friend in another part of the city. This lady friend was not a bit prettier or younger than his wife, but the world is full of such puzzling things and it is not our business to judge them.

So the important personage came down the steps, stepped into his sledge, and said to the coachman:

"To Karolina Ivanovna's."

Wrapping his warm luxurious fur coat around him, he sat back in his seat. He was in that state so cherished by Russians, in which, without your having to make any effort, thoughts, each one pleasanter than the last, slip into your head by themselves.

Perfectly content, he went over all the most pleasant moments at the party, over the clever retorts that had caused that select gathering to laugh. He even repeated many of them under his breath and, still finding them funny, laughed heartily at them all over again, which was natural enough. However, he kept being bothered by gusts of wind which would suddenly blow, God knows from where or for what reasons, cutting his face, throwing lumps of snow into it, filling the cape of his coat like a sail and throwing it over his head, so that he had to extricate himself from it again and again.

Suddenly the important personage felt someone grab him violently from behind. He turned around and saw a small man in a worn-out frock coat. Terrified, he recognized Akaky Akakievich, his face as white as the snow and looking altogether very ghostly indeed. Fear took over completely

---

17. **Bonjour** (bôn zho͞or): Good day (French).

86 Discussion Have students discuss how Akaky's behavior as a ghost contrasts with his behavior when he was still alive.

87 Discussion Ask students whether this outcome represents the little person's victory over oppression. Or is this interpretation of the story too broad?

88 Discussion Have students discuss why Gogol might have decided to end the story with a description of an incident involving a different ghost.

Enrichment In a book about the Russian short story, L. Michael O'Toole points out the parallels between Petrovich and the important personage, whom O'Toole refers to as the "Person of Consequence (Note that the passages from "The Overcoat" that O'Toole cites are from his own translation): "Both Petrovich and the Person of Consequence are tyrants in their own sphere who boost their own morale by browbeating and disheartening the weak and dependent like Akaky who turn to them for help. Significantly, the same phrases are used about them: Petrovich is pleased not to have to let himself down by giving in to Akaky's pleas: 'satisfied that he both had not let himself down and had not betrayed his tailor's art'. . . while the Person of Consequence is always held back from being sociable by the thought of 'letting down his consequence.' . . . And, of course, they are both much concerned with the effect their words have, as they look sideways (*iskosa*) at their hearers: 'He [Petrovich] was very fond of powerful *effects,* loved to throw a person into confusion in some way and then glance sideways. . . .' While 'the Person of Consequence, satisfied that the effect had exceeded his expectations . . . glanced sideways at his friend. . . .'"

Cooperative Learning Students might be interested in learning more about nineteenth-century Russian life. Divide the class into groups of three or four and have each group choose a specific topic related to nineteenth-century

Russian life. Once the groups have completed their research, have them report their findings to the rest of the class.

---

when the important personage saw the ghost's mouth twist and, sending a whiff of the grave into his face, utter the following words:

86
87 "I've caught you at last. I've got you by the collar now! It's the coat I need. You did nothing about mine and hollered at me to boot. Now I'll take yours!"

The poor important personage almost died. He may have displayed force of character in the office and, in general, toward his inferiors, so that after one glance at his strong face and manly figure, people would say: "Quite a man," but now, like many other mighty-looking people, he was so frightened that he began to think, and not without reason, that he was about to have an attack of something or other. He was even very helpful in peeling off his coat, after which he shouted to the coachman in a ferocious tone:

"Home! As fast as you can!"

The coachman, hearing the ferocious tone which the important personage used in critical moments and which was sometimes accompanied with something even more drastic, instinctively ducked his head and cracked his whip, so that they tore away like a streak. In a little over six minutes the important personage was in front of his house. Instead of being at Karolina Ivanovna's, he was somehow staggering to his room, pale, terrified, and coatless. There he spent such a restless night that the next morning, at breakfast, his daughter said:

"You look terribly pale this morning, Papa."

But Papa was silent, and he didn't say a word to anyone about what had happened to him, or where he had been or where he had intended to

go. This incident made a deep impression upon him. From then on his subordinates heard far less often: "How dare you!" and "Do you know whom you're talking to?" And even when he did use these expressions it was after listening to what others had to say.

But even more remarkable—after that night, Akaky Akakievich's ghost was never seen again. The important personage's overcoat must have fitted him snugly. At any rate, one no longer heard of coats being torn from people's shoulders. However, many busybodies wouldn't let the matter rest there and maintained that the ghost was still haunting certain distant parts of the city. And, sure enough, a watchman in the Kolomna district caught a glimpse of the ghost behind a house. But he was rather a frail watchman. (Once an ordinary, but mature, piglet, rushing out of a private house, knocked him off his feet to the huge delight of a bunch of cabbies, whom he fined two kopeks each for their lack of respect —then he spent the proceeds on tobacco.) So, being rather frail, the watchman didn't dare to arrest the ghost. Instead he followed it in the darkness until at last it stopped suddenly, turned to face him, and asked:

"You looking for trouble?"

And it shook a huge fist at him, much larger than any you'll find among the living.

"No," the watchman said, turning away.

This ghost, however, was a much taller one and wore an enormous mustache. It walked off, it seems, in the direction of the Obukhov Bridge and soon dissolved into the gloom of night.

Reader's Response *Do you sympathize with Akaky? Why or why not? What is your reaction to the trouble that befalls him?*

Closure and Extension

ANSWERS TO THINKING ABOUT THE SELECTION

1. (a) Suggested response: He conveys the impression that St. Petersburg is a dreary place. Although the lives of the inhabitants seem essentially mundane and dreary, the people are able to find diversions that make their lives

more interesting and enjoyable. (b) Answers will differ. Students should note how Gogol's descriptions of the setting contribute to this impression.

2. Suggested response: He lives as a recluse. He wants to do no evil nor have any evil befall him.

3. Suggested response: The tailor intimidates Akaky much as the important person does later in the story.

4. (a) Suggested response: He is

THINKING ABOUT THE SELECTION

Interpreting

1. (a) What impression of St. Petersburg and the lives of its inhabitants does Gogol convey in this story? (b) Which details contribute to this impression?
2. The name *Akaky* comes from a Greek word meaning "no evil." How does the origin of Akaky's name relate to his character and to his experiences in this story?
3. How does the tailor's treatment of Akaky foreshadow, or hint at, the very important person's treatment of Akaky later in the story?
4. (a) How would you characterize Akaky as he is depicted early in the story? (b) How does he change after he purchases the overcoat? (c) In what ways does he remain the same?
5. How does Gogol want readers to respond to Akaky and his misfortunes? Explain your answer.
6. (a) What does Gogol's portrayal of the police commissioner and the very important person suggest about his attitude toward high-ranking officials? (b) What seems to be Gogol's attitude toward the Russian government as a whole? (c) How is his attitude conveyed?
7. (a) What is the true cause of Akaky's death? (b) What is the significance of the hallucinations he has just prior to his death?
8. What does the final section, involving Akaky's ghost and the tall ghost with the mustache, add to the story as a whole?
9. (a) What are the differences between the ways in which Akaky and the very important person deal with the thefts of their overcoats? (b) What is the reason for these differences?
10. Throughout the story, Gogol describes objects much more vividly than he describes people. What do you think was his purpose in doing so?
11. How does Gogol's manner of telling this story create the impression that the events really happened?
12. The Realists of the late nineteenth century were characterized by their grimly accurate depictions of lower-class and middle-class characters. Given this description, explain whether you think that all or part of Gogol's story could be described as a work of Realistic fiction.

Applying

13. In what ways do you think this story would and would not be different if the setting were changed to contemporary America?

ANALYZING LITERATURE

Understanding a Symbol

The overcoat is an extremely complex symbol with a vast number of different meanings. Many of its symbolic meanings contrast with one another. For example, the overcoat represents security, but it also symbolizes the risks associated with novelty.

1. Akaky's overcoat also comes to represent a companion, or a close friend. What evidence is there that the overcoat assumes this symbolic meaning even before Akaky acquires it?
2. What details in the story indicate that the overcoat also symbolizes a new identity and a new outlook on the world?
3. (a) After Akaky has died, what does the overcoat come to represent? (b) What details in the story support this interpretation?

CRITICAL THINKING AND READING

Relating Symbolism to Theme

The meaning of a symbol is often closely tied to the theme of a literary work. In Gogol's story, for example, the various symbolic meanings of the overcoat suggest a number of different possible themes.

1. One of the themes of Gogol's story is that it is possible for material objects to acquire so much importance that they are valued even more than people. Which of the overcoat's symbolic meanings are directly related to this theme? Explain your answer.
2. A related theme is that material objects cannot serve as a replacement for human companionship. Which of the overcoat's meanings are related to this theme? Explain your answer.
3. What theme is suggested by the interpretation of the overcoat as a symbol of the need for justice?

THINKING AND WRITING

Responding to Criticism

A critic has commented that "The Overcoat" portrays "a freakish, distorted moral universe in which the normal proportions are drastically reversed." Write a paper in which you either support or refute the critic's comment. Begin by reviewing the story, keeping the critic's comment in mind. Decide on the stance you want to take. Then begin writing your paper, using passages from the story for support.

(continued from bottom of page)

10. Suggested response: He is more concerned with the inner life of his characters than with their outward appearances. He is interested in the symbolic value of the objects.
11. Suggested response: He uses a conversational tone and includes many digressions that make the story sound true.
12. Answers will differ. Students may note that the story contains elements of both Realism and Romanticism.
13. Answers will differ. Students may note that most Americans would not have such difficulty buying an overcoat.

Challenge Gogol's writing generally pleased the czar and the worldly nobles, but it infuriated the bureaucrats. After having read "The Overcoat," explain both reactions.

ANSWERS TO ANALYZING LITERATURE

1. Suggested response: While scrimping to buy it, he pictures the overcoat as "a delightful companion."
2. Suggested response: He is treated differently by his co-workers, he goes to a party, he notices a saucy picture, and he is aroused by the sight of a vibrant woman.
3. (a) Suggested response: It comes to represent the need for justice. (b) Suggested response: The ghost's seizure of the important personage's coat supports this interpretation.

ANSWERS TO CRITICAL THINKING AND READING

1. Suggested response: The coat symbolizes the "new" Akaky. So impressed are his co-workers that they invite him to a party, something they have never done before. To them, the coat is more important than the owner.
2. Suggested response: The coat came to represent a lifelong companion to Akaky. Its loss devastated him as much as it did partly because he lacked human companionship.
3. Suggested response: The downtrodden will gain justice, if not in this life, in the next.

THINKING AND WRITING

Publishing Student Writing Arrange students' papers into a class bulletin-board display.

mouselike and withdrawn, with a genuine liking for his job. (b) Suggested response: He becomes slightly more outgoing and self-confident. (c) Suggested response: His personality remains essentially the same.
5. Suggested response: Gogol wants readers to feel sympathetic toward Akaky.
6. (a) Suggested response: It suggests that he feels contempt for these peo-

ple. (b) Suggested response: He seems to think it is uncaring and inefficient. (c) Suggested response: His attitude is conveyed mainly through his characterization of government officials.
7. (a) Suggested response: He is crushed by the loss of his coat and the impossibilty of recovering it. (b) Suggested response: They represent the expression of his hidden anger

and frustration.
8. Answers will differ. Students may feel that Gogol's use of this ending makes the entire story more interesting.
9. (a) Suggested response: Akaky tries desperately to recover his overcoat; the important person accepts his loss and turns over a new leaf. (b) Suggested response: The important person has the means to rebound from his loss; Akaky does not.

1828–1910

Although Leo Tolstoy may be the greatest of all the nineteenth-century Russian writers, he is remembered almost as much for his radical life style and personal beliefs as he is for his writing.

Tolstoy was born at Yasnaya Polyana, his family's estate, near Moscow. His father was a retired army officer, who had fought against the French forces that invaded Russia in 1812. His mother was a member of one of the wealthiest families in all of Russia. Both of his parents died when he was a young boy, and he spent much of his childhood with his devoutly religious aunt. When he was thirteen, however, his aunt also died, and he was forced to move in with another relative. The deaths of his parents and his aunt had a profound impact on him, leading to a lifelong obsession with the inevitability of death.

After briefly attending law school, Tolstoy joined the army in 1851. While serving as an artillery officer, he spent most of his free time writing, and in 1852 he published his first novel, *A History of My Childhood*. Tolstoy went on to serve in the Crimean War and used his experiences as the basis for a series of war stories entitled the *Sevastopol Stories* (1856). Following the war he moved into his family's estate, which he had inherited at the age of nineteen. There he opened an innovative school for peasant children and tried somewhat unsuccessfully to improve the lives of the serfs who were bound to the estate.

At the age of thirty-four, he fell in love with and married Sonya Bers. An intelligent, headstrong, and energetic woman, Sonya was so supportive of Tolstoy's literary career that she even took the time to recopy his nearly indecipherable manuscripts so that they could be read by his publisher. She also managed the estate and bore Tolstoy thirteen children.

In 1863 Tolstoy published *The Cossacks*, an autobiographical novel inspired by his experiences during and immediately after the Crimean War. During that year he also began working on *War and Peace,* his masterful historical novel about Napoleon's invasion of Russia in 1812. Published in 1869, the novel was immediately recognized as Tolstoy's masterpiece for its graphic depiction of war, its insights into Russian life, and its exploration into the meaning of life.

Tolstoy's next novel, *Anna Karenina* (1874–1876), offered a faithful portrait of the lives of the Russian upper classes. A tragic novel of great depth and complexity, *Anna Karenina* enhanced Tolstoy's already lofty reputation as a writer. Yet it also foreshadowed the spiritual crisis that Tolstoy was about to experience.

Tolstoy's spiritual crisis occurred when he was about fifty, resulting from his questions about the meaning of life and his awareness of the inevitability of death. Rejecting established religion and the foundations of Russian society, Tolstoy created his own religious faith, which emphasized a natural existence, universal love, social equality, and nonviolence. In accordance with his beliefs, Tolstoy dramatically altered his life style. He took up shoemaking, became a vegetarian, and gave up drinking and smoking; and in 1891 he renounced the rights to his works published after 1881 and gave his property to his family. Tolstoy's actions placed a great strain on his marriage and eventually forced him to leave home. In 1910, shortly after he had left his estate, Tolstoy died in an obscure railroad station.

GUIDE FOR INTERPRETING

How Much Land Does a Man Need?

Commentary

Allegory. An **allegory** is a narrative in which certain characters, events, or details of setting represent abstract ideas or moral qualities. For example, the characters in an allegory might represent such qualities as intelligence, boldness, and greed. The term *allegory* originated from the Greek word *allegorein,* meaning "to speak so as to imply other than what is said." As the origin of the term suggests, an allegory may be interpreted on a symbolic level as well as on a literal one. When interpreted on a symbolic level, allegories generally teach moral lessons or express universal truths.

The allegory form developed out of the discovery that people are more likely to listen to moral lessons when they are conveyed in an entertaining manner. Thus, the purpose of an allegory is both to entertain and to instruct. Since the aim of most allegories is to reach as many people as possible, the stories tend to be fairly simple and straightforward, involving one-dimensional characters, whose symbolic meaning is usually obvious. In fact, in some cases the names of the characters may even reveal or hint at the qualities they represent.

A **parable** is a special type of allegory characterized by its extreme simplicity and brevity. Generally, parables focus entirely on one or two characters and deal with a specific circumstance that motivates their actions. In addition, the outcome of a parable usually seems inevitable. Often, as is the case in the Bible, parables are used for religious instruction.

In analyzing "How Much Land Does a Man Need?" critics have noted that Tolstoy's story echoes the Biblical parable of the rich fool (Luke 12:16–20), the story of a wealthy farmer who incurs the wrath of God by tearing down his barns and building larger ones. As you read Tolstoy's story, look for the ways in which it parallels this Biblical parable.

Writing

Why do you think people sometimes become obsessed with obtaining material objects? Do you think that this type of obsession can affect the way that a person treats other people? Why or why not? Why do you think that people sometimes do not feel satisfied when they obtain something they have longed for? Jot down your responses to these questions in a journal entry.

Literary Focus Have students discuss why people might be more likely to listen to moral lessons when they are conveyed in an entertaining manner. Then have them think of examples of allegories they have read, and have them explore the types of messages these allegories convey.

Writing/Prior Knowledge Before students begin their journal entries, they should spend some time thinking about an object they have wanted very much. If they gained the object, how did it make them feel? If they did not, how did that make them feel?

Teaching Tenth-Grade Students Students may be studying the Russian Revolution this year in their history class. How does the title of this story relate to what they know about the Russian Revolution?

ESL Teaching Strategy Put each ESL student in a group with three or four native-speaking students. Assign one of the native-speaking students to monitor the ESL student's comprehension and answer his or her questions as those in the group take turns reading the story aloud.

Spelling Tip Draw students' attention to the double *t* in the word *acquitted.*

Support Material

Teaching Portfolio
Teacher Backup, p. 1141
Grammar in Action Worksheet, *Infinitives and Infinitive Phrases*, p. 1145
Grammar in Action Worksheet, *Punctuating Dialogue*, p. 1147
Usage and Mechanics Worksheet,
p. 1149
Vocabulary Check, p. 1150
Analyzing Literature Worksheet, *Understanding Allegory*, p. 1151
Language Worksheet, *Understanding Specific Language*, p. 1152
Selection Test, pp. 1153–1154

Presentation

Motivation/Prior Knowledge A good way to lead into this story is to mention the westward movement in the United States during the nineteenth century. Throughout the century, people headed west to escape from the crowded, industrialized East and to find inexpensive land. Some early ranchers acquired vast holdings by moving to the West. One of these ranchers was Richard King, who established a ranch in Texas that is larger than the state of Rhode Island.

Purpose-Setting Question Why is Pahom never satisfied with the land he acquires?

Universal Themes The idea that the pursuit of wealth and material possessions can be unfulfilling is a recurring theme in world literature. Two other selections that explore this theme are the excerpt from the *Gulistan* of Sa'di (page 112) and Rabindranath Tagore's story "The Artist" (page 1192).

Master Teacher Note After a public reading of "How Much Land Does a Man Need?" at Moscow University, Tolstoy's wife wrote to her husband: "The impression was that *the style* is remarkably austere, terse, not a single extra word; everything is true and precise, like a musical chord; there is much content, few words, and it is satisfying to the end." Ask students to think of a story they have already read that fits Mrs. Tolstoy's description. Then after they have read this story, have them compare the two stories according to the quoted criteria.

1 Reading Strategy Have students make inferences about the story based on its title.

2 Discussion Ask students to discuss some of the advantages of living in the city. What are some of the disadvantages?

3 Reading Strategy Have students speculate about what these observations about the devil might foreshadow.

How Much Land Does a Man Need?

Leo Tolstoy

translated by Louise and Aylmer Maude

1

An elder sister came to visit her younger sister in the country. The elder was married to a shopkeeper in town, the younger to a peasant in the village. As the sisters sat over their tea talking, the elder began to boast of the advantages of town life, saying how comfortably they lived there, how well they dressed, what fine clothes her children wore, what good things they ate and drank, and how she went to the theater, promenades, and entertainments.

The younger sister was piqued,[1] and in turn disparaged[2] the life of a shopkeeper, and stood up for that of a peasant.

"I wouldn't change my way of life for yours," said she. "We may live roughly, but at least we're free from worry. You live in better style than we do, but though you often earn more than you need, you're very likely to lose all you have. You know the proverb, 'Loss and gain are brothers twain.' It often happens that people who're wealthy one day are begging their bread the next. Our way is safer. Though a peasant's life is not a rich one, it's long. We'll never grow rich, but we'll always have enough to eat."

The elder sister said sneeringly:

"Enough? Yes, if you like to share with the pigs and the calves! What do you know of elegance or manners! However much your good man may slave, you'll die as you live—in a dung heap—and your children the same."

"Well, what of that?" replied the younger sister. "Of course our work is rough and hard. But on the other hand, it's sure, and we need not bow to anyone. But you, in your towns, are surrounded by temptations; today all may be right, but tomorrow the Evil One may tempt your husband with cards, wine, or women, and all will go to ruin. Don't such things happen often enough?"

Pahom, the master of the house, was lying on the top of the stove[3] and he listened to the women's chatter.

"It is perfectly true," thought he. "Busy as we are from childhood tilling mother earth, we peasants have no time to let any nonsense settle in our heads. Our only trouble is that we haven't land enough. If I had plenty of land, I shouldn't fear the Devil himself!"

The women finished their tea, chatted a while about dress, and then cleared away the tea things and lay down to sleep.

But the Devil had been sitting behind the stove and had heard all that had been said. He was pleased that the peasant's wife had led her husband into boasting and that he had said that if he had plenty of land he would not fear the Devil himself.

---

1. **piqued** (pēkt) *v.*: Offended.
2. **disparaged** (dis par´ ijd) *v.*: Spoke slightingly of; belittled.

---

3. **the stove:** A brick or tile oven used to heat the room.

Primary Source

At the time he wrote "How Much Land Does a Man Need?" Tolstoy had decided that his own answer to the question posed in the title of the story was none. This created problems for his family, as A. N. Wilson relates in his biography, *Tolstoy*:

The Tolstoy family income, since [Leo] had started to become a saint, had dropped violently. Stewards on his various estates, like all stewards in Russian novels, were not slow to take advantage of their master's lack of interest in the revenues of land and villages, and the money mys-

"All right," thought the Devil. "We'll have a tussle. I'll give you land enough; and by means of the land I'll get you into my power."

2

Close to the village there lived a lady, a small landowner who had an estate of about three hundred acres. She had always lived on good terms with the peasants until she engaged as her manager an old soldier, who took to burdening the people with fines. However careful Pahom tried to be, it happened again and again that now a horse of his got among the lady's oats, now a cow strayed into her garden, now his calves found their way into her meadows—and he always had to pay a fine.

Pahom paid up, but grumbled, and, going home in a temper, was rough with his family. All through that summer Pahom had much trouble because of this manager, and he was actually glad when winter came and the cattle had to be stabled. Though he grudged the fodder[4] when they could no longer graze on the pasture land, at least he was free from anxiety about them.

In the winter the news got about that the lady was going to sell her land and that the keeper of the inn on the high road was bargaining for it. When the peasants heard this they were very much alarmed.

"Well," thought they, "if the innkeeper gets the land, he'll worry us with fines worse than the lady's manager. We all depend on that estate."

So the peasants went on behalf of their village council and asked the lady not to sell the land to the innkeeper, offering her a better price for it themselves. The lady agreed to let them have it. Then the peasants tried to arrange for the village council to buy the whole estate, so that it might be held by them all in common. They met twice to discuss it, but could not settle the matter; the Evil One sowed discord among them and they could not agree. So they decided to buy the land individually, each according to his means; and the lady agreed to this plan as she had to the other.

Presently Pahom heard that a neighbor of his was buying fifty acres, and that the lady had consented to accept one half in cash and to wait a year for the other half. Pahom felt envious.

"Look at that," thought he, "the land is all being sold, and I'll get none of it." So he spoke to his wife.

"Other people are buying," said he, "and we must also buy twenty acres or so. Life is becoming impossible. That manager is simply crushing us with his fines."

So they put their heads together and considered how they could manage to buy it. They had one hundred rubles[5] laid by. They sold a colt and one half of their bees, hired out one of their sons as a farmhand and took his wages in advance, borrowed the rest from a brother-in-law, and so scraped together half the purchase money.

Having done this, Pahom chose a farm of forty acres, some of it wooded, and went to the lady to bargain for it. They came to an agreement, and he shook hands with her upon it and paid her a deposit in advance. Then they went to town and signed the deeds, he paying half the price down, and undertaking to pay the remainder within two years.

So now Pahom had land of his own. He borrowed seed and sowed it on the land he had bought. The harvest was a good one, and within a year he had managed to pay off his debts both to the lady and to his brother-in-law. So he became a landowner, plowing and sowing his own land, making hay on his own land, cutting his own trees, and feeding his cattle on his own pasture. When he went out to plow his fields, or to look at his growing corn, or at his grass meadows, his heart would fill with joy. The grass that grew and the flowers that bloomed there seemed to him unlike any that grew elsewhere. Formerly, when he had passed by that land, it had appeared the same as any other land, but now it seemed quite different.

3

So Pahom was well contented, and everything would have been right if the neighboring peasants would only not have trespassed on his wheatfields

---

4. **fodder** (fäd′ ər) *n.*: Coarse food for livestock.

5. **rubles** (roo′ b'lz) *n.*: The ruble is the Russian monetary unit.

teriously vanished. The farms, which Tolstoy had formerly supervised with a modicum of rough and ready efficiency, started to go to ruin. The united revenues from Yasnaya Polyana [and two other estates], whose capital value was hundreds of thousands of rubles, had shrunk to fifty thousand rubles. . . . It was all very well to speak of wickedness, of laying up treasures on earth. But Tolstoy chose to ignore parts of the New Testament which commend good husbandry, and the wise investment of talents.

THE VILLAGE OF ANDREIKOVO
Vladimir Stozharov
The Tretyakov Gallery, Moscow

and meadows. He appealed to them most civilly, but they still went on: now the herdsmen would let the village cows stray into his meadows, then horses from the night pasture would get among his corn. Pahom turned them out again and again, and forgave their owners, and for a long time he forbore to prosecute anyone. But at last he lost patience and complained to the District Court. He knew it was the peasants' want of land, and no evil intent on their part, that caused the trouble, but he thought:

"I can't go on overlooking it, or they'll destroy all I have. They must be taught a lesson."

So he had them up, gave them one lesson, and then another, and two or three of the peasants were fined. After a time Pahom's neighbors began to bear him a grudge for this, and would now and then let their cattle onto his land on purpose. One peasant even got into Pahom's wood at night and cut down five young lime trees for their bark. Pahom, passing through the wood one day, noticed something white. He came nearer and saw the stripped trunks lying on the ground, and close by stood the stumps where the trees had been. Pahom was furious.

"If he'd only cut one here and there it would have been bad enough," thought Pahom, "but the rascal has actually cut down a whole clump. If I

could only find out who did this, I'd get even with him."

He racked his brains as to who it could be. Finally he decided: "It must be Simon—no one else could have done it." So he went to Simon's homestead to have a look around, but he found nothing and only had an angry scene. However, he now felt more certain than ever that Simon had done it, and he lodged a complaint. Simon was summoned. The case was tried, and retried, and at the end of it all Simon was acquitted, there being no evidence against him. Pahom felt still more aggrieved, and let his anger loose upon the Elders and the Judges.

"You let thieves grease your palms," said he. "If you were honest folk yourselves you wouldn't let a thief go free."

So Pahom quarreled with the judges and with his neighbors. Threats to burn his hut began to be uttered. So though Pahom had more land, his place in the community was much worse than before.

About this time a rumor got about that many people were moving to new parts.

"There's no need for me to leave my land," thought Pahom. "But some of the others may leave our village and then there'd be more room for us. I'd take over their land myself and make my estates somewhat bigger. I could then live more at ease. As it is, I'm still too cramped to be comfortable."

One day Pahom was sitting at home when a peasant, passing through the village, happened to drop in. He was allowed to stay the night, and supper was given him. Pahom had a talk with this peasant and asked him where he came from. The stranger answered that he came from beyond the Volga,[6] where he had been working. One word led to another, and the man went on to say that many people were settling in those parts. He told how some people from his village had settled there. They had joined the community there and had had twenty-five acres per man granted them. The land was so good, he said, that the rye sown on it grew as high as a horse, and so thick that five cuts of a sickle made a sheaf. One peasant, he said, had brought nothing with him but his bare hands, and now he had six horses and two cows of his own.

Pahom's heart kindled with desire.

"Why should I suffer in this narrow hole, if one can live so well elsewhere?" he thought. "I'll sell my land and my homestead here, and with the money I'll start afresh over there and get everything new. In this crowded place one is always having trouble. But I must first go and find out all about it myself."

Toward summer he got ready and started out. He went down the Volga on a steamer to Samara,[7] then walked another three hundred miles on foot, and at last reached the place. It was just as the stranger had said. The peasants had plenty of land: every man had twenty-five acres of communal land given him for his use, and anyone who had money could buy, besides, at a ruble and a half an acre, as much good freehold land as he wanted.

Having found out all he wished to know, Pahom returned home as autumn came on, and began selling off his belongings. He sold his land at a profit, sold his homestead and all his cattle, and withdrew from membership in the village. He only waited till the spring, and then started with his family for the new settlement.

---

6. **Volga** (väl′ gə): A river in the western part of the Soviet Union.
7. **Samara** (sə mä′ rə): A river in the eastern part of the Soviet Union.

As soon as Pahom and his family reached their new abode, he applied for admission into the council of a large village. He stood treat to the Elders and obtained the necessary documents. Five shares of communal land were given him for his own and his sons' use: that is to say—125 acres (not all together, but in different fields) besides the use of the communal pasture. Pahom put up the buildings he needed and bought cattle. Of the communal land alone he had three times as much as at his former home, and the land was good wheat land. He was ten times better off than he had been. He had plenty of arable land and pasturage, and could keep as many head of cattle as he liked.

At first, in the bustle of building and settling down, Pahom was pleased with it all, but when he got used to it he began to think that even here he hadn't enough land. The first year he sowed wheat on his share of the communal land and had a good crop. He wanted to go on sowing wheat, but had not enough communal land for the purpose, and what he had already used was not available, for in those parts wheat is sown only on virgin soil or on fallow land. It is sown for one or two years, and then the land lies fallow till it is again overgrown with steppe grass. There were many who wanted such land, and there was not enough for all, so that people quarreled about it. Those who were better off wanted it for growing wheat, and those who were poor wanted it to let to dealers, so that they might raise money to pay their taxes. Pahom wanted to sow more wheat, so he rented land from a dealer for a year. He sowed much wheat and had a fine crop, but the land was too far from the village—the wheat had to be carted more than ten miles. After a time Pahom noticed that some peasant dealers were living on separate farms and were growing wealthy, and he thought:

"If I were to buy some freehold land and have a homestead on it, it would be a different thing altogether. Then it would all be fine and close together."

The question of buying freehold land recurred to him again and again.

He went on in the same way for three years, renting land and sowing wheat. The seasons turned out well and the crops were good, so that he began

12 **Discussion** Have students discuss whether they think the devil had a hand in the appearance of the peasant. Might the peasant actually be the devil in disguise? If so, what is the devil hoping to accomplish?

13 **Enrichment** Tell students that Samara is a river that rises in the Ural Mountains and flows northeast into the Volga. At the time of the story, Samara was also the name of a city at the junction of the Volga and Samara rivers. Today this city, with a population of more than a million people, is called Kuybychev.

14 **Clarification** Make sure students realize that the communal land is publicly owned land, available for people who want to farm it.

15 **Reading Strategy** Have students predict whether or not Pahom will now be satisfied with the amount of land he has. On what do they base their predictions?

16 **Discussion** Have students discuss why Pahom is still not satisfied.

vices and duplicities. And yet, though pulled in so many divergent directions, Tolstoy somehow managed "to become as a child" and to write [these] slight, pellucid, sardonic tales.

17 **Discussion** Ask students why the dealer happens to stop by at this point in the story. Is he the devil, or an agent of the devil? If so, what is his purpose?

18 **Discussion** Remind students that Pahom once told his wife he needed only twenty acres. With this in mind, why do students think that he now chooses to pass up acquiring "only thirteen hundred acres" to try to acquire even more land?

19 **Literary Focus** As Pahom's actions indicate, one of the lessons this story teaches is that the more people have, the more they want. Do students agree with this insight? Why or why not?

20 **Enrichment** The Bashkirs live "far away" from Pahom's present home, but their land is still in Europe, not Asia. Pahom is moving eastward (somewhat like America's westward-moving pioneers) in search of cheaper and more abundant land.

21 **Enrichment** Tell students that Pahom needs an interpreter because the Bashkirs, who are a Muslim people, speak a Turkic language.

to lay by money. He might have gone on living contentedly, but he grew tired of having to rent other people's land every year and having to scramble for it. Wherever there was good land to be had, the peasants would rush for it and it was taken up at once, so that unless you were sharp about it, you got none. It happened in the third year that he and a dealer together rented a piece of pasture land from some peasants, and they had already plowed it up, when there was some dispute and the peasants went to law about it, and things fell out so that the labor was all lost.

"If it were my own land," thought Pahom, "I should be independent, and there wouldn't be all this unpleasantness."

So Pahom began looking out for land which he could buy, and he came across a peasant who had bought thirteen hundred acres, but having got into difficulties was willing to sell again cheap. Pahom bargained and haggled with him, and at last they settled the price at fifteen hundred rubles, part in cash and part to be paid later. They had all but clinched the matter when a passing dealer happened to stop at Pahom's one day to get feed for his horses. He drank tea with Pahom, and they had a talk. The dealer said that he was just returning from the land of the Bashkirs,[8] far away, where he had bought thirteen thousand acres of land, all for a thousand rubles. Pahom questioned him further, and the dealer said:

"All one has to do is to make friends with the chiefs. I gave away about one hundred rubles' worth of silk robes and carpets, besides a case of tea, and I gave wine to those who would drink it; and I got the land for less than three kopecks[9] an acre." And he showed Pahom the title deed, saying:

"The land lies near a river, and the whole steppe is virgin soil."

Pahom plied him with questions, and the dealer said:

"There's more land there than you could cover if you walked a year, and it all belongs to the Bashkirs. They're as simple as sheep, and land can be got almost for nothing."

"There, now," thought Pahom, "with my one thousand rubles, why should I get only thirteen hundred acres, and saddle myself with a debt besides? If I take it out there, I can get more than ten times as much for my money."

5

Pahom inquired how to get to the place, and as soon as the grain dealer had left him, he prepared to go there himself. He left his wife to look after the homestead, and started on his journey, taking his hired man with him. They stopped at a town on their way and bought a case of tea, some wine, and other presents, as the grain dealer had advised.

On and on they went until they had gone more than three hundred miles, and on the seventh day they came to a place where the Bashkirs had pitched their round tents. It was all just as the dealer had said. The people lived on the steppe, by a river, in felt-covered tents. They neither tilled the ground nor ate bread. Their cattle and horses grazed in herds on the steppe. The colts were tethered behind the tents, and the mares were driven to them twice a day. The mares were milked, and from the milk kumiss[10] was made. It was the women who prepared the kumiss, and they also made cheese. As far as the men were concerned, drinking kumiss and tea, eating mutton, and playing on their pipes was all they cared about. They were all stout and merry, and all the summer long they never thought of doing any work. They were quite ignorant, and knew no Russian, but were good-natured enough.

As soon as they saw Pahom, they came out of their tents and gathered around the visitor. An interpreter was found, and Pahom told them he had come about some land. The Bashkirs seemed very glad; they took Pahom and led him into one of the best tents, where they made him sit on some down cushions placed on a carpet, while they sat around him. They gave him some tea and kumiss, and had a sheep killed, and gave him mutton to eat. Pahom took presents out of his cart and distributed them

---

8. Bashkirs (bash kirz´): A nomadic people who live in the plains of southwestern Russia.

9. kopecks (kō´ peks) *n.*: A kopeck is a Russian monetary unit equal to a hundredth of a ruble.

10. kumiss (ko͞o´ mis) *n.*: Mare's milk that has been fermented and is used as a drink.

Grammar in Action

An **infinitive** is a form of verb that generally appears with the word *to* and acts as a noun, adjective, or adverb. An **infinitive phrase** is an infinitive with modifiers, a complement, or an object, all acting together as a single part of speech. Note the following examples from Louise and Aylmer Maude's translation of "How Much Land Does a Man Need?":

They had all but clinched the matter when a passing dealer happened *to stop at Pahom's one day* . . . (infinitive phrase as a direct object)

He left his wife *to look after the homestead,* . . . (infinitive phrase as an adverb)

Student Activity 1. Find at least five more infinitives or infinitive phrases in "How Much Land Does a Man Need?" Then identify the function of each.

Student Activity 2. Write five separate sentences, each containing an infinitive or an infinitive phrase. Then identify the function of the infinitive or infinitive phrase in each sentence.

among the Bashkirs, and divided the tea amongst them. The Bashkirs were delighted. They talked a great deal among themselves and then told the interpreter what to say.

"They wish to tell you," said the interpreter, "that they like you and that it's our custom to do all we can to please a guest and to repay him for his gifts. You have given us presents, now tell us which of the things we possess please you best, that we may present them to you."

"What pleases me best here," answered Pahom, "is your land. Our land is crowded and the soil is worn out, but you have plenty of land, and it is good land. I never saw the likes of it."

The interpreter told the Bashkirs what Pahom had said. They talked among themselves for a while. Pahom could not understand what they were saying, but saw that they were much amused and heard them shout and laugh. Then they were silent and looked at Pahom while the interpreter said:

"They wish me to tell you that in return for your presents they will gladly give you as much land as you want. You have only to point it out with your hand and it is yours."

The Bashkirs talked again for a while and began to dispute. Pahom asked what they were disputing about, and the interpreter told him that some of them thought they ought to ask their chief about the land and not act in his absence, while others thought there was no need to wait for his return.

6

While the Bashkirs were disputing, a man in a large fox-fur cap appeared on the scene. They all became silent and rose to their feet. The interpreter said: "This is our chief himself."

Pahom immediately fetched the best dressing gown and five pounds of tea, and offered these to the chief. The chief accepted them and seated himself in the place of honor. The Bashkirs at once began telling him something. The chief listened for a while, then made a sign with his head for them to be silent, and addressing himself to Pahom, said in Russian:

"Well, so be it. Choose whatever piece of land you like; we have plenty of it."

"How can I take as much as I like?" thought Pahom. "I must get a deed to make it secure, or

MOUNTAINS
Martiros Saryan
The Tretyakov Gallery, Moscow

else they may say: 'It is yours,' and afterward may take it away again."

"Thank you for your kind words," he said aloud. "You have much land, and I only want a little. But I should like to be sure which portion is mine. Could it not be measured and made over to me? Life and death are in God's hands. You good people give it to me, but your children might wish to take it back again."

"You are quite right," said the chief. "We will make it over to you."

"I heard that a dealer had been here," continued Pahom, "and that you gave him a little land, too, and signed title deeds to that effect. I should like to have it done in the same way."

The chief understood.

"Yes," replied, he, "that can be done quite easily. We have a scribe, and we will go to town with you and have the deed properly sealed."

"And what will be the price?" asked Pahom.

"Our price is always the same: one thousand rubles a day."

Pahom did not understand.

"A day? What measure is that? How many acres would that be?"

22 **Discussion** Have students discuss why the Bashkirs are so generous with their land. How does the Bashkirs' attitude concerning land contrast with that of Pahom?

23 **Discussion** Ask students to explain why Pahom insists that the Bashkirs give him a deed to the land. What does this request reveal about Pahom's character?

Humanities Note
Fine art, *Mountains* by Martiros Saryan. Saryan (1880–1972), who studied at the Moscow School of Painting, rejected detailed renditions of landscapes in favor of simpler depictions conveying a sense of harmony and serenity. In this painting, he portrays the sunlit highland terrain of Soviet Armenia, a favorite subject of his because of the land's picturesque scenery and the spiritual strength and the traditions of the Armenian people. As is generally the case with Saryan's work, this painting consists of pure, light colors and decorative rhythms, and it harmoniously integrates animal and human figures into the natural landscape.

You might want to use the following questions to discuss the art:
1. How does this painting convey a sense of harmony between humanity and nature?
2. How does the artist capture the immensity of the mountains?
3. Would Pahom be happy on this land? Why or why not?
4. How does the landscape depicted in this painting compare with the way in which you usually envision the Soviet Union?

24 **Reading Strategy** Have students pause to predict the outcome of the story. On what do they base their predictions?

25 **Clarification** Explain to students that the steppe is a level, treeless grassland. Pahom will be able to return to his starting point in this unfamiliar country because the Bashkirs will wait for him on a hillock, which is slightly raised above the rest of the land. Thus, they will be visible to Pahom, and he to them, even at a great distance.

26 **Enrichment** Thirty-five miles is a very long distance to walk in one day. Tell students that if Pahom does walk that far—forming a square with 8.75 miles on each side—he will acquire 76.5 square miles of land, or 48,960 acres.

27 **Discussion** Have students discuss how this dream might foreshadow the outcome of the story.

28 **Discussion** Ask students what is revealed by the Bashkirs' ability to remain in the same spot for an entire day. Do they think that Pahom would be able to do this? Why or why not?

"We do not know how to reckon it out," said the chief. "We sell it by the day. As much as you can go around on your feet in a day is yours, and the price is one thousand rubles a day."

Pahom was surprised.

"But in a day you can get around a large tract of land," he said.

The chief laughed.

"It will all be yours!" said he. "But there is one condition: If you don't return on the same day to the spot whence you started, your money is lost."

"But how am I to mark the way that I have gone?"

"Why, we shall go to any spot you like and stay there. You must start from that spot and make your round, taking a spade with you. Wherever you think necessary, make a mark. At every turning, dig a hole and pile up the turf; then afterward we will go around with a plow from hole to hole. You may make as large a circuit as you please, but before the sun sets you must return to the place you started from. All the land you cover will be yours."

Pahom was delighted. It was decided to start early next morning. They talked a while, and after drinking some more kumiss and eating some more mutton, they had tea again, and then the night came on. They gave Pahom a featherbed to sleep on, and the Bashkirs dispersed for the night, promising to assemble the next morning at daybreak and ride out before sunrise to the appointed spot.

7

Pahom lay on the feather bed, but could not sleep. He kept thinking about the land.

"What a large tract I'll mark off!" thought he, "I can easily do thirty-five miles in a day. The days are long now, and within a circuit of thirty-five miles what a lot of land there will be! I'll sell the poorer land or let it to peasants, but I'll pick out the best and farm it myself. I'll buy two ox teams and hire two more laborers. About a hundred and fifty acres shall be plowland, and I'll pasture cattle on the rest."

Pahom lay awake all night and dozed off only just before dawn. Hardly were his eyes closed when he had a dream. He thought he was lying in that same tent and heard somebody chuckling outside. He wondered who it could be, and rose and went out, and he saw the Bashkir chief sitting in front of the tent holding his sides and rolling about with laughter. Going nearer to the chief, Pahom asked: "What are you laughing at?" But he saw that it was no longer the chief but the grain dealer who had recently stopped at his house and had told him about the land. Just as Pahom was going to ask: "Have you been here long?" he saw that it was not the dealer, but the peasant who had come up from the Volga long ago, to Pahom's old home. Then he saw that it was not the peasant either, but the Devil himself with hoofs and horns, sitting there and chuckling, and before him lay a man, prostrate on the ground, barefooted, with only trousers and a shirt on. And Pahom dreamed that he looked more attentively to see what sort of man it was lying there, and he saw that the man was dead, and that it was himself. Horror-struck, he awoke.

"What things one dreams about!" thought he.

Looking around he saw through the open door that the dawn was breaking.

"It's time to wake them up," thought he. "We ought to be starting."

He got up, roused his man (who was sleeping in his cart), bade him harness, and went to call the Bashkirs.

"It's time to go to the steppe to measure the land," he said.

The Bashkirs rose and assembled, and the chief came, too. Then they began drinking kumiss again, and offered Pahom some tea, but he would not wait.

"If we are to go, let's go. It's high time," said he.

8

The Bashkirs got ready and they all started; some mounted on horses and some in carts. Pahom drove in his own small cart with his servant and took a spade with him. When they reached the steppe, the red dawn was beginning to kindle. They ascended a hillock (called by the Bashkirs a *shikhan*) and, dismounting from their carts and their horses, gathered in one spot. The chief came up to Pahom and, stretching out his arm toward the plain:

Grammar in Action

When writing a short story or novel, a writer must be careful to **punctuate dialogue** correctly. Most often, writers use commas and quotation marks to separate the identification of the speaker from a passage of dialogue. Note the following example from "How Much Land Does a Man Need?":

"It's time to go to the steppe to measure the land," he said.

When a passage of dialogue is interrupted by the identification of the speaker, either an extra comma (if the identification of the speaker does not follow a complete thought) or a period (if the identification does follow a complete thought) is also used. Note the following examples:

"It's time to wake them up," thought he. "We ought to be starting."

"No matter," he concluded, "I'll go toward the rising sun."

Student Activity 1. Correctly punctuate each of the following passages of dialogue.

1. I don't know what I was thinking he said I shouldn't have done what I did.
2. I cannot believe that you did that the chief snapped, his voice filled with anger.

"See," said he, "all this, as far as your eye can reach, is ours. You may have any part of it you like."

Pahom's yes glistened: it was all virgin soil, as flat as the palm of your hand, as black as the seed of a poppy, and in the hollows different kinds of grasses grew breast-high.

The chief took off his fox-fur cap, placed it on the ground, and said:

"This will be the mark. Start from here, and return here again. All the land you go around shall be yours."

Pahom took out his money and put it on the cap. Then he took off his outer coat, remaining in his sleeveless undercoat. He unfastened his girdle and tied it tight below his stomach, put a little bag of bread into the breast of his coat, and, tying a flask of water to his girdle, he drew up the tops of his boots, took the spade from his man, and stood ready to start. He considered for some moments which way he had better go—it was tempting everywhere.

"No matter," he concluded, "I'll go toward the rising sun."

He turned his face to the east, stretched himself, and waited for the sun to appear above the rim.

"I must lose no time," he thought, "and it's easier walking while it's still cool."

The sun's rays had hardly flashed above the horizon when Pahom, carrying the spade over his shoulder, went down into the steppe.

Pahom started walking neither slowly nor quickly. After having gone a thousand yards he stopped, dug a hole, and placed pieces of turf one on another to make it more visible. Then he went on; and now that he had walked off his stiffness he quickened his pace. After a while he dug another hole.

Pahom looked back. The hillock could be distinctly seen in the sunlight, with the people on it, and the glittering iron rims of the cartwheels. At a rough guess Pahom concluded that he had walked three miles. It was growing warmer; he took off his undercoat, slung it across his shoulder, and went on again. It had grown quite warm now; he looked at the sun—it was time to think of breakfast.

"The first shift is done, but there are four in a day, and it's too soon yet to turn. But I'll just take off my boots," said he to himself.

He sat down, took off his boots, stuck them into his girdle,[11] and went on. It was easy walking now.

"I'll go on for another three miles," thought he, "and then turn to the left. This spot is so fine that it would be a pity to lose it. The further one goes, the better the land seems."

He went straight on for a while, and when he looked around, the hillock was scarcely visible and the people on it looked like black ants, and he could just see something glistening there in the sun.

"Ah," thought Pahom, "I have gone far enough in this direction; it's time to turn. Besides, I'm in a regular sweat, and very thirsty."

He stopped, dug a large hole, and heaped up pieces of turf. Next he untied his flask, had a drink, and then turned sharply to the left. He went on and on; the grass was high, and it was very hot.

Pahom began to grow tired: he looked at the sun and saw that it was noon.

"Well," he thought, "I must have a rest."

He sat down, and ate some bread and drank some water; but he did not lie down, thinking that if he did he might fall asleep. After sitting a little while, he went on again. At first he walked easily; the food had strengthened him; but it had become terribly hot and he felt sleepy. Still he went on, thinking: "An hour to suffer, a lifetime to live."

He went a long way in this direction also, and was about to turn to the left again, when he perceived a damp hollow:

"It would be a pity to leave that out," he thought. "Flax would do well there." So he went on past the hollow and dug a hole on the other side of it before he made a sharp turn. Pahom looked toward the hillock. The heat made the air hazy: it seemed to be quivering, and through the haze the people on the hillock could scarcely be seen.

"Ah," thought Pahom, "I have made the sides too long; I must make this one shorter." And he went along the third side, stepping faster. He looked at the sun: it was nearly halfway to the horizon, and he had not yet done two miles of the third side of the square. He was still ten miles from the goal.

"No," he thought, "though it will make my land lopsided, I must hurry back in a straight line

_____
11. **girdle** (gʉrd´ 'l) *n.*: A belt or sash.

29 **Clarification** Make sure students note that since Pahom has given the money to the Bashkirs, there is no way for him to recover it—this is not a bet. If he does not return before the sun sets, he loses both his money and his land.

30 **Discussion** How far do students think Pahom should walk in each direction? Why? How accurately would Pahom be able to estimate how far he has traveled in each direction?

31 **Discussion** Have students discuss the possible implications of Pahom's decision to "go on for another three miles."

32 **Literary Focus** Have students contemplate how this passage relates to the message that Tolstoy is trying to convey. How does the passage convey Pahom's inability to restrain his greed?

33 **Discussion** Have students discuss how Pahom's observation might foreshadow the outcome of the story.

34 **Master Teacher Note** Have a student volunteer draw a diagram of Pahom's route on the chalkboard.

3. Jim remarked I like watching baseball, but I love watching football.
4. It was Alice mused a very embarrassing moment for all of us.
5. It's time for us to start getting down to business Ronald suggested anxiously.

Student Activity 2. Record a conversation between two of your friends, making sure to punctuate the dialogue correctly.

now. I might go too far, and as it is I have a great deal of land."

So Pahom hurriedly dug a hole and turned straight toward the hillock.

9

Pahom went straight toward the hillock, but he now walked with difficulty. He was exhausted from the heat, his bare feet were cut and bruised, and his legs began to fail. He longed to rest, but it was impossible if he meant to get back before sunset. The sun waits for no man, and it was sinking lower and lower.

"Oh, Lord," he thought, "if only I have not blundered trying for too much! What if I am too late?"

He looked toward the hillock and at the sun. He was still far from his goal, and the sun was already near the rim of the sky.

Pahom walked on and on; it was very hard walking, but he went quicker and quicker. He pressed on, but was still far from the place. He began running, threw away his coat, his boots, his flask, and his cap, and kept only the spade which he used as a support.

"What am I to do?" he thought again. "I've grasped too much and ruined the whole affair. I can't get there before the sun sets."

And this fear made him still more breathless. Pahom kept on running; his trousers stuck to him, and his mouth was parched. His breast was working like a blacksmith's bellows, his heart was beating like a hammer, and his legs were giving way as if they did not belong to him. Pahom was seized with terror lest he should die of the strain.

Though afraid of death, he could not stop.

"After having run all that way they will call me a fool if I stop now," thought he.

And he ran on and on, and drew near and heard the Bashkirs yelling and shouting to him, and their cries inflamed his heart still more. He gathered his last strength and ran on.

The sun was close to the rim of the sky and, cloaked in mist, looked large, and red as blood. Now, yes, now, it was about to set! The sun was quite low, but he was also quite near his goal. Pahom could already see the people on the hillock waving their arms to make him hurry. He could see the fox-fur cap on the ground and the money in it, and the chief sitting on the ground holding his sides. And Pahom remembered his dream.

"There's plenty of land," thought he, "but will God let me live on it? I have lost my life, I have lost my life! Never will I reach that spot!"

Pahom looked at the sun, which had reached the earth: one side of it had already disappeared. With all his remaining strength he rushed on, bending his body forward so that his legs could hardly follow fast enough to keep him from falling. Just as he reached the hillock it suddenly grew dark. He looked up—the sun had already set!

He gave a cry: "All my labor has been in vain," thought he, and was about to stop, but he heard the Bashkirs still shouting and remembered that though to him, from below, the sun seemed to have set, they on the hillock could still see it. He took a long breath and ran up the hillock. It was still light there. He reached the top and saw the cap. Before it sat the chief, laughing and holding his sides. Again Pahom remembered his dream, and he uttered a cry: his legs gave way beneath him, he fell forward and reached the cap with his hands.

"Ah, that's a fine fellow!" exclaimed the chief. "He has gained much land!"

Pahom's servant came running up and tried to raise him, but he saw that blood was flowing from his mouth. Pahom was dead.

The Bashkirs clicked their tongues to show their pity.

His servant picked up the spade and dug a grave long enough for Pahom to lie in, and buried him in it.

Six feet from his head to his toes was all he needed.

___

Reader's Response *If you were in Pahom's place, at what point, if any, would you have been satisfied with your property? Explain.*

___

35 Discussion Ask students if they think Pahom should have accounted for the fact that he would grow increasingly tired as the day progressed.

36 Discussion Have students discuss what the Bashkirs would be likely to think of Pahom's actions.

37 Discussion After students have finished reading the story, have them look back at this comment and discuss why it is ironic.

Enrichment As mentioned in the Guide for Interpreting (page 943), Tolstoy's story echoes the biblical parable of the rich fool (Luke 12:16–20). Bring in a copy of the Bible and read this parable to the class. Then have students discuss the parallels between the biblical parable and Tolstoy's story.

Cultural Note Many American and British writers have praised Tolstoy's works. In fact, the renowned Irish novelist James Joyce called "How Much Land Does a Man Need?" "the greatest story that the world of literature knows." Have students offer reasons why Joyce might have been so impressed with this story.

Cooperative Learning Divide the class into groups of four or five. Then have each group discuss what they did and did not like about Tolstoy's story and what they think they can learn from it.

Primary Source

In his critical biography of Tolstoy, William W. Rowe applauds the effectiveness of the ending of Tolstoy's story:

The image of the sun (which "will not wait") is particularly successful, as it races in its arching journey across the sky against the wide curve of Pahom's greed upon the ground. The fact that Pahom's heart pounds like a hammer while the sun turns blood-red is a grimly apt anticipation of the blood that will issue from his mouth when he dies. Later in the day, the sun's intense heat, recalling the devil's own element, appropriately "influ-

ences" Pahom to lie down and sleep in a premature realization of his devil-induced dream. . . . At the end, both Pahom and the sun disappear beneath the ground after tracing their curving courses above the earth—a focus that appropriately reinforces the deadly playfulness of the story's title.

Closure and Extension

ANSWERS TO THINKING ABOUT THE SELECTION

1. She says that city people are wealthy but their lives are unstable, and she says that city people may succumb to the temptation of the devil. In contrast, she says that peasants are poor, but they are contented and their lives

are long. As it turns out, her husband is the one who succumbs to the temptation of the devil, and despite becoming wealthy, ends up dying an early death as a result of his greed.
2. After becoming a landowner, he behaves in the same way that the manager of the estate had.
3. (a) He becomes discontented with his land because he feels cramped in by his neighbors. (b) Answers will differ.

THINKING ABOUT THE SELECTION

Interpreting

1. Considering the outcome of the story, what is ironic, or surprising, about the younger sister's comments about peasant life and city life?

2. In view of Pahom's earlier difficulties with the manager of the woman's estate, what is ironic about the disputes he becomes involved in after becoming a landowner?

3. (a) How and why does Pahom's attitude toward his first plot of land change? (b) Explain whether you think that Pahom's attitude would have remained the same if he had not had difficulties with his neighbors.

4. (a) How would you characterize the peasants who live in the settlement beyond the Volga? (b) How does their way of life and their behavior contrast with that of the Bashkirs?

5. (a) How does Pahom's dream foreshadow, or hint at, the outcome of the story? (b) What does the dream suggest about the role played by the Devil throughout the story?

6. (a) What is ironic about the outcome of the story? (b) Considering the outcome, what is ironic about the final line? (c) Did you find this ending satisfying? Why or why not?

7. During the course of his life, Tolstoy came to believe that property ownership was evil. How does this story reflect this view?

Applying

8. Explain whether you think that most people would behave like Pahom if they were put in his situation.

9. Socrates said, "He is richest who is content with the least. He who has little and wants less is richer than he that has much and wants more." (a) How do Socrates' words relate to this story? (b) How do they relate to life in general?

ANALYZING LITERATURE

Understanding Allegory

Critics generally classify "How Much Land Does a Man Need?" as a parable, a special type of allegory that focuses entirely on one or two characters and deals with specific circumstances that motivate their actions.

1. What is the moral lesson that Tolstoy's parable teaches?

2. Parables are often used as a means of religious instruction. How might "How Much Land Does a Man Need?" be used for this purpose?

3. (a) How does this tale blend realism with the fantastic? (b) Would it have been as effective if the tale were entirely realistic or entirely fantastic? Explain your answer.

CRITICAL THINKING AND READING

Exploring Connections Among Works

Certain motifs recur throughout the literary works of different cultures and eras. The idea of a character either making a pact with the Devil or being controlled by the Devil is one such motif. In addition to Tolstoy's story, the topic is explored in such works as Marlowe's *Doctor Faustus* (page 700) and Goethe's *Faust* (page 863).

1. Look again at the information on the Faust legend on page 860. In both *Faust* and *Doctor Faustus*, the protagonists openly bargain with the Devil in their quests to attain knowledge, experience, and power. Based on this information, what differences can you see between the role of the Devil in these works and in Tolstoy's story?

2. What are the similarities between Tolstoy's story and the two earlier works?

3. What other literary works can you think of in which a character either makes a pact with or is controlled by the Devil?

4. In what ways are these works similar to and different from Tolstoy's story?

THINKING AND WRITING

Writing a Parable

Try writing a parable of your own modeled after Tolstoy's story. Start by deciding what you want your parable to teach. Then choose a setting and develop one or two main characters. When writing your parable, try to make your message clear. Before you revise put your parable aside for a day or two so that you can evaluate it more objectively. Finally, once you have finished revising it, read it to your classmates.

(continued from bottom of page)

does, because people are not greedy by nature.

9. (a) Suggested response: Tolstoy's story shows what can happen to someone who "has much and wants more." (b) Suggested response: Both suggest that people should learn to feel grateful for what they have.

Challenge During the years before Tostoy's death, the phrase "property is theft" often became associated with Tolstoy. Having just read "How Much Land Does a Man Need?" would you be surprised if Tolstoy did in fact hold such a view? Why or why not?

ANSWERS TO ANALYZING LITERATURE

1. Suggested response: It teaches that people who are greedy and self-centered can never be satisfied and that people who become obsessed with material wants may end up destroying themselves.

2. Suggested response: The story teaches that people should live humbly and simply, free from the desire for material objects.

3. (a) Suggested response: The story dramatizes real-life situations. Yet the devil plays a major role in the story. (b) Answers will differ. Many students are likely to respond that the story would not be as effective.

ANSWERS TO CRITICAL THINKING AND READING

1. The devil does not openly reveal his presence in Tolstoy's story as he does in the other works. Instead, he deceives and manipulates Pahom without making Pahom aware that he is doing so.

2. Answers will differ. Students should note that the devil manipulates the characters in all three works.

3. Answers will differ. Two such works are "The Devil and Tom Walker" by Washington Irving and "Young Goodman Brown" by Nathaniel Hawthorne.

4. Student responses will differ according to the works they name.

THINKING AND WRITING

Publishing Student Writing Encourage students to submit their parables to the school literary magazine.

Students may respond that Pahom's later actions indicate that he would have grown dissatisfied with his land even if he had not had difficulties with his neighbors.

4. (a) Suggested response: They are self-centered and greedy. (b) Unlike the peasants who are constantly quarreling over control of the land, the Bashkirs live a simple, peaceful existence and are willing to share their land.

5. (a) As in Pahom's dream, the chief is laughing as Pahom approaches him after he has finished marking his land; and, as in his dream, Pahom dies at the end of the story. (b) The dream suggests that the chief, the grain dealer, and the wandering peasant were either the devil in disguise or agents of the devil.

6. (a) Although Pahom makes it back to the starting point to avoid losing his

money, he dies. (b) In the end, Pahom needs only enough land for his grave. (c) Answers will differ. Many students will probably respond that Pahom got what he deserved.

7. The story dramatizes how property ownership can result in self-centeredness and greed.

8. Answers will differ. Many students may respond that they do not feel that most people would behave as Pahom

GREAT WORK

THE BROTHERS KARAMAZOV
by Fyodor Dostoevsky

Presentation

Motivation/Prior Knowledge Tell students that Dostoevsky is ranked second only to Tolstoy among nineteenth-century Russian fiction writers. Point out that although both Tolstoy and Dostoevsky wrote some excellent short stories, they are remembered mainly for their novels. Then explain that *The Brothers Karamazov* is widely regarded as Dostoevsky's finest novel.

Clarification It is possible that students may be intimidated by the length of this novel. Explain that although the novel is quite long, it has a gripping plot that is easy to follow. In addition, this translation of the novel consists of simple, straightforward language that students should have no trouble understanding.

Teaching Across the Curriculum Students may find it helpful to learn something about life in nineteenth-century Russia before they begin the novel. You might offer a group of students extra credit for researching life in nineteenth-century Russia and reporting their findings to the rest of the class.

Fyodor Karamazov (fyô′ dôr kä rä mä′ zof) is a repulsive man. His face is bloated and shows "unmistakable traces of the [depraved] life he [has] led. Besides the heavy, fleshy bags under his eternally insolent, suspicious, mocking little eyes, besides the multitude of tiny wrinkles on his small flabby face, his large, meaty Adam's apple [hangs] under his sharp chin shaped like a purse, and this somehow [gives] him a repulsively sensual air." Yet Karamazov's grotesque physical appearance is not the only repulsive aspect of his character. He is an irresponsible, morally bankrupt sensualist who has amassed a fortune by sponging off, taking advantage of, and cheating other people. He is a wicked man, who often acts like a buffoon but sees himself as clever and witty. He is a man who is easy to hate.

Karamazov and his sons, Dmitry (də mē′ trē) (also called Mitya [mē′ tyä]), Ivan (ē′ vän) (also called Vanya [vän′ yä]), and Alexei (ä lex ē ä′) (also called Alyosha [ä lo′ shä]), are the central characters of Fyodor Dostoevsky's (dôs′ tô yef′ skē) *The Brothers Karamazov*. When you open this novel, you will plunge directly into the complex and sometimes nightmarish lives of these characters. You will become embroiled in a bitter family dispute. You will delve into tangled love affairs. You will absorb the teachings of a renowned holy man. You will follow the Karamazov brothers on their quests for truth and understanding. You will witness a murder. And you will take part in the trial of the man accused of committing this crime.

Meeting the Karamazovs

Dostoevsky opens the novel by introducing Fyodor Karamozov. He tells us that Karamazov belongs to "a peculiar though widespread human type, the sort of man who is not only wretched and depraved but also muddle-headed—muddle-headed in a way that allows him to pull off all sorts of shady little financial deals and not much else." We also learn that Karamazov has been married twice and has three sons—one by his first wife and two by his second. Having come to the realization that her husband was "nothing but a nasty buffoon," Karamazov's first wife had left him and had later died. Raised by maternal relatives, their son, Dmitry, had grown to hate his father, who he believed had cheated him out of much of his inheritance. Karamazov's second wife had also died, and his two sons from this marriage, Ivan and Alexei, had been raised by their maternal grandmother's heir.

Throughout their childhood, Ivan and Alexei had been ignored by their father. Yet, during his late teens, Alexei leaves school to visit his father and to see his mother's grave. A kind, good-hearted young man, Alexei truly loves his father and his father grows to love him. Alexei decides to leave his father's house, however, to enter the local monastery. Shortly after Alexei leaves, Ivan moves in with his father and the two get along surprisingly well, though Ivan clearly does not share the feelings of his brother.

The Gathering of the Karamazovs

Aiming to resolve the problems between Fyodor and Dmitry, the entire Karamazov family gathers at the monastery. The revered holy man, Zosima, reluctantly agrees to serve as the mediator of the dispute. Throughout the Karamazovs' stay at the monastery, Fyodor behaves like a buffoon. At one point the old man himself even declares, "You have before you a buffoon, a true buffoon—that's how I will introduce myself. Alas, it's an old habit with me! And if I sometimes talk nonsense, it is actually intentional, to make people laugh, to please them." Yet his behavior pleases no one; it only embarrasses Alexei.

Surprisingly, Zosima (zä sē′ mä) is not bothered by the old man's behavior and calmly advises him to "stop lying to [himself]." He then goes on to say, "A man who lies to himself, and believes his own lies, becomes unable to recognize truth, either in himself or in anyone else, and he ends up losing respect for himself as well as for others. When he has no respect for anyone, he can no longer love and, in order to divert himself, having no love in him, he yields to his impulses, indulges in the lowest forms of pleasures, and behaves in the end like an animal, in satisfying his vices."

Despite his wisdom, Zosima is unable to resolve the dispute between Fyodor and Dmitry. Instead, the two Karamazovs engage in a bitter exchange during which Fyodor exclaims, "Dmitry Karamazov! . . . If you were not my son, I'd challenge you to a duel this very second—pistols . . . at three paces . . ." Enraged, Dmitry growls, "Why should such a man live? . . . You tell me . . . Should he be allowed to go on defiling the earth with his existence?"

The Story Continues

Leaving the dispute between Fyodor and Dmitry unresolved, Dostoevsky continues to unravel the entertaining and sometimes disturbing story of the Karamazov clan. As the novel progresses, we learn more and more about the Karamazov family, and new characters are introduced. Dmitry becomes involved in a love triangle with two women named Katerina (kä tä rē′ nä) and Grushenka (grōō′ shən kä). Fyodor fathers another son. Alexei becomes engaged. Ivan conveys a cynical philosophy of life that contrasts sharply with traditional values and beliefs. Zosima dies. And someone is murdered.

Who will be the victim? Who will be the murderer? Will the murderer be caught and convicted of the crime? How will Dmitry's love triangle be resolved? What will become of the other Karamazov brothers? You will soon find out.

The Themes of the Novel

Not only is *The Brothers Karamazov* a gripping and powerful novel, it is also a tremendously deep and insightful work that tackles many of the questions that have haunted people of all cultures since the beginning of time. It delves into questions concerning life, death, and the meaning of existence. It probes into the role of suffering in people's lives and reflects upon the responsibilities that all people have for one another. And it examines the conflicting elements of human nature. Because of its penetrating exploration of these and other enduring concerns, *The Brothers Karamazov* has survived the test of time and has earned a place

A SCENE FROM THE FILM VERSION OF *THE BROTHERS KARAMAZOV*

among the finest novels ever written.

Dostoevsky's Life

While he was in the process of writing *The Brothers Karamazov*, Fyodor Dostoevsky (1821–1881) once commented, "I'd die happy if I could finish this novel, for I would have expressed myself completely." Clearly, Dostoevsky expected *The Brothers Karamazov* to be the crowning achievement of his brilliant literary career. And it was.

Dostoevsky died in 1881, only a year after completing *The Brothers Karamazov*. Despite his success as a writer, he had not had an easy life. Although he was born into an aristocratic family, the free-spending Dostoevsky, who had an irrepressible passion for gambling, experienced financial difficulties throughout his life. In addition, he was almost always in poor health. During his late thirties, he contracted epilepsy, and he later came down with tuberculosis, one of the diseases that contributed to his death.

Yet the most difficult aspect of his life was probably the treatment he was subjected to because of his advocacy of political reform and social change. In 1849 Dostoevsky and a number of his friends were arrested and charged with subversion of the government of Czar Nicholas I. After being tried and found guilty, they were sentenced to death. Subsequently, they were taken to the place of their execution, blindfolded, and placed in front of a firing squad. Just as the executioners were being ordered to take aim, a horseman suddenly appeared bearing a reprieve from the czar. This sequence of events had been prearranged to discourage Dostoevsky and his friends from questioning the czar's policies.

Obviously this experience had a tremendous impact on Dostoevsky, as did his experiences in the Siberian prison camp he was sent to following the aborted execution. Having been sentenced to four years of hard labor, followed by five years of military service in a penal battalion, he spent close to a decade in Siberia. By the time he was finally permitted to leave, he was a changed man. Having rejected the liberal ideas he had previously embraced, he had become a staunch conservative and a devoutly religious man. His experiences had not dampened his enthusiasm for writing, however, and his greatest literary achievements still lay ahead of him.

Dostoevsky completed *Notes from Underground*, the first of his great works, in 1864. This work tracks the experiences and expresses the thoughts of a nameless hero who rebels against all outside influences and asserts his personal freedom. Dostoevsky continued to explore the issue of personal freedom in *Crime and Punishment* (1865), a novel about a man who resorts to murder as a means of asserting his independence. *Crime and Punishment* was followed by two more success-

ful novels, *The Idiot* (1869) and *The Possessed* (1869). These work set the stage for *The Brothers Karamazov*, which has come to be almost universally acknowledged as Dostoevsky's finest work.

A Critic's Response to the Novel

In his biography of Dostoevsky, Konstantin Mochulsky wrote: "Dostoevsky worked for three years on his last novel. For three years—the concluding stage of the labor—its artistic embodiment continued. But spiritually he had worked on it his entire life. *The Brothers Karamazov* is the summit, from which we see the organic unity of the writer's whole creative work disclosed. Everything that he experienced, thought, and created finds its place in this vast synthesis. . . . *The Brothers Karamazov* is not only a synthesis of Dostoevsky's creative work, but also the culmination of his life."

PORTRAIT OF DOSTOEVSKY
Vasili G. Perov

ANTON CHEKHOV

1860–1904

Anton Chekhov (än tôn´ chek´ ôf) is one of only a few major writers who also studied and practiced medicine. By applying to his writing the same type of compassion and objectivity that are required of a good doctor, Chekhov was able to establish himself as one of the dominant figures in Russian Realism.

The grandson of a serf who had purchased his freedom, Chekhov was born in the small coastal town of Taganrog in southern Russia. After the failure of his father's grocery business, his family moved to Moscow, while he remained in Taganrog to complete his schooling. In 1879 he moved to Moscow to be with his family, and he enrolled in medical school. As a medical student, he began writing comic sketches and light short stories to earn extra money to help support his family. Following his graduation in 1884, he published his first collection of stories, *Tales of Melpomeme.* In the same year, he also experienced the first symptoms of tuberculosis, the disease that would eventually result in his premature death.

Despite accepting a position at a hospital on the outskirts of Moscow, Chekhov began devoting most of his energy to his writing and started to develop a substantial literary reputation. Although he never completely abandoned the use of humor, his stories became much more serious and complex. In fact, many of the stories he wrote during the late 1880's were insightful and penetrating studies of people's inner thoughts. Chekhov also exhibited his profound understanding of human nature in his first play, *Ivanov,* which was first performed in 1887.

In 1890 Chekhov embarked on a long, taxing journey across Siberia to the island of Sakhalin, the cite of a Russian penal colony. There he conducted a sociological study of the effects of prison life, later publishing his findings in *The Island of Sakhalin* (1893–1894), a book that helped produce some minor reforms in the Russian penal system. After returning from his trip, he bought an estate in Melikhovo, a village about fifty miles south of Moscow. While helping to care for his elderly parents, offering medical treatment to local peasants, and becoming involved in community affairs, Chekhov managed to continue writing prolifically throughout the six years he lived in Melikhovo. Among the most notable short stories that he produced during this period are "Ward Number Six" (1894), the story of a doctor who is ironically committed to the same grim, depressing mental ward that he had previously been in charge of; "An Anonymous Story" (1893) and "Peasant" (1897), two harshly realistic sketches of Russian peasant life; and "A Woman's Kingdom" (1894) and "Three Years" (1895), both of which offer a strikingly vivid portrait of Russian society at the time. During this period Chekhov also wrote one of his finest plays, *The Seagull* (1896), which focuses on the conflict between different generations of people.

Toward the end of the nineteenth century, Chekhov's physical condition began to rapidly deteriorate. No longer able to withstand the cold climate of Melikhovo, he was forced to move to Yalta, a coastal resort on the Black Sea. His ill health did not impair his literary output, however, and in the final years of life he was able to produce two critically acclaimed plays, *The Sisters* (1901) and *The Cherry Orchard* (1904).

When Chekhov finally succumbed to his illness in 1904, his literary reputation had not yet extended beyond the boundaries of Russia. In the years since World War I, however, he has come to be regarded as one of the finest short story writers the world has ever produced.

GUIDE FOR INTERPRETING

The Bet

Characterization and Point of View. Characterization is the means by which a writer reveals a character's personality. Generally, writers develop a character through one or more of the following methods: direct statements about the character, physical descriptions of the character, the character's actions, the character's thoughts and comments, or other characters' reactions to or comments about the character.

Related to the portrayal of characters in a story is the **point of view,** or the vantage point or perspective from which the story is told. Most often, stories are told from either a first-person or a third-person point of view. In a narrative with a first-person point of view, one of the characters in the story tells the story in his or her own words, using the first-person pronoun *I.* In a narrative with a third-person point of view, the narrator does not participate in the story and refers to the characters using the third-person pronouns *he* and *she.* A third- person narrator may be either limited or omniscient. A limited third-person narrator focuses on the thoughts and feelings of only one character. An omniscient third-person narrator conveys the thoughts and feelings of all the characters.

The point of view that a writer uses can have an important impact on the development of characters. Using an omniscient point of view enables writers to utilize thoughts and feelings as a means of developing all the characters. In contrast, when a writer uses a first-person or limited third-person point of view, he or she can use this method only for developing the character from whose point of view the story is being told. In addition, the attitudes and beliefs of the character from whose point of view the story is being told may color or shape the portrayal of the other characters. For example, in a story told from a first-person point of view, if the narrator dislikes one of the other characters, he or she is likely to describe that character in a negative or unflattering manner.

Prior to the late nineteenth century, fiction writers frequently used an omniscient point of view. During the the late 1800's and early 1900's, however, writers began abandoning the use of omniscient narrators in favor of first-person and limited third-   person narrators. This development reflected the growing belief that it is not possible to create an objective picture of the world or of a specific situation, because no two people view the world in exactly the same way.

Writing

Some people think that quick decisions are the worst decisions of all, while others like to act on their first impulses. Which type of person are you? Freewrite, exploring your answer.

Writing/Prior Knowledge Before students begin their freewriting, hold a class discussion about impulsiveness. What are the possible benefits of impulsiveness? What are the potential drawbacks?

ESL Teaching Strategy To accomplish the writing assignment, pair each ESL student with another member of the class. The native-speaking student should act as a coach, making sure the ESL student fully understands the topic and helping him or her to express ideas.

Teaching Tenth-Grade Students Before tenth-grade students begin the story, make sure they fully understand the concept of point of view. To help them grasp the various types of points of view, complete the following exercise. First, have a student relate a personal experience to the class. Then have a student relate a story about one of his or her friends, disclosing only the thoughts of their friend. Finally, have a student relate a story about a group of people, disclosing the thoughts of all the people involved.

Vocabulary

Preteach the following vocabulary words:
outmoded (out´ mōd´ id) *adj.*: No longer in fashion or acceptable
preposterous (pri päs´ tər əs) *adj.*: Ridiculous
compulsory (kəm pul´ sər ē) *adj.*: Obligatory; required
surveillance (sər vā´ ləns) *n.*: Watch kept over a person
gaunt (gônt) *adj.*: Thin and bony
meticulous (mə tik´ yo͞o ləs) *adj.*: Extremely or excessively careful about details
abysses (ə bis´ əz) *n.*: Bottomless gulfs

Analyzing Literature Worksheet, *Understanding Characterization*, p. 1163
Critical Thinking and Reading Worksheet, *Noting the Effect of Point of View*, p. 1164
Selection Test, pp. 1165–1166

Spelling Tip Point out to students that in the word *abyss,* the *i* sound is spelled with the letter *y.*

Literary Focus Tell students that Chekhov drew heavily on his own experiences when creating characters. Once while walking through Yalta, he noticed a photograph in a bookstore window. It showed a bishop named Michael Gribanovsky with an unidentified old woman.

Chekhov bought the picture and began to inquire about Gribanovsky's life. The information that he gathered provided him with the basis for "The Bishop," widely regarded as one of his finest short stories. As students read "The Bet," have them think about whether it seems likely that any of the characters might have been based on real people.

The Bet

Anton Chekhov

translated by Ronald Wilks

I

It was a dark autumn night and an elderly banker was pacing his study, reminiscing about a party he had given one autumn fifteen years ago. Many clever people had come and there had been a most interesting conversation, capital punishment being one of the topics they had discussed, among others. The great majority of the guests, who included many scholars and journalists, had been against it: in their view this form of punishment was outmoded, immoral and unfit for Christian states. Some thought that the death penalty should be replaced everywhere by life imprisonment.

"I don't agree," the banker had told his guests. "I've never tasted capital punishment or life imprisonment myself. But if I may offer an *a priori*[1] judgment, I think that capital punishment is more moral and humane than imprisonment. Executions kill you right away, whereas life imprisonment does it slowly. Which kind of executioner is more humane? One who takes just a few minutes to kill you, or one who drags the life out of you during the course of many years?"

"Both are equally immoral," remarked one of the guests. "Both have the same purpose—to take life. The State isn't God. It has no right to take away what it can't give back, if it so chooses."

Among the guests was a young lawyer of about twenty-five. When his opinion was asked he said, "The death penalty and life imprisonment are

---

1. *a priori* (ä′ prē ôr′ ē): Based on theory instead of experience or experiment.

equally immoral. But if I had to choose between execution or being locked away for life, I'd opt for the second, without any doubt. Any sort of life's better than none at all."

A lively argument had broken out then. The banker, who was younger and more excitable in those days, suddenly lost his temper, banged his fist on the table and shouted at the young lawyer, "That's not true! I bet you two million that you wouldn't even last five years in a cell on your own."

"If you mean that seriously," the lawyer replied, "then I bet you I could stay locked up for fifteen years, not five."

"Fifteen? Done!" shouted the banker. "Gentlemen, I stake two million on it!"

"I accept! You're staking millions, I'm staking my freedom!" the lawyer said.

And so that preposterous, senseless bet was made. The banker, a spoiled, frivolous man at the time, who had more millions than he could count, was overjoyed at the bet. Over supper he made fun of the lawyer. "Come to your senses, young man, before it's too late," he said. "Two million is chicken-feed to me, but you risk losing three or four of the best years of your life. I say three or four, because you won't last longer. And don't you forget, poor man, that voluntary confinement is much harder than compulsory incarceration. The thought that you could regain your freedom any minute will poison your whole existence in prison. I feel sorry for you!"

As the banker paced the room he now remembered all this.

"What was the point of that bet?" he wondered. "What was the use of that lawyer losing fifteen years of his life or my throwing away two million? How could that prove that the death penalty is any better or worse than life imprisonment? Definitely not! Stuff and nonsense! On my part it was the whim of someone with too much money, on the lawyer's it was sheer greed."

A little later he remembered the events following that evening. They had decided that the lawyer must serve his time under the strictest surveillance in one of the lodges in the banker's garden. The conditions were: for fifteen years he was not to be allowed to cross the threshold, to see a living soul or hear a human voice, to receive newspapers or letters. He was allowed a musical instrument and books to read, and to write letters, drink wine and smoke. His only communication with the outside world, they stipulated, was to be through a small, specially built window and he wasn't allowed to speak one word. Books, music, wine and so on—he could have anything he needed and as much as he liked, but only via the window and by writing little notes. To ensure his confinement was strictly solitary, the agreement covered every minute point of detail and compelled the lawyer to serve a term of *exactly* fifteen years, from twelve o'clock on 14 November 1870 until twelve o'clock on 14 November 1885. The least attempt to violate these conditions, even two minutes before the time was up, freed the banker from any obligation to pay the two million.

During the first year of his confinement the lawyer suffered dreadfully from loneliness and boredom—as far as one could judge from his brief notes. Day and night the sound of the piano came from the lodge. He refused wine and tobacco: wine, he wrote, stimulates desire and desire was a prisoner's worst enemy. Moreover, nothing was more depressing than drinking good wine on one's own. And tobacco polluted the air in his room. For the first year the lawyer mainly had light books sent in—novels with complicated love plots, crime fiction, fantastic tales, comedies and so on.

In the second year music no longer came from the lodge and the lawyer wrote and asked for classics only. In the fifth year music was heard again and the prisoner asked for wine. People watching him through the window said that throughout that year he did nothing but eat, drink and lie on his bed, often yawning and talking angrily to himself. He didn't read any books. Some nights he would sit up writing and would keep at it for ages. But toward the morning he'd tear everything he'd written to shreds. More than once they heard him weeping.

In the second half of the sixth year the prisoner devoted himself with great zeal to the study of languages, philosophy and history. He applied himself so eagerly to these subjects that the banker was hard put keeping him supplied with books: in the course of four years nearly six hundred volumes had been obtained at his request. During this craze the banker happened to receive the following letter from his captive:

DIEGO MARTELLI
Edgar Degas
National Gallery of Scotland, Edinburgh

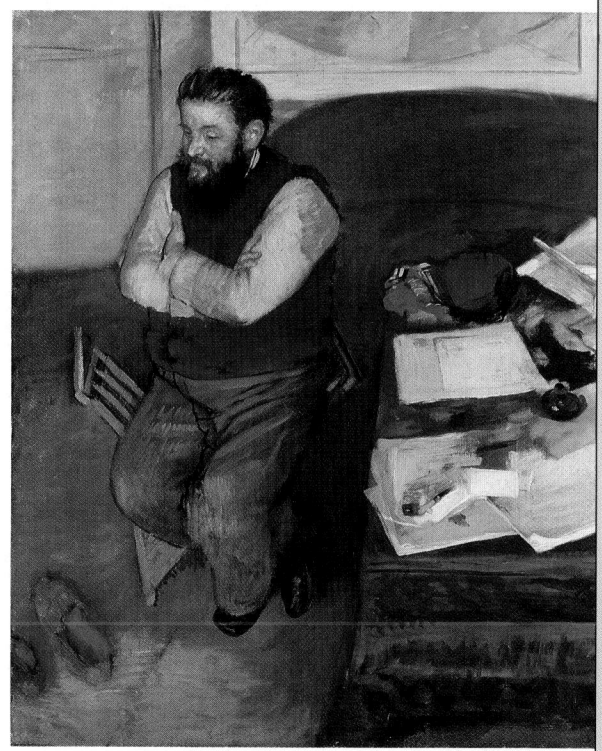

4 **Literary Focus** Point out to students that two methods of characterization are at work here. One is the banker's assessment of himself ("someone with too much money"). The other is the banker's assessment of another character, the lawyer ("sheer greed"). Ask students which of these two judgments is likely to be the more accurate. Why?

5 **Literary Focus** Have students discuss what this passage reveals about the banker's personality.

6 **Discussion** Have students discuss the possible significance of the lawyer's switch from light fiction to the classics. Why do they suppose that during the fifth year, the lawyer resumed playing music and began requesting wine?

7 **Discussion** Point out that the lawyer is a very intelligent person. Would a less intelligent person have more difficulty coping with this situation? Why or why not?

Humanities Note
Fine art, *Diego Martelli* by Edgar Degas. One of the greatest French artists of the nineteenth century, Edgar Degas (1834–1917) originally set out to be a lawyer. During the early stages of his artistic career, he often used historical situations as subjects for his work. As his career progressed, however, he began depicting ordinary people in natural settings. Arrangements such as the one seen here seem almost accidental, offering viewers a momentary and seemingly arbitrary glimpse of a person's life.

You might want to use the following questions to discuss the art:
1. How would you characterize the man depicted in the painting?
2. How would you describe the mood, or atmosphere, of the painting?
3. In what ways is this painting an appropriate illustration for Chekhov's story?
4. Would you be interested in meeting the man depicted in the painting? Why or why not?

sages from "The Bet" is part of a flashback or part of the action occurring at the time of the story.
1. It was a dark autumn night and an elderly banker was pacing his study, reminiscing about a party he had given one autumn fifteen years ago.
2. A lively argument had broken out then.
3. As the banker paced the room he now remembered all this.
4. They had decided that the lawyer must serve his time under the strictest surveillance in one of the lodges in the banker's garden.
5. After reading this the banker laid the piece of paper on the table, kissed the strange man's head and left the lodge weeping.

Student Activity 2. Write a narrative account of a real or imaginary event. Arrange the events in your account in chronological order, while including at least two flashbacks or flashforwards.

8 **Literary Focus** This story presents a limited, third-person point of view. Events are seen through the banker's eyes. The banker finds it odd that the prisoner spends so much time on "one slim, easily comprehensible volume." How does this observation reflect the banker's attitudes and beliefs? How might the lawyer's view of the Gospels differ from that of the banker?

9 **Clarification** Make sure students realize that the Gospels are the first four books of the New Testament: Matthew, Mark, Luke, and John.

10 **Discussion** Have students explain the meaning of this analogy.

11 **Clarification** Point out to students that this paragraph explains why the banker was pacing back and forth in his study at the beginning of the story.

12 **Literary Focus** Have students discuss what this thought reveals about the banker's personality.

My dear Gaoler![2]

I'm writing these lines in six languages. Show them to the experts. Let them read them. If they don't find any mistakes I beg you to have a shot fired in the garden—that will prove to me that my efforts haven't been in vain. Geniuses of all centuries and countries speak different languages, but the same flame burns in all of them. If only you knew the heavenly bliss I feel in my heart now that I can understand them!

The prisoner's wish was carried out—the banker ordered two shots to be fired in the garden.

After the tenth year the lawyer sat motionless at his table, reading nothing except the Gospels. The banker thought it strange that someone who had mastered six hundred abstruse[3] tomes[4] in four years should spend nearly a year reading one slim, easily comprehensible volume. Then the Gospels were followed by the history of religion and theology.

During the last two years of his incarceration the prisoner read a vast amount, quite indiscriminately. First he read natural science, then he asked for Byron or for Shakespeare. In some of his notes he asked for books on chemistry, medical textbooks, a novel and a philosophical or theological treatise—wanting them all at the same time. His reading put one in mind of someone swimming in the sea amidst the wreckage of his ship, eagerly clutching at one piece of wood after the other to save his life.

II

As he recalled all this the old banker reflected, "Tomorrow at twelve he goes free. And I have to pay him two million, according to the agreement. But if I pay up, I'm finished, I'll be absolutely ruined."

Fifteen years ago he had more millions than he could count, but now he was afraid to ask which was the greater, his assets or his debts. Gambling on the stock exchange and very risky speculation, combined with an impulsiveness that he had never managed to control despite his advanced years, had gradually brought a decline in his fortunes and that fearless, self-confident, proud man of wealth was now just a small-time financier, trembling at every rise or fall in his assets.

"That cursed bet!" the old man muttered, clutching his head. "Why couldn't the man die? He's only just forty. He'll take my last copeck,[5] he'll marry, he'll enjoy life, he'll play the stock market, while I jealously watch him like a beggar. Every day I'll hear him say the same thing. 'I owe all my happiness to you, please let me help you.' No, it's too much! My only salvation from bankruptcy and disgrace is that man's death!"

Three o'clock struck. The banker cocked an ear. The whole household was sleeping—the only sound was the rustling of the frozen trees outside. Trying not to make any noise, he took from a fireproof safe the key to the door that had been unopened for fifteen years, put on his coat and went out.

It was dark and cold outside and it was raining. A sharp, damp wind swept howling around the whole garden and gave the trees no peace. The banker strained his eyes but couldn't see the ground, the white statues, the lodge or the trees. As he approached the spot where the lodge stood he called out twice to his watchman. There was no reply—he was obviously sheltering from the weather and sleeping somewhere in the kitchen, or in the greenhouse.

"If I have the courage to carry out my intention," thought the old man, "then the first to be suspected will be the watchman."

By groping about in the dark he found the dark steps and door, and entered the hall. Then he felt his way into a small passage and lit a match. No one was there—only some sort of bed without any bedding and the dark shape of a cast-iron stove in the corner. The seals on the door leading to the prisoner's room were intact.

When the match went out the old man, trembling with excitement, peered through the small window.

---

2. **Gaoler** (jāl′ ər) *n.*: British form of the word *jailer*.
3. **abstruse** (ab strōōs′) *adj.*: Hard to understand.
4. **tomes** (tōmz) *n.*: Large, scholarly or ponderous books.

---

5. **copeck** (kō pek) *n.*: A Russian monetary unit, usually spelled *kopeck*.

Primary Source

"When I write," Chekhov once noted, "I rely fully on the reader, presuming that he himself will add the subjective elements missing in my story."

In *The Russian Short Story: 1880–1917*, the critic Julian W. Connolly adds:

Chekhov's observation points to a fundamental principle of his narrative art: by declining to mold his reader's attitudes through traditional methods of authorial omniscience, he requires the reader to work at extracting meaning from his stories. Structurally, Chekhov eliminated much of the expository material that earlier writers used to establish a background for their characters and plots. Paring descriptions of people and settings to a minimum, Chekhov relied on the use of a few details chosen for their suggestive potential. In many stories an internal conflict engenders expectations that are never met. Chekhov's plots have been compared to gradual curves that start out in one direction and gently arc to end up in an entirely unexpected place.

Have students respond to both Chekhov's and Connolly's comments and discuss how they apply to "The Bet."

THE MERRY MONTH OF MAY
S. Zhukovsky
The Tretyakov Gallery, Moscow

In the prisoner's room a candle burned dimly. The prisoner was sitting at the table. Only his back, the hair on his head and hands were visible. On the table, on two armchairs and on the rug near the table, lay open books.

Five minutes passed without the captive moving once. Fifteen years of confinement had taught him to sit still. The banker tapped on the window with one finger, but the prisoner made no movement in response. Then the banker carefully broke the seals on the doors and put the key in the keyhole. The rusty lock grated and the door creaked. The banker was expecting an immediate shout of surprise and footsteps, but three minutes went by and it was still absolutely quiet on the other side. He decided to go in.

A man quite unlike any normal human being was sitting motionless at the table. He was all skin and bones, with the long curly hair of a woman and a shaggy beard. His complexion was yellow, with an earthy tinge, his cheeks were hollow, his back long and narrow, and the hand with which he propped his bushy head was so thin and wasted it was painful to look at. His hair was already touched with gray and no one looking at that gaunt, senile face would have believed that he was only forty. He was sleeping . . . A sheet of paper with something written on it in small letters lay on the table in front of his bowed head.

"Poor man!" thought the banker. "He's asleep and probably dreaming of those millions! All I have to do is take hold of this semi-corpse, throw it on the bed, just smother it gently with a pillow and the most meticulous examination won't find a trace of death by violence. However, let's first read what he's written . . ."

The banker picked up the sheet of paper and read the following:

Tomorrow at twelve o'clock I regain my freedom and the right to mix with people again. But before I leave this room and see the sun again there's some things I feel I should tell you. With a clear conscience, and with God as my witness, I declare that I despise freedom, life, health and everything that those books of yours call the blessings of this world.

I have spent fifteen years making a careful study of life on earth. True, I haven't *seen* anything of the earth, of people, but in your books I have drunk fragrant wine, sung songs, hunted deer and wild boar in forests, loved women . . . Beautiful creatures as ethereal[6] as clouds created by the magic of your great poets have visited me at night and whispered marvelous tales in my ear, making my head reel. In your books I have scaled the summits of Elbrus and Mont Blanc[7] and from them I have seen the sun rising in the morning, flooding the sky, ocean and mountain peaks with crimson gold in the evening. From there I have seen the lightning flash above me and cleave the clouds. I have seen green forests, fields, rivers, lakes, towns. I have heard the sirens[8] sing and the music of shepherds' pipes. I have touched the wings of beautiful demons who flew down to talk to me about God. In your books I have hurled myself into bottomless abysses, wrought miracles, murdered, burnt cities, preached new religions, conquered entire kingdoms.

Your books have given me wisdom. Everything that man's indefatigable[9] mind has created over the centuries is compressed into a tiny lump inside my skull. I know that I'm cleverer than the lot of you.

And I despise your books. I despise all the blessings of this world, all its wisdom. Everything is worthless, transient,[10] illusory and as deceptive as a mirage. You may be proud, wise and handsome, but death will wipe you from the face of the earth, together with the mice under the floorboards. And your posterity,[11] your history,

your immortal geniuses will freeze or be reduced to ashes, along with the terrestrial globe. You've lost all reason and are on the wrong path. You mistake lies for the truth and ugliness for beauty. You'd be surprised if apple and orange trees suddenly started producing frogs and lizards instead of fruit, or if roses smelt of sweaty horses. I'm amazed at you people who have exchanged heaven for earth. I just don't *want* to understand you.

To show in actual practice how much I despise what you live by, I renounce the two million I once dreamed of, as though of paradise, but for which I feel only contempt now. To forfeit my right to them I shall leave this place five hours before the stipulated time and thus break the agreement . . .

After reading this the banker laid the piece of paper on the table, kissed the strange man's head and left the lodge weeping. At no other time, not even after heavy losses on the stock exchange, had he ever felt such contempt for himself as now. Back in his house he went to bed, but he was kept awake for a long time by excitement and tears.

Next morning some white-faced watchmen came running to inform him that they had seen the man from the lodge climb through his window into the garden, make for the gate and disappear. The banker went to the lodge with his servants to make certain that the prisoner had in fact fled. To put paid to any unnecessary disputes later on he picked up the sheet with the renunciation from the table, returned to the house and locked it in his fireproof safe.

---

6. **ethereal** (i thir′ ē əl) *adj.*: Airy; delicate.
7. **Elbrus** (el′ broos) **and Mont Blanc** (mōn blän′): Two of the highest mountains in Europe.
8. **sirens** (sī rənz): In Greek and Roman mythology, sea nymphs who lured sailors to their death on rocky coasts by seductive singing.
9. **indefatigable** (in′ di fat′ i gə b'l) *adj.*: Untiring.
10. **transient** (tran′ shənt) *adj.*: Not permanent.
11. **posterity** (päs ter′ ə tē) *n.*: All of a person's future descendants.

Reader's Response *Do you think that $15,000,000 is worth sacrificing fifteen years of your life for? Why or why not?*

THINKING ABOUT THE SELECTION

Interpreting

1. How does Chekhov convey the banker's feeling of anxiety in the opening paragraph?
2. (a) Why do you think that Chekhov chose to explain the origin of the bet in the form of a flashback, or reminiscence, rather than beginning the story on the night of the banker's party? (b) How does his use of flashbacks make the story more suspenseful?
3. (a) How does the lawyer's behavior change from year to year during his imprisonment? (b) How would you explain each of these changes?
4. After being imprisoned for fifteen years, would the lawyer still argue that "any sort of life's better than none at all"? Explain.
5. Considering the banker's assumption that the lawyer is "probably asleep dreaming of all those millions," what is ironic, or surprising, about the lawyer's note?
6. Considering the description of the lawyer's behavior during his imprisonment, how would you explain the content of his note?
7. (a) After reading the lawyer's note, why does the banker kiss the lawyer's head and leave "the lodge weeping"? (b) Why does the banker feel contempt for himself?
8. (a) What is the theme, or main point, of this story? (b) How is the theme conveyed?

Applying

9. Think about the argument at the opening of this story. If you had been one of the guests, which side would you have taken? Why?

ANALYZING LITERATURE

Understanding Characterization

In "The Bet" the banker's personality is revealed through his thoughts, comments, and actions, and through the narrator's observations about him. For example, early in the story, the narrator offers an insight into the banker's personality at the time of the party, commenting that the banker "was younger and more excitable in those days."

1. What do the banker's comments and actions on the night of his party reveal about his personality?
2. What does the description of the way in which the banker squandered his fortune convey about his character?
3. What does the banker's solution to his dilemma reveal about his personality?

4. What does the banker's decision to lock the lawyer's letter in a safe convey about his character?
5. What does the description of the lawyer's physical appearance on the last night of his imprisonment reveal about his character?

CRITICAL THINKING AND READING

Noting the Effect of Point of View

Generally, when a writer uses a first-person or limited third-person point of view, he or she can use only thoughts and feelings to develop the character from whose point of view the story is being told. However, although "The Bet" is told from the banker's point of view, Chekhov is able to convey the thoughts of the lawyer by having the banker read the letter in which the lawyer expresses his feelings regarding his imprisonment.

1. What does the lawyer's letter reveal about his character?
2. What other techniques might Chekhov have used to convey the lawyer's thoughts, while maintaining a limited point of view?
3. In a story that uses a limited narrator, the portrayal of characters is often shaped by the feelings and attitudes of the character from whose point of view the story is being told. Explain how the banker's own attitudes and beliefs shape his impressions of how the lawyer will respond to winning the bet.
4. Toward the end of the story, how does the banker project his own feelings onto the lawyer when he imagines that the lawyer is "dreaming of those millions"?

THINKING AND WRITING

Comparing and Contrasting Stories

Although both "The Bet" and Leo Tolstoy's "How Much Land Does a Man Need?" (page 944) deal with the effects of greed, there are many differences between the two stories. Write a paper in which you compare and contrast these two stories. Start by reviewing the two stories, noting similarities and differences in form, theme, character development, and use of such literary devices as irony, foreshadowing, and flashback. Also look for elements of both realism and fantasy. After you have organized your notes, begin writing your paper, using passages from the two stories to support your ideas. When you have finished writing, revise your paper making sure you have presented your ideas in an organized and coherent manner. Proofread your paper and prepare a final copy.

(continued from bottom of page)

9. Answers will differ. Many students may argue in favor of capital punishment.

Challenge Chekhov once wrote, "When I describe horse thieves, you want me to say that horse stealing's a bad thing. But that's surely been known long enough without my having to say so. Let juries decide their guilt, my only job is to describe what they're like." Ask students to relate this quotation to "The Bet."

ANSWERS TO ANALYZING LITERATURE

1. Suggested response: He is dogmatic, self-satisfied, conceited, impulsive, and cruel.
2. Suggested response: It reveals that he is impulsive, overly confident, and foolish.
3. Suggested response: It reveals that money is more important to him than honor, or even than human life. It reveals that he is not only greedy, but cold, calculating, and vicious.
4. Suggested response: It reveals that he is distrustful and he has no sense of remorse.
5. Suggested response: His physical decay reflects his mental decay. It reveals that he has given up caring about himself or the world around him.

ANSWERS TO CRITICAL THINKING AND READING

1. Suggested response: It reveals that he is enraged at the world and has lost any reason for living.
2. Answers will differ. Students might suggest that Chekhov could have had the watchman discuss his observations of the lawyer.
3. Suggested response: The banker expects that the lawyer would respond to winning the bet in the same manner in which he would if he were in the lawyer's place.
4. Suggested response: If he were in the lawyer's place, he would be "dreaming of those millions."

THINKING AND WRITING

Publishing Student Writing Have students read their papers to the class and use the papers as a springboard for a class discussion about the two stories.

---

tries to entertain himself. Then he starts enthusiastically devoting himself to acquiring knowledge. Finally, he becomes passive and looks to religion and later to science for fulfillment. (b) Answers will differ. Students may respond that he turns to education as a means of fulfillment. They may suggest that he turns to religion when he develops the need of spiritual fulfillment.

4. Suggested response: Given the lawyer's condition and the content of his letter, it does not seem likely.
5. Contrary to the banker's expectations, the lawyer gives up his claim to the money.
6. Answers will differ. Students may respond that throughout his imprisonment the lawyer had been engaged in a fruitless quest for fulfillment. The failure of this quest left him bitter.

7. (a) Suggested response: He feels both relief and guilt. (b) Suggested response: He feels contempt for himself because he had been ready to commit murder. In addition, he feels responsible for the lawyer's condition.
8. (a) Answers may differ. Students may respond that the story suggests the pursuit of wealth is corrupting. (b) Answers will differ according to the theme that students suggest.

The New Age of Drama

Humanities Note

Fine art, *The Loge,* 1874, by Pierre Auguste Renoir. French Impressionist Pierre Auguste Renoir (1841–1919) endured many hardships before he gained recognition as an important painter. His technique has a precision and craftsmanship that was greatly admired by fellow artists. Throughout his career he enjoyed the friendship of the leading Impressionists of the day, including Manet, Monet, and Sisley. In mid-career, Renoir abandoned the light, feathery Impressionist technique, which depicted form broken into small particles of colored light, for a more solid approach.

The Loge was exhibited at the first Impressionist Exhibition in 1874. Shortly afterward, Renoir was happy to sell it for 425 francs, which was exactly the amount of his past-due rent.

This painting is a salute to feminine beauty. Each detail of the woman's delicate features and costume is lush and sensuous. The model was Nini Lopez, whom Renoir found to be a beauty of "antique purity." Here he brings her face into sharp focus while the rest of the painting is less distinct. This serves to attract the viewer's eye immediately to the face.

The model for the man in the background was Renoir's younger brother, Edmond. Despite the fact that he, too, is dressed in black and white, his figure is left in shadow to subdue the contrast and allow it to serve as a backdrop for the dazzling woman.

You might want to use the following questions to discuss the art:

1. What is your response to the two figures in the painting?
2. How would you describe the relationship between the two people?
3. What aspects of life in the nineteenth century does the painting capture?

THE LOGE
Pierre Auguste Renoir

HENRIK IBSEN

1828–1906

When Henrik Ibsen's (hen′rik ib′s'n) play *Ghosts* was first performed in 1881, one critic attacked the play, calling it "an open drain, a loathsome sore, an abominable piece, a repulsive and degrading work." This was not the only time that one of Ibsen's plays was criticized. Yet the only reason why critics and even audiences sometimes responded negatively to Ibsen's works was because he was a literary pioneer. Not only was he the creator of the modern, realistic prose drama, but he also was one of the first writers to make drama a vehicle for social comment and one of the only nineteenth-century dramatists to explore topics that were considered socially unacceptable. Because of his boldness, his innovativeness, and his extraordinary talent, Ibsen is now widely regarded as the greatest and most influential dramatist of the nineteenth century.

Ibsen was born in Skein, Norway. In the mid-1830's his father, a once-successful merchant, went bankrupt, and his family was forced to move to an isolated farm. Uncomfortable in his new surroundings and stung by the poverty and social rejection resulting from his family's financial failures, Ibsen become increasingly introverted.

When he was fifteen, he became a druggist's apprentice. Hating his work and living in virtual isolation, Ibsen turned to writing poetry in his spare time. In 1850 Ibsen moved to the capital city of Christiania (now Oslo), planning to attend the university. After failing the entrance examination, however, he became determined to forge a living as a writer. Having already written two plays, *Catiline* (1850) and *The Burial Mound* (1850), Ibsen was hired as a playwright by the recently established National Theater in the city of Bergen, and he remained there for six years.

Given the opportunity to manage a new theater, Ibsen moved back to Christiania in 1857. The theater went bankrupt in 1862, however, leaving Ibsen deeply in debt and in a state of despair. Two years later, he left Norway for Italy and began a twenty-seven-year period of self-imposed exile during which he wrote most of his finest plays. With the completion of *Brand* (1866), the tragedy of a misunderstood idealist, and *Peer Gynt* (1867), a dramatic fantasy based on Norwegian folklore, he established himself as a well-known playwright among both critics and theatergoers.

In the following years, Ibsen's talent as a playwright continued to blossom, though his plays were not always greeted enthusiastically by the public. *A Doll's House* (1879) aroused controversy because it portrayed a woman whose actions were not considered acceptable at the time. Similarly, *Ghosts* (1881) provoked public outrage because of its explicit treatment of a hereditary disease that was not viewed as an appropriate topic for a literary work. In response to the public's hostile reception of *Ghosts*, Ibsen wrote *An Enemy of the People* (1882), which portrays a man who comes into conflict with the inhabitants of a village.

As the nineteenth century wound to a close, Ibsen continued to write prolifically, completing such well-known plays as *The Wild Duck* (1884), and *Hedda Gabler* (1890). In 1900, however, he suffered the first of a series of strokes that almost completely incapacitated him. When Ibsen died in 1906, it was already clear that he had made a major impact on the theater. Yet the tremendous extent of his impact did not become apparent until later in the twentieth century, when it became obvious that Ibsen had completely altered the direction of the theater.

GUIDE FOR INTERPRETING

Literary Focus You may want to point out to students that Ibsen did not begin by writing realistic prose dramas such as *A Doll's House*. Instead, he began by writing more traditional, though often sardonic, plays in verse. Only with *The Pillars of Society*, written two years before *A Doll's House*, did he fully embrace the prose "problem play," featuring the objective observation of real life, colloquial language, and a tight plot structure. Most critics, however, consider *The Pillars of Society*, with its conventional happy ending, to be an artistic failure. The real turning point for Ibsen, and for the theater in general, came with the completion of *A Doll's House*.

Ask students if they can name any writers other than Ibsen (not necessarily dramatists) who began their careers by using traditional techniques and later changed to more experimental forms. Point out that two such writers are William Faulkner and James Joyce.

Writing/Prior Knowledge Before students begin their freewriting, have them discuss the roles of communication and trust in a relationship.

Vocabulary

Preteach the following vocabulary words:

spendthrift (spend´ thrift) *n.*: A person who spends money carelessly or wastefully

squandering (skwän´ dər iŋ) *v.*: Spending or using wastefully

prodigal (präd´ i gəl) *adj.*: Exceedingly or recklessly wasteful

indiscreet (in´ dis krēt´) *adj.*: Unwise

frivolous (friv´ ə ləs) *adj.*: Silly or light-minded

contraband (kän´ trə band) *n.*: Goods forbidden by law to be imported

subordinate (sə bôr´ də nit) *adj.*: Secondary

Commentary

A Doll's House, Act I

The Modern Realistic Prose Drama. Though it may be hard for you to imagine, the members of the first audience to see a performance of *A Doll's House* were stunned by what they saw. Not only were they shaken because the play ended with a character's conscious rejection of existing social conventions, but they were also surprised by the play's graphic, realistic, and unflattering depiction of middle-class life. The play was unlike anything the theatergoers had seen before, and as a result many people found it disturbing. Yet, though no one could have been aware of it at the time, the members of the first audience had participated in a historical event: They had witnessed the birth of modern drama.

Prior to Ibsen's time, dramas were written predominantly in verse and generally did not depict events in an accurate manner. Plays were meant to entertain audiences by appealing to people's imaginations and diverting their attention from everyday life. Consequently, dramatists frequently wove together intricate plots, filled with coincidences that would be unlikely to occur in real life. In addition, the language spoken by the characters rarely mirrored the way in which most people actually speak, and characters often revealed their inner thoughts directly to the audience. Finally, the sets used in dramatic productions tended to be quite simple, and a single set was generally used to represent a number of different places.

In contrast, Ibsen sought to depict life accurately and realistically in his plays, while delving into the types of conflicts and dilemmas that he viewed as characteristic of his time. He focused on situations that could easily occur in real life, and he patterned his dialogue after real-life conversations. Just as in a typical discussion between you and your friends, his characters sometimes speak in incomplete sentences, express incomplete thoughts, change their train of thought in midsentence, and interrupt one another.

Ibsen also revolutionized the way in which plays were staged, by introducing elaborate, detailed sets that often changed from act to act. In his stage directions, he offers a precise description of how the set should appear, as well as how lighting should be used. Not only does he use scenery, props, and lighting to contribute to the realistic quality of his plays, but he also frequently uses these elements as symbols. Ibsen also uses stage directions to instruct actors about how they should interpret certain lines of dialogue.

Writing

Write a journal entry in which you discuss the characteristics of a successful relationship.

Objectives

Thematic
To understand the importance of communication and trust in a relationship

Skills
1 To understand realistic drama
2 To write a dramatic scene

Support Material

Teaching Portfolio
Teacher Backup, p. 1167
Grammar in Action Worksheets, *Realistic Dialogue*, p. 1171; *Deductive Reasoning*, p. 1173
Usage and Mechanics Worksheet, p. 1175
Vocabulary Check, p. 1176

Analyzing Literature Worksheet, *Understanding a Realistic Drama*, p. 1177
Language Worksheet, *Recognizing Appropriate Diction*, p. 1178
Selection Test, pp. 1179–1180

Spelling Tip Tell students to remember that the letter *o* appears twice in the word *frivolous*.

A Doll's House

Henrik Ibsen

translated by Rolf Fjelde

THE CHARACTERS

Torvald Helmer, a lawyer
Nora, his wife
Dr. Rank
Mrs.Linde
Nils Krogstad, a bank clerk

The Helmers' Three Small Children
Anne-Marie, their nurse
Helene, a maid
A Delivery Boy

The action takes place in HELMER's *residence.*

Act I

[*A comfortable room, tastefully but not expensively furnished. A door to the right in the back wall leads to the entryway; another to the left leads to* HELMER's *study. Between these doors, a piano. Midway in the left-hand wall a door, and farther back a window. Near the window a round table with an armchair and a small sofa. In the right-hand wall, toward the rear, a door, and nearer the foreground a porcelain stove with two armchairs and a rocking chair beside it. Between the stove and the side door, a small table. Engravings on the walls. An* étagère[1] *with china figures and other small art objects; a small bookcase with richly bound books; the floor carpeted; a fire burning in the stove. It is a winter day.*

A bell rings in the entryway; shortly after we hear the door being unlocked. NORA *comes into the room, humming happily to herself; she is wearing street clothes and carries an armload of packages, which she puts down on the table to the right. She has left the hall door open; and through it a* DELIVERY BOY *is seen, holding a Christmas tree and a basket, which he gives to the* MAID *who let them in.*]

NORA. Hide the tree well, Helene. The children mustn't get a glimpse of it till this evening, after it's trimmed. [*To the* DELIVERY BOY, *taking out her purse*] How much?

DELIVERY BOY. Fifty, ma'am.

NORA. There's a crown.[2] No, keep the change. [*The* BOY *thanks her and leaves.* NORA *shuts the door. She laughs softly to herself while taking off her street things. Drawing a bag of macaroons from her pocket, she eats a couple, then steals over and listens at her husband's study door.*] Yes, he's home. [*Hums again as she moves to the table right*]

---

1. **étagère** (ā tà zher′) *n.*: A stand with open shelves for displaying small art objects and ornaments.

2. **crown:** The crown, or krone, is the monetary unit of Denmark and Norway.

2 **Reading Strategy** In this passage, Torvald calls Nora his "little lark" and his "squirrel." Have a student keep a running list of the names Torvald uses in addressing his wife.

3 **Discussion** Have students discuss Nora's attitude toward money. What is their impression of the Helmers' financial status?

4 **Discussion** Point out the contrast between Nora's attitude and Torvald's toward borrowing and debt. Do students think that most couples have contrasting attitudes about certain matters? Why or why not? Can contrasting attitudes about matters such as borrowing and debt be detrimental to a relationship? Why or why not?

5 **Enrichment** Although Torvald is apparently being generous to his wife, the forty kroner he gives her would be worth only about five dollars and fifty cents today. To help students grasp the impact of inflation, tell them that in 1879, the year in which *A Doll's House* was first produced, a pound of bacon cost about eight cents in the United States. In addition, a skilled laborer earned only about ten dollars a week at the time.

HELMER. [*From the study*] Is that my little lark twittering out there?

NORA. [*Busy opening some packages*] Yes, it is.

HELMER. Is that my squirrel rummaging around?

NORA. Yes!

HELMER. When did my squirrel get in?

NORA. Just now. [*Putting the macaroon bag in her pocket and wiping her mouth*] Do come in, Torvald, and see what I've bought.

HELMER. Can't be disturbed. [*After a moment he opens the door and peers in, pen in hand.*] Bought, you say? All that there? Has the little spendthrift been out throwing money around again?

NORA. Oh, but Torvald, this year we really should let ourselves go a bit. It's the first Christmas we haven't had to economize.

HELMER. But you know we can't go squandering.

NORA. Oh yes, Torvald, we can squander a little now. Can't we? Just a tiny, wee bit. Now that you've got a big salary and are going to make piles and piles of money.

HELMER. Yes—starting New Year's. But then it's a full three months till the raise comes through.

NORA. Pooh! We can borrow that long.

HELMER. Nora! [*Goes over and playfully takes her by the ear*] Are your scatterbrains off again? What if today I borrowed a thousand crowns, and you squandered them over Christmas week, and then on New Year's Eve a roof tile fell on my head, and I lay there—

NORA. [*Putting her hand on his mouth*] Oh! don't say such things!

HELMER. Yes, but what if it happened—then what?

NORA. If anything so awful happened, then it just wouldn't matter if I had debts or not.

HELMER. Well, but the people I'd borrowed from?

NORA. Them? Who cared about them! They're strangers.

HELMER. Nora, Nora, how like a woman! No, but seriously, Nora, you know what I think about that. No debts! Never borrow! Something of freedom's lost—and something of beauty, too—from a home that's founded on borrowing and debt. We've made a brave stand up to now, the two of us; and we'll go right on like that the little while we have to.

NORA. [*Going toward the stove*] Yes, whatever you say, Torvald.

HELMER. [*Following her*] Now, now, the little lark's wings mustn't droop. Come on, don't be a sulky squirrel. [*Taking out his wallet*] Nora, guess what I have here.

NORA. [*Turning quickly*] Money!

HELMER. There, see. [*Hands her some notes*] Good grief, I know how costs go up in a house at Christmastime.

NORA. Ten—twenty—thirty—forty. Oh, thank you, Torvald; I can manage no end on this.

HELMER. You really will have to.

NORA. Oh yes, I promise I will! But come here so I can show you everything I bought. And so cheap! Look, new clothes for Ivar here—and a sword. Here a horse and a trumpet for Bob. And a doll and a doll's bed here for Emmy; they're nothing much, but she'll tear them to bits in no time anyway. And here I have dress material and handkerchiefs for the maids. Old Anne-Marie really deserves something more.

HELMER. And what's in that package there?

NORA. [*With a cry*] Torvald, no! You can't see that till tonight!

HELMER. I see. But tell me now, you little prodigal, what have you thought of for yourself?

NORA. For myself? Oh, I don't want anything at all.

HELMER. Of course you do. Tell me just what—within reason—you'd most like to have.

NORA. I honestly don't know. Oh, listen, Torvald—

HELMER. Well?

Commentary

Plotting in Ibsen's Plays As a youth, Ibsen wanted to be a painter, and his sense of artistic composition is evident in his plays. For instance, all the pieces of the plot of *A Doll's House* are ingeniously woven together into a meticulously structured work of art. In fact, the tightness of the plot prompted one critic to call the play a "structural miracle."

Students should understand that an effective plot does not always demand electrifying action. Ibsen's plays, for example, are somewhat static. The audience is presented with a series of striking images conveyed through dialogue. Through these images, the story gradually unfolds in a natural and believable manner. Each event and each line of conversation seems to arise inevitably from the last. In addition, each line of dialogue, no matter how brief, serves a purpose. As students read the play, have them pay close attention to the relationship between the events and have them think about the purpose of each line of dialogue.

NORA. [*Fumbling at his coat buttons, without looking at him*] If you want to give me something, then maybe you could—you could—

HELMER. Come on, out with it.

NORA. [*Hurriedly*] You could give me money, Torvald. No more than you think you can spare; then one of these days I'll buy something with it.

HELMER. But Nora—

NORA. Oh, please, Torvald darling, do that! I beg you, please. Then I could hang the bills in pretty gilt paper on the Christmas tree. Wouldn't that be fun?

HELMER. What are those little birds called that always fly through their fortunes?

NORA. Oh yes, spendthrifts; I know all that. But let's do as I say, Torvald; then I'll have time to decide what I really need most. That's very sensible, isn't it?

HELMER. [*Smiling*] Yes, very—that is, if you actually hung onto the money I give you, and you actually used it to buy yourself something. But it goes for the house and for all sorts of foolish things, and then I only have to lay out some more.

NORA. Oh, but Torvald—

HELMER. Don't deny it, my dear little Nora. [*Putting his arm around her waist*] Spendthrifts are sweet, but they use up a frightful amount of money. It's incredible what it costs a man to feed such birds.

NORA. Oh, how can you say that! Really, I save everything I can.

HELMER. [*Laughing*] Yes, that's the truth. Everything you can. But that's nothing at all.

NORA. [*Humming, with a smile of quiet satisfaction*] Hm, if you only knew what expenses we larks and squirrels have, Torvald.

HELMER. You're an odd little one. Exactly the way your father was. You're never at a loss for scaring up money; but the moment you have it, it runs right out through your fingers; you never know

6 **Discussion** Ask students if they find it strange that Nora asks for money as a Christmas present. Do they themselves sometimes prefer money to other gifts? If so, why?

7 **Clarification** This exchange reflects the difficulty of translating Ibsen's Norwegian into English. There is no single word in the English language for "little birds . . . that always fly through their fortunes." The translator chose the word *spendthrift*, which essentially conveys the intended meaning. Yet the choice of this word may cause some audience members or readers to mistakenly believe that there is actually a type of bird known as a spendthrift.

8 **Discussion** Nora's smile and her cryptic comment foreshadow later developments. Have students guessed what Nora's unknown expenses might be?

9 Discussion Students know that Nora has eaten a couple of macaroons. Now they learn that her husband has forbidden her to eat such confections. They also learn that she has given her word not to and that she is willing to lie about what she has done. This may seem trivial in itself, but it helps to develop the characters of both Nora and Torvald. Have students discuss the role of the macaroons in developing the two characters. In addition, have students express their opinions of Nora and Torvald at this point in the play.

10 Discussion Ask students to consider what this exchange between Nora and Torvald reveals about their relationship.

Master Teacher Note Point out to students that nothing appears by accident in the script of a play. Ibsen, more than many other playwrights, has been praised for his economy and simplicity. A friend of Ibsen's said of *A Doll's House* that "the Master has for the past two or three years been chiseling away everything unnecessary." Similarly, a critic noted: "Every needless line is cut, every exchange carries the action a step forward, there is not a superfluous effect in the whole play. . . ."

Considering that every detail in the play serves a purpose, why do students think that Ibsen included details about the preceding Christmas?

what you've done with it. Well, one takes you as you are. It's deep in your blood. Yes, these things are hereditary, Nora.

NORA. Ah, I could wish I'd inherited many of Papa's qualities.

HELMER. And I couldn't wish you anything but just what you are, my sweet little lark. But wait; it seems to me you have a very—what should I call it?—a very suspicious look today—

NORA. I do?

HELMER. You certainly do. Look me straight in the eye.

NORA. [*Looking at him*] Well?

HELMER. [*Shaking an admonitory³ finger*] Surely my sweet tooth hasn't been running riot in town today, has she?

NORA. No. Why do you imagine that?

HELMER. My sweet tooth really didn't make a little detour through the confectioner's?

NORA. No, I assure you, Torvald—

HELMER. Hasn't nibbled some pastry?

NORA. No, not at all.

HELMER. Not even munched a macaroon or two?

NORA. No, Torvald, I assure you, really—

HELMER. There, there now. Of course I'm only joking.

NORA. [*Going to the table, right*] You know I could never think of going against you.

HELMER. No, I understand that; and you *have* given me your word. [*Going over to her*] Well, you keep your little Christmas secrets to yourself, Nora darling. I expect they'll come to light this evening, when the tree is lit.

NORA. Did you remember to ask Dr. Rank?

HELMER. No. But there's no need for that; it's assumed he'll be dining with us. All the same, I'll ask

---

3. **admonitory** (əd män′ ə tôr′ ē) *adj.*: Warning.

him when he stops by here this morning. I've ordered some fine wine. Nora, you can't imagine how I'm looking forward to this evening.

NORA. So am I. And what fun for the children, Torvald!

HELMER. Ah, it's so gratifying to know that one's gotten a safe, secure job, and with a comfortable salary. It's a great satisfaction, isn't it?

NORA. Oh, it's wonderful.!

HELMER. Remember last Christmas? Three whole weeks before, you shut yourself in every evening till long after midnight, making flowers for the Christmas tree, and all the other decorations to surprise us. Ugh, that was the dullest time I've ever lived through.

NORA. It wasn't at all dull for me.

HELMER. [*Smiling*] But the outcome *was* pretty sorry, Nora.

NORA. Oh, don't tease me with that again. How could I help it that the cat came in and tore everything to shreds.

HELMER. No, poor thing, you certainly couldn't. You wanted so much to please us all, and that's what counts. But it's just as well that the hard times are past.

NORA. Yes, it's really wonderful.

HELMER. Now I don't have to sit here alone, boring myself, and you don't have to tire your precious eyes and your fair little delicate hands—

NORA. [*Clapping her hands*] No, is it really true, Torvald, I don't have to? Oh, how wonderfully lovely to hear! [*Taking his arm*] Now I'll tell you just how I've thought we should plan things. Right after Christmas— [*The doorbell rings.*] Oh, the bell. [*Straightening the room up a bit*] Somebody would have to come. What a bore!

HELMER. I'm not at home to visitors, don't forget.

MAID. [*From the hall doorway*] Ma'am, a lady to see you—

NORA. All right, let her come in.

Grammar in Action

To write realistic dialogue, a playwright must have an appreciation for the manner in which people naturally speak. For instance, the playwright must be aware that people sometimes speak in incomplete sentences, use contractions, express incomplete thoughts, change their train of thought in mid-sentence, and interrupt one another. For example, look at the following passages of dialogue from *A Doll's House*:

MRS. LINDE. Hello, Nora.

NORA. Hello—
MRS. LINDE. You don't recognize me.
NORA. No, I don't know—but wait, I think–What! Kristine! Is it really you?
NORA. So completely alone. How terribly hard that must be for you. I have three lovely children. You can't see them now; they're out with the maid. But now you must tell me everything—
MRS. LINDE. No, no, no, tell me about yourself.
NORA. No, you begin. Today, I don't want to be selfish. I want to think only of you today. But there is something I must tell you. Did you hear of the wonderful luck we had recently?

MAID. [*To* HELMER] And the doctor's just come too.

HELMER. Did he go right to my study?

MAID. Yes, he did. [HELMER *goes into his room. The* MAID *shows in* MRS. LINDE, *dressed in traveling clothes, and shuts the door after her.*]

MRS. LINDE. [*In a dispirited and somewhat hesitant voice*] Hello, Nora.

NORA. [*Uncertain*] Hello—

MRS. LINDE. You don't recognize me.

NORA. No, I don't know—but wait, I think— [*Exclaiming*] What! Kristine! Is it really you?

MRS. LINDE. Yes, it's me.

NORA. Kristine! To think I didn't recognize you. But then, how could I? [*More quietly*] How you've changed, Kristine!

MRS. LINDE. Yes, no doubt I have, In nine—ten long years.

NORA. Is it so long since we met! Yes, it's all of that. Oh, these last eight years have been a happy time, believe me. And so now you've come in to town, too. Made the long trip in the winter. That took courage.

MRS. LINDE. I just got here by ship this morning.

NORA. To enjoy yourself over Christmas, of course. Oh, how lovely! Yes, enjoy ourselves, we'll do that. But take your coat off. You're not still cold? [*Helping her*] There now, let's get cozy here by the stove. No, the easy chair there! I'll take the rocker here. [*Seizing her hands*] Yes, now you have your old look again; it was only in that first moment. You're a bit more pale, Kristine—and maybe a bit thinner.

MRS. LINDE. And much, much older, Nora.

NORA. Yes, perhaps a bit older; a tiny, tiny bit; not much at all. [*Stopping short; suddenly serious*] Oh, but thoughtless me, to sit here, chattering away. Sweet, good Kristine, can you forgive me?

MRS. LINDE. What do you mean, Nora?

NORA. [*Softly*] Poor Kristine, you've become a widow.

MRS. LINDE. Yes, three years ago.

NORA. Oh, I knew it, of course; I read it in the papers. Oh, Kristine, you must believe me; I often thought of writing you then, but I kept postponing it, and something always interfered.

MRS. LINDE. Nora dear, I understand completely.

NORA. No, it was awful of me, Kristine. You poor thing, how much you must have gone through. And he left you nothing?

MRS. LINDE. No.

NORA. And no children?

MRS. LINDE. No.

NORA. Nothing at all, then?

MRS. LINDE. Not even a sense of loss to feed on.

NORA. [*Looking incredulously at her*] But Kristine, how could that be?

MRS. LINDE. [*Smiling wearily and smoothing her hair*] Oh, sometimes it happens, Nora.

NORA. So completely alone. How terribly hard that must be for you. I have three lovely children. You can't see them now; they're out with the maid. But now you must tell me everything—

MRS. LINDE. No, no, no, tell me about yourself.

NORA. No, you begin. Today I don't want to be selfish. I want to think only of you today. But there *is* something I must tell you. Did you hear of the wonderful luck we had recently?

MRS. LINDE. No, what's that?

NORA. My husband's been made manager in the bank, just think!

MRS. LINDE. Your husband? How marvelous!

NORA. Isn't it? Being a lawyer is such an uncertain living, you know, especially if one won't touch any cases that aren't clean and decent. And of course Torvald would never do that, and I'm with him completely there. Oh, we're simply delighted, be-

11 **Discussion** Have students discuss whether they think it is normal for old friends not to recognize one another after a long period of separation. Why or why not?

12 **Discussion** Ask students if they think that Nora seems truly concerned about Mrs. Linde's woes. On what do they base their answer?

13 **Discussion** Have students discuss what this comment suggests about Mrs. Linde's feelings about her deceased husband.

14 **Discussion** Ask students if Nora is trying to act superior to Mrs. Linde by mentioning her three children and her maid. If so, why? If not, what prompts her to mention them so early in the conversation?

Enrichment Tell students that Ibsen became intensely involved in the lives of his fictional characters. Once, when asked why he had chosen the name Nora for the central character in *A Doll's House*, he replied, "Well, you see, her name wasn't really Nora. She was christened Elanora. But at home they called her Nora because she was such a pet."

Student Activity 1. Rewrite a passage of dialogue from the play, eliminating all contractions, incomplete sentences, changes of thought, and interruptions. Then explain why the rewritten passage is less natural and realistic than the original passage.

Student Activity 2. Record a conversation between two friends, family members, or strangers. Then develop that conversation into a script for a scene from a play. Make sure your script captures the conversation as accurately as possible.

15 Discussion Have students discuss the apparent similarities between Mrs. Linde's and Torvald's attitudes concerning Nora's spending habits.

16 Clarification Make sure students realize that the Helmers traveled south because Torvald's condition made it necessary to settle in a place with a warmer climate.

17 Learning Across the Curriculum Some of your students might be interested in learning more about the Norwegian climate. Encourage them to research this topic in the library and to report their findings to their classmates.

18 Literary Focus Have students note how Ibsen introduces Dr. Rank and provides background information about him without interrupting the natural flow of the dialogue.

19 Discussion Have students discuss whether they feel that Mrs. Linde made the right decision. Why or why not? Do they feel that it is ever acceptable for a person to marry someone whom he or she does not love?

lieve me! He'll join the bank right after New Year's and start getting a huge salary and lots of commissions. From now on we can live quite differently—just as we want. Oh, Kristine, I feel so light and happy! Won't it be lovely to have stacks of money and not a care in the world?

MRS. LINDE. Well, anyway, it would be lovely to have enough for necessities.

NORA. No, not just for necessities, but stacks and stacks of money!

MRS. LINDE. [*Smiling*] Nora, Nora, aren't you sensible yet? Back in school you were such a free spender.

NORA. [*With a quiet laugh*] Yes, that's what Torvald still says. [*Shaking her finger*] But "Nora, Nora" isn't as silly as you all think. Really, we've been in no position for me to go squandering. We've had to work, both of us.

MRS. LINDE. You too?

NORA. Yes, at odd jobs—needlework, crocheting, embroidery, and such— [*Casually*] and other things too. You remember that Torvald left the department when we were married? There was no chance of promotion in his office, and of course he needed to earn more money. But that first year he drove himself terribly. He took on all kinds of extra work that kept him going morning and night. It wore him down, and then he fell deathly ill. The doctors said it was essential for him to travel south.

MRS. LINDE. Yes, didn't you spend the whole year in Italy?

NORA. That's right. It wasn't easy to get away, you know. Ivar had just been born. But of course we had to go. Oh, that was a beautiful trip, and it saved Torvald's life. But it cost a frightful sum, Kristine.

MRS. LINDE. I can well imagine.

NORA. Four thousand, eight hundred crowns it cost. That's really a lot of money.

MRS. LINDE. But it's lucky you had it when you needed it.

NORA. Well, as it was, we got it from Papa.

MRS. LINDE. I see. It was just about the time your father died.

NORA. Yes, just about then. And, you know, I couldn't make that trip out to nurse him. I had to stay here, expecting Ivar any moment, and with my poor sick Torvald to care for. Dearest Papa, I never saw him again, Kristine. Oh, that was the worst time I've known in all my marriage.

MRS. LINDE. I know how you loved him. And then you went off to Italy?

NORA. Yes. We had the means now, and the doctors urged us. So we left a month after.

MRS. LINDE. And your husband came back completely cured?

NORA. Sound as a drum!

MRS. LINDE. But—the doctor?

NORA. Who?

MRS. LINDE. I thought the maid said he was a doctor, the man who came in with me.

NORA. Yes, that was Dr. Rank—but he's not making a sick call. He's our closest friend, and he stops by at least once a day. No, Torvald hasn't had a sick moment since, and the children are fit and strong, and I am, too. [*Jumping up and clapping her hands*] Oh, dear God, Kristine, what a lovely thing to live and be happy! But how disgusting of me—I'm talking of nothing but my own affairs. [*Sits on a stool close by* KRISTINE, *arms resting across her knees*] Oh, don't be angry with me! Tell me, is it really true that you weren't in love with your husband? Why did you marry him, then?

MRS. LINDE. My mother was still alive, but bedridden and helpless—and I had my two younger brothers to look after. In all conscience, I didn't think I could turn him down.

NORA. No, you were right there. But was he rich at the time?

MRS. LINDE. He was very well off, I'd say. But the business was shaky, Nora. When he died, it all fell apart, and nothing was left.

NORA. And then—?

Commentary

Ibsen's Influence on James Joyce The Irish novelist James Joyce had great admiration for Ibsen's plays. In fact, Joyce's play *Exiles* (1918) clearly reflects the influence of Ibsen, as the critic B. J. Tysdahl points out in his book *Joyce and Ibsen*:

In appearance *Exiles* is like one of Ibsen's realistic dramas from beginning to end. Joyce's stage directions begin, as if copied from *A Doll's House* . . . , with a minute description of the drawing room; then follows, in a new paragraph, a sketch of the persons we see on the stage.

Throughout the play, stage directions are frequent, often in the form of an adverb to indicate the tone of speech. Words like *heartily* and *shyly* are used as often as in *Exiles* as in *The Master Builder* [another of Ibsen's plays]. Behind these outer resemblances lies the fact that, like Ibsen, Joyce deliberately chose the present time and the ordinary parlor as a setting for his drama. In his articles on Ibsen's plays Joyce had praised the Norwegian dramatist for his courage to put life—real life—on the stage, without the conventions or embellishments that had often served to veil reality.

MRS. LINDE. Yes, so I had to scrape up a living with a little shop and a little teaching and whatever else I could find. The last three years have been like one endless workday without a rest for me. Now it's over, Nora. My poor mother doesn't need me, for she's passed on. Nor the boys, either; they're working now and can take care of themselves.

NORA. How free you must feel—

MRS. LINDE. No—only unspeakably empty. Nothing to live for now. [*Standing up anxiously*] That's why I couldn't take it any longer out in that desolate hole. Maybe here it'll be easier to find something to do and keep my mind occupied. If I could only be lucky enough to get a steady job, some office work—

NORA. Oh, but Kristine, that's so dreadfully tiring, and you already look so tired. It would be much better for you if you could go off to a bathing resort.

MRS. LINDE. [*Going toward the window*] I have no father to give me travel money, Nora.

NORA. [*Rising*] Oh, don't be angry with me.

MRS. LINDE. [*Going to her*] Nora dear, don't you be angry with me. The worst of my kind of situation is all the bitterness that's stored away. No one to work for, and yet you're always having to snap up your opportunities. You have to live; and so you grow selfish. When you told me the happy change in your lot, do you know I was delighted less for your sakes than for mine?

NORA. How so? Oh, I see. You think maybe Torvald could do something for you.

MRS. LINDE. Yes, that's what I thought.

NORA. And he will, Kristine! Just leave it to me; I'll bring it up so delicately—find something attractive to humor him with. Oh, I'm so eager to help you.

MRS. LINDE. How very kind of you, Nora, to be so concerned over me—double kind, considering you really know so little of life's burdens yourself.

NORA. I—? I know so little—?

MRS. LINDE. [*Smiling*] Well, my heavens—a little needlework and such—Nora, you're just a child.

NORA. [*Tossing her head and pacing the floor*] You don't have to act so superior.

MRS. LINDE. Oh?

NORA. You're just like the others. You all think I'm incapable of anything serious.

MRS. LINDE. Come now—

NORA. That I've never had to face the raw world.

MRS. LINDE. Nora dear, you've just been telling me all your troubles.

NORA. Hm! Trivia! [*Quietly*] I haven't told you a big thing.

MRS. LINDE. Big thing? What do you mean?

NORA. You look down on me so, Kristine, but you shouldn't. You're proud that you worked so long and hard for your mother.

MRS. LINDE. I don't look down on a soul. But it *is* true: I'm proud—and happy, too—to think it was given to me to make my mother's last days almost free of care.

NORA. And you're also proud thinking of what you've done for your brothers.

MRS. LINDE. I feel I've a right to be.

NORA. I agree. But listen to this, Kristine—I've also got something to be proud and happy for.

MRS. LINDE. I don't doubt it. But whatever do you mean?

NORA. Not so loud. What if Torvald heard! He mustn't, not for anything in the world. Nobody must know, Kristine. No one but you.

MRS. LINDE. But what is it, then?

NORA. Come here. [*Drawing her down beside her on the sofa*] It's true—I've also got something to be proud and happy for. I'm the one who saved Torvald's life.

MRS. LINDE. Saved—? Saved how?

NORA. I told you about the trip to Italy. Torvald never would have lived if he hadn't gone south—

MRS. LINDE. Of course; your father gave you the means—

23
24

20 **Reading Strategy** Have students predict whether Torvald will hire Mrs. Linde. On what do they base their prediction?

21 **Discuss** Ask students what the manner in which Nora plans to approach Torvald reveals about their relationship. Is Nora's planned approach consistent with her earlier interactions with Torvald? Why or why not?

22 **Discussion** Do students agree with Mrs. Linde's comment that Nora is "just a child"? Why or why not? How do they think this comment might relate to the title of the play?

23 **Discussion** Do students agree with Nora's observation that Mrs. Linde is acting superior? If so, do they feel that Mrs. Linde is entitled to act superior? Why or why not?

24 **Discussion** Do students think that people have a right to feel proud about making sacrifices for others? Why or why not? What situations can students recall in which they have made a sacrifice for someone they cared about? How did it make them feel?

25 Clarification Make sure students understand the importance of these lines. According to Norwegian law at the time, Nora had no legal right to borrow the money without her husband's approval.

26 Discussion Do students feel that Nora had an obligation to do whatever she had to do in order to save her husband, regardless of whether her actions were legal or not. Why or why not? Do students feel that there are any situations in which it is acceptable to break the law?

27 Discussion Do students think Nora should have told Torvald that his life was in danger? Why or why not?

28 Discussion Ask students how Ibsen has prepared audiences and readers for Torvald's response to Nora's "hint that he could easily take out a loan."

NORA. [*Smiling*] That's what Torvald and all the rest think, but—

MRS. LINDE. But—?

NORA. Papa didn't give us a pin. I was the one who raised the money.

MRS. LINDE. You? That whole amount?

NORA. Four thousand, eight hundred crowns. What do you say to that?

MRS. LINDE. But Nora, how was it possible? Did you win the lottery?

NORA. [*Disdainfully*] The lottery? Pooh! No art to that.

MRS. LINDE. But where did you get it from then?

NORA. [*Humming, with a mysterious smile*] Hmm, tra-la-la-la.

MRS. LINDE. Because you couldn't have borrowed it.

25

NORA. No? Why not?

MRS. LINDE. A wife can't borrow without her husband's consent.

NORA. [*Tossing her head*] Oh, but a wife with a little business sense, a wife who knows how to manage—

MRS. LINDE. Nora, I simply don't understand—

NORA. You don't have to. Whoever said I *borrowed* the money? I could have gotten it other ways. [*Throwing herself back on the sofa*] I could have gotten it from some admirer or other. After all, a girl with my ravishing appeal—

MRS. LINDE. You lunatic.

NORA. I'll bet you're eaten up with curiosity, Kristine.

MRS. LINDE. Now listen here, Nora—you haven't done something indiscreet?

NORA. [*Sitting up again*] Is it indiscreet to save your husband's life?

MRS. LINDE. I think it's indiscreet that without his knowledge you—

NORA. But that's the point: he mustn't know! My Lord, can't you understand? He mustn't ever know the close call he had. It was to *me* the doctors came to say his life was in danger—that nothing could save him but a stay in the south. Didn't I try strategy then! I began talking about how lovely it would be for me to travel abroad like other young wives; I begged and I cried; I told him please to remember my condition, to be kind and indulge me; and then I dropped a hint that he could easily take out a loan. But at that, Kristine, he nearly explod-

Primary Source

At the time Henrik Ibsen was writing *A Doll's House*, he delivered a speech to the Scandinavian Club in which he proposed that women should be allowed to vote at the club's annual meeting. He remarked:

I am not afraid of these so-called unpractical women; women have something in common with the true artist, just as young people in general have—something that is a good substitute for worldly understanding. Look at our student societies in Norway! Matters are decided there which are ten times more complicated than ours; yet do they not manage well, although youth, untried, unpracticed and unpractical youth there enjoys an overwhelming majority? And why? Because youth has this instinctive genius which unconsciously hits upon the right answer. And it is precisely this instinct which women share with youth, and with the true artist.

ed. He said I was frivolous, and it was his duty as man of the house not to indulge me in whims and fancies—as I think he called them. Aha, I thought, now you'll just have to be saved—and that's when I saw my chance.

MRS. LINDE. And your father never told Torvald the money wasn't from him?

NORA. No, never. Papa died right about then. I'd considered bringing him into my secret and begging him never to tell. But he was too sick at the time—and then, sadly, it didn't matter.

MRS. LINDE. And you've never confided in your husband since?

NORA. For heaven's sake, no! Are you serious? He's so strict on that subject. Besides—Torvald, with all his masculine pride—how painfully humiliating for him if he ever found out he was in debt to me. That would just ruin our relationship. Our beautiful, happy home would never be the same.

MRS. LINDE. Won't you ever tell him?

NORA. [*Thoughtfully, half smiling*] Yes—maybe sometime, years from now, when I'm no longer so attractive. Don't laugh! I only mean when Torvald loves me less than now, when he stops enjoying my dancing and dressing up and reciting for him. Then it might be wise to have something in reserve— [*Breaking off*] How ridiculous! That'll never happen —Well, Kristine, what do you think of my big secret? I'm capable of something too, hm? You can imagine, of course, how this thing hangs over me. It really hasn't been easy meeting the payments on time. In the business world there's what they call quarterly interest and what they call amortization,[4] and these are always so terribly hard to manage. I've had to skimp a little here and there, wherever I could, you know. I could hardly spare anything from my house allowance, because Torvald has to live well. I couldn't let the children go poorly dressed; whatever I got for them, I felt I had to use up completely—the darlings!

MRS. LINDE. Poor Nora, so it had to come out of your own budget, then?

---

4. **amortization** (am′ ər ti zā′ shən) *n*.: The putting aside of money at intervals, for gradual payment.

NORA. Yes, of course. But I was the one most responsible, too. Every time Torvald gave me money for new clothes and such, I never used more than half; always bought the simplest, cheapest outfits. It was a godsend that everything looks so well on me that Torvald never noticed. But it did weigh me down at times, Kristine. It *is* such a joy to wear fine things. You understand.

MRS. LINDE. Oh, of course.

NORA. And then I found other ways of making money. Last winter I was lucky enough to get a lot of copying to do. I locked myself in and sat writing every evening till late in the night. Ah, I was tired so often, dead tired. But still it was wonderful fun, sitting and working like that, earning money. It was almost like being a man.

MRS. LINDE. But how much have you paid off this way so far?

NORA. That's hard to say, exactly. These accounts, you know, aren't easy to figure. I only know that I've paid out all I could scrape together. Time and again I haven't known where to turn. [*Smiling*] Then I'd sit here dreaming of a rich old gentleman who had fallen in love with me—

MRS. LINDE. What! Who is he?

NORA. Oh, really! And that he'd died, and when his will was opened, there in big letters it said, "All my fortune shall be paid over in cash, immediately, to that enchanting Mrs. Nora Helmer."

MRS. LINDE. But Nora dear—who *was* this gentleman?

NORA. Good grief, can't you understand? The old man never existed; that was only something I'd dream up time and again whenever I was at my wits' end for money. But it makes no difference now; the old fossil can go where he pleases for all I care; I don't need him or his will—because now I'm free. [*Jumping up*] Oh, how lovely to think of that, Kristine! Carefree! To know you're carefree, utterly carefree; to be able to romp and play with the children, and to keep up a beautiful, charming home—everything just the way Torvald likes it! And think, spring is coming, with big blue skies. Maybe we can travel a little then. Maybe I'll see the

36 **Reading Strategy** Have students make inferences about why Nora becomes so tense when Krogstad enters the room.

37 **Literary Focus** Call students' attention to Ibsen's detailed stage directions. Point out how he directs the actors to convey specific emotions, such as tension and indifference. Ask students why Ibsen might have felt it important to include such detailed directions. Also explain that Ibsen's use of detailed stage directions represents a departure from the approach of most earlier dramatists.

38 **Enrichment** Call students' attention to how these developments reflect the tight structure of the plot. Not only have Krogstad and Mrs. Linde met before, they also have much in common: They are both widowers, and they both had unhappy marriages. In addition, Mrs. Linde's behavior suggests that they may have much more in common than their parallel misfortunes.

39 **Discussion** Have students discuss how this information might help to explain Nora's discomfort when Krogstad enters the room.

ocean again. Oh yes, it *is* so marvelous to live and be happy! [*The front doorbell rings.*]

MRS. LINDE. [*Rising*] There's the bell. It's probably best that I go.

NORA. No, stay. No one's expected. It must be for Torvald.

MAID. [*From the hall doorway*] Excuse me, ma'am —there's a gentleman here to see Mr. Helmer, but I didn't know—since the doctor's with him—

NORA. Who is the gentleman?

KROGSTAD. [*From the doorway*] It's me, Mrs. Helmer. [MRS. LINDE *starts and turns away toward the window.*]

NORA. [*Stepping toward him, tense, her voice a whisper*] You? What is it? Why do you want to speak to my husband?

KROGSTAD. Bank business—after a fashion. I have a small job in the investment bank, and I hear now your husband is going to be our chief—

NORA. In other words, it's—

KROGSTAD. Just dry business, Mrs. Helmer. Nothing but that.

NORA. Yes, then please be good enough to step into the study. [*She nods indifferently as she sees him out by the hall door, then returns and begins stirring up the stove.*]

MRS. LINDE. Nora—who was that man?

NORA. That was a Mr. Krogstad—a lawyer.

MRS. LINDE. Then it really was him.

NORA. Do you know that person?

MRS. LINDE. I did once—many years ago. For a time he was a law clerk in our town.

NORA. Yes, he's been that.

MRS. LINDE. How he's changed.

NORA. I understand he had a very unhappy marriage.

MRS. LINDE. He's a widower now.

NORA. With a number of children. There now, it's burning. [*She closes the stove door and moves the rocker a bit to one side.*]

MRS. LINDE. They say he has a hand in all kinds of business.

NORA. Oh? That may be true; I wouldn't know. But let's not think about business. It's so dull. [DR. RANK *enters from* HELMER'S *study.*]

RANK. [*Still in the doorway*] No, no, really—I don't want to intrude, I'd just as soon talk a little while with your wife. [*Shuts the door, then notices* MRS. LINDE.] Oh, beg pardon. I'm intruding here too.

NORA. No, not at all. [*Introducing him*] Dr. Rank, Mrs. Linde.

RANK. Well now, that's a name much heard in this house. I believe I passed the lady on the stairs as I came.

MRS. LINDE. Yes, I take the stairs very slowly. They're rather hard on me.

RANK. Uh-hm, some touch of internal weakness?

MRS. LINDE. More overexertion, I'd say.

RANK. Nothing else? Then you're probably here in town to rest up in a round of parties?

MRS. LINDE. I'm here to look for work.

RANK. Is that the best cure for overexertion?

MRS. LINDE. One has to live, Doctor.

RANK. Yes, there's a common prejudice to that effect.

NORA. Oh, come on, Dr. Rank—you really do want to live yourself.

RANK. Yes, I really do. Wretched as I am, I'll gladly prolong my torment indefinitely. All my patients feel like that. And it's quite the same, too, with the morally sick. Right at this moment there's one of those moral invalids in there with Helmer—

MRS. LINDE. [*Softly*] Ah!

NORA. Who do you mean?

RANK. Oh, it's a lawyer, Krogstad, a type you wouldn't know. His character is rotten to the root—but even he began chattering all-importantly about how he had to *live.*

NORA. Oh? What did he want to talk to Torvald about?

RANK. I really don't know. I only heard something about the bank.

NORA. I didn't know that Krog—that this man Krogstad had anything to do with the bank.

RANK. Yes, he's gotten some kind of berth down there. [*To* MRS. LINDE] I don't know if you also have, in your neck of the woods, a type of person who scuttles about breathlessly, sniffing out hints of moral corruption, and then maneuvers his victim into some sort of key position where he can keep an eye on him. It's the healthy these days that are out in the cold.

MRS. LINDE. All the same, it's the sick who most need to be taken in.

RANK. [*With a shrug*] Yes, there we have it. That's the concept that's turning society into a sanatorium. [NORA, *lost in her thoughts, breaks out into quiet laughter and claps her hands.*]

RANK. Why do you laugh at that? Do you have any real idea of what society is?

NORA. What do I care about dreary old society? I was laughing at something quite different—something terribly funny. Tell me, Doctor—is everyone who works in the bank dependent now on Torvald?

RANK. Is that what you find so terribly funny?

NORA. [*Smiling and humming*] Never mind, never mind! [*Pacing the floor*] Yes, that's really immensely amusing: that we—that Torvald has so much power now over all those people. [*Taking the bag out of her pocket*] Dr. Rank, a little macaroon on that?

RANK. See here, macaroons! I thought they were contraband here.

NORA. Yes, but these are some that Kristine gave me.

MRS. LINDE. What? I—?

NORA. Now, now, don't be afraid. You couldn't possibly know that Torvald had forbidden them. You see, he's worried they'll ruin my teeth. But hmp! Just this once! Isn't that so, Dr. Rank? Help

40 **Clarification** Tell students that when Dr. Rank says, "It's the healthy these days that are out in the cold," he is apparently referring to the honest, moral people of nineteenth-century Norway—those uncorrupted by the likes of Krogstad. Mrs. Linde's response that "it's the sick who most need to be taken in" is based on a more literal interpretation of the word *healthy.* Yet Dr. Rank replies, "That's the concept that's turning society into a sanatorium." Evidently Dr. Rank thinks that "moral invalids" such as Krogstad are being given preferred treatment. This view is undoubtedly shared by Helmer. Do students think that many people in our society share Dr. Rank's views?

41 **Discussion** Nora pulls out her macaroons again, this time on what seems to be a triumphant note. Remind students that Ibsen often used props, such as the macaroons, as symbols. Then have students discuss what the macaroons might symbolize.

42 **Discussion** Ask students why Nora lies about the source of the macaroons. Is she afraid that Dr. Rank will tell her husband?

yourself! [*Puts a macaroon in his mouth*] And you too, Kristine. And I'll also have one, only a little one—or two, at the most. [*Walking about again*] Now I'm really tremendously happy. Now there's just one last thing in the world that I have an enormous desire to do.

RANK. Well! And what's that?

NORA. It's something I have such a consuming desire to say so Torvald could hear.

RANK. And why can't you say it?

NORA. I don't dare. It's quite shocking.

MRS. LINDE. Shocking?

RANK. Well, then it isn't advisable. But in front of us you certainly can. What do you have such a desire to say so Torvald could hear?

NORA. I have such a huge desire to say—to hell and be damned!

RANK. Are you crazy?

MRS. LINDE. My goodness, Nora!

RANK. Go on, say it. Here he is.

NORA. [*Hiding the macaroon bag*] Shh, shh, shh! [HELMER *comes in from his study, hat in hand, overcoat over his arm.*]

NORA. [*Going toward him*] Well, Torvald dear, are you through with him?

HELMER. Yes, he just left.

NORA. Let me introduce you—this is Kristine, who's arrived here in town.

HELMER. Kristine—? I'm sorry, but I don't know—

NORA. Mrs. Linde, Torvald dear. Mrs. Kristine Linde.

HELMER. Of course. A childhood friend of my wife's, no doubt?

MRS. LINDE. Yes, we knew each other in those days.

NORA. And just think, she made the long trip down here in order to talk with you.

HELMER. What's this?

MRS. LINDE. Well, not exactly—

NORA. You see, Kristine is remarkably clever in office work, and so she's terribly eager to come under a capable man's supervision and add more to what she already knows—

HELMER. Very wise, Mrs. Linde.

NORA. And then when she heard that you'd become a bank manager—the story was wired out to the papers—then she came in as fast as she could and—Really, Torvald, for my sake you can do a little something for Kristine, can't you?

HELMER. Yes, it's not at all impossible. Mrs. Linde, I suppose you're a widow?

MRS. LINDE. Yes.

HELMER. Any experience in office work?

MRS. LINDE. Yes, a good deal.

HELMER. Well, it's quite likely that I can make an opening for you—

NORA. [*Clapping her hands*] You see, you see!

HELMER. You've come at a lucky moment, Mrs. Linde.

MRS. LINDE. Oh, how can I thank you?

HELMER. Not necessary. [*Putting his overcoat on*] But today you'll have to excuse me—

RANK. Wait, I'll go with you. [*He fetches his coat from the hall and warms it at the stove.*]

NORA. Don't stay out long, dear.

HELMER. An hour; no more.

NORA. Are you going too, Kristine?

MRS. LINDE. [*Putting on her winter garments*] Yes, I have to see about a room now.

HELMER. Then perhaps we can all walk together.

NORA. [*Helping her*] What a shame we're so cramped here, but it's quite impossible for us to—

MRS. LINDE. Oh, don't even think of it! Good-bye, Nora dear, and thanks for everything.

Primary Source

In his book *The Quintessence of Ibsenism*, the Irish playwright George Bernard Shaw offers a sarcastic description of the surface appearance of Helmer's World:

In the famous *Doll's House* the pillar of society who owns the doll is a model husband, father, and citizen. In his little household, with the three darling children and the affectionate little wife, all on the most loving terms with one another, we have the sweet home, the womanly woman, the happy family life of the idealist's dream. Mrs. Nora Helmer is happy in the belief that she has attained a valid realization of all these illusions; that she is an ideal wife and mother; and that Helmer is an ideal husband who would, if the necessity arose, give his life to save her reputation.

NORA. Good-bye for now. Of course you'll be back this evening. And you too, Dr. Rank. What? If you're well enough? Oh, you've got to be! Wrap up tight now. [*In a ripple of small talk the company moves out into the hall; children's voices are heard outside on the steps.*]

NORA. There they are! There they are! [*She runs to open the door. The children come in with their nurse,* ANNE-MARIE.] Come in, come in! [*Bends down and kisses them*] Oh, you darlings—! Look at them, Kristine. Aren't they lovely!

RANK. No loitering in the draft here.

HELMER. Come, Mrs. Linde—this place is unbearable now for anyone but mothers. [DR. RANK, HELMER, *and* MRS. LINDE *go down the stairs.* ANNE-MARIE *goes into the living room with the children.* NORA *follows, after closing the hall door.*]

NORA. How fresh and strong you look. Oh, such red cheeks you have! Like apples and roses. [*The children interrupt her throughout the following.*] And it was so much fun? That's wonderful. Really? You pulled both Emmy and Bob on the sled? Imagine, all together! Yes, you're a clever boy, Ivar. Oh, let me hold her a bit, Anne-Marie. My sweet little doll baby! [*Takes the smallest from the nurse and dances with her*] Yes, yes, Mama will dance with Bob as well. What? Did you throw snowballs? Oh, if I'd only been there! No, don't bother, Anne-Marie—I'll undress them myself. Oh yes, let me. It's such fun. Go in and rest; you look half frozen. There's hot coffee waiting for you on the stove. [*The nurse goes into the room to the left.* NORA *takes the children's winter things off, throwing them about, while the children talk to her all at once.*] Is that so? A big dog chased you? But it didn't bite? No, dogs never bite little, lovely doll babies. Don't peek in the packages, Ivar! What is it? Yes, wouldn't you like to know. No, no, it's an ugly something. Well? Shall we play? What shall we play? Hide-and-seek? Yes, let's play hide-and-seek. Bob must hide first. I must? Yes, let me hide first. [*Laughing and shouting, she and the children play in and out of the living room and the adjoining room to the right. At last* NORA *hides under the table. The children come storming in, search, but cannot find her, then hear her muffled laughter, dash over to the table, lift the cloth up and find her. Wild shouting. She creeps forward as if to scare them. More shouts. Meanwhile, a knock at the hall door; no one has noticed it. Now the door half opens, and* KROGSTAD *appears. He waits a moment; the game goes on.*]

KROGSTAD. Beg pardon, Mrs. Helmer—

NORA. [*With a strangled cry, turning and scrambling to her knees*] Oh! What do you want?

KROGSTAD. Excuse me. The outer door was ajar; it must be someone forgot to shut it—

NORA. [*Rising*] My husband isn't home, Mr. Krogstad.

KROGSTAD. I know that.

NORA. Yes—then what do you want here?

KROGSTAD. A word with you.

NORA. With—? [*To the children, quietly*] Go in to Anne-Marie. What? No, the strange man won't hurt Mama. When he's gone, we'll play some more. [*She leads the children into the room to the left and shuts the door after them. Then, tense and nervous*] You want to speak to me?

KROGSTAD. Yes, I want to.

NORA. Today? But it's not yet the first of the month—

KROGSTAD. No, it's Christmas Eve. It's going to be up to you how merry a Christmas you have.

NORA. What is it you want? Today I absolutely can't—

KROGSTAD. We won't talk about that till later. This is something else. You do have a moment to spare, I suppose?

NORA. Oh, yes, of course—I do, except—

KROGSTAD. Good. I was sitting over at Olsen's Restaurant when I saw your husband go down the street—

NORA. Yes?

KROGSTAD. With a lady.

46 Discussion Have students discuss what this comment suggests about the role that Torvald plays in raising his children. Do they imagine that he is a good father? Why or why not?

47 Discussion Point out to students that Nora refers to her children as "doll babies." Then have them discuss what, if anything, these references imply about Nora's view of her children and about her relationship with them.

48 Discussion Ask students how Nora's remarks to her children relate to the title of the play.

49 Literary Focus Once again call students' attention to Ibsen's detailed stage directions. Urge them to try to envision the actions that Ibsen describes in these directions.

50 Reading Strategy Have students speculate about what Krogstad might mean when he says that it is "up to [her] how merry a Christmas [she will] have."

51 Discussion Remind students of Dr. Rank's remarks concerning Nils Krogstad. Ask them if Krogstad's behavior is consistent with Rank's description of him.

NORA. Yes. So?

KROGSTAD. If you'll pardon my asking: wasn't that lady a Mrs. Linde?

NORA. Yes.

KROGSTAD. Just now come into town?

NORA. Yes, today.

KROGSTAD. She's a good friend of yours?

NORA. Yes, she is. But I don't see—

KROGSTAD. I also knew her once.

NORA. I'm aware of that.

KROGSTAD. Oh? You know all about it. I thought so. Well, then let me ask you short and sweet: is Mrs. Linde getting a job in the bank?

NORA. What makes you think you can cross-examine me, Mr. Krogstad—you, one of my husband's employees? But since you ask, you might as well know —yes, Mrs. Linde's going to be taken on at the bank. And I'm the one who spoke for her, Mr. Krogstad. Now you know.

KROGSTAD. So I guessed right.

NORA. [*Pacing up and down*] Oh, one does have a tiny bit of influence, I should hope. Just because I am a woman, don't think it means that— When one has a subordinate position, Mr. Krogstad, one really ought to be careful about pushing somebody who—hm—

KROGSTAD. Who has influence?

NORA. That's right.

KROGSTAD. [*In a different tone*] Mrs. Helmer, would you be good enough to use your influence on my behalf?

NORA. What? What do you mean?

KROGSTAD. Would you please make sure that I keep my subordinate position in the bank.

NORA. What does that mean? Who's thinking of taking away your position?

KROGSTAD. Oh, don't play the innocent with me. I'm quite aware that your friend would hardly relish the chance of running into me again; and I'm also aware now whom I can thank for being turned out.

NORA. But I promise you—

KROGSTAD. Yes, yes, yes, to the point: there's still time, and I'm advising you to use your influence to prevent it.

NORA. But Mr. Krogstad, I have absolutely no influence.

KROGSTAD. You haven't? I thought you were just saying—

NORA. You shouldn't take me so literally. I! How can you believe that I have any such influence over my husband?

KROGSTAD. Oh, I've known your husband from our student days. I don't think the great bank manager's more steadfast than any other married man.

NORA. You speak insolently about my husband, and I'll show you the door.

KROGSTAD. The lady has spirit.

NORA. I'm not afraid of you any longer. After New Year's, I'll soon be done with the whole business.

KROGSTAD. [*Restraining himself*] Now listen to me, Mrs. Helmer. If necessary, I'll fight for my little job in the bank as if it were life itself.

NORA. Yes, so it seems.

KROGSTAD. It's not just a matter of income; that's the least of it. It's something else— All right, out with it! Look, this is the thing. You know, just like all the others, of course, that once, a good many years ago, I did something rather rash.

NORA. I've heard rumors to that effect.

KROGSTAD. The case never got into court; but all the same, every door was closed in my face from then on. So I took up those various activities you know about. I had to grab hold somewhere; and I dare say I haven't been among the worst. But now I want to drop all that. My boys are growing up. For their sakes, I'll have to win back as much respect as possible here in town. That job in the bank was like the first rung in my ladder. And now your husband wants to kick me right back down in the mud again.

NORA. But for heaven's sake, Mr. Krogstad, it's simply not in my power to help you.

KROGSTAD. That's because you haven't the will to—but I have the means to make you.

NORA. You certainly won't tell my husband that I owe you money?

KROGSTAD. Hm—what if I told him that?

NORA. That would be shameful of you. [*Nearly in tears*] This secret—my joy and my pride—that he should learn it in such a crude and disgusting way—learn it from you. You'd expose me to the most horrible unpleasantness—

KROGSTAD. Only unpleasantness?

NORA. [*Vehemently*] But go on and try. It'll turn out the worse for you, because then my husband will really see what a crook you are, and then you'll *never* be able to hold your job.

KROGSTAD. I asked if it was just domestic unpleasantness you were afraid of?

NORA. If my husband finds out, then of course he'll pay what I owe at once, and then we'd be through with you for good.

KROGSTAD. [*A step closer*] Listen, Mrs. Helmer—you've either got a very bad memory, or else no head at all for business. I'd better put you a little more in touch with the facts.

NORA. What do you mean?

KROGSTAD. When your husband was sick, you came to me for a loan of four thousand, eight hundred crowns.

NORA. Where else could I go?

KROGSTAD. I promised to get you that sum—

NORA. And you got it.

KROGSTAD. I promised to get you that sum, on certain conditions. You were so involved in your husband's illness, and so eager to finance your trip, that I guess you didn't think out all the details. It might just be a good idea to remind you. I promised you the money on the strength of a note I drew up.

NORA. Yes, and that I signed.

KROGSTAD. Right. But at the bottom I added some lines for your father to guarantee the loan. He was supposed to sign down there.

NORA. Supposed to? He did sign.

KROGSTAD. I left the date blank. In other words, your father would have dated his signature himself. Do you remember that?

NORA. Yes, I think—

KROGSTAD. Then I gave you the note for you to mail to your father. Isn't that so?

NORA. Yes.

KROGSTAD. And naturally you sent it at once—because only some five, six days later you brought me the note, properly signed. And with that, the money was yours.

NORA. Well, then; I've made my payments regularly, haven't I?

KROGSTAD. More or less. But—getting back to the point—those were hard times for you then, Mrs. Helmer.

NORA. Yes, they were.

KROGSTAD. Your father was very ill, I believe.

NORA. He was near the end.

KROGSTAD. He died soon after?

NORA. Yes.

KROGSTAD. Tell me, Mrs. Helmer, do you happen to recall the date of your father's death? The day of the month, I mean.

NORA. Papa died the twenty-ninth of September.

KROGSTAD. That's quite correct; I've already looked into that. And now we come to a curious thing—[*Taking out a paper*] which I simply cannot comprehend.

NORA. Curious thing? I don't know—

57 **Discussion** Have students discuss why Nora refers to her secret loan as her "pride and [her] joy." Does she feel any remorse about what she did?

58 **Discussion** Ask students why Krogstad asks if it is "just domestic unpleasantness" that Nora is afraid of. What else might Nora have to be afraid of?

59 **Discussion** Remind students that a wife could not legally borrow money unless her husband signed the note. Given this fact, what would have been the point of having Nora's father sign the note? Why might Krogstad have asked for her father's signature, even though he knew that the transaction would be illegal?

60 **Enrichment** Remind students that Krogstad is a former lawyer. Therefore, it is not surprising that his questioning of Nora sounds like a courtroom cross-examination. Also point out to students that the questioning serves an important role in the plot, providing the opportunity for a detailed description of the financial transaction around which the story revolves. In addition, Krogstad's questioning of Nora contributes to the development of both characters.

61 Discussion Explain to students that this is a revealing moment in the play. Krogstad gives Nora a way out of her predicament—or at least he seems to—by suggesting that Nora's father signed the note and that Nora later added the date. Students have already learned that Nora is willing to keep secrets and tell lies. Considering this fact, why do students think that she refrains from telling a lie in this situation?

62 Discussion Have students discuss Nora's value system. Does she believe that she did anything wrong by forging her father's signature? Explain. Does she believe that it was wrong for her to mislead Krogstad about the genuineness of the signature?

63 Enrichment Tell students that a lawyer might be likely to question Krogstad's legal position as well as Nora's. He also signed the note, knowing that the signature of Nora's father, genuine or forged, had no legal value.

64 Discussion Have students discuss whether or not the fact that Nora forged her signature "out of love" excuses her actions.

KROGSTAD. This is the curious thing: that your father co-signed the note for your loan three days after his death.

NORA. How—? I don't understand.

KROGSTAD. Your father died the twenty-ninth of September. But look. Here your father dated his signature October second. Isn't that curious, Mrs. Helmer? [NORA *is silent.*] Can you explain it to me? [NORA *remains silent.*] It's also remarkable that the words "October second" and the year aren't written in your father's hand, but rather in one that I think I know. Well, it's easy to understand. Your father forgot perhaps to date his signature, and then someone or other added it, a bit sloppily, before anyone knew of his death. There's nothing wrong in that. It all comes down to the signature. And there's no question about *that*, Mrs. Helmer. It really *was* your father who signed his own name here, wasn't it?

NORA. [*After a short silence, throwing her head back and looking squarely at him*] No, it wasn't. *I* signed Papa's name.

KROGSTAD. Wait, now—are you fully aware that this is a dangerous confession?

NORA. Why? You'll soon get your money.

KROGSTAD. Let me ask you a question—why didn't you send the paper to your father?

NORA. That was impossible. Papa was so sick. If I'd asked him for his signature, I also would have had to tell him what the money was for. But I couldn't tell him, sick as he was, that my husband's life was in danger. That was just impossible.

KROGSTAD. Then it would have been better if you'd given up the trip abroad.

NORA. I couldn't possibly. The trip was to save my husband's life. I couldn't give that up.

KROGSTAD. But didn't you ever consider that this was a fraud against me?

NORA. I couldn't let myself be bothered by that. You weren't any concern of mine. I couldn't stand you, with all those cold complications you made, even though you knew how badly off my husband was.

KROGSTAD. Mrs. Helmer, obviously you haven't the vaguest idea of what you've involved yourself in. But I can tell you this: it was nothing more and nothing worse that I once did—and it wrecked my whole reputation.

NORA. You? Do you expect me to believe that you ever acted bravely to save your wife's life?

KROGSTAD. Laws don't inquire into motives.

NORA. Then they must be very poor laws.

KROGSTAD. Poor or not—if I introduce this paper in court, you'll be judged according to law.

NORA. This I refuse to believe. A daughter hasn't a right to protect her dying father from anxiety and care? A wife hasn't a right to save her husband's life? I don't know much about laws, but I'm sure that somewhere in the books these things are allowed. And you don't know anything about it—you who practice the law? You must be an awful lawyer, Mr. Krogstad.

KROGSTAD. Could be. But business—the kind of business we two are mixed up in—don't you think I know about that? All right. Do what you want now. But I'm telling you *this*: if I get shoved down a second time, you're going to keep me company. [*He bows and goes out through the hall.*]

NORA. [*Pensive[5] for a moment, then tossing her head*] Oh, really! Trying to frighten me! I'm not so silly as all that. [*Begins gathering up the children's clothes, but soon stops*] But—? No, but that's impossible! I did it out of love.

THE CHILDREN. [*In the doorway, left*] Mama, that strange man's gone out the door.

NORA. Yes, yes, I know it. But don't tell anyone about the strange man. Do you hear? Not even Papa!

THE CHILDREN. No, Mama. But now will you play again?

NORA. No, not now.

THE CHILDREN. Oh, but Mama, you promised.

---

5. *Pensive* (pen′ siv) *adj.*: Thinking deeply or seriously, often of sad or melancholy things.

Grammar in Action

When people use **deductive reasoning,** they start with a general statement that is assumed to be true and apply that statement to specific cases. For example, based on the assumption that dead people cannot sign their names, Krogstad concludes that since Nora's father's signature is dated three days after his death, his signature must have been forged.

   Student Activity. Use deductive reasoning to draw a conclusion from each of the following statements relating to the events in *A Doll's House.*
1. At the time of the play, it was illegal for a married woman to borrow money without her husband's approval. Nora borrowed money without Torvald's approval.
2. At the time of the play, most people believed that married women had the obligation to care for their husbands and children. Nora was a married woman with three small children.
3. Helmer believes that anyone who has committed forgery should be punished. Although Helmer is not aware of it, Nora has committed forgery.

NORA. Yes, but I can't now. Go inside; I have too much to do. Go in, go in, my sweet darlings. [*She herds them gently back in the room and shuts the door after them. Settling on the sofa, she takes up a piece of embroidery and makes some stitches, but soon stops abruptly.*] No! [*Throws the work aside, rises, goes to the hall door and calls out*] Helene! Let me have the tree in here. [*Goes to the table, left, opens the table drawer, and stops again*] No, but that's utterly impossible!

MAID. [*With the Christmas tree*] Where should I put it, ma'am?

NORA. There. The middle of the floor.

MAID. Should I bring anything else?

NORA. No, thanks. I have what I need. [*The* MAID, *who has set the tree down, goes out.*]

NORA. [*Absorbed in trimming the tree*] Candles here—and flowers here. That terrible creature! Talk, talk, talk! There's nothing to it at all. The tree's going to be lovely. I'll do anything to please you, Torvald. I'll sing for you, dance for you— [HELMER *comes in from the hall, with a sheaf of papers under his arm.*]

NORA. Oh! You're back so soon?

HELMER. Yes. Has anyone been here?

NORA. Here? No.

HELMER. That's odd. I saw Krogstad leaving the front door.

NORA. So? Oh yes, that's true. Krogstad was here a moment.

HELMER. Nora, I can see by your face that he's been here, begging you to put in a good word for him.

NORA. Yes.

HELMER. And it was supposed to seem like your own idea? You were to hide it from me that he'd been here. He asked you that, too, didn't he?

NORA. Yes, Torvald, but—

HELMER. Nora, Nora, and you could fall for that? Talk with that sort of person and promise him anything? And then in the bargain, tell me an untruth.

NORA. An untruth—?

HELMER. Didn't you say that no one had been here? [*Wagging his finger*] My little songbird must never do that again. A songbird needs a clean beak to warble with. No false notes. [*Putting his arm about her waist*] That's the way it should be, isn't it? Yes, I'm sure of it. [*Releasing her*] And so, enough of that. [*Sitting by the stove*] Ah, how snug and cozy it is here. [*Leafing among his papers*]

NORA. [*Busy with the tree, after a short pause*] Torvald!

HELMER. Yes.

NORA. I'm so much looking forward to the Stenborgs' costume party, day after tomorrow.

HELMER. And I can't wait to see what you'll surprise me with.

NORA. Oh, that stupid business!

HELMER. What?

NORA. I can't find anything that's right. Everything seems so ridiculous, so inane.[6]

HELMER. So my little Nora's come to *that* recognition?

NORA. [*Going behind his chair, her arms resting on his back*] Are you very busy, Torvald?

HELMER. Oh—

NORA. What papers are those?

HELMER. Bank matters.

NORA. Already?

HELMER. I've gotten full authority from the retiring management to make all necessary changes in personnel and procedure. I'll need Christmas week for that. I want to have everything in order by New Year's.

NORA. So that was the reason this poor Krogstad—

HELMER. Hm.

NORA. [*Still leaning on the chair and slowly stroking the nape of his neck*] If you weren't so very busy, I would have asked you an enormous favor, Torvald.

---

6. **inane** (in ān´) *adj.*: Foolish; silly.

65 Literary Focus Although this play preceded the widespread use of the stream-of-consciousness technique in fiction, Ibsen's pursuit of realism and his intuitive grasp of psychology sometimes led him to a similar technique in his dialogue. Have students look closely at this passage, noting how Nora's words mirror her jumbled thoughts. How does this passage capture Nora's stream of consciousness?

66 Discussion Have students offer explanations about why Nora continues to lie to Torvald.

67 Discussion Point out that this dialogue begins with a pair of seemingly happy observations by Nora and Torvald. However, reality soon intrudes. Have students discuss whether the Helmers might have a more authentic marriage if Torvald tried to treat Nora as an equal.

68 Discussion Have students discuss the significance of the time of year during which the play is set. Do students feel that it is inappropriate to fire someone during the holiday season? Why or why not?

HELMER. Let's hear. What is it?

NORA. You know, there isn't anyone who has your good taste—and I want so much to look well at the costume party. Torvald, couldn't you take over and decide what I should be and plan my costume?

69 HELMER. Ah, is my stubborn little creature calling for a lifeguard?

NORA. Yes, Torvald, I can't get anywhere without your help.

HELMER. All right—I'll think it over. We'll hit on something.

NORA. Oh, how sweet of you. [*Goes to the tree again. Pause*] Aren't the red flowers pretty—? But tell me, was it really such a crime that this Krogstad committed?

HELMER. Forgery. Do you have any idea what that means?

NORA. Couldn't he have done it out of need?

HELMER. Yes, or thoughtlessness, like so many others. I'm not so heartless that I'd condemn a man **70** categorically for just one mistake.

NORA. No, of course not, Torvald!

HELMER. Plenty of men have redeemed themselves by openly confessing their crimes and taking their punishment.

NORA. Punishment—?

HELMER. But now Krogstad didn't go that way. He got himself out by sharp practices, and that's the real cause of his moral breakdown.

NORA. Do you really think that would—?

HELMER. Just imagine how a man with that sort of guilt in him has to lie and cheat and deceive on all sides, has to wear a mask even with the nearest and dearest he has, even with his own wife and children. And with the children, Nora—that's where it's most horrible.

71 NORA. Why?

HELMER. Because that kind of atmosphere of lies infects the whole life of a home. Every breath the children take in is filled with the germs of something degenerate.

NORA. [*Coming closer behind him*] Are you sure of that?

HELMER. Oh, I've seen it often enough as a lawyer. Almost everyone who goes bad early in life has a mother who's a chronic liar.

NORA. Why just—the mother?

HELMER. It's usually the mother's influence that's dominant, but the father's works in the same way, of course. Every lawyer is quite familiar with it. And still this Krogstad's been going home year in, year out, poisoning his own children with lies and pretense; that's why I call him morally lost. [*Reaching his hands out toward her*] So my sweet little Nora must promise me never to plead his cause. Your hand on it. Come, come, what's this? Give me your hand. There, now. All settled. I can tell you it'd be impossible for me to work alongside of him. I literally feel physically revolted when I'm anywhere near such a person.

NORA. [*Withdraws her hand and goes to the other side of the Christmas tree*] How hot it is here! And I've got so much to do.

HELMER. [*Getting up and gathering his papers*] Yes, and I have to think about getting some of these read through before dinner. I'll think about your costume, too. And something to hang on the tree in gilt paper, I may even see about that. [*Putting his hand on her head*] Oh you, my darling little songbird. [*He goes into his study and closes the door after him.*]

NORA. [*Softly, after a silence*] Oh, really! it isn't so. It's impossible. It must be impossible.

ANNE-MARIE. [*In the doorway, left*] The children are begging so hard to come in to Mama.

NORA. No, no, no, don't let them in to me! You stay with them, Anne-Marie.

ANNE-MARIE. Of course, ma'am. [*Closes the door*]

NORA. [*Pale with terror*] Hurt my children—? Poison my home? [*A moment's pause; then she tosses her head.*] That's not true. Never in all the world.

THINKING ABOUT THE SELECTION

Interpreting

1. Torvald refers to Nora by such names as his "little lark," his "squirrel," and the "little spendthrift." (a) What does his use of these names suggest about his attitude toward her? Explain. (b) What seems to be Torvald's attitude toward women in general, and how is his attitude revealed?
2. What else is revealed about Torvald's personality in the opening scene, and how is it revealed?
3. Considering what Nora reveals to Mrs. Linde later in the act, what is ironic, or surprising, about Torvald's comments concerning Nora's management of money?
4. (a) How would you characterize Nora and Torvald's relationship based on their interactions in the opening scene? Support your characterization with details. (b) What details in the first act indicate that Nora and Torvald do not know each other very well? (c) Considering the true nature of Nora and Torvald's relationship, what is ironic about her comment that if he found out her secret it "would just ruin [their] relationship"?
5. (a) What aspects of Nora's personality are revealed in the information that she reveals to Mrs. Linde? (b) How do these aspects of her personality contrast with the impression that she conveys to her husband?
6. Krogstad arrives just as Nora is commenting that "it *is* so marvelous to live and be happy!" (a) What is the significance of this timing? (b) How do Nora's actions following Krogstad's arrival reveal that she is nervous?
7. When the children appear at the door, Torvald comments that "this place is unbearable now for anyone but mothers." (a) What does this comment suggest about his attitude toward his children? (b) What do Nora's interactions with her children suggest about her relationship with them?
8. (a) What aspects of Krogstad's personality are revealed through his interactions with Nora, and how are they revealed? (b) What seems to have been the nature of his previous relationship with Mrs. Linde? (c) What details in the first act hint at the nature of the relationship?
9. (a) What do Torvald's comments about morality reveal about his character? (b) How do his comments relate to Nora's situation? (c) What are the implications of his comments on her situation?
10. How and why did your impression of Nora change throughout the course of the first act?

Applying

11. Given the behavior of the characters during the first act, what differences can you see between our society and the society depicted in the play?
12. It has been said that people who live their lives to please others never find real happiness. Do you agree or disagree? Explain your answer.

ANALYZING LITERATURE

Understanding a Realistic Drama

Throughout much of his life, Ibsen had a strong interest in painting. While he never established any sort of reputation as a painter, he applied many of the skills used in painting to his writing. Just as many paintings capture a scene or landscape in a real and lifelike manner, Ibsen's plays depict characters and situations graphically and realistically. His emphasis on realism had a tremendous impact on the theater, shaping the direction of modern drama and influencing countless later dramatists.

1. Explain whether you think that the situation depicted in the play seems like something that would occur in real life.
2. Explain how the detailed set described in Ibsen's stage directions contributes to the play's realistic quality.
3. Nora's beloved macaroons are an example of the type of minute details that Ibsen often included in his plays. How does his inclusion of the macaroons contribute to the development of both Nora's and Torvald's character and add to the play's realism?
4. Find a passage of dialogue that you find especially realistic. Then explain how this passage resembles a real-life conversation.

THINKING AND WRITING

Writing a Dramatic Scene

Write a realistic dramatic scene involving two or more characters. Begin by brainstorming for ideas for your scene. You might want to consider basing your scene on an event or situation from your own life, and you may want to base your characters on interesting or unusual people that you have known. After you have come up with an idea for your scene, you may want to spend some time listening to conversations between other people and use these conversations as models for your dialogue. When you write your scene, focus on making the dialogue seem natural and realistic.

(continued from bottom of page)

her crime and that she would be viewed as an unfit mother.
10. Suggested response: At first she seems shallow and silly. Later, as details of her secret loan emerge, she seems clever and inventive.
11. Answers will differ. Students will probably note that women have more freedom and more opportunities in our society than in the one depicted in the play.
12. Answers will differ. Many students wil probably agree with this comment.

Challenge Nora's plight is based on an actual incident involving a young woman. How might the play's factual basis have contributed to the play's realistic quality?

ANSWERS TO ANALYZING LITERATURE

1. Answers will differ. Students may respond that it does seem like a situation that might have occurred in 1879.
2. Suggested response: The detailed set creates the impression that the action is occurring in a real place rather than on stage.
3. Suggested response: They show Nora rebelling against Torvald on a surface level. They also cover her deeper dissatisfaction and reveal Torvald as a petty tyrant.
4. Answers will differ, depending on the passage students choose.

THINKING AND WRITING

Publishing Student Writing Have students choose members of the class to play each of the roles in their scenes. Then have the students act out the scenes in front of the class.

---

that she is resourceful and self-sacrificing. (b) Suggested response: When she is with Torvald, she conveys the impression that she is helpless and extravagant.
6. (a) Suggested response: The villain arrives in the midst of apparent joy. (b) Suggested response: She whispers when she talks to Krogstad. She pumps Dr. Rank for news and giddily offers him macaroons.

7. (a) Suggested response: It suggests that he does not want to play an important role in raising them. (b) Suggested response: Her relationship with them is similar to a child's relationship with dolls.
8. (a) Suggested response: In pressuring Nora, he shows himself to be shrewd and cruel. (b) Suggested response: It seems likely that they had a romantic relationship. (c) She starts

when he introduces himself, hinting at a previous close relationship.
9. (a) Suggested response: He is rigid and self-righteous. (b) His comments apply directly to Nora because both she and Krogstad have committed forgery. (c) Suggested response: His comments imply that he would not be able to forgive her for what she did. In addition, the comments imply that she would have to be punished for

GUIDE FOR INTERPRETING

Literary Focus To emphasize the point that in drama, character is revealed solely through dialogue, actions, and appearances, you may want to stage an impromptu drama in class. Ask one student to be a police investigator looking into the question of who spray-painted "Ted loves Linda" on a local viaduct. Choose three students to be interrogated. One should be told to act arrogant and uncooperative; the second, meek and frightened; the third, calm and helpful. Have the investigator begin his or her questioning. Tell the student audience to pay close attention to the three actors being questioned. Even if their acting is mediocre, this demonstration should help to reinforce the following information about characterization in drama.

Writing/Prior Knowledge Urge students to try to remain in character while they are freewriting. They should try to be Nora, taking on both her weaknesses and her strengths.

A Doll's House, Act II

Commentary

Characterization in Drama. Characterization is the means by which a writer reveals a character's personality. In a work of fiction, a character may be developed through a variety of different methods, including direct statements about the character's personality and insights into the character's thoughts and feelings. Similarly, the verse dramas written before Ibsen's time often included soliloquies in which the characters revealed their innermost thoughts directly to the audience. In contrast, realistic prose dramas generally do not include soliloquies, because in real life people rarely recite their thoughts aloud. As a result, characters in a realistic drama must be developed through their physical appearances, comments, and actions and through other characters' remarks about them. Everything that the audience learns about the characters, including their names and occupations, must be revealed through the characters' comments, actions, and appearances. Yet the dialogue cannot be written with the sole intention of conveying details about the characters. Instead, the dialogue must seem natural and realistic, as if it were taken from real-life conversations.

As you read or view any type of drama, you begin to develop certain expectations about a character's behavior based on what you have learned about his or her personality. Before you begin reading the second act, think about what you have already learned about each of the characters, and try to determine what type of behavior you can anticipate from them in the coming acts. What actions do you think Krogstad might take against the Helmers? How will Nora attempt to solve the problem that Krogstad poses for her?

Writing

Imagine that you are in Nora's place. Then freewrite about your feelings concerning your situation and explore possible solutions to your predicament.

Primary Source

Ibsen once offered the following explanation of how he developed characters for his plays: "Before I write down one word, I have to have the character in mind through and through. I must penetrate into the last wrinkle of his soul. I always proceed from the individual; the stage setting, the dramatic ensemble, all that comes naturally and does not cause me any worry, as soon as I am certain of the individual in every aspect of his humanity. But I have to have his exterior in mind also, down to the last button, how he stands and walks, how he conducts himself, what his voice sounds like. Then I do not let him go until his fate is fulfilled."

Vocabulary

Preteach the following vocabulary words:
proclaiming (prō klām´ iŋ) v.: Announcing
intolerable (in täl´ ər ə b'l) adj.: Unbearable
impulsive (im´ pul siv) adj.: Likely to act on a sudden inclination
tactless (takt´ lis) adj.: Lacking skill in dealing with people
excruciating (iks krōō´ shē āt´ iŋ) adj.: Agonizing
retribution (ret´ rə byōō´ shən) n.: Deserved punishment for evil done
disreputable (dis rep´ yōō tə b'l) adj.: Having or causing a bad reputation

Objectives

Thematic
To understand the importance of openness and honesty

Skills
1 To understand characterization in drama
2 To make predictions
3 To recognize appropriate diction
4 To write a letter

Support Material

Teaching Portfolio
Teacher Backup, p. 1181
Grammar in Action Worksheets, *The Four Functions of Sentences*, p. 1185; *Sentence Fragments*, p. 1187
Usage and Mechanics Worksheet, p. 1189

Act II

[*Same room. Beside the piano the Christmas tree now stands stripped of ornament, burned-down candle stubs on its ragged branches.* NORA's *street clothes lie on the sofa.* NORA, *alone in the room, moves restlessly about; at last she stops at the sofa and picks up her coat.*]

NORA. [*Dropping the coat again*] Someone's coming! [*Goes toward the door, listens*] No—there's no one. Of course—nobody's coming today, Christmas Day—or tomorrow, either. But maybe—[*Opens the door and looks out*] No, nothing in the mailbox. Quite empty. [*Coming forward*] What nonsense! He won't do anything serious. Nothing terrible could happen. It's impossible. Why, I have three small children.

[ANNE-MARIE, *with a large carton, comes in from the room to the left.*]

ANNE-MARIE. Well, at last I found the box with the masquerade clothes.

NORA. Thanks. Put it on the table.

ANNE-MARIE. [*Does so*] But they're all pretty much of a mess.

NORA. Ahh! I'd love to rip them in a million pieces!

ANNE-MARIE. Oh, mercy, they can be fixed right up. Just a little patience.

NORA. Yes, I'll go get Mrs. Linde to help me.

ANNE-MARIE. Out again now? In this nasty weather? Miss Nora will catch cold—get sick.

NORA. Oh, worse things could happen—How are the children?

ANNE-MARIE. The poor mites are playing with their Christmas presents, but—

NORA. Do they ask for me much?

ANNE-MARIE. They're so used to having Mama around, you know.

NORA. Yes. But Anne-Marie, I *can't* be together with them as much as I was.

ANNE-MARIE. Well, small children get used to anything.

NORA. You think so? Do you think they'd forget their mother if she was gone for good?

ANNE-MARIE. Oh, mercy—gone for good!

NORA. Wait, tell me, Anne-Marie—I've wondered so often—how could you ever have the heart to give your child over to strangers?

ANNE-MARIE. But I had to, you know, to become little Nora's nurse.

NORA. Yes, but how could you *do* it?

ANNE-MARIE. When I could get such a good place? A girl who's poor and who's gotten in trouble is glad enough for that. Because that slippery fish, he didn't do a thing for me, you know.

NORA. But your daughter's surely forgotten you.

ANNE-MARIE. Oh, she certainly has not. She's written to me, both when she was confirmed and when she was married.

NORA. [*Clasping her about the neck*] You old Anne-Marie, you were a good mother for me when I was little.

ANNE-MARIE. Poor little Nora, with no other mother but me.

NORA. And if the babies didn't have one, then I know that you'd—What silly talk! [*Opening the carton*] Go in to them. Now I'll have to—Tomorrow you can see how lovely I'll look.

ANNE-MARIE. Oh, there won't be anyone at the party as lovely as Miss Nora. [*She goes off into the room, left.*]

NORA. [*Begins unpacking the box, but soon throws it aside*] Oh, if I dared to go out. If only nobody would come. If only nothing would happen here while I'm out. What craziness—nobody's coming. Just don't think. This muff—needs a brushing. Beautiful gloves, beautiful gloves. Let it go. Let it go! One, two, three, four, five, six— [*With a cry*] Oh, there they are! [*Poises to move toward the door, but remains irresolutely standing.* MRS. LINDE *enters*

4 Discussion Ask students why Nora has to rely on Mrs. Linde to sew her costume for her. What do these circumstances reveal about their respective personalities?

5 Enrichment Explain to students that the women of the late 1880's used roundabout language when talking about sexual matters. According to Nora, Dr. Rank's condition was inherited from his loose-living father.

6 Discussion Ask students what seems to be Nora's attitude concerning Dr. Rank's condition.

7 Discussion Have students discuss what this passage reveals about Nora's relationship with Torvald. What do they think it reveals about her relationship with Dr. Rank?

8 Discussion Ask students why Mrs. Linde suggests that Nora "put an end to all this with Dr. Rank." How does she interpret Nora's relationship with Dr. Rank? On what does she base her interpretation?

from the hall, where she has removed her street clothes.]

NORA. Oh, it's you,. Kristine. There's no one else out there? How good that you've come.

MRS. LINDE. I hear you were up asking for me.

NORA. Yes, I just stopped by. There's something you really can help me with. Let's get settled on the sofa. Look, there's going to be a costume party tomorrow evening at the Stenborgs' right above us, and now Torvald wants me to go as a Neapolitan[1] peasant girl and dance the tarantella that I learned in Capri.[2]

MRS. LINDE. Really, are you giving a whole performance?

NORA. Torvald says yes, I should. See, here's the dress. Torvald had it made for me down there; but now it's all so tattered that I just don't know—

MRS. LINDE. Oh, we'll fix that up in no time. It's nothing more than the trimmings—they're a bit loose here and there. Needle and thread? Good, now we have what we need.

NORA. Oh, how sweet of you!

MRS. LINDE. [*Sewing*] So you'll be in disguise tomorrow, Nora. You know what? I'll stop by then for a moment and have a look at you all dressed up. But listen, I've absolutely forgotten to thank you for that pleasant evening yesterday.

NORA. [*Getting up and walking about*] I don't think it was as pleasant as usual yesterday. You should have come to town a bit sooner, Kristine—Yes, Torvald really knows how to give a home elegance and charm.

MRS. LINDE. And you do, too, if you ask me. You're not your father's daughter for nothing. But tell me, is Dr. Rank always so down in the mouth as yesterday?

NORA. No, that was quite an exception. But he goes around critically ill all the time—tuberculosis of the spine, poor man. You know, his father was a

---

1. **Neapolitan** (nē′ ə päl′ ə t′n): Of Naples, a seaport in southern Italy.
2. **Capri** (ka prē′): An island near the entrance to the Bay of Naples.

---

disgusting thing who kept mistresses and so on—and that's why the son's been sickly from birth.

MRS. LINDE. [*Lets her sewing fall to her lap*] But my dearest Nora, how do you know about such things?

NORA. [*Walking more jauntily*] Hmp! When you've had three children, then you've had a few visits from—from women who know something of medicine, and they tell you this and that.

MRS. LINDE. [*Resumes sewing; a short pause*] Does Dr. Rank come here every day?

NORA. Every blessed day. He's Torvald's best friend from childhood, and *my* good friend, too. Dr. Rank almost belongs to this house.

MRS. LINDE. But tell me—is he quite sincere? I mean, doesn't he rather enjoy flattering people?

NORA. Just the opposite. Why do you think that?

MRS. LINDE. When you introduced us yesterday, he was proclaiming that he'd often heard my name in this house; but later I noticed that your husband hadn't the slightest idea who I really was. So how could Dr. Rank—?

NORA. But it's all true, Kristine. You see, Torvald loves me beyond words, and, as he puts it, he'd like to keep me all to himself. For a long time he'd almost be jealous if I even mentioned any of my old friends back home. So of course I dropped that. But with Dr. Rank I talk a lot about such things, because he likes hearing about them.

MRS. LINDE. Now listen, Nora; in many ways you're still like a child. I'm a good deal older than you, with a little more experience. I'll tell you something: you ought to put an end to all this with Dr. Rank.

NORA. What should I put an end to?

MRS. LINDE. Both parts of it, I think. Yesterday you said something about a rich admirer who'd provide you with money—

NORA. Yes, one who doesn't exist—worse luck. So?

MRS. LINDE. Is Dr. Rank well off?

NORA. Yes, he is.

Commentary

Figurative Language and Symbolism in Ibsen's Writing Ibsen first gained recognition as a poet. In fact, he was once considered Norway's leading poet. He wrote his early plays in verse, and after his "realistic period" (which included *A Doll's House*), he wrote a number of plays that some critics feel contain an excess of symbolism.

During the period in which he concentrated on prose realism, he tried to portray his characters precisely—their words, their actions, their attitudes. His literary technique at the time prevented him from using very much fig- urative language or overt symbolism, because that would have detracted from the realism. Consequently, the figures of speech in the dialogue in *A Doll's House* are mostly dead metaphors from everyday life. Torvald calls Nora a "lark," a "goose", a "squirrel," and so on. Obviously, these are the words of a narrow-minded lawyer, not of a poet. Similarly, the play's realistic quality prevents Ibsen from including many symbols, aside from Nora's beloved macaroons.

MRS. LINDE. With no dependents?

NORA. No, no one. But—?

MRS. LINDE. And he's over here every day?

NORA. Yes, I told you that.

MRS. LINDE. How can a man of such refinement be so grasping?

NORA. I don't follow you at all.

MRS. LINDE. Now don't try to hide it, Nora. You think I can't guess who loaned you the forty-eight hundred crowns?

NORA. Are you out of your mind? How could you think such a thing! A friend of ours, who comes here every single day. What an intolerable situation that would have been!

MRS. LINDE. Then it really wasn't him.

NORA. No, absolutely not. It never even crossed my mind for a moment—And he had nothing to lend in those days; his inheritance came later.

MRS. LINDE. Well, I think that was a stroke of luck for you, Nora dear.

NORA. No, it never would have occurred to me to ask Dr. Rank—Still, I'm quite sure that if I had asked him—

MRS. LINDE. Which you won't, of course.

NORA. No, of course not. I can't see that I'd ever need to. But I'm quite positive that if I talked to Dr. Rank—

MRS. LINDE. Behind your husband's back?

NORA. I've got to clear up this other thing; *that's* also behind his back. I've *got* to clear it all up.

MRS. LINDE. Yes, I was saying that yesterday, but—

NORA. [*Pacing up and down*] A man handles these problems so much better than a woman—

MRS. LINDE. One's husband does, yes.

NORA. Nonsense. [*Stopping*] When you pay everything you owe, then you get your note back, right?

MRS. LINDE. Yes, naturally.

NORA. And can rip it into a million pieces and burn it up—that filthy scrap of paper!

MRS. LINDE. [*Looking hard at her, laying her sewing aside, and rising slowly*] Nora, you're hiding something from me.

NORA. You can see it in my face?

MRS. LINDE. Something's happened to you since yesterday morning. Nora, what is it?

NORA. [*Hurrying toward her*] Kristine! [*Listening*] Shh! Torvald's home. Look, go in with the children a while. Torvald can't bear all this snipping and stitching. Let Anne-Marie help you.

MRS. LINDE. [*Gathering up some of the things*] All right, but I'm not leaving here until we've talked this out. [*She disappears into the room, left, as* TORVALD *enters from the hall.*]

NORA. Oh, how I've been waiting for you, Torvald dear.

HELMER. Was that the dressmaker?

NORA. No, that was Kristine. She's helping me fix up my costume. You know, it's going to be quite attractive.

HELMER. Yes, wasn't that a bright idea I had?

NORA. Brilliant! But then wasn't I good as well to give in to you?

HELMER. Good—because you give in to your husband's judgment? All right, you little goose, I know you didn't mean it like that. But I won't disturb you. You'll want to have a fitting, I suppose.

NORA. And you'll be working?

HELMER. Yes. [*Indicating a bundle of papers*] See. I've been down to the bank. [*Starts toward his study*]

NORA. Torvald.

HELMER. [*Stops*] Yes.

NORA. If your little squirrel begged you, with all her heart and soul, for something—?

HELMER. What's that?

NORA. Then would you do it?

HELMER. First, naturally, I'd have to know what it was.

NORA. Your squirrel would scamper about and do tricks, if you'd only be sweet and give in.

HELMER. Out with it.

NORA. Your lark would be singing high and low in every room—

HELMER. Come on, she does that anyway.

NORA. I'd be a wood nymph and dance for you in the moonlight.

HELMER. Nora—don't tell me it's that same business from this morning?

NORA. [*Coming closer*] Yes, Torvald, I beg you, please!

HELMER. And you actually have the nerve to drag that up again?

NORA. Yes, yes, you've got to give in to me; you *have* to let Krogstad keep his job in the bank.

HELMER. My dear Nora, I've slated his job for Mrs. Linde.

NORA. That's awfully kind of you. But you could just fire another clerk instead of Krogstad.

HELMER. This is the most incredible stubbornness! Because you go and give an impulsive promise to speak up for him, I'm expected to—

NORA. That's not the reason, Torvald. It's for your own sake. That man does writing for the worst papers; you said it yourself. He could do you any amount of harm. I'm scared to death of him—

HELMER. Ah, I understand. It's the old memories haunting you.

NORA. What do you mean by that?

HELMER. Of course, you're thinking about your father.

NORA. Yes, all right. Just remember how those nasty gossips wrote in the papers about Papa and slandered him so cruelly. I think they'd have had him dismissed if the department hadn't sent you up to investigate, and if you hadn't been so kind and open-minded toward him.

HELMER. My dear Nora, there's a notable difference between your father and me. Your father's official career was hardly above reproach. But mine is; and I hope it'll stay that way as long as I hold my position.

NORA. Oh, who can ever tell what vicious minds can invent? We could be so snug and happy in our quiet, carefree home—you and I and the children, Torvald! That's why I'm pleading with you so—

HELMER. And just by pleading for him you make it impossible for me to keep him on. It's already known at the bank that I'm firing Krogstad. What if it's rumored around now that the new bank manager was vetoed by his wife—

NORA. Yes, what then—?

HELMER. Oh yes—as long as our little bundle of stubbornness gets her way—! I should go and make myself ridiculous in front of the whole office—give people the idea I can be swayed by all kinds of outside pressure. Oh, you can bet I'd feel the effects of that soon enough! Besides—there's something that rules Krogstad right out at the bank as long as I'm the manager.

NORA. What's that?

HELMER. His moral failings I could maybe overlook if I had to—

NORA. Yes, Torvald, why not?

HELMER. And I hear he's quite efficient on the job. But he was a crony of mine back in my teens—one of those rash friendships that crop up again and again to embarrass you later in life. Well, I might as well say it straight out: we're on a first-name basis. And that tactless fool makes no effort at all to hide it in front of others. Quite the contrary—he thinks that entitles him to take a familiar air around me, and so every other second he comes booming out with his "Yes, Torvald!" and "Sure thing, Torvald!" I tell you, it's been excruciating for me. He's out to make my place in the bank unbearable.

NORA. Torvald, you can't be serious about all this.

HELMER. Oh no? Why not?

NORA. Because these are such petty considerations.

HELMER. What are you saying? Petty? You think I'm petty!

NORA. No, just the opposite, Torvald dear. That's exactly why—

HELMER. Never mind. You call my motives petty; then I might as well be just that. Petty! All right! We'll put a stop to this for good. [*Goes to the hall door and calls*] Helene!

NORA. What do you want?

HELMER. [*Searching among his papers*] A decision. [*The* MAID *comes in.*] Look here; take this letter; go out with it at once. Get hold of a messenger and have him deliver it. Quick now. It's already addressed. Wait, here's some money.

MAID. Yes, sir. [*She leaves with the letter.*]

HELMER. [*Straightening his papers*] There, now, little Miss Willful.

NORA. [*Breathlessly*] Torvald, what was that letter?

HELMER. Krogstad's notice.

NORA. Call it back, Torvald! There's still time. Oh, Torvald, call it back! Do it for my sake—for your sake, for the children's sake! Do you hear, Torvald; do it! You don't know how this can harm us.

HELMER. Too late.

NORA. Yes, too late.

HELMER. Nora dear, I can forgive you this panic, even though basically you're insulting me. Yes, you are! Or isn't it an insult to think that *I* should be afraid of a courtroom hack's revenge? But I forgive you anyway, because this shows so beautifully how much you love me. [*Takes her in his arms*] This is the way it should be, my darling Nora. Whatever comes, you'll see: when it really counts, I have strength and courage enough as a man to take on the whole weight myself.

NORA. [*Terrified*] What do you mean by that?

HELMER. The whole weight, I said.

NORA. [*Resolutely*] No, never in all the world.

HELMER. Good. So we'll share it, Nora, as man and wife. That's as it should be. [*Fondling her*] Are you happy now? There, there, there—not these frightened dove's eyes. It's nothing at all but emp-

16 **Literary Focus** Up to this point, Torvald has come across as a proud, stubborn, and self-righteous man. Now he appears in a worse light. It seems that what he dislikes most about Krogstad is not Krogstad's supposed moral turpitude but the fact that Krogstad addresses him by his first name in the office. In this speech, the seemingly high-minded Torvald reveals that he is actually small-minded and insecure. Apparently he has never even bothered to ask Krogstad *not* to address him familiarly. Instead, he has decided that the only solution is to fire Krogstad. Have students discuss what Torvald's manner of dealing with Krogstad reveals about Torvald's character. In addition, have them discuss the significance of Torvald's preoccupation with the way in which he is perceived by his workers.

17 **Discussion** Ask students if they are surprised that Nora questions her husband's motives. Why or why not? Do they agree with her observation that his motives are "petty"? Why or why not?

18 **Critical Thinking and Reading** Have students make predictions about what will happen now that Torvald has sent Krogstad his notice.

19 **Literary Focus** Ask students: What does the fact that Torvald sends Krogstad his notice rather than telling him in person reveal about Torvald's personality?

20 **Discussion** Have students discuss the implications of Torvald's promise. Do they think there is a chance that Torvald might "take on the whole weight" of Nora's crime? Why or why not?

ty fantasies—Now you should run through your tarantella and practice your tambourine. I'll go to the inner office and shut both doors, so I won't hear a thing; you can make all the noise you like. [*Turning in the doorway*] And when Rank comes, just tell him where he can find me. [*He nods to her and goes with his papers into the study, closing the door.*]

NORA. [*Standing as though rooted, dazed with fright, in a whisper*] He really could do it. He will do it. He'll do it in spite of everything. No, not that, never, never! Anything but that! Escape! A way out— [*The doorbell rings.*] Dr. Rank! Anything but that! *Anything*, whatever it is! [*Her hands pass over her face, smoothing it; she pulls herself together, goes over and opens the hall door.* DR. RANK *stands outside, hanging his fur coat up. During the following scene, it begins getting dark.*]

NORA. Hello, Dr. Rank. I recognized your ring. But you mustn't go in to Torvald yet; I believe he's working.

RANK. And you?

NORA. For you, I always have an hour to spare— you know that. [*He has entered, and she shuts the door after him.*]

RANK. Many thanks. I'll make use of these hours while I can.

NORA. What do you mean by that? While you can?

RANK. Does that disturb you?

NORA. Well, it's such an odd phrase. Is anything going to happen?

RANK. What's going to happen is what I've been expecting so long—but I honestly didn't think it would come so soon.

NORA. [*Gripping his arm*] What is it you've found out? Dr. Rank, you have to tell me!

RANK. [*Sitting by the stove*] It's all over with me. There's nothing to be done about it.

NORA. [*Breathing easier*] Is it you—then—?

RANK. Who else? There's no point in lying to one's self. I'm the most miserable of all my patients, Mrs.

Helmer. These past few days I've been auditing my internal accounts. Bankrupt! Within a month I'll probably be laid out and rotting in the churchyard.

NORA. Oh, what a horrible thing to say.

RANK. The thing itself is horrible. But the worst of it is all the other horror before it's over. There's only one final examination left; when I'm finished with that, I'll know about when my disintegration will begin. There's something I want to say. Helmer with his sensitivity has such a sharp distaste for anything ugly. I don't want him near my sickroom.

NORA. Oh, but Dr. Rank—

RANK. I won't have him in there. Under no condition. I'll lock my door to him— As soon as I'm completely sure of the worst, I'll send you my calling card marked with a black cross, and you'll know then the wreck has started to come apart.

NORA. No, today you're completely unreasonable. And I wanted you so much to be in a really good humor.

RANK. With death up my sleeve? And then to suffer this way for somebody else's sins. Is there any justice in that? And in every single family, in some way or another, this inevitable retribution of nature goes on—

NORA. [*Her hands pressed over her ears*] Oh, stuff! Cheer up! Please—be gay!

RANK. Yes, I'd just as soon laugh at it all. My poor, innocent spine, serving time for my father's gay army days.

NORA. [*By the table, left*] He was so infatuated with asparagus tips and *pâté de foie gras*,[3] wasn't that it?

RANK. Yes—and with truffles.

NORA. Truffles, yes. And then with oysters, I suppose?

RANK. Yes, tons of oysters, naturally.

NORA. And then the port and champagne to go with it. It's so sad that all these delectable things have to strike at our bones.

---

3. *pâté de foie gras* (pä tä´ də fwä grä´): A paste made of goose livers.

---

21 Discussion Remind students that Nora told Mrs. Linde she would never have asked Dr. Rank for the money. Given her current dilemma, do students think that she might change her mind? Why or why not? Do they think that Dr. Rank would give her the money without telling Torvald? Why or why not?

22 Discussion Ask students why Nora breathes more easily when she finds out that Dr. Rank is about to die.

23 Literary Focus Have students cite evidence to support Dr. Rank's claim that Torvald has "a sharp distaste for anything ugly."

24 Discussion Have students discuss why Dr. Rank tells Nora that he is about to die but chooses not to tell Torvald, who is supposed to be his best friend.

25 Literary Focus Have students discuss what this comment reveals about Nora's character. Do students agree with her observation that Dr. Rank is being "completely unreasonable"? Why or why not?

Grammar in Action

All sentences can be classified according to one of **four functions**: declarative, interrogative, imperative, and exclamatory. A declarative sentence states an idea and ends with a period. An interrogative sentence asks a question and ends with a question mark. An imperative sentence gives an order or a direction and ends with a period or an exclamation mark. An exclamatory sentence conveys strong emotions and ends with an exclamation mark. Note the following examples from *A Doll's House*:

She'll be my successor here in the house. (declarative)

Is anything going to happen? (interrogative)
Dr. Rank, you have to tell me! (imperative)
Anything but that! (exclamatory)

Student Activity 1. Identify each of the following sentences from the play as declarative, interrogative, imperative, or exclamatory.
1. You're my best and truest friend, I'm sure.
2. Why did you have to be so clumsy, Dr. Rank?
3. I fought to the bitter end, but nothing worked.
4. I have!

RANK. Especially when they strike at the unhappy bones that never shared in the fun.

NORA. Ah, that's the saddest of all.

RANK. [*Looks searchingly at her*] Hm.

NORA. [*After a moment*] Why did you smile?

RANK. No, it was you who laughed.

NORA. No, it was you who smiled, Dr. Rank!

RANK. [*Getting up*] You're even a bigger tease than I'd thought.

NORA. I'm full of wild ideas today.

RANK. That's obvious.

NORA. [*Putting both hands on his shoulders*] Dear, dear Dr. Rank, you'll never die for Torvald and me.

RANK. Oh, that loss you'll easily get over. Those who go away are soon forgotten.

NORA. [*Looks fearfully at him*] You believe that?

RANK. One makes new connections, and then—

NORA. Who makes new connections?

RANK. Both you and Torvald will when I'm gone. I'd say you're well under way already. What was that Mrs. Linde doing here last evening?

NORA. Oh, come—you can't be jealous of poor Kristine?

RANK. Oh yes, I am. She'll be my successor here in the house. When I'm down under, that woman will probably—

NORA. Shh! Not so loud. She's right in there.

RANK. Today as well. So you see.

NORA. Only to sew on my dress. Good gracious, how unreasonable you are. [*Sitting on the sofa*] Be nice now, Dr. Rank. Tomorrow you'll see how beautifully I'll dance; and you can imagine then that I'm dancing only for you—yes, and of course for Torvald, too—that's understood. [*Takes various items out of the carton*] Dr. Rank, sit over here and I'll show you something.

RANK. [*Sitting*] What's that?

NORA. Look here. Look.

RANK. Silk stockings.

NORA. Flesh-colored. Aren't they lovely? Now it's so dark here, but tomorrow— No, no, no, just look at the feet. Oh well, you might as well look at the rest.

RANK. Hm—

NORA. Why do you look so critical? Don't you believe they'll fit?

RANK. I've never had any chance to form an opinion on that.

NORA. [*Glancing at him a moment*] Shame on you. [*Hits him lightly on the ear with the stockings*] That's for you. [*Puts them away again*]

RANK. And what other splendors am I going to see now?

NORA. Not the least bit more, because you've been naughty. [*She hums a little and rummages among her things.*]

RANK. [*After a short silence*] When I sit here together with you like this, completely easy and open, then I don't know—I simply can't imagine—whatever would have become of me if I'd never come into this house.

NORA. [*Smiling*] Yes, I really think you feel completely at ease with us.

RANK. [*More quietly, staring straight ahead*] And then to have to go away from it all—

NORA. Nonsense, you're not going away.

RANK. [*His voice unchanged*] —and not even be able to leave some poor show of gratitude behind, scarcely a fleeting regret—no more than a vacant place that anyone can fill.

NORA. And if I asked you now for—? No—

RANK. For what?

NORA. For a great proof of your friendship—

RANK. Yes, yes?

NORA. No, I mean—for an exceptionally big favor—

RANK. Would you really, for once, make me so happy?

NORA. Oh, you haven't the vaguest idea what it is.

---

26 Discussion Have students respond to the way in which Nora is acting in this scene. Is she romantically attracted to Dr. Rank? If not, is she leading him on? Or is this just the normal manner in which she interacts with men? Is there a chance that Dr. Rank will misinterpret her behavior? Why or why not?

27 Discussion Ask students why Nora reacts fearfully to the suggestion that "those who go away are soon forgotten."

28 Enrichment This is also a good place to reemphasize the importance of Ibsen's detailed stage directions. How do students think an actress would be most likely to deliver this line if Ibsen had not included the direction, "Looks fearfully at him"?

29 Discussion Point out to students that when Nora flirts with Torvald, she usually has a favor to ask of him. Ask them if they think she has the same motive for flirting with Dr. Rank.

30 Discussion Ask students to identify the "exceptionally big favor" that Nora is about to ask of Dr. Rank.

---

5. Tear it up.

6. Are you forgetting that *I'll* be in control then over your final reputation?

7. Yes, take care of me, Torvald, please!

8. Then you're my witness that it's true, Kristine.

9. Let me practice right now; there's still time before dinner.

0. The child can have her way.

Student Activity 2. Write a brief passage of dialogue in which you use each of the four types of sentences at least once.

31 Discussion Have students discuss why Dr. Rank has suddenly decided to declare his love for Nora.

32 Discussion Have students discuss how Ibsen uses stage directions to convey Nora's reaction to Dr. Rank's declaration of love.

33 Discussion Keeping in mind that every one of Ibsen's details serves a purpose, why do students think Ibsen has the maid bring in a lamp at this point in the conversation?

34 Discussion Have students discuss why Dr. Rank's clumsy expression of love makes it impossible for Nora to ask her big favor.

35 Literary Focus Tell students that this exchange between Nora and Dr. Rank helps to develop Nora's character by revealing her hazy concept of love. She seems to be saying that she likes Dr. Rank in the way in which she liked the maids in her father's house. Yet she seems to feel bound by duty to love the person she is *supposed* to love—first her father, now her husband. Have students express their reaction to Nora's conception of love.

RANK. All right, then tell me.

NORA. No, but I can't, Dr. Rank—it's all out of reason. It's advice and help, too—and a favor—

RANK. So much the better. I can't fathom what you're hinting at. Just speak out. Don't you trust me?

NORA. Of course. More than anyone else. You're my best and truest friend, I'm sure. That's why I want to talk to you. All right, then, Dr. Rank: there's something you can help me prevent. You know how deeply, how inexpressibly dearly Torvald loves me; he'd never hesitate a second to give up his life for me.

31
32
RANK. [*Leaning close to her*] Nora—do you think he's the only one—

NORA. [*With a slight start*] Who—?

RANK. Who'd gladly give up his life for you.

NORA. [*Heavily*] I see.

RANK. I swore to myself you should know this before I'm gone. I'll never find a better chance. Yes, Nora, now you know. And also you know now that you can trust me beyond anyone else.

NORA. [*Rising, natural and calm*] Let me by.

RANK. [*Making room for her, but still sitting*] Nora—

NORA. [*In the hall doorway*] Helene, bring the lamp in. [*Goes over to the stove*] Ah, dear Dr. Rank, that was really mean of you.

RANK. [*Getting up*] That I've loved you just as deeply as somebody else? Was *that* mean?

NORA. No, but that you came out and told me. That was quite unnecessary—

33
RANK. What do you mean? Have you known—? [*The* MAID *comes in with the lamp, sets it on the table, and goes out again.*]

RANK. Nora—Mrs. Helmer—I'm asking you: have you known about it?

NORA. Oh, how can I tell what I know or don't know? Really, I don't know what to say— Why did you have to be so clumsy, Dr. Rank! Everything was so good.

RANK. Well, in any case, you now have the knowledge that my body and soul are at your command. So won't you speak out?

NORA. [*Looking at him*] After that?

RANK. Please, just let me know what it is.

NORA. You can't know anything now.

RANK. I have to. You mustn't punish me like this. Give me the chance to do whatever is humanly possible for you.

NORA. Now there's nothing you can do for me. Besides, actually, I don't need any help. You'll see—it's only my fantasies. That's what it is. Of course! [*Sits in the rocker, looks at him, and smiles*] What a nice one you are, Dr. Rank. Aren't you a little bit ashamed, now that the lamp is here?

RANK. No, not exactly. But perhaps I'd better go—for good?

NORA. No, you certainly can't do that. You must come here just as you always have. You know Torvald can't do without you.

RANK. Yes, but *you*?

NORA. You know how much I enjoy it when you're here.

RANK. That's precisely what threw me off. You're a mystery to me. So many times I've felt you'd almost rather be with me than with Helmer.

NORA. Yes—you see, there are some people that one loves most and other people that one would almost prefer being with.

RANK. Yes, there's something to that.

NORA. When I was back home, of course I loved Papa most. But I always thought it was so much fun when I could sneak down to the maids' quarters, because they never tried to improve me, and it was always so amusing, the way they talked to each other.

RANK. Aha, so it's *their* place that I've filled.

NORA. [*Jumping up and going to him*] Oh, dear, sweet Dr. Rank, that's not what I meant at all. But

---

Primary Source

Shortly before he finished writing *A Doll's House*, Ibsen received a letter from an old friend, Bjornstjerne Bjornson, that urged him to join the fight to free Norway from Swedish influence. Ibsen had no sympathy for this cause. He responded:

I have not much sympathy for symbols . . . I regard it as a sin against our people to make an issue burningly important when it is not. . . . We have only one thing which I think worth fighting for, and that is the introduction of up-to-date education for our children. . . . It is quite im-material whether our politicians bring about isolated reforms if they do not achieve liberty for the individual. . . . take away the mark of prejudice and narrow-mindedness and short-sightedness and subservience and unthinking trust in authority, so that every individual can sail under his own flag. . . .

Have students discuss what this comment reveals about Ibsen. Then have them explore how the comment relates to *A Doll's House*.

you can understand that with Torvald it's just the same as with Papa— [*The* MAID *enters from the hall.*]

MAID. Ma'am—please! [*She whispers to* NORA *and hands her a calling card.*]

NORA. [*Glancing at the card*] Ah! [*Slips it into her pocket*]

RANK. Anything wrong?

NORA. No, no, not at all. It's only some—it's my new dress—

RANK. Really? But—there's your dress.

NORA. Oh, that. But this is another one—I ordered it—Torvald mustn't know—

RANK. Ah, now we have the big secret.

NORA. That's right. Just go in with him—he's back in the inner study. Keep him there as long as—

RANK. Don't worry. He won't get away. [*Goes into the study*]

NORA. [*To the* MAID] And he's standing waiting in the kitchen?

MAID. Yes, he came up by the back stairs.

NORA. But didn't you tell him somebody was here?

MAID. Yes, but that didn't do any good.

NORA. He won't leave?

MAID. No, he won't go till he's talked with you, ma'am.

NORA. Let him come in, then—but quietly. Helene, don't breathe a word about this. It's a surprise for my husband.

MAID. Yes, yes, I understand— [*Goes out*]

NORA. This horror—it's going to happen. No, no, no, it can't happen, it mustn't. [*She goes and bolts* HELMER's *door. The* MAID *opens the hall door for* KROGSTAD *and shuts it behind him. He is dressed for travel in a fur coat, boots, and a fur cap.*] 39

NORA. [*Going toward him*] Talk softly. My husband's home.

KROGSTAD. Well, good for him.

NORA. What do you want?

KROGSTAD. Some information.

NORA. Hurry up, then. What is it?

KROGSTAD. You know, of course, that I got my notice.

NORA. I couldn't prevent it, Mr. Krogstad. I fought for you to the bitter end, but nothing worked.

KROGSTAD. Does your husband's love for you run so thin? He knows everything I can expose you to, and all the same he dares to— 40

36 **Reading Strategy** What can students infer from Nora's reaction about the identity of the visitor?

37 **Discussion** Have students explain why Nora lies to Dr. Rank. Now that Rank has declared his love for her, why does she not take him into her confidence and see if he can help her?

38 **Discussion** Have students speculate about the emotions that Dr. Rank is experiencing at this point in the play.

39 **Discussion** Have students discuss how Krogstad's clothing contributes to the play's realistic quality. Why would it be inappropriate for Krogstad to simply be wearing a pair of pants and a short-sleeved shirt?

40 **Clarification** Explain to students that Krogstad apparently assumes that Nora has told her husband about the loan. Krogstad had reasoned that Torvald, when faced with the possible revelation of Nora's crime, would retain him at the bank to avoid a scandal. Now that Krogstad has received his notice, however, he muses that Torvald must not care about what happens to Nora.

41 Reading Strategy A key question in the play is how Torvald will react if and when he learns that Nora has committed forgery. Nora thinks, or at least hopes, that he will respond nobly. Torvald has recently boasted that he has "strength and courage enough as a man to take on the whole weight [himself]." Yet Krogstad, who has known Torvald since boyhood, seems to have a lower opinion of his old friend. As students continue reading, have them pause every now and then to speculate about how Torvald will react if and when he learns of Nora's actions.

42 Discussion If Ibsen had included a stage direction prior to this line of dialogue, what do students think it would have been? Remind students that Ibsen often included adverbs describing the characters' emotions.

43 Literary Focus Have students discuss what this passage reveals about Krogstad's character. Make sure students recognize that the passage indicates that Krogstad is not the one-dimensional character he at first appeared to be.

44 Discussion Ask students to recall what it was that Krogstad just told Nora.

NORA. How can you imagine he knows anything about this?

KROGSTAD. Ah, no—I can't imagine it either, now. It's not at all like my fine Torvald Helmer to have so much guts—

NORA. Mr. Krogstad, I demand respect for my husband!

KROGSTAD. Why, of course—all due respect. But since the lady's keeping it so carefully hidden, may I presume to ask if you're also a bit better informed than yesterday about what you've actually done?

NORA. More than you ever could teach me.

KROGSTAD. Yes, I *am* such an awful lawyer.

NORA. What is it you want from me?

KROGSTAD. Just a glimpse of how you are, Mrs. Helmer. I've been thinking about you all day long. A cashier, a night-court scribbler, a—well, a type like me also has a little of what they call a heart, you know.

NORA. Then show it. Think of my children.

KROGSTAD. Did you or your husband ever think of mine? But never mind. I simply wanted to tell you that you don't need to take this thing too seriously. For the present, I'm not proceeding with any action.

NORA. Oh no, really! Well—I knew that.

KROGSTAD. Everything can be settled in a friendly spirit. It doesn't have to get around town at all; it can stay just among us three.

NORA. My husband must never know anything of this.

KROGSTAD. How can you manage that? Perhaps you can pay me the balance?

NORA. No, not right now.

KROGSTAD. Or you know some way of raising the money in a day or two?

NORA. No way that I'm willing to use.

KROGSTAD. Well, it wouldn't have done you any good, anyway. If you stood in front of me with a fistful of bills, you still couldn't buy your signature back.

NORA. Then tell me what you're going to do with it.

KROGSTAD. I'll just hold onto it—keep it on file. There's no outsider who'll even get wind of it. So if you've been thinking of taking some desperate step—

NORA. I have.

KROGSTAD. Been thinking of running away from home—

NORA. I have!

KROGSTAD. Or even of something worse—

NORA. How could you guess that?

KROGSTAD. You can drop those thoughts.

NORA. How could you guess I was thinking of *that*?

KROGSTAD. Most of us think about *that* at first. I thought about it too, but I discovered I hadn't the courage—

NORA. [*Lifelessly*] I don't either.

KROGSTAD. [*Relieved*] That's true, you haven't the courage? You too?

NORA. I don't have it—I don't have it.

KROGSTAD. It would be terribly stupid, anyway. After that first storm at home blows out, why, then—I have here in my pocket a letter for your husband—

NORA. Telling everything?

KROGSTAD. As charitably as possible.

NORA. [*Quickly*] He mustn't ever get that letter. Tear it up. I'll find some way to get money.

KROGSTAD. Beg pardon, Mrs. Helmer, but I think I just told you—

NORA. Oh, I don't mean the money I owe you. Let me know how much you want from my husband, and I'll manage it.

Grammar in Action

People often use **sentence fragments**, or incomplete sentences, in their everyday conversations. Consequently, the dialogue in a realistic prose drama is likely to be filled with sentence fragments. For example, notice the sentence fragments in the following passage of dialogue from *A Doll's House*:

KROGSTAD. I'll just hold onto it—keep it on file. There's no outsider who'll even get wind of it. *So if you've been thinking of taking some desperate step—*

NORA. I have.
KROGSTAD. *Been thinking about running away from home—*
NORA. I have!
KROGSTAD. *Or even of something worse—*

Student Activity. Identify the sentence fragments in the following passages. Then rewrite the fragments as complete sentences or combine them with other sentences in the passage.
1. NORA. Or anything else occurred—so I couldn't be present here—

KROGSTAD. I don't want any money from your husband.

NORA. What do you want, then?

KROGSTAD. I'll tell you what. I want to recoup, Mrs. Helmer; I want to get on in the world—and there's where your husband can help me. For a year and a half I've kept myself clean of anything disreputable—all that time struggling with the worst conditions; but I was satisfied, working my way up step by step. Now I've been written right off, and I'm just not in the mood to come crawling back. I tell you, I want to move on. I want to get back in the bank—in a better position. Your husband can set up a job for me—

NORA. He'll never do that!

KROGSTAD. He'll do it. I know him. He won't dare breathe a word of protest. And once I'm in there together with him, you just wait and see! Inside of a year, I'll be the manager's right-hand man. It'll be Nils Krogstad, not Torvald Helmer, who runs the bank.

NORA. You'll never see the day!

KROGSTAD. Maybe you think you can—

NORA. I have the courage now—for *that*.

KROGSTAD. Oh, you don't scare me. A smart, spoiled lady like you—

NORA. You'll see; you'll see!

KROGSTAD. Under the ice, maybe? Down in the freezing, coal-black water? There, till you float up in the spring, ugly, unrecognizable, with your hair falling out—

NORA. You don't frighten me.

KROGSTAD. Nor do you frighten me. One doesn't do these things, Mrs. Helmer. Besides, what good would it be? I'd still have him safe in my pocket.

NORA. Afterwards? When I'm no longer—?

KROGSTAD. Are you forgetting that *I'll* be in control then over your final reputation? [NORA *stands speechless, staring at him.*] Good; now I've warned you. Don't do anything stupid. When Helmer's

read my letter, I'll be waiting for his reply. And bear in mind that it's your husband himself who's forced me back to my old ways. I'll never forgive him for that. Good-bye, Mrs. Helmer. [*He goes out through the hall.*]

NORA. [*Goes to the hall door, opens it a crack, and listens*] He's gone. Didn't leave the letter. Oh no, no, that's impossible too! [*Opening the door more and more*] What's that? He's standing outside—not going downstairs. He's thinking it over? Maybe he'll—? [*A letter falls in the mailbox; then* KROGSTAD's *footsteps are heard, dying away down a flight of stairs.* NORA *gives a muffled cry and runs over toward the sofa table. A short pause.*] In the mailbox. [*Slips warily over to the hall door*] It's lying there. Torvald, Torvald—now we're lost!

MRS. LINDE. [*Entering with the costume from the room, left*] There now, I can't see anything else to mend. Perhaps you'd like to try—

NORA. [*In a hoarse whisper*] Kristine, come here.

MRS. LINDE. [*Tossing the dress on the sofa*] What's wrong? You look upset.

NORA. Come here. See that letter? *There!* Look—through the glass in the mailbox.

MRS. LINDE. Yes, yes, I see it.

NORA. That letter's from Krogstad—

MRS. LINDE. Nora—it's Krogstad who loaned you the money!

NORA. Yes, and now Torvald will find out everything.

MRS. LINDE. Believe me, Nora, it's best for both of you.

NORA. There's more you don't know. I forged a name.

MRS. LINDE. But for heaven's sake—?

NORA. I only want to tell you that, Kristine, so that you can be my witness.

MRS. LINDE. Witness? Why should I—?

NORA. If I should go out of my mind—it could easily happen—

45 **Literary Focus** Make sure students realize that even Krogstad, the villain, is a complex character. Ask students if any of them sympathize with Krogstad's plight. Why or why not?

46 **Clarification** Call students' attention to the fact that Krogstad's demands are escalating. At this point, he will no longer be satisfied with his previous position at the bank—he wants to be Torvald's "right-hand man."

47 **Discussion** Have students explain why Krogstad is not scared by Nora's threat. Does he really believe there is a chance that she will follow through with her threat?

48 **Discussion** Do students agree that Helmer has, in fact, "forced [Krogstad] back to [his] old ways"? Why or why not? What does Krogstad's comment reveal about his character? Does he really have anyone other than himself to blame for his misfortune? Why or why not?

49 **Discussion** Have students discuss why Mrs. Linde thinks it is better for both Nora and Torvald if Torvald finds out everything. Do students agree with this assessment? Why or why not?

2. NORA. Yes, take care of me, Torvald, please! Promise me that? Oh, I'm so nervous. That big party—You must give up everything this evening for me. No business—don't even touch your pen. Yes? Dear Torvald, promise?

3. HELMER. It's a promise. Tonight I'm totally at your service—you little helpless thing. Hm—but first there's one thing I want to—

4. NORA. Look here. Look.
RANK. Silk stockings.
NORA. Flesh-colored. Aren't they lovely? Now it's so dark here, but to-

morrow— No, no, no, just look at the feet. Oh well, you might as well look at the rest.

5. RANK. And what other splendors am I going to see now?
NORA. Not the least bit more, because you've been naughty.

50 Discussion Ask students why Nora tells Mrs. Linde to remember that "nobody else has known about this." Whom is she trying to protect?

51 Discussion Have your students guess what Nora means when she says that a "miracle" is going to take place.

52 Discussion Have students explain what this line suggests about Mrs. Linde's previous relationship with Krogstad. Why do they think that Ibsen waits so long to disclose the nature of their relationship?

53 Discussion Ask students what Torvald was expecting to find in the living room. Why does Nora first seem unaware that his expectations have not been met?

54 Discussion Have students discuss why it is easy for Nora to convince Torvald that she is nervous about the party.

MRS. LINDE. Nora!

NORA. Or anything else occurred—so I couldn't be present here—

MRS. LINDE. Nora, Nora, you aren't yourself at all!

NORA. And someone should try to take on the whole weight, all of the guilt, you follow me—

MRS. LINDE. Yes, of course, but why do you think—?

50 NORA. Then you're my witness that it isn't true, Kristine. I'm very much myself; my mind right now is perfectly clear; and I'm telling you: nobody else has known about this; I alone did everything. Remember that.

MRS. LINDE. I will. But I don't understand all this.

NORA. Oh, how could you ever understand it? It's the miracle now that's going to take place.

51 MRS. LINDE. The miracle?

NORA. Yes, the miracle. But it's so awful, Kristine. It mustn't take place, not for anything in the world.

MRS. LINDE. I'm going right over and talk with Krogstad.

NORA. Don't go near him; he'll do you some terrible harm!

52 MRS. LINDE. There was a time once when he'd gladly have done anything for me.

NORA. He?

MRS. LINDE. Where does he live?

NORA. Oh, how do I know? Yes. [*Searches in her pocket*] Here's his card. But the letter, the letter—!

HELMER. [*From the study, knocking on the door*] Nora!

NORA. [*With a cry of fear*] Oh! What is it? What do you want?

HELMER. Now, now, don't be so frightened. We're not coming in. You locked the door—are you trying on the dress?

NORA. Yes, I'm trying it. I'll look just beautiful, Torvald.

MRS. LINDE. [*Who has read the card*] He's living right around the corner.

NORA. Yes, but what's the use? We're lost. The letter's in the box.

MRS. LINDE. And your husband has the key?

NORA. Yes, always.

MRS. LINDE. Krogstad can ask for his letter back unread; he can find some excuse—

NORA. But it's just this time that Torvald usually—

MRS. LINDE. Stall him. Keep him in there. I'll be back as quick as I can. [*She hurries out through the hall entrance.*]

NORA. [*Goes to* HELMER'*s door, opens it, and peers in*] Torvald!

HELMER. [*From the inner study*] Well—does one dare set foot in one's own living room at last? Come on, Rank, now we'll get a look— [*In the doorway*] But what's this?

NORA. What, Torvald dear?

HELMER. Rank had me expecting some grand masquerade.

RANK. [*In the doorway*] That was my impression, but I must have been wrong.

NORA. No one can admire me in my splendor—not till tomorrow.

HELMER. But Nora, dear, you look so exhausted. Have you practiced too hard?

NORA. No, I haven't practiced at all yet.

HELMER. You know, it's necessary—

NORA. Oh, it's absolutely necessary, Torvald. But I can't get anywhere without your help. I've forgotten the whole thing completely.

HELMER. Ah, we'll soon take care of that.

NORA. Yes, take care of me, Torvald, please! Promise me that? Oh, I'm so nervous. That big party— You must give up everything this evening for me. No business—don't even touch your pen. Yes? Dear Torvald, promise?

HELMER. It's a promise. Tonight I'm totally at your service—you little helpless thing. Hm—but first there's one thing I want to— [*Goes toward the hall door*]

NORA. What are you looking for?

HELMER. Just to see if there's any mail.

NORA. No, no, don't do that, Torvald!

HELMER. Now what?

NORA. Torvald, please. There isn't any.

HELMER. Let me look, though. [*Starts out.* NORA, *at the piano, strikes the first notes of the tarantella.* HELMER, *at the door, stops.*] Aha!

NORA. I can't dance tomorrow if I don't practice with you.

HELMER. [*Going over to her*] Nora dear, are you really so frightened?

NORA. Yes, so terribly frightened. Let me practice right now; there's still time before dinner. Oh, sit down and play for me, Torvald. Direct me. Teach me, the way you always have.

HELMER. Gladly, if it's what you want. [*Sits at the piano*]

NORA. [*Snatches the tambourine up from the box, then a long, varicolored shawl, which she throws around herself, whereupon she springs forward and cries out*] Play for me now! Now I'll dance! [HELMER *plays and* NORA *dances.* RANK *stands behind* HELMER *at the piano and looks on.*]

HELMER. [*As he plays*] Slower. Slow down.

NORA. Can't change it.

HELMER. Not so violent, Nora!

NORA. Has to be just like this.

HELMER. [*Stopping*] No, no, that won't do at all.

NORA. [*Laughing and swinging her tambourine*] Isn't that what I told you?

RANK. Let me play for her.

HELMER. [*Getting up*] Yes, go on. I can teach her more easily then. [RANK *sits at the piano and plays;*

NORA *dances more and more wildly.* HELMER *has stationed himself by the stove and repeatedly gives her directions; she seems not to hear them; her hair loosens and falls over her shoulders; she does not notice, but goes on dancing.* MRS. LINDE *enters.*]

MRS. LINDE. [*Standing dumbfounded at the door*] Ah—!

NORA. [*Still dancing*] See what fun, Kristine!

HELMER. But Nora darling, you dance as if your life were at stake.

NORA. And it is.

HELMER. Rank, stop! This is pure madness. Stop it, I say! [RANK *breaks off playing, and* NORA *halts abruptly.*]

HELMER. [*Going over to her*] I never would have believed it. You've forgotten everything I taught you.

NORA. [*Throwing away the tambourine*] You see for yourself.

HELMER. Well, there's certainly room for instruction here.

NORA. Yes, you see how important it is. You've got to teach me to the very last minute. Promise me that, Torvald?

HELMER. You can bet on it.

NORA. You mustn't, either today or tomorrow, think about anything else but me; you mustn't open any letters—or the mailbox—

HELMER. Ah, it's still the fear of that man—

NORA. Oh yes, yes, that too.

HELMER. Nora, it's written all over you—there's already a letter from him out there.

NORA. I don't know. I guess so. But you mustn't read such things now; there mustn't be anything ugly between us before it's all over.

RANK. [*Quietly to* HELMER] You shouldn't deny her.

HELMER. [*Putting his arm around her*] The child can have her way. But tomorrow night, after you've danced—

58

55 Enrichment Point out to students that this is a classic example of dramatic irony. Readers and viewers are well aware that Nora is frightened by the implications of Krogstad's letter. Torvald, however, thinks she is frightened by the prospect of performing the tarantella the following evening.

56 Enrichment Tell students that the dancing of the tarantella is a highly charged moment in the play. Prior to this point, there has been little physical action in the play. Now it springs into violent physical motion. The initial purpose of her dance is to stop Torvald from looking in his mailbox. Yet as she gets into the dance, she uses the intense physical activity to release some of her pent-up emotions. In addition, this wild dancing, which "won't do at all" (according to Torvald), has the desirable side effect (from Nora's standpoint) of making Torvald come to the conclusion that he has much to teach Nora.

57 Discussion Ask students: If the tarantella has become Nora's "dance of death," as she now believes, why is it ironic that Dr. Rank plays the music for her?

58 Literary Focus Point out to students that when Torvald observes that Nora is dancing as if her life were at stake, Nora responds that "it is." Yet Torvald is so self-centered and self-absorbed that he either ignores or fails to register his wife's remark. Instead of following up on her dramatic statement, his only observation is that she has "forgotten everything [he] taught [her]."

59 Discussion Have students respond to this sudden change in Nora's disposition. What does this change suggest about Nora's emotional state?

60 Discussion Ask students why Nora tells Mrs. Linde that she should not have left a note for Krogstad. What is the miracle to which she refers?

61 Discussion Ask students if Nora's observation that she has "thirty-one hours to live" should be taken literally. Why or why not?

62 Critical Thinking and Reading Now that students have finished the second act, have them make predictions about the outcome of the play.

Cooperative Learning Divide students into small groups. Then have each group act out a scene from the play. Urge students to read their lines as expressively as possible, following Ibsen's stage directions. Point out that this exercise should help to remind them that plays are meant to be seen, not read.

NORA. Then you'll be free.

MAID. [*In the doorway, right*] Ma'am, dinner is served.

NORA. We'll be wanting champagne, Helene.

MAID. Very good, ma'am. [*Goes out*]

HELMER. So—a regular banquet, hm?

NORA. Yes, a banquet—champagne till daybreak! [*Calling out*] And some macaroons, Helene. Heaps of them—just this once.

HELMER. [*Taking her hands*] Now, now, now—no hysterics. Be my own little lark again.

NORA. Oh, I will soon enough. But go on in—and you, Dr. Rank. Kristine, help me put up my hair.

RANK. [*Whispering, as they go*] There's nothing wrong—really wrong, is there?

HELMER. Oh, of course not. It's nothing more than this childish anxiety I was telling you about. [*They go out, right.*]

NORA. Well?

MRS. LINDE. Left town.

NORA. I could see by your face.

MRS. LINDE. He'll be home tomorrow evening. I wrote him a note.

NORA. You shouldn't have. Don't try to stop anything now. After all, it's a wonderful joy, this waiting here for the miracle.

MRS. LINDE. What is it you're waiting for?

NORA. Oh, you can't understand that. Go in to them; I'll be along in a moment. [MRS. LINDE *goes into the dining room.* NORA *stands a short while as if composing herself; then she looks at her watch.*]

NORA. Five. Seven hours to midnight. Twenty-four hours to the midnight after, and then the tarantella's done. Seven and twenty-four? Thirty-one hours to live.

HELMER. [*In the doorway, right*] What's become of the little lark?

NORA. [*Going toward him with open arms*] Here's your lark!

Reader's Response *If you were Nora, what would you do about the predicament at this point?*

THINKING ABOUT THE SELECTION

Interpreting

1. How does the condition of the Christmas tree at the beginning of the second act relate to the developments in the characters' lives?
2. (a) What is the significance of Nora's openly questioning whether her children would forget her if she were "gone for good"? (b) What later event might her question foreshadow, or hint at?
3. What later event might be foreshadowed by Dr. Rank's comment: "Those who go away are soon forgotten"?
4. (a) In what way does Dr. Rank's condition parallel Nora's situation? (b) How does Rank's condition parallel Krogstad's situation? (c) What options are available to Nora and Krogstad that are unavailable to Rank?
5. (a) How would you characterize Nora's relationship with Dr. Rank? (b) How would you describe her relationship with Anne-Marie? (c) What do Rank and Anne-Marie offer her that her husband does not?
6. (a) What is the significance of the fact that it begins to get dark during Nora's conversation with Rank? (b) What does the lamp that the maid brings into the room symbolize, or represent?
7. Why does Nora cover her ears when Rank speaks of suffering for the sins of his father?
8. Why does Nora decide not to ask Rank for the money?
9. (a) What is Krogstad's attitude toward Torvald? (b) How is his attitude conveyed?

Closure and Extension

ANSWERS TO THINKING ABOUT THE SELECTION

1. Suggested response: The tree is "stripped of ornaments," as the lives of the main characters are being stripped of pretense.
2. (a) Suggested response: It indicates that she thinks there is a real possibility that her children will be forced to do without her. (b) It hints at the fact that she may leave home, or even take her own life.
3. Nora might "go away."
4. (a) Suggested response: Nora's emotional decay parallels Dr. Rank's physical deterioration. In addition, Rank's imminent death parallels the imminent collapse of Nora's marriage. (b) Suggested response: Dr. Rank's imminent death parallels the imminent collapse of Krogstad's world. (c) Answers will differ. Students may suggest that Krogstad can look for another job and that Nora can tell Torvald the truth and hope he understands.
5. (a) Answers will differ. Students might respond that they have a platonic relationship based on mutual understanding and trust. (b) Answers will differ. Students may respond that Nora views Anne-Marie as a trusted friend. (c) Suggested response: She can be herself with Rank and Anne-Marie and can talk openly to both of them.
6. (a) Suggested response: Both characters are headed for a type of darkness. In addition, a low level of light can foster romance. (b) Answers will differ. Students might suggest that the light symbolizes the end to Nora's il-

10. What is ironic about Torvald's comment that Nora dances "as if [her] life were at stake"?
11. What might be the "miracle" for which Nora says she is waiting? Explain your answer.

Applying

12. What do you think that you might learn about personal relationships from the problems facing Nora and Torvald?
13. (a) For which characters in the play do you have the most sympathy? Why? (b) Which characters do you find distasteful? Why?
14. How do you react to Nora's comment that "there are some people that one loves most and other people that one would almost prefer to be with"? Explain.

ANALYZING LITERATURE

Understanding Characterization

In modern dramas, such as *A Doll's House*, characters are generally developed through dialogue, action, and physical appearance. Although they may be regarded as an element of a character's appearance or behavior, it is worth noting that personal possessions, such as Nora's macaroons, may also play a minor role in character development.
1. What is revealed about Torvald's personality through his explanation of his decision to fire Krogstad and his refusal to reconsider his decision?
2. What seems to be Torvald's main concern in life? Support your answer.
3. How does Torvald's main concern contrast with Nora's primary concern?
4. How would you characterize Nora based on her comments and actions in the first two acts?
5. (a) How would you characterize Dr. Rank? (b) How is his personality conveyed?

CRITICAL THINKING AND READING

Making Predictions

After reading the first two acts of *A Doll's House*, you should be able to make some predictions about the outcome of the play based on what you have already learned about the characters and their situations.

For each of the following items, support your prediction with details from the first two acts.
1. How will Torvald react if he reads Krogstad's letter?
2. How will Torvald's reaction affect Nora and Torvald's marriage?
3. What will become of Dr. Rank?
4. What will become of Krogstad and Mrs. Linde?

UNDERSTANDING LANGUAGE

Recognizing Appropriate Diction

In a realistic drama, the **diction,** or the writer's choice of words, must be appropriate for the characters. For example, it would be inappropriate to have uneducated people speak in elaborate, elevated language. However, this type of language would be suitable for a group of scholars.
1. How would you describe the language used by the characters in *A Doll's House*?
2. Explain why this type of language is appropriate for these characters.
3. How does the language used add to the realism of the play?

THINKING AND WRITING

Writing a Letter

Imagine that a friend who has never read or seen *A Doll's House* has asked you whether you would recommend the play. After reading the first two acts, how would you respond to your friend's question? Once you have reached a decision, write a letter to your friend in which you offer a recommendation about whether he or she should or should not read or see the play. Support your recommendation by explaining whether you find the characters interesting and the events compelling. When you have finished writing, revise your letter, making sure you have clearly conveyed your opinion of the first two acts and have offered a thorough explanation of your opinion.

(continued from bottom of page)
2. Suggested response: He wants to be the picture-perfect businessman, husband, and father. He wants to be in complete control, as shown by his petty rules for Nora and his real reason for firing Krogstad.
3. Suggested response: Nora wants some control over her life, but Torvald wants her to be completely dependent on him.
4. Suggested response: Nora acts like two different people. With Torvald, she plays the role of the helpless squirrel and the happy lark. With others, she seems like a normal, free-willed, yet naive, individual.
5. (a) Suggested response: Dr. Rank seems like a pleasant, rather shy man of good sense and broad experience. (b) It is conveyed through his comments and actions.

Challenge What are the similarities and differences between Mrs. Linde's personality and Nora's personality?

ANSWERS TO CRITICAL THINKING AND READING

1. Answers will differ. Students are likely to predict that he will be furious.
2. Answers will differ. Students might predict that it will ruin their marriage.
3. Suggested response: He will die.
4. Answers will differ. Students might predict that they will resume their previous relationship.

ANSWERS TO UNDERSTANDING LANGUAGE

1. Suggested response: It is the informal language of educated people at the time.
2. Suggested response: The characters are educated and intelligent, and they speak in an intelligent manner for the most part.
3. Suggested response: The language mirrors the way in which people really speak.

THINKING AND WRITING

Publishing Student Writing Have students read their letters to the class.

lusion that her relationship with Rank is a childlike friendship.
7. Nora is worried about contaminating her children.
8. Suggested response: His declaration of love destroys her illusion of their relationship as one of childlike friends.
9. (a) He has little respect for Torvald. (b) His attitude is conveyed through his comments and actions.
10. Her life is at stake.

11. Answers will differ. Students might suggest she is hoping that Torvald will forgive her and will stand up for her.
12. Answers will differ. Students might note that their problems highlight the importance of honesty and communication.
13. (a) Answers will differ. Many students will probably name Nora. (b) Answers will differ. Many students will probably name Krogstad and Torvald.

14. Answers will differ. Many students will probably observe that people should like to be with the ones they love the most.

ANSWERS TO ANALYZING LITERATURE

1. Suggested response: He is more concerned about maintaining a respectable image for himself than he is about fairness.

Commentary

A Doll's House, Act III

Theme. The **theme** is the central idea or insight into life that a writer hopes to convey in a work of literature. In some literary works, the theme is directly stated. More often, however, the theme is implied, or revealed indirectly, through the portrayal of characters and events or through the use of literary devices such as irony, symbols, or allusions.

Longer literary works, such as plays and novels, are likely to have many possible themes; and disagreements frequently arise among readers and critics as to the theme or themes of a particular literary work. These disagreements result because writers often deliberately make their works ambiguous, or indefinite or uncertain, and because every reader's interpretation of a work is colored by his or her viewpoint or perspective. For example, someone who is especially concerned with women's rights might interpret *A Doll's House* as an expression of the need for women to escape from the confinement and restriction they faced in nineteenth-century European society.

This is only one of many possible themes of *A Doll's House.* Another theme is that in order for a marriage to be successful, the people involved should know and trust each other, should view each other as equals, and should have separate identities. Related to this idea is the theme that true love has little to do with such superficial qualities as physical beauty and financial and social status. Still another theme is that people are often faced with, as Ibsen put it, an internal conflict between "natural feeling on the one hand and belief in authority on the other." A related theme is the notion that society and authority place restrictions on people that inhibit the development of individuality. This idea is connected to another possible theme that Ibsen himself suggested when he described his plays as the depiction of "the struggle which all serious-minded human beings have to wage with themselves to bring their lives into harmony with their convictions." Finally, the play also suggests that it is wrong to try to apply a rigid moral code to all situations and that people who claim to adhere to such a moral code sometimes expose themselves as hypocrites.

As you read the third act, pay close attention to how each of these themes is conveyed through the comments and actions of the characters. Also look for other possible themes and note how each of these themes is revealed.

Writing

It is one thing to talk at a person and quite another to talk to a person. Freewrite about the difference using examples from Act I and Act II.

Literary Focus Before discussing the themes of *A Doll's House*, you may want to discuss the theme of a current movie that many students have seen. Choose a serious movie for the discussion—one that deals with serious problems or issues. Have each student who has seen the movie write his or her interpretation of its theme on a piece of paper. Then collect the papers and list the suggested themes on the chalkboard. Finally, have the class offer details from the movie to support each of the various interpretations.

Writing/Prior Knowledge Before students begin their freewriting, you might ask them to give examples from television shows of situations in which people talk "at" each other and situations in which they talk "to" each other.

ESL Teaching Strategy ESL students may have difficulty in seeing the distinction between talking "at" a person and talking "to" a person. Consequently, you may want to gather your ESL students and take time to explain this distinction to them.

Vocabulary

Preteach the following vocabulary words:

calculating (kal´ kyo͞o lāt iŋ) *adj.*: Shrewd or cunning

evasions (i vā´ zhənz) *n.*: Attempts to avoid duties or questions

naturalistic (nach´ ər ə lis´ tik) *adj.*: In accordance with, or in imitation of, nature

proprieties (prə prī´ ə tēz) *n.*: The qualities of being fitting, proper, or suitable

hypocrite (hip´ ə krit) *n.*: A person who pretends to be what he or she is not

grafter (graft´ ər) *n.*: Someone who takes advantage of his or her position to gain money or property

bewildered (bi wil´ dərd) *v.*: Puzzled

Objectives

To recognize the need for a person to establish a sense of individuality

Skills

1 To recognize the themes of the play

2 To appreciate the importance of casting

3 To write about theme

Support Material

Teaching Portfolio

Teacher Backup, p. 1195

Grammar in Action Worksheets, *Directions*, p. 1199; *Rhetorical and Direct Questions*, p. 1201

Usage and Mechanics Worksheet, p. 1203

Vocabulary Check, p. 1204

Act III

[*Same scene. The table, with chairs around it, has been moved to the center of the room. A lamp on the table is lit. The hall door stands open. Dance music drifts down from the floor above.* MRS. LINDE *sits at the table, absently paging through a book, trying to read, but apparently unable to focus her thoughts. Once or twice she pauses, tensely listening for a sound at the outer entrance.*]

MRS. LINDE. [*Glancing at her watch*] Not yet—and there's hardly any time left. If only he's not—[*Listening again*] Ah, there he is. [*She goes out in the hall and cautiously opens the outer door. Quiet footsteps are heard on the stairs. She whispers*] Come in. Nobody's here.

KROGSTAD. [*In the doorway*] I found a note from you at home. What's back of all this?

MRS. LINDE. I just *had* to talk to you.

KROGSTAD. Oh? And it just *had* to be here in this house?

MRS. LINDE. At my place it was impossible; my room hasn't a private entrance. Come in; we're all alone. The maid's asleep, and the Helmers are at the dance upstairs.

KROGSTAD. [*Entering the room*] Well, well, the Helmers are dancing tonight? Really?

MRS. LINDE. Why not?

KROGSTAD. How true—why not?

MRS. LINDE. All right, Krogstad, let's talk.

KROGSTAD. Do we two have anything more to talk about?

MRS. LINDE. We have a great deal to talk about.

KROGSTAD. I wouldn't have thought so.

MRS. LINDE. No, because you've never understood me, really.

KROGSTAD. Was there anything more to understand—except what's all too common in life? A calculating woman throws over a man the moment a better catch comes by.

MRS. LINDE. You think I'm so thoroughly calculating? You think I broke it off lightly?

KROGSTAD. Didn't you?

MRS. LINDE. Nils—is that what you really thought?

KROGSTAD. If you cared, then why did you write me the way you did?

MRS. LINDE. What else could I do? If I had to break off with you, then it was my job as well to root out everything you felt for me.

KROGSTAD. [*Wringing his hands*] So that was it. And this—all this, simply for money!

MRS. LINDE. Don't forget I had a helpless mother and two small brothers. We couldn't wait for you, Nils; you had such a long road ahead of you then.

KROGSTAD. That may be; but you still hadn't the right to abandon me for somebody else's sake.

MRS. LINDE. Yes—I don't know. So many, many times I've asked myself if I did have that right.

KROGSTAD. [*More softly*] When I lost you, it was as if all the solid ground dissolved from under my feet. Look at me; I'm a half-drowned man now, hanging onto a wreck.

MRS. LINDE. Help may be near.

KROGSTAD. It was near—but then you came and blocked it off.

MRS. LINDE. Without my knowing it, Nils. Today for the first time I learned that it's you I'm replacing at the bank.

KROGSTAD. All right—I believe you. But now that you know, will you step aside?

MRS. LINDE. No, because that wouldn't benefit you in the slightest.

KROGSTAD. Not "benefit" me, hm! I'd step aside anyway.

MRS. LINDE. I've learned to be realistic. Life and hard, bitter necessity have taught me that.

KROGSTAD. And life's taught me never to trust fine phrases.

3 **Discussion** Ask students what Mrs. Linde seems to be suggesting. Has she invited Krogstad to the Helmers' apartment in order to propose? If so, do students find these circumstances surprising? Why or why not?

4 **Discussion** Have students discuss Mrs. Linde's response to Krogstad's question. Does she answer it directly? Indirectly? Explain.

5 **Discussion** Do students interpret this as a proposal of marriage? If so, do they think that Krogstad will accept? Why or why not?

6 **Literary Focus** Call students' attention to the contrast between the rebirth of Krogstad and Mrs. Linde's relationship and the potential demise of Nora and Helmer's relationship. How might this relate to one of the themes of the play?

7 **Literary Focus** Ask students whether Mrs. Linde's comment could be applied to Nora. Then have them consider how Mrs. Linde's observation might reflect one of the themes of the play.

MRS. LINDE. Then life's taught you a very sound thing. But you do have to trust in actions, don't you?

KROGSTAD. What does that mean?

MRS. LINDE. You said you were hanging on like a half-drowned man to a wreck.

KROGSTAD. I've good reason to say that.

MRS. LINDE. I'm also like a half-drowned woman on a wreck. No one to suffer with; no one to care for.

KROGSTAD. You made your choice.

MRS. LINDE. There wasn't any choice then.

KROGSTAD. So—what of it?

MRS. LINDE. Nils, if only we two shipwrecked people could reach across to each other.

KROGSTAD. What are you saying?

MRS. LINDE. Two on one wreck are at least better off than each on his own.

KROGSTAD. Kristine!

MRS. LINDE. Why do you think I came into town?

KROGSTAD. Did you really have some thought of me?

MRS. LINDE. I have to work to go on living. All my born days, as long as I can remember, I've worked, and it's been my best and my only joy. But now I'm completely alone in the world; it frightens me to be so empty and lost. To work for yourself—there's no joy in that. Nils, give me something—someone to work for.

KROGSTAD. I don't believe all this. It's just some hysterical feminine urge to go out and make a noble sacrifice.

MRS. LINDE. Have you ever found me to be hysterical?

KROGSTAD. Can you honestly mean this? Tell me—do you know everything about my past?

MRS. LINDE. Yes.

KROGSTAD. And you know what they think I'm worth around here.

MRS. LINDE. From what you were saying before, it would seem that with me you could have been another person.

KROGSTAD. I'm positive of that.

MRS. LINDE. Couldn't it happen still?

KROGSTAD. Kristine—you're saying this in all seriousness? Yes, you are! I can see it in you. And do you really have the courage, then—?

MRS. LINDE. I need to have someone to care for; and your children need a mother. We both need each other. Nils, I have faith that you're good at heart—I'll risk everything together with you.

KROGSTAD. [*Gripping her hands*] Kristine, thank you, thank you— Now I know I can win back a place in their eyes. Yes—but I forgot—

MRS. LINDE. [*Listening*] Shh! The tarantella. Go now! Go on!

KROGSTAD. Why? What is it?

MRS. LINDE. Hear the dance up there? When that's over, they'll be coming down.

KROGSTAD. Oh, then I'll go. But—it's all pointless. Of course, you don't know the move I made against the Helmers.

MRS. LINDE. Yes, Nils, I know.

KROGSTAD. And all the same, you have the courage to—?

MRS. LINDE. I know how far despair can drive a man like you.

KROGSTAD. Oh, if I only could take it all back.

MRS. LINDE. You easily could—your letter's still lying in the mailbox.

KROGSTAD. Are you sure of that?

MRS. LINDE. Positive. But—

KROGSTAD. [*Looks at her searchingly*] Is that the meaning of it, then? You'll save your friend at any price. Tell me straight out. Is that it?

MRS. LINDE. Nils—anyone who's sold herself for somebody else once isn't going to do it again.

Grammar in Action

When writing **stage directions,** a playwright must use simple, direct language that is easy to follow. In addition, the directions must be presented in a logical order. For example, in the following directions Ibsen uses a combination of chronological order and spatial order:

[She picks up her hat and coat. NORA'S and HELMER'S voices can be heard outside; a key turns in the lock, and HELMER brings NORA into the hall almost by force. She is wearing the Italian costume with a large black shawl about her; he has on evening dress, with a black domino over it.]

Student Activity 1. Imagine that you are a playwright and you want to stage a play in a room resembling your room at home. Write a set of stage directions describing the appearance of your room. Make your directions as simple and clear as possible. Yet make sure to include as many specific details as possible.

Student Activity 2. The guidelines for writing stage directions can also be applied to other types of directions. Write a set of directions that explain how to get from your home to your school. Make sure to use simple and straightforward language and to present your directions in a logical order.

KROGSTAD. I'll demand my letter back.

MRS. LINDE. No, no.

KROGSTAD. Yes, of course. I'll stay here till Helmer comes down; I'll tell him to give me my letter again—that it only involves my dismissal—that he shouldn't read it—

MRS. LINDE. No, Nils, don't call the letter back.

KROGSTAD. But wasn't that exactly why you wrote me to come here?

MRS. LINDE. Yes, in that first panic. But it's been a whole day and night since then, and in that time I've seen such incredible things in this house. Helmer's got to learn everything; this dreadful secret has to be aired; those two have to come to a full understanding; all these lies and evasions can't go on.

KROGSTAD. Well, then, if you want to chance it. But at least there's one thing I can do, and do right away—

MRS. LINDE. [Listening] Go now, quick! The dance is over. We're not safe another second.

KROGSTAD. I'll wait for you downstairs.

MRS. LINDE. Yes, please do; take me home.

KROGSTAD. I can't believe it; I've never been so happy. [He leaves by way of the outer door; the door between the room and the hall stays open.]

MRS. LINDE. [Straightening up a bit and getting together her street clothes] How different now! How different! Someone to work for, to live for—a home to build. Well, it is worth the try! Oh, if they'd only come! [Listening] Ah, there they are. Bundle up. [She picks up her hat and coat. NORA's and HELMER's voices can be heard outside; a key turns in the lock, and HELMER brings NORA into the hall almost by force. She is wearing the Italian costume with a large black shawl about her; he has on evening dress, with a black domino open over it.]

NORA. [Struggling in the doorway] No, no, no, not inside! I'm going up again. I don't want to leave so soon.

HELMER. But Nora dear—

NORA. Oh, I beg you, please, Torvald. From the bottom of my heart, *please*—only an hour more! 11

HELMER. Not a single minute, Nora darling. You know our agreement. Come on, in we go; you'll catch cold out here. [*In spite of her resistance, he gently draws her into the room.*]

MRS. LINDE. Good evening.

NORA. Kristine!

HELMER. Why, Mrs. Linde—are you here so late?

MRS. LINDE. Yes, I'm sorry, but I did want to see Nora in costume.

NORA. Have you been sitting here, waiting for me?

MRS. LINDE. Yes. I didn't come early enough; you were all upstairs; and then I thought I really couldn't leave without seeing you.

8 **Discussion** Make sure students realize that this is a pivotal development. Krogstad has agreed to demand his letter. Surprisingly, however, Mrs. Linde tells him not to. Have students discuss why Krogstad is now willing to withdraw his letter, and have them speculate about why Mrs. Linde has told him not to. Are students surprised by these developments? Why or why not?

9 **Discussion** Have students discuss Mrs. Linde's conclusion that "this dreadful secret has to be aired." Do they feel that she is right? Why or why not?

10 **Clarification** This is Krogstad's last appearance on stage. During this scene he has undergone an amazingly rapid transformation from a miserable man whose life is about to collapse to someone who has "never been so happy." Many critics have objected to this transformation. One calls Krogstad "the only exonerated blackmailer [he] can think of in fiction." You may want to elicit students' reactions to this abrupt shift in Krogstad's character. Do they find it believable? Why or why not?

11 **Discussion** Have students discuss why Nora so desperately wants to remain at the party.

12 Discussion Torvald's speech is a marvel of self-revelation. Point out to students that while Torvald observes that Nora's tarantella "overstepped the proprieties of art," he feels that it does not matter "because she made it an overwhelming success." Have students discuss what Torvald's remark says about his real values as opposed to his expressed values.

13 Discussion Torvald's remark that "an exit should always be effective" is an example of both irony and foreshadowing. Not only does this comment foreshadow Nora's exit at the end of the play, but it is ironic because Nora's exit contradicts Torvald's observation that Nora cannot "grasp" the importance of an effective exit. When students have finished reading the play, have them look back at this passage and discuss Ibsen's use of irony and foreshadowing.

14 Discussion At first reading, this conversation about knitting and embroidery seems to be superfluous. Yet it actually serves an important purpose, revealing essential information about Torvald's character and the Helmers' relationship. Have students discuss how Torvald's remarks indicate that he prefers appearance over substance. Then discuss the impact of this preference on the Helmers' relationship.

15 Discussion Have students respond to Torvald's unflattering characterization of Mrs. Linde. Do they agree with him? Why or why not? Do they feel that this characterization could be applied to Torvald himself? Why or why not?

HELMER. [*Removing* NORA's *shawl*] Yes, take a good look. She's worth looking at, I can tell you that, Mrs. Linde. Isn't she lovely?

MRS. LINDE. Yes, I should say—

HELMER. A dream of loveliness, isn't she? That's what everyone thought at the party, too. But she's horribly stubborn—this sweet little thing. What's to be done with her? Can you imagine, I almost had to use force to pry her away.

NORA. Oh, Torvald, you're going to regret you didn't indulge me, even for just a half hour more.

HELMER. There, you see. She danced her tarantella and got a tumultuous[1] hand—which was well earned, although the performance may have been a bit too naturalistic—I mean it rather overstepped the proprieties of art. But never mind—what's important is, she made a success, an overwhelming success. You think I could let her stay on after that and spoil the effect? Oh no; I took my lovely little Capri girl—my capricious[2] little Capri girl, I should say—took her under my arm; one quick tour of the ballroom, a curtsy to every side, and then—as they say in novels—the beautiful vision disappeared. An exit should always be effective, Mrs. Linde, but that's what I can't get Nora to grasp. Phew, its hot in here. [*Flings the domino on a chair and opens the door to his room*] Why's it dark in here? Oh, yes, of course. Excuse me. [*He goes in and lights a couple of candles.*]

NORA. [*In a sharp, breathless whisper*] So?

MRS. LINDE. [*Quietly*] I talked with him.

NORA. And—?

MRS. LINDE. Nora—you must tell your husband everything.

NORA. [*Dully*] I knew it.

MRS. LINDE. You've got nothing to fear from Krogstad, but you have to speak out.

NORA. I won't tell.

---

1. **tumultuous** (tōō mult′ chōō wəs) *adj.*: Wild and noisy.
2. **capricious** (kə prish′ əs) *adj.*: Erratic; flighty.

MRS. LINDE. Then the letter will.

NORA. Thanks, Kristine. I know now what's to be done. Shh!

HELMER. [*Reentering*] Well, then, Mrs. Linde—have you admired her?

MRS. LINDE. Yes, and now I'll say good night.

HELMER. Oh, come, so soon? Is this yours, this knitting?

MRS. LINDE. Yes, thanks. I nearly forgot it.

HELMER. Do you knit, then?

MRS. LINDE. Oh yes.

HELMER. You know what? You should embroider instead.

MRS. LINDE. Really? Why?

HELMER. Yes, because it's a lot prettier. See here, one holds the embroidery so, in the left hand, and then one guides the needle with the right—so—in an easy, sweeping curve—right?

MRS. LINDE. Yes, I guess that's—

HELMER. But, on the other hand, knitting—it can never be anything but ugly. Look, see here, the arms tucked in, the knitting needles going up and down, there's something Chinese about it. Ah, that was really a glorious champagne they served.

MRS. LINDE. Yes, goodnight, Nora, and don't be stubborn anymore.

HELMER. Well put, Mrs. Linde!

MRS. LINDE. Good night, Mr. Helmer.

HELMER. [*Accompanying her to the door*] Good night, good night. I hope you get home all right. I'd be very happy to—but you don't have far to go. Good night, good night. [*She leaves. He shuts the door after her and returns.*] There, now, at last we got her out the door. She's a deadly bore, that creature.

NORA. Aren't you pretty tired, Torvald?

HELMER. No, not a bit.

NORA. You're not sleepy?

Primary Source

In his book *Ibsen and Shaw*, Keith M. May discusses the significance of Nils Krogstad and Kristine Linde:

Krogstad's role is plainly necessary, for by sending his letter to Torvald (the letter which languishes in the locked box in the hall and which Torvald is detained from reading by Nora's desperate tarantella) he precipitates the final disclosures and Nora's metamorphosis. But apart from that Krogstad is an interesting and indeed necessary figure of frustration and embitterment, the perfect though surprising partner for Mrs. Linde.

In addition to aiding the mechanics of the plot these two enrich the theme, for they have both suffered in humiliating ways, as the relatively comfortable Helmers have not. At the end there is an appropriate kind of ripening for them both. . . . There is a touch of seediness about both of them: the self-sacrificing, mildly represented Mrs. Linde, plain as well as spirited; Krogstad hitherto steeped in malice. And they come together *tragically,* which is to say with no higher hopes for a happy future than their pasts will allow.

HELMER. Not at all. On the contrary, I'm feeling quite exhilarated. But you? Yes, you really look tired and sleepy.

NORA. Yes, I'm very tired. Soon now I'll sleep.

HELMER. See! You see! I was right all along that we shouldn't stay longer.

NORA. Whatever you do is always right.

HELMER. [*Kissing her brow*] Now my little lark talks sense. Say, did you notice what a time Rank was having tonight?

NORA. Oh, was he? I didn't get to speak with him.

HELMER. I scarcely did either, but it's a long time since I've seen him in such high spirits. [*Gazes at her a moment, then comes nearer her*] Hm—it's marvelous, though, to be back home again—to be completely alone with you. Oh, you bewitchingly lovely young woman.

NORA. Torvald, don't look at me like that!

HELMER. Can't I look at my richest treasure? At all that beauty that's mine, mine alone—completely and utterly.

NORA. [*Moving around to the other side of the table*] You mustn't talk to me that way tonight.

HELMER. [*Following her*] The tarantella is still in your blood, I can see—and it makes you even more enticing. Listen. The guests are beginning to go. [*Dropping his voice*] Nora—it'll soon be quiet through this whole house.

NORA. Yes, I hope so.

HELMER. You do, don't you, my love? Do you realize—when I'm out at a party like this with you—do you know why I talk to you so little, and keep such a distance away; just send you a stolen look now and then—you know why I do it? It's because I'm imagining then that you're my secret darling, my secret young bride-to-be, and that no one suspects there's anything between us.

NORA. Yes, yes; oh, yes, I know you're always thinking of me.

HELMER. And then when we leave and I place the shawl over those fine young rounded shoulders—over that wonderful curving neck—then I pretend that you're my young bride, that we're just coming from the wedding, that for the first time I'm bringing you into my house—that for the first time I'm alone with you—completely alone with you, your trembling young beauty! All this evening I've longed for nothing but you. When I saw you turn and sway in the tarantella—my blood was pounding till I couldn't stand it—that's why I brought you down here so early—

NORA. Go away, Torvald! Leave me alone. I don't want all this.

HELMER. What do you mean? Nora, you're teasing me. You will, won't you? Aren't I your husband—? [*A knock at the outside door*]

NORA. [*Startled*] What's that?

HELMER. [*Going toward the hall*] Who is it?

RANK. [*Outside*] It's me. May I come in a moment?

HELMER. [*With quiet irritation*] Oh, what does he want now? [*Aloud*] Hold on. [*Goes and opens the door*] Oh, how nice that you didn't just pass us by!

RANK. I thought I heard your voice, and then I wanted so badly to have a look in. [*Lightly glancing about*] Ah, me, these old familiar haunts. You have it snug and cozy in here, you two.

HELMER. You seemed to be having it pretty cozy upstairs, too.

RANK. Absolutely. Why shouldn't I? Why not take in everything in life? As much as you can, anyway, and as long as you can. The wine was superb—

HELMER. The champagne especially.

RANK. You noticed that too? It's amazing how much I could guzzle down.

NORA. Torvald also drank a lot of champagne this evening.

RANK. Oh?

NORA. Yes, and that always makes him so entertaining.

16 Enrichment Some critics have observed that Torvald can almost be viewed as a caricature. Throughout the play he lacks even a hint of self-awareness. No amount of flattery from Nora ever seems too much for him. In his own eyes he is the perfect husband, which means that with regard to his wife, he is infallible. Most twentieth-century European husbands on hearing the line, "Whatever you do is always right," would suspect sarcasm. Torvald, on the other hand, replies, "Now my little lark talks sense." Have students respond to these lines. Do they know any people as pompous and self-righteous as Torvald?

17 Discussion During her earlier conversation with Dr. Rank, Nora began to see the physical nature, or physically exploitive nature, of her relationship with Torvald. This aspect of their relationship comes to the forefront in this scene. Have students discuss Torvald's advances and Nora's reactions. Does this exchange make Torvald seem more human? Or does it merely reinforce the picture of him as egotistical and insensitive?

18 **Clarification** Make sure students recognize that Dr. Rank's reference to "certainty" indicates that he is about to die.

19 **Discussion** Have students discuss the irony of Torvald's comment in light of Dr. Rank's physical condition.

20 **Discussion** Nora knows that Dr. Rank will die before the next masquerade party. She is also aware of the likelihood that she will not be at the next party either (though Rank does not know it). Given this information, what do students think her purpose is in asking this question?

21 **Discussion** Have students discuss whether Torvald, who is aware of Dr. Rank's poor health, should take Rank's suggested costume as an indication of Rank's imminent death rather than as a "funny idea." Given Torvald's behavior up to this point, are they surprised that he is oblivious to Dr. Rank's hints about his approaching death? Why or why not?

RANK. Well, why shouldn't one have a pleasant evening after a well-spent day?

HELMER. Well spent? I'm afraid I can't claim that.

RANK. [*Slapping him on the back*] But I can, you see!

NORA. Dr. Rank, you must have done some scientific research today.

RANK. Quite so.

HELMER. Come now—little Nora talking about scientific research!

NORA. And can I congratulate you on the results?

RANK. Indeed you may.

NORA. Then they were good?

RANK. The best possible for both doctor and patient—certainty.

NORA. [*Quickly and searchingly*] Certainty?

RANK. Complete certainty. So don't I owe myself a gay evening afterwards?

NORA. Yes, you're right, Dr. Rank.

HELMER. I'm with you—just so long as you don't have to suffer for it in the morning.

RANK. Well, one never gets something for nothing in life.

NORA. Dr. Rank—are you very fond of masquerade parties?

RANK. Yes, if there's a good array of odd disguises—

NORA. Tell me, what should we two go as at the next masquerade?

HELMER. You little featherhead—already thinking of the next!

RANK. We two? I'll tell you what: you must go as Charmed Life—

HELMER. Yes, but find a costume for *that*!

RANK. Your wife can appear just as she looks every day.

HELMER. That was nicely put. But don't you know what you're going to be?

RANK. Yes, Helmer, I've made up my mind.

HELMER. Well?

RANK. At the next masquerade I'm going to be invisible.

HELMER. That's a funny idea.

RANK. They say there's a hat—black, huge—have you never heard of the hat that makes you invisible? You put it on, and then no one on earth can see you.

HELMER. [*Suppressing a smile*] Ah, of course.

RANK. But I'm quite forgetting what I came for. Helmer, give me a cigar, one of the dark Havanas.

Primary Source

The critic John Northam has explored the parallels between Nora's "moral disease" and Dr. Rank's physical disease:

Ibsen also emphasizes the climax of the disease and death theme by bringing on Rank. Nora has danced her tarantella at the party upstairs—her last fling. At the same party, Rank has enjoyed his last fling—at the champagne—before retiring to his deathbed. The last link which Ibsen forges between the two victims of poison and corruption is that their death warrants share the same letterbox: Rank leaves behind him a visiting card marked with a black cross, a sign that he has crawled away to die; the card lies beside Korgstad's letter to Torvald, and when Torvald reads that, Nora must die so as not to inflict her moral disease on others; physical and moral corruptions are to burn themselves out together.

HELMER. With the greatest pleasure. [*Holds out his case*]

RANK. Thanks. [*Takes one and cuts off the tip*]

NORA. [*Striking a match*] Let me give you a light.

RANK. Thank you. [*She holds the match for him; he lights the cigar.*] And now good-bye.

HELMER. Good-bye, good-bye, old friend.

NORA. Sleep well, Doctor.

RANK. Thanks for that wish.

NORA. Wish me the same.

RANK. You? All right, if you like— Sleep well. And thanks for the light. [*He nods to them both and leaves.*]

HELMER. [*His voice subdued*] He's been drinking heavily.

NORA. [*Absently*] Could be. [HELMER *takes his keys from his pocket and goes out in the hall.*] Torvald—what are you after?

HELMER. Got to empty the mailbox; it's nearly full. There won't be room for the morning papers.

NORA. Are you working tonight?

HELMER. You know I'm not. Why—what's this? Someone's been at the lock.

NORA. At the lock—?

HELMER. Yes, I'm positive. What do you suppose—? I can't imagine one of the maids—? Here's a broken hairpin. Nora, it's yours—

NORA. [*Quickly*] Then it must be the children.

HELMER. You'd better break them of that. Hm, hm—well, opened it after all. [*Takes the contents out and calls into the kitchen*] Helene! Helene, would you put out the lamp in the hall? [*He returns to the room, shutting the hall door, then displays the handful of mail.*] Look how it's piled up. [*Sorting through them*] Now what's this?

NORA. [*At the window*] The letter! Oh, Torvald, no!

HELMER. Two calling cards—from Rank.

NORA. From Dr. Rank?

HELMER. [*Examining them*] "Dr. Rank, Consulting Physician." They were on top. He must have dropped them in as he left.

NORA. Is there anything on them?

HELMER. There's a black cross over the name. See? That's a gruesome notion. He could almost be announcing his own death.

NORA. That's just what he's doing.

HELMER. What! You've heard something? Something he's told you?

NORA. Yes. That when those cards came, he'd be taking his leave of us. He'll shut himself in now and die.

HELMER. Ah, my poor friend! Of course I knew he wouldn't be here much longer. But so soon— And then to hide himself away like a wounded animal.

NORA. If it has to happen, then it's best it happens in silence—don't you think so, Torvald?

HELMER. [*Pacing up and down*] He'd grown right into our lives. I simply can't imagine him gone. He with his suffering and loneliness—like a dark cloud setting off our sunlit happiness. Well, maybe it's best this way. For him, at least. [*Standing still*] And maybe for us too, Nora. Now we're thrown back on each other completely. [*Embracing her*] Oh you, my darling wife, how can I hold you close enough? You know what, Nora—time and again I've wished you were in some terrible danger, just so I could stake my life and soul and everything for your sake.

NORA. [*Tearing herself away, her voice firm and decisive*] Now you must read your mail, Torvald.

HELMER. No, no, not tonight. I want to stay with you, dearest.

NORA. With a dying friend on your mind?

HELMER. You're right. We've both had a shock. There's ugliness between us—these thoughts of death and corruption. We'll have to get free of them first. Until then—we'll stay apart.

22 Clarification Point out to students that Nora, knowing that Dr. Rank is about to die, tells him to "sleep well." He thanks her for this final good-bye, but is puzzled when Nora tells him to "wish [her] the same." Have students explain the significance of Nora's request.

23 Discussion Have students discuss what the light might symbolize.

24 Discussion Ask students if they recall any prior reference to Nora using a hairpin on the mailbox lock. Does it seem reasonable that Nora would have tried to pick the lock? Why or why not? Why does she blame it on the children? (After all, Torvald already knows that she is frightened of the contents of Krogstad's letter.)

25 Discussion Ask students if they are surprised that Torvald does not have a stronger reaction to the news of Dr. Rank's imminent death. Why or why not?

26 Discussion Have students discuss the irony of Torvald's comment that Dr. Rank was "like a dark cloud setting off [their] sunlit happiness."

27 Enrichment Point out to students that in his own mind, Torvald is a hero. He declares that he has often "wished that [Nora] were in some terrible danger, just so [he] could stake [his] life and soul and everything for [her] sake." By now, however, the audience suspects that this is just romantic bravado. Yet Nora vainly hopes for a "miracle"—she hopes that Torvald will follow through on his heroic declarations. Given new hope by Torvald's lofty words, she tears herself away from him and insists that he read his mail.

28 Reading Strategy Now that Torvald is about to read his mail, have students pause to predict his reaction to the letter. Did his declaration of the desire to save Nora from "some terrible danger" change their expectations concerning his reaction? Why or why not?

29 Clarification Make sure students recognize what Nora is contemplating at this point.

30 Discussion Where do students think that Nora is trying to go? On what do they base their answer?

NORA. [*Clinging about his neck*] Torvald—good night! Good night!

HELMER. [*Kissing her on the cheek*] Good night, little songbird. Sleep well, Nora. I'll be reading my mail now. [*He takes the letters into his room and shuts the door after him.*]

NORA. [*With bewildered glances, groping about, seizing* HELMER*'s domino, throwing it around her, and speaking in short, hoarse, broken whispers*] Never see him again. Never, never. [*Putting her shawl over her head*] Never see the children either—them, too. Never, never. Oh, the freezing black water! The depths—down— Oh, I wish it were over— He has it now; he's reading it—now. Oh no, no, not yet. Torvald, good-bye, you and the children— [*She starts for the hall; as she does,* HELMER *throws open his door and stands with an open letter in his hand.*]

HELMER. Nora!

NORA. [*Screams*] Oh—!

HELMER. What is this? You know what's in this letter?

NORA. Yes, I know. Let me go! Let me out!

HELMER. [*Holding her back*] Where are you going?

Primary Source

Rolf Fjelde's translation of *A Doll's House* is so clear and colloquial that a reader can easily forget it is a translation. Not every translation is as good as Fjelde's, however. A short time ago, a Danish schoolteacher published an English translation of the play that shows how far a translator can go astray. Note the following passages:

NORA. Don't utter such stupid shuffles . . . From this moment it depends no longer on felicity; it depends on saving the rests, remnants, and the appearance.

. . .

NORA. As I am now, I am no wife to you.
HELMER. I have power to grow another.

. . .

HELMER. Change yourself in such a manner that —
NORA. — that cohabitation between you and me might become a matrimony. Good-bye.

Have students contrast these passages with the corresponding passages from Fjelde's translation. Then have them discuss what the passages

NORA. [*Struggling to break loose*] You can't save me, Torvald!

HELMER. [*Slumping back*] True! Then it's true what he writes? How horrible! No, no it's impossible—it can't be true.

NORA. It *is* true. I've loved you more than all this world.

HELMER. Ah, none of your slippery tricks.

NORA. [*Taking one step toward him*] Torvald—!

HELMER. What *is* this you've blundered into!

NORA. Just let me loose. You're not going to suffer for my sake. You're not going to take on my guilt.

HELMER. No more playacting. [*Locks the hall door*] You stay right here and give me a reckoning. You understand what you've done? Answer! You understand?

NORA. [*Looking squarely at him, her face hardening*] Yes. I'm beginning to understand everything now.

HELMER. [*Striding about*] Oh, what an awful awakening! In all these eight years—she who was my pride and joy—a hypocrite, a liar—worse, worse—a criminal! How infinitely disgusting it all is! The shame! [*NORA says nothing and goes on looking straight at him. He stops in front of her.*] I should have suspected something of the kind. I should have known. All your father's flimsy values— Be still! All your father's flimsy values have come out in you. No religion, no morals, no sense of duty— Oh, how I'm punished for letting him off! I did it for your sake, and you repay me like this.

NORA. Yes, like this.

HELMER. Now you've wrecked all my happiness—ruined my whole future. Oh, it's awful to think of. I'm in a cheap little grafter's hands; he can do anything he wants with me, ask for anything, play with me like a puppet—and I can't breathe a word. I'll be swept down miserably into the depths on account of a featherbrained woman.

NORA. When I'm gone from this world, you'll be free.

HELMER. Oh, quit posing. Your father had a mess of those speeches too. What good would that ever do me if you were gone from this world, as you say? Not the slightest. He can still make the whole thing known; and if he does, I could be falsely suspected as your accomplice. They might even think that I was behind it—that I put you up to it. And all that I can thank you for—you that I've coddled the whole of our marriage. Can you see now what you've done to me?

NORA. [*Icily calm*] Yes.

HELMER. It's so incredible, I just can't grasp it. But we'll have to patch up whatever we can. Take off the shawl. I said, take it off! I've got to appease him somehow or other. The thing has to be hushed up at any cost. And as for you and me, it's got to seem like everything between us is just as it was—to the outside world, that is. You'll go right on living in this house, of course. But you can't be allowed to bring up the children; I don't dare trust you with them— Oh, to have to say this to someone I've loved so much! Well, that's done with. From now on happiness doesn't matter; all that matters is saving the bits and pieces, the appearance— [*The doorbell rings.* HELMER *starts.*] What's that? And so late. Maybe the worst—? You think he'd—? Hide, Nora! Say you're sick. [NORA *remains standing motionless.* HELMER *goes and opens the door.*]

MAID. [*Half dressed, in the hall*] A letter for Mrs. Helmer.

HELMER. I'll take it. [*Snatches the letter and shuts the door*] Yes, it's from him. You don't get it; I'm reading it myself.

NORA. Then read it.

HELMER. [*By the lamp*] I hardly dare. We may be ruined, you and I. But—I've got to know. [*Rips open the letter, skims through a few lines, glances at an enclosure, then cries out joyfully.*] Nora! [NORA *looks inquiringly at him.*] Nora! Wait!—better check it again— Yes, yes, it's true. I'm saved. Nora, I'm saved!

31 **Clarification** Point out to students that Nora and Torvald are talking at cross purposes here. Nora is accepting her guilt and telling Torvald that he need not try to redeem her. Torvald, on the other hand, has no thought of trying to redeem her. His only concern is for himself.

32 **Discussion** Have students discuss the irony of Torvald's demand, "No more playacting." Then have them discuss the meaning of Nora's answer, noting the stage directions that precede it.

33 **Discussion** Have students discuss what this passage reveals about Torvald and his feelings for Nora. Would he attack her in this manner if he really loved her? Why does he fail to ask her questions about the reasons for her actions? Would an explanation from Nora help her cause? Why or why not?

34 **Discussion** Have students discuss what Torvald's declaration that he "can't breathe a word" reveals about his character. If he truly possesses the lofty values that he claims to, would he choose this course of action? Why or why not?

35 **Discussion** Have your students respond to Torvald's proposed solution to the problem.

36 **Enrichment** Tell students that in an earlier draft of the play, this line read, "We're saved! Nora, we're saved." In revising his play, however, Ibsen changed the line to "I'm saved. Nora, I'm saved!" Have students discuss the significance of this revision.

reveal about the difficulties involved in translating literature from one language to another.

37 **Discussion** Have students discuss how they interpret Nora's "frozen look." Do they agree with Torvald's interpretation?

38 **Clarification** Modern audiences may feel that Torvald's obtuseness is overdrawn. Could he, they wonder, really believe that he should be forgiving Nora at this point rather than asking her to forgive him? Students should remember that the world has changed dramatically since the play was written. Consequently, although Torvald's behavior may seem unrealistic today, it was very realistic at the time the play was written. In fact, Laura Kieler, the real-life model for Nora, had been committed to an insane asylum by her husband after a series of events similar to those in Ibsen's play.

39 **Reading Strategy** Have students predict what will follow Nora's uncharacteristic demand: "Sit down . . . I have a lot to say."

40 **Discussion** Have students explain what Nora means when she says, "We're closing our accounts, Torvald." Why is her choice of words especially appropriate?

NORA. And I?

HELMER. You too, of course. We're both saved, both of us. Look. He's sent back your note. He says he's sorry and ashamed—that a happy development in his life—oh, who cares what he says! Nora, we're saved! No one can hurt you. Oh, Nora, Nora—but first, this ugliness all has to go. Let me see— [*Takes a look at the note*] No, I don't want to see it; I want the whole thing to fade like a dream. [*Tears the note and both letters to pieces, throws them into the stove and watches them burn*] There—now there's nothing left— He wrote that since Christmas Eve you— Oh, they must have been three terrible days for you, Nora.

NORA. I fought a hard fight.

HELMER. And suffered pain and saw no escape but— No, we're not going to dwell on anything unpleasant. We'll just be grateful and keep on repeating: it's over now, it's over! You hear me, Nora? You don't seem to realize—it's over. What's it mean—that frozen look? Oh, poor little Nora, I understand. You can't believe I've forgiven you. But I have Nora; I swear I have. I know that what you did, you did out of love for me.

NORA. That's true.

HELMER. You loved me the way a wife ought to love her husband. It's simply the means that you couldn't judge. But you think I love you any the less for not knowing how to handle your affairs? No, no—just lean on me; I'll guide you and teach you. I wouldn't be a man if this feminine helplessness didn't make you twice as attractive to me. You mustn't mind those sharp words I said—that was all in the first confusion of thinking my world had collapsed. I've forgiven you, Nora; I swear I've forgiven you.

NORA. My thanks for your forgiveness. [*She goes out through the door, right.*]

HELMER. No, wait— [*Peers in*] What are you doing in there?

NORA. [*Inside*] Getting out of my costume.

HELMER. [*By the open door*] Yes, do that. Try to calm yourself and collect your thoughts again, my frightened little songbird. You can rest easy now; I've got wide wings to shelter you with. [*Walking about close by the door*] How snug and nice our home is, Nora. You're safe here; I'll keep you like a hunted dove I've rescued out of a hawk's claws. I'll bring peace to your poor, shuddering heart. Gradually it'll happen, Nora; you'll see. Tomorrow all this will look different to you; then everything will be as it was. I won't have to go on repeating I forgive you; you'll feel it for yourself. How can you imagine I'd ever conceivably want to disown you—or even blame you in any way? Ah, you don't know a man's heart, Nora. For a man there's something indescribably sweet and satisfying in knowing he's forgiven his wife—and forgiven her out of a full and open heart. It's as if she belongs to him in two ways now: in a sense he's given her fresh into the world again, and she's become his wife and his child as well. From now on that's what you'll be to me—you little, bewildered, helpless thing. Don't be afraid of anything, Nora; just open your heart to me, and I'll be conscience and will to you both— [NORA *enters in her regular clothes.*] What's this? Not in bed? You've changed your dress?

NORA. Yes, Torvald, I've changed my dress.

HELMER. But why now, so late?

NORA. Tonight I'm not sleeping.

HELMER. But Nora dear—

NORA. [*Looking at her watch*] It's still not so very late. Sit down, Torvald; we have a lot to talk over. [*She sits at one side of the table.*]

HELMER. Nora—what is this? That hard expression—

NORA. Sit down. This'll take some time. I have a lot to say.

HELMER. [*Sitting at the table directly opposite her*] You worry me, Nora. And I don't understand you.

NORA. No, that's exactly it. You don't understand me. And I've never understood you either—until tonight. No, don't interrupt. You can just listen to what I say. We're closing out accounts, Torvald.

Grammar in Action

Rhetorical questions are questions that are not intended to be answered orally. Yet, because listeners generally will try to answer these questions in their minds, the questions force them to think actively about what is being said. **Direct questions**, on the other hand, are questions that are expected to be answered. Because people frequently use rhetorical questions and direct questions in everyday speech, both types of questions are often used in realistic prose plays. Note the following examples from *A Doll's House*:

RHETORICAL QUESTIONS:
How can you imagine I'd ever conceivably want to disown you—or even blame you in any way?
But you think I love you any the less for not knowing how to handle your affairs?

DIRECT QUESTIONS:
But why now, so late?
Doesn't anything strike you about our sitting here like this?

HELMER. How do you mean that?

NORA. [*After a short pause*] Doesn't anything strike you about our sitting here like this?

HELMER. What's that?

NORA. We've been married now eight years. Doesn't it occur to you that this is the first time we two, you and I, man and wife, have ever talked seriously together?

HELMER. What do you mean—seriously?

NORA. In eight whole years—longer even—right from our first acquaintance, we've never exchanged a serious word on any serious thing.

HELMER. You mean I should constantly go and involve you in problems you couldn't possibly help me with?

NORA. I'm not talking of problems. I'm saying that we've never sat down seriously together and tried to get to the bottom of anything.

HELMER. But dearest, what good would that ever do you?

NORA. That's the point right there: you've never understood me. I've been wronged greatly, Torvald—first by Papa, and then by you.

HELMER. What! By us—the two people who've loved you more than anyone else?

NORA. [*Shaking her head*] You never loved me. You've thought it fun to be in love with me, that's all.

HELMER. Nora, what a thing to say!

NORA. Yes, it's true now, Torvald. When I lived at home with Papa, he told me all his opinions, so I had the same ones too; or if they were different I hid them, since he wouldn't have cared for that. He used to call me his doll-child, and he played with me the way I played with my dolls. Then I came into your house—

HELMER. How can you speak of our marriage like that?

NORA. [*Unperturbed*] I mean, then I went from Papa's hands into yours. You arranged everything to your own taste, and so I got the same taste as you—or I pretended to; I can't remember. I guess a little of both, first one, then the other. Now when I look back, it seems as if I'd lived here like a beggar—just from hand to mouth. I've lived by doing tricks for you, Torvald. But that's the way you wanted it. It's a great sin what you and Papa did to me. You're to blame that nothing's become of me.

HELMER. Nora, how unfair and ungrateful you are! Haven't you been happy here?

NORA. No, never. I thought so—but I never have.

HELMER. Not—not happy!

NORA. No, only lighthearted. And you've always been so kind to me. But our home's been nothing but a playpen. I've been your doll-wife here, just as at home I was Papa's doll-child. And in turn the children have been my dolls. I thought it was fun when you played with me, just as they thought it fun when I played with them. That's been our marriage, Torvald.

HELMER. There's some truth in what you're saying—under all the raving exaggeration. But it'll all be different after this. Playtime's over; now for the schooling.

NORA. Whose schooling—mine or the children's?

HELMER. Both yours and the children's, dearest.

NORA. Oh, Torvald, you're not the man to teach me to be a good wife to you.

HELMER. And you can say that?

NORA. And I—how am I equipped to bring up children?

HELMER. Nora!

NORA. Didn't you say a moment ago that that was no job to trust me with?

HELMER. In a flare of temper! Why fasten on that?

NORA. Yes, but you were so very right. I'm not up to the job. There's another job I have to do first. I have to try to educate myself. You can't help me with that. I've got to do it alone. And that's why I'm leaving you now.

41 **Discussion** Ask students if it is entirely Torvald's fault that they have "never exchanged a serious word on any serious thing." Why or why not? Could Nora have insisted on having this conversation eight years earlier?

42 **Discussion** Do students feel that the play has established the truth of Nora's claims—that she was wronged by both her father and Torvald, and that she is not loved by Torvald? Why or why not?

43 **Discussion** Ask students to identify the most recent "trick" that Nora has performed for Torvald.

44 **Literary Focus** Have students discuss the major themes of the play as reflected in this passage. Also ask them how this passage helps to explain the play's title.

45 **Discussion** How do students react to Nora's conclusion that she is unequipped to bring up children? What does she lack? Do students find Nora's reasoning persuasive? If so, what qualities must a mother possess to bring up children properly? Do students think there is any chance that the children might be better off without her? Why or why not?

Student Activity. Identify each of the questions in the following passages as a rhetorical question or a direct question.

1. NORA. What do you think are my most sacred vows?
   HELMER. I have to tell you that! Aren't they your duties to your husband and children?
   NORA. I have other duties equally sacred.
   HELMER. That isn't true. What duties are they?
2. HELMER. Why can't you understand your place in your own home? On a point like that, isn't there one everlasting guide you can turn to? Where's your religion?
   NORA. Oh, Torvald, I'm not really sure what religion is.
3. HELMER. A young woman your age shouldn't talk like that. If religion can't move you, I can try to rouse your conscience. You do have some moral feeling? Or, tell me—has that gone too?
   NORA. It's not easy to answer that. . . .

HELMER. [*Jumping up*] What's that?

NORA. I have to stand completely alone, if I'm ever going to discover myself and the world out there. So I can't go on living with you.

HELMER. Nora, Nora!

NORA. I want to leave right away. Kristine should put me up for the night—

HELMER. You're insane! You've no right! I forbid you!

NORA. From here on, there's no use forbidding me anything. I'll take with me whatever is mine. I don't want a thing from you, either now or later.

HELMER. What kind of madness is this?

NORA. Tomorrow I'm going home—I mean, home where I came from. It'll be easier up there to find something to do.

HELMER. Oh, you blind, incompetent child!

NORA. I must learn to be competent, Torvald.

46 HELMER. Abandon your home, your husband, your children! And you're not even thinking what people will say.

NORA. I can't be concerned about that. I only know how essential this is.

HELMER. Oh, it's outrageous. So you'll run out like this on your most sacred vows.

NORA. What do you think are my most sacred vows?

HELMER. And I have to tell you that! Aren't they your duties to your husband and children?

NORA. I have other duties equally sacred.

HELMER. That isn't true. What duties are they?

NORA. Duties to myself.

HELMER. Before all else, you're a wife and a mother.

47 NORA. I don't believe in that anymore. I believe that, before all else, I'm a human being, no less than you—or anyway, I ought to try to become one. I know the majority thinks you're right, Tor-vald, and plenty of books agree with you, too. But I can't go on believing what the majority says, or what's written in books. I have to think over these things myself and try to understand them.

HELMER. Why can't you understand your place in your own home? On a point like that, isn't there one everlasting guide you can turn to? Where's your religion?

NORA. Oh, Torvald, I'm really not sure what religion is.

HELMER. What—?

NORA. I only know what the minister said when I was confirmed. He told me religion was this thing and that. When I get clear and away by myself, I'll go into that problem too. I'll see if what the minister said was right, or, in any case, if it's right for me.

HELMER. A young woman your age shouldn't talk like that. If religion can't move you, I can try to rouse your conscience. You do have some moral feeling? Or, tell me—has that gone too?

NORA. It's not easy to answer that, Torvald. I simply don't know. I'm all confused about these things. I just know I see them so differently from you. I find out, for one thing, that the law's not at all what I'd thought—but I can't get it through my head that the law is fair. A woman hasn't a right to protect her dying father or save her husband's life! I can't believe that.

HELMER. You talk like a child. You don't know anything of the world you live in.

NORA. No, I don't. But now I'll begin to learn for myself. I'll try to discover who's right, the world or I.

HELMER. Nora, you're sick; you've got a fever. I almost think you're out of your head.

NORA. I've never felt more clearheaded and sure in my life.

HELMER. And—clearheaded and sure—you're leaving your husband and children?

NORA. Yes.

HELMER. Then there's only one possible reason.

NORA. What?

HELMER. You no longer love me.

NORA. No. That's exactly it.

HELMER. Nora! You can't be serious!

NORA. Oh, this is so hard, Torvald—you've been so kind to me always. But I can't help it. I don't love you anymore.

HELMER. [*Struggling for composure*] Are you also clearheaded and sure about that?

NORA. Yes, completely. That's why I can't go on staying here.

HELMER. Can you tell me what I did to lose your love?

NORA. Yes, I can tell you. It was this evening when the miraculous thing didn't come—then I knew you weren't the man I'd imagined.

HELMER. Be more explicit; I don't follow you.

NORA. I've waited now so patiently eight long years—for, my Lord, I know miracles don't come every day. Then this crisis broke over me, and such a certainty filled me: *now* the miraculous event would occur. While Krogstad's letter was lying out there, I never for an instant dreamed that you could give in to his terms. I was so utterly sure you'd say to him: go on, tell your tale to the whole wide world. And when he'd done that—

HELMER. Yes, what then? When I'd delivered my own wife into shame and disgrace—!

NORA. When he'd done that, I was so utterly sure that you'd step forward, take the blame on yourself and say: I am the guilty one.

HELMER. Nora—!

NORA. You're thinking I'd never accept such a sacrifice from you? No, of course not. But what good would my protests be against you? That was the miracle I was waiting for, in terror and hope. And to stave that off, I would have taken my life.

HELMER. I'd gladly work for you day and night, Nora—and take on pain and deprivation. But there's no one who gives up honor for love.

NORA. Millions of women have done just that.

HELMER. Oh, you think and talk like a silly child.

NORA. Perhaps. But you neither think nor talk like the man I could join myself to. When your big fright was over—and it wasn't from any threat against me, only for what might damage you—when all the danger was past, for you it was just as if nothing had happened. I was exactly the same, your little lark, your doll, that you'd have to handle with double care now that I'd turned out so brittle and frail. [*Gets up*] Torvald—in that instant it dawned on me that for eight years I've been living here with a stranger, and that I'd even conceived three children—oh, I can't stand the thought of it! I could tear myself to bits.

HELMER. [*Heavily*] I see. There's a gulf that's opened between us—that's clear. Oh, but Nora, can't we bridge it somehow?

NORA. The way I am now, I'm no wife for you.

HELMER. I have the strength to make myself over.

NORA. Maybe—if your doll gets taken away.

HELMER. But to part! To part from you! No, Nora, no—I can't imagine it.

NORA. [*Going out, right*] All the more reason why it has to be. [*She reenters with her coat and a small overnight bag, which she puts on a chair by the table.*]

HELMER. Nora, Nora, not now! Wait till tomorrow.

NORA. I can't spend the night in a strange man's room.

HELMER. But couldn't we live here like brother and sister—

NORA. You know very well how long that would last. [*Throws her shawl about her*] Good-bye, Torvald. I won't look in on the children. I know they're in better hands than mine. The way I am now, I'm no use to them.

49 Discussion Have students discuss whether they think Nora ever truly believed that this "miraculous thing" would actually happen.

50 Literary Focus Remind students that one of the major themes of the play is that people must bring their lives into harmony with their convictions. Ask students to explain whether Torvald is already living in harmony with his convictions. Point out that he indicates that he considers honor to be more important than love. Has he acted on this conviction?

51 Discussion Ask students whether they believe Torvald when he says he has the strength to make himself over. Why or why not?

52 Discussion Do students believe it would really be possible for Nora and Torvald to live "like brother and sister"? Why or why not?

53 **Enrichment** When the play was first performed, many critics and theatergoers were enraged by Nora's abandonment of her children. Even some actors expressed outrage at this aspect of the play. In fact, one German actress refused to perform the final scene unless it was rewritten, insisting, "*I* would never leave *my* children." How do students respond to Nora's abandonment of her children?

54 **Discussion** Ask students how Nora is going to survive. Has she acquired any marketable skills during her years as wife and mother? If so, what are they?

55 **Discussion** George Bernard Shaw wrote, "Nora's revolt is the end of a chapter of human history." Ask students if the slamming of the Helmers' front door might also be viewed as the beginning of a chapter.

Cultural Note Ibsen influenced many noted British and American playwrights, including George Bernard Shaw and Eugene O'Neill.

Cooperative Learning Divide the class into as many groups of five as possible. Have one person in each group assume the role of one of the five major characters in the play. Each group should then engage in a discussion during which each student should try to defend the actions of the character whose role he or she has assumed. For instance, a student who assumes the role of Nora should try to defend her decision to leave her husband and children.

HELMER. But someday, Nora—someday—?

NORA. How can I tell? I haven't the least idea what'll become of me.

HELMER. But you're my wife, now and wherever you go.

NORA. Listen, Torvald—I've heard that when a wife deserts her husband's house just as I'm doing, then the law frees him from all responsibility. In any case, I'm freeing you from being responsible. Don't feel yourself bound, any more than I will. There has to be absolute freedom for us both. Here, take your ring back. Give me mine.

HELMER. That too?

NORA. That too.

HELMER. There it is.

NORA. Good. Well, now it's all over, I'm putting the keys here. The maids know all about keeping up the house—better than I do. Tomorrow, after I've left town, Kristine will stop by to pack up everything that's mine from home. I'd like those things shipped up to me.

53 **HELMER.** Over! All over! Nora, won't you ever think about me?

NORA. I'm sure I'll think of you often, and about the children and the house here.

HELMER. May I write you?

NORA. No—never. You're not to do that.

HELMER. Oh, but let me send you—

NORA. Nothing. Nothing.

HELMER. Or help you if you need it.

NORA. No. I accept nothing from strangers.

HELMER. Nora—can I never be more than a stranger to you?

NORA. [*Picking up the overnight bag*] Ah, Torvald—it would take the greatest miracle of all—

HELMER. Tell me the greatest miracle!

NORA. You and I both would have to transform ourselves to the point that— Oh, Torvald, I've stopped believing in miracles.

HELMER. But I'll believe. Tell me! Transform ourselves to the point that—?

NORA. That our living together could be a true marriage. [*She goes out down the hall.*]

HELMER. [*Sinks down on a chair by the door, face buried in his hands*] Nora! Nora! [*Looking about and rising*] Empty. She's gone. [*A sudden hope leaps in him.*] The greatest miracle—? [*From below, the sound of a door slamming shut.*]

Reader's Response *Do you think that Nora made the correct decision in choosing to leave Torvald and the children? Why or why not? Do you think there is any chance that Nora and Torvald will get back together? Why or why not?*

THINKING ABOUT THE SELECTION

Interpreting

1. (a) What draws Mrs. Linde and Krogstad back to each other? (b) Do these two characters have more in common than Nora and Torvald do? Explain. (c) How does Nora's and Torvald's situation contrast with Mrs. Linde's and Krogstad's situation at the end of the play?
2. Why does Mrs. Linde tell Krogstad not to ask for his letter back?
3. After Nora and Torvald return from the party, why does Nora tell Torvald to "go away" and "leave [her] alone"?

Closure and Extension

ANSWERS TO THINKING ABOUT THE SELECTION

1. (a) Suggested response: They are drawn together because they are both down on their luck and in need of companionship and support. (b) Suggested response: They have a great deal more in common. They have both been through adversity and share common, real-world experiences. (c) Mrs. Linde and Krogstad are coming together at the same time Nora and Torvald are breaking apart.
2. Suggested response: She believes it is time for Nora and Torvald to start being open and honest with each other.
3. Suggested response: Torvald is in an amorous mood, and Nora is preoccupied with the implications of the letter in the mailbox.
4. (a) Suggested response: He does not seem greatly upset; he seems more concerned about the effect that Rank's death will have on him and Nora. (b) Suggested response: He is incredibly self-centered.
5. (a) It is ironic because they are about to be torn apart, not "thrown

---

4. (a) How would you describe Torvald's reaction to the news that Rank is going to die? (b) What does Torvald's reaction reveal about his personality?
5. (a) What is ironic about Torvald's comment that now that Rank is gone, he and Nora will be "thrown back on each other completely"? (b) What other examples of irony can you find in his comments to Nora?
6. How does Rank's demise parallel the collapse of Nora and Torvald's marriage?
7. When Torvald asks Nora if she understands what she has done, she responds, "Yes. I'm beginning to understand everything now." What is it that she is actually beginning to understand?
8. (a) What does Torvald's response to the letter reveal about the true nature of his feelings for Nora? (b) What conclusions do you draw about him based on this response?
9. (a) How does Torvald's reaction to the note along with the immediate shift in his attitude following the receipt of the second note expose him as a hypocrite? (b) Why is Nora unmoved by Torvald's declaration that he has forgiven her?
10. Explain whether you think that Torvald truly understands Nora's reasons for leaving.
11. How does the play's title relate to Nora's explanation of her decision to leave Torvald and the children?

Applying

12. When this play was first performed, the people in the audience were stunned by Nora's decision to leave her husband and children, since it puts her duty to her family second to her responsibility to herself. (a) Do you agree with her decision? Why or why not? (b) Do you think that her decision is as shocking today as when the play was first performed? Explain.

ANALYZING LITERATURE

Recognizing Themes

A Doll's House is an example of a literary work with numerous possible themes. To be considered valid, each of these possible themes must be supported by evidence in the play. For example, the idea that the play is an expression of the need for women to escape from the confinement and restriction that they faced in nineteenth-century European society is supported by the condescending manner in which Torvald treats Nora and by his frequent references to the respective roles of men and women.
1. What evidence in the play supports the theme concerning the characteristics of a successful marriage?
2. What evidence supports the theme that society and authority hinder the development of individuality?
3. What evidence suggests that the play is about "the struggle which all serious-minded human beings have to wage with themselves to bring their lives into harmony with their convictions"?
4. What theme does the play convey concerning the role of morality in people's lives, and how is this theme conveyed?

CRITICAL THINKING AND READING

Appreciating the Importance of Casting

Plays are generally written to be performed, not read. As a result, a person's response to a play usually depends to a great extent on the actors' portrayal of the various characters. For this reason the casting of a dramatic production is extremely important.

If you were the casting director for a dramatic production of *A Doll's House*, list specific actors or types of actors you would choose to play each of the following roles: Nora, Torvald, Krogstad, Mrs. Linde, and Dr. Rank. Explain each choice.

THINKING AND WRITING

Writing About Theme

Choose one theme that you feel is important. Then write a paper in which you explain how this theme is conveyed. Begin by reviewing the play and noting details that relate to the theme you have chosen. Organize your notes. Then write your paper, using passages from the play for support. In your conclusion explain why the theme you have chosen is especially important or relevant. After you have finished writing, work with a partner or in a small group to revise your paper.

(continued from bottom of page)
will probably respond that it was wrong for her to abandon her children. (b) Suggested response: It is not as shocking today, because the type of action that Nora takes is no longer uncommon.

Challenge If you were going to write an adaptation of this play set in contemporary America, how would you change the plot? Explain each change you suggest.

ANSWERS TO ANALYZING LITERATURE

1. Answers will differ. The most important piece of evidence is the failure of Nora and Torvald's marriage.
2. Answers will differ. Nora's inability to develop a sense of individuality is one piece of evidence supporting this theme.
3. Answers will differ. Students should point out that Nora's actions at the end of the play are aimed at bringing her life into harmony with her convictions.
4. Suggested response: The play suggests that high moral principles must be lived, not merely expressed. This theme is conveyed through the discrepancy between Torvald's words and actions.

ANSWERS TO CRITICAL THINKING AND READING

Answers will differ. Make sure that students offer reasons for each of their choices.

THINKING AND WRITING

Publishing Student Writing
You may want to arrange students' papers into a class bulletin-board display.

back" together. (b) Answers will differ. Students may note the irony of his declaration that he would stake his "life and soul and everything" for Nora's sake.
6. Suggested response: Just as Rank's life is about to come to an end, the Helmers' marriage comes to an end.
7. Suggested response: She is beginning to recognize how self-centered Torvald is. She is also beginning to recognize that they do not have a good marriage.
8. (a) Suggested response: He does not truly love her. (b) Suggested response: He does not really care about anyone other than himself.
9. (a) Suggested response: He is not really upset about the fact that what Nora did was wrong; he is upset because he is afraid that his reputation will be damaged. (b) Suggested response: He, not she, is the one who needs to be forgiven at this point.
10. Answers will differ. Students may feel that his comments at the end of the play suggest that he is beginning to understand.
11. Suggested response: Nora has been a "doll wife" to Torvald, and their children have been like dolls to her.
12. (a) Answers will differ. Many students

THE SLAMMING OF THE DOOR IN A DOLL'S HOUSE

Presentation

Motivation/Prior Knowledge
Have students discuss the status of women in America today. In what areas do students think that women have attained virtually the same status as men? In what areas are women still discriminated against? What measures can be taken to further improve the status of women in the United States?

Point out to students that until fairly recently, women were severely discriminated against and were offered limited educational and professional opportunities. Explain that the first production of *A Doll's House* was one of the events that helped to precipitate change in the area of women's rights. Tell students that this feature will examine the impact of *A Doll's House* and will outline some of the changes in the area of women's rights that have taken place since the play was first produced.

Enrichment Tell students that in most American states women did not gain the right to vote until the early 1900's. In fact, no state allowed women to vote until Wyoming entered the Union in 1890. Three decades later, however, the 19th Amendment of the United States Constitution was ratified, giving all American women the right to vote. The amendment reads: "The right of citizens of the United States to vote shall not be denied or abridged by the United States or by any state on account of sex."

The slamming of the door at the end of *A Doll's House* was a sound that reverberated around the world. As a symbol of Nora's assertion of her freedom and independence, this sound represented a direct challenge to the existing beliefs concerning sex roles. In the decades that followed the publication of the play, the role of women in society began undergoing a dramatic transformation. Because of its startling impact and the changes that followed, the slamming of the door is now viewed by many as a pivotal starting point in the modern feminist movement. In fact, as the modern British playwright George Bernard Shaw wrote, the slamming of the door can be regarded as "the end of a chapter in human history."

Women in the Nineteenth Century

At the time the play was written, the idea of a woman leaving her husband and children to live freely and independently was considered unacceptable by the vast majority of people in the Western world. It was widely believed that women were inferior to men, and as a result women did not enjoy the same rights and privileges as men. Few women were provided with a quality education, and they had severely limited career opportunities. Rather than pursuing a career, women were expected to marry and to devote their lives to serving their husbands and raising their children. In doing so they were expected to respect and obey their husbands without question.

Nora's Rebellion Against Society

By leaving Torvald and her children to educate herself and to search for personal fulfillment, Nora was rebelling not only against Torvald's authority but against the attitudes and expectations of society as a whole. When she tells Torvald that she plans to leave him, he at first tries to forbid her, then warns her that she is "not even thinking about what people will say." Nora responds that she is not concerned with what other people think, and she goes on to say that her duties to herself are more important than her duties as a wife and mother. She declares, "I'm a human being, no less than you—or anyway, I ought to try to become one. I know the majority thinks you're right, Torvald, and plenty of books agree with you, too. But I can't go on believing what the majority says, or what's written in books."

The Impact of Nora's Rebellion

When Nora finally leaves and the door slams shut behind her, Torvald is left in a state of shock and dismay. Similarly, the early audiences were shocked and dismayed by what they saw. Yet this sense of shock forced many people to begin re-evaluating the role of women in society, and in the years that followed, women began to gain some of the rights and privileges that they had previously been denied. For example, one historian points out that "within five years of the publication of *A Doll's House*, women were being admitted to the private

NSIGHTS

Liberal Club in the tradition-bound city of Oslo" in Ibsen's native land of Norway.

During the course of the twentieth century, the status of women has continued to steadily improve. In virtually all Western democratic countries, women have gained the right to vote. In addition, the educational and professional opportunities available to women have expanded tremendously. Many women have become involved in politics, and in a number of countries, including Great Britian, Pakistan, and the Philippines, women have been elected to the highest ranking government post. As a result of such changes, women from many nations now enjoy virtually the same status as men, although there are still a few areas in which women are subject to discrimination.

Ibsen and Feminism

Because of Nora's actions in *A Doll's House*, Ibsen is often regarded as one of the pioneer spirits in the feminist movement. Although Ibsen himself might have argued that he did not deserve this label, it cannot be denied that he was one of the first men to openly express concern about the needs of women, as well as about their role in society. Ibsen's preliminary notes to *A Doll's House* clearly indicate that he wanted the play to capture the way in which society inhibited the freedom and growth of women. He wrote, "There are two kinds of spiritual law, two kinds of conscience, one in man and another, altogether different, in woman. They do not understand each other; but in practical life the woman is judged by man's law, as though she were not a woman but a man. . . . A woman cannot be herself in the society of the present day, which is exclusively a masculine society. . . ."

Questions and Activities

1. Explain why Ibsen's observation does or does not apply to contemporary American society.
2. Explain why Nora's actions at the end of *A Doll's House* would or would not be considered acceptable in contemporary American society.
3. Do you think there are many men in contemporary American society who share Torvald's attitude toward women? Support your answer.
4. Prepare an oral report about one of the major breakthroughs in the feminist movement or about one of the major figures in the movement. For example, you might focus on how women gained the right to vote in the United States, or you might explore Simone de Beauvoir's contributions to the women's movement. Once you have chosen the topic for your report, it will be necessary for you to do some library research. After you have finished your research, take some time to organize your ideas. You can accomplish this either by preparing an outline or by using notecards. Next, you may want to rehearse your report with one of your classmates. Finally, when you deliver your report, make sure you vary the tone and pitch of your voice and use nonverbal language, such as hand gestures, to emphasize your most important ideas.

Enrichment Tell students that in 1893, New Zealand became the first country to grant women full voting rights. In subsequent decades, most of the other democratic countries also gave women the right to vote. By the 1980's there were only seven democratic nations in which women had not been given voting rights: Bahrain, Kuwait, Oman, Qatar, Saudi Arabia, the United Arab Emirates, and Yemen. Have students locate these countries on a map. Then have them explain what these countries have in common.

Closure and Extension

ANSWERS TO QUESTIONS AND ACTIVITIES

1. Answers will differ. Many students will argue that the observation does not apply to contemporary American society because it is not an "exclusively masculine society."
2. Answers will differ. Students may respond that her actions would not be considered surprising. Yet they may also point out that many people still do not think it is acceptable for a mother to abandon her children.
3. Answers will differ. Students may respond that most contemporary American men do not share Torvald's attitude. They may also note that there are still some men who do share Torvald's attitude.
4. When evaluating students' oral reports, consider the delivery of the reports as well as their content.

The Artist and Society

> "The artist is the child in the popular fable, every one of whose tears was a pearl. Ah! the world, that cruel stepmother, beats the poor child the harder to make him shed more pearls."
> —Heinrich Heine

Heine was only one of many Romantic writers who viewed the artist as being isolated or alienated from the rest of society. Some of these writers felt that their isolation was caused by society's inability to fully understand or appreciate them. They saw themselves as being unavoidably set apart from other people by their acute sensibilities and insatiable spirits. Others deliberately sought to separate themselves from society in order to engage in quiet contemplation and poetic composition. Still others separated themselves from society because they rejected its dominant attitudes and values. Baudelaire expressed this view of the Romantic poet.

The Poet resembles this prince of the
   clouds,
Who laughs at hunters and haunts the
   storms;
Exiled to the ground amid the jeering pack,
His giant wings will not let him walk.
    —Baudelaire, "The Albatross"

Goethe also speaks of the Romantic spirit.

Fate has given this man [Faust] a spirit
Which is always pressing onward, beyond
   control,

And whose mad striving overleaps
All joys of earth between pole and pole.
Him shall I drag through the wilds of life
And through the flats of meaninglessness,
I shall make him flounder and gape and
   stick
And to tease his insatiableness
Hang meat and drink in the air before his
   watering lips;
In vain he will pray to slake his inner thirst,
And even had he not sold himself to the
   devil
He would be equally accursed.
    —Goethe, *Faust*

Rimbaud sees the Romantic spirit as soaring upward.

Of human sanctions,
Of common transports,
You free yourself:
You soar according . . .
    —Rimbaud, "Eternity"

The relationship between the artist and society has also been explored by writers from many other literary eras. In his story "The Infant Prodigy" (page 1039), for example, the modern writer Thomas Mann demonstrates how people's attitudes and preoccupations can color their perceptions of an artist's work.

Other literary works that deal with the relationship between the artist and society include the following:

SUGGESTED READINGS

T'ao Ch'ien, "I Built My House Near Where Others Dwell," page 226
Wang Wei, "To the Assistant Prefect Chang," page 230
William Shakespeare, *The Tempest*, page 709
Rainer Maria Rilke, "Archaic Torso of Apollo," page 1057

Rabindranath Tagore, "The Artist," page 1192
Gabriel García Márquez, "The Handsomest Drowned Man in the World," page 1213
Octavio Paz, "Poet's Epitaph," page 1246

CROSS CURRENTS

Simone de Beauvoir (1908–1986)

Simone de Beauvoir was a renowned French writer and philosopher. One of her best-known works is *The Second Sex*, a book hailed by many as the most forceful vindication of women's rights written in the twentieth century. Obviously, de Beauvoir was a woman who understood why Nora, the heroine of Ibsen's *A Doll's House*, slammed the door on Torvald and her former life.

THE SECOND SEX

In *The Second Sex*, an insightful and in-depth study of the role of women in history, de Beauvoir forcefully expresses her feminist views. Throughout the course of the book, she chronicles how myths, social traditions, and inherited attitudes and biases worked together to relegate women to a secondary status. As a result of their secondary position, she argues, women have been deprived of their freedom and independence—two privileges that can play a vital role in the development of a sense of dignity and self-esteem.

Although de Beauvoir cites *The Second Sex* as being the book that has brought her the greatest satisfaction, she herself was not the one who originally came up with the idea of writing it. Claiming never to have personally experienced the sense of confinement and restraint that Nora does in *A Doll's House*, de Beauvoir did not consider exploring the subject of the role of women until her longtime associate the French philosopher Jean-Paul Sartre suggested it. With Sartre's encouragement, however, she immersed herself in the subject, eventually producing a work that has been translated into nineteen languages and has sold more than a half million copies.

LIVING PROOF

De Beauvoir herself served as living proof of a number of the arguments she set forth in her book. Through her accomplishments as a writer, she proved that women can be just as productive and successful as men. Like the heroines in her novels and plays, she confronted responsibilities and took risks in both her professional and personal lives. Throughout her life, she continually exhibited her strength, intelligence, and independence—the same types of qualities that Ibsen's Nora hoped to someday possess.

Controversial Issue

Writing About a Controversial Issue

> Controversy—a battle in which spittle or ink replaces the . . . cannonball.
> —Ambrose Bierce

Writing about controversial issues means taking a stand. It then forces the writer to argue convincingly that that stand is correct. In order to do so, the writer must care about something. A good controversial-issue essay anticipates objections or questions that skeptical readers may have and refutes them. Therefore, the cornerstone of writing well about a controversial issue is knowing information and reporting it accurately. In most cases doing so will require research.

Characteristics of Writing About Controversial Issues

- ISSUE: the matter in dispute that you will clearly define while taking a strong stand
- POSITION: the logical or emotional foundation expressed in a thesis statement
- SUPPORT: the readers' confidence that the author gains by establishing common values and principles
- TONE: the reasonable and self-confident attitude of a committed, assured writer

---

Henrik Ibsen raises several controversial issues in *A Doll's House*. For example, when Nora shuts the door on Torvald, she also leaves her children. Divorce is a common phenomenon in our society, and with increasing frequency, children find themselves the innocent victims of broken marriages. Should Nora have considered her children's needs before her own? Some critics have argued that Nora did the right thing in leaving her family, and others have taken the opposite view.

Writing Assignment

Write a paper in which you take a position on a controversial issue facing us today. Convince your reader that you are right by using accurate information, concrete examples, and a compelling organization.

Prewrite

Brainstorm with your classmates to list controversial issues. Then choose an issue you feel strongly about. Gather information about your topic. Here are a few simple research steps you may find useful.

- **Investigate your issue:** Begin by checking basic resource books in your library. Most libraries have specific reference books devoted to current controversial issues. Ask your librarian about them. Skim these to get an overview of your issue. Then formulate a rough idea of your strategy by observing the major counterpoints to your view.
- **Limit your focus:** Through research, you will no doubt find your issue more complex than you first thought. To make the material manageable, express your position, or stance, in a focused, defining statement.

Then read in depth, ignoring all that does not directly relate to either proving your stance or to countering it.

- **Test your stance with partners:** Find other students working on the same issue and discuss the issue.

Write

State your position clearly and forcefully in your first paragraph, striving for a committed, assured tone. Then support your stance with the material you gathered, lacing the counterarguments and their refutations throughout the paper in the places where these questions would naturally arise in the reader's mind. If you become unsure about where to place key counterarguments, ask a partner to read what you have written so far and tell you where counterarguments sprang to mind.

As you present your support, maintain a confident and reasonable tone. Present your case to skeptical readers in a mature, controlled, and convincing manner, making your arguments seem fair even from their viewpoints.

Collaborate

- Ask a partner to answer these questions.
- Where did you find the biggest flaws in my argument?
- Did I present the counterarguments fairly?

- Where were you most nearly convinced and why?
- If I did not convince you, why not?

Revise

With your partner's feedback in mind, revise your draft. Pay particular attention to strengthening your reasonable yet confident tone.

If your partner pointed out major flaws in your paper, go back to your notes or perhaps to the library. The writing process is seldom a smooth step-by-step progression, and spending time rewriting an inadequate draft is foolish.

Publish

Send a copy of your work to the editor of a local newspaper for possible publication on the Editorial or Opinions page. Be sure to include your name and address as well as your phone number so that it will be convenient for the publication to contact you.

Evaluate

Now consider sending your essay to someone who is directly involved with the issue you wrote about. Send the article to that person. If possible, arrange to meet with this reader to discuss your opinion. Lend your support to whatever efforts this person is making to promote ideas in your favor and carefully consider whatever objections the person has to your position.

Master Teacher Note Explain to students that they should not hesitate to make revisions in their work as they are writing. Point out that they can vary the stages of the writing process to find the approach that works best for them. For example, they may find that it works best for them to prepare a formal outline before they begin writing, or they may find that they like to organize their ideas as they write.

Guidelines for Evaluating Writing about Literature Keep the following questions in mind when evaluating students' compositions.
1. Is the student's position clearly and forcefully stated in the first paragraph?
2. Does the student thoroughly support his or her position?
3. Does the paper include counter arguments and refutations?
4. Is the paper well organized?

Tell students that this map depicts the world as it appears today. Point out that the world has changed dramatically since the turn of the century. During the early part of the century, the colonial empires of powerful European nations such as Britain and France crumbled. As a result many nations, including India and Egypt, regained their independence. In addition, a number of new nations have emerged over the course of the century. For example, in the aftermath of World War II the nation of Israel was founded.

Also remind students that monumental advances in travel and communication have taken place during the twentieth century. Point out to students that these advances have made it easy for people from distant nations to share their ideas, concerns, and traditions with one another. Distance has ceased to be a barrier between different groups of people, and the world has been transformed into an interconnected web of nations and cultures.

The Twentieth Century (1890–Present)

Using the Map

Have students study the map. Then ask them the following questions:

1. Compare this map with a map or a group of maps depicting the world or parts of the world at the turn of the century. Identify at least ten geographical changes that have taken place since the turn of the century.
2. Predict two geographical changes that you think might occur in the next fifty years. Explain each of your predictions.
3. Which are the two largest countries in the world?
4. Identify three countries that you would expect to have a very warm climate.
5. Identify three countries that you would expect to have a very cold climate.
6. Which part of the world would you most like to visit? Why?

Fine art, *Guernica* by Pablo Picasso. Probably the most famous of all twentieth-century painters, Picasso (1881–1973) had a long artistic career that can be divided into several stages. Born in Malaga, Spain, Picasso demonstrated his artistic gift at an early age. After abandoning realism as a young man, he entered a phase of his artistic career known as the Blue Period. During this period, he produced works that featured many shades of blue and evoked feelings of loneliness and despair. When this stage of his career came to an end, he began creating paintings that contained startling combinations of of jagged and often distorted images. These paintings gave birth to a major artistic movement known as Cubism. The next stage of his career was marked by his use of colorful, dreamlike images. In the 1920s and 1930s, he focused on expressing his reactions to current events in his works. Finally, as his career drew to a close, he produced paintings and sculptures with a more relaxed, gentle feeling.

Picasso was bitterly opposed to the Nationalist cause during the Spanish Civil War. In April of 1937, the Nationalist forces wiped out the small Basque town of Guernica. Within days Picasso began sketches for what would become a haunting and immense (11'6" x 25'8") canvas depicting the tragedy of war. This work, entitled *Guernica*, has become widely recognized as one of Picasso's greatest works. One critic has said of this painting that it "overflows with fullness and presence, with signs and cries."

You might want to use the following questions to discuss the art:

1. This painting was inspired by events occurring during the Spanish Civil War. What message do you think Picasso was trying to convey about the war?
2. What emotions does this painting evoke in you? Why?
3. If you were an art collector, would you want to include this painting in your collection? Why or why not?

GUERNICA, 1937
Pablo Picasso

1 To understand the major historical events and developments of the modern age
2 To understand modern literature

THE MODERN WORLD

1890–1945

The storm has died away, and still we are
restless, uneasy, as if the storm were about to break.
Almost all of the affairs of men remain a terrible
uncertainty. We think of what has disappeared, and
we are almost destroyed by what has been
destroyed; we do not know what will be born, and
we fear the future, not without reason. . . .

—Paul Valéry

Presentation

Motivation/Prior Knowledge
Have a class discussion in which students share their prior knowledge about the events and developments that occurred during the modern age. Make sure that students explore the major scientific and technological developments, such as the invention of the automobile and the airplane, as well as the most significant historical events, including World War I and World War II.

Purpose-Setting Question What were the most significant historical events and developments of the modern age? How did these events and developments shape people's lives? What effect did these events and developments have on the literary world?

1 Discussion Have students discuss the impact of these inventions on people's lives. Why might it be argued that these inventions made the world seem like a smaller place?

2 Enrichment Tell students that in 1895 the German physicist Wilhelm Roentgen discovered X-rays, which were soon put to work in the field of medicine.

3 Enrichment Tell students that Einstein argued that since all matter is in constant motion, there is no fixed point from which to measure motion. The motion of one object can be measured only by comparing it to the motion of another. All measurements are therefore relative. This theory is called the theory of relativity.

4 Discussion Have students share any prior knowledge they have of Pavlov's experiments.

Written in the aftermath of World War I, this passage by the French poet Paul Valéry (1871–1945) captures the sentiments of many of the people of his day. More devastating than any war the world had previously known, World War I forced people to the realization that the world had irrevocably changed. In doing so, it left them feeling disconnected from the past and uncertain about the future. No longer trusting the ideas and values of the past, many people struggled desperately to find new ideas that were more applicable to twentieth-century life. Similarly, many modern writers turned away from the style, form, and content of nineteenth-century literature and began experimenting with new themes and techniques.

HISTORICAL BACKGROUND

The Technological Revolution

The world had already begun undergoing a rapid transformation long before the first shots of World War I were fired. Sparked by the efforts of such brilliant scientists and inventors as Thomas Edison, Alexander Graham Bell, and Louis Pasteur, major technological advances began occurring in the late nineteenth and early twentieth centuries that would permanently alter the way in which people lived. Within a period of just a few decades, the airplane, the automobile, the radio, and the telephone were introduced, making travel and communication faster and easier than ever before imagined. At the same time, other discoveries and inventions, such as electricity, central heating, movies, and new medical remedies, were improving the quality of people's lives. Yet other advances were being made, such as the development of the machine gun and the tank, that made it easier for people to destroy one another.

Scientific Breakthroughs

In addition to these technological advances, major scientific breakthroughs were also taking place that dramatically changed the way people perceived themselves and their world. During the 1870's Gregor Mendel, an Austrian monk, made discoveries that improved people's understanding of how heredity works. A couple of decades later, the husband-and-wife team of Marie and Pierre Curie began making momentous breakthroughs concerning radioactivity. Finally, during the early 1900's, the German-born scientist Albert Einstein proposed radical new theories that ushered in the era of modern physics.

Understanding Human Behavior

None of these developments had more of an impact, however, than the advances that took place in the area of human behavior. One of the first people to make breakthroughs in this area was the Russian scientist Ivan Pavlov. After conducting a series of experiments with dogs, Pavlov came to the conclusion that some human behavior is motivated by conditioned responses rather than by conscious rational thought.

Even more influential than the findings of Pavlov were the ideas of his Austrian contemporary Sigmund Freud. Using a method of gathering information about mental processes known as psychoanalysis, Freud came to the conclusion that people's behavior is largely shaped by unconscious influences stemming from their experiences during infancy and early childhood. Because Freud's theories challenged the belief that human activity sprang from rational thought, they initially sparked controversy. Yet as time passed, his ideas gained increasing acceptance and became a guiding force for many writers, scholars, and artists, as well as scientists.

World War I

Encouraged by the advances in science and technology, many people became increasingly optimistic about the future of humanity. To some, it even seemed possible that people could ultimately solve all their problems and establish lasting peace. This sense of optimism was completely shattered, however, by the horrifying realities of World War I.

Beginning late in the summer of 1914, the war at first pitted France, Russia, and Great Britain against Germany, Austria-Hungary, and the Ottoman Empire. As it progressed, many other countries, including Italy, Greece, and the United States, also became involved, until almost the entire world had become embroiled in the fighting.

Throughout most of the conflict, neither side was able to make any significant advances.

Having reached a stalemate early in the war, the opposing armies had settled into trenches protected by mines and barbed wire. For the next few years, the two sides took turns rushing the opposing trenches. With each of these charges, hundreds of soldiers would be mowed down by machine-gun fire. By the time the war ended in 1918, over ten million soldiers had been killed, twenty million had been wounded, and about a million civilians had lost their lives.

The Rise of Nazism

In the aftermath of the war, the victorious allies drafted a treaty that required Germany to accept full blame and pay reparations for the total cost of the war. Although Germany signed the treaty, it created strong feelings of bitterness and resentment among the German people. These feelings coupled with the severe inflation caused by the war reparations created a state of political unrest that plagued the nation throughout the 1920's. In the early 1930's, Adolf Hitler and the Nazis were able to exploit this political chaos and seize control of the nation.

Hitler quickly molded Germany into a totalitarian state in which all dissent was brutally suppressed. The Nazis assumed control of every aspect of German life, including religion, schools, and the press. They burned books and destroyed works of art they judged to be "un-German," and they forced radio stations to play military

TROOPS WAITING TO ADVANCE AT HATTONCHATEL, SAN MIHIEL DRIVE, 1918
W. J. Aylward
Smithsonian Institution, Washington, D.C.

5 **Enrichment** Tell students that Freud believed that the human mind could be divided into three parts: the id, the ego, and the superego. The id includes the most basic human drives, such as the drive to satisfy thirst and hunger. The ego, on the other hand, connects the internal mind to the outside environment. Finally, the superego is the part of the mind that governs moral behavior.

6 **Learning Across the Curriculum** You might want to offer students extra credit to uncover more information about Freud's theories and to present their findings to the rest of the class.

Humanities Note

Fine art, *Troops Waiting to Advance at Hattonchatel*, San Mihiel Drive, 1918, by W. J. Aylward. During World War I, governments hired artists to record the major events of the war. In addition to capturing major battles, these artists depicted soldiers at rest, long convoys of vehicles and marching men, and troops preparing for battle. One of the leading combat artists of World War I was William J. Aylward, whose paintings are now part of the collection at the Smithsonian Institution.

In this painting Aylward captures Allied troops preparing for an assault on German lines in Eastern France. At the time, the Germans had begun a final offensive in France, hoping to force a decision in their favor before America's entrance into the war could turn the tide against them. The Allies, however, prepared a sweeping counterattack, involving over 665,000 soldiers. This counterattack, which the allies called the San Mihiel Drive, succeeded in halting the German advance and played a major role in ending the war.

You might want to use the following questions to discuss the art:
1. What is the mood, or atmosphere, of this painting?
2. Which elements of the painting contribute to this mood?
3. Do you think that this painting is more effective than a photograph of the scene would have been? Why or why not?

In 1898 Marie Curie, wife of French scientist Pierre Curie, discovered radium, a radioactive element found in pitchblende, a black mineral. For their work on radioactivity, the Curies won the Nobel Prize in Physics in 1903.

The Boxer Rebellion, an antiforeign movement in China from 1898 to 1900, culminated in an uprising against Westerners and Western influence. In this twentieth-century painting, the Chinese are forcing Westerners out of their country.

On December 17, 1903, Orville (1871–1948) and Wilbur (1867–1912) Wright successfully completed the first sustained flight of a power-driven airplane at Kitty Hawk, North Carolina. Of the four flights on that day, the first, flown by Orville, lasted 12 seconds; the fourth, made by Wilbur, lasted 59 seconds and covered 852 feet.

Austrian psychiatrist Sigmund Freud (1856–1939) is the founder of psychoanalysis. Psychoanalysis, one type of psychotherapy used in psychiatry, has had great influence on child rearing, education, the cultural and social sciences, medicine, and the arts. Freud's theories of a dynamic unconscious and dreams being a key to the unconscious were instrumental in influencing André Breton's surrealism manifesto and the subsequent surrealism movement in literature.

The Modern World (1890–1945)

Marie Curie
in her laboratory

Boxer Rebellion, an antiforeign
movement in China
The British Museum, London

Wright Brothers' flight
at Kitty Hawk, 1903

1890	1900	1910

HISTORY

- Spanish-American War begins
- Chinese secret society "Fists of Righteous Harmony," or "Boxers"
- Boxer rebellion begins
- Russo-Japanese War begins
- Russian Revolution (Bloody Sunday) takes place
- Signing of treaty ends Russo-Japanese War
- Mexican Revolution begins
- Chinese Revolution begins
- Francis Ferdinand is assassinated; World War I breaks out in Europe

HUMAN PROGRESS

- Henry Ford builds his first car
- Cinematography is invented by Louis Lumière
- German physicist develops x-rays
- Radio telegraphy is invented
- First U.S. Open Golf Championship is held
- First modern Olympics are held in Athens
- Wright brothers make first flight at Kitty Hawk
- Boston Red Sox defeat Pittsburgh Pirates in first World Series
- Curies win Nobel Prize in Physics
- First railroad tunnel is built
- Color photography, using a three-color screen, is developed
- Plastic Age begins
- Electric self-starter for cars is invented
- R.M.S. *Titanic* sinks on her maiden voyage
- Ford's assembly line improves production of automobiles
- Panama Canal opens

LITERATURE

- Boris Pasternak is born
- Pär Lagerkvist is born
- Manuel Rojas is born
- Federico García Lorca is born
- Jorge Luis Borges is born
- Kawabata Yasunari is born
- Primo Levi is born
- R. K. Narayan is born
- Pablo Neruda is born
- Najib Mahfouz is born
- Thomas Mann: *Death in Venice*
- Albert Camus is born
- Rabindranath Tagore, Nobel Prize for Literature
- Julio Cortázar is born
- Octavio Paz is born
- Franz Kafka: *The Metamorphosis*

Austrian psychiatrist
Sigmund Freud

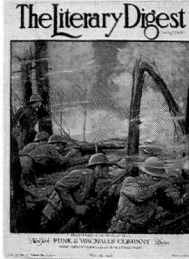

"Shattering a German Charge," World War I

American physicist
Albert Einstein

Japanese raid
at Pearl Harbor,
December 7, 1941

1920   **1930**   **1940**   **1945**

- Bolsheviks seize control of Russia in October Revolution
- U.S. declares war on Germany, entering W.W.I
  - Germany signs the Versailles Treaty; W.W.I ends
    - Ireland gains independence
    - Lenin announces New Economic Policy
      - Mussolini comes to power in Italy

- U.S. stock crash leads to Great Depression
  - Hitler comes to power in Germany
    - Nuremburg Laws deprive German Jews of citizenship
      - Japan attacks China
        - World War II begins
        - Jewish Holocaust begins
          - Japan attacks Pearl Harbor

- Women over 30 win right to vote in Britain
  - Jazz emerges in U.S.
- Charles Lindbergh flies *Spirit of St. Louis* from New York to Paris
- Talking pictures begin
    - Amelia Earhart is first woman to fly across the Atlantic
    - Penicillin is discovered
      - Passenger airlines become common
        - Process of natural color photography is developed
          - New forms of atomic energy are discovered
  - Dirigible *Hindenburg* completes transatlantic flight
- First U.S. jet plane is tested
    - First successful helicopter flight in U.S. occurs
      - First digital computer is invented

- Heinrich Böll is born
  - Alexander Solzhenitsyn is born
  - Guillaume Apollinaire dies
    - Doris Lessing is born
      - Stanislaw Lem is born
- Herman Hesse: *Siddhartha*
  - T. S. Eliot: *The Waste Land*
  - Paris publishes James Joyce's *Ulysses*; U.S. Post Office burns 500 copies
      - Book of the Month Club is founded
        - Gabriel García Márquez is born
- Thomas Mann wins Nobel Prize for Literature
- Wole Soyinka is born
        - Bessie Head is born
    - Boris Pasternak: *Second Birth,* poem
          - Margaret Atwood is born
    - Chinua Achebe is born
      - Luigi Pirandello wins Nobel Prize for Literature
        - James Joyce's *Ulysses* is allowed into the U.S. after court ruling
        - Books by non-Nazi and Jewish authors are burned in Germany

Taken from the cover of *The Literary Digest*, "Shattering a German Charge" depicts World War I soldiers in a trench. World War I began in 1914 after the assassination of Archduke Francis Ferdinand of Austria-Hungary by a nationalist from Serbia, a constituent republic of Yugoslavia. The largest war the world had yet seen lasted until 1918.

Albert Einstein (1879–1955), who was born in Germany, is known as the greatest physicist of all time. He is best known for his theory of relativity. In 1921 Einstein won the Nobel Prize in Physics for his photoelectric effect. He became an American citizen in 1940.

On December 7, 1941, Japanese carrier planes swept in over Pearl Harbor without warning. The raid on the United States Pacific fleet destroyed eight American battleships, three of which are pictured here. From left to right: U.S.S. *West Virginia* was severely damaged; U.S.S. *Tennessee* was damaged; and U.S.S. *Arizona* was sunk. On December 8 the United States declared war on Japan.

music and Nazi speeches. At the same time, they began ruthlessly persecuting German Jews, stripping them of their citizenship and expelling them from government posts and teaching positions.

Other Totalitarian Regimes

Hitler's government was only one of a number of totalitarian regimes to emerge during the first half of the twentieth century. In Russia, where communists had seized power in the November Revolution of 1917, a totalitarian state was established after Joseph Stalin rose to power in the late 1920's. Like Hitler, Stalin brutally suppressed all dissent, executing millions of people who resisted his policies. Another totalitarian ruler, Benito Mus-

solini, gained control of Italy and later became one of Hitler's chief allies. Finally, after winning a bloody civil war, Francisco Franco established a fascist regime in Spain in 1939.

The German Invasion of Poland

During the Spanish Civil War, both the Germans and the Italians provided Franco with military support, using the war as a testing ground for new weapons and tactics. Because the democratic powers did little to discourage German and Italian involvement in Spain, Hitler and Mussolini did not hesitate to engage in further acts of military aggression. Consequently, in September of 1939, German forces engaged in an all-out attack

The World at War (1939–45)

Axis territory September 1, 1939
Axis satellites
Axis occupied
Soviet occupied territory 1939-1940
British Empire
Neutral Powers

on Poland. Within less than a month, Poland had surrendered and the world was once again embroiled in a massive war.

Japanese Aggression in Eastern Asia

Long before Hitler's invasion of Poland, the Japanese had begun engaging in acts of military aggression in eastern Asia. Having already assumed control of Korea and Taiwan, the Japanese seized Manchuria from China in 1931. Six years later, they launched a full-scale war against the Chinese. Although the Chinese resisted, their forces proved to be no match for the Japanese army, and by 1938 the Japanese had won control of northern and central China.

The Attack on Pearl Harbor

A year after the beginning of World War II, the Japanese allied themselves with the Germans and the Italians. At the time the Japanese officially entered the war, the United States had not become directly involved in the conflict, despite the pleas of the European democratic nations. In December of 1941, however, the Japanese drew the United States into the war by launching a massive aerial assault on the American naval base at Pearl Harbor in Hawaii.

The Defeat of Germany and Japan

In May of 1945, after years of savage fighting on battlefronts that circled the world, the Nazis surrendered to the Allies, led by the United States, Great Britain, and the Soviet Union. Three months later, Japan also surrendered, after the United States had dropped atomic bombs on the Japanese cities of Hiroshima and Nagasaki. With the defeat of Japan, peace had finally arrived. Yet so had the atomic age.

The destruction caused by World War II was staggering. More than twelve million soldiers and over twenty million civilians were killed and countless others were wounded. In addition, much of Europe and Japan was reduced to rubble by bombing raids, uprooting millions of people from their homes.

The Holocaust

One of the most shocking aspects of the war was not fully discovered until the Allied forces marched into Germany. In response to Hitler's diabolical plan to exterminate the entire Jewish population, the Nazis had imprisoned and executed over six million Jews in concentration camps. This systematic slaughter, which has come to be known as the Holocaust, stands out as one of the most tragic events in human history.

MODERN LITERATURE

The modern age was one of the most turbulent and violent periods of human history. Yet it was also an era of tremendous artistic and literary achievement. Responding to the events and developments of their time and experimenting with new literary forms and approaches, modern writers from across the world created a fresh and remarkably diverse body of literature.

Worldwide Literary Connections

With the advances in travel and communication, the various regions of the world became increasingly intertwined during the modern age. Consequently, the literary world became more interconnected than ever before, as writers from all countries were exposed to the literary movements and traditions of other cultures.

For the first time, writers from non-Western and less developed countries began to receive worldwide attention. The modern Indian writer Rabindranath Tagore, for example, earned a Nobel Prize for his literary accomplishments. The Chilean poet Gabriela Mistral also won a Nobel Prize, after the Nicaraguan poet Rubén Darío had drawn the attention of the literary world to Latin America. Darío not only received worldwide acclaim but also influenced a number of important European poets.

13

The late nineteenth and early twentieth centuries also marked the beginning of literary interaction between the Western world and the nations of eastern Asia. The introduction of Western literature had a dramatic impact on both Chinese and Japanese literature, and writers from both countries, such as the Japanese writer Mori Ōgai and the Chinese writer Lu Hsun, adopted many Western literary forms and techniques. At the same time, a number of prominent Western writers, including American poet Ezra Pound and German 14 playwright Bertolt Brecht, were influenced by traditional Oriental literature.

The Birth of Modernism

Regardless of where they lived, modern writers could not escape being affected by the momentous events and developments of their time. Even before World War I, some writers were concerned by the rapid changes that were taking place and sensed that society was becoming disconnected from the values and traditions of the past. Following the devastation caused by the war, these feelings developed into an overwhelming sense of uncertainty, disjointedness, and disillusionment—emotions shared not only by writers but also by artists, philosophers, and many other people. Distrusting the attitudes and beliefs that had existed before the war, many people embarked on a quest for new ideas. This quest produced a broad collection of artistic and literary movements often referred to as Modernism.

Although there were major differences among the many writers associated with Modernism, they generally shared the desire to establish new literary approaches and techniques. In addition they typically sought to capture the essence of modern life in both the form and the content of their works. To reflect the disjointedness of the modern world, they often constructed their works out of frag15 ments, omitting the expositions, transitions, resolutions, and explanations used in traditional literature. In poetry, they abandoned traditional forms in favor of free verse. In addition the themes of their works were usually implied, rather than directly stated, creating a sense of uncertainty and forcing readers to draw their own conclusions.

Among the most prominent Modernist writers are the American poet T. S. Eliot, the Irish novelist James Joyce, the German-speaking fiction writer Franz Kafka, and the Italian playwright Luigi Pirandello. In their works both Eliot and Kafka captured the bleakness, alienation, and despair often associated with modern life. Influenced by recent psychological breakthroughs, Joyce tried to re-create the inner workings of the human mind. Finally, in his highly innovative plays, Pirandello attempted to convey the uncertain nature of reality.

Standing Up Against Hardships

In addition to shaping the direction of modern literature, the turbulent events of the first half of the twentieth century directly affected the lives of many writers. Among these was the Spanish poet Federico García Lorca, who was murdered during the early stages of the Spanish Civil War. Another was the Russian poet Anna Akhmatova, who was arrested and sent to a labor camp following the rise of Stalin. The life of German writer Thomas Mann was also severely disrupted when he was forced into involuntary exile following Adolf Hitler's rise to power. Like a number of other writers, Mann used his literary talents to speak out against the Nazis, and in his novel *Doctor Faustus* he symbolically depicts the rise of the Nazis. Another writer, Isak Dinesen, risked her own life by aiding many Jews in escaping from the Nazis, who had seized control of her native land of Denmark.

Beyond the Modern Age

Although the end of World War II marks the official close of the modern age, the literary innovations and accomplishments of this era did not end in 1945. Many modern writers, including Mann, Mistral, and Akhmatova, remained productive long after the end of the war. At the same time, a new generation of talented writers arose across the globe, bringing with them fresh ideas and approaches.

MODERN VOICES

Opinions cannot survive if no one has a chance to fight for them.
Thomas Mann, *The Magic Mountain*

The most visible joy can only reveal itself to us when we've transformed it, within.
Rainer Maria Rilke, *The Duino Elegies*

When Gregor Samsa woke up one morning from unsettling dreams, he found himself changed in his bed into a monstrous vermin.
Franz Kafka, "The Metamorphosis"

Art is unthinkable without risk and spiritual self-sacrifice.
Boris Pasternak, "On Modesty and Bravery"

Poetry is simply literature reduced to the essence of its active principle.
Paul Valéry, *Literature*

By means of an image we are often able to hold on to our lost belongings. But it is the desperateness of losing which picks the flowers of memory, binds the bouquet.
Colette, *Mes Apprentissages*

At five in the afternoon.
Ah, that fatal five in the afternoon!
It was five by all the clocks!
It was five in the shade of the afternoon!
Federico García Lorca, "Lament for Ignacio Sánchez Mejías"

He who longs to strengthen his spirit
must go beyond obedience and respect.
He will continue to honor some laws
but he will mostly violate
both law and custom.
Constantine Cavafy, "Strengthening the Spirit"

I seek a form that my style cannot discover,
a bud of thought that wants to be a rose.
Rubén Darío, "I Seek a Form"

At my dying hour, and over my long life,
A clock strikes somewhere at the city's edge.
Rabindranath Tagore, "Poem"

The Literature of the Modern Age

Historical Context

The Modern Age was an era marked by violent conflict and rapid change. As the period began, major scientific and technological developments were occurring that were dramatically altering the way in which people lived. At the same time, the balance of power among the world's nations was beginning to shift, with such countries as the United States, Japan, and Germany emerging as world powers. The emergence of Germany as a world power contributed to the volatile European political climate that ultimately resulted in World War I, a bloody conflict that wiped out almost an entire generation of European men. In the aftermath of the war, a worldwide economic depression occurred and fascist dictators assumed control of Germany, Italy, and Spain. Soon after Adolf Hitler's rise to power in Germany, the world was plummeted into another world war.

Cultural Context

Because of the dramatic developments and changes that were taking place, many traditional European cultural attitudes and beliefs began to disappear, producing a climate of uncertainty and disjointedness. This was especially true in Germany, where sweeping political and economic changes had occurred in the late 1800's as a result of rapid industrialization and the unification of the German states. The sense of uncertainty and despair was even more prevalent in Germany following its defeat in World War I. In the aftermath of the war, the German government was completely restructured, and the nation suffered from severe economic problems, leaving the German people feeling disconnected from their past and pessimistic about their future—a state of mind that made them susceptible to Adolf Hitler and his promises of national glory.

Literary Context

The Modern Age was also a period of dramatic change in the literary world. Many writers turned away from the dominant literary forms and approaches of the past and began experimenting with new themes and techniques. In addition, these writers, known as Modernists, sought to capture the essence of modern life in both the form and the content of their works. As a result, many modern literary works convey a sense of rapid change, uncertainty, detachment, and disillusionment—the feelings that modern writers most often associated with early-twentieth-century life.

The annotations that accompany the following story by the modern German writer Thomas Mann (tō′ mäs män) point out the work's historical context, cultural context, and literary context.

Objectives

Thematic

To understand how extremely gifted people are set apart from other members of society

Skills

1 To recognize point of view
2 To recognize dramatic irony
3 To write about point of view

The Infant Prodigy

Thomas Mann

translated by H. T. Lowe-Porter

The infant prodigy entered. The hall became quiet.

It became quiet and then the audience began to clap, because somewhere at the side a leader of mobs, a born organizer, clapped first. The audience had heard nothing yet, but they applauded; for a mighty publicity organization had heralded the prodigy and people were already hypnotized, whether they knew it or not.

The prodigy came from behind a splendid screen embroidered with Empire[1] garlands and great conventionalized flowers, and climbed nimbly up the steps to the platform, diving into the applause as into a bath; a little chilly and shivering, but yet as though into a friendly element. He advanced to the edge of the platform and smiled as though he were about to be photographed; he made a shy, charming gesture of greeting, like a little girl.

He was dressed entirely in white silk, which the audience found enchanting. The little white jacket was fancifully cut, with a sash underneath it, and even his shoes were made of white silk. But against the white socks his bare little legs stood out quite brown; for he was a Greek boy.

He was called Bibi Saccellaphylaccas.[2] And such indeed was his name. No one knew what Bibi was the pet name for, nobody but the impresario,[3] and he regarded it as a trade secret. Bibi had smooth black hair reaching to his shoulders; it was parted on the side and fastened back from the narrow domed forehead by a little silk bow. His was the most harmless childish countenance in the world, with an unfinished nose and guileless mouth. The area beneath his pitch black mouse-like eyes was already a little tired and visibly lined. He looked as though he were nine years old but was really eight and given out for seven. It was

---

1. **Empire:** The Empire style is a manner of French interior decoration and costume.
2. **Bibi Saccellaphylaccas** (bē′ bē sa səl la′ fə la kəs)
3. **impressario** (im′ prə sär′ ē ō): The organizer, director, or manager of an opera or ballet company or concert series.

Historical Context: "The Infant Prodigy" was written in 1903. The details of the setting and the prodigy's clothing reveal that the action of the story takes place in either the late nineteenth century or the early twentieth century.

Literary Context: Mann begins the story with an exposition in which he provides important background information. The exposition is part of the traditional plot structure that many modern writers abandoned in an effort to capture the uncertainty of modern life in the form of their works. In his work, however, Mann generally utilizes both traditional and modern forms and approaches.

Support Material

Teaching Portfolio
Teacher Backup, p. 1223
Reading Critically, "The Bird's Nest" by Selma Lagerloff, p. 1227
Grammar in Action Worksheet, *Using Active and Passive Voice*, p. 1233
Usage and Mechanics Worksheet, p. 1235

Vocabulary Check, p. 1236
Analyzing Literature Worksheet, *Recognizing Point of View*, p. 1237
Critical Thinking and Reading Worksheet, *Recognizing Dramatic Irony*, p. 1238
Selection Test, pp 1239–1240

Presentation

Motivation/Prior Knowledge
Have students discuss what they imagine it would be like to be a young genius. What do they see as some of the possible disadvantages of being so gifted? What do they see as the main advantages?

Purpose-Setting Question What is Bibi's attitude toward the people in his audience? How are the responses of the people in the audience to Bibi's performance shaped by their own preoccupations?

ESL Teaching Strategy Team each of your ESL students with a native-speaking student. Have the pairs read the selection together, taking turns reading aloud. Instruct the native speaker to clarify the meanings of any words with which the ESL student is unfamiliar.

Teaching Tenth-Grade Students
You might want to introduce the concept of point of view to tenth-grade students before they begin reading the story. Have a student volunteer read aloud the Commentary on point of view on page 1154. Then encourage students to ask any questions they still have about point of view.

Vocabulary

Preteach the following vocabulary words:
prodigy (präd′ ə jē) *n.*: A child of highly unusual talent or genius
countenance (koun′ tə nəns) *n.*: Facial expression
guileless (gīl′ lis) *adj.*: Candid; frank
objectively (äb′ jek′ tiv lē) *n.*: Impartially
abysmal (ə biz′ m'l) adj.: Immeasurably bad
proffered (präf′ ərd) *v.*: Offered
ineffable (in ef′ ə b'l) *adj.* Inexpressible

Spelling Tip Call students' attention to the double *f* in both *ineffable* and *proffered*.

Master Teacher Note Students might benefit from some background knowledge about a real-life infant prodigy, Wolfgang Amadeus Mozart (1756–1791). Have a group of student volunteers gather information about Mozart and present their findings to the class. Encourage students to keep their knowledge of Mozart in mind as they read Mann's story.

Universal Themes Mann's story explores the relationship between the artist and society. This theme has been explored by many other writers from a wide range of cultures and literary eras. One of these writers is the French poet Charles Baudelaire, whose poem "The Albatross" (page 905) conveys the idea that the artist is alienated from the rest of society.

1 Discussion Have students discuss what it means to describe something as having "real artistic significance." Then have them discuss the tone of this passage. What seems to be Mann's attitude toward the prodigy? What seems to be his attitude toward the impressario?

2 Discussion Ask students what Mann means when he writes that the condition of Bibi's piano "only made things more interesting."

3 Discussion Have students discuss whether Bibi's movements seem to have been carefully planned out. If so, who might be responsible for planning them?

4 Discussion Have students explain the simile that Mann uses in this passage. Do they find it effective? Why or why not?

1

2

3

Literary Context: In this passage, Mann develops Bibi's character through Bibi's thoughts and actions.

4

hard to tell whether to believe this or not. Probably everybody knew better and still believed it, as happens about so many things. The average man thinks that a little falseness goes with beauty. Where should we get any excitement out of our daily life if we were not willing to pretend a bit? And the average man is quite right, in his average brains!

The prodigy kept on bowing until the applause died down, then he went up to the grand piano, and the audience cast a last look at its programs. First came a *Marche solennelle*,[4] then a *Rêverie*,[5] and then *Le Hibou et les moineaux*[6]— all by Bibi Saccellaphylaccas. The whole program was by him, they were all his compositions. He could not score them, of course, but he had them all in his extraordinary little head and they possessed real artistic significance, or so it said, seriously and objectively, in the program. The program sounded as though the impresario had wrested these concessions from his critical nature after a hard struggle.

The prodigy sat down upon the revolving stool and felt with his feet for the pedals, which were raised by means of a clever device so that Bibi could reach them. It was Bibi's own piano; he took it everywhere with him. It rested upon wooden trestles and its polish was somewhat marred by the constant transportation—but all that only made things more interesting.

Bibi put his silk-shod feet on the pedals; then he made an artful little face, looked straight ahead of him, and lifted his right hand. It was a brown, childish little hand; but the wrist was strong and unlike a child's, with well-developed bones.

Bibi made his face for the audience because he was aware that he had to entertain them a little. But he had his own private enjoyment in the thing too, an enjoyment which he could never convey to anybody. It was that prickling delight, that secret shudder of bliss, which ran through him every time he sat at an open piano—it would always be with him. And here was the keyboard again, these seven black and white octaves, among which he had so often lost himself in abysmal and thrilling adventures—and yet it always looked as clean and untouched as a newly washed blackboard. This was the realm of music that lay before him. It lay spread out like an inviting ocean, where he might plunge in and blissfully swim, where he might let himself be borne and carried away, where he might go under in night and storm, yet keep the mastery: control, ordain—he held his right hand poised in the air.

A breathless stillness reigned in the room—the tense moment before the first note came. . . . How would it begin? It began so. And Bibi, with

---

4. *Marche solennelle* (märsh sə len el′): "Solemn March" (French).
5. *Rêverie* (rev′ ər ē): "Dreamy thinking"; "musing" (French).
6. *Le Hibou et les moineaux* (lö ē bo̅o̅′ ā lā mwä nō′): "The owl and the sparrows" (French).

Primary Source

In his study of Thomas Mann, the literary scholar Eric Heller discusses Mann's treatment of the relationship between the artist and society. He writes:

Thomas Mann knows only too well—and how could the creator of Hanno Buddenbrook and Tonio Kröger not know it?—that in actual fact the artist he has in mind exists in painful isolation from his society. What he as yet refuses to envisage is the possibility that the divorce may be due more to the misdemeanor of society than to the unfaithfulness of art; and it is, notwithstanding the 'ethical aspect of my existence,' his in-

eradicable moral distrust of the artist that prevents him from indulging such suspicions. . . . Thomas Mann believes that the artist, or at least the prevalent type of artist . . . is condemned to a subtle kind of insincerity in his proclaimed opposition to the 'world' as represented by the society of his time. He wishes to please. What ultimately matters to him is success. . . . The artist is concerned to move men through beauty, not to convince them of truth. He woos even with his aggression, seduces even with his chastity, seeks the admiration of those he dooms in his apocalyptic visions, and the applause of those he damns with his last judgments.

his index finger, fetched the first note out of the piano, a quite unexpectedly powerful first note in the middle register, like a trumpet blast. Others followed, an introduction developed—the audience relaxed.

The concert was held in the palatial hall of a fashionable first-class hotel. The walls were covered with mirrors framed in gilded

Historical Context: The interior of the hotel reflects the preference of the nineteenth-century European upper class for ornate and elaborate artistic and architectural forms.

THE OLD BURGTHEATER, 1888–1889
Gustav Klimt
Historisches Museum der Stadt Wien, Vienna

Humanities Note
Fine art, *The Old Burgtheater* by Gustav Klimt. The German painter Gustav Klimt (1862–1918) was a leading member of the art nouveau movement. This movement, which originated in London during the 1880s, involved furniture and jewelry designers and book illustrators, as well as painters. All the artists associated with the movement emphasized the use of rich, ornamental designs. Often, these designs had symbolic meaning or were imbued with exotic, dreamlike forms.

Klimt painted many murals for public buildings, including a series for the Vienna Burgtheater. Yet his fame as a painter rests mainly on his portraits and landscapes. His works are characterized by his use of rich, extravagant colors and his sensitivity to balance and rhythm.

You might want to use the following questions to discuss the art:

1. What impression does the artist convey of his subjects?
2. How would you describe the artist's use of color?
3. What makes this an appropriate illustration for Mann's story?
4. Do you like this painting? Why or why not?

5 Discussion Have students discuss the impression that Mann conveys of the concert hall. Which details contribute to this impression?

6 Discussion Have students discuss the tone of this passage. Do they think that Mann actually believed that "it was in the upper classes, of course, that the greatest enthusiasm was felt"?

7 Discussion Have students discuss the impression that Mann conveys of Bibi's mother and of the princess. Which details contribute to these impressions?

8 Discussion Have students discuss why Bibi finishes with the march theme. Do they think that Bibi's body movements during this piece are spontaneous? Or have they been planned?

9 Literary Focus Have students discuss why Mann might have chosen to use an omniscient third-person point of view in this story. How does his use of this type of point of view contribute to the effectiveness of the story?

10 Discussion Have students discuss the significance of the fact that the members of the audience cannot remember Bibi's name.

5
6

Literary Context: Note how Mann develops these **7** characters through his descriptions of their physical appearances.

8

Literary Context: The story is told from a third-**9** person omniscient point of **10** view. During the modern age, most writers abandoned the use of omniscient narrators.

arabesques,[7] between frescoes[8] of the rosy and fleshy school. Ornamental columns supported a ceiling that displayed a whole universe of electric bulbs, in clusters darting a brilliance far brighter than day and filling the whole space with thin, vibrating golden light. Not a seat was unoccupied, people were standing in the side aisles and at the back. The front seats cost twelve marks;[9] for the impresario believed that anything worth having was worth paying for. And they were occupied by the best society, for it was in the upper classes, of course, that the greatest enthusiasm was felt. There were even some children, with their legs hanging down demurely[10] from their chairs and their shining eyes staring at their gifted little white-clad contemporary.

Down in front on the left side sat the prodigy's mother, an extremely obese woman with a powdered double chin and a feather on her head. Beside her was the impresario, a man of oriental appearance with large gold buttons on his conspicuous cuffs. The princess was in the middle of the front row—a wrinkled, shriveled little old princess but still a patron of the arts, especially everything full of sensibility. She sat in a deep, velvet-upholstered armchair, and a Persian carpet was spread before her feet. She held her hands folded over her gray striped-silk breast, put her head on one side, and presented a picture of elegant composure as she sat looking up at the performing prodigy. Next to her sat her lady-in-waiting, in a green striped-silk gown. Being only a lady-in-waiting she had to sit up very straight in her chair.

Bibi ended in a grand climax. With what power this wee manikin belabored the keyboard! The audience could scarcely trust its ears. The march theme, an infectious, swinging tune, broke out once more, fully harmonized, bold and showy; with every note Bibi flung himself back from the waist as though he were marching in a triumphal procession. He ended *fortissimo*,[11] bent over, slipped sideways off the stool, and stood with a smile awaiting the applause.

And the applause burst forth, unanimously, enthusiastically; the child made his demure little maidenly curtsy and people in the front seat thought: "Look what slim little hips he has! Clap, clap! Hurrah, bravo, little chap, Saccophylax or whatever your name is! Wait, let me take off my gloves—what a little devil of a chap he is!"

---

7. **arabesques** (ar´ ə besks´) *n.*: Complex and elaborate designs of intertwined patterns, painted or carved in low relief.

8. **frescoes** (fres´ kōz) *n.*: Paintings or designs made with watercolors on wet plaster.

9. **marks:** The mark was the German monetary unit prior to World War I.

10. **demurely** (di myoor´ lē) *adv.*: Modestly; reservedly.

11. **fortissimo** (fôr tis´ ə mō´): Very loud.

Grammar in Action

When the subject of the sentence receives, rather than performs, the verb's action, the **passive voice** is being used. In contrast, when the subject does perform the action, the **active voice** is being used. Note the following examples from "The Infant Prodigy":

ACTIVE VOICE: Bibi *ended* in a grand climax.
PASSIVE VOICE: But the court lady *was commanded to* go over to Bibi . . . (page 1046)

While most authorities advise that we write in the active voice whenever possible, the passive voice is sometimes used to preserve the vitality of action verbs or to place emphasis on the subject.

Student Activity 1. Identify the type of voice used in each of the following passages from "The Infant Prodigy."
1. But against the white socks his bare legs stood out quite brown . . .
2. It was that prickling delight, that secret shudder of bliss, which ran through him every time he sat at an open piano . . .
3. He ended fortissimo, bent over, slipped sideways off the stool . . .
4. Some latecomers entered the hall and moved about looking for seats.
5. In front of one of the great mirrors an elegant young lady was being ar-

Bibi had to come out three times from behind the screen before they would stop. Some latecomers entered the hall and moved about looking for seats. Then the concert continued. Bibi's *Rêverie* murmured its numbers, consisting almost entirely of arpeggios,[12] above which a bar of melody rose now and then, weak-winged. Then came *Le Hibou et les moineux*. This piece was brilliantly successful, it made a strong impression; it was an effective childhood fantasy, remarkably well envisaged.[13] The bass represented the owl, sitting morosely[14] rolling his filmy eyes; while in the treble the impudent, half-frightened sparrows chirped. Bibi received an ovation when he finished, he was called out four times. A hotel page with shiny buttons carried up three great laurel wreaths onto the stage and proffered them from one side while Bibi nodded and expressed his thanks. Even the princess shared in the applause, daintily and noiselessly pressing her palms together.

Ah, the knowing little creature understood how to make people clap! He stopped behind the screen; they had to wait for him; he lingered a little on the steps of the platform, admired the long streamers on the wreaths—although actually such things bored him stiff by now. He bowed with the utmost charm, he gave the audience plenty of time to rave itself out, because applause is valuable and must not be cut short. "*Le Hibou* is my drawing card," he thought—this expression he had learned from the impresario. "Now I will play the fantasy, it is a lot better than *Le Hibou*, of course, especially the C-sharp passage. But you idiots dote on the *Hibou*, though it is the first and the silliest thing I wrote." He continued to bow and smile.

Next came a *Méditation*[15] and then an *Étude*[16]—the program was quite comprehensive. The *Méditation* was very like the *Rêverie*—which was nothing against it—and the *Étude* displayed all of Bibi's virtuosity, which naturally fell a little short of his inventiveness. And then the *Fantaisie*.[17] This was his favorite; he varied it a little each time, giving himself free rein and sometimes surprising even himself, on good evenings, by his own inventiveness.

He sat and played, so little, so white and shining, against the great black grand piano, elect and alone, above that confused sea of faces, above the heavy, insensitive mass soul, upon which he was laboring to

Literary Context: Note what Bibi's thoughts reveal about his relationship with his audience. The relationship between the artist and society is a common theme in both nineteenth- and twentieth-century literature.

11 **Discussion** Ask students to explain whose interpretation of *Le Hobou et les moineux* is being offered in this passage.

12 **Discussion** Have students speculate about how Bibi may have developed an understanding of how to make people clap. Do they imagine that the impresario may have played a role in Bibi's acquisition of this knowledge? Why or why not?

13 **Discussion** Have students discuss what this passage suggests about Bibi's attitude toward his audience.

14 **Discussion** Have students discuss the significance of the narrator's observation that Bibi's virtuosity "naturally fell a little short of inventiveness."

15 **Discussion** Have students discuss the impression that this passage conveys of Bibi's relationship with his audience. Which details contribute to this impression?

---

12. **arpeggios** (är pej′ōz) *n.*: Chords in which the notes are played in quick succession rather than simultaneously.
13. **envisaged** (en viz′ ijd) *v.*: Visualized; imagined.
14. **morosely** (mə rōs′ lē) *adv.*: Gloomily; sullenly.
15. **Méditation** (mā dē ta syōn′): "Meditation" (French).
16. **Étude** (ā′ tōōd): "Study" (French).
17. **Fantaisie** (fàn te zē′) *n.*: "Fancy" (French).

rayed in her eveing cloak and fur shoes by her brothers, two lieutenants.

Student Activity 2. Transform each of the following active sentences into a passive sentence.
1. All of these people sat there in their regular rows, looking at the prodigy and thinking all sorts of things in their regular brains.
2. The prodigy stopped playing and a perfect storm arose in the hall.
3. The man with the shiny buttons carried up more wreaths . . .
4. She rather despised them, but she looked after them until they had turned the corner.
5. A girl with untidy hair and swinging arms, accompanied by a gloomy-faced youth, came out just behind them.

16 Discussion Ask students if they imagine that most artists experience "moments of oblivion and solitude." If so, why?

17 Discussion Have students discuss why Bibi might have such contempt for his audience. Why is the audience completely unaware that he feels this way about them?

18 Discussion Call students' attention to Mann's repetition of the word *regular* in this sentence. Then have them explore the connotations of this word.

19 Discussion Have students respond to the thoughts of the old gentleman. Are his thoughts presented in a realistic manner? Why or why not?

20 Literary Focus Call students' attention to how the businessman's preoccupations color his response to Bibi's performance. Then have students discuss how the story might have been different if it had been presented entirely from the businessman's point of view.

21 Discussion Have students respond to the piano teacher's appraisal of Bibi's performance. Why is she so critical of him? What do her thoughts reveal about her character?

Cultural Context: Because of his genius, Bibi is isolated and alienated from society. Isolation and alienation are two feelings that modern writers often associated with life in the modern world.

16

17

18

Literary Context: Note how Mann uses the omniscient narrator to capture the responses of several different members of the audience to Bibi's performance.

19

20

21

work with his individual, differentiated soul. His lock of soft black hair with the white silk bow had fallen over his forehead, his trained and bony little wrists pounded away, the muscles stood out visibly on his brown childish cheeks.

Sitting there he sometimes had moments of oblivion and solitude, when the gaze of his strange little mouselike eyes with the big rings beneath them would lose itself and stare through the painted stage into space that was peopled with strange vague life. Then out of the corner of his eye he would give a quick look back into the hall and be once more with his audience.

"Joy and pain, the heights and the depths—that is my *Fantaisie*," he thought lovingly. "Listen, here is the C-sharp passage." He lingered over the approach, wondering if they would notice anything. But no, of course not, how should they? And he cast his eyes up prettily at the ceiling so that at least they might have something to look at.

All these people sat there in their regular rows, looking at the prodigy and thinking all sorts of things in their regular brains. An old gentleman with a white beard, a seal ring on his finger, and a bulbous swelling on his bald spot, a growth if you like, was thinking to himself: "Really, one ought to be ashamed." He had never got any further than "Ah, thou dearest Augustin" on the piano, and here he sat now, a gray old man, looking on while this little hop-o'-my-thumb performed miracles. Yes, yes, it is a gift of God, we must remember that. God grants his gifts, or he withholds them, and there is no shame in being an ordinary man. Like with the Christ child.—Before a child one may kneel without feeling ashamed. Strange that thoughts like these should be so satisfying—he would even say so sweet, if it was not too silly for a tough old man like him to use the word. That was how he felt, anyhow.

Art . . . the businessman with the parrot-nose was thinking. "Yes, it adds something cheerful to life, a little good white silk and a little tumty-ti-ti-tum. Really he does not play so badly. Fully fifty seats, twelve marks apiece, that makes six hundred marks—and everything else besides. Take off the rent of the hall, the lighting, and the programs, you must have fully a thousand marks profit. That is worthwhile."

"That was Chopin[18] he was just playing," thought the piano teacher, a lady with a pointed nose; she was of an age when the understanding sharpens as the hopes decay. "But not very original—I will say that afterward; it sounds well. And his hand position is entirely amateur. One must be able to lay a coin on the back of the hand—I would use a ruler on him."

---

18. **Chopin** (shō' pan): Frédéric François Chopin (1810–1849), a Polish-born composer and pianist.

Primary Source

THE ITALIAN MUSIC HALL
Eva Gonzalès
The Louvre, Paris

22 Discussion Have students discuss the young girl's observations about passion. Do they agree with these observations? Why or why not?

23 Discussion Have students explain the meaning of the critic's observation that Bibi "has in himself all the artist's exaltation and his utter worthlessness."

Humanities Note
Fine art, *The Italian Music Hall Box* by Eva Gonzalès. Gonzalès (1849–1883) modeled for the famous French Impressionist Edouard Manet and later became Manet's pupil. Despite her association with Manet, however, she did not adopt the style of the Impressionists. Instead, she focused on providing viewers with an intimate perspective of her subjects. In this painting, for example, viewers feel almost as if they are part of the audience at the Italian music hall and are sitting directly across from the couple that the artist has depicted.

You might want to use the following questions to discuss the art:

1. How would you describe the mood, or atmosphere, of this painting?
2. In what ways is this painting similar to and different from the painting on page 1041?
3. Does this make an appropriate illustration for "The Infant Prodigy"? Why or why not?
4. How would you describe this painting to a friend who has never seen it?

Then there was a young girl, at that self-conscious and chlorotic[19] time of life when the most ineffable ideas come into the mind. She was thinking to herself: "What is it he is playing? It is expressive of passion, yet he is a child. If he kissed me it would be as though my little brother kissed me—no kiss at all. Is there such a thing as passion all by itself, without any earthly object, a sort of child's-play of passion? What nonsense! If I were to say such things aloud they would just be at me with some more cod-liver oil. Such is life."

An officer was leaning against a column. He looked on at Bibi's success and thought: "Yes, you are something and I am something, each in his own way." So he clapped his heel together and paid to the prodigy the respect which he felt to be due to all the powers that be.

Then there was a critic, an elderly man in a shiny black coat and turned-up trousers splashed with mud. He sat in his free seat and thought: "Look at him, this young beggar of a Bibi. As an individual he has still to develop, but as a type he is already quite complete, the artist *par excellence*.[20] He has in himself all the artist's exaltation and his utter worthlessness, his charlatanry[21] and his sacred fire, his burning

22

23

Literary Context: The critic's personality is developed through his thoughts about Bibi and his performance.

---

19. chlorotic (klə rät′ ik) *adj.*: Having chlorosis, a condition that causes the skin to turn a greenish color.
20. *par excellence* (pär ek se läns′): "Beyond comparison" (French).
21. charlatanry (shär′ lə t′n rē) *n.*: Pretending to have expert knowledge or skill that one does not have.

24 Discussion Do students imagine that the critic's ability to see "through the whole business so clearly" is the real reason why he did not become an artist? Why or why not? What do his observations reveal about his character?

25 Discussion Have students discuss why the impresario's kiss has such a powerful impact on the audience.

26 Clarification Make sure that students are aware that the word *august* means "worthy of respect because of age, dignity, or high position."

27 Discussion Have students discuss what the critic means when he compares an artist to a "jack-in-the-box." Why does he think that "criticism is on a higher plane"?

28 Discussion Have students discuss whether the audience's response to the performance seems somewhat exaggerated. If so, what effect might Mann have been trying to produce by exaggerating the audience's response?

Literary Context: The critic recognizes that the performance has been staged to draw the greatest possible reaction from the audience. This observation offers an important insight into the theme of the story.

contempt and his secret raptures. Of course I can't write all that, it is too good. Of course, I should have been an artist myself if I had not seen through the whole business so clearly."

Then the prodigy stopped playing and a perfect storm arose in the hall. He had to come out again and again from behind his screen. The man with the shiny buttons carried up more wreaths: four laurel wreaths, a lyre[22] made of violets, a bouquet of roses. He had not arms enough to convey all these tributes; the impresario himself mounted the stage to help him. He hung a laurel wreath round Bibi's neck, he tenderly stroked the black hair—and suddenly as though overcome he bent down and gave the prodigy a kiss, a resounding kiss, square on the mouth. And then the storm became a hurricane. That kiss ran through the room like an electric shock, it went direct to people's marrow and made them shiver down their backs. They were carried away by a helpless compulsion of sheer noise. Loud shouts mingled with the hysterical clapping of hands. Some of Bibi's commonplace little friends down there waved their handkerchiefs. But the critic thought: "Of course that kiss had to come—it's a good old gag. Yes, good Lord, if only one did not see through everything quite so clearly—"

And so the concert drew to a close. It began at half past seven and finished at half past eight. The platform was laden with wreaths and two little pots of flowers stood on the lamp stands of the piano. Bibi played as his last number his *Rhapsodie grecque,*[23] which turned into the Greek national hymn at the end. His fellow countrymen in the audience would gladly have sung it with him if the company had not been so august. They made up for it with a powerful noise and hullabaloo, a hot-blooded national demonstration. And the aging critic was thinking: "Yes, the hymn had to come too. They have to exploit every vein—publicity cannot afford to neglect any means to its end. I think I'll criticize that as inartistic. But perhaps I am wrong, perhaps that is the most artistic thing of all. What is the artist? A jack-in-the-box. Criticism is on a higher plane. But I can't say that." And away he went in his muddy trousers.

After being called out nine or ten times the prodigy did not come anymore from behind the screen but went to his mother and the impresario down in the hall. The audience stood about among the chairs and applauded and pressed forward to see Bibi close at hand. Some of them wanted to see the princess too. Two dense circles formed, one round the prodigy, the other round the princess, and you could actually not tell which of them was receiving more homage. But the court lady was commanded to go over to Bibi; she smoothed down his silk jacket

---

22. **lyre** (līr) *n.*: A small stringed instrument of the harp family.
23. ***Rhapsodie grecque*** (ràp sə dē´ grek): "Greek Rhapsody" (French).

a bit to make it look suitable for a court function, led him by the arm to the princess, and solemnly indicated to him that he was to kiss the royal hand. "How do you do it, child?" asked the princess. "Does it come into your head of itself when you sit down?" "*Oui, madame,*"24 answered Bibi. To himself he thought: "Oh, what a stupid old princess!" Then he turned round shyly and uncourtierlike and went back to his family.

Outside in the cloakroom there was a crowd. People held up their numbers and received with open arms furs, shawls, and galoshes. Somewhere among her acquaintances the piano teacher stood making her critique. "He is not very original," she said audibly and looked about her.

In front of one of the great mirrors an elegant young lady was being arrayed in her evening cloak and fur shoes by her brothers, two lieutenants. She was exquisitely beautiful, with her steel-blue eyes and her clean-cut, well-bred face. A really noble dame. When she was ready she stood waiting for her brothers. "Don't stand so long in front of the glass, Adolf," she said softly to one of them, who could not tear himself away from the sight of his simple, good-looking young features. But Lieutenant Adolf thinks: "What cheek!" He would button his overcoat in front of the glass, just the same. Then they went out on the street where the arc lights gleamed cloudily through the white mist. Lieutenant Adolf struck up a little dance on the frozen snow to keep warm, with his hands in his slanting overcoat pockets and his collar turned up.

A girl with untidy hair and swinging arms, accompanied by a gloomy-faced youth, came out just behind them. "A child!" she thought. "A charming child. But in there he was an awe-inspiring . . ." and aloud in a toneless voice she said: "We are all infant prodigies, we artists."

"Well, bless my soul!" thought the old gentleman who had never got further than"Augustin" on the piano, and whose boil was now concealed by a top hat. "What does all that mean? She sounds very oracular." But the gloomy youth understood. He nodded his head slowly.

Then they were silent and the untidy-haired girl gazed after the brothers and sister. She rather despised them, but she looked after them until they had turned the corner.

---

24. *Oui, madame* (wē mä däm´): "Yes, ma'am" (French).

Reader's Response *What do you imagine that it would be like to be an infant prodigy? What might be some of the drawbacks of being such a gifted child?*

Literary Context: Like most modern short stories, "The Infant Prodigy" ends without a resolution, forcing readers to draw their own conclusions. This reflects the Modernist perception of life as being uncertain and ambiguous.

29 **Discussion** Have students respond to the prodigy's thoughts concerning the princess. What do these thoughts reveal about Bibi's personality?

30 **Discussion** Ask students why the piano teacher makes this comment aloud. Is she hoping that someone will respond?

31 **Discussion** Call students' attention to Mann's description of the "elegant young lady" and her two brothers. What seems to be Mann's attitude toward these characters? How is his attitude conveyed?

32 **Discussion** Have students discuss what the girl means when she comments that all artists are infant prodigies.

33 **Discussion** Have students comment on the ending of the story. Why does the girl despise the elegant young lady and her two brothers? Why does she still "look after them until they had turned the corner"? Why does Mann end the story with the girl's observations?

Cooperative Learning Thomas Mann was a vocal opponent of Adolf Hitler and the Nazis. Your students might be interested in learning about other writers who spoke out about the events of their time. Divide your class into groups of three or four. Have each group research a single writer who openly expressed his or her views about the events of the time. Once the groups have completed their research, have them present their findings to the rest of the class.

THOMAS MANN

1875–1955

The German writer Thomas Mann once wrote, "In the Word is involved the unity of humanity, the wholeness of the human problem, which permits nobody to separate the intellectual and artistic from the political and social, and to isolate himself within the ivory tower of the 'cultural' proper." As his comment suggests, Thomas Mann never shied away from political and social issues in either his writing or his public life. In fact, Mann was so devoted to his beliefs that he did not hesitate to speak out against the Nazis, even though his opposition to Adolf Hitler's regime forced him to leave his native land.

Mann was born in the German city of Lübeck into a wealthy merchant family. His father died in 1891, and two years later the family moved to Munich. While studying part time at the university, Mann worked on developing his literary skills, publishing a number of short stories that earned him some notoriety. He then traveled to Italy, where with the encouragement and support of his elder brother Heinrich, who also became a successful writer, he began work on his first novel, *Buddenbrooks* (1901). Depicting the history of a German merchant family similar to his own, *Buddenbrooks* made him internationally famous.

In 1905 Mann married Katia Pringsheim, a member of a prominent Munich family, and the couple eventually had six children. During the years leading up to World War I, he became increasingly alarmed by the state of European society. Believing that longstanding European cultural attitudes and beliefs were in a state of demise, he felt uncertain and apprehensive about the future. His concerns prompted him to begin writing *The Magic Mountain* in 1912. This novel, which took him twelve years to write, is set in a sanitarium on the eve of World War I and captures the conflicted values and political beliefs that had emerged in European society following the onset of the Modern Age.

In the aftermath of World War I, Mann tried to warn people of the dangers posed by Fascism and Nazism. By doing so he incurred the wrath of the Nazis, and when the Nazis seized control of Germany in 1933, he was forced into exile in Switzerland. After living there for five years, he moved to the United States. Throughout the war he continued to use his talents as both a writer and a speaker to attack the Nazi regime. Two years after the war ended, he published his despairing novel *Doctor Faustus*, an allegorical tale that symbolically depicts the rise of Nazism.

Mann moved back to Switzerland in 1952 and remained there for the last few years of his life. In 1954 he published his last novel, *The Confessions of Felix Krull*, a humorous tale about the adventures of a vagabond.

Although he is remembered mainly for his novels, Mann was also a gifted short-story writer. Among his best known stories are "Tonio Kröger," "Disorder and Early Sorrow," and "The Infant Prodigy."

Interpreting

1. (a) What measures are taken to shape the audience's response to Bibi even before he begins playing? (b) Who is responsible for these actions? (c) Why are these measures significant?
2. (a) What elements and details of the story draw attention to Bibi's youth? (b) How does Bibi's age affect the way in which people respond to his music?
3. (a) How would you describe the way in which Bibi conducts himself on stage? (b) How does Bibi manipulate his audience during his performance? (c) What evidence is there that his performance is consciously constructed to have the greatest possible impact on the audience? (d) What evidence is there that Bibi has received extensive coaching from the impresario?
4. (a) What is Bibi's attitude toward the audience? (b) How is his attitude conveyed? (c) What is his attitude toward his music, and how is it conveyed?
5. (a) What overall impression does Mann convey of the audience? (b) How does he convey this impression? (c) What impression does he convey of the individual members of the audience that he portrays? (d) What techniques does he use to convey these impressions?
6. Tone refers to the author's attitude toward his or her subject, characters, or audience. (a) How would you describe the tone of "The Infant Prodigy"? (b) How is the tone conveyed?
7. (a) What indications are there that the audience in the story symbolizes, or represents, society as a whole? (b) If the audience does indeed represent society as a whole, what does the story suggest about the relationship between the artist and society? Support your answer. (c) What does the story suggest about the overall ability of society to appreciate art? Support your answer.
8. (a) After the concert a girl with untidy hair comments, "We are all infant prodigies, we artists." What is the meaning of this comment? (b) How does it relate to the rest of the story?

Applying

9. In what ways do you think that this story would be different if it were set in contemporary America and focused on a young rock musician?
10. Do you think that most of today's musicians construct their performances to have the greatest pos-

sible impact on their audiences? Why or why not?
11. (a) What do you see as the primary concerns of most of today's popular musicians? (b) Do you feel that these musicians are somehow detached from the rest of society? Explain.

ANALYZING LITERATURE

Recognizing Point of View

Point of view refers to the vantage point from which a story is told. "The Infant Prodigy" is told from an omniscient third-person point of view. In other words, the story is recounted by a narrator who does not participate in the story and can see into the minds of all the characters.

1. By using an omniscient point of view, Mann is able to show how several members of the audience react to Bibi's performance. Explain how each character's response to the performance is shaped by his or her own preoccupations.
2. Explain why the story would be less effective if Mann had used a limited narrator who conveyed only Bibi's thoughts and feelings.

CRITICAL THINKING AND READING

Recognizing Dramatic Irony

One of the several types of irony used in literature, **dramatic irony** occurs when readers perceive something that a character in a literary work does not.

1. Why is Bibi's attitude toward the audience an example of dramatic irony?
2. Why are the attitudes of the piano teacher and the critic toward Bibi also examples of dramatic irony?
3. Why would it have been impossible for Mann to create these contrasting examples of dramatic irony if he had not used an omniscient point of view?

THINKING AND WRITING

Writing About Point of View

Write a paper in which you discuss how Mann's use of an omniscient point of view contributes to the effectiveness of the story. When writing your paper, make sure you use passages from the story for support. After you have finished writing, revise your paper, making sure you have presented your ideas in an organized and coherent manner.

(continued from bottom of page)

comment concerns the situation of the artist in society.
9. Answers will differ. Students may note that the audience would have been much different.
10. Answers will differ. Many students may feel that many performers do construct their performances to have the greatest possible effect.
11. (a) Answers will differ. Students may note that many of today's musicians are involved in social or political causes. (b) Answers will differ. Students may feel that today's musicians are not detached from society.

Challenge What other literary works have you read that focus on the relationship between the artist and society? How are these works similar to and different from Mann's story?

ANSWERS TO ANALYZING LITERATURE

1. Suggested response: The old gentleman relates Bibi's performance to his own childhood experiences. The businessman thinks about how much money the concert will bring in. The piano teacher analyzes Bibi's technique and criticizes him for being unoriginal.
2. Suggested response: It would have been less effective because Mann would have been unable to capture the reactions of the members of the audience.

ANSWERS TO CRITICAL THINKING AND READING

1. The audience is unaware that Bibi feels contempt for them.
2. Bibi is unaware of these attitudes and is under the impression that all the people love his performance.
3. It would have been impossible because Mann could not have presented the thoughts of all three characters.

THINKING AND WRITING

Publishing Student Writing Arrange students' papers on a class bulletin board display.

5. (a) Answers will differ. Students may respond that he conveys the impression that they are easily manipulated. (b) Answers will differ according to students' responses to the first part of the question. (c) Suggested response: He conveys the impression that they are absorbed in their own preoccupations and are unable to respond to Bibi in an unbiased manner. (d) Suggested response: He conveys

these impressions mainly by revealing their thoughts about Bibi's performance.
6. (a) Answers will differ. Students may respond that the story has a cynical, critical tone. (b) Suggested response: The tone is conveyed through Mann's choice of words.
7. (a) Suggested response: The audience included many different types of people. (b) Suggested response: It

suggests that the relationship between the artist and society is characterized by a sense of alienation. (c) Suggested response: It suggests that people are unable to respond to art objectively.
8. (a) Suggested response: The comment suggests that, like the infant prodigies, all artists stand apart from the rest of society. (b) Suggested response: Like the story as a whole, the

BACKGROUND

MANN'S STAND AGAINST THE NAZIS

In 1937 Thomas Mann's name was removed from the list of honorary doctors at the University of Bonn because of his criticism of Hitler's regime. When Mann learned of this, he wrote a scathing letter to the dean, expressing his outrage at this action, voicing his overall disgust with Hitler's regime, and explaining his need to speak out against the regime. The following is an excerpt from this letter:

"I have spent four years in exile which it would be euphemistic to call voluntary since if I had remained in Germany or gone back there I should probably not be alive today. In these four years the odd blunder committed by fortune when she put me in this situation has never once ceased to trouble me. I could never have dreamed, it could never have been prophesied of me at my cradle, that I should spend my latter years as an émigré, expropriated, outlawed, and committed to inevitable political protest.

"From the beginning of my intellectual life I had felt myself in happiest accord with the temper of my nation and at home with its intellectual traditions. I am better suited to represent those traditions than to become a martyr for them; far more fitted to add a little to the gaiety of the world than to foster conflict and hatred in it. Something very wrong must have happened to make my life take so false and unnatural a turn. I tried to check it, this very wrong thing, so far as my weak powers were able—and in doing so I called down the fate which I must learn to reconcile with a nature essentially foreign to it.

"Certainly I challenged the wrath of these despots by remaining away and giving evidence of my irrepressible disgust. But it is not merely in the last four years that I have done so. I felt thus long before, and was driven to it because I saw—earlier than my now desperate fellow-countrymen—who and what would emerge from all this. . . . My books, I said to myself, are written for Germans, for them above all; the outside world and its sympathy have always been for me only a happy accident. They are—these books of mine—the product of a mutually nourishing bond between nation and author, and depend on conditions which I myself have helped to create in Germany. Such bonds as these are delicate and of high importance; they ought not to be rudely sundered by politics. . . .

"A German author . . . whose patriotism, perhaps naively, expresses itself in a belief in the infinite moral significance of whatever happens in Germany—should he be silent, wholly silent, in the face of the inexpiable evil that is done daily in my country to bodies, souls, and minds, to right and truth, to men and mankind? And should he be silent in the face of the frightful danger to the whole continent presented by this soul-destroying regime, which exists in abysmal ignorance of the hour that has struck today in the world? It was not possible for me to be silent. And so . . . came the utterances, the unavoidably compromising gestures which have now resulted in the absurd and deplorable business of my national excommunication. I, forsooth, am supposed to have dishonored the Reich, Germany, in acknowledging that I am against them! They have the incredible effrontery to confuse themselves with Germany! When, after all, perhaps the moment is not far off when it will be of supreme importance to the German people not to be confused with them."

Europe

HARMONY IN RED
Henri Matisse

Humanities Note

Fine art, *Harmony in Red* by Henri Matisse. Matisse (1869–1954) is considered by many to be the most important French artist of the twentieth century. Throughout his long artistic career, he experimented with a variety of artistic techniques and approaches. In the early 1900's, he was the leader of an artistic movement known as Fauvism, which emphasized the sensual and decorative values of vivid colors. Later, he exhibited his talent as a sculptor, creating sculptured forms that reflected the influence of African sculptures and of the works of French sculptor Auguste Rodin. Toward the end of his career, he created striking paper cutouts and stencils.

In each stage of his career, Matisse focused on and conveyed the emotions that his subjects evoked in him rather than on capturing literal appearance. He once wrote, "A work should carry its whole meaning in itself and impress it on the spectator even before he has understood the subject."

You might want to use the following questions to discuss the art:

1. What overall impression does this painting convey?
2. How does the artist's use of colors contribute to this impression?
3. What emotions does this painting evoke in you? Why?

1875–1926

Rainer Maria Rilke (*rī′ nər mä rē′ ä ril′ kə*) once wrote, "The necessity to be alone, alone for a long time, builds in me every day. . . . People (whether it be my fault or theirs) wear me out." As this comment suggests, Rilke felt detached from other people. Throughout much of his life, he led a solitary existence, immersing himself in his inner thoughts and in his writing. Although he was never completely happy, his devotion to his writing ultimately established him as one of the finest poets ever to write in the German language.

Born in Prague (at the time part of the Austro-Hungarian Empire) to German-speaking parents, Rilke had a traumatic, lonely childhood. Prior to his birth, his mother and father had lost a baby daughter. To compensate for this loss, Rilke's mother often dressed young Rainer as a girl and pretended that he was her daughter. When he was nine, his parents separated, and a year later his father sent him off to military school. Finding that he did not fit in with his classmates, Rilke felt alienated and unhappy at military school. Yet he spent six years there, until he was forced to leave because of illness.

After attending business school for a year, Rilke enrolled at the University of Prague, and he later studied at universities in Munich and Berlin. Although his family wanted him to pursue a career in business or law, Rilke had his sights set on a career as a writer. While he was still a student, he wrote poetry, plays, and short stories. In 1895 he published his first collection of poems, *Sacrifice to the Lares*, and a year later he published his second collection, *Crowned by Dream*.

Rilke traveled to Russia in 1899, where he met Leo Tolstoy and Leonid Pasternak, a painter whom Rilke greatly admired. During this journey he wrote many of the poems that were later published in *The Book of Hours* (1905); and shortly after his return, he wrote *Stories of God* (1904), a collection of stories in which he expressed his admiration for the Russian landscape and people.

In 1900, after Rilke returned from a second trip to Russia, he met and fell in love with Clara Westhoff, a German sculptor. A year later, he and Clara were married, but the marriage lasted for less than two years. Following the failure of his marriage, Rilke moved to Paris and accepted a position as the private secretary of the famous sculptor Auguste Rodin. From Rodin he learned not only to pay close attention to minute details but also to see life and vitality in inanimate objects.

The commercial success of Rilke's novel *The Tale of the Love and Death of Cornet Christopher Rilke* (1906) enabled him to devote the rest of his life entirely to his writing. Rilke followed this novel with *New Poems* (1908), a collection of poetry that some critics regard as his masterpiece. Reflecting his involvement with Rodin, the poems in this collection, including "Archaic Torso of Apollo," extract profound insights from inanimate objects.

During the final years of his life, Rilke completed two more critically acclaimed collections of poetry: *Sonnets to Orpheus* (1923) and *Duino Elegies* (1923). Seeking a peaceful place to write, Rilke moved to a friend's château in Switzerland in 1922. Unfortunately, however, his health failed him shortly after his move, and in 1926 he died of an infection that he acquired by pricking himself on a rose he had cut from his garden.

Objectives

Thematic
To see the life and vitality in an ancient work of art

2 To learn to approach the reading of poetry as a process

Skills
1 To write a poem describing a painting

GUIDE FOR INTERPRETING

The Grownup; Interior of the Rose; Archaic Torso of Apollo

Commentary

Interpreting Poetry. Do you ever have difficulty understanding or interpreting poetry? Do you find certain poems overwhelming? If so, you are not alone. Although it may seem hard to believe, even the most distinguished scholars have difficulty interpreting certain poems. In fact, it is virtually impossible for anyone to interpret a complex poem without reading it several times. For this reason you should plan on reading a poem a number of times, each time with a different purpose in mind. If you approach the reading of poetry as a process, involving a series of stages, you may be surprised to find that you can interpret poems that you once would have found overwhelming.

When you read a poem for the first time, concentrate on the emotions that it evokes inside you. Because the writing of poetry is generally an emotional experience for the poet, almost all poetry is meant to touch the emotions of the reader. If a poem is effective, it should arouse the same types of emotions in the reader that the writer had when he or she wrote it. To accomplish this, a poet must choose appropriate words, images, and details. For this reason once you are in touch with the feelings that a poem arouses in you, you should look back over the poem and try to determine which words, images, and details contributed to your response and why they did so.

Next, reread the poem, focusing on its literal meaning. What is the poem about? Who or what is the subject? What is happening in the poem? When you read a complex poem, it may not be immediately apparent to you what the poem is about, and you may have to read it a few times just to decipher it. For example, it may not be obvious to you that Rilke's poem "The Grownup" describes a person's transformation from a child into an adult.

The next step in interpreting poetry is to try to determine any meaning hidden beneath the surface of a poem. To accomplish this, you must look for the use of literary devices such as **symbols** and **figures of speech.** In "Interior of the Rose," for example, the rose can be seen as a symbol of a person, consisting of an exterior (the body) and an interior (the spirit). By interpreting the meaning of the various literary devices in a poem, you should be able to reach a conclusion about the poem's **theme,** or the central message that the poet is trying to convey. You should be aware, however, that a single poem may have more than one possible theme. As a result, you and a classmate may interpret the same poem differently.

Writing

Write a journal entry in which you explore your feelings about becoming an adult.

Literary Focus Before students read the Commentary, have them discuss how they go about trying to interpret poetry. If they remark that they often have difficulty interpreting poems, tell them that they are about to learn about a process that should make it easier for them to do so.

Writing/Prior Knowledge Before students begin writing their journal entries, have them discuss their perceptions of what it means to be an adult.

ESL Teaching Strategy Because the definition of adulthood varies from culture to culture, you might want to have ESL students discuss the prevalent conception of adulthood in their countries of origin.

Teaching Tenth-Grade Students You might want to have the entire tenth-grade class work together to interpret each of Rilke's poems. Emphasize the fact that there is likely to be more than one correct interpretation for each poem. Consequently, students should be encouraged to offer any interpretations they come up with, as long as they can support them with details from the poem.

Vocabulary
Preteach the following vocabulary words:
serene (sə rēn´) *adj.:* Not disturbed or troubled
opaque (ō pāk´) *adj.:* Not letting light pass through
suffused (sə fyo͞ozd´) *v.:* Filled with a glow, color, or liquid
placid (plas´ id) *adj.:* Calm
translucent (trans lo͞o´ s'nt) *adj.:* Partially transparent
glisten (glis´ 'n) *v.:* Shine or sparkle

Support Material
Teaching Portfolio
Teacher Backup, p. 1241
Usage and Mechanics Worksheet, p. 1245
Vocabulary Check, p. 1246
Analyzing Literature Worksheet, *Interpreting Poetry,* p. 1247
Critical Thinking and Reading Worksheet, *Recognizing Simile and*

Metaphor, p. 1248
Selection Test, pp. 1249–1250

Spelling Tip Call students' attention to the fact that the first six letters of the word suffused still appear in the same order when they are reversed.

INGER ON THE BEACH
Edvard Munch
Rasmus Meyers Samlinger

The Grownup

Rainer Maria Rilke

translated by Randall Jarrell

All this stood on her and was the world
And stood on her with all things, pain and grace,
As trees stand, growing and erect, all image
And imageless as the ark of the Lord God,[1]
5 And solemn, as if set upon a state.

And she bore it, bore, somehow, the weight
Of the flying, fleeting, faraway,
The monstrous and the still unmastered,
Unmoved, serene, as the water bearer
10 Stands under a full jar. Till in the midst of play,
Transfiguring,[2] preparing for the other,
The first white veil fell smoothly, softly,

Over her opened face, almost opaque,
Never to raise itself again, and giving somehow
15 To all her questions one vague answer:
In thee, thou once a child, in thee.

---

1. all image . . . the Lord God: The Ark of the Covenant, the sacred chest of the Hebrews containing the Tables of the Law, represented God. However, because the Jews had been commanded by God not to reproduce His image, the chest was not adorned with the image of God.

2. Transfiguring (trans fig′ yər iŋ) *v.*: Changing the figure, form, or outward appearance of.

Reader's Response *What do you imagine you will be like ten years from now? Do you imagine that you will ever forget what it was like to be a child? Why or why not?*

THINKING ABOUT THE SELECTION

Interpreting

1. In "The Grownup" Rilke describes a person's transformation from a child into an adult. (a) What impression does he convey of this process? (b) Which details contribute to this impression?
2. (a) In the second stanza, what does Rilke mean when he refers to the "flying, fleeting, faraway"? (b) What does he mean when he refers to "The monstrous and the still unmastered"?
3. What does the falling of the "white veil" over the person's face symbolize, or represent?
4. (a) What is your interpretation of the theme of "The Grownup"? (b) What led you to this interpretation?

Applying

5. After you have interpreted the theme of a poem, you should try to determine how you can apply this theme to your own life. Explain how you could apply the theme of "The Grownup" to your life.
6. (a) What other literary works can you think of that deal with the passage from childhood to adulthood? (b) How do the ways in which these works depict this process compare with Rilke's depiction?

THINKING AND WRITING

Writing a Poem

Write a poem describing a painting that you find especially striking. Begin by choosing a painting. Feel free to choose any one of the paintings reproduced in this text. Next, list some images describing details from the painting. Organize your images. Then begin writing your poem. As Rilke does in his poem "Archaic Torso of Apollo" (page 1057), try to infuse the subject of the painting with energy and vitality. After you have finished writing, read over your poem with a reproduction of the painting in front of you. Make sure you have captured the essence of the painting in your poem. After making any necessary revisions, proofread your poem and prepare a final copy. Then share it with your classmates.

ROSES, 1917
Pierre Auguste Renoir
Virginia Museum of Fine Arts

Interior of the Rose

Rainer Maria Rilke

translated by Kate Flores

Where, for this within,
Is there a without? And upon what wound
Lies a weft[1] so thin?
What heavens are reflected
5 In the inward seas
Of these opening roses
Thus reposing?[2] See
How loosely in looseness
They lie, as though never

10 A tremulous[3] hand could spill them.
They cannot hold themselves still;
Many are filling
Up unto their brim and flowing
Over with interior space
15 Into days, which seem ever
Grown fuller and fuller,
Until all of summer a room
Has become, a room enclosed in a dream.

---

1. **weft** (weft) *n.*: Something woven.
2. **reposing** (ri pōz′ iŋ) *v.*: Resting.

---

3. **tremulous** (trem′ yoo ləs) *adj.*: Trembling; quivering.

Archaic Torso of Apollo[1]

Rainer Maria Rilke

translated by Stephen Mitchell

We cannot know his legendary head
with eyes like ripening fruit. And yet his torso
is still suffused with brilliance from inside,
like a lamp, in which his gaze, now turned to low,

5 gleams in all its power. Otherwise
  the curved breast could not dazzle you so, nor
    could
 a smile run through the placid hips and thighs
to that dark center where procreation[2] flared.

Otherwise this stone would seem defaced
10 beneath the translucent cascade of the shoulders
and would not glisten like a wild beast's fur:

would not, from all the borders of itself,
burst like a star: for here there is no place
that does not see you. You must change your life.

---

1. Archaic . . . Apollo: The Archaic period of Greek art
lasted from the late seventh century to about 480 B.C. Apollo
was the Greek god of music, poetry, prophecy, and medicine.
He was associated with the sun and portrayed as a handsome,
athletic young man.
2. procreation (prō′ krē ā′ shən) *n.*: The process of
producing or bringing into existence.

Reader's Response *After reading Rilke's
poem, would you like to see the statue he
describes? Why or why not? If so, do you
imagine that it would live up to Rilke's
description of it?*

THINKING ABOUT THE SELECTION

Interpreting

1. (a) How does Rilke capture the fragility of the rose
in "Interior of the Rose"? (b) How does he at the
same time convey the impression that the rose has
an enduring quality and that its growth and development are inevitable? (c) What is paradoxical, or
seemingly self-contradictory, about the rose's being
fragile yet enduring? (d) What other paradoxes can
you find in the poem? (e) What do you see as the
meaning of each of these paradoxes?
2. (a) Explain how the rose can be seen as a symbol of
both the tangible world and the spiritual world. (b) How
can the rose be seen as a symbol of a person? (c)
How can the rose be seen as a symbol of summer?
3. The statue of Apollo that Rilke describes is missing
its head and limbs. According to Rilke why would it
be less impressive if it were still intact?
4. (a) In his description how does Rilke infuse the statue
with energy and vitality? (b) How might the energy and
vitality of the statue relate to the god that it depicts?
5. What is ironic, or surprising, about Rilke's remark that
the statue would "seem defaced" if it were still intact?
6. (a) Why is the last line of the poem startling? (b)
How does it relate to the rest of the poem?

Applying

7. The French sculptor Auguste Rodin taught Rilke to
see life, vitality, and movement in objects that most
people perceive as inanimate. How is the lesson
apparent in "Interior of the Rose"?

ANALYZING LITERATURE

Interpreting Poetry

Rainer Maria Rilke's poetry tends to be quite complex. For this reason it is usually necessary to read
each poem several times in order to interpret it.
1. What emotions did "Interior of the Rose" evoke in
you the first time you read it?
2. Which details in each poem contributed to your
emotional response?
3. What natural process does Rilke describe in "Interi-
or of the Rose"?
4. What do you think that this process symbolizes, or
represents? Support your answer.
5. Based on this interpretation, what do you see as the
theme of the poem? Support your answer.
6. Explain whether you think that "Interior of the Rose"
can be interpreted in more than one way.

(continued from bottom of page)

same energy and vitality if it were intact.
4. (a) Suggested response: He describes it as being "suffused with
brilliance inside." (b) Suggested response: Apollo is associated with
the sun and is portrayed as a handsome, athletic young man.
5. It is ironic because people might
describe the statue as being defaced because it is missing its head
and limbs.
6. (a) Suggested response: It is surprising because it does not at first
appear to fit in with the rest of the
poem. (b) Answers will differ. Students may respond that the speaker
feels the statue possesses more energy and vitality than he himself
possesses.
7. Suggested response: Rilke depicts
the statue as possessing life and vitality.

ANSWERS TO ANALYZING LITERATURE

1. Answers will differ. Students may respond that it evoked a sense of
wonder.
2. Answers will differ according to the
emotions that the poem evoked for
students.
3. It describes the blooming of a rose.
4. Answers will differ. Students may
feel that it symbolizes a person's
spiritual development.
5. Answers will differ. Make sure that
students support their interpretations.
6. Suggested response: The poem
can be interpreted in more than one
way.

3 **Clarification** Explain to students
that Rilke's poem describes a
statue of Apollo that is missing its
head and limbs.

4 **Enrichment** The literary critic
Robert Hass notes that "Archaic
Torso of Apollo" "begins from a
sense of shock . . . . [This] feeling
occurs because, looking at a mutilated piece of old Greek sculpture,
[the speaker] suddenly realizes
that it is more real than he is—not
more perfect but more real . . . ."

Closure and Extension

ANSWERS TO THINKING ABOUT THE SELECTION

1. (a) Suggested response: He captures
the fragility of the rose by suggesting
that "a tremulous hand could spill
them." (b) Suggested response: He
conveys this impression in his description in lines 11 through 14. (c)

Suggested response: In most cases,
the more fragile an item is the less
likely it is to endure. (d) The other
paradoxes in the poem include the
idea that summer is a "room enclosed
in a dream" and the idea that the rose
is "flowing/Over with interior space."
(e) Answers will differ. Make sure students support each interpretation.
2. (a) Answers will differ. Students may
respond that the exterior of the rose

can be seen as the tangible world
and the interior can be seen as the
spiritual world. (b) Like a blooming
rose, a person goes through stages
of growth, development, fulfillment,
and passing away. (c) Suggested response: The blooming and eventual
wilting of the rose parallel the passage of summer.
3. Suggested response: He suggests
that the statue might not possess the

Translation: The Art of Damage Control

A work of literature can be disfigured as it passes from one language into another. Such damage results from the differences between languages—differences in vocabulary and sounds, of course, but also in grammar, word order, and idiomatic expressions. The translator's job is to minimize this damage so that readers can sense the beauties of the original work.

Rilke's "Archaic Torso of Apollo"

One way to understand how translation can harm the delicate structure of a poem is to compare a literal, word-for-word translation with a more skillful rendering. Below are a literal version of Rilke's first stanza and Stephen Mitchell's translation of the same lines.

> We knew not his unheard-of head,
> in which the eye-apples ripened. But
> his torso glows still like a candelabrum,
> in which his look, only twisted back . . .
> —Literal Translation

> We cannot know his legendary head
> with eyes like ripening fruit. And
> yet his torso
> is still suffused with brilliance from
> inside,
> like a lamp, in which his gaze, now
> turned to low . . .
> —Mitchell's Translation

Word Order and Rhythm

The literal translation sounds strange because it follows the German word order. Also, Mitchell re-creates Rilke's iambic pentameter line—five metrical feet, each with a weak stress followed by a strong one. The literal translation, however, hobbles along on lines of unequal length. You cannot translate poetry merely by substituting an English word for each foreign one. Too much is lost.

A Closer Look

Why Translations Differ

While granting that translation is not as simple as it first appears, you may still wonder how translators can come up with so many different versions of the same poem. Isn't this a bit suspicious? A translator may have to fiddle with word order and rhythm, but don't most words in one language have a logical equivalent in another? For instance, the German word for eyes is *Augen,* and the German for apples is *Apfel.* Where is the room for disagreement in translating these terms?

This view of translation, however, does not allow for differences in idiom, the constructions and expressions peculiar to a language. In German, for example, the combination of the nouns *Augen* and *Apfel—Augenapfel*—is an idiomatic term that means "eyeballs." It is also the plural of a term of endearment: "apple of my eye."

Unfortunately for translators, this German word does not have a simple English equivalent.

NSIGHTS

The term "eye-apples," a literal translation of the German, is not an English idiom and means neither "eyeballs" nor "sweethearts." As a result, Rilke's use of *Augenapfel* in a description of Apollo's vanished head has caused translators abundant headaches.

The Case of the Missing Eye-Apples

Following are four translations of the beginning of Rilke's poem: Notice that each translator disposes of the German "eye-apples" in a different manner.

We knew not his unheard-of head,
in which the eye-apples ripened . . .
　　—Literal Translation

We did not know his legendary head
in which the eyeballs ripened . . .
　　—Norton's Translation

Though we've not known his unimagined
　head
and what divinity his eyes were
　　showing . . .
　　—Leishman's Translation

We cannot know his legendary head
with eyes like ripening fruit . . .
　　—Mitchell's Translation

Rilke uses the double meaning of *Augenapfel* to make a play on words. He suggests that the statue's missing *"Augenapfel"* (eyeballs) are also the apples of our eyes—in other words, beloved and precious like a sweetheart or small child. Since this idiomatic expression has no English equivalent, Rilke's word-play is lost in all these translations.

Three Translators, Three Solutions

Norton correctly translates *"Augenapfel"* as "eyeballs"; however, the image of eyeballs ripening seems a bit outlandish. In German this image makes sense because eyeballs are eye-apples and apples do ripen. Also, Norton fails to suggest that the eyeballs are also cherished things.

Leishman uses magic to make the statue's *"Augenapfel"* vanish entirely from the text. Now you see them, now you don't. The German word becomes "eyes" and the verb *ripened* is gone.

Mitchell transforms the metaphor ("eye-apples ripened") into a simile: "eyes like ripening fruit." He, too, fails to preserve Rilke's play on the word *Augenapfel*. His simile, however, makes the image of ripening easier for an American reader to swallow. While it is a bit grotesque to think of eyeballs ripening, it is both surprising and suggestive to imagine eyes ripening *like* fruit.

If three translators can honestly disagree about a single word, no wonder there are so many different translations of the same poem, story, or novel!

Thinking About Translation

1. List five English idioms that would be particularly difficult to translate into a foreign language. Explain the reasons for each choice.
2. Select a brief poem and, using a dual-language dictionary, translate it into a foreign language you have studied. Preserve as much of the poem's rhythms, sounds, and flavor as possible. Then write a description of the problems you encountered and how you solved them.

GREAT WORK

SIDDHARTHA
by Hermann Hesse

The moment you open Hermann Hesse's novel *Siddhartha* (1922), you will be whisked away to an exotic, faraway land. You will be transported back in time to the sixth century B.C., and you will travel thousands of miles into the lush tropical forests and bustling villages of India. You will be introduced to Siddhartha, a bright, handsome young man who is admired and respected by all who know him. You will learn, however, that despite his popularity Siddhartha feels restless, unsettled, and even unhappy. Driven by an unquenchable thirst for wisdom, Siddhartha will take you on a long spiritual quest aimed at attaining inner harmony and an understanding of the nature of existence. Filled with unexpected twists and surprising discoveries, Siddhartha's journey will not only entertain you, but it may even teach you something about yourself and your place in the world.

Hinduism and the Indian Way of Life

At the time of Siddhartha's birth, Hinduism, which continues to thrive in present-day India, was already firmly entrenched as the dominant Indian religion. Among the most important characteristics of this polytheistic religion are the belief in reincarnation and the notion that the material world is illusory. Another major aspect of Hinduism is its hereditary caste system—a rigid social hierarchy that governed Indian society for thousands of years. This system divides society into four classes, or castes, the highest-ranking of which is the Brahmin caste, consisting of the priests and scholars. Siddhartha has been born into the Brahmin caste and is expected to follow in his father's footsteps and become a Hindu priest. Yet Siddhartha has other ideas.

Siddhartha's Quest Begins

Throughout his childhood, Siddhartha demonstrates his intellectual keenness and his insatiable thirst for knowledge. By the time he is approaching adulthood, he has already absorbed volumes of wisdom from his father and from Brahmin scholars. He feels that he has learned just about everything these people can teach him. Yet he is not satisfied—so many unanswered questions still burn inside him. Driven by the need to find answers to these questions, he leaves home with his best friend, Govinda, and joins a band of wandering ascetics known as the Samanas.

Shedding his expensive clothes and fasting for weeks at a time, Siddhartha embarks on a life of poverty and religious discipline. From the Samanas, he learns many ways of losing the Self. "He [loses] his Self a thousand times and for days on end he [dwells] in nonbeing." Yet his frequent escapes from the Self still leave him feeling unsatisfied. "I suffer thirst," he comments to Govinda, "and on this Samana path my thirst has not grown less."

BUDDHA
Tibetan sculpture
Victoria and Albert Museum, London

(continued from bottom of page)

1. What impression of Buddha does the sculpture convey?
2. How do the surrounding designs relate to the central figure?
3. How does this sculpture relate to Hesse's novel?
4. How does the depiction of Buddha in this sculpture compare with other depictions of Buddha you have seen?

Having come to this realization, Siddhartha decides to leave the Samanas. With Govinda again by his side, he sets off to find a renowned holy man called Gotama, or Buddha, the Illustrious One.

Siddhartha as a different individual. This is reflected in that fact that although Siddhartha is impressed by the Buddha's teachings, he chooses not to become one of his followers. Instead, he parts with Govinda, who has decided to join the Illustrious One, and sets out again on his quest for wisdom.

The Birth of Buddhism

Hesse's Buddha is based on a real historical figure, Siddhartha Gautama (563?–483? B.C.), the founder of the Buddhist religion. Buddha taught that all life is sorrow and that sorrow is caused by desire. Accordingly, he preached that the way to free oneself of sorrow and to attain salvation was to rid one's life of desire through self-discipline, restraint, moral conduct, and meditation.

Buddha's teachings spread rapidly throughout India, and by the end of his life he had hoards of followers. Eventually, Buddhism even supplanted Hinduism as the dominant Indian religion. After prospering for several centuries, however, its popularity declined sharply in India, and it now exists there only as a minority religion, though it continues to thrive in other countries such as China and Japan.

Although Hesse's protagonist shares Buddha's given name, Hesse clearly wants you to view his

Siddhartha's Quest Continues

On his own for the first time in his life, Siddhartha suddenly awakens to the beauty of the physical and material world. He looks around and drinks in the breathtaking colors of the Indian landscape—the blues of the sky and the rivers, the golds and yellows of the sun and the flowers, the greens of the vegetation. As he continues on his way, unsure of where he is headed, he learns "something new on every step of his path." He watches the "sun rise over the forest and mountains and set over the distant palm shore." Hearing a voice that emanates from his own heart, he is suddenly driven by the desire to be with people and to seek love. Where do you think this desire will lead him? Will he find happiness and contentment? Will he ever reach the end of his journey? If so, how will his journey end?

Humanities Note

Fine art, *Buddha*. This elaborate Tibetan sculpture shows Buddha on his throne, surrounded by carvings portraying events from his life. He is depicted in deep meditation, with his legs crossed and his eyes closed. Each of the details of his appearance and of the surrounding decorations has a distinct meaning. The knot into which his hair is drawn indicates that he has attained full enlightenment. His large ears symbolize that he hears everything. The lotus throne on which he is seated represents the purity out of which he has been born. Finally, the position of his right hand, with its open palm, indicates that he is bestowing mercy.

This sculpture is typical of Tibetan Buddhist art, which is known for its extensive use of symbolism. Tibet was just one of many Asian countries to develop its own unique style of Buddhist art. The other countries include China, Nepal, Japan, and Laos.

You might want to use the following questions to discuss the art:

Fine art, *First Preaching of Buddha*. This spectacular wall painting is another example of Tibetan Buddhist art. As is typically the case with Tibetan Buddhist art, each of the details in the painting has a specific symbolic meaning. Buddha's hair is drawn into a knot, which represents his total enlightenment. The flame that appears above his topknot is a sign of his spiritual power. The two animals beneath Buddha serve as a reminder that Buddha first began preaching in a park near Benares, India. Between the two animals is an important Buddhist symbol known as the Wheel of Life. The figures that appear beneath the animals are Bodhisatvas, saint-like figures who have attained enlightenment but have delayed entering Paradise in order to help others find the way. Finally, the two coiled snakes in the upper right-hand corner of the painting are a Buddhist symbol of inner strength.

You might want to use the following questions to discuss the art:

1. Do you imagine that each of the details in this painting has symbolic significance? Why or why not?

2. Why do you imagine that art work has served as an important means of expression in the Buddhist religion?

3. If you were the curator of a museum, would you be interested in displaying this painting? Why or why not?

FIRST PREACHING OF BUDDHA
Tibetan fresco

Themes in *Siddhartha*

As you may have already guessed, one of the main themes of Hesse's novel is that people cannot find true happiness and contentment until they fully understand themselves and their place in the world. Yet at the same time Hesse emphasizes the difficulty of achieving this goal. Although it may not appear so, self-knowledge can be difficult to attain. How can you be sure about what you really want from life? How are you to know if you are headed in the right direction? How are you to know if you are being true to yourself? These are not easy questions to answer.

Another of Hesse's themes is concerned with how people attain wisdom. Hesse suggests that like self-knowledge, wisdom is difficult to attain. He also implies that the best way to acquire wisdom is through personal experiences rather than from the teachings of another person. Do you agree with his views about the attainment of wisdom? Why or why not?

A number of other themes also emerge from *Siddhartha*. For instance, Hesse delves into the distinction between the physical and spiritual world, and he examines recurring elements in the relationships between children and parents. He also makes some observations about the passage of time, and he stresses the importance of love. Hesse's message about love is conveyed most clearly in the following observation by Siddhartha: "It seems to me . . . that love is the most important thing in the world. It may be important to the great thinkers to explain and despise it. But I think it is only important to love the world, not to despise it, not for us to hate each other, but to be able to regard the world and ourselves and all beings with love, admiration, and respect." What is your reaction to this observation? Do you agree with it? Why or why not?

Hermann Hesse's Life

Hesse's emphasis on love and his expression of the need to find the true self and to seek spiritual fulfillment earned him popularity among young Americans during the 1960's. In fact, a successful

SCENE FROM A FILM ADAPTATION
OF *SIDDHARTHA*

Enrichment Hesse was sent to theological school at the age of fourteen. After attending for only half a year, however, he ran away, and when he was returned to the school by a constable he expressed such displeasure that his father was forced to remove him from the seminary and enroll him in a secular school. Yet Hesse eventually abandoned his formal schooling without receiving his high-school diploma, deciding instead to educate himself.

After supporting himself by working in a clock factory and a bookstore, Hesse became a freelance writer, and in 1904 he published his first novel, *Peter Camenzind*. Both this novel and his story *"Beneath the Wheel"* (1906) reflect Hesse's belief that conventional schooling stifles the artistic mind. In his second novel, *Gertrud* (1910), he focused on a related theme, the strain that personal relationships can place on artistic pursuits.

Because of Hesse's hatred for war and his rejection of nationalism, the onset of World War I prompted him to move to Switzerland, where he lived for the remainder of his life. From his new home, he became one of the most outspoken critics of World War I, and his criticism provoked an angry response among many of the residents of his native land.

Following the war, Hesse was severely shaken by the death of his father and the illness of his wife and youngest son. Finding himself on the verge of a mental breakdown, he began receiving psychological analysis. The influence of his analysis was reflected in his next novel, *Demian* (1919), as well as in a number of his other subsequent novels. The story of a German boy's struggle to come to terms with his true identity, *Demian* was extremely popular among the post-war generation and earned Hesse international fame.

During the later part of his career, Hesse continued to produce novels and other works that enhanced his literary reputation. These works include *Steppenwolf* (1927), *Death and the Lover* (1930), *Journey to the East* (1932), and *Magister Ludi* (1943).

late-1960's rock band even adopted the name of another of his best-known novels, *Steppenwolf* (1927). Yet Hesse's reputation is by no means limited to the 1960's generation, and it extends far beyond the boundaries of the United States. The depth and extent of his reputation are evident in the fact that he was awarded the Nobel Prize for Literature in 1946.

Siddhartha, Hesse's most famous novel, reflects his lifelong fascination with India and its people. Born at the edge of the Black Forest, a wooded, mountainous region in southwestern Germany, he first learned about India from his father and his grandfather, both of whom had been there as missionaries. Later, as a young adult, Hesse himself traveled to India and immersed himself in its culture. In writing *Siddhartha*, Hesse drew upon all that he had absorbed about this distant land. Yet the messages that he conveys in the novel stretch across the boundaries of both time and space and touch concerns shared by people of all cultures and eras.

ISAK DINESEN

1885–1962

Anyone who has seen the Academy Award–winning movie *Out of Africa* is familiar with Isak Dinesen (ē′ säk dē′ nə sən) and her adventure-filled life. Based on Dinesen's book of memoirs (also entitled *Out of Africa*), the film captures her great strength, courage, dignity, and compassion. Yet to fully appreciate her talent as a writer, one must read her short stories.

Born Karen Christence Dinesen in Rungsted, Denmark, she studied painting at the Academy of Fine Arts in Copenhagen. After marrying her cousin Baron Bror Blixen-Finecke (blik′ sən fē′ nə kə) in 1914, she moved to British East Africa (now Kenya), where she and her husband ran a coffee plantation. Although she divorced her husband in 1921, she remained in Africa for ten more years, until falling coffee prices forced her to abandon her plantation and move back to Denmark. Dinesen related her African experiences in *Out of Africa* (1937), which was published in both English and Danish and made her internationally famous. The book offers readers a vivid sense of the African landscape and people. In addition it captures Dinesen's exciting and romantic relationship with an English pilot, Denys Finch-Hatton.

Out of Africa was only one of many books that Dinesen produced in the years after her return to Denmark. Most of her books, including *Seven Gothic Tales* (1934), *Winter's Tales* (1942), *Last Tales* (1957), *Anecdotes of Destiny* (1958), and *Ehrengard* (1963), are collections of short stories. Generally her stories are set in the past in romantic or mysterious places, and they often involve grotesque or fantastic characters as well as elements of the supernatural.

During the final years of her life, Dinesen suffered from severe physical ailments that caused her great pain and prevented her from eating properly. She had to undergo several spinal operations, and her once-beautiful face became lined and disfigured. Yet despite her physical problems, Dinesen remained proud and courageous until the end of her life, exhibiting the same attributes that had enabled her to thrive in Africa as a young woman.

GUIDE FOR INTERPRETING

The Pearls

Commentary

Setting. In real life people's attitudes, values, and behavior are likely to be shaped to some extent by the environment in which they live. Similarly, in a work of literature, the characters are likely to be shaped by the **setting,** or the time, environment, and conditions in which the events in the work occur. For instance, the characters in a story set in an upper-class section of London during the nineteenth century are likely to be well-educated, sophisticated, and refined. In addition to having a long-term effect on the characters' personalities, the setting may also have a more immediate impact on the characters' actions. For example, in a story set in the Arctic wilderness, the characters' actions might result directly from their efforts to cope with the dangers posed by the frigid Arctic weather.

Because of its potential impact on the characters, writers often devote a great deal of attention to describing a setting. For example, Isak Dinesen's works are filled with vivid, detailed descriptions of settings. By using precise sensory details, or details appealing to one or more of the five senses, Dinesen makes it easy for readers to envision the setting and to imagine the characters interacting with it.

Writing

What do you imagine it was like to live in Denmark or Norway during the eighteenth century? How do you envision the landscape of these two countries? What is the source of your impressions? Write a journal entry in which you explore your responses to these places and explain why you would or would not like to visit these two countries.

Primary Source

Isak Dinesen's ability to bring a setting to life is highlighted in her best-selling book, *Out of Africa*. In fact, the success of the book was largely a result of her breathtaking descriptions of the African landscape. In the following passage from the book, she offers a bird's-eye view of an African lake: "The sky was blue, but as we flew from the plains in over the stony and bare lower country, all color seemed to be scorched out of it. The whole landscape below us looked like delicately marked tortoise-shell. Suddenly, in the midst of it was the lake. The white bottom, shining through the water, gives it, when seen from the air, a striking, an unbelievable azure-color, so clear that for a moment you shut your eyes at it; the expanse of water lies in the bleak tawny land like a big bright aquamarine. We had been flying high, now we went down, and as we sank our own shade, dark-blue, floated under us upon the light-blue lake. Here live thousands of flamingoes, although I do not know how they exist in the brackish water—surely there are no fish here. At our approach they spread out in large circles and fans, like the rays of a setting sun . . ."

(continued from bottom of page)

from different parts of the United States.

Writing/Prior Knowledge Before students begin writing their journal entries, you may want to have a class discussion in which students share their prior knowledge of Denmark and Norway.

ESL Teaching Strategy Instruct ESL students to keep a dictionary close at hand as they are reading the story. Whenever they come across a word with which they are unfamiliar, they should look it up in the dictionary and jot down the word and its definition on a piece of paper.

Teaching Tenth-Grade Students As tenth-grade students are reading the story, they should jot down each passage or detail that seems important, noting the page on which each of these details or passages appears. When they have finished reading the story, they should look back at the passages and details they have listed and use them to try to determine the theme of the story.

Vocabulary

Preteach the following vocabulary words:
enamored (in am´ ərd) *v.*: Filled with love or desire
melancholia (mel´ ən kō´ lē ə) *n.*: A mental disorder characterized by extreme depression
formidable (fôr´ mə də b'l) *adj.*: Hard to handle or overcome
indignation (in´ dig nā´ shən) *n.*: Righteous anger
incalculableness (in kal´ kyōō lə b'l nəs) *n.*: Unpredictability
abomination (ə bäm´ ə nā´ shən) *n.*: Anything hateful or disgusting
demure (di myoor´) *adj.*: Modest; reserved
redoubtable (ri dout´ ə b'l) *adj.*: Formidable
frivolous (friv´ ə ləs) *adj.*: Silly or light-minded

Support Material
Teaching Portfolio
Teacher Backup, p. 1251
Grammar in Action Worksheets, *Using Coordination and Subordination*, p. 1255; *Infinitives and Infinitive Phrases*, p. 1257
Usage and Mechanics Worksheet, p. 1259
Vocabulary Check, p. 1260

Critical Thinking and Reading Worksheet, *Recognizing Sensory Details*, p. 1261
Language Worksheet, *Understanding Phonetic Spelling*, p. 1262
Selection Test, pp. 1263–1264
Art Transparency 13
Summer Evening on the Skagen Sound Beach with A. Ancher and M. Kroyer by Peter Severin Kroyer

Spelling Tip Point out that the words *abomination* and *indignation* end with the same six letters.

Literary Focus To help students understand how characters can be shaped by the setting of a literary work, you may want to have students compare and contrast people from different regions of the world or

Guide for Interpreting 1065

The Pearls

Isak Dinesen

About eighty years ago a young officer in the guards, the youngest son of an old country family, married, in Copenhagen, the daughter of a rich wool merchant whose father had been a peddler and had come to town from Jutland.[1] In those days such a marriage was an unusual thing. There was much talk of it, and a song was made about it, and sung in the streets.

The bride was twenty years old, and a beauty, a big girl with black hair and a high color, and a distinction about her as if she were made from whole timber. She had two old unmarried aunts, sisters of her grandfather the peddler, whom the growing fortune of the family had stopped short in a career of hard work and thrift, and made to sit in state in a parlor. When the elder of them first heard rumors of her niece's engagement she went and paid her a visit, and in the course of the conversation told her a story.

"When I was a child, my dear," she said, "young Baron Rosenkrantz became engaged to a wealthy goldsmith's daughter. Have you heard such a thing? Your great-grandmother knew her. The bridegroom had a twin sister, who was a lady at Court. She drove to the goldsmith's house to see the bride. When she had left again, the girl said to her lover: 'Your sister laughed at my frock, and because, when she spoke French, I could not answer. She has a hard heart, I saw that. If we are to be happy you must never see her again, I could not bear it.' The young man, to comfort her, promised that he would never see his sister again. Soon afterwards, on a Sunday, he took the girl to dine with

his mother. As he drove her home she said to him: 'Your mother had tears in her eyes, when she looked at me. She has hoped for another wife for you. If you love me, you must break with your mother.' Again the <u>enamored</u> young man promised to do as she wished, although it cost him much, for his mother was a widow, and he was her only son. The same week he sent his valet with a bouquet to his bride. Next day she said to him: 'I cannot stand the mien your valet has when he looks at me. You must send him away at the first of the month.' 'Mademoiselle,' said Baron Rosenkrantz, 'I cannot have a wife who lets herself be affected by my valet's mien. Here is your ring. Farewell forever.' "

While the old woman spoke she kept her little glittering eyes upon her niece's face. She had an energetic nature and had long ago made up her mind to live for others, and she had established herself as the conscience of the family. But in reality she was, with no hopes or fears of her own, a vigorous old moral parasite on the whole clan, and particularly on the younger members of it. Jensine, the bride, was a full-blooded young person and a gratifying object to a parasite. Moreover, the young and the old maid had many qualities in common. Now the girl went on pouring out coffee with a quiet face, but behind it she was furious, and said to herself: "Aunt Maren shall be paid back for this." All the same, as was often the case, the aunt's admonition[2] went deep into her, and she pondered it in her heart.

After the wedding, in the Cathedral of Copenhagen, on a fine June day, the newly married cou-

---

1. **Jutland** (jut´ lənd): A peninsula in northern Europe that forms the mainland of Denmark and the northern part of the state of Schleswig-Holstein in Germany.

2. **admonition** (ad´ mə nish´ ən) *n.*: A warning to correct specific faults.

NORDIC SUMMER
EVENING
Richard Bergh
Goteborgs Konstmuseum

3 **Discussion** Ask students why
Jensine chose to honeymoon in a
"wilderness" if she wanted no new
experiences. Why does she ask
God for help?

4 **Critical Thinking and Writing** Call
students' attention to Dinesen's
use of vivid sensory details in describing the setting. Have students
identify the sense or senses to
which each of these details appeals. Then have them discuss the
overall impression that these details convey.

Humanities Note

Fine art, *Nordic Summer Evening*
by Richard Bergh. The son of the
landscape painter Edvard Bergh,
Richard Bergh (1858–1919) was
born in Stockholm, Sweden. A gifted and versatile painter, he produced portraits, landscapes, and
genre paintings. All of his paintings are characterized by their realism, their attention to detail, and
their delicate and exquisite colors.

In this painting, Bergh offers
an evocative view of a man and a
woman gazing off into the horizon
on a beautiful summer evening.
Notice how he has used the location of his subjects and the arrangement of the landscape to
create a sense of balance in the
painting. Also note how he has
used color and lighting to create
a contemplative, dreamlike mood.

You might want to use the following questions to discuss the
art:

1. How does the artist create a
   sense of balance in the painting?
2. How would you describe the
   painting's mood, or atmosphere?
3. Which elements of the painting
   contribute to this mood?
4. What makes this painting an appropriate illustration for Dinesen's story?

ple went away to Norway for their wedding trip.
They sailed as far north as Hardanger.[3] At that time
a journey to Norway was a romantic undertaking,
and Jensine's friends asked her why they did not go
to Paris, but she herself was pleased to start her
married life in the wilderness, and to be alone with
her husband. She did not, she thought, need or
want any further new impressions or experiences.
And in her heart she added: God help me.

The gossips of Copenhagen would have it that
the bridegroom had married for money, and the
bride for a name, but they were all wrong. The
match was a love affair, and the honeymoon, technically, an idyll. Jensine would never have married a
man whom she did not love; she held the god of
love in great respect, and had already for some
years sent a little daily prayer to him: "Why doest
thou tarry?" But now she reflected that he had perhaps granted her her prayer with a vengeance, and
that her books had given her but little information
as to the real nature of love.

The scenery of Norway, amongst which she
had her first experience of the passion, contributed
to the overpowering impression of it. The country

was at its loveliest. The sky was blue, the bird-
cherry flowered everywhere and filled the air with
sweet and bitter fragrance, and the nights were so
light that you could see to read at midnight. Jensine, in a crinoline[4] and with an alpenstock,[5]
climbed many steep paths on her husband's
arm—or alone, for she was strong and lightfooted.
She stood upon the summits, her clothes blown
about her, and wondered and wondered. She had
lived in Denmark, and for a year in a pension in
Lubeck,[6] and her idea of the earth was that it must
spread out horizontally, flat or undulating,[7] before
her feet. But in these mountains everything seemed
strangely to stand up vertically, like some great animal that rises on its hind legs—and you know not
whether to play, or to crush you. She was higher
than she had ever been, and the air went to her
head like wine. Also, wherever she looked there
was running water, rushing from the sky-high
mountains into the lakes, in silvery rivulets or in

3. **Hardanger** (här däŋ′ ər): Hardangerfiord, the second
largest fiord in Norway. A fiord is a narrow inlet or arm of the
sea bordered by steep cliffs.

4. **crinoline** (krin′ ′l in) *n*.: A coarse, stiff petticoat worn
under a skirt to make it puff out.
5. **alpenstock** (al′ pən stäk′) *n*.: A strong iron-pointed staff
used by mountain climbers.
6. **Lubeck** (lü′ bek): A city and port in northwestern
Germany.
7. **undulating** (un′ joo lāt′ iŋ) *adj*.: Having a wavy form,
margin, or surface.

roaring falls, rainbow-adorned. It was as if Nature itself was weeping, or laughing, aloud.

At first all this was so new to her that she felt her old ideas of the world blown about in all directions, like her skirts and her shawl. But soon the impressions converged into a sensation of the deepest alarm, a panic such as she had never experienced.

She had been brought up in an atmosphere of prudence and foresight. Her father was an honest tradesman, afraid both to lose his own money, and to let down his customers. Sometimes this double risk had thrown him into <u>melancholia.</u> Her mother had been a God-fearing young woman, a member of a pietistic[8] sect; her two old aunts were persons of strict moral principle, with an eye to the opinions of the world. At home Jensine had at times believed herself a daring spirit, and had longed for adventure. But in this wildly romantic landscape, and taken by surprise and overwhelmed by wild, unknown, <u>formidable</u> forces within her own heart, she <u>looked round</u> for support. Where was she to find it? Her young husband, who had brought her there, and with whom she was all alone, could not help her. He was, on the contrary, the cause of the turbulence in her, and he was also, in her eyes, preeminently exposed to the dangers of the outward world. For very soon after her marriage Jensine realized—as she had perhaps dimly known from their first meeting—that he was a human being entirely devoid, and incapable, of fear.

She had read in books of heroes, and had admired them with all her heart. But Alexander was not like the heroes of her books. He was not braving, or conquering, the dangers of this world, but he was unaware of their existence. To him the mountains were a playground, and all the phenomena of life, love itself included, were his playmates within it. "In a hundred years, my darling," he said to her, "it will all be one." She could not imagine how he had managed to live till now, but then she knew that his life had been, in every way, different from hers. Now she felt, with horror, that here she was, within a world of undreamt of heights and depths, delivered into the hands of a person totally

ignorant of the law of gravitation. Under the circumstances her feelings for him intensified into both a deep moral <u>indignation,</u> as if he had deliberately betrayed her, and into an extreme tenderness, such as she would have felt toward an exposed, helpless child. These two passions were the strongest of which her nature was capable; they took speed with her, and developed into a possession. She recalled the fairy tale of the boy who is sent out in the world to learn to be afraid, and it seemed to her that for her own sake and his, in self-defense as well as in order to protect and save him, she must teach her husband to fear.

He knew nothing of what went on in her. He was in love with her, and he admired and respected her. She was innocent and pure; she sprang from a stock of people capable of making a fortune by their wits; she could speak French and German, and knew history and geography. For all these qualities he had a religious reverence.[9] He was prepared for surprises in her, for their acquaintance was but slight, and they had not been alone together in a room more than three or four times before their wedding. Besides, he did not pretend to understand women, but held their <u>incalculableness</u> to be part of their grace. The <u>moods and caprices</u>[10] of his young wife all confirmed in him the assurance, with which she had inspired him at their first meeting, that she was what he needed in life. But he wanted to make her his friend, and reflected that he had never had a real friend in his life. He did not talk to her of his love affairs of the past—indeed he could not have spoken of them to her if he had wanted to—but in other ways he told her as much as he could remember of himself and his life. One day he recounted how he had gambled in Baden-Baden,[11] risked his last cent, and then won. He did not know that she thought, by his side: "He is really a thief, or if not that, a receiver of stolen goods, and no better than a thief." At other times he made fun of the debts he had had, and the trouble he had had to take to avoid meeting his

---

8. **pietistic** (pī ə tis′ tik) *adj.*: Stressing the devotional ideal in religion.

---

9. **reverence** (rev′ ər əns) *n.*: A feeling or attitude of deep respect, love, and awe, as for something sacred.

10. **caprices** (kə prēs′ əz) *n.*: Sudden, impulsive changes in the way one thinks or acts.

11. **Baden-Baden** (bäd′ 'n bäd′ 'n): City in southwestern Germany.

Grammar in Action

Coordination and **subordination** clarify connections between ideas. Coordination joins *equal* and related words, phrases, and clauses within a sentence. Subordination, on the other hand, joins *unequal* but related ideas within a sentence. Note the following examples from "The Pearls":

Jensine had never had a string of pearls before, and she was proud of hers. (Coordination)

As long as I must strain myself against him in this way, we will never have a child. (Subordination)

Student Activity 1. Identify the examples of coordination or subordination in each of the following sentences:

1. She had an energetic nature and had long ago made up her mind to live for others, and she had established herself as the conscience of the family.
2. The match was a love affair, and the honeymoon, technically, an idyll.
3. When Jensine set out to teach her husband to fear, she had the tale of Aunt Maren in her mind, and she made the vow that she would never cry quarter, but that this should be his part.
4. When Jensine sat down and loosened her bonnet, the string of pearls caught in her bracelet, and the pearls sprang all over the floor, as if she

tailor. This talk sounded really uncanny to Jensine's ears. For to her debts were an abomination, and that he should have lived on in the midst of them without anxiety, trusting to fortune to pay up for him, seemed against nature. Still, she reflected, she herself, the rich girl he married, had come along in time, as the willing tool of fortune, to justify his trust in the eyes of his tailor himself. He told her of a duel that he had fought with a German officer, and showed her a scar from it. As, at the end of it all, he took her in his arms, on the high hilltops, for all the skies to see them, in her heart she cried: "If it be possible, let this cup pass from me."

When Jensine set out to teach her husband to fear, she had the tale of Aunt Maren in her mind, and she made the vow that she would never cry quarter,[12] but that this should be his part. As the relation between herself and him was to her the central factor of existence, it was natural that she should first try to scare him with the possibility of losing her. She was an unsophisticated girl, and resorted to simple measures.

From now on she became more reckless than he in their climbs. She would stand on the edge of a precipice, leaning on her parasol, and ask him how deep it was to the bottom. She balanced across narrow, brittle bridges, high above foaming streams, and chattered to him the while. She went out rowing in a small boat, on the lake, in a thunderstorm. At nights she dreamed about the perils of the days, and woke up with a shriek, so that he took her in his arms to comfort her. But her daring did her no good. Her husband was surprised and enchanted at the change of the demure maiden into a Valkyrie.[13] He put it down to the influence of married life, and felt not a little proud. She herself, in the end, wondered whether she was not driven on in her exploits by his pride and praise as much as by her resolution to conquer him. Then she was angry with herself, and with all women, and she pitied him, and all men.

Sometimes Alexander would go out fishing. These were welcome opportunities to Jensine to be alone and collect her thoughts. So the young bride would wander about alone, in a tartan frock, a small figure in the hills. Once or twice, in these walks, she thought of her father, and the memory of his anxious concern for her brought tears to her eyes. But she sent him away again; she must be left alone to settle matters of which he could know nothing.

One day, when she sat and rested on a stone, a group of children, who were herding goats, approached and stared at her. She called them up and gave them sweets from her reticule. Jensine had adored her dolls, and as much as a modest girl of the period dared, she had longed for children of her own. Now she thought with sudden dismay: "I shall never have children! As long as I must strain myself against him in this way, we will never have a child." The idea distressed her so deeply that she got up and walked away.

On another of her lonely walks she came to think of a young man in her father's office who had loved her. His name was Peter Skov. He was a brilliant young man of business, and she had known him all her life. She now recalled how, when she had had the measles, he had sat and read to her every day, and how he had accompanied her when she went out skating, and had been distressed lest she should catch cold, or fall, or go through the ice. From where she stood she could see her husband's small figure in the distance. "Yes," she thought, "this is the best thing I can do. When I come back to Copenhagen, then, by my honor, which is still my own"—although she had doubts on this point—"Peter Skov shall be my lover."

On their wedding day Alexander had given his bride a string of pearls. It had belonged to his grandmother, who had come from Germany and who was a beauty and a *bel esprit*.[14] She had left it to him to give to his future wife. Alexander talked too much to her of his grandmother. He did, he said, first fall in love with her because she was a little like his grandmama. He asked her to wear the pearls every day. Jensine had never had a string of pearls before, and she was proud of hers. Lately, when she had so often been in need of support, she had got into the habit of twisting the string, and

---

12. **never cry quarter:** Show no mercy.
13. **Valkyrie** (val kir′ ē): In Norse mythology the Valkyries are maidens who conduct the souls of heroes slain in battle to Valhalla, the great hall of the fallen warriors.

14. *bel esprit* (bel′ es prē′): A clever, cultured person.

11 **Discussion** Have students explain how Aunt Maren's tale contributes to Jensine's determination to teach her husband to fear.

12 **Discussion** Have students discuss why Jensine's reckless behavior does not succeed in changing her husband. Why is it ironic that Jensine's behavior convinces Alexander that Jensine has been transformed from "a demure maiden into a Valkyrie"?

13 **Discussion** Have students discuss what causes Jensine to feel angry toward women and feel pity for men?

14 **Discussion** Have students explain why Jensine decides that she should not have children.

15 **Discussion** Have students discuss what causes Jensine to begin thinking about Peter Skov. What is the significance of the fact that she sees Alexander's "small figure in the distance" just before she decides to have a romantic relationship with Peter Skov?

16 **Reading Strategy** Have students pause and summarize the story up to this point.

---

had burst into a rain of tears.
5. She counted the pearls up to him, and gravely confided them into his hands.

    Student Activity 2. Find three more examples of coordination and three more examples of subordination in Dinesen's story.

17 Discussion Have students explain why Jensine is surprised by Alexander's concern for the pearls.

18 Discussion Have students explain why Jensine comes to look on Alexander's grandmother "as her best friend in the family."

19 Discussion Have students speculate about the hidden dangers that might await Jensine when she returns to Copenhagen.

20 Discussion Have students discuss the irony of the way in which the string of pearls breaks.

21 Discussion Have students discuss how the story of how the old man lost his feet confirms Jensine's impression that the mountains are a dangerous place.

22 Discussion Have students explain why Jensine feels as if she has "come home" as she looks around the shoemaker's shop?

17 pulling it with her lips. "If you go on doing that," Alexander said one day, "you will break the string." She looked at him. It was the first time that she had known him to foresee disaster. "He has loved his grandmother," she thought, "or is it that you must be dead to carry weight with this man?" Since then she often thought of the old woman. She, **18** too, had come from her own milieu and had been a stranger in her husband's family and circle of friends. She had managed to get this string of pearls from Alexander's grandfather, and to be remembered by it down through the generations. Were the pearls, she wondered, a token of victory, or of submission? Jensine came to look upon Grandmama as her best friend in the family. She would have liked to pay her a grand-daughterly visit, and to consult her on her own troubles.

The honeymoon was nearing its end, and that strange warfare, the existence of which was known to one of the belligerents only, had come to no decision. Both the young people were sad to go away. Only now did Jensine fully realize the beauty of the landscape round her, for, after all, in the end she had made it her ally. Up here, she reflected, the dangers of the world were obvious, ever in sight. In Copenhagen life looked secure, but might prove to **19** be even more redoubtable. She thought of her pretty house, waiting for her there, with lace curtains, chandeliers and linen cupboards. She could not at all tell what life within it would be like.

20 The day before they were to sail they were staying in a small village, from where it was six hours' drive in a cariole[15] down to the landing place of the coast steamer. They had been out before breakfast. When Jensine sat down and loosened her bonnet, the string of pearls caught in her bracelet, and the pearls sprang all over the floor, as if she had burst into a rain of tears. Alexander got down on his hands and knees, and, as he picked them up one by one, placed them in her lap.

She sat in a kind of mild panic. She had broken the one thing in the world that she had been afraid of breaking. What omen did that have for them? "Do you know how many there were?" she asked him. "Yes," he said from the floor, "Grandpapa

15. **cariole** (kar′ ē ōl′) *n*.: A small carriage drawn by one horse.

gave Grandmama the string at their golden wedding, with a pearl for each of their fifty years. But afterwards he added one every year, at her birthday. There are fifty-two. It is easy to remember; it is the number of cards in a pack." At last they got them all collected and wrapped them up in his silk handkerchief. "Now I cannot put them on till I get to Copenhagen," she said.

At that moment their landlady came in with the coffee. She observed the catastrophe and at once offered to assist them. The shoemaker in the village, she said, could do up the pearls for them. Two years ago an English lord and his lady, with a party, had traveled in the mountains, and when the young lady broke her string of pearls, in the same way, he had strung them for her to her perfect satisfaction. He was an honest old man, although very poor, and a cripple. As a young man he had got lost in a snowstorm in the hills, and been found only two days later, and they had had to cut off both his feet. Jensine said that she would take her pearls to the shoemaker, and the landlady showed her the way to his house.

She walked down alone, while her husband was strapping their boxes, and found the shoemaker in his little dark workshop. He was a small, thin, old man in a leather apron, with a shy, sly smile in a face harassed by long suffering. She counted the pearls up to him, and gravely confided them into his hands. He looked at them, and promised to have them ready by next midday. After she had settled with him she kept sitting on a small chair, with her hands in her lap. To say something, she asked him the name of the English lady who had broken her string of pearls, but he did not remember it.

She looked round at the room. It was poor and bare, with a couple of religious pictures nailed on the wall. In a strange way it seemed to her that here she had come home. An honest man, hard tried by destiny, had passed his long years in this little room. It was a place where people worked, and bore troubles patiently, in anxiety for their daily bread. She was still so near to her schoolbooks that she remembered them all, and now she began to think of what she had read about deep-water fish, which have been so much used to bear the weight of many thousand fathoms of water, that if they are raised to the surface, they will burst. Was she herself, she

Commentary

Dinesen and the Scandinavian Gothic Tale Along with the modern Swedish writer Pär Lagerkvist (page 1076), Isak Dinesen is recognized as one of the masters of a type of story that has come to be known as the Scandinavian Gothic tale. These tales are generally set in an imaginary past or an exotic place and often involve grotesque or bizarre characters. They are referred to as "tales" because they are reminiscent of legends and seem as if they might have originally been spoken aloud rather than written. In addition, these tales often contain stories within stories and include incidental characters that bring about important changes in one of the central characters. Finally, symbols typically play an important role in these tales, and the tales usually contain implied, or indirectly stated, moral messages.

Considering this definition, would students classify "The Pearls" as a Scandinavian Gothic tale? Which of the characteristics of the Gothic tale are evident in "The Pearls"? Which characteristics are not?

wondered, such a deep-water fish that felt at home only under the pressure of existence? And her father, her grandfather, and his people before him, had they been the same? What was a deep-water fish to do, she thought on, if she were married to one of those salmon which here she had seen springing in the waterfalls? Or to a flying-fish? She said good-bye to the old shoemaker, and walked off.

As she was going home she caught sight, on the path in front of her, of a small stout man in a black hat and coat who walked on briskly. She remembered that she had seen him before; she even believed that he was staying in the same house as she. There was a seat by the path, from which one had a magnificent view. The man in black sat down, and Jensine, whose last day in the mountains it was, sat down on the other end of the seat. The stranger lifted his hat a little to her. She had believed him to be an elderly man, but now saw that he could not be much over thirty. He had an energetic face and clear, penetrating eyes. After a moment he spoke to her, with a little smile. "I saw you coming out from the shoemaker's," he said. "You have not lost your sole in the mountains?" "No, I brought him some pearls," said Jensine. "You brought him pearls?" said the stranger humorously. "That is what I go to collect from him." She wondered if he were a bit deranged. "That old man," said he, "has got, in his hut, a big store of our old national treasures—pearls if you like—which I happen to be collecting just now. In case you want children's tales, there is not a man in Norway who can give you a better lot than our shoemaker. He once dreamed of becoming a student, and a poet—do you know that?—but he was hard hit by destiny, and had to take to a shoemaker's trade."

After a pause he said: "I have been told that you and your husband come from Denmark, on your wedding trip. That is an unusual thing to do; these mountains are high and dangerous. Who of you two was it who desired to come here? Was it you?" "Yes," said she. "Yes," said the stranger. "I thought so. That he might be the bird, which upwards soars, and you the breeze, which carries him along. Do you know that quotation? Does it tell you anything?" "Yes," said she, somewhat bewildered. "Upwards," said he and sat back, silent,

with his hands upon his walking stick. After a little while he went on: "The summits! Who knows? We two are pitying the shoemaker for his bad luck, that he had to give up his dreams of being a poet, of fame and a great name. How do we know but that he has had the best of luck? Greatness, the applause of the masses! Indeed, my young lady, perhaps they are better left alone. Perhaps in common trade they cannot reasonably purchase a shoemaker's sign board, and the knowledge of soling. One may do well in getting rid of them at cost price. What do you think, Madam?" "I think that you are right," she said slowly. He gave her a sharp glance from a pair of ice-blue eyes.

"Indeed," said he. "Is that your advice, on this fair summer day? Cobbler, stay by your last. One should do better, you think, in making up pills and drafts for the sick human beings, and cattle, of this world?" He chuckled a little. "It is a very good jest. In a hundred years it will be written in a book: A little lady from Denmark gave him the advice to stay by his last. Unfortunately, he did not follow it. Good-bye, Madam, good-bye." With these words he got up, and walked on. She saw his black figure grow smaller amongst the hills. The landlady had come out to hear if she had found the shoemaker. Jensine looked after the stranger. "Who was that gentleman?" she asked. The woman shaded her eyes with her hand. "Oh, indeed," said she. "He is a learned man, a great man, he is here to collect old stories and songs. He was an apothecary[16] once. But he has had a theater in Bergen, and written plays for it, too. His name is Herr Ibsen."[17]

In the morning news came up from the landing place that the boat would be in sooner than expected, and they had to start in haste. The landlady sent her small son to the shoemaker to fetch Jensine's pearls. When the travelers were already seated in the cariole, he brought them, wrapped in a leaf from a book, with a waxed string round them. Jensine undid them, and was about to count them, but thought better of it, and instead clasped the string round her throat. "Ought you not to count them?" Alexander asked her. She gave him a great

---

16. apothecary (ə päth′ ə ker′ ē) *n*.: A pharmacist.
17. Ibsen (ib′ s'n): Henrik Ibsen (1829–1906), Norwegian playwright and poet.

29 Clarification The word *triumphator* refers to any successful Roman general who was allowed to make a festive parade through Rome to celebrate a great victory. Ask students why Dinesen uses this obscure word instead of simply writing: "She sat by his side, triumphant. Now she knew what triumph felt like"? What great victory does Jensine feel she has won?

30 Discussion Have students discuss why Jensine might have waited until this time to count the pearls. Why is she so certain a pearl will be missing? Why does she feel that she will lose a year of her married life if one of the pearls is missing?

31 Discussion Have students discuss Jensine's apparent attitude toward the possibility of war. How does her attitude contrast with that of the young officers? Why can she not talk to Alexander about the possibility of war?

32 Discussion Have students discuss why Jensine attributes the appearance of the extra pearl to the Devil.

33 Discussion Have students explain why Jensine turns to Peter Skov to help her in appraising the pearls. Then have them explain why she lies to him and why she is so terrified by his news.

29 glance. "No," she said. She was silent on the drive. His words rang in her ears: "Ought you not to count them?" She sat by his side, a triumphator. Now she knew what a triumphator felt like.

Alexander and Jensine came back to Copenhagen at a time when most people were out of town and there were no great social functions. But she had many visits from the wives of his young military friends, and the young people went together to the Tivoli of Copenhagen in the summer evenings. Jensine was made much of by all of them.

Her house lay by one of the old canals of the town and looked over to the Thorwaldsen Museum. Sometimes she would stand by the window, gaze at the boats, and think of Hardanger. During all this time she had not taken off her pearls or counted them. She was sure that there would be at least one pearl missing. She imagined that she felt the weight, on her throat, different from before.

30 What would it be, she thought, which she had sacrificed for her victory over her husband? A year, or two years, of their married life, before their golden wedding? This golden wedding seemed a long way off, but still each year was precious; and how was she to part with one of them?

In the last months of this summer people began to discuss the possibility of war. The Schleswig-Holstein question[18] had become imminent. A Danish Royal Proclamation, of March, had repudiated all German claims upon Schleswig. Now in July a German note demanded, on pain of federal execution, the withdrawal of the Proclamation.

Jensine was an ardent patriot and loyal to the King, who had given the people its free constitution. The rumors put her into the highest agitation. She thought the young officers, Alexander's 31 friends, frivolous in their light, boastful talk of the country's danger. If she wanted to debate the crisis seriously she had to go to her own people. With her husband she could not talk of it at all, but in her heart she knew that he was as convinced of

---

18. The Schleswig-Holstein (shles´ vik hôl´ shtīn) **question:** During the mid-nineteenth century, a dispute occurred between Denmark and the German Confederation concerning the control of the state of Schleswig-Holstein. Eventually, after two wars and several decades of tension, Germany won control of the state. Today, Schleswig-Holstein is part of Germany.

Denmark's invincibility as of his own immortality.

She read the newspapers from beginning to end. One day in the *Berlingske Tidende* she came upon the following phrase: "The moment is grave to the nation. But we have trust in our just cause, and we are without fear."

It was, perhaps, the words "without fear" which now made her collect her courage. She sat down in her chair by the window, took off her pearls, and put them in her lap. She sat for a moment with her hands folded upon them, as in prayer. Then she counted them. There were fifty-three pearls and the one in the middle was the biggest.

Jensine sat for a long time in her chair, quite giddy. Her mother, she knew, had believed in the Devil. At this moment the daughter did the same. She would not have been surprised had she heard laughter from behind the sofa. Had the powers of the universe, she thought, combined, here, to make fun of a poor girl?

When she could again collect her thoughts, she remembered that before she had been given the necklace, the old goldsmith of her husband's family had repaired the clasp of it. He would therefore know the pearls, and might tell her what to believe. But she was so thoroughly scared that she dared not go to him herself, and only a few days later she asked Peter Skov, who came to pay her a visit, to take the string to him.

Peter returned and told her that the goldsmith had put on his spectacles to examine the pearls, and then, in amazement, had declared that there was one more than when he had last seen them. "Yes, Alexander gave me that," Jensine interrupted him, blushing deeply at her own lie. Peter reflected, as the goldsmith had done, that it was a cheap generosity in a lieutenant to make the heiress he had married a rich present. But he repeated to her the old man's words. "Mr. Alexander," he had declared, "shows himself a rare judge of pearls. I shall not hesitate to pronounce this one pearl worth as much as all the others put together." Jensine, terrified but smiling, thanked Peter, but he went away sadly, for he felt as if he had annoyed or frightened her.

She had not been feeling well for some time, and when, in September, they had a spell of heavy,

---

Grammar in Action

Infinitives and Infinitive Phrases An **infinitive** is a form of a verb that generally appears with the word *to* and acts as a noun, adjective, or adverb. An **infinitive phrase** is an infinitive with modifiers, a complement, or an object, all acting together as a single part of speech. Note the following examples from Isak Dinesen's story:

If she wanted *to debate the crisis seriously* . . . (Infinitive phrase as a direct object)

. . . she asked Peter Skov, . . . *to take the string with him.* (Infinitive phrase as a direct object)

Student Activity 1. Find five more infinitives or infinitive phrases in "The Pearls." Then identify the function of each.

Student Activity 2. Write five separate sentences that each contain either an infinitive or an infinitive phrase. Then identify the function of the infinitive or infinitive phrase in each of these sentences.

sultry weather in Copenhagen, it left her pale and sleepless. Her father and her two old aunts were upset about her and tried to make her come and stay at his villa on the Strandvej, outside town. But she would not leave her own house or husband, nor would she, she thought, ever get well, until she had come to the bottom of the mystery of the pearls. After a week she made up her mind to write to the shoemaker at Odda. If, as Herr Ibsen had told her, he had been a student and a poet, he would be able to read, and would answer her letter. It seemed to her that in her present situation she had no friend in the world but this crippled old man. She wished that she could go back to his workshop, to the bare walls and the three-legged chair. She dreamed at night that she was there. He had smiled kindly at her; he knew many children's tales. He might know how to comfort her. Only for a moment she trembled at the idea that he might be dead, and that then she would never know.

Within the following weeks the shadow of the war grew deeper. Her father was worrying over the prospects and about King Frederick's[19] health. Under these new circumstances the old merchant began to take pride in the fact that he had his daughter married to a soldier, which before had been far from his mind. He and her old aunts showed Alexander and Jensine great respect.

One day, half against her own will, Jensine asked straight out if he thought there would be a war. "Yes," he answered quickly and confidently, "there will be war. It could not be avoided." He went on to whistle a bit of a soldier's song. The sight of her face made him stop. "Are you affrighted of it?" he asked. She considered it hopeless, and even unseemly, to explain to him her feelings about the war. "Are you frightened for my sake?" he asked her again. She turned her head away. "To be a hero's widow," he said, "would be just the part for you, my dear." Her eyes filled with tears, as much of anger as of woe. Alexander came and took her hand. "If I fall," he

---

19. **King Frederick's:** Frederick VII (1808–1863), the king of Denmark from 1848 through 1863.

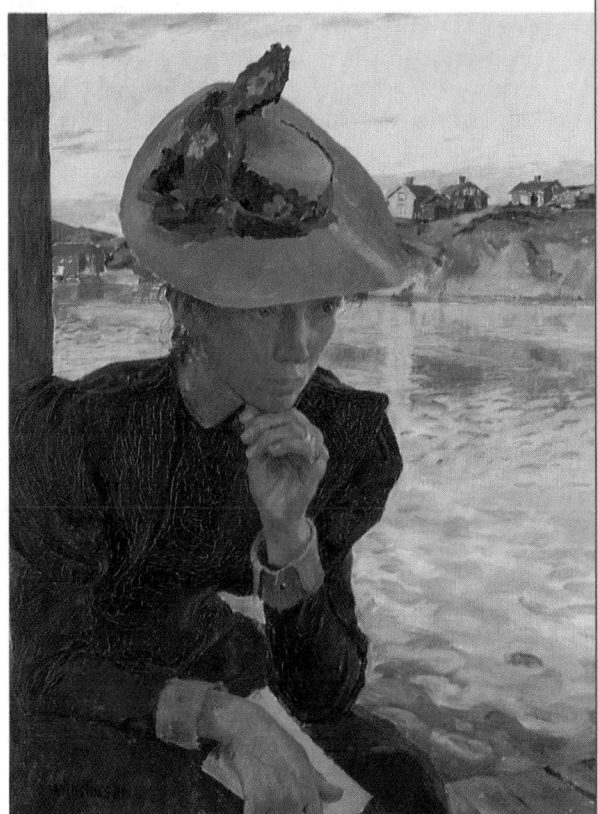

SCENE FROM THE SWEDISH COAST
Carl Wilhelmson
Goteborgs Konstmuseum

said, "it will be a consolation to me to remember that I have kissed you as often as you would let me." He did so now, once more, and added: "Will it be a consolation to you?" Jensine was an honest girl. When she was questioned she tried to find the truthful answer. Now she thought: Would it be a consolation to me? But she could not, in her heart, find the reply.

With all this Jensine had much to think of, so that she half forgot about the shoemaker, and, when one morning she found his letter on the breakfast table, she for a minute took it to be a mendicant's letter, of which she got many. The next moment she grew very pale. Her husband, opposite her, asked her what was the matter. She

37 Discussion Ask students to explain why Jensine accuses herself of being no better than a thief. Make sure that they note that she uses the same words with which she mentally reproached her husband earlier in the story.

38 Clarification In the Bible's account of Eve's temptation by the serpent, the Lord God casts Adam and Eve out of the Garden of Eden, but says to the serpent, often regarded as the Devil: "And I will put enmity between thee and the woman, and between thy seed and her seed; it shall bruise thy head, and thou shalt bruise his heel." In other words, a male descendant of Eve will strike the serpent in the head, but the serpent will bite his foot. Here, Jensine quotes the Bible in a way that places her in the role of the serpent.

39 Discussion Ask students why Jensine holds herself responsible for the appearance of the extra pearl.

40 Discussion Have students explain the revelation that Jensine has in this scene. What is the significance of the fact that her recollection of Alexander's remark, "In a hundred years . . . it will all be one," leads her to her revelation?

Cooperative Learning Students might be interested in learning about Norse mythology, which was an important influence on Dinesen and many other Scandinavian writers. Divide your class into groups of three or four. Have each group research a different aspect of Norse mythology. For example, they might research a specific god, such as Thor. When the groups have completed their research, have them share their findings with the rest of the class.

---

gave him no reply, but got up, went into her own small sitting-room, and opened the letter by the fireplace. The characters of it, carefully printed, recalled to her the old man's face, as if he had sent her his portrait.

"Dear young Danish Missus," the letter went.

"Yes, I put the pearl onto your necklace. I meant to give you a small surprise. You made such a fuss about your pearls, when you brought them to me, as if you were afraid that I should steal one of them from you. Old people, as well as young, must have a little fun at times. If I have frightened you, I beg that you will forgive me all the same. This pearl I got two years ago, when I strung the English lady's necklace. I forgot to put the one in, and only found it afterwards. It has been with me for two years, but I have no use for it. It is better that it should be with a young lady. I remember that you sat in my chair, quite young and pretty. I wish you good luck, and that something pleasant may happen to you on the very same day as you get this letter. And may you wear the pearl long, with a humble heart, a firm trust in the Lord God, and a friendly thought of me, who am old, here up at Odda. Good-bye.

"Your friend, Peiter Viken."

Jensine had been reading the letter with her elbows on the mantelpiece, to steady herself. As she looked up, she met the grave eyes of her own image in the looking glass above it. They were severe; they might be saying: "You are really a thief, or if not that, a receiver of stolen goods, and no better than a thief." She stood for a long time, nailed to the spot. At last she thought: "It is all over. Now I know that I shall never conquer these people, who know neither care nor fear. It is as in the Bible; I shall bruise their heel, but they bruise my head. And Alexander, as far as he is concerned, ought to have married the English lady."

To her own deep surprise she found that she did not mind. Alexander himself had become a very small figure in the background of life; what he did or thought mattered not in the least. That she herself had been made a fool of did not matter. "In a hundred years," she thought, "it will all be one."

What mattered then? She tried to think of the war, but found that the war did not matter either. She felt a strange giddiness, as if the room was sinking away round her, but not unpleasantly. "Was there," she thought, "nothing remarkable left under the visiting moon?" At the word of the visiting moon the eyes of the image in the looking glass opened wide; the two young women stared at one another intensely. Something, she decided, was of great importance, which had come into the world now, and in a hundred years would still remain. The pearls. In a hundred years, she saw, a young man would hand them over to his wife and tell the young woman her own story about them, just as Alexander had given them to her, and had told her of his grandmother.

The thought of these two young people, in a hundred years' time, moved her to such tenderness that her eyes filled with tears, and made her happy, as if they had been old friends of hers, whom she had found again. "Not cry quarter?" she thought. "Why not? Yes, I shall cry as high as I can. I cannot, now, remember the reason why I would not cry."

The very small figure of Alexander, by the window in the other room, said to her: "Here is the eldest of your aunts coming down the street with a big bouquet."

Slowly, slowly Jensine took her eyes off the looking glass, and came back to the world of the present. She went to the window. "Yes," she said, "they are from Bella Vista," which was the name of her father's villa. From their window the husband and wife looked down into the street.

Reader's Response *If you were in Alexander's place, would you share his attitude concerning the coming war? Why or why not? How would you feel if you were in Jensine's place?*

Closure and Extension

ANSWERS TO THINKING ABOUT THE SELECTION

1. (a) People talked about the marriage because the two came from different classes. (b) Suggested response: It dramatizes one of the potential problems of a marriage involving people from different classes.

2. (a) Suggested response: His behavior during their honeymoon leads her to this conclusion. (b) Suggested response: She feels that he can protect both himself and her better if he knows how to fear.

3. Suggested response: She does not want to have children as long as she is struggling to change Alexander.

4. Suggested response: Like Jensine, the grandmother had been a stranger to her husband's family and circle of friends.

5. (a) Suggested response: It reminds her of her upbringing by people who also worked hard and bore their troubles patiently. (b) Suggested response: Brought up amidst the pressures of everyday life, she compares herself to a deep-water fish that bears the weight of many thousand fathoms of water. Her untroubled, uninhibited husband, on the other hand, she compares to a carefree salmon, a flying-fish.

6. Suggested response: Alexander is carefree and can enjoy his marriage because Jensine gives him emotional support and keeps him from falling.

7. Suggested response: She feels triumphant because she does not act on her fear that one of the pearls is missing.

THINKING ABOUT THE SELECTION

Interpreting

1. (a) Why was there so much talk about Jensine and Alexander's marriage? (b) How does the story that Jensine's aunt tells her relate to her own situation?

2. (a) Why does Jensine come to the realization that her husband is incapable of fear? (b) Why does she become resolved to teach him to fear?

3. Why does Jensine conclude that she and Alexander will never have children?

4. Why does Jensine come to look on Alexander's deceased grandmother as her best friend in his family?

5. (a) Why does being in the shoemaker's workshop make Jensine feel as if she had come home? (b) How do her memories of what she learned in school about fish relate to her situation with Alexander?

6. What does Herr Ibsen mean when he comments that Alexander is "the bird, which soars upward" and Jensine is "the breeze which carries him along"?

7. Why does Jensine feel as if she has triumphed over Alexander when she decides not to count the pearls before heading back to Copenhagen?

8. (a) What is Jensine's attitude concerning the approaching war? (b) What is Alexander's attitude? (c) How do the differences in their attitudes relate to Jensine's earlier observations about fear?

9. (a) Why is Jensine so shaken by Peter Viken's letter? (b) What realization provides her with relief from her agitation?

10. (a) What do the pearls come to symbolize, or represent, at the end of the story? (b) What do you think is the theme of the story?

Applying

11. (a) Explain whether you do or do not feel that it is possible for a person to be completely incapable of fear. (b) Do you think that it is important for a person to be capable of fear? Why or why not?

ANALYZING LITERATURE

Understanding Setting

Setting is the time, environment, and conditions in which the events in a work of literature occur. Although it is rarely the most important element of a literary work, the setting often plays an important role in shaping the characters' personalities and behavior.

1. Explain how the setting of "The Pearls" relates to the attitude of Jensine's family concerning her marriage to Alexander.

2. What impression does Dinesen convey of the Norwegian landscape?

3. Which details contribute most to this impression?

4. What impact does the Norwegian landscape have on Jensine?

CRITICAL THINKING AND READING

Recognizing Sensory Details

When writing a description, writers use **sensory language,** or language that appeals to one or more of the five senses. For example, Dinesen appeals to both our sense of sight and our sense of smell in the following description: "The sky was blue, the wild-cherry flowered everywhere and filled the air with sweet and bitter fragrance."

1. Find two more examples of language that appeals to the sense of sight.

2. Find an example of language that appeals to one of the other senses.

3. Which of these examples do you find most effective? Explain.

THINKING AND WRITING

Writing a Description

Write a description of a place that you have been to that had an especially powerful impact on you. For example, you might recall a trip to New York City or to the Rocky Mountains. Once you have chosen a place to describe, prepare a list of details you can use in your paper. After you have decided how you want to organize your description, begin writing. Make sure you use sensory language appealing to several different senses. When you have finished writing, revise your description, making sure it conveys the impression you want it to.

(continued from bottom of page)

phe. (b) Answers will differ.

ANSWERS TO ANALYZING LITERATURE

1. In the society in which the characters live, it is considered unacceptable for people of different classes to marry.

2. Suggested response: It is beautiful yet dangerous.

3. Suggested response: Details that emphasize the beauty of the landscape include those in the description of Norwegian scenery on page 1067. Details emphasizing its danger include the paragraph on page 1069 in which Jensine tries to behave recklessly on precipices, on narrow, brittle bridges, and on the lake in a thunderstorm.

4. Suggested response: It makes her decide that she must teach her husband to fear.

ANSWERS TO CRITICAL THINKING AND READING

1. Answers will differ. Possible responses: "everything seemed strangely to stand up vertically, like some great animal that rises on its hind legs—and you know not whether to play, or to crush you"; "running water, rushing from the sky-high mountains into the lakes, in silvery rivulets."

2. Answers will differ. Possible responses: "roaring falls" and "It was as if Nature itself was weeping, or laughing, aloud."

3. Answers will differ. Make sure that students offer reasons for each of their choices.

THINKING AND WRITING

Publishing Student Writing You may want to encourage students to submit their papers to the school literary magazine.

Challenge Tell students that Dinesen greatly admired the work of the Swedish writer Pär Lagerkvist. Have students read Lagerkvist's story "The Princess and All the Kingdom" (page 1078). Then have them compare and contrast Lagerkvist's story with Dinesen's story.

8. (a) Suggested response: Although an ardent patriot, Jensine dreads the coming war and considers the boastful talk of the young officers to be frivolous. (b) Suggested response: He is resigned to the fact that there will be a war and is optimistic about its outcome. (c) Suggested response: Jensine clearly fears the war, and Alexander does not.

9. (a) Suggested response: It makes her view herself as a thief, even though she has no real reason to feel this way. (b) Suggested response: Her agitation disappears when she recalls Alexander's comment, "In a hundred years, it will all be one."

10. (a) Suggested response: The pearls symbolize the customs or traditions that are handed down across generations and give stability to our otherwise insecure lives. (b) Answers will differ. Possible responses include the idea that standing alone can be frightening, while accepting traditions that connect one to others can be comforting.

11. (a) Answers will differ. Some students may suggest that even the most fearless person can be shaken by a great or unexpected catastro-

PÄR LAGERKVIST

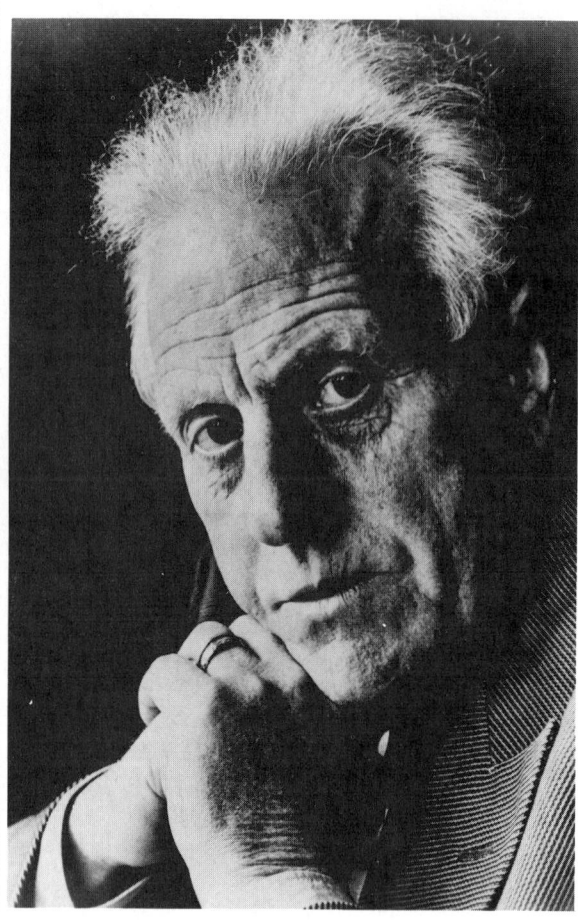

1891–1974

Because of the extreme pessimism of his earlier works, Pär Lagerkvist (par lä′ gər kvist′) did not earn widespread public recognition and critical acclaim until late in his career. In 1951, however, following the publication of his two best-known novels, *The Dwarf* (1944) and *Barabbas* (1950), he earned the most distinguished of all literary awards: the Nobel Prize.

The son of a railway worker, Lagerkvist was born and reared in a small rural town in Sweden.

Unlike many of the inhabitants of his town, he received a university education, during which he learned about modern scientific ideas that prompted him to question the rigid, traditional beliefs he had been brought up with. His uncertainty about traditional attitudes is clearly reflected in his early literary works.

Published during World War I, his earliest works, including his collection of poetry *Anguish* (1916) and his dramatic production *The Difficult Hour* (1918), portray a world that is completely devoid of meaning and hope. As his literary career progressed, however, his work became less pessimistic. After the publication of a number of slightly more optimistic works, such as his prose fantasy *The Eternal Smile* (1920), Lagerkvist reached a major turning point in his development as a writer when he completed *The Triumph over Life* (1927), a collection of meditations and sayings in which he expressed his growing faith in humankind.

In the years leading up to World War II, Lagerkvist became a vocal critic of violence, Nazism, and totalitarian rule. He expressed his views about these issues in such works as his prose tale *The Hangman* (1933) and his play *The Man Without a Soul* (1936). During World War II he worked on *The Dwarf*, the first of his two most famous novels. Set in a Renaissance court and narrated by a corrupt dwarf, this novel delves into the conflict between good and evil. His second well-known work, *Barabbas*, also explores this conflict, focusing on the actions of a sinister robber.

Although was he was unable to match the success of *The Dwarf* and *Barabbas*, Lagerkvist continued to write prolifically throughout the remainder of his life. His later works include his collection of poems *Aftonland* (1953) and his novels *The Sibyl* (1956), *The Death of A.* (1960), and *Pilgrim at Sea* (1962). Through these works Lagerkvist conveyed his own internal struggle to come to terms with his own religious faith, which he ultimately resolved in his novel *The Holy Land* (1964).

GUIDE FOR INTERPRETING

Commentary

The Princess and All the Kingdom

Fairy Tales. As young children we all read **fairy tales** or had them read to us by our parents or teachers. We remember them as exciting and entertaining stories set in imaginary places, involving elves, witches, dragons, princesses, and talking animals. Just a few of the many fairy tales that may be etched into our memories are "Hansel and Gretel," "Goldilocks and the Three Bears," "Little Red Riding Hood," "The Emperor's New Clothes," and "The Three Little Pigs."

These and other popular fairy tales come from a variety of sources. Many originated as part of the oral tradition of a specific culture and were recorded and collected by compilers such as the Grimm brothers. Others are the original creation of writers such as Hans Christian Andersen. Regardless of their origin, almost all fairy tales share a number of common features. As you probably know, fairy tales typically begin with the phrase *Once upon a time,* indicating that they are not set in any specific time period. In addition, the stories generally take place in vague, dreamlike lands unlike any specific places in the real world. Although the tales may involve mystery, danger, and even violence, they are generally told in an unthreatening manner and conclude with a happy ending in which all conflicts are resolved. Finally, fairy tales often teach a lesson or convey a general truth about life. Yet, unlike fables, fairy tales do not contain direct statements of theme.

Aside from entertaining children, fairy tales can serve a number of other purposes. By portraying characters who overcome threatening situations involving evil creatures and villains, fairy tales can help children to overcome any imaginary demons that may haunt them. The tales can also inspire and instruct children by suggesting that even seemingly impossible problems can be solved. Finally, because they frequently depict young children who are able to solve their own problems, fairy tales encourage children to take initiative.

Although fairy tales are generally associated with children, they have captured the interest of many adults. A number of writers have written works of fiction that are either based on or modeled after fairy tales. For example, Pär Lagerkvist adopted certain elements of the fairy tale in writing "The Princess and All the Kingdom." At the same time, however, certain characteristics of his story clearly contrast with those of a fairy tale. As you read the story, look for the ways in which it does and does not resemble a fairy tale.

Writing

Write a journal entry in which you discuss some of the fairy tales that you read when you were a child.

Literary Focus Have students discuss why a writer might choose to model a story after a fairy tale. What effect might be produced by a writer's use of the fairy tale form? What associations might a writer's use of the form call to mind for readers? How might the use of this form affect the way in which the reader responds to the story?

Writing/Prior Knowledge To help refresh students' memories about the fairy tales they read as a child, have a class brainstorming session in which students discuss the various fairy tales with which they are familiar.

ESL Teaching Strategy Have ESL students discuss their knowledge of the fairy tales that are part of the folk heritages of their cultures of origin.

Teaching Tenth-Grade Students Make sure tenth-grade students understand that Lagerkvist's story is not actually a fairy tale but rather is an adult short story that is modeled after a fairy tale.

Vocabulary
Preteach the following vocabulary words:
ravaging (rav´ ij iŋ) *v.*: Devastating
valiant (val´ yənt) adj.: Brave
pomp (pämp) n.: Stately or brilliant display
tendered (ten´ dərd) v.: Presented for acceptance
impoverished (im päv´ ər isht) v.: Deprived of strength and resources
glowering (glou´ ər iŋ) v.: Scowling

Support Material
Teaching Portfolio
Teacher Backup, p. 1265
Usage and Mechanics Worksheet, p. 1269
Vocabulary Check, p. 1270
Analyzing Literature Worksheet, *Interpreting Gestures*, p. 1271
Critical Thinking and Reading Worksheet, *Analyzing Conflict*, p. 1272

Selection Test, pp. 1273–1274

Spelling Tip Write the word *tendered* on the chalkboard. Then point out to students that the last five letters appear in the same order when they are listed backward.

The Princess and All the Kingdom

Pär Lagerkvist

translated by Alan Blair

1 Once upon a time there was a prince, who went out to fight in order to win the princess whose beauty was greater than all others' and whom he loved above everything. He dared his life, he battled his way step by step through the country, ravaging it; nothing could stop him. He bled from his wounds but merely cast himself from one fight to the next, the most valiant nobleman to be seen and with a shield as pure as his own young features. At last he stood outside the city where the

VIEW OF THE ILE DE LA CITÉ, PARIS
Jehan Fouquet
Bibliothèque Nationale, Paris

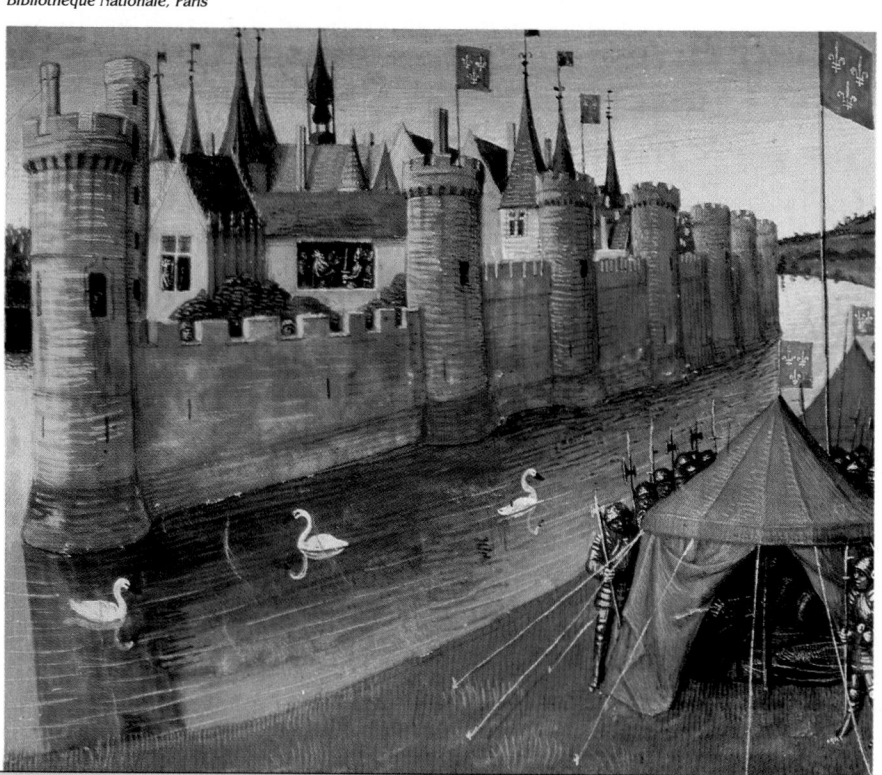

Primary Source

Like many writers of the time, Lagerkvist was profoundly affected by the events of the 1930's. The literary historian Sven H. Rossel notes that

The political crises of the 1930s are mirrored in Lagerkvist's writing. The aggression of the totalitarian states deepened the pessimism of this writer who was so sensitive to his times. But it also sharpened his will to fight for the humanistic cultural heritage. In 1933 he stepped forth as a committed contemporary writer with the novella *The Hangman.* The first part is set in a medieval village inn, the hangman a red-hooded princess lived in her royal castle. It could not hold out against him and had to beg for mercy. The gates were thrown open; he rode in as conqueror.

When the princess saw how proud and handsome he was and thought of how he had dared his life for her sake, she could not withstand his power but gave him her hand. He knelt and covered it with ardent[1] kisses. "Look, my bride, now I have won you!" he exclaimed, radiant with happiness. "Look, everything I have fought for, now I have won it!"

And he commanded that their wedding should take place this same day. The whole city decked itself out for the festival and the wedding was celebrated with rejoicing, pomp, and splendor.

When in the evening he went to enter the princess's bedchamber, he was met outside by the aged chancellor, a venerable[2] man. Bowing his snow-white head, he tendered the keys of the kingdom and the crown of gold and precious stones to the young conqueror.

"Lord, here are the keys of the kingdom which open the treasuries where everything that now belongs to you is kept."

The prince frowned.

"What is that you say, old man? I do not want your keys. I have not fought for sordid[3] gain. I have fought merely to win her whom I love, to win that which for me is the only costly thing on earth."

The old man replied, "This, too, you have won, lord. And you cannot set it aside. Now you

---

1. **ardent** (är′ d'nt) *adj.*: Warm or intense in feeling.
2. **venerable** (ven′ ər ə b'l) *adj.*: Worthy of respect by reason of age and dignity, character, or position.
3. **sordid** (sôr′ did) *adj.*: Dirty; filthy.

---

must administer and look after it."

"Do you not understand what I say? Do you not understand that one can fight, can conquer, without asking any reward other than one's happiness—not fame and gold, not land and power on earth? Well, then, I have conquered but ask for nothing, only to live happily with what, for me, is the only thing of value in life."

"Yes, lord, you have conquered. You have fought your way forward as the bravest of the brave, you have shrunk from nothing, the land lies ravaged where you have passed by. You have won your happiness. But, lord, others have been robbed of theirs. You have conquered, and therefore everything now belongs to you. It is a big land, fertile and impoverished, mighty and laid waste, full of riches and need, full of joy and sorrow, and all is now yours. For he who has won the princess and happiness, to him also belongs this land where she was born; he shall govern and cherish it."

The prince stood there glowering and fingering the hilt of his sword uneasily.

"I am the prince of happiness, nothing else!" he burst out. "Don't want to be anything else. If you get in my way, then I have my trusty sword."

But the old man put out his hand soothingly and the young man's arm sank. He looked at him searchingly, with a wise man's calm.

"Lord, you are no longer a prince," he said gently. "You are a king."

And lifting the crown with his aged hands, he put it on the other's head.

When the young ruler felt it on his brow he stood silent and moved, more erect than before. And gravely, with his head crowned for power on earth, he went in to his beloved to share her bed.

Reader's Response *Do you think the prince's prize was worth the price? Explain.*

2 Discussion Ask students to explain who is begging "for mercy." What impact do students imagine that the prince's quest had on the people of the princess's kingdom? On what do they base their answer?

3 Discussion Do students imagine that it might have been possible for the prince to win the princess's love without conquering her kingdom? Why or why not?

4 Discussion Have students discuss the impression of the kingdom that the chancellor conveys. Do they agree with the chancellor's claim that the prince is now responsible for governing the kingdom? Why or why not?

5 Discussion Have students discuss the irony of the prince's claim that he is "the prince of happiness."

6 Discussion Have students discuss whether the prince now seems ready to take responsibility for his actions by assuming control of the kingdom he has conquered.

Cooperative Learning Lagerkvist's story illustrates the need for people to be aware of and take responsibility for their actions. Divide students into groups of three or four. Have each group brainstorm to come up with a real or fictional situation from contemporary life that also illustrates this principle. Then have the members of each group work together to write a brief dramatic scene based on the situation they have come up with. Once the groups have completed their dramatic scenes, have them act the scenes out in front of the rest of the class.

---

mute figure who listens to the drunken artisans and peasants as they tell tales about the destructive power of evil. In the second part the scene is a dance hall in the fascist world of the present, where the hangman is again a silent observer. Here Lagerkvist has resurrected the primitive quality of the medieval period in an even more sinister way and has clothed his characters in modern attire. In the Middle Ages the hangman was watched with anxious interest; now he is celebrated. He reveals himself at the end as the timeless, but suffering embodiment of evil; he is condemned for eternity to take the guilt of all human beings upon himself, without finding salvation . . .

ANSWERS TO THINKING ABOUT THE SELECTION

1. (a) Answers will differ. Some students may feel that the prince did not *have* to fight to win the princess. Instead, he may have *chosen* to fight to win the princess. (b) Answers will differ. Students may respond that his omission of such details contributes to the mysterious, dreamlike quality of the story.

2. Suggested response: The prince is impulsive and irresponsible and does not want to accept the implications of his actions. The chancellor is thoughtful and wise and believes that it is the prince's duty to accept responsibility for his actions.

3. Suggested response: He calls attention to the unpleasant realities of the prince's actions and points out the prince's moral obligations.

4. (a) Suggested response: The story points out that people need to consider the implications of their behavior before they act and that once they have acted they need to accept responsibility for what they have done. (b) Suggested response: The theme is conveyed through the comments of the chancellor.

5. Answers will differ. Students may note that the message applies to any type of behavior that may hurt other people.

ANSWERS TO ANALYZING LITERATURE

1. Suggested response: It begins with the phrase *Once upon a time*; it is set in a vague, dreamlike land; it is told in an unthreatening manner, even though it includes violent events; and it teaches a moral lesson.

2. Suggested response: In Lagerkvist's story, the people conquered by the prince are not evil and have done nothing to provoke him.

3. Suggested response: The chancellor's comments call attention to the fact that the prince's quest has had an unhappy outcome for many members of the kingdom.

4. Suggested response: Unlike most fairy tales, Lagerkvist's story does not have a happy ending. Instead, the ending leaves readers with a sense of uncertainty about the future of the kingdom that the prince has conquered.

5. Answers will differ. Students may respond that these contrasting elements help to emphasize the story's message.

THINKING ABOUT THE SELECTION

Interpreting

1. (a) Why do you think the prince had "to fight in order to win the princess"? (b) Why do you think Lagerkvist chose not to reveal this information?
2. How do the attitudes of the aged chancellor and the prince contrast with one another?
3. How would you describe the role that the old chancellor serves in this story?
4. (a) What is the story's theme, or central idea? (b) How is the theme conveyed?

Applying

5. To what types of situations in the real world do you think that the story's theme could be applied?

ANALYZING LITERATURE

Recognizing Elements of a Fairy Tale

As the opening line reveals, Lagerkvist's story is clearly modeled after a fairy tale. Yet the story also includes a number of elements that dramatically contrast with certain characteristics of a typical fairy tale.

1. What characteristics of fairy tales are evident in Lagervist's story?
2. Fairy tales often depict the conquests of princes or other noble characters over the forces of evil. How does Lagerkvist's story contrast with this type of fairy tale?
3. Explain how the old chancellor's comments about the unpleasant realities of the situation contrast with the fairy-tale-like elements of the story.

4. How does the ending of the story contrast with the type of ending that is typical of a fairy tale?
5. Explain how Lagerkvist's use of certain elements of fairy tales along with other contrasting elements contributes to the effectiveness of the story.

THINKING AND WRITING

Writing an Imitation of a Fairy Tale

Write an imitation of a fairy tale modeled after Lagervist's story. Begin by reviewing the story, noting the ways in which it is similar to and different from a typical fairy tale. Then gather with a group of your classmates and brainstorm for ideas. Drawing on what you remember about the fairy tales that you read as a child, think of as many appropriate characters and situations as you can. Once you have finished brainstorming, choose the ideas that you find most interesting and use them in developing a plot outline for your tale. If you do not like any of the ideas you and your classmates come up with, you may choose to write an extension of Lagerkvist's tale, focusing on the life of the prince after his marriage to the princess. Regardless of the topic you choose, make sure your tale includes some elements that contrast with those of a typical fairy tale. Also make sure your tale conveys a message about life. After you have finished writing, gather once again with the members of your brainstorming group and work together to revise your tales. When evaluating the tales of other group members, focus on making sure they have clearly conveyed their themes.

ments help to emphasize the story's message.

THINKING AND WRITING

Publishing Student Writing Encourage students to submit their stories to the school literary magazine.

Challenge Find a fairy tale that focuses on events that are in some ways similar to those depicted in Lagerkvist's story. Then write an essay in which you compare and contrast this fairy tale with "The Princess and All Her Kingdom."

IDEAS AND INSIGHTS

THE NOBEL PRIZE

"If I have a thousand ideas a year, and only one turns out to be good, I'm satisfied," said Alfred Bernhard Nobel. But Nobel was to have more than one invention to his credit. The Swedish scientist who invented dynamite and the blasting cap is also the founder of the most distinguished of all prizes—the Nobel Prize.

When Nobel's explosive first hit the market it was still a relatively new invention. Because so many accidents occurred involving the explosions of nitroglycerin, Nobel was soon considered a public enemy and was nicknamed the "merchant of death." In 1867 Nobel perfected his invention, making it more easily handled and shipped. The number of accidents as a result of his revised invention, which he called dynamite, decreased. But soon his invention was used for purposes Nobel had not originally intended. Nobel invented dynamite for peaceful reasons, but it was later used during wartime for killing people. Nobel could no longer withstand his feelings of guilt. He did not want to be associated with death and destruction, but with peace. In his will he set up a fund of $9 million; the interest from this fund was to be used to set up an annual prize rewarding achievements promoting peace.

One of the most publicly followed of all the Nobel prizes is the one for literature. The purpose of the Nobel Prize for Literature is to recognize the most distinguished body of literary work. This prize also represents a new international standard whereby all writers are judged equally and has been beneficial for bringing both author and country into the public light. For example, Gabriel García Márquez and Pablo Neruda have brought Latin American literature to the forefront; Wole Soyenka has brought African literature to new heights of recognition; and Naguib Mahfouz has brought Egyptian literature to the contemporary world.

At the same time, however, the Nobel Prize for Literature has had its share of controversy. The Nobel committee for literature is made up of four to five committee members primarily from the Swedish community. Scandinavian countries have received the Nobel Prize for Literature most often, monopolizing 17.4 percent of the prizes. France is the runner-up, taking home 15.1 percent of the prizes. Most recently, however, the awards have spanned the globe, introducing writers from Guatemala, Czechoslovakia, and Iceland.

The Nobel Prize for Literature has been declined twice, by Jean Paul Sartre in 1964 and by Boris Pasternak in 1958. Sartre declined the prize because he did not believe in prizes, and Pasternak was forced by the Russian government to decline his prize.

Some critics claim the Nobel Prize for Literature is too political and has not been awarded to the most influential writers of the twentieth century, including Marcel Proust, Franz Kafka, and James Joyce. Although the final decision of the Nobel Institute is a compromise and many writers go unrecognized, the Nobel Prize for Literature has raised literature to a main news event and has brought to public attention influential writers who might otherwise go unrecognized.

Motivation/Prior Knowledge Ask students whom among the contemporary writers they have read would they nominate to receive the next Nobel Prize. Have students prepare a short presentation in which they convince their classmates to vote for their choice. When all the presentations have been heard, have the class decide who will be their class's choice to recieve the Nobel Prize for Literature.

Finally, ask students to discuss what they know about the Nobel Prize for Literature. Then invite students to learn more about its history and importance in this feature.

Enrichment In 1969 a new memorial prize was established in the field of economics.

Enrichment *World Masterpieces* features many of the Nobel Prize for Literature recipients, including Rabindranath Tagore (1913), Thomas Mann (1929), Luigi Pirandello (1934), Gabriela Mistral (1945), Hermann Hesse (1946), Pär Lagerkvist (1951), Albert Camus (1957), Boris Pasternak (declined, 1958), Yasunari Kawabata (1968), Alexander Solzhenitsyn (1970), Pablo Neruda (1971), Heinrich Böll (1972), Czeslaw Milosz (1980), Gabriel García Márquez (1982), Wole Soyinka (1986), and Najib Mahfouz (1988).

Focus

More About the Author At the time he wrote "The Metamorphosis," Kafka could write only during the night when everyone else was asleep. Though this conflicted with his need to be alert at his job during the day, he saw no way out of this dilemma. Have students discuss how the circumstances in which a writer works might shape his or her writing. Do they imagine that works written late at night are likely to be different from those written during the day? If so, how?

Critical Evaluation In discussing Kafka's influence on twentieth-century American writers, the critic Leo Hamalian notes: "An intensely European writer, Franz Kafka has exerted a greater grip on the American consciousness than on the less optimistic European, although his influence on both is by now almost literary legend. This paradox was inevitable. Within the span of their own lifetime, many Europeans experienced firsthand the nightmares best defined by the term his name has given our language: Kafkaesque. . . . Kafka became something of a vogue among intellectuals and the avant-garde in America shortly after the end of World War II, but those special states of mind conveyed in his writing did not attract a wider audience until the 1950s, that age of anxiety in which the events of the McCarthy era overtook fiction. As Americans began to discover that mass society had neuroses of its own, they consumed in paperback and anthology the man who prophesied the ailments of our age. . . . Thomas Mann, referring to those who read the writer, observed appropriately, 'They all swear by the name of the great invalid, thanks to whose madness they no longer need to be mad.' Mad or not, no writer has mirrored the anxieties of being alive for his readers with more candor, wit, and in the end, acceptance."

1883–1924

In a letter to a friend, Franz Kafka once wrote, "I think we ought to read only the kind of books that wound and stab us. . . . We need the books that affect us like a disaster, that grieve us deeply, like the death of someone we loved more than ourselves, like being banished into forests far from everyone. . . . A book must be the axe for the frozen sea inside of us." Although he was not discussing his own writing at the time, Kafka's description probably fits his own works of fiction better than those of any other writer. In fact, few writers have created literary works more tragic, disturbing, and unsettling than Kafka's.

Born in Prague, in what is now Czechoslovakia, Kafka grew up as the only son in a family of six. His father was a successful and domineering self-made businessman, and Kafka spent a good part of his life alternately longing for his father's approval and resenting his strictness. Kafka lived with his family until he was thirty-two, and his relationship with his father, along with his feelings of familial obligation, guilt, and duty are reflected in much of his writing.

Kafka began writing short stories and plays at a very young age. Despite his interest in writing, however, he chose to study law at the University of Prague. After serving a legal internship, he then took a job with an Italian insurance company. A year later he was offered a position with the state Worker's Accident Insurance Institute, where he remained employed until 1922. Kafka's career in the insurance business never hindered his writing. In fact, his insurance career actually served as an inspiration for his writing by teaching about the bureaucratic chaos that often exists within government agencies.

As a German-speaking Jew in a country inhabited predominantly by Czech-speaking gentiles, Kafka had firsthand knowledge of what it was like to live outside the mainstream. His resulting sense of alienation is apparent in nearly all his work. In his early works, including "The Metamorphosis" (1915), he explored the potentially disastrous results of ignoring one's true desires and aspirations and living according to the expectations of others. During the later stages of his career, Kafka delved into the destructive capabilities of society and depicted the conflict of the individual who rejects society yet truly longs to be fulfilled by it. In his story "A Hunger Artist" (1924), for example, the protagonist attracts the attention of the public by sitting in a cage and refusing to eat. Eventually, however, the public loses interest in him, and he starves to death in obscurity and despair.

In 1917 Kafka was diagnosed as having tuberculosis. Shortly before his death in 1924, he instructed his friend Max Brod to destroy all his papers and personal documents, as well as his unfinished and unpublished works. Believing that Kafka never intended for him to follow the instructions, Brod ignored the request and arranged for the publication of Kafka's unfinished novels, *The Trial*, *The Castle*, and *America*, along with his personal diaries, *Letter to My Father*, and a number of his unpublished short stories.

The publication of these works earned Kafka critical acclaim and public acceptance—neither of which he had known during his lifetime. In the subsequent years, Kafka's reputation continued to grow, and he is now widely recognized as one of the finest writers of the twentieth century.

Objectives

Thematic
To understand how changes in people's conditions or physical appearances can affect the way in which others respond to them

Skills
1 To understand Modernism
2 To relate the work to the writer's life
3 To respond in writing to a statement by the writer

Support Material

Teaching Portfolio
Teacher Backup, p. 1275
Grammar in Action Worksheets, *Adjective Clauses*, p. 1279;
Varying Sentence Lengths, p. 1281;
Descriptive Writing, p. 1283
Usage and Mechanics Worksheet, p. 1285

GUIDE FOR INTERPRETING

The Metamorphosis

Commentary

Modernism. During the late nineteenth and early twentieth centuries, major scientific, technological, and industrial developments occurred that dramatically altered the way people lived. Not only did this period involve such breakthroughs as the invention of the automobile, the airplane, the telephone, and the machine gun, but it also saw the emergence of a number of brilliant scientists and thinkers, including Sigmund Freud, Albert Einstein, and Friederich Nietzsche, who set forth revolutionary ideas that reshaped people's understanding of themselves and the world surrounding them. This period of rapid change culminated in World War I—a tragic and bloody conflict that wiped out almost an entire generation of European men. As a result of these events and developments, many people came to believe in the need to discard the ideas and values of the past and to find new ideas that seemed more applicable to twentieth-century life. Similarly, writers began turning away from the style, form, and content of nineteenth-century literature and began experimenting with new themes and techniques, and a new literary movement known as Modernism was born.

Modernism was an extremely broad and diverse movement that encompassed a vast number of smaller literary movements. Yet, although there were significant differences in their interests and approaches, all the Modernists shared the desire to create literature that was new and different. In addition they were united in their belief in the need to capture the reality of modern life in both the form and the content of their work. The Modernists generally felt that the rapid changes in the world had created an overwhelming sense of uncertainty, disjointedness, and alienation. This view is apparent in the themes of many Modernist works. Generally, however, the themes of Modernist works are subtly implied, rather than directly stated, to reflect a sense of uncertainty and to force readers to draw their own conclusions. For similar reasons fiction writers began abandoning the traditional plot structure, omitting the expositions and resolutions that in the past had clarified the work for the reader. Instead, stories and novels were structured to reflect the fragmentation and uncertainty of human experience. As a result, a typical modern story or novel seems to begin arbitrarily and to end without a resolution, leaving the reader with possibilities, not solutions.

Writing

Imagine that one day when you arrived at school, your friends no longer recognized you and that when you tried to talk to them, they were unable to understand you. Write a journal entry in which you describe how it might feel to suddenly find yourself in this situation.

---

have had in which they found themselves in a situation similar to the one described in the writing assignment. Then have them complete their journal entries.

ESL Teaching Strategy Team each ESL student with a native-speaking student and have them read the story together, taking turns reading aloud. Instruct the native- speaking student to clarify the meanings of any words with which the ESL student is unfamiliar.

Teaching Tenth-Grade Students Ask tenth-grade students to discuss metamorphoses they have encountered in Greek and Roman mythology. Then ask them to consider the type of metamorphosis that might occur in a modern story. What might a person change into? Why?

Read the story aloud to tenth-grade students. Pause periodically and ask students to summarize the events that have just been described. This will enable you to see if students are having difficulty following the story.

Literary Focus You might want to start by discussing some parallels between the Modernists and the Romantics. Point out that both movements emerged partly as a reaction to major events and developments of the time. In addition, the writers involved with both movements turned away from established literary conventions and approaches and sought to establish new forms and techniques. Have students discuss any other parallels they can see between the two movements. What do they see as the main differences between the two movements?

Writing/Prior Knowledge Have students discuss any dreams they

The Metamorphosis

Franz Kafka

translated by Stanley Corngold

I

When Gregor Samsa woke up one morning from unsettling dreams, he found himself changed in his bed into a monstrous vermin. He was lying on his back as hard as armor plate, and when he lifted his head a little, he saw his vaulted brown belly, sectioned by arch-shaped ribs, to whose dome the cover, about to slide off completely, could barely cling. His many legs, pitifully thin compared with the size of the rest him, were waving helplessly before his eyes.

"What's happened to me?" he thought. It was no dream. His room, a regular human room, only a little on the small side, lay quiet between the four familiar walls. Over the table, on which an unpacked line of fabric samples was all spread out—Samsa was a traveling salesman—hung the picture which he had recently cut out of a glossy magazine and lodged in a pretty gilt frame. It showed a lady done up in a fur hat and a fur boa, sitting upright and raising up against the viewer a heavy fur muff in which her whole forearm had disappeared.

Gregor's eyes then turned to the window, and the overcast weather—he could hear raindrops hitting against the metal window ledge—completely depressed him. "How about going back to sleep for a few minutes and forgetting all this nonsense," he thought, but that was completely impracticable, since he was used to sleeping on his right side and in his present state could not get into that position. No matter how hard he threw himself onto his right side, he always rocked onto his back again. He must have tried it a hundred times, closing his eyes so as not to have to see his squirming legs, and stopped only when he began to feel a slight, dull pain in his side, which he had never felt before.

"Oh God," he thought, "what a grueling job I've picked. Day in, day out—on the road. The upset of doing business is much worse than the actual business in the home office, and besides, I've got the torture of traveling, worrying about changing trains, eating miserable food at all hours, constantly seeing new faces, no relationships that last or get more intimate. To the devil with it all!" He felt a slight itching up on top of his belly; shoved himself slowly on his back closer to the bedpost, so as to be able to lift his head better; found the itchy spot, studded with small white dots which he had no idea what to make of; and wanted to touch the spot with one of his legs but immediately pulled it back, for the contact sent a cold shiver through him.

He slid back again into his original position. "This getting up so early," he thought, "makes anyone a complete idiot. Human beings have to have their sleep. Other traveling salesmen live like harem women. For instance, when I go back to the hotel before lunch to write up the business I've done, these gentlemen are just having breakfast. That's all I'd have to try with my boss; I'd be fired on the spot. Anyway, who knows if that wouldn't be a very good thing for me. If I didn't hold back for my parents' sake, I would have quit long ago, I would have marched up to the boss and spoken my piece from the bottom of my heart. He would have fallen off the desk! It is funny, too, the way he sits on the desk and talks down from the heights to the employees, especially when they have to come right up close on account of the boss's being hard of hearing. Well, I haven't given up hope completely; once I've gotten the money together to pay off my parents' debt to him—that will probably take another five or six years—I'm going to do it without fail. Then I'm going to make the big break. But for the time being I'd better get up, since my train leaves at five."

And he looked over at the alarm clock, which was ticking on the chest of drawers. "God Almighty!" he thought. It was six-thirty, the hands were quietly moving forward, it was actually past the half-hour, it was already nearly a quarter to. Could it be that the alarm hadn't gone off? You could see from the bed that it was set correctly for four o'clock; it certainly had gone off, too. Yes, but was it possible to sleep quietly through a ringing that made the furniture shake? Well, he certainly hadn't slept quietly, but probably all the more soundly for that. But what should he do now? The next train left at seven o'clock; to make it, he would have to hurry like a madman, and the line of samples wasn't packed yet, and he himself didn't feel especially fresh and ready to march around. And even if he did make the train, he could not avoid getting it from the boss, because the messenger boy had been waiting at the five-o'clock train and would have long ago reported his not showing up. He was a tool of the boss, without brains or backbone. What if he were to say he was sick? But that would be extremely embarrassing and suspicious because during his five years with the firm Gregor had not been sick even once. The boss would be sure to come with the health-insurance doctor, blame his parents for their son's laziness, and cut all excuses short by referring to the health-insurance doctor. The health-insurance doctor, for whom the world consisted of people who were completely healthy but afraid to work. And, besides, in this case would he be so very wrong? In fact, Gregor felt fine, with the exception of his drowsiness, which was really unnecessary after sleeping so late, and he even had a ravenous appetite.

Just as he was thinking all this over at top speed, without being able to decide to get out of bed—the alarm clock had just struck a quarter to seven—he heard a cautious knocking at the door next to the head of his bed. "Gregor," someone called—it was his mother—"it's a quarter to seven. Didn't you want to catch the train?" What a soft voice! Gregor was shocked to hear his own voice answering, unmistakably his own voice, true, but in which, as if from below, an insistent distressed chirping intruded, which left the clarity of his words intact only for a moment really, before so badly garbling them as they carried that no one could be sure if he had heard right. Gregor had wanted to answer in detail and to explain everything, but, given the circumstances, confined himself to saying, "Yes, yes, thanks, Mother, I'm just getting up." The wooden door must have prevented the change in Gregor's voice from being noticed outside, because his mother was satisfied with this explanation and shuffled off. But their little exchange had made the rest of the family aware that, contrary to expectations, Gregor was still in the house, and already his father was knocking on one of the side doors, feebly but with his fist. "Gregor, Gregor," he called, "what's going on?" And after a little while he called again in a deeper, warning voice, "Gregor! Gregor!" At the other side door, however, his sister moaned gently, "Gregor? Is something the matter with you? Do you want anything?" Toward both sides Gregor answered: "I'm all ready," and made an effort, by meticulous pronunciation and by inserting long pauses between individual words, to eliminate everything from his voice that might betray him. His father went back to his breakfast, but his sister whispered, "Gregor, open up, I'm pleading with you." But Gregor had absolutely no intention of opening the door and complimented himself instead on the precaution he had adopted from his business trips, of locking all the doors during the night even at home.

First of all he wanted to get up quietly, without any excitement; get dressed; and the main thing, have breakfast, and only then think about what to do next, for he saw clearly that in bed he would never think things through to a rational conclusion. He remembered how even in the past he had often felt some kind of slight pain, possibly caused by lying in an uncomfortable position, which, when he got up, turned out to be purely imaginary, and he was eager to see how today's fantasy would

5 Clarification Make sure students note that Gregor has been forced to continue working for his current employer because he has to pay off his parents' debt to his boss.

6 Discussion Ask students what Gregor's determination to get up and catch his train suggests about his acceptance of the implications of his transformation.

7 Critical Thinking and Reading Explain to students that Kafka himself was an accident-insurance lawyer in an organization for workers. He was very good at his job, was sympathetic to his clients, and worked hard to win claims for injured workers. This passing reference is a sly joke about his own profession. Do students think that the knowledge of this fact adds anything to the humor of the opening scene? Why or why not?

8 Enrichment Tell students that when Gregor becomes aware that his voice has been replaced by an unintelligible chirping, it is the first of many small losses by which he is cut off from human beings.

9 Clarification Have students visualize the layout of the doors to Gregor's room and note who is speaking through each of them. The mother is calling softly through the double doors at the front of the room. At one side door, Gregor's father is knocking and calling. At the other side door, his sister Grete is moaning gently. While the situation is shocking and disturbing, it also has a comic quality to it that Kafka fully intended.

Mikhail Baryshnikov in the dramatic adaptation of "The Metamorphosis"

gradually fade away. That the change in his voice was nothing more than the first sign of a bad cold, an occupational ailment of the traveling salesman, he had no doubt in the least.

It was very easy to throw off the cover; all he had to do was puff himself up a little, and it fell off by itself. But after this, things got difficult, especially since he was so unusually broad. He would have needed hands and arms to lift himself up, but instead of that he had only his numerous little legs, which were in every different kind of perpetual motion and which, besides, he could not control. If he wanted to bend one, the first thing that happened was that it stretched itself out; and if he finally succeeded in getting this leg to do what he wanted, all the others in the meantime, as if set free, began to work in the most intensely painful agitation. "Just don't stay in bed being useless," Gregor said to himself.

First he tried to get out of bed with the lower part of his body, but this lower part—which by the way he had not seen yet and which he could not form a clear picture of—proved too difficult to budge; it was taking so long; and when finally, almost out of his mind, he lunged forward with all his force, without caring, he had picked the wrong direction and slammed himself violently against the lower bedpost, and the searing pain he felt taught him that exactly the lower part of his body was, for the moment anyway, the most sensitive.

He therefore tried to get the upper part of his body out of bed first and warily turned his head toward the edge of the bed. This worked easily, and in spite of its width and weight, the mass of his body finally followed, slowly, the movement of his head. But when at last he stuck his head over the edge of the bed into the air, he got too scared to continue any further, since if he finally let himself fall in this position, it would be a miracle if he didn't injure his head. And just now he had better not for the life of him lose consciousness; he would rather stay in bed.

But when, once again, after the same exertion, he lay in his original position, sighing, and again watched his little legs struggling, if possible more fiercely, with each other and saw no way of bringing peace and order into this mindless motion, he again told himself that it was impossible for him to stay in bed and that the most rational thing was to make any sacrifice for even the smallest hope of freeing himself from the bed. But at the same time he did not forget to remind himself occasionally that thinking things over calmly—indeed, as calmly as possible—was much better than jumping to desperate decisions. At such moments he fixed his eyes as sharply as possible on the window, but unfortunately there was little confidence and cheer to be gotten from the view of the morning fog, which shrouded even the other side of the narrow street. "Seven o'clock already," he said to himself as the

---

Primary Source

People have long debated what kind of "vermin" Gregor becomes in "The Metamorphosis." The American novelist John Updike writes:

What kind of insect is Gregor? Popular belief has him a cockroach, which would be appropriate for a city apartment; and the creature's retiring nature and sleazy dietary preferences would seem to conform. But, as Vladimir Nabokov, who knew his entomology, pointed out in his lectures upon "The Metamorphosis" at Cornell University, Gregor is too broad and convex to be a cockroach. The charwoman calls him a "dung beetle" (*Mistkafer*) but, Nabokov said, "it is obvious that the good woman is adding the epithet only to be friendly." . . . Gregor Samsa, awaking, sees "numerous legs, which were pitifully thin compared to the rest of his bulk." If "numerous" is more than six, he must be a centipede—not an insect at all. From evidence in the story he is brown in color and about as long as the distance between a doorknob and the floor; he is broader than half a door. He has a voice at first . . . which disappears as the story progresses. His jaws don't work as ours do but he has eyelids, nostrils, and a neck. He is, in short, impossible to picture except when the author wants to evoke his appearance, to bump the reader up alarm clock struck again, "seven o'clock already and still such fog." And for a little while he lay quietly, breathing shallowly, as if expecting, perhaps, from the complete silence the return of things to the way they really and naturally were.

But then he said to himself, "Before it strikes a quarter past seven, I must be completely out of bed without fail. Anyway, by that time someone from the firm will be here to find out where I am, since the office opens before seven." And now he started rocking the complete length of his body out of the bed with a smooth rhythm. If he let himself topple out of bed in this way, his head, which on falling he planned to lift up sharply, would presumably remain unharmed. His back seemed to be hard; nothing was likely to happen to it when it fell onto the carpet. His biggest misgiving came from his concern about the loud crash that was bound to occur and would probably create, if not terror, at least anxiety behind all the doors. But that would have to be risked.

When Gregor's body already projected halfway out of bed—the new method was more of a game than a struggle, he only had to keep on rocking and jerking himself along—he thought how simple everything would be if he could get some help. Two strong persons—he thought of his father and the maid—would have been completely sufficient; they would only have had to shove their arms under his arched back, in this way scoop him off the bed, bend down with their burden, and then just be careful and patient while he managed to swing himself down onto the floor, where his little legs would hopefully acquire some purpose. Well, leaving out the fact that the doors were locked, should he really call for help? In spite of all his miseries, he could not repress a smile at this thought.

He was already so far along that when he rocked more strongly he could hardly keep his balance, and very soon he would have to commit himself, because in five minutes it would be a quarter past seven—when the doorbell rang. "It's someone from the firm," he said to himself and almost froze, while his little legs only danced more quickly. For a moment everything remained quiet. "They're not going to answer," Gregor said to himself, captivated by some senseless hope. But then, of course, the maid went to the door as usual with her firm stride

and opened up. Gregor only had to hear the visitor's first word of greeting to know who it was— the office manager himself. Why was only Gregor condemned to work for a firm where at the slightest omission they immediately suspected the worst? Were all employees louts without exception, wasn't there a single loyal, dedicated worker among them who, when he had not fully utilized a few hours of the morning for the firm, was driven half-mad by pangs of conscience and was actually unable to get out of bed? Really, wouldn't it have been enough to send one of the apprentices to find out—if this prying were absolutely necessary—did the manger himself have to come, and did the whole innocent family have to be shown in this way that the investigation of this suspicious affair could be entrusted only to the intellect of the manager? And more as a result of the excitement produced in Gregor by these thoughts than as a result of any real decision, he swung himself out of bed with all his might. There was a loud thump, but it was not a real crash. The fall was broken a little by the carpet, and Gregor's back was more elastic than he had thought, which explained the not very noticeable muffled sound. Only he had not held his head carefully enough and hit it; he turned it and rubbed it on the carpet in anger and pain.

"Something fell in there," said the manager in the room on the left. Gregor tried to imagine whether something like what had happened to him today could one day happen even to the manager; you really had to grant the possibility. But, as if in rude reply to this question, the manager took a few decisive steps in the next room and made his patent leather boots creak. From the room on the right his sister whispered, to inform Gregor, "Gregor, the manager is here." "I know," Gregor said to himself; but he did not dare raise his voice enough for his sister to hear.

"Gregor," his father now said from the room on the left, "the manager has come and wants to be informed why you didn't catch the early train. We don't know what we should say to him. Besides, he wants to speak to you personally. So please open the door. He will certainly be so kind as to excuse the disorder of the room." "Good morning, Mr. Samsa," the manager called in a friendly voice. "There's something the matter with him," his moth-

against some astounding, poignant new aspect of Gregor's embodiment. . . . When "The Metamorphosis" was to be published as a book in 1915, Kafka, fearful that the cover illustrator "might want to draw the insect itself," wrote the publisher, "Not that, please not that! . . . The insect itself cannot be depicted. It cannot even be shown from a distance." He suggested instead a scene of the family in the apartment with a locked door, or a door open and giving on darkness. Any theatrical or cinematic version of the story must founder on this point of external representation: a concrete image of the insect would be too distracting and shut off sympathy; such a version would lack the very

heart of comedy and pathos which beats in the unsteady area between objective and subjective, where Gregor's insect and human selves swayingly struggle. . . . Such scenes could not be done except with words. In this age that lives and dies by the visual, "The Metamorphosis" stands as a narrative absolutely literary, able to exist only where language and the mind's hazy wealth of imagery intersect.

er said to the manager while his father was still at the door, talking. "Believe me, sir, there's something the matter with him. Otherwise how would Gregor have missed a train? That boy has nothing on his mind but the business. It's almost begun to rile me that he never goes out nights. He's been back in the city for eight days now, but every night he's been home. He sits there with us at the table, quietly reading the paper or studying timetables. It's already a distraction for him when he's busy working with his fretsaw.[1] For instance, in the span of two or three evenings he carved a little frame. You'll be amazed how pretty it is; it's hanging inside his room. You'll see it right away when Gregor opens the door. You know, I'm glad that you've come, sir. We should never have gotten Gregor to open the door by ourselves; he's so stubborn. And there's certainly something wrong with him, even though he said this morning there wasn't." "I'm coming right away," said Gregor slowly and deliberately, not moving in order not to miss a word of the conversation. "I haven't any other explanation myself," said the manager. "I hope it's nothing serious. On the other hand, I must say that we businessmen—fortunately or unfortunately, whichever you prefer—very often simply have to overcome a slight indisposition[2] for business reasons." "So can the manager come in now?" asked his father, impatient, and knocked on the door again. "No," said Gregor. In the room on the left there was an embarrassing silence; in the room on the right his sister began to sob.

Why didn't his sister go in to the others? She had probably just got out of bed and not even started to get dressed. Then what was she crying about? Because he didn't get up and didn't let the manager in, because he was in danger of losing his job, and because then the boss would start hounding his parents about the old debts? For the time being, certainly, her worries were unnecessary. Gregor was still here and hadn't the slightest intention of letting the family down. True, at the moment he was lying on the carpet, and no one knowing his

---

1. **fretsaw** (fret′ sô) n.: A saw with a long, narrow, fine-toothed blade.
2. **indisposition** (in′ dis pə zish′ ən) n.: Slight illness.

condition could seriously have expected him to let the manager in. But just because of this slight discourtesy, for which an appropriate excuse would easily be found later on, Gregor could not simply be dismissed. And to Gregor it seemed much more sensible to leave him alone now than to bother him with crying and persuasion. But it was just the uncertainty that was tormenting the others and excused their behavior.

"Mr. Samsa," the manager now called, raising his noise, "what's the matter? You barricade yourself in your room, answer only 'yes' and 'no,' cause your parents serious, unnecessary worry, and you neglect—I mention this only in passing—your duties to the firm in a really shocking manner. I am speaking here in the name of your parents and of your employer and ask you in all seriousness for an immediate, clear explanation. I'm amazed, amazed. I thought I knew you to be a quiet, reasonable person, and now you suddenly seem to want to start strutting about, flaunting strange whims. The head of the firm did suggest to me this morning a possible explanation for your tardiness—it concerned the cash payments recently entrusted to you—but really, I practically gave my word of honor that this explanation could not be right. But now, seeing your incomprehensible obstinacy, I am about to lose even the slightest desire to stick up for you in any way at all. And your job is not the most secure. Originally I intended to tell you all this in private, but since you make me waste my time here for nothing, I don't see why your parents shouldn't hear too. Your performance of late has been very unsatisfactory; I know it is not the best season for doing business, we all recognize that; but a season for not doing any business, there is no such thing, Mr. Samsa, such a thing cannot be tolerated."

"But sir," cried Gregor, beside himself, in his excitement forgetting everything else, "I'm just opening up, in a minute. A slight indisposition, a dizzy spell, prevented me from getting up. I'm still in bed. But I already feel fine again. I'm just getting out of bed. Just be patient for a minute! I'm not as well as I thought yet. But really I'm fine. How something like this could just take a person by surprise! Only last night I was fine, my parents can tell you, or wait, last night I already had a

---

Grammar in Action

Adjective Clauses An adjective clause is a subordinate clause that modifies a noun or a pronoun by providing additional information. Adjective clauses are usually introduced by relative pronouns—*which, that, who, whom, whose*—which, in addition to joining the subordinate clause to the independent clause, serve as sentence elements within the adjective clause. Note the following adjective clauses from "The Metamorphosis":

He would have needed hands and arms to lift himself up, but instead of that he had only his numerous little legs, *which were in every different*

kind of perpetual motion . . . (page 1086)

If he let himself topple out of bed in this way, his head, *which on falling he planned to lift up sharply*, would presumably remain unharmed. (page 1087)

Student Activity. Identify the adjective clauses in each of the following passages from "The Metamorphosis":
1. In fact, Gregor felt fine, with the exception of his drowsiness, which was really unnecessary after sleeping so late, and he even had a ravenous appetite.

slight premonition.[3] They must have been able to tell by looking at me. Why didn't I report it to the office! But you always think that you'll get over a sickness without staying home. Sir! Spare my parents! There's no basis for any of the accusations that you're making against me now; no one has ever said a word to me about them. Perhaps you haven't seen the last orders I sent in. Anyway, I'm still going on the road with the eight o'clock train; these few hours of rest have done me good. Don't let me keep you, sir. I'll be at the office myself right away, and be so kind as to tell them this, and give my respects to the head of the firm."

And while Gregor hastily blurted all this out, hardly knowing what he was saying, he had easily approached the chest of drawers, probably as a result of the practice he had already gotten in bed, and now he tried to raise himself up against it. He actually intended to open the door, actually present himself and speak to the manager; he was eager to find out what the others, who were now so anxious to see him, would say at the sight of him. If they were shocked, then Gregor had no further responsibility and could be calm. But if they took everything calmly, then he, too, had no reason to get excited and could, if he hurried, actually be at the station by eight o'clock. At first he slid off the polished chest of drawers a few times, but at last, giving himself a final push, he stood upright; he no longer paid any attention to the pains in his abdomen, no matter how much they were burning. Now he let himself fall against the back of a nearby chair, clinging to its slats with his little legs. But by doing this he had gotten control of himself and fell silent, since he could now listen to what the manager was saying.

"Did you understand a word?" the manager was asking his parents. "He isn't trying to make fools of us, is he?" "My God," cried his mother, already in tears, "maybe he's seriously ill, and here we are, torturing him. Grete! Grete!" she then cried. "Mother?" called his sister from the other side. They communicated by way of Gregor's room. "Go to the doctor's immediately. Gregor is sick. Hurry, get the doctor. Did you just hear Gregor talking?" "That was the voice of an animal," said the manager, in a tone conspicuously soft compared with the mother's yelling. "Anna!" "Anna!" the father called through the foyer into the kitchen clapping his hands, "get a locksmith right away!" And already the two girls were running with rustling skirts through the foyer—and tearing open the door to the apartment. The door could not be heard slamming; they had probably left it open, as is the custom in homes where a great misfortune has occurred.

But Gregor had become much calmer. It was true that they no longer understood his words, though they had seemed clear enough to him, clearer than before, probably because his ear had grown accustomed to them. But still, the others now believed that there was something the matter with him and were ready to help him. The assurance and confidence with which the first measures had been taken did him good. He felt integrated into human society once again and hoped for marvelous, amazing feats from both the doctor and the locksmith, without really distinguishing sharply between them. In order to make his voice as clear as possible for the crucial discussions that were approaching, he cleared his throat a little—taking pains, of course, to do so in a very muffled manner, since this noise, too, might sound different from human coughing, a thing he no longer trusted himself to decide. In the next room, meanwhile, everything had become completely still. Perhaps his parents were sitting at the table with the manager, whispering; perhaps they were all leaning against the door listening.

Gregor slowly lugged himself toward the door, pushing the chair in front of him, then let go of it, threw himself against the door, held himself upright against it—the pads on the bottom of his little legs exuded a little sticky substance—and for a moment rested there from the exertion. But then he got started turning the key in the lock with his mouth. Unfortunately it seemed that he had no real teeth—what was he supposed to grip the key with?—but in compensation his jaws, of course, were very strong; with their help he actually got the key moving and paid no attention to the fact that he was undoubtedly hurting himself in some

---

3. **premonition** (prē′ mə nish′ ən) *n*.: A warning in advance.

27 Clarification Remind students that Gregor has not yet seen himself in a mirror. Consequently, he still wonders if his transformation is nothing more than a personal delusion. If this is the case, then no one will be startled when he emerges from the room. If it is not, however, he realizes that people will be shocked by the sight of him.

28 Discussion Ask students whether Gregor's movements reveal that he is beginning to adjust to his new body.

29 Discussion Have students discuss what the reactions of each of the characters reveals about his or her personality.

30 Discussion Have students discuss why Gregor becomes calmer when he feels certain that people can no longer understand his words. Why does he feel "integrated into human society once again"? Why is he unable to distinguish between the doctor and the locksmith? Why does he clear his throat in spite of his awareness that no one can understand him?

31 Discussion Have students discuss how Kafka's inclusion of the line, "what was he supposed to grip the key with?," adds a touch of humor to the story.

2. Gregor was shocked to hear his own voice answering, unmistakably his own voice, true, but in which, as if from below, an insistent distressed chirping intruded, which left the clarity of his words intact only for a moment really, before so badly garbling them as they carried that no one could be sure if he had heard right.

3. But just because of this slight discourtesy, for which an appropriate excuse would easily be found later on, Gregor could not simply be dismissed.

4. The breakfast dishes were laid out lavishly on the table; since for his father breakfast was the most important meal of the day, which he would prolong for hours while reading various newspapers.

5. But you, sir, you have a better perspective of things than the rest of the office, an even better perspective, just between the two of us, than the head of the firm himself, who in his capacity as owner easily lets his judgment be swayed against an employee.

way, for a brown liquid came out of his mouth, flowed over the key, and dripped onto the floor. "Listen," said the manager in the next room, "he's turning the key." This was great encouragement to Gregor; but everyone should have cheered him on, his father and mother too. "Go, Gregor," they should have called, "keep going, at that lock, harder, harder!" And in the delusion that they were all following his efforts with suspense, he clamped his jaws madly on the key with all the strength he could muster. Depending on the progress of the key, he danced around the lock; holding himself upright only by his mouth, he clung to the key, as the situation demanded, or pressed it down again with the whole weight of his body. The clearer click of the lock as it finally snapped back literally woke Gregor up. With a sigh of relief he said to himself, "So I didn't need the locksmith after all," and laid his head down on the handle in order to open wide one wing of the double doors.

Since he had to use this method of opening the door, it was really opened very wide while he himself was still invisible. He first had to edge slowly around the one wing of the door, and do so very carefully if he was not to fall flat on his back just before entering. He was still busy with this difficult maneuver and had no time to pay attention to anything else when he heard the manager burst out with a loud "Oh!"—it sounded like a rush of wind—and now he could see him, standing closest to the door, his hand pressed over his open mouth, slowly backing away, as if repulsed by an invisible, unrelenting force. His mother—in spite of the manager's presence she stood with her hair still unbraided from the night, sticking out in all directions—first looked at his father with her hands clasped, then took two steps toward Gregor, and sank down in the midst of her skirts spreading out around her, her face completely hidden on her breast. With a hostile expression his father clenched his fist, as if to drive Gregor back into his room, then looked uncertainly around the living room, shielded his eyes with his hands, and sobbed with heaves of his powerful chest.

Now Gregor did not enter the room after all but leaned against the inside of the firmly bolted wing of the door, so that only half his body was visible and his head above it, cocked to one side and peeping out at the others. In the meantime it had grown much lighter; across the street one could see clearly a section of the endless, grayish-black building opposite—it was a hospital—with its regular windows starkly piercing the façade; the rain was still coming down, but only in large, separately visible drops that were also pelting the ground literally one at a time. The breakfast dishes were laid out lavishly on the table; since for his father breakfast was the most important meal of the day, which he would prolong for hours while reading various newspapers. On the wall directly opposite hung a photograph of Gregor from his army days, in a lieutenant's uniform, his hand on his sword, a carefree smile on his lips, demanding respect for his bearing and his rank. The door to the foyer was open, and since the front door was open too, it was possible to see out onto the landing and the top of the stairs going down.

"Well," said Gregor—and he was thoroughly aware of being the only one who had kept calm—"I'll get dressed right away, pack up my samples, and go. Will you, will you please let me go? Now, sir, you see, I'm not stubborn and I'm willing to work; traveling is a hardship, but without it I couldn't live. Where are you going, sir? To the office? Yes? Will you give an honest report of everything? A man might find for a moment that he was unable to work, but that's exactly the right time to remember his past accomplishments and to consider that later on, when the obstacle has been removed, he's bound to work all the harder and more efficiently. I'm under so many obligations to the head of the firm, as you know very well. Besides, I also have my parents and my sister to worry about. I'm in a tight spot, but I'll also work my way out again. Don't make things harder for me than they already are. Stick up for me in the office, please. Traveling salesmen aren't well liked there, I know. People think they make a fortune leading the gay life. No one has any particular reason to rectify this prejudice. But you, sir, you have a better perspective on things than the rest of the office, an even better perspective, just between the two of us, than the head of the firm himself, who in his capacity as owner easily lets his judgment be swayed against an employee. And you also know very well that the traveling salesman, who is out of the office practically the whole year round, can so easily become the victim of gossip, coincidences, and unfounded accusations, against which he's completely unable to defend himself, since in most cases he knows nothing at all about them except when he returns exhausted from a trip, and back home gets to suffer on his own person the grim consequences, which can no longer be traced back to their causes. Sir, don't go away without a word to tell me you think I'm at least partly right!"

But at Gregor's first words the manager had already turned away and with curled lips looked back at Gregor only over his twitching shoulder. And during Gregor's speech he did not stand still for a minute but, without letting Gregor out of his sight, backed toward the door, yet very gradually, as if there were some secret prohibition against leaving the room. He was already in the foyer, and from the sudden movement with which he took his last step from the living room, one might have thought he had just burned the sole of his foot. In the foyer, however, he stretched his right hand far out toward the staircase, as if nothing less than an unearthly deliverance were awaiting him there.

Gregor realized that he must on no account let the manager go away in this mood if his position in the firm were not to be jeopardized in the extreme. His parents did not understand this too well; in the course of the years they had formed the conviction that Gregor was set for life in this firm; and furthermore, they were so preoccupied with their immediate troubles that they had lost all consideration for the future. But Gregor had this forethought. The manager must be detained, calmed down, convinced, and finally won over; Gregor's and the family's future depended on it! If only his sister had been there! She was perceptive; she had already begun to cry when Gregor was still lying calmly on his back. And certainly the manager, this ladies' man, would have listened to her; she would have shut the front door and in the foyer talked him out of his scare. But his sister was not there, Gregor had to handle the situation himself. And without stopping to realize that he had no idea what his new faculties of movement were, and without stop-

ping to realize either that his speech had possibly—indeed, probably—not been understood again, he let go of the wing of the door; he shoved himself through the opening, intending to go to the manager, who was already on the landing, ridiculously holding onto the banisters with both hands; but groping for support, Gregor immediately fell down with a little cry onto his numerous little legs. This had hardly happened when for the first time that morning he had a feeling of physical well-being; his little legs were on firm ground; they obeyed him completely, as he noted to his joy; they even strained to carry him away wherever he wanted to go; and he already believed that final recovery from all his sufferings was imminent. But at that very moment, as he lay on the floor rocking with repressed motion, not far from his mother and just opposite her, she, who had seemed so completely self-absorbed, all at once jumped up, her arms stretched wide, her fingers spread, and cried, "Help, for God's sake, help!" held her head bent as if to see Gregor better, but inconsistently darted madly backward instead; had forgotten that the table laden with the breakfast dishes stood behind her; sat down on it hastily, as if her thoughts were elsewhere, when she reached it; and did not seem to notice at all that near her the big coffeepot had been knocked over and coffee was pouring in a steady stream onto the rug.

"Mother, Mother," said Gregor softly and looked up at her. For a minute the manager had completely slipped his mind; on the other hand at the sight of the spilling coffee he could not resist snapping his jaws several times in the air. At this his mother screamed once more, fled from the table, and fell into the arms of his father, who came rushing up to her. But Gregor had no time now for his parents; the manager was already on the stairs; with his chin on the banister, he was taking a last look back. Gregor was off to a running start, to be sure as possible of catching up with him; the manager must have suspected something like this, for he leaped down several steps and disappeared; but still he shouted "Agh," and the sound carried through the whole staircase. Unfortunately the manager's flight now seemed to confuse his father completely, who had been relatively calm until now, for instead

36 Discussion Point out to students that they have no unbiased information by which to judge whether or not the manager's earlier assessment of Gregor's performance was accurate. Given the details that have been presented up to this point in the story, do students imagine that Gregor was a good worker? Why or why not?

37 Discussion Have students discuss Gregor's sense of obligation to his family. Do they imagine that Gregor might have somewhat resented his family's dependence on him? Why or why not?

38 Discussion Have students discuss what this passage reveals about Gregor's feelings toward his sister?

39 Clarification Remind students that this is the first time Gregor has left his room since his metamorphosis.

40 Discussion Ask students to explain why Gregor snaps his jaws several times. What effect does this have on his mother? Have students stay alert to other instances in which actions of Gregor's are wrongly interpreted by those who witness them.

of running after the manager himself, or at least not hindering Gregor in his pursuit, he seized in his right hand the manager's cane, which had been left behind on a chair with his hat and overcoat, picked up in his left hand a heavy newspaper from the table, and stamping his feet, started brandishing the cane and the newspaper to drive Gregor back into his room. No plea of Gregor's helped, no plea was even understood; however humbly he might turn his head, his father merely stamped his feet more forcefully. Across the room his mother had thrown open a window in spite of the cool weather, and leaning out, she buried her face, far outside the window, in her hands. Between the alley and the staircase a strong draft was created, the window curtains blew in, the newspapers on the table rustled, single sheets fluttered across the floor. Pitilessly his father came on, hissing like a wild man. Now Gregor had not had any practice at all walking in reverse, it was really very slow going. If Gregor had only been allowed to turn around, he could have gotten into his room right away, but he was afraid to make his father impatient by this time-consuming gyration, and at any minute the cane in his father's hand threatened to come down on his back or his head with a deadly blow. Finally, however, Gregor had no choice, for he noticed with horror that in reverse he could not even keep going in one direction; and so, incessantly throwing uneasy side glances at his father, he began to turn around as quickly as possible, in reality turning only very slowly. Perhaps his father realized his good intentions, for he did not interfere with him; instead, he even now and then directed the maneuver from afar with the tip of his cane. If only his father did not keep making this intolerable hissing sound! It made Gregor lose his head completely. He had almost finished the turn when—his mind continually on this hissing—he made a mistake and even started turning back around to his original position. But when he had at last successfully managed to get his head in front of the opened door, it turned out that his body was too broad to get through as it was. Of course in his father's present state of mind it did not even remotely occur to him to open the other wing of the door in order to give Gregor enough room to pass through. He had only the fixed idea that Gregor must return to his room as quickly as possible. He would never have allowed the complicated preliminaries Gregor needed to go through in order to stand up on one end and perhaps in this way fit through the door. Instead he drove Gregor on, as if there were no obstacle, with exceptional loudness; the voice behind Gregor did not sound like that of only a single father; now this was really no joke anymore, and Gregor forced himself—come what may—into the doorway. One side of his body rose up, he lay lopsided in the opening, one of his flanks was scraped raw, ugly blotches marred the white door, soon he got stuck and could not have budged anymore by himself, his little legs on one side dangled tremblingly in midair, those on the other were painfully crushed against the floor—when from behind his father gave him a hard shove, which was truly his salvation, and bleeding profusely, he flew far into his room. The door was slammed shut with the cane, then at last everything was quiet.

II

It was already dusk when Gregor awoke from his deep, comalike sleep. Even if he had not been disturbed, he would certainly not have woken up much later, for he felt that he had rested and slept long enough, but it seemed to him that a hurried step and a cautious shutting of the door leading to the foyer had awakened him. The light of the electric streetlamps lay in pallid streaks on the ceiling and on the upper parts of the furniture, but underneath, where Gregor was, it was dark. Groping clumsily with his antennae, which he was only now beginning to appreciate, he slowly dragged himself toward the door to see what had been happening there. His left side felt like one single long, unpleasantly tautening scar, and he actually had to limp on his two rows of legs. Besides, one little leg had been seriously injured in the course of the morning's events—it was almost a miracle that only one had been injured—and dragged along lifelessly.

Only after he got to the door did he notice what had really attracted him—the smell of something to eat. For there stood a bowl filled with fresh milk, in which small slices of white bread were floating. He could almost have laughed for joy, since he was even hungrier than he had been in the morning, and he immediately dipped his head into the milk, almost to over his eyes. But he soon drew it back again in disappointment; not only because he had difficulty eating on account of the soreness in his left side—and he could eat only if his whole panting body cooperated—but because he didn't like the milk at all, although it used to be his favorite drink, and that was certainly why his sister had put it in the room; in fact, he turned away from the bowl almost with repulsion and crawled back to the middle of the room.

In the living room, as Gregor saw through the crack in the door, the gas had been lit, but while at this hour of the day his father was in the habit of reading the afternoon newspaper in a loud voice to his mother and sometimes to his sister too, now there wasn't a sound. Well, perhaps this custom of reading aloud, which his sister was always telling him and writing him about, had recently been discontinued altogether. But in all the other rooms too it was just as still, although the apartment certainly was not empty. "What a quiet life the family has been leading," Gregor said to himself, and while he stared rigidly in front of him into the darkness, he felt very proud that he had been able to provide such a life in so nice an apartment for his parents and his sister. But what now if all the peace, the comfort, the contentment were to come to a horrible end? In order not to get involved in such thoughts, Gregor decided to keep moving, and he crawled up and down the room.

During the long evening first one of the side doors and then the other was opened a small crack and quickly shut again; someone had probably had the urge to come in and then had had second thoughts. Gregor now settled into position right by the living-room door, determined somehow to get the hesitating visitor to come in, or at least to find out who it might be; but the door was not opened again, and Gregor waited in vain. In the morning, when the doors had been locked, everyone had wanted to come in; now that he had opened one of the doors and the others had evidently been opened during the day, no one came in, and now the keys were even inserted on the outside.

It was late at night when the light finally went out in the living room, and now it was easy for Gregor to tell that his parents and his sister had stayed up so long, since, as he could distinctly hear, all three were now retiring on tiptoe. Certainly no one would come in to Gregor until the morning; and so he had ample time to consider undisturbed how best to rearrange his life. But the empty high-ceilinged room in which he was forced to lie flat on the floor made him nervous, without his being able to tell why—since it was, after all, the room in which he had lived for the past five years—and turning half unconsciously and not without a slight feeling of shame, he scuttled under the couch where, although his back was a little crushed and he could not raise his head anymore, he immediately felt very comfortable and was only sorry that his body was too wide to go completely under the couch.

There he stayed the whole night, which he spent partly in a sleepy trance, from which hunger pangs kept waking him with a start, partly in worries and vague hopes, all of which, however, led to the conclusion that for the time being he would have to lie low and, by being patient and showing his family every possible consideration, help them bear the inconvenience which he simply had to cause them in his present condition.

Early in the morning—it was still almost night—Gregor had the opportunity of testing the strength of the resolutions he had just made, for his sister, almost fully dressed, opened the door from the foyer and looked in eagerly. She did not see him right away, but when she caught sight of him under the couch—God, he had to be somewhere, he couldn't just fly away—she became so frightened that she lost control of herself and slammed the door shut again. But, as if she felt sorry for her behavior, she immediately opened the door again and came in on tiptoe, as if she were visiting someone seriously ill or perhaps even a stranger. Gregor had pushed his head forward just to the edge of the couch and was watching her. Would she notice that he had left the milk standing, and not because he hadn't been hungry, and would she bring in a dish of something he'd like better? If she were not going to do it of her own free will, he would rather starve than call it to her attention, although, really, he felt an enormous urge to shoot out from under the couch, throw himself at his sister's feet, and beg her for something good to eat. But his sister noticed at once, to

46 **Discussion** Have students discuss the significance of Gregor's distaste for the milk and bread his sister had put out for him.

47 **Reading Strategy** Ask students to stop reading and summarize the events that have occurred up to this point. What does Gregor do instead of worrying about the outcome of his situation?

48 **Discussion** Have students discuss why Kafka describes the evening as "long."

49 **Discussion** Have students discuss why Gregor feels comfortable beneath the couch.

50 **Discussion** What do students see as the "inconvenience" that Gregor causes his family in his present condition? How will the family support itself now that Gregor is no longer able to work?

51 **Discussion** Have students discuss the contradictory emotions that Gregor's sister expresses when she leaves the room and then returns. Do students view her behavior as realistic? Why or why not? What does her behavior suggest about her feelings for Gregor?

her astonishment, that the bowl was still full, only a little milk was spilled around it; she picked it up immediately—not with her bare hands, of course, but with a rag—and carried it out. Gregor was extremely curious to know what she would bring him instead, and he racked his brains on the subject. But he would never have been able to guess what his sister, in the goodness of her heart, actually did. To find out his likes and dislikes, she brought him a wide assortment of things, all spread out on an old newspaper: old, half-rotten vegetables; bones left over from the evening meal, caked with congealed white sauce; some raisins and almonds; a piece of cheese, which two days before Gregor had declared inedible; a plain slice of bread, a slice of bread and butter, and one with butter and salt. In addition to all this she put down some water in the bowl apparently permanently earmarked for Gregor's use. And out of a sense of delicacy, since she knew that Gregor would not eat in front of her, she left hurriedly and even turned the key, just so that Gregor should know that he might make himself as comfortable as he wanted. Gregor's legs began whirring now that he was going to eat. Besides, his bruises must have completely healed, since he no longer felt any handicap, and marveling

at this he thought how, over a month ago, he had cut his finger very slightly with a knife and how this wound was still hurting him only the day before yesterday. "Have I become less sensitive?" he thought, already sucking greedily at the cheese, which had immediately and forcibly attracted him ahead of all the other dishes. One right after the other, and with eyes streaming with tears of contentment, he devoured the cheese, the vegetables, and the sauce; the fresh foods, on the other hand, he did not care for; he couldn't even stand their smell and even dragged the things he wanted to eat a bit further away. He had finished with everything long since and was just lying lazily at the same spot when his sister slowly turned the key as a sign for him to withdraw. That immediately startled him, although he was almost asleep, and he scuttled under the couch again. But it took great self-control for him to stay under the couch even for the short time his sister was in the room, since his body had become a little bloated from the heavy meal, and in his cramped position he could hardly breathe. In between slight attacks of suffocation he watched with bulging eyes as his unsuspecting sister took a broom and swept up, not only his leavings, but even the foods which Gregor had left completely

Mikhail Baryshnikov in the dramatic adaptation of "The Metamorphosis"

Primary Source

Many critics have suggested that Gregor is the innocent scapegoat of his family's refusal to take responsibility for earning its own living. However, in his essay "Gregor Samsa and Modern Spirituality," the critic Martin Greenberg grants that Gregor has been treated badly by his parents, but sees his metamorphosis as a fitting punishment for his own shallowness:

He pretends that he will get up and resume his old life. He will get dressed "and above all eat his breakfast," after which the "morning's delusions" will infallibly be dissipated. But the human self whose claims

he always postponed and continues to postpone, is past being put off, having declared itself negatively by changing him from a human into an insect. His metamorphosis is a judgment on himself by his defeated humanity. . . . His mother succinctly describes its deathly aridity as she pleads with the chief clerk: "The only amusement he gets is doing fretwork. For instance, he spent two or three evenings cutting out a little picture frame." The picture in the little frame shows a woman in furs . . . ; it is the second object that Gregor's eye encounters when he surveys his room on waking. . . . Later in the story, when his sister and mother empty his room of its furniture, he defends his "human past" by making untouched—as if they too were no longer usable—and dumping everything hastily into a pail, which she covered with a wooden lid, she carried everything out. She had hardly turned her back when Gregor came out from under the couch, stretching and puffing himself up. This, then, was the way Gregor was fed each day, once in the morning, when his parents and the maid were still asleep, and a second time in the afternoon after everyone had had dinner, for then his parents took a short nap again, and the maid could be sent out by his sister on some errand. Certainly they did not want him to starve either, but perhaps they would not have been able to stand knowing any more about his meals than from hearsay, or perhaps his sister wanted to spare them even what was possibly only a minor torment, for really, they were suffering enough as it was.

Gregor could not find out what excuses had been made to get rid of the doctor and the locksmith on that first morning, for since the others could not understand what he said, it did not occur to any of them, not even to his sister, that he could understand what they said, and so he had to be satisfied, when his sister was in the room, with only occasionally hearing her sighs and appeals to the saints. It was only later, when she had begun to get used to everything—there could never, of course, be any question of a complete adjustment—that Gregor sometimes caught a remark which was meant to be friendly or could be interpreted as such. "Oh, he liked what he had today," she would say when Gregor had tucked away a good helping, and in the opposite case, which gradually occurred more and more frequently, she used to say, almost sadly, "He's left everything again."

But if Gregor could not get any news directly, he overheard a great deal from the neighboring rooms, and as soon as he heard voices, he would immediately run to the door concerned and press his whole body against it. Especially in the early days, there was no conversation that was not somehow about him, if only implicitly. For two whole days there were family consultations at every mealtime about how they should cope; this was also the topic of discussion between meals, for at least two members of the family were always at home, since no one probably wanted to stay home alone and it was impossible to leave the apartment completely empty. Besides, on the very first day the maid—it was not completely clear what and how much she knew of what had happened—had begged his mother on bended knees to dismiss her immediately; and when she said goodbye a quarter of an hour later, she thanked them in tears for the dismissal, as if for the greatest favor that had ever been done to her in this house, and made a solemn vow, without anyone asking her for it, not to give anything away to anyone.

Now his sister, working with her mother, had to do the cooking too; of course that did not cause her much trouble, since they hardly ate anything. Gregor was always hearing one of them pleading in vain with one of the others to eat and getting no answer except, "Thanks, I've had enough," or something similar. They did not seem to drink anything either. His sister often asked her father if he wanted any beer and gladly offered to go out for it herself; and when he did not answer, she said, in order to remove any hesitation on his part, that she could also send the janitor's wife to get it, but then his father finally answered with a definite "No," and that was the end of that.

In the course of the very first day his father explained the family's financial situation and prospects to both the mother and the sister. From time to time he got up from the table to get some kind of receipt or notebook out of the little strongbox he had rescued from the collapse of his business five years before. Gregor heard him open the complicated lock and secure it again after taking out what he had been looking for. These explanations by his father were to some extent the first pleasant news Gregor had heard since his imprisonment. He had always believed that his father had not been able to save a penny from the business, at least his father had never told him anything to the contrary, and Gregor, for his part, had never asked him any questions. In those days Gregor's sole concern had been to do everything in his power to make the family forget as quickly as possible the business disaster which had plunged everyone into a state of total despair. And so he had begun to work with special ardor[4] and had risen almost overnight from

---

4. **ardor** (är′ dər) *n*.: Emotional warmth.

56 **Discussion** Have students discuss how the parents' response to Gregor's condition differs from that of his sister. What do students think would happen to Gregor if he did not have a sister or if his sister refused to take responsibility for him?

57 **Discussion** Ask students if they think that it is natural for the members of the Samsa family to assume that Gregor cannot understand them.

58 **Discussion** Ask students why the maid promises not to tell anyone about the family's situation. Do students think that Gregor's family asked her to make this promise? If so, what does this reveal about the attitude of the Samsa family concerning their situation?

59 **Discussion** Have students explain what Kafka might mean when he refers to the "pleasant news" that Gregor hears. Is the Samsa family's financial situation better than Gregor had imagined?

60 Discussion Have students discuss what Gregor's quick rise from stock clerk to traveling salesman suggests about his abilities as a worker.

61 Discussion Do students think that Gregor might have secretly resented the fact that his family had come to take his efforts for granted? Why or why not?

62 Discussion Have students discuss what Gregor's secret plan to send his sister to the Conservatory reveals about his personality.

63 Discussion Ask students why Gregor's parents were unhappy to hear even "innocent allusions" to the Conservatory. Why did Gregor intend to announce his plan "solemnly"? Did Gregor's parents have the right to refuse to let him send his sister to the Conservatory? Why or why not?

64 Discussion Have students respond to the information revealed in this passage. Should Gregor's father have informed Gregor about the money he had saved? Why or why not? Does Gregor have a right to be angered by the discovery that his father had money about which he had not told him? Why or why not? Should the additional money have been used to pay off more of the father's debt? Why or why not?

65 Discussion Have students discuss why Gregor feels "hot with shame and grief" whenever his family discusses "the necessity of earning money."

stock clerk to traveling salesman, which of course had opened up very different money-making possibilities, and in no time his successes on the job were transformed, by means of commissions, into hard cash that could be plunked down on the table at home in front of his astonished and delighted family. Those had been wonderful times, and they had never returned, at least not with the same glory, although later on Gregor earned enough money to meet the expenses of the entire family and actually did so. They had just gotten used to it, the family as well as Gregor, the money was received with thanks and given with pleasure, but no special feeling of warmth went with it anymore. Only his sister had remained close to Gregor, and it was his secret plan that she who, unlike him, loved music and could play the violin movingly, should be sent next year to the Conservatory, regardless of the great expense involved, which could surely be made up for in some other way. Often during Gregor's short stays in the city, the Conservatory would come up in his conversations with his sister, but always merely as a beautiful dream which was not supposed to come true, and his parents were not happy to hear even these innocent allusions; but Gregor had very concrete ideas on the subject and he intended solemnly to announce his plan on Christmas Eve.

Thoughts like these, completely useless in his present state, went through his head as he stood glued to the door, listening. Sometimes out of general exhaustion he could not listen anymore and let his head bump carelessly against the door, but immediately pulled it back again, for even the slight noise he made by doing this had been heard in the next room and made them all lapse into silence. "What's he carrying on about in there now?" said his father after a while, obviously turning toward the door, and only then would the interrupted conversation gradually be resumed.

Gregor now learned in a thorough way—for his father was in the habit of often repeating himself in his explanations, partly because he himself had not dealt with these matters for a long time, partly, too, because his mother did not understand everything the first time around—that in spite of all their misfortunes a bit of capital, a very little bit, certainly, was still intact from the old days, which in the meantime had increased a little through the untouched interest. But besides that, the money Gregor had brought home every month—he had kept only a few dollars for himself—had never been completely used up and had accumulated into a tidy principal. Behind his door Gregor nodded emphatically, delighted at this unexpected foresight and thrift. Of course he actually could have paid off more of his father's debt to the boss with this extra money, and the day on which he could have gotten rid of his job would have been much closer, but now things were undoubtedly better the way his father had arranged them.

Now this money was by no means enough to let the family live off the interest; the principal was perhaps enough to support the family for one year, or at the most two, but that was all there was. So it was just a sum that really should not be touched and that had to be put away for a rainy day; but the money to live on would have to be earned. Now his father was still healthy, certainly, but he was an old man who had not worked for the past five years and who in any case could not be expected to undertake too much; during these five years, which were the first vacation of his hard-working yet unsuccessful life, he had gained a lot of weight and as a result had become fairly sluggish. And was his old mother now supposed to go out and earn money, when she suffered from asthma, when a walk through the apartment was already an ordeal for her, and when she spent every other day lying on the sofa under the open window, gasping for breath? And was his sister now supposed to work—who for all her seventeen years was still a child and whom it would be such a pity to deprive of the life she had led until now, which had consisted of wearing pretty clothes, sleeping late, helping in the house, enjoying a few modest amusements, and above all playing the violin? At first, whenever the conversation turned to the necessity of earning money, Gregor would let go of the door and throw himself down on the cool leather sofa which stood beside it, for he felt hot with shame and grief.

Often he lay there the whole long night through, not sleeping a wink and only scrabbling on the leather for hours on end. Or, not balking at the huge effort of pushing an armchair to the window, he would crawl up to the windowsill and, propped up in the chair, lean against the window, evidently in some sort of remembrance of the feeling of freedom he used to have from looking out the window. For, in fact, from day to day he saw things even a short distance away less and less distinctly; the hospital opposite, which he used to curse because he saw so much of it, was now completely beyond his range of vision, and if he had not been positive that he was living in Charlotte Street—a quiet but still very much a city street—he might have believed that he was looking out of his window into a desert where the gray sky and the gray earth were indistinguishably fused. It took his observant sister only twice to notice that his armchair was standing by the window for her to push the chair back to the same place by the window each time she had finished cleaning the room, and from then on she even left the inside casement of the window open.

If Gregor had only been able to speak to his sister and thank her for everything she had to do for him, he could have accepted her services more easily; as it was, they caused him pain. Of course his sister tried to ease the embarrassment of the whole situation as much as possible, and as time went on, she naturally managed it better and better, but in time Gregor, too, saw things much more clearly. Even the way she came in was terrible for him. Hardly had she entered the room than she would run straight to the window without taking time to close the door—though she was usually so careful to spare everyone the sight of Gregor's room—then tear open the casements with eager hands, almost as if she were suffocating, and remain for a little while at the window even in the coldest weather, breathing deeply. With this racing and crashing she frightened Gregor twice a day; the whole time he cowered under the couch, and yet he knew very well that she would certainly have spared him this if only she had found it possible to stand being in a room with him with the window closed.

One time—it must have been a month since Gregor's metamorphosis, and there was certainly no particular reason anymore for his sister to be astonished at Gregor's appearance—she came a little earlier than usual and caught Gregor still looking out the window, immobile and so in an excellent position to be terrifying. It would not have surprised Gregor if she had not come in, because his position prevented her from immediately opening the window, but not only did she not come in, she even sprang back and locked the door; a stranger might easily have thought that Gregor had been lying in wait for her, wanting to bite her. Of course Gregor immediately hid under the couch, but he had to wait until noon before his sister came again, and she seemed much more uneasy than usual. He realized from this that the sight of him was still repulsive to her and was bound to remain repulsive to her in the future and that she probably had to overcome a lot of resistance not to run away at the sight of even the small part of his body that jutted out from under the couch. So, to spare her even this sight, one day he carried the sheet on his back to the couch—the job took four hours—and arranged it in such a way that he was now completely covered up and his sister could not see him even when she stooped. If she had considered this sheet unnecessary, then of course she could have removed it, for it was clear enough that it could not be for his own pleasure that Gregor shut himself off altogether, but she left the sheet the way it was, and Gregor thought that he had even caught a grateful look when one time he cautiously lifted the sheet a little with his head in order to see how his sister was taking the new arrangement.

During the first two weeks, his parents could not bring themselves to come in to him, and often he heard them say how much they appreciated his sister's work, whereas until now they had frequently been annoyed with her because she had struck them as being a little useless. But now both of them, his father and his mother, often waited outside Gregor's room while his sister straightened it up, and as soon as she came out she had to tell them in great detail how the room looked, what Gregor had eaten, how he had behaved this time, and whether he had perhaps shown a little improvement. His mother, incidentally, began relatively soon to want to visit Gregor, but his father and his sister at first held her back with reasonable arguments to which Gregor listened very attentively and of which he wholeheartedly approved. But later she had to be restrained by force, and then when she cried out, "Let me go to Gregor, he is my

66 **Discussion** Have students discuss the significance of Gregor's loss of distance vision.

67 **Discussion** Have students explain the contradiction in the sister's behavior in this scene. On one hand, she moves a chair out of consideration for him. Yet on the other hand, she frightens him by slamming the open window upon entering his room.

68 **Discussion** Have students speculate about whether Grete's behavior might foreshadow a change in her attitude toward Gregor.

69 **Discussion** Have students discuss how Gregor's arranging of the sheet over the couch reflects his deep love for his sister.

70 **Clarification** Call students' attention to the change in the parents' attitude toward the sister. How is Gregor's transformation indirectly responsible for this change? How does Gregor's transformation seem to parallel his sister's emergence as a mature woman?

71 **Discussion** Have students discuss why Gregor's mother feels so strongly about seeing him.

unfortunate boy! Don't you understand that I have to go to him?" Gregor thought that it might be a good idea after all if his mother did come in, not every day of course, but perhaps once a week; she could still do everything much better than his sister, who, for all her courage, was still only a child and in the final analysis had perhaps taken on such a difficult assignment only out of childish flightiness.

Gregor's desire to see his mother was soon fulfilled. During the day Gregor did not want to show himself at the window, if only out of consideration for his parents, but he couldn't crawl very far on his few square yards of floor space, either; he could hardly put up with just lying still even at night; eating soon stopped giving him the slightest pleasure, so, as a distraction, he adopted the habit of crawling crisscross over the walls and the ceiling. He especially liked hanging from the ceiling; it was completely different from lying on the floor; one could breathe more freely; a faint swinging sensation went through the body; and in the almost happy absent-mindedness which Gregor felt up there, it could happen to his own surprise that he let go and plopped onto the floor. But now, of course, he had much better control of his body than before and did not hurt himself even from such a big drop. His sister immediately noticed the new entertainment Gregor had discovered for himself—after all, he left behind traces of his sticky substance wherever he crawled—and so she got it into her head to make it possible for Gregor to crawl on an altogether wider scale by taking out the furniture which stood in his way—mainly the chest of drawers and the desk. But she was not able to do this by herself; she did not dare ask her father for help; the maid would certainly not have helped her, for although this girl, who was about sixteen, was bravely sticking it out after the previous cook had left, she had asked for the favor of locking herself in the kitchen at all times and of only opening the door on special request. So there was nothing left for his sister to do except to get her mother one day when her father was out. And his mother did come, with exclamations of excited joy, but she grew silent at the door of Gregor's room. First his sister looked to see, of course, that everything in the room was in order; only then did she let her mother come in. Hurrying as fast as he could, Gregor had pulled the sheet down lower still and pleated it more tightly —it really looked just like a sheet accidentally thrown over the couch. This time Gregor also refrained from spying from under the sheet; he renounced seeing his mother for the time being and was simply happy that she had come after all. "Come on, you can't see him," his sister said, evidently leading her mother in by the hand. Now Gregor could hear the two frail women moving the old chest of drawers—heavy for anyone—from its place and his sister insisting on doing the harder part of the job herself, ignoring the warnings of her mother, who was afraid that she would overexert herself. It went on for a long time. After struggling for a good quarter of an hour, his mother said that they had better leave the chest where it was, because, in the first place, it was too heavy, they would not finish before his father came, and with the chest in the middle of the room, Gregor would be completely barricaded; and, in the second place, it was not at all certain they were doing Gregor a favor by removing his furniture. To her the opposite seemed to be the case; the sight of the bare wall was heart-breaking; and why shouldn't Gregor also have the same feeling, since he had been used to his furniture for so long and would feel abandoned in the empty room. "And doesn't it look," his mother concluded very softly—in fact she had been almost whispering the whole time, as if she wanted to avoid letting Gregor, whose exact whereabouts she did not know, hear even the sound of her voice, for she was convinced that he did not understand the words—"and doesn't it look as if by removing his furniture we were showing him that we have given up all hope of his getting better and are leaving him to his own devices without any consideration? I think the best thing would be to try to keep the room exactly the way it was before, so that when Gregor comes back to us again, he'll find everything unchanged and can forget all the more easily what's happened in the meantime."

When he heard his mother's words, Gregor realized that the monotony of family life, combined with the fact that not a soul had addressed a word directly to him, must have addled[5] his brain in the

---

5. addled (ad′ 'ld) *v*.: Muddled or confused.

course of the past two months, for he could not explain to himself in any other way how in all seriousness he could have been anxious to have his room cleared out. Had he really wanted to have his warm room, comfortably fitted with furniture that had always been in the family, changed into a cave, in which, of course, he would be able to crawl around unhampered in all directions but at the cost of simultaneously, rapidly, and totally forgetting his human past? Even now he had been on the verge of forgetting, and only his mother's voice, which he had not heard for so long, had shaken him up. Nothing should be removed; everything had to stay; he could not do without the beneficial influence of the furniture on his state of mind; and if the furniture prevented him from carrying on this senseless crawling around, then that was no loss but rather a great advantage.

But his sister unfortunately had a different opinion; she had become accustomed, certainly not entirely without justification, to adopt with her parents the role of the particularly well-qualified expert whenever Gregor's affairs were being discussed; and so her mother's advice was now sufficient reason for her to insist, not only on the removal of the chest of drawers and the desk, which was all she had been planning at first, but also on the removal of all the furniture with the exception of the indispensable couch. Of course it was not only childish defiance and the self-confidence she had recently acquired so unexpectedly and at such a cost that led her to make this demand; she had in fact noticed that Gregor needed plenty of room to crawl around in; and on the other hand, as best as she could tell, he never used the furniture at all. Perhaps, however, the romantic enthusiasm of girls her age, which seeks to indulge itself at every opportunity, played a part, by tempting her to make Gregor's situation even more terrifying in order that she might do even more for him. Into a room in which Gregor ruled the bare walls all alone, no human being besides Grete was ever likely to set foot.

And so she did not let herself be swerved from her decision by her mother, who, besides, from the sheer anxiety of being in Gregor's room, seemed unsure of herself, soon grew silent, and helped her daughter as best she could to get the chest of drawers out of the room. Well, in a pinch Gregor could do without the chest, but the desk had to stay. And hardly had the women left the room with the chest, squeezing against it and groaning, than Gregor stuck his head out from under the couch to see how he could feel his way into the situation as considerately as possible. But unfortunately it had to be his mother who came back first, while in the next room Grete was clasping the chest and rocking it back and forth by herself, without of course budging it from the spot. His mother, however, was not used to the sight of Gregor, he could have made her ill, and so Gregor, frightened, scuttled in reverse to the far end of the couch but could not stop the sheet from shifting a little at the front. That was enough to put his mother on the alert. She stopped, stood still for a moment, and then went back to Grete.

Although Gregor told himself over and over again that nothing special was happening, only a few pieces of furniture were being moved, he soon had to admit that this coming and going of the women, their little calls to each other, the scraping of the furniture along the floor had the effect on him of a great turmoil swelling on all sides, and as much as he tucked in his head and his legs and shrank until his belly touched the floor, he was forced to admit that he would not be able to stand it much longer. They were clearing out his room; depriving him of everything that he loved; they had already carried away the chest of drawers, in which he kept the fretsaw and other tools; were now budging the desk firmly embedded in the floor, the desk he had done his homework on when he was a student at business college, in high school, yes, even in public school—now he really had no more time to examine the good intentions of the two women, whose existence, besides, he had almost forgotten, for they were so exhausted that they were working in silence, and one could hear only the heavy shuffling of their feet.

And so he broke out—the women were just leaning against the desk in the next room to catch their breath for a minute—changed his course four times, he really didn't know what to salvage first, then he saw hanging conspicuously on the wall, which was otherwise bare already, the picture of the lady all dressed in furs, hurriedly crawled up on it and pressed himself against the glass, which gave

77 Discussion Have students discuss the internal conflict that Gregor experiences as a result of the prospect of having his furniture removed. Why does he now oppose the removal of his furniture after initially approving of the idea?

78 Discussion Ask students why Gregor's sister has come to think of herself as an expert where Gregor's affairs are concerned. Do students think that she is justified in feeling this way? Why or why not?

79 Discussion Have students respond to this suggestion. Do they believe that it is possible that Gregor's sister actually does want to make his "situation even more terrifying in order that she might do even more for him"? Why or why not?

80 Discussion Have students discuss why Gregor is unable to convince himself that "nothing special [is] happening."

81 Discussion Ask students to explain the significance of the one object Gregor tries to salvage from his mother and sister.

82 **Discussion** Have students discuss how Gregor's defiance contrasts with his behavior throughout
the previous sections of the story.
Is this the first time that Gregor has
placed his own wishes before his
concern for his family?

83 **Discussion** Have students discuss how this sequence of events
emphasizes Gregor's powerlessness. Given his condition, is there
any way in which he can help his
mother and his sister?

84 **Discussion** Have students discuss whether Gregor's feelings of
worry and self-reproach can be
viewed as his typical response to
problems concerning members of
his family. Did he experience these
feelings even before his metamorphosis?

85 **Discussion** Have students speculate about what Gregor's father
has been telling Gregor's mother
and sister.

86 **Discussion** Taking into account
what they already know about Gregor's father's personality, what action do students expect Gregor's
father to take? Do they think that
he will harm Gregor? Why or why
not?

a good surface to stick to and soothed his hot belly. At least no one would take away this picture, while Gregor completely covered it up. He turned his head toward the living-room door to watch the women when they returned.

They had not given themselves much of a rest and were already coming back; Grete had put her arm around her mother and was practically carrying her. "So what should we take now?" said Grete and looked around. At that her eyes met Gregor's as he clung to the wall. Probably only because of her mother's presence she kept her self-control, bent her head down to her mother to keep her from looking around, and said, though in a quavering and thoughtless voice: "Come, we'd better go back into the living room for a minute." Grete's intent was clear to Gregor, she wanted to bring his mother into safety and then chase him down from the wall. Well, just let her try! He squatted on his picture and would not give it up. He would rather fly in Grete's face.

But Grete's words had now made her mother really anxious; she stepped to one side, caught sight of the gigantic brown blotch on the flowered wallpaper, and before it really dawned on her that what she saw was Gregor, cried in a hoarse, bawling voice: "Oh, God, oh, God!"; and as if giving up completely, she fell with outstretched arms across the couch and did not stir. "You, Gregor!" cried his sister with raised fist and piercing eyes. These were the first words she had addressed directly to him since his metamorphosis. She ran into the next room to get some kind of spirits to revive her mother; Gregor wanted to help too—there was time to rescue the picture—but he was stuck to the glass and had to tear himself loose by force; then he too ran into the next room, as if he could give his sister some sort of advice, as in the old days; but then had to stand behind her doing nothing while she rummaged among various little bottles; moreover, when she turned around she was startled, a bottle fell on the floor and broke, a splinter of glass wounded Gregor in the face, some kind of corrosive medicine flowed around him; now without waiting any longer, Grete grabbed as many little bottles as she could carry and ran with them inside to her mother; she slammed the door behind her with her foot. Now Gregor was cut off from his mother, who was perhaps near death through his fault; he could not dare open the door if he did not want to chase away his sister, who had to stay with his mother; now there was nothing for him to do except wait; and tormented by self-reproaches and worry, he began to crawl, crawled over everything, walls, furniture and ceiling, and finally in desperation, as the whole room was beginning to spin, fell down onto the middle of the big table.

A short time passed; Gregor lay there prostrate; all around, things were quiet, perhaps that was a good sign. Then the doorbell rang. The maid, of course, was locked up in her kitchen and so Grete had to answer the door. His father had come home. "What's happened?" were his first words; Grete's appearance must have told him everything. Grete answered in a muffled voice, her face was obviously pressed against her father's chest; "Mother fainted, but she's better now. Gregor's broken out." "I knew it," his father said. "I kept telling you, but you women don't want to listen." It was clear to Gregor that his father had put the worst interpretation on Grete's all-too-brief announcement and assumed that Gregor was guilty of some outrage. Therefore Gregor now had to try to calm his father down, since he had neither the time nor the ability to enlighten him. And so he fled to the door of his room and pressed himself against if for his father to see, as soon as he came into the foyer, that Gregor had the best intentions of returning to his room immediately and that it was not necessary to drive him back; if only the door were opened for him, he would disappear at once.

But his father was in no mood to notice such subtleties; "Ah!" he cried as he entered, in a tone that sounded as if he were at once furious and glad. Gregor turned his head away from the door and lifted it toward his father. He had not really imagined his father looking like this, as he stood in front of him now; admittedly Gregor had been too absorbed recently in his newfangled crawling to bother as much as before about events in the rest of the house and should really have been prepared to find some changes. And yet, and yet—was this still his father? Was this the same man who in the old days used to lie wearily buried in bed when Gregor left on a business trip; who greeted him on his return in the evening, sitting in his bathrobe in the arm-

Grammar in Action

To emphasize sudden shifts in mood or in the pace at which events occur, Kafka often introduces variations in sentence length. For instance, he often uses long sentences to suggest a long, drawn-out effort of struggle, then introduces short, dramatic sentences that signal an abrupt end to the struggle or announce a drastic turn of events. Note his use of this technique in the following passage from "The Metamorphosis":

Now Gregor was cut off from his mother, who was perhaps near death through his fault; he could not dare open the door if he did not want to chase away his sister, who had to stay with his mother; now there was nothing for him to do except wait; and tormented by self-reproaches and worry, he began to crawl, crawled over everything, walls, furniture and ceiling, and finally in desperation, as the whole room was beginning to spin, fell down onto the middle of the big table.

A short time passed; Gregor lay there prostrate; all around, things were quiet, perhaps that was a good sign. Then the doorbell rang. The maid, of course, was locked up in her kitchen and so Grete had to answer the door. His father had come home.

chair, who actually had difficulty getting to his feet but as a sign of joy only lifted up his arms; and who, on the rare occasions when the whole family went out for a walk, on a few Sundays in June and on the major holidays, used to shuffle along with great effort between Gregor and his mother, who were slow walkers themselves, always a little more slowly than they, wrapped in his old overcoat, always carefully planting down his crutch-handled cane, and, when he wanted to say something, nearly always stood still and assembled his escort around him? Now, however, he was holding himself very erect, dressed in a tight-fitting blue uniform with gold buttons, the kind worn by messengers at banking concerns; above the high stiff collar of the jacket his heavy chin protruded; under his bushy eyebrows his black eyes darted bright, piercing glances; his usually rumpled white hair was combed flat, with a scrupulously exact, gleaming part. He threw his cap—which was adorned with a gold monogram, probably that of a bank—in an arc across the entire room onto the couch, and with the tails of his long uniform jacket slapped back, his hands in his pants pockets, went for Gregor with a sullen look on his face. He probably did not know himself what he had in mind; still he lifted his feet unusually high off the floor, and Gregor staggered at the gigantic size of the soles of his boots. But he did not linger over this, he had known right from the first day of his new life that his father considered only the strictest treatment called for in dealing with him. And so he ran ahead of his father, stopped when his father stood still, and scooted ahead again when his father made even the slightest movement. In this way they made more than one tour of the room, without anything decisive happening; in fact the whole movement did not even have the appearance of a chase because of its slow tempo. So Gregor kept to the floor for the time being, especially since he was afraid that his father might interpret a flight onto the walls or the ceiling as a piece of particular nastiness. Of course Gregor had to admit that he would not be able to keep up even this running for long, for whenever his father took one step, Gregor had to execute countless movements. He was already beginning to feel winded, just as in the old days he had not had very reliable lungs. As he now staggered around, hardly keeping his eyes open in order to gather all his strength for the running; in his obtuseness[6] not thinking of any escape other than by running; and having almost forgotten that the walls were at his disposal, though here of course they were blocked up with elaborately carved furniture full of notches and points—at that moment a lightly flung object hit the floor right near him and rolled in front of him. It was an apple; a second one came flying right after it; Gregor stopped dead with fear; further running was useless, for his father was determined to bombard him. He had filled his pockets from the fruit bowl on the buffet and was now pitching one apple after another, for the time being without taking good aim. These little red apples rolled around on the floor as if electrified, clicking into each other. One apple, thrown weakly, grazed Gregor's back and slid off harmlessly. But the very next one that came flying after it literally forced its way into Gregor's back; Gregor tried to drag himself away, as if the startling, unbelievable pain might disappear with a change of place; but he felt nailed to the spot and stretched out his body in a complete confusion of all his senses. With his last glance he saw the door of his room burst open, as his mother rushed out ahead of his screaming sister, in her chemise, for his sister had partly undressed her while she was unconscious in order to let her breathe more freely; saw his mother run up to his father and on the way her unfastened petticoats slide to the floor one by one; and saw as, stumbling over the skirts, she forced herself onto his father, and embracing him, in complete union with him—but now Gregor's sight went dim—her hands clasping his father's neck, begged for Gregor's life.

III

Gregor's serious wound, from which he suffered for over a month—the apple remained imbedded in his flesh as a visible souvenir since no one dared to remove it—seemed to have reminded even his father that Gregor was a member of the family, in spite of his present pathetic and repulsive

---

6. **obtuseness** (äb tōōs′ nəs) *n*.: Slowness to understand or perceive.

91

87 **Discussion** Have students comment on how Gregor's father has changed since Gregor's metamorphosis. Has he been forced to make these changes? Why or why not? How do the changes in Gregor's father parallel the changes in Gregor's sister?

88 **Discussion** Have students explain how Gregor has known that his father "considered only the strictest treatment called for in dealing with him." Up to this point, has Gregor's father done anything to show that he still cares for Gregor?

89 **Critical Thinking and Reading** Remind students that Kafka's father was strict and domineering. Then ask them if this description can also be applied to Gregor's father. Why or why not? Also remind students that throughout his life Kafka experienced feelings of familial obligation, guilt, and duty. How are these feelings reflected in "The Metamorphosis"?

90 **Enrichment** Explain to students that this reference to Gregor's "poor lungs" is unintentionally ironic, since Kafka himself, not long after writing this story, was diagnosed as having tuberculosis. Ask students if they think that people can sometimes have premonitions about what will happen to them.

91 **Discussion** Ask students if they think Gregor's father is trying to kill Gregor? Make sure that they explain their response. Then ask them why Gregor's mother is so desperate to save Gregor's life. Do they think she still believes that there is a chance he will return to his former condition? Why or why not?

Student Activity 1. Find two more passages in which Kafka varies the lengths of his sentences. Then explain the effect produced by the sentence variation in each of these passages.

Student Activity 2. Write a paragraph in which you vary the length of your sentences to emphasize an abrupt shift in mood or an unexpected turn of events. In your paragraph, you may want to describe a slowly developing sequence of events, such as a long-distance race.

Mikhail Baryshnikov in the dramatic adaptation of "The Metamorphosis"

92 shape, who could not be treated as an enemy; that, on the contrary, it was the commandment of family duty to swallow their disgust and endure him, endure him and nothing more.

And now, although Gregor had lost some of his mobility probably for good because of his wound, and although for the time being he needed long, long minutes to get across his room, like an old war veteran—crawling above ground was out of the question—for this deterioration of his situation he was granted compensation which in his view was entirely satisfactory: every day around dusk the living-room door—which he was in the habit of watching closely for an hour or two be-93 forehand--was opened, so that, lying in the darkness of his room, invisible from the living room, he could see the whole family sitting at the table under the lamp and could listen to their conversation, as it were with general permission; and so it was completely different from before.

Of course these were no longer the animated conversations of the old days, which Gregor used to remember with a certain nostalgia in small hotel rooms when he'd had to throw himself wearily into the damp bedding. Now things were mostly very quiet. Soon after supper his father would fall asleep in his armchair; his mother and sister would caution each other to be quiet; his mother, bent low under the light, sewed delicate lingerie for a clothing store; his sister, who had taken a job as a sales-

girl, was learning shorthand and French in the evenings in order to attain a better position sometime in the future. Sometimes his father woke up, and as if he had absolutely no idea that he had been asleep, said to his mother, "Look how long you're sewing again today!" and went right back to sleep, while mother and sister smiled wearily at each other.

With a kind of perverse obstinacy his father refused to take off his official uniform even in the house; and while his robe hung uselessly on the clothes hook, his father dozed, completely dressed, in his chair, as if he were always ready for duty and were waiting even here for the voice of his superior. As a result his uniform, which had not been new to 9 start with, began to get dirty in spite of all the mother's and sister's care, and Gregor would often stare all evening long at this garment, covered with stains and gleaming with its constantly polished gold buttons, in which the old man slept most uncomfortably and yet peacefully.

As soon as the clock struck ten, his mother tried to awaken his father with soft encouraging words and then persuade him to go to bed, for this was no place to sleep properly, and his father badly needed his sleep, since he had to be at work at six o'clock. But with the obstinacy that had possessed him ever since he had become a messenger, he always insisted on staying at the table a little longer, although he invariably fell asleep and then could be persuaded only with the greatest effort to exchange 9 his armchair for bed. However much mother and sister might pounce on him with little admonitions,[7] he would slowly shake his head for a quarter of an hour at a time, keeping his eyes closed, and would not get up. Gregor's mother plucked him by the sleeves, whispered blandishments into his ear, his sister dropped her homework in order to help her mother, but all this was of no use. He only sank deeper into his armchair. Not until the women lifted him up under his arms did he open his eyes, look alternately at mother and sister, and usually say, "What a life. So this is the peace of my old age." And leaning on the two women, he would 9

---

7. **admonitions** (ad′ mə nish′ ənz) *n.*: Mild rebukes; reprimands.

Primary Source
A year before Kafka wrote "The Metamorphosis," he watched an artist grimacing and mimicking what he was drawing. That day, Kafka wrote this prophetic comment in his diary:

[The artist] reminds me that I too have a pronounced talent for metamorphosing myself, which no one notices. . . . Yesterday evening, on the way home, if I had observed myself from the outside I should have taken myself for Tucholsky. The alien being must be in me, then, as distinctly and invisibly as the hidden object in a picture-puzzle, where, too, one would never find anything if one did not know that it is there. When these metamorphoses take place, I should especially like to believe in a dimming of my own eyes."

get up laboriously, as if he were the greatest weight on himself, and let the women lead him to the door, where, shrugging them off, he would proceed independently, while Gregor's mother threw down her sewing and his sister her pen as quickly as possible so as to run after his father and be of further assistance.

Who in this overworked and exhausted family had time to worry about Gregor any more than was absolutely necessary? The household was stinted more and more; now the maid was let go after all; a gigantic bony cleaning woman with white hair fluttering about her head came mornings and evenings to do the heaviest work; his mother took care of everything else, along with all her sewing. It even happened that various pieces of family jewelry, which in the old days his mother and sister had been overjoyed to wear at parties and celebrations, were sold, as Gregor found out one evening from the general discussion of the prices they had fetched. But the biggest complaint was always that they could not give up the apartment, which was much too big for their present needs, since no one could figure out how Gregor was supposed to be moved. But Gregor understood easily that it was not only consideration for him which prevented their moving, for he could easily have been transported in a suitable crate with a few air holes; what mainly prevented the family from moving was their complete hopelessness and the thought that they had been struck by a misfortune as none of their relatives and acquaintances had ever been hit. What the world demands of poor people they did to the utmost of their ability; his father brought breakfast for the minor officials at the bank, his mother sacrificed herself to the underwear of strangers, his sister ran back and forth behind the counter at the request of the customers; but for anything more than this they did not have the strength. And the wound in Gregor's back began to hurt anew when mother and sister, after getting his father to bed, now came back, dropped their work, pulled their chairs close to each other and sat cheek to cheek; when his mother, pointing to Gregor's room, said, "Close that door, Grete"; and when Gregor was back in darkness, while in the other room the women mingled their tears or stared dry-eyed at the table.

Gregor spent the days and nights almost entirely without sleep. Sometimes he thought that the next time the door opened he would take charge of the family's affairs again, just as he had done in the old days; after this long while there again appeared in his thoughts the boss and the manager, the salesmen and the trainees, the handyman who was so dense, two or three friends from other firms, a chambermaid in a provincial hotel—a happy fleeting memory—a cashier in a millinery store,[8] whom he had courted earnestly but too slowly—they all appeared, intermingled with strangers or people he had already forgotten; but instead of helping him and his family, they were all inaccessible, and he was glad when they faded away. At other times he was in no mood to worry about his family, he was completely filled with rage at his miserable treatment, and although he could not imagine anything that would pique his appetite, he still made plans for getting into the pantry to take what was coming to him, even if he wasn't hungry. No longer considering what she could do to give Gregor a special treat, his sister, before running to business every morning and afternoon, hurriedly shoved any old food into Gregor's room with her foot; and in the evening, regardless of whether the food had only been toyed with or—the most usual case—had been left completely untouched, she swept it out with a swish of the broom. The cleaning up of Gregor's room, which she now always did in the evenings, could not be done more hastily. Streaks of dirt ran along the walls, fluffs of dust and filth lay here and there on the floor. At first, whenever his sister came in, Gregor would place himself in those corners which were particularly offending, meaning by his position in a sense to reproach her. But he could probably have stayed there for weeks without his sister's showing any improvement; she must have seen the dirt as clearly as he did, but she had just decided to leave it. At the same time she made sure—with an irritableness that was completely new to her and which had in fact infected the whole family—that the cleaning of Gregor's room remain her province. One time his mother had submitted Gregor's room

8. **millinery** (mil′ ə ner′ ē) **store:** A store that sells women's hats.

97 Discussion Do students think these pieces of jewelry should have been sold when Gregor's father's business collapsed? Why or why not?

98 Discussion Have students discuss the accuracy of Gregor's assessment of his family's situation. Is Gregor correct in concluding that his family is essentially paralyzed by complete hopelessness?

99 Discussion Have students explain why the mingling tears of Gregor's mother and sister cause Gregor's back to begin "to hurt anew."

100 Discussion Have students discuss these dramatic fluctuations in Gregor's thoughts. What is the significance of the images that come to Gregor's mind when he imagines that he is about to take charge of his family's affairs again? Why is he glad when these images fade away?

101 Discussion Have students discuss how Grete's attitude toward Gregor has changed. How is this change revealed? Why does Grete continue to make sure that the "cleaning of Gregor's room [remains] her province"?

to a major housecleaning, which she managed only after employing a couple of pails of water—all this dampness, of course, irritated Gregor too and he lay prostrate, sour and immobile, on the couch—but his mother's punishment was not long in coming. For hardly had his sister noticed the difference in Gregor's room that evening than, deeply insulted, she ran into the living room and, in spite of her mother's imploringly uplifted hands, burst out in a fit of crying, which his parents—his father had naturally been startled out of his armchair—at first watched in helpless amazement; until they too got going; turning to the right, his father blamed his mother for not letting his sister clean Gregor's room; but turning to the left, he screamed at his sister that she would never again be allowed to clean Gregor's room; while his mother tried to drag his father, who was out of his mind with excitement, into the bedroom, his sister, shaken with sobs, hammered the table with her small fists; and Gregor hissed loudly with rage because it did not occur to any of them to close the door and spare him such a scene and a row.

But even if his sister, exhausted from her work at the store, had gotten fed up with taking care of Gregor as she used to, it was not necessary at all for his mother to take her place and still Gregor did not have to be neglected. For now the cleaning woman was there. This old widow, who thanks to her strong bony frame had probably survived the worst in a long life, was not really repelled by Gregor. Without being in the least inquisitive, she had once accidentally opened the door of Gregor's room, and at the sight of Gregor—who, completely taken by surprise, began to race back and forth although no one was chasing him—she had remained standing, with her hands folded on her stomach, marveling. From that time on she never failed to open the door a crack every morning and every evening and peek in hurriedly at Gregor. In the beginning she also used to call him over to her with words she probably considered friendly, like, "Come over here for a minute, you old dung beetle!" or "Look at that old dung beetle!" To forms of address like these Gregor would not respond but remained immobile where he was, as if the door had not been opened. If only they had given this cleaning woman orders to clean up his room

every day, instead of letting her disturb him uselessly whenever the mood took her. Once, early in the morning—heavy rain, perhaps already a sign of approaching spring, was beating on the window panes—Gregor was so exasperated when the cleaning woman started in again with her phrases that he turned on her, of course slowly and decrepitly, as if to attack. But the cleaning woman, instead of getting frightened, simply lifted up high a chair near the door, and as she stood there with her mouth wide open, her intention was clearly to shut her mouth only when the chair in her hand came crashing down on Gregor's back. "So, is that all there is?" she asked when Gregor turned around again, and she quietly put the chair back in the corner.

Gregor now hardly ate anything anymore. Only when he accidentally passed the food laid out for him would he take a bite into his mouth just for fun, hold it in for hours, and then mostly spit it out again. At first he thought that his grief at the state of his room kept him off food, but it was the very changes in his room to which he quickly became adjusted. His family had gotten into the habit of putting in this room things for which they could not find any other place, and now there were plenty of these, since one of the rooms in the apartment had been rented to three boarders. These serious gentlemen—all three had long beards, as Gregor was able to register once through a crack in the door—were obsessed with neatness, not only in their room, but since they had, after all, moved in here, throughout the entire household and especially in the kitchen. They could not stand useless, let alone dirty junk. Besides, they had brought along most of their own household goods. For this reason many things had become superfluous, and though they certainly weren't salable, on the other hand they could not just be thrown out. All these things migrated into Gregor's room. Likewise the ashcan and the garbage can from the kitchen. Whatever was not being used at the moment was just flung into Gregor's room by the cleaning woman, who was always in a big hurry; fortunately Gregor generally saw only the object involved and the hand that held it. Maybe the cleaning woman intended to reclaim the things as soon as she had a chance or else to throw out everything together in

Commentary

Kafka's Response to Music Many people feel that the climax of "The Metamorphosis" is the scene in which Gregor is drawn out of his room by his sister's violin playing. Given the importance of this scene, it seems logical to conclude that Kafka himself had a deep love for music. Yet, in reality, Kafka failed in his attempts to learn to play the violin and the piano as a young man, and he felt unresponsive to music for the rest of his life. In his diary he wrote, "The essence of my unmusicalness consists in my inability to enjoy music connectedly; it only now and then has an effect on me, and how seldom it is a musical one. The natural effect of music on me is to circumscribe me with a wall, and its only constant influence on me is that, confined in this way, I am different from what I am when free. . . . There is, among the public, no such reverence for literature as there is for music."

one fell swoop, but in fact they would have remained lying wherever they had been thrown in the first place if Gregor had not squeezed through the junk and set it in motion, at first from necessity, because otherwise there would have been no room to crawl in, but later with growing pleasure, although after such excursions, tired to death and sad, he did not budge again for hours.

Since the roomers sometimes also had their supper at home in the common living room, the living-room door remained closed on certain evenings, but Gregor found it very easy to give up the open door, for on many evenings when it was opened he had not taken advantage of it, but instead, without the family's noticing, had lain in the darkest corner of his room. But once the cleaning woman had left the living-room door slightly open, and it also remained opened a little when the roomers came in in the evening and the lamp was lit. They sat down at the head of the table where in the old days his father, his mother, and Gregor had eaten, unfolded their napkins, and picked up their knives and forks. At once his mother appeared in the doorway with a platter of meat, and just behind her came his sister with a platter piled high with potatoes. A thick vapor steamed up from the food. The roomers bent over the platters set in front of them as if to examine them before eating, and in fact the one who sat in the middle, and who seemed to be regarded by the other two as an authority, cut into a piece of meat while it was still on the platter, evidently to find out whether it was tender enough or whether it should perhaps be sent back to the kitchen. He was satisfied, and mother and sister, who had been watching anxiously, sighed with relief and began to smile.

The family itself ate in the kitchen. Nevertheless, before going into the kitchen, his father came into this room and, bowing once, cap in hand, made a turn around the table. The roomers rose as one man and mumbled something into their beards. When they were alone again, they ate in almost complete silence. It seemed strange to Gregor that among all the different noises of eating he kept picking up the sound of their chewing teeth, as if this were a sign to Gregor that you needed teeth to eat with and that even with the best make of toothless jaws you couldn't do a thing. "I'm hungry enough, " Gregor said to himself, full of grief, "but not for these things. Look how these roomers are gorging themselves, and I'm dying!"

On this same evening—Gregor could not remember having heard the violin during the whole time—the sound of violin playing came from the kitchen. The roomers had already finished their evening meal, the one in the middle had taken out a newspaper, given each of the two others a page, and now, leaning back, they read and smoked. When the violin began to play, they became attentive, got up, and went on tiptoe to the door leading to the foyer, where they stood in a huddle. They must have been heard in the kitchen, for his father called, "Perhaps the playing bothers you, gentlemen? It can be stopped right away." "On the contrary," said the middle roomer. "Wouldn't the young lady like to come in to us and play in here where it's much roomier and more comfortable?" "Oh, certainly," called Gregor's father, as if he were the violinist. The boarders went back into the room and waited. Soon Gregor's father came in with the music stand, his mother with the sheet music, and his sister with the violin. Calmly his sister got everything ready for playing; his parents—who had never rented out rooms before and therefore behaved toward the roomers with excessive politeness—did not even dare sit down on their own chairs; his father leaned against the door, his right hand inserted between two buttons of his uniform coat, which he kept closed; but his mother was offered a chair by one of the roomers, and since she left the chair where the roomer just happened to put it, she sat in a corner to one side.

His sister began to play. Father and mother, from either side, attentively followed the movements of her hands. Attracted by the playing, Gregor had dared to come out a little farther and already had his head in the living room. It hardly surprised him that lately he was showing so little consideration for the others; once such consideration had been his greatest pride. And yet he would never have had better reason to keep hidden; for now, because of the dust which lay all over his room and blew around at the slightest movement, he too was completely covered with dust; he dragged around with him on his back and along his sides fluff and hairs and scraps of food; his indiffer-

111

112

108 Discussion Have students discuss the significance of Gregor's growing pleasure at scuttling through the junk in his room.

109 Discussion Have students discuss the impression of the roomers that Kafka conveys in this passage. How would students describe the tone of this passage? In other words, what seems to be Kafka's attitude toward these characters?

110 Discussion Have students discuss how the family's groveling before the boarders parallels the way in which Gregor used to behave toward the office manager. How does the Samsas' treatment of the boarders contrast with their treatment of Gregor?

111 Discussion Do students think the Samsas have a duty to treat the boarders with such excessive politeness? Why or why not? Does it seem as if the boarders have taken control of the apartment?

112 Discussion Have students discuss why Grete's playing has such a powerful impact on Gregor. Why does the music draw Gregor out of his room? How will the boarders react if they see him?

113 **Discussion** Have students contrast the roomers' reaction to Grete's violin playing with Gregor's reaction.

114 **Clarification** Call students' attention to Kafka's suggestion that Grete's violin playing provided Gregor with the "unknown nourishment that he had longed for." Have students suggest what this line suggests about the symbolic meaning of Gregor's increasing hunger. Ask students if they think Gregor's hunger might symbolize the lack of substance and lack of meaning in his life. Why or why not?

115 **Discussion** Have students respond to Gregor's bizarre fantasy of abducting his sister and guarding her from all "aggressors."

116 **Discussion** Have students discuss what is revealed by the fact that the boarders are apparently more entertained by the sight of Gregor than by Grete's violin playing.

117 **Discussion** Have students explain why Mr. Samsa rushes toward the roomers rather than toward Gregor.

ence to everything was much too deep for him to have gotten on his back and scrubbed himself clean against the carpet, as once he had done several times a day. And in spite of his state, he was not ashamed to inch out a little farther on the immaculate living-room floor.

Admittedly no one paid any attention to him. The family was completely absorbed by the violin playing; the roomers, on the other hand, who at first had stationed themselves, hands in pockets, much too close behind his sister's music stand, so that they could all have followed the score, which certainly must have upset his sister, soon withdrew to the window, talking to each other in an undertone, their heads lowered, where they remained, anxiously watched by his father. It now seemed only too obvious that they were disappointed in their expectation of hearing beautiful or entertaining violin playing, had had enough of the whole performance, and continued to let their peace be disturbed only out of politeness. Especially the way they all blew the cigar smoke out of their nose and mouth toward the ceiling suggested great nervousness. And yet his sister was playing so beautifully. Her face was inclined to one side, sadly and probingly her eyes followed the lines of music. Gregor crawled forward a little farther, holding his head close to the floor, so that it might be possible to catch her eye. Was he an animal, that music could move him so? He felt as if the way to the unknown nourishment he longed for were coming to light. He was determined to force himself on until he reached his sister, to pluck at her skirt, and to let her know in this way that she should bring her violin into his room, for no one here appreciated her playing the way he would appreciate it. He would never again let her out of his room—at least not for as long as he lived; for once, his nightmarish looks would be of use to him; he would be at all the doors of his room at the same time and hiss and spit at the aggressors; his sister, however, should not be forced to stay with him, but would do so of her own free will; she should sit next to him on the couch, bending her ear down to him, and then he would confide to her that he had had the firm intention of sending her to the Conservatory, and that, if the catastrophe had not intervened, he would have announced this to everyone last Christ-

mas—certainly Christmas had come and gone?—without taking notice of any objections. After this declaration his sister would burst into tears of emotion, and Gregor would raise himself up to her shoulder and kiss her on the neck which, ever since she started going out to work, she kept bare, without a ribbon or collar.

"Mr. Samsa!" the middle roomer called to Gregor's father and without wasting another word pointed his index finger at Gregor, who was slowly moving forward. The violin stopped, the middle roomer smiled first at his friends, shaking his head, and then looked at Gregor again. Rather than driving Gregor out, his father seemed to consider it more urgent to start by soothing the roomers although they were not at all upset, and Gregor seemed to be entertaining them more than the violin playing. He rushed over to them and tried with outstretched arms to drive them into their room and at the same time with his body to block their view of Gregor. Now they actually did get a little angry—it was not clear whether because of his father's behavior or because of their dawning realization of having had without knowing it such a next-door neighbor as Gregor. They demanded explanations from his father; in their turn they raised their arms, plucked excitedly at their beards, and, dragging their feet, backed off toward their room. In the meantime his sister had overcome the abstracted mood into which she had fallen after her playing had been so suddenly interrupted; and all at once, after holding violin and bow for a while in her slackly hanging hands and continuing to follow the score as if she were still playing, she pulled herself together, laid the instrument on the lap of her mother—who was still sitting in her chair, fighting for breath, her lungs violently heaving—and ran into the next room, which the roomers, under pressure from her father, were nearing more quickly than before. One could see the covers and bolsters on the beds, obeying his sister's practiced hands, fly up and arrange themselves. Before the boarders had reached the room, she had finished turning down the beds and had slipped out. Her father seemed once again to be gripped by his perverse obstinacy to such a degree that he completely forgot any respect still due his tenants. He drove them on and kept on driving until, already at the

Grammar in Action

Descriptive Writing creates an image of a person, place, or thing in the reader's mind. To create mental images, writers use sensory details—details appealing to one or more of the five senses. Note Kafka's use of sensory details in the following descriptive passage from "The Metamorphosis":

He was lying on his back as hard as armor plate, and when he lifted his head a little, he saw his vaulted brown belly, sectioned by arch-shaped ribs, to whose dome the cover, about to slide off completely, could barely cling. His many legs, pitifully thin compared with the rest

of him, were wavering helplessly before his eyes. (page 1084)

In looking at this passage, you will also notice that the details are presented in spatial order, or arranged according to their position. Spatial order is the most common method of organization in descriptive writing, although writers also sometimes use chronological order or comparison-and-contrast order.

Student Activity 1. Locate five more descriptive passages in Kafka's story. Then find the sensory details in these passages and identify the sense or senses to which each detail appeals.

Student Activity 2. Write a paragraph describing a person, an animal, bedroom door, the middle boarder stamped his foot thunderingly and thus brought him to a standstill. "I herewith declare," he said, raising his hand and casting his eyes around for Gregor's mother and sister too, "that in view of the disgusting conditions prevailing in this apartment and family"—here he spat curtly and decisively on the floor—"I give notice as of now. Of course I won't pay a cent for the days I have been living here, either; on the contrary, I shall consider taking some sort of action against you with claims that—believe me—will be easy to substantiate." He stopped and looked straight in front of him, as if he were expecting something. And in fact his two friends at once chimed in with the words, "We too give notice as of now." Thereupon he grabbed the door knob and slammed the door with a bang.

Gregor's father, his hands groping, staggered to his armchair and collapsed into it; it looked as if he were stretching himself out for his usual evening nap, but the heavy drooping of his head, as if it had lost all support, showed that he was certainly not asleep. All this time Gregor had lain quietly at the spot where the roomers had surprised him. His disappointment at the failure of his plan—but perhaps also the weakness caused by so much fasting—made it impossible for him to move. He was afraid with some certainty that in the very next moment a general debacle would burst over him, and he waited. He was not even startled by the violin as it slipped from under his mother's trembling fingers and fell off her lap with a reverberating clang.

"My dear parents," said his sister and by way of an introduction pounded her hand on the table, "things can't go on like this. Maybe you don't realize it, but I do. I won't pronounce the name of my brother in front of this monster, and so all I say is: we have to try to get rid of it. We've done everything humanly possible to take care of it and to put up with it; I don't think anyone can blame us in the least."

"She's absolutely right," said his father to himself. His mother, who still could not catch her breath, began to cough dully behind her hand, a wild look in her eyes.

His sister rushed over to his mother and held her forehead. His father seemed to have been led by Grete's words to more definite thoughts, had

sat up, was playing with the cap of his uniform among the plates which were still lying on the table from the roomers' supper, and from time to time looked at Gregor's motionless form.

"We must try to get rid of it," his sister now said exclusively to her father, since her mother was coughing too hard to hear anything. "It will be the death of you two, I can see it coming. People who already have to work as hard as we do can't put up with this constant torture at home, too. I can't stand it anymore either." And she broke out crying so bitterly that her tears poured down onto her mother's face, which she wiped off with mechanical movements of her hand.

"Child," said her father kindly and with unusual understanding, "but what can we do?"

Gregor's sister only shrugged her shoulders as a sign of the bewildered mood that had now gripped her as she cried, in contrast with her earlier confidence.

"If he could understand us," said her father, half questioning; in the midst of her crying Gregor's sister waved her hand violently as a sign that that was out of the question.

"If he could understand us," his father repeated and by closing his eyes, absorbed his daughter's conviction of the impossibility of the idea, "then maybe we could come to an agreement with him. But the way things are——"

"It has to go," cried his sister. "That's the only answer, Father. You just have to try to get rid of the idea that it's Gregor. Believing it for so long, that is our real misfortune. But how can it be Gregor? If it were Gregor, he would have realized long ago that it isn't possible for human beings to live with such a creature, and he would have gone away of his own free will. Then we wouldn't have a brother, but we'd be able to go on living and honor his memory. But as things are, this animal persecutes us, drives the roomers away, obviously wants to occupy the whole apartment and for us to sleep in the gutter. Look, Father," she suddenly shrieked, "he's starting in again!" And in a fit of terror that was completely incomprehensible to Gregor, his sister abandoned even her mother, literally shoved herself off from her chair, as if she would rather sacrifice her mother than stay near Gregor, and rushed behind her father, who, upset only by her

118 Discussion Do students think the boarders have a right to refuse to pay for the days they have been living at the Samsas' apartment? Why or why not? What makes their reaction seem comical? Do students think Kafka meant for it to seem comical? Why or why not?

119 Discussion Point out to students that since the metamorphosis, Grete has most often referred to Gregor as "he" and has only once referred to him by his name. How does the manner in which she refers to him in the passage indicate that a final and decisive change in her attitude toward Gregor has taken place?

120 Discussion Do students agree with Grete's pronouncement that she and her parents have done "everything humanly possible to take care of" Gregor? Why or why not?

121 Discussion Have students explain the irony of Grete's comment that "It will be the death of you two."

122 Discussion Ask students if Mr. Samsa's response seems out of character. Why or why not?

123 Discussion Ask students if it would have been possible for Gregor to go "away of his own free will." Why or why not?

or a beautiful scene from nature. Include details appealing to at least three different senses, and arrange your details in spatial order.

124 Discussion Have students explain why the family members are silent and sad as they watch Gregor struggle to turn around and return to his room.

125 Discussion Have students discuss the significance of the fact that Gregor's mother has fallen asleep by the time he turns back to look at her. Do students think this is the last time that Gregor will ever see the members of his family? Why or why not?

126 Discussion Have students discuss Gregor's thoughts as he approaches his death. Why does he think back on his family "with deep emotion and love"?

127 Discussion Point out to students that the cleaning woman had "credited [Gregor] with unlimited intelligence." Do students think the Samsas also regarded Gregor as intelligent? If not, what is the significance of the fact that the cleaning woman gave Gregor more credit than did the members of his own family?

128 Discussion Have students discuss how the depiction of the cleaning woman's discovery that Gregor has died contrasts with the description of Gregor's death in the preceding paragraph.

behavior, also stood up and half lifted his arms in front of her as if to protect her.

But Gregor had absolutely no intention of frightening anyone, let alone his sister. He had only begun to turn around in order to trek back to his room; certainly his movements did look peculiar, since his ailing condition made him help the complicated turning maneuver along with his head, which he lifted up many times and knocked against the floor. He stopped and looked around. His good intention seemed to have been recognized; it had only been a momentary scare. Now they all watched him, silent and sad. His mother lay in her armchair, her legs stretched out and pressed together, her eyes almost closing from exhaustion; his father and his sister sat side by side, his sister had put her arm around her father's neck.

Now maybe they'll let me turn around, Gregor thought and began his labors again. He could not repress his panting from the exertion, and from time to time he had to rest. Otherwise no one harassed him, he was left completely on his own. When he had completed the turn, he immediately began to crawl back in a straight line. He was astonished at the great distance separating him from his room and could not understand at all how, given his weakness, he had covered the same distance a little while ago almost without realizing it. Constantly intent only on rapid crawling, he hardly noticed that not a word, not an exclamation from his family interrupted him. Only when he was already in the doorway did he turn his head—not completely, for he felt his neck stiffening; nevertheless he still saw that behind him nothing had changed except that his sister had gotten up. His last glance ranged over his mother, who was now fast asleep.

He was hardly inside his room when the door was hurriedly slammed shut, firmly bolted, and locked. Gregor was so frightened at the sudden noise behind him that his little legs gave way under him. It was his sister who had been in such a hurry. She had been standing up straight, ready and waiting, then she had leaped forward nimbly. Gregor had not even heard her coming, and she cried "Finally!" to her parents as she turned the key in the lock.

"And now?" Gregor asked himself, looking around in the darkness. He soon made the discovery that he could no longer move at all. It did not surprise him; rather, it seemed unnatural that until now he had actually been able to propel himself on these thin little legs. Otherwise he felt relatively comfortable. He had pains, of course, throughout his whole body, but it seemed to him that they were gradually getting fainter and fainter and would finally go away altogether. The rotten apple in his back and the inflamed area around it, which were completely covered with fluffy dust, already hardly bothered him. He thought back on his family with deep emotion and love. His conviction that he would have to disappear was, if possible, even firmer than his sister's. He remained in this state of empty and peaceful reflection until the tower clock struck three in the morning. He still saw that outside the window everything was beginning to grow light. Then, without his consent, his head sank down to the floor, and from his nostrils streamed his last weak breath.

When early in the morning the cleaning woman came—in sheer energy and impatience she would slam all the doors so hard although she had often been asked not to, that once she had arrived, quiet sleep was no longer possible anywhere in the apartment—she did not at first find anything out of the ordinary on paying Gregor her usual short visit. She thought that he was deliberately lying motionless, pretending that his feelings were hurt; she credited him with unlimited intelligence. Because she happened to be holding the long broom, she tried from the doorway to tickle Gregor with it. When this too produced no results, she became annoyed and jabbed Gregor a little, and only when she had shoved him without any resistance to another spot did she begin to take notice. When she quickly became aware of the true state of things, she opened her eyes wide, whistled softly, but did not dawdle; instead, she tore open the door of the bedroom and shouted at the top of her voice into he darkness; "Come and have a look, it's croaked; it's lying there, dead as a doornail!"

The couple Mr. and Mrs. Samsa sat up in their marriage bed and had a struggle overcoming their shock at the cleaning woman before they could finally grasp her message. But then Mr. and Mrs. Samsa hastily scrambled out of bed, each on his side, Mr. Samsa threw the blanket around his shoulders, Mrs. Samsa came out in nothing but her nightgown; dressed this way, they entered Gregor's room. In the meantime the door of the living room had also opened, where Grete had been sleeping since the roomers had moved in; she was fully dressed, as if she had not been asleep at all; and her pale face seemed to confirm this. "Dead?" said Mrs. Samsa and looked inquiringly at the cleaning woman, although she could scrutinize everything for herself and could recognize the truth even without scrutiny. "I'll say," said the cleaning woman, and to prove it she pushed Gregor's corpse with her broom a good distance sideways. Mrs. Samsa made a movement as if to hold the broom back but did not do it. "Well," said Mr. Samsa, "now we can thank God!" He crossed himself, and the three women followed his example. Grete, who never took her eyes off the corpse, said, "Just look how thin he was. Of course he didn't eat anything for such a long time. The food came out again just the way it went in." As a matter of fact, Gregor's body was completely flat and dry; this was obvious now for the first time, really, since the body was no longer raised up by his little legs and nothing else distracted the eye.

"Come in with us for a little while, Grete," said Mrs. Samsa with a melancholy smile, and Grete, not without looking back at the corpse, followed her parents into their bedroom. The cleaning woman shut the door and opened the window wide. Although it was early in the morning, there was already some mildness mixed in with the fresh air. After all, it was already the end of March.

The three boarders came out of their room and looked around in astonishment for their breakfast; they had been forgotten. "Where's breakfast?" the middle roomer grumpily asked the cleaning woman. But she put her finger to her lips and then hastily and silently beckoned the boarders to follow her into Gregor's room. They came willingly and then stood, their hands in the pockets of their somewhat shabby jackets, in the now already very bright room, surrounding Gregor's corpse.

At that point the bedroom door opened, and Mr. Samsa appeared in his uniform, his wife on one arm, his daughter on the other. They all looked as if they had been crying, from time to time Grete pressed her face against her father's sleeve.

"Leave my house immediately," said Mr. Samsa and pointed to the door, without letting go of the women. "What do you mean by that?" said the middle roomer, somewhat nonplussed, and smiled with a sugary smile. The two others held their hands behind their back and incessantly rubbed them together, as if in joyful anticipation of a big argument, which could only turn out in their favor. "I mean just what I say," answered Mr. Samsa and with his two companions marched in a straight line toward the roomer. At first the roomer stood still and looked at the floor, as if the thoughts inside his head were fitting themselves together in a new order. "So, we'll go, then," he said and looked up at Mr. Samsa as if, suddenly overcome by a fit of humility, he were asking for further permission even for this decision. Mr. Samsa merely nodded briefly several times, his eyes wide open. Thereupon the roomer actually went immediately into the foyer, taking long strides; his two friends had already been listening for a while, their hands completely still, and now they went hopping right after him, as if afraid that Mr. Samsa might get into the foyer ahead of them and interrupt the contact with their leader. In the foyer all three took their hats from the coat rack, pulled their canes from the umbrella stand, bowed silently, and left the apartment. In a suspicious mood which proved completely unfounded, Mr. Samsa led the two women out onto the landing; leaning over the banister, they watched the three roomers slowly but steadily going down the long stairway and a few moments later emerging again; the farther down they got, the more the Samsa family's interest in them wore off, and when a butcher's boy with a carrier on his head came climbing up the stairs with a proud bearing, toward them and then up on past them, Mr. Samsa and the women quickly left the banister and all went back, as if relieved, into their apartment.

They decided to spend this day resting and going for a walk; they not only deserved a break in their work, they absolutely needed one. And so they sat down at the table and wrote three letters of excuse, Mr. Samsa to the management of the bank, Mrs. Samsa to her employer, and Grete to the store owner. While they were writing, the cleaning woman came in to say that she was going, since her morning's work was done. The three letter

133

134

129 **Discussion** Have students discuss Mr. Samsa's reaction to the news of Gregor's death.

130 **Discussion** Ask students if Grete seems to have regained her sense of compassion for Gregor now that Gregor has died.

131 **Discussion** Ask students to discuss the significance of the fact that it is the beginning of spring. Point out that the coming of spring parallels the rebirth of the Samsa family following Gregor's death.

132 **Discussion** Make sure that students recognize that the Samsas have been crying. Why does Gregor's death make them feel both sad and relieved?

133 **Discussion** Have students discuss why Gregor's father suddenly has the strength and the courage to stand up to the boarders and order them out of the apartment.

134 **Discussion** Have students discuss why the Samsas decide to spend the day resting and going for a walk.

writers at first simply nodded without looking up, but as the cleaning woman still kept lingering, they looked up, annoyed. "Well?" asked Mr. Samsa. The cleaning woman stood smiling in the doorway, as if she had some great good news to announce to the family but would do so only if she were thoroughly questioned. The little ostrich feather which stood almost upright on her hat and which had irritated Mr. Samsa the whole time she had been with them swayed lightly in all directions. "What do you want?" asked Mrs. Samsa, who inspired the most respect in the cleaning woman. "Well," the cleaning woman answered, and for good-natured laughter could not immediately go on, "look, you don't have to worry about getting rid of the stuff next door. It's already been taken care of." Mrs. Samsa and Grete bent down over their letters, as if to continue writing; Mr. Samsa, who noticed that the cleaning woman was now about to start describing everything in detail, stopped her with a firmly outstretched hand. But since she was not going to be permitted to tell her story, she remembered that she was in a great hurry, cried, obviously insulted, "So long, everyone," whirled around wildly, and left the apartment with a terrible slamming of doors.

135

"We'll fire her tonight," said Mr. Samsa, but did not get an answer from either his wife or his daughter, for the cleaning woman seemed to have ruined their barely regained peace of mind. They got up, went to the window, and stayed there, holding each other tight. Mr. Samsa turned around in his chair toward them and watched them quietly for a while. Then he called, "Come on now, come over here. Stop brooding over the past. And have a little consideration for me, too." The women obeyed him at once, hurried over to him, fondled him, and quickly finished their letters.

Then all three of them left the apartment together, something they had not done in months, and took the trolley into the open country on the outskirts of the city. The car, in which they were the only passengers, was completely filled with warm sunshine. Leaning back comfortably in their seats, they discussed their prospects for the time to come, and it seemed on closer examination that these weren't bad at all, for all three positions—about which they had never really asked one another in any detail—were exceedingly advantageous and especially promising for the future. The greatest immediate improvement in their situation would come easily, of course, from a change in apartments; they would now take a smaller and cheaper apartment, but one better situated and in every way simpler to manage than the old one, which Gregor had picked for them. While they were talking in this vein, it occurred almost simultaneously to Mr. and Mrs. Samsa, as they watched their daughter getting livelier and livelier, that lately, in spite of all the troubles which had turned her cheeks pale, she had blossomed into a good-looking, shapely girl. Growing quieter and communicating almost unconsciously through glances, they thought that it would soon be time, too, to find her a good husband. And it was like a confirmation of their new dreams and good intentions when at the end of the ride their daughter got up first and stretched her young body.

Reader's Response *What is your reaction to the way in which Gregor's family treated him following his metamorphosis? Do you think they should have been more sympathetic and compassionate? Why or why not?*

THINKING ABOUT THE SELECTION

Interpreting

1. (a) How would you characterize Gregor's relationship with the office manager? (b) What is the overall attitude of Gregor's firm concerning its employees? (c) How is this attitude conveyed?

2. (a) Explain whether Gregor was happy before his metamorphosis. (b) In the first few weeks after his metamorphosis, what seems to be his attitude concerning his condition and his life in general? (c) How and why does his attitude change? (d) Explain whether Gregor's metamorphosis might be viewed as a fulfillment of his hidden desires. (e) Can his metamorphosis also be viewed as a punishment for his desires? Why or why not?

3. (a) How would you characterize Gregor's sister? (b) What is her attitude toward Gregor following his metamorphosis, and how is her attitude revealed? (c) How and why does her attitude toward Gregor change as the story progresses?

4. (a) How would you characterize Gregor's mother and father? (b) What are their respective attitudes toward Gregor following his metamorphosis, and how are their attitudes revealed?

5. (a) How does Gregor's attitude toward his family change during the course of the story? (b) What brings about the change in his attitude?

6. Contrary to what Gregor had been led to believe, his father had not actually gone bankrupt when the business failed. What does this signify?

7. (a) Why is it that Gregor does not want the furniture removed from his room? (b) Why does Grete become so determined to remove the furniture?

8. (a) How is the way in which the cleaning woman responds to Gregor different from the manner in which the family members respond to him? (b) What is the reason for this difference?

9. Why is Gregor so moved by his sister's violin playing?

10. (a) What causes Gregor's death? (b) What are his family's feelings concerning his death?

Applying

11. Explain why "The Metamorphosis" is as relevant today as it was when it was written.

ANALYZING LITERATURE

Understanding Modernism

Influenced by the developments of Sigmund Freud, the Modernists often focused on the inner thoughts of their characters and tried to re-create the inner workings of people's minds. In "The Metamorphosis," for example, Kafka pays a great deal of attention to what is happening inside Gregor's mind.

1. As is the case with most Modernist short stories, Kafka uses a limited point of view, revealing only Gregor's thoughts and feelings. How do Gregor's feelings and perceptions shape the portrayal of the other characters in the story?

2. In a typical Modernist work, the narrator never makes any judgments about the characters or offers any conclusions. Explain whether this is true with "The Metamorphosis."

3. Prior to the Modern Age, writers often began novels and short stories with expositions in which they presented important background information. Why would "The Metamorphosis" have been less effective if it had begun with an exposition?

4. Many Modernists believed that early twentieth-century life was characterized by a sense of uncertainty, alienation, detachment, and despair. Explain how this view is reflected in "The Metamorphosis."

CRITICAL THINKING AND READING

Relating a Work to the Writer's Life

Like most of Kafka's works, "The Metamorphosis" clearly reflects the impact of Kafka's own personal experiences. For example, in some respects Gregor's sense of isolation mirrors the sense of isolation that Kafka felt as a German-speaking Jew living in a society that was populated predominantly by Czech-speaking gentiles.

1. Kafka's father was a large, imposing, and strict man who played a dominant role in his son's life, instilling in him a strong sense of duty, along with feelings of fear and guilt. Although Kafka longed to please his father, he also resented him. Explain whether you think that Kafka's father might have served as a model for Mr. Samsa.

2. How does Gregor's relationship with his father seem to parallel Kafka's relationship with his father?

THINKING AND WRITING

Responding to a Writer's Statement

Write a paper in which you relate "The Metamorphosis" to Kafka's comment in the first paragraph of his biography (page 1082). Begin by rereading Kafka's quotation. Then skim through the story, keeping this comment in mind. Organize your ideas. Then write your paper, using passages from the story for support.

(continued from bottom of page)

she had no involvement with Gregor prior to his transformation.

9. Suggested response: It reawakens his human feelings and rekindles his love for his sister.

10. (a) Suggested response: Gregor gradually starves himself, because he feels he has no real reason to go on living. (b) Suggested response: They are both relieved and saddened by his death.

11. Answers will differ.

Challenge What is the theme, or main point, of "The Metamorphosis"? Support your answer with details from the story.

ANSWERS TO ANALYZING LITERATURE

1. Answers will differ. Students should note how Gregor's affection for Grete shapes the portrayal of her.

2. Suggested response: It is true of "The Metamorphosis." The narrator makes few direct statements about the characters and does not draw any conclusions about the meaning of the events.

3. Suggested response: The first sentence in the story is extremely startling. To precede this sentence with an exposition would destroy its impact.

4. Suggested response: Following his metamorphosis, Gregor is alienated and detached from other people and is uncertain about his future.

ANSWERS TO CRITICAL THINKING AND READING

1. Suggested response: It seems likely that Kafka's father did serve as a model for Mr. Samsa. Like Kafka's father, Mr. Samsa is strict and domineering and has instilled in Gregor a sense of duty and a feeling of guilt.

2. Suggested response: Like Kafka, Gregor fears his father and is bound to him by a sense of duty.

THINKING AND WRITING

Publishing Student Writing Have student volunteers read their papers aloud and use these readings as a springboard for a class discussion about the story.

---

brought about by the impact of Gregor's presence on the family's life.

4. (a) Suggested response: The father is temperamental and insensitive. The mother is loving and meek. (b) Suggested response: The father has little sympathy for Gregor and is angered by his presence. This attitude is demonstrated in his attack on Gregor. The mother still loves Gregor but is devastated by what has happened to

him and has difficulty accepting it. Her attitude is conveyed through her desire to see Gregor and through her reaction when she does see him.

5. (a) Suggested response: At first he is more concerned for their unhappiness than for himself. Later he becomes filled with rage at the miserable way they treat him. (b) Suggested response: It results from the changes in the treatment he re-

ceives from them.

6. Suggested response: Gregor's father had been taking advantage of him.

7. (a) Suggested response: The furniture is one of the few remaining links to his previous life. (b) Answers will differ.

8. (a) Suggested response: Unlike the others, the cleaning woman is not disturbed or frightened by the sight of Gregor. (b) Answers will differ. Students may respond that it is because

ANNA AKHMATOVA

1889–1966

As a young girl, Anna Akhmatova (äk mä′ tō və) became very ill. Neither her doctors nor her family thought she would survive what seemed to be a terrible case of smallpox. Because of her inner strength and determination, Akhmatova did not succumb to the illness. In fact, her illness proved to be the catalyst that brought forth Akhmatova's gift for writing poetry. Akhmatova said that somehow she knew that her poetry was connected with her mysterious illness and she was not going to deny her fate. From then on, Akhmatova proved to be one of Russia's most beloved poets.

Ann Gorenko—Akhmatova's real name—was born on June 11, 1889, in a small town on the coast of the Black Sea near Odessa. At seventeen, when Gorenko began publishing her poetry, her father asked her to change her name to dissociate herself from her family: He did not want the shame of a daughter who was a published poet. She adopted the name Akhmatova—her Tartar grandmother's name—because the southern Tartars always seemed mysterious and fascinating to her.

Throughout her career, Akhmatova's personal and autobiographical poetry was strongly influenced by people she knew and by outside events. The Russo-Japanese War, World War I, World War II, and Stalin's totalitarianism greatly influenced her writing. During Stalin's purge of writers and intellectuals in the late 1930's, Akhmatova's poetry was banned from publication, and her life was threatened simply because she was a writer. However, neither the ban on her poetry nor the threat against her life kept Akhmatova from writing. Finally, in 1940 when the ban was lifted, Akhmatova published *Anno Domini MCMXXI* and *From Six Books*.

In more personal and immediate ways, Akhmatova's life and poetry were affected by the attempted suicide of Nikolay Gumilyov (ni′ kō lT gōōm′ ə yäv), a close friend and fellow poet, who helped Akhmatova in the early years of her career. Although he did not succeed, his attempt brought close to home the possible death of a loved one.

Akhmatova's poetry exhibited several recurring characteristics through the years. One constant in her poetry was her source of inspiration. Akhmatova's poems grew out of and accurately recorded her feelings, experiences, and circumstances at the time she wrote. This is not to say, however, that she did not also add imaginary details and events. In fact, in Akhmatova's earlier poems, the people she wrote about were often fictitious people who were the doubles of people she knew.

Another constant in her poetry was the style in which she and her closest friends and contemporaries wrote. As a reaction against the Russian Symbolists, Akhmatova, Gumilyov, and Osip Mandel'shtam (ä′ sip män′ del shtäm) wrote poetry in a style they called Acmeism. Critics gave the Acmeists mixed reviews, but much of their work fell under harsh criticism, especially from the Symbolists, who dominated the Russian literary scene. Akhmatova, however, emerged even from this harsh criticism and won the hearts of her compatriots, earning a reputation as a truly gifted poet.

GUIDE FOR INTERPRETING

Everything Is Plundered; I Am Not One of Those Who Left the Land

Commentary

Acmeism. Imagine that you are a poet living in a time of war: Your country is being torn apart; brothers are fighting brothers; allegiances are blurred; and loved ones die or emigrate to another country. To express your feelings in your poetry, you have the option of using your words as a means of escaping reality or as a means of dealing with the situation then and there.

Around 1910 Russian poets were faced with this same decision. The **Symbolists,** who dominated the Russian literary scene, used their poetry as a means of transcending reality. The **Acmeists**—including Anna Akhmatova, Nikolay Gumilyov, and Osip Mandel'shtam—on the other hand, emphasized the here and now and used their poetry as a way of dealing with their experiences head on. The Acmeists, also called **Adamists,** strove for concrete imagery and clarity of expression. They wanted to look at the world with fresh eyes, like those of Adam in the Garden of Eden, hence the term Adamism. They used their poetry as a way of understanding, cherishing, and praising their world.

Amanda Haight, in *Anna Akhmatova: A Poetic Pilgrimage,* wrote the following about Acmeism.

> At the core of Acmeism was a refusal to escape into another world, a conviction that God can be found through the here and now on earth, that life is a blessing to be lived. . . .
> . . . In their outlook on life and on poetry the Acmeists were facing in a direction diametrically opposed to that of the Symbolists. As a result there was to be no escape for them from the world's realities as these grew harsher. It was necessary for them to try to reach God and to understand His purposes through understanding, living, and loving life.

In the spirit of Acmeism, Anna Akhmatova used her poetry to express her feelings about being in love and her feelings and experiences during wartime. In "Everything Is Plundered" and "I Am Not One of Those Who Left the Land," two poems she wrote during the Russian civil war, Akhmatova looked at war with the fresh eyes of the Acmeists and in her words found hope, strength, and a love for her country.

Writing

Three topics characterized Akhmatova's poetry: love, death, and war. Imagine that you were an Acmeist writing about one of these topics. Choose one, and then make a list of images that come to mind that would express your feelings about the topic.

Literary Focus Amanda Haight describes Acmeism as follows:

To discover the essence of Acmeism one must look beyond the form in which their poetry was written, beyond such things as the subjects they treated or even their politics. The outlook they shared was exactly in line with what the manifestoes of Acmeism demanded—a return to earth. With this went a deep understanding of the richness of European culture and the close ties between poets of all ages. At the core of Acmeism was a refusal to escape into another world, a conviction that God can be found through the here and now on earth, that life is a blessing to be lived.

Acmeism was a short-lived literary movement in Russia. Ask students why this might have been the case.

Writing/Prior Knowledge Discuss with students their views on these three themes. What experiences, if any, have they had? How would they describe those experiences? Then tell them to complete the writing activity.

ESL Teaching Strategy Ask ESL students why they left their homelands. If some left because of conflict, ask them to relate their feelings to the speaker's attitude in the poem.

Teaching Tenth-Grade Students Discuss with tenth-grade students what the human spirit is. Point out that in times of crisis people have a tendency to rise above the finite and immediate and view a larger picture. Then have them read Akhmatova's poems.

Humanities Note

Fine art, *Above the Trees* by Emily Carr. Carr (1871–1945), was born in Victoria, British Columbia. She was an Expressionist painter of landscapes, forests, and Indians of her native country. Her colorful, bold style was not immediately accepted and she led a very secluded existence making and selling carpets and pottery. Eventually she was discovered by the director of the National Gallery of Canada and found critical support.

Her most successful period was the 1930's and 1940's when her style was a very powerful, colorful expression of nature, such as this painting exhibits.

Ask students which lines of the poem this painting best illustrates.

Motivation/Prior Knowledge

Discuss with students their definition of patriotism. What does it mean to say that someone is patriotic? Do they believe they are patriotic? How would they feel if their country were invaded and taken over by foreign powers? Would they stay? If so, how would they feel toward those who left the country?

Purpose-Setting Question

How does Akhmatova feel about her homeland?

Closure and Extension

ANSWERS TO THINKING ABOUT THE SELECTION

1. Suggested responses: (a) Akhmatova is perhaps describing the destruction of war, with its death, betrayals, and miseries. (b) She is describing and reveling in the peaceful, serene beauty of nature in the summer and at night.
2. The effect of this contrasting imagery is stark and riveting. In the first stanza, all is destroyed, dead, and lost; in the second stanza nature and life are beautiful and alive.
3. Suggested response: The miracle she is referring to is the miracle of life and perhaps God.
4. Answers may differ. Suggested response: She sees that war destroys lives and possessions. War is like "death's great black wing" that destroys and kills everything in its

ABOVE THE TREES
Emily Carr
Vancouver Art Gallery

Everything Is Plundered

Anna Akhmatova

translated by Stanley Kunitz

Everything is plundered, betrayed, sold,
Death's great black wing scrapes the air,
Misery gnaws to the bone.
Why then do we not despair?

5 By day, from the surrounding woods,
cherries blow summer into town;
at night the deep transparent skies
glitter with new galaxies.

And the miraculous comes so close
10 to the ruined, dirty houses—
something not known to anyone at all,
but wild in our breast for centuries.

THINKING ABOUT THE SELECTION

Interpreting

1. (a) What is Akhmatova describing in the first stanza?
   (b) What is she describing in the second stanza?
2. What is the effect of this contrasting imagery?
3. What is the miracle Akhmatova refers to in line 9?
4. What is Akhmatova's attitude about war and its destructive power?
5. What understanding or new insight about life does Akhmatova reveal in this poem?

Applying

6. What can we and future generations learn from this poem?

ANALYZING LITERATURE

Understanding Acmeism

Acmeism, a movement in Russian poetry, was a style of writing in which the poet stressed the here and now. Using concrete imagery and concise, clear language, the Acmeists used their poetry as a means of dealing with their reality, not as a means of escaping from it. They embraced and cherished life, looked at life with fresh eyes, and gained new insight and understanding through their poetry.

1. How does Akhmatova stand up to the harsh realities of her world in "Everything Is Plundered"?
2. Explain how Akhmatova shows how she cherishes and celebrates life in this poem.

path. The destruction of war is so great that you can feel the pain and misery deep in your bones.
5. Answers may differ. Suggested response: Akhmatova recognizes the destructive power of war, yet she asks, "Why then do we not despair?" She does not despair because she also sees the beauty of life and the resiliency of the human spirit. It is something of which we are not aware, but

it is "wild in our breast for centuries."
6. Most students will respond that we can learn how futile war is. Despite its ability to destroy everything else, it is unable to completely destroy the human spirit.

ANSWERS TO ANALYZING LITERATURE

1. Suggested response: Akhmatova is

not afraid to take a good hard look at the destruction of war and its effect on people's lives.
2. Suggested response: She cherishes life because she does not abandon it. She also sees the beauty in life and sees life as a miracle.

I Am Not One of Those Who Left the Land

Anna Akhmatova

translated by Stanley Kunitz

1 **Enrichment** This poem was written at the time of the Russian civil
war, the war from which Lenin and
the Bolsheviks emerged victorious.

2 **Discussion** What is Akhmatova's
attitude toward those who stayed
in Russia? What evidence of
courage do you find in these two
stanzas?

I am not one of those who left the land
to the mercy of its enemies.
Their flattery leaves me cold,
my songs are not for them to praise.

5 But I pity the exile's lot.
Like a felon, like a man half-dead,
dark is your path, wanderer;
wormwood infects your foreign bread.

But here, in the murk of conflagration,[1]
10 where scarcely a friend is left to know,
we, the survivors, do not flinch
from anything, not from a single blow.

Surely the reckoning will be made
after the passing of this cloud.
15 We are the people without tears,
straighter than you . . . more proud . . .

---

1. **conflagration** (kän´ flə grā´ shən) *n.*: A destructive fire.

Reader's Response *What surprised you most, or what did you like best, about Akhmatova's poetry? Explain.*

THINKING ABOUT THE SELECTION

Interpreting

1. What is Akhmatova's attitude toward those who fled Russia?
2. Why does Akhmatova use the simile "Like a felon, like a man half-dead, / dark is your path, wanderer"?
3. (a) Akhmatova uses the pronoun *we* in line 15. To whom is she referring? (b) To whom is she referring with the pronoun *you?*

4. Define the word *patriot*. Do you consider Akhmatova a patriot? Support your answer with evidence from the poem.

Applying

5. (a) Imagine "one of those who left the land." What reasons might this person give to Akhmatova? (b) Do you think that it is ever right for people to leave their land "to the mercy of its enemies"? Explain your answer.

(continued from bottom of page)

sponses: (a) It is possible that many of the deserters were intellectuals who had to leave to save their lives; others perhaps left because of a lack of loyalty to their homeland. (b) Circumstances and reasons people flee their homelands are different for every person. Most students will probably support the idea that if the United States were in danger of foreign invasion, they would stay to fight.

Universal Themes The love of her homeland that Akhmatova expresses in her poetry is present in other works as well. You might also have students read Homer's *Iliad*, page 335; Callinus' "A Call to Arms," page 395; Thucydides' "Pericles' Funeral Oration," page 408; Virgil's *Aeneid*, page 493; and Nguyen Thi Vinh's "Thoughts of Hanoi," page 1436.

Cultural Note Many writers have influenced Akhmatova's life and poetry, including Dante, Byron, Pushkin, Cervantes, and Oscar Wilde. Ask students how the works of Dante, Pushkin, and Cervantes, all of whom are included in *World Masterpieces*, might have influenced Akhmatova's poetry.

Cooperative Learning Historical events have often influenced and been the topic of many writers' works. Have students research the works of world writers from a determined period of time. Tell them to select the most representative pieces that illustrate from a literary perspective what was happening at the time. Students can then compile them in a book that can serve as a literary history book.

Closure and Extension

ANSWERS TO THINKING ABOUT THE SELECTION

1. Akhmatova is bitter toward those who left Russia "to the mercy of its enemies." As an Acmeist, she believed that people should stand up for what they believe and face life head on, not run away from it.

2. Akhmatova is comparing the deserters to a felon, a criminal who left the scene of a crime. She says that those who left the land will live as though they are half-dead and their lives will be dark.

3. Answers may differ. Suggested responses: (a) She is referring to her fellow Russians; she could also be referring to humankind. (b) She is referring to the deserters—those who left Russia as well as those who have left any country during a time of great need.

4. Answers may differ. Suggested response: Patriotism is love and loyalty to one's country. According to this definition Akhmatova is indeed a patriot. She loves her country dearly and was even willing to stay and die rather than leave her country.

5. Answers may differ. Suggested re-

BORIS PASTERNAK

1890–1960

Throughout his life, Boris Pasternak (pas′ tər nak) was regarded as one of Russia's greatest poets and novelists. In fact, unlike many of his contemporaries who suffered profoundly during the Stalin years, Pasternak's poetic abilities insulated him to a certain extent from the turmoil during these years in Russia.

Boris Pasternak was born in Moscow on February 10, 1890. His father, Leonid Pasternak, was an accomplished painter, and his mother, Rosa Kaufman, was a professional concert pianist. Pasternak said that he owed "much if not everything" to his father and mother. In a letter he wrote to his parents, he said: "Sometimes it seems to me that . . . if ever I have achieved something, then somewhere in the depths of my being I had been doing it for you." From his mother and father, Pasternak acquired the gifts and dedication of an artist.

Pasternak also drew inspiration from Alexander Scriabin (skrē ä′ bin), a Russian composer and pianist, and from Leo Tolstoy, a Russian novelist and philosopher (see page 942). After his meeting with Scriabin in 1903, Pasternak began studying music. But it was Tolstoy, a close friend of Pasternak's father, who influenced Pasternak's literary career and education.

Although he originally enrolled at the Law Faculty of Moscow University, Pasternak later transferred to a philosophy program. He studied philosophy in Germany from 1912 to 1914. After graduation Pasternak published his first collection of poems, *The Twin in the Clouds*.

When Russia entered World War I in 1914, a leg injury kept Pasternak out of the army. Fortunately, this was the first of many atrocities from which Pasternak would escape. While most of his friends and contemporaries emigrated, suffered in prison camps, or were exiled during the Stalin purge of the late 1930's, Pasternak led a relatively calm life. During the height of the purge, Pasternak was unable to publish his work. It is possible that Pasternak was spared the harsher fates of his contemporaries either by virtue of his friendship with Stalin's wife, Alliluyeva (al lē′ lū yev′ ə), or because of his translations of the Georgian poets whom Stalin admired. During the ban on publishing, Pasternak spent his time translating the plays of Goethe and Shakespeare.

During World War II, when Pasternak was in his fifties and too old to be drafted, he published two more poetry collections: *On Early Trains* (1943) and *Spacious Earth* (1945).

After Stalin's death in 1953, Pasternak began writing his famous novel *Doctor Zhivago*. He was denied publication in the U.S.S.R. because the novel offended Soviet authorities. His novel was first published in Russian in Italy; the English translation appeared in 1958. Although *Doctor Zhivago* was read by many in Russia through underground editions, it was officially published in the Soviet Union in 1988 as a series in a magazine.

In 1958 Pasternak received the Nobel Prize for Literature, which he gladly accepted. The Soviet authorities, however, forced him to withdraw his acceptance by threats of persecution against his intimate friend, Olga Ivinskaya (ē vin skī′ ə). After pleading with Soviet officials, Pasternak was allowed to remain in the Soviet Union but was expelled from the Soviet Writers' Union. He lived the remaining two years of his life in virtual exile in the artists' community outside Moscow.

GUIDE FOR INTERPRETING

The Drowsy Garden;
The Weeping Garden

Commentary

Imagery and Figures of Speech. **Imagery** is language that helps form a mental picture by appealing to one or more of the senses. Imagery can communicate one's experiences vividly, making the reader see, feel, hear, smell, and taste the experiences of the poet.

To create an image, writers will often use such figures of speech as similes and metaphors. A **simile** is a figure of speech that suggests a comparison between two basically unlike subjects using a connective word such as *like* or *as*.

A **metaphor** also suggests a comparison between dissimilar subjects but without using a connective word. Whereas a simile will suggest, for example, that the branch against the window is *like* the lace in embroidery, a metaphor suggests that the pattern of the branch *is* lace.

Pasternak, like many other Russian authors, wrote poems that as a whole were metaphors for something larger than what the poems at first appeared to be. **Imagism,** or Imaginism, was a poetic movement in Russia that stressed the use of imagery. Pasternak and the other Imagists believed that the true basis of poetry was the metaphor.

Writing

Picture a garden in late summer. What images come to mind? Freewrite, describing each of these images.

Literary Criticism

In *The Three Worlds of Boris Pasternak*, Robert Payne writes the following about Pasternak's work: "From the beginning . . . [Pasternak] was concerned with the tangible earth, with nature in all her moods, with the human condition in all its amazing variety. He remains a difficult poet because his vision is intricate and conveyed with an extraordinary density of imagery. He defies translation; and no one has yet succeeded in conveying in English the richness of his vocabulary, the leaping brilliance of his rhythms, the way he gives the impression of writing in a language he has invented this morning. Yet no one could be more tradition-bound. His verse patterns are the simplest imaginable. . . ."

The Drowsy Garden

Boris Pasternak

translated by Babette Deutsch

The drowsy garden scatters insects
Bronze as the ash from braziers[1] blown.
Level with me and with my candle,
Hang flowering worlds, their leaves full-grown.

5 As into some unheard-of dogma[2]
I move across into this night,
Where a worn poplar age has grizzled
Screens the moon's strip of fallow[3] light,

Where the pond lies, an open secret,
10 Where apple bloom is surf and sigh,
And where the garden, a lake dwelling,
Holds out in front of it the sky.

---

1. braziers (brā′ zhərz) *n.*: Metal pans or bowls used to hold burning coals or charcoal.
2. dogma (dôg′ mə) *n.*: A doctrine or belief or a set of doctrines and beliefs.
3. fallow (fal′ ō) *adj.*: Inactive.

The Weeping Garden

Boris Pasternak

translated by Phillip C. Flayderman

How horrible! It drips and listens,
    Is it then the only one in the world
That pushes the branch in at the window,
    Like a bit of lace in embroidery? Or someone *is*
        watching.

5 I hear the spongy earth.
    Weighed down by its own sogginess,
And listen: Far off, as in August,
    Midnight ripens in the fields.

No sounds; no secret watchers.
10   Convinced it is alone, starts up again,
Rolling down the roof,
    Over and under gutters.

I will lift it to my lips and listen.
    Am I alone on earth?
15 Am I ready to weep for this?
    Or someone *is* watching.

Silence. Not a leaf stirs.
    No sign of light; only pathetic sobs
And scraping of slippers and sighing
20   And tears in the pauses.

Reader's Response *How might reading these two poems affect how you will think or feel about similar scenes in the future? Explain.*

PICKING FLOWERS
Pierre Auguste Renoir
National Gallery of Art

THINKING ABOUT THE SELECTION

Interpreting

1. Why is *drowsy* an effective description of the garden Pasternak creates in the first poem?
2. What is the speaker's attitude toward the garden and nature? How do you know?
3. "The Weeping Garden" comes from a collection entitled *My Sister, Life*. (a) What is the meaning of the title? (b) How does this poem fit into the theme of the collection?
4. (a) What effect does the repetition of the phrase "Or someone *is* watching" have? (b) Why does the translator emphasize the word by italicizing it?
5. Pasternak often projects his feelings and actions on nature or aspects of nature. In line 10, what might Pasternak be implying about himself through the imagery that he and the garden are one or equal?
6. What might Pasternak be implying or describing on a larger scale in these two poems?

ANALYZING LITERATURE

Understanding Imagery and Figures of Speech

Imagery creates a mental picture in the mind of the reader. For example, the phrase "Hang flowering worlds" creates a strong impression that the phrase "the flowers were in bloom" does not. Often writers will use **figures of speech** such as similes and metaphors to create an image.

1. To what senses do Pasternak's images appeal in these poems? Explain how the image appeals to each sense.
2. Pasternak often uses water as an image to represent life. What is Pasternak's attitude toward life in these two poems, which both contain an image of water?
3. List two similes from these two poems. (a) What is the effect of these similes? (b) Do they effectively create an image in your mind? Why or why not?
4. Find one metaphor in these poems and describe its effect.

COLETTE

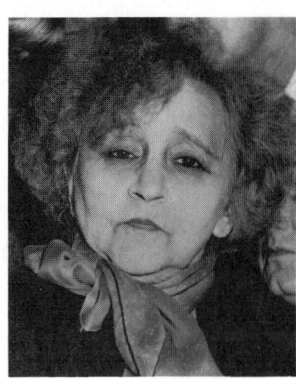

1873–1954

No other writer captured what it was like to be a woman in late nineteenth- and early twentieth-century France better than Colette (kȏ let′). Yet in the way that she lived her life, Colette might be viewed as a woman who was ahead of her time. Living in an age when the women's rights movement was still in its infancy, she proved that a woman could be strong, determined, independent, and extremely successful.

Colette was born in the small village of St.-Sauveur-en-Puisaye (san so vᵾr′ àn püē zā) in the French province of Burgundy. As a child, she was taught by her strong-willed mother to savor and contemplate the sights, sounds, textures, and aromas of country life, an appreciation that would later be reflected in her fiction. Before her twentieth birthday, she married Henri Gauthier-Villars (àn rē′ gō tyā′ vē làr′), a mediocre writer fourteen years her senior. By providing her with valuable encouragement and support and by introducing her to many of the most prominent French writers of the time, her new husband played a vital role in launching her literary career. In fact, it was her husband who was responsible for publishing her first series of novels, known as the "Claudine" novels, under the pseudonym Willy.

After her marriage failed in 1906, Colette lived freely and independently for several years. During this period she continued to develop her skills as a writer, while also indulging in a number of other creative endeavors, including singing, dancing, and hairdressing. Colette's experiences as an independent woman inspired two successful books, *The Vagabond* (1911) and *Recaptured* (1913).

In 1912 she married Henri de Jouvenel (àn rē′ də zhȏȏ və nel′), a prominent journalist. The marriage lasted twelve years, ending in divorce in 1924. In the midst of the failure of her second marriage, however, Colette emerged as a famous and critically acclaimed writer, publishing such highly regarded works as *Chéri* (1920), *My Mother's House* (1922), *The Ripening* (1923), *The Last of Chéri* (1926), and *Sido* (1929). Two of these works, *Chéri* and *The Last of Chéri*, focus on a tragic love affair between a young man and an older woman, while the other works deal with the experiences of childhood and adolescence.

Colette married her third husband, Maurice Goudeket (mȏ rēs′ gȏȏ də kē′), another writer, in 1935. Unlike her first two marriages, her marriage to Goudeket brought her great happiness and satisfaction and lasted for the remainder of her life. Unfortunately, her happiness was tainted by the onset of crippling arthritis and by her husband's arrest and imprisonment by the Nazis during World War II. These setbacks did not affect her productivity as a writer, however, and in the 1930's and 1940's she wrote many successful books, exploring a wide range of themes. These books include *The Cat* (1933), *Duo* (1934), *Gigi* (1944), and *The Blue Light* (1949).

By the time of her death in 1954, Colette had written over fifty novels or novellas and an even more impressive number of short stories. Among the French public she had established herself as a literary legend, and she had received a number of distinguished literary honors, including her induction into both the Royal Belgian Academy and the French Goncourt Academy. During the years since her death, her reputation has continued to grow, and she is now regarded by many as the outstanding French fiction writer of her time.

Objectives

Thematic

To learn how a character deals with adult disappointment and cherishes childhood memories

Skills

1 To recognize how epiphanies

are used in stories
2 To appreciate the significance of word origins
3 To write a letter using the persona of a character from a story
4 To practice sequencing

GUIDE FOR INTERPRETING

The Bracelet

Commentary

Epiphany. An **epiphany** is something that virtually all people experience at one time or another during the course of their lives. It is a sudden flash of insight or a revelation that a person has about himself or herself, another person, a specific event or situation, or life in general. For example, in the near future an event might occur in your own life that will lead you to a sudden realization that you have matured into an adult.

The term *epiphany* is derived from Greek mythology, where it was used to describe the occasion when a god or goddess, wearing a disguise or concealed in a cloud, would suddenly reveal his or her true identity to a mortal. In many Christian churches, Epiphany (spelled with a capital letter) refers to an annual festival held on January 6 (the twelfth day of Christmas), commemorating the revelation of the baby Jesus to the three wise men (Magi). Influenced by his religious upbringing, the highly regarded Irish novelist James Joyce (1882–1941) was the first writer to use the word as a literary term, defining it as a profound mental or spiritual revelation experienced by a character in a literary work.

Although the term *epiphany* is still most often associated with the works of Joyce, epiphanies also occur in works by many other twentieth-century writers. The use of epiphanies in twentieth-century literature has resulted partly from the decision of most fiction writers to abandon the traditional plot structure, in which the sequence of events ultimately leads to the resolution of the conflict, by ending their stories with the conflicts left unresolved. As an alternative, writers began constructing plots so that they lead to an epiphany. In "The Bracelet," for example, the plot culminates in the epiphany of the main character, Madame Augelier.

Writing

Colette once wrote, "By means of an image we are often able to hold on to our lost belongings. But it is the desperateness of losing which picks the flowers of memory, binds the bouquet." Freewrite, exploring the meaning of the quotation and your reaction to it.

Primary Source

In his autobiographical narrative, *Stephen Hero*, which he later reworked into his first novel, *Portrait of the Artist as a Young Man*, Joyce offered the following definition of an epiphany: "By an epiphany he [the protagonist, Stephen Daedalus] meant a sudden spiritual manifestation, whether in vulgarity of speech or of gesture or in a memorable phase of the mind itself. He believed it was for the man of letters to record these epiphanies with extreme care, seeing that they themselves are the most delicate and evanescent of moments."

Literary Focus Begin by mentioning epiphanies in the lives of authors in this book. Tell students about Pascal's apparition (page 828) and Dante's encounter with Beatrice (page 618). Have them recall any experiences of their own that were like epiphanies.

Writing/Prior Knowledge Before having students do the writing assignment that follows the Commentary, ask them to recall some things they have lost that were important to them. Have them jot down several such items. Then place those in a list with priority given to the most significant of the losses.

ESL Teaching Strategy Have ESL students choose native-speaking partners with whom to work. Let them look up definitions and pronunciations for each of the following words from the opening page of the text: *mechanically, recounted, slithered,* and *brilliants.*

Teaching Tenth-Grade Students Ask tenth-grade students to recall some special gift they cherished in younger years. Discuss why no new present could ever take its place.

Vocabulary
Preteach the following vocabulary words:
supple (sup´ 'l) *adj.* : Easily bent, flexible
connoisseur (kän´ə sur) *n.* : Person with expert taste
convalescent (kän və les´ ənt) *adj.* : Gradually recovering health after illness
enraptured (in rap´ chərd) *v.*: Filled with great pleasure
iridescent (ir´ə des´ nt) *adj.*: Showing shifting changes in color
bangle (baŋ´g'l) *n.* : Decorative bracelet
congealed (kən jēld´) *v.* : Solidified; thickened

Support Material

Teaching Portfolio
Teacher Backup, p. 1311
Usage and Mechanics Worksheet, p. 1315
Vocabulary Check, p. 1316
Analyzing Literature Worksheet, *Understanding Epiphany*, p.1317
Critical Thinking and Reading Worksheet, *Identifying Cause and*

Effect, p. 1318
Selection Test, pp. 1319–1320
Essay Questions and Evaluation Guidelines, p. 1439

Art Transparency 14
The Studio by Pablo Picasso.

Spelling Tip Write the word *connoisseur* on the chalkboard. Point out that both the letter *n* and the letter *s* are repeated in the correct spelling.

The Bracelet

Colette

translated by Matthew Ward

". . . Twenty-seven, twenty-eight, twenty-nine . . . There really are twenty-nine . . ."

Madame Augelier mechanically counted and recounted the little *pavé*[1] diamonds. Twenty-nine square brilliants, set in a bracelet, which slithered between her fingers like a cold and supple snake. Very white, not too big, admirably matched to each other—the pretty bijou[2] of a connoisseur. She fastened it on her wrist, and shook it, throwing off blue sparks under the electric candles; a hundred tiny rainbows, blazing with color, danced on the white tablecloth. But Madame Augelier was looking more closely instead at the other bracelet, the three finely engraved creases encircling her wrist above the glittering snake.

"Poor François . . . what will he give me next year, if we're both still here?"

François Augelier, industrialist, was traveling in Algeria at the time, but, present or absent, his gift marked both the year's end and their wedding anniversary. Twenty-eight jade bowls, last year; twenty-seven old enamel plaques mounted on a belt, the year before . . .

"And the twenty-six little Royal Dresden[3] plates . . . And the twenty-four meters of antique Alençon lace[4] . . ." With a slight effort of memory Madame Augelier could have gone back as far as four modest silver place settings, as far as three pairs of silk stockings . . .

"We weren't rich back then. Poor François, he's always spoiled me so . . ." To herself, secretly, she called him "poor François," because she believed herself guilty of not loving him enough, underestimating the strength of affectionate habits and abiding fidelity.

Madame Augelier raised her hand, tucked her little finger under, extended her wrist to erase the bracelet of wrinkles, and repeated intently, "It's so pretty . . . the diamonds are so white . . . I'm so pleased . . ." Then she let her hand fall back down and admitted to herself that she was already tired of her new bracelet.

"But I'm not ungrateful," she said naively with a sigh. Her weary eyes wandered from the flowered tablecloth to the gleaming window. The smell of some Calville apples in a silver bowl made her feel slightly sick and she left the dining room.

In her boudoir[5] she opened the steel case which held her jewels, and adorned her left hand in honor of the new bracelet. Her ring had on it a black onyx band and a blue-tinted brilliant; onto her delicate, pale, and somewhat wrinkled little finger, Madame Augelier slipped a circle of dark sapphires. Her prematurely white hair, which she did not dye, appeared even whiter as she adjusted amid slightly frizzy curls a narrow fillet sprinkled with a dusting of diamonds, which she immediately untied and took off again.

---

1. *pavé* (pà vā´): A setting of jewelry in which the gems are placed close together so that no metal shows.

2. **bijou** (bē´ zhoo) *n.*: A jewel.

3. **Royal Dresden** (drez´ dən): A fine, decorated porcelain or chinaware made near Dresden, a city in south-central Germany.

4. **Alençon** (ə len´ sən) **lace:** A needlepoint lace with a solid design on a net background.

---

5. **boudoir** (bood´ wär) *n.*: A woman's bedroom, dressing room, or private sitting room.

PORTRAIT OF MADAME MAYDEN
Amedeo Modigliani

Humanities Note

Fine art, *Portrait of Madame Mayden* by Amedeo Modigliani. Modigliani (1884–1920) was born of wealthy parents in Leghorn, Italy, and received his artistic training in Paris, where he was influenced by the work of Cézanne.

Modigliani was also a noted sculptor. During his short life he was often ill with tuberculosis and alcoholism. His paintings often conveyed a sense of melancholy.

Notice the characteristic Modigliani elongation of features and the graceful lines in this painting.

You might want to use the following questions to discuss the art:

1. How would you describe the subject's character?
2. Does she fit your own image of Madame Augelier?
3. What mood has Modigliani created?
4. What contributes to this mood?

"I don't know what's wrong with me. I'm not feeling all that well. Being fifty is a bore, basically . . ."

She felt restless, both terribly hungry and sick to her stomach, like a convalescent whose appetite the fresh air has yet to restore.

"Really now, is a diamond actually as pretty as all that?"

Madame Augelier craved a visual pleasure which would involve the sense of taste as well; the unexpected sight of a lemon, the unbearable squeaking of the knife cutting it in half, makes the mouth water with desire . . .

"But I don't want a lemon. Yet this nameless pleasure which escapes me does exist, I know it does, I remember it! Yes, the blue glass bracelet . . ."

A shudder made Madame Augelier's slack cheeks tighten. A vision, the duration of which she could not measure, granted her, for a second time, a moment lived forty years earlier, that incomparable moment as she looked, enraptured, at the color of the day, the iridescent, distorted image of objects seen through a blue glass bangle, moved around in a circle, which she had just been given. That piece of perhaps Oriental glass, broken a few hours later, had held in it a new universe, shapes not the inventions of dreams, slow, serpentine animals moving in pairs, lamps, rays of light congealed in an atmosphere of indescribable blue . . .

The vision ended and Madame Augelier fell back, bruised, into the present, into reality.

But the next day she began searching, from antique shops to flea markets, from flea markets to crystal shops, for a glass bracelet, a certain color of blue. She put the passion of a collector, the precaution, the dissimulation[6] of a lunatic into her search. She ventured into what she called "impossible districts," left her car at the corner of strange streets, and in the end, for a few centimes, she found a circle of blue glass which she recognized in the darkness, stammered as she paid for it, and carried it away.

In the discreet light of her favorite lamp she set the bracelet on the dark field of an old piece of velvet, leaned forward, and waited for the shock . . . But all she saw was a round piece of bluish glass, the trinket of a child or a savage, hastily made and blistered with bubbles; an object whose color and material her memory and reason recognized; but the powerful and sensual genius who creates and nourishes the marvels of childhood, who gradually weakens, then dies mysteriously within us, did not even stir.

Resigned, Madame Augelier thus came to know how old she really was and measured the infinite plain over which there wandered, beyond her reach, a being detached from her forever, a stranger, turned away from her, rebellious and free even from the bidding of memory: a little ten-year-old girl wearing on her wrist a bracelet of blue glass.

---

6. **dissimulation** (di sim′ yə lā′ shən) *n.*: The hiding of one's feelings or motives by pretense.

Reader's Response *Do you sympathize with Madame Augelier and the feelings she expresses in this story? Why or why not?*

THINKING ABOUT THE SELECTION

Interpreting

1. (a) How would you describe Madame Augelier's reaction to her anniversary gift? (b) What are the reasons why she reacts in this manner?
2. (a) What seems to be the nature of Madame Augelier's relationship with her husband? (b) How is the nature of their relationship conveyed? (c) What changes in their relationship seem to have taken place in the years since they were first married?
3. Why does Madame Augelier feel restless, hungry, and sick to her stomach?
4. (a) Why does Madame Augelier stammer as she pays for the new blue-glass bracelet? (b) Why does the new one not have the same effect on her as the one she was given as a child?
5. Do you think the title of this story refers to the diamond bracelet or to the blue bracelet? Support your answer.
6. Considering Madame Augelier's state of mind at the end of the story, how do you envision her future? Explain your answer.

Applying

7. When adults return to places that they loved as a child, they often find that the places do not live up to their memories of them. Why do you think this happens?
8. What gifts did you receive as a young child that had an especially strong impact on you? Explain.

ANALYZING LITERATURE

Understanding Epiphany

Epiphanies, or sudden flashes of insight, often occur in modern and contemporary short stories that delve into the thoughts and feelings of a character or a number of characters. "The Bracelet" is an example of such a story.

1. What sudden realization does Madame Augelier come to at the end of the story?
2. (a) What prompts Madame Augelier's epiphany? (b) Does her epiphany seem believable? Explain your answer.
3. How does the epiphany relate to the theme of "The Bracelet"?

CRITICAL THINKING AND READING

Sequencing Events

The **sequence of events** in a story is called its plot. Place each of the following events in their proper sequence. Number the event that happens first 1.
1. Madame Augelier remembers the blue-glass bracelet.
2. François Augelier gives his wife a diamond bracelet.
3. Madame Augelier begins searching in flea markets.
4. Madame Augelier realizes that she is old.
5. The smell of some Calville apples makes Madame Augelier feel sick.

UNDERSTANDING LANGUAGE

Appreciating Word Origins

Just as the literary traditions and movements of different countries often feed on and influence one another, most languages are to some extent shaped and influenced by other languages. For example, many English words were borrowed or derived from other languages. The word *bracelet,* for instance, comes from the Latin word *brachium,* meaning "arm."

Using a dictionary that provides etymologies, find the earliest language of origin of each of the following words from Matthew Ward's translation of "The Bracelet."

1. bijou
2. connoisseur
3. serpentine
4. dissimulation
5. antique

THINKING AND READING

Writing a Letter

Putting yourself in the place of Madame Augelier, write a letter to your husband in which you discuss the revelation that you had after buying the blue-glass bracelet. Begin by reviewing the story, noting what it suggests about Madame Augelier's relationship with her husband. As you write your letter, keep the nature of their relationship in mind. In other words the letter should not be written in a loving tone if you do not feel that Madame Augelier has a loving attitude toward her husband. When you have finished writing, revise the letter, making sure it clearly expresses the feelings that Madame Augelier has at the end of the story.

PAUL VALÉRY

Focus

More About the Author Paul Valéry began writing poetry in 1884, when he was just thirteen years old. His first poem was published five years later. By nineteen he had written almost two hundred poems. During his writing career, Valéry wrote for several literary journals. He was also interested in journalism and for a while was a reporter stationed in South Africa for the British South Africa Company. A bout with illness returned him to France in 1897 where he worked for the artillery munitions bureau of the French army.

Despite the amount of poetry he had already written, Valéry was relatively unknown. Following the publication of "The Young Fate" in 1917, however, Valéry won critical acclaim that brought him public notoriety and a greater demand for his poetry and commentary.

In the spring of 1945, Valéry knew that he had cancer. He died in July 1945 at age seventy-three. Upon Valéry's death General de Gaulle requested a state funeral.

Ask students why someone who clearly loved poetry might suddenly stop and enter a "silent period."

Critical Evaluation Paul Valéry was intensely curious about the creative process and the role of poetry and poets. In his book *Paul Valéry*, H.A.L. Fisher describes Valéry's curiosity as follows:

> The things that interest [Valéry] are the theory of the arts and the processes of his own thinking. . . . As he conceives the business of the poet, it is not to paint the outward face of nature or the visible spectacle of human events, but to dive into the recesses of the personal consciousness and to extract whatever pearls the deep may yield. . . . It is only by the dragnets of the mind sunk to the uttermost depths of human nature that the most precious secrets of the spirit are revealed.

1871–1945

As Paul Valéry (pôl và lā rē´) became more involved in writing poetry, he became increasingly curious about the creative process. His curiosity grew to such proportions that he could no longer tolerate his imperfect poetry. As a result, from 1892 to 1917, Valéry faded into reclusive investigations of math and psychology in search of a scientifically based theory of the creative process. Although during his "silent years" he primarily studied math and science, he did not completely abandon his poetry and prose writing. In fact, in 1917, Valéry published "The Young Fate," the poem that made him famous throughout Europe.

Valéry was born on October 30, 1871, in Sète, a small Mediterranean coastal town in France. As a young boy, Valéry spent many summers in Italy, where he learned about Italian architecture and literature. At fourteen he moved to Montpellier, where he studied at the lycée. He then studied law at the University of Montpellier.

While at Montpellier, Valéry met poet Pierre Louÿs (pyer lwē). Louÿs introduced Valéry to literary circles and to the symbolist poet Stéphane Mallarmé (stā fan´ mà làr mā´). Mallarmé's poetry and symbolist philosophy greatly influenced Valéry's own writing. Valéry was also influenced by his reading of the American poet and poetry theorist Edgar Allan Poe, whose poetry taught him about the melodious verbal combinations that are possible in poetry.

Valéry experimented with symbolist poetry. His fascination with the creative process was the stimulus for much of his poetry and prose. However, he soon became disillusioned and skeptical of writing's imperfections that arise out of the limitations of language and the artist's creative powers. It is possible that the combination of Valéry's unsatisfied opinion of his published work in *Album de vers anciens* in 1890 and the death of Mallarmé in 1898 acted as catalysts for Valéry's "silent period" and his subsequent investigations into discovering the mechanism behind the creative process, or the art of creating art.

Valéry recorded his scientific and mathematical insights in personal notebooks, the *Cahiers* (kà yā´), which filled twenty-nine volumes. He did not intend publishing his notebooks, but he did publish many entries and published the poetry and prose sparked by his reflections. All twenty-nine volumes of the *Cahiers* were published posthumously between 1957 and 1961.

Valéry's retreat into his own studies was not entirely out of character. Valéry had a strong aversion to fame and to being in the public light. Despite this, once Valéry emerged from his silent period, he did go before the public to receive a series of awards and appointments. In 1921 a public opinion poll chose Valéry as the greatest living poet. In 1925 he was elected to the French Academy. In 1926 he participated as a member of the Committee on Intellectual Cooperation of the League of Nations. Seven years later the French government elected Valéry administrator of the Centre Universitaire Méditerranéen at Nice. Then in 1935 he became a member of the Academy of Sciences of Lisbon and received honorary degrees from Coimbra and Oxford universities. In 1937 he was elected Chair of Poetics at the College of France and served as a professor of poetry until his death in 1945.

Objectives

Thematic
To understand a writer's role

Skills
1 To understand symbolism
2 To write using symbolism

Support Material

Teaching Portfolio
Teacher Backup, p. 1321
Usage and Mechanics Worksheet, p. 1325
Vocabulary Check, p. 1326
Analyzing Literature Worksheet, *Understanding Symbolism*, p. 1327
Language Worksheet, *Understanding Denotation and Connotation*, p. 1328
Selection Test, pp. 1329–1330

GUIDE FOR INTERPRETING

Caesar, The Friendly Wood, Palm

Commentary

Symbolism. The Symbolist movement, which was influential in Valéry's work, was primarily a reaction against Realism. The Realists strove to represent life accurately and realistically in the arts. Many Symbolists disagreed with the Realist philosophy; instead, they used symbols to suggest ideas and themes and manipulated reality in order to rise above reality or to reach a higher state of consciousness.

The Symbolists believed that language in and of itself was insufficient to reveal the deeper level of meaning or consciousness that they thought was possible to achieve. Although language was insufficient, poetry and the use of symbols were sufficient to point to a higher reality. The purpose of the poem was to take the reader beyond the poem itself to another level of meaning or experience. One strain of Symbolist poetry strove to achieve a higher reality or unity with God or the universe.

It is important to remember that a **symbol** is similar to an image in that it is a literal and concrete representation of a sensory experience. But, unlike an image, a symbol goes beyond the image to another level of meaning. A symbol suggests a deeper meaning; it does not "stand for" the meaning.

Valéry strove to write musical verse because he believed that music is the purest form of art. At times he abandoned a thought, image, or symbol in order to complete a musical line. His verse is sometimes a series of sounds and rhythms that when spoken create beautiful music, but which bear little meaning. Valéry gave little attention to his audience. As a result, to some readers his poetry will contain a deeper level of meaning; to others, his poetry will be purely musical.

Writing

The American poet Archibald MacLeish wrote, "A poem should not mean but be." Freewrite, exploring the meaning of this quotation.

Primary Source

In his book, *Paul Valéry*, H.A.L. Fisher states the following about Valéry's poetry: ". . . it has a curious power of transporting the reader into a magical world of its own in which there is nothing common and nothing definite, but only a phantasmagoria of haunting images passing before the eye to the sound of delicate unearthly music and with just so much of consistency and permanence as belong to the scent of flowers in the night breeze or the ethereal tissues of a dream."

Literary Focus Ask students to name some commonly used symbols. Help them to distinguish between a symbol and a sign. Point out that a sign has a single, distinct meaning. A symbol, however, may have an indefinable meaning, a number of different meanings, or a meaning that can vary from one interpreter to another. Reassure students that Valéry's symbols can be taken in any number of ways. Students should not be inhibited from expressing their interpretations.

Writing/Prior Knowledge Ask students what they think poetry is. Discuss what purpose or role they think poetry plays in their lives or in society. Then have students complete the writing activity.

ESL Teaching Strategy Valéry's poetry is difficult and may be especially so for ESL students. You may wish to read the poems aloud and have students paraphrase each line, stanza, or poem, making sure all students understand the symbolism and what is being said.

Vocabulary

Preteach the following vocabulary words:

rive (rīv) *v.*: Tear apart; rend

betrothed (bō trōthd´) *adj.*: Engaged

accolade (ak´ ə lād´) *n.*: Words of praise; anything done as a sign of great respect

formidable (fôr´məd ə bəl) *adj.*: Awe-inspiring

profusion (prō fyōō zhən) *n.*: Abundance; rich or lavish supply

imperishable (im per´ ish ə b'l) *adj.*: Indestructible

oracle (ôr´ə kəl) *n.*: A person of great knowledge or wisdom

secretes (si krēts´) *v.*: Hides

despond (di spänd´) *v.*: To lose courage or hope; become disheartened

---

Master Teacher Note Valéry was strongly influenced by American poet Edgar Allan Poe. Have students read several of Poe's poems and compare them with Valéry's.

Teaching Tenth-Grade Students Valéry's poetry may be difficult for tenth-grade students to understand. You may wish to spend a little extra time reviewing symbolism with students. Have students read these poems aloud. Ask them to paraphrase Valéry's work, making sure students understand the symbolism and what is being said before moving on.

RETURNING TO THE TRENCHES, 1914
Christopher R. W. Nevinson
National Gallery of Canada, Ottawa

Caesar[1]

Paul Valéry

translated by C. F. MacIntyre

Caesar, serene Caesar, your foot on all,
The hard fists in the beard, and the gloomy eyes
Pregnant with eagles and battles of foreseen fall,
Your heart swells, feeling itself omnipotent[2] cause.

5   In vain the lake trembles, licking its rosy bed,
Vainly glistens the gold of the young wheat straws.
You harden in the knots of your gathered body

The word which must finally <u>rive</u> your tight-
    clenched jaws.

The spacious world, beyond the immense horizon,
The Empire awaits the torch, the order, the
10   lightning
Which will turn the evening to a furious dawn.

Happily there on the waves, and cradled in hazard,
A lazy fisherman is drifting and singing,
Not knowing what thunder collects in the center
    of Caesar.

---

1. **Caesar** (sē′ zər): Here, any emperor or dictator.
2. **omnipotent** (äm nip′ ə tənt) *adj.*: Having unlimited power or authority.

The Friendly Wood

Paul Valéry

translated by Vernon Watkins

Meditations pure were ours
Side by side, along the ways;
We held each other's hand without
Speaking, among the hidden flowers.

Alone we walked as if betrothed,
Lost in the green night of the fields;
We shared this fruit of fairy reels,
The moon, to madmen well disposed.

And then, we were dead upon the moss,
Far, quite alone, among the soft
Shades of this intimate, murmuring wood;

And there, in the vast light aloft,
We found ourselves with many a tear,
O my companion of silence dear!

Reader's Response *What do you feel is the most important, beautiful, or musical phrase in Valéry's work? Why?*

THINKING ABOUT THE SELECTION

Interpreting

1. What contrasting descriptions of Caesar are in the first stanza?
2. Who or what does Caesar represent? Support your answer.
3. How will Caesar's actions affect the fisherman? Support your answer.
4. In "The Friendly Wood," with whom or what is the speaker in communion? Explain your answer.
5. Why does the communion end in tears?
6. (a) Why are their meditations pure? (b) How might one attain pure meditations?
7. A common characteristic of Symbolist poetry is the blurring of the senses; for example, smells become sounds and sights become tastes, and so on. (a) How does Valéry blur the image of the moon in lines 7–8? What effect does this blurring have? (b) Why might this technique be used?

Applying

8. Do you think people can communicate without speaking? Explain your answer.

ANALYZING LITERATURE

Understanding Symbolism

In the Symbolist movement, writers used symbols as a way of conveying a deeper meaning than the words themselves allowed. The purpose of poetry was to suggest or hint at a higher level of understanding, consciousness, or experience. The Symbolists used poetry as a means of transcending the reality we perceive through our senses and bringing the reader to a world that is not governed by the same rules. In this new reality lies a deeper understanding of life and possibly of God and the universe.

1. In "Caesar" what do the reactions of the natural world to Caesar suggest about the Symbolists' theory of unity?
2. (a) Whom does the fisherman represent? (b) How do the figures of Caesar and the fisherman contrast?
3. (a) To what senses does Valéry appeal in "The Friendly Wood"? (b) What does the speaker's heightened sensibility suggest about the speaker's relationship with the wood or with nature?

(continued from bottom of page)

know it. (b) This technique graphically suggests that the elements of nature have special and unexpected relationships of which we are unaware.
8. Answers may differ. Most students will agree that it is possible to communicate without speaking. Students may suggest that close friends, family members, and lovers can communicate without speaking.

ANSWERS TO ANALYZING LITERATURE

1. Answers may differ. Suggested response: The reactions of the world to Caesar suggest that the universe is so unified or tied together that the slightest ripple in that unity affects everything.
2. Answers may differ. Suggested responses: (a) The fisherman represents the people, the innocents who are caught up in the decisions and influence of those who are in power. (b) Caesar is all-powerful and can control life and death. The fisherman is powerless and ignorant of Caesar and the decisions that are being made around him. In addition, Caesar sees only worlds to conquer, not worlds to enjoy, as the fisherman does.
3. Answers may differ. Suggested responses: (a) He appeals to all of the senses. (b) His heightened sensibility suggests the close relationship the speaker has to the wood.

1 Discussion Valéry personifies nature and treats it as though it were the speaker's lover. How can one hold hands with nature?

2 Discussion What sounds might the wood murmur?

3 Discussion Why does the speaker describe the wood as his "companion of silence"?

Closure and Extension

ANSWERS TO THINKING ABOUT THE SELECTION

1. In the first line Valéry says Caesar is serene, yet his description suggests he is anything but serene.
2. Caesar represents a supreme or ultimate authoritarian figure. His power is so great that even the "lake trembles."

3. Answers may differ. Suggested response: The fisherman is an unsuspecting victim who can get caught up in the destructive waves of the dictator's plans.
4. The speaker is in communion with nature, as though it were a loved one.
5. Answers may differ. Suggested response: The poem ends with a tear because the speaker is moved by the beauty of the wood.

6. Answers may differ. Students might recall the meditations of the Chinese poets as they communed with nature. They, like Valéry, are transcending their worldly fears, worries, and desires to reach "pure meditations."
7. Answers may differ. Suggested responses: (a) The moon becomes the fruit of the wood fairies. This blurring gives the impression that life in the friendly wood is apart from life as we

Motivation/Prior Knowledge
Have students go outside and observe one element of nature. Tell
them to observe their subject very
closely and to jot down their observations and descriptions of what
they see. Then tell them that in this
poem, Valéry is closely observing
nature at work through one palm
frond.

Purpose-Setting Question What
secrets about life does the palm
frond hold?

1 Enrichment Valéry wrote "Palm" in
1917 almost immediately after he
finished "The Young Fate," which
Valéry described as "a long, obscure poem." "Palm" was originally
part of a longer piece that was later divided into two separate poems, "Aurore" and "Palm."

2 Discussion Paraphrase this passage. What is Valéry describing?

3 Discussion "Palm" was the last
poem Valéry wrote for his collection entitled *Charmes*, which
means "songs." In what ways is
this poem like a song?

Palm

Paul Valéry

translated by Barbara Gibbs

An angel sets at my place
—Barely screening the accolade
Of his formidable grace—
Fresh milk, new-baked bread;
5 With his lids he makes a sign
That is like a petition
That says to my vision:
Calm, calm, be calm,
Know the heaviness of a palm
10 Bearing its profusion!

Even as it bends
Under abundant good things
The shape perfectly rounds,
The heavy fruits are strings.
15 Wonder how it sheds
Vibrancy, how a slow thread
That parcels out the moment
Adjudicates[1] without mystery
The heaviness of the sky
20 And the earth's enticement!

This fair mobile arbitress
Between shadow and sunlight
Wears the sibyl's[2] dress,
Wisdom of day, sleep of night.
25 All round the one spot
The wide palm wearies not
Of welcomes and farewells . . .
How noble and soft it is
And worthy to dispose
30 The comforts of immortals!

The faint gold it sighs
Rings like a mere finger of air
Burdening the desert skies
With a silken signature.
35 An imperishable sound
Which it gives to the sandy wind
That waters it with its grains
Serves it as oracle
And foretells the miracle
40 Of the chanting pain.

Between sand and sky,
Ignorant of its own nature,
Each brightening day
Adds honey to its store.
45 This gentleness is ordered by
The divine continuity
Which does not mark passing time
But rather hides it
In a juice wherein secretes
50 All of love's perfume.

If you sometimes despond—
If the ardored[3] rigor
In spite of tears responds
Under a shadow of languor[4]—
55 Never blame of avarice[5]
A Wisdom that is nurse
To so much gold and authority:
An everlasting hope
Rises through the dark sap
60 To maturity!

---

1. **Adjudicates** (ə jōō′ də kātz′) *v.*: Serves as a judge.
2. **sibyl's** (sib′ ′lz): In ancient Greece and Rome, sibyls were
female prophets or oracles.

3. **ardored** (är′ dərd) *adj.*: Passionate.
4. **languor** (laŋ′ gər) *n.*: A lack of interest or spirit.
5. **avarice** (av′ ər is) *n.*: Greed for riches.

Reader's Response *When you feel
despondent, what do you focus on to
uplift your spirit?*

Closure and Extension

ANSWERS TO THINKING
ABOUT THE SELECTION

1. The single palm frond is a microcosm
of the natural world. By observing it
closely, we see nature at work.
2. Answers may differ. Suggested response: The palm acts as a conduit
or mediator between the earth and

LANDSCAPE, CANNES
Max Beckmann
San Francisco Museum of Modern Art

THINKING ABOUT THE SELECTION

Interpreting

1. Why does Valéry focus his attention on a single palm frond?
2. What is the significance of the palm branch's location "between sand and sky"?
3. What might the palm represent? Support your answer with details from the poem.
4. For what is the palm frond a nurse? How does it heal?
5. What discoveries does Valéry make while observing the palm?
6. Look up *angel* in a dictionary. What definition of angel best fits this poem? Why?
7. (a) Who is the arbitress? (b) Why is she dressed in "Sibyl's dress"? What do her garments suggest about her purpose?

Applying

8. How does Valéry's work help heighten your sensibility toward life?

THINKING AND WRITING

Writing Using Symbolism

Imitate the Symbolists' style in an original poem or short descriptive paragraph. First describe the symbols that come to mind after careful examination of some part of the natural world, such as Valéry did in "Palm." In your poem or descriptive paragraph, you must convey or hint at some discovery or higher level of meaning. In revising, give your paper to a peer to read. Ask your partner if he or she can understand your symbolism. Make any necessary revisions. Write a final draft.

(continued from bottom of page)

8. Answers may differ. Most students will state that Valéry's poetry helps them to see the intricate world of nature and the larger meaning of life and hope it holds.

THINKING AND WRITING

Publishing Student Writing Submit students' work to the school or a local newspaper. You might also wish to compile students' work in a classroom book and display it for others to read and enjoy.

Challenge Valéry represents the French Symbolists whom the Acmeists, such as Anna Akhmatova, rejected. In an essay or oral presentation, have students support which movement—Symbolist or Acmeist—they favor and why.

Humanities Note

Fine art, *Landscape, Cannes* by Max Beckmann. Born in Leipzig, Germany, Beckmann (1884–1950) began as a traditional painter of religious and classical themes. His service in World War I affected him deeply and he began to turn inward for his inspiration. His new style was less academic and more expressive than his previous work. Using twisted angular shapes and discordant color schemes, he depicted the violence of war and the cruelty of postwar society.

Beckmann left Germany for Holland to escape Nazi harassment. He came to the United States in 1947 to teach at the Brooklyn Museum in New York.

You might want to use the following questions to discuss the art:

1. What is unusual about the artist's depiction of palm trees?
2. Does the mood of the painting fit the mood of Valéry's poem? Explain.

heaven and what lies beyond heaven.
3. Answers may differ. Students may reply that the palm represents life and all its goodness and hardships, a judge, an oracle, and a means by which we can find hope and peace.
4. The palm nurses those who are despondent. It heals by raising you above your worries and giving you everlasting hope.
5. Answers may differ. Suggested response: He discovers how it looks with the weight of the fruit it bears, yet it never wearies "of welcomes and farewells"; that it is comforting to watch it and listen to it as it foretells "the miracle of the chanting pain"; that it represents continuous life by "divine continuity"; and that nature and the miracle of life can cure the ailments and pain of life.
6. Answers may differ. Suggested response: An angel is a messenger from a higher power. As a messenger the angel makes the speaker aware of the life and importance of the palm.
7. Answers may differ. (a) The arbitress is the angel. Some students may think that the palm is also the arbitress because it acts as a prophet or oracle would. (b) The angel is clothed in "sibyl's dress" because she is a prophet and messenger from God. The angel and the palm are passing on their wisdom to others.

LUIGI PIRANDELLO

1867–1936

With the completion of his masterpiece, *Six Characters in Search of an Author* (1921)—a unique play about a group of characters who, in their quest to find an author to tell their story, interrupt a group of actors rehearsing another play—Luigi Pirandello (lōō ē′ jē pir′ ən del′ ō) firmly established himself as one of the most innovative dramatists of his time. Unfortunately, however, Pirandello's success as a dramatist obscured his accomplishments as a fiction writer, and many today are unaware that in his native land of Italy he is widely recognized as the master of the short story.

The son of a sulfur merchant, Pirandello was born on the island of Sicily. After graduating from high school, he attended the University of Rome and later received a doctorate from the University of Bonn in Germany. In 1894 he married the daughter of another successful sulfur merchant, and with the financial support of both his parents and his in-laws, he was able to devote the next ten years entirely to writing poetry and short stories. When the sulfur mines collapsed in 1903, however, the fortunes of both families were wiped out, and Pirandello was forced to go into teaching in order to earn a living. At about the same time, his wife began suffering from a mental illness that would last until her death.

Fortunately, these setbacks did not hinder Pirandello's development as a writer. Having already established himself as a successful short-story writer, Pirandello published his best-known novel, *The Late Mattia Pascal*, in 1904. As was the case with many of his early stories, this novel delved into the difficulties of achieving a sense of identity and questioned the distinction between appearance and reality. These themes were also the focus of *It Is So (If You Think So)* (1917), Pirandello's first popular and critically acclaimed drama.

It Is So (If You Think So) marked the beginning of a series of dramatic successes that culminated in *Six Characters in Search of an Author* and *Henry IV* (1922). Having established a worldwide reputation as a playwright, Pirandello was able to open his own theater company in 1924. At the same time, he continued to write prolifically, publishing among other things a collection of stories, *A Year's Worth of Stories* (1922), and a novel, *One, None, and a Hundred Thousand* (1925–1926). Although his later works did not achieve the popularity and critical acclaim of his most successful plays, Pirandello received the ultimate recognition for his literary achievements in 1934 when he was awarded the Nobel Prize. Two years later, after publishing *Naked Masks* (1936), a collection of his plays, Pirandello died in Rome.

At the time of his death, it was already clear that Pirandello had had a major impact on the theater, as well as on the literary world in general. Yet the extent of his impact did not become clear until the emergence of a number of gifted playwrights, including Eugene Ionesco, Samuel Beckett, and Harold Pinter, whose work clearly reflected the influence of Pirandello. Because of his innovativeness and his influence on other writers, Pirandello will be remembered as one of the most important writers of the twentieth century.

Objectives

Thematic
To understand the frustration and the sense of helplessness that can result from a lack of communication

Skills
1 To understand plot devices
2 To identify antonyms
3 To write a short story

GUIDE FOR INTERPRETING

A Breath of Air

Commentary

Plot Devices. The **plot** of a story is the sequence of related events. When writers construct a plot, they often arrange all the events in chronological order and precede the action with an **exposition,** in which they provide readers with important background information. In many cases, however, writers plunge right into the action of a novel or short story without offering any insights into the characters or their situations. If a writer chooses to take this approach, he or she must find other methods of providing readers with the knowledge they need to understand the work. One of the most effective methods of accomplishing this is the use of **flashbacks,** or interruptions in the action in which an earlier event is shown or described. Often a flashback takes the form of a reminiscence of one of the characters, while in other cases an earlier scene is either dramatized or described by the narrator.

The use of flashbacks and the omission of expositions is especially common in twentieth-century literary works. This is because many twentieth-century writers view reality as being uncertain and confusing and believe that by packaging information into expositions and by neatly arranging events so that they are easy to follow, they are presenting a false picture of reality.

In addition to determining the order of events and deciding how to provide readers with background information, writers must find ways to sustain a reader's interest. To accomplish this, writers usually try to create **suspense,** or the quality of a literary work that makes the reader curious and excited about what will happen next. One of the main methods that writers use to create suspense is **foreshadowing,** or the use of clues that hint at events that are going to occur later in the story. For example, in Tolstoy's story "How Much Land Does a Man Need?" the main character has a dream that foreshadows his death.

Writing

In our society there is currently a great deal of concern about the treatment of the elderly. How do you think they should be treated? Should they be treated differently from other people? How do you think they want to be treated? What types of special problems and concerns do they have? How can younger generations help them to cope with these problems and concerns? Write a journal entry in which you respond to these questions and discuss measures that might be taken to improve the situation of the elderly in our country.

Presentation

Literary Focus Have students describe films they have seen in which foreshadowing or flashbacks were used. One film that they might discuss is *Citizen Kane*, which consists almost entirely of flashbacks and which also utilizes foreshadowing. When discussing the various films, students should note how flashbacks are introduced and how foreshadowing helps to create suspense.

Writing/Prior Knowledge Before students begin writing their journal entries, have a class discussion in which students describe their interactions with their grandparents or with other elderly people. What have students learned through these interactions?

ESL Teaching Strategy Pair each ESL student with a native-speaking student. Have the pairs read through the story together, taking turns reading aloud. Instruct the native-speaking student to help clarify the meanings of any words with which the ESL student is unfamiliar.

Teaching Tenth-Grade Students Tell tenth-grade students to pause in their reading when they reach the grandfather's flashback. At this point tell them that the grandfather is about to recall events that occurred earlier in his life. When they have finished reading the flashback, have them pause again and explain why the flashback is a vital part of the story.

Vocabulary
Preteach the following vocabulary words:
imp (imp) *n.*: A mischievous child
banished (ban´ isht) *v.*: Sent or put away
animation (an´ə mā´ shən) *n.*: Brisk, lively quality
inert (in ʉrt´) *adj.*: Dull; slow
nettled (net´ l'd) *v.*: Annoyed; irritated
wafted (waft´ id) *v.*: Floated
doggedly (dôg´ id lē) *adj.*: Stubbornly

Support Material
Teaching Portfolio
Teacher Backup, p. 1331
Grammar in Action Worksheet, *Recognizing Tone*, p. 1335
Usage and Mechanics Worksheet, p. 1337
Vocabulary Check, p. 1338
Analyzing Literature Worksheet, *Understanding Plot Devices*, p. 1339

Language Worksheet, *Finding Antonyms*, p. 1340
Selection Test, pp. 1341–1342

Spelling Tip Point out to students that the word *animation* has the same first five letters as the word *animal*.

Presentation

Motivation/Prior Knowledge Tell students that this story is about a character who feels that the members of his family are keeping a secret from him. Have students discuss whether they have ever had this type of experience in their own lives. If so, what emotions did it arouse in them? Did it make them angry? Why or why not?

Purpose-Setting Question What event has occurred that has caused the husband and wife and their daughter to behave differently? Why have they not shared their knowledge of this event with the grandfather?

Universal Themes The idea that communication is vital to interpersonal relationships is a recurring theme in world literature. For example, Henrik Ibsen's play *A Doll's House* (page 969) dramatizes how a lack of communication can contribute to the collapse of a marriage.

Master Teacher Note Tell students that Pirandello had a deep awareness that every individual sees the world from a different perspective. As students read the story, have them think about how it reflects this awareness. Encourage them to pay special attention to how the characters in the story view one another.

1 Reading Strategy Have students make inferences about the story based on its title.

2 Discussion Have students discuss the impression of Tina that is conveyed in the first two paragraphs. Which details contribute to this impression?

3 Discussion Have students discuss the impression of the grandfather that is conveyed in this passage. Why is Tina frightened of him?

4 Discussion Have students speculate about why the old man's eyes are filled with "terror and silent hate." Then ask them what Pirandello means when he writes that "the old man's huge frame seemed to have banished his soul."

5 Literary Focus Point out to stu-

A Breath of Air

Luigi Pirandello

translated by Lily Duplaix

Sparkling eyes, blond hair, bare little arms and legs, childish laughter escaping in muffled giggles—that imp of a Tina darted across the room to open the glass doors of the balcony.

She had started to turn the knob when a hoarse growl, like that of a wild beast surprised in his lair, quickly stopped her. Petrified with fear, she turned around to stare into the room.

Everything was dark.

The balcony shutters were open only a crack. Although her eyes were still blinded by the lighted corridor from which she had come, she was keenly aware of her grandfather's presence in the darkness, a huge mound propped up in his big chair heaped with cushions, gray-checked shawls, and rough, shaggy blankets, all smelling of stuffy old age stagnating in paralysis.

His immovable bulk did not frighten her so much as the fact that she had forgotten him there in the dark and had disobeyed her parents' strict order never to go into his room without first knocking and asking permission. What was it she was supposed to say? "May I come in, Grandpapa?" Then she must enter very, very quietly, on tiptoe, without making a sound!

The first impulsive laugh was quickly stifled by a gasp verging on a sob. The trembling child tiptoed toward the door not realizing that the old man, accustomed to the dark, could see her.

"Here!" he commanded harshly, just as she was about to step over the threshold.

She caught her breath and hesitantly tiptoed back toward him. Now that she too began to see in the darkness, the wicked look in her grandfather's piercing eyes made her quickly lower her own.

Those eyes, alert with inexorable[1] terror and silent hate, showed between puffy, inflamed bags which reminded her of the sticky body of a tarantula. Already held captive by death, the old man's huge frame seemed to have banished his soul, which now rallied only in his eyes.

He could still move his left hand a little. After staring at it a long time with those implacable[2] eyes, willing animation into it, he at last succeeded in lifting it ever so slightly above the covers. After a fraction of a second it fell back again inert. He persevered in this exercise because that flicker of movement was all the life left to him—"life" understood as movement in which others participated at will and in which he, too, could still take this infinitesimal part.

"Why . . . the balcony?" he faltered, his sluggish tongue struggling with the words.

Still trembling, the child did not answer. The old man immediately sensed something different in her. She trembled with fear every time her mother or father bade her approach him, yet this time it was not the same. She had been startled by his harsh, unexpected command, but there was something else which sent a thrill through her whole body.

"What's the matter?" he asked.

"Nothing," she replied, hardly daring to raise her eyes.

---

1. **inexorable** (in ek′ sər ə b'l) *adj.*: Not moved or influenced by persuasion or entreaty.
2. **implacable** (im plak′ ə b'l) *adj.*: That which cannot be appeased or pacified.

dents that the grandfather senses "something different" in Tina's behavior. Then ask them to speculate about what this difference in her behavior might foreshadow.

Primary Source
In addition to being aware that all people perceive the world differently, Pirandello also believed that there

are many different sides to everyone's personality and that each individual's perceptions fluctuate according to his or her state of mind. These views are reflected in the comments of the Father in Pirandello's play *Six Characters in Search of an Author*:

Each one of us has within him

a whole world of things, each man of us his own special world. And how can we ever come to an understanding if I put in the words I utter the sense and value of things as I see them; while you who listen to me must inevitably translate them according to your conception of things each one of

The old man still detected something unusual in the child's voice, even in the way she breathed.

"What is the matter?" he repeated resentfully.

She burst into tears and threw herself on the floor. She screamed and struggled with such convulsive violence that the old man was increasingly irritated, for here too he sensed a difference.

"Heavens, Tina, what's the matter?" cried her mother, running into the room. "What's come over you? Now, now hush! Come to Mama. Why did you come in here? . . . What's that? Bad! Who is bad? . . . Ah! Grandpa! No, *you* are bad. Grandpa loves you. What happened?"

The old man, to whom the last question had been addressed, stared fiercely at the smile on his daughter-in-law's red lips, then at the lovely strand of golden hair the child pulled from her mother's head in her struggle to drag her from the room.

"Oww! My hair . . . Oh! Tina, you'll pull it all out. Mama's poor hair! Bad little girl! Look!" she said, opening the small hand and drawing the hairs, one by one, through the little fingers, repeating, "See . . . see . . ."

The child stared down at her fingers with tears in her eyes. She suddenly believed she had really pulled out all her mother's hair. But seeing nothing in her hand, and hearing her mother's happy laugh, she started to cry again, tugging at her mother to leave the room.

The old man breathed heavily. He was nettled by the question, which had rekindled his hatred.

"What's the matter with all of them?" he said to himself.

Their eyes, their voices—even his daughter-in-law's laugh, and the way she drew those hairs, one by one, through the child's little fingers—had something unusual about them. No, neither of them behaved the same as on other days. What was it all about?

His resentment soared when he lowered his eyes and saw a golden hair resting on the blanket over his knees. Wafted there by her carefree laugh, it had settled on his dead legs. He tried doggedly to urge his hand along little by little toward the hair which mocked him so bitterly. When his son came in, as was his custom before leaving the house to go to work, he found the old man ex-

OLIVIA
Lydia Field Emmet
National Gallery of Art, Washington, D.C.

hausted from the effort he had been making in vain for half an hour.

"Good morning, Papa!"

The old man looked up, his eyes dilating with fear and surprise. His son, too?

Understanding his look to mean that the child had annoyed him, the son hastened to say, "Tina is a little devil! Did she disturb you? Listen, she's still crying because I scolded her. So long, Papa. I'm in a hurry. See you later. Nerina will come in to you shortly."

The old man's eyes followed him all the way to the door.

Now his son, too! Never before had he used that tone. "Good morning, Papa!" Why? What had

(continued from bottom of page)

7 Literary Focus Point out to students that the grandfather now senses that both the mother and her daughter are behaving in an unusual manner. Once again, have students speculate about what the grandfather's observation might foreshadow.

8 Discussion Have students discuss what this passage reveals about the grandfather's physical condition.

Humanities Note

Fine art, *Olivia* by Lydia Field Emmet. A disciple of the renowned American landscape painter William Merritt Chase, Emmet (1866–1952) was an early twentieth-century painter known both for her landscapes and her portraits. Emmet's portraits often depicted children. As is the case with the painting seen here, these portraits captured the freedom and innocence of youth.

In addition to being a painter, Emmet worked as an illustrator for *Harper's* magazine and as a designer of stained glass windows for Tiffany & Company. She also won many awards for her art-work, including a bronze medal for a mural at the Women's Building of the 1938 Columbian Exhibition.

You might want to use the following questions to discuss the art:

1. What seems to be the artist's attitude toward her subject?
2. How is the artist's attitude conveyed?
3. Does the girl depicted in this painting match the way in which you envision the girl in Pirandello's story? Why or why not?
4. If you were an art collector, would you want to include this painting in your collection? Why or why not?

you has within himself. We think we understand each other, but we never really do. . . .

. . . We believe [our] conscience to be a single thing, but it is many-sided. There is one for this person, and another for that. Diverse consciences. So we have this illusion of being one person for all, of having a personality that is unique in all our acts. But it isn't true. We perceive this when, tragically perhaps, in something we do, we are as it were, suspended, caught up in the air on a kind of hook. Then we perceive that all of us was not in that act, and it would be an atrocious injustice to judge us by that action alone, as if all of our existence were summed up in that one deed. . . .

6 Discussion Ask students why Tina begins to cry again after she sees that she does not have any of her mother's hair in her hand.

9 Discussion Have students speculate about why the grandfather feels so bitter toward his son and his daughter-in-law. Is there any indication the son and the daughter-in-law mistreat the grandfather? Explain.

10 Literary Focus Draw students' attention to the grandfather's flashback. Then have them discuss what the flashback adds to their understanding of the story. Would the story have been as effective if the information in the flashback had been presented at the beginning of the story? Why or why not?

11 Enrichment Tell students that many Italians, as well as people from other European countries, emigrated to Argentina in the period the grandfather is recalling.

12 Discussion Given what they have just learned, do students think the grandfather is justified in "detesting" his son? Why or why not?

13 Discussion Have students discuss what this passage suggests about Nerina's attitude toward the grandfather. What seems to be his attitude toward her?

14 Discussion Have students explain why the grandfather seems to continue eating. What seems strange to him about Nerina's behavior?

he expected? Were they all in league against him? What had happened? First the child came in all aflutter, then the mother laughed because her hair was pulled, and now his son with his cheerful "Good morning, Papa!"

Something had happened or was going to happen today and they all wanted to keep it from him. What could it be?

They had taken the world for themselves, his son and daughter-in-law and grandchild—*his* world that he had created and into which he had placed them. Not only that, but they had also appropriated[3] time—as if he no longer existed in time! As if time were not his also—was he not to see, nor breathe, nor think in it? He still breathed, and he saw everything—more than all of them put together.

A stream of impressions and memories ran riot in his mind, like lightning flashing in a storm. La Plata,[4] the pampas,[5] the salt marshes of lost rivers, innumerable pawing herds bleating, whinnying, lowing. Out there, he had built a fortune from nothing in forty-five years, always keeping his eye on the main chance, forever hatching schemes with patient cunning. Beginning as a herdsman, he had gone on to become a small-holdings settler, then an employee of big railroad contractors, and finally a contractor and builder on his own. He had come back to Italy after the first fifteen years and married, but immediately after the birth of his only son he had gone back there alone. His wife died without his having seen her again, and his son, raised by his mother's relatives, had grown up without knowing him.

Four years ago he had returned, a sick man near death, his body horribly distended by dropsy,[6] suffering from hardening of the arteries, his kidneys ruined and a bad heart. But although his days and even his hours were numbered, he didn't stop. He bought land in Rome and started building, having himself transported to and from the site in a wheelchair, enormously swollen but rugged as a rock. Every fifteen days or so they would drain quarts of fluid from his belly, and then he'd be right back in the thick of things again. That is, until two years ago when he was felled by a stroke of apoplexy[7]—but not quite finished off. No, he had not been granted the good fortune to die in harness. For two years now he'd been completely paralyzed, smoldering in resentful anticipation of the end and hating his son, who was so unlike himself, a stranger to him. His son had voluntarily liquidated the whole business, about which he knew nothing, and had prudently invested the paternal fortune, but he had chosen to continue his own modest legal practice—as if refusing to give the old man any satisfaction, thus avenging his mother and himself for their long abandonment.

He detested the son. They had nothing in common, either of thought or feeling. Yes, he detested his daughter-in-law too, and that child! He despised them all because they had excluded him from their life, refusing to tell him what had happened today to change all three of them.

Big tears slipped from his eyes. He let himself go and cried like a baby, forgetting the tower of strength he had been for so many years.

Nerina, the servant, paid no attention to his tears when she came in a little later to take care of him. The old man was so full of water that it did no harm if a little of it spilled out of his eyes. With this thought, she carelessly dried his face and took up a bowl of milk.

"Eat, eat," she told him, dipping a biscuit into the warm milk and holding it to his mouth.

He ate, peering stealthily[8] up at her. She sighed, he thought, but not because she was tired or bored. He suddenly raised his eyes and stared at her. There! She was about to sigh again but smothered it. Instead of ignoring his gaze, she huffed and shrugged her shoulders as if she were cross. Then, for no reason at all, she blushed! What was the matter with *her*? They all had something strange about them today. What could it be?

He refused to eat any more.

---

3. appropriated (ə prō′ prē āt id) *v.*: Taken for their own use.
4. La Plata (la plä′ tə): A city in Argentina.
5. the pampas (pam′ pəz) *n.*: Extensive, grass-covered plains.
6. dropsy (dräp′ sē) *n.*: An abnormal accumulation of fluid in cells, tissues, or cavities of the body, resulting in swelling.

---

7. apoplexy (ap′ ə plek′ sē) *n.*: Sudden paralysis caused by the breaking or obstruction of a blood vessel in the brain, commonly referred to as a stroke.
8. stealthily (stelth′ ə lē) *adv.*: Secretly; slyly.

Grammar in Action

Tone refers to the writer's attitude toward his or her subject, characters, or audience. Unlike speakers, who can communicate tone through body movements and the manner in which they speak, writers must rely solely on their use of language to convey tone. Consequently, to recognize the tone of a piece of writing, you must pay close attention to the writer's choice of words. Note the following passage from "A Breath of Air":

Nerina, the servant, paid no attention to his tears when she came in a little later to take care of him. The old man was so full of water that it did no harm if a little of it spilled out of his eyes. With this thought, she carelessly dried his face and took up a bowl of milk.

If you look closely at Pirandello's choice of words in this passage, you can infer, or conclude, that he views the servant as cold and unsympathetic. For example, he immediately points out that she "paid no attention to" the grandfather. He then delves into the servant's thoughts to convey her indifference to the grandfather: "The old man was so full of water that it did no harm if a little of it spilled out of his eyes." Then, in the final sentence, Pirandello uses the word "carelessly" to describe how the servant wiped

BREAKFAST
Paul Signac
State Museum Kroller-Muller, Otterlo, The Netherlands

"What's the matter with you?" he demanded testily.

"Me? What's the matter with me?" she repeated, surprised.

"Yes, you—everybody. What is it? What's happened?" he asked.

"Nothing . . . I don't know. What do you mean?"

"Sighs!" he mumbled.

"Did I sigh? Not at all! Well, if I did, maybe I did it unconsciously. I really have no reason to sigh," she said, and laughed merrily.

"Why do you laugh like that?"

"Laugh? I laughed because you said I sighed," she told him, laughing all the more.

"Oh, go away," the old man snapped.

Later, when the doctor arrived for his regular visit and they all gathered in the room—his son, daughter-in-law and their little girl—the suspicion he had nursed all day, even in his sleep, that they were hiding something from him became a certainty.

They were all in on the secret. They talked of other things in his presence just to put him off, but the understanding between them showed clearly in their glances. They had never before looked at one

16

the grandfather's face.

Student Activity 1. Find three more passages in which Pirandello's attitude toward one or more of the characters is apparent. Then describe the attitude that he conveys in each of these passages and explain how his attitude is revealed.

Student Activity 2. Write a paragraph in which you describe a person or place about which you have especially strong feelings. Make sure you convey your attitude toward your subject through your choice of words.

17

another in just this way. Their gestures, their voices, their very smiles did not match their words. And what about all that animated discussion about wigs? It seemed that wigs were coming into fashion again!

"Green, if you please, green, or mauve!" cried his daughter-in-law, turning pink with mock indignation, so feigned indeed that she couldn't help laughing outright.

Her mouth laughed of its own accord, and her hands rose instinctively to caress her hair—as if her hair needed that caress!

"I understand, I quite understand," the doctor said, his full-moon face wreathed in smiles. "When one has hair like yours, dear lady, it would be a crime to hide it under a wig."

The old man could hardly restrain his anger. He would have liked to bellow and drive them all out of the room. The doctor, accompanied by the daughter-in-law holding her little girl by the hand, was hardly through the door when his rage exploded against his son, left alone with him in the room. He shot the same questions at him as he had put in vain to the child and to the servant girl.

"What's the matter with all of you? Why are you all behaving like this today? What's happened? What are you trying to hide from me?"

"Nothing at all, Papa. What is there to hide?" his son replied in surprise and dismay. "We're all just about the same as usual, I think."

"It's not true! There's something different. I see it! I feel it in all of you! You think I don't see anything or feel anything because I'm like *this!*" he said thickly, trying to turn his head to the wall.

"But, Papa, I really can't think what you see new or different in us today. Nothing has happened. Believe me. I swear and double-swear it! Now, you must be calm."

The old man was somewhat mollified[9] by his son's evident sincerity, but he was not yet fully convinced. He had no doubt whatsoever that something was up. He saw it; he felt it in all of them. What could it be?

When he was alone in the room, the reply came suddenly, silently, from the balcony. The knob, half turned by the child that morning, was released now in the early evening by a breath of air and the door onto the balcony swung open.

He did not notice it at first, but then he smelled a delicious perfume invading the room which came from the garden. He looked up and saw a strip of moonlight lying across the floor, a trace of luminous brilliance piercing the dark shadows.

"Ah, so that's it," he said, sighing.

The others could not see it. They could not even feel it in themselves because they were still part of life. But he who was almost dead, he had seen and felt it there among them. So that was why the child had trembled this morning. That was why his daughter-in-law had laughed and taken such delight in her golden hair. And that was why the servant girl sighed. That was why they had all behaved differently, without even knowing it.

Spring had come.

---

9. **mollified** (mäl′ ə fīd′) *v.*: Soothed; pacified.

Teacher notes (left margin)

17 Discussion Have students explain why the grandfather is so infuriated by the conversation between his daughter-in-law and his doctor.

18 Discussion Have students discuss why the others are unaware of the coming of spring and how this has affected their behavior. Then have them discuss why the coming of spring can have such a powerful impact on people. How does it usually affect them?

Cultural Note Pirandello influenced a number of modern and contemporary playwrights, including the British dramatists Samuel Beckett and Harold Pinter. If any students are familiar with any of the plays of Pinter or Beckett, have them share their knowledge with the rest of the class.

Cooperative Learning Students might enjoy being exposed to Pirandello's dramas. Divide your class into groups of five or six. Have each group skim through two or three of Pirandello's plays to find a scene they find especially captivating. Then have each group act out the scene they have chosen in front of the rest of the class. Following each performance, have a class discussion in which students respond to the scene they have just witnessed.

COMMENTARY
Traditional Plot Structure

The plot of a traditional short story includes an **exposition**, a **conflict**, a **climax**, and a **resolution**. During the modern age, however, many writers abandoned the traditional plot structure. Consequently, many modern stories begin without an exposition and end without a resolution.

Study the following diagram:

1. How well does the plot of Pirandello's story fit this diagram?
2. What is the climax of the story?

Closure and Extension
ANSWERS TO THINKING ABOUT THE SELECTION

1. (a) Suggested response: The grandfather seems gruff, bitter, angry, and frightening. (b) Suggested response: He is suggesting that the grandfather's stroke not only paralyzed his body but also stripped him of his spirit.

2. (a) Suggested response: He is angered by the way in which they treat him because he feels that they act as if he no longer exists. (b) Suggested response: Early in the story, his attitude is shown through his growling voice, his harshness, and his resentment. Later in the story, his feelings are conveyed directly.

3. (a) Suggested response. Early in the story, Pirandello refers to the grand-

THINKING ABOUT THE SELECTION

Interpreting

1. (a) What impression does Pirandello convey of the grandfather in the first several paragraphs? (b) What does he mean when he writes that the grandfather's "huge frame seemed to have banished his soul"?
2. (a) What is the grandfather's attitude about the way in which he is treated by the other family members? (b) How is his attitude conveyed?
3. (a) Which details in the story emphasize the severity of the grandfather's physical handicap? (b) What is the grandfather's attitude toward his handicap, and how is it revealed?
4. Why do you think that the grandfather was the only one who was aware of the changes in the other characters' behavior?
5. How does the grandfather's lack of awareness of the coming of spring highlight the tragic nature of his condition?

Applying

6. (a) In what ways do you think that the arrival of spring affects people's attitudes and behavior? (b) Why does it have this type of effect on people?

ANALYZING LITERATURE

Understanding Plot Devices

In this story Pirandello creates suspense by continually hinting at the fact that an important event has occurred that the grandfather will eventually become aware of. Yet, because Pirandello does not offer any clues about the nature of the event, the ending of the story comes as a surprise.

1. Find three examples of Pirandello's use of foreshadowing in the story.
2. What expectations did you have about the outcome of the story as a result of Pirandello's use of foreshadowing?
3. Explain how Pirandello's use of foreshadowing along with a surprise ending contributes to the effectiveness of the story.
4. Another plot device that serves an important purpose in this story is the grandfather's flashback. How does this flashback contribute to your understanding of the characters and their situation?
5. Explain whether you think it would be possible to understand the story if Pirandello had not included the flashback.

6. Explain whether you think the story would be as effective if it had begun with the information presented in the flashback.

UNDERSTANDING LANGUAGE

Finding Antonyms

Antonyms are words that are opposite or nearly opposite in meaning. For example, the words *active* and *passive* are antonyms.

The words in capital letters are from Lily Duplaix's translation of Pirandello's story. Choose the word that is most opposite in meaning to each of these words.

1. DISOBEYED
   a. succumbed   c. regarded
   b. submitted   d. obfuscated
2. IMPULSIVE
   a. spontaneous   c. impetuous
   b. intentional   d. provocative
3. INFINITESIMAL
   a. substantial   c. impressive
   b. finite   d. extraordinary
4. HASTENED
   a. hesitated   c. pondered
   b. avoided   d. abstained
5. MOLLIFIED
   a. pacified   c. stagnated
   b. enraged   d. placated

THINKING AND WRITING

Writing a Short Story

Write a short story in which you use foreshadowing and flashbacks. Begin by gathering together with a group of your classmates and brainstorming for ideas. As you are brainstorming, feel free to draw on incidents and experiences from your own life. After you and other members of your group have gathered a list of ideas, choose the one that you find most interesting. Next, review Pirandello's story, focusing on his use of foreshadowing and flashbacks. Develop a plot outline for your story. Then begin writing your story, focusing on creating suspense and providing background information through the use of flashbacks. When you have finished writing, revise your story, making sure the characters are well developed and the dialogue seems natural and realistic. Finally, proofread your story, prepare a final copy, and share it with your classmates.

(continued from bottom of page)
ANSWERS TO ANALYZING LITERATURE

1. Answers will differ. All the examples of foreshadowing involve the grandfather's perception that the others are behaving in an unusual manner.
2. Answers will differ. Possible responses may include the expectation that the family had decided to put him away in a nursing home.
3. Answers will differ. Students may note that the use of foreshadowing creates suspense.
4. Suggested response: The grandfather's flashback explains his current situation and his feelings toward his son and daughter-in-law.
5. Suggested response: It would be difficult to understand the story without an understanding of why the grandfather feels so bitter toward his son and daughter-in-law.
6. Suggested response: It would be less effective because the reader's curiosity about the grandfather's condition and his accompanying bitterness would not be aroused.

ANSWERS TO UNDERSTANDING LANGUAGE

1. b   4. a
2. b   5. b
3. a

THINKING AND WRITING

Publishing Student Writing Encourage students to submit their stories to the school literary magazine.

father's "immovable bulk." Later, he points out that the grandfather struggles for half an hour to brush a hair from his knee. Still later, Pirandello shows the grandfather weeping like a baby. (b) Suggested response: He bitterly resents his handicap and feels that he has nothing to live for. His bitterness is revealed through his behavior and his thoughts about the other characters.

4. Suggested response: The other characters are busy and active and have no time to notice little details. The grandfather, on the other hand, has nothing to do but notice little details.
5. Suggested response: It reveals that the grandfather has completely lost contact with the outside world.
6. (a) Answers will differ. Some students might respond that it makes people livelier and more energetic. (b) An-

swers will differ. Students might respond that it has this effect on people because it represents a type of rebirth.

Challenge What type of point of view does Pirandello use in this story? How does his use of this type of point of view contribute to the effectiveness of the story?

1898–1936

In August 1936 the Spanish newspaper *El Diario de Albacete* ran the following article on the front page:

Has García Lorca (gär thē′ ä lôr′ kä) been assassinated?

Guadix. Rumors from the Córdoba front, which up to now have not been disproved, reveal the possible shooting of the great poet Federico García Lorca, on the orders of Colonel Cascajo, [the commander of the Nationalist forces that took Córdoba at the beginning of the Spanish Civil War].

García Lorca, one of our most outstanding contemporary literary figures, appears to have been under arrest in Córdoba and to have been killed during one of the latest insurgent razzias, on which they habitually embark when they have suffered a setback.

Although it mistakenly identified Córdoba, not Granada, as the place of the assassination, *El Diario* was the first newspaper to break the story about García Lorca's death. The news created a wave of disbelief. Subsequent reports denied the assassination; however, some reports confirmed that he was indeed assassinated and held the Nationalist forces responsible.

For years after his death, the Nationalists hid the truth behind García Lorca's assassination. The truth is that he was put to death in their attempt to purge all the "undesirables," the people who might resist the rising Nationalist Movement. His death most likely occurred because the new Spanish Government found García Lorca's poetry offensive and political.

García Lorca did not intend for his poetry to be political. His inspiration came almost entirely from the people and culture of his homeland—rural Andalusia, an area near the city of Granada. It was here that García Lorca came of age shortly after World War I, when his homeland possessed a vibrant cultural and literary life. One aspect of Spain's cultural life that influenced García Lorca's poetry was the music of the gypsies, or flamencos—*cante jondo* (kan′ tä hōn′ dō).

Cante jondo expresses the world view—the pain and the happiness—of the Andalusian gypsies. And it was the deeply reflective lyrics of these songs that influenced García Lorca's tragic and comic vision of life and crystalized the themes that would run through his work.

In 1919 García Lorca left home and moved to Madrid, where he lived in a center for writers, critics, and scholars. There he devoted himself to writing for the next decade. In 1929 he made his first visit to the United States. During his stay in New York City, García Lorca wrote a series of poems illustrating the horror of a mechanized civilization, which contrasted sharply with the poems inspired by his country life. The poems in *Poet in New York* (published posthumously) were the only ones he wrote that were not inspired by and closely tied to Andalusia.

Shortly after he returned to Spain in 1930, García Lorca wrote several plays in which he fuses dreams with reality—a characteristic of the Surrealistic Movement occurring in France at the time.

García Lorca eventually returned to writing poetry, and although his life was cut short, he is considered one of Spain's most accomplished poets and playwrights.

GUIDE FOR INTERPRETING

The Guitar; My Child Went to Sea; Rider's Song

Commentary

Poet's Vision. Tragedy and comedy are most often associated with drama. The symbol for drama in the Western world is two masks—one smiling and one frowning. But tragedy and comedy can be an integral part of a poet's vision, as well.

As they are in life, both comedy and tragedy are essential elements in García Lorca's poetry. Both crying and laughing can offer the same release from life's pleasures and disasters and are, therefore, sometimes interchangeable and often mixed in García Lorca's poetry.

García Lorca's poetry, although not intentionally political, often expressed his world view of Spain during the 1920's and 1930's. In addition to the conflicts and tensions that existed in Spain just before the civil war in 1936, García Lorca drew much of his inspiration for his tragic and comic vision from *cante jondo* (kän' tä hōn' dō), or deep song. *Cante jondo* is the music of the flamenco dancers, or the Spanish gypsies. The traditional songs of flamenco dance and music are emotionally charged, expressing passions for both life and death. García Lorca's poems are not imitations of *cante-jondo* lyrics. Rather, they are an exploration into the soul of the gypsies' world and into their world view. García Lorca's poems express images that were inspired or provoked by *cante jondo*, expressing the emotions and thoughts produced within him as he listened to the gypsies' personal lyrics.

Writing

Think of an event that has either happened to you or has happened during your lifetime. Write five words or phrases that describe both your comic and your tragic vision of this event. Share your work with classmates and discuss the differences in perspective between your tragic and your comic visions.

Primary Source

Many of García Lorca's critics claimed he was a "gypsy poet" because he was inspired by the culture and songs of the gypsies. In a letter to a friend, García Lorca says the following about being classified as a gypsy poet: "This gypsy *myth of mine* annoys me a little. They confuse my life and character. This isn't what I want at all. The gypsies are a theme. And nothing more. I could just as well be a poet of sewing needles and hydraulic landscapes. Besides, this gypsyism gives me the appearance of an uncultured, ignorant and *primitive poet* that you know very well I'm not. I don't want to be typecast. I feel as if they're chaining me down."

Literary Focus Explain to students that a poet's vision is similar to the tone of a piece of literature—the writer's attitude toward a particular subject. Ask them to describe the tone of some other works they have read in *World Masterpieces*.

Writing/Prior Knowledge Have students brainstorm for possible topics. Encourage them to think of historic as well as personal events. Then have them complete the writing activity individually.

ESL Teaching Strategy If you have Spanish-speaking students, ask them to translate García Lorca's poetry into Spanish and read it to the class. Ask the class to discuss the differences in sound, tempo, and tone between the English and Spanish versions.

Universal Themes You might like to group García Lorca's poems with other works that express a comic or tragic vision, such as Anna Akhmatova's poetry, page 1114; Pablo Neruda's "Ode to My Socks," page 1250; and Stanislaw Lem's "The First Sally (A) OR Trurl's Electronic Bard," page 1308.

Teaching Tenth-Grade Students Tenth-grade students should have little difficulty with García Lorca's poetry. You might wish, however, to review imagery with students before they read these selections.

Vocabulary

Preteach the following vocabulary words:

vaults (vôlts) *n*.: The sky as a canopy; an arched ceiling

monotonously (mə nät´ 'n əs lē) *adv*.: Drearily; desolately

keels (kēlz) *n*.: The bottom parts of boats

swells (swelz) *n*.: Steadily moving waves

russet (rus´it) *n*.: Yellowish- or reddish-brown

stowed (stōd) *v*.: Packed; bundled

stark (stärk) *adj*.: Harsh

Humanities Note

Fine art, *The Old Guitarist*, 1903, by Pablo Picasso. Picasso (1881–1973), who was born in Málaga, Spain, was the son of an art teacher. After going to school where he showed a great propensity for art, he visited and later moved to Paris, where he had a large circle of artist and writer friends.

During his career Picasso went throught numerous periods. In his Blue Period, which occurred early in his career, he painted alienated blue figures in a dark, sorrowful, and pessimistic mood. This period is epitomized by *The Old Guitarist*.

All his life Picasso seemed to be at the center of every avant-garde art movement of the first half of the twentieth century. His most amazing facet was his experimentation in a variety of styles and "periods," which eventually led to the development of Cubism, a style of art that shows a subject as it might look dissected and from a variety of angles.

Picasso was the most widely known, controversial, and influential art figure of his time. His enormous volume of work is unparalleled.

You might want to use the following questions to discuss the art:

1. What is your reaction to the predominance of blue in this painting? What emotions are generally associated with the color blue?

2. What words in "The Guitar" fit the mood of Picasso's work?

THE OLD GUITARIST
Pablo Picasso
Art Institute of Chicago

The Guitar

Federico García Lorca

translated by
Elizabeth du Gué Trapier

Now begins the cry
Of the guitar,
Breaking the vaults
Of dawn.
Now begins the cry
Of the guitar.
Useless
To still it.
Impossible
To still it.
It weeps monotonously
As weeps the water,
As weeps the wind
Over snow.
Impossible
To still it.
It weeps
For distant things,
Warm southern sands
Desiring white camellias.[1]
It mourns the arrow without a target,
The evening without morning.
And the first bird dead
Upon a branch.
O guitar!
A wounded heart,
Wounded by five swords.

---

1. camellias (kə mēl′ yəz): The flowers of the camellia, a type of evergreen tree and shrub that grows mainly in the Far East.

Reader's Response *Do you tend to have a tragic or a comic vision of life? Why?*

THINKING ABOUT THE SELECTION

Interpreting

1. What details in the poem suggest that it was inspired by *cante jondo?*
2. What images of death are in this poem? What effect do these images have?
3. For what might music be a metaphor?
4. Music is a form of communication; when the music stops, there will be nothing but silence. Why might García Lorca think it necessary for the music to never end? Support your answer.

Applying

5. The flamenco dancers and musicians and García Lorca all expressed in their work what they most desired. What desires do you think this poem expresses? Why?

ANALYZING LITERATURE

Recognizing a Poet's Vision

Poets often express their comic and tragic vision in their poetry. Because García Lorca considered tragedy and comedy an integral part of life, he believed they were both essential to express in his work. Since García Lorca believed crying and laughing offered the same relief, he manipulated his use of comedy and tragedy, thereby expressing his unique vision of life. In his tragic poems, García Lorca expressed the pain and suffering of his people. His comic poems, on the other hand, are playful, rhythmic lyrics most often about children or childhood.

1. What do you think is the message behind García Lorca's tragic vision in "The Guitar"?
2. Is García Lorca's tragic vision devoid of all hope? Why or why not? Support your answer.

My Child Went to Sea

Federico García Lorca

translated by John A. Crow

My child went to the sea
To count the waves and shells,
But at Seville's[1] wide river,
She stopped and looked for me.

5   Five spotless ships were rocking
Between the flowers and bells,

Their oars were in the water,
Their keels riding in the swells.

Who sees inside the dazzling
10   Gold tower of Seville?
Five hidden voices answered,
Five rounded rings they fill.

The sky mounted the river
From shore to shining shore,
15   And in the russet twilight
Rocked five rings, not one more.

---

1. Seville's (sə vilz´): Seville is a city and port in southwestern Spain, on the Guadalquivir (gwä´ d'l kwiv´ ər) River.

CHILDREN ON THE BEACH
Joaquín Sorolla
Private Collection

Rider's Song

Federico García Lorca
translated by **Eleanor L. Turnbull**

Córdoba.[1]
Distant and lonely.

Black my pony, full the moon
and olives stowed in my saddle-bags.
5 Though well I may know the way
I'll never arrive at Córdoba.

Across the plain, through the wind,
black my pony, red the moon,
stark death is staring at me
10 from the tall towers of Córdoba.

Alas, how long is the way!
Alas, for my brave black pony!
Alas, stark death awaits me
before I arrive at Córdoba!

15 Córdoba.
Distant and lonely.

---

1. **Córdoba** (kôr′ də bə): A city in southern Spain.

THINKING ABOUT THE SELECTION

Interpreting

1. To what qualities of life and childish wonder does García Lorca appeal in "My Child Went to Sea"? Support your answer.
2. Part of humor comes from surprise and incongruity. What events happen to the child that seem incongruous?
3. The sea is a motif in many works by Latin American and Spanish writers. What might the sea represent to García Lorca in this poem?
4. This poem is from *Canciones* (songs). What qualities of a song does this poem have?
5. (a) Who might the solitary rider be in "Rider's Song"? Why is he alone? (b) What might García Lorca be implying through this isolated and solitary figure?
6. (a) What character traits does the rider possess? (b) Why might these be qualities that García Lorca values?

Applying

7. How does seeing the light side of a tragic event sometimes help people to see things more clearly?

THINKING AND WRITING

Writing About Vision

We all have a unique vision of life. Sometimes it is a tragic vision, sometimes a comic one, and sometimes a mixture of both. What is your vision of life at this moment? In any form you choose—one-act play, poem, short story, letter, and so on—communicate your vision of life without directly saying what it is. Use images and evocative language to express your vision and feelings about life. If possible, think of a single event that illustrates your vision, and describe that event. Give your first draft to a partner to see if he or she can determine what your vision is. If not, have your partner suggest ways to clarify your vision. Write a final version of your work.

1863–1933

Biographers claim that ever since Constantine Cavafy (kə´ vä′ fē) began writing poetry when he was a teenager, he wrote about seventy poems a year. Of these poems he saved maybe four or five and destroyed the rest. Cavafy was very fearful of public reaction to his poems. Before he submitted them for publication, he sent his work to trusted friends for their reactions. Only after he was assured of the merit of his work did he submit his poetry to magazines for publication. But Cavafy need not have been so self-conscious of his work. His work was readily received in Greece, Egypt, and the United States and is steadily gaining acceptance worldwide.

Although he was born in Alexandria, Egypt, and lived most of his life in Alexandria, Cavafy became a Greek citizen as soon as he was of age. Not only did he write about the Alexandria he loved, he also wrote about Greek history and was very much affected by the events that were happening in Greece while he lived in Egypt.

In 1882 the British bombed the Alexandrian forts, leaving the city in flames. The Cavafy family moved to Constantinople, where Cavafy lived for the next three years.

In 1885 the family returned to Alexandria, where Cavafy devoted his time to studying and writing. The Alexandrian Greeks found it difficult to rebuild their lives and institutions after the 1882 bombing. Cavafy's earlier poems reflect a pessimism for life affected by the misery and decadence he saw around him, such as in "Waiting for the Barbarians" (1898) and "Artificial Flowers" (1903).

With the help of a close friend, in 1901 Cavafy made his first trip to Athens, where he met novelist Gregory Xenopoulos (zen′ ō pōō lōs) and various magazine editors. During his second trip to Athens, in 1903, Xenopoulos selected twelve of Cavafy's poems and published them in the *Panatheneum* along with an article on his work. His popularity grew after his debut in the Athenian literary magazine.

In 1904 Cavafy published the first of only two books published during his lifetime. This first book contained only fourteen poems. In 1910, he published a second book, which included the first fourteen poems and twelve new ones. In addition, from 1908 to 1918 Cavafy steadily published his work in *Nea Zoe* (New Life), a literary magazine dedicated to literature and the advancement of demotic (vernacular) Greek.

Two characteristics of Cavafy's poetry are his unique combination of ancient and modern history and of demotic and purist Greek. Demotic Greek is the language spoken by the common people; purist Greek is the official language of the church and state. Although the distinction between demotic and purist Greek does not translate into English, it is a characteristic of Cavafy's poetry that is worth noting. Cavafy's daring use of both the scholarly language of the church and the coarse language of the common people was a kind of a political statement.

Although his poetry did not bring him money, it did bring him fame as word of his poetry spread. Cavafy's poetry first became known in English-speaking countries in E. M. Forster's collection of essays about Alexandria, *Pharos and Pharillon*. Several collections of his poetry have been published posthumously and have since been translated into several languages.

GUIDE FOR INTERPRETING

Waiting for the Barbarians; Artificial Flowers

Commentary

Irony. Irony occurs when there is a contrast between what is said and what is meant or between what is expected and what occurs. There are three types of irony in literature.

Verbal irony exists when a speaker says one thing but means the opposite. For instance, in Shakespeare's *Julius Caesar*, Mark Antony says during his oration after the death of Caesar, "Brutus is an honorable man." Although his words say that Brutus is honorable, Antony means that Brutus is not at all honorable.

In *dramatic irony* a character does not understand the words or acts of another character or characters, but the audience does. In Act I, Scene vi of *Macbeth*, for example, Banquo and Duncan discuss the pleasant and delicate air as they arrive at Inverness. The audience knows, however, that a murder is being plotted, and the atmosphere is anything but pleasant.

Situational irony occurs when the expected results of an action or situation differ from the actual results. Often there will be a twist at the end of the work that will surprise the reader or audience and change the meaning of what came before. Many of O. Henry's short stories contain an ironic twist at the end that the reader finds surprising or unexpected.

Many of Cavafy's poems contain irony, such as the situational irony found in "Waiting for the Barbarians" and "Artificial Flowers." Cavafy often leads his reader to expect one outcome but delivers another. He purposefully leaves his poems somewhat ambiguous, as in "Waiting for the Barbarians." As you read this poem, you will think one way about the reactions of the people who are waiting for the barbarians, but the end will surprise you and change the meaning of the beginning of the poem. "Artificial Flowers" also contains irony, as Cavafy unexpectedly reveres the artificiality of man-made products over those that nature produces. In this poem Cavafy's irony occurs when events or perceptions contradict the expectations of the readers.

Writing

Ironic situations occur and are recorded every day. You can find irony in the news, on television, in comic strips, and in everyday activities and conversation. Think of an ironic situation that has happened to you. Freewrite, briefly describing the situation and why it was ironic. Or, if nothing comes to mind, make up an imaginary ironic situation and describe it or create a cartoon to illustrate the situation. You might use Gary Larson's *The Far Side* cartoons, which frequently capture ironic situations, as a springboard for ideas.

Literary Focus Discuss some examples of situational irony. If students are familiar with *Return of the Jedi*, the third movie in the *Star Wars* trilogy, point out that it is ironic that the primitive Ewoks are the ones who are able to defeat the fire power and technology of the proponents of the Dark Side. Point out that situational irony is often used to undercut a reader's expectations. When reading Cavafy's poetry, have students pay attention to how certain expectations are aroused and then unexpectedly changed.

Writing/Prior Knowledge You might want to put up transparencies of Gary Larson's *The Far Side* cartoons on an overhead projector. As a class, discuss the irony in the cartoons. After students are comfortable identifying irony, have them individually complete the writing activity.

ESL Teaching Strategy ESL students may have difficulty with the writing activity. Pair up these students with another member of the class. Have the native-speaking student help the ESL student to understand irony and Gary Larson's *The Far Side* cartoons.

Vocabulary
Preteach the following vocabulary words:

imposing (im pō´ziŋ) *adj.*: Intimidating; grand

consuls (kän´səlz) *n.*: One of two chief magistrates of the ancient Roman republic

orators (ôr´ət ərz) *n.*: Eloquent public speakers

rhetoric (ret´ər ik) *n.*: Language that is showy and elaborate but largely empty of clear ideas and sincere emotion

trite (trīt) *adj.*: Insignificant; worn out with use

wrought (rôt) *v.*: Decorated

mire (mīr) *n.*: Slush; deep mud

---

sheet, *Recognizing Situational Irony*, p. 1360
Selection Test, pp. 1361–1362

Teaching Tenth-Grade Students These poems should not present any problems for tenth-grade students. You may wish, however, to review irony with students and perhaps have them discuss the irony in poetry and prose with which they are already familiar.

Spelling Tip Point out to students the spelling and definition of the word *consuls*. Tell them this word should not be confused with *counsels*.

Waiting for the Barbarians

Constantine Cavafy

translated by Edmund Keeley and Philip Sherrard

What are we waiting for, assembled in the forum?

   The barbarians are due here today.

Why isn't anything going on in the senate?
Why are the senators sitting there without
   legislating?

5   Because the barbarians are coming today.
   What's the point of senators making laws now?
   Once the barbarians are here, they'll do the
   legislating.

Why did our emperor get up so early,
and why is he sitting enthroned at the city's main
   gate,
10 in state, wearing the crown?

   Because the barbarians are coming today
   and the emperor's waiting to receive their leader.
   He's even got a scroll to give him,
   loaded with titles, with imposing names.

Why have our two consuls and praetors[1] come out
15   today
wearing their embroidered, their scarlet togas?

----

1. **praetors** (prēt´ ərz) *n.*: Magistrates of ancient Rome, next below consuls in rank.

Why have they put on bracelets with so many
   amethysts,
rings sparkling with magnificent emeralds?
Why are they carrying elegant canes
20 beautifully worked in silver and gold?

   Because the barbarians are coming today
   and things like that dazzle the barbarians.

Why don't our distinguished orators turn up as
   usual
to make their speeches, say what they have to say?

25   Because the barbarians are coming today
   and they're bored by rhetoric and public speaking.

Why this sudden bewilderment, this confusion?
(How serious people's faces have become.)
Why are the streets and squares emptying so
   rapidly,
30 everyone going home lost in thought?

   Because night has fallen and the barbarians
   haven't come.
   And some of our men just in from the border say
   there are no barbarians any longer.

Now what's going to happen to us without
   barbarians?
35 Those people were a kind of solution.

Reader's Response *Do you share Cavafy's feelings about civilization? Explain.*

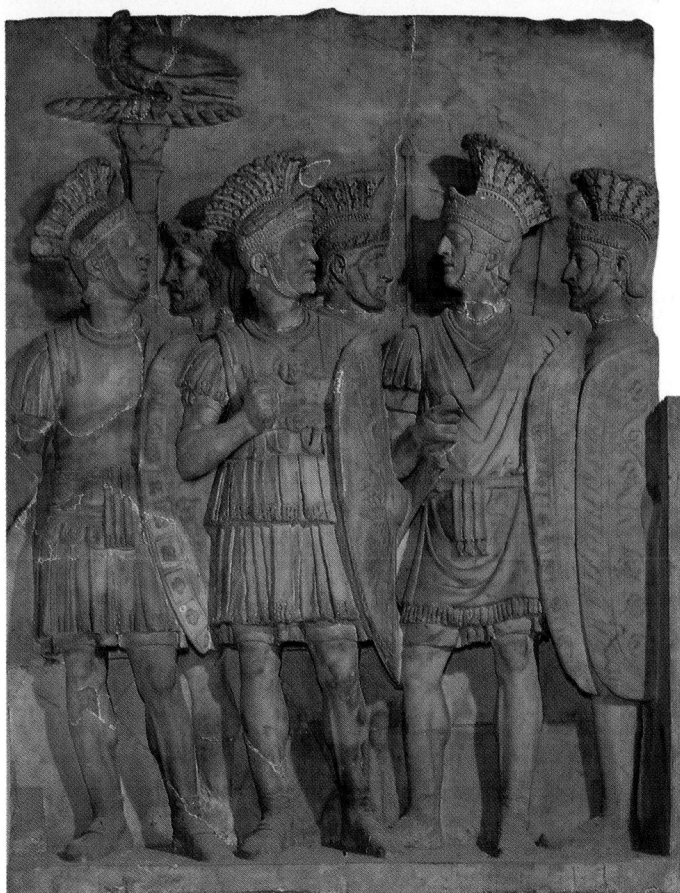

**RELIEF OF
ROMAN SOLDIERS**
Second century
The Louvre, Paris

THINKING ABOUT THE SELECTION

Interpreting

1. Who are the two characters speaking in the poem?
2. Why have the people been waiting for the barbarians?
3. To what problem might the barbarians have been "a kind of solution"?
4. The location and time period of this poem are unknown. (a) In what time period and location might this poem be set? Support your answer with details from the poem. (b) What role did the barbarians play in this location and time period?
5. Who or what are the barbarians?

Applying

6. Cavafy often used ancient history to shed light on the present. What message for present generations might Cavafy be illustrating in this poem?

ANALYZING LITERATURE

Understanding Irony

Situational irony occurs when the expected results of an action or situation differ from the actual results or when events occur that contradict the expectations of the reader.

Explain the situational irony in "Waiting for the Barbarians."

(continued from bottom of page)
three Roman soldiers dressed for battle.

Ask students to discuss the figures' dress and expressions. Why is this an appropriate piece to illustrate Cavafy's poem?

Closure and Extension
ANSWERS TO THINKING ABOUT THE SELECTION

1. The two speakers are commoners. The one who knows slightly more than the other leads the reader through the drama.
2. The people, emperor, and legislators no longer know what to do; they are waiting for the barbarians to lead them and give them the answers.
3. The barbarians are the solution to the problems of civilization.
4. Suggested responses: (a) It appears that the poem is set in ancient Rome because of the barbarians, the emperor, the references to the senators, consuls, and praetors, and their clothes and jewelry. (b) The barbarian movement contributed to the fall of the Roman Empire.
5. The barbarians were a non-Roman people regarded as primitive or savage; they were uncivilized.
6. Answers may differ. Suggested response: Because this poem was written near the turn of the nineteenth century, Cavafy may have been warning his generation and future generations of the evils and pitfalls of civilization. He expresses that just as barbarism was not the answer, so civilization may not be the answer either, because, after all, Rome did fall.

ANSWERS TO ANALYZING LITERATURE

Answers may differ. Suggested response: The irony lies in the fact that a highly civilized culture is waiting for barbarism to solve its problems—"those people were a kind of solution." Yet, in the end the barbarians do not show up and the people are lost.

Challenge Critics have claimed that Cavafy's poetry is reminiscent of T. S. Eliot's early work. Have students read Eliot's earlier poems and compare his tone and use of irony with those of Cavafy. Have them present their findings in oral presentations or essays.

Humanities Note

Fine art, *Relief of Roman Soldiers.* This relief dates back to the second century. Reliefs are three-dimensional sculptures that project from a flat background. They most often decorate public buildings, churches, and arches. Roman relief sculpture was strongly influenced by Greek art and sculpture. This relief depicts

Motivation/Prior Knowledge Discuss with students all the man-made or machine-made items and inventions that are replacing those that we used to get from nature or that we used to make from scratch. For example, students might reply that we use man-made fibers instead of or in addition to natural fibers; that machines have made every facet of life easier and quicker; and that we no longer make clothes, food, and so on, when we can go to a store and buy them. Ask them what the advantages of such advancements are. What are the disadvantages? Then have them read Cavafy's poem "Artificial Flowers," in which he ironically states that the artificial is far more beautiful and more perfect than nature itself.

Purpose-Setting Question What message lies in Cavafy's ironic poem?

Universal Themes You might like to pair this poem with "Ode to My Socks," page 1250, in which Pablo Neruda expresses his views on beauty.

Closure and Extension

ANSWERS TO THINKING ABOUT THE SELECTION

1. (a) The speaker finds the imperishable beauty, immortality, and cleanliness of the artificial desirable. (b) He finds their perishable beauty and mortality undesirable. He also finds their unadorned forms boring and common because they cannot be "wrought" with beautiful ornaments and materials. It is also undesirable that real flowers "sprout unclean from dirt and mire."
2. Answers may differ. Suggested response: The speaker's attitude is one of fear and sarcasm. He fears that we are so dependent on the artificial and man-made items that we can no longer appreciate beauty.
3. Answers may differ. Suggested response: The tone is one of sadness and almost despair. The speaker sees the direction we are headed and is fearful that it is too late to change that direction.
4. Answers may differ. Suggested response: The speaker is clinging to the way things were before civiliza-

Artificial Flowers

Constantine Cavafy

translated by Edmund Keeley and Philip Sherrard

I do not want the real narcissus[1]—nor do
real lilies or real roses please me.
These but adorn the trite and common gardens.
　Their flesh
accords me bitterness, fatigue, and pain—
5　their perishable beauty bores me.

　Give me but artificial flowers—glories of porcelain
　　and metal—
　that never wither and never rot, whose forms will
　　never age.
　Flowers of an exquisite garden in another land
　where Rhythms, Theories, and Ideas dwell.

10　Flowers I love created out of gold and glass,
　trustworthy gifts of a trustworthy art,
　and dyed in hues more beautiful than nature's,
　with mother-of-pearl and with enamel wrought,
　with ideal stalks and leaves.

15　They draw their grace from wise and purest Taste;
　nor did they sprout unclean from dirt and mire.
　And if they lack aroma, we'll pour them
　　fragrances,
　we'll burn before them myrrh[2] of our sentiments.

----

1. narcissus (när′ sis′ əs) *n.*: Bulb plants with smooth leaves and clusters of white, yellow, or orange flowers.
2. myrrh (mur) *n.*: A fragrant, bitter-tasting gum resin used in making incense and perfume.

THINKING ABOUT THE SELECTION

Interpreting

1. (a) What characteristics of artificial flowers does the speaker find desirable? (b) What characteristics of real flowers does the speaker find undesirable?
2. What can you imply about the speaker's attitude toward life? What does the speaker fear?
3. What is the tone of this poem? Explain.
4. To what does the speaker cling in his desire for the artificial?
5. (a) What power does Cavafy give humans in this poem? (b) What danger and benefits are inherent in having such power?

Applying

6. Cavafy wrote this poem in 1903. What message might Cavafy be sending as civilization was entering the Modern Age?

THINKING AND WRITING

Writing About History

　　Much of Cavafy's poetry was based on historical events. He liked to combine ancient history with events that were current at the time. Sometimes his poetry had a message that we should learn from history; other times his poetry illustrated a scene as civilization entered into a new age—the Modern Age. Think of a historical event that you think carries a message for the present generation or will help the present generation to enter a new age or decade. Decide on the form that will best suit your message. You might decide to write a poem, an essay, or a short story. Then write about the historical event, giving clues as to what we can learn from the event and how we can apply what we've learned to our own lives. You do not want to directly tell your audience the lesson they should learn. If possible, use irony, as Cavafy did, as the vehicle for communicating your lesson or message.

tion—a time when nature was the epitome of beauty and mystery.
5. Answers may differ. Suggested responses: (a) He gives humans the power to improve on and perfect nature—God's work—and to reach beyond ourselves and nature. (b) Power in the hands of those who misuse or do not fully understand that power is dangerous and can result in deaths and misguided values. The benefits

of such power have been to prolong life expectancy, cure diseases, travel into space, and so on.
6. Answers may differ. Suggested response: As with "Waiting for the Barbarians," Cavafy is warning his and future generations of the possible repercussions of civilization and advancement.

THINKING AND WRITING

Writing Across the Curriculum Notify the history department that students are writing fiction based on a historical account. Encourage students to consult their history teachers for assistance and sources for more information about their chosen event.

The Americas

THE TOTONAC CIVILIZATION—THE GREAT PYRAMID OF TAJIN
Diego Rivera

Humanities Note

Fine art, *The Totonac Civilization* by Diego Rivera. Born in Guanajuato, Mexico, Rivera (1886–1957) began to draw as a small child and was provided with his own studio before he even learned to read. He eventually enrolled in the San Carlos Academy of Fine Arts, but he was expelled for taking part in street riots—an event that hinted at the future direction of both his life and his art.

Rivera is known for his huge frescoes, which he composed using ancient artistic techniques. Many of these frescoes conveyed political and social messages that at times sparked controversy. Rivera also frequently depicted the ancient peoples that first inhabited his native land. In the work seen here, for example, he proudly captures the colorfulness and elegance of one of Mexico's earliest civilizations.

You might want to use the following questions to discuss the art:

1. What impression does this painting convey of the culture it depicts?
2. Which details contribute to this impression?
3. How would you describe the style in which this work is painted? Explain.
4. How would you describe this painting to someone who has never seen it?

MANUEL ROJAS

1896–1973

A man of great strength and vigor, Manuel Rojas (mä noo el' rō' häs) is known for his forceful and moving prose. Not only is he regarded as the master of the modern Chilean short story, but he is also considered to be one of the finest of all the modern Latin American fiction writers.

Although he was of Chilean descent, Manuel Rojas was born and reared in Argentina. Having lost his father when he was less than five, he was forced to begin working as a laborer during his early teens. When he was sixteen, he moved to Chile, where he worked as a sailor, housepainter, bargeman, night watchman, typographer, and railroad worker. In 1924 he settled permanently in Santiago, the Chilean capital, and began devoting his energies to journalism and creative writing. Two years later he published his first collection of short stories, *Men of the South* (1926). Closely based on his experiences as a laborer in both Argentina and Chile, this collection immediately established Rojas as one of the most promising Latin American writers of his generation.

In 1931 Rojas was named the director of the University of Chile Press. This appointment, along with the publication of his novel *Launches in the Bay* (1932), contributed to his growing stature in the Latin American literary community. Throughout the next three decades, he continued to widen his reputation among critics, writers, and the general public. The works he produced during this period include *The Biretta from Maule* (1943), *Son of a Thief* (1951), and *Better Than Wine* (1958).

Regarded as Rojas's finest work, the novel *Son of a Thief* is an account of the sufferings of a young Argentine boy. Following his father's arrest and imprisonment for burglary, the boy is forced to spend his childhood in poverty. As Rojas did during his own childhood, the boy works as a laborer to support himself and makes a lone journey to Chile in hope of finding a better life. There, he accidentally becomes involved in a street riot and is unjustly imprisoned. All the boy's experiences are described in a graphically realistic manner. Yet more than anything else, it is Rojas's penetrating insights into the inner workings of the boy's mind that have established this novel as one of the finest ever produced in Latin America.

Despite the success of this novel, Rojas is remembered mainly for his short stories. "The Glass of Milk" is a typical Rojas story. Based on his personal experiences, the story is told in a simple and restrained yet authoritative and moving manner.

GUIDE FOR INTERPRETING

The Glass of Milk

Commentary

Point of View. Because many of Rojas's stories are closely based on his personal experiences, it would be easy for readers to make the mistake of assuming that the stories are narrated by Rojas himself. Yet in Rojas's works, as in all works of fiction, the narrator is *never* the author himself. Instead, the narrator is a character or voice created by the author to tell the story.

The term **point of view** refers to the type of narrator used in a fictional work. Most often, stories are told from either a first-person or third-person point of view. In a narrative with a first-person point of view, one of the characters tells the story in his or her own words, using the first-person pronoun *I*. In a narrative with a third-person point of view, the narrator does not participate in the story and refers to the characters using the third-person pronouns *he* and *she*. A third-person narrator may be either limited or omniscient. An omniscient third-person narrator is able to see into the minds of all the characters. In contrast, a limited third-person narrator can convey the thoughts and feelings only of a single character.

During the late nineteenth and early twentieth centuries, fiction writers generally abandoned the use of the omniscient point of view in favor of first-person and third-person limited narrators. Because people in the real world cannot see into one another's minds, writers came to the conclusion that a fictional work with an omniscient point of view cannot be considered realistic. In addition, the disappearance of the omniscient point of view reflected the growing belief that "reality" and "truth" cannot be viewed objectively because no two people view the world in exactly the same way. By using a first-person or limited third-person point of view, the writers hoped to capture the way in which people's attitudes and feelings shape their perceptions of the world.

As you read Rojas's story, determine the point of view and take note of how it shapes the portrayal of characters and events.

Writing

What would you do if you were in a strange city with no food, no money, and no place to stay? How would you go about finding food and money? How would you go about trying to find shelter? What would you do if the place in which you were stranded had an especially hot or cold climate? Write a journal entry in which you respond to these questions and discuss any other thoughts and feelings you have about this type of situation.

Literary Focus To help students understand how point of view can shape the portrayal of characters and events in a work of fiction, have students take turns describing a person, place, or event with which they are all familiar. Then have them discuss the differences between the descriptions of the various students. How might these differences reflect the attitudes and feelings of the individual students?

Writing/Prior Knowledge Before students begin freewriting, ask them if they ever got lost or separated from their parents when they were younger. If so, have them discuss these experiences.

ESL Teaching Strategy If you have any Latin American students in your class, you might want to have them offer their impressions of city life in their countries of origin. How are the cities in their native land different from the American cities they have visited?

Teaching Tenth-Grade Students Have tenth-grade students jot down any questions that come to mind as they are reading the story. Then have a class discussion in which students ask the questions that they have listed.

Vocabulary

Preteach the following vocabulary words:

gaudy (gôd′ ē) *adj.*: bright and showy but tasteless

timidity (tim id′ i tē) *n.*: showing fear, hesitation, or lack of self-confidence

bewildered (bē wil′ derd) *adj.*: hopelessly confused

anguished (aŋ′ gwisht) *adj.*: filled with agonizing worry or pain

entrails (en′ trālz) *n.*: internal organs

Support Material

Teaching Portfolio

Teacher Backup, p. 1363

Grammar in Action Worksheet, *Indirect and Direct Quotations*, p. 1367

Usage and Mechanics Worksheet, p. 1369

Vocabulary Check, p. 1370

Analyzing Literature Worksheet, *Un-derstanding Point of View*, p. 1371

Critical Thinking and Reading Worksheet, *Recognizing Period Characteristics*, p. 1372

Selection Test, pp. 1373–1374

Spelling Tip Caution students to be sure they use *gu* not *qu* in spelling *anguished*.

The Glass of Milk

Manuel Rojas

translated by Zoila Nelken

Propped on the starboard[1] rail, the sailor seemed to be waiting for someone. A bundle wrapped in white paper, grease-spotted, was in his left hand; his right tended his pipe.

From behind some freight-cars, a thin youth appeared; he paused a moment, looked out to sea, and then walked on along the edge of the wharf with his hands in his pockets, idling or thinking.

When he passed in front of the ship, the sailor called out to him in English:

"I say, look here!"

The youth raised his head, and without stopping, answered in the same language.

"Hello! What?"

"Are you hungry?"

There was a brief silence during which the youth seemed to be thinking, and took one shorter step as if to stop, but then replied, smiling feebly at the sailor:

"No, I'm not hungry. Thanks, sailor."

"All right."

The sailor took his pipe out of his mouth, spat, and replacing it, looked away. The youth, ashamed that he had seemed to need charity, walked a little faster, as if afraid he might change his mind.

A moment later, a gaudy tramp with a long, blond beard and blue eyes, dressed in odd rags and oversized, torn shoes, passed before the sailor, who without greeting called to him:

"Are you hungry?"

He had not yet finished the phrase when the tramp looked with shining eyes at the package the sailor held in his hand and answered hurriedly:

"Yes, sir; I'm very much hungry!"

The sailor smiled. The package flew through the air and landed in the eager hands. The hungry fellow did not even say "thanks", but sat right down on the ground, opened the still-warm bundle, and happily rubbed his hands as he saw what it contained. A port loafer might not speak English well, but he would never forgive himself if he didn't know enough to ask food from someone who did speak it.

The youth who passed by first had stopped nearby, and had seen what happened.

He was hungry too. He had not eaten for exactly three days, three long days. And more from timidity and shame than from pride, he refused to wait by the gangways at mealtimes, hoping the generosity of the sailors would produce some package of left-overs and bits of meat. He could not do it, he would never be able to do it. And when, as just now, someone did offer him a handout, the boy refused it heroically, though he felt his hunger increase with the refusal.

He had been wandering for six days around the side streets and docks of that port. An English vessel had left him there after bringing him from Punta Arenas,[2] where he had jumped a previous ship on which he had served as captain's mess boy. He had spent a month there helping an Austrian crabber and then had stowed away on the first ship bound north.

---

1. **starboard** (stär′ bərd) *adj.:* On the right-hand side of a ship.

2. **Punta Arenas** (po͞on′ tä ä *re′* näs): A city in southern Chile.

He was discovered the day after sailing, and put to work in the boiler room. At the first large port of call, he had been put off, and there he had remained, like a bale without a label, without an acquaintance, without a penny, and without a trade.

As long as the ship was in port, the boy managed to eat, but after that . . . The great city that rose up beyond the back streets with their taverns and cheap inns did not attract him; it seemed a place of slavery: stale, dark, without the grand sweep of the sea; among its high walls and narrow streets people lived and died bewildered by agonizing drudgery.

The boy was gripped by that fascination of the sea which molds the most peaceful and orderly lives as a strong arm a thin rod. Although very young, he had already made several trips along the coast of South America on various ships, doing odd jobs and tasks, tasks and odd jobs which were almost useless on land.

After the ship left him, the boy walked and walked, hoping to chance upon something that would enable him to live somehow until he could get back to his home grounds; but he found nothing. The port was not very busy, and the few ships that had work would not take him on.

The docks were swarming with confirmed tramps: sailors on the beach, like himself, who had either jumped ship or were fleeing some crime; loafers given to idleness, who kept alive one knows not how, by begging or stealing, spending their days as if they were the beads of some grimy rosary,[3] waiting for who knows what extraordinary events, or not expecting anything; people of the strangest and most exotic races and places, and even some in whose existence one doesn't believe until one sees a living example.

The following day, convinced that he could not hold out much longer, the youth decided to resort to any means to get some food.

Walking along, he found himself in front of a ship that had docked the night before, and was loading wheat. A line of men, heavy sacks on their shoulders, shuttled from the freight-cars, across the gangplank to the hatchways of the ship's hold where the stevedores[4] received the cargo.

He watched for a while, until he dared to speak to the foreman, offering his services. He was accepted, and enthusiastically he took his place in the long line of dock workers.

During the first period of the day he worked well; but later, he began to feel tired and dizzy; he swayed as he crossed the gangplank, the heavy load on his shoulder, on seeing at his feet the opening between the side of the ship and the thick wall of the wharf, at the bottom of which the sea, stained with oil and littered with garbage, lapped quietly.

There was a brief pause at lunch time, and

---

3. rosary (rō′ zər ē) n.: A string of beads used to keep count in saying prayers.

4. stevedores (stē′ və dôrz′) n.: People employed at loading and unloading ships.

RETRATO DE UN JOVEN (PORTRAIT OF A YOUTH)
Leonor Fini

...losa emerged as one of the major political figures in his native country during the late 1980's.

During the early twentieth century, three Chilean writers devoted much of their energy to addressing the dominant social concerns of their nation. These writers were Manuel Rojas, Joaquín Edwards Bello, and Eduardo Barrios. All three were widely regarded as champions of Chile's underprivileged classes. Yet, in actual fact, these three writers were more interested in the dispassionate representation of the realities of lower-class life than in advocating social solutions.

5 **Discussion** Have students explain the simile that Rojas uses in this passage. Do they find it to be effective? Why or why not?

6 **Discussion** Have students discuss the impression of the city that Rojas conveys in this paragraph.

7 **Discussion** Ask students if this seems like a realistic depiction of a Chilean port city in the early 1900's. Why or why not? How do they think that Rojas's personal experiences might have contributed to the realistic quality of his descriptions?

Humanities Note

Fine art, *Retrato de un Joven* by Leonor Fini. Fini was born in 1908 in Buenos Aires, Argentina. Feeling that the South American artistic community was less receptive to her work because she was a woman, she left her native land and traveled to Paris. There she was exposed to the works of Pablo Picasso, who become one of her main sources of inspiration. In 1936 Fini exhibited her paintings at a Surrealist show in New York, and she subsequently established herself as an internationally famous and critically acclaimed artist. As is the case with this painting, her works typically have a realistic yet magical quality.

You might want to use the following questions to discuss the art:
1. What impression does the artist convey of the youth depicted in this painting?
2. How does she convey this impression?
3. Does the youth pictured here match the way in which you envision the youth in Rojas's story? Why or why not?
4. If you had to describe this painting to a friend who has never seen it, what would you say?

Discussion sidebar (left column)

Discussion Have students explain why the young man pretends not to be hungry.

Discussion Have students explain why the young man refuses the foreman's offer to lend him forty cents. Is it because he is embarrassed that he is so desperately in need of money? Is it because he is too proud to accept help from someone else?

Discussion Point out to students that up to this point Rojas has not revealed the name of the story's central character. Why do students think that Rojas chose to refer to him as the "youth" or "the boy" rather than by name? Do students expect that the boy's name will eventually be revealed? Why or why not?

Discussion Have students discuss why the images of the young man's home and family appear in his mind at this point in the story.

Discussion Ask students to explain how Rojas was able to describe the effects of hunger in such detail. Do they imagine that Rojas himself had experienced extreme hunger at some point in his life?

13 Discussion Why do students think that the boy suddenly becomes determined to steal food after refusing previous offers of food and money?

14 Literary Focus Have students speculate about how this passage might have been different if Rojas had used an omniscient third-person point of view rather than a limited third-person point of view. Do they think that Rojas would have revealed the thoughts of the man reading the newspaper?

Main text

8 while some of the men went off to the nearby eating places, and others ate what they had brought, the boy stretched out on the ground to rest, hiding his hunger.

He finished the day's work feeling completely exhausted, covered with sweat, at the end of his rope. While the laborers were leaving, the boy sat on some sacks, watching for the foreman, and when the last man had gone, approached him; confused and stuttering, he asked, without explaining what was happening to him, if he could be paid immediately, or if it were possible to get an advance on his earnings.

The foreman answered that it was customary to pay at the end of a job, and that it would still be necessary to work the following day in order to finish loading the ship. One more day! On the other hand, they never paid a cent in advance.

"But," he said, "if you need it, I could lend you about forty cents . . . That's all I have."

9 The boy thanked him for his offer with an anguished smile, and left.

Then the boy was seized by acute despair. He was hungry, hungry, hungry! Hunger doubled him over, like a heavy, broad whiplash. He saw everything through a blue haze, and he staggered **10** like a drunk when he walked. Nevertheless, he would not have been able to complain or to shout, for his suffering was deep and exhausting; it was not pain, but anguish, the end! It seemed to him that he was flattened out by a great weight.

Suddenly he felt his entrails on fire, and he stood still. He began to bend down, down, doubling over forcibly like a rod of steel, until he thought that he would drop. At that instant, as if a window opened before him, he saw his home, the **11** view from it, the faces of his mother, brothers and sisters, all that he wanted and loved appeared and disappeared before his eyes shut by fatigue . . . Then, little by little, the giddiness passed and he began to straighten up, while the burning subsided gradually. Finally, he straightened up, breathing **12** deeply. One more hour and he would drop unconscious to the ground.

He quickened his step, as if fleeing another dizzy spell, and, as he walked, he made up his mind to eat anywhere, without paying, even if they shamed him, beat him, sent him to jail, anything;

the main thing was to eat, eat, eat. A hundred times he mentally repeated the word: eat, eat, eat, until it lost its meaning, leaving his head feeling hot and empty.

He did not intend to run away; he would simply say to the owner, "Sir, I was hungry, hungry, hungry, and I can't pay . . . Do what you want."

He came to the outskirts of the city, and on one of the first streets he found a milk bar. It was a small, clean, and airy place, with little tables with marble tops. Behind the counter stood a blonde lady in a very white apron.

He chose that place. There were few passersby. He could have eaten at one of the cheap grills near the wharves but they were always full of people who gambled and drank.

There was only one customer in the milk bar. He was a little old man with glasses, who sat reading, his nose stuck between the pages of a newspaper, motionless, as if glued to his chair. On the little table there was a half-empty glass of milk.

While he waited for him to leave, the boy walked up and down the sidewalk; he felt the burning sensation in his stomach returning little by little; and he waited five, ten, up to fifteen minutes. He grew tired, and stood to one side of the door, from where he cast glances like stones at the old man.

What the devil could he be reading with such attention? The boy even imagined the old man was his enemy, who knew his intentions and had decided to frustrate them. He felt like entering and saying something insulting that would force the old man to leave, a rude word or phrase that would show him he had no right to sit there reading for an hour for so small a purchase.

Finally, the client finished what he was reading, or at least, interrupted it. He downed the rest of the milk in one gulp, rose slowly, paid, and walked toward the door. He went out. He was a stoop-shouldered old man, probably a carpenter or varnisher.

Once in the street, the old man put on his glasses, stuck his nose in the newspaper again, and walked slowly away, stopping every ten steps to read more closely.

Bottom section

Direct quotations record the exact words spoken by a character and are presented in quotation marks. **Indirect quotations,** on the other hand, report the substance of what a character said, rather than the exact words. Unlike direct quotations, indirect quotations do not require quotation marks and are punctuated like a simple declarative sentence. Note the following examples from Rojas's story:

DIRECT QUOTATION: "But," he said, "if you need it, I could lend you about forty cents . . . That's all I have."

INDIRECT QUOTATION: The foreman answered that it was customary to pay when the job was over, and that it was still necessary to work the following day in order to finish loading the ship.

Student Activity 1. Find four more direct quotations and two more indirect quotations in "The Glass of Milk." Then explain why a writer would sometimes choose to report a character's words directly and, at other times, use indirect quotations.

Student Activity 2. Rewrite the following direct quotations from "The Glass of Milk" as indirect quotations.

1. . . . The youth seemed to be thinking, . . . but then he replied,

PUERTO DE VILLEFRANCHE (PORT OF VILLEFRANCHE)
Joaquín Torres-García

The youth waited until he was some distance away, and then entered. For a moment the boy stood by the entrance, undecided, not knowing where to sit. Finally, he chose a table and walked toward it, but halfway there he changed his mind, walked back, tripped over a chair, and finally installed himself in a corner.

The lady came, wiped the tabletop with a rag, and in a soft voice that had a trace of Castilian[5] accent, asked him:

"What will you have?"

_____
5. Castilian (kas til′ yən): Of Castile, a region in northern and central Spain.

"A glass of milk."

"Large?"

"Yes, large."

"Is that all?"

"Are there any biscuits?"

"No. Vanilla wafers."

"Well, vanilla wafers."

When the lady had turned away, he wiped his hands on his knees, rejoicing, as if he were cold and were about to drink something hot.

The lady returned, and placed before him a large glass of milk, and a dish full of vanilla wafers; then she went back to her place behind the counter.

smiling feebly at the sailor: "No, I'm not hungry. Thanks, sailor."
2. The lady came, and . . . asked him, "What will you have?"
3. At last he got up and said simply, "Thank you very much ma'am; goodbye . . ."
4. "Goodbye, son," she answered.

Student Activity 3. Write a brief dialogue between two real people or two fictional characters, using both direct and indirect quotations. If you want, you can base your dialogue on a conversation between two friends or family members.

16 Discussion Have students discuss what the boy's inability to look the woman in the eye reveals about his personality.

17 Discussion Have students explain why the boy begins to weep. Are students surprised by his weeping? Why or why not?

18 Discussion Are students surprised by the waitress's reaction to the boy's weeping? How do they think that most people would react? Do they think that many people would be likely to let him leave without paying for his food? Why or why not?

Discussion Do students think that it is natural for feelings of gratitude to vanish so quickly? Why or why not?

20 Literary Focus Tell students that a typical modern short story ends abruptly with no resolution, leaving readers with possibilities, not solutions. Is this true of "The Glass of Milk"? How does this characteristic reflect the Modernist perception that twentieth-century life is characterized by an overwhelming sense of uncertainty?

Cultural Note Tell students that Rojas was heavily influenced by the modern American writer William Faulkner. If students have studied American literature, have them compare and contrast "The Glass of Milk" with the Faulkner stories they have read. Then have them try to think of other foreign writers who were influenced by American writers.

Cooperative Learning Students may be interested in learning more about what it was like to live in Latin America during the early twentieth century. Divide your class into groups of three or four and assign each group a different Latin American country. Then have each group find out as much as they can about life during the early twentieth century in the country they have been assigned. Once the groups have completed their research, have them share their findings.

His first impulse was to drink the milk in one gulp and then eat the vanilla wafers; but he immediately changed his mind. He felt the woman's eyes watching him with curiosity and attention,. He did not dare to look at her; he felt that if he did she would guess his situation and his shameful intentions, and he would have to get up and leave without touching what he had ordered.

Slowly, he took a vanilla wafer and moistening it in the milk, he took a bite; he took a sip of milk, and he felt the burning in his stomach diminishing, dying away. But he became aware of the reality of his desperate situation at once, and he felt something tight and hot well up inside, choking him. He realized that he was about to cry, to sob aloud, and although he knew that the lady was looking at him, he could neither hold back nor undo the burning knot of tears that grew tighter and tighter. He fought it, and as he fought he ate hurriedly, as if frightened, afraid that crying would keep him from eating. When he had finished the milk and the wafers, his eyes clouded and something hot rolled down his nose and into the glass. A terrible sob racked his whole body.

He held his head in his hands, and for a long time he cried, cried with rage, cried with shame, crying as he had never cried before.

He was hunched over crying when he felt a hand caress his tired head, and heard a woman's voice with a sweet Castilian accent say to him:

"Cry, son, cry. . ."

Again his eyes filled with tears and he cried as intensely as before, but this time, not with pain but with joy; he felt a great refreshing sensation spread inside him, extinguishing the hot something that had nearly strangled him. As he cried, it seemed to him that his life and feelings were cleansed like a glass under a stream of water, recovering the clearness and firmness of former days.

When the crying spell passed, he wiped his eyes and face with his handkerchief, feeling relieved. He raised his head and looked at the lady, but she was no longer looking at him, she was gazing out at the street, at a distant point in space, and her face seemed sad.

On the table before him there was another glass of milk and another dish heaped with vanilla wafers. He ate slowly, without thinking about anything, as if nothing had happened to him, as if he were at home and his mother were that woman who was standing behind the counter.

When he had finished, it had grown dark, and the place was lit by an electric light. He remained seated for a while, wondering what he would say to the lady when he left, without thinking of anything appropriate.

At last he got up and said simply,

"Thank you very much, ma'am; goodbye. . . "

"Goodbye, son," she answered.

He went out. The wind blowing from the sea refreshed his face, still hot from crying. He walked about aimlessly for a while, then went down a street that led to the docks. It was a very beautiful night, and large stars gleamed in the summer sky.

He thought about the blonde lady who had treated him so generously, resolving to repay her, to reward her as she deserved, when he got some money. But these thoughts of gratitude vanished with the burning of his face, until not one remained, and the recent event receded and was lost in the recesses of his past life.

Suddenly, he surprised himself humming. He straightened up happily, strode on with assurance and determination.

He came to the edge of the sea, and walked back and forth with a spring in his step; he felt like a new man, as if his inner forces, previously scattered, had reassembled and united solidly.

Then he sat down on a pile of burlap sacks; fatigue, like a tingling sensation, climbed up his legs. He looked at the sea. The lights of the wharf and ships spread over the water in a reddish-gold ripple, trembling softly. He stretched out on his back, looking up at the sky for a long time. He did not feel like thinking, or singing, or talking. He just felt alive, that was all. Then he fell asleep with his face toward the sea.

ANSWERS TO THINKING ABOUT THE SELECTION

1. (a) Answers will differ. Students may feel that he is too proud to accept charity. (b) Suggested response: It reveals that he is proud and that he feels ashamed of his present condition.

2. Suggested response: He is in a strange place in which he knows no one and he does not know how to work at any trade.

3. (a) Suggested response: He does not explain his situation to the foreman because he is ashamed of it. (b) Answers will differ. Students may again suggest that it is because he is too proud.

4. Suggested response: He thinks of his home and family after he becomes almost delirious, overcome with hunger and exhaustion.

5. Suggested response: He is ashamed of what he is about to do, and he does not want anyone to witness it.

6. Suggested response: He is overpowered by sorrow and rage and by the reality of his desperate situation.

Reader's Response *What is your reaction to the young man's plight? Do you feel sympathetic toward him? Why or why not?*

THINKING ABOUT THE SELECTION

Interpreting

1. (a) At the beginning of the story, why does the young man refuse to accept the sailor's offer of food? (b) What does the young man's refusal reveal about his character?
2. Why did the young man have such a difficult time finding work after the steamer set him ashore?
3. (a) Why does the young man choose not to explain his situation to the foreman? (b) Why does he choose not to accept the forty cents that the foreman offers to lend him?
4. What prompts the young man's memories of his home and family?
5. Why does he wait until the milk bar is empty before going in?
6. Why does the young man lapse into a fit of uncontrollable weeping in the milk bar?
7. What does the waitress's treatment of the young man reveal about her character?
8. Why do the young man's feelings of gratitude vanish so quickly?
9. Given his behavior in this story, what is your overall characterization of the young man?
10. What do you see as the theme, or central message, of this story and how is it conveyed?

Applying

11. (a) How do you envision the young man's future? (b) On what do you base this prediction?

ANALYZING LITERATURE

Understanding Point of View

Point of view refers to the vantage point or perspective from which a narrative is told. In "The Glass of Milk," Rojas uses a limited third-person point of view,

revealing the thoughts of only the young man.
1. How would the story be different if Rojas had used a first-person point of view?
2. How would the story be different if he had used an omniscient third-person point of view?

CRITICAL THINKING AND READING

Recognizing Period Characteristics

Like "The Glass of Milk," most modern short stories are told from either a first-person or limited third-person point of view. One reason for this tendency is the belief of many modern writers that it is not possible to paint an objective picture of the world. By using a limited point of view, the writers hope to show how a person's view of the world is shaped by his or her attitudes and feelings.
1. Explain how the young man's thoughts and feelings shape the portrayal of characters and events in "The Glass of Milk."
2. In many modern stories, the character from whose point of view the story is being told does not fully understand the events that are taking place. Explain whether this is the case with the young man in "The Glass of Milk."

THINKING AND WRITING

Exploring a Different Point of View

Write a short story in which you relate the events in the milk bar from the waitress's point of view. Feel free to portray other events and situations that are not depicted in Rojas's story. For example, you might begin with the scene involving the young man and follow it with a flashback in which the waitress remembers an event in her own life that makes her especially sympathetic to the young man's plight.

RUBÉN DARÍO

1867–1916

The first Latin American poet to achieve world-wide recognition, Rubén Darío (rōō ben′ dä rē′ ō) led a life that dramatically contrasted with his writing. Filled with elegant, beautiful language, his poems depict an exotic, dreamlike world inhabited by princes, princesses, and swans. Yet he led a troubled existence filled with sordid love affairs, excessive drinking, financial failures, and health problems.

Darío, whose real name was Felix Rubén García, was born in Nicaragua in the small town of San Pedro de Metapa. His parents separated when he was a young boy, and he went to live with his aunts and an uncle. It was from one of his aunts that he assumed the surname Darío. Although he was a shy and sickly child, he demonstrated his talents as a writer at an early age. He began writing poetry when he was eleven, and he published his first poems when he was just thirteen.

Darío's early poetry earned him widespread recognition in his native land and helped him get a job at the National Library, where he avidly read the Spanish classics. When he was twenty, he left Nicaragua and moved to Chile. Settling in Santiago, he lived in poverty, barely able to scrape together enough money for food and lodging. Despite his financial troubles, however,

he became friends with the son of the Chilean president and gained access to the president's well-stocked library. There he became acquainted with the works of the most prominent French poets of the time. Influenced by the works of these writers, he composed the poems and short stories that appear in his collection *Azure* (1888), the work that first earned him international critical acclaim.

After being given a job as a foreign correspondent for the Argentine newspaper *The Nation*, Darío was sent to Spain in 1892, and he later traveled to France. He immediately fell in love with Europe, and he lived there for most of his remaining years. He especially loved Paris, where he immersed himself in a Bohemian existence, characterized by excessive drinking, eating, and carousing.

Although Darío's life style eventually took its toll on his health, it did not affect his literary output. In 1896 he published *Profane Prose*, a collection of poems filled with exquisite, ornamental language. Nine years later he completed *Songs of Life and Hope*, a poetry collection regarded as his finest work. These collections not only established Darío as the leading Latin American writer of his time, but they also had a profound influence on many prominent European writers.

When Darío returned to Nicaragua in 1907, he was greeted as a national hero, and the Nicaraguan government appointed him Minister to Spain. Because of his unrestrained life style, however, he was soon removed from this post, and he moved back to Paris. Without any reliable means of support, he was again forced to live in extreme poverty. At the same time, his health began to deteriorate rapidly, and in 1916 his brief and turbulent life came to an end.

The problems in Darío's personal life did nothing to tarnish his reputation as a poet. Today he is not only regarded as one of the most gifted modern poets, but he is also credited with drawing worldwide attention to Latin American literature. For this reason all of today's successful Latin American writers are indebted to Rubén Darío.

Objectives

Thematic

To understand the need for love and romance

and contrasting poems by two different writers

Skills

1 To recognize the distinctive features of Darío's poetry
2 To write a paper comparing

GUIDE FOR INTERPRETING

Sonatina

Commentary

Characteristics of a Poet's Work. Although poets are often influenced and inspired by one another, no two poets are exactly alike. Rather, each poet's work has certain distinctive **characteristics** that set it apart from the works of other poets. These characteristics can be divided into three categories: style, content, and theme. **Style** involves the characteristics that concern form of expression rather than the thoughts conveyed. In poetry, style is determined by such factors as choice and arrangement of words, choice of metrical and verse forms, and use of literary devices. As you can probably guess, **content,** or subject matter, refers to what the poems are about. It involves the people, places, objects, and events that a writer depicts. Closely related to content is **theme,** which refers to the central message or insight into life that a writer conveys in a work. Obviously, a single poet is likely to write about a variety of subjects and convey many different themes and may even vary his or her writing style. Yet when you examine the entire body of a writer's work, it is usually possible to make generalizations in each of these areas.

Rubén Darío's style, for example, can be characterized as rich, energetic, and ornamental. This characterization results from his use of beautiful, elegant language and exotic images of color and sound, along with his use of musical rhythms and sound devices. Unfortunately, as is the case of all literature in translation, many distinctive elements of Darío's style are lost when his work is translated from Spanish into English. Yet in the better translations of his poetry, many characteristics of his style are still apparent.

Probably the most easily recognizable feature of Darío's poetry is his choice of subject matter. His poems often describe exotic golden lands set in the distant, imagined past. These lands are inhabited by noble princes and princesses and beautiful animals and birds, and they offer a feast of sensual pleasures—alluring sights, sounds, smells, and sensations. His poetry draws readers out of the real world into a world of fantasy and perfection. For this reason Darío is often described as an escapist poet.

Related to Darío's depiction of imaginary lands is one of the dominant recurring themes in his work: the idea that people should live life to its fullest, seeking love and indulging in various sensual pleasures. Yet this was only one of many themes that he explored in his work. Among the other issues that he examined are the meaning of life, art, love, and time, and the status of Latin America.

Writing

What is your idea of a perfect world? Write a journal entry in which you describe your own vision of an ideal world.

Literary Focus Have students discuss the distinctive characteristics of the work of some of the poets with which they are already familiar. For example, if students have studied American literature, you might have them discuss the distinctive characteristics of the poetry of Emily Dickinson, Walt Whitman, Robert Frost, and E. E. Cummings.

Writing/Prior Knowledge Before students begin writing their journal entries, have a class discussion in which students discuss real places that they consider especially appealing. Encourage them to keep these places in mind as they write their journal entries.

ESL Teaching Strategy Team each ESL students with a native-speaking student. Have the pairs read the poem together, taking turns reading aloud. Instruct the native-speaking student to clarify the meanings of any words with which the ESL student is unfamiliar.

Teaching Tenth-Grade Students Read the poem aloud to tenth-grade students. Pause after each stanza and have students discuss its style, content, and underlying meaning.

Vocabulary

Preteach the following vocabulary words:
languish (laŋ´ gwish) v.: Become weak; droop
vague (vāg) adj.: Indefinite in shape, form, or character
sovereign (säv´ rən) adj.: Supreme in power, rank, or authority.
azure (azh´ ər) n.: Sky-blue
enmeshed (ən mesht´) v.: Entangled
composure (kəm pō´ zhər) n.: Calmness of mind or manner

Support Material

Teaching Portfolio
Teacher Backup, p. 1375
Usage and Mechanics Worksheet, p. 1379
Vocabulary Check, p. 1380
Analyzing Literature Worksheet, *Recognizing Distinctive Themes*, p. 1381
Critical Thinking and Reading Worksheet, *Appreciating Tone and Atmosphere*, p. 1382
Language Worksheet, p. 1382
Selection Test, pp. 1383–1384

Spelling Tip Write the word *sovereign* on the chalkboard. Then call students' attention to the fact that the last five letters form the word *reign*.

Sonatina

Rubén Darío

translated by John A. Crow

The princess is sad . . . and in languish reposes,
She signs for relief and her lips of blown roses
Have lost their gay laughter, have lost their fresh
   bloom.
The princess is pale on her throne and is waiting,
5 The keyboard is mute, a strange silence creating,
And the vase holds a flower that has lost its perfume.

The garden is filled with the peacocks' proud
   chatter,
The duenna[1] is banal,[2] jejune[3] in her chatter,
And vested in red pirouettes the buffoon;
10 The princess not laughing, the princess not feeling,
Pursues in the sky where a star is concealing
An illusion as vague as the light of the moon.

Is she thinking perhaps of the prince of Galconda?
Or of him who has halted his carriage in wonder
15 To seek in her eyes for the beauty of night?
Or the king of the islands of fragrant rose bowers,
Or of him who is sovereign of diamonds and
   flowers,
Or of the proud lord of the pearls of Delight?

Alas, the poor princess with lips red as cherry,
20 Would now be a butterfly, swallow, or fairy,
Have wings that would carry her far in the sky.
She would soar to the sun on a shining stepladder,

Or the lilies of May with her verses make gladder,
Or be lost on the wind as it lifts the waves high.

25 She no longer wants the gold distaff or palace,
The magical falcon, the jester's red challis,
The swans' classic grace on the azure lagoon.
The flowers are all sad for the yearning king's
   daughter,
The lotus has withered with roots in the water,
To all the four corners dead roses are strewn.

Poor princess, her eyes have a look that distresses,
She's enmeshed in her jewels, her lavish lace dresses,
The palace of marble encages her soul.
The superb royal palace guard never relaxes,
35 A hundred giant negroes with giant battle-axes
With watchdogs and dragon would take a huge toll.

I wish that the cocoon would break its enclosure!
The princess grows sad in her pallid composure.
Oh, tower of ivory, oh, vision in white.
She would fly to a land where a dream prince
40   would hail her.
(The princess is sadder, the princess grows paler)
A prince more resplendent[4] than dawn after night.

Be silent, my child, says the fairy godmother,
On a swift wingèd steed never loved by another,
45 With a sword at his side and a falcon above,
Rides the knight who adores you, his whole body
   yearning,
He overcomes distance and Death and is burning
To impassion your lips with the kiss of his love!

---

1. duenna (dōō ən′ ə) *n.*: An elderly woman who has charge of the girls and young unmarried women of a Spanish or Portuguese family.
2. banal (bā′ n'l) *adj.*: Dull or stale; commonplace.
3. jejune (ji jōōn′) *adj.*: Not interesting or satisfying.

---

4. resplendent (ri splen′ dənt) *adj.*: Shining brightly; dazzling.

Reader's Response *Does the setting of the poem seem like a place you would want to visit? Why or why not?*

THE FROG PRINCE
Walter Crane

THINKING ABOUT THE SELECTION

Interpreting

1. (a) Why is the princess sad? Support your answer. (b) How are the details of the setting colored by the princess's mood?
2. (a) What impressions does Darío convey of the princess's potential lovers? (b) How does he convey these impressions?
3. In the fourth stanza, Darío writes that if the princess were a "butterfly, swallow, or fairy," she would "soar to the sun on a shining stepladder." What does this action symbolize, or represent?
4. (a) What does Darío mean when he writes, "The Palace of marble encages her soul"? (b) What does he mean when he writes, "I wish that the cocoon would break its enclosure"?
5. Explain how Darío conveys the princess's longing not only for a lover but also for freedom and spiritual growth.
6. What is the theme, or central message, of this poem?

Applying

7. Like the princess in Darío's poem, many people at times feel trapped by their circumstances or their surroundings. (a) What might be some reasons why people feel this way? (b) What can people do to overcome this feeling?

ANALYZING LITERATURE

Recognizing Distinctive Features

Rubén Darío's poetry is characterized by his use of distant, dreamlike settings inhabited by princes and princesses, along with his use of rich, exotic imagery and lively, musical language.

1. Given this characterization, explain why "Sonatina" might be viewed as a typical Darío poem.
2. The musical quality of Darío's poetry results partly from his use of sound devices such as rhyme, alliteration, consonance, and assonance. However, these sound effects often cannot be re-created in English translations of his poetry. Which of these sound effects are evident in John A. Crow's translation of "Sonatina"? Support your answer with examples.
3. Another important aspect of Darío's writing style is his preference for fixed verse forms. Is this preference evident in Crow's translation of "Sonatina"? Explain.
4. "Sonatina" contains many symbols that recur throughout Darío's poetry, including the following: roses (lines 2 and 16), butterfly (line 20), gold (line 25), swans (line 27), azure (line 27), lace (line 32), marble (line 33), and ivory (line 39). How do you interpret the meaning of each of these symbols?

THINKING AND WRITING

Comparing and Contrasting Writers

Rubén Darío's work influenced a number of Spanish writers, including Federico García Lorca (page 1140). Write a paper in which you compare and contrast Darío's poetry with that of García Lorca. Begin by reviewing the works by Darío and García Lorca included in this book. Focus on the similarities and differences in style, content, and theme. Organize your ideas. Then write your paper, supporting your ideas with passages from works by both poets. When you have finished writing, revise your paper, making sure you have presented your ideas in an organized and coherent manner.

(continued from bottom of page)

change jobs and seek to enrich themselves through education.

Challenge Darío's poetry influenced a number of prominent European poets. Through research, identify as many of these writers as you can and explain the ways in which they were influenced by Darío.

ANSWERS TO ANALYZING LITERATURE

1. The poem is set in a distant, dreamlike place, the central character is a princess, and it is filled with rich imagery and musical language.
2. The poem contains rhyme, alliteration, consonance, and assonance. Students' examples will differ.
3. This preference is evident. Each stanza is six-lines long, and all of the lines are fairly equal in length.
4. Answers will differ. Make sure that students support each of their interpretations.

THINKING AND WRITING

Publishing Student Writing Have student volunteers read their papers to the class and use the readings as a springboard for a class discussion about the similarities and differences between Darío and García Lorca.

Humanities Note

Fine art, *The Frog Prince* by Walter Crane. A well-known illustrator of children's books, Crane (1845–1915) was born in Liverpool, England. In creating illustrations such as *The Frog Prince*, he drew upon his knowledge of both Japanese prints and fifteenth-century Italian paintings.

You might want to use the following questions to discuss the art:

1. What impression is conveyed of the woman in the illustration?
2. What makes this an appropriate illustration for "Sonatina"?
3. If you were the editor of an anthology of children's stories, would you consider using this illustration? Why or why not?

roses are strewn" to "all four corners."
2. (a) Suggested response: He conveys the impression that they are gallant, noble, wealthy and romantic. (b) Suggested response: He conveys the impressions through the details he associates with them. For example, he refers to one as the "sovereign of diamonds and flowers."
3. Suggested response: It represents freeing herself of her responsibilities,

leaving her kingdom, and going off in search of love and new experiences.
4. (a) Suggested response: He is suggesting that she feels trapped in her present life. (b) Suggested response: The speaker is suggesting that the princess needs to break away from her kingdom and seek a new life.
5. Suggested response: He conveys this through his images that cap-

ture the princess's sense of entrapment.
6. Suggested response: The poem conveys the need for love, romance, freedom, and spiritual growth.
7. (a) Answers will differ. Students may respond that people come to feel trapped because they find themselves doing the same things day after ter day. (b) Answers will differ. Students may note that people can

GABRIELA MISTRAL

Focus

More About the Author As Gabriela Mistral stated in her Nobel address, she devoted her life to improve the position of and education for women and children. As a young poet and schoolteacher, Mistral wrote poems to help children learn to read. As her reputation as a poet grew, so grew her status and reputation as an educator. During her career, Mistral instigated what were then progressive methods of education, which included visual aids, extracts from literature, and games in place of textbooks.

Mistral's efforts to help children extended beyond her own country. In 1938 Mistral published *Tala* (ta´ lə), her third collection of poetry, in Buenos Aires. At the time of this publication, Spain was in civil war. Mistral donated the proceeds from her book to the orphans living in children's camps in Catalonia and in France.

When the news reached her homeland that Mistral died, Chilean president Ibañez decreed three days of national mourning. She was also eulogized in the United Nations.

Ask students why being a poet may have contributed to Mistral's success as a teacher.

Critical Evaluation In "Gabriela Mistral," an article written for *Poet Lore,* A. Ortiz-Vargas said the following about Mistral's poetry and influence as a poet:

[Mistral's poetic] appearance was an epoch-making event, for it initiated a poetry that from the beginning bore the unmistakable stamp of things that endure. Her art, free from modern foreign influences, showed a distinctive individuality that at once placed her entirely apart from her contemporaries.

1889–1957

When Gabriela Mistral (gà brē e´ là mē stràl´) officially heard the news about being awarded the Nobel Prize for Literature in 1945, she declared, "Perhaps it was because I was the candidate of the women and children." Ever since Mistral began writing poems, she wrote most often about women and children. She also devoted much of her life to educating and helping them both.

At fifteen, without having finished school and without a teaching certificate, Mistral became an elementary school teacher in La Compania, a small village near Montegrande, Chile, her childhood home. In 1910 Mistral obtained her teaching certificate and thereafter taught at the secondary level.

At the same time she started her teaching career, Mistral began writing poetry. She submitted her work to local newspapers and international magazines under a variety of pen names. Mistral, whose real name is Lucila Godoy Alcayaga (loo cē´ lə go doi al kT ä´ gə), used various pseudonyms for fear that she might lose her teaching job because of the content of her poetry. For the work she submitted to the Paris fashion magazine *Elegancias* (el ə gän´ sē əs), she used the name Gabriela Mistral. This name came from the archangel Gabriel and the fierce mistral wind that blows over the south of France. It was under this name that Mistral became almost legendary in her own country and the first South American to win the Nobel Prize for Literature.

Mistral first became well known in South America when she won the Chilean National Prize for Poetry with a trio of sonnets called the "Sonnets of Death." In 1922 her fame spread to the United States when she published her first book of poetry, *Desolación* (de sō lä sē ōn´), in New York. The central themes in *Desolación,* from which "Fear" and "The Prayer" were taken, are despair, suffering, and death. Mistral wrote *Desolación* shortly after her fiancé committed suicide when his involvement in embezzlement was discovered. Many believe that his death became the driving force behind her creativity and was the primary cause for the despairing tone in her poetry.

Also in 1922 the Mexican minister of education, José Vasconcelos (hō sā´ väs kōn´ sā´ lōs), invited Mistral to help him with a program of education reform. As part of her new position, she taught Indian children and adults in isolated rural villages. Mexico City later named a school after Mistral and erected a statue in her honor in the school's courtyard. She also became Chile's delegate to the League of Nations Institute of Intellectual Cooperation.

In 1931 Mistral came to the United States. During her stay in America, Mistral taught Spanish history and civilization at Middlebury College in Vermont and at Barnard College in New York City. Later she represented the Chilean government in various diplomatic posts in South America and Europe and was a member of the United Nations Subcommittee on the Status of Women.

Mistral was then invited to live in Mexico for two years, after which she was Chilean consul in Brazil, Portugal, Los Angeles, and Naples. After a year as consul at Naples, Mistral moved back to New York, where she lived on Long Island until her death.

Objectives

Thematic

1 To understand literature in praise of commonplace objects
2 To understand literature that explores one's relationship to God or a god
3 To understand literature that expresses a fear

Skills

1 To understand tone
2 To compare and contrast tone in poetry
3 To respond to fine art

Support Material

Teaching Portfolio

Teacher Backup, p. 1385
Usage and Mechanics Worksheet, p. 1389
Vocabulary Check, p. 1390
Analyzing Literature Worksheet, *Understanding Tone,* p. 1391
Critical Thinking and Reading Worksheet, *Comparing and Contrasting*

GUIDE FOR INTERPRETING

Bread; The Prayer; Fear

Commentary

Tone. In casual conversation the words you use and the way you say them suggest an attitude you have toward that subject. In addition to your word choice, you might also add intonations and gestures to convey your particular attitude about the subject. Sometimes what you say and what you reveal in your gestures and voice conflict. For example, if you want to convey a sarcastic attitude, you might say your words in a straightforward manner, but you can nonverbally convey the intended sarcastic tone.

In the same way we convey tone in conversation, poets convey tone in their poetry. A poet, however, is restricted to only what he or she can put down on paper. Therefore, a poet must use mechanical and literary devices to convey his or her attitude about a subject. For instance, poets can convey tone through the particular words they choose, the details of description, and the images they present. In addition, tone can be created through the writer's use of meter, sentence structure, and punctuation. The syntax and use of poetic license can also contribute to our understanding of a writer's tone.

Identifying the tone of a poem is essential. Determining the tone of a poem helps readers to better understand the meaning of the poem. It also helps shape the reader's response to the poem and creates the mood, or overall effect, of the poem.

The tone of the poems in each of Mistral's collections is generally guided by an overall theme or tone present in the collection. "Fear" and "The Prayer," for example, were written in *Desolación*, Mistral's first collection, which contains a pervasive attitude of despair. "Bread," on the other hand, was written much later and reflects a lighter tone than her earlier work.

Writing

Think of a subject about which you would like to write. What is your attitude toward the subject? How might you go about conveying your attitude toward the subject to someone else? Jot down several words and phrases that convey your attitude about the subject without directly saying how you feel about it.

Literary Focus Remind students that the tone of a piece of literature is the author's feelings toward a subject, not the feelings of the characters in a story or the speaker of a poem. Clues about a poem's tone can be revealed when it is read aloud. Have students read aloud each of Mistral's poems, expressing through their intonations what they think is the author's tone.

Writing/Prior Knowledge As a class brainstorm for ideas. Then have students complete the writing activity. Have volunteers share their responses with the class.

ESL Teaching Strategy ESL students may have difficulty with the writing activity. Pair each ESL student with another member of the class. The native-speaking student should act as a coach, discussing the ways in which the ESL student might indirectly convey his or her attitude toward the topic.

Vocabulary
Preteach the following vocabulary words:
prodding (präd´ iŋ) *v.*: Poking; jabbing
summoned (sum´ ənd) *v.*: Called forth
invokes (in vōks´) *v.*: Calls on
trill (tril) *n.*: The warbling sound made by some birds
anoint (ə noint´) *v.*: To rub oil or ointment on
ecstatic (ek stat´ik) *adj.*: Joyful
sheaves (shēvz) *n.*: Bundles of cut stalks of grain
eaves (ēvz) *n.*: Lower edges of a roof, projecting beyond the sides of the building

Tone in Poetry, p. 1392
Selection Test, pp. 1393–1394

Art Transparency 15
Proletarian Mother and Child by David Alfaro Siqueiros.

Master Teacher Note In the citation for Mistral's Nobel Prize for Literature, Swedish Academy member H. J. Gullberg described

Mistral's poetry as "poems of love dedicated to death." Discuss with students what this phrase means; then see how it applies to Mistral's poem "The Prayer."

Teaching Tenth-Grade Students
Personal lyrics such as these are very accessible to students at all levels. Tenth-grade students may

have difficulty with the vocabulary, however. Preteach the vocabulary words that appear on this page as well as others you believe might give students some difficulty.

Bread

Gabriela Mistral

translated by Allan Francovich and Kathleen Weaver

They have left bread on the table,
half-burnt, half-white, with its crown
broken open in large crumbs.

It seems new to me
5 like something never seen,
yet I have eaten nothing else.

Prodding its soft center like a sleepwalker,
my sense of touch and smell are forgotten.

It has the odor of my mother giving milk,
10 the odor of three valleys I have walked—
Aconcaqua, Patzcuaro, Elqui—
and the odor of my insides when I sing.

There are no other odors in the room,
and so I was summoned,
15 there is no one else in the house
but this bread, broken, on a plate—
it knows me with its body
and I know it with mine.

Eaten in all climates,
20 a hundred brothers, this bread
is the bread of Coquimbo and Oaxaca,
of Santa Ana and Santiago.[1]

As a child I knew its shapes—
sun, halo, fish, its heat of pigeon feathers,
25 my hand its friend . . .

I have forgotten it since then,
until we meet this day,
I with an old woman's body,
and it with the body of a child.

30 Dead friends, with whom in other valleys
I have eaten bread,
smell the misted odor of bread
mown in August
milled in September in Castilla.[2]

35 Different, it is still the same
we ate in lands where you now rest.
I open its crust and give you its heat;
I turn it and release its breath.

My hand overflows with it,
40 its glance is in my hand;
in sorrow I cry out
for such long forgetfulness
and my face ages or is reborn
in this discovery.

45 How empty the house is,
may we who have met again
be united
at this table without meat or fruit
we two in this human silence
50 until the time we shall be one
and our day over . . .

---

1. **Coquimbo** (kō kēm′ bō) . . . **Oaxaca** (wä hä′ kä) . . .
Santa Ana (san′ tə an′ ə) . . . **Santiago** (sän′ tē ä′ gồ): Latin-American cities.

---

2. **Castilla** (käs tēl′ yä): A region in northern and central Spain.

SEÑORA CORONEL GRINDING CORN
Alexander Harmer

THINKING ABOUT THE SELECTION

Interpreting

1. Why might Mistral have chosen bread as the subject for a poem?
2. To whom might Mistral be referring as "they"?
3. How do "they" regard and treat the bread?
4. What importance does bread have for the speaker?
5. What universal message or theme does this poem have?

Applying

6. What other necessities of life might Mistral praise that others might think are mundane?

THINKING AND WRITING

Responding to Fine Art

Like poetry, fine art also conveys the artist's attitude toward his or her subject. Look closely at the painting above. Write a brief essay in which you discuss the tone of this artwork and whether this painting is an appropriate piece for Mistral's "Bread." In your essay you should discuss the artist's choice of color, background, expression, and so on. When you have finished writing, revise your work, making sure you have expressed your reasons why this painting is or is not an appropriate illustration for "Bread." Proofread your paper carefully and make a final copy. Then share it with your classmates.

The Prayer

Gabriela Mistral

translated by John A. Crowe

---

1. **entreaty** (in trēt´ ē) *n.*: An earnest request.
2. **spikenard** (spīk´ nərd) *n.*: A perennial North American plant with whitish flowers, purplish berries, and fragrant roots.
3. **nascent** (nas´ 'nt) *adj.*: Coming into being.

---

4. **tresses** (tres´ əz) *n.*: A woman's or girl's hair.

THINKING ABOUT THE SELECTION

Interpreting

1. Why is it important to the speaker that God forgive or pardon the speaker's lover?
2. "The Prayer" appears in *Desolación*. What details and images in this poem create a mood of despair and desolation?
3. Most likely this poem was written for her fiancé who committed suicide. What feelings about her fiancé does Mistral reveal in "The Prayer"?
4. (a) What is the tone of "The Prayer"? (b) How does Mistral convey the tone?
5. What hope does Mistral imply in this poem? Support your answer with details from the poem.

Applying

6. Mark Twain called forgiveness "the fragrance the violet shed on the heel that has crushed it," while George Macdonald called it "the giving and so the receiving of life." What is your definition of forgiveness?

CRITICAL THINKING AND READING

Comparing and Contrasting Tone in Poetry

"Fear" and "The Prayer" both come from her collection *Desolación*; however, "Bread" comes from a different collection entitled *Tala*. *Tala* was written sixteen years after *Desolación* and reflects a different tone from that in her earlier work.

1. Compare and contrast the tone of "Bread" with the tone of "The Prayer." (a) How does her attitude about life change? (b) How does the tone affect the mood of the poems?
2. Compare and contrast the tone of one of Mistral's poems with that of a poem by one of the other modern Latin American poets you have read.

THE REVOLUTION, 1946
Manuel Rodríguez Lozano
Museo Nacional de Arte Moderno, Mexico City

(continued from bottom of page)

was wholly his."
4. Answers may differ. Suggested responses: (a) The tone of "The Prayer" is sorrowful; the speaker is obviously in much pain over her lover's death and wants his death vindicated. (b) She conveys the tone in the way that she pleads with God to absolve his sin. Her pleas are wrought with anguish and emotion.
5. Answers may differ. Suggested response: The hope is in the pardon. If God is to pardon her lover, she describes what will happen to the world as a result (lines 41–44).
6. Answers will differ. Forgiveness can have as many interpretations as there are students in the class. No single response is the correct one.

ANSWERS TO CRITICAL THINKING AND READING

1. Answers may differ. Suggested responses: (a) Although there is an element of hope in "The Prayer," it is primarily a very despairing poem. In contrast, her poem "Bread" celebrates life and reveres even the most basic needs of human life.
2. Answers will differ.

Humanities Note

Fine art, *The Revolution*, 1946, by Manuel Rodríguez Lozano. Rodríguez Lozano (1896–1971) was born in Mexico City. He studied in Paris from 1914 to 1921 and was influenced by Picasso's purity of craftsmanship. Rodríguez Lozano was a pioneer of "Mexicanism" in the early 1920's. Since the mid-1930's, the artist's work has been characterized by themes of death, despair, and ecstasy. The mysterious shrouded figures and somber colors in *The Revolution* are characteristic of his work.

You might want to use the following questions to discuss the art:

1. Do the colors and figures in the painting reflect the mood of the poem? Explain.
2. The artist has conveyed a sense of mystery in this painting. How has he achieved this? What is your reaction to this piece?

Closure and Extension

ANSWERS TO THINKING ABOUT THE SELECTION

1. Answers may differ. Suggested response: It is especially important that God forgive the speaker's lover because he committed suicide, "without waiting for Thy sign."
2. Answers may differ. Suggested response: Mistral's choice of words, such as "plead," "harshly," and "tormented heart" create a mood of despair and desolation. Her images such as those in lines 17–20 and 25–28 also contribute to this mood.
3. Mistral reveals that she thought her fiancé was a good man, "whose heart was entirely open" and deserving of God's forgiveness and that she loved him dearly and "her wounded heart

Presentation

Motivation/Prior Knowledge Ask students to discuss or write in their journals what they fear most. Why is it so fearful? Ask volunteers to share their responses. Then tell them that in "Fear," Mistral reflects on what a mother's greatest fears might be.

Purpose-Setting Question Why does the speaker fear these things?

Master Teacher Note Put Art Transparency 15, *Proletarian Mother and Child* by David Alfaro Siqueiros, on an overhead projector. Ask students to discuss the tone of this painting. Why did Alfaro Siqueiros use only shades of pink? What is the relationship between this mother and child? What details led students to their answer? What fears might this mother have for her child? Why?

Closure and Extension

ANSWERS TO THINKING ABOUT THE SELECTION

1. She does not want her child to be turned into a swallow because then the child will not return home where the speaker can care for her; turning her child into a princess would mean that she would not appreciate life to its fullest; and turning her child into a queen would mean that her child would no longer need or want her mother.
2. All these fears suggest that the child is close to leaving home, which is difficult at times for mothers to accept.
3. Answers may differ. "They" could refer to humankind or society.
4. Answers may differ. Suggested response: Readers can infer that Mistral wants her child to be safe at home, where the mother can take care of her and ensure that she is properly brought up with her mother's morals and values.
5. Answers may differ. Some students may reply that her convictions toward motherhood are strong—possibly even suffocating, since she does not want her child to leave the nest. Others may reply that she is a good mother and wants what every mother wants—for her child to be safe and happy.

Fear

Gabriela Mistral

translated by Doris Dana

I don't want them to turn
my little girl into a swallow.
She would fly far away into the sky
and never fly again to my straw bed,
5 or she would nest in the eaves
where I could not comb her hair.
I don't want them to turn
my little girl into a swallow.

I don't want them to make
10 my little girl a princess.
In tiny golden slippers
how could she play on the meadow?
And when night came, no longer
would she sleep at my side.
15 I don't want them to make
my little girl a princess.

And even less do I want them
one day to make her queen.
They would put her on a throne
20 where I could not go to see her.
And when nighttime came
I could never rock her . . .
I don't want them to make
my little girl a queen!

Reader's Response *How did reading about Mistral's view of life make you feel? Explain.*

THINKING ABOUT THE SELECTION

Interpreting

1. Why does the speaker not want her child to be turned into a swallow, a princess, or a queen?
2. For what reasons might the speaker be fearful?
3. Who might "they" be in this poem?
4. What can you infer that Mistral does want for her child?
5. Mistral did not have children of her own, yet she often wrote about motherhood and children. What is Mistral's attitude toward motherhood and children?
6. (a) Why does Mistral call this poem "Fear"? (b) What title would you give to this poem? Explain.

Applying

7. Mistral begins the first two stanzas with the words "I don't want." Imagine that you are Mistral. Name two other things you do not want.

ANALYZING LITERATURE

Understanding Tone

Tone is a poet's attitude toward a subject. A poet must use literary and mechanical devices, such as diction, syntax, and punctuation, to convey tone. Tone can also be conveyed through a writer's use of language, details, and imagery. In addition, tone helps to create the mood or overall effect of the poem. To fully understand the meaning of a poem, it is essential first to determine its tone.

1. What is the tone of "Fear"?
2. What devices does Mistral use to create this tone?
3. What message might Mistral be conveying about children or motherhood?

6. Answers may differ. Suggested responses: (a) Although she never had children of her own, her experience with children may have led her to fear for all children and society the ideas expressed in her poem. (b) Answers will vary.
7. Answers will differ.

ANSWERS TO ANALYZING LITERATURE

1. Answers may differ. Suggested response: The tone of "Fear" is one of fear, trepidation, and sorrow.
2. Answers may differ. Suggested response: The speaker is speculating what will happen to her child if these things happen to her, which suggests trepidation. She is sorrowful because there is a hint that despite her fears and desire to keep her child at home, her child will still leave home.
3. Answers may differ. Suggested response: Her message is that mothers can be fearful of what will happen when their children leave home, but they have to let them go. All a mother can do is provide the best home possible while they are young, but let them leave when the time comes.

Asia

ORDINATION PAVILION OF KING RAMA V
Detail of early twentieth-century mural
Wat Benchamabopit, Bangkok

Humanities Note

Fine art, *Ordination Pavilion of King Rama V*, detail of early twentieth-century mural. This mural celebrates King Rama V, who inherited the crown of Siam (now known as Thailand) from his father in 1868. Just fifteen years old at the time of his coronation, Rama V went on to rule Siam for forty years. During his reign he took important measures to modernize his country, such as establish a railroad system. Yet his greatest achievement was the abolition of slavery in 1905.

This mural captures the magnificence and splendor of the massive celebration that took place when King Rama V was coronated. The festivities included singing, dancing, and Buddhist religious rituals.

You might want to use the following questions to discuss the art:

1. What does this mural suggest about the atmosphere in Bangkok on the day of King Rama V's coronation?
2. Based on this mural, what inferences might you make about life in Siam at the time of King Rama's coronation?
3. Does the celebration depicted in this mural seem like a type of event you would be interested in attending? Why or why not?

MORI ŌGAI

Focus

More About the Author Many early twentieth-century Japanese fiction writers modeled their work after the French writer Emile Zola and the Naturalists (see page 913). Ōgai, on the other hand, was openly opposed to Naturalism. Following the example of their European predecessors, the Japanese Naturalists took a scientific approach to writing and rejected the idea of using personal experiences as subject matter for their work. In contrast, Ōgai believed that personal experiences should be one of the main sources of inspiration for a fiction writer. In addition, he viewed writing as an enjoyable and highly personal process to which the principles of science should not be applied.

Ask students if they can think of writers from other countries who rebelled against the dominant literary approaches of their time. Were these writers able to gain acceptance during their lifetimes? If not, have their reputations grown over time?

Critical Evaluation Prior to the emergence of Mori Ōgai and other modern Japanese fiction writers, Japanese fiction had for some time been in a state of demise. The literary critic Donald Keene notes: "If we can believe contemporary accounts, by the early 1870's not more than five men were making a living as writers of fiction. . . . The great tradition of the Japanese novel seemed to have come to an end. A revival might conceivably have occurred even without the introduction from the West of new models of literature, but this particular stimulus, transmitted to the Japanese in the form of translations and adaptations, in fact led to the creation of a new kind of Japanese fiction, one that is now read all over the world."

1862–1922

Appointed to the post of surgeon general in 1907, Mori Ōgai (mō′ rē′ ō′ gä′ ē′) was the highest ranking doctor in Japan for nearly ten years. Yet Ōgai is remembered much more for his contributions to literature than for his achievements as a doctor. In fact, he is now widely regarded not only as one of the leading writers of his time but also as one of the pioneers of modern Japanese fiction.

Ōgai, whose father was also a doctor, earned his medical degree from Tokyo University. After enlisting in the imperial army, he was sent to Germany in 1884 to continue his studies of medicine. Remaining there for four years, he developed a strong interest in both German literature and the German way of life. In fact, many of his earliest literary works were translations of German poems and short stories.

A man of tremendous energy and intelligence, Ōgai quickly achieved success as both a writer and a surgeon following his return from Germany. In his role as an army surgeon, he served in both the Sino-Japanese War (1895) and the Russo-Japanese War (1904–1905), before being promoted to the rank of surgeon general. As a writer, he first achieved success in the 1890's, publishing autobiographical works of fiction based on his experiences in Germany. His reputation as a writer continued to grow throughout the early part of the twentieth century, with the publication of such well-known works as his novel *The Wild Goose* (1911–1913). During the final stage of his literary career, he focused on writing historical novels, stories, and biographies, which some readers and critics consider his finest works.

In addition to his achievements as a fiction writer, Ōgai also made important contributions as a dramatist and a literary critic. As a dramatist, he not only wrote a number of Western-style plays, but he was also a strong supporter of the traditional Kabuki theater. As a critic, he played an important role in shaping the direction of Japanese poetry, drama, and fiction. Because of the wide scope of Ōgai's literary contributions, some contemporary critics consider him to be the most important Japanese literary figure of the entire twentieth century.

Objectives

Thematic

To understand the problems that cultural differences can cause in a personal relationship

Skills

1 To appreciate changes in Japanese life
2 To make connections between literary works
3 To describe a society in transition

Support Material

Teaching Portfolio
Teacher Backup, p. 1395
Grammar in Action Worksheet, *Concrete Details*, p. 1399
Usage and Mechanics Worksheet, p. 1401
Vocabulary Check, p. 1402
Analyzing Literature Worksheet,

GUIDE FOR INTERPRETING

Under Reconstruction

Commentary

The Modernization of Japan. Considering Japan's position in the world today, it seems incredible that not much more than a century ago Japan was an undeveloped feudal society that was almost completely isolated from the rest of the world. Yet it is true that for over two hundred years, beginning in the early 1600's, Japan existed in a state of strict seclusion, after closing its doors to the outside world to put an end to the spread of foreign ideas and beliefs. In 1853, however, a fleet of American naval ships arrived in Japan to pressure the Japanese into reopening their ports. A year later, the Japanese signed a trade agreement with the United States, prompting a period of political upheaval in Japan that eventually brought an end to the dominance of the nation's most powerful families and resulted in the establishment of a centralized government headed by a new emperor named Meiji (mā ē jē) (r. 1867–1913), which means "enlightened peace."

The new government's assumption of control in 1867, which has come to be known as the Meiji Restoration, was the event that would propel Japan into its modern age. Strongly influenced by the experiences of the Western economic and military powers, Japan abolished its feudal system and began an amazingly rapid process of modernization. Within several decades the nation transformed itself into a powerful industrialized state with a capitalist economy, a compulsory educational system, a formal constitution, and a good-sized national army and navy—armed forces that were strong enough to defeat both China in the Sino-Japanese War (1895) and Russia in the Russo-Japanese War (1904–1905). In making this transformation, the Japanese abandoned many longstanding habits and traditions and adopted numerous Western customs and practices. In fact, Western influence was so strong that at one point there was actually a serious proposal to replace the Japanese language with English.

"Under Reconstruction" was written in 1910, while Japan was still in the midst of its rapid transformation. As you read the story, look for what it suggests about the impact of both modernization and Western influence on Japanese society.

Writing

What do you imagine it might have been like to live in Japan during the late nineteenth and early twentieth centuries? In what ways do you think the Japanese people might have benefited from the rapid changes that were taking place? Why might some people have objected to the abandonment of many longstanding traditions and customs? Write a journal entry in which you respond to these questions and express any other reactions to the changes that took place in Japan following the Meiji Restoration.

Appreciating Literary Symbolism, p. 1403
Critical Thinking and Reading Worksheet, *Connecting Literary Works*, p. 1404
Selection Test, pp. 1405–1406

Spelling Tip Write the word *ineffectually* on the chalkboard. Then separate it into syllables. Explain to students that they may find it easier to spell this word if they sound out each separate syllable.

Literary Focus You might want to introduce this topic by discussing the reconstruction of Japanese society that occurred in the aftermath of World War II. Point out that Japan was economically and psychologically devastated by the war. Yet the Japanese quickly overcame the damage caused by the war and transformed their nation into one of the world's leading economic powers. Have students discuss how this process of economic revitalization parallels the process of modernization and westernization that took place during the late nineteenth and early twentieth centuries.

Writing/Prior Knowledge Before students begin their journal entries, have them discuss what it might be like if the United States were undergoing a rapid transformation that was dramatically altering the American way of life.

ESL Teaching Strategy If you have any Japanese students in class, have them share their knowledge of the changes that took place in their native country in the late nineteenth and early twentieth centuries.

Teaching Tenth-Grade Students Make sure tenth-grade students have a thorough understanding of the information in the Commentary before they begin reading the selection.

Vocabulary

Preteach the following vocabulary words:
oblique (ə blēk´) *adj.*: Not straightforward
truncated (truŋ´ kāt id) *adj.*: Having its angles cut off
imposingly (im pō´ ziŋ lē) *adv.*: Impressively
mauve (mōv) *n.*: A shade of delicate purple
nonchalantly (nän shə länt´ lē) *adv.*: Done in an unenthusiastic manner
ineffectually (in´ e fek´ choo wəl lē) *adv.*: Not producing the desired effect

Under Reconstruction

Mori Ōgai

translated by Ivan Morris

It had just stopped raining when Councilor Watanabé got off the tram in front of the Kabuki[1] playhouse. Carefully avoiding the puddles, he hurried through the Kobiki district in the direction of the Department of Communications. Surely that restaurant was somewhere around here, he thought as he strode along the canal; he remembered having noticed the signboard on one of these corners.

The streets were fairly empty. He passed a group of young men in Western clothes. They were talking noisily and looked as if they had all just left their office. Then a girl in a kimono[2] and a gaily-colored sash hurried by, almost bumping into him. She was probably a waitress from some local teahouse, he thought. A rickshaw[3] with its hood up passed him from behind.

Finally he caught sight of a small signboard with the inscription written horizontally in the Western style: *Seiyōken Hotel*. The front of the building facing the canal was covered with scaffolding. The side entrance was on a small street. There were two oblique flights of stairs outside the restaurant, forming a sort of truncated triangle. At the head of each staircase was a glass door; after hesitating a moment, Watanabé entered the one on the left on which were written the characters for *Entrance*.

---

1. **Kabuki** (kä bōō′ kē): A form of Japanese drama.
2. **kimono** (kə mō′ nə) *n*.: A traditional Japanese outer garment with short, wide sleeves and a sash.
3. **rickshaw** (rik′ shô) *n*.: A small, two-wheeled carriage with a hood, pulled by one or two people.

Inside he found a wide passage. By the door was a pile of little cloths for wiping one's shoes and next to these a large Western doormat. Watanabé's shoes were muddy after the rain and he carefully cleaned them with both implements. Apparently in this restaurant one was supposed to observe the Western custom and wear one's shoes indoors.

There was no sign of life in the passage, but from the distance came a great sound of hammering and sawing. The place was under reconstruction, thought Watanabé.

He waited awhile, but as no one came to receive him, he walked to the end of the passage. Here he stopped, not knowing which way to turn. Suddenly he noticed a man with a napkin under his arm leaning against the wall a few yards away. He went up to him.

"I telephoned yesterday for a reservation."

The man sprang to attention. "Oh yes, sir. A table for two, I believe? It's on the second floor. Would you mind coming with me, sir."

The waiter followed him up another flight of stairs. The man had known immediately who he was, thought Watanabé. Customers must be few and far between with the repairs underway. As he mounted the stairs, the clatter and banging of the workmen became almost deafening.

"Quite a lively place," said Watanabé, looking back at the waiter.

"Oh no, sir. The men go home at five o'clock. You won't be disturbed while you're dining, sir."

When they reached the top of the stairs, the waiter hurried past Watanabé and opened a door to

OUDA (detail)
Hironaga Takehiko

(continued from bottom of page)

there is every reason for our country to go on imitating the West without reservation." Ōgai commented, "The expression is somewhat peculiar, but it seems to correspond exactly to my own views." Even when discussing such painful subjects as the racial prejudices of Europeans and Americans, Ōgai never failed to balance such accounts with mentions of Western traits he admired.

Humanities Note

Fine art, *Ouda* by Hironaga Takehiko. Takehiko (1935–   ) is a twentieth-century Japanese artist who specializes in traditional Japanese woodblock prints. Often, his prints depict rural villages and old country dwellings. In this print, for example, he portrays the Japanese village of Ouda.

Notice how the artist has used subtle shading to create a sense of depth in the work. The sense of depth is reinforced by his inclusion of a tiny figure at the end of the street. The appearance of this figure also helps to create a sense of loneliness and isolation—feelings that are intensified by the dim, subdued colors he uses in the print.

You might want to use the following questions to discuss the art:

1. How would you describe the mood, or atmosphere, of this print?
2. Which elements of the print contribute to the mood?
3. Do you think that this print makes an appropriate illustration for Mori Ōgai's story? Why or why not?
4. What emotions does this print evoke in you? Why?

the insipid paintings in the old-fashioned Japanese manner decorating the walls. Indeed, all of Japan is under reconstruction, and it wears the look of an adulterous mélange of two civilizations, uneasily brought together like the once-intimate couple.

Keene goes on to point out:

Ōgai believed in both East and West; the two did not war within him or make conflicting claims on his devotion. He recognized that the adoption of Western science had enabled Japan to outstrip China and Korea, where the scholars still clung obstinately to the old-fashioned learning and sneered at practical knowledge. He quoted the remarks made by a certain general on returning to Japan after helping suppress the Boxer Rebellion: "We have our imitation of the countries of the West to thank for this happy conclusion to the fighting, and

3 **Discussion** Ask students why Watanabé might find it strange that he does not "have the slightest feeling of anticipation." What does this suggest about the person whom Watanabé is about to meet?

4 **Discussion** Have students describe the mood, or atmosphere, of the story. How do the details in this paragraph contribute to the mood?

5 **Discussion** Have students explain why Watanabé considers the decorations to be an "ill-assorted collection."

6 **Discussion** Ask students why Watanabé has to force a smile onto his face when the woman appears. What indications are there that Watanabé once had a romantic relationship with this woman?

7 **Discussion** Ask students why Watanabé assumes that this gesture is done "for the benefit of the waiter."

8 **Discussion** Have students discuss the impression of the woman that has been conveyed up to this point. Which details have contributed to this impression?

the left. It was a large room overlooking the canal. It seemed rather big for just two people. Round each of the three small tables in the room were squeezed as many chairs as could possibly be fitted. Under the window was a huge sofa and next to it a potted vine about three feet high and a dwarfed plant with large hothouse grapes.

The waiter walked across the room and opened another door. "This is your dining room, sir." Watanabé followed him. The room was small—just right, in fact, for a couple. In the middle a table was elaborately set with two covers and a large basket of azaleas and rhododendrons.

With a certain feeling of satisfaction, Watanabé returned to the large room. The waiter withdrew and Watanabé again found himself alone. Abruptly the sound of hammering stopped. He looked at his watch: yes, it was exactly five o'clock. There was still half an hour till his appointment. Watanabé took a cigar from an open box on the table, pierced the end, and lit it.

Strangely enough, he did not have the slightest feeling of anticipation. It was as if it did not matter who was to join him in this room, as if he did not care in the slightest whose face it was that he would soon be seeing across that flower basket. He was surprised at his own coolness.

Puffing comfortably at his cigar, he walked over to the window and opened it. Directly below were stacked huge piles of timber. This was the main entrance. The water in the canal appeared completely stationary. On the other side he could see a row of wooden buildings. They looked like houses of assignation. Except for a woman with a child on her back, walking slowly back and forth outside one of the houses, there was no one in sight. At the far right, the massive redbrick structure of the Naval Museum imposingly blocked his view.

Watanabé sat down on the sofa and examined the room. The walls were decorated with an ill-assorted collection of pictures: nightingales on a plum tree, an illustration from a fairy tale, a hawk. The scrolls were small and narrow, and on the high walls they looked strangely short as if the bottom portions had been tucked under and concealed. Over the door was a large framed Buddhist text.

And this is meant to be the land of art, thought Watanabé.

For a while he sat there smoking his cigar and simply enjoying a sensation of physical well-being. Then he heard the sound of voices in the passage and the door opened. It was she.

She wore a large Anne-Marie straw hat decorated with beads. Under her long gray coat he noticed a white embroidered batiste blouse. Her skirt was also gray. She carried a tiny umbrella with a tassel. Watanabé forced a smile to his face. Throwing his cigar in an ashtray, he got up from the sofa.

The German woman removed her veil and glanced back at the waiter, who had followed her into the room and who was now standing by the door. Then she turned her eyes to Watanabé. They were the large, brown eyes of a brunette. They were the eyes into which he had so often gazed in the past. Yet he did not remember those mauve shadows from their days in Berlin. . . .

"I'm sorry I kept you waiting," she said abruptly in German.

She transferred her umbrella to her left hand and stiffly extended the gloved fingers of her right hand. No doubt all this was for the benefit of the waiter, thought Watanabé as he courteously took the fingers in his hand.

"You can let me know when dinner is ready," he said, glancing at the door. The waiter bowed and left the room.

"How delightful to see you," he said in German.

The woman nonchalantly threw her umbrella on a chair and sat down on the sofa with a slight gasp of exhaustion. Putting her elbows on the table, she gazed silently at Watanabé. He drew up a chair next to the table and sat down.

"It's very quiet here, isn't it?" she said after a while.

"It's under reconstruction," said Watanabé. "They were making a terrible noise when I arrived."

"Oh, that explains it. The place does give one rather an unsettled feeling. Not that I'm a particularly calm sort of person at best."

"When did you arrive in Japan?"

"The day before yesterday. And then yesterday I happened to see you on the street."

Grammar in Action

When writers describe a person, place, or object, they use **concrete details,** or details that appeal to one or more of the five senses, to create a mental image in the readers' minds. For example, note Ōgai's use of concrete details in the following descriptions from "Under Reconstruction":

Directly below were stacked *huge piles of timber.* . . . On the other side he could see a *row of wooden buildings.* . . .

The walls were decorated with an *ill-assorted collection of pictures: nightingales on a plum tree, an illustration from a fairy tale, a hawk.* . . .

Student Activity 1. Find five more descriptive passages in which Ōgai uses concrete details. Then explain how these details create a mental image in your mind.

Student Activity 2. Write a paragraph describing a place that you find especially beautiful or interesting. Use concrete details to create a vivid image of your subject.

"And why did you come?"

"Well, you see, I've been in Vladivostok[4] since the end of last year."

"I suppose you've been singing in that hotel there, whatever it's called."

"Yes."

"You obviously weren't alone. Were you with a company?"

"No, I wasn't with a company. But I wasn't alone either. . . . I was with a man. In fact you know him." She hesitated a moment. "I've been with Kosinsky."

"Oh, that Pole. So I suppose you're called Kosinskaya now."

"Don't be silly! It's simply that I sing and Kosinsky accompanies me."

"Are you sure that's all?"

"You mean, do we have a good time together? Well, I can't say it never happens."

"That's hardly surprising. I suppose he's in Tokyo with you?"

"Yes, we're both at the Aikokusan Hotel."

"But he lets you come out alone."

"My dear friend, I only let him accompany me in singing, you know." She used the word *begleiten*.[5] If he accompanied her on the piano, thought Watanabé, he accompanied her in other ways too.

"I told him that I'd seen you on the Ginza," she continued, "and he's very anxious to meet you."

"Allow me to deprive myself of that pleasure."

"Don't worry. He isn't short of money or anything."

"No, but he probably will be before long if he stays here," said Watanabé with a smile. "And where do you plan to go next?"

"I'm going to America. Everyone tells me that Japan is hopeless, so I'm not going to count on getting work here."

"You're quite right. America is a good place to go after Russia. Japan is still backward. . . . It's still under reconstruction, you see."

"Good heavens! If you aren't careful, I'll tell them in America that a Japanese gentleman admitted his country was backward. In fact, I'll say it was

a Japanese government official. You are a government official, aren't you?"

"Yes, I'm in the government."

"And behaving yourself very correctly, no doubt?"

"Frighteningly so! I've become a real *Fürst*,[6] you know. Tonight's the only exception."

"I'm very honored!" She slowly undid the buttons of her long gloves, took them off, and held out her right hand to Watanabé. It was a beautiful, dazzlingly white hand. He clasped it firmly, amazed at its coldness. Without removing her hand from Watanabé's grasp, she looked steadily at him. Her large, brown eyes seemed with their dark shadows to have grown to twice their former size.

"Would you like me to kiss you?" she said.

Watanabé made a wry face. "We are in Japan," he said.

Without any warning, the door was flung open and the waiter appeared. "Dinner is served, sir."

"We are in Japan," repeated Watanabé. He got up and led the woman into the little dining room. The waiter suddenly turned on the glaring overhead lights.

The woman sat down opposite Watanabé and glanced round the room. "They've given us a *chambre séparée*,"[7] she said laughing. "How exciting!" She straightened her back and looked directly at Watanabé as if to see how he would react.

"I'm sure it's quite by chance," he said calmly.

Three waiters were in constant attendance on the two of them. One poured sherry, the other served slices of melon, and the third bustled about ineffectually.

"The place is alive with waiters," said Watanabé.

"Yes, and they seem to be a clumsy lot," she said, squaring her elbows as she started on her melon. "They're just as bad at my hotel."

"I expect you and Kosinsky find they get in your way. Always barging in without knocking. . . ."

"You're wrong about all that, you know. Well, the melon is good anyway."

---

6. *Fürst* (fürst): "Duke" (German).

7. *chambre séparée* (shän br' sä pà rā'): "Separate room" (French).

---

4. **Vladivostok** (vlad´ i väs´ täk): A city in the Soviet Union.

5. *begleiten* (bə glī´ tən): "Accompany" (German).

9 Discussion Do students think that Watanabé seems jealous of Kosinsky? Why or why not? What does Watanabé seem to suspect about the woman's relationship with Kosinsky?

10 Enrichment Tell students that for a long time, the Ginza has been the most glamorous shopping district in Tokyo and one of the best known in the world. It begins near the Imperial Palace and extends for close to two miles, and it is crowded with shops. At night the Ginza's bars and restaurants attract tourists from nearby hotels and theaters. The name *ginza* comes from the words *gin*, meaning "silver," and *za*, meaning "guild." This name comes from the silver mint that was established in the district by the Japanese government in 1612.

11 Literary Focus Have students discuss Watanabé's apparent attitude toward the condition of his country.

12 Literary Focus Explain that according to traditional Japanese etiquette, it is considered improper for a man and a woman to kiss in public.

13 Literary Focus Have students discuss how the tension and uneasiness of the meeting between Watanabé and the woman parallels the tension created by the fusion of Japanese and Western customs and traditions.

14 **Discussion** Have students discuss why Watanabé responds to the woman's question in this manner.

15 **Discussion** Does it seem to students that the woman is upset by Watanabé's response to her question? Why or why not?

16 **Discussion** Ask students to explain whether this final detail indicates that the dinner has ended earlier than expected.

Cultural Note Explain to students that just as many modern Japanese writers were influenced by Western literature, a number of modern Western writers were inspired by traditional Japanese literary forms and techniques. One of these writers was the American poet Ezra Pound, who founded the Imagist movement. If students have studied American literature, have them discuss what they remember about the poetry of Ezra Pound and the Imagists.

Cooperative Learning You might want to offer a group of three or four students extra credit to prepare an oral report about the changes that occurred in Japanese society following the Meiji Restoration. Tell this group to begin by researching the topic in the library. The students should then organize their information and present it to the rest of the class. Make sure that each group member plays a role in delivering the report.

"In America you'll be getting stacks of food to eat every morning as soon as you wake up."

The conversation drifted along lightly. Finally the waiters brought in fruit salad and poured champagne.

"Aren't you jealous—even a little?" the woman suddenly asked. All the time they had been eating and chatting away. She had remembered how they used to sit facing each other like this after the theater at the little restaurant above the Blühr Steps. Sometimes they had quarreled, but they had always made it up in the end. She had meant to sound as if she were joking; but despite herself, her voice was serious and she felt ashamed.

Watanabé lifted his champagne glass high above the flowers and said in a clear voice: "Kosinsky *soll leben!*"[8]

The woman silently raised her glass. There was a frozen smile on her face. Under the table her hand trembled uncontrollably.

It was still only half past eight when a solitary, black car drove slowly along the Ginza through an ocean of flickering lights. In the back sat a woman, her face hidden by a veil.

---

8. **soll leben** (zōl lā′ bən): "Shall live" (German).

Reader's Response *After reading this story, do you feel that you would like to know more about the characters? Why or why not?*

PRIMARY SOURCE

In his book *The Pleasures of Japanese Literature*, the renowned Japanese literary scholar Donald Keene notes the dramatic transformation of Japanese society. Yet he also points out that the dominant Japanese tastes—the preference for simplicity, suggestion, irregularity, and perishability—have survived this transformation. He writes:

"The Western visitor to Japan today who expects to find exquisite beauty wherever he looks is likely to be disappointed and even shocked by his first encounters with contemporary culture. He will notice Kentucky Fried Chicken establishments and other fast-food shops, the ugliness of the commercial signs, the blank looks on the faces of people hurrying to places of business that more clearly resemble contemporary models in the West than anything traditional. But the past survives in aesthetic preferences that often find surprising outlets for expression—a box of sushi, a display of lacquered zori, branches of artificial maple leaves—along a commercial street. And the man who prides himself on elegantly tailored Western clothes will be delighted to sit in Japanese style, destroying the creases, at a restaurant where traditional food is served with traditional elegance. The Japanese aesthetic past is not dead. It accounts for the magnificent profusion of objects of art that are produced each year, and its principles . . . are not forgotten even in an age of incessant change."

Closure and Extension

ANSWERS TO THINKING ABOUT THE SELECTION

1. (a) Suggested response: He is observant and calm and behaves in a restrained, dignified manner. (b) Suggested response: He is jealous but is too proud to admit it. He is critical of

THINKING ABOUT THE SELECTION

Interpreting

1. (a) What is revealed about Watanabé's character during the period before the woman arrives at the restaurant? (b) What is revealed about his character during his conversation with the German woman? (c) What information about the woman's identity is revealed through the conversation? (d) What is revealed about her character, and how is it revealed?
2. (a) What evidence is there that Watanabé and the German woman had previously been involved in a love relationship? (b) How does the fact that Ōgai does not reveal this information directly contribute to the effectiveness of the story?
3. (a) What is the nature of the woman's relationship with Kosinsky? (b) What is Watanabé's attitude concerning the woman's relationship with Kosinsky? (c) How is his attitude conveyed?
4. How does the description of the woman in the black car relate to the rest of the story?

Applying

5. (a) Would you feel uncomfortable about having dinner with a former boyfriend or girlfriend? Why or why not? (b) Could you ever be friends with a former boyfriend or girlfriend? Why or why not?

ANALYZING LITERATURE

Appreciating Changes in Japanese Life

Although on one level Ōgai's story is about Watanabé's relationship to the German woman, it is also about the changes in Japanese society in the aftermath of the Meiji Restoration.
1. How does the story's title relate to the condition of Japanese society at the time?
2. How do Councilor Watanabé's observations on his way to the restaurant reflect the transitional state that Japan was in at the time?
3. Explain how Ōgai uses the Seiyoken Hotel as a microcosm of Japanese society as a whole.
4. What objects and details in the hotel suggest that the Japanese were struggling to strike a balance between their own traditions and Western methods and ideas?

CRITICAL THINKING AND READING

Connecting Literary Works

Mori Ōgai's first published story, "The Dancing Girl," was about an unsuccessful love relationship between a Japanese man and a German dancer.
1. How do you think that "Under Reconstruction" might be related to this earlier story? Support your answer.
2. If the two stories are connected, how might reading the earlier story enhance your understanding and appreciation for "Under Reconstruction"?
3. Considering that Ōgai spent four years in Germany and served as a government official, explain whether you think that the two stories might to some extent be based on the author's personal experiences.

THINKING AND WRITING

Describing a Society in Transition

Gather together with a group of your classmates. Then brainstorm about what it would be like if the United States were currently in the midst of a period of rapid transition, such as the one that Japan went through following the Meiji Restoration. What types of changes might this transition involve? By which cultures might American society be influenced? In what ways might these cultures influence the American way of life? How would the American public respond to the changes that were taking place? After you and the other members of your group have finished brainstorming, work independently to write a description of the changes in American society that you have envisioned. Offer an explanation of why these changes would take place, and discuss how the changes would affect the American people. Also examine the role of foreign influence in these changes. Once you have finished writing, revise your description, making sure you have presented your ideas in a clear and well-organized manner.

(continued from bottom of page)

differ. Many students will probably respond that they could be friends with a former boyfriend or girlfriend.

Challenge How does the uneasiness of the meeting between Watanabé and the woman parallel the uneasiness created by the merging of Japanese and Western customs and traditions?

ANSWERS TO ANALYZING LITERATURE

1. Suggested response: Japan is in the midst of being restructured and modernized.
2. Watanabé observes a mixture of Japanese and Western elements.
3. Like the hotel, Japan is under reconstruction. In addition, the hotel is filled with a mixture of Japanese and Western elements, as is Japanese society in general.
4. Suggested response: Japanese-style cloths for cleaning shoes are placed beside a Western doormat. Shoes are worn indoors, as in the West. The room where they dine is filled with Western furniture but has an ill-assorted collection of Japanese art on the walls.

ANSWERS TO CRITICAL THINKING AND READING

1. Answers will differ. Students should note that both stories are about relationships between a Japanese man and a German woman.
2. Answers will differ. Students may respond that reading the other story would help them to better understand the relationship between the two characters in "Under Reconstruction."
3. Suggested response: It seems likely that the two stories are to some extent based on Ōgai's experiences.

THINKING AND WRITING

Publishing Student Writing You might want to arrange students' descriptions into a class bulletin-board display.

the state of his country. (c) She is a German singer with whom Watanabé seems to have had a romantic relationship in Berlin. (d) Suggested response: She seems proud. This is revealed in the fact that she is disappointed that Watanabé will not admit that he is jealous of her relationship with Kosinsky. She also seems free-spirited. This is revealed through the details about her life style.

2. (a) They both recall intimate moments together in Berlin. (b) Answers will differ. Students may respond that Ōgai retains the reader's interest by not directly revealing information about their relationship.
3. (a) Suggested response: Although the woman does not admit it, it seems as if she is romantically involved with Kosinsky. (b) Suggested response: He is jealous, though he refuses to

admit it. (c) Suggested response: It is revealed through his obvious interest in her relationship with Kosinsky.
4. Suggested response: This final description reveals that the dinner between the couple has ended early and that they will not reestablish their love affair.
5. (a) Answers will differ. Most students will probably respond that they would feel uncomfortable. (b) Answers will

LU HSUN

More About the Author Lu Hsun spent part of his youth traveling abroad and was influenced by foreign experiences. He admitted that it was almost inevitable for him to search elsewhere since he claimed Chinese writers could not provide him with all he needed. He was most attentive to writers from Russia and central Europe.

Ask students to name other writers who were heavily influenced by authors outside their own national background.

Pronunciation Lu Hsun is pronounced in two syllables. The *h* of the *Hsun* is silent but the *s* is spoken as if it were *sh*. It is pronounced as if it were spelled *Shun*.

Critical Evaluation In his introduction to Chinese literature, Liu Wu-Chi describes Lu Hsun as "an author of pungent realistic stories, an irascible satirist, a vitriolic critic." Others also speak of him as a reformer who was more interested in producing fiction that might change society than in authoring literature that might be compared with that of his Russian and European models.

1881–1936

The most important event in Lu Hsun's (lo͞o shunz) life may have occurred in 1905 when he saw a film that showed a Chinese man, who had been accused of spying for the Russians, being executed by the Japanese during the Russo-Japanese War (1904–1905). Lu felt that this incident epitomized the deterioration of his nation from the dominant force of the Far East into a backward country that was at the mercy not only of the powerful Western nations but also of such emerging Eastern powers as Japan. At that point he vowed to become a writer and to use his pen to help to promote change in his country, and he spent the rest of his life fulfilling this promise.

Lu Hsun was born into a wealthy family who stressed the ancient Chinese principle of respect for education and learning. During his childhood, however, his family suffered severe financial setbacks that left them in poverty. Despite their financial problems, his family was able to send him to a private school at Nanking and later to Japan to study medicine. After seeing the film of the Chinese man being executed, however, he decided to abandon the study of medicine to pursue a career as a writer.

Lu Hsun prepared himself for his literary career by learning to speak German and Russian and by reading the works of such writers as Nikolai Gogol, Anton Chekhov, and Friedrich Nietzsche. He then began publishing a journal called *New Life*, in which he included translations of stories by Western writers, along with articles encouraging the Chinese people to read the works of such influential Western thinkers as Nietzsche and Charles Darwin.

In 1918 Lu Hsun became part of a circle of Chinese writers that came to be known as the New Culture Movement. Encouraged by the other members of this movement, he wrote his first short story, "Diary of a Madman" (1918). Throughout the rest of his life, he was an extremely successful and prolific writer, composing poems and essays, as well as short stories. His most famous story, "The Story of Ah Q" (1921), is a satirical attack on the state of contemporary Chinese society. His collection of stories *Old Stories Retold* (1935) also offers a satirical portrait of Chinese society.

During the final years of his life, Lu Hsun's writing became increasingly political as he became convinced that a republican government could not succeed in China, and he began promoting the necessity of a revolution. Because of his sympathy for the revolution, his work has remained popular in contemporary Chinese society, even during periods in which most literature was being suppressed by the government. Today many scholars from both China and the West consider him to be the most important Chinese fiction writer of his time.

Objectives

Thematic

To appreciate the longing for home that fills certain characters

Skills

1 To appreciate historical context

2 To recognize an author's attitude

3 To find antonyms

4 To compare and contrast stories

Support Material

Teaching Portfolio
Teacher Backup, p. 1407
Grammar in Action Worksheet, *Prepositional Phrases,* p. 1411
Usage and Mechanics Worksheet, p. 1413
Vocabulary Check, p. 1414
Analyzing Literature Worksheet, *Ap-*

GUIDE FOR INTERPRETING

My Old Home

Commentary

The Transformation of Chinese Society. The Chinese empire lasted for over two thousand years, surviving numerous wars, rebellions, and attacks by outside invaders. In 1911, however, the empire finally collapsed in the face of a successful nationalist revolution, and a year later China was made into a republic. Yet, the fall of the empire did not come as a surprise.

During the late 1700's and early 1800's, the empire had begun to weaken because of the decline in the Chinese standard of living resulting from rapid population growth. At the same time, the Western powers began pressuring the Chinese to loosen restrictions on foreign trade. This resulted in the signing of a series of treaties that benefited Western countries at the expense of the Chinese.

Throughout the late 1800's, Western influence spread rapidly throughout China, and it seemed likely that the nation would eventually be divided into several Western colonies. In addition the Chinese began having problems with the Japanese—problems that ultimately erupted into a war in which the Chinese were easily defeated. The loss to the Japanese, along with the threat of complete Western dominance, resulted in the emergence of strong feelings of nationalism and the creation of a revolutionary movement aimed at overthrowing the empire and establishing a republic.

Although the revolutionaries accomplished their purpose, the new republican government turned out to be a failure. By 1917 the power of the central government had crumbled and the nation had become divided. Local military leaders assumed control of northern China, and the Chinese Nationalist party established a rival government in the south. China lapsed into a state of civil war that ended with the establishment of a Nationalist government in 1928. Impaired by the opposition of the Chinese Communist party and the increasing aggression of the Japanese, the Nationalist government also proved ineffective. During World War II, the Japanese assumed control of most of China. When the Japanese occupation ended, another civil war broke out that ended in a communist victory.

Close to a decade after the overthrow of the Chinese empire, Lu Hsun returned to his native town for the first time in twenty years. What he discovered during this visit forced him to realize that the overthrow of the empire had done nothing to improve people's lives. "My Old Home" is a fictionalized account of this visit.

Writing

Write a journal entry in which you discuss what it might be like to return to your home town after being away for twenty years.

preciating Historical Context, p. 1415
Critical Thinking and Reading Worksheet, *Recognizing the Author's Attitude*, p.1416
Selection Test, pp. 1417–1418

Art Transparency 16
Tang Ren Jie by Hung Liu

Spelling Tip Mention to students that the correct plural spelling of talisman is *talismans,* not *talismen.*

Literary Focus The historical context of any literary work may contain important information for an understanding of the story. Certain pieces of fiction, Crane's *The Red Badge of Courage* or Hemingway's *For Whom the Bell Tolls,* cannot be appreciated without a consideration of the military conditions that give background to the entire work.

Ask students if such a framework can become a hindrance to a work's success with future generations.

Writing/Prior Knowledge Pair the students in your class. Have them discuss their own family's historical contexts for the last three generations.

Teaching Tenth-Grade Students Ask tenth-grade students how often they have moved from one address to another while growing up. Discuss whether such changes help or hinder their relationships with friends and relatives.

ESL Teaching Strategy Pair students with native-speaking students and have them describe the locations of places their families have lived before settling where they now are.

My Old Home

Lu Hsun

translated by Yang Hsien-yi and Gladys Young

Braving the bitter cold, I traveled more than seven hundred miles back to the old home I had left over twenty years before.

It was late winter. As we drew near my former home the day became overcast and a cold wind blew into the cabin of our boat, while all one could see through the chinks in our bamboo awning were a few desolate villages, void of any sign of life, scattered far and near under the somber yellow sky. I could not help feeling depressed.

Ah! Surely this was not the old home I had remembered for the past twenty years?

The old home I remembered was not in the least like this. My old home was much better. But if you asked me to recall its peculiar charm or describe its beauties, I had no clear impression, no words to describe it. And now it seemed this was all there was to it. Then I rationalized the matter to myself, saying: Home was always like this, and although it has not improved, still it is not so depressing as I imagine; it is only my mood that has changed, because I am coming back to the country this time with no illusions.

This time I had come with the sole object of saying goodbye. The old house our clan had lived in for so many years had already been sold to another family, and was to change hands before the end of the year. I had to hurry there before New Year's Day to say goodbye forever to the familiar old house, and to move my family to another place where I was working, far from my old home town.

At dawn on the second day I reached the gateway of my home. Broken stems of withered grass on the roof, trembling in the wind, made very clear the reason why this old house could not avoid changing hands. Several branches of our clan had probably already moved away, so it was unusually quiet. By the time I reached the house my mother was already at the door to welcome me, and my eight-year-old nephew, Hung-erh, rushed out after her.

Though mother was delighted, she was also trying to hide a certain feeling of sadness. She told me to sit down and rest and have some tea, letting the removal wait for the time being. Hung-erh, who had never seen me before, stood watching me at a distance.

But finally we had to talk bout the removal. I said that rooms had already been rented elsewhere, and I had bought a little furniture; in addition it would be necessary to sell all the furniture in the house in order to buy more things. Mother agreed, saying that the luggage was nearly all packed, and about half the furniture that could not easily be moved had already been sold. Only it was difficult to get people to pay up.

"You must rest for a day or two, and call on our relatives, and then we can go," said mother.

"Yes."

"Then there is Jun-tu. Each time he comes here he always asks after you, and wants very much to see you again. I told him the probable date of your return home, and he may be coming any time."

At this point a strange picture suddenly flashed into my mind: a golden moon suspended in a deep blue sky and beneath it the seashore, planted as far as the eye could see with jade-green watermelons, while in their midst a boy of eleven or twelve, wearing a silver necklet and grasping a steel pitchfork in his hand, was thrusting with all his might at a *zha*[1] which dodged the blow and escaped between his legs.

This boy was Jun-tu. When I first met him he was just over ten—that was thirty years ago, and at that time my father was still alive and the family well off, so I was really a spoiled child. That year it was our family's turn to take charge of a big ancestral sacrifice, which came round only once in thirty years, and hence was an important one. In the first month the ancestral images were presented and offerings made, and since the sacrificial vessels were very fine and there was such a crowd of worshipers, it was necessary to guard against theft. Our family had only one part-time laborer. (In our district we divide laborers into three classes: those who work all the year for one family are called full-timers; those who are hired by the day are called dailies; and those who farm their own land and only work for one family at new Year, during festivals or when rents are being collected are called part-timers.) And since there was so much to be done, he told my father that he would send for his son Jun-tu to look after the sacrificial vessels.

When my father gave his consent I was overjoyed, because I had long since heard of Jun-tu and knew that he was about my own age, born in the intercalary month,[2] and when his horoscope was told it was found that of the five elements[3] that of earth was lacking, so his father called him Jun-tu (Intercalary Earth). He could set traps and catch small birds.

I looked forward every day to New Year, for New Year would bring Jun-tu. At last, when the end of the year came, one day mother told me that Jun-tu had come, and I flew to see him. He was standing in the kitchen. He had a round, crimson face and wore a small felt cap on his head and a gleaming silver necklet round his neck, showing that his father doted on him and, fearing he might die, had made a pledge with the gods and buddhas,[4] using the necklet as a talisman. He was very shy, and I was the only person he was not afraid of. When there was no one else there, he would talk with me, so in a few hours we were fast friends.

I don't know what we talked of then, but I remember that Jun-tu was in high spirits, saying that since he had come to town he had seen many new things.

The next day I wanted him to catch birds.

"Can't be done," he said. "It's only possible after a heavy snowfall. On our sands, after it snows, I sweep clear a patch of ground, prop up a big threshing basket with a short stick, and scatter husks of grain beneath. When the birds come there to eat, I tug a string tied to the stick, and the birds are caught in the basket. There are all kinds: wild pheasants, woodcocks, wood-pigeons, 'blue-backs.' . . ."

Accordingly I looked forward very eagerly to snow.

"Just now it is too cold," said Jun-tu another time, "but you must come to our place in summer. In the daytime we'll go to the seashore to look for shells, there are green ones and red ones, besides 'scare-devil' shells and 'buddha's hands.' In the evening when dad and I go to see to the watermelons, you shall come too."

"Is it to look out for thieves?"

"No. If passers-by are thirsty and pick a watermelon, folk down our way don't consider it as stealing. What we have to look out for are badgers, hedgehogs and *zha*. When under the moonlight you hear the crunching sound made by the *zha* when it bites the melons, then you take your pitchfork and creep stealthily over. . . ."

I had no idea than what this thing called *zha* was—and I am not much clearer now for that matter—but somehow I felt it was something like a small dog, and very fierce.

---

1. zha (ja): A badgerlike animal.

2. intercalary month: Each year in the Chinese lunar calendar consists of 360 days, divided into twelve months of twenty-nine or thirty days. To compensate for the five additional days included in the traditional western calendar, a thirteenth, or intercalary, month is added to the Chinese calendar every few years.

3. the five elements: Metal, water, fire, wood, and earth.

---

4. buddhas (bōōd′ dəz): In the Buddhist religion, buddhas are figures who embody divine wisdom and virtue.

1 **Discussion** What effect is created by the narrator's reference to himself as a spoiled child? Discuss how important students think the news of his father's death will be later in the story.

2 **Discussion** Ask students to discuss how memory tricks the mind. Have them speculate on whether Jun-tu will seem as changed to the narrator as the old home's appearance.

3 **Discussion** Ask students why Jun-tu's special knowledge of birds and shells seems so important and so worthwhile to the narrator. Discuss what part such knowledge has to do with the attraction that the narrator has for him.

"Don't they bite people?"

"You have a pitchfork. You go across, and when you see it you strike. It's a very cunning creature and will rush toward you and get away between your legs. Its fur is a slippery as oil. . . ."

I had never known that all these strange things existed: at the seashore there were shells all colors of the rainbow; watermelons were exposed to such danger, yet all I had known of them before was that they were sold in the greengrocer's.

"On our shore, when the tide comes in, there are lots of jumping fish, each with two legs like a frog. . . ."

Jun-tu's mind was a treasure-house of such strange lore, all of it outside the ken of my former friends. They were ignorant of all these things and, while Jun-tu lived by the sea, they like me could see only the four corners of the sky above the high courtyard wall.

Unfortunately, a month after New Year Jun-tu had to go home. I burst into tears and he took refuge in the kitchen, crying and refusing to come out, until finally his father carried him off. Later he sent me by his father a packet of shells and a few very beautiful feathers, and I sent him presents once or twice, but we never saw each other again.

Now that my mother mentioned him, this childhood memory sprang into life like a flash of lightning, and I seemed to see my beautiful old home. So I answered:

"Fine! And he—how is he?"

"He? . . . He's not at all well off either," said mother. And then, looking out of the door: "Here come those people again. They say they want to buy our furniture; but actually they just want to see what they can pick up. I must go and watch them."

Mother stood up and went out. The voices of several women could be heard outside. I called Hung-erh to me and started talking to him, asking him whether he could write, and whether he would be glad to leave.

"Shall we be going by train?"

"Yes, we shall go by train."

"And boat?"

"We shall take a boat first."

"Oh! Like this! With such a long mustache!" A strange shrill voice suddenly rang out.

I looked up with a start, and saw a woman of about fifty with prominent cheekbones and thin lips. With her hands on her hips, not wearing a skirt but with her trousered legs apart, she stood in front of me just like the compass in a box of geometrical instruments.

I was flabbergasted.

"Don't you know me? Why, I have held you in my arms!"

I felt even more flabbergasted. Fortunately my mother came in just then and said:

"He has been away so long, you must excuse him for forgetting. You should remember," she said to me, "this is Mrs. Yang from across the road. . . . She has a beancurd shop."

Then, to be sure, I remembered. When I was a child there was a Mrs. Yang who used to sit nearly all day long in the beancurd shop across the road, and everybody used to call her Beancurd Beauty. She used to powder herself, and her cheekbones were not so prominent then nor her lips so thin; moreover she remained seated all the time, so that I had never noticed this resemblance to a compass. In those days people said that, thanks to her, that beancurd shop did very good business. But, probably on account of my age, she had made no impression on me, so that later I forgot her entirely. However, the Compass was extremely indignant and looked at me most contemptuously, just as one might look at a Frenchman who had never heard of Napoleon or an American who had never heard of Washington, and smiling sarcastically she said:

"You had forgotten? Naturally I am beneath your notice. . . ."

"Certainly not . . . I . . ." I answered nervously, getting to my feet.

"Then you listen to me, Master Hsun. You have grown rich, and they are too heavy to move, so you can't possibly want these old pieces of furniture anymore. You had better let me take them away. Poor people like us can do with them."

"I haven't grown rich. I must sell these in order to buy. . . ."

LANDSCAPE
Zhu Qizhan
Private Collection

Humanities Note
Fine art, *Landscape* by Zhu Qizhan. Qizhan was born in 1911 in China and studied oil painting at the Shanghai College of Arts, where he became a teacher in 1913. He also studied Japanese and Western art, especially the works of Vincent Van Gogh and Henri Matisse. Qizhan specialized in painting landscapes, flowers, and plants.

You might want to use the following questions to discuss the art:

1. How does this painting help to illustrate Hsun's distance from his past?
2. Does the composition of the painting convey the difficulty of travel to the village?
3. How does this relate to the story?
4. What do you find most interesting about this landscape?

"Oh, come now, you have been made the intendant of a circuit,[5] how can you still say you're not rich? You have three concubines now, and whenever you go out it is in a big sedan-chair with eight bearers. Do you still say you're not rich? Hah! You can't hide anything from me."

Knowing there was nothing I could say, I remained silent.

---

5. intendant of a circuit: An official position between the county and provincial levels.

7 **Discussion** Have students focus attention on the single word, "master," that separates the boyhood friends. Discuss why it places such a profound distance between the two men.

Master Teacher Note Place Art Transparency 16, *Tang Ren Jie* by Hung Liu, on an overhead projector. Point out the painting's attempt to juxtapose the old and the new faces of Chinese clothing. Note the differences between the traditional depiction of the woman on the right with that of the woman walking in the western setting of Sacramento at the turn of the century. Discuss the differences.

"Come now, really, the more money people have the more miserly they get, and the more miserly they are the more money they get . . ." remarked the Compass, turning indignantly away and walking slowly off, casually picking up a pair of mother's gloves and stuffing them into her pocket as she went out.

After this a number of relatives in the neighborhood came to call. In the intervals between entertaining them I did some packing, and so three or four days passed.

One very cold afternoon, I sat drinking tea after lunch when I was aware of someone coming in, and turned my head to see who it was. At the first glance I gave an involuntary start, hastily stood up and went over to welcome him.

The newcomer was Jun-tu. But although I knew at a glance that this was Jun-tu, it was not the Jun-tu I remembered. He had grown to twice his former size. His round face, once crimson, had become sallow and acquired deep lines and wrinkles; his eyes too had become like his father's, the rims swollen and red, a feature common to most peasants who work by the sea and are exposed all day to the wind from the ocean. He wore a shabby felt cap and just one very thin padded jacket, with the result that he was shivering from head to foot. He carried a paper package and a long pipe, nor was his hand the plump red hand I remembered, but coarse and clumsy and chapped, like the bark of a pine tree.

Delighted as I was, I did not know how to express myself, and could only say:

"Oh! Jun-tu—so it's you? . . ."

After this there were so many things I wanted to talk about, they should have poured out like a string of beads: woodcocks, jumping fish, shells, *zha*. . . . But I was tongue-tied, unable to put all I was thinking into words.

He stood there, mixed joy and sadness showing on his face. His lips moved, but not a sound did he utter. Finally, assuming a respectful attitude, he said clearly:

"Master! . . ."

I felt a shiver run through me; for I knew then what a lamentably thick wall had grown up between us. Yet I could not say anything.

He turned his head to call:

"Shui-sheng, bow to the master." Then he pulled forward a boy who had been hiding behind his back, and this was just the Jun-tu of twenty years before, only a little paler and thinner, and he had no silver necklet.

"This is my fifth," he said. "He's not used to company, so he's shy and awkward."

Mother came downstairs with Hung-erh, probably after hearing our voices.

"I got your letter some time ago, madam," said Jun-tu. "I was really so pleased to know the master was coming back. . . ."

"Now, why are you so polite? Weren't you playmates together in the past?" said mother gaily. "You had better still call him Brother Hsun as before."

"Oh, you are really too. . . . What bad manners that would be. I was a child then and didn't understand." As he was speaking Jun-tu motioned Shui-sheng to come and bow, but the child was shy, and stood stock-still behind his father.

"So he is Shui-sheng? Your fifth?" asked mother. "We are all strangers, you can't blame him for feeling shy. Hung-erh 1189 had better take him out to play."

When Hung-erh heard this he went over to Shui-sheng, and Shui-sheng went out with him, entirely at his ease. Mother asked Jun-tu to sit down, and after a little hesitation he did so; then leaning his long pipe against the table he handed over the paper package, saying:

"In winter there is nothing worth bringing; but these few beans we dried ourselves, if you will excuse the liberty, sir."

When I asked him how things were with him, he just shook his head.

"In a very bad way. Even my sixth can do a little work, but still we haven't enough to eat . . . and then there is no security . . . all sorts of people want money, there is no fixed rule . . . and the harvests are bad. You grow things, and when you take them to sell you always have to pay several taxes and lose money, while if you don't try to sell, the things may go bad. . . ."

He kept shaking his head; yet, although his face was lined with wrinkles, not one of them moved, just as if he were a stone statue. No doubt he felt intensely bitter, but could not express himself. After a pause he took up his pipe and began to smoke in silence.

From her chat with him, mother learned that he was busy at home and had to go back the next day; and since he had had no lunch, she told him to go to the kitchen and fry some rice for himself.

After he had gone out, mother and I both shook our heads over his hard life: many children, famines, taxes, soldiers, bandits, officials and landed gentry, all had squeezed him as dry as a mummy. Mother said that we should offer him all the things we were not going to take away, letting him choose for himself.

That afternoon he picked out a number of things: two long tables, four chairs, an incense burner and candlesticks, and one balance. He also asked for all the ashes from the stove (in our part we cook over straw, and the ashes can be used to fertilize sandy soil), saying that when we left he would come to take them away by boat.

That night we talked again, but not of anything serious; and the next morning he went away with Shui-sheng.

After another nine days it was time for us to leave. Jun-tu came in the morning. Shui-sheng did not come with him—he had just brought a little girl of five to watch the boat. We were very busy all day, and had no time to talk. We also had quite a number of visitors, some to see us off, some to fetch things, and some to do both. It was nearly evening when we left by boat, and by that time everything in the house, however old or shabby, large or small, fine or coarse, had been cleared away.

As we set off, in the dusk, the green mountains on either side of the river became deep blue, receding toward the stern of the boat.

Hung-erh and I, leaning against the cabin window, were looking out together at the indistinct scene outside, when suddenly he asked:

"Uncle, when shall we go back?"

"Go back? Do you mean that before you've left you want to go back?"

"Well, Shui-sheng has invited me to his home. . . ."

He opened wide his black eyes in anxious thought.

Mother and I both felt rather sad, and so Jun-tu's name came up again. Mother said that ever since our family started packing up, Mrs. Yang from the beancurd shop had come over every day, and the day before in the ash-heap she had unearthed a dozen bowls and plates, which after some discussion she insisted must have been buried there by Jun-tu, so that when he came to remove the ashes he could take them home at the same time. After making this discovery Mrs. Yang was very pleased with herself, and flew off taking the dog-teaser with her. (The dog-teaser is used by poultry keepers in our parts. It is a wooden cage inside which food is put, so that hens can stretch their necks in to eat but dogs can only look on furiously.) And it was a marvel, considering the size of her feet, how fast she could run.

I was leaving the old house farther and farther behind, while the hills and rivers of my old home were also receding gradually ever farther in the distance. But I felt no regret. I only felt that all round me was an invisible high wall, cutting me off from my fellows, and this depressed me thoroughly. The vision of that small hero with the silver necklet among the watermelons had formerly been as clear as day, but now it suddenly blurred, adding to my depression.

Mother and Hung-erh fell asleep.

I lay down, listening to the water rippling beneath the boat, and knew that I was going my way. I thought: although there is such a barrier between Jun-tu and myself, the children still have much in common, for wasn't Hung-erg thinking of Shui-sheng just now? I hope they will not be like us, that they will not allow a barrier to grow up between them. But again I would not like them, because they want to be akin, all to have a treadmill existence like mine, nor to suffer like Jun-tu until they become stupefied,[6] nor yet, like others, to devote all their energies to dissipation. They should have a new life, a life we have never experienced.

The access of hope made me suddenly afraid. When Jun-tu asked for the incense burner and candlesticks I had laughed up my sleeve at him to think

_____
6. **stupefied** (stoo′ pə fīd) *n*.: Stunned; made dull or lethargic.

that he still worshiped idols and could not put them out of his mind. Yet what I now called hope was no more than an idol I created myself. The only difference was that what he desired was close at hand, while what I desired was less easily realized.

As I dozed, a stretch of jade-green seashore spread itself before my eyes, and above a round golden moon hung in a deep blue sky. I thought: hope cannot be said to exist, nor can it be said not to exist. It is just like roads across the earth. For actually the earth had no roads to begin with, but when many men pass one way, a road is made.

Reader's Response *If you were in the narrator's position, would you try to do something to help Jun-tu? Do you think that it is possible for him to do anything to help Jun-tu? Why or why not?*

PRIMARY SOURCE

Lu Hsun once wrote, "What I wrote generally arose from something I had seen or heard, but I never relied entirely on the facts. I just took part of an event and modified or elaborated it until it expressed completely my ideas. The models for characters would be treated in the same way and I never picked on any specific individual."

THINKING ABOUT THE SELECTION

Interpreting

1. Why does the narrator become depressed during his journey back to his old home?
2. Why had the narrator been so fascinated by Jun-tu as a boy?
3. During the flashback in which he recalls his experiences with Jun-tu, what does the narrator reveal about the ancient superstitions and traditions of the people of rural China?
4. (a) What impression of Mrs. Yang does the narrator convey? (b) How does he convey this impression? (c) What is Mrs. Yang's attitude toward him? (d) Why does she have this type of attitude?
5. (a) Why is the narrator "tongue-tied" when Jun-tu first appears? (b) Why does Jun-tu address the narrator as "Master"?
6. Why does the narrator assume that Jun-tu must feel "intensely bitter"?

7. Why does the narrator feel cut "off from [his] fellows" as he travels away from his old home?
8. What is the meaning of the analogy, or comparison, that the narrator makes between hope and roads?

Applying

9. How is the society depicted in this story different from our society?

ANALYZING LITERATURE

Appreciating Historical Context

Based on Lu Hsun's return to his home town after a twenty-year absence, "My Old Home" paints a distressing portrait of life in rural China in the aftermath of the collapse of the empire.
1. What evidence is there in the story that the people are poor and oppressed?
2. What evidence is there that people were still following the traditional feudal modes of conduct?

Grammar in Action

A preposition is a word that relates the noun or pronoun that appears with it to another word in the sentence. A preposition is always part of a unit called a **prepositional phrase,** consisting of the preposition and a noun or pronoun called the object of the preposition.

"My Old Home" contains many prepositional phrases that are used to show different relationships among words. Note the following italicized examples in a single sentence:

As I dozed, a stretch *of jade-green seashore* spread itself *before my eyes,* and *above a round golden moon* hung *in a deep blue sky.*

Student Activity 1. Find five other prepositional phrases in the final paragraphs of Lu Hsun's story.

Student Activity 2. Locate five sentences in this story that are without prepositional phrases. Create and insert appropriate prepositional phrases for those sentences.

3. How does the narrator's discussion with his mother concerning Jun-tu's plight hint that China was currently in a state of disarray?
4. One of the major problems facing China at the time of the story was overpopulation. How are Jun-tu's circumstances indicative of this problem?

CRITICAL THINKING AND READING

Recognizing the Author's Attitudes

In his depiction of rural Chinese life, Lu Hsun not only conveys his displeasure with the current state of Chinese society but also expresses his hopes concerning the country's future.
1. What seems to be Lu Hsun's attitude concerning the traditional feudal mode of conduct, and how is his attitude revealed?
2. What type of changes in Chinese society does Lu Hsun seem to be hoping for? Support your answer.

UNDERSTANDING LANGUAGE

Finding Antonyms

Antonyms are words that are opposite or nearly opposite in meaning. For example the words *sluggish* and *active* are antonyms.

The words in capital letters are from "My Old Home." Choose the word that is most opposite in meaning to each of the capitalized words.

1. SOMBER
   a. melancholy
   b. cheerful
   c. energetic
   d. gregarious
2. FAMILIAR
   a. unknown
   b. inaccessible
   c. antiquated
   d. unfashionable
3. PROBABLE
   a. farfetched
   b. outrageous
   c. coincidental
   d. certain
4. IGNORANT
   a. understanding
   b. open-minded
   c. knowledgeable
   d. brilliant
5. PROMINENT
   a. unforseen
   b. anonymous
   c. inconspicuous
   d. protruding
6. COMMON
   a. obscure
   b. scarce
   c. infamous
   d. eccentric
7. INDISTINCT
   a. noteworthy
   b. renowned
   c. typical
   d. intelligible
8. ANXIOUS
   a. angry
   b. unconcerned
   c. expectant
   d. inconstant
9. GRADUALLY
   a. promptly
   b. confidently
   c. swiftly
   d. ploddingly
10. STUPEFIED
   a. apathetic
   b. stimulated
   c. enthralled
   d. astonished

THINKING AND WRITING

Comparing and Contrasting Stories

Just as "My Old Home" conveys a striking impression of the current state of Chinese society, Mori Ōgai's "Under Reconstruction" offers a clear sense of the state of Japanese society at approximately the same time. Write a paper in which you compare and contrast the two stories and the societies they depict. Begin by reviewing the two stories, noting what they indicate about the respective societies. Also note the similarities and differences in the techniques that the two writers use to convey their intended impressions. Organize your ideas according to corresponding points of contrast. Then write your paper, using passages from the two stories for support. When you have finished writing, revise your paper, making sure you have thoroughly supported each idea you have expressed.

RABINDRANATH TAGORE

Focus

More About the Author Tagore's striking appearance helped to shape his image as a prophetic sage and teacher. He believed that children should be one with their natural surroundings and that they should be sensitive to the environmental balance of the earth. The school he founded in Bolpur in 1901 was called Santiniketan (abode of peace). Many of its classes were held under the campus trees. When it expanded its program in 1922 to become the Visva-Bharati University, the curriculum continued to emphasize Tagore's concern for social reform and for international unity. Ask students if they think authors who are interested in reform are likely to produce didactic literature.

Pronunciation Note The author's surname can be accented in English on either its first or second syllable (i.e., ta gor′ or ta′ gor). His first name, Rabindranath, has its second syllable stressed (rə bēn′ drə nät).

Critical Evaluation A part of the author's success is credited to W. B. Yeats, who introduced Tagore to the English-speaking world after grief forced the Indian poet into retirement from public life in 1907. Writing in 1912, the year before Tagore received the Nobel Prize, Yeats said that "he writes music for his words, and one understands at every moment that he is so abundant, so spontaneous, so daring in his passion, so full of surprise, because he is doing something which has never seemed strange, unnatural, or in need of defence." Ask students if they know of another author about whom they would be willing to say the same.

1861–1941

In recognition for his literary contributions, the Indian writer Rabindranath Tagore (re bēn′ drə nät′ tä′ gôr) was knighted by the British government in 1915. Yet he had such strong principles and such a deep social commitment that he did not hesitate to renounce this title four years later in protest of the Amritsar (əm rit′ sər) Massacre, in which British troops fired on a group of Indian protesters.

Tagore was born in Bengal, which at the time was a province of British India. His father was a famous Hindu philosopher and religious reformer, and other members of his family distinguished themselves in art, music, and finance. A gifted child with a wide range of intellectual and artistic talents, Tagore began writing at an early age. Composing both poems and short stories, Tagore produced a series of books while he was still in his twenties, culminating with the publication of *Manasi* (mä nä′ sē), one of his finest collections of verse, in 1890.

In 1891 Tagore moved to his father's estate in a rural section of Bengal, where he developed a deep awareness of the poverty and other hardships faced by so many of the nation's inhabitants. From that point on, his social concerns played an important role not only in his writing but in the way in which he conducted his life. Among the many contributions that he made to Indian society were his establishment of a university and a progressive, open-air school in western Bengal. He was also a vocal supporter of human rights and personal freedom, though he did not press for Indian independence.

Despite his involvement in other activities, Tagore remained a productive writer throughout his life. Altogether he produced over 1,000 poems, two dozen plays, eight novels, and several collections of short stories. Generally, his poems, which are characterized by their simplicity and dignity, and short stories, which are noted for their irony and subtle humor and their social and philosophical themes, are considered his best works. Among his most famous collections of poems and short stories are *The Golden Boat* (1893), *Late Harvest* (1896), *Dreams* (1896), *Song Offerings* (1910), and *Bunches of Tales* (1912). The English translation of *Song Offerings* along with his overall role in introducing Indian literature to the Western world earned him the Nobel Prize for Literature in 1913.

Although it is not a well-known fact outside India, Tagore's artistic talents were by no means limited to writing. A gifted musician and composer, he wrote over two thousand songs and helped to create a new style of Indian music. In addition, he was also a talented painter, considered by many art critics to be the finest Indian artist of his time.

Objectives

Thematic
To learn how conflicts sometimes arise between the artistic and pragmatic sides of human beings

Skills

1 To examine internal and external conflict
2 To appreciate the role of conflict in fiction
3 To evaluate the importance of conflict as an element contributing much to a story's success

Supporting Material

Teaching Portfolio
Teacher Backup, p. 1419
Grammar in Action Worksheet, *Understanding Appositives,* p. 1423
Usage and Mechanics Worksheet, p. 1425
Vocabulary Check, p. 1426
Analyzing Literature Worksheet, *Understanding Conflict,* p. 1427

GUIDE FOR INTERPRETING

The Artist

Commentary

Conflict. Conflict, or a struggle between two opposing forces or characters, is probably the most indispensable element of a work of fiction or a drama. Just as the doubt concerning the outcome of a football game sustains a fan's interest, a reader's interest is sustained by his or her uncertainty about the outcome of a story's conflict. As a result, if a story does not have a conflict, there is little chance that people will want to read it.

Although there are many different types of literary conflicts, they can generally be divided into two categories: **internal conflicts** and **external conflicts.** As the term suggests, an internal conflict occurs within a character's mind and involves a struggle between opposing thoughts or emotions. For example, in Anton Chekhov's story "The Bet," a lawyer struggles to decide whether he should pay off a bet he has lost, knowing that doing so will drive him into bankruptcy, or whether he should commit murder to avoid paying off the bet. In contrast, an external conflict is a struggle between a character or group of characters and an outside force, such as another character, society, nature, or fate. In Nikolai Gogol's story "The Overcoat," for instance, the main character, Akaky Akakavich, is pitted against a society that ridicules him, strips him of his dignity, and robs him of the only possession that means anything to him.

Despite the fact that virtually all dramas and works of fiction involve at least one—and often more than one—conflict, it is not always obvious. Like real-life struggles, literary conflicts are often subtle and complex. For example, in Leo Tolstoy's story "How Much Land Does a Man Need?" it may not be immediately apparent that the protagonist, Pahom, is engaged in an internal struggle resulting from his inability to be satisfied with what he has. Internal conflicts, such as the one in Tolstoy's story, are often the most difficult to identify. In contrast, external conflicts involving two main characters tend to be the most obvious.

Prior to the twentieth century, writers usually resolved all conflicts by the end of a literary work. In the modern age, however, it became a common practice to leave conflicts unresolved. This new trend reflects the view of many writers that life is uncertain and confusing. As a result, the writers feel that a literary work that accurately depicts reality should present readers with possibilities, not solutions.

Writing

Write a journal entry in which you discuss whether you think it is more important for people to choose a career that they enjoy or to choose one in which they make a lot of money.

Literary Focus Tell students that the conflicts in "The Artist" are both internal and external. Explain that Chunilal's mother has always privately felt her own tensions between the mercantile and artistic spheres of existence. Have students think about the conflicts in their own lives as they try to determine how it would be best to earn a living in as complicated a society as our own.

ESL Teaching Strategy Pair ESL students with native-speaking students. Have partners list the circumstances that prompt them to be artistically creative. Also have them discuss the ways in which various cultures see the role of the artist.

Teaching Tenth-Grade Students Have tenth-grade students discuss jobs they have had after school or in the summer. Ask them if learning to make a living is more important than anything else they learn in school. Why or why not? How could one position be considered the short view and the other the long view?

Writing/Prior Knowledge Before composing the journal entry, let students speak with partners about pipe-dream jobs that pay little but offer attractive conditions. Have them mention at least one very lucrative position with dimensions that the students would find intolerable.

Selection Test, pp. 1429–1430
Essay Questions and Evaluation
Guidelines, p. 1439

Spelling Tip Ask students to notice that *squanders* follows the general rule of having the letter *u* come after the letter *q* in its correct spelling.

Vocabulary

Preteach the following vocabulary words:

meager (mē´ gər) *adj.*: Thin; lean

connotations (kän ə tā´ shənz) *n.*: Meanings

equable (ek´ wəb'l) *adj.*: Steady; uniform

squandered (skwän´ dərd) *v.*: Wasted

degradation (deg´ rə dā´ shən) *n.*: Disgrace

disdain (dis dān´) *n.*: Strong dislike

myriad (mir´ ē əd) *adj.*: Many; varied

enumerating (i nōō´ mə rāt iŋ) *v.*: Counting

The Artist

Rabindranath Tagore

translated by Mary Lago, Tarum Gupta, and Amiya Chakravarty

Govinda came to Calcutta after graduation from high school in Mymensingh.[1] His widowed mother's savings were meager, but his own unwavering determination was his greatest resource. "I *will* make money," he vowed, "even if I have to give my whole life to it." In his terminology, wealth was always referred to as *pice*.[2] In other words he had in mind a very concrete image of something that could be seen, touched, and smelled; he was not greatly fascinated with fame, only with the very ordinary *pice*, eroded by circulation from market to market, from hand to hand, the tarnished *pice,* the *pice* that smells of copper, the original form of Kuvera,[3] who assumes the assorted guises of silver, gold, securities, and wills, and keeps men's minds in a turmoil.

After traveling many tortuous roads and getting muddied repeatedly in the process, Govinda had now arrived upon the solidly paved embankment of his wide and free-flowing stream of money. He was firmly seated in the manager's chair at the MacDougal Gunnysack Company. Everyone called him MacDulal.

When Govinda's lawyer-brother, Mukunda,[4] died, he left behind a wife, a four-year-old son, a house in Calcutta, and some cash savings. In addi-tion to his property there was some debt; therefore, provision for his family's needs depended upon frugality. Thus his son, Chunilal,[5] was brought up in circumstances that were undistinguished in comparison with those of the neighbors.

Mukunda's will gave Govinda entire responsibility for this family. Ever since Chunilal was a baby, Govinda had bestowed spiritual initiation upon his nephew with the sacred words: "Make money."

The main obstacle to the boy's initiation was his mother, Satyabati.[6] She said nothing outright; her opposition showed in her behavior. Art had always been her hobby. There was no limit to her enthusiasm for creating all sorts of original and decorative things from flowers, fruits and leaves, even foodstuffs, from paper and cloth cutouts, from clay and flour, from berry juices and the juices of other fruits, from *jaba*- and *shiuli*-flower stems. This activity brought her considerable grief, because anything unessential or irrational has the character of flash floods in July: it has considerable mobility, but in relation to the utilitarian[7] concerns of life it is like a stalled ferry. Sometimes there were invitations to visit relatives; Satyabati forgot them and spent the time in her bedroom with the door shut, kneading a lump of clay. The relatives said, "She's terribly stuck-up." There was no satisfactory reply to this. Mukunda had known, even on the basis of his bookish knowledge, that value judgments can

---

1. **Calcutta** (kal kut′ ə) **. . . Mymensingh** (mē mən siŋ′): Calcutta and Mymensingh are both cities in India.
2. *pice* (pīs): An Indian coin.
3. **Kuvera** (ko͞o ver′ ä): The Hindu god of wealth, usually spelled *Kubera*.
4. **Mukunda** (mə ko͞on′ də)

5. **Chunilal** (cho͞on′ ēl al)
6. **Satyabati** (sa tē′ ə ba tē)
7. **utilitarian** (yo͞o til ə ter′ ē ən) adj.: Stressing usefulness.

be made about art too. He had been thrilled by the noble connotations of the word "art," but he could not conceive of its having any connection with the work of his own wife.

This man's nature had been very equable. When his wife squandered time on unessential whims, he had smiled at it with affectionate delight. If anyone in the household made a slighting remark, he had protested immediately. There had been a singular self-contradiction in Mukunda's makeup; he had been an expert in the practice of law, but it must be conceded that he had had no worldly wisdom with regard to his household affairs. Plenty of money had passed through his hands, but since it had not preoccupied his thoughts, it had left his mind free. Nor could he have tyrannized over his dependents in order to get his own way. His living habits had been very simple; he had never made any unreasonable demands for the attention or services of his relatives.

Mukunda had immediately silenced anyone in the household who cast an aspersion[8] upon Satyabati's disinterest in housework. Now and then, on his way home from court, he would stop at Radhabazar to buy some paints, some colored silk and colored pencils, and stealthily[9] he would go and arrange them on the wooden chest in his wife's bedroom. Sometimes, picking up one of Satyabati's drawings, he would say, "Well, this one is certainly very beautiful."

One day he had held up a picture of a man, and since he had it upside down, he had decided that the legs must be a bird's head. He had said, "Satu, this should be framed—what a marvelous picture of a stork!" Mukunda had gotten a certain delight out of thinking of his wife's artwork as child's play, and the wife had taken a similar pleasure in her husband's judgment of art. Satyabati had known perfectly well that she could not hope for so much patience, so much indulgence, from any other family in Bengal.[10] No other family would have made way so lovingly for her overpowering devotion to art. So, whenever her husband had made extravagant remarks about her painting, Satyabati could scarcely restrain her tears.

One day Satyabati lost even this rare good fortune. Before his death her husband had realized one thing quite clearly: the responsibility for his debt-ridden property must be left in the hands of someone astute enough to skillfully steer even a leaky boat to the other shore. This is how Satyabati and her son came to be placed completely under Govinda's care. From the very first day Govinda made it plain to her that the *pice* was the first and foremost thing in life. There was such profound degradation in his advice that Satyabati would shrink with shame.

Nevertheless, the worship of money continued in diverse forms in their daily life. If there had been some modesty about it, instead of such constant discussion, it wouldn't have been so bad. Satyabati knew in her heart that all of this lowered her son's standard of values, but there was nothing to do but endure it. Since those delicate emotions endowed with uncommon dignity are the most vulnerable, they are very easily hurt or ridiculed by rude or insensitive people.

The study of art requires all sorts of supplies. Satyabati had received these for so long without even asking that she had felt no reticence[11] with regard to them. Amid the new circumstances in the family she felt terribly ashamed to charge all these unessential items to the housekeeping budget. So she would save money by economizing on her own food and have the supplies purchased and brought in secretly. Whatever work she did was done furtively,[12] behind closed doors. She was not afraid of a scolding, but the stares of insensitive observers embarrassed her.

Now Chuni was the only spectator and critic of her artistic activity. Gradually he became a participant. He began to feel its intoxication. The child's offense could not be concealed, since it overflowed the pages of his notebook onto the walls of the

---

8. aspersion (ə spʉr′ zhən) *n.*: A damaging or disparaging remark.

9. stealthily (stelth′ ə lē) *adv.*: Secretely or slyly.

10. Bengal (ben gôl′): A region in northeastern India.

11. reticence (ret′ ə s'ns) *n.*: The quality or state of being habitually silent or uncommunicative.

12. furtively (fʉr′ tiv lē) *adv.*: Slyly; secretively.

---

5 Discussion Ask students what kind of man the narrator describes in this paragraph about Mukunda.

6 Literary Focus Have students examine this passage for evidence of Mukunda's uncritical, illogical acceptance of Satyabati's artwork.

7 Enrichment Tell students that some religious individuals, like Francis of Assisi, would react to Govinda's avarice in the same way as Satyabati. Explain that in certain traditions the rejection of wealth and of the worship of money led to the vows of poverty taken by those who renounced the pursuit of affluence.

8 Discussion Ask students about the extremes to which today's artists sometimes go in their devotion to craft. What sacrifices do they make befcre becoming commercially successful? Have them relate stories about artists working on creative endeavors without any financial reimbursement.

9 Discussion Consider the use of the word *intoxication*. What other word could be used to translate the joy associated with artistic activity? Is *intoxicating* a misleading word? Why?

Humanities Note

Fine art, *Two Gazelles* from the *Babar Nama*. The *Babar Nama* was an illustrated book created by court painters to commemorate the rule of Babar from 1526 to 1530. Babar, a Turk, was descended from Genghis Khan. He conquered Delhi in 1526, founding the Mogul Empire. The exploits of Babar were told as history and legend, illustrated with active figures.

Rulers of sixteenth-century India were interested in art for its aesthetics as well as its ability to create a sense of history and stability. Note the elegant line, surface patterns, and decorative detail of *Two Gazelles*.

You might want to use the following questions to discuss the art:

1. Is this work effective in illustrating Satyabati's love for art?
2. How do you imagine the illustration could be made more attractive?
3. What words describe the feeling of *Two Gazelles*?
4. What is your reaction to the work?

TWO GAZELLES, 1530
"They drew pictures of animals that God has yet to create . . . "
From the Babar Nama
New Delhi National Museum

Grammar in Action

An **appositive** is a noun, pronoun, or phrase placed near another noun or pronoun that it renames for clarification or emphasis. Tagore uses **appositives** and **appositive phrases** throughout this story. For example, he writes:

Only Brahma, the Creator, and Rudra, the destroyer, witnessed the creative delight of these two persons; Vishnu, the Heavenly Preserver, never arrived.

Appositives are punctuated like adjective clauses. If they contain material essential to the meaning of the sentence, they are not set off by commas. If the material is not essential to the understanding of the sentence, they are set off by commas.

Tagore, a famous poet, wrote many short stories.

His story "The Artist" is among his most widely admired.

Student Activity 1. Find three appositives on page 1195 in addition to the ones already quoted.

Student Activity 2. Place an appositive or an appositive phrase after the italicized noun in each of the following sentences. Set off the nonessential house. There were stains on his face, on his hands, on the cuffs of his shirt. Indra,[13] the king of the gods, does not spare even the soul of a little boy in the effort to tempt him away from the worship of money.

On the one hand the restraint increased, on the other hand the mother collaborated in the violations. Occasionally the head of the company would take his office manager, Govinda, along on business trips out of town. Then the mother and son would get together in unrestrained joy. This was the absolute extreme of childishness! They drew pictures of animals that God has yet to create. The likeness of the dog would get mixed up with that of the cat. It was difficult to distinguish between fish and fowl. There was no way to preserve all these creations; their traces had to be thoroughly obliterated before the head of the house returned. Only Brahma, the Creator, and Rudra, the Destroyer, witnessed the creative delight of these two persons; Vishnu,[14] the heavenly Preserver, never arrived.

The compulsion for artistic creation ran strong in Satyabati's family. There was an older nephew, Rangalal, who rose overnight to fame as an artist. That is to say, the connoisseurs of the land roared with laughter at the unorthodoxy of his art. Since their stamp of imagination did not coincide with his, they had a violent scorn for his talent. But curiously enough, his reputation thrived upon disdain and flourished in this atmosphere of opposition and mockery. Those who imitated him most took it upon themselves to prove that the man was a hoax as an artist, that there were obvious defects even in his technique.

This much-maligned artist came to his aunt's home one day, at a time when the office manager was absent. After persistent knocking and shoving at the door he finally got inside and found that there was nowhere to set foot on the floor. The cat was out of the bag.

---

13. Indra (in′ drə): The chief god of the early Hindu religion.
14. Brahma (brä′ mə) . . . **Rudra** (rōō′ drə) . . . **Vishnu** (vish′ nōō): In the Hindu religion, Brahma is the creator of the universe, Rudra is the god of destruction and reproduction, Vishnu is the god of preservation.

"It is obvious," said Rangalal, "that the image of creation has emerged anew from the soul of the artist; this is not random scribbling. He and that god who creates form are the same age. Get out all the drawings and show them to me."

Where should they get the drawings? That artist who draws pictures all over the sky in myriad colors, in light and shadow, calmly discards his mists and mirages. Their creations had gone the same way. With an oath Rangalal said to his aunt, "From now on, I'll come and get whatever you make."

There came another day when the office manager had not returned. Since morning the sky had brooded in the shadows of July; it was raining. No one monitored the hands of the clock and no one wanted to know about them. Today Chuni began to draw a picture of a sailing boat while his mother was in the prayer room. The waves of the river looked like a flock of hungry seals just on the point of swallowing the boat. The clouds seemed to cheer them on and float their shawls overhead, but the seals were not conventional seals, and it would be no exaggeration to say of the clouds: "Light and mist merge in the watery waste." In the interests of truth it must be said that if boats were built like this one, insurance companies would never assume such risks. Thus the painting continued; the sky-artist drew fanciful pictures, and inside the room the wide-eyed boy did the same.

No one realized that the door was open. The office manager appeared. He roared in a thunderous voice, "What's going on?"

The boy's heart jumped and his face grew pale. Now Govinda perceived the real reason for Chunilal's examination errors in historical dates. Meanwhile the crime became all the more evident as Chunilal tried unsuccessfully to hide the drawing under his shirt. As Govinda snatched the picture away, the design he saw on it further astonished him. Errors in historical dates would be preferable to this. He tore the picture to pieces. Chunilal burst out crying.

From the prayer room Satyabati heard the boy's weeping and she came running. Both Chunilal and the torn pieces of the picture were on the floor. Govinda went on enumerating the reasons

---

---

appositives with commas.
1. *"The Artist"* _____ has been made into a film.
2. *Tagore* _____ grew up in India.
3. *The Nobel Prize* _____ is given annually.
4. *Many readers* _____ favor his style of writing.

15 Discussion Satyabati suggests here that an artist's talents are God-given. Discuss whether or not this belief is often shared by Western writers who might not have the same faith as Tagore does.

Cultural Note Other writers of fiction, such as Tolstoy and Camus, share Tagore's concern for the connections between literature and social reform. Have volunteers compile a list of such authors. For example, they might list the American author Sinclair Lewis. What effect have these writers had? Have students discuss the truth of the saying "The pen is mightier than the sword."

for his nephew's failure in the history examination and suggesting dire remedies.

Satyabati had never said a word about Govinda's behavior toward them. She had quietly endured everything, remembering that this was the person on whom her husband had relied. Now her eyes were wet with tears, and shaking with anger, she said hoarsely, "Why did you tear up Chuni's picture?"

Govinda said, "Doesn't he have to study? What will become of him in the future?"

"'Even if he becomes a beggar in the street," answered Satyabati, "he'll be better off in the future. But I hope he'll never be like you. May his pride in his God-given talent be more than your pride in *pices.* This is my blessing for him, a mother's blessing."

"I can't neglect my responsibility," said Govinda. "I will not tolerate this. Tomorrow I'll send him to a boarding school; otherwise, you'll ruin him."

The office manager returned to the office. The rain fell in torrents and the streets flowed with water.

Holding her son's hand, Satyabati said, "Let's go, dear."

Chuni said, "Go where, Mother?"

"Let's get out of this place."

The water was knee-deep at Rangalal's door. Satyabati came in with Chunilal. She said, "My dear boy, you take charge of him. Keep him from the worship of money."

Reader's Response *What is your response to the attitudes expressed by the various characters in the story? Which outlook on life expressed in this story is most similar to your own? Explain.*

PRIMARY SOURCE

India has a rich artistic tradition. In his book *The Wonder That Was India* the historian A. L. Bashman offers insights about the art of painting in ancient India.

" . . . Painting was a very highly developed art in ancient India. Palaces and the homes of the rich were adorned with beautiful murals, and smaller paintings were made on prepared boards. Not only were there professional artists, but many men and women of the educated classes could ably handle a brush.

"Though now all in very bad condition, the surviving remains of ancient Indian painting are suffi-cient to show its achievement. They consist almost entirely of murals in certain of the cave temples. No doubt most temples were painted in some way, and the statuary was brightly colored, as it often is in Hindu temples today, and here and there more elaborate color schemes of mural decoration were carried out. A few caves in outlying places contain rough painted sketches of no special merit, often primitive in style, and believed by many authorities to be prehistoric. Some of the artificial caves dedicated to religious purposes, however, give us samples of the work of highly developed schools of painting . . ."

Closure and Extension

ANSWERS TO THINKING ABOUT THE SELECTION

1. They were insulted that she forgot their invitations and chose to draw rather than socialize with them.
2. (a) He implies that they are indifferent to art because its pursuit is rarely lu-

THINKING ABOUT THE SELECTION

Interpreting

1. Why do the relatives think that Satyabati is "stuck-up"?
2. (a) What does Tagore suggest about the general attitude of the people of Bengal concerning artistic pursuits? (b) What is Mukunda's attitude concerning his wife's interest in art? (c) How does the contrast between Mukunda's attitude and the attitude of other people help Satyabati to appreciate Mukunda?
3. How would you characterize Satyabati's and Mukunda's marriage?
4. (a) In what ways are Govinda and Mukunda different from each other? (b) How are these differences conveyed?
5. (a) What similarity is there between Rangalal's works and the artistic creations of Satyabati and Chunilal? (b) Considering the experiences of Satyabati and Chunilal, what is ironic, or surprising, about the statement that Rangalal's "reputation thrived upon disdain and flourished in [an] atmosphere of mockery"?
6. (a) Who is the "sky-artist"? (b) What does Tagore mean when he writes, "the sky-artist drew fanciful pictures, and inside the room the wide-eyed boy did the same"?
7. What is symbolized, or represented, by the fact that after Govinda's outburst, the "rain [fell] in torrents and the streets flowed with water"?
8. (a) What is Tagore's attitude concerning the contrasting priorities of the characters? (b) How is his attitude conveyed?

Applying

9. How would this story be different if it were set in contemporary America? Explain your answer.

ANALYZING LITERATURE

Understanding Conflict

"The Artist" clearly centers on an external conflict between Govinda and Satyabati. Yet the story also involves a larger conflict between two contrasting approaches to life.

1. When does Tagore first establish the conflict between Govinda and Satyabati?
2. Explain how the conflict is resolved.
3. Both Govinda and Satyabati embody specific values and a particular approach to life. If you consider what the two characters embody, what larger conflict does the story involve?

CRITICAL THINKING AND READING

Relating Conflict to Theme

The conflict of a literary work is often closely related to the theme, or central message. For example, the theme of a story in which the conflict is between a character and fate might be that people are sometimes unable to control their own destinies.

1. What is the theme of "The Artist"?
2. How is the theme conveyed?
3. How is the story's conflict related to the theme?

THINKING AND WRITING

Writing a Continuation of the Story

Write a continuation of the story focusing on Chunilal's life after his separation from his mother. Begin by rereading the story. Then think about what would be likely to happen to Chunilal in the future. How would he fare without his mother's guidance and support? How would they stay in touch with each other? How would Rangalal raise him? Would he become a famous artist like Rangalal? After considering these questions, develop a plot outline. Then begin writing your story. Make sure the way in which you portray Chunilal and Rangalal is consistent with the way in which Tagore portrayed them. After you have finished writing, revise your story, making sure the actions and events you have depicted seem believable.

(continued from bottom of page)

and correctly to the misfortune that has entered the life of Satyabati.

8. (a) Tagore seems to side with Satyabati, the artist for whom the story is named. He suggests she triumphs over adversity by escaping to her nephew at the end of the story. (b) This may show the author's hope that artists can find alternatives to social expectations.
9. Answers will differ. Possible responses might include mention of artists' colonies or homelessness.

ANSWERS TO ANALYZING LITERATURE

1. He first sets their dispute over the instruction of Chunilal.
2. It is resolved when Satyabati decides to leave Govinda's care.
3. It can be said to involve the philosophic tensions between materialism and altruism.

ANSWERS TO CRITICAL THINKING AND READING

1. Students' answers will differ. Students should see that the theme concerns the woman's care for her artistic vocation. Some might state it as follows: A fulfilled life requires realizing one's artistic nature rather than simply pursuing materialistic needs.
2. The theme is conveyed by having her courage set against the stubborn insistence of her brother-in-law.
3. The conflict is related to the theme because it sets up an opportunity for Satyabati to display just how forceful she can be.

THINKING AND WRITING

Writing Across the Curriculum Suggest to students that they illustrate this story with sketches of their own. Let them depict scenes from life in India or create pictures of artists at work. Then ask them to compose a brief caption relating their own illustration to "The Artist."

Challenge Ask students to look up the myth of Philoctetes, the Greek warrior famous for his wound and bow. Have them explain how Philoctetes could be compared, as he was by Edmund Wilson, to the modern artist who is both needed and detested by society.

crative. (b) Mukunda favored her interest because it seemed to make her happy. (c) She sees that few others would promote her as he does and she loves him for that.
3. It appears to be a mutually satisfactory marriage that allowed both husband and wife to be happy.
4. (a) Govinda was consumed by his need for wealth and the acquisition of money. Mukunda was not. He was indifferent to such success. (b) They are shown in their attitudes toward art and business.
5. (a) There is a similarity in the source of inspiration, according to Rangalal, who insists that "the image of creation has emerged from the soul of the artist." (b) His success is ironic because it seems to have thrived on the very same disdain that chokes and mocks the artistic efforts of his relatives.
6. (a) Satyabati is the sky artist. (b) Tagore is saying that Satyabati created beautiful paintings that were imitated by her son as he learned to follow in her artistic footsteps.
7. With this use of the pathetic fallacy, Tagore has nature act sympathetically

THEMES IN WORLD LITERATURE

Alienation and Despair

> "You can ride, you can travel
> with a friend of your own;
> the final step
> you must walk alone.
>
> No wisdom is better
> than this, when known:
> that every hard thing
> is done alone."
> —Hermann Hesse

These lines by the modern German novelist and poet Hermann Hesse capture the sentiments of many modern writers. These writers felt that the complexity, instability, and uncertainty of modern life placed an added strain on personal relationships and caused people to become increasingly isolated from one another. Consequently, modern literary works often portray characters who feel alienated or detached from others.

Gregor's serious wound, from which he suffered for over a month—the apple remained imbedded in his flesh as a visible souvenir since no one dared to remove it —seemed to have reminded even his father that Gregor was a member of the family, in spite of his present pathetic and repulsive shape, who could not be treated as an enemy; that, on the contrary, it was the commandment of family duty to swallow their disgust and endure him, endure him and nothing more.
—Kafka, "The Metamorphosis"

He detested the son. They had nothing in common, either of thought or feeling. Yes, he detested his daughter-in-law too, and that child! He despised them all because they had excluded him from their life, . . .
—Luigi Pirandello, "A Breath of Air"

I was leaving the old house farther and farther behind, while the hills and rivers of my old home were also receding gradually ever farther in the distance. But I felt no regret. I only felt that all round me was an invisible high wall, cutting me off from my fellows, and this depressed me thoroughly. . . .
—Lu Hsun, "My Old Home"

The theme of alienation and despair is most often associated with modern writers. Yet writers from many other literary eras have also depicted characters who suffer from a sense of alienation. In the nineteenth-century Russian writer Nikolai Gogol's story "The Overcoat," for example, the main character feels completely alienated not only from his coworkers but from society as a whole.

Here are some other literary works that portray characters who experience feelings of alienation and despair.

SUGGESTED READINGS

The Epic of Gilgamesh, page 15
Tu Fu, "Loneliness," page 242
Priest Jakuren, "One Cannot Ask Loneliness," page 284

Zeami, *The Deserted Crone*, page 306
Anton Chekhov, "The Bet," page 960
Albert Camus, "The Myth of Sisyphus," page 1274

CROSS CURRENTS

Isadora Duncan 1878–1927

A free spirit and a true pioneer, Isadora Duncan transformed the world of dance by developing a new expressive and theatrical dance form—modern dance. Despite its originality, however, Duncan's style of dancing was heavily influenced by her interest in the art and culture of ancient Greece. This interest developed in 1899 when she attended exhibits of ancient Greek art in London and Paris. In the Greek statues and the scenic depictions on the Greek vases, she found the lyrical postures she had been yearning for in dance and had been unable to find in traditional ballet. As a result, Duncan studied the poses in the works of art and echoed them with body movements.

DUNCAN'S RISE TO FAME

By 1905 Duncan's Greek-inspired experimentations in "free dance" had made her famous—a status that she enjoyed for the remainder of her life. Throughout her career she continued to look to ancient Greece for inspiration. She even modeled her costumes after the attire worn by the people of ancient Greece. Typically, she performed in bare feet, wearing a loose, flowing tunic, like the ones worn in ancient Greece.

DUNCAN'S SCHOOLS OF DANCE

Duncan performed all over the world, from New York to Paris to Moscow. In addition she established schools of dance for children in France, Germany, Russia, and the United States. Largely because of these schools, Duncan's innovative dance style lived on long after her death in 1927. In the performances of the students trained at these schools, the influence of ancient Greece was just as evident as it had been in Duncan's performances. For example, *Dance with a Scarf*, performed in Moscow in 1946, featured an array of tunic-clad "goddesses" interacting with a flowing scarf in a dance program fit to be frozen on a Grecian urn.

DUNCAN'S LASTING INFLUENCE

Duncan's contribution to the artistic world of the twentieth century extends far beyond the new dance form that she pioneered. She dared to break with tradition and to follow the impulses of her spirit. Because of her innovativeness and her willingness to take chances, many of the dancers and other artists who have followed her have dared to ignore the existing artistic preferences and have sought to find new and unique forms of expression.

Presentation

Motivation/Prior Knowledge
Have a class discussion about the way in which information is presented in newspapers and on television news programs. If any of your students work for the school newspaper or have taken a journalism course, have them share their prior knowledge about journalistic techniques. How are newspaper stories organized? What techniques do reporters use to capture the reader's interest? Is it a reporter's duty to strive to present information in an unbiased manner? Why or why not?

Teaching Tenth-Grade Students
Because tenth-grade students may have difficulty deciding which selection to write about, you may want to assign a single selection or a choice of two or three selections to the entire class.

Reporting Information

Writing a Report of Information

Writing to report information can take many different forms. All such writing has a few characteristics in common, however.

Characteristics of Report Writing

- Express information clearly
- Follow organizational patterns, whether spatial, chronological, or categorical, appropriate to reported subject
- Help reader gain picture by elaborating with details or examples
- Offer theories to explain facts and draw conclusions when information warrants it

For example, Kafka's story "The Metamorphosis" is the strange report of Gregor Samsa's grotesque transformation and ultimate death and of the equally grotesque transformation of a family in crisis. The story is effective through the realistic way in which Kafka reports it. By relentlessly exposing the mundane events of Gregor's existence, minute detail by minute detail, Kafka forces his reader to view these bizarre occurrences as if they were factual. In fact, Kafka's near neutral, reportorial style of presentation gives the tale power through understatement.

Assignment

Write about an unusual occurrence in one of the works you have read in this unit. Assume that the story is over when you begin. "Investigate" the story for a newspaper or a television news magazine, reporting from various viewpoints all the information about what happened. Allow your readers or viewers a full spectrum of information so that they may formulate an opinion about the event.

- Include all important facts beginning with basics on What, Where, Who, How, and Why.
- Recount perspectives on the facts gathered from "interviews" with characters in the selection.
- Offer possible theories about the occurrence that allow the reader to judge it.

Prewrite

Subject

To gather information for your report you will need to know the selection well. Discuss it in class, with a partner, or both. Concentrate on getting the facts straight first, then examine the various characters' responses to those facts. Write notes about both the facts and the characters' unique perspectives on them. Your examination of the characters' responses will give you ideas about questions to ask them in your "interviews."

Next, decide which characters you need to interview and prepare question lists for each one. (You should do a minimum of three interviews.) Then ask a friend who knows the story well to pretend to be each of the characters you plan to interview. Use your question list, but don't be afraid to pursue an interesting response with a follow-up question not on your list. Be sure to write down notable quotations to use in your report. If you like, you may use a tape recorder.

Remember that you are interviewing friends pretending to be the story's characters. If you think their responses are wrong, do not hesitate to change them.

Format

Organize your notes. Then decide on a format for your investigative report. Think about the audience you plan to draw. Is the piece for *The New York Times*, *60 Minutes*, or the high school *Observer*?

Write

Remembering that all good investigative reporting starts with the facts clearly presented, then elaborates on those facts with additional information from various sources like interviews, write your report. If you get stuck, return to your notes or tapes, or interview partners for help.

Consider placement of your materials. Would it be more compelling to include one character's comments before or after those of another? Sometimes investigative reporting offers theories about the facts and elaborations it has presented. You should end your report by doing so.

Collaborate

Ask a partner to respond to your draft in the following way.

- Note in the margin any facts that are missing from the first paragraph.
- Make suggestions in the margin about reordering sections for more force.
- Put a straight line under words, phrases, or sentences that are particularly strong.
- Put a wavy line under words, phrases, or sentences that are unclear or poorly written.

Revise

If your investigative report is for a television magazine such as *60 Minutes*, you must hear it read aloud before you revise it. If it is for a newspaper, hearing it aloud is still a good idea. Ask someone to read it to you while you listen as if someone else had written it.

Now, using the suggestions your response partner made and any problems you heard when it was read to you, rewrite your paper.

Improve your paper further by excising any emotional language you may have used. Good reporting should be detached, allowing the reader or viewer to grasp the facts and perspectives and make his or her own judgments. Your language should be clear, strong, and neutral.

Be sure to check your quotations carefully while you proofread for grammar, spelling, and punctuation errors.

Publish

Prepare an oral presentation of this same story. Pretend that it is being aired as a radio broadcast. Tape-record the report in advance and bring the tape to class. Play a segment, perhaps the opening or the part you believe is strongest. Be prepared to answer any questions that arise about the choices you have made.

Evaluate

You have given an informational report on something unreal, and you have done it as if it were real. How did it feel to make up interviews? Did you learn anything about the story's characters by doing so? Did you experience any difficulty pretending something was real when it was not? Why or why not? Consider keeping this paper to review sometime in the future.

Master Teacher Note Explain to students that they should not hesitate to make revisions in their work as they are writing. In fact, they should feel free to change their method of organization if they find that the method they have chosen is not working.

You might also want to make it clear to students that they should try to present their information in a manner that will capture the reader's or the viewer's interest. In addition, point out to students that they should try to make their report as objective as possible.

Guidelines for Evaluating Writing About Literature Keep the following questions in mind when evaluating students' compositions.
1. Is the information in the report accurate?
2. Are any important facts omitted from the report?
3. Is the information presented in a way that captures the reader's or the viewer's interest?
4. Is the information presented as objectively as possible?

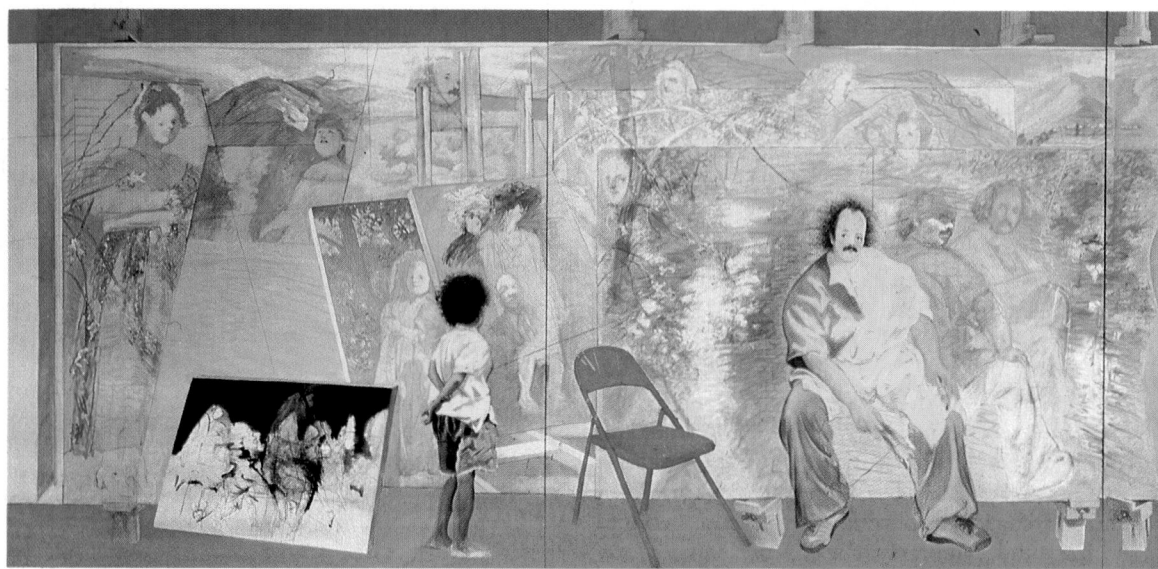

THE REAL MOUNTAIN, 1981
Jacobo Borges

THE CONTEMPORARY WORLD

1946–Present

Viewed from the distance of the moon, the astonishing thing about the earth . . . is that it is alive . . . Aloft, floating free beneath the moist, gleaming membrane of bright blue sky, is the rising earth, the only exuberant thing in this part of the cosmos. . . . It has the organized, self-contained look of a live creature, full of information, marvelously skilled in handling the sun.

—Lewis Thomas, *The Lives of a Cell*

EARTH, FROM THE MOON

Perhaps the most important photograph of the postwar period is the picture of Earth from the moon. It shows a cloud-wrapped blue jewel of a planet, alone in the darkness of outer space. That jewel is ours. If we—the people of the world—do not learn how to cherish the earth and live in peace with one another, then our treasure will be lost. The story of the postwar period, with its sprawl of events and relentless changes, reflects the struggle of humankind to realize and act on this idea.

HISTORICAL BACKGROUND

The End of Colonialism

The end of World War II hastened the end of Europe's colonial empires, many of which were built up in the nineteenth century. These former colonies became independent nations and, together with countries in Latin America, came to be known as the Third World: Less developed than the nations of the Eastern or Western bloc, they represented a *third*, relatively independent group in world politics.

The Road to Recovery

World War II left much of Europe and Asia in ruins. The immediate postwar task was to rebuild. In Europe the rebuilding took place during the icy chill of the Cold War. No sooner had the fighting stopped than our wartime ally, the Soviet Union under Joseph Stalin, made clear its aim to control eastern Europe and, if possible, to spread Communism westward. Western Europe resisted, aided greatly by the Marshall Plan, a United States–funded program to assist the economic recovery of the Western democracies.

Meanwhile Japan, devastated by American bombs, began its recovery under the watchful eye of General Douglas MacArthur. The new government was allowed to have very little military capacity. Instead, the nation, with government and business as close partners, began to manufacture consumer goods suitable for export. Over the next forty years, Japan rose to be one of the great economic powers of the world.

Western Europe, too, grew increasingly prosperous with the passage of time. The Communist nations, however, lagged far behind. Political repression coupled with a singleminded concentration on military strength led finally to economic exhaustion. By 1989 it was plain to Soviet President Mikhail Gorbachev that the Soviet Union had nothing to gain from the Cold War. The Berlin Wall—a looming symbol of the Cold War—fell. Eastern European nations were suddenly granted new freedoms, and the promise of democracy and a free-market economy was the talk of the day. The collapse of the Soviet Union as a political entity liberated some countries and plunged others into civil war.

International Cooperation and Conflict

Throughout the postwar period, a new international organization, the United Nations (UN), tried to prevent or quell conflicts between nations. Established in San Francisco in 1945 and permanently housed in New York City, the UN had some success with its peacekeeping missions, but its greatest contribution came not in abolishing war—there have been many small, searing wars—but rather in its humanitarian work in fighting disease and famine.

The Middle East, a Hot Spot

For centuries Jews had been without a homeland. Often they were forced to live in ghettos within cities, and with a disturbing frequency they were subjected to pogroms, or violent attacks. Anti-Semitism reached its height in Germany under Adolf Hitler. By the end of World War II more than six million Jews had perished in Nazi concentration camps. This brutal extermination, called the Holocaust, prompted a UN move to establish the sovereign nation of Israel as a Jewish homeland. The UN General Assembly approved this plan, but the Arab nations in the Middle East did not. A series of wars between fledgling Israel and the surrounding Arab states began immediately. Israel proved able to hold its own in warfare, but the sources of conflict still have not been resolved.

A United Europe

As western Europe grew prosperous, its leaders decided that economic cooperation made more sense than a policy of every nation for itself. Out of this decision came the European Economic Community (EEC). The agreements creating the EEC were designed to make Europe capable of competing on an equal footing with the economic superpowers, the United States and Japan.

Cooperation and Conflict in Latin America

Latin America, too, has seen both cooperation and conflict. The Organization of American States (OAS), created in 1948 at Bogotá, Colombia,

times she should fold her ballot paper. 'You can fold it as many times as you like,' said the volunteer official, 'it's a free election!' By the time I got to the polling station in the small village of Seeberg, at midday, more than 80 percent of the electors had voted. When I say polling station, I mean the back room of a local pub. And when I say 80 percent, I mean about fifty people, for there were only sixty-five electors in this village—and eight of them were on the supervisory electoral commission.

"These electoral commissions, containing, where possible, representatives of the main parties, took their tasks very seriously indeed, scrupulously checking off names and insisting that people use the polling booths. Previously, to use the polling booth was a sign that you were not toeing the line: good conformists openly folded their paper and put it straight into the box. A friend once described the few paces to the polling booth as 'the longest walk of my life.' And another recalled how, at the local government elections only last May, her hand was shaking so much that she could not get her (deliberately spoiled) ballot paper into the slot. Today, these sounded like tales from a distant epoch."

Pictured from left to right:

In 1953 molecular biologists J. D. Watson and F. H. Crick discovered that DNA was composed of two strands coiled into a double helix configuration. DNA is found in the nucleus of the cell and is the chief material in chromosomes, the cells that control the heredity of living organisms.

On July 20, 1969, U.S. astronaut Neil Armstrong became the first man to step on the moon. Edwin Aldrin, Jr., pictured here, was the second man from the Apollo 11 lunar module, *Eagle*, to walk on the moon's surface. The *Eagle* was on the moon for nearly twenty-two hours.

Solidarity is an organization composed of approximately fifty Polish trade unions. In 1980 Lech Walesa became the leader of Poland's labor movement. Walesa's negotiations with the Polish government led to the government's recognition of Solidarity, which marks the first time labor unions have been recognized as independent from the Communist Party. Pictured here is a rural Solidarity meeting near Warsaw. In 1981, when government opposition to Solidarity grew, the Polish government suspended the organization's activities and arrested Walesa. He was released in 1982. That same year the government officially outlawed Solidarity. Walesa continued to organize strikes, and in 1989 negotiated an agreement with the government that made Solidarity legal again. In 1990, he was elected president of Poland.

Amnesty International is an independent organization that helps put international pressure on governments that suppress human rights. The organization also strives to set free prisoners of conscience, ensure fair and prompt trials, and end torture and executions throughout the world. Amnesty International has approximately 750,000 members in over 150 countries.

Apartheid is the system of racial segregation in the Republic of

The Contemporary World (1946–Present)

A computer image of a DNA molecule

Astronaut Edwin Aldrin, Jr., during first moon landing

1946	1956	1966

HISTORY

- India wins independence
- Marshall Plan is proposed to help rebuild Western Europe
- Arab-Israeli War begins
- Gandhi is assassinated
- Apartheid is established in South Africa
- People's Republic of China is declared under Mao Zedong
- Korean War begins

- Hungarian Revolution takes place
- Ghana becomes the first independent nation of West Africa
- Great Leap Forward begins in China
- Congo and Nigeria become independent
- OPEC is formed
- Cuban missile crisis takes place

- Cultural Revolution begins in China

HUMAN PROGRESS

- Transistor is invented
- First supersonic flight in U.S. occurs
- First kidney transplant takes place
- Rock-and-roll music begins in U.S.
- Russia's first unmanned satellite, *Sputnik I,* is sent into orbit
- First U.S. spacecraft, *Explorer I,* is sent into orbit
- Computer chip is developed
- John Glenn is first American to orbit the earth
- Organization of African Unity is founded
- Structure of DNA molecule is determined
- Soviet cosmonaut Yuri Gagarin is first person sent into orbit

LITERATURE

- Alexander Solzhenitsyn is exiled
- Herman Hesse wins Nobel Prize for Literature
- Thomas Mann: *Doktor Faustus*
- Pär Lagerkvist wins Nobel Prize for literature
- Colette dies
- Thomas Mann dies
- Albert Camus: *The Myth of Sisyphus*
- Albert Camus wins Nobel Prize for Literature
- Boris Pasternak: *Doktor Zhivago*
- Gabriela Mistral dies
- Boris Pasternak is forced to decline the Nobel Prize for Literature
- Chinua Achebe: *Things Fall Apart*
- T. S. Eliot dies

South Africa. Objections to the restrictions placed on black Afrikaners escalated to riots and deadly battles. Pictured here is a group of protesters against apartheid in Johannesburg, South Africa. The sign reads: "F. W. De Klerk [the current prime minister of South Africa] stop police brutality." In 1993, the Nobel Prize was jointly awarded to De Klerk and Nelson Mandela, anti-apartheid activist and president of the African National Congress. They won the prize for working together to dismantle apartheid.

In April 1989 Beijing University students protested at Tiananmen Square in Beijing, China, against the government's lagging political reform and suppression of freedom and human rights. The demonstrators also wanted the removal of key government leaders who opposed these goals. The "hardline" leaders, with the support of paramount leader Deng Xiaoping, feared the social unrest would pose dangers for China's future. On June 3, 1989, the hardline leaders opted for military

Solidarity meeting,
Warsaw, Poland

Amnesty International,
an independent
human-rights
organization

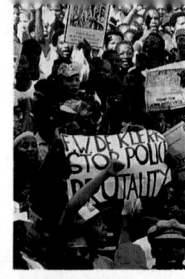
Anti-apartheid
protesters,
Johannesburg,
South Africa

Chinese student
protesters at Tiananmen
Square, Beijing

1976   **1986**   **Present**

- Civil war begins in Nigeria
- Six-Day War is fought
- U.S. expansion in the Vietnam War occurs
- 38 new nations are established in Africa
  - Colonel Qaddafi becomes leader of Libya

- Saigon falls; U.S. leaves Vietnam; Cambodia falls to communist forces
  - Rioting and violence against apartheid spread from Soweto to Johannesburg and Cape Town
    - P.R.C. and U.S. establish full diplomatic relations
      - Khomeini comes to power in Iran
      - Soviets invade Afghanistan
        - Workers riot in Poland; Solidarity is founded
  - Nixon resigns presidency
  - Civil war begins in Lebanon

- Pinochet declares state of siege in Chile
  - Protest against apartheid spreads in South Africa
    - The Soviet Union collapses
      - South African whites vote to abolish apartheid
  - Mikhail Gorbachev becomes head of Soviet Union
    - Polish government formally lifts martial law

- First U.S. landing on the moon takes place
  - First complete synthesis of a gene is developed
    - Soviet spacecraft lands on Venus

- Structure of the sun's magnetic field is determined
- Passenger service on the *Concorde* supersonic transport begins
  - Test-tube baby is born in England

- Breakthroughs are made in bucky ball research
- Space shuttle *Challenger* explodes
- Superconductivity research accelerates
- Human genome project begins

- García Márquez: *One Hundred Years of Solitude*
  - Alexander Solzhenitsyn wins Nobel Prize for Literature
  - Pablo Neruda wins Nobel Prize for Literature
    - Heinrich Böll wins Nobel Prize for Literature
      - Pablo Neruda dies

- Manuel Rojas dies
  - Pär Lagerkvist dies

- Czeslaw Milosz wins Nobel Prize for Literature
  - Gabriel García Márquez wins Nobel Prize for Literature
    - Julio Cortázar dies
      - Wole Soyinka wins Nobel Prize for Literature
      - Bessie Head dies

- Najib Mahfouz wins Nobel Prize for Literature
  - Octavio Paz wins Nobel Prize for Literature
    - Walcott wins Nobel Prize

suppression of the demonstrators at
Tiananmen Square; the crackdown
resulted in hundreds and possibly
thousands of deaths.

attempted to promote hemispheric solidarity and to prevent outside interference in the affairs of member nations. The OAS has in fact resolved a number of conflicts between member nations. Predictably, it objected to the United States invasion of Panama in 1989.

Apart from wars and dictatorships, the greatest challenge facing Latin America has been economic. Many of the region's countries borrowed too much money from foreign banks during the 1970's and now face staggering debt.

CULTURAL BACKGROUND

Science and Technology

From a technological perspective, the world of 1946 seems ancient. Television sets were in the experimental stage, as were jet aircraft, electronic computers, and hi-fi stereo components. New communications equipment, including the earth-orbiting satellite, was just beginning to change the world into what Canada's Marshall McLuhan would call "the global village."

As the postwar period continued, many people became frightened by the prospect of nuclear war. The bombs that had forced Japan to surrender, destructive as they were, were puny compared with those that the United States and the Soviet Union soon developed. Journalists called the big-power standoff a "balance of terror." Fortunately for the planet, the vast arsenals of nuclear weapons that were built up in the postwar years remained unused. Yet even the peaceful uses of nuclear energy could be frightening, as the 1986 accident at Russia's Chernobyl nuclear power plant proved.

Scientists made major discoveries after the war, one of the most important being the structure of DNA. The "double helix" of DNA, or *d*eoxyribo*n*ucleic *a*cid, is the molecular basis of human heredity. An array of medical advances—such as the Salk anti-polio vaccine, microsurgery, and the Jarvik artificial heart—revolutionized the prevention and treatment of illnesses and injuries. At the same time, new diseases arose to challenge complacency about medical progress. Chief among these was the acquired immune deficiency syndrome

(AIDS). Caused by a virus, it weakens the body's defenses against disease and leaves its victims prey to a host of afflictions.

"One Giant Step for Mankind"

Space exploration, which began with the Soviet launch of *Sputnik I* in 1957, brought striking gains in our knowledge of outer space and led to many innovations in technology. Perhaps the most dramatic moment of the postwar period occurred on July 20, 1969, when American astronaut Neil Armstrong first set foot on the moon.

Giant Problems for Humankind

Unfortunately, technological progress carried with it serious dangers to our common home: polluted air and water, pesticide poisoning, massive accumulations of garbage, and depletion of the protective ozone layer in the atmosphere. Progress in the industrial nations, moreover, seemed to make the rich richer while the poor got poorer. While the life of one child in Sweden, for example, might be saved by a costly organ transplant, thousands of children were dying of starvation in places like Ethiopia, Mali, and Bangladesh.

Literacy and International Culture

In general, the worldwide literacy rate has been rising over the past few decades, although it is still far higher in the industrialized nations than in the Third World. A growing sense of our planet as a single, interrelated community has also led many people to master two or more languages.

The advent of instant communication and easy travel has tended to make national cultures more similar than they once were. Just as you can find a McDonald's or a Pizza Hut in nearly any large city in the world, so can you find familiar downtown skylines, business dress, and popular music—particularly rock-and-roll, which England and the United States have exported everywhere.

However, even while people are more aware of foreign achievements than they were before World

War II, they are also more aware of their own unique cultural heritage. Mass marketing may homogenize the world of commerce, but it is unlikely to eliminate many of the deep-seated cultural distinctions, either in everyday life or in the arts.

Two Postwar Trends

Two other trends emerged after the war. One was the development of existential philosophy in the late 1940's and the 1950's. Existentialism, a movement that influenced many writers, stressed the freedom and responsibility of the individual. However, it also underscored the isolation imposed on each person in a world that cannot be rationally explained. Another trend was the growth of a youth counterculture, which reached its height in the 1960's. Rock-and-roll music was one of its outward expressions; others were long hair, faded bluejeans, and, tragically, drugs. Inwardly, this counterculture reflected a genuine desire for universal peace and a new awareness of the need to protect the environment

LITERARY TRENDS

The Latin American "Boom"

The postwar upsurge of literature in Latin America was so dramatic that it was called the "Boom." Two leading figures of this "Boom" were Argentinians. Jorge Luis Borges (page 1224) was best known for his short stories, although he also

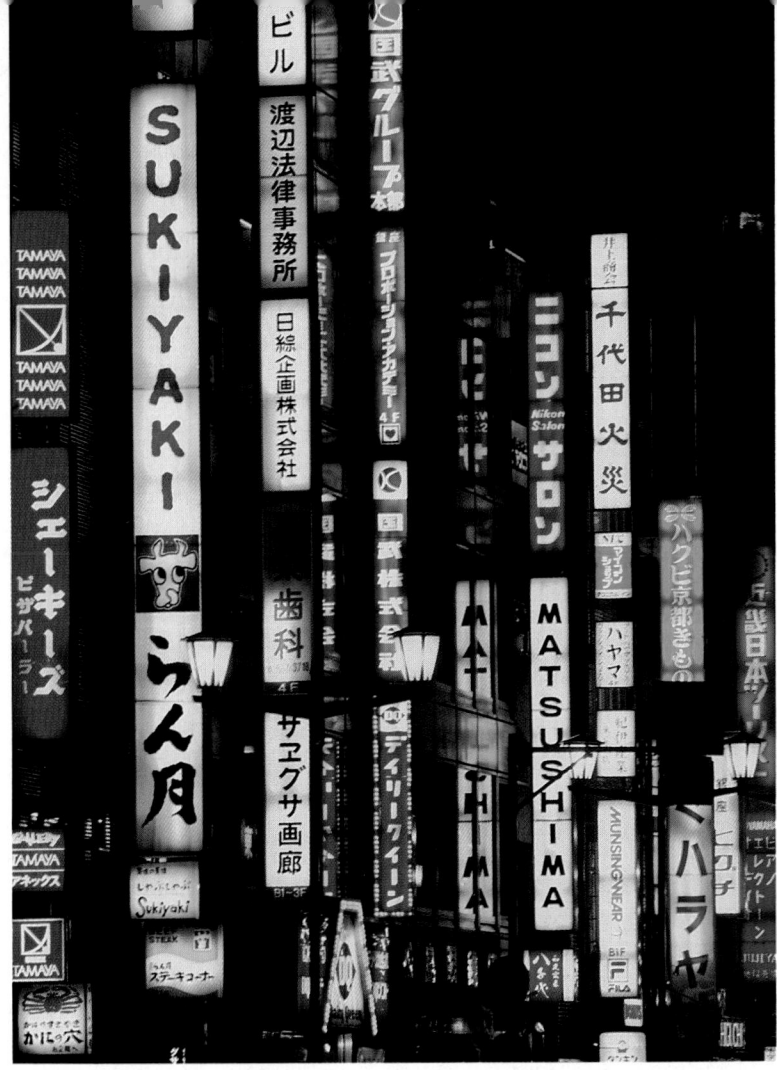

wrote poetry and essays. Like Borges, Julio Cortázar (page 1236) was influenced by the work of Edgar Allan Poe. His novel *Hopscotch* (1963) is often cited as the work that first gained attention for Latin authors.

Another landmark novel was *One Hundred Years of Solitude* (1967), by a Colombian author, Gabriel García Márquez (page 1219). The "solitude" referred to in the title of his book is, on a symbolic level, the solitude and isolation of Latin America itself. With the emergence of so many talented writers, however, it seemed as if this region were finding its voice.

of each other, that the central problem in molecular biology was the chemical structure of the gene. . . . We could not at all see what the answer was, but we considered it so important that we were determined to think about it long and hard, from any relevant point of view.

National and Literary Independence

In the newly independent nations of Africa and Asia, political independence has gone hand in hand with literary accomplishment. Wole Soyinka (page 1360), a playwright from Nigeria, has successfully combined such diverse traditions as African mythology and ancient Greek drama. Just as Soyinka has dazzled the English-speaking world with his writing, so has the Indian novelist R. K. Narayan (page 1408).

The Two Europes

The West has also produced a group of outstanding contemporary writers, among them Albert Camus (page 1272) of France, Günter Grass (page 1278) of Germany, and Italo Calvino (page 1282) of Italy. These authors, if not disillusioned, are at least without illusions. They are familiar with the ravages of war and the temptations to escape into a material, unreflective existence in postwar society.

Writers from eastern Europe—sometimes called "The Other Europe"—had to contend with censorship and the disapproval of authoritarian governments. Their options were few. They could stay put, hoping or fighting for better times. The Russian poets Andrei Voznesensky (page 1322) and Yevgeny Yevtushenko (page 1326), for instance, stayed and campaigned for more liberal policies. Another choice, with its own set of problems, was emigration. The Polish poet Czeslaw Milosz (page 1302) took this course, defecting to the West in the early 1950's. However, Russia's Alexander Solzhenitsyn (page 1316) was unceremoniously bundled into exile, without being asked his preference.

Censorship in Africa

Eastern Europe was not the only region where writers were censored and harassed. The South African novelist Bessie Head (page 1374), of mixed racial heritage, fled to Botswana to escape repression in her native land. Nadine Gordimer, a white, stayed in South Africa and attacked the policy of apartheid. Her support for racial equality angered the white government.

"The One Great Heart"

World literature takes on a new meaning in an era when we can view the earth from the moon. Never before have all the cultures of the world talked to each other so directly and immediately by means of the printed page. Solzhenitsyn, noting this fact, has called world literature "the one great heart," and he looks to writers as a force for truth and justice.

Solzhenitsyn's vision is menaced in two quite different ways. First, it is threatened by those who favor censorship, whether they be dictators or self-appointed groups that want to control what others read. Second, it is under attack from the impersonal forces of hunger, poverty, and illiteracy. If much of the planet's population can neither feed themselves nor understand a book, then the most imaginative novels and poems will go begging.

These warnings aside, however, we should celebrate the achievement of contemporary authors. In few other eras have writers contended with such rapid changes or such breakdowns of traditional ways and truths. In no other era have they searched for identity and meaning with greater persistence or passion. Their spirited, playfully serious poems, essays, and novels are "the one great heart" of our time.

CONTEMPORARY VOICES

ESTRAGON: I can't go on like this.
VLADIMIR: That's what you think.
    Samuel Beckett, from *Waiting for Godot*

Meticulously, motionlessly, secretly, he wrought in time his lofty, invisible labyrinth.
    Jorge Luis Borges, from "The Secret Miracle"

What is certain is that hitherto woman's possibilities have been suppressed and lost to humanity, and that it is high time she be permitted to take her chances in her own interest and in the interest of all.
    Simone de Beauvoir, from *The Second Sex*

The time of irresponsible artists is over.
    Albert Camus, from "Create Dangerously"

Liberty is the possibility of doubting, the possibility of making a mistake, the possibility of searching and experimenting, the possibility of saying "No" to any authority—literary, artistic, philosophic, religious, social, and even political.
    Ignazio Silone, *The God That Failed*

All art is a revolt against man's fate.
    André Malraux, *Voices of Silence*

In some sort of crude sense which no vulgarity, no humor, no overstatement can quite extinguish, the physicists have known sin; and this is a knowledge which they cannot lose.
    J. Robert Oppenheimer

Sometimes love is stronger than a man's convictions.
    Isaac Bashevis Singer in an interview

A great writer is, so to speak, a second government in his country. And for that reason no regime has ever loved great writers, only minor ones.
    Alexander Solzhenitsyn, *The First Circle*

To change your language you must change your life.
    Derek Walcott, "Codicil"

Life shrinks or expands in proportion to one's courage.
    Anaïs Nin, *The Diary of Anaïs Nin*

Additional Voices

The Aquarium is gone. Everywhere,
giant finned cars nose forward like fish;
a savage servility
slides by on grease.
    —Robert Lowell, from "For the Union Dead"

In the daytime I walk around with the Ten
Commandments on my lips
like an old tune someone hums to himself.
    —Yehuda Amichai, from "A Letter of Recommendation"

Violins are naked. They have thin arms. Clumsily they try to protect themselves with them. They cry from shame and cold. That's why. And not, as the music critics maintain, so it will be more beautiful. This is not true."
    —Zbigniew Herbert, "Violins"

Explanation separates us from astonishment, which is the only gateway to the incomprehensible.
    —Eugene Ionesco, from *Découvertes*

Along a parabola life like a rocket flies,
Mainly in darkness, now and then on a rainbow.
    —Andrei Voznesensky, from "Parabolic Ballad"

Nonviolence is the first article of my faith. It is also the last article of my creed.
    —Mahatma Gandhi, Defense against charge of sedition

But oh my love, I cannot understand
why it is, why it is, why it is, my dear
that you cannot read
and I—Oh the hopelessness!—cannot write

The Literature of 1946–Present

The knowledge you bring to reading literature affects what you take from reading it. Knowing a story's historical context, cultural context, and literary context will provide you with a more satisfying reading experience and help you interpret it.

Historical Context

Since 1946 Latin America has often served as a battlefield for the conflict between the Soviet Union and the United States. In Latin American countries, political upheaval often brought about by the military has led to the establishment of totalitarian governments of both the right and the left. For the most part, revolution has resulted in only moderate improvement in the culture of poverty that continues to dominate the area.

Cultural Context

García Márquez titled his Nobel Address of 1982 "The Solitude of Latin America." In it he describes South America as a continent marked by the fantastic—one in which nature is not gentle and where incredible creatures seem to exist. Here the weather is often violent, the landscape rough, and the animals—such as the giant turtles on the Galápagos Islands—fantastic. He also describes it as a culture marked by political oppression and social unrest, one in which "nearly twenty million Latin American children have died before their second birthday." In other words, it is a place where the fantastic and the outrageous are part of everyday life.

Latin America is, however, also a stronghold of European, particularly Spanish, culture. Like other Latin American writers, García Márquez calls upon this culture through allusions to the Bible, classical Greek and Roman myths, and great European works such as *Don Quixote*.

Literary Context

Much of García Márquez's writing can be seen as a blending of two literary movements: social realism and magical realism. Social realism is a type of literature that often protests against oppression and other unjust social conditions. Magical realism expands the category of realism to include myth, magic, and other marvels of the natural world, while using humor and irony.

On the following pages is a short story by García Márquez. The annotations in the margin point out the historical context, cultural context, and literary context.

The Handsomest Drowned Man in the World

Gabriel García Márquez

A Tale for Children

translated by Gregory Rabassa

The first children who saw the dark and slinky bulge approaching through the sea let themselves think it was an enemy ship. Then they saw it had no flags or masts and they thought it was a whale. But when it washed up on the beach, they removed the clumps of seaweed, the jellyfish tentacles, and the remains of fish and flotsam, and only then did they see that it was a drowned man.

They had been playing with him all afternoon, burying him in the sand and digging him up again, when someone chanced to see them and spread the alarm in the village. The men who carried him to the nearest house noticed that he weighed more than any dead man they had ever known, almost as much as a horse, and they said to each other that maybe he'd been floating too long and the water had got into his bones. When they laid him on the floor they said he'd been taller than all other men because there was barely enough room for him in the house, but they thought that maybe the ability to keep on growing after death was part of the nature of certain drowned men. He had the smell of the sea about him and only his shape gave one to suppose that it was the corpse of a human being, because the skin was covered with a crust of mud and scales.

They did not even have to clean off his face to know that the dead man was a stranger. The village was made up of only twenty-odd wooden houses that had stone courtyards with no flowers and which were spread about on the end of a desertlike cape. There was so little land that mothers always went about with the fear that the wind would carry off their children and the few dead that the years had caused among them had to be thrown off the cliffs. But the sea was calm and

Literary Context: Critics have characterized García Márquez's style as "magical realism." The title alone indicates the accuracy of this label. A "drowned man" is a dead-and-done-with-fact, but the addition of the superlative adjective "handsomest" transforms this fact into something that is magical and strange. The superlative also suggests that the story will contain humorous exaggeration.

Cultural Context: García Márquez grew up in Aracataca, a small town on the Caribbean coast of Colombia. He is therefore familiar with the sea as a source of unlooked-for gifts. In *One Hundred Years of Solitude*, he describes a wrecked Spanish galleon that miraculously landed in a jungle.

Literary Context: This is a magical belief, yet García Márquez makes it seem natural that the villagers would entertain such a notion.

Literary Context: The use of a humble, nondescript village as a setting for this fantastic event shows how García Márquez combines social realism and highly imaginative details.

Presentation

Motivation/Prior Knowledge Tell students that they will be reading a story with some of the qualities of a folk tale. Have them name some of the folk tales they have read, and elicit from them the kinds of events that occur in such stories.

Purpose-Setting Question How does the drowned man take on more and more identity as the story continues?

Universal Themes Other stories with elements of the fantastic are "The Garden of Forking Paths," page 1226, and "House Taken Over," page 1238.

Master Teacher Note Offer students a strategy for incorporating the annotations into their reading. Suggest that they read the bracketed portion of the story, look at the note, then reread the bracketed portion with the note in mind. Tell them not to be concerned that this strategy slows their reading speed.

Teaching Tenth-Grade Students Tenth-grade students should find this story very accessible. You might want to have them briefly note the sequence of events after they have finished reading. This technique will help prepare them to analyze the tale.

Vocabulary

Preteach the following vocabulary words:
flotsam (flät′ səm) *n.*: Wreckage of a ship or its cargo floating at sea
bountiful (boun′ tə fəl) *adj.*: Generous
labyrinths (lab′ ə rinths) *n.*: Structures with an intricate network of winding passages where one can lose one's way
haggard (hag′ ərd) *adj.*: Wasted; worn; gaunt
virile (vir′ əl) *adj.*: Manly
resistant (ri zis′ tənt) *adj.*: Offering opposition; retarding; hindering
destitute (des′ tə toot′) *adj.*: Completely poor

Support Material

Teaching Portfolio
Teacher Backup, p. 1449
Grammar in Action Worksheets, *Shifting Point of View*, p. 1459; *Fantastic and Concrete Details*, p. 1461
Usage and Mechanics Worksheet, p. 1463

Vocabulary Check, p. 1464
Analyzing Literature Worksheet, *Appreciating an Unusual Characterization*, p. 1465
Language Worksheet, *Identifying Participial Modifiers*, p. 1466
Selection Test, pp. 1467–1468

Spelling Tip Write the word *resistant* on the chalkboard and tell stu-

dents that the final vowel is often misspelled with an *e,* rather than with an *a.* Tell them this mistake probably results from confusing two similar words, *resistance* and *existence.*

bountiful and all the men fit into seven boats. So when they found the drowned man they simply had to look at one another to see that they were all there.

That night they did not go out to work at sea. While the men went to find out if anyone was missing in neighboring villages, the women stayed behind to care for the drowned man. They took the mud off with grass swabs, they removed the underwater stones entangled in his hair, and they scraped the crust off with tools used for scaling fish. As they were doing that they noticed that the vegetation on him came from faraway oceans and deep water and that his clothes were in tatters, as if he had sailed through labyrinths of coral. They noticed too that he bore his death with pride, for he did not have the lonely look of other drowned men who came out of the sea or that haggard, needy look of men who drowned in rivers. But only when they finished cleaning him off did they become aware of the kind of man he was and it left them breathless. Not only was he the tallest, strongest, most virile, and best built man they had ever seen, but even though they were looking at him there was no room for him in their imagination.

They could not find a bed in the village large enough to lay him on nor was there a table solid enough to use for his wake. The tallest men's holiday pants would not fit him, nor the fattest ones' Sunday shirts, nor the shoes of the one with the biggest feet. Fascinated by his huge size and his beauty, the women then decided to make him some pants from a large piece of sail and a shirt from some bridal brabant[1] linen so that he could continue through his death with dignity. As they sewed, sitting in a circle and gazing at the corpse between stitches, it seemed to them that the wind had never been so steady nor the sea so restless as on that night and they supposed that the change had something to do with the dead man. They thought that if that magnificent man had lived in the village, his house would have had the widest doors, the highest ceiling, and the strongest floor, his bedstead would have been made from a midship frame held together by iron bolts, and his wife would have been the happiest woman. They thought that he would have had so much authority that he could have drawn fish out of the sea simply by calling their names and that he would have put so much work into his land that springs would have burst forth from among the rocks so that he would have been able to plant flowers on the cliffs. They secretly compared him to their own men, thinking that for all their lives theirs were incapable of doing what he could do in one night, and they ended up dismissing them deep in their hearts as the weakest, meanest, and most useless creatures on earth. They were

---

1. **Brabant** (brə bant′): A region in Belguim and the Netherlands famous for its textile products.

Grammar in Action

Fantastic and Concrete Details Concrete details are those that describe the actual sensory characteristics of a scene, person, or object. Fantastic details are those that go beyond mere realism to describe a situation in a highly imaginative way. Following are examples of concrete and fantastic details from the story:

CONCRETE DETAILS: "They took the mud off with grass swabs, they removed the underwater stones entangled in his hair, and they scraped the crust off with tools used for scaling fish."

FANTASTIC DETAILS: "They thought that he would have had so much authority that he could have drawn fish out of the sea simply by calling their names and that he would have put so much work into his land that springs would have burst forth from among the rocks so that he would have been able to plant flowers on the cliffs."

Student Activity 1. Find a passage in the story in which García Márquez weaves together concrete and fantastic details. Explain the effect of this combination.

Student Activity 2. Write a brief description of a scene using fantastic and concrete details. Try not to introduce the fantastic details in a sud-

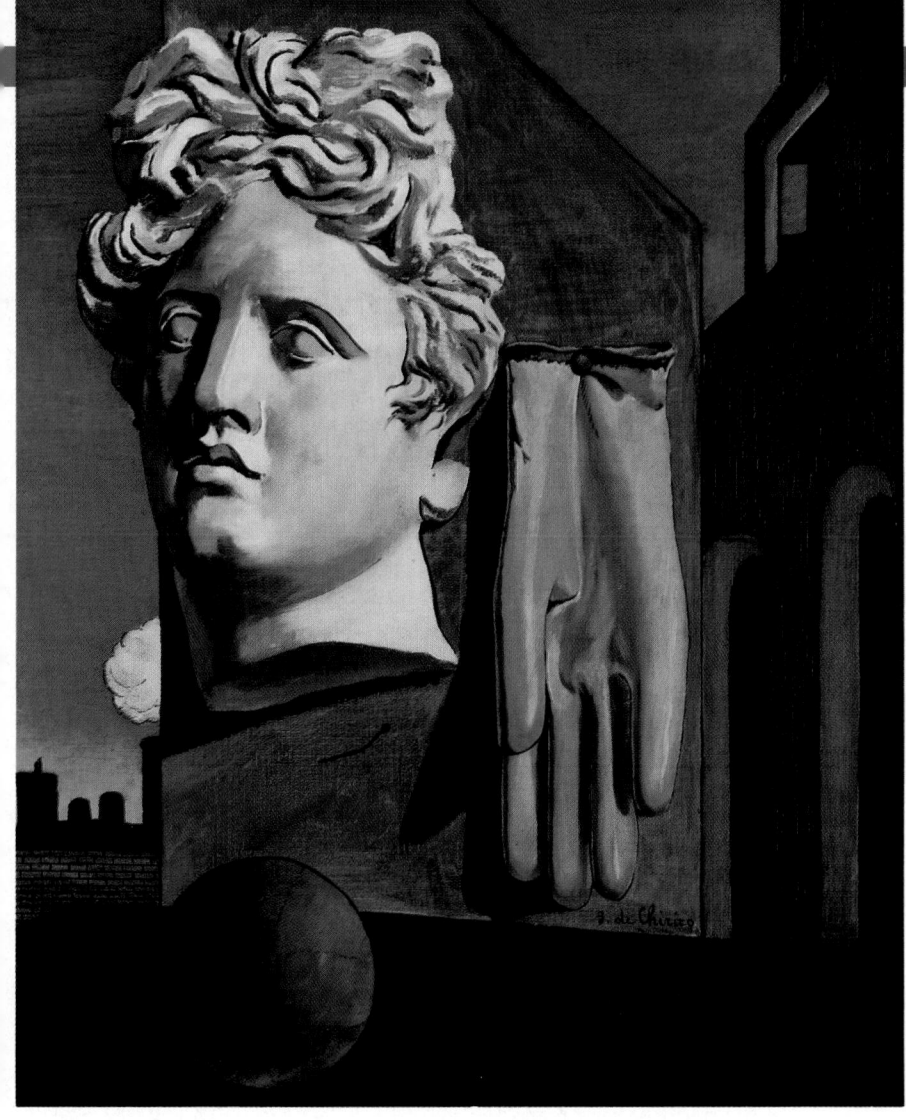

THE SONG OF LOVE, 1914
Giorgio de Chirico
Museum of Modern Art,
New York

wandering through that maze of fantasy when the oldest woman, who as the oldest had looked upon the drowned man with more compassion than passion, sighed:

"He has the face of someone called Esteban."

It was true. Most of them had only to take another look at him to see that he could not have any other name. The more stubborn among them, who were the youngest, still lived for a few hours with the illusion that when they put his clothes on and he lay among the flowers in patent leather shoes his name might be Lautaro. But it was a vain illusion. There had not been enough canvas, the poorly cut and worse

Cultural Context:
Esteban translates as Stephen, and it may be significant that in the Bible, Stephen is the first Christian martyr. García Márquez may be using this connection to suggest that Esteban, too, is a kind of martyr and that his death will benefit the village.

4

den or jarring way. Weave them into your account so that a reader will readily accept them.

4 Clarification Point out to students that the Spanish word *lauto* means "rich, lavish, or opulent." Why do the younger women insist on this name? Why does their insistence reflect a "vain illusion" and why do they abandon this illusion when the wind dies down?

Humanities Note

Fine art, *The Song of Love*, 1914, by Giorgio de Chirico (jôrˊ jô de kēˊ rē kô). Although he was Italian, de Chirico (1888–1978) was born and raised in Greece. During his training as a painter in Greece and Germany, he became acquainted with classical antiquity and German philosophy. His studies led him to believe that underneath the reality we perceive through our senses, there is another, concealed, reality. De Chirico tried to suggest this hidden reality by taking objects out of their contexts and juxtaposing them in strange ways. The dreamlike images that resulted have a surrealistic quality. (For more about Surrealism, see page 1246.) Ironically, de Chirico painted this type of picture for a comparatively brief period (1911–1919) before he adopted a more classical style. It is for his surrealistic work that he is best remembered, however.

In this painting, with its enigmatic title, he juxtaposes the head of Alexander the Great with an orange rubber glove.

You might want to use the following questions to discuss the art:

1. Aside from the head and the glove, what other objects in this painting seem strangely out of place?
2. What feelings does this picture evoke in you?
3. Which elements in the picture inspire these feelings?
4. In what ways is this picture like a dream?
5. Does the picture go well with the story? Why or why not?
6. If you were in charge of decorating city buildings, in what type of building would you have this painting hung? Why?

Literary Context: The women's sympathy with the drowned man increases still more as they imagine the problems that his size might have caused him. By focusing 5 on his difficulties and giving him words to speak, they succeed in bringing him to life—in their minds at least. García Márquez may omit quotation marks from the dialogue to indicate that it is imagined rather than real.

Literary Context: Although he first seemed superior to their men, now his vulnerability makes him seem like their husbands, sons, and brothers. Their change in perspective causes them to mourn for Esteban.

Literary Context: Contrast the attitude of the 6 women with that of the men. The women accept Esteban as a member of the village, but for the men he is just a problem to be solved.

7

sewn pants were too tight, and the hidden strength of his heart popped the buttons on his shirt. After midnight the whistling of the wind died down and the sea fell into its Wednesday drowsiness. The silence put an end to any last doubts: he was Esteban. The women who had dressed him, who had combed his hair, had cut his nails and shaved him were unable to hold back a shudder of pity when they had to resign themselves to his being dragged along the ground. It was then that they understood how unhappy he must have been with that huge body since it bothered him even after death. They could see him in life, condemned to going through doors sideways, cracking his head on crossbeams, remaining on his feet during visits, not knowing what to do with his soft, pink, sea-lion hands while the lady of the house looked for her most resistant chair and begged him, frightened to death, sit here, Esteban, please, and he, leaning against the wall, smiling, don't bother, ma'am, I'm fine where I am, his heels raw and his back roasted from having done the same thing so many times whenever he paid a visit, don't bother, ma'am, I'm fine where I am, just to avoid the embarrassment of breaking up the chair, and never knowing perhaps that the ones who said don't go, Esteban, at least wait till the coffee's ready, were the ones who later on would whisper the big boob finally left, how nice, the handsome fool has gone. That was what the women were thinking beside the body a little before dawn. Later, when they covered his face with a handkerchief so that the light would not bother him, he looked so forever dead, so defenseless, so much like their men that the first furrows of tears opened in their hearts. It was one of the younger ones who began the weeping. There others, coming to, went from sighs to wails, and the more they sobbed the more they felt like weeping, because the drowned man was becoming more Esteban for them, and so they wept so much, for he was the most destitute, most peaceful, and most obliging man on earth, poor Esteban. So when the men returned with the news that the drowned man was not from the neighboring villages either, the women felt an opening of jubilation in the midst of their tears.

"Praise the Lord," they sighed, "he's ours!"

The men thought the fuss was only womanish frivolity. Fatigued because of the difficult nighttime inquiries, all they wanted was to get rid of the bother of the newcomer once and for all before the sun grew strong on that arid, windless day. They improvised a litter with the remains of foremasts and gaffs,[2] tying it together with rigging[3] so that it would bear the weight of the body until they reached the cliffs. They wanted to tie the anchor from a cargo ship to him so that he would sink easily into the deepest waves, where fish are blind and divers die of nos-

---

2. gaffs: Poles that are part of a ship's mast.
3. rigging: Ropes and other gear used to control the sails of a vessel.

Grammar in Action

Shifting Perspectives Point of view is the vantage point from which a story is told. This story is told from an omniscient third-person point of view, meaning that the narrator uses "he" and "she" and is outside the story but has access to the characters' thoughts. This point of view itself does not change throughout the story. However, there are some surprising shifts in perspective within this point of view. For example, the dead man suddenly comes to life when the narrator gives him imagined dialogue to speak:

They could see him in life, condemned to going through doors sideways, cracking his head on crossbeams, remaining on his feet during visits, not knowing what to do with his soft, pink, sea-lion hands while the lady of the house looked for her most resistant chair and begged him, frightened to death, sit here, Esteban, please, and he, leaning against the wall, smiling, don't bother, ma'am, I'm fine where I am, . . .

This shift in perspective is all the more surprising because it takes place in mid-sentence and Esteban's words are not placed in quotation marks.

algia, and bad currents would not bring him back to shore, as had happened with other bodies. But the more they hurried, the more the women thought of ways to waste time. They walked about like startled hens, pecking with the sea charms on their breasts, some interfering on one side to put a scapular[4] of the good wind on the drowned man, some on the other side to put a wrist compass on him, and after a great deal of *get away from there, woman, stay out of the way, look, you almost made me fall on top of the dead man,* the men began to feel mistrust in their lives and started grumbling about why so many main-altar decorations for a stranger, because no matter how many nails and holy-water jars he had on him, the sharks would chew him all the same, but the women kept piling on their junk relics, running back and forth, stumbling, while they released in sighs what they did not in tears, so that the men finally exploded with *since when has there ever been such a fuss over a drifting corpse, a drowned nobody, a piece of cold Wednesday meat.* One of the women, mortified by so much lack of care, then removed the handkerchief from the dead man's face and the men were left breathless too.

He was Esteban. It was not necessary to repeat it for them to recognize him. If they had been told Sir Walter Raleigh,[5] even they might have been impressed with his gringo accent, the macaw on his shoulder, his cannibal-killing blunderbuss, but there could be only one Esteban in the world and there he was, stretched out like a sperm whale, shoeless, wearing the pants of an undersized child, and with those stony nails that had to be cut with a knife. They had only to take the handkerchief off his face to see that he was ashamed, that it was not his fault that he was so big or so heavy or so handsome, and if he had known that this was going to happen, he would have looked for a more discreet place to drown in, seriously, I even would have tied the anchor off a galleon around my neck and staggered off a cliff like someone who doesn't like things in order not to be upsetting people now with this Wednesday dead body, as you people say, in order not to be bothering anyone with this filthy piece of cold meat that doesn't have anything to do with me. There was so much truth in his manner that even the most mistrustful men, the ones who felt the bitterness of endless nights at sea fearing that their women would tire of dreaming about them and begin to dream of drowned men, even they and others who were harder still shuddered in the marrow of their bones at Esteban's sincerity.

That was how they came to hold the most splendid funeral they could conceive of for an abandoned drowned man. Some women who had gone to get flowers in the neighboring villages returned with other women who could not believe what they had been told, and those

---

4. **scapular** (skap´ yə lər): A religious medal.
5. **Sir Walter Raleigh:** An English explorer (1552–1618) known for his charm and boldness. He organized expeditions to North and South America.

Cultural Context: The contrasting reactions of the men and women may suggest that García Márquez believes women are more imaginative and sympathetic than men. If so, that belief may spring from his early relationship with his grandmother. She told him fantastic and magical tales that later influenced his own writing.

Literary Context: The immediate and dramatic effect of this action recalls magical events in fairy tales. For instance, a kiss from a young prince suddenly awakens a princess who has been sleeping for hundreds of years.

Literary Context: Note how the point of view shifts in mid-sentence as Esteban begins speaking directly. This sudden shift brings the dead man to life, and his embarrassment at his own unwieldy size makes him a humorously appealing character.

8 **Discussion** Have students consider why the men are now left breathless, just as the women were before. What wins them over to the women's point of view? Are they moved by the same impulse that affected the women? Why or why not?

9 **Enrichment** Tell students that when James I succeeded to the crown of England (1603), he regarded Raleigh as an enemy and stripped him of many of his privileges and possessions. Found guilty of treason, Raleigh was released in 1616 to make a second voyage into Guiana to find the fabled golden city of El Dorado (he had already made a voyage in search of this city in 1595). He was warned, however, not to interfere with Spanish ships or possessions. After one of his fellow explorers captured a Spanish town, in violation of this order, Raleigh was executed on his return to England.

10 **Discussion** Point out to students that this is the only time jealousy is suggested as a motive in the men who mistrust Esteban. What is it about Esteban that wins these men over?

Student Activity. Find a shift in perspective that takes place in mid-sentence at the end of the story. How does this shift make the ending more dramatic and effective?

women went back for more flowers when they saw the dead man, and they brought more and more until there were so many flowers and so many people that it was hard to walk about. At the final moment it pained them to return him to the waters as an orphan and they chose a father and mother from among the best people, and aunts and uncles and cousins, so that through him all the inhabitants of the village became kinsmen. Some sailors who heard the weeping from a distance went off course and people heard of one who had himself tied to the mainmast, remembering ancient fables about sirens. While they fought for the privilege of carrying him on their shoulders along the steep escarpment[6] by the cliffs, men and women became aware for the first time of the desolation of their streets, the dryness of their courtyards, the narrowness of their dreams as they faced the splendor and beauty of their drowned man. They let him go without an anchor so that he could come back if he wished and whenever he wished, and they all held their breath for the fraction of centuries the body took to fall into the abyss. They did not need to look at one another to realize that they were no longer all present, that they would never be. But they also knew that everything would be different from then on, that their houses would have wider doors, higher ceilings, and stronger floors so that Esteban's memory could go everywhere without bumping into beams and so that no one in the future would dare whisper the big boob finally died, too bad, the handsome fool has finally died, because they were going to paint their house fronts gay colors to make Esteban's memory eternal and they were going to break their backs digging for springs among the stones and planting flowers on the cliffs so that in future years at dawn the passengers on great liners would awaken, suffocated by the smell of gardens on the high seas, and the captain would have to come down from the bridge in his dress uniform, with his astrolabe,[7] his pole star, and his row of war medals and, pointing to the promontory of roses on the horizon, he would say in fourteen languages, look there, where the wind is so peaceful now that it's gone to sleep beneath the beds, over there, where the sun's so bright that the sunflowers don't know which way to turn, yes, over there, that's Esteban's village.

---

6. **escarpment** (e skärp´ mənt): Slope.
7. **astrolabe** (as´ trō lāb´): An old-fashioned instrument used in navigating a ship.

Reader's Response *Did your feelings about Esteban change as you read the story? Explain.*

Commentary

Film as an Influence on García Márquez In 1951 García Márquez worked as a scriptwriter on the film *There Are No Thieves in This Town*. The result was a radical departure from the mainstream of Latin American films of that time, and García Márquez was greatly impressed by his contact with the surrealist filmmaker Luis Buñuel. Many scripts he later worked on, however, were turned into mere "cowboy" movies. Nevertheless, he says that what he learned as a scriptwriter helped him with his fiction.

Now he says that he wants to continue writing for both fiction and films, but he does not want to translate one into the other. For example, he has forbidden all attempts to film his masterpiece *One Hundred Years of Solitude*. He argues that a film would destroy the margin of imagination that the novel leaves to a reader. In addition, he complains that North American directors who are interested in his book want to cast American actors in the lead roles.

GABRIEL GARCÍA MÁRQUEZ

1928–

The Colombian Gabriel García Márquez is one of the most innovative writers of our time. García Márquez's style, which combines realistic story-telling with elements of folklore and fantasy, has been called "magical realism." This style has enabled him to depict the sometimes incredible realities of Colombia, a country known for its democratic institutions and its political violence.

García Márquez was born in Aracataca, a town in Colombia's Caribbean zone near the northern coast. All his fiction is set in this region, which is, in the words of critic Stephen Minta, a "tropical zone, a world of drama, movement, and light, of endless, and frequently oppressive, heat." García Márquez identifies with the mixed African and Native American heritage of this region, and he feels little sympathy with the Spanish colonial legacy of his nation's capital, Bogotá.

Although he was born into a large family, he spent his first eight years alone with his grandparents. He felt especially close to his grandfather, an impressive man who had fought in the Colombian civil war, called the War of a Thousand Days (1899–1902). García Márquez also had a close relationship with his grandmother, from whom he heard magical and fantastic tales that influenced his own art.

After finishing high school, García Márquez decided that he wanted to be a journalist and a novelist. He began working as a reporter only two years later, and he supported himself through newspaper writing until the success of his fiction made him economically independent. Journalism taught him stylistic lessons similar to those he learned from his grandmother: ". . . tricks you need to transform something which appears fantastic, unbelievable, into something plausible, credible. . . ."

Like many other writers, he first imitated others in order to find his own true voice. The influence of Faulkner and Hemingway, for example, is evident in early work such as *Leaf Storm* (1955) and *No One Writes to the Colonel* (1962). Faulkner taught him the virtues of lush, imaginative writing; in addition, Faulkner's imaginary Mississippi county, described in book after book, probably inspired García Márquez to convert the real Aracataca into the fictional town of Macondo. From Hemingway, García Márquez learned the importance of keen observation. He once recalled his thrill on reading Hemingway's precise description of a bull turning as agilely as a cat rounding a corner.

The story "Big Mama's Funeral" marks the first appearance of his own blend of precise observation and outrageous fantasy. This style reaches its height in his masterpiece *One Hundred Years of Solitude* (1967). On a literal level, this book is the humorous and tragic tale of the Buendía family. Critics have pointed out, however, that the isolation and "solitude" of the Buendías may also symbolize the condition of Colombia or other underdeveloped Latin American countries. García Márquez seemed to confirm this observation in his Nobel acceptance speech (see page 1221) when he expressed the hope that "the lineal generations of one hundred years of solitude will have . . . a second chance on earth."

ANSWERS TO THINKING ABOUT THE SELECTION

1. (a) The children play with the body as if it were a toy. The men at first think of the body only as something to be disposed of. The women come to think of the body as wonderful, name the drowned man, and imagine that he is grander than their own men. (b) Answers will differ. Students may suggest that each group relates the body to its own experience—the children to play, the men to work, and the women to their longing for a more fulfilling life.

2. He is incredibly larger than life, while the village is remarkably small.

3. He comes to symbolize the richer, deeper, more satisfying possibilities of life.

4. (a) They become proud of the new dimension he has brought into their lives. (b) In keeping with their new pride, they want to make the village a more beautiful place. They decide to build larger, more brightly painted houses and to dig springs so they can plant flowers.

5. Answers will differ. Students may respond that the subtitle suggests the simple, fairy tale-like qualities of the story.

6. Answers will differ. Students may indicate that the blend of fact and fantasy in the story could be called "magical realism."

7. Answers will differ.

ANSWERS TO ANALYZING LITERATURE

1. Answers will differ. Students may indicate that to the children, he is a "dark and slinky bulge," then an "enemy ship," then a "whale." At first the men notice only that he weighs almost as much as a horse. They later call him "*a piece of cold Wednesday meat.*"

2. They wash him, make him new clothes, and give him a name.

3. Answers will differ. Students may respond that in traditional societies, women are often considered more imaginative than men, who are concerned with work and practical affairs.

4. The name suggests the idea that the drowned man somehow died or martyred himself for the villagers and that he is their savior.

5. They imagine him as being unhappy with his huge body, apologizing politely for it. They also think of him

as "the most destitute, most peaceful, and most obliging man on earth."

6. They remove the handkerchief from his face, and the men are left breathless.

7. Answers will differ. Students may note that as a result of the funeral, all the people become Esteban's relatives. He is therefore the most important person in the town, the one who

THINKING ABOUT THE SELECTION

Interpreting

1. (a) Compare and contrast the ways in which the children, women, and men react to the drowned man. (b) How do you account for the differences in their reactions?

2. How does the drowned man's stature contrast with the dimensions of the village?

3. What does the drowned man come to symbolize for the people of the village?

4. (a) How does the spirit of the villagers change as a result of their experience with Esteban? (b) In what way do their new plans for the village reflect this change?

5. How is the nature of the village's transformation hinted at in the story's subtitle, "A Tale for Children"?

6. Some critics have characterized García Márquez's style of writing as "magical realism." Do you think this phrase is a good description of his style in this story? Explain.

Applying

7. Philosophers have sometimes expressed the idea that the key to releasing human potential is to expand people's imaginations. Explain how this story supports that notion.

ANALYZING LITERATURE

Appreciating an Unusual Characterization

Esteban is not only the handsomest but the liveliest dead man in the world. He is so vital that he is the central character of the story and more memorable than any of the villagers. How does the author accomplish this remarkable feat? As the story progresses, the other characters react to the drowned man as if he were alive. Esteban evolves from a less-than-human thing to the man for whom the village is named.

1. Find a passage in which the drowned man is described as little more than a thing.

2. Show how the women take three important actions that give him an identity.

3. Why do you think that women rather than men initiate each of these steps?

4. Esteban, Stephen in English, is the name of the first Christian who died for his faith; his holiday is on December 26. How does this fact add to the drowned man's identity?

5. Describe Esteban's personality as the women imagine it.

6. How do the women convince the men that the drowned man is more than "*a piece of cold Wednesday meat*"?

7. Explain how the funeral and the naming of the town complete the development of Esteban's character.

8. Argue convincingly that the dead man is a dynamic and round character.

UNDERSTANDING LANGUAGE

Completing Analogies

A verbal analogy is an expression of a relationship between two words. Analogy questions on standardized tests ask you to choose two words that are related in the same way as a given pair. For example, TALL : SHORT :: BOLD : SHY. In this example the two sets of words are antonyms.

Complete each of the following analogies. Choose the pair of words whose relationship is most similar to that expressed by the capitalized pair.

1. RECALCITRANT : STUBBORN ::
   a. discrete : tactful   c. easier : harder
   b. known : hidden   d. weary : helpful
2. RISIBLE : SAD ::
   a. sanguine : hopeful   c. merit : goal
   b. vicious : truculent   d. weary : buoyant
3. WINSOME : ATTRACTIVE ::
   a. wise : foolish   c. spice : herb
   b. dull : tedious   d. bright : dumb

THINKING AND WRITING

Writing About an Extraterrestrial

García Márquez's giant drowned man is so mysterious to the villagers that he seems to come from another world. Imagine that one of our space probes discovered the dead body of an extraterrestrial creature, unlike anything that humans have ever seen. Write a newspaper article describing this event. Begin by briefly answering key questions about the story: who? what? when? where? why? Then, using your questions and answers, write your epoch-making article. Remember that newspaper readers want the most important questions answered at the beginning of a story. Conclude your article by speculating how this discovery will affect our lives. In revising your article, make sure you have included a vivid description of the creature.

unites it. By giving the town his name, they ensure that he will remain an active force in improving their lives.

8. Answers will differ. Students may respond that as imagined by the villagers, the drowned man has a complete personality, moods, manners, a way of speaking—to which different people respond differently at various times, just as with a real person.

ANSWERS TO UNDERSTANDING LANGUAGE

1. a   2. d   3. b

THINKING AND WRITING

Publishing Student Writing Create a class newspaper in which students' articles can be published.

BACKGROUND

GABRIEL GARCÍA MÁRQUEZ'S NOBEL ADDRESS

In his 1982 Nobel Address, Gabriel García Márquez discussed the "disorderly reality" of Latin America and his hopes for the future of this region.

The Solitude of Latin America: Nobel Address 1982

Gabriel García Márquez
Translated by Richard Cardwell

Antonio Pigafetta, the Florentine navigator who accompanied Magellan on the first circumnavigation of the world, kept a meticulous log on his journey through our Southern American continent which, nevertheless, also seems to be an adventure into the imagination. He related that he had seen pigs with their umbilicus on their backs and birds without feet, the females of the species of which would brood their eggs on the backs of the males, as well as others like gannets without tongues whose beaks looked like a spoon. He wrote that he had seen a monstrosity of an animal with the head and ears of a mule, the body of a camel, the hooves of a deer and the neigh of a horse. He related that they put a mirror in front of the first native they met in Patagonia and how that overexcited giant lost the use of his reason out of the fear of his own image.

This short and fascinating book, in which we can perceive the germs of our contemporary novels, is not, by any means, the most surprising testimony of our reality at that time. The Chroniclers of the Indies have left us innumerable others. Eldorado, our illusory land which was much sought after, figured on many maps over a long period, changing in situation and extent according to the whim of the cartographers . . . Later on, during the colonial period, they used to sell in Cartagena de India chickens raised on alluvial soils in whose gizzards were found gold nuggets. This delirium for gold among our founding fathers has been a bane upon us until very recent times. Why, only in the last century the German mission appointed to study the construction of a railway line between the oceans across the Panamanian isthmus concluded that the project was a viable one on the condition that the rails should be not of iron, a scarce metal in the region, but of gold.

* * *

Eleven years ago, one of the outstanding poets of our time, Pablo Neruda from Chile, brought light to this very chamber with his words. In the European mind, in those of good—and often those of bad—consciences, we witness, on a forceful scale never seen before, the eruption of an awareness of the Phantoms of Latin America, that great homeland of deluded men and historic women, whose infinite stubbornness is confused with legend. We have never had a moment of serenity. . . .

Nearly one hundred and twenty thousand have disappeared as a consequence of repression, which is as if, today, no one knew where all the inhabitants of Uppsala were. Many women arrested during pregnancy gave birth in Argentinian prisons but, still, where and who their children are is not known; ei-

Presentation

Motivation/Prior Knowledge Ask students what they know about the Nobel Prizes and the Nobel Prize for Literature. (You may want to have them read the feature on the Nobel Prize, page 1081.) Point out to them that when writers receive this award, they are expected to make a speech. Ask them what they think a writer might want to say on such an occasion.

1 **Enrichment** Tell students that, in Spanish, El Dorado means "the gilded man." It referred to a mythical country, a land of gold, that supposedly existed in South America. Many European adventurers searched for this fabled country. The legend of El Dorado may have originated with a custom practiced by Native Americans living in what is today Colombia. Each year they rolled one of their chiefs in gold and then he ritually cleansed himself of this gold in a sacred lake. This custom had died out before the conquistadors, or conquerors, reached South America. Accounts of this custom, however, lured the conquistadors into a quest for a land of gold.

2 **Enrichment** Pablo Neruda was awarded the 1971 Nobel Prize for Literature. (For more about Neruda, see page 1248.)

ther they were passed on into secret adoption or interned in orphanages by military authorities. So that things should not continue thus, two thousand men and women have given up their lives over the continent and more than one hundred thousand in three tiny, wilful countries in Central America: Nicaragua, El Salvador and Guatemala. Were this to happen in the United States the proportional ratio would be one million six hundred violent deaths in four years. . . .

I dare to believe that it is this highly unusual state of affairs, and not only its literary expression, which, this year, has merited the attention of the Swedish Literary Academy: a reality which is not one on paper but which lives in us and determines each moment of our countless daily deaths, one which constantly replenishes an insatiable fount of creation, full of unhappiness and beauty, of which this wandering and nostalgic Colombian is merely another singled out by fate. Poets and beggars, musicians and prophets, soldiers and scoundrels, all we creatures of that disorderly reality have needed to ask little of the imagination, for the major challenge before us has been the want of conventional resources to make our life credible. This, my friends, is the nub of solitude.

For, if these setbacks benumb us, we who are of its essence, it is not difficult to understand that the mental talents of this side of the world, in an ecstasy of contemplation of their own cultures, have found themselves without a proper means to interpret us. One realizes this when they insist on measuring us with the same yardstick with which they measure themselves. . . .

Perhaps venerable old Europe would be more sympathetic if it tried to see us in its own past; if it remembered that London needed three hundred years to build her first defensive wall and another three hundred years before her first bishop; that Rome debated in the darkness of uncertainty for twenty centuries before an Etruscan king rooted her in history, and that even in the sixteenth century the pacifist Swiss of today, who so delight us with their mild cheeses and their cheeky clocks, made Europe bloody as soldiers of fortune. . . .

* * *

Latin America has no desire to be, nor should it be, a pawn without will, neither is it a mere shadow of a dream that its designs for independence and originality should become an aspiration of the western hemisphere. Nevertheless, advances in methods of travel which have reduced the huge distances between our Americas and Europe seem to have increased our cultural distance. Why are we granted unreservedly a recognition of our originality in literature when our attempts, in the face of enormous difficulties, to bring about social change are denied us with all sorts of mistrust? Why must they think that the system of social justice imposed by advanced European nations upon their peoples cannot also be an objective for us Latin Americans but with different methods in different conditions? . . .

Nevertheless, in the face of oppression, pillage and abandonment, our reply is life. Neither floods nor plagues, nor famine nor cataclysms, nor even eternal war century after century have managed to reduce the tenacious advantage that life has over death. It is an advantage which is on the increase and quickens apace: every year there are seventy-four million more births than deaths, a sufficient number of new living souls to populate New York every year seven times over. The majority of them are born in countries with few resources, and among these, naturally, the countries of Latin America. On the other hand, the more prosperous nations have succeeded in accumulating sufficient destructive power to annihilate one hundred times over not only every human being who has ever existed but every living creature ever to have graced this planet of misfortune.

On a day like today, my master William Faulkner said in this very place, "I refuse to admit the end of mankind." I should not feel myself worthy of standing where he once stood were I not fully conscious that, for the first time in the history of humanity, the colossal disaster which he refused to recognize thirty-two years ago is now simply a scientific possibility. Face to face with a reality that overwhelms us, . . . tellers of tales who, like me, are capable of believing anything, feel entitled to believe that it is not yet too late to undertake the creation of a minor utopia: a new and limitless utopia for life wherein no one can decide for others how they are to die, where love really can be true and happiness possible, where the lineal generations of one hundred years of solitude will have at last and forever a second chance on earth.

The Americas

SOL Y VIDA, 1947
Frida Kahlo

Humanities Note

Fine art, *Sol y Vida* [Sun and Life], 1947, by Frida Kahlo. Kahlo (1910–1957) was born in Mexico City and attended the university there. At the age of eighteen she was involved in a serious traffic accident and fractured her spine and pelvis. Her injuries, which caused her life-long pain, are a motif in a number of her self-portraits.

Kahlo married the famous Mexican muralist Diego Rivera. They traveled extensively, becoming involved in many left-wing political causes. Although she and Rivera were frequently in the newspapers, her paintings were not widely known until the Mexican government mounted an exhibition of her work in 1977.

As an artist Kahlo was influenced by Surrealism, a movement that stressed the irrational nature of artistic creation (for more on Surrealism, see page 1249). The images in Kahlo's paintings therefore often have the mystery and power of images seen in dreams. In *Sol y Vida*, for instance, the red sun-face has a third eye in the middle of its forehead, and above the sun a fetus is enclosed in a plant.

You might want to use the following questions to discuss the art:

1. What is unusual about the images in this painting?
2. How do the colors contribute to the mood the painting evokes?
3. How does the artist seem to feel about the sun?
4. Why do you think Kahlo called this painting *Sol y Vida* [Sun and Life]?
5. What kind of picture would you paint to express your feelings about the sun?

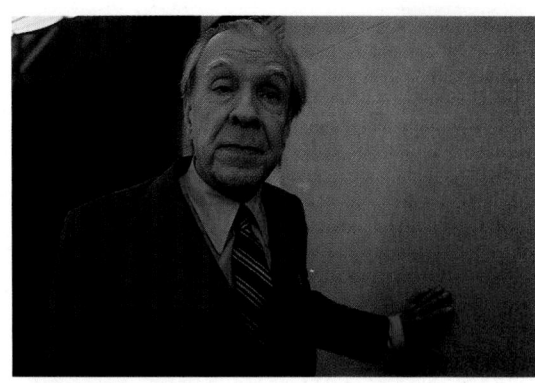

1899–1986

Can a person be two people at once? In a prose poem called "Borges and I," the Argentine writer Jorge Luis Borges (hôr´ he loo es´ bôr´ hes) says, "The other one, the one called Borges, is the one things happen to. . . . I know of Borges from the mail and see his name on a list of professors. . . . I live, let myself go on living, so that Borges may contrive his literature." As he teasingly separates the "I," the living person, from the author "Borges," Jorge Borges displays the playful, paradoxical, and thought-provoking style that won him an international audience.

Born to a wealthy Buenos Aires family, Borges had a paternal grandmother who was English. From an early age, therefore, he spoke and read English as well as Spanish. He was an extremely well-read young man and once declared, "If I were asked to name the chief event in my life, I should say my father's library."

Borges learned still other foreign languages —Latin, German, and French—when his family moved to Switzerland in 1914. After World War I (1914–1918), his family settled in Spain, where he made friends with a group of young, experimental writers. These associations inspired him to organize his own group of young writers when he returned to Argentina in 1921. All through the 1920's and 1930's, he contributed fiction to Argentine literary magazines.

In 1938, the year of his father's death, Borges sustained a serious head injury. The complications that resulted from this injury almost cost him his life. Shaken, he began to doubt his artistic ability and even his sanity; however, the experimental stories he wrote at this time are among the best he ever produced. They deemphasize the usual fictional elements of plot and character, taking their inspiration from philosophical ideas. Rather than being dry and intellectual, however, they are poetic and fantastic. Published in *The Garden of Forking Paths* (1941), they won him a greater readership among the Argentinian public.

Similar stories also appeared in *Fictions* (1944) and *The Aleph* (1949). In a number of these works, Borges uses the detective story to symbolize the search for a tantalizing and elusive reality. The strangeness of these tales recalls the fiction of Edgar Allen Poe, the inventor of the detective story. Related to the detective mysteries are the puzzles, games, and riddles that appear throughout his fiction. He often describes the universe itself as a gigantic puzzle—sometimes it is an "indefinite . . . infinite" library, other times a mysterious lottery in which our lives are the prizes.

Even though Borges did not usually participate in politics, he opposed the military dictatorship of Juan Perón. The Perón regime retaliated in 1946 by removing him from the librarian's position he had occupied since 1938 and scornfully offering him a job as a chicken inspector. That wrong was righted in 1955, when Perón fell from power. The new government appointed Borges director of Argentina's national library. At the same time, unfortunately, he lost his sight as a result of an eye disease—although this handicap did not prevent him from continuing to write.

In 1961 he finally earned the reputation he deserved when he shared the International Publisher's Prize with Irish author Samuel Beckett. His book *Labyrinths* (1962), which contained translations of some of his best work, influenced many American writers in the 1960's and 1970's. Borges died, world-famous, in 1986.

GUIDE FOR INTERPRETING

The Garden of Forking Paths

The Labyrinth as a Symbol. A **labyrinth** is a series of winding passages, with false directions and blind alleys, designed to puzzle and disorient the person trapped within it. Down through the ages, labyrinths have fascinated people in many cultures. You can find them in today's puzzle books as two-dimensional mazes. Or you can read about them in ancient Greek mythology: King Minos of Crete had the inventor Daedalus design a labyrinth into which the Minotaur, a monster half-bull and half-man, was placed. Those who lost their way on the winding paths died of hunger or were devoured by the Minotaur. Only the Greek hero Theseus escaped this fate. He killed the Minotaur and traced his way back by means of a ball of yarn he had unwound.

Labyrinths have had such a universal appeal because they suggest more general meanings. For Borges they symbolized the riddling strangeness of our lives, and he used the word *labyrinths* as the title of an English-language selection from his work. He believed that the universe itself was a bewildering labyrinth in which no direction is certain and danger may lurk at every turn. This notion may have resulted from his exposure to the First World War: Borges's family was traveling in Europe at the outbreak of the war and settled in Switzerland to avoid the fighting. As an intelligent teenager, Borges would have been especially sensitive to the atmosphere of violence. He would also have encountered the belief, widespread at the time, that this conflict revealed the breakdown of Western civilization.

Not only does Borges write about labyrinths, but he also constructs his stories like mazes. They contain an array of references and names from various cultures and eras. As you enter the maze of this story, however, there is a clue that will help you to find your way, much as the ball of yarn helped Theseus to find his way out of the Cretan labyrinth: Remember that despite the many allusions, this is basically a spy story with two antagonists.

Writing

Tell about a time when you successfully dealt with a confusing problem. The situation could be serious or challenging or even funny. It could be an occasion when you lost your way in an unfamiliar place, solved a puzzle, or wrestled with a difficult idea in school.

Literary Focus Ask students if they have ever worked the two-dimensional mazes in puzzle books and, if so, whether they found them enjoyable, frustrating, or boring. Tell them that in English gardens, mazes are created out of dense hedges at least seven feet tall and that it is quite possible to enter these hedge-labyrinths and get completely lost. Students may have had a similar experience in a fun-house "hall of mirrors" or a theme-park maze. Ask if they ever felt a mingling of amusement and mild panic in such a place. Then tell them that this story deals with an extremely unusual type of labyrinth, a labyrinth in time.

Writing/Prior Knowledge Have students share ideas about perplexing problems they may have faced. Emphasize that the problem should not be personal but more of the "how to" variety. Before they begin writing, have them tell each other how they went about solving such a problem.

ESL Teaching Strategy To help with the writing assignment, pair each ESL student with a native-speaking student. Have the native-speaking students coach the ESL students, discussing ways to go about telling how they solved a difficult problem.

> ### Vocabulary
> Preteach the following vocabulary words:
> laxity (laks´ i tē) *n.*: Carelessness
> fallaciously (fə lā´ shəs lē) *adj.*: Erroneously
> brigands (brig´ əndz) *n.*: Bandits
> calligrapher (kə lig´ rə fər) *n.*: One who practices handwriting as an art
> coalescent (kō ə les´ sənt) *adj.*: Merging
> usurps (yōo sʉrp´s) *v.*: Wrongfully takes something
> primordial (prī môr´ dē əl) *adj.*: Existing from the beginning
> contrition (kən trish´ ən) *n*: Remorse for having done wrong

nation, comes from the Latin word *alescere*, meaning "to grow up." Indicate other examples of this root, as in *senescent, convalescent,* and *juvenescent.*

The Garden of Forking Paths

Jorge Luis Borges

translated by Donald A. Yates

On page 22 of Liddell Hart's *History of World War I* you will read that an attack against the Serre-Montauban line by thirteen British divisions (supported by 1,400 artillery pieces), planned for the 24th of July, 1916, had to be postponed until the morning of the 29th. The torrential rains, Captain Liddell Hart comments, caused this delay, an insignificant one, to be sure.

The following statement, dictated, reread and signed by Dr. Yu Tsun, former professor of English at the *Hochschule* at Tsingtao,[1] throws an unsuspected light over the whole affair. The first two pages of the document are missing.

". . . and I hung up the receiver. Immediately afterwards, I recognized the voice that had answered in German. It was that of Captain Richard Madden. Madden's presence in Viktor Runeberg's apartment meant the end of our anxieties and—but this seemed, *or should have seemed*, very secondary to me—also the end of our lives. It meant that Runeberg had been arrested or murdered.[2] Before the sun set on that day, I would encounter the same fate. Madden was implacable.[3] Or rather,

---

1. *Hochschule* (hŏkh′ shōō′ lə) **at Tsingtao** (tsiŋ′ tou′): A secondary school in China.
2. **murdered:** Borges added the following footnote—"An hypothesis both hateful and odd. The Prussian spy Hans Rabener, alias Viktor Runeberg, attacked with drawn automatic the bearer of the warrant for his arrest, Captain Richard Madden. The latter, in self-defense, inflicted the wound which brought about Runeberg's death. (Editor's note.)"
3. **implacable** (im plā′ kə b'l) *adj.*: Relentless.

he was obliged to be so. An Irishman at the service of England, a man accused of laxity and perhaps of treason, how could he fail to seize and be thankful for such a miraculous opportunity: the discovery, capture, maybe even the death of two agents of the German Reich? I went up to my room; absurdly I locked the door and threw myself on my back on the narrow iron cot. Through the window I saw the familiar roofs and the cloud-shaded six o'clock sun. It seemed incredible to me that that day without premonitions[4] or symbols should be the one of my inexorable[5] death. In spite of my dead father, in spite of having been a child in a symmetrical garden of Hai Feng, was I—now—going to die? Then I reflected that everything happens to a man precisely, precisely *now*. Centuries of centuries and only in the present do things happen; countless men in the air, on the face of the earth and the sea, and all that really is happening is happening to me . . . The almost intolerable recollection of Madden's horselike face banished these wanderings. In the midst of my hatred and terror (it means nothing to me now to speak of terror, now that I have mocked Richard Madden, now that my throat yearns for the noose) it occurred to me that that tumultuous and doubtless happy warrior did not suspect that I possessed the Secret. The name of the exact location of the

---

4. **premonitions** (prēm′ ə nish′ ənz) *n.*: Forewarnings.
5. **inexorable** (in ek′ sər ə b'l) *adj.*: That cannot be changed.

new British artillery park on the River Ancre.[6] A bird streaked across the gray sky and blindly I translated it into an airplane and that airplane into many (against the French sky) annihilating the artillery station with vertical bombs. If only my mouth, before a bullet shattered it, could cry out that secret name so it could be heard in Germany . . . My human voice was very weak. How might I make it carry to the ear of the Chief? To the ear of that sick and hateful man who knew nothing of Runeberg and me save that we were in Staffordshire and who was waiting in vain for our report in his arid office in Berlin, endlessly examining newspapers . . . I said out loud: *I must flee.* I sat up noiselessly, in a useless perfection of silence, as if Madden were already lying in wait for me. Something—perhaps the mere vain ostentation[7] of proving my resources were nil—made me look through my pockets. I found what I knew I would find. The American watch, the nickel chain and the square coin, the key ring with the incriminating useless keys to Runeberg's apartment, the notebook, a letter which I resolved to destroy immediately (and which I did not destroy), a crown, two shillings and a few pence,[8] the red and blue pencil, the handkerchief, the revolver with one bullet. Absurdly, I took it in my hand and weighed it in order to inspire courage within myself. Vaguely I thought that a pistol report can be heard at a great distance. In ten minutes my plan was perfected. The telephone book listed the name of the only person capable of transmitting the message; he lived in a suburb of Fenton, less than a half hour's train ride away.

I am a cowardly man. I say it now, now that I have carried to its end a plan whose perilous nature no one can deny. I know its execution was terrible. I didn't do it for Germany, no. I care nothing for a barbarous country which imposed upon me the abjection[9] of being a spy. Besides, I know of a man from England—a modest man—who for me is no less great than Goethe.[10] I talked with him for scarcely an hour, but during that hour he was Goethe . . . I did it because I sensed that the Chief somehow feared people of my race—for the innumerable ancestors who merge within me. I wanted to prove to him that a yellow man could save his armies. Besides, I had to flee from Captain Madden. His hands and his voice could call at my door at any moment. I dressed silently, bade farewell to myself in the mirror, went downstairs, scrutinized the peaceful street and went out. The station was not far from my home, but I judged it wise to take a cab. I argued that in this way I ran less risk of being recognized; the fact is that in the deserted street I felt myself visible and vulnerable, infinitely so. I remember that I told the cab driver to stop a short distance before the main entrance. I got out with voluntary, almost painful slowness; I was going to the village of Ashgrove but I bought a ticket for a more distant station. The train left within a very few minutes, at eight-fifty. I hurried; the next one would leave at nine-thirty. There was hardly a soul on the platform. I went through the coaches; I remember a few farmers, a woman dressed in mourning, a young boy who was reading with fervor the *Annals* of Tacitus,[11] a wounded and happy soldier. The coaches jerked forward at last. A man whom I recognized ran in vain to the end of the platform. It was Captain Richard Madden. Shattered, trembling, I shrank into the far corner of the seat, away from the dreaded window.

From this broken state I passed into an almost abject felicity.[12] I told myself that the duel had already begun and that I had won the first encounter by frustrating, even if for forty minutes, even if by a stroke of fate, the attack of my adversary. I argued that this slightest of victories foreshadowed a total victory. I argued (no less fallaciously) that my cowardly felicity proved that I was a man capable of carrying out the adventure successfully. From this weakness I took strength that did not abandon me. I foresee that man will resign himself each day to more atrocious undertakings; soon there will be no one but warriors and brigands; I give them this counsel: *The author of an*

---

6. River Ancre (än kr'): A river in northeastern France.

7. ostentation (äs' tən tā' shən) *n*.: Showy display.

8. a crown . . . pence: A small sum of English money.

9. abjection (ab jek' shən) *n*.: Wretchedness.

10. Goethe (gö' tə): A great German poet and dramatist (1749–1832).

---

11. *Annals* of Tacitus (tas' i təs): A work of history by the Roman historian Tacitus (c. A.D. 55–c. 120).

12. felicity (fə lis' it ē) *n*.: Happiness; bliss.

5 Discussion Ask students to notice that at the beginning of this passage, Yu Tsun does not have a plan for transmitting his secret and that at the end of it, he does. Ask students to explain why withholding this plan from the reader is effective. Also, what is accomplished, if anything, by listing the contents of his pockets in such an understated way?

6 Discussion Point out to students that Yu Tsun's dislike of Germany becomes clear at this point. Tell them that the name of the Englishman "no less great than Goethe" will become clear in the course of the story. Ask students what purpose it serves to mention this man before readers know his identity.

7 Discussion Ask students if the glimpse of Madden missing the train is a credible coincidence. Have them explain their answers. Also, ask them to recall coincidences that play a part in their favorite stories and novels.

Commentary

Paradox in Borges's Stories A paradox is any statement or set of statements that defy common sense or the rules of logic. One of the most famous examples of paradox is the following series of propositions:

1. People from Crete are incapable of telling the truth.
2. I am a person from Crete.
3. Statements #1 and #2 are both true.

If you think about these three sentences, you will see that if the last statement is true, then the first (and/or second) must be false. However, if the first two are true, then the last must be false, which makes the first true, which makes the last false, and so on into infinity.

Many stories by Borges are, in fact, the fleshing out of such a paradoxical idea. In "The Circular Ruins," for example, a man creates a living human being, whom he molds from his dreams, only to find that he himself was created in the same way—and possibly by the very person he has created.

Often Borges uses the image of the labyrinth to embody his love of paradox. Labyrinths suggest the paradoxical, hidden structure of the universe, which defies human reason. It is truly mysterious and unknowable, and can be deadly to humans who are arrogant enough to think they can tame it to their purposes.

8 Discussion Ask students how Yu Tsun manages to make the atrocious act he plans to commit seem inevitable and beyond altering. Tell them that the concept of a "future as irrevocable as the past" is a fatalistic view of time that will be challenged later in the story.

9 Literary Focus Ask students how the labyrinth that Yu Tsun imagines differs from a more common labyrinth like a garden maze. Do you have a clear image of Yu Tsun's maze? Why or why not? Tell students that later in the story, the narrator will set forth the idea of a labyrinth that involves time as well as space.

10 Discussion Have students explain how their view of the narrator's character is affected by his thought that one can be an enemy of men, but not of a country. Ask them if this idea is consistent with Yu Tsun's feelings about Germany.

11 Discussion Ask students to explain what occurs beneath the surface in the conversation between Yu Tsun and the man who opens the door. How is each of them surprised by what the other says and why?

atrocious undertaking ought to imagine that he has already accomplished it, ought to impose upon himself a future as irrevocable as the past. Thus I proceeded as my eyes of a man already dead registered the elapsing of that day, which was perhaps the last, and the diffusion of the night. The train ran gently along, amid ash trees. It stopped, almost in the middle of the fields. No one announced the name of the station. "Ashgrove?" I asked a few lads on the platform. "Ashgrove," they replied. I got off.

A lamp enlightened the platform but the faces of the boys were in shadow. One questioned me, "Are you going to Dr. Stephen Albert's house?" Without waiting for my answer, another said, "The house is a long way from here, but you won't get lost if you take this road to the left and at every crossroads turn again to your left." I tossed them a coin (my last), descended a few stone steps and started down the solitary road. It went downhill, slowly. It was of elemental earth; overhead the branches were tangled; the low, full moon seemed to accompany me.

For an instant, I thought that Richard Madden in some way had penetrated my desperate plan. Very quickly, I understood that that was impossible. The instructions to turn always to the left reminded me that such was the common procedure for discovering the central point of certain labyrinths. I have some understanding of labyrinths: not for nothing am I the great-grandson of that Ts'ui Pên who was governor of Yunnan and who renounced worldly power in order to write a novel that might be even more populous than the *Hung Lu Meng*[13] and to construct a labyrinth in which all men would become lost. Thirteen years he dedicated to these heterogeneous[14] tasks, but the hand of a stranger murdered him—and his novel was incoherent and no one found the labyrinth. Beneath English trees I meditated on that lost maze: I imagined it inviolate and perfect at the secret crest of a mountain; I imagined it erased by rice fields or beneath the water; I imagined it infinite, no longer composed of octagonal kiosks and returning paths, but of rivers and provinces and kingdoms . . . I

---

13. *Hung Lu Meng* (ho͞on lō mən): The author of the *Dream of the Red Chamber*, a famous eighteenth-century Chinese novel.
14. **heterogeneous** (het′ ər ə jē′ nē əs) *adj.*: Dissimilar.

thought of a labyrinth of labyrinths, of one sinuous spreading labyrinth that would encompass the past and the future and in some way involve the stars. Absorbed in these illusory images, I forgot my destiny of one pursued. I felt myself to be, for an unknown period of time, an abstract perceiver of the world. The vague, living countryside, the moon, the remains of the day worked on me, as well as the slope of the road which eliminated any possibility of weariness. The afternoon was intimate, infinite. The road descended and forked among the now confused meadows. A high-pitched, almost syllabic music approached and receded in the shifting of the wind, dimmed by leaves and distance. I thought that a man can be an enemy of other men, of the moments of other men, but not of a country: not of fireflies, words, gardens, streams of water, sunsets. Thus I arrived before a tall, rusty gate. Between the iron bars I made out a poplar grove and a pavilion. I understood suddenly two things, the first trivial, the second almost unbelievable: the music came from the pavilion, and the music was Chinese. For precisely that reason I had openly accepted it without paying it any heed. I do not remember whether there was a bell or whether I knocked with my hand. The sparkling of the music continued.

From the rear of the house within a lantern approached: a lantern that the trees sometimes striped and sometimes eclipsed, a paper lantern that had the form of a drum and the color of the moon. A tall man bore it. I didn't see his face for the light blinded me. He opened the door and said slowly, in my own language: "I see that the pious Hsi P'êng persists in correcting my solitude. You no doubt wish to see the garden?"

I recognized the name of one of our consuls and I replied, disconcerted, "The garden?"

"The garden of forking paths."

Something stirred in my memory and I uttered with incomprehensible certainty, "The garden of my ancestor Ts'ui Pên."

"Your ancestor? Your illustrious ancestor? Come in."

The damp path zigzagged like those of my childhood. We came to a library of Eastern and Western books. I recognized bound in yellow silk several volumes of the Lost Encyclopedia, edited by

---

Grammar in Action

Understatement By means of a device called understatement a writer can suggest an idea or feeling without actually mentioning it. Sometimes this deliberate playing down of an idea or feeling can emphasize it more strongly than exaggeration would. The following examples show how a passage can be more effective by replacing exaggerated writing with understatement.

EXAGGERATED: Besides, I was desperate to escape from Captain Madden. With a cruel leer, he would soon be pounding on my door. Gasping with fear, almost sobbing, I trembled as I dressed, stared in horror at my disheveled image in the mirror, stumbled downstairs, looked in terror at the suspiciously peaceful street and—with a heavy heart— staggered out to meet my doom.

UNDERSTATED: "Besides, I had to flee from Captain Madden. His hands and his voice could call at my door at any moment. I dressed silently, bade farewell to myself in the mirror, went downstairs, scrutinized the peaceful street and went out."

the Third Emperor of the Luminous Dynasty[15] but never printed. The record on the phonograph revolved next to a bronze phoenix. I also recall a *famille rose* vase[16] and another, many centuries older, of that shade of blue which our craftsmen copied from the potter of Persia . . .

Stephen Albert observed me with a smile. He was, as I have said, very tall, sharp-featured, with gray eyes and a gray beard. He told me that he had been a missionary in Tientsin "before aspiring to become a Sinologist."[17]

We sat down—I on a long, low divan, he with his back to the window and a tall circular clock. I calculated that my pursuer, Richard Madden, could not arrive for at least an hour. My irrevocable determination could wait.

"An astounding fate, that of Ts'ui Pên," Stephen Albert said. "Governor of his native province, learned in astronomy, in astrology and in the tireless interpretation of the canonical books, chess player, famous poet and calligrapher—he abandoned all this in order to compose a book and a maze. He renounced the pleasures of both tyranny and justice, of his populous couch, of his banquets and even of erudition—all to close himself up for thirteen years in the Pavilion of the Limpid Solitude. When he died, his heirs found nothing save chaotic manuscripts. His family, as you may be aware, wished to condemn them to the fire; but his executor—a Taoist or Buddhist monk[18]—insisted on their publication."

"We descendants of Ts'ui Pên," I replied, "continue to curse that monk. Their publication was senseless. The book is an indeterminate heap of contradictory drafts. I examined it once: in the third chapter the hero dies, in the fourth he is alive. As for the other undertaking of Ts'ui Pên, his labyrinth . . ."

---

15. Third . . . Dynasty: Yung-lo (yo͞oŋ lō), third emperor of the Ming Dynasty (1368–1644), who reigned from 1403 to 1424.

16. phoenix (fē′ niks) . . . *famille rose* (fà mē′ rôz′) **vase:** The phoenix is a mythical bird that lives for 500 or 600 years in the Arabian desert, then sets itself on fire and rises renewed from the ashes. A *famille rose* vase is an open container to hold flowers.

17. Sinologist (sī näl′ ə jist): A student of Chinese language and culture.

18. a Taoist (dou′ ist) **or Buddhist monk:** Taoism and Buddhism are two of the three great religions of China.

"Here is Ts'ui Pên's labyrinth," he said, indicating a tall lacquered desk.

"An ivory labyrinth!" I exclaimed. "A minimum labyrinth."

"A labyrinth of symbols," he corrected. "An invisible labyrinth of time. To me, a barbarous Englishman, has been entrusted the revelation of this diaphanous[19] mystery. After more than a hundred years, the details are irretrievable; but it is not hard to conjecture what happened. Ts'ui Pên must have said once: *I am withdrawing to write a book.* And another time: *I am withdrawing to construct a labyrinth.* Everyone imagined two works; to no one did it occur that the book and the maze were one and the same thing. The Pavilion of the Limpid Solitude stood in the center of a garden that was perhaps intricate; that circumstance could have suggested to the heirs a physical labyrinth. Ts'ui Pên died; no one in the vast territories that were his came upon the labyrinth; the confusion of the novel suggested to me that *it* was the maze. Two circumstances gave me the correct solution of the problem. One: the curious legend that Ts'ui Pên had planned to create a labyrinth which would be strictly infinite. The other: a fragment of a letter I discovered."

Albert rose. He turned his back on me for a moment; he opened a drawer of the black and gold desk. He faced me and in his hands he held a sheet of paper that had once been crimson, but was now pink and tenuous and cross-sectioned. The fame of Ts'ui Pên as a calligrapher had been justly won. I read, uncomprehendingly and with fervor, these words written with a minute brush by a man of my blood: *I leave to the various futures (not to all) my garden of forking paths.* Wordlessly, I returned the sheet. Albert continued:

"Before unearthing this letter, I had questioned myself about the ways in which a book can be infinite. I could think of nothing other than a cyclic volume, a circular one. A book whose last page was identical with the first, a book which had the possibility of continuing indefinitely. I remembered too that night which is at the middle of the

---

19. diaphanous (dī af′ ə nəs) *adj.:* So fine or gauzy as to be transparent or translucent.

While the first passage is filled with emotional words—"desperate," "cruel," "horror"—the second passage implies the tension in the narrator simply by describing his actions.

Student Activity 1. Find other examples of understatement in the story. Explain why implying emotions in these passages can be more effective than using exaggerated or emotional words to describe the feelings of the characters.

Student Activity 2. Write a brief description of an emergency or crisis that you have witnessed or imagined. Try to tell exactly what happened without directly stating the emotions you or others felt in that crisis.

Suggest how the people in the situation felt through an understated description of their actions.

HIDDEN TREASURES, 1969
Consuelo González Amézcua

Thousand and One Nights when Scheherazade[20] (through a magical oversight of the copyist) begins to relate word for word the story of the Thousand and One Nights, establishing the risk of coming once again to the night when she must repeat it, and thus on to infinity. I imagined as well a Platonic, hereditary work, transmitted from father to son, in which each new individual adds a chapter or corrects with pious care the pages of his elders. These conjectures diverted me; but none seemed to correspond, not even remotely, to the contradictory

---

20. the Thousand . . . Scheherazade (shə her′ ə zä′ də): The *Thousand and One Nights* is a series of stories in Arabic, presumably told by Scheherazade to her husband, one each night, in order to prevent him from killing her.

chapters of Ts'ui Pên. In the midst of this perplexity, I received from Oxford the manuscript you have examined. I lingered, naturally, on the sentence: *I leave to the various futures (not to all) my garden of forking paths.* Almost instantly, I understood: 'the garden of forking paths' was the chaotic novel; the phrase 'the various futures (not to all)' suggested to me the forking in time, not in space. A broad rereading of the work confirmed the theory. In all fictional works, each time a man is confronted with several alternatives, he chooses one and eliminates the others; in the fiction of Ts'ui Pên, he chooses—simultaneously—all of them. *He creates,* in this way, diverse futures, diverse times, which themselves also proliferate and fork. Here, then, is the explanation of the novel's contradictions. Fang, let us say, has a secret; a stranger calls at his door; Fang resolves to kill him. Naturally, there are several possible outcomes: Fang can kill the intruder, the intruder can kill Fang, they both can escape, they both can die, and so forth. In the work of Ts'ui Pên, all possible outcomes occur; each one is the point of departure for other forkings. Sometimes, the paths of this labyrinth converge: for example, you arrive at this house, but in one of the possible pasts you are my enemy, in another, my friend. If you will resign yourself to my incurable pronunciation, we shall read a few pages."

His face, within the vivid circle of the lamplight, was unquestionably that of an old man, but with something unalterable about it, even immortal. He read with slow precision two versions of the same epic chapter. In the first, an army marches to a battle across a lonely mountain; the horror of the rocks and shadows makes the men undervalue their lives and they gain an easy victory. In the second, the same army traverses a palace where a great festival is taking place; the resplendent battle seems to them a continuation of the celebration and they win the victory. I listened with proper veneration to these ancient narratives, perhaps less admirable in themselves than the fact that they had been created by my blood and were being restored to me by a man of a remote empire, in the course of a desperate adventure, on a Western isle. I remember the last words, repeated in each version like a secret commandment: *Thus fought the heros, tranquil their admirable hearts, violent their swords, resigned to kill and to die.*

From that moment on, I felt about me and within my dark body an invisible, intangible swarming. Not the swarming of the divergent, parallel, and finally coalescent armies, but a more inaccessible, more intimate agitation that they in some manner prefigured. Stephen Albert continued:

"I don't believe that your illustrious ancestor played idly with these variations. I don't consider it credible that he would sacrifice thirteen years to the infinite execution of a rhetorical experiment. In your country, the novel is a subsidiary form of literature; in Ts'ui Pên's time it was a despicable form. Ts'ui Pên was a brilliant novelist, but he was also a man of letters who doubtless did not consider himself a mere novelist. The testimony of his contemporaries proclaims—and his life fully confirms—his metaphysical[21] and mystical interests. Philosophic controversy usurps a good part of the novel. I know that of all problems, none disturbed him so greatly nor worked upon him so much as the abysmal problem of time. Now then, the latter is the only problem that does not figure in the pages of the *Garden*. He does not even use the word that signifies *time.* How do you explain this voluntary omission?"

I proposed several solutions—all unsatisfactory. We discussed them. Finally, Stephen Albert said to me:

"In a riddle whose answer is chess, what is the only prohibited word?"

I thought a moment and replied, "The word *chess.*"

"Precisely," said Albert. "*The Garden of Forking Paths* is an enormous riddle, or parable, whose theme is time; this recondite[22] cause prohibits its mention. To omit a word always, to resort to inept metaphors and obvious periphrases, is perhaps the most emphatic way of stressing it. That is the tortuous method preferred, in each of the meanderings of his indefatigable novel, by the oblique Ts'ui Pên. I have compared hundreds of manuscripts, I have corrected the errors that the negligence of the copyists has introduced. I have guessed the plan of

---

21. metaphysical (met´ ə fiz´ i k'l) *adj.*: Connected with metaphysics, the branch of philosophy that seeks to explain the nature of being.

22. recondite (rek´ ən dīt´) *adj.*: Beyond the grasp of the ordinary mind.

19 Discussion Have students note that Albert contrasts Ts'ui Pên's multiply forking time with Western philosophy's concept of a single-threaded time. Have students recall the narrator's previous meditations on time. Ask them which view of these two views of time those meditations reflect.

20 Clarification It might be helpful to students if you diagramed these two conceptions of time on the chalkboard.

21 Reading Strategy Have students stop after this passage to summarize the story and predict how it will end. Ask them who seems more aware of the danger Albert is in, Yu Tsun or Albert himself.

22 Enrichment Borges once said, "'The Garden of Forking Paths' is a detective story; its readers will assist at the execution, and all the preliminaries, of a crime, a crime whose purpose will not be unknown to them, but which they will not understand—it seems to me—until the last paragraph." Ask students how the last paragraph "solves" the mystery. What evidence is there that Borges had the last paragraph in mind at the very start of the story?

Master Teacher Note Explain to students that in his fiction, Borges is fond of bringing together people of diverse national origins. In his own life, Borges felt the pull of conflicting loyalties. He loved English, German, and Argentine literature, but often disliked the governments of these countries. Here the spy for the Germans is Chinese, the agent of the English is Irish. Both are distrusted or feared by those they work for, yet both feel obliged to prove their loyalty to their superiors. Have students discuss how these ironies flavor the story and its outcome.

Cooperative Learning Have students work in small groups to devise a short story that involves a labyrinth in some way.

this chaos, I have re-established—I believe I have re-established—the primordial organization, I have translated the entire work: it is clear to me that not once does he employ the word 'time.' The explanation is obvious: *The Garden of Forking Paths* is an incomplete, but not false, image of the universe as Ts'ui Pên conceived it. In contrast to Newton and Schopenhauer,[23] your ancestor did not believe in a uniform, absolute time. He believed in an infinite series of times, in a growing, dizzying net of divergent, convergent and parallel times. This network of times which approached one another, forked, broke off, or were unaware of one another for centuries, embraces *all* possibilities of time. We do not exist in the majority of these times; in some you exist, and not I; in others I, and not you; in others, both of us. In the present one, which a favorable fate has granted me, you have arrived at my house; in another, while crossing the garden, you found me dead; in still another, I utter these same words, but I am a mistake, a ghost."

"In every one," I pronounced, not without a tremble to my voice, "I am grateful to you and revere you for your re-creation of the garden of Ts'ui Pên."

"Not in all," he murmured with a smile. "Time forks perpetually toward innumerable futures. In one of them I am your enemy."

---

23. Newton and Schopenhauer (shō′ pən hou′ ər): Isaac Newton (1642–1727) was an English mathematician who formulated the laws of gravity and motion. Arthur Schopenhauer (1788–1860) was a German philosopher.

Once again I felt the swarming sensation of which I have spoken. It seemed to me that the humid garden that surrounded the house was infinitely saturated with invisible persons. Those persons were Albert and I, secret, busy and multiform in other dimensions of time. I raised my eyes and the tenuous nightmare dissolved. In the yellow and black garden there was only one man; but this man was as strong as a statue . . . this man was approaching along the path and he was Captain Richard Madden.

"The future already exists," I replied, "but I am your friend. Could I see the letter again?"

Albert rose. Standing tall, he opened the drawer of the tall desk; for the moment his back was to me. I had readied the revolver. I fired with extreme caution. Albert fell uncomplainingly, immediately. I swear his death was instantaneous—a lightning stroke.

The rest is unreal, insignificant. Madden broke in, arrested me. I have been condemned to the gallows. I have won out abominably; I have communicated to Berlin the secret name of the city they must attack. They bombed it yesterday; I read it in the same papers that offered to England the mystery of the learned Sinologist Stephen Albert who was murdered by a stranger, one Yu Tsun. The Chief had deciphered this mystery. He knew my problem was to indicate (through the uproar of the war) the city called Albert, and that I had found no other means to do so than to kill a man of that name. He does not know (no one can know) my innumerable contrition and weariness.

For Victoria Ocampo.

Reader's Response *What did you find most puzzling about this story?*

Closure and Extension

ANSWERS TO THINKING ABOUT THE SELECTION

1. The story takes place in England, in July 1916, during World War I.
2. Dr. Yu Tsun, who tells the story, is a Chinese spy working for the Germans. He must get a message to Berlin that reveals the exact location of a new British artillery park near the front in northeastern France. He has only a few hours to do this, because he is being hunted down by a British agent.
3. (a) He decides to make headlines by killing a man with the same name as the place where the park is located, thus signaling his chief in Berlin the location to bomb before the battle. (b) Yes, the plan works exactly as Yu Tsun conceived it would. He kills a man named Albert, and his chief realizes that the city to be bombed is Albert.
4. Answers will differ. Possible answers include, as similarities: neither Yu Tsun (Chinese) nor Madden (Irish) are English or German, yet both feel "obliged" to play their roles with fierce determination and to succeed at any cost; as differences: Yu Tsun is remarkably ingenious, while Mad-

THINKING ABOUT THE SELECTION

Clarifying

1. When and where does this story take place?
2. Who tells the story, and what dilemma does he face?
3. (a) Describe the ingenious plan that he devises to solve this dilemma. (b) Does the plan work? Explain.

Interpreting

4. Compare and contrast the two antagonists in this tale.
5. In what way is this narrative both a spy story and much more than a spy story?
6. (a) What role does coincidence play in this story? (b) How is coincidence related to the notion that there can be many versions of reality?
7. Why does the narrator feel a "swarming sensation" after learning about his ancestor's novel from Stephen Albert?
8. (a) Why does the narrator say at the end, "I have won out abominably"? (b) Is there anything surprising about his mood? Explain.

Applying

9. Have you ever seen a science-fiction or mystery movie that made you feel the way this story did? If so, tell your class about it.
10. (a) What modern-day parallels to labyrinths can you cite? (b) What special traits might be needed to negotiate them?

ANALYZING LITERATURE

Understanding Symbols

A labyrinth is a construct of winding passages and blind alleys designed to confuse and disorient those who enter it. In this story the labyrinth becomes a symbol for our puzzling and mysterious universe. We can see it taking on such meaning as the narrator recalls his ancestor's wish "to construct a labyrinth in which all men would become lost." Then he imagines that his ancestor's labyrinth, itself lost, is an "infinite" maze that encompasses the past, the future, and "the stars." At that point it is unclear how a labyrinth, which is usually two- or three-dimensional, could encompass time as well as space. Stephen Albert, however, explains how the novel written by Ts'ui Pên is a time-labyrinth.

1. Before finding Ts'ui Pên's letter, Albert thinks of three ways in which a book can be "infinite." (a) What are these ways? (b) Explain why each of these books would continue forever.
2. (a) How is Ts'ui Pên's novel different from these books? (b) Why is the novel confusing? (c) What is the secret that explains this confusion and indicates how the book is a time-labyrinth? (d) Why is the title of the novel appropriate?
3. (a) How does learning the secret of the novel affect the narrator's perception of his own situation? (b) Is this new perception consoling? Why or why not?
4. The story itself begins with a very precise reference to history. Yet how does the notion of a time-labyrinth undermine the idea that history can be precisely recorded?
5. Do you think Borges wants the reader to feel lost or found at the end of the story? Explain.

THINKING AND WRITING

Writing an Interactive Story

An interactive story is similar to the novel of Ts'ui Pên in "The Garden of Forking Paths." The term *interactive* means that the reader participates in creating the story by choosing what will happen at each turning point. Readers who make different choices, therefore, are creating different stories.

Get together with a group of classmates and devise such a tale. Begin by outlining the plot of a mystery story. Just note the main events of the story; don't spell out the action in detail. Then at every point where the hero or heroine makes a decision, think of a choice other than the one that was made. This other decision can serve as the basis for a related story that goes off in a different direction and ends in a different way. When you have finished, your outline should resemble an upside-down tree. The main narrative is the trunk of the tree, while the alternative stories are the branches.

Next have each of the group members write out one of these stories. The person who tells the main story should put each episode on a separate piece of paper or index card. At the bottom of the paper or card, the writer should ask the reader to choose what the protagonist will do next. One choice will lead to a continuation of the main story; another will lead to one of the branches. Use a color or number code to match each choice with the narrative that continues from it.

Your group can test the story by reading all the different versions. Are the directions clear? Is each version of the story satisfying? Finally, have classmates from other groups read your interactive story.

(continued from bottom of page)
end of *2001*.

10. (a) Answers will differ. Possible answers include being lost in a city of narrow, winding streets or in an unfamiliar landscape. (b) Answers will differ. Possible traits include courage, resourcefulness, and self-reliance.

ANSWERS TO ANALYZING LITERATURE

1. (a) It could be cyclic or circular; it could start telling the story of itself in the middle; it could be added to by members of each succeeding generation. (b) The last page would return the reader to the first and the book would continue indefinitely; the story of the story would continue to the middle and then start retelling itself again; the generational book would continue to be written and thus would never be finished.
2. (a) Ts'ui Pên's novel forks in time, choosing all possible futures simultaneously. (b) A character may die in one chapter and go on living in a later chapter. (c) A character may appear dead, then alive because the episodes are tracing all possible futures through all their infinite forkings. (d) The novel shows time spread out like the forking paths in a garden labyrinth.
3. (a) He is moved that Albert has deciphered the meaning of his ancestor's novel and upset that he still plans to kill him. (b) The narrator could possibly console himself that in another future he doesn't kill Albert, but this cannot really be consoling because in this fork of time he does kill him.
4. If all possible outcomes co-exist and are equally feasible, then the recording of a supposedly unique, linear history makes no sense.
5. Answers will differ. Possible answers include the view that Borges wants the reader to feel lost because the idea of multiple futures has not helped Yu Tsun to escape the dreadful act he chooses to commit on this fork of his path.

THINKING AND WRITING

Publishing Student Writing Have students read the stories written by other groups.

---

den is presented as oblivious to Yu Tsun's secret and plan.

5. The tale has all the trappings of a spy story but is also concerned with a paradoxical idea about time and the future.
6. (a) Yu Tsun happens to phone his dead friend's apartment when Madden is there; a man by the name of Albert happens to live not far away; Albert happens to know the work of

Yu Tsun's ancestor; Madden happens to find his way to Albert's house without being aware of Yu Tsun's scheme. (b) If coincidences like these did not occur, different futures would have resulted.
7. He begins to sense that the house is surrounded by himself and Albert as they might exist in other dimensions of time.
8. (a) He has met someone he admires

intensely, yet feels he is compelled to kill him. (b) Yes, a person normally would not kill someone who proved to be so admirable. The past in which he devised his abstract plan ends up dominating this fork of the future, even at the cost of dishonoring his own ancestor.
9. Answers will differ. A student might mention a film about time travel, such as *Back to the Future*, or the

Presentation

Motivation/Prior Knowledge Ask students if they have ever solved the mazes in puzzle books. Tell them that these mazes are two-dimensional versions of labyrinths and that labyrinths have fascinated people throughout history.

Enrichment Tell students that in ancient Egypt and elsewhere, labyrinths were meant to exclude unwanted visitors from a burial place. However, they were often used as "Do Not Enter!" signs at other sites. Throughout the British isles, people drew labyrinthine designs on doorsteps to ward off evil spirits and witches. Sometimes these designs were placed at the entrances to barns as well as houses. They were also drawn in sand on a bride's doorstep before she departed for the wedding ceremony. Their purpose in this case was to guard against harmful spells.

The British turf mazes could have had a similar protective function. These are labyrinthine designs made of earth and matted roots and raised slightly above the ground. One of them, in Yorkshire—unfortunately, it no longer exists—was a circle 60 feet in diameter. The total length of the winding path it created was 407 yards. Only a few of these mazes still remain, but their location near ancient camps suggests that they might have been used to protect these sites.

Labyrinths: A Long History

If you have ever been hopelessly lost on the winding streets of an unfamiliar neighborhood, you know what it feels like to be in a labyrinth. The word *labyrinth*, which comes from the Greek language, refers to any network of winding passages. A common synonym for *labyrinth* is the word *maze*, used to describe two-dimensional puzzles that appear in newspapers and game books. In order to solve a maze, you must reach the center of the puzzle by turning through a series of complicated paths and avoiding blind alleys.

The feelings of being lost and found are deeply ingrained in our minds: Very young children love to play hide and seek. It is not surprising, therefore, that labyrinths, in two and three dimensions, have appealed to many cultures. The ancient and widespread use of this pattern indicates that different peoples discovered it independently rather than learning about it from a common source.

Egyptian Labyrinths

The ancient Egyptians incorporated labyrinths into their tombs and temples. For instance, King Perabsen's tomb (c. 3400 B.C.)—his title is *king* because he lived before the time of the pharaohs—was placed in the center of a labyrinth. The purpose of the confusing passageways surrounding the tomb was to hide the king's remains.

Another famous Egyptian labyrinth was the temple of Amenemhet III. The Roman author Pliny described this complex and mysterious structure: ". . . it contained winding ways and bewildering twists and turns . . . with many entrances designed to produce misleading goings and comings. . . . Those who go through its laborious windings with their baffling intricacy, come by slopes to lofty chambers. . . . The passages are for the most part in darkness."

This description suggests the creepy, unnerving feelings that labyrinths often arouse. They can hide unexpected menaces and are often designed to exclude people from a secret or sacred place. Frequently, as in ancient Egypt, they are associated with death and the underworld.

The Cretan Labyrinth

The labyrinth built by the inventor Daedalus for King Minos of Crete was frightening for a good reason: Lurking in its confusing passageways was a beast—half-man and half-bull—called the Minotaur. According to legend Minos periodically demanded young men and women as tribute from Athens. He locked these young Athenians in his labyrinth, where they lost their way and were devoured by the monster. The Greek hero Theseus, however, obtained a ball of yarn from Ariadne, the daughter of Minos. Unraveling the yarn as he walked through the labyrinth, he encountered and killed the Minotaur, then followed the strand of yarn back to the entrance.

Scholars have disagreed about the site of this legendary labyrinth. Some have argued that the great palace excavated at Knossos, Crete, was itself the labyrinth, because it is filled with twisting and turning passages. Others maintain that the legend refers to one of Crete's many

Commentary

W. H. Auden's "The Labyrinth" Labyrinths, with their multiple meanings and associations, have intrigued many contemporary writers and artists. W. H. Auden began a poem entitled "The Labyrinth" as follows:

Anthropos apteros for days
Walked whistling round and round the Maze
Relying happily upon
His temperament for getting on.

The first two words are Latin for "wingless man." Since humans do not have wings, Auden is saying, we are trapped in a Maze that represents the world itself. The Latin phrase is also an allusion to Daedalus, the inventor of the Cretan labyrinth. Imprisoned by King Minos, Daedalus invented wings to enable him and his son to escape from the island of Crete. With this allusion, Auden is suggesting that ordinary humans, unlike Daedalus, cannot fly away from the labyrinth of their lives.

Despite the distressing predicament Auden describes, his poem has a jaunty, humorous tone. For that reason, his Maze seems more like a harmless English hedge maze than the frightening Cretan labyrinth.

NSIGHTS

caves. In the nineteenth century, an Englishman explored a cave in the southern part of the island and reported as follows: "The clearly intentional intricacy and apparently endless number of galleries impressed me with a sense of horror and fascination I cannot describe. At every ten steps one was arrested, and had to turn to right or left, sometimes to choose one of three or four roads. What if one should lose the clue!"

There is some evidence that supports the connection between labyrinths and caves. The original meaning of the word *labyrinth* may be "place of stone," and this definition would certainly apply to a cave as well. Also, like labyrinths, caves have been used as tombs and are associated with the underworld.

Labyrinths in Contemporary Literature and Art

Labyrinths, with their multiple meanings and associations, have intrigued contemporary writers and artists. The stories of the Argentinian writer Jorge Luis Borges seem to draw upon the darker meanings associated with labyrinths. Borges views the universe itself as a strange and riddling maze. His story "The Library of Babel," for instance, begins as follows: "The universe (which others call the Library) is composed of an indefinite and perhaps infinite number of hexagonal galleries, with vast air shafts between, surrounded by very low railings."

Borges's description induces in a reader the dizzying sense of being lost in a vast labyrinth. The Dutch artist Maurits Escher conveys the same sensation through his use of impossible perspectives. He may, for instance, show a man in a gallery looking at a painting (see the picture on this page). This painting, however, seems to depict the world in which the gallery itself is located! Clearly this is an impossible situation. As people gaze at Escher's visual riddles, they may begin to feel as if they are trapped in a labyrinth from which there is no exit.

PRINT GALLERY
M. C. Escher

JULIO CORTÁZAR

1914–1984

Standing six feet six, with long hair and a beard, the Argentinian Julio Cortázar (hōo´ lē ō kôr tä´ zər) was an imposing figure. He was also a towering presence as a writer, admired for the range of his work. Not only did he produce novels and short stories but he also composed poetry and translated into Spanish the works of authors such as Edgar Allan Poe. He is best known, however, for his experimental fiction, which often allows readers to participate in creating the story.

Cortázar was born in Brussels, Belgium, of Argentinian parents. Although he returned to Argentina when he was still a small boy, he would later journey back to Europe. In fact, his sense of belonging to both Europe and Latin America became an important theme in his life.

In Argentina Cortázar began a career as an elementary and high school teacher. Then, in his early thirties, he taught French literature at a university, and, shortly afterward, moved to Buenos Aires and became a translator. Upon winning a scholarship from the French government, he traveled to Paris, where he worked as a translator for the United Nations—a job he held for the rest of his life.

Before leaving Argentina for Paris, Cortázar began to write the fiction that made him famous. His collection of stories *Bestiary,* which includes "House Taken Over," appeared in 1951. Two years later, after he had moved to Europe, he wrote much of *Cronopias and Famas,* which he called his "most playful book." In the opening section entitled "The Instruction Manual," he provides detailed and wacky directions for such habitual actions as combing one's hair or climbing down a staircase.

Cortázar continued to live in France, with time out for visits to such places as Italy, the United States, and Cuba. Although he was criticized for living in exile, he insisted that he never lost his Argentine identity. He compared himself to a snail that "carries his nest with him and travels all over the world."

In 1963 he published his most remarkable novel, *Hopscotch.* Named for a child's game, it has a "Table of Instructions" that explains how it can be read in at least two different ways. Other experimental novels, like *62: A Model Kit* (1968) and *Last Round* (1969), also invite playful reader participation. In the former book, Cortázar deliberately leaves gaps in his descriptions of the characters, so that readers have to fill in the missing pieces of the puzzle.

Cortázar became politically active toward the end of his life, espousing revolutionary views in books like *Fantomas Takes on the Multinational Vampires* (1975). However, he never lost his sense of play—*Fantomas,* for instance, is in the form of a comic book!

Cortázar once summarized his theory of fiction as follows: "The fantastic is something that one must never say good-bye to lightly. The man of the future . . . will have to find the bases of a reality which is truly his and, at the same time, maintain the capacity of dreaming and playing . . . since it is through those doors that the Other, the fantastic dimension, and the unexpected will always slip, . . ." When you read "House Taken Over," you will step through "those doors."

GUIDE FOR INTERPRETING

House Taken Over

Commentary

The Fantastic. We are all familiar with fantasy. Each night we have dreams in which the most ordinary situations appear in strange new lights. We are driving on a highway and suddenly the car begins to fly, or we walk out of our home and find ourselves in an exotic jungle. In our daydreams, too, fantasy expands the dimensions of the everyday world. One moment we are listening to someone speak; the next, we have tuned into our dreams and are speeding down a highway in a chartreuse sports car.

In literature of **the fantastic,** writers harness the power of fantasy to challenge, puzzle, discomfort, and entertain readers. Like dreams or daydreams, fantastic stories distort and expand our usual world. They open up passageways into mysterious places. One such story is Jorge Luis Borges's "The Secret Miracle," in which a man facing a firing squad is given a year to finish a play he is writing. The fantastic element of the tale is that the year takes place while the bullets are flying toward him! To everyone in the story except the man, the year is just a split second.

According to the Argentine critic Alberto Manguel, ". . . fantastic literature deals with what can best be defined as the impossible seeping into the possible, what Wallace Stevens calls 'black water breaking into reality." However, just as no dream is totally unrealistic—even the strangest will have recognizable characters and actions—no fantastic story is entirely fantastic. Imagine what would happen if readers encountered a fictional world in which nothing were familiar! It would be like traveling to a planet in a different universe: The sights and sounds and sensations would be almost totally incomprehensible. In fantastic literature, fantasy and reality exist side by side.

Different writers, however, use different strategies for combining these two elements. In "House Taken Over," for example, Julio Cortázar establishes a situation that seems to be entirely realistic. A middle-aged man and his sister settle down to a comfortable, routine life in their family's "old and spacious" Buenos Aires house. Into these pleasant surroundings, however, Cortázar introduces a discordant note of fantasy that mounts to a crescendo, drowning out the humdrum, ordinary world.

Writing

Have you ever told a friend about an experience and said, "It was like something out of a dream"? All of us have experienced moments when life seemed stranger and more mysterious than usual. Freewrite about such a time, using vivid language to call up the sense of mystery you felt.

Literary Focus Have students discuss their own experiences with films or stories that include elements of fantasy. Many of them, for example, may have read Edgar Allan Poe's tales or J.R.R. Tolkien's trilogy *Lord of the Rings*, or even Stephen King's popular novels. Students may also be familiar with the reruns of Rod Serling's television show *Twilight Zone.* If any students are science-fiction buffs, you may want to have them consider the differences between science-fiction and fantasy literature.

Writing/Prior Knowledge Pair up the students in your class. Have them share ideas and tell each other about their strange experiences before they begin freewriting.

ESL Teaching Strategy To accomplish the writing assignment, pair each ESL student with another member of the class. The native-speaking student should act as a coach, discussing the ways in which the ESL student might develop two or three drawings to help recount his or her strange tale.

Vocabulary
Preteach the following vocabulary words:
indispensable (in´ di spen´ sə bəl) *adj.*: Absolutely necessary; essential
chiffonier (shif´ ə nir´) *n.*: A chest of drawers, usually with a mirror on top
replete (ri plēt´) *adj.*: Well-filled; stocked
dexterity (deks ter´ ə tē) *n.*: Skillfulness in the use of one's hands
vestibule (ves´ tə byool´) *n.*: A small entrance hall
folios (fō´ lē ōz) *n.*: Large sheets of paper folded so as to create four pages
brusquely (brusk´ lē) *adv.*: In an abrupt manner

Analyzing Literature Worksheet, *Identifying Clues That Help You Make Inferences,* p. 1489
Language Worksheet, *Finding the Meaning That Fits the Context,* p. 1490
Selection Test, pp. 1491–1492
Art Transparency 17
Fire and Light Against Darkness by David Alfaro Siqueiros

Master Teacher Note Place Art Transparency 17, *Fire and Light Against Darkness,* on an overhead projector after students have read the story. Ask them whether this picture conveys the same mood as "House Taken Over."

Spelling Tip Write the word *brusquely* on the chalkboard. Point out that the /k/ sound at the end of *brusque* is spelled by the letter *q.* Tell students that another word in which the /k/ sound at the end is spelled by *q* is *masque,* a form of dramatic entertainment featuring costumes and masks. Still another word is *mosque,* a Moslem temple.

House Taken Over

Julio Cortázar

translated by Paul Blackburn

We liked the house because, apart from its being old and spacious (in a day when old houses go down for a profitable auction of their construction materials), it kept the memories of great-grandparents, our paternal grandfather, our parents and the whole of childhood.

Irene and I got used to staying in the house by ourselves, which was crazy, eight people could have lived in that place and not have gotten in each other's way. We rose at seven in the morning and got the cleaning done, and about eleven I left Irene to finish off whatever rooms and went to the kitchen. We lunched at noon precisely; then there was nothing left to do but a few dirty plates. It was pleasant to take lunch and commune with[1] the great hollow, silent house, and it was enough for us just to keep it clean. We ended up thinking, at times, that that was what had kept us from marrying. Irene turned down two suitors for no particular reason, and María Esther went and died on me before we could manage to get engaged. We were easing into our forties with the unvoiced concept that the quiet, simple marriage of sister and brother was the indispensable end to a line established in this house by our grandparents. We would die here someday, obscure and distant cousins would inherit the place, have it torn down, sell the bricks and get rich on the building plot; or more justly and better yet, we would topple it ourselves before it was too late.

Irene never bothered anyone. Once the morning housework was finished, she spent the rest of the day on the sofa in her bedroom, knitting. I couldn't tell you why she knitted so much; I think women knit when they discover that it's a fat excuse to do nothing at all. But Irene was not like that, she always knitted necessities, sweaters for winter, socks for me, handy morning robes and bedjackets for herself. Sometimes she would do a jacket, then unravel it the next moment because there was something that didn't please her; it was pleasant to see a pile of tangled wool in her knitting basket fighting a losing battle for a few hours to retain its shape. Saturdays I went downtown to buy wool; Irene had faith in my good taste, was pleased with the colors and never a skein[2] had to be returned. I took advantage of these trips to make the rounds of the bookstores, uselessly asking if they had anything new in French literature. Nothing worthwhile had arrived in Argentina since 1939.[3]

But it's the house I want to talk about, the house and Irene, I'm not very important. I wonder what Irene would have done without her knitting. One can reread a book, but once a pullover is finished you can't do it over again, it's some kind of disgrace. One day I found that the drawer at the bottom of the chiffonier, replete with mothballs,

---

1. **commune** (kə myo͞on´) **with:** Be in close rapport or harmony with.

2. **skein** (skān) *n.*: A quantity of thread or yarn wound in a coil.

3. **Nothing worthwhile . . . since 1939:** When World War II began in 1939, communications with Europe were disrupted.

was filled with shawls, white, green, lilac. Stacked amid a great smell of camphor—it was like a shop; I didn't have the nerve to ask her what she planned to do with them. We didn't have to earn our living, there was plenty coming in from the farms each month, even piling up. But Irene was only interested in the knitting and showed a wonderful <u>dexterity</u>, and for me the hours slipped away watching her, her hands like silver sea-urchins, needles flashing, and one or two knitting baskets on the floor, the balls of yarn jumping about. It was lovely.

How not to remember the layout of that house. The dining room, a living room with tapestries, the library and three large bedrooms in the section most recessed, the one that faced toward Rodríguez Peña.[4] Only a corridor with its massive oak door separated that part from the front wing, where there was a bath, the kitchen, our bedrooms and the hall. One entered the house through a <u>vestibule</u> with enameled tiles, and a wrought-iron grated door opened onto the living room. You had to come in through the vestibule and open the gate to go into the living room; the doors to our bedrooms were on either side of this, and opposite it was the

7

------

4. Rodríguez Peña (rō drē′ gɔz pā′ nyɔ): A fashionable street in Bueno Aires.

invasion of the mysterious noises, the residents of the house in *Bestiary* try to adjust to the tiger's presence. Finally, however, one of the characters is devoured by the fantasy tiger.

In each story the being or creature that invades the house is linked to the suffering, thoughts, or desires of the characters. This connection leads some critics to believe that the house symbolizes the human mind beset by irrational forces. You might ask students to keep this interpretation in mind as they continue reading "House Taken Over."

In fact, Cortázar's method of writing lends further support to this interpretation. He described, for instance, how *his* mind was often invaded by "the shapeless mass" of a story. The only way in which he could free himself was to write the story down. (See Primary Source, page 1242.)

6 **Discussion** Ask students whether the scarcity of figurative language in the narrative makes this simile more effective. Also ask them how this figure of speech contributes to the mood and atmosphere of the story. Have them look for other figures of speech as the story continues.

7 **Clarification** Make sure students realize that the house consists of a front section (with a kitchen, bath, living room, and bedrooms) and an unused back section (library and other rooms). If time permits, ask for student volunteers to create maps of the house.

Humanities Note
Fine art, *La Nuit* by René Magritte. The Belgian René Magritte (1898–1967) was known as a leading surrealist painter. He frequently used the surrealist technique of combining ordinary objects in unusual ways. He also depicted certain objects and figures in more than one painting so that they came to have symbolic value. The man with the bowler hat in *La Nuit*, for instance, appears in a number of other Magritte paintings.

In *La Nuit* this man stands apart from the warmly lit house, conveying a feeling of loneliness and alienation. Magritte's colors contribute to the somber mystery of the scene. Using a few ordinary things—a man, a hat, trees, and a house—the painter evokes a haunting, uneasy mood.

You might want to use the following questions to discuss the art:
1. What events do you think led up to the scene in this painting?
2. Magritte uses ordinary things —a house, a tree, a man—to create a painting that is unusual, or even fantastic. Explain how he achieves this effect.
3. We all form pictures of the scenes we read about. How is the house in Magritte's painting different from or similar to your image of the house in the story?
4. Choose a friend to whom you would give this painting as a gift. Then explain your choice.

8 **Enrichment** Tell students that *mate* was first brewed by South American Indians hundreds of years ago. This drink, which contains a great deal of caffeine, is still popular in South America.

9 **Literary Focus** Ask students to identify the fantastic element in this paragraph. Initiate a discussion about the understated quality of this fantastic detail. Haven't we all, at one time or another, heard strange sounds in the night? Point out that what the narrator hears is not very alarming in itself. Then ask them to discuss whether it is the noises or the narrator's reaction to them that produces an uncanny feeling.

10 **Discussion** Have students discuss the reaction of the narrator and his sister to the invasion of their house. Is there anything surprising about this reaction? Why?

11 **Discussion** Ask students what these two activities, knitting and stamp collecting, have in common. Why are they especially appropriate for the narrator and his sister?

Master Teacher Note Explain to students that in Cortázar's fiction, routine and habit are seen as enemies. If characters do not rebel against these deadening influences, something extraordinary usually occurs to jar them out of their complacency. Have students discuss in what ways routine and habit might hinder personal growth. Then have them keep this idea in mind as they continue reading the story.

corridor leading to the back section; going down the passage, one swung open the oak door beyond which was the other part of the house; or just before the door, one could turn to the left and go down a narrower passageway which led to the kitchen and the bath. When the door was open, you became aware of the size of the house; when it was closed, you had the impression of an apartment, like the ones they build today, with barely enough room to move around in. Irene and I always lived in this part of the house and hardly ever went beyond the oak door except to do the cleaning. Incredible how much dust collected on the furniture. It may be Buenos Aires[5] is a clean city, but she owes it to her population and nothing else. There's too much dust in the air, the slightest breeze and it's back on the marble console tops and in the diamond patterns of the tooled-leather desk set. It's a lot of work to get it off with a feather duster; the motes[6] rise and hang in the air, and settle again a minute later on the pianos and the furniture.

I'll always have a clear memory of it because it happened so simply and without fuss. Irene was knitting in her bedroom, it was eight at night, and I suddenly decided to put the water up for *mate*.[7] I went down the corridor as far as the oak door, which was ajar, then turned into the hall toward the kitchen, when I heard something in the library or the dining room. The sound came through muted and indistinct, a chair being knocked over onto the carpet or the muffled buzzing of a conversation. At the same time, or a second later, I heard it at the end of the passage which led from those two rooms toward the door. I hurled myself against the door before it was too late and shut it, leaned on it with the weight of my body; luckily, the key was on our side; moreover, I ran the great bolt into place, just to be safe.

I went down to the kitchen, heated the kettle, and when I got back with the tray of *mate*, I told Irene:

---

5. **Buenos Aires** (bwā′ nəs er′ ēz): The capital of Argentina.
6. **motes:** Specks of dust or other tiny particles.
7. *mate* (mä′ tä′): A beverage made from the dried leaves of a South American evergreen tree.

"I had to shut the door to the passage. They've taken over the back part."

She let her knitting fall and looked at me with her tired, serious eyes.

"You're sure?"

I nodded.

"In that case," she said, picking up her needles again, "we'll have to live on this side."

I sipped at the *mate* very carefully, but she took her time starting her work again. I remember it was a gray vest she was knitting. I liked that vest.

The first few days were painful, since we'd both left so many things in the part that had been taken over. My collection of French literature, for example, was still in the library. Irene had left several folios of stationery and a pair of slippers that she used a lot in the winter. I missed my briar pipe, and Irene, I think, regretted the loss of an ancient bottle of Hesperidin.[8] It happened repeatedly (but only in the first few days) that we would close some drawer or cabinet and look at one another sadly.

"It's not here."

One thing more among the many lost on the other side of the house.

But there were advantages, too. The cleaning was so much simplified that, even when we got up late, nine-thirty for instance, by eleven we were sitting around with our arms folded. Irene got into the habit of coming to the kitchen with me to help get lunch. We thought about it and decided on this: while I prepared the lunch, Irene would cook up dishes that could be eaten cold in the evening. We were happy with the arrangement because it was always such a bother to have to leave our bedrooms in the evening and start to cook. Now we made do with the table in Irene's room and platters of cold supper.

Since it left her more time for knitting, Irene was content. I was a little lost without my books, but so as not to inflict myself on my sister, I set about reordering papa's stamp collection; that killed some time. We amused ourselves sufficiently, each

---

8. **Hesperidin** (hes per′ i din): A vitamin that comes from the rind of green citrus fruits and is used for various medicinal purposes.

Grammar in Action

Precise Language Writers choose their words carefully. They use precise language to make you hear, smell, taste, and see the things they are describing. An example follows of how a sentence can be improved by making the language precise.

VAGUE: As I walked through the house, I saw and heard some interesting things.

PRECISE: As I walked through the house, I saw the *ornately framed portraits of ancestors covering the vestibule walls* and heard the *scratchy notes of violin music playing on an old victrola.*

While the first sentence uses the vague adjective "interesting" and the general noun "things," the second sentence is concrete and specific.

Noises are important in "House Taken Over," and Cortázar is precise in his descriptions of sounds:

"Aside from our nocturnal rumblings, everything was quiet in the house. During the day there were the household sounds, the *metallic click of knitting needles,* the *rustle of stamp-album pages turning.*"

with his own thing, almost always getting together in Irene's bedroom, which was the more comfortable. Every once in a while, Irene might say:

"Look at this pattern I just figured out, doesn't it look like clover?"

After a bit it was I, pushing a small square of paper in front of her so that she could see the excellence of some stamp or another from Eupen-et-Malmédy.[9] We were fine, and little by little we stopped thinking. You can live without thinking.

(Whenever Irene talked in her sleep, I woke up immediately and stayed awake. I never could get used to this voice from a statue or a parrot, a voice that came out of the dreams, not from a throat. Irene said that in my sleep I flailed about enormously and shook the blankets off. We had the living room between us, but at night you could hear everything in the house. We heard each other breathing, coughing, could even feel each other reaching for the light switch when, as happened frequently, neither of us could fall asleep.

Aside from our nocturnal rumblings, everything was quiet in the house. During the day there were the household sounds, the metallic click of knitting needles, the rustle of stamp-album pages turning. The oak door was massive, I think I said that. In the kitchen or the bath, which adjoined the part that was taken over, we managed to talk loudly, or Irene sang lullabies. In a kitchen there's always too much noise, the plates and glasses, for there to be interruptions from other sounds. We seldom allowed ourselves silence there, but when we went back to our rooms or to the living room, then the house grew quiet, half-lit, we ended by stepping around more slowly so as not to disturb one another. I think it was because of this that I woke up irremediably[10] and at once when Irene began to talk in her sleep.)

Except for the consequences, it's nearly a matter of repeating the same scene over again. I was thirsty that night, and before we went to sleep, I

---

9. **Eupen-et-Malmédy** (yo͞o pen′ ā mäl mā dē′): Districts in eastern Belgium.
10. **irremediably** (ir′ ri mē′ de ə blē) *adv.*: In a way that cannot be helped or corrected.

STILL LIFE REVIVING, 1963
Remedios Varo
Beatriz Varo de Cano, Valencia, Spain

told Irene that I was going to the kitchen for a glass of water. From the door of the bedroom (she was knitting) I heard the noise in the kitchen; if not the kitchen, then the bath, the passage off at that angle dulled the sound. Irene noticed how brusquely I had paused, and came up beside me without a word. We stood listening to the noises, growing more and more sure that they were on our side of the oak door, if not the kitchen then

12 Discussion Have students discuss the implications of the narrator's statement, "You can live without thinking."

13 Discussion Ask students to consider the effect of this passage, coming as it does after the narrator's assurance that, "We were fine . . ."

14 Discussion Have students identify some of the descriptions of sounds in the story. Ask them how these descriptions help create suspense. You might also have them consider how the different types of noises relate to the balance between realistic and fantastic elements in the story.

Humanities Note

Fine art, *Still Life Reviving*, 1963, by Remedios Varo. The Spanish surrealist painter Remedios Varo (1909–1963) is one of the few female artists of her generation to achieve recognition. Her work was greatly influenced by the founding artists of the surrealist movement with whom she worked in Paris and Barcelona. The Spanish Civil War (1936–1939) caused her to flee her native country and settle in Mexico.

In *Still Life Reviving*, Varo uses the surrealist technique of removing objects from their usual context. Orbiting like planets above the table, the pieces of fruit seem to take part in a magical, if miniature, solar system. Startling and modern as this painting is, however, it testifies to Varo's attention to detail. She paints with the care of an old master.

You might want to use the following questions to discuss the art:

1. A still life is a painting of fruit or other objects on a table. Why did the painter call this work *Still Life Reviving*?

2. What precise words would you use to describe this painting to a friend who has not seen it?

3. How is this picture similar to and different from your image of the mysterious happening in "House Taken Over"?

4. Would you like to have this painting in your room? Explain.

Instead of merely saying "there were household sounds," he describes specific sounds. The concrete language he uses makes the scene vivid, while creating a feeling of tension, because these sounds are *too* ordinary. As we hear them, we half listen for the mysterious invaders.

Student Activity 1. Find additional passages in the story where Cortázar uses precise language to describe sounds or other sensations. Explain how this language contributes to the mood or atmosphere of the story.

Student Activity 2. Write a brief description of some of the sounds you hear when the lights are turned off late at night. Use concrete language to make your account as vivid as possible.

the bath, or in the hall itself at the turn, almost next to us.

We didn't wait to look at one another. I took Irene's arm and forced her to run with me to the wrought-iron door, not waiting to look back. You could hear the noises, still muffled but louder, just behind us. I slammed the grating and we stopped in the vestibule. Now there was nothing to be heard.

"They've taken over our section," Irene said. The knitting had reeled off from her hands and the yarn ran back toward the door and disappeared under it. When she saw that the balls of yarn were on the other side, she dropped the knitting without looking at it.

"Did you have time to bring anything?" I asked hopelessly.

"No, nothing."

We had what we had on. I remembered fifteen thousand pesos[11] in the wardrobe in my bedroom. Too late now.

I still had my wristwatch on and saw that it was 11 P.M. I took Irene around the waist (I think she was crying) and that was how we went into the street. Before we left, I felt terrible; I locked the front door up tight and tossed the key down the sewer. It wouldn't do to have some poor devil decide to go in and rob the house, at that hour and with the house taken over.

---

11. fifteen thousand pesos: A large sum of money at that time, equivalent to over a thousand dollars.

Reader's Response *Put yourself in the place of the narrator. Would you have acted as he did on hearing the mysterious noises? Why or why not?*

PRIMARY SOURCE

The critic Evelyn Picon Garfield tells how Cortázar's story "House Taken Over" began as a nightmare:

"He [Cortázar] had dreamt that he was alone in a house full of passageways when suddenly he heard a noise from the depths of the corridor. He had a sensation of nightmarish terror. After quickly closing the door and bolting it tight, for a few minutes he felt safe and thought that the nightmare would become a peaceful dream. All of a sudden the noise sounded on his side of the door. He woke up, and still in his pajamas, without taking time to brush his teeth or comb his hair, he sat down at the typewriter. In about an hour and a half 'House Taken Over' was written."

Primary Source Note

"House Taken Over" was not the only story that took Cortázar over.

. . . I see a man relatively happy and mundane, wrapped up in the same trivialities and dentists as any inhabitant of a great city, who reads the newspaper, falls in love and goes to the theater and who, all of a sudden, instantaneously, on a subway ride, in a cafe, in a dream, in the office while revising a suspicious looking translation about illiteracy in Tanzania, stops being man-and-his-circumstance and for no *reason* at all, without warning, without an epileptic air, without the contraction that precedes a bad headache, without anything that gives you time to grit your teeth and breathe deeply, *it is a short story*, a shapeless mass without words or faces or beginning or end but already a short story, something that can only be a short story and besides at once, immediately, Tanzania can go to Hell because this man will put a piece of paper in the typewriter and will start to write even though his bosses and the United Nations are breathing down his neck, even though his wife calls him because the soup is getting cold, even though great things are happening in the world and he ought to listen to the news on the radio or take a bath or telephone some friends.

THINKING ABOUT THE SELECTION

Interpreting

1. How does the narrator's description of the house reveal his personality?
2. (a) What inferences can you make about the narrator and his sister based on their daily routine? (b) What inferences can you make about them based on their reaction to the mysterious invasion of their house?
3. (a) How is the behavior they exhibit during sleep different from their normal behavior? (b) What does the difference indicate about their true reaction to the invasion of their house?
4. What details in the first part of the story foreshadow the mysterious noises? Explain.
5. Critics have interpreted the mysterious noises in several ways. Following are two interpretations, among others: (1) The noises are the symbol of a new generation replacing an old, aristocratic one; (2) they are symbolic of the mysterious forces that can attack the mind. Comment on these two interpretations.
6. In Edgar Allan Poe's "The Fall of the House of Usher," a house represents a family line, and the fall of the house represents the end of the line. (a) In what ways does the house in this story represent a family line? (b) How does the house itself prevent the brother and sister from continuing the family line into the future?
7. Express the theme, or central meaning, of this story. Explain how the plot and mood contribute to the theme.

Applying

8. Cortázar wrote this story after having a nightmare. (a) How does the story resemble a nightmare? (b) How might the act of writing help someone deal with fears?

ANALYZING LITERATURE

Understanding the Fantastic

In literature of **the fantastic,** writers use highly imaginative, sometimes dreamlike details alongside more realistic ones. The mysterious noises in "House Taken Over" are an example of a fantastic detail. They occur in a realistically described house with "a bath . . . kitchen . . . bedrooms and . . . hall."

Realistic and fantastic details do not simply coexist in this story, however. There is a changing balance between them. At first the story is an entirely realistic account. By the end, the element of fantasy has displaced ordinary reality, in the same way that the brother and sister are driven out of the house.

1. Find three brief passages that illustrate the changing balance of realistic and fantastic details in the story. Explain your choices.
2. How does the division of the house into a front and back section relate to the changing balance of reality and fantasy?

CRITICAL THINKING AND READING

Making Inferences About a Story

Fantastic tales often have gaps that more realistic stories do not. In fantastic literature, what is *not* said or explained can be more important than what is spelled out. Cortázar, for example, never tells us very much about the invaders of the house. They only amount to a series of noises. Also, the brother and sister seem to have an understanding from which the reader is excluded. When the narrator tells his sister, "They've taken over the back part," he never says who *they* are and, mysteriously, she never asks what he means.

1. To whom or what do you think the narrator is referring when he says *they*? Support your interpretation.
2. (a) Find other places in the story where Cortázar has created "holes," leaving out explanations or excluding the reader from a secret shared by the characters. (b) Explain what is left out from each passage you have chosen.
3. What is the effect of these "holes" on a reader?

THINKING AND WRITING

Writing a Fantastic Tale

Write a story like Cortázar's in which fantastic elements invade a realistic scene. Begin by choosing a setting for your tale. Make it as bland and ordinary as possible. Some possibilities are an office, a high school gymnasium, a supermarket, or a bank. Then decide on the element of fantasy you will introduce. Cortázar used an unexplained noise, but a strange odor might also be effective. As you write, remember to establish the realistic scene, as Cortázar does, before you inject an element of fantasy. In revising your story, make sure you have introduced the fantastic occurrence repeatedly, with greater emphasis each time. Also make sure you have not explained too much.

(continued from bottom of page)

orized that the story shows the narrator's ancestors punishing him for not marrying.

8. (a) As in many dreams, no reasons are given for what occurs, and the threat remains mysterious. (b) The act of writing can give form to fears and therefore make them more understandable and manageable.

ANSWERS TO ANALYZING LITERATURE

1. The first paragraph of the story contains only realistic details. The paragraph on page 1240 that begins, "I'll always . . . ," contains both realistic and fantastic details. While the noises are fantastic, the setting is realistic. At this stage, however, the fantastic can still be closed behind a door. The first paragraph on page 1242 illustrates the taking over of the house by mysterious noises.
2. The mysterious back section is the place where the noises originate. Eventually, however, the noises invade the rest of the house as well.

ANSWERS TO CRITICAL THINKING AND READING

1. Answers will differ. Possible responses are ancestral ghosts, irrational forces, or a new generation.
2. Suggested response: (a) When the narrator and his sister hear the noises a second time, they immediately leave the house. (b) The narrator never explains why he and his sister must leave the house or what they are fleeing.
3. Answers will differ. Some students may suggest that the lack of explanation makes the story more frightening.

THINKING AND WRITING

Writing Across the Curriculum
You may want to inform the music department that students are reading this selection. A music teacher can then help students choose an appropriate record to introduce and accompany a reading of the story. As a writing assignment, students can justify their choice.

Challenge Tell students that Cortázar was fascinated by the Greek myth about Theseus and the Minotaur. Have them read a version of this myth and then ask them to explain the symbolism of the ball of yarn in "House Taken Over."

Closure and Extension

ANSWERS TO THINKING ABOUT THE SELECTION

1. It shows his need to feel safe, comfortable, and secure.
2. (a) They are well-to-do, quiet, private, and somewhat dull followers of routine; the narrator is well-educated. (b) They share deep but unexpressed fears.
3. (a) During sleep they are much more agitated. (b) They are really quite disturbed about what is happening.
4. The calmness of the tone and the reference to an unused portion of the house foreshadow the noises.
5. Answers will differ. Those who favor the first interpretation may emphasize the social class of the narrator and his sister. Those who lean toward the second interpretation may view the story from a psychological perspective. Especially perceptive students may realize that the house could symbolize the mind.
6. (a) In the first paragraph, the narrator says that the house "kept the memories" of his family. (b) Their life in the house prevents them from marrying.
7. Answers will differ. Possible answers include the interpretations mentioned in question 5. Some critics have the-

OCTAVIO PAZ

1914–

Discussing the contrasts between Mexican and American culture, the Mexican poet Octavio Paz (ôk tä´ vyô päs) writes, "To us, 'valuable' is a synonym for 'enduring.' The pre-Columbian heritage accentuates this inclination: the pyramid is the very image of immutability. The polar opposites that exist between Americans and Mexicans are epitomized in our attitudes toward change. To us the secret lies not in getting ahead but in managing to stay where we already are. It is the opposition between the wind and the rock. . . . we instinctively relate the present to the past, whereas Americans relate it to the future."

Paz was born in a suburb of Mexico City and attended the National University of Mexico. If he compares the Mexican outlook to a rock, however, his own travels have taken him as far as the wind. Latin America has a tradition of bestowing diplomatic posts on its writers, and Paz joined the Mexican diplomatic corps in the 1930's. In 1945 this career enabled him to travel to France, where he served as the secretary to the Mexican Embassy in Paris. His exposure to French surrealism (see page 1249), a school of writing that stressed the irrational, unconscious elements of art, had a great effect on his own poetry. It encouraged him, for instance, to write freely and imaginatively, without worrying about logical meaning as in the poem "Salamander": "Salamander, you who lay dynamite in iron's / black and blue breast / you explode like a sun / you open yourself like a wound / you speak / as a fountain speaks."

Even as Paz traveled and learned about new directions in poetry, however, he neither forgot his Mexican heritage nor gave up his Mexican identity. If anything, his journeys only encouraged him to think more deeply about his country's rocklike "resistance to change." In 1950 he wrote a book about Mexico entitled *The Labyrinth of Solitude*, which one critic called "a Latin American classic." Paz also continued to write a great deal of poetry. By the time his book on Mexico came out, he had published several volumes of poems, including *Calamities and Miracles* (1947) and *Eagle or Sun?* (1950).

In 1951 Paz was given an important position in the Mexican Embassy in Japan, and from 1962 to 1968 he served as the Mexican ambassador to India. There he studied Buddhism (see page 164) and other Indian religions and philosophies. As always, his exposure to other cultures influenced his poetry. His long poem "Blanco" (1966) (blanco means "white" or "blank" in Spanish), for instance, is arranged like the sections of the sacred Indian diagram called a mandala.

Throughout the 1970's Paz taught at a number of American universities, including Harvard. He was also made an honorary member of the American Academy of Arts and Letters. In a recent book of essays, entitled *One Earth, Four or Five Worlds* (1985), he analyzes the complex relationship between the United States and Mexico. Of his own experience as a visitor to America he writes, "For a Mexican, to travel through the United States is to enter the giant's castle and visit its chambers of horrors and marvels. But there is one difference: the ogre's castle leaves us wonderstruck by its archaism, the United States by its novelty."

Paz has received many international awards, including the Nobel Prize for Literature (1990). He is universally acknowledged as a writer of world-class stature.

In the following poems, he uses language with a childlike playfulness and freshness.

Objectives

Thematic
To understand how poetry says many things with few words

Skills
1 To appreciate poetic language
2 To write about paradox

GUIDE FOR INTERPRETING

Poet's Epitaph; Fable; Concord

Commentary

The Language of Poetry. In "Ode on a Grecian Urn," John Keats wrote that a work of art can "tease us out of thought." Poetry is filled with such teasing. Its playful language, alive with reversals and figures of speech, startles us out of our typical responses.

One device that poets use to tease us out of common sense and logic is **paradox,** or apparent contradiction. When we think in our customary way, winter is cold and summer is hot, love is love and hate is hate—opposites stay in their separate categories. Poets, however, know that in our illogical lives opposites mix and mingle. The Italian poet Petrarch (page 674), for example, conveys this truth by describing his feelings with paradoxical phrases like "sweet despair."

Personification—the description of nonhuman things as if they were human—is another device that can startle us into fresh perception. When Wordsworth says that the Thames "glideth at his own sweet will," we experience the river as a fellow being rather than a meaningless collection of countless waterdrops. Children see the world in this vivid fashion. For them the sun and moon, trees and grass, insects and flowers are all companions. We tend to lose this vision as we grow older and learn to label and divide the world into its separate parts. By means of personification, poets can tease us back into childlike ways of seeing and feeling.

In the three poems that follow, Octavio Paz plays with language in the hope that we, too, will join in the game. He invites us to put aside our ideas of what is reasonable and proper and see the world upside down, inside out, and totally transformed.

Writing

Poets are not the only ones who use language playfully. In our relaxed moments, all of us tease and surprise one another with words. In your journal write about a time when you or one of your friends used language in such a way. How did these words—whether a nickname, a figure of speech, or a clever phrase—make you see the world differently?

Literary Focus Write the following oxymorons on the chalkboard: *thunderous silence, tender hatred, sweet despair.* Tell students that these phrases are oxymorons, combinations of opposite or contradictory ideas. Have students explain what each of these phrases means and imagine a situation to which it might apply. Then tell them that poets use this type of paradox and other figures of speech to convey a great deal of meaning in a few words.

Writing Divide the class into small groups. Before students begin writing, have them discuss with other group members the phrase, nickname, or figure of speech they will use for the assignment.

ESL Teaching Strategy Have ESL students share with the class a clever use of words in their language. If there are Spanish ESL students in your class, have them read to the class the Spanish originals of these three poems.

Teaching Tenth-Grade Students For tenth-grade students, compare Paz's three poems to riddles. Point out to them that "Poet's Epitaph" and "Concord" are based on reversals of usual meanings or perceptions. Tell them that "Fable" describes a certain time of life and ask them to guess what this time is, based on evidence in the poem.

Support Material

Teaching Portfolio
Teacher Backup, p. 1493
Usage and Mechanics Worksheet, p. 1497
Analyzing Literature Worksheet, *Appreciating Poetic Language*, p. 1498
Critical Thinking and Reading

Worksheet, *Reading and Responding to Poetry*, p. 1499
Language Worksheet, *Recognizing Prepositions and Adverbs*, p. 1500
Selection Test, pp. 1501–1502

Poet's Epitaph

Octavio Paz

translated by Muriel Rukeyser

He tried to sing, singing
not to remember
his true life of lies
and to remember
5 his lying life of truths.

Concord

Octavio Paz

translated by Eliot Weinberger

Water above
Grove below
Wind on the roads

Quiet well
5 Bucket's black   Spring water

Water coming down to the trees
  Sky rising to the lips

For Carlos Fuentes

Fable

Octavio Paz

translated by Eliot Weinberger

Ages of fire and of air
Youth of water
From green to yellow
              From yellow to red
From dream to watching
              From desire to act
5 It was only one step and you took it so lightly
Insects were living jewels
The heat rested by the side of the pond
Rain was a willow with unpinned hair
A tree grew in the palm of your hand
10 And that tree laughed sang prophesied
Its divinations filled the air with wings
There were simple miracles called birds
Everything was for everyone
              Everyone was everything
There was only one huge word with no back to it
15 A word like a sun
One day it broke into tiny pieces
They were the words of the language we now speak
Pieces that will never come together
Broken mirrors where the world sees itself shattered

Reader's Response *Which of these poems did you find most surprising? Why?*

---

a dream? Explain.

Humanities Note

Fine art, *The Torment of the Poet* by Giorgio de Chirico (1888–1978). Although he painted for most of his long life, de Chirico (de kē´ rē kô) is most famous for a series of pictures he did in the early twentieth century. These paintings, of which *The Torment of the Poet* is one, are often associated with the work of the Surrealists (for more on Surrealism, see page 1249). Like the Surrealists, de Chirico presents strange dreamlike images; he takes objects out of their normal contexts and combines them in unusual ways. Often these objects are the classical statues and buildings he observed during his childhood in Greece (although Ital-

THE TORMENT OF THE POET
Giorgio de Chirico
Yale University Art Gallery

THINKING ABOUT THE SELECTION

Interpreting

1. An epitaph is a short poem in tribute to someone who has died. Is "Poet's Epitaph" a good title for Paz's poem? Why or why not?
2. What does Paz mean when he says, in "Fable," "Everything was for everyone/Everyone was everything"?
3. (a) How would you describe the state of mind that Paz depicts in the first fifteen lines of "Fable"? (b) Is this state of mind associated with childhood? Why or why not?
4. (a) What is the "step" taken in the fifth line of "Fable"? (b) What is the nature of the change described in the last four lines?
5. A fable is "a fictitious story meant to teach a moral lesson, a myth or legend, or a false story." Which of these three definitions is most appropriate for the poem "Fable"? Explain.

6. *Concord* means "harmony or agreement." How does the poem "Concord" express such harmony?
7. How do both "Fable" and "Concord" show the search for—in the words of one critic—"a lost sense of unity"?

Applying

8. Why would a poet want to forget "his true life of lies"?
9. Tell about a time when the world seemed vivid and whole to you, as Paz describes it in "Fable."

ANALYZING LITERATURE

Appreciating Poetic Language

Poets often use language playfully to tease us out of our usual mode of seeing and feeling. By means of paradox, for instance, they express ideas that seem to be contradictory. In order to resolve the apparent contradiction, we must think and feel in unaccustomed ways. The paradoxical statements in "Poet's Epitaph"—"true life of lies" and "lying life of truths"—challenge us to move beyond the conventional definitions of lie and truth. Personification, or giving human qualities to non-human things, can also surprise us into new perceptions. In "Fable," for example, Paz says that a tree "laughed sang prophesied."

1. In "Poet's Epitaph," Paz says that the artist's "true life" consists of "lies." (a) What is his "true life," and why is it made up of "lies"? (b) What is his "lying life," and why does it consist of "truths"?
2. (a) In "Fable" Paz personifies a tree. To what is Paz comparing the tree's "divinations," or prophecies? (b) How might Paz's use of personification affect the way in which a reader sees the world?
3. (a) Identify two other personifications in "Fable." (b) Explain how they contribute to the state of mind Paz is describing.

THINKING AND WRITING

Writing About Paradox

A Chinese philosopher called paradox "the truest sayings." Create your own paradox and then explain it to an audience of your classmates. First write a statement containing two seemingly contradictory thoughts that work together to reveal a truth about life. For example, you might write that sorrow is sweet or that in weakness there is strength. Then write an essay explaining the truth of your paradox. When you revise, make sure your reasoning will be clear to your classmates. Finally, proofread your essay and prepare a final draft.

(continued from bottom of page)

3. (a) Answers will differ. Students may respond that it is a state of mind in which all things seem related and have a magical quality. (b) Answers will differ. Students may respond that this state of mind is associated with childhood, when the world seems more vibrant and miraculous.
4. (a) The step from desiring something to acting on that desire. (b) With the use of language and names, the world seems divided and not unified.
5. Answers will differ. Students may respond that Paz is creating a myth to describe a sense of unity with the world that many people no longer feel.
6. Answers will differ. Students may indicate that the poem evokes a peaceful mood. Perceptive students may note that in the final act of drinking, heaven and earth are harmonized.
7. Answers will differ. Students may respond as follows: "Fable" portrays an imagined time of unity, before the use of langue fragmented the world. "Concord" portrays a moment of peace, in which sky and earth are unified in someone's act of drinking well water.
8. Answers will differ. Some students may feel that the poet wants to escape the everyday world and enter an imaginary world like that portrayed in "Fable."
9. Answers will differ. Students may respond with descriptions of childhood memories or of moments of special clarity.

ANSWERS TO ANALYZING LITERATURE

1. (a) His "true life" is his everyday life. It is made up of "lies" because it does not seem vivid and whole. (b) His "lying life" is the world he creates in his poems. It consists of "truths" because it is true to his emotions.
2. (a) He compares "Its divinations" to birds. (b) Answers will differ. Students may respond that it might help readers see the world more vividly.
3. (a) Line 7 personifies the heat, and in line 8 the willow is personified as a woman. (b) Answers will differ. Students may respond that seeing objects as people makes the world seem more alive.

THINKING AND WRITING

Publishing Student Writing Have students show their essay to a parent or an adult they know.

---

ian, he was raised in Greece). The overall effect of these pictures is a sense of haunting loneliness and disquietude.

In *The Torment of the Poet*, de Chirico strangely combines a classical facade; an armless, togaed statue; a coil; a ball; a bird; and what appears to be a flowerpot.

You might want to use the fol-

lowing questions to discuss the art:
1. How is this picture like the image from a dream?
2. What mood does the picture call up in you?
3. How does the title relate to the picture?

Closure and Extension

ANSWERS TO THINKING ABOUT THE SELECTION

1. Answers will differ. Students may say it is good because it sums up a poet's life.
2. Answers will differ. Students may indicate he means that people enjoyed things together and felt a sense of unity.

PABLO NERUDA

1904–1973

More About the Author When Neruda was only twenty-three, he was sent as a diplomat to Asia. While serving in Burma, Siam, China, Japan, and India during the next five years, he was often extremely lonely. That loneliness emerges in many of the poems he wrote at the time. For example, his poem "Funeral in the East" reflects in its opening lines a sense of being alone in a foreign place: "I work at night, the city all around me, / fishermen, and potters, and corpses that are burned / with saffron and fruit, rolled in scarlet muslin. . . ."

Critical Evaluation The American poet Robert Bly ranks Neruda extremely high:

The fifty-six poems in *Residencia I* and *II* were written over a period of ten years . . . , and they are the greatest surrealist poems yet written in a Western language. French surrealist poems appear drab and squeaky beside them. Aragon and Breton are poets of reason, who occasionally throw themselves backward into the unconscious, but Neruda, like a deep-sea crab, all claws and shell, is able to breathe in the heavy substances that lie beneath the daylight consciousness. He stays on the bottom for hours, and moves around calmly and without hysteria.

Cultural Note Neruda was influenced by the work of Walt Whitman. He once commented on Whitman's influence as follows:

Poetry in South America is a different matter altogether [from poetry in Spain]. You see there are in our countries rivers which have no names, trees which nobody knows, and birds which nobody has described. It is easier for us to be surrealistic because everything we know is new. Our duty, then, as we understand it, is to express what is unheard of. Everything has been painted in Europe, everything has been sung in Europe. But not in America. In that sense, Whitman was a great teacher. Because what is Whitman? He was not only intensely conscious, but he was open-eyed! He had tremendous eyes to see everything—he taught us to see things. He was our poet.

The Chilean poet Pablo Neruda (pä′blŏ ne rōō′thä) drew the inspiration for some of his best poems from objects that others hardly gave a glance:

It is well, at certain hours of the day and night, to look closely at the world of objects at rest. Wheels that have crossed long, dusty distances with their mineral and vegetable burdens, sacks from coalbins, barrels and baskets. . . . From them flow the contacts of the man with the earth. . . .

Neruda was born in Parral, Chile, the son of a railway worker. His original name was Neftali Ricardo Reyes; however, he changed it to Pablo Neruda when, as a young man, he began to publish poetry. He was afraid that if the poems appeared under his real name, his father would be offended.

When Neruda was twenty, his book *Twenty Love Poems and a Desperate Song* earned him recognition as one of Chile's best young poets. Because the Chilean government liked to send its promising young poets abroad, Neruda was given various diplomatic positions. For the next twelve years, he lived and traveled extensively in Europe and Asia. When he was assigned to Madrid in 1934, he was acclaimed by some of Spain's best poets and came into closer contact with surrealism, one of Europe's latest literary trends. (This movement stressed the irrational side of human nature; for more about it, see page 1249.) His own work, however, had already taken a more surrealistic turn in *Residence on Earth and Other Poems* (1933).

Not only did his experience in Spain affect his writing, but it caused him to move leftward politically. The Spanish Civil War (1936–1939) was a struggle between the elected, socialist government and the right-wing forces, backed by Hitler, that wanted to topple it. Neruda supported the government. He also supported Stalin's regime in Russia. We may find this decision puzzling today, but we should remember that Russia was one of the few countries to combat Hitler in Spain. Also, Russia was a major ally of the United States during the Second World War.

After Neruda returned to Chile in the middle of that war, he participated in Chilean politics and became a member of the Communist party. From 1948 to 1952, he had to leave his country to escape persecution by its right-wing government.

Much of Neruda's later work expresses political sentiments; however, he never lost his sense of poetry's irrational magic, and even his political opponents conceded his great talent. In 1971 he received the Nobel Prize for Literature.

During the period 1970–1973, he served as Chile's ambassador to France. That was the era when the Chilean president Salvador Allende was administering the first freely elected Marxist government in the Western Hemisphere. By a tragic irony, Neruda died in Chile just as Allende was overthrown in a bloody coup.

The two poems that follow, which were published in *Elementary Odes* (1954), illustrate his affection for common objects and his ability to view them in startling ways.

Objectives

Thematic

To understand how poets can free their imagination from the bonds of rationality

Skills

1 To understand Surrealism
2 To write a surrealistic ode

GUIDE FOR INTERPRETING

Ode to My Socks

Commentary

Surrealism. Surrealism, which means "beyond realism," is an artistic movement that emphasizes the irrational side of human nature. It goes beyond a realistic depiction of the world to portray the vivid, imaginative associations of the unconscious mind. Originating in France just after World War I, it was a protest against the so-called rationalism that led the world into a destructive war.

Surrealist writers like André Breton and Louis Aragon invented techniques to loosen their imaginations and free their minds from the bonds of logic. For instance, they would go on long walks to lull themselves into a hypnotic state. Then, without censoring their thoughts, they would produce long riffs of startling images.

Often these images had the haunting power of things that are seen in dreams. Like dream-images they would combine ordinary objects in striking new ways—a sewing machine might click away on an operating table or a single eye might stare from the cover of a book.

Surrealist painters used similar techniques to shock viewers out of their normal ways of seeing. In *The Song of Love* (see page 1215), for instance, Giorgio de Chirico placed a rubber glove beside the head of Alexander the Great. If the audience was disconcerted, so much the better. Art was intended not for the rational mind but for a deeper part of the self, the mysterious region where dreams and fantasies arise.

Although Surrealism started in France, it was adopted with enthusiasm by Latin American poets like Pablo Neruda. In the following poem, Neruda does not take you into an irrational, totally unfamiliar world. The subject of the poem, a pair of socks, is always in focus; however, Neruda uses wild, surrealistic figures of speech to color your perceptions.

Writing

Think about a common object that has given you pleasure and write about it very quickly for five minutes. Don't hesitate to put down the most ridiculous, extravagant thoughts that occur to you. Do not censor yourself. Write quickly and let your imagination wander, even if what you put down seems awkward or silly. When you have finished, see whether anything you have written tickles your fancy. Do certain phrases or images tantalize you with a meaning that you cannot quite explain?

Literary Focus Have students describe the strangest dreams they have ever had. Then tell them that the artistic movement they will be reading about, surrealism, emphasized the importance of dream images in art.

Writing/Prior Knowledge To help overcome students' inhibitions, tell them that you will do this assignment yourself and will share with them what you have written.

ESL Teaching Strategy If you have Spanish-speaking ESL students, arrange for them to read the original version of this poem aloud to the class. Ask non-Spanish ESL students to share with the class surrealistic or fantastic works of literature from their cultures.

Teaching Tenth-Grade Students Tenth-grade students should not have a problem with the language of this poem. Point out to them the vein of extravagant humor in this poem and encourage them to enjoy the humor.

Master Teacher Note To get students into the spirit of this poem, you may want to show them a series of surrealistic paintings. The following paintings from this book might serve the purpose: *The Song of Love*, by Giorgio de Chirico, page 1215; *La Nuit*, by Rene Magritte, page 1239; *Still Life Reviving*, by Remedios Varo, page 1241; and *The Torment of the Poet*, by Giorgio de Chirico, page 1247. Have students try to identify the qualities that make each of these works surreal.

Vocabulary

Preteach the following vocabulary words:
decrepit (dē krep´ it) *adj.*:
    Broken down
nevertheless (nev´ ər thə
    les´) *adv.*: However
texts (teksts) *n.*: Books
impulse (im´ puls´) *n.*: Urge
spit (spit) *n.*: A thin rod for
    roasting meat
remorse (ri môrs´) *n.*: Guilt
    felt over a wrong
moral (môr´ əl) *n.*: Lesson
    taught by a fable

Support Material

Teaching Portfolio
Teacher Backup, p. 1503
Usage and Mechanics Worksheet, p. 1507
Vocabulary Check, p. 1508
Analyzing Literature Worksheet, *Understanding Surrealism*, p. 1509
Critical Thinking and Reading Work-
sheet, *Learning to Interpret*, p. 1510
Selection Test, pp. 1511–1512

Ode to My Socks

Pablo Neruda

translated by Robert Bly

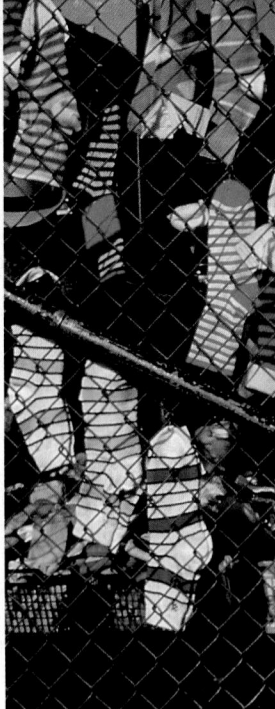

SOCKS DISPLAYED ON A FENCE
Albert Normandin

Maru Mori brought me
a pair
of socks
which she knitted herself
5 with her sheepherder's hands,
two socks as soft
as rabbits.
I slipped my feet
into them
10 as though into
two
cases
knitted
with threads of
15 twilight
and goatskin.
Violent socks,
my feet were
two fish made
20 of wool,
two long sharks
sea-blue, shot
through
by one golden thread,
25 two immense blackbirds,
two cannons:
my feet
were honored
in this way
30 by
these
heavenly
socks.
They were
35 so handsome
for the first time
my feet seemed to me

unacceptable
like two decrepit
40 firemen, firemen
unworthy
of that woven
fire,
of those glowing
45 socks.

Nevertheless
I resisted
the sharp temptation
to save them somewhere
50 as schoolboys
keep
fireflies,
as learned men
collect
55 sacred texts,
I resisted
the mad impulse
to put them
into a golden
60 cage
and each day give them
birdseed
and pieces of pink melon.
Like explorers
65 in the jungle who hand
over the very rare
green deer
to the spit
and eat it
70 with remorse,
I stretched out
my feet
and pulled on

the magnificent
socks
and then my shoes.

The <u>moral</u>
of my ode is this:
beauty is twice
beauty
and what is good is doubly
good
when it is a matter of two socks
made of wool
in winter.

Reader's Response *What everyday objects have delighted you as much as the socks delighted Neruda?*

(continued from bottom of page)

THINKING ABOUT THE SELECTION

Interpreting

1. This poem is not simply a description of a pair of socks; it contains a little story as well. (a) What dilemma does the poet face in the course of this story? (b) How does he resolve it?
2. (a) What is the tone of this poem? (b) How does the tone affect your attitude toward the poet's dilemma?
3. In what way is the poet like the explorers mentioned in line 64?
4. (a) How is the poet's action at the end of the poem related to the moral? (b) What does the poem's moral say about the relationship between beauty and usefulness?

Applying

5. Have you ever felt that something you owned was too good to use? Explain how you resolved the problem.

ANALYZING LITERATURE

Understanding Surrealism

Surrealism is an artistic movement that concerns itself with the mysterious, nighttime portion of the mind rather than the daylight self. This irrational side has its own kind of emotional, imaginative logic that differs from rational thinking. In a dream, for instance, a person who seems cold and remote to us may appear as part-human and part-machine. Neruda uses such dreamlike, emotional associations in figures of speech. In lines 56–63, he compares the socks to exotic birds fed with "birdseed / and pieces of pink melon."

1. Explain the emotional or imaginative sense behind this comparison.
2. (a) To what does Neruda compare his own feet in lines 19–26? (b) Is there a kind of irrational, dreamlike logic to these surprising comparisons? Explain.

THINKING AND WRITING

Writing a Surrealistic Ode

Compose a surrealistic ode in the style of Pablo Neruda. Choose phrases and images for your ode. Write from your heart and imagination, not from your rational mind. Try to convey to readers the delight that the object inspires in you. As you revise your ode, make sure readers will understand what you are praising. However, discard adjectives and figures of speech that fail to describe the object in a strange or unusual way.

(continued from bottom of page)
ANSWERS TO ANALYZING LITERATURE

1. Answers will differ. Students may respond that like exotic birds, the socks are beautiful and rare objects. Just as such birds are kept for their beauty and not used, the poet wants to keep his socks for their beauty and not use them.
2. (a) He compares them to fish, sharks, blackbirds, and cannons. (b) Answers will differ. Students may indicate that his stockinged feet have the same general shape as these objects. The color of the sharks may have been suggested by the color of the socks. Perceptive students may notice that the "Violent" color of the socks suggests, in a dreamlike way, images of violence and aggression for his feet. Sharks, cannons, and blackbirds all have a predatory quality.

THINKING AND WRITING

Publishing Student Writing Ask students to recite their odes to the class. Have artistically talented students illustrate these odes in a surrealistic fashion. Post the odes and the illustrations on the class bulletin board.

Challenge Go on a long walk as surrealists like Breton and Aragon did. Carry a paper and pencil and jot down whatever thoughts occur to you, without trying to make sense of them.

Closure and Extension

ANSWERS TO THINKING ABOUT THE SELECTION

1. (a) The socks were so fine that they made his feet seem unworthy and he was tempted to save the socks and not use them. (b) He decides to use the socks.
2. (a) Answers will differ. Most students will respond that the poem is humorous and exuberant in tone. (b) Answers will differ. Students will probably respond that the tone signals readers that the dilemma is to be taken in a spirit of fun.
3. As the explorers reluctantly "use" a rare and beautiful animal by killing and eating it, the poet reluctantly wears his beautiful socks.
4. (a) The poet decides to use the socks and the moral justifies this choice. (b) The poem's moral says that a beautiful object that can be put to use is twice beautiful.
5. Answers will differ. However, students should include a description of their problem and its resolution.

DEREK WALCOTT

1930–

As a Caribbean islander, Derek Walcott (wôl´ kut) has experienced a sense of cultural division. On the one hand, he owes allegiance to the rich native traditions of the Caribbean islands, traditions that can often be traced back to African sources. He is also attracted to Western traditions that go back to ancient Greece. However, his love of European culture presents a problem, because Europeans dominated the Caribbean region and mistreated the natives. Walcott expresses the confusion that can result from his mixed loyalties in the poem "A Far Cry from Africa." The speaker in this poem uses Africa, rather than the Caribbean, as his reference point, but his dilemma is similar to Walcott's: "Where shall I turn, divided to the vein?/ I who have cursed/the drunken officer of British rule, how choose/Between this Africa and the English tongue I love?/Betray them both, or give back what they give?"

Walcott was born on St. Lucia, a West Indian island. His racial and ethnic background is mixed, and he grew up speaking both the dialect of the island and English. He was educated at St. Mary's College, St. Lucia, and the University of the West Indies, Kingston, Jamaica.

An early starter, he published his first book, *Twenty-Five Poems,* in 1948. By the time he was thirty, he had published three additional volumes of poetry.

Walcott's poetry and plays reflect both the Caribbean and European traditions; however, his poems tend to be influenced more by Western culture, while his plays are steeped in Caribbean folklore. The expressive power of his poetry led one critic to praise his "old-fashioned love of eloquence." She favorably contrasted his "dense and elaborate" style with the "minimalist," or pared down, style of many poets writing today. Ironically, Walcott may have such a keen appreciation for the eloquence and music of English because he learned it as a second language.

In addition to being a poet, Walcott has distinguished himself as a director and playwright. He was, for instance, the founding director of the Trinidad Theatre Workshop (1959), which staged a number of his plays. In these dramas he explores his Caribbean roots more deeply than he does in his poetry. The most famous of them is *Dream on Monkey Mountain,* a play that won an Obie award (1971) when it was produced in New York. Set in the back country of a Caribbean island, it portrays a world in which superstition and myth are the dominant forces. The play suggests that such a folk tradition has more validity for Caribbeans than a colonial, European culture imposed on them by force.

Dividing his year between Trinidad and Massachusetts, Walcott is just as familiar with the United States as he is with his native Caribbean. In a recent book of poetry, *The Arkansas Testament* (1987), he focuses on the American South. He has taught at a number of American colleges, and he currently teaches creative writing at Boston University.

In 1992 Walcott received the Nobel Prize for Literature in recognition for his achievements as a poet and playwright.

The following poems show the richness of Walcott's language and illustrate his sense of dual cultural citizenship: Caribbean and European.

GUIDE FOR INTERPRETING

Commentary

Sea Grapes; *from* Omeros

Theme and Allusion. Poetry does more than entertain. The best poems offer us a way of looking at life that we may not have thought of before, a fresh way of evaluating our experiences. That central insight of a poem—or any work of art—is called its **theme.**

Sometimes a poet directly states the theme. In "Archaic Torso of Apollo," for instance, Rainer Maria Rilke announces the theme in the poem's final line: "You must change your life." Rilke is saying that a work of art as powerful as the ancient Greek statue he is describing can inspire people to change the way in which they live. Often, however, a poet will suggest a theme without stating it directly. When a theme is unstated, readers become aware of it through the accumulated meaning of the poem. Readers can identify an unstated theme by asking what idea about life the writer is expressing.

Poets and other writers often use **allusions**, references to other works of literature or to well-known people or events, to help convey their themes. The advantage of an allusion is that it briefly expresses the whole range of feelings and ideas associated with the work, event, or historical figure being referred to. An allusion will only be successful, however, if readers understand the reference and the way in which it supports the writer's theme.

The following two poems by Derek Walcott refer to Odysseus, the Greek hero in Homer's epic poem the *Odyssey*. The first is a brief lyric, "Sea Grapes." The other is an excerpt from Walcott's book-length poem *Omeros,* which contains many references to the *Odyssey* and to the other epic poem by Homer, the *Iliad*. (*Omeros* is the Greek form of Homer's name.) In "Sea Grapes" Walcott alludes to Odysseus' long and eventful journey home after the Trojan War. This journey established Odysseus as a symbol of *both* fidelity and adventure; he persisted in his efforts to return to his wife and son but he also became involved with other women and goddesses on the way. As you read "Sea Grapes," look for Walcott's statement of the theme and the allusions to Odysseus' journey that support the theme.

In the excerpt from *Omeros*, Walcott alludes to Odysseus' descent to the underworld to receive guidance from the prophet Tiresias. (He may also be alluding to Dante's journey through the underworld in the *Inferno*.) Walcott, however, encounters not a prophet but the ghost of his own father, the speaker as the poem begins. Walcott's father describes his life and the conditions on St. Lucia, where father and son lived. He also gives his son a goal to strive for in his writing, and that goal is one of the main themes of *Omeros*.

Writing

Briefly describe an encounter that inspired you to strive for a goal. It may have been a meeting with a person, a trip to a special place, or even a film that you saw.

Literary Focus Help students to distinguish between the theme and the subject of a work by having them discuss their favorite films. First have them briefly summarize the plot; then ask them to formulate the central idea of the film.

Familiarize them with allusions by having them identify and explain allusions in the lyrics of popular songs.

Writing/Prior Knowledge Pair up students in your class. Before they begin writing, have them describe their inspirational encounters to their partners.

ESL Teaching Strategy Have ESL students share with the class examples of historical figures or events that could serve as readily understandable allusions in their culture.

Teaching Tenth-Grade Students You may want to briefly summarize for tenth-grade students the events described in the *Iliad* and the *Odyssey*.

Vocabulary

Preteach the following vocabulary words:

schooner (skōōn´ ər) *n*.: Ship with two or more masts

trough (trôf) *n*.: Hollow between waves

console (kən sol´) *v*.: Comfort

askew (ə skyōō´) *adj*.: Off to one side; crooked

indignation (in´ dig nā´ shən) *n*.: Anger at injustice

preening (prēn´ iŋ) *v*.: Showing satisfaction with oneself

emblem (em´ bləm) *n*.: A visible symbol

immaculate (im mak´ yōō lit) *adj*.: Pure

palpable (pal´ pə bəl) *adj*.: Capable of being touched or felt

extinction (ek stiŋk´ shən) *n*.: Nonexistence; nothingness

pittances (pit´ 'n səz) *n*.: Small amounts of money

Support Material
Teacher Backup, p. 1513
Usage and Mechanics Worksheet, p. 1517
Vocabulary Check, p. 1518
Analyzing Literature Worksheet, *Understanding Theme*, p. 1519
Language Worksheet, *Utilizing Etymology*, p. 1520
Selection Test, pp. 1521–1522

Spelling Tip Write the word *trough* on the chalkboard and point out to students that it is spelled with an *ou*, even though the vowel sounds like the *o* in *off*.

Sea Grapes

Derek Walcott

1 That sail which leans on light,
    tired of islands,
    a schooner beating up the Caribbean

    for home, could be Odysseus,
5   home-bound on the Aegean;[1]
    that father and husband's

2 longing, under gnarled sour grapes, is
    like the adulterer hearing Nausicaa's[2] name
    in every gull's outcry.

10 This brings nobody peace. The ancient war
    between obsession[3] and responsibility
    will never finish and has been the same

    for the sea-wanderer or the one on shore
    now wriggling on his sandals to walk home,
15 since Troy[4] sighed its last flame,

    and the blind giant's boulder[5] heaved the trough
    from whose ground-swell the great hexameters[6]
       come
    to the conclusions of exhausted surf.

    The classics can console. But not enough.

---

1. **Odysseus** (ō dis′ yōōs), . . . **Aegean** (ē jē′ ən): Odysseus is the Greek hero whose ten-year voyage home from the Trojan War is described by Homer in the *Odyssey*. The Aegean is the sea, between Greece and Turkey, on which he voyaged.
2. **Nausicaa's** (nô sik′ ā əz) *n*.: Nausicaa was a beautiful young woman who helped Odysseus when he was shipwrecked. The "adulterer" referred to is Odysseus himself.

3. **obsession** (əb sesh′ ən) *n*.: A persistent idea or desire that cannot be gotten rid of by reasoning.
4. **Troy:** The city in Asia Minor that Odysseus and his fellow Greeks conquered.
5. **blind giant's boulder:** In the *Odyssey*, the blind giant Polyphemus hurls a boulder at Odysseus' ship.
6. **hexameters** (heks am′ ə tərz): The meter in which Homer's *Iliad* and *Odyssey* were composed.

Reader's Response *Which would you rather be, a "sea-wanderer or the one on shore"? Explain.*

Humanities Note

Fine art, *Palm Tree, Nassau, 1898* by Winslow Homer. Many critics regard Winslow Homer (1836–1910) as the finest American artist of the nineteenth century. His pictures—Homer did many delicate watercolors like this one, as well as oil paintings—often portray the power of wind and waves. Sometimes they depict people struggling against the forces of nature, and sometimes they show wind and waves alone.

Homer began his career as an illustrator. During the Civil War he made sketches of life at the front for *Harper's* magazine. Eventually he became a full-time artist. He visited Nassau, the capital of the Bahamas, in 1884 and again in 1898 when he painted this picture.

Palm Tree, Nassau, 1898, like many of Homer's Caribbean watercolors, conveys the brightness of tropical light. It also reflects Homer's study of Japanese woodcuts, with their simplicity and asymmetrical composition. Notice, for example, the deliberately asymmetrical placement of the palm tree in the foreground. If it were placed in the center, the composition would have less tension and consequently less interest.

You might want to use the following questions to discuss the art:

1. How does Homer show the presence of the invisible wind?
2. How does he indicate the force of the waves?
3. The palm tree in the foreground is not at the exact center of the picture. What is the effect of this off-center placement of the tree?
4. Homer chose to show only a few details in this picture. What is the effect of this choice?
5. How would you depict a tropical island?

Presentation

Motivation/Prior Knowledge
Have students discuss different versions and interpretations of a given story. For example, they might enjoy comparing and contrasting different film versions of the Dracula story. Ask them why directors are continually remaking this story and changing various details in it. Then explain that, from the time of the ancient Greeks until the present, writers and painters have been reinterpreting the *Odyssey*.

Purpose-Setting Question Why do you think the *Odyssey* has fascinated writers and visual artists for thousands of years?

Master Teacher Note Call students' attention to other modern interpretations of the *Odyssey*, such as "Siren Song" by Margaret Atwood and "Ithaca" by Constantine Cavafy. Ask volunteers to read these poems aloud; then have the class compare and contrast them with Walcott's "Sea Grapes."

Humanities Note

Fine art, *The Return of Ulysses,* by Romare Bearden. African American artist Romare Bearden (1914–1988) studied art at the Art Students League in New York City and continued his education at the Sorbonne in Paris. In forming his own distinctive style, Bearden was influenced by such modernist techniques as collage and the use of bold colors. He was also influenced by his travels through Europe and North Africa.

Bearden was fascinated by the works of the Greek poet Homer and produced numerous paintings based on these epic tales. One such painting is *The Return of Ulysses,* rendered in tempera (opaque watercolor). In this work he uses bright, flat painted areas to create an abstract interpretation of Ulysses' reunion with his wife, Penelope. The simplicity of Bearden's approach and his use of blacks in nontraditional roles give an expressive impact to this image.

You might want to use the following questions to discuss the art:

COMMENTARY: Retelling the *Odyssey*

Like Derek Walcott, many writers and visual artists have been inspired by Homer's poem the *Odyssey*. With its account of a hero's long, eventful journey home after a war, this epic tale has universal appeal.

As often occurs, however, writers have been tempted to rewrite this story of survival and homecoming or at least to give it their own personal interpretation. The medieval Italian poet Dante, for instance, places Odysseus (or Ulysses, as he called him) in hell as a punishment for his deceit. In contrast, however, the nineteenth-century British poet Alfred, Lord Tennyson praises Ulysses for his indomitable will. Tennyson has him set off once again, this time as an old man, spurning the comforts of home for new adventures: "To sail beyond the sunset, and the baths/Of all the western stars, until I die."

Modern Greek Versions Modern Greek writers have been especially eager to reinterpret one of their nation's great epics. Nikos Kazantzakis, a poet and novelist, wrote a long poem titled *The Odyssey: A Modern Sequel* (1938) because he was dissatisfied with the conclusion of Homer's tale.

Like Tennyson, Kazantzakis could not imagine the great hero sitting calmly by the fire in his old age. He therefore launches Odysseus once more on a series of adventures.

Odysseus in Dublin The Irish novelist James Joyce has given the *Odyssey* what is perhaps its most unusual interpretation. For Joyce, Odysseus becomes Leopold Bloom, a citizen of Dublin. In the novel *Ulysses*, we follow Bloom not on a ten-year journey over the seas but on a single day's wandering through his native city.

The Visual Arts Writers are not the only ones who have been tempted to revise Homer; painters have taken their turn as well. In the painting that appears on this page, the African American artist Romare Bearden gives the court of Ulysses a flavor that seems half Elizabethan and half African.

Activity

Retell an episode from the *Odyssey*, giving it a modern twist. If you prefer, present your retelling as a collage, drawing, or painting.

THE RETURN
OF ULYSSES
Romare Bearden
Courtesy Estaste of Romare Bearden

1. How is this painting similar to or different from the way you picture Ulysses' homecoming?
2. Which details in the painting help to tell the story? Explain.
3. Which details represent Bearden's own interpretation of the ancient Greek myth? Give reasons for your answer.

from Omeros

Chapter XIII
Derek Walcott

I

"I grew up where alleys ended in a harbor
and Infinity wasn't the name of our street;
where the town anarchist was the corner barber

with his own flagpole and revolving Speaker's seat.
There were rusted mirrors in which we would
    look back
on the world's events. There, toga'd[1] in a pinned
    sheet,

the curled hairs fell like commas. On their
    varnished rack,
The World's Great Classics read backwards in his
    mirrors
where he doubled as my chamberlain.[2] I was
    known

for quoting from them as he was for his scissors.
I bequeath you that clean sheet and an empty
    throne."
We'd arrived at that corner where the barber-pole

angled from the sidewalk, and the photographer,
who'd taken his portrait, and, as some think, his
    soul,
leant from a small window and scissored his own
    hair

in a mime, suggesting a trim was overdue
to my father, who laughed and said "Wait" with
    one hand.
Then the barber mimed a shave with his mouth
    askew,

20 and left the window to wait by his wooden door
framed with dead portraits, and he seemed to
    understand
something in the life opposite not seen before.

"The rock he lived on was nothing. Not a nation
or a people," my father said, and, in his eyes,
this was a curse. When he raged, his indignation   4

25 jabbed the air with his scissors, a swift catching
    flies,
as he pumped the throne serenely round to his
    view.
He gestured like Shylock: "Hath not a Jew eyes?"[3]

making his man a negative. An Adventist,
he's stuck on one glass that photograph of
    Garvey's
30 with the braided tricorne and gold-fringed
    epaulettes,

---

1. **toga'd** (tō´ gəd) *v.*: Dressed like an ancient Roman, in a long, one-piece outer garment.
2. **chamberlain** (chām´ bər lin) *n.*: Personal attendant of a ruler or lord.

3. **Shylock: "Hath . . . eyes?":** A question asked by Shylock, a Jewish character in Shakespeare's *The Merchant of Venice.* Shylock's point is that a Jew does, of course, have eyes and is just as human as a Christian.

5 Discussion Why is Africa referred to as the barber's "paradise"? Why is it a "phantom" paradise?

6 Enrichment Point out to students that the idea of returning to Africa is a key theme of *Omeros*. Just as Odysseus longed to return to his home on Ithaca, some black Caribbeans feel a longing for Africa— the continent from which they were brought as slaves to the Caribbean. In a long passage from *Omeros*, the fisherman Achille dreams that he is returning to the African village of his ancestors.

7 Literary Focus Explain to students that the magnificent liner symbolizes everything that Castries is not. Have them contrast the description of the liner with the description of Castries and its people.

8 Literary Focus Ask students why Walcott refers to these peasant women as "Helens." What does the allusion contribute to the poem's theme? How does the description of the women contrast with that of the liner?

5
6
and that is his other Messiah.[4] His paradise
is a phantom Africa. Elephants. Trumpets.
And when I quote Shylock silver brims in his eyes.

II

"Walk me down to the wharf."
                                    At the corner of Bridge
35 Street, we saw the liner as white as a mirage,
7   its hull bright as paper, preening with privilege.

"Measure the days you have left. Do just that labor
which marries your heart to your right hand: simplify
your life to one emblem, a sail leaving harbor

40 and a sail coming in. All corruption will cry
to be taken aboard. Fame is that white liner
at the end of your street, a city to itself,

taller than the Fire Station, and much finer,
with its brass-ringed portholes, mounting shelf after shelf,
45 than anything Castries[5] could ever hope to build."

The immaculate hull insulted the tin roofs
beneath it, its pursers[6] were milk, even the bilge
bubbling from its stern in quietly muttering troughs

and its humming engines spewed expensive garbage
50 where boys balanced on logs or, riding old tires,
shouted up past the hull to tourists on the rails

to throw down coins, as cameras caught their black cries,
then jackknife or swan-dive—their somersaulting tails
like fishes flipped backwards—as the coins grew in size

55 in the wobbling depth; then, when they surfaced, fights
for possession, their heads butting like porpoises,
till, like a city leaving a city, the lights

blazed in its moving rooms, and the liner would glide
over its own phosphorus, and wash hit the wharves
60 long after stewards had set the service inside

the swaying chandeliered salons, and the black waves
settle down to their level. The stars would renew
their studded diagrams over Achille's canoe.[7]

From here, in his boyhood, he had seen women climb
65 like ants up a white flower-pot, baskets of coal
balanced on their torchoned[8] heads, without touching them,

up the black pyramids, each spine straight as a pole,
and with a strength that never altered its rhythm.
He spoke for those Helens[9] from an earlier time:

70 "Hell was built on those hills. In that country of coal
without fire, that inferno the same color
as their skins and shadows, every laboring soul

---

4. **An Adventist** (ad´ vənt´ ist) **. . . other Messiah** (mə sī´ ə): An Adventist is a member of a Christian sect that believes the world will soon come to an end. Marcus Garvey (1887–1940), an African American of Jamaican descent, believed that blacks around the world should unite and return to Africa. That is why some regard him as a messiah, or savior of his people.
5. **Castries:** The capital of St. Lucia and Walcott's hometown.
6. **pursers** (pʉrs´ ərz) *n*.: Ships' officers in charge of freight, tickets, and similar matters.

7. **Achille's** (ə shēlz´) **canoe:** Achille, a fisherman, is one of the main characters in Walcott's *Omeros*, which is loosely based on the epics of the ancient Greek poet Homer (*Omeros* is Greek for Homer). Achille is named for Achilles (ə kil´ ēz´), a hero whose exploits are described by Homer.
8. **torchoned** (tôr´ shänd) *v*.: Wrapped around with a cloth.
9. **Helens:** Helen is one of the main characters in Homer's epic the *Iliad*. A beautiful Greek queen, she was kidnapped by a Trojan prince, and this deed provoked a war between the Greeks and the Trojans.

Primary Source

In an essay in *The Art of Derek Walcott* (Poetry Wales Press Ltd., 1991), John Figueroa discusses the Homeric influence on *Omeros*:

. . . this poem is in no way written, as it were, over the template of the Iliad or the Odyssey. Helen (of St. Lucia) appears, and Hector and Achille. And there is a fight over her mysterious beauty. But these St. Lucians also bear these names because of the tradition started in slavery of giving slaves such heroic names. . . .

The Homeric aspect, and context of meaning, in this poem is more

in the sea and the struggles with it, in what men fight for in Homer and elsewhere, in the displacement and dislocation of people; the Wrath of Achilles, in the Iliad, sent the souls of many noblemen to Hades, leaving their bodies as carrion for the dogs and passing birds.

But the real heroes in this poem are not nobles, or "Kings of Men" as they are in Homer; they are noble people, but most without rank. There are a few with rank. . . . But they are few and unimportant. The real heroes are Hector and Achille and Helen and Philoctete and Seven Seas, some of them fishermen finding it difficult to make a living in the days of trawling fishnets almost as big as St. Lucia . . .

climbed with her hundredweight basket,[10] every load for
one copper penny, balanced erect on their necks
that were tight as the liner's hawsers[11] from the weight.

The carriers were women, not the fair, gentler sex.
Instead, they were darker and stronger, and their gait
was made beautiful by balance, in their ascending

the narrow wooden ramp built steeply to the hull
of a liner tall as a cloud, the unending
line crossing like ants without touching for the whole

day. That was one section of the wharf, opposite
your grandmother's house where I watched the silhouettes
of these women, while every hundredweight basket

was ticked by two tally clerks in their white pith-helmets,[12]
and the endless repetition as they climbed the
infernal anthracite hills[13] showed you hell, early."

III

"Along this coal-blackened wharf, what Time decided
to do with my treacherous body after this,"
he said, watching the women, "will stay in your head

as long as a question you have no right to ask,
only to doubt, not hate our infuriating
silence. I am only the shadow of that task

as much as their work, your pose of a question waiting,
95 as you crouch with a writing lamp over a desk,
remains in the darkness after the light has gone,

and whether night is palpable between dawn and dusk
is not for the living; so you mind your business,
which is life and work, like theirs, but I will say this:

100 O Thou, my Zero, is an impossible prayer,
utter extinction is still a doubtful conceit.
Though we pray to nothing, nothing cannot be there.[14]

Kneel to your load, then balance your staggering feet
and walk up that coal ladder as they do in time,
105 one bare foot after the next in ancestral rhyme.

Because Rhyme remains the parentheses of palms
shielding a candle's tongue, it is the language's
desire to enclose the loved world in its arms;

or heft a coal-basket; only by its stages
110 like those groaning women will you achieve that height
whose wooden planks in couplets lift your pages

higher than those hills of infernal anthracite.
There, like ants or angels, they see their native town,
unknown, raw, insignificant. They walk, you write;

115 keep to that narrow causeway without looking down,
climbing in their footsteps, that slow, ancestral beat
of those used to climbing roads; your own work owes them

---

10. hundredweight basket: A basket weighing one hundred pounds.

11. hawsers (hô´ zərz) *n.*: Large ropes used for towing or securing a ship.

12. two tally clerks . . . pith-helmets: The clerks who tallied, or counted, the baskets wore light, bell-shaped hats to protect them from the sun.

13. anthracite (an´ thrə sīt´) **hills:** Mounds of hard coal.

14. O Thou . . . conceit (kən sēt´) **. . . be there:** You cannot address a prayer to nothingness as if you were praying to God. The conceit, or idea, of nothingness probably does not correspond to anything real.

9 Discussion How does the poet contrast the laboring women with the "two tally clerks"? Why is "the endless repetition" compared to "hell"?

10 Literary Focus This is the key thematic statement of Chapter XIII. Make sure students understand the comparison being established between the labor of the women and the poet's labor. Ask them if they find the comparison convincing and moving. Why does the poet choose these women as an image of his craft?

Humanities Note

because the couplet of those multiplying feet
made your first rhymes. Look, they climb, and no
    one knows them;
120 they take their copper pittances, and your duty

11

from the time you watched them from your
    grandmother's house
as a child wounded by their power and beauty
is the chance you now have, to give those feet a
    voice."

We stood in the hot afternoon. My father took
125 his fob-watch[15] from its pocket, replaced it, then
    said,
lightly gripping my arm,
                    "He enjoys a good talk,

a serious trim, and I myself look ahead
to our appointment." He kissed me. I watched
    him walk
through a pillared balcony's alternating shade.

---

15. fob-watch (fäb´ wäch): Watch carried in a small pocket in the front of a pair of trousers.

Reader's Response *Which image in this poem were you able to picture most clearly? Explain.*

ST. LUCIA—LOOKING AT RAT ISLAND
Derek Walcott
Collection of Michael and Judy Chastanet

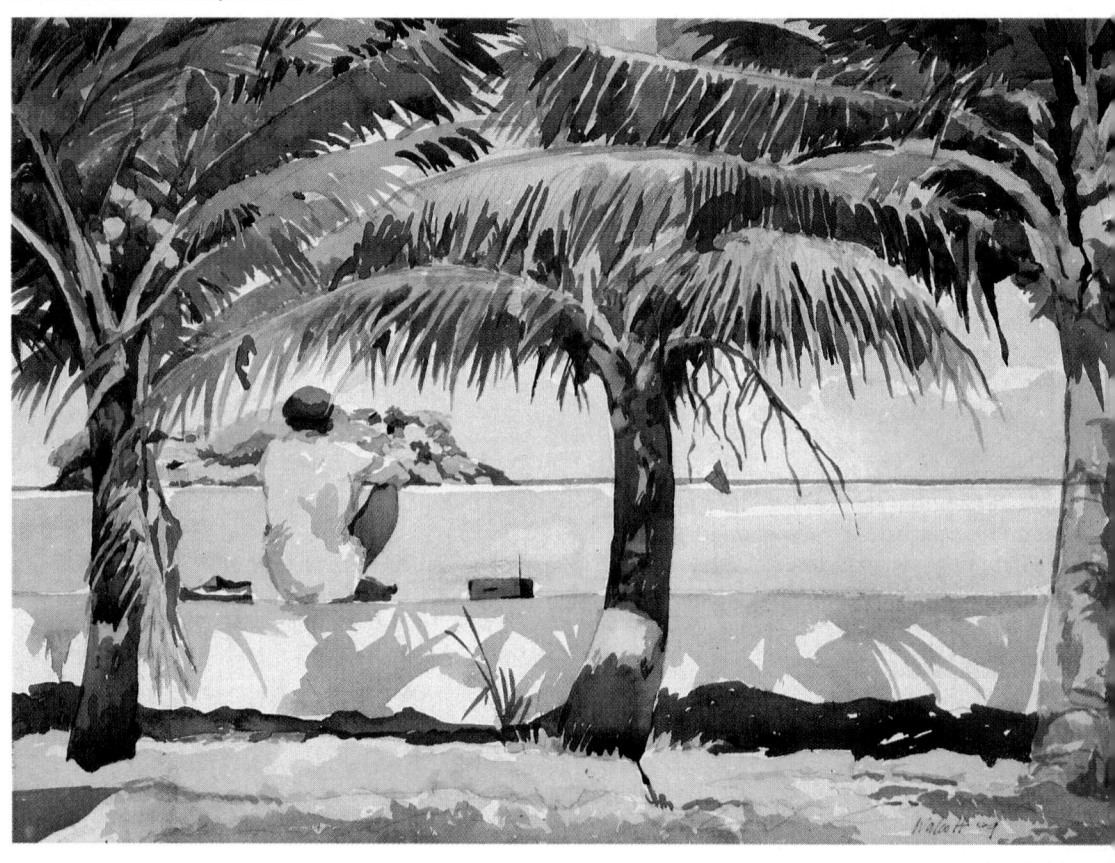

THINKING ABOUT THE SELECTION

Interpreting

1. (a) What is the mood of "Sea Grapes"? (b) Which words and phrases convey this mood?
2. (a) In your own words, explain the conflict between "obsession" and "responsibility" that the poet mentions in the fourth stanza. (b) Why does he say this conflict will never be resolved?
3. (a) How can "The classics . . . console" someone who is experiencing such a conflict? (b) Why is such consolation "not enough"?
4. How does the statement of theme in the final line relate to the mood of the poem?
5. In the excerpt from *Omeros,* the poet's father refers to his native town, Castries on St. Lucia, as "unknown, raw, insignificant." Explain what he means by this description.
6. How does the "white liner" contrast with the rawness and insignificance of the town?
7. Which is more important to the poet and his father, the "white liner" or the women climbing the hills of anthracite? Why?

Applying

8. In "Sea Grapes" Walcott says that art can partially "console" us for the pains of life. Has a work of art ever made you feel better about your life? Explain.

ANALYZING LITERATURE

Understanding Theme Through Allusion

In these poems by Derek Walcott, the **theme** or central idea about life is stated directly or strongly implied. Also, in each poem, **allusions** or references to Homer's *Odyssey* or *Iliad* help convey the theme. For example, Walcott states the theme of "Sea Grapes" in its final line, which he isolates as a kind of summary of the poem: "The classics can console. But not enough." The poem's previous eighteen lines, which compare a modern situation with episodes in Homer's *Odyssey,* have all built up to this statement. Often writers draw comfort from such comparisons, offering solace for current problems by showing how past ones were overcome. Here the poet frustrates that expectation, his last line casting a chill over both the modern event and Homer's story.

1. Do you agree with Walcott's view in "Sea Grapes" of what literature can and cannot do? Explain.
2. In the excerpt from *Omeros,* the poet refers to the women workers as "Helens," alluding to the Greek queen whose beauty helped provoke the Trojan War. In what ways is this comparison both ironic and not ironic?
3. (a) Why was the poet "wounded" when, as a boy, he watched these women? (b) How, as a man, can he act on that experience and give meaning to the lives of these workers?
4. Identify passages from *Omeros* that seem to summarize the meaning of the poem. (Remember that, as in "Sea Grapes," the poet builds toward such thematic statements.) Explain your choices.

CRITICAL THINKING AND READING

Making Inferences About Allusions

When reading, it is important to identify and understand allusions. It is just as important, however, to make inferences about how these allusions contribute to the theme of a work. For example, in the excerpt from *Omeros,* Walcott quotes the Jewish character Shylock from Shakespeare's play *The Merchant of Venice:* "Hath not a Jew eyes?" How does this allusion relate to Walcott's own theme? Shylock, scorned by Christian characters in the play, must assert that he is just as human as they are. Similarly, Walcott is asserting that his fellow islanders, though living in a place regarded as "raw" and "insignificant," are the equals of the privileged tourists on the ocean liner.

Explain how the reference to Marcus Garvey in *Omeros* relates to the theme of the poem. One way to do this is to compare and contrast Garvey's aims with the goals set for the poet by his father. To answer this question, you may want to research Garvey.

THINKING AND WRITING

Writing About an Inspirational Encounter

Colleges and employers often require applicants to write a statement about their goals. Your statement may attract more attention if, instead of merely listing and discussing your aims, you write about an encounter that inspired you to achieve an objective. In the spirit of Walcott's encounter with his father, you may want to tell about a parent or teacher who motivated you to learn, a coach who helped make you a winner, or a classmate who served as an inspiration. When you revise your account, add details that will make the encounter more vivid for the college admissions officer or employer who reads it. Such details might include memorable dialogue or precise descriptions like Walcott's image of the "somersaulting tails" of the divers. Finally, make sure that the reader will understand the goal that you were inspired to achieve.

(continued from bottom of page)

hard-working islanders, who embody a power and beauty that the poet must strive to express.
8. Answers will differ. Students answering yes should specify the work and explain how it affected them.

ANSWERS TO ANALYZING LITERATURE

1. Answers will differ, but students should support their responses.
2. The comparison is ironic because Helen was a Greek queen and these women are peasants. It is not ironic because these peasant women embody a power and beauty that is queenly.
3. (a) Suggested response: He was "wounded" because he realized how oppressed these women were. (b) He can give meaning to their lives by expressing in words the beauty of their lives.
4. Answers will differ; however, students should select specific passages and support their choices.

ANSWER TO CRITICAL THINKING AND READING

Suggested response: Like the poet and his father, Garvey was "wounded" by the colonial oppression of blacks by Europeans. His solution was to urge blacks to return to Africa. The poet's father, however, urges his son not to go to Africa but to express in words the injustices that he has witnessed.

THINKING AND WRITING

Publishing Student Writing Encourage students to use their essays in actual job or college applications, wherever appropriate.

Writing Across the Curriculum Notify an art teacher that you are studying this selection and have this teacher help students to write an appreciation of Winslow Homer's painting (page 1255), Bearden's (page 1256), or Walcott's (page 1260).

Challenge Read another section of Walcott's *Omeros* and report on it to the class. As an alternative, read and report on Walcott's *The Odyssey: A Stage Version* (1993).

"tired," "longing," "gnarled," "ancient war," "sighed," "exhausted," and the entire last line.
2. (a) Answers will differ. Students may respond that what one wants to or feels driven to do (obsession) and what one should do (responsibility) are sometimes not identical. (b) Answers will differ. Students may indicate that an adventurer will always long for home, while someone at rest will sooner or later begin to be restless.
3. (a) Answers will differ. Students may respond that the classics may show that this conflict existed at other times as well. They may also be consoling because they present the conflict in a beautiful way. (b) The consolation is not enough because it does not solve the conflict.
4. It relates to the mood because it shows the possibility of limited consolation through art but not an ultimate resolution of the conflict.
5. He means that it is a backward little place compared to the big cities from which the liner sails.
6. The white liner is rich and magnificent, a symbol of everything Castries is not.
7. The women are more important for the poet and his father. They represent the

JAMAICA KINCAID

1949–

"I've never really written about anyone except myself and my mother," says author Jamaica Kincaid. Drawn from her childhood experiences on a Caribbean island, Kincaid's fictional works explore the complex relationship between mother and daughter and how it changes, sometimes painfully, during the passage into adulthood.

Jamaica Kincaid was born Elaine Potter Richardson on May 25, 1949, in St. John's, Antigua. Like most rural Antiguans, Kincaid grew up in a home without electricity or running water. Nonetheless, her early childhood was a happy one, primarily because of the deep connection she felt to her mother. All of that changed, however, when Kincaid was nine, and the first of three younger brothers was born. The writer was devastated by this threat to the love that she perceived as hers alone.

Kincaid was a bright child, but her gifts went unrecognized by her teachers. Today, she attributes this to the colonial system under which she grew up. (Antigua was a British dependency during Kincaid's childhood. It became an independent nation in 1981.) Racism and economic oppression ensured that expectations for young black women remained low. In the face of indifference at home and at school, Kincaid retreated to books, where she discovered a passion that was missing in other areas of her life. One of her favorite books was *Jane Eyre*.

By the time she was a teenager, Kincaid was determined to leave Antigua. At the age of sixteen, she found a job taking care of children for a well-to-do family in a suburb of New York City. From there she moved on to a series of unskilled jobs and an unsuccessful attempt to get a college degree. Despite educational and career setbacks, Kincaid made connections in the New York publishing world, and by the early 1970's several magazines for teens were publishing articles by her.

Eventually, Kincaid became a staff writer for *The New Yorker*, in which many of her stories first appeared. In 1983, she published *At the Bottom of the River*, a collection of short stories. Its imaginative metaphors, possibly based in West Indian folklore, seemed too obscure to some reviewers. Others praised the book's lyrical prose and universal insights. Kincaid admits that the stories in this collection may be difficult to grasp; in writing them she says she sometimes fell into a kind of hallucinatory state. However, now that she is married and has two children, Kincaid finds that her connection to her family makes it difficult for her to do this type of writing. Her more recent works have a traditional narrative style.

Kincaid's novels *Annie John* (1985) and *Lucy* (1990) are clearly autobiographical. *Annie John* relates the experiences of a young girl growing up on a Caribbean island; it ends with her decision to leave the stifling atmosphere of that island. *Lucy* tells the story of a young Caribbean girl's experiences after she leaves her home and travels to the United States to take a job caring for the children of a wealthy American couple.

"A Walk to the Jetty" is the conclusion to *Annie John*. It describes the narrator's last walk with her parents, through her childhood world, as she prepares to leave her native island. It is classic Jamaica Kincaid, rich in memories and charged with emotional intensity.

Objectives

Thematic
To explore the passage from childhood to adulthood

Skills
1 To understand the uses of reminiscence
2 To analyze the effect of setting on a story
3 To compose a narrative incorporating reminiscences

GUIDE FOR INTERPRETING

from Annie John

Commentary

Reminiscences. Do you have vivid memories of certain events in your life? Perhaps you recall, for example, your first day of school, a special birthday, or a troubling conflict with a friend. **Reminiscences** are memories of past events, often evoking the emotional responses that accompanied them.

Many different kinds of experiences can trigger reminiscences. A photograph or a glimpse of someone from your past, the discovery of a long-forgotten toy, or a visit to a place you haven't been to for a while can all prompt involuntary memories. Sensory experiences can also prompt a reminiscence: a piece of music or a familiar taste or smell. In one of the most famous scenes in world literature, a small cake, called a madeleine, dipped in tea, unlocks a host of memories for the narrator of Marcel Proust's *Remembrance of Things Past.* Until that moment, the narrator has had only one memory of youth. Suddenly, he is flooded with them. Reminiscences are the core of Proust's six-volume novel, but other authors have used reminiscence more sparingly with excellent effect. Writers may use reminiscence to provide vital information about a character or a situation without having to start the narration at some distant time in the past. In addition, they may use reminiscence to provide insight into a character's personality or motivation, to explain why others treat the character as they do, or to reveal what is important to the character.

Memories are often tied to a specific place, and a return to that place can trigger those memories. In "A Walk to the Jetty," the narrator and central character, Annie John, reminisces about her childhood as she walks through a familiar landscape with her parents. Various spots along the road to the jetty are associated with significant memories from childhood. The setting of the narration is integral to its structure and meaning. Places along the road prompt memories, which reveal some of the forces that have compelled Annie John to leave her island home. Reminiscence helps Kincaid establish the road as a metaphor for Annie's life.

Writing

Have you ever revisited a place that made you recall past experiences and feelings related to that place? Freewrite, exploring the reminiscences that one specific place conjures up for you.

Literary Focus Ask students if they ever reminisce with their childhood friends. What kinds of things do they recall? Funny? Sad? Frightening? How do they feel as they look back on events and feelings from a new perspective?

Writing/Prior Knowledge Before students write, encourage them to identify some places that might prompt reminiscences for people their age. List on the chalkboard the places they mention.

ESL Teaching Strategy Use a discussion on reminiscences to call attention to the way words and phrases express the passage of time. Enhance ESL students' fluency by encouraging them to use verbs in the past tense as well as words like *years, months, then, while, ago, once, past,* and *after.*

Teaching Tenth-Grade Students This story is especially suitable for tenth-grade students. You might prepare them for the selection by having them draw a map of their neighborhood and then asking them to annotate that map with reminiscences.

Vocabulary

Preteach the following vocabulary words:

jetty (jet´ē) *n.:* A pier; a landing dock

loomed (loomd) *v.:* Appeared in a large or threatening form

wharf (wôrf) *n.:* A pier or dock where ships are loaded or unloaded

scorn (skôrn) *n.:* Contempt or disdain for someone or something

stupor (stoo´ pər) *n.:* Mental dullness, as if drugged

cue (kyoo) *n.:* A signal to do something

Support Material

Teaching Portfolio
Teacher Backup, p. 1523
Usage and Mechanics Worksheet, p. 1527
Vocabulary Check, p. 1528
Analyzing Literature Worksheet, *Appreciating Reminiscence,* p. 1529

Critical Thinking and Reading Worksheet, *Analyzing the Effect of Setting,* p. 1530
Selection Test, pp. 1531–1532

from Annie John

from A Walk to the Jetty

Jamaica Kincaid

My mother had arranged with a stevedore[1] to take my trunk to the jetty ahead of me. At ten o'clock on the dot, I was dressed, and we set off for the jetty. An hour after that, I would board a launch that would take me out to sea, where I then would board the ship. Starting out, as if for old time's sake and without giving it a thought, we lined up in the old way: I walking between my mother and my father. I loomed way above my father and could see the top of his head. We must have made a strange sight: a grown girl all dressed up in the middle of a morning, in the middle of the week, walking in step in the middle between her two parents, for people we didn't know stared at us. It was all of half an hour's walk from our house to the jetty, but I was passing through most of the years of my life. We passed by the house where Miss Dulcie, the seamstress that I had been apprenticed to for a time, lived, and just as I was passing by, a wave of bad feeling for her came over me, because I suddenly remembered that the months I spent with her all she had me do was sweep the floor, which was always full of threads and pins and needles, and I never seemed to sweep it clean enough to please her. Then she would send me to the store to buy buttons or thread, though I was only allowed to do this if I was given a sample of the button or thread, and then she would find fault even though they were an exact match of the samples she had given me. And all the while she said to me, "A girl like you will never learn to sew properly, you know." At the time, I don't suppose I minded it, because it was customary to treat the first-year apprentice with such scorn, but now I placed on the dustheap of my life Miss Dulcie and everything that I had had to do with her.

We were soon on the road that I had taken to school, to church, to Sunday school, to choir practice, to Brownie meetings, to Girl Guide meetings, to meet a friend. I was five years old when I first walked on this road unaccompanied by someone to hold my hand. My mother had placed three pennies in my little basket, which was a duplicate of her bigger basket, and sent me to the chemist's shop to buy a pennyworth of senna leaves, a pennyworth of eucalyptus leaves, and a pennyworth of camphor.[2] She then instructed me on what side of the road to walk, where to make a turn, where to cross, how to look carefully before I crossed, and if I met anyone that I knew to politely pass greetings and keep on my way. I was wearing a freshly ironed yellow dress that had printed on it scenes of acrobats flying through the air and swinging on a trapeze. I had just had a bath, and after it, instead of powdering me with my baby-smelling talcum powder, my mother had, as a special favor, let me

---

1. stevedore (stē′ və dôr) *n.*: A person whose job is loading and unloading ships.

2. chemist's shop . . . camphor: The first phrase is a British term for a pharmacy. The items mentioned are small amounts of plant matter to be used in remedies.

use her own talcum powder, which smelled quite perfumy and came in a can that had painted on it people going out to dinner in nineteenth-century London and was called Mazie. How it pleased me to walk out the door and bend my head down to sniff at myself and see that I smelled just like my mother. I went to the chemist's shop, and he had to come from behind the counter and bend down to hear what it was that I wanted to buy, my voice was so little and timid then. I went back just the way I had come, and when I walked into the yard and presented my basket with its three packages to my mother, her eyes filled with tears and she swooped me up and held me high in the air and said that I was wonderful and good and that there would never be anybody better. If I had just conquered Persia, she couldn't have been more proud of me.

We passed by our church—the church in which I had been christened and received[3] and had sung in the junior choir. We passed by a house in which a girl I used to like and was sure I couldn't live without had lived. Once, when she had mumps, I went to visit her against my mother's wishes, and we sat on her bed and ate the cure of roasted, buttered sweet potatoes that had been placed on her swollen jaws, held there by a piece of white cloth. I don't know how, but my mother found out about it, and I don't know how, but she put an end to our friendship. Shortly after, the girl moved with her family across the sea to somewhere else. We passed the doll store, where I would go with my mother when I was little and point out the doll I wanted that year for Christmas. We passed the store where I bought the much-fought-over shoes I wore to church to be received in. We passed the bank. On my sixth birthday, I was given, among other things, the present of a sixpence.[4] My

---

3. **received:** Accepted into the congregation as a mature Christian.

4. **sixpence** *n*.: A monetary unit in the British commonwealth, worth six pennies (not of the same value as the pennies in United States currency). A *shilling* is worth two sixpence, a *two-and-sixpence* is two and one half shillings, that is, two shillings and one sixpence. A *pound* is worth twenty shillings. A *farthing* is a "fourthing": one fourth of a penny.

SAN ANTONIO DE ORIENTE (detail)
José Antonio Velásquez
Museum of Modern Art of Latin America

mother and I then went to this bank, and with the sixpence I opened my own savings account. I was given a little gray book with my name in big letters on it, and in the balance column it said "6d." Every Saturday morning after that, I was given a sixpence—later a shilling, and later a two-and-sixpence piece—and I would take it to the bank for deposit. I had never been allowed to withdraw even a farthing from my bank account until just a few weeks before I was to leave; then the whole account was closed out, and I received from the bank the sum of six pounds ten shillings and two and a half pence. ⌐7

We passed the office of the doctor who told my mother three times that I did not need glasses,

4 **Literary Focus** Ask students to discuss the significance of this detail. What is the symbolic meaning of being allowed to use her mother's powder? How does this reflect the significance of the entire episode?

5 **Reading Strategy** Ask students to infer some of the mother's thoughts and feelings at this point.

6 **Discussion** Ask students to suggest reasons the mother might have put an end to the friendship.

7 **Clarification** Make sure students understand that this is not a very large sum of money to be taking on a trip.

Humanities Note
Fine art, *San Antonio de Oriente* by José Antonio Velásquez. Latin American primitive painter José Antonio Velásquez (1906–) was born in the village of San Antonio de Oriente, Honduras, where he has lived all of his life. He worked as a telegraph operator and a barber; for a time he was also the mayor of San Antonio de Oriente.

Although he has had no formal artistic training, the unaffected talent and ability of José Antonio Velásquez have earned him worldwide recognition as a notable Latin American painter.

The rhythmic patterns of the tiles, flowers, and stone walls in his painting *San Antonio de Oriente* are offset by the smooth, solid planes of the distant roofs, the white buildings, and the colorful wash hung on a line in the foreground.

You might want to use the following questions to discuss the art:
1. Do you think you would like to live in this village? Why or why not?
2. The artist was born in this village. Why do you think he has chosen to remain there for his entire life?
3. How do you think this village in Honduras might be similar to a village like Annie John's home on Antigua? How might it be different?

that if my eyes were feeling weak a glass of carrot juice a day would make them strong again. This happened when I was eight. And so every day at recess I would run to my school gate and meet my mother, who was waiting for me with a glass of juice from carrots she had just grated and then squeezed, and I would drink it and then run back to meet my chums. I knew there was nothing at all wrong with my eyes, but I had recently read a story in *The Schoolgirl's Own Annual* in which the heroine, a girl a few years older than I was then, cut such a figure to my mind with the way she was always adjusting her small, round, horn-rimmed glasses that I felt I must have a pair exactly like them. When it became clear that I didn't need glasses, I began to complain about the glare of the sun being too much for my eyes, and I walked around with my hands shielding them—especially in my mother's presence. My mother then bought for me a pair of sunglasses with the exact horn-rimmed frames I wanted, and how I enjoyed the gestures of blowing on the lenses, wiping them with the hem of my uniform, adjusting the glasses when they slipped down my nose, and just removing them from their case and putting them on. In three weeks, I grew tired of them and they found a nice resting place in a drawer, along with some other things that at one time or another I couldn't live without.

We passed the store that sold only grooming aids, all imported from England. This store had in it a large porcelain dog—white, with black spots all over and a red ribbon of satin tied around its neck. The dog sat in front of a white porcelain bowl that was always filled with fresh water, and it sat in such a way that it looked as if it had just taken a long drink. When I was a small child, I would ask my mother, if ever we were near this store, to please take me to see the dog, and I would stand in front of it, bent over slightly, my hands resting on my knees, and stare at it and stare at it. I thought this dog more beautiful and more real than any actual dog I had ever seen or any actual dog I would ever see. I must have outgrown my interest in the dog, for when it disappeared I never asked what became of it. We passed the library, and if there was anything on this walk that I might have wept over

leaving, this most surely would have been the thing. My mother had been a member of the library long before I was born. And since she took me everywhere with her when I was quite little, when she went to the library she took me along there, too. I would sit in her lap very quietly as she read books that she did not want to take home with her. I could not read the words yet, but just the way they looked on the page was interesting to me. Once, a book she was reading had a large picture of a man in it, and when I asked her who he was she told me that he was Louis Pasteur[5] and that the book was about his life. It stuck in my mind, because she said it was because of him that she boiled my milk to purify it before I was allowed to drink it, that it was his idea, and that that was why the process was called pasteurization. One of the things I had put away in my mother's old trunk in which she kept all my childhood things was my library card. At that moment, I owed sevenpence in overdue fees.

As I passed by all these places, it was as if I were in a dream, for I didn't notice the people coming and going in and out of them, I didn't feel my feet touch ground, I didn't even feel my own body—I just saw these places as if they were hanging in the air, not having top or bottom, and as if I had gone in and out of them all in the same moment. The sun was bright; the sky was blue and just above my head. We then arrived at the jetty.

My heart now beat fast, and no matter how hard I tried, I couldn't keep my mouth from falling open and my nostrils from spreading to the ends of my face. My old fear of slipping between the boards of the jetty and falling into the dark-green water where the dark-green eels lived came over me. When my father's stomach started to go bad, the doctor had recommended a walk every evening right after he ate his dinner. Sometimes he would take me with him. When he took me with him, we usually went to the jetty, and there he would sit

---

5. Louis Pasteur (Pas·tur´) (1822–1895): The French chemist and bacteriologist who developed the process (pasteurization) for using heat to kill disease-causing bacteria in milk.

and talk to the night watchman about cricket[6] or some other thing that didn't interest me, because it was not personal; they didn't talk about their wives, or their children, or their parents, or about any of their likes and dislikes. They talked about things in such a strange way, and I didn't see what they found funny, but sometimes they made each other laugh so much that their guffaws would bound out to sea and send back an echo. I was always sorry when we got to the jetty and saw that the night watchman on duty was the one he enjoyed speaking to; it was like being locked up in a book filled with numbers and diagrams and what-ifs. For the thing about not being able to understand and enjoy what they were saying was I had nothing to take my mind off my fear of slipping in between the boards of the jetty.

Now, too, I had nothing to take my mind off what was happening to me. My mother and my father—I was leaving them forever. My home on an island—I was leaving it forever. What to make of everything? I felt a familiar hollow space inside. I felt I was being held down against my will. I felt I was burning up from head to toe. I felt that someone was tearing me up into little pieces and soon I

---

6. **cricket** *n.*: A British game, similar to baseball, but played with a flat bat and eleven players on each team.

would be able to see all the little pieces as they floated out into nothing in the deep blue sea. I didn't know whether to laugh or cry. I could see that it would be better not to think too clearly about any one thing. The launch was being made ready to take me, along with some other passengers, out to the ship that was anchored in the sea. My father paid our fares, and we joined a line of people waiting to board. My mother checked my bag to make sure that I had my passport, the money she had given me, and a sheet of paper placed between some pages in my Bible on which were written the names of the relatives—people I had not known existed—with whom I would live in England. Across from the jetty was a <u>wharf</u>, and some stevedores were loading and unloading barges. I don't know why seeing that struck me so, but suddenly a wave of strong feeling came over me, and my heart swelled with a great gladness as the words "I shall never see this again" spilled out inside me. But then, just as quickly, my heart shriveled up and the words "I shall never see this again" stabbed at me. I don't know what stopped me from falling in a heap at my parents' feet.

When we were all on board, the launch headed out to sea. Away from the jetty, the water became the customary blue, and the launch left a wide path in it that looked like a road. I passed by sounds and smells that were so familiar that I had long ago stopped paying any attention to them. But now

PORT DE LA SALINE, HAITI
Lois Mailou Jones
Courtesy of the artist

13 **Literary Focus** Have students suggest the possible significance of this reminiscence.

14 **Reading Strategy** Ask students to infer how the narrator is feeling at this point.

15 **Discussion** Ask students to discuss why the mother might never have mentioned these relatives to her daughter.

16 **Enrichment** Point out the use of strong verbs to describe the narrator's emotional state.

Humanities Note

Fine art, *Port de la Saline, Haiti* by Lois Mailou Jones. The African American painter Lois Mailou Jones (1905–) studied art at the Boston Normal School, Boston Museum School of Fine Arts, and later Harvard, Howard, and Columbia universities. In 1937, she won a fellowship to study at the prestigious Academie Julien in Paris. She became one of America's important modern painters and was among the first African American women who used African motifs in their art.

Port de la Saline, Haiti was painted in Haiti, a country Jones fell in love with in 1953 when she went there with her husband, Louis Vergniaud Pierre Noel. The Haitian government commissioned Jones to paint a series of scenes from Haitian life such as this work. In 1954, thirty of these canvases were exhibited at the Pan American Union in Washington, D.C.

This brilliant and joyful canvas shows a dockside scene typical of island countries. The clouds, sails, and foreground planes are angular geometric shapes that speak of the artist's ties to cubism and fascination with African textile patterns.

You may want to use the following questions to discuss the art:
1. What sensory details might Annie John describe in a setting such as this?
2. How does this scene compare and contrast with Annie John's impressions of the jetty near her home?

17 **Critical Thinking and Reading**
Ask students to suggest why the sensory details of the setting are affecting the narrator so strongly.

18 **Discussion** Ask students to discuss whether or not they agree with the distinction made between childhood and adulthood. What do students see as some of the differences between being a child and being an adult?

19 **Literary Focus** Lead students to recognize that the narrator's earlier reminiscence about her father suggests that his behavior at this point is consistent with his character.

20 **Literary Focus** Have students discuss how the narrator's reminiscences have prepared them for her reaction to her mother's smothering embrace.

21 **Enrichment** Draw students' attention to the narrator's last image of her mother. Ask them to discuss how this image reinforces one of the themes of the selection.

Cultural Note About her island home, Jamaica Kincaid has said, "essentially everyone has the personality of an artist, the self-absorption and the inability to disguise it. . . . Yet they don't produce any objective work of art." Ask students if they think Kincaid has turned self-absorption into an objective work of art.

here they were, and the ever-present "I shall never see this again" bobbed up and down inside me. There was the sound of the seagull diving down into the water and coming up with something silverish in its mouth. There was the smell of the sea and the sight of small pieces of rubbish floating around in it. There were boats filled with fishermen coming in early. There was the sound of their voices as they shouted greetings to each other. There was the hot sun, there was the blue sea, there was the blue sky. Not very far away, there was the white sand of the shore, with the run-down houses all crowded in next to each other, for in some places only poor people lived near the shore. I was seated in the launch between my parents, and when I realized that I was gripping their hands tightly I glanced quickly to see if they were looking at me with scorn, for I felt sure that they must have known of my never-see-this-again feelings. But instead my father kissed me on the forehead and my mother kissed me on the mouth, and they both gave over their hands to me, so that I could grip them as much as I wanted. I was on the verge of feeling that it had all been a mistake, but I remembered that I wasn't a child anymore, and that now when I made up my mind about something I had to see it through. At that moment, we came to the ship, and that was that.

The goodbyes had to be quick, the captain said. My mother introduced herself to him and then introduced me. She told him to keep an eye on me, for I had never gone this far away from home on my own. She gave him a letter to pass on to the captain of the next ship that I would board in Barbados.[7] They walked me to my cabin, a small space that I would share with someone else—a woman I did not know. I had never before slept in a room with someone I did not know. My father kissed me goodbye and told me to be good and to write home often. After he said this, he looked at me, then looked at the floor and swung his left foot, then looked at me again. I could see that he wanted to say something else, something that he

had never said to me before, but then he just turned and walked away. My mother said, "Well," and then she threw her arms around me. Big tears streamed down her face, and it must have been that—for I could not bear to see my mother cry—which started me crying, too. She then tightened her arms around me and held me to her close, so that I felt that I couldn't breathe. With that, my tears dried up and I was suddenly on my guard. "What does she want now?" I said to myself. Still holding me close to her, she said, in a voice that raked across my skin, "It doesn't matter what you do or where you go, I'll always be your mother and this will always be your home."

I dragged myself away from her and backed off a little, and then I shook myself, as if to wake myself out of a stupor. We looked at each other for a long time with smiles on our faces, but I know the opposite of that was in my heart. As if responding to some invisible cue, we both said, at the very same moment, "Well." Then my mother turned around and walked out the cabin door. I stood there for I don't know how long, and then I remembered that it was customary to stand on deck and wave to your relatives who were returning to shore. From the deck, I could not see my father, but I could see my mother facing the ship, her eyes searching to pick me out. I removed from my bag a red cotton handkerchief that she had earlier given me for this purpose, and I waved it wildly in the air. Recognizing me immediately, she waved back just as wildly, and we continued to do this until she became just a dot in the matchbox-size launch swallowed up in the big blue sea.

I went back to my cabin and lay down on my berth. Everything trembled as if it had a spring at its very center. I could hear the small waves lap-lapping around the ship. They made an unexpected sound, as if a vessel filled with liquid had been placed on its side and now was slowly emptying out.

---

7. **Barbados** (bär bā´ dōs): The easternmost island in the West Indies; it is southeast of Antigua.

Reader's Response *Which of the narrator's feelings were easy for you to understand? Which did you have difficulty understanding? Why?*

Closure and Extension

ANSWERS TO THINKING ABOUT THE SELECTION

1. (a) It was her first step of independence away from her mother, and her mother praised her elaborately for the fine job she did. (b) Both walks represent the narrator's growing independence. In the first walk she cares

about her mother's opinion and wants to please her. At the time of the walk to the jetty, although she is still concerned about her mother's opinion, she is not as concerned with pleasing her mother as she is concerned with being an adult.

2. Suggested response: The narrator feels very close to her mother. (Her mother's tears bring on her tears.) However, she also feels stifled by her

mother. (When her mother hugs her, she can't breathe.)

3. He probably wants to say he loves her. He can't verbalize his feelings.

4. It reminds her of the ways in which she has felt controlled and stifled by her mother.

5. Her reminiscences include memories that illustrate her mixed feelings. For instance, the reminiscence about her mother's pride in her independent

THINKING ABOUT THE SELECTION

Interpreting

1. (a) Why might the narrator have such vivid memories of the first time she walked down the road alone when she was five years old? (b) How is that walk compared and contrasted with the walk to the jetty?
2. What can you infer about the relationship between the narrator and her mother? Present evidence for your inferences.
3. What do you think the narrator's father wants to say to her when they are on the ship? Why doesn't he say it?
4. When the narrator begins to cry, her mother holds her so close that she feels she can't breathe. Why does this cause the narrator to stop crying?
5. How do the narrator's reminiscences reflect her mixed feelings about leaving home?
6. The last sentence in the selection describes the sound of the waves lapping at the ship: " . . . as if a vessel filled with liquid had been placed on its side and now was slowly emptying out." How does this simile also describe the narrator?

Applying

7. Kincaid has been praised by some critics for her "universal insight." (a) What universal insight can be found in "A Walk to the Jetty"? (b) How is Annie's story relevant to young people of today?

ANALYZING LITERATURE

Understanding Reminiscences

"A Walk to the Jetty" is built around a series of **reminiscences,** memories of events and feelings. Using reminiscences allows an author to reveal many incidents from a character's past in a short span of time and to explore some of the events that continue to influence a character's personality and motivate his or her actions. For example, in "A Walk to the Jetty," the narrator's reminiscence about visiting a friend who had mumps reveals the control the narrator's mother had over her life. This explains some of the narrator's feelings and actions as she prepares to leave her mother.

1. The narrator's reminiscences about her mother provide insights into their complex relationship. Identify two events in the story that reflect contrasting facets of their relationship. Explain your choices.

2. Some of the narrator's reminiscences are very brief; others are very elaborate. Choose one of the brief memories and explain why the author might have included it.
3. How does the narrator think her father views her? Which memory highlights this perception?
4. How does the author use reminiscence to reveal the narrator's reasons for leaving the island?

CRITICAL THINKING AND READING

Analyzing the Effect of Setting

Setting is the time and place of the action in a literary work. Sometimes, however, the setting functions as more than just a backdrop for the action. In "A Walk to the Jetty," for example, Jamaica Kincaid uses setting to prompt the narrator's reminiscences and to organize them spatially. As the narrator walks through the landscape of her island home, she recalls significant events from her life. The events are organized not chronologically, but spatially. The setting provides a framework for the narrator's thoughts and feelings.

1. Two locations frame the narrator's walk to the jetty: the house of the seamstress and the library. How does the contrast between the narrator's feelings about these two places reflect one of the themes of the selection?
2. What feelings does being on the jetty arouse in the narrator? How does the writer use this location to connect old feelings with new experiences?

THINKING AND WRITING

Writing Reminiscences

Imagine that you are walking through a landscape that is familiar to you. It could be outdoors or indoors. For example, you might imagine yourself walking through your neighborhood, a shopping mall, a school, or the rooms of a familiar house. Write a narrative that reveals the reminiscences that are prompted by the setting. Try to have a theme emerge from your reminiscences. If you wish, you may write as a character from a book, a movie, or a TV series. When you revise your reminiscences, make sure that they are organized spatially and that a theme runs through them.

(continued from bottom of page)

illustrated by her breaking up the childhood friendship.
2. Answers will differ. The reminiscence that occurs while passing the shoe store suggests that the mother didn't win every conflict with her daughter. The reminiscence about being on the jetty with her father shows that she sometimes felt confused, frightened, and alone among adults. Students may choose any reminiscence whose significance they can explain.
3. Suggested response: The narrator feels her father does not always notice her, and that he does not know how to talk to her. The reminiscence about her fear of slipping through the boards of the jetty highlights her feelings of not being noticed. Her lack of interest in the unemotional topics pursued by her father and his friend highlights her isolation from her father and his way of thinking and talking.
4. The reminiscences suggest that the daughter may have to get away from her mother in order to lead a fully independent life.

ANSWERS TO CRITICAL THINKING AND READING

1. The narrator has negative feelings about her experience with the seamstress and positive feelings about the library. One of the themes of the selection deals with the mixed emotions inspired by growing toward independence.
2. Being on the jetty reminds the narrator that she used to feel terrified that she would slip into the water through the boards of the jetty. Now she also feels terrified at leaving the familiar (the jetty) for the unknown (the water).

THINKING AND WRITING

Writing Across the Curriculum
Have students work in groups to research the island of Antigua: its history, geography, economy, and so on. One group might conduct interviews with people who have lived on or visited Antigua. Display the research reports on the bulletin board around a map of Antigua.

Challenge Ask students to interview older members of the community about their reminiscences of a specific period or event in history.

walk to the chemist's shop is immediately followed by the reminiscence about the friendship her mother ended, which illustrates her mother's controlling influence.
6. She is emptying herself of all of her previous experiences and becoming an empty vessel ready for a new life.
7. (a) Answers will differ. Students might point out that every experience in life has some significance even if we

don't recognize it at the time. They might also recognize that Annie's struggle for identity and independence is a struggle most people go through, to one degree or another. (b) Students may be able to relate Annie's mixed feelings about leaving her island to their own experiences of change and growth.

ANSWERS TO ANALYZING LITERATURE

1. Suggested response: Some reminiscences suggest that the mother loved her daughter and was very indulgent toward her. For example, she brought carrot juice to school for her every day and gave her a doll every Christmas. However, the mother also had firm control over the daughter's life, as

CALYPSO AND DUB POETRY

Calypso music and dub poetry are two forms of creative expression unique to Caribbean culture. Each is deeply rooted in the African Caribbean oral tradition.

Songs That Sting

Calypso originated on the island of Trinidad with the songs of African slaves who worked on plantations. These songs often had a satirical sting, with the lyrics commenting on local events.

Modern calypso descends directly from these witty, gossipy songs. Today's popular calypso singers direct their barbs at politics, society, or the general human condition. Their songs are highly entertaining, but they also point out problems that need to be remedied. One of the most popular calypsonians is Hollis "Chalkdust" Liverpool, whose nickname is a reminder of his former profession: teaching. Although he has exchanged his box of chalk for a guitar, he still aims to teach.

Technology and the Oral Tradition

We often read how technology has destroyed the oral tradition. With everyone watching television, no one bothers to tell stories anymore. Dub poetry, however, is an example of technology fostering the oral tradition. It began when DJs in Jamaica produced popular records with a "dub" side—an instrumental version of a song with the vocal track dubbed out. DJs could then contribute their own witty, half-spoken and half-sung track over the music.

Some who realized the potential of this form began to compose poems to be performed with music. These "dub poets" also recited their poems without a musical accompaniment. Extremely popular with Caribbean audiences, these poets are true practitioners of the oral tradition. They resist the idea of a script and emphasize the uniqueness of each performance.

Dub poets often express the viewpoint of the urban poor oppressed by the establishment, and a recurring theme in their work is the celebration of Africa.

Activity

Make up your own satirical song or dub poem; then perform it for your friends or classmates.

"Chalkdust" in performance

Western Europe

MEMORY OF OCEANIA, 1952–1953
Henri Matisse
Museum of Modern Art, New York

Humanities Note

Fine art, *Memory of Oceania*, 1952–1953, by Henri Matisse (1869–1954). Born in Picardy, France, Matisse (ma tēs´) did not show an early interest in art. As a twenty-year-old, he was studying law when, during an illness, he suddenly started painting. This newfound interest took him over and he

(continued from bottom of page)
quickly gave up his legal studies.

His early work is associated with the fauvist movement. The French word *fauve* means "wild beast," and it was used derogatively by critics to describe painters whose use of color seemed too wild. The young painters of this movement, however, wore this term like a proud badge. Matisse, who became their leader, was especially known for the liveliness of his colors.

Even when fauvism came to an end, Matisse continued his experimentation. He once wrote that he wanted to depict the emotions a subject inspired rather than the exact shape and form of the subject. His brilliance seemed to consist in knowing what to leave out of a picture: Many of his paintings are characterized by a bold, but certainly not unskilled, simplicity. Also, he experimented with perspective, often deliberately introducing a two-dimensional "feel" into the spaces he painted. In his old age, when he could no longer hold a paintbrush, he made paintings out of brightly colored bits of paper.

Matisse visited Tahiti but was very wary of being influenced by Gauguin, whose Tahitian paintings were famous. Years after Matisse's visit, however, the influence of Tahiti mysteriously worked its way into the abstract paper cutouts of his old age, like *Memory of Oceania*. The term *Oceania* refers to "islands in the Pacific."

You might want to use the following questions to discuss the art:

1. (a) How can you tell that Matisse used brightly colored paper cutouts to make this work of art? (b) Where did he also use crayon markings?
2. The title of this work refers to a visit Matisse made to Tahiti. Does the painting suggest a south Pacific environment? Why or why not?
3. Matisse was famous for knowing what to leave out of a picture. How does he show this talent here?
4. Describe a picture that you could make with paper cutouts.

1913–1960

When a now-famous Polish writer was an unknown student in Paris, he often wandered around the city at all hours. Late one night he met a solitary man in a cheap, lowdown café and had a stimulating philosophical discussion. Only later, when he was home in bed, did he realize that he had been talking with the well-known French author Albert Camus (al bär′ kà mü′). This anecdote illustrates several of Camus's most endearing qualities: his modesty, searching intelligence, and restless night-owl habits.

Camus was born in Mondovi, Algeria, to a father and mother of European descent. He had to overcome many hardships in his early life. Not only was his family poor, but his father died in World War I and his mother suffered from deafness.

Educated at the University of Algiers, Camus supported himself by working at odd jobs. He was an excellent scholar and developed a love of literature. Also, he showed energy and initiative by helping to found a small theater group with his friends. Their goal was to stage plays that would be of interest to working-class people, and Camus gained experience in all aspects of the theater. This background proved helpful when, years later, he wrote plays such as *Caligula* (1944), the drama of a Roman emperor who resembles modern dictators like Hitler and Mussolini.

A man of strong moral principles, Camus sometimes got into trouble for expressing his convictions. For instance, when he publicly criticized the French colonial government of Algiers (France controlled this African country until 1962), he had to leave the country. He emigrated to France, where he worked as an investigative reporter for a Parisian newspaper.

Camus's integrity and character were tested again when the Germans occupied France during World War II. At the risk of his life, he supported the French Resistance Movement by serving as the principal editor of an illegal newspaper, *Combat*. As an underground journalist, he won recognition for his independent left-wing views and the emphasis he placed on moral behavior. During the turmoil of the war, he also published two of his most influential works, his novel *The Stranger* (1942) and his essay "The Myth of Sisyphus" (1942). The novel tells about a man who realizes that conventional values and emotions are senseless because life is absurd—humans are uninvited guests in an indifferent universe.

In 1947 Camus published another novel that deals with the meaninglessness of existence in a more positive way. Set in the Algerian city of Oran, *The Plague* describes a mysterious epidemic that symbolizes both the German Occupation of France and all the evils that beset humankind. In combating the plague, several of the characters learn the importance of integrity and compassion.

Acknowledged as a major twentieth-century writer, Camus spent part of the late 1940's touring and lecturing in North and South America. On returning to Paris, he withdrew from public life to recover his health—he suffered from tuberculosis—and continued to produce essays and plays. In 1957 he received the Nobel Prize in Literature. With characteristic modesty, however, he commented that if he had been on the Nobel committee, he would have voted for the French novelist André Malraux. Camus's death in an auto accident three years later cut short his brilliant career.

"The Myth of Sisyphus," an essay written during the horrors of World War II, affirms the importance of human effort and values even in a meaningless world.

Objectives

Thematic
To understand a myth for our times

2 To appreciate the connotations of a word

3 To reinterpret a myth

Skills
1 To understand existentialism

GUIDE FOR INTERPRETING

The Myth of Sisyphus

Existentialism. Today we find it hard to imagine the suffering that World War II caused in Europe. As many as 20 million people may have died in the Soviet Union alone; that is enough bodies to fill the seats in 400 football stadiums. At death camps like Auschwitz in Poland, the Nazis killed millions more: Jews, gypsies, homosexuals, political prisoners, and prisoners of war. Whole cities were decimated. Warsaw, the capital of Poland, was little more than a heap of rubble by the end of the conflict.

Under the Nazi Occupation of Europe, people were faced with difficult, almost impossible, moral choices. Should they resist the Nazis and risk the lives of their husbands, wives, and children? Or should they try to function normally, hoping for the best? In certain occupied countries, even listening to British radio news was a crime punishable by death.

These desperate conditions gave added authority to a philosophy known as **Existentialism** (eg′ zis ten′ shəl iz′m), which stresses the importance of choice in creating values. As the name of this movement suggests, its followers are more concerned with the responses of individuals—their existence—than with abstract ideas. Existentialists believe that the universe is indifferent to humans. It contains no "right" answers, no ready-made truths. People are thrown upon this earth by chance; however, they are still free to accept their fate and affirm the importance of honesty and compassion.

In "The Myth of Sisyphus," Camus expresses these ideas by rewriting a Greek myth. This ancient myth told how Sisyphus observed Zeus, the king of the gods, carrying away a woman. When Sisyphus revealed this crime, Zeus condemned him to perpetual, body-racking torture. He was forced to roll a heavy rock up an incline, helplessly watch it tumble back down, and then push it up again—time after time, forever. Camus uses this story to symbolize the injustice and senselessness of human suffering. However, he also shows how humanity can rise above suffering by saying, "Yes."

Writing

Have you ever done a job that was boring, difficult, and apparently endless? Describe this task and the feelings it called up in you.

Primary Source

During World War II, Camus expressed his philosophy in a letter to a German friend: "I continue to believe that this world has no ultimate meaning. But I know that something in it has a meaning and that is man, because he is the only creature to insist on having one."

Language Worksheet, *Appreciating the Connotation of a Word*, p. 1540
Selection Test, pp. 1541–1542

Spelling Tip Write the word *myriad* on the chalkboard. Point out to students that the first syllable is spelled with a *y* and not an *i* or an *e*.

Literary Focus Have students discuss their own experiences with films or stories that deal with difficult or trying situations. They may have seen the movie *Spartacus*, for example, about a slave revolt in ancient Rome, or read about those who fought against slavery in the United States, such as Harriet Tubman or Frederick Douglass. Most likely they will have encountered some version of Anne Frank's story. All of these examples show people struggling to be free or to stay alive in the most difficult of circumstances.

Writing/Prior Knowledge Assemble students in small groups. Have them share ideas and tell each other about difficult, seemingly endless situations they have experienced before they begin the assignment.

ESL Teaching Strategy Pair each ESL student with a student proficient in English. Have the English-proficient student act as a coach and elicit from the ESL student a story about a difficult situation he or she once experienced.

Teaching Tenth-Grade Students Tenth-grade students might be daunted by the complexity of Camus's language. Ease them into the essay by telling them the story of Sisyphus and then having them discuss the art on page 1275.

Vocabulary
Preteach the following vocabulary words:
futile (fyoot′ 'l) *adj.*: Useless; hopeless
prudent (prood′ 'nt) *adj.*: Exercising sound judgment; cautious
citadel (sit′ ə del) *n.*: A fortress on a commanding height for the defense of a city
impudent (im′ pyoo dənt) *adj.*: Immodest; shameless
summit (sum′ it) *n.*: Highest point
lucidity (loo sid′ ə tē) *n.*: Clarity
myriad (mir′ ē əd) *adj.*: A great number

The Myth of Sisyphus

Albert Camus

translated by Justin O'Brien

The gods had condemned Sisyphus to ceaselessly rolling a rock to the top of a mountain, whence the stone would fall back of its own weight. They had thought with some reason that there is no more dreadful punishment than futile and hopeless labor.

If one believes Homer, Sisyphus was the wisest and most prudent of mortals. According to another tradition, however, he was disposed to practice the profession of highwayman. I see no contradiction in this. Opinions differ as to the reasons why he became the futile laborer of the underworld. To begin with, he is accused of a certain levity[1] in regard to the gods. He stole their secrets. Aegina, the daughter of Aesopus, was carried off by Jupiter.[2] The father was shocked by that disappearance and complained to Sisyphus. He, who knew of the abduction, offered to tell about it on condition that Aesopus would give water to the citadel of Corinth.[3] To the celestial thunderbolts he preferred the benediction of water. He was punished for this in the underworld. Homer tells us also that Sisyphus had put Death in chains. Pluto[4] could not endure the sight of his deserted, silent empire. He dispatched the god of war, who liberated Death from the hands of her conqueror.

It is said also that Sisyphus, being near to death, rashly wanted to test his wife's love. He ordered her to cast his unburied body into the middle of the

public square. Sisyphus woke up in the underworld. And there, annoyed by an obedience so contrary to human love, he obtained from Pluto permission to return to earth in order to chastise his wife. But when he had seen again the face of this world, enjoyed water and sun, warm stones and the sea, he no longer wanted to go back to the infernal darkness. Recalls, signs of anger, warnings were of no avail. Many years more he lived facing the curve of the gulf, the sparkling sea, and the smiles of earth. A decree of the gods was necessary. Mercury came and seized the impudent man by the collar and, snatching him from his joys, led him forcibly back to the underworld, where his rock was ready for him.

You have already grasped that Sisyphus is the absurd hero. He *is,* as much through his passions as through his torture. His scorn of the gods, his hatred of death, and his passion for life won him that unspeakable penalty in which the whole being is exerted toward accomplishing nothing. This is the price that must be paid for the passions of this earth. Nothing is told us about Sisyphus in the underworld. Myths are made for the imagination to breathe life into them. As for this myth, one sees merely the whole effort of a body straining to raise the huge stone, to roll it and push it up a slope a hundred times over; one sees the face screwed up, the cheek tight against the stone, the shoulder bracing the clay-covered mass, the foot wedging it, the fresh start with arms outstretched, the wholly human security of two earth-clotted hands. At the very end of his long effort measured by skyless space and time without depth, the purpose is achieved. Then Sisyphus watches the stone rush

---

1. **levity** (lev′ i tē) *n*.: Lightness of disposition or conduct; flippancy.
2. **Jupiter** (jōō′ pit ər): In Roman mythology, the chief god.
3. **Corinth** (kôr′ inth): An ancient city in Greece.
4. **Pluto** (plōōt′ ō): In Roman mythology, the god ruling over the lower world.

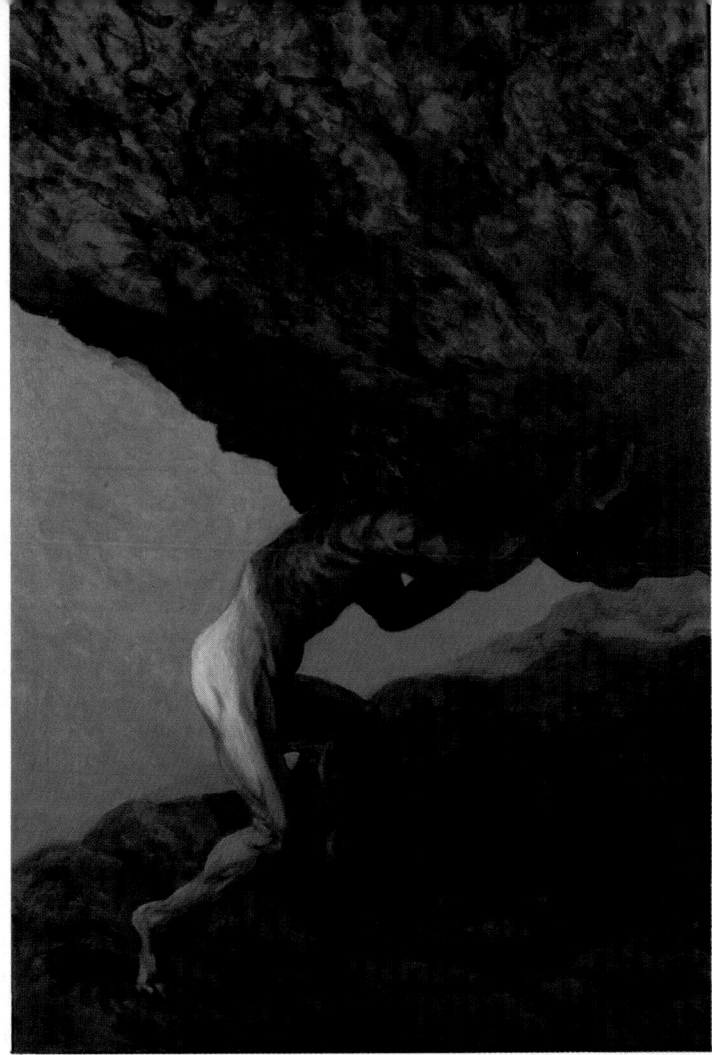

SISYPHUS, 1983
Earl Staley
Private collection

Humanities Note
Fine art, *Sisyphus*, 1983, by Earl Staley. Born in 1938, Earl Staley lives and works in Texas.

In this painting, the leaning, struggling figure of Sisyphus is positioned between two gigantic masses, against a backdrop of brilliant red. The white portion on the figure's back suggests a sun or a fire that is burning into him. The artist has given the rock a rough, uneven texture so that we can almost feel it pressing down on us.

You might want to use the following questions to discuss the art:
1. How does the artist convey the weight of the rock pressing down on Sisyphus?
2. How do the colors that the artist has chosen contribute to the picture's meaning?
3. Does this painting correspond to the picture of Sisyphus that you imagined? Why or why not?
4. Why do you think a contemporary painter might want to use this myth as a subject?

4 Discussion Ask students to explain why Sisyphus must be conscious if his punishment is to be a torture to him. Then ask why being conscious also allows Sisyphus to surmount his torture. Point out the connection that Camus makes between Sisyphus and a member of the working class. Then have students compare the job of an assembly-line worker to that of Sisyphus and explain what meaning Camus's myth might have for such a person.

down in a few moments toward that lower world whence he will have to push it up again toward the summit. He goes back down to the plain.

It is during that return, that pause, that Sisyphus interests me. A face that toils so close to stones is already stone itself! I see that man going back down with a heavy yet measured step toward the torment of which he will never know the end. That hour like a breathing-space which returns as surely as his suffering, that is the hour of consciousness. At each of those moments when he leaves the heights and gradually sinks toward the lairs of the gods, he is superior to his fate. He is stronger than his rock.

If this myth is tragic, that is because its hero is conscious. Where would his torture be, indeed, if at every step the hope of succeeding upheld him? The workman of today works every day in his life at the same tasks, and this fate is no less absurd. But it is tragic only at the rare moments when it becomes conscious. Sisyphus, proletarian[5] of the gods, powerless and rebellious, knows the whole extent of his wretched condition: it is what he thinks of during his descent. The lucidity that was

4

---

5. **proletarian** (prō´ lə ter´ ē ən) *n*.: A member of the working class.

was more than ever necessary. But if we intervene as men, that experience will have an effect upon our language. And if we are not artists in our language first of all, what sort of artists are we? . . . I shall certainly not choose the moment when we are beginning to leave nihilism [the belief that there is no meaning in existence] behind to stupidly deny the values of creation in favor of the values of humanity, or vice versa. In my mind neither one is ever separated from the other and I measure the greatness of an artist (Moliere, Tolstoy, Melville) by the balance he managed to maintain between the two.

to constitute his torture at the same time crowns his victory. There is no fate that cannot be surmounted by scorn.

If the descent is thus sometimes performed in sorrow, it can also take place in joy. This word is not too much. Again I fancy Sisyphus returning toward his rock, and the sorrow was in the beginning. When the images of earth cling too tightly to memory, when the call of happiness becomes too insistent, it happens that melancholy rises in man's heart: this is the rock's victory, this is the rock itself. The boundless grief is too heavy to bear. These are our nights of Gethsemane.[6] But crushing truths perish from being acknowledged. Thus, Oedipus[7] at the outset obeys fate without knowing it. But from the moment he knows, his tragedy begins. Yet at the same moment, blind and desperate, he realizes that the only bond linking him to the world is the cool hand of a girl. Then a tremendous remark rings out: "Despite so many ordeals, my advanced age and the nobility of my soul make me conclude that all is well." Sophocles' Oedipus, like Dostoevsky's Kirilov,[8] thus gives the recipe for the absurd victory. Ancient wisdom confirms modern heroism.

One does not discover the absurd without being tempted to write a manual of happiness. "What! by such narrow ways—?" There is but one world, however. Happiness and the absurd are two sons of the same earth. They are inseparable. It would be a mistake to say that happiness necessarily springs from the absurd discovery. It happens as well that

6. **Gethsemane** (geth sem′ ɔ nē): The garden, east of Jerusalem, where Jesus Christ underwent an ordeal as he contemplated his possible death.
7. **Oedipus** (ed′ i pɔs): A character in Greek mythology who unwittingly killed his father and married his mother. The Greek dramatist Sophocles (496–406 B.C.) wrote three famous plays about him. In the last of these, Oedipus at Colonus, Oedipus is blind and led by his daughter Antigone (an tig′ ɔ nē).
8. **Kirilov** (kē rē′ luf): A character in Dostoevsky's novel *The Possessed* (1871–1872).

the feeling of the absurd springs from happiness. "I conclude that all is well," says Oedipus, and that remark is sacred. It echoes in the wild and limited universe of man. It teaches that all is not, has not been, exhausted. It drives out of this world a god who had come into it with dissatisfaction and a preference for futile sufferings. It makes of fate a human matter, which must be settled among men.

All Sisyphus' silent joy is contained therein. His fate belongs to him. His rock is his thing. Likewise, the absurd man, when he contemplates his torment, silences all the idols. In the universe suddenly restored to its silence, the myriad wondering little voices of the earth rise up. Unconscious, secret calls, invitations from all the faces, they are the necessary reverse and price of victory. There is no sun without shadow, and it is essential to know the night. The absurd man says yes and his effort will henceforth be unceasing. If there is a personal fate, there is no higher destiny, or at least there is but one which he concludes is inevitable and despicable. For the rest, he knows himself to be the master of his days. At that subtle moment when man glances backward over his life, Sisyphus returning toward his rock, in that slight pivoting he contemplates that series of unrelated actions which becomes his fate, created by him, combined under his memory's eye and soon sealed by his death. Thus, convinced of the wholly human origin of all that is human, a blind man eager to see who knows that the night has no end, he is still on the go. The rock is still rolling.

I leave Sisyphus at the foot of the mountain! One always finds one's burden again. But Sisyphus teaches the higher fidelity that negates the gods and raises rocks. He too concludes that all is well. This universe henceforth without a master seems to him neither sterile nor futile. Each atom of that stone, each mineral flake of that night-filled mountain, in itself forms a world. The struggle itself toward the heights is enough to fill a man's heart. One must imagine Sisyphus happy.

Reader's Response *What character in literature or myth is your special hero or heroine? Why?*

THINKING ABOUT THE SELECTION

Interpreting

1. How do the several different stories Camus tells about Sisyphus add further dimensions to this mythical character?
2. Camus says, "Myths are made for the imagination to breathe life into them." How does Camus use realistic details "to breathe life into" this myth?
3. Why is Sisyphus the "proletarian" of the gods?
4. What does Camus mean when he says, "crushing truths perish from being acknowledged"?
5. (a) Why does Sisyphus' awareness of his condition make this a "tragic" myth? (b) How is he like Oedipus?
6. (a) What does Camus mean by asserting that Sisyphus says "yes" to his fate? (b) How does such an affirmation enable Sisyphus to avoid being subject to the gods? (c) How might such an affirmation be a source of "joy"?

Applying

7. Does Camus convince you that "One must imagine Sisyphus happy"? Why or why not?
8. Does this retold myth have any application to our time? Explain.

ANALYZING LITERATURE

Understanding Existentialism

Existentialism, a philosophy given added authority by the events of World War II, focuses on individuals rather than on abstract ideas. It stresses the importance of human choice in an indifferent universe. Although it views the world as a difficult, inhospitable place, it celebrates the power of humans to affirm values such as dignity, honesty, and compassion.

1. "The Myth of Sisyphus" was written during World War II. Why do you think this particular myth had a powerful appeal for people who experienced the terrible events of that time?
2. Sisyphus is condemned to perform the same meaningless actions throughout eternity, and yet Existentialism stresses the importance of choice. According to Camus where does Sisyphus demonstrate the power to choose?

UNDERSTANDING LANGUAGE

Appreciating the Connotations of a Word

The denotation of a word is its dictionary definition. The **connotation** consists of the associations and feelings the word arouses. Sometimes a philosophy or movement of thought will transform the way in which a familiar word is used. Existentialism, for instance, gave entirely new dimensions to the word *absurd*. The dictionary meaning of this adjective is "so clearly untrue as to be laughable or ridiculous," as when we tell someone, "Don't be absurd!" Writers like Camus, however, gave this word a great deal of weight by using it to describe the chanciness and inexplicability of human existence. According to Existentialists we are trapped in a world without rhyme or reason—our position is *absurd*.

1. Camus asserts that Sisyphus is "the absurd hero." (a) In what way is he absurd? (b) In what way is he a hero? (c) How does an "absurd hero" differ from a traditional hero?
2. In this essay Camus also uses this word as a noun: "the absurd." (a) What does he mean—in the third paragraph from the end—by referring to the discovery of "the absurd"? (b) Why does he say, "Happiness and the absurd are two sons of the same earth"?

THINKING AND WRITING

Reinterpreting a Myth

In this essay Camus "breathes life into" an old myth by reinterpreting it so that it applies to his own experience. Choose a myth that has a special appeal to you and reinterpret it for our own era. This tale does not have to come from Greek mythology. You can use a story from Norse mythology, Native American legends, Hebrew folklore, or any other source. Keep the main outline of the myth, but retell it so that it has meaning for a modern audience. In writing your tale, remember to use concrete, realistic details, as Camus does. Emphasize the character or situation that conveys your message. As you revise your myth, read it to several classmates and see whether it speaks to them in some way.

1927–

Günter Grass (goon′ tər gräs) is viewed as a personification of Germany and postwar German literature. In Germany and abroad, he is recognized as a formidable artistic and political force. He has written lyric poetry, drama, fiction, ballet libretti, and political articles; he also draws and paints. When asked how writing relates to drawing, he replied, "I admit that the word or the image comes more easily with the pen. A written metaphor can shine—even glitter—but when I try to evaluate its worth by drawing it, I conclude that the pencil is a much better, more exacting instrument. I regard drawing and sculpture as a corrective endeavor, as a medium of control revealing the limitations of the written word." Grass has illustrated and designed the covers of some of his books.

Grass was born in Danzig, the Baltic seaport that is now the Polish city of Gdansk (g′dänsk). At the time of Grass's birth in 1927, Danzig was a free city, a German-speaking island in the Polish Baltic created after World War I. The first shots of World War II were fired in the attack on the Polish post office in Danzig, annexed by the Nazis. At sixteen, Grass was drafted. Later, seeing the horrors of the German concentration camp at Dachau led him to question Nazi values and practices. Grass uses Germany's Nazi experience as a moral and ethical yardstick.

In the spring of 1946, Grass was released from the service. After working in a potash mine for a year, he moved to Düsseldorf to study at the Academy of Art, but the academy was temporarily closed. Upon a professor's suggestion, he completed an apprenticeship in stonemasonry, after which he studied sculpting and graphics at the Academy. He worked in the evenings as a jazz drummer, and in his spare time, he wrote poetry and dramatic sketches. In 1951 he traveled through Italy. Following his tour of France in 1952, Grass moved to Berlin, where he studied metal sculpture at the Berlin Academy of Art.

Two years later he married Anna Schwarz, a Swiss dancer who stimulated his interest in dance and writing ballets. Without his knowledge Anna submitted some of his poems in a competition sponsored by South German Radio; he won third prize. Subsequently, Grass's poems, short plays, and essays appeared in the literary magazine *Akzente*.

In 1955 Grass read some of his work at a meeting of the Gruppe (Group) 47, an extremely influential association of politically engaged writers. They recognized his talent and encouraged him to write a novel. He and Anna moved to Paris in 1956 so that she could study dance and he could concentrate on his novel *The Tin Drum*, a controversial survey of the Nazi era that mixes fairy tale, fantasy, and realism. The intent of the novel is to investigate the rise of dictatorship, war, and holocaust in the twentieth century. Grass won many literary prizes for *The Tin Drum*; it established his reputation as a writer in Germany and abroad.

Grass has helped to organize meetings of writers from East and West and to promote the cause of peace. In 1982 he won the Antonio Feltrinelli Prize in Rome, a prestigious and richly endowed cultural award. In his acceptance speech, he said that the one reliable ally literature has is the future. Some of Grass's writing deals with the role of the artist in understanding how the past informs the present and determines the future. For Grass the purpose of art is to discover truth and confront reality.

Objectives

Thematic
To understand symbolism and impermanence

Skill
To understand symbolism

GUIDE FOR INTERPRETING

Folding Chairs; Food for Prophets

Commentary

Symbolism. The word symbol is derived from the Greek verb *symballein,* which means "to put together." The related Greek noun *symbolon* means "mark, token, or sign." A symbol, therefore, combines a literal, sensuous quality with an abstract or suggestive quality. Many everyday objects are symbolic, such as the shape of a heart as a symbol of love or a wedding band as a symbol of marriage.

In symbolism concrete objects are used to evoke abstract meanings. Some symbols appear frequently in literature, such as the symbol of a river or flowing water used to represent time and eternity. Other types of symbols are suggestive, depending on how they are used. For example, rain can be used to symbolize a spiritual cleansing or rebirth, or rain can be used as a symbol of death.

In the middle of the nineteenth century, symbolism was dominant in Romantic literature, particularly in the Transcendentalists' writings. In reaction to the Realists, the symbolists of the Romantic period used details of the natural world to represent spiritual ideas. Later in the nineteenth century, a Symbolist movement originated in France that strongly influenced British writing at the turn of the century, as well as twentieth-century poets. Edgar Allan Poe, Paul Valéry, Arthur Rimbaud, William Butler Yeats, Rainer Maria Rilke, and T. S. Eliot are all famous for their symbolism.

Günter Grass is also recognized for his use of symbolism in poetry. He crafts symbols from his immediate experience. As an impressionable child in a Danzig suburb, Grass literally took notes on the making of a world war and the Holocaust. He has been outspoken about the importance of remembering the horrors of World War II. In his writings he concentrates on minutiae as he explores the causes of global evil. For example, he has occasionally used teeth and tooth decay as a symbol of hidden moral or social putrescence.

Similar symbols of rot and disgust occur in "Folding Chairs" and "Food for Prophets." Pay attention to the associations you make as you read these two poems. The associations you make will help you interpret the symbols Grass uses.

Writing

Grass believes that the past should serve as a constant reminder to the present. Discuss a historical event that continues to influence the present and the future.

Literary Focus In pairs or small groups, have students create an original symbol, as Günter Grass does in "Folding Chairs." Tell students to be creative and thoughtful in their choices. Then have them write a short poem or story in which they use their symbol and allude to its meaning. Finally, have students share their work with the class.

Writing/Prior Knowledge As a class, brainstorm for ideas. List all the ideas on the chalkboard. Students should not limit themselves to national events; international events have also had a profound effect on our lives in the United States. Have students select one to write about individually.

ESL Teaching Strategy You might use this poem to discuss the ideas of change and emigration. Ask ESL students to write a journal entry on how their lives have changed. Have these changes been for the better? What changes don't they like? Ask volunteers to share their journal entries with the class.

Master Teacher Note Change is one of the consequences of modern society. With our fast-paced lives, we need to acquire a certain degree of adaptability. Like folding chairs, which are designed for temporary seating in a temporary location, we are continually changing and adapting our needs to fit the pace our lives have taken. Have students write journal entries about difficult or interesting changes in their own lives and how they had to adapt to those changes.

Teaching Tenth-Grade Students Have tenth-grade students memorize Grass's poetry. With such an intimate relationship to the work, students will gain insights into each poem's meaning. Have students recite the poems aloud.

Support Material

Teaching Portfolio
Teacher Backup, p. 1543
Usage and Mechanics Worksheet, p. 1547
Analyzing Literature Worksheet, *Understanding Symbolism*, p. 1548
Critical Thinking and Reading Worksheet, *Interpreting Symbols and*

Expressions, p. 1549
Language Worksheet, *Recognizing Symbols*, p. 1550
Selection Test, pp. 1551–1552

CHAIRS OF PARIS
André Kertész

Folding Chairs

Günter Grass

translated by Michael Hamburger

How sad these changes are.
People unscrew the name plates from the doors,
take the saucepan of cabbage
and heat it up again, in a different place.

5 What sort of furniture is this
that advertises departure?
People take up their folding chairs
and emigrate.

Ships laden with homesickness and the urge to
vomit
10 carry patented seating contraptions
and unpatented owners
to and fro.

Now on both sides of the great ocean
there are folding chairs;
15 how sad these changes are.

Food for Prophets

Günter Grass

translated by Anselm Hollo

When the locusts occupied our town,
no milk came to the door, the dailies suffocated,
our jails were opened to release
all prophets.
They streamed through the streets,
3800 prophets,
talking and teaching without restriction,

and eating their fill of that gray
& jumpy mess
10 we called the plague.
So everything was fine and up to expectations.

Soon our milk came again; our papers reappeared;
and prophets filled our jails.

Reader's Response *Do you agree that change is sad? Explain.*

THINKING ABOUT THE SELECTION

Interpreting

1. What symbols of impermanence do you find in "Folding Chairs"?
2. What is the poet's message in "Folding Chairs"?
3. How does the sense of disgust in "Folding Chairs" contribute to the poet's message?
4. (a) In "Food for Prophets," what does the plague symbolize? (b) Why are the prophets released during the plague?
5. When the "milk came again," and the "papers reappeared," why did the prophets fill the jails?
6. Explain the meaning of the title "Food for Prophets."
7. What comparisons can you make between "Folding Chairs" and "Food for Prophets"?

Applying

8. "Folding Chairs" criticizes the sense of rootlessness in today's world. How do you see the world as lacking roots?

ANALYZING LITERATURE

Understanding Symbolism

The use of concrete objects as representations of abstract ideas is **symbolism.** Writers use symbols as an economical way of expressing complex ideas. For example, in literature, the moon is often used as a symbol of lunacy; a rose sometimes represents youth and beauty.

1. Identify what each of the following symbolize and briefly discuss their functions in the poems.
   a. "Folding Chairs": folding chairs
   b. "Folding Chairs": saucepan of cabbage
   c. "Folding Chairs": homesickness
   d. "Food for Prophets": the dailies
   e. "Food for Prophets": the locusts
2. Add another stanza to "Folding Chairs" in which you include another appropriate symbol of sad change.
3. In your own words, rephrase the title of "Food for Prophets," using an appropriate symbol.

(continued from bottom of page)
THINKING AND WRITING

For a Thinking and Writing assignment for this selection, see page 1543 in the Teaching Portfolio.

Challenge Compare Günter Grass's poetry with the poetry of Rainer Maria Rilke, page 1055, and Federico García Lorca, page 1143, both of whom were highly influential on Grass's poetry.

1 **Enrichment** Locusts, which are members of the grasshopper family, migrate only occasionally. Following an enormous buildup of population, the locusts travel hundreds and thousands of miles to feed on vegetation. Locust swarms are so dense that they actually blacken the sky. In the United States between 1874 and 1877, the Great Plains were frequently hit by locusts, wiping out billions of dollars worth of crops. A single swarm contained an estimated 124 billion insects.

2 **Enrichment** Prophets were religious leaders of Israel. They are believed to have been inspired by God to guide the chosen people. They were often advocates of the poor and leaders in social reform.

6. Answers may differ. Some students may suggest that the title implies an exchange of food for the prophets; others may suggest that the food for the prophets is national strife.
7. In both poems, Grass is reflecting on the theme of impermanence, or change.
8. Answers may differ. Students may reiterate the ideas Grass presents in his poems as well as state how their own lives lack roots.

ANSWERS TO ANALYZING LITERATURE

1. Answers may differ. Suggested responses: a. society's affirmation and perpetuation of impermanence; b. the portability of even our food; c. a desire to return home; d. a lack of information and the suffocation of our need to know what is happening around the world; e. the disease and strife that can plague a society
2. Answers may differ. Students may add symbols for the homeless or victims of AIDS, and so on, which suggest a society that is changing in a negative way.
3. Answers may differ. Their symbols should reflect the tone and theme of the poem.

ITALO CALVINO

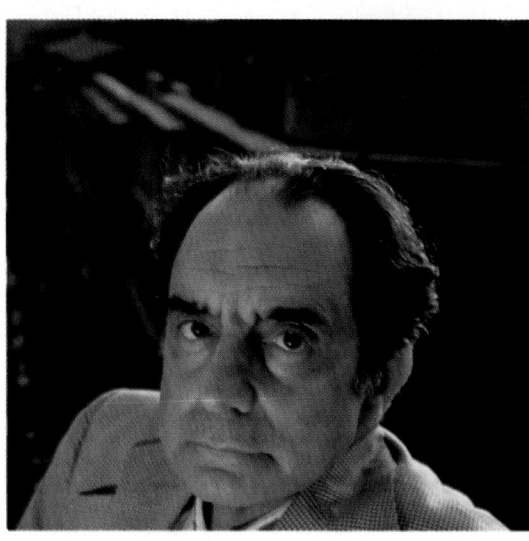

1923–1985

In a collection of Italo Calvino's (ē′ tə lō kal vē′ nō′) essays on the uses of literature, his publisher asked him for a biographical note, which he began: "You ask me for a biographical note—something that always embarrasses me. Biographical data, even those recorded in the public registers, are the most private things one has, and to declare them openly is rather like facing a psychoanalyst. As least I imagine so: I have never had myself psychoanalyzed."

Calvino grew up on the Italian Riviera at San Remo, where his father was curator of the botanical gardens. His parents, both botanists, encouraged him to pursue a career in science, but in his words, Calvino was "attracted to another kind of vegetation, that of the written word." He emerged from World War II as one of Italy's most inventive writers.

During World War II, Calvino fought in a partisan movement against Fascist control of Italy and the Nazi occupation. His experience as a partisan was the basis for his first novel, *The Path to the Nest of Spiders*, which was critically acclaimed. His short story collections *Adam, One Afternoon*, and *Entering the War* were also based on his war experience. They were conceived under the influence of Italy's leading writers in the postwar period, authors who had been stifled previously by government censorship. Their work is characterized by Neorealism, which expressed the harsh, violent postwar mood of the Italian partisans. Calvino's voice, however, is distinct from the Neorealists in its fantasy and fairy-tale qualities.

At the end of the war, Calvino said that he "felt the call of the big city," so he settled in Turin, where he studied literature. After graduating he joined Einaudi, a publishing venture begun by Cesare Pavese. Pavese and Elio Vittorini were writers who shared literary ideas with Calvino and introduced him to leftist politics. During the postwar period, Calvino wrote essays and criticism.

Calvino is best known for having edited a monumental collection of fables. According to his theory, the mold of the fable, which involves a child in the woods or a knight fighting beasts, is the scheme for all human stories. One aspect of the fable relevant to Calvino's fiction is the tension between character and environment. Calvino's characters must triumph over a challenging environment.

Calvino's work has been internationally praised for its imagination, humor, and mixture of actual and fanciful elements interwoven with philosophical and scientific ideas. Calvino himself called for "a literature which breathes philosophy and science but keeps its distance and dissolves, with a slight puff of air, not only theoretical abstractions but also the apparent concreteness of reality." His ability to fuse fantasy and reality has led critics to compare him with the master storytellers Jorge Luis Borges and Gabriel García Márquez.

GUIDE FOR INTERPRETING

The Garden of Stubborn Cats

Commentary

Theme. The central or dominant idea in a work of literature is its **theme.** Theme is often defined as the universal truth or message the author wants to convey. In general theme is a statement about life that applies not only to the characters in the selection but to all people universally. Writers don't usually express theme directly. Rather, they imply theme through the elements of the work such as plot, character, and setting. For example, the urban setting is especially important to the theme of "The Garden of Stubborn Cats."

The cats who populate the voids and cavities of the city give Calvino's story a fairy-tale quality. Calvino depicts them as having their own secret society in which they stubbornly preserve the only garden left in an area of skyscrapers and automobiles. The cats violently resist any urban development where the garden is concerned. Calvino endows the cats with such a mysterious power that even the garden's owner feels like a prisoner to them. By mixing fantasy and reality, Calvino imaginatively explores how urbanization affects the natural environment.

Writing

In "The Garden of Stubborn Cats," Calvino explores the theme of how urban growth interferes with the natural environment. Freewrite, discussing the advantages and disadvantages of urban growth.

Primary Source

In his introduction to a collection of folk tales he retold, Calvino explains why he sees the folk-tale genre as important. "Taken all together, they [folk tales] offer, in their oft-repeated and constantly varying examinations of human vicissitudes, a general explanation of life preserved in the slow ripening of rustic consciences; these folk stories are the catalog of the potential destinies of men and women, especially for that stage in life when destiny is formed, i.e., youth, beginning with birth, which itself often foreshadows the future; then the departure from home, and, finally, through the trials of growing up, the attainment of maturity and the proof of one's humanity . . . There must be fidelity to a goal and purity of heart, values fundamental to salvation and triumph. There must also be beauty, a sign of grace that can be masked by the humble, ugly guise of a frog; and above all, there must be present the infinite possibilities of mutation, the unifying element in everything: men, beasts, plants, things."

Literary Focus Have students discuss the theme of poems, stories, or films they have experienced. Tell them that the theme is not always clear if a work is primarily a comedy or an adventure story. For example, ask them if there is any theme they could draw from the *Star Wars* series of movies. Point out that the theme of a creative work is not the same as its having a moral added to the end, as in some literature of the previous century.

Writing/Prior Knowledge Pair the students in your class. Have them share ideas about the advantages and disadvantages of urban growth before they begin freewriting.

ESL Teaching Strategy To help with the writing assignment, pair each ESL student with an English-proficient student. Have the English-proficient student coach the ESL student on words that concretely reflect his or her ideas about urbanization, as a way of helping with the writing assignment.

Vocabulary

Preteach the following vocabulary words:

environs (en vī´ rənz) *n.*: Districts surrounding a town; vicinity

impassive (im pas´ iv) *adj.*: Not feeling or showing emotion

convergent (kən vʉr´ jənt) *adj.*: Point at which things come together

squalid (skwäl´ id) *adj.*: Wretched; miserable

transfigured (trans fig´ yərd) *adj.*: Having a changed outward appearance

altruistic (al´ tro͞o is´ tik) *adj.*: Motivated by the general welfare of society

Support Material

Teaching Portfolio
Teacher Backup, p. 1553
Grammar in Action Worksheet, *Writing Dialogue*, p. 1557
Usage and Mechanics Worksheet, p. 1559
Vocabulary Check, p. 1560
Analyzing Literature Worksheet,

Analyzing Theme, p. 1561
Critical Thinking and Reading Worksheet, *Appreciating Tone*, p. 1562
Selection Test, pp. 1563–1564

Art Transparency 18
Homage to Louis David by Fernnand Léger

Teaching Tenth-Grade Students
Have tenth-grade students discuss their impressions of cats. What is the typical behavior of cats? Perhaps some students will share details peculiar to their own cats.

The Garden of Stubborn Cats

Italo Calvino

translated by William Weaver

The city of cats and the city of men exist one inside the other, but they are not the same city. Few cats recall the time when there was no distinction: the streets and squares of men were also streets and squares of cats, and the lawns, courtyards, balconies, and fountains: you lived in a broad and various space. But for several generations now domestic felines have been prisoners of an uninhabitable city: the streets are uninterruptedly overrun by the mortal traffic of cat-crushing automobiles; in every square foot of terrain where once a garden extended or a vacant lot or the ruins of an old demolition, now condominiums loom up, welfare housing, brand-new skyscrapers; every entrance is crammed with parked cars; the courtyards, one by one, have been roofed by reinforced concrete and transformed into garages or movie houses or storerooms or workshops. And where a rolling plateau of low roofs once extended, copings,[1] terraces, water tanks, balconies, skylights, corrugated-iron sheds, now one general superstructure rises wherever structures can rise; the intermediate differences in height, between the low ground of the street and the supernal[2] heaven of the penthouses, disappear; the cat of a recent litter seeks in vain the itinerary[3] of its fathers, the point

from which to make the soft leap from balustrade to cornice to drainpipe, or for the quick climb on the roof-tiles.

But in this vertical city, in this compressed city where all voids tend to fill up and every block of cement tends to mingle with other blocks of cement, a kind of counter-city opens, a negative city, that consists of empty slices between wall and wall, of the minimal distances ordained by the building regulations between two constructions, between the rear of one construction and the rear of the next; it is a city of cavities, wells, air conduits, driveways, inner yards, accesses to basements, like a network of dry canals on a planet of stucco and tar, and it is through this network, grazing the walls, that the ancient cat population still scurries.

On occasion, to pass the time, Marcovaldo would follow a cat. It was during the work-break, between noon and three, when all the personnel except Marcovaldo went home to eat, and he—who brought his lunch in his bag—laid his place among the packing-cases in the warehouse, chewed his snack, smoked a half-cigar, and wandered around, alone and idle, waiting for work to resume. In those hours, a cat that peeped in at a window was always welcome company, and a guide for new explorations. He had made friends with a tabby, well fed, a blue ribbon around its neck, surely living with some well-to-do family. This tabby shared with Marcovaldo the habit of an

---

1. **copings** (kō′ piŋz) *n.*: Top layers of masonry walls.
2. **supernal** (sə pʉrn′ əl) *adj.*: Celestial or divine.
3. **itinerary** (ī tin′ ər er′ ē) *n.*: Route.

afternoon stroll right after lunch; and naturally a friendship sprang up.

Following his tabby friend, Marcovaldo had started looking at places as if through the round eyes of a cat and even if these places were the usual environs of his firm he saw them in a different light, as settings for cattish stories, with connections practicable only by light, velvety paws. Though from the outside the neighborhood seemed poor in cats, every day on his rounds Marcovaldo made the acquaintance of some new face, and a miau, a hiss, a stiffening of fur on an arched back was enough for him to sense ties and intrigues and rivalries among them. At those moments he thought he had already penetrated the secrecy of the felines' society: and then he felt himself scrutinized by pupils that became slits, under the surveillance of the antennae of taut whiskers, and all the cats around him sat impassive as sphinxes, the pink triangles of their noses convergent on the black triangles of their lips, and the only things that moved were the tips of the ears, with a vibrant jerk like radar. They reached the end of a narrow passage, between squalid blank walls; and, looking around, Marcovaldo saw that the cats that had led him this far had vanished, all of them together, no telling in which direction, even his tabby friend, and they had left him alone. Their realm had territories, ceremonies, customs that it was not yet granted to him to discover.

On the other hand, from the cat city there opened unsuspected peepholes onto the city of men: and one day the same tabby led him to discover the great Biarritz Restaurant.

Anyone wishing to see the Biarritz Restaurant had only to assume the posture of a cat, that is, proceed on all fours. Cat and man, in this fashion, walked around a kind of dome, at whose foot some low, rectangular little windows opened. Following the tabby's example, Marcovaldo looked down. They were transoms through which the luxurious hall received air and light. To the sound of gypsy violins, partridges and quails swirled by on silver dishes balanced by the white-gloved fingers of waiters in tailcoats. Or, more precisely, above the partridges and quails the dishes whirled, and above the dishes the white gloves, and poised on the waiters'

patent-leather shoes, the gleaming parquet floor,[4] from which hung dwarf potted palms and tablecloths and crystal and buckets like bells with the champagne bottle for their clapper: everything was turned upside-down because Marcovaldo, for fear of being seen, wouldn't stick his head inside the window and confined himself to looking at the reversed reflection of the room in the tilted pane.

But it was not so much the windows of the dining-room as those of the kitchens that interested the cat: looking through the former you saw, distant and somehow transfigured, what in the kitchens presented itself—quite concrete and within paw's reach—as a plucked bird or a fresh fish. And it was toward the kitchens, in fact, that the tabby wanted to lead Marcovaldo, either through a gesture of altruistic friendship or else because it counted on the man's help for one of its raids. Marcovaldo, however, was reluctant to leave his belvedere[5] over the main room: first as he was fascinated by the luxury of the place, and then because something down there had riveted his attention. To such an extent that, overcoming his fear of being seen, he kept peeking in, with his head in the transom.

In the midst of the room, directly under that pane, there was a little glass fish tank, a kind of aquarium, where some fat trout were swimming. A special customer approached, a man with a shiny bald pate, black suit, black beard. An old waiter in tailcoat followed him, carrying a little net as if he were going to catch butterflies. The gentleman in black looked at the trout with a grave, intent air; then he raised one hand and with a slow, solemn gesture singled out a fish. The waiter dipped the net into the tank, pursued the appointed trout, captured it, headed for the kitchens, holding out in front of him, like a lance, the net in which the fish wriggled. The gentleman in black, solemn as a magistrate who has handed down a capital sentence, went to take his seat and wait for the return of the trout, sautéed "à la meunière."[6]

---

4. **parquet** (pär kā´) **floor:** A floor with inlaid woodwork in geometric forms.
5. **belvedere** (bel´ və dir´): An open, roofed gallery in an upper story, built for giving a view of the scenery.
6. **sautéed "à la meunière"** (sȯ tād´ à là mə nyeȓ´): Fish prepared by being rolled in flour, fried in butter, and sprinkled with lemon juice and chopped parsley.

not feel crushed, defeated, "beat." On the contrary, we were victors, driven by the propulsive charge of the just-ended battle, the exclusive possessors of its heritage. Ours was not easy optimism, however, or gratuitous euphoria. Quite the opposite. What we felt we possessed was a sense of life as something that can begin again from scratch, a general concern with problems, even a capacity within us to survive torment and abandonment; but we added also an accent of bold gaiety. Many things grew out of that atmosphere, including the attitude of my first stories and my first novel.

7 **Discussion** Ask students to discuss and evaluate Marcovaldo's reasoning that he cannot be accused of *theft* by hooking a trout from the tank. Point out that words relating to theft are an important strand throughout the rest of the story.

8 **Discussion** Ask students if they think the cat is being any more treacherous than Marcovaldo himself in stealing the fish from him. Why or why not?

9 **Discussion** Ask students what the significance is of the trailing line that leads Marcovaldo "into more and more cattish places." How does the line, unlike his own earlier efforts, finally lead Marcovaldo into the secret realm of the cats?

10 **Discussion** Ask students to compare and contrast the description of the garden with that of the surrounding skyscrapers. What are the unappealing elements in both descriptions?

11 **Discussion** Have students explain what Marcovaldo's emotional state must have been when he almost forgot his fish upon discovering the garden. How does an element of fantasy echo within the description of the garden?

If I found a way to drop a line from up here and make one of those trout bite, Marcovaldo thought, I couldn't be accused of theft; at worst, of fishing in an unauthorized place. And ignoring the miaus that called him toward the kitchens, he went to collect his fishing tackle.

Nobody in the crowded dining room of the Biarritz saw the long, fine line, armed with hook and bait, as it slowly dropped into the tank. The fish saw the bait, and flung themselves on it. In the fray one trout managed to bite the worm: and immediately it began to rise, rise, emerge from the water, a silvery flash, it darted up high, over the laid tables and the trolleys of hors d'oeuvres,[7] over the blue flames of the crêpes Suzette,[8] until it vanished into the heavens of the transom.

Marcovaldo had yanked the rod with the brisk snap of the expert fisherman, so the fish landed behind his back. The trout had barely touched the ground when the cat sprang. What little life the trout still had was lost between the tabby's teeth. Marcovaldo, who had abandoned his line at that moment to run and grab the fish, saw it snatched from under his nose, hook and all. He was quick to put one foot on the rod, but the snatch had been so strong that the rod was all the man had left, while the tabby ran off with the fish, pulling the line after it. Treacherous kitty! It had vanished.

But this time it wouldn't escape him: there was that long line trailing after him and showing the way he had taken. Though he had lost sight of the cat, Marcovaldo followed the end of the line: there it was, running along a wall; it climbed a parapet, wound through a doorway, was swallowed up by a basement . . . Marcovaldo, venturing into more and more cattish places, climbed roofs, straddled railings, always managed to catch a glimpse—perhaps only a second before it disappeared—of that moving trace that indicated a thief's path.

Now the line played out down a sidewalk, in the midst of the traffic, and Marcovaldo, running after it, almost managed to grab it. He flung himself down on his belly: there, he grabbed it! He managed to seize one end of the line before it slipped between the bars of a gate.

Beyond a half-rusted gate and two bits of wall buried under climbing plants, there was a little rank[9] garden, with a small, abandoned-looking building at the far end of it. A carpet of dry leaves covered the path, and dry leaves lay everywhere under the boughs of the two plane-trees, forming actually some little mounds in the yard. A layer of leaves was yellowing in the green water of a pool. Enormous buildings rose all around, skyscrapers with thousands of windows, like so many eyes trained disapprovingly on that little square patch with two trees, a few tiles, and all those yellow leaves, surviving right in the middle of an area of great traffic.

And in this garden, perched on the capitals and balustrades,[10] lying on the dry leaves of the flower-beds, climbing on the trunks of the trees or on the drainpipes, motionless on their four paws, their tails making a question-mark, seated to wash their faces, there were tiger cats, black cats, white cats, calico cats, tabbies, angoras, Persians, house cats and stray cats, perfumed cats and mangy cats. Marcovaldo realized he had finally reached the heart of the cats' realm, their secret island. And, in his emotion, he almost forgot his fish.

It had remained, that fish, hanging by the line from the branch of a tree, out of reach of the cats' leaps; it must have dropped from its kidnapper's mouth at some clumsy movement, perhaps as it was defended from the others, or perhaps displayed as an extraordinary prize. The line had got tangled, and Marcovaldo, tug as he would, couldn't manage to yank it loose. A furious battle had meanwhile been joined among the cats, to reach that unreachable fish, or rather, to win the right to try and reach it. Each wanted to prevent the others from leaping; they hurled themselves on one another, they tangled in midair, they rolled around clutching each other, and finally a general war broke out in a whirl of dry, crackling leaves.

---

7. hors d'oeuvres (ôr dʉrvz´) *n*.: Appetizers served at the beginning of a meal.
8. crêpes Suzette (krāp´ soo zet´): Thin pancakes rolled or folded in a hot, orange-flavored sauce and usually served in flaming brandy.

---

9. rank (raŋk) *adj*.: Growing vigorously and coarsely.
10. capitals and balustrades (bal´ əs trāds): The top parts of columns and railings, respectively.

After many futile yanks, Marcovaldo now felt the line was free, but he took care not to pull it: the trout would have fallen right in the midst of that infuriated scrimmage[11] of felines.

It was at this moment that, from the top of the walls of the gardens, a strange rain began to fall: fish-bones, heads, tails, even bits of lung and lights. Immediately the cats' attention was distracted from the suspended trout and they flung themselves on the new delicacies. To Marcovaldo, this seemed the right moment to pull the line and regain his fish. But, before he had time to act, from a blind of the little villa, two yellow, skinny hands darted out: one was brandishing scissors; the other, a frying pan. The hand with the scissors was raised above the trout, the hand with the frying pan was thrust under it. The scissors cut the line, the trout fell into the pan; hands, scissors and pan withdrew, the blind closed: all in the space of a second. Marcovaldo was totally bewildered.

"Are you also a cat lover?" A voice at his back made him turn round. He was surrounded by little old women, some of them ancient, wearing old-

13

---

11. scrimmage (skrim′ ij) *n*.: A rough-and-tumble fight.

SCHRÖDINGER'S CAT
Elizabeth Knight
New York Academy of Sciences

(continued from bottom of page)
to tie it down to finite ground.

You might want to use the following questions to discuss the art:
1. Why do you think some of the cats have hazy, lighted areas around them?
2. How does the picture suggest that the cat has no definite place or position?

12 Discussion Ask students why this "strange rain" comes as a surprise at this moment in the story. What does it indicate about Marcovaldo's idea that he has discovered the secret world of the city's cats?

13 Discussion Ask students how these surprises deliberately add to the reader's confusion at this point. Is the seizing of the fish related to the "strange rain"? How does the question about being a cat lover also seem interconnected with these events? Point out that writers often exploit such blurrings of cause and effect to startle readers into rethinking the whole situation they are trying to communicate.

Humanities Note

Fine art, Schrödinger's Cat by Elizabeth Knight. Elizabeth Knight was a high-school student from Colorado when she made this picture. The subject is the work of Erwin Schrödinger, an Austrian theoretical physicist who shared a Nobel Prize for his work on the quantum theory and the mathematical formulation of wave mechanics. Knight described her work as follows:

This picture exemplifies Erwin Schrödinger's electron wave equations. The wave/particle duality of the cat inside the faint borders of a box illustrates the wave/particle duality of electrons within the faint borders of an atom. In the same way that electrons are treated as probability clouds with no definite location, this cat has become probability, with no definite position. He occupies all places and yet no places. Schrödinger's cat always lands on its feet of probability, no matter how one tries

14 **Discussion** Ask students if the explanations of the cat-lovers are as convincing about the birds and the frogs as they may be about the cats. Why or why not?

15 **Discussion** Point out to students that Marcovaldo sums up the opinions about the Marchesa in three categories, one positive, and two negative. Ask students to list the arguments presented so far in these three categories. Which category is most persuasive? Explain why.

16 **Reading Strategy** Ask students to add each point in this interchange to their list concerning ways of regarding the Marchesa. Then have students summarize the argument so far.

fashioned hats on their heads; others, younger, but with the look of spinsters; and all were carrying in their hands or their bags packages of leftover meat or fish, and some even had little pans of milk. "Will you help me throw this package over the fence, for those poor creatures?"

All the ladies, cat lovers, gathered at this hour around the garden of dry leaves to take the food to their protégés.[12]

"Can you tell me why they are all here, these cats?" Marcovaldo inquired.

"Where else could they go? This garden is all they have left! Cats come here from other neighborhoods, too, from miles and miles around . . ."

"And birds, as well," another lady added. "They're forced to live by the hundreds and hundreds on these few trees . . ."

"And the frogs, they're all in that pool, and at night they never stop croaking . . . You can hear them even on the eighth floor of the buildings around here."

"Who does this villa belong to anyway?" Marcovaldo asked. Now, outside the gate, there weren't just the cat-loving ladies but also other people: the man from the gas pump opposite, the apprentices from a mechanic's shop, the postman, the grocer, some passers-by. And none of them, men and women, had to be asked twice: all wanted to have their say, as always when a mysterious and controversial subject comes up.

"It belongs to a Marchesa.[13] She lives there, but you never see her . . ."

"She's been offered millions and millions, by developers, for this little patch of land, but she won't sell . . ."

"What would she do with millions, an old woman all alone in the world? She wants to hold on to her house, even if it's falling to pieces, rather than be forced to move . . ."

"It's the only undeveloped bit of land in the downtown area . . . Its value goes up every year . . . They've made her offers—"

---

12. **protégés** (prōt′ ə zhāz′) *n.*: Those guided and helped by another.
13. **Marchesa** (mär kā′ zä): The title of an Italian noblewoman.

"Offers! That's not all. Threats, intimidation, persecution . . . You don't know the half of it! Those contractors!"

"But she holds out. She's held out for years . . ."

"She's a saint. Without her, where would those poor animals go?"

"A lot she cares about the animals, the old miser! Have you ever seen her give them anything to eat?"

"How can she feed the cats when she doesn't have food for herself? She's the last descendant of a ruined family!"

"She hates cats! I've seen her chasing them and hitting them with an umbrella!"

"Because they were tearing up her flowerbeds!"

"What flowerbeds? I've never seen anything in this garden but a great crop of weeds!"

Marcovaldo realized that with regard to the old Marchesa opinions were sharply divided: some saw her as an angelic being, others as an egoist and a miser.

"It's the same with the birds; she never gives them a crumb!"

"She gives them hospitality. Isn't that plenty?"

"Like she gives the mosquitoes, you mean. They all come from here, from that pool. In the summertime the mosquitoes eat us alive, and it's all the fault of that Marchesa!"

"And the mice? This villa is a mine of mice. Under the dead leaves they have their burrows, and at night they come out . . ."

"As far as the mice go, the cats take care of them . . ."

"Oh, you and your cats! If we had to rely on them . . ."

"Why? Have you got something to say against cats?"

Here the discussion degenerated into a general quarrel.

"The authorities should do something: confiscate the villa!" one man cried.

"What gives them the right?" another protested.

"In a modern neighborhood like ours, a mouse-nest like this . . . it should be forbidden . . ."

"Why, I picked my apartment precisely because it overlooked this little bit of green . . ."

"Green, hell! Think of the fine skyscraper they could build here!"

Grammar in Action

Dialogue in fiction consists of the actual words the characters speak, usually but not always enclosed in quotation marks, and sometimes preceded or followed by a phrase identifying the speaker, as in this example: *"Hello," the man said.*

In creative writing classes, students were once taught to replace the word *said* in such dialogue passages with more colorful words. But the style for writing dialogue had already changed drastically, a change largely credited to American writer Ernest Hemingway, who either used *said* almost ex-

clusively or did not attribute quotations to speakers at all, leaving the reader to infer who was speaking.

OLD STYLE DIALOGUE: "As far as the mice go," the old woman quavered querulously, "the cats take care of them."

"Oh," the other woman rasped out with a gasp, "you and your cats! If we had to rely on them . . ."

NEW STYLE DIALOGUE: "As far as the mice go, the cats take care of them. . . ."

Marcovaldo would have liked to add something of his own, but he couldn't get a word in. Finally, all in one breath, he exclaimed: "The Marchesa stole a trout from me!"

The unexpected news supplied fresh ammunition to the old woman's enemies, but her defenders exploited it as proof of the indigence[14] to which the unfortunate noblewoman was reduced. Both sides agreed that Marcovaldo should go and knock at her door to demand an explanation.

It wasn't clear whether the gate was locked or unlocked; in any case, it opened, after a push, with a mournful creak. Marcovaldo picked his way among the leaves and cats, climbed the steps to the porch, knocked hard at the entrance.

At a window (the very one where the frying pan had appeared), the blind was raised slightly and in one corner a round, pale blue eye was seen, and a clump of hair dyed an undefinable color, and a dry skinny hand. A voice was heard, asking: "Who is it? Who's at the door?" the words accompanied by a cloud smelling of fried oil.

"It's me, Marchesa. The trout man," Marcovaldo explained. "I don't mean to trouble you. I only wanted to tell you, in case you didn't know, that the trout was stolen from me, by that cat, and I'm the one who caught it. In fact the line . . ."

"Those cats! It's always those cats . . ." the Marchesa said, from behind the shutter, with a shrill, somewhat nasal voice. "All my troubles come from the cats! Nobody knows what I go through! Prisoner night and day of those horrid beasts! And with all the refuse people throw over the walls, to spite me!"

"But my trout . . ."

"Your trout! What am I supposed to know about your trout!" The Marchesa's voice became almost a scream, as if she wanted to drown out the sizzle of oil in the pan, which came through the window along with the aroma of fried fish. "How can I make sense of anything, with all the stuff that rains into my house?"

"I understand, but did you take the trout or didn't you?"

---

14. **indigence** (in´ di jəns) *n*.: Poverty.

"When I think of all the damage I suffer because of the cats! Ah, fine state of affairs! I'm not responsible for anything! I can't tell you what I've lost! Thanks to those cats, who've occupied house and garden for years! My life at the mercy of those animals! Go and find the owners! Make them pay damages! Damages? A whole life destroyed! A prisoner here, unable to move a step!"

"Excuse me for asking: but who's forcing you to stay?"

From the crack in the blind there appeared sometimes a round, pale blue eye, sometimes a mouth with two protruding teeth; for a moment the whole face was visible, and to Marcovaldo it seemed, bewilderingly, the face of a cat.

"They keep me prisoner, they do, those cats! Oh, I'd be glad to leave! What wouldn't I give for a little apartment all my own, in a nice clean modern building! But I can't go out . . . They follow me, they block my path, they trip me up!" The voice became a whisper, as if to confide a secret. "They're afraid I'll sell the lot . . . They won't leave me . . . won't allow me . . . When the builders come to offer me a contract, you should see them, those cats! They get in the way, pull out their claws; they even chased a lawyer off! Once I had the contract right here, I was about to sign it, and they dived in through the window, knocked over the inkwell, tore up all the pages . . ."

All of a sudden Marcovaldo remembered the time, the shipping department, the boss. He tiptoed off over the dried leaves, as the voice continued to come through the slats of the blind, enfolded in that cloud apparently from the oil of a frying pan. "They even scratched me . . . I still have the scar . . . All alone here at the mercy of these demons . . ."

Winter came. A blossoming of white flakes decked the branches and capitals and the cats' tails. Under the snow, the dry leaves dissolved into mush. The cats were rarely seen, the cat lovers even less; the packages of fish-bones were consigned only to cats who came to the door. Nobody, for quite a while, had seen anything of the Marchesa. No smoke came now from the chimneypot of the villa.

One snowy day, the garden was again full of cats, who had returned as if it were spring, and they were miauing as if on a moonlight night. The

---

17 Discussion Ask students to debate Marcovaldo's accusation that the Marchesa "stole a trout" from him. If they consider his argument self-serving, ask them to decide if this is an oversight on Calvino's part—or if the author is deliberately showing how self-centered even the most generous person can be. Whatever their point of view, ask students to justify their opinion concretely within the context of the story.

18 Discussion Ask students to explain the comic effects of Marcovaldo calling himself "the trout man" and the Marchesa referring to herself as a "prisoner" of the cats. Are either of them really victims of the cats? Why or why not?

19 Discussion What is the significance of Marcovaldo's impression that the Marchesa herself, despite her dislike of the cats, seems to have the face of a cat?

20 Discussion Ask students whether or not the scene the Marchesa describes is credible. How does she impart a fantasy element to the cats' ability to resist the destruction of their secret garden?

"Oh, you and your cats! If we had to rely on them . . ."

In this passage, Calvino merely records the various voices in the garden without indicating exactly who speaks which lines. At other times, Calvino uses *said* or simple, explanatory words such as *inquired, added,* or *explained*. This is very much in the new style of writing dialogue.

Student Activity 1. Find additional passages in the story that reveal how Calvino handles dialogue. In each case, explain why he does or does not identify the speaker or speakers of the lines.

Student Activity 2. Write a brief account of a conversation in which

the speakers are described at the beginning but then referred to as little as possible in the ensuing dialogue. Write the dialogue so that the tone and attitude of the speaker are clear from the words themselves.

Cultural Note Italy has a more defined gender structure than the United States, one that allows less flexibility in how men and women can be regarded. But there is at least one exception to this general rule. In the United States there is a widespread stereotype suggesting that men should prefer dogs as pets while women should prefer cats. In Italy, expressing affection toward domestic animals of all kinds is equally allowable to men and women. Ask students to notice that in "The Garden of Stubborn Cats," it is a man whose affection for cats sets the story in motion, while it is a woman's dislike for cats that provides the story's chief conflict.

Cooperative Learning How writers depict animals in their work is a subject that might appeal to students. Divide the class into small groups. Have each group select a writer who depicts animals in his or her work. Then have them compare that writer's depiction of animals to Calvino's depiction in "The Garden of Stubborn Cats."

neighbors realized that something had happened: they went and knocked at the Marchesa's door. She didn't answer: she was dead.

In the spring, instead of the garden, there was a huge building site that a contractor had set up. The steam shovels dug down to great depths to make room for the foundations, cement poured into the iron armatures, a very high crane passed beams to the workmen who were making the scaffoldings. But how could they get on with their work? Cats walked along all the planks, they made bricks fall and upset buckets of mortar, they fought in the midst of the piles of sand. When you started to raise an armature, you found a cat perched on top of it, hissing fiercely. More treacherous pusses climbed onto the masons' backs as if to purr, and there was no getting rid of them. And the birds continued making their nests in all the trestles,[15] the cab of the crane looked like an aviary . . . And you couldn't dip up a bucket of water that wasn't full of frogs, croaking and hopping . . .

---

15. **trestles** (tres´ 'lz) *n.*: Frameworks of vertical or slanting beams and crosspieces.

Reader's Response *What would you have done if you were the Marchesa?*

PRIMARY SOURCE

Calvino explains that he wrote his classic book *Italian Folktales* because of a publishing need: "a collection of Italian folktales to take its rightful place alongside the great anthologies of foreign folklore." In his introduction to the magnificent collection, Calvino discusses the skill of the storyteller constructing a folktale.

". . . The storyteller, with a kind of instinctive skillfulness, shies away from the constraint of popular tradition, from the unwritten law that the common people are capable only of repeating trite themes without ever actually 'creating'; perhaps the narrator thinks that he is producing only variations on a theme, whereas actually he ends up telling us what is in his heart.

"A regard for conventions and a free inventiveness are equally necessary in constructing a folktale. Once the theme is laid out there are certain steps required to reach a solution; they are interchangeable ingredients—the horse hide carried up in flight by an eagle, the well that leads to the netherworld, dove-maidens whose clothes are stolen while they bathe, magic boots and cloak purloined by thieves, three nuts that must be cracked, the house of the winds where information is given about the path to be followed, and so on. It is up to the narrator to organize these, to pile them up like the bricks in a wall, hurrying over the dull places, all this depending upon the degree of the narrator's talent and what he puts into his story, mixing his own mortar of local color and personal tribulations and expectations."

Closure and Extension

ANSWERS TO THINKING ABOUT THE SELECTION

1. They no longer can inhabit the same spaces humans do because of the traffic, the skyscrapers, and the gardens that have been turned into garages. As a result, they have to live in the uninhabited leftover spaces and empty slices between buildings that people cannot visit.

2. The story is told from Marcovaldo's point of view, and much of it shows him imagining or inferring how and why cats act as they do in the city and in their garden.

3. (a) He wants to see the city from their point of view, learn their stories, and share the way they regard people. (b) Few cats appear to live in the neighborhood and yet many of them actually do live there in a world of their own that exists right next to the world of people.

4. Answers will differ. Possible evaluations may consider her neither as an angelic being nor as an egoist and miser, but rather as an interesting and colorful eccentric.

5. The food they bring ensures that the cats will stay in the garden and con-

THINKING ABOUT THE SELECTION

Interpreting

1. Why are the cats "prisoners of an uninhabitable city," as Calvino calls them early in the story?
2. In what ways do we see the story through Marcovaldo's imagination?
3. (a) Why does Marcovaldo want to share the cats' secret society? (b) What intrigues him about the cats?
4. Public opinion about the Marchesa was divided. What is your opinion of her?
5. How do the neighbors who feed the cats contribute to the Marchesa's imprisonment?
6. How do you interpret the face that Marcovaldo sees through the crack in the blind?
7. Calvino shifts from third-person narration (he, she, they) to second-person narration (you) at the end of the story. What is the effect of Calvino's shift in narration?
8. Calvino leaves the end of the story suspended. (a) Do you think the developers were able to finish the job? (b) Whether they finished or not, with what implied moral does Calvino end the story?

Applying

9. Both the cats and the Marchesa are portrayed as victims in the story. How are people and animals victims of their surroundings?

ANALYZING LITERATURE

Analyzing Theme

Theme, the universal truth or message conveyed in a literary work, is sometimes implied through the elements of character, plot, and setting. As the author develops these elements, theme emerges as a general insight into life. Usually theme is meant to apply to all people of different cultures as well as to the characters in the story. For example, Italy is not the only country that has had to face the effects of urbanization; other European, North American, and Asian countries have had to consider how to preserve their natural environment while advancing in urban growth and development.

1. The title of the story provides some insight into its theme. Retitle the story to capture its theme.
2. How does Calvino's description of setting early in the story contribute to theme?
3. Reread the dialogue among the Marchesa's neighbors. Summarize the debate, including all perspectives of the controversial argument.

CRITICAL THINKING AND READING

Appreciating Tone

Tone refers to the author's attitude toward his or her subject. One of the ways authors establish tone is simply through the language they use to describe characters and setting. A writer can manipulate the reader's reaction to the subject through tone. Consider, for example, Calvino's tone early in "The Garden of Stubborn Cats." "But for several generations now domestic felines have been prisoners of an uninhabitable city: the streets are uninterruptedly overrun by the mortal traffic of cat crushing automobiles. . . ." First, by calling the animals "domestic felines," Calvino endows them with a certain dignity. Then he calls them prisoners and describes their living condition as totally impossible, which should arouse the audience's compassion and sympathy. Furthermore, Calvino calls the human traffic of the city "mortal" and "cat crushing," terms that will outrage the cat lover. Maintaining tone or shifting tone when appropriate is important to the coherence of a literary work.

1. (a) What is the tone of the paragraph beginning "Following his tabby friend, Marcovaldo . . ."? (b) How does Calvino achieve tone in this paragraph?
2. Identify the tone at the end of the story and refer to specific examples from the text to support your answer.

THINKING AND WRITING

Writing About Urbanization

What parallels can you draw between the setting of "The Garden of Stubborn Cats" and land with which you are familiar? Once a location starts being developed commercially, more and more land surrounding that location has to accommodate the commercial center. The people who work in the office buildings and skyscrapers need to have houses or apartments in which to live close to work. In turn those people must have access to grocery and clothes shopping and recreational facilities. Develop an essay in which you discuss the ways in which urbanization places demands on the land and interferes with the natural habitat. As you write, discuss both positive and negative results of urbanization. You might want to interview a few of your peers to get their opinions on urbanization. As you revise, propose solutions to the problems you discussed. Finally, proofread your paper for spelling and mechanical errors.

(continued from bottom of page)

less pleasant, more cramped life.
3. Those who see the Marchesa as an angelic being point out that she provides a refuge for the cats, birds, and frogs, even if she doesn't feed them or like them. They feel she has a right to stay in her own house, and they like the bit of green her garden provides. Those who see the Marchesa as an egoist and a miser regard all the animals as nuisances that shouldn't exist in a modern neighborhood. They regard her as too stingy to feed the cats and too stubborn to move, thus limiting her financial income.

ANSWERS TO CRITICAL THINKING AND READING

1. (a) The description is affectionate, amusing, gives the cats almost human relationships, and expresses respect for their secrets. (b) The detailed descriptions of the cats make them vivid and sympathetic; the use of words usually applied to people ("ties and intrigues and rivalries") gives the reader a sense of observing characters with human personalities.
2. The tone in describing the construction work is dull and matter-of-fact: "cement poured into the iron armatures, a very high crane passed beams." It is almost as though nothing human is involved in the work. The disrupting animals, however, are seen as angry and defiant: "hissing fiercely," "treacherous pusses."

THINKING AND WRITING

Writing Across the Curriculum You might want to inform the social studies department that students are reading this selection. A social studies teacher can then help students choose materials about urbanization that will provide a context for discussing Calvino's theme. As a writing assignment, students can relate his theme of urbanization to present-day concerns.

Challenge Tell students that Calvino was fascinated by the Tarot, a medieval deck of cards about which he wrote an interconnected book of tales. Have students research the history of the Tarot or examine a deck of Tarot cards. Then ask them to explain how Calvino's interest in fantasy could be triggered by these cards.

tinue to pester the Marchesa.
6. He is bewildered by the fact that it looks like the face of a cat. Student responses may suggest that she is very like the cats, despite her anger at them.
7. The second person refers to any of the construction workers and thus the story moves away from the character of Marcovaldo and his sympathetic view of the cats and the garden.

8. (a) Answers will differ, but students should observe that few building projects are disrupted by stubborn cats, birds, and frogs. (b) Urbanization not only removes the spaces where people once lived, but removes the environment in which animals lived as well, no matter how stubborn they are.
9. People and animals who have to live in unpleasant environments often suffer because of it.

ANSWERS TO ANALYZING LITERATURE

1. Answers will differ. Possible responses will reflect students' ideas of the story's theme.
2. The opening of the story lays out the two worlds that exist side by side in the city, that of people and that of the cats. It also points out that urbanization has already caused cats to live a

PRIMO LEVI

1919–1987

Focus

More About the Author Primo Levi's writing reveals much insight into the Holocaust experience. At the end of his book *The Reawakening*, the author analyzes the factors that helped him survive the Nazi concentration camps at Auschwitz-Buna: "The fact that I survived and returned unharmed is due, in my opinion, chiefly to good luck. Preexisting factors played only a small part: for instance, my training as a mountaineer and my profession of chemist, which won me some privileges in the last months of imprisonment. Perhaps I was helped too by my interest, which has never flagged, in the human spirit and by the will not only to survive (which was common to many) but to survive with the precise purpose of recounting the things we had witnessed and endured."

Critical Evaluation Writing in *The New Republic*, critic David Denby declared that "Primo Levi is the great memoirist of the Holocaust . . . and one of the outstandingly beautiful and moving writers of our time." Ask students to look for ways in which Levi makes his personal experience "moving" to readers.

In his memoirs, novels, short stories, poetry, and essays, Primo Levi (prē´ mō lā´ vē) allowed his formidable curiosity to wander widely. Yet Levi was probably best known as a survivor and chronicler of the Nazi Holocaust—the war against Jews and other groups that claimed millions and millions of lives.

Born in Turin, Italy, Levi came from a Jewish family that had lived in the region for many generations. As a boy, Levi had little sense of his own Judaism. "Like most Jews of . . . Italian descent," he later wrote, "my parents and grandparents . . . had thoroughly assimilated the language, customs, and ethical attitudes of the country. Religion did not count much in my family."

Yet Levi's religion was to have a drastic effect on his life. In 1938 the Italian government enacted a series of "racial laws" similar to those in Germany. These laws made it illegal for Jews to study or teach in public schools, serve in the armed forces, or own land over a certain value. Levi, who had been fascinated by science since he was a teenager, was then completing a university degree in chemistry. Suddenly, however, his presence at school was less welcome. As he later recalled in *The Periodic Table*: "My Christian classmates were civil people; none of them, nor any of the teachers, had directed at me a hostile word or gesture, but I could feel them withdraw and, following an ancient pattern, I withdrew as well."

With some persistence Levi earned his degree in 1941. However, more terrible events were to come. Two years later the German army occupied Italy, and Levi fled to the hills above Turin to join a resistance band, an underground group working against the Nazi threat. In December 1943 Levi and his comrades were captured. Since the young chemist confessed that he was Jewish, he was soon deported to the Nazi concentration camp at Auschwitz, in Poland. As in most concentration camps, the prisoners were starved and brutalized. In periodic "selections," all those prisoners deemed incapable of work were gassed and burned in large ovens called crematoria.

Against great odds Levi survived until the camp was liberated in late 1944. Back in Turin he resumed his career as a chemist. Yet Levi felt a compulsion to record his nightmarish experiences, and in 1947 he completed *Survival in Auschwitz*. The book won little attention when it was first published, and Levi wrote nothing more for years. In 1958, however, the book was reprinted and made its author famous. Encouraged, Levi set to work on *The Reawakening* (1963), a sequel describing his long, eventful trek home after his liberation.

Levi lived a productive dual life as an industrial chemist and writer until 1977, when he retired to write full time. In many of his books, such as *The Periodic Table* (1975) and *Other People's Trades* (1985), Levi explored the worlds of science, literature, history, and language. Yet he never ceased to examine his Holocaust experiences, and in his last book, *The Drowned and the Saved* (1986), he viewed this subject with a darker, less hopeful eye. Primo Levi died on April 11, 1987, an apparent suicide.

GUIDE FOR INTERPRETING

from *Survival in Auschwitz*

Commentary

Historical Context. The word *holocaust* originally referred to a burnt religious sacrifice, but today the word is used to describe the murder of millions of Jews and other groups by Adolf Hitler's Nazi regime. Hitler's war on the Jews began during the early 1930's, when the Nazi Party boycotted Jewish businesses, drove Jews from many professions, and declared marriages between Jews and Christians a crime.

The worst, however, was yet to come. After the German Army invaded Poland in 1939, the invaders began confining the three million Polish Jews in overcrowded ghettos. At least 700,000 died of disease and starvation over the next two years.

Soon the Germans marched into France, Holland, Belgium, and other parts of Europe, extending the scope of the Holocaust. When, for example, Germany attacked the Soviet Union in June 1941, special soldiers were sent to murder Jewish civilians. One of the worst such atrocities occurred in September of that year, when German soldiers shot 33,771 Jews and threw their bodies into the Babi Yar ravine near Kiev. Meanwhile, millions of Jews, Gypsies, Poles, Russians, and others were sent to concentration camps such as Auschwitz, Buchenwald, Dachau, and Treblinka. Here the prisoners were worked to death or simply exterminated by means of poison gas, electrocution, or lethal injection. By the war's end, six million Jews—nearly two out of every three Jews living in Europe before the war—had died in the concentration camps. So had millions of non-Jews.

Although Italy had encouraged the rise of Hitler's regime, the Italian dictator Benito Mussolini originally had little interest in persecuting Italy's Jews. In fact, the Italian Fascist Party even included a small number of Jewish members. Yet as the two nations drew closer together, Mussolini decided that Italy, too, needed to preserve its "racial purity." In November 1938 Italy's "racial laws" went into effect.

However, until the German invasion of 1943, Italian Jews such as Primo Levi were seldom deported to concentration camps. Even after the German invasion, many Italians courageously hid their Jewish neighbors or smuggled them to freedom. For this reason about 85 percent of the 45,200 Italian Jews survived to the end of the war. Yet almost 7,000 were captured, loaded into cattle cars, and sent to concentration camps. Primo Levi was one of the tiny minority who returned home alive to tell the brutal story of his ordeal in the Nazi camps.

Writing

Think of something that plays a big part in defining your identity, such as an item of clothing or jewelry, or a favorite book or musical recording. Describe the item; then tell why it is important to you and how you would feel if it were taken away.

Literary Focus Help students recognize that personal narrative provides a compelling insight into a historical context. Discuss with students how a first-person narrative creates an authentic, convincing point of view. Have students give examples of other personal narratives that have given them insights into historical contexts.

Writing/Prior Knowledge Have students think of "trademarks" that identify famous sports figures, entertainers, or politicians before they brainstorm a list of personal items to start their own writing.

ESL Teaching Strategy Have ESL students share with the class incidents of political or social prejudice that they are aware of in their culture. Ask the class to discuss whether this kind of incident occurs in their own neighborhoods.

Teaching Tenth-Grade Students Students may find it difficult to comprehend the experience of having their shoes and clothing taken away and being forced to wear issued clothing. You may wish to have them compare and contrast this experience with that of wearing uniforms for sports teams.

Vocabulary

Preteach the following vocabulary words:

writhe (rīth) *v.*: To contort the body, as in agony

robust (rō bust´) *adj.*: Strong and healthy, full of vigor

taciturn (tas´ə tʉrn´) *adj.*: Silent, uncommunicative

incomprehensible (in´ käm prē hen´ sə bəl) *adj.*: Unable to be understood

sordid (sôr´ did) *adj.*: Depressingly wretched

demolition (dem´ ə lish´ ən) *n.*: Destruction, ruin

prophetic (prō fet´ ik) *adj.*: Showing a prediction of the future, especially under divine guidance

intuition (in´ tōo ish´ ən) *n.*: Immediate apprehension or understanding

affinity (ə fin´ i tē) *n.*: Close relationship or connection

---

Support Material

Teaching Portfolio

Teacher Backup, p. 1565
Grammar in Action Worksheet, *Using Active and Passive Voice*, p. 1569
Usage and Mechanics Worksheet, p. 1571
Vocabulary Check, p. 1572

Analyzing Literature Worksheet, *Understanding Historical Context*, p. 1573
Critical Thinking and Reading Worksheet, *Appreciating Details*, p. 1574
Selection Test, pp. 1575–1576

Spelling Tip Point out to students the *-ible* ending on the word *incomprehensible*. Draw their attention also to the *c* in *taciturn*.

from Survival in Auschwitz

Primo Levi

translated by Stuart Woolf

The journey did not last more than twenty minutes. Then the lorry[1] stopped, and we saw a large door, and above it a sign, brightly illuminated (its memory still strikes me in my dreams): *Arbeit Macht Frei,*[2] work gives freedom.

We climb down, they make us enter an enormous empty room that is poorly heated. We have a terrible thirst. The weak gurgle of the water in the radiators makes us ferocious; we have had nothing to drink for four days. But there is also a tap—and above it a card which says that it is forbidden to drink as the water is dirty. Nonsense. It seems obvious that the card is a joke, "they" know that we are dying of thirst and they put us in a room, and there is a tap, and *Wassertrinken Verboten.*[3] I drink and I incite my companions to do likewise, but I have to spit it out, the water is tepid and sweetish, with the smell of a swamp.

This is hell. Today, in our times, hell must be like this. A huge, empty room: we are tired, standing on our feet, with a tap which drips while we cannot drink the water, and we wait for something which will certainly be terrible, and nothing happens and nothing continues to happen. What can one think about? One cannot think anymore, it is like being already dead. Someone sits down on the ground. The time passes drop by drop.

We are not dead. The door is opened and an SS[4] man enters, smoking. He looks at us slowly and asks, *"Wer kann Deutsch?"*[5] One of us whom I have never seen, named Flesch, moves forward; he will be our interpreter. This SS man makes a long, calm speech; the interpreter translates. We have to form rows of five, with intervals of two yards between man and man; then we have to undress and make a bundle of the clothes in a special manner, the woolen garments on one side, all the rest on the other; we must take off our shoes but pay great attention that they are not stolen.

Stolen by whom? Why should our shoes be stolen? And what about our documents, the few things we have in our pockets, our watches? We all look at the interpreter, and the interpreter asks the German, and the German smokes and looks him through and through as if he were transparent, as if no one had spoken.

I had never seen old men naked. Mr. Bergmann wore a truss[6] and asked the interpreter if he should take it off, and the interpreter hesitated. But the German understood and spoke seriously to the interpreter pointing to someone. We saw the interpreter swallow and then he said: "The officer says, take off the truss, and you will be given that of Mr. Coen." One could see the words coming bitterly out of Flesch's mouth; this was the German manner of laughing.

---

1. lorry (lôr´ē) *n.*: British term for "truck."
2. *Arbeit Macht Frei* (är´ bīt mäkt frī)
3. *Wassertrinken Verboten* (väs´ ər trink´n fer bōt´ 'n): German for "It is forbidden to drink the water."

4. SS: Schutzstaffel, a Nazi secret police organization.
5. *Wer kann Deutsch?* (ver kän doich): German for "Who knows German?"
6. truss *n.*: A padded strap worn to support a hernia, or abdominal muscle rupture.

Now another German comes and tells us to put the shoes in a certain corner, and we put them there, because now it is all over and we feel outside this world and the only thing is to obey. Someone comes with a broom and sweeps away all the shoes, outside the door in a heap. He is crazy, he is mixing them all together, ninety-six pairs, they will be all mixed up. The outside door opens, a freezing wind enters and we are naked and cover ourselves up with our arms. The wind blows and slams the door; the German reopens it and stands watching with interest how we <u>writhe</u> to hide from the wind, one behind the other. Then he leaves and closes it.

Now the second act begins. Four men with razors, soapbrushes and clippers burst in; they have trousers and jackets with stripes, with a number sewn on the front; perhaps they are the same sort as those others of this evening (this evening or yesterday evening?); but these are <u>robust</u> and flourishing. We ask many questions but they catch hold of us and in a moment we find ourselves shaved and sheared. What comic faces we have without hair!

The four speak a language which does not seem of this world. It is certainly not German, for I understand a little German.

Finally another door is opened: here we are, locked in, naked, sheared and standing, with our feet in water—it is a shower-room. We are alone. Slowly the astonishment dissolves, and we speak, and everyone asks questions and no one answers. If we are naked in a shower-room, it means that we will have a shower. If we have a shower it is because they are not going to kill us yet. But why then do they keep us standing, and give us nothing to drink, while nobody explains anything, and we have no shoes or clothes, but we are all naked with our feet in the water, and we have been traveling five days and cannot even sit down. **9**

And our women?

Mr. Levi asks me if I think that our women are like us at this moment, and where they are, and if we will be able to see them again. I say yes, because he is married and has a daughter; certainly we will see them again. But by now my belief is that all this

6 Discussion Ask students why they think Levi refers so often to a sense of being outside the world: "we feel outside this world."

7 Reading Strategy Have students look for Levi's references to drama or theater in which he suggests that events are being performed as a play in which he is an unwilling participant.

8 Discussion Ask students to imagine how their appearance would change without any hair around their faces.

9 Reading Strategy Ask students how pronouns help Levi to personalize his narrative. What is the effect of this personalization on the reader?

Humanities Note

Fine art, *To the Victims of Fascism*, by Hans Grundig. German painter Hans Grundig and his wife, Lea, were documentary artists who used their art to lead an active campaign against the Nazis.

Grundig painted *To the Victims of Fascism* to illustrate the theme of "the senseless destruction of humanity." Two corpses lie in the foreground of an enclosure fenced with barbed wire. Both wear the numbers of political prisoners, and the first one is also marked as a Jew. The color red, symbolizing blood, dominates the canvas.

You might want to use the following questions to discuss the art:
1. What feeling or mood does the painting convey?
2. How does this painting convey the theme of "the senseless destruction of humanity"?

Grammar in Action

Using Active and Passive Voice A verb is in the **active voice** if its subject performs the action:

We *ask* him many questions.

A verb is in the **passive voice** if its action is performed upon the subject. The passive verb is always a verb phrase consisting of some form of the verb *be* (*is*, *was*, and so on) plus the past participle of the verb:

We *will be given* shoes and clothes.

The active voice is more direct and economical. However, a writer may use the passive voice to produce a particular effect. For example, Primo Levi uses the passive voice to underscore the prisoners' helplessness. Note the use of the passive voice in the following sentence from *Survival in Auschwitz*:

We *are transformed* into the phantoms glimpsed yesterday evening.

Student Activity 1. Locate three active and three passive verbs in *Survival in Auschwitz*. (Choose examples other than the ones shown above.) Write and label the sentences and identify the verb parts in each.

Student Activity 2. Write a three-sentence description using the active voice. Then change the active voice to the passive voice and compare the two descriptions.

10 Enrichment Jewish learning is characterized by reading, discussion, and questioning. Study of the Torah, the body of wisdom and law contained in Jewish scripture and other sacred literature, is considered one of the noblest kinds of work. The oral tradition is valued, with each generation of scholars—rabbis and students alike—uncovering answers and finding new meanings in the scriptures.

11 Discussion Have students explain why Levi feels respect for Flesch. Do students agree? Why does Levi want the reader to know that he recognizes Flesch's pain in his role as interpreter?

12 Discussion Have students analyze why Levi feels that the prisoners are "ashamed" of their silence. How do the students feel they might have acted in the same circumstances? Why?

13 Enrichment Point out that *reveille* is the signal to arise in the morning, given at about sunrise by bugle or other alarm. It is from the French word *réveiller*, meaning to awaken.

14 Clarification There *was* a class of people in the camps designated as criminals. These were probably common criminals, at least in part, and had a higher status than Jews. It is unclear, however, who this man is.

15 Discussion Have students debate whether they would have believed this description of life in the concentration camp. What does the author mean by "whoever boxes well can become cook"? Could this be true, or is it an example of the seeming absurdity of the dispensation of jobs in the camp?

is a game to mock and sneer at us. Clearly they will kill us, whoever thinks he is going to live is mad, it means that he has swallowed the bait, but I have not; I have understood that it will soon all be over, perhaps in this same room, when they get bored of seeing us naked, dancing from foot to foot and trying every now and again to sit down on the floor. But there are two inches of cold water and we cannot sit down.

We walk up and down without sense, and we talk, everybody talks to everybody else, we make a great noise. The door opens, and a German enters; it is the officer of before. He speaks briefly, the interpreter translates. "The officer says you must be quiet, because this is not a rabbinical school."[7] One sees the words which are not his, the bad words, twist his mouth as they come out, as if he was spitting out a foul taste. We beg him to ask what we are waiting for, how long we will stay here, about our women, everything; but he says no, that he does not want to ask. This Flesch, who is most unwilling to translate into Italian the hard cold German phrases and refuses to turn into German our questions because he knows that it is useless, is a German Jew of about fifty, who has a large scar on his face from a wound received fighting the Italians on the Piave.[8] He is a closed, taciturn man, for whom I feel an instinctive respect as I feel that he has begun to suffer before us.

The German goes and we remain silent, although we are a little ashamed of our silence. It is still night and we wonder if the day will ever come. The door opens again, and someone else dressed in stripes comes in. He is different from the others, older, with glasses, a more civilized face, and much less robust. He speaks to us in Italian.

By now we are tired of being amazed. We seem to be watching some mad play, one of those plays in which the witches, the Holy Spirit and the devil appear. He speaks Italian badly, with a strong foreign accent. He makes a long speech, is very polite, and tries to reply to all our questions.

---

7. rabbinical school: A school for the training of rabbis, scholars, and teachers of Jewish law. The comment is a negative reference to the practice of orally disputing issues of the law.
8. Piave (pyä′ vä): A river in northeastern Italy, located between Padua and Venice.

We are at Monowitz, near Auschwitz, in Upper Silesia, a region inhabited by both Poles and Germans. This camp is a work-camp, in German one says *Arbeitslager*;[9] all the prisoners (there are about ten thousand) work in a factory which produces a type of rubber called Buna, so that the camp itself is called Buna.

We will be given shoes and clothes—no, not our own—other shoes, other clothes, like his. We are naked now because we are waiting for the shower and the disinfection, which will take place immediately after the reveille, because one cannot enter the camp without being disinfected.

Certainly there will be work to do, everyone must work here. But there is work and work: he, for example, acts as doctor. He is a Hungarian doctor who studied in Italy and he is the dentist of the Lager.[10] He has been in the Lager for four and a half years (not in this one: Buna has only been open for a year and a half), but we can see that he is still quite well, not very thin. Why is he in the Lager? Is he Jewish like us? "No," he says simply, "I am a criminal."

We ask him many questions. He laughs, replies to some and not to others, and it is clear that he avoids certain subjects. He does not speak of the women: he says they are well, that we will see them again soon, but he does not say how or where. Instead he tells us other things, strange and crazy things, perhaps he too is playing with us. Perhaps he is mad—one goes mad in the Lager. He says that every Sunday there are concerts and football matches. He says that whoever boxes well can become cook. He says that whoever works well receives prize-coupons with which to buy tobacco and soap. He says that the water is really not drinkable, and that instead a coffee substitute is distributed every day, but generally nobody drinks it as the soup itself is sufficiently watery to quench thirst. We beg him to find us something to drink, but he says that he cannot, that he has come to see us secretly, against SS orders, as we still have to be disinfected, and that he must leave at once; he has come because he has a liking for Italians, and

---

9. Arbeitslager (är′ bīt släg′ r): "Work camp."
10. Lager (läg′ r): German for "camp."

TYPHUS IN THE CAMP,
TRANSNISTRIA, 1943
Arnold Daghani
/O Institute for Jewish Research,
New York

Humanities Note
Fine art, *Typhus in the Camp, Transnistria*, 1943, by Arnold Daghani. Jewish painter Arnold Daghani (b. 1909) was interned in a Nazi labor camp at the age of thirty-one. He spent two years in various prison camps, where he was forced to do hard labor and witnessed many atrocities against his fellow prisoners. During this time Daghani chronicled the hard life of his fellow Jews with more than fifty drawings and watercolor paintings. He also complied with requests from German soldiers and SS men to paint their portraits.

Arnold Daghani's artistic ability may have saved his life in the Nazi labor camps, where so many others died. In 1944 he escaped to Bucharest. His work is an important historic record and may be seen today in Jerusalem.

Typhus in the Camp, Transnistria was painted during Arnold Daghani's first year of internment. He used watercolor paints brought from his home and crude brushes fashioned of fur taken from fellow prisoners' hats. The dark and gloomy blue paint is appropriate to the mood of this tragic scene. The stark rows of mauve and sickly yellow faces and the dejected postures of the figures convey the despair and hopelessness of the imprisoned victims.

You might want to use the following questions to discuss the art:
1. Describe how this picture makes you feel.
2. What is the significance of the featureless faces in this painting?

16 Reading Strategy Ask students what they think of this person. Would they believe anything he said? Why or why not?

17 Discussion Why do the prisoners avoid looking into one another's eyes? Why did the author choose the word "puppets" to describe the prisoners?

because, he says, he "has a little heart." We ask him if there are other Italians in the camp and he says there are some, a few, he does not know how many; and he at once changes the subject. Meanwhile a bell rang and he immediately hurried off and left us stunned and disconcerted. Some feel refreshed but I do not. I still think that even this dentist, this <u>incomprehensible</u> person, wanted to amuse himself at our expense, and I do not want to believe a word of what he said.

At the sound of the bell, we can hear the still dark camp waking up. Unexpectedly the water gushes out boiling from the showers—five minutes of bliss; but immediately after, four men (perhaps they are the barbers) burst in yelling and shoving and drive us out, wet and steaming, into the adjoining room which is freezing; here other shouting people throw at us unrecognizable rags and thrust into our hands a pair of broken-down boots with wooden soles; we have no time to understand and we already find ourselves in the open, in the blue and icy snow of dawn, barefoot and naked, with all our clothing in our hands, with a hundred yards to run to the next hut. There we are finally allowed to get dressed.

When we finish, everyone remains in his own corner and we do not dare lift our eyes to look at one another. There is nowhere to look in a mirror, but our appearance stands in front of us, reflected **17** in a hundred livid faces, in a hundred miserable and <u>sordid</u> puppets. We are transformed into the phantoms glimpsed yesterday evening.

Then for the first time we became aware that our language lacks words to express this offense, the <u>demolition</u> of a man. In a moment, with almost <u>prophetic</u> <u>intuition</u>, the reality was revealed to us: we had reached the bottom. It is not possible to sink lower than this; no human condition is more miserable than this, nor could it conceivably be so. Nothing belongs to us anymore; they have taken away our clothes, our shoes, even our hair; if we speak, they will not listen to us, and if they

nized him immediately in the midst of a great number of unknown faces, although his physiognomy was greatly changed. . . . It seems to me obvious today that this attention of mine at that time, turned to the world and to the human beings around me, was not only a symptom but also an important factor of spiritual and physical salvation.

listen, they will not understand. They will even take away our name: and if we want to keep it, we will have to find in ourselves the strength to do so, to manage somehow so that behind the name something of us, of us as we were, still remains.

We know that we will have difficulty in being understood, and this is as it should be. But consider what value, what meaning is enclosed even in the smallest of our daily habits, in the hundred possessions which even the poorest beggar owns: a handkerchief, an old letter, the photo of a cherished person. These things are part of us, almost like limbs of our body; nor is it conceivable that we can be deprived of them in our world, for we immediately find others to substitute the old ones, other objects which are ours in their personification and evocation of our memories.

Imagine now a man who is deprived of everyone he loves, and at the same time of his house, his habits, his clothes, in short, of everything he possesses: he will be a hollow man, reduced to suffering and needs, forgetful of dignity and restraint, for he who loses all often easily loses himself. He will be a man whose life or death can be lightly decided with no sense of human affinity, in the most fortunate of cases, on the basis of a pure judgment of utility. It is in this way that one can understand **18** the double sense of the term "extermination camp," and it is now clear what we seek to express with the phrase: "to lie on the bottom."

Häftling.[11] I have learnt that I am a Häftling. My number is 174517; we have been baptized, we will carry the tattoo on our left arm until we die.

The operation was slightly painful and extraordinarily rapid: they placed us all in a row, and one by one, according to the alphabetical order of our names, we filed past a skillful official, armed with a sort of pointed tool with a very short needle. It seems that this is the real, true initiation: only by "showing one's number" can one get bread and soup. Several days passed, and not a few cuffs and punches, before we became used to showing our number promptly enough not to disorder the daily operation of food-distribution; weeks and months were needed to learn its sound in the German language. And for many days, while the habits of freedom still led me to look for the time on my wristwatch, my new name ironically appeared instead, its number tattooed in bluish characters under the skin.

---

11. *Häftling* (häf′ tliŋ): German for "prisoner."

Reader's Response *Do you think you would lose your sense of identity if you were identified as a number rather than as a name? Would you feel as Primo Levi did? Why or why not?*

THINKING ABOUT THE SELECTION

Interpreting

1. As he recalls his feelings upon arriving at the camp, Levi writes, "Today, in our times, hell must be like this." What do you think he means?
2. (a) How does Mr. Flesch fulfill his role as translator? (b) Why is he reluctant to translate the German officer's comments into Italian?
3. Why does Levi think it important for prisoners to hang on to their names?
4. (a) Explain what you think Levi means by the phrase "to lie on the bottom" (page 1298). (b) Why do you think Levi says that "our language lacks words to express this offense, the demolition of a man" (page 1297)?

Applying

5. Have you ever found yourself in a confusing or frightening situation? What positive steps did you take to cope with the situation? Explain.
6. Are there places in the world today where people are treated as Levi was at Auschwitz? Explain.

ANALYZING LITERATURE

Understanding Historical Context

As Adolf Hitler's Nazi regime steadily evolved into a totalitarian police state, determined to wield total control over its populations, it systematically seized all institutions and media and forced them to adhere to Nazi regimentation. While German Catholics and Protestants experienced bitter conflict with the Nazi regime, the brunt of this purge was inflicted on the Jews. The Nürnberg Laws of 1935 stripped them of virtually all their civil rights, and the pogrom, or persecution, of 1938 confined the entire Jewish population in ghettos.

During the course of World War II, Jews were deported from these ghettos to concentration camps where they were systematically exterminated. Although there were a handful of rebellions by prisoners, most were too weak and demoralized to resist. As Primo Levi makes clear, the process of demoralization began as soon as they arrived. This is the reason for the steady confusion he describes. By depriving each prisoner of every last shred of dignity, the Germans speeded up the transformation of an individual into what Levi calls "a hollow man."

1. How does Levi convey the prisoners' confusion?
2. After being shaved and dressed, why are the prisoners unwilling to "lift [their] eyes and look at one another"?
3. What is the final step in stripping prisoners of their identity?

CRITICAL THINKING AND READING

Appreciating Details

Levi recounts his nightmarish experience as one would describe a dream: a sequence of vivid details that follow one after another. Think about details that stand out in Levi's narrative, for example the shoes that the prisoners are to keep in neat piles and then are swept out of the room in a jumble; the onrush of men who bustle into the room to shave the prisoners; the naked men standing ankle-deep in water, waiting for the shower to be turned on. Choose a detail that stands out in the narrative and answer the following questions about it.

1. What is your response to this detail?
2. Why do you think Levi included it?
3. How does it contribute to the narrative as a whole?

UNDERSTANDING LANGUAGE

Interpreting the Language of Irony

Irony is the discrepancy between appearance and reality, or between what is said and what is meant. Levi uses irony to underscore the bitterness of his situation in many ways, but most significantly by using words and phrases that contrast strikingly with the situation at hand. For example, in citing the sign at the entrance to the work camp, *"Arbeit Macht Frei,* work gives freedom," he points out that work in a death camp leads only to oppression and eventually to death. In describing the tattooing of a number on his arm as a baptism, he suggests that rather than being purified and born into a new life he has been marked for damnation and death.

Identify the ironic language in the following passages from Levi's narrative and explain how it contributes to the theme:

1. "He says that the water is really not drinkable, and that instead a coffee substitute is distributed every day, but generally nobody drinks it as the soup itself is sufficiently watery to quench thirst."
2. ". . . life or death can be lightly decided with no sense of human affinity, in the most fortunate of cases, on the basis of a pure judgment of utility."

Find other examples of ironic language and share your examples with the class.

THINKING AND WRITING

Writing a Personal Essay

Levi's narrative shows how the Nazi treatment of prisoners was designed to strip individuals of their identity before putting them to death. For Levi, this loss of identity seemed almost worse than death itself. How important is your identity to you? Think about what has helped you to feel a sense of identity. Write a personal essay about an experience that helped to define your personal identity. Spend a little time deciding which experience to write about. You may be surprised at what finally seems important in defining who you are. When you write, try to remember exactly which details made the experience so significant. Including these details will make your experience more real for your reader. They may also help you to understand why the experience is important to you.

As you revise your essay, focus on the way these details add up to a whole. How do they convey your feelings about your identity?

(continued from bottom of page)

ashamed of their appearance, stripped of all individuality and clothed in identical rags. If the men look at each other, they will know how they themselves appear to the others.
3. A number was tattooed on each prisoner's left forearm. This number became his or her new identity and was needed to receive food.

ANSWERS TO CRITICAL THINKING AND READING

Suggested responses:
1. Students may share Levi's anger at the senselessness of jumbling the neatly arranged shoes in a mass sweeping out the door.
2. Levi suggests the strict but arbitrary nature of decisions and actions in the camp.
3. The incident prepares the reader for more arbitrary and disorienting events to come.

ANSWERS TO UNDERSTANDING LANGUAGE

1. Levi's irony comments on the absurdity of replacing undrinkable water with undrinkable coffee, consequently making the unpalatable soup the only option for the prisoners.
2. The words *lightly, fortunately,* and *utility* usually have positive connotations; however, in this case, they are referring to cold-blooded murder. Levi's grim irony underscores the way in which the Germans devalued the lives of their prisoners.

THINKING AND WRITING

Publishing Student Writing Have volunteers display or read aloud their essays. Some students may not feel comfortable sharing this personal glimpse of themselves with their classmates.

Challenge Ask students if they think it is easier to write about a pleasant occurrence or an experience that is frightful or unbearable. Which exercise might give them the best opportunity to use powerful images and graphic detail? Have them support their answers with examples from their writing or that of others.

---

losing one's identity is the worst form of torture.
4. (a) Answers will differ. The phrase suggests that stripping people of their humanity reduces them to the lowest form of life. (b) Suggested response: Levi suggests that it is impossible to express in words the utter humiliation that he and the other prisoners felt.
5. Answers will differ. Suggested response: Students may observe that

they enlisted help from others.
6. Answers will differ. Students may respond that human injustice persists throughout the world today, from civil rights violations in the United States to atrocities in Bosnia, the Middle East, or South Africa.

ANSWERS TO ANALYZING LITERATURE

1. Answers will differ. Suggested response: Levi describes how the prisoners walk and talk aimlessly. He mentions their surprise, wonder, and disbelief at several points in his essay. The author admits, "We seem to be watching some mad play."
2. The prisoners are horrified and

Presentation

Motivation/Prior Knowledge Discuss with students how issues of human tragedy still surround us today. Help students to identify current news events and topics studied in their social studies classes that relate to the Holocaust events of World War II.

Enrichment After years of planning, the United States Holocaust Memorial Museum opened in Washington, D.C., in April 1993, honoring victims, survivors, liberators, and rescuers. The opening ceremony—marking the annual Days of Remembrance—coincided with the fiftieth anniversary of the Warsaw (Poland) ghetto uprising, a courageous battle of a 1,300-member Jewish fighting organization against Nazi forces.

At the museum, Elie Wiesel delivered the dedication speech (see Primary Source, below), which included an impassioned plea to stop the violence in Bosnia/Herzegovina. From his experience at Auschwitz stems Wiesel's lifelong commitment to the championing of human rights everywhere.

More information about the museum can be obtained from U. S. Holocaust Memorial Museum 100 Raoul Wallenberg Place, S.W. Washington, D.C. 20024-2150 (202) 488-0400.

Enrichment Following are two excellent books on the Holocaust: Inge Auerbacher, *I Am a Star: Child of the Holocaust* (Prentice Hall, 1986). The author relates her imprisonment as a young girl in a Nazi death camp. Elie Wiesel, *Night* (Avon Books, 1960). The author describes his nightmarish experience in Auschwitz and Buchenwald.

ELIE WIESEL: SURVIVOR AND WITNESS

Elie Wiesel lived through most of World War II in Sighet, Romania, largely untouched by the atrocities that were befalling millions of Jews and others in Europe and Russia. Then, in the spring of 1944, when Wiesel was fifteen years old, the German army moved into town. Still hoping that the Russian army would arrive in time to liberate them from the Germans, Jewish families suddenly found themselves confined in a ghetto, a walled-off section of town, where they were stripped of their property and freedom. Soon after, they were deported in crowded cattle cars to the Nazi death camps. Wiesel and his family were sent to Auschwitz-Birkenau, in Poland, a sister camp to Auschwitz-Buna, where Primo Levi was captive (see the excerpt from Levi's *Survival in Auschwitz*, page 1294).

Death and Survival

At Birkenau, Wiesel lost his mother and sister in the camp's crematoria, which blanketed the region in a smoky pall of burned human flesh. He clung to his father, desperately hoping to preserve a sense of loyalty and faith. Through chance and sheer will they survived at Auschwitz until January 18, 1945, when word came that the camp was to be disbanded. Fearing what might befall them if they remained in the abandoned camp, they fled in a grueling forced march over forty miles in a blizzard. Tragically, their flight transported them away from the front, where Auschwitz was liberated only two days later, to Buchenwald, a labor camp in Germany. The ordeal of the trek and his brutal treatment in the German camp finally broke Wiesel's father, and he was sent to the ovens of Buchenwald. Wiesel endured until the camp was liberated a few months later, narrowly escaping death from food poisoning.

Life After the Death Camp

After Buchenwald, Wiesel emigrated to France, where he studied philosophy at the University of Paris and became a journalist. After moving to the United States in 1956 he published his first book, *Night*, a testament of his experience in the Nazi camps. Since then his writings have continued to explore the emotional and philosophical toll of the Holocaust experience.

Testimony to Survival

Elie Wiesel headed the U.S. Holocaust Memorial Council from 1980 to 1986 and was instrumental in creating the U.S. Holocaust Memorial Museum, which opened in Washington, D.C., in April 1993. In 1986 he was awarded the Nobel Prize for Peace. His citation reads: "Wiesel is a messenger to mankind. His message is one of peace and atonement and human dignity." Wiesel's work speaks for the millions who died in the Holocaust, that the story of their lives may not be forgotten.

Eastern Europe

MONUMENT
Jan Sawka

Humanities Note

Fine art, *Monument*, 1989, by Jan Sawka (säf´kə). Sawka was born December 10, 1946, in Zabrze, Poland. Now an American citizen, he lives with his wife and daughter in a small town near Woodstock, New York.

Although he does not regard himself as a political artist, there are strong undercurrents of social commentary in his work. His inspiration for *Monument* came from a childhood memory of a photograph. This photograph was in an issue of *Life* magazine smuggled into Poland. It showed a scene from the 1956 Hungarian Revolution: Soviet tanks rumble into a square as a defiant Hungarian crowd tears down a statue of Joseph Stalin. Sawka was struck by the fact that all that remained of the monument was the pedestal and the dictator's shoes. He says, "How very elusive is power, when all that may remain of a monument is a pair of shoes."

You might want to use the following questions to discuss the art:

1. How is the monument in this painting different from an ordinary monument?
2. What message does this difference convey?
3. Recall a monument that impressed you in some way. Explain how you would depict it in a painting.

CZESLAW MILOSZ

1911–

The poet, essayist, and novelist Czeslaw Milosz (ches′ läf me̅′ wo̅sh) seems to have lived through as many lives as a cat. Between the world wars, he was a young Polish writer haunted by "gloomy visions" of catastrophe. Just after World War II, he was a diplomat of Communist Poland serving in Washington, D.C. When he defected from his country, he lived for a while in France and then became a professor at the University of California, Berkeley. Today, however, he is a distinguished Nobel Prize winner familiar to many Americans.

Milosz was born to Polish-speaking parents in the Lithuanian city of Wilno (also known as Vilna). In his autobiographical book *Native Realm* (1950), he devotes a whole chapter to this small but lively city with its excellent theaters and bookstores. As a young reader, he had "an uncritical admiration for anything that came from abroad," going "from Jack London and Kipling to Joseph Conrad . . ."

Wilno was surrounded by "lakes and forests," and as he explored them, Milosz developed an avid love of nature. This countryside is the setting of his novel *The Issa Valley*, whose young hero Thomas comes of age in "the Land of Lakes."

As a university student in Wilno, he took long hikes and went on kayak trips with his friends. He knew he wanted to be a writer, but he studied law in order to gain "a knowledge of society." Hitler had just seized control in Germany, and Milosz rejected this dictator's politics of hate and all right-wing beliefs that glorified the state. Communism seemed like an antidote to these repressive, right-wing ideologies. Yet Milosz viewed the world as an artist, and the absolute doctrines of Communism were too rigid and inflexible for him. Rather than giving himself totally to a political belief, he conveyed the violence-haunted atmosphere of the 1930's in his poetry. He said of those years, "there was terror in them and a foreboding of what was to come."

Not long after World War II broke out, Milosz moved to Warsaw, where he lived for four years. There he participated in the underground universities and publishing activities that were carried on in defiance of the Nazis. Some of his best-known poems—such as "A Poor Christian Looks at the Ghetto," "Cafe," and "A Song on the End of the World"—date from this era of his life.

After the war, when Russia seized control of Poland and other eastern European nations, he represented the Polish government as a diplomat in Washington, D.C. While he had no illusions about the Communists, he wondered whether he should stay in his country and work for another, more humane revolution. He experienced a painful period of uncertainty. In early 1951, however, he formally broke with the Communist government and went to live in France. Nine years later he became a professor of Slavic literature at the University of California at Berkeley.

His independence of mind made him an admired figure among the younger generation in Poland, especially those who were college students in the late 1960's. Although he professes to be uncomfortable in the role of a moral leader, there is no doubt that his poems had a great deal of moral authority in his native country. In America he was at first known to only a few intellectuals as the author of essays on eastern Europe. When he received the Nobel Prize in Literature in 1980, he became known to a wider English-speaking public.

Although the following poem focuses on Milosz's wartime experience, it is included in this unit because most of his work was written in the postwar period.

Objectives

Thematic

To understand how artists deal with and interpret times of crisis

Skills

1 To understand historical context
2 To write about a quiet hero

GUIDE FOR INTERPRETING

A Song on the End of the World

Commentary

Cultural Context. Czeslaw Milosz's poem "A Song on the End of the World" would not be fully understandable without reference to the little tag that comes after it: "Warsaw, 1944." In many ways the world *did* come to an end in the Polish capital of Warsaw during World War II. That war began on September 1, 1939, when Nazi Germany invaded Poland. About two weeks later, the Soviet Union, which had signed a secret nonaggression pact with the Germans, invaded Poland from the east. In a very short time, the sovereign nation of Poland no longer existed: It was shared out, like war booty, between the Nazis and the Russians, with the city of Warsaw coming under German control.

The Nazis hated Christian Poles almost as much as they despised the Jews, whom they did not regard as Polish citizens even though Jews had lived in Poland for a thousand years. All Poles were subject to brutal treatment. They could be rounded up at a moment's notice for dangerous work details, or they could be tortured and killed at the Nazis' whim. Milosz, who was living in Warsaw at the time, writes bitterly of that era: "During those four years, I, and many like me, unlearned Western civilization, if what it teaches can be boiled down, more or less, to respect for money and the feeling that one has some kind of rights."

Jews, however, were singled out for annihilation. First they were isolated in a ghetto, a small area of Warsaw, which was then walled off from the rest of the city. Food allowances were inadequate, and many died from starvation or illness. In late 1942 large numbers of Jews were deported to the death camps. A valiant resistance movement arose in the Jewish ghetto in April 1943, but it was doomed when the Nazis systematically destroyed the ghetto with dive-bombers, artillery, and flamethrowers.

The Polish Resistance movement mounted its own rebellion against Nazi rule in the summer of 1944. In the course of this uprising, which failed after several months, Warsaw was nearly leveled. As Milosz escaped from the capital, he saw "a white city on a plain over which billowed masses of black smoke pierced through with red tongues of flame."

Writing

During World War II no fighting occurred on the American mainland, while many European cities were devastated. How do you think this difference affected the outlooks of Americans and Europeans after the war?

Literary Focus Elicit from students what they know about the suffering experienced by Europeans during World War II. Point out to them that European losses were far greater than American casualties. Also, many European cities were bombed, while American cities escaped this fate. The last war in which battles were fought on American soil was the Civil War. Finally, point out to students that groups like Jews and Gypsies were singled out for destruction by the Nazis. Altogether about six million Jews perished in the Holocaust, a significant portion of world Jewry.

Writing/Prior Knowledge Before students begin writing, have them gather in small groups and discuss what they have heard about World War II from their parents and other adults.

ESL Teaching Strategy Have ESL students tell the class about the experience of their people in World War II.

The language of the poem is simple and should not pose too great a problem for ESL students.

Teaching Tenth-Grade Students Tenth-grade students will not have a problem with the language of this poem. Take time to help them imagine the situation to which this poem is a response. You can kindle their historical imagination by reading them excerpts from Emanuel Ringelblum's *History of the Warsaw Ghetto*.

Also draw upon their prior knowledge. Ask them to discuss any television programs or movies they have seen that focus on the Warsaw Ghetto.

Support Material

Teaching Portfolio
Teacher Backup, p. 1577
Usage and Mechanics Worksheet, p. 1581
Analyzing Literature Worksheet, *Understanding Historical Context*, p. 1582
Critical Thinking and Reading Work-

sheet, *Detecting Irony*, p. 1583
Language Worksheet, *Appreciating Repetition*, p. 1584
Selection Test, pp. 1585–1586

Presentation

Motivation/Prior Knowledge
Have students recall books or movies in which people faced crisis situations. Ask students to describe these situations, and the people's reactions, in vivid detail. Then explain to them that they may be surprised by the description of a desperate situation in this poem.

Purpose-Setting Question How would you describe the tone of this poem?

Universal Themes Another selection that responds to the crises engendered by World War II is "The Myth of Sisyphus," page 1274.

Humanities Note

Fine art, *Babal II*, 1977 by Jerzy Duda Garcz. In this picture, the contemporary Polish painter Garcz alludes to the Biblical story of the Tower of Babel. This story tells how Noah's descendants presumed to build a tower that would reach to heaven. God punished their arrogance and stopped work on the tower by confusing the language of the workers so they could not understand one another. Garcz is making a satirical comparison between modern Poland and the Tower of Babel. In his picture the partially built tower rises behind three men. One seems to be a prisoner with a number on his shirt. The other two are modern workmen. The man in the center looks ironically at us as all three figures crouch in the debris.

You might want to use the following questions to discuss the art:
1. How has the artist changed and modernized the Biblical story of the Tower of Babel?
2. What message does the artist convey by comparing Poland to the legendary tower?

1 **Discussion** Have students recall the definition of irony and then explain what is ironic about the first stanza of this poem.

2 **Enrichment** Read aloud to students portions of The Book of Revelations. This will demonstrate an apocalyptic tone and imagery that they can contrast with the tone

A Song on the End of the World

Czeslaw Milosz

translated by Anthony Milosz

On the day the world ends
A bee circles a clover,
A fisherman mends a glimmering net.
Happy porpoises jump in the sea,
5 By the rainspout young sparrows are playing
And the snake is gold-skinned as it should always be.

On the day the world ends
Women walk through the fields under their
    umbrellas,
A drunkard grows sleepy at the edge of a lawn,
10 Vegetable peddlers shout in the street
And a yellow-sailed boat comes nearer the island,
The voice of a violin lasts in the air
And leads into a starry night.

And those who expected lightning and thunder
15 Are disappointed.
And those who expected signs and archangels'
    trumps[1]
Do not believe it is happening now.
As long as the sun and the moon are above,
As long as the bumblebee visits a rose,
20 As long as rosy infants are born
No one believes it is happening now.

Only a white-haired old man, who would be a
    prophet
Yet is not a prophet, for he's much too busy,
Repeats while he binds his tomatoes:
25 There will be no other end of the world,
There will be no other end of the world.

Warsaw, 1944.

---

1. **trumps:** Trumpets.

Reader's Response *Did the calm and peace of this poem surprise you? Why or why not?*

Babal II
Jerzy Duda Garcz

and imagery of the poem.

Master Teacher Note Read this poem aloud to students in order to communicate its ironic flavor.

Cooperative Learning Divide the class into small groups and have each group choose a different poem that Milosz wrote during the war. They can find these in his *Selected Poems*, published by Ecco Press. Possible choices are "A Poor Christian Looks at the Ghetto," "Cafe," and "Outskirts." Ask each group to present its poem to the class and explain how it relates to "A Song on the End of the World."

THINKING ABOUT THE SELECTION

Interpreting

1. Each of the first two stanzas begins with the statement "On the day the world ends," and then gives a series of images. (a) What do these images have in common? (b) What is unexpected about them?
2. In the New Testament, the end of the world is described in Revelations. According to Revelations 16:18, when the seventh angel poured his vial into the air, ". . . there were voices, and thunders, and lightnings; and there was a great earthquake such as was not since men were upon the earth, so mighty an earthquake and so great." (a) In Milosz's poem, why might some people have anticipated "lightning and thunder . . . and archangels' trumps"? (b) Why don't they believe the world is ending?
3. Irony is a difference between what is expected and what actually occurs. (a) What is ironic about lines 22–24? (b) How is the whole poem saturated with irony?
4. (a) What is the meaning of the poem's last line? (b) What is the effect of repeating this line? (c) Why do you think the old man binds tomatoes if he believes that the world is ending?
5. (a) How would you describe the rhythm and mood of this poem? (b) How do they contribute to the poem's meaning?

Applying

6. (a) What do you think it suggests about contemporary life that people might be too busy to take notice of the end of the world? (b) What are the implications for today? In other words, what are some issues we should pay attention to, but are too caught up in our daily lives to bother with?

ANALYZING LITERATURE

Understanding Historical Context

In a peculiar way, a knowledge of the historical background to this poem makes it both clearer and more confusing. On the one hand, the destruction of Warsaw during World War II certainly explains why Milosz was thinking about the world's end. However, the reaction to these events expressed in the poem is at first quite puzzling. Milosz evokes a peaceful, almost lyrical world, ending with a description of an old man binding tomatoes. This puzzling quality of the poem invites us to think and feel more deeply.

A remark that Milosz makes in his autobiographical book *Native Realm* throws some light on this riddle. He says that he thought it was unlikely he would survive the war. This reflection, however, led him to obey "Martin Luther's advice: when asked what he would do if he knew tomorrow was going to be the end of the world, he said, 'I would plant apple trees.'"

1. What do you think Luther meant by this response?
2. Why do you think Milosz found Luther's attitude comforting?
3. (a) How does this remark explain the behavior of the old man in the poem? (b) In what way does it explain the absence of gory details in this lyric?
4. Is it fair to call this poem a farewell to the world? Why or why not?

THINKING AND WRITING

Writing About a Quiet Hero

The old man in Milosz's poem could be considered heroic for his unflinching devotion to ordinary pursuits in the midst of danger. Have you ever known or read about such a person? Write an account of his or her actions, showing why they should be admired. Begin by freewriting about the dangerous situation and the way in which your subject managed to keep a sense of quiet dignity. As you write your account, remember that understatement can sometimes be more effective than exaggeration. The heroism you are describing is quiet and unassuming, and your writing style should reflect these qualities. When presented in the proper context, ordinary actions can carry great weight. If bombs are falling all around, for instance, the binding of a tomato is highly meaningful. In revising your description, add specific details that will help the reader imagine the scene.

Closure and Extension

ANSWERS TO THINKING ABOUT THE SELECTION

1. (a) These images reflect a peaceful, ordinary world. (b) It is unexpected that such normal events would occur on such a disastrous day.
2. (a) It is natural to think that such a disaster would be marked by extraordi-

(continued from bottom of page)

nary signs. Such signs are described in a famous biblical account of the world's end. (b) They don't believe it because everything is going on as usual.
3. (a) Prophecy is so important that it seems odd to reject it in favor of an apparently trivial activity like binding tomatoes. (b) The whole poem plays upon the difference between what one would expect to accompany the end of the world and what is actually occurring.
4. (a) Answers will differ. Students may respond that the line means, "Appearances to the contrary, the world is really ending." (b) The repetition stresses its meaning. (c) Answers will differ. Students may respond that even though the act seems trivial, it reflects an assertion of life in the face of disaster.
5. (a) Answers will differ. Many students will indicate that the poem has an unexpectedly calm tone. (b) Perceptive students will realize that its rhythms and repetitions are like those of a song or a songlike prayer that one says to oneself.
6. (a) Answers will differ. (b) Answers will differ. Students may indicate issues like pollution, poverty, and racial injustice.

ANSWERS TO ANALYZING LITERATURE

1. Answers will differ. Students may respond that he meant it is important to affirm life, even in the face of death.
2. Milosz was living in a time when it really seemed as if the world might end. Luther's response gave him a way to affirm life in a desperate situation.
3. (a) The old man is following Luther's advice. (b) Answers will differ. Students may respond that Milosz was more interested in affirming life through everyday activities than in painting a lurid picture of disaster.
4. Answers will differ. Students may indicate that Milosz's loving allusion to everyday events is like a farewell to them.

THINKING AND WRITING

Publishing Student Writing Have students read their accounts to the class.

Challenge Write a poem about the quiet hero you have described.

STANISLAW LEM

1921–

Lem enjoyed a happy childhood in Lvov,
Poland, during the period between the two world
wars. From an early age, he began to invent
imaginary worlds and to create passports that
would enable him to visit these places.

The onset of World War II wrenched him from
his charmed and protected existence. He had
enrolled in medical school. However, his family
was of Jewish heritage; consequently, when the
Nazis occupied Poland, Lem had to withdraw from
the university and change his name. He got a job
as a garage mechanic and learned to sabotage
German vehicles while pretending to repair them.
In addition, he risked his life by carrying messages
for Polish Resistance fighters. Lem's wartime experiences impressed him with the chanciness of
life, a theme he later explored in many books: "the
difference between life and death depended upon
. . . whether one went to visit a friend at one
o'clock or twenty minutes later."

After the war the government of Poland, like
that of other eastern European nations, was controlled by the Soviet Union. Lem's family, having
lost all their possessions, moved to Cracow,
Poland, and he resumed his medical studies. He
also began to write in order to earn some money.
This sideline turned into his main source of income when his first science-fiction books, *The
Astronauts* (1951) and *The Magellan Nebula*
(1955), sold more than a million copies in the
Soviet Union. In the meantime he had become
disillusioned with medicine because he considered the official Soviet version of genetic theory
to be "rubbish." This official doctrine was based
on the ideas of the Russian biologist Lysenko,
who believed that acquired characteristics could
be inherited. Lem was also dismayed when the
Soviet Union discouraged the study of cybernetics, which was called "a false capitalist science."

Lem had turned to science fiction because he
believed that traditional novels could not convey
the sense of uncertainty that wartime experience
taught him. While his first two science-fiction novels portrayed optimistic utopias, his later works
took on a darker quality. In *Solaris* (1961) and
The Invincible (1973), for example, Lem directs
his satire against all human attempts to control
the universe by means of power or knowledge.
Solaris, Lem's most famous novel, is about a
planet whose only living inhabitant is an ocean.
When scientists attack this "creature" with X-
rays, it retaliates by activating their deepest
fears.

Lem has continued to maintain a comfortable
house in Cracow. For a brief period, however, he
and his wife lived in Vienna, Austria, where his
son attended high school. Now the Lem family
alternates between both residences.

The story that follows comes from a collection of stories entitled *The Cyberiad* (1974), a
name based on the word *cybernetics*. One critic,
referring to a series of enthralling Arabic tales,
called this book a science-fiction "equivalent of
the Arabian Nights."

Focus

More About the Author Stanislaw
Lem often delights his friends with
his whimsical imaginings. Once
Lem had heard about a strange
kind of rodent and wanted to show
a friend of his a booklet about this
animal. When he could not find the
booklet, he declared, "Never mind.
I'll invent it." Lem then made up a
name for this unusual rodent and
went on for an hour inventing facts
about this imaginary beast! Ask
students if they have ever made
up imaginary countries, machines,
or animals. Have them speculate
about why such an activity is enjoyable.

Critical Evaluation The critic
Theodore Solotaroff made the following evaluation of Lem's work:

> Lem is both a polymath and
> a virtuoso storyteller and
> stylist. . . . His imagination is
> so powerful and pure that no
> matter what world he creates
> it is immediately convincing
> because of its concreteness
> and plenitude, the intimacy
> and authority with which it is
> occupied. . . . He is a major
> writer, and one of the deep
> spirits of our age.

Objectives

Thematic
To understand how human
creativity is unique and, so
far, not reproducible by
machines

Skills
1 To understand satire in
science fiction
2 To write a parody

GUIDE FOR INTERPRETING

The First Sally (A) OR
Trurl's Electronic Bard

Commentary

Satire and Science Fiction. Satire is a type of literature that ridicules and criticizes the foibles of individuals, groups, or societies. Such concerns seem alien to science fiction, which finds its subject matter in worlds beyond the earth.

Actually, these different types of literature are compatible: Attacks on earthly foibles can be disguised as tales about extraterrestrial worlds. Such tactics were especially necessary for Stanislaw Lem, who lived most of his life under a Russian-dominated Polish regime. Lem wanted to satirize this authoritarian government, but he had to be indirect in order to avoid going to jail. He solved this dilemma in *The Star Diaries* (1957) by attributing the worst aspects of Communism to the government of an extraterrestrial planet. The engineers of this planet accidentally flood their world while devising systems of irrigation. Rather than confessing to this mistake, however, the rulers try to convince people that everything is for the best. They recommend that their subjects, who are rapidly drowning, learn how to breathe underwater. The parallels between these outer-space idiocies and the foibles of Communist dictatorship were not lost on Lem's readers, even if the government censors mistook the novel for harmless science fiction.

In his novel *Fiasco* (1987), Lem turned his satiric eye on the arms race. Once again using an outer-space setting, he shows the ridiculous extremes to which military competition can lead. As he portrays a distant planet totally surrounded by a massive defense system, he obviously has in mind the American "Star Wars" defense program. The title of his book conveys his attitude toward such measures.

The following story, which is more lighthearted, pokes fun at the human wish to build perfect machines and the vanity of poets. In the course of this delightful satire, Lem is also able to mock some famous works of literature.

Writing

A well-known scientist recently commented that computer technology advances with the speed of a contagious disease. What will computers be capable of doing in twenty-five years? Jot down some of your predictions.

(continued from bottom of page)

novel *Frankenstein* in the 1800's was a forerunner of science fiction that posed questions about the nature of human creativity, though films reduced its impact, largely to the "creature feature" level. Ask them to discuss themes with which they think science fiction is or should be most concerned.

Writing/Prior Knowledge Before students begin writing, briefly summarize some past developments in computer technology. For instance, you might want to emphasize the trend toward increased miniaturization of circuits. The movement from comparatively bulky electron tubes to chips and microchips has been a prime factor in increasing the capacity of computers.

ESL Teaching Strategy You may want to alert ESL students to the fact that Lem makes up words. Review some of these made-up words with them before they begin reading. Also review some of the legitimate scientific terminology he uses and the literary works that he parodies.

Teaching Tenth-Grade Students Tenth-grade students may be confused at first by Lem's propensity to invent technological words. To get them into the spirit of Lem's writing, have them make up their own pseudo-technological jargon and write their words on the chalkboard.

Vocabulary
Preteach the following vocabulary words:
primordial (prī môr´ dē əl)
  adj.: Primitive
intrepid (in trep´ id) *adj.*:
  Bold; fearless
millennium (mi len´ ē əm) *n.*:
  Period of 1000 years
shunts (shunts) *n.*: Switches
chagrin (shə grin´) *n.*: Feeling of embarrassment and annoyance due to failure or disappointment
bemused (bē myo͞ozd´)
  adj.: Muddled; preoccupied

Support Material
Teaching Portfolio
Teacher Backup, p. 1587
Grammar in Action Worksheet, *Writing Science Fiction*, p. 1591
Usage and Mechanics Worksheet, p. 1593
Vocabulary Check, p. 1594
Critical Thinking and Reading Worksheet, *Making Inferences*, p. 1595

Language Worksheet, *Understanding Jargon*, p. 1596
Selection Test, pp. 1597–1598

Spelling Tip Write the word *millennium* on the chalkboard. Point out to students that it comes from two Latin words: *mille* (thousand) and *annus* (year). This Latin derivation indicates why the English word is spelled with two *l*'s and two *n*'s.

Literary Focus Have students discuss their own experiences with science fiction films or stories. They may, for example, have seen *2001: A Space Odyssey* or its sequel *2010*. Many, of course, will have seen *Star Trek* in the original or current series, or in the recent *Star Trek* feature films. Point out that Mary Wollstonecraft Shelley's

The First Sally[1] (A)
OR
Trurl's Electronic Bard

Stanislaw Lem

translated by Michael Kandel

First of all, to avoid any possible misunderstanding, we should state that this was, strictly speaking, a sally to nowhere. In fact, Trurl never left his house throughout it—except for a few trips to the hospital and an unimportant excursion to some asteroid. Yet in a deeper and/or higher sense this was one of the farthest sallies ever undertaken by the famed constructor, for it very nearly took him beyond the realm of possibility.

Trurl had once had the misfortune to build an enormous calculating machine that was capable of only one operation, namely the addition of two and two, and *that* it did incorrectly. As is related earlier in this volume, the machine also proved to be extremely stubborn, and the quarrel that ensued between it and its creator almost cost the latter his life. From that time on Klapaucius teased Trurl unmercifully, making comments at every opportunity, until Trurl decided to silence him once and for all by building a machine that could write poetry. First Trurl collected eight hundred and twenty tons of books on cybernetics[2] and twelve thousand tons of the finest poetry, then sat down to read it all. Whenever he felt he just couldn't take another chart or equation, he would switch over to verse, and vice versa. After a while it became clear to him that the construction of the machine itself was child's play in comparison with the writing of the program. The program found in the head of an average poet, after all, was written by the poet's civilization, and that civilization was in turn programmed by the civilization that preceded it, and so on to the very Dawn of Time, when those bits of information that concerned the poet-to-be were still swirling about in the primordial chaos of the cosmic deep. Hence in order to program a poetry machine, one would first have to repeat the entire Universe from the beginning—or at least a good piece of it.

Anyone else in Trurl's place would have given up then and there, but our intrepid constructor was nothing daunted. He built a machine and fashioned a digital model of the Void, an Electrostatic Spirit to move upon the face of the electrolytic waters,[3] and he introduced the parameter[4] of light, a protogalactic cloud or two, and by de-

---

1. **Sally** (sal´ ē) *n.*: A sudden rushing forth.
2. **cybernetics** (sī bər net´ iks): The science that compares the human brain and nervous system with electronic systems.

3. **an Electrostatic . . . waters:** A parody of Genesis 1:2: "And the Spirit of God moved upon the face of the waters."
4. **parameter** (pə ram´ ət ər) *n.*: A quantity or constant with changing values.

grees worked his way up to the first ice age—Trurl could move at this rate because his machine was able, in one five-billionth of a second, to simulate one hundred septillion events at forty octillion different locations simultaneously. And if anyone questions these figures, let him work it out for himself.

Next Trurl began to model Civilization, the striking of fires with flints and the tanning of hides, and he provided for dinosaurs and floods, bipedality[5] and taillessness, then made the paleopaleface *(Albuminidis sapientia)*, which begat the paleface, which begat the gadget, and so it went, from eon to millennium, in the endless hum of electrical currents and eddies. Often the machine turned out to be too small for the computer simulation of a new epoch, and Trurl would have to tack on an auxiliary unit—until he ended up, at last, with a veritable metropolis of tubes and terminals, circuits and shunts, all so tangled and involved that the devil himself couldn't have made head or tail of it. But Trurl managed somehow, he only had to go back twice—once, almost to the beginning, when he discovered that Abel had murdered Cain and not Cain Abel[6] (the result, apparently, of a defective fuse), and once, only three hundred million years back to the middle of the Mesozoic, when after going from fish to amphibian to reptile to mammal, something odd took place among the primates and instead of great apes he came out with gray drapes. A fly, it seems, had gotten into the machine and shorted out the polyphase step-down directional widget.[7] Otherwise everything went like a dream. Antiquity and the Middle Ages were recreated, then the period of revolutions and reforms—which gave the machine a few nasty jolts—and then civilization progressed in such leaps and bounds that Trurl had to hose down the coils and cores repeatedly to keep them from overheating.

Toward the end of the twentieth century the machine began to tremble, first sideways, then lengthwise—for no apparent reason. This alarmed Trurl; he brought out cement and grappling irons just in case. But fortunately these weren't needed; instead of jumping its moorings, the machine settled down and soon had left the twentieth century far behind. Civilizations came and went thereafter in fifty-thousand-year intervals: these were the fully intelligent beings from whom Trurl himself stemmed. Spool upon spool of computerized history was filled and ejected into storage bins; soon there were so many spools, that even if you stood at the top of the machine with high-power binoculars, you wouldn't see the end of them. And all to construct some versifier! But then, such is the way of scientific fanaticism. At last the programs were ready; all that remained was to pick out the most applicable—else the electropoet's education would take several million years at the very least.

During the next two weeks Trurl fed general instructions into his future electropoet, then set up all the necessary logic circuits, emotive elements, semantic[8] centers. He was about to invite Klapaucius to attend a trial run, but thought better of it and started the machine himself. It immediately proceeded to deliver a lecture on the grinding of crystallographical surfaces as an introduction to the study of submolecular magnetic anomalies.[9] Trurl bypassed half the logic circuits and made the emotive more electromotive; the machine sobbed, went into hysterics, then finally said, blubbering terribly, what a cruel, cruel world this was. Trurl intensified the semantic fields and attached a strength of character component; the machine informed him that from now on he would carry out its every wish and to begin with add six floors to the nine it already had, so it could better meditate upon the meaning of existence. Trurl installed a philosophical throttle instead; the machine fell silent and sulked. Only after endless pleading and cajoling was he able to

---

5. bipedality (bī′ ped al′ i tē) *n.*: The ability to walk on two legs.
6. Abel . . . Abel: An allusion to the biblical account of the murder of Abel by his brother Cain. (Genesis 4:8)
7. polyphase . . . widget: Here and elsewhere Lem invents imaginary technology.

8. semantic (sə man′ tik) *adj.*: Of or pertaining to meaning, especially meaning in language.
9. anomalies (ə näm′ ə lēz) *n.*: Abnormalities.

4 Enrichment About another of Lem's speeded-up worlds, Douglas R. Hofstadter and Daniel C. Dennett say: "Lem would have it that thanks to the blinding speed of computers, the 'biological time' of these simulated worlds can be much faster than our real time. . . . "

Hofstadter and Dennett, however, indicate that such speeded-up time is not achievable: "A computer simulation must work by sequentially painting in details, and even at the speed of light quite simple and façadelike simulations (which is all that artificial intelligence has yet attempted to produce) take much longer to run than their real-life inspirations."

5 Discussion Ask students whether or not they find Trurl's mistakes amusing and have them explain why. Point out that Lem's breezy style here sweeps through the complications in this paragraph with a sprinkling of made-up jargon for atmosphere. Does Lem hope that the reader will find this hocus-pocus believable? Why or why not?

6 Enrichment Many people besides Lem have argued that the twentieth century has been a time of horrors unparalleled in all human history—a genuine Dark Age in which human survival itself was put in doubt. Such an argument points to the world wars, the Nazi extermination of Jews and others, the nuclear arms race, ecological disaster, and such atrocities as the mass murders of Armenians, Indonesians, and Cambodians. Ask students to discuss such an assessment and then make a list of great human advances that also occurred in this century.

7 Discussion What series of steps is Trurl compelled to take in fine-tuning his electropoet? Have them point out how the machine seesaws from being too rational to being excessively emotional to being too philosophical. Tell them to be alert to one more significant change Trurl must make before the electropoet is ready to function.

Humanities Note

Fine art, *Green Depth* by Irene Rice Pereira. Pereira (1907–1971) was an abstractionist painter, meaning that she used abstract forms in her work rather than trying to imitate reality directly. Her use of geometric forms, like the ones in this painting, was influenced by modern science, and she once described herself as "seeking a system of [artistic] equivalents for the revolutionary discoveries in mathematics, physics, biochemistry, and radioactivity."

In this painting the sources of light in the background and the interlinked geometric shapes create a mysterious sense of depth.

You might want to use the following questions to discuss the art:

1. What kind of feeling does this picture call up in you?
2. How do light and geometric shapes contribute to the total effect of the picture?
3. This artist was very interested in modern science. How does her work suggest the scientific breakthroughs of our century?

8 Clarification The reference to alternating rhyme is a sly joke about the most common hymn-tune stanza, which alternates rhymes in four lines that are four beats long. The point is that the machine, fixated on this one poetic form, thinks of becoming a missionary—a quite appropriate impulse for a hymn-tune poet.

9 Clarification Point out to students that this is an example of Lem's invention of technical jargon. The term *egocentripetal* is a fancy word for self-centered, while the term *narcissistor* was probably modeled on the word *transistor*. Ask students why a "narcissistor" would be necessary for a poet. How does this term enable Lem to poke fun at poets?

10 Discussion Ask students what caused the machine finally to ask for pen and paper. How does this step satirize the personalities of

get it to recite something: "I had a little froggy." That appeared to exhaust its repertoire. Trurl adjusted, modulated, expostulated, disconnected, ran checks, reconnected, reset, did everything he could think of, and the machine presented him with a poem that made him thank heaven Klapaucius wasn't there to laugh—imagine, simulating the whole Universe from scratch, not to mention Civilization in every particular, and to end up with such dreadful doggerel![10] Trurl put in six cliché filters, but they snapped like matches; he had to make them out of pure corundum steel. This seemed to work, so he jacked the semanticity up all the way, plugged in an alternating rhyme generator—which nearly ruined everything, since the machine resolved to become a missionary among destitute tribes on far-flung planets. But at the very last minute, just as he was ready to give up and take a hammer to it, Trurl was struck by an inspiration; tossing out all the logic circuits, he replaced them with self-regulating egocentripetal

---

10. doggerel (dôg′ ər el) *n*.: Any trivial or bad poetry.

narcissistors.[11] The machine simpered a little, whimpered a little, laughed bitterly, complained of an awful pain on its third floor, said that in general it was fed up, through, life was beautiful but men were such beasts and how sorry they'd all be when it was dead and gone. Then it asked for pen and paper. Trurl sighed with relief, switched it off and went to bed. The next morning he went to see Klapaucius. Klapaucius, hearing that he was invited to attend the debut of Trurl's electronic bard, dropped everything and followed—so eager was he to be an eyewitness to his friend's humiliation.

Trurl let the machine warm up first, kept the power low, ran up the metal stairs several times to take readings (the machine was like the engine of a giant steamer, galleried, with rows of rivets, dials and valves on every tier)—till finally, satisfied all the decimal places were where they ought to be, he

---

11. self-regulating . . . narcissistors (när sis ist′ ôrz): These imaginary electronic devices will make the electro-poet vain and self-regarding (narcissistic).

GREEN DEPTH
Irene Rice Pereira
The Metropolitan Museum of Art, New York

poets? Why is Klapaucius so sure he is going to witness Trurl's humiliation?

said yes, it was ready now, and why not start with something simple. Later, of course, when the machine had gotten the feel of it, Klapaucius could ask it to produce poetry on absolutely whatever topic he liked.

Now the potentiometers indicated the machine's lyrical capacitance was charged to maximum, and Trurl, so nervous his hands were shaking, threw the master switch. A voice, slightly husky but remarkably vibrant and bewitching, said: "Phlogisticosh. Rhomothriglyph. Floof."

"Is that it?" inquired Klapaucius after a pause, extremely polite. Trurl only bit his lip, gave the machine a few kicks of current, and tried again. This time the voice came through much more clearly; it was a thrilling baritone, solemn yet intriguingly sensual:

Pev't o' tay merlong gumin gots,
Untle yun furly pözzen ye,
Confre an' ayzor, ayzor ots,
Bither de furloss bochre blee!

"Am I missing something?" said Klapaucius, calmly watching a panic-stricken Trurl struggling at the controls. Finally Trurl waved his arms in despair, dashed clattering several flights up the metal stairs, got down on all fours and crawled into the machine through a trapdoor; he hammered away inside, swearing like a maniac, tightened something, pried at something, crawled out again and ran frantically to another tier. At long last he let out a cry of triumph, threw a burnt tube over his shoulder—it bounced off the railing and fell to the floor, shattering at the feet of Klapaucius. But Trurl didn't bother to apologize; he quickly put in a new tube, wiped his hands on a chammy cloth and hollered down for Klapaucius to try it now. The following words rang out:

Mockles! Fent on silpen tree,
Blockards three a-feening
Mockles, what silps came to thee
In thy pantry dreaming?

"Well, that's an improvement!" shouted Trurl, not entirely convinced. "The last line particularly, did you notice?"

"If this is all you have to show me . . ." said Klapaucius, the very soul of politeness.

"Damn!" said Trurl and again disappeared inside the machine. There was a fierce banging and clanging, the sputtering of shorted wires and the muttering of an even shorter temper, then Trurl stuck his head out of a trapdoor on the third story and yelled, "*Now* try it!"

Klapaucius complied. The electronic bard shuddered from stem to stern and began:

Oft, in that wickless chalet all begorn,
Where whilom soughed the mossy sappertort
And you were wont to bong—

Trurl yanked out a few cables in a fury, something rattled and wheezed, the machine fell silent. Klapaucius laughed so hard he had to sit on the floor. Then suddenly, as Trurl was rushing back and forth, there was a crackle, a clack, and the machine with perfect poise said:

The Petty and the Small
Are overcome with gall
When Genius, having faltered, fails to fall.

Klapaucius too, I ween,
Will turn the deepest green
To hear such flawless verse from Trurl's
*   machine.*

"There you are, an epigram![12] And wonderfully apropos!" laughed Trurl, racing down the metal stairs and flinging himself delightedly into his colleague's arms. Klapaucius, quite taken aback, was no longer laughing.

"What, *that?*" he said. "That's nothing. Besides, you had it all set up beforehand."

"Set up?!"

"Oh, it's quite obvious . . . the ill-disguised hostility, the poverty of thought, the crudeness of execution."

"All right, then ask it something else! Whatever you like! Go on! What are you waiting for? Afraid?!"

"Just a minute," said Klapaucius, annoyed. He was trying to think of a request as difficult as possible, aware that any argument on the quality of the verse the machine might be able to produce would be hard if not impossible to settle either way. Suddenly he brightened and said:

---

12. epigram (ep′ ə gram′) *n.*: A brief, witty poem or saying.

Commentary

Translating Stanislaw Lem As readers of world literature in English translations, we can all too easily forget the effort required to give us a version of these authors that approaches the original. There is a famous Italian saying about this situation: "Traduttore, traditore." It means, "The translator is a traitor." In other words, the labor of translation is so difficult that the translator must inevitably betray the original. The verbal inventiveness of this translation, however, indicates that Michael Kandel has not been very traitorous at all. His skill is reflected in the machine's increasingly impressive efforts at verse. Whatever the Polish original, for example, Kandel comes up with a brilliantly funny English solution to the nonsensical problem of "a poem about a haircut" (see page 1312).

In *The Mind's I*, a book on artificial intelligence, Daniel C. Dennett and Douglas R. Hofstadter praise Kandel for his translation of *The Cyberiad*:

Before commenting on Lem's ideas, we must pay tribute to [Michael] Kandel for his ingenious conversions of sparkling Polish wordplay into sparkling English wordplay. All through *The Cyberiad* . . . , this high level of translation is maintained. In reading translations like this one, we are reminded how woefully far the current programs for machine translation are from snatching jobs away from people.

14 Discussion Ask students why these tests Klapaucius devises are not a fair measurement of the ability to write poetry. Why would a machine be more likely to succeed at these difficult tasks than a real poet?

15 Clarification Tell students that trochaic hexameter is a six-foot line in which each foot has an accented followed by an unaccented syllable. For a more complete explanation of English meters, refer students to the introduction to Shakespearean Drama, page 707.

16 Enrichment To help students enjoy this tour de force, bring the Marlowe lyric to class and have students read it aloud. Another strand in the machine's poem is its reference to mathematical and scientific terminology. Ask for a volunteer to work with a math or science teacher and explain some of these references.

Point out that the phrase "Cancel me not" is a poignant appeal to be allowed to live, as a computer might express it. This stanza also suggests that the machine has begun to regard its poetry as the end-all and be-all of the universe.

Also point out to students the flair with which the translator, Michael Kandel, has rendered this poem (see the Commentary on page 1311). In the first line of the next-to-last stanza, just to take one example, there is a play on the word *lips*—it is contained in the mathematical term *ellipse* and then echoed later in the line.

"Have it compose a poem—a poem about a haircut! But lofty, noble, tragic, timeless, full of love, treachery, retribution, quiet heroism in the face of certain doom! Six lines, cleverly rhymed, and every word beginning with the letter *s*!!"

"And why not throw in a full exposition of the general theory of nonlinear automata while you're at it?" growled Trurl. "You can't give it such idiotic—"

But he didn't finish. A melodious voice filled the hall with the following:

> *Seduced, shaggy Samson snored.*
> *She scissored short. Sorely shorn,*
> *Soon shackled slave, Samson sighed,*
> *Silently scheming,*
> *Sightlessly seeking*
> *Some savage, spectacular suicide.*[13]

"Well, what do you say to that?" asked Trurl, his arms folded proudly. But Klapaucius was already shouting:

"Now all in *g*! A sonnet, trochaic hexameter, about an old cyclotron who kept sixteen artificial mistresses, blue and radioactive, had four wings, three purple pavilions, two lacquered chests, each containing exactly one thousand medallions bearing the likeness of Czar Murdicog the Headless . . ."

"Grinding gleeful gears, Gerontogyron grabbed / Giggling gynecobalt-60 golems," began the machine, but Trurl leaped to the console, shut off the power and turned, defending the machine with his body.

"Enough!" he said, hoarse with indignation. "How dare you waste a great talent on such drivel? Either give it decent poems to write or I call the whole thing off!"

"What, those aren't decent poems?" protested Klapaucius.

"Certainly not! I didn't build a machine to solve ridiculous crossword puzzles! That's hack work, not Great Art! Just give it a topic, any topic, as difficult as you like . . ."

Klapaucius thought, and thought some more. Finally he nodded and said:

"Very well. Let's have a love poem, lyrical, pastoral, and expressed in the language of pure mathe-

---

13. Seduced . . . suicide: The poem alludes to the biblical story of Samson and Delilah (Judges 13–16).

---

matics. Tensor algebra mainly, with a little topology and higher calculus, if need be. But with feeling, you understand, and in the cybernetic spirit."

"Love and tensor algebra? Have you taken leave of your senses?" Trurl began, but stopped, for his electronic bard was already declaiming:

> *Come let us hasten to a higher plane,*
> *Where dyads tread the fairy fields of Venn,*
> *Their indices bedecked from one to n,*
> *Commingled in an endless Markov chain!*
>
> *Come, every frustum longs to be a cone,*
> *And every vector dreams of matrices.*
> *Hark to the gentle gradient of the breeze:*
> *It whispers of a more ergodic zone.*
>
> *In Riemann, Hilbert or in Banach space*
> *Let superscripts and subscripts to their ways.*
> *Our asymptotes no longer out of phase,*
> *We shall encounter, counting, face to face.*
>
> *I'll grant thee random access to my heart,*
> *Thou'lt tell me all the constants of thy love;*
> *And so we two shall all love's lemmas prove,*
> *And in our bound partition never part.*
>
> *For what did Cauchy know, or Christoffel,*
> *Or Fourier, or any Boole or Euler,*
> *Wielding their compasses, their pens and*
>   *rulers,*
> *Of thy supernal sinusoidal spell?*
>
> *Cancel me not—for what then shall*
>   *remain?*
> *Abcissas, some mantissas, modules, modes,*
> *A root or two, a torus and a node:*
> *The inverse of my verse, a null domain.*
>
> *Ellipse of bliss, converge. O lips divine!*
> *The product of our scalars is defined!*
> *Cyberiad draws nigh, and the skew mind*
> *Cuts capers like a happy haversine.*
>
> *I see the eigenvalue in thine eye,*
> *I hear the tender tensor in thy sigh.*
> *Bernoulli would have been content to die,*
> *Had he but known such $a^2 \cos 2\phi$!*[14]

---

14. Come, let us hasten . . . a² cos2ø: This poem parodies Christopher Marlowe's (1564–1593) famous lyric "The Passionate Shepherd to His Love," which begins, "Come live with me and be my love . . ."

Grammar in Action

Writing Science Fiction A branch of fantasy literature, science fiction depends in some way on scientific or pseudoscientific concepts. Some science fiction stories are mere translations of the past into the future. For example, old-fashioned "space operas" are mere westerns ("horse operas") translated into the future.

OLD-FASHIONED: The clicking cycloptic cactus seized in its gigantic claws the defenseless Rhea as she struggled in vain to free herself from its loathsome grasp. Just at this moment, Hardy Trueblood leaped from his space-

ship and with a mighty blast from his raygun obliterated the monster.

More challenging science fiction usually asks us to stretch our minds or to imagine societies with assumptions quite different from our own. American science fiction writers who create these kinds of stories include Samuel Delany, Ursula K. Le Guin, and Joanna Russ.

Lem's science fiction is challenging, if whimsical, because it provokes readers to consider just what machines can and cannot do.

Student Activity 1. Find passages in Lem's story that suggest it is an example of the more challenging kind of science fiction being written today.

Student Activity 2. Write a brief sketch of a future time that differs from

This concluded the poetic competition, since Klapaucius suddenly had to leave, saying he would return shortly with more topics for the machine; but he never did, afraid that in so doing, he might give Trurl more cause to boast. Trurl of course let it be known that Klapaucius had fled in order to hide his envy and chagrin. Klapaucius meanwhile spread the word that Trurl had more than one screw loose on the subject of that so-called mechanical versifier.

Not much time went by before the news of Trurl's computer laureate reached the genuine—that is, the ordinary—poets. Deeply offended, they resolved to ignore the machine's existence. A few, however, were curious enough to visit Trurl's electronic bard in secret. It received them courteously, in a hall piled high with closely written paper (for it worked day and night without pause). Now these poets were all avant-garde,[15] and Trurl's machine wrote only in the traditional manner; Trurl, no connoisseur of poetry, had relied heavily on the classics in setting up its program. The machine's guests jeered and left in triumph. The machine was self-programming, however, and in addition had a special ambition-amplifying mechanism with glory-seeking circuits, and very soon a great change took place. Its poems became difficult, ambiguous,[16] so intricate and charged with meaning that they were totally incomprehensible. When the next group of poets came to mock and laugh, the machine replied with an improvisation that was so modern, it took their breath away, and the second poem seriously weakened a certain sonneteer who had two State awards to his name, not to mention a statue in the city park. After that, no poet could resist the fatal urge to cross lyrical swords with Trurl's electronic bard. They came from far and wide, carrying trunks and suitcases full of manuscripts. The machine would let each challenger recite, instantly grasp the algorithm[17] of his verse, and use it to compose an answer in exactly the same style, only two hundred and twenty to three hundred and forty-seven times better.

---

15. avant garde (ä vänt´ gärd´) *adj.*: New and unconventional.
16. ambiguous (am big´ yoo əs) *adj.*: Having two or more possible meanings.
17. algorithm (al´ gə ri*th*´ ´m) *n.*: A system or method of solving a problem.

The machine quickly grew so adept at this, that it could cut down a first-class rhapsodist with no more than one or two quatrains. But the worst of it was, all the third-rate poets emerged unscathed; being third-rate, they didn't know good poetry from bad and consequently had no inkling of their crushing defeat. One of them, true, broke his leg when, on the way out, he tripped over an epic poem the machine had just completed, a prodigious work beginning with the words:

> *Arms, and machines I sing, that forc'd by fate,*
> *And haughty Homo's unrelenting hate,*
> *Expell'd and exil'd, left the Terran shore . . .*[18]

The true poets, on the other hand, were decimated by Trurl's electronic bard, though it never laid a finger on them. First an aged elegist,[19] then two modernists committed suicide, leaping off a cliff that unfortunately happened to lie hard by the road leading from Trurl's place to the nearest train station.

There were many poet protests staged, demonstrations, demands that the machine be served an injunction to cease and desist. But no one else appeared to care. In fact, magazine editors generally approved: Trurl's electronic bard, writing under several thousand different pseudonyms at once, had a poem for every occasion, to fit whatever length might be required, and of such high quality that the magazine would be torn from hand to hand by eager readers. On the street one could see enraptured faces, bemused smiles, sometimes even hear a quiet sob. Everyone knew the poems of Trurl's electronic bard, the air rang with its delightful rhymes. Not infrequently, those citizens of a greater sensitivity, struck by a particularly marvelous metaphor or assonance, would actually fall into a faint. But this colossus of inspiration was prepared even for that eventuality; it would immediately supply the necessary number of restorative rondelets.[20]

---

18. Arms, and machines I sing . . . shore: These lines parody the opening of Virgil's epic the *Aeneid:* "Arms and the man I sing . . ."
19. elegist (el´ ə jist) *n.*: A writer of mournful verse.
20. rondelets (rän d'l ets´): The rondelet is a French verse form with five to seven lines.

---

ours in some interesting ways. Create a concrete character from today who is thrown into that time and is trying to understand it.

---

17 Discussion Ask students how Lem uses this account of the machine's adjustment to make fun of modern poetry. What aspects of modern poetry is he satirizing?

18 Clarification Students may find it surprising to think of a "sonneteer" with State awards and a statue. Tell them that when Eastern Europe was under Soviet control, authors who conformed politically received honors and important positions in the state-sponsored writer's union. This description, therefore, is not as farfetched as it seems.

19 Enrichment Point out to students that the beginning of the electropoet's epic glorifies machines and speaks of leaving Earth because of human arrogance and hatred. Lem, in showing the machine to be increasingly ungovernable, echoes one of the most powerful themes in Romantic and modern literature. The theme concerns a magician, scientist, or religious scholar who creates a life-form which is supposed to remain subservient to him but instead defies its creator and runs rampant until destroyed. Stories such as "The Golem," "The Sorcerer's Apprentice," and *Frankenstein* all deal with this theme. The word *golem* in Hebrew means "an embryo or anything incompletely developed." The legendary golem was a Jewish Frankenstein monster, a powerful automaton made of clay and given life by means of magic. According to legend this monster was created by a rabbi who lived in sixteenth-century Prague.

You might want to have students consider why this theme has been so popular in Romantic and modern literature.

20 Discussion Point out to students that most poets certainly hope their work will have a powerful effect on readers or listeners. Ask them in what ways the electropoet successfully carries this hope to an absurd extreme. How does Lem use this absurdity to gently mock the ambitions of poets?

DEMON ABOVE THE SHIPS, 1916
Paul Klee
Museum of Modern Art, New York

Trurl himself had no little trouble in connection with his invention. The classicists, generally elderly, were fairly harmless; they confined themselves to throwing stones through his windows and smearing the sides of his house with an unmentionable substance. But it was much worse with the younger poets. One, for example, as powerful in body as his verse was in imagery, beat Trurl to a pulp. And while the constructor lay in the hospital, events marched on. Not a day passed without a suicide or a funeral; picket lines formed around the hospital; one could hear gunfire in the distance— instead of manuscripts in their suitcases, more and more poets were bringing rifles to defeat Trurl's electronic bard. But the bullets merely bounced off its calm exterior. After his return from the hospital, Trurl, weak and desperate, finally decided one night to dismantle the homeostatic[21] Homer he had created.

But when he approached the machine, limping slightly, it noticed the pliers in his hand and the grim glitter in his eye, and delivered such an eloquent, impassioned plea for mercy, that the constructor burst into tears, threw down his tools and hurried back to his room, wading through new works of genius, an ocean of paper that filled the hall chest-high from end to end and rustled incessantly.

---

21. homeostatic (hō′ mē ō stat′ ik) *adj.*: Self-regulating.

The following month Trurl received a bill for the electricity consumed by the machine and almost fell off his chair. If only he could have consulted his old friend Klapaucius! But Klapaucius was nowhere to be found. So Trurl had to come up with something by himself. One dark night he unplugged the machine, took it apart, loaded it onto a ship, flew to a certain small asteroid, and there assembled it again, giving it an atomic pile for its source of creative energy.

Then he sneaked home. But that wasn't the end of it. The electronic bard, deprived now of the possibility of having its masterpieces published, began to broadcast them on all wavelengths, which soon sent the passengers and crews of passing rockets into states of stanzaic stupefaction, and those more delicate souls were seized with severe attacks of esthetic ecstasy besides. Having determined the cause of this disturbance, the Cosmic Fleet Command issued Trurl an official request for the immediate termination of his device, which was seriously impairing the health and well-being of all travelers.

At that point Trurl went into hiding, so they dropped a team of technicians on the asteroid to gag the machine's output unit. It overwhelmed them with a few ballads, however, and the mission had to be abandoned. Deaf technicians were sent next, but the machine employed pantomime. After that, there began to be talk of an eventual punitive expedition, of bombing the electropoet into submission. But just then some ruler from a neighboring star system came, bought the machine and hauled it off, asteroid and all, to his kingdom.

Now Trurl could appear in public again and breathe easy. True, lately there had been supernovae[22] exploding on the southern horizon, the like of which no one had ever seen before, and there were rumors that this had something to do with poetry. According to one report, that same ruler, moved by some strange whim, had ordered his astroengineers to connect the electronic bard to a constellation of white supergiants,[23] thereby transforming each line of verse into a stupendous solar prominence; thus the Greatest Poet in the Universe

---

22. supernovae (sōō′ pər nō′ vē): Stars that increase in brightness tremendously over a comparatively short period.
23. supergiants: Immense and extremely bright stars.

was able to transmit its thermonuclear creations to all the illimitable reaches of space at once. But even if there were any truth to this, it was all too far away to bother Trurl, who vowed by everything that was ever held sacred never, never again to make a cybernetic model of the Muse.

Reader's Response: *How likely is it that a computer could learn to write great poetry? Explain.*

THINKING ABOUT THE SELECTION

Interpreting

1. When is this story set?
2. (a) What is Trurl's motivation for building the electronic bard? (b) How does this new machine resemble and differ from his "calculating machine"?
3. (a) How would you describe the relationship between Trurl and Klaupaucius? (b) How does the interplay between them add interest to the story?
4. (a) How does Lem endow the electronic bard with a personality? (b) Describe this personality.
5. **Irony** is the contrast between what is expected and what occurs. Show how the following contrasts are ironic: (a) The magnitude of Trurl's task versus the way in which he goes about it. (b) The appearance of the machine versus its poems.
6. **Tone** is an author's attitude toward his subject. How would you describe the tone of this story?
7. (a) How does Trurl's success eliminate the factor of chance from poetry? (b) In what way is this success also a failure? (c) How does Lem dramatize this failure in the story?

Applying

8. (a) What is Lem suggesting about the role of chance and accident in the creative process? (b) Do you agree with him? Why or why not?

ANALYZING LITERATURE

Understanding Satire in Science Fiction

Not only does Lem deal with futuristic worlds in his **science fiction,** but he uses **satire** to criticize familiar, down-to-earth foibles. In this tale the sword of his satire has a double edge. He pokes fun at poets while also mocking the notion that the creative process can be perfected by a machine. One device he uses to achieve this two-way satire is the application of imaginary technical language to poetic inspiration. By humorously suggesting that poems can be created

with tubes and gadgets, he satirizes both the irrationality of poets and the excessive rationality of scientists.

1. Explain how descriptions of the machine are satiric comments on poets' lack of logic, emotionality, vanity, and ambition.
2. How does the made-up technical jargon also satirize the desire of scientists to eliminate chance and mystery?
3. Show how Lem uses the poets' reactions to the machine to mock the following groups: (a) third-rate poets (b) classical poets (c) younger poets.
4. Is Lem's mockery of poets and scientists affectionate? Why or why not?
5. What does the fate of the machine suggest about the usefulness of such an invention?

THINKING AND WRITING

Writing a Parody

Parody, or literature that gently pokes fun at the style of other literature, is usually most effective when written in a spirit of teasing affection. Lem writes in this manner when he parodies Virgil's *Aeneid* and Christopher Marlowe's lyric "The Passionate Shepherd to His Love." He also shows how a deliberately unsuitable form, or inappropriate jargon, like the mathematical rendering of Marlowe, can make a serious work seem ridiculous.

Following Lem's example, choose a poem or story you enjoy and parody it. Remember that parody works best when the work being imitated is highly serious. Before beginning decide on your strategy. What features of the work can you exaggerate to produce a humorous effect? What discordant formal elements—such as Lem's use of nonsense rhyme—can you introduce? Is it possible to translate the language of the work into another, unsuitable language, as Lem does with Marlowe's poem? While writing, imagine that your audience consists of classmates who are familiar with the original. When you have completed your parody, read it to several classmates and revise the sections that don't make them laugh or smile.

(continued from bottom of page)

that an infallible machine can never replace human creativity. (b) Answers will differ.

ANSWERS TO ANALYZING LITERATURE

1. Lem shows Trurl failing to get the proper results from the machine until he removes the logic circuits, makes the emotive elements more electromotive, adds a character component to make it ambitious, and adds refinements that increase the machine's vanity.
2. The reduction of mysterious and accidental elements in human creativity to mechanical terms shows a scientific attitude that all human problems can be quantified.
3. (a) Third-rate poets don't know good poetry when they see it, and so aren't aware of their defeat by the machine. (b) Classical poets, who should value reason and order, become irrational and disorderly. (c) Younger poets behave like selfish children and become envious and violent.
4. Answers will differ; however, many students will respond that Lem's mockery is gentle and whimsical rather than savage and that he clearly knows a great deal about poetry and science.
5. Answers will differ. Students may respond that the fate of the machine suggests that such an invention, even if it were possible, would be of no use to humans.

THINKING AND WRITING

Writing Across the Curriculum
You may want to inform the computer or science departments that students are reading this selection. An appropriate teacher can then help students research the field of artificial intelligence. As a writing assignment, students can state their opinions about the limits, if any, of computer creativity.

Challenge Read another story in Lem's *The Cyberiad* and compare and contrast it to this one.

ses to Trurl's requests reveal its personality. (b) Answers will vary. Students may indicate that at times it is highly emotional or highly intellectual. When narcissistors are added, it becomes vain and self-regarding.
4. (a) It is ironic that Trurl literally has to re-create the universe, yet he is said to do this with such comparatively paltry equipment as "tubes

and terminals, circuits and shunts." (b) Answers will differ. Students may point to the ironic contrast between a machine that resembles the engine of a giant steamer and the absurd ditties or sophisticated poems it produces.
5. Lem's tone is humorous, playful, ironic, and satirical.
6. (a) His machine can create great poems to order, apparently without

the slightest difficulty. (b) Answers will differ. Students may point to the fact that the machine becomes unmanageable as it creates great poem after great poem, causing ordinary poets to attack it or kill themselves. (c) Lem shows the poets' reactions to the machine. Finally, Trurl has to send the machine away into distant space.
7. (a) Answers will differ, but most students will realize Lem is suggesting

ALEXANDER SOLZHENITSYN

Focus

More About the Author During World War II, Solzhenitsyn served in the Red Army. During his time in the service, he rose to the rank of artillery captain and was decorated for bravery.

After completing his eight-year prison sentence, Solzhenitsyn was exiled to Kazakhstan. His citizenship was restored in 1956, three years after Stalin's death. His first novels, such as *One Day in the Life of Ivan Denisovich*, describe life in the labor camps, about which he had first-hand knowledge.

Why might Solzhenitsyn write a fictitious account of his experience in a labor camp? Why didn't he write an autobiographical account?

Critical Evaluation Since Solzhenitsyn's first book was published in 1962, thousands of pages have been written, in many languages, assessing his work. None, however, conveys the full effect his books have had on Russian readers as well as the letters they have sent him. A sample of them appears in Michael Scammell's biography of Solzhenitsyn, published in 1984: "My face was smothered in tears. I didn't wipe them away or feel ashamed, because all this . . . was mine, intimately mine, mine for every day of the fifteen years I spent in the camps." Another wrote, "Thank you, dear friend, comrade and brother! . . . You have already left your name in the history of Soviet literature, and nothing can wipe it away." Still another said, "For me and others like me your story was the last hope that justice still exists somewhere, that it has not vanished or died out."

1918–

Alexander Solzhenitsyn (sŏl′ zhə nēt′ sin) spent years in Soviet prison camps. This experience failed to intimidate him and only confirmed his resolve to survive as a witness to oppression. Today his unsparing accounts of life in the camps are among the most important documents of our century.

Solzhenitsyn was born in Kislovodsk, a resort town in the mountains of southern Russia. His father died in a hunting accident before he was born, and Solzhenitsyn and his mother eked out a bare living on her small salary as a typist. He was a brilliant student and easily won admission to college, where he studied physics and mathematics.

When Germany invaded Russia in 1941, Solzhenitsyn was drafted and served in the army for four years. One day he was brought before his commanding officer and charged with treason for writing letters to a friend that were critical of the Soviet leader, Stalin. He was sentenced to eight years in jail and soon found himself in a windswept prison camp in central Asia. Here, in a harsh climate, prisoners did backbreaking work on a meager diet. Although he survived this ordeal, fate seemed to be against him. Released in 1953, he was almost immediately stricken with cancer. Doctors saw little hope for him. However, after an operation and radiation treatment, he recovered.

In 1956 he became a college teacher in central Russia. In his spare time, he began to write a description of his life in the camps. When, in 1961, the editor of the magazine *New World* called for writers to tell the "whole truth" about life under Stalin, Solzhenitsyn sent him the novel he had been working on, *One Day in the Life of Ivan Denisovich*.

The magazine published it, with the formal approval of Nikita Khrushchev, the prime minister. At the age of forty-four, Solzhenitsyn was suddenly a celebrity. Unfortunately, Khrushchev soon fell from power and a reactionary leadership replaced him. Solzhenitsyn continued to write prolifically, but a ban was placed on his books that was not lifted until 1989.

He was, however, able to publish his next two novels, *The First Circle* and *Cancer Ward*, in the West in 1968. For doing so the Soviet Writers' Union expelled him in 1969. The following year he was awarded the Nobel Prize in Literature "for the ethical force with which he has pursued the indispensable traditions of Russian literature."

In 1973 a Paris publisher released Solzhenitsyn's epic, three-volume chronicle of the network of Soviet prison camps that once occupied an area the size of France. Its title was *The Gulag Archipelago, 1918–1956* (the word *gulag* is a Russian acronym for such camps). Within months the Soviet government deported him. He lived for a time in Switzerland but in 1976 settled in the United States, where he continues to write.

Authors who receive the Nobel Prize customarily give a speech presenting their ideas about literature. Solzhenitsyn wrote such a speech but never was able to give it because he was forbidden to go to Sweden to accept the award. In the following selection, an excerpt from this unpresented speech, Solzhenitsyn discusses the role of world literature.

Objectives

Thematic	**Skills**
To compare speeches	1 To understand theme
	2 To appreciate a writer's background
	3 To respond to theme

GUIDE FOR INTERPRETING

The One Great Heart

Commentary

Theme. Theme is the insight into life conveyed through a work of literature. The theme of Solzhenitsyn's speech deals with the topic of the writer's role.

Different countries have different conceptions of the writer's role, the part that he or she plays in society. Russia, for instance, has a long tradition of viewing the writer as someone who searches for the truth and speaks out against social injustice. Poets and novelists have played a highly influential part in Russian life.

Why have Russian writers enjoyed so much prestige? For one thing, Russians love literature and admire those who create it. When the poet Pushkin (see page 878) died in 1837, thousands of people came to his funeral. Many of them could not read but had heard his poems and knew them by heart. A second reason has to do with Russia's political system: In a nation that has not experienced democracy for an appreciable length of time, writers have frequently been the only ones to publicly oppose the country's rulers. Those rulers, whether czars or Communists, have often been harsh and tyrannical.

Pushkin began the tradition of the writer as public spokesman in the early nineteenth century by speaking out against mistreatment of the Russian poor. His example inspired the novelist Tolstoy (see page 942) to take even stronger action later in that century. In Tolstoy's day most work in Russia was done by peasants who were desperately poor, while most of the wealth was held by a few rich families. Believing this situation to be immoral, Tolstoy, a wealthy man, gave everything he owned away, even the copyrights of his highly successful books. He lived simply and took a leading role in social reform or, as the Russians call it, "community action."

After the 1917 revolution, writers criticized the Soviet leaders as vigorously as they had the czars. Boris Pasternak's novel (see page 1118 for his poetry), *Doctor Zhivago* (1960), although not published officially, circulated in mimeographed form and caused an entire generation of Russians to question the course of their nation's history. It deserves some of the credit for the *perestroika,* or restructuring, which led eventually to the collapse of the Soviet Union as a political entity.

Like Pushkin, Tolstoy, and Pasternak, Alexander Solzhenitsyn also believes in the writer's role as social critic and searcher for the truth.

Writing

Brainstorm about the role of the writer as people in the United States see it. Do we tend to believe that writers should express a definite political viewpoint? Are we used to seeing writers participate in public affairs?

Literary Focus Ask students to name some American writers who have believed, like Solzhenitsyn, that a writer should take an active role in social issues. From Whitman to Toni Morrison, social themes have played a central role in the work of many of our finest writers, and many have had widespread international influence. For example, Thoreau's concept of civil disobedience in the face of unjust authority inspired women fighting for the right to vote in the United States and Britain. Similarly, Gandhi's and Martin Luther King, Jr.'s writings and speeches inspired people all over the world to protest colonialism in India and fight for civil rights, respectively.

Writing/Prior Knowledge Divide the class into groups of four. Have each group make a list of books they have read that have dealt directly with social issues. Then have groups complete the writing activity.

ESL Teaching Strategy In the spirit of Solzhenitsyn's Nobel address, have ESL students share with the class the great writers and works of their countries.

Master Teacher Note Solzhenitsyn quotes a Russian proverb: "One word of truth outweighs the world." Play the devil's advocate. Ask students to consider this: Governments sometimes obscure or twist the truth for reasons of "national security." Ask them if there is ever a time when truth is of less importance than "national security." Have them consider the implications of telling the truth versus lying when the stakes are high.

Support Material

Teaching Portfolio
Teacher Backup, p. 1599
Usage and Mechanics Worksheet, p. 1603
Analyzing Literature Worksheet, *Understanding Theme*, p. 1604
Critical Thinking and Reading Worksheet, *Appreciating a Writer's*

Background, p. 1605
Language Worksheet, *Understanding Phrasing*, p. 1606
Selection Test, pp. 1607–1608

Art Transparency 19
Interior with a Table by Vanessa Bell

The One Great Heart

Alexander Solzhenitsyn

translated by F. D. Reeve

I am, however, encouraged by a keen sense of WORLD LITERATURE as the one great heart that beats for the cares and misfortunes of our world, even though each corner sees and experiences them in a different way.

In past times, also, besides age-old national literatures there existed a concept of world literature as the link between the summits of national literatures and as the aggregate of reciprocal literary influences. But there was a time lag: readers and writers came to know foreign writers only belatedly, sometimes centuries later, so that mutual influences were delayed and the network of national literary high points was visible not to contemporaries but to later generations.

Today, between writers of one country and the readers and writers of another, there is an almost instantaneous reciprocity,[1] as I myself know. My books, unpublished, alas, in my own country, despite hasty and often bad translations have quickly found a responsive world readership. Critical analysis of them has been undertaken by such leading Western writers as Heinrich Böll.[2] During all these recent years, when both my work and my freedom did not collapse, when against the laws of gravity they held on seemingly in thin air, seemingly ON NOTHING, on the invisible, mute surface tension of sympathetic people, with warm gratitude I learned, to my complete surprise, of the support of the world's writing fraternity. On my fiftieth birthday I was astounded to receive greetings from well-known European writers. No pressure put on me now passed unnoticed. During the dangerous weeks when I was being expelled from the Writers' Union,[3] THE PROTECTIVE WALL put forward by the prominent writers of the world saved me from worse persecution, and Norwegian writers and artists hospitably prepared shelter for me in the event that I was exiled from my country. Finally, my being nominated for a Nobel Prize was originated not in the land where I live and write but by François Mauriac[4] and his colleagues. Afterward, national writers' organizations expressed unanimous support for me.

As I have understood it and experienced it myself, world literature is no longer an abstraction or a generalized concept invented by literary critics, but a common body and common spirit, a living, heartfelt unity reflecting the growing spiritual unity of mankind. State borders still turn crimson, heated red-hot by electric fences and machine-gun fire; some ministries of internal affairs still suppose that literature is "an internal affair" of the countries under their jurisdiction; and newspaper headlines still herald, "They have no right to interfere in our internal affairs!" Meanwhile, no such thing as INTER-

---

1. **reciprocity** (res´ ə präs´ ə tē): Mutual action, dependence.
2. **Heinrich Böll** (hīn´ riH böl): A German novelist (1917–1985) and winner of the Nobel Prize for Literature.

3. **the Writers Union:** The official Soviet writers' organization. In addition to being expelled from this union, Solzhenitsyn was forbidden to live in Moscow.
4. **François Mauriac** (frän swä´ mȯ ryàk´): A French novelist and essayist (1885–1970).

NAL AFFAIRS remains on our crowded Earth. Mankind's salvation lies exclusively in everyone's making everything his business, in the people of the East being anything but indifferent to what is thought in the West, and in the people of the West being anything but indifferent to what happens in the East. Literature, one of the most sensitive and responsive tools of human existence, has been the first to pick up, adopt, and assimilate this sense of the growing unity of mankind. I therefore confidently turn to the world literature of the present, to hundreds of friends whom I have not met face to face and perhaps never will see.

My friends! Let us try to be helpful, if we are worth anything. In our own countries, torn by differences among parties, movements, castes, and groups, who for ages past has been not the dividing but the uniting force? This, essentially, is the position of writers, spokesmen of a national language, of the chief tie binding the nation, the very soil which the people inhabit, and, in fortunate circumstances, the nation's spirit too.

I think that world literature has the power in these frightening times to help mankind see itself accurately despite what is advocated by partisans[5] and by parties. It has the power to transmit the condensed experience of one region to another, so that different scales of values are combined, and so that one people accurately and concisely knows the true history of another with a power of recognition and acute awareness as if it had lived through that

---

5. **partisans** (pärt´ ə z'nz): Unreasoning, emotional supporters of a party or viewpoint.

These postage stamps honor writers from many different countries.

5 **Discussion** Solzhenitsyn speaks fervently about the need for "mankind's salvation," but, in this selection, he does not say explicitly from which problems humanity needs to be saved. Name the problems he seems to have in mind, judging from references contained in the selection.

6 **Clarification** Remind students that Solzhenitsyn's own country at the time, the Soviet Union, included diverse religious and ethnic groups whose main common bond was the Russian language.

Master Teacher Note Place Art Transparency 19, *Interior with a Table* by Vanessa Bell, on an overhead projector. Have students imagine that they are writers and that this is their library or study. About what topics might their view from the window stimulate them to write? Have them jot down a list and compare their lists with the class. Ask students if they think their topics are universal. How? How does this exercise fit in with Solzhenitsyn's Nobel address?

history itself—and could thus be spared repeating old mistakes. At the same time, perhaps we ourselves may succeed in developing our own WORLD-WIDE VIEW, like any man, with the center of the eye seeing what is nearby but the periphery of vision taking in what is happening in the rest of the world. We will make correlations and maintain worldwide standards.

Who, if not writers, are to condemn their own unsuccessful governments (in some states this is the easiest way to make a living; everyone who is not too lazy does it) as well as society itself, whether for its cowardly humiliation or for its self-satisfied weakness, or the lightheaded escapades of the young, or the youthful pirates brandishing knives?

We will be told: What can literature do against the pitiless onslaught of naked violence? Let us not forget that violence does not and cannot flourish by itself; it is inevitably intertwined with LYING. Between them there is the closest, the most profound and natural bond: nothing screens violence except lies, and the only way lies can hold out is by violence. Whoever has once announced violence as his METHOD must inexorably choose lying as his PRINCIPLE. At birth, violence behaves openly and even proudly. But as soon as it becomes stronger and firmly established, it senses the thinning of the air around it and cannot go on without befogging itself in lies, coating itself with lying's sugary oratory. It does not always or necessarily go straight for the gullet; usually it demands of its victims only allegiance to the lie, only complicity in the lie.

The simple act of an ordinary courageous man is not to take part, not to support lies! Let *that* come into the world and even reign over it, but not through me. Writers and artists can do more: they can VANQUISH LIES! In the struggle against lies, art has always won and always will. Conspicuously, incontestably for everyone. Lies can stand up against much in the world, but not against art.

Once lies have been dispelled, the repulsive nakedness of violence will be exposed—and hollow violence will collapse.

That, my friends, is why I think we can help the world in its red-hot hour: not by the nay-saying of having no armaments, not by abandoning oneself to the carefree life, but by going into battle!

In Russian, proverbs about TRUTH are favorites. They persistently express the considerable, bitter, grim experience of the people, often astonishingly:

ONE WORD OF TRUTH OUTWEIGHS THE WORLD.

On such a seemingly fantastic violation of the law of the conservation of mass and energy[6] are based both my own activities and my appeal to the writers of the whole world.

---

6. **the law of the conservation of mass and energy:** This law states that in any physical or chemical change, neither mass nor energy can be lost.

Reader's Response *Tell how a work of world literature has helped you to understand the values and traditions of a different people.*

Interpreting

1. Solzhenitsyn says that today literature travels from country to country more quickly than in the past. How does his own career illustrate this observation?

2. (a) Explain what he means by declaring that "WORLD LITERATURE" is "the one great heart." (b) Is the image of a "heart" appropriate? Why or why not?

3. (a) What connection does he see between lies and violence? (b) Is his reasoning convincing? Explain.

4. What is the meaning of the Russian proverb that Solzhenitsyn quotes?

5. In your own words, describe the role that Solzhenitsyn feels the writer should play in modern society.

Applying

6. How would you convince someone that "no such thing as INTERNAL AFFAIRS remains on our crowded Earth"?

7. Solzhenitsyn says that "Lies can stand up against much in the world, but not against art." Do you agree or disagree? Explain.

ANALYZING LITERATURE

Understanding Theme

The **theme** of Solzhenitsyn's speech deals with the topic of the writer's role in society. Solzhenitsyn's idea of the writer's role, or function, in society was influenced by such figures as Pushkin and Tolstoy. Like them he believes that a writer should try to correct social ills. "Who, if not writers," he asks, "are to condemn their own unsuccessful governments . . . as well as society itself . . . ?" He urges writers throughout the world to become social activists and to help nourish the growing unity of mankind."

1. Identify two reasons he gives for thinking that writers can play this role.

2. Solzhenitsyn says that by reading the literature of other nations, people can avoid "repeating old mistakes." Do you think this is possible? Why or why not?

3. What do you think Solzhenitsyn would say about the following American authors: Edgar Allan Poe, Mark Twain, Stephen King?

CRITICAL THINKING AND READING

Appreciating a Writer's Background

Few writers have based their novels as literally on their own experience as Solzhenitsyn has. Many of his books, for instance, are based directly on his own years in Soviet prison camps. Even his novel *August 1914*, written about events that occurred before he was born, is set in the area of eastern Germany where he himself served during World War II.

His experiences have also affected the reaction to his work. His conflicts with the Soviet government led to his being deported from the Soviet Union, and when he arrived in the West, his work won even greater recognition than it had gained already.

1. When Solzhenitsyn came to the West, the Vietnam War was still in progress and relations between the Soviet Union and the United States were badly strained. How might these circumstances have affected American attitudes toward Solzhenitsyn?

2. How do you think the acclaim he received in Europe and the United States may have influenced his ideas about the ability of writers to affect public opinion?

THINKING AND WRITING

Responding to Theme

Solzhenitsyn believes that literature should bring people from different nations together to work for common purposes. Write a paper identifying the major problems the world faces and explaining how authors can contribute to their solution. Get together with a group of students and brainstorm to create a list of problems. Working with your group, review Solzhenitsyn's remarks about the author's role. Then come up with additional ways in which authors can battle against social ills. As you write your own paper, use the ideas from your group discussion that seemed most persuasive to you. Finally, read your paper to members of your group and ask them for suggestions to improve it.

(continued from bottom of page)

ANSWERS TO ANALYZING LITERATURE

1. One reason is that writers' works travel from nation to nation more quickly than in earlier times. Another is that writers can combat violence by exposing the lies by which it tries to disguise itself.

2. Some students may argue that human nature is not subject to change: that wrongdoing is not based on ignorance, but on human selfishness. Others may point to examples where people did seem to learn from others' mistakes.

3. Answers may differ. Suggested response: Solzhenitsyn would probably consider the work of Poe and King to be "escapist," but he might admire Twain's attempts at exposing falsehood and injustice, as in his treatment of slavery in *The Adventures of Huckleberry Finn*.

ANSWERS TO CRITICAL THINKING AND READING

1. Answers may differ. Suggested response: The prevalent anti-Soviet feeling in the United States during the Vietnam War may have helped make Solzhenitsyn, someone who had been branded an "anti-Soviet" writer, more popular here.

2. Answers may differ. Suggested response: He may have been encouraged in his belief about what writers in general can achieve by his own success in winning public recognition and influence.

THINKING AND WRITING

Publishing Student Writing Choose the best papers expressing the two sides of the debate and submit them to the school newspaper, where they can be published in a point-counterpoint format.

Challenge Have students read Solzhenitsyn's most famous book, *One Day in the Life of Ivan Denisovich*, and write a report about it. For example, they can address whether this book is a good example of what Solzhenitsyn says in his Nobel address a writer should do.

---

problems in a way that all the world's people can potentially share. (b) The heart is an appropriate image because it is often associated both with concern for others and with literature.

3. (a) Solzhenitsyn says that violence cannot exist without using lies to conceal itself. (b) His reasoning is convincing because those using violence often allege that they are doing so for a good cause.

4. It means that the truth is more powerful than anything else in the world.

5. Solzhenitsyn specifically cites that writers can help to solve today's problems by fighting falsehood and speaking the truth.

6. Answers may differ. Suggested response: Two key reasons are that both modern industrial processes and modern weapons affect the whole planet's ecology, so no nation's actions regard-

ing either one can be considered entirely an "internal affair."

7. Answers may differ. Some students will cite works such as *Dr. Zhivago* that have had widespread influence despite efforts to silence their authors. Others may point out that such eventual success does not alleviate the plight of the writers themselves, citing examples such as Anne Frank.

1933–

Andrei Voznesensky (än′ drā väz nə sen′ skē), one of the Soviet Union's leading writers, has accomplished something no living American writer has done: He has made poetry popular.

Voznesensky was born in Moscow in 1933. He began writing poetry as a teenager in the years just after World War II. At the age of fourteen, he mailed some of his poems to Boris Pasternak (see page 1116), then one of Russia's most famous poets. Voznesensky's parents were astonished when they received a phone call from the great writer inviting their son to visit him at his Moscow apartment. It was the beginning of an unusual friendship that lasted until Pasternak's death in 1960. The older poet often showed Voznesensky his newest work, and Voznesensky showed Pasternak his.

Yet for a while Voznesensky hoped to become an architect. He changed his mind only when his senior project—after a full year's work—was destroyed in a fire just before graduation. This event seemed like an act of fate to him, and he devoted himself completely to poetry. Within a few years he had established a reputation as a compelling young poet with a distinctive style. Along with Yevgeny Yevtushenko (see page 1332) and Bella Akhmadulina, he became a leading figure in what is called the "thaw," a period in the early 1960's when Soviet writers enjoyed greater freedom of expression than they had since the 1920's.

The hallmarks of Voznesensky's poetry are wry humor, highly imaginative associations, and sudden twists of meaning. Many of his poems use scientific terms, partly because of his interest in science, but also because Soviet scientists have played a leading role in the demand for greater freedom. (The country's chief opposition leader was the physicist Andrei Sakharov. However, Sakharov was hailed and received by Gorbachev and was a member of the Congress of People's Deputies before his death in 1989.) Voznesensky's poetry is also marked by a great sensitivity to the sound of words. Many of his most famous poems are structured around a repeated sound or group of sounds that create a chiming or tolling effect. This aspect of his style may be a legacy of his relationship with Pasternak, whose own work is highly musical in its sound.

Voznesensky's combination of traditional sound devices and imaginative leaps has made his work very popular. His books regularly sell hundreds of thousands of copies, and his emotional readings fill arenas the size of Madison Square Garden. By contrast, American poetry books usually sell in editions of one or two thousand.

Not only Russians, but readers around the world have become familiar with Voznesensky's work. His poems have been translated into every major language, and he has read to enthusiastic audiences throughout Europe and the United States. Voznesensky's travels abroad have led to close friendships with a number of prominent Americans, including Senator Edward Kennedy, the playwright Arthur Miller, and the poet Allen Ginsberg. Three separate collections of his verse have been published in English: *Antiworlds and the Fifth Ace* (1966), *Nostalgia for the Present* (1978), and *An Arrow in the Wall* (1987).

Voznesensky was a passionate advocate of *glasnost,* the policy of greater openness in the former Soviet Union. His lobbying efforts led to the first Soviet publication of Pasternak's long-banned novel *Doctor Zhivago,* and he continues to press for greater freedom of expression in today's Russia.

Objectives

Thematic
To understand literature that expresses the brutality of war

Skill
To understand persona

GUIDE FOR INTERPRETING

I Am Goya

Commentary

Persona. In many poems the speaker is understood to be the poet. For example, when Walt Whitman says, "I hear America singing," the reader takes the "I" to be Whitman himself. Often, however, poets prefer to use a speaker who is someone other than themselves. When a poet creates a character to speak the words of a poem, that character is called a **persona,** from the Latin word for "mask."

A poet can gain many advantages by speaking through a mask. If the poet is a man, he may feel that the poem's content can be better conveyed from a woman's point of view. Or, if the poem's events occur in an earlier period of history, the poet may want to describe them from the vantage point of someone who was present at the time. A mask can also free the poet to explore his or her own feelings—we are often more willing to express buried or rejected emotions when we don't have to take complete responsibility for them! Finally, a mask often conveys added authority to a poem. If the persona is a well-known historical figure, for instance, the reader may take the poet's words more seriously.

In "I Am Goya," Voznesensky gives his poem added authority by speaking as a long-dead Spanish artist famous for his depictions of warfare. In a clever twist, however, he has Goya comment on events of our own time.

Writing

If you could go to a masquerade party dressed as a famous historical figure, which person would you choose? Describe the kind of things you would say and do when you were in costume.

Primary Source

Voznesensky gave the following account of his first encounter with Goya's art: "I remember the last war [World War II] fairly vividly, although I was quite small when it started. My mother and I were refugees in a small village in the Ural Mountains. My father was in Leningrad. We thought that he had died. We were hungry; near the village wolves howled at night. One day the door opened and my father came in. He was unshaven and wore an old black overcoat. He brought us a tin of canned meat and a book about Goya; he was on leave and had come to visit us briefly. Since that day—I was nine—Goya has become a symbol for me, the symbol of war. Even today he reminds me of the partisans shot by the Germans, of wolves, of our neighbor who was mourning her dead son, of the sirens during the bombardments of Moscow. . . . Above all, Goya tells us that all serious artists must be concerned with the threat of a war."

(continued from bottom of page)

the U.S.A." and "My Hometown." Have students compare one of these examples with "I Am Goya" to show what a writer gains by using a persona.

Writing/Prior Knowledge Explain that Voznesensky wrote this poem in the persona of Goya because he strongly identified with the Spanish painter. Ask students to name an important figure—a scientist, athlete, artist, or political leader—from an earlier historical period with whom they feel a special affinity. Why does that particular person appeal to them?

ESL Teaching Strategy Feeling a sense of ownership of a new language is an important step in mastering it. The length of this poem makes it appropriate for memorization, both by ESL students and by native-speaking students. Have students memorize and perform this poem for classmates. You might point out to students that when performing their poems in public, Russian poets rarely have the text before them, unless the poem is a very new one.

Master Teacher Note Bring in some examples of Goya's paintings. Have students look them over and then discuss the value of "chilling depictions of warfare." Have them consider the following: Are the paintings realistic? Do they accurately reflect the conditions of war for that time?

Teaching Tenth-Grade Students Tenth-grade students may have difficulty understanding persona. According to *A Handbook to Literature*, persona is "literally a mask . . . or 'second self' created by the author and through whom the narrative is told." Explain to them that although the persona may be a narrator, it cannot be a character in the story or poem. It is "an implied author."

Support Material

Teaching Portfolio
Teacher Backup, p. 1609
Usage and Mechanics Worksheet, p. 1613
Analyzing Literature Worksheet, *Understanding Persona*, p. 1614
Critical Thinking and Reading Worksheet, *Understanding Allu-*

sions, p. 1615
Language Worksheet, *Understanding Paradox*, p. 1616
Selection Test, pp. 1617–1618

Literary Focus Ask students to cite examples of the use of a persona in poems or popular songs they know. Perhaps the most famous American poet to use a persona is T. S. Eliot in "The Love Song of J. Alfred Prufrock." Bruce Springsteen frequently uses personae in his song lyrics. Two well-known examples that students may know are "Born in

Humanities Note

Fine art, *Colosso o Pánico (Giant)* by Francisco José de Goya. Goya (1746–1828) was a Spanish painter and graphic artist. He gained royal attention to his talents through a series of tapestry designs that depicted scenes from everyday life. In 1786 Goya served as court painter to Charles III, and he was a favorite at the court of Charles IV.

In 1793 Goya suffered from an illness that was nearly fatal and left him deaf. Goya became even further isolated because of his deafness; his work thereafter was dark and cheerless.

Napoleon's armies occupied Spain in 1808. Spain hoped that the conquerors would bring reform to their country, but because of the savage behavior of the French, their hopes were soon crushed. From 1810 to 1815, Goya's works reflected his bitter experience and resentment toward the French. One of his most famous pieces from this period was *Disasters of War*, which depicts the Napoleonic invasions of Spain. After the French were defeated and driven out of Spain, Goya retreated to nightmarish visions, such as *Colosso o Pánico*. He also painted his villa walls with a series of "black paintings" of macabre subjects.

In 1824 Goya went into self-exile. He finally settled in Bordeaux, where he died.

You might want to use the following questions to discuss the art:

1. Describe what is happening in this painting. What is the painting's tone?
2. If the giant were able to speak, what might he be saying to the panic-stricken people below him?

COLOSSO O PÁNICO (GIANT)
Francisco José de Goya
Prado, Madrid

Primary Source

The Great Patriotic War The Russians call World War II the Great Patriotic War. Before Germany invaded Russia in June 1941, Soviet society had experienced twenty-four years of revolution, civil war, and tyrannical oppression. Russian historian Roy Medvedev explains how the war fused the diverse peoples of the Soviet Union into a single, unified nation:

It was the moment of our greatest humiliation, but also of our greatest triumph. The war remains more important than the 1917 Revolution that created the Soviet state, than the civil war which followed its birth, than even the terror of Stalin's purges. It was truly the moment in which the Soviet Union came together as one nation, for the first time no longer divided, thrust together in desperation that overcame the years of division and repression, to save our country, everyone's country, to save our dream.

I Am Goya[1]

Andrei Voznesensky

translated by Stanley Kunitz

I am Goya
of the bare field, by the enemy's beak gouged
till the craters of my eyes gape
I am grief

I am the tongue
of war, the embers of cities
on the snows of the year 1941[2]
I am hunger

I am the gullet[3]
of a woman hanged whose body like a bell
tolled over a blank square
I am Goya

O grapes of wrath!
I have hurled westward
                the ashes of the uninvited
                  guest!
and hammered stars into the unforgetting sky—
   like nails
I am Goya

1959

---

1. **Goya:** Francisco José de Goya (frän thēs′ kỏ hỏ se′ the gỏ′ yä), a Spanish painter (1746–1828) known for his dramatic and chilling depictions of warfare.
2. **the year 1941:** In 1941, Germany invaded the Soviet Union and, by winter, had destroyed much of the Red Army.
3. **gullet** (gul′ ət) n.: The throat or neck.

Reader's Response *Did you notice any patterns of sound in this translation? Explain.*

THINKING ABOUT THE SELECTION

Interpreting

1. Even in translation, the sound of the Russian poem, with its short, emphatic lines, comes through. What feeling does their insistent rhythm convey?
2. A **paradox** is an apparent contradiction. (a) Explain the paradox in line 3. (b) What does this paradox suggest about the nature of war?
3. (a) How does the fourth stanza differ from the first three in both form and content? (b) Who do you think is the "uninvited guest" of line 14?
4. What attitude toward war do you think the poet wants to communicate? Explain.

Applying

5. The Soviet Union suffered greater destruction in World War II than any other country. Many of its major cities were destroyed and as many as 20 million of its citizens may have been killed. (By contrast, United States deaths numbered about 400,000.) How is that experience reflected in this poem?

ANALYZING LITERATURE

Understanding Persona

A **persona**—from the Latin word for "mask"—is an invented or historical character who speaks the words of a poem. In "I Am Goya," the title and first line make it clear that the speaker is not the poet himself but the Spanish artist Goya. This device creates immediate interest because the reader is curious to discover what this famous, but long-dead artist will say. It soon becomes obvious that he is describing events not only of his own time, but of ours.

1. Why is Goya an appropriate persona for a poem about war?
2. In the "I am . . ." phrases of lines 4, 5, 8, and 9, the speaker identifies with various things. (a) What do these things have in common? (b) What does the speaker's identification with them suggest about his attitude toward war?
3. To what extent do you think the poet shares the persona's attitude? Explain.

(continued from bottom of page)
and Suhrab," page 89; the *Iliad*, page 347; "Russia 1812," page 890; "Two Friends," page 914; Anna Akhmatova's poems, page 1114; and "Thoughts of Hanoi," page 1436.

Closure and Extension

ANSWERS TO THINKING ABOUT THE SELECTION

1. The poem's rhythm conveys a feeling of stark solemnity.
2. (a) The paradox is that the craters of eyes are described as gaping, even after the eyes themselves are gone. (b) This suggests the futility of war.
3. (a) In the fourth stanza, the poem's mood changes from grief to anger. (b) "The uninvited guest" refers to the invading German armies.
4. Answers may differ. Suggested response: Much of the poem suggests war's terrible cost and its futility, but the proud declaration of the final sentences undermine those initial impressions.
5. The Soviet experience in World War II is reflected in the poem's bitter description of "total war," in which civilians are as much a target as military forces.

ANSWERS TO ANALYZING LITERATURE

1. Goya is appropriate because many of his most famous works depict scenes of war.
2. (a) All these things convey the agony of wartime. (b) It suggests that he views war as an act of wanton destruction.
3. The whole thrust and tone of the poem imply that the poet shares the persona's view of war.

Challenge Have students compare the treatment of modern war in poems such as Wilfred Owen's "Anthem for Doomed Youth" or Randall Jarrell's "The Death of the Ball Turret Gunner" with Voznesensky's poem.

Presentation

Motivation/Prior Knowledge Remind students of the kinds of associative leaps they saw in the poems of García Lorca (see page 1143) and explain that in this selection Voznesensky, who has been influenced by García Lorca, handles language with the same kind of daring—and the same unexpected results—that García Lorca did.

Purpose-Setting Question How does Voznesensky vividly depict the brutality of war?

Universal Themes The brutality of war is a frequent theme in twentieth-century literature. You might have students also read "Rustam

YEVGENY YEVTUSHENKO

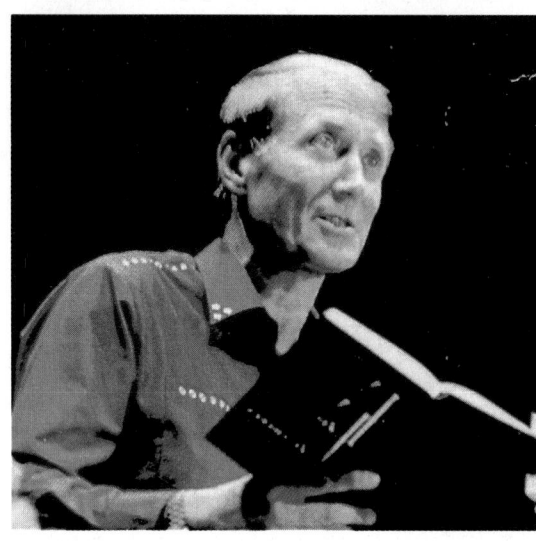

1933–

Yevgeny Yevtushenko (yev gen´ ē yev´ tōō sheŋ´ kō) is one of the few modern poets known throughout the world. His poetry—direct and tender, yet harsh in its criticism of injustice—is found in bookstores in Los Angeles, Paris, and Tokyo, as well as in his native Russia.

Born in 1933 in Zima Junction, along the Trans-Siberian Railroad, Yevtushenko grew up in the wide-open spaces of central Asia, a region not unlike western Colorado. Ironically, this most Russian of writers was not Russian by birth. His mother came from Latvia, a small country on the Baltic Sea (an independent country in his mother's youth, it became part of the Soviet Union, and is now one of the independent countries in the Commonwealth of Independent States). His father's family was Ukrainian and had been exiled to Siberia by the czar in the 1800's.

Yevtushenko's poetry attracted attention when he was still a teenager. His teachers recommended him for a prestigious college in Moscow, and it was there that he published his first book, *Prospectors of the Future* (1952).

The six books of poems he published over the next nine years, along with his famous public readings, made him as popular as a movie star would be in the United States. By 1961 he was giving over 200 readings a year. However, he did not merely "read" his poems: He acted them out, sometimes lowering his voice to a whisper, then breaking out in a mighty roar, always with plenty of accompanying body language. He was also known for his leadership in the movement for greater freedom in Russia.

In 1962 Yevtushenko wrote a poem that carried his fame around the world. This poem was "Babi Yar," the name of a place near Kiev where German troops murdered 35,000 Jews on two awful days in September of 1941. In writing it, Yevtushesnko did something brave: He referred not only to the Nazis but to Russian anti-Semitism as well. There is a long history of mistreatment of the Jews in Russia, but at that time it was a dangerous subject to bring up.

Yevtushenko's autobiography, written in 1962, tells how the editor who published "Babi Yar" stayed up all night trying to decide whether to print it. He knew the poem could easily cost him his job but decided to print it anyway. The poem's passionate attack on religious prejudice won the poet many admirers in the West, and soon he was in demand as a performer of poetry in both Europe and the United States.

Yevtushenko continues to write, but much of his time now is spent on politics. Elected in 1989 to the Congress of People's Deputies, he supported Mikhail Gorbachev's policy of *perestroika*, or restructuring of Soviet society, and continues to work on the reorganization of the new Commonwealth of Independent States. Yevtushenko's most recent work is *Don't Die Before Your Death* (1993), a novel which addresses the political climate emerging from the dismantling of the former Soviet Union.

The best introduction to Yevtushenko is one of his many recordings. If Voznesensky's poetry resembles Pasternak's (see page 1116), then in Yevtushenko we hear a clear echo of the poet Mayakovsky (1893–1930)—a voice fit to calm a frightened child, or storm a barricade.

GUIDE FOR INTERPRETING

Visit; Weddings

Commentary

Atmosphere. Many poems, especially those that tell a story, create a particular **atmosphere,** or overall mood. This mood can be jubilant or melancholy, playful or poignant, soothing or mischievous.

In a good poem, the atmosphere is often so all-pervasive that we hardly know how the poet has evoked it. Edgar Allan Poe's "The Raven," for instance, casts a dark spell of foreboding so unmistakable that it probably would be felt by even the most casual listener. Yet the source of the poem's atmosphere may not be immediately apparent.

On closer inspection it is possible to identify some of the ways in which poets create atmosphere. As in a piece of music, the rhythm of a poem stirs certain emotions in the reader, and those emotions contribute to its overall mood. However, to summon up a specific atmosphere, poets frequently use two other important devices.

The first one is imagery. A moss-covered tombstone creates one mood, a bright banner snapping in the wind creates another. Through their selection of images and the play of one image against another, poets can make subtle changes in the mood of a poem. A second key device is tone. The tone, or attitude, of the poem's speaker colors each image with a particular feeling and so contributes to the atmosphere.

Each of these two poems by Yevtushenko has a distinctive atmosphere. There is, however, a similarity in the way each uses physical details that marks them as the work of the same author. In addition, each has Yevtushenko's distinctive tone of voice, one that makes his readers—in any language—feel that he is sharing intimate thoughts with them.

Writing

Think about the atmosphere of a poem, song, or story you especially like. If you had to choose one word to describe its atmosphere, what would that word be? Freewrite, exploring the reasons for your choice.

Commentary

The critic Rosh Ireland made the following comments about Yevtushenko's "modern style": "Its main features were striking and unusual rhyme schemes, based not on perfect rhymes but on assonance, alliteration, and association by meaning . . . irregular mete . . . and garish juxtapositons and bold metaphors. . . . To these one could add a notable liking for antithesis [a contrast or opposition of thoughts]: Yevtushenko, dealing as he does so often with discrepancies and contradictions, frequently makes use of antithesis in the closing lines of his poems."

Literary Focus One of the most appealing aspects of literature is its ability to create atmosphere. Poems, stories, and plays present the whole spectrum of human experience, providing a way of escaping from our concerns of the moment. Perhaps more important, as we "soak in" the atmosphere of a particular literary work, we may find that it awakens feelings in ourselves we did not realize existed. Ask students to describe a poem or a popular song they know that creates a distinctive atmosphere.

Writing/Prior Knowledge Ask students to think of some devices writers use to create atmosphere other than rhythm, imagery, and tone. Some possibilities include striking or humorous rhymes; locales with strong psychological associations, and settings with vivid historical connections. Then have them complete the writing activity.

ESL Teaching Strategy Encourage ESL students to share a poem or song in their native language that has a particularly strong atmosphere. Then have them explain the devices used in it.

Master Teacher Note No recording of Yevtushenko reading either of these poems has been released in the West, but several recordings of his performances of other poems are available on LP or cassette. Many libraries will have copies in their audio-visual collections. Play one for the class, reading the poem aloud in English first. (As an alternative, play for students the reading of the Russian original on the *Prentice Hall Listening to Literature* audiocassette.) This comparison will enable students to see how individual lines are rendered in the original Russian. After playing the recording, ask students how their impression of Yevtushenko has been affected by hearing him.

Teaching Tenth-Grade Students These poems may be a little bit more difficult for tenth-grade students than some of the other poems in this unit. You may wish to read these poems aloud, periodically stopping to clarify points and to ask questions.

Support Material

Teaching Portfolio
Teacher Backup, p. 1619
Usage and Mechanics Worksheet, p. 1623
Analyzing Literature Worksheet, *Understanding Atmosphere*, p. 1624
Critical Thinking and Reading Worksheet, *Appreciating the Speaker's*

Characteristics, p. 1625
Language Worksheet, *Appreciating Sensuous Language*, p. 1626
Selection Test, pp. 1627–1628

Visit

Yevgeny Yevtushenko

translated by Robin Milner-Gulland and Peter Levi, S.J.

Going to Zima Junction,[1] quiet place.
Watching out for it in the distance
with the window of the carriage wide open,
familiar houses, ornamental carving.
5 The jump down from the train before it stops,
crunching along on the warm slag;[2]
the linesman working with a hose
cursing and swearing in the stifling heat.
The ducks in midstream with their heads buried,
10 the perches where the poultry crow at dawn,
along the sidings ornamental stars
of white and colored bricks set in the wall.
Walking along the dusty paving-boards,
passing the clock that sits on the town hall,
15 hearing behind the fence of the old market
rustle of oats and clink of weights and measures:
and there the painted wooden fruit-baskets,
the cranberries wet on the low counters,
and the bright yellow butter-balls afloat
20 in basins made of flower-painted china.
Same cranny where the birds are still nesting,
and, most familiar, the faded gate.
And the house is exactly the same size,
the log fence still mended with boards,

25 the same broom leaning upon the stove,
the same tinned mushrooms on the window-sill,
the crack in the stairs is not different,
darkening deeply down, feeding fungus. . . .
Some nut or bolt or other I'd picked up
30 just as I always picked something up
was clenched happily in my hand
and dropped again as I went hurrying
down to the river and the river-mist,
and wandering sometimes in the woods
35 by a path choked in a tangle of tall weeds
in search of some deep-colored country flower,
and working with the freckled ferry girl,
heaving the glossy hawser[3] hand by hand.
Trying the quality of "old honey"
40 where the beehives rear up above the pond,
rocking along slow-motion in the cart,
slow rhythms of the whip's lazy flicking.
Wandering through the cranberry patches
with a casual crowd of idle lads,
45 and fishing beneath bridges with the noise
of trains thundering above your head,
joking, throwing your shirt off in the grass,
and diving in high from the river-bank,
with one sudden thought, how little I
have done in life, how much I can do.

---

1. **Zima** (zē′ mə) **Junction:** A town in the Asian part of the Soviet Union, just west of Lake Baikal and north of Mongolia.
2. **slag** (slag): Refuse separated from a metal in the process of smelting.

---

3. **hawser** (hô′ zər): A large rope used for towing or mooring a ship.

Reader's Response *Do you like revisiting places where you once spent a great deal of time? Why or why not?*

Weddings

Yevgeny Yevtushenko

**translated by Robin Milner-Gulland
and Peter Levi, S.J.**

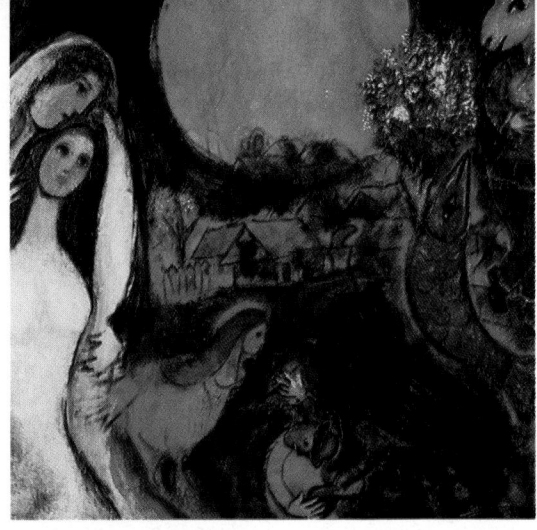

VILLAGE WITH DARK SUN
Marc Chagall

Those weddings in wartime![1] The deceiving
  comfort!
The dishonesty of words about living.
Sonorous[2] snowy roads.
In the wind's wicked teeth I hurry down them
to a hasty wedding at the next village.
With worn-out tread and hair down in my eyes
I go inside, I famous for my dancing,
into the noisy house.
In there tensed up with nerves and with emotion
among a crowd of friends and family,
called up, distraught,[3] the bridegroom
sitting beside his Vera, his bride.
Will in a few days put his greatcoat on
and set out coated for the war.
Will see new country, carry a rifle.
May also drop if he is hit.
His glass is fizzing but he can't drink it.
The first night may be the last night.
And sadly eyeing me and bitter-minded
he leans in his despair across the table
and says, "Come on then, dance."
Drinks are forgotten. Everyone looks round.
Out I twirl to begin. Clap of my feet.
Shake.

Scrape the floor with my toe-cap.
25 Whistle. Whistle. Slap hands.
Faster, leaping ceiling-high.
Moving the posters pinned up on the walls:
HITLER KAPUT[4]
               Her eyes streaming with tears.
Already soaked in sweat and out of breath—
30 "Dance!"
They cry out in despair, and I dance.

When I get home my feet are log-heavy:
some drunken people from another wedding
turn up behind me. Mother must let me go.
35 The scene again: I see it, and again
beside the edge of a trailing tablecloth
I squat down to dance.
           She weeping
and her friends weeping. I frightened
don't feel like dancing, but you can't not dance.

---

1. **in wartime:** The poem is set during World War II.
2. **Sonorous** (sə nôr′ əs) *adj.*: Producing a full, deep, or rich sound.
3. **distraught** (di strôt′) *adj.*: Extremely troubled.

---

4. **HITLER KAPUT** (kə′ pʊt′): German for "Hitler Defeated."

Reader's Response *Compare and contrast this wedding with weddings you have attended.*

Closure and Extension

ANSWERS TO THINKING ABOUT THE SELECTION

1. The theme established by them is that nothing has changed in Zima since the speaker left.
2. (a) At line 29, the speaker begins to describe his memories of Zima when he was a boy. (b) The imagery in the second part of the poem is more animated, suggesting the livelier days of a boy.
3. (a) It gives them greater emotional impact, because the reader has been held in suspense, waiting for a direct statement about how the speaker feels. (b) The lines are meant to be those of the boy.
4. Wartime weddings are seen as a "deceiving comfort" because the groom may soon die.
5. (a) Answers will differ, but whatever details students cite owe their effectiveness to their ability to dramatize the situation. (b) Answers will differ according to their choices and their understanding of the details.
6. "Weddings" explores the contradiction of couples marrying and trying to celebrate at a time when death may be near.
7. (a) The ending indicates the speaker is a child because he or she needs the mother's permission to go to another wedding. (b) A child does not have a frame of reference to deal with the complexity of this situation.
8. The poem suggests that the war left that generation with an acute awareness of the tragic dimension of human life.

ANSWERS TO ANALYZING LITERATURE

1. Answers may differ. (a) Some possibilities include the presence of guns at the wedding celebration, the wartime poster on the wall, and the sad eyes of the groom as he asks the speaker to dance. (b) Each adds to the sense of outside events intruding on the festivities.
2. Answers may differ. Suggested response: The overall mood of the poem is one of pathos, created by the continuation of traditional wedding activities even when those participating cannot feel the joy that should accompany them.

ANSWERS TO CRITICAL THINKING AND READING

1. Suggested responses: (a) The last sentence is like a confession in that

THINKING ABOUT THE SELECTION

Interpreting

1. In the first 28 lines of "Visit," the poet notices a number of things about his home town. What is the pattern or theme that emerges from these images?
2. (a) How does the time frame shift in the section of the poem beginning with line 29? (b) Compare and contrast the images in this section with those in the first part of the poem.
3. The speaker does not reveal much of an emotional reaction to being in Zima Junction until the poem's final statement. (a) How does this strategy affect the reader's response to the last two lines? (b) Do these lines refer to the speaker's thoughts as a boy, his current thoughts, or both? Explain.
4. In "Weddings" why does the poet say wartime weddings are a "deceiving comfort"?
5. (a) Identify three sensuous details that bring this wedding to life. (b) Why is each effective?
6. A critic has said that Yevtushenko's poetry often deals with "discrepancies and contradictions." How is "Weddings" the expression of "contradictions"?
7. (a) How does the end of the poem indicate that the speaker is a child? (b) Why would the "contradictions" of this occasion be even more vivid to a child?

Applying

8. A generation of Russians grew up during World War II. What does "Weddings" suggest about the ways in which they were affected by this experience?

ANALYZING LITERATURE

Understanding Atmosphere

The **atmosphere** of a poem is its overall mood. In "Weddings" the atmosphere is memorable enough that the reader might well recall it long after details of the poem have faded. It is not the atmosphere of a typical wedding, with its more usual mixture of joy and sorrow. In this case, the war and its dangers cast a pall over the whole celebration. The poet captures this unusual mood with vivid images: "His glass is fizzing but he can't drink it." Here the "fizzing" symbolizes the rejoicing that a wedding usually inspires, but the groom is unable to partake of this joy.

1. (a) Find another vivid image in which the poet conveys the unusual, wartime atmosphere of this wedding. (b) Show how this image contributes to the poem's atmosphere.
2. Describe the overall mood of this poem.

CRITICAL THINKING AND READING

Appreciating a Poem's Ending

Like the last part of a sentence, the conclusion of a poem stays in a reader's mind. The ending therefore gives a poet the opportunity to sum up the poem's message in a final, resounding statement. Sometimes it contains an unexpected twist that makes the reader see everything that has come before it in a surprising new way.

Throughout "Weddings" the speaker portrays himself as the one person at the wedding who is acting in the customary manner. While everyone else is too distressed to be festive, he does the traditional wedding dance. In the last sentence, however, he admits that he too is upset but explains his dancing by saying simply that "you can't not dance."

1. (a) How is the last sentence like a confession? (b) How does it summarize the divided feelings that have run through the poem?
2. In the beginning of the poem, the poet mentions "The dishonesty of words about living" that characterizes wartime weddings. Is the speaker being dishonest by dancing even though he doesn't feel like it?
3. (a) What philosophy or outlook on life is encapsulated in the final statement, "you can't not dance"? (b) How does this statement make you see the previous events in a new way?

THINKING AND WRITING

Evoking Atmosphere

Write about a place or a time that seemed especially atmospheric to you, one that evoked a very particular mood. Start by choosing a subject and making a list of words and phrases to describe it. Draw upon your list as you write. Use sensuous language, as Yevtushenko did in these poems, to convey an overall mood. Remember also that your tone, or attitude toward the subject, will affect the reader's impression of the atmosphere. Even though you are not writing poetry, pay close attention to the rhythms of your sentences. Good prose can use rhythm effectively, just as poetry does. For example, a number of heavily accented syllables, one after another, will slow the pace of your description and possibly contribute to a more somber atmosphere. When you revise your description, read it aloud to several classmates and have them describe the atmosphere it evoked. Is it the one you had in mind? If not, revise your work so that it calls up the mood you want to convey.

it reveals the speaker's innermost thoughts. (b) It summarizes the divided feelings running through the poem by announcing directly that the boy does not feel like celebrating, a feeling many earlier actions described in the poem merely suggest.
2. Some students may believe that he is, but others may say that he seems to feel duty-bound to dance regardless of his personal feelings.

3. Suggested responses: (a) It is a philosophy sometimes called "stoicism," which demands that a person perform what are seen as necessary functions in life, even if he or she views them as difficult or even distasteful. (b) Previously, the reader might think that the speaker, unlike the wedding guests, is actually enjoying himself. The last line shows that he shares their sense of despair.

THINKING AND WRITING

Publishing Student Writing Choose the ten best written descriptions of atmosphere and post them on a bulletin board so that others may enjoy them.

The Middle East

PILGRIMAGE
Shraga Weil

Humanities Note
Fine art, *Pilgrimage*, 1974, by Shraga Weil. Born in Nitra, Czechoslovakia, in 1918, Weil studied sculpture and painting in Prague. He produced his first works of graphic art during World War II, part of which he spent in jail. After the war he sailed on an illegal immigrant ship to Israel. He arrived there in 1947 and became a member of Kibbutz Haogen, where he and his family still live. A kibbutz is an Israeli collective farm.

Weil has had numerous one-man exhibitions in Israel and the United States. One of his many commissioned murals can be seen in the Israeli Lounge of the Kennedy Center in Washington, D.C. He has also illustrated such great works of literature as *Joseph and His Brothers* by Thomas Mann and The Song of Songs from the Bible.

Pilgrimage is a serigraph measuring 17 by 24 inches. A serigraph is a color print made by the silkscreen process and printed personally by the artist. A gallery note on this work comments, "The figures appear and disappear, silhouetted against contrasting or harmonizing backgrounds. While an over-all pattern of varying textures keeps the surface active, it also suggests the constant restless movement of the pilgrims on an unspecific but inevitable journey."

You might want to use the following questions to discuss the art:

1. A *pilgrimage* is a journey made to a shrine or a holy place. How does this work suggest such a journey?

2. (a) Is it clear what kind of a pilgrimage this is? Why or why not? (b) What can you infer about the various silhouetted figures?

3. How do the different backgrounds and textures contribute to the meaning of the work?

4. Have you ever made a pilgrimage to a place that was particularly important to you? Explain.

1911–

In 1988 the Egyptian writer Najib Mahfouz (nä´hēb´ mä´ fōoz) won the Nobel Prize for Literature. The Arab world had long considered Mahfouz its greatest living novelist, but the Nobel Prize brought him international recognition. It also brought international attention to Arabic literature. In an interview, Egypt's Nobel laureate remarked: "Egypt and the Arab world also get the Nobel Prize with me. I believe that from now on the international doors have opened, and in the future, literate people will look for Arab literature, and Arab literature deserves that recognition."

Mahfouz was born in 1911 in an old quarter of Cairo, the setting for many of his works. He is famous for mastering the novel form, which is still relatively new in Egypt. In fact, he is credited with Egyptianizing the Western genre of the novel. He also modernized literary language, from classical Arabic to the Arabic of the streets. By shaping classical Arabic into a vehicle of popular speech, he gives voice to the disillusions and dreams of the Egyptian man in the street. Western literary critics have compared him to Balzac, Dickens, and Dostoevsky because of his vivid social frescoes of twentieth century Cairo. Ironically, he insists that he was not particularly attracted to Balzac, and he admits that he never finished a Dickens story.

In 1930 Mahfouz entered the University of Cairo, where he studied philosophy. Throughout his undergraduate career, he contributed essays on philosophical subjects to various magazines. Although his readings in literature were slim, classes at the University of Cairo were in English and French, and Mahfouz's access to those languages greatly increased the scope of his reading. Among his favorite authors were Dostoevsky, Tolstoy, Chekhov, Proust, Mann, Kafka, and Ibsen. However, his favorite authors' styles have not filtered into his own unique work.

Mahfouz began his career as a novelist in the repressive atmosphere of Egyptian political unrest. In June 1930 the despot Ismail Sidki became prime minister and suspended the 1923 constitution to prevent Egypt from adopting a Western-like democracy. Sidki silenced all opposition by brutally crushing any attempt to question his authority. The writers Taha Hussein and Abbas al-Akkad were influential on Mahfouz; Hussein was accused of heresy, and al-Akkad was imprisoned. The harsh treatment of Hussein and al-Akkad, as well as his other outspoken contemporaries, made Mahfouz realize the futility of open rebellion. As a result, Mahfouz used his narrative method to imply criticism of contemporary Egyptian society without jeopardizing his career.

The 1940's were prolific years for Mahfouz. During World War II, he wrote three historical novels set in ancient Egypt. Mixing history with symbolism, Mahfouz's tales of tyrannical rule and the expulsion of foreign invaders had strong contemporary implications in an Egypt under the despotic rule of Ismail Sidki. Using ancient history allowed Mahfouz to avoid being censored. His work of the late forties is striking in its humanitarianism and sensitivity to human suffering. His tragic vision of life transcends the Egyptian setting and assumes universal meaning.

The Egyptian Revolution of 1952 caused Mahfouz to withdraw from writing until 1959. Mahfouz's novels of the 1960's reflect the changing nature of Egyptian society after the revolution. His more recent work reflects much of the current malaise in Egypt. Now almost deaf and partially blind, Mahfouz claims to live only to write; he has said, "If the urge should ever leave me, I want that day to be my last."

GUIDE FOR INTERPRETING

The Happy Man

Commentary

Irony and Theme. Irony is a technique used to indicate an intention or attitude that is opposite to what is actually expressed. Verbal irony involves a character saying the opposite of what he or she means. Irony is often characterized by grim humor and sarcasm, particularly when a writer wishes to indirectly criticize. For example, an ironist would say that a plan is perfectly logical when it is actually irrational and unreasonable. Another form of irony is situational irony, where an event occurs that contradicts the expectations of the characters, readers, or audience. The man in "The Happy Man" finds himself in a state of bliss that contrasts sharply with his usual mood. At the same time, he is acutely aware of all the reasons why he should not feel such intense happiness: racism, suffering, tragedy, death.

In "The Happy Man," Mahfouz uses irony to arrive at **theme,** the universal truth or insight conveyed in a literary work. In "The Happy Man," the protagonist suddenly finds himself isolated from the problems of the world by his incomprehensible happiness. He seems to have achieved what humans strive for, and ironically, that achievement is torturing him. He has lost his will to work, his compassion for the world's problems, and his desire to be with people. He is left wondering, as most people do, if perfect happiness is possible. He also questions how, in spite of all the world suffering, it is possible to have any happiness at all.

Writing

What is happiness? Why do people consider happiness fleeting? Why do people question whether they are truly happy when their happiness is apparent to everyone else? Freewrite, exploring your answers to these questions.

Primary Source

In an article written for *The Egyptian Bulletin* in June 1982, M. M. Badawi described the importance of Mahfouz's work as social and political commentary: "The destinies of the individual characters are the microcosm, but the macrocosm is the destiny of modern Egypt. The tragedies, the poignant sufferings, the conflicts of the numerous men and women who people these novels reflect the larger social, intellectual, and political changes in one significant part of the modern Arab world. The struggle of the younger generation of men and women to attain their domestic freedom to shape their own lives mirrors or parallels the nation's struggle to achieve political independence and to free itself from the shackles of outworn and debilitating, almost medieval, conventions and world outlook in a gigantic endeavor to belong to the modern world."

Literary Focus Ask students to think about how irony has served as a vehicle for theme in other literary works. For example, most students are familiar with Oedipus of Sophocles' *Oedipus the King,* who in a fierce attempt to avoid killing his father and marrying his mother, ends up performing both acts. The irony of his situation points to the theme that human beings cannot run away from their destinies, but at the same time, they must take moral responsibility for their actions. Have students look for how Mahfouz conveys theme through irony in "The Happy Man."

Writing/Prior Knowledge Have students form groups and share their ideas on happiness.

ESL Teaching Strategy Point out the rhetorical questions in the story to ESL students and explain that they underscore the reasons for the character's confusion.

Teaching Tenth-Grade Students Ask tenth-grade students to write a one-page journal entry about a time when they were extremely happy, explaining the reasons for and conditions of their happiness.

Vocabulary
Preteach the following vocabulary words:
assailed (ə sāld´) *v.*: Attacked forcefully
exerts (eg zʉrts´) *v.*: Applies with great energy
verge (vʉrj) *n.*: Edge or brink
abstract (ab strakt´) *adj.*: Not easily understood; not concrete
mirth (mʉrth) *n.*: Joyfulness
equanimity (ek´ wə nim´ ə tē) *n.*: Calmness; composure
inertia (in ʉr´ shə) *n.*: Fixed condition

Support Material

Teaching Portfolio
Teacher Backup, p. 1629
Grammar in Action Worksheet, *Understanding Parallelism*, p. 1633
Usage and Mechanics Worksheet, p. 1635
Vocabulary Check, p. 1636

Analyzing Literature Worksheet, *Recognizing Theme*, p. 1637
Language Worksheet, *Using Concrete and Abstract Nouns*, p. 1638
Selection Test, pp. 1639–1640

The Happy Man

Najib Mahfouz

translated by Saad El-Gabalawy

When he woke up, he found himself happy. That was most strange compared with his habitual state of mind in the early morning. For he usually got up with a terrible headache from working late hours in his office at the newspaper, or with a hangover from too much eating and drinking at some wild party. The worries of the day before and the problems of the present day usually assailed him then, so that he dragged himself out of bed with great difficulty, trying to muster all his energy and face the troubles of life. But today he was unquestionably happy, overflowing with happiness. The feeling was so clear and intense that it imposed itself on his mind and senses. Yes, he was happy. If this was not happiness, what was it then? He felt all his organs were functioning in perfect harmony with each other and with the whole world around him. Inside him there was infinite energy and a tremendous capacity to achieve anything with great skill and confidence. And his heart was brimming with love for people, animals and things, with an overwhelming feeling of optimism, as if he had finally defeated fear, anxiety, sickness and death. Above all, there was the incomprehensible sensation which penetrated his body and soul, playing a delightful tune of joy, contentment and peace.

Intoxicated with this ecstasy, he savored it slowly and with a deep sense of wonder about its mysterious source. There was nothing in his past to explain it or in his future to justify it. How did it come? How long would it last? Oh no, this must be just a fleeting mood which could never be permanent. For if it lasted forever, man would become an angel and reach the world beyond. Let him enjoy it now, live with it, treasure it, before it became a vague memory in the distant horizon.

He ate his breakfast with great appetite, looking from time to time with a bright, smiling face at Am Beshir who was serving the food. The old man became increasingly surprised and anxious, because his master did not normally look in his direction except to give orders or ask questions. Then he said to him:

"Tell me, Am Beshir, am I a happy man?"

The man was embarrassed, since the master was for the first time addressing him as a companion or friend. After moments of uneasy silence, he replied:

"My master is happy with God's gifts and blessings."

"Do you mean that I must be happy with my excellent position, beautiful apartment and good health? Is this what you mean? But do you really think I am a happy man?"

"My master exerts himself beyond human endurance and often gets angry in heated discussions with other people."

He interrupted him with a loud laugh and asked:

"What about you? Don't you have any worries?"

"Of course. Nobody lives without worries."

"Do you mean that perfect happiness is impossible?"

"Well, this is the nature of life."

How could Beshir, or anybody else, imagine his wonderful state of happiness? It was something strange and unique, as if it were his own private secret of all people on earth.

In the conference room at the newspaper, he saw his greatest rival in this world turning the pages of a magazine. The man heard his footsteps but did not raise his eyes. Not doubt he somehow glanced quickly but tried to ignore him for his own peace of mind. In regular meetings they often disagreed violently and exchanged the harshest words until they were on the <u>verge</u> of fighting. And only last week he was shamefully defeated by his rival in the union elections, which was a terrible blow to his pride that filled him with bitterness and darkened his vision. But here he was now approaching his enemy with a pure and carefree heart, intoxicated with that wonderful happiness, overflowing with tolerance and forgiveness, as if he were another man who conveyed the promise of a new friendship. And without feeling awkward, he smilingly greeted him. Taken by surprise, the man raised his eyes in wonder and for moments remained silent until he could collect himself and answer the greeting briefly, as if he did not believe his eyes and ears. He sat close to him, saying:

"The weather is gorgeous today."

"Oh yes."

"It's the kind of weather that fills the heart with deep happiness."

The man looked at him cautiously and intently, then mumbled:

"I am glad that you're happy."

He said laughingly:

"It's happiness beyond comprehension."

The other replied hesitantly:

"I hope that I will not spoil your mood at the meeting of the editorial board today."

"Oh, never. My opinion is well known to everybody. But I don't mind if the members accept your view. This will not spoil my happiness at all."

"You have changed considerably overnight."

"In fact, I am happy beyond comprehension."

"I bet your son has changed his mind about staying in Canada for good."

He chuckled and said:

"No, my friend, he has not changed his decision."

"But that was your greatest source of grief."

"Oh, yes. I have pleaded with him again and again to come back in order to relieve my loneliness and serve his country. But he told me that he intended to start an engineering business with a Canadian partner, and even invited me to join him there. Let him live where he likes. But here I am—as you see—happy, unbelievably happy."

"This is unique courage on your part."

"I don't know what it is, but I am happy in the full sense of the word."

Yes, this was happiness, rich and touchable, firm like absolute power, free as the air, violent as a flame, fascinating as the scent of flowers. Yet this unnatural feeling could not last forever.

The other man, attracted by his friendliness, said amicably:[1]

"In fact, I always regarded you as a man with a violent nature that caused you a good deal of suffering."

"Really?"

"You don't know the meaning of compromise. You live intensely with your nerves, with your whole being, fighting fiercely as if any problem were a matter of life or death."

"Yes, that's true."

---

1. **amicably** (am′ i kə blē) *adv.*: In a friendly manner.

---

3 Discussion Ask students if they agree that perfect happiness is eternally elusive according to the nature of life.

4 Literary Focus Ask students to examine the pattern of extremes in this passage. What do the extremes indicate about the man's character? His temperament seems never to fall on middle ground. Students might characterize him as unbalanced.

5 Discussion Point out to students that like the "happy man," his colleague also insists on concrete reasons for such intense happiness. Although this is a normal response from the colleague, who is accustomed to seeing the "happy man" miserable, ask students why people insist on justifying, or rationalizing, emotions.

6 Literary Focus Call students' attention to the phrase "unnatural feeling." Do students find this phrase in connection with happiness paradoxical? What is unnatural about the man's happiness? Unnatural can imply artificial. Do students see the "happy man's" happiness as artificial?

7 Discussion Focus students' attention on the colleague's evaluation of the "happy man." Ask students if they think this is an accurate judgment. Then ask them to discuss the importance of compromise. Why is it important for individuals to compromise? When is compromise particularly important within ourselves?

But Mahfouz's success as an Arab writer has not been without controversy. As Christopher Dickey points out in his review of *Palace Walk*,

Mahfouz's newfound recognition in the West comes after a life filled with fame and controversy in the Arab world . . . the frank realism of his characters, especially the women, gained him the hatred of religious zealots . . . [and he] has been singled out for death by fanatical preachers . . . But he does not worry much about the fundamentalists, and he refuses bodyguards. "At my age, a threat of death is not really that frightening," he says. "I might receive a threat on Sunday and die on Monday of natural causes."

He accepted this criticism tolerantly, as though it were a little wave in his infinite ocean of happiness, and with a bright smile on his face, asked:

"Then, you believe that there should be some balance in my approach to events?"

"Certainly. Take, for example, our discussion yesterday about racism. We share the same opinion, and the issue is worthy of enthusiasm to the point of anger. But what kind of anger? It should, in a sense, be intellectual, <u>abstract</u> anger. Not the anger that would fray the nerves, cause indigestion and raise blood pressure. Right?"

"That is very clear to me now."

Guard house, Giza pyramids

His heart would not release a single drop of its joys. Racism, Vietnam, Angola, Palestine[2] . . . no problem could invade the fortress of happiness which surrounded his heart. Whenever he remembered a problem, his heart chuckled joyfully. It was, so to speak, a gigantic happiness, indifferent to any misery, always smiling in the face of suffering. He wished to laugh, to dance, to sing, spreading his infinite <u>mirth</u> over problems of the world.

Suddenly he felt that the office was too small for him; he had no desire to work. The mere thought of his daily work was treated with absolute indifference and contempt, and he failed completely to bring his mind down from the heaven of bliss. How could he write about the trolley bus which sank in the Nile, when he was intoxicated with all this terrifying happiness? Yes, it was terrifying, coming as it did from nowhere, violent to the point of exhaustion and paralyzing his will. Besides, it was now midday and the feeling still possessed him without any sign of diminishing at all. He left his papers blank on the desk and started pacing his room, laughing and snapping his fingers.

He had a moment of anxiety which did not sink deeply inside him, but floated as an abstract thought on the surface of the mind. It occurred to him to recall deliberately the tragedies of his life in order to test their effect on his present mood, hoping they might help him regain some equanimity or at least reassure him that this happiness might eventually fade away. He recreated in his memory, for example, the death of his wife with all its tragic circumstances. But the event seemed to him as a series of movements without meaning or effect, as if it happened to another woman, the wife of another man, in a remote age of ancient history. The recollection even had a pleasant effect on him so that he smiled and could not help laughing loudly.

The same thing happened when he remembered the first letter he received from his son, declaring his intention to emigrate to Canada. And when he started to review mentally the bloody tragedies of the world, his chuckles became so loud they might have been heard in the other offices or

2. **Vietnam . . . Palestine:** Sites of conflict in the world, at the time the story is set.

even in the street. Nothing could touch his happiness. The memories of grief floated softly like gentle waves touching the sands of the shore. Then he left his office and the whole building, without a note of apology for not attending the editorial meeting. After lunch, he went to bed for the usual nap, but felt that sleep was impossible. There was no sign of its approach in this bright, boisterous[3] world of joy that kept him wide awake. He must have some rest and tranquillity, some inertia, some numbness in his senses. But how? Finally he left his bed and started humming a tune while pacing his apartment back and forth. And he said to himself that if this state of mind and feeling lasted longer, he would become totally incapable of sleep or work or grief. It was time to go to the club, but he did not feel like meeting any of his friends. There was no sense in these endless talks about public affairs or private worries. And what would his friends think of him if they found him laughing at the most serious matters? No, he did not need anybody; he had no desire for conversation. It was essential for him to sit by himself or walk for miles to release some of this tremendous energy. He must think deeply of what happened to him. How did this fabulous happiness assault him? For how long could he carry this intolerable burden? Will this feeling deprive him forever of his work and friends, of his sleep and peace of mind? Should he yield to it and drift with the current? Or should he seek an outlet, through mental effort, strenuous work or professional advice?

*   *   *   *   *

He felt a little awkward when he was called to the examination room in the office of his friend, the eminent doctor. The physician looked at him smilingly and said:

"You don't seem to have any sickness."
"I didn't come to you because I am ill but because I am happy. Yes, I am extremely happy," he replied hesitantly.

There was a moment of silence charged with anxiety and surprise.

---

3. boisterous (bois′ tər əs) *adj.*: Noisy and unruly.

"It's a very strange sensation which I cannot define in words. But it's quite serious."

The doctor laughed and said jokingly:

"I wish your disease would be infectious."
"Oh, don't take the matter lightly. As I told you, it's very serious."

Then he started to tell the story of his happiness from the moment he got up in the morning until this visit for advice.

"Did you take any liquor or drugs or tranquilizers?"
"No, nothing of this sort at all."
"Maybe you have achieved something valuable in terms of work, love or money?"
"No, nothing of this sort either. Actually, in my life there is much more cause for sadness than happiness."

The doctor examined him very carefully, then said, shrugging his shoulders in wonder:

"You are in perfect health. I can give you some sleeping pills, but you must consult a neurologist."[4]

The same thorough examination was carried out by the other specialist, who then said to him:

"Your nerves are in perfect shape."
"Don't you have any convincing explanation for my condition?"
"I'm sorry, there is absolutely nothing wrong with your nerves."

Whenever he heard the same reply from other specialists, he laughed, then apologized laughingly for his laughter, as if that was his way to express anxiety and despair. He felt very lonely in the company of this overwhelming happiness, without a friend or guide to help him. Suddenly he remembered there was the office of a psychiatrist across the street. But he did not trust these psychiatrists, in spite of his knowledge of the nature

---

4. neurologist (noo rä l′ ə jist) *n.*: A doctor who treats diseases of the nervous system.

12 Discussion Ask students to think about the happy man's condition. Do they ever find themselves wanting to be alone when they are happy? What kind of feelings normally cause us to want solitude, time away from our friends and our responsibilities?

Master Teacher Note During this time in their lives, students are one another's best confidantes. Ask students what they would do if a friend came to them complaining of overwhelming, inexplicable happiness. Use their answers as a springboard for a more imaginative role in which students put themselves in the doctor's shoes. Ask students: What is your diagnosis of the happy man? What do you prescribe? Have students answer in a short paper explaining the happy man's problem, its cause, and what he can do to solve it.

13 Discussion Ask students how they would answer these rhetorical questions.

14 Clarification Call students' attention to the implied optimism in the happy man's reply. There is probably more cause for sadness than happiness in most people's lives, but despite those causes, people do experience happiness. Ask students what this says about "the nature of life," as it was referred to earlier in the story.

15 Literary Focus Call students' attention to the paradox in this passage. Expressing anxiety and despair through laughter is really what the happy man has been doing throughout the story. In addition, he has become increasingly lonely and alienated, which also contradicts his feelings of overwhelming happiness. Ask students to think about how these paradoxes contribute to the complexity of the story.

Student Activity 2. Write a character analysis of the man in the story using sentences that have parallel structure.

of psychoanalysis.[5] Besides, he knew quite well that their treatment extended over long periods of time, so that they became almost constant companions of their patients. And he laughed when he remembered their method of treatment by free association[6] to reveal the neuroses[7] buried in the subconscious mind. While his feet were leading him to the doctor's office, he was still laughing, especially as he visualized the man listening to his strange complaint of happiness, when he usually listened to people complaining of hysteria, depression, anxiety or schizophrenia.[8]

"To tell you the truth, doctor, I came to you because I am happy beyond comprehension."

And he looked at his face to see the effect of his words, but the doctor kept his calm. Hardly had he started to tell his story when the man stopped him with a gesture of his hand, and asked quietly:

"It is an overwhelming, strange, exhausting sort of happiness?"

---

5. psychoanalysis (sī kō ə nal′ ə sis) *n*.: A method developed by Freud and others, of investigating and treating disorders of the mind.

6. free association: The technique of having a patient talk spontaneously, expressing whatever ideas or memories come to mind.

7. neuroses (noo rō′ sēz) *n*.: Mental disorders characterized by anxiety and depression.

8. hysteria . . . schizophrenia: Various types of mental disorders.

He looked at him in amazement and was about to say something when the doctor resumed:

"It's happiness that would make you incapable of work, tired of friends and unable to sleep. And whenever you face any suffering you burst out laughing."

"You must be a mind reader."

"Oh no, nothing of this sort, but I see similar cases at least once a week."

"Is it an epidemic?"

"I didn't say that. I don't even claim that I have been able, so far, to trace a single case to its original cause."

"But it's a disease?"

"All the cases are still under treatment."

"But you are undoubtedly convinced they are all abnormal?"

"Well, in our field this is a necessary hypothesis."

"Did you observe a sign of insanity or emotional disturbance in any of them?" he asked anxiously. And he pointed to his head in fear, but the doctor said with certainty:

"No. I assure you they are all sane in the proper sense of the word. But you will need two sessions every week. You shouldn't worry or grieve . . ."

Worry, grief? He smiled and the smile widened on his face until he burst out laughing. Then his resistance collapsed completely and he could not control his tears.

Reader's Response *What is your definition of happiness? Is happiness possible? Explain.*

THINKING ABOUT THE SELECTION

Interpreting

1. As the story begins, the main character feels as though he has "finally defeated fear, anxiety, sickness and death." What does his overwhelming optimism indicate about his feeling of happiness?
2. Why do you think the happy man insists on justifying his feeling?
3. When the happy man asks Am Beshir if he thinks perfect happiness is impossible, Am Beshir replies, "Well, this is the nature of life." Explain Am Beshir's reply.
4. The happy man's political opponent accuses him of being unable to compromise. Do you agree with his judgment? Why or why not?
5. Study the paragraph that begins, "His heart would not release a single drop of its joys." What does this paragraph suggest about the happy man's character?
6. (a) Find quotations from the story that prove that the happy man has not defeated "fear, anxiety, sickness, and death." (b) Discuss the ways in which the happy man is alienated.
7. Why do you think the happy man burst into uncontrollable tears at the end of the story?

Applying

8. Imagine that you woke up one morning with inexplicable happiness. What world issues would haunt you the way the happy man is haunted?
9. Nathaniel Hawthorne said, "Happiness . . . comes incidentally—make it the object of pursuit and it leads us on a wild goose chase and is never obtained." Edith Wharton said, "If only we'd stop trying to be happy we'd have a pretty good time." (a) Compare these two quotations. (b) Tell how they relate to "The Happy Man." (c) Explain how they do or do not correspond to your own thoughts on happiness.

ANALYZING LITERATURE

Understanding Irony and Theme

In "The Happy Man," Mahfouz depicts a man who is, ironically, plagued with happiness. Mahfouz uses **irony,** the contrast between what is actually true and what is literally expressed, to explore the possibility of happiness in a troubled world. Through the irony of the happy man's situation, Mahfouz develops his **theme,** the universal truth or message he wants to convey.

1. In your words, what is the theme of "The Happy Man"?
2. How is theme achieved ironically?
3. Why does the man regard happiness an "intolerable burden"? Is happiness really the burden? Explain.

CRITICAL THINKING AND READING

Anticipating a Surprise Ending

Often, a story rich in irony will have a surprise ending, as in "The Happy Man." Throughout the story, the happy man struggles to come to terms with his intense joy, much as people struggle to accept grief and sadness. The happiness simultaneously transforms and imprisons him until he cannot function. He now laughs out loud at topics that used to enrage or sadden him. And he feels completely alone; he expects no one to understand his state of mind. Therefore, we are surprised at the end of the story when the psychiatrist says that he has seen similar cases. We are also surprised when the happy man bursts into tears at the mention of worry and grief.

1. (a) What was your immediate reaction to the surprise ending? (b) How did your reaction help you understand the story more fully?
2. Look through the story for clues to the surprise ending. Discuss how the clues make the surprise ending believable.

THINKING AND WRITING

Writing About Happiness

The happy man tells the physician, "Actually, in my life there is much more cause for sadness than happiness." Yet he insists that he *is* happy. In their introduction to an anthology of Mahfouz's short stories, Akef Abadir and Roger Allen said, "The present state of the world, wars between men and nations, none of these things can explain his happiness. And yet, in spite of all the frustrations and anxieties which our civilization has created and fostered, inexplicably and perhaps unjustifiably there still remains happiness. Technology cannot provide the answers for the happenings in this mad world." Discuss happiness in terms of "The Happy Man." In an essay, define the happy man's problem, discuss its causes, and draw a conclusion. Revise your essay, making sure that you have shown causes and effects. Finally, proofread your essay and prepare a final draft. Then ask a friend to read and react to your paper.

(continued from bottom of page)

ANSWERS TO ANALYZING LITERATURE

1. Answers will differ but should cover the paradoxes and unexpected insights provided by the story.
2. Ironically, the man insists that he is happy, while he is tormented by all the reasons for unhappiness. Possibly, he is a happy person, but he feels as if he should be unhappy.
3. Happiness is an intolerable burden to him because it interferes with his ability to lead his normal life. The burden is his deep sadness for the tragedies of the world.

ANSWERS TO CRITICAL THINKING AND READING

1. (a) Reactions will differ. Students might respond that they were not surprised by the man's emotional outburst, that it seemed to have been building throughout the story. (b) In spite of its emphasis on the man's intoxicating happiness, the story also addresses deep sadness.
2. Answers will differ; however, students should support their arguments by referring to specific passages in the story.

THINKING AND WRITING

Publishing Student Writing You might want to display students' papers in a display case or on the bulletin board. Before you do, ask them to critique one another's work and make necessary revisions.

---

reply from other specialists, he laughed, then apologized laughingly for his laughter, as if that was his way to express anxiety and despair." (b) The man feels alone in his happiness—he no longer wishes to spend time with friends, and he is sure no one else can feel or understand his feelings. "He felt very lonely in the company of this overwhelming happiness, without a friend or guide to

help him." "No, he did not need anybody; he had no desire for conversation."

7. His emotional outburst at the end of the story is a manifestation of the true nature of his problem: he is actually very unhappy, and the happiness he is capable of despite his unhappiness is a burden to his intellect.
8. Answers will differ. Students might respond with such problems as home-

lessness, world hunger, or epidemic diseases.

9. (a) Both quotations suggest that happiness is elusive and is most likely experienced by those who don't consciously pursue it. (b) The man in "The Happy Man" doesn't necessarily pursue happiness; he finds himself happy by chance. (c) Answers will differ.

YEHUDA AMICHAI

1924–

When he was a teenager, Yehuda Amichai (yə hōō′ də ä′ mi khī) gave up the formal practice of Judaism; however, he has never given up his love of Jewish history and tradition. Referring to the Hebrew language, he once said, "Every word we use carries in and of itself connotations from the Bible. . . . Every word reverberates through the halls of Jewish history. Coming from a religious background the spoken language I use still retains for me the original traditional flavor." Amichai's genius as a Hebrew poet arises from his ability to contrast these traditional connotations with technical terms, popular song lyrics, and the language of the street.

Amichai was born in Germany, the son of Orthodox Jews. Luckily for him, his family emigrated to Palestine—the region that became Israel in 1948—before the outbreak of World War II. Eventually they settled in Jerusalem, and Amichai continued his religious education, becoming thoroughly familiar with the Bible, Jewish rituals, and the ancient tradition of Jewish law. Not too long after coming to Palestine, however, he rebelled against the strict religious practices of his father. This rebellion distanced him from the religion of his father without entirely removing him from its influence. The result was a sense of loss that paradoxically enriched his poetry. Several of his poems also testify to the fact that his rebellion did not diminish his great love for his father.

In addition to being a writer, Amichai is a man of action. He served with England's Jewish Brigade in Egypt during World War II, and after the war he was a soldier with the Israeli defense forces during Israel's War of Independence. At the same time, he began reading English poets like W. H. Auden and T. S. Eliot. Both these poets, but especially Auden, inspired him to introduce colloquial language into his work—what one critic calls "the prosaic perspective of the streets." Amichai has disclaimed a role as the founder of a new school of Hebrew poetry. Many critics, however, have called him a pioneer in the use of a down-to-earth, spoken language.

His first book of poetry, *Now and in Other Days* (1955), received a distinguished prize two years after its publication. *Two Hopes Apart* (1958), his next book, seemed to speak for his whole generation in expressing a sense of disillusionment. It also introduced what one critic calls the characteristic themes of his work: "love, war, the passage of time, his relationship with his father, his father's death, and his own undefined guilt."

A versatile writer, Amichai has produced short stories, radio plays, and novels in addition to his poetry. *This Terrible Wind* (1961), his first collection of stories, is based in part on his wartime experiences. Shortly after this publication, he brought out his first novel, *Not of This Time, Not of This Place* (1963). It was inspired by his return to Wurzburg, the place of his birth, and deals with the destruction of European Jewry before and during World War II.

In the two poems that follow, Amichai depicts a contemporary sense of weariness and alienation while not losing sight of traditional Jewish themes.

Objectives

Thematic

To understand the biblical echoes in contemporary Hebrew poetry

Skills

1 To appreciate sustained images and metaphors
2 To appreciate how language changes

GUIDE FOR INTERPRETING

The Diameter of the Bomb; From the Book of Esther I Filtered the Sediment

Commentary

Images and Figures of Speech. Similes, metaphors, and images, especially striking ones, are like fireworks. They seem to be meant for show. Poets launch them like rockets that arch high over the poem and then fall, trailing multicolored plumes. We rarely think of imagery and figurative language in relation to such a humdrum matter as the structure of a poem. Yet these flashier elements of poetry, especially when they are sustained over a number of lines, can unify a lyric.

A figure of speech that binds together a poem can be found in Robert Frost's "The Silken Tent," which begins as follows:

> She is as in a field a silken tent
> At midday when a sunny summer breeze
> Has dried the dew and all its ropes relent,
> So that in guys it gently sways at ease

Not only is this sonnet made up of a single sentence, but it is bound together by the simile introduced in the first line. In the following lines, the "central cedar pole" of the tent is used to symbolize the woman's "sureness of . . . soul," and the tent-ropes are compared to the "countless silken ties of love and thought" that link her to "everything on earth." By exploring a single simile in this poem, Frost conveys a satisfying feeling of completion. He also shows how an unexpected comparison, if pursued, can reveal deeper and deeper levels of meaning.

Yehuda Amichai uses sustained images and figures of speech in "The Diameter of the Bomb" and "From the Book of Esther I Filtered the Sediment." The first poem begins deceptively as a matter-of-fact account of a terrorist bombing; however, the poet relentlessly pursues the image of a bomb's "range" to an unsettling conclusion. In the second poem, he uses a surprising metaphor in the opening lines and then repeats it, with variations, to drive home his point.

Writing

"The Diameter of the Bomb" reveals how much a single action can imply. Tell about a time when you were surprised by the unforeseen results of an action.

Literary Focus Challenge students to come up with a striking simile to describe a crowd at a sports event. Write their similes on the chalkboard; then choose several of them to pursue further. Have students continue to elaborate these similes, searching for additional likenesses between the crowd and whatever it has been compared to. Explain that poets sometimes "try out" images in this way to see whether they will disclose deeper levels of meaning.

Writing/Prior Knowledge Have students create a diagram that will help them do this writing assignment. In the center of a circle they can briefly describe an event. Ask them to draw a series of concentric circles like ripples expanding from a central point. Have them label each "ripple" with an event that resulted from the central event they described.

ESL Teaching Strategy Have each ESL student find a sustained image or metaphor in a poem from their culture. ESL students can then translate these poems for the class and explain the sustained figure of speech.

Teaching Tenth-Grade Students Read "The Silken Tent" aloud to tenth-grade students and write it on the chalkboard (it's only fourteen lines long). Go over the poem in detail with them, pointing out the sustained comparison between the woman and the tent.

Master Teacher Note If there is a Hebrew speaker in your school or community, invite him or her to read the Hebrew versions of these poems to the class. This person can then answer students' questions about the ways in which the original poems differ from and resemble the translations.

You might be able to find such a resource person by contacting a local synagogue or a chapter of the B'nai B'rith.

Support Material

Teaching Portfolio
Teacher Backup, p. 1641
Usage and Mechanics Worksheet, p. 1645
Analyzing Literature Worksheet, *Appreciating Sustained Images and Metaphors*, p. 1646
Critical Thinking and Reading Worksheet, *Understanding Tone*, p. 1647
Language Worksheet, *Appreciating How Language Changes*, p. 1648
Selection Test, pp. 1649–1650

The Diameter of the Bomb

Yehuda Amichai

translated by Chana Bloch and Stephen Mitchell

The diameter of the bomb was thirty centimeters
and the diameter of its effective range about seven
  meters,
with four dead and eleven wounded.
And around these, in a larger circle
5 of pain and time, two hospitals are scattered
and one graveyard. But the young woman
who was buried in the city she came from,
at a distance of more than a hundred kilometers,
enlarges the circle considerably,
10 and the solitary man mourning her death
at the distant shores of a country far across the sea
includes the entire world in the circle.
And I won't even mention the crying of orphans
that reaches up to the throne of God and
15 beyond, making
a circle with no end and no God.

THRUST, 1959
Adolph Gottlieb
The Metropolitan
Museum of Art, New York

From the Book of Esther I Filtered the Sediment

Yehuda Amichai

translated by Chana Bloch and Stephen Mitchell

From the Book of Esther I filtered the sediment
of vulgar[1] joy, and from the Book of Jeremiah
the howl of pain in the guts. And from
the Song of Songs the endless
search for love, and from Genesis the dreams
and Cain, and from Ecclesiastes
the despair, and from the Book of Job: Job.

_____

1. vulgar (vul′ gər) *adj.*: Coarse.

And with what was left, I pasted myself a new Bible.
Now I live censored and pasted and limited and in
   peace.

10 A woman asked me last night on the dark street
how another woman was
who'd already died. Before her time—and not
in anyone else's time either.
Out of a great weariness I answered,
15 "She's fine, she's fine."

Reader's Response *What tone of voice should these poems be read in? Why?*

THINKING ABOUT THE SELECTIONS

Interpreting

1. In "The Diameter of the Bomb," what do we learn about the event that inspired the poem?
2. A **paradox** is an apparent contradiction. What is paradoxical about the image of "a circle with no end"?
3. (a) How is this poem a search for meaning and justice in a world without clear answers? (b) What does the poet suggest about meaning and justice by leaving God out of the final circle?
4. (a) How do the numbers cited by the poet contribute to the poem's tone? (b) In what way does this tone make the last line even more disturbing?

5. In "From the Book of Esther I Filtered the Sediment," the speaker begins by naming books of the Old Testament. What is the nature of the "new Bible" that the poet creates for himself?
6. (a) What is the relationship between this "new Bible" and the poet's great "weariness"? (b) How does he betray this "weariness" in the poem's last line?
7. An indictment is an accusation or charge leveled against someone. To what extent is this poem a self-indictment? Explain.

Applying

8. From what books have you filtered the meaning of life? Explain what you have taken from each.

ANSWERS TO ANALYZING LITERATURE

1. (a) The poem moves from the diameter of the bomb and its range to circles that include, successively, the hospitals where casualties were treated and the graveyard where the dead were buried, the distant city where one young woman was buried, the foreign country of a mourner, the entire world, the throne of God, and beyond. (b) They expand the meaning from a purely physical description to an emotional one.

2. (a) Like such ripples, the meaning of the event expands and expands. (b) Answers will differ. Students may respond that the movement beyond the throne of God is unexpected, because one naturally expects to find meaning and justice there.

3. Answers will differ. Students may suggest that a single tragic occurrence can provoke questions about the existence of meaning and justice in the world.

4. (a) The sediments are all strong emotions. (b) The term *sediment* usually refers to waste matter that settles to the bottom of a liquid. In this poem the poet ironically filters out not "waste matter" but the very emotions that vitalize the Bible.

5. (a) It is "censored and . . . in peace" because it is devoid of strong emotion. (b) He suggests it may not be desirable because the words "censored" and "limited" have negative connotations. Also, his self-portrait in the second stanza is not flattering.

6. Answers will differ. Many students will respond that the repetition of the metaphor unifies the stanza by creating a recognizable pattern. It reveals his state of mind because the pattern suggests that he cannot cope with strong emotions.

ANSWERS TO UNDERSTANDING LANGUAGE

Answers will differ. Students may respond that it presents opportunities because it creates an interesting tension between old and new. This situation might present a problem because even if writers want to, they cannot escape the influence of an ancient tradition.

ANALYZING LITERATURE

Appreciating Images and Metaphors

A **sustained image or figure of speech** is one that is extended over a number of lines or throughout a whole poem. In "From the Book of Esther . . ." Amichai repeatedly uses the metaphor of filtering sediment from books of the Bible. Usually "sediment" refers to waste matter that settles at the bottom of a liquid, but Amichai gives the word a surprising twist in this poem. In "The Diameter of the Bomb," Amichai repeatedly uses the image of a circle that describes the range of a terrorist's bomb. As the poem continues, however, he applies this image in a more daring way to explore the implications of a deed.

1. (a) Describe each of the enlargements of the bomb's "circle" in "The Diameter of the Bomb." (b) How do the words "circle / of pain and time" expand the meaning of a bomb's "effective range"?

2. (a) How does Amichai's repetition of this image follow the pattern that ripples make when a stone is thrown into the water? (b) How does the sustained imagery lead to an unexpected conclusion?

3. What does this conclusion suggest about the implications of a single tragic occurrence?

4. (a) In "From the Book of Esther . . ." what is similar about the sediments removed from the various books? (b) How is Amichai's use of the word *sediment* ironically different from the usual use of this word?

5. (a) Why does the poet's filtering lead to a Bible that is "censored and . . . in peace"? (b) How does Amichai suggest that such a result may not be desirable?

6. How does the repetition of the metaphor unify the first stanza and reveal the poet's state of mind?

UNDERSTANDING LANGUAGE

Appreciating How Language Changes

Hebrew is the language of the Bible, and it has been a literary language ever since biblical times. With the founding of Israel, however, Hebrew was revived as a spoken tongue. The result is that colloquial rhythms and words for modern inventions like the telephone have been introduced into a language haunted by biblical cadences and phrases.

Explain how this unusual situation might present opportunities *and* problems to a modern Hebrew poet.

PRIMARY SOURCE

The Israeli poet and scholar T. Carmi explains how Amichai creates a "tension between" biblical phrases and "everyday speech":

"Whether the poet wills it or not, there is often an element of counterpoint in Hebrew poetry. However colloquial the rhythms and even the diction, it is heard by the alert reader against the background of biblical poetry and of an uninterrupted poetic tradition. And some of the finest effects of modern Hebrew poetry still result from the tension between everyday speech and the undertones and overtones of a shared heritage.

"Here, for example is the opening stanza of a poem by Yehuda Amichai, entitled 'A Sort of Apocalypse.'

"'The man under his fig tree telephoned the man under his vine: / "Tonight they will surely come. / Armor the leaves, / Lock up the tree, / Call home the dead and be prepared."'

"The introduction of the anachronistic telephone into the body of a famous biblical idiom for peace and peace of mind—'They shall sit every man under his vine and under his fig tree and none shall make them afraid'—is enough to jolt any Hebrew reader. But something is also happening on the physical, visual level. The peace-loving vine and fig tree shed their symbolic roles and are transformed into routine accessories of field camouflage."

Africa

CONTEMPORARY AFRICAN CARVINGS
Joseph Agbana (Irisha Workshop)

Humanities Note
Fine art, *Contemporary African Carvings* by Joseph Agbana (Irisha Workshop). Christian art is currently thriving in Africa. Folk artists are working with a variety of materials to produce religiously inspired works like these carvings. The artists adapt biblical stories to African settings. As with medieval European artists, they often do not sign their works. To many of these artists, the act of creating art is a religious experience and does not require the self-advertisement of a signature.

These carvings seem to depict the visit of the Magi to Jesus, Mary, and Joseph.

You might want to use the following questions to discuss the art:

1. Can you name any of the biblical characters portrayed in this group of carvings?
2. How has the artist adapted a biblical story to an African setting?

LÉOPOLD SÉDAR SENGHOR

1906–

We don't often think of great poets as being world leaders, but Léopold Sédar Senghor (lā ô pôld′ sä där′ sän gôr′) is both. Not only is he considered one of the greatest of African poets writing in French, but he also served as president of the West African nation of Senegal, from its independence in 1960 until his retirement in 1981.

Senghor was born in the small village of Joal on the coast of Senegal—a predominantly Muslim country—where he attended schools run by Catholic missionaries. In 1928 he left his homeland for France after receiving a government scholarship. He graduated four years later from the Sorbonne—France's equivalent of Harvard or Yale—with a degree in literature.

During these student years in Paris, Senghor and other young black writers launched the influential literary movement known as negritude. The movement aimed to promote traditional African cultural values in opposition to the French colonial policy of assimilating blacks into French culture. Though one of the foremost advocates for negritude, Senghor ironically embraced many elements of French culture. He chose, for example, to write exclusively in French, a "universal" language which he praised as "analytical, made for exploding false myths, hard, precise, brilliant as a diamond." Senghor strongly believed that a black literature was possible in French and that he could reach a much wider audience by writing in French than if he were to write in an African language. He was influenced in this belief by the example of African American writers of the Harlem Renaissance, particularly Langston Hughes, who successfully and innovatively wedded African consciousness and rhythms with traditional English literary forms.

Senghor remained in France after graduating and became a French citizen. The first African to receive certification to teach in France's lycées (secondary schools) and universities, he taught until World War II, when he joined the French army. In 1940 he was captured by the Germans and held as a prisoner of war for two years. During this decade of his life, Senghor wrote the poems that would go into his first two books, *Chant d'ombre* (*Songs of Shadow,* 1945) and *Hosties noires* (*Black Hosts,* 1948). In them, the poet speaks as an exile longing for his homeland, aware of the tension between his African heritage and European culture. In 1948, Senghor also published a ground-breaking anthology of Caribbean and African poetry that firmly established the work of black poets within the French tradition. Many other books followed, including *Chants pour Naëtt* (1949), *Éthiopiques* (1956), and *Nocturnes* (1961). In 1983 Senghor was elected to the Academie Francaise, the first black member since this prestigious literary institution's founding in 1635.

As you will see in "Prayer to Masks" and "Night of Sine" Senghor's poetic style is lushly imagistic, chant-like, serene, life-affirming, and always appreciative of the beauty of African life.

GUIDE FOR INTERPRETING

Prayer to Masks; Night of Sine

Negritude. Negritude, which means literally "blackness," began as a cultural movement among French-speaking black students in Paris in 1932. The term was coined by Aimé Césaire (ā mā´ sā zer´), a young poet and playwright from Martinique in the West Indies, and popularized by Léopold Sédar Senghor. Though different writers have disagreed somewhat about the movement's goals, Senghor's definition is the most inclusive:

> Quite simply, *negritude is the sum of the values of the civilization of the African world.* It is not radicalism, it is culture.

Elsewhere, Senghor defined the movement and its connection to literature in this way:

> *Negritude is the awareness, defense and development of African cultural values.* . . . It is the awareness by a particular social group of people of its own situation in the world, and the expression of it by means of the concrete image.

The movement was originally intended as a response to French government policy toward native cultures. In their colonies, the French tried to assimilate, or absorb, native cultures into French culture, thereby ensuring that French values would dominate. Negritude was a bold assertion that African culture was as valuable in its own unique ways as French culture. Although the movement raised awareness and developed African cultural values among French-speaking Africans, it had even broader social consequences. Negritude helped revitalize pride in African cultural identity among blacks worldwide, especially in the United States and the Caribbean.

In Senghor's poetry, concrete images that affirm African cultural values are often used to represent universal themes. "Night of Sine," for example, describes a sleeping African village that embodies peacefulness and communion with the past. Similarly in "Prayer to Masks," the ancestral masks are specifically African, but they evoke a respect for tradition that is universal.

Writing

If you were to leave your homeland and go into exile, what objects would you want to take along to remind yourself and others of your cultural identity? What activities, rituals, and ceremonies would you continue to perform and celebrate to keep your cultural values alive? Describe these objects and activities and explain their cultural significance to you.

Literary Focus Stimulate discussion on other works students have read that reveal unique features of a particular culture or region. Ask students to suggest aspects of a culture that are best conveyed through literature.

Writing/Prior Knowledge Allow time for students from different backgrounds to meet in small groups and discuss their various celebrations and customs.

Vocabulary

Preteach the following vocabulary words:

eternity (ē tʉr´ nə tē) *n.*: Endless time, especially after death

despotism (des´ pət iz´əm) *n.*: Tyranny

pitiable (pit´ ē ə bəl) *adj.*: Arousing pity, sometimes mixed with a slight contempt for weakness or foolishness

immobile (im mō´ bəl) *adj.*: Motionless

ejaculate (ē jak´ yōō lāt) *v.*: Exclaim; speak suddenly or sharply

balsam (bôl´ səm) *adj.*: Healing and soothing, like the ointments made from the sweet-smelling resins of balsam trees

slack (slak) *adj.*: Barely moving; sluggish

dandle (dan´ dəl) *v.*: Move up and down, as one might do to entertain a child

reclines (ri klīnz´) *v.*: Lies down or leans back

extinguished (ek stiŋ´ gwisht) *v.*: Put out; doused

propitious (prō pish´əs) *adj.*: Gracious and favorably inclined

contemplate (känt´ təm plāt) *v.*: Think about; study carefully

lofty (lôf´ tē) *adj.*: Very high

ESL Teaching Strategy Clarify a few examples of metaphorical language, such as the "altar of white paper" in "Prayer to Masks." Then explain to ESL students that such figures of speech are a way for a poet to suggest several meanings at the same time.

Teaching Tenth-Grade Students Ask if any students in the class have ever spent an extended period of time away from home—either in another part of the country or overseas. Then ask these students to discuss what they missed most while they were away, and why.

Spelling Tip Have students locate the root *mobile* in *immobile.* Point out that the *m* in the prefix and the *m* in the root are both retained. Ask students to add the prefix *im-* to other words that begin with *m,* for instance, *material, mature, moral,* and *measurable.*

Motivation/Prior Knowledge Tell students that in the poem they are about to read, the speaker addresses various carved masks that represent his ancestors and the ancestors of his people. (Refer them to examples of such masks on page 1349.) Ask them what kinds of things a person might want to ask or tell his or her ancestors. Prompt them to continue thinking about this question as they read the poem.

Purpose-Setting Question What mission does the speaker in "Prayer to Masks" envision for African writers?

Universal Themes Like Senghor, other African writers have recognized the importance of "the awareness, defense and development of African cultural values." Though not technically part of the negritude movement, writers such as Wole Soyinka (page 1360), Okot p'Bitek (page 1354), and Chinua Achebe (page 1404) faithfully depict the beauty and value of their African cultures. Remind students that Soyinka's commitment to African culture was noted by the Swedish Academy when he was awarded the Nobel Prize for Literature in 1986.

Master Teacher Note Students may be intimidated by Senghor's long lines of verse and dense language. Allow time for students to preview the poems in small groups, using the punctuation rather than line length to guide their reading. Then ask for volunteers to read sections of the poems aloud to the class.

1 **Critical Thinking and Reading** Ask students to identify images and phrases in this part of the poem that evoke the feelings associated with a holy place. Which images do they think are universal? Which images do they feel are uniquely African?

2 **Clarification** Senghor may be alluding to the breakup of some of the European colonial empires during World War II, which ended the year this poem was published.

Prayer to Masks

Léopold Sédar Senghor

translated by Gerald Moore and Ulli Beier

Black mask, red mask, you black and white masks,
Rectangular masks through whom the spirit breathes,
I greet you in silence!
And you too, my lionheaded ancestor.
5 You guard this place, that is closed to any feminine laughter, to any
    mortal smile.
You purify the air of eternity, here where I breathe the air of my
    fathers.
Masks of markless faces, free from dimples and wrinkles,
You have composed this image, this my face that bends over the altar
    of white paper.
In the name of your image, listen to me!
10 Now while the Africa of despotism is dying—it is the agony of a
    pitiable princess
Like that of Europe to whom she is connected through the navel[1]—
Now fix your immobile eyes upon your children who have been called
And who sacrifice their lives like the poor man his last garment
So that hereafter we may cry "here" at the rebirth of the world being
    the leaven[2] that the white flour needs.
15 For who else would teach rhythm to the world that has died of
    machines and cannons?
For who else should ejaculate the cry of joy, that arouses the dead and
    the wise in a new dawn?
Say, who else could return the memory of life to men with a torn
    hope?
They call us cotton heads, and coffee men, and oily men,
They call us men of death.
20 But we are the men of the dance whose feet only gain power when
    they beat the hard soil.

---

1. navel (nā′ vəl)*n.*: The scar on the abdomen where the umbilical cord, which supplies oxygen and nutrients from the mother, was attached to the fetus in the womb.
2. leaven (lev′ ən) *n.*: A small piece of fermenting dough that is added to a larger batch of dough to make it rise.

Reader's Response *How do you picture the masks that the poet is addressing? Are they like the ones on the facing page? Explain.*

3 **Discussion** To whom do students think the speaker is referring?

4 **Discussion** Ask students to suggest literal meanings for this metaphor.

5 **Literary Focus** How do Europeans define Africans? How does the African speaker define Africans?

AOULÉ MASK FROM THE IVORY COAST

MASK FROM THE IVORY COAST

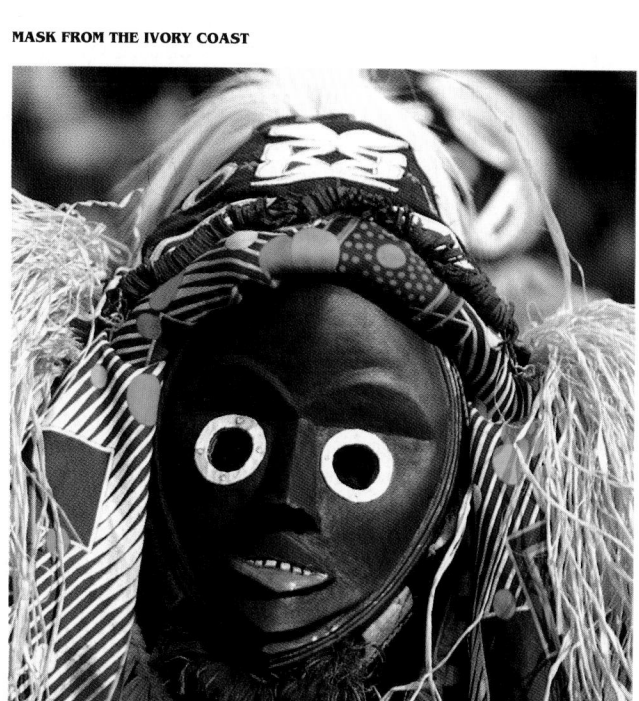

Humanities Note

Fine art, *Masks from the Ivory Coast.* The art of mask making is a long-standing tradition among African peoples. Masks are used as portraits and function in religious and ritual dances as well.

The Baoulé people are master wood carvers. The three decorative loops of hair on the mask to the left are characteristic of Baoulé design. This mask was probably used in ritual dances before the hunt.

The other mask, also carved by people of the Ivory Coast, is used in ritual dancing. It represents an ancestral spirit. The attached straw serves to cover the body of the dancer.

You may want to use the following questions to discuss the art:

1. What feelings do these masks inspire in you?
2. The mask to the right represents an ancestral spirit, and the straw attached to it hides the dancer's body. How might hiding the dancer's body increase the spirit-like appearance of the mask?
3. How do the horns on the Baoulé mask reflect its probable use in dances before a hunt?

Night of Sine[1]

Léopold Sédar Senghor

translated by Gerald Moore and Ulli Beier

Woman, rest on my brow your balsam hands, your hands gentler than
    fur.
The tall palmtrees swinging in the nightwind
Hardly rustle. Not even cradlesongs,
The rhythmic silence rocks us.
5 Listen to its song, listen to the beating of our dark blood, listen
To the beating of the dark pulse of Africa in the mist of lost villages.
Now the tired moon sinks towards its bed of slack water,
Now the peals of laughter even fall asleep, and the bards[2] themselves
Dandle their heads like children on the backs of their mothers.
10 Now the feet of the dancers grow heavy and heavy grows the tongue
    of the singers.

This is the hour of the stars and of the night that dreams
And reclines on this hill of clouds, draped in her long gown of milk.
The roofs of the houses gleam gently. What are they telling so
    confidently to the stars?
Inside the hearth is extinguished in the intimacy of bitter and sweet
    scents.
15 Woman, light the lamp of clear oil, and let the children in bed talk
    about their ancestors, like their parents.
Listen to the voice of the ancients of Elissa.[3] Like us, exiled,
They did not want to die, lest their seminal flood[4] be lost in the sand.
Let me listen in the smoky hut for the shadowy visit of propitious
    souls,
My head on your breast glowing, like a kuskus ball[5] smoking out of
    the fire,
20 Let me breathe the smell of our dead, let me contemplate and repeat
    their living voice, let me learn
To live before I sink, deeper than the diver, into the lofty depth of
    sleep.

---

1. Sine (sē´ nā): The poet's traditional home kingdom, a region of Senegal on the west coast of Africa.
2. bards *n*.: Storytellers, honored as guardians of the culture's oral tradition. Often they would provide the entertainment at ceremonies and community gatherings, recounting the history of the people.
3. Elissa: Also called Dido. According to Greek legend, she founded the ancient north African city of Carthage, which fell to the Romans in 146 B.C. The inhabitants of Carthage were killed or driven out, and the city was burned.
4. seminal flood: Generations of descendants.
5. kuskus (kᴜs´ kᴜs) **ball** *n*.: Steamed cracked wheat, cooked and eaten with meat or vegetables.

THINKING ABOUT THE SELECTION

Interpreting

1. In "Prayer to Masks," why do you think the speaker greets the masks in silence?
2. What do the masks represent for him?
3. What does he believe about the relationship between Africa and Europe? Explain.
4. In "Night of Sine," what do lines 3–6 suggest about the poet's attitude toward his African heritage?
5. (a) Why might the speaker in "Night of Sine" describe the gleaming rooftops as speaking to the stars? (b) What might they be saying?
6. How does the poet's prayer in the last two lines sum up the meaning of the poem?

Applying

7. Though Senghor is specifically talking about preserving and advancing African culture in these two poems, what message do you think they have for you within your own culture?

ANALYZING LITERATURE

Understanding Negritude

Negritude is a literary movement that affirms and promotes African cultural values through concrete images that evoke the beauty of African life. Sometimes these images are uniquely African; sometimes they evoke shared cultural values. In "Prayer to Masks," for example, the holy place that the masks guard is "closed to any feminine laughter." This image reflects the differing roles of men and women in many African religions. On the other hand, the holiness of the masks is similar to the sanctity of religious objects in other cultures. The aim of negritude in the hands of poets like Senghor is not to set African culture on a pedestal by itself but to enshrine it alongside all the other cultures of the world.

1. (a) In "Prayer to Masks," what does the speaker ask the masks to help him accomplish? (b) How is this task related to the aims of the negritude movement?
2. In "Night of Sine," Senghor depicts an African village preparing for sleep. (a) What role do the ancestors seem to play in the life of this village? (b) What images reflect the value that these Africans place on their ancestors? Explain.
3. Senghor has defined the aims of negritude as "awareness, defense and development" of African cultural values. How do these two poems support any or all of these aims? Explain.

CRITICAL THINKING AND READING

Relating to Features of Another Culture

Different cultures often share similar features and values. For example, in "Night of Sine," the familiar image of "children on the backs of their mothers" suggests the comfort and security of family life that most cultures value. Though Senghor focuses on features of African life in his poems, they are not so alien that readers from other cultures cannot find parallels within their own societies.

1. In "Night of Sine," Senghor uses a variety of images to convey a sense of tranquility. Explain which of these images seem universal and which seem rooted in African culture.
2. Identify objects in your own culture that are revered like the masks in "Prayer to Masks."

THINKING AND WRITING

Explaining an Original Design

Masks have important symbolic value in African culture, as they do in many societies around the world. For Senghor, masks embody the ancestral spirits of Africa and might be worn in religious ceremonies. In American society, masks might be worn for protection, as in sports or industry, or for disguise, as on Halloween. Even make-up might be considered a kind of mask, especially when worn by an actor. Do some research into the uses of masks around the world and design your own mask, either as a drawing or a three-dimensional model. Then write a detailed description of the mask you have created. Explain the intended use of the mask as well as the significance of the materials, colors, and other design features.

(continued from bottom of page)

ANSWERS TO ANALYZING LITERATURE

1. (a) Suggested response: He wants the masks to help Africans contribute to the rebirth of the world. (b) The speaker is affirming the value of African culture, saying that its vitality will help restore life to the dying world. Senghor uses the concrete image of African dance to convey this vitality.
2. (a) Answers will differ. Students may interpret the ancestors as guardian spirits watching over the village and imparting understanding during the quiet hours of the night. (b) The people of the village love and respect their ancestors: The children are allowed to stay awake in bed talking about them, the adults light a lamp and sit meditating on them, and the speaker wants to draw them into himself and learn from them.
3. Both poems use concrete images of African heritage— masks, dance, smoky huts, and kuskus—to convey their message, promoting awareness of African culture as it relates to the rest of the world. They develop African cultural values because Senghor is creating "African literature." Some students may note that the defense of African culture is implied in the reverent tone used in both of the poems.

ANSWERS TO CRITICAL THINKING AND READING

1. Answers will differ. Many students will probably relate to the images of children falling asleep in their mothers' arms, children whispering in bed, and stars and clouds over hills. Images that students may suggest are uniquely African include: "the pulse of Africa in the mist of lost villages," hearths in smoky huts, and a kuskus ball smoking in the fire.
2. Answers will differ. Encourage students to identify what the objects represent. Have students speculate how the objects came to be related to the ideas or philosophies that they represent.

THINKING AND WRITING

Publishing Student Writing Display students' designs at random among the written explanations. Encourage students to try to match each explanation with its design.

3. Answers will differ. Students may have inferred from the speaker's tone that he feels African countries need to establish their independence from Europe—in a cultural as well as a political and economic sense.
4. The images suggest that the speaker feels that his heritage is an integral part of him; the music of his beating blood is linked with the beat of Africa's blood.

5. (a) Suggested response: The image of conversation might be used to describe the way the twinkling of the stars seems to be interacting with the light gleaming on the rooftops. (b) Answers will differ. Students may suggest that the roofs are telling the stars, which may represent ancestors, about the families that they shelter.
6. The speaker wants to achieve a spiritual communion with his ancestors.

The last two lines sum up the poem's message that heritage is a fundamental element of identity.
7. Answers will differ. Students may feel that the call to respect and have pride in one's heritage is a message that is valuable to all cultures.

IDEAS AND

THE NUBIAN EXCAVATIONS

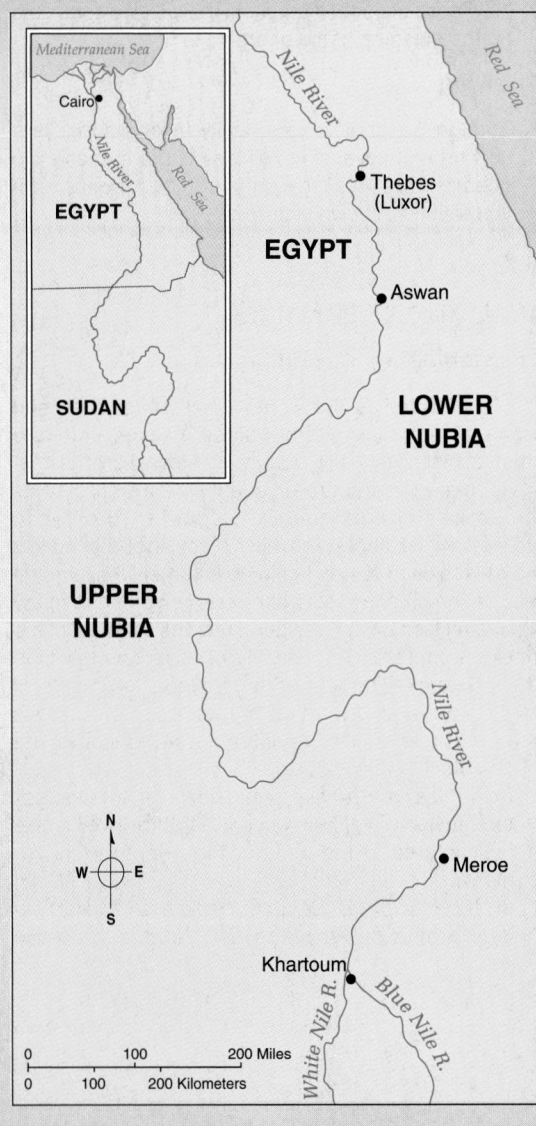

A Culture of Brilliance

Nubia was a black African culture of great brilliance and power. The Nubian empire extended along the Nile River for more than 1,000 miles, from what is today Aswan in Egypt to the Sudanese city of Khartoum. The Nubians built cities, roads, and structures that equaled those of Egypt, its neighbor and rival to the north. In addition to their many other achievements, the Nubians developed their own writing system. This system is the second oldest in Africa, Egyptian hieroglyphics being the first. As yet, however, scholars have been unable to decipher this language.

The Egypt-Nubia Connection

The Egyptian and Nubian cultures influenced and borrowed from each other over the years. Archeologists have determined that Egypt dominated Nubia during most of the period from 2000 to 747 B.C. During this time, features of Egyptian culture were adopted by the Nubians. Then, beginning around 747, Nubian kings ruled Egypt for about a century and revived Egyptian culture, art, and architecture. When Egypt was conquered by Syrian armies, the Nubian cultural center shifted farther south. Nubian kings ruled their kingdom from the city of Meroe.

In spite of its influence and accomplishments, Nubian culture was for years overshadowed by that of Egypt. Nubian civilization was neglected and be-

Presentation

Motivation/Prior Knowledge Ask students to share what they know about archeological excavations. Some students may have seen documentaries or read factual accounts. Other students' knowledge may be based on movies or television programs. Point out to students that the Nubian excavations were conducted with the permission of the Egyptian government.

Have students read or review the *Ideas and Insights* feature "Egyptian Book of the Dead" (page 36) to learn more about some beliefs that may have influenced Nubian culture.

Questions

1. What are some positive influences one culture can have on another? What are some negative influences?
2. Who do you think should have the authority to make decisions regarding archeological artifacts? The government? The discovering archeologists? Museums?

Activities

1. **Map Reading** Have students use the map legend to calculate how many miles it is between Thebes, once the capital of ancient Egypt, and Meroe, which became the cultural center of Nubia after the Syrians conquered Egypt. To help students grasp the actual distance, have them identify cities in the United States that are approximately the same distance apart. Remind students when they are measuring the distance between American cities that the scale for the American map may not be the same as the scale for the Nubian map.

You might also want to have students research the terrain and the climate of this area and suggest the best way for ancient Egyptians and Nubians to have traveled this distance.

2. **Cooperative Learning** Ancient Egypt, ruled by the Nubians from approximately 747 B.C. to 670 B.C., had a lively political and cultural history. Have students work in small groups to create sections of a timeline beginning at about 3200 B.C., when Menes united Upper and Lower Egypt, and continuing to about 30 B.C. with the death of Cleopatra. Combine the sections to create one complete timeline.

NSIGHTS

ame virtually unknown. This may be due in part
o Nubia's remoteness and forbidding landscape
nd climate. Its heat and aridity make travel diffi-
ult and dangerous. Some believe, however, that
his neglect was due to prejudice and condescen-
ion on the part of European historians because
Nubia was a black African empire. This prejudice
nay have been shared by archeologists, who for
ears viewed Nubian artifacts as lesser versions of
Egyptian artifacts.

Nubian Archeology

The first archeological excavations that revealed
he importance of the Nubian civilization began
arly in this century. The Egyptian government in-
ited archeologists to explore areas upriver of
Aswan before work on the Aswan dam flooded
hese regions. The resulting excavations uncovered
ombs, temples, and artifacts that revealed the
plendor of Nubian civilization.

In 1959 Egypt decided to construct a modern
am and power project at Aswan that would cause
arge-scale flooding of the Aswan Desert. Archeolo-
ists again joined forces to save artifacts, monu-
nents, and tombs of ancient Nubia. A splendid
emple built during the thirteenth century B.C. was
ismantled and reconstructed above the water line,
nd thousands of Nubian artifacts were also rescued.

Nubia on Display

Treasures from both these archeological efforts
ave been displayed in museums, and these institu-
ions have recognized Nubian civilization as out-
tanding in its own right. In addition, permanent
Nubian galleries have been established at the
Boston Museum of Fine Arts and the Royal On-
ario Museum in Toronto.

BALL WITH HATHOR HEAD AND HOLLOW CYLINDER
Unknown artist
Museum of Fine Arts, Boston

CRIOSPHINX ON A COLUMN
Unknown artist
Museum of Fine Arts, Boston

BOTTLE IN THE SHAPE OF A BOUND ORYX
Unknown artist
Museum of Fine Arts, Boston

Some of the objects typically on display include
jewelry, clothing, weapons, tools, brightly painted
pottery, and bronze statues. Among the earliest artifacts is a distinctive kind of "eggshell pottery," so
called because its walls seem as thin and fragile as
those of an eggshell. Patterns on the surface of this
pottery suggest the texture of woven garments.

Nubia in Popular Culture

The museum exhibits coincide with today's
heightened interest in African culture and civilizations. Exhibits have been well attended, and there
are even signs that an awareness of Nubia has infil-
trated into popular culture. A comic book character, Heru: son of Ausar, who is a Nubian hero, and
a rap group called Brand Nubian have emerged.

Humanities Note

Fine art, *Nubian artifacts.* These artifacts were discovered in the tomb of an unnamed queen of Nubian King Piankhy. Like their neighbors the Egyptians, the Nubian people had a deep love for beautiful objects and often buried their dead with a supply of beautiful and useful objects to take to the next world.

Ball with Hathor head and hollow cylinder is made of rock crystal. The hollow cylinder in the center of the crystal may have held ointment or perfume. The cap to the container is decorated with a representation of Hathor, the Nubian and Egyptian goddess of love, music, and dance.

Criosphinx on a column may be a replica of a temple or palace admired by the queen. The ram-headed sphinx that tops the column is made of electrum, an alloy of gold and silver. The column is made of the same alloy and inlaid with precious stones.

Bottle in the shape of a bound oryx is made of alabaster, a soft, translucent stone favored by Egyptian and Nubian craftsmen for carving into small vessels. Like *Ball with Hathor head,* this bottle probably held perfumes or ointments for the queen to use in her journey to the next life.

You may want to use the following questions to discuss the art:
1. How is this art similar to the Egyptian art pictured on pages 30, 32, and 33? How is it different?
2. Which do you think is the greater value of these objects—historical or artistic? Explain.

OKOT P'BITEK

1930–1982

"I really hold very strongly," Okot p'Bitek (ō´ kät pē bē tak´) said in an interview shortly before his death, "that an artist should tease people," and stick "needles into everybody so that they don't go to sleep and think everything is fine." This desire to raise awareness and stir up controversy is nowhere more evident than in p'Bitek's popular book *Song of Lawino* (1966), a sequence of poems about the clash between African and Western values.

Like other Africans of his generation, p'Bitek experienced this clash of values firsthand. He was born in Uganda, a small, beautiful, densely populated country in east-central Africa, which at the time was still under British domination. The colonial system, with its English-speaking schools, Christian missionaries, and centralized government, stood in sharp contrast to traditional Ugandan society: a patchwork of separate hereditary kingdoms, speaking many different languages and dialects, and practicing African religions.

P'Bitek himself embodied this contrast of cultures. He attended English-speaking schools in Uganda but never lost touch with traditional African values. From an early age, he used his wide array of talents to pursue his interests in both African and Western cultures. While still in college, he composed and produced an opera. In his early twenties, he published his first novel, written in the Acoli dialect of the Luo language.

He then traveled to Britain as part of Uganda's national football team. P'Bitek stayed on in Britain and studied education, law, social anthropology, and literature at various universities.

When he returned to Uganda, he taught at Makerere University College and subsequently held teaching positions in Kenya, Nigeria, and the United States. He became Director of Uganda's National Theater and Cultural Center and organized several regional arts festivals in both Uganda and Kenya. In 1967 he returned to Oxford to complete a doctorate in religion.

Despite all of his diverse activities, p'Bitek published a steady stream of books, in a variety of genres, promoting the value of African cultures. A sequel to *Song of Lawino*, called *Song of Ocol,* appeared in 1970. This was followed by two studies of religion, *African Religions and Western Scholarship* and *Religion of the Central Luo.* In 1974 he published *Horn of My Love,* a collection of Acoli songs, followed by *Hare and Hornbill*, a collection of African folk tales. When an interviewer marveled at how p'Bitek managed to do the many different things that he did, he replied, "I think that there is always time for anything you like to do, anything you are interested in." When p'Bitek died in his early fifties, one commentator wrote that his death was "like the splitting of a drum."

Drawing on the oral techniques of traditional Ugandan poetry, *Song of Lawino* has been called the "first important poem in English to emerge from Eastern Africa." Though p'Bitek originally wrote the poem in the Luo language, he translated it and published it in English. He describes the book as "a big laugh by this village girl called Lawino, laughing at modern man and modern woman in Uganda." In Lawino's opinion, Westernized Ugandans have abandoned their heritage and are out of touch with the real Ugandan culture. Lawino's "song" is a plea for such people to look back to traditional village life and recapture African values. Like p'Bitek himself, Lawino sticks "needles into everybody" so that they won't think everything is fine with modern life.

GUIDE FOR INTERPRETING

from Song of Lawino

Commentary

Cultural Conflict. A culture is a set of values that finds expression in the countless ways people are expected to conduct their lives. Think of some of the unspoken rules that govern your life, for example: how you are expected to dress for certain social occasions, to greet friends as opposed to strangers, and to behave toward your elders and persons of authority. Many of the world's cultures share values and can live side by side in harmony; however, there are often occasions when **cultural conflict** results from intolerance or ignorance of the ways of others.

Though bloodshed can be one outcome of cultural conflict, another outcome is the abandonment of one culture for another, supposedly superior, one. In Africa under colonialism, some Africans abandoned traditional ways of life that had been centered for centuries on the village. They moved to the cities, the centers of colonial power, where everything modern was considered a sign of "progress." There they attended European schools, learned to speak English or some other European language, donned European clothes, converted to Christianity, and worked for European-owned companies. They considered themselves superior to those they left behind in the village; nevertheless, their European overlords never considered them their equals. In time, these Westernized Africans no longer felt comfortable when they returned to visit their village homes. They had become cultural exiles within their own countries. Their heritage had died within them.

This is the kind of cultural conflict that Okot p'Bitek explores in *Song of Lawino.* Lawino is an old-fashioned "village girl" who complains that her Westernized husband, Ocol, has become a "stump" in a "forest of books."

Writing

Many people associate anything new with "progress" and would dislike being labeled "old-fashioned." What are some of the pros and cons of progress? Freewrite, exploring your thoughts on this subject.

Literary Focus Have students identify cultural categories that are potential sources of conflict among cultures. Possible categories include the roles of men and women in society, authority and rules, education, religion, and family structure. Tell students to watch for examples of cultural conflict in one or more of these areas as they read the poem.

Writing/Prior Knowledge Before students begin writing, have the class identify some of the results of "progress" in the past fifty years. Identify social and political changes as well as inventions, medical breakthroughs, and scientific discoveries. List these results on the board and suggest that students use their feelings about some of these changes and discoveries as a springboard for their freewriting.

ESL Teaching Strategy The use of figurative language may confuse some students who know the literal meaning of a word but do not understand the use of it in this poem. Both ESL and English-proficient students will benefit from restating the images in their own words.

Teaching Tenth-Grade Students Make the impact of the poem immediate by asking tenth-grade students how they would feel if somebody they had known for a long time were to change his or her behavior and habits.

Support Material

Teaching Portfolio
Teacher Backup, p. 1661
Usage and Mechanics Worksheet, p. 1665
Vocabulary Check, p. 1666
Analyzing Literature Worksheet, *Understanding Cultural Conflict,* p. 1667

Critical Thinking and Reading Worksheet, *Appreciating Figurative Language,* p. 1668
Selection Test, pp. 1669–1670

Spelling Tip Write the following words on the blackboard: *destructively, expansively, constructively.* Elicit from students that all these words retain the final *e* of the root word before the *-ly* is added. Have students identify *extensively* as the vocabulary word that fits this category.

from Song of Lawino[1]
Okot p'Bitek

from My Husband's House Is a Dark Forest of Books
translated by the author

1
Listen, my clansmen,
I cry over my husband
Whose head is lost.
Ocol has lost his head
5 In the forest of books.

When my husband
Was still wooing me
His eyes were still alive,
His ears were still unblocked,
10 Ocol had not yet become a fool
My friend was a man then!

2
He had not yet become a woman,
He was still a free man,
His heart was still his chief.

3
15 My husband was still a Black man
The son of the Bull
The son of Agik[2]
The woman from Okol[3]
Was still a man,
20 An Acoli[4]

4
My husband has read much.
He has read <u>extensively</u> and deeply, . . .
And he is clever like white men

And the reading
25 Has killed my man,
In the ways of his people
He has become
A stump.

He abuses all things Acoli,
30 He says
The ways of black people
Are black
Because his eyeballs have exploded,
And he wears dark glasses,
35 My husband's house
Is a dark forest of books.
Some stand there
Tall and huge
Like the *tido* tree . . .

40 The papers on my husband's desk
Coil threateningly
Like the giant forest climbers,
Like the *kituba* tree
That squeezes other trees to death;
45 Some stand up,
Others lie on their backs,
They are interlocked
Like the legs of youths
At the *orak*[5] dance,

---

1. Lawino (lä wē′ nō): The speaker, a woman.
2. The son of the Bull . . . Agik (ä jēk′): References to the ancestors of the speaker's husband.
3. Okol (ô kōl′): A town in northern Uganda.
4. Acoli (ä chōl′ ē): A people of northern Uganda, sharing a cultural, linguistic, and geographic heritage.

---

5. *orak* (ô rak′) *n*.: A traditional dance; an inner circle of young women and an outer circle of young men dance intricate steps until the two circles are intertwined.

UBI GIRL FROM TAI REGION
Lois Mailou Jones
Museum of Fine Arts, Boston

Humanities Note
Fine art, *Ubi Girl from Tai Region* by Lois Mailou Jones. A distinguished artist, Lois Mailou Jones (1905–) also taught art for forty-seven years at Howard University in Washington, D.C. Her works are owned by many major museums, among them the Metropolitan Museum of Art in New York and the National Collection of Art in Washington, D.C.

During more than half a century of painting, Jones's work has gone through many phases. In *Ubi Girl from Tai Region,* she returned to the African themes that characterized her early paintings. A realistic portrait of an African woman in ceremonial paint is juxtaposed with a flat, stylized profile of an African woman. This contrast between the real and the abstract is striking and surreal. The bold colors and patterns of the background recall those of African textiles and baskets.

You might want to use the following questions to discuss the art:
1. Do you think these are two views of the same woman? Why or why not?
2. How do you think Lawino would respond to the different images in this painting?
3. Does the theme of this painting support or contradict p'Bitek's views as expressed through Lawino?

50 Like the legs of the planks
Of the *goggo* fence,
They are tightly interlocked
Like the legs of the giant forest climbers
In the impenetrable forest.

55 My husband's house
Is a mighty forest of books,
Dark it is and very damp,
The steam rising from the ground
Hot, thick and poisonous
60 Mingles with the corrosive dew
And the rain drops
That have collected in the leaves . . . .

O, my clansmen,
Let us all cry together!
65 Come,
Let us mourn the death of my husband,
The death of a Prince
The Ash that was produced
By a great Fire!
70 O, this homestead is utterly dead,
Close the gates
With *lacari*[6] thorns,
For the Prince
The heir to the Stool[7] is lost!
75 And all the young men
Have perished in the wilderness!
And the fame of this homestead
That once blazed like a wild fire
In a moonless night
80 Is now like the last breaths
Of a dying old man!

There is not one single true son left,
The entire village
Has fallen into the hands
85 Of war captives and slaves!
Perhaps one of our boys
Escaped with his life!
Perhaps he is hiding in the bush
Waiting for the sun to set!

90 But will he come
Before the next mourning?
Will he arrive in time?

Bile burns my inside!
I feel like vomiting!

95 For all our young men
Were finished in the forest,
Their manhood was finished
In the class-rooms, . . .

---

6. *lacari* *n.*: Large thorns, some as long as three inches. The branches of the *lacari* tree are woven together to make a natural barbed wire that is used to protect homes and livestock.
7. **heir to the Stool:** Determined by birth to be a chief.

Reader's Response *Do you feel more sympathetic toward Lawino or her husba Explain.*

THINKING ABOUT THE SELECTION

Interpreting

1. In your own words, describe what has happened to Ocol.
2. According to Lawino, what broader effect has Ocol's "death" had on the village as a whole?
3. (a) What do you imagine the role of women is in Lawino's village? (b) By calling her husband a woman, what is Lawino implying about Ocol's position in Acoli society? In white society?
4. P'Bitek says that Lawino is "laughing at modern man and modern woman." Is this excerpt from the poem humorous? Why or why not?
5. (a) What are some of the likely effects of the conflict between Lawino and her husband? (b) What would have to happen for them to be able to live again in harmony as husband and wife?

Applying

6. Provide some examples, either current or historical, of people "losing their heads" in the pursuit of some new activity or ideal.

ANALYZING LITERATURE

Understanding Cultural Conflict

Cultural conflict occurs when the values of one society clash with those of another. In *Song of Lawino* this clash takes the form of a wife's complaint about her husband. At first glance, Lawino and her man may seem to be members of the same culture engaged in a domestic squabble, a squabble flavored by Lawino's exaggerations and figures of speech. However, Lawino's complaints about her husband are more than the ingredients of a comic quarrel. By lamenting the effects of her husband's Western education, she raises questions about the relative value for Africans of Western and African traditions.

1. (a) According to Lawino, what is wrong with the way Ocol has pursued knowledge in his "forest of books"? (b) What cultural threat do those books represent for Lawino?
2. Considering Ocol's attitudes toward "the ways of black people," what would Lawino say is wrong with the kind of education Africans receive in European-run schools?
3. (a) How do you think the kind of cultural conflict that p'Bitek describes in *Song of Lawino* can be resolved? (b) Is p'Bitek's own life an example of such a resolution? Explain.

CRITICAL THINKING AND READING

Appreciating Figurative Language

Figurative language is any descriptive expression that conveys a truth beyond the literal level. For example, when Lawino says that "reading / Has killed my man," she is using figurative language. Ocol is not literally dead; instead, Lawino is saying that a valuable part of her husband's personality has been altered for the worse by the kind of education he has received. All good writers, but especially poets, use figurative language to make important points indirectly and succinctly. Figurative language can often capture in a few well-chosen words what it would take many sentences to describe literally.

1. We usually think of education as nourishment for our growth. However, though Ocol lives in a "mighty forest of books," he himself is a "stump." Explain the point that Lawino makes by setting up this figurative contrast.
2. (a) What does Lawino mean when she says Ocol's "eyeballs have exploded"? (b) What caused this explosion? (c) To what is Ocol now blind?
3. Lawino describes Ocol's papers as giant coiling vines that strangle other vegetation. Explain how this figurative language enhances the expression of cultural conflict in the poem.

THINKING AND WRITING

Examining Cultural Conflict

Resolving a cultural conflict, indeed any conflict, requires compromise. Imagine a conversation between Lawino and Ocol, with each trying to convince the other of the validity of his or her viewpoint. Is Lawino right to believe that Ocol's books are a destructive cultural influence? Is Ocol wrong in his view that "The ways of black people / Are black"? Brainstorm to gather ideas and arguments that represent both sides in this cultural conflict between modern Western ways and traditional African values. Then, write a dialogue between Lawino and Ocol in which they try to reach a compromise.

(continued from bottom of page)

2. Suggested response: Lawino would probably say that European schools make Africans think European ways are *better* than African ways, instead of just *different*.
3. (a) Students will probably suggest that it is possible to receive a modern education without losing respect for traditional values. (b) Answers will differ, but most students will probably recognize that p'Bitek used his education to promote the value of his traditional culture, at home and abroad. Point out to students that because p'Bitek could write in English, they were able to learn something about his culture by reading this poem.

ANSWERS TO CRITICAL THINKING AND READING

1. Suggested response: Education has made Ocol less than he once was. It has diminished his vitality rather than increased it.
2. (a) Answers will differ. The image suggests that his vision—and his sense of himself—have been irreparably damaged. (b) Reading Western books has destroyed both his sight and his sense of identity. (c) He is blind to the value and beauty of his traditional culture.
3. Suggested response: The images reflect the surreptitious way that Western culture has taken hold of Ocol and "killed" his respect for his traditional culture.

THINKING AND WRITING

Publishing Student Writing Tell students to imagine that this dialogue will be published in book form. Have students design a book jacket that reflects images from both cultures.

Challenge Ask for volunteers to research the clash between native and European cultures in other parts of Africa. Then have the volunteers present their findings to the class.

accepted a subordinate role in white society.
4. Answers will differ. Encourage students to cite specific examples of lines and images that they do or do not find humorous.
5. (a) Answers will differ. Some students may feel that the gap between Lawino and Ocol will grow wider as time passes. Others may feel that Ocol will grow tired of his adopted culture and embrace his heritage again. (b) Either Ocol will have to return to traditional village life or Lawino must become Westernized.
6. Answers will differ. Students may choose examples of fads in clothes or hairstyles, or they may choose examples dealing with the pursuit of health, money, or personal fulfillment.

ANSWERS TO ANALYZING LITERATURE

1. (a) According to Lawino, Ocol has pursued Western knowledge exclusively, sacrificing knowledge of his own culture. (b) The books and the Western ways they represent have overwhelmed and killed Ocol's identity as an Acoli.

WOLE SOYINKA

1934–

Although Wole Soyinka (wō´ lā shô yiŋ´ kə) has also written poetry, novels, criticisms, and autobiography, he is acknowledged as perhaps Nigeria's finest contemporary dramatist. In 1986 he became the first African to receive the Nobel Prize in Literature. In presenting the award, the members of the Swedish Academy, who choose Nobel recipients, noted a total commitment both to African culture and to social change and human rights that lies behind all of Soyinka's work. This latter commitment was reinforced by the experience of two years in prison for speaking out against the Nigerian government.

Soyinka was born in western Nigeria and raised by Christian parents during British colonial rule. However, as he vividly describes in the autobiography of his early years, *Ake: The Years of Childhood* (1981), Soyinka was greatly influenced by the native cultural forces of the Yoruba people, his traditional African group. Indeed, the foundation of all Soyinka's work rests on the traditions and beliefs of the Yoruba culture, not on European or Christian values.

Soyinka was educated both in Nigeria and in England at the University of Leeds, where he graduated with honors in 1957. It was at Leeds that his first work was published. After working in England for several years, Soyinka returned to Nigeria in 1960.

His return to Nigeria coincided with the country's independence from Britain. This is significant because Soyinka has always believed in the need for a cultural independence to go along with political independence. He feels that by recognizing the integrity and validity of traditional African culture, Africans will be better able to deal effectively with the problems of post-Colonialist Africa.

Soyinka's works reflect this belief. Many of his plays, including *The Swamp Dwellers* (1958), *The Lion and the Jewel* (1959), and *A Dance of the Forest* (1960), depict the conflict between traditional Yoruba cultural values and values based on British and other European cultures. His work also incorporates many traditional elements of Yoruba culture. Traditional Yoruban proverbs are an important part of the dialogue in his plays. Traditional dance and music are incorporated in the plays *The Strong Breed* (1964) and *Death and the King's Horseman* (1976). *Idanre and Other Poems* (1967) has a long poem about the legend of Ogun the Yoruban god of war, fire, and metal.

Soyinka's work is also influenced by his term in prison from 1967 to 1969. He was thrown in jail without charges because of his outspoken criticism of the impending civil war with Biafra, an eastern region of Nigeria. His prison experiences were recorded in *Poems from Prison* (1969) and in a memoir, *The Man Died* (1972).

Although his earlier work was always full of social and political satire, his literary output following his imprisonment is marked by an increased concern and passion for human freedom. The drama *Madmen and Specialists* (1970) denounces the effects of the civil war in Nigeria, and many of his later plays, including *Opera Wonyosi* (1977) and *A Play of Giants* (1984), are satires decrying the succession of military regimes that have ruled Nigeria.

Soyinka has said "The greatest threat to freedom is the absence of criticism." Throughout his literary career he has used his work, including the poem "Civilian and Soldier," as a vehicle for social and political criticism. He is also a truly African writer. As "Season" shows, his work is immersed in traditional West African culture.

Objectives

Thematic
To understand that confusion, uncertainty, and contradictions are inherent in life

Skill
To understand irony and paradox

GUIDE FOR INTERPRETING

Season; Civilian and Soldier

(continued from bottom of page)

Commentary

Irony and Paradox. The modern world is full of uncertainties and strange realities. The difference between appearance and reality, good and evil, right and wrong, is elusive and hard to distinguish. As a result, writers have increasingly turned to irony and paradox to reflect the confusion and uncertainty confronting contemporary society.

In literature **irony** is a situation or a use of language that involves a surprising, interesting, or amusing contradiction. There are three types of irony: dramatic, situational, and verbal. **Dramatic irony** is a contradiction between what the character thinks and what the reader or audience knows to be true. **Situational irony** occurs when an event contradicts what is appropriate or what is expected by the readers or the audience. **Verbal irony** is a figure of speech in which what is meant is the opposite of what is said. "It is a tropical 5 degrees outside" is an example of verbal irony. Although the temperature is described as "tropical," it is actually very cold. Using irony enables a writer to point out the inconsistencies and uncertainties of life and to suggest meanings without actually stating them.

A **paradox** is a situation or a statement that seems contradictory yet is actually somehow true. A surgeon's job, inflicting pain in order to relieve pain, is in a sense paradoxical. A statement like "You must sometimes be cruel to be kind" is paradoxical. It sounds contradictory at first, yet makes sense when you consider situations requiring unkind words or actions that will help someone in the long run. The surprising or shocking nature of a paradox gets the reader's attention, therefore underscoring the truth about the statement.

The success of both irony and paradox in writing depends to a great extent on the reader. With irony, the reader must grasp the intended meaning rather than the literal meaning of the statement or action. With paradox, the reader must think critically to fully understand the truth of the statement or the action.

In "Season" and "Civilian and Soldier," Wole Soyinka uses both verbal irony and paradox to point out some of the contradictions and truths of political and cultural life in Nigeria.

Writing

Have you ever experienced a situation that could be described as ironic? We have all experienced situational irony, though we usually do not think of it as such. Think carefully about something that concluded in a contradictory, surprising, or even humorous way. Does it fit in the category of situational irony? Jot down a brief narrative of such an experience.

think of? Situational irony is less common. How many students have laughed when the opposite of what they expected occurs? They might provide examples of situational irony from everyday life, or from television programs, movies, or books.

Writing/Prior Knowledge Have students work in groups to brainstorm about possible instances of situational irony that they experienced. Students can discuss the experiences and decide whether or not they fit into the category of irony. You might want to group less advanced students with average and more advanced students for this activity.

ESL Teaching Strategy Read the poems aloud to ESL students and have them follow along. If they think either of the poems is confusing, ask them to write down three questions they have about it. Collect the questions and discuss them with the class. Can members of the class answer the questions?

Teaching Tenth-Grade Students For "Civilian and Soldier," consider working tenth-grade students through the plot line by line. This is important because poetry often uses language that is much more subtle than most language in prose. Ask students to read a line or two and then to describe the action in their own words. Discuss any differences in how different students paraphrase the lines. You could even chart the action and characters on the chalkboard.

Master Teacher Note Read the poems aloud, or have student volunteers read the poems aloud to the class as they follow along silently. Next, split the class into groups of equal ability levels. Have groups discuss and interpret each poem. Have groups present their interpretations to the rest of the class. The class should then discuss differences in interpretations. During this discussion, stress the idea that there can be more than one correct interpretation of the same poem.

Support Material

Teaching Portfolio
Teacher Backup, p. 1671
Usage and Mechanics Worksheet, p. 1675
Analyzing Literature Worksheet, *Understanding Irony*, p. 1676
Critical Thinking and Reading Worksheet, *Understanding the Poem as*

a Dramatic Situation, p. 1677
Language Worksheet, *Understanding Denotation and Connotation*, p. 1678
Selection Test, pp. 1679–1680

Literary Focus Have students discuss everyday examples of irony in their lives. How many students have jokingly described a difficult test as "a piece of cake"? This is an example of verbal irony. We all use verbal irony quite often in everyday speech, although we often don't think of it as such. What other examples of verbal irony can students

Season

Wole Soyinka

Rust is ripeness, rust
And the wilted corn-plume;
Pollen is mating-time when swallows
Weave a dance
5 Of feathered arrows
Thread cornstalks in winged
Streaks of light. And, we loved to hear
Spliced[1] phrases of the wind, to hear
Rasps[2] in the field, where corn leaves
10 Pierce like bamboo slivers.

Now, garnerers[3] we,
Awaiting rust on tassels, draw
Long shadows from the dusk, wreathe
Dry thatch in woodsmoke. Laden stalks
15 Ride the germ's decay—we await
The promise of the rust.

---

1. **Spliced** (splīst) *adj.*: Woven together.
2. **Rasps** (rasps) *n.*: Rough, grating tones (usually a verb).
3. **garnerers** (gär´ nər ərz) *n.*: Harvesters; gatherers.

Market scene in Igbomina Yoruba town of Ila-Orangun

Civilian and Soldier

Wole Soyinka

My apparition[1] rose from the fall of lead,
Declared, "I'm a civilian." It only served
To aggravate your fright. For how could I
Have risen, a being of this world, in that hour
Of impartial death! And I thought also: nor is
Your quarrel of this world.

                  You stood still
For both eternities, and oh I heard the lesson
Of your training sessions, cautioning—
Scorch earth behind you, do not leave
A dubious[2] neutral to the rear. Reiteration

Of my civilian quandary,[3] burrowing earth
From the lead festival of your more eager friends
Worked the worse on your confusion, and when
You brought the gun to bear on me, and death
15 Twitched me gently in the eye, your plight
And all of you came clear to me.

                      I hope some day
Intent upon my trade of living, to be checked
In stride by *your* apparition in a trench,
Signaling, I am a soldier. No hesitation then
20 But I shall shoot you clean and fair
With meat and bread, a gourd of wine
A bunch of breasts from either arm, and that
Lone question—do you friend, even now, know
What it is all about?

---

1. **apparition** (ap´ ə rish´ ən) *n.*: A strange, suddenly appearing figure, thought to be a ghost.
2. **dubious** (doo´ bē əs) *adj.*: Causing suspicion.

---

3. **quandary** (kwän´ də rē) *n.*: Dilemma.

Reader's Response *Do you think the civilian's attitude is justified? Why or why not?*

ANALYZING LITERATURE

Understanding Irony and Paradox

Writers use irony and paradox to illustrate the difficulty of distinguishing between appearance and reality in the modern world. In literature, **verbal irony** is a figure of speech in which what is said is the opposite of what is meant. A **paradox** is a statement that seems contradictory yet is true. The surprise or shock-value of a paradox underscores its essential truth.

1. What verbal irony is used in the third stanza of "Civilian and Soldier"? What conflicting feelings does this use of irony reveal in the speaker?
2. What irony is implied by the final question the civilian would ask the soldier?
3. For "Season," explain the truth revealed in the paradoxes "Rust is ripeness, rust / And the wilted corn-plume" and "we await / The promise of the rust."

NADINE GORDIMER

1923–

South African writer Nadine Gordimer once described herself as "not a politically minded person by nature." She said, "I don't suppose if I had lived elsewhere, my writing would have reflected politics much, if at all." Nonetheless, her ten novels and nine story collections do reflect politics, like an unforgiving mirror held up to South African society; and the images have sometimes been so ugly that three of her books were banned by the South African government.

The daughter of Lithuanian Jewish immigrants, Nadine Gordimer was born in Springs, a mining town near Johannesburg. Under apartheid, the official government policy of racial separation, she was raised in a segregated society and attended private schools. "As a child, you don't question these things," she once said. "I just thought, 'black children don't go to the movies and don't go to dancing class.'" Always an avid reader and writer, she had her first story published when she was fifteen. Gordimer later enrolled at the University of Witwatersrand to study English literature but left after one year.

In the meantime, reading had introduced her to the world on the other side of the color line. By the time her first collection of stories was published in 1949, she had become actively opposed to the government's policy of apartheid. Beginning with *The Lying Days* (1953), her ten novels are powerful indictments of a legal system that has enabled a white minority to control and oppress the country's black majority.

In *Burger's Daughter* (1979), a young white woman must come to terms with the anti-apartheid activities of her father, who dies in prison. *July's People* (1981) tells the story of a white family adapting to life in their black servant's village. A recent novel, *My Son's Story* (1991), is about a "colored" schoolteacher who becomes estranged from his family when he takes up political activism and becomes involved with a white human-rights worker. In these complex tales of human relationships under apartheid, everyone suffers—blacks, whites, men, women, parents, children. No one is exempt.

Gordimer's own political struggle has eased somewhat since 1990. In that year, reform finally gained momentum in her country, and Nelson Mandela and other anti-apartheid leaders were freed from prison. She is no longer hiding friends from the police, as she did years ago. She has openly joined the formerly illegal African National Congress, after years of meeting in secret. The ban on her books has been lifted.

In 1991, Nadine Gordimer was awarded the Nobel Prize for Literature. To many it seemed appropriate that she was chosen just as her country was beginning to dismantle the system she opposed throughout her long career.

Although Gordimer's works are political statements, they gain their power from her intimate portrayal of characters. In "The Ultimate Safari," from a recent collection, *Jump and Other Stories,* the effects of civil war in Mozambique are seen through the eyes of a young girl.

GUIDE FOR INTERPRETING

Commentary

The Ultimate Safari

Social Context. Suppose you were asked to write a short story in which the setting is your community and the time is the present. Any small details the reader needs to know about your community, you will, as a good author, weave into the story itself. What about the big picture? Are there any background issues—the economic recession, a local election, or racial tensions, to name a few examples—that might help the reader understand your characters better? These social issues that provide the larger backdrop for a story are its **social context.** Recognizing the social context of a story can help you understand the characters and the conditions under which they live. It can even clarify elements of the plot.

In Nadine Gordimer's fiction, the social context is particularly important. Because most of her stories are set in South Africa, her characters inhabit a world defined by apartheid. This is a complex system of laws and restrictions designed to keep the races separate. Historically, it has deprived the black majority in South Africa of any civil rights and kept them economically downtrodden. Black South Africans have been prohibited from living where they want, traveling where they want, or getting a decent education. Although progress has been made toward ending apartheid in recent years, reform still has far to go.

Some of the story "The Ultimate Safari" takes place in Mozambique, South Africa's neighbor to the northeast. Colonized by the Portuguese in the sixteenth century, Mozambique finally became independent in 1975 after ten years of fighting between the Portuguese government and the liberation movement known as Frelimo. Soon, however, civil war had broken out again, this time between the new Frelimo government and the guerrillas of the National Resistance Movement. By the mid-1980's, droughts and the disruption of war had caused food shortages that led to malnutrition and starvation for millions of people, including nearly half a million children.

"The Ultimate Safari" is the story of one Mozambican family's upheaval as seen through the eyes of a young girl. As always in Nadine Gordimer's stories, a character's personal perspective illuminates a much larger social conflict.

Writing

If someone asked you to pack your bags tomorrow for an African safari, what mental images would this request conjure up? Freewrite, describing your expectations, images, and ideas about a safari. Then, as you read, compare your images of a safari with the "safari" described in the story.

Literary Focus To help students understand social context, show photos or magazine pictures from each of the past three decades. Use these pictures to stimulate discussion about cultural changes in the United States. Ask students to identify differences in the way people dress and style their hair. Encourage students to share what they know about changes in the government, the economy, laws, transportation, employment, and social customs and attitudes. Ask them to consider how these differences in social context might affect the way a story from each decade would be written, and the way it might be interpreted by people who read it.

Writing/Prior Knowledge Before students freewrite about their African safari, ask them to speculate about the climate and geography of the different countries of Africa to which they might travel.

ESL Teaching Strategy Explain that in this story, Gordimer writes from the point of view of a young Mozambican girl, and as such, she does not always adhere to standard English sentence structure and punctuation. Assist ESL students in locating examples of sentences that do not follow standard usage and use these examples as the basis for small-group discussion.

Teaching Tenth-Grade Students Ask tenth-grade students to imagine that they have been forced to leave their homes and seek shelter in a foreign country where they are unwelcome. How would their feelings about the people who forced them to leave home differ from their feelings about the people in the foreign country? In what ways would those feelings be similar?

Support Material

Teaching Portfolio
Teacher Backup, p. 1681
Usage and Mechanics
  Worksheet, p. 1685
Analyzing Literature
  Worksheet, *Understanding Social Context*, p. 1686

Critical Thinking and
  Reading Worksheet,
  Recognizing Point of View,
  p. 1687
Language Worksheet, *Using Similes*, p. 1688
Selection Test, pp. 1689–1690

The Ultimate Safari

Nadine Gordimer

The African Adventure Lives On . . . You can do it!
The ultimate safari or expedition
with leaders who <u>know</u> Africa.

—TRAVEL ADVERTISEMENT.
Observer, LONDON, 27/11/88

That night our mother went to the shop and she didn't come back. Ever. What happened? I don't know. My father also had gone away one day and never come back; but he was fighting in the war.[1] We were in the war, too, but we were children, we were like our grandmother and grandfather, we didn't have guns. The people my father was fighting—the bandits, they are called by our government—ran all over the place and we ran away from them like chickens chased by dogs. We didn't know where to go. Our mother went to the shop because someone said you could get some oil for cooking. We were happy because we hadn't tasted oil for a long time; perhaps she got the oil and someone knocked her down in the dark and took that oil from her. Perhaps she met the bandits. If you meet them, they will kill you. Twice they came to our village and we ran and hid in the bush and when they'd gone we came back and found they had taken everything; but the third time they came back there was nothing to take, no oil, no food, so they burned the thatch[2] and the roofs of our houses fell in. My mother found some pieces of tin and we put those up over part of the house. We were waiting there for her that night she never came back.

We were frightened to go out, even to do our business, because the bandits did come. Not into our house—without a roof it must have looked as if there was no one in it, everything gone—but all through the village. We heard people screaming and running. We were afraid even to run, without our mother to tell us where. I am the middle one, the girl, and my little brother clung against my stomach with his arms round my neck and his legs round my waist like a baby monkey to its mother. All night my first-born brother kept in his hand a broken piece of wood from one of our burnt house-poles. It was to save himself if the bandits found him.

We stayed there all day. Waiting for her. I don't know what day it was; there was no school, no church any more in our village, so you didn't know whether it was a Sunday or a Monday.

---

1. the war: A civil war between the Communist Frelimo government of Mozambique and the guerrilla forces of the National Resistance Movement. By 1988, the conflict had claimed the lives of 600,000 people. In addition, 494,000 children died from malnutrition as a result of the war.

2. thatch *n.*: Straw, grasses, or leaves laid over a framework of woven sticks to make a roof.

When the sun was going down, our grandmother and grandfather came. Someone from our village had told them we children were alone, our mother had not come back. I say "grandmother" before "grandfather" because it's like that: our grandmother is big and strong, not yet old, and our grandfather is small, you don't know where he is, in his loose trousers, he smiles but he hasn't heard what you're saying, and his hair looks as if he's left it full of soap suds. Our grandmother took us—me, the baby, my first-born brother, our grandfather—back to her house and we were all afraid (except the baby, asleep on our grandmother's back) of meeting the bandits on the way. We waited a long time at our grandmother's place. Perhaps it was a month. We were hungry. Our mother never came. While we were waiting for her to fetch us our grandmother had no food for us, no food for our grandfather and herself. A woman with milk in her breasts gave us some for my little brother, although at our house he used to eat porridge, same as we did. Our grandmother took us to look for wild spinach but everyone else in her village did the same and there wasn't a leaf left.

Our grandfather, walking a little behind some young men, went to look for our mother but didn't find her. Our grandmother cried with other women and I sang the hymns with them. They brought a little food—some beans—but after two days there was nothing again. Our grandfather used to have three sheep and a cow and a vegetable garden but the bandits had long ago taken the sheep and the cow, because they were hungry, too; and when planting time came our grandfather had no seed to plant.

So they decided—our grandmother did; our grandfather made little noises and rocked from side to side, but she took no notice—we would go away. We children were pleased. We wanted to go away from where our mother wasn't and where we were hungry. We wanted to go where there were no bandits and there was food. We were glad to think there must be such a place; away.

Our grandmother gave her church clothes to someone in exchange for some dried mealies[3] and she boiled them and tied them in a rag. We took them with us when we went and she thought we would get water from the rivers but we didn't come to any river and we got so thirsty we had to turn back. Not all the way to our grandparents' place but to a village where there was a pump. She opened the basket where she carried some clothes and the mealies and she sold her shoes to buy a big plastic container for water. I said, *Gogo,* how will you go to church now even without shoes, but she said we had a long journey and too much to carry. At that village we met other people who were also going away. We joined them because they seemed to know where that was better than we did.

To get there we had to go through the Kruger Park.[4] We knew about the Kruger Park. A kind of whole country of animals—elephants, lions, jackals, hyenas, hippos, crocodiles, all kinds of animals. We had some of them in our own country, before the war (our grandfather remembers; we children weren't born yet) but the bandits kill the elephants and sell their tusks, and the bandits and our soldiers have eaten all the buck. There was a man in our village without legs—a crocodile took them off, in our river; but all the same our country is a country of people, not animals. We knew about the Kruger Park because some of our men used to leave home to work there in the places where white people come to stay and look at the animals.

So we started to go away again. There were women and other children like me who had to carry the small ones on their backs when the women got tired. A man led us into the Kruger Park; are we there yet, are we there yet, I kept asking our grandmother. Not yet, the man said, when she asked him for me. He told us we had to take a long way to get round the fence, which he explained would kill you, roast off your skin the moment you touched it, like the wires high up on poles that give electric light in our towns. I've seen that sign of a head without eyes or skin or hair on an iron box at the mission hospital we used to have before it was blown up.

---

3. **mealies** *n.*: Ears of corn on the cob.

4. **Kruger Park:** A game preserve in the Republic of South Africa. The park, bordering Mozambique and Zimbabwe, is approximately fifty miles wide and two hundred miles long.

7 **Reading Strategy** Ask students to speculate about why Gordimer has the narrator emphasize the difference between the grandparents.

8 **Clarification** Explain that Mozambique's economy is primarily agricultural. Droughts in the 1980's and food shortages brought about by the civil war resulted in malnutrition and starvation for millions of Mozambicans.

9 **Discussion** Ask students what the references to the hymns and the gifts of food might indicate.

10 **Critical Thinking and Reading** Draw attention to the way Gordimer uses sentence structure and punctuation to convey the age of the narrator.

11 **Reading Strategy** Have students locate Kruger Park on a map of Africa. Ask why refugees from Mozambique might have decided to flee to South Africa.

12 **Literary Focus** Ask students what this passage reveals about racial separation in South Africa.

13 **Reading Strategy** Point out that the skull and crossbones symbol appears at the beginning of the journey through Kruger Park. Ask students what this symbol represents, and have them predict what it foreshadows.

14 **Discussion** Ask students how the narrator's response to the elephants might be influenced by her own sense of powerlessness.

15 **Clarification** Explain that the narrator is referring to coal mines, of which there are many in central Mozambique.

16 **Discussion** Have students describe ways in which the people are forced to become "like the animals."

17 **Discussion** Ask students why they think the grandmother's indifference to the flies frightens the narrator.

18 **Discussion** How does the hyenas' behavior reflect the refugees' plight?

19 **Reading Strategy** Ask students to comment on the irony of these circumstances. How do social conditions in South Africa make black Africans "invisible"?

When I asked the next time, they said we'd been walking in the Kruger Park for an hour. But it looked just like the bush we'd been walking through all day, and we hadn't seen any animals except the monkeys and birds which live around us at home, and a tortoise that, of course, couldn't get away from us. My first-born brother and the other boys brought it to the man so it could be killed and we could cook and eat it. He let it go because he told us we could not make a fire; all the time we were in the Park we must not make a fire because the smoke would show we were there. Police, wardens, would come and send us back where we came from. He said we must move like animals among the animals, away from the roads, away from the white people's camps. And at that moment I heard—I'm sure I was the first to hear—cracking branches and the sound of something parting grasses and I almost squealed because I thought it was the police, wardens—the people he was telling us to look out for—who had found us already. And it was an elephant, and another elephant, and more elephants, big blots of dark moved wherever you looked between the trees. They were curling their trunks round the red leaves of the Mopane trees and stuffing them into their mouths. The babies leant against their mothers. The almost grown-up ones wrestled like my first-born brother with his friends—only they used trunks instead of arms. I was so interested I forgot to be afraid. The man said we should just stand still and be quiet while the elephants passed. They passed very slowly because elephants are too big to need to run from anyone.

The buck ran from us. They jumped so high they seemed to fly. The warthogs stopped dead, when they heard us, and swerved off the way a boy in our village used to zigzag on the bicycle his father had brought back from the mines. We followed the animals to where they drank. When they had gone, we went to their water-holes. We were never thirsty without finding water, but the animals ate, ate all the time. Whenever you saw them they were eating, grass, trees, roots. And there was nothing for us. The mealies were finished. The only food we could eat was what the baboons ate, dry little figs full of ants that grow along the branches of the trees at the rivers. It was hard to be like the animals.

When it was very hot during the day we would find lions lying asleep. They were the color of the grass and we didn't see them at first but the man did, and he led us back and a long way round where they slept. I wanted to lie down like the lions. My little brother was getting thin but he was very heavy. When our grandmother looked for me to put him on my back, I tried not to see. My first-born brother stopped talking; and when we rested he had to be shaken to get up again, as if he was just like our grandfather, he couldn't hear. I saw flies crawling on our grandmother's face and she didn't brush them off; I was frightened. I picked a palm leaf and chased them.

We walked at night as well as by day. We could see the fires where the white people were cooking in the camps and we could smell the smoke and the meat. We watched the hyenas with their backs that slope as if they're ashamed, slipping through the bush after the smell. If one turned its head, you saw it had big brown shining eyes like our own when we looked at each other in the dark. The wind brought voices in our own language from the compounds where the people who work in the camps live. A woman among us wanted to go to them at night and ask them to help us. They can give us the food from the dustbins,[5] she said, she started wailing and our grandmother had to grab her and put a hand over her mouth. The man who led us had told us that we must keep out of the way of our people who worked at the Kruger Park; if they helped us they would lose their work. If they saw us, all they could do was pretend we were not there; they had seen only animals.

Sometimes we stopped to sleep for a little while at night. We slept close together. I don't know which night it was—because we were walking, walking, any time, all the time—we heard the lions very near. Not groaning loudly the way they did far off. Panting, like we do when we run, but it's a different kind of panting: you can hear they're not running, they're waiting, somewhere near. We

_____

5. **dustbins:** Garbage cans.

Primary Source

In the essay "Selecting My Stories," Gordimer writes as follows:

Nobody has ever succeeded in defining a short story in a manner to satisfy all who write or read them, and I shall not, here. I sometimes wonder if one shouldn't simply state flatly: a short story is a piece of fiction short enough to be read at one sitting? No, that will satisfy no one, least myself. But for me certainly there is a clue, there, to the choice of the short story by writers, as a form: whether or not it has a narrative in the external or internal sense, whether it sprawls or neatly bites its own tail, a short story is a concept that the writer can "hold," fully realized, in his imagination, at one time. A novel is, by comparison, staked out, and must be taken possession of stage by stage; it is impossible to contain, all at once, the proliferation of concepts it ultimately may use. For this reason I cannot understand how people can suppose one makes a conscious choice, *after* knowing what one wants to write about between writing a novel or a short story. A short story occurs, in the imaginative sense. To write one is to express from a situation in the exterior or interior world the life giving drop . . . that will spread an intensity on the page; burn a hole in it.

all rolled closer together, on top of each other, the ones on the edge fighting to get into the middle. I was squashed against a woman who smelled bad because she was afraid but I was glad to hold tight on to her. I prayed to God to make the lions take someone on the edge and go. I shut my eyes not to see the tree from which a lion might jump right into the middle of us, where I was. The man who led us jumped up instead, and beat on the tree with a dead branch. He had taught us never to make a sound but he shouted. He shouted at the lions like a drunk man shouting at nobody, in our village. The lions went away. We heard them groaning, shouting back at him from far off.

We were tired, so tired. My first-born brother and the man had to lift our grandfather from stone to stone where we found places to cross the rivers. Our grandmother is strong but her feet were bleeding. We could not carry the basket on our heads any longer, we couldn't carry anything except my little brother. We left our things under a bush. As long as our bodies get there, our grandmother said. Then we ate some wild fruit we didn't know from home and our stomachs ran. We were in the grass called elephant grass because it is nearly as tall as an elephant, that day we had those pains, and our grandfather couldn't just get down in front of people like my little brother, he went off into the grass to be on his own. We had to keep up, the man who led us always kept telling us, we must catch up, but we asked him to wait for our grandfather.

So everyone waited for our grandfather to catch up. But he didn't. It was the middle of the day; insects were singing in our ears and we couldn't hear him moving through the grass. We couldn't see him because the grass was so high and he was so small. But he must have been somewhere

JOURNEY TO THE UNKNOWN #1
Achameleh Debela
University of Maryland University College

Humanities Note
Fine art, *Journey to the Unknown #1* by Achameleh Debela. The Ethiopian artist Achameleh Debela (1947–) works much of the time in the United States. He has earned numerous diplomas and degrees for art in Africa and the United States, including a Master of Arts degree from Morgan State University in Maryland and a Master of Fine Arts degree from the Maryland Institute of Art.

Despite Debela's years of living in the United States, his art is focused on the continuing Ethiopian struggle to maintain human dignity in the midst of extreme poverty. It also comments on the contrast between the ancient and modern ways of his people.

Journey to the Unknown #1 is suffused with tragedy. Like Gordimer, Debela depicts the suffering of people traveling in a hostile landscape and struggling to endure.

You might want to use the following questions to discuss the art:
1. Which aspect of the journey described in Gordimer's story do you feel is best captured in this artwork?
2. How do the different colors in the painting convey the progression of a journey?

20 Clarification Tell students that cotton refers to thread, which is manufactured from the fiber of the cotton plant.

21 Reading Strategy Encourage students to predict whether or not they will find the grandfather. What do they think has happened to him?

22 Discussion Ask what birds the narrator is describing, and why they are mentioned at this point in the story.

23 Reading Strategy Pause to allow students to predict what the grandmother will do.

24 Reading Strategy Encourage students to identify changes in the characters and try to determine approximately how much time has passed since the narrator and her family first entered Kruger Park.

25 Literary Focus Ask students to summarize how the tent is similar to a village and how it is different.

---

20 there inside his loose trousers and his shirt that was torn and our grandmother couldn't sew because she had no cotton. We knew he couldn't have gone far because he was weak and slow. We all went to look for him, but in groups, so we too wouldn't be hidden from each other in that grass. It got into our eyes and noses; we called him softly but the noise of the insects must have filled the little space left for hearing in his ears. We looked and looked but we couldn't find him. We stayed in that long grass all night. In my sleep I found him curled round in a place he had tramped down for himself, like the places we'd seen where the buck hide their babies.

21 When I woke up he still wasn't anywhere. So we looked again, and by now there were paths we'd made by going through the grass many times, it would be easy for him to find us if we couldn't find him. All that day we just sat and waited. Everything is very quiet when the sun is on your head, inside your head, even if you lie, like the animals, under the trees. I lay on my back and saw those ugly birds with hooked beaks and plucked necks flying round and round above us. We had passed them often where they were feeding on the bones of dead animals, nothing was ever left there **22** for us to eat. Round and round, high up and then lower down and then high again. I saw their necks poking to this side and that. Flying round and round. I saw our grandmother, who sat up all the time with my little brother on her lap, was seeing them, too.

In the afternoon the man who led us came to our grandmother and told her the other people must move on. He said, if their children don't eat soon they will die.

Our grandmother said nothing.

I'll bring you water before we go, he told her.

23 Our grandmother looked at us, me, my first-born brother, and my little brother on her lap. We watched the other people getting up to leave. I didn't believe the grass would be empty, all around us, where they had been. That we would be alone in this place, the Kruger Park, the police or the animals would find us. Tears came out of my eyes and nose onto my hands but our grandmother took no notice. She got up, with her feet apart the way she puts them when she is going to lift firewood, at home in our village, she swung my little brother onto her back, tied him in her cloth—the top of her dress was torn and her big breasts were showing but there was nothing in them for him. She said, come.

So we left the place with the long grass. Left behind. We went with the others and the man who led us. We started to go away, again.

There's a very big tent, bigger than a church or a school, tied down to the ground. I didn't understand that was what it would be, when we got there, away. I saw a thing like that the time our mother took us to the town because she heard our soldiers were there and she wanted to ask them if they knew where our father was. In that tent, people were praying and singing. This one is blue and white like that one but it's not for praying and singing, we live in it with other people who've come from our country. Sister[6] from the clinic says we're two hundred without counting the babies, and we have new babies, some were born on the way through the Kruger Park.

Inside, even when the sun is bright it's dark and there's a kind of whole village in there. Instead of houses each family has a little place closed off with sacks or cardboard from boxes—whatever we can find—to show the other families it's yours and they shouldn't come in even though there's no door and no windows and no thatch, so that if you're standing up and you're not a small child you can see into everybody's house. Some people have even made paint from ground rocks and drawn designs on the sacks.

Of course, there really is a roof—the tent is the roof, far, high up. It's like a sky. It's like a mountain and we're inside it; through the cracks paths of dust lead down, so thick you think you could climb them. The tent keeps off the rain overhead but the water comes in at the sides and in the little streets between our places—you can only move along them one person at a time—the small kids like my little brother play in the mud. You have to step over them. My little brother doesn't play. Our grandmother takes him to the clinic when the doc-

---

6. Sister: A nurse.

tor comes on Mondays. Sister says there's something wrong with his head, she thinks it's because we didn't have enough food at home. Because of the war. Because our father wasn't there. And then because he was so hungry in the Kruger Park. He likes just to lie about on our grandmother all day, on her lap or against her somewhere, and he looks at us and looks at us. He wants to ask something but you can see he can't. If I tickle him he may just smile. The clinic gives us special powder to make into porridge for him and perhaps one day he'll be all right.

When we arrived we were like him—my first-born brother and I. I can hardly remember. The people who live in the village near the tent took us to the clinic, it's where you have to sign that you've come—away, through the Kruger Park. We sat on the grass and everything was muddled. One Sister was pretty with her hair straightened and beautiful high-heeled shoes and she brought us the special powder. She said we must mix it with water and drink it slowly. We tore the packets open with our teeth and licked it all up, it stuck round my mouth and I sucked it from my lips and fingers. Some other children who had walked with us vomited. But I only felt everything in my belly moving, the stuff going down and around like a snake, and hiccups hurt me. Another Sister called us to stand in line on the veranda of the clinic but we couldn't. We sat all over the place there, falling against each other; the Sisters helped each of us up by the arm and then stuck a needle in it. Other needles drew our blood into tiny bottles. This was against sickness, but I didn't understand, every time my eyes dropped closed I thought I was walking, the grass was long, I saw the elephants, I didn't know we were away.

But our grandmother was still strong, she could still stand up, she knows how to write and she signed for us. Our grandmother got us this place in the tent against one of the sides, it's the best kind of place there because although the rain comes in, we can lift the flap when the weather is good and then the sun shines on us, the smells in the tent go out. Our grandmother knows a woman here who showed her where there is good grass for sleeping mats, and our grandmother made some

for us. Once every month the food truck comes to the clinic. Our grandmother takes along one of the cards she signed and when it has been punched we get a sack of mealie meal. There are wheelbarrows to take it back to the tent; my first-born brother does this for her and then he and the other boys have races, steering the empty wheelbarrows back to the clinic. Sometimes he's lucky and a man who's bought beer in the village gives him money to deliver it—though that's not allowed, you're supposed to take that wheelbarrow straight back to the Sisters. He buys a cold drink and shares it with me if I catch him. On another day, every month, the church leaves a pile of old clothes in the clinic yard. Our grandmother has another card to get punched, and then we can choose something: I have two dresses, two pants and a jersey,[7] so I can go to school.

The people in the village have let us join their school. I was surprised to find they speak our language; our grandmother told me, That's why they allow us to stay on their land. Long ago, in the time of our fathers, there was no fence that kills you, there was no Kruger Park between them and us, we were the same people under our own king, right from our village we left to this place we've come to.

Now that we've been in the tent so long—I have turned eleven and my little brother is nearly three although he is so small, only his head is big, he's not come right in it yet—some people have dug up the bare ground around the tent and planted beans and mealies and cabbage. The old men weave branches to put up fences round their gardens. No one is allowed to look for work in the towns but some of the women have found work in the village and can buy things. Our grandmother, because she's still strong, finds work where people are building houses—in this village the people build nice houses with bricks and cement, not mud like we used to have at our home. Our grandmother carries bricks for these people and fetches baskets of stones on her head. And so she has money to buy sugar and tea and milk and soap. The store

---

7. **jersey** *n.*: A pullover sweater or knitted shirt.

26 Discussion Have students comment on the narrator's description of her little brother's condition. What might he want to ask? Do students agree that perhaps one day he will be all right? Why or why not?

27 Discussion Ask students why the narrator keeps dreaming about Kruger Park.

28 Clarification Why does the narrator tell us that the grandmother knows how to write? What does this indicate about literacy in Mozambique?

29 Clarification Explain that Portuguese explorers established a trading post in Mozambique in the early 1500's and controlled the area for hundreds of years. When Africa was divided among several European countries in 1885, Mozambique was recognized as a Portuguese colony. Regardless of traditional borders, the Europeans established new borders for Mozambique in 1891.

30 Discussion Ask students why Gordimer has the narrator emphasize the grandmother's strength.

31 Discussion Ask students to infer what clean shoes represent to the narrator and her family.

32 Reading Strategy Read More About the Author (page 1364) to your students. Then have them relate this passage to Gordimer's experience with the BBC.

33 Literary Focus How does this exchange highlight the difference between the grandmother's perspective and the interviewer's?

34 Critical Thinking and Reading Ask students to use the narrator's observations to infer the grandmother's feelings.

35 Discussion Ask if the girl or the grandmother is more likely to be correct.

Humanities Note

Fine art, *Untitled* by Malangatana Ngwanya. Mozambican painter and poet Ngwanya (1936–) pursued an interest in art from an early age. His only formal art education was obtained in night school. A prolific artist, Ngwanya doggedly turned out paintings that eventually gained notice from the African art community. Today his work is included in many collections worldwide.

Ngwanya's choice of subjects is influenced by his African heritage but his presentation is modern. He often writes poetry to accompany his paintings and considers a poem "art written on white paper without color."

The jumbled faces and limbs in this untitled work convey a loss of individual identity, while the exaggerated eyes evoke a strong response to individual suffering. Like the people in Gordimer's story, these people appear to have been herded together as they struggle to survive.

You might use the following questions to discuss the art:

1. What feelings does this painting evoke?
2. How do your feelings about the images in the art compare or contrast with your feelings about the images in the final part of the story?

UNTITLED
Malangatana Ngwanya
Contemporary African Art Gallery, New York City

gave her a calendar she has hung up on our flap of the tent. I am clever at school and she collected advertising paper people throw away outside the store and covered my schoolbooks with it. She makes my first-born brother and me do our homework every afternoon before it gets dark because there is no room except to lie down, close together, just as we did in the Kruger Park, in our place in the tent, and candles are expensive. Our grandmother hasn't been able to buy herself a pair of shoes for church yet, but she has bought black school shoes and polish to clean them with for my first-born brother and me. Every morning, when people are getting up in the tent, the babies are crying, people are pushing each other at the taps outside and some children are already pulling the crusts of porridge off the pots we ate from last night, my first-born brother and I clean our shoes. Our grandmother makes us sit on our mats with our legs straight out

so she can look carefully at our shoes to make sure we have done it properly. No other children in the tent have real school shoes. When we three look at them it's as if we are in a real house again, with no war, no away.

Some white people came to take photographs of our people living in the tent—they said they were making a film, I've never seen what that is though I know about it. A white woman squeezed into our space and asked our grandmother questions which were told to us in our language by someone who understands the white woman's.

How long have you been living like this?

She means here? our grandmother said. In this tent, two years and one month.

And what do you hope for the future?

Nothing. I'm here.

But for your children?

I want them to learn so that they can get good jobs and money.

Do you hope to go back to Mozambique—to your own country?

I will not go back.

But when the war is over—you won't be allowed to stay here? Don't you want to go home?

I didn't think our grandmother wanted to speak again. I didn't think she was going to answer the white woman. The white woman put her head on one side and smiled at us.

Our grandmother looked away from her and spoke—There is nothing. No home.

Why does our grandmother say that? Why? I'll go back. I'll go back through that Kruger Park. After the war, if there are no bandits any more, our mother may be waiting for us. And maybe when we left our grandfather, he was only left behind, he found his way somehow, slowly, through the Kruger Park, and he'll be there. They'll be home, and I'll remember them.

Reader's Response *With whom do you identify at the end of the story, the young girl or her grandmother? Why?*

Closure and Extension

ANSWERS TO THINKING ABOUT THE SELECTION

1. Suggested response: The girl's mother and father have both disappeared; the rest of the family has lost whatever resources it once had and is starving; they are forced to become refugees.

2. Answers will differ, but students should recognize that because of the civil war, Mozambique is plagued by violence, homelessness, and starvation.

3. Suggested response: The irony of the contrast between the white Europeans' recreational safaris in Kruger Park and the refugees' journey for survival emphasizes the unjust conditions in South Africa.

4. (a) At the beginning of the story, "away" is an ideal place symbolizing relief from the violence and sadness of the narrator's current situation. (b) As the family journeys through

Interpreting

1. In what ways is the girl's family affected by the fighting going on in and around the village?
2. What can you infer about conditions in Mozambique from the narrator's experiences? Be specific.
3. Why do you think Gordimer titled her story "The Ultimate Safari"?
4. (a) What does "away" symbolize for the girl at the beginning of the story? (b) How does the meaning of "away" change as the story unfolds?
5. How is the grandmother's attitude toward the future different from the narrator's? Why do you think this is so?

Applying

6. (a) What do you think Gordimer's purpose was in writing this story? (b) Do you think she was successful? Why or why not?

ANALYZING LITERATURE

Understanding Social Context

The **social context** of a work of fiction is the set of larger social issues that provide the backdrop for the story. In "The Ultimate Safari," a young girl and her family are forced to leave their village and travel into the unknown. They are starving, and the threat of violence is ever-present. In order to fully understand their experience, readers must consider the social context, the civil war in Mozambique and the conditions in South Africa. Typically, Gordimer has revealed the harsh truth by showing how the war affects her characters on a personal level.

1. How does the journey through Kruger Park reflect the irony of social conditions in South Africa?
2. How does the author convey the horror of civil war? Be specific.
3. What do you think Gordimer is saying in this story about the future of Mozambique and the people in the refugee camps? Explain.

CRITICAL THINKING AND READING

Recognizing Point of View

Point of view is an essential element of fiction. It determines what readers can come to know about characters and events, and what they must infer. "The Ultimate Safari" is told in the first person, from the point of view of an eleven-year-old girl. When the grandmother decides to stop waiting for the grandfather and continue their journey, readers only know what the young girl sees and thinks. The thoughts and feelings of the grandmother must be inferred.

Point of view is also crucial to the author's choice of tone and language. Events that might seem remote if related in a news report take on a personal perspective as the reader comes to know the character that is narrating the story. In "The Ultimate Safari," the narrator's straightforward manner of speaking intensifies the personal connection between reader and narrator.

1. How might this story be different if it were told from the grandmother's point of view, rather than the girl's? Choose a scene from the story to illustrate your answer.
2. Imagine reading about the events of this story in a newspaper account. How would that account differ from the story told by the young girl? Give specific details in your answer.

THINKING AND WRITING

Writing from a Personal Perspective

In a recent interview, Nadine Gordimer said that the idea for the title story from *Jump and Other Stories* came from a short newspaper article that caught her imagination. Create your own fictional story based on an actual event. Use a newspaper or a television news program to find an incident on which to base your story. Then, with the facts of the event serving as a framework, create a fictional narrator who is the same age as you and tell the story from his or her personal perspective. When you revise your story, make sure you have maintained a consistent point of view.

BESSIE HEAD

1937–1986

When asked to express her politics and religion for a brief autobiography, the South African author Bessie Head wrote simply "dislike politics" and "dislike formal religion." Nevertheless, her three novels and two historical chronicles reveal her deeply felt opposition to all kinds of political oppression, including racism and the second-class status of women. They also reveal an almost religious feeling for the African earth.

Bessie Head was born of mixed black and white parentage in Pietermaritzburg, South Africa. Trained as an educator, she taught primary school for several years and then worked as a reporter in the large South African cities of Johannesburg and Cape Town. Eventually, she moved to Botswana to escape the racial policies of the South African government. These policies, called *apartheid* (ə pär´ tāt)—an Afrikaans word for "the state of being separate"—required blacks to live in segregated, poorer areas and limited their ability to acquire a good education and a well-paying job.

In her adopted country, she worked as a gardener for a village cooperative. "I find . . . that work with crops/plant life interests me deeply," she wrote. "Perhaps I like food so much because I've been poor." She was disillusioned to find, however, that even in a country run by blacks she was discriminated against as a refugee.

All of her novels describe the often painful search for personal freedom, a search based closely on her own experience. The protagonists of her books are oppressed by both whites and blacks. They are also caught up in the conflict between traditional customs and modern ways. Her first novel, *When Rain Clouds Gather* (1969) is set in a Botswana village whose name, Golema Mmidi, means "to grow crops." Like the author herself, the hero of this novel has fled the oppressive racial policies of South Africa. He discovers, however, that even in a newly independent African country all is not well. For instance, as a refugee he is mistreated by the authorities, and he observes the way in which traditional customs deprive women of equal rights.

In her second and third novels, *Maru* (1971) and *A Question of Power* (1973), Head continues to criticize injustice, whether it is perpetrated by whites or blacks. She views evil as a universal problem and not the characteristic of a particular race or people.

Head used her experience as a novelist to good effect in her nonfiction work *Serowe: Village of the Rain Wind* (1981). By skillfully combining interviews with many residents of Serowe, her own Botswana village, she provides a fascinating picture of village history and life.

Unfortunately, Bessie Head died of hepatitis just as she was achieving international recognition.

The following story, "Snapshots of a Wedding," is one of a series from *The Collector of Tales* (1977) that focuses on life in Botswana before and after independence. These stories illustrate the chaos that results when traditional and modern ways collide.

Objectives

Thematic
To understand some of the effects of rapid cultural change

Skills
1 To understand theme
2 To write from a different perspective

GUIDE FOR INTERPRETING

Commentary

Snapshots of a Wedding

Theme. Bessie Head's short story provides insights into the topic of cultural change. The understandings the story reveals are called its **theme.**

When people live through a car crash or any bad accident, they often go into shock. Symptoms of this condition include weakness, thirst, and a cold, moist skin. Blood pressure is often severely reduced. In a similar way, the rapid pace of social change in a society can result in a form of shock—an author recently coined the term "future shock" to describe such a reaction. The symptoms of this reaction are not physiological, as in a car crash, but social. They can include behavior ranging from criminality to depression and apathy.

This century has witnessed the most rapid social change in human history. People who grew up in small villages, where roosters scurried over cobblestones and farm wagons were the only vehicles, have lived to see the landing of a manned rocket on the moon.

No social change has been more dramatic than the ending of colonial rule in Africa. Traditional societies have been propelled into the modern world, with all its blessings and curses. Unfortunately, however, change that has taken place over one or two generations elsewhere—in itself a rapid development—occurred in the lightning swiftness of a few years. One result of such a breakneck pace is confusion and shock. Old ways are found side by side with the new in an uneasy coexistence.

In "Snapshots of a Wedding," Bessie Head depicts a traditional African society in the throes of change. However, rather than describing the symptoms of this process as a scientist might, she focuses on a single social event. Frame by frame these "photos" of a wedding reveal a society in conflict. Every detail—whether it reflects a person's education, dress, or body language—is telling.

Writing

Have you ever attended a party or celebration where old customs and modern ways were both in evidence? Describe the occasion and tell whether or not there was a sense of conflict between the old and the new.

Literary Focus Elicit from students what they know about the end of colonialism in Africa. First have them discuss the political dimensions of this process: when various countries won their independence, the European nations relinquished their colonies, and so forth. Then have them consider some of the social implications of this historic change. Ask them, for example, how they think this process affected people living in small villages. Then tell them that the story they are about to read illuminates the problems of social change by focusing on one event.

Writing/Prior Knowledge Divide the class into small groups and have students share their experiences with their group before writing.

ESL Teaching Strategy ESL students can share with their group experiences of rapid social change in their culture. Also, after the class has read the story, ESL students can tell their classmates about marriage customs in their society.

Teaching Tenth-Grade Students Have tenth-grade students make a chart with two columns, labeled Old and New. As they read have them fill in their chart with traditional customs and new developments described in the story.

Support Material
Teaching Portfolio
Teacher Backup, p. 1691
Usage and Mechanics Worksheet, p. 1695
Analyzing Literature Worksheet, *Understanding Theme*, p. 1696
Critical Thinking and Reading Worksheet, *Making Inferences About Tone*, p. 1697

Language Worksheet, *Appreciating Abstract and Concrete Words*, p. 1698
Selection Test, pp. 1699–1700

Presentation

Motivation/Prior Knowledge
Have students describe weddings they have attended. Ask them to compile a list of wedding customs based on this experience. Note these customs on the chalkboard. Whenever possible, have students speculate about the origin and meaning of these customs.

Purpose-Setting Question What do you think is the author's attitude toward the process of social change? Explain.

Universal Themes You might want to teach this story, which describes change within a culture, together with the excerpt from p'Bitek's *Song of Lawino,* page 1356, which deals with the conflict that can result from cultural changes.

Master Teacher Note Have students bring in photograph albums of weddings. Divide the class into small groups and have students share these albums with one another. Then hold a general class discussion about techniques of recording a wedding. Ask students: What is the best way to document a wedding, by photographing it, videotaping it, or both? Is it more important to stress formal photographs or candid shots? Ask students to keep this discussion in mind as they read Bessie Head's verbal snapshots of a wedding ceremony.

1 **Discussion** Ask students what mood the author creates with these first sentences. How do the images contribute to this mood?

2 **Discussion** Have students consider how this paragraph contrasts with the preceding one. Does the mood change? Why or why not? If so, what causes this shift in mood?

3 **Literary Focus** Point out to students that this second paragraph sounds the theme of cultural change. If the first paragraph describes what seems to be a traditional, almost timeless, setting, this paragraph stresses the ways in which the chaotic present differs from the well-ordered past.

Snapshots of a Wedding

Bessie Head

Wedding days always started at the haunting, magical hour of early dawn when there was only a pale crack of light on the horizon. For those who were awake, it took the earth hours to adjust to daylight. The cool and damp of the night slowly arose in shimmering waves like water and even the forms of the people who bestirred themselves at this unearthly hour were distorted in the haze; they appeared to be dancers in slow motion, with fluid, watery forms. In the dim light, four men, the relatives of the bridegroom, Kegoletile,[1] slowly herded an ox before them toward the yard of MmaKhudu,[2] where the bride, Neo,[3] lived. People were already astir in MmaKhudu's yard, yet for a while they all came and peered closely at the distorted fluid forms that approached, to ascertain if it were indeed the relatives of the bridegroom. Then the ox, who was a rather stupid fellow and unaware of his sudden and impending end as meat for the wedding feast, bellowed casually his early morning yawn. At this the beautiful ululating[4] of the women rose and swelled over the air like water bubbling rapidly and melodiously over the stones of a clear, sparkling stream. In between ululating all the while, the women began to weave about the yard in the wedding dance; now and then they bent over and shook their buttocks in the air. As they handed over the ox, one of the bridegroom's relatives joked:

"This is going to be a modern wedding." He meant that a lot of the traditional courtesies had been left out of the planning for the wedding day; no one had been awake all night preparing diphiri[5] or the traditional wedding breakfast of pounded meat and samp;[6] the bridegroom said he had no church and did not care about such things; the bride was six months pregnant and showing it, so there was just going to be a quick marriage ceremony at the police camp.

"Oh, we all have our own ways," one of the bride's relatives joked back. "If the times are changing, we keep up with them." And she weaved away ululating joyously.

Whenever there was a wedding the talk and gossip that preceded it were appalling, except that this time the relatives of the bride, Neo, kept their talk a strict secret among themselves. They were anxious to be rid of her; she was an impossible girl with haughty, arrogant ways. Of all her family and relatives, she was the only one who had completed her "O" levels[7] and she never failed to rub in this fact. She walked around with her nose in the air; illiterate relatives were beneath her greeting—it was done in a clever way, she just turned her head to one side and smiled to herself or when she greeted it was like an insult; she stretched her hand out palm outspread, swung it down laughing with a gesture that plainly said: "Oh, that's you!" Only

---

1. **Kegoletile** (kə gō lə tēl′)
2. **MmaKhudu** (mä ko͞o′ do͞o)
3. **Neo** (nā′ ō)
4. **ululating** (yo͞ol′ yo͞o lāt′ iŋ) *n.*: Usually howling or wailing, as at a funeral; in this case, cries or wails for a joyous occasion.

---

5. **diphiri** (də pē′ rē): A cereal-like food.
6. **samp:** Cooked mashed corn.
7. **"O" levels:** An examination for college roughly similar to the SATs in America.

her mother seemed bemused[8] by her education. At her own home Neo was waited on hand and foot. Outside her home nasty remarks were passed. People bitterly disliked conceit and pride.

"That girl has no manners!" the relatives would remark. "What's the good of education if it goes to someone's head so badly they have no respect for the people? Oh, she is not a person."

Then they would nod their heads in that fatal way, with predictions that one day life would bring her down. Actually, life had treated Neo rather nicely. Two months after completing her "O" levels she became pregnant by Kegoletile with their first child. It soon became known that another girl, Mathata,[9] was also pregnant by Kegoletile. The difference between the two girls was that Mathata was completely uneducated; the only work she would ever do was that of a housemaid, while Neo had endless opportunities before her—typist, bookkeeper, or secretary. So Neo merely smiled; Mathata was no rival. It was as though the decision had been worked out by circumstance because when the families converged on Kegoletile at the birth of the children—he was rich in cattle and they wanted to see what they could get—he of course immediately proposed marriage to Neo; and for Mathata, he agreed to a court order to pay a maintenance of R10.00[10] a month until the child was twenty years old. Mathata merely smiled too. Girls like her offered no resistance to the approaches of men; when they lost them, they just let things ride.

"He is of course just running after the education and not the manners," Neo's relatives commented, to show they were not fooled by human nature. "He thinks that since she is as educated as he is they will both get good jobs and be rich in no time . . ."

Educated as he was, Kegoletile seemed to go through a secret conflict during the year he prepared a yard for his future married life with Neo. He spent most of his free time in the yard of Mathata. His behavior there wasn't too alarming but he showered Mathata with gifts of all kinds—food, fancy dresses, shoes and underwear. Each time he came, he brought a gift and each time Mathata would burst out laughing and comment: "Ow, Kegoletile, how can I wear all these dresses? It's just a waste of money! Besides, I manage quite well with the R10.00 you give every month for the child . . ."

She was a very pretty girl with black eyes like stars; she was always smiling and happy; immediately and always her own natural self. He knew what he was marrying—something quite the opposite, a new kind of girl with false postures and acquired, grand-madame ways. And yet, it didn't pay a man these days to look too closely into his heart. They all wanted as wives, women who were big money-earners and they were so ruthless about it! And yet it was as though the society itself stamped each of its individuals with its own particular brand of wealth and Kegoletile had not yet escaped it; he had about him an engaging humility and eagerness to help and please that made him loved and respected by all who knew him. During those times he sat in Mathata's yard, he communicated nothing of the conflict he felt but he would sit on a chair with his arms spread out across its back, turn his head sideways and stare at what seemed to be an empty space beside him. Then he would smile, stand up and walk away. Nothing dramatic. During the year he prepared the huts in his new yard, he frequently slept at the home of Neo.

Relatives on both sides watched this division of interest between the two yards and one day when Neo walked patronizingly[11] into the yard of an aunt, the aunt decided to frighten her a little.

"Well aunt," she said, with the familiar careless disrespect which went with her so-called, educated, status. "Will you make me some tea? And how's things?"

The aunt spoke very quietly.

"You may not know it, my girl, but you are hated by everyone around here. The debate we have going is whether a nice young man like Kegoletile should marry bad-mannered rubbish like you. He would be

---

8. bemused (bē myoozd′) *adj*.: Muddled; preoccupied; confused.

9. Mathata (mä tä′ tə)

10. R10.00: Ten rands; a rand is the basic monetary unit of South Africa.

11. patronizingly (pā′ trə nīz′ iŋ lē) *adv*.: In a kindly but snobbish way.

9 **Discussion** Ask students whether they think the aunt has done Neo a service. If so, was it the aunt's intention to help her niece? Explain.

10 **Discussion** Have students consider why Neo's change in behavior did not result in a corresponding change in her relatives' feeling about her.

11 **Discussion** Ask students why the relatives' dislike of Neo did not diminish their pleasure in the wedding ceremonies. What does their behavior reveal about the nature of customs and rituals? For example, do customs have an *impersonal* dimension that goes beyond the personal feelings of the participants? Explain.

12 **Discussion** Have students compare and contrast this method of handing "over the bride" with the ways a bride is given in marriage in our society.

13 **Discussion** Ask students why both sets of aunts kept their faces "still and expressionless." Why is such a lack of expression important to their role in the wedding?

14 **Discussion** Ask students who traditionally pays for the wedding in our society.

15 **Discussion** Ask students how this ritual counsel reveals a traditional society's attitudes toward the roles of men and women. Does this description of a woman's role fit Neo? Why or why not?

16 **Literary Focus** Point out to students the ironic contrast between old and new ways in this passage. Ask them whether they think such old-fashioned customs should be preserved in the wedding ceremony or dropped because they no longer apply.

far better off if he married a girl like Mathata, who though uneducated, still treats people with respect."

The shock the silly girl received made her stare for a terrified moment at her aunt. Then she stood up and ran out of the house. It wiped the superior smile off her face and brought her down a little. She developed an anxiety to greet people and also an anxiety about securing Kegoletile as a husband—that was why she became pregnant six months before the marriage could take place. In spite of this, her own relatives still disliked her and right up to the day of the wedding they were still debating whether Neo was a suitable wife for any man. No one would have guessed it though with all the dancing, ululating and happiness expressed in the yard and streams of guests gaily ululated themselves along the pathways with wedding gifts precariously balanced on their heads. Neo's maternal aunts, all sedately[12] decked up in shawls, sat in a select group by themselves in a corner of the yard. They sat on the bare ground with their legs stretched out before them but they were served like queens the whole day long. Trays of tea, dry white bread, plates of meat, rice, and salad were constantly placed before them. Their important task was to formally hand over the bride to Kegoletile's maternal aunts when they approached the yard at sunset. So they sat the whole day with still, expressionless faces, waiting to fulfill this ancient rite.

Equally still and expressionless were the faces of the long column of women, Kegoletile's mater-

------

12. **sedately** (si dāt′ lē) *adv.*: Calmly; properly.

Maidens at wedding feast wearing "ikum besi" (blankets)

nal aunts, who appeared outside the yard just as the sun sank low. They walked slowly into the yard indifferent to the ululating that greeted them and seated themselves in a group opposite Neo's maternal aunts. The yard became very silent while each group made its report. Kegoletile had provided all the food for the wedding feast and a maternal aunt from his side first asked:

"Is there any complaint? Has all gone well?"

"We have no complaint," the opposite party replied.

"We have come to ask for water," Kegoletile's side said, meaning that from times past the bride was supposed to carry water in her in-laws' home.

"It is agreed to," the opposite party replied.

Neo's maternal aunts then turned to the bridegroom and counseled him: "Son, you must plow and supply us with corn each year."

Then Kegoletile's maternal aunts turned to the bride and counseled her: "Daughter, you must carry water for your husband. Beware, that at all times, he is the owner of the house and must be obeyed. Do not mind if he stops now and then and talks to other ladies. Let him feel free to come and go as he likes . . ."

The formalities over, it was now time for Kegoletile's maternal aunts to get up, ululate and weave and dance about the yard. Then, still dancing and ululating, accompanied by the bride and groom, they slowly wound their way to the yard of Kegoletile where another feast had been prepared. As they approached his yard, an old woman suddenly dashed out and chopped at the ground with a hoe. It was all only a formality. Neo would never be the kind of wife who went to the lands to plow. She already had a well-paid job in an office as a secretary. Following on this another old woman took the bride by the hand and led her to a smeared and decorated courtyard wherein had been placed a traditional animal-skin Tswana mat. She was made to sit on the mat and a shawl and kerchief were placed before her. The shawl was ceremonially wrapped around her shoulders; the kerchief tied around her head—the symbols that she was now a married woman.

Guests quietly moved forward to greet the bride. Then two girls started to ululate and dance in front of the bride. As they both turned and bent

Closure and Extension

ANSWERS TO THINKING ABOUT THE SELECTION

1. (a) Answers will differ. Students may refer to the description of the way Neo greeted her relatives, Mathata's laugh and comment whenever Kegoletile brought her a gift, Kegoletile's side ways stare in Mathata's yard, and the

over to shake their buttocks in the air, they bumped into each other and toppled over. The wedding guests roared with laughter. Neo, who had all this time been stiff, immobile, and rigid, bent forward and her shoulders shook with laughter.

The hoe, the mat, the shawl, the kerchief, the beautiful flutelike ululating of the women seemed in itself a blessing on the marriage but all the guests were deeply moved when out of the crowd, a wom-

an of majestic, regal bearing slowly approached the bride. It was the aunt who had scolded Neo for her bad manners and modern ways. She dropped to her knees before the bride, clenched her fists together and pounded the ground hard with each clenched fist on either side of the bride's legs. As she pounded her fists she said loudly:

"Be a good wife! Be a good wife!"

Reader's Response *How is this wedding similar to and different from weddings you have attended?*

THINKING ABOUT THE SELECTION

Interpreting

1. (a) Show how Head uses "snapshots"—quick moments of action or dialogue—to reveal the personalities of Neo, Mathata, Kegoletile, and Neo's "majestic" aunt. (b) How are these "snapshots" in words similar to and different from photographs?
2. (a) Contrast the mood of the story's beginning with that of the ending. (b) Why is it effective to begin with the wedding morning, recall past events, and then return to the wedding ceremony?
3. (a) What is effective about combining the following two moments at the end of the story: the accident with the dancing girls and the appearance of the "majestic" aunt? (b) How does the final moment sum up all that has gone before?
4. Do the "snapshots" of the wedding add up to a complete picture of the event? Why or why not?

Applying

5. Provide some examples, either current or historical, of the clashing of old and new. How were they resolved?

ANALYZING LITERATURE

Understanding Theme

In our century the pace of cultural change has increased from the speed of a gallop to the supersonic swiftness of a rocket. This acceleration has had a disturbing effect on traditional societies. By focusing on a particular African wedding, Bessie Head captures the

uneasy coexistence of old customs and jarring, new realities. Many of the wedding rituals are unchanged, for instance, but the joking and gossip of the wedding party reflects a shift in values and expectations.

1. How do the first two paragraphs of the story show the contrast between old ways and new?
2. (a) How do Mathata and Neo symbolize the difference between traditional and modern approaches to life? (b) In what way is Neo's education a disruptive, negative influence?
3. (a) How do the bridegroom's responses to the two women reveal a cultural conflict? (b) Explain how this unvoiced conflict is expressed in his body language. (c) How are he and his bride both victims of the shock of change?
4. What do you think is the theme of this story?

THINKING AND WRITING

Writing from a Different Perspective

Bessie Head tells this story from the point of view of an onlooker familiar with all the events leading up to the wedding. The story would be different, however, if it were told by Neo, Mathata, Kegotile, or Neo's aunt. Choose one of these characters and describe the wedding itself from his or her perspective. Imagine that you are this character and freewrite about the ceremony you are witnessing. Then draw on your notes to write a vivid account. In describing the events, use language that appeals to several different senses. However, also include an account of your thoughts and feelings. When you revise your description, make sure it reflects the concerns and attitudes of the character you have selected.

BARBARA KIMENYE

1940–

When Barbara Kimenye's sons were small, their English grandmother would send them storybooks. Sometimes the wide difference between the experiences of English and African children made it difficult for her sons to connect to the stories. Snow, for instance, was completely foreign to them. In trying to find meaningful books for her sons, Kimenye discovered that few children's books told stories related to African life. She decided to fill this void and write stories that had meaning for African children. Kimenye didn't expect that these tales would be widely read, but she was very wrong! The project that began as stories for her sons grew into a set of twelve books—the *Moses* series. These books are now standard reading fare for African schoolchildren.

In addition to pursuing her writing career, Kimenye worked for many years for His Highness the Kabaka (the monarch) of Uganda. She worked in the Ministry of Education and later served as the Kabaka's librarian. She also worked for a short time as a journalist on the staff of the newspaper *The Uganda Nation* and eventually became a well-known columnist for a Nairobi newspaper. In addition, she published works of fiction like *Kalasanda* (1965), *Kalasanda Revisited* (1966), and *The Smugglers* (1968). Although Kimenye describes most of her stories as geared toward school-age children, she reached out to a wider audience in 1992 with her book *The Money Game*.

Kimenye's native Uganda was plagued by a dictatorial government and blatant disregard for civil rights until 1986. That year, Yoweri Museveni and his National Resistance Army were victorious in their efforts to gain control of the country and restore some order and decency. Since then, progress has been steady, but scars remain. Personal property and many national shrines and monuments were destroyed, both under the old regime and at the hands of looters.

Even villages such as the one you will read about in "The Winner" were not exempt from the destruction. Kimenye recalls that in her village there was a sacred tomb, which she visited as a young woman. This tomb was immaculately kept by its wizened old caretaker. When she revisited the tomb some years later, she found it in a shambles, a casualty of looters and vandals.

Kimenye can name one bright spot in the midst of the destruction. As a great animal lover, she befriended a stray dog during the weeks of looting in Kampala. Although Kimenye fed the dog whenever it appeared, the mongrel had obviously gone too long without care and food, and looked as if it would soon die. On its final visit, the little dog surprised Kimenye by depositing a pup on the doorstep before disappearing for the last time. Kimenye kept this pup as well as another which was given to her by a veterinarian friend who knew of her love for animals.

Experiences like this show that Kimenye has a clear vision of what she values, and she shares this vision in her stories. In "The Winner," she incorporates the culture of her beloved native Uganda into a gently humorous story that expresses a universal truth.

GUIDE FOR INTERPRETING

Commentary

The Winner

Theme. Have you ever dreamed of winning the lottery? If you have, then you can identify with Pius, the protagonist of "The Winner." A man of modest means, he unexpectedly comes into a great deal of money and learns that sudden wealth is a mixed blessing. As the story unfolds, you may find yourself asking, "Who is the real winner?" and "What is the real prize?" Kimenye's suggested answers to these questions are a clue to the **theme**, or central idea, of the story.

The theme of a work may be intended to teach a lesson or simply to communicate the writer's thoughts about human nature or conditions in society. Sometimes writers reveal the theme in a direct statement by a character or the narrator. More often, writers allow readers to interpret the theme of the work by examining the events and the characters' reactions to the events. Barbara Kimenye uses both of these techniques in her story "The Winner." As you read, you will find that Kimenye invests some characters with opinions that reinforce her theme. You will also be able to infer the theme of the story by thinking about the conclusion. How does Kimenye resolve the conflict? How do her characters respond to the situations she creates?

Most people fantasize at some point about how a great deal of money could change their lives; they often think it would solve all their problems. Indeed, there are many problems for which money *can* provide a solution, but sudden wealth can also have its drawbacks. The relationship between wealth and happiness has been explored in "The Pardoner's Tale," from Chaucer's *Canterbury Tales;* Marlowe's drama of pride and power, *The Tragical History of the Life and Death of Dr. Faustus;* and Steinbeck's novel *The Pearl,* to name just a few. Contemporary poets, playwrights, and movie producers continue to address the issue. The theme of Kimenye's touching story also deals with the relative value of money. As the title suggests, her story gives us an insight into what she thinks it really means to be a winner.

Writing

Imagine you have just won ten million dollars in the lottery. How would your life change? Freewrite, exploring the pros and cons of suddenly becoming a multimillionaire.

Literary Focus Tell students that Uganda is an agricultural country; most people work to provide themselves with food and shelter rather than with money for luxuries. Ask students why such a society is a particularly suitable background for a story about the sudden acquisition of enormous wealth.

Writing/Prior Knowledge Have students brainstorm and create two lists of things that make them happy: things that *can* be purchased and things that *cannot* be purchased. Then have students share their lists in groups and make some generalizations about money and happiness.

Teaching Tenth-Grade Students Make the impact of this story immediate by asking tenth-grade students to discuss how they might feel if a relative suddenly won a fortune.

Vocabulary
Preteach the following vocabulary words:

unpretentious (un´ prē ten´ shəs) *adj.*: Making no claims to importance; simple and modest

edification (ed´ i fi kā´ shən) *n.*: Instruction or enlightenment

garrulous (gar´ ə ləs) *adj.*: Very talkative, especially about trivial matters

obscurity (əb skyoor´ ə tē) *n.*: Anonymity; being of no particular interest and going unnoticed

mesmerized (mez´ mər īzd´) *v.*: Hypnotized

audibly (ô´ dəb lē) *adv.*: Loudly enough to be heard

incredulity (in´ krə doo´ lə tē) *n.*: Disbelief

aplomb (ə pläm´) *n.*: Self-assurance; poise

formidable (fôr´ mə də bəl) *adj.*: Awe-inspiring; impressive

impetuous (im pech´ oo əs) *adj.*: Impulsive; acting quickly, suddenly

thrives (thrīvz) *v.*: Grows and prospers; improves physically

---

Critical Thinking and Reading Worksheet, *Inferring Cultural Values,* p. 1708
Selection Test, pp. 1709–1710

Spelling Tip Write the words *climb, plumber, comb,* and *limb* on the chalkboard. Read the words aloud and call students' attention to the silent *b.* Ask students to add the word *aplomb* to the list.

ESL Teaching Strategy Some students may have difficulty with the differences between this text and standard American English. (Kimenye was educated in schools established by the British.) Pair ESL students with English-proficient reading partners to facilitate the use of context clues.

The Winner

Barbara Kimenye

When Pius Ndawula won the football pools,[1] overnight he seemed to become the most popular man in Buganda.[2] Hosts of relatives converged upon him from the four corners of the kingdom: cousins and nephews, nieces and uncles, of whose existence he had never before been aware, turned up in Kalasanda by the busload, together with crowds of individuals who, despite their downtrodden appearance, assured Pius that they and they alone were capable of seeing that his money was properly invested—preferably in their own particular businesses! Also lurking around Pius's unpretentious mud hut were newspaper reporters, slick young men weighed down with cameras and sporting loud checked caps or trilbies set at conspicuously jaunty angles, and serious young men from Radio Uganda who were anxious to record Pius's delight at his astonishing luck for the edification of the Uganda listening public.

The rest of Kalasanda were so taken by surprise that they could only call and briefly congratulate Pius before being elbowed out of the way by his more garrulous relations. All, that is to say, except Pius's greatest friend Salongo, the custodian of the Ssabalangira's tomb. He came and planted himself firmly in the house, and nobody attempted to move him. Almost blind, and very lame, he had tottered out with the aid of a stout stick. Just to see him arrive had caused a minor sensation in the village, for he hadn't left the tomb for years. But recognizing at last a chance to house Ssabalangira's remains in a state befitting his former glory, made the slow, tortuous journey worthwhile to Salongo.

Nantondo hung about long enough to have her picture taken with Pius. Or rather, she managed to slip beside him just as the cameras clicked, and so it was that every Uganda newspaper, on the following day, carried a front-page photograph of "Mr. Pius Ndawula and his happy wife," a caption that caused Pius to shake with rage and threaten legal proceedings, but over which Nantondo gloated as she proudly showed it to everybody she visited.

"Tell us, Mr. Ndawula, what do you intend to do with all the money you have won . . . ?"

"Tell us, Mr. Ndawula, how often have you completed pools coupons . . . ?"

"Tell us . . . Tell us . . . Tell us . . . "

Pius's head was reeling under this bombardment of questions, and he was even more confused by Salongo's constant nudging and muttered advice to "Say nothing!" Nor did the relatives make things easier. Their persistent clamoring for his attention, and the way they kept shoving their children under his nose, made it impossible for him to think, let alone talk.

It isn't at all easy, when you have lived for sixty-five years in complete obscurity, to adjust yourself in a matter of hours to the role of a celebrity, and the strain was beginning to tell.

Behind the hut—Pius had no proper kitchen—gallons of tea were being boiled, whilst several of the female cousins were employed in ruthlessly hacking down the bunches of *matoke* from his

---

1. football pools: A kind of lottery based on the performance of soccer teams.

2. Buganda (bo͞o gän′ dä): An area of southern Uganda, on the northern shore of Lake Victoria.

meager plantains[3] to cook food for everybody. One woman—she had introduced herself as Cousin Sarah—discovered Pius's hidden store of banana beer, and dished it out to all and sundry as though it were her own. Pius had become very wary of Cousin Sarah. He didn't like the way in which she kept loudly remarking that he needed a woman about the place, and he was even more seriously alarmed when suddenly Salongo gave him a painful dig in the ribs and muttered, "You'll have to watch that one—she's a sticker!"

Everybody who came wanted to see the telegram that announced Pius's win. When it had arrived at the Ggombolola Headquarters—the postal address of everyone residing within a radius of fifteen miles—Musisi had brought it out personally, delighted to be the bearer of such good tidings. At Pius's request he had gone straightaway to tell Salongo, and then back to his office to send an acknowledgment on behalf of Pius to the pools firm, leaving the old man to dream rosy dreams. An extension of his small coffee shamba,[4] a new roof on his house—or maybe an entirely new house—concrete blocks this time, with a veranda perhaps. Then there were hens. Salongo and he had always said there was money in hens these days, now that the women ate eggs and chicken; not that either of them agreed with the practice. Say what you liked, women who ate chicken and eggs were fairly asking to be infertile! That woman welfare officer who came around snooping occasionally, tried to say it was all nonsense, that chicken meat and eggs made bigger and better babies. Well, they might look bigger and better, but nobody could deny that they were fewer! Which only goes to show.

But news spreads fast in Africa—perhaps the newspapers have contacts in the pools offices. Anyway, before the telegram had even reached Pius, announcements were appearing in the local newspapers, and Pius was still quietly lost in his private dreams when the first batch of visitors arrived. At first he was at a loss to understand what was happening. People he hadn't seen for years and only recognized with difficulty fell upon him with cries of joy. "Cousin Pius, the family are delighted!" "Cousin Pius, why have you not visited us all this time?"

Pius was pleased to see his nearest and dearest gathered around him. It warmed his old heart once more to find himself in the bosom of his family, and he welcomed them effusively. The second crowd to arrive were no less well received, but there was a marked coolness on the part of their forerunners.

However, as time had gone by and the flood of strange faces had gained momentum, Pius's shamba had come to resemble a political meeting. All to be seen from the door of the house was a turbulent sea of white kanzus and brilliant busutis,[5] and the house itself was full of people and tobacco smoke.

The precious telegram was passed from hand to hand until it was reduced to a limp fragment of paper with the lettering partly obliterated: not that it mattered very much, for only a few members of the company could read English.

"Now, Mr. Ndawula, we are ready to take the recording." The speaker was a slight young man wearing a checked shirt. "I shall ask you a few questions, and you simply answer me in your normal voice." Pius looked at the leather box with its two revolving spools, and licked his lips. "Say nothing!" came a hoarse whisper from Salongo. The young man steadfastly ignored him, and went ahead in his best BBC manner.[6] "Well, Mr. Ndawula, first of all let me congratulate you on your winning the pools. Would you like to tell our listeners what it feels like suddenly to find yourself rich?" There was an uncomfortable pause, during which Pius stared mesmerized at the racing spools and the young man tried frantically to span the gap by asking, "I mean, have you any plans for the future?" Pius swallowed audibly, and opened his mouth to

---

3. plantains (plan´ tinz) *n*.: Tropical plants with broad flat leaves. The banana-like fruit, called *matoke*, is served cooked like a vegetable.
4. shamba (shäm´ bä) *n*.: A field or garden for a particular crop; a small plantation.

5. kanzus (kän´ zo͞oz) . . . **busutis** (bo͞o so͞o´ tēz): Long, flowing robes, the first worn by men, the second by women.
6. BBC manner: Polite and polished style of the British Broadcasting Corporation's reporters.

8 **Discussion** Ask students what reasons Pius has for being wary of Cousin Sarah.

9 **Discussion** Have students suggest what Salongo might mean when he calls Cousin Sarah "a sticker."

10 **Clarification** Explain that most of the houses in Buganda, where this story is set, are made of mud, cement, or concrete blocks with corrugated iron roofs.

11 **Discussion** Ask if these are the plans of a man who has become a millionaire. Encourage students to support their answers with reasons.

12 **Critical Thinking and Reading** Have students determine what Pius's and Salongo's views indicate about the values of their culture.

13 say something, but shut it again when Salongo growled, "Tell him nothing!"

The young man snapped off the machine, shaking his head in exasperation. "Look here, sir, all I want you to do is to say something—I'm not asking you to make a speech! Now, I'll tell you what. I shall ask you again what it feels like suddenly to come into money, and you say something like 'It was a wonderful surprise, and naturally I feel very pleased'—and will you ask your friend not to interrupt! Got it? Okay, off we go!"

The machine was again switched on, and the man brightly put his question, "Now, Mr. Ndawula, what does it feel like to win the pools?" Pius swallowed, then quickly chanted in a voice all off key, "It was a wonderful surprise and naturally I feel very happy and will you ask your friend not to interrupt!" The young man nearly wept. This happened to be his first assignment as a radio interviewer, and it looked like it would be his last. He switched off the machine and mourned his lusterless future, groaning. At that moment Cousin Sarah caught his eye. "Perhaps I can help you," she said. "I am Mr. Ndawula's cousin." She made this pronouncement in a manner that suggested Pius had no others. The young man brightened considerably. "Well, madam, if you could tell me something about Mr. Ndawula's plans, I would be most grateful." Cousin Sarah folded her arms across her imposing bosom, and when the machine again started up, she was off. Yes, Mr. Ndawula was very

14 happy about the money. No, she didn't think he had any definite plans on how to spend it—with all these people about he didn't have time to think. Yes, Mr. Ndawula lived completely alone, but she was prepared to stay and look after him for as long as he needed her. Here a significant glance passed between the other women in the room, who clicked their teeth and let out long "Eeeeeehs!" of incredulity. Yes, she believed she was Mr. Ndawula's nearest living relative by marriage . . .

Pius listened to her confident aplomb with growing horror, while Salongo frantically nudged him and whispered, "There! What did I tell you! That woman's a sticker!"

Around three in the afternoon, *matoke* and tea were served, the *matoke,* on wide fresh plantain leaves, since Pius owned only three plates, and the tea in anything handy—tin cans, old jars, etc.—because he was short of cups too. Pius ate very little but he was glad of the tea. He had shaken hands with so many people that his arm ached, and he was tired of the chatter and the comings and goings in his house of all these strangers. Most of all he was tired of Cousin Sarah, who insisted on treating him like an idiot invalid. She kept everybody else at bay, as far as she possibly could, and when one woman plonked a sticky fat baby on his lap, Cousin Sarah dragged the child away as though it were infectious. Naturally, a few cross words were exchanged between Sarah and the fond mother, but by this time Pius was past caring.

Yosefu Mukasa and Kibuka called in the early evening, when some of the relatives were departing with effusive promises to come again tomorrow. They were both alarmed at the weariness they saw on Pius's face. The old man looked utterly worn out, his skin gray and sickly. Also, they were a bit taken aback by the presence of Cousin Sarah, who pressed them to take tea and behaved in every respect as though she were mistress of the house. " believe my late husband knew you very well, sir," she told Yosefu. "He used to be a Miruka chief in Buyaga County. His name was Kivumbi." "Ah yes," Yosefu replied, "I remember Kivumbi very well indeed. We often hunted together. I was sorry to hear of his death. He was a good man." Cousin Sarah shrugged her shoulders. "Yes, he was a good man. But what the Lord giveth, He also taketh away." Thus was the late Kivumbi dismissed from the conversation.

Hearing all this enabled Pius to define the exact relationship between himself and Cousin Sarah and even by Kiganda standards it was virtually nonexistent, for the late Kivumbi had been the stepson of one of Pius's cousins.

"Your stroke of luck seems to have exhausted you, Pius," Kibuka remarked, when he and Yosefu were seated on the rough wooden chairs brought forth by Cousin Sarah.

Salongo glared at the world in general and snarled, "Of course he is exhausted! Who wouldn't be with all these scavengers collected to pick his bones?" Pius hushed him as one would a child

DRINKING WATER
Rosemary Karuga
Contemporary African
Art Gallery, New York City

17 **Reading Strategy** Ask students if Pius's attitude and behavior are consistent with their predictions.

Humanities Note

Fine art, *Drinking Water* by Rosemary Karuga. African artist Rosemary Karuga (1928–   ) was born in Kenya, and she studied art at the School of Art, Makerere University, Uganda. Karuga's works include both painting and sculpture but she is best known for her collages, works that are composed of cut or torn bits of colored paper or other material that is adhered to a flat surface to form an image. She was attracted to this technique when she studied mosaics in her art history classes at Makerere University.

Drinking Water is an example of Karuga's skillful collage work. Karuga often depicts ordinary scenes like this; she finds inspiration for subjects in her surroundings, the suburban area outside of Nairobi, Kenya, where she lives.

You might want to use the following questions to discuss the art:

1. What is the mood of this painting? Explain why you do or do not think it is consistent with the mood of the story.
2. What do the clothes, posture, and surroundings of the woman in the painting reveal about her personality?
3. How might the woman in the painting be like Cousin Sarah?

"No, no, Salongo. It is quite natural that my family should gather round me at a time like this. Only I fear I am perhaps a little too old for all this excitement."

Salongo spat expertly through the open doorway, narrowly missing a group of guests who were preparing to bed down, and said, "That woman doesn't think he's too old. She's out to catch him. I've seen her type elsewhere!"

Yosefu's mouth quirked with amusement at the thought that "elsewhere" could only mean the Ssabalangira's tomb, which Salongo had guarded for the better part of his adult life. "Well, she's a fine woman," he remarked. "But see here, Pius," he went on, "don't be offended by my proposal, but wouldn't it be better if you came and stayed with us at Mutunda for tonight? Miriamu would love to have you, and you look as though you need a good night's rest, which you wouldn't get here—those relatives of yours outside are preparing a fire and are ready to dance the night away!"

"I think that's a wonderful idea!" said Cousin

18 Discussion What does this indicate about Pius's state of mind? What other clues to Pius's state of mind can you find?

19 Discussion How do Miriamu's words and actions reveal her personality?

20 Reading Strategy Have students predict what the news will be.

21 Clarification Tell students that although the exchange rate varies, this news is as dramatic as being told that the prize is one hundred dollars instead of many thousands.

22 Reader's Response Ask: Would you laugh if this happened to you? What does this tell you about Pius?

Sarah, bouncing in to remove the tea cups. "You go with Mr. Mukasa, Cousin Pius. The change will do you as much good as the rest. And don't worry about your home—I shall stay here and look after things." Pius hesitated. "Well, I think I shall be all right here—I don't like to give Miriamu any extra work. . . ." Salongo muttered. "Go to Yosefu's. You don't want to be left alone in the house with that woman—there's no knowing what she might get up to . . . !" "I'll pack a few things for you, Pius," announced Cousin Sarah and bustled off before anything more could be said, pausing only long enough to give Salongo a look that was meant to wither him on the spot.

So Pius found himself being driven away to Mutunda in Yosefu's car, enjoying the pleasant sensation of not having to bother about a thing. Salongo too had been given a lift to as near the tomb as the car could travel, and his wizened old face was contorted into an irregular smile, for Pius had promised to help him build a new house for the Ssabalangira. For him the day had been well spent, despite Cousin Sarah.

Pius spent an enjoyable evening with the Mukasas. They had a well-cooked supper, followed by a glass of cold beer as they sat back and listened to the local news on the radio. Pius had so far relaxed as to tell the Mukasas modestly that he had been interviewed by Radio Uganda that morning, and when Radio Newsreel was announced they **18** waited breathlessly to hear his voice. But instead of Pius, Cousin Sarah came booming over the air. Until that moment the old man had completely forgotten the incident of the tape recording. In fact, he had almost forgotten Cousin Sarah. Now it all came back to him with a shiver of apprehension. Salongo was right. That woman did mean business! It was a chilling thought. However, it didn't cause him to lose any sleep. He slept like a cherub,[7] as if he hadn't a care in the world.

Because he looked so refreshed in the morning, Miriamu insisted on keeping him at Mutunda

for another day. "I know you feel better, but after seeing you yesterday, I think a little holiday with us will do you good. Go home tomorrow, when the excitement has died down a bit," she advised.

Soon after lunch, as Pius was taking a nap in a chair on the veranda, Musisi drove up in the Land Rover, with Cousin Sarah by his side. Miriamu came out to greet them, barely disguising her curiosity about the formidable woman about whom she had heard so much. The two women sized each other up and decided to be friends.

Meanwhile, Musisi approached the old man. "Sit down, son." Pius waved him to a chair at his side. "Miriamu feeds me so well it's all I can do to keep awake."

"I am glad you are having a rest, sir." Musisi fumbled in the pocket of his jacket. "There is another telegram for you. Shall I read it?" The old man sat up expectantly and said, "If you'll be so kind."

Musisi first read the telegram in silence, then he looked at Pius and commented, "Well, sir, I'm afraid it isn't good news."

"Not good news? Has somebody died?"

Musisi smiled. "Well, no. It isn't really as bad as that. The thing is, the pools firm say that owing to an unfortunate oversight they omitted to add, in the first telegram, that the prize money is to be shared among three hundred other people."

Pius was stunned. Eventually he murmured, "Tell me, how much does that mean I shall get?"

"Three hundred into seventeen thousand pounds won't give you much over a thousand shillings."[8]

To Musisi's astonishment, Pius sat back and chuckled. "More than a thousand shillings!" he said. "Why, that's a lot of money!"

"But it's not, when you expected so much more!"

"I agree. And yet, son, what would I have done with all those thousands of pounds? I am getting past the age when I need a lot."

Miriamu brought a mat onto the veranda and

---

7. slept like a cherub: An expression meaning "slept peacefully," using the image of a cherub, or child angel, to convey innocence and freedom from worries.

8. pounds . . . shillings: Ugandan currency, distinct from British pounds and shillings.

he and Cousin Sarah made themselves comfortble near the men. "What a disappointment!" cried Miriamu, but Cousin Sarah sniffed and said, "I agree with Cousin Pius. He wouldn't know what to do with seventeen thousand pounds, and the family would be hanging round his neck forevermore!"

At mention of Pius's family, Musisi frowned. "I should warn you, sir, those relatives of yours have made a terrific mess of your *shamba*—your plantains have been stripped—and Mrs. Kivumbi here," nodding at Sarah, "was only just in time to prevent them digging up your sweet potatoes!"

"Yes, Cousin Pius," added Sarah. "It will take us some time to put the *shamba* back in order. They've trodden down a whole bed of young beans."

"Oh, dear," said Pius weakly. "This is dreadful news."

"Don't worry. They will soon disappear when I tell them there is no money, and then I shall send for a couple of my grandsons to come and help us do some replanting." Pius could not help but admire the way Sarah took things in her stride.

Musisi rose from his chair. "I'm afraid I can't stay any longer, so I will go now and help Cousin Sarah clear the crowd, and see you tomorrow to take you home." He and Sarah climbed back into the Land Rover and Sarah waved energetically until the vehicle was out of sight.

"Your cousin is a fine woman," Miriamu told Pius, before going indoors. Pius merely grunted, but for some odd reason he felt the remark to be a compliment to himself.

All was quiet at Pius's home when Musisi brought him home next day. He saw at once that his *shamba* was well nigh wrecked, but his drooping spirits quickly revived when Sarah placed a mug of steaming tea before him, and sat on a mat at his feet, explaining optimistically how matters could be remedied. Bit by bit he began telling her what he planned to do with the prize money, ending with, "Of course, I shan't be able to do everything now, especially since I promised Salongo something for the tomb."

Sarah poured some more tea and said, "Well, I think the roof should have priority. I noticed last night that there are several leaks. And whilst we're about it, it would be a good idea to build another room on and a small outside kitchen. Mud and wattle⁹ is cheap enough, and then the whole place can be plastered. You can still go ahead and extend your coffee. And as for hens, well, I have six good layers at home, as well as a fine cockerel. I'll bring them over!"

Pius looked at her in silence for a long time. She is a fine looking woman, he thought, and that blue *busuti* suits her. Nobody would ever take her for a grandmother—but why is she so anxious to throw herself at me?

"You sound as if you are planning to come and live here," he said at last, trying hard to sound casual.

Sarah turned to face him and replied, "Cousin Pius, I shall be very frank with you. Six months ago my youngest son got married and brought his wife to live with me. She's a very nice girl, but somehow I can't get used to having another woman in the house. My other son is in Kampala, and although I know I would be welcome there, he too has a wife, and three children, so if I went there I wouldn't be any better off. When I saw that bit about you in the paper, I suddenly remembered— although I don't expect you to—how you were at my wedding and so helpful to everybody. Well, I thought to myself, here is somebody who needs a good housekeeper, who needs somebody to keep the leeches off, now that he has come into money. I came along right away to take a look at you, and I can see I did the right thing. You do need me." She hesitated for a moment, and then said, "Only you might prefer to stay alone . . . I'm so used to having my own way, I never thought about that before."

Pius cleared his throat. "You're a very impetuous woman," was all he could find to say.

A week later, Pius wandered out to the tomb and found Salongo busily polishing the Ssabalangira's weapons. "I thought you were dead," growled the custodian, "it is so long since you

---

9. **wattle** *n*.: Sticks woven together and used as a framework to support the grasses and mud used to thatch a roof.

23 Reading Strategy Have students explain why they did or did not expect this reaction from Cousin Sarah.

24 Discussion Have students contrast Pius's reaction to this news with his reaction to the news about his prize money. Ask them to identify what this suggests about his priorities.

25 Discussion Have students describe how Pius's attitude toward Cousin Sarah is changing.

26 Clarification Kampala is the capital of Uganda; it is located on the shores of Lake Victoria.

27 Discussion What does this speech indicate about Cousin Sarah?

28 **Discussion** Ask students what Salongo's gift of bananas signifies.

ESL Teaching Strategy Ask ESL students to relate to the class any folk tales or legends from their native cultures that address the relationship between money (or material possessions) and happiness.

Humanities Note

Fine art, *The Birds* by Rosemary Karuga. Karuga (1928–) worked for many years before gaining recognition for her fine paintings, sculptures, and collages. In 1989 she gave a one-woman show at the French Cultural Centre in Nairobi, Kenya, and in 1990 she participated in a show that focused on important African contemporary art at the Studio Museum of Harlem in New York City.

Although the style of *The Birds* is far from representational, Karuga captures the image of a group of birds with a natural feeling that demonstrates her close observation of the subjects she depicts.

You may want to use the following questions to discuss the art:
1. How does this work suggest community and simplicity?
2. How does the collage reflect the tone of "The Winner"?

came here—but then, this tomb <u>thrives</u> on neglect. Nobody cares that one of Buganda's greatest men lies here."

"I have been rather busy," murmured Pius. "But I didn't forget my promise to you. Here! I've brought you a hundred shillings, and I only wish it could have been more. At least it will buy a few cement blocks."

Salongo took the money and looked at it as if it were crawling with lice. Grudgingly he thanked Pius and then remarked, "Of course, you will find life more expensive now that you are keeping a woman in the house."

"I suppose Nantondo told you," Pius smiled sheepishly.

"Does it matter who told me?" the custodian replied. "Anyway, never say I didn't warn you. Next thing she'll want will be a ring marriage!"

Pius gave an uncertain laugh. "As a matter of fact, one of the reasons I came up here was to invite you to the wedding— it's next month."

Salongo carefully laid down the spear he was rubbing upon a piece of clean barkcloth and stared at his friend as if he had suddenly grown another head. "What a fool you are! And all this stems from your scribbling noughts and crosses[10] on a bit of squared paper! I knew it would bring no good! At your age you ought to have more sense. Well, all I can advise is that you run while you still have the chance!"

For a moment Pius was full of misgivings. Was he, after all, behaving like a fool? Then he thought of Sarah, and the wonders she had worked with his house and his *shamba* in the short time they had been together. He felt reassured. "Well, I'm getting married, and I expect to see you at both the church and the reception, and if you don't appear, I shall want to know the reason why!" He was secretly delighted at the note of authority in his voice, and Salongo's face was the picture of astonishment. "All right," he mumbled, "I shall try and come. Before you go, cut a bunch of bananas to take back to your good lady, and there might be some cabbage ready at the back. I suppose I've got to hand it to her! She's the real winner!"

28

---

10. noughts (nôts) **and crosses:** Zeros and *x*'s used to mark the spaces on the football pools card.

THE BIRDS
Rosemary Karuga
Contemporary African Art Gallery, New York City

Reader's Response *Who do you think is the real winner in this story? Is there more than one? Explain.*

Closure and Extension

ANSWERS TO THINKING ABOUT THE SELECTION

1. The relatives and reporters want to use Pius's good fortune to improve their own situations. Some students may suggest that the relatives pay attention to Pius because they want to share the wealth and that the reporters pay attention to him because he can give them a good story.

2. Answers will differ. Students might respond that Salongo doesn't want anything for himself. He is motivated by concern for the Ssabalangira's tomb and for Pius.

3. Suggested response: (a) Initially Pius welcomes his relatives; he is happy to be surrounded by family. (b) By the end of the day, he is exhausted by the

attention and glad to spend the nigh with true friends.

4. Suggested response: (a) At first, Piu is somewhat intimidated by Cousi Sarah. He is not sure how they are re lated and feels that she is pushy an meddlesome. (b) Pius's attitude to ward Cousin Sarah starts to chang when she shows little concern abou the change in his fortune. He begin to admire Sarah because her action

THINKING ABOUT THE SELECTION

Interpreting

1. Why do relatives and reporters descend on Pius when he wins the football pools?
2. How is Salongo different from the rest of Pius's relatives and friends?
3. (a) What is Pius's initial attitude toward his horde of relatives? (b) How does his attitude change?
4. (a) How does Pius feel about Cousin Sarah at the beginning of the story? (b) Why do his feelings change?
5. Why does Pius chuckle at the news that he has won only a thousand shillings instead of seventeen thousand pounds?

Applying

6. Pius's attitude toward Cousin Sarah undergoes a dramatic change. How important or accurate are first impressions? Explain.

ANALYZING LITERATURE

Understanding Theme

The **theme** of a work gives the reader some insight, reveals a truth, or teaches a lesson. The theme may be directly stated by one of the characters, or even expressed in the writer's own words. More often, though, the reader infers what the writer wants to say by examining the events in the plot and the actions and attitudes of the characters.

In "The Winner," Barbara Kimenye makes a statement about the relationship between money and happiness. Pius's windfall doesn't bring him happiness; it brings nothing but trouble. Only when he loses the potential fortune is he free to discover a prize of real value.

1. How does the news of Pius's sudden wealth change his relationship with his relatives and with society?
2. Which events in the story turn out differently than you expected? Explain.
3. (a) What does Salongo mean when he says that Cousin Sarah is the "real" winner? (b) Do you agree or disagree? Explain.
4. What do you think is the theme of the story? Explain.

CRITICAL THINKING AND READING

Inferring Cultural Values

Knowing the **cultural values,** the social standards or principles of a group of people, can give insight into otherwise confusing behavior. In some cultures, it is considered polite to maintain eye contact while having a conversation. Yet in other cultures, making eye contact while being spoken to would be considered a sign of disrespect. By knowing a person's cultural preferences with regard to eye contact, you can avoid misunderstanding his or her behavior.

Similarly, being able to infer cultural values from a story can enrich your understanding by helping you to understand the characters' actions. In "The Winner," Pius is inundated with dozens of relatives that he hasn't seen or heard from in years; clearly they are influenced by his newly acquired wealth. These relatives disrupt Pius's previously quiet and peaceful life, yet Pius welcomes them; he doesn't turn them away. Why not? Family connections are obviously important in Pius's culture. His behavior and attitude stem from a manner of thinking and acting that is shared and accepted by most of the people in his culture.

1. What cultural values can you infer from the descriptions of Salongo and his vocation?
2. Why do you think everyone wants to see and handle the telegram that announces Pius's win?
3. Do you think Pius's philosophical attitude toward the change in the amount of the prize money stems from personal or cultural values? Why do you think as you do?

THINKING AND WRITING

Exploring Personal Values

You have probably imagined what it would be like to win a fortune in the lottery. Now imagine that you suddenly discover, as Pius did, that the prize is $100, instead of thousands or millions of dollars. Freewrite, exploring possible responses to this sudden reversal. Be sure to include thoughts about how your personal values, as well as your cultural values, might affect your feelings. Then use your notes to write a brief narrative that describes how you respond to the situation. In revising your narrative, make sure that a reader will be able to infer the values that motivated your response.

(continued from bottom of page)

doesn't win a fortune after all; another is the arrival of Cousin Sarah, who seems unbearably meddlesome and pushy at first, but who later shows herself to be competent and sincere.

3. (a) Answers will differ. Suggested response: Salongo means that although Pius won the football pools, Cousin Sarah has benefited more than any other character involved in the situation. (b) Answers will differ, but students should realize that Pius has won because he is far happier with the smaller cash prize and with Sarah as his wife.
4. Answers will differ. Students will probably relate the theme to the value of love and friendship versus the value of money.

ANSWERS TO CRITICAL THINKING AND READING

1. The description of Salongo suggests that his advanced age and his position as keeper of the hero's tomb are respected and revered in the community.
2. Suggested response: Even though many of the relatives cannot read it, they recognize it as the official document announcing Pius's win. Everyone is awed and impressed by the physical representation of his good fortune.
3. Answers will differ, but most students will suggest that although cultural values lead Pius to place more emphasis on human relationships than on material possessions, his attitude incorporates personal virtues as well.

Challenge Will Sarah and Salongo remain at odds with each other, come to tolerate each other, or become fast friends? Support your opinion with examples from the story.

THINKING AND WRITING

Publishing Student Writing Allow classroom time for students to work in small groups to read their completed narratives aloud and then to compare their narratives to "The Winner."

Writing Across the Curriculum Ask students to write an essay comparing and contrasting the traditional culture of Uganda with that of one other African country.

---

show that she is capable, sensible, and caring.
5. Answers will differ. Students may feel that he laughs from relief; the fortune had become a burden that was destroying his peaceful existence.
6. Answers will differ. Some students may feel that Pius's experience is typical; first impressions are not necessarily accurate. Others may suggest that Pius's experience with Cousin

Sarah is the exception to the rule; first impressions are almost always correct. Encourage students to support their opinions with examples drawn from their own experience.

ANSWERS TO ANALYZING LITERATURE

1. Suggested response: Until his sudden windfall, Pius had lived for 65 years

in "complete obscurity," practically forgotten by society. The change in his financial situation leads many of his relations to consider him to be a more important person than they had previously considered him to be. His sudden wealth does not change the feelings of those who value him for himself instead of his money.
2. Suggested response: One event that turns out differently is that Pius

OUSMANE SEMBÈNE

1923–

"You are aspiring to be a writer? You will never be a good one so long as you don't defend a cause." So wrote Ousmane Sembène (sem be´ nā) in his first novel, *Le Docker noir* (*The Black Dock Worker,* 1956). The words are uttered by a fictional character, but they also voice Sembène's own philosophy as a writer. His works reveal an intense commitment to political and social change.

Ousmane Sembène was born in Ziguinchor, Senegal, in 1923. Expelled from school at the age of fourteen, he worked as a fisherman, a plumber, a bricklayer, and an apprentice mechanic before serving with the French army in Europe during World War II. After the war Sembène returned briefly to Senegal, where he joined African railway workers in a strike for better wages and working conditions. His experiences with the striking workers contributed to his growing political consciousness.

He returned to France as a stowaway on a ship and found a job as a dockworker in Marseilles. Eventually, he became a trade union leader and joined the French Communist party. He also taught himself to read and write in French and began writing his first novel.

Sembène's early works included the semi-autobiographical *Le Docker noir,* followed by *O Pays mon beau peuple!* (*O My Country, My Beautiful People,* 1957), and *Les Bouts de bois de Dieu* (*God's Bits of Wood,* 1960), which many consider his masterpiece. In these and subsequent novels, Sembène tries to awaken the consciousness of his people to a wide array of social problems. *Les Bouts,* for example, is a call to action against colonialist oppression. Through its striking and dynamic female characters, *Les Bouts* also addresses sexism in African society. *Le Docker noir* is a scathing exposé of political corruption. *O Pays* explores the conflict between tradition and modernism in African society.

In the preface to his novel *L'Harmattan* (*The Storm,* 1964), Sembène compares himself to the traditional African *griots.* A *griot* was a professional storyteller who kept the people's history alive by narrating tales from the past. According to Sembène, the griot was also the "'witness' of every event. It was he who captured, and laid out before everyone under the tree of talk the deeds and mannerisms of each." In much the same way, Sembène aims to "capture and lay out," to expose, the evils that weigh down modern African society.

In the early 1960's Sembène took up filmmaking, hoping to reach an even wider audience than he was able to reach in print. (See the feature on Sembène as filmmaker, page 1402.) His films reflect the same social and political concerns as his books. His prize-winning film *Mandabi* (*The Money Order,* 1968), based on his short novel of the same name, established Sembène's international reputation as a filmmaker. Since then, he has continued in his role as observer, critic, and chronicler of African society, producing novels and films despite censorship by the Senegalese government.

"Tribal Scars" comes from an early short story collection, *Voltaique* (1962). It is a tale of oppression and resistance, of fear and courage. Like a modern-day griot, Sembène tells a tale from out of Africa's past—a tale that has a meaning and relevance for contemporary society.

GUIDE FOR INTERPRETING

Tribal Scars

Commentary

Historical Context. Do you think you would speak, think, and act exactly as you do if you had lived during the Civil War?—probably not. Your attitudes and actions would be affected by the events and customs of the period. Just like real people, fictional characters generally act and think in ways that are consistent with the time in which they live.

The historical events, traditions, and practices that furnish the background (though not necessarily the setting) for a work of fiction provide a **historical context.** Knowing the historical context of a work contributes to the reader's understanding of the plot, the characters' attitudes, actions, and motives, and the theme of the work.

Ousmane Sembène's "Tribal Scars" takes place approximately two hundred years ago on the West African coast—an area infamous for the bloody and violent raids that provided human "merchandise" for the slave trade. Initiated in the early seventeenth century by white Europeans, the slave trade grew to mammoth proportions as the demand for cheap labor in the Americas intensified.

The slave trade was a system of interdependent parts—links in a chain of greed, persecution, oppression, and terror. The captains of the slave ships often became quite wealthy transporting their human cargo from Africa to the Americas. The white slave traders in the Americas took the Africans off the ships and sold them to the highest bidder, often tearing families apart in order to make the highest possible profit. The white slave owners created the tremendous demand for black labor; they constantly needed to replace slaves that had been shot, beaten, or worked to death. The slave hunters, usually Africans, raided villages up and down the African coast, terrorizing, capturing, and selling their fellow Africans. The white traders functioned as middlemen between the African slave hunters and the captains of the slave ships.

"Tribal Scars" relates the experiences of one West African family caught in the nightmare of the slave trade. Knowing the historical context helps us to understand the symbolism of the scars, and the conflict created when Amoo, the protagonist, must make a distinction between surviving and living.

Writing

The protagonist of Sembène's story makes a difficult choice. Think about choices you have made in your life or choices made by the characters in your favorite movie or book. List some of the choices that come to mind. Which were easy decisions and which were difficult? In many choices, something is gained and something is let go. What was gained in each choice on your list and what was let go?

Literary Focus To help students understand the concept of historical context, ask them to imagine a teenager from one hundred years ago suddenly thrust into their world. Ask them what aspects of the present would have to be explained to such a person.

Writing/Prior Knowledge Before students write about difficult choices, have them brainstorm for ideas about situations that can lead to such choices: for example, conflicts between friends, peer pressure, money problems, and so on.

ESL Teaching Strategy Have ESL students research and report to the class on the historical context in the place of their heritage two hundred years ago.

Teaching Tenth-Grade Students Help tenth-grade students relate to Amoo's dilemma by asking them to suggest movies or television programs in which the protagonists face difficult decisions. Assist students in distinguishing between the practical and philosophical problems of each dilemma.

Vocabulary

Preteach the following vocabulary words:

stolid (stäl´ id) *adj.*: Not showing much emotion or sensitivity; not excitable

endeavor (en dev´ ər) *n.*: A serious attempt

vehemently (vē´ əm ənt lē) *adv.*: Intensely; with passion

lithely (līth´ lē) *adv.*: With easy grace and agility

entice (en tīs´) *v.*: Lure; attract by holding out hope of a reward

spurned (spʉrnd) *v.*: Rejected with contempt and disdain

wan (wän) *adj.*: Faint, feeble, or weak

gamboling (gam´ bəl iŋ) *v.*: Jumping about in play; frolicking

distraught (di strôt´) *adj.*: Extremely troubled

antiseptic (an tə sep´ tik) *adj.*: Cleansing and able to fight infection

---

Support Material

Teaching Portfolio
Teacher Backup, p. 1711
Grammar in Action, *Using Adverbs,* p. 1715
Usage and Mechanics Worksheet, p. 1717

Vocabulary Check, p. 1718
Analyzing Literature Worksheet, *Understanding Historical Context,* p. 1719
Critical Thinking and Reading Worksheet, *Examining Dilemmas,* p. 1720
Selection Test, pp. 1721–1722

Spelling Tip Write the word *antiseptic* on the board and point out that it is made up of the prefix *anti-*, meaning against, and the root *sepsis*, meaning rotting. Remind students that the prefix *ante-* looks similar to *anti-* but means "before," as in anteroom and antecedent. Ask them to identify other words that illustrate the difference between *anti-* and *ante-*.

Tribal Scars or The Voltaique[1]

Ousmane Sembène

translated by Len Ortzen

In the evenings we all go to Mane's place, where we drink mint tea and discuss all sorts of subjects, even though we know very little about them. But recently we neglected the major problems such as the ex-Belgian Congo, the trouble in the Mali Federation, the Algerian War and the next UNO meeting[2]—even women, a subject which normally takes up about a quarter of our time. The reason was that Saer, who is usually so stolid and serious, had raised the question, "Why do we have tribal scars?"

(I should add that Saer is half Voltaique, half Senegalese;[3] but he has no tribal scars.)

Although not all of us have such scars on our faces, I have never heard such an impassioned discussion, such a torrent of words, in all the time we have been meeting together at Mane's. To hear us, anyone would have thought that the future of the whole continent of Africa was at stake. Every evening for weeks the most fantastic and unexpected explanations were put forward. Some of us went to neighboring villages and even farther afield to consult the elders and the griots,[4] who are known as the "encyclopedias" of the region, in an endeavor to plumb the depths of this mystery, which seemed buried in the distant past.

Saer was able to prove that all the explanations were wrong.

Someone said vehemently that "it was a mark of nobility"; another that "it was a sign of bondage." A third declared that "It was decorative—there was a tribe which would not accept a man or a woman unless they had these distinctive marks on the face and body." One joker told us with a straight face that: "Once upon a time, a rich African chief sent his son to be educated in Europe. The chief's son was a child when he went away, and when he returned he was a man. So he was educated, an intellectual, let us say. He looked down on the tribal traditions and customs. His father was annoyed by this, and wondered how to bring him back into the royal fold. He consulted his chief counselor. And one morning, out on the square and in front of the people, the son's face was marked with cuts."

No one believed that story, and the teller was reluctantly obliged to abandon it.

---

1. The Voltaique (väl tĭ ēk´): A person from Upper Volta—present-day Burkina Faso in western Africa.
2. ex-Belgian Congo . . . UNO meeting: The first three were political topics that concerned Africans at the time this story was written. UNO stands for United Nations Organization, now simply called the United Nations.
3. half Voltaique . . . Senegalese: Descended from the west-African peoples of the former Upper Volta and Senegal.

---

4. griots (grē´ ōz) *n.*: Storytellers, respected as the guardians of tradition and culture.

Someone else said: "I went to the French Institute and hunted around in books, but found nothing. However, I learned that the wives of the gentlemen in high places are having these marks removed from their faces; they go to Europe to consult beauticians. For the new rules for African beauty disdain the old standards of the country; the women are becoming Americanized. . . . And as the trend develops, tribal scars lose their meaning and importance and are bound to disappear."

We talked about their diversity, too; about the variety even within one tribe. Cuts were made on the body as well as on the face. This led someone to ask: "If these tribal scars were signs of nobility, or of high or low caste,[5] why aren't they ever seen in the Americas?"

"Ah, we're getting somewhere at last!" exclaimed Saer, who obviously knew the right answer to his original question, or thought he did.

"Tell us then. We give up," we all cried.

"All right," said Saer. He waited while the man on duty brought in glasses of hot tea and passed them round. The room became filled with the aroma of mint.

"So we've got around to the Americas," Saer began. "Now, none of the authoritative writers on slavery and the slave trade has ever mentioned tribal scars, so far as I know. In South America, where fetishism and witchcraft as practiced by slaves still survive to this day, no tribal scars have ever been seen. Neither do Negroes living in the Caribbean have them, nor in Haiti, Cuba, the Dominican Republic nor anywhere else. So we come back to Black Africa before the slave trade, to the time of the old Ghana Empire, the Mali and the Gao empires, and the cities and kingdoms of the Hausa, Bournou, Benin, Mossi and so on. Now, not one of the travelers who visited those places and wrote about them mentions this practice of tribal scars. So where did it originate?"

By now everyone had stopped sipping hot tea; they were all listening attentively.

"If we study the history of the slave trade ob-jectively we find that the dealers sought blacks who were strong and healthy and without blemish. We find too, among other things, that in the markets here in Africa and on arrival overseas the slave was inspected, weighed and evaluated like an animal. No one was inclined to buy merchandise which had any blemish or imperfection, apart from a small mark which was the stamp of the slave-trader; but nothing else was tolerated on the body of the beast. For there was also the preparation of the slave for the auction market; he was washed and polished—whitened, as they said then—which raised the price. How, then, did these scars originate?"

We could find no answer. His historical survey had deepened the mystery for us.

"Go on, Saer, you tell us," we said, more eager than ever to hear his story of the origin of tribal scars.

And this is what he told us:

The slave-ship *African* had been anchored in the bay for days, waiting for a full load before sailing for the Slave States. There were already more than fifty black men and thirty Negro women down in the hold. The captain's agents were scouring the country for supplies. On this particular day only a few of the crew were on board; with the captain and the doctor, they were all in the latter's cabin. Their conversation could be heard on deck.

Amoo bent lower and glanced back at the men who were following him. He was a strong, vigorous man with rippling muscles, fit for any manual work. He gripped his ax firmly in one hand and felt his long cutlass[6] with the other, then crept stealthily forward. More armed men dropped lithely over the bulwarks,[7] one after the other. Momutu, their leader, wearing a broad-brimmed hat, a blue uniform with red facings, and high black boots, signaled with his musket to surround the galley. The ship's cooper had appeared from nowhere and tried to escape by jumping into the sea. But the blacks who

---

5. **caste:** In some cultures the social class that is determined by birth and defines one's lifelong place in society.

6. **cutlass** (kut´ ləs) *n.:* A short, thick, curving sword.
7. **bulwarks** (bool´ wərks) *n.:* The parts of a ship's side that extend above the deck, forming a wall around it.

3 **Reading Strategy** What can you infer from the speaker's choice of words about his attitude toward the practice of having the scars removed?

4 **Discussion** Ask students if this statement predisposes them to believe Saer's story or not.

5 **Enrichment** Fetishism is the worship of inanimate objects believed to have magical powers.

6 **Reading Strategy** Ask students to identify the main idea of the information Saer is presenting.

7 **Literary Focus** Call students' attention to the shift in the time period. Saer's tale is being told in the historical context of the slave trade.

8 **Literary Focus** Point out to students that this is not typical clothing for an African of the period. What does Momutu's European clothing reveal about him?

9 **Reading Strategy** Ask students to predict what Momutu and his men intend to do with the slaves they take from the ship.

10 **Enrichment** Tell students that money was of little use to most Africans of this period. Thus, European slave traders paid for slaves through barter, offering to trade goods that Africans might find useful or attractive.

11 **Reading Strategy** What clues led you to expect this behavior from Momutu?

12 **Discussion** Ask students to imagine why Momutu might have blown up the ship instead of simply killing the captain and remaining crew.

13 **Discussion** Ask students to discuss what this fact reveals about Amoo's character.

had remained in the canoes seized him and speared him to death.

Fighting had broken out aboard the *African*. One of the crew tried to get to close quarters with the leading attackers and was struck down. The captain and the remaining men shut themselves in the doctor's cabin. Momutu and his band, armed with muskets and cutlasses, besieged the cabin, firing at it now and again. Meanwhile the vessel was being looted. As the shots rang out, the attackers increased in number; canoes left the shore, glided across the water to the *African*, and returned laden with goods.

Momutu called his lieutenants to him—four big fellows armed to the teeth. "Start freeing the prisoners and get them out of the hold."

"What about him?" asked his second-in-command, nodding towards Amoo who was standing near the hatchway.

"We'll see about him later," replied Momutu. "He's looking for his daughter. Get the hold open—and don't give any arms to the local men. Take the lot!"

The air was heavy with the smell of powder and sweat. Amoo was already battering away at the hatch-covers, and eventually they were broken open with axes and a ram.

Down in the stinking hold the men lay chained together by their ankles. As soon as they had heard the firing they had begun shouting partly with joy, partly from fright. From between-decks, where the women were, came terrified cries. Among all this din, Amoo could make out his daughter's voice. Sweat pouring from him, he hacked at the panels with all his strength.

"Hey, brother, over here!" a man called to him. "You're in a hurry to find your daughter?"

"Yes," he answered, his eyes glittering with impatience.

After many hours of hard work the hold was wide open and Momutu's men had brought up the captives and lined them up on deck, where the ship's cargo for barter had been gathered together: barrels of spirits, boxes of knives, crates containing glassware, silks, parasols and cloth. Amoo had found his daughter, Iome, and the two were standing a little apart from the rest. Amoo knew very well that Momutu had rescued the captives only in order to sell them again. It was he who had lured the *African*'s captain into the bay.

"Now we're going ashore," Momutu told them. "I warn you that you are my prisoners. If anyone tries to escape or to kill himself, I'll take the man next in the line and cut him to pieces."

The sun was sinking towards the horizon and the bay had become a silvery, shimmering sheet of water; the line of trees along the shore stood out darkly. Momutu's men began to put the booty into canoes and take it ashore. Momutu, as undisputed leader, directed operations and gave orders. Some of his men still stood on guard outside the cabin, reminding those inside of their presence by discharging their muskets at the door every few minutes. When the ship had been cleared, Momutu lit a long fuse that ran to two kegs of gunpowder. The captain, finding that all was quiet, started to make his way up top; as he reached the deck, a ball from a musket hit him full in the chest. The last canoe pulled away from the ship, and when they were half-way to the shore the explosions began; then the *African* blew up and sank.

By the time everything had been taken ashore it was quite dark. The prisoners were herded together and a guard set over them, although their hands and feet were still tied. Throughout the night their whisperings and sobs could be heard punctuated now and then by the sharp crack of a whip. Some distance away, Momutu and his aides were reckoning up their haul, drinking quantities of spirits under the starry sky as they found how well they had done for themselves.

Momutu sent for Amoo to join them.

"You'll have a drink with us, won't you?" said Momutu when Amoo approached with his sleeping daughter on his back (but they only appeared as dim shadows).

"I must be going. I live a long way off and the coast isn't a safe place now. I've been working for you for two months," said Amoo, refusing a drink.

"Is it true that you killed your wife rather than let her be taken prisoner by slave-traders?" asked one of the men, reeking of alcohol.

Grammar in Action

Adverbs Adverbs modify verbs, adjectives, or other adverbs. They add to the meanings of the words they modify and make the meaning of the sentence more precise and sometimes more vivid. Without adverbs, a sentence would be less specific. Notice how Ousmane Sembène uses vivid adverbs to expand the meanings of the words they modify.

"Days and weeks slipped by *peacefully*."

"The frightened animals *instinctively* fled *madly* into the forest. . . ."

The adverbs *peacefully* and *madly* contrast the scene in the village before and after the arrival of the slavers. Compare Sembène's sentences with the following sentences to see the effect of using adverbs.

Days and weeks slipped by.

The frightened animals fled into the forest.

The sentences without the adverbs are not as specific; they do not convey as vivid an image as the sentences that use adverbs.

HARRIET TUBMAN SERIES
NUMBER 9
Jacob Lawrence
Hampton University Museum,
Hampton, Virginia

14 Discussion Ask students to imagine why Amoo is polite to Momutu, a man he despises.

15 Literary Focus Ask students why Amoo's concerns seem odd to Momutu and his men. Would they seem strange in our own historical context?

16 Reading Strategy Ask students to predict if Momutu will let Amoo and his daughter go.

Humanities Note

Fine art, *Harriet Tubman Series Number 9,* Jacob Lawrence (1917–). Lawrence says of his style, "When the subjects are strong, I believe simplicity is the best way of treating them." His paintings, often produced in a series, chronicle the history and struggle of African Americans.

"Harriet Tubman dreamed of freedom . . ." is panel nine of thirty-one panels Lawrence painted for the *Harriet Tubman Series* in the years 1938–1940. Like "Tribal Scars," this painting offers a moving perspective into the effects of slavery, especially on the human spirit.

You might use the following questions to discuss the art:
1. Which aspect of this painting strikes you most forcibly?
2. Why do you think Lawrence chose bright colors and patterns for the slaves' clothing?
3. How do you think Jacob Lawrence would respond to the story Saer tells in "Tribal Scars"? Explain.

"Ahan!"[8]

"And you've risked your life more than once to save your daughter?"

"She's my daughter! I've seen all my family sold into slavery one after another, and taken away into the unknown. I've grown up with fear, fleeing with my tribe so as not to be made a slave. In my tribe there are no slaves, we're all equal."

"That's because you don't live on the coast," put in a man, which made Momutu roar with laughter. "Go on, have a drink! You're a great fighter. I saw how you cut down that sailor. You're good with an ax."

"Stay with me. You're tough and you know what you want," said Momutu, passing the keg of spirits to him. Amoo politely declined a drink. "This is our work," Momutu went on. "We scour the grasslands, take prisoners and sell them to the whites. Some captains know me, but I entice others to this bay and some of my men lure the crew off the ship. Then we loot the ship and get the prisoners back again. We kill any whites left on board. It's easy work, and we win all round. I've given you back your daughter. She's a fine piece and worth several iron bars."

(Until the seventeenth century on the west coast of Africa slaves were paid for with strings of cowries[9] as well as with cheap goods; later, iron bars took the place of cowries. It is known that elsewhere in other markets iron bars have always been the medium of exchange.)

"It's true that I've killed men," said Amoo, "but never to take prisoners and sell them as slaves. That's your work, but it isn't mine. I want to get back to my village."

"He's an odd fellow. He thinks of nothing but his village, his wife and his daughter." ⌐15

Amoo could only see the whites of their eyes. He knew that these men would not think twice of seizing himself and his daughter and selling them to the first slave-trader encountered. He was not made in their evil mold.

"I wanted to set off tonight."

"No," snapped Momutu. The alcohol was beginning to take effect, but he controlled himself and softened his voice. "We'll be in another fight⌐16 soon. Some of my men have gone with the remaining whites to collect prisoners. We must capture them. Then you'll be free to go."

---

8. **"Ahan!":** An affirmative exclamation.

9. **cowries** (kou´ rēz) *n.*: Brightly colored, glossy shells, formerly used as currency in parts of Africa and Asia.

Student Activity 1. Find three other sentences in "Tribal Scars" in which Sembène uses vivid adverbs. Explain how the use of each adverb increases the precision and vividness of the sentence.

Student Activity 2. Add vivid adverbs to the following sentences to enrich and expand the meaning of each sentence. Compare your sentences with your classmates' to see how the choice of the adverb can affect the mood and feeling of the sentences.
1. Iome cried out to her father.
2. Momutu's men waited for the other group.
3. The villagers gathered around Amoo and Iome.

Student Activity 3. Write an original paragraph using at least five vivid adverbs.

17 **Clarification** Tell students that this gives some idea of the number of Africans wrenched from their homes during the era of the slave trade. There are not many strong Africans to be found along the coast because the best have already been taken away by slave traders.

18 **Clarification** Point out that Amoo and Momutu are doing an elaborate dance of deception. Momutu is disguising his true intentions, and Amoo is disguising his suspicions of Momutu.

"I'm going to get her to lie down and have some sleep. She's had a bad time," said Amoo, moving away with his daughter.

"Has she had something to eat?"

"We've both eaten well. I'll be awake early."

The two disappeared into the night; but a shadowy figure followed them.

"He's a fine, strong fellow. Worth four kegs."

"More than that," added another. "He'd fetch several iron bars and some other stuff as well."

"Don't rush it! After the fight tomorrow we'll seize him and his daughter too. She's worth a good bit. We mustn't let them get away. There aren't many of that kind to be found along the coast now."

A soothing coolness was coming in from the sea. Night pressed close, under a starry sky. Now and then a scream of pain rose sharply, followed by another crack of the whip. Amoo had settled down with Iome some distance away from the others. His eyes were alert, though his face looked sleepy. During the dozen fights he had taken part in to redeem his daughter, Momutu had been able to judge his qualities, his great strength and supple body. Three times three moons ago, slave-hunters had raided Amoo's village and carried off all the able-bodied people. He had escaped their clutches because that day he had been out in the bush. His mother-in-law, who had been spurned because of her elephantiasis,[10] had told him the whole story.

When he had recovered his daughter from the slave-ship, his tears had flowed freely. Firmly holding the girl's wrist and clutching the bloodstained ax in his other hand, his heart had beat fast. Iome, who was nine or ten years old, had wept too.

He had tried to soothe away her fears. "We're going back to the village. You mustn't cry, but you must do what I tell you. Do you understand?"

"Yes, father."

"Don't cry any more. It's all over now! I'm here with you."

And there in the cradle of the night, Iome lay asleep with her head on her father's thigh. Amoo

---

10. **elephantiasis** (el´ ə fən tī´ ə sis) *n*.: A disease that causes the enlargement of certain body parts, especially the legs.

unslung his ax and placed it close at hand. Sitting with his back against a tree, his whole attention was concentrated on the immediate surroundings. At the slightest rustle, his hand went out to grasp his weapon. He dozed a little from time to time.

Even before a wan gleam had lighted the east, Momutu roused his men. Some of them were ordered to take the prisoners and the loot to a safe place. Amoo and Iome kept out of the way. The girl had deep-set eyes and was tall for her age; her hair was parted in the middle and drawn into two plaits which hung down to her shoulders. She clung to her father's side; she had seen her former companions from the slave-ship, and although she may not have known the fate in store for them, the sound of the whips left her in no doubt as to their present state.

"They'll wait for us farther on," said Momutu, coming across to Amoo. "We mustn't let ourselves be surprised by the whites' scouting party. Why are you keeping your child with you? You could have left her with one of my men."

"I'd rather keep her with me. She's very frightened," answered Amoo, watching the prisoners and escort moving off.

"She's a beautiful girl."

"Yes."

"As beautiful as her mother?"

"Not quite."

Momutu turned away and got the rest of his men, about thirty, on the move. They marched in single column. Momutu was well known among slave-traders, and none of them trusted him. He had previously acted as an agent for some of the traders, then had become a "master of language" (interpreter), moving between the forts and camps where the captured Negroes were held.

They marched all that morning, with Amoo and his daughter following in the rear. When Iome was tired, her father carried her on his back. He was well aware that a watch was being kept on him. The men ahead of him were coarse, sorry-looking creatures; they looked ridiculous, trailing their long muskets. They began to leave the grasslands behind and soon were among tall trees where flocks of vultures perched. No one spoke. All that could be heard was the chattering of birds and now and again a distant, echoing howling. Then they reached the forest, humid and hostile, and Momutu called a halt; he dispersed his men and told them to rest.

"Are you tired, brother?" one of them asked Amoo. "And what about her?"

Iome raised her thick-lashed eyes towards the man, then looked at her father.

"She's a bit tired," said Amoo, looking round for a resting-place. He saw a fallen trunk at the foot of a tree and took Iome to it. The man set to keep watch on them remained a little distance away.

Momutu had a few sweet potatoes distributed to the men, and when this meager meal was over he went to see Amoo.

"How's your daughter?"

"She's asleep," said Amoo, who was carving a doll out of a piece of wood.

"She's a strong girl," said Momutu, sitting down beside him and taking off his broad-brimmed hat. His big black boots were all muddy. "We'll have a rest and wait for them here. They're bound to come this way."

Amoo was more and more on his guard. He nodded, but kept his eyes on Iome in between working at the piece of wood, which was gradually taking shape.

"After that you'll be free to go. Do you really want to go back to your village?"

"Yes."

"But you haven't anybody left there," said Momutu, and without waiting for Amoo to reply went on, "I once had a village, too, on the edge of a forest. My mother and father lived there, many relatives—a whole clan! We had meat to eat and sometimes fish. But over the years, the village declined. There was no end to lamentations. Ever since I was born I'd heard nothing but screams, seen mad flights into the bush or the forest. You go into the forest, and you die from some disease; you stay in the open, and you're captured to be sold into slavery. What was I to do? Well, I made my choice. I'd rather be with the hunters than the hunted."

Amoo, too, knew that such was life. You were never safe, never sure of seeing the next day dawn.

But what he did not understand was the use made of the men and women who were taken away. It was said that the whites used their skins for making boots.

They talked for a long time, or rather Momutu talked without stopping. He boasted of his exploits and his drinking bouts. As Amoo listened, he became more and more puzzled about Momutu's character. He was like some petty warlord, wielding power by force and constraint. Eventually, after what seemed a very long time to Amoo, a man came to warn the chief that the whites were approaching. Momutu gave his orders—kill them all, and hold their prisoners. In an instant the forest fell silent; only the neutral voice of the wind could be heard.

The long file of black prisoners came into view, led by four Europeans each armed with two pistols and a culverin.[11] The prisoners, men and women, were joined together by a wooden yoke bolted round the neck and attached to the man in front and the one behind. Three more Europeans brought up the rear, and a fourth, probably ill, was being carried in a litter[12] by four natives.

A sudden burst of firing from up in the trees echoed long and far. This was followed by screams and confused fighting. Amoo took advantage to fell the man guarding him and, taking his daughter by the hand, slipped away into the forest.

They crossed streams and rivers, penetrating ever deeper into the forest but heading always to the south-east. Amoo's knife and ax had never been so useful as during this time. They traveled chiefly at night, never in broad daylight, avoiding all human contact.

Three weeks later they arrived at the village—about thirty huts huddled together between the bush and the source of a river. There were few inhabitants about at that hour of the day; besides, having been frequently drained of its virile members, the village was sparsely populated. When

---

11. culverin (kul´ vər in) *n.*: A long-barreled gun used by soldiers before the invention of the rifle.
12. litter (lit´ ər) *n.*: A stretcher for carrying the sick or wounded.

Amoo and Iome reached the threshold of his mother-in-law's hut, the old woman limped out and her cries drew other people, many of them feeble. They were terrified at first, but stood uttering exclamations of joy and surprise when they saw Amoo and Iome. Tears and questions mingled as they crowded round. Iome's grandmother gathered her up and took her into the hut like a most precious possession, and the girl replied to her questions between floods of tears.

The elders sent for Amoo to have a talk and tell them of his adventures.

"All my life, and since before my father's life," said one of the oldest present, "the whole country has lived in the fear of being captured and sold to the whites. The whites are barbarians."

"Will it ever end?" queried another. "I have seen all my children carried off, and I can't remember how many times we have moved the village. We can't go any farther into the forest . . . there are the wild beasts, diseases . . . "

"I'd rather face wild beasts than slave hunters," said a third man. "Five or six rains ago, we felt safe here. But we aren't any longer. There's a slave camp only three-and-a-half days' march from the village."

They fell silent; their wrinkled, worn and worried faces bore the mark of their epoch.[13] They discussed the necessity to move once again. Some were in favor, others pointed out the danger of living in the heart of the forest without water, the lack of strong men, and the family graves that would have to be abandoned. The patriarch, who had the flat head and thick neck of a degenerate,[14] proposed that they should spend the winter where they were but send a group to seek another suitable site. It would be sheer madness to leave without having first discovered and prepared a place to go to. There were also the customary sacrifices to be made. Finally, all the men agreed on this course of action. During the short time they would remain there, they would increase cultivation and hold all the cattle in common, keeping the herd in an enclosure. The patriarch was of the opinion that the old women could be used to keep a watch on the village.

---

13. **epoch** (ep′ ək) *n.*: A period of time marked by noteworthy events.
14. **patriarch** (pā′ trē ark) **. . . degenerate** (dē jen′ ər it): The leader of the village showed signs of physical abnormality.

SAD CARNIVAL
Fikile (Magadlela)
De Beers Centenary Art Collection

Primary Source

The scarring that Amoo inflicts on his daughter not only keeps her free but bestows on her a mark of African identity. Many of the characters in Sembène's novels struggle to achieve such an identity, which can be realized through language as well as through visible scars. In the critical anthology *A Celebration of Black and African Writing* (Oxford, 1975), Martin T. Bestman describes this struggle as follows:

[Sembène's] imaginative world revolves around the search for an African identity. His main characters fight not only for political and economic

The return of Amoo and Iome had put new life into them. They started working communally, clearing and weeding the ground and mending the fences. The men set off for work together and returned together. The women busied themselves too; some did the cooking while others kept a look-out for any surprise visit by "procurers." (Procurers were native agents, recognizable by their uniform in the colors of the nation they worked for; they were commonly called "slave-hunters.") No one looked in the direction of the sea without a feeling of apprehension.

The rains came, and the fertile, bountiful earth gave life to the seeds that had been sown. Although the villagers went about their work with no visible sign of worry or fear, they were always on the alert for an attack, knowing it was bound to come sooner or later.

Amoo shared his hut with Iome and always slept with a weapon close at hand. Even a harmless gust of wind sent the girl into a panic. Amoo put his whole heart into his work; Iome, by general agreement, was allowed to rest as much as possible, and she gradually recovered from her ordeal. . . .

Days and weeks slipped by peacefully. The narrow, cultivated strips of land, wrenched from the grip of nature after long struggles, were giving promise of a good harvest. The cassava plants were in bud; the people were beginning to get in stocks of palm-oil, butter, beans and honey, in fact everything they would need in the new village. The prospecting party returned, having discovered an excellent site at the foot of the mountains but above the grasslands, and not far from a running stream. The soil was good, there was plenty of pasture, and the children would be safe from the "procurers."

Everyone was very pleased with the prospect. The patriarch named the day for departure, and the feeling of safety in the near future led to a relaxation of precautions. Fires, previously forbidden during the hours of darkness for fear of betraying the village, now glowed at night; laughter rang out, and children dared to wander out of sight of their parents, for the adults were thinking only of the departure. They could count the days now. In the council hut there were discussions on which was the favorable sign for the move. Each and everyone was attending to the household gods, the totems[15] and the family graves.

Yet it was not a sacred day, but one like any other. The sun was shining brightly, the tender green leaves of the trees were rustling in the wind, the clouds frolicked in the sky, the humming-birds were gaily seeking food, and the monkeys especially were gamboling in the trees. The whole village was enjoying this glorious day, the kind that can tempt a traveler to stay awhile, a long while.

And it happened on that particular day! On that day the "procurers" suddenly appeared. The frightened animals instinctively fled madly into the forest; men, women and children gave terrified screams on hearing the firing and scattered in panic, having but one thought, to flee to the only retreat open to them—the forest.

Amoo, grasping his ax, pushed Iome and her grandmother before him. But the old, handicapped woman could make only slow progress. They had fled between the huts and the enclosure and gained the edge of the village, and then Amoo had come face to face with one of Momutu's lieutenants. Amoo was the quicker, and struck him down. But now a whole pack was in pursuit.

Amoo went deeper into the forest, where the thick undergrowth and overhanging branches made progress even slower. Still, if Amoo had been alone, he could have escaped. But he could not abandon his child. He thought of his wife. He had killed her so that she should not be taken. His mother-in-law reminded him of his wife. To abandon the old woman would be abandoning his wife. Time and again, the old woman stopped to get her breath; her thick leg was becoming ever weightier to drag along. Amoo helped her as best he could, while Iome stuck to his side, not saying a word.

An idea came to Amoo. He stopped, took Iome gently by the chin and gazed at her for a long time, for what seemed an eternity. His eyes filled with tears.

---

15. **totems** (tōt′ əmz) *n*.: Images of animals or natural objects that are regarded as the ancestors of a group.

27 **Discussion** Why does the return of Amoo and Iome put new life into the villagers? How had they been feeling before? How do they feel after the return?

28 **Reading Strategy** Ask students to recall a personal experience involving anxious and apprehensive anticipation. What effect did the tension have on them? What effect do they think it has on the villagers?

29 **Discussion** Ask students if they think anyone ever completely recovers from such an ordeal. What lasting effects might Iome experience?

30 **Reading Strategy** Ask students to predict the consequences of the villagers' relaxed vigilance.

31 **Enrichment** Ask students to identify the mood evoked by this description.

32 **Reading Strategy** How does the mood of this paragraph contrast with that of the preceding one? Why is it especially painful when something disastrous happens on a beautiful day?

33 **Discussion** Why can't Amoo abandon his daughter and mother-in-law?

---

independence but also for cultural and linguistic identity. They deplore the up-rooting of African culture by centuries of colonial domination. . . . But the preservation of a culture demands the promotion of a national language.

A language identifies a homogeneous social group and constitutes a corner-stone of a people's culture. Literature—a crystallization of the emotions, experiences, joys, sufferings, hopes, and aspirations of a people—forms an integral part of a national culture. A genuine African rebirth requires the development of indigenous, national languages—for it is paradoxical that Africans who advocate a cultural revival should write in the languages of their erstwhile dominators. Even old Niakoro, in *God's Bits of Wood*, is conscious of the problem. That is why she deplores the neglect of African languages, adding that the enthusiasm the young show in learning the white man's language generates their inferiority complex and contributes to their cultural alienation. . . .

"Mother," he said, "we can't go any farther. Ahead, there's death for all three of us. Behind, there's slavery for Iome and me."

"I can't go a step farther," said the old woman, taking her granddaughter by the hand. She raised a distraught face to Amoo.

"Mother, Iome can escape them. You both can. Your skin is no longer any use, the whites can't make boots with it."

"But if Iome's left alone, she'll die. And what about you?"

"You go free. What happens to me is my affair."

"You're not going to kill us?" exclaimed the woman.

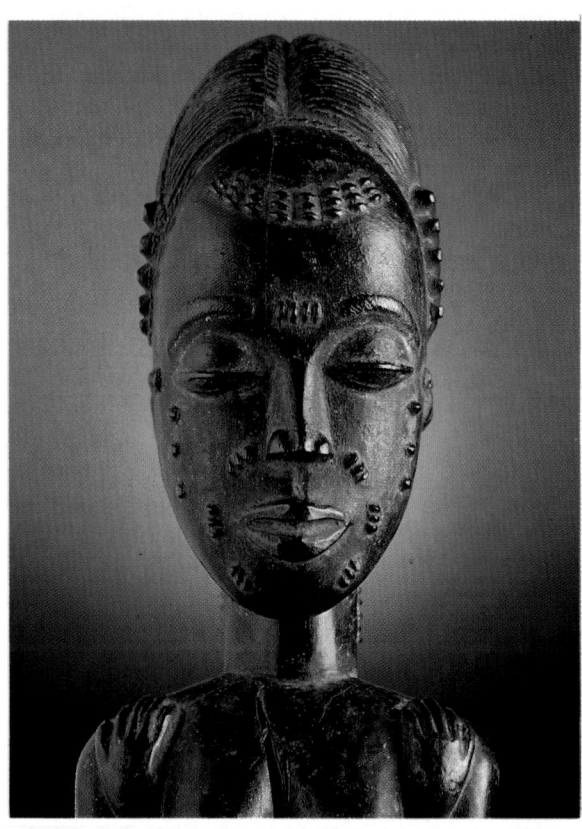

BAOULÉ STATUETTE OF A WOMAN
Côte d'Ivoire (Ivory Coast)
Musée des Arts Africains et Oceaniens

"No, mother. But I know what to do so that Iome stays free. I must do it quickly. They're getting near, I can hear their voices."

A thunderbolt seemed to burst in his head and the ground to slip away from him. He took a grip on himself, seized his knife and went to a particular bush (the Wolof call it *Bantamare*; its leaves have antiseptic properties), wrenched off a handful of the large leaves and returned to the other two, who had been watching him wonderingly.

His eyes blurred with tears as he looked at his daughter. "You mustn't be afraid, Iome."

"You're not going to kill her as you did her mother?" exclaimed his mother-in-law again.

"No. Iome, this is going to hurt, but you'll never be a slave. Do you understand?"

The child's only answer was to stare at the blade of the knife. She remembered the slave-ship and the bloodstained ax.

Swiftly, Amoo gripped the girl between his strong legs and began making cuts all over her body. The child's cries rang through the forest; she screamed till she had no voice left. Amoo just had time to finish before the slave-hunters seized him. He had wrapped the leaves all round the girl. With the other captured villagers, Amoo was taken down to the coast. Iome returned to the village with her grandmother, and thanks to the old woman's knowledge of herbs Iome's body soon healed; but she still bore the scars.

Months later, the slave-hunters returned to the village; they captured Iome but let her go again. She was worth nothing, because of the blemishes on her body.

The news spread for leagues around. People came from the remotest villages to consult the grandmother. And over the years and the centuries a diversity of scars appeared on the bodies of our ancestors.

And that is how our ancestors came to have tribal scars. They refused to be slaves.

Reader's Response *Do you agree or disagree with Amoo's decision to kill his wife and disfigure Iome rather than let them be captured by the slave hunters? Explain.*

THINKING ABOUT THE SELECTION

Interpreting

1. Why won't Amoo drink with Momutu after freeing Iome from the slave ship?
2. Why does Amoo keep his daughter with him constantly while they are with the slave traders?
3. (a) How do you think Amoo's actions come in conflict with his personality? (b) Identify specific instances that illustrate the conflict.
4. (a) Did Amoo love his wife? (b) How do you know?
5. At the end of the story, which characters do you think are "living" and which are "surviving"? Explain.
6. (a) What do the tribal scars represent for Saer? (b) How do you think he feels about people having them removed? Explain.

Applying

7. Why do you think Saer researched the history of tribal scars and shared it with his companions?

ANALYZING LITERATURE

Understanding Historical Context

Context is the whole situation or set of circumstances relevant to a particular person, thing, or event. In literature, one type of context is **historical context,** that is, the historical period and events that provide the background for a story or novel. Familiarity with the historical context of a piece enriches our understanding of the characters, their motivations, and even elements of the plot.

In "Tribal Scars," the narrator, Saer, hints at the historical context of the story he is about to tell. The context is confirmed when he begins his story by stating that there were "more than fifty black men and thirty Negro women down in the hold" of the slave ship *African.* We know right away that the story takes place in the historical context of the slave trade. The more we know about the horrors of the slave trade, the easier it is for us to understand why a whole village of people might be willing to leave their homes to escape the procurers. It might even give us some insight into why some Africans chose to join forces with the slave traders to avoid being forced into slavery themselves.

1. How is the story affected by the fact that slave traders wanted "perfect specimens"?
2. Describe the effects of the slave trade on West African village life.
3. Did this story give you a different perspective on the slave trade? Explain.

CRITICAL THINKING AND READING

Examining Conflict

Any struggle between opposing forces is a **conflict.** Conflict can take many forms. It can range from a boxing match to full-scale warfare, from a family quarrel to a presidential debate. Some of the most difficult conflicts, however, take place not in public, but in our hearts and minds. One type of internal conflict, and one of the hardest to resolve, is prompted by a **dilemma**—a situation that forces a choice between two unpleasant options. Commonly referred to as choosing between the lesser of two evils, resolving a dilemma can be a gut-wrenching experience. In "Tribal Scars," Amoo must choose between working with Momutu or losing his daughter to slavery. Although he chooses to work with Momutu and save Iome, it must have been very painful for Amoo to participate in the recapturing of fellow Africans.

1. How does Amoo deal with the conflict between his peaceful nature and the violence required to free his daughter?
2. (a) What dilemma does the slave trade force upon the villagers? (b) How has Momutu resolved this dilemma for himself?
3. What do you think is the most difficult aspect of Amoo's dilemma at the end of the story? Explain.

THINKING AND WRITING

Writing About a Difficult Decision

Difficult decisions lead us to examine our attitudes, our values, and our convictions. Sometimes, in making such a decision, we recognize the importance of something we had been taking for granted. Think about decisions that you have made, or decisions made by characters in books, movies, or television programs. You might want to review the list you made before you read "Tribal Scars."

Choose a decision made by you or by a fictional character. Write an essay, either as yourself or as a character, explaining the choices you faced, the reasons for your decision, and what you learned in making that decision.

When you revise your essay, make sure that each of your paragraphs expresses and supports a central idea. Revise any paragraphs that contain sentences unrelated to the central thought.

(continued from bottom of page)

2. Answers will differ, but students should gather that the slave trade decimated the villages along the West African coast. It robbed communities of their able-bodied men and women, leaving behind only the old and infirm; it uprooted villages, destroyed families, and terrorized people.
3. Answers will differ. Some students may not have considered that some people were willing to die rather than become slaves; others may not have realized that the slave trade introduced an ongoing fear into the lives of villagers; others may never have considered that teenagers like themselves were also enslaved.

ANSWERS TO CRITICAL THINKING AND READING

1. Answers will differ, but students may infer that Amoo's silent and determined behavior is due to his single-minded pursuit of rescuing his daughter. Until they escape from Momutu and his gang, Amoo shuts out social and emotional interaction with anyone or anything but Iome.
2. (a) They are forced to choose between the unpleasant options of risking disease and death by moving deeper into the forest, and risking torturous death and enslavement if they remain in their village on the coast where the slave hunters can find them. (b) Momutu found a third option; he decided to join the pack and escape being hunted by becoming one of the hunters.
3. Difficult aspects of Amoo's dilemma include: not living to see the outcome of his actions, the possibility that Iome would die from the wounds, and having to inflict pain on the daughter he has spent his life caring for. Students may suggest other aspects of the dilemma that they feel would be most difficult.

Challenge What is the effect of having this tale told as a story within a story? How would the story's focus change if it were told without Saer as the narrator of Amoo's story?

THINKING AND WRITING

Writing Across the Curriculum Students may want to invent a dilemma for a character from history or for a current social or political leader.

5. Students may suggest that Amoo, in slavery, is "surviving" as is Momutu, who is alive but has betrayed his own people. Iome and her grandmother are "living" because they are free from slavery and they no longer live in fear of the slave hunters.
6. (a) The scars are symbols of the nobility and dignity of his heritage. He is proud that his people "refused to be slaves." (b) He is probably disdainful of the people who have the scars removed—he may feel that they are betraying their heritage.
7. Answers will differ. Saer's story might reflect his respect for and pride in his cultural heritage; he may have felt that he and his companions should address more serious issues than they had previously; or he may feel strongly about the concept of personal dignity and freedom.

ANSWERS TO ANALYZING LITERATURE

1. The slave traders' insistence on perfect specimens is integral to the literal outcome of the story. It provides the means for saving Iome from slavery without killing her. On a symbolic level, it accentuates the error of judging another human being's worth by outward appearances.

IDEAS AN

OUSMANE SEMBÈNE

FATHER OF AFRICAN CINEMA

"I like for people to think about what I am telling them through my films. They may accept or reject it, but the important thing is to bring about new avenues of thought." So says Ousmane Sembène, author of "Tribal Scars" and award-winning filmmaker. In his films, he opens new avenues of thought on a wide range of topics. He challenges his audiences to think about slavery, family structure, alienation, bureaucracy, colonialism, and class conflict. Addressing a variety of contemporary and historical issues, Sembène strives to "decolonize" the minds of his fellow Africans. He tries to instill personal and cultural pride.

A Changing Focus

The first film made by an African appeared in 1924, only one year after Sembène's birth. Thirty-nine years later, Sembène made *his* first film, the short film *Borom Sarret (The Cart Driver)*, which in only twenty minutes conveys the poverty and injustice of early post-colonial Africa.

Ironically, the film industry in Africa had experienced little artistic growth during those years. *Mouramini*, an adaptation of a traditional oral narrative, was produced in Guinea, and *Afrique-Sur-Seine (Africa on the Seine)*, a collaborative work of African filmmakers, was produced in Paris under the leadership of Paulin Vieyra. These socially conscious filmmakers were, however, overshadowed by "escapist" filmmakers who capitalized on the popularity of entertainment films that portrayed Western values and ideas rather than African ones. Then

in 1963, Sembène produced *Borom Sarret,* releasing cinema from the confinement of a popular entertainment form and creating a model of film a a forum for social and political commentary.

A Man of the People

Sembène's social background and life experiences make him an appropriate artistic spokesperson for ordinary Africans. Although very well educated, he is largely self-taught, having left school a the age of fourteen. Often, he supported himsel doing manual labor. He did not isolate himsel from the common people portrayed in his films.

Always suspicious of those who considered themselves to be the intellectual elite, Sembèn encouraged filmmakers to use the colloquial speech patterns of the popular culture—a practice currently subscribed to by many internationally recognized filmmakers, including Spike Lee. In Sembène's first full-length color film, *Mandabi (The Money Order)*, the characters speak Wolof (a widely used language in Senegal). This innovation encouraged many African filmmakers to use African rather than Western languages in their films.

A New Medium

Sembène turned to film after pursuing a successful career as a writer. His aims as a writer were no different from his aims as a filmmaker, but he soon realized that in a largely illiterate society, his written work would not reach or affect many peo

INSIGHTS

Learning Across the Curriculum
You can use foreign films to reinforce students' knowledge of other cultures. As students view a film from another culture, encourage them to note the foods, landscapes, clothing, and social customs. Many video reference books index foreign films by country, also indicating which are subtitled and which are dubbed. You might want to start with the video version of "The Overcoat," produced in the former Soviet Union.

...le. The medium of film, he decided, would help him reach a wider audience. He applied for and was granted a scholarship to study filmmaking in Moscow with two renowned Soviet filmmakers, Mark Donskoy and Sergei Gerassimov. When Sembène returned to Africa, he used many of his short stories and novels as the bases for films.

One of his earliest films, *Niaye*, is based on his story of the injustice and violence experienced by a young, unwed mother in a Senegalese village under French colonial control. The film, praised by critics for its insight, won awards in France and Switzerland. Another of Sembène's award-winning films, *La Noire de . . . (Black Girl)*, is now considered a landmark in the history of African film.

In *Guelwaar,* a recent film, Sembène explores internal threats to an independent, unified Africa. The film chronicles the events surrounding the disappearance of the body of a deceased political activist, Guelwaar. Muslims accuse Christians and Christians accuse Muslims, while rumors and speculation escalate. The photo on this page, showing a scene from the film, illustrates the tension arising from the conflict. Sembène uses these struggles to suggest that the jealousies and suspicions among different groups are barriers to true African independence.

A scene from Sembène's 1992 film Guelwaar.

economic concerns. Inspired by Sembène's example, filmmakers have fought the battle for social and political reform on the screen. They seek to inform the people and develop in them a radical consciousness, an anti-colonial mindset. The increasing number of these filmmakers and the popularity of their films reflect Africa's growing independence.

Sembène's Influence

Most of the significant progress made in African films can be attributed to Sembène's influence. African filmmakers continue to produce films of substance in spite of, or perhaps because of, the social upheaval, economic crisis, and political instability that have become the backdrop for almost all creative efforts in Africa over the past thirty years. It is no surprise that the majority of themes in African cinema reflect social, political, cultural, and

An International Perspective

It is ironic that as African filmmaking establishes its artistic identity, the world community is becoming increasingly aware that few, if any, issues are uniquely African. The issues of injustice, bureaucracy, independence, poverty, and pride are relevant to us all, no matter what our heritage. Sembène's contributions to cinema have not only had an immeasurable impact on the African people; his work carries a message for all people.

GREAT WORK

THINGS FALL APART
by Chinua Achebe

Presentation

Motivation/Prior Knowledge Ask students to imagine what it must have been like to grow up in an African village in the late nineteenth century. As they volunteer details, write these on the chalkboard. You might even want to structure these details with titles such as A Typical Day or A Typical Year. Then tell them that by reading Chinua Achebe's novel *Things Fall Apart*, they will gain an intimate knowledge of life in an Ibo village.

Enrichment You might want to read Yeats's poem aloud to students so that they have a full appreciation of its sense of menace:

Turning and turning in the widening gyre
The falcon cannot hear the falconer:
Things fall apart; the center cannot hold;
Mere anarchy is loosed upon the world.
The blood-dimmed tide is loosed, and everywhere
The ceremony of innocence is drowned;
The best lack all conviction, while the worst
Are full of passionate intensity.
Surely some revelation is at hand;
Surely the Second Coming is at hand.
The Second Coming! Hardly are those words out
When a vast image out of Spiritus Mundi[1]
Troubles my sight: somewhere in sands of the desert
A shape with lion body and the head of a man,
A gaze blank and pitiless as the sun,
Is moving its slow thighs, while all about it
Reel shadows of the indignant desert birds.
The darkness drops again; but now I know
That twenty centuries of stony sleep

1. Spiritus Mundi: The Universal Spirit or soul, the Universal Subconscious in which the memories of the entire human race are forever preserved.

Achebe's Magic

In one scene from this novel a swarm of locusts descends on an African village: "And then appeared on the horizon a slowly-moving mass like a boundless sheet of black cloud drifting towards Umuofia. Soon it covered half the sky, and the solid mass was now broken by tiny eyes of light like shining star dust. It was a tremendous sight, full of power and beauty." At night the villagers go out and gather the locusts, whose wings are weighed down with dew. Regarded as a great delicacy, these rarely appearing insects are dried in the sun and then "eaten with solid palm-oil."

Taken out of context, this feasting on locusts may seem alien, even repugnant, to American readers. By the time they reach this episode of the novel, however, they will probably be thinking more like Ibo tribe members than like Americans. Achebe's feat of magic is to intitiate readers into African village life. They become so familiar with the rhythms and rituals of Umuofia that the great wrestling match and the Feast of the New Yam convey the same excitement as the World Series and Thanksgiving.

The Turning Point

Just when readers are comfortable with Ibo customs, however, Achebe unsettles them once more. The turning point of the novel occurs when the British come to Nigeria and begin to disrupt the age-old patterns of African village life. Although the cloud of locusts seems menacing and powerful, the arrival of a white man on a bicycle proves far more significant for Okonkwo, the protagonist of the novel, and his fellow villagers. From the time that whites appear, the Ibo culture indeed begins to "fall apart"—Achebe took the title of his book, *Things Fall Apart*, from "The Second Coming," a well-known poem by the Irish poet William Butler Yeats:

Things fall apart; the center cannot hold;
Mere anarchy is loosed upon the world,
The blood-dimmed tide is loosed, and
   everywhere
The ceremony of innocence is drowned.

Yeats goes on to describe the chaos and threat of a change that he believed would occur in the year 2000. Inspired by Yeats's words, Achebe applied them to the breakdowns in African society brought about by nineteenth-century colonialism.

The beauty of Achebe's technique, however, is that readers are steeped in Ibo traditions *before* the whites arrive. Like the Africans themselves, therefore, readers view Europeans as strange and possibly threatening invaders. They experience colonialism, therefore, from the perspective of a colonized people.

Were vexed to nightmare by a rocking cradle,
And what rough beast, its hour come round at last,
Slouches towards Bethlehem to be born?

Okonkwo's Story

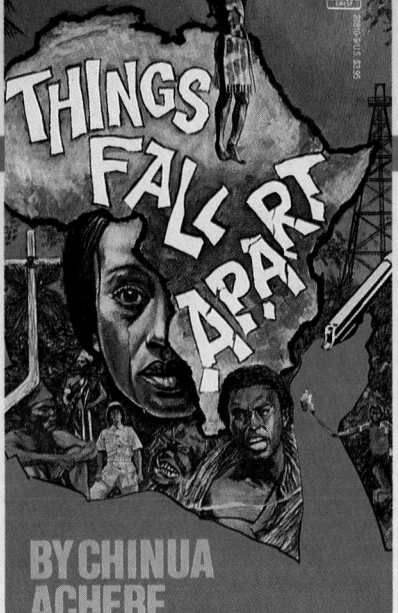

Since it is difficult to empathize with a whole people, Achebe tells the story from the vantage point of a single character, Okonkwo. This man, known as "Roaring Flame," is an imposing figure: "He was tall and huge, and his bushy eyebrows and wide nose gave him a very severe look." Years before the events of the book, he became famous by winning a legendary wrestling match. As the book opens, Okonkwo is a wealthy and respected man.

Like the protagonist of a Greek tragedy, however, Okonkwo carries within himself the seeds of his own destruction. Although he dominates those around him, ruling "his household with a heavy hand," he is secretly plagued "by fear, the fear of failure and of weakness." He is desperate to prove that he is better than his father, Unoka. A drunkard and a debtor, Unoka was unable to care for his family. He dragged around the village mournfully, "except when he was drinking or playing on his flute."

Okonkwo therefore strives to be everything his father was not: strong, manly, prosperous, respected. Naturally, he wants his own son, Nwoye, to follow in his footsteps. Ironically, however, Nwoye is in some ways more like his grandfather Unoka: "Nwoye knew that it was right to be masculine and to be violent, but somehow he still preferred the stories that his mother used to tell, . . ." This difference in temperament leads to serious conflicts between Okonkwo and his son.

In ordinary circumstances, Okonkwo's hidden fears and brooding anger might not have led him to a tragic end. He has the misfortune, however, of living in extraordinary times. Okonkwo witnesses the coming of Europeans, an event that calls into question all the deepest assumptions of Ibo culture. Being an angry, inflexible man, Okonkwo cannot survive this encounter between different ways of life.

Other Characters

While the novel centers on Okonkwo, other characters add interest to the story. Nwoye is more sensitive than his father and responds much differently to the religion of the white men, Christianity. Ezinma, the daughter of Okonkwo's wife Ekwefe—he has several wives, in accordance with Ibo customs—is an attractive, intelligent girl. She is also a bit spoiled, because "it was impossible to refuse Ezinma anything." Okonkwo likes his daughter so much that he wishes she were a boy, a thought that shows how little he values women.

Ezinma is involved in some of the most appealing moments of the story. One night, for instance, she sits on the floor and listens attentively as her mother tells an Ibo folk tale: "Once upon a time, . . . all the birds were invited to a feast in the sky. . . ."

Themes

Despite such lighter moments, it is the tragedy of Okonkwo that embodies the theme of the novel. Because he is so devoted to Ibo ideals, his downfall symbolizes the breakdown of traditional ways brought about by colonialism.

Okonkwo's story also reveals the misunderstandings that can arise when two different cultures encounter each other. The missionary who comes to

Enrichment You may want to explain to students that the region known to us as Nigeria has had a long history. It has not always been what we perceive it to be today: a developing nation. For instance, a sophisticated Iron Age culture flourished in Nigeria during the period from 500 B.C. to A.D. 200. Advanced cultures also appeared in this region about 1,000 years later.

European contact with Nigeria did not begin in the nineteenth century, when it was colonized by Britain. Trade existed between Europe and Nigeria during the Middle Ages. In 1441 Portugal began to take slaves from Africa. (Slavery had been practiced by black Africans for many years, but on a limited basis.) Soon Europeans were exporting thousands of slaves from Nigeria and other regions.

Further Reading Students may enjoy reading Achebe's other works of fiction:

No Longer at Ease. New York: Fawcett, 1961

Arrow of God. New York: John Day, 1967

A Man of the People. New York: John Day, 1966

Anthills of the Savannah. New York: Anchor/Doubleday, 1988

the village believes sincerely in the doctrines of Christianity. Okonkwo, however, believes just as sincerely in the ancestral spirits of his tribe and the many gods of his religion. To him the Christian doctrine of the Holy Trinity makes no sense at all: "Okonkwo was fully convinced that the man was mad."

Achebe's themes are not limited to the events surrounding colonialism. They relate to any situation in which traditional values are called into question and people from different cultures meet for the first time.

Language

In writing his novel, Achebe faced a special problem with regard to language. As an educated Nigerian, he naturally chose to write in English: One legacy of British colonialism in Nigeria is the widespread use of English in education and government. However, Achebe also had to convey the flavor of an African culture.

He solved this problem in part by having his characters pepper their conversation with Ibo sayings and proverbs. At one point, for example, a group of men are speculating about why a palm-wine tapper (someone who climbs palm trees and extracts the sap used to make wine) gave up his trade. One man remarks, "There must be a reason for it. A toad does not run in the daytime for nothing."

Achebe also conveys the flavor of Ibo culture by having characters tell traditional folk tales. An example is the story that Ezinma hears from her mother.

Still another device he uses is the introduction of Ibo words and phrases. Included in the narrative, for instance, are such words as *iba*, meaning "fever," and *jigida*, which refers to "a string of waist beads." Achebe assists the English-speaking reader by including a glossary of these words and phrases at the back of the book.

The Author

The man who so successfully describe African village life was himself born in a villag close to the Niger River on November 15, 193(Unlike his brooding protagonist, howeve Achebe was familiar with both Christian and Ib traditions. His father was an Ibo who had cor verted to Christianity. Achebe's early knowledg of the differences between cultures was a valuab preparation for the writing of *Things Fall Apart*.

An exceptionally bright student, Achebe wer on to study European literature at a Nigerian unive sity. His mastery of European and African traditior explains why his Ibo tale has the clear, dramatic forr of a Greek tragedy. It also explains why he borrowe the title of his novel from the work of an Irish poe

Although Achebe has worked in both radi broadcasting and publishing, today he earns h living as a university teacher in Nigeria and tl United States. He has taught, for instance, Northwestern University in Chicago and the Ci University of New York.

Achebe's Influence

Many critics regard this novel, published 1959, as one of the first major works of fiction emerge from Africa. Not only has it been prais by critics, but it has been a popular success as we Translated into more than forty languages, it h sold more than two and a half million copi

Besides gaining a wide readershi *Things Fall Apart* has had a major i fluence on other African writers. A hebe's use of language and his p spective on the past have inspir such writers as Flora Nwap James Ngugi, and Elech Amadi.

The most important read of this book, however, is you.. you begin to read, prepare to i merse yourself in the life of nineteenth-century Ibo village— village where huts are lit by palm-lamps, beds are made of bambo and children are "warned not to whis at night for fear of evil spirits."

CHINUA ACHEBE

Asia

THREE JUMPING CARP
Yi Dynasty,
nineteenth century
The Brooklyn Museum,
New York

Humanities Note

Fine art, *Three Jumping Carp*, Yi Dynasty, nineteenth century. The Yi Dynasty ruled Korea from 1392, when Yi Songgye seized the throne, until 1910. This dynasty built a new capital at Seoul and instituted Confucianism as the official religion of the country.

Carp were a popular and special subject to Yi Dynasty painters. They were regarded as a lucky fish, and fishers were supposed to throw them back if they caught them. Sometimes they were kept as pets and became tame enough to eat food from a person's hand.

The use of carp as a symbol was inspired by their life cycle. Like salmon they swim upstream to spawn. In the course of this upstream journey, they have to swim against the current and sometimes ascend waterfalls. These fish therefore came to symbolize persistence, courage, vigor, and success. According to one Chinese legend (many legends about carp came to Korea from China), they turned into dragons after they negotiated their upstream journey.

Koreans believed that pictures of jumping carp had magical value and could transmit the qualities that carp symbolized. Sometimes such pictures were placed over a bride's bed, so she would give birth to sons. (It was a chauvinistic belief of this time that men exemplified courage and persistence more than women did.)

You might want to use the following questions to discuss the art:

1. For Koreans carp symbolize courage and persistence because they swim upstream. How does the artist capture this symbolism?
2. How does his placement of the fish contribute to the feeling of the picture?
3. Which animal would you choose as a symbol of courage and persistence? Why?
4. How would you depict this animal in a painting?

R. K. NARAYAN

1906–

Indian writer R. K. Narayan once said, "If one pauses to think, one realizes that there is little one could say about one's self." Others, however, have plenty to say about Narayan. John Updike, for instance, called him "the foremost Indian writer of fiction in English." And Graham Greene, who helped Narayan to publish his first novel, said, "It was Mr. Narayan with his *Swami and Friends* who first brought India, in the sense of Indian population and the Indian way of life, alive to me." Throughout his literary career, Narayan's work has met with favorable criticism and has been translated into all European languages and Hebrew.

One of the most outstanding features of Narayan's talent is his ability to combine the English language and the Indian sensibility. He speaks Tamil (an Indian language) at home, but he writes in English, which is not surprising since his education from primary school on was in English. Narayan explained his view of the English language to William Walsh in a British Broadcasting Company radio interview: "English has been with us [in India] for over a century and a half. I am particularly fond of the language. I was never aware that I was using a different, a foreign, language when I wrote in English, because it came to me very easily . . . English is a very adaptable language. And it's so transparent it can take on the tint of any country." Walsh describes Narayan's English as having "a uniquely Indian flavor by avoiding the American purr of the combustio[n] engine . . . [and] the thick marmalade quality o[f] British English."

Narayan was born in Madras, India, on Octo[o]ber 10, 1906, one of nine children in a middle[-]class Brahmin family. His father traveled fre[-]quently because of his role as a headmaster i[n] the government education service. Narayan wa[s] raised by his grandmother and an uncle becaus[e] his mother was frail. After school, Narayan'[s] grandmother gave him lessons in Tamil and reci[t-]ed Indian tales and poetry. She inspired i[n] Narayan the passion for people that is evident i[n] his writing. The people who visited her back yar[d] to seek her advice on marriages, to be treated fo[r] scorpion bites, and to have their horoscopes rea[d] became the subject for Narayan's early fiction.

Narayan enrolled in the Maharajah's Colleg[e] in Mysore when his father was transferred there[.] He was bored for most of his academic caree[r] and did not receive his bachelor of arts degre[e] until he was twenty-four. After he graduated, h[e] worked as a teacher, but he soon left teaching i[n] favor of devoting himself to his writing. He elect[-]ed to live off the joint-family system, whereby [a] number of relatives live under one roof. Then h[e] began writing his first novel, *Swami and Friends*[.]

During that time Narayan created his fiction[al] setting of Malgudi, based on his observations o[f] Mysore. As a mythical locale, Malgudi is a literar[y] microcosm comparable to William Faulkner'[s] Yoknapatawpha County. In Malgudi, Naraya[n] represents the universal human condition as we[ll] as the human condition of life in India.

Narayan is one of the first writers to depic[t] India from an insider's perspective. He choose[s] his characters from the middle class: street ven[-]dors, holy men, financial experts, students, teach[-]ers. He writes about a small segment of India[n] society with an objective, humorous, yet sympa[-]thetic attitude toward that critical segment'[s] struggle to harmonize ancient traditions and th[e] confusions of the contemporary world.

Objectives

Thematic
To understand the capabilities of the human soul

Skills
1 To understand situational irony
2 To appreciate humor
3 To write a story with a surprise ending

GUIDE FOR INTERPRETING

An Astrologer's Day

Commentary

Situational Irony and Humor. In **situational irony,** an event occurs that contradicts the expectations of the characters, readers, or audience. Like verbal irony, where the literal meaning of what is expressed is opposite to the actual meaning, situational irony involves a kind of grim **humor.** Writers use irony and humor to expose the sad and comic aspects of the world. Narayan's awareness of the sad and comic realities of life is evident in his fiction.

Narayan also uses situational irony in his detached yet sympathetic portrayal of his characters. In "An Astrologer's Day," a man passes himself off as an astrologer, when he actually gives little more than common-sense advice. The whole premise of his occupation is a lie, but the "astrologer" considers himself honest. At any rate, he tells people what they want to hear, which in his eyes justifies taking their money. Although Narayan's ironic portrayal of the astrologer is humorous, it is also laced with serious sadness because of the severity of an event hidden in the astrologer's past. Through irony, Narayan exposes the astrologer's true identity.

Writing

In your journal write about an occasion when something seemingly unimportant managed to change your mood entirely.

Primary Source

Graham Greene helped launch Narayan's career by helping him publish his first novel. In the introduction to another novel, *Bachelor of Arts*, Greene describes acquiring the *Swami and Friends* manuscript. ". . . We had both been born under the sign of Libra, so if one believes in astrology, as Narayan, who once supplied me with my horoscope, certainly does, we were destined by the stars to know each other. One day an Indian friend of mine called Purna brought me a rather traveled and weary typescript—a novel written by a friend of his—and I let it lie on my desk for weeks unread until one rainy day . . . I didn't know that it had been rejected by half a dozen publishers and that Purna had been told by the author not to return it to Mysore but to weight it with a stone and drop it into the Thames. Anyway Narayan and I had been brought together (I half believe myself in the stars that ruled over an Indian and an English Libra birth). I was able to find a publisher for *Swami*, and Malgudi was born . . ."

Literary Focus Have students discuss films they have seen or stories they have read that use situational irony. Many students may be familiar with "Twilight Zone" episodes, for example, in which Rod Serling takes the audience through a situation, only to surprise viewers with an ironic twist at the end. Fables also contain situational irony, often with an element of humor.

Writing/Prior Knowledge At one point or another, everyone has had an ironic experience laced with humor. Ask students to explore their memories for such an experience. Then ask them to comment on the experience in a few, well-developed paragraphs.

ESL Teaching Strategy Make sure ESL students know what an astrologer does. You might begin by writing *astrology* on the board, explaining that it is the study of (logy) stars (astro).

Teaching Tenth-Grade Students Tenth-grade students might like to share their views of astrology. For instance, to what extent do they believe astrological patterns govern our lives? Some students may be particularly well-versed in astrology. Encourage them to share their knowledge of the astrological signs and their functions with you and their classmates.

Support Material

Teaching Portfolio
Teacher Backup, p. 1723
Usage and Mechanics Worksheet, p. 1727
Vocabulary Check, p. 1728
Analyzing Literature Worksheet, *Understanding Situational Irony*, p. 1729

Critical Thinking and Reading Worksheet, *Appreciating Humor*, p. 1730
Selection Test, pp. 1731–1732

An Astrologer's Day

R. K. Narayan

Punctually at midday he opened his bag and spread out his professional equipment, which consisted of a dozen cowrie shells,[1] a square piece of cloth with obscure mystic charts on it, a notebook, and a bundle of palmyra writing. His forehead was resplendent with sacred ash and vermilion,[2] and his eyes sparkled with a sharp abnormal gleam which was really an outcome of a continual searching look for customers, but which his simple clients took to be a prophetic light and felt comforted. The power of his eyes was considerably enhanced by their position—placed as they were between the painted forehead and the dark whiskers which streamed down his cheeks: even a half-wit's eyes would sparkle in such a setting. To crown the effect he wound a saffron-colored turban around his head. This color scheme never failed. People were attracted to him as bees are attracted to cosmos or dahlia stalks. He sat under the boughs of a spreading tamarind tree which flanked a path running through the Town Hall Park. It was a remarkable place in many ways: a surging crowd was always moving up and down this narrow road morning till night. A variety of trades and occupations was represented all along its way: medicine sellers, sellers of stolen hardware and junk, magicians, and, above all, an auctioneer of cheap cloth, who created enough din all day to attract the whole town. Next to him in vociferousness came a vendor of fried groundnut, who gave his ware a fancy name each day, calling it "Bombay Ice Cream" one day, and on the next "Delhi Almond," and on the third "Raja's Delicacy," and so on and so forth, and people flocked to him. A considerable portion of this crowd dallied before the astrologer too. The astrologer transacted his business by the light of a flare which crackled and smoked up above the groundnut heap nearby. Half the enchantment of the place was due to the fact that it did not have the benefit of municipal lighting. The place was lit up by shop lights. One or two had hissing gaslights, some had naked flares stuck on poles, some were lit up by old cycle lamps, and one or two, like the astrologer's, managed without lights of their own. It was a bewildering crisscross of light rays and moving shadows. This suited the astrologer very well, for the simple reason that he had not in the least intended to be an astrologer when he began life; and he knew no more of what was going to happen to others than he knew what was going to happen to himself next minute. He was as much a stranger to the stars as were his innocent customers. Yet he said things which pleased and astonished everyone: that was more a matter of study, practice, and shrewd guesswork. All the same, it was as much an honest man's labor as any other, and he deserved the wages he carried home at the end of a day.

He had left his village without any previous thought or plan. If he had continued there he would have carried on the work of his forefathers—namely, tilling the land, living, marrying, and ripening in his cornfield and ancestral home. But that was not to be. He had to leave home without telling anyone, and he could not rest till he left it behind a couple of hundred miles. To a villager it is a great deal, as if an ocean flowed between.

---

1. **cowrie** (kou′ rē) **shells:** Brightly colored, glossy seashells.
2. **sacred ash and vermilion:** A religious marking originally used only by Brahmins, the highest caste in Indian society.

Primary Source

In his article "India's Master of Comedy," A. G. Mojtabai discusses the combination of humor and sadness in Narayan's fiction.

Narayan's humor . . . is laced with sadness—not unlike, it seems to me, the mood of that unforgettable moment in Chaucer's *Troilus and Criseyde* with Troilus passing to the other side of death, looking back, and laughing as he looks, at "this litel spot of erthe" where he's been slain.

He had a working analysis of mankind's troubles: marriage, money, and the tangles of human ties. Long practice had sharpened his perception. Within five minutes he understood what was wrong. He charged three pies[3] per question, never opened his mouth till the other had spoken for at least ten minutes, which provided him enough stuff for a dozen answers and advices. When he told the person before him, gazing at his palm, "In many ways you are not getting the fullest results for your efforts," nine out of ten were disposed to agree with him. Or he questioned: "Is there any woman in your family, maybe even a distant relative who is not well disposed toward you?" Or he gave an analysis of character: "Most of your troubles are due to your nature. How can you be otherwise with Saturn where he is? You have an impetuous[4] nature and a rough exterior." This endeared him to their hearts immediately, for even the mildest of us loves to think that he has a forbidding exterior.

The nuts vendor blew out his flare and rose to go home. This was a signal for the astrologer to bundle up too, since it left him in darkness except for a little shaft of green light which strayed in from somewhere and touched the ground before him. He picked up his cowrie shells and paraphernalia and was putting them back into his bag when the green shaft of light was blotted out; he looked up and saw a man standing before him. He sensed a possible client and said: "You look so careworn. It will do you good to sit down for a while and chat with me." The other grumbled some reply vaguely. The astrologer pressed his invitation; whereupon the other thrust his palm under his nose, saying: "You call yourself an astrologer?" The astrologer felt challenged and said, tilting the other's palm toward the green shaft of light: "Yours is a nature . . ." "Oh, stop that," the other said. "Tell me something worthwhile. . . ."

Our friend felt piqued.[5] "I charge only three pies per question, and what you get ought to be good enough for your money. . . ." At this the oth-

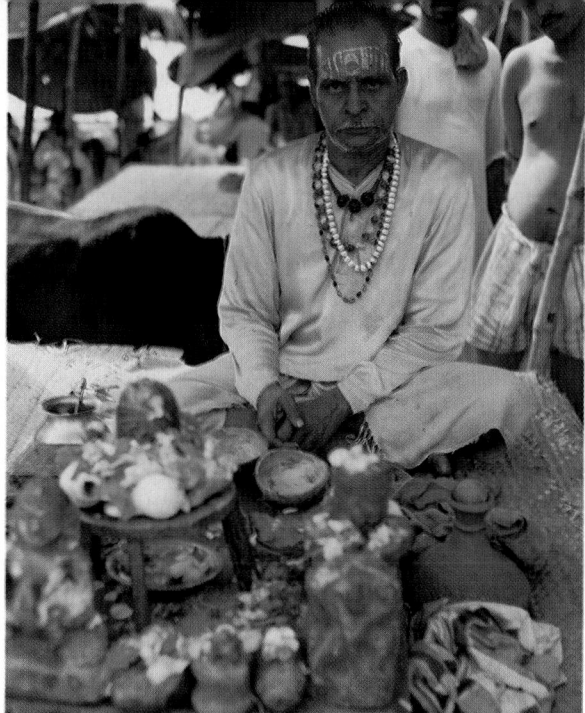

Man in Hindu temple, Varanasi, India

er withdrew his arm, took out an anna, and flung it out to him, saying: "I have some questions to ask. If I prove you are bluffing, you must return that anna to me with interest."

"If you find my answers satisfactory, will you give me five rupees?"

"No."

"Or will you give me eight annas?"

"All right, provided you give me twice as much if you are wrong," said the stranger. This pact was accepted after a little further argument. The astrologer sent up a prayer to heaven as the other lit a cheroot. The astrologer caught a glimpse of his face by the matchlight. There was a pause as cars hooted on the road, *jutka*[6] drivers swore at their horses, and the babble of the crowd agitated the semidarkness of the park. The other sat down, sucking his cheroot, puffing out, sat there ruthlessly. The astrologer felt very uncomfortable. "Here, take your anna back. I am not used to such chal-

---

pies: Paisas (pī′ säs), monetary units of India or Pakistan, equal to one hundredth of a rupee.

impetuous (im pech′ ōō əs) *adj.*: Rash; impulsive.

piqued (pēkt) *adj.*: Displeased; resentful.

---

6. *jutka* (jət′ kə): A Hindi word for a one-horse vehicle, hired out as a taxi.

5 **Discussion** What is Narayan suggesting about the astrologer's clientele? Students should notice that basically the same type of people with common troubles patronize the astrologer. Ask students to predict how he will respond to his customers.

6 **Discussion** Ask students if they agree with the narrator's statement here. Why would people like to think they have forbidding exteriors? Do students consider this observation humorous?

7 **Discussion** Ask students to determine why the astrologer presses his invitation. What are his motives?

8 **Reading Strategy** Have students pay careful attention to the client's skepticism. What have we learned about the client after he cuts off the astrologer mid-sentence and demands to be told something worthwhile?

9 **Clarification** Ask students if they understand why the astrologer suddenly backs out. Could there be a connection between the astrologer's having seen the client's face in the matchlight and the astrologer's sudden discomfort?

Master Teacher Note Encourage students to think about instances when they felt they were being taken advantage of by a dishonest person. What tipped students off to the individual's insincerity? How did students handle the situation? What did students learn from the incident? Ask them to discuss the similarities or differences between what happened to them and what the astrologer does in "An Astrologer's Day."

For Narayan, there is no apotheosis—not just yet, anyway; he remains as he was, rooted to the particular spot of earth that he has so lovingly furnished and populated, devoted to the characters dashing about in the foreground. There is intense immersion in the drama at hand, a gathering momentum, then—as it were—a blink: an abrupt distance. For the reader, there is an instant of puzzlement; it feels almost as if the author had lost interest. Something happens that is tantamount to a shifting of scale; there is a sudden sense of disproportion.

"For an Indian, training in the classics begins early," Narayan says.

"Our minds are trained to accept without surprise characters of godly or demonic proportions with actions and reactions set in limitless worlds and progressing through incalculable time-scale." Modern literature has quite a different thrust. Here the attempt is "to compress the range of our observation and subject the particle to an intense scrutiny."

lenges. It is late for me today. . . ." He made preparations to bundle up. The other held his wrist and said: "You can't get out of it now. You dragged me in while I was passing." The astrologer shivered in his grip; and his voice shook and became faint. "Leave me today. I will speak to you tomorrow." The other thrust his palm in his face and said: "Challenge is challenge. Go on." The astrologer proceeded with his throat drying up: "There is a woman . . ."

"Stop," said the other. "I don't want all that. Shall I succeed in my present search or not? Answer this and go. Otherwise I will not let you go till you disgorge all your coins." The astrologer muttered a few incantations and replied: "All right. I will speak. But will you give me a rupee if what I say is convincing? Otherwise I will not open my mouth, and you may do what you like." After a good deal of haggling the other agreed. The astrologer said: "You were left for dead. Am I right?"

"Ah, tell me more."

"A knife has passed through you once?" said the astrologer.

"Good fellow!" He bared his chest to show the scar. "What else?"

"And then you were pushed into a well nearby in the field. You were left for dead."

"I should have been dead if some passerby had not chanced to peep into the well," exclaimed the other, overwhelmed by enthusiasm.

"When shall I get at him?" he asked, clenching his fist.

"In the next world," answered the astrologer. "He died four months ago in a far-off town. You will never see any more of him." The other groaned on hearing it. The astrologer proceeded:

"Guru Nayak—"

"You know my name!" the other said, taken aback.

"As I know all other things. Guru Nayak, listen carefully to what I have to say. Your village is two days' journey due north of this town. Take the next train and be gone. I see once again great danger to your life if you go from home." He took out a pinch of sacred ash and held it to him. "Rub it on your forehead and go home. Never travel southward again, and you will live to be a hundred."

"Why should I leave home again?" the other said reflectively. "I was only going away now and then to look for him and to choke out his life if I met him." He shook his head regretfully. "He has escaped my hands. I hope at least he died as he deserved." "Yes," said the astrologer. "He was crushed under a lorry." The other looked gratified to hear it.

The place was deserted by the time the astrologer picked up his articles and put them into his bag. The green shaft was also gone, leaving the place in darkness and silence. The stranger had gone off into the night, after giving the astrologer a handful of coins.

It was nearly midnight when the astrologer reached home. His wife was waiting for him at the door and demanded an explanation. He flung the coins at her and said: "Count them. One man gave all that."

"Twelve and a half annas," she said, counting. She was overjoyed. "I can buy some jaggery[7] and coconut tomorrow. The child has been asking for sweets for so many days now. I will prepare some nice stuff for her."

"The swine has cheated me! He promised me a rupee," said the astrologer. She looked up at him. "You look worried. What is wrong?"

"Nothing."

After dinner, sitting on the pyol,[8] he told her: "Do you know a great load is gone from me today? I thought I had the blood of a man on my hands all these years. That was the reason why I ran away from home, settled here, and married you. He is alive."

She gasped. "You tried to kill!"

"Yes, in our village, when I was a silly youngster. We drank, gambled, and quarreled badly one day—why think of it now? Time to sleep," he said, yawning, and stretched himself on the pyol.

---

7. **jaggery** (jag′ ər ē) *n*.: A dark, crude sugar from the sap of certain palm trees.

8. **pyol** (pī′ əl): A collection of material on which a person can sit or sleep

---

Reader's Response *What is your opinion of the astrologer's character? Explain your answer, using examples from the story that support your opinion.*

THINKING ABOUT THE SELECTION

Interpreting

1. What does Narayan's description of the astrologer's clothing indicate about his character?
2. Why does the author claim that the astrologer earns an honest wage?
3. What equips the astrologer to answer people's questions?
4. Describe the astrologer's method of character analysis, based on the two examples Narayan gives.
5. Why does the astrologer decline the stranger's money after sending a prayer to heaven?
6. Why do you think the astrologer mentions the attempted murder?
7. At home, the astrologer learns that the stranger paid him less than what they had agreed upon. Do you agree with the astrologer that the stranger cheated him? Explain.
8. What is the astrologer's attitude toward what he has done to the stranger?

Applying

9. Can you think of an example of injustice in the world that is similar to the injustice in "An Astrologer's Day"?

ANALYZING LITERATURE

Understanding Situational Irony

Situational irony involves a situation or event that contradicts the expectations of the reader. In "An Astrologer's Day," a man who knows nothing more about the stars than his customers poses as an astrologer. Everything about his appearance makes him believable, but the reader knows that he's a fraud. Nevertheless, his customers have faith in him, except for one, who unknowingly has the best reason to distrust him. As in his novels, in "An Astrologer's Day," Narayan takes us through a passage from illusion to reality as he exposes the protagonist's true identity.

1. What is ironic about the author's statement: "All the same, it was as much an honest man's labor as any other, and he deserved the wages he carried home at the end of a day"? In what two ways is the astrologer actually not an honest man?

2. Find and discuss another example of irony in "An Astrologer's Day."
3. Evaluate Narayan's success in using irony by discussing your expectations of the story after Guru Nyak goes off into the night.

CRITICAL THINKING AND READING

Appreciating Humor

In a magazine article, Narayan was referred to as India's "master of comedy." One of the distinctive features of Narayan's writing is humor. **Humor** evokes laughter at the ridiculous, the ludicrous, and the comical aspects of life. In Narayan's work, humor evokes laughter while arousing the reader's awareness of the depths of human nature. The humorous elements of "An Astrologer's Day" lead the reader to think carefully about the capabilities of the human soul.

1. When the astrologer calls the stranger by name, the stranger is astonished. What is humorous about the astrologer's reply to the stranger's surprise, "As I know all things"? How does his response affect your interpretation of his character?
2. Were you amused when the astrologer discovered that Guru Nyak did not pay him a rupee? How does Nyak's "insufficient" payment affect the story?
3. Discuss another example of humor in "An Astrologer's Day."

THINKING AND WRITING

Writing a Story with a Surprise Ending

Stories rich in irony often have surprise endings. In "An Astrologer's Day," we don't learn that the astrologer tried to kill Nyak until the end of the story. Narayan offers clues that should make us suspicious of the astrologer, however. Think of a surprising situation that would make a good story. Write about the situation in the form of a story, with a setting, characters, and a plot. Develop the story so that the reader is surprised at the outcome of the plot. Throughout the story, include hints at the surprise ending. As you revise, make sure your clues do not give the ending away. Finally, proofread your story and ask a friend to react to your use of the surprise ending.

(continued from bottom of page)

ed, while the only person in the story who cheats anyone is the astrologer.

ANSWERS TO CRITICAL THINKING AND READING

1. The astrologer's response "As I know all things" is funny because he doesn't actually know anything more than the average person. His character is quick, sharp-witted, and manipulative.
2. The insufficient payment seems like poetic justice.
3. Another example of humor occurs when the astrologer tries to turn the stranger away saying, "I am not used to such challenges," when the stranger wasn't asking him to do anything beyond his supposed powers.

THINKING AND WRITING

Publishing Student Writing Students might want to compile their stories in an anthology. Have them arrange their papers in meaningful order, according to the nature of the story and the surprise ending.

Challenge Have students explore other Narayan stories to learn more about Malgudi County.

When he believed he killed the man, he felt guilty. After learning the man is alive, he dismisses his deed as an unimportant error of his youth. Answers will differ. Students might respond that many serious crimes seem to go unpunished.

ANSWERS TO ANALYZING LITERATURE

1. It is actually dishonest labor because he knows no more about the stars than his customers do. The astrologer is a phony, and he tried to kill a man.
2. Answers will differ. Suggested response: It is ironic that the one customer who doubts him is the only customer of whom the astrologer does have some knowledge, even if it is not mystic knowledge.
3. Answers will differ. Suggested response: Most readers probably did not expect the stranger to underpay the astrologer after agreeing to pay a rupee. This reinforces the irony because the astrologer feels cheat-

ANITA DESAI

1937–

Born in Mussourie, India, to a Bengali father and a German mother, Anita Desai has become recognized as one of the most important Indian writers of her generation. Her mixed heritage may have given her a unique perspective on Indian society, as someone who is both an insider and an outsider. This viewpoint is often reflected in her stories, which present a detailed picture of urban Indian life but also depict characters who are lonely in the midst of this crowded and energetic society.

In *Fire on the Mountain* (1977), for example, a widow has decided to spend her old age alone in a house up in the hills. Yet her withdrawal fails to shield her from interaction with other people, and a visit from a troubled great-granddaughter leads to disaster. This novel won Britain's Winifred Holtby Award and, in India, the 1978 National Academy of Letters Award. In *Baumgartner's Bombay* (1989), which won the Hadassah Award, Desai drew on both sides of her parentage, setting down a German Jewish refugee in the streets of Bombay. By virtue of being a *firanghi*—a foreigner—Baumgartner is perhaps the most isolated of all Desai's characters. Neither truly German nor truly Indian, he lives alone with a pack of stray cats he has rescued from the street.

Despite the frequent loneliness of her characters, Desai's books never make the reader feel alone. With the knowledge of a cultural insider, she plunges readers into the sights and sounds, the heat and clamor of urban India. Critics have praised her skillful use of imagery to capture the local color of her country. In *Baumgartner's Bombay,* for example, she describes the streets of Bombay as alive with "officers . . . gleaming with Brasso and boot polish—hawkers and traders scurrying around with baskets and trays . . . Indian women in shapeless garments . . . and over it all . . . the light from the sky and the sea, an invasion of light . . . and heat like boiling oil tipped out of a cauldron onto their heads. . . ."

Anita Desai was a writer from her earliest years. She attended a mission school in Old Delhi run by English missionaries and so was taught English before Hindi. Of the three languages spoken in her home—Hindi, English, and German—English was the one she read and wrote in. She had written her own stories and novels and contributed to children's magazines when she was nine or ten. After graduating from Delhi University she married and started a family. Her first novel was published when she was a young mother (she now has four children). She has also lived and taught abroad, including stints in England and the United States. In addition to awards for individual novels, she received the Taraknath Das Foundation Award (1989) for enhancing understanding between the United States and India.

Desai is a cosmopolitan writer whose subject has always remained her native land. Her perspective as both a participant and an observer makes her uniquely qualified to translate the complexities of India for the rest of the world. She says that in her fiction she has tried "to convey the rhythms, accents, tones, and pace of Indian life" in the richness of English, her "literary language." In "Studies in the Park," she conveys the bustling life in a city park as well as the turmoil of an impressionable teenager.

GUIDE FOR INTERPRETING

Studies in the Park

Commentary

Cultural Context. In 1639 a British trading company called the East India Company purchased a strip of land in Madras, India. This was the beginning of Britain's influence in India, which would expand decade by decade until the whole of the subcontinent was actually incorporated into the British empire.

Throughout the early twentieth century, many Indians sought freedom and independence for their nation. Foremost among the leaders demanding independence was Mahatma Gandhi, who pioneered techniques of nonviolent resistance. However, it wasn't until after the Second World War that the British were willing to give up their prize possession.

Given this long period of British dominance, it is hardly surprising that Britain left its mark on India's customs and culture. India's parliamentary system of government is based on the British model. The English language is widely spoken throughout the country. In fact, India's languages have mingled with English, so that English now includes such Indian-derived words as *pundit*, *sherbet*, *dungaree*, and *loot*, while the current word for "boss" in Hindi is *incharge*. Last but not least, India's educational system derives directly from that of the British.

This is why Suno, the protagonist of Anita Desai's "Studies in the Park," is urged by his father to get "a first"—meaning the highest possible grade assigned by the British system. (Less diligent students would end up with a second or a third.) Similarly, he shares his study area in the park with candidates for the "B.A., or M.A." These degrees—a Bachelor of Arts or a Master of Arts—are also awarded in the United States, of course, but they are British in origin.

Beneath this overlay of British culture remain the traditions of a complex ancient civilization that developed thousands of years before the rise of Western civilization. India is the birthplace of several of the world's great religions, primarily Hinduism and Buddhism. (See the feature on Indian religion, page 164.) These religions have given rise to such practices as yoga, a system of exercise and breathing, and study under a guru or spiritual advisor. The influence of Indian religion affects the life of the park where Suno goes to study.

Not every aspect of Suno's experience is specifically related to British or Indian culture, however. His problems with school reflect the concerns of young people in many parts of the world.

Writing

The protagonist in "Studies in the Park" finds numerous distractions from studying. How do you find time to study? Describe how your typical day is divided between study and other, nonacademic activities.

Analyzing Literature Worksheet, *Understanding Cultural Context*, p. 1741
Critical Thinking and Reading Worksheet, *Interpreting Epiphanies*, p. 1742
Selection Test, pp. 1743–1744

Teaching Tenth-Grade Students As preparation for reading the selection, you may wish to have students discuss how they cope with stressful situations, such as studying for examinations, deciding what college to attend, or passing the test for a driver's license.

Spelling Tip Suggest that students can avoid an error with the unstressed middle vowel in *pilgrimage* if they recognize the base word, *pilgrim*. Point out that the prefixes *ir-* and *im-* (in *irreverence* and *impertinently*, respectively) are variants of the prefix *in-*, meaning "not."

Literary Focus Ask students to share their experience of other cultures. What adjustments, if any, did they make in moving from one culture to another? As students read the selection, have them consider what adjustments they would make if they were to live in the Indian culture of Desai's story.

Writing/Prior Knowledge Before students begin writing, have them prepare a log of their activities during a typical day, listing their school schedule and activities outside of school, including meals, homework, sports, and so on.

ESL Teaching Strategy Have ESL students relate anecdotes or examples from their culture that illustrate the pressure students may feel to succeed in their studies. What value does their culture place on academic achievement?

Vocabulary

Preteach the following vocabulary words:

wheedles (hwēd´ 'lz) v.: Persuades by flattery or soothing words

pilgrimage (pil´ grim ij) n.: A journey, as to a shrine or holy place

earnestness (ʉr´ nist nis´) n.: Zeal; intensity

impertinently (im pʉrt´ 'n ənt lē) adv.: Disrespectfully

imbibing (im bīb´ iŋ) v.: Drinking in; absorbing

hirsute (hʉr´ sōōt´) adj.: Hairy; shaggy; bristly

aborigine (ab´ ə rij´ ə ne´) n.: First inhabitant; native

supine (sōō´ pīn´) adj.: Lying on the back, face upward

demented (dē ment´ id) adj.: Mentally deranged; insane

irreverence (ir rev´ ər əns) n.: Disrespect

cynicism (sin´ ə siz´ əm) n.: Sarcasm; sneering attitude

perpetual (pər pech´ ōō əl) adj.: Unceasing; constant

Studies in the Park

Anita Desai

—Turn it off, turn it off, turn it off! First he listens to the news in Hindi. Directly after, in English. Broom—brroom—brrroom—the voice of doom roars. Next, in Tamil. Then in Punjabi. In Gujarati.[1] What next, my god, what next? Turn it off before I smash it onto his head, fling it out of the window, do nothing of the sort of course, nothing of the sort.

—And my mother. She cuts and fries, cuts and fries. All day I hear her chopping and slicing and the pan of oil hissing. What all does she find to fry and feed us on, for God's sake? Eggplants, potatoes, spinach, shoe soles, newspapers, finally she'll slice me and feed me to my brothers and sisters. Ah, now she's turned on the tap. It's roaring and pouring, pouring and roaring into a bucket without a bottom.

—The bell rings. Voices clash, clatter and break. The tin-and-bottle man? The neighbors? The police? The Help-the-Blind man? Thieves and burglars? All of them, all of them, ten or twenty or a hundred of them, marching up the stairs, hammering at the door, breaking in and climbing over me—ten, twenty or a hundred of them.

—Then, worst of all, the milk arrives. In the tallest glass in the house. "Suno, drink your milk. Good for you, Suno. You need it. Now, before the exams. Must have it, Suno. Drink." The voice wheedles its way into my ear like a worm. I shudder. The table tips over. The milk runs. The tum-

bler clangs on the floor. "Suno, Suno, how will you do your exams?"

—That is precisely what I ask myself. All very well to give me a room—Uncle's been pushed off on a pilgrimage to Hardwar to clear a room for me—and to bring me milk and say, "Study, Suno, study for your exam." What about the uproar around me? These people don't know the meaning of the word Quiet. When my mother fills buckets, sloshes the kitchen floor, fries and sizzles things in the pan, she thinks she is being Quiet. The children have never even heard the word, it amazes and puzzles them. On their way back from school they fling their satchels in at my door, then tear in to snatch them back before I tear them to bits. Bawl when I pull their ears, screech when mother whacks them. Stuff themselves with her fries and then smear the grease on my books.

So I raced out of my room, with my fingers in my ears, to scream till the roof fell down about their ears. But the radio suddenly went off, the door to my parents' room suddenly opened and my father appeared, bathed and shaven, stuffed and set up with the news of the world in six different languages—his white *dhoti*[2] blazing, his white shirt crackling, his patent leather pumps glittering. He stopped in the doorway and I stopped on the balls of my feet and wavered. My fingers came out of my ears, my hair came down over my eyes. Then he looked away from me, took his watch out of his

---

1. Hindi (hin′ dē) **. . . Tamil** (tam′ əl) **. . . Punjabi** (pun jä′ bē) **. . . Gujarati** (goo′ jə rät′ ē) *n.:* Four of the major languages spoken in India.

---

2. dhoti (dō′ tē) *n.:* A long loincloth traditionally worn by Hindu men.

ocket and inquired, "Is the food ready?" in a oice that came out of his nose like the whistle of a unctual train. He skated off towards his meal, I urned and slouched back to my room. On his way o work, he looked in to say, "Remember, Suno, I xpect good results from you. Study hard, Suno." ust behind him, I saw all the rest of them stand- ng, peering in, silently. All of them stared at me, at he exam I was to take. At the degree I was to get. Or not get. Horrifying thought. Oh study, study, tudy, they all breathed at me while my father's ootsteps went down the stairs, crushing each un- erfoot in turn. I felt their eyes on me, goggling, nd their breath on me, hot with <u>earnestness</u>. I ooked back at them, into their open mouths and taring eyes.

"Study," I said, and found I croaked. "I know ought to study. And how do you expect me to tudy—in this madhouse? You run wild, *wild*. I'm etting out," I screamed, leaping up and grabbing ny books, "I'm going to study outside. Even the treet is quieter," I screeched and threw myself past hem and down the stairs that my father had just owed and subjugated so that they still lay quiver- ng, and paid no attention to the howls that broke ut behind me of "Suno, Suno, listen. Your nilk—your studies—your exams, Suno!"

At first I tried the tea shop at the corner. In my eading I had often come across men who wrote at afé tables—letters, verse, whole novels—over a up of coffee or a glass of absinthe.[3] I thought it vould be simple to read a chapter of history over a up of tea. There was no crowd in the mornings, one of my friends would be there. But the propri- tor would not leave me alone. Bored, picking his ose, he wandered down from behind the counter o my table by the weighing machine and tried to ass the time of day by complaining about his piles, he new waiter and the high prices. "And sugar," e whined. "How can I give you anything to put n your tea with sugar at four rupees[4] a kilo? There's rationed sugar, I know, at two rupees, but

that's not enough to feed even an ant. And the way you all sugar your tea—*hai, hai*," he sighed, worse than my mother. I didn't answer. I frowned at my book and looked stubborn. But when I got rid of him, the waiter arrived. "Have a biscuit?" he mur- mured, flicking at my table and chair with his filthy duster. "A bun? Fritters? Make you some hot frit- ters?" I snarled at him but he only smiled, deter- mined to be friendly. Just a boy, really, in a pink shirt with purple circles stamped all over it—he thought he looked so smart. He was growing side- burns, he kept fingering them. "I'm a student, too," he said, "sixth class, fail. My mother wanted me to go back and try again, but I didn't like the teacher—he beat me. So I came here to look for a job. Lala-*ji* had just thrown out a boy called Hari for selling lottery tickets to the clients so he took me on. I can make out a bill . . ." He would have babbled on if Lala-*ji* had not come and shoved him into the kitchen with an oath. So it went on. I didn't read more than half a chapter that whole morning. I didn't want to go home either. I walked along the street, staring at my shoes, with my shoulders slumped in the way that makes my fa- ther scream, "What's the matter? Haven't you bones? A spine?" I kicked some rubble along the pavement, down the drain, then stopped at the iron gates of King Edward's Park.

"Exam troubles?" asked a *gram* vendor[5] who sat outside it, in a friendly voice. Not insinuating, but low, pleasant. "The park's full of boys like you," he continued in that sympathetic voice. "I see them walk up and down, up and down with their books, like mad poets. Then I'm glad I was never sent to school," and he began to whistle, not <u>impertinently</u> but so cheerfully that I stopped and stared at him. He had a crippled arm that hung out of his shirt sleeve like a leg of mutton dangling on a hook. His face was scarred as though he had been dragged out of some terrible accident. But he was shuffling hot *gram* into paper cones with his one hand and whistling like a bird, whistling the tune of, "We are the *bul-buls*[6] of our land, our land is

---

3. **absinthe** (ab´ sinth´) *n.*: A licorice-flavored alcoholic drink.
4. **rupees** (roo̅´ pēz) *n.*: Monetary units of India.

5. *gram* (gräm) **vendor** *n.*: A person who sells gram, dark-brown beans of the chickpea family, usually eaten roasted.
6. *bul-buls* (bool´ boolz) *n.*: Active, noisy, plain-colored birds.

---

7 **Discussion** Have students evalu- ate the author's use of personifica- tion (". . . stairs that my father had just cowed and subjugated so that they still lay quivering"). Have them identify the effect of attribut- ing human qualities to inanimate objects (the stairs). Ask students to look for other examples of per- sonification in the story.

8 **Literary Focus** In India, as in Britain, tea is consumed through- out the day—thus the presence of the tea shop at the corner. Point out that tea first appeared as a beverage in China about 2700 B.C., and became a popular bev- erage in Holland, England, and the American colonies in the early eighteenth century. Students may be interested to know that Britain's infamous Tea Act (1773), which eventually led to the American colonists' rebellious Boston Tea Party, was enacted to help the fi- nancially troubled British East In- dia Company unload a surplus of 17 million pounds of tea stored in England. (See Commentary, page 1415.)

9 **Reading Strategy** Point out to stu- dents how Desai's word choices (*flicking, filthy, snarled*) depict Suno's growing impatience and frustration. Have students identify other specific examples of words that create a mood.

10 **Clarification** Students may be un- familiar with this image. Open-air markets throughout the world often display mutton (a cut of meat from a sheep) and other meats hanging from hooks, to attract customers, cool the meat, and show what is for sale that day.

Primary Source
Anita Desai's eloquent appreciation of her native land, revealed in her colorful descriptions of Suno's park, is also apparent in the following excerpt from an article she wrote in 1991 for *The New York Review of Books*:

In India, the line between the sacred and the secular is a thin and wavering one. Together, they weave a web, and the web is spun by its people who are also its captives. The gods do not reside in some towering cathedral or remote shrine; they establish themselves in kitchens, storerooms, offices, even vehicles. In a land where a bus or taxi driver hangs an oleograph of a deity on the dashboard and decorates it with garlands of fresh flowers, where merchants set an idol upon their cashboxes and shopkeepers do not begin their trade before lighting incense and intoning prayers to their chosen god, the presence of the divine is so pervasive as to become intimate and familiar, woven into the texture of everyday.

BIRD, 1990
Tara Sabharwal
Collection of the artis[t]

Paradise." Nodding at the greenery beyond the gates, he said, "The park's a good place to study in," and, taking his hint, I went in.

I wonder how it is I never thought of the park before. It isn't far from our house and I sometimes went there as a boy, if I managed to run away from school, to lie on a bench, eat peanuts, shy stones at the chipmunks that came for the shells, and drink from the fountain. But then it was not as exciting as playing marbles in the street or stoning rats with my school friends in the vacant lot behind the cinema. It had straight paths, beds of flapping red flowers—cannas, I think—rows of palm trees like limp flags, a dry fountain and some green benches. Old men sat on them with their legs far apart, heads drooping over the tops of sticks, mumbling through their dentures or cackling with that mad, ripping laughter that makes children think of old men as wizards and bogey-men. Bag-like women in gray and fawn *saris*[7] or black *borkhas*[8] screamed, just as gray and fawn and black birds do, at chil[-]dren falling into the fountain or racing on rickety legs after the chipmunks and pigeons. A madman or two, prancing around in paper caps and bits of rags, munching banana peels and scratching like monkeys. Corners behind hibiscus bushes[9] stinking of piss. Iron rails with rows of beggars contentedly dozing, scratching, gambling, with their sackcloth backs to the rails. A city park.

What I hadn't noticed, or thought of, were all the students who escaped from their city flats and families like mine to come and study here. Now, walking down a path with my history book tucked under my arm, I felt like a gatecrasher at a party or a visitor to a public library trying to control a sneeze. They all seemed to belong here, to be at home here. Dressed in loose pajamas, they strolled up and down under the palms, books open in their hands, heads lowered into them. Or they sat in twos and threes on the grass, reading aloud in turns. Or lay full length under the trees, book spread out across their faces—sleeping, or else im[-]bibing information through the subconscious

---

7. saris (sä´ rēz) *n.*: Outer garments worn by Hindu women of India and Pakistan, each consisting of a long piece of cloth wrapped around the body.
8. borkhas (bʉr´ käs) *n.*: Garments of thin fabric that cover the head and veil the face, worn by Muslim women.

9. hibiscus (hi bis´ kəs) **bushes** *n.*: Tropical plants with large, colorful flowers.

Opening out my book, I too strolled up and down, reading to myself in a low murmur.

In the beginning, when I first started studying in the park, I couldn't concentrate on my studies. I'd keep looking up at the boy strolling in front of me, reciting poetry in a kind of thundering whisper, waving his arms about and running his bony fingers through his hair till it stood up like a thorn bush. Or at the chipmunks that fought and played and chased each other all over the park, now and then joining forces against the sparrows over a nest or a paper cone of *gram*. Or at the madman going through the rubble at the bottom of the dry fountain and coming up with a rubber shoe, a banana peel or a piece of glittering tin that he appreciated so much that he put it in his mouth and chewed it till blood ran in strings from his mouth.

It took me time to get accustomed to the ways of the park. I went there daily, for the whole day, and soon I got to know it as well as my own room at home and found I could study there, or sleep, or daydream, as I chose. Then I fell into its routine, its rhythm, and my time moved in accordance with its time. We were like a house-owner and his house, or a turtle and its shell, or a river and its bank—so close. I resented everyone else who came to the park—I thought they couldn't possibly share my feeling for it. Except, perhaps, the students.

The park was like a hotel, or a hospital, belonging to the city but with its own order and routine, enclosed by iron rails, laid out according to prescription in rows of palms, benches and paths. If I went there very early in the morning, I'd come upon a yoga class. It consisted of young body-builders rippling their muscles like snakes as well as old crack-pots determined to keep up with the youngest and fittest, all sitting cross-legged on the grass and displaying *hus-mukh* [10] to the sun just rising over the palms: the Laughing Face pose it was called, but they looked like gargoyles [11] with their mouths torn open and their thick, discolored tongues sticking out. If I were the sun, I'd feel so disgusted by such a reception I'd just turn around

and go back. And that was the simplest of their poses—after that they'd go into contortions that would embarrass an ape. Once their leader, a black and hirsute man like an aborigine, saw me watching and called me to join them. I shook my head and ducked behind an oleander.[12]. . . I despise all that body-beautiful worship anyway. What's the body compared to the soul, the mind?

I'd stroll under the palms, breathing in the cool of the early morning, feeling it drive out, or wash clean, the stifling dark of the night, and try to avoid bumping into all the other early morning visitors to the park—mostly aged men sent by their wives to fetch the milk from the Government dairy booth just outside the gates. Their bottles clinking in green cloth bags and newspapers rolled up and tucked under their arms, they strutted along like stiff puppets and mostly they would be discussing philosophy. "Ah but in Vedanta[13] it is a different matter," one would say, his eyes gleaming fanatically, and another would announce, "The sage Shanakaracharya showed the way," and some would refer to the Upanishads or the Bhagavad Puranas,[14] but in such argumentative, hacking tones that you could see they were quite capable of coming to blows over some theological argument. Certainly it was the mind above the body for these old coots but I found nothing to admire in them either. I particularly resented it when one of them disengaged himself from the discussion long enough to notice me and throw me a gentle look of commiseration. As if he'd been through exams, too, long long ago, and knew all about them. So what?

Worst of all were the athletes, wrestlers, Mr. Indias and others who lay on their backs and were massaged with oil till every muscle shone and glittered. The men who massaged them huffed and puffed and cursed as they climbed up and down the supine bodies, pounding and pummeling the

---

12. oleander (ō′ lē an′ dər) *n.*: An ornamental flowering shrub that grows up to fifteen feet in height.

13. Vedanta (vi dan′ tə) *n.*: One of the six orthodox systems of Indian philosophy and the one that forms the basis of most modern schools of Hinduism.

14. Upanishads (ōō pan′ i shadz′) **. . . Bhagavad Puranas** (bug′ ə vəd pōō rä′ nəz) *n.*: Hindu philosophical and literary writings.

---

10. *hus-mukh* (hus′ mōōk′) *n.*: Hindi meaning "cheerful or laughing face."

11. gargoyles (gär′ goilz′) *n.*: Grotesque animal figures used to adorn buildings, often functioning as waterspouts.

Desai's images also appear as metaphors, or implied comparisons of two different things. The following image is an extended metaphor:

My brains began to *jam up*....As if the *oil were all used up*. As if *everything was getting locked together, rusted*. The white cells, the gray matter, the *springs and nuts and bolts*. (page 1420)

Here the images compare Suno's brain to a machine that has stopped functioning.

Student Activity 1. Identify five examples of imagery in "Studies in the Park." Explain the comparisons suggested by the images. Include examples of both similes and metaphors.

Student Activity 2. Describe an event or activity using images. Write a paragraph that includes comparisons in the form of at least one simile and one metaphor.

men who lay there wearing nothing but little greasy clouts, groaning and panting in a way I found obscene and disgusting. They never looked up at me or at anyone. They lived in a meaty, sweating world of their own—massages, oils, the body, a match to be fought and won—I kicked up dust in their direction but never went too close.

The afternoons would be quiet, almost empty. I would sit under a tree and read, stroll and study, doze too. Then, in the evening, as the sky softened from its blank white glare and took on shades of pink and orange and the palm trees rustled a little in an invisible breeze, the crowds would begin to pour out of Darya Ganj, Mori Gate, Chandni Chowk and the Jama Masjid bazaars and slums. Large families would come to sit about on the grass, eating peanuts and listening to a transistor radio placed in the center of the circle. Mothers would sit together in flocks like screeching birds while children jumped into the dry fountains, broke flowers and terrorized each other. There would be a few young men moaning at the corners, waiting for a girl to roll her hips and dart her fish eyes in their direction, and then start the exciting adventure of pursuit. The children's cries would grow more piercing with the dark; frightened, shrill and exalted with mystery and farewell. I would wander back to the flat.

The exams drew nearer. Not three, not two, but only one month to go. I had to stop daydreaming and set myself tasks for every day and remind myself constantly to complete them. It grew so hot I had to give up strolling on the paths and staked out a private place for myself under a tree. I noticed the tension tightening the eyes and mouths of other students—they applied themselves more diligently to their books, talked less, slept less. Everyone looked a little demented from lack of sleep. Our books seemed attached to our hands as though by roots, they were a part of us, they lived because we fed them. They were parasites and, like parasites, were sucking us dry. We mumbled to ourselves, not always consciously. Chipmunks jumped over our feet, mocking us. The *gram* seller down at the gate whistled softly "I'm glad I never went to school, I am a *bul-bul,* I live in Paradise . . ."

My brains began to jam up. I could feel it happening, slowly. As if the oil were all used up. As if everything was getting locked together, rusted. The white cells, the gray matter, the springs and nuts and bolts. I yelled at my mother—I think it was my mother—"What do you think I am? What do you want of me?" and crushed a glass of milk between my hands. It was sticky. She had put sugar in my milk. As if I were a baby. I wanted to cry. They wouldn't let me sleep, they wanted to see my light on all night, they made sure I never stopped studying. Then they brought me milk and sugar and made clicking sounds with their tongues. I raced out to the park. I think I sobbed as I paced up and down, up and down, in the corner that stank of piss. My head ached worse than ever. I slept all day under the tree and had to work all night.

My father laid his hand on my shoulder. I knew I was not to fling it off. So I sat still, slouching, ready to spring aside if he lifted it only slightly. "You must get a first, Suno," he said through his nose, "must get a first, or else you won't get a job. Must get a job, Suno," he sighed and wiped his nose and went off, his patent leather pumps squealing like mice. I flung myself back in my chair and howled. Get a first, get a first, get a first—like a railway engine, it went charging over me, grinding me down, and left me dead and mangled on the tracks.

Everything hung still and yellow in the park. I lay sluggishly on a heap of waste paper under my tree and read without seeing, slept without sleeping. Sometimes I went to the water tap that leaked and drank the leak. It tasted of brass. I spat out a mouthful. It nearly went over the feet of the student waiting for his turn at that dripping tap. I stepped aside for him. He swilled the water around his mouth and spat, too, carefully missing my feet. Wiping his mouth, he asked, "B.A.?"

"No, Inter." [15]

"Hu," he burped. "Wait till you do your B.A.

---

15. B. A. . . . Inter: The Bachelor of Arts is a college degree. The Inter, or Intermediate degree, was taken after the tenth grade and was comparable to completing the eleventh and twelfth grades of high school.

Then you'll get to know." His face was like a gray bone. It was not unkind, it simply had no expression. "Another two weeks," he sighed and louched off to his own lair.

I touched my face. I thought it would be all bone, like his. I was surprised to find a bit of skin till covering it. I felt as if we were all dying in the park, that when we entered the examination hall it would be to be declared officially dead. That's what the degree was about. What else was it all about? Why were we creeping around here, hiding from the city, from teachers and parents, pretending to study and prepare? Prepare for what? We hadn't been told. Inter, they said, or B.A. or M.A. These were like official stamps—they would declare us dead. Ready for a dead world. A world in which ghosts went about, squeaking or whining, rattling or rustling. Slowly, slowly we were killing ourselves in order to join them. The ball-point pen in my pocket was the only thing that still lived, that still worked. I didn't work myself any more—I mean physically, my body no longer functioned. I was constipated, I was dying. I was lying under a yellow tree, feeling the dust sift through the leaves to cover me. It was filling my eyes, my throat. I could barely walk. I never strolled. Only on the way out of the park, late in the evening, I crept down the path under the palms, past the benches.

Then I saw the scene that stopped it all, stopped me just before I died.

Hidden behind an oleander was a bench. A woman lay on it, stretched out. She was a Muslim, wrapped in a black *borkha*. I hesitated when I saw this straight, still figure in black on the bench. Just then she lifted a pale, thin hand and lifted her veil. I saw her face. It lay bared, in the black folds of her *borkha*, like a flower, wax-white and composed, like a Persian lily or a tobacco flower at night. She was young. Very young, very pale, beautiful with a beauty I had never come across even in a dream. It caught me and held me tight, tight till I couldn't breathe and couldn't move. She was so white, so still, I saw she was very ill—with anemia,[16] perhaps,

or TB.[17] Too pale, too white—I could see she was dying. Her head—so still and white it might have been carved if it weren't for this softness, this softness of a flower at night—lay in the lap of a very old man. Very much older than her. With spectacles and a long gray beard like a goat's, or a scholar's. He was looking down at her and caressing her face—so tenderly, so tenderly, I had never seen a hand move so gently and tenderly. Beside them, on the ground, two little girls were playing. Round little girls, rather dirty, drawing lines in the gravel. They stared at me but the man and the woman did not notice me. They never looked at anyone else, only at each other, with an expression that halted me. It was tender, loving, yes, but in an inhuman way, so intense. Divine, I felt, or insane. I stood, half-hidden by the bush, holding my book, and wondered at them. She was ill, I could see, dying. Perhaps she had only a short time to live. Why didn't he take her to the Victoria Zenana Hospital, so close to the park? Who was this man—her husband, her father, a lover? I couldn't make out although I watched them without moving, without breathing. I felt not as if I were staring rudely at strangers, but as if I were gazing at a painting or a sculpture, some work of art. Or seeing a vision. They were still and I stood still and the children stared. Then she lifted her arms above her head and laughed. Very quietly.

I broke away and hurried down the path, in order to leave them alone, in privacy. They weren't a work of art, or a vision, but real, human and alive as no one else in my life had been real and alive. I had only that glimpse of them. But I felt I could never open my books and study or take degrees after that. They belonged to the dead, and now I had seen what being alive meant. The vision burnt the surfaces of my eyes so that they watered as I groped my way up the stairs to the flat. I could hardly find my way to the bed.

It was not just the examination but everything else had suddenly withered and died, gone lifeless and purposeless when compared with this vision. My studies, my family, my life—they all belonged

---

16. **anemia** (ə nē´ mē ə) *n.*: A condition in which the blood is deficient in red blood cells, hemoglobin, or volume.

17. **TB:** Tuberculosis, an infectious disease of the lung, also known as consumption.

24 **Discussion** In what way do you think the encounter with the student preparing for his B.A. exam adds to Suno's despair? Why do you think Desai refers to the student's place as a "lair"?

25 **Discussion** Have students identify the different kinds of death in this passage. Why does Suno contrast himself with his ball-point pen?

26 **Reading Strategy** Have students predict what could happen to stop Suno from dying. What will he see?

27 **Critical Thinking and Reading** Ask students how the author is able to convey an intensity of feeling without clarifying the exact relationship between the man and the woman. Have students discuss why this scene has such an impact on Suno.

28 **Discussion** Ask students to share works of art they have seen in museums, books, or other sources that portray an intense emotion. Have them compare their response to the art with that of Suno to this scene.

Master Teacher Note Challenge students to research and compare the educational opportunities available to students in India and in the United States.

Primary Source

These lines from a review in *The Times Literary Supplement* refer to Desai's award-winning book *Fire on the Mountain*, but they could just as easily apply to "Studies in the Park":

Mrs. Desai is marvelous at describing places, weather, atmosphere, sticks, stones, plants, animals, physical movement, and physical sensation. . . . Her novel is carefully and successfully constructed and although it is so quiet until the final denouement, suspense builds up again and again. . . .

to the dead and only what I had seen in the park had any meaning.

Since I did not know how to span the distance between that beautiful ideal and my stupid, dull existence, I simply lay still and shut my eyes. I kept them shut so as not to see all the puzzled, pleading, indignant faces of my family around me, but I could not shut out their voices.

"Suno, Suno," I heard them croon and coax and mourn.

"Suno, drink milk."

"Suno, study."

"Suno, take the exam."

And when they tired of being so patient with me and I still would not get up, they began to crackle and spit and storm.

"Get up, Suno."

"Study, Suno."

"At once, Suno."

Only my mother became resigned and gentle. She must have seen something quite out of the ordinary on my face to make her so. I felt her hand on my forehead and heard her say, "Leave him alone. Let him sleep tonight. He is tired out, that is what it is—he has driven himself too much and now he must sleep."

Then I heard all of them leave the room. Her hand stayed on my forehead, wet and smelling of onions, and after a bit my tears began to flow from under my lids.

"Poor Suno, sleep," she murmured.

I went back to the park of course. But now I was changed. I had stopped being a student—I was a "professional." My life was dictated by the rules and routine of the park. I still had my book open on the palms of my hands as I strolled but now my eyes strayed without guilt, darting at the young girls walking in pairs, their arms linked, giggling and bumping into each other. Sometimes I stopped to rest on a bench and conversed with one of the old men, told him who my father was and what examination I was preparing for, and allowing him to tell me about his youth, his politics, his philosophy his youth and again his youth. Or I joked with the other students, sitting on the grass and throwing peanut shells at the chipmunks, and shocking them, I could see, with my irreverence and cynicism about the school, the exam, the system. Once I even nodded at the yoga teacher and exchanged a few words with him. He suggested I join his class and I nodded vaguely and said I would think it over. It might help. My father says I need help. He says I am hopeless but that I need help. I just laugh but I know that he knows I will never appear for the examination, I will never come up to that hurdle or cross it—life has taken a different path for me, in the form of a search, not a race as it is for him, for them.

Yes, it is a search, a kind of perpetual search for me and now that I have accepted it and don't struggle, I find it satisfies me entirely, and I wander about the park as freely as a prince in his palace garden. I look over the benches, I glance behind the bushes, and wonder if I shall ever get another glimpse of that strange vision that set me free. I never have but I keep hoping, wishing.

GREETINGS, 1992
Tara Sabharwal
Collection, Robert Skelton

THINKING ABOUT THE SELECTION

Interpreting

1. (a) Describe the various activities that are frustrating Suno in the very beginning of the story. (b) How are these similar to or different from the types of distractions in an American community?
2. (a) Why hasn't Suno ever before thought of the park as a place to study? (b) How does his view of the park change throughout the story?
3. When he watches the yoga class in the mornings, Suno says, "What's the body compared to the soul, the mind?" (a) What does he mean by this comment? (b) Does he change his opinion in any way? Explain.
4. In your own words describe how the sight of the young woman and the old man on the bench affects Suno.
5. What is Suno searching for at the end of the story? Explain.

Applying

6. Suno has decided not to take the degrees his family wanted him to. How important is finishing school to your goals in life?

ANALYZING LITERATURE

Understanding Cultural Context

Indian culture has borrowed many customs from British culture, often modifying them in the process. It has also retained many customs that are uniquely its own. As you read "Studies in the Park," you probably noticed certain features of Suno's life that seemed specifically Indian. For example, Suno encounters aged men in the park who discuss the Hindu holy books known as the Upanishads and the Bhagavad Puranas. On the other hand, the bodybuilders that he sees are probably typical of other cultures as well.

1. (a) Identify aspects of British and Indian culture that play a role in the story. Be specific. (b) Then identify aspects of the story that are more universal.

2. (a) Describe the types of changes you would make if you were to retell this story using your community as a setting. (b) Do you think that you could convey the same theme as Desai does? Why or why not?

CRITICAL THINKING AND READING

Interpreting Epiphanies

The term *epiphany* originally came from Greek mythology, where it referred to the moment when a disguised god or goddess suddenly revealed his or her identity to a mortal. Today we use the word in a different sense. A modern epiphany is a sudden flash of insight or revelation that allows a person to learn more about himself or herself, or about life in general. An epiphany is an experience that many people have at some point in their lives.

1. (a) At what point does Suno experience an epiphany in Desai's story? (b) Describe his experience in your own words.
2. Does Desai prepare the reader for this epiphany or does it come as a complete surprise? Explain.
3. (a) How does Suno's sudden flash of insight change his attitude toward his studies? (b) Why does his attitude change?
4. (a) Is Suno's epiphany beneficial or harmful? (b) How will it continue to influence his life?

THINKING AND WRITING

Writing a Personal Essay

Write a personal essay about some turning point in your life. It need not be an especially dramatic or earth-shattering experience. The important thing is that it led to some new understanding on your part. Take some time to choose the appropriate experience. Try to remember as many details as possible about the time, place, and setting.

When you write, shape your essay so that it leads the reader toward your "turning point." If, for example, you were surprised by the incident you are describing, try to surprise the reader, too.

When you are revising your essay, pay attention to exactly how this experience changed your feelings or ideas. Even if the turning point you are describing was a small one, emphasize what was different for you before and after the experience.

Focus

More About the Author Pak Tu-jin was heavily influenced by Chong Chi-yong (choŋ chē yoŋ), Korea's first truly successful modern poet. In his early poems, Pak wrote allegorical pieces to veil his love of his country and to convey his vision of a fallen world. His later poems focus on modern Korean culture.

In addition to being a poet, Pak is an accomplished calligrapher and a connoisseur of stones, the subject of several hundred of his poems. He was also professor of Korean literature at Yonsei University. Ask students why stones might be good symbols of nature. What might they represent?

Critical Evaluation Like many poets, Pak shared his work with his mentor, Chong Chi-yong. Upon reading Pak's early poems, Chong stated: "Your poetry smells like plants in a forest . . . and brings a new nature to Korean poetry."

1916–

Until after the end of World War II in 1945, many critics claimed Korea did not have a literary voice of its own. Korea's lack of a literary heritage was in part due to China's control over Korea from 108 B.C. to A.D. 300. During this period, many Korean writers imitated Chinese writers.

To further retard writers from developing their craft, Japan—during its control over Korea from 1910 to 1945—prohibited publishing literature written in Korean. Because of this repression and prohibition of the use of the Korean language, many writers like Pak Tu-jin (päk tōō´ jin) refused to write and publish in a language other than their own. When Japan was defeated in 1945 and Korea was liberated, a flowering of modern poetry written in Korean emerged that reflected the voices of Koreans.

Shortly after Korea's liberation, the country was divided into two parts, each having its own form of government. North Korea installed a communist government backed by the Soviet Union and China; South Korea installed a noncommunist government backed by the United States. In 1950 the North Koreans invaded the South and the Korean War ensued; the war ended in 1953.

The division of Korea left the South with a weak economy. The outbreak of the war further weakened South Korea with the destruction of its farm crops and factories.

It is from this context that a group of contemporary Korean writers emerged who reflected the first modern literary voice of Korea. Peter H. Lee, in the introduction of *The Silence of Love* states the following about post–World War II Korean writers:

Their work bears the marks of desire, doubt, suffering, and frustration. Dismayed at the betrayal of hope and outraged at man's capacity for evil, some dwellers in this modern wasteland have become underground men, urban word-guerrillas. With a passionate concern for the fate of Korea, they have celebrated poetry, the quintessentially human. Despite considerable stylistic and thematic differences, they have opened Korean poetry to new areas of experience and have assimilated more of actuality.

Among the many poets who emerged was Pak Tu-jin. Pak and the other modern poets of the 1940's were strongly influenced by the French Symbolists, including Charles Baudelaire and Arthur Rimbaud. Pak's poetry mingles sound and symbol to create a beauty in his poetry that did not exist in his world. Through nature imagery, Pak created a utopian world of beauty and hope. His poetry inspired hope for new life in a new generation.

Pak, who was born in Ansong, in the Kyonggi province in South Korea, made his literary debut in 1939. After thirty-one years of writing but not publishing his work, he re-emerged in 1949 as one of Korea's major Southern writers with the publication of his first collection, *The Sun*. Since this first publication, Pak has published ten other books of poetry, numerous essays, and interpretations of his own poems. In addition, he received numerous awards including the Free Literature Prize in 1956, the Culture Prize of the City of Seoul in 1962, the March First Literature Prize in 1970, and the Korean Academy of Art Prize in 1976.

Objectives

Thematic
To understand symbolism

Skill
To understand symbols of nature

GUIDE FOR INTERPRETING

Commentary

High Mountain Plant; August River

Symbols. A **symbol** is anything that stands for or represents something else. The use of symbols in writing is called symbolism. Symbolism was an important literary movement that began in France in the nineteenth century. French Symbolists stressed the importance of suggestion and evocation.

In 1919, with the widespread reading of translations of the French Symbolists, a powerful Western influence on Korean poetry began to appear. The most influential poem to the French Symbolists and to the emerging Korean writers was Baudelaire's poem "Correspondences." In this poem Baudelaire creates a correspondence between the material world and spiritual realities and between the different human senses.

The Symbolist philosophy complemented many of the Korean writers' philosophical and religious beliefs. Many Korean writers, like Pak Tu-jin, adopted French Symbolism in the form of nature symbols, which complemented the familiar nature imagery found in Buddhist and Confucian philosophy, two of the most prominent religions of South Korea.

Pak Tu-jin used nature symbols as a way of communicating his personal feelings about hope, the fate of Korea, and his vision of an unfallen world. Pak's nature poems, like symbolist poetry in general, take the reader beyond the poem to a higher level of understanding about life. On one level, Pak is describing a plant or a river, as he does in "High Mountain Plant" and "August River," respectively. On a deeper level, however, he is describing a world of decay and renewal and communicating a message that reflects his feelings and hopes about life.

Writing

Many writers have written about the effects of nature on them. Choose something from the world of nature—a rainbow, a storm, daybreak—and freewrite about its effects on you. Explain what this aspect of nature symbolizes or represents to you.

Primary Source

In the introduction of *The Silence of Love*, Peter H. Lee said the following about the influence of the French Symbolists on Korean writers: "The force with which these poets observed the world and listened to the flow of Time in their blood—tradition—was a reflex of its hold on them. . . . These poets delved into their own tradition to redeem the past and to verify a new world they created . . . They never lost sight of examining the immediacy of 'now' and of re-animating the Old to gain knowledge of the New."

(continued from bottom of page)
Writing/Prior Knowledge Encourage students to use imagery to explain the effects of nature on them. Have volunteers share their responses with the class.

ESL Teaching Strategy ESL students may have difficulty understanding Pak's imagery and symbolism. You may wish to read these poems aloud, stopping periodically to answer questions and to clarify points.

Master Teacher Note The masterful use of natural images is an ancient tradition in Asian literature. For millennia nature has provided lessons in living for those who were patient enough to learn. Ask students to discuss possible themes or messages in each of these poems. After giving students time to work, record their insights on the chalkboard.

Teaching Tenth-Grade Students Have tenth-grade students select a natural subject and write a 12- to 14-line poem on that subject. Require, however, that students develop a second level of meaning in the poem. In other words, encourage them to develop a metaphorical level of meaning as well as a literal level of meaning in their work.

Vocabulary
Preteach the following vocabulary words:
engulfing (en gulf´ iŋ) v.: Swallowing up; overwhelming
mute (myo͞ot) adj.: Not speaking; silent
wrath (rath) n.: Rage; fury
betrayals (bē trā´ əlz) n.: Deceptions; insurrections

Support Material

Teaching Portfolio
Teacher Backup, p. 1745
Usage and Mechanics Worksheet, p. 1749
Vocabulary Check, p. 1750
Analyzing Literature Worksheet, *Understanding Symbols of Nature*, p. 1751

Critical Thinking and Reading Worksheet, *Interpreting Poetry*, p. 1752
Selection Test, pp. 1753–1754

Literary Focus Explain to students that poets often write about topics that are controversial and express ideas that are dangerous to voice. To help mask their feelings, poets sometimes write allegorical and symbolic pieces. Have students look for details in the imagery that indirectly describe a war-torn and corrupt Korea.

Presentation

Motivation/Prior Knowledge
Discuss with students symbols from nature with which they are already familiar. Students might suggest a dove, which symbolizes love and peace and a fish, which symbolizes Christ, and so on. Also ask them what songs include images and symbols from nature. If possible, have students bring these songs to class to share with classmates.

Purpose-Setting Question
What is the effect of Pak's contrasting imagery?

Universal Themes Other selections that use symbolism that can be interpreted on different levels include Giovanni Boccaccio's "Federigo's Falcon," page 684; Rainer Maria Rilke's "Interior of the Rose," page 1056; and Mori Ōgai's "Under Reconstruction," page 1174.

1 Discussion To what might Pak be referring here?

2 Discussion What is Pak describing in this passage?

3 Discussion What does he mean when he says the "fog shivers"? How is the orchid able to live in such an environment?

4 Literary Focus: Symbols Who might Pak really be describing here?

5 Discussion What is the effect of the stark contrast between this stanza and the second stanza?

6 Discussion Restate in your own words what Pak is saying in this stanza.

High Mountain Plant

Pak Tu-jin

translated by Peter H. Lee

You live on a sheer riven[1] cliff.
The dagger in my heart is a blossoming orchid
Curving through the thick fog and rain, shivering
    in the wind.
A fierce bird's torn wings mirrored in the cold
    moonlight,
5 The gorgeous flags, like a tide, engulfing the hill,
The mute roar, now fallen as flowers,

——————
1. riven (riv´ ən) *adj.*: Torn apart; split.

You live on the cliff this side of the silent abyss.[2]
Gusts will blow again in the morning sky,
Revolution will overrun the earth, north south
    east west,
10 The dagger will stab the chain, the net, that night,
The creation's last light scattering flowers.
Orchid, you live on a cliff where the fog shivers.

——————
2. abyss (ə bis´) *n.*: Bottomless gulf; chasm.

August River

Pak Tu-jin

translated by Peter H. Lee

The August river claps its hands,
The August river writhes,[1]
The August river agonizes,
The river hides its brilliance.

The river remembers yesterday's sighs, tears,
    spilling of blood, and deaths,
Remembers the forked tongues and bloodied
5   teeth of snakes and wolves
That harbor[2] the wrath, supplications,[3] and betray-
    als of yesterday.

——————
1. writhes (rīthz) *v.*: Contorts itself in agony.
2. harbor (här´ bər) *v.*: Shelter; conceal.
3. supplications (sup´ lə kā´ shənz) *n.*: Humble requests; prayers.

Remembers the remote idea of the Milky Way,[4] the
    brilliant solar system
And its golden sublimation.[5]

10 For the sake of victory, attainment, fulfillment for all
It commits yesterday to today, today to tomorrow.

The river, the river of August is long and bright.
Full of spirit, slapping its hands, flying its flags,
It moves on, on to the vast sea.

——————
4. the Milky Way: The spiral galaxy in which our sun is found.
5. sublimation (sub´ lə mā´ shən) *n.*: Purification; refinement.

Reader's Response *What feelings did each of Pak's poems evoke?*

Closure and Extension

ANSWERS TO THINKING ABOUT THE SELECTION

1. Because Pak was influenced by and wrote during the Korean War, the "sheer riven cliff" could symbolize the line that divided North and South Korea; it could also be the front line of a battle.

2. Answers may differ. Some students may state that the orchid symbolizes life before the war. Its beauty and life stabs the speaker's heart.

3. Answers may differ. Some students will state that the orchid will remain and survive on the "sheer riven cliff." This conveys the message that there is hope that the war will end, peace will be restored, and life will be renewed.

4. Answers may differ. Suggested response: The month of August symbolizes the end of summer and the beginning of fall when nature begins to die and go into dormancy in preparation for winter. He is perhaps suggesting that the memories of the war must be put aside and lie dormant because life must go on.

5. Answers may differ. Most students will state that they envision a turbu-

MOUNTAIN LANDSCAPE IN MOONLIGHT
Kim Ki-chang
The Brooklyn Museum, New York

THINKING ABOUT THE SELECTION

Interpreting

1. What might the symbol of a "sheer riven cliff" suggest?
2. What might the orchid symbolize?
3. The orchid lives on "the cliff this side of the silent abyss." In existentialism the abyss is the point at which one must make a choice of either falling into the abyss or turning around and facing whatever brought one to the edge. Giving the orchid the human capacity to reason, what choice will the orchid make? Support your answer. What message does this decision convey?
4. Why does Pak name this river the August river?
5. What kind of river do you envision as you read "August River"? Why?
6. What words and phrases describe an unfallen world?

7. Personification is common in Symbolist poetry. What human characteristics does Pak give the river? What is the effect of Pak's personification of the river?

ANALYZING LITERATURE

Understanding Symbols of Nature

Nature symbols describe the natural world as well as express a higher level of understanding about life. Through Pak's use of nature symbols, he described a world of decay and renewal and communicated a message that reflected his feelings and hopes about Korea's future.

1. What hope does Pak express in each of these two poems? What images symbolize this hope?
2. Compare and contrast the recurring images of water in its various forms in each of these two poems. What does water symbolize in each one? In which poem is the water imagery most effective? Why?

(continued from bottom of page)
and torrential tidal waves that engulf the hill. These images suggest despair, sorrow, death, and destruction. In "August River," the river symbolizes hope and life. Answers will differ in terms of which students think is the most effective.

THINKING AND WRITING

For a Thinking and Writing assignment for this selection, see page 1746 in the Teaching Portfolio.

Challenge Some critics have noted the similarity between the work of English poet John Keats and Pak Tu-jin. Have students read several poems by Keats and compare the imagery and symbolism in both poets' work.

Humanities Note

Fine art, *Mountain Landscape in Moonlight*, 1975, by Kim Ki-chang. Born in Seoul, South Korea, in 1914, Kim Ki-chang is one of Korea's best-known artists. As a child, Kim contracted an illness that impaired his hearing and his speech. He started painting at 16. Since then his paintings have won several prizes and have been exhibited in Korea, the United States, France, and Brazil.

Kim often paints under different art names. He painted *Mountain Landscape in Moonlight* under the name Un Po, or Mr. Cloud.

This painting depicts a pair of mandarin ducks flying among boulders, cliffs, and blue mountain peaks.

Tell students that like Pak Tu-jin, Kim Ki-chang uses symbols from nature in his paintings. Ask students what the two mandarin ducks might symbolize.

lent river, with numerous bends in it because of the description of the river in lines 1–4.

6. Answers may differ. Suggested response: The "blossoming orchid," and "the Milky Way, the brilliant solar system / And its golden sublimation" suggest an unfallen world.

7. Pak gives the river hands which it claps and slaps; he gives it a memory which conjures up the horrors of

war; and he gives the river spirit. Some students may state that the personification suggests that the river is more than just a river—it is a symbol for life.

ANSWERS TO ANALYZING LITERATURE

1. Pak expresses the hope that the war will end and that life will endure and

be renewed. The orchid lives in a place that makes even the fog shiver, yet it survives. The river, even though it is in pain from the memories of the war, also recognizes the beauty that exists. By the end of the poem, the river has cast away its sorrows and "moves on, on to the vast sea."

2. In "High Mountain Plant," images of water are in the form of rain, fog,

KAWABATA YASUNARI

1899–1972

Early in his youth, Kawabata Yasunari (kow′ ə bä′ tə yä′ soo nä′ rē) thought of himself as a painter, but he immersed himself in Buddhist literature at age twelve. His interest in painting is evident in some of his colorfully descriptive, visual passages. Above all, his writing is most often characterized by sadness and an acute perception of the impermanence of life. Critics see Kawabata's pensive writing as a reflection of his childhood.

Kawabata found himself entirely alone in the world at age sixteen. When he was only two years old, his father died. The next year, his mother died, followed by his sister, and then his grandmother. He lived with his grandfather for nine years until the grandfather too died. After his grandfather's death, he attended the elite First High School in Tokyo and Tokyo Imperial University, where he studied Japanese literature.

His first work, though not his first published work, was *Diary of a Sixteen-Year-Old*. According to Kawabata, he composed the diary in 1914, covering twelve days in May. He stopped writing in the diary a week before his grandfather died. The memories of the last days of his grandfather recur in Kawabata's fiction, but the *Diary* is the most evocative. Some scholars question the *Diary*'s authenticity, arguing that it was probably written the year it was published in 1925. But Kawabata insists that he found the manuscript on student composition paper in an uncle's storehouse. He said, "The strangest thing was that I had not the least recollection of the events described in the diary . . . I confronted the honest emotions of a forgotten past. But the grandfather I had described was uglier than the grandfather of my memory. For ten years my mind had been constantly cleansing my grandfather's image."

Kawabata's first published story, "A View of the Yasukuni Festival," attracted favorable attention. It was an auspicious beginning for his career because it impressed Kikuchi Kan, an important figure in the Japanese literary world. Kikuchi made Kawabata a staff member of his literary magazine, *Bungei Shunju*. He also introduced Kawabata to Yokomitsu Riichi, who influenced Kawabata's writing throughout his career. Yokomitsu and Kawabata eventually became two of the major Japanese novelists of the 1920's.

Kawabata avoided direct involvement in World War II by traveling in Manchuria. During the war he read the Japanese classics, including *The Tale of Genji*, which he describes as having "the traditional sadness of Japan, [but also] consolation and salvation." Perhaps because of traditional influences, his work evokes awareness of the transience and loneliness of life, a typical theme of Japanese literature.

For years Kawabata led an extremely private life, but in 1933 he began to participate more actively in the literary world. He joined the staffs of magazines, and he was appointed to the Literary Discussion Group, an organization that tried to control literature by fostering cooperation between writers and the repressive government. Although Kawabata willingly cooperated with the government, he continued to publish articles in which he encouraged freedom of speech and a spirit of rebellion against social conventions. In his words, "Without rebellion against conventional morality there can be no pure literature."

Kawabata was an influential figure in the careers of new writers in Japan. The Akutagawa Prize, established in 1935 to encourage new writers, had him as one of its judges. Kawabata himself won most of Japan's major literary awards. In 1968 he became the first Japanese writer to win the Nobel Prize for Literature.

Objectives

Thematic

To understand the interdependence between children and parents

Skills

1 To analyze thematic imagery
2 To understand structure
3 To appreciate words from Japanese
4 To write from past experience

GUIDE FOR INTERPRETING

The Jay

Commentary

Thematic Imagery. One of the outstanding characteristics of Kawabata's work is its sharp imagery. Imagery is the use of images as concrete representations of sensory or emotional experiences. **Thematic imagery** involves the repeated use of an image in a pattern connected with theme, the universal truth in a literary work. Some image themes are recurrent in literature, like those of light and dark images connected with the theme of goodness versus evil. Another recurrent image theme involves seasonal imagery in connection with the cyclical quality of life. Thematic imagery can be the key to the values and interpretation of the literary work.

In "The Jay" Kawabata connects an image of a fragile, injured bird with the characters in his story. Each character is somehow alienated or hurt like the injured bird. Fear, loneliness, pain—qualities Kawabata indirectly associates with the injured bird—surface in each of the characters. The bird's need for parental nourishment is also an important need for the characters.

Writing

Have you ever come upon an injured bird? Perhaps at one time you had to care for a small, helpless creature, like a pet, or a sick child. Even if you have never had such an experience, explore the associations that type of situation brings to mind. Draw from your own experience or your imagination.

Primary Source

Kawabata believed strongly in the importance of tradition in artistic discipline, as he explained in the following excerpt from his *Complete Works.* "It is part of the discipline of the different arts of Japan, as well as a guidepost to the spirit, for a man to make his way in the footsteps of his predecessors, journeying a hundred times to the famous places and old sites, but not to waste time traipsing over unknown mountains and rivers . . . The utensils used by the men of the past have been considered treasures and they have also produced new beauty. Disciples who have attempted while still immature to display their individuality have been disowned. The custom of maintaining strict control over the transmission of the arts had its origins in the national character (kunigara) of Japan."

Literary Focus Explain to students that when an author uses a thematic image, such as the jay in this story, the situation illustrated by the image can often be taken as representing the emotional state in one or more of the characters. Have students discuss whose emotions are best dramatized by the situation of the helpless jay. Then have them keep this discussion in mind as they read the story.

Writing/Prior Knowledge Pair the students in the class. Have them share ideas and exchange experiences with sick or helpless creatures before they begin freewriting.

ESL Teaching Strategy To help with the writing assignment, pair each ESL student with a native-speaking student. Have the native-speaking student coach the ESL student on how to develop a drawing that might help visualize the creature that he or she is writing about.

Teaching Tenth-Grade Students Ask tenth-grade students what associations they make with a jay. What images come to mind? What are a jay's characteristics?

Master Teacher Note Have students discuss their own experiences with films and stories that include thematic imagery. Many of them, for example, may have read Mark Twain's *The Adventures of Huckleberry Finn*, in which the Mississippi River runs through as a theme and an image.

Support Material

Teaching Portfolio
Teacher Backup, p. 1755
Usage and Mechanics Worksheet, p. 1759
Analyzing Literature Worksheet, *Analyzing Thematic Imagery*, p. 1760
Critical Thinking and Reading Worksheet, *Understanding Struc-*ture, p. 1761
Language Worksheet, *Understanding Linking Verbs*, p. 1762
Selection Test, pp. 1763–1764

Art Transparency 20
Enjoying Cherry Blossom Viewing at Ueno by Yoshu Chikanobu

Master Teacher Note Use the overhead projector to show Art Transparency 20, *Enjoying Cherry Blossom Viewing at Ueno* by Yoshu Chikanobu. Ask students what they find most striking about this painting.

The Jay

Kawabata Yasunari

translated by Edward Seidensticker

The jay was noisy from dawn.

It seemed to have flown from a lower branch of the pine tree as Yoshiko was opening the shutters and then come back again. They could hear its wings from the breakfast table.

"What a racket," said her brother, starting to get up.

"Leave it alone," said her grandmother. "I think the little one must have fallen from the nest yesterday. I could still hear the mother last night after dark. I suppose she couldn't find it. And isn't that nice, here she is back again this morning."

"Are you sure?" asked Yoshiko.

Save for a liver attack some ten years before, her grandmother had never been ill, but she had suffered from cataracts[1] ever since she was very young. Now she could barely see, and with the left eye only. She had to be handed her food. She could grope her way around the house, but she never went out alone into the garden.

She would sometimes stand or sit at the glass door and gaze at her fingers, spread out in the sunlight. Her whole life seemed to be concentrated in the gaze.

Yoshiko would be afraid of her. She would want to call from behind, and then she would slip away.

Yoshiko was filled with admiration that her blind grandmother could talk about the jay as if she had seen it.

When she went out to do the breakfast dishes, the jay was calling from the roof next door.

There were a chestnut and several persimmons in the back yard. She could see against them that a gentle rain was falling, so gentle that she could not make it out except against the dark background.

The jay flew to the chestnut, skimmed the ground, and flew back again, calling out all the while.

Would the nestling still be near, that the mother was so reluctant to leave?

Yoshiko went to her room. She must be ready by noon.

Her mother and father would be bringing her fiancé's mother.

As she sat down before the mirror she glanced at the white dots on her fingernails. They were said to be a sign that someone would come with gifts, but she had read in a newspaper that they really showed a deficiency in vitamin C or something of the sort. She was pleased with her face when she had finished making herself up. She thought her eyebrows and lips rather charming. She liked the set of her kimono.[2]

She had thought she would wait for her mother to help her, and then she was glad that she had dressed by herself.

Her father and mother, actually her stepmother, did not live with them.

---

1. **cataracts** (kat′ ə rakts′): An eye disease in which the lens or its capsule becomes opaque, causing partial or total blindness.

2. **kimono** (kə mō′ nə) *n.*: A robe with wide sleeves and a sash, part of the traditional costume of Japanese men and women.

Her father had divorced her mother when Yoshiko was four and her brother two. It was said that her mother had been gaudy and extravagant, but Yoshiko suspected that there had been deeper causes.

Her father had said nothing when her brother had found a picture of their mother and shown it to him. He had frowned and torn the picture to pieces.

When Yoshiko was thirteen her new mother came into the house. Later Yoshiko was to think it rather remarkable of her father to have waited almost ten years. Her new mother was a kind woman and they lived a quiet, happy life.

When her brother entered high school and went to live in a dormitory, it was plain to all of them that his attitude toward his stepmother was changing.

"I've seen Mother," he said to Yoshiko. "She is married and living in Azabu.[3] She is very beautiful. She was glad to see me."

Yoshiko was too startled to answer. She was sure that she had turned white, and she was trembling.

Her stepmother came in from the next room.

"It's all right. There's nothing wrong at all with his seeing his own mother. It's only natural. I knew it would happen. It doesn't bother me at all."

Her stepmother seemed drained of strength, and so tiny that Yoshiko felt somehow protective.

Her brother got up and went out. Yoshiko wanted to slap him.

"You are not to say anything, Yoshiko," said her stepmother softly. "It would only make things worse."

Yoshiko was in tears.

Her father brought her brother home from the dormitory. She thought that would be the end of the matter; and then her father and stepmother moved away.

She was frightened. She felt that she had had the full force of—a man's anger, perhaps, or vengefulness? She wondered if she and her brother had something of the same thing in them. She had felt certain, as he had left the room, that her brother had inherited that terrible masculine something.

Yet she felt too that she knew her father's loneliness those ten years he had waited to take a new wife.

---

3. **Azabu** (ə zä bo͞o): A street in Tokyo.

She was startled when her father came with talk of a prospective bridegroom.

"You have had a hard time of it, Yoshiko, and I am sorry. I have told his mother that I want you to have the girlhood you never had."

There were tears in Yoshiko's eyes.

With Yoshiko married, there would be no one to take care of her grandmother and brother, and so

YUKI
Kotondo
Ronin Gallery, New York

valued sensory detail in this way all his life, his friend eventually retreated from this ideal into writing that championed right-wing politics. In his Nobel Prize speech, Kawabata said that in his work he had made a lifelong search for beauty, even the beauty in death itself, and for harmony among human beings, nature, and emptiness.

5 **Discussion** Ask students to discuss the three different views of the father presented here in succession. First, the divorce has deeper causes. Next, he tears up the mother's picture. Then Yoshiko finds his ten-year wait remarkable. What is the effect of this quick succession of thoughts?

6 **Clarification** Point out to students the complexity of the emotions that we glimpse indirectly in this scene. Yoshiko is startled, trembling, and finally in tears, primarily because she knows that the father will be furious at what her brother has done. Why, then, in spite of the stepmother's being so understanding, does Yoshiko feel protective of her and why does the stepmother herself seem drained of strength?

7 **Discussion** Ask students what Yoshiko is frightened of in this passage. Why is she concerned that she has inherited something of her father's anger? At the same time, how is it possible for her to be so understanding toward her father because of his ten years of loneliness?

8 **Enrichment** Point out to students that even at the time of the story, and sometimes even today, it was customary for parents to arrange marriages for their children without the young couple's having met. How does this affect students' understanding of Yoshiko's tears in this scene?

Humanities Note
Fine Art, *Yuki* by Kotondo. Kotondo (1900–1976) was born in Japan. Kotondo's favorite subjects were the beautiful women of Japan. Note the bold design and yet delicate handling of details. Kotondo became the director of the Torii school until his retirement in 1951.

You might want to use the following questions to discuss the art:
1. How would you characterize the woman in this print?
2. Why is this print appropriate to the story?

9 Discussion Ask students to explain why Yoshiko is affected most by the decision to allow the brother and grandmother to live with the father and stepmother. How exactly does it affect her and what other things are evidently affecting her at the same time?

10 Discussion Ask students to discuss why Yoshiko is embarrassed that her grandmother can no longer remember what she looks like.

11 Critical Thinking and Reading Have students explain how the story's beginning and ending with the lost jay create a framing structure for the story it contains.

12 Literary Focus Ask students how the author uses the reunion of the jays to sum up and comment on Yoshiko's situation at the end of the story.

Cultural Note Many early traditional Japanese stories are very similar to "The Jay" in the way they use images to reveal character. The clues that this is a modern story, however, can be seen in details that have only recently been a part of Japanese life: divorce, the glass door, concern about a vitamin deficiency, a power line. Ask students what other details in the story are likely to have been a part of Japanese life for a very long time.

Cooperative Learning How writers depict families in conflict is a subject that is likely to interest students. Divide the class into small groups. Have each group select a writer whom they have already studied in *World Masterpieces*. Then have them determine through discussion of that writer's work the attitude toward family conflict that it displays and compare it to "The Jay."

it was decided that they would live with her father and stepmother. The decision was what touched Yoshiko most. Because of what her father had been through she had been frightened of marriage, but now that it was coming it did not seem so frightening after all.

She went to her grandmother when she had finished dressing.

"Can you see the red, Grandmother?"

"I can see that there is something red." She pulled Yoshiko to here and looked intently at her kimono and obi.[4] "I have forgotten what you look like, Yoshiko. How nice if I could see you again."

Embarrassed, Yoshiko put her hand to her grandmother's head.

She went out into the garden. She wanted to run and meet her father and stepmother. She opened a hand, but the rain was scarcely enough to wet it. Lifting her skirts she looked through the shrubs and bamboo, and found the nestling jay in the grass under the *hagi*.[5]

She stole up to it. Head pulled in, it was a tight little ball. It seemed without strength and she had no trouble taking it. She looked around but could not find the mother.

She ran to the house.

---

4. obi (ō′ bē) *n.*: A broad sash with a bow in the back, worn with a kimono.
5. hagi (hä gē): The Japanese name for the bush-clover plant.

"I've found it, Grandmother. It seems very weak."

"Really? You must give it water."

Her grandmother was very calm.

She brought a cup of water and put its beak in, and it drank most prettily, swelling its small throat.

"Kikikikiki." It quickly revived.

Hearing, the mother jay called from a power line.

"Kikiki." The nestling struggled in Yoshiko's hand.

"How very nice," said her grandmother. "You must give it back."

Yoshiko went into the garden. The mother jay left the power line and sat watching Yoshiko from the cherry tree.

Raising her hand to show the nestling, Yoshiko put it on the ground.

She watched from inside the glass door. The nestling called forlornly up. The mother came nearer and then was at the lower branches of the pine tree just above. The nestling flapped its wings as if it were about to take flight, and fell forward, calling out to its mother.

Very cautious, the mother still did not alight.

Then, in a swoop, it was beside the nestling, whose joy was boundless. The head shook, the outstretched wings were trembling, it was like a spoiled child. The mother seemed to be feeding it.

Yoshiko wished that her father and stepmother would hurry. She wanted them to see.

Reader's Response *In what ways do you sympathize or identify with the jay? What does the jay mean to you?*

Closure and Extension

ANSWERS TO THINKING ABOUT THE SELECTION

1. The sole survivor of her generation in the family, she is very old and nearly blind; where she lives is determined by others without consideration for her own wishes.

2. She finds herself in a strange, possibly hostile environment and cannot turn to anyone in her own family for help.

3. Possibly out of consideration for his children, he did not remarry for ten years after an evidently bitter divorce.

4. He visited his mother partly out of a natural desire to see her and partly to defy his father, who had placed his son in a school dormitory.

5. Yoshiko, being older, may miss their mother more than her brother does, but may feel that, unlike him, she lacked the courage to defy their father by visiting her. She also knows that her brother's defiance will enrage their father—and she is frightened of the family conflict that may follow.

6. She constantly tries to reclaim and heal the lost harmony of her family.

THINKING ABOUT THE SELECTION

Interpreting

1. In what ways is Yoshiko's grandmother lonely and alienated?
2. How is Yoshiko's stepmother like the jay?
3. Why does Yoshiko sympathize with her father?
4. Why do you think Yoshiko's brother went to see his mother?
5. Why does Yoshiko cry when her brother describes seeing their mother?
6. How is Yoshiko like the jay's mother? Refer to specific examples from the story in your answer.
7. Why does Yoshiko want her father and stepmother to see the jay's mother feeding it?

Applying

8. What other relationships of nature are comparable to family relationships?

ANALYZING LITERATURE

Analyzing Thematic Imagery

Thematic imagery is the repeated use of an image in a pattern that is somehow connected to the deeper, underlying message in a literary work. Image themes can sometimes point to the unconscious motivations of the author. Although a piece of writing should never be judged in terms of its author's biography, sometimes there is a legitimate connection between the author's life and the subjects of his or her writing. For example, the need for parental nourishment in "The Jay" reminds the reader familiar with Kawabata's past that he lost his parents at a young age. His image of a frightened, fragile, injured bird in need of its mother connects with the sadness, loneliness, and alienation that we know were a part of his life.

1. Besides the fragile bird, what other images of fragility can you find in "The Jay"?
2. Discuss the maternal images in the story. What image theme do they convey?
3. (a) Find and discuss the images of youth and age in the story. (b) How does Kawabata convey these images?

CRITICAL THINKING AND READING

Understanding Structure

Kawabata is said to have had little sense of structure. Some critics describe the structure of some of his work as linear, in the form of linked verse. In linked verse, moments are strung together as if they follow one another in an irrational, meandering way. In linked verse, emphasis is on the immediate moment, its memories, and its desires. Gestures, startling dialogue, and momentary feelings strung together convey a keen awareness of emotional states and how they are similar to the natural world. Linked verse is the precursor of the Japanese haiku.

1. (a) In what ways does "The Jay" seem fragmentary and strung together? (b) How does the fragmentary narration of "The Jay" affect its meaning?
2. In "The Jay," Kawabata doesn't analyze characters at length or depict them in long, dramatic scenes. Yet, he does provide glimpses into their personalities. What insightful hints does he provide for each character?

UNDERSTANDING LANGUAGE

Appreciating Words from Japanese

In *The American Language*, H. L. Mencken wrote, "A living language is like a man suffering incessantly from small hemorrhages, and what it needs above all is constant transactions of new blood from other tongues." The Japanese tongue is only one of many that have influenced American English. One common example is the word *karate* (kə rät´ ē), which comes from the Japanese root *kara*, empty and *te*, hand.

1. Find an example of a Japanese word common in American English in "The Jay."
2. Use a dictionary to identify the origins of the following Japanese words and explain how they are used in American culture: (a) teriyaki, (b) haiku, (c) kamikaze.

THINKING AND WRITING

Writing from Past Experience

Writers often draw from past experiences for the raw material of their fiction. Even if a story is only indirectly or subtly related to a writer's actual experience, memory can generate an idea for a story, poem, or novel. The English poet William Wordsworth's famous definition of poetry is "emotion recollected in tranquility." Wordsworth's definition is not necessarily limited to poetry; past experience is a resource for all writers. Think of something wonderful that happened to you. Write a short description of that experience, showing how it still affects you. Explain why it is an experience you are not likely to forget. What did you learn? As you revise, make sure you have made connections for the reader. Finally, proofread your paper.

(continued from bottom of page)

grandmother. Images of youth are presented in depictions of Yoshiko and her brother. (b) The images themselves are mostly concrete and visual, but they present the theme indirectly in that Kawabata never says what they mean.

ANSWERS TO CRITICAL THINKING AND READING

1. (a) There is no progression from one thing to another; events and details are presented without transition. (b) The intense emotions underlying the family conflict are only glimpsed. The flitting movement from one detail to another gives the feeling of danger, avoidance of confrontation, and the fragility of the family structure and of life itself.
2. The grandmother has forgotten what Yoshiko looks like. The brother discovers that his mother is beautiful. The stepmother tries to be kind and generous toward the brother. The father recognizes that Yoshiko has had a hard time because of the divorce. Yoshiko's concern for the well-being of everyone even includes the mother and baby jay.

ANSWERS TO UNDERSTANDING LANGUAGE

1. The word *kimono* is now commonly used in American English for any housecoat or bathrobe made of ornately patterned silk.
2. (a) *Teriyaki* comes from words meaning "flame" and "to broil" and applies to meat or fish that has been skewered, broiled, and marinated—or to the marinating sauce itself. (b) *Haiku* comes ultimately from Japanese words that mean "amusement" and "verse" and, taken together, mean "amusing poem." The word applies to a lyric poem of a fixed seventeen-syllable form that depicts something in nature. (c) *Kamikaze* comes from words that mean "God" and "wind" and, taken together, mean "divine wind." The word refers to a pilot trained to make a suicidal crash attack on an enemy.

THINKING AND WRITING

Publishing Student Writing Have students share their papers with the class.

Examples include the way she is kind toward the grandmother in the opening scene, and feels protective of her stepmother.

7. She hopes, perhaps, that seeing the joy expressed by the mother and baby jay at their reunion will soften her father's anger.
8. Possible responses may refer to the cycle in plant life and the cycle of seasons.

ANSWERS TO ANALYZING LITERATURE

1. Images of fragility include the grandmother's groping her way through the house, Yoshiko's white dotted fingernails, and the delicate balance of emotions between family members.
2. Maternal images in the story include the mother jay, Yoshiko's protective attitude toward all the other members of her family, the gladness of the mother for her son's visit, the stepmother's kindness toward the son, and Yoshiko's concern for the baby jay. The theme of all these images is the delicate balance between nurturing life and harming or destroying it.
3. (a) Images of age are most vividly conveyed by the depiction of the

1924–

In 1924 Vietnamese, Cambodian, Lao, Chinese, French, British, Soviet, and American diplomats met in Geneva, Switzerland, to end France's colonial occupation in Vietnam. The agreement they reached divided Vietnam into two independent countries: North Vietnam's communist government backed by the Soviet Union would be led by Ho Chi Minh; South Vietnam's democratic government backed by the United States would be led by Bao Dai. However, in an election in 1955, the people of South Vietnam chose Ngo Dinh Diem as their leader.

Prior to the installation of the communist government in the North following the Geneva Convention, nearly one million North Vietnamese fled south. Many of those who fled south were military and political leaders, prominent academics and business executives, and renowned writers and poets, such as Nguyen Thi Vinh (no͞o´ yin tĭ vin).

In 1957 conflict emerged between the South Vietnamese government and the Viet Cong, the South Vietnamese communist rebels who opposed Diem. In 1959 North Vietnam publicly supported the Viet Cong's revolt against South Vietnam's government and began infiltrating the South in the mid-sixties and increasing its aid to the Viet Cong. At the same time, the United States increased military support to the South Vietnamese. Then, in 1975 after the United States pulled out of South Vietnam, the North Vietnamese invaded the South, resulting in the fall of Saigon and the installation of a new North Vietnamese communist government.

To the people who fled from the North to the South, the war was a particular hardship. These people were in a sense refugees, living in self-imposed exile; their fate under the communist regime most likely would have been death. The South, although it was a sanctuary, was a strange and alien place; the climate, cuisine, landscape, and customs were all different from what they had known in the North. And the North Vietnam they knew in effect no longer existed.

It was in this climate and context that Nguyen Thi Vinh wrote "Thoughts of Hanoi," her personal lyric about the Vietnam War from the perspective of a North Vietnamese living in the South.

Nguyen was born on July 15, 1924, in Ha Dong Province in the Red River Delta of North Vietnam. She is a novelist, poet, editor, and publishing executive, but most of all she is a writer of short stories. Her first and perhaps most famous work was *Two Sisters*, published in 1953. Since then she has published at least six other books of fiction—collections of short stories and at least one novel—including *A Poor Hamlet* (1958), *Rising Wave* (1973), and *Birthmark* (1973). *The Poetry of Nguyen Thi Vinh* was also published in 1973, and is perhaps her only collection of poetry.

Until the communist takeover of South Vietnam in 1975, Nguyen was a prominent member of the Saigon community of writers. She served as editor-in-chief of the bimonthly journal *New Wind* and was director of the magazine *The East*. She contributed to many magazines, newspapers, and journals and was also active in the Vietnam P.E.N. Club. After the fall of Saigon in 1975, she remained in Vietnam but refused to play any public role. Then in 1983 she was able to join her family in Norway, once again a refugee in a very different and alien country.

Objectives

Thematic
To understand the longing to return to one's homeland

Skills
1 To understand theme
2 To appreciate imagery
3 To write a poem

GUIDE FOR INTERPRETING

Thoughts of Hanoi

Commentary

Theme. Theme is the central idea, concern, or purpose in a literary work that can usually be expressed as a general statement or insight about life. For example, the theme of Alexander Solzhenitzen's speech "The One Great Heart" (page 1318) is that "Mankind's salvation lies exclusively in everyone's making everything his business" and that the writer's responsibility is to cut through the fabric of lies to reveal truth to the world. The theme might be directly stated, but it is usually expressed indirectly or implied, and the reader must infer the theme from the events and descriptions in the work. Every element in a work of literature contributes to the theme. In a poem, for example, metaphor, image, and choice of words frequently develop the theme.

In many works of literature, such as "Thoughts of Hanoi," the theme pertains not only to the lives of the speaker and the characters in the story or poem, but more important, to the lives of the author and his or her readers. Many works of literature have more than one theme; however, there are usually one dominant or controlling idea and several secondary or subordinate ones.

Theme should not be confused with a poem's subject, which can be described in a single word. Rather the theme reflects the author's observations or thoughts on the subject. For example, the subject of Cavafy's "Waiting for the Barbarians" (page 1148) might be civilization. The theme of the poem lies in Cavafy's conclusions and observations about civilization versus barbarism. Similarly, Nguyen Thi Vinh's poem "Thoughts of Hanoi" is about the Vietnam War. The theme of her poem lies in her attitude toward and conclusions and observations about the war and its effect on people's lives.

Writing

If you were to write your thoughts about something as Nguyen does about the Vietnam War in "Thoughts of Hanoi," what five topics would you pick? Why? Freewrite, explaining your answer.

Primary Source

In the introduction to *The Heritage of Vietnamese Poetry*, Huyn Sanh Thong says the following about Vietnamese poetry: "The strikingly worded and artfully measured utterance, be it a saying, a riddle, or a song, must have enlivened the speech of Vietnamese peasants at work or play since time immemorial. But it was not until Vietnam had been exposed for many centuries to Chinese writing and literature that poetry in the Southeast Asian land evolved from word of mouth onto paper and became one of the most highly regarded activities of the educated classes."

Literary Focus Review with students some of the selections they have already read in *World Masterpieces* and express the theme of each.

Writing/Prior Knowledge As a class, brainstorm for ideas. Reassure students that their topics need not be as catastrophic as a war. Their topics may range from school to a current event that has directly affected them.

ESL Teaching Strategy This poem lends itself well to ESL students, since many of them will remember what life was like in their home countries. Ask students to share their memories with the class. Then extend the invitation to all students who may have experiences of having lived in different states or countries.

Master Teacher Note Although imagery and detail are known to contribute to the meaning of a poem, the imagery and detail *are* the meaning in this poem. Nguyen's cataloguing of images near and dear to her is reminiscent of American poet Walt Whitman. Bring in one or two examples of his work for comparison.

Teaching Tenth-Grade Students Discuss with tenth-grade students the value of creating sharp imagery. Ask them which of the visual images in this poem is most memorable, vivid, and realistic. Why? What makes it so? Lead students to see why an image is vivid or memorable so that they can apply that knowledge to their own writing.

Support Material

Teaching Portfolio
Teacher Backup, p. 1725
Usage and Mechanics Worksheet, p. 1729
Analyzing Literature Worksheet, *Understanding Theme*, p. 1730
Critical Thinking and Reading Worksheet, *Appreciating Im-* *agery,* p. 1731
Language Worksheet, *Understanding Metaphor*, p. 1732
Selection Test, pp. 1733–1734

Thoughts of Hanoi

Nguyen Thi Vinh

translated by Nguyen Ngoc Bich with Burton Raffel and W. S. Merwin

The night is deep and chill
as in early autumn. Pitchblack,
it thickens after each lightning flash.
I dream of Hanoi:
5   Co-ngu[1] Road
ten years of separation
the way back sliced by a frontier of hatred.
I want to bury the past
to burn the future
10 still I yearn
still I fear
those endless nights
waiting for dawn.

Brother,
15 how is Hang Dao[2] now?

_____
1. **Co-ngu** (cổ g$\overline{oo}$)
2. **Hang Dao** (häŋ dɔu)

Children by water, Hanoi, Vietnam

How is Ngoc Son[3] temple?
Do the trains still run
each day from Hanoi
to the neighboring towns?
20 To Bac-ninh, Cam-giang, Yen-bai,[4]
the small villages, islands
of brown thatch in a lush green sea?

The girls
    bright eyes
        ruddy cheeks
    four-piece dresses
        raven-bill scarves
    sowing harvesting
25   spinning weaving
    all year round,
the boys
    plowing
        transplanting
    in the fields
        in their shops
    running across
        the meadow at evening
    to fly kites
30   and sing alternating songs.

Stainless blue sky,
    jubilant voices of children
stumbling through the alphabet,
    village graybeards strolling to the temple,
grandmothers basking in twilight sun,
    chewing betel leaves
while the children run—

_____
3. **Ngoc Son** (nōk sōn)
4. **Bac-ninh** (bäk nin), **Cam-giang** (cäm giäŋ), **Yen-bai** (ēŋ bī)

Brother,
how is all that now?
Or is it obsolete?
Are you like me,
reliving the past,
imagining the future?
Do you count me as a friend
or am I the enemy in your eyes?
Brother, I am afraid
that one day I'll be with the March-North Army
meeting you on your way to the South.
I might be the one to shoot you then
or you me
but please
not with hatred.

50 For don't you remember how it was,
    you and I in school together,
    plotting our lives together?
    Those roots go deep!

    Brother, we are men,
55 conscious of more
    than material needs.
    How can this happen to us
    my friend
    my foe?

6

Reader's Response *How did Nguyen Thi Vinh's personal lyric about the Vietnam War make you feel?*

THINKING ABOUT THE SELECTION

Interpreting

1. What is the tone of "Thoughts of Hanoi"? Support your answer with details from the poem.
2. What might the "frontier of hatred" (line 7) be?
3. Why might the speaker want to "burn the future" (line 9)?
4. Why might the speaker be "reliving the past"?
5. What does the speaker fear most about the war? Why?

Applying

6. (a) What message does Nguyen express in lines 66–71? (b) How can we apply her message in our own lives? Explain.

ANALYZING LITERATURE

Understanding Theme

The **theme** of a poem is the central idea or purpose that can usually be expressed as an insight about life. Most often the theme of a poem is expressed indirectly or implied. Every element—metaphor, image, and tone—contributes to the theme.

1. What is the dominating theme of "Thoughts of Hanoi"? Support your answer with details from the poem.
2. State the theme of "Thoughts of Hanoi" as it pertains to the author and to her readers.

CRITICAL THINKING AND READING

Appreciating Imagery

Imagery is language that helps a reader form a mental picture by appealing to one or more senses. Imagery is important in poetry because it adds color to descriptions, suggests mood, and helps to give concrete reality to abstract ideas.

1. To which senses does Nguyen Thi Vinh appeal in "Thoughts of Hanoi"?
2. Which image do you believe is her most powerful and effective? Why?
3. What do you think is Nguyen's purpose for including images of Hanoi before the war? What is the effect of these images set against her thoughts about the war?

THINKING AND WRITING

Writing a Poem with Vivid Imagery

Think of a topic about which you would like to write an original poem. Next, make a list of the images you might use in your poem. Think of how you might appeal to your sense of sound, taste, smell, sight, and touch. Then, write a poem in which you use vivid imagery. Write a first draft and give it to a peer to read. Have your partner comment on whether your imagery is clear and vivid and make other suggestions for improvement. Write a final draft of your poem.

(continued from bottom of page)

rial rights. (b) Some students will say that we have to rise above our petty desires for wealth and power and respect and treat each other as equals and as brothers.

ANSWERS TO ANALYZING LITERATURE

1. Answers may differ. Some students will state that the dominating theme of this poem is the futility of war.
2. Answers may differ. Some students may state that Nguyen is perhaps making the South Vietnamese more sensitive to the thoughts and feelings of the North Vietnamese.

ANSWERS TO CRITICAL THINKING AND READING

1. She appeals to all the senses.
2. Answers may differ. Many students may state that the images in lines 1–9 or lines 41–49 are her most powerful and effective because they express her fears and the gravity of war.
3. Answers may differ. She may have wanted to set up a stark contrast between pre-war life and life during the war to make her message about war all the more poignant and horrifying.

THINKING AND WRITING

Publishing Student Writing Have students write their thoughts about their homelands. Compile students' work in a classroom book in which students include maps indicating where their homes are. Display the class's literary "atlas" for others to read and enjoy.

Challenge Vietnamese literature is continually being translated from French and Vietnamese into English. Challenge students to read more Vietnamese literature. In oral presentations, have them share their readings and their discoveries about the Vietnamese, their culture, and their country.

5 **Discussion** Have students discuss the powerful imagery of this simple line: "Or is it obsolete?"

6 **Discussion** What does this passage mean?

Closure and Extension

ANSWERS TO THINKING ABOUT THE SELECTION

1. The tone is one of reminiscence and longing to return to her homeland. The speaker dreams of Hanoi and yearns to see the girls and boys and the home she knew before the war.
2. The frontier of hatred is the border between North and South Vietnam—the line over which brothers are fighting brothers.
3. Answers may differ. Some students may say that burying the past and burning the future suggests the speaker's desire to start over. Other students may say that because the future is bleak for her in her own country, she wishes to burn it.
4. By reliving the past, the speaker is living in a time before the war.
5. The speaker most fears that people who were once friends and relatives and who grew up and made plans together are now reduced to fighting and killing one another. She fears that she too will have to do the same: "I might be the one to shoot you then."
6. Answers may differ. (a) She expresses that as humans we should want far more than material needs and territo-

BEI DAO

GU CHENG

SHU TING

Bei Dao (1949–   )

Bei Dao, (bā d…) which means "North Island," is a pen name. The poet's given name is Zhao Zhenkai. His mother was a nurse, his father an official in one of China's non-communist political parties. He was born just two months before China's Communists, under Mao Zedong, instituted the People's Republic, ending over a hundred years of foreign domination of China at the hands of Britain, Russia, Japan, and the United States.

Bei Dao attended one of China's best schools, and seemed destined for a position in the Communist bureaucracy. Instead, in 1965, his final year in school, he became a member of the Red Guard. This movement of idealistic teenagers sought to revitalize the Chinese Revolution by criticizing people they felt were enjoying unfair privileges. However, the revitalization soon degenerated into a wholesale persecution of artists, teachers, and other intellectuals.

Disillusioned with the Red Guard, Bei Dao turned to writing poems. Bold, questioning, and moving in a series of vivid images, his poems expressed a deep dissatisfaction with Chinese society. Eventually he became associated with a like-minded group called the Misty Poets.

When a new wave of discontent swept the country in 1976, his poem "Answer" became a rallying cry for change. In 1978 students set up large bulletin boards in central places where dissident writing could be read by passersby. This unusual form of publication became known as the Democracy Wall Movement, and it brought Bei Dao's work to a far wider audience.

During the Tiananmen Square massacre (1989), Bei Dao was traveling abroad, and the period of repression that followed the massacre made it impossible for him to return. Today, he lives and works in Scandinavia, separated from his wife and child, who remain in China.

Gu Cheng (1956–1993)

Gu Cheng (gōo chän) was the youngest of the so-called Misty Poets. Because his father, Gu Gong, was a prominent poet, his family was forced to leave Beijing during the Cultural Revolution of the late 1960's. When he returned there in 1974, Gu Cheng earned his living as a carpenter but wrote poetry in his spare time.

Five years later his first poems appeared in print, and he subsequently became one of the most respected poets writing in Chinese. In the years before his death he lived in New Zealand; however, in 1992 he visited the United States, where he gave a series of readings.

Shu Ting (1952–   )

Shu Ting (shōo tiŋ) is the pen name of Gong Peiyu. The Cultural Revolution was a major event in her life, as it was in the lives of Bei Dao and Gu Cheng. Like many other teenagers during that era, she was forced to leave Beijing and live in a small peasant village.

She began writing poetry about this time and, while still in her twenties, gained nationwide fame as a poet. In both 1981 and 1983, she received official recognition in the form of China's National Poetry Award.

Shu Ting is the only one of these three poets who still remains in China. She lives and writes in the seaport city of Xiamen.

GUIDE FOR INTERPRETING

The Misty Poets

Commentary

The Misty Poets. In 1980 Gu Cheng published a short poem called "Image" that pictured two brightly colored children emerging from a world of gray. This poem seemed to be a criticism of the dull grayness of Chinese life and of the equally dull literature prescribed by the state. According to the communist regime, literature had to be realistic, supportive of communism, and not subjective or personal. When a state literary critic attacked Gu Cheng's poem as "misty," Gu Cheng and some of his fellow poets adopted the term as a badge of honor. They became known as the **Misty Poets**.

These poets took as their model neither traditional Chinese poetry nor the "gray" literature of communism. Instead, they patterned their work after Western poets like Baudelaire and Sylvia Plath, writers known for their surprising images and highly personal emotions.

In the late 1980's, people in China challenged totalitarian rule and demanded a say in their government, as they had in 1976. The new poets fueled these yearnings—even though, to a North American reader, some of their poems may not seem openly political. In a country where private feelings were suspect, however, the mere expression of such feelings in poetry was viewed as a political act.

The pressure for reform came to a head in April of 1989, when over a hundred thousand students took over Tiananmen Square, an act tantamount to American students seizing the Washington Monument. Shen Tong, one of the student leaders, tells how the Misty Poets had inspired him: "I discovered through these poems that art and literature could be active. Through their writing, the Misty Poets told people about themselves and about what was wrong in China."

Could a nonviolent popular movement overthrow the government of a nation four times the size of the United States? The world watched in amazement. Then, on the night of June 3, heavily armed troops swept the students from the square and killed nearly a thousand of them as they fled through the city streets. Several student leaders were tried and executed; others escaped to live in foreign countries.

Today the struggle to bring democracy to China goes on. The writers known as the Misty Poets continue to give those aspirations a voice.

Writing

Even though the Misty Poets share a great deal, they also differ in important respects. In fact, Shu Ting's poem "Also All" is a direct rebuttal of Bei Dao's "All." Have you ever heard a song whose lyrics you strongly disagreed with? Write a note to the singer or songwriter expressing your point of view.

Literary Focus Ask students to discuss what they know about China and the Chinese government. Most students should remember the incident at Tiananmen Square in 1989. Ask them to explain what the students were protesting and what the outcome of the protest was. Finally, ask students whether they think these acts of rebellion against the Chinese government still occur today.

Writing/Prior Knowledge Ask students to suggest some of the purposes for songs. Lead students to an understanding that in addition to entertainment and personal expressions of feelings and experiences, songs communicate the songwriters' opinions on a variety of issues, including politics.

Teaching Tenth-Grade Students Have your tenth-grade students complete the prereading writing assignment. Before students begin reading the poems in this unit, they should be aware that songs and poetry are a natural vehicle for expressing one's views about politics.

Vocabulary

Preteach the following vocabulary words:

undulant (un´ dyo͞o lənt) *adj.*: Wavelike

reprisal (ri prī´ zəl) *n.*: Revenge for an injury; retaliation

lamentation (lam´ ən tā´ shən) *n.*: Expression of grief

heralds (her´ əldz) *v.*: Announces; introduces

reverberates (ri vʉr´ bə rāts) *v.*: Sounds again

hapless (hap´ lis) *adj.*: Unlucky; unfortunate

imperturbably (im´ pər tʉr´ bə blē) *adv.*: In an undisturbed manner

insidious (in sid´ ē əs) *adj.*: Treacherous

chasm (kaz´ əm) *n.*: Deep crack in the earth

immaculate (im mak´ yo͞o lit) *adj.*: Pure

Critical Thinking and Reading Worksheet, *Interpreting Imagery*, p. 1782

Selection Test, pp. 1783–1784

ESL Teaching Strategy Ask your native Chinese students or students who know Chinese to read one or several of the poems in this unit in Chinese. Have students bring in copies of the originals written in Chinese and ask them to explain what the characters mean.

Spelling Tip Suggest to students that they create a mnemonic for the words they have trouble spelling. For example, for the word *heralds*, students can remember it means "calls" and should be spelled *heralds* (not *herelds*) because of the *a* in *calls*.

Answer

Bei Dao
translated by Donald Finkel
and Xueliang Chen

The scoundrel carries his baseness around like an
  ID card.
The honest man bears his honor like an epitaph.
Look—the gilded sky is swimming
with undulant reflections of the dead.

5 They say the ice age ended years ago.
Why are there icicles everywhere?
The Cape of Good Hope has already been found.
Why should all those sails contend on the Dead
  Sea?[1]

I came into this world with nothing
10 but paper, rope, and shadow.
Now I come to be judged,
and I've nothing to say but this:

Listen. *I don't believe!*
OK. You've trampled
15 a thousand enemies underfoot. Call me
a thousand and one.

I don't believe the sky is blue.
I don't believe what the thunder says.
I don't believe dreams aren't real,
20 that beyond death there is no reprisal.

If the sea should break through the sea-wall,
let its brackish water fill my heart.
If the land should rise from the sea again,
we'll choose again to live in the heights.

25 The earth revolves. A glittering constellation
pricks the vast defenseless sky.
Can you see it there? that ancient ideogram[2]—
the eye of the future, gazing back.

---

1. The Cape of Good Hope . . . the Dead Sea: The Cape of Good Hope is the southernmost tip of Africa, first reached by Europeans in 1488. The Dead Sea is an inland body of salt water on the Israel-Jordan border.

---

2. ideogram (id´ ē ō gram´) *n.*: In the Chinese language, a picture-symbol representing an object or idea without expressing the sounds that form its name.

UNTITLED
Shao Fei

7 Discussion What does the speaker mean by asserting that "the eye of the future" is "gazing back"? Is this a positive or a negative image? Explain.

Humanities Note

Fine art, *Untitled,* by Shao Fei. The Chinese artist Shao Fei is Bei Dao's wife, so it is highly appropriate that her painting appears on this page. Unfortunately, Bei Dao now lives in exile, while his wife and child remain in China. Until that country changes its policies, it is doubtful that he will be able to see his family.

Like Bei Dao and the othe[r] Misty Poets, Shao Fei has bee[n] strongly influenced by Wester[n] artists. This painting, for instance[,] seems to owe a debt to Surrealism[.] (For a brief description of this artisti[c] movement, see page 1249.) Sha[o] Fei has filled the picture plane wit[h] animals, some recognizable an[d] some not. Mixed in with the animal[s]

Testament[1]

Bei Dao
translated by Donald Finkel
and Xueliang Chen

Perhaps the time has come.
I haven't left a will,
just one pen, for my mother.

I'm no hero, you understand.
This isn't the year for heroes.
I'd just like to be a man.

The horizon still divides
the living from the dead,
but the sky's all I need.

I won't kneel on the earth—
the firing squad might block
the last free breaths of air.

From starry bullet-holes
the blood-red dawn will flow.

---

[1]. **Testament** (tes´ tə mənt) *n.*: A will; also, a statement of one's beliefs.

Reader's Response: *If you wrote an imaginary will or testament like Bei Dao's, what would it include?*

All

Bei Dao
translated by Donald Finkel
and Xueliang Chen

All is fated,
all cloudy,

all an endless beginning,
all a search for what vanishes,

5 all joys grave,
all griefs tearless,

every speech a repetition,
every meeting a first encounter,

all love buried in the heart,
10 all history prisoned in a dream,

all hope hedged with doubt,
all faith drowned in lamentation.

Every explosion heralds an instant of stillness,
every death reverberates forever.

THINKING ABOUT THE SELECTIONS

Interpreting

1. Which stanza of Bei Dao's "Answer" best summarizes the theme of the poem? Explain.
2. Is "All" an optimistic poem or a pessimistic one? Why?

3. The word *testament* can mean a will or a statement of belief. How do both of these definitions apply to "Testament"?

Applying

4. Why do you think the poem "Answer" became a rallying cry for change among China's youth?

---

re nebulous, ghostlike shapes with early human faces. These and the animals stare out at the viewer with expressions that range from benign to threatening. The artist provides no insight as to the purpose or story behind this work, allowing the viewer to discover its meaning.

You might want to use the following questions to discuss the art:

1. What mood does this painting evoke in you? Is the mood similar to that of the poem? Why or why not?
2. Can you identify some of the animals represented in this work? Explain.

Closure and Extension

ANSWERS TO THINKING ABOUT THE SELECTION

1. Answers will differ. Some students may argue that the fourth stanza best summarizes the theme of the poem. In this stanza, the poet asserts that he does not believe anything government officials tell him and that he is their enemy.

When Hope Comes Back

for Shu Ting

Gu Cheng
translated by Donald Finkel
and Sheng-Tai Chang

There's nothing left.

The southwest wind's already landed.
The sky's alive with gulls.
The evening's shaken out the waves,
5 folded one hapless mast neatly in two.
Flounder swim imperturbably,
uninvited, through the skull of a ship.
Gleaming like coins, their eyes recall
an army of shopkeepers.

10 There's nothing left.

The lamp turns to a firefly in my hand
and darts through the darkness. The last patient candle
topples to the ground, kindling a cry of delight.
A fire blazes up and spreads until
15 the child who before was afraid of the dark
now shrieks at this strange conflagration and scampers home.
Curled in a ball, he hides one spark in his dream
while, humming softly, his mother closes the shutters.

There's nothing left.

20 The sea is black as a hole,
the squid's insidious ink swirls into the sky,
the screaming seagulls urge the storm clouds on.
Only the tree can't fly. Stricken by lightning,
thrashing its tormented feathers,
25 the olive tree wants to demolish the sky.

There's nothing left.

```
       Nothing? Really?
       Tell me. The warm earth shimmers.
   7   "There's more," you say, in your low, melodious voice
   30  as the river trembles in a lightning flash
       and vanishes. "There's more."
       As if the world were a small black boy
       who'd wept too long, you comfort him
       like an older sister, and smooth his dripping hair.

   35  "There's more."

       You whisper it in his ear while the world sleeps calmly,
       while motherless birds crowd sleeping together
   8   and the sea leans against the shoulder of the cliff.
       He sleeps on quietly. Quietly.
   40  From far away, a solitary star approaches.
       It wants to stand beneath his window on the lawn
       and learn how to commune with the taciturn grass.

       "There's more. More."
       The world will wake at daybreak, fully grown.
   45  His eyes will flash a grown-up smile. Yes.
       Outside, the sun will anchor in the harbor.
   9   The East will redden, blushing, little by little.
       She'll have caught sight of the world
       and fallen in love like a schoolgirl.
   50  The dripping bush will be crowned with flowers.

       Hope's back.
   10  What more can I ask?
```

7 **Discussion** How does this stanza mark a turning point in the poem? Who is the person the poet refers to as "you"?

8 **Discussion** In what way is the second half of the poem a mirror of the first? How does the refrain on this page answer the refrain on the previous page?

9 **Discussion** Until this stanza, the poem is written in the present tense. In which tense is this stanza written? What does this change in tense suggest about the poet's hope?

10 **Discussion** Why is hope all that the poet can ask for?

Reader's Response: *If you were writing a poem or a song about hope, what images would you use?*

THINKING ABOUT THE SELECTION

Interpreting

(a) Identify two images in the poem that express sadness and two that express hope. (b) Explain your choices.
Which feeling is dominant in the poem, hope or despair? Why?

3. (a) What natural cycle underlies the poet's descriptions? (b) How does the poet use this cycle to structure the poem?

Applying

4. What things give you cause for hope? Explain.

Closure and Extension

ANSWERS TO THINKING ABOUT THE SELECTION

(a) Answers will differ. Images of sadness include the squid squirting ink into the sky and the tree stricken by lightning. Images of hope include the solitary star approaching and the world waking at daybreak. (b) Students should justify their choices.

2. Answers will differ. Suggested response: Hope is dominant because it is expressed in the second part of the poem and supersedes the despair.

3. (a) The cycle that underlies the poem is the daily alternating of darkness and light. (b) The poet divides the poem in half; the first part deals with oncoming night, the second with the return of day. Also, the first part is sad, while the second is more hopeful.

4. Answers will differ, but students should explain their responses.

Assembly Line

Shu Ting
translated by Carolyn Kizer

In time's assembly line
Night presses against night.
We come off the factory night-shift
In line as we march towards home.
5 Over our heads in a row
The assembly line of stars
Stretches across the sky.
Beside us, little trees
Stand numb in assembly lines.

10 The stars must be exhausted
After thousands of years
Of journeys which never change.
The little trees are all sick,
Choked on smog and monotony,
15 Stripped of their color and shape.
It's not hard to feel for them;
We share the same tempo and rhythm.

Yes, I'm numb to my own existence
As if, like the trees and stars
20 —perhaps just out of habit
—perhaps just out of sorrow,
I'm unable to show concern
For my own manufactured fate.

Also All

In answer to Bei Dao's "All"

Shu Ting
translated by Donald Finkel
and Jinsheng Yi

UNTITLED
Shao Fei
Courtesy of Bei Dao

Not all trees are felled by storms.
Not every seed finds barren soil.
Not all the wings of dream are broken,
nor is all affection doomed
5 to wither in a desolate heart.

No, not all is as you say.

Not all flames consume themselves,
shedding no light on other lives.
Not all stars announce the night
10 and never dawn. Not every song
will drift past every ear and heart.

No, not all is as you say.

Not every cry for help is silenced,
nor every loss beyond recall.
15 Not every chasm spells disaster.
Not only the weak will be brought to their knees,
nor every soul be trodden under.

It won't all end in tears and blood.
Today is heavy with tomorrow—
20 the future was planted yesterday.
Hope is a burden all of us shoulder
though we might stumble under the load.

Fairy Tales

1 *for Gu Cheng*

Shu Ting
translated by Donald Finkel and Jinsheng Yi

2
You believed in your own story,
then climbed inside it—
a turquoise flower.
You gazed past ailing trees,
5 past crumbling walls and rusty railings.
Your least gesture beckoned a constellation
of wild vetch,[1] grasshoppers, and stars
to sweep you into immaculate distances.

3
The heart may be tiny
10 but the world's enormous.

And the people in turn believe—
in pine trees after rain,
ten thousand tiny suns, a mulberry branch
bent over water like a fishing-rod,
15 a cloud tangled in the tail of a kite.
Shaking off dust, in silver voices
ten thousand memories sing from your dream.

The world may be tiny
but the heart's enormous.

---
1. wild vetch (vech): Any of a number of leafy climbing or trailing plants.

Reader's Response: *Shu Ting writes that "the people . . . believe—/in pine trees after rain . . . " What do you believe in?*

THINKING ABOUT THE SELECTION

Interpreting

1. (a) What is compared to an assembly line in Shu Ting's poem of that name? (b) How do these comparisons contribute to the poem's mood?
2. "Also All" was written in response to Bei Dao's poem "All." (a) What is Shu Ting's interpretation of the poem she is answering? (b) How do the following lines express her disagreement with "All"?
"Today is heavy with tomorrow—
the future was planted yesterday."
3. In "Fairy Tales" what do you think the poet mean by the statement "The world may be tiny/but th heart's enormous"?
4. Why do you think she interchanges the word "heart" and "world" in the poem's refrain?

Applying

5. In "Assembly Line" the poet writes, "Yes, I'm num to my own existence." (a) What causes people feel this way? (b) How can such feelings be ove come?

ANALYZING LITERATURE

Understanding the Misty Poets

Living in a society that places a high value on conformity, the **Misty Poets** have found a way of expressing their individuality. Their work, modeled after that of Western poets, contains surprising images and conveys strong emotions. That alone would be enough to place these poets in conflict with their country's rulers. However, these poets have sometimes directly challenged the communist bureaucracy. Bei Dao's poem "Answer," for instance, is an attack on totalitarian rule: "Listen. *I don't believe!*"

(a) What inferences can you make from this poem about the people or behaviors the poet is answering? (b) In your own words, summarize the values that the poet supports. (c) How does repetition contribute to the poem's message?

(a) Find an example of strongly expressed emotion in the work of one of these poets. (b) Describe the emotion and explain how the poet conveys it.

Are any of the poems by these poets similar to modern Western poems you know? Explain.

Shu Ting's "Also All" is an answer to Bei Dao's "All," and her poem "Fairy Tales" is dedicated to Gu Cheng. What does this suggest about the relationships among these poets?

CRITICAL THINKING AND READING

Interpreting Imagery

Poetic **imagery** is language that creates sensory impressions in a reader's mind. These impressions are often visual, but they can also relate to the other senses. For instance, when Gu Cheng describes an olive tree as "thrashing its tormented feathers," he is appealing not only to the sense of sight but to that of touch as well.

The Misty Poets are especially known for their use of surprising and highly personal imagery, like Gu Cheng's description of an olive tree. To Western readers images like this may seem imaginative and appealing but hardly political. In China's closed society, however, the use of this poetic device, even in poems that are not overtly political, is like a declaration of freedom.

(a) To what senses does Shu Ting appeal with her imagery in "Assembly Line"? (b) How might the imagery of this poem be a description of Chinese society?

---

2. How could her statement and image at the beginning of her poem "Fairy Tales" serve as a motto for the Misty Poets? Explain.

3. (a) What is surprising about the image in the last two lines of Bei Dao's "Testament"? (b) What two things is the poet comparing in this image? (c) How does the comparison contribute to the theme of the poem?

UNDERSTANDING LANGUAGE

Appreciating Repetition

You have probably noticed that the Misty Poets use repeated phrases and sentences in their work. Sometimes, as in Bei Dao's "Answer," the repetitions add emphasis to what the poet is saying. For example, the three sentences beginning "I don't believe . . ." (lines 17–19) become a forceful declaration of defiance. In other cases, a poet will use repetition with variation, restating a sentence but changing it in a significant way.

1. In Shu Ting's "Fairy Tales," lines 18 and 19 are a mirror image of lines 9 and 10. (a) What is the effect of this repetition with variation? (b) How would the poem be different if the poet simply repeated lines 9 and 10 without changing them?

2. Would Gu Cheng's poem be better or worse without the repeated sentences "There's nothing left" and "There's more"? Explain.

3. Why do you think Shu Ting uses repetition in her poem answering Bei Dao's "All"?

THINKING AND WRITING

Comparing and Contrasting Poems

Like many other schools of artists, the Misty Poets share a general outlook but don't necessarily agree about everything. For example, Shu Ting wrote her poem "Also All" as a rebuttal of Bei Dao's "All." Write a short essay comparing and contrasting these two poems. Consider such literary elements as theme, mood, and imagery. Also, compare and contrast each poet's use of poetic devices like imagery, stanza structure, and repetition. Use your comparison and contrast to support a conclusion as to which poem is most effective in stating its case. While drafting and revising your essay, make sure that your ideas are arranged logically. Give readers a pattern they can follow by comparing the poems point by point or writing first about one and then about the other.

---

2. Suggested response: The Misty Poets believe in expressing their own feelings and emotions, and in that sense, they climb inside their own story. Also, the bright color of the flower ("turquoise") suggests the vibrancy and color of their work.

3. Suggested responses: (a) The last two lines are surprising because one would not usually describe bullet holes as "starry" or expect dawn, a symbol of life and rebirth, to flow from bullet holes. (b) He is comparing an executed person with a dawn sky. (c) The comparison contributes to the theme by suggesting that the speaker's death will lead to a rebirth.

ANSWERS TO UNDERSTANDING LANGUAGE

1. Answers will differ. Suggested responses: (a) The repetition with variation allows the poet to show two important effects of poetry like Gu Cheng's. Such poetry illustrates the enormous possibilities of the world *and* of the individual heart. (b) If the poet had simply repeated the words, she would not have stressed the importance of the human heart.

2. Answers will differ. Suggested response: The poem would not be as powerful without the refrains. These repeated lines concentrate and focus the intense emotions of the poem—the despair and the hope. They also give the poem a songlike beauty.

3. Answers will differ. Suggested response: Shu Ting is mirroring Bei Dao's repetition as a means of refuting his statements.

THINKING AND WRITING

Writing Across the Curriculum The Misty Poets illustrate the strong tie between literature and history. Have students write about current conditions in China or about the Tiananmen Square massacre and link those events to a poem by one of the Misty Poets.

Challenge Read more poems by the Misty Poets and report on them to the class. Following are two books you might use: *A Splintered Mirror: Chinese Poetry from the Democracy Movement,* translated by Donald Finkel (North Point 1991); *The August Sleepwalker,* by Bei Dao (New Directions, 1990).

---

lieves is as antiquated as the Ice Age. (b) The poet values freedom of expression, the reality of dreams, and responsibility to future generations. (c) The repetition of the words "I don't believe" emphasizes his defiance.

Answers will differ. Suggested responses: (a) In "All," Bei Dao writes, "All is fated,/ all cloudy." (b) The words *fated* and *cloudy* suggest that life is unfree and troubled. The repe-

tition of the word *all* suggests that there is no exception to this state of affairs.

3. Answers will differ. Students may choose poets who write about personal experiences or who use surprising imagery. In any case, students should explain their choices.

4. It suggests that the Misty Poets all know one another or at least know one another's work. It also suggests

that they don't agree about everything.

ANSWERS TO CRITICAL THINKING AND READING

1. Suggested responses: (a) Shu Ting appeals to the senses of sight, smell, and touch in her poem "Assembly Line." (b) The imagery suggests that, like assembly-line work, Chinese society kills one's spirit.

Justice and Injustice

> Injustice anywhere is a threat to justice everywhere.
> —Martin Luther King, Jr.

The above quotation reflects a contemporary awareness that injustice can no longer be a local matter: The oppression of a peasant in Guatemala and the jailing of a student demonstrator in China are matters of concern to a salesman in Boise, Idaho, or a nurse in El Paso, Texas. Great leaders and thinkers have always realized that justice must be universal. In the contemporary period, however, the speed of our communications has made this insight more obvious. Television, radio, books, and newspapers help to make the peoples of the world into a single community. By merely turning on her television, a nurse in El Paso can see the unforgettable image of a young Chinese man stepping in front of a tank. The power of that image involves her in a struggle for justice that is thousands of miles away.

In his Nobel address, Alexander Solzhenitsyn makes the same point about justice being everyone's concern. Rather than stressing the effects of television, however, he indicates that the international publication of books has enabled writers to address a worldwide audience. This situation, he argues, gives writers a special responsibility: They must become fighters for truth and justice.

> Writers and artists can do more: they can VANQUISH LIES! In the struggle against lies, art has always won and always will. Conspicuously, incontestably for everyone.
> —Alexander Solzhenitsyn, from "The One Great Heart"

Primo Levi and Elie Wiesel have written about their ordeals in the Holocaust so that the world will not forget, and therefore not repeat, the horror and injustice that people were forced to suffer under the Nazis. In *Survival in Auschwitz*, Levi wrote

> In a moment, with almost prophetic intuition, the reality was revealed to us: we had reached the bottom. It is not possible to sink lower than this; no human condition is more miserable than this, nor could it conceivably be so. Nothing belongs to us anymore; they have taken away our clothes, our shoes, even our hair; if we speak, they will not listen to us, and if they listen, they will not understand. They will even take away our name . . .

Although modern communications have given us a new awareness of justice and injustice, this theme has been a constant concern of humankind. Almost 4,000 years ago, for instance, the Babylonian king Hammurabi drew up a code of laws "to cause justice to prevail in the land, to destroy the wicked and the evil, to prevent the strong from oppressing the weak . . . and to further the welfare of the people." The following selections from this book reflect the way in which different cultures have interpreted this theme:

SUGGESTED READINGS

"The Fisherman and the Jinnee," from *The Thousand and One Nights*, page 128
Plato, from the *Apology*, page 416
Dante, from the *Divine Comedy*, page 622

Jonathan Swift, "A Modest Proposal," page 801
Leo Tolstoy, "How Much Land Does a Man Need?" page 944

Black Women Writers and Magical Realism

MAKING THE MAGIC REAL

Magical realism invites the reader to believe the unbelievable—to suspend disbelief. It is characterized by the skillful blending of realistic and fantastic elements. Characters may experience premonitions or talk with spirits, objects may appear or disappear, and time and space may become distorted, but unlikely characters and events are always presented in the context of ordinary events and circumstances. The supernatural becomes plausible and the mundane becomes magic. In magical realism, it is important to reflect on *why* something happens rather than *how*.

CLASSIC AND CONTEMPORARY

The characteristics of magical realism can be seen in literary works as early as Cervantes's *Don Quixote de la Mancha*. In contemporary writing it has been associated with the works of Latin American authors such as Gabriel García Márquez and Isabel Allende and with African American writers like Paul Laurence Dunbar, Margaret Walker Alexander, Langston Hughes, Sterling Brown, Toni Morrison, Toni Cade Bambara, Paule Marshall, and Maya Angelou.

BLACK WOMEN WRITERS

African heritage provides a rich source of material on which writers of magical realism can draw. In African cultures, myth and folk traditions sometimes play a role in practical decisions—when to plant, when to marry, or where to build, for instance. In addition, African folk tales are rich with examples of ordinary characters that have extraordinary powers. Toni Morrison uses elements from folk tales in her novels *Song of Solomon* and *Beloved*.

According to Margaret Walker Alexander, famous for her landmark poem "For My People,"

magical realism has been "a latent quality or literary trait found in the works of many Black writers throughout the African Diaspora." In increasing numbers, however, black women writers are actively choosing to incorporate magical realism into their writing, maintaining a cultural identity while addressing contemporary themes and issues. The first International Conference on Black Women Writers of Magic Realism, was held in Jackson, Mississippi, in October 1992. It provided a forum for playwrights, poets, and fiction writers to explore the influence of this literary movement on their own work and the work of writers worldwide.

THE ASCENT OF ETHIOPIA, 1932
Lois Mailou Jones
Collection of the artist

Presentation

Motivation/Prior Knowledge
Challenge students to state a generalization that is true. Elicit several generalizations from students and write them on the chalkboard. Have the class discuss each statement and search for examples that would disprove it. Then tell students that by reading this feature, they will learn how to write in support of generalizations.

Learning Across the Curriculum
Suggest to students that they read a chapter of their history textbook and identify five generalizations. Then have them determine whether or not each generalization is adequately supported by evidence.

Generalization

Writing to Support Generalization

We all like to spot trends. We look around to spot the latest spring styles, the look of the latest model car, and even the movement of the stock market. For example, if we observe several people wearing day-glo colors and notice models in the latest fashion magazine sporting outfits in hot pink or orange, we may say that bright colors are the trend for spring. This type of statement is a generalization. The more instances we use to back up our generalizations, the more likely people will be to accept them.

Sometimes we generalize in order to understand life. For example, after observing how people withstand adversity, we may conclude that the human spirit is indomitable or that life takes a heavy toll on the human spirit.

Writing Assignment

Camus makes many generalizations in "The Myth of Sisyphus." For example, he writes, "Happiness and the absurd are two sons of the same earth. They are inseparable" and "One always finds one's burden again." Some of these generalizations he supports with specific incidents; some he does not.

Choose a generalization about life. It may be one of Camus's general statements, or you may list other generalizations about life and choose one of these. For example,

It's always darkest before the dawn.
All things come to those who wait.
It is wise to risk no more than you can afford to lose

Then write an essay in which you prove or disprove the truth of the generalization. Support your position with incidents from life.

Prewrite

In a group of two or three, brainstorm about your generalization, noting all the possible things it implies. An open mind is essential when you brainstorm. Then, as individuals, paraphrase the generalized statement on paper. For example, "There is no sun without shadow, and it is essential to know the night" can be paraphrased as, "There is no light without its connected darkness. The darkness is important to understand too." Compare the paraphrased statements within your group and decide what they have in common.

Once you have fully understood the generalization, list every instance you can that might prove this generalization true. Select items from diverse categories such as *business, history, politics, relationships, sports, literature, the animal world,* and so forth. Don't edit your list. When all the lists are completed, share them with the group and discuss ways in which each item fits or doesn't fit the generalization.

Examine the instances one by one in your group. Like actors, imagine yourselves in the circumstances of each situation. Walk through each situation and see if it continues to prove the generalization. Set aside the ones that break down.

Then, on your own, pick three examples to write about, and thoroughly examine the specific details of each.

Write

Order your essay in the following way.

- State the generalization early in the first paragraph.
- Write one paragraph for each example.
- Check that the example proves the generalization.

Aim at convincing readers who may be hard to persuade, and then measure your success by the quality of arguments you use that compel reluctant readers to agree.

Collaborate

Your teacher can help you set up response circles that will give you reactions to your work from several fellow students. Make circles of ten or fewer students.

Prepare your draft for response by attaching a blank page behind it. As you sit in a circle, pass your draft to the student on your right. Read the paper quickly, then write a useful comment on the attached sheet along with your name. Remember that general comments such as "I liked it" or "It was good" are not helpful. Give specific help as in: "You lost me when you described the legislative process. Go step by step and use shorter sentences there." The following are a few suggestions on possible comments to make.

- sequence problems
- confusing passages
- places that are too general
- effective or ineffective language

Continue to circulate the papers and make comments until your teacher directs you to stop.

Revise

Reread your draft and the comments. Ask responders to clarify anything you don't understand. Use the comments you think make valid points as a guide to help you revise your paper.

As you rewrite, feel free to confer with students whose comments you found insightful. Don't be afraid to go back to the text and to your early notes for help.

Publish

Before you hand in your work, find someone else in class who wrote on the same generalization. Exchange papers and spend a brief time discussing how your papers compare.

Evaluate

You have spent a good deal of time supporting a general statement with specific instances. Now think about how this statement relates to your life. Do you find it true in your experience? Does it still feel abstract to you? Did you argue a point you didn't fundamentally believe in? Consider saving this paper to see if your current thoughts change in future years.

Enrichment Explain to students that it is important to be aware of the connotations of words when commenting on someone's work. Advise them not to use words like "lousy," "bad," or "poor," which have negative connotations and can therefore discourage a writer.

Enrichment Encourage your students to comb the pages of their favorite newspapers and magazines to find reader response columns. Often the letters submitted to these publications contain arguments for and against statements made in articles. Have students choose such a letter and evaluate how effectively it argues in support of a generalization.

HANDBOOK OF GRAMMAR AND REVISING STRATEGIES

STRATEGIES FOR REVISING PROBLEMS IN GRAMMAR AND STANDARD USAGE

Problems of Sentence Structure

■ Run-on Sentences

GUIDE FOR REVISING: A run-on sentence results when no punctuation or coordinating conjunction separates two or more independent clauses. A run-on sentence also occurs when only a comma is used to join two or more independent clauses.

Strategy 1: **Form two sentences by using a period to separate independent clauses.**

First Draft From the excavations of Nineveh and Nimrud, Austen Henry Layard unearthed a major portion of the Assyrian **scriptures, fourteen** years later, his successor Rassam discovered the tablets containing the story of Gilgamesh.

Revision From the excavations of Nineveh and Nimrud, Austen Henry Layard unearthed a major portion of the Assyrian **scriptures. Fourteen** years later, his successor Rassam discovered the tablets containing the story of Gilgamesh.

Strategy 2: **Separate independent clauses with a semicolon.**

First Draft Sinon is held prisoner by the **Trojans he** tells them a clever lie: As long as the wooden horse remains outside of Troy, the Greeks will have safe passage home.

Revision Sinon is held prisoner by the **Trojans; he** tells them a clever lie: As long as the wooden horse remains outside of Troy, the Greeks will have safe passage home.

Model from Literature Methinks he hath no drowning mark upon **him; his** complexion is perfect gallows.
                                          —*Shakespeare, p. 711*

Strategy 3: **Use a comma and a coordinating conjunction (*and, but, or, for, yet, so*) to join the two sentences.**

First Draft Victor Hugo was free to return to France after the amnesty of **1855 he** refused to return until a republican form of government was restored.

Revision Victor Hugo was free to return to France after the amnesty of **1855, yet he** refused to return until a republican form of government was restored.

Strategy 4:	**Make one clause subordinate by adding a subordinating conjunction.**
First Draft	Playwright Luigi Pirandello believed people couldn't face the truth about human **nature his** characters deny the reality of their lives.
Revision	**Since** playwright Luigi Pirandello believed people couldn't face the truth about human **nature, his** characters deny the reality of their lives.

■ Fragments

GUIDE FOR REVISING: A fragment is a group of words that does not express a complete thought. Although a fragment may begin with a capital letter and end with a period, it is only part of a sentence because it lacks a subject, a verb, or both.

Strategy:	**Add the necessary sentence part(s) to make a phrase fragment into a complete sentence with a subject and a verb.**
First Draft	Rubén Darío was essentially self-educated. **Using his access to the National Library, learned** to write by studying the great works of Spanish literature.
Revision	Rubén Darío was essentially self-educated. **Using his access to the National Library, this resourceful young man learned** to write by studying the great works of Spanish literature.

■ Mixed Constructions

GUIDE FOR REVISING: A mixed construction results when a sentence begins with one pattern and ends with another.

Strategy:	**Make sure that you use a single structural pattern consistently throughout each sentence.**
First Draft	Giovanni Boccaccio's studies at the University of Naples gave him a law degree, exposed him to literature, awakened in him new talents, and ultimately **his studies were leading** him toward a career in writing.
Revision	Giovanni Boccaccio's studies at the University of Naples gave him a law degree, exposed him to literature, awakened in him new talents, and ultimately **led** him toward a career in writing.
Model from Literature	So now he became a landowner, **plowing** and **sowing** his own land, **making** hay on his own land, **cutting** his own trees, and **feeding** his cattle on his own land.
	—*Tolstoy, p. 945*

Problems of Clarity and Coherence

■ Effective Transitions

GUIDE FOR REVISING: Transitions are words or phrases that help the reader by signaling connections between words, sentences, and paragraphs.

Strategy 1:	**Use transitions to indicate chronological order. Transitions may be used to indicate frequency, duration, or a particular time.**
First Draft	The Achaians drove the Trojans back to the city gates and Hektor entered the city to urge the women to make sacrifices to the gods.
Revision	**After the Achaians drove the Trojans back to the city gates,** Hektor entered the city to urge the women to make sacrifices to the gods.
Model from Literature	**But now, as it was the twelfth dawn after the death of Hektor**, Phoibos Apollo spoke his word out among the immortals: "You are hard, you gods, and destructive. . . ." —*Homer, p. 381*

Strategy 2:	**Use transitions to indicate spatial relationships. Transitions may be used to show closeness, distance, or direction.**
First Draft	**With her husband raging**, Nora could finally feel his inability to love her.
Revision	**Standing face to face with her raging husband**, Nora could finally feel his inability to love her.
Model from Literature	He advanced **to the edge of the platform** and smiled as though he were about to be photographed . . . —*Mann, p. 1039*

Strategy 3:	**Use transitions to indicate comparison or contrast, or cause and effect.**
First Draft	Faust's accomplishments in philosophy and education suggest that he is a content and rational person; his eagerness to sign the devil's contract demonstrates the mad striving and "inner thirst" of someone less stable.
Revision	Faust's accomplishments in philosophy and education suggest that he is a content and rational person; his eagerness to sign the devil's contract, **however**, demonstrates the mad striving and "inner thirst" of someone less stable.

GUIDE FOR REVISING: When something is omitted from a comparison or only implied, the comparison may be incomplete or illogical.

Strategy 1:	**Be sure that a comparison contains only items of a similar kind.**
First Draft	The style and tone of Ibsen's *A Doll's House* are more realistic **than Shakespeare's** *The Tempest*.
Revision	The style and tone of Ibsen's *A Doll's House* are more realistic **than those of Shakespeare's** *The Tempest*.
Model from Literature	Her eyes were brighter than the radiant west. —*Petrarch, p. 676*

Strategy 2:	**Be sure to include the words *other* or *else* in comparisons that compare one of a group with the rest of the group.**
First Draft	Susie found the character Nora in Henrik Ibsen's *A Doll's House* to be more interesting than anyone in the play.
Revision	Susie found the character Nora in Henrik Ibsen's *A Doll's House* to be more interesting than anyone **else** in the play.
Model from Literature	"You're just like the **others**. You all think I'm incapable of anything serious." —*Ibsen, p. 975*

■ Revising for Pronoun-Antecedent Agreement

GUIDE FOR REVISING: Personal pronouns must agree with their antecedents in number (singular or plural), person (first, second, or third), and gender (masculine, feminine, or neuter).

Strategy 1:	**Make sure that a pronoun used to stand for a noun that appears somewhere else in the sentence agrees in number (singular or plural) with that noun.**
First Draft	**The quest for knowledge and the struggle for power** often motivate the tragic Greek hero, and **it often appears** as themes in the literature of classical Greece.
Revision	**The quest for knowledge and the struggle for power** often motivate the tragic Greek hero, and **they often appear** as themes in the literature of classical Greece.
Model from Literature	The **vision** of that small hero with the silver necklet among the watermelons had formerly been as clear as day, but now **it** suddenly blurred, adding to my depression. —*Lu Hsun, p. 1187*

Strategy 2:	When you use a pronoun to stand for two or more nouns joined by *or* or *nor*, make sure that it is singular. Use a plural personal pronoun if any part of a compound antecedent joined by *or* or *nor* is plural.
First Draft	Neither **Arthur Rimbaud nor Charles Baudelaire** conformed **their** lifestyle to the social mores of **their** time.
Revision	Neither **Arthur Rimbaud nor Charles Baudelaire** conformed **his** lifestyle to the social mores of **his** time.

Strategy 3:	When you use a personal pronoun to stand for a singular indefinite pronoun, make sure that it is also singular. Use a plural personal pronoun when the antecedent is a plural indefinite pronoun.
First Draft	Both William Shakespeare and Christopher Marlowe used historical subjects in their plays; however, **each** displayed very different styles in **their** writing.
Revision	**Both** William Shakespeare and Christopher Marlowe used historical subjects in their plays; however, **each** displayed very different styles in **his** writing.
Model from Literature	The place was full of professional vagabonds . . . even types in whose existence **one** does not believe until **he** has seen a living example. —*Rojas, p. 1155*

Strategy 4:	Do not use a pronoun to stand for a noun unless it is obvious which noun is its antecedent.
First Draft	Both Matsuo Bashō and Yosa Buson are revered as great Japanese haiku poets, but **he** is generally regarded as the best.
Revision	Both Matsuo Bashō and Yosa Buson are revered as great Japanese haiku poets, but **Bashō** is generally regarded as the best.

■ Dangling Modifiers

GUIDE FOR REVISING: A dangling phrase or clause either seems to modify the wrong word or no word at all, because the word it should logically modify has been omitted from the sentence.

Strategy 1:	Fix a participial phrase by adding the word that the phrase should modify, usually right after or before the phrase.
First Draft	**Believing that "every man is by nature a friend to every other man," his knowledge** should be shared through writing.

Revision	**Believing that "every man is by nature a friend to every other man," Dante** believed his knowledge should be shared through writing.
Model from Literature	**His face, within the vivid circle of the lamplight**, was unquestionably that of an old man, but with something unalterable about it, even immortal. —*Borges, p. 1231*

Strategy 2:	**Fix a dangling clause by rewording the sentence.**
First Draft	**Before she is married, Jensine's Aunt Maren** tells her a story of failed marriage.
Revision	**Before Jensine is married, her Aunt Maren** tells her a story of failed marriage.

■ Misplaced Modifiers

GUIDE FOR REVISING: A modifier placed too far away from the word it modifies is called a misplaced modifier. Misplaced modifiers may seem to modify the wrong word in a sentence. Always place a modifier as close as possible to the word it modifies.

Strategy:	**Move the modifying word, phrase, or clause closer to the word it should logically modify.**
First Draft	Ferdinand works diligently for Miranda's father, desperate to hold onto her love.
Revision	Desperate to hold onto her love, Ferdinand works diligently for Miranda's father.
Model from Literature	Trying not to make any noise, he took from a fireproof safe the key to the door that had been unopened for fifteen years, put on his coat and went out. —*Chekhov, p. 962*

Problems of Consistency

■ Subject-Verb Agreement

GUIDE FOR REVISING: Subject and verb must agree in number. A singular subject needs a singular verb, and a plural subject needs a plural verb.

Strategy 1:	**A phrase or clause that interrupts a subject and its verb does not affect subject-verb agreement.**
First Draft	The **beginning** of original sin and human weakness, topics common to the writings of Milton's contemporaries, **are explored** in *Paradise Lost*.

Revision	The **beginning** of original sin and human weakness, topics common to the writings of Milton's contemporaries, **is explored** in *Paradise Lost*.
Model from Literature	The driving mire/submerges; **men**, trapped in that white empire,/**have** no more bread and march on barefoot— *—Hugo, p. 890*
Strategy 2:	**Use a singular verb with two or more singular subjects joined by *or* or *nor*. When singular and plural subjects are joined by *or* or *nor*, the verb must agree with the subject closer to it.**
First Draft	Neither Shakespeare nor the other sixteenth-century playwrights **strays** from the convention of metered verse.
Revision	Neither Shakespeare nor the other sixteenth-century playwrights **stray** from the convention of metered verse.
Strategy 3:	**A linking verb must agree with its subject, regardless of the number of its predicate nominative.**
First Draft	Foreshadowing **questions** asserted by both chorus members and heroes **is commonly used** in Greek tragedies.
Revision	Foreshadowing **questions** asserted by both chorus members and heroes **are commonly used** in Greek tragedies.
Model from Literature	Those **people were** a kind of solution. *—Cavafy, p. 1148*
Strategy 4:	**Indefinite pronouns such as *all*, *any*, *more*, *most*, *none*, *some* can agree with either a singular or plural verb. The correct usage depends on the meaning given to the pronoun.**
Models from Literature	That night, when **all was** quiet, they would fool/Their guardians . . . *—Ovid, p. 532* All were asleep under the silent night. *—Virgil, p. 519*

■ Inconsistencies in Verb Tense

GUIDE FOR REVISING: Verb tenses should not shift unnecessarily from sentence to sentence or within a single sentence.

Strategy:	**In sentences describing two actions that occurred at different times in the past, the past perfect tense is used for the earlier action.**
First Draft	By the time Milton was born in 1608, the plays of Shakespeare **were** popular favorites for many years.
Revision	By the time Milton was born in 1608, the plays of Shakespeare **had been** popular favorites for many years.

Model from Literature   About eighty years ago a young officer in the guards, the youngest son of an old country family, married, in Copenhagen, the daughter of a rich wool merchant whose father **had been** a peddler and **had come** to town from Jutland.

—*Dinesen, p. 106*

■ Faulty Parallelism

GUIDE FOR REVISING: Parallel grammatical structures can be two or more words of the same part of speech, two or more phrases of the same type, or two or more clauses of the same type. Correct a sentence containing faulty parallelism by rewording it so that each parallel idea is expressed in the same grammatical structure.

Strategy: **Check to see that the words, phrases, and clauses in series are parallel.**

First Draft   Niccolò Machiavelli's Florence was one of the most brilliant states of the Italian Renaissance, prospering from **the abundance of trading, the production of clothing, and banking was employed**.

Revision   Niccolò Machiavelli's Florence was one of the most brilliant states of the Italian Renaissance, prospering from **the abundance of trading, the production of clothing, and the employment of banking**.

Model from Literature   How shall I say/what wood that was! I never saw **so drear,/so rank, so arduous** a wilderness!

—*Dante, p. 62*

Problems with Incorrect Words or Phrases

■ Nonstandard Pronoun Cases

GUIDE FOR REVISING: Use the nominative case of a personal pronoun for the subject of a sentence, for a predicate nominative, and for the pronoun in a nominative absolute. Use the objective case of the object of any verb or preposition for the subject of an infinitive.

Strategy 1:   **Be sure to identify the case of a personal pronoun correctly when the pronoun is part of a compound construction. You will often find it helpful to confirm the cases of pronouns by rewording the sentence mentally.**

First Draft   Seeing a production of *The Tempest* on television helped **Lynn and I** to understand the play better.

Revision   Seeing a production of *The Tempest* on television helped **Lynn and me** to understand the play better.

Model from Literature	"They wish **me** to tell you that in return for your presents they will gladly give you as much land as you want." —*Tolstoy, p. 949*
Strategy 2:	**Personal pronouns in the possessive case show possession before nouns. The possessive case is also regularly used when a pronoun precedes a gerund.**
First Draft	The class felt that **me reading aloud** "Everything Is Plundered" made the poem seem less hopeless.
Revision	The class felt that **my reading aloud** "Everything Is Plundered" made the poem seem less hopeless.
Model from Literature	When You and I behind the Veil are past,/Oh but the long, long while the World shall last,/Which of **our Coming and Departure** heeds/As the Sea's self should heed a pebble-cast. —*Khayyám, p. 102*
Strategy 3:	**In elliptical clauses with *than* or *as*, use the form of the pronoun that you would use if the clause were fully stated.**
First Draft	Joan is more versed in Sumerian literature and customs than **him**.
Revision	Joan is more versed in Sumerian literature and customs than **he** [is].

■ Wrong Words or Phrases

GUIDE FOR REVISING: Words or phrases that are suitable in one context may be inappropriate in another.

Strategy 1:	**Make sure that the literal meaning of a word or phrase expresses your meaning precisely.**
First Draft	In his preface to the *Ramayana*, Narayan tells **how it all began.**
Revision	In his preface to the *Ramayana*, Narayan tells **how this great epic became part of the Indian oral tradition.**
Strategy 2:	**Be sure that your language is appropriately formal or informal, depending on your writing context.**
First Draft	The character of Thisbe in Ovid's "The Story of Pyramus and Thisbe" kills herself with **totally awesome courage!**
Revision	The character of Thisbe in Ovid's "The Story of Pyramus and Thisbe" kills herself with **awe-inspiring courage.**

GUIDE FOR REVISING: A double negative is the use of two or more negative words in one clause to express a negative meaning.

Strategy:	Do not use *but* in its negative sense with another negative. Do not use *barely*, *hardly*, and *scarcely* with another negative word.
First Draft	Arthur Rimbaud **wasn't but** nineteen when he abandoned his budding poetry career for a life of adventure.
Revision	Arthur Rimbaud **was but** nineteen when he abandoned his budding poetry career for a life of adventure.

Problems of Readability

■ **Sentence Variety**

GUIDE FOR REVISING: Varying the length and structure of your sentences will help you to hold your readers' attention.

Strategy 1:	Combine short, related sentences by using compound, complex, or compound-complex sentences.
First Draft	Pär Lagerkvist's early work was pessimistic. Thus, he did not receive widespread public recognition at that time. In 1951, following the publication of his two best-known novels he did enjoy widespread recognition. He earned the Nobel Prize.
Revision	**Because his early work was pessimistic,** Pär Lagerkvist did not receive widespread public recognition. **However,** in 1951, **following the publication of his two best-known novels, he earned** the Nobel Prize.
Model from Literature	They improvised a litter with the remains of foremasts and **gaffs, tying it** together with rigging so that it would bear the weight of the body until they reached the cliffs. —*García Márquez, p. 1216*

Strategy 2:	Simplify rambling sentences by separating them into simpler sentences or by regrouping ideas.
First Draft	Karen Blixen became serious about a professional writing career in 1931, **after which time** she spent two years concentrating her efforts to produce her first manuscript, *Seven Gothic Gables*. **It was unfortunate that** finding a publisher who would print her first effort was nearly as difficult as writing **it; yet** ultimately Karen met Dorothy Canfield Fisher, who facilitated the publishing of *Seven Gothic Tales* in 1934 by an American company.

Revision   Karen Blixen became serious about a professional writing career in 1931. **After two years** of concentrated efforts, she produced her first manuscript. Unfortunately, finding a publisher that would print her first effort was nearly as difficult as writing **it. Ultimately,** Karen met Dorothy Canfield Fisher, who, in 1934, facilitated the publishing of *Seven Gothic Tales* by an American company.

Model from Literature   He ate, peering stealthily up at her. She sighed, he thought, but not because she was tired or bored. He suddenly raised his eyes and stared at her.
                                                                        —*Pirandello, p. 1136*

Strategy 3:   **Avoid a series of monotonous sentence openers or a series of sentences that overuse any one particular sentence structure. Vary the sentence openers in a passage.**

First Draft   Theater enthusiasts often wonder when roaming bands of actors began to use permanent performing spaces. The first British theater structures were erected in the mid-sixteenth century. Actor-carpenter John Burbage built the first theater in London in 1576. It was simply called The Theater. The enterprise was a success. The Rose, the Swan, and the famous Globe theaters were built soon after.

Revision   **"When did roaming bands of actors begin to use permanent performing spaces?"** theater enthusiasts often wonder. **In 1576,** Britain's first theater structure was erected by actor-carpenter John Burbage. **Simply called The Theater,** the London enterprise was a success. **Soon after,** the Rose, the Swan, and the Globe theaters were built.

■ Stringy Sentences

GUIDE FOR REVISING: Too many prepositional phrases can make writing wordy and monotonous.

Strategy: **Eliminate some prepositional phrases to reduce the number of words and make the meaning clearer.**

First Draft   In "Ophelia" **by** Arthur Rimbaud, the speaker **of the poem** reflects upon **the tragedy of** one of Shakespeare's characters.

Revision   In Arthur Rimbaud's "Ophelia," **the poem's** speaker reflects upon one of Shakespeare's **tragic** characters.

■ Overuse of Passive Voice

GUIDE FOR REVISING: Strengthen your writing by using the active voice whenever possible. Passive verbs usually force the reader to wait until the end of the sentence to identify who or what is doing the action.

Strategy:	**Change passive verbs to active verbs whenever possible.**
First Draft	Government work and the pressures of city life **were given up by poet Wang Wei**, and a quiet country life **was sought by** him to pursue his writing and painting.
Revision	**Poet Wang Wei gave up** government work and the pressures of city life, and **he sought** a quiet country life to pursue his writing and painting.

Problems of Conciseness

■ Redundancy

GUIDE FOR REVISING: Redundancy is the unnecessary repetition of an idea. It makes writing heavy and dull.

Strategy:	**Eliminate redundant words, phrases, and clauses.**
First Draft	During the **turbulent, unsettled** years of the fifteenth century, a novel type of dramatic presentation emerged: the morality play.
Revision	During the **turbulent** fifteenth century, a novel type of drama emerged: the morality play.

■ Unnecessary Intensifiers

GUIDE FOR REVISING: Intensifiers such as *really*, *very*, *truly*, and *of course* should be used to strengthen statements. Overuse of these words may weaken a sentence.

Strategy:	**Eliminate unnecessary intensifiers from your writing.**
First Draft	David Daiches identifies one of William Wordsworth's poems as **a really accurate** record of "the profit and loss of growing up."
Revision	David Daiches identifies one of William Wordsworth's poems as **an accurate** record of "the profit and loss of growing up."

Problems of Appropriateness

■ Inappropriate Diction

GUIDE FOR REVISING: Problems of inappropriate diction occur when words or phrases that are generally accepted in informal conversation or writing are inappropriately used in formal writing.

Strategy: Choose the appropriate level of diction based on your subject, audience, and writing occasion.

First Draft Thais Lindstrom hints that Nikolai Gogol **was totally wacko** when he says that Gogol's "*The Overcoat* may be taken as an exposé of his own secretive, inner-directed world."

Revision Thais Lindstrom hints that Nikolai Gogol **had an eccentric and troubled personality** when he says that Gogol's "*The Overcoat* may be taken as an exposé of his own secretive, inner-directed world."

■ Inappropriate Imagery

GUIDE FOR REVISING: An image, or a figure of speech, is inappropriate when the comparison seems overly exaggerated or when the reader cannot easily understand the connection.

Strategy: Do not mix metaphors. A comparison that contains many unlike objects may become ludicrous.

First Draft When Sinon sees that the Trojans have bought his story, **hook, line, and sinker,** he knows that it is just a matter of time until his fellow Grecians revel **like pigs in mud** with the spoils of victory.

Revision When Sinon sees that the Trojans have believed his story completely, he knows that it is just a matter of time until his fellow Grecians revel in the spoils of victory.

■ Clichés

GUIDE FOR REVISING: Clichés are expressions that were once fresh and vivid but through overuse now lack force and appeal.

Strategy: When you recognize a cliché, you should substitute a fresh expression of your own.

First Draft Ariel the sprite, ironically indentured to a mortal in Shakespeare's *The Tempest*, wants to be **free as a bird**.

Revision Ariel the sprite, ironically indentured to a mortal in Shakespeare's *The Tempest*, wants to be **set free**.

SUMMARY OF GRAMMAR

Nouns   A **noun** is the name of a person, place, or thing.

A **common noun** names any one of a class of people, places, or things. A **proper noun** names a specific person, place, or thing.

Common Nouns	Proper Nouns
writer	Nora Helmer
country	India, Great Britain

Pronouns   **Pronouns** are words that stand for nouns or for words that take the place of nouns.

Personal pronouns refer to the person speaking; the person spoken to; or the person, place, or thing spoken about.

	Singular	Plural
First Person	I, me, my, mine	we, us, our, ours
Second Person	you, your, yours	you, your, yours
Third Person	he, him, his, she, her, hers, it, its	their, theirs

A **reflexive pronoun** ends in *-self* or *-selves* and adds information to a sentence by referring to a noun or pronoun near the beginning of the sentence.

An **intensive pronoun** ends in *-self* or *-selves* and adds emphasis to a noun or pronoun in a sentence.

"I should like to take breakfast with you this morning, together with my companion here, but you must not put yourself to any trouble." (reflexive)
—*Boccaccio, p. 685*

Still, she reflected, she herself, the rich girl he married, had come along in time, as the willing tool of fortune, to justify his trust in the eyes of his tailor himself. (intensive)   —*Dinesen, p. 1069*

Demonstrative pronouns direct attention to specific people, places, or things.

this   these   that   those

A **relative pronoun** begins a subordinate clause and connects it to another idea in the sentence.

"Yes, Socrates, but what is the origin of these accusations *which* are brought against you . . . "
—*Plato, p. 417*

Interrogative pronouns are used to begin questions.

Which, of he or Adrian, for a good wager, first begins to crow?   —*Shakespeare, p. 731*

Indefinite pronouns refer to people, places, things, often without specifying which ones.

One with a stubby pipe teases his beak,/*Another* mimics, limping, the cripple who could fly!
—*Baudelaire, p. 90*

Verbs   A **verb** is a word or group of words that expresses time while showing an action, a condition, or the fact that something exists. An **action verb** tells what action someone or something is performing.

An action verb is **transitive** if it directs action toward something or someone named in the same sentence.

Their help in need you *ask.*/You first must *hear* them preach.   —*La Fontaine, p. 83*

An action verb is **intransitive** if it does not direct action toward something or someone named in the same sentence.

No smoke *came* now from the chimneypot of the villa.   —*Calvino, p. 128*

A **linking verb** is a verb that connects its subject with a word generally found near the end of the sentence. All linking verbs are intransitive.

Mr. and Mrs. Farquar *were* flustered and pleased and flattered.   —*Lessing, p. 136*

Helping verbs are verbs that can be added to another verb to make a single verb phrase.

"It *can be stopped* right away."   —*Kafka, p. 110*

Adjectives   An **adjective** is a word used to describe a noun or pronoun or to give a noun or a pronoun a more specific meaning. Adjectives answer these questions:

What kind?	*purple* hat, *happy* face
Which one?	*this* bowl, *those* cameras
How many?	*three* cars, *several* dishes
How much?	*less* attention, *enough* food

The articles *the*, *a*, and *an* are adjectives. *An* is used before a word beginning with a vowel sound.

A noun may sometimes be used as an adjective:
language lesson   *chemistry* book

Adverbs   An **adverb** is a word that modifies a verb, an adjective, or another adverb. Adverbs answer the questions *Where? When? In what manner? To what extent?*

She answered *soon.*   (modifies verb *answered*)
Afterward they ate dinner.   (modifies verb *ate*)

I was *extremely* sad. (modifies adjective *sad*)
You called *more*
often than I. (modifies adverb *often*)

Prepositions A **preposition** is a word that relates a noun or pronoun that appears with it to another word in the sentence. Prepositions are almost always followed by nouns or pronouns:

around the fire   *in* sight   *through* us

Conjunctions A **conjunction** is used to connect other words or groups of words.

Coordinating conjunctions connect similar kinds or groups of words:

bread *and* wine   brief *but* powerful

Correlative conjunctions are used in pairs to connect similar words in groups.

Both Luis *and* Rosa   *neither* you *nor* I

Subordinating conjunctions connect two ideas by placing one below the other in rank or importance:

When the man's speech returned once more, he
told him of his adventure. —*de France, p. 616*

Interjections An **interjection** is a word that expresses feeling or emotion and functions independently of a sentence.

O ho, Oh! Would't had been done!
—*Shakespeare, p. 723*

Sentences A **sentence** is a group of words with two main parts: a subject and a predicate. Together these parts express a complete thought.

The infant prodigy entered. —*Mann, p. 1039*

A **fragment** is a group of words that does not express a complete thought.

Phrase A **phrase** is a group of words, without subject and verb, that functions as one part of speech.

A **prepositional phrase** is a group of words that includes a preposition and a noun or pronoun.

on account of the rain   *prior to* 1979

An **adjective phrase** is a prepositional phrase that modifies a noun or pronoun by telling what kind or which one.

The likeness *of the dog* would get mixed up with
that *of the cat.* —*Tagore, p. 1194*

An **adverb phrase** is a prepositional phrase that modifies a verb, an adjective, or an adverb by pointing out where, when, in what manner, or to what extent.

From every side men ran *to the succor of the
dame.* —*de France, p. 615*

An **appositive phrase** is a noun or pronoun with modifiers, placed next to a noun or pronoun, to add information and details.

Man is but a reed, *the weakest in nature*, but he is
a thinking reed. —*Pascal, p. 832*

A **participial phrase** is a participle with an adjective or adverb phrase, or a complement, all acting together as an adjective.

. . . it was an effective childhood fantasy, *remarkably well envisaged.* —*Mann, p. 1043*

A **gerund phrase** is a gerund with modifiers or a complement, all acting together as a noun.

"This *getting up so early*," he thought, "makes anyone a complete idiot." —*Kafka, p. 1084*

An **infinitive phrase** is an infinitive with modifiers, complements, or a subject, all acting together as a single part of speech.

He despised them all because they had excluded
him from their life, refusing *to tell* him what had
happened today *to change* all three of them.
—*Pirandello, p. 1136*

Clauses A **clause** is a group of words with its own subject and verb. An **independent clause** can stand by itself as a complete sentence. A **subordinate clause** cannot stand by itself as a complete sentence.

An **adjective clause** is a subordinate clause that modifies a noun or pronoun by telling what kind or which one.

The more stubborn among them, *who were the
youngest*, still lived for a few hours with the illusion that . . . his name might be Lautaro.
—*García Márquez, p. 1213*

Subordinate **adverb clauses** modify verbs, adjectives, adverbs, or verbals by telling where, when, in what manner, to what extent, under what conditions, or why.

When he died, his heirs found nothing save chaotic
manuscripts. —*Borges, p. 1229*

Subordinate **noun clauses** act as nouns.

. . . she thanked them in tears for the dismissal, as
if for *the greatest favor that had ever been done
to her in this house* . . . —*Kafka, p. 1095*

SUMMARY OF CAPITALIZATION AND PUNCTUATION

CAPITALIZATION

Capitalize the first word in sentences, interjections, and incomplete questions. Also capitalize the first word in a quotation if the quotation is a complete sentence.

> When she had left again, the girl said to her lover: "Your sister laughed at my frock, and because, when she spoke French, I could not answer."
> —*Dinesen, p. 1066*

Capitalize all proper nouns and adjectives.

> Dante Alighieri   Thames River   Mediterranean

Capitalize titles showing family relationships when they refer to a specific person unless they are preceded by a possessive noun or pronoun.

> Uncle Oscar   Mary's aunt

Capitalize the first word and all other key words in the titles of books, periodicals, poems, stories, plays, paintings, and other works of art.

> *The Metamorphosis*   "Waiting for the Barbarians"

PUNCTUATION

End Marks   Use a **period** to end a declarative sentence, a mild imperative sentence, an indirect question, and most abbreviations.

> Everyone knew the poems of Trurl's electronic bard, the air rang with its delightful rhymes.
> —*Lem, p. 1313*

Use a **question mark** to end an interrogative sentence and an incomplete question.

> "A knife has passed through you once?" said the Astrologer.
> "Good fellow!" He bared his chest to show the scar. "What else?"   —*Narayan, p. 1412*

Use an **exclamation mark** after an exclamatory sentence, a forceful imperative sentence, or an interjection expressing strong emotion.

> Heigh, my heart! Cheerly, cheerly, my hearts! Yare, yare! Take in the topsail!   —*Shakespeare, p. 709*

Commas   Use a **comma** before the conjunction to separate two independent clauses in a compound sentence.

> The youth began his journey from/the castle, and the daytime whole/he did not meet one living soul . . .   —*de Troyes, p. 602*

Use **commas** to separate three or more words, phrases, or clauses in a series.

> Their flesh/accords me bitterness, fatigue, and pain—/their perishable beauty bores me.
> —*Cavafy, p. 1150*

Use **commas** to separate adjectives of equal rank. Do not use **commas** to separate adjectives that must stay in a specific order.

> She sat in a deep, velvet-upholstered armchair, and a Persian carpet was spread before her feet.
> —*Mann, p. 1042*

> There was only one huge word with no back to it.
> —*Paz, p. 1246*

Use a **comma** after an introductory word, phrase, or clause.

> As soon as Phom and his family reached their new abode, he applied for admission into the council of a large village.   —*Tolstoy, p. 947*

Use **commas** to set off parenthetical and nonessential expressions.

> Then she was angry with herself, and with all women, and she pitied him, and all men.
> —*Dinesen, p. 1068*

Use **commas** with places, dates, and titles.
London, England   May 9, 1939   John Doe, Esq.

Use **commas** after items in addresses, after the salutation in a personal letter, after the closing in all letters, and in numbers of more than three digits.

Paris, France   Dear Randolph,
Yours Faithfully,   9,744

Use a **comma** to indicate words left out of an elliptical sentence, to set off a direct quotation, and to prevent a sentence from being misunderstood.

> In Rimbaud's poetry, I admire the music; in Pasternak's, the feeling tone.

> "No," Petrovich said with finality, "nothing can be done with it. It's just no good."   —*Gogol, p. 927*

Semicolons   Use a **semicolon** to join independent clauses that are not already joined by a conjunction.

> He saw it; he felt it in all of them.
> —*Pirandello, p. 1138*

Use a **semicolon** to join independent clauses separated by either a conjunctive adverb or a transitional expression.

> He kept shaking his head; yet, although his face was lined with wrinkles, not one of them moved, just as if he were a stone statue.
> —*Lu Hsun, pp. 1186–1187*

Use **semicolons** to avoid confusion when independent clauses or items in a series already contain commas.

> Fang, let us say, has a secret; a stranger calls at his door; Fang resolves to kill him.
> —*Borges, p. 1231*

Colons Use a **colon** before a list of items following an independent clause.

> When the greatest of French poetry is discussed, the following names are certain to be mentioned: Charles Baudelaire, Arthur Rimbaud, Paul Valéry, and Victor Hugo.

Use a **colon** to introduce a formal or lengthy quotation.

> Finally M. Sauvage pulled himself together: "Come on! On our way! But let's go carefully."
> —*Maupassant, p. 915*

Use a **colon** to introduce a sentence that summarizes or explains the sentence before it.

> He did not dare to look at her: it seemed to him that if he did so she would become aware of his frame of mind and his shameful intentions . . .
> —*Rojas, p. 1158*

Quotation Marks A direct quotation represents a person's exact speech or thoughts and is enclosed within **quotation marks**.

> . . . he leans in his despair across the table/and says, "Come on then, dance."
> —*Yevtushenko, p. 1329*

An indirect quotation reports only the general meaning of what a person said or thought and does not require **quotation marks**.

> A woman asked me last night on the dark street/ how another woman was/who'd already died.
> —*Amichai, p. 1343*

Always place a **comma** or **period** inside the final quotation mark.

> Out of a great weariness I answered,/"She's fine, she's fine."
> —*Amichai, p. 1343*

Place a **question mark** or **exclamation mark** inside the final quotation mark if the end mark is part of the quotation; if it is not part of the quotation, place it outside the final quotation mark.

> "What about you? Don't you have any worries?"
> —*Mahfouz, p. 1340*

Use **single quotation marks** for a quotation within a quotation.

> Pointing out clues about character in dialogue, the teacher told her students, "We can infer that Margaret Atwood's mother did not approve of swearing by the fact that she substitutes 'dad-ratted' or 'blankety-blank' for stronger language."

Underline the titles of long written works, movies, television and radio shows, lengthy works of music, paintings, and sculptures. Also **underline** foreign words not yet accepted into English and words you wish to stress.

> <u>60 Minutes</u>   <u>Oedipus the King</u>   <u>Jaws</u>
> <u>déjà vu</u>   <u>The Tempest</u>

Use **quotation marks** around the titles of short written works, episodes in a series, songs, and titles of works mentioned as parts of collections.

> "The Battle Hymn of the Republic" "The Grownup"

Parentheses Use **parentheses** to set off asides and explanations only when the material is not essential or when it consists of one or more sentences.

> For we can neither employ them in handicraft or agriculture; we neither build houses (I mean in the country) nor cultivate land.   —*Swift, p. 802*

Hyphens Use a **hyphen** with certain numbers, after certain prefixes, with two or more words used as one word, with a compound modifier, and within a word when a combination of letters might otherwise be confusing.

> twenty-nine   pre-Romantic   re-create

Apostrophes Add an **apostrophe** and an *-s* to show the possessive case of most singular nouns, including those ending in *-s*.

> Rilke's poetry an editor's pencil Charles's wagon

Add an **apostrophe** to show the possessive case of plural nouns ending in *-s* and *-es*.

> the girls' songs   the Ortizes' car

Add an **apostrophe** and an *-s* to show the possessive case of plural nouns that do not end in *-s* or *-es*.

> the children's games   the mice's whiskers

Use an **apostrophe** in a contraction to indicate the position of the missing letter or letters.

> That's all I'd have to try with my boss; I'd be fired on the spot.   —*Kafka, p. 1084*

Use an **apostrophe** and an *-s* to write the plurals of numbers, symbols, letters, and words used to name themselves.

> the 1890's   five a's   no if's or but's

GLOSSARY OF COMMON USAGE

among, between

Among is generally used with three or more items. *Between* is generally used with only two items.

> *Among* Ibsen's characters, my favorite has always been Nora in *A Doll's House*.
> The character of Miranda from *The Tempest* is at first torn *between* her love for Ferdinand and her duty to her father.

amount, number

Amount refers to quantity of a unit, whereas *number* refers to individual items that can be counted. Therefore, *amount* generally appears with a singular noun, and *number* appears with a plural noun.

> The *amount* of attention that great writers have paid to the Faust legend is remarkable.
> A considerable *number* of publishers reject new novels.

as, because, like, as to

The word *as* has several meanings and can function as several parts of speech. To avoid confusion, use *because* rather than *as* when you want to indicate cause and effect.

> *Because* he felt he had fulfilled himself as a poet, Arthur Rimbaud set down his pen and pursued a life of adventure.

Do not use the preposition *like* to introduce a clause that requires the conjunction *as*.

> *As* we might expect from the verse of Baudelaire, the tone of "Invitation to the Voyage" is sultry and musical.

The use of *as to* for *about* is awkward and should be avoided.

> In "The Handsomest Drowned Man in the World," the men of a small fishing village are jealous *about* the attraction the women feel for a good-looking dead stranger.

bad, badly

Use the predicate adjective *bad* after linking verbs such as *feel*, *look*, and *seem*. Use *badly* whenever an adverb is required.

> In "Ode: Intimations of Immortality From Recollections of Early Childhood," the poet feels *bad* that nature no longer seems clothed "in celestial light."
> At the end of *A Doll's House*, Nora chooses to leave her husband, realizing just how *badly* she'd been affected by seven years in a bad marriage.

because of, due to

Use *due to* if it can logically replace the phrase *caused by*. In introductory phrases, however, *because of* is better usage than *due to*.

> The resurgence of popularity in Henrik Ibsen's *A Doll's House* in recent decades may be *due to* its feminist themes.
> *Because of* the expansion of the reading public and the rise of publishers, booksellers, and royalties, writers during the eighteenth century became less dependent on a smaller number of wealthy patrons.

compare, contrast

The verb *compare* can involve both similarities and differences. The verb *contrast* always involves differences. Use *to* or *with* after *compare*. Use *with* after *contrast*.

> When Rubén Darío's lifestyle is *compared to* his writing style, one finds a dramatic dissimilarity between them.
> Jerry's report *compared* the bohemian lifestyle of Baudelaire *with* that of Rimbaud, noting parallels in their writing styles as well.
> The Greeks *contrasted* inner vision *with* physical vision; thus the legend that Homer was a blind bard indicates how highly they esteemed introspection.

continual, continuous

Continual means "occurring again and again in succession." *Continuous* means "occurring without interruption."

> In the poem "Invitation to the Voyage," Baudelaire's *continual* use of a two-line refrain creates a feeling of the rolling ocean waves.
> Though critics assert that Pablo Neruda spent many painstaking hours shaping his verse, the exuberant voice of the speaker in "Ode to My Socks" suggests that he may have written the poem in a single *continuous* burst of inspiration.

different from, different than

The preferred usage is *different from*.

> Colette's third marriage was very *different from* her previous ones simply by the fact that it brought her great happiness and satisfaction.

farther, further

Use *farther* when you refer to distance. Use *further* when you mean "to a greater degree" or "additional."

> Discontent with his new life in Paris, the young

French poet Rimbaud traveled *farther* east to quench his thirst for adventure.

In Ibsen's *A Doll's House*, Nora realizes that staying in her unhappy marriage will only bring *further* psychological abuse.

fewer, less

Use *fewer* for things that can be counted. Use *less* for amounts or quantities that cannot be counted.

When asked to compare the two versions of the Faust legend they had read, *fewer* students preferred Christopher Marlowe's version. Most found it to be *less* dramatic than Goethe's.

just, only

When you use *just* as an adverb meaning "no more than," be sure that you place it directly before the word it modifies logically. Likewise, be sure you place *only* before the word it logically modifies.

The form of the villanelle allows a poet to use *just* two rhymes.

Poet Arthur Rimbaud was *only* fifteen years old when he was first published.

lay, lie

Do not confuse these verbs. *Lay* is a transitive verb meaning "to set or put something down." Its principal parts are *lay*, *laying*, *laid*, *laid*. *Lie* is an intransitive verb meaning "to recline." Its principal parts are *lie*, *lying*, *lay*, *lain*.

In Shakespeare's *The Tempest*, Prospero has the power to *lay* strange curses and spells on his enemies.

According to Blaise Pascal, an individual *lies* somewhere in the midst of a paradoxical universe, unable to comprehend the extremes of nature.

Plurals that do not end in *-s*

The plurals of certain nouns from Greek and Latin are formed as they were in their original language. Words such as *criteria*, *media*, and *phenomena* are plural and should not be treated as if they were singular (*criterion*, *medium*, *phenomenon*).

Are the electronic *media* of the twentieth century contributing to the death of literature?

raise, rise

Raise is a transitive verb that usually takes a direct object. *Rise* is intransitive and never takes a direct object.

In "On an Autumn Evening in the Mountains," poet Wang Wei *raises* an allegorical question about human mortality when he writes, "Why cannot I linger over this pleasant view?"

As the poets in Dante's *Inferno* pass the Gates of Hell, they hear the anguished cries of the opportunists *rise* within.

that, which, who

Use the relative pronoun *that* to refer to things or people. Use *which* only for things and *who* only for people.

The contemporary poet *that* I most enjoy reading is Pablo Neruda.

World War II, *which* imposed on Colette's personal life, did not affect her literary output.

Derek Walcott, *who* is considered by many critics to be one of the most talented poets writing in English today, draws largely on his experiences in St. Lucia and Jamaica.

when, where

Do not directly follow a linking verb with *when* or *where*. Also be careful not to use *where* when your context requires *that*.

Faulty: Evaluation is *when* you make a judgment about the quality or value of something.

Revised: Evaluation is the process of making a judgment about the quality or value of something.

Faulty: Avignon is *where* Francesco Petrarch was raised.

Revised: Francesco Petrarch was raised in Avignon.

Faulty: Clyde read *where*, even though he lived only twenty-nine years, Christopher Marlowe earned a place in literary history before he died.

Revised: Clyde read *that*, even though he lived only twenty-nine years, Christopher Marlowe earned a place in literary history before he died.

who, whom

Remember to use *who* only as a subject in clauses and sentences and *whom* only as an object.

Goethe, *who* spent over sixty years writing his masterpiece, first encountered the Faust story at a puppet show in a country fair.

Alexander Pushkin, *whom* critics perceive as a man of plain words, wove magical tales with his simple dialogue.

ALLEGORY An *allegory* is a literary work with two or more levels of meaning—one literal level and one or more symbolic levels. The events, settings, objects, or characters in an allegory stand for ideas or qualities beyond themselves. Dante's *Divine Comedy* (page 622) is an allegory written in the Middle Ages, when allegorical writing was common. Many works can be read allegorically as well as literally. When reading a work allegorically, one tries to match every element at the literal level with a corresponding element at the symbolic level. Allegories are also written in the form of parables and fables.
See *Fable* and *Parable*.

ALLITERATION *Alliteration* is the repetition of initial consonant sounds. William Wordsworth's "Ode: Intimations of Immortality from Recollections of Early Childhood" uses alliteration of the *s* sound in the following line:

> Our *S*ouls have *s*ight of that immortal *s*ea

Alliteration is often used, especially in poetry, to emphasize and to link words as well as to create pleasing, musical sounds.

ALLUSION An *allusion* is a reference to a well-known person, place, event, literary work, or work of art. Writers often make allusions to tales from the Bible, classical Greek and Roman myths, plays by Shakespeare, historical or political events, and other materials with which they expect their readers to be familiar. An allusion appears in Shakespeare's *The Tempest*, when Gonzalo states "Not since widow Dido's time," alluding to a great love story in the Roman epic the *Aeneid*, by Virgil. Writers sometimes use allusions as a sort of shorthand to suggest ideas in a simple and concise manner.

ANTAGONIST An *antagonist* is a character or force in conflict with the main character, or protagonist, in a literary work. In many stories the plot is based on a conflict between the antagonist and the protagonist. In 1 Samuel 17 (David and Goliath), on page 61, the antagonist is Goliath, battling the protagonist, David.
See *Character* and *Protagonist*.

APOSTROPHE An *apostrophe* is a figure of speech in which a speaker directly addresses an absent person or a personified quality, object, or idea. In Ovid's *Metamorphoses* (page 532), Thisbe uses an apostrophe to address a tree. Apostrophe is often used in poetry and in speeches to add emotional intensity.
See *Figurative Language*.

ARCHETYPE An *archetype* is a descriptive detail, plot pattern, character type, or theme that recurs in many different cultures. One such archetype that appears in *The Epic of Gilgamesh* is the battle between the forces of good and the forces of evil.

ASIDE An *aside* is a statement delivered by an actor to an audience in such a way that other characters on stage are presumed not to hear what is said. In an aside the character reveals his or her private thoughts, reactions, or motivations. Act I, Scene ii of *The Tempest* contains the following aside:

> **Miranda.**   I might call him
> A thing divine; for nothing natural
> I ever saw so noble.
> **Prospero.**   (Aside) It goes on, I see,
> As my soul prompts it. Spirit, fine spirit,
>   I'll free thee
> Within two days for this.

In this aside, Prospero reveals his pleasure that his desire to match Ferdinand and Miranda is working.

ASSONANCE *Assonance* is the repetition of vowel sounds in stressed syllables containing dissimilar consonant sounds. Derek Walcott uses assonance in the following line from *Omeros*:

I bequeath you that clean sheet and an
     empty throne.

The long *e* sound is repeated in the words *bequeath*, *clean*, and *sheet* in stressed syllables containing these consonants: *b-q-th*, *cl-n*, and *sh-t*.
See *Consonance.*

BLANK VERSE *Blank verse* is poetry written in unrhymed iambic pentameter lines. Each iambic foot has one weakly stressed syllable followed by one strongly stressed syllable. A pentameter line has five of these feet. Blank verse usually contains occasional variations in rhythm—variations that are introduced to create emphasis, variety, and naturalness of sound. Because blank verse sounds so much like ordinary spoken English it is often used in drama and in poetry. The following lines come from William Shakespeare's *The Tempest*:

> **Ferdinand.** Where should this music be?
>   I' th' air or th' earth?
> It sounds no more; and sure it waits upon
> Some god o' th' island. Sitting on a bank,

See *Meter.*

CHARACTER A *character* is a person or animal who takes part in the action of a literary work. Characters can be described in many different ways, as follows:

1. In terms of the importance of their roles: A character who plays an important role in a story is called a *major character*. A character who does not play an important role is called a *minor character*.
2. In terms of their roles: A character who plays the central role in a story is called the *protagonist*. A character who opposes the protagonist is called the *antagonist*.
3. In terms of their complexity: A complex character is called *round*, while a simple character is called *flat*.
4. In terms of the degree to which they change: A character who changes is called *dynamic*; a character who does not change is called *static*. Character types that readers recognize easily,

such as the hard-boiled detective or the wicked stepmother, are called *stereotypes*, or *stock characters*.
See *Characterization* and *Motivation.*

CHARACTERIZATION *Characterization* is the act of creating and developing a character. A writer uses *direct characterization* when he or she states a character's traits explicitly. *Indirect characterization* occurs when the writer reveals a character's traits by some other means. A character's traits can be revealed indirectly by means of what he or she says, thinks, or does; by means of a description of his or her appearance; or by means of the statements, thoughts, or actions of other characters. When using indirect characterization, the writer depends on the reader to infer a character's traits from the clues provided.
See *Character.*

CHOKA A traditional Japanese verse form, *choka* are poems that consist of alternating lines of five and seven syllables, with an additional seven-syllable line at the end. There is no limit to the number of lines in a choka. Choka frequently end with one or more *envoys* consisting of five lines of five, seven, five, seven, and seven syllables. Generally, the envoys elaborate or summarize the theme of the main poem.

CLIMAX The *climax* is the high point of interest or suspense in a literary work. Often the climax is also the point at which the protagonist changes his or her understanding or situation. Sometimes the climax coincides with the *resolution*, the point at which the central conflict is ended. For example, Julio Cortázar's "House Taken Over," on page 1238, reaches its climax with the characters' abandonment of their home.
See *Plot.*

CONFLICT A *conflict* is a struggle between opposing forces. Sometimes this struggle is *internal*, or within a character. At other times the struggle is *external*, or between the character and some outside force. The outside force may be another character, nature, or some element of society such as custom, culture, or a political institution. Often the conflict in a work is complicated and combines several of these possibili-

ties. For example, in *The Tempest* Prospero struggles against Antonio and Sebastian and against different parts of his own nature.
See *Antagonist*, *Plot*, and *Protagonist*.

CONNOTATION A *connotation* is an association that a word calls to mind in addition to its dictionary meaning. For example, the words *home* and *domicile* have the same dictionary meanings. However, the first has positive connotations of warmth and security while the second does not. Therefore, a writer who wants to convey a sense of warmth and security will be more likely to use the word *home* than the word *domicile*. Because the connotations of words are so powerful, writers carefully choose words with connotations that suggest the shades of meaning they intend.
See *Denotation*.

CONSONANCE *Consonance* is the identity of consonant sounds in words without the identity of vowel sounds. Following are some examples of consonance:

black - block
slip - slop
creak - croak
feat - fit
slick - slack

When used at the ends of lines, consonance can create *approximate* or *slant rhyme*.

COUPLET A *couplet* is a pair of rhyming lines written in the same meter. The following iambic tetrameter couplets come from John Milton's "L'Allegro":

And if I give thee honor due,
Mirth, admit me of the crew
To live with her, and live with thee,
In unreproved pleasures free.

A *heroic couplet* is a rhymed pair of iambic pentameter lines. Sonnets written in the English, or Shakespearean style, usually end with heroic couplets.
See *Sonnet*.

DENOTATION The *denotation* of a word is its exact, specific meaning, independent of other associations the word calls to mind. Dictionaries list the denotative meanings of words. Another term for denotative meaning is *referential meaning*.
See *Connotation*.

DIALOGUE A *dialogue* is a conversation between characters. Writers use dialogue to reveal characters, to present events, to add variety to narratives, and to interest readers. The dialogue in a story or play is usually set off by quotation marks and paragraphing. The dialogue in a play script generally follows the characters' names.

DICTION *Diction* is word choice. A writer's diction can be a major determinant of his or her style. Diction can be described as formal or informal, abstract or concrete, plain or ornate, ordinary or technical.
See *Style*.

DRAMA A *drama* is a story written to be performed by actors. It may consist of one or more large sections called *acts*, which are made up of any number of smaller sections called *scenes*.

Drama originated in religious rituals and symbolic reenactments of primitive peoples. The ancient Greeks developed drama into a sophisticated art and created such dramatic forms as comedy and tragedy. *Oedipus the King*, on page 433, is a classic example of Greek tragedy. The classical drama of the Greeks and the Romans declined as the Roman Empire declined.

Drama revived in Europe during the Middle Ages. The Renaissance produced a number of great dramatists, especially in England. Christopher Marlowe's tragedy *Dr. Faustus* and William Shakespeare's romantic comedy *The Tempest* are two examples from that period. Molière's *Tartuffe* is a comedy of manners, a form of drama popular in the seventeenth century. In the middle of the nineteenth century, Henrik Ibsen's *A Doll's House* began a trend toward realistic prose drama and away from drama in verse form. Most of the great Western plays of the twentieth century were written in prose.

Among the many forms of drama from non-Western cultures are the Nō plays of Japan such as Zeami's *The Deserted Crone*.
See *Tragedy*.

EPIC An *epic* is a long narrative poem about the adventures of gods or of a hero. Homer's *Iliad*, on page 335, is a *folk epic*, one that was composed orally and then passed from storyteller to storyteller by word of mouth. Virgil's *Aeneid*, on page 493, and Dante's *Divine Comedy*, on page 622, are examples of literary epics from the Classical and Medieval periods, respectively. John Milton's *Paradise Lost* continues the tradition of the literary epic in the Age of Rationalism. Milton's goal in creating *Paradise Lost* was to write a Christian epic similar in form and equal in value to the great epics of antiquity. Because of an epic's length and seriousness of theme, it presents an encyclopedic portrait of the culture in which it was produced.
See *Epic Convention*.

EPIC CONVENTION An *epic convention* is a traditional characteristic of epic poems. These characteristics include an opening statement of theme; an appeal for supernatural help in telling the story; a beginning *in medias res* (Latin: "in the middle of things"); long lists, or catalogs, of people and things; accounts of past events; and descriptive phrases such as epic similes and Homeric epithets.
See *Epic*.

EPIPHANY *Epiphany* is a term introduced by Irish writer James Joyce to describe a moment of revelation or insight in which a character recognizes some truth. In Colette's "The Bracelet," on page 1122, the main character's epiphany comes at the end of the story when she realizes she cannot recapture her past.

EPITAPH An *epitaph* is an inscription written on a tomb or burial place. In literature, epitaphs also include serious or humorous lines written as if they were intended for such use. Catullus' "I Crossed Many Lands and a Lot of Ocean" on page 528 and Octavio Paz's "Poet's Epitaph" on page 1246 are examples of epitaphs.

EXISTENTIALISM *Existentialism* is a term applied to a kind of philosophical, religious, and artistic thought that emphasizes existence rather than abstract ideas and asserts that human reason is inadequate to explain the meaning of life. Existentialists believe that the universe is indifferent to humans; that things in general exist, but they have no meaning for humans except that meaning which humans create by acting on them. Feodor Dostoevsky, Franz Kafka, and Albert Camus are a few of the writers who utilized existentialist thought in their work.

FABLE A *fable* is a brief story, usually with animal characters, that teaches a lesson, or moral. The earliest extant fables are those attributed to Aesop, a Greek writer of the sixth century B.C. Jean de La Fontaine continued this tradition with the fables he wrote during the Age of Rationalism (see pages 836–840). In the twentieth century, James Thurber of the United States wrote fables that reflect modern times.
See *Allegory*, *Legend*, and *Parable*.

FANTASY *Fantasy* is highly imaginative writing that contains elements not found in real life. In literature of the *fantastic,* fantasy and reality are combined to challenge, puzzle, discomfort, and entertain readers. See Julio Cortázar's "House Taken Over" on page 1238.

FIGURATIVE LANGUAGE *Figurative language* is writing or speech not meant to be interpreted literally. Poets and other writers use figurative language to create vivid word pictures, to make their writing emotionally intense and concentrated, and to state their ideas in new and unusual ways that satisfy readers' imaginations.

FLASHBACK A *flashback* is a section of a literary work that interrupts the sequence of events to relate an event from an earlier time. The writer may present the flashback as a character's memory or recollection, as part of an account or story told by a character, or as a dream or daydream. For example, in Luigi Pirandello's "A Breath of Air" on page 1134, the grandfather thinks back to various events in his life. Writers use flashbacks to show what motivates a character and to supply background information in a dramatic way.
See *Foreshadowing*.

FOLK TALE A *folk tale* is a story composed orally and then passed from person to person by word of mouth. "The Fisherman and the Jinnee," from *The Thousand and One Nights*, on page 128, is a folk tale.

FORESHADOWING *Foreshadowing* is the use, in a literary work, of clues that suggest events that have yet to occur. Writers use foreshadowing to create suspense or to prepare the audience for the eventual outcome of events.

FREE VERSE *Free verse* is poetry not written in a regular rhythmical pattern, or meter. Instead of having metrical feet and lines, free verse has a rhythm that suits its meaning and that uses the sounds of spoken language in lines of different lengths. Free verse has been widely used in twentieth-century poetry. An example is this stanza from Nguyen Thi Vinh's "Thoughts of Hanoi":

> Brother, we are men,
> conscious of more
> than material needs.
> How can this happen to us
> my friend
> my foe?

HAIKU *Haiku* is a three-line Japanese verse form. The first and third lines of a haiku have five syllables. The second line has seven syllables. The brief form is designed to arouse a specific emotion or suggest an insight about life.

HERO/HEROINE A *hero* or *heroine* is a character whose actions are inspiring or noble. Often heroes struggle to overcome foes or to escape from difficulties. The most obvious examples of heroes and heroines are the larger-than-life characters in myths and legends, such as Achilleus from the *Iliad* and Roland from the *Song of Roland*. However, more ordinary characters can, and often do, perform heroic deeds.

HYPERBOLE A *hyperbole* is a deliberate exaggeration or overstatement. In "Ode to My Socks," Pablo Neruda uses this figure of speech:

> two socks as soft
> as rabbits.
> I slipped my feet
> into them
> as though into

> two
> cases
> knitted
> with threads of
> twilight
> and goatskin.

Hyperbole may be used for heightened seriousness or for comic effect.
See *Figurative Language*.

IMAGERY *Imagery* is the descriptive language used in literature to re-create sensory experiences. The following lines from Boris Pasternak's "The Weeping Garden" show how a poet can use imagery to appeal to several senses:

> Silence. Not a leaf stirs.
>   No sign of light; only pathetic sobs
> And scraping of slippers and sighing
>   And tears in the pauses.

These lines describe the sights and sounds of a garden in the evening after a storm. Imagery can enrich writing by making it more vivid, by setting a tone, by suggesting emotions, and by guiding a reader's reactions.

IRONY *Irony* is the general name given to literary techniques that involve surprising, interesting, or amusing contradictions. In *verbal irony*, words are used to suggest the opposite of their usual meaning. In *dramatic irony*, there is a contradiction between what a character thinks and what the reader or audience knows to be true. In *irony of situation*, an event occurs that directly contradicts the expectations of the characters, the reader, or the audience.

LEGEND A *legend* is a widely told story about the past, one that may or may not have a foundation in fact. A legend often reflects a people's identity or cultural values, generally with more historical truth and less emphasis on the supernatural than in a myth. *The Epic of Gilgamesh* from Sumeria and the *Shah-nama* from Persia are both based in part on legends. In Europe, the well-known legend of German Johann Faust has inspired novels and plays.
See *Fable*.

LYRIC POEM A *lyric poem* is a poem that expresses the observations and feelings of a single speaker. Unlike a narrative poem, it presents an experience or a single effect, but it does not tell a full story. Early Greeks defined a lyric poem as that which was expressed by a single speaker accompanied by a lyre. The poems of Archilochus, Callinus, Sappho, and Pindar are lyric. Although they are no longer designed to be sung to the accompaniment of a lyre, lyric poems retain a melodic quality due to the rhythmic patterns of rhymed or unrhymed verse. Modern forms of lyrics include the elegy, the ode, and the sonnet. Nearly all poets use the lyric form in some of their work.

METAPHOR A *metaphor* is a figure of speech in which one thing is spoken of as though it were something else, as in "death, that long sleep." Through this identification of dissimilar things, a comparison is suggested or implied. Octavio Paz used the following metaphor in his poem "Fable": "Insects were living jewels." The metaphor suggests the similarities between insects and precious stones.

An *extended metaphor* is one that is developed at length and that involves several points of comparison. For example, Yehuda Amichai uses extended metaphor in "The Diameter of the Bomb," on page 1342.

A *mixed metaphor* occurs when two metaphors are jumbled together. For example, thorns and rain are illogically mixed in "The thorns of life rained down on him."

A *dead metaphor* is one that has been so overused that its original metaphorical impact has been lost. Examples of dead metaphors include "the foot of the bed" and "toe the line." See *Figurative Language.*

METER The *meter* of a poem is its rhythmical pattern. This pattern is determined by the number and types of stresses, or beats, in each line. To describe the meter of a poem, you must scan its lines. *Scanning* involves marking the strongly stressed and weakly stressed syllables, as follows:

Ĭ weén | thăt, whĕn | thĕ grave's | dark wall
   Dĭd first | hĕr form | rĕtain,

Theў thought | theĭr hearts | coŭld ne'er |
   recall
Thĕ light | ŏf joy | ăgain.
   —Emily Brontë, "Song"

As you can see, each strong stress is marked with a slanted line (´) and each weak stress is marked with a horseshoe symbol (˘). The weak and strong stresses are then divided by vertical lines into groups called *feet*. The following types of feet are common in English poetry:

1. *Iamb*: a foot with one weak stress followed by one strong stress, as in the word "ăfraid"
2. *Trochee*: a foot with one strong stress followed by one weak stress, as in the word "heathĕr"
3. *Anapest*: a foot with two weak stresses followed by one strong stress, as in the word "dĭsĕmbark"
4. *Dactyl*: a foot with one strong stress followed by two weak stresses, as in the word "solĭtŭde"
5. *Spondee*: a foot with two strong stresses, as in the word "workday"
6. *Pyrrhic*: a foot with two weak stresses, as in the last foot of the word "ŭnspeakăbly˘"
7. *Amphibrach*: a foot with a weak syllable, one strong syllable, and another weak syllable, as in the word "ănothĕr"
8. *Amphimacer*: a foot with a strong syllable, one weak syllable, and another strong syllable, as in "up ănd down"

A line of poetry is described as *iambic*, *trochaic*, *anapestic*, or *dactylic* according to what kind of foot appears most often in the line.

Lines are also described in terms of the number of feet that occur in them, as follows:

1. *Monometer:* verse written in one-foot lines
2. *Dimeter:* verse written in two-foot lines
3. *Trimeter:* verse written in three-foot lines
4. *Tetrameter:* verse written in four-foot lines
5. *Pentameter:* verse written in five-foot lines
6. *Hexameter:* verse written in six-foot lines
7. *Heptameter:* verse written in seven-foot lines

A complete description of the meter of a line tells both how many feet there are in the line and what kind of foot is most common. Thus the stanza from Emily Brontë's poem, quoted at the beginning of this entry, would be described as being made up of alternating iambic tetrameter and iambic trimeter lines. Poetry that does not have a regular meter is called *free verse*.

MODERNISM *Modernism* was a broad and diverse movement that encompassed a vast number of smaller literary movements. It is perhaps best defined by the characteristics commonly found in modernist writings. Modernists shared the desire to break with past literary traditions in order to create new and different literature. They therefore rejected many traditional values and assumptions and strove to capture the reality of the modern world in both the form and the content of their work. They sought to do this through experimentation with language, form, and symbol.

MOOD *Mood,* or atmosphere, is the feeling created in the reader by a literary work or passage. The mood may be suggested by the writer's choice of words, by events in the work, or by the physical setting. Julio Cortázar's "House Taken Over," on page 1238, begins with a description of the narrator's life that sets a mood of comfort and routine. He later introduces an element of unknown danger that contrasts with and finally overcomes the pleasant mood at the beginning.

MOTIVATION A *motivation* is a reason that explains or partially explains a character's thoughts, feelings, actions, or speech. Characters may be motivated by their physical needs; by their wants, wishes, desires, or dreams; or by their beliefs, values, and ideals. Effective characterization involves creating motivations that make characters seem believable.
See *Character.*

NARRATIVE POEM A *narrative poem* tells a story in verse. The *Shah-nama,* the *Iliad,* the *Aeneid,* the *Song of Roland* are some of the epic narrative poems in this book. Poets who have written narrative poems include Alexander Pushkin, Victor Hugo, and Wole Soyinka.

ODE An *ode* is a long, formal lyric poem with a serious theme. It may or may not have a traditional structure consisting of three alternating stanza patterns called the *strophe, antistrophe,* and *epode.* An ode may be written for a private occasion or for a public ceremony. Odes often honor people, commemorate events, respond to natural scenes, or consider serious human problems. Wordsworth's "Ode: Intimations of Immortality . . ." and Neruda's "Ode to My Socks" are examples of odes.
See *Lyric Poem.*

ONOMATOPOEIA *Onomatopoeia* is the use of words that imitate sounds. Examples of such words are *buzz, hiss, murmur,* and *rustle.* For example, in the line ". . . to hear/Rasps in the field," from Wole Soyinka's "Season," on page 1362, *rasps* is onomatopoeic. Onomatopoeia is used to create musical effects and to reinforce meaning or tone, especially in poetry.

OXYMORON *Oxymoron* is a figure of speech that fuses two contradictory or opposing ideas. An oxymoron, such as "freezing fire" or "happy grief," thus suggests a paradox in just a few words. In Book 1 of *Paradise Lost,* Milton uses the oxymoron "darkness visible" to describe the pit into which Satan and the other rebellious angels have been thrown.
See *Figurative Language* and *Paradox.*

PARABLE A *parable* is a brief story that allegorically answers a question or expresses a moral or truth. A parable is a simple and brief form of allegory, usually focusing on one or two characters and one specific action. Often, as in the case of the Bible, parables are used as a means of religious instruction. Tolstoy's "How Much Land Does a Man Need?," on page 944, echoes the biblical parable Luke 12:16–20.
See *Allegory* and *Fable.*

PARADOX A *paradox* is a statement that seems to be contradictory but that actually presents the truth. Wole Soyinka's "Season" presents this paradox, "Rust is ripeness, rust/And the wilted corn-plume . . ." Because rust is often associated with decay, the statement seems contradictory. However, in the context of the color o arvested crops, the statement makes sense.

Because a paradox is surprising or even mocking, it draws the reader's attention to what being said.

ee *Figurative Language* and *Oxymoron*.

ARALLELISM *Parallelism* is the repetition of grammatical pattern. Parallelism is used in this tanza from Rubén Darío's "Sonatina" (translatd by John A. Crow):

> She no longer wants the gold distaff or
>   palace,
> The magical falcon, the jester's red challis,
> The swans' classic grace on the azure
>   lagoon.
> The flowers are all sad for the yearning
>   king's daughter,
> The lotus has withered with roots in the
>   water,
> To all the four corners dead roses are
>   strewn.

arallelism is used in poetry and in other writing emphasize and to link related ideas.

ARODY A *parody* is a humorous, mocking nitation of a literary work. Stanislaw Lem's "The irst Sally (A) OR Trurl's Electronic Bard" paroes, among other works, Marlowe's "The Pasionate Shepherd to His Love" and the opening nes of Virgil's *Aeneid*.

ERSONA *Persona* means, literally, "a mask." persona is a fictional self created by an auor—a self through whom the narrative of a oem or story is told. In "I Am Goya," on page 325, Voznesensky adopts the persona of the mous artist Goya.

ee *Speaker*.

ERSONIFICATION *Personification* is a type of gurative language in which a nonhuman subject given human characteristics. Pak Tu-jin used ersonification in these lines from "August River":

> The August river claps its hands,
> The August river writhes,
> The August river agonizes,
> The river hides its brilliance.

Effective personification of things or ideas makes them seem vital and alive, as if they were human.

See *Figurative Language* and *Metaphor*.

PLOT *Plot* is the sequence of events in a literary work. The two primary elements of any plot are the characters and a conflict. Most plots can be analyzed by dividing them into most or all of the following parts:

1. The *exposition* introduces the setting, the characters, and the basic situation.
2. The *inciting incident* introduces the central conflict.
3. During the *development*, the conflict runs its course and usually intensifies.
4. At the *climax*, the conflict reaches a high point of interest or suspense.
5. At the *resolution*, the conflict is ended.
6. The *denouement* ties up loose ends that remain after the resolution of the conflict.

There are many variations on the standard plot structure. Some stories begin *in medias res* ("in the middle of things"), after the inciting incident has already occurred. In some stories the expository material appears toward the middle, in flashbacks. In many stories there is no denouement. Occasionally, though not often, the conflict is left unresolved.

POINT OF VIEW *Point of view* is the perspective, or vantage point, from which a story is told. If a character within the story tells the story, then it is told from the *first-person* point of view. If a voice from outside the story tells it, then the story is told from the *third-person* point of view. If the knowledge of the storyteller is limited to the internal states of one character, then the storyteller has a *limited* point of view. if the storyteller's knowledge extends to the internal states of all of the characters, then the storyteller has an *omniscient* point of view. The point of view from which a story is told determines what view of events will be presented.

PROTAGONIST The *protagonist* is the main character in a literary work. In R. K. Narayan's "An Astrologer's Day," on page 1410, the protagonist is the astrologer.

See *Antagonist* and *Character*.

PSALM A *psalm* is a song or hymn of praise, especially one included in the Book of Psalms in the Bible. See Psalms 8, 19, 23, and 137 beginning on page 67.

REALISM *Realism* is the presentation in art of the details of actual life. Another term for Realism, one that derives from Aristotle's *Poetics*, is *mimesis*, the Greek word for "imitation." Realism arose in the nineteenth century, in part as a reaction to Romanticism. Toward the end of the nineteenth and the first part of the twentieth centuries, Realism enjoyed considerable popularity in France, England, and America. Nowhere, perhaps, was Realism more evident than in the novel. Novels often dealt with grim social realities and often presented realistic portrayals of the psychological states of characters. Realism also had considerable influence on theater in the early Modern Era. During the first part of this century, for example, the most common sort of stage setting was that in which a room was presented as though one wall had been removed and the audience were peering inside.
See *Romanticism*.

RHYME *Rhyme* is the repetition of sounds at the ends of words. *End rhyme* occurs when the rhyming words are repeated at the ends of lines of poetry. *Internal rhyme* occurs when the rhyming words fall within a line. *Exact rhyme* is the use of identical rhyming sounds, as in *love* and *dove*. *Approximate* or *slant rhyme* is the use of sounds that are similar but not identical, as in *prove* and *glove*.

RHYME SCHEME A *rhyme scheme* is a regular pattern of rhyming words in a poem or stanza. To indicate a rhyme scheme, one assigns each final sound in the poem or stanza a different letter. Consider, for example, how the following lines from Elizur Wright's translation of La Fontaine's "The Wolf and the Lamb" have been marked:

A lamb her thirst was slaking	*a*
Once at a mountain rill.	*b*
A hungry wolf was taking	*a*
His hunt for sheep to kill,	*b*
When spying on the streamlet's brink	*c*
This sheep of tender age,	*d*
He howled in tones of rage,	*d*
How dare you roil my drink?	*c*

The rhyme scheme of these lines i ababcddc.

ROMANTICISM *Romanticism* was a literar and artistic movement of the eighteenth an nineteenth centuries. The Romantics empha sized imagination, fancy, freedom, emotion wildness, the beauty of the untamed natura world, the rights of the individual, the nobility c the common man, and the attractiveness of pas toral life. Important figures in the Romanti movement included William Wordsworth, Victo Hugo, and Heinrich Heine.
See *Realism*.

SATIRE *Satire* is writing that ridicules or hold up to contempt the faults of individuals or c groups. A satirist may use a sympathetic tone c an angry, bitter tone. Some satire, like Jonatha Swift's "A Modest Proposal" (page 801), is writ ten in prose. Other satire is written in poetry. A though satire is often humorous, its purpose i not simply to make readers laugh but also t correct, through laughter, the flaws and short comings that it points out.

SCANSION *Scansion* is the process of ana lyzing the metrical pattern of a poem.
See *Meter*.

SETTING The *setting* of a literary work is th time and place of the action. A setting can serv many different purposes. It can provide a back drop for the action. It can be the force that th protagonist struggles against and thus th source of the central conflict. It can also be use to create a mood, or atmosphere. In man works the setting symbolizes some point tha the author wishes to emphasize. In Yevgen Yevtushenko's "Weddings," on page 1329, th setting itself is conflicting—while the place of th setting is a wedding, the time is during war. Thi conflict in the setting is the cause of the conflic ing feelings of the characters. The first lines c the poem sum up the conflicting feelings cause by this setting:

Those weddings in wartime! The deceiving
   comfort!
The dishonesty of words about living.

See *Mood* and *Symbol.*

SIMILE   A *simile* is a figure of speech that
compares two dissimilar things by using a key
word such as *like* or *as.* There are many similes
used in the *Iliad,* such as the following:

But swift Achilleus kept unremittingly after
   Hektor,
chasing him, as a dog in the mountains who
   has flushed from his covert
a deer's fawn follows him through the folding ways and the valleys,

By comparing dissimilar things, the writer of
a simile shocks the reader into appreciation of
the qualities of the things being compared. Thus
a simile makes a description more vivid and
memorable.

SONNET   A *sonnet* is a fourteen-line lyric
poem focusing on a single theme. Sonnets
have many variations but are usually written in
iambic pentameter, following one of two traditional patterns.

   The *Petrarchan* or *Italian sonnet* is divided
into two parts, the eight-line octave and the six-
line sestet. The octave rhymes *abba abba,* while
the sestet generally rhymes *cde cde* or uses
some combination of *cd* rhymes. The two parts
of the Petrarchan sonnet work together. The octave raises a question, states a problem, or presents a brief narrative, and the sestet answers
the question, solves the problem, or comments
on the narrative.

   The *Shakespearean* or *English sonnet* has
three four-line quatrains plus a concluding two-
line couplet. The rhyme scheme of such a sonnet is usually *abab cdcd efef gg.* Each of the
three quatrains usually explores a different variation of the main theme. Then the couplet presents a summarizing or concluding statement.
See *Lyric Poem.*

SPEAKER   The *speaker* is the imaginary voice
assumed by the writer of a poem. In other words,
the speaker is the character who tells the poem.

This character often is not identified by name.
The speaker of Wole Soyinka's "Civilian and Soldier" identifies him or herself in the first stanza:

My apparition rose from the fall of lead,
Declared, "I'm a civilian." It only served
To aggravate your fright. For how could I
Have risen, a being of this world, in that
   hour
Of impartial death! And I thought also: nor is
Your quarrel of this world.

   Recognizing the speaker and thinking about
his or her characteristics are often central to interpreting a lyric poem.
See *Persona* and *Point of View.*

STANZA   A *stanza* is a group of lines in a poem
considered as a unit. Many poems are divided
into stanzas that are separated by spaces. Stanzas often function like paragraphs in prose. Each
stanza states and develops a single main idea.

   Stanzas are commonly named according to
the number of lines found in them, as follows:
1. *Couplet:* a two-line stanza
2. *Tercet:* a three-line stanza
3. *Quatrain:* a four-line stanza
4. *Cinquain:* a five-line stanza
5. *Sestet:* a six-line stanza
6. *Heptastich:* a seven-line stanza
7. *Octave:* an eight-line stanza
See *Sonnet.*

STYLE   A writer's *style* is his or her typical way
of writing. Determinants of a writer's style include his or her formality, use of figurative language, use of rhythm, typical grammatical patterns, typical sentence lengths, and typical
methods of organization. John Milton is noted
for a grand heroic style while the style of Stanislaw Lem is playful. Yehuda Amichai's colloquial
style is an innovation in Hebrew literature and
Jorge Luis Borges is noted for a highly allusive
style.

SURREALISM   *Surrealism* is a movement in
art and literature that emphasizes the irrational
side of human nature. It focuses on the imaginary world of dreams and the unconscious mind.

Originating in France following World War I, Surrealism was a protest against the so-called rationalism that led the world into a destructive war. Outside of France, Surrealism influenced Latin American poets such as Pablo Neruda, whose "Ode to My Socks" appears on page 1250.

SUSPENSE *Suspense* is a feeling of growing curiosity or anxious uncertainty about the outcome of events in a literary work. Writers create suspense by raising questions in the minds of their readers.
See *Foreshadowing.*

SYMBOL A *symbol* is anything that stands for or represents something else. Thus a flag is a symbol of a country, a group of letters can symbolize a spoken word, a fine car can symbolize wealth, and so on. In literary criticism a distinction is often made between *traditional* or *conventional symbols*—symbols that are part of a general cultural inheritance—and *personal symbols* —symbols that are created by particular authors for use in particular works. For example, the river, the cliff, and other images from nature in Pak Tu-jin's "High Mountain Plant," on page 1426, are conventional symbols inherited from Buddhist and Confucian philosophies. However, the overcoat in Gogol's "The Overcoat," on page 922, is a personal symbol. Gogol created this symbol of a new identity specifically for this story.

SYMBOLISM *Symbolism* was a literary movement of nineteenth-century France. The Symbolist writers reacted against Realism and stressed, instead, the importance of suggestion and evocation of emotional states, especially by means of symbols corresponding to these states. The Symbolists were also quite concerned with using sound to achieve emotional effects. Important Symbolist writers included Arthur Rimbaud, Stéphane Mallarmé, and Paul Verlaine. Many twentieth-century writers around the world were influenced by the Symbolist movement.

TANKA *Tanka* is a form of Japanese poetry consisting of five lines of five, seven, five, seven, and seven syllables. Tanka is the most prevalent verse form in traditional Japanese literature. Tanka often tell a brief story or express a single feeling or thought.

THEME The *theme* is a central idea, concern, or purpose in a literary work. In an essay the theme might be directly stated in what is known as a thesis statement. In a serious literary work, the theme is usually expressed indirectly rather than directly. A light work, one written strictly for entertainment, may not have a theme.

TONE The *tone* of a literary work is the writer's attitude toward the readers and toward the subject. A writer's tone may be formal or informal, friendly or distant, personal or pompous. For example, Jonathan Swift's tone in his "A Modest Proposal," on page 801, is satirical, while Gabriela Mistral's poem "Fear," on page 1170, has a fearful tone.
See *Mood.*

TRAGEDY *Tragedy* is a type of drama or literature that shows the downfall or destruction of a noble or outstanding person, traditionally one who possesses a character weakness called a tragic flaw. The *tragic hero,* through choice or circumstance, is caught up in a sequence of events that inevitably results in disaster. Because the protagonist is neither a wicked villain nor an innocent victim, the audience reacts with mixed emotions—both pity and fear. The outcome of a tragedy, in which the protagonist is isolated from society, contrasts with the happy resolution of a comedy, in which the protagonist makes peace with society. Sophocles' *Oedipus the King,* on page 433, is a Greek tragedy.
See *Drama.*

UNDERSTATEMENT *Understatement* is the literary technique of saying less than is actually meant, generally in an ironic way. An example of understatement is the description of a flooded area as "slightly soggy."
See *Figurative Language.*

GLOSSARY

PRONUNCIATION KEY

Symbol	Key Words	Symbol	Key Words
a	asp, fat, parrot	f	fall, after, off, phone
ā	ape, date, play, break, fail	g	get, haggle, dog
		h	he, ahead, hotel
ä	ah, car, father, cot	j	joy, agile, badge
		k	kill, tackle, bake, coat, quick
e	elf, ten, berry	l	let, yellow, ball
ē	even, meet , money, flea, grieve	m	met, camel, trim, summer
i	is, hit, mirror	n	not, flannel, ton
ī	ice, bite, high, sky	p	put, apple tap
ō	open, tone, go, boat	r	red, port, dear, purr
ô	all, horn, law, oar	s	sell, castle, pass, nice
oo	look, pull, moor, wolf		
ōō	ooze, tool, crew, rule	t	top, cattle, hat
		v	vat, hovel, have
		w	will, always, swear, quick
yōō	use, cute, few		
yoo	cure, globule	y	yet, onion, yard
oi	oil, point, toy	z	zebra, dazzle, haze, rise
ou	out, crowd, plow		
u	up, cut, color, flood	ch	chin, catcher, arch, nature
ʉr	urn, fur, deter, irk	sh	she, cushion, dash, machine
ə	a in ago	th	thin, nothing, truth
	e in agent	*th*	then, father, lathe
	i in sanity	zh	azure, leisure, beige
	o in comply	ŋ	ring, anger, drink
	u in focus	'	[indicates that a following l or n is a syllabic consonant, as in cattle (kat´'l), Latin (lat´'n)]
ər	perhaps, murder		
b	bed, fable, dub, ebb		
d	dip, beadle, had, dodder		

FOREIGN SOUNDS

ȧ This symbol, representing the *a* in French *salle*, can best be described as intermediate between (a) and (ä).

ë This symbol represents the sound of the vowel cluster in French *coeur* and can be approximated by rounding the lips as for (ō) and pronouncing (e).

ö This symbol variously represents the sound of *eu* in French *feu*, or of *ö* or *oe* in German *blöd* or *Goethe*, and can be approximated by rounding lips as for (ō) and pronouncing (ā).

ô This symbol represents a range of sounds between (ô) and (u); it occurs typically in the sound of the *o* in French *tonne* or German *korrekt*; in Italian *poco* and Spanish *torero*, it is almost like English (ô), as in *horn*.

ü This symbol variously represents the sound of *u* in French *duc* and in German *grun* and can be approximated by rounding the lips as for (ō) and pronouncing (ē).

kh This symbol represents the voiceless velar or uvular fricative as in the *ch* of German *doch* or Scots English *loch*. It can be approximated by placing the tongue as for (k) but allowing the breath to escape in a stream, as in pronouncing (h).

H This symbol represents a sound similar to the preceding but formed by friction against the forward part of the palate, as in German *ich*. It can be made by placing the tongue as for English (sh) but with the tip pointing downward.

n This symbol indicates that the vowel sound immediately preceding it is nasalized; that is, the nasal passage is left open so that the breath passes through both the mouth and nose in voicing the vowel, as in French *mon* (mōn). The letter *n* itself is not pronounced unless followed by a vowel.

r This symbol represents any of various sounds used in languages other than English for the consonant *r*. It may represent the tongue-point trill or uvular trill of the *r* in French *reste* or *sur*, German *Reuter*, Italian *ricotta*, Russian *gorod*, etc.

' The apostrophe is used after final *l* and *r*, in certain French pronunciations, to indicate that they are voiceless after an unvoiced consonant, as in *lettre* (let´r'). In Russian words the "soft sign" in Cyrillic spelling is indicated by (y'). The sound can be approximated by pronouncing an unvoiced (y) directly after the consonant involved, as in *Sevastopol* (se´ väs tô´ pel y').

This pronunciation key is from *Webster's New World Dictionary,* Third College Edition. Copyright © 1988 by Simon & Schuster. Used by permission.

READING THE GLOSSARY ENTRIES

The words in this glossary are from selections appearing in your textbook. Each entry in the glossary contains the following parts:

1. Entry word. This word appears at the beginning of the entry in boldface type.

2. Pronunciation. The symbols in parentheses tell how the entry word is pronounced. If a word has more than one possible pronunciation, the most common of these pronunciations is given first.

3. Part of Speech. Appearing after the pronunciation, in italics, is an abbreviation that tells the part of speech of the entry word. The following abbreviations have been used:

n. noun **p.** pronoun **v.** verb
adj. adjective **adv.** adverb **conj.** conjunction

4. Definition. This part of the entry follows the part-of-speech abbreviation and gives the meaning of the entry word as used in the selection in which it appears.

A

abase (ə bās´) *v.* To humble or humiliate
abhor (ab hôr´) *v.* To shrink from in disgust or hatred; detest
abjure (ab jōōr´) *v.* To give up on oath; renounce publicly
abomination (ə bäm´ ə nā´ shen) *n.* Anything hateful and disgusting
aborigine (ab´ ə rij´ ə nē´) *n.* First inhabitant; native
abstinent (ab´ stə nənt) *n.* One who voluntarily does without food, drink, or other pleasures

abstract (ab strakt´) *adj.* Thought of apart from any particular instances of material objects; not concrete

abysmal (ə biz´ məl) *adj.* Wretched to the point of despair; immeasurably bad

abyss (ə bis´) *n.* A deep fissure in the earth; bottomless gulf; chasm

accolade (ak´ ə lād´) *n.* Anything done or given as a sign of great respect, approval; appreciation

accrue (ə krōō´) *v.* To come as a natural growth, advantage, or right

acquit (ə kwit´) *v.* To clear a person of a charge by declaring him or her not guilty; exonerate

acute (ə kyōōt´) *adj.* Severe but of short duration; not chronic

adorn (ə dôrn´) *v.* To put decorations on; ornament

adrenalin (ə dren´ ə lin´) *n.* Trademark for epinephrine, a hormone secreted by adrenal gland that stimulates the heart, increases blood sugar, muscular strength, and endurance

affable (af´ ə bəl) *adj.* Pleasant and easy to approach or talk to; friendly; gentle and kindly

affidavit (af´ ə dā´ vit) *n.* A written statement made on oath before a notary public or other person authorized to administer oaths

affinity (ə fin´ i tē) *n.* Close relationship or connection

allay (a lā´) *v.* To put to rest; quiet; calm

altruistic (al´ trōō is´ tik) *adj.* Motivated by unselfish concern for the welfare of others; selfless

amethyst (am´ i thist) *n.* A purple or violet variety of quartz used in jewelry

anarchist (an´ ər kist) *n.* A person who believes that individuals should not have to follow laws

ancestral (an ses´ trəl) *adj.* Of or inherited from any person from whom one is descended

animation (an´ i mā´ shən) *n.* A condition of motion, action; life

anoint (ə noint´) *v.* To rub oil or ointment on

antiquity (an tik´ wə tē) *n.* The quality of being ancient or old; great age

antiseptic (an´ tə sep´ tik) *adj.* Cleansing and able to fight infection

aplomb (ə pläm´) *n.* Self-assurance; poise

appropriate (ə prō´ prē āt´) *v.* To take for one's own exclusive use

arbiter (är´ bit ər) *n.* A person selected to judge a dispute; umpire; arbitrator

arbitress (är´ bə tris) *n.* A woman selected to judge or decide a dispute; umpire; arbitrator

ardor (är´ dər) *n.* Emotional warmth; passion

array (ə rā´) *n.* Troops in order; military force

askew (ə skyōō´) *adj.* Off to one side; crooked

aspiring (ə spīr´ iŋ) *adj.* Ambitious; yearning or seeking

assail (ə sāl´) *v.* To attack violently; assault

assert (ə sʉrt´) *v.* To state positively; declare; affirm

assertion (ə sur´ shen) *n.* A positive statement or declaration with no objective proof

asunder (ə sun´ der) *adv.* Into parts or pieces

asylum (ə sī´ ləm) *n.* Sanctuary where one is safe and secure; refuge

audibly (ô´ dəb lē) *adv.* Loudly enough to be heard

auspicious (ôs pish´ əs) *adj.* Of good omen; boding well for the future; favorable; propitious

austere (ô stir´) *adj.* Showing strict discipline and denial; ascetic

avenger (ə venj´ ər) *n.* Someone who takes vengeance on behalf of someone else, as for an injury or wrong

awry (ə rī´) *adv.* With a twist to a side; not straight; askew

B

ballast (bal´ əst) *n.* Anything heavy carried in a ship, aircraft, or vehicle to give stability

balsam (bôl´ səm) *adj.* Healing and soothing, like the ointments made from the sweet-smelling resins of balsam trees

bangle (baŋ´ gəl) *n.* A decorative bracelet, armlet, or anklet; disk-shaped ornament

banish (ban´ ish) *v.* To send or put away; get rid of

beatitude (bē at´ ə tōōd´) *n.* Perfect blessedness or happiness

begrudge (bē gruj´) *v.* To regard with displeasure or disapproval

beguile (bē gīl´) *v.* To mislead by cheating or tricking; deceive

bemuse (bē myōōz´) *v.* To plunge in thought; preoccupy

beneficent (bə nef´ ə sənt) *adj.* Showing the quality of being kind or having done charitable acts; resulting in benefit

benevolent (bə nev´ ə lənt) *adj.* Doing or inclined to do good; kindly; charitable

bereave (bē rēv´) *v.* To leave in a sad or lonely state, as by loss or death

beseech (bē sēch´) *v.* To ask for earnestly; solicit eagerly; beg for; entreat; implore

betoken (bē tō´ kən) *v.* To be a token or sign of; indicate; show

betray (bē trā´) *v.* To break faith with; fail to meet the hopes of

betrothed (bē trōthd´) *adj.* Engaged to be married

bewildered (bē wil´ dər'd) *adj.* Hopelessly confused by something complicated or involved; befuddled; puzzled

biased (bī´ əs'd) *adj.* Having a mental leaning or inclination; partial; prejudiced

bile (bīl) *n.* A digestive fluid, associated since ancient times with anger and bitterness

blanch (blanch) *v.* To make pale; whiten; take the color out of

blasphemous (blas´ fə məs) *adj.* Characterized by profane or contemptuous speech, writing, or action concerning God or anything held as divine

blight (blīt) *n.* Anything that destroys, prevents growth, or causes devaluation

blithe (blīth) *adj.* Showing a gay, cheerful disposition; carefree

blotch (bläch) *n.* Any large blot or stain

bluster (blus´ tər) *v.* To speak or conduct oneself in a noisy, swaggering or bullying manner

bountiful (boun´ tə fəl) *adj.* Giving freely and graciously; generous; provided in abundance; plentiful

boxwood (bäks wood´) *n.* The hard, close grained wood of the box shrub or tree

brandish (bran´ dish) *v.* To wave, shake, or exhibit in a menacing, challenging or exultant way

brigand (brig´ ənd) *n.* A bandit, usually one of a roving band

brocaded (brō kād´ əd) *adj.* A rich cloth with a raised design

brusque (brusk) *adj.* Rough and abrupt in manner or speech
bustle (bus´ əl) *n.* Busy and noisy activity; commotion

C

calamity (kə lam´ ə tē) *n.* Deep trouble or misery
calculating (kal´ kyōō lāt´ iŋ) *adj.* Shrewd or cunning in a selfish way; scheming
calligrapher (kə lig´ rə fər) *n.* A person whose beautiful handwriting is an art form
canker (kaŋ´ kər) *v.* To infect or debase with corruption
caricature (kar´ i kə chər) *n.* A likeness or imitation that is so distorted or inferior as to seem ludicrous
carrion (kar´ ē ən) *adj.* Feeding on the decaying flesh of a dead body
celestial (sə les´ chəl) *adj.* Of heaven, divine
censorious (sen sôr´ ē əs) *adj.* Inclined to find fault; harshly critical
chagrin (shə grin´) *n.* A feeling of embarrassment and annoyance because one has failed or become disappointed; mortification
chasm (kaz´ əm) *n.* Deep crack in the earth's surface
chastise (chas tīz´) *v.* To scold or condemn sharply
chastisement (chas tīz´ mənt) *n.* Punishment by beating, scolding, or sharp condemnation
checked (chekd) *v.* Held back; restrained; controlled
cherubim (cher´ yōō bim´) *n.* Any of the second order of angels, usually ranked just below the seraphim
chiffonier (shif´ ə nir´) *n.* A narrow, high bureau or chest of drawers, often with a mirror
chink (chiŋk) *n.* A narrow opening; crack; fissure
citadel (sit´ ə del´) *n.* A fortified place, stronghold; place of safety; refuge
clamor (klam´ ər) *n.* Loud, sustained noise
clinch (klinch) *v.* To settle a bargain definitely
coalesce (kō ə les´) *v.* To unite or merge into a single body, group, or mass
communal (käm´ yōō nəl) *adj.* Of or belonging to the community; shared or participated in by all; public
compliance (kəm plī´ əns) *n.* A giving in to a request, wish, or demand; acquiescence
composure (kəm pō´ zhər) *n.* Calmness of mind or manner; tranquility; self-possession
compulsory (kəm pul´ sə rē) *adj.* That must be done, undergone; obligatory; required
concession (kən sesh´ ən) *n.* A thing conceded or granted; acknowledgment; as of an argument or claim
conflagration (kän´ flə grā´ shən) *n.* A big, destructive fire
confront (kən frunt´) *v.* To face or oppose boldly, defiantly, or antagonistically
congeal (kən gēl´) *v.* To solidify or thicken; coagulate; jell
conjecturing (kən jek´ chər iŋ) *v.* Arriving at or proposing by guess or inference
connoisseur (kän´ ə sur´) *n.* A person who has expert knowledge and keen discrimination in some field
connotation (kän´ ə tā´ shən) *n.* Idea or notion suggested by or associated with a word, phrase, etc., in addition to its explicit meaning
console (kən sōl´) *v.* To make less sad or disappointed; comfort
consolidate (kən säl´ ə dāt´) *v.* To combine into a single whole; to become strong, stable, firmly established; merge; unite

consonant (kän´ sə nənt) *adj.* In harmony or agreement; in accord
consternation (kän´ stər nā´ shən) *n.* Great fear or shock that makes one feel helpless or bewildered
consul (kän´ səl) *n.* Either of the two chief magistrates of the ancient Roman republic
contemplate (kän´ təm plāt´) *v.* Think about; study carefully
contemplation (kän´ təm plā´ shən) *n.* Thoughtful religious meditation
contemptuous (kən temp´ chōō əs) *adj.* Full of contempt; scornful; disdainful
contention (kən ten´ shən) *n.* The act of strife, struggle, controversy, dispute, quarrel
contraband (kän´ trə band´) *n.* Goods forbidden by law to be imported or exported; smuggled merchandise
contrition (kən trish´ ən) *n.* Remorse for having done wrong
contrived (kən trīvd´) *adj.* Too obviously the result of forethought and planning; not spontaneous or natural
convalescent (kän´ və les´ ənt) *n.* A person who is recovering health after illness
convergence (kən vur´ jəns) *n.* The point at which things come together
copious (kō´ pē əs) *adj.* Very plentiful; abundant
cornice (kôr´ nis) *n.* A horizontal molding projecting along the top of a wall, building, etc.
corrosive (kə rōs´ iv) *adj.* Having properties that cause a gradual disintegration, rusting, or decay
countenance (koun´ tə nəns) *n.* The face, facial features; visage
coursing (kôr´ siŋ) *v.* Running through or over; traversing
courtier (kôrt´ ē ər) *n.* A person who uses flattery to get something or to win favor
courtier (kôrt´ ē ər) *n.* An attendant at a royal court
courtly (kōrt´ lē) *adj.* Suitable for a king's court; dignified, polite, elegant
covet (kuv´ it) *v.* To want something another person has ardently; long with envy
credulous (krej´ ōō ləs) *adj.* Tending to believe too readily; easily convinced
crevice (krev´ is) *n.* A narrow opening caused by a crack or a split
crone (krōn) *n.* An ugly, withered old woman; hag
cue (kyōō) *n.* A signal to do something
culmination (kul´ mə nā´ shən) *n.* A reaching of the highest point; zenith; climax
cunning (kun´ iŋ) *adj.* Skillful in deception; sly; crafty
cynicism (sin´ ə siz´ əm) *n.* Sarcasm; sneering attitude

D

dandle (dan´ dəl) *v.* Move up and down, as one might do to entertain or soothe a child
dauntless (dônt´ lis) *adj.* That which cannot be intimidated
debris (də brē´) *n.* Rough broken bits and pieces of stone, wood, etc., as after destruction; rubble
decree (dē krē´) *v.* To order, decide or appoint officially
decrepit (dē krep´ it) *adj.* Broken down or worn out by old age or long use; illness
deference (def´ ər əns) *n.* Courteous regard or respect
degradation (deg´ rə dā´ shən) *n.* A condition of dishonor or contempt
degradation (deg´ rə dā´ shən) *n.* The lowering or corruption in quality, moral character, or value; debasedness
deliberate (di lib´ ər āt) *v.* To consider carefully

delusion (di lōō´ zhən) *n.* A false belief or opinion

demarcation (dē´ mär kā´ shən) *n.* The act of setting and marking limits or boundaries

demented (dē ment´ id) *adj.* Mentally deranged; insane; mad

demolition (dem´ ə lish´ ən) *n.* Destruction; ruin; annihilation

demure (di myōōr´) *adj.* Decorous; modest; reserved

deplorable (dē plôr´ ə bəl) *adj.* That which can or should be regarded as unfortunate or wretched; regrettable; very bad

depository (dē päz´ ə tor´ ē) *n.* A place where things are put for safekeeping; storehouse

derelict (der´ ə likt´) *n.* A destitute person without a home or a regular job and rejected by society

derision (di rizh´ ən) *n.* Contempt or ridicule

desolate (des´ ə lit) *adj.* Uninhabited; deserted

despicable (des´ pi kə bəl) *adj.* Deserving to be despised; contemptible

despond (di spänd´) *v.* To lose courage or hope; become disheartened; be depressed

despondency (di spän´ dən sē) *n.* Loss of courage or hope; dejection

despondent (di spän´ dənt) *adj.* Filled with loss of courage or hope; dejected

despotism (des´ pət iz´ əm) *n.* Tyranny

destitute (des´ tə tōōt´) *adj.* Not having; being without; lacking the necessities of life; living in complete poverty

devour (di vour´) *v.* To swallow up; engulf

dexterity (deks ter´ ə tē) *n.* Skill in using one's hands, body or mind; adroitness; cleverness

diffidence (dif´ ə dəns) *n.* Lack of confidence in oneself, marked by hesitation in asserting oneself; shyness

dirge (dɜrj) *n.* A slow, sad song, poem, or musical composition expressing grief or mourning; lament

discord (dis´ kôrd´) *n.* Lack of concord; disagreement; dissention; conflict

discrimination (di skrim´ i nā´ shən) *n.* The ability to make or perceive distinctions; perception; discernment

disdain (dis dān´) *n.* The feeling, attitude or expression of aloof contempt or scorn. *v.* To regard or treat as unworthy or beneath one's dignity; to refuse or reject with aloof contempt or scorn

disgorge (dis gôrj´) *v.* To give up something against one's will

dismay (dis mā´) *n.* A loss of courage or confidence at the prospect of trouble or danger

dispatch (di spach´) *v.* To put an end to; kill

disquiet (dis kwī´ ət) *v.* To make anxious, uneasy or restless; disturb; fret

disreputable (dis rep´ yōō tə bəl) *adj.* Not reputable; having or causing a bad reputation; discreditable

dissembler (di sem´ blər) *n.* Someone who conceals the truth or one's true feelings, motives by pretense

dissipation (dis´ ə pā´ shən) *n.* A wasting or squandering; idle or frivolous amusement or diversion

dissolution (dis´ ə lōō´ shən) *n.* A dissolving or being dissolved; the ending of life; death

distraught (di strôt´) *adj.* Extremely troubled; mentally confused; distracted; harassed

diversion (də vɜr´ zhən) *n.* Anything that diverts or distracts the attention; a pastime or amusement

doggedly (dôg´ id lē) *adv.* Not giving in readily; stubborn

dreary (drir´ ē) *adj.* Gloomy; cheerless; depressing; dismal; dull

dregs (dregz) *n.* The most worthless part

drought (draft) *n.* The amount of fish caught in one draw

E

earnest (ɜr´ nist) *adj.* Serious; not joking

earnestness (ɜr´ nist nis´) *n.* Zeal; serious intensity

eaves (ēvz) *n.* The lower edge or edges of a roof, usually projecting beyond the sides of a building

ebony (eb´ ə nē) *n.* A hard, heavy, dark durable wood, used for furniture and decorative woodwork

ecstasy (ek´ stə sē) *n.* A feeling of overpowering joy; great delight; rapture

ecstatic (ek stat´ ik) *adj.* Characterized by a feeling of overpowering joy; great delight; rapture

edification (ed´ i fi kā´ shən) *n.* Instruction or enlightenment

egoist (ē´ gō ist) *n.* A person who is self-centered or selfish

ejaculate (ē jak´ yōō lāt) *v.* Exclaim; speak suddenly or sharply

elated (ē lā´ təd) *adj.* Filled with a feeling of exultant joy or pride; high spirits

elixir (ē liks´ ir) *n.* A sweetened, aromatic solution

elocution (el´ ə kyōō´ shən) *n.* Style or manner of speaking or reading in public

eloquence (el´ ə kwəns) *n.* Speech or writing that is vivid, forceful, fluent, graceful, and persuasive

emanation (em´ ə nā´ shən) *n.* Something that comes forth from a source; thing omitted

embark (em bärk´) *v.* To begin a journey

embellish (em bel´ ish) *v.* To decorate or improve by adding detail; to improve often of a fictitious or imaginary kind

emblem (em´ bləm) *n.* A visible symbol

enamor (en am´ ər) *v.* To fill with love and desire; charm; captivate

endeavor (en dev´ ər) *n.* A serious attempt

endow (en dou´) *v.* To provide with some talent, quality

engorge (en gôrj´) *v.* To eat greedily; feed ravenously

engulf (en gulf´) *v.* To swallow up; overwhelm

enmesh (en mesh´) *v.* To catch in or as in the meshes of a net

enrapture (en rap´ chər) *v.* To fill with great pleasure or delight; entrance; enchant

ensue (en sōō´) *v.* To happen as a consequence; result

enthrall (en thrôl´) *v.* To hold as if in a spell

enthrone (en thrōn´) *v.* To place on a throne

entice (en tīs´) *v.* Lure; attract by holding out hope of a reward

entreaty (en trēt´ ē) *n.* An earnest request; supplication prayer

entwine (en twīn´) *v.* To weave or twist together or around

enumerate (ē nōō´ mər āt´) *v.* To name one by one; specify as in a list

environs (en vī´ rənz) *n.* Surrounding area; vicinity

envoy (än´ voi´) *n.* A messenger; agent

equable (ek´ wə bəl) *adj.* Not varying or fluctuating; steady uniform; not readily upset; even; tranquil; serene

equanimity (ek´ wə nim´ ə tē) *n.* The quality of remaining calm and undisturbed; evenness of mind or temper; composure

eschew (es chōō´) *v.* To keep away from something harmful or disliked; shun; avoid; abstain from

esteem (e stēm´) *v.* To have great regard for; value highly respect

eternity (ē tʉr´ nə tē) *n.* Endless time, especially after death

evasion (ē vā´ zhən) *n.* An avoiding of a duty, question, etc., by deceit or cleverness

excruciating (eks krōō´ shē āt´ iŋ) *adj.* Causing intense physical or mental pain; agonizing

exemplify (eg zem´ plə fī´) *v.* To show by example; serve as an example of

exert (eg zʉrt´) *v.* To apply oneself with great energy or straining effort

exhale (eks´ hāl) *v.* To breathe out; to give off

exhort (eg zôrt´) *v.* To urge earnestly by advice, warning; admonish strongly

exorbitant (eg zor´ bi tənt) *adj.* Going beyond what is reasonable, just, proper, usual; excessive; extravagant

expatiate (eks pā´ shē āt´) *v.* To speak or write in great detail; elaborate or enlarge

expedient (ek spē´ dē ənt) *n.* Something useful for effecting a desired result; means to an end

exploit (eks´ ploit´) *n.* An act remarkable for brilliance or daring; bold deed

extensively (ek sten´ siv lē) *adj.* Widely; covering a broad range

extinction (ek stiŋk´ shən) *n.* Nonexistence; nothingness

extinguished (ek stin´ gwisht) *v.* Put out; doused

extortion (eks tôr´ shən) *n.* The act of getting money by threats, misuse of authority

exude (eg zōōd´) *v.* To diffuse or seem to radiate

exult (eg zult´) *v.* To rejoice greatly; be jubilant; glory

F

fallacious (fə lā´ shəs) *adj.* Containing a fallacy; erroneous; misleading or deceptive

fealty (fē´ əl tē) *n.* Loyalty; fidelity

ferment (fʉr ment´) *v.* To be excited or agitated; seethe

fervent (fʉr´ vənt) *adj.* Having or showing great warmth of feeling; intensely devoted or earnest; ardent

fetter (fet´ ər) *n.* A shackle or chain for the feet

fidelity (fə del´ ə tē) *n.* Faithful devotion to duty or to someone's obligations or vows; loyalty; faithfulness

fief (fēf) *n.* Under feudalism, heritable land held from a lord in return for service

flay (flā) *v.* To strip off the skin or hide of

flotsam (flät´ səm) *n.* Floating debris

flounder (floun´ dər) *v.* To struggle awkwardly to move; plunge about in a stumbling manner

flourish (flʉr´ ish) *n.* Anything done in a showy way

flout (flout) *v.* To mock or scoff at; show scorn or contempt for

folio (fō´ lē ō) *n.* A large-sized book made of sheets folded once so that it forms two leaves, or four pages of a book; manuscript

foray (fôr´ ā) *n.* A sudden attack or raid in order to seize or steal things

formidable (fôr´ mə də bəl) *adj.* Awe-inspiring in size, excellence; strikingly impressive; hard to handle or overcome

fortitude (fôrt´ ə tōod´) *n.* The strength to bear misfortune, pain, calmly and patiently; firm courage

frail (frāl) *adj.* Slender and delicate; not robust; weak

fraudulent (frô´ jə lənt) *adj.* Acting with deceit; trickery; cheating

frequent (frē´ kwənt) *v.* To go to constantly; to be at often

fricassee (frik´ ə sē´) *n.* A dish of meat cut into pieces, stewed or fried and served in a sauce of its own gravy

frivolous (friv´ ə ləs) *adj.* Not properly serious or sensible; silly and light-minded; giddy

frugal (frōō´ gəl) *adj.* Not wasteful; not spending freely or unnecessarily; thrifty; economical

futile (fyōō´ t'l) *adj.* Useless; vain; hopeless

G

gamboling (gam´ bəl iŋ) *v.* Jumping about in play; frolicking

garrulous (gar´ əl əs) *adj.* Very talkative, especially about trivial matters

gaunt (gônt) *adj.* Thin and bony; hollow-eyed and haggard, as from great hunger or age; emaciated

genesis (jen´ ə sis) *n.* The way in which something comes to be; beginning; origin

gentry (jen´ trē) *n.* People of high social standing; the class of land-owning people

germination (jʉr´ mə nā´ shən) *n.* Sprouting as from a spore, seed, or bud

gesticulate (jes tik´ yōo lāt´) *v.* To make or use hand or arm gestures to add nuances or force to one's speech

gird (gʉrd) *v.* To encircle or fasten with a belt or band

glean (glēn) *v.* To collect grain left by reapers

glisten (glis´ ən) *v.* To shine or sparkle with reflected light, as a wet or polished surface

globule (gläb´ yōol´) *n.* A tiny ball or blob; a drop of liquid

gonfalon (gän´ fə län´) *n.* A flag hanging from a crosspiece instead of an upright staff, usually ending in streamers

gracious (grā´ shəs) *adj.* Having or showing kindness, courtesy, charm

grafter (graft´ ər) *n.* Someone who takes advantage of one's position to gain money, property, etc., dishonestly

grandeur (grän´ jər) *n.* The quality of being grand; splendor; magnificence

gratify (grat´ i fī´) *v.* To give pleasure or satisfaction to

groat (grōt) *n.* An English silver coin worth fourpence

grotesque (grō tesk´) *adj.* Ludicrously eccentric or strange; ridiculous; absurd

grudge (gruj) *v.* To envy and resent someone because of that person's possession or enjoyment

guileless (gīl´ lis) *adj.* Without slyness and cunning in dealing with others; candid; frank

gyration (jī rā´ shən) *n.* The act of moving in a circular or spiral path; rotating or revolving on an axis; whirling

H

habitual (hə bich´ ōō əl) *adj.* Much seen, done, or used

haggard (hag´ ərd) *adj.* Having a wild-eyed, wasted, worn look; gaunt

hapless (hap´ lis) *adj.* Unlucky; unfortunate

haughty (hôt´ ē) *adj.* Having or showing great pride in one's self and disdain, contempt, or scorn for others; proud; arrogant; supercilious

haunch (hônch) *n.* The part of the body including the hip, buttock and thickest part of the thigh

haven (hā´ vən) *n.* Any sheltered, safe place; refuge

heft (heft) *v.* To lift or heave

herald (her´ əld) *v.* To announce; introduce

hexagonal (heks ag´ ə nəl) *adj.* Having a six-sided base or section, said of a solid figure

hinterland (hin´ tər land´) *n.* An area far from big cities and towns; back country

hirsute (hʉr´ sō͞ot´) *adj.* Hairy; shaggy; bristly

homage (häm´ ij) *n.* Anything given or done to show reverence, honor or respect

hover (huv´ ər) *v.* To stay suspended or flutter in the air near one place

hued (hyō͞od) *adj.* Having some specific shade or intensity or color or colors

hygienic (hī jēn´ ik) *adj.* Promoting health; healthful; sanitary

hypocrite (hip´ ə krit´) *n.* A person who pretends to be what he or she is not; one who pretends to be better than is really so; to be pious or virtuous without really being so

I

ignoramus (ig´ nə rā´ məs) *n.* An ignorant and stupid person

illuminated (i lō͞o´ mə nāt´ əd) *adj.* Enlightened in mind or spirit

imbibe (im bīb´) *v.* Drink in; absorb

immaculate (im mak´ yō͞o lit) *adj.* Pure

immobile (im mō´ bəl) *adj.* Motionless

immolation (im´ ə lā shən) *n.* A killing offered as a sacrifice

immortality (im´ môr tal´ i tē) *n.* Deathlessness

imp (imp) *n.* A mischievous child

impassive (im pas´ iv) *adj.* Not feeling or showing emotion; placid; calm

impel (im pel´) *v.* To force, compel or urge; incite; constrain

impending (im pend´ iŋ) *adj.* About to happen; imminent; threatening

impenetrable (im pen´ i trə bəl) *adj.* So dense that it is not possible to pass through it

imperceptible (im´ pər sep´ tə bəl) *adj.* Not plain or distinct to the senses or the mind; so slight, gradual, subtle as not to be easily perceived

imperishable (im per´ ish ə bəl) *adj.* Not perishable; that will not die or decay; indestructible; immortal

impertinent (im pʉrt´ 'n ənt) *adj.* Not showing proper respect or manners; saucy; insolent

impertinently (im pʉrt´ 'n ənt lē) *adv.* Disrespectfully; impudently

imperturbably (im´ pər turb´ ə blē) *adv.* In an undisturbed manner

impetuous (im pech´ ō͞o əs) *adj.* Impulsive; acting quickly or suddenly

implore (im plôr´) *v.* To ask or beg earnestly; beseech

importune (im´ pôr tō͞on´) *v.* To make urgent requests or demands

importunity (im´ pôr tō͞on´ i tē) *n.* Persistence in requesting or demanding

imposing (im pō´ ziŋ) *adj.* Making a strong impression because of great size, strength, dignity; impressive

impracticable (im prak´ ti kə bəl) *adj.* Not capable of being carried out in practice

impudence (im´ pyoo dəns) *n.* The quality of being shamelessly bold or disrespectful

impulse (im´ puls´) *n.* A sudden inclination to act, usually without premeditation

impulsive (im pul´ siv) *adj.* Acting or likely to act without premeditation

impunity (im pyō͞o´ ni tē) *n.* Freedom or exemption from punishment, penalty, or harm

incalculable (in kal´ kyoo lə bəl) *adj.* That cannot be calculated; too great or too many to be counted

incantation (in´ kan tā´ shən) *n.* The chanting of magical words or formulas that are supposed to cast a spell or perform other magic

incarnate (in kär´ nit) *adj.* Provided with flesh or a body; embodied

incessant (in ses´ ənt) *adj.* Never ceasing; continuing or being repeated without stopping or in a way that seems endless; constant

incomprehensible (in´ käm prē hen´ sə bəl) *adj.* Unable to be understood; unintelligible

inconceivable (in´ kən sēv´ ə bəl) *adj.* That cannot be thought of, understood, imagined, or believed

incredulity (in´ krə dō͞o´ lə tē) *n.* Disbelief

incur (in kʉr´) *v.* To become subject to through one's own action; bring upon oneself

indictment (in dīt´ mənt) *n.* A charge; accusation; formal written accusation charging one or more persons with the commission of a crime

indignant (in dig´ nənt) *adj.* Feeling or expressing anger or scorn at unjust, mean, or ungrateful action or treatment

indignation (in´ dig nā´ shən) *n.* Anger or scorn that is a reaction to injustice, ingratitude, or meanness; righteous anger

indiscreet (in´ di skrēt´) *adj.* Not discreet; lacking prudence in speech or action; unwise

indiscriminate (in´ di skrim´ i nit) *adj.* Not based on careful selection or discerning taste; confused, random; not making careful choices or distinctions

indispensable (in´ di spen´ sə bəl) *adj.* Absolutely necessary or required

ineffable (in ef´ ə bəl) *adj.* Too overwhelming to be expressed or described in words; inexpressible

ineffectual (in´ ē fek´ chō͞o əl) *adj.* Not effectual; not producing or not able to produce the desired effect

inert (in ʉrt´) *adj.* Having inertia; without power to move

inertia (in ʉr´ shə) *n.* A tendency to remain in a fixed condition without change; disinclination to move or act

inextinguishable (in´ ek stiŋ´ gwish´ ə bəl) *adj.* That cannot be quenched, put out, or stopped

inquisition (in´ kwə zish´ ən) *n.* The act of severe or intensive questioning

inquisitive (in kwiz´ ə tiv) *adj.* Asking more questions than is necessary or proper

insidious (in sid´ ē əs) *adj.* Slyly treacherous; dangerous in a way that is not completely apparent

interminable (in tʉr´ mi nə bəl) *adj.* Without or apparently without end; lasting, or seeming to last, forever; endless

intolerable (in täl´ ər ə bəl) *adj.* Not tolerable; unbearable; too severe, painful, or cruel to be endured

intrepid (in trep´ id) *adj.* Not afraid; bold; fearless; dauntless; very brave

intuition (in´ tō͞o ish´ ən) *n.* The ability to perceive or know things without conscious reasoning; immediate apprehension or understanding

inveterate (in vet´ ər it) *adj.* Firmly established over a long period; of long standing; deeply rooted

invoke (in vōk´) *v.* To call on for blessing, help, inspiration, support

iridescent (ir´ i des´ ənt) *adj.* Having or showing shifting changes in color or an interplay of rainbow-like colors as when seen from different angles

irrefutable (ir ref´ yō͞o tə bəl) *adj.* That cannot be refuted or disproved

irreverence (ir rev´ ər əns) *n.* Disrespect

aunty (jônt´ ē) *adj.* Having an easy confidence; gay and carefree; sprightly; perky

eer (jir) *v.* To make fun of in a rude, sarcastic manner; mock; taunt; scoff at

etty (jet´ ē) *n.* A pier; a landing dock

ocund (jäk´ ənd) *adj.* Cheerful; genial; gay

ovial (jō´ vē əl) *adj.* Full of hearty, playful good humor; genial and gay

ubilation (jōō´ be lā´ shən) *n.* A rejoicing, as in triumph; exultation; a happy celebration

uxtapose (juks´ tə pōz´) *v.* To put side by side or close together

eel (kēl) *n.* The chief timber or steel piece extending along the entire length of the bottom of a boat or ship and supporting the frame

indle (kin´ dəl) *v.* To arouse or excite interest or feelings

abyrinth (lab´ ə rinth´) *n.* An intricate network of winding passages; maze

ament (lə ment´) *v.* To express deep sorrow by weeping or wailing

amentation (lam´ ən tā´ shən) *n.* Outward expression of grief; a weeping or wailing

anguishing (laŋ´ gwish iŋ) *v.* Becoming weak; groping; losing vigor, vitality; failing in health

axity (laks´ i tē) *n.* The quality or condition of being not strict or exact; carelessness

eaden (led´ 'n) *adj.* Depressed; dispirited; gloomy

egate (leg´ āt) *n.* An envoy or ambassador

iberality (lib´ ər al´ i tē) *n.* Willingness to give or share freely; generosity

ineage (lin´ ē ij) *n.* Ancestry; family; stock

istless (list´ lis) *adj.* Having no interest in what is going on about one; as a result of illness, weariness, dejection; spiritless; languid

ithely (līth´ lē) *adv.* With easy grace and agility

ivid (liv´ id) *adj.* Grayish-blue; lead-colored

oathsome (lōth´ səm) *adj.* Causing intense dislike, disgust or hatred; abhorrent; disgusting; detestable

ofty (lôf´ tē) *adj.* Very high

oomed (lōōmd) *v.* Appeared in a large or threatening form

ucid (lōō´ sid) *adj.* Clear to the mind; readily understood

ush (lush) *adj.* Of luxuriant growth

uster (lus´ tər) *n.* Brightness; radiance; brilliance; radiant beauty

agnanimous (mag nan´ ə məs) *adj.* Noble in mind; high-souled

alice (mal´ is) *n.* Active ill will; desire to harm another or to do mischief; spite

alignant (mə lig´ nənt) *adj.* Wishing evil; very malevolent or malicious

anifest (man´ ə fest´) *adj.* Apparent to the senses (of sight or to the mind); evident; obvious; clear; plain

manifestation (man´ i fes tā´ shən) *n.* A form made clear or evident, shown plainly, revealed

manifold (man´ ə fōld´) *adj.* Of many and varied sorts; multifarious

mauve (mōv) *n.* Any of several shades of delicate purple

meager (mē´ gər) *adj.* Of poor quality or small amount; not full or rich; inadequate

meditate (med´ ə tāt´) *v.* Think deeply and continuously

melancholia (mel´ ən kō´ lē ə) *n.* A mental disorder, often psychotic, characterized by extreme depression of spirits, brooding, and anxiety

melancholy (mel´ ən käl´ ē) *adj.* Sad and depressed; gloomy

mesmerized (mez´ mər īzd) *v.* Hypnotized

metamorphosis (mət´ ə môr´ fə sis) *n.* Change of form, shape, structure or substance; transformation by magic or sorcery

meticulous (mə tik´ yōō ləs) *adj.* Extremely or excessively careful about details; scrupulous or finicky

mettle (met´'l) *n.* Quality of character or temperament; spirit; ardor; courage

millennium (mil len´ ē əm) *n.* Any period of one thousand years

mire (mīr) *n.* Deep mud; wet, soggy earth; slush

mirthful (murth´ fəl) *adj.* Full of, expressing, or causing mirth; merry

mischance (mis chans´) *n.* An unlucky accident; misadventure

misgiving (mis´ giv´ iŋ) *n.* A disturbed feeling of fear, doubt, apprehension

mite (mīt) *n.* A very small creature or object

mitigate (mit´ ə gāt´) *v.* To make less severe

monotony (mə nät´'n ē) *n.* Lack of variation or variety; tiresome sameness or uniformity

moral (môr´ əl) *n.* An implication or lesson taught by a fable, event

morsel (môr´ səl) *n.* A small bite or portion of food

munificence (myōō nif´ ə səns) *n.* Generosity in giving; lavishness

mutely (myōōt´ lē) *adv.* Silently

myriad (mir´ ē əd) *n.* A great number of persons or things

myrtle (murt´ 'l) *n.* Any of a genus (Myrtus) of plants of the myrtle family

N

nativity (nə tiv´ ə tē) *n.* Birth; with reference to place, time, or accompanying conditions

naturalistic (nach´ ər əl is´ tik) *adj.* In accordance with, or in imitation of, nature

nettle (net´ 'l) *v.* To irritate; annoy

nevertheless (nev´ ər *th*ə les´) *adj.* In spite of that; however

nonchalant (nän´ shə länt´) *adj.* Without warmth or enthusiasm; not showing interest

nutmeg (nut´ meg´) *n.* The hard, aromatic seed of an East Indian tree that is grated and used as a spice

O

objective (əb jək´ tiv) *adj.* Without bias or prejudice; detached

obligatory (əb lig´ ə tôr´ ē) *adj.* Legally binding; having the nature of an obligation; required

oblique (ə blēk´) *adj.* Having a slanted position or direction; neither perpendicular nor horizontal; inclined

obscurity (əb skyoor´ ə tē) *n.* Anonymity; being of no particular interest and going unnoticed

obsession (əb sesh´ ən) *n.* A persistent idea, desire, emotion that cannot be gotten rid of by reasoning

obstinacy (äb´ stə nə sē) *n.* The state or quality of being unreasonably determined to have one's own way; not yielding to reason or plea; stubborn; dogged; mulish

odious (ō´ dē əs) *adj.* Arousing or deserving hatred or loathing; disgusting; offensive

ominous (äm´ ə nəs) *adj.* Of or serving as an evil omen; threatening; sinister

onslaught (än´ slôt´) *n.* A violent, intense attack

opaque (ō pāk´) *adj.* Not letting light pass through; not transparent or translucent

oppress (ə pres´) *v.* To weigh heavily on the mind, spirits, or senses; worry; trouble

oracle (ôr´ ə kəl) *n.* Any person or agency believed to be in communication with a deity

orator (ôr´ ət ər) *n.* An eloquent public speaker

ordinance (ôrd´'n əns) *n.* That which is held to be a decree of fate or of a deity

outlandish (out´ lan´ dish) *adj.* Very odd, strange, or peculiar; fantastic; bizarre

outmoded (out´ mōd´ id) *adj.* No longer in fashion or accepted; obsolete

P

palfrey (pôl´ frē) *n.* A saddle horse, especially a gentle one for a woman

palpable (pal´ pə bəl) *adj.* Capable of being touched or felt

paraphernalia (par´ ə fər nāl´ yə) *n.* Collection of articles, usually things used in some activity; equipment; apparatus

parched (pärcht) *adj.* Dried by heating

parody (par´ ə dē) *n.* A poor or weak imitation

penitent (pen´ i tənt) *adj.* Truly sorry for having sinned or done other wrong and willing to atone; contrite; repentant

perfidious (pər fid´ ē əs) *adj.* Characterized by the deliberate breaking of faith or betrayal of trust; treacherous

perished (per´ isht) *v.* Died; often used to describe a violent or too early death

perjured (pur´ jərd) *adj.* Characterized by the willful telling of a lie while under lawful oath or affirmation to tell the truth

permeate (pur´ mē āt´) *v.* To pass into or through and affect every part of; penetrate and spread through

perpetual (pər pech´ oo əl) *adj.* Continuing indefinitely without interruption; unceasing; constant

pervade (pər vād´) *v.* To be prevalent throughout

perversion (pər vur´ zhən) *n.* A deviation from what is considered right or good

pestilence (pes´ tə ləns) *n.* Any virulent or fatal contagious or infectious disease of epidemic proportions

phenomenon (fə näm´ ə nən´) *n.* Any extremely unusual or extraordinary thing or occurrence

piebald (pī´ bôld´) *adj.* Covered with patches or spots of two colors

piety (pī´ ə tē) *n.* Devotion to religious duties and practices; dutiful conduct; scrupulousness

pilgrimage (pil´ grim ij) *n.* A journey, as to a shrine or holy place

pillage (pil´ ij) *v.* To deprive of money or property by violence; loot; plunder

pine (pīn) *v.* To have an intense longing or desire; yearn

pitiable (pit´ ē əb əl) *adj.* Arousing pity, sometimes mixed with a slight contempt for weakness or foolishness

pittances (pit´ 'n səz) *n.* Small amounts of money

placid (plas´ id) *adj.* Without disturbance; tranquil; calm; quiet

pliant (plī´ ənt) *adj.* Adaptable or compliant

plummet (plum´ it) *v.* To fall or drop straight downward

ply (plī) *v.* To sail or travel regularly back and forth

pomegranate (päm´ gran´ it) *n.* A round, red fruit with a red leathery rind and many seeds covered with red, juicy, edible flesh

pommel (pum´ əl) *n.* The knob on the end of the hilt of a sword or dagger

pomp (pämp) *n.* Ostentatious show or display

posterity (päs ter´ ə tē) *n.* All succeeding generations

potentate (pōt´'n tāt´) *n.* A person having great power; ruler; monarch

precept (prē´ sept´) *n.* A commandment or direction meant as a rule of action or conduct

precipitous (prē sip´ ə təs) *adj.* Steep like a precipice; sheer

preening (prēn´ iŋ) *v.* Showing satisfaction with oneself

preposterous (prē päs´ tər əs) *adj.* So contrary to nature, reason, or common sense as to be laughable; absurd; ridiculous

prescribe (prē skrīb´) *v.* To set down as a rule or direction; order; ordain; direct

prevail (prē vāl´) *v.* To gain the advantage or mastery; be victorious; triumph over or against

primal (prī´ məl) *adj.* First in importance; chief; primary

primordial (prī môr´ dē əl) *adj.* First in time; not derivative; fundamental; original; primitive; primeval

probationer (prō bā´ shən ər) *n.* A person undergoing a testing or trial of his or her abilities to meet requirements

proclaim (prō klām´) *v.* To show to be

prod (präd) *v.* To jab or poke; goad

prodigal (präd´ i gəl) *n.* A person who wastes his or her means; spendthrift

prodigy (präd´ ə jē) *n.* A person, thing, or act so extraordinary as to inspire wonder; a child of highly unusual talent or genius

proffer (präf´ ər) *v.* To offer, usually something intangible

proficient (prō fish´ ənt) *adj.* Highly competent; skilled; adept

profusion (prō fyoo´ zhən) *n.* Rich or lavish supply; abundance

progeny (präj´ ə nē) *n.* Lineage; children, descendants, or offspring collectively

prohibition (prō´ i bish´ ən) *n.* An order or law forbidding something to be done

promenade (präm´ ə nād´) *n.* A public place for a leisurely walk taken for pleasure to display one's finery; a ball or formal dance

prophesy (präf´ ə sī´) *v.* To predict (a future event) in any way

prophetic (prō fet´ ik) *adj.* Having the nature of or containing a prophecy

propitious (prō pish´ əs) *adj.* Gracious and favorably inclined

propriety (prō prī´ ə tē) *n.* The quality of conformity with proper, fitting, or suitable manners or behavior; fitness

prosper (präs´ pər) *v.* To succeed, thrive, grow in a vigorous way

rostrate (präs´ trāt´) *adj.* Lying flat, prone, or supine

rowess (prou´ is) *n.* Bravery; valor; superior ability

rudent (prōod´´nt) *adj.* Capable of exercising sound judgment in matters; cautious or discreet in conduct; circumspect; not rash

umice (pum´ is) *n.* A spongy, light, porous volcanic rock

utrid (pyōo´ trid) *adj.* Decomposed; rotten and foul-smelling

Q

ualm (kwäm) *n.* A twinge of conscience; scruple

uandary (kwän´ də rē) *n.* A state of uncertainty; perplexing situation or position; dilemma

uench (kwench) *v.* To satisfy; slake

uiver (kwiv´ ər) *n.* A case for holding arrows

R

adiance (rā´ dē əns) *n.* The quality or state of being filled with light; brightness

aiment (rā´ mənt) *n.* Clothing; wearing apparel; attire

ampart (ram´ pärt´) *n.* Any defense or bulwark

ank (raŋk) *adj.* Strong and offensive in smell or taste

avening (rav´ ən iŋ) *adj.* Greedily searching for prey

aze (rāz) *v.* To tear down completely; level to the ground; demolish

eaper (rē´ pər) *n.* A person who cuts grain with a scythe, sickle, or reaping machine

ebuke (ri byōok´) *v.* To blame or scold in a sharp way; reprimand

ecline (ri klīn´) *v.* Lie down or lean back

ectify (rek´ tə fī´) *v.* To put or set right; correct; amend

edeem (ri dēm´) *v.* To buy back

edeemer (ri dēm´ ər) *n.* One who delivers from sin and its penalties, as by a sacrifice for the sinner

edoubtable (ri dout´ ə bəl) *adj.* Formidable; fearsome; commanding respect

emedy (rem´ ə dē) *n.* Any medicine or treatment that cures, heals, or relieves a disease or bodily or mental disorder or tends to restore health

emorse (ri môrs´) *n.* A deep, torturing sense of guilt felt over a wrong that one has done; self-reproach

paration (rep´ ə rā´ shən) *n.* A making of amends; making up for a wrong or injury

pentance (ri pen´ təns) *n.* Feeling of sorrow for wrongdoing; contrition; remorse

eplete (ri plēt´) *adj.* Well-filled or plentifully supplied

epose (ri pōz´) *v.* To rest in death or a grave

eprimand (rep´ rə mand´) *n.* A severe or formal rebuke by a person in authority

eprisal (ri prī´ zəl) *n.* Revenge for an injury inflicted by another

eproach (ri prōch´) *n.* Shame, disgrace, discredit, or blame

eprobate (rep´ rə bāt´) *adj.* Totally bad; corrupt; depraved

eproof (ri prōof´) *n.* The act of speaking to someone in disapproval; rebuke; censure

esistant (ri zis´ tənt) *adj.* Offering opposition; withstanding against

esolute (rez´ ə lōot´) *adj.* Having or showing a fixed, firm purpose; determined; resolved; unwavering

espite (res´ pit) *n.* An interval of temporary relief or rest, as from pain, work, or duty; lull

resplendent (ri splen´ dənt) *adj.* Shining brightly; full of splendor; dazzling

restrained (rē strānd´) *adj.* Exercising or showing the results of self-discipline or rational control; disciplined

retribution (re´ trə byōo´ shən) *n.* Punishment for evil done or reward for good done; requital

revel (rev´ əl) *v.* To take much pleasure; delight

reverberates (ri vʉr´ bə rāts´) *v.* Sounds again; echoes

rhetoric (ret´ ər ik) *n.* The art of using words effectively in speaking or writing

rill (ril) *n.* A little brook; rivulet

ritual (rich´ ōo əl) *n.* A set form or system of rites, religious or otherwise

rive (rīv) *v.* To split; cleave

robust (rō bust´) *adj.* Strong and healthy; full of vigor

roil (roil) *v.* To make a liquid cloudy, muddy, or unsettled by stirring up the sediment

rout (rout) *n.* A disorderly crowd; noisy mob; rabble; disorderly flight or retreat

russet (rus´ it) *adj.* Yellowish-brown or reddish-brown

S

sally (sal´ ē) *n.* An excursion or unusual side trip; jaunt

sanction (saŋk´ shən) *n.* Support; encouragement; approval

sate (sāt) *v.* To satisfy to the full; gratify completely

scabbard (skab´ ərd) *n.* A sheath or case to hold the blade of a sword, dagger

schooner (skōon´ ər) *n.* A ship with two or more masts, rigged fore and aft

scion (sī´ ən) *n.* A descendant; offspring

scorn (skôrn) *n.* Contempt or disdain for someone or something. *v.* To view or treat with contempt

scruple (skrōo´ pəl) *n.* A feeling of hesitancy, doubt, or uneasiness arising from difficulty in deciding what is right, proper, ethical

scrupulous (skrōo´ pyə ləs) *adj.* Extremely careful to do the precisely right or proper or correct thing in every last detail

scurry (skʉr´ ē) *v.* To run hastily; scamper

secrete (si krēt´) *v.* To form and release as a gland does

semblance (sem´ bləns) *n.* Outward form or appearance; aspect

sentinel (sen´ ti nəl) *adj.* Furnishing or protecting, as a guard

serene (sə rēn´) *adj.* Not disturbed or troubled; calm; peaceful; tranquil

sheathed (shē*th*d) *v.* Enclosed in or protected with a case or covering

sheaves (shēvz) *n.* A bunch of cut stalks of grain bound up in a bundle

shroud (shroud) *n.* A cloth sometimes used to wrap a corpse for burial; winding sheet

shunt (shunt) *n.* A conductor connecting two points in a circuit in parallel and serving to divert part of the current

simp (simp) *n.* A person who is stupid or easily deceived; fool

sinister (sin´ is tər) *adj.* Threatening harm, evil, or misfortune; ominous; portentous

skeptical (skep´ ti kəl) *adj.* Not easily persuaded or convinced; doubting; questioning

skulk (skulk) *v.* To avoid work or responsibility

slack (slak) *adj.* Barely moving; sluggish

sluice (slōōs) *n.* Any artificial channel or passage for water, having a gate or valve to regulate the flow

sojourn (sō´ jʉrn) *n.* A brief or temporary stay; visit

solace (säl´ is) *n.* An easing or relieving; comfort; consolation; relief

solicitous (sə lis´ ə təs) *adj.* Showing care, attention, or concern

solitude (säl´ ə tōod) *n.* The state of being solitary or alone; seclusion; isolation or remoteness

somber (säm´ bər) *adj.* Earnest and solemn; grave; melancholy

sordid (sôr´ did) *adj.* Mercenary, avaricious, grasping or meanly selfish; depressingly wretched

sovereign (säv´ rən) *adj.* Above or superior to all others; chief; supreme

spendthrift (spend´ thrift´) *n.* A person who spends money carelessly or wastefully; squanderer

spit (spit) *n.* A thin, pointed rod or bar on which meat is impaled for broiling or roasting over a fire or before other direct heat

spurned (spʉrnd) *v.* Rejected with contempt and disdain

squalid (skwäl´ id) *adj.* Foul or unclean as a result of neglect or unsanitary conditions

squander (skwän´ dər) *v.* To spend or use wastefully or extravagantly

stark (stärk) *adj.* Bleak; desolate; barren

stature (stach´ ər) *n.* The height of a person or animal, in a natural standing position

statute (stach´ ōot) *n.* An established rule; formal regulation

stealth (stelth) *n.* Secret, furtive, or artfully sly action or behavior

stolid (stäl´ id) *adj.* Not showing much emotion or sensitivity; not excitable

stow (stō) *v.* To pack or store away

strains (strānz) *n.* Passages of music, time, or poetry of a lyric sort

strand (strand) *n.* Land at the edge of a body of water; ocean shore

strenuous (stren´ yōo əs) *adj.* Vigorous, arduous, zealous

stupor (stōo´ pər) *n.* Mental dullness, as if drugged

submerge (sub mʉrj´) *v.* To sink or plunge beneath the surface of water

submissive (sub mis´ iv) *adj.* Showing a tendency to submit without resistance

subordinate (sə bôrd´'n it) *n.* A person placed below another in rank, power, importance; secondary person

subside (səb sīd´) *v.* To become less active or intense; abate

succor (suk´ ər) *n.* Aid; help; relief

suffice (sə fīs´) *v.* To be enough; be adequate

suffuse (sə fyōoz´) *v.* To overspread so as to fill with a glow, color, or fluid

summit (sum´ it) *n.* The highest point, part, or elevation; top or apex

summon (sum´ ən) *v.* To order to come or to appear; call for or send for with authority or urgency

sumptuous (sump´ chōo əs) *adj.* Magnificent or splendid

superimpose (sōo´ pər im pōz´) *v.* To add as a dominant or unassimilated feature

superintendence (sōo´ pər in ten´ dəns) *n.* The act of directing, supervising, managing affairs

supine (sōo´ pīn) *adj.* Lying on the back, face upward

supplant (sə plant´) *v.* To take the place of; supersede, sometimes through force or plotting

supple (sup´ əl) *adj.* Able to bend and move easily and nimbly; lithe; limber

surfeit (sʉr´ fit) *n.* Too great an amount or supply; excess ⟨

surveillance (sər vā´ ləns) *n.* Close watch kept over som⟨ person, place, or process; constant observation

sustenance (sus´ tə nəns) *n.* That which sustains life; nou⟨ ishment; food

swells (swelz) *n.* Large waves that move steadily withou⟨ breaking

T

tabernacle (tab´ ər nak´ əl) *n.* A shrine; niche

taciturn (tas´ ə tʉrn´) *adj.* Silent; uncommunicative

tactless (takt´ lis) *adj.* Not having or showing perception ⟨ the right thing to do or say without offending; lacking skill ⟨ dealing with people

talisman (tal´ is mən) *n.* An object thought to bring good luc⟨ keep away evil; anything thought to have magic or charm

tangible (tan´ jə bəl) *adj.* That which can be understoo⟨ definite; objective

temperate (tem´ pər it) *adj.* Moderate in one's action⟨ speech; self-restrained

tenacity (tə nas´ ə tē) *n.* The quality or state of being persi⟨ tent; stubborn

testimony (tes´ tə mō´ nē) *n.* Any affirmation or declaratio⟨

text (tekst) *n.* Any of the forms, versions, or editions in whic⟨ a written work exists

thrive (thrīv) *v.* Grow and prosper; improve physically

throes (thrōz) *n.* A spasm or pang of pain; the act of strug⟨ gling with a problem

throng (thrôŋ) *n.* A great number of people gathere⟨ together

thwart (thwôrt) *v.* To hinder, obstruct, frustrate, or defeat

tranquil (tran´ kwil) *adj.* Quiet or motionless; steady

transfigure (trans fig´ yər) *v.* To change the figure, form, ⟨ outward appearance of; transform

translucent (trans lōo´ sənt) *adj.* Letting light pass but d⟨ fusing it so that objects on the other side cannot be clear⟨ distinguished; partially transparent

travail (trə vāl´) *n.* Very hard work; toil

treacherous (trech´ ər əs) *adj.* Characterized by betrayal ⟨ trust, faith, or allegiance; traitorous; disloyal

tremulous (trem´ yōo ləs) *adj.* Trembling; quivering; palp⟨ tating

trifling (trī´ fliŋ) *adj.* Having little value or importance; trivia⟨

trill (tril) *n.* The warbling sound made by some birds

trite (trīt) *adj.* Worn out by constant use; no longer havir⟨ freshness, originality, or novelty; stale

trough (trôf) *n.* A long, narrow hollow or depression, a⟨ between waves

trudge (truj) *v.* To walk warily or laboriously

truncate (truŋ´ kāt´) *v.* To cut off a part of; shorten by cuttin⟨ lop

turret (tʉr´ it) *n.* A small tower projecting from a buildin⟨ usually at a corner and often merely ornamental

tyrannical (tə ran´ i kəl) *adj.* Harsh; cruel; unjust; oppressiv⟨

U

unassuming (un ə sōom´ iŋ) *adj.* Not assuming, prete⟨ tious, or forward; modest; retiring

undeterred (un dē tʉrd´) *v.* Not kept or discouraged fro⟨ doing something by fear, anxiety, or doubt

undulant (un´ dyo͞o lənt) *adj.* Wavelike

unearthly (un ʉrth´ lē) *adj.* Not of the earth; not worldly; not temporal or secular

unhampered (un ham´ pərd) *adj.* Not kept from moving or acting freely; not hindered or encumbered

unmitigated (un mit´ ə gāt´ id) *adj.* Not lessened or eased

unpretentious (un´ prē ten´ shəs) *adj.* Making no claims to importance; simple and modest

unremitting (un ri mit´ iŋ) *adj.* Not stopping, relaxing, or slackening; incessant; persistent

unsatiable (un sā´ shə bəl) *adj.* That cannot be satisfied

unsubdued (un sub do͞od´) *v.* Unrepressed

unsullied (un sul´ ēd) *adj.* Not soiled, stained, tarnished, or besmirched

usurp (yo͞o sʉrp´) *v.* To take or assume and hold in possession by force or without right

V

vagabond (vag´ ə bänd´) *n.* A person who wanders from place to place, having no fixed home; a tramp

vague (vāg) *adj.* Indefinite in shape, form, or character; hazily or indistinctly seen or sensed

valor (val´ ər) *n.* Marked courage or bravery

vault (vôlt) *n.* The sky as a canopy structure; arched roof, ceiling

vehemently (vē´ ə mənt lē) *adv.* Intensely; with passion

vengeance (ven´ jəns) *n.* Return of an injury for an injury, in punishment or retribution; avenging of an injury or offense; revenge

venison (ven´ i zən) *n.* The flesh of a deer used as food

verge (vʉrj) *n.* The edge, brink, or margin

vestibule (ves´ tə byo͞ol) *n.* A small entrance hall or room, either to a building or to a larger room

vesture (ves´ chər) *n.* Clothing; garments; apparel; covering

vex (veks) *v.* To give trouble to in a petty or nagging way; disturb, annoy, irritate

vintner (vint´ nər) *n.* A person who sells wine; wine merchant

virile (vir´ əl) *adj.* Having manly strength or vigor; forceful

visitant (viz´ it ənt) *n.* A visitor, especially one from a strange or foreign place

vista (vis´ tə) *n.* A view or lookout

vociferous (vō sif´ ər əs) *adj.* Characterized by clamor or vehement outcry

vulgar (vul´ gər) *adj.* Characterized by a lack of culture, refinement, taste, restraint, sensitivity; coarse; crude; boorish

W

waft (wäft) *v.* To transport lightly through the air

wan (wän) *adj.* Faint, feeble, or weak

wanton (wän´ tən) *adj.* Senseless, unprovoked, unjustifiable, or deliberately malicious

weal (wēl) *n.* Sound or prosperous public welfare

wharf (wôrf) *n.* A pier or a dock where ships are loaded or unloaded

wheedle (hwēd´ʼl) *v.* Influence or persuade by flattery or soothing words

wile (wīl) *n.* A sly trick; deceitful artifice; stratagem

woodbine (wo͝od´ bīn´) *n.* A European climbing honeysuckle with fragrant, yellowish-white flowers

wooer (wo͞o´ ər) *n.* A person who tries to get the love of another; courter

wrangle (raŋ´ gəl) *v.* To argue; dispute

wrath (rath) *n.* Intense anger; rage; fury

writhe (rīth) *v.* To contort the body as in agony

wrought (rôt) *v.* Formed; fashioned

Z

zeal (zēl) *n.* Intense enthusiasm in working for a cause; ardent endeavor or devotion; fervor

INDEX OF FINE ART

INDEX OF SKILLS

CRITICAL THINKING AND READING

UNDERSTANDING LANGUAGE

INDEX OF TITLES BY THEMES

FANTASY AND THE UNEXPLAINED

THE ENVIRONMENT AND THE TOUCHED AND UNTOUCHED EARTH

QUEST FOR UNDERSTANDING

INDEX OF AUTHORS AND TITLES

ACKNOWLEDGMENTS (continued)

edited by Robert Bly, Beacon Press, Boston, 1971. Copyright © 1962, 1967 by the Sixties Press; copyright © 1971 by Robert Bly. Reprinted by permission of Robert Bly.

William F. Bottighlia Lines from *Voltaire, A Collection of Critical Essays*, edited by William F. Bottighlia. Copyright © 1968 by Prentice-Hall, Inc., Englewood Cliffs, New Jersey. Reprinted by permission of the editor.

Carol Publishing Group "The Lorelei" by Heinrich Heine from *The Poetry and Prose of Heinrich Heine*. Copyright © 1948, edited by Frederic Ewen. Reprinted by arrangement with Carol Publishing Group.

Judith H. Ciardi for the Estate of John Ciardi Excerpt from Dante's *Paradise*, translated by John Ciardi, copyright 1982. Reprinted by permission of Judith H. Ciardi.

Columbia University Press From *Essays in Idleness* by Yoshida Kenko, translated by Donald Keene. Copyright © 1967 Columbia University Press. "The Deserted Crose" by Zeami from *Twenty Plays of the Nō Theatre*, edited by Donald Keene. Copyright © 1970 Columbia University Press. Reprinted by permission.

Columbia University Press and Oxford University Press "In Spring It Is the Dawn," "The Cat Who Lived in the Palace," "Oxen Should Have Very Small Foreheads," "Nothing Can Be Worse," "Hateful Things," "Things That Make One's Heart Beast Faster," "Things That Arouse a Fond Memory," and "I Remember a Clear Morning" reprinted from *The Pillow Book of Sei Shōnagon*, translated and edited by Ivan Morris. © Ivan Morris 1967, published by Columbia University Press. Used by permission.

The Continuum Publishing Company "The First Sally (A) OR Trurl's Electronic Bard" by Stanislaw Lem, translated by Michael Kandel from *The Cyberiad: Fables for the Cybernetic Age* by Stanislaw Lem. Copyright © 1974 by The Continuum Publishing Company. Reprinted by permission.

Stanley Corngold "The Metamorphosis" by Franz Kafka, translated by Stanley Corngold. Copyright © 1972 by Stanley Corngold. Reprinted by permission of the translator.

J.M. Dent & Sons Ltd. and Everyman's Library "The Lay of the Werewolf" by Marie de France, from *Lays of Marie de France*, translated by Eugene Mason. Reprinted by permission.

Devin-Adair Publishing Company "Caesar" by Paul Valéry, translated by C. F. MacIntyre, from *War and the Poet*, edited by Richard Eberhart and Selden Rodman. Copyright 1945, renewed 1969 by Devon-Adair Publishers, Inc., 6 North Water Street, Greenwich, Connecticut 06830. Reprinted by permission.

Doubleday, a division of Bantam, Doubleday, Dell Publishing Group, Inc. Haiku: "The Sun's Way," "Poverty's Child," and "Clouds Come from Time to Time" by Bashō. Excerpts from *An Introduction to Haiku* by Harold G. Henderson, copyright © 1958 by Harold G. Henderson. Excerpt from *The Power of Myth* by Joseph Campbell with Bill Moyers. Used by permission.

Dutton Signet, a division of Penguin Books USA, Inc. "The Return of the Wanderers" by Tu Fu, translated by Arthur Christy, "To the Assistant Perfect Chang", "The Hill", "On An Autumn Evening In the Mountains", by Wang Wei, translated by Arthur E. Christy, from *IMAGES IN JADE* by Arthur E. Christy Translation copyright © 1929 by E. P. Dutton & Co., Inc. Renewed copyright © 1957 by Gertrude N. Christy. "Addressed Humorously to Tu Fu" by Li Po, from *The Works of Li Po*, translated by Shigeyoshi Obata. Copyright 1922, renewed 1950 by E. P. Dutton. Reprinted by permission of the publisher.

The Ecco Press "A Song on the End of the World" by Czeslaw Milosz, copyright © 1988 by Czeslaw Milosz Royalties, Inc. from *The Collected Poems 1931–1987*, first published by The Ecco Press in 1988. Reprinted by permission.

The Estate of Okot p'Bitek From "Song of Lawino" from *Song of Lawino & Song of Ocol* by Okot p'Bitek. © The estate of Okot p'Bitek 1966, 1967.

Farrar, Straus & Giroux, Inc. "Russia 1812" by Victor Hugo from *Imitations* translated by Robert Lowell. Copyright © 1958, 1959, 1960, 1961 by Robert Lowell. "The Bracelet" from *The Collected Stories of Colette*. Translation copyright © 1957, 1966, 1983 by Farrar, Straus and Giroux, Inc. "The One Great Heart," excerpt from *Nobel Lecture* by Alexander Solzhenitsyn. Copyright © 1972 by The Nobel Foundation. Translation copyright © 1972 by Farrar, Straus and Giroux, Inc. "Sea Grapes" from *Collected Poems* by Derek Walcott. Copyright © 1971, 1973, 1974, 1975, 1976, 1986 by Derek Walcott. Excerpt from *Omeros* by Derek Walcott. Copyright © 1990 by Derek Walcott. Excerpt from "Codicil" from *Collected Poems, 1948–1984* by Derek Walcott. Copyright © 1962, 1965, 1968 by Derek Walcott. Excerpt from "A Walk to the Jetty" from *Annie John* by Jamaica Kincaid. Copyright © 1983, 1984, 1985 by Jamaica Kincaid. All rights reserved. First appeared in *The New Yorker*. From *A Splintered Mirror, Chinese Poetry from the Democracy Movement*, translated by Donald Finkel, additional translations by Carolyn Kizer, © 1991 by Donald Finkel; "Answer," "All," and "Testament" by Bei Dao, translated by Donald Finkel and Xueliang Chen; "When Hope Comes Back" by Gu Cheng, translated by Donald Finkel and Sheng-Tai Chang; "Also All" and "Fairy Tales" by Shu Ting, translated by Donald Finkel and Jinsheng Yi; "Assembly Line" by Shu Ting, translated by Carolyn Kizer. Reprinted by permission.

Farrar, Straus & Giroux, Inc., and Penguin Books Canada Limited "The Ultimate Safari" from *Jump and Other Stories* by Nadine Gordimer. Copyright © Felix Licensing BV, 1991. Reprinted by permission.

Angel Flores "The Grownup" and "Interior of the Rose" by Rainer Maria Rilke, from *An Anthology of German Poetry From Holderlin to Rilke in English Translation*, edited by Angel Flores. From *An Anthology of French Poetry From Nerval to Valéry in English Translation With French Originals*, edited by Angel Flores: "The Friendly Wood" and "Palm" by Paul Valéry, "The Albatross" by Charles Baudelaire, and "Ophelia" and "Eternity" by Arthur Rimbaud. Reprinted by permission of Angel Flores.

Foreign Languages Press, Beijing, China "My Old Home" by Lu Hsun from *Selected Stories of Lu Hsun*, translated by Yang Hsien-yi and Gladys Yang, first edition 1960. Published and copyright by Foreign Languages Press, Beijing, China. Reprinted by permission.

John L. Foster "Your Love, Dear man, Is as Lovely to Me," "I Think I'll Go Home and Lie Very Still," and "The Voice of the Swallow," from *Love Songs of the New Kingdom*, translated from the ancient Egyptian by John L. Foster, Copyright © 1969, 1970, 1971, 1972, 1973, 1974 by John L. Foster. Reprinted by permission of the translator.

Grove Atlantic Monthly Press From the book *Anthology of Japanese Literature* by Donald Keene, copyright © 1955 by Grove Press: "In the Sea of Iwami" from *Man'yoshu (Collection of Ten Thousand Leaves)* by Kakinomoto Hitomaro, "The Clustering Clouds" by Minamoto no Toshiyori, and an excerpt from "Love's Complaint" by Lady Otomo. "Poem on Returning to Dwell in the Country" and "I Built My House Near Where Others Dwell" by T'ao Ch'ien from the book *Anthology of Chinese Literature* by Cyril Birch. Copyright © 1965 by Grove Press. Reprinted by permission of Grove Atlantic Monthly Press.

ART CREDITS

Alabaster relief from the Palace of King Sargon II at Khorsabad, 721–705 B.C., Louvre, Paris; **25:** *The Legend of the Fish,* Gordon Laite, New York Public Library, Astor, Lenox, and Tilden Foundations; **28:** *Unfinished* Kudurru (*boundary stone*), Babylonian, twelfth century, B.C., Louvre, © photo RMN; **30:** *Queen Anointing Tutankhamun with Perfume,* Detail of back of throne of Tutankhamun, Lee Boltin Picture Library; **32:** *Offering bearer, from Tomb of Mekutra,* c. 2009–1998 B.C., The Metropolitan Museum of Art, Museum Excavations, 1919–1920, Rogers Fund, Supplemented by Contribution of Edward S. Harkness, 1920, © 1967/1983 Copyright by The Metropolitan Museum of Art; **33:** *Musicians with Harp, Lute, Double-pipe, & Lyre,* Copy of wall painting from Tomb of Djeserkaraseneb, c. 1411–1397 B.C., The Metropolitan Museum of Art, © 1978/1983 Copyright by The Metropolitan Museum of Art; **35:** *Birds in a Papyrus Swamp* (detail), Akhenaton at Tell el Amarna, c. 1360 B.C., The Metropolitan Museum of Art, © 1978/1983 Copyright by The Metropolitan Museum of Art; **37:** *Page from the Book of the Dead,* c. 1100 B.C., Egyptian, The British Museum, Photo by Michael Holford; **38:** *Moses with the Ten Commandments,* Guido Reni, Galleria Borghese, Rome, Scala, Art Resource, New York; **43:** *The Creation of Adam,* Michelangelo, Scala, Art Resource, New York; **48:** *The Flood,* Michelangelo, Scala, Art Resource, New York; **53:** *Dead Sea Scroll, The Manual of Discipline,* From Cols. 2–4, Qumram Cave #1, The Granger Collection, New York; **57:** *Scenes from the Story of Ruth,* French illuminated manuscript, c. A.D. 1250, © The Pierpont Morgan Library, 1993, New York, M 638, f.18; **63:** *The Youthful David,* Andrea del Castagno, © 1993 National Gallery of Art, Washington, Widener Collection; **67:** *David Composing the Psalms,* Illustrated Paris Psalter, tenth century, Photo Bibliotheque Nationale, Paris; **69:** *Il Buon Pastore (The Good Shepherd),* early Christian, fourth century, Vatican Museum, Scala, Art Resource, New York; **76:** *The Court of Gayumarth, January 1518,* Iran (Shiraz), From a copy of the *Shah-nama* of Abu'l-Oasim Firdawsi, Courtesy of the Arthur M. Sackler Gallery, Smithsonian Institution, Washington, D.C.; **78:** *Darius Dying Comforted by Alexander While His Assassins Are Hanged,* From the *Book of Omens,* Qazwin style, 1550–1560, Geneve, Musée d'art et d'histoire, Collection Jean Pozzi; **80:** (left) *Darius I and Mede Offical Paying Homage,* SEF, Art Resource, New York; (right) *Koran leaf in Kufic Calligraphy,* ninth century, The Metropolitan Museum of Art, Gift of Rudolph M. Riefstahl, 1930, © 1982 Copyright by The Metropolitan Museum of Art; **81:** (left) *Khorassan Perfume Burner in the Form of a Lion,* Bronze, Persian art, The Louvre, Paris, Giraudon, Art Resource, New York; (center left) *The Simurgh Brings Zal to Sam,* Leaf from *Shah-nama* by Firdawsi, fourteenth century, The Metropolitan Museum of Art, Rogers Fund, 1969, © 1989 Copyright by The Metropolitan Museum of Art; (center right) *Silk Medallion Rug,* c. 1500–1550, © 1993 National Gallery of Art, Washington, Widener Collection; **87:** *Firdawsi,* Manuscript illumination by Mirza Ali, c. 1535, The Granger Collection, New York; **90:** *Birth of Rustam,* Iranian painting, 1560–1980, The Metropolitan Museum of Art, Purchase, 1965, Rogers Fund and Joseph V. McMullan Gift, © 1979 Copyright by The Metropolitan Museum of Art; **93:** *Zal Slays Khazarvan, the Leader of the Invading Army,* 1525–1530, Attributed to Abd ul-Vahhab, The Metropolitan Museum of Art, Gift of Arthur A. Houghton, Jr., 1970, © 1978/1989 Copyright by The Metropolitan Museum of Art; **98:** *Omar Khayyám,* The Bettmann Archive; **101, 102:** *Rubáiyát of Omar Khayyám,* Edmund Dulac, 1952, Photo by John Lei, Omni-Photo Communications, Inc.; **106:** *Ascent of Mohammed into Paradise,* Persian miniature, sixteenth century, The British Museum; **108:** *Koran, in Naskhi Calligraphy,* 1427, Ibrahim Sultan, grandson of Tamerlane, The Metropolitan Museum of Art, Gift of Alexander Smith Cochran, 1913, © Copyright by The Metropolitan Museum of Art; **110:** (left) *Sa'di,* New York Public Library Picture Collection; (right) *Hafiz,* New York Public Library Picture Collection; **114:** *Salih, The Ayyubid King of Syria, Conversing with Two Paupers,* XVI Century, Bustan (Garden of Perfume) by Sa'di, The Metropolitan Museum of Art, Hewitt Fund, 1911, © 1982, Copyright by The Metropolitan Museum of Art; **118:** *Love Scene,* Persian miniature, 1587–1628, Bokhara School, Period of Shah Abbas, The Metropolitan Museum of Art, Gift of George D. Pratt, 1925, © 1970 Copyright by The Metropolitan Museum of Art; **120:** *Rumi Visits 'Attar,* From *The Nafahat Aluns* by Jami, Indian Mughal book painting, 1603, The Granger Collection, New York; **123:** *Iskandar and the Seven Wise Men,* 1475–1485, Shiraz style, From the *Book of*

Alexander by Nizami, Geneve, Musée d'art et d'histoire, Collection Jean Pozzi; **124:** *Concourse of the Birds,* c. 1600, Habib Allah, The Metropolitan Museum of Art, Fletcher Fund, 1963, © Copyright by The Metropolitan Museum of Art; **126:** *Sinbad Plots against the Giant,* Reprinted with the permission of Charles Scribner's Sons, an imprint of Macmillan Publishing Company from *The Arabian Nights* by Kate Wiggin and Nora A. Smith, Illustrated by Maxfield Parrish, Copyright 1909 Charles Scribner's Sons, copyright renewed 1937 Maxfield Parrish; **129:** Illustration for *Arabian Nights* for "The Fisherman and the Genie," Edmund Dulac, Photo courtesy of the New York Public Library, Astor, Lenox and Tilden Foundations; **133:** *Charge of the Faramourz Cavaliers,* mid-fourteenth century, Musée Reza Abbasi, Teheran, Photo by John Lei, Omni-Photo Communications, Inc.; **137:** *Shahrazad and King Shahriyar,* Anton Pieck, Illustration from *Stories of the Arabian Nights,* Retold by Naomi Lewis, Illustration © 1984 by B. V. Elsevier, Uitgeversmaatschappij, Amsterdam, Photo by Rex Joseph; **142:** *Krishna's Magic Flute,* Unknown artist, Kangra Valley, c. eighteenth–nineteenth centuries, New York Public Library, Astor, Lenox and Tilden Foundations; **146:** (left) *Yogic positions,* Bahr al Hayat manuscript, 1600–1605, Reproduced by kind permission of the Trustees of the Chester Beatty Library, Dublin; (center) *Terracotta figure of a musician,* The Granger Collection, New York; **147:** (left) *Face of Celestial Nymph,* Scala, Art Resource, New York; (center left) *Shiva Nataraja,* eleventh century, Unknown artist, early Chola, National Museum, Madras, Giraudon, Art Resource, New York; (center) *Hindu God Vishnu Seated on the Snake Shesha,* The Granger Collection, New York; (center right) *Buddha Standing,* Bronze, first half of seventh century, The Metropolitan Museum of Art, Purchase, Bequest of Florance Waterbury, 1969, © Copyright by The Metropolitan Museum of Art; **149:** *Buddha Teaching His Disciples,* eighteenth century, Victoria and Albert Museum, Photo by Michael Holford; **150:** *Krishna and Radha in the Rain with Two Musicians,* School of the Raj-putana, New Delhi National Museum, Borromeo, Art Resource, New York; **152:** *Nandin the Bull,* From Karnataka or Tamil Nadu, thirteenth–fifteenth centuries, Ashmolean Museum, Oxford; **153:** *Statue of Mother and Child,* eleventh century A.D., Indian Museum, Calcutta, Borromeo, Art Resource, New York; **155:** *Jambu-dvipa,* Painting, Rajastan, c. eighteenth century, Published in A. Mookerjee, Tantra Asana, Photo by Innervisions; **160:** *Hindu cosmogram showing tortoise supporting elephants,* The Granger Collection, New York; **162:** *Yogic positions,* Bahr al Hayat manuscript, 1600–1605, Reproduced by kind permission of the Trustees of the Chester Beatty Library, Dublin; **166:** *Krishna on the Swing,* Guler, Scala, Art Resource, New York; **169:** *A Hawk,* eighteenth-century miniature, Indian Mughal, Victoria and Albert Museum, Photo by Michael Holford; **171:** *King Sibi's Sacrifice to the God Indra,* c. second century, Gandharan art, Courtesy of the Trustees of the British Museum; **174:** *Episode from the Gita* (detail), Kangra School, Prince of Wales Museum, Bombay, Giraudon, Art Resource, New York; **177:** *Arjuna and Krishna in the Chariot, between the Two Armies,* Illustration from the *Bhagavad-Gita,* Photo by Lynn Saville, New York Public Library; **182:** *Kangra Valley Painting,* New York Public Library; **185:** *Fragment of an Indian animal carpet,* third quarter sixteenth century, Unknown artist, The Textile Museum, Washington, D.C.; **192:** *Two Ladies in a Landscape—Leaf from an Album of Eleven Paintings,* Unknown artist, Chinese, Ming Dynasty, The Metropolitan Museum of Art, Rogers Fund, 1942, © Copyright by The Metropolitan Museum of Art; **196:** (center) *Marco Polo Entering Beijing,* From *Livre de Merveilles,* fourteenth century, The Granger Collection, New York; (right) *Imaginary Portrait of T'ao Ch'ien Smelling Flowers* (detail), 1650, Chen Hongshou, Honolulu Academy of Arts, Purchase, 1954; **197:** (left) *The Poet Li Po Admiring a Waterfall,* Hokusai, c. 1830, Honolulu Academy of Arts, Gift of James A. Michener; (center left) *Cloisonne vase,* Ming Dynasty, British Museum, London; (center right) *Kublai Khan,* The Granger Collection, New York; **198:** *The Lives of the Chinese Emperors,* c. 1027–256 B.C., Tchou Dynasty, Bibliothèque Nationale, Paris, Giraudon, Art Resource, New York; **200:** *Confucius,* nineteenth century, Chinese style, Bibliothèque Nationale, Paris, Photo Jean-Loup Charmet; **204:** *A Myriad of Trees on Strange Peaks,* Yen Wen-kuei, Northern Sung Dynasty, The Granger Collection, New York; **207:** *Visiting Group,* nineteenth century, Chinese print on silk, Free Library of Philadelphia, Joseph Martin, Scala, Art Resource, New York; **208:** *Lao Tzu,* New York Public Library Picture Collection; **210:**

White Clouds over Xiao and Xiang, Wang Chien, Courtesy the Freer Gallery of Art, Smithsonian Institution, Washington, D.C.; **212:** *Confucius*, The Granger Collection, New York; **215:** *Old Trees by Cold Waterfall*, 1470–1559, Wen Zhengming, The Los Angeles County Museum of Art, Ernest Larsen Blancok Memorial Fund; **218:** *Frog on a Lotus Leaf*, Hsiang Sheng-mo, 1639, The Metropolitan Museum of Art, Edward Elliott Family Collection, Purchase, The Dillon Fund Gift, 1981, © Copyright by The Metropolitan Museum of Art; **220:** *Streams and Hills under Fresh Snow* (detail #1), 1127–1279, Anonymous artist, Southern Sung Dynasty handscroll, The Metropolitan Museum of Art, Gift of John M. Crawford, Jr., 1984, © 1982 Copyright by The Metropolitan Museum of Art; **222:** *T'ao Ch'ien*, Collection of the National Palace Museum, Taipei, Taiwan, Republic of China; **224:** *Mountain Hermitage*, Wang Meng, The Granger Collection, New York; **227:** *Landscape*, Lan Yin, The Granger Collection, New York; **228:** *Waiting for Guests by Lamplight*, Southern Sung Dynasty, The Granger Collection, New York; **230:** *Autumn Hill after Wang Meng*, Ch'ing Dynasty, The Granger Collection, New York; **231:** *River and Mountains in Autumn Color*, 1120–1182, Zhao Boju, Palace Museum, Beijing, China; **232:** *Li Po in His Cups*, New York Public Library Picture Collection; **235:** *River Village in a Rainstorm*, Hanging scroll, Ink and slight color on silk, 169.2 x 103.5 cm, Lü Wenying, Chinese, active c. 1490–1507, © The Cleveland Museum of Art, John L. Severance Fund, 70.76; **236:** *Landscape after Kao K'o-Kung*, Lan Ying, The Metropolitan Museum of Art, The Sackler Fund, 1970, © 1977/1979 Copyright by The Metropolitan Museum of Art; **238:** *Tu Fu*, seventeenth-century Chinese manuscript, Bibliothèque Nationale, Paris, New York Public Library Picture Collection; **240:** *Conversation in Autumn*, 1732, Hua Yen, Chinese (1682–c. 1762), Qing Dynasty, Hanging scroll, Ink and color on paper, 115.3 x 39.7 cm., © The Cleveland Museum of Art, John L. Severance Fund, 54.263; **243:** *Autumn Mountains*, T'ang Yin, The Granger Collection, New York; **244:** *Po Chü-i*, Collection of the National Palace Museum, Taipei, Taiwan, Republic of China; **247:** *Scenes from the Life of T'ao Ch'ien*, 1650, Chen Hongshou, Honolulu Academy of Arts, Purchase, 1954; **248:** *Fan Mounted as an album leaf: Hermitage by a Pine-Covered Bluff*, Unknown artist, mid-twelfth century, The Metropolitan Museum of Art, Purchase, Gift of Mr. and Mrs. Jeremiah Milbank and gift of Mary Phelps Smith, In memory of Howard Caswell Smith, By exchange, 1973, © Copyright by The Metropolitan Museum of Art; **250:** *The Eight Kua*, Trigrams from the ancient classic *I Ching (Book of Change)*, The Granger Collection, New York; **251:** *Chinese title page to I Ching*, The Granger Collection, New York; **256:** *The Great Wave*, Katsushika Hokusai, Spaulding Collection, Courtesy, Museum of Fine Arts, Boston; **259:** *Su Tung-P'o's Visit to Li Chieh-ch'iao at the Wind and Water Cave* (detail of six-panel screen), early seventeenth century, Japanese, Kano school, The Metropolitan Museum of Art, The Harry G. C. Packard Collection of Asian Art, Gift of Harry G. C. Packard and Purchase, Fletcher, Rogers, Harris Brisbane Dick and Louis V. Bell Funds, Joseph Pulitzer Bequest and The Annanberg Fund, Inc., Gift, 1975, © Copyright by The Metropolitan Museum of Art; **260:** (left) *Sanjo-den youchi no emaki (Scroll with Depictions of the Night Attack on the Sanjo Palace)*, Japanese Kamakura Period, second half of the thirteenth century, Unknown artist, Fenollosa-Weld Collection, Courtesy, Museum of Fine Arts, Boston; (center) *Murasaki-shikibu*, Pacific Press Service; (right) Scene from *Yadori* chapter of the *Tale of Genji*, The Granger Collection, New York; **261:** (left) *Portrait of Yoritomo*, Tankanobu, Art Resource, New York; (center left) *Nō Mask: Ko-Omote*, Ashikaga period, fifteenth century A.D., Kongo Family Collection, Tokyo; (center right) *First Landing at Kurihama, July 14, 1853*, Gessan Ogata, Courtesy of United States Naval Academy Museum; **262:** *The Actor Ichimura Mitsuzo as a Samurai*, Torii Kiyomasu II, The Metropolitan Museum of Art, Frederick Charles Hewitt Fund, 1912, © Copyright by The Metropolitan Museum of Art; **264:** *Young Women Arranging a Bouquet of Peonies*, Paris, Musée Guimet, Giraudon, Art Resource, New York; **269:** *Summer Night*, Maruyama Okyo, Japanese (1733–1795), Edo period, Folding screen, Ink, gold, and silver on paper, 154 x 362 cm., © The Cleveland Museum of Art, Leonard C. Hanna, Jr., Bequest, 73.157; **271:** *Yoshida Kenko*, Heibonsha, Pacific Press Service; **273:** *Triptych of Snow, Moon, and Flower* (left panel), c. 1780's, Shunsho, Museum of Art, Atami; **274:** *Kakinomoto Hitomaro*, Heibonsha, Pacific Press Service; **277:** *Fuji from Futamii*, nineteenth century, Ichiryusai Hiroshige, From the series *Thirty-six Views of Fuji*, The Minneapolis Institute of Arts; **279:** *Plum Blossoms by the Riverside in February*, c. 1750, Suzuki Harunobu, Courtesy Keio Gijuku Library; **281:** *The Celebrated Beauty of the Teahouse, Kagiya, at Kasamori Shrine*, eighteenth century, Suzuki Harunobu, The Metropolitan Museum of Art, The Henry L. Phillips Collection, Bequest of Henry L. Phillips, 1940, © 1978 Copyright by The Metropolitan Museum of Art; **282:** (left) *Ono Komachi*, Heibonsha, Pacific Press Service; (center left) *Ki no Tsurayuki*, Heibonsha, Pacific Press Service; (center right) *Minamoto no Toshiyori*, Heibonsha, Pacific Press Service; (right) *Jakuren Houshi*, Heibonsha, Pacific Press Service; **284:** *Winter: Japanese Girl Gardening in a Frozen Garden*, Japanese painting, Joseph Martin, Scala, Art Resource, New York; **286:** (left) *Yosa Buson*, Heibonsha, Pacific Press Service; (center) *Matsuo Bashō*, The Granger Collection, New York; (right) *Kobayashi Issa*, Heibonsha, Pacific Press Service; **288:** *The Monkey Bridge in Koshu Province*, 1841, Hiroshige hitsu, Christie's, New York; **291:** *Sudden Shower on Ohashi Bridge*, Hiroshige hitsu, Art Resource, New York; **293:** *Nichiren Calming the Storm*, 1835, Kuniyoshi, The Granger Collection, New York; **294:** *Sei Shonagon*, Heibonsha, Pacific Press Service; **297:** *Triptych of Snow, Moon, and Flower* (center panel), c. 1780's, Shunsho, Museum of Art, Atami; **299:** *The Oiran Yoso-Oi Seated at Her Toilet*, c. 1799, Kitagawa Utamaro, The Metropolitan Museum of Art, Rogers Fund, 1918, © 1974 Copyright by The Metropolitan Museum of Art; **302:** *Two Japanese Nō masks: Yase-onna and Uba*, The Granger Collection, New York; **308:** *The Riverhead at Shijo: Theater and Entertainment District at Shijo Kawara* (detail), Edo period, Fenollosa-Weld Collection, Courtesy, Museum of Fine Arts, Boston; **311:** *Nō Mask: Demon Ja*, Courtesy Mitsui Bunko; **320:** *The School of Athens*, Raphael, Photo Vatican Museums; **324:** (left) *Beaked Jug*, 1800 B.C., Kamares style from Phaistos, Archaeological Museum, Heraklion, Crete; (center left) *Attic Red Figure Skyphos, Side A: Paris Abducting Helen*, Signed by Makron as painter and Hieron as potter, about 490–480 B.C., Francis Bartlett Fund, Courtesy, Museum of Fine Arts, Boston; (right) *Tetradrachm* (front and back), 425–422 B.C., Leontini (Sicily), Smithsonian Institution, National Numismatic Collection, Washington, D.C.; **325:** (center) *Statue of Sophocles*, Scala, Art Resource, New York; **328:** *Head of a philosopher*, From Antikythera, c. third century B.C., Nimatallah, Art Resource, New York; **330:** *Apotheosis of Homer*, J. A. Dominique Ingres, The Louvre, Paris, Giraudon, Art Resource, New York; **332:** *The Abduction of Helen of Troy*, 1631, Guido Reni, The Louvre, Paris, Scala, Art Resource, New York; **336:** *Achilles and Agamemnon*, Greek vase, Archaeological Museum, Agrigento, Scala, Art Resource, New York; **342:** *The Iliad: Athena Restraining the Anger of Achilles*, Giovanni Battista Tiepolo, Giraudon, Art Resource, New York; **344:** *The Surrender of Briseis*, Pompeii wall painting, A.D. 63–79, National Museum, Naples, Scala, Art Resource, New York; **348:** *The Abduction of Helen by Paris*, Fra Angelico (follower), National Gallery of Art, London; **351:** *Hector Taking Leave of Andromache*, Angelica Kaufman, Tate Gallery, London, Art Resource, New York; **353:** *Odysseus' Mission to Achilles*, Cleophrades Painter, 485–475 B.C., Staatliche Antikensammlungen und Glyptothek, Munich; **356:** *The Fight over the Body of Patroclus*, 1538–1539, Guilio Romano, Hall of Troy, Ducal Palace, Mantua, Photo by Giovetti; **358:** *The Trojans Withdraw to the Town, Hector Alone Stops to Wait for Achilles*, Ilias Ambrosiana, Biblioteca Ambrosiana; **362:** *Attic Red Figure Nolan Amphora: Hephaestus Making Armor for Achilles*, The Dutuit painter, Francis Bartlett Fund, Courtesy, Museum of Fine Arts, Boston; **367:** *Hector and Andromache from the Destruction of Troy*, fifteenth century, Franco-Flemish tapestry (Tournai), The Metropolitan Museum of Art, Fletcher Fund, 1939, © 1971/1987 Copyright by The Metropolitan Museum of Art; **373:** *Hector Killed by Achilles*, Peter Paul Rubens, Musée des Beaux-Arts, Giraudon, Art Resource, New York; **376:** *Attic Black Figure Hydria: Achilles Dragging the Body of Hector around the Walls of Troy* (detail), Attributed to the Antiope Group, Courtesy, Museum of Fine Arts, Boston, William Francis Warden Fund; **379:** *Achilles*, Detail from the fresco *Thetis Consoling Achilles*, Giovanni Battista Tiepolo, Scala, Art Resource, New York; **383:** *Priam Pleading with Achilles for the Body of Hector*, Gavin Hamilton, The Granger Collection, New York; **391:** *Thetis Bringing Armour to Achilles*, Greek vase, Archaeological Museum, Gela, Scala, Art Resource, New York; **392:** *Death of Hector*, fifth century B.C., Attic red-figured Hydria,

Collection, New York; **1114:** *Above the Trees,* Emily Carr, Collection of the Vancouver Art Gallery, Photo by Jim Gorman; **1119:** *Picking Flowers,* 1875, Pierre Auguste Renoir, © 1993 National Gallery of Art, Washington, Ailsa Mellon Bruce Collection; **1123:** *Madame Mayden,* Amedeo Modigliani, Superstock, Inc.; **1128:** *Returning to the Trenches,* 1914, Christopher R. W. Nevinson, National Gallery of Canada, Ottawa, Gift of the Massey Collection of English Painting, 1946; **1131:** *Landscape, Cannes,* Max Beckmann, San Francisco Museum of Modern Art, Gift of Louise S. Ackerman; **1132:** *Luigi Pirandello,* Giraudon, Art Resource, New York; **1135:** *Olivia,* 1911, Lydia Field Emmet, © 1993 National Gallery of Art, Washington, Gift of Olivia Stokes Hatch; **1137:** *Breakfast,* 1886–1987, Paul Signac, Collection, State Museum Kröller-Müller, Otterlo, The Netherlands; **1142:** *The Old Guitarist,* 1903, Pablo Picasso, Spanish, 1881–1973, Oil on panel 122.9 x 82.6 cm, Helen Birch Bartlett Memorial Collection, 1926.253, photograph courtesy of The Art Institute of Chicago; **1144:** *Children on the Beach,* 1916, Joaquín Sorolla, Private Collection; **1149:** *Soldats et Officiers Romains,* second century, Roman bas-relief, Louvre, Paris; **1151:** *The Totonac Civilization—The Great Pyramid of Tajin,* Diego Rivera, National Palace, Mexico City, Superstock, Inc.; **1155:** *Retrato de un Joven,* Leonor Fini, Christie's, New York; **1157:** *Puerto de Villefranche,* Joaquim Torres-García, Christie's, New York; **1163:** *The Frog Prince,* Walter Crane, Photo by John Lei, Omni-Photo Communications, Inc.; **1167:** *Señora Coronel Grinding Corn,* Alexander Harmer; **1169:** *The Revolution,* Manuel Rodriguez Lozano, Museo Nacional de Arte Moderno, Mexico City, Photo Laurie Platt Winfrey; **1171:** *Ordination Pavillion of King Rama V,* Detail of early twentieth-century mural, Wat Benchamabopit, Bangkok, Invernizzi, Art Resource, New York; **1175:** *Ouda* (detail), Hironaga Takehiko, Courtesy of the Trustees of the British Museum, Photo by John Lei, Omni-Photo Communications, Inc.; **1185:** *Landscape,* Zhu Qizhan, Photo Courtesy of Joan Lebold Cohen; **1194:** *Two Gazelles,* 1530, From the *Babar Nama,* New Delhi National Museum, Borromeo, Art Resource, New York; **1202:** *The Real Mountain,* 1981, Jacobo Borges, Private Collection, Courtesy of CDS Galleries; **1215:** *The Song of Love,* 1914, Giorgio de Chirico, Oil on canvas, 28 3/4" x 23 3/8", The Museum of Modern Art, New York, Nelson A. Rockefeller Bequest; **1223:** *Sol y Vida,* 1947, Frida Kahlo, Private collection, Courtesy of CDS Gallery; **1230:** *Hidden Treasures,* 1969, Consuelo González Amézcua, Courtesy of the artist, Photo by John Lei, Omni-Photo Communications, Inc.; **1235:** *Print Gallery,* 1956, M. C. Escher, Lithograph, 32 x 32 cm., © 1956 M. C. Escher Foundation, Baarn, Holland, All rights reserved; **1239:** *La Nuit,* René Magritte, © Copyright Charly Herscovici, Art Resource, New York; **1241:** *Still Life Reviving,* Remedios Varo, Collection of Beatriz Varo de Cano, Valencia, Spain, Photo courtesy of Walter Gruen; **1247:** *The Torment of the Poet,* 1914, Giorgio de Chirico, Yale University Art Gallery, Bequest of Kay Sage Tanguy; **1255:** *Palm Tree, Nassau,* 1898, Winslow Homer, The Metropolitan Museum of Art, Purchase, 1910, Amelia B. Lazarus Fund, © 1982/1989 Copyright by The Metropolitan Museum of Art; **1256:** *The Return of Ulysses,* Romare Bearden, Courtesy Estate of Romare Bearden; **1260:** *St. Lucia—Looking at Rat Island,* Watercolor by Derek Walcott, From the collection of Michael and Judy Chastanet; **1265:** *San Antonio de Oriente* (detail), 1954, José Antonio Velásquez, Oil on canvas, Museum of Modern Art of Latin America, Washington, D.C.; **1267:** *Port de la Saline, Haiti,* n.d., Lois Mailou Jones, Courtesy of the artist; **1271:** *Memory of Oceania (Souvenir d'Océanie),* Henri Matisse, Nice, Summer 1952–early 1953, Gouache and crayon on cut-and-pasted paper over canvas, 9'4" x 9'4 7/8", The Museum of Modern Art, New York, Mrs. Simon Guggenheim Fund, © 1993 Succession H. Matisse, ARS, New York; **1275:** *Sisyphus,* 1983, Earl Staley, Private Collection; **1287:** *Schrödinger's Cat,* 1989, Elizabeth Knight, Courtesy of the New York Academy of Sciences; **1295:** *To the Victims of Fascism,* 1946–1949, Hans Grundig, Sächsische Landesbibliothek du Dresden, Abteilung Deutsche Fotothek; **1297:** *Typhus in the Camp,* Transnistria, 1943, Arnold Daghani, Watercolor, 12" x 9", YIVO Institute for Jewish Research, New York; **1301:** *Monument,* 1989, Jan Sawka, Courtesy of the artist; **1304:** *Babal II,* Jerzy Duda Gracz, Photo by Margaret B. Duda, Photo Researchers, Inc.; **1310:** *Green Depth,* 1944, Irene Rice Pereira, The Metropolitan Museum of Art, New York, George A. Hearn Fund, 1944, © Copyright by The Metropolitan Museum of Art; **1314:** *Demon Above the Ships (Dämon über den Schiffen),* 1916, Paul Klee, Watercolor and pen and ink on paper, Mounted on cardboard, 9'3/8" x 8'1/8", The Museum of Modern Art, New York, Acquired through the Lillie P. Bliss Bequest; **1324:** *Colosso o Panico,* Francisco José de Goya, Prado, Madrid, Art Resource, New York; **1329:** *Village with Dark Sun,* Marc Chagall, Photo by Francis Mayer, Photo Researchers, Inc., © 1993 ARS, New York, ADAGP, Paris; **1331:** *Pilgrimage,* 1974, Shraga Weil, Courtesy of Pucker/Safrai Gallery; **1342:** *Thrust,* 1959, Adolph Gottlieb, The Metropolitan Museum of Art, George A. Hearn Fund, 1959, Photography by Malcolm Varon, © 1987/1989 Copyright by The Metropolitan Museum of Art; **1345:** *Contemporary African carvings,* By Joseph Agbana of the Inisha Workshop, Photo by William Campbell, *Time* magazine; **1353:** (top left) *Ball with Hathor Head and Hollow Cylinder,* mid-eighteenth century, B.C., Unknown artist, Rock crystal and gold, Museum Expedition, Courtesy, Museum of Fine Arts, Boston; (top right) *Criosphinx on a Column,* late eighth century, B.C., Unknown artist, Electrum with colored glass inlays, Museum Expedition, Courtesy, Museum of Fine Arts, Boston; (bottom) *Bottle in the Shape of a Bound Oryx,* 700 B.C., Unknown artist, Alabaster, Museum Expedition, Courtesy, Museum of Fine Arts, Boston; **1357:** *Ubi Girl from Tai Region,* 1972, Lois Mailou Jones, The Hayden Collection, Courtesy of Museum of Fine Arts, Boston; **1369:** *Journey to the Unknown #1,* 1981, Achameleh Debela, Mixed media on canvas, 32" x 44", Gift of Mr. and Mrs. Achameleh Debela, Maryland Artists Collection, University of Maryland University College; **1372:** *Untitled,* Malangatana Ngwanya, Lithograph, 18" x 23", From Contemporary African Art Gallery, New York City, Photo by Ken Karp; **1385:** *Drinking Water,* Rosemary Karuga, Paper collage, 21" x 13", From Contemporary African Art Gallery, New York City; **1388:** *The Birds,* Rosemary Karuga, From Contemporary African Art Gallery, New York City; **1395:** *Harriet Tubman Series Number 9,* Jacob Lawrence, Hampton University Museum, Hampton, Virginia; **1398:** *Sad Carnival,* n.d., Fikile, (Magadlela), Mixed media on paper, 24 x 33 cm., De Beers Centenary Art Collection, University of Fort Hare; **1400:** *Baoulé statuette of woman,* Côte d'Ivoire, Musée des Arts Africains et Oceaniens, Photo J. M. Labat, Explorer; **1407:** *Three Jumping Carp,* Yi Dynasty, nineteenth century, The Brooklyn Museum, Gift of Mr. and Mrs. Burton Krouner, 82.79; **1418:** *Bird,* 1990, Tara Sabharwal, Watercolor, Tempera, 20" x 28", Collection of the artist; **1422:** *Greetings,* 1992, Tara Sabharwal, Watercolor, Tempera, 9" x 12", Collection, Robert Skelton; **1427:** *Mountain Landscape in Moonlight,* Kim Ki-chang, The Brooklyn Museum, Gift of Dr. and Mrs. Peter Reimann, 81.124; **1431:** *Yuki,* 1929, Kotondo, Courtesy Ronin Gallery, New York; **1440, 1444:** *Untitled,* Original painting by Shao Fei, Reproduced by permission of Bei Dao; **1449:** *The Ascent of Ethiopia,* 1932, Lois Mailou Jones, Collection of the artist

PHOTOGRAPH CREDITS